American Constitutional Law

American Constitutional Law
by Louis Fisher and Katy J. Harriger
is available in two formats:

SINGLE-VOLUME HARDCOVER EDITION
American Constitutional Law

TWO-VOLUME PAPERBACK EDITION

VOLUME 1
Constitutional Structures
Separated Powers and Federalism

VOLUME 2
Constitutional Rights
Civil Rights and Civil Liberties

American Constitutional Law
Tenth Edition

Louis Fisher
Katy J. Harriger

CAROLINA ACADEMIC PRESS
Durham, North Carolina

Copyright © 2013 by Louis Fisher and Katy J. Harriger.
All rights reserved.

ISBN 978-1-61163-352-8

Library of Congress Cataloging-in-Publication Data

Fisher, Louis.
American constitutional law / Louis Fisher and Katy J. Harriger. --Tenth edition.
    pages cm
Includes bibliographical references and index.
ISBN 978-1-61163-352-8 (hardback : alk. paper) -- ISBN 978-1-61163-353-5 (volume 1, pbk. : alk. paper) -- ISBN 978-1-61163-354-2 (volume 2, pbk. : alk. paper)
1. Constitutional law--United States. 2. Civil rights--United States. I. Harriger, Katy J. (Katy Jean) II. Title.

KF4550.F568 2013
342.73--dc23   2013001261

Carolina Academic Press
700 Kent Street
Durham, North Carolina 27701
Telephone (919) 489-7486
Fax (919) 493-5668
E-mail cap@cap-press.com

Printed in the United States of America

To The Constitution Project — Louis Fisher

In memory of my father, Russell E. Harriger (1923–2010) — Katy J. Harriger

Summary of Contents

Contents

About the Authors

LOUIS FISHER received his B.S. from the College of William and Mary and his Ph.D. from the New School for Social Research. After teaching political science at Queens College, he joined the Congressional Research Service of the Library of Congress in 1970, where he served as Senior Specialist in Separation of Powers. On March 6, 2006, he joined the Law Library of the Library of Congress as Specialist in Constitutional Law. Upon his retirement from the Library in August 2010, he joined The Constitution Project as scholar in residence. He has testified before congressional committees more than 50 times on such issues as war powers, state secrets, NSA surveillance, Congress and the Constitution, executive lobbying, executive privilege, committee subpoenas, impoundment of funds, legislative vetoes, the item veto, the pocket veto, presidential reorganization authority, recess appointments, executive spending discretion, the congressional budget process, the Balanced Budget Amendment, biennial budgeting, covert spending, and CIA whistleblowing. During 1987 he served as Research Director for the House Iran-Contra Committee.

His twenty books, listed on his webpage at http://loufisher.org, include *Constitutional Conflicts between Congress and the President* (5th ed., 2007), *Constitutional Dialogues* (1988), *Presidential War Power* (2d ed. 2004), *The Constitution and 9/11: Recurring Threats to America's Freedoms* (2008), *Defending Congress and the Constitution* (2011), and *The Law of the Executive Branch: Presidential Power* (2013).

Dr. Fisher has been active with CEELI (Central and East European Law Initiative) of the American Bar Association, traveling to Bulgaria, Albania, and Hungary to lend assistance to constitution writers. In addition to these trips abroad, he participated in CEELI conferences in Washington, D.C., involving delegations from Lithuania, Romania, and Russia, and has served on CEELI "working groups" on Armenia and Belarus. He traveled to Russia in 1992 as part of a CRS delegation to assist on questions of separation of powers and federalism and to Ukraine in 1993 to participate in an election law conference.

His specialties include constitutional law, war powers, state secrets, budget policy, executive-legislative relations, and judicial-congressional relations. He is the author of more than 450 articles in law reviews, political science journals, encyclopedias, books, magazines, and newspapers. He has been invited to speak in Albania, Australia, Belgium, Bulgaria, Canada, the Czech Republic, China, Denmark, England, France, Germany, Greece, Israel, Japan, Macedonia, Malaysia, Mexico, the Netherlands, Oman, the Philippines, Poland, Romania, Russia, Slovenia, South Korea, Sweden, Taiwan, Ukraine, and United Arab Emirates.

KATY J. HARRIGER received her B.A. in Political Science from Edinboro State College in Pennsylvania and her M.A. and Ph.D. in Political Science from the University of Connecticut. She is a Professor of Political Science and chair of that department at Wake Forest University where she teaches courses in American Constitutional Law, American politics, judicial process, and democracy and citizenship. She has testified before Congress and been a frequent media commentator on issues related to the use of independent counsel and political influences on the Department of Justice. Dr. Harriger is the editor of *Separation of Powers: Commentary and Documents,* (Congressional Quarterly Press

2003), the author of *The Special Prosecutor in American Politics.* 2nd ed., revised (University Press of Kansas, 2000), and *Independent Justice: The Federal Special Prosecutor in American Politics* (University Press of Kansas, 1992), as well as a number of articles about constitutional law issues in journals and law reviews. Most recently she co-authored, with Jill J. McMillan, *Speaking of Politics: Preparing College Students for Democratic Citizenship through Deliberative Dialogue* (Kettering Foundation Press, 2007). At Wake Forest, Harriger has been the recipient of the Reid Doyle Prize for Excellence in Teaching (1988), the John Reinhardt Distinguished Teaching Award (2002), and the Schoonmaker Award for Community Service (2006).

Acknowledgments

This book, in gestation for years, has many contributors and abettors. With the publication of the eighth edition, Katy J. Harriger joined as co-author. She brings to the task a strong background in constitutional law and separation of powers and many years of classroom experience and professional activity on legal issues. David Gray Adler, co-author of the seventh edition, offered extensive analytical contributions and in previous editions provided careful, thoughtful reviews.

Morton Rosenberg of the Congressional Research Service lent a guiding hand, giving encouragement and insightful observations. In reviewing the manuscript and selections for readings, he was the major source of counsel and enlightenment. Other friends and colleagues who offered important advice and comments include Susan Burgess, Phillip J. Cooper, Neal Devins, Murray Dry, Roger Garcia, Jerry Goldman, Nancy Kassop, Jacob Landynski, Leonard W. Levy, Robert Meltz, Wayne Moore, Ronald Moe, Christopher Pyle, Jeremy Rabkin, Harold Relyea, William Ross, Jay Shampansky, Gordon Silverstein, Mitchel Sollenberger, Charles Tiefer, and Stephen Wasby.

It is my pleasure to dedicate the book to The Constitution Project, which I have worked with for more than a decade on a number of issues, including war powers and the state secrets privilege. Its expertise, analytical skills, and nonpartisan approach contribute to an informed and professional debate on key questions of constitutional law. Upon my retirement from government in late August 2010, I worked even more closely with The Constitution Project as Scholar in Residence and am proud to be among its supporters.

Louis Fisher

After many years of teaching American Constitutional Law using this textbook, it has been a privilege and a pleasure to work with Lou Fisher on recent editions. I have always been drawn to this text because it recognizes that constitutional law is made through a dynamic dialogic political process rather than simply by nine Supreme Court justices. This seems a particularly important lesson to understand, for political science and law students alike, in a time when the popular understandings of constitutional politics and issues are so shallow and often misinformed. I dedicate the book to my late father, Russell E. Harriger, who always encouraged and supported my endeavors, even when he disagreed with me (which in the area of constitutional law was early and often).

I am thankful for the help of student research assistant Taylor Williams, who has been enormously helpful in keeping me up to date with contemporary developments in the law. Keith Sipe, Tim Colton, and the rest of the staff at Carolina Academic Press, were amiable, helpful and professional in bringing this project to fruition. We express our thanks and gratitude to them for all of their efforts.

Katy J. Harriger

Introduction

To accommodate the leading cases on constitutional law, textbooks concentrate on court decisions and overlook the political, historical, and social framework in which these decisions are handed down. Constitutional law is thus reduced to the judicial exercise of divining the meaning of textual provisions. The larger process, including judicial as well as nonjudicial actors, is ignored. The consequence, as noted by one law professor, is the absence of a "comprehensive course on constitutional law in any meaningful sense in American law schools."[1]

The political process must be understood because it establishes the boundaries for judicial activity and influences the substance of specific decisions, if not immediately then within a few years. This book keeps legal issues in a broad political context. Cases should not be torn from their environment. A purely legalistic approach to constitutional law misses the constant, creative interplay between the judiciary and the political branches. The Supreme Court is not the exclusive source of constitutional law. It is not the sole or even dominant agency in deciding constitutional questions. The Constitution is interpreted initially by a private citizen, legislator, or executive official. Someone from the private or public sector decides that an action violates the Constitution; political pressures build in ways to reshape fundamental constitutional doctrines.

Books on constitutional law usually focus exclusively on Supreme Court decisions and stress its doctrines, as though lower courts and elected officials are unimportant. Other studies describe constitutional decision making as lacking in legal principle, based on low-level political haggling by various actors. We see an open and vigorous system struggling to produce principled constitutional law. Principles are important. Constitutional interpretations are not supposed to be idiosyncratic events or the result of a political free-for-all. If they were, our devotion to the rule of law would be either absurd or a matter of whimsy.

It is traditional to focus on constitutional rather than statutory interpretation, and yet the boundaries between these categories are unclear. Issues of constitutional dimension usually form a backdrop to "statutory" questions. Preoccupation with the Supreme Court as the principal or final arbiter of constitutional questions fosters a misleading impression. A dominant business of the Court is statutory construction, and through that function it interacts with other branches of government in a process that refines the meaning of the Constitution.

This study treats the Supreme Court and lower courts as one branch of a political system with a difficult but necessary task to perform. They often share with the legislature and the executive the responsibility for defining political values, resolving political conflict, and protecting the political process. Through commentary and reading selections, we try to bridge the artificial gap in the literature that separates law from politics. Lord Radcliffe advised that "we cannot learn law by learning law." Law must be "a part of history, a part of economics and sociology, a part of ethics and a philosophy of life. It is not strong enough in itself to be a philosophy in itself."[2]

---

1. W. Michael Reisman, "International Incidents: Introduction to a New Genre in the Study of International Law," 10 Yale J. Int'l L. 1, 8 n.13 (1984).
2. Lord Radcliffe, The Law & Its Compass 92–93 (1960).

A Note on Citations. The introductory essays to each chapter contain many citations to court cases, public laws, congressional reports, and floor debates. The number of these citations may seem confusing and even overwhelming. We want to encourage the reader to consult these documents and develop a richer appreciation of the complex process that shapes constitutional law. Repeated citations to federal statutes help underscore the ongoing role of Congress and the executive branch in constitutional interpretation. To permit deeper exploration of certain issues, either for a term paper or scholarly research, footnotes contain leads to supplementary cases. Bibliographies are provided for each chapter. The appendices include a glossary of legal terms and a primer on researching the law.

If the coverage is too detailed, the instructor may always advise students to skip some of the material. Another option is to ask the student to understand two or three departures from a general doctrine, such as the famous *Miranda* warning developed by the Warren Court but whittled away by the Burger and Rehnquist Courts. Even if a student is initially stunned by the complexity of constitutional law, it is better to be aware of the delicate shadings that exist than to believe that the Court paints with bold, permanent strokes.

At various points in the chapters, we give examples where state courts, refusing to follow the lead of the Supreme Court, conferred greater constitutional rights than available at the federal level. These are examples only. They could have been multiplied many times over. No one should assume that rulings from the Supreme Court represent the last word on constitutional law, even for lower courts.

Compared to other texts, this book offers much more in the way of citations to earlier decisions. We do this for several reasons. The citations allow the reader to research areas in greater depth. They also highlight the process of trial and error used by the Court to clarify constitutional principles. Concentration on contemporary cases would obscure the Court's record of veering down side roads, backtracking, and reversing direction. Focusing on landmark cases prevents the reader from understanding the *development* of constitutional law: the dizzying exceptions to "settled" doctrines, the laborious manner in which the Court struggles to fix the meaning of the Constitution, the twists and turns, the detours and dead ends. Describing major cases without these tangled patterns would presume an orderly and static system that mocks the dynamic, fitful, creative, and consensus-building process that exists. No one branch of government prevails. The process is polyarchal, not hierarchical. The latter, perhaps attractive for architectural structures, is inconsistent with our aspiration for self-government.

In all court cases and other documents included as readings, footnotes have been deleted. For the introductory essays, reference works are abbreviated as follows:

Comp. Gen.	Decisions of the Comptroller General.
Elliot	Jonathan Elliot, ed., The Debates in the Several State Conventions, on the Adoption of the Federal Constitution (5 vols., Washington, D.C., 1836–1845).
Farrand	Max Farrand, ed., The Records of the Federal Convention of 1787 (4 vols., New Haven: Yale University Press, 1937).
Fisher	Constitutional Conflicts between Congress and the President (5th ed. 2007).
Landmark Briefs	Landmark Briefs and Arguments of the Supreme Court of the United States: Constitutional Law. Gerald Gunther and Gerhard Casper, eds. University Publications of America.
O.L.C.	Office of Legal Counsel Opinions, U.S. Department of Justice.
Op. Att'y Gen.	Opinions of the Attorney General.
Richardson	James D. Richardson, ed., A Compilation of the Messages and Papers of the Presidents (20 vols., New York: Bureau of National Literature, 1897–1925).
Wkly Comp. Pres. Doc.	Weekly Compilation of Presidential Documents, published each week by the Government Printing Office from 1965 to 2009: available online.

American Constitutional Law

1

Constitutional Politics

For those who teach and study constitutional law, the relationship between the judiciary and politics remains an awkward issue. Technical details of a decision have a way of driving out the political events that generate a case and influence its disposition. To infuse law with dignity, majesty, and perhaps a touch of mystery, it is tempting to separate the courts from the rest of government and make unrealistic claims of judicial independence. Similarly, studies exaggerate the extent to which the Supreme Court supplies the "last word" on constitutional law. The elected branches and the general public necessarily share in that complex, sensitive task.

Legal scholars who explored the law-politics relationship early in the twentieth century did so against the warnings of traditional leaders of the legal profession. To speak the truth, or even search for it, threatened judicial symbols and concepts of long standing. In 1914, when legal philosopher Morris Raphael Cohen began describing how judges make law, his colleagues warned of dire consequences. The deans of major law schools advised him that his findings, although unquestionably correct, might invite even greater recourse to "judicial legislation."

Undeterred by these cautionary words, Cohen had "an abiding conviction that to recognize the truth and adjust oneself to it is in the end the easiest and most advisable course." He denied that the law is a "closed, independent system having nothing to do with economic, political, social, or philosophical science." If courts were in fact constantly making and remaking the law, it became "of the utmost social importance that the law should be made in accordance with the best available information, which it is the object of science to supply." Morris R. Cohen, Law and the Social Order 380–81 n.86 (1933).

Constitutional Principles

The chapter title "Constitutional Politics" is meant to underscore two values: the interplay between law and politics and the core principles that define constitutional government. Political judgments and accommodations must respect those principles and be subordinate to them. If public policy were merely the end result of compromises reached by the three branches of government, we would have politics but no constitution. The period after the terrorist attacks of 9/11 represents one period in American history where government pursued policies at the cost of constitutional liberties. In previous years, the country also lost sight of fundamental principles and violated the rights of citizens and aliens.

What are the overarching values of the U.S. Constitution? The framers were heavily influenced by the Enlightenment and its belief that individuals have the capacity to develop and participate in self-government. In America they would be citizens, not "subjects" of a monarch. A purpose of the U.S. Constitution is to protect the dignity and worth of individuals, enabling them to promote their skills and talents. James Madison believed that an individual "has property in his opinions and in the free communication of them." Property included religious opinions, personal safety and liberty, and the "free use of his faculties and free choice of the objects on which to employ them." Flowing from those fundamental, inherent values were the rights of free speech, free press, religious liberty, and protection against arbitrary arrest and seizure of property. Conscience, he said, "is the most sacred of all property." Invading someone's conscience was a greater violation than invading a person's home.

3

From British history, the framers held that individuals have a right to be tried in open court, upon specific charges, and with full access to evidence presented by prosecutors. Procedural safeguards were needed to curb arbitrary imprisonment. Secret trials and secret evidence were abhorrent. Defendants had the right to confront accusers and gain access to legal counsel. Juries and grand juries represented a potential check on government abuse. American colonies and states included the privilege against self-incrimination in their charters and constitutions. Evidence against the accused could not be obtained by coercive methods.

These rights and liberties were protected by the structure of government, including separation of powers and the system of checks and balances. The framers did not trust in human nature. Concentrating government authority in one place invited the abuse of power. In Federalist No. 4, John Jay explained why the power to place the country in a state of war was vested in Congress, not the President. A study of history demonstrated that executives regularly committed their country to military adventures not for national interest but for reasons of fame, glory, and ambition, leading to calamitous loss of life and treasure. It was the practice of an executive to engage in wars "not sanctified by justice or the voice and interests of his people." The period after World War II has underscored the dangers to constitutional democracy when unchecked power is concentrated in the executive branch.

Madison also depended on a self-checking mechanism within the regular political process. In Federalist No. 10, he analyzed what should be done about "factions," which he understood to mean citizens whose interests were adverse to that of the community. He rejected any effort to destroy the liberty that made factions possible, or attempt to make everyone think the same way. Some of the passions of factions would be filtered through a representative system. Another important check was to increase the size of the republic so that factions would tend to neutralize each other. These safeguards would help protect minority rights.

Mechanical Jurisprudence

For more than a century, the legal profession claimed that judges "found" the law rather than made it. This doctrine of mechanical jurisprudence, joined with the supposed nonpolitical nature of the judiciary, offered convenient reasons for separating courts from the rest of government. A perceptive essay by political scientist C. Herman Pritchett noted that the disciplines of law and political science drifted apart for semantic, philosophical, and practical reasons: "Law is a prestigious symbol, whereas politics tends to be a dirty word. Law is stability; politics is chaos. Law is impersonal; politics is personal. Law is given; politics is free choice. Law is reason; politics is prejudice and self-interest. Law is justice; politics is who gets there first with the most." Joel B. Grossman and Joseph Tanenhaus, eds., Frontiers of Judicial Research 31 (1969). With options drawn in that manner, no wonder courts looked attractive. A famous example of mechanical jurisprudence is the claim by Justice Owen Roberts that when an act of Congress "is appropriately challenged in the courts as not conforming to the constitutional mandate the judicial branch of the Government has only one duty, — to lay the article of the Constitution which is invoked beside the statute which is challenged and to decide whether the latter squares with the former." United States v. Butler, 297 U.S. 1, 62 (1936).

U.S. constitutional law is often taught as a progression from two distinct legal cultures. The first was "legal formalism" from the 1870s to the 1920s, during which time judges supposedly developed law by logical and mechanical deduction. That model was replaced in the 1920s and 1930s by "legal realists" who argued that judges construct legal justifications to support their personal preferences. In a study published in 2010, Brian Tamanaha debunks the doctrinal purity of those two schools, explaining that legal realists existed from the 1870s to the 1920s. Articles published over that period regularly and plainly spoke about "judicial legislation." Moreover, legal realism after 1920 did not usher in a round of freewheeling, subjective court rulings. Brian Z. Tamanaha, Beyond the Formalist-Realist Divide (Princeton University Press, 2010).

Chief Justice Warren believed that law could be distinguished from politics. Progress in politics "could be made and most often was made by compromising and taking half a loaf where a whole loaf could not be obtained." He insisted that the "opposite is true so far as the judicial process was concerned." Through the judicial process, "and particularly in the Supreme Court, the basic ingredient of decision is principle, and it should not be compromised and parceled out a little in one case, a little more in another, until eventually someone receives the full benefit." The Memoirs of Earl Warren 6 (1977).

Yet the piecemeal approach applies quite well to the judicial process. The Supreme Court prefers to avoid general rules that exceed the necessities of a particular case. Especially in the realm of constitutional law, it recognizes the "embarrassment" that may result from formulating rules or deciding questions "beyond the necessities of the immediate issue." Euclid v. Ambler Co., 272 U.S. 365, 397 (1926). Compromise, expediency, and ad hoc action are no strangers to a multimember court that gropes incrementally toward a consensus and decision. The desegregation case, *Brown v. Board of Education* (1954), was preceded by two decades of halting progress toward the eventual abandonment of the "separate but equal" doctrine enunciated by the Supreme Court in 1896. After he left the Court, Potter Stewart reflected on the judicial decision to exclude from the courtroom evidence that had been illegally obtained: "Looking back, the exclusionary rule seems a bit jerry-built—like a roller coaster track constructed while the roller coaster sped along. Each new piece of track was attached hastily and imperfectly to the one before it, just in time to prevent the roller coaster from crashing, but without an opportunity to measure the curves and dips preceding it or to contemplate the twists and turns that inevitably lay ahead." 83 Colum. L. Rev. 1365, 1366 (1983).

A. LITIGATION AS A POLITICAL PROCESS

Throughout the twentieth century, cases decided by federal courts embodied issues that were of vital importance to individual citizens, corporations and trade unions, and the elected branches of government. The Court moved from narrow nineteenth-century questions of private law (estates, trusts, admiralty, real property, contracts, and commercial law) to contemporary issues of public law (federal regulation, criminal law, individual liberties, equal protection, and federal taxation). The period after World War II is generally considered a high-water mark in judicial policymaking. Decisions with nationwide impact affected desegregation in 1954, reapportionment and school prayers in 1962, criminal justice in the 1960s, and abortion from 1973 onward.

Although members of Congress criticize "judicial activism," they do their part to encourage judicial policymaking. Congress passes statutes that give standing to litigants, provide fees for attorneys, and establish separate agencies (such as the Legal Services Corporation) to initiate suits on broad public issues. Instead of merely resolving private disputes between private individuals, courts develop and articulate public values on major social, economic, and political questions. Increasingly, their decisions are prospective rather than retrospective. Judges actively participate in negotiating a resolution and maintain their involvement after issuing an initial decree. Courts do more than resolve private disputes between litigants according to the principles of law. "As a result, courts are inevitably cast in an affirmative, political—activist, if you must—role, a role that contrasts with the passive umpireship we are taught to expect." Abram Chayes, "Public Law Litigation and the Burger Court," 96 Harv. L. Rev. 4, 4 (1982). This activist role has been criticized by those who believe that federal judges lack both the legitimacy and the capacity to decide questions of broad social policy (see box on next page).

Justices of the Supreme Court sometimes encourage the belief that a gulf separates law from politics. Chief Justice John Marshall insisted that "Questions in their nature political ... can never be made in this court." Marbury v. Madison, 5 U.S. 137, 170 (1803). In that very same decision, however, he established a precedent of far-reaching political importance: the power of the judiciary to review and overturn the actions of Congress and the executive. As noted by one scholar, Marshall "more closely associated the art of judging with the positive qualities of impartiality and disinterestedness,

Judicial Capacity for Making Social Policy

[There is a] growing recognition that there are elements of overstatement in the case against judicial review. The courts are more democratically accountable, through a variety of formal and informal mechanisms, than they have been accused of being. Equally important, the other branches are in many ways less democratically accountable than they in turn were said to be by those who emphasized the special disabilities under which judges labor....

As the debate over the democratic character of judicial review wanes, there is another set of issues in the offing. It relates not to legitimacy but to capacity, not to whether the courts *should* perform certain tasks but to whether they *can* perform them competently.

Of course, legitimacy and capacity are related. A court wholly without capacity may forfeit its claim to legitimacy. A court wholly without legitimacy will soon suffer from diminished capacity....

[Judicial capacity is limited by five factors: (1) adjudication is so focused by the particular litigants that other alternatives and remedies are overlooked; (2) the piecemeal nature of adjudication leads to incremental decisionmaking that pushes to the side related issues; (3) judges must await the capricious timing of litigants; (4) fact-finding in adjudication is ill-adapted to the ascertainment of social facts and results in reduced understanding and abstract rulings; and (5) adjudication makes no provision for policy review and little for future consequences.]

SOURCE: Donald L. Horowitz, The Courts and Social Policy 18, 34–56 (1977).

and yet he had made his office a vehicle for the expression of his views about the proper foundations of American government." G. Edward White, The American Judicial Tradition 35 (1976).

During his days as law school professor, Felix Frankfurter referred to constitutional law as "applied politics." Archibald MacLeish and E. F. Prichard, eds., Law and Politics 6 (1962). "The simple truth of the matter," he said, "is that decisions of the Court denying or sanctioning the exercise of federal power, as in the first child labor case, largely involve a judgment about practical matters, and not at all any esoteric knowledge of the Constitution." Id. at 12. He regarded courts as "less than ever technical expounders of technical provisions of the Constitution. They are arbiters of the economic and social life of vast regions and at times of the whole country." Felix Frankfurter and James M. Landis, The Business of the Supreme Court 173 (1928).

Once on the bench, however, Frankfurter insisted that a dichotomy exists between law and politics. Refusing to take a reapportionment case in 1946, he said it was "hostile to a democratic system to involve the judiciary in the politics of the people." Colegrove v. Green, 328 U.S. 549, 553–54 (1946). In *Baker* v. *Carr* (1962) the Supreme Court liberated itself from this narrow holding and has demonstrated throughout its history an awareness of the political system in which it operates daily. Writing in 1921, Justice Cardozo dismissed the idea that judges "stand aloof" from the "great tides and currents" that engulf the rest of mankind (see box on next page). Although the Supreme Court is an independent branch, it is not isolated. It is buffeted by the same social winds that press upon the executive and legislative branches.

From the late nineteenth century to the 1930s, the courts struck down a number of federal and state efforts to ameliorate industrial conditions. Laws that established maximum hours or minimum wages were declared an unconstitutional interference with the "liberty of contract." Lawyers from the corporate sector helped translate the philosophy of laissez-faire into legal terms and constitutional doctrine. These judicial rulings were so spiced with conservative business values that Justice Holmes protested that cases were "decided upon an economic theory which a large part of the country does not entertain." He chided his brethren: "The Fourteenth Amendment does not enact Mr. Herbert Spencer's Social Statics." Lochner v. New York, 198 U.S. 45, 75 (1905). When it was evident that the

Cardozo on Judicial Process

I do not doubt the grandeur of the conception which lifts [judges] into the realm of pure reason, above and beyond the sweep of perturbing and deflecting forces. None the less, if there is anything of reality in my analysis of the judicial process, they do not stand aloof on these chill and distant heights; and we shall not help the cause of truth by acting and speaking as if they do. The great tides and currents which engulf the rest of men do not turn aside in their course and pass the judges by. We like to figure to ourselves the processes of justice as coldly objective and impersonal. The law, conceived of as a real existence, dwelling apart and alone, speaks, through the voices of priests and ministers, the words which they have no choice except to utter. That is an ideal of objective truth toward which every system of jurisprudence tends. It is an ideal of which great publicists and judges have spoken as of something possible to attain.... It has a lofty sound; it is well and finely said; but it can never be more than partly true. [John] Marshall's own career is a conspicuous illustration of the fact that the ideal is beyond the reach of human faculties to attain. He gave to the constitution of the United States the impress of his own mind; and the form of our constitutional law is what it is, because he moulded it while it was still plastic and malleable in the fire of his own intense convictions.

SOURCE: Benjamin N. Cardozo, The Nature of the Judicial Process 168–70 (1921).

country would no longer tolerate interference by the courts, the judiciary retreated. After retiring from the Court, Justice Roberts explained why the judiciary chose to step back and allow the expansion of national power over economic conditions: "Looking back, it is difficult to see how the Court could have resisted the popular urge for uniform standards throughout the country—for what in effect was a unified economy." Owen J. Roberts, The Court and the Constitution 61 (1951).

To associate litigation with economic and social forces is not meant to treat adjudication as just another form of politics. Judges make policy, but not in the same manner as legislators and executives. Unlike the elected branches, the judiciary is not expected to satisfy the needs of the majority. Although judges have an opportunity to engage in their own form of lobbying, they are not supposed to participate in ex parte meetings open to only one party—privileges routinely exercised by legislators and administrators. Most lobbying of the executive and legislative branches is open and direct; lobbying the judiciary is filtered through legal briefs, professional meetings, and law review articles. The executive and legislative branches have elaborate mechanisms for handling public relations, self-promotion, and contacts with the press. For the most part, judges release their opinions and remain silent. If executive officials and legislators are criticized in the press, they can respond in kind. Judges, with rare exceptions, take their lumps without retaliation.

Operations of the political branches can resemble those of the courts. Although responsive to majoritarian pressures, Congress and the President are also sensitive to minority rights and can protect those rights as well as, if not better than, the courts. Since the days of President Franklin D. Roosevelt, executive orders and congressional statutes have advanced the cause of civil rights. Many religious freedoms are the result of statutes passed by Congress and the states. The political branches are more at liberty to engage in ad hoc actions, but they usually follow general principles and precedents of their own and feel an obligation to present a reasoned explanation for their decisions.

B. LOBBYING THE COURTS

Private organizations accept litigation as part of the political process. They may conclude that their interests will be better served through court action than through the legislative and executive branches.

Thurgood Marshall on Group Pressures

In last year's address, Justice Clark spoke to you of one of the most basic institutions for the attainment of justice—the courts. I speak to you tonight of another "institution" essential to the attainment of justice, an institution perhaps even more basic. No matter how solemn and profound the declarations of principle contained in our charter of government, no matter how dedicated and independent our judiciary, true justice can only be obtained through the actions of committed individuals, individuals acting both independently and through organized groups.

... As we move into the future, the role formerly filled for the most part by individuals will have to be filled to an increasingly large degree by organized group practice....

My message can be aptly illustrated by the history of the Civil War amendments, a history in which I was in recent years fortunate enough to have played a small part. That history demonstrates that mere declarations of rights have not been sufficient to secure justice. It further illustrates that true progress can only be made by organized effort. The rights guaranteed by our Constitution are not self-enforcing; they can be made meaningful only by legislative or judicial action. As we shall see, legislation does not pass itself and the courts cannot act in the absence of a controversy. Organized, committed effort is necessary to promote legislation and institute legal action on any significant scale.

SOURCE: Thurgood Marshall, "Group Action in the Pursuit of Justice," 44 N.Y.U. L. Rev. 661, 662–63 (1969).

In 1963 Justice Brennan called litigation "a form of political expression." Groups unable to achieve their objectives through the electoral process often turn to the judiciary: "under the conditions of modern government, litigation may well be the sole practicable avenue open to a minority to petition for redress of grievances." NAACP v. Button, 371 U.S. 415, 429–30 (1963). It could also be said that under the conditions of modern government, appeals to the elected branches may well be the sole practicable avenue open to a minority after being rebuffed in the courts. For groups such as the National Association for the Advancement of Colored People (NAACP) and the American Civil Liberties Union (ACLU), litigation is not merely a technique for resolving private differences. It is a form of political action. In re Primus, 436 U.S. 412, 428 (1978). In an article in 1969, Justice Thurgood Marshall explained the importance of individual and group efforts to pressure courts and the elected branches (see box above).

The use of litigation in the 1940s and 1950s to shape social policy led to broader public participation and produced fundamental changes in the amicus curiae (friend of the court) brief. Originally, such briefs permitted third parties, without any direct interest in the case, to bring certain facts to the attention of the court to avoid judicial error. Over the years it lost this innocent quality and became an instrument used by private groups to advance their cause. The amicus curiae brief moved "from neutrality to partisanship, from friendship to advocacy." Samuel Krislov, 72 Yale L. J. 694 (1963). The briefs are now regularly used as part of the interest group struggle in the courts. The number of amicus briefs increased so rapidly that the Supreme Court adopted a rule in November 1949 to control their filing. With the exception of government units, all parties must consent to the filing of an amicus brief. If a party objects, the applicant must request the Court's permission to file.

The political nature of litigation is underscored by many familiar examples. Through dozens of court actions, the Jehovah's Witnesses secured such rights as the refusal to salute or pledge allegiance to the American flag, the right to solicit from house to house, and the right to preach in the streets without a license. The NAACP created a Legal Defense and Educational Fund to pursue rights denied blacks by Congress and state legislatures. A series of victories in the courts established basic rights for blacks in voting, housing, education, and jury service. The National Consumers' League channeled its resources into litigation and won important protections for factory workers. The American Liberty League, organized by conservative businessmen, turned to litigation in an effort to prevent the enactment of economic regulation by Congress.

Through the publication of articles, books, and commission reports, authors hope to influence a future court decision. Reliance on this body of literature has been of deep concern to many legislators who fear that the judiciary indiscriminately considers "unknown, unrecognized and nonauthoritative text books, law review articles, and other writings of propaganda artists and lobbyists." 103 Cong. Rec. 16160 (1957). The author of this statement, Congressman Wright Patman, complained that the Supreme Court had turned increasingly for guidance to private publications and studies promoted by the administration. The research was designed, he said, not to study an issue objectively but to advance the particular views of private interests trying, through the medium of publication, to influence the judiciary's disposition of public-policy questions. Experts have pointed out that the members of these study committees and commissions are aware that lawyers will cite the reports in their briefs "and that the real impact of this might very well be in the decisions made by courts and administrative agencies." Id. at 16167 (Prof. Louis B. Schwartz).

The practice of citing professional journals goes back at least to Justice Brandeis in the 1920s. Other Justices, like Cardozo and Stone, adopted this technique as a way of keeping law current with changes in American society. Brandeis's opinions introduced a new meaning to the word *authority*. He believed that an opinion "derives its authority, just as law derives its existence, from all the facts of life. The judge is free to draw upon these facts wherever he can find them, if only they are helpful." Chester A. Newland, 48 Geo. L. J. 105, 140 (1959).

C. THE EXECUTIVE IN COURT

The Judiciary Act of 1789 established an Attorney General to prosecute and conduct all suits in the Supreme Court concerning the government. This office represented Congress as well as the President. Despite some ambiguity in the original statute as to whether the Attorney General was an executive officer in the same sense as the heads of the State, Treasury, and War Departments, the first Attorney General (Edmund Randolph) attended Cabinet meetings and was early identified as an administrative official.

Unlike the heads of the executive departments, who received full-time salaries, the Attorney General received a nominal sum and was expected to maintain a private practice to supplement his income. Randolph complained that he was "a sort of mongrel between the State and the U.S.; called an officer of some rank under the latter, and yet thrust out to get a livelihood in the former, — perhaps in a petty mayor's or county court." Leonard D. White, The Federalists 164–65 (1948). The staff of the Attorney General was so small that outside counsel had to be hired to conduct the government's business in court. Partly to do away with this expense, in 1870 Congress established a Justice Department and created the office of Solicitor General to assist the Attorney General. To the Solicitor General fell the primary responsibility of representing the federal government in court.

The Solicitor General

Contemporary duties of the Solicitor General are broad-ranging. After consulting agency officials, the Solicitor General conducts (or assigns and supervises) Supreme Court cases, including appeals, petitions regarding certiorari, and the preparation of briefs and arguments; authorizes or declines to authorize appeals by the federal government to appellate courts; authorizes the filing of amicus briefs by the government in all appellate courts; and may authorize intervention by the government in cases involving the constitutionality of acts of Congress (see box on next page). The Supreme Court recognizes the Solicitor General's "traditional role in conducting and controlling all Supreme Court lit-

Duties of Solicitor General

The following-described matters are assigned to, and shall be conducted, handled, or supervised by, the Solicitor General, in consultation with each agency or official concerned:

(a) Conducting, or assigning and supervising, all Supreme Court cases, including appeals, petitions for and in opposition to certiorari, briefs and arguments, and ... settlement thereof.

(b) Determining whether, and to what extent, appeals will be taken by the Government to all appellate courts (including petitions for rehearing *en banc* and petitions to such courts for the issuance of extraordinary writs) and ... advising on the approval of settlements of cases in which

he had determined that an appeal would be taken.

(c) Determining whether a brief *amicus curiae* will be filed by the Government, or whether the Government will intervene, in any appellate court.

(d) Assisting the Attorney General, the Deputy Attorney General and the Associate Attorney General in the development of broad Department program policy.

. . .

The Solicitor General may in consultation with each agency or official concerned, authorize intervention by the Government in cases involving the constitutionality of acts of Congress.

Source: 28 C.F.R. §§ 0.20–0.21.

igation on behalf of the United States and its agencies." FEC v. NRA Political Victory Fund, 513 U.S. 88, 93 (1994).

The cases that flow through the office of Solicitor General raise complex and specialized issues, but, as a former Solicitor General remarked, the incumbent "must try to discover the social tensions, the reverberations of strife and passion, the political issues, the clashes of interest that are dressed up in technical legal forms." Simon E. Sobeloff, 41 A.B.A.J. 229, 279 (1955). To discharge that responsibility, the Solicitor General juggles several conflicting assignments. As the federal government's lawyer, the Solicitor General is an advocate but is also positioned to play a somewhat detached role. By entering only at the appellate level, the Solicitor General does not begin with the same emotional attachment as do the original parties in district court (including agency attorneys). The Solicitor General must also decide, out of a multitude of cases requested by the agencies, which ones deserve the attention of the Supreme Court.

Because of the frequency of appearances before the Supreme Court, the Solicitor General has been characterized as the Court's "ninth-and-a-half" member and serves many functions for the Court:

> The Supreme Court's frequent invitation to the Solicitor General to participate as amicus in constitutional cases is one indication of his useful role. The Solicitor General and his staff have unparalleled experience in constitutional litigation. Their access to and knowledge of the government apparatus not only enable them to inform the Court of factors unknown to private parties, but also to proffer statutory grounds for a decision avoiding the constitutional issues raised. The Solicitor General may indicate the relationship of the case to others pending on the docket, or the particular infirmities or strengths of the case for resolving constitutional or statutory issues. Knowing the Justices' proclivities, the Solicitor General may be able to offer a compromise solution that can gain a majority vote of the Court. The Supreme Court, lacking an extensive staff of its own, often benefits from the Solicitor General's impartial and sophisticated analysis of such constitutional cases. 78 Yale L. J. 1442, 1480 (1969).

The long-term and "impartial" objectives of the Solicitor General compete with, and are sometimes subordinated to, the particular and immediate needs of the President. This relationship is especially common in the field of national security. In arguing cases involving the discharge of federal employees, exclusion and deportation of aliens, and actions against conscientious objectors, Solicitors General in the past have shown little sympathy for fundamental notions of individual liberties or due process. Kathryn Mickle Werdeger, "The Solicitor General and Administrative Due Process," 36 G.W. L. Rev. 481 (1968).

Attorneys General and Solicitors General are legal officers, operating as members of the bar and officers of the court. However, they are also executive officials responsible to the President. As underscored by the actions against Japanese Americans during World War II, Justice Department attorneys at times swallow their doubts and defend government actions that seem to them not merely unwise but unconstitutional. Under these conditions, constitutional issues are subordinated to the task of behaving as the "President's lawyers." Peter H. Irons, Justice at War 350–61 (1982). Rex Lee, Solicitor General during the Reagan administration, said that one of his duties was "to represent his client, the president of the United States. One of the ways to implement the president's policies is through positions taken in court. When I have that opportunity, I'm going to take it." 69 A.B.A.J. 734, 736 (1983). If a Solicitor General becomes too partisan, there is risk of losing the trust and confidence of the Supreme Court.

There is often friction between the Justice Department and the White House. For example, during the Carter presidency, Attorney General Bell complained about White House interference in litigation that involved questions of church-state separation, affirmative action, and civil rights. Vice President Mondale, his aide Bert Carp, domestic adviser Stuart Eizenstat, and other White House officials treated many of these matters as broad policy questions rather than technical legal issues. In one case, after the Justice Department had taken a position on a church-state question, President Carter responded to political considerations and personally intervened to overrule the decision. Griffin B. Bell, Taking Care of the Law 24–25 (1982).

The Tide of Public Opinion

Efforts to subordinate constitutional principles to political tactics can backfire against the President. Faced with a nationwide strike in 1952, President Truman decided to attack the steel companies and work informally with the labor unions rather than invoke the Taft-Hartley Act, which he had vetoed. When that strategy failed, he seized the steel mills and claimed that he could act "for whatever is for the best of the country." Public Papers of the Presidents, 1952, at 273. Realizing that his definition of presidential authority had shocked the country because it raised questions about his power to seize even the press and the radio, he hastily explained that his powers were derived from the Constitution and that individual rights were protected. Id. at 301.

In district court, however, the Justice Department told Judge Pine that the courts had no power to constrain the President. Presidential power could be curbed only by the ballot box or impeachment. This audacious and ill-advised presentation provoked the judiciary to act boldly to reject a sweeping and dangerous theory of inherent executive authority (see reading on Steel Seizure Case). The political climate invited a rebuff to presidential power. As Chief Justice Rehnquist noted in 1987, the Steel Seizure Case was "one of those celebrated constitutional issues where what might be called the tide of public opinion suddenly began to run against the government, for a number of reasons, and that this tide of public opinion had a considerable influence on the Court." William H. Rehnquist, The Supreme Court 95 (1987). Justice Robert Jackson spoke perceptively about the impact of public opinion (see box on next page).

Control Over Litigation

The Justice Department has made a concerted effort to retain exclusive control over agency litigation policy. Loss of authority to the agencies can produce an incoherent and ineffective strategy in court. Some of the legal setbacks of the New Deal can be traced to the splintering of litigating authority in

Justice Jackson on Public Opinion

The judge who would resolve uncertainties of interpretation by conscious deference to public opinion will find new pitfalls in his path. Is there any more reliable test of prevalence of a public opinion or will than the election returns? That certainly is its legal manifestation, and I see no reason to believe that judges have better understanding of it than those the public has elected to represent them. To the extent that public opinion of the hour is admitted to the process of constitutional interpretation, the basis for judicial review of legislative action disappears. If interpretation is not to be a mere following of election returns but a legal process, the utmost deference that courts can consciously pay to political trends is a strong, but rebuttable, presumption in favor of the constitutionality of action by the political branches.

Exclude as far as humanly possible the pressures of group opinion, but let us not deceive ourselves: long-sustained public opinion does influence the process of constitutional interpretation. Each new member of the ever-changing personnel of our courts brings to his task the assumptions and accustomed thought of a later period. The practical play of the forces of politics is such that judicial power has often delayed but never permanently defeated the persistent will of a substantial majority. Judicial review in practice therefore has proved less an obstacle to majority rule than the followers of Mr. Jefferson feared and less a guaranty of the *status quo* than the followers of Mr. Hamilton hoped.

Source: Vital Speeches, No. 24, Vol. XIX, at 761 (October 1, 1953).

the Roosevelt administration. The Justice Department had to compete with autonomous efforts by the Interior Department and other agencies. Peter H. Irons, The New Deal Lawyers (1982).

The tremendous growth of litigation since the 1930s has made decentralization inevitable. Congress has given several agencies independent litigating authority and the Justice Department regularly enters into special agreements called Memoranda of Understanding (MOUs), which allow agencies to litigate certain types of cases at the district and appellate levels. In 1994 the Supreme Court held that the Federal Election Commission did not have general statutory authority to appeal its cases to the Supreme Court. Like other agencies, it must receive the Solicitor General's authorization. The FEC does have statutory authority to seek appeal from the Supreme Court in the specific area of presidential election funds. FEC v. NRA Political Victory Fund, 513 U.S. 88 (1994).

Steel Seizure Case of 1952:
Oral Argument Before the District Court

On April 24, 1952, in oral argument before U.S. District Judge David A. Pine, Assistant Attorney General Holmes Baldridge presented the government's case in defense of the seizure of steel companies by Secretary of Commerce Charles Sawyer. Judge Pine's decision, declaring the seizure illegal, was later affirmed by the Supreme Court. The following excerpt of the oral argument comes from House Document No. 534 (Part I), 82d Cong., 2d Sess. (1952), pp. 362–63, 371–73.

Mr. Baldridge: Our position is that there is no power in the Courts to restrain the President and, as I say, Secretary Sawyer is the alter ego of the President and not subject to injunctive order of the Court.

The Court: If the President directs Mr. Sawyer to take you into custody, right now, and have you executed in the morning you say there is no power by which the Court may intervene even by habeas corpus?

Mr. Baldridge: If there are statutes protecting me I would have a remedy.

The Court: What statute would protect you?

Mr. Baldridge: I do not recall any at the moment.

The Court: But on the question of the deprivation of your rights you have the Fifth Amendment; that is what protects you.

I would like an answer to that—what about that?

Mr. Baldridge: Well, as I was going to point out in a little while—

The Court (interposing): I will give you a chance to think about that overnight and you may answer me tomorrow....

The Court: Now, Mr. Attorney General, it is getting near the time when we shall have to stop. I wonder if you would give me such assistance as you can before we stop so that I can think about your viewpoint overnight, as to your power, or as to your client's power.

As I understand it, you do not assert any statutory power.

Mr. Baldridge: That is correct.

The Court: And you do not assert any express constitutional power.

Mr. Baldridge: Well, your Honor, we base the President's power on Sections 1, 2 and 3 of Article II of the Constitution, and whatever inherent, implied or residual powers may flow therefrom.

We do not propose to get into a discussion of semantics with counsel for plaintiffs. We say that when an emergency situation in this country arises that is of such importance to the entire welfare of the country that something has to be done about it and has to be done now, and there is no statutory provision for handling the matter, that it is the duty of the Executive to step in and protect the national security and the national interests. We say that Article II of the Constitution, which provides that the Executive power of the Government shall reside in the President, that he shall faithfully execute the laws of the office and he shall be Commander-in-Chief of the Army and of the Navy and that he shall take care that the laws be faithfully executed, are sufficient to permit him to meet any national emergency that might arise, be it peace time, technical war time, or actual war time.

The Court: So you contend the Executive has unlimited power in time of an emergency?

Mr. Baldridge: He has the power to take such action as is necessary to meet the emergency.

The Court: If the emergency is great, it is unlimited, is it?

Mr. Baldridge: I suppose if you carry it to its logical conclusion, that is true. But I do want to point out that there are two limitations on the Executive power. One is the ballot box and the other is impeachment.

The Court: Then, as I understand it, you claim that in time of emergency the Executive has this great power.

Mr. Baldridge: That is correct.

The Court: And that the Executive determines the emergencies and the Courts cannot even review whether it is an emergency.

Mr. Baldridge: That is correct.

D. CONGRESSIONAL DUTIES

During the nineteenth century it was not unusual for members of Congress to maintain a flourishing business in the federal courts. Daniel Webster is the most prominent example of a member of Congress with a dual career as lawyer and legislator. While serving in Congress as a Representative and a Senator, he delivered forceful arguments in major cases before the Supreme Court, which at that time was located in a chamber beneath the Senate. Congressmen supplemented their incomes by "duck[ing] into the lower chamber, so to speak, for a lucrative hour or two. After all, should not those who made laws help interpret them?" Maurice G. Baxter, Daniel Webster & the Supreme Court 31 (1966).

Although Congress depends on the Justice Department to protect its interests, members of Congress may intervene on an individual basis. In a 1926 case, involving the President's power to remove executive officials, the Supreme Court invited Senator George Wharton Pepper to serve as amicus curiae. His oral argument and an extract of his brief, together with those of the appellant and the Solicitor General, are printed immediately before the Court's opinion. Myers v. United States, 272 U.S. 52, 65–88 (1926).

During the impoundment disputes of the Nixon administration, members of Congress submitted an amicus brief on behalf of the plaintiff suing the administration. State Highway Commission of Missouri v. Volpe, 479 F.2d 1099 n.1 (8th Cir. 1973). In the abortion case eventually decided by the

POLITICAL DYNAMICS OF CONSTITUTIONAL LAW

Supreme Court in 1980, the district court permitted Senator James L. Buckley, Senator Jesse A. Helms, and Congressman Henry J. Hyde to intervene as defendants. Harris v. McRae, 448 U.S. 297, 303 (1980). The Ninth Circuit invited both the House and the Senate to submit briefs concerning a legislative veto used by Congress in deportation cases. When the case reached the Supreme Court, both Houses of Congress intervened to protect their interests and participated before the Court during oral argument. INS v. Chadha, 462 U.S. 919 (1983). The attorneys for Congress defended the legislative veto, but in a separate brief nine members of the House of Representatives urged the Supreme Court to declare the legislative veto unconstitutional.

Legislative precedents in the House and the Senate do not permit the Speaker or the Chair to rule on questions of constitutionality. Points of order, raising the issue of unconstitutional provisions, are referred to the full chamber for decision. In the Senate, a member may raise a point of order that a bill or an amendment is legislation that changes the Constitution. If there is substantial doubt within Congress concerning the constitutionality of a provision, legislators can place within the bill a procedure authorizing expedited review by the courts. Examples include the Federal Election Campaign Act amendments of 1974. 86 Stat. 1285, §315. Two years later the Supreme Court declared the contested provision unconstitutional. Buckley v. Valeo, 424 U.S. 1 (1976). A similar procedure was placed in the Gramm-Rudman-Hollings Act of 1985. 99 Stat. 1098, §274 (1985). The provision in question was struck down a year later. Bowsher v. Synar, 478 U.S. 714 (1986).

Standing for Members

A striking development over the past decade is the frequency with which members of Congress take issues directly to the courts for resolution. Senator Edward M. Kennedy was successful at both the district court and appellate court levels in challenging Nixon's attempt to use the pocket veto during brief recesses of the House and Senate. Kennedy v. Sampson, 364 F.Supp. 1075 (D.D.C. 1973); Kennedy v. Sampson, 511 F.2d 430 (D.C. Cir. 1974). As a result of those lower court decisions, the Ford administration announced that it would use the pocket veto only during the final adjournment at the end of a Congress. 121 Cong. Rec. 41884 (1975); 122 Cong. Rec. 11202 (1976). Senator Kennedy was successful because his prerogative to vote (to override a presidential veto) had been denied by the pocket veto.

Other members of Congress have been unsuccessful when they have tried to achieve political goals from the courts that are available through the regular legislative process. In such cases the members have been told by the courts that (1) they lack standing to sue, (2) the issue is not ripe for adjudication, or (3) the matter is a "political question" to be decided by Congress and the President. Legislators must overcome the standing hurdles (faced by any litigant) by showing that (1) they have suffered injury, (2) the interests are within the zone protected by the statute or constitutional provision, (3) the injury is caused by the challenged action, and (4) the injury can be redressed by a favorable court decision. Legislators face an additional obstacle. If they suffer from an injury that can be redressed by colleagues acting through the regular legislative process, a court will instruct the lawmakers to use the institutional powers available to them.

Throughout these cases, there is a general wariness on the part of judges that the controversy is really not between Congress and the executive. Rather, it is one group of legislators pitted against another. Federal judges may suspect that members of Congress turn to the courts because they have been unable to attract sufficient votes from colleagues to pass a bill. When judges believe that legislators have failed to make use of remedies available within Congress, they have been denied standing to resolve the issue in court. It was partly on that basis that the Supreme Court in 1997 denied standing to some members of Congress who had challenged the constitutionality of the Line Item Veto Act of 1996. RAINES v. BYRD, 521 U.S. 811 (1997). There may be other disputes that members of Congress could legitimately bring to court (see box).

Over the last half century, members of Congress have become concerned about the refusal of the Justice Department to defend the constitutionality of certain statutory provisions. Sometimes the De-

---

Standing for Members

The item veto case was relatively easy for the Court to sidestep. To the extent that there was injury to Congress, it was self-administered. If surrendering some of its spending power to the President was repugnant, members of Congress had plenty of ways to recover the power: repeal the statute, add subsequent restrictions to the President's power, or write bills and committee reports in such a way that the President had fewer opportunities to cancel an item.

The item veto case was particularly weak for Congress. As the Court noted at the end of *Raines v. Byrd* (1997), Congress had not authorized Senator Byrd and his colleagues to bring the suit. In fact, both Houses of Congress had filed briefs opposing their action.

On other constitutional disputes, the President causes the injury and Congress has few or no institutional remedies. One example is the *Kennedy* pocket veto case. Because President Nixon did not return the vetoed bill to Congress, legislators had no options other than to pass the bill again and remain in session to prevent a pocket veto. Another dispute that might be litigated is the war power. Suppose Congress prohibited the President from engaging in a particular military action and the President vetoed the bill. If Congress lacked the two-thirds majority needed in each chamber to override the veto, could members bring the issue to the Court, having exhausted all legislative remedies? Without a judicial check, a President could initiate and continue a war so long as he retained a one-third plus one minority in either chamber to prevent the override. Would a court tackle that constitutional issue?

partment took this position after deciding that a statute infringed on presidential power or was so patently unconstitutional that it could not be defended, as in the bill of attainder case in 1946. United States v. Lovett, 328 U.S. 303 (1946). Because of statutory language, the Attorney General must now report to Congress whenever the Justice Department does not intend to defend the constitutionality of a law passed by Congress. These reports specify the statutory provision and contain a detailed explanation by the Department for calling the provision unconstitutional.

Congress has always been able to hire private counsel to defend itself, as it did in the civil action brought against it by Congressman Adam Clayton Powell in the 1960s. Yet there was no established procedure for Congress to defend its statutes when the Justice Department chose not to do so. The institutional interests of Congress, as noted by the Senate Committee on Governmental Affairs in 1977, made it "inappropriate as a matter of principle and of the constitutional separation of powers for the legislative branch to rely upon and entrust the defense of its vital constitutional powers to the advocate for the executive branch, the Attorney General." S. Rept. No. 170, 95th Cong., 1st Sess. 11. The committee recalled that in two cases involving the power of Congress to investigate, the Justice Department withdrew its representation of Congress just as the litigation reached the Supreme Court, after having represented Congress in the district and appellate courts. Id. at 12.

As part of the Ethics in Government Act of 1978, the Senate established an Office of Senate Legal Counsel. The Senate Legal Counsel and the Deputy Legal Counsel are appointed by the President pro tempore of the Senate from among recommendations submitted by the majority and minority leaders of the Senate. The principal duty of the Counsel is to defend the Senate or a committee, subcommittee, member, officer, or employee of the Senate when directed by two-thirds of the members of the Joint Leadership Group or by the adoption of a Senate resolution. Individual Senators may initiate suits on their own. In the House of Representatives, the Office of General Counsel handles litigation that involves members, House officers, and staff.

Raines v. Byrd

521 U.S. 811 (1997)

The Line Item Veto Act of 1996 provided that any member of Congress may bring a lawsuit to challenge the constitutionality of the statute. Senator Robert C. Byrd and five other legislators sued under this provision, a district judge held that the statute violated the Constitution, and the matter was brought directly to the Supreme Court.

CHIEF JUSTICE REHNQUIST delivered the opinion of the Court.

The District Court for the District of Columbia declared the Line Item Veto Act unconstitutional. On this direct appeal, we hold that appellees lack standing to bring this suit, and therefore direct that the judgment of the District Court be vacated and the complaint dismissed....

II

Under Article III, § 2 of the Constitution, the federal courts have jurisdiction over this dispute between appellants and appellees only if it is a "case" or "controversy." This is a "bedrock requirement." ... As we said in Simon v. Eastern Ky. Welfare Rights Organization, 426 U.S. 26, 37 (1976), "No principle is more fundamental to the judiciary's proper role in

our system of government than the constitutional limitation of federal-court jurisdiction to actual cases or controversies."

... In the light of this overriding and time-honored concern about keeping the judiciary's power within its proper constitutional sphere, we must put aside the natural urge to proceed directly to the merits of this important dispute and to "settle" it for the sake of convenience and efficiency. Instead, we must carefully inquire as to whether appellees have met their burden of establishing that their claimed injury is personal, particularized, concrete, and otherwise judicially cognizable.

III

We have never had occasion to rule on the question of legislative standing presented here. In Powell *v. McCormack*, 395 U.S. 486, 496, 512–514 (1969), we held that a Member of Congress' constitutional challenge to his exclusion from the House of Representatives (and his consequent loss of salary) presented an Article III case or controversy. But *Powell* does not help appellees. First, appellees have not been singled out for specially unfavorable treatment as opposed to other Members of their respective bodies. Their claim is that the Act causes a type of institutional injury (the diminution of legislative power), which necessarily damages all Members of Congress and both Houses of Congress equally.... Second, appellees do not claim that they have been deprived of something to which they *personally* are entitled—such as their seats as Members of Congress after their constituents had elected *them*. Rather, appellees' claim of standing is based on a loss of political power, not loss of any private right, which would make the injury more concrete. Unlike the injury claimed by Congressman Adam Clayton Powell, the injury claimed by the Members of Congress here is not claimed in any private capacity but solely because they are Members of Congress.... If one of the Members were to retire tomorrow, he would no longer have a claim; the claim would be possessed by his successor instead. The claimed injury thus runs (in a sense) with the Member's seat, a seat which the Member holds (it may quite arguably be said) as trustee for his constituents, not as a prerogative of personal power....

[*The Court also distinguishes the item veto suit from an earlier case, Coleman v. Miller, 307 U.S. 433 (1939), in which the Court had upheld standing for state legislators who had claimed an institutional injury. But in this state case, twenty of Kansas' forty state senators voted not to ratify the proposed Child Labor Amendment to the Federal Constitution. With the vote deadlocked 20 to 20, the amendment ordinarily would not have been ratified. However, the state's lieutenant governor, the presiding officer of the state senate, cast a deciding vote in favor of the amendment and it was deemed ratified. The twenty senators who had voted against the amendment, joined by a 21st senator and three state house members, filed an action to prevent ratification by the state. Senator Byrd and his colleagues could not argue that their votes on the Line Item Veto Act had not been given full effect. As the Court noted: "They simply lost that vote."*]

There would be nothing irrational about a system which granted standing in these cases; some European constitutional courts operate under one or another variant of such a regime [*allowing legislators to take constitutional questions to the courts*].... But

it is obviously not the regime that has obtained under our Constitution to date. Our regime contemplates a more restricted role for Article III courts....

IV

In sum, appellees have alleged no injury to themselves as individuals (contra *Powell*), the institutional injury they allege is wholly abstract and widely dispersed (contra *Coleman*), and their attempt to litigate this dispute at this time and in this form is contrary to historical experience. We attach some importance to the fact that appellees have not been authorized to represent their respective Houses of Congress in this action, and indeed both Houses actively oppose their suit.... We also note that our conclusion neither deprives Members of Congress of an adequate remedy (since they may repeal the Act or exempt appropriations bills from its reach), nor forecloses the Act from constitutional challenge (by someone who suffers judicially cognizable injury as a result of the Act)....

JUSTICE SOUTER, concurring in the judgment, with whom JUSTICE GINSBURG joins, concurring.

. . .

JUSTICE STEVENS, dissenting.

The Line Item Veto Act purports to establish a procedure for the creation of laws that are truncated versions of bills that have been passed by the Congress and presented to the President for signature. If the procedure were valid, it would deny every Senator and every Representative any opportunity to vote for or against the truncated measure that survives the exercise of the President's cancellation authority. Because the opportunity to cast such votes is a right guaranteed by the text of the Constitution, I think it clear that the persons who are deprived of that right by the Act have standing to challenge its constitutionality. Moreover, because the impairment of that constitutional right has an immediate impact on their official powers, in my judgment they need not wait until after the President has exercised his cancellation authority to bring suit. Finally, the same reason that the respondents have standing provides a sufficient basis for concluding that the statute is unconstitutional.

. . .

Assuming for the moment that this procedure is constitutionally permissible, and that the President will from time to time exercise the power to cancel portions of a just-enacted-law, it follows that the statute deprives every Senator and every Representative of the right to vote for or against measure that may become law. The appellees cast their challenge to the constitutionality of the Act in a slightly different way. Their complaint asserted that the Act "alter[s] the legal and practical effect of all votes they may cast on bills containing such separately vetoable items" and "divest[s] the[m] of their constitutional role in the repeal of legislation." Complaint ¶ 14. These two claimed injuries are at best the same as the injury on which I rest my analysis....

JUSTICE BREYER, dissenting.

· · ·

I concede that there would be no case or controversy here were the dispute before us not truly adversary, or were it not concrete and focused. But the interests that the parties assert are genuine and opposing, and the parties are therefore truly adverse.... Moreover, as JUSTICE STEVENS points out, the harm that the plaintiffs suffer (on their view of the law) consists in part of the systematic abandonment of laws for which a majority voted, in part of the creation of other laws in violation of procedural rights which (they say) the Constitution provides them, and in part of the consequent and immediate impediment to their ability to do the job that the Constitution requires them to do....

In sum, I do not believe that the Court can find this case nonjusticiable without overruling *Coleman*. Since it does not do so, I need not decide whether the systematic nature, seriousness, and immediacy of the harm would make this dispute constitutionally justiciable even in *Coleman*'s absence. Rather, I can and would find this case justiciable on *Coleman*'s authority. I add that because the majority has decided that this dispute is not now justiciable and has expressed no view on the merits of the appeal, I shall not discuss the merits either, but reserve them for future argument.

E. JUDGE AS LAWMAKER

From the common law of England to the decisions of American courts, judge-made law has been a fact of life. Lawmaking by legislatures was a late development in our history, and one that judges opposed because of its blunt and imprecise quality. It is disingenuous to pretend that judges "find" the law rather than "make" it. Jeremiah Smith, who taught law at Harvard after a career on the New Hampshire Supreme Court, was refreshingly candid on this point. When asked "Do judges make law?" he responded: "'Course they do. Made some myself." Paul A. Freund, The Supreme Court of the United States 28 (1961). Few statutes or constitutional provisions are clear in meaning. Judicial interpretation, broadly exercised, becomes a substitute for legislation. Because judges fill in the "interstices" of law, Holmes said he recognized "without hesitation that judges do and must legislate." Southern Pacific Co. v. Jensen, 244 U.S. 205, 221 (1917).

There have been periods when judicial lawmaking became so flagrant and arbitrary that it provoked biting criticism. At the end of the nineteenth century, after legislative attempts to regulate the economy were frustrated by Supreme Court decisions, certain members of the Court condemned what they regarded as a judicial assumption of power. When the Court in 1890 decided that the judiciary, not the legislature, was the final arbiter in regulating railroad fares, freight rates, and other charges on the public, Justice Bradley's dissent considered this an arrogation of authority the Court had no right to make. Chicago, Milwaukee & St. Paul R.R. Co. v. Minnesota, 134 U.S. 418, 462–63 (1890). In the Income Tax Case of 1895, Justice White's dissent accused his brethren of amending the Constitution by judicial fiat. For more than a century the federal government and constitutional scholars had confined the definition of direct tax to capitation and land taxes. The Court decided to add a third category: the income tax. White said that the Constitution should have been amended directly rather than by the judiciary. Pollock v. Farmers' Home & Trust Col, 157 U.S. 429, 639 (1895). It took a constitutional amendment—the Sixteenth—to override the Court.

Dissenting in a 1904 case, Justice Harlan charged that the court "entrenches upon the domain of the legislative department.... It has made, not declared, law." Schick v. United States, 195 U.S. 65, 99 (1904). In an antitrust decision in 1911 he assailed the Court for converting the formula of the Sherman Act from restraint of trade to "rule of reason." Borrowing language from an earlier decision, he charged that the Court had read into the Act *"by way of judicial legislation an exception that is not placed there by the lawmaking branch of the Government,* and this is to be done upon the theory that the impolicy of such legislation is so clear that it cannot be supposed Congress intended the natural import of the language it used. This *we cannot and ought not to do....*" By mere interpretation, he said, the Court had modified an act of Congress and deprived it of its force in combating monopoly practices. The most ominous part of the decision for Harlan was "the usurpation by the judicial branch of the Government of the functions of the legislative department." Standard Oil v. United States, 221 U.S. 1, 88, 99, 103 (1911).

Contemporary Issues

The judiciary plays an active legislative role by interpreting such general concepts as "equal protection" and "due process." The abortion decision of *Roe* v. *Wade* (1973) represents for many scholars a spectacular example of judicial legislation. Writing for the majority, Justice Blackmun declared that during the first three months (trimester) of pregnancy a physician, after consulting with the woman, is free to perform an abortion without interference by the state. During the second trimester, the state may regulate and even prevent abortion except where it is necessary to preserve the life or health of the mother. The state's interest expands during the third trimester. In one of the two dissents, Justice Rehnquist said that the Court's "conscious weighing of competing factors ... is far more appropriate to a legislative judgment than to a judicial one." Roe v. Wade, 410 U.S. at 173. After almost two decades of criticism, in 1992 the Court abandoned its trimester analysis. Planned Parenthood v. Casey, 505 U.S. 833 (1992).

If the weighing of competing factors constitutes an act of lawmaking, the courts do little else. Questions of federalism and the commerce power turn on the competing interests of the federal government and the states. The courts regularly balance the government's national security interests against the rights of individual freedom. The needs of law enforcement collide with the rights to privacy. A judge's decision to close a trial conflicts with the right of the press and the public to attend. The power of Congress to investigate the executive branch must be weighed against the President's privilege to withhold information.

In addition to this level of involvement, federal judges act on issues that are within the jurisdiction of Congress and could have been addressed through the regular legislative process. Justice Powell noted that much of the expanded role of the Warren Court "was a reaction to the sluggishness of the legislative branch in addressing urgent needs for reform." 62 A.B.A.J. 1454, 1455 (1976). There are other pressures on judges to legislate. If one section or provision of a statute is unconstitutional, courts may decide to "sever" that portion while retaining the balance of the statute. Such decisions require courts to judge whether the altered statute, as redesigned by the judiciary, is consistent with legislative objectives. Judicial rewriting can provoke comments from colleagues that the majority opinion erred by "simply deleting the crucial statutory language and using the words that remain as the raw materials for a new statute of his own making." Regan v. Time, Inc., 468 U.S. 641, 673 (1984). Justice Harlan once complained that the Court, in the name of interpreting the will of Congress, had resorted to "judicial surgery" to remove an offending section, so transforming the statute that the Court performed "a lobotomy." Welsh v. United States, 398 U.S. 333, 351 (1970).

F. JUDGE AS ADMINISTRATOR

Judicial lawmaking is a venerable and long-debated topic. A more contemporary issue, linked to the public-law litigation explosion, concerns judges who actually *administer* a political system to protect legal rights. Attorney General William French Smith offered this criticism in 1981:

... federal courts have attempted to restructure entire school systems in desegregation cases—

and to maintain continuing review over basic administrative decisions. They have asserted similar control over entire prison systems and public housing projects. They have restructured the employment criteria to be used by American business and government — even to the extent of mandating numerical results based upon race or gender. No area seems immune from judicial administration. At least one federal judge even attempted to administer a local sewer system. 21 Judges' Journal 4, 7 (Winter 1982).

Involvement in administrative affairs is not a totally new phenomenon for the courts. Nineteenth-century judges reviewed dismissals of federal employees, ordered administrators to carry out "ministerial" (nondiscretionary) duties, and decided questions about the liability of federal officials subjected to lawsuits. With the rise of federal regulatory commissions toward the end of the nineteenth century and the early decades of the twentieth, federal courts became involved in reviewing agency rulemaking and adjudication.

The Administrative Procedure Act (APA) of 1946 provides that any person suffering legal wrong because of agency action is entitled to judicial review. The reviewing court "shall decide all relevant questions of law, interpret constitutional and statutory provisions, and determine the meaning or applicability of the terms of any agency action." Courts shall hold unlawful and set aside agency actions found to be arbitrary, capricious, an abuse of discretion, or contrary to law; contrary to constitutional right, power, privilege, or immunity; or unsupported by substantial evidence in cases subject to formal rulemaking. Although courts often defer to agency expertise and grant a presumption of regularity in favor of the federal government, judges may also require agencies to take a "hard look" at the decisions entrusted to their jurisdiction and insist on adequate documentation to support the agency's determinations.

The breadth of judicial administration is reflected in the efforts of District Judge W. Arthur Garrity, Jr., to desegregate the Boston school system. In 1975 he placed South Boston High School in temporary receivership under a supervisor appointed by him. His ruling came after more than a decade of racial discrimination by the local school board. Barry Stuart Roberts, 12 N.E. L. Rev. 55 (1976). Another federal judge, seeking to promote school desegregation in Wilmington, Delaware, "set a tax rate for the school district, ordered state payments to the district, required new training programs for teachers and administrators, mandated specific curricular offerings, ordered the reassignment of staff and called for the development of an 'appropriate human relations program'...." Terry W. Hartle, 41 Pub. Adm. Rev. 595, 599 (1981). Because of opposition from citizens and elected officials, judges gradually withdrew their involvement in school desegregation.

District Judge Frank M. Johnson, Jr., was deeply involved for more than a decade in administering certain institutions in Alabama. "The history of Alabama," he explained, "is replete with instances of state officials who could have chosen one of any number of courses to alleviate unconstitutional conditions but who chose instead to do nothing but punt the problem to the courts." Steven Brill, New York Magazine, April 26, 1976, at 38. Because of the failure of state officials to correct shocking deficiencies in state prisons, mental hospitals, and institutions for the retarded, Johnson repeatedly found violations of the Eighth and Fourteenth Amendments. He graphically described the conditions: "the evidence reflected that one resident was scalded to death when a fellow resident hosed water from one of the bath facilities on him; another died as a result of the insertion of a running water hose into his rectum by a working resident who was cleaning him; one died when soapy water was forced into his mouth; another died of a self-administered overdose of inadequately stored drugs; and authorities restrained another resident in a straightjacket for *nine years* to prevent him from sucking his hands and fingers." Frank M. Johnson, "The Constitution and the Federal District Judge," 54 Tex. L. Rev. 903 (1976).

Rather than devise specific steps to improve conditions, Johnson at first directed the state to design its own plan for upgrading the system to meet constitutional standards. After two deadlines passed without acceptable progress, Johnson intervened to define the minimal constitutional standards. The story suggests a solitary judge pitted against the state, but other parties intervened in the suit, including the Justice Department, the American Psychological Association, the American Orthopsychiatric Association, and the American Civil Liberties Union. Wyatt v. Stickney, 334 F.Supp. 1341 (M.D. Ala. 1971). Johnson was able to forge an effective alliance of state officials and private citizens to bring pressure on the legislature and the governor. A case of "judicial activism"? It is difficult to make that claim when the attorney for the state of Alabama admitted in open court that every prisoner in the state system was subjected to cruel and inhuman treatment within the meaning of the Eighth Amendment. Pugh v. Locke, 406 F.Supp. 318, 322, 329 & n.13 (M.D. Ala. 1976).

G. INDEPENDENT STATE ACTION

By interpreting their own constitutions and statutes, states can reach constitutional decisions that are markedly different from U.S. Supreme Court rulings. The federal Constitution provides only a minimum, or a floor, for the protection of individual rights and liberties. As noted by the U.S. Supreme Court, each state has the "sovereign right to adopt in its own Constitution individual liberties more expansive than those conferred by the Federal Constitution." PruneYard Shopping Center v. Robins, 447 U.S. 74, 81 (1980). When states want to express these independent views, they must make clear that their rulings depend exclusively on the constitution and laws of the state. If state courts base their decisions on "bona fide separate, adequate and independent grounds," the U.S. Supreme Court will not undertake a review. Michigan v. Long, 463 U.S. 1032 (1983). Under these circumstances, the "final word" on state constitutional law rests with the states, not the U.S. Supreme Court (see box).

Many of the so-called innovations by the U.S. Supreme Court were established first at the state level. Thus, in 1914 the Court ruled that papers illegally seized by federal officers had to be excluded in federal court as evidence (the exclusionary rule). Some states had already adopted that policy. When the Court applied the exclusionary rule to all of the states in 1961, it acknowledged that states were

---

A State Court Analyzes "Plain View"

In 1980 the Supreme Court of Washington held that a university police officer had exceeded his authority in seizing incriminating evidence in a student's room. The officer stopped the student who was carrying a bottle of gin and appeared to be under age. The student asked permission to return to his dormitory room to retrieve his identification card and the officer followed. From an open doorway the officer noticed what appeared to be marijuana seeds and a pipe. He entered the room, confirmed that the seeds were marijuana, and concluded that the pipe smelled of marijuana. The Supreme Court of Washington held that the evidence had been obtained illegally and could not be admitted at the trial. State v. Chrisman, 619 P.2d 971 (Wash. 1980).

The U.S. Supreme Court reversed the state court decision, holding that its "plain view" doctrine permits a law enforcement officer to seize incriminating evidence or contraband "when it is discovered in a place where the officer has a right to be." Washington v. Chrisman, 455 U.S. 1, 6 (1982). The case was returned to the state court for "further proceedings not inconsistent with this opinion."

In fact, on this next go-round the Supreme Court of Washington refused to accept the plain-view analysis offered by the U.S. Supreme Court. Whereas its 1980 decision had cited several federal decisions, this time the Supreme Court of Washington based its reasoning "solely and exclusively on the constitution and laws of the state of Washington." It concluded that it was right the first time and excluded the evidence. State v. Chrisman, 676 P.2d 419 (Wash. 1984).

moving increasingly in that direction anyway. Even now, the exclusionary rule leaves plenty of room for independent state action. Evidence admissible in federal court is not necessarily admissible in state court. In 1984, when the Supreme Court held that evidence resulting from a defective search warrant can be admitted if police believe they are acting in "good faith," this relaxed standard was later rejected by a number of state courts (see box in Chapter 14, Section E).

State independence is also strengthened by more explicit language in their constitutions. Although the Supreme Court has accepted the use of public funds for sectarian schools to pay for such expenses as transportation and textbooks, many state courts have denied this type of assistance because of highly restrictive language in their constitutions that prohibits the appropriation of public funds for any religious worship or instruction (see box in Chapter 12, Section D). Similarly, state constitutions are often far more explicit in protecting the rights of speech, assembly, and privacy. By interpreting this language, state courts can issue rulings that depart dramatically from U.S. Supreme Court doctrines. Independent constitutional interpretations by the states can satisfy the values we place on diversity, pluralism, representative government, and a distrust of centralized authority.

By participating in ballot initiatives in state elections, citizens regularly offer judgments on sensitive and controversial constitutional issues. In the state of Washington, voters in 1997 rejected a measure to legalize the medical use of marijuana, rejected a law requiring trigger locks on handguns and safety courses for owners, and rejected a proposal that barred job discrimination based on sexual orientation. Voters in Houston, Texas, rejected a measure to repeal affirmative action. Citizens in Orange County, California, supported a local school board's decision to drop bilingual education. The New York Times, November 11, 1997, at A28. In 1998, voters in California supported Proposition 227, which is designed to abolish bilingual education after no more than a year of intensive immersion in English. In a ballot initiative in 2000, California voters limited marriage to the union between man and woman, thereby excluding gay couples. In 2006, Arizonans rejected a similar amendment to their constitution. The issue of gay marriages returned to California in 2008, pitting the courts against the voters (see Chapter 17 for details).

H. WHO HAS THE "LAST WORD"?

The notion that the Constitution is somehow equivalent to Supreme Court decisions is a curious product of the twentieth century. One searches previous periods in vain for evidence that the judiciary enjoyed a monopoly on constitutional law. Nevertheless, students in undergraduate, graduate, and law schools are taught that the Court announces the "last word" on what the Constitution means. In 1992 Chief Justice Rehnquist wrote: "We rightly think of our courts as the final voice in the interpretation of our Constitution, and therefore tend to think of constitutional law in terms of cases decided by the courts." William H. Rehnquist, Grand Inquests 278 (1992). Law courses concentrate almost exclusively on case law, rather than exploring the complex (and far more interesting) process that involves the three branches of the national government, the states, and the general public.

This book develops the theme of coordinate construction—the opportunity for all three branches to interpret and shape the Constitution. That process is heavily influenced by pressures brought to bear by the public and organized interest groups, as well as by leadership and initiatives from state governments. The courts are an important element, but not the only one, in maintaining a constitutional order. Throughout this book there are many examples that explain the dynamic, open process of constitutional interpretation, which is constantly shaped by a combination of judicial and nonjudicial forces. If private organizations find the courts unreceptive to their arguments, they will turn to executive and legislative bodies, either at the federal or the state level.

The constitutionality of the Sedition Act of 1798 was never determined by the courts. Instead, it was decided by the people in the national elections of 1800, which drove the Federalist party out of

Jefferson and the Sedition Act

... I discharged every person under punishment or prosecution under the sedition law, because I considered, and now consider, that law to be a nullity, as absolute and as palpable as if Congress had ordered us to fall down and worship a golden image; and that it was as much my duty to arrest its execution in every stage, as it would have been to have rescued from the fiery furnace those who should have been cast into it for refusing to worship the image. It was accordingly done in every instance, without asking what the offenders had done, or against whom they had offended, but whether the pains they were suffering were inflicted under the pretended sedition law. (Jefferson to Mrs. John Adams, July 22, 1804).

You seem to think it devolved on the judges to decide on the validity of the sedition law. But nothing in the Constitution has given them a right to decide for the Executive, more than to the Executive to decide for them. Both magistrates are equally independent in the sphere of action assigned to them. The judges, believing the law constitutional, had a right to pass a sentence of fine and imprisonment; because the power was placed in their hands by the Constitution. But the executive, believing the law to be unconstitutional, were bound to remit the execution of it; because that power has been confided to them by the Constitution. That instrument meant that its co-ordinate branches should be checks on each other. But the opinion which gives to the judges the right to decide what laws are constitutional, and what not, not only for themselves in their own sphere of action, but for the legislature and executive also, in their spheres, would make the judiciary a despotic branch.... (Jefferson to Mrs. Adams, September 11, 1804).

---

office and into oblivion. President Jefferson called the Sedition Act a "nullity" and pardoned every person prosecuted under it (see box above). He believed that prosecution for seditious libel could be done only by the states, not the federal government. Later, Congress pronounced the statute "unconstitutional, null, and void," and appropriated funds to reimburse those who had been subjected to fines (see reading). The Supreme Court later acknowledged that the Sedition Act was struck down not by a court of law but by "the court of history." New York Times Co. v. Sullivan, 376 U.S. 254, 276 (1964).

President Andrew Jackson, who inherited some of the Jeffersonian distrust toward the judiciary, disagreed sharply with John Marshall on both personal and policy grounds. Every public officer, he said in 1832, took an oath to support the Constitution "as he understands it, and not as it is understood by others." The opinion of judges "has no more authority over Congress than the opinion of Congress has over the judges, and on that point the President is independent of both" (reading by Jackson). However, Jackson appreciated the value of judicial independence. He saw the courts as natural allies in his fight against the Nullifiers, who wanted to release the states from judgments of federal courts. Richard P. Longaker, 71 Pol. Sci. Q. 341, 358–61 (1956). Jackson's theory of the President's independent duty to interpret the Constitution provoked a sharp debate in the Senate (see reading).

In 1857, the Supreme Court held that Dred Scott (and all other black slaves and their descendants) was not a citizen of the United States or of Missouri. Chief Justice Taney refused to allow contemporary social beliefs to change the meaning of the constitution by making blacks citizens. Taney also ruled that Congress was without power to prevent the spread of slavery to the territories in the West. Dred Scott v. Sandford, 19 How. 393 (1857). During debates in a Senate race a year later, Abraham Lincoln repudiated the larger policy questions decided by the Court (see reading). In his first inaugural address, Lincoln acknowledged that Supreme Court rulings are binding on the parties to a suit and are "entitled to very high respect and consideration in all parallel cases by all other departments of the government." At the same time, he said that "if the policy of the Government upon vital questions affecting the whole people is to be irrevocably fixed by decisions of the Supreme Court, the instant they are made in ordinary litigation between parties in personal actions the people will have ceased to be their own rulers, having to that extent practically resigned their Government into the hands of that eminent tribunal."

These exchanges and volleys between the Court and the political system continue in our time. For example, during the 1970s and early 1980s, it appeared that courts were sympathetic to the arguments of those who were pro-choice on the issue of abortion. Consequently, the pro-choice community concentrated on litigation while the pro-life group appealed to the legislatures, the President, and governors. By the end of the 1980s, as a result of appointments by Presidents Nixon, Ford, Reagan, and Bush, the Supreme Court indicated that it would give less protection to the interests sought by the pro-choice organizations. Consequently, they now turned to Congress for support. On June 27, 1991, the National Abortion Rights Action League (NARAL) sent a "Supreme Court Alert" to its membership, calling attention to the abortion restrictions being enacted in the states and through regulations issued by the Bush administration. NARAL, which had relied on the courts in the past, now stated: "Clearly Congress is our Court of Last Resort. All hopes of protecting our constitutional right to choose depends upon our elected representatives in Congress responding to the will of the American people." The American Civil Liberties Union, which had also depended heavily on litigation, sounded a similar theme: "Congress is increasingly asked to look at these [constitutional] issues because there is nobody else. It is now the court of last resort." W. John Moore, "In Whose Court?," National Journal, Oct. 5, 1991, at 2400. The question "who shall interpret" the Constitution is explored in the final reading by Walter F. Murphy.

Congress Responds to the Sedition Act

The Federalists passed the Alien and Sedition Acts of 1798 to silence domestic opponents of governmental policy. Thomas Jefferson regarded the Sedition Act as unconstitutional, although federal judges did not find it so. After his election as President in 1800, he used his executive authority to discharge whoever had been punished or prosecuted under the Sedition Act. In 1840 Congress passed a private bill to reimburse the heirs of Matthew Lyon, who had been prosecuted under the Sedition Act (6 Stat. 802, c. 45). The committee report accompanying the bill stated that the Sedition Act was "unconstitutional, null, and void" (H. Rept. No. 86, 26th Cong., 1st Sess.).

That in the month of October, 1798, the late Matthew Lyon, the father of the petitioners, at the circuit court held at Rutland, in the State of Vermont, was indicted and found guilty of having printed and published what was alleged to be a libel against Mr. John Adams, the then President of the United States. The alleged libel was in the following words, to wit: "As to the Executive, when I shall see the effects of that power bent on the promotion of the comfort, the happiness, and accommodation of the people, that Executive shall have my zealous and uniform support. But whenever I shall, on the part of our Executive, see every consideration of public welfare swallowed up in a continual grasp for power, in an unbounded thirst for ridiculous pomp, foolish adulation, and selfish avarice — when I shall behold men of real merit daily turned

out of office for no other cause than independency of sentiment — when I shall see men of firmness, merit, years, abilities, and experience, discarded in their applications for office, for fear they possess that independence, and men of meanness preferred for the ease with which they can take up and advocate opinions, the consequence of which they know but little of — when I shall see the sacred name of religion employed as a State engine to make mankind hate and persecute each other, I shall not be their humble advocate!" The second count in the indictment, on which the said Matthew Lyon was convicted, charged him with printing and publishing a seditious writing or libel, entitled "Copy of a letter from an American diplomatic character in France (Mr. Joel Barlow) to a member of Congress in Philadelphia," which was in the following words, to wit: "The misunderstanding between the two Governments has become extremely alarming; confidence is completely destroyed; mistrusts, jealousies, and a disposition to a wrong attribution of motives, are so apparent as to require the utmost caution in every word and action that are to come from your Executive—I mean if your object is to avoid hostilities. Had this truth been understood with you before the recall of Monroe—before the coming and second coming of Pinckney; had it guided the pens that wrote the bullying speech of your President, and stupid answer of your Senate, at the opening of Congress in November last, I should probably have had no occasion to address you this letter. But when we found him borrowing the language of Edmund Burke, and telling the world that, although he should succeed in treating with the French, there was no dependence to be placed in any of their engagements; that their religion and morality were at an end, and they had turned pirates and plunderers, and that it would be necessary to be perpetually armed against them, though you are at peace; we wondered that the answer of both Houses had not been an order to send him to the mad-house. Instead of this, the Senate have echoed the speech with more servility than ever George the Third experienced from either House of Parliament."

The court deemed both the publications above recited libellous, under the 2d section of the act commonly called the sedition law, passed the 4th July, 1798; which section is as follows, viz: *"And be it further enacted.* That if any person shall write, print, utter, or publish, or shall cause or procure to be written, printed, uttered, or published, or shall knowingly and wilfully assist or aid in writing, printing, uttering, or publishing, any false, scandalous, and malicious writing or writings, against the Government of the United States, or either House of the Congress of the United States, or of the President of the United States, with an intent to defame the said Government, or either House of the said Congress, or the President, or to bring them, or either of them, into contempt or disre-

spect, or to excite against them, or either or any of them, the hatred of the good people of the United States, &c., then such person, being thereof convicted before any court of the United States having jurisdiction thereof, shall be punished by a fine not exceeding two thousand dollars, and by imprisonment not exceeding two years."

Upon this indictment Matthew Lyon was convicted, and sentenced by the court to be imprisoned for four months; to pay a fine of one thousand dollars, and the costs of the prosecution, taxed at sixty dollars and ninety-six cents; and to stand committed until the fine and costs were paid: which were paid, as appears by the exemplification of the record of the said trial and proceedings, now in the archives of this House.

The committee are of opinion that the law above recited was unconstitutional, null, and void, passed under a mistaken exercise of undelegated power, and that the mistake ought to be corrected by returning the fine so obtained, with interest thereon, to the legal representatives of Matthew Lyon.

The committee do not deem it necessary to discuss at length the character of that law, or to assign all the reasons, however demonstrative, that have induced the conviction of its unconstitutionality. No question connected with the liberty of the press ever excited a more universal and intense interest—ever received so acute, able, long-continued, and elaborate investigation—was ever more generally understood, or so conclusively settled by the concurring opinions of all parties, after the heated political contests of the day had passed away. All that now remains to be done by the representatives of a people who condemned this act of their agents as unauthorized, and transcending their grant of power, to place beyond question, doubt, or cavil, that mandate of the constitution prohibiting Congress from abridging the liberty of the press, and to discharge an honest, just, moral, and honorable obligation, is to refund from the Treasury the fine thus illegally and wrongfully obtained from one of their citizens: for which purpose the committee herewith report a bill.

Jackson's Veto of the Bank Bill*

President Andrew Jackson received a bill in 1832 to renew the Bank of the United States. Although the bill had been passed by Congress, and the constitutionality of the Bank had been

---

* SOURCE: The full veto message appears in 3 Messages and Papers of the Presidents 1139–43 (Richardson ed.).

upheld by the Supreme Court in *McCulloch* v. *Maryland* (1819), Jackson exercised his veto. His veto message of July 10, 1832, explains the independence of the President in determining constitutional questions notwithstanding the judgments reached by the legislative and judicial branches.

To the Senate:

The bill "to modify and continue" the act entitled "An act to incorporate the subscribers to the Bank of the United States" was presented to me on the 4th July instant. Having considered it with that solemn regard to the principles of the Constitution which the day was calculated to inspire, and come to the conclusion that it ought not to become a law, I herewith return it to the Senate, in which it originated, with my objections.

A bank of the United States is in many respects convenient for the Government and useful to the people. Entertaining this opinion, and deeply impressed with the belief that some of the powers and privileges possessed by the existing bank are unauthorized by the Constitution, subversive of the rights of the States, and dangerous to the liberties of the people, I felt it my duty at an early period of my Administration to call the attention of Congress to the practicability of organizing an institution combining all its advantages and obviating these objections. I sincerely regret that in the act before me I can perceive none of those modifications of the bank charter which are necessary, in my opinion, to make it compatible with justice, with sound policy, or with the Constitution of our country.

[*Jackson states his objections that various features of the bill grant monopoly and exclusive privileges to the rich at the expense of the poor. He also regarded the Bank as injurious to the states.*]

It is maintained by the advocates of the bank that its constitutionality in all its features ought to be considered as settled by precedent and by the decision of the Supreme Court. To this conclusion I can not assent. Mere precedent is a dangerous source of authority, and should not be regarded as deciding questions of constitutional power except where the acquiescence of the people and the States can be considered as well settled. So far from this being the case on this subject, an argument against the bank might be based on precedent. One Congress, in 1791, decided in favor of a bank; another, in 1811, decided against it. One Congress, in 1815, decided against a bank; another, in 1816, decided in its favor. Prior to the present Congress, therefore, the precedents drawn from that source were equal. If we resort to the States, the expressions of legislative, judicial, and executive opinions against the bank have been probably to those in its favor as 4 to 1. There is nothing in precedent, therefore, which, if its authority were admitted, ought to weigh in favor of the act before me.

If the opinion of the Supreme Court covered the whole ground of this act, it ought not to control the coordinate authorities of this Government. The Congress, the Executive, and the Court, must each for itself be guided by its own opinion of the Constitution. Each public officer who takes an oath to support the Constitution swears that he will support it as he understands it, and not as it is understood by others. It is as much the duty of the House of Representatives, of the Senate, and of the President to decide upon the constitutionality of any bill or resolution which may be presented to them for passage or approval as it is of the supreme judges when it may be brought before them for judicial decision. The opinion of the judges has no more authority over Congress than the opinion of Congress has over the judges, and on that point the President is independent of both. The authority of the Supreme Court must not, therefore, be permitted to control the Congress or the Executive when acting in their legislative capacities, but to have only such influence as the force of their reasoning may deserve.

. . .

The Senate Debates Jackson's Veto Message*

President Jackson's veto of the Bank of the United States reached the Senate on July 10, 1832. Before sustaining the veto, the Senate engaged in a major debate on the substantive reasons

* Source: *Congressional Debates,* 22nd Cong. 1st Sess. 1231–44 (1832).

given by Jackson in opposing the Bank. Several Senators also concentrated on the legitimacy of the veto itself. Did the President have the power to veto a proposal that had been previously passed by Congress, signed by a President (Madison), and upheld by the Supreme Court (in *McCulloch* v. *Maryland*)? Senator Daniel Webster argued that Jackson had no such right. Senator Hugh Lawson White strongly defended Jackson's action.

[*Senator Webster:*] Does the President, then, reject the authority of all precedent, except what is suitable to his own purposes to use? And does he use, without stint or measure, all precedents which may augment his own power, or gratify his wishes? But if the President thinks lightly of the authority of Congress, in construing the constitution, he thinks still more lightly of the authority of the Supreme Court. He asserts a right of individual judgment on constitutional questions, which is totally inconsistent with any proper administration of the Government, or any regular execution of the laws. Social disorder, entire uncertainty in regard to individual rights and individual duties, the cessation of legal authority, confusion, the dissolution of free Government—all these are the inevitable consequences of the principles adopted by the message, whenever they shall be carried to their full extent. Hitherto it has been thought that the final decision of constitutional questions belonged to the supreme judicial tribunal. The very nature of free Government, it has been supposed, enjoins this: and our constitution, moreover, has been understood so to provide, clearly and expressly. It is true that each branch of the Legislature has an undoubted right, in the exercise of its functions, to consider the constitutionality of a law proposed to be passed. This is naturally a part of its duty, and neither branch can be compelled to pass any law, or do any other act, which it deems to be beyond the reach of its constitutional power. The President has the same right when a bill is presented for his approval; for he is, doubtless, bound to consider, in all cases, whether such bill be compatible with the constitution, and whether he can approve it consistently with his oath of office. But when a law has been passed by Congress, and approved by the President, it is now no longer in the power, either of the same President, or his successors, to say whether the law is constitutional or not. He is not at liberty to disregard it: he is not at liberty to feel or to affect "constitutional scruples," and to sit in judgment himself on the validity of a statute of the Government, and to nullify it if he so chooses. After a law has passed through all the requisite forms: after it has received the requisite legislative sanction and the Executive approval, the question of its constitutionality then becomes a judicial question, and a judicial question alone. In the courts, that question may be raised, argued, and adjudged; it can be adjudged nowhere else.

. . .

[*Senator White:*] The honorable Senator argues that the constitution has constituted the Supreme Court a tribunal to decide great constitutional questions, such as this, and that, when they have done so, the question is put at rest, and every other department of the Government must acquiesce. This doctrine I deny. The constitution vests "the judicial power in a Supreme Court, and in such inferior courts as Congress may from time to time ordain and establish." Whenever a suit is commenced and prosecuted in the courts of the United States, of which they have jurisdiction, and such suit is decided by the Supreme Court, as that is the court of the last resort, its decision is final and conclusive between the parties. But as an authority, it does not bind either the Congress or the President of the United States. If either of these co-ordinate departments is afterwards called upon to perform an official act, and conscientiously believe the performance of that act will be a violation of the constitution, they are not bound to perform it, but, on the contrary, are as much at liberty to decline acting, as if no such decision had been made. In examining the extent of their constitutional power, the opinion of so enlightened a tribunal as our Supreme Court has been, and I hope ever will be, will always be entitled to great weight; and, without doubt, either Congress or the President would always be disposed, in a doubtful case, to think its decisions correct; but I hope neither will ever view them as authority binding upon them. They ought to examine the extent of their constitutional powers for themselves; and when they have had access to all sources of information within their reach, and given to every thing its due weight, if they are satisfied the constitution has not given a power to do the act required, I insist they ought to refrain from doing it.

... Each coordinate department, within its appropriate sphere of action, must judge of its own powers, when called upon to do its official duties; and if either blindly follows the others, without forming an opinion for itself, an essential check against the exercise of unconstitutional power is destroyed. A mistake by Congress in passing an act, inconsistent with the constitution, followed by a like mistake by the Supreme Court, in deciding such act to be constitutional, might be attended with the most fatal consequences. Let each department judge for itself, and we are safe. If different interpretations are put upon the constitution by the different departments, the people is the tribunal to settle the dispute....

Lincoln's Critique of *Dred Scott*

On July 17, 1858, at Springfield, Illinois, Abraham Lincoln responded to the Supreme Court's decision in *Dred Scott* v. *Sandford* (1857). At the same time, he rejected the defense of that decision by his opponent for the U.S. Senate, Stephen A. Douglas. Lincoln carefully identified the portion of the decision he regarded as legally binding. He considered major parts of the decision a nullity, to be left to political resolution outside the courts.

Does Judge Douglas, when he says that several of the past years of his life have been devoted to the question of "popular sovereignty," and that all the remainder of his life shall be devoted to it, does he mean to say that he has been devoting his life to securing to the people of the territories the right to exclude slavery from the territories? If he means so to say, he means to deceive; because he and every one knows that the decision of the Supreme Court, which he approves and makes especial ground of attack upon me for disapproving, forbids the people of a territory to exclude slavery. This covers the whole ground, from the settlement of a territory till it reaches the degree of maturity entitling it to form a State Constitution. So far as all that ground is concerned, the Judge is not sustaining popular sovereignty, but absolutely opposing it....

Now, as to the Dred Scott decision; for upon that he makes his last point at me. He boldly takes ground in favor of that decision.

This is one-half the onslaught, and one-third of the entire plan of the campaign. I am opposed to that decision in a certain sense, but not in the sense which he puts on it. I say that in so far as it decided in favor of Dred Scott's master and against Dred Scott and his family, I do not propose to disturb or resist the decision.

I never have proposed to do any such thing. I think, that in respect for judicial authority, my humble history would not suffer in a comparison with that of Judge Douglas. He would have the citizen conform his vote to that decision; the Member of Congress, his; the President, his use of the veto power. He would make it a rule of political action for the people and all the departments of the government. I would not. By resisting it as a political rule, I disturb no right of property, create no disorder, excite no mobs.

. . .

... I shall read from a letter written by Mr. Jefferson in 1820.... It seems he had been presented by a gentleman of the name of Jarvis with a book, or essay, or periodical, called the "Republican," and he was writing in acknowledgement of the present, and noting some of its contents. After expressing the hope that the work will produce a favorable effect upon the minds of the young, he proceeds to say:

"That it will have this tendency may be expected, and for that reason I feel an urgency to note what I deem an error in it, the more requiring notice as your opinion is strengthened by that of many others. You seem in pages 84 and 148, to consider the judges as the ultimate arbiters of all constitutional questions—a very dangerous doctrine indeed and one which would place us under the despotism of an oligarchy. Our judges are as honest as other men, and not more so. They have, with others, the same passions for party, for power, and the privilege of their corps. Their maxim is, "boni judicis est ampliare jurisdictionem'; and their power is the more dangerous as they are in office for life, and not responsible, as the other functionaries are, to the elective control. The Constitution has erected no such single tribunal, knowing that to whatever hands confided, with the corruptions of time and party, its members would become despots. It has more wisely made all the departments co-equal and co-sovereign within themselves."

Thus we see the power claimed for the Supreme Court by Judge Douglas, Mr. Jefferson holds, would reduce us to the despotism of an oligarchy.

Now, I have said no more than this—in fact, never quite so much as this—at least I am sustained by Mr. Jefferson.

. . .

One more thing. Last night Judge Douglas tormented himself with horrors about my disposition to make negroes perfectly equal with white men in social and political relations. He did not stop to show that I have said any such thing, or that it legitimately follows from any thing I have said, but he rushes on with his assertions. I adhere to the Declaration of Independence. If Judge Douglas and his friends are not willing to stand by it, let them come up and amend it. Let them make it read that all men are created equal except negroes. Let us have it decided, whether the Declaration of Independence, in this blessed year of 1858, shall be thus amended.

. . .

My declarations upon this subject of negro slav-

ery may be misrepresented, but can not be misunderstood. I have said that I do not understand the Declaration to mean that all men were created equal in all respects. They are not our equal in color; but I suppose that it does mean to declare that all men are equal in some respects; they are equal in their right to "life, liberty, and the pursuit of happiness." Certainly the negro is not our equal in color — perhaps not in many other respects; still, in the right to put into his mouth the bread that his own hands have earned, he is the equal of every other man, white or black. In pointing out that more has been given you, you can not be justified in taking away the little which has been given him. All I ask for the negro is that if you do not like him, let him alone. If God gave him but little, that little let him enjoy.

Walter F. Murphy
Who Shall Interpret?*

So entrenched is the belief that the U.S. Supreme Court is the ultimate interpreter of the Constitution that the independent contributions of the other branches and the states are largely overlooked in the legal literature. In this essay, political scientist Walter Murphy explores the tradition of departmentalism: the responsibility of all three branches to interpret and apply the Constitution.

I. INTRODUCTION

… It is a fact of American political life that all public officials, from presidents to local police, often have to interpret the Constitution. Every public official takes an oath to uphold the Constitution, and the terms of the constitutional document are often broad. Deciding what policies government may legitimately pursue, whether to enact, sign, veto, or enforce a law, all create problems of interpretation. Even if one believes judges are the ultimate constitutional interpreters, government cannot halt and await a judicial decision whenever a constitutional problem arises.

The oath is also one that millions of private citizens have taken, and the Preamble lodges responsibility for the Constitution in "the people of the United States." Thus, it is fair for "the people," as its ultimate source of authority, to have an interpretive role. Indeed, one can plausibly argue, they have the duty, when they vote or utilize other means to influ-

ence public policy, to judge candidates' records and promises about constitutional interpretation.

. . .

II. WHO SHALL INTERPRET
THE CONSTITUTION?

The plain words of the document contain several different messages about WHO shall interpret. In conferring on Congress authority to make "all laws necessary and proper" to carry out powers delegated to the national government, Article I, Sec. 8, clearly implies that Congress (with the participation of the president since he is part of the legislative process) shall make judgments about the Constitution's meaning, for what laws are "proper" under the Constitution are sometimes far from manifest. There are similar terms in the Thirteenth, Fourteenth, Fifteenth, Nineteenth, Twenty-third, Twenty-fourth, and Twenty-sixth amendments.

* SOURCE: Walter F. Murphy, "Who Shall Interpret? The Quest for the Ultimate Constitutional Interpreter," 48 Review of Politics 401 (1986).

In requiring the president to "preserve, protect, and defend the Constitution," Article II adds to his interpretive responsibilities. He could hardly fulfill those tasks without interpreting the Constitution to determine if it was being threatened or how to protect it....

The logic of institutional history as well as the words of the constitutional document also enmesh judges in constitutional interpretation. By extending "the judicial power" "to all cases, in law and equity, arising under this Constitution," Article III commands courts to participate in the interpretive process, as judges before and since John Marshall have modestly conceded.

But there is not a word in these clauses about whose views should prevail if the branches disagree....

III. WHO IS THE AUTHORITATIVE INTERPRETER: THREE COMPETING THEORIES

Three principal theories claim to produce an answer to the question of WHO is the ultimate interpreter: judicial supremacy, legislative supremacy, and departmentalism. All, however, draw heavily on democratic theory; and much of the debate rests on the possibility of an appeal to "the people," though never so directly as in Jefferson's plan for national conventions.

A. Judicial Supremacy

Judicial supremacy is the most familiar theory. Its usual justification rests on the textual and functional grounds Marshall used in *Marbury v. Madison* (1803) for judicial review: (1) Article VI says the Constitution is law; (2) "it is emphatically the province and duty of the judicial department to say what the law is"; and thus (3) judicial review must be an integral part of the political system. Then follows a long step from judicial review — the authority of a court, when deciding cases, to refuse to give force to an act of a coordinate branch of government — to judicial supremacy, the obligation of coordinate officials not only to obey that ruling but to follow its reasoning in future deliberations....

On the other hand: (1) no constitutional text "expressly confine[s]" interpretation to the judiciary; (2) judicial review says nothing about the obligation of other branches of government to obey a court's decision or follow its reasoning; ...

B. Legislative Supremacy

Systematic assertions of legislative supremacy in constitutional interpretation have been infrequent, though they have at times been vigorously pushed, as after the Civil War when the Radical Republicans dominated Congress, impeached the president, and curbed the Court. Early on, some Jeffersonians had also pressed for congressional supremacy. Caesar Rodney of Delaware wrote in 1803: "Judicial supremacy may be made to bow before the strong arm of Legislative authority. We shall discover who is master of the ship." Threats of impeachment so frightened John Marshall that he was ready to modify judicial review:

[T]he modern doctrine of impeachment should yield to an appellate jurisdiction in the legislature. A reversal of those legal opinions deemed unsound by the legislature would certainly better comport with the mildness of our character than a removal of the Judge who has rendered them unknowing of his fault.

This proposal has been several times revised — usually with the appellate jurisdiction resting in the Senate alone — but, of course, has never been adopted.

At bottom, any claim that congressional interpretation should prevail over judicial rests on legislators' connections to the people....

On the other hand, constitutionalism is wary of arguments that allow popularly elected officials final authority to define substantive rights....

C. Departmentalism

No president has ever pressed a claim to supremacy in constitutional interpretation. On the other hand, some presidents, like many legislators, have asserted equality.

Madison's position shifted as he faced various crises, but in the early days of the Republic he was clearly a departmentalist. His theory of allowing different social interests to dominate particular institutions and of pitting ambition against ambition and power against power pushes toward stalemates that can only be overcome by compromise, not adjudication. As he told the First Congress:

There is not one Government ... in the United States, in which provision is made for a particular authority to determine the limits of the constitutional division of power between the branches of the Government. In all systems, there are points which must be adjusted by the departments themselves, to which no one of them is competent.

. . .

V. CONCLUSION

The question of WHO shall interpret poses one of the fundamental problems with which any coherent constitutional theory must come to grips. The sort of analysis suggested here transforms the question from one that yields a universally applicable response, into a more complex set of queries about degrees of deference one institution owes another under varying circumstances. What emerges is a modified version of departmentalism.

. . .

There is a magnetic attraction to the notion of an ultimate constitutional interpreter, just as there is a magnetic pull to the idea of some passkey to constitutional interpretation that will, if properly turned, always open the door to truth, justice, and the American way. But finality, as Disraeli reminded us, "is not the language of politics." James Madison would have agreed.

NOTES AND QUESTIONS

1. Assume it is true, as Justice Robert H. Jackson observed in a speech on October 1, 1953 (fifth box in this chapter), that "long-sustained public opinion does influence the process of constitutional interpretation." Assume, as well, that Chief Justice Rehnquist was correct in his observation that the "tide of public opinion" had exerted "considerable influence" on the Court's ruling in the Steel Seizure Case. Do you think the Court should take account of public opinion in its deliberations? If so, how should the Court discern the state of public opinion? What are the implications of this interpretive approach for constitutional government?

2. Should majoritarian preferences outweigh minority rights? Does judicial consideration of public opinion promote republican values? Is it a desirable approach? Consider Justice Jackson's criticism: "To the extent that public opinion of the hour is admitted to the process of constitutional interpretation, the basis for judicial review of legislative action disappears."

3. On what basis did Thomas Jefferson and Abraham Lincoln subscribe to the doctrine of coordinate construction? What do you consider to be the strengths and weaknesses of their reasoning? How would you respond to Jefferson's warning of judicial supremacy: "[If the Supreme Court is the ultimate arbiter,] the constitution . . . is a mere thing of wax in the hands of the judiciary, which they may twist and shape into any form they please."

4. If each of the three branches has the "right" and authority to interpret the constitution, who has the "last word"?

5. After the terrorist attacks of 9/11, Congress enacted some restrictions, such as prohibitions against torture. Should Presidents in their statements signing the bill be able to indicate that they may ignore the statutory language by relying on "inherent" powers available in Article II?

SELECTED READINGS

BAKER, NANCY. Conflicting Loyalties: Law and Politics in the Attorney General's Office, 1789–1990. Lawrence, Kansas: University Press of Kansas, 1992.

BALL, HOWARD. Courts and Politics: The Federal Judicial System. Englewood Cliffs, N.J.: Prentice-Hall, 1980.

BAMBURGER, MICHAEL A. Reckless Legislation: How Lawmakers Ignore the Constitution. New Brunswick, N.J.: Rutgers University Press, 2000.

CAMPBELL, TOM. Separation of Powers in Practice. Stanford, Cal.: Stanford University Press, 2004.

CAPLAN, LINCOLN. The Tenth Justice: The Solicitor General and the Rule of Law. New York: Knopf, 1987.

CHAYES, ABRAM. "The Role of the Judge in Public Law Litigation." 89 Harvard Law Review 1281 (1976).

CLAYTON, CORNELL W. The Politics of Justice: The Attorney General and the Making of Legal Policy. New York: M. E. Sharpe, Inc., 1992.

COOPER, PHILLIP J. Hard Judicial Choices: Federal District Court Judges and State and Local Officials. New York: Oxford University Press, 1988.

DEVINS, NEAL. Shaping Constitutional Values: Elected Government, the Supreme Court, and the Abortion Debate. Baltimore, Md.: Johns Hopkins University Press, 1996.

———, ed. Elected Branch Influences in Constitutional Decisionmaking, 56 Law & Contemporary Problems (Autumn 1993).

———and LOUIS FISHER. The Democratic Constitution. New York: Oxford University Press, 2004.

EPSTEIN, LEE. Conservatives in Court. Knoxville: University of Tennessee Press, 1985.

FISHER, LOUIS. "Social Influences on Constitutional Law." 15 Journal of Political Science 7 (1987).

———. The Supreme Court and Congress: Rival Interpretations. Washington, D.C.: CQ Press, 2009.

———. "Constitutional Interpretation by Members of Congress." 63 North Carolina Law Review 707 (1985).

———. "Is the Solicitor General an Executive or a Judicial Agent? Caplan's Tenth Justice," 15 Law & Social Inquiry 305 (1990).

———. "The Judge as Manager," The Public Manager, Fall 1996, pp. 7–10.

———. Constitutional Dialogues: Interpretation as Political Process. Princeton, N.J.: Princeton University Press, 1988.

FISHER, LOUIS AND NEAL DEVINS. Political Dynamics of Constitutional Law. St. Paul, Minn.: Thomson-West Publishing, 5th ed. 2011.

GINGER, ANN FAGAN. "Litigation as a Form of Political Action." 9 Wayne Law Review 458 (1963).

GRIFFITH, J. A. G. The Politics of the Judiciary. Glasgow: Fontana Press, 1985.

HARRIMAN, LINDA, AND JEFFREY D. STRAUSSMAN. "Do Judges Determine Budget Decisions? Federal Court Decisions in Prison Reform and State Spending for Corrections." 43 Public Administration Review 343 (1983).

HODDER-WILLIAMS, RICHARD. The Politics of the U.S. Supreme Court. London: George Allen & Unwin, 1980.

KMIEC, DOUGLAS W. The Attorney General's Lawyer: Inside the Meese Justice Department. New York: Praeger, 1992.

LASSER, WILLIAM. The Limits of Judicial Power: The Supreme Court in American Politics. Chapel Hill: University of North Carolina Press, 1988.

LATHAM, EARL. "The Supreme Court as a Political Institution." 31 Minnesota Law Review 205 (1947).

MURPHY, WALTER, AND C. HERMAN PRITCHETT, eds. Courts, Judges, and Politics. New York: Random House, 2002.

NEIER, ARYEH. Only Judgment: The Limits of Litigation in Social Change. Middletown, Conn.: Wesleyan University Press, 1982.

O'BRIEN, DAVID M. Storm Center: The Supreme Court in American Politics. New York: Norton, 1986.

O'CONNOR, KAREN, AND LEE EPSTEIN. "Amicus Curiae Participation in U.S. Supreme Court Litigation: An Appraisal of Hakman's "Forklore."" 16 Law and Society Review 311 (1981–1982).

PELTASON, JACK. Federal Courts in the Political Process. New York: Random House, 1955.

PICKERILL, J. MITCHEL. Constitutional Deliberation in Congress. Durham, N.C.: Duke University Press, 2004.

ROSENBLUM, VICTOR G. Law as a Political Instrument. New York: Random House, 1955.

SALOKAR, REBECCA MAE. The Solicitor General: The Politics of Law. Philadelphia: Temple University Press, 1992.

VOSE, CLEMENT E. Caucasians Only: The Supreme Court, the NAACP, and the Restrictive Covenant Cases. Berkeley: University of California Press, 1959.

WHITTINGTON, KEITH E. Constitutional Construction: Divided Powers and Constitutional Meaning. Cambridge, Mass.: Harvard University Press, 1999.

2

The Doctrine of Judicial Review

Judicial review in America survives a number of nagging, unanswered questions. By what right do life-tenured judges invalidate policies adopted by popularly elected officials? If judicial review is of such crucial importance in safeguarding a written constitution, why did the framers omit it? Why is it based on implied, rather than explicit, power? If judicial review is essential to protect constitutional freedoms, how do other democratic nations survive without it?

At some point, judicial review assumes the characteristics of lawmaking. Constitutional interpretation is more than a technical exercise or display of judicial erudition. The power to interpret the law is the power to make the law. Judicial review can be another name for judicial legislation. As Bishop Hoadly announced in 1717: "Whoever hath an absolute authority to interpret any written or spoken laws, it is he who is truly the lawgiver, to all intents and purposes, and not the person who first wrote or spoke them." James Bradley Thayer, 7 Harv. L. Rev. 129, 152 (1893).

Judicial review includes many activities. Courts may overturn a government action, find support for it, or refuse to rule at all. Judicial review applies to Congress, the chief executive, administrative agencies, state legislatures, and rulings of state courts. Although the holding of the Supreme Court is of utmost importance, it often serves as but one stage of an ongoing constitutional process shared with lower courts, the executive branch, the legislature, and the general public.

A. SOURCES OF JUDICIAL REVIEW AUTHORITY

When the chief executive or legislators make unpopular decisions, the voters may jettison them at the next election. The ballot box represents a periodic test of the legitimacy of elected officers, a reaffirmation of authority they are quite happy to cite. The federal judiciary, however, cannot draw legitimacy from elections. When judges announce an unpopular decision, citizens want to know on what authority courts may overturn the judgments of elected officials who also take an oath to uphold the Constitution. Judges must be able to cite persuasive and authoritative sources: constitutional language, pre-*Marbury* precedents, principles announced by the Marshall Court, or convincing evidence that has accumulated since that time.

Constitutional Language

Article III, Section 1, of the Constitution provides that "The judicial Power of the United States, shall be vested in one Supreme Court, and in such inferior Courts as the Congress may from time to time ordain and establish." Section 2 extends the judicial power to various cases and controversies, but there is no specific grant of power to declare an act of Congress, the President, or state government unconstitutional. The absence of an explicit grant is not conclusive. An implied power may exist. For example, although the Constitution provides no authority for the President to assert executive privilege, remove appointees from office, issue executive orders with the force of law, or enter into international agreements without the advice and consent of the Senate, the Supreme Court has considered those powers implicit in Article II.[1] Similarly, the Court has found an implied power for Congress to investigate, issue subpoenas, and exercise the power of contempt.[2]

The power of judicial review might be drawn from three sources. First, courts need judicial review to strike down actions by the elected branches that threaten judicial independence. For example, suppose that Congress passed legislation that reduced the salary of judges, in direct violation of Article III, Section 1, which provides that federal judges shall receive a compensation "which shall not be diminished during their Continuance in Office." Invalidating such statutes would be consistent with the system of checks and balances that encourages each branch to fight off encroachments.

Second, under Article III, Section 2, the judicial power extends to all cases "*arising under this Constitution,* the Laws of the United States, and Treaties made" (emphasis added). In most of the early drafts of the Constitution, the language *arising under* applied only to laws passed by Congress. When William Samuel Johnson moved to insert the words *this Constitution and the* before the word *Laws,* James Madison objected, stating that he "doubted whether it was not going too far to extend the jurisdiction of the Court generally to cases arising Under the Constitution, & whether it ought to be limited to cases of a Judiciary Nature. The right of expounding the Constitution in cases of this nature ought not to be given to that Department." Johnson's motion was agreed to without further discussion, "it being generally supposed that the jurisdiction given was constructively limited to cases of a Judiciary nature." 2 Farrand 430.

An intriguing bit of legislative history, but what did the framers mean by cases of a "judiciary nature"? However defined, evidently it was something less than full-blown judicial review. At the Virginia ratifying convention, Madison interpreted "arising under" to justify judicial review only against the states. 3 Elliot 532. Alexander Hamilton made the same point in Federalist No. 80. Under these readings, the purpose of judicial review was to control the states and protect federalism. It was not intended to control Congress and the President.

Third, the power of judicial review might be drawn from the Supremacy Clause in Article VI, which provides that the Constitution, federal laws "made in Pursuance thereof," and all treaties shall be the supreme law of the land, and "the Judges in every State shall be bound thereby, any Thing in the Constitution or Laws of any State to the Contrary notwithstanding." At a minimum, the Supremacy Clause requires federal courts to review the actions of state governments. It might also invite review of congressional statutes that are not "in pursuance" of the Constitution. However, judicial review over the coequal branches of Congress and the President represents a major leap and demands greater evidence. Justice Holmes once remarked: "I do not think the United States would come to an end if [the Supreme Court] lost [its] power to declare an act of Congress void. I do think the Union would be imperiled if we could not make that declaration as to the laws of the several States." Collected Legal Papers · 295–96 (1920).

The Pre-*Marbury* Precedents

Several precedents for judicial review, established in the years before *Marbury,* prepared the way for Marshall's famous statement in 1803 that it is "emphatically the province and duty of the judicial department to say what the law is." Marbury v. Madison, 5 U.S. (1 Cr.) 137, 177 (1803). British efforts in the 1760s to reestablish control over America provoked accusations by colonists that the laws of Parliament had violated the "common law" and the "law of reason" and were therefore void. Those arguments became important ingredients in the case presented to a "candid world" in the Declaration of Independence.

---

1. United States v. Nixon, 418 U.S. 683 (1974) (executive privilege); Myers v. United States, 272 U.S. 52 (1926) (removal power); Contractors Ass'n of Eastern Pa. v. Secretary of Labor, 442 F.2d 159 (3d Cir. 1971), cert. denied, 404 U.S. 854 (1971) (executive orders); and Dames & Moore v. Regan, 453 U.S. 654 (1981) (executive agreements).

2. McGrain v. Daugherty, 273 U.S. 135 (1927) (investigations); Eastland v. United States Servicemen's Fund, 421 U.S. 491, 505 (1975) (subpoenas); Anderson v. Dunn, 19 U.S. (6 Wheat.) 204, 228 (1821) (contempt power).

James Otis and Fundamental Law

This writ is against the fundamental principles of law. The privilege of the House. A man who is quiet, is as secure in his house, as a prince in his castle — notwithstanding all his debts and civil processes of any kind. But —

For flagrant crimes and in cases of great public necessity, the privilege may be infringed on. For felonies an officer may break upon process and oath, that is, by a special warrant to search such a house, sworn to be suspected, and good grounds of suspicion appearing....

As to Acts of Parliament. An act against the Constitution is void; an act against natural equity is void; and if an act of Parliament should be made, in the very words of this petition, it would be void. The executive Courts must pass such acts into disuse.

SOURCE: The Works of John Adams (Charles Francis Adams, ed.), Vol. II, pp. 521–22. See also pp. 523–25.

The best-known American challenge to an act of Parliament came in 1761 when James Otis argued the writs of assistance case in Boston. He claimed that British customs officials were not empowered by Parliament to use general search warrants. Even if Parliament had authorized the writs of assistance, Otis said that the statute would be "against the Constitution," "against natural equity," and therefore void (see box). In 1766 a Virginia court held the Stamp Act unconstitutional. On the eve of the Declaration of Independence, a Massachusetts judge instructed the jury to treat acts of Parliament that violated fundamental law as "void" and "inoperative." Edward S. Corwin, The Doctrine of Judicial Review 32 (1914).

The proposition that courts could void an act of Parliament appears in an opinion by Chief Justice Coke in 1610. He said that when an act of Parliament "is against common right and reason, or repugnant, or impossible to be performed, the common law will controul it, and adjudge such Act to be void." Dr. Bonham's Case, 77 Eng. Rep. 646, 652. A few British judges in the seventeenth and eighteenth centuries cited Coke's argument, but the principle of judicial review never took root on English soil. Day v. Savadge, 80 Eng. Rep. 235, 237 (1614); The City of London v. Wood, 88 Eng. Rep. 1592, 1602 (1702). In 1884 the Supreme Court noted: "notwithstanding what was attributed to Lord Coke in *Bonham's Case* ... the omnipotence of Parliament over the common law was absolute, even against common right and reason." Hurtado v. California, 110 U.S. 516, 531 (1884).

For their understanding of British law the framers relied mainly on Blackstone's *Commentaries,* which states the case for parliamentary supremacy with singular clarity. For those who believed that acts of Parliament contrary to reason were void, he offered this advice:

> But if the parliament will positively enact a thing to be done which is unreasonable, I know of no power that can control it: and the examples usually alleged in support of this sense of the rule do none of them prove, that, where the main object of a statute is unreasonable, the judges are at liberty to reject it; for that were to set the judicial power above that of the legislature, which would be subversive of all government. Blackstone, Commentaries, Book One, § 3, at 91 (Oxford 1775).

Although *Dr. Bonham's Case* provides inadequate support for the American concept of judicial review, it was accepted as good law and precedent by those who wanted to break with England. Intellectual justifications were needed to neutralize the appearance of impetuous and impulsive behavior by the American colonists. However, "voiding" the acts of Parliament did not automatically deliver the power of judicial review to American courts, especially those at the national level.

From independence to the framing of the Constitution, some of the state judges challenged the acts of their legislatures. Although scholars disagree on the strength of those precedents, decisions providing support for the theory of judicial review were handed down by judges in Virginia, New Jersey, New York, Connecticut, Rhode Island, and North Carolina. The language used by judges in holding state laws invalid was often more bold than the results they achieved. Charles Grove Haines, The American Doctrine of Judicial Supremacy 88–120 (1932).

B. THE FRAMERS' INTENT

By the time of the convention, some of the framers expected judicial review to be part of the new government. In reading their statements at the convention and during the ratification debates, it is important to keep their thoughts in context and recognize conflicting statements. The framers did not have a clear or fully developed theory of judicial review.

The framers wanted to replace the Articles of Confederation to make the central government more effective, resolve disputes among the states over legal and monetary systems, and limit legislative abuses. Each goal depended on the structure and power of the federal judiciary. Instead of the legislative supremacy that prevailed under the Articles of Confederation, the new Congress would be only one of three coordinate and coequal branches. Both the Virginia Plan, presented by Edmund Randolph, and the New Jersey Plan, advocated by William Paterson, called for the creation of an independent judiciary headed by a Supreme Court. Although the new judicial article left undecided such questions as whether to create lower federal courts or rely solely on state courts, it did grant broad authority to the Supreme Court.

The framers were worried that 13 sets of state courts would announce contradictory rulings on matters of national concern. In Federalist No. 80, Alexander Hamilton said that 13 independent courts of final jurisdiction "over the same causes, arising upon the same laws, is a hydra in government from which nothing but contradiction and confusion can proceed." The convention responded to that problem by adopting the Supremacy Clause. Judicial review over presidential and congressional actions, however, was a subject of much greater delicacy. By 1787 the framers had become alarmed about legislative overreaching. In Federalist No. 48, James Madison wrote that the "legislative department is everywhere extending the sphere of its activity and drawing all power into its impetuous vortex." Several delegates to the Philadelphia Convention expressed the same concern. 1 Farrand 254 (Wilson) and 2 Farrand 35 (Madison), 110 (Madison), and 288 (Mercer). However, giving the courts the final say over congressional acts was an extremely radical notion.

A common pastime of constitutional scholars is counting the heads of framers who favored judicial review. Depending on which year he wrote, Edward S. Corwin vacillated on the statistics, ranging from a high of 17 framers to a low of five or six. Leonard D. Levy, ed., Judicial Review and the Supreme Court 3–4 (1967). Corwin uttered this scholar's lament in 1937 when he testified on the court-packing plan: "These people who say the framers intended [judicial review] are talking nonsense; and the people who say they did not intend it are talking nonsense. There is evidence on both sides." Senate Committee on the Judiciary, "Reorganization of the Federal Judiciary" (Part 2), 75th Cong., 1st Sess. 176 (1937). Other studies on the judiciary were flavored by a crusading spirit, designed either to "prove" the legitimacy of judicial review or to chop away at its foundations.[3] The issue remains unsettled; this very ambiguity adds some constraint to judicial activism.

Council of Revision

Judicial review was discussed at the convention as a means of checking Congress and the states. The most important debate was over the veto of legislation passed by Congress. Randolph proposed a Council of Revision consisting of the "Executive and a convenient number of the National Judiciary ... with authority to examine every act of the National Legislature before it shall operate, & every act of

---

3. For support of judicial review, see Charles A. Beard, The Supreme Court and the Constitution (1912), and Raoul Berger, Congress v. The Supreme Court (1969). Critics include Louis B. Boudin, Government by Judiciary (1932), and William W. Crosskey, Politics and the Constitution (1953).

a particular Legislature before a Negative thereon shall be final; and that the dissent of the said Council shall amount to a rejection, unless the Act of the National Legislature be again passed...." 1 Farrand 21. Some commentators accept the elimination of the revisionary council as proof that the framers rejected judicial review. However, one of the arguments against the Council was the *availability* of judicial review. As reported by Madison: "Mr. Gerry doubts whether the Judiciary ought to form a part of it, as they will have a sufficient check agst. encroachments on their own department by their exposition of the laws, which involved a power of deciding on their Constitutionality. In some States the Judges had <actually> set aside laws as being agst. the Constitution. This was done too with general approbation." Id. at 97. Here is a clue of judicial review being exercised in cases of a "judiciary nature." The Court needed power to strike down congressional legislation that threatened the integrity or existence of the judiciary. Rufus King supported Gerry's argument after observing that the Justices of the Supreme Court "ought to be able to expound the law as it should come before them, free from the bias of having participated in its formation." This comment provides broader support for judicial review, whereas Gerry appeared to restrict it to legislative encroachments.

Congress Vetoing State Legislation

After debating a congressional veto over proposed state legislation, that idea was rejected for two reasons. The addition of the Supremacy Clause would presumably handle any conflicts between national law and state legislation. Moreover, the state courts could exercise judicial review to control legislative excesses. They "would not consider as valid any law contravening the Authority of the Union," and if such laws were not set aside by the judiciary they "may be repealed by a Nationl. law." 2 Farrand 27–28 (Sherman and Morris). Madison later said that a law "violating a constitution established by the people themselves, would be considered by the Judges as null & void." Id. at 93. These statements were clearly limited to judicial review at the *state,* not the national, level. A year later, writing to Thomas Jefferson, Madison denied that the Constitution empowered the Court to strike down acts of Congress (see box). His comments support fluidity, not finality.

James Wilson, soon to be a member of the Supreme Court, defended the concept of judicial review at the Pennsylvania ratification convention. He said the legislature would be "kept within its prescribed bounds" by the judiciary. 2 Elliot 445. At the Connecticut ratifying convention, Oliver

---

James Madison on Judicial Review

A revisionary power [by the Council of Revision] is meant as a check to precipitate, to unjust, and to unconstitutional laws. These important ends would it is conceded be more effectually secured, without disarming the Legislature of its requisite authority, by requiring bills to be separately communicated to the Exec. & Judic'y depts. If either of these object, let 2/3, if both 3/4 of each House be necessary to overrule the objection; and if either or both protest agst a bill as violating the Constitution, let it moreover be suspended notwithstanding the overruling proportion of the [legislative] Assembly, until there shall have been a subsequent election of the [House of Deputies] and a re-passage of the bill by 2/3 or 3/4 of both Houses as the case may be. It sd not be allowed the Judges or [the] Executive to pronounce a law thus enacted unconstitu'l & invalid.

In the State Constitutions & indeed in the Fed'l one also, no provision is made for the case of a disagreement in expounding them; and as the Courts are generally the last in making [the] decision, it results to them by refusing or not refusing to execute a law, to stamp it with its final character. This makes the Judiciary Dept paramount in fact to the Legislature, which was never intended and can never be proper.

SOURCE: 5 Writings of James Madison 294 (Hunt ed. 1904).

Ellsworth (destined to be the third Chief Justice of the Supreme Court) expected federal judges to void any legislative acts that were contrary to the Constitution. Id. at 196; see also Samuel Adams's comments in Massachusetts, id. at 131. At the Virginia ratifying convention, John Marshall anticipated that the federal judiciary would strike down unconstitutional legislative acts. Id. at 553; see also George Nicholas, id. at 443. The context of these remarks suggests that the availability of judicial review was used to reassure the states that national power would be held in check.

Federalists and Anti-Federalists

The *Federalist Papers* include several essays that speak strongly for judicial review. The principal essay, Hamilton's Federalist No. 78 (see reading), is designed partly to allay state fears about the power of the central government. The Antifederalists, as expressed in Letter XI of Brutus, worried that judicial review at the national level would weaken the powers of the states, Congress, and the President. Any errors committed by federal courts could not be "corrected by any power above them, if any such power there be." From the decisions of federal courts there appeared to be "no appeal." How could Congress set aside a judgment if those courts "are authorized by the constitution to decide in the last resort"? The impeachment power, Brutus argued, would be an unlikely check on judicial errors. Herbert J. Storing, ed., The Anti-Federalist 163–65 (1985 ed.).

Hamilton's effort to rebut these concerns, in Federalist No. 78, were later borrowed by John Marshall to buttress his *Marbury* opinion. Hamilton's enthusiasm is somewhat suspect; he appears to have been a late convert to the cause of judicial review. His plan of government presented to the 1787 convention did not grant this power to the judiciary. 1 Farrand 282–93, 302–11; 3 Farrand 617–30. State laws contrary to the Constitution would be "utterly void," but the judiciary is not identified as the voiding agency. 1 Farrand 293.

The New Government

In the years between ratification and *Marbury* v. *Madison,* the issue of judicial review was debated often in Congress, but not with any consistency. When Madison introduced the Bill of Rights in the House of Representatives, he predicted that once they were incorporated into the Constitution, "independent tribunals of justice will consider themselves in a peculiar manner the guardians of those rights; they will be an impenetrable bulwark against every assumption of power in the Legislative or Executive." 1 Annals of Congress 439 (June 8, 1789). But nine days later, during debate on the President's removal power, Madison denied that Congress should defer to the courts on this constitutional issue. He begged to know on what principle could it be contended "that any one department draws from the Constitution greater powers than another, in marking out the limits of the powers of the several departments?" If questions arose on the boundaries between the branches, he did not see "that any one of these independent departments has more right than another to declare their sentiments on that point." Id. at 500 (June 17, 1789). In 1791, when proponents of a national bank cited judicial review as a possible check on unconstitutional legislation, Madison was unpersuaded and voted against the bank. 3 Annals of Congress 1978–79 (February 4, 1791).

Alexander Hamilton, Federalist No. 78

We proceed now to an examination of the judiciary department of the proposed government.

In unfolding the defects of the existing Confederation, the utility and necessity of a federal judicature have been clearly pointed out....

Whoever attentively considers the different departments of power must perceive, that, in a government in which they are separated from each other, the judiciary, from the nature of its functions, will always be the least dangerous to the political rights of the Constitution; because it will be least in a capacity to annoy or injure them. The Executive not only dispenses the honors, but holds the sword of the community. The legislature not only commands the purse, but prescribes the rules by which the duties and rights of every citizen are to be regulated. The judiciary, on the contrary, has no influence over either the sword or the purse; no direction either of the strength or of the wealth of the society; and can take no active resolution whatever. It may truly be said to have neither FORCE nor WILL, but merely judgment; and must ultimately depend upon the aid of the executive arm even for the efficacy of its judgments....

The complete independence of the courts of justice is peculiarly essential in a limited Constitution. By a limited Constitution, I understand one which contains certain specified exceptions to the legislative authority; such, for instance, as that it shall pass no bills of attainder, no *ex-post-facto* laws, and the like. Limitations of this kind can be preserved in practice no other way than through the medium of courts of justice, whose duty it must be to declare all acts contrary to the manifest tenor of the Constitution void. Without this, all the reservations of particular rights or privileges would amount to nothing.

Some perplexity respecting the rights of the courts to pronounce legislative acts void, because contrary to the constitution, has arisen from an imagination that the doctrine would imply a superiority of the judiciary to the legislative power. It is urged that the authority which can declare the acts of another void, must necessarily be superior to the one whose acts may be declared void. As this doctrine is of great importance in all the American constitutions, a brief discussion of the ground on which it rests cannot be unacceptable.

There is no position which depends on clearer principles, than that every act of a delegated authority, contrary to the tenor of the commission under which it is exercised, is void. No legislative act, therefore, contrary to the Constitution, can be valid. To deny this, would be to affirm, that the deputy is greater than his principal; that the servant is above his master; that the representatives of the people are superior to the people themselves; that men acting by virtue of powers, may do not only what their powers do not authorize, but what they forbid.

If it be said that the legislative body are themselves the constitutional judges of their own powers, and that the construction they put upon them is conclusive upon the other departments, it may be answered, that this cannot be the natural presumption, where it is not to be collected from any particular provisions in the Constitution. It is not otherwise to be supposed, that the Constitution could intend to enable the representatives of the people to substitute their *will* to that of their constituents. It is far more rational to suppose, that the courts were designed to be an intermediate body between the people and the legislature, in order, among other things, to keep the latter within the limits assigned to their authority. The interpretation of the laws is the proper and peculiar province of the courts. A constitution is, in fact, and must be regarded by the judges, as a fundamental law. It therefore belongs to them to ascertain its meaning, as well as the meaning of any particular act proceeding from the legislative body. If there should happen to be an irreconcilable variance between the two, that which has the superior obligation and validity ought, of course, to be preferred; or, in other words, the Constitution ought to be preferred to the statute, the intention of the people to the intention of their agents.

Nor does this conclusion by any means suppose a superiority of the judicial to the legislative power. It only supposes that the power of the people is superior to both; and that where the will of the legislature, declared in its statutes, stands in opposition to that of the people, declared in the Constitution, the judges ought to be governed by the latter rather than the former. They ought to regulate their decisions by the fundamental laws, rather than by those which are not fundamental....

This independence of the judges is equally requisite to guard the Constitution and the rights of individuals from the effects of those ill humors, which the arts of designing men, or the influence of particular conjunctures, sometimes disseminate among the people themselves, and which, though they speedily give place to better information, and more deliberate reflection, have a tendency, in the meantime, to occasion dangerous innovations in the government, and serious oppressions of the minor party in the community.

C. THE ROAD TO *MARBURY*

Federal courts reviewed both national and state legislation prior to the 1803 decision *Marbury*. In 1792, three circuit courts held divergent views on an act of Congress that appointed federal judges to serve as commissioners for claims settlement. Their decisions could be set aside by the Secretary of War. One of the courts agreed to serve. The other two believed that the statute was "unwarranted" because it required federal judges to perform nonjudicial duties and to render what was essentially an advisory (instead of binding) opinion. The Supreme Court postponed decision until the next term; by that time Congress had repealed the offending sections and removed the Secretary's authority to veto decisions rendered by judges. Hayburn's Case, 2 Dall. 409 (1792). See 1 Stat. 243 (1792) and 1 Stat. 324 (1793). In 1794, a year after Congress repaired the statute, the Supreme Court decided that the original statute would have been unconstitutional if it sought to impose nonjudicial duties on the circuit courts. United States v. Yale Todd, 13 How. 52 (1794). The use of this case (not published until 1851) as a precedent for judicial review is rendered suspect by the fact that the statutory provision no longer existed.

Between 1791 and 1799, federal courts began to challenge and strike down a number of state laws. 1 Charles Warren, The Supreme Court in United States History 65–69 (1937). With regard to national legislation, in 1796 the Supreme Court *upheld* a congressional statute that imposed a tax on carriages. If the Court had authority to uphold an act of Congress, presumably it had authority to strike one down. Justice Chase said it was unnecessary "*at this time,* for me to determine, whether this court, *constitutionally* possesses the power to declare an act of Congress *void* ... but if the court have such power, I am free to declare, that I will never exercise it, *but in a very clear case.*" Hylton v. United States, 3 Dall. 171, 175 (1796) (emphasis in original). Two years later the Court upheld the constitutionality of another congressional act, this time involving the process of constitutional amendment. Hollingsworth v. Virginia, 3 Dall. 378 (1798).

Three other cases between 1795 and 1800 explored the authority of federal judges to declare state acts unconstitutional. In the first case, a circuit court decided that a Pennsylvania law was unconstitutional and void. Vanhorne's Lessee v. Dorrance, 2 Dall. 304 (1795). In 1798, Supreme Court Justices offered differing views on the existence and scope of judicial review (see box). In the third case, Justice Chase said that even if it were agreed that a statute contrary to the Constitution would be void, "it still remains a question, where the power resides to declare it void?" The "general opinion," he said, is that the Supreme Court could declare an act of Congress unconstitutional, "but there is no adjudication of the Supreme Court itself upon the point." Cooper v. Telfair, 4 Dall. 14, 19 (1800).

From 1789 to 1802, eleven state judiciaries exercised judicial review over state statutes. Charles Grove Haines, The American Doctrine of Judicial Supremacy, at 148–64. The assertion of power by the national judiciary against coequal branches was much more cautious, and yet even the Jefferson-

---

Supreme Court Justices Inquire: May We Void a Legislative Act?

JUSTICE CHASE. Without giving an opinion, at this time whether this Court has jurisdiction to decide that any law made by Congress, contrary to the Constitution of the *United States* is void; I am fully satisfied that this court has no *jurisdiction* to determine that any law of any state *Legislature,* contrary to the Constitution of such *state,* is void....

I am under a necessity to give a *construction,* or explanation of the words, "*ex post facto law,*" because they have not any certain meaning attached

to them. But I will not go farther than I feel myself bound to do; and if I ever exercise the jurisdiction I will not decide *any law to be void, but in a very clear case.*

JUSTICE IREDELL. If any act of Congress, or of the Legislature of a state, violates those constitutional provisions, it is unquestionably void; though, I admit, that as the authority to declare it void is of delicate and awful nature, the Court will never resort to that authority, but in a clear and urgent case.

SOURCE: Calder v. Bull, 3 Dall. 386, 392, 395, 399 (1798).

ian Republicans rebuked the federal courts for not striking down the repressive Alien and Sedition Acts of 1798. 1 Warren, The Supreme Court in United States History, at 215. In that same year Jefferson looked to the courts to protect basic rights: "the laws of the land, administered by upright judges, would protect you from any exercise of power unauthorized by the Constitution of the United States." 10 Writings of Thomas Jefferson 61 (Memorial ed. 1903).

Marshall Court Foundations

By 1801 the Supreme Court had yet to solidify its powers. It had upheld the constitutionality of a congressional statute. In a series of dicta, it gingerly explored the theory that it could hold one unconstitutional. In four bold decisions from 1803 to 1821, the Court held that it had the power to determine the constitutionality of statutes passed by Congress and state legislatures, as well as authority to review judgments by state courts in cases raising federal questions.

The election of 1800 marked a pivotal point for the nation. Although formally neutral between Britain and France, America split into two warring camps. The Federalist party was pro-British; the Jeffersonian Republicans sympathized with the French. Efforts by the Adams administration to limit Republican criticism led to the Alien and Sedition Acts, further exacerbating partisan strife. When the Jeffersonians swept the elections of 1800, the Federalists looked for ways to salvage their dwindling political power.

Early in 1801, with a few weeks remaining for the Federalist Congress, two bills were passed to create a number of federal judges and justices of the peace in the District of Columbia. 2 Stat. 89, 103 (1801). Within a matter of days, President John Adams nominated Federalists to the new posts, much to the outrage of Republicans. John Marshall was at that point serving as Secretary of State, although he had already been appointed to the Supreme Court for the next term. The commissions of office were processed, sent to the Senate, and confirmed. Some of the commissions, William Marbury's among them, were never delivered.

In taking office as President, Thomas Jefferson ordered that the commissions be withheld. The administration also urged Congress to repeal the Circuit Court Act (with its additional judgeships) and to block the anticipated 1802 term of the Supreme Court. Congress complied. 2 Stat. 132, 156 (1802). Partisan bitterness increased in the spring of 1801 when two Federalist judges instructed a district attorney to prosecute a newspaper that had published an attack on the judiciary. The jury refused to indict, but the Republicans saw this as additional evidence that the Federalists were engaged in a national conspiracy.[4] As part of a counterattack, the House of Representatives impeached District Judge John Pickering (a Federalist) and the Senate removed him. Congress contemplated the removal of Justice Samuel Chase from the Supreme Court and seemed poised to remove other Federalist judges, including John Marshall.

In this tense political climate, William Marbury and his colleagues appealed to the former Attorney General, Charles Lee, for legal assistance. Lee brought the action directly to the Supreme Court under Section 13 of the Judiciary Act of 1789, which empowered the Court to issue writs of mandamus "in cases warranted by the principles and usages of law, to any courts appointed, or persons holding office, under the authority of the United States." Lee argued that the Court had jurisdiction under Section 13 because Madison was a person holding office (Secretary of State) under the authority of the United States. He asked the Court to issue a writ of mandamus, ordering Madison to deliver the commissions.

Marshall's options were circumscribed by one overpowering fact: whatever technical ground he might use to rule against the administration, any order directing Madison to deliver the commissions was sure to be ignored. If the Court's order could be dismissed with impunity, the judiciary's power

---

4. George Lee Haskins and Herbert A. Johnson, 2 History of the Supreme Court of the United States: Foundations of Power: John Marshall 161–62 (1981).

and prestige would suffer greatly. As Chief Justice Burger noted: "The Court could stand hard blows, but not ridicule, and the ale house would rock with hilarious laughter" had Marshall issued a mandamus ignored by Jefferson.[5] Marshall chose a tactic he used in future years. He would appear to absorb a short-term defeat in exchange for a long-term victory. The decision has been called "a masterwork of indirection, a brilliant example of Marshall's capacity to sidestep danger while seeking to court it, to advance in one direction while his opponents are looking in another." Robert G. McCloskey, The American Supreme Court 40 (1960).

The opinion acknowledged the merits of Marbury's case but denied that the Court had power to issue the mandamus. Through a strained reading, Marshall concluded that Section 13 expanded the original jurisdiction of the Court and thereby violated Article III of the Constitution. He maintained that Congress could alter the boundaries only of appellate jurisdiction and that if a statute conflicted with the Constitution it was the duty of judges, who took an oath to support the Constitution, to strike down the offending law. MARBURY v. MADISON, 5 U.S. (1 Cr.) 137 (1803).

The decision in *Marbury* has stimulated a number of critiques. Marshall's analysis of original and appellate jurisdiction is less than compelling. He could have read Section 13 to connect mandamus action to appellate jurisdiction. Even if he related it to original jurisdiction, the Constitution did not explicitly prohibit Congress from adding to original jurisdiction. Furthermore, if the Court did indeed lack jurisdiction, why did Marshall reach further and explore the merits of Marbury's claim and expound on novel questions of judicial authority? Finally, given his previous involvement in the matter, there were strong grounds for Marshall to disqualify himself (see reading by Van Alstyne).

Encircled by hostile political forces, Marshall decided to strike boldly for judicial independence. Instead of citing historical and legal precedents, all of which could have been challenged and picked apart by his opponents, Marshall reached to a higher plane and grounded his case on what appeared to be self-evident, universal principles. His decision seems to march logically and inexorably toward the only possible conclusion. *Marbury* v. *Madison* is famous for the proposition that the Court is supreme on constitutional questions, but it stands for a much more modest claim. Chief Justice Marshall stated that it is "emphatically the province and duty of the judicial department to say what the law is." 5 U.S. (1 Cr.) 137, 177 (1803). So it is, but the same can be said for Congress. Surely it is the province and duty of Congress to say what the law is. The Court in 1803 lacked the power to dictate to Congress or to the President.

Did Marshall believe that the Court was supreme on questions of constitutionality? Probably not. His behavior during the impeachment hearings of Judge Pickering and Justice Chase suggest that he was quite willing to share constitutional interpretations with the coequal branches. *Marbury* was issued on February 24, 1803. The House impeached Pickering on March 2, 1803, and the Senate convicted him on March 12, 1804. As soon as the House had impeached Pickering, it turned its guns on Chase. Under these precarious circumstances, Marshall wrote to Chase on January 23, 1805, suggesting that members of Congress did not have to impeach judges whenever they objected to their judicial opinions. Instead, Congress could simply review and reverse objectionable decisions through the legislative process. Marshall's letter to Chase is somewhat ambiguous. He could have been referring to reversals of statutory interpretation, not constitutional interpretation, but given the temper of the times the latter seems more likely (see box on next page).

Stuart v. Laird

One week after issuing *Marbury*, the Court handed down an important case that further defined how the judiciary and the elected branches shape the meaning of the Constitution. Unfortunately, this second case receives little attention or appreciation. It concerned the decision of the Jeffersonian Con-

---

5. Warren E. Burger, "The Doctrine of Judicial Review: Mr. Marshall, Mr. Jefferson, and Mr. Marbury," in Mark W. Cannon and David M. O'Brien, eds., Views From the Bench 14 (1985).

Marshall Writes to Chase

Jan. 23, 1805

My dear Sir

. . .

Admitting it to be true that on legal principles Colo. Taylors testimony was admissible, it certainly constitutes a very extraordinary ground for an impeachment. According to the antient doctrine a jury finding a verdict against the law of the case was liable to an attaint; & the amount of the present doctrine seems to be that a Judge giving a legal opinion contrary to the opinion of the legislature is liable to impeachment.

As, for convenience & humanity the old doctrine of attaint has yielded to the silent, moderate but not less operative influence of new trials, I think the modern doctrine of impeachment should yield to an appellate jurisdiction in the legislature. A reversal of those legal opinions deemed unsound by the legislature would certainly better comport with the mildness of our character than [*would*] a removal of the Judge who has rendered them unknowing of his fault.

. . .

J. Marshall

SOURCE: 3 Albert J. Beveridge, The Life of John Marshall 177 (1919). Marshall dated the letter January 23, 1804, but modern scholarship fixes the date a year later; 6 The Papers of John Marshall 348 n.1 (Hobson ed. 1990). Like the rest of us, Marshall forgot to switch to the new year.

gress to repeal the Circuit Court Act passed in the waning days of Federalist control. The statute created 16 new judgeships. They were quickly nominated by President Adams and confirmed by the Senate. Did the Jeffersonians have authority to abolish courts with Article III judges entitled to lifetime terms? Federalists found it repugnant that Congress could not take a judge out of the office (save by impeachment) but could take the office out of the judge.

Would the Court invoke its newfound strength of judicial review by invalidating the repeal law? Such action would greatly intensify congressional efforts to impeach and remove Federalist judges. Facing that reality, the Court held that the issue of circuit judges had been settled by congressional action in 1789 when it created circuit courts and required Supreme Court Justices to "ride circuit." The Court deferred to the constitutional judgment of Congress. The 1789 statute had "fixed the construction" of the Constitution (see box in Chapter 4, Section A). The final voice on constitutional meaning in this case went to the elected branches. Stuart v. Laird, 5 U.S. (1 Cr.) 299 (1803).

Developments after *Marbury*

The power to strike down a congressional statute was not used again until 1857, when the Court tackled the issue of slavery. Dred Scott v. Sandford, 60 U.S. (19 How.) 393. Judicial review of state actions, however, was more frequent. In two sets of decisions, the Court established its authority to review state statutes and state judicial decisions.

United States v. *Peters* (1809) and *Fletcher* v. *Peck* (1810) were decided in a difficult political period. Some states, reacting against the growth of national power, threatened secession and nullification. Richard Peters, a federal judge in Pennsylvania, discovered that state officials refused to obey a decree he had issued. The state legislature passed a law declaring the decree a usurpation of power and ordered the governor to resist any attempt to enforce it. Chief Justice Marshall issued a mandamus, ordering enforcement on the ground that state legislatures cannot interfere with the operation of the federal judicial process. United States v. Peters, 9 U.S. (5 Cr.) 115 (1809). The governor called out the militia to prevent a federal marshal from executing the court order. He also sought President Madison's assistance, but the state's resistance collapsed when Madison replied that the President "is not only unauthorized to prevent the execution of a decree sanctioned by the Supreme Court of the

United States, but is expressly enjoined, by statute, to carry into effect any such decree where opposition may be made to it." Annals of Congress, 11th Cong., 2269.

In *Fletcher* v. *Peck*, the Court struck down an act of a state legislature as unconstitutional. Several land companies had obtained a huge land grant at a bargain price from the Georgia legislature by offering bribes to a number of lawmakers. After elections, the new legislature revoked the land grant. In the meantime, innocent third parties had bought property from the corrupt land companies. Some of the purchasers challenged the revocation, claiming impairment of the obligations of a contract protected by Article I, Section 10, of the Constitution. Justice Marshall, recognizing the delicate task of reviewing state legislation, concluded that the revocation did constitute a violation of the Impairments Clause. Fletcher v. Peck, 10 U.S. (6 Cr.) 87, 136–39 (1810) (see reading in Chapter 9).

A second pair of cases was decided after the War of 1812, following a substantial change in the Supreme Court's membership. The most important addition was Joseph Story. Though appointed by James Madison, he became as ardent a defender of national interests as Marshall. He wrote the decision that established the Court's authority to review state court decisions involving federal questions. MARTIN v. HUNTER'S LESSEE, 1 Wheat. 304 (1816). The dispute in *Martin* was between two private parties. In 1821, with a state as one of the parties, Marshall solidified the relationship of the Court to state courts and breathed new life into the Supremacy Clause. COHENS v. VIRGINIA, 6 Wheat. 264 (1821).

Marbury v. Madison

5 U.S. (1 Cr.) 137 (1803)

William Marbury and several colleagues were nominated by President John Adams to be justices of the peace in the District of Columbia. The Senate confirmed their names. Adams signed their commissions, and the seal of the United States was affixed to the commissions. However, in the confusion of the remaining days of the Adams administration, some of the commissions, including Marbury's, were not delivered. When President Thomas Jefferson entered office, he ordered that the commissions not be delivered. Marbury sued the Secretary of State, James Madison. The opinion in this case is written by Chief Justice John Marshall.

Opinion of the Court.

At the last term on the affidavits then read and filed with the clerk, a rule was granted in this case, requiring the secretary of state to show cause why a *mandamus* should not issue, directing him to deliver to William Marbury his commission as a justice of the peace for the county of Washington, in the district of Columbia.

No cause has been shown, and the present motion is for a *mandamus*....

The first object of inquiry is,

1st. Has the applicant a right to the commission he demands?

. . .

It appears, from the affidavits, that ... a commission for William Marbury, as a justice of peace for the county of Washington, was signed by John Adams, then President of the United States; after which the seal of the United States was affixed to it;

but the commission has never reached the person for whom it was made out....

The last act to be done by the president is the signature of the commission. He has then acted on the advice and consent of the senate to his own nomination. The time for deliberation has then passed. He has decided. His judgment, on the advice and consent of the senate concurring with his nomination, has been made, and the officer is appointed. This appointment is evidenced by an open, unequivocal act; and being the last act required from the person making it, necessarily excludes the idea of its being, so far as respects the appointment, an inchoate and incomplete transaction....

The commission being signed, the subsequent duty of the secretary of state is prescribed by law, and not to be guided by the will of the president. He is to affix the seal of the United States to the commission, and is to record it.

This is not a proceeding which may be varied, if the judgment of the executive shall suggest one more eligible; but is a precise course accurately marked out by law, and is to be strictly pursued. It is the duty of the secretary of state to conform to the law, and in this he is an officer of the United States, bound to obey the laws. He acts, in this respect, as has been very properly stated at the bar, under the authority of law, and not by the instructions of the president. It is a ministerial act which the law enjoins on a particular officer for a particular purpose....

Mr. Marbury, then, since his commission was signed by the president, and sealed by the secretary of state, was appointed; and as the law creating the office, gave the officer a right to hold for five years, independent of the executive, the appointment was not revocable, but vested in the officer legal rights, which are protected by the laws of his country.

To withhold his commission, therefore, is an act deemed by the court not warranted by law, but violative of a vested legal right.

This brings us to the second inquiry; which is,

2dly, If he has a right, and that right has been violated, do the laws of his country afford him a remedy?

The very essence of civil liberty certainly consists in the right of every individual to claim the protection of the laws, whenever he receives an injury. One of the first duties of government is to afford that protection....

The government of the United States has been emphatically termed a government of laws, and not of men. It will certainly cease to deserve this high appellation, if the laws furnish no remedy for the violation of a vested legal right....

By the constitution of the United States, the president is invested with certain important political powers, in the exercise of which he is to use his own discretion, and is accountable only to his country in his political character and to his own conscience. To aid him in the performance of these duties, he is authorized to appoint certain officers, who act by his authority, and in conformity with his orders.

In such cases, their acts are his acts; and whatever opinion may be entertained of the manner in which executive discretion may be used, still there exists, and can exist, no power to control that discretion. The subjects are political. They respect the nation, not individual rights, and being intrusted to the executive, the decision of the executive is conclusive.... The acts of such an officer, as an officer, can never be examinable by the courts.

But when the legislature proceeds to impose on that officer other duties; when he is directed peremptorily to perform certain acts; when the rights of individuals are dependent on the performance of those acts; he is so far the officer of the law; is amenable to the laws for his conduct; and cannot at his discretion sport away the vested rights of others.

The conclusion from this reasoning is, that where the heads of departments are the political or confidential agents of the executive, merely to execute the will of the president, or rather to act in cases in which the executive possesses a constitutional or legal discretion, nothing can be more perfectly clear than that their acts are only politically examinable. But where a specific duty is assigned by law, and individual rights depend upon the performance of that duty, it seems equally clear that the individual who considers himself injured, has a right to resort to the laws of his country for a remedy....

The question whether a right has vested or not, is, in its nature, judicial, and must be tried by the judicial authority....

It is, then, the opinion of the court,

1st. That by signing the commission of Mr. Marbury, the President of the United States appointed him a justice of peace for the county of Washington, in the district of Columbia; and that the seal of the United States, affixed thereto by the secretary of state, is conclusive testimony of the verity of the signature, and of the completion of the appointment; and that the appointment conferred on him a legal right to the office for the space of five years.

2dly. That, having this legal title to the office, he has a consequent right to the commission; a refusal to deliver which is a plain violation of that right, for which the laws of his country afford him a remedy.

It remains to be inquired whether,

3dly. He is entitled to the remedy for which he applies. This depends on,

1st. The nature of the writ applied for; and,

2dly. The power of this court.

1st. The nature of the writ....

The [1789] act to establish the judicial courts of the United States authorizes [in Section 13] the supreme court "to issue writs of *mandamus,* in cases warranted by the principles and usages of law, to any courts appointed, or persons holding office, under the authority of the United States."

The secretary of state, being a person holding an office under the authority of the United States, is precisely within the letter of the description; and if this court is not authorized to issue a writ of *mandamus* to such an officer, it must be because the law is unconstitutional, and therefore absolutely incapable of conferring the authority, and assigning the duties which its words purport to confer and assign.

[Marshall analyzed two types of jurisdiction granted to the Court: "In all Cases affecting Ambassadors, other public Ministers and Consuls, and those in which a State shall be a Party," the Court "shall have original Jurisdiction." In all other cases the Court "shall have appellate Jurisdiction, both as to Law and Fact, with such Exceptions, and under such Regulations as the Court shall make." Reading those two categories as exclusive and ignoring the authority of Congress to make exceptions, Marshall regarded Marbury's case as not one of original jurisdiction as specified in the Constitution. Neither was it appellate because no lower court had acted.]

This original and supreme will organizes the government, and assigns to different departments their respective powers. It may either stop here, or establish certain limits not to be transcended by those departments.

The government of the United States is of the latter description. The powers of the legislature are defined and limited; and that those limits may not be mistaken, or forgotten, the constitution is written. To what purpose are powers limited, and to what purpose is that limitation committed to writing, if these limits may, at any time, be passed by those intended to be restrained? The distinction between a government with limited and unlimited powers is abolished, if those limits do not confine the persons on whom they are imposed, and if acts prohibited and acts allowed, are of equal obligation. It is a proposition too plain to be contested, that the constitution controls any legislative act repugnant to it; or, that the legislature may alter the constitution by an ordinary act.

Between these alternatives there is no middle ground. The constitution is either a superior paramount law, unchangeable by ordinary means, or it is on a level with ordinary legislative acts, and, like other acts, is alterable when the legislature shall please to alter it.

If the former part of the alternative be true, then a legislative act contrary to the constitution is not law: if the latter part be true, then written constitutions are absurd attempts, on the part of the people, to limit a power in its own nature illimitable.

Certainly all those who have framed written constitutions contemplate them as forming the fundamental and paramount law of the nation, and, consequently, the theory of every such government must be, that an act of the legislature, repugnant to the constitution, is void.

This theory is essentially attached to a written constitution, and, is consequently, to be considered, by this court, as one of the fundamental principles of our society. It is not therefore to be lost sight of in the further consideration of this subject.

If an act of the legislature, repugnant to the constitution, is void, does it, notwithstanding its invalidity, bind the courts, and oblige them to give it effect? Or, in other words, though it be not law, does it constitute a rule as operative as if it was a law? This would be to overthrow in fact what was established in theory; and would seem, at first view, an absurdity too gross to be insisted on. It shall, however, receive a more attentive consideration.

It is emphatically the province and duty of the judicial department to say what the law is. Those who apply the rule to particular cases, must of necessity expound and interpret that rule. If two laws conflict with each other, the courts must decide on the operation of each.

So if a law be in opposition to the constitution; if both the law and the constitution apply to a particular case, so that the court must either decide that case conformably to the law, disregarding the constitution; or conformably to the constitution, disregarding the law; the court must determine which of these conflicting rules governs the case. This is of the very essence of judicial duty.

If, then, the courts are to regard the constitution, and the constitution is superior to any ordinary act of the legislature, the constitution, and not such ordinary act, must govern the case to which they both apply.

Those, then, who controvert the principle that the constitution is to be considered, in court, as a paramount law, are reduced to the necessity of maintaining that courts must close their eyes on the constitution, and see only the law.

This doctrine would subvert the very foundation of all written constitutions. It would declare that an act which, according to the principles and theory of our government, is entirely void, is yet, in practice, completely obligatory. It would declare that if the legislature shall do what is expressly forbidden, such act, notwithstanding the express prohibition, is in reality effectual. It would be giving to the legislature a practical and real omnipotence, with the same breath which professes to restrict their powers within narrow limits. It is prescribing limits, and declaring that those limits may be passed at pleasure.

That it thus reduces to nothing what we have deemed the greatest improvement on political institutions, a written constitution, would of itself be sufficient, in America, where written constitutions have been viewed with so much reverence, for rejecting the construction. But the peculiar expressions of the constitution of the United States furnish additional arguments in favour of its rejection.

The judicial power of the United States is extended to all cases arising under the constitution.

Could it be the intention of those who gave this

power, to say that in using it the constitution should not be looked into? That a case arising under the constitution should be decided without examining the instrument under which it arises?

This is too extravagant to be maintained.

In some cases, then, the constitution must be looked into by the judges. And if they can open it at all, what part of it are they forbidden to read or to obey?

There are many other parts of the constitution which serve to illustrate this subject.

It is declared that "no tax or duty shall be laid on articles exported from any state." Suppose a duty on the export of cotton, of tobacco, or of flour; and a suit instituted to recover it. Ought judgment to be rendered in such a case? ought the judges to close their eyes on the constitution, and only see the law?

The constitution declares "that no bill of attainder or *ex post facto* law shall be passed."

If, however, such a bill should be passed, and a person should be prosecuted under it; must the court condemn to death those victims whom the constitution endeavours to preserve?

"No person," says the constitution, "shall be convicted of treason unless on the testimony of two witnesses to the same overt act, or on confession in open court."

Here the language of the constitution is addressed especially to the courts. It prescribes, directly for them, a rule of evidence not to be departed from. If the legislature should change that rule, and declare *one* witness, or a confession *out* of court, sufficient for conviction, must the constitutional principle yield to the legislative act?

From these, and many other selections which might be made, it is apparent, that the framers of the constitution contemplated that instrument as a rule for the government of *courts,* as well as of the legislature.

Why otherwise does it direct the judges to take an oath to support it? This oath certainly applies in an especial manner, to their conduct in their official character. How immoral to impose it on them, if they were to be used as the instruments, and the knowing instruments, for violating what they swear to support!

The oath of office, too, imposed by the legislature, is completely demonstrative of the legislative opinion on this subject. It is in these words: "I do solemnly swear that I will administer justice without respect to persons, and do equal right to the poor and to the rich; and that I will faithfully and impartially discharge all the duties incumbent on me as * * * * * *, according to the best of my abilities and understanding, agreeably to *the constitution* and laws of the United States."

Why does a judge swear to discharge his duties agreeably to the constitution of the United States, if that constitution forms no rule for his government? if it is closed upon him, and cannot be inspected by him?

If such be the real state of things, this is worse than solemn mockery. To prescribe, or, to take this oath, becomes equally a crime.

It is also not entirely unworthy of observation, that in declaring what shall be the *supreme* law of the land, the *constitution* itself is first mentioned; and not the laws of the United States generally, but those only which shall be made in *pursuance* of the constitution, have that rank.

Thus, the particular phraseology of the constitution of the United States confirms and strengthens the principle, supposed to be essential to all written constitutions, that a law repugnant to the constitution is void; and that *courts,* as well as other departments, are bound by that instrument.

The rule must be discharged.

William W. Van Alstyne[*]
A Critical Guide to *Marbury* v. *Madison*

The Court declares that the "first" issue presented by the case is: "Has the applicant a right to the commission he demands?" At least two criticisms of this beginning have been made. Both arise in answer to the question: Was Marbury's entitlement to the commission he demanded really the

issue which the Court should have examined first? Arguably, it was not.

Surely the Court ought first determine whether it has any authority to decide any issues whatever respecting the merits of the case, *i.e.,* it should first resolve the preliminary question of its own jurisdic-

[*] SOURCE: 1969 Duke L. J. 1. Footnotes omitted.

tion. The Court's jurisdiction was ostensibly based on section 13 of the Judiciary Act of 1789 which Marbury alleged to empower the Court to issue a writ of mandamus in this sort of case. But if the Act did not in fact provide for such jurisdiction, or if it were invalid in attempting to provide for such jurisdiction, the Court would be without proper authority to consider the merits of Marbury's claim....

... [T]here is clearly an "issue" of sorts which preceded any of those touched upon in the opinion. Specifically, it would appear that Marshall should have recused himself in view of his substantial involvement in the background of this controversy. Remember, too, that the Court thought it important to establish whether Marbury's commission had already been signed and sealed before it was withdrawn — to determine whether Marbury's interest had "vested" and whether Madison was refusing to carry out a merely ministerial duty, or whether the commission was sufficiently incomplete that matters of executive discretion were involved. Proof of the status of Marbury's commission not only involved circumstances within the Chief Justice's personal knowledge, it was furnished in the Supreme Court by Marshall's own younger brother who had been with him in his office when, as Secretary of State, he had made out the commissions. Arguably the first issue, then, was the appropriateness of Marshall's participation in the decision.

MARBURY'S "RIGHT" TO THE COMMISSION

On the basis of the Act of 1801 providing for the appointment of justices of the peace for a five-year term plus findings of fact that the appointment had "vested," the Court held that Marbury had a "right" to the commission. The Act itself was based on the power of Congress granted by the Constitution in Article I, section 8, clause 17, "to exercise Legislation in all Cases whatsoever, over" the District of Columbia. Marshall concludes that once the commission had been signed and sealed by President Adams, Marbury's claim to the office was complete.

Marshall reasonably could have concluded, however, that no interest actually "vested" in Marbury prior to actual delivery of the commission. Jefferson evidently thought that the better conclusion, subsequently insisting that Marshall's decision on this point was a "perversion of law," and maintaining that "if there is any principle of law never yet contradicted, it is that delivery is one of the essentials to the validity of the deed." Even if Jefferson overstated the law, and even assuming authority could be found urging that certain interests "vest" prior to delivery, it would not necessarily be dispositive of this

case. The Court is reviewing an aspect of executive power and passing judgment upon the propriety of conduct by a coordinate branch of government here, a consideration not present in an ordinary civil suit between private litigants....

STATUTORY INTERPRETATION

Certainly the first question is the following one of statutory interpretation which was just barely treated in the opinion: Did section 13 of the Judiciary Act authorize this action to originate in the Supreme Court? The section provides:

"And be it further enacted, That the Supreme Court shall have exclusive jurisdiction of all controversies of a civil nature, where a state is a party, except between a state and its citizens; and except also between a state and citizens of other states, or aliens, in which latter case it shall have original but not exclusive jurisdiction. And shall have exclusively all such jurisdiction of suits or proceedings against ambassadors, or other public ministers, or their domestics, or domestic servants, as a court of law can have or exercise consistently with the law of nations; and original, but not exclusive jurisdiction of all suits brought by ambassadors, or other public ministers, or in which a consul, or vice consul, shall be a party. And the trial of issues in fact in the Supreme Court, in all actions at law against citizens of the United States, shall be by jury. The Supreme Court shall also have appellate jurisdiction from the circuit courts and courts of the several states, in the cases herein after specially provided for; and shall have power to issue writs of prohibition to the district courts, when proceeding as courts of admiralty and maritime jurisdiction, and writs of *mandamus,* in cases warranted by the principles and usages of law, to any courts appointed, or persons holding office, under the authority of the United States."

Marshall quotes only the fragment at the end, perfunctorily notes that Madison holds office under the authority of the United States and therefore "is precisely within the letter of the description," and since he has already established that mandamus would otherwise be an appropriate remedy he quickly concludes that section 13 purports to authorize this case. But there is no discussion of whether this section *confers* original jurisdiction over suits seeking mandamus against persons holding office under the authority of the United States, or whether it merely authorizes mandamus to be so employed by the Court in cases properly *on appeal* or in aid of its original jurisdiction in cases involving foreign ministers or states. If it means only the latter, and if Marbury has no other basis for commencing his case in the Supreme Court, then the Court should simply dismiss the case for want of (statutory) jurisdiction and it need not, and ought not, examine the constitutionality of section 13 under some other construction. An argument can be made, of course, that section 13 did not attempt to grant original jurisdiction in Marbury's case.

The section opens by describing the Court's original jurisdiction and then moves on to describe appellate jurisdiction ("hereinafter specially provided for"). Textually, the provision regarding mandamus says nothing expressly as to whether it is part of original or appellate jurisdiction or both, and the clause itself does not speak at all of "conferring jurisdiction" on the court. The grant of "power" to issue the writ, however, is juxtaposed with the section of appellate jurisdiction and, in fact, follows the general description of appellate jurisdiction in the same sentence, being separated only by a semicolon. No textual mangling is required to confine it to appellate jurisdiction. Moreover, no mangling is required even if it attaches both to original and to appellate jurisdiction, not as an enlargement of either, but simply as a specification of power which the Court is authorized to use in cases which are *otherwise* appropriately under consideration. Since this case is not otherwise within the specified type of original jurisdiction (*e.g.*, it is not a case in which a state is a party or a case against an ambassador), it should be dismissed....

JUDICIAL REVIEW

Assuming that section 13 of the Judiciary Act of 1789 does confer original jurisdiction in this case, is its constitutionality subject to judicial review? Marshall initially responds to this question, which, of course, is the issue which has made the case of historic importance, by posing his own rhetorical question: "whether an Act repugnant to the Constitution can become the law of the land." That it cannot is clear, he says, from the following considerations.

The people in an exercise of their "original right," established the government pursuant to a written constitution which defines and limits the powers of the legislature. A "legislative act contrary to the constitution is not law," therefore, as it is contrary to the original and supreme will which organized the legislature itself.

· · ·

That the Constitution is a "written" one yields little or nothing as to whether acts of Congress may be given the force of positive law notwithstanding the opinion of judges, the executive, a minority or majority of the population, or even of Congress itself (assuming that Congress might sometimes be pressed by political forces to adopt a law against its belief that it lacked power to do so) that such Acts are repugnant to the Constitution. That this is so is clear enough simply from the fact that even in Marshall's time (and to a great extent today), a number of nations maintained written constitutions and yet gave national legislative acts the full force of positive law without providing any constitutional check to guarantee the compatibility of those acts with their constitutions.

This observation, moreover, leads to the conclusion that Marshall presents a false dilemma in insisting that "[t]he constitution is *either* a superior paramount law, unchangeable by ordinary means, *or* it is on a level with ordinary legislative acts, and, like other acts, is alterable when the legislature shall please to alter it." Remember, the question he has posed is "whether an Act repugnant to the Constitution can become the law of the land." The question is not whether Congress can alter the Constitution by means other than those provided by Article V, and the case raises no issue concerning an alteration of any provision in the Constitution. We may assume that Congress cannot, by simple act, alter the Constitution and still we may maintain that an act which the Court or someone else *believes* to be repugnant to the Constitution shall be given the full force of positive law until repealed. Again, this is the situation which prevails in many other countries, and no absurdity is felt to exist where such a condition obtains.

· · ·

Martin v. Hunter's Lessee

14 U.S. (1 Wheat.) 304 (1816)

A state district court upheld Martin's land claim, which was based on a treaty between America and Great Britain. The Virginia Court of Appeals, the highest court in that state, regarded the issue as solely one of state law and reversed the district court. The conflict escalated when the U.S. Supreme Court set aside the state ruling and the state court refused to obey. The Virginia

Court of Appeals claimed that the Supreme Court had no authority to review its judgment, and to the extent that Section 25 of the Judiciary Act of 1789 attempted to extend the appellate jurisdiction of the Supreme Court to the state courts, the statute was unconstitutional. Chief Justice Marshall did not participate since he had earlier served as attorney for one of the parties.

STORY, J., delivered the opinion of the court.

. . .

The constitution of the United States was ordained and established, not by the states in their sovereign capacities, but emphatically, as the preamble of the constitution declares, by "the People of the United States." There can be no doubt, that it was competent to the people to invest the general government with all the powers which they might deem proper and necessary; to extend or restrain these powers according to their own good pleasure, and to give them a paramount and supreme authority. As little doubt can there be, that the people had a right to prohibit to the states the exercise of any powers which were, in their judgment, incompatible with the objects of the general compact; to make the powers of the state governments, in given cases, subordinate to those of the nation, or to reserve to themselves those sovereign authorities which they might not choose to delegate to either. The constitution was not, therefore, necessarily carved out of existing state sovereignties, nor a surrender of powers already existing in state institutions, for the powers of the states depend upon their own constitutions; and the people of every state had the right to modify and restrain them, according to their own views of policy or principle. On the other hand, it is perfectly clear, that the sovereign powers vested in the state governments, by their respective constitutions, remained unaltered and unimpaired, except so far as they were granted to the government of the United States. . . .

. . . The constitution was for a new government, organized with new substantive powers, and not a mere supplementary charter to a government already existing. The confederation was a compact between states; and its structure and powers were wholly unlike those of the national government. The constitution was an act of the people of the United States to supersede the confederation, and not to be engrafted on it, as a stock through which it was to receive life and nourishment. . . .

This leads us to the consideration of the great question, as to the nature and extent of the appellate jurisdiction of the United States. We have already seen, that appellate jurisdiction is given by the constitution to the supreme court, in all cases where it has not original jurisdiction; subject, however, to such exceptions and regulations as congress may prescribe. It is, therefore, capable of embracing every case enumerated in the constitution, which is not exclusively to be decided by way of original jurisdiction. But the exercise of appellate jurisdiction is far from being limited, by the terms of the constitution, to the supreme court. . . .

As, then, by the terms of the constitution, the appellate jurisdiction is not limited as to the supreme court, and as to this court, it may be exercised in all other cases than those of which it has original cognisance, what is there to restrain its exercise over state tribunals, in the enumerated cases? The appellate power is not limited by the terms of the third article to any particular courts. The words are, "the judicial power (which includes appellate power) shall extend to all cases," &c., and "in all other cases before mentioned the supreme court shall have appellate jurisdiction." It is the case, then, and not the court, that gives the jurisdiction. . . .

If the constitution meant to limit the appellate jurisdiction to cases pending in the courts of the United States, it would necessarily follow, that the jurisdiction of these courts would, in all the cases enumerated in the constitution, be exclusive of state tribunals. How, otherwise, could the jurisdiction extend to *all* cases arising under the constitution, laws and treaties of the United States, or to *all* cases of admiralty and maritime jurisdiction? If some of these cases might be entertained by state tribunals, and no appellate jurisdiction as to them should exist, then the appellate power would not extend to *all*, but to *some*, cases. . . .

But it is plain, that the framers of the constitution did contemplate that cases within the judicial cognisance of the United States, not only might, but would, arise in the state courts, in the exercise of their ordinary jurisdiction. With this view, the sixth article declares, that "this constitution, and the laws of the United States which shall be made in pursuance thereof, and all treaties made, or which shall be made, under the authority of the United States, shall be the supreme law of the land, and the judges in every state shall be bound thereby, anything in the constitution or laws of any state to the contrary notwithstanding." It is obvious, that this obligation is imperative upon the state judges, in their official, and not merely in their private, capacities. From the very nature of their judicial duties, they would be called upon to pronounce the law applicable to the case in judgment. They were not to decide merely according to the laws or constitution of the state, but according to the constitution, laws and treaties of the United States—"the supreme law of the land."...

. . .

It has been argued, that such an appellate jurisdiction over state courts is inconsistent with the genius of our governments, and the spirit of the constitution. That the latter was never designed to act upon state sovereignties, but only upon the people, and that if the power exists, it will materially impair the sovereignty of the states, and the independence of their courts. We cannot yield to the force of this reasoning; it assumes principles which we cannot admit, and draws conclusions to which we do not yield our assent.

... The courts of the United States can, without question, revise the proceedings of the executive and legislative authorities of the states, and if they are found to be contrary to the constitution, may declare them to be of no legal validity. Surely, the exercise of the same right over judicial tribunals is not a higher or more dangerous act of sovereign power.

Nor can such a right be deemed to impair the independence of state judges. It is assuming the very ground in controversy, to assert that they possess an absolute independence of the United States. In respect to the powers granted to the United States, they are not independent; they are expressly bound to obedience, by the letter of the constitution; and if they should unintentionally transcend their authority, or misconstrue the constitution, there is no more reason for giving their judgments an absolute and irresistible force, than for giving it to the acts of the other co-ordinate departments of state sovereignty....

It is further argued, that no great public mischief can result from a construction which shall limit the appellate power of the United States to cases in their own courts: first, because state judges are bound by an oath to support the constitution of the United States, and must be presumed to be men of learning and integrity; and secondly, because congress must have an unquestionable right [to] remove all cases within the scope of the judicial power from the state courts to the courts of the United States, at any time before final judgment, though not after final judgment. As to the first reason—admitting that the

judges of the state courts are, and always will be, of as much learning, integrity and wisdom, as those of the courts of the United States (which we very cheerfully admit), it does not aid the argument. It is manifest, that the constitution has proceeded upon a theory of its own, and given or withheld powers according to the judgment of the American people, by whom it was adopted. We can only construe its powers, and cannot inquire into the policy or principles which induced the grant of them. The constitution has presumed (whether rightly or wrongly, we do not inquire), that state attachments, state prejudices, state jealousies, and state interests, might sometimes obstruct, or control, or be supposed to obstruct or control, the regular administration of justice....

This is not all. A motive of another kind, perfectly compatible with the most sincere respect for state tribunals, might induce the grant of appellate power over their decisions. That motive is the importance, and even necessity of uniformity of decisions throughout the whole United States, upon all subjects within the purview of the constitution. Judges of equal learning and integrity, in different states, might differently interpret the statute, or a treaty of the United States, or even the constitution itself: if there were no revising authority to control these jarring and discordant judgments, and harmonize them into uniformity, the laws, the treaties and the constitution of the United States would be different, in different states, and might, perhaps, never have precisely the same construction, obligation or efficiency, in any two states....

On the whole, the court are of opinion, that the appellate power of the United States does extend to cases pending in the state courts; and that the 25th section of the judiciary act, which authorizes the exercise of this jurisdiction in the specified cases, by a writ of error, is supported by the letter and spirit of the constitution. We find no clause in that instrument which limits this power; and we dare not interpose a limitation, where the people have not been disposed to create one.

. . .

It is the opinion of the whole court, that the judgment of the court of appeals of Virginia, rendered on the mandate in this cause, be reversed, and the judgment of the district court, held at Winchester, be, and the same is hereby affirmed.

Cohens v. Virginia

19 U.S. (6 Wheat.) 264 (1821)

This case involved the question of Supreme Court jurisdiction to review a criminal case in which the state itself was a party. The Cohens brothers were convicted by a Virginia court for selling lottery tickets, contrary to state law. The lottery had been established by an act of Congress to operate in the District of Columbia. The Cohens argued that state courts had no jurisdiction to review a congressional statute. The Virginia Court of Appeals, the state's highest court, rejected that defense and denied that the Supreme Court had power under the Constitution to review its ruling. Section 25 of the Judiciary Act of 1789 was again at issue.

Mr. Chief Justice MARSHALL delivered the opinion of the Court.

. . .

The counsel who opened the cause said, that the want of jurisdiction was shown by the subject matter of the case. The counsel who followed him said, that jurisdiction was not given by the judiciary act. The Court has bestowed all its attention on the arguments of both gentlemen, and supposes that their tendency is to show that this Court has no jurisdiction of the case, or, in other words, has no right to review the judgment of the State Court, because neither the constitution nor any law of the United States has been violated by that judgment.

The questions presented to the Court by the two first points made at the bar are of great magnitude, and may be truly said vitally to affect the Union. They exclude the inquiry whether the constitution and laws of the United States have been violated by the judgment which the plaintiffs in error seek to review; and maintain that, admitting such violation, it is not in the power of the government to apply a corrective. They maintain that the nation does not possess a department capable of restraining peaceably, and by authority of law, any attempts which may be made, by a part, against the legitimate powers of the whole; and that the government is reduced to the alternative of submitting to such attempts, or of resisting them by force. They maintain that the constitution of the United States has provided no tribunal for the final construction of itself, or of the laws or treaties of the nation; but that this power may be exercised in the last resort by the Courts of every State in the Union. That the constitution, laws, and treaties, may receive as many constructions as there are States; and that this is not a mischief, or, if a mischief, is irremediable....

1st. The first question to be considered is, whether the jurisdiction of this Court is excluded by the character of the parties, one of them being a State, and the other a citizen of that State?

The second section of the third article of the constitution defines the extent of the judicial power of the United States. Jurisdiction is given to the Courts of the Union in two classes of cases. In the first, their jurisdiction depends on the character of the cause, whoever may be the parties. This class comprehends "all cases in law and equity arising under this constitution, the laws of the United States, and treaties made, or which shall be made, under their authority." This clause extends the jurisdiction of the Court to all the cases described, without making in its terms any exception whatever, and without any regard to the condition of the party. If there be any exception, it is to be implied against the express words of the article.

In the second class, the jurisdiction depends entirely on the character of the parties. In this are comprehended "controversies between two or more States, between a State and citizens of another State," "and between a State and foreign States, citizens or subjects." If these be the parties, it is entirely unimportant what may be the subject of controversy. Be it what it may, these parties have a constitutional right to come into the Courts of the Union.

. . .

When we consider the situation of the government of the Union and of a State, in relation to each other; the nature of our constitution; the subordination of the State governments to that constitution; the great purpose for which jurisdiction over all cases arising under the constitution and laws of the United States, is confided to the judicial department; are we at liberty to insert in this general grant, an exception of those cases in which a State may be a party? Will the spirit of the constitution justify this attempt to control its words? We think it will not. We think a case arising under the constitution or laws of the United States, is cognizable in the Courts of the Union, whoever may be the parties to that case.

Had any doubt existed with respect to the just construction of this part of the section, that doubt would have been removed by the enumeration of those cases to which the jurisdiction of the federal Courts is extended, in consequence of the character of the parties.

... It would be hazarding too much to assert, that the judicatures of the States will be exempt from the prejudices by which the legislatures and people are influenced, and will constitute perfectly impartial tribunals. In many States the judges are dependent for office and for salary on the will of the legislature. The constitution of the United States furnishes no security against the universal adoption of this principle. When we observe the importance which that constitution attaches to the independence of judges, we are the less inclined to suppose that it can have intended to leave these constitutional questions to tribunals where this independence may not exist, in all cases where a State shall prosecute an individual who claims the protection of an act of Congress. These prosecutions may take place even without a legislative act. A person making a seizure under an act of Congress, may be indicted as a trespasser, if force has been employed, and of this a jury may judge. How extensive may be the mischief if the first decisions in such cases should be final! ...

It is most true that this Court will not take jurisdiction if it should not: but it is equally true, that it must take jurisdiction if it should. The judiciary cannot, as the legislature may, avoid a measure because it approaches the confines of the constitution. We cannot pass it by because it is doubtful. With whatever doubts, with whatever difficulties, a case may be attended, we must decide it, if it be brought before us. We have no more right to decline the exercise of jurisdiction which is given, than to usurp that which is not given. The one or the other would be treason to the constitution. Questions may occur which we would gladly avoid; but we cannot avoid them. All we can do is, to exercise our best judgment, and conscientiously to perform our duty. In doing this, on the present occasion, we find this tribunal invested with appellate jurisdiction in *all* cases arising under the constitution and laws of the United States. We find no exception to this grant, and we cannot insert one....

2d. The second objection to the jurisdiction of the Court is, that its appellate power cannot be exercised, in any case, over the judgment of a State Court.

This objection is sustained chiefly by arguments drawn from the supposed total separation of the judiciary of a State from that of the Union, and their entire independence of each other. The argument considers the federal judiciary as completely foreign to that of a State; and as being no more connected with it in any respect whatever, than the Court of a foreign State....

That the United States form, for many, and for most important purposes, a single nation, has not yet been denied. In war, we are one people. In making peace, we are one people. In all commercial regulations, we are one and the same people. In many other respects, the American people are one, and the government which is alone capable of controlling and managing their interests in all these respects, is the government of the Union....

In a government so constituted, is it unreasonable that the judicial power should be competent to give efficacy to the constitutional laws of the legislature? That department can decide on the validity of the constitution or law of a State, if it be repugnant to the constitution or to a law of the United States. Is it unreasonable that it should also be empowered to decide on the judgment of a State tribunal enforcing such unconstitutional law? Is it so very unreasonable as to furnish a justification for controlling the words of the constitution?

We think it is not. We think that in a government acknowledgedly supreme, with respect to objects of vital interest to the nation, there is nothing inconsistent with sound reason, nothing incompatible with the nature of government, in making all its departments supreme, so far as respects those objects, and so far as is necessary to their attainment. The exercise of the appellate power over those judgments of the State tribunals which may contravene the constitution or laws of the United States, is, we believe, essential to the attainment of those objects....

3d. We come now to the third objection, which, though differently stated by the counsel, is substantially the same. One gentleman has said that the judiciary act does not give jurisdiction in the case.

The cause was argued in the State Court, on a case agreed by the parties, which states the prosecution under a law for selling lottery tickets, which is set forth, and further states the act of Congress by which the City of Washington was authorized to establish the lottery. It then states that the lottery was regularly established by virtue of the act, and concludes with referring to the Court the questions, whether the act of Congress be valid? whether, on its just construction, it constitutes a bar to the prosecution? and, whether the act of Assembly, on which the prosecution is founded, be not itself invalid? These questions were decided against the operation of the act of Congress, and in favour of the operation of the act of the State.

If the 25th section of the judiciary act be inspected, it will at once be perceived that it comprehends expressly the case under consideration....

After having bestowed upon this question the most deliberate consideration of which we are capable, the Court is unanimously of opinion, that the objections to its jurisdiction are not sustained, and that the motion ought to be overruled.

Motion denied.

[*Having ruled against Virginia's motion to dismiss the*

case for want of jurisdiction, the Court heard arguments on the merits of the Cohens' claim that the congressional sponsorship of the lottery barred a state prosecution for the sale of tickets. The Court affirmed the Virginia conviction by reasoning that the congressional statute was not a piece of national legislation but rather an exercise of congressional power over the District of Columbia. As local legislation, the lottery law did not override state penal laws.]

D. CONSTRAINTS ON JUDICIAL REVIEW

By the time he visited America in the 1830s, Alexis de Tocqueville could write of judicial review: "I am aware that a similar right has been sometimes claimed, but claimed in vain, by courts of justice in other countries, but in America it is recognized by all the authorities; and not a party, not so much as an individual, is found to contest it." 1 Alexis de Tocqueville, Democracy in America 100 (Bradley ed. 1951). In fact, judicial review was sharply challenged at every level of government and society. State courts and state legislatures regularly disputed the jurisdiction of the Supreme Court, not only up to the Civil War but afterward as well. Charles Warren, 47 Am. L. Rev. 1, 161 (1913).

Justice John Gibson's dissent in *Eakin* v. *Raub* (1825) represents a trenchant rebuttal of Marshall's position on judicial review. Gibson, a Pennsylvania judge, conceded that the Supremacy Clause required judges to strike down state laws in conflict with the federal Constitution, but he rejected judicial review as a means of policing Congress and the President. Although a constitution is superior to a statute, that fact alone did not elevate judges to be the sole interpreters. The oath to support the Constitution was not unique to judges. Political branches had an equal right to put a construction on the Constitution. If a legislature were to abuse its powers and overstep the boundaries established by the Constitution, Gibson preferred that correction come at the hands of the people. Judicial errors were more difficult to correct, for they required constitutional amendment or a change in the court's membership. EAKIN v. RAUB, 12 S. & R. 330, 343 (Pa. 1825). In subsequent years, Gibson resigned himself to a more generous definition of judicial review. Norris v. Clymer, 2 Pa. 277, 281 (1845).

Concern about judicial overreaching prompted some judges to advocate a philosophy of self-restraint. To temper criticism, they offered to presume the validity of government actions and to uphold the legislature in doubtful cases. Fletcher v. Peck, 10 U.S. 87, 128 (1810); Dartmouth College v. Woodward, 17 U.S. 517, 625 (1819). Similar guidelines were issued when reviewing lower court decisions. Judges comfortable with the legitimacy of judicial review wielded the power actively and aggressively. In a veto message in 1832, President Jackson vigorously asserted his own independent authority in interpreting the Constitution, even in the face of a contrary Supreme Court opinion. Similarly, President Lincoln sharply rejected the belief in judicial supremacy regarding constitutional analysis (see readings in Chapter 1, Section H).

A major challenge to judicial review arose late in the nineteenth century when federal judges began to impose their philosophies of economic laissez-faire. Repeatedly the courts struck down state and federal statutes designed to alleviate economic hardship. Legislative efforts to deal with monopoly, prices, minimum wages, maximum work hours, and organized labor were either rejected by the courts or severely restricted. The philosophy of judicial restraint, the presumption of legislative validity, and avoidance of decisions based on the wisdom of government action seemed virtually abandoned. The judges reached outside the Constitution to discover a "liberty of contract" that narrowed the scope of interstate commerce and the taxing power. These decisions stood in the path of progressive legislation and threatened effective government. Justice Stone lectured his colleagues in 1936 that

Learned Hand on Judicial Restraint

... [W]hen the Constitution emerged from the Convention in September, 1787, the structure of the proposed government, if one looked to the text, gave no ground for inferring that the decisions of the Supreme Court, and *a fortiori* of the lower courts, were to be authoritative upon the Executive and the Legislature. Each of the three "departments" was an agency of a sovereign, the "People of the United States." Each was responsible to that sovereign, but not to one another; indeed, their "Separation" was still regarded as a condition of free government, whatever we may think of that notion now....

Each one of us must in the end choose for himself how far he would like to leave our collective fate to the wayward vagaries of popular assemblies. No one can fail to recognize the perils to which the last forty years have exposed such governments.... For myself it would be most irksome to be ruled by a bevy of Platonic Guardians, even if I knew how to choose them, which I assuredly do not. If they were in charge, I should miss the stimulus of living in a society where I have, at least theoretically, some part in the direction of public affairs. Of course I know how illusory would be the belief that my vote determined anything; but nevertheless when I go to the polls I have a satisfaction in the sense that we are all engaged in a common venture.

SOURCE: Learned Hand, The Bill of Rights 27–28, 73–74 (1958).

courts "are not the only agency of government that must be assumed to have capacity to govern." United States v. Butler, 297 U.S. 1, 87 (1936).

Changes in the composition of the Supreme Court after 1937 removed the judicial impediment to economic regulation. The era of "substantive due process" appeared to be over. However, the Warren Court sparked another round of debate over judicial review, this time raising the claim that courts had tilted in a liberal direction. The opinions outlawing desegregation, requiring legislative reapportionment, providing right of counsel, and announcing novel constitutional rights of association and privacy—all supported the weak and politically disfranchised.

Activism vs. Self-Restraint

Critics who had called for judicial self-restraint during the 1930s now found themselves applauding the substantive results of the activist Warren Court. Others warned that the Court risked losing popular support by issuing broad decisions in social and political areas. Reacting against Judge Learned Hand's plea in 1958 for judicial restraint (see box), Herbert Wechsler maintained that the issue was not whether judges possessed judicial review but rather how they *exercised* that authority. He objected to what he regarded as idiosyncratic, ad hoc, and poorly reasoned decisions and urged the courts to follow principled rules, deciding on grounds of "adequate neutrality and generality, tested not only by the instant application but by others that the principles imply." 73 Harv. L. Rev. 1, 15 (1959).

Many scholars agree that the Warren Court's opinions should have been better crafted to clarify statements of principles. If a majority opinion simply announced a result without adequately explaining the underlying argument, the courts would rule by fiat and decree. However, the concept of "neutral principles" has remained elusive and confusing. It appears to run counter to Holmes's dictum: "The life of the law has not been logic: it has been experience." The Common Law 1 (1881). In such areas as separation of church and state, separation of powers, and search-and-seizure operations, it is difficult to discover general principles that guide the Court. The judicial process has been characterized by starts and stops, direction and redirection, trial and error. Others point out that an insistence on principled decisions might prevent judges from discovering novel responses for unprecedented conditions. Charles E. Clark, 49 Va. L. Rev. 660, 665 (1963). Rigid adherence to fixed principles would prevent the tactical use of threshold arguments (such as standing, mootness, and ripeness) needed to protect the Court's prestige and effectiveness.

The post-Warren Court years were marked by continued controversy over the scope of judicial decisions. Presidents used rulings on such contentious issues as school desegregation, the death penalty, criminal procedures, and abortion as political rallying points. Courts were accused of deciding too many cases and overtaxing their institutional capacity. They were urged to limit court access in order to divert issues from the courthouse to the legislative arena.

Despite President Nixon's vow to nominate "strict constructionists" to the bench, the Court continued to play an activist role. It created a constitutional right of "commercial free speech," struck down death-penalty statutes, initiated busing to overcome segregated schools, began the process of reversing sex discrimination, and authored the abortion decision of *Roe* v. *Wade*. Many commentators viewed the abortion case as a revival of the era of "substantive due process" that prevailed before 1937. The Court's decision against the legislative veto, Justice White noted, struck down in "one fell swoop provisions in more laws enacted by Congress than the Court has cumulatively invalidated in its history." INS v. Chadha, 462 U.S. 919, 1002 (1983). Conservatives were disappointed that the Rehnquist Court, like the Burger Court, maintained an activist role. The conditions that encourage judicial activism were explored by Justice Powell in a revealing interview in 1979 (see Powell reading).

Judicial Review and Democracy

Some critics of contemporary courts argue that the main objection to judicial review is that it runs counter to American democratic values. One study advised judges to limit their work to supporting broad participation in the democratic process and protecting minority rights. John Hart Ely, Democracy and Distrust (1980). Another study endorsed judicial review for protecting individual rights but proposed that the courts withdraw from almost all areas of federalism and separation of powers. Jesse H. Choper, Judicial Review and the National Political Process (1980).

It is tempting, but misleading, to call judicial review anti-democratic. The Constitution establishes a limited republic, not a direct or pure democracy. Popular sentiment is filtered through a system of representation. Majority vote is limited by various restrictions in the Constitution: candidates must be a certain age, Presidents may not serve a third term—regardless of what the people want. Although states range in population from less than a million to more than twenty million, each state receives the same number of Senators. Filibusters conducted by a minority of Senators can prevent the Senate from acting. Majority rule is further constrained by checks and balances, separation of powers, federalism, a bicameral legislature, and the Bill of Rights.

To the extent that the judiciary protects constitutional principles, it upholds the values of the people who drafted and ratified the Constitution. Throughout much of its history, however, the judiciary gave little support to civil liberties or civil rights. The record of the first century and a half does provides little evidence of judicial support for individual liberties. Henry W. Edgerton, 22 Corn. L. Q. 299 (1937). In a number of contemporary cases on reapportionment, the right of association, and the "white primary" cases, it can be argued that the Supreme Court opened the door to broader public participation in the political process. In many ways the contemporary judiciary has helped strengthen democracy. Through its decisions, it performs an informing function previously associated with legislative bodies.

The judiciary performs other positive, legitimizing functions. Actions by executive and legislative officials are contested and brought before the courts for review. When upheld, citizens can see some standard at work other than the power of majorities and the raw force of politics. Alexander Bickel wrote: "The Court's prestige, the spell it casts as a symbol, enables it to entrench and solidify measures that may have been tentative in the conception or that are on the verge of abandonment in the execution." 75 Harv. L. Rev. 40, 48 (1961). But what happens when the Court faces a repressive executive or legislative action? If judges lend their support, as in the curfew and imprisonment of Japanese-Americans during World War II, the reputation of the judiciary as the guarantor of constitutional liberties is tarnished.

When the judiciary seems out of step with the elected branches and the public, there are many methods available to legislators and executives to invoke court-curbing pressures. Presidential appointments and Senate confirmations supply a steady stream of influence by popularly elected public officials. Court decisions can be overturned by constitutional amendment, a process that is directly controlled by national and state legislatures. Short of such drastic remedies, judges generally remain sensitive and responsive to public opinion, notwithstanding traditional claims of judicial isolation from political forces (see the final chapter).

Statutory Restrictions on Judicial Review

By adopting explicit language in statutes, Congress may prohibit judicial review of agency actions. Thus, legislation in 1885 stated that decisions by the accounting officers of the Treasury Department regarding claims for property were to be treated as final determinations "and shall never thereafter be reopened or considered." A unanimous Court held that the statute conferred exclusive and final jurisdiction on the Treasury Department and that federal courts had no power to exercise judicial review over the agency's judgment. United States v. Babcock, 250 U.S. 328 (1919). Most decisions by the Secretary of Veterans Affairs on "questions of law and fact" affecting veterans' benefits "shall be final and conclusive and may not be reviewed by any other official or by any court...." 38 U.S.C. 511. The Court accepts the prohibition of judicial review on these questions of benefits or claims, providing there is no constitutional issue. Johnson v. Robison, 415 U.S. 361, 366–67 (1974). Legislation in 1988 subjected certain actions by the Department of Veterans Affairs to judicial review. 102 Stat. 4105 (1988). Under this authority, the Supreme Court decided a veteran's case in 1994. Brown v. Gardner, 513 U.S. 115 (1994).

The Administrative Procedure Act (APA) prohibits judicial review over agency action "committed to agency discretion by law." 5 U.S.C. §701(a)(2). When the Supreme Court determines that an agency action falls within that scope, it acknowledges that judicial review does not apply. Lincoln v. Vigil, 508 U.S. 182 (1993). If there is no explicit statutory language that precludes judicial review, courts will presume that federal court jurisdiction exists to hear challenges to agency procedures. McNary v. Haitian Refugee Center, Inc., 498 U.S. 479 (1991). Congress may authorize the Attorney General to make temporary orders that are not subject to judicial review. Touby v. United States, 500 U.S. 160 (1991).

In 1994 the Supreme Court again acknowledged the limits of judicial review. The Defense Base Closure and Realignment Act of 1990 established a commission to recommend the closing of unnecessary military bases. A unanimous Court ruled that commission recommendations were not a "final agency action" under the APA since the ultimate decision on closure rests with the President. Therefore the recommendations are not reviewable by the courts. "Where a statute, such as the 1990 Act, commits decisionmaking to the discretion of the President, judicial review of the President's action is not available." Dalton v. Specter, 511 U.S. 462, 477 (1994). An amendment by Senator Arlen Specter to subject base closures to judicial review was rejected a month later. 140 Cong. Rec. 14078–90, 14092–93 (1994). Two years earlier the Court had held that presidential actions are not reviewable under the APA because the President is not an "agency." Franklin v. Massachusetts, 505 U.S. 788 (1992).

Other executive actions are not subject to judicial review. When the Attorney General decides not to go to the special division of federal judges for the appointment of an independent counsel, that decision is not reviewable "in any court." 28 U.S.C. 592(f). See Dellums v. Smith, 797 F.2d 817, 823 (9th Cir. 1986); Banzhaf v. Smith, 737 F.2d 1167 (D.C. Cir. 1984). In 1999, Congress decided not to reauthorize the independent counsel statute.

Eakin v. Raub: Gibson's Dissent

12 S. & R. 330 (Pa. 1825)

In this case, the Supreme Court of Pennsylvania reviews the constitutionality of a law passed by the state legislature. In a dissenting opinion, Justice John Gibson acknowledged that the Supremacy Clause required federal and state judges to invalidate state laws in conflict with the U.S. Constitution, but denied that the same power gave judges the right to invalidate actions by the legislative and executive branches unrelated to the Supremacy Clause. Gibson's dissent represents one of the most coherent critiques of Chief Justice Marshall's reasoning in *Marbury* v. *Madison*.

GIBSON, J., dissenting. [*He questions the general power of courts to hold legislative acts unconstitutional.*] But it is said, that without [*the changes insisted on by the Supreme Court of Pennsylvania*], the latter act would be unconstitutional; and, instead of controverting this, I will avail myself of it, to express an opinion which I have deliberately formed, on the abstract right of the judiciary to declare an unconstitutional act of the legislature void. It seems to me, there is a plain difference, hitherto unnoticed, between acts that are repugnant to the constitution of the particular state, and acts that are repugnant to the constitution of the *United States;* my opinion being, that the judiciary is bound to execute the former, but not the latter. I shall hereafter attempt to explain this difference, by pointing out the particular provisions in the constitution of the *United States,* on which it depends. I am aware, that a right to declare all unconstitutional acts void, without distinction as to either constitution, is generally held as a professional dogma; but I apprehend, rather as a matter of faith than of reason. I admit, that I once embraced the same doctrine, but without examination, and I shall, therefore, state the arguments that impelled me to abandon it, with great respect for those by whom it is still maintained. But I may premise, that it is not a little remarkable, that although the right in question has all along been claimed by the judiciary, no judge has ventured to discuss it, except Chief Justice MARSHALL (in *Marbury* v. *Madison*, 1 *Cranch* 176); and if the argument of a jurist so distinguished for the strength of his ratiocinative powers be found inconclusive, it may fairly be set down to the weakness of the position which he attempts to defend....

The constitution of *Pennsylvania* contains no express grant of political powers to the judiciary. But to establish a grant by implication, the constitution is said to be a law of superior obligation; and consequently, that if it were to come into collision with an act of the legislature, the latter would have to give way; this is conceded. But it is a fallacy, to suppose, that they can come into collision *before the judiciary.* ...

The constitution and the *right* of the legislature to pass the act, may be in collision; but is that a legitimate subject for judicial determination? If it be, the judiciary must be a peculiar organ, to revise the proceedings of the legislature, and to correct its mistakes; and in what part of the constitution are we to look for this proud preeminence? Viewing the matter in the opposite direction, what would be thought of an act of assembly in which it should be declared that the supreme court had, in a particular case, put a wrong construction on the constitution of the *United States,* and that the judgment should therefore be reversed? It would, doubtless, be thought a usurpation of judicial power. But it is by no means clear, that to declare a law void, which has been enacted according to the forms prescribed in the constitution, is not a usurpation of legislative power. It is an act of sovereignty; and sovereignty and legislative power are said by Sir William *Blackstone* to be convertible terms. It is the business of the judiciary, to interpret the laws, not scan the authority of the lawgiver; and without the latter, it cannot take cognisance of a collision between a law and the constitution. So that, to affirm that the judiciary has a right to judge of the existence of such collision, is to take for granted the very thing to be proved....

But it has been said to be emphatically the business of the judiciary, to ascertain and pronounce what the law is; and that this necessarily involves a consideration of the constitution. It does so: but how far? If the judiciary will inquire into anything beside the form of enactment, where shall it stop? ...

... [L]et it be supposed that the power to declare a law unconstitutional has been exercised. What is to be done? The legislature must acquiesce, although it may think the construction of the judiciary wrong. But why must it acquiesce? Only because it is bound to pay that respect to every other organ of the government, which it has a right to exact from each of them in turn. This is the argument. But it will not be pretended, that the legislature has not, at least, an equal right with the judiciary to put a construction on the constitution; nor that either of them is infallible; nor that either ought to be required to surrender its judgment to the other.... I take it, then, the legislature is entitled to all the deference that is due to the judiciary; that its acts are, in no case, to be treated as *ipso facto* void, except where they would produce a revolution in the government; and that, to avoid them, requires the act of some tribunal competent, under the constitution (if any such there be), to pass on their validity. All that remains, therefore, is, to inquire whether the judiciary or the people are that tribunal.

Now, as the judiciary is not expressly constituted for that purpose, it must derive whatever authority of the sort it may possess, from the reasonableness and fitness of the thing. But, in theory, all the organs of the government are of equal capacity; or, if not equal, each must be supposed to have superior capacity only for those things which peculiarly belong to it; and as legislation peculiarly involves the consideration of those limitations which are put on the law-making power, and the interpretation of the laws when made, involves only the construction of the laws themselves, it follows, that the construction of the constitution, in this particular, belongs to the legislature, which ought, therefore, to be taken to have superior capacity to judge of the constitutionality of its own acts. But suppose, all to be of equal capacity, in every respect, why should one exercise a controlling power over the rest? That the judiciary is of superior rank, has never been pretended, although it has been said to be coordinate....

But the judges are sworn to support the constitution, and are they not bound by it as the law of the land? ... The oath to support the constitution is not peculiar to the judges, but is taken indiscriminately by every officer of the government.... The official oath, then, relates only to the official conduct of the officer, and does not prove that he ought to stray from the path of his ordinary business, to search for violations of duty in the business of others; nor does it, as supposed, define the powers of the officer.

. . .

But it has been said, that this construction would deprive the citizen of the advantages which are peculiar to a written constitution, by at once declaring the power of the legislature, in practice, to be illimitable....

... I am of opinion, that it rests with the people,

in whom full and absolute sovereign power resides, to correct abuses in legislation, by instructing their representatives to repeal the obnoxious act. What is wanting to plenary power in the government, is reserved by the people, for their own immediate use; and to redress an infringement of their rights in this respect, would seem to be an accessory of the power thus reserved. It might, perhaps, have been better to vest the power in the judiciary; as it might be expected, that its habits of deliberation, and the aid derived from the arguments of counsel, would more frequently lead to accurate conclusions. On the other hand, the judiciary is not infallible; and an error by it would admit of no remedy but a more distinct expression of the public will, through the extraordinary medium of a convention; whereas, an error by the legislature admits of a remedy by an exertion of the same will, in the ordinary exercise of the right of suffrage—a mode better calculated to attain the end, without popular excitement. It may be said, the people would probably not notice an error of their representatives. But they would as probably do so, as notice an error of the judiciary; and beside, it is a *postulate* in the theory of our government, and the very basis of the superstructure, that the people are wise, virtuous, and competent to manage their own affairs....

. . .

But in regard to an act of assembly, which is found to be in collision with the constitution, laws or treaties of the *United States,* I take the duty of the judiciary to be exactly the reverse. By becoming parties to the federal constitution, the states have agreed to several limitations of their individual sovereignty, to enforce which, it was thought to be absolutely necessary, to prevent them from giving effect to laws in violation of those limitations, through the instrumentality of their own judges. Accordingly, it is declared in the fifth article and second section of the federal constitution, that "This constitution, and the laws of the *United States* which shall be made in pursuance thereof, and all treaties made, or which shall be made under the authority of the *United States,* shall be the *supreme* law of the land; and the *judges* in every *state* shall be BOUND thereby; anything in the *laws* or *constitution* of any *state* to the contrary notwithstanding."

This is an express grant of a political power, and it is conclusive, to show that no law of inferior obligation, as every state law must necessarily be, can be executed at the expense of the constitution, laws or treaties of the *United States.* ...

The Boundaries of Judicial Review:
Interview with Justice Powell

In an extraordinarily candid interview in 1979, Justice Lewis F. Powell discussed with Professor Harry M. Clor some of the considerations that determine the scope of judicial review and the reasons for judicial activism. The interview was published in the *Kenyon College Alumni Bulletin* (Summer 1979).

CLOR: I would like to begin with a rather broad and somewhat philosophic question. We can get more specific later on as you choose. This is a question about the role of the federal judiciary and particularly the Supreme Court in the American system of constitutional democracy. Do you see the Court as primarily a political institution, sharing responsibility for governing and making of public policy, or do you see it having a rather narrower function, simply to interpret the Constitution and the law?

POWELL: The judicial branch of government in the United States, of course, is a political branch in the broad sense. In view of the special role it has in our system, the Supreme Court is more than just an ordinary court. It is empowered to decide whether the other two branches of government live within the Constitution. You perhaps would know more accurately than I, but I do not think there is any other country in the world in which the judiciary has the power to invalidate decisions made by the legislative bodies of the country, both federal and state, and by the executive branch also. That's a rather awesome power and it's one that makes our system and our Court distinctive. A good many of the questions that involve constitutionality of statutes, and executive branch conduct, fairly can be viewed as political in the broadest sense. I suppose one could say our function, in that sense and to that degree, is politically oriented, yet basically we think of ourselves as judges guided by the Constitution as the law of the land.

CLOR: It is sometimes said that a certain judge or justice is a judicial statesman, or has acted in a statesmanlike way, which seems to suggest that something more is involved than just reading or interpreting the text of the Constitution or a law. Do you think there is such a thing as judicial statesmanship?

POWELL: Possibly, though in a limited sense. The Constitution was framed in rather sweeping language, some of which is susceptible to interpretations that not only *may* change but *have* changed over the decades. The clauses that people think about more frequently in this connection are the due process and equal protection clauses, the commerce clause and a number of other quite general phrases.

The Court has to give meaning to those provisions of the Constitution, particularly the Bill of Rights, and as history demonstrates the views taken by the Court in one era do not necessarily survive a different era. That has happened with a good deal of frequency. The Constitution has been described, properly I think, as a sort of living political organism. The Court has helped, by its decisions, to keep the Constitution abreast of the vast changes that occur in the life of our nation.

CLOR: Do you think that judicial statesmanship, to the extent that there is such a thing, consists primarily of insight into the needs or demands of the times or into the changing conditions to which Constitutional clauses are to be applied?

POWELL: I'd rather not phrase it quite that way. It's well to bear in mind that the Court is composed of judges who are elected for life. We, therefore, are not directly responsible to the people in any political sense. This is both an asset and perhaps a liability. It could mean that the Court could move too far away from our democratic system. I don't think the Court has done that. Perhaps on very rare occasions. Yet, our independence does give the Court a freedom to make decisions that perhaps are necessary for our society, decisions that the legislative branch may be reluctant to make. The classic case that comes to mind is *Brown* v. *Board of Education*. The Congress had adequate authority under the Constitution to enact the sort of legislation that has been adopted since *Brown*. But it was the Supreme Court that finally decided in 1954 that segregation in our society must come to an end....

CLOR: One thing that fascinates me about the desegregation decision of *Brown* v. *Board of Education* is that the Court interpreted the equal protection clause quite differently from the earlier interpretation in 1896 of *Plessy* v. *Ferguson*. The Court virtually reversed its interpretation of the equal protection clause. How do you do that, Mr. Justice Powell?

POWELL: The Court has felt far freer to reverse Constitutional decisions than it has to reverse the interpretation of statutes. The Court's peculiar responsibility is to decide what the Constitution means. This country had moved a long ways by 1954 from the public mores and public perceptions that existed at the time of *Plessy* v. *Ferguson*. If you read the history of the post-Civil War, civil rights legislation, legislation that enacted Section 1983 of the statute which now produces a vast amount of litigation, I think you would have a hard time justifying the decision of our Court in 1954. One would have to strain to find an intention on the part of the Congress in 1866, and again in 1870 and 1871, to provide that there should be integration in education. Of course, there weren't very many public schools, but if the Court had gone strictly by what the Congress had intended, or probably intended, it would have reaffirmed *Plessy* v. *Ferguson*.

· · ·

... The point I am making is that the Supreme Court perceived that vast changes had occurred not only in the United States but worldwide. It was long overdue to bring our Negro citizens into full citizenship.

CLOR: Does that mean the Court was remaking the Constitution, reading into the equal protection clause a meaning that it did not originally have?

POWELL: The Court cannot rely solely on what the founding fathers intended, or even on congressional intent when the Fourteenth Amendment was adopted. Conditions change as our country matures....

... As a matter of fact—and I don't assert this myself, but you've seen it in print—a good many people think the legislative branch bucks tough decisions to the judicial branch by drawing statutes in quite general and vague terms. Thus, a role sometimes viewed as legislative—I would not say "aristocratic"—is thrust upon us.

CLOR: The Congress hands the tough problem to the Court?

POWELL: It has been said a number of times that Congress does that, and perhaps if I were there I'd think it was a good idea on some issues. In this way members of Congress do not have to go on record on a tough issue.

· · ·

E. METHODS OF CONSTITUTIONAL INTERPRETATION

Justice Jackson once remarked that "[n]othing has more perplexed generations of conscientious judges than the search in juridical science, philosophy and practice for objective and impersonal criteria for solution of politico-legal questions put to our courts." Vital Speeches, No. 24, Vol. XIX, at 759 (October 1, 1953). No completely satisfactory guide to judicial interpretation has ever been fashioned. Jerome Frank, in his classic, Law and the Modern Mind, 6th ed., XXIV (1963), wrote of a Freudian "yearning for an unattainable legal certainty," which resembled a "young child's father-dependence and the grown-up's resultant tendency to hanker after father-substitutes." Different techniques are available, including a dependence on foreign influences, literalism, originalism, natural law, history, national consensus, and an eclectic approach.

Foreign Influences

Decisions by federal courts are often influenced by foreign law and international pressures. In the Desegregation Case of 1954, both the State Department and the Justice Department urged the Supreme Court to take the case and strike down the "separate but equal" doctrine. Much of their argument took into account the opportunity of the Soviet Union to highlight the hypocrisy of U.S. democracy to prevent black students from attending school with white students. As the government's brief explained to the Court, racial discrimination in the United States "furnishes grist for the Communist propaganda mills, and its raises doubts even among friendly nations as to the intensity of our devotion to the democratic faith" (reading in Chapter 15, Section C).

International pressures are well understood. Every nation lives in a fishbowl. Following decisions by courts in other countries, however, is more controversial. There is sharp disagreement on this practice. The House Judiciary Committee held hearings in 2005 on H. Res. 97, a resolution expressing the sense of the House that judicial determinations regarding the meaning of the U.S. Constitution should not be based on "judgments, laws, or pronouncements of foreign institutions unless such foreign judgments, laws, or pronouncements inform an understanding of the original meaning of the Constitution of the United States." The resolution singled out *Lawrence v. Texas*, 539 U.S. 558 (2003), which struck down Texas's ban on private consensual sex between adults of the same sex. In looking for authority, the Court cited a report submitted to the British Parliament in 1957, a decision by the European Court of Human Rights, and the European Convention on Human Rights. On March 1, 2005, in *Roper v. Simmons*, 543 U.S. 551 (2005), the Court held unconstitutional the death penalty for offenders under the age of 18, relying in part on a UN convention contained in other international covenants: "The opinion of the world community, while not controlling our outcome, does provide respected and significant confirmation for our own conclusions." Id. at 578.

Literalism

Advocates of strict constructionism argue that judges should enforce only those norms that are stated in the Constitution. Literalism is helpful on some issues (two Senators per state, minimum age of 35 for a President, and so forth), but those issues are so easy they do not provoke lawsuits. Other language in the Constitution is more vexing, such as the general phrases "due process" and "equal protection." Moreover, it would be inappropriate to take some phrases literally. In 1987 the Supreme Court noted that "it is well settled that the prohibition against impairing the obligation of contracts [Art. I, § 10] is not to be read literally." Keystone Bituminous Coal Assn. v. DeBenedictis, 480 U.S. 470, 502 (1987).

In fact, literalism may be self-defeating. The point is illustrated in Pufendorf's reference to an ancient Bolognian law which provided that "whoever drew blood in the streets should be punished with utmost severity." Enforcement of the statute would have punished a physician for treating a man who had fallen in the street from a fit. Jerome Frank, Courts on Trial: Myth and Reality in American Justice 298 (1949). As Judge Learned Hand observed, it is "one of the surest indexes of a mature and developed jurisprudence not to make a fortress out of a dictionary; but to remember that statutes always have some purpose or object to accomplish, whose sympathetic and imaginative discovery is the surest guide to their meaning." Cabell v. Markham, 148 F. 2d 737, 739 (2d Cir. 1945). Linguistic precision is seldom attainable. In 1898, James Bradley Thayer wrote of a dream world, "that lawyer's paradise where all words have a fixed, precisely ascertained meaning; where men express their purposes not only with accuracy, but with fulness; and where, if the writer has been careful, a lawyer, having a document before him, may sit in his chair, inspect the text, and answer all questions without raising his eyes." But, as Jerome Frank observed, "there is no Paradise." Frank, Courts on Trial 299.

Although some politicians equate strict constructionism with conservative law-and-order views, it can be applied equally well to liberal support for individual rights and religious freedom. Likewise, strict constructionism does not always mean judicial restraint. It can be synonymous, and often is, with judicial activism. Arthur J. Goldberg, Equal Justice 35–63 (1971). An example is the legislative veto case of 1983, which used strict constructionism with a vengeance to invalidate dozens of statutory provisions. INS v. Chadha, 462 U.S. 919 (1983).

Extreme literalists demand that textual ambiguities be resolved solely by constitutional amendment instead of judicial interpretation. Although the literalist approach may have some superficial appeal, its impracticalities as Jerome Frank and Learned Hand pointed out, are immense. Madison went to great lengths in Federalist No. 44 to point out that a constitution, to survive, must be phrased in general terms. He offered his comments to support the Necessary and Proper Clause of Article I, Section 8, which had been attacked for its vague grant of power to Congress. He said that the framers might have copied the Articles of Confederation, which prohibited the exercise of any power not *expressly* delegated by the states, or they might have attempted to enumerate congressional powers. The first alternative risked leaving the national government with insufficient power, whereas the second meant "a complete digest of laws on every subject to which the Constitution relates; accommodated not only to the existing state of things, but to all the possible changes which futurity may produce...."

Marshall on Constitutional Interpretation

... A constitution, to contain an accurate detail of all the subdivisions of which its great powers will admit, and of all the means by which they may be carried into execution, would partake of the prolixity of a legal code, and could scarcely be embraced by the human mind. It would probably never be understood by the public. Its nature, therefore, requires, that only its great outlines should be marked, its important objects designated, and the minor ingredients which compose those objects be deduced from the nature of the objects themselves.... In considering this question, then, we must never forget, that it is *a constitution* we are expounding.

· · ·

Let this be done in the case under consideration. The subject is the execution of those great powers on which the welfare of a nation essentially depends. It must have been the intention of those who gave these powers, to insure, as far as human prudence could insure, their beneficial execution. This could not be done by confiding the choice of means to such narrow limits as not to leave it in the power of Congress to adopt any which might be appropriate, and which were conducive to the end. This provision is made in a constitution intended to endure for ages to come, and, consequently, to be adapted to the various *crises* of human affairs. To have prescribed the means by which government should, in all future time, execute its powers, would have been to change, entirely, the character of the instrument, and give it the properties of a legal code....

· · ·

We admit, as all must admit, that the powers of the government are limited, and that its limits are not to be transcended. But we think the sound construction of the constitution must allow to the national legislature that discretion, with respect to the means by which the powers it confers are to be carried into execution, which will enable that body to perform the high duties assigned to it, in the manner most beneficial to the people. Let the end be legitimate, let it be within the scope of the constitution, and all means which are appropriate, which are plainly adapted to that end, which are not prohibited, but consist with the letter and spirit of the constitution, are constitutional.

SOURCE: McCulloch v. Maryland, 17 U.S. 315, 407, 415, 421 (1819).

In 1819 Chief Justice John Marshall advanced the same argument in *McCulloch* v. *Maryland* (see box).

Chief Justice Taney, in *Dred Scott*, authored what is widely regarded as one of the major self-inflicted wounds on the Supreme Court. He did so by insisting that the meaning of "citizens" in Article III was restricted to what it meant in 1787: "No one, we presume, supposes that any change in public opinion or feeling, in relation to this unfortunate race [of blacks], in the civilized nations of Europe or in this country, should induce the court to give to the words of the Constitution a more liberal construction in their favor than they were intended to bear when the instrument was framed and adopted.... [Constitutional language] must be construed now as it was understood at the time of its adoption. It is not only the same in words, but the same in meaning...." Dred Scott v. Sandford, 60 U.S. at 426 (1857).

Justice Holmes rejected that type of reasoning. To him, a word "is not a crystal, transparent and unchanged, it is the skin of a living thought and may vary greatly in color and content according to the circumstances and the time in which it is used." Towne v. Eisner, 245 U.S. 418, 425 (1918). Moreover, a literalist is at sea when two commands of the Constitution, such as free press and fair trial, collide. How is one constitutional principle to be balanced against another? What guides the Court in deciding between civil rights and state rights? When does government regulation give way to individual privacy? What weight should be given to protect a free press against searches and seizures by law enforcement officers? Where in the Constitution do we find answers to conflicts between workers and employers? Do certain rights, such as those enumerated in the First Amendment, have a "preferred" status?[6] Even if they do, are those rights subordinated to the needs of the government during time of national emergency?

Originalism

Attorney General Edwin Meese III, in a speech in 1985, advocated a "Jurisprudence of Original Intention." He argued that judges should restrict themselves to the original meaning of constitutional provisions. Justice Brennan, in a speech later that year, rejected the search for the framers' intent as "little more than arrogance cloaked as humility" (see reading).

Originalism, sometimes called interpretivism, involves a search for the intentions or purposes of those who wrote the Constitution. Judges generally try to interpret the Constitution in accordance with the framers' intent, so far as that is possible, but in sifting through conflicting evidence they may reach different conclusions. In 2008, all nine Justices of the Supreme Court looked to the intention of the Second Amendment in determining the constitutionality of a District of Columbia law that restricted handguns in the home. Yet the Court still split apart, 5 to 4, in interpreting the amendment. District of Columbia v. Heller, 554 U.S. 570 (2008).

How are the intentions of the framers determined? Are the records of the Constitutional Convention reliable? Not entirely. What weight should be attached to the remarks of the framers? How much importance should be attributed to the views of those who ratified the Constitution? Thomas Jefferson promised as President to administer the Constitution "according to the safe and *honest* meaning contemplated by the *plain understanding of the people at the time of its adoption*—a meaning to be found in the explanations of those who advocated, not those who opposed it." 4 Elliot 446 (emphasis in original).

In 1803, Justice Paterson, himself a framer, held for the Court that a congressional interpretation of the Constitution, contemporaneous with the framing of the document fixed the meaning of the clause in question on the ground that early Congresses contained many members of the Philadelphia Convention who best knew the meaning of the Constitution. Stuart v. Laird, 5 U.S. (1 Cr.) 299 (1803). In 1827, Justice William Johnson stated that the "contemporaries of the Constitution have claims to our deference ... because they had the best opportunities of informing ourselves of the understanding of the framers of the Constitution, and of the sense put upon it by the people, when it was adopted by them." Ogden v. Saunders, 25 U.S. (12 Wheat.) 212, 270, 290 (1827). Yet advocates of Originalism are reminded that efforts by the Supreme Court to introduce historical evidence have been criticized by some historians as mere law-office efforts: special pleading for a particular point of view. Alfred H. Kelly, 1965 Sup. Ct. Rev. 119. Justice Jackson said despairingly at one point: "Just what our forefathers did envision, or would have envisioned had they foreseen modern conditions, must be divined from material almost as enigmatic as the dreams Joseph was called upon to interpret for Pharaoh." Youngstown Co. v. Sawyer, 343 U.S. 579, 624 (1952). Still, he did not hesitate in this case to rule that fundamental principles promoted by the framers prohibited President Truman from invoking "inherent" powers to seize steel mills to prosecute the war in Korea.

Natural Law

Judges sometimes reach outside the Constitution to discover fundamental or universal principles to guide their decisions. This natural law approach, however, remains a continuing source of dispute. Writing in *Calder* v. *Bull* (1798), Justice Iredell urged his colleagues to base their decisions on constitutional grounds rather than on mere declarations of opinions regarding the laws of nature, which "are regulated by no fixed standard" (see box on next page).

---

6. . Palko v. Connecticut, 302 U.S. 319, 326–27 (1937); Marsh v. Alabama, 326 U.S. 501, 509 (1946); Kovacs v. Cooper, 336 U.S. 77, 106 (1949) (Rutledge, J., dissenting).

Justice Iredell on Natural Law

If, then, a government, composed of legislative, executive and judicial departments, were established, by a constitution which imposed no limits on the legislative power, the consequence would inevitably be, that whatever the legislative power chose to enact, would be lawfully enacted, and the judicial power could never interpose to pronounce it void. It is true, that some speculative jurists have held, that a legislative act against natural justice must, in itself, be void; but I cannot think that, under such a government any court of justice would possess a power to declare it so....

... If ... the legislature of the Union, or the legislature of any member of the Union, shall pass a law, within the general scope of their constitutional power, the court cannot pronounce it to be void, merely because it is, in their judgment, contrary to the principles of natural justice. The ideas of natural justice are regulated by no fixed standard: the ablest and the purest men have differed upon the subject; and all that the court could properly say, in such an event, would be, that the legislature (possessed of an equal right of opinion) had passed an act which, in the opinion of the judges, was inconsistent with the abstract principles of natural justice....

SOURCE: Calder v. Bull, 3 U.S. at 398–99 (1798).

Justices react defensively to the charge that they merely read their own predilections into the Constitution, especially when interpreting such vague phrases as "due process," "equal protection," "unreasonable searches and seizures," and "cruel and unusual punishments." Nevertheless, Justices who oppose the death penalty argue that it violates the "human dignity" protected by the Constitution and is "no longer morally tolerable in our civilized society."[7] The law of defamation has been drawn not just from the First Amendment but from "our basic concept of the essential dignity and worth of every human being—a concept at the root of any decent system of ordered liberty." Rosenblatt v. Baer, 383 U.S. 75, 92 (1966).

Justice Frankfurter, remembered as the champion of judicial restraint, objected to those who called the interpretation of "due process" a mere matter of judicial caprice. Notwithstanding his general doctrine, he struck down actions that "shock the conscience" and "offend the community's sense of fair play and decency." Justice Black, a perennial critic of these opinions, charged that Frankfurter derived his standards basically from natural law, not constitutional law, and that such methods allowed judges to propound their own personal philosophies (see readings). In fact, the Constitution does have a "higher law" heritage.[8] From the very start, federal judges recognized that "there are certain great principles of justice, whose authority is universally acknowledged, that ought not to be entirely disregarded." Fletcher v. Peck, 10 U.S. 87, 132 (1810).

Historical Development

To shed further light on constitutional meaning, judges turn to historical analysis. Justice O'Connor has said that when the intent of the framers is unclear, "we must employ both history and reason in our analysis." Wallace v. Jaffree, 472 U.S. 38, 81 (1985). Legal historian Willard Hurst regarded the general political, economic, and social history of the United States as "legally competent and relevant evidence for the interpretation of the Constitution." Edmond Cahn, ed., Supreme Court and Supreme

---

7. Furman v. Georgia, 408 U.S. 238, 270 (1972) (Brennan, J., dissenting); Gregg v. Georgia, 428 U.S. 153, 229 (1976) (Brennan, J., dissenting).

8. Edward S. Corwin, The "Higher Law" Background of American Constitutional Law (1928); J. A. C. Grant, "The Natural Law Background of Due Process," 31 Colum. L. Rev. 56 (1931).

Law 56 (1954). The meaning of "interstate commerce" could not be restricted to the methods of commerce available at the time the Constitution was adopted. The phrase had to keep pace with the progress of the country, extending from stagecoaches to steamboats, from railroads to the telegraph. Pensacola Telegraph Co. v. Western Union Telegraph Co., 96 U.S. 1, 9 (1877).

More than a century of practice became a justification for supporting the exercise of presidential power over the public lands despite the absence of any express or statutory authority: "long continued practice, known to and acquiesced in by Congress, would raise a presumption ... of a recognised administrative power of the Executive in the management of the public lands."[9] Justice Holmes, writing in 1920, said that a case before the Court has to be considered "in the light of our whole experience and not merely in that of what was said a hundred years ago." Missouri v. Holland, 252 U.S. 416, 433 (1920). Holmes also remarked that "a page of history is worth a volume of logic." New York Trust Co. v. Eisner, 256 U.S. 345, 349 (1921). Death penalty cases are decided not by the meaning of the Eighth Amendment in 1791 but by "the evolving standards of decency that mark the progress of a maturing society." Trop v. Dulles, 356 U.S. 86, 101 (1958).

The judiciary has been influenced by the prevailing views of social scientists, be they conservative or liberal. It has been customary for the Court to go outside the legal record and take judicial notice of writings by experts. The philosophy of Social Darwinism in the late nineteenth and twentieth centuries supplied part of the theoretical justification for a laissez-faire state. This doctrine, reshaped in the hands of judges, helped support their opposition to social and economic regulation. In time, laissez-faire principles were challenged by the "Brandeis brief," which introduced social and economic facts to justify regulation of factory and working conditions. The use of extralegal data helped undermine the Court's reliance on abstract reasoning about "liberty of contract." Paul L. Rosen, The Supreme Court and Social Science 23–101 (1972). Eventually, lawyers on both sides learned how to put together a Brandeis brief to support their case. Today, it is not unusual in a particular case for dozens of individuals and groups to submit briefs that identify facts and precedents to guide the courts.

National Consensus

At times the Supreme Court will interpret the Constitution in terms of trends that develop in the states. It looks not to the text of the Constitution, framers' intent, or natural law, but rather to how *other people in the country* (particularly at the state level) are interpreting constitutional rights. For example, in 1977 the Court held that death is a disproportionate punishment for the crime of raping an adult woman. Coker v. Georgia, 433 U.S. 584 (1977). In deciding death penalty cases, it said that "attention must be given to the public attitudes concerning a particular sentence—history and precedent, legislative attitudes, and the response of juries reflected in their sentencing decisions." Id. at 592.

At no time in the past 50 years had a majority of states authorized death as a punishment for rape. In 1925, 18 states, the District of Columbia, and the federal government authorized capital punishment for the rape of an adult female. By 1971, that number had declined to 16 states plus the federal government. When states had to rewrite death penalty laws after the Court in *Furman* v. *Georgia* (1972) invalidated existing laws on capital punishment, only three (Georgia, North Carolina, and Louisiana) decided to reinstate the death penalty for rape. Louisiana and North Carolina, responding to court challenges, reenacted the death penalty for murder but not for rape. This process of reconsideration by the states helped convince the Court that the penalty of death for rape was disproportionate.

---

9. United States v. Midwest Oil Co., 236 U.S. 459, 472–74 (1915). See also Charles E. Miller, The Supreme Court and the Uses of History (1969); Paul Brest, "The Misconceived Quest for the Original Understanding," 60 B.U.L. Rev. 204 (1980); Frederick Bernays Wiener, Uses and Abuses of Legal History (1962); Sister Marie Carolyn Klinkhamer, "The Use of History in the Supreme Court, 1789–1935," 36 U. Det. L. J. 553 (1959); John Woodford, "The Blinding Light: The Uses of History in Constitutional Interpretation," 31 U. Chi. L. Rev. 502 (1964).

In 1989, the Court was asked to decide whether a state could sentence to death someone who is mentally retarded. The individual sentenced to die argued that "there is an emerging national consensus against executing the mentally retarded." Penry v. Lynaugh, 492 U.S. 302, 329 (1989). However, only one state (Georgia) at the time this case was litigated banned the execution of retarded persons found guilty of a capital offense. A Maryland statute adopting the same policy was scheduled to take effect on July 1, 1989. In the Court's view, "the two state statutes prohibiting execution of the mentally retarded ... do not provide sufficient evidence at present of a natural consensus." Id. at 334.

By 2002, the Court decided that a sufficient number of states had moved toward prohibiting capital punishment for the retarded, making the practice no longer constitutional. Atkins v. Virginia, 536 U.S. 304 (2002). The two states that prohibited death penalties for the retarded had now grown to 18. Under pressure to reverse its 1989 ruling, the Court "asked whether there is reason to disagree with the judgment reached by the citizenry and its legislators." The Court said that "today our society views mentally retarded offenders as categorically less culpable than the average criminal." The practice of executing the retarded had declined to the point where the Court said "it is fair to say that a national consensus has developed against it." In 2008, the Court's relied on its understanding of "national consensus" to strike down the death penalty for someone convicted of raping an eight-year-old girl. Kennedy v. Louisiana, 554 U.S. 407 (2008). What began as a process of the Court looking to individual state practices for guidance has gradually changed. Each time the Court "nationalizes" a constitutional value it inhibits states from making independent judgments. The decentralized and state-driven mechanism is increasingly centralized and made rigid by the Court.

Eclecticism

If the Constitution is to guide future generations, there must be some flexibility in applying its language. Speaking of a New Deal dispute over the Contract Clause, the Supreme Court observed:

> It is no answer to say that this public need was not apprehended a century ago, or to insist that what the provision of the Constitution meant to the vision of that day it must mean to the vision of our time. If by the statement that what the Constitution meant at the time of its adoption it means to-day, it is intended to say that the great clauses of the Constitution must be confined to the interpretation which the framers, with the conditions and outlook of their time, would have placed upon them, the statement carries its own refutation. Home Bldg. & Loan Ass'n v. Blaisdell, 290 U.S. 398, 442–43 (1934).

In interpreting the Constitution, we look partly at the "judicial gloss" added by the courts. It is the responsibility of the judiciary to interpret the law, and under the doctrine of stare decisis (stand by the precedents) judges try to honor prior rulings. Nevertheless, sufficient variations and discord among existing precedents allow any number of directions for future decisions. Which elements of an opinion were essential for the result and therefore binding on subsequent courts? Which were peripheral (obiter dicta)? At what point do we comb concurring and dissenting opinions?

Judges hold different views about the doctrine of stare decisis. Some are more willing than others to break with prior holdings. The Supreme Court's practice is to apply stare decisis less rigidly to constitutional than to nonconstitutional cases. Glidden Co. v. Zdanok, 370 U.S. 530, 543 (1962). If the Court "errs" on nonconstitutional matters, legislatures may respond by passing a new statute. Errors of constitutional dimension, however, are more difficult to fix. Burnet v. Coronado Oil & Gas Co., 285 U.S. 393, 406–07 (1932). Continuity is important for statutory law, for it permits citizens to arrange their business and personal affairs with confidence. Courts should not disturb this sense of security and stability by needlessly disrupting the law. National Bank v. Whitney, 103 U.S. 99, 102 (1880). But errors of constitutional doctrine require correction. In the words of Justice Douglas, judges swear to support and defend the Constitution, "not the gloss which his predecessors may have put on it." 49 Colum. L. Rev. 735, 736 (1949).

Justice Owen Roberts once complained that the Court's change of views "tends to bring adjudications of this tribunal into the same class as a restricted railroad ticket, good for this day and train only." Smith v. Allwright, 321 U.S. 649, 669 (1944). Justice Stewart argued that even if he believed the Court decided wrongly and he dissented at the time, subsequent rulings should be governed by what the majority decided. Donovan v. Dewey, 452 U.S. 594, 609 (1981). Many judges, however, would consider it irresponsible if they failed to correct a previous decision containing a mistake in constitutional law. The initial embarrassment of having the Court reverse itself is more than offset by the enhanced reputation of a Court willing to acknowledge its own errors. Justice Jackson declined to bind himself "hand and foot" to prior decisions, even when they were his own. He saw "no reason why I should be consciously wrong today because I was unconsciously wrong yesterday." Massachusetts v. United States, 333 U.S. 611, 639–40 (1948). Two years later, he penned an elegant justification for rejecting prior opinions that have lost their persuasive quality (see Jackson reading).

Outright reversal of a ruling is rare. More frequent is the practice of ignoring a precedent or "distinguishing" it from the pending case. These silent or tacit overrulings prompted Justice Black to remark of such cases: "Their interment is tactfully accomplished, without ceremony, eulogy, or report of their demise." Hood & Sons v. Du Mond, 336 U.S. 525, 555 (1949). Judges may argue that the current facts are different or simply reinterpret the precedent. Such techniques avoid the costs of overruling a precedent but also produce conflicting case law and uncertainty for those who must obey, interpret, enforce, and practice law.

After reviewing the various approaches to constitutional interpretation, Justice Cardozo described the judge's task as an eclectic exercise that blends in varying proportions the methods of philosophy, history, tradition, logic, and sociology. Rules are replaced by working hypotheses. The Nature of the Judicial Process (1921). The pressure of deadlines eliminates many options. Time, political constraints, and other limitations often make it impossible for judges to examine the entire record, pursue promising leads, review all the precedents, and produce original research. For those and other reasons, judicial decisions should be treated not as final utterances but as works in progress.

Philip Bobbitt identified a broad range of techniques used by judges to interpret the Constitution. He suggested that if someone took colored pencils to mark through passages of a Supreme Court opinion, using a different color for each technique, the reader would end up with a multicolored document. Constitutional Fate 93–94 (1982).

The Doctrine of Original Intent:
Attorney General Meese versus Justice Brennan[*]

Reliance on the framers' intent to interpret the Constitution has been debated almost continuously. A particularly interesting exchange of views occurred in 1985. Attorney General Edwin Meese III, in a speech to the American Bar Association on July 9, 1985, advocated a "Jurisprudence of Original Intention." He insisted that the only legitimate method of constitutional interpretation consists of resurrecting the original meaning of constitutional provisions. In a speech delivered at Georgetown University on October 12, 1985, Justice William J. Brennan, Jr., rejected primary dependence on original intent. The task of judges, he said, is to adapt the Constitution to current problems and current needs.

Attorney General Meese: The intended role of the judiciary generally, and the Supreme Court in particular, was to serve as the "bulwark of a limited constitution." The Founders believed that judges

---

* SOURCE: 27 South Texas Law Review 433–66 (1986). Footnotes omitted.

would not fail to regard the Constitution as fundamental law and would regulate their decisions by it. As the "faithful guardians of the Constitution," the judges were expected to resist any political effort to depart from the literal provisions of the Constitution. The standard of interpretation applied by the judiciary must focus on the text and the drafter's original intent.

. . .

In considering these areas of adjudication—Federalism, criminal law, and religion—one may conclude that far too many of the Court's opinions were, on the whole, mere policy choices rather than articulations of constitutional principle. The voting blocs and the arguments all reveal a greater allegiance to what the Court thinks constitutes sound public policy rather than a deference to what the Constitution, its text and intention, may demand.

One may also say that until there emerges a coherent jurisprudential stance, the work of the Court will continue in this ad hoc fashion. But that is not to argue for just *any* jurisprudence. In my opinion, a drift back toward the radical egalitarianism and expansive civil libertarianism of the Warren Court would once again be a threat to the notion of a limited but energetic government.

What, then, should a constitutional jurisprudence actually be? It should be a *jurisprudence of original intention.* By seeking to judge policies in light of principles, rather than remold principles in light of policies, the Court could avoid both the charge of incoherence *and* the charge of being either too conservative or too liberal.

A jurisprudence seriously aimed at the explication of original intention would produce defensible principles of government that would not be tainted by ideological predilection.

This belief in a *jurisprudence of original intention* also reflects a deeply rooted commitment to the idea of democracy. The Constitution represents the consent of the governed to the structures and powers of the government. The Constitution is the fundamental will of the people; that is the reason the Constitution is the fundamental law. To allow the courts to govern simply by what it views at the time as fair and decent, is a scheme of government no longer popular; the idea of democracy has suffered. The permanence of the Constitution has been weakened. A constitution that is viewed as only what the judges say it is, is no longer a constitution in the true sense of the term.

Those who framed the Constitution chose their words carefully; they debated at great length the most minute points. The language they chose meant something. It is incumbent upon the Court to determine what that meaning was. This is not a shockingly new theory; nor is it arcane or archaic.

. . .

Our belief is that only the sense in which the Constitution was accepted and ratified by the nation, and only the sense in which laws were drafted and passed provide a solid foundation for adjudication. Any other standard suffers the defect of pouring new meaning into old words, thus creating new powers and new rights totally at odds with the logic of our Constitution and its commitment to the rule of law.

Justice Brennan:

The amended Constitution of the United States entrenches the Bill of Rights and the Civil War amendments and draws sustenance from the bedrock principles of another great text, the Magna Carta. So fashioned, the Constitution embodies the aspiration to social justice, brotherhood, and human dignity that brought this nation into being. The Declaration of Independence, the Constitution, and the Bill of Rights solemnly committed the United States to be a country where the dignity and rights of all persons were equal before all authority. In all candor we must concede that part of this egalitarianism in America has been more pretension than realized fact. But we are an aspiring people, a people with faith in progress. Our amended Constitution is the lodestar for our aspirations. Like every text worth reading, it is not crystalline. The phrasing is broad and the limitations of its provisions are not clearly marked. Its majestic generalities and ennobling pronouncements are both luminous and obscure. This ambiguity, of course, calls forth interpretation, the interaction of reader and text. The encounter with the constitutional text has been, in many senses, my life's work. What is it we do when we interpret the Constitution? I will attempt to elucidate my approach to the text as well as my substantive interpretation.

. . .

… Our commitment to self-governance in a representative democracy must be reconciled with vesting in electorally unaccountable Justices the power to invalidate the expressed desires of representative bodies on the ground of inconsistency with higher law. Because judicial power resides in the authority to give meaning to the Constitution, the debate is really a debate about how to read the text, about constraints on what is legitimate interpretation.

There are those who find legitimacy in fidelity to what they call "the intentions of the Framers." In its most doctrinaire incarnation, this view demands that Justices discern exactly what the Framers thought about the question under consideration and simply follow that intention in resolving the case before them. It is a view that feigns self-effacing deference to the specific judgments of those who forged our original social compact. But in truth it is little more than arrogance cloaked as humility. It is arrogant to pretend that from our vantage we can gauge accurately the intent of the Framers on application of principle to specific, contemporary questions. All too often, sources of potential enlightenment such as records of the ratification debates provide sparse or ambiguous evidence of the original intention. Typically, all that can be gleaned is that the Framers themselves did not agree about the application or meaning of particular constitutional provisions and hid their differences in cloaks of generality. Indeed, it is far from clear whose intention is relevant—that of the drafters, the congressional disputants, or the ratifiers in the states—or even whether the idea of an original intention is a coherent way of thinking about a jointly drafted document drawing its authority from a general assent of the states. Apart from the problematic nature of the sources, our distance of two centuries cannot but work as a prism refracting all we perceive. One cannot help but speculate that the chorus of lamentations calling for interpretation faithful to "original intention"—and proposing nullification of interpretations that fail this quick litmus test—must inevitably come from persons who have no familiarity with the historical record.

. . .

Current Justices read the Constitution in the only way that we can: as twentieth-century Americans. We look to the history of the time of framing and to the intervening history of interpretation. But the ultimate question must be: What do the words of the text mean in our time? For the genius of the Constitution rests not in any static meaning it might have had in a world that is dead and gone, but in the adaptability of its great principles to cope with current problems and current needs....

The Natural Law Debate:
Frankfurter Against Black

In *Rochin* v. *California*, 342 U.S. 165 (1952), Justice Frankfurter overturned the actions of law enforcement officers who took a narcotics suspect to the hospital where an emetic was forced into his stomach against his will. He vomited two capsules containing morphine, and they were later admitted in evidence that led to his conviction. Frankfurter relied on the Due Process Clause of the Fourteenth Amendment to reverse the conviction. In a concurrence, Justice Black criticized Frankfurter for invoking natural law. Later, in *Griswold* v. *Connecticut*, 381 U.S. 479 (1965), in a case that struck down a state law banning contraceptives, Black's dissent summed up his views on the natural law approach.

Mr. Justice Frankfurter delivered the opinion of the Court.

... Regard for the requirements of the Due Process Clause "inescapably imposes upon this Court an exercise of judgment upon the whole course of the proceedings [resulting in a conviction] in order to ascertain whether they offend those canons of decency and fairness which express the notions of justice of English-speaking peoples even toward those charged with the most heinous offenses." *Malinski* v. *New York, supra,* at 416–417. These standards of justice are not authoritatively formulated anywhere as though they were specifics. Due process of law is a summarized constitutional guarantee of respect for those personal immunities which, as Mr. Justice Cardozo twice wrote for the Court, are "so rooted in the traditions and conscience of our people as to be ranked as fundamental"... or are "implicit in the concept of ordered liberty."...

The vague contours of the Due Process Clause do not leave judges at large. We may not draw on our merely personal and private notions and disregard the limits that bind judges in their judicial function.

Even though the concept of due process of law is not final and fixed, these limits are derived from considerations that are fused in the whole nature of our judicial process....

Due process of law thus conceived is not to be derided as resort to a revival of "natural law." To believe that this judicial exercise of judgment could be avoided by freezing "due process of law" at some fixed stage of time or thought is to suggest that the most important aspect of constitutional adjudication is a function for inanimate machines and not for judges, for whom the independence safeguarded by Article III of the Constitution was designed and who are presumably guided by established standards of judicial behavior. Even cybernetics has not yet made that haughty claim. To practice the requisite detachment and to achieve sufficient objectivity no doubt demands of judges the habit of self-discipline and self-criticism, incertitude that one's own views are incontestable and alert tolerance toward views not shared. But these are precisely the presuppositions of our judicial process. They are precisely the qualities society has a right to expect from those entrusted with ultimate judicial power.

. . .

Applying these general considerations to the circumstances of the present case, we are compelled to conclude that the proceedings by which this conviction was obtained do more than offend some fastidious squeamishness or private sentimentalism about combatting crime too energetically. This is conduct that shocks the conscience. Illegally breaking into the privacy of the petitioner, the struggle to open his mouth and remove what was there, the forcible extraction of his stomach's contents — this course of proceeding by agents of government to obtain evidence is bound to offend even hardened sensibilities. They are methods too close to the rack and the screw to permit of constitutional differentiation....

Mr. Justice Black, concurring.

. . .

What the majority hold is that the Due Process Clause empowers this Court to nullify any state law if its application "shocks the conscience," offends "a sense of justice" or runs counter to the "decencies of civilized conduct." The majority emphasize that these statements do not refer to their own consciences or to their senses of justice and decency. For we are told that "we may not draw on our merely personal and private notions"; our judg-

ment must be grounded on "considerations deeply rooted in reason and in the compelling traditions of the legal profession." We are further admonished to measure the validity of state practices, not by our reason, or by the traditions of the legal profession, but by "the community's sense of fair play and decency"; by the "traditions and conscience of our people"; or by "those canons of decency and fairness which express the notions of justice of English-speaking peoples." These canons are made necessary, it is said, because of "interests of society pushing in opposite directions."

If the Due Process Clause does vest this Court with such unlimited power to invalidate laws, I am still in doubt as to why we should consider only the notions of English-speaking peoples to determine what are immutable and fundamental principles of justice. Moreover, one may well ask what avenues of investigation are open to discover "canons" of conduct so universally favored that this Court should write them into the Constitution? All we are told is that the discovery must be made by an "evaluation based on a disinterested inquiry pursued in the spirit of science, on a balanced order of facts." ...

Mr. Justice Black [*dissenting in* Griswold].

The due process argument which my Brothers Harlan and White adopt here is based, as their opinions indicate, on the premise that this Court is vested with power to invalidate all state laws that it considers to be arbitrary, capricious, unreasonable, or oppressive, or on this Court's belief that a particular state law under scrutiny has no "rational or justifying" purpose, or is offensive to a "sense of fairness and justice." If these formulas based on "natural justice," or others which mean the same thing, are to prevail, they require judges to determine what is or is not constitutional on the basis of their own appraisal of what laws are unwise or unnecessary. The power to make such decisions is of course that of a legislative body....

... And so, I cannot rely on the Due Process Clause or the Ninth Amendment or any mysterious and uncertain natural law concept as a reason for striking down this state law. The Due Process Clause with an "arbitrary and capricious" or "shocking to the conscience" formula was liberally used by this Court to strike down economic legislation in the early decades of this century, threatening, many people thought, the tranquility and stability of the Nation. See, *e.g., Lochner* v. *New York,* 198 U. S. 45. That formula, based on subjective considerations of "natural justice," is no less dangerous when used to enforce this Court's views about personal rights than those about economic rights....

Stare Decisis

In the interest of consistency and predictability, judges prefer to decide cases in accordance with past rulings. This doctrine of stare decisis (stand by the precedents) has particular force when applied to statutory interpretation, but decisions are regularly reviewed and revised to take into account recent developments, new information, and better understanding. In a concurring opinion in *McGrath* v. *Kristensen,* 340 U.S. 162 (1950), Justice Jackson offered a candid, personal, and amusing justification for parting company with opinions that seem, upon reflection, unconvincing.

MR. JUSTICE JACKSON, concurring.

I concur in the judgment and opinion of the Court. But since it is contrary to an opinion which, as Attorney General, I rendered in 1940, I owe some word of explanation. 39 Op. Atty. Gen. 504. I am entitled to say of that opinion what any discriminating reader must think of it—that it was as foggy as the statute the Attorney General was asked to interpret. It left the difficult borderline questions posed by the Secretary of War unanswered, covering its lack of precision with generalities which, however, gave off overtones of assurance that the Act applied to nearly every alien from a neutral country caught in the United States under almost any circumstances which required him to stay overnight.

The opinion did not at all consider aspects of our diplomatic history, which I now think, and should think I would then have thought, ought to be considered in applying any conscription Act to aliens.

. . .

Precedent, however, is not lacking for ways by which a judge may recede from a prior opinion that has proven untenable and perhaps misled others. See Chief Justice Taney, *License Cases,* 5 How. 504, recanting views he had pressed upon the Court as Attorney General of Maryland in *Brown* v. *Maryland,* 12 Wheat. 419. Baron Bramwell extricated himself from a somewhat similar embarrassment by saying, "The matter does not appear to me now as it appears to have appeared to me then." *Andrews* v. *Styrap,* 26 L. T. R. (N.S.) 704, 706. And Mr. Justice Story, accounting for his contradiction of his own former opinion, quite properly put the matter: "My own error, however, can furnish no ground for its being adopted by this Court...." *United States* v. *Gooding,* 12 Wheat. 460, 478. Perhaps Dr. Johnson really went to the heart of the matter when he explained a blunder in his dictionary—"Ignorance, sir, ignorance." But an escape less self-depreciating was taken by Lord Westbury, who, it is said, rebuffed a barrister's reliance upon an earlier opinion of his Lordship: "I can only say that I am amazed that a man of my intelligence should have been guilty of giving such an opinion." If there are other ways of gracefully and good-naturedly surrendering former views to a better considered position, I invoke them all.

NOTES AND QUESTIONS

1. The omission in the text of the Constitution of any reference to the power of judicial review has triggered a great debate on several fronts. If the framers intended the courts to exercise the power, why didn't they enumerate it in the Constitution? Did they simply assume the availability of judicial review? How do you compare the merits of Alexander Hamilton's Federalist No. 78 and the competing views of Brutus in his critique of judicial power?

2. In your view, did Chief Justice Marshall's opinion in *Marbury v. Madison* claim for the judiciary the final word on questions involving merely its own power, or did he assert the broader claim that the Court possessed the authority to rule on the constitutionality of the acts of coordinate departments as well?

3. Did Judge Gibson provide an effective critique of Marshall's reasoning in his dissent in *Eakin v. Raub?* Which of his arguments seem to you compelling?

4. In 1986, Attorney General Ed Meese III delivered a speech at Tulane University in which he challenged the last-word doctrine. His speech drew charges that he had exhibited disrespect for the Court,

but which is more important: the text of the Constitution or the Court's interpretation of it? How would you answer that question?

5. Scholars have long debated the compatibility of judicial review and democracy. Is the promotion of democracy a responsibility of the judicial department? How should it best pursue that objective?

SELECTED READINGS

AGRESTO, JOHN. The Supreme Court and Constitutional Democracy. Ithaca, N.Y.: Cornell University Press, 1984.

ALFANGE, DEAN, JR. "On Judicial Policymaking and Constitutional Change: Another Look at the 'Original Intent' Theory of Constitutional Interpretation." 5 Hastings Constitutional Law Quarterly 603 (1978).

———. "Marbury v. Madison and Original Understandings of Judicial Review: In Defense of Traditional Wisdom," 1993 Supreme Court Review 329.

BERGER, RAOUL. Congress v. The Supreme Court. Cambridge, Mass.: Harvard University Press, 1969.

BICKEL, ALEXANDER M. The Least Dangerous Branch. New York: Bobbs-Merrill, 1962.

BISHIN, WILLIAM R. "Judicial Review in Democratic Theory." 50 Southern California Law Review 1099 (1977).

BLACK, CHARLES L., JR. The People and the Court. New York: Macmillan, 1960.

BREYER, STEPHEN. Making Our Democracy Work: A Judge's View. New York: Alfred A. Knopf, 2010.

CARR, ROBERT K. The Supreme Court and Judicial Review. New York: Farrar and Rinehart, 1942.

COMMAGER, HENRY STEELE. Majority Rule and Minority Rights. New York: Oxford University Press, 1943.

CORWIN, EDWARD S. The Doctrine of Judicial Review. Princeton, N.J.: Princeton University Press, 1914.

———. Court over Constitution. Princeton, N.J.: Princeton University Press, 1938.

DAHL, ROBERT A. "Decision-Making in a Democracy: The Role of the Supreme Court as a National Policy-Maker." 6 Journal of Public Law 279 (1957).

ENGEL, STEPHEN M. American Politicians Confront the Court: Opposition Politics and Changing Responses to Judicial Power. New York: Cambridge University Press, 2011.

FISHER, LOUIS. "Methods of Constitutional Interpretation: The Limits of Original Intent." 18 Cumberland Law Review 43 (1987–1988).

———. "The Curious Belief in Judicial Supremacy." 25 Suffolk University Law Review 85 (1991).

———. "Interpreting the Constitution: More Than What the Supreme Court Says," Extensions, Fall 2008, 15–19.

HAINES, CHARLES GROVES. The American Doctrine of Judicial Supremacy. Berkeley: University of California Press, 1932.

JAFFE, LOUIS L. "The Right to Judicial Review." 71 Harvard Law Review 401, 769 (1958).

KURLAND, PHILIP B. Politics, the Constitution, and the Warren Court. Chicago: University of Chicago Press, 1970.

LEVY, LEONARD W. Original Intent and the Framers' Constitution. New York: Macmillan, 1988.

MILLER, ARTHUR S., AND RONALD F. HOWELL. "The Myth of Neutrality in Constitutional Adjudication." 27 University of Chicago Law Review 661 (1960).

NELSON, WILLIAM E. "Changing Conceptions of Judicial Review: The Evolution of Constitutional Theory in the States, 1790–1860." 120 University of Pennsylvania Law Review 1166 (1972).

O'BRIEN, DAVID M. "Judicial Review and Constitutional Politics: Theory and Practice." 48 University of Chicago Law Review 1052 (1981).

POLLAK, LOUIS H. "Racial Discrimination and Judicial Integrity: A Reply to Professor Wechsler." 108 University of Pennsylvania Law Review 1 (1959).

SCALIA, ANTONIN. A Matter of Interpretation: Federal Courts and the Law. Princeton, N.J.: Princeton University Press, 1997.

SNOWISS, SYLVIA. Judicial Review and the Law of the Constitution. New Haven, Conn.: Yale University Press, 1990.

WELLINGTON, HARRY H. "The Nature of Judicial Review." 91 Yale Law Journal 486 (1982).

WOLFE, CHRISTOPHER. The Rise of Modern Judicial Review. New York: Basic Books, 1986.

WRIGHT, J. SKELLY. "The Role of the Supreme Court in a Democratic Society—Judicial Activism or Restraint." 54 Cornell Law Review 1 (1968).

———. "Professor Bickel, the Scholarly Tradition, and the Supreme Court." 84 Harvard Law Review 769 (1971).

3

Threshold Requirements: Husbanding Power and Prestige

The scope of judicial review is circumscribed by rules of self-restraint fashioned by judges. Various court doctrines sketch out the minimum conditions needed to adjudicate a case. These thresholds (or "gatekeeping rules") do more than limit access by litigants. They shield judges from cases that threaten their independence and institutional effectiveness. They ration scarce judicial resources and postpone or avoid decisions on politically sensitive issues.

Chief Justice Marshall suggested that the boundaries for judicial action were quite fixed: "It is most true that this Court will not take jurisdiction if it should not: but it is equally true, that it must take jurisdiction if it should." Cohens v. Virginia, 6 Wheat. 264, 404 (1821). The record of the judiciary, however, is quite different. What the Court should or should not accept is largely a matter of judicial discretion. Reflecting on his work at the Supreme Court, Justice Brandeis confided: "The most important thing we do is not doing." Alexander M. Bickel, The Unpublished Opinions of Mr. Justice Brandeis 17 (1957). The deliberate withholding of judicial power often reflects the fact that courts lack ballot-box legitimacy. While often couched in technical jargon, jurisdictional requirements implicate fundamental questions of democratic theory.

Judges invoke access rules to promote the adversary system, preserve public support, avoid conflicts with other branches of government, and provide flexibility of action for the judiciary. The doctrines used to pursue those goals include justiciability, standing, mootness, ripeness, political questions, and prudential considerations, all of which help protect an unelected and unrepresentative judiciary. Although efforts are made to distinguish these doctrines, inevitably they overlap. As noted by the Supreme Court: "The standing question thus bears close affinity to questions of ripeness — whether the harm asserted has matured sufficiently to warrant judicial intervention — and of mootness — whether the occasion for judicial intervention persists." Warth v. Seldin, 422 U.S. 490, 499 n.10 (1975).

A. CASES AND CONTROVERSIES

Article III of the Constitution limits the jurisdiction of federal courts to "cases" and "controversies." Courts must determine that they have jurisdiction to hear the case. Jurisdiction is granted both by the Constitution and by statute. Even after accepting jurisdiction, courts may decide that the subject matter is inappropriate for judicial consideration — what the courts call "nonjusticiable." This latter concept, at times synonymous with "political questions," is used to avoid collisions with Congress and the President. Baker v. Carr, 369 U.S. 186, 198, 208–34 (1962). It is also applied more broadly to cover issues outside the separation of powers. Flast v. Cohen, 392 U.S. 83, 95 (1968).

As a way to minimize error, miscalculation, and political conflict, courts adopt guidelines to avoid judgment on a large number of constitutional questions. These guidelines only provide very broad direction for judicial activity. If judges want to ignore them, they can. However, the rules supply a convenient list of justifications for refusing to decide a case. ASHWANDER v. TVA, 297 U.S. 288 (1936).

To resolve a legal claim, courts need to know that parties have been adversely affected. Abstract or hypothetical questions, removed from a concrete factual setting, prevent courts from reaching an informed judgment. The words "cases" and "controversies" limit the federal courts "to questions presented in an adversary context and in a form historically viewed as capable of resolution through the judicial process." Flast v. Cohen, 392 U.S. at 95.

Adverseness

The adversary system seeks truth by having judges and juries observe a contest between two sets of professional advocates. It assumes that two antagonistic parties, each with a sufficient stake in the outcome, will marshal the best arguments to defend their interests. This clash between rival parties "sharpens the presentation of issues upon which the court so largely depends for illumination of difficult constitutional questions." Baker v. Carr, 369 U.S. at 204. A case brought by two parties with the same interest loses its adversary character. South Spring Gold Co. v. Amador Gold Co., 145 U.S. 300 (1892). Nor is there adverseness when two attorneys bring a collusive or "friendly suit" or when both parties agree on a constitutional issue and want the same result.[1] In an 1883 case involving a woman's right to practice law, Mrs. Bradwell's attorney pleaded her case but no one appeared for the other side. The court record simply states: "No opposing counsel." Bradwell v. State, 83 U.S. (16 Wall.) 130, 137 (1883).

Courts occasionally consider a case even when both parties agree on the issue. In *United States* v. *Lovett* (1946), the Justice Department agreed with the plaintiff that a provision in a congressional statute was unconstitutional as a forbidden bill of attainder. To protect its interests, Congress passed legislation to create a special counsel. Functioning officially as amicus curiae, the counsel in effect served as counsel for Congress to assure adverseness. 328 U.S. 303, 304 (1946). In other cases the courts have appointed a special counsel to create an adversary proceeding. Granville-Smith v. Granville-Smith, 349 U.S. 1, 4 (1955).

During the battle over the Watergate tapes, President Nixon's lawyers argued in court that a case or controversy did not exist because Special Prosecutor Leon Jaworski "was an employee of the executive branch and Nixon was his boss." The judge in that trial, John Sirica, remarked: "any fool could see that a more genuine controversy couldn't be imagined." John J. Sirica, To Set the Record Straight 224 (1979).

There appeared to be lack of adverseness in the legislative veto case decided by the Supreme Court in 1983. The plaintiff, Jagdish Rai Chadha, sued the Immigration and Naturalization Service (INS), charging that its statutory procedure for deportation was unconstitutional. The government agreed with his position. The Ninth Circuit asked the House of Representatives and the Senate to file briefs as amici curiae. To the House, Chadha's case lacked adverseness because both parties found the statute invalid. Moreover, an appearance as amicus did not supply adverseness to create a case or controversy. The court rejected this reasoning because it would "implicitly approve the untenable result that all agencies could insulate unconstitutional orders and procedures from appellate review simply by agreeing that what they did was unconstitutional." Chadha v. INS, 634 F.2d 408, 420 (9th Cir. 1980).

In affirming the judgment of the Ninth Circuit, the Supreme Court also refused to regard the case as a "friendly, non-adversary, proceeding" between Chadha and the INS. As the Court noted, it would be "a curious result if, in the administration of justice, a person could be denied access to the courts because the Attorney General of the United States agreed with the legal arguments asserted by the individual." From the moment of Congress's formal intervention as amicus, adverseness was "beyond

---

1. United States v. Johnson, 319 U.S. 302 (1943). See also Lord v. Veazie, 49 U.S. 251 (1850), in which the plaintiff and defendant had the same interest, and Moore v. Board of Education, 402 U.S. 47 (1971). In some cases the Court will allow a president to sue his or her own company because the board of directors, backed by stockholders, voted against the president to create adverseness. Carter v. Carter Coal Co., 298 U.S. 238, 286–87 (1936).

doubt." Even prior to intervention there was "adequate Art. III adverseness." INS v. Chadha, 462 U.S. 919, 939 (1983).

[See also "Lack of Adversary Process" in Chapter 5, Section C.]

Advisory Opinions

The case or controversy requirement was tested in 1790 when Secretary of the Treasury Alexander Hamilton sought the advice of Chief Justice John Jay about a pending legal issue. Resolutions adopted by the Virginia House of Representatives had challenged the right of the national government to assume state debts. Hamilton regarded this resistance as "the first symptom of a spirit which must either be killed or it will kill the Constitution of the United States" and urged that the "collective weight" of the three branches be employed to repudiate the resolutions. Jay replied that it was inadvisable for the Court to join such action. 1 Charles Warren, Supreme Court in United States History 52–53 (1937). Similar efforts by Secretary of State Thomas Jefferson in 1793 to obtain advisory opinions were rebuffed by the Court. The Justices considered it improper to make extrajudicial decisions, noting that the Constitution gives the President the express power to obtain opinions from the heads of the executive departments (see box).

This same period, however, yields conflicting evidence. Chief Justice Jay and his colleagues on the Court advised President Washington in 1790 that the statutory requirement for them to "ride circuit" (travel around the country hearing appellate cases) was unconstitutional. Robert A. Dahlquist, 14 Sw. U. L. Rev. 46, 50–54 (1983). And in *Hayburn's Case* (1792), three circuit courts explained to President Washington their constitutional objections to a statute passed by Congress.[2] In both of these disputes, the interests of the courts were directly involved: having to ride circuit and perform nonjudicial duties.

The Supreme Court's formal position on advisory opinions appeared in 1911. Congress had authorized certain Indians to bring suit to determine the constitutionality of a statute. They were given expedited treatment by the Court of Claims and a right of appeal to the Supreme Court. Justice Day

---

Chief Justice Jay Explains the Court's Position on Issuing Advisory Opinions

We have considered the previous question stated in a letter written by your direction to us by the Secretary of State on the 18th of last month, [regarding] the lines of separation drawn by the Constitution between the three departments of the government. These being in certain respects checks upon each other, and our being judges of a court in the last resort, are considerations which afford strong arguments against the propriety of our extra-judicially deciding the questions alluded to, especially as the power given by the Constitu-

tion to the President, of calling on the heads of departments for opinions, seems to have been *purposely* as well as expressly united to the *executive* departments.

We exceedingly regret every event that may cause embarrassment to your administration, but we derive consolation from the reflection that your judgment will discern what is right, and that your usual prudence, decision, and firmness will surmount every obstacle to the preservation of the rights, peace, and dignity of the United States.

3 The Correspondence and Public Papers of John Jay 488–89 (H. Johnston ed. 1890) (emphasis in original). August 8, 1793.

---

2. U.S. (2 Dall.) at 410–14 nn (1792). The statute was constitutionally objectionable because judicial decisions could be set aside by the Secretary of War, in effect converting a judicial decision into a mere advisory opinion. For similar reasons, the Court has opposed procedures that make its decisions dependent on executive and legislative actions before being carried out; Gordon v. United States, 117 U.S. 697 (1864).

reviewed earlier instances in which federal judges decided that Congress could not impose nonjudicial duties on the courts. The suit, even though authorized by Congress, did not create a case or controversy between adverse parties. It was an effort to obtain the Court's opinion on the validity of congressional statutes. Day said it was inappropriate for the judiciary "to give opinions in the nature of advice concerning legislative action, a function never conferred upon it by the Constitution and against the exercise of which this court has steadily set its face from the beginning." Muskrat v. United States, 219 U.S. 346, 362 (1911). In 1948, the Court voiced constitutional objections to a statute that allowed the President to override the judgment of a federal court. The procedure amounted to "an advisory opinion in its most obnoxious form." C. & S. Air Lines v. Waterman Corp., 333 U.S. 103, 113–14 (1948).

Nevertheless, judges find ways to offer advice to the political branches. A number have met with Presidents, legislators, and agency administrators to discuss matters that were being, or could be, litigated. Walter Murphy, The Elements of Judicial Strategy 132–55 (1964). As a nonjudicial function, the Judicial Conference performs an advisory role by commenting on pending legislation. In their off-bench activities, federal judges have offered advice about the constitutionality of legislative proposals. After the Supreme Court in *INS* v. *Chadha* (1983) struck down the legislative veto, D.C. Circuit Judge Abner J. Mikva told a House committee that he did not think "there is any question" that a joint resolution of approval or disapproval, as a substitute for the discredited one-House and two-House vetoes, "would pass constitutional muster."[3]

Even in the course of writing an opinion, judges often resort to dicta to advise executive and legislative officers. In a 1978 case, Chief Justice Burger rejected a number of procedural attempts to postpone adjudication of the Price-Anderson Act. He said that any delay in interpreting the statute would frustrate one of its key purposes: "the elimination of doubts concerning the scope of private liability in the event of major nuclear accident." All parties would be adversely affected, he claimed, by deferring a decision. Duke Power Co. v. Carolina Environmental Study Group, 438 U.S. 59, 82 (1978). Justice Stevens admitted that the decision would serve the national interest by removing doubts concerning the constitutionality of the statute, but he did not include among judicial functions the duty to provide advisory opinions on important subjects:

> We are not statesmen; we are judges. When it is necessary to resolve a constitutional issue in the adjudication of an actual case or controversy, it is our duty to do so. But whenever we are persuaded by reasons of expediency to engage in the business of giving legal advice, we chip away a part of the foundation of our independence and our strength. Id. at 103 (concurring opinion).

A year later, Justice Stevens and three colleagues accused the Court of rendering an advisory opinion for the state of Massachusetts. In defense, Justice Powell explained that his decision merely provided "some guidance" to the state legislators. This exchange took place in two intriguing footnotes. See BELLOTTI v. BAIRD, 443 U.S. 622 (1979). In 1994, a concurrence by Justice O'Connor offered suggestions to New York State on how to create a school district for a religious minority without running into constitutional problems. Board of Ed. of Kiryas Joel v. Grumet, 512 U.S. 687, 717 (1994). Justices may decide to express concerns about a dispute in a manner that "encourages" Congress to revisit a statute to clarify it. Brogan v. United States, 522 U.S. 398, 408–18 (1998) (Ginsburg, J., concurring op., joined by Souter, J.).

Declaratory Judgments

Parties uncertain of their legal rights want courts to determine those rights before injury is done. Otherwise, they might have to violate a law to bring a test case or forgo possible rights because of a fear of litigation. By issuing "declaratory judgments," courts can offer preventive relief. In 1928, Repre-

---

3. "Legislative Veto After Chadha," hearings before the House Committee on Rules, 98th Cong., 2d Sess. 600 (1984).

sentative Ralph Gilbert explained the advantages of declaratory judgments: "Under the present law you take a step in the dark and then turn on the light to see if you stepped into a hole. Under the declaratory law you turn on the light and then take a step." 69 Cong. Rec. 2030 (1928). Unlike other judgments, declaratory relief decides only legal rights; it does not determine damages or the right to coercive relief. To avoid the ban on advisory opinions, such judgments are limited to actual controversies. Also, declaratory judgments (unlike advisory opinions) are binding on the parties.

Before 1934, declaratory judgments had been issued by Great Britain, India, Scotland, Canada, Australia, and other nations. More than two dozen American states had adopted the practice. H. Rept. No. 1264, 73d Cong., 2d Sess. 1 (1934). Federal courts had also issued what were in effect declaratory judgments, because they determined rights and duties before a law was violated and even before a law had taken effect. Pierce v. Society of Sisters, 268 U.S. 510, 525 (1925); Village of Euclid v. Ambler Realty Co., 272 U.S. 365 (1926). To remove the legal uncertainty, Congress in 1934 passed the Declaratory Judgments Act. In "a case of actual controversy," it gives federal courts the power to declare "the rights and other legal relations of any interested party seeking such declaration, whether or not further relief is or could be sought. Any such declaration shall have the force and effect of a final judgment or decree and be reviewable as such." 48 Stat. 955 (1934); 28 U.S.C. § 2201. In a unanimous decision, the Supreme Court upheld the constitutionality of this statute. Aetna Life Insurance Co. v. Haworth, 300 U.S. 227 (1937).

Ashwander v. TVA
(The Brandeis Rules)

297 U.S. 288 (1936)

In a concurring opinion, Justice Brandeis reviewed the rules used by the courts to limit their exercise of judicial review. The rules are designed to avoid needless and potentially damaging (for the judiciary) conflicts with Congress.

The Court has frequently called attention to the "great gravity and delicacy" of its function in passing upon the validity of an act of Congress; and has restricted exercise of this function by rigid insistence that the jurisdiction of federal courts is limited to actual cases and controversies; and that they have no power to give advisory opinions. On this ground it has in recent years ordered the dismissal of several suits challenging the constitutionality of important acts of Congress....

The Court developed, for its own governance in the cases confessedly within its jurisdiction, a series of rules under which it has avoided passing upon a large part of all the constitutional questions pressed upon it for decision. They are:

1. The Court will not pass upon the constitutionality of legislation in a friendly, non-adversary, proceeding, declining because to decide such questions "is legitimate only in the last resort, and as a necessity in the determination of real, earnest and vital controversy between individuals. It never was the thought that, by means of a friendly suit, a party

beaten in the legislature could transfer to the courts an inquiry as to the constitutionality of the legislative act." ...

2. The Court will not "anticipate a question of constitutional law in advance of the necessity of deciding it." ...

3. The Court will not "formulate a rule of constitutional law broader than is required by the precise facts to which it is to be applied." ...

4. The Court will not pass upon a constitutional question although properly presented by the record, if there is also present some other ground upon which the case may be disposed of. This rule has found most varied application. Thus, if a case can be decided on either of two grounds, one involving a constitutional question, the other a question of statutory construction or general law, the Court will decide only the latter. ... Appeals from the highest court of a state challenging its decision of a question under the Federal Constitution are frequently dismissed because the judgment can be sustained on an independent state ground. ...

5. The Court will not pass upon the validity of a statute upon complaint of one who fails to show that he is injured by its operation....

6. The Court will not pass upon the constitutionality of a statute at the instance of one who has availed himself of its benefits.

7. "When the validity of an act of the Congress is drawn in question, and even if a serious doubt of constitutionality is raised, it is a cardinal principle that this Court will first ascertain whether a construction of the statute is fairly possible by which the question may be avoided." ...

Bellotti v. Baird (Advisory Opinions)

443 U.S. 622 (1979)

A Massachusetts statute required parental consent before an abortion could be performed on an unmarried woman under the age of eighteen. If one or both parents refused, a judge could order the abortion "for good cause shown." The Court held that the statute unduly burdened the right to seek an abortion because it gave a judge the right to disapprove an abortion for a mature minor and required parental consultation or notification in every instance. Writing for the Court, Justice Powell suggested to Massachusetts what would be an acceptable judicial bypass procedure. Justice Stevens, joined by Justices Brennan, Marshall, and Blackmun, wrote a footnote that called Powell's opinion, in effect an advisory opinion. Powell prepared a footnote of his own to justify the direction he had given.

JUSTICE STEVENS:

Until and unless Massachusetts or another State enacts a less restrictive statutory scheme, this Court has no occasion to render an advisory opinion on the constitutionality of such a scheme. A real statute—rather than a mere outline of a possible statute—and a real case or controversy may well present questions that appear quite different from the hypothetical questions MR. JUSTICE POWELL has elected to address. Indeed, there is a certain irony in his suggestion that a statute that is intended to vindicate "the special interest of the State in encouraging an unmarried pregnant minor to seek the advice of her parents in making the important decision whether or not to bear a child," see *ante*, at 639, need not require notice to the parents of the minor's intended decision. That irony makes me wonder whether any legislature concerned with parental consultation would, in the absence of today's advisory opinion, have enacted a statute comparable to the one my Brethren have discussed.

JUSTICE POWELL:

The opinion of MR. JUSTICE STEVENS, concurring in the judgment, joined by three Members of the Court, characterizes this opinion as "advisory" and the questions it addresses as "hypothetical." Apparently, this is criticism of our attempt to provide some guidance as to how a State constitutionally may provide for adult involvement—either by parents or a state official such as a judge—in the abor-

tion decisions of minors. In view of the importance of the issue raised, and the protracted litigation to which these parties already have been subjected, we think it would be irresponsible simply to invalidate § 12S without stating our views as to the controlling principles.

The statute before us today is the same one that was here in *Bellotti I*. The issues it presents were not then deemed "hypothetical." In a unanimous opinion, we remanded the case with directions that appropriate questions be certified to the Supreme Judicial Court of Massachusetts "concerning the meaning of [§ 12S] and the procedure it imposes." 428 U.S., at 151. We directed that this be done because, as stated in the opinion, we thought the construction of § 12S urged by appellants would "avoid or substantially modify the federal constitutional challenge to the statute." *Id.*, at 148. The central feature of § 12S was its provision that a state-court judge could make the ultimate decision, when necessary, as to the exercise by a minor of the right to an abortion. See *id.*, at 145. We held that this "would be fundamentally different from a statute that creates a 'parental veto' [of the kind rejected in *Danforth*.]" *Ibid.* (footnote omitted). Thus, all Members of the Court agreed that providing for decisionmaking authority in a judge was not the kind of veto power held invalid in *Danforth*. The basic issues that were before us in *Bellotti I* remain in the case, sharpened by the construction of § 12S by the Supreme Judicial Court.

B. STANDING TO SUE

To satisfy the requirements of a case or controversy, parties bringing an action must have standing to sue. "Generalizations about standing to sue," Justice Douglas said with customary bluntness, "are largely worthless as such." Data Processing Service v. Camp, 397 U.S. 150, 151 (1970). Judges frequently accuse one another of circular reasoning. After the Supreme Court announced that the requirements of standing are met if a taxpayer has the "requisite personal stake in the outcome" of his or her suit, Justice Harlan chided the Court: "This does not, of course, resolve the standing problem; it merely restates it." Flast v. Cohen, 392 U.S. at 121 (dissenting opinion).

The reader forewarned, here are some generalizations. To demonstrate standing, parties must show injury to a legally protected interest, an injury that is real rather than abstract or hypothetical. O'Shea v. Littleton, 414 U.S. 488, 494 (1974). Injuries may be economic or noneconomic. Data Processing Service v. Camp, 397 U.S. at 154. They may be actual or threatened.[4] Injuries may afflict organizations as well as persons. Havens Realty Corp. v. Coleman, 455 U.S. 363, 379 n.19 (1982); Warth v. Seldin, 422 U.S. at 511. A "threatened" injury can be close cousin to the hypothetical. Five members of the Supreme Court in 1973 held that *allegations* of injury were sufficient to establish standing. Proof of actual injury was not necessary.[5] On the other hand, actual injury may be inadequate to establish standing if the Court wishes to defer to the states. City of Los Angeles v. Lyons, 461 U.S. 95 (1983). Occasionally, the Court summarizes the main elements of standing (see box).

Individuals, functioning in the role of private attorneys general, may have standing as "representatives of the public interest." Scenic Hudson Preservation Conf. v. FPC, 354 F.2d 608, 615–16 (2d Cir. 1965). This principle sometimes permits one party to assert the rights of third parties (*jus tertii*). Third-party suits (sometimes called "next-friend" standing) require special circumstances, such as someone intervening because a prisoner is mentally incompetent to represent himself. Coalition of Clergy, Lawyers & Professors v. Bush, 310 F.3d 1153, 1157–60 (9th Cir. 2002), citing Whitmore v. Arkansas, 495 U.S. 149, 161–64 (1990). Federal courts are reluctant to resolve a controversy on the basis of the rights of third persons who are not parties to the litigation. "The courts depend on effective advocacy, and therefore should prefer to construe legal rights only when the most effective advo-

---

The Elements of Standing

Lujan v. Defenders of Wildlife, 504 U.S. 555, 560–61 (1992): Over the years, our cases have established that the irreducible constitutional minimum of standing contains three elements. First, the plaintiff must have suffered an "injury in fact"—an invasion of a legally protected interest which is (a) concrete and particularized, see [*Allen* v. *Wright*, 468 U.S.] at 756; *Warth* v. *Seldin*, 422 U.S. 490, 508 (1975); *Sierra Club* v. *Morton*, 405 U.S. 727, 740–741, n. 16 (1972); and (b) "actual or imminent, not 'conjectural' or 'hypothetical,'" *Whitmore* [v. *Arkansas*], 495 U.S., at 155 (quoting *Los Angeles* v. *Lyons*, 461 U.S. 95, 102 (1983)). Second, there must be a causal connection between the injury and the conduct complained of—the injury has to be "fairly ... trace[able] to the challenged action of the defendant, and not ... th[e] result [of] the independent action of some third party not before the court." *Simon* v. *Eastern Kentucky Welfare Rights Org.*, 426 U.S. 26, 41–42 (1976). Third, it must be "likely," as opposed to merely "speculative," that the injury will be "redressed by a favorable decision." *Id.*, at 38, 43.

---

4. Linda R.S. v. Richard D., 410 U.S. 614, 617 (1973); Gladstone, Realtors v. Village of Bellwood, 441 U.S. 91, 99 (1979); Muller Optical Co. v. EEOC, 574 F.Supp. 946, 950 (W.D. Tenn. 1983).

5. United States v. SCRAP, 412 U.S. 669 (1973). Justice Stewart was satisfied with an "attenuated line of causation" linking litigant to an injury; id. at 688. Justices Blackmun and Brennan accepted allegations of harm as sufficient; id. at 699. Justice Douglas agreed with their position; id. at 703. Justice Marshall agreed with the holding on standing; id. at 724.

cates of those rights are before them." Singleton v. Wulff, 428 U.S. 106, 113–14 (1976). When genuine obstacles prevent a third party from appearing in court (such as the need to maintain anonymity to avoid the loss of rights), the courts allow exceptions.[6]

Courts recognize that Congress can, by statute, confer standing upon an individual or a group, and courts may defer to Congress on such matters.[7] "Citizen suits" may be brought by private individuals to enforce federal laws, such as the Clean Water Act. Friends of Earth v. Laidlaw Environmental Servs., 528 U.S. 167 (2000). However, such statutory phrases as "any person aggrieved" or "adversely affected" allow the courts broad discretion in interpreting what Congress means by *standing*. Furthermore, Congress cannot compel the courts to grant standing for a suit that, in the opinion of judges, lacks the necessary ingredients of a case or controversy. Congressional efforts to confer standing are limited by the judiciary's exclusive responsibility to determine Article III requirements.[8] There is a fundamental difference between Article I statutory standing and Article III constitutional standing. In addition to the standing requirements of Article III (injury, etc.), the Court adopts a "prudential standing" rule that can favor not only the plaintiff seeking relief but also judicial power to referee disputes.[9]

Courts raise and lower the standing barrier depending on circumstances. In 1923, an individual taxpayer was denied standing to challenge the constitutionality of a federal statute that provided appropriations to the states for maternal and infant care. The taxpayer claimed that Congress had exceeded its Article I powers and had invaded territory reserved to the states by the Tenth Amendment. The Supreme Court decided that a federal taxpayer's interest in financing the program was "comparatively minute and indeterminable," and the effect on future taxation "so remote, fluctuating and uncertain" that there was no possibility of a direct injury to confer standing. FROTHINGHAM v. MELLON, 262 U.S. 447, 487 (1923). As explained below, the Court found it necessary to revisit this reasoning.

The *Flast* Doctrine

The Court in *Frothingham* understood that any effort to lower the barrier for standing would mean increased casework for the judiciary. Other taxpayers could challenge federal statutes involving the outlay of public funds. Greater recourse to litigation might bring the administrative process to a standstill, as each disappointed party looked automatically to the courts for relief. Critics objected to the 1923 decision because it was unclear whether the Court had announced a constitutional bar to taxpayer suits (compelled by Article III limitations on federal court jurisdiction) or had temporarily imposed a rule of self-restraint to be lifted in the future. In later years the Supreme Court admitted that *Frothingham* could be read either way. Flast v. Cohen, 392 U.S. at 92–93.

The Justice Department interpreted *Frothingham* as an absolute prohibition on taxpayer suits. The Supreme Court discarded that notion in a 1968 suit that involved a taxpayer's challenge to the use of public funds for religious schools. An absolute prohibition would put the government in the position of conceding that a taxpayer lacked standing "even if Congress engaged in such palpably unconstitu-

---

6. NAACP v. Alabama, 357 U.S. 449 (1958). See also Singleton v. Wulff, 428 U.S. at 114–16, and Note, "Standing to Assert Constitutional Jus Tertii," 88 Harv. L. Rev. 423 (1974). For a rejection of third-party suits, in this case involving one death row inmate attempting to intervene for another, see Whitmore v. Arkansas, 495 U.S. 149 (1990).

7. Sierra Club v. Morton, 405 U.S. 727, 732 n.3 (1972); Trafficante v. Metropolitan Life Ins., 409 U.S. 205, 209 (1972); Linda R.S. v. Richard D., 410 U.S. at 617 n.3; Warth v. Seldin, 422 U.S. at 501.

8. Data Processing Service v. Camp, 397 U.S. at 154; Simon v. Eastern Kentucky Welfare Rights Org., 426 U.S. 26, 41 n.22 (1976). For a strict reading of statutory authorization to bring suit, see Bread PAC v. FEC, 455 U.S. 577 (1982).

9. Here the courts determine whether the interest sought to be protected by the plaintiffs is *arguably* within the "zone of interests" to be protected by statute. The test is not whether a statute specifically intends to benefit a plaintiff; it is enough to find that the plaintiff's interests are arguably protected. National Credit Union Admin. v. First National Bank & Trust Co., 522 U.S. 479, 488–99 (1998); FEC v. Akins, 524 U.S. 11, 19–26 (1998).

The Party/Issue Dichotomy in *Flast*

The effort of the Court to distinguish between party and issue in *Flast* lost its crispness when the Justices tried to explain why Mrs. Flast had standing and Mrs. Frothingham did not.. The Court looked to the substantive issues to determine whether a logical "nexus" existed between the status asserted and the claim adjudicated. The Court identified two aspects of nexus: (1) "the taxpayer must establish a logical link between his or her status and the legislative statute attacked," and (2) the taxpayer must connect his or her status with "the precise nature of the constitutional infringement alleged." 392 U.S. at 102. The Court concluded that both Frothingham and Flast satisfied the first but only Flast satisfied the second. Justice

Harlan dissented, unable to understand how the Court could classify the Article I/Tenth Amendment position in *Frothingham* as too general, while accepting the First Amendment/Establishment Clause in *Flast* as sufficiently "precise."

The Court decided that it was time to retreat from the absolute barrier of *Frothingham* even if it could not adequately explain why. The party/issue distinction was unpersuasive. Even the questions of party and injury had become muddled. Did Mrs. Flast have to be a taxpayer to bring suit? Could she have had standing if she lived on interest from tax-exempt bonds and was therefore unable to show injury or a monetary stake? Such fundamental questions were left unanswered.

---

tional conduct as providing funds for the construction of churches for particular sects." FLAST v. COHEN, 392 U.S. 83, 98 n.17. The Court decided to liberalize the rule on standing but only at the cost of creating substantial doctrinal confusion. It claimed that standing focuses on the party, not the issue: "when standing is placed in issue in a case, the question is whether the person whose standing is challenged is a proper party to request an adjudication of a particular issue and not whether the issue is justiciable." Id. at 99–100. This distinction between party and issue was very unclear (see box). By lowering the barrier for standing, the Supreme Court not only encouraged more lawsuits but invited collisions with other branches of government. As noted in the next section, Supreme Court Justices regularly challenge the usefulness and value of *Flast*. Chapter 12 explains that *Flast* was greatly weakened in 2011 by the Supreme Court when it ruled that litigants lacked standing to challenge tax credits that benefited religious schools. Arizona Christian School Tuition Organization v. Winn, 563 U.S. ___ (2011).

Separation of Powers Concerns

In 1972, the Burger Court raised the barrier to standing. It denied standing to an environmental group that wanted to prevent construction of a ski resort in a national park. The Court was deeply split, four Justices arrayed against three. Sierra Club v. Morton, 405 U.S. 727 (1972). In that same year it refused to decide whether the Army's surveillance of domestic activities constituted a chilling effect on First Amendment liberties. A majority of five Justices, with four dissenting, held that there was insufficient evidence of a direct injury to present a case for resolution in the courts.[10]

The close link between standing, issue, and limiting collisions with other branches is highlighted by a 1974 decision in which the Supreme Court denied standing to a taxpayer who challenged the constitutionality of covert spending by the Central Intelligence Agency. The Court specifically looked at the issues raised before dismissing the case on standing, even though the constitutional provision (the Statement and Account Clause) is quite as "precise" as the Establishment Clause at stake in *Flast*. More

---

10. Laird v. Tatum, 408 U.S. 1 (1972). Curiously, a year later the Court gave standing to five law students to bring an environmental suit against the Interstate Commerce Commission; United States v. SCRAP, 412 U.S. 669 (1973). Evidently, standing *does* depend on the issue.

to the point, the Court noted that relief was available through the regular political process. What was dismissed on standing appeared to turn basically on questions of separation of power.[11] UNITED STATES v. RICHARDSON, 418 U.S. 166 (1974). In concurring in this 5 to 4 opinion, Justice Powell urged the Court to abandon *Flast*'s two-part "nexus" test as hopeless and warned that a failure by the judiciary to exercise self-restraint might provoke retaliation by the political branches. A relaxed standing policy, he said, would expand judicial power: "It seems to be inescapable that allowing unrestricted taxpayer or citizen standing would significantly alter the allocation of power at the national level, with a shift away from a democratic form of government." In 1997, under pressure of a lawsuit, the CIA released a figure of $26.6 billion for the budget of the intelligence community. Of that amount, the CIA portion was about $3 billion. In 1998, the CIA voluntarily released a figure of $26.7 billion for the community's budget, but in 1999 it again refused to disclose the aggregate budget. A lawsuit to obtain the budget total by invoking the Freedom of Information Act was dismissed in 1999. Aftergood v. CIA, Civ. No. 98-2107(TFH) (D.D.C. 1999). In 2007, Congress required the administration to disclose the aggregate budget of the intelligence community. 121 Stat. 335 (2007). On October 30, 2007, the administration released the aggregate amount of $43.5 billion for fiscal year 2007. Adding intelligence funds from the military services pushes the total beyond $50 billion.

The connection between standing and sensitive political issues was evident in 1975 when the Court announced that the inquiry into standing "involves both constitutional limitations on federal-court jurisdiction and prudential limitations on its exercise.... In both dimensions it is founded in concern about the proper—and properly limited—role of the courts in a democratic society." Warth v. Seldin, 422 U.S. at 498. Prudential rules of standing are not constitutionally required, but they "serve to limit the role of the courts in resolving public disputes." Id. at 500. In a dissenting opinion joined by Justices White and Marshall, Justice Brennan picked additional holes in the Court's doctrine that standing was unrelated to the issue being litigated:

> While the Court gives lip service to the principle, often repeated in recent years, that "standing in no way depends on the merits of the plaintiff's contention that particular conduct is illegal," ... in fact the opinion, which tosses out of court almost every conceivable kind of plaintiff who could be injured by the activity claimed to be unconstitutional, can be explained only by an indefensible hostility to the claim on the merits.

The *Flast* doctrine was further shaken by *Valley Forge College* v. *Americans United* (1982), which denied plaintiffs standing to challenge the transfer of federal property to a Christian college. Justice Rehnquist, writing for the Court, first argued that the plaintiffs could not sue as taxpayers because the land was transferred under the Property Clause, not the Taxing and Spending Clause. He then denied that the Establishment Clause gave citizens a personal constitutional right to bring suit. Four Justices dissented, accusing the majority of using a "threshold question" to decide substantive issues and obfuscate legal rights. Valley Forge College v. Americans United, 454 U.S. 464 (1982). In 1984, the Court relied on separation of powers analysis to deny standing to black parents who challenged the government's desegregation policy. ALLEN v. WRIGHT, 468 U.S. 737 (1984).

In 1997, the Supreme Court issued an important decision regarding standing for members of Congress. Senator Robert C. Byrd and five other legislators brought suit to challenge the constitutionality of the Line Item Veto Act of 1996. Although Congress had by statute authorized such a lawsuit by members of Congress, the Court unanimously held that the lawmakers lacked standing. The decision pointed out that Senator Byrd and his five colleagues were simply on the losing end of a vote to give the President a form of item-veto authority, and that both Houses of Congress had filed a brief up-

---

11. See also Schlesinger v. Reservists to Stop the War, 418 U.S. 208 (1974), which denied plaintiffs standing to challenge the constitutionality of members of Congress who served in the military reserves, in apparent conflict with the Ineligibility Clause.

holding the constitutionality of the statute. The effect of the decision was to advise legislators who lose during the legislative process to seek remedies within Congress rather than turn to the courts for relief. Raines v. Byrd, 521 U.S. 811 (1997). See the reading for this case in Chapter One. A year later, when standing was established for two private plaintiffs, the Court declared the statute unconstitutional. Clinton v. City of New York, 524 U.S. 417 (1998). The reading for this decision appears in Chapter 6. Much of the confusion about the standing doctrine has its source in the Court's habit of spinning abstract theories that are, at bottom, techniques of pushing matters to the states and the elected branches.

In 2007, the Court appeared to partially revive *Frothingham* by placing strict limits on *Flast*. The case involved a presidential executive order that created a White House office to assist faith-based communities. The Court suggested that a plaintiff might have had standing if Congress had established the office, but not when the initiative came from the executive branch, even when the funds for the office came from congressional appropriations. Depending on how one wants to count the votes, the decision was either 5 to 4 or 3–2–4. Justices Scalia and Thomas concurred with the plurality of three but said it was time to overrule *Flast*. The plurality declined to go that far. Hein v. Freedom From Religion Foundation, 551 U.S. 557 (2007). This case is also discussed in Chapter 12.

Frothingham v. Mellon

262 U.S. 447 (1923)

The Commonwealth of Massachusetts and a taxpayer, Harriet Frothingham, challenged the constitutionality of a federal statute that provided funds to the states for maternal and infant care. They claimed that this use of the appropriations power exceeded the authority of Congress and invaded state power. The Court concluded that neither party had sufficient standing to bring this type of lawsuit.

MR. JUSTICE SUTHERLAND delivered the opinion of the Court.

These cases were argued and will be considered and disposed of together. The first is an original suit in this Court. The other was brought in the Supreme Court of the District of Columbia.... Both cases challenge the constitutionality of the Act of November 23, 1921, c. 135, 42 Stat. 224, commonly called the Maternity Act. Briefly, it provides for an initial appropriation and thereafter annual appropriations for a period of five years, to be apportioned among such of the several States as shall accept and comply with its provisions, for the purpose of coöperating with them to reduce maternal and infant mortality and protect the health of mothers and infants. It creates a bureau to administer the act in coöperation with state agencies, which are required to make such reports concerning their operations and expenditures as may be prescribed by the federal bureau. Whenever that bureau shall determine that funds have not been properly expended in respect of any State, payments may be withheld.

It is asserted that these appropriations are for purposes not national, but local to the States, and together with numerous similar appropriations con-

stitute an effective means of inducing the States to yield a portion of their sovereign rights.... In the *Frothingham* case plaintiff alleges that the effect of the statute will be to take her property, under the guise of taxation, without due process of law.

We have reached the conclusion that the cases must be disposed of for want of jurisdiction without considering the merits of the constitutional questions.

In the first case, the State of Massachusetts presents no justiciable controversy either in its own behalf or as the representative of its citizens. The appellant in the second suit has no such interest in the subject-matter, nor is any such injury inflicted or threatened, as will enable her to sue.

First. The State of Massachusetts in its own behalf, in effect, complains that the act in question invades the local concerns of the State, and is a usurpation of power, viz: the power of local self government reserved to the States.

Probably, it would be sufficient to point out that the powers of the State are not invaded, since the statute imposes no obligation but simply extends an option which the State is free to accept or reject. But we do not rest here. Under Article III, §2, of the Constitution, the judicial power of this Court extends "to controversies ... between a State and citizens of another State" and the Court has original jurisdiction "in all cases ... in which a State shall be party." The effect of this is not to confer jurisdiction upon the Court merely because a State is a party, but only where it is a party to a proceeding of judicial cognizance. Proceedings not of a justiciable character are outside the contemplation of the constitutional grant....

We come next to consider whether the suit may be maintained by the State as the representative of its citizens. To this the answer is not doubtful. We need not go so far as to say that a State may never intervene by suit to protect its citizens against any form of enforcement of unconstitutional acts of Congress; but we are clear that the right to do so does not arise here. Ordinarily, at least, the only way in which a State may afford protection to its citizens in such cases is through the enforcement of its own criminal statutes, where that is appropriate, or by opening its courts to the injured persons for the maintenance of civil suits or actions. But the citizens of Massachusetts are also citizens of the United States. It cannot be conceded that a State, as *parens patriae,* may institute judicial proceedings to protect citizens of the United States from the operation of the statutes thereof....

Second. The attack upon the statute in the *Frothingham* case is, generally, the same, but this plaintiff alleges in addition that she is a taxpayer of the United States; and her contention, though not clear, seems to be that the effect of the appropriations complained of will be to increase the burden of future taxation and thereby take her property without due process of law. The right of a taxpayer to enjoin the execution of a federal appropriation act, on the ground that it is invalid and will result in taxation for illegal purposes, has never been passed upon by this Court. In cases where it was presented, the question has either been allowed to pass *sub silentio* or the determination of it expressly withheld....

... But the relation of a taxpayer of the United States to the Federal Government is very different. His interest in the moneys of the Treasury—partly realized from taxation and partly from other sources—is shared with millions of others; is comparatively minute and indeterminable; and the effect upon future taxation, of any payment out of the funds, so remote, fluctuating and uncertain, that no basis is afforded for an appeal to the preventive powers of a court of equity.

The administration of any statute, likely to produce additional taxation to be imposed upon a vast number of taxpayers, the extent of whose several liability is indefinite and constantly changing, is essentially a matter of public and not of individual concern. If one taxpayer may champion and litigate such a cause, then every other taxpayer may do the same, not only in respect of the statute here under review but also in respect of every other appropriation act and statute whose administration requires the outlay of public money, and whose validity may be questioned. The bare suggestion of such a result, with its attendant inconveniences, goes far to sustain the conclusion which we have reached, that a suit of this character cannot be maintained....

The functions of government under our system are apportioned. To the legislative department has been committed the duty of making laws; to the executive the duty of executing them; and to the judiciary the duty of interpreting and applying them in cases properly brought before the courts. The general rule is that neither department may invade the province of the other and neither may control, direct or restrain the action of the other.... We have no power *per se* to review and annul acts of Congress on the ground that they are unconstitutional. That question may be considered only when the justification for some direct injury suffered or threatened, presenting a justiciable issue, is made to rest upon such an act.... Here the parties plaintiff have no such case. Looking through forms of words to the substance of their complaint, it is merely that officials of the executive department of the government are executing and will execute an act of Congress asserted to be unconstitutional; and this we are asked to prevent. To do so would be not to decide a judicial controversy, but to assume a position of authority over the governmental acts of another and co-equal department, an authority which plainly we do not possess.

No. 24, Original, dismissed.
No. 962 affirmed.

Flast v. Cohen

392 U.S. 83 (1968)

Taxpayers challenged the Elementary and Secondary Education Act of 1965 on the ground that it used federal funds to finance instruction and the purchase of educational materials for use in

religious and sectarian schools, in violation of the Establishment and Free Exercise Clauses. A three-judge court ruled, on the basis of *Frothingham* v. *Mellon* (1923), that the taxpayers lacked standing to bring the suit. Florence Flast and other taxpayers brought this suit against Wilbur Cohen, Secretary of Health, Education and Welfare.

MR. CHIEF JUSTICE WARREN delivered the opinion of the Court.

In *Frothingham* v. *Mellon,* 262 U.S. 447 (1923), this Court ruled that a federal taxpayer is without standing to challenge the constitutionality of a federal statute. That ruling has stood for 45 years as an impenetrable barrier to suits against Acts of Congress brought by individuals who can assert only the interest of federal taxpayers. In this case, we must decide whether the *Frothingham* barrier should be lowered when a taxpayer attacks a federal statute on the ground that it violates the Establishment and Free Exercise Clauses of the First Amendment.

Appellants filed suit in the United States District Court for the Southern District of New York to enjoin the allegedly unconstitutional expenditure of federal funds under Titles I and II of the Elementary and Secondary Education Act of 1965, ... The complaint alleged that the seven appellants had as a common attribute that "each pay[s] income taxes of the United States," and it is clear from the complaint that the appellants were resting their standing to maintain the action solely on their status as federal taxpayers....

The gravamen of the appellants' complaint was that federal funds appropriated under the Act were being used to finance instruction in reading, arithmetic, and other subjects in religious schools, and to purchase textbooks and other instructional materials for use in such schools. Such expenditures were alleged to be in contravention of the Establishment and Free Exercise Clauses of the First Amendment. Appellants' constitutional attack focused on the statutory criteria which state and local authorities must meet to be eligible for federal grants under the Act.... The specific criterion ... attacked by the appellants is the requirement

"that, to the extent consistent with the number of educationally deprived children in the school district of the local educational agency who are enrolled in private elementary and secondary schools, such agency has made provision for including special educational services and arrangements (such as dual enrollment, educational radio and television, and mobile educational services and equipment) in which such children can participate...." 20 U.S.C. § 241e (a)(2).

... A State wishing to participate in the program must submit a plan to the Commissioner [*of Education*] for approval, and the plan must

"provide assurance that to the extent consistent with law such library resources, textbooks, and other instructional materials will be provided on an equitable basis for the use of children and teachers in private elementary and secondary schools in the State...."

. . .

II.

This Court first faced squarely the question whether a litigant asserting only his status as a taxpayer has standing to maintain a suit in a federal court in *Frothingham* v. *Mellon, supra,* and that decision must be the starting point for analysis in this case.... The Court noted that a federal taxpayer's "interest in the moneys of the Treasury ... is comparatively minute and indeterminable" and that "the effect upon future taxation, of any payment out of the [Treasury's] funds, ... [is] remote, fluctuating and uncertain." *Id.,* at 487. As a result, the Court ruled that the taxpayer had failed to allege the type of "direct injury" necessary to confer standing. *Id.,* at 488.

Although the barrier *Frothingham* erected against federal taxpayer suits has never been breached, the decision has been the source of some confusion and the object of considerable criticism. The confusion has developed as commentators have tried to determine whether *Frothingham* establishes a constitutional bar to taxpayer suits or whether the Court was simply imposing a rule of self-restraint which was not constitutionally compelled. The conflicting viewpoints are reflected in the arguments made to this Court by the parties in this case. The Government has pressed upon us the view that *Frothingham* announced a constitutional rule, compelled by the Article III limitations on federal court jurisdiction and grounded in considerations of the doctrine of separation of powers. Appellants, however, insist that *Frothingham* expressed no more than a policy of judicial self-restraint which can be disregarded when compelling reasons for assuming jurisdiction over a taxpayer's suit exist. The opinion delivered in *Frothingham* can be read to support either position....

To the extent that *Frothingham* has been viewed as resting on policy considerations, it has been criticized as depending on assumptions not consistent with modern conditions. For example, some commentators have pointed out that a number of corporate taxpayers today have a federal tax liability running into hundreds of millions of dollars, and such taxpayers have a far greater monetary stake in the Federal Treasury than they do in any municipal treasury. To some degree, the fear expressed in *Frothingham* that allowing one taxpayer to sue would inundate the federal courts with countless similar suits has been mitigated by the ready availability of the devices of class actions and joinder under the Federal Rules of Civil Procedure, adopted subsequent to the decision in *Frothingham.* Whatever the merits of the current debate over *Frothingham,* its very existence suggests that we should undertake a fresh examination of the limitations upon standing to sue in a federal court and the application of those limitations to taxpayer suits.

III.

The jurisdiction of federal courts is defined and limited by Article III of the Constitution. In terms relevant to the question for decision in this case, the judicial power of federal courts is constitutionally restricted to "cases" and "controversies." As is so often the situation in constitutional adjudication, those two words have an iceberg quality, containing beneath their surface simplicity submerged complexities which go to the very heart of our constitutional form of government. Embodied in the words "cases" and "controversies" are two complementary but somewhat different limitations. In part those words limit the business of federal courts to questions presented in an adversary context and in a form historically viewed as capable of resolution through the judicial process. And in part those words define the role assigned to the judiciary in a tripartite allocation of power to assure that the federal courts will not intrude into areas committed to the other branches of government....

... [T]he Government's position is that the constitutional scheme of separation of powers, and the deference owed by the federal judiciary to the other two branches of government within that scheme, present an absolute bar to taxpayer suits challenging the validity of federal spending programs. The Government views such suits as involving no more than the mere disagreement by the taxpayer "with the uses to which tax money is put." According to the Government, the resolution of such disagreements is committed to other branches of the Federal Government and not to the judiciary. Consequently, the Government contends that, under no

circumstances, should standing be conferred on federal taxpayers to challenge a federal taxing or spending program. [*At this point the Court observes, in a footnote:* "The logic of the Government's argument would compel it to concede that a taxpayer would lack standing even if Congress engaged in such palpably unconstitutional conduct as providing funds for the construction of churches for particular sects."] An analysis of the function served by standing limitations compels a rejection of the Government's position.

..[The fundamental aspect of standing is that it focuses on the party seeking to get his complaint before a federal court and not on the issues he wishes to have adjudicated. The "gist of the question of standing" is whether the party seeking relief has "alleged such a personal stake in the outcome of the controversy as to assure that concrete adverseness which sharpens the presentation of issues upon which the court so largely depends for illumination of difficult constitutional questions." *Baker* v. *Carr,* 369 U.S. 186, 204 (1962). In other words, when standing is placed in issue in a case, the question is whether the person whose standing is challenged is a proper party to request an adjudication of a particular issue and not whether the issue itself is justiciable. Thus, a party may have standing in a particular case, but the federal court may nevertheless decline to pass on the merits of the case because, for example, it presents a political question....]

When the emphasis in the standing problem is placed on whether the person invoking a federal court's jurisdiction is a proper party to maintain the action, the weakness of the Government's argument in this case becomes apparent. The question whether a particular person is a proper party to maintain the action does not, by its own force, raise separation of powers problems related to improper judicial interference in areas committed to other branches of the Federal Government. Such problems arise, if at all, only from the substantive issues the individual seeks to have adjudicated.... A taxpayer may or may not have the requisite personal stake in the outcome, depending upon the circumstances of the particular case. Therefore, we find no absolute bar in Article III to suits by federal taxpayers challenging allegedly unconstitutional federal taxing and spending programs. There remains, however, the problem of determining the circumstances under which a federal taxpayer will be deemed to have the personal stake and interest that impart the necessary concrete adverseness to such litigation so that standing can be conferred on the taxpayer *qua* taxpayer consistent with the constitutional limitations of Article III.

IV.

The various rules of standing applied by federal courts have not been developed in the abstract.... However, our decisions establish that, in ruling on standing, it is both appropriate and necessary to look to the substantive issues for another purpose, namely, to determine whether there is a logical nexus between the status asserted and the claim sought to be adjudicated....

The nexus demanded of federal taxpayers has two aspects to it. First, the taxpayer must establish a logical link between that status and the type of legislative enactment attacked.... Secondly, the taxpayer must establish a nexus between that status and the precise nature of the constitutional infringement alleged. Under this requirement, the taxpayer must show that the challenged enactment exceeds specific constitutional limitations imposed upon the exercise of the congressional taxing and spending power and not simply that the enactment is generally beyond the powers delegated to Congress by Art. I, § 8. When both nexuses are established, the litigant will have shown a taxpayer's stake in the outcome of the controversy and will be a proper and appropriate party to invoke a federal court's jurisdiction.

The taxpayer-appellants in this case have satisfied both nexuses to support their claim of standing under the test we announce today. Their constitutional challenge is made to an exercise by Congress of its power under Art. I, § 8, to spend for the general welfare, and the challenged program involves a substantial expenditure of federal tax funds. In addition, appellants have alleged that the challenged expenditures violate the Establishment and Free Exercise Clauses of the First Amendment. Our history vividly illustrates that one of the specific evils feared by those who drafted the Establishment Clause and fought for its adoption was that the taxing and spending power would be used to favor one religion over another or to support religion in general.

. . .

The allegations of the taxpayer in *Frothingham* v. *Mellon, supra*, were quite different from those made in this case, and the result in *Frothingham* is consistent with the test of taxpayer standing announced today. The taxpayer in *Frothingham* attacked a federal spending program and she, therefore, established the first nexus required. However, she lacked standing because her constitutional attack was not based on an allegation that Congress, in enacting the Maternity Act of 1921, had breached a specific limitation upon its taxing and spending power. The tax-payer in *Frothingham* alleged essentially that Congress, by enacting the challenged statute, had exceeded the general powers delegated to it by Art. I, § 8, and that Congress had thereby invaded the legislative province reserved to the States by the Tenth Amendment. To be sure, Mrs. Frothingham made the additional allegation that her tax liability would be increased as a result of the allegedly unconstitutional enactment, and she framed that allegation in terms of a deprivation of property without due process of law. However, the Due Process Clause of the Fifth Amendment does not protect taxpayers against increases in tax liability, and the taxpayer in *Frothingham* failed to make any additional claim that the harm she alleged resulted from a breach by Congress of the specific constitutional limitations imposed upon an exercise of the taxing and spending power....

. . .

Mr. Justice Douglas, concurring.

While I have joined the opinion of the Court, I do not think that the test it lays down is a durable one for the reasons stated by my Brother Harlan.... It would therefore be the part of wisdom, as I see the problem, to be rid of *Frothingham* here and now.

. . .

Mr. Justice Stewart, concurring.

I join the judgment and opinion of the Court, which I understand to hold only that a federal taxpayer has standing to assert that a specific expenditure of federal funds violates the Establishment Clause of the First Amendment....

Mr. Justice Fortas, concurring.

I would confine the ruling in this case to the proposition that a taxpayer may maintain a suit to challenge the validity of a federal expenditure on the ground that the expenditure violates the Establishment Clause....

Mr. Justice Harlan, dissenting.

The problems presented by this case are narrow and relatively abstract, but the principles by which they must be resolved involve nothing less than the proper functioning of the federal courts, and so run to the roots of our constitutional system. The nub of my view is that the end result of *Frothingham* v. *Mellon*, 262 U.S. 447, was correct, even though, like others, I do not subscribe to all of its reasoning and premises. Although I therefore agree with certain of the conclusions reached today by the Court, I cannot accept the standing doctrine that it substitutes for *Frothingham*, for it seems to me that this new doctrine rests on premises that do not withstand analysis. Accordingly, I respectfully dissent.

. . .

United States v. Richardson

418 U.S. 166 (1974)

William B. Richardson, a taxpayer, sued to obtain the expenditures of the Central Intelligence Agency, which are not publicly reported. He claimed that covert funding violated the Statement and Account Clause. In the majority opinion, which denied standing, Chief Justice Burger tried to preserve the doctrines set forth in *Flast* v. *Cohen*. Justice Powell, concurring, urged that the two-part "nexus" test in *Flast* be abandoned as intellectually incoherent.

Mr. Chief Justice Burger delivered the opinion of the Court.

We granted certiorari in this case to determine whether the respondent has standing to bring an action as a federal taxpayer alleging that certain provisions concerning public reporting of expenditures under the Central Intelligence Agency Act of 1949 ... violate Art. I, § 9, cl. 7, of the Constitution which provides:

"No Money shall be drawn from the Treasury, but in Consequence of Appropriations made by Law; and a regular Statement and Account of the Receipts and Expenditures of all public Money shall be published from time to time."

. . .

Although the recent holding of the Court in *Flast* v. *Cohen* ... is a starting point in an examination of respondent's claim to prosecute this suit as a taxpayer, that case must be read with reference to its principal predecessor, *Frothingham* v. *Mellon*, 262 U.S. 447 (1923). In *Frothingham*, the injury alleged was that the congressional enactment challenged as unconstitutional would, if implemented, increase the complainant's future federal income taxes. Denying standing, the *Frothingham* Court rested on the "comparatively minute[,] remote, fluctuating and uncertain," *id.*, at 487, impact on the taxpayer, and the failure to allege the kind of direct injury required for standing.

. . .

II

Although the Court made it very explicit in *Flast* that a "fundamental aspect of standing" is that it focuses primarily on the *party* seeking to get his complaint before the federal court rather than "on the is-

sues he wishes to have adjudicated," *id.*, at 99, it made equally clear that

"in ruling on [taxpayer] standing, it is both appropriate and necessary to look to the substantive issues for another purpose, namely, to determine whether there is a logical nexus between the status asserted and the claim sought to be adjudicated." *Id.*, at 102.

We therefore turn to an examination of the issues sought to be raised by respondent's complaint to determine whether he is "a proper and appropriate party to invoke federal judicial power," *ibid.*, with respect to those issues.

We need not and do not reach the merits of the constitutional attack on the statute; our inquiry into the "substantive issues" is for the limited purpose indicated above. The mere recital of the respondent's claims and an examination of the statute under attack demonstrate how far he falls short of the standing criteria of *Flast* and how neatly he falls within the *Frothingham* holding left undisturbed....

Mr. Justice Powell, concurring.

I join the opinion of the Court because I am in accord with most of its analysis, particularly insofar as it relies on traditional barriers against federal taxpayer or citizen standing. And I agree that *Flast* v. *Cohen*, 392 U.S. 83 (1968), which set the boundaries for the arguments of the parties before us, is the most directly relevant precedent and quite correctly absorbs a major portion of the Court's attention. I write solely to indicate that I would go further than the Court and would lay to rest the approach undertaken in *Flast*. I would not overrule *Flast* on its facts, because it is now settled that federal taxpayer standing exists in Establishment Clause cases. I would not, however, perpetuate the doctrinal confusion inherent in the *Flast* two-part "nexus" test. That test is not a reliable indicator of when a federal taxpayer has standing, and it has no sound relationship to the question whether such a plaintiff, with no other interest at stake, should be allowed to bring suit against one of the branches of the Federal Government. In my opinion, it should be abandoned.

I

My difficulties with *Flast* are several. The opinion purports to separate the question of standing from the merits, *id.*, at 99–101, yet it abruptly returns to the substantive issues raised by a plaintiff for the purpose of determining "whether there is a logical nexus between the status asserted and the claim sought to be adjudicated." *Id.*, at 102. Similarly, the opinion distinguishes between constitutional and prudential limits on standing. *Id.*, at 92–94, 97. I find it impossible, however, to determine whether the two-part "nexus" test created in *Flast* amounts to a constitutional or a prudential limitation, because it has no meaningful connection with the Court's statement of the bare-minimum constitutional requirements for standing.

. . .

Relying on history, the Court [in *Flast*] identified the Establishment Clause as a specific constitutional limitation upon the exercise by Congress of the taxing and spending power conferred by Art. I, § 8.... On the other hand, the Tenth Amendment, and apparently the Due Process Clause of the Fifth Amendment, were determined not to be such "specific" limitations. The bases for these determinations are not wholly clear, but it appears that the Court found the Tenth Amendment addressed to the interests of the States, rather than of taxpayers, and the Due Process Clause no protection against increases in tax liability. *Id.*, at 105.

In my opinion, Mr. Justice Harlan's critique of the *Flast* "nexus" test is unanswerable. As he pointed out, "the Court's standard for the determination of standing [*i.e.*, sufficiently concrete adverseness] and its criteria for the satisfaction of that standard are entirely unrelated." *Id.*, at 122....

The ambiguities inherent in the *Flast* "nexus" limitations on federal taxpayer standing are illustrated by this case. There can be little doubt about respondent's fervor in pursuing his case, both within administrative channels and at every level of the federal courts. The intensity of his interest appears to bear no relationship to the fact that, literally speaking, he is not challenging directly a congressional exercise of the taxing and spending power. On the other hand, if the involvement of the taxing and spending power has some relevance, it requires no great leap in reasoning to conclude that the Statement and Account Clause, Art. I, § 9, cl. 7, on which respondent relies, is inextricably linked to that power. And that Clause might well be seen as a "specific" limitation on congressional spending. Indeed, it could be viewed as the most democratic of limitations. Thus, although the Court's application of *Flast* to the instant case is probably literally correct, adherence to the *Flast* test in this instance suggests, as does *Flast* itself, that the test is not a sound or logical limitation on standing.

The lack of real meaning and of principled content in the *Flast* "nexus" test renders it likely that it will in time collapse of its own weight, as MR. JUSTICE DOUGLAS predicted in his concurring opinion in that case. 392 U.S., at 107....

Relaxation of standing requirements is directly related to the expansion of judicial power. It seems to me inescapable that allowing unrestricted taxpayer or citizen standing would significantly alter the allocation of power at the national level, with a shift away from a democratic form of government. I also believe that repeated and essentially head-on confrontations between the life-tenured branch and the representative branches of government will not, in the long run, be beneficial to either. The public confidence essential to the former and the vitality critical to the latter may well erode if we do not exercise self-restraint in the utilization of our power to negative the actions of the other branches. We should be ever mindful of the contradictions that would arise if a democracy were to permit general oversight of the elected branches of government by a nonrepresentative, and in large measure insulated, judicial branch....

The power recognized in *Marbury* v. *Madison*, 1 Cranch 137 (1803), is a potent one. Its prudent use seems to me incompatible with unlimited notions of taxpayer and citizen standing. Were we to utilize this power as indiscriminately as is now being urged, we may witness efforts by the representative branches drastically to curb its use....

. . .

MR. JUSTICE DOUGLAS, dissenting.

. . .

From the history of the [Statement and Account Clause] it is apparent that the Framers inserted it in the Constitution to give the public knowledge of the way public funds are expended. No one has a greater "personal stake" in policing this protective measure than a taxpayer. Indeed, if a taxpayer may not raise the question, who may do so? The Court states that discretion to release information is in the first instance "committed to the surveillance of Congress," and that the right of the citizenry to information under Art. I, § 9, cl. 7, cannot be enforced directly, but only through the "[s]low, cumbersome, and unresponsive" electoral process. One has only to read constitutional history to realize that statement would shock Mason and Madison. Congress of course has discretion; but to say that it has the power to read the clause out of the Constitution when it comes to one or two or three agencies is astounding....

MR. JUSTICE STEWART, with whom MR. JUSTICE MARSHALL, joins, dissenting.

... I believe that Richardson had standing to bring this action. Accordingly, I would affirm the judgment of the Court of Appeals.

MR. JUSTICE BRENNAN, dissenting [*at 235*].

... [Richardson's] complaint, properly construed, alleged that the violations caused him injury not only in respect of his right as a citizen to know how Congress was spending the public fisc, but also in respect of his right as a voter to receive information to aid his decision how and for whom to vote. These claims may ultimately fail on the merits, but Richardson has "standing" to assert them.

Allen v. Wright

468 U.S. 737 (1984)

Inez Wright and several other black parents had children attending public schools in districts that were undergoing desegregation. They brought this nationwide class action against the federal government, alleging that the Internal Revenue Service (1) had not adopted sufficient standards and procedures to fulfill its obligation to deny tax-exempt status to racially discriminatory private schools, and (2) had thereby harmed the parents and interfered with their children's opportunity to receive an education in desegregated public schools. W. Wayne Allen, the head of a private school identified in the complaint, intervened as a defendant. With an eye to the separation of powers doctrine, the Court held that the parents lacked standing to sue.

JUSTICE O'CONNOR delivered the opinion of the Court.

[II.A]

Article III of the Constitution confines the federal courts to adjudicating actual "cases" and "controversies." As the Court explained in *Valley Forge Christian College v. Americans United for Separation of Church and State, Inc.*, 454 U.S. 464, 471–476 (1982), the "case or controversy" requirement defines with respect to the Judicial Branch the idea of separation of powers on which the Federal Government is founded. The several doctrines that have grown up to elaborate that requirement are "founded in concern about the proper—and properly limited—role of the courts in a democratic society." *Warth v. Seldin*, 422 U.S. 490, 498 (1975).

"All of the doctrines that cluster about Article III—not only standing but mootness, ripeness, political question, and the like—relate in part, and in different though overlapping ways, to an idea, which is more than an intuition but less than a rigorous and explicit theory, about the constitutional and prudential limits to the powers of an unelected, unrepresentative judiciary in our kind of government." *Vander Jagt v. O'Neill*, 226 U.S. App. D.C. 14, 26–27, 699 F.2d 1166, 1178–1179 (1983) (Bork, J., concurring).

The case-or-controversy doctrines state fundamental limits on federal judicial power in our system of government.

The Art. III doctrine that requires a litigant to have "standing" to invoke the power of a federal court is perhaps the most important of these doctrines....

... [T]he law of Art. III standing is built on a single basic idea—the idea of separation of powers....

Determining standing in a particular case may be facilitated by clarifying principles or even clear rules developed in prior cases. Typically, however, the standing inquiry requires careful judicial examination of a complaint's allegations to ascertain whether the particular plaintiff is entitled to an adjudication of the particular claims asserted. Is the injury too abstract, or otherwise not appropriate, to be considered judicially cognizable? Is the line of causation between the illegal conduct and injury too attenuated? Is the prospect of obtaining relief from the injury as a result of a favorable ruling too speculative? These questions and any others relevant to the standing inquiry must be answered by reference to the Art. III notion that federal courts may exercise power only "in the last resort, and as a necessity," *Chicago & Grand Trunk R. Co. v. Wellman*, 143 U.S. 339, 345 (1892), and only when adjudication is "consistent with a system of separated powers and [the dispute is one] traditionally thought to be capable of resolution through the judicial process," *Flast v. Cohen*, 392 U.S. 83, 97 (1968). See *Valley Forge*, 454 U.S., at 472–473.

B

Respondents allege two injuries in their complaint to support their standing to bring this lawsuit. First, they say that they are harmed directly by the mere fact of Government financial aid to discriminatory private schools. Second, they say that the federal tax exemptions to racially discriminatory private schools in their communities impair their ability to have their public schools desegregated....

... We conclude that neither suffices to support respondents' standing. The first fails under clear precedents of this Court because it does not constitute judicially cognizable injury. The second fails because the alleged injury is not fairly traceable to the assertedly unlawful conduct of the IRS.

1

Respondent's first claim of injury can be interpreted in two ways. It might be a claim simply to have the Government avoid the violation of law alleged in respondents' complaint. Alternatively, it might be a claim of stigmatic injury, or denigration, suffered by all members of a racial group when the Government discriminates on the basis of race. Under neither interpretation is this claim of injury judicially cognizable.

. . .

The consequences of recognizing respondents' standing on the basis of their first claim of injury illustrate why our cases plainly hold that such injury is not judicially cognizable. If the abstract stigmatic injury were cognizable, standing would extend nationwide to all members of the particular racial groups against which the Government was alleged to be discriminating by its grant of a tax exemption to

a racially discriminatory school, regardless of the location of that school. All such persons could claim the same sort of abstract stigmatic injury respondents assert in their first claim of injury. A black person in Hawaii could challenge the grant of a tax exemption to a racially discriminatory school in Maine. Recognition of standing in such circumstances would transform the federal courts into "no more than a vehicle for the vindication of the value interest of concerned bystanders." *United States v. SCRAP*, 412 U.S. 669, 687 (1973). Constitutional limits on the role of the federal courts preclude such a transformation.

2

It is in their complaint's second claim of injury that respondents allege harm to a concrete, personal interest that can support standing in some circumstances. The injury they identify—their children's diminished ability to receive an education in a racially integrated school—is, beyond any doubt, not only judicially cognizable but, as shown by cases from *Brown v. Board of Education*, 347 U.S. 483 (1954), to *Bob Jones University v. United States*, 461 U.S. 574 (1983), one of the most serious injuries recognized in our legal system. Despite the constitutional importance of curing the injury alleged by respondents, however, the federal judiciary may not redress it unless standing requirements are met. In this case, respondents' second claim of injury cannot support standing because the injury alleged is not fairly traceable to the Government conduct respondents challenge as unlawful.

The illegal conduct challenged by respondents is the IRS's grant of tax exemptions to some racially discriminatory schools. The line of causation between that conduct and desegregation of respondents' schools is attenuated at best. From the perspective of the IRS, the injury to respondents is highly indirect and "results from the independent action of some third party not before the court," *Simon v. Eastern Kentucky Welfare Rights Org.*, 426 U.S., at 42. As the Court pointed out in *Warth v. Seldin*, 422 U.S., at 505, "the indirectness of the injury ... may make it substantially more difficult to meet the minimum requirement of Art. III...."

The diminished ability of respondents' children to receive a desegregated education would be fairly traceable to unlawful IRS grants of tax exemptions only if there were enough racially discriminatory private schools receiving tax exemptions in respondents' communities for withdrawal of those exemptions to make an appreciable difference in public school integration. Respondents have made no such allegation. It is, first, uncertain how many racially discriminatory private schools are in fact receiving tax exemptions. Moreover, it is entirely speculative, as respondents themselves conceded in the Court of Appeals ... whether withdrawal of a tax exemption from any particular school would lead the school to change its policies. See 480 F.Supp., at 796. It is just as speculative whether any given parent of a child attending such a private school would decide to transfer the child to public school as a result of any changes in education or financial policy made by the private school once it was threatened with loss of tax-exempt status. It is also pure speculation whether, in a particular community, a large enough number of the numerous relevant school officials and parents would reach decisions that collectively would have a significant impact on the racial composition of the public schools.

The links in the chain of causation between the challenged Government conduct and the asserted injury are far too weak for the chain as a whole to sustain respondents' standing....

... The Constitution, after all, assigns to the Executive Branch, and not to the Judicial Branch, the duty to "take Care that the Laws be faithfully executed." U.S. Const., Art. II, § 3. We could not recognize respondents' standing in this case without running afoul of that structural principle.

. . .

JUSTICE MARSHALL took no part in the decision of these cases.

JUSTICE BRENNAN, dissenting.

. . .

JUSTICE STEVENS, with whom JUSTICE BLACKMUN joins, dissenting....

C. MOOTNESS

Litigants able to establish standing at the outset of a case may find their personal stake diluted or eliminated by subsequent events. Because of a change in law or facts, the case or controversy may disappear and leave insufficient adverseness to guide the courts. If the action that triggered the complaint ceases, a court may have no means of granting relief.[12]

A case is not mooted simply because one party discontinues a contested action. Judicial review cannot be circumvented merely through a strategy of starts and stops. If the controversy is likely to reappear, judicial scrutiny "ought not to be, as they might be, defeated, by short term orders, capable of repetition, yet evading review...."[13] Complaints about an election process, even after a particular election is over, may remain a continuing controversy that requires decision by the courts. Moore v. Ogilvie, 394 U.S. 814, 816 (1969).

If the judiciary is unprepared or unwilling to decide an issue, mootness is one avenue of escape. In 1952 the Supreme Court held that a public school Bible-reading case was moot because the child had graduated by the time the case had reached the Supreme Court. Although other students would be subjected to the same school policy in the future, the Court declared that "no decision we could render now would protect any rights she may once have had, and this Court does not sit to decide arguments after events have put them to rest." Doremus v. Board of Education, 342 U.S. 429, 433 (1952).

---

12. California v. San Pablo and Tulare Railroad Co., 149 U.S. 308 (1893); Jones v. Montague, 194 U.S. 147 (1904); Richardson v. McChesney, 218 U.S. 487 (1910). See also Sidney A. Diamond, "Federal Jurisdiction to Decide Moot Cases," 94 U. Pa. L. Rev. 125 (1946); United States v. Hamburg-American Co., 239 U.S. 466 (1916); United States v. Alaska S.S. Co., 253 U.S. 113 (1920); Brockington v. Rhodes, 396 U.S. 41 (1969); Hall v. Beals, 396 U.S. 45 (1969); Lewis v. Continental Bank Corp., 494 U.S. 472 (1990).

13. Southern Pacific Terminal Co. v. ICC, 219 U.S. 498, 515 (1911). See Washington v. Harper, 494 U.S. 210 (1990); United States v. Phosphate Export Corp., 393 U.S. 199, 203 (1968) and United States v. W. T. Grant Co., 345 U.S. 629, 632 (1953).

The Mootness Doctrine

The Court's refusal to hear moot cases was initially grounded in the common law doctrine that courts lack power to decide abstract questions in cases where no dispute exists. Courts have traditionally declined to hear cases in which neither party stands to gain or lose by a decision, on the theory that the state should not "be burdened with the expense of trying such unsubstantial controversies." Over the past decade, however, the Court has based its mootness decisions specifically on the case or controversy requirement of article III of the Constitution, a broad limitation which maintains the separation of powers by "assur[ing] that the federal courts will not intrude into areas committed to the other branches of government." The doctrine that courts will not hear moot cases thus serves two complementary purposes: it prevents the useless expenditure of judicial resources and assures that the courts will not intrude prematurely into policymaking in a manner that will unnecessarily constrain the other branches of government.

Note, "The Mootness Doctrine in the Supreme Court," 88 Harv. L. Rev. 373, 374–76 (1974) (footnotes omitted).

In a 1974 case, a white student denied admission to a law school claimed that the school's affirmative action policy discriminated against him, allowing minorities with lower test scores to enter. He was admitted after winning in trial court. By the time the case reached the Supreme Court he was in his third and final year. The school assured the Court that he would be allowed to complete his legal studies regardless of the disposition of the case. The Court refused to reach the merits of the case, considering it moot. Four Justices dissented, predicting (correctly) that the issue would inevitably return to the Supreme Court. DeFUNIS v. ODEGAARD, 416 U.S. 312 (1974). Within a few years another case challenging a university's affirmative action program found its way to the Supreme Court, and this time the Court confronted the merits. Regents of the University of California v. Bakke, 438 U.S. 265 (1978). For reading on *Bakke*, see Chapter 15.

In *Roe v. Wade* (1973), plaintiffs argued that the Texas criminal abortion laws were unconstitutionally vague and infringed upon their right of privacy. The laws prohibited abortion except on medical advice to save the mother's life. Texas responded that one of the suits, brought by a pregnant single woman, was moot because her pregnancy had terminated. Justice Blackmun, writing for the majority, rejected that position:

> But when, as here, pregnancy is a significant fact in the litigation, the normal 266-day human gestation period is so short that the pregnancy will come to term before the usual appellate process is complete. If that termination makes a case moot, pregnancy litigation seldom will survive much beyond the trial stage, and appellate review will be effectively denied. Our law should not be that rigid. Pregnancy often comes more than once to the same woman, and in the general population, if man is to survive, it will always be with us. Pregnancy provides a classic justification for a conclusion of nonmootness. It truly could be "capable of repetition, yet evading review." Roe v. Wade, 410 U.S. 113, 125 (1973).

In 1984, the Supreme Court had an opportunity to dismiss as moot an affirmative action case involving a court order for the dismissal or demotion of white employees who had more seniority than black employees who were retained. All white employees laid off as a result of the order were restored to duty a month later. Those demoted were later offered their old positions. Those facts did not prevent the Supreme Court from deciding the case and reversing the lower court actions. Firefighters v. Stotts, 467 U.S. 561, 568–72 (1984). Although some of the dissenters accused the majority of issuing an advisory opinion, the Court was evidently ready and willing to circumscribe the reach of affirmative action. The twists and turns of the mootness doctrine reflect the Court's effort to maintain a proper relationship with the other political branches.

In 2000, the Court held that the closing of a nude dancing club did not render the case moot. The city still needed to know whether its ordinance proscribing nudity in public places was constitutional and could be enforced. City of Erie v. Pap's A.M., 529 U.S. 277 (2000). Mootness standards are also explored in Knox v. Service Employees, 567 U.S. ___ (2012) and Turner v. Rogers, 564 U.S. ___ (2011).

DeFunis v. Odegaard

416 U.S. 312 (1974)

Marco DeFunis, Jr., was denied admission to the University of Washington Law School, although his test scores were higher than those of some of the minorities admitted. He was accepted after a trial court found in his favor and was in his third and final year when the case reached the Supreme Court. The question was whether the case should be dismissed on grounds of mootness.

PER CURIAM

In 1971 the petitioner Marco DeFunis, Jr., applied for admission as a first-year student at the University of Washington Law School, a state-operated institution. The size of the incoming first-year class was to be limited to 150 persons, and the Law School received some 1,600 applications for these 150 places. DeFunis was eventually notified that he had been denied admission. He thereupon commenced this suit in a Washington trial court, contending that the procedures and criteria employed by the Law School Admissions Committee invidiously discriminated against him on account of his race in violation of the Equal Protection Clause of the Fourteenth Amendment to the United States Constitution.

DeFunis brought the suit on behalf of himself alone, and not as the representative of any class, against the various respondents, who are officers, faculty members, and members of the Board of Regents of the University of Washington. He asked the trial court to issue a mandatory injunction commanding the respondents to admit him as a member of the first-year class entering in September 1971, on the ground that the Law School admissions policy had resulted in the unconstitutional denial of his application for admission. The trial court agreed with his claim and granted the requested relief. DeFunis was, accordingly, admitted to the Law School and began his legal studies there in the fall of 1971. On appeal, the Washington Supreme Court reversed the judgment of the trial court and held that the Law School admissions policy did not violate the Constitution. By this time DeFunis was in his second year at the Law School.

He then petitioned this Court for a writ of certiorari, and MR. JUSTICE DOUGLAS, as Circuit Justice, stayed the judgment of the Washington Supreme Court pending the "final disposition of the case by this Court." By virtue of this stay, DeFunis has remained in law school, and was in the first term of his third and final year when this Court first considered his certiorari petition in the fall of 1973. Because of our concern that DeFunis' third-year standing in the Law School might have rendered this case moot, we requested the parties to brief the question of mootness before we acted on the petition. In response, both sides contended that the case was not moot. The respondents indicated that, if the decision of the Washington Supreme Court were permitted to stand, the petitioner could complete the term for which he was then enrolled but would have to apply to the faculty for permission to continue in the school before he could register for another term.

We granted the petition for certiorari on November 19, 1973, 414 U.S. 1038. The case was in due course orally argued on February 26, 1974.

In response to questions raised from the bench during the oral argument, counsel for the petitioner has informed the Court that DeFunis has now registered "for his final quarter in law school." Counsel for the respondents have made clear that the Law School will not in any way seek to abrogate this registration. In light of DeFunis' recent registration for the last quarter of his final law school year, and the Law School's assurance that his registration is fully effective, the insistent question again arises whether this case is not moot, and to that question we now turn.

The starting point for analysis is the familiar proposition that "federal courts are without power to decide questions that cannot affect the rights of litigants in the case before them." *North Carolina* v. *Rice,* 404 U.S. 244, 246 (1971).... Although as a matter of Washington state law it appears that this case would be saved from mootness by "the great public interest in the continuing issues raised by this appeal," 82 Wash.2d 11, 23 n. 6, 507 P.2d 1169, 1177 n.6 (1973), the fact remains that under Art. III "[e]ven in cases arising in the state courts, the question of mootness is a federal one which a federal court must resolve before it assumes jurisdiction." *North Carolina* v. *Rice, supra,* at 246.

The respondents have represented that, without regard to the ultimate resolution of the issues in this case, DeFunis will remain a student in the Law School for the duration of any term in which he has already enrolled. Since he has now registered for his final term, it is evident that he will be given an opportunity to complete all academic and other requirements for graduation, and, if he does so, will receive his diploma regardless of any decision this Court might reach on the merits of this case. In short, all parties agree that DeFunis is now entitled to complete his legal studies at the University of Washington and to receive his degree from that institution. A determination by this Court of the legal issues tendered by the parties is no longer necessary to compel that result, and could not serve to prevent it. DeFunis did not cast his suit as a class action, and the only remedy he requested was an injunction commanding his admission to the Law School. He was not only accorded that remedy, but he now has also been irrevocably admitted to the final term of the final year of the Law School course. The controversy between the parties has thus clearly ceased to be "definite and concrete" and no longer "touch[es] the legal relations of parties having adverse legal interests." *Aetna Life Ins. Co.* v. *Haworth,* 300 U.S. 227, 240–241 (1937).

... [J]ust because this particular case did not reach the Court until the eve of the petitioner's graduation from law school, it hardly follows that the issue he raises will in the future evade review. If the admissions procedures of the Law School remain unchanged, there is no reason to suppose that a subsequent case attacking those procedures will not come with relative speed to this Court, now that the Supreme Court of Washington has spoken....

... [T]he judgment of the Supreme Court of Washington is vacated, and the cause is remanded for such proceedings as by that court may be deemed appropriate.

It is so ordered.

[Justice Douglas prepared a separate dissent.]

Mr. Justice Brennan, with whom Mr. Justice Douglas, Mr. Justice White, and Mr. Justice Marshall concur, dissenting.

I respectfully dissent. Many weeks of the school term remain, and petitioner may not receive his degree despite respondents' assurances that petitioner will be allowed to complete this term's schooling regardless of our decision. Any number of unexpected events — illness, economic necessity, even academic failure — might prevent his graduation at the end of the term. Were that misfortune to befall, and were petitioner required to register for yet another term, the prospect that he would again face the hurdle of the admissions policy is real, not fanciful; for respondents warn that "Mr. DeFunis would have to take some appropriate action to request continued admission for the remainder of his law school education, and *some discretionary action by the University on such request would have to be taken.*" Respondents' Memorandum on the Question of Mootness 3–4 (emphasis supplied). Thus, respondents' assurances have not dissipated the possibility that petitioner might once again have to run the gantlet of the University's allegedly unlawful admissions policy....

Moreover, in endeavoring to dispose of this case as moot, the Court clearly disserves the public interest. The constitutional issues which are avoided today concern vast numbers of people, organizations, and colleges and universities, as evidenced by the filing of twenty-six *amicus curiae* briefs. Few constitutional questions in recent history have stirred as much debate, and they will not disappear. They must inevitably return to the federal courts and ultimately again to this Court. Cf. *Richardson* v. *Wright,* 405 U.S. 208, 212 (1972) (dissenting opinion). Because avoidance of repetitious litigation serves the public interest, that inevitability counsels against mootness determinations, as here, not compelled by the record....

D. RIPENESS

Just as a case brought too late can be moot, a case brought too early may not yet be ripe. Sometimes this results from a failure to exhaust administrative and state remedies. Plaintiffs must show that they

---

The Ripeness Doctrine

... The injunctive and declaratory judgment remedies are discretionary, and courts traditionally have been reluctant to apply them to administrative determinations unless these arise in the context of a controversy "ripe" for judicial resolution. Without undertaking to survey the intricacies of the ripeness doctrine it is fair to say that its basic rationale is to prevent the courts, through avoidance of premature adjudication, from entangling themselves in abstract disagreements over administrative policies, and also to protect the agencies from judicial interference until an administrative decision has been formalized and its effects felt in a concrete way by the challenging parties. The problem is best seen in a twofold aspect, requiring us to evaluate both the fitness of the issues for judicial decision and the hardship to the parties of withholding court consideration.

SOURCE: Abbott Laboratories v. Gardner, 387 U.S. 136, 148–49 (1967) (footnotes omitted).

---

have explored all avenues of relief before turning to the federal courts. Premature consideration by the courts does more than create unnecessary workload. It deprives judges of information needed for informed adjudication and forces them to deal at an abstract, speculative, and hypothetical level. The ripeness doctrine encourages settlement in the administrative arena (see box).

Ripeness was at issue in a 1947 case brought by twelve federal employees against the Civil Service Commission. They wanted to prevent the Commission from enforcing a section of the Hatch Act that prohibited them from taking "any active part in political management or in political campaigns." The federal workers complained that the statute deprived them of their First Amendment rights of speech, press, and assembly. The Supreme Court regarded the employees' fears of losing their jobs as too speculative:

> The power of courts, and ultimately of this Court, to pass upon the constitutionality of acts of Congress arises only when the interests of litigants require the use of this judicial authority for their protection against actual interference. A hypothetical threat is not enough. We can only speculate as to the kinds of political activity the appellants desire to engage in or as to the contents of their proposed public statements or the circumstances of their publication. It would not accord with judicial responsibility to adjudge, in a matter involving constitutionality, between the freedom of the individual and the requirements of public order except when definite rights appear upon the one side and definite prejudicial interferences upon the other. United Public Workers v. Mitchell, 330 U.S. 75, 90 (1947).

The situation of one of the federal employees, George P. Poole, was not hypothetical. He faced dismissal unless he could refute the charges of the Commission that his political activities had violated the Hatch Act. Accepting his suit as a justiciable case, the Court held that disciplinary action under the Hatch Act would not violate the Constitution. Justices Black and Douglas dissented, believing that the Court should have heard the cases of all twelve litigants. The threat of discharge, they said, was real rather than fanciful, immediate not remote. Douglas observed:

> ... [T]o require these employees first to suffer the hardship of a discharge is not only to make them incur a penalty; it makes inadequate, if not wholly illusory, any legal remedy which they might have. Men who must sacrifice their means of livelihood in order to test their rights to their jobs must either pursue prolonged and expensive litigation as unemployed persons or pull up their roots, change their life careers, and seek employment in other fields.

The issue of preventive relief often splits the courts. Should judges rule on a statute before its sanctions are invoked? A decision might offer relief to threatened individuals, but it also requires the courts to rule in advance of a concrete case or controversy. It forces judgments on hypothetical situations that raise remote and abstract issues. And yet judicial inaction can lead to irreparable harm to individuals once the statute is enforced. Longshoremen's Union v. Boyd, 347 U.S. 222, 224–26 (1954). Judicial review may be both necessary and appropriate to protect individuals before an agency enforces a regulation.[14]

The extreme point is reached when a suit lingers so long in the courts that it becomes "overripe." Justice Black described a case that bounced around for ten years before the Supreme Court sent it back to the lower courts "because of the staleness of the record." Hugo L. Black, A Constitutional Faith 17 (1968).

Marking Time

As with mootness, disposing of a case on the ground of ripeness may delay but not necessarily avoid decision. In 1943 and 1961 the Supreme Court refused to rule on the constitutionality of Connecticut laws that prohibited married couples from using contraceptives or physicians from giving advice about their use. Tileston v. Ullman, 318 U.S. 44 (1943); Poe v. Ullman, 367 U.S. 497 (1961). Because the record suggested that the state was unlikely to prosecute offenders, the Court held that it lacked jurisdiction to decide hypothetical cases. In the 1961 case, the Court ignored the fact that the state had closed several birth control clinics. POE v. ULLMAN, 367 U.S. 497 (1961). After that decision, the state arrested physicians who had operated a birth control clinic in New Haven. They were found guilty and fined $100 each. In 1965 the Supreme Court held that they had standing and declared the Connecticut statute invalid under the "penumbra" of the Bill of Rights. Griswold v. Connecticut, 381 U.S. 479 (1965).

"Ripeness" may provide the means to sidestep momentarily a socially sensitive issue. Immediately after the Court had decided *Brown* v. *Board of Education* in 1954, it was faced with the constitutionality of a Virginia miscegenation statute. To strike down a law banning interracial marriages would stimulate the fears of critics of the decision who predicted that integrated schools would lead to "mongrelization" of the white race. The Court returned the case to the lower courts by citing the "inadequacy of the record" and the lack of a "properly-presented federal question." Naim v. Naim, 350 U.S. 891 (1955); 350 U.S. 985 (1956). In essence, the Court decided to buy some time. Years later, after the principle of desegregation had been safely established and Congress had passed the Civil Rights Act of 1964, the Court struck down the Virginia statute. Loving v. Virginia, 388 U.S. 1 (1967).

Judicial doctrine and political practicalities were joined in a 1978 case involving a congressional limitation on liability for accidents by private nuclear plants. A "hypothetical" issue, to be sure, but it was intuitively unappealing to insist that the courts await a nuclear catastrophe before deciding. The Court was satisfied that the test of ripeness had been met by two effects already evident from the operation of nuclear power plants: the emission of small quantities of radiation in the air and water, and an increase in the temperature of two lakes used for recreational purposes.[15]

---

14. Abbott Laboratories v. Gardner, 387 U.S. 136 (1967). See also Toilet Goods Assn. v. Gardner, 387 U.S. 158 (1967) and Gardner v. Toilet Goods Assn., 387 U.S. 167 (1967).

15. Duke Power Co. v. Carolina Environment Study Group, 438 U.S. 69, 72–74, 81–82 (1978). Also on the need for courts to avoid premature decisions: Renne v. Geary, 501 U.S. 312 (1991); Socialist Labor Party v. Gilligan, 406 U.S. 583 (1972); Adler v. Board of Education, 342 U.S. 485, 497–508 (Frankfurter, J., dissenting).

Poe v. Ullman

367 U.S. 497 (1961)

A married couple, a married woman, and a doctor sued for declaratory relief against the threatened enforcement of Connecticut's birth control laws that prohibited married couples from using contraceptives and physicians from advising married couples about their use. Paul and Pauline Poe are the fictitious names of the plaintiffs, threatened with prosecution by the state's attorney, Abraham S. Ullman.

MR. JUSTICE FRANKFURTER announced the judgment of the Court and an opinion in which THE CHIEF JUSTICE, MR. JUSTICE CLARK and MR. JUSTICE WHITTAKER join.

These appeals challenge the constitutionality, under the Fourteenth Amendment, of Connecticut statutes which, as authoritatively construed by the Connecticut Supreme Court of Errors, prohibit the use of contraceptive devices and the giving of medical advice in the use of such devices. In proceedings seeking declarations of law, not on review of convictions for violation of the statutes, that court has ruled that these statutes would be applicable in the case of married couples and even under claim that conception would constitute a serious threat to the health or life of the female spouse....

... The State's Attorney intends to prosecute offenses against the State's laws, and claims that the giving of contraceptive advice and the use of contraceptive devices would be offenses forbidden by Conn. Gen. Stat. Rev., 1958, §§ 53-32 and 54-196....

Appellants' complaints in these declaratory judgment proceedings do not clearly, and certainly do not in terms, allege that appellee Ullman threatens to prosecute them for use of, or for giving advice concerning, contraceptive devices. The allegations are merely that, in the course of his public duty, he intends to prosecute any offenses against Connecticut law, and that he claims that use of and advice concerning contraceptives would constitute offenses. The lack of immediacy of the threat described by these allegations might alone raise serious questions of non-justiciability of appellants' claims. See *United Public Workers* v. *Mitchell*, 330 U.S. 75, 88. But even were we to read the allegations to convey a clear threat of imminent prosecutions, we are not bound to accept as true all that is alleged on the face of the complaint and admitted, technically, by demurrer, any more than the Court is bound by stipulation of the parties. *Swift & Co.* v. *Hocking Valley R. Co.,* 243 U.S. 281, 289. Formal agreement between parties that collides with plausibility is too fragile a foundation for indulging in constitutional adjudication.

The Connecticut law prohibiting the use of contraceptives has been on the State's books since 1879. Conn. Acts 1879, c. 78. During the more than three-quarters of a century since its enactment, a prosecution for its violation seems never to have been initiated, save in *State* v. *Nelson,* 126 Conn. 412, 11 A.2d 856....

The fact that Connecticut has not chosen to press the enforcement of this statute deprives these controversies of the immediacy which is an indispensable condition of constitutional adjudication. This Court cannot be umpire to debates concerning harmless, empty shadows. To find it necessary to pass on these statutes now, in order to protect appellants from the hazards of prosecution, would be to close our eyes to reality....

Justiciability is of course not a legal concept with a fixed content or susceptible of scientific verification. Its utilization is the resultant of many subtle pressures, including the appropriateness of the issues for decision by this Court and the actual hardship to the litigants of denying them the relief sought. Both these factors justify withholding adjudication of the constitutional issue raised under the circumstances and in the manner in which they are now before the Court.

Dismissed.

MR. JUSTICE BLACK dissents because he believes that the constitutional questions should be reached and decided.

MR. JUSTICE BRENNAN, concurring in the judgment....

MR. JUSTICE DOUGLAS dissenting....

A public clinic dispensing birth-control information has indeed been closed by the State. Doctors and a nurse working in that clinic were arrested by the police and charged with advising married women on the use of contraceptives. That litigation produced *State* v. *Nelson,* 126 Conn. 412, 11 A.2d 856, which upheld these statutes. That same police raid on the clinic resulted in the seizure of a quantity of the clinic's contraception literature and medical equipment and supplies. The legality of that seizure was in question in *State* v. *Certain Contraceptive Materials,* 126 Conn. 428, 11 A.2d 863.

... At oral argument, counsel for appellants confirmed that the clinics are still closed. In response to a question from the bench, he affirmed that "no public or private clinic" has dared give birth-control advice since the decision in the *Nelson* case....

When the Court goes outside the record to determine that Connecticut has adopted "The undeviating policy of nullification ... of its anticontraceptive laws," it selects a particularly poor case in which to exercise such a novel power. This is not a law which is a dead letter. Twice since 1940, Connecticut has re-enacted these laws as part of general statutory revisions. Consistently, bills to remove the statutes from the books have been rejected by the legislature. In short, the statutes—far from being the accidental left-overs of another era—are the center of a continuing controversy in the State....

What are these people—doctor and patients—to do? Flout the law and go to prison? Violate the law surreptitiously and hope they will not get caught? By today's decision we leave them no other alternatives. It is not the choice they need have under the regime of the declaratory judgment and our constitutional system. It is not the choice worthy of a civilized society. A sick wife, a concerned husband, a conscientious doctor seek a dignified, discrete, orderly answer to the critical problem confronting them. We should not turn them away and make them flout the law and get arrested to have their constitutional rights determined....

Mr. Justice Harlan, dissenting.

I am compelled, with all respect, to dissent from the dismissal of these appeals. In my view the course which the Court has taken does violence to established concepts of "justiciability," and unjustifiably leaves these appellants under the threat of unconstitutional prosecution.

... Nor can I regard as "chimerical" the fear of enforcement of these provisions that seems to have caused the disappearance of at least nine birth-control clinics. In short, I fear that the Court has indulged in a bit of sleight of hand to be rid of this case....

. . .

Mr. Justice Stewart dissenting....

E. POLITICAL QUESTIONS

The "political question" doctrine survives partly on circular reasoning. Chief Justice Marshall claimed that "Questions in their nature political ... can never be made in this court." Marbury v. Madison, 5 U.S. (1 Cr.) 137, at 170 (1803). Yet every question that reaches a court is, by its very nature, political. Justice Holmes, hearing a litigant claim that a question concerning a party primary was nonjusticiable because of its political character, said that such an objection "is little more than a play upon words." Nixon v. Herndon, 273 U.S. 536, 540 (1927).

Definitional problems are legion. After refusing to decide a war powers case in 1968, a federal judge declared: "Though it is not always a simple matter to define the meaning of the term 'political question,' it is generally used to encompass all questions outside the sphere of judicial power." Velvel v. Johnson, 287 F.Supp. 846, 850 (D. Kans. 1968). That definition recalls this dictionary entry: "violins are small cellos, and cellos are large violins." Roche, 49 Am. Pol. Sci. Rev. 762, 768 (1955).

Beyond questions of definition, there is some doubt whether a political question doctrine even exists in the sense that courts refuse to adjudicate certain issues. After reviewing political question cases, Louis Henkin concluded: "the Court does not refuse judicial review; it exercises it. It is not dismissing the case or the issue as nonjusticiable; it adjudicates it. It is not refusing to pass on the power of the political branches; it passes upon it, only to affirm that they had the power which had been challenged and that nothing in the Constitution prohibited the particular exercise of it." Henkin, 85 Yale L. J. 597, 606 (1976). In 1962, the Court identified six areas that are generally classified as political questions. BAKER v. CARR, 369 U.S. 186 (1962) (see box on the next page).

The first criterion is "a textually demonstrable constitutional commitment of the issue to a coordinate political department." However, the very question of whether an issue has been textually committed to a coordinate branch requires judicial interpretation. Powell v. McCormack, 395 U.S. 486,

Criteria for Political Questions

1. A textually demonstrable constitutional commitment of the issue to a coordinate political department.

2. A lack of judicially discoverable and manageable standards for resolving it.

3. The impossibility of deciding without an initial policy determination of a kind clearly for nonjudicial discretion.

4. The impossibility of a court's undertaking independent resolution without expressing lack of the respect due coordinate branches of government.

5. An unusual need for unquestioning adherence to a political decision already made.

6. The potentiality of embarrassment from multifarious pronouncements by various departments on one question.

Baker v. Carr, 369 U.S. 186, 217 (1962).

519 (1969). Moreover, the fact that an area *is* committed to Congress or the President does not automatically produce a political question. As the Supreme Court has noted, "virtually every challenge to the constitutionality of a statute would be a political question" under that reasoning. INS v. Chadha, 462 U.S. 919, 941 (1983). The Court further pointed out:

> It is correct that this controversy may, in a sense, be termed "political." But the presence of constitutional issues with significant political overtones does not automatically invoke the political question doctrine. Resolution of litigation challenging the constitutional authority of one of the three branches cannot be evaded by courts because the issues have political implications in the sense urged by Congress. *Marbury* v. *Madison,* 1 Cranch 137 (1803), was also a "political" case, involving as it did claims under a judicial commission alleged to have been duly signed by the President but not delivered. Id. at 942–43.

During the Vietnam War period, several students at Kent State University in Ohio were killed after the governor had called out the National Guard. The students sought injunctive relief to prevent the governor from taking such actions in the future and to prevent the Guard from future violations of students' constitutional rights. Basically, the students wanted the courts to supervise the future training and operations of the Guard. The Supreme Court regarded those duties as vested solely in Congress by Art. I, Sec. 8, Cl. 16, which empowers Congress to provide "for organizing, arming, and disciplining the Militia, and for governing such Part of them as may be employed in the Service of the United States, reserving to the States respectively, the Appointment of the Officers, and the Authority of training the Militia according to the discipline prescribed by Congress." The Court said that such actions were meant to be exercised by the political branches: "it is difficult to conceive of an area of governmental activity in which the courts have less competence." Gilligan v. Morgan, 413 U.S. 1, 10 (1973).

The Court agreed that the concept of political questions was not of fixed content, and that "nonjusticiable" voting rights cases came to be accepted by the courts. But those cases, it said, "represented the Court's efforts to strengthen the political system by assuring a higher level of fairness and responsiveness to the political processes, not the assumption of a continuing judicial review of substantive political judgments entrusted expressly to the coordinate branches of government." Id. at 11. The judiciary accepts the exclusive responsibility of Congress to determine whether a state satisfies the language of Article IV, Section 4, which requires that the United States "shall guarantee to every State in this Union a Republican Form of Government." Luther v. Borden, 7 How. 1 (1849). In 1993 the Court held that the particular procedure used by the Senate to try impeachments, including the use of a committee to take testimony and gather evidence, is a nonjusticiable political question. Some of the Justices, however, were reluctant to say that Senate procedures for trying impeachments could never be reviewed by the courts. NIXON v. UNITED STATES, 506 U.S. 224 (1993).

The second criterion in *Baker* v. *Carr* is "a lack of judicially discoverable and manageable standards for resolving" a dispute. One example comes from a 1939 case. Thirteen years had elapsed before Kansas ratified the Child Labor Amendment. Was that too long a time for state action? The Court decided that it lacked statutory and constitutional criteria for judicial determination. The question of a reasonable time involved "an appraisal of a great variety of relevant conditions, political, social and economic, which can hardly be said to be within the appropriate range of evidence receivable in a court of justice...." Coleman v. Miller, 307 U.S. 433, 453 (1939).

Certain matters of foreign policy are too sensitive for the courts to handle. When President Carter terminated the defense treaty with Taiwan, Senator Goldwater asked the courts to declare the termination invalid. The case reached the Supreme Court a few weeks before the scheduled termination. Justice Rehnquist attracted three other colleagues to his position that the issue represented a nonjusticiable political question. The Court was being asked to settle a dispute between the executive and legislative branches, "each of which has resources available to protect and assert its interests, resources not available to private litigants outside the judicial forum." Goldwater v. Carter, 444 U.S. 996, 1004 (1979). (See the reading on *Goldwater* v. *Carter* in Chapter 7.)

In 2001, a federal appellate court was asked to decide whether the North American Free Trade Agreement (NAFTA) was a "treaty" requiring Senate ratification pursuant to the Treaty Clause. It had been passed as a regular bill and submitted to the President for his signature. The court held that there were no standards available to the judiciary to decide whether one procedure was superior to the other. The issue represented a nonjusticiable political question. Made in the USA Foundation v. United States, 242 F.3d 1300 (11th Cir. 2001), cert. denied, sub nom. United Steelworkers of America, AFL-CIO, CLC, et al., 534 U.S. 1039 (2001).

The third criterion is "the impossibility of deciding without an initial policy determination of a kind clearly for nonjudicial discretion." This criterion is laced with circularity and basically restates the issue. It would cover reapportionment in 1946 but not after 1962 (Colegrove v. Green, 328 U.S. 549 and Baker v. Carr, 369 U.S. 186).

The fourth criterion: "the impossibility of a court's undertaking independent resolution without expressing lack of the respect due coordinate branches of government." This factor offers little guidance in resolving particular controversies. Whether in the Nixon tapes case (*United States* v. *Nixon*) or the exclusion of Adam Clayton Powell by the House of Representatives (*Powell* v. *McCormack*), the Court's judgment often challenges and overrides decisions made by coordinate branches (see box on the next page). Disrespect, in that sense, cannot be sufficient reason for creating a political question: "If it were, *every* judicial resolution of a constitutional challenge to a congressional enactment would be impermissible." United States v. Munoz-Flores, 495 U.S. 385, 390–91 (1990) (emphasis in original).

Criterion five: "an unusual need for unquestioning adherence to a political decision already made." Professor Henkin said that he did not know "of any case from which Justice Brennan might have derived such a principle." 85 Yale L. J. at 605–06 n.26. Some recent possibilities might include President Carter's termination of the Taiwan defense treaty and his handling of Iranian assets.[16]

The sixth criterion: "the potentiality of embarrassment from multifarious pronouncements by various departments on one question." Despite this guideline, the Supreme Court told the House of Rep-

---

16. Goldwater v. Carter, 444 U.S. 996 (1979); Dames & Moore v. Regan, 453 U.S. 654 (1981). See also Idaho v. Freeman, 529 F.Supp. 1107, 1140–41 (D. Idaho 1981), regarding Idaho's rescission of its vote to ratify the Equal Rights Amendment.

The Exclusion of Adam Clayton Powell

Adam Clayton Powell, a black Democrat from New York, served for 22 years in Congress and chaired the House Education and Labor Committee. He was re-elected in 1966 by a three-to-one majority, despite press reports that he had misallocated public funds and was unlawfully abusing the privileges of his office. He had also been held in criminal contempt of New York state courts in connection with a defamation suit against him.

Rather than expel Powell, a constitutional procedure that requires a two-thirds majority, the House decided on January 10, 1967 to postpone the seating of Powell until a special committee could investigate his conduct. On March 1, the committee unanimously recommended that Powell be seated and then publicly censured and fined. The committee proposed this intermediate solution rather than risk an almost certain confrontation with the courts by excluding Powell.

In a fighting mood, the House decided that the courts would not intervene because of the political question. The committee's proposal failed by a vote of 202 to 222. A vote to exclude Powell passed by the overwhelming margin of 307 to 115.

The D.C. Circuit upheld the exclusion. Writing for the court was Warren Burger, who a year later would become Chief Justice of the Supreme Court. Burger wanted to avoid a collision course with Congress. That courts "encounter some problems for which they can supply no solution is not invariably an occasion for regret or concern; this is an essential limitation in a system of divided powers." Powell v. McCormack, 395 F.2d 577, 605 (D.C. Cir. 1968).

When the case was taken to the Supreme Court, the House claimed "exclusive power" over the seating of members. In oral argument, House counsel Bruce Bromley insisted that the Court had no authority to restrain House action, no matter how audacious or unconstitutional. He claimed that "clearly unconstitutional, clearly improper" action would not be subject to judicial review. Yet in this confrontation the Supreme Court declared that Congress had overstepped its authority by excluding someone on factors other than the three qualifications specified in the Constitution: age, citizenship, and residency requirements. Powell v. McCormack, 395 U.S. 486 (1969). (See reading in Chapter 6.)

---

resentatives that Adam Clayton Powell should be seated. However, this criterion retains usefulness in matters regarding the recognition of foreign governments, political boundaries, envoys, the dates for beginning and ending wars, calling out the militia, and an alien's eligibility for federal benefits.[17]

Rules of self-restraint are part of the complex process of drawing limits on judicial power. Some scholars argue that prudence dictates restrictions on judicial activity. Others warn that the contemporary Court has confused the concept of justiciability and abdicated its duty to decide proper cases and controversies. The use of threshold requirements to avoid or delay judicial decision has sparked a number of lively debates, particularly one between Alexander M. Bickel and Gerald Gunther (see reading).

Baker v. Carr

369 U.S. 186 (1962)

In this case, in which the Supreme Court accepts jurisdiction over the apportionment of legislative seats, the Court offers criteria for determining whether a case falls within the category of a "political question."

---

17. Recognizing foreign governments: Rose v. Himely, 4 Cr. 241 (1808); Gelston v. Hoyt, 3 Wheat. 246 (1818). Political boundaries: Foster v. Neilson, 2 Pet. 253 (1829); Williams v. Suffolk Insurance Co., 13 Pet. 415 (1839). Envoys: Ex parte Hitz, 111 U.S. 766 (1884). Beginning and ending wars: Martin v. Mott, 12 Wheat. 19 (1827); Commercial Trust Co. v. Miller, 262 U.S. 51 (1923). Calling out the militia: Martin v. Mott, 12 Wheat. 19 (1827). Federal benefits: Mathews v. Diaz, 426 U.S. 67, 81–84 (1976).

Mr. Justice Brennan delivered the opinion of the Court....

Our discussion, even at the price of extending this opinion, requires review of a number of political question cases, in order to expose the attributes of the doctrine—attributes which, in various settings, diverge, combine, appear, and disappear in seeming disorderliness. Since that review is undertaken solely to demonstrate that neither singly nor collectively do these cases support a conclusion that this apportionment case is nonjusticiable, we of course do not explore their implications in other contexts. That review reveals that in the Guaranty Clause cases and in the other "political question" cases, it is the relationship between the judiciary and the coordinate branches of the Federal Government, and not the federal judiciary's relationship to the States, which gives rise to the "political question."

We have said that "In determining whether a question falls within [the political question] category, the appropriateness under our system of government of attributing finality to the action of the political departments and also the lack of satisfactory criteria for a judicial determination are dominant considerations." *Coleman* v. *Miller,* 307 U. S. 433, 454–455. The nonjusticiability of a political question is primarily a function of the separation of powers. Much confusion results from the capacity of the "political question" label to obscure the need for case-by-case inquiry. Deciding whether a matter has in any measure been committed by the Constitution to another branch of government, or whether the action of that branch exceeds whatever authority has been committed, is itself a delicate exercise in constitutional interpretation, and is a responsibility of this Court as ultimate interpreter of the Constitution. To demonstrate this requires no less than to analyze representative cases and to infer from them the analytical threads that make up the political question doctrine. We shall then show that none of those threads catches this case.

Foreign relations: There are sweeping statements to the effect that all questions touching foreign relations are political questions. Not only does resolution of such issues frequently turn on standards that defy judicial application, or involve the exercise of a discretion demonstrably committed to the executive or legislature; but many such questions uniquely demand single-voiced statement of the Government's views. Yet it is error to suppose that every case or controversy which touches foreign relations lies beyond judicial cognizance....

While recognition of foreign governments so strongly defies judicial treatment that without executive recognition a foreign state has been called "a republic of whose existence we know nothing," and the judiciary ordinarily follows the executive as to which nation has sovereignty over disputed territory, once sovereignty over an area is politically determined and declared, courts may examine the resulting status and decide independently whether a statute applies to that area. Similarly, recognition of belligerency abroad is an executive responsibility, but if the executive proclamations fall short of an explicit answer, a court may construe them seeking, for example, to determine whether the situation is such that statutes designed to assure American neutrality have become operative. *The Three Friends,* 166 U.S. 1, 63, 66....

Dates of duration of hostilities: Though it has been stated broadly that "the power which declared the necessity is the power to declare its cessation, and what the cessation requires," *Commercial Trust Co.* v. *Miller,* 262 U.S. 51, 57, here too analysis reveals isolable reasons for the presence of political questions, underlying this Court's refusal to review the political departments' determination of when or whether a war has ended. Dominant is the need for finality in the political determination, for emergency's nature demands "A prompt and unhesitating obedience," *Martin* v. *Mott,* 12 Wheat. 19, 30 (calling up of militia). Moreover, "the cessation of hostilities does not necessarily end the war power. It was stated in *Hamilton* v. *Kentucky Distilleries & W. Co.,* 251 U.S. 146, 161, that the war power includes the power 'to remedy the evils which have arisen from its rise and progress' and continues during that emergency. *Stewart* v. *Kahn,* 11 Wall, 493, 507." *Fleming* v. *Mohawk Wrecking Co.,* 331 U.S. 111, 116. But deference rests on reason, not habit....

Validity of enactments: In *Coleman* v. *Miller, supra,* this Court held that the questions of how long a proposed amendment to the Federal Constitution remained open to ratification, and what effect a prior rejection had on a subsequent ratification, were committed to congressional resolution and involved criteria of decision that necessarily escaped the judicial grasp. Similar considerations apply to the enacting process: "The respect due to coequal and independent departments," and the need for finality and certainty about the status of a statute contribute to judicial reluctance to inquire whether, as passed, it complied with all requisite formalities. *Field* v. *Clark,* 143 U.S. 649, 672, 676–677; see *Leser* v. *Garnett,* 258 U.S. 130, 137. But it is not true that courts will never delve into a legislature's records upon such a quest: If the enrolled statute lacks an effective date, a court will not hesitate to seek it in the legislative journals in order to preserve the enactment. *Gardner* v. *The Collector,* 6 Wall. 499. The political question doctrine, a tool of maintenance of governmental order, will not be so applied as to promote only disorder.

The status of Indian tribes: This Court's deference to the political departments in determining whether Indians are recognized as a tribe, while it reflects familiar attributes of political questions, *United States* v. *Holliday,* 3 Wall. 407, 419, also has a unique element in that "the relation of the Indians to the United States is marked by peculiar and cardinal distinctions which exist no where else.... [The Indians are] domestic dependent nations ... in a state of pupilage. Their relation to the United States resembles that of a ward to his guardian." *The Cherokee Nation* v. *Georgia,* 5 Pet. 1, 16, 17. Yet, here too, there is no blanket rule.... "[I]t is not meant ... that Congress may bring a community or body of people within the range of this power by arbitrarily calling them an Indian tribe...." *United States* v. *Sandoval,* 231 U.S. 28, 46. Able to discern what is "distinctly Indian," *ibid.,* the courts will strike down any heedless extension of that label. They will not stand impotent before an obvious instance of a manifestly unauthorized exercise of power.

It is apparent that several formulations which vary slightly according to the settings in which the questions arise may describe a political question, although each has one or more elements which identify it as essentially a function of the separation of powers. Prominent on the surface of any case held to involve a political question is found a textually demonstrable constitutional commitment of the issue to a coordinate political department; or a lack of judicially discoverable and manageable standards for resolving it; or the impossibility of deciding without an initial policy determination of a kind clearly for nonjudicial discretion; or the impossibility of a court's undertaking independent resolution without expressing lack of the respect due coordinate branches of government; or an unusual need for unquestioning adherence to a political decision already made; or the potentiality of embarrassment from multifarious pronouncements by various departments on one question.

Unless one of these formulations is inextricable from the case at bar, there should be no dismissal for nonjusticiability on the ground of a political question's presence. The doctrine of which we treat is one of "political questions," not one of "political cases." The courts cannot reject as "no law suit" a bona fide controversy as to whether some action denominated "political" exceeds constitutional authority. The cases we have reviewed show the necessity for discriminating inquiry into the precise facts and posture of the particular case, and the impossibility of resolution by any semantic cataloguing.

But it is argued that this case shares the characteristics of decisions that constitute a category not yet considered, cases concerning the Constitution's guaranty, in Art. IV, ' 4, of a republican form of government....

Republican form of government: Luther v. *Borden,* 7 How. 1, though in form simply an action for damages for trespass was, as Daniel Webster said in opening the argument for the defense, "an unusual case." The defendants, admitting an otherwise tortious breaking and entering, sought to justify their action on the ground that they were agents of the established lawful government of Rhode Island, which State was then under martial law to defend itself from active insurrection; that the plaintiff was engaged in that insurrection; and that they entered under orders to arrest the plaintiff....

Clearly, several factors were thought by the Court in *Luther* to make the question there "political": the commitment to the other branches of the decision as to which is the lawful state government; the unambiguous action by the President, in recognizing the charter government as the lawful authority; the need for finality in the executive's decision; and the lack of criteria by which a court could determine which form of government was republican.

Nixon v. United States

506 U.S. 224 (1993)

Walter L. Nixon, Jr., a federal district judge, was convicted of federal crimes and sentenced to prison. The House of Representatives adopted articles of impeachment against him and the Senate, following Rule XI, sent the matter to a committee of Senators to hear evidence and report that evidence to the full Senate. After the Senate voted to convict Nixon, he sued on the ground that Senate Rule XI violates the constitutional language that places upon the Senate, and not a committee of the Senate, to "have the sole Power to try all Impeachments." A district court and appellate court held that his claim was nonjusticiable.

CHIEF JUSTICE REHNQUIST delivered the opinion of the Court.

. . .

A controversy is nonjusticiable — *i.e.*, involves a political question — where there is "a textually demonstrable constitutional commitment of the issue to a coordinate political department; or a lack of judicially discoverable and manageable standards for resolving it...." *Baker v. Carr*, 369 U.S. 186, 217 (1962). But the courts must, in the first instance, interpret the text in question and determine whether and to what extent the issue is textually committed. See *ibid.; Powell v. McCormack*, 396 U.S. 486, 519 (1969). As the discussion that follows makes clear, the concept of a textual commitment to a coordinate political department is not completely separate from the concept of a lack of judicially discoverable and manageable standards for resolving it; the lack of judicially manageable standards may strengthen the conclusion that there is a textually demonstrable commitment to a coordinate branch.

In this case, we must examine Art I, §3, cl. 6, to determine the scope of authority conferred upon the Senate by the Framers regarding impeachment. It provides:

"The Senate shall have the sole Power to try all Impeachments. When sitting for that Purpose, they shall be on Oath or Affirmation. When the President of the United States is tried, the Chief Justice shall preside: And no Person shall be convicted without the Concurrence of two thirds of the Members present."

The language and structure of this Clause are revealing. The first sentence is a grant of authority to the Senate, and the word "sole" indicates that this authority is reposed in the Senate and nowhere else. The next two sentences specify requirements to which the Senate proceedings shall conform: The Senate shall be on oath or affirmation, a two-thirds vote is required to convict, and when the President is tried the Chief Justice shall preside.

Petitioner argues that the word "try" in the first sentence imposes by implication an additional requirement on the Senate in that the proceedings must be in the nature of a judicial trial. From there petitioner goes on to argue that this limitation precludes the Senate from delegating to a select committee the task of hearing the testimony of witnesses, as was done pursuant to Senate Rule XI. "'[T]ry' means more than simply 'vote on' or 'review' or 'judge.' In 1787 and today, trying a case means hearing the evidence, not scanning a cold record." Brief for Petitioner 25. Petitioner concludes from this that courts may review whether or not the Senate "tried" him before convicting him.

There are several difficulties with this position which lead us ultimately to reject it. The word "try," both in 1787 and later, has considerably broader meanings than those to which petitioner would limit it. Older dictionaries define try as "[t]o examine" or "[t]o examine as a judge." See 2 S. Johnson, A Dictionary of the English Language (1785). In more modern usage the term has various meanings. For example, try can mean "to examine or investigate judicially," "to conduct the trial of," or "to put to the test by experiment, investigation, or trial." Webster's Third New International Dictionary 2457 (1971). Petitioner submits that "try," as contained in T. Sheridan, Dictionary of the English Language (1796), means "to examine as a judge; to bring before a judicial tribunal." Based on the variety of definitions, however, we cannot say that the Framers used the word "try" as an implied limitation on the method by which the Senate might proceed in trying impeachments....

... We think that the word "sole" is of considerable significance. Indeed, the word "sole" appears only one other time in the Constitution — with respect to the House of Representatives' "*sole* Power of Impeachment." Art. I, §2, cl. 5 (emphasis added). The commonsense meaning of the word "sole" is that the Senate alone shall have authority to determine whether an individual should be acquitted or convicted. The dictionary definition bears this out. "Sole" is defined as "having no companion," "solitary," "being the only one," and "functioning ... independently and without assistance or interference." Webster's Third New International Dictionary 2168 (1971). If the courts may review the actions of the Senate in order to determine whether that body "tried" an impeached official, it is difficult to see how the Senate would be "functioning ... independently and without assistance or interference."

. . .

The Framers labored over the question of where the impeachment power should lie. Significantly, in at least two considered scenarios the power was placed with the Federal Judiciary. See 1 Farrand 21–22 (Virginia Plan); *id.*, at 244 (New Jersey Plan).

Indeed, James Madison and the Committee of Detail proposed that the Supreme Court should have the power to determine impeachments. See 2 *id.*, at 551 (Madison); *id.*, at 178–179, 186 (Committee of Detail). Despite these proposals, the Convention ultimately decided that the Senate would have "the sole Power to try all Impeachments." Art. I, § 3, cl. 6. According to Alexander Hamilton, the Senate was the "most fit depositary of this important trust" because its Members are representatives of the people. See The Federalist No. 65, p. 440 (J. Cooke ed. 1961). The Supreme Court was not the proper body because the Framers "doubted whether the members of that tribunal would, at all times, be endowed with so eminent a portion of fortitude as would be called for in the execution of so difficult a task" or whether the Court "would possess the degree of credit and authority" to carry out its judgment if it conflicted with the accusation brought by the Legislature—the people's representative. See *id.*, at 441. In addition, the Framers believed the Court was too small in number: "The awful discretion, which a court of impeachments must necessarily have, to doom to honor or to infamy the most confidential and the most distinguished characters of the community, forbids the commitment of the trust to a small number of persons." Id., at 441–442.

There are two additional reasons why the Judiciary, and the Supreme Court in particular, were not chosen to have any role in impeachments. First, the Framers recognized that most likely there would be two sets of proceedings for individuals who commit impeachable offenses—the impeachment trial and a separate criminal trial. In fact, the Constitution explicitly provides for two separate proceedings. See Art. I, § 3, cl. 7. The Framers deliberately separated the two forums to avoid raising the specter of bias and to ensure independent judgments....

Second, judicial review would be inconsistent with the Framers' insistence that our system be one of checks and balances. In our constitutional system, impeachment was designed to be the *only* check on the Judicial Branch by the Legislature....

... Nixon's argument would place final reviewing authority with respect to impeachments in the hands of the same body that the impeachment process is meant to regulate.

. . .

In addition to the textual commitment argument, we are persuaded that the lack of finality and the difficulty of fashioning relief counsel against justiciability. See *Baker v. Carr,* 369 U.S., at 210. We agree with the Court of Appeals that opening the door of judicial review to the procedures used by the Senate in trying impeachments would "expose the political life of the country to months, or perhaps years, of chaos."... This lack of finality would manifest itself most dramatically if the President were impeached. The legitimacy of any successor, and hence his effectiveness, would be impaired severely, not merely while the judicial process was running its course, but during any retrial that a differently constituted Senate might conduct if its first judgment of conviction were invalidated. Equally uncertain is the question of what relief a court may give other than simply setting aside the judgment of conviction. Could it order the reinstatement of a convicted federal judge, or order Congress to create an additional judgeship if the seat had been filled in the interim?

. . .

For the foregoing reasons, the judgment of the Court of Appeals is

Affirmed

JUSTICE STEVENS, concurring.

For me, the debate about the strength of the inferences to be drawn from the use of the words "sole" and "try" is far less significant than the central fact that the Framers decided to assign the impeachment power to the Legislative Branch.... Respect for a coordinate branch of the Government forecloses any assumption that improbable hypotheticals like those mentioned by JUSTICE WHITE and JUSTICE BLACKMUN will ever occur....

JUSTICE WHITE, with whom JUSTICE BLACKMUN joins, concurring in the judgment.

Petitioner contends that the method by which the Senate convicted him on two articles of impeachment violates Art. I, § 3, cl. 6, of the Constitution, which mandates that the Senate "try" impeachments. The Court is of the view that the Constitution forbids us even to consider his contention. I find no such prohibition and would therefore reach the merits of the claim. I concur in the judgment because the Senate fulfilled its constitutional obligation to "try" petitioner.

I

... I would prefer not to announce an unreviewable discretion in the Senate to ignore completely the constitutional direction to "try" impeachment cases. When asked at oral argument whether that direction would be satisfied if, after a House vote to impeach, the Senate, without any procedure whatsoever, unanimously found the accused guilty of being "a bad guy," counsel for the United States answered that the Government's theory "leads me to answer that question yes." Tr. of Oral Arg. 51. Especially in light of this advice from the Solicitor General, I would not issue an invitation to the Senate to find an excuse, in the name of other pressing business, to be dismissive of its critical role in the impeachment process....

[II. A]

... While the majority rejects petitioner's justiciability argument as espousing a view "inconsistent with the Framers' insistence that our system be one of checks and balances," *ante*, at 234, it is the Court's finding of nonjusticiability that truly upsets the Framers' careful design. In a truly balanced system, impeachments tried by the Senate would serve as a means of controlling the largely unaccountable Judiciary, even as judicial review would ensure that the Senate adhered to a minimal set of procedural standards in conducting impeachment trials.

B

The majority also contends that the term "try"

does not present a judicially manageable standard....

... Were the Senate, for example, to adopt the practice of automatically entering a judgment of conviction whenever articles of impeachment were delivered from the House, it is quite clear that the Senate will have failed to "try" impeachments....

JUSTICE SOUTER, concurring in the judgment.

. . .

[*Although Souter regards the Court as correct in dismissing this particular dispute as a political question, he can*] envision different and unusual circumstances that might justify a more searching review of impeachment proceedings. If the Senate were to act in a manner seriously threatening the integrity of its results, convicting, say, upon a coin toss, or upon a summary determination that an officer of the United States was simply "'a bad guy,'" *ante*, at 239 (White, J., concurring in judgment), judicial interference might well be appropriate....

Virtues and Vices: Bickel versus Gunther

In a foreword entitled "The Passive Virtues," written for the 1960 term of the Supreme Court and published in the *Harvard Law Review* in 1961, Alexander M. Bickel urged the Court to avoid adjudication by making greater use of its doctrines on standing, case and controversy, ripeness, and political questions. A rebuttal, "The Subtle Vices of the 'Passive Virtues'—A Comment on Principle and Expediency in Judicial Review," was prepared by Gerald Gunther and published in the January 1964 issue of the *Columbia Law Review*.

ALEXANDER M. BICKEL:

. . .

It would seem ... to follow from *Marbury* v. *Madison* that, except as stated, "all Cases" are justiciable and must be heard. Indeed Marshall, assuming the tone of absolute assertion that he deemed suitable when the Court's basic powers were in issue, said in *Cohens* v. *Virginia*:

"It is most true that this court will not take jurisdiction if it should not; but it is equally true, that it must take jurisdiction if it should. The judiciary cannot, as the legislature may, avoid a measure because it approaches the confines of the constitution. We cannot pass it by because it is doubtful. With whatever doubts, with whatever difficulties, a case may be attended, we must decide it if it be brought before us. We have no more right to decline the exercise of jurisdiction which is given, than to usurp

that which is not given. The one or the other would be treason to the constitution."

But the doctrines of standing and case and controversy have in time come to mean also something entirely unrelated to the reasoning of *Marbury* v. *Madison*. They have encompassed numerous instances in which the Court did nothing else but to "decline the exercise of jurisdiction which is given...." And to this end they have been abetted by, or used interchangeably (and rather unanalytically) with, other doctrines, such as "ripeness" and "political question." This has caused great difficulties for those who would rest the institution of judicial review on the foundation of the opinion in *Marbury* v. *Madison*, or even on an independent, more scrupulous but quite similar process of deduction from the constitutional text.

. . .

... [O]nly by means of a play on words can the broad discretion that the courts have in fact exercised be turned into an act of constitutional interpretation. The political-question doctrine simply resists being domesticated in this fashion. There is something different about it, in kind, not in degree, from the general "interpretive process"; something greatly more flexible, something of prudence, not construction and not principle. And it is something that cannot exist within the four corners of *Marbury* v. *Madison*.

· · ·

I have tried to show that the Supreme Court's well-established if imperfectly understood practice of declining on occasion to exercise the power of judicial review is difficult to reconcile with the strict-constructionist conception of the foundation of that power. If this were all what is called merely academic, it would be none the worse for it. Actually, however, important consequences are in play. Of course, no concept, strict-, loose-, or medium-constructionist, can get around the sheer necessity of limiting each year's business to what nine men can fruitfully deal with. But strict-constructionist compunctions cause the techniques for meeting this necessity to be viewed with misgiving and to be encumbered with fictive explanations. So are other techniques of avoiding adjudication, and I would suggest that herein lies at least part of the reason for the confusion and lack of direction that has characterized their development. Some of the confusion may be in the eye of the beholder, but not all....

Quite obviously, no society, certainly not a large and heterogeneous one, can fail in time to explode if it is deprived of the arts of compromise, if it knows no ways to muddle through. No good society can be unprincipled; and no viable society can be principle-ridden. But it is not true in our society that we are generally governed wholly by principle in some matters and indulge a rule of expediency exclusively in others. There is no such neat dividing line. There are exceptions, some of which are delineated by the political-question doctrine. Most often, however, and as often as not in matters of the widest and deepest concern such as the racial problem, both requirements exist most imperatively side by side: guiding principle and expedient compromise. The role of principle, when it cannot be the inflexible governing rule, is to affect the tendency of policies of expediency. And it is a potent role....

It follows that the techniques and allied devices for staying the Court's hand, as is avowedly true at least of certiorari, cannot themselves be principled in the sense in which we have a right to expect adjudications on the merits to be principled. They mark the point at which the Court gives the electoral institutions their head and itself stays out of politics, and there is nothing paradoxical in finding that here the Court is most a political animal. But this is not to concede unchanneled, undirected, unchartered discretion. It is not to concede judgment proceeding from impulse, hunch, sentiment, predilection, inarticulable and unreasoned. The antithesis of principle in an institution that represents decency and reason is not whim, nor even expediency, but prudence....

GERALD GUNTHER:

· · ·

Principle and reason are hard taskmasters. Insistence on these essential ingredients is Bickel's starting point; but, as he contemplates their impact on the judicial process, unpalatable consequences loom ever larger. He cannot bear to abandon the requirement of principle in constitutional adjudication; he cannot bear the inexpedient results of unflinching adherence to principle. He is put to an excruciating choice; his response is to avoid the choice, to seek escape routes.

He derives the philosophic basis for his ingenious solution from his contemplation of American democracy at large: "No good society can be unprincipled; and no viable society can be principle-ridden.... Our democratic system of government exists in this Lincolnian tension between principle and expediency, and within its judicial review must play its role." These cosmic observations may be sound; but their relevance and utility as applied to a specific process and institution, to judicial review and the Supreme Court, are questionable. And the inferences Bickel draws ultimately fail to satisfy: they rest on faulty perceptions of the adjudicatory process; and they yield guidelines which invite not accommodation but surrender of principle to expediency....

Bickel's ambitious survey of the avoidance techniques, his "passive virtues," is the most comprehensive we have had, and his examination of this tangled field is of significance quite independent of his purposes....

The result is a strange mixture. He covers an enormous range of techniques; he describes and applies his concepts with skill; he offers some fresh insights and much helpful clarification; yet the total product is essentially unpersuasive, profoundly disturbing, and ultimately subversive of the very values it professes to serve. Two major flaws, I submit, help to explain why so many superior parts add up to such an unsatisfying whole. First, the discrete analyses of the varied avoidance devices are too much influenced by Bickel's underlying premises and overriding purposes: in his anxiety to enlarge Court discretion not to adjudicate, some of the techniques are subjected to greater strains than they can bear. Second, as Bickel criticized some commentators as neo-realists, so it can be said that he suffers from the neo-Brandeisian fallacy: invoking the well-known *Ashwander* statement by Brandeis, regarding avoidance of constitutional questions in adjudication, to assert an amorphous authority to withhold adjudication altogether—a power far broader than any suggested by the examples given by Brandeis, a discretion far wider than any that can be independently justified....

Of course the Court often may and should avoid "passing upon a large part of all of the constitutional questions pressed upon it for decision." Four of the seven Brandeis rules involve well-known instances of such avoidance—avoidance only of some or all of the constitutional questions argued, *not* avoidance of all decision on the merits of the case. Thus, when the Court does not "formulate a rule of constitutional law broader than is required by the precise facts," it merely narrows the constitutional ground of decision, but does not even avoid all constitutional decision. Similarly, when the Court does not decide a constitutional question presented by the case because there is a nonconstitutional ground "upon which the case may be disposed of," it only avoids constitutional decision, not a decision on the merits of the case. Nor, of course, does the Court withhold adjudication of the case when it makes a ruling on the constitutionality of a federal law unnecessary by finding a construction of the statute which is "fairly possible" and which avoids the constitutional doubts. These are all in a sense avoidance devices, and Bickel includes these and similar ones in his catalogue of techniques—but they are devices which go to the choice of the ground of decision of a case, not devices which avoid decision on the merits, not devices which "decline to exercise" the jurisdiction to decide....

F. EQUITABLE DISCRETION

As Justice Brennan observed in *Baker v. Carr*, the political question doctrine is "essentially a function of the separation of powers," designed to restrain courts "from inappropriate interference in the business of the other branches of Government." See also Nixon v. United States, 506 U.S. 224, 252 (1993); United States v. Munoz-Flores, 495 U.S. 385, 394 (1990). The same may be said of the doctrine of equitable discretion, often invoked by courts as a "companion" to the political question doctrine. Equitable discretion has been utilized by courts, particularly in foreign affairs cases, to dismiss claims against the executive brought by members of Congress, when members have an effective in-House remedy for their alleged injuries.

Congressional lawsuits may arise if a disappointed minority in either the House or the Senate is unable to move its chamber to act against a claimed presidential usurpation, and seeks relief from the Court. The doctrine of equitable discretion may be invoked to deny relief. Justice Powell provided the rationale in a concurring opinion in *Goldwater v. Carter*: "If the Congress chooses not to confront the President, it is not our task to do so." 444 U.S. 996, 998 (1979). See also Crockett v. Reagan, 558 F.Supp. 893, 898–99 (D.D.C. 1982); aff'd per curiam, 720 F.2d 1355 (D.C. Cir. 1983); Riegle v. FOMC, 656 F.2d 873, 879 (D.C. Cir. 1981), cert. denied, 454 U.S. 1082 (1981).

NOTES AND QUESTIONS

1. Suppose, for the sake of argument that Chief Justice Marshall really did assert, in *Marbury v. Madison*, that the Supreme Court is the "final arbiter" of the meaning of the Constitution. Is the "final word" principle reconcilable with the political question doctrine? Does the political question doctrine leave the last word to the courts or to the political branches?

2. Louis Henkin concluded that there is no political question "doctrine." Henkin, "Is there a Polit-

ical Question Doctrine?" 85 Yale L. J. 597, 622–23 (1976). Is he correct? If so, what are the courts doing when they characterize a case as a "nonjusticiable" political question?

3. Should the Court abstain from ruling in a case in which a remedy seems unavailing or likely to invite sharp conflict with a coordinate branch? Was there a remedy in *Nixon v. United States*? Could the Court have ordered reinstatement of Judge Nixon if it had determined that the Senate had abused its powers? Charles Black observed: "If the Supreme Court [were] to order reinstatement of an impeached and convicted president there would be [a] very grave and quite legitimate doubt whether that decree had any title to being obeyed, or whether it was [as] widely outside judicial jurisdiction as would be a judicial order to Congress to increase the penalty for counterfeiting. To cite the most frightening consequence, our military commanders would have to decide for themselves which president they were bound to obey. [It] would be most unfortunate if the notion got about that the Senate's verdict was somewhat tentative." Charles Black, Jr., Impeachment: A Handbook 61–62 (1974).

4. In *Cohens v. Virginia* (1821), Chief Justice Marshall wrote: "It is most true that this Court will not take jurisdiction if it should not: but it is equally true, that it must take jurisdiction if it should." He said the Court had "no more right to decline the exercise of jurisdiction which is given, than to usurp that which is not given." What exceptions to that policy did the Court later develop? What insights were provided by Alexander Bickel and Gerald Gunther?

SELECTED READINGS

ALBERT, LEE A. "Justiciability and Theories of Judicial Review: A Remote Relationship." 50 Southern California Law Review 1139 (1977).

BRILMAYER, LEA. "The Jurisprudence of Article III: Perspectives on the 'Case or Controversy' Requirement." 93 Harvard Law Review 297 (1979).

CONDON, DANIEL PATRICK. "The Generalized Grievance Restriction: Prudential Restraint or Constitutional Mandate?" 70 Georgetown Law Journal 1157 (1982).

HUGHES, GRAHAM. "Civil Disobedience and the Political Question Doctrine." 43 New York University Law Review 1 (1968).

JACKSON, R. BROOKE. "The Political Question Doctrine: Where Does It Stand After Powell v. McCormack, O'Brien v. Brown, and Gilligan v. Morgan?" 44 University of Colorado Law Review 477 (1973).

KATES, DON B., JR., AND WILLIAM T. BARKER. "Mootness in Judicial Proceedings: Toward a Coherent Theory." 62 California Law Review 1385 (1974).

LOGAN, DAVID A. "Standing to Sue: A Proposed Separation of Powers Analysis." 1984 Wisconsin Law Review 37.

MONAGHAN, HENRY P. "Constitutional Adjudication: The Who and When." 82 Yale Law Journal 1363 (1973).

MORRISON, HENRY P. "Rights Without Remedies: The Burger Court Takes the Federal Courts Out of the Business of Protecting Federal Rights." 30 Rutgers Law Review 841 (1977).

MOURTADA-SABBAH AND BRUCE E. CAIN, EDS. The Political Question Doctrine and the Supreme Court of the United States. Lanham, Md.: Lexington Books, 2007.

NAGEL, ROBERT F. "Political Law, Legalistic Politics: A Recent History of the Political Question Doctrine." 56 University of Chicago Law Review 643 (1989).

NICHOL, GENE R., JR. "Causation as a Standing Requirement: The Unprincipled Use of Judicial Restraint." 69 Kentucky Law Journal 185 (1980).

ORREN, KAREN. "Standing to Sue: Interest Group Conflict in the Federal Courts." 70 American Political Science Review 723 (1976).

POST, CHARLES GORDON, JR. The Supreme Court and Political Questions. Baltimore: The Johns Hopkins Press, 1936.

RADCLIFFE, JAMES E. The Case-or-Controversy Provision. University Park: Pennsylvania State University Press, 1978.

ROSENBLUM, VICTOR G. "Justiciability and Justice: Elements of Restraint and Indifference." 15 Catholic University Law Review 141 (1966).

SCALIA, ANTONIN. "The Doctrine of Standing as an Essential Element of the Separation of Powers." 17 Suffolk University Law Review 881 (1983).

SCHARPF, FRITZ W. "Judicial Review and the Political Question: A Functional Analysis." 75 Yale Law Journal 517 (1966).

SCOTT, KENNETH E. "Standing in the Supreme Court — A Functional Analysis." 86 Harvard Law Review 645 (1973).

SEDLER, ROBERT ALLEN. "Standing and the Burger Court: An Analysis and Some Proposals for Legislative Reform." 30 Rutgers Law Review 863 (1977).

STRUM, PHILIPPA. The Supreme Court and "Political Questions." University: University of Alabama Press, 1974.

TIGAR, MICHAEL E. "Judicial Power, the 'Political Question Doctrine,' and Foreign Relations." 17 UCLA Law Review 1135 (1970).

TUCKER, EDWIN W. "The Metamorphosis of the Standing to Sue Doctrine." 17 New York Law Forum 911 (1972).

TUSHNET, MARK V. "The Sociology of Article III: A Response to Professor Brilmayer." 93 Harvard Law Review 1698 (1980).

4

Judicial Organization

Questions of judicial organization may seem far afield from constitutional law. However, organizational issues ultimately present questions of power. This chapter identifies the tangible constraints that operate on the judiciary: the power of Congress to create and monitor the federal court system, including the creation of legislative and specialized courts; the President's power to nominate judges and the Senate's power to confirm; questions of tenure, removal, and compensation of federal judges; and the extent to which judges can lobby for their causes.

A. FEDERAL COURT SYSTEM

Long before the American colonies declared their separation from England, the idea of an independent judiciary had secured a firm foothold among the framers. The Act of Settlement, passed by England in 1701, contributed to judicial autonomy by guaranteeing tenure for judges during good behavior. The power to constitute courts in the American colonies, however, was vested in the governor and council (creatures of the King). The assemblies were allowed to create courts only for small causes, subject always to the King's veto.[1]

The principle of judicial independence appears in several sections of the Declaration of Independence. The American framers accused the King of "obstruct[ing] the Administration of Justice, by refusing his Assent to Laws for establishing Judiciary Powers." Because of disputes between the British Crown and several of the colonies, laws establishing courts of justice were struck down repeatedly, sometimes eliminating courts for long stretches of time. Edward Dumbauld, The Declaration of Independence and What It Means Today 108–12 (1950). The Declaration of Independence criticized the King for making judges "dependent on his Will alone, for the Tenure of their Offices, and the Amount and Payment of Their Salaries." The policy of colonial judges serving at the King's pleasure provoked bitter resistance in New York, New Jersey, Pennsylvania, North Carolina, South Carolina, and Massachusetts, where colonial legislatures wanted judges to have tenure during good behavior. Id. at 112–15. Following the break with England, several American colonies included tenure and salary provisions in their constitutions to secure judicial independence.

Setting Up Federal Courts

After the colonies cut ties with England, state governments authorized vessels to prey on British shipping. A judicial system was needed to dispose of "prizes" (property captured at sea). State admiralty courts made the initial determination, but appeals beyond that level required the attention of the Continental Congress. From 1776 to 1780, appeals were handled first by temporary committees and then by a standing committee, until Congress, in May 1780, created a Court of Appeals in Cases of Capture. This tribunal, the first national judiciary, took direction from the Continental Congress and

---

1. Julius Goebel, Jr., 1 History of the Supreme Court of the United States: Antecedents and Beginnings 12–13 (1971).

even from the Secretary for Foreign Affairs.[2] The Court of Appeals continued to function until delegates arrived at Philadelphia in May 1787 to draft a new constitution.

The delegates to the Philadelphia Convention recognized the need for executive and judicial independence. They explored the possibility of setting up a Council of Revision, consisting of the executive and "a convenient number of the National Judiciary," to examine all bills from the legislature before they became law. Rejection by the Council could be overridden by the legislature. 1 Farrand 21. The convention turned down the proposal because the delegates wanted the Supreme Court to interpret the law without any prior participation. Id. at 97–98. The framers decided to vest the veto power exclusively in the President.

Article III of the Constitution created a separate judicial branch. The judges, both of the Supreme and inferior courts, "shall hold their Offices during good Behaviour, and shall, at stated Times, receive for their Services, a Compensation, which shall not be diminished during their Continuance in Office." The Constitution vests the judicial power of the United States "in one supreme Court, and in such inferior Courts as the Congress may from time to time ordain and establish." The word "may" implies that the establishment of lower courts is discretionary, and some members of the First Congress proposed to do only the minimum: staff and fund the Supreme Court and rely on the states for trial courts. The Judiciary Bill of 1789, as first drafted by the Senate, opted for federal trial (district) courts. An amendment to restrict those courts to cases of admiralty and maritime matters (like the Court of Appeals in Cases of Capture) was rejected. Warren, 37 Harv. L. Rev. 49, 67 (1923).

There were similar efforts in the House of Representatives to limit inferior courts to questions of admiralty. 1 Annals of Cong. 762, 777–78. These proposals, too, were unsuccessful. Although there was some resistance to federal district courts, the House rejected the idea of relying on state courts. Id. at 783. Madison warned that the courts in many states "cannot be trusted with the execution of Federal laws." Because of limited tenure and possible salary reductions, some courts were too dependent on state legislatures. Making federal laws dependent on these courts, Madison said, "would throw us back into all the embarrassments which characterized our former situation." Id. at 812–13. By a vote of 31 to 11, the House decisively rejected a motion to establish only State Courts of Admiralty with no federal district courts. Id. at 834.

Creating Circuit Courts

The Judiciary Act of 1789 provided for a Chief Justice and five Associate Justices for the Supreme Court. It divided the United States into thirteen districts, with a federal judge for each district, and created three circuits to handle appellate cases: the eastern, middle, and southern circuits. The circuit courts met twice a year in each district and consisted of any two Justices of the Supreme Court and one district judge from that circuit. District judges could not vote in any case of appeal or error from their own decisions. Section 25 of the Judiciary Act solidified federal control over the states by conferring upon the Supreme Court a supervisory role over state courts.

The Justices of the Supreme Court complained bitterly about their circuit court duties. In addition to handling cases on the Court's docket, Justices had to "ride circuit" by traveling around the country to hear appellate cases in their circuit. Riding circuit was an arduous and hazardous enterprise. Participation in circuit cases had another drawback: a Justice might have to review his own decision if the case reached the Supreme Court. All six Justices appealed to President Washington and Congress to reduce their labors. Congress offered modest relief in 1793 by allowing the attendance of only one Justice for the holding of circuit court. 1 Am. State Papers 24, 52 (1834); 1 Stat. 333 (1793).

With six Justices to cover three circuits, each Justice now had to ride circuit only once a year. Pressure for relief resulted in the controversial Judiciary Act of 1801, which divided the country into six

---

2. Id. at 178–79; Henry J. Bourguignon, The First Federal Court: The Federal Appellate Prize Court of the American Revolution (1977).

Congress "Fixes" the Meaning of the Constitution

[Congress passed legislation in 1802 to repeal the Judiciary Act of the previous year, in effect abolishing sixteen circuit judges and their salaries. A case challenging the right of Congress to abolish the circuit courts reached the Supreme Court in 1803, but Justice Paterson, writing for the Court, declined to overturn the statute.]

... Congress have constitutional authority to establish, from time to time, such inferior tribunals as they may think proper; and to transfer a cause from one such tribunal to another. In this last particular, there are no words in the constitution to prohibit or restrain the exercise of legislative power....

2d. Another reason for reversal is, that the judges of the supreme court have no right to sit as circuit judges, not being appointed as such, or, in other words, that they ought to have distinct commissions for that purpose. To this objection, which is of recent date, it is sufficient to observe, that practice, and acquiescence under it, for a period of several years, commencing with the organization of the judicial system, affords an irresistible answer, and has indeed fixed the construction. It is a contemporary interpretation of the most forcible nature. This practical exposition is too strong and obstinate to be shaken or controlled. Of course, the question is at rest, and ought not now to be disturbed.

SOURCE: Stuart v. Laird, 5 U.S. (1 Cr.) 299, 308 (1803).

circuits and promised to terminate circuit riding by creating sixteen circuit judges. Following the election of Thomas Jefferson as the next President, President John Adams elevated six district judges to those positions and named three Senators and one Representative to the vacant district judgeships. Farrand, 5 Am. Hist. Rev. 682 (1900); 2 Stat. 89, §7 (1801).

Although the creation of circuit judges had been proposed for several years, the statute creating them was not signed until the closing days of the Adams administration. After President Adams hastily filled the positions and allotted them to loyal Federalists, the Jeffersonians condemned the "midnight judges bill" as unconscionable. They accused the Federalists of trying to accomplish through judicial appointments what had just been denied them in the national election. The Judiciary Act of 1801 reduced the number of Supreme Court Justices from six to five, effective with the next vacancy. The reduction might have been justified because the work of the Justices had been cut back by eliminating circuit duties. Moreover, five Justices would avoid the possibility of tie votes. The Jeffersonians interpreted the statute less charitably. The reduction decreased Jefferson's opportunity to appoint his own candidate to the High Court. The new Congress promptly repealed the Judiciary Act of 1801 (see box).

Changes in the Number of Justices

The size of the Supreme Court fluctuated throughout the nineteenth century, keeping pace with the addition of new circuits. A seventh Justice was added in 1807 after the creation of a new judicial circuit. The size of the Supreme Court rose to nine in 1837, reflecting the westward expansion, and to ten by 1863 (to accommodate the Pacific Circuit). Three years later Congress lowered the permanent size of the Court to seven, although the membership never fell below eight. The reduction is often interpreted as a slap against President Andrew Johnson, depriving him of an opportunity to fill vacancies. The Radical Republicans feared that his appointees to the Court would oppose Reconstruction policies. S. Rept. No. 711, 75th Cong., 1st Sess. 13 (1937). His nomination of Henry Stanbery as an Associate Justice had to be withdrawn because Congress reduced the Court's size. However, Johnson signed the bill, and its legislative history does not suggest an attack on the Court. In fact, Chief Jus-

THE THIRTEEN FEDERAL JUDICIAL COURTS

tice Salmon P. Chase, in pursuit of higher salaries for the Supreme Court, supported a reduction to seven members.[3] Legislation in 1869 brought the Court back to its present size of nine members.

Appellate Courts

A major step in judicial reorganization occurred in 1891 when Congress created a separate system of appellate courts, producing three tiers: district (trial) courts, circuit (appellate) courts, and the Supreme Court. A comprehensive "Judges Bill" in 1925 gave the Supreme Court greater discretion to grant or deny petitions of appeal from the lower courts.

In 1891 there were nine circuit courts of appeals. The Tenth Circuit, split from the Eighth, appeared in 1929. When the workload of the Fifth Circuit grew too large, Congress divided it in 1981, forming the Eleventh Circuit. Together with the D.C. Circuit, that made twelve courts of appeals. In 1982 Congress established the Court of Appeals for the Federal Circuit (CAFC), which inherited the work of the Court of Customs and Patent Appeals and reviewed cases coming from the U.S. Claims Court (later renamed Court of Federal Claims). Unlike the other twelve circuits, which cover a specific geographical area and possess general jurisdiction, the CAFC is nationwide and limited in subject matter jurisdiction (see map).

---

3. Charles Fairman, 6 History of the Supreme Court of the United States: Reconstruction and Reunion 163–71 (1971); Cong. Globe, 39th Cong. 3909 (July 18, 1866); Stanley I. Kutler, Judicial Power and Reconstruction Politics 48–63 (1968). As a U.S. Senator, Chase had proposed that no vacancies be filled until the Court's membership fell to six. He justified this smaller number because of reduced duties once Justices were relieved of their responsibilities for riding circuit. Cong. Globe, 33d Cong., 2d Sess. 216–17 (1855).

Three-Judge Courts

As a means of expediting action, Congress submits some disputes to a three-judge court consisting of a mix of district and appellate judges. 28 U.S.C. § 2284. Initially, these courts were established to limit the interference of federal courts with state statutes. Instead of allowing a single federal district judge to nullify a state law, Congress required three federal judges (including at least one circuit judge) to hear applications to enjoin the enforcement of state statutes on constitutional grounds. Their determinations are appealable directly to the Supreme Court. Three-judge courts place an administrative burden on the federal judiciary, requiring three judges to do what might be done by one. In 1976 Congress eliminated three-judge courts for certain disputes. 90 Stat. 1119. Over the years, the jurisdiction of three-judge courts has been cut substantially. Gressman, Geller, Shapiro, Bishop, and Hartnett, Supreme Court Practice 89–92, 99–121 (9th ed. 2007).

Other Judicial Bodies

Congress has established several organizations to help the judiciary. In 1922, it created the Judicial Conference to coordinate the legislative requests and administrative actions of the federal courts. It had been the responsibility of the Justice Department to handle the administrative needs of the courts (including their budgets), creating an obvious separation of powers problem. In 1939, Congress established the Administrative Office of the United States Courts to take care of the managerial, research, statistical, and budgetary needs of the national judiciary. Also in 1939, Congress created judicial councils in each circuit to supervise the work of judges. In 1967, Congress created a Federal Judicial Center to study methods of improving judicial administration.

B. LEGISLATIVE AND SPECIALIZED COURTS

In addition to "constitutional courts" established by Congress pursuant to Article III of the Constitution, Congress creates Article I courts to carry out legislative duties. Drawing on various sections of the Constitution, Congress has set up territorial courts, legislative courts, military courts, and the courts of the District of Columbia. Judges sitting on those courts are not entitled to the rights of life tenure and irreducible compensation guaranteed to Article III federal judges.

Territorial Courts

Section 3 of Article IV gives Congress the power "to dispose of and make all needful Rules and Regulations respecting the Territory or other Property belonging to the United States." After Spain ceded Florida to the United States in 1819, Congress established a territorial government in Florida and its legislature created a court system that gave judges a term of four years. This system was challenged as a violation of the requirement in Article III that judges serve for life "during good Behaviour." The Supreme Court ruled that the territorial courts of Florida were not constitutional courts; they were legislative courts.[4]

Under its authority to govern territories, Congress established district courts in Puerto Rico, Guam, the Virgin Islands, the former Canal Zone, and the Northern Mariana Islands. The district court of Puerto Rico is classified as an Article III federal district court. Its judges hold office during

---

4. American Ins. Co. v. Canter, 26 U.S. (1 Pet.) 511, 545 (1828). Also on territorial courts see Benner v. Porter, 9 How. 235 (1850); Hornbuckle v. Toombs, 18 Wall. 648 (1874); Reynolds v. United States, 98 U.S. 145 (1878); The "City of Panama," 101 U.S. 453 (1880); and Romeu v. Todd, 206 U.S. 358 (1907).

Is It Legislative or Judicial?

Two centuries of statutory activity illustrate the broad range of options available to Congress in handling the adjudication of certain federal questions. It may choose to resolve disputes within its own chambers, as it did initially with federal claims. In legislating on claims, it can create outside bodies and call on them to investigate and make nonbinding recommendations. Congress may decide to shift adjudicatory issues to executive agencies, as it did with the Board of General Appraisers. Finally, it can vest them in adjudicatory bodies and designate whether those courts should have Article I or Article III status. In cases brought before them, federal courts monitor these designations to assure that they comply with constitutional principles. Functions of government therefore float from one branch to another as Congress searches for the most effective means of discharging its duties. What is "legislative" at one stage becomes "administrative" at another and "judicial" still later.

---

good behavior; territorial judges serve eight- or ten-year terms. Similar to territorial courts are the consular courts established by Congress to carry out the constitutional powers regarding treaties and commerce with foreign nations. Ex parte Bakelite Corp., 279 U.S. 438, 451 (1929).

Legislative Courts

Congress has established a number of Article I legislative courts. It created the Court of Claims in 1855 to help Congress handle the large number of claims presented by citizens against the United States. The responsibility for determining these claims "belongs primarily to Congress as an incident of its power to pay the debts of the United States." Ex parte Bakelite, 279 U.S. at 452. Initially, the Court of Claims performed an advisory role but subsequent statutes made some of its judgments binding. Gradually, the Court of Claims changed from an investigative to an adjudicatory body. In 1953, Congress made the Court of Claims an Article III court, giving it the constitutional protections of tenure and irreducible salary. 67 Stat. 226 (1953). However, legislation in 1982 gave the judges of the Claims Court a 14-year term, returning them to the status of an Article I Court. 96 Stat. 25 (1982). Legislation in 1992 changed its name to the Court of Federal Claims.

The United States Customs Court also illustrates the congressional need to delegate some of its constitutional responsibilities to judicial bodies. In 1890, Congress established within the Department of Treasury a Board of General Appraisers to review the decisions of appraisers and collectors at U.S. ports. In 1926 the Board was replaced by the United States Customs Court and in 1956 Congress made the Customs Court an Article III court. Its name was changed in 1980 to the Court of International Trade. 70 Stat. 532 (1956); 94 Stat. 1727 (1980).

Congress created a Court of Customs Appeal in 1909 to review final decisions of the Board of General Appraisers. The Court was established pursuant to the power of Congress to lay and collect duties on imports. Ex parte Bakelite, 279 U.S. at 458–59. The statute had been silent about judicial tenure. Congress granted the judges life tenure in 1930. 46 Stat. 590, 762 (1930). In 1958 Congress changed the court (by now called the Court of Customs and Patent Appeals) to an Article III court. Legislation in 1982 folded this court into the Court of Appeals for the Federal Circuit. 72 Stat. 848 (1958); 96 Stat. 25 (1982). These statutes illustrate the choices available to Congress in handling adjudicatory issues (see box).

Congress created a United States tax court in 1924 as the Board of Tax Appeals, placed within the Treasury Department as "an independent agency in the executive branch of the Government." 43 Stat. 338 (1924). Legislation in 1942 and 1969 changed the name of the Board to the "Tax Court of the United States" and gave it Article I status, 56 Stat. 957 (1942); 83 Stat. 30 (1969). Judges serve 15-year terms. All decisions of the Tax Court, other than small tax cases, are subject to review by the United States Court of Appeals and by the Supreme Court.

Military Courts

A third class of specialized courts derives from the power of Congress under Article I, Section 8, to "make Rules for the Government and Regulation of the land and naval Forces." Congress decided that criminal behavior in the military shall be tried by court-martial proceedings, not by courts established under Article III. The U.S. Court of Appeals for the Armed Forces, composed of five judges with 15-year terms, is an Article I court. Military courts need not satisfy all of the procedural protections offered by Article III courts.[5]

In 1969, the Supreme Court attempted to subject certain military questions to the jurisdiction of civilian courts. It held that a crime must be "service connected" to be under military jurisdiction. O'Callahan v. Parker, 395 U.S. 258 (1969). The service-connected doctrine became so confusing that the Court abandoned it in 1987. Jurisdiction of a court-martial now depends solely on the accused's status as a member of the armed forces. Solorio v. United States, 483 U.S. 435 (1987). Thus, the rights of servicemen result from action by Congress, not the courts. For additional material on military commissions (or military tribunals) see Chapter 7.

Article II Courts

The executive branch has created a number of courts to administer justice in territories occupied by U.S. armed forces. Frequently these take the form of military tribunals (Chapter 7). The President's power to establish these courts is subject to legislative and judicial checks. A recent example of an Article II court is the United States Court for Berlin, created in 1955 but not activated until 1979. The case produced a major collision between the State Department, which regarded the court as an instrument of American foreign policy, and the Article III judge who presided and insisted on full independence. United States v. Tiede, 86 F.R.D. 227 (U.S. Ct. Berlin 1979). See Louis Fisher, "Hijack in Berlin," Legal Times, July 2, 2004, at 50–51, and David J. Bederman, "Article II Courts," 44 Mercer L. Rev. 825 (1993).

District of Columbia Courts

Under Article I, Section 8, Congress exercises "exclusive Legislation in all Cases whatsoever, over such District." Initially, the Supreme Court regarded the District of Columbia courts as legislative, not constitutional.[6] In 1933 the Court reasoned that because the District was formed from territory belonging to Maryland and Virginia, District inhabitants should continue to enjoy their former constitutional rights and protections. D.C. courts were therefore considered constitutional courts established under Article III. O'Donoghue v. United States, 289 U.S. 516 (1933). There are two types of D.C. courts: federal courts (the U.S. District Court for the District of Columbia and the U.S. Court of Appeals for the D.C. Circuit) and local courts for the District (the Superior Court and the D.C. Court of Appeals). The former are Article III Courts; the latter can have Article I characteristics. The Court compared a District resident to that of a citizen in any other state charged with violating a state criminal law. Citizens in the D.C. courts are "no more disadvantaged and no more entitled to an Art. III

---

5. Palmore v. United States, 411 U.S. 389, 404 (1973). See Toth v. Quarles, 350 U.S. 11, 17–18 (1955).

6. Keller v. Potomac Electric Power Co., 261 U.S. 428, 441–43 (1923); Postum Cereal Co. v. Calif. Fig Nut Co., 272 U.S. 693, 700 (1927); Ex parte Bakelite Corp., 279 U.S. 438, 450 (1929); Federal Radio Comm'n v. Gen'l Elec. Co., 281 U.S. 464, 468 (1930).

ROUTES TO THE SUPREME COURT

judge than any other citizen of any of the 50 States who is tried for a strictly local crime." Palmore v. United States, 411 U.S. 389, 410 (1973).

Bankruptcy Courts

The demarcation between Article I and Article III courts remains a source of disagreement among Justices of the Supreme Court. In 1978, in an effort to handle thousands of bankruptcy cases, Congress established a bankruptcy court in each federal district. The judges of those courts were appointed by the President (subject to Senate advice and consent) for 14-year terms and could be removed by the judicial council of the circuit. Their salaries could be decreased by Congress.

In 1982, the Supreme Court denied that Congress could establish specialized courts to carry out every one of its Article I powers. Although Congress has constitutional authority under Article I, Section 8, to establish "uniform Laws on the subject of Bankruptcies throughout the United States," this authority did not permit Congress to rely on a non-Article III court. Such reasoning, said the Court, "threatens to supplant completely our system of adjudication in independent Art. III tribunals and replace it with a system of 'specialized' legislative courts." The Court concluded that the Bankruptcy Act of 1978 had removed essential attributes of judicial power from the Article III district court and vested them in a non-Article III body. Northern Pipeline Const. Co. v. Marathon Pipe Line Co., 458 U.S. 50 (1982). Two years later, Congress passed legislation to reinstate the bankruptcy courts. The bankruptcy judges were made adjuncts of the district courts and given 14-year terms. 98 Stat. 2704 (1984).

The strict ruling on bankruptcy judges should not obscure the extent of adjudication that takes place outside Article III courts. In 1985 a unanimous Court upheld the arbitration provision of the Federal Insecticide, Fungicide, and Rodenticide Act. The Court decided that agency adjudication posed only a minimum threat to Article III judicial powers: "practical attention to substance rather than doctrinaire reliance on formal categories should inform application of Article III." Thomas v. Union Carbide Agric. Products Co., 473 U.S. 568, 587 (1985). A year later, the Court upheld another case of agency adjudication, again declining to "adopt formalistic and unbending rules." Commodity Futures Trading Comm'n v. Schor, 478 U.S. 833, 851 (1986).

Magistrates

In 1976 Congress created the office of U.S. magistrate to replace the earlier office of U.S. commissioner. Magistrates are appointed by district judges to serve for fixed terms. Their salaries, set by the Judicial Conference pursuant to statute, may be diminished by Congress. Magistrates are not Article III judges; they serve "as an integral part" of the U.S. District Court to hear and determine procedural motions, to hear motions for dismissal and for summary judgment, and to serve as special masters to research particular issues. In 1980 the Supreme Court upheld the authority of magistrates to conduct an evidentiary hearing, provided that the district judge makes a de novo (new) determination when the magistrate's findings or recommendations are contested. United States v. Raddatz, 447 U.S. 667 (1980).

C. THE APPOINTMENT PROCESS

The delegates at the Constitutional Convention condemned the British system of executive appointment, associating it with official corruption and debasement of the judiciary. At first they placed the power to select judges with Congress. Next, they considered vesting that responsibility solely in the Senate. Only late in the convention did they settle on joint action by the President and the Senate. 1 Farrand 21, 63, 119–28, 232–33; 2 Farrand 41–44, 80–83, 121. The President, under Article II of the Constitution, shall nominate "and by and with the Advice and Consent of the Senate, shall appoint ... Judges of the supreme Court." The Constitution also permits Congress to vest the appointment of "inferior officers" in the President alone, in the courts, or in the heads of the executive departments.

Subjecting federal judges to presidential nomination and Senate confirmation creates an intensely political process. From an early date, Senators wielded considerable power in choosing nominees for federal judgeships. Members of the Supreme Court (such as Chief Justice Taft) have lobbied vigorously for their candidates. Other sectors of government are active. Private organizations participate. The American Bar Association (ABA) plays an important role. Its influence increased during the Truman administration when it established a special committee to judge the professional qualifications of candidates submitted by the Attorney General.

In 2001, the Bush White House advised the ABA that it would no longer receive advance notice of judicial nominees. However, the Senate Judiciary Committee continues to rely on ABA evaluations. In 2009, President Obama agreed to submit names to the ABA before sending judicial nominees to the Senate. For detailed analysis: Mitchel A. Sollenberger, Judicial Appointments and Democratic Controls (2011). At face value, the Constitution appears to give the President the exclusive power over nominations ("he shall nominate"). However, many public officials and private citizens participate actively and influentially in the pre-nomination process. Mitchel A. Sollenberger, The President Shall Nominate: How Congress Trumps Executive Power (2008).

In 1989, the Supreme Court received a challenge to ABA's participation in the nomination process for federal judges. The ABA had refused a request from a foundation for the names of potential nominees it was reviewing and for the reports and minutes of its meetings. The request was brought under the Federal Advisory Committee Act (FACA). A district court decided that applying FACA to the ABA would unconstitutionally infringe on the President's Article II authority to nominate federal judges and would violate the principle of separation of powers. The Supreme Court held FACA did not apply to ABA's advisory relationship. Public Citizen v. Department of Justice, 491 U.S. 440 (1989).

Nominating Panels

President Carter altered the selection process for appellate judges by establishing nominating panels. They were directed to recommend five candidates for each vacancy, allowing the President to select the nominee. As part of an accommodation, Senators continued to control nominations for district judges, although some opted for a panel system. When President Reagan took office, he abolished the judicial nominating commissions for appellate judges. During subsequent administrations, the nominating process for selecting federal judges followed a variety of practices: screening committees or panels to help Senators choose a nominee, recommendations from the state bar or lawyers associations, and an informal structure for interviewing and recommending candidates for judgeships.

How Nominations Affect Judicial Policy

The power to nominate Supreme Court Justices can produce sudden shifts in judicial policy. Slight changes in the composition of the Supreme Court have reversed previous rulings. In 1870 the Court reviewed a congressional statute that treated paper money as legal tender for discharging prior debts. Voting 4 to 3, the Court declared the statute unconstitutional. The partisanship that raged throughout the post-Civil War period did not bypass the courts. The four Justices in the majority were Democrats; the three dissenters were Republicans. In the lower federal courts, almost every Democratic judge pronounced the statute unconstitutional; nearly every Republican judge sustained it. Hepburn v. Griswold, 8 Wall. (75 U.S.) 603 (1870); Fairman, 54 Harv. L. Rev. 1128, 1131 (1941).

The retirement of Justice Grier and the authorization by Congress the previous year of a new Justice allowed President Grant to appoint two new members. His first appointments were ill-starred. The Senate rejected his Attorney General, Ebenezer Hoar, while his second nominee, Edwin Stanton, died four days after being confirmed. Those nominations were made before the Court's decision. Grant had reason to believe that his next two appointments, submitted after the decision, would support the statute. William Strong, as a member of the Supreme Court of Pennsylvania, had already sustained the Legal Tender Act. Joseph P. Bradley appeared to be no less sympathetic. Fifteen months after the Legal Tender Act had been declared unconstitutional, the reconstituted Court upheld the Act by a 5–4 margin. Strong and Bradley joined the original three dissenters to form the majority; the four Justices who decided the case in 1870 now found themselves in the minority. Legal Tender Cases, 12 Wall. (79 U.S.) 457 (1871).

The transition from the Warren Court to the Burger Court also produced reversals of prior decisions (or efforts by the Court to "distinguish" prior holdings from current judicial policy). In 1971, a 5 to 4 majority—including two newcomers, Chief Justice Burger and Justice Blackmun—upheld a statutory procedure that stripped an individual of citizenship. The Court thus narrowed earlier holdings that citizenship could not be taken away unless voluntarily renounced. Justice Black objected that protections for American citizenship "should not be blown around by every passing political wind that changes the composition of this Court." Rogers v. Bellei, 401 U.S. 815, 837 (1971). No doubt Black was frustrated by policy shifts from the Warren Court to the Burger Court, but he himself had been part of the Roosevelt nominations after 1937 that helped chart a new course in constitutional interpretation. Changes in the Court's composition enable it to incorporate contemporary ideas and attitudes.

The Senate's Confirmation Record

The Senate has refused to confirm almost one out of every five presidential nominations to the Supreme Court. Twenty-five nominees have either been rejected, had their names submitted without Senate action, or been forced to withdraw. Most of those actions (eighteen) occurred before 1900. After the Senate rejected John J. Parker in 1930, confirmation of Supreme Court nominees seemed an automatic step. That pattern ended in 1968 when the Senate refused to advance Associate Justice Abe Fortas to the position of Chief Justice. Fortas, subjected to embarrassing questions about his acceptance of fees from private parties, eventually asked President Johnson to withdraw his nomination. Homer Thornberry, picked by Johnson to fill Fortas's seat as Associate Justice, withdrew his name. A year later, with impeachment proceedings gearing up against him amidst charges of financial and personal improprieties, Fortas resigned from the Court.

The Supreme Court remained embroiled in political controversy in 1969 when the Senate rejected Nixon's nomination of Clement F. Haynsworth, Jr., to the Supreme Court. The ethical test applied by Republicans against Fortas was now used by Democrats against Haynsworth. A year later, the Senate rejected Nixon's next nominee, G. Harrold Carswell, who lacked the qualifications needed for Associate Justice. Nixon finally nominated Harry A. Blackmun, who was confirmed by a unanimous vote.

Probing a Nominee's Views

The emphasis given by Nixon to the sociopolitical views of judicial candidates helps underscore the entanglement of law and politics. Senators, too, in expressing their advice and consent, feel at liberty to evaluate a nominee's political and constitutional philosophy in order to maintain a balance of views on the Court.[7]

As shown by the 1981 hearings on the nomination of Sandra Day O'Connor to the Court, her personal and judicial philosophy on the exceedingly sensitive issue of abortion became a matter of recurrent interest to Senators and one on which she was willing to state her views (see reading). Her willingness to discuss why she opposed abortion "as a matter of birth control or otherwise" contrasts with very different responses from Clarence Thomas and Ruth Bader Ginsburg during their confirmation hearings. At his hearings in 1991, Thomas was asked to comment on the position in *Roe v. Wade* that it is a woman's right to decide to terminate a pregnancy. He declined to discuss the issue: "I do not think that at this time that I could maintain my impartiality as a member of the judiciary and comment on that specific case" (page 127, Part 1, of hearings). Most nominees offer similar responses, regarding it as improper to discuss an issue that is likely to come before the Court. However, in hearings in 1993, Ruth Bader Ginsburg did not hesitate to express her view about a woman's right to choose (see box on the next page).

The Senate's rejection of two nominees by Nixon to the Supreme Court was duplicated in 1987. President Reagan nominated Judge Robert H. Bork, a conservative member of the D.C. Circuit, to replace the more moderate Justice Powell. Everyone recognized the nomination as pivotal, especially after Reagan's selection of O'Connor in 1981, Antonin Scalia in 1986, and the elevation of Rehnquist as Chief Justice in 1986. Powell, a centrist, had supplied a swing vote on the Burger Court. The addition of Bork threatened to reverse a number of important decisions.

Major groups in the country mounted an intensive campaign against Bork, whose writings and speeches contained provocative views on civil rights, women's rights, the First Amendment, abortion, privacy, reapportionment, and criminal law. Four members of the ABA committee found him "not qualified." One voted "not opposed" (meaning minimally qualified and not among the best available). Bork did not fare well during the hearings and the White House committed a number of tactical blunders, such as trying to paint Bork as a moderate. The Senate voted 58 to 42 to reject him.

To replace Bork, Reagan turned to Judge Douglas H. Ginsburg of the D.C. Circuit. The nomination unraveled almost hour by hour because of Ginsburg's modest credentials and questions about conflicts of interest while he served in the Justice Department. When he admitted smoking marijuana into his thirties, as a professor of law, conservative support for his nomination took flight. The disclosure was particularly damaging because of Reagan's strong campaign against drugs and the administration's heavy emphasis on law and order. Within nine days of the nomination, Reagan received Ginsburg's request to withdraw his name. The next nominee, Judge Anthony Kennedy of the Ninth Circuit, sailed through the confirmation process without difficulty.

Another bruising battle occurred in 1991, when President George H. W. Bush nominated Clarence Thomas to replace Justice Thurgood Marshall. After sensational hearings in which Anita F. Hill tes-

---

7. Senate Committee on the Judiciary, "Advice and Consent on Supreme Court Nominations," 94th Cong., 2d Sess. (Committee Print 1976). See L. A. Powe, Jr., "The Senate and the Court: Questioning a Nominee," 54 Tex. L. Rev. 891 (1976).

Ruth Bader Ginsburg on Abortion

Judge GINSBURG.... you asked me about my thinking on equal protection versus individual autonomy. My answer is that both are implicated. The decision whether or not to bear a child is central to a woman's life, to her well-being and dignity. It is a decision she must make for herself. When Government controls that decision for her, she is being treated as less than a fully adult human responsible for her own choices.

Senator [Hank] BROWN.... With regard to the equal protection argument, though, since this may well confer a right to choose on the woman, or could, would it also follow that the father would be entitled to a right to choose in this regard or [possess] some rights in this regard?

Judge GINSBURG. That was an issue left open in *Roe v. Wade* (1973). But if I recall correctly, it was put to rest in *Casey* (1992). In that recent decision, the Court dealt with a series of regulations. It upheld most of them, but it struck down one requiring notice to the husband....

The *Casey* majority understood that marriage and family life is not always all we might wish them to be. There are women whose physical safety, even their lives, would be endangered, if the law required them to notify their partner....

Senator BROWN. I was concerned that if the equal protection argument were relied on to ensure a right to choose, then looking for a sex-blind standard in this regard might also then convey rights in the father to this decision. Do you see that as following logically from the rights that can be conferred on the mother?

Judge GINSBURG. I will rest my answer on the *Casey* decision, which recognizes that it is her body, her life, and men, to that extent, are not similarly situated. They don't bear the child.

Senator BROWN. So the rights are not equal in this regard, because the interests are not equal?

Judge GINSBURG. It is essential to woman's equality with man that she be the decisionmaker, that her choice be controlling....

SOURCE: "Nomination of Ruth Bader Ginsburg, To Be Associate Justice of the Supreme Court of the United States," hearings before the Senate Committee on the Judiciary, 103d Cong., 1st Sess. 207 (1993).

---

tified on alleged sexual harassment by Thomas when he served as chairman of the Equal Employment Opportunity Commission, the Senate confirmed him by the close vote of 52 to 48. Clinton's nominees encountered little opposition. Ruth Bader Ginsburg was confirmed by a vote of 96 to 3 and Stephen Breyer by a vote of 87 to 9.

From Roberts to Kagan

Two nominations by George W. Bush encountered greater opposition. John Roberts was confirmed as Chief Justice with a vote of 78–22; the margin for Samuel Alito as Associate Justice was more narrow, 58–42. During his confirmation hearing, Roberts' prepared statement said that judges "are like umpires. Umpires don't make the rules, they apply them. The role of an umpire and a judge is critical. They make sure everybody plays by the rules, but it is a limited role. Nobody ever went to a ball game to see the umpire.... I will remember that it's my job to call balls and strikes, and not to pitch or bat." "Confirmation Hearing on the Nomination of John G. Robert, Jr. to be Chief Justice of the United States," hearing before the Senate Committee on the Judiciary, 109th Cong., 1st Sess. 55–56 (2005). For comments on the baseball analogy by Senators, see pp. 46, 184–86, 256–57, 266–67, 279.

In baseball, the strike zone is defined by the width of the home plate and the height from the shoulders down to the knees. The U.S. Constitution has some clear strike zones, including a two-thirds majority for veto overrides, the age of at least 35 to be President, a six-year term for Senators, and the requirement of two witnesses to prove treason. What is the strike zone for equal protection of the laws, freedom of speech, free exercise of religion, due process of law, unreasonable searches and seizures, cruel and unusual punishments, and other constitutional values?

On May 26, 2009, President Barack Obama announced his choice of Judge Sonia Sotomayor to be Associate Justice. He spoke about the importance "of the limits of the judicial role, an understanding that a judge's job is to interpret, not make, law." During subsequent Senate hearings, Sotomayor repeated the same standard for judges: to apply law, not make it. Few observers of constitutional law could accept that description. Federal courts, especially the Supreme Court, are continually creating new rules that apply to broad classes of people.

President Obama's next nominee to the Court, Elena Kagan, was questioned at a Senate Judiciary hearing on June 30, 2010 about the baseball analogy. Regarding it as correct in some respects, she cautioned that "like all metaphors, it does have its limits." She expressed concern that it "might suggest to some people that law is a kind of robotic enterprise, that there is a kind of automatic quality to it, that it's easy, that we just sort of stand there and we say ball and strike and everything is clear-cut, that there is no judgment in the process. I do think that that's not right, and it is especially not right at the Supreme Court level."

Recess Appointments

The Senate is denied a role in the confirmation process when the President makes recess appointments, including to the Supreme Court. Under Article II, Section 2, the President "shall have Power to fill up all Vacancies that may happen during the Recess of the Senate, by granting Commissions which may expire at the End of their next Session." During the 1950s, President Eisenhower placed three men on the Supreme Court while the Senate recessed: Earl Warren, William J. Brennan, Jr., and Potter Stewart. All three joined the Court and participated in decisions before the Senate had an opportunity to review their qualifications and vote on their confirmation. In each case, the Senate gave its advice and consent, but the experience convinced most Senators that the procedure was unhealthy both for the Senate and the Court. How could federal judges serving under a recess appointment maintain total independence of mind? The anticipation of questions by a Senate committee during confirmation hearings might influence the direction and content of a nominee's decision. Similarly, a recess appointee could shade an opinion to attract White House support for a lifetime appointment.

In 1960, Senator Philip Hart introduced a resolution to discourage recess appointments to the courts. The Senate passed the resolution, 48 to 37, voting essentially along party lines. The resolution stated that the making of recess appointments to the Supreme Court may be inconsistent with the interests of the Court, the nominee, litigants before the Court, and the people of the United States. Such appointments should "not be made except under unusual circumstances and for the purpose of preventing or ending a demonstrable breakdown in the administration of the Court's business." 106 Cong. Rec. 18130–45 (1960). Although the resolution is not legally binding, no President after Eisenhower has made recess appointments to the Supreme Court.

The President's constitutional authority to make recess appointments to federal courts was upheld in 1985. United States v. Woodley, 751 F.2d 1008 (9th Cir. 1985), cert. denied, 475 U.S. 1048 (1986). However, the dissenters noted that although there have been approximately 300 judicial recess appointments since 1789, there had been only one such appointment since 1964. A second recess appointment of a federal judge occurred on December 27, 2000, when President Clinton placed Roger L. Gregory on the Fourth Circuit. President George W. Bush nominated Gregory for a life term on July 20, 2001, and the Senate confirmed him. President Bush made two recess appointments to federal appellate courts: Charles Pickering to the Fifth Circuit on January 16, 2004, and William Pryor to the Eleventh Circuit on February 20, 2004.

The fact that courts sanction the use of judicial recess appointments does not mean that the elected branches are obliged to accept the practice as constitutionally acceptable. The decision of the appellate court in 1985 functions more like an advisory opinion: It is constitutional if the elected branches want to do it. The final word on whether judges are placed on the courts on a recess basis lies with the President and the Senate. The Senate has a powerful role because it can decide to automatically deny a life term to any judge who receives a recess appointment. It could adopt a resolution stating that any individual placed on an Article III court on a recess basis would be denied any Senate action if named later for a lifetime appointment.

Nomination Hearings of Sandra Day O'Connor

During the 1981 hearings on the nomination of Sandra Day O'Connor to be Associate Justice of the Supreme Court, Senators were interested in learning about the personal and philosophical views of the first woman nominated to the High Bench. Although the Senators wanted a nominee who would possess certain general qualities—integrity, honesty, technical knowledge, and proper judicial temperament—they also probed her position on the highly controversial issue of abortion, a question that had been decided already by the Court and was likely to be relitigated in the future. The selections below come from "Nomination of Sandra Day O'Connor," hearings before the Senate Committee on the Judiciary, 97th Cong., 1st Sess., September 9, 1981, pp. 60–63.

The CHAIRMAN [*Strom Thurmond*]. Judge O'Connor, there has been much discussion regarding your views on the subject of abortion. Would you discuss your philosophy on abortion, both personal and judicial, and explain your actions as a State senator in Arizona on certain specific matters: First, your 1970 committee vote in favor of House bill No. 20, which would have repealed Arizona's felony statutes on abortion. Then I have three other instances I will inquire about.

Judge O'CONNOR. Very well. May I preface my response by saying that the personal views and philosophies, in my view, of a Supreme Court Justice and indeed any judge should be set aside insofar as it is possible to do that in resolving matters that come before the Court.

Issues that come before the Court should be resolved based on the facts of that particular case or matter and on the law applicable to those facts, and any constitutional principles applicable to those facts. They should not be based on the personal views and ideology of the judge with regard to that particular matter or issue.

Now, having explained that, I would like to say that my own view in the area of abortion is that I am opposed to it as a matter of birth control or otherwise. The subject of abortion is a valid one, in my view, for legislative action subject to any constitutional restraints or limitations.

I think a great deal has been written about my vote in a Senate Judiciary Committee in 1970 on a bill called House bill No. 20, which would have repealed Arizona's abortion statutes. Now in reviewing that, I would like to state first of all that that vote occurred some 11 years ago, to be exact, and was one which was not easily recalled by me, Mr. Chairman.

In fact, the committee records when I looked them up did not reflect my vote nor that of other members, with one exception.

It was necessary for me, then, to eventually take time to look at news media accounts and determine from a contemporary article a reflection of the vote on that particular occasion. The bill did not go to the floor of the Senate for a vote; it was held in the Senate Caucus and the committee vote was a vote which would have taken it out of that committee with a recommendation to the full Senate.

The bill is one which concerned a repeal of Arizona's then statutes which made it a felony, punishable by from 2 to 5 years in prison, for anyone providing any substance or means to procure a miscarriage unless it was necessary to save the life of the mother. It would have, for example, subjected anyone who assisted a young woman who, for instance, was a rape victim in securing a D. & C. procedure within hours or even days of that rape.

At that time I believed that some change in Arizona statutes was appropriate, and had a bill been presented to me that was less sweeping than House bill No. 20, I would have supported that. It was not, and the news accounts reflect that I supported the committee action in putting the bill out of committee, where it then died in the caucus.

I would say that my own knowledge and awareness of the issues and concerns that many people have about the question of abortion has increased since those days. It was not the subject of a great deal of public attention or concern at the time it came before the committee in 1970. I would not have voted, I think, Mr. Chairman, for a simple repeal thereafter.

The CHAIRMAN. Now the second instance was your cosponsorship in 1973 of Senate bill No. 1190, which would have provided family planning services, including surgical procedures, even for minors without parental consent.

Judge O'CONNOR. Senate bill No. 1190 in 1973 was a bill in which the prime sponsor was from the city of Tucson, and it had nine other cosigners on the bill. I was one of those cosigners.

I viewed the bill as a bill which did not deal with abortion but which would have established as a State policy in Arizona, a policy of encouraging the availability of contraceptive information to people generally. The bill at the time, I think, was rather loosely drafted, and I can understand why some might read it and say, "What does this mean?"

That did not particularly concern me at the time because I knew that the bill would go through the committee process and be amended substantially before we would see it again....

The CHAIRMAN. The third instance, your 1974 vote against House Concurrent Memorial No. 2002, which urged Congress to pass a constitutional amendment against abortion.

Judge O'CONNOR. Mr. Chairman, as you perhaps recall, the *Rowe* [sic] v. *Wade* decision was handed down in 1973. I would like to mention that in that year following that decision, when concerns began to be expressed, I requested the preparation in 1973 of Senate bill No. 1333 which gave hospitals and physicians and employees the right not to participate in or contribute to any abortion proceeding if they chose not to do so and objected, notwithstanding their employment. That bill did pass the State Senate and became law.

The following year, in 1974, less than a year following the *Rowe* [sic] v. *Wade* decision, a House Memorial was introduced in the Arizona House of Representatives. It would have urged Congress to amend the Constitution to provide that the word person in the 5th and 14th amendments applies to the unborn at every stage of development, except in an emergency when there is a reasonable medical certainty that continuation of the pregnancy would cause the death of the mother. The amendment was further amended in the Senate Judiciary Committee.

I did not support the memorial at that time, either in committee or in the caucus.

· · ·

I voted against it, Mr. Chairman, because I was not sure at that time that we had given the proper amount of reflection or consideration to what action, if any, was appropriate by way of a constitutional amendment in connection with the *Rowe* [sic] v. *Wade* decision.

· · ·

The CHAIRMAN. Now the last instance is concerning a vote in 1974 against a successful amendment to a stadium construction bill which limited the availability of abortions.

Judge O'CONNOR. Also in 1974, which was an active year in the Arizona Legislature with regard to the issue of abortion, the Senate had originated a bill that allowed the University of Arizona to issue bonds to expand its football stadium. That bill passed the State Senate and went to the House of Representatives.

In the House it was amended to add a nongermane rider which would have prohibited the performance of abortions in any facility under the jurisdiction of the Arizona Board of Regents. When the measure returned to the Senate, at that time I was the Senate majority leader and I was very concerned because the whole subject had become one that was controversial within our own membership.

I was concerned as majority leader that we not encourage a practice of the addition of nongermane riders to Senate bills which we had passed without that kind of a provision. Indeed, Arizona's constitution has a provision which prohibits the putting together of bills or measures or riders dealing with more than one subject. I did oppose the addition by the House of the nongermane rider when it came back.

It might be of interest, though, to know, Mr. Chairman, that also in 1974 there was another Senate bill which would have provided for a medical assistance program for the medically needy. That was Senate bill No. 1165. It contained a provision that no benefits would be provided for abortions except when deemed medically necessary to save the life of the mother, or where the pregnancy had resulted from rape, incest, or criminal action. I supported that bill together with that provision and the measure did pass and become law....

D. TENURE, REMOVAL, AND COMPENSATION

Under Article III of the Constitution, judges "both of the supreme and inferior Courts, shall hold their Offices during good Behaviour." Article I gives the House of Representatives the sole power of impeachment and the Senate the sole power to try all impeachments. A two-thirds majority of the Senate is required for conviction. Judges may be removed from office "on Impeachment for, and Conviction of, Treason, Bribery, or other high Crimes and Misdemeanors."

The impeachment process is cumbersome and suitable only for grave offenses. However, the need to remove judges for lesser offenses has long been recognized. In Federalist No. 79, Alexander Hamilton said that "insanity, without any formal or express provision, may be safely pronounced to be a virtual disqualification" for federal judges. If insanity is a basis for removal, what of senility, incompetence, disability, alcoholism, laziness, and other deficiencies that may fall short of an impeachable offense?

19th Century Removal Efforts

The first example of a federal judge impeached and removed from office occurred in 1803 in the case of John Pickering. He was charged with misconduct in a trial and for being on the bench while intoxicated. Supreme Court Justice Samuel Chase was impeached in 1804 but acquitted. Actions were brought against a number of other federal judges, many of whom preferred to resign from office rather than defend themselves against the charges. Shipley, 35 Law & Contemp. Prob. 178, 190–91 (1970). Still other federal judges withdrew quietly from the bench before prosecutors could launch a full-scale investigation. Joseph Borkin, The Corrupt Judge (1962).

To encourage aged and infirm judges to leave the bench, Congress passed legislation in 1869 to authorize the payment of full salary to any federal judge who resigned at or after age 70 with at least ten years' service on the bench. 16 Stat. 44, §5 (1869). For Justices with less than ten years, Congress has passed special statutes to provide full retirement benefits. 22 Stat. 2 (1882); Fairman, 51 Harv. L. Rev. 397 (1938).

Article I judges, such as territorial judges, have been removed by Presidents; these judges are not entitled to life tenure.[8] Article III judges are immune from removal, other than by impeachment. Nevertheless, they are subject to prosecution by the Justice Department for criminal offenses. The First Congress passed legislation providing that judges convicted of accepting a bribe "shall forever be disqualified to hold any office of honour, trust or profit under the United States." 1 Stat. 117, §21 (1790). Moreover, any federal judge who engages in the practice of law "is guilty of a high misdemeanor." 28 U.S.C. §454.

Contemporary Removals

Criminal prosecutions have been used to drive corrupt judges from the bench. In 1973 Judge Otto Kerner, Jr., of the Seventh Circuit was found guilty of bribery, perjury, tax evasion, and other crimes, most of which occurred during his previous service as governor of Illinois. On appeal, Kerner argued that the Constitution provides only one way to remove a judge: impeachment. The Seventh Circuit decided that judicial immunity does not exempt judges from the operation of criminal laws and affirmed Kerner's conviction. United States v. Isaacs, 493 F.2d 1124 (7th Cir. 1974).

Kerner's prosecution largely concerned his actions before joining the bench. A different issue arose in the early 1980s when the Justice Department charged U.S. District Judge Alcee L. Hastings with criminal activities while sitting as a judge. The Eleventh Circuit decided in 1982 that Hastings could be prosecuted. United States v. Hastings, 681 F.2d 706 (11th Cir. 1982), cert. denied, 459 U.S. 1203 (1983). After a jury acquitted Hastings in 1983, a judicial inquiry panel conducted its own investiga-

---

8. United States v. Guthrie, 58 U.S. (17 How.) 284, 288–89 (1854); 5 Op. Att'y Gen. 288, 291 (1851); and McAllister v. United States, 141 U.S. 174 (1891).

tion into charges of misconduct. Hastings claimed that this inquiry undermined his independence as a federal judge, but the investigative and disciplinary procedure was upheld by the courts.[9]

As explained later in this section, Hastings was impeached and removed by Congress. In 1984 U.S. District Judge Harry Claiborne was found guilty of income tax evasion. Two years later he was impeached and removed. In 1986 U.S. District Judge Walter L. Nixon, Jr., of Mississippi was convicted of lying to a federal grand jury; in 1989 he was impeached and removed. In 2009, the impeachment process was used against two federal judges: G. Thomas Porteous of Louisiana and Samuel B. Kent of Texas. Kent, after he was impeached by the House, resigned from office. Porteous was impeached in 2010 and removed the same year.

Ineligibility Clause

Once nominated and appointed to the bench, a few judges have been vulnerable to the charge that they violated the "ineligibility clause" of the Constitution. Article I, Section 6, Clause 2, provides that no Senator or Representative "shall, during the Time for which he was elected, be appointed to any Civil Office under the Authority of the United States, which shall have been created, or the Emoluments whereof shall have been encreased during such time." Hugo Black's nomination to the Supreme Court in 1937 was challenged because a retirement system for the judiciary had been enacted that year while Black served as U.S. Senator. The Supreme Court avoided the constitutional issue by holding that the plaintiff lacked standing to bring suit. Ex parte Levitt, 302 U.S. 633 (1937).

A more recent challenge concerned Abner Mikva, a member of Congress nominated by President Carter to the D.C. Circuit. Working through Senator James McClure, who served as plaintiff, the National Rifle Association argued that the salaries of federal judges had been increased during Mikva's term in Congress. A three-judge court ruled that McClure lacked standing to challenge the validity of an appointment of a federal judge. The court said that McClure and his colleagues had an opportunity to vote against Mikva's confirmation. Senators on the losing side could not then ask the judiciary to reverse the Senate's action. McClure v. Carter, 513 F.Supp. 265 (D. Idaho 1981), aff'd sub nom. McClure v. Reagan, 454 U.S. 1025 (1981).

Judicial Council Sanctions

Statutory procedures are available for judges to retire on grounds of disability. If a judge fails to certify to the President his disability, a majority of the members of the judicial council of his circuit may sign a certificate of disability and submit it to the President. Once the President finds that the judge is "unable to discharge efficiently all the duties of his office by reason of permanent mental or physical disability," and that an additional judge is needed, the President may make the appointment with the advice and consent of the Senate. 28 U.S.C. § 372(b). Under this procedure the "disabled" judge remains in office.

Each judicial council is authorized to make all necessary orders for the effective administration of court business. Judges "shall promptly carry into effect all orders of the judicial council." 28 U.S.C. § 332(d)(2). The judicial council for the Tenth Circuit relied on this provision in the 1960s to order Judge Stephen S. Chandler of the Western District of Oklahoma to "take no action whatsoever in any case or proceeding now or hereafter pending in his court." The order did not remove Chandler from office; instead, it removed the office from him. In 1966 the Supreme Court denied an application to stay the council's order. Chandler v. Judicial Council, 382 U.S. 1003 (1966). The judicial council later modified its order, allowing Chandler to retain his cases but withholding any new assignments. The

---

9. Hastings v. Judicial Conference of United States, 593 F.Supp. 1371 (D.D.C. 1984); In the Matter of Certain Complaints Under Investigation, 783 F.2d 1488 (11th Cir. 1986).

Judicial Councils Investigating Judges

... [W]e believe that Congress [in the 1980 statute] could reasonably have determined that some internal procedure for investigating complaints against members of the judiciary was not only in the public interest but was important to the continued independence of the judiciary as a whole. Judges have very substantial powers and are supported at public expense. Today, some kind of complaint procedure exists with respect to state judges in every state in the union. The judiciary as a whole, including the colleagues of complained-against judges, has an interest in seeing that non-frivolous complaints are looked into, to the end that the judge, and the system he exemplifies, be exonerated or, if not, that the public perceive that the system has undertaken to police itself, within constitutional limits, of course. Absent any form of judicial complaint procedure, courts would be virtually alone among public and professional occupations in lacking a means to clean house. The increase in the number of judges coupled with the increase in the complexity of judicial work and of courts, all suggest that some mechanism for looking into complaints is necessary and reasonable, if only to enable the courts themselves to sort out their own shortcomings and make the necessary administrative adjustments. In fact, a credible internal complaint procedure can be viewed as essential to maintaining the institutional independence of the courts. If judges cannot or will not keep their own house in order, pressures from the public and legislature might result in withdrawal of needed financial support or in the creation of investigatory mechanisms outside the judicial branch which, to a greater degree than the Act, would threaten judicial independence. Considerations of this sort were at the heart of the present legislation.

SOURCE: In the Matter of Certain Complaints Under Investigation, 783 F.2d 1488, 1507 (11th Cir. 1986).

Supreme Court denied a motion by Chandler to nullify the new order. Chandler v. Judicial Council, 398 U.S. 74 (1970).

By 1979 all judicial councils had implemented rules for the processing of complaints against federal judges. Building on this system, Congress passed legislation in 1980 that assigns to the councils the responsibility for investigating charges against judges. The statute contemplates charges of inefficiency or ineffectiveness resulting from mental or physical disability (conditions that may not be impeachable). The legislation does not encompass complaints regarding the merits of a decision or the conduct of judges unconnected with their judicial duties.[10] The 1980 statute was upheld by a district court in 1984 and by the Eleventh Circuit in 1986. The latter court argued that investigation by judicial councils *increased* judicial independence (see box).[11]

The statute also allows a judicial council, after determining that a judge has engaged in conduct constituting one or more grounds for impeachment, to certify this determination for the Judicial Conference, which may then present a report to the House of Representatives for possible impeachment proceedings. This statutory procedure was upheld by a federal appellate court in 1987. Hastings v. Judicial Conference of United States, 829 F.2d 91 (D.C. Cir. 1987). The Judicial Conference invoked the statute in 1987 to vote unanimously for a recommendation to the House of Representatives that it consider impeaching U.S. District Court Judge Hastings. A year later, the House acted to impeach him, and in 1989 he was removed by the Senate.

---

10. 94 Stat. 2035 (1980). See S. Rept. No. 362, 96th Cong., 1st Sess. (1979) and H. Rept. No. 1313, 96th Cong., 2d Sess. (1980).

11. Hastings v. Judicial Conference of the United States, 593 F.Supp. 1371 (D.D.C. 1984). This decision was vacated in part and remanded in Hastings v. Judicial Conference of the United States, 770 F.2d 1093 (D.C. Cir. 1985). The appellate court ruled that the question of constitutionality of the 1980 statute was premature. The Eleventh Circuit not only upheld the statute but regarded it as a means of protecting judicial independence. In the Matter of Certain Complaints Under Investigation, 783 F.2d 1488 (11th Cir. 1986).

Judges Nixon and Hastings continued to challenge their removals. Nixon brought an action claiming that his conviction in the Senate was void because he was not granted a trial before the full Senate. Instead, he was first examined by a twelve-member Senate committee. The lower courts held that the Senate's procedure was not justiciable. Nixon v. United States, 744 F.Supp. 9 (D.D.C. 1990); Nixon v. United States, 938 F.2d 239 (D.C. Cir. 1991). To the surprise of many, the Supreme Court granted cert to hear the case. Later, a federal district judge reviewed a similar complaint by Judge Hastings and decided that the Senate procedure violated elementary notions of fairness and due process associated with a trial. Hastings v. United States, 802 F.Supp. 491 (D.D.C. 1992). In 1993 the Supreme Court held that the Senate had sole discretion to choose the procedures to be used for impeachment, including the use of a committee to take testimony and gather evidence. Nixon v. United States, 506 U.S. 224 (1993). (This decision appears as a reading in Chapter 3, in the section on political questions.)

U.S. District Court Judge Robert Aguilar was convicted of illegally disclosing a wiretap. Although an appellate court reversed that conviction, Aguilar's conviction was reinstated by the Supreme Court in 1995. United States v. Aguilar, 515 U.S. 593 (1995). In 1996, the Justice Department dropped the charges in return for Aguilar's resignation. Legal Times, July 8, 1996, at 8.

In 2002, the Supreme Court denied cert to a case involving an action by the Judicial Council of the Fifth Circuit, which reprimanded a federal district judge and suspended him from hearing new cases for a year because of "intemperate, abusive and intimidating" treatment of lawyers and other judges. McBryde v. Committee to Review Circuit Council Conduct, 264 F.3d 52 (D.C. Cir. 2001), cert. denied, 537 U.S. 821 (2002).

Compensation

Judicial independence would count for little if the salaries of judges could be cut by legislators. Federal judges appointed to Article III courts are entitled to a compensation "which shall not be diminished during their Continuance in Office." In Federalist No. 79, Hamilton said that next to permanency in office "nothing can contribute more to the independence of the judges than a fixed provision for their support.... In the general course of human nature, a power over a man's subsistence amounts to a power over his will." That principle had been embodied in the Declaration of Independence, which attacked the British King for making colonial judges "dependent on his Will alone, for the Tenure of their Offices, and the Amount and Payment of their Salaries."

The No-Diminution Clause of the Constitution was challenged in 1802 when Congress repealed the Judiciary Act of the previous year. The effect was to abolish 16 circuit judges and their salaries. Supporters of the repeal argued that it was irrational to expect a judge to hold office during good behavior and to continue receiving payment if the office no longer existed. A salary could not exist without an office. A case challenging the right of Congress to abolish the circuit courts reached the Supreme Court in 1803, but the Court declined to overturn the statute. Stuart v. Laird, 5 U.S. (1 Cr.) 298 (1803).

In 1920, the Supreme Court held that a federal income tax levied against Article III judges unconstitutionally diminished their salaries. Justice Holmes, in a dissent that would later become the majority position, denied that the No-Diminution Clause relieved federal judges "from the ordinary duties of a citizen." To require someone from the judicial branch to pay taxes like other people "cannot possibly be made an instrument to attack his independence as a judge." Evans v. Gore, 253 U.S. 245, 265 (1920). Nineteen years later the Supreme Court held that a federal tax could be applied to Article III judges. O'Malley v. Woodrough, 307 U.S. 277 (1939).

Nothing in this line of cases prevents Congress from giving judges a smaller pay raise than other federal employees or no increase at all. In 1964 members of Congress raised their pay by $7,500 while limiting the increase for Supreme Court Justices to $4,500. The legislative debate suggests that some members of Congress may have wanted to use the power of the purse to penalize the Court for its recent decisions. However, the smaller raise for the judiciary could be justified on other grounds: the more generous retirement system for the courts, the need for members of Congress to maintain two residences, and the extra costs they bear in traveling home to see constituents. 110 Cong. Rec. 17912, 18032–33 (1964).

As a way to protest their salary levels, 140 federal judges brought an action in the 1970s to argue that their salaries had been diminished unconstitutionally because pay had not kept pace with inflation. The courts dismissed this claim as meritless. Atkins v. United States, 556 F.2d 1028 (Ct. Cl. 1977), cert. denied, 434 U.S. 1009 (1978). Another case arose when Congress, in four consecutive years (1976–1979), passed statutes to stop or reduce scheduled cost-of-living increases for all federal employees, including judges. A number of federal judges filed suit, claiming that these actions violated the No-Diminution Clause. In 1980 the Supreme Court held that Congress, under the provisions of the salary statutes, could disapprove scheduled pay increases for the judiciary provided it acted before October 1 of a new fiscal year (when they automatically took effect). The Court allowed two of the statutory actions taken prior to October 1 and struck down two others that came too late. United States v. Will, 449 U.S. 200 (1980).

As a result of this decision, judicial salaries moved well ahead of executive and legislative pay schedules. Congress retaliated in 1981 by passing legislation to require specific congressional authorization before any future pay raise for federal judges could take effect. The language effectively eliminated future automatic increases for the judiciary. 95 Stat. 1200, § 140 (1981). A subsequent statute allowed judicial salaries to be increased unless Congress, within a 30-day period, passed a joint resolution of disapproval. 99 Stat. 1322, § 135 (1985). Congress used that procedure in 1989 to defeat a substantial raise for all federal officials, including judges. Later that year, however, it passed legislation that authorized pay increases for all three branches. 103 Stat. 1763–71 (1989).

Beginning in 1994, members of Congress denied themselves a cost-of-living increase. Since federal district judges are tied to the same salary as a member of Congress, the effect was to deny increases for the judiciary as well. Congress denied itself those increases in 1995 and 1996. When Congress voted itself a pay raise in 1997, it neglected to include judges. "Congress, but Not Judiciary, Receives an Increase in Pay," The New York Times, October 21, 1997, at A23. The following month Congress included a cost-of-living increase for federal judges. 111 Stat. 2493, § 306 (1997).

In 1998, federal judges went to court to win a cost-of-living pay increase and prevailed in district court. Williams v. United States, 48 F.Supp.2d 52 (D.D.C. 1999). However, that victory was overturned two years later by the U.S. Court of Appeals for the Federal Circuit. The Supreme Court denied cert on March 4, 2002. Williams v. United States, 240 F.3d 1019 (Fed. Cir. 2001), cert. denied, 535 U.S. 911 (2002).

State judges have been denied regular pay increases. On June 11, 2008, a New York court reviewed the record of the governor's office and the legislative branch in depriving the judiciary of a salary adjustment for almost a decade. It decided that the refusal to act demonstrated an abuse of power and an unconstitutional interference with the independence of the judiciary. Inaction amounted to a 30% decrease in judicial salaries. Having so held, the court expected the two elected branches to take the appropriate remedial steps within 90 days. Larabee v. Governor of the State of New York, 2008 N.Y., Slip Op 28217. In 2010, the New York Court of Appeals held that the legislative and executive branches had undermined the independence of the judicial branch by tying the pay raise of judges to unrelated legislation, including bills to increase the salaries of legislators. In August 2011, a state commission decided to increase the pay of New York State judges by 27 percent over a three-year period. N.Y. Times, August 27, 2011, at A17.

E. JUDICIAL LOBBYING

To preserve their reputation for impartiality, objectivity, and independence, judges traditionally abstain from political activities that are the daily fare of executives and legislators. Judicial activities, both on and off the bench, are expected to be free from impropriety and the *appearance* of impropriety.

This principle is strained by the manner of recruiting judges. Before coming to the bench, most judges have been active in legislatures, government agencies, and other political activities. They are unlikely, upon confirmation, to behave like a cloistered judge. Nor should they. Legislation often has a direct bearing on the courts, justifying the active participation of judges at the bill-drafting and congressional-hearing stages. Canon 4 of the American Bar Association's Code of Judicial Conduct permits a judge to "appear at a public hearing before an executive or legislative body or official on matters concerning the law, the legal system, and the administration of justice," and they may "otherwise consult with an executive or legislative body or official, but only on matters concerning the administration of justice" and never by casting doubt on their capacity to decide impartially any issue that may come before them. See 2 O.L.C. 30 (1978).

Frankfurter's Activities

With the 1982 release of *The Brandeis/Frankfurter Connection* by Bruce Allen Murphy, the public learned that Justice Brandeis, over a period of years, had secretly paid more than $50,000 to Felix Frankfurter to advance Brandeis's political agenda. The financial arrangement ended when Brandeis left the Court in 1939. Frankfurter joined the Court that year and remained deeply enmeshed in politics. He drafted legislative proposals for the Roosevelt administration, helped staff the upper echelons of the War Department, and assisted Roosevelt's reelection campaign in 1940.

The details of Frankfurter's activities were particularly ironic. As a member of the Court, he described himself as a "political eunuch," claiming that the Court "has no excuse for being unless it's a monastery." In 1944 he confided to a friend that "I have an austere and even sacerdotal view of the position of a judge on this Court, and that means I have nothing to say on matters that come within a thousand miles of what may fairly be called politics." Murphy, The Brandeis/Frankfurter Connection 9, 259–69. In a dissenting opinion, Frankfurter insisted that the authority of the Supreme Court depended on its "complete detachment, in fact and in appearance, from political entanglements." Baker v. Carr, 369 U.S. 186, 267 (1962). Despite such protestations, few Justices have been as politically active as Frankfurter.

Other Justices also participated in off-the-bench activities. The contacts between Brandeis and President Franklin D. Roosevelt had already been noted in the literature.[12] Taft, Frankfurter, Byrnes, and Fortas, while on the Court, met frequently with Presidents and discussed public issues.[13]

Other Political Activities

Much earlier examples illustrate the difficulty that some members of the Supreme Court have had in drawing a line between law and politics. During the Court's first two decades, individual Justices campaigned for political candidates, ran for political office, and accepted political duties that came their way. Chief Justice John Jay was sent as special envoy to negotiate a treaty with England. Chief Justice Oliver Ellsworth followed that precedent by negotiating a treaty with France. Murphy, The Brandeis/Frankfurter Connection 345–63.

After Chief Justice Marshall issued his decision in *McCulloch* v. *Maryland* (1819), arguing in favor of broad implied powers for the federal government, a series of anonymous articles appeared in a

---

12. Philippa Strum, "Justice Brandeis and President Roosevelt," reprinted in Walter F. Murphy and C. Herman Pritchett, eds., Courts, Judges, and Politics 187–90 (1979).

13. See Max Freedman, ed., Roosevelt and Frankfurter: Their Correspondence (1967); John P. MacKenzie, The Appearance of Justice 1–33 (1974); and "Nonjudicial Activities of Supreme Court Justices and Other Federal Judges," hearings before the Senate Committee on the Judiciary, 91st Cong., 1st Sess. (1969).

Richmond newspaper attacking the decision and championing states' rights. The first few critiques were probably written by William Brockenbrough, a state judge from Virginia. Marshall could not bear to let the charges go unanswered. Working through his colleague Justice Bushrod Washington, Marshall penned a number of anonymous rebuttals (signed "A Friend of the Union") and published them in a Philadelphia newspaper. Four more critiques appeared in the Richmond newspaper, this time by Judge Spencer Roane of the Virginia Court of Appeals (using the pseudonym Hampden). Marshall answered those as well, signing them "A Friend of the Constitution." Gerald Gunther, ed., John Marshall's Defense of *McCulloch* v. *Maryland* (1969). Justice Story, while serving for more than 20 years as president of a Massachusetts branch of the United States Bank, tried to influence Treasury Department officials to secure large deposits in his bank and helped Daniel Webster draft a reply to President Jackson's veto of the Bank's charter in 1832.[14]

Several Justices have agreed to accept presidential requests to head national commissions to study politically controversial matters. In December 1941, President Roosevelt named Justice Owen Roberts to chair a commission to investigate the Japanese attack on Pearl Harbor. Roberts' performance was subject to harsh critiques. Martin V. Melosi, The Shadow of Pearl Harbor 31–46, 97–98 (1977); Gordon W. Prange, At Dawn We Slept 592–604 (1981). Chief Justice Earl Warren, after voicing substantial objections to serving as head of a commission to investigate the assassination of President John F. Kennedy, agreed to do so. Earl Warren, The Memoirs of Earl Warren 356 (1977). See Wendy E. Ackerman, "Separation of Powers and Judicial Service on Presidential Commissions," 53 U. Chi. L. Rev. 993 (1986).

Many avenues are available to Justices who want to affect the course of political events. Public addresses, law review articles, and contacts with reporters, scholars, and magazine writers are methods of extending judicial influence beyond official actions. The Chief Justice prepares an annual "year-ender," summing up the problems, needs, and accomplishments of federal courts. He also delivers an annual report on the state of the judiciary, sometimes using these forums to criticize Congress for its actions and inactions. Proposals have been introduced for an annual "State of the Judiciary" address, to be delivered by the Chief Justice to a joint session of Congress. This proposal passed the Senate in 1980, but the House took no action. 126 Cong. Rec. 23397 (1980).

Judicial Conference

The Judicial Conference is the principal institutional body for preparing a legislative agenda. The organization dates back to 1922, when Congress directed the Chief Justice to call an annual conference of the senior circuit judges. The objective was to make a comprehensive survey of cases pending before the federal courts: their number and character, cases disposed of, and backlog. The potential for judicial lobbying did not go unnoticed. Representative Clarence F. Lea predicted that the Conference "will become the propaganda organization for legislation for the benefit of the Federal judiciary." 62 Cong. Rec. 203 (1921).

As the law now reads, the Chief Justice submits to Congress "an annual report of the proceedings of the Judicial Conference and its recommendations for legislation." 28 U.S.C. § 331 (2000). These reports are prepared for the spring and fall meetings of the Conference. Because the meetings are largely devoted to administrative and legislative matters rather than judicial duties, there has been pressure to open them to the public. Opponents of this reform proposal concede that the Conference is a creature of Congress and subject to further statutory change, but they argue that the principle of judicial independence should protect the proceedings of the Judicial Conference. The Conference came under fire in 1984 for improper lobbying, including a private group called the Federal Judges Association, but a GAO investigation found no legal violation. 63 Comp. Gen. 624 (1984).

---

14. G. Edward White, The American Political Tradition 41 (1976); Gerald T. Dunne, Justice Joseph Story and the Rise of the Supreme Court 301–02, 328–31 (1970).

Rehnquist Lobbies the House

Chief Justice William H. Rehnquist yesterday took the unusual step of asking House members to reject a Senate-passed provision that would make most handgun murders a federal crime that carries the death penalty.

Rehnquist's lobbying effort against two provisions of the Senate's crime bill came as the House Judiciary Committee prepared for a drafting session Monday on its version of anti-crime legislation.

The Senate bill would authorize prosecution of handgun murders as federal crimes punishable by death. The provision introduced by Sen. Alfonse D'Amato (R-N.Y.) would apply to all murders committed with handguns that moved across state lines....

A statement accompanying Rehnquist's letter said the D'Amato amendments "will swamp the federal courts with routine cases that states are better equipped to handle, and will weaken the ability of the federal courts effectively to deal with difficult criminal cases that present uniquely federal issues."...

SOURCE: "Rehnquist Asks House Members to Reject Senate Handgun Bill," Washington Post, September 21, 1991, at A2.

Chief Justice Initiatives

The lobbying activities of Chief Justice Burger attracted press attention in 1978. On the eve of a Senate vote on the bankruptcy bill, he called Senator Dennis DeConcini and several other members of the Senate Judiciary Committee. DeConcini told reporters that Burger accused him of being "irresponsible" for supporting the legislation and said that the bill "was a political sale and he was going to the President and have him veto it." Calling the charge "a slap in the face of the entire Senate," DeConcini described Burger as being "very, very irate and rude." He "just screamed at me" and "not only lobbied, but pressured and attempted to be intimidating."[15] Representative Don Edwards, head of the House subcommittee responsible for the bankruptcy bill, said that he welcomed the views of judges but only when presented in "a scholarly, judicious way, in writing or in hearings, not in telephone calls once a bill has gone to the floor."[16]

Within a month, while accepting an award in New York City, Burger defended his participation in the legislative process (see Burger reading). He also resisted activities he viewed as inappropriate. In 1981, a number of federal judges wanted to form an association to lobby Congress for higher salaries and fringe benefits. Interested judges would contribute $200 and list the members of Congress they felt comfortable contacting about judicial salaries. Burger advised the judges that the position of the federal judiciary should be expressed through the Judicial Conference.[17]

Chief Justice Rehnquist took a leading role in advocating legislation to reform appellate procedures for the death penalty. In 1989, instead of waiting for the Judicial Conference to submit its report and recommendations to Congress, Rehnquist took the initiative in sending to Congress a report prepared by a committee of federal judges he had appointed. Some judges interpreted his move as an end run around the Judicial Conference. Rehnquist's effort to expedite the legislative process was unsuccessful; serious divisions continued within Congress and the Judicial Conference on the proper legislative remedy. In 1991, Rehnquist intervened to ask members of the House of Representatives to reject a handgun bill because it would strain the federal courts (see box). In 2000, he urged Congress to end an eleven-year ban on speaking honoraria for federal judges.

---

15. "Senator Slams Burger on Move to Thwart Bill," National Law Journal, October 16, 1978; "Burger Wants Judges to Speak Up to Congress," Washington Post, October 26, 1978, at A13.

16. "Lobbying by Burger Provokes Criticism," New York Times, November 19, 1978, at 39.

17. "U.S. Judges Want Lobby; Burger Against Proposal," National Law Journal, June 29, 1981, at 2, 10.

Burger on Judicial Lobbying

On October 25, 1978, while accepting the Fordham-Stein Award in New York City, Chief Justice Burger delivered the following remarks on the proper boundaries of judicial intervention in the legislative process.

. . .

From time to time the question comes up as to whether the activities of those of our profession who are judges and who try to see that the needs of the courts are met in some way violate the concept of separation of powers.

I hope that you will not mind if I reflect with you tonight on the real meaning of the separation of powers in our tripartite constitutional system—and what it does not mean.

Justice Jackson had some relevant observations on this subject:

"While the Constitution diffuses power the better to secure liberty, it also contemplates that practice will integrate the dispersed powers into a workable government. It enjoins upon its branches separateness but interdependence, autonomy but reciprocity."

The separation of powers concept was never remotely intended to preclude cooperation, coordination, communication and joint efforts by the members of each branch with the members of the others. Examples of this are legion: The executive, represented by the Solicitor General, volunteers, or is invited by the Supreme Court, to file briefs advising the Supreme Court on questions of law. This happens countless times each term. Members of the Congress—sometimes singly, sometimes a dozen or more of them together—file briefs *amicus curiae* before the Court, advising us how a matter should be decided. These briefs are always welcomed by the Court.

We all remember that President Washington formally asked the Supreme Court for advice on certain policy questions but wisely the Court decided that it would not advise him on such matters. Justices have come to realize that they should avoid advising Presidents and the Congress on substantive policy questions but on matters relating to the courts there must be joint consultation. The separation of powers does not preclude such consultation.

From the beginning of the republic, members of the Congress have appeared as advocates before the Supreme Court. Indeed, they have been some of our great advocates, from Daniel Webster, Henry Clay and John Quincy Adams, and later William Seward. Webster was a Senator when he argued the famous *Dartmouth College* case. In more recent times other Senators, including Sam Ervin and William Saxbe, have appeared.

To be sure, there is a great and necessary tradition of insulation of judges and Justices from political activities generally. But participation in legislative and executive decisions which affect the judicial system is an absolute obligation of judges, as it is of lawyers. One manifestation of the desirable aloofness of judges from controversy is found in the tradition that they do not answer criticism or respond to attacks, no matter how scurrilous or unwarranted. But reasons for refusing to answer attacks must not be used as reasons to abdicate responsibility when Congress is legislating on matters directly affecting the courts. Indeed, the contrary is most emphatically true.

It is entirely appropriate for judges to comment upon issues which affect the courts. The Judicial Conference of the United States and the Administrative Office of the United States Courts receive requests from Congress from fifty to one hundred times each year to comment on pending bills.

Historically, the most valuable judicial improvements are made when the judiciary makes proposals and consults with Congress. Indeed, even after Congress acts, the President regularly requests the views of the Judicial Conference before he passes on legislation which relates to the federal courts. This has been going on for nearly two hundred years. It was more than forty years ago that Congress created the Judicial Conference of the United States, which as you know is made up of twenty-five judges from district courts, courts of appeals and special courts. It made the Chief Justice of the United States the chairman of that Conference. It meets approximately five or six days each year. It has committees dealing with special subjects—a committee on court administration, a committee on appellate rules, on criminal rules, on civil rules, on bankruptcy, on magistrates and similar subjects. These committees regularly confer with Congress and its staffs and the executive branch.

In creating the Judicial Conference, it was contemplated that the Conference would comment on legislation directly affecting the operation of the federal judicial system. The Conference has been doing that routinely for more than forty years. Any notion, therefore, that each of these branches should remain in solitary isolation or logic-tight compartments has no basis in reason, law, history or tradition....

NOTES AND QUESTIONS

1. The framers of the Constitution provided structural mechanisms such as tenure during "good Behavior" and protection from salary cuts as a means of promoting judicial independence. Still, the combination of presidential nomination and Senate confirmation of judges assures an intensely political process. Should Senators "defer" to presidential choices? If not, what independent standards should the Senate impose?

2. What degree of judicial independence is appropriate in a democratic republic? Given the confirmation process and the type of cases decided by the judiciary, can it be anything other than a "political" branch? When should federal judges, lacking ballot-box legitimacy, push legal and constitutional issues to the elected branches and the public for resolution?

3. Various individuals and organizations influence the selection of judges. Do you believe it is appropriate for a sitting member of the Court to suggest to the President names of potential nominees? May it be argued that, by reason of their experience and expertise, that sitting Justices are better equipped than most to make such suggestions?

4. In recent confirmation hearings, nominees to the Supreme Court typically claim they will approach issues with "an open mind" and they have "no agenda." Yet Presidents routinely search for nominees to promote specific values and principles. How realistic is it to expect nominees, once on the Bench, to treat each legal dispute independently and without reference to a broader framework?

5. What level of judicial lobbying is appropriate? When does it undermine the reputation and integrity of the judiciary?

SELECTED READINGS

ABRAHAM, HENRY J. Justices and Presidents: A Political History of Appointments to the Supreme Court. New York: Oxford University Press, 1974.

BALL, HOWARD. Courts and Politics: The Federal Judicial System. Englewood Cliffs, N.J.: Prentice-Hall, 1980.

BLACK, CHARLES L., JR. "A Note on Senatorial Consideration of Supreme Court Nominees." 79 Yale Law Journal 657 (1970).

BUSHNELL, ELEANORE. Crimes, Follies, and Misfortunes: The Federal Impeachment Trials. Champaign, Ill.: University of Illinois Press, 1992.

CARP, ROBERT A., AND C. K. ROWLAND. Policymaking and Politics in the Federal District Courts. Knoxville: University of Tennessee Press, 1983.

CHASE, HAROLD W. Federal Judges: The Appointing Process. Minneapolis: University of Minnesota, 1972.

DANELSKI, DAVID J. A Supreme Court Justice Is Appointed. New York: Random House, 1964.

EARLY, STEPHEN T., JR. Constitutional Courts of the U.S. Totowa, N.J.: Littlefield, Adams, 1977.

FISH, PETER GRAHAM. The Politics of Federal Judicial Administration. Princeton, N.J.: Princeton University Press, 1973.

GERHARDT, MICHAEL J. The Federal Impeachment Process: A Constitutional and Historical Analysis. Princeton University Press, 1996.

GROSSMAN, JOEL B. Lawyers and Judges: The ABA and the Politics of Judicial Selection. New York: Wiley, 1965.

HARRIS, JOSEPH P. The Advice and Consent of the Senate. Berkeley: University of California Press, 1953.

HAYNES, EVAN. The Selection and Tenure of Judges. Newark, N.J.: National Conference of Judicial Councils, 1944.

HOWARD, J. WOODFORD, JR. Courts of Appeals in the Federal Judicial System. Princeton, N.J.: Princeton University Press, 1981.

HULBARY, WILLIAM E., AND THOMAS G. WALKER. "The Supreme Court Selection Process: Presidential Motivations and Judicial Performance." 33 Western Political Quarterly 185 (1980).

KAHN, MICHAEL A. "The Politics of the Appointment Process: An Analysis of Why Learned Hand Was Never Appointed to the Supreme Court." 25 Stanford Law Review 251 (1973).

KURLAND, PHILIP B. "The Constitution and the Tenure of Federal Judges: Some Notes From History." 36 University of Chicago Law Review 665 (1969).

MASON, ALPHEUS THOMAS. "Extra-Judicial Work for Judges: The Views of Chief Justice Stone." 67 Harvard Law Review 193 (1953).

MURPHY, WALTER. "In His Own Image: Mr. Chief Justice Taft and Supreme Court Appointments." 1961 Supreme Court Review 159.

REHNQUIST, WILLIAM H. Grand Inquests: The Historical Impeachments of Justice Samuel Chase and President Andrew Johnson. New York: Morrow & Co., 1992.

SCHMIDHAUSER, JOHN R. "The Justices of the Supreme Court: A Collective Portrait." 3 Midwest Journal of Political Science 1 (1959).

———. Judges and Justices: The Federal Appellate Judiciary. Boston: Little, Brown, 1979.

SCIGLIANO, ROBERT. The Supreme Court and the Presidency. New York: The Free Press, 1971.

SOLLENBERGER, MITCHEL A. Judicial Appointments and Democratic Controls. Durham: Carolina Academic Press, 2011.

TRIBE, LAURENCE H. God Save This Honorable Court. New York: Random House, 1985.

WHEELER, RUSSELL. "Extrajudicial Activities of the Early Supreme Court." 1973 Supreme Court Review 123.

WINTERS, GLENN R., ed. Selected Readings: Judicial Selection and Tenure. Chicago: American Judicature Society, 1973.

5

Decision Making: Process and Strategy

Publication of *The Brethren: Inside the Supreme Court* in 1979 promised a rare glimpse into the inner sanctum of the Supreme Court. The authors claimed that for nearly two centuries the Supreme Court had made its decisions "in absolute secrecy." In fact, the deliberative process of the Court had been studied and scrutinized from the start. Scholars have access to internal memoranda, conference notes, diaries, draft opinions, and correspondence by the Justices. Members of the Court and their law clerks publish widely. Drawing on those materials, we have a fairly detailed picture of the process that Justices use to make decisions.[1]

The Supreme Court begins its term on the first Monday in October and ends in late June or early July of the following year. A term is designated by the October date. For example, the 2010 term began October 4, 2010. Over a period of approximately nine months, the Court selects cases, hears oral argument, writes opinions, and announces decisions. After recessing for the summer, the Justices continue to review petitions in preparation for the new term and decide emergency petitions brought to their attention. Although decisions by the Supreme Court require a quorum of six, in certain cases individual Justices may stay the enforcement of lower court orders and give aggrieved parties time to petition the full Court for review. Each Justice performs other duties when assigned to one of their judicial circuits.

On rare occasions the Court convenes in the summer in special session to deal with urgent matters. For example, the Court met on July 29–30, 1942, to hear argument for nine hours on the Nazi saboteur case. Ex parte Quirin, 317 U.S. 1 (1942). On June 18, 1953, it considered Justice Douglas' stay in the execution of Ethel and Julius Rosenberg, convicted of delivering atomic bomb information to the then Soviet Union. On the following day the Court vacated the stay and the Rosenbergs were executed hours later. Another special session occurred on August 28, 1958, when the Court convened to consider a lower court order enforcing a desegregation plan for Little Rock High School. The Court unanimously upheld the lower court on September 12, three days before the school's scheduled opening. Cooper v. Aaron, 358 U.S. 1 (1958). On July 8, 1974, the Court held oral argument on the Watergate tapes case, deciding on July 24 that President Nixon had to surrender the tapes to prosecutors. United States v. Nixon, 418 U.S. 683 (1974). He resigned from office on August 9.

---

1. Bob Woodward and Scott Armstrong, The Brethren: Inside the Supreme Court 1 (1979). Of many commendable studies published before *The Brethren,* special note should be made of J. Woodford Howard, Jr., Mr. Justice Murphy 231–496 (1968); Walter F. Murphy, Elements of Judicial Strategy (1964); and Alpheus Thomas Mason, Harlan Fiske Stone: Pillar of the Law (1956). See also H. W. Perry, Jr., Deciding to Decide: Agenda Setting in the United States Supreme Court (1991); Bernard Schwartz, Decision: How the Supreme Court Decides Cases (1996); Edward Lazarus, Closed Chambers: The First Eyewitness Account of the Epic Struggles Inside the Supreme Court (1998); Jeffrey Toobin, The Nine: Inside the Secret World of the Supreme Court (2007).

A. JURISDICTION: ORIGINAL AND APPELLATE

The Constitution assigns to the Supreme Court judicial power in "all Cases, in Law and Equity, arising under this Constitution, the Laws of the United States, and Treaties made, or which shall be made under their Authority...." The types of cases identified in the Constitution affect (1) ambassadors, other public ministers, and consuls; (2) admiralty and maritime controversies; (3) controversies in which the United States is a party; and (4) controversies between two or more states, between a state and a citizen of another state, between citizens of different states, between citizens of the same state claiming lands under grants of different states, and between a state (or its citizens) and foreign states, citizens, or subjects.

This jurisdiction is divided between original and appellate. In all cases affecting ambassadors, other public ministers, and consuls, and those in which a state is a party, the Supreme Court has original jurisdiction. These cases may be taken directly to the Court without action by lower courts. Only rarely does a case of original jurisdiction concern ambassadors, diplomats, and consuls. Most of the cases involve litigation between states, such as disputes over boundaries and water rights. In the early days, original cases were tried before a jury in the Supreme Court. Georgia v. Brailsford, 3 U.S. (3 Dall.) 1 (1794). That practice was soon abandoned.

"Original" appears to imply exclusivity, suggesting that what is granted by the Constitution cannot be abridged or altered by Congress. Nevertheless, Congress has passed legislation that divides original jurisdiction into two categories: (1) original and exclusive jurisdiction, and (2) original but not exclusive jurisdiction. 28 U.S.C. § 1251. For the latter, lower federal courts share concurrent jurisdiction.

Congress has restricted the jurisdiction of federal courts by establishing criteria for "federal questions." Until 1980, certain federal court cases required at least $10,000 in dispute. The purpose was to reduce case congestion in federal courts. That amount was eliminated in 1980. 94 Stat. 2369. Congress wanted to resolve the anomaly faced by persons whose rights had been violated but were barred from the courts because they had not suffered a sufficient economic injury. Congress has established a dollar threshold of $75,000 for "diversity" jurisdiction (where federal courts consider cases involving state law if the parties are from different states). 28 U.S.C. § 1332.

Court jurisdiction may seem like a technical matter of interest only to specialists and practitioners of the law, but jurisdiction translates into political power. A question of jurisdiction provoked the first constitutional amendment adopted after the Bill of Rights. In 1793 the Court held that states could be sued in federal courts by citizens of another state. Chisholm v. Georgia, 2 Dall. (2 U.S.) 419. The public outcry was so deep and swift that the Eleventh Amendment, overriding *Chisholm*, passed both Houses of Congress in 1794 and was ratified in 1795. (Congressional efforts to withdraw jurisdiction from the courts are covered in the final chapter, "Efforts to Curb the Court.")

Dockets

Each year the Supreme Court receives about 9,000 petitions for review. A few cases concern original jurisdiction and are placed on the Original Docket. Original jurisdiction is used sparingly to protect the Court's workload with its appellate docket. The Court is especially reluctant to become a court of first instance and assume the fact-finding function of a trial court, a task for which the Court considers itself "ill-equipped." Ohio v. Wyandotte, 401 U.S. 493, 498 (1971). To assist in the handling of its original jurisdiction docket, the Court usually appoints special masters to study an issue and present recommendations.

Cases reach the Supreme Court by one of four routes. First, some parties come to the Court as a matter of statutory right. Congress has passed a number of statutes that provide for direct appeal, preferred treatment, and expedited action. In recent years, however, Congress has begun converting some of these statutes to discretionary review. H. Rept. No. 824 (Part 1), 97th Cong., 2d Sess. 6 (1982). After the Court urged Congress to grant even greater discretion, Congress passed legislation in 1988 to substantially eliminate the Court's mandatory or obligatory jurisdiction. 102 Stat. 662 (1988). To handle its workload, the Court often disposes of cases without written opinion.

Writs of certiorari are a second route to the Supreme Court. By "granting cert" the Court calls up the records of a lower court, a decision that is wholly discretionary.

Third, petitions for review are submitted by indigents, including prison inmates, sometimes in the form of handwritten notes. These requests, called *in forma pauperis* (in the manner of a pauper), numbered a few dozen in 1930 but now range in the thousands each term. To discourage nuisance suits by indigents who file dozens of petitions and motions, the Court can require indigents to pay the normal $300 filing fee when they seek "extraordinary writs" in excess of normal requests. In re Sindram, 498 U.S. 177 (1991). Subsequently, the Court changed its rules to allow it to reject filings by indigents if filings are frivolous or malicious (Rule 39.8).

Fourth, an appellate court may submit a writ of certification to seek instruction on a question of law. 28 U.S.C. § 1254. This procedure is seldom used, for it forces the Court to decide questions of law without the guidance of findings and conclusions by the lower courts.

B. THE WRIT OF CERTIORARI

The Supreme Court controls its workload largely by exercising discretionary authority over cases coming to it for review. The discretionary writ of certiorari was initiated by the Evarts Act of 1891 and the Judicial Code of 1911, but the primary source of discretion awaited the "Judges Bill" of 1925. That statute eliminated direct review by the Supreme Court of decisions in the district courts and greatly expanded the use of the writ of certiorari. 43 Stat. 936 (1925).

Most of the decisions of the Supreme Court involve "cert" denials. Under Rule 10 of the Supreme Court, a review on writ of certiorari "is not a matter of right, but of judicial discretion" and will be granted "only for compelling reasons." Among the reasons listed in Rule 10 are conflicts among federal courts of appeals, between a federal court of appeals and a state court of last resort, and over federal questions decided by different state courts of last resort. Justices look for cases that pose questions of general importance: broad issues on the administration of the law, substantive constitutional questions, the construction of important federal statutes, and serious questions of public law. In a 1949 address, Chief Justice Vinson advised lawyers who prepare cert petitions to spend "a little less time discussing the merits of their cases and a little more time demonstrating why it is important that the Court should hear them.... If [a petition for certiorari] only succeeds in demonstrating that the decision below may be erroneous, it has not fulfilled its purpose." 69 S.Ct. vi (1949). Lawyers learn how to get the Court's attention (reading by Lauter).

Other factors explain why the Court grants cert. The literature on "cue theory" points to a key ingredient: the federal government's decision to seek review. The Court relies heavily on the seasoned judgment of the Solicitor General to bring only those cases that merit appeal. When that factor combines with other elements (the presence of a civil liberty issue, conflict between circuits, a lower court decision in which judges are divided), granting a petition is even more likely (see box on next page).

At various times in its history, the Court has accepted an issue from a lower court because it appeared that the executive and legislative branches were unwilling to act. An appellate judge said that "waiting for the legislature is not productive. The legislature doesn't legislate. Courts have had to do a good deal of stuff that would be better for the legislature to have done. But it's better for courts to do them than no one." J. Woodford Howard, Jr., Courts of Appeals in the Federal Judicial System 163 n. (1981). Presumably the same attitude prevailed on the Supreme Court, but only recently have its members publicly admitted this function. Justice Powell said that judicial independence gives the Court "a freedom to make decisions that perhaps are necessary for our society, decisions that the legislative branch may be reluctant to make." Kenyon College Alumni Bulletin, Summer 1979, at 15. Jus-

Major Reasons for Granting Cert

1. Conflicts among federal appellate courts.

2. Conflicts between federal courts and state courts.

3. State or federal court's holding congressional statute unconstitutional.

4. Substantial constitutional, legal, or political issue.

5. Construction of important federal statute.

6. Submission of a petition by the Solicitor General.

7. Flagrant or egregious abuse of justice in the lower courts.

tice Blackmun elaborated on that point in 1982. Asked whether desegregation was an example of where the courts had to do more because other branches did less, he replied:

> Well, one can come up with a lot of possible examples. That is one. One man, one vote is another one. And many of the sex discrimination cases perhaps are others. If one goes back twenty-five years, certainly things are different because of judicial intervention. I can remember when I was a law clerk a case came up concerning the possibility of a federal judge intervening in the administration of a prison and it was unheard of in those days. That was a problem for the prison administrative authorities. And now, of course, in recent years—and by that I mean twenty years anyway—there have been many instances where the courts, in effect, have taken constitutional rights inside the prison doors.... "A Justice Speaks Out: A Conversation with Harry A. Blackmun," Cable News Network, Inc., conducted November 25, 1982, at 10–11.

Of the approximately 9,000 cases received each year, less than one hundred are accepted for oral argument and full opinions. In other words, more than 98 percent of all petitions are denied. In evaluating the petitions, Justices dismiss many as frivolous and "dead-list" them (denying them "cert") without further deliberation. In recent years the Court has replaced the "dead list" with a "discuss list," which includes the cases deemed worthy of discussion. Any Justice can request that a case be added to the discuss list. Examples of frivolous petitions include: "Are Negroes in fact Indians and therefore entitled to Indians' exemptions from federal income taxes?"; "Are the federal income tax laws unconstitutional insofar as they do not provide a deduction for depletion of the human body?"; and "Does a ban on drivers turning right on a red light constitute an unreasonable burden on interstate commerce?" Brennan, 40 U. Chi. L. Rev. 473, 478 (1973). When an appeal or petition for writ of certiorari is frivolous, the Supreme Court may award appropriate damages or costs to the party sued (Rule 42.2).

Screening Cert Petitions

Justices try to avoid cases where the legal issue is overpowered by emotional ingredients. When the Court reviewed cert petitions in 1975 to clarify the rights available to criminal defendants, it deliberately passed over the petition of someone who had been convicted of strangling, raping, and beheading a woman, followed by an attempt to skin her. Liva Baker, Miranda 105 (1983). It would have been poor judgment for the Court to announce legal principles in the midst of such gruesome circumstances.

Justices depend on their law clerks to prepare memoranda that summarize the facts of a case and recommend acceptance or rejection. Most Justices participate in a "cert pool" to divvy up the work. They meet at a Friday conference to discuss and vote on the petitions that survive initial review. A single Justice may set a case for decision at conference. As a symbol of unity, Justices shake hands upon entering the conference room. These gestures preserve an atmosphere of civility in an institution com-pelled to deal with some of the most fractious issues in society. Maintaining a measure of collegiality among nine strong personalities is no small feat.

To preserve confidentiality in the conference room, only the Justices are present. The junior Jus-tice sits closest to the door, receiving and delivering messages that flow in and out of the room. Some political scientists reported that the rectangular table in the conference room had been chopped into three pieces by Chief Justice Burger and converted into an inverted U, supposedly to prevent the lib-eral Douglas from sitting opposite him in direct confrontation. Justice Powell reassured his readers in 1975 that the conference table "retains its pristine shape; there has been no hacking or sawing; the justices occupy their seats in the traditional order of seniority."[2] Visitors to the room find the table intact.

The Chief Justice begins the discussion of each case. He summarizes the facts, analyzes the law, and announces his proposed vote. He is followed by the other Justices, in order of seniority, from the senior Associate Justice down to the newest Justice. Before the Warren Court, voting was done in the opposite manner: the junior Justice voted first and the Chief Justice last. Toward the end of his service, Warren persuaded the Justices to vote in the same order as they had spoken.[3] Four votes are needed to grant certiorari. There have been cases where the Court grants cert and later, on the basis of changed circumstances, dismisses the writ of certiorari as "improvidently granted." Dis-missing a case in this manner is sometimes called "digging a case" (dig—dismissed as improvidently granted).

Granting cert involves some tactical decisions by Justices. If five Justices are rigidly opposed, the four in favor of granting cert may decide against hearing the case because they know they will lose on the merits. If three Justices feel strongly that cert should be granted, sometimes another Justice will add the fourth vote ("join three"). For "defensive denials," Justices prefer to let some cases at lower levels, even if decided badly, remain as a precedent only for a single circuit, instead of compounding the legal situation with a decision by the Supreme Court. If the Court is in transition from a liberal to a conservative body, a remaining liberal Justice may engage in defensive denials to prevent the Court from overturning liberal precedents. H. W. Perry, Jr., Deciding to Decide 98, 166–70, 198–207 (1991).

Justices address a wide range of complex cases at each conference. They keep a docket sheet to record each step of the process from deciding to hear a case to postconference voting. Conference notes provide a summary record of the arguments of each Justice on the merits of the case. Whoever is selected to draft the opinion can review the conference notes and weave an argument that will at-tract the maximum number of votes. At any point, however, votes may be changed before the opin-ion of the Court reaches its final stage.

In denying cert, the Court seldom offers an explanation. When it does, the reason is usually brief if not cryptic. More light is shed when Justices write a dissenting opinion on cert denials. This prac-tice, which has grown significantly in recent decades, complicates the Court's traditional position that cert denial means a refusal to take a case and nothing more. Darr v. Burford, 339 U.S. 200, 226 (1950). If dissenting Justices strongly voice their reasons and argue the merits, it may appear that the major-ity denying cert considered and rejected those arguments. Justices often differ on the significance to

---

2. Lewis F. Powell, Jr., "Myths and Misconceptions About the Supreme Court," 61 A.B.A.J. 1344 (1975). See Glendon Schubert, Judicial Policy Making 134 (1977) and Howard Ball, Courts and Politics 254 (1980). For a discussion of some of the practices in conference, see William H. Rehnquist, "Sunshine in the Third Branch," 16 Washburn L. J. 559 (1977).

3. Walter F. Murphy and C. Herman Pritchett, eds., Courts, Judges, and Politics 657 (1979). This account is supported by a 1982 interview with Justice Blackmun; "A Justice Speaks Out: A Conversation with Harry A. Blackmun," Cable News Network, Inc., conducted November 25, 1982, at 21. In a 1963 article, Justice Brennan stated that voting began with the junior Justice; William J. Brennan, Jr., "Inside View of the High Court," New York Times Magazine, October 6, 1963, at 100. Justice Clark, in 1956, also said that the junior Justice voted first, 19 F.R.D. 303, 307, as did Justice Frankfurter in 1953, "Chief Justices I Have Known," 39 Va. L. Rev. 883, 903.

be attached to dissents on cert denials.[4] Speculation as to intent is hazardous. Even when Justices think that a lower court is wrong, they may vote to deny an application simply because they regard the federal question as insubstantial, poorly timed for review, or inappropriate because of the need for judicial restraint.

David Lauter
Certiorari Strategies

In the following article, "The Fine Art of Creating a Certiorari Petition," Lauter explains the considerations of obtaining four votes for a successful cert petition. The article appeared in the *National Law Journal*, December 10, 1984.

Several years ago, Bruce J. Ennis, then legal director of the American Civil Liberties Union, wrote a law review article about how to write a brief for the Supreme Court.

The theme of the piece was that a lawyer should not write for an abstract court, but should concentrate on catching the attention of each of the nine justices who actually will be reviewing the case.

Last week, Mr. Ennis ... provided an object lesson on how the job is done, persuading the Supreme Court to grant certiorari in a libel case involving a candidate for U.S. attorney, a man who didn't like him and a letter to President Reagan. *McDonald* v. *Smith*, 84476.

The letter, written in 1980 by Robert McDonald, Mr. Ennis' client, told the president that he should not appoint David I. Smith to the U.S. attorney's job in Greensboro, N.C. Mr. Smith did not get the job, found out about the letter and sued for libel.

Mr. Ennis' argument, so far unsuccessful in federal district court and the 4th U.S. Circuit Court of Appeals, is that Mr. McDonald should be absolutely immune from civil liability for the letter under the First Amendment right to "petition the Government for a redress of grievances." The decisions rejecting that argument appear to be the first times the issue has been considered in federal court.

Mr. Ennis started out with the assumption that Justices William J. Brennan Jr. and Thurgood Marshall, who have been sympathetic to defense claims in libel cases, might be interested in hearing the case. Then he set about trying to find two more votes.

First, he noted, "the court has sort of gotten interested in libel issues again. From a law clerk's perspective it's a very juicy question and I thought the law clerks would push it."

The petition for certiorari made a particular point of emphasizing the venerable nature of the petition clause, arguing that the right to petition is far older than the rights of free speech and press. That argument, Mr. Ennis noted, was specially designed to appeal to the interest that several of the justices have in history. Justices John Paul Stevens and Lewis F. Powell Jr. frequently mention historical antecedents in their opinions as does Chief Justice Warren E. Burger.

In addition, the case posed an unusual conflict between state- and federal-court interpretations of constitutional law that Mr. Ennis hoped would appeal to several other justices.

Two state high courts within the 4th Circuit — West Virginia and Maryland — have held that petitions to the government cannot be the basis for a civil suit. With the 4th Circuit holding the other way, Mr. Ennis' petition argued, federal district courts in those two states sitting in diversity actions would be forced to follow the law of the circuit, rejecting the law of the state, implying "a premise that federal courts have greater wisdom, or at least authority, in interpreting the federal Constitution than do state courts."

"Justice [Sandra Day] O'Connor has written law review articles about the need to allow state court judges to make decisions," Mr. Ennis noted, hoping that argument might particularly appeal to her. In addition, Justice William H. Rehnquist might be interested in the federalism aspect of the argument, he said.

---

4. See differing views of Justices Blackmun and Marshall in United States v. Kras, 409 U.S. 434, 443, 460–61 (1973). Justices Stevens, Brennan, and Stewart objected when the Court gave a brief reason for denying cert ("for failure to file petition within time provided"); County of Sonoma v. Isbell, 439 U.S. 996 (1978). See also Peter Linzer, "The Meaning of Certiorari Denials," 79 Colum. L. Rev. 1127 (1979).

Having now gotten the court's attention, Mr. Ennis, of course, faces the more difficult matter of winning the case. "It's a long way to go to convince this court to grant a new absolute right," he said.

C. FROM ORAL ARGUMENT TO DECISION

After a case receives four votes from Justices, it is transferred to the oral argument list. If Justices conclude that a question is clearly controlled by one of the Court's earlier decisions, they may summarily dispose of a lower court decision without oral argument or full briefing. One form of summary disposition is a per curiam opinion that grants cert but disposes of the merits without giving parties an opportunity to file briefs or argue before the Court. In 1980, for example, the Court decided a case involving press and speech restrictions on former government employees without hearing oral argument. Snepp v. United States, 444 U.S. 507. Summary disposition carries the risk of depriving the Court of crucial information. It can also suggest a "rush to judgment."

The Pentagon papers case of 1971 moved through the courts with extraordinary speed. Beginning with the *New York Times*'s publication of a secret Pentagon study on the origins and conduct of the Vietnam War, only 17 days were consumed for action by two district courts, two appellate courts, and the Supreme Court. The *New York Times*'s petitions and motions were filed with the Supreme Court on June 24 at about 11 A.M. The government filed its motion later that evening. Oral argument took place on June 26. The record in the *Times* case did not arrive until 7 or 8 P.M. the previous evening. The briefs of the parties were received less than two hours before oral argument. Four days later the Court announced its decision, upholding the right of the press to publish material from the Pentagon study. Despite protests from several Justices, the Court moved quickly to protect the First Amendment right of the press to publish without prior restraint. New York Times v. United States, 403 U.S. 713 (1971).

Lack of Adversary Process

We expect the Supreme Court to hear arguments from both sides of a dispute to properly inform itself (see "Adverseness" in Chapter 3, Section A). Justices receive briefs from opposing parties and most likely numerous amici briefs from interested individuals and organizations. Litigants appear in open court to present their positions. Yet at times this process can be highly abridged, removing the safeguards and informing function of the adversary system.

Several examples of this abbreviated process appeared in 2012. On February 17, the Court decided to grant a stay on a campaign finance case from Montana. It was stayed "pending the timely filing and disposition of a petition for a writ of certiorari." In a separate statement, Justices Ginsburg and Breyer noted that Montana's experience and experience elsewhere questioned the Court's position in *Citizens United* (2010) that independent expenditures by corporations "do not give rise to corruption or the appearance of corruption." By granting cert, they argued, the Court would have an opportunity to consider whether, "in light of the huge sums currently deployed to buy candidates' allegiance, *Citizens United* should continue to hold sway."

In 1912, Montana passed a Corrupt Practices Act in response to influence-buying by copper interests. In 2011, the Montana Supreme Court reviewed the circumstances that led the state to adopt statutory restrictions on corporate expenditures. Those restrictions were in conflict with *Citizens United*, which was based on no evidentiary record. Taking the case and hearing argument from both sides would have permitted the Court to decide whether Montana had a right, under its constitution, to curb corporate spending. However, in a short per curiam the Court said: "The question presented in this case is whether the holding in *Citizens United* applies to the Montana state law. There can be no serious doubt that it does. See U.S. Const., Art. VI, cl. 2." American Tradition Partnership, Inc. v. Bullock, 567 U.S. ___ (2012). Clause 2 of Article VI states that the U.S. Constitution "shall be the supreme Law of the Land; and the Judges in every State shall be bound thereby, any Thing in the Constitution or Laws of any States to the Contrary notwithstanding." Nothing in Clause 2 wholly denies states the possibility of adopting laws that vary from standards announced by the Supreme Court (see Chapter 1, Section G).

A second Supreme Court decision in 2012 also illustrates how the adversary process can be curtailed. The case involved a California law that permitted public sector employees in a bargaining unit to decide by majority vote to create an "agency shop" under which employees would be represented by a union. Employees who chose not to join the union would pay an annual amount for "chargeable expenses" (the cost of nonpolitical union services related to collective bargaining). The Court held that the public-sector union's treatment of nonmembers ran afoul of the First Amendment. Knox v. Service Employees, 567 U.S. ___ (2012).

Four Justices objected to the Court's willingness to address constitutional issues that exceeded the scope of questions presented, briefed, and argued. Sotomayor and Ginsburg made that point in their concurrence, adding that the majority broke the Court's rules. Rule 14.1(a) provides: "Only the questions set out in the petition [for certiorari], or fairly included therein, will be considered by the Court." They regarded the lack of adversarial presentations as "both unfair and unwise." In a dissent, Breyer and Kagan noted that none of the briefs argued this particular issue, nor was the issue explored during oral argument. No party asked that the question be examined, and it was not fully argued in the lower courts. Breyer and Kagan acknowledged that the principles of stare decisis are not absolute, but "the Court cannot be right when it departs from those principles without benefit of argument in a matter of such importance."

The adversary process is also weakened when judges and their clerks perform independent research, reaching out to studies and authorities never mentioned in briefs and therefore beyond the capacity of litigants to check for errors and misconceptions. Robert Barnes, "When justices call on research engines," Washington Post, July 9, 2012, at A17.

Oral Argument

In preparation for oral argument, counsel for each side submits briefs and records that are distributed to each Justice. The Court hears oral argument in public session from Monday through Thursday, listening to cases from 10 A.M. to noon and from 1 to 3 P.M. On some days it is only from 10 to noon. Usually one hour is set aside for each case. Although briefs are important, members of the judiciary have noted that there are some judges "who listen better than they read and who are more receptive to the spoken than the written word." Harlan, 41 Corn. L. Q. 6 (1955). The impressions they receive during oral argument often carry with them into the conference room at the end of the week. Oral argument allows judges to explore with counsel key issues left undeveloped in the briefs.

During oral argument, the Chief Justice sits in the center of a raised bench with the senior Associate Justice to his right and the next ranking Justice to his left. Other Justices are arrayed by seniority alternately to his right and left, leaving the most junior Justice positioned farthest to his left. Some Justices rely on a "bench memorandum" prepared by law clerks to digest the facts and arguments of both sides and provide guidance during the questioning of counsel. Judicial styles differ at oral argument. Justice Douglas asked few questions and regarded many of the ones put forth by colleagues as attempts to lobby Justices for votes rather than to illuminate issues. William O. Douglas, The Court Years 181 (1981). On the current Court, Clarence Thomas is known for keeping silent while Antonin Scalia, Ruth Bader Ginsburg, and other Justices participate actively.

Writing Opinions

The number of full opinions each year is now less than 80, down from the 150 annual rate of the 1980s (see figures on workload on the next page and Table 5.1 at the end of the chapter). The length of opin-

SUPREME COURT'S WORKLOAD (2010–2011 TERM)

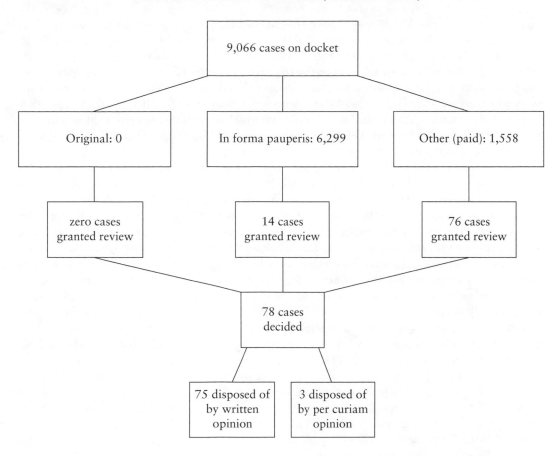

9,066 cases on docket

Original: 0   In forma pauperis: 6,299   Other (paid): 1,558

zero cases granted review   14 cases granted review   76 cases granted review

78 cases decided

75 disposed of by written opinion   3 disposed of by per curiam opinion

SOURCE: U.S. Supreme Court

ions has grown dramatically: about four times longer than in the 1950s. To divide the time between hearing cases and writing opinions, the Court alternates between several weeks of oral argument and several weeks of recess to write opinions and study appeals and cert petitions. If the Chief Justice has voted with the majority in conference, he assigns the majority opinion either to himself or to another Justice. When the Chief Justice is in the minority, the senior Justice voting with the majority assigns the case. The dissenters decide who shall write the dissenting opinion. Each Justice may write a separate opinion, concurrence, or dissent.

Although Justices are appointed for life and are immune from periodic campaigning for electoral office, they know that the ability to write acceptable opinions depends on sensitivity to the public. This consideration affects the assignment of opinions. In 1944, Chief Justice Stone initially assigned the Texas "white primary" case to Justice Frankfurter. Justice Jackson shared his misgivings with both Frankfurter and Stone, suggesting that because of "Southern sensibilities" it was unwise to have a Vienna-born Jew, raised in New England (the seat of the abolition movement), write the majority opinion striking down the Texas statute. With Frankfurter's consent, Stone transferred the assignment to Stanley Reed, a native-born Protestant and old-line Kentuckian. Reed was a Democrat of long-standing, whereas Frankfurter's past ties to the Democratic party were suspect. Alpheus T. Mason, Harlan Fiske Stone: Pillar of the Law 614–15 (1968).

Recusal

Under English common law, judges could be disqualified for direct interest in a case but never for bias. Such an admission would have conceded the capacity for partiality or favoritism in a judge. Frank, 56 Yale L. J. 605, 609–10 (1947); Forer, 73 Harv. L. Rev. 1325, 1327 (1960). Many of the early Justices on the Supreme Court failed to recuse (remove) themselves from cases that, under today's standards, would call for disqualification. Justice Story decided cases involving the Bank of the United States while serving as president of a Massachusetts branch of it. Chief Justice Marshall wrote *Marbury* v. *Madison* after serving as the Secretary of State who had neglected to deliver the commission of office. However, Marshall withdrew from *Stuart* v. *Laird*, 5 U.S. (1 Cr.) 299 (1803) because he had tried the case earlier in the circuit court.

Based on statutory guidelines, court decisions, judicial codes, and personal standards, judges withdraw from certain cases when they have a personal bias, when they previously served as counsel in the matter in controversy, and for other stated (and unstated) reasons. 28 U.S.C. §§ 144, 455. Judges disqualify themselves to maintain the appearance of impartiality and due process. Chief Justice Stone and Justice Jackson did not take part in a 1942 decision because as former Attorneys General they had helped prosecute the case. United States v. Bethlehem Steel Corp., 315 U.S. 289, 309 (1942).

Justice Jackson shocked the country in June 1946 by issuing a blistering attack on Justice Black. This extraordinary public revelation of a bitter feud between two members of the Supreme Court had its origins in a 1945 decision in which Black was part of a 5 to 4 majority upholding the right of coal miners. Jewell Ridge Coal Corp. v. Local No. 6167, 325 U.S. 161 (1945). Jackson's dissent in that case quoted from a Senate debate in 1937 to show that Black, as a Senator, provided legislative history contrary to the majority's decision. It was also known that the chief counsel for the miners in the 1945 case was Black's former law partner.

The coal company petitioned for a rehearing, asking whether Black could render impartial justice given his connection with the legislation and the chief counsel. All members of the Court agreed that the motion for a rehearing should be denied, because the decision to disqualify oneself is purely a personal judgment to be made by each Justice. However, Jackson did not want to imply, by silence, that everyone on the Court supported Black's decision. When the Court denied the motion, Jackson wrote a concurring opinion, explaining that disqualification was not a decision for the full Court. Each Justice had to make that determination for himself. Frankfurter joined Jackson's concurrence. Jewell Ridge Coal Corp. v. Local No. 6167, 325 U.S. 897 (1945). Black's supporters were outraged by the concurrence because it drew attention to the issue of disqualification.

A newspaper article in May 1946 reported that Black regarded Jackson's concurrence as a gratuitous insult and a slur on Black's honor. The dispute intensified with the pending selection of a Chief Justice. Jackson hoped to be named; Black was dead-set against it. According to the newspaper story, Black threatened to resign if President Truman selected Jackson as Chief Justice. Fleeson, "Supreme Court Feud," [Washington] Evening Star, May 16, 1946, at A15. Black refused to comment on these newspaper stories.

While Jackson was in Nuremberg serving as Special Prosecutor for the Nazi trials, Truman nominated Fred Vinson to be Chief Justice. Jackson believed that Black played a hand in denying him the promotion. From Nuremberg, Jackson cabled the Judiciary Committees to elaborate on the 1945 dispute. He said that after he announced his decision to write a concurrence on the petition for a rehearing, Black became "very angry" and said that any opinion that discussed the subject at all would mean "a declaration of war." Jackson told Black that he would "not stand for any more of his bullying and that, whatever I would otherwise do, I would now have to write my opinion to keep self-respect in the face of threats." Alluding to rumors that had been published critical of his role, Jackson remarked: "If war is declared on me I propose to wage it with the weapons of the open warrior, not those of the stealthy assassin." Jackson warned that if Black failed to disqualify himself in comparable situations in the future, "I will make my Jewell Ridge opinion look like a letter of recommendation by comparison." New York Times, June 11, 1946, at 2.

Justice Rehnquist was asked to recuse himself from a case because he had earlier testified on the subject while serving as an official in the Justice Department. In a memorandum, Rehnquist agreed that disqualification would have been required had he signed a pleading or brief in the case or actively participated in it. In two earlier cases he withdrew for those reasons. Laird v. Tatum, 409 U.S. 824, 828–29 (1972). However, he disagreed that testimony or the expression of one's views were adequate grounds for recusal. He also pointed out that disqualification of a Supreme Court Justice presents problems that do not exist in a lower court where one judge may substitute for another. Id. at 837–38. This issue resurfaced in 1986 during Rehnquist's nomination hearings to be Chief Justice.

In 2004, Justice Scalia was pressured to recuse himself from a case involving Vice President Cheney. The two had gone duck hunting together, and Scalia had traveled on Cheney's government plane to the hunting camp in Louisiana. Scalia did not save any money from Cheney's offer, because Scalia bought a round-trip ticket and returned home by commercial aircraft. Scalia reasoned that recusal would be appropriate if the personal fortune or personal freedom of a friend was at stake, but not when a case concerned Cheney's *official* action. Cheney v. U.S. District Court, 541 U.S. 913 (2004).

A decision by the Supreme Court in 2009 concerned the failure of a state judge to recuse himself from a case in which one of the parties had earlier contributed campaign funds to his successful reelection. A 5–4 Court held that, in the circumstances of the case, due process required recusal. The dissenting Justices (Roberts, Scalia, Thomas, Alito) warned that the decision would invite other lawsuits and erode public confidence in judicial impartiality. Caperton v. A.T. Massey Coal Co., 556 U.S. 868 (2009).

Drafting Opinions

The process of writing opinions begins with the briefs prepared by opposing counsel, research by law clerks and library staff, and the knowledge that Justices acquire from decades of experience in public and private life. Drafts are printed within the Court building and circulated among the Justices. Comments are written on the drafts; memorandums are exchanged. Often, a forceful dissent may persuade members of the majority to change their position, creating a new majority from the old dissenting position. Chief Justice Vinson once remarked that an opinion circulated as a dissent "sometimes has so much in logic, reason, and authority to support it that it becomes the opinion of the Court." 69 S.Ct. x (1949). Draft opinions may be so influential in modifying the Court's final decision that they are never published. Alexander M. Bickel, The Unpublished Opinions of Mr. Justice Brandeis (1967). The threat of a dissent can force changes in the majority opinion.

The role of law clerks is sometimes described in lavish terms, as though they largely write the opinions. Because of the growing importance of law clerks, Senator John Stennis suggested (perhaps whimsically) that it might be appropriate to subject them to confirmation by the Senate. 104 Cong. Rec. 8107–08 (1958). Publication of *The Brethren: Inside the Supreme Court* in 1979 catapulted clerks to a seemingly pivotal role in making judicial policy. However, this study depended heavily on interviews with clerks who no doubt found it irresistible to magnify their contributions to public law. Edward Lazarus, a former Supreme Court law clerk, claimed that Justices "yield great and excessive power to immature, ideologically driven clerks, who in turn use that power to manipulate their bosses and the institution they ostensibly serve." Edward Lazarus, Closed Chambers 6 (1998).

Judges in the prime of life are not likely to defer to the opinions of clerks fresh out of law school, however much the clerks may stimulate new ideas and approaches. Clerks come and go, but the persistence in decisions of a unique writing style is compelling evidence that judges do their own work. Nevertheless, clerks do more than check footnotes, locate citations from law reviews and other sources, review cert petitions, and perform minor editing tasks. Depending on the judge they work for, they might be asked to prepare a "prototype or aspirant opinion" to guide the thinking of the court. Frank M. Coffin, The Ways of a Judge 69 (1980). Because of heavy court workload, judges usually ask clerks to write the preliminary draft of an opinion (see Coffin reading).

Personal Values and Attitudes

The legal profession no longer seriously argues that it is the duty of a judge to place a constitutional provision next to a challenged statute to see whether the latter squares with the former. United States v. Butler, 297 U.S. 1, 62 (1936). Still, the belief that judges, in the act of deciding, are able to put aside their personal value systems retains a following. Justice Frankfurter made an eloquent plea for this concept of judicial deliberation:

> It is asked with sophomoric brightness, does a man cease to be himself when he becomes a Justice? Does he change his character by putting on a gown? No, he does not change his character. He brings his whole experience, his training, his outlook, his social, intellectual and moral environment with him when he takes a seat on the Supreme Bench. But a judge worth his salt is in the grip of his function. The intellectual habits of self-discipline which govern his mind are as much a part of him as the influence of the interest he may have represented at the bar, often much more so. 98 Proceedings Am. Phil. Soc. 233, 238 (1954).

It would be superficial to suggest that judges use their office simply to disseminate personal views, but decisions of individual judges flow at least in part from their own values and attitudes. Justice Miller, who served on the Supreme Court from 1862 to 1890, despaired of the fixed views and predispositions of those on the bench: "It is vain to contend with judges who have been at the bar the advocates for forty years of rail road companies, and all the forms of associated capital, when they are called upon to decide cases where such interests are in contest. All their training, all their feelings are from the start in favor of those who need no such influence." Charles Fairman, Mr. Justice Miller and the Supreme Court 374 (1939).

Although the votes of judges cannot be predicted with mathematical accuracy, attorneys are sophisticated enough to engage in "forum shopping" to find the court or circuit that augurs best for their client. Judicial independence and objectivity remain important values in the administration of justice, but by now it is routine to recognize definite alignments and alliances among judges. Even members of the judiciary acknowledge the existence of blocs. When Justice Blackmun joined the Supreme Court, he calculated that there were two Justices on the right, two on the left, and "five of us in the center." "A Justice Speaks Out: A Conversation with Harry A. Blackmun," Cable News Network, Inc., conducted November 25, 1982, at 22. Justice O'Connor's appearance in 1981 added another conservative voice to that of Chief Justice Burger and Justice Rehnquist. Blackmun, meanwhile, now found himself voting more frequently with the liberal bloc of Justices Brennan and Marshall. Blocs are not necessarily stable. They change over time and vary with the issue. During the Burger Court, Justices Blackmun, Powell, Stevens, and White formed part of a "floating center," casting the votes necessary to build a majority by joining either with the liberal votes of Brennan and Marshall or the conservative wing of Burger, O'Connor, and Rehnquist.

By the early 1990s, O'Connor was often associated with a moderate center consisting of Kennedy and Souter. Blackmun and Stevens formed a more liberal bloc, while Scalia and Thomas were identified as conservatives. After President Clinton's appointments of Ruth Bader Ginsburg and Stephen Breyer, the Court divided largely along the lines of five conservatives (Rehnquist, O'Connor, Scalia, Kennedy, and Thomas) and four moderate-liberals (Stevens, Souter, Ginsburg, and Breyer). Several Justices operated in the center, adding a fifth vote with one side to form a majority. O'Connor played that role on the Rehnquist Court; Kennedy functions that way with the Roberts Court. The addition of Sonia Sotomayor and Elena Kagan (replacing David Souter and John Paul Stevens) leaves the Court with five Justices in the conservative wing (Roberts, Thomas, Kennedy, Scalia, Alito) and four in the liberal-moderate wing (Ginsburg, Breyer, Sotomayor, Kagan).

Communicating Clearly

Members of the judiciary sometimes complain that their decisions are distorted by the press. Mistakes and misconceptions by reporters are likely, given the time pressures between the announcement of a decision and the deadlines imposed by newspapers, magazines, and broadcast services. These pressures have been partly relieved by several changes over the past few decades. In 1965 the Supreme Court, instead of handing down all opinions on "Decision Monday," began delivering some of its decisions on other days of the week. The Court also started meeting at 10 A.M. rather than noon; these extra hours eased deadlines for reporters. To assure more accurate and sophisticated coverage, major newspapers and wire services began selecting reporters with law degrees or special training in the law.

Some of the "distortions" in the press come from Justices who use careless language in their opinions. When the Supreme Court announced the School Prayer Decision in 1962, Justice Douglas's concurrence suggested that the decision would cover ceremonial observances of a religious nature, such as the Court's traditional invocation when it convenes and the offering of a daily prayer by a chaplain in Congress. Engel v. Vitale, 370 U.S. 421, 439–42 (1962). Such speculations, well beyond the issue before the Court, helped fuel public confusion and outrage. When opinions contain sharp crossfire between Justices, "news reporters and the public at large are likely to lose sight of the law in what appears (to the uninitiated at least) to be a battle of men and not of law." Newland, 17 West. Pol. Q. 15, 24–25 (1964). The prayer case was also grossly misrepresented by the president of the American Bar Association, who weighed in with the warning that the decision would require elimination of the motto "In God We Trust" from all coins. Id. at 28.

The judiciary's ability to communicate accurately to the public requires a writing style that is precise and economical. Opinion writers should use familiar words and short sentences, emphasizing simplicity, clarity, brevity, and a direct and vigorous style. Justice Jackson gloried in the "short Saxon word that pierces the mind like a spear and the simple figure that lights the understanding." 37 A.B.A.J. 801, 863–64 (1951). Nevertheless, judges have personal idiosyncrasies that produce affectation, ornate prose, and verbosity. Ambiguity is also likely when several strong-minded individuals must agree on a single statement.

In deciding a particular case, judges often stray from the central issue and add extraneous matter in the form of obiter dicta. Because these remarks are not necessary to the basic decision, they are not binding as legal precedent. Nevertheless, they can serve as the functional equivalent of an advisory opinion, supplying guidance to the future direction of legal thinking. It is not unusual for dicta, over time, to be treated as the decision.

Coherence and "principled decision making" are difficult virtues to achieve for a multi-membered Court that operates necessarily as a committee, attempting to stitch together a decision that can attract a majority. Compromises are needed. The difficulty is compounded by the practice of moving a step at a time, responding to the concrete case at hand. As noted by one scholar, the Court "is in the unenviable posture of a committee attempting to draft a horse by placing very short lines on a very large drawing-board at irregular intervals during which the membership of the committee constantly changes." Amsterdam, 58 Minn. L. Rev. 349, 350 (1974).

Finality of Decisions

Decisions by federal courts may embody broad policies of commerce, slavery and other issues that provoke other branches to restrict and reverse judicial judgments. The general rule is that the outcome of an individual case — for a particular litigant — is accepted by Congress and the President, but not necessarily the larger public policy. For example, Abraham Lincoln challenged the political judgments in *Dred Scott* v. *Sandford* without proposing to "disturb or resist the decision" regarding Dred Scott or Dred Scott's master (see reading in Chapter 1). The overarching issue—such as slavery or abortion—requires continuing debate in a democratic society.

Writing in 2003, Justice O'Connor challenged the notion that a decision by the Supreme Court on a controversial issue settles it. Instead, she described a "dynamic dialogue" between the Court and the American public: "No one, it seems, considers the Supreme Court decision in *Roe* v. *Wade* to have settled the issue for all time. Such intense debate by citizens is as it should be. A nation that docilely and unthinkingly approved every Supreme Court decision as infallible and immutable would, I believe, have severely disappointed our founders." Sandra Day O'Connor, The Majesty of the Law 45 (2003).

Frank M. Coffin
The Process of Writing a Decision*

Every important appellate court decision is made by a group of equals. This fact reflects the shrewd judgment of the architects of our state and federal judicial systems that an appellate judge is no wiser than a trial judge. His only claim to superior judgment lies in numbers; three, five, seven, or nine heads are usually better than one....

There is intimacy, continuity, and dynamism in the relations among judges, at least on the smaller courts. They do not come together just to vote. They interact with each other, influence each other, and have each other in mind almost from the time they first read briefs for the next session of court. In a sense, the relationship among judges who differ in their values and views is a bargaining one, yet it is a continuing negotiation, where each player lays his cards on the table just as soon as he discovers what cards he has. There is, on a serene court, no suggestion that anyone seeks to manipulate anyone else.

In short, there is a difference between arriving at a yes or no decision through majority vote and working up an opinion on a close case so that three or more judges of different sensitivities, values, and backgrounds can join not only in the result, but in the rationale, tone, nuances, and reservations. Although the task of building toward a unanimous opinion, or even of carpentering a majority, demands a certain amount of sacrifice of ego and substantive concession, collegiality has its solid satisfactions. One quickly realizes that he is not the only source of useful insights. He learns to rejoice when he sees an opinion he has written measurably strengthened by the suggestion of one of his colleagues. Then, too, decisions are sometimes unpleasant, hard, risky, controversial, when the public

and the press are hot and quick in their criticism. On such occasions, the comfort of collegiality is a pearl of no little worth.

THE INTENSITY OF INDIVIDUAL INVOLVEMENT

One of the paradoxes about appellate courts is that there can coexist the kind of intimate collegiality I have sketched and a profound, almost antique individualism. Indeed, perhaps the collegiality is the more enduring because it feeds on, cherishes, and respects the individualism nourished by appellate courts. In any case I make so bold as to say that in this supertechnical, industrialized, computerized, organized age, appellate courts are among the last redoubts of individual work.

While reliance on machines and staff proliferates apace in corporations, legislatures, and executive bureaucracies, the appellate judge still lives and works in his chamber with his law clerks. Although, unlike his predecessor, he can no longer write the first draft of every opinion, he is, as we shall see, in the very heart of creation of every opinion at every stage.

The kind of individualism I refer to is not the individualism of style, flair, or color, though these, happily, are not absent. Rather, every work product of an appellate court, a judicial opinion, bears the individual trademarks of, and is freighted with, the personal scrutiny and reflection of each member to a greater extent than that of any other collegial body....

Perhaps there are appellate judges who, on hearing the essential facts of such a case, can confidently announce a sound decision without pause. I have seen professors in the classroom so respond; also panelists, lecturers, and cocktail-party pundits. But

---

* SOURCE: From Frank M. Coffin, The Ways of a Judge: Reflections from the Federal Appellate Bench (Boston: Houghton Mifflin, 1980), pp. 57–63. When this book was published, Coffin was Chief Judge of the First Circuit.

I am thankful that nothing said under such circumstances affects the rights of parties. Judges do have their share of excellent talkers. The best of them are called brilliant. Brilliance, however, seems to me more associated with the pyrotechnics of speech and writing; as the word suggests, it has to do with how thoughts can be made to shine and sparkle. Sound decision, on the other hand, is more than result; it is an edifice made up of rationale, tone, and direction. It is faithful to the past, settles the present, and foreshadows the future. Such a decision is rarely made quickly.

I see decision-making as neither a process that results in an early conviction based on instant exposure to competing briefs nor one in which the judge keeps an open mind through briefs, discussion in chambers, argument, and conference, and then summons up the will to decide. I see the process, rather, as a series of shifting biases. It is much like tracing the source of a river, following various minor tributaries, which are found to rise in swamps, returning to the channel, which narrows as one goes upstream.

One reads a good brief from the appellant; the position seems reasonable. But a good brief from appellee, bolstered perhaps by a trial judge's opinion, seems incontrovertible. Discussion with the law clerks in chambers casts doubt on any tentative position. Any such doubt may be demolished by oral argument, only to give rise to a new bias, which in turn may be shaken by the postargument conference among the judges. As research and writing reveal new problems, the tentative disposition of the panel of judges may appear wrong. The opinion is written and circulated, producing reactions from the other judges, which again change the thrust, the rationale, or even the result. Only when the process has ended can one say that the decision has been made, after as many as seven turns in the road. The guarantee of a judge's impartiality lies not in suspending judgment throughout the process but in recognizing that each successive judgment is tentative, fragile, and likely to be modified or set aside as a consequence of deepened insight. The nonlawyer looks on the judge as a model of decisiveness. The truth is more likely that the appellate judge in a difficult case is committed to the unpleasant state of prolonged indecisiveness.

D. UNANIMITY AND DISSENT

The Supreme Court initially followed the British practice of allowing each Justice to write opinions seriatim (in a series). Rather than announce a single opinion representing the collective position of the majority, the Justices delivered separate statements. Before John Marshall's appointment as Chief Justice, the Court had begun to deliver an opinion for the entire Court rather than a string of seriatim opinions. Marshall reinforced that direction, believing that a single decision strengthened the Court's power and dignity. He selected one Justice (often himself) to write the majority opinion. Dissents were rare. Jefferson delivered a stinging rebuke to the Chief Justice for departing from seriatim decisions: "An opinion is huddled up in conclave, perhaps by a majority of one, delivered as if unanimous, and with the silent acquiescence of lazy or timid associates, by a crafty chief judge, who sophisticates the law to his own mind, by the turn of his own reasoning." 15 Writings of Thomas Jefferson 298 (Memorial ed. 1904).

Jefferson's critique was written in 1820, about two decades after Marshall had joined the Court, and appeared to be triggered by Marshall's broad nationalist ruling in *McCulloch* v. *Maryland* (1819). Seriatim opinions had offered a definite benefit: each Justice was accountable for articulating the rationale behind a decision. However, Marshall wanted the Court to develop an institutional view, moving away from personal positions to a more generalized principle for the majority.

Dissents became more frequent in later years of the Marshall Court and under future Chief Justices. At various times throughout history, however, members of the Court have placed a premium on unanimity. In 1922 Justice McReynolds wrote a majority opinion that provoked dissents from Brandeis, Clarke, and Pitney. Chief Justice Taft scheduled a reargument, and by the time he wrote the new majority opinion, Clarke and Pitney had retired. Taft sought Brandeis's views and eventually produced a unanimous opinion, with which McReynolds concurred.[5]

---

5. Alpheus Thomas Mason, "William Howard Taft," in Leon Friedman and Fred L. Israel, eds., 3 The Justices of the United States Supreme Court 2114 (1969), and Alexander M. Bickel, The Unpublished Opinions of Mr. Justice Brandeis, at 11–113. The case was Sonneborn Bros. v. Cureton, 262 U.S. 506 (1923).

Concurrences and Per Curiams

At the urging of colleagues who fear that dissents will damage the corporate reputation of the Supreme Court, Justices have been willing to convert a dissent into a concurring opinion. Labeling it a concurrence, however, is often an inadequate mask to cover the dissenting view.[6] It is not unusual for Justices to concur in the judgment or result while shredding the logic, reasoning, and precedents contained in the opinion of the Court.[7] Justices also withhold dissents when the case is less significant to them. Such accommodations create a reservoir of good will, promote institutional harmony, and allow the acquiescent Justice to call upon a colleague at some future time for reciprocal favors — perhaps a fourth vote to grant certiorari. Walter F. Murphy, Elements of Judicial Strategy 52–53 (1964).

During preparation for *Brown* v. *Board of Education,* members of the Court felt strongly that unanimity was crucial in building public acceptance for desegregation. Discreet pressure was applied to Justices to ward off concurring and dissenting opinions. Chief Justice Warren realized that once a Justice had announced his position, it would be more difficult for him to change his thinking, "so we decided that we could dispense with our usual custom of formally expressing our individual views at the first conference and would confine ourselves for a time to informal discussion of the briefs, the arguments made at the hearing, and our own independent research for each conference day, reserving our final opinions until the discussions were concluded." Warren, 239 Atlantic Monthly 35–36 (April 1977). By following this process, the Court agreed unanimously that the "separate but equal" doctrine had no place in public education.

In earlier rulings, the Court relied on per curiam opinions (unsigned opinions "for the court") to reduce friction. This technique permitted the Justices to present a united front and avoid details or legal interpretations that might have fractured the Court and communicated more information to the public than the Court thought prudent. In one of the early racial discrimination cases before *Brown,* Justice Frankfurter explained in a letter to Chief Justice Vinson that the per curiam "should set forth as briefly and as unargumentatively as possible" the Court's position. "In short," Frankfurter wrote, "our *per cur.* should avoid every possibility of serving as a target for contention. . . ." Hutchinson, 68 Geo. L. J. 1, 9 (1979).

In the Nazi Saboteur Case of 1942, the Supreme Court chose to issue a per curiam upholding the jurisdiction of a military tribunal, leading to the execution of six men. Not until three months later did the Court release a full decision setting forth the legal reasoning. Ex parte Quirin, 317 U.S. 1 (1942). This two-step procedure so damaged the Court's reputation that when it had an opportunity in 1953 to follow that precedent with the case of Julius and Ethel Rosenberg, it chose not to. Louis Fisher, Nazi Saboteurs on Trial 68–79, 108–34 (2003). In 2004, a dissent by Justices Scalia and Stevens referred to *Quirin* as "not this Court's finest hour." Hamdi v. Rumseld, 542 U.S. 507 (2004).

Unanimity to Make a Point

When Governor Orval Faubus and the Arkansas legislature fought to retain the state's system of segregated schools, the Supreme Court reaffirmed the principle it had enunciated in 1954. To underscore its unanimity, the names of all nine Justices were listed, including the three who had joined the Court since 1954. Frankfurter frustrated this strategy by insisting on a separate concurrence, agreeing to file it a week after the Court released its opinion. Cooper v. Aaron, 358 U.S. 1 (1958). Warren, Black, and Brennan were furious. Frankfurter's only justification for the extra statement was that he felt a spe-

---

6. Justice Murphy, under the urgings of colleagues, changed his dissent in *Hirabayashi* v. *United States* to a concurrence. See Murphy, supra note 1, at 46–47, and Howard, supra note 1, at 302–09.

7. Murphy v. Waterfront Comm'n, 378 U.S. 52, 80–92 (1964) (Harlan, J., concurring); Warden v. Hayden, 387 U.S. 294, 310–12 (Fortas, J., and Warren, C. J., concurring) (1967); Argersinger v. Hamlin, 407 U.S. 25, 41–44 (1972) (Burger, C. J., concurring) and 44–46 (Powell, J., concurring, joined by Rehnquist, J.).

cial responsibility to lecture Southern lawyers and law professors who had been his students at Harvard Law School. Bernard Schwartz, Super Chief 302–03 (1983).

In 1974, with President Nixon threatening to defy any judicial effort to make him surrender the Watergate tapes, the Supreme Court once again produced a unanimous ruling. United States v. Nixon, 418 U.S. 683 (1974). By forging a united front and rejecting Nixon's broad claim of executive privilege, the Court played a crucial role in bringing about his resignation. However, the very process of generating a unanimous opinion invited generalization at so high a plane, accompanied by wholly unnecessary dicta, that the result obfuscated the law of executive privilege.[8] This is an ever-present risk. Attracting a few additional votes may dilute legal principles to such an extent that some Justices in the original majority may decide to write concurring or even dissenting opinions.

Unanimity can help prepare the public for important rulings. In other situations, however, a multiplicity of opinions may be enlightening. In *Youngstown Co.* v. *Sawyer* (1952), every member of the six-man majority wrote a separate opinion discussing the limits of presidential power in time of emergency. The country was therefore privy to nuances and complexities that would have been obscured by a broad ruling satisfactory to the majority. Multiplicity gave room for sophisticated explorations of the source and scope of executive powers but also added uncertainty about constitutional principles. Concurring opinions may anticipate future developments in the direction of law.

Plurality Opinions

With the growth in the number of cases that determine constitutional issues, separate concurring and dissenting opinions have increased dramatically. Justice Rehnquist suggested that it "may well be that the nature of constitutional adjudication invites, at least, if it does not require, more separate opinions than does adjudication of issues of law in other areas." Rehnquist, 59 A.B.A.J. 361, 363 (1973). Of special concern is the Court's inability to prepare a decision that attracts a majority of the Justices. Instead, the Court delivers a plurality opinion that creates confusion in the lower courts and other branches of government. The number of plurality opinions by the Burger Court exceeded the number of all previous Courts. Note, 94 Harv. L. Rev. 1127 (1981); Davis & Reynolds, 1974 Duke L. J. 59.

In 1977, the Supreme Court announced a rule for determining the meaning of a plurality holding. Borrowing language from *Gregg v. Georgia*, 428 U.S. 153 (1976), the Court stated: "When a fragmented Court decides a case and no single rationale explaining the result enjoys the assent of five Justices, 'the holding of the Court may be viewed as that position taken by those Members who concurred in the judgments on the narrowest grounds....'" Marks v. United States, 430 U.S. 188, 193 (1977). A scholar, after studying the application of the *Marks* rule, concluded that it was "insupportable and should be rejected." Mark Alan Thurmon, "When the Supreme Court Divides: Reconsidering the Precedential Value of Supreme Court Plurality Decisions," 42 Duke L. J. 419, 421 (1992).

Dissents

Shortly before returning to the Supreme Court, this time as Chief Justice, Charles Evans Hughes wrote eloquently on the deliberative process of the judiciary. He recognized that a dissenting opinion can damage the appearance of justice that the public needs in a court of last resort. However, he felt it far more injurious to obtain unanimity by concealing genuine differences and personal convictions (see box on next page). Following this tradition, Justice Douglas said that "[c]ertainty and unanimity in the law are possible both under the fascist and communist systems. They are not only possible; they are indispensable...." (see Douglas reading).

Dissents may force the majority to clarify and tighten its opinion. They can also serve as a precur-

---

8. Louis Henkin, "Executive Privilege: Mr. Nixon Loses but the Presidency Largely Prevails," 22 UCLA L. Rev. 40 (1974); William Van Alstyne, "A Political and Constitutional Review of *United States* v. *Nixon*," 22 UCLA L. Rev. 116 (1974).

Charles Evans Hughes on Dissent

There are some who think it desirable that dissents should not be disclosed as they detract from the force of the judgment. Undoubtedly, they do. When unanimity can be obtained without sacrifice of conviction, it strongly commends the decision to public confidence. But unanimity which is merely formal, which is recorded at the expense of strong, conflicting views, is not desirable in a court of last resort, whatever may be the effect upon public opinion at the time. This is so because what must ultimately sustain the court in public confidence is the character and independence of the judges. They are not there simply to decide cases, but to decide them as they think they should be decided, and while it may be regrettable that they cannot always agree, it is better that their independence should be maintained and recognized than that unanimity should be secured through its sacrifice. This does not mean that a judge should be swift to dissent, or that he should dissent for the sake of self-exploitation or because of a lack of that capacity for cooperation which is of the essence of any group action, whether judicial or otherwise. Independence does not mean cantankerousness and a judge may be a strong judge without being an impossible person. Nothing is more distressing on any bench than the exhibition of a captious, impatient, querulous spirit. We are fortunately free from this in our highest courts in Nation and State, much freer than in some of the days gone by. Dissenting opinions enable a judge to express his individuality. He is not under the compulsion of speaking for the court and thus of securing the concurrence of a majority. In dissenting, he is a free lance. A dissent in a court of last resort is an appeal to the brooding spirit of the law, to the intelligence of a future day, when a later decision may possibly correct the error into which the dissenting judge believes the court to have been betrayed.

SOURCE: Charles Evans Hughes, The Supreme Court of the United States 67–68 (1928).

sor for a future majority holding. Justice Harlan's dissents in the *Civil Rights Cases* (1883), in *Plessy* v. *Ferguson* (1895), and in other race cases offered a broad interpretation of the Fourteenth Amendment in protecting the rights of blacks. His doctrine gained strength in some of the lower courts more than a half century later and foreshadowed the eventual overruling of *Plessy*. The dissents of Justice Holmes, especially in economic regulation cases, later carried the day for the Court. Justice Stone was a lone dissenter in the first flag-salute case in 1940, involving the religious freedoms of Jehovah's Witnesses. Two years later, three Justices from the majority (Black, Douglas, and Murphy) publicly announced that the decision "was wrongly decided." The following year, the Court reversed its 1940 ruling, vindicating Stone's position.[9] In 1942 the Court split 6 to 3, deciding that indigent defendants did not have a right to counsel in state court for all felonies. By 1963 the position of the three dissenters had been elevated to the majority position. Betts v. Brady, 316 U.S. 455, 474 (1942); Gideon v. Wainwright, 372 U.S. 335 (1963).

For a judicial body, dissent carries substantial costs. Justice Edward D. White, himself dissenting in an 1895 opinion, said that the "only purpose which an elaborate dissent can accomplish, if any, is to weaken the effect of the opinion of the majority, and thus engender want of confidence in the conclusions of courts of last resort." Pollock v. Farmers' Loan & Trust Co., 157 U.S. 429, 608 (1895). Dissents detract from institutional unity and may exacerbate tensions within a court, which is by nature a collegial body. Those tensions are heightened by sarcastic dissents that question the integrity or intellectual ability of a fellow judge. Dissents can be especially irresponsible when they confuse or distort the holding of the Court (see Jackson reading).

---

9. Minersville School District v. Gobitis, 310 U.S. 586 (1940); Jones v. Opelika, 316 U.S. 584, 624 (1942); West Virginia Board of Education v. Barnette, 319 U.S. 624 (1943).

Some members of the judiciary feel a special obligation to express their dissent when constitutional questions are at stake. Said Justice Moody in a 1908 dissent:

Under ordinary circumstances, where the judgment rests exclusively, as it does here, upon a mere interpretation of the words of a law, which may be readily changed by the lawmaking branches of the Government, if they be so minded, a difference of opinion may well be left without expression. But where the judgment is a judicial condemnation of an act of a coordinate branch of our Government it is so grave a step that no member of the court can escape his own responsibility, or be justified in suppressing his own views, if unhappily they have not found expression in those of his associates. The Employers' Liability Cases, 207 U.S. 463, 504–05 (1908).

The choice between writing a dissent and joining the majority remains an individual matter. Although Justice Harlan dissented in *Miranda* v. *Arizona*, 384 U.S. 436 (1966), the principle of stare decisis and the goal of institutional continuity and cohesiveness prompted him to acquiesce in future applications of *Miranda*. Orozco v. Texas, 394 U.S. 324, 328 (1969). Other Justices persist with their dissents.

William O. Douglas
The Dissent: A Safeguard of Democracy*

All of us in recent years have heard and read many criticisms of the dissenting or concurring opinion. Separate opinions have often been deplored. Courts have been severely criticized for tolerating them. And that is why I rise to their defense.

* * *

SEARCH FOR CERTAINTY

Holmes, perhaps better than anyone either before or after him, pointed out how illusory was the lawyer's search for certainty. Law is not what has been or is—law in the lawyer's sense is the prediction of things to come, the prediction of what decree will be written by designated judges on specified facts. In layman's language law is the prediction of what will happen to you if you do certain things. This was the lesson Holmes taught; and every lawyer on reflection knows that it is sound.

There are many reasons why this is so. No matter how clear and precise the code or other legal rule may be, the proof may be surrounded with doubt. And even though the proof is clear to the advocate, the credibility of the witnesses may raise serious questions for judge or jury. Uncertainty is increased when new and difficult problems under ambiguous statutes arise....

These are the things that Holmes summed up when he described the lawyer's continuing and uncertain search for certainty. They indeed suggest why philosophers of the democratic faith will rejoice in the uncertainty of the law and find strength and glory in it.

Certainty and unanimity in the law are possible both under the fascist and communist systems. They are not only possible; they are indispensable; for complete subservience to the political regime is a *sine qua non* to judicial survival under either system. One cannot imagine the courts of Hitler engaged in a public debate over the principles of Der Fuehrer, with a minority of one or four deploring or denouncing the principles themselves. One cannot imagine a judge of a Communist court dissenting against the decrees of the Kremlin.

Disagreement among judges is as true to the character of democracy as freedom of speech itself. The dissenting opinion is as genuinely American as Otis' denunciation of the general warrants, as Thomas Paine's, Thomas Jefferson's, or James Madison's briefs for civil liberties....

LEGISLATIVE PROCESS ONE OF COMPROMISE

Those who have followed the legislative process can produce examples on end. That process is one of compromise—of qualifying absolutes, of creating

---

* SOURCE: Journal of the American Judicature Society, Vol. 32, pp. 104–07 (December 1948). Justice Douglas served on the Supreme Court from 1939 to 1975.

exceptions to general rules. At times the process of compromise or conciliation involves well-nigh impossible adjustments. The clash of ideas may be so violent that a meeting of the minds seems out of the question. Where such cleavage is great and involves major issues, it may even tear a society apart. By the same token it can stop the legislative process or render it impotent, and thus deprive society of lawful and nonviolent means and methods of solving its problems. When the breach between the *pros* and *cons* is not too great, the legislative process functions. Even then, the compromise between competing ideas that emerges in the final legislation may be more apparent than real. For the legislative solution is often to write two opposing ideas into a statute. Without that solution enactment of the measure might, indeed, be impossible.

INTERPRETATION HAS LEGISLATIVE CHARACTERISTICS

And so the bill becomes the law and the law arrives before judges for interpretation. The battle that raged before the legislature is now transferred to the court. The passage of the legislation quieted the conflict only temporarily. It breaks out anew in the process of interpretation in the courts. A storm hits the court room, and the advocates take up the fight where the legislators left off. The same cleavage that appeared in legislative halls now shows up among the judges. Each side has eminent authority for its

view since two conflicting ideas found their way into the legislation. It is therefore easy for judge or lawyer or editor to accuse the judge, who takes the opposing view, of usurping the role of the legislature. A more honest, a more objective view would concede that interpretation has legislative as well as judicial characteristics. It cannot be otherwise where the legislature has left the choice of competing theories or ideas to the judges.

* * *

STARE DECISIS HAS SMALL PLACE IN CONSTITUTIONAL LAW

When we move to constitutional questions, uncertainty necessarily increases. A judge who is asked to construe or interpret the Constitution often rejects the gloss which his predecessors have put on it. For the gloss may, in his view, offend the spirit of the Constitution or do violence to it. That has been the experience of this generation and of all those that have preceded. It will likewise be the experience of those which follow. And so it should be. For it is the Constitution which we have sworn to defend, not some predecessor's interpretation of it. *Stare decisis* has small place in constitutional law. The Constitution was written for all time and all ages. It would lose its great character and become feeble, if it were allowed to become encrusted with narrow, legalistic notions that dominated the thinking of one generation.

Robert H. Jackson
The Limitation of Dissent*

In argued cases, conferences are followed by the preparation and circulation of opinions by Justices designated by the Chief Justice when he is with the prevailing view and, if not, by the senior Associate who is. But any Justice is free to write as he will, and there may be one or more opinions concurring in the result but reaching it by different reasons, and there may be a dissenting opinion or opinions....

The dissenting opinion strives to undermine the Court's reasoning and discredit its result. At its best, the dissent, as Mr. Hughes said, is "an appeal to the brooding spirit of the law, to the intelligence of a future day...." But Judge Cardozo has written:

"... Comparatively speaking at least, the dissenter is irresponsible. The spokesman of the court is cau-

tious, timid, fearful of the vivid word, the heightened phrase. He dreams of an unworthy brood of scions, the spawn of careless *dicta*, disowned by the *ratio decidendi*, to which all legitimate offspring must be able to trace their lineage. The result is to cramp and paralyze. One fears to say anything when the peril of misunderstanding puts a warning finger to the lips. Not so, however, the dissenter.... For the moment, he is the gladiator making a last stand against the lions. The poor man must be forgiven a freedom of expression, tinged at rare moments with a touch of bitterness, which magnanimity as well as caution would reject for one triumphant."

Dissent has a popular appeal, for it is an underdog judge pleading for an underdog litigant. Of

---

* SOURCE: From Justice Jackson's book, The Supreme Court in the American System of Government 16–19 (1955). Footnotes omitted.

course, one party or the other must always be underdog in a lawsuit, the purpose of which really is to determine which one it shall be. But the tradition of great dissents built around such names as Holmes, Brandeis, Cardozo, and Stone is not due to the frequency or multiplicity of their dissents, but to their quality and the importance of the few cases in which they carried their disagreement beyond the conference table. Also, quite contrary to the popular notion, relatively few of all the dissents recorded in the Supreme Court have later become law, although some of these are of great importance.

There has been much undiscriminating eulogy of dissenting opinions. It is said they clarify the issues. Often they do the exact opposite. The technique of the dissenter often is to exaggerate the holding of the Court beyond the meaning of the majority and then to blast away at the excess. So the poor lawyer with a similar case does not know whether the majority opinion meant what it seemed to say or what the minority said it meant. Then, too, dissenters frequently force the majority to take positions more extreme than was originally intended. The classic example is the *Dred Scott Case,* in which Chief Justice Taney's extreme statements were absent in his original draft and were inserted only after Mr. Justice McLean, then a more than passive candidate for the presidency, raised the issue in dissent.

The *right of dissent* is a valuable one. Wisely used on well-chosen occasions, it has been of great service to the profession and to the law. But there is nothing good, for either the Court or the dissenter, in dissenting per se. Each dissenting opinion is a confession of failure to convince the writer's colleagues, and the true test of a judge is his influence in leading, not in opposing, his court.

E. CASELOAD BURDENS

The number of cases submitted to the Supreme Court increased dramatically in the twentieth century. In this era of "rights consciousness," individuals and organizations went to court either to secure rights or to enforce rights already established by statute. The creation of additional district and appellate judgeships allows more plaintiffs and attorneys to enter the courts. Further adding to workload are dozens of statutes passed by Congress creating new causes of action, providing expedited methods of appeal, imposing duties on the judiciary, and awarding fees for attorneys.

In 1971, Chief Justice Burger appointed a group to study the growing caseload of the Supreme Court. Called the Freund Committee, the group recommended that Congress establish a seven-member National Court of Appeals to screen petitions filed with the Supreme Court and to certify 400 or so cases considered the most worthy. The Supreme Court would select from that list, but no appeal would be permitted from the cases rejected by the National Court of Appeals. The Committee's recommendation paralleled those announced earlier by Burger. U.S. News & World Report, December 14, 1970, at 43. The previous Chief Justice, Earl Warren, criticized the Committee's screening idea as a naive proposal from people who were unfamiliar with the Court's decisional process. He also objected to giving the National Court limited power to resolve conflicting decisions among the circuits. Warren, 28 Record Ass'n Bar of the City of N.Y. 627, 637, 642 (1973).

A second study, prepared by the Hruska Commission, was released in 1975. It, too, proposed a National Court of Appeals, but not to screen cases for the Supreme Court. A new court would be established to handle cases referred to it by the Supreme Court or appellate courts. In 1983, Chief Justice Burger offered his own version of a National Court of Appeals. He suggested a temporary court, drawn from appellate judges in each circuit, to resolve conflicts between appellate courts. A major restructuring of the judicial system, he warned, was necessary to "avoid a breakdown of the system — or of some of the justices." Washington Post, February 7, 1983, at A1.

The Court's docket is largely discretionary; to that extent its workload is self-imposed and self-inflicted. Workload increases when the Court reaches out to decide matters that might have been left to state courts or to the regular political process. In 1985 Justice Stevens (joined by Justices Brennan and Marshall) noted in dissent:

> Much of the Court's "burdensome" workload is a product of its own aggressiveness in this area [*of Fourth Amendment cases*]. By promoting the Supreme Court of the United States as the High

TABLE 5.1 CASES DECIDED BY THE SUPREME COURT 1984–2012

	Disposed of by Signed Opinion	Disposed of by Per Curiam Opinion
1984–1985	159	11
1985–1986	161	10
1986–1987	164	10
1987–1988	151	9
1988–1989	156	12
1989–1990	143	3
1990–1991	121	4
1991–1992	120	3
1992–1993	111	4
1993–1994	93	6
1994–1995	91	3
1995–1996	87	3
1996–1997	87	3
1997–1998	93	1
1998–1999	84	4
1999–2000	81	2
2000–2001	87	4
2001–2002	85	3
2002–2003	79	5
2003–2004	89	2
2004–2005	85	2
2005–2006	82	5
2006–2007	74	4
2007–2008	72	2
2008–2009	74	4
2009–2010	77	4
2010–2011	75	3
2011–2012	73	3

Magistrate for every warrantless search and seizure, this practice has burdened the argument docket with cases presenting fact bound errors of minimal significance. It has also encouraged state legal officers to file petitions for certiorari in even the most frivolous search and seizure cases. California v. Carney, 471 U.S. 386, 396 (1985).

Justice Stevens made a similar point in two cases decided in 1990. Florida v. Wells, 495 U.S. 1, 12–13 (1990); Minnesota v. Olson, 495 U.S. 91, 101–02 (1990).

Justice Brennan consistently criticized proposals to allow a special court to screen cases for the Supreme Court. He called the screening function "second to none in importance." Brennan, 40 U. Chi. L. Rev. 473, 477 (1973). From his perspective, the dissenting opinions in denying cert represent an important foundation for the development of legal doctrine and the formation of future majority positions. He would not delegate to a separate court the responsibility for screening cases, a process he called "inherently subjective" in nature and one that helps educate Justices on contemporary issues. Id. at 480–81.

Workload problems could be relieved by withdrawing some nonjudicial duties from the Court. At present, the Chief Justice is a member of the Board of Regents of the Smithsonian Institution. He is also a trustee of the National Gallery of Art and of the Joseph H. Hirshhorn Museum and Sculpture

Garden. He is responsible for appointing someone from the judicial branch to the National Historical Publications and Records Commission. Carrying out these extraneous duties seems to belie the claim that the Court is pressed to the limit with its caseload. In recent years, the Court decides far fewer cases than in the past (see Table 5.1).

NOTES AND QUESTIONS

1. Considerable debate surrounds the question of the relevance and utility of oral argument. Justice William O. Douglas believed "oral arguments win or lose a case," while Chief Justice Earl Warren thought they were "not highly persuasive." Quoted in Henry Abraham, The Judicial Process 203 (4th ed. 1980). What do you see as the purpose of oral argument?

2. Scholars agree that when it comes to the Court's opinion that the choice of the opinion writer is crucial to the result, for any one of several reasons. Lee Epstein and Jack Knight, The Choices Justices Make 125–37 (1998). By tailoring an opinion narrowly or broadly, how might that establish the initial legal and policy preferences over which Justices will negotiate, bargain and fight?

3. An opinion may be made more "palatable" to the public if it is written by a particular Justice. For example, Chief Justice Harlan Fiske Stone assigned to Justice Hugo Black, a prominent civil libertarian, the task of writing the opinion in Korematsu v. United States, in which the Court authorized the detention of Japanese-Americans, two-thirds of them U.S. citizens. Chief Justice Warren assigned Mapp v. Ohio, in which the Court created the exclusionary rule, to Justice Tom Clark, a former attorney general. David M. O'Brien, Storm Center 303–04 (4th ed. 1996).

4. Chief Justice John Marshall sought to build the Court's prestige. Toward that end, he abandoned the Court's practice of issuing seriatim opinions and implemented the practice of issuing a majority opinion, that is, an institutional opinion. He also discouraged dissenting opinions as a means of creating consensus on the Court. To what extent do individual opinions, particularly dissents, help shape constitutional law?

5. Do dissenting and concurring opinions undermine public respect for the Court as an institution? Dissents represent a method of undercutting the Court's opinion. Do you suppose that the threat of a dissent is an effective tool for judicial bargaining? Consider the dissent as a means of persuading the majority to narrow its holding. How often do dissents later become the "law of the land" or provoke legislative action? Justice John Marshall Harlan's famous dissent in Plessy v. Ferguson (1896) was vindicated in Brown v. Board of Education (1954). Justice James Iredell's dissent in Chisholm v. Georgia (1793) encouraged adoption of the Eleventh Amendment, which overturned the Court's opinion.

SELECTED READINGS

BARTH, ALAN. Prophets with Honor: Great Dissents and Great Dissenters in the Supreme Court. New York: Knopf, 1974.

CASPER, GERHARD, AND RICHARD A. POSNER. The Workload of the Supreme Court. Chicago: American Bar Foundation, 1976.

EPSTEIN, LEE AND JACK KNIGHT. The Choices Justices Make. Washington, D.C.: CQ Press, 1998.

ESTREICHER, SAMUEL, AND JOHN SEXTON. Redefining the Supreme Court's Role. New Haven: Yale University Press, 1986.

FRANK, JOHN P. Marble Palace: The Supreme Court in American Life. New York: Knopf, 1958.

HART, HENRY M., JR. "Foreword: The Time Chart of the Justices." 73 Harvard Law Review 84 (1959).

HARTNETT, EDWARD A. "Questioning Certiorari: Some Reflections Seventy-Five Years After the Judges' Bill." 100 Columbia Law Review 1643 (2000).

HELLMAN, ARTHUR D. "Caseload, Conflicts, and Decisional Capacity: Does the Supreme Court Need Help?" 67 Judicature 29 (1983).

HOWARD, J. WOODFORD, JR. Mr. Justice Murphy. Princeton, N.J.: Princeton University Press, 1968.

LAZARUS, EDWARD. Closed Chambers. New York: Times Books (1998).

MASON, ALPHEUS THOMAS. Harlan Fiske Stone: Pillar of the Law. New York: Viking, 1956.

MILLER, ARTHUR SELWYN, AND D. S. SASTRI. "Secrecy and the Supreme Court—On the Need for Piercing the Red Velour Curtain." 22 Buffalo Law Review 799 (1973). See also accompanying comments by Eugene Gressman; Joel B. Grossman; J. Woodford Howard, Jr.; Walter Probert; Glendon Schubert; and Roland Young.

MURPHY, WALTER F. Elements of Judicial Strategy. Chicago: University of Chicago Press, 1964.

NEWLAND, CHESTER A. "Personal Assistants to Supreme Court Justices: The Law Clerks." 40 Oregon Law Review 299 (1961).

O'BRIEN, DAVID M. Storm Center: The Supreme Court in American Politics. New York: Norton, 6th ed., 2002.

——, ed. Judges on Judging: Views from the Bench. Chatham, N.J.: Chatham House Publishers, 2d ed., 2004.

PELTASON, JACK W. Federal Courts in the Political Process. New York: Random House, 1955.

PERRY, H. W., JR. Deciding to Decide: Agenda Setting in the United States Supreme Court. Cambridge: Harvard University Press, 1991.

PROVINE, DORIS MARIE. Case Selection in the United States Supreme Court. Chicago: University of Chicago Press, 1980.

RICHARDSON, RICHARD J., AND KENNETH N. VINES. The Politics of Federal Courts: Lower Courts in the United States. Boston: Little, Brown, 1970.

ROHDE, DAVID W., AND HAROLD J. SPAETH. Supreme Court Decision Making. San Francisco: W. H. Freeman, 1976.

SCHWARTZ, BERNARD. Decision: How the Supreme Court Decides Cases. New York: Oxford University Press, 1996.

SEGAL, JEFFREY A. AND HAROLD J. SPAETH. The Supreme Court and the Attitudinal Model Revisited. Cambridge: Cambridge University Press, 2002.

SPAETH, HAROLD J. Supreme Court Policy Making. San Francisco: W. H. Freeman, 1979.

STERN, ROBERT L., EUGENE GRESSMAN, AND STEPHEN M. SHAPIRO. Supreme Court Practice, 7th ed. Washington, D.C.: The Bureau of National Affairs, 1993.

SUNSTEIN, CASS. One Case at a Time: Judicial Minimalism on the Supreme Court. Cambridge, Mass.: Harvard University Press, 1999.

ULMER, S. SIDNEY. "Bricolage and Assorted Thoughts on Working in the Papers of the Supreme Court Justices." 35 Journal of Politics 286 (1973).

WESTIN, ALAN F., ed. The Supreme Court: Views from Inside. New York: Norton, 1961.

——. An Autobiography of the Supreme Court. New York: Macmillan, 1963.

WILKINSON, J. HARVIE, III. Serving Justice: A Supreme Court Clerk's View. New York: Charterhouse, 1974.

WOODWARD, BOB, AND SCOTT ARMSTRONG. The Brethren: Inside the Supreme Court. New York: Simon and Schuster, 1979.

6

Separation of Powers: Domestic Conflicts

The doctrine of separation of powers, as applied in the United States, is difficult to grasp. In both theory and practice it teems with subtleties, ironies, and apparent contradictions. Just what the framers intended remains a subject of continuing dispute, spawning a vast literature with varying interpretations. Even if we could agree on the "framers' intent," the relationships among the three branches of government have changed fundamentally in two centuries to produce novel arrangements and peculiar overlappings. Chapters 6 and 7 cover these general principles as well as specific clashes and controversies.

A. THE SEPARATION DOCTRINE

Critics of separated powers in America claim that this political system produces intolerable deadlocks and inefficiency, especially for a twenty-first century government expected to exercise worldwide responsibilities. However, there is no necessary link between separated powers and inefficiency. The framers did not adopt a separation of powers to obstruct government. They wanted to create a system in 1787 that would operate more effectively and efficiently than the discredited Articles of Confederation, written in 1777 and ratified in 1781.

From One Branch to Three

Only one branch of national government existed before 1787: the Continental Congress. There was no executive or judiciary. Members of the Congress had to legislate and then serve on committees to administer and adjudicate what they had passed. Within a few years, the system proved to be so exhausting, inept, and embarrassing that it became necessary to delegate administrative and judicial duties to outside bodies. To relieve committees of administrative details, Congress turned to boards staffed by people outside the legislature. When those multiheaded boards failed to supply energy and accountability, Congress appointed single executive officers in 1781 to run the executive departments. These departments supplied a vital link in administrative structures between the Continental Congress and the national government established in 1787. Louis Fisher, President and Congress 1–27, 253–70 (1972).

The Continental Congress also established the beginnings of a national judiciary by setting up Courts of Admiralty to decide all controversies over naval captures and the distribution of war prizes. In 1780 Congress created the Court of Appeals in Cases of Capture, which functioned until its last session on May 16, 1787, at the State House in Philadelphia across the hall from the room in which delegates were assembling for the Constitutional Convention.

Separation for Efficiency and Liberty

This separation of legislative, executive, and judicial functions reflects the framers' search for more efficient government. The separation was driven principally by events, not theory. In a striking phrase, the historian Francis Wharton said that the Constitution "did not make this distribution of power. It would be more proper to say that this distribution of power made the Constitution of the United States." 1 Francis Wharton, The Revolutionary Diplomatic Correspondence of the United States 663 (1889). Justice Brandeis spoke a half-truth when he claimed that the doctrine of separated powers was "adopted by the Convention of 1787, not to promote efficiency but to preclude the exercise of arbitrary power." Myers v. United States, 272 U.S. 52, 293 (1926). Efficiency was a key objective.

It is often said that powers are separated to preserve liberties. It is equally true that a rigid separation can *destroy* liberties. The historic swings in France between executive and legislative dominance demonstrate the danger of extreme separation. The French constitutions of 1791 and 1848, based on a pure separation of powers, ended in absolutism and reaction. M.J.C. Vile, Constitutionalism and the Separation of Powers 176–211 (1967). The framers wanted to avoid political fragmentation and paralysis of power. They knew that a rigid adherence to separated powers "in all cases would be subversive of the efficiency of the government, and result in the destruction of the public liberties." 2 Joseph Story, Commentaries on the Constitution of the United States 12 (1970 ed.). Justice Jackson described the complex elements that coexist in America's separation doctrine: "While the Constitution diffuses power the better to secure liberty, it also contemplates that practice will integrate the dispersed powers into a workable government. It enjoins upon its branches separateness but interdependence, autonomy but reciprocity." Youngstown Co. v. Sawyer, 343 U.S. 579, 635 (1952).

Implied Separation

Although the separation of powers doctrine is not expressly stated in the Constitution, it is implied in the allocation of legislative powers to the Congress in Article I, executive powers to the President in Article II, and judicial powers to the Supreme Court in Article III. Several provisions help reinforce the separation. Article I, Section 6, prohibits members of either House of Congress from holding any other civil office (the *Incompatibility Clause*). This provision has been difficult to litigate. In 1974 the Court denied standing to plaintiffs who challenged the right of members of Congress to hold a commission in the armed forces reserves. Schlesinger v. Reservists to Stop the War, 418 U.S. 208 (1974). The meaning of that clause is therefore left to the elected branches. Article I, Section 6, also prohibits members of Congress from being appointed to any federal office created during their term of office, or to any federal position whose salary has been increased during their term of office (the *Ineligibility Clause*). The framers were aware that members of the British Parliament had been corrupted by appointments to office from the Crown, but they were reluctant to exclude qualified and able people from public office. 1 Farrand 379–82, 386–90; 2 Farrand 283–84, 489–92.

To reconcile these conflicting goals, Congress has at times reduced the salary of an executive position to permit someone from the House or the Senate to be appointed to the post. For example, after Congress had increased the salary of the Secretary of State from $8,000 to $12,000, President Taft wanted to name Senator Philander Knox to that office in 1909. A special bill was drafted to reduce the compensation of the Secretary of State to the original figure. The bill inspired heated debate in the House of Representatives, 43 Cong. Rec. 2390–2404, 2408–15, but was enacted into law. 35 Stat. 626. Knox was then nominated by President Taft and confirmed by the Senate. A similar situation arose in 1973 concerning the nomination of Senator William Saxbe as Attorney General after Congress had increased the salary of that office from $35,000 to $60,000. Legislation was enacted to keep Saxbe's compensation at $35,000. 87 Stat. 697 (1973). Floor debate illustrates how Congress engages in constitutional interpretation (see reading on Ineligibility Clause). Building on these precedents, Congress passed legislation in 1980 (94 Stat. 343) and in 1993 (107 Stat. 4) to permit Senator Ed Muskie to become Secretary of State and Senator Lloyd Bentsen to become Secretary of the Treasury. Similarly, it passed legislation in 2008 to permit Senator Hillary Clinton to be Secretary of State (122 Stat. 5036). An effort to challenge the constitutionality of her appointment as a violation of the Ineligibility Clause was dismissed for lack of standing. Rodearmel v. Clinton, 666 F.Supp.2d 123 (D.D.C. 2009), dismissed by the Supreme Court on June 7, 2010 for want of jurisdiction.

Other safeguards for the separation doctrine exist. Congress is prohibited from reducing the compensation of the President and members of the judiciary. United States v. Will, 449 U.S. 200 (1980). The Speech or Debate Clause, covered later in this chapter, provides legislative immunity to protect members of Congress from executive or judicial harassment and intimidation.

Explicit Sharing

Several sections of the Constitution produce combinations, not separations, of the branches. The President may veto legislation, subject to a two-thirds override vote of each house of Congress. Some of the Anti-Federalists objected that the veto allowed the President to encroach upon the legislature. Alexander Hamilton, in Federalist No. 73, defended the qualified veto on two grounds: it protected the President's office against legislative "depredations," and it served as a check on bad laws. In signing legislation into law, Presidents often interpret provisions of a bill to avoid what they consider to be constitutional infirmities. This practice is not without controversy. Critics of President George W. Bush objected to the frequency of his signing statements asserting broad claims of presidential power. While not as frequent, President Barak Obama continued the practice during his presidency (see readings on signing statements).

Presidents also exercise a "pocket veto." The Constitution provides that any bill not returned by the President within ten days (Sundays excepted) shall become law unless the adjournment by Congress prevents the bill's return. In such cases, the bill does not become law and is pocket vetoed. Several decisions effectively eliminated the use of a pocket veto *during* a congressional session.[1] The power to pocket veto a bill *between* the first and second sessions reached the Supreme Court but was dismissed in 1987 as moot. Barnes v. Kline, 759 F.2d 21 (D.C. Cir. 1985); Burke v. Barnes, 479 U.S. 361 (1987). This is another constitutional issue that requires interpretation by the elected branches. Of course there is no question about the President's power to invoke the pocket veto at the end of the second session when Congress adjourns.

The Constitution contains other overlapping of power. The President nominates officers and judges, but the Senate confirms. The President submits treaties that the Senate must approve. The House of Representatives may impeach executive and judicial officers, subject to the Senate's conviction in a trial presided over by the Chief Justice (for presidential impeachment). The courts decide criminal cases, but the President may pardon offenders. These mixtures led to complaints by several delegates at the state ratifying conventions. They objected that the branches of government had been intermingled instead of being kept separate. By the time of the Philadelphia Convention, however, the doctrine of separated powers had been overtaken by the system of checks and balances. One contemporary pamphleteer dismissed the separation doctrine, in its pure form, as a "hackneyed principle" and a "trite maxim." M.J.C. Vile, Constitutionalism and the Separation of Powers 153.

Madison devoted several of the essays in his *Federalist Papers* to the need for overlapping powers, claiming that the concept was superior to the impracticable partitioning of powers demanded by some of the Anti-Federalists (see readings). Alexander Hamilton, in Federalist No. 75, defended the combination of the executive with the Senate in the treaty process and bristled at "the trite topic of the intermixture of powers." Opponents were not satisfied. Three states — Virginia, North Carolina, and Pennsylvania — wanted a separation clause added to the national Bill of Rights. They proposed that

---

1. Kennedy v. Sampson, 511 F.2d 430 (D.C. Cir. 1974); Wright v. United States, 302 U.S. 583 (1938). See also The Pocket Veto Case, 279 U.S. 655 (1929).

Is the Federal Government One of Enumerated Powers?

In exercising its power of judicial review, the Supreme Court frequently claims that the federal government is one of enumerated powers. In 1995, while striking down a congressional effort to regulate guns in schoolyards, it said: "We start with first principles. The Constitution creates a Federal Government of enumerated powers." United States v. Lopez, 514 U.S. 549, 552 (1995). Two years later, in invalidating the Religious Freedom Restoration Act, the Court announced: "Under our Constitution, the Federal Government is one of enumerated powers." Boerne v. Flores, 521 U.S. 507, 516 (1997).

Yet the federal government clearly exercises powers that are not enumerated, including the Court's own power of judicial review. Over the years, the Court has recognized a number of implied powers for all three branches. A more accurate statement would be that the federal government is one of enumerated powers plus those that are implied in the enumeration or considered necessary for the effective functioning of government.

Article I, Section 5, provides that each House of Congress "may determine the Rules of its Proceedings [and] punish its Members for disorderly Behaviour." Article II, Section 2, states that the President "may require the Opinion, in writing, of the principal Officer in each of the executive Departments." Does any one doubt that Congress and the President could exercise those powers even if not enumerated?

Why does the Court speak about enumerated powers? Is it to impress upon the public that the federal government is subject to limits and that the Court is available to police the boundaries? Wouldn't that goal be satisfied by saying that the federal government is one of limited powers, which is surely the case? In these assertions about enumerated powers, is there risk that the Court may mislead the public and appear to be simplistic and false about fundamental principles?

neither branch could exercise the powers vested in the others. Congress rejected that proposal as well as a substitute amendment to make the three departments "separate and distinct."[2]

Enumerated and Implied Powers

Strict constructionists treat the American Constitution as one of enumerated powers. They oppose the notion of implied powers, powers derived from custom, or any other power not explicitly granted to one of the three branches. Although there is legitimate concern about the scope of implied powers, all three branches find it necessary to exercise powers not stated in the Constitution. Congress has the power to investigate as a necessary function of its legislative power; the President has the power to remove certain administrative officials to maintain executive accountability and responsibility; the Supreme Court has acquired the power to review legislative, executive, and state actions on questions of federal constitutionality. Nevertheless, the Court frequently insists that the federal government "is one of enumerated powers" (see box).

The framers recognized the need for implied powers. Madison noted in Federalist No. 44: "No axiom is more clearly established in law, or in reason, than that whenever the end is required, the means are authorized; whenever a general power to do a thing is given, every particular power necessary for doing it is included." Congress is granted not merely the enumerated powers found within Article I but is also authorized to "make all Laws which shall be necessary and proper for carrying into Execution the foregoing Powers, and all other Powers vested by this Constitution in the Government

---

2. Proposed by three states: 3 Elliot 280; 4 Elliot 116, 121; John Bach McMaster and Frederick D. Stone, eds., Pennsylvania and the Federal Constitution 475–77 (1888). Amendment language: Edward Dumbauld, The Bill of Rights and What It Means Today 174–75, 183, 199 (1957). Rejection: 1 Annals of Congress 435–36 (June 8, 1789) and 789–90 (August 18, 1789); 1 Senate Journals 64, 73–74 (1820).

of the United States, or in any Department or Officer thereof." The history of the Tenth Amendment underscores the need for implied powers (see section "Tenth Amendment" early in Chapter 8).[3]

The boundaries between the three branches of government are also strongly affected by the role of custom and acquiescence. When one branch engages in a certain practice and the other branches acquiesce, the practice gains legitimacy and can fix the meaning of the Constitution. Stuart v. Laird, 5 U.S. (1 Cr.) 299, 309 (1803). The President's power to remove officials was upheld in a 1903 ruling based largely on the "universal practice of the government for over a century." Shurtleff v. United States, 189 U.S. 311, 316 (1903). See also United States v. Midwest Oil Co., 236 U.S. 459, 469–71 (1915). Justice Frankfurter explained how executive power can grow when unchallenged: "A systematic, unbroken executive practice, long pursued to the knowledge of the Congress and never before questioned, engaged in by Presidents who have also sworn to uphold the Constitution, making as it were such exercise of power part of the structure of our government, may be treated as a gloss on 'executive Power' vested in the President by § 1 of Art. II." Youngstown Co. v. Sawyer, 343 U.S. 579, 610–11 (1952) (concurring opinion).[4]

Inherent Powers

Implied powers are drawn reasonably from enumerated powers and are therefore anchored in the Constitution. "Inherent" powers, by definition, are not drawn from express or enumerated powers. The powers are said to "inhere" in a person or an office. It has been argued that inherent powers are so intrinsic to an office that they are not subject to the constitutional system of checks and balances. Several Presidents have claimed the right to exercise inherent powers. On each occasion they have been rebuffed by Congress, the courts, or both: Truman trying to seize mills in 1952 to prosecute the war in Korea, Nixon refusing to spend appropriated funds ("impoundment"), Nixon conducting warrantless domestic surveillance, and Bush after the 9/11 terrorists attacks creating military tribunals without first obtaining authority from Congress. Louis Fisher, "Invoking Inherent Powers: A Primer," 37 Pres. Stud. Q. 1 (2007).

Congress Interprets the Ineligibility Clause

During debate in 1973, Congress interpreted the Ineligibility (or Emoluments) Clause, which provides that no Senator or Representative shall, during the time for which he or she is elected, be appointed to any civil office "the Emoluments whereof shall have been encreased during such time." President Nixon wanted to nominate Senator William Saxbe to be Attorney General. Because of the constitutional prohibition, legislation was introduced with the support of the administration. The debate is an excellent example of the choice between the literal language of the Constitution and going behind the language to determine the framers' intent. The debate below occurred in the Senate on November 28, 1973, and can be found at 119 Cong. Rec. 38315–49. Senator Hiram Fong defended the bill; Senator Robert C. Byrd opposed it.

MR. FONG. Mr. President, S. 2673 is a very simple bill. It merely sets the compensation and emoluments of the Office of Attorney General at that which existed on January 1, 1969. The proposed nomination of our colleague, Senator WILLIAM SAXBE, to the office of Attorney General has raised

---

3. Implied powers have been upheld in such cases as In re Neagle, 135 U.S. 1 (1890), which recognized the President's authority to assign a U.S. marshal to protect a threatened federal judge, and In re Debs, 158 U.S. 1 (1895), supporting presidential use of military force to break a railroad strike.

4. The failure of Congress to repeal or revise a grant of statutory authority in the face of administrative interpretation has been held by the courts as "persuasive evidence" that the interpretation was intended by Congress. Zemel v. Rusk, 381 U.S. 1, 11 (1965). See also Dames & Moore v. Regan; 453 U.S. 654, 678–88 (1981); Norwegian Nitrogen Co. v. United States, 288 U.S. 294, 313 (1933); Costanzo v. Tillinghast, 287 U.S. 341, 345 (1932).

the question of the eligibility of a Member of Congress for appointment to a high executive office when the emoluments of that office have been increased during the term of the Member.

Senator SAXBE was elected a Senator from the State of Ohio. He took his oath January 4, 1969, and commenced his term of office....

The President transmitted to Congress on January 15, 1969, recommendations which included the increase of the salary of the Attorney General from $35,000 to $60,000 a year. On February 4, 1969, the Senate defeated Senate Resolution No. 82, which would have disapproved the Presidential recommendation. Senator SAXBE voted with the majority.

The pay raise, including that of the Attorney General, became effective shortly thereafter.

This is the increased emolument now making Senator SAXBE ineligible for appointment to the Office of Attorney General.

S. 2673 is designed to reduce the emolument of the Office of Attorney General to what it was at the time Senator SAXBE took office as Senator in 1969 and thus remove his ineligibility for appointment to that office.

. . .

2. APPOINTMENT TO OFFICE WHERE EMOLUMENT INCREASED

The relevant portion of the clause where an emolument has been increased states:

"No Senator or Representative shall, during the Time for which he was elected, be appointed to any civil Office under the Authority of the United States ... the Emoluments whereof shall have been encreased during such time;" ...

What has been permissible under this portion of this clause?

[*Senator Fong explains that in two earlier instances, Senators were permitted to accept a Cabinet position although the salary of the Cabinet position had been increased during their term in office. In one case, Senator Morrill was confirmed for Secretary of State in 1876 after Congress had increased Cabinet officers from $8,000 to $10,000 in 1873 and reduced the salary a year later to $8,000. There was no challenge to his eligibility to serve. In 1909, Senator Knox was appointed Secretary of State after the salary for that position had been increased from $8,000 to $12,000 while Knox served as Senator. The Senate reduced Knox's salary as Secretary of State to what it was before his Senate term commenced and before the increase in pay.*]

. . .

The [*Ineligibility Clause*] ... was intended mainly to prevent two evils:

First. To protect legislators from unscrupulous executives using the enticement of public office to influence the actions of the legislators, and

Second. To avoid legislators viewing their election to Congress as a stepping stone to lucrative public office and utilizing their positions in the legislature as a means of creating offices or increasing the compensation of the offices they seek.

This being so, clearly the intent was not to prevent able and qualified Members of Congress from taking civil office.

Surely, the action of this Congress in reducing the emolument of the office of Attorney General from $60,000 to $35,000 cannot be said to be corruptive of the Members of this Congress nor can it be said that Senator SAXBE used his $42,500 Senate office as a stepping stone to a $35,000 office of Attorney General.

. . .

Mr. ROBERT C. BYRD. Mr. President, I yield myself such time as I may require.

... [I]t seems clear beyond doubt that the proposed nomination of Mr. SAXBE, would fly squarely into the face of the prohibition contained in article I, section 6, clause 2 of the Constitution ...

Clearly, the emoluments of the Office of Attorney General were increased from $35,000 to $60,000 during the term for which Mr. SAXBE was elected— which term will not expire until January 3, 1975.

. . .

We, as legislators, have a responsibility to consider the constitutional aspects of the actions we take in the performance of our senatorial duties. We cannot be fully responsive to the high calling of our office by simply saying, "We will act to do thus and so; leave it to the courts to determine the constitutional rectitude of what we have done."

Ours is a higher duty. It is a duty that requires us—especially when great constitutional questions confront us in the first instance and on the first impression—to examine and to determine, according to our best lights, the constitutionality of actions we are called upon to take.

The nomination of Mr. SAXBE, under the circumstances peculiar to the nomination, fits almost squarely as a constitutional question heretofore essentially untested and unexplored.

Returning now to the matter before us: Can the constitutional bar be lifted by legislation? I say not.

. . .

[The Senate passed the bill, 75 to 16, and the House passed it on December 3. It became law on December 10, 1973 (P.L. 93-178, 87 Stat. 697)].

Presidential Signing Statements and Congressional Response

When signing a bill into law, Presidents have adopted the practice of offering interpretations of various provisions in the bill to bring about what the President and his advisers consider a constitutional result. In 2006 a controversy erupted when a reporter for the Boston Globe published an article detailing the extensive use by President George W. Bush of signing statements asserting broad presidential powers. Below is a statement by President Bush on December 30, 2005, signing a defense appropriation bill that prohibited cruel, inhuman, or degrading treatment or punishment of persons held in U.S. custody. The purpose of the legislation was to prohibit torture of detainees. Following that is a signing statement by President Obama on December 31, 2011 regarding a defense appropriations bill that contained provisions that limited his ability to try detainees in the federal courts rather than in military tribunals. Finally, the statements are followed by a bill proposed in the House of Representatives in response to the practice.

. . .

Statement by the President on H.R. 2863

Today, I have signed into law H.R. 2863, the "Department of Defense, Emergency Supplemental Appropriations to Address Hurricanes in the Gulf of Mexico, and Pandemic Influenza Act, 2006." The Act provides resources needed to fight the war on terror, help citizens of the Gulf States recover from devastating hurricanes, and protect Americans from a potential influenza pandemic.

Sections 8007, 8011, and 8093 of the Act prohibit the use of funds to initiate a special access program, a new overseas installation, or a new start program, unless the congressional defense committees receive advance notices. The Supreme Court of the United States has stated that the President's authority to classify and control access to information bearing on the national security flows from the Constitution and does not depend upon a legislative grant of authority. Although the advance notice contemplated by sections 8007, 8011, and 8093 can be provided in most situations as a matter of comity, situations may arise, especially in wartime, in which the President must act promptly under his constitutional grants of executive power and authority as Commander in Chief of the Armed Forces while protecting certain extraordinarily sensitive national security information. The executive branch shall construe these sections in a manner consistent with the constitutional authority of the President.

. . .

The executive branch shall construe Title X in Division A of the Act, relating to detainees, in a manner consistent with the constitutional authority of the President to supervise the unitary executive branch and as Commander in Chief and consistent with the constitutional limitations on the judicial power, which will assist in achieving the shared objective of the Congress and the President, evidenced in Title X, of protecting the American people from further terrorist attacks.…
George W. Bush
The White House
December 30, 2005

Statement by the President on H.R. 1540

Today I have signed into law H.R. 1540, the "National Defense Authorization Act for Fiscal Year 2012." I have signed the Act chiefly because it authorizes funding for the defense of the United States and its interests abroad, crucial services for service members and their families, and vital national security programs that must be renewed.

. . .

[Despite the administration's successful national defense efforts] some in Congress continue to insist upon restricting the options available to our counterterrorism professionals and interfering with the very operations that have kept us safe. My Administration has consistently opposed such measures.… Moving forward, my Administration will interpret and implement the provisions described below in a manner that best preserves the flexibility on which our safety depends and upholds the values on which this country was founded....

. . .

Section 1022 seeks to require military custody for a narrow category of non-citizen detainees who are "captured in the course of hostilities authorized by the Authorization for Use of Military Force." This section is ill-conceived and will do nothing to improve the security of the United States. The executive branch already has the authority to detain in military custody those members of al-Qa'ida who are captured in the course of hostilities ... and as Commander in Chief I have directed the military to do so where appropriate. I reject any approach that would mandate military custody where law enforcement provides the best method of incapacitating a terrorist threat.... I have signed the bill because I believe that this section can be interpreted and applied in a manner that avoids undue harm to our current operations.

. . .

Other provisions in this bill above could interfere with my constitutional foreign affairs powers ... my Administration will also interpret and implement [the section requiring the president to provide notice to Congress before sharing any information about the ballistic missile defense with Russia] in a manner that does not interfere with the President's constitutional authority to conduct foreign affairs and avoids the undue disclosure of sensitive diplomatic communications. [Other sections] could be read to require the disclosure of sensitive diplomatic communications and national security secrets.... [S]hould any application of these provisions conflict with my constitutional authorities, I will treat the provisions as non-binding.

. . .

Barack Obama
The White House
December 31, 2011

. . .

Response in Congress to Signing Statement Controversy

Congresswoman Sheila Jackson Lee of Texas introduced the following bill in 2007, (and again in 2009), objecting to presidential use of signing statements to assert authority:

110TH CONGRESS
1ST SESSION
H. R. 264

To prevent the President from encroaching upon the Congressional prerogative to make laws, and for other purposes.

. . .

A BILL

To prevent the President from encroaching upon the Congressional prerogative to make laws, and for other purposes.

-Be it enacted by the Senate and House of Representatives of the United States of America in Congress assembled,

SECTION 1. SHORT TITLE.

-This Act may be cited as the 'Congressional Lawmaking Authority Protection Act of 2007'.

SEC. 2. FINDINGS AND PURPOSES.

-(a) Findings- The Congress makes the following findings:

-(1) The Framers of the Constitution understood that the power to make laws is such an awesome power that they intended it to be exercised by the most democratic branch of government.

-(2) To ensure that the lawmaking power would be exercised by the branch of government that is the closest and most accountable to the people the Constitution provides that 'All legislative power herein granted shall be vested in a Congress of the United States, which shall consist of a Senate and House of Representatives.'

-(3) The Constitution limits the role of the President in the lawmaking process to—

-(A) giving Congress information on the State of the Union;

-(B) recommending to Congress for consideration such measures as the President deems necessary and expedient; and

-(C) approving or vetoing bills and joint resolutions presented to him for signature.

-(4) Statements made by the President contemporaneously with the signing of a bill or joint resolution that express the President's interpretation of the scope, constitutionality, and intent of Congress in enacting the bill or joint resolution presented for signature encroach upon the power to make laws that the Framers vested solely in the Congress.

-(5) According to a May 5, 2006, editorial in the New York Times, the current President of the United States has issued more than 750 'presidential signing statements' declaring he would not do what the laws required, the most notorious example of which is the signing statement issued by the President asserting he was not bound by the Congressional ban on the torture of prisoners.

-(6) On June 5, 2006, the American Bar Association created a 10-member Blue-Ribbon Task Force on Presidential Signing Statements and the Separation of Powers Doctrine' to take a balanced, scholarly look at the use and implications of signing statements, and to propose appropriate ABA policy consistent with the ABA's commitment to safeguarding the rule of law and the separation of powers in our system of government.

-(7) On July 24, 2006, the Task Force determined that signing statements that signal the president's intent to disregard laws adopted by Congress undermine the separation of powers by depriving Congress of the opportunity to override a veto, and by shutting off policy debate between the two branches of government. According to the Task Force, such presidential signing statements operate as a 'line item veto,' which the U.S. Supreme Court has ruled unconstitutional. The Task Force strongly recommended the Congress to enact appropriate legislation to ensure that such presidential

signing statements do not undermine the rule of law and the constitutional system of separation of powers.

-(b) Purposes- The purposes of this Act are—

-(1) to preserve the separation of powers intended by the Framers by preventing the President from encroaching upon the Congressional prerogative to make law; and

-(2) to ensure that no Federal or State executive or independent agency, and no Federal or State judge, can attach legal significance to any presidential signing statement when construing any law enacted by the Congress.

SEC. 3. LIMITATION ON USE OF FUNDS.

-(a) Limitation on Use of Funds—None of the funds made available to the Executive Office of the President, or to any Executive agency (as defined in section 105 of title 5 of the United States Code), from any source may be used to produce, publish, or disseminate any statement made by the President contemporaneously with the signing of any bill or joint resolution presented for signing by the President.

-(b) Application of Limitation—Subsection (a) shall apply only to statements made by the President regarding the bill or joint resolution presented for signing that contradict, or are inconsistent with, the intent of Congress in enacting the bill or joint resolution or that otherwise encroach upon the Congressional prerogative to make laws.

SEC. 4. CONSTRUCTION AND APPLICATION OF ACTS OF CONGRESS.

-For purposes of construing or applying any Act enacted by the Congress, a governmental entity shall not take into consideration any statement made by the President contemporaneously with the President's signing of the bill or joint resolution that becomes such Act.

Madison's Analysis of the Separation Doctrine

Some Anti-Federalists were astonished to find in the draft Constitution a variety of overlappings among the three branches of government: the President's power to veto legislation, the Senate's involvement in treaties and appointments, and other features of what we now call the system of checks and balances. In Federalist Nos. 47, 48, and 51, James Madison refutes these objections by reviewing the British Constitution, the theory of Montesquieu, and the practices adopted by the American states, all for the purpose of demonstrating that checks and balances are necessary to give the three branches adequate power to resist encroachments.

FEDERALIST NO. 47

Having reviewed the general form of the pro-

posed government and the general mass of power allotted to it, I proceed to examine the particular structure of this government, and the distribution of this mass of power among its constituent parts.

One of the principal objections inculcated by the more respectable adversaries to the Constitution, is its supposed violation of the political maxim, that the legislative, executive, and judiciary departments ought to be separate and distinct. In the structure of the federal government, no regard, it is said, seems to have been paid to this essential precaution in favor of liberty. The several departments of power are distributed and blended in such a manner as at once to destroy all symmetry and beauty of form, and to expose some of the essential parts of the edifice to the danger of being crushed by the disproportionate weight of other parts.

No political truth is certainly of greater intrinsic value, or is stamped with the authority of more enlightened patrons of liberty, than that on which the objection is founded. The accumulation of all powers, legislative, executive, and judiciary, in the same hands, whether of one, a few, or many, and whether hereditary, self-appointed, or elective, may justly be pronounced the very definition of tyranny. Were the federal Constitution, therefore, really chargeable with the accumulation of power, or with a mixture of powers, having a dangerous tendency to such an accumulation, no further arguments would be necessary to inspire a universal reprobation of the system. I persuade myself, however, that it will be made apparent to every one, that the charge cannot be supported, and that the maxim on which it relies has been totally misconceived and misapplied....

The oracle who is always consulted and cited on this subject is the celebrated Montesquieu. If he be not the author of this invaluable precept in the science of politics, he has the merit at least of displaying and recommending it most effectually to the attention of mankind. Let us endeavor, in the first place, to ascertain his meaning on this point.

The British Constitution was to Montesquieu what Homer has been to the didactic writers on epic poetry....

On the slightest view of the British Constitution, we must perceive that the legislative, executive, and judiciary departments are by no means totally separate and distinct from each other. The executive magistrate forms an integral part of the legislative authority. He alone has the prerogative of making treaties with foreign sovereigns, which, when made, have, under certain limitations, the force of legislative acts. All the members of the judiciary department are appointed by him, can be removed by him on the address of the two Houses of Parliament, and form, when he pleases to consult them, one of his

constitutional councils. One branch of the legislative department forms also a great constitutional council to the executive chief, as, on another hand, it is the sole depositary of judicial power in cases of impeachment, and is invested with the supreme appellate jurisdiction in all other cases. The judges, again, are so far connected with the legislative department as often to attend and participate in its deliberations, though not admitted to a legislative vote.

From these facts, by which Montesquieu was guided, it may clearly be inferred that, in saying "There can be no liberty where the legislative and executive powers are united in the same person, or body of magistrates," or, "if the power of judging be not separated from the legislative and executive powers," he did not mean that these departments ought to have no *partial agency* in, or no *control* over, the acts of each other. His meaning, as his own words import, and still more conclusively as illustrated by the example in his eye, can amount to no more than this, that where the *whole* power of one department is exercised by the same hands which possess the *whole* power of another department, the fundamental principles of a free constitution are subverted....

If we look into the constitutions of the several States, we find that, notwithstanding the emphatical and, in some instances, the unqualified terms in which this axiom has been laid down, there is not a single instance in which the several departments of power have been kept absolutely separate and distinct.

[*Here Madison proceeds, state by state, to explain how the state constitutions mix the three powers of government.*]

FEDERALIST NO. 48

It was shown in the last paper that the political apothegm there examined does not require that the legislative, executive, and judiciary departments should be wholly unconnected with each other. I shall undertake, in the next place, to show that unless these departments be so far connected and blended as to give to each a constitutional control over the others, the degree of separation which the maxim requires, as essential to a free government, can never in practice be duly maintained.

It is agreed on all sides, that the powers properly belonging to one of the departments ought not to be directly and completely administered by either of the other departments. It is equally evident, that none of them ought to possess, directly or indirectly, an overruling influence over the others, in the administration of their respective powers. It will not be denied, that power is of an encroaching nature, and that it ought to be effectually restrained from passing the limits assigned to it. After discriminating, therefore, in theory, the several classes of power, as they may in their nature be legislative, executive, or judiciary, the next and most difficult task is to provide some practical security for each, against the invasion of the others. What this security ought to be, is the great problem to be solved.

Will it be sufficient to mark, with precision, the boundaries of these departments, in the constitution of the government, and to trust to these parchment barriers against the encroaching spirit of power? This is the security which appears to have been principally relied on by the compilers of most of the American constitutions. But experience assures us, that the efficacy of the provision has been greatly overrated; and that some more adequate defence is indispensably necessary for the more feeble, against the more powerful, members of the government. The legislative department is everywhere extending the sphere of its activity, and drawing all power into its impetuous vortex.

[*Starting with Virginia, Madison details various examples of legislative usurpations of executive and judicial power. He also cites instances of executive encroachments.*]

FEDERALIST NO. 51

To what expedient, then, shall we finally resort, for maintaining in practice the necessary partition of power among the several departments, as laid down in the Constitution? The only answer that can be given is, that as all these exterior provisions are found to be inadequate, the defect must be supplied, by so contriving the interior structure of the government as that its several constituent parts may, by their mutual relations, be the means of keeping each other in their proper places....

In order to lay a due foundation for that separate and distinct exercise of the different powers of government, which to a certain extent is admitted on all hands to be essential to the preservation of liberty, it is evident that each department should have a will of its own; and consequently should be so constituted that the members of each should have as little agency as possible in the appointment of the members of the others....

It is equally evident, that the members of each department should be as little dependent as possible on those of the others, for the emoluments annexed to their offices. Were the executive magistrate, or the judges, not independent of the legislature in this particular, their independence in every other would be merely nominal.

But the great security against a gradual concentration of the several powers in the same department, consists in giving to those who administer each department the necessary constitutional means and personal motives to resist encroachments of the others. The provision for defence must in this, as in all other cases, be made commensurate to the danger of attack. Ambition must be made to counteract ambition. The interest of the man must be connected with the constitutional rights of the place. It may be a reflection on human nature, that such devices should be necessary to control the abuses of government. But what is government itself, but the greatest of all reflections on human nature? If men were angels, no government would be necessary. If angels were to govern men, neither external nor internal controls on government would be necessary. In framing a government which is to be administered by men over men, the great difficulty lies in this: you must first enable the government to control the governed; and in the next place oblige it to control itself. A dependence on the people is, no doubt, the primary control on the government; but experience has taught mankind the necessity of auxiliary precautions.

B. PRESIDENTIAL POWER

Scholars have long debated the nature of executive power, viewing it in historical, philosophical, political, and constitutional terms. Do the words "executive power" in Article II suggest a grant to the President of broad, discretionary authority, of all powers conceivably executive in nature? Or is the executive power clause a reference to the subsequent enumeration of presidential power? In Federalist Nos. 69 and 70, Alexander Hamilton offered his views on the nature of executive power and compared it to the more comprehensive grant of power for the English king (see reading).

In a concurring opinion, Justice Robert H. Jackson denied that the executive power "is a grant in bulk of all conceivable power." Youngstown Co. v. Sawyer, 343 U.S. 579, 641 (1952). Yet it is widely acknowledged that the President possesses powers beyond those that are enumerated. For functional purposes, he enjoys some implied powers. As part of his administrative responsibilities and his duty to faithfully execute the laws under the Take Care Clause of Article II, he may exercise the power to remove executive officials. Myers v. United States, 272 U.S. 52 (1926). Similarly, the Court has recognized a limited executive privilege to retain information within the executive branch, as an attribute of the President's duties and responsibilities. United States v. Nixon, 418 U.S. 683 (1974).

Prerogative

Quite apart from the concept of enumerated and implied powers, as properly grounded in the Constitution, do Presidents possess an extraconstitutional authority or prerogative power? May they act in response to an emergency—in the absence of law or even in conflict with it—for the public good? In 1936, Justice George Sutherland asserted that authority over foreign affairs is not dependent upon a grant from the Constitution since the powers of external sovereignty are derived from the English Crown. United States v. Curtiss-Wright, 299 U.S. 304, 315–16 (1936). When President Harry S. Truman seized the steel mills in 1952, he invoked emergency powers and claimed that he could act "for whatever is for the best of the country." Public Papers of the Presidents, 1952–53, at 273. That interpretation was emphatically rejected by the Supreme Court. Youngstown Co. v. Sawyer, 343 U.S. 579 (1952).

Some scholars, embracing the claim of extraconstitutional executive powers, have located its modern expression in the Lockean Prerogative. Edward S. Corwin, The President: Office and Powers, 1787–1948, at 6–7, 10, 15–16, 182 (3rd rev. ed. 1948). In the second of his *Two Treatises of Civil Government* published in 1690, John Locke stated that prerogative was the power "to act according to discretion, for the public good, without the prescription of the law and sometimes even against it." The executive does not possess the legal authority to act, but because he is perhaps best-positioned and best-equipped to act, he may choose to respond to the emergency, much like the man who pulls down "an innocent Man's House to stop the Fire, when the next to it is burning." Locke, Second Treatise, § 159. Neither the good citizen nor the executive acts under the color of law in the case of emergency; they simply act and accept the consequences. They can be spared punishment through exoneration from the legislature in the way of retroactive authorization or by a pardon. If a President's explanation is unsatisfactory he may be impeached.

The method of retroactive authorization or indemnity maintains constitutional government: the legislature and not the executive is the lawmaker. There is no evidence that the framers of the Constitution intended to incorporate the Lockean Prerogative in the Constitution. When President Lincoln took extraordinary actions at the start of the Civil War while Congress was in recess, he acknowledged that some of his actions may have lacked legal authority and therefore turned to Congress for retroactive approval (see "Lincoln's Initiatives" in Chapter 7).

Hamilton on Executive Power

In several essays in *The Federalist*, Alexander Hamilton hoped to allay the fears that the framers had defined executive power too broadly. In Federalist No. 69, he compared the power of the President to the much larger prerogatives of the King of England. How does contemporary presidential power compare with Hamilton's analysis? In Federalist No. 70, he defended energy in the executive as not only a leading characteristic of good government but also consistent with republican principles.

FEDERALIST NO. 69

I PROCEED now to trace the real characters of the proposed Executive, as they are marked out in the plan of the convention. This will serve to place in a strong light the unfairness of the representations which have been made in regard to it.

. . .

That magistrate is to be elected for *four* years; and is to be reeligible as often as the people of the United States shall think him worthy of their confidence. In these circumstances there is a total dissimilitude between *him* and a king of Great Britain, who in an *hereditary* monarch, possessing the crown as a patrimony descendible to his heirs forever; but there is a close analogy between *him* and a governor of New York, who is elected for *three* years, and is reeligible without limitation or intermission....

The President of the United States would be liable to be impeached, tried, and, upon conviction of treason, bribery, or other high crimes or misdemeanors, removed from office; and would afterwards be liable to prosecution and punishment in the ordinary course of law. The person of the king of Great Britain is sacred and inviolable; there is no constitutional tribunal to which he is amenable; no punishment to which he can be subjected without involving the crisis of a national revolution....

The President of the United States is to have power to return a bill, which shall have passed the two branches of the legislature, for reconsideration; and the bill so returned is to become a law, if, upon that reconsideration, it be approved by two thirds of both houses. The king of Great Britain, on his part, has an absolute negative upon the acts of the two houses of Parliament....

The President is to be the "commander-in-chief of the army and navy of the United States, and of the militia of the several States, when called into the actual service of the United States...." In most of these particulars, the power of the President will resemble equally that of the king of Great Britain and of the governor of New York. The most material points of difference are these:—*First.* The President will have only the occasional command of such part of the militia of the nation as by legislative provision may be called into the actual service of the Union. The king of Great Britain and the governor of New York have at all times the entire command of all the militia within their several jurisdictions. In this article, therefore, the power of the President would be inferior to that of either the monarch or the governor. *Second.* The President is to be commander-in-chief of the army and navy of the United States. In this respect his authority would be nominally the same with that of the king of Great Britain, but in substance much inferior to it. It would amount to nothing more than the supreme command and direction of the military and naval forces, as first General and admiral of the Confederacy; while that of the British king extends to the *declaring* of war and to the *raising* and *regulating* of fleets and armies,—all which, by the Constitution under consideration, would appertain to the legislature....

The President is to have power, with the advice and consent of the Senate, to make treaties, provided two thirds of the senators present concur. The king of Great Britain is the sole and absolute representative of the nation in all foreign transactions. He can of his own accord make treaties of peace, commerce, alliance, and of every other description....

The President is also to be authorized to receive ambassadors and other public ministers. This, though it has been a rich theme of declamation, is more a matter of dignity than of authority....

The President is to nominate, and, *with the advice and consent of the Senate,* to appoint ambassadors and other public ministers, judges of the Supreme Court, and in general all officers of the United States established by law, and whose appointments are not otherwise provided for by the Constitution. The king of Great Britain is emphatically and truly styled the fountain of honor. He not only appoints to all offices, but can create offices. He can confer titles of nobility at pleasure; and has the disposal of an immense number of church preferments. There is evidently a great inferiority in the power of the President, in this particular, to that of the British king; ...

FEDERALIST NO. 70

THERE is an idea, which is not without its advocates, that a vigorous Executive is inconsistent with the genius of republican government. The enlightened well-wishers to this species of government must at least hope that the supposition is destitute of foundation; since they can never admit its truth, without at the same time admitting the condemnation of their own principles. Energy in the Executive is a leading character in the definition of good government. It is essential to the protection of the community against foreign attacks; it is not less essential to the steady administration of the laws; to the protection of property against those irregular and high-handed combinations which sometimes interrupt the ordinary course of justice; to the security of liberty against the enterprises and assaults of ambition, of faction, and of anarchy....

There can be no need, however, to multiply arguments or examples on this head. A feeble Executive implies a feeble execution of the government. A feeble execution is but another phrase for a bad execution; and a government ill executed, whatever it may be in theory, must be, in practice, a bad government.

Taking it for granted, therefore, that all men of sense will agree in the necessity of an energetic Executive, it will only remain to inquire, what are the ingredients which constitute this energy? ...

The ingredients which constitute energy in the Executive are, unity; duration; an adequate provision for its support; competent powers.

The ingredients which constitute safety in the republican sense are, a due dependence on the people; a due responsibility.

. . .

That unity is conducive to energy will not be disputed. Decision, activity, secrecy, and dispatch will generally characterize the proceedings of one man in a much more eminent degree than the proceedings of any greater number; and in proportion as the number is increased, these qualities will be diminished.

C. CREATING THE EXECUTIVE DEPARTMENTS

The Constitution established only a shell for government. It was left to the First Congress, by statute, to create executive departments and lower federal courts. In so doing, it necessarily debated and decided a number of fundamental constitutional issues. At that time, there was neither a functioning judiciary nor federal judicial precedents. From 1789 to the present, it has been primarily the responsibility of Congress to determine the structure of government, the powers and functions of agencies, limitations on the President's power, the qualifications of appointees, and the level of funding. But as presidential power expanded, so too did efforts to resist congressional attempts to limit presidential control of executive officers. Contemporary advocates for a strong presidency argue that the Framers intended to create a "unitary executive" without the divided control that is characteristic of the modern administrative state. Calabresi and Yoo, The Unitary Executive (2008). Other scholars have challenged this notion, characterizing the theory as one that undermines the separation of powers. MacKenzie, Absolute Power: How the Unitary Executive is Undermining the Constitution (2008). The history of the development of the federal government administrative structure tends to support the claims for congressional authority.

Since each department had to be created by statute, the First Congress could have placed departments under a single individual or a board of commissioners. The experience under the Articles of Confederation convinced most legislators that the board system lacked responsibility, energy, and order. The House of Representatives in 1789 voted for single executives to head the departments. Congress treated the Secretary of Foreign Affairs and the Secretary of War as executive officials, which had been the practice under the Articles. In contrast, Congress regarded the Secretary of the Treasury partly as a *legislative* agent, reflecting the mixed record during the Articles when the duties shifted back and forth between a Superintendent of Finance and a Board of Treasury. However, the first Secretary of the Treasury, Alexander Hamilton, performed essentially as an arm of the President, not Congress, and so it has been ever since. Under President Andrew Jackson, Congress tried to treat the Secretary of the Treasury as a legislative agent. Jackson eventually prevailed by arguing that the Secretary was "wholly an executive officer," but he had to remove two Secretaries of the Treasury to effectuate his policy and was censured by the Senate for his action. Three years later the Senate ordered its resolution of censure expunged from the record. Louis Fisher, Constitutional Conflicts Between Congress and the President 54 (2007).

Hybrid Officers

Some of the officers within the Treasury Department had duties that were not wholly executive in nature. During debate on the Department in 1789, Madison admitted that the comptroller's office "seemed to bear a strong affinity" to the legislative branch, while its settlement and adjustment of legal claims "partake too much of the Judicial capacity to be blended with the Executive" (see box on next page). When Congress created the General Accounting Office (GAO) in 1921, it transferred to it not

Madison Describing Independence of Comptroller's Office

It will be necessary, said he, to consider the nature of this office, to enable us to come to a right decision on the subject; in analyzing its properties, we shall discover they are not purely of an Executive nature. It seems to me that they partake of a Judiciary quality as well as Executive; perhaps the latter obtains in the greater degree. The principal duty seems to be deciding upon the lawfulness and justice of the claims and accounts subsisting between the United States and particular citizens; this partakes strongly of a judicial char-

acter, and there may be strong reasons why an officer of this kind should not hold his office at the pleasure of the Executive branch of the Government.

... I question very much whether [the President] can or ought to have any interference in the settling and adjusting the legal claims of individuals against the United States. The necessary examination and decision in such cases partake too much of the Judicial capacity to be blended with the Executive....

Source: 1 Annals of Congress 611–12, 614 (1789).

---

merely the powers and duties of the comptroller but even the personnel. GAO has been called a mixed agency: "legislative" when it audits accounts and investigates programs, and "executive" when it approves payments and settles and adjusts accounts.[5]

This hybrid status was attacked by the Reagan administration in 1985 but the GAO's powers were upheld in several lower court decisions.[6] The confrontation heightened at the end of 1985 when Congress passed the Gramm-Rudman-Hollings Act. The statute, which attempted to reduce federal deficits, authorized the Comptroller General under certain circumstances to order program cuts to be carried out by the President through a "sequestration" process. The administration claimed that Congress could not give executive duties to a legislative officer. The Supreme Court in 1986 agreed that the Comptroller General's sequestration duties were unconstitutional because Congress could not vest executive functions in an officer removable by Congress. BOWSHER v. SYNAR, 478 U.S. 714 (1986).

Take Care Clause

What is the President's authority to supervise officers within the executive branch? A careless reading of the Constitution gives the President the power to execute the laws. In fact, he is to "take Care that the Laws be faithfully executed" (Article II, Section 3). What happens if a statute places the execution of a program outside his control? Does this violate the principle of responsibility and accountability vested in a single executive? The short answer is that the heads of executive departments function only in part as political agents of the President. They also perform legal duties assigned to them by Congress.

In 1803, Chief Justice Marshall distinguished between two types of duties for a Cabinet head: ministerial and discretionary. The first duty allows Congress to direct a Secretary to carry out certain activities. The second duty is owed to the President alone. When a Secretary performs the first duty he is bound to obey the laws: "He acts ... under the authority of law, and not by the instructions of the

---

5. United States ex rel. Brookfield Const. Co., Inc. v. Stewart, 234 F.Supp. 94, 99–100 (D.D.C. 1964), aff'd, 339 F.2d 754 (D.C. Cir. 1964).

6. See Ameron, Inc. v. U.S. Army Corps of Engineers, 607 F.Supp. 962 (D. N.J. 1985); 610 F.Supp. 750 (D. N.J. 1985); 787 F.2d 875 (3d Cir. 1986); 809 F.2d 979 (3d Cir. 1986). The statute was also upheld in Lear Siegler, Inc. v. Lehman, 842 F.2d 1102 (9th Cir. 1988). In response to a Justice Department request, the Supreme Court agreed to dismiss its writ of certiorari. 488 U.S. 918 (1988).

president. It is a ministerial act which the law enjoins on a particular officer for a particular purpose." Marbury v. Madison, 5 U.S. (1 Cr.) 137, 157 (1803). The dispute over ministerial duties reappeared in 1838. Congress could mandate that certain payments be made, and neither the head of the executive department nor the President could deny or control these ministerial acts. Kendall v. United States, 37 U.S. 522 (1838).[7]

In 1854, the Attorney General stated that when laws "define what is to be done by a given head of department, and how he is to do it, there the President's discretion stops...." 6 Op. Att'y Gen. 326, 341. Opinions by Attorneys General advised various Presidents of substantial political and legal constraints on their ability to intervene in certain departmental matters (see Attorney General reading). The President is responsible for seeing that administrative officers faithfully perform their duties, "but the statutes regulate and prescribe these duties, and he has no more power to add to, or subtract from, the duties imposed upon subordinate executive and administrative officers by the law, than those officers have to add or subtract from his duties."[8] Departmental heads recognize the limitations that prevent them from interfering with decisions by administrative law judges (ALJs). Nash v. Califano, 613 F.2d 10 (2d Cir. 1980).

Federal courts invoked the ministerial-discretionary distinction on a regular basis during the Nixon administration to force the release of impounded funds. Cabinet heads were ordered to allocate or obligate funds. Berends v. Butz, 357 F.Supp. 143 (D. Minn. 1973); Train v. City of New York, 420 U.S. 35 (1975). Statutory duties also apply to the President. In 1974 an appellate court held that President Nixon had violated the law by refusing to carry out a statute on federal pay. He was directed to either submit to Congress the pay plan proposed by a salary commission or his own alternative plan. National Treasury Employees Union v. Nixon, 492 F.2d 587 (D.C. Cir. 1974).

The Department of Justice offers a classic case study of the tensions inherent in executive control of law enforcement. As presidential appointees, officers like the Attorney General and U.S. Attorneys serve at the pleasure of the President and are expected to advance the policy objectives of the President. On the other hand, as key federal law enforcement officers they are also expected to "take care" that the laws are faithfully executed regardless of political considerations. The controversy that erupted in 2007 over the firing of a number of U.S. Attorneys illustrated this tension. While everyone acknowledged that the President had the authority to remove these attorneys at his discretion, the concern that they were removed for illegitimate political reasons led to extensive press coverage, congressional hearings, and ultimately, the resignation of Attorney General Alberto Gonzales.

The meaning of the "take care" provision, and the amount of executive discretion in law enforcement, was also called into question several times during the Obama administration. In 2011 the Department of Justice announced that it would no longer defend the 1996 Defense of Marriage Act in court, having concluded that where same-sex couples were legally married in their state, the federal law violated the equal protection component of the Fifth Amendment due process clause. Congressional supporters of the Act accused the administration of shirking its constitutional duty to defend the laws Congress passes. Similar criticism was launched at Obama's decision in 2012 to stop deportation of and allow work permits for undocumented young people who were brought to the country illegally by their parents. The president's defenders argued that the decision was well within the discretion given the executive in enforcing the law.

---

7. See also United States v. Schurz, 102 U.S. 378 (1880); United States v. Price, 116 U.S. 43 (1885); United States v. Louisville, 169 U.S. 249 (1898); and Clackamus County, Ore. v. McKay, 219 F.2d 479, 496 (D.C. Cir. 1954), vacated as moot, 349 U.S. 909 (1955).

8. 19 Op. Att'y Gen. 685, 686–87 (1890). See also 1 Op. Att'y Gen. 624 (1823); 1 Op. Att'y Gen. 636 (1824); 1 Op. Att'y Gen. 678 (1824); 1 Op. Att'y Gen. 705 (1825); 1 Op. Att'y Gen. 706 (1825); 2 Op. Att'y Gen. 480 (1831); 2 Op. Att'y Gen. 507 (1832); 2 Op. Att'y Gen. 544 (1832); 4 Op. Att'y Gen. 515 (1846); 5 Op. Att'y Gen. 287 (1851); 10 Op. Att'y Gen. 526 (1863); 11 Op. Att'y Gen. 14 (1864); 13 Op. Att'y Gen. 28 (1869); 18 Op. Att'y Gen. 31 (1884).

Independent Commissions

Beginning in 1887, Congress created independent regulatory commissions and gave them some autonomy from presidential control. The Interstate Commerce Commission (ICC) was the first of these creatures, and since that time Congress has established other independent bodies, including the Federal Reserve System (1913), the Federal Trade Commission (1914), the Securities and Exchange Commission (1934), and the Commodity Futures Trading Commission (1975).

Compared to the single administrators who head the executive departments, commissions are multimember (collegial) bodies that are headed by at least three commissioners. Independence is secured in three ways: (1) the terms of the commissioners are staggered to insulate them from presidential elections, (2) the President's power to remove commissioners is limited by specified statutory grounds, and (3) restrictions are placed on the number of commissioners who may belong to the same political party.

Independent commissions often carry out judicial duties, which helps explain why commissions are collegial bodies. Just as we want appellate courts to consist of more than one judge to protect against "the idiosyncrasies of a single individual," so do we want agencies that adjudicate to be multimember. Kenneth Culp Davis, Administrative Law of the Seventies 15 (1976). Even if the functions of these commissions were transferred to the regular executive departments, the judicial functions would still be set apart and insulated from presidential control.

Another odd body created by Congress is the U.S. Sentencing Commission, established in 1984 "as an independent commission in the judicial branch of the United States." Because of serious disparities among the sentences imposed by federal judges for similar offenses, this commission is responsible for devising more equitable sentencing guidelines. The seven voting members are appointed by the President with the advice and consent of the Senate. At least three members are federal judges. The chairman of the Commission and other members are subject to removal by the President "only for neglect of duty or malfeasance in office or for other good cause shown." Of course, the President may only remove judges from the Commission, not from their judicial positions. The Supreme Court, voting 8 to 1, upheld the Commission against a number of challenges. It concluded that Congress had not delegated excessive legislative power to the Commission, nor had it violated separation of power principles by placing the Commission in the judicial branch and requiring federal judges to serve on the Commission and share their authority with non-judges. Furthermore, it was not a constitutional violation to limit presidential removal for cause only. Mistretta v. United States, 488 U.S. 361 (1989).

Independent Counsel

Following the scandals of the Watergate period, Congress passed legislation in 1978 to establish an independent "special prosecutor" to investigate charges against the President, the Vice President, and high-level executive branch officials. Congress concluded that the Attorney General, as a key member of the President's cabinet, might face a conflict of interest in trying to prosecute a suspected top official. The special prosecutor, later called independent counsel, could be removed by the President only for "good cause" and was appointed by a special panel of federal judges.

The Justice Department attacked the statute as unconstitutional because it vested part of law enforcement in an officer not appointed by the President. Moreover, the removal feature was seen as an impermissible restriction on presidential power. However, the Supreme Court voted 7 to 1 to sustain the independent counsel. MORRISON v. OLSON, 487 U.S. 654 (1988). Although the independent counsel statute was reauthorized by Congress in 1994 for five years, objections continued to be voiced, both on policy and constitutional grounds. If Congress reauthorized the statute, could the President veto the bill on constitutional grounds after the procedure had been upheld by the Court in *Morrison* (see box on next page)?

Each time Congress reauthorized the independent counsel statute—in 1983, 1987, and 1994— substantial reforms were adopted. Even with these changes, no doubt the potential for abuse is great

Could the President Use Constitutional Grounds to Veto an Independent Counsel Bill?

Suppose you work in the White House Counsel office and the President receives a bill to reauthorize the independent counsel statute. He tells you he has serious reservations about the bill, not merely policy concerns but constitutional issues as well. He concludes that the exercise of prosecuting authority by the independent counsel encroaches upon executive power and his obligations under the Constitution.

You remind him that the Supreme Court considered those issues in *Morrison* and yet upheld the statute on constitutional grounds. He reminds you that President Jackson vetoed the U.S. Bank bill despite *McCulloch* and says he does not feel bound by Court rulings when it comes to invoking the veto power to protect the prerogatives of his office. He feels an obligation to defend his own institution, regardless of what Congress or the courts do. In drafting his veto message, can you use constitutional arguments or has that issue already been settled by the Court's decision? For that matter, could Congress, in considering a bill to reauthorize the independent counsel, vote it down on constitutional grounds?

for any prosecutor, including those in the Justice Department. When the office of independent counsel expired in 1999, Congress did not renew it.

The record of the independent counsel law does not support the general claim that these individuals inevitably target a particular person and use unlimited funds to indict him. From 1978 to 1999, independent counsels conducted 20 investigations. No indictments were brought in twelve of the cases. When indictments and convictions were obtained, as with probes into corruption in executive departments (Housing and Urban Development, Agriculture) or the Iran-Contra affair, the abuses were great and needed correction. Complaints have been made about the time that some investigations take and the level of expenditures (especially Lawrence Walsh's investigation of Iran-Contra and Kenneth Starr's investigation of Whitewater and other matters), but much of the delay and cost come from the complexity of the issues and the withholding of key documents by the administration. Some form of independent counsel—whether statutory or not—is needed because there are activities (particularly White House and presidential) that cannot be investigated by the Justice Department without creating an unacceptable conflict of interest.

On December 30, 2003, Acting Attorney General James B. Comey appointed Patrick J. Fitzgerald as special counsel to investigate the leak from the Bush White House of the name of a CIA employee, Valerie Plame. In 2005 a grand jury indicted I. Lewis "Scooter" Libby, assistant to the Vice President, for perjury and making false statements in the investigation and in 2007 a jury found him guilty. Later that year President Bush, in the exercise of his pardon power, commuted Libby's prison sentence, leaving in place the conviction. Although Special Counsel Fitzgerald had been appointed by the executive, he was nonetheless criticized in the same way independent counsels had been under the Ethics Act provisions. Given the high political stakes in criminal investigations of top-level executive branch officials, it seems inevitable that prosecutors of these investigations will face challenges to their authority. Katy Harriger, "Executive Power and Prosecution: Lessons from the Libby Trial and the U.S. Attorney Firings," 38 Pres. Stud. Q. 491 (2008).

Bowsher v. Synar

478 U.S. 714 (1986)

In an effort to control the budget deficits that had mushroomed during the Reagan administration, Congress passed the Gramm-Rudman-Hollings Act in 1985. The statute established a mul-

tiyear schedule designed to bring the federal deficit to zero by 1991. If Congress and the President failed to abide by the statutory schedule, automatic cuts (called "sequestration") would occur. Under the sequestration process, the Comptroller General would receive budget estimates from the Office of Management and Budget (OMB) and the Congressional Budget Office (CBO) and proceed to draft the sequestration order, to be signed and issued by the President without change. A three-judge federal district court in 1986 held that the statute was unconstitutional as a violation of the separation of powers doctrine because the Comptroller General is removable only by a joint resolution initiated by Congress or by impeachment. Congressman Mike Synar filed the suit attacking the constitutionality of the Act. One of the defendants was Charles A. Bowsher, the Comptroller General.

CHIEF JUSTICE BURGER delivered the opinion of the Court.

The question presented by these appeals is whether the assignment by Congress to the Comptroller General of the United States of certain functions under the Balanced Budget and Emergency Deficit Control Act of 1985 violates the doctrine of separation of powers.

· · ·

III

We noted recently that "[t]he Constitution sought to divide the delegated powers of the new Federal Government into three defined categories, Legislative, Executive, and Judicial." *INS* v. *Chadha*, 462 U.S. 919, 951 (1983). The declared purpose of separating and dividing the powers of government, of course, was to "diffus[e] power the better to secure liberty." *Youngstown Sheet & Tube Co.* v. *Sawyer*, 343 U.S. 579, 635 (1952) (Jackson, J., concurring). Justice Jackson's words echo the famous warning of Montesquieu, quoted by James Madison in The Federalist No. 47, that "'there can be no liberty where the legislative and executive powers are united in the same person, or body of magistrates'...."

The Constitution does not contemplate an active role for Congress in the supervision of officers charged with the execution of the laws it enacts. The President appoints "Officers of the United States" with the "Advice and Consent of the Senate...." Article II, § 2. Once the appointment has been made and confirmed, however, the Constitution explicitly provides for removal of Officers of the United States by Congress only upon impeachment by the House of Representatives and conviction by the Senate. An impeachment by the House and trial by the Senate can rest only on "Treason, Bribery or other high Crimes and Misdemeanors." Article II, § 4. A direct congressional role in the removal of officers charged with the execution of the laws beyond this limited one is inconsistent with separation of powers.

This was made clear in debate in the First Congress in 1789. [*The Court summarizes the holdings in Myers v. United States, 272 U.S. 52 (1926), Humphrey's Executor v. United States, 295 U.S. 602 (1935), and Weiner v. United States, 357 U.S. 349 (1958).*]

In light of these precedents, we conclude that Congress cannot reserve for itself the power of removal of an officer charged with the execution of the laws except by impeachment. To permit the execution of the laws to be vested in an officer answerable only to Congress would, in practical terms, reserve in Congress control over the execution of the laws....

· · ·

IV

Appellants urge that the Comptroller General performs his duties independently and is not subservient to Congress. We agree with the District Court that this contention does not bear close scrutiny.

The critical factor lies in the provisions of the statute defining the Comptroller General's office relating to removability. Although the Comptroller General is nominated by the President from a list of three individuals recommended by the Speaker of the House of Representatives and the President pro tempore of the Senate, see 31 U.S.C. § 703(a)(2), and confirmed by the Senate, he is removable only at the initiative of Congress. He may be removed not only by impeachment but also by Joint Resolution of Congress "at any time" resting on any one of the following bases:

"(i) permanent disability;

"(ii) inefficiency;

"(iii) neglect of duty;

"(iv) malfeasance; or

"(v) a felony or conduct involving moral turpitude." 31 U.S.C. § 703(e)(1).

* * *

... The statute permits removal for "inefficiency,"

"neglect of duty," or "malfeasance." These terms are very broad and, as interpreted by Congress, could sustain removal of a Comptroller General for any number of actual or perceived transgressions of the legislative will....

... In constitutional terms, the removal powers over the Comptroller General's office dictate that he will be subservient to Congress.

. . .

Against this background, we see no escape from the conclusion that, because Congress had retained removal authority over the Comptroller General, he may not be entrusted with executive powers. The remaining question is whether the Comptroller General has been assigned such powers in the Balanced Budget and Emergency Deficit Control Act of 1985.

V

The primary responsibility of the Comptroller General under the instant Act is the preparation of a "report." This report must contain detailed estimates of projected federal revenues and expenditures. The report must also specify the reductions, if any, necessary to reduce the deficit to the target for the appropriate fiscal year. The reductions must be set forth on a program-by-program basis.

. . .

... [W]e view these functions as plainly entailing execution of the law in constitutional terms. Interpreting a law enacted by Congress to implement the legislative mandate is the very essence of "execution" of the law. Under § 251, the Comptroller General must exercise judgment concerning facts that affect the application of the Act. He must also interpret the provisions of the Act to determine precisely what budgetary calculations are required. Decisions of that kind are typically made by officers charged with executing a statute. ... [A]s *Chadha* makes clear, once Congress makes its choice in enacting legislation, its participation ends. Congress can thereafter control the execution of its enactment only indirectly—by passing new legislation. *Chadha*, 462 U.S., at 958. By placing the responsibility for execution of the Balanced Budget and Emergency Deficit Control Act in the hands of an officer who is subject to removal only by itself, Congress in effect has retained control over the execution of the Act and has intruded into the executive function. The Constitution does not permit such intrusion.

VI

[*Appellants argued that rather than strike down the*

sequestration powers of the Comptroller General, the Court should nullify the provision of the Budget and Accounting Act of 1921 giving Congress authority to remove the Comptroller General. The Court rejected this option, concluding that this might make the Comptroller General subservient to the President, a result not intended by Congress.]

VII

No one can doubt that Congress and the President are confronted with fiscal and economic problems of unprecedented magnitude, but "the fact that a given law or procedure is efficient, convenient, and useful in facilitating functions of government, standing alone, will not save it if it is contrary to the Constitution. Convenience and efficiency are not the primary objectives—or the hallmarks—of democratic government ..." *Chadha, supra,* 462 U.S., at 944.

We conclude the District Court correctly held that the powers vested in the Comptroller General under § 251 violate the command of the Constitution that the Congress play no direct role in the execution of the laws. Accordingly, the judgment and order of the District Court are affirmed.

Our judgment is stayed for a period not to exceed 60 days to permit Congress to implement the fallback provisions.

JUSTICE STEVENS, with whom JUSTICE MARSHALL joins, concurring in the judgment.

[*They disagree that the power of Congress to remove the Comptroller General "represents the primary constitutional evil." They disagree also on the attempt to label the functions assigned to the Comptroller General as "executive." They view the statute as unconstitutional because it allows Congress, through the agency of the Comptroller General, to make policy that binds the nation without following the procedures mandated by Article I: passage of a bill by both Houses and presentment of the bill to the President. Stevens and Marshall also reject the premise in the majority opinion that a definite line distinguishes executive power from legislative power.*]

. . .

JUSTICE WHITE dissenting.

The Court, acting in the name of separation of powers, takes upon itself to strike down the Gramm-Rudman-Hollings Act, one of the most novel and far-reaching legislative responses to a national crisis since the New Deal. The basis of the Court's action is a solitary provision of another statute that was passed over sixty years ago and has lain dormant since that time. I cannot concur in the Court's action. Like the Court, I will not purport to speak to the wisdom of the policies incorporated in the legislation the Court invalidates; that is a matter for the Congress and the Executive, *both* of which expressed their assent to the statute barely half a year ago. I will, however, address the wisdom of the Court's willingness to interpose its distressingly formalistic view of separation of powers as a bar to the attainment of governmental objectives through the means chosen by the Congress and the President in the legislative process established by the Constitution. Twice in the past four years I have expressed my view that the Court's recent efforts to police the separation of powers have rested on untenable constitutional propositions leading to regrettable results. See *Northern Pipeline Construction Co.* v. *Marathon Pipe Line Co.,* 458 U.S. 50, 92–118 (1982) (WHITE, J., dissenting); *INS* v. *Chadha,* 462 U.S. 919, 967–1003. (WHITE, J., dissenting). Today's result is even more misguided....

JUSTICE BLACKMUN dissenting.

The Court may be correct when it says that Congress cannot constitutionally exercise removal authority over an official vested with the budget-reduction powers that § 251 of the Balanced Budget and Emergency Deficit Control Act of 1985 gives to the Comptroller General. This, however, is not because "the removal powers over the Comptroller General's office dictate that he will be subservient to Congress," *ante,* at 730; I agree with JUSTICE WHITE that any such claim is unrealistic. Furthermore, I think it is clear under *Humphrey's Executor* v. *United States,* 295 U.S. 602 (1935), that "executive" powers of the kind delegated to the Comptroller General under the Deficit Control Act need not be exercised by an officer who serves at the President's pleasure; Congress certainly could prescribe the standards and procedures for removing the Comptroller General....

Attorney General Opinion on Ministerial Duties

As early as *Marbury* v. *Madison* (1803), the Supreme Court distinguished between two types of executive duties: ministerial and discretionary. For the latter, the duty of an executive official and adviser is to the President alone. For ministerial actions, the duty is to the statute. Beginning in 1823, Attorneys General regularly informed Presidents that they had no authority to interfere with certain statutory duties assigned by Congress to executive officers. The opinion below, by Attorney General William Wirt in 1823 (1 Op. Att'y Gen. 624), explains the law on ministerial duties to President Monroe.

SIR: I have examined the case of Major Joseph Wheaton, submitted by you for my opinion; and would proceed at once to the expression of an opinion on the merits of his claims, but that there is a preliminary inquiry which must be first made, and as to which I beg leave to ask your direction; and that is, whether it is proper for you to interfere in this case at all? I will suggest the considerations which strike me as rendering it improper.

I. It appears to me that you have no power to interfere.

The constitution of the United States requires the President, in general terms, to take care that the laws be faithfully executed; that is, it places the officers engaged in the execution of the laws under his general superintendence: he is to see that they do their duty faithfully; and on their failure, to cause them to be displaced, prosecuted, or impeached, according to the nature of the case. In case of forcible resistance to the laws, too, so as to require the interposition of the power of the government to overcome

the illegal resistance, he is to see that that power be furnished. But it could never have been the intention of the constitution, in assigning this general power to the President to take care that the laws be executed, that he should in person execute the laws himself. For example: if a marshal should either refuse to serve process altogether, or serve it irregularly, that the President should correct the irregularity, or supply the omission, by executing the process in person. To interpret this clause of the constitution so as to throw upon the President the duty of a personal interference in every specific case of an alleged or defective execution of the laws, and to call upon him to perform such duties himself, would be not only to require him to perform an impossibility himself, but to take upon himself the responsibility of all the subordinate executive officers of the government—a construction too absurd to be seriously contended for. But the requisition of the constitution is, that he shall *take care* that the *laws* be executed. If the laws, then, require a particular officer by name to perform a duty, not only is that officer bound to perform it, but no other officer can perform it without a violation of the law; and were the President to perform it, he would not only be not taking care that the laws were faithfully executed, but he would be violating them himself. The constitution assigns to Congress the power of designating the duties of particular officers: the President is only required to take care that they execute them faithfully....

Let us carry this principle to the laws which regulate the settlement of public accounts. In the original organization of the Treasury Department (vol. 2, Laws U.S., p. 48,) the duties of the officers are designated specifically. There was one Auditor and one Comptroller. The duty of the Auditor is declared to be to receive all public accounts; and, after examination, to certify the balance, and transmit the accounts, with the vouchers and certificate, to the Comptroller, for his decision thereon; with this *proviso:* that if any person be dissatisfied therewith, he may within six months appeal to the Comptroller against such settlement. Here the right of appeal stops; there is no proviso for an appeal to the President. With regard to the Comptroller, it directs that it shall be his duty to superintend the adjustment and preservation of all public accounts; to examine all accounts settled by the Auditor, and certify the balances arising thereon to the Register: no right of appeal from his decision to the President....

It would be strange, indeed, if it were otherwise. The office of President is ordained for very different purposes than that of settling individual accounts. The constitution has committed to him the care of the great interests of the nation, in all its foreign and domestic relations. [*For example, the President is charged with being the Commander in Chief, granting pardons, selecting ambassadors, making treaties, and so forth.*] How will it be possible for the President to perform these great duties, if he is also to exercise the appellate power of revising and correcting the settlement of all the individual accounts which pass through the hands of the accounting officers? ...

Morrison v. Olson

487 U.S. 654 (1988)

The Ethics in Government Act of 1978, as amended, created an "independent counsel" to investigate high-ranking officials in the executive branch. Under the provisions of the statute, if the Attorney General concluded that the actions of an official exceeded a certain threshold that required additional investigation, he or she applied to a panel of three federal judges who were authorized to appoint an independent counsel and to define the counsel's prosecutorial jurisdiction. The Attorney General could remove the independent counsel only "for cause." In this lawsuit, Independent Counsel Alexia Morrison investigated Theodore B. Olson, a former official with the Department of Justice. He was accused of giving false and misleading testimony to Congress. The statute was declared unconstitutional by a divided (2 to 1) panel of the D.C. Circuit.

CHIEF JUSTICE REHNQUIST delivered the opinion of the Court.

This case presents us with a challenge to the independent counsel provisions of the Ethics in Government Act of 1978, 28 U.S.C.A. §§ 49, 591 *et seq.* (1982 ed., Supp. V). We hold today that these provisions of the Act do not violate the Appointments Clause of the Constitution, Art. II, § 2, cl. 2, or the limitations of Article III, nor do they impermissibly interfere with the President's authority under Article II in violation of the constitutional principle of separation of powers.

I

[*In this section the Court reviews the statutory*

arrangement for the appointment and removal of independent counsels.]

. . .

III

The Appointments Clause of Article II reads as follows:

"[The President] shall nominate, and by and with the Advice and Consent of the Senate, shall appoint Ambassadors, other public Ministers and Consuls, Judges of the Supreme Court, and all other Officers of the United States, whose Appointments are not herein otherwise provided for, and which shall be established by Law: but the Congress may by

Law vest the Appointment of such inferior Officers, as they think proper, in the President alone, in the Courts of Law, or in the Heads of Departments." U.S. Const., Art. II, § 2, cl. 2.

The parties do not dispute that "[t]he Constitution for purposes of appointment ... divides all its officers into two classes." *United States* v. *Germaine,* 99 U.S. (9 Otto) 508, 509 (1879). As we stated in *Buckley* v. *Valeo,* 424 U.S. 1, 132 (1976), "[p]rincipal officers are selected by the President with the advice and consent of the Senate. Inferior officers Congress may allow to be appointed by the President alone, by the heads of departments, or by the Judiciary." The initial question is, accordingly, whether appellant is an "inferior" or a "principal" officer. If she is the latter, as the Court of Appeals concluded, then the Act is in violation of the Appointments Clause.

The line between "inferior" and "principal" officers is one that is far from clear, and the Framers provided little guidance into where it should be drawn.... We need not attempt here to decide exactly where the line falls between the two types of officers, because in our view appellant clearly falls on the "inferior officer" side of that line. Several factors lead to this conclusion.

First, appellant is subject to removal by a higher Executive Branch official. Although appellant may not be "subordinate" to the Attorney General (and the President) insofar as she possesses a degree of independent discretion to exercise the powers delegated to her under the Act, the fact that she can be removed by the Attorney General indicates that she is to some degree "inferior" in rank and authority. Second, appellant is empowered by the Act to perform only certain, limited duties. An independent counsel's role is restricted primarily to investigation and, if appropriate, prosecution for certain federal crimes.... [T]his grant of authority does not include any authority to formulate policy for the Government or the Executive Branch....

Third, appellant's office is limited in jurisdiction. Not only is the Act itself restricted in applicability to certain federal officials suspected of certain serious federal crimes, but an independent counsel can only act within the scope of the jurisdiction that has been granted by the Special Division pursuant to a request by the Attorney General. Finally, appellant's office is limited in tenure. There is concededly no time limit on the appointment of a particular counsel. Nonetheless, the office of independent counsel is "temporary" in the sense that an independent counsel is appointed essentially to accomplish a single task, and when that task is over the office is termi-

nated, either by the counsel herself or by action of the Special Division.... In our view, these factors ... are sufficient to establish that appellant is an "inferior" officer in the constitutional sense.

. . .

This does not, however, end our inquiry under the Appointments Clause. Appellees argue that even if appellant is an "inferior" officer, the Clause does not empower Congress to place the power to appoint such an officer outside the Executive Branch. They contend that the Clause does not contemplate congressional authorization of "interbranch appointments," in which an officer of one branch is appointed by officers of another branch. The relevant language of the Appointments Clause is worth repeating. It reads: " ... but the Congress may by Law vest the Appointment of such inferior Officers, as they think proper, in the President alone, in the courts of Law, or in the Heads of Departments." On its face, the language of this "excepting clause" admits of no limitation on interbranch appointments. Indeed, the inclusion of "as they think proper" seems clearly to give Congress significant discretion to determine whether it is "proper" to vest the appointment of, for example, executive officials in the "courts of Law." ...

We do not mean to say that Congress' power to provide for interbranch appointments of "inferior officers" is unlimited. In addition to separation of powers concerns, which would arise if such provisions for appointment had the potential to impair the constitutional functions assigned to one of the branches, [precedent suggests]that Congress' decision to vest the appointment power in the courts would be improper if there was some "incongruity" between the functions normally performed by the courts and the performance of their duty to appoint....

IV

Appellees next contend that the powers vested in the Special Division by the Act conflict with Article III of the Constitution.... As a general rule, we have broadly stated that "executive or administrative duties of a nonjudicial nature may not be imposed on judges holding office under Art. III of the Constitution." *Buckley,* 424 U.S., at 123.... The purpose of this limitation is to help ensure the independence of the Judicial Branch and to prevent the judiciary from encroaching into areas reserved for the other branches....

Most importantly, the Act vests in the Special Division the power to choose who will serve as independent counsel and the power to define his or her jurisdiction. § 593(b). Clearly, once it is accepted that the Appointments Clause gives Congress the power to vest the appointment of officials such as the independent counsel in the "courts of Law," there can be no Article III objection to the Special Division's exercise of that power, as the power itself derives from the Appointments Clause, a source of authority for judicial action that is independent of Article III....

We are more doubtful about the special Division's power to terminate the office of the independent counsel pursuant to § 596(b)(2)....

... As we see it, "termination" may occur only when the duties of the counsel are truly "completed" or "so substantially completed" that there remains no need for any continuing action by the independent counsel. It is basically a device for removing from the public payroll an independent counsel who has served her purpose, but is unwilling to acknowledge the fact. So construed, the Special Division's power to terminate does not pose a sufficient threat of judicial intrusion into matters that are more properly within the Executive's authority to require that the Act be invalidated as inconsistent with Article III.

. . .

V

We now turn to consider whether the Act is invalid under the constitutional principle of separation of powers. Two related issues must be addressed: The first is whether the provision of the Act restricting the Attorney General's power to remove the independent counsel to only those instances in which he can show "good cause," taken by itself, impermissibly interferes with the President's exercise of his constitutionally appointed functions. The second is whether, taken as a whole, the Act violates the separation of powers by reducing the President's ability to control the prosecutorial powers wielded by the independent counsel.

A

. . .

Unlike both *Bowsher* and *Myers,* this case does not involve an attempt by Congress itself to gain a role in the removal of executive officials other than its established powers of impeachment and conviction. The Act instead puts the removal power squarely in the hands of the Executive Branch; an independent counsel may be removed from office, "only by the personal action of the Attorney General,

and only for good cause." ... In our view, the removal provisions of the Act make this case more analogous to *Humphrey's Executor* v. *United States,* 295 U.S. 602 (1935), and *Wiener* v. *United States,* 357 U.S. 349 (1958), than to *Myers* or *Bowsher.*

. . .

Although the counsel exercises no small amount of discretion and judgment in deciding how to carry out her duties under the Act, we simply do not see how the President's need to control the exercise of that discretion is so central to the functioning of the Executive Branch as to require as a matter of constitutional law that the counsel be terminable at will by the President.

. . .

B

The final question to be addressed is whether the Act, taken as a whole, violates the principle of separation of powers by unduly interfering with the role of the Executive Branch....

We observe first that this case does not involve an attempt by Congress to increase its own powers at the expense of the Executive Branch.... Unlike some of our previous cases, most recently *Bowsher* v. *Synar,* this case simply does not pose a "dange[r] of congressional usurpation of Executive Branch functions." 478 U.S., at 727; see also *INS* v. *Chadha,* 462 U.S. 919, 958 (1983)....

Similarly, we do not think that the Act works any *judicial* usurpation of properly executive functions. As should be apparent from our discussion of the Appointments Clause above, the power to appoint inferior officers such as independent counsels is not in itself an "executive" function in the constitutional sense, at least when Congress has exercised its power to vest the appointment of an inferior office in the "courts of Law." ...

... It is undeniable that the Act reduces the amount of control or supervision that the Attorney General and, through him, the President exercises over the investigation and prosecution of a certain class of alleged criminal activity.... Nonetheless, the Act does give the Attorney General several means of supervising or controlling the prosecutorial powers that may be wielded by an independent counsel. Most importantly, the Attorney General retains the power to remove the counsel for "good cause," ... Notwithstanding the fact that the counsel is to some degree "independent" and free from Executive supervision to a greater extent than other federal prosecutors, in our view these features of the Act give the

Executive Branch sufficient control over the independent counsel to ensure that the President is able to perform his constitutionally assigned duties.

. . .

Reversed.

Justice Kennedy took no part in the consideration or decision of this case.

Justice Scalia, dissenting.

... [T]he founders conspicuously and very consciously declined to sap the executive's strength in the same way they had weakened the legislature: by dividing the executive power. Proposals to have multiple executives, or a council of advisors with separate authority were rejected....

. . .

II

. . .

"The executive Power shall be vested in a President of the United States."

As I described at the outset of this opinion, this does not mean *some of* the executive power, but *all of* the executive power. It seems to me, therefore, that the decision of the Court of Appeals invalidating the present statute must be upheld on funda-

mental separation-of-powers principles if the following two questions are answered affirmatively: (1) Is the conduct of a criminal prosecution (and of an investigation to decide whether to prosecute) the exercise of purely executive power? (2) Does the statute deprive the President of the United States of exclusive control over the exercise of that power? Surprising to say, the Court appears to concede an affirmative answer to both questions, but seeks to avoid the inevitable conclusion that since the statute vests some purely executive power in a person who is not the President of the United States it is void.

. . .

As for the second question, whether the statute before us deprives the President of exclusive control over that quintessentially executive activity: The Court does not, and could not possibly, assert that it does not. That is indeed the whole object of the statute. Instead, the Court points out that the President, through his Attorney General, has at least *some* control. That concession is alone enough to invalidate the statute....

... It is not for us to determine, and we have never presumed to determine, how much of the purely executive powers of government must be within the full control of the President. The Constitution prescribes that they *all* are....

D. APPOINTMENTS AND REMOVALS

Three steps are required to fill offices created by Congress: (1) nomination by the President, (2) confirmation by the Senate, and (3) commissioning of the appointee by the President. For lesser officers, the Constitution permits Congress to dispense with the confirmation process and place the power of appointment directly in the President, the courts, or department heads.

In legal theory, the power to nominate is the "sole act of the president" and "completely voluntary." Marbury v. Madison, 5 U.S. at 155. Theoretically, Congress cannot designate the person to fill the office it creates. United States v. Ferreira, 54 U.S. (13 How.) 39, 50–51 (1852); Myers v. United States, 272 U.S. at 128. Nevertheless, it can stipulate the qualifications of appointees, and legislators frequently select the names of judges, U.S. attorneys, and marshals for their state. In such cases, the roles are reversed: Congress nominates and the President "advises and consents." If the names submitted by Congress are unacceptable, the White House and the Justice Department can insist on substitute recommendations. Interest groups and professional organizations are also active in submitting names for consideration and evaluating those who are nominated. Senators can also thwart the president's nominations by refusing to schedule hearings and votes, something that has happened with increasing frequency with judicial nominees.

There are limits to congressional intervention. In 1976, the Supreme Court reviewed a statute giving Congress the power to appoint four members to the Federal Election Commission, which monitors the financing and conduct of congressional and presidential elections. All six voting members (including two nominated by the President) required confirmation by the majority of *both* Houses of Congress. The Court ruled that Congress could not select officers responsible for carrying out exec-

Congressional Appointment of Executive Officials That Investigate

[*President Reagan's statement on signing the U.S. Commission on Civil Rights Act of 1983*]:

I have signed today H.R. 2230, establishing a new Commission on Civil Rights....

The bill I have signed today is, of course, a product of negotiation and compromise. While, as noted, I am pleased that the Commission has been re-created so that it may continue the missions assigned to it, the Department of Justice has raised concerns as to the constitutional implications of certain provisions of this legislation. I have appended a recitation of these reservations.

. . .

Statement by the Department of Justice

... The basic purpose of the old Commission on Civil Rights — to investigate, study, appraise, and report on discrimination — would be maintained, and most of its current authorities would remain intact. However, because half of the members of the Commission will be appointed by the Congress, the Constitution does not permit the Commission to exercise responsibilities that may be performed only by "Officers of the United States" who are appointed in accordance with the Appointments Clause of the United States Constitution (Article II, Section 2, clause 2). Therefore, it should be clear that although the Commission will continue to perform investigative and informative functions, it may not exercise enforcement, regulatory, or other executive responsibilities that may be performed only by officers of the United States.

SOURCE: Public Papers of the Presidents, 1983 (II), at 1634–35.

utive and judicial duties. Such functions could be exercised only by "Officers of the United States" appointed pursuant to Article II, Section 2, Clause 2. For the Court, this meant either one of two constitutional options: nomination by the President, subject to the advice and consent of the Senate; or vesting the appointment power in the President alone, in the courts of law, or in department heads. Congress took the first option when it rewrote the statute. The decision explains how the appointment process is related to presidential responsibility and the separation doctrine. BUCKLEY v. VALEO, 424 U.S. 1 (1976).[9]

In *Buckley* v. *Valeo*, the Court noted that if an agency's powers are "essentially of an investigative and informative nature," Congress can appoint the agency officials. In reauthorizing the Civil Rights Commission in 1983, Congress passed legislation that gave it the right to appoint four of the eight members of the Commission. The President appointed the remaining four. 97 Stat. 1301 (1983). In signing the bill, President Reagan acknowledged that Congress operated within its powers because the essential functions of the Civil Rights Commission were investigative (see box).

Recess Appointments

The framers recognized that the Senate would not always be in session to give advice and consent to presidential nominations. To cover these periods, the President is authorized to make recess appointments: "The President shall have Power to fill up all Vacancies that may happen during the Recess of the Senate, by granting Commissions which shall expire at the End of their next Session" (Article II, Section 3, Clause 3). "Happen" is interpreted broadly to mean "happen to exist," even if a

---

9. For subsequent analyses of the Appointments Clause, see Olympic Federal Savings and Loan Assn. v. Director, Office of Thrift Supervision, 732 F.Supp. 1183 (D.D.C. 1990), Freytag v. Commissioner, 501 U.S. 868 (1991), and Edmond v. United States, 520 U.S. 661 (1997).

vacancy occurs while the Senate is in session. 1 Op. Att'y Gen. 631 (1823). The meaning of "recess" remains uncertain. The Justice Department has stated that adjournments "for 5 or even 10 days" are too short to justify the use of the recess power. 3 Op. Att'y Gen. 20, 25 (1921); 3 O.L.C. 311, 314 (1979). In recent years, however, the department has argued in briefs that recess appointments might be justified for recesses in excess of three days.

The question of what constitutes a "recess" for the purposes of such an appointment may well be decided in court. In early January of 2012, before the scheduled return of Congress on January 23rd, President Obama made recess appointments to the new Consumer Financial Protection Bureau and to the National Labor Relations Board. The administration claimed that the "pro forma" sessions that the Senate had been holding over the holiday vacation (where one Senator shows up every few days) were not real work sessions and that in truth, the Senate was in recess (See OLC Recess Appointments reading). Three business groups opposed to the nominations attempted to challenge the appointments as part of an existing suit over an NLRB rule, but a federal district court rejected that attempt. It seems likely that cases will be filed once the agencies issue regulations, but whether federal courts want to wade into this political dispute over what constitutes a recess remains to be seen.

In 1863, when it appeared that Presidents were abusing the power to make recess appointments and were deliberately circumventing the Senate's confirmation role, Congress passed legislation to prohibit the use of funds to pay the salary of anyone appointed during a Senate recess to fill a vacancy that existed "while the Senate was in session and is by law required to be filled by and with the advice and consent of the Senate, until such appointee shall have been confirmed by the Senate." 12 Stat. 646 (1863). The law was liberalized in 1940 to permit payment under three conditions. 54 Stat. 751 (1940); 5 U.S.C. § 5503. Legislation has also been passed to prohibit funds to pay the salary of any recess appointee who is later rejected by the Senate. E.g., 113 Stat. 467, § 609 (1999); Fisher, Constitutional Conflicts between Congress and the President 38–45. See also the section, "Recess Appointments" in Chapter 4.

Removing Officials

Although the Constitution provides no express authority for the President to remove officials in the executive branch, it was agreed by the First Congress that responsible government requires the President to dismiss incompetent, corrupt, or unreliable administrators. If anything by nature is executive, Madison said, "it must be that power which is employed in superintending and seeing that the laws are faithfully executed." 1 Annals of Congress 500 (June 17, 1789).

The debates of 1789 were interpreted by Chief Justice Taft to leave not the "slightest doubt" that the power to remove officers appointed by the President and confirmed by the Senate is "vested in the President alone." MYERS v. UNITED STATES, 272 U.S. at 114. Taft reached too far; the debates reveal deep divisions among House members and close votes on the Senate side. Fisher, Constitutional Conflicts between Congress and the President, 49–54. Moreover, the debates in 1789 focused on the President's power to remove the Secretary of Foreign Affairs, which Congress conceded to be an agent of the President and executive in nature. Madison anticipated other types of officers in the executive branch who might have a mix of legislative and judicial duties, requiring greater independence from the President. 1 Annals of Congress 611–14 (June 29, 1789). See box in Section C of this chapter. Congress can place statutory limitations on the removal power. Before Taft made his sweeping claim, the Supreme Court had recognized that Congress could specify the grounds for removal. Shurtleff v. United States, 189 U.S. 311 (1903).

A balance must be struck between the President's authority to remove executive officials and Congress's power under the Necessary and Proper Clause to create an office and attach conditions to it. Taft's decision was later modified to permit Congress to limit the President's power to remove commissioners with quasi-legislative and quasi-judicial powers. HUMPHREY'S EXECUTOR v. UNITED

STATES 295 U.S. 602 (1935); Wiener v. United States, 357 U.S. 349 (1958). Depending on statutory language or commitments by the President and his subordinates to maintain an officer's independence, presidential power to remove officers may face other constraints.[10]

New removal power issues were raised in 2002 by the creation of the Public Company Accounting Oversight Board (PCAOB) in the Sarbanes-Oxley Act. The PCAOB was created in the wake of the Enron and WorldCom scandals to investigate and provide oversight of firms that conduct audits of large corporations. The Securities and Exchange Commission makes the appointments, and is authorized to remove board members for "good cause." An accounting firm challenged the constitutionality of the process by which board members were appointed. A federal district court dismissed the case and the U.S. Court of Appeals for the DC Circuit affirmed that decision in a 2–1 vote, finding that *Humphrey's Executor* and *Morrison* were controlling. A vigorous dissent by Judge Brett Kavanaugh contended that "On the removal issue, the majority opinion views this case as *Humphrey's Executor* redux. But this case is *Humphrey's Executor* squared." Basing his argument on the "unitary executive" view of the presidency, he noted that "the President is two levels of for-cause removal away from Board members, a previously unheard-of restriction on and attenuation of the President's authority over executive officers." Free Enterprise Fund v. Public Company Accounting Oversight Bd., et al., 537 F.3d 667 (D.C. Cir. 2008). In 2010 a divided (5–4) Supreme Court reversed in part and affirmed in part the appellate court's decision, finding the double for-cause removal restrictions unconstitutional but finding the SEC's appointment of the Board acceptable and severing the "for cause" removal restrictions from the rest of the Act. FREE ENTERPRISE FUND v. PUBLIC COMPANY ACCOUNTING OVERSIGHT BOARD, 561 U.S. ___ (2010). Beyond the occasional lawsuit are the more frequent interventions by Congress. Congress may remove an individual by abolishing the office. A term of office created by one statute can be reduced or eliminated by a subsequent statute, requiring the discharge of a federal employee. Crenshaw v. United States, 134 U.S. 99 (1890). Through the passage of nonbinding resolutions, committee investigations, the contempt power, and other pressures, Congress can precipitate a person's resignation or removal. Congress also intervenes to *protect* an officeholder, particularly a "whistleblower" who alerts Congress to agency deficiencies. Lawmakers intervene for reasons of simple justice and to keep open the channels of communication between agencies and Congress. Louis Fisher, "Congress and the Removal Power," 10 Congress & the Presidency 63 (1983).

Buckley v. Valeo

424 U.S. 1 (1976)

As part of the Federal Election Campaign Act amendments of 1974, which responded to the scandals during the presidential election of 1972, Congress enacted a number of reforms, including the creation of the Federal Election Commission (FEC). Because Congress appointed some of the commissioners, the Supreme Court reviewed the framers' intent with respect to the Appointments Clause and the separation of powers theory. The case also involved First Amendment challenges to the limits placed on campaign spending, although that part of the opinion is not excerpted here. Senator James Buckley was one of several plaintiffs who brought this action against Francis Valeo, Secretary of the Senate.

---

10. Nader v. Bork, 366 F.Supp. 104 (D.D.C. 1973); Borders v. Reagan, 518 F.Supp. 250 (D.D.C. 1981); Stephen Gettinger, "The Power Struggle Over Federal Parole," 8 Corrections Magazine 41 (1982); Berry v. Reagan, Civil Action No. 83-3182 (D.D.C. November 14, 1983).

PER CURIAM.

These appeals present constitutional challenges to the key provisions of the Federal Election Campaign Act of 1971 (Act), and related provisions of the Internal Revenue Code of 1954, all as amended in 1974.

. . .

IV. THE FEDERAL ELECTION COMMISSION

The 1974 amendments to the Act create an eight-member Federal Election Commission (Commission) and vest in it primary and substantial responsibility for administering and enforcing the Act. The question that we address in this portion of the opinion is whether, in view of the manner in which a majority of its members are appointed, the Commission may under the Constitution exercise the powers conferred upon it....

... the Commission is given extensive rulemaking and adjudicative powers....

The body in which this authority is reposed consists of eight members. The Secretary of the Senate and the Clerk of the House of Representatives are *ex officio* members of the Commission without the right to vote. Two members are appointed by the President *pro tempore* of the Senate "upon the recommendations of the majority leader of the Senate and the minority leader of the Senate." Two more are to be appointed by the Speaker of the House of Representatives, likewise upon the recommendations of its respective majority and minority leaders. The remaining two members are appointed by the President. Each of the six voting members of the Commission must be confirmed by the majority of both Houses of Congress, and each of the three appointing authorities is forbidden to choose both of their appointees from the same political party.

. . .

[*After concluding that the Commission's composition was ripe for review, the Court analyzed the substantive issues.*]

B. The Merits

Appellants urge that since Congress has given the Commission wide-ranging rulemaking and enforcement powers with respect to the substantive provisions of the Act, Congress is precluded under the principle of separation of powers from vesting in itself the authority to appoint those who will exercise such authority. Their argument is based on the language of Art. II, § 2, cl. 2, of the Constitution, which provides in pertinent part as follows:

"[The President] shall nominate, and by and with the Advice and Consent of the Senate, shall appoint ... all other Officers of the United States, whose Appointments are not herein otherwise provided for, and which shall be established by Law: but the Congress may by Law vest the Appointment of such inferior Officers, as they think proper, in the President alone, in the Courts of Law, or in the Heads of Departments."

Appellants' argument is that this provision is the exclusive method by which those charged with executing the laws of the United States may be chosen. Congress, they assert, cannot have it both ways. If the Legislature wishes the Commission to exercise all of the conferred powers, then its members are in fact "Officers of the United States" and must be appointed under the Appointments Clause. But if Congress insists upon retaining the power to appoint, then the members of the Commission may not discharge those many functions of the Commission which can be performed only by "Officers of the United States," as that term must be construed within the doctrine of separation of powers.

Appellee Commission and *amici* in support of the Commission urge that the Framers of the Constitution, while mindful of the need for checks and balances among the three branches of the National Government, had no intention of denying to the Legislative Branch authority to appoint its own officers. Congress, either under the Appointments Clause or under its grants of substantive legislative authority and the Necessary and Proper Clause in Art. I, is in their view empowered to provide for the appointment to the Commission in the manner which it did because the Commission is performing "appropriate legislative functions."

. . .

1. SEPARATION OF POWERS

... Our inquiry of necessity touches upon the fundamental principles of the Government established by the Framers of the Constitution, and all litigants and all of the courts which have addressed themselves to the matter start on common ground in the recognition of the intent of the Framers that the powers of the three great branches of the National Government be largely separate from one another.

... [T]he Constitution by no means contemplates total separation of each of these three essential branches of Government.... The men who met in Philadelphia in the summer of 1787 were practical statesmen, experienced in politics, who viewed the principle of separation of powers as a vital check against tyranny. But they likewise saw that a hermetic sealing off of the three branches of Government from one another would preclude the establishment of a Nation capable of governing itself effectively.

. . .

2. THE APPOINTMENTS CLAUSE

The principle of separation of powers was not simply an abstract generalization in the minds of the Framers: it was woven into the document that they drafted in Philadelphia in the summer of 1787....

The Appointments Clause could, of course, be read as merely dealing with etiquette or protocol in describing "Officers of the United States," but the drafters had a less frivolous purpose in mind....

We think that the term "Officers of the United States" ... is a term intended to have substantive meaning. We think its fair import is that any appointee exercising significant authority pursuant to the laws of the United States is an "Officer of the United States," and must, therefore, be appointed in the manner prescribed by § 2, cl. 2, of that Article.

. . .

Although two members of the Commission are initially selected by the President, his nominations are subject to confirmation not merely by the Senate, but by the House of Representatives as well. The remaining four voting members of the Commission are appointed by the President *pro tempore* of the Senate and by the Speaker of the House. While the second part of the Clause authorizes Congress to vest the appointment of the officers described in that part in "the Courts of Law, or in the Heads of Departments," neither the Speaker of the House nor the President *pro tempore* of the Senate comes within this language.

The phrase "Heads of Departments," used as it is in conjunction with the phrase "Courts of Law," suggests that the Departments referred to are themselves in the Executive Branch or at least have some connection with that branch. While the Clause expressly authorizes Congress to vest the appointment of certain officers in the "Courts of Law," the absence of similar language to include Congress must mean that neither Congress nor its officers were included within the language "Heads of Departments" in this part of cl. 2.

Thus with respect to four of the six voting members of the Commission, neither the President, the head of any department, nor the Judiciary has any voice in their selection.

. . .

3. THE COMMISSION'S POWERS

... Our previous description of the statutory provisions ... disclosed that the Commission's powers fall generally into three categories: functions relating to the flow of necessary information—receipt, dissemination, and investigation; functions with respect to the Commission's task of fleshing out the statute—rulemaking and advisory opinions; and functions necessary to ensure compliance with the statute and rules—informal procedures, administrative determinations and hearings, and civil suits.

Insofar as the powers confided in the Commission are essentially of an investigative and informative nature, falling in the same general category as those powers which Congress might delegate to one of its own committees, there can be no question that the Commission as presently constituted may exercise them....

But when we go beyond this type of authority to the more substantial powers exercised by the Commission, we reach a different result. The Commission's enforcement power, exemplified by its discretionary power to seek judicial relief, is authority that cannot possibly be regarded as merely in aid of the legislative function of Congress. A lawsuit is the ultimate remedy for a breach of the law, and it is to the President, and not to the Congress, that the Constitution entrusts the responsibility to "take Care that the Laws be faithfully executed." Art. II, § 3.

. . .

We hold that these provisions of the Act, vesting in the Commission primary responsibility for conducting civil litigation in the courts of the United States for vindicating public rights, violate Art. II, § 2, cl. 2, of the Constitution. Such functions may be discharged only by persons who are "Officers of the United States" within the language of that section.

. . .

Mr. Justice Stevens took no part in the consideration or decision of these cases.

. . .

Mr. Chief Justice Burger, concurring in part and dissenting in part.

. . .

Mr. Justice White, concurring in part and dissenting in part.

. . .

[Justices Marshall, Blackmun, and Rehnquist wrote separate opinions, concurring in part and dissenting in part, but concurred in the Court's opinion on FEC appointments.]

OLC Memo on President Obama's Recess Appointments (2012)

The Office of Legal Counsel of the Department of Justice provided the following memo as legal justification for President Obama's January 2012 recess appointments to the Consumer Financial Protection Bureau and the National Labor Relations Board. Because of their dislike for these agencies, Senate Republicans had been blocking efforts to confirm Obama appointments to them. In 2007 during the George W. Bush Administration, Senate Democrats had begun the practice of using pro forma sessions during recesses in order to block recess appointments by Bush. Once these appointees make a decision that creates a true case or controversy, the issue of whether or not the appointments are constitutional is likely to end up in court.

January 6, 2012

MEMORANDUM OPINION FOR THE COUNSEL TO THE PRESIDENT

On December 17, 2011, the Senate agreed by unanimous consent to "adjourn and convene for pro forma sessions only, with no business conducted," every Tuesday and Friday between that date and January 23, 2012.... During that period, on January 3, 2012, the Senate convened one such pro forma session to begin the second session of the 112th Congress and adjourned less than a minute later under its prior agreement.... You asked whether the President has authority under the Recess Appointments Clause ... to make recess appointments during the period between January 3 and January 23 notwithstanding the convening of periodic pro forma sessions. We advised you that he does. This opinion memorializes and elaborates on that advice.

. . .

II.

To address the President's authority to make recess appointments during a recess including pro forma sessions, we consider two distinct issues: The first is whether the President has authority to make a recess appointment during the recess at issue here, an intrasession recess of twenty days. We conclude that he does. The opinions of the Attorney General and this Office, historical practice, and the limited judicial authority that exists all provide strong support for that conclusion.

Thereafter, we consider whether the President is disabled from making an appointment when the recess is punctuated by periodic pro forma sessions at which Congress has declared in advance that no business is to be conducted. Based primarily on the traditional understanding that the Recess Appointments Clause is to be given a practical construction focusing on the Senate's ability to provide advice and consent on nominations, we conclude that while Congress can prevent the President from making recess appointments by remaining continuously in session and available to receive and act on nominations, it cannot do so by conducting pro forma sessions during a recess. The question is a novel one, and the substantial arguments on each side create some litigation risk for such appointments....

A.

. . .

Under a framework first articulated by Attorney General Daugherty in 1921, and subsequently reaffirmed and applied by several opinions of the Attorney General and this Office, the "constitutional test for whether a recess appointment is permissible is whether the adjournment of the Senate is of such a duration that the Senate could 'not receive communications from the President or participate as a body in making appointments'" ... Although "the line of demarcation can not be accurately drawn" in determining whether an intrasession recess is of sufficient length to permit the President to make a recess appointment, "the President is necessarily vested with a large, although not unlimited, discretion to determine when there is a real and genuine recess making it impossible for him to receive the advice and consent of the Senate."

We have little doubt that a twenty-day recess may give rise to presidential authority to make recess appointments. Attorneys General and this Office have repeatedly affirmed the President's authority to make recess appointments during intrasession recesses of similar or shorter length.

. . .

B.

[This section addresses the question of whether the pro forma sessions interrupt the length of the intrasession, making the adjournment periods too brief for the President to exercise his recess appointment power.]

1.

The Appointments Clause of the Constitution provides that the President "shall nominate and by and with the Advice and Consent of the Senate, shall appoint Ambassadors, other public Ministers and Consuls, Judges of the supreme Court, and all other Officers of the United States." ... The Recess Appointments Clause immediately follows and confers on the President the "Power to fill up all Vacancies that may happen during the Recess of the Senate, by granting Commissions which shall expire at the End of their next Session." ... The clause was adopted at the Constitutional Convention without debate.... Alexander Hamilton described the Clause in *The Federalist* as providing a "supplement" to the President's appointment power, establishing an "auxiliary method of appointment, in cases to which the general method was inadequate."... The Clause was necessary because "it would have been improper to oblige [the Senate] to be continually in session for the appointment of officers," and it "might be necessary for the public service to fill [vacancies] without delay." ...

. . .

Subsequent Attorneys General and, later, this Office have continued to place central importance on the Senate's availability to give advice and consent. In his seminal opinion concluding that a significant intrasession adjournment is a "recess" in which recess appointments can be made, Attorney General Daugherty focused on this point: "Regardless of whether the Senate has adjourned or recessed, the real question ... is whether *in a practical* sense the Senate is in session so that its *advice and consent can be obtained.*" ... Thus, in determining whether an intrasession adjournment constitutes a recess in the constitutional sense, the touchstone is "its *practical effect: viz.,* whether or not the Senate is *capable of exercising its constitutional function* of advising and consenting to executive nominations."

. . .

2.

Guided by these principles, we conclude that the President may determine that pro forma sessions at

which no business is to be conducted do not interrupt a Senate recess for purposes of the Recess Appointments Clause. Our conclusion rests on three considerations.

First, both the Framers' original understanding of the Recess Appointments Clause and the longstanding views of the Executive and Legislative Branches support the conclusion that the President may make recess appointments when he determines that, as a practical matter, the Senate is not available to give advice and consent to executive nominations....

. . .

Second, allowing the Senate to prevent the President from exercising his authority under the Recess Appointments Clause by holding pro forma sessions would be inconsistent with both the purpose of the Clause and historical practice in analogous situations.... If the Senate can avoid a "Recess of the Senate" under the Clause by having a single Member "gavel in" before an empty chamber, then the Senate can preclude the President from making recess appointments even when, as a practical matter, it is unavailable to fulfill its constitutional role in the appointment process for a significant period of time. The purpose of the Clause is better served by a construction that permits the President to make recess appointments when the Senate is unavailable to advise and consent for lengthy periods....

. . .

Third, permitting the Senate to prevent the President from making recess appointments through pro forma sessions would raise constitutional separation of powers concerns. To preserve the constitutional balance of powers, the Supreme Court has held that congressional action is invalid if it "'undermine[s] the powers of the Executive Branch,' or 'disrupts the proper balance between the coordinate branches [by] prevent[ing] the Executive Branch from accomplishing its constitutionally assigned functions."[*Citing Morrison v. Olson*]....

. . .

3.

[This section considers the counterarguments, which the OLC concludes "do not overcome the conclusion presented above." These arguments include (1)the past use of pro forma sessions to conduct "housekeeping" matters, which the OLC considers not analogous to using them to stop the president from exercising his constitutional authority to make recess appointments,

(2) the Senate's Article I power to "determine the Rules of its Proceedings," an argument weakened by the fact that the Supreme Court has held that in exercising this power the Senate may not "ignore constitutional restraints," in this case by preventing the president from exercising his constitutional authority; (3) recent uses of pro forma sessions to pass meaningful legislation suggesting that the Senate is available to meet its constitutional duties during this time, which the OLC distinguishes from this instance because the Senate stated publically that there was to be "no business conducted" during this recess; (4) Supreme Court precedent regarding the President's ability to use the "pocket veto" during recess periods, distinguished from the recess appointment issue by the fact that the ability to receive messages from the President is different from the ability to provide advice and consent.]

III.

In our judgment, the text of the Constitution and precedent and practice thereunder support the conclusion that the convening of periodic pro forma sessions in which no business is to be conducted does not have the legal effect of interrupting an intrasession recess otherwise long enough to qualify as a "Recess of the Senate" under the Recess Appointments Clause. In this context, the President therefore has discretion to conclude that the Senate is unavailable to perform its advise-and-consent function and to exercise his power to make recess appointments.

/s/
VIRGINIA A. SEITZ
Assistant Attorney General

Myers v. United States

272 U.S. 52 (1926)

A statute of 1876 provided that postmasters of the first, second, and third classes shall be appointed and may be removed by the President "by and with the advice and consent of the Senate." President Wilson removed Frank S. Myers, a postmaster of the first class, without seeking or obtaining Senate approval. The constitutional question was whether Congress could interfere with or restrict the President's power of removal, which the Solicitor General and the heirs of Myers argued was essential to preserve the President's responsibility as chief executive officer. The issue of the removal power was limited to officers subject to Senate confirmation.

MR. CHIEF JUSTICE TAFT delivered the opinion of the Court.

This case presents the question whether under the Constitution the President has the exclusive power of removing executive officers of the United States whom he has appointed by and with the advice and consent of the Senate.

Myers, appellant's intestate, was on July 21, 1917, appointed by the President, by and with the advice and consent of the Senate, to be a postmaster of the first class at Portland, Oregon, for a term of four years. On January 20, 1920, Myers' resignation was demanded. He refused the demand. On February 2, 1920, he was removed from office by order of the Postmaster General, acting by direction of the President....

By the 6th section of the Act of Congress of July 12, 1876, 19 Stat. 80, 81, c. 179, under which Myers was appointed with the advice and consent of the Senate as a first-class postmaster, it is provided that

"Postmasters of the first, second and third classes shall be appointed and may be removed by the Pres-

ident by and with the advice and consent of the Senate and shall hold their offices for four years unless sooner removed or suspended according to law."

The Senate did not consent to the President's removal of Myers during his term....

The question where the power of removal of executive officers appointed by the President by and with the advice and consent of the Senate was vested, was presented early in the first session of the First Congress. There is no express provision respecting removals in the Constitution, except as Section 4 of Article II ... provides for removal from office by impeachment. The subject was not discussed in the Constitutional Convention. Under the Articles of Confederation, Congress was given the power of appointing certain executive officers of the Confederation, and during the Revolution and while the Articles were given effect, Congress exercised the power of removal....

Consideration of the executive power was initiated in the Constitutional Convention by the seventh resolution in the Virginia Plan, introduced by

Edmund Randolph. 1 Farrand, Records of the Federal Convention, 21. It gave to the Executive "all the executive powers of the Congress under the Confederation," which would seem therefore to have intended to include the power of removal which had been exercised by that body as incident to the power of appointment.

[*Later modifications vested executive power in a single person, elected by an electoral college, with the power to appoint officers and the duty to see that all laws are faithfully observed.*]

In the House of Representatives of the First Congress, on Tuesday, May 18, 1789, Mr. Madison moved in the Committee of the Whole that there should be established three executive departments—one of Foreign Affairs, another of the Treasury, and a third of War—at the head of each of which there should be a Secretary, to be appointed by the President by and with the advice and consent of the Senate, and to be removable by the President. The committee agreed to the establishment of a Department of Foreign Affairs, but a discussion ensued as to making the Secretary removable by the President. 1 Annals of Congress, 370, 371. "The question was now taken and carried, by a considerable majority, in favor of declaring the power of removal to be in the President." 1 Annals of Congress, 383.

On June 16, 1789, the House resolved itself into a Committee of the Whole on a bill proposed by Mr. Madison for establishing an executive department to be denominated the Department of Foreign Affairs, in which the first clause, after stating the title of the officer and describing his duties, had these words: "to be removable from office by the President of the United States." 1 Annals of Congress, 455. After a very full discussion the question was put: shall the words "to be removable by the President" be struck out? It was determined in the negative—yeas 20, nays 34. 1 Annals of Congress, 576.

On June 22, in the renewal of the discussion, "Mr. Benson moved to amend the bill, by altering the second clause, so as to imply the power of removal to be in the President alone...." 1 Annals of Congress, 578.

"Mr. Benson stated that his objection to the clause 'to be removable by the President' arose from an idea that the power of removal by the President hereafter might appear to be exercised by virtue of a legislative grant only, and consequently be subjected to legislative instability, when he was well satisfied in his own mind that it was fixed by a fair legislative construction of the Constitution." ...

Mr. Madison admitted the objection made by the gentleman near him (Mr. Benson) to the words in the bill. He said: "They certainly may be construed to imply a legislative grant of the power. He wished everything like ambiguity expunged, and the sense of the House explicitly declared, and therefore seconded the motion." ...

Mr. Benson's first amendment ... was then approved by a vote of thirty to eighteen. 1 Annals of Congress, 580. Mr. Benson then moved to strike out in the first clause the words "to be removable by the President," in pursuance of the purpose he had already declared, and this second motion of his was carried by a vote of thirty-one to nineteen. 1 Annals of Congress, 585.

The bill as amended was ordered to be engrossed, and read the third time the next day, June 24, 1789, and was then passed by a vote of twenty-nine to twenty-two, and the Clerk was directed to carry the bill to the Senate and desire their concurrence. 1 Annals of Congress, 591.

It is very clear from this history that the exact question which the House voted upon was whether it should recognize and declare the power of the President under the Constitution to remove the Secretary of Foreign Affairs without the advice and consent of the Senate. That was what the vote was taken for. Some effort has been made to question whether the decision carries the result claimed for it, but there is not the slightest doubt, after an examination of the record, that the vote was, and was intended to be, a legislative declaration that the power to remove officers appointed by the President and the Senate vested in the President alone, and until the Johnson Impeachment trial in 1868, its meaning was not doubted even by those who questioned its soundness.

... After the bill as amended had passed the House, it was sent to the Senate, where it was discussed in secret session, without report. The critical vote there was upon the striking out of the clause recognizing and affirming the unrestricted power of the President to remove. The Senate divided by ten to ten, requiring the deciding vote of the Vice-President, John Adams, who voted against striking out, and in favor of the passage of the bill as it had left the House. Ten of the Senators had been in the Constitutional Convention, and of them six voted that the power of removal was in the President alone. The bill having passed as it came from the House was signed by President Washington and became a law. Act of July 27, 1789, 1 Stat. 28, c.4.

[*Taft summarizes the reasons advanced by Madison*

and his associates for vesting the removal power in the President: the need to separate the legislature from the executive functions; the intention to create a strong President; the use of the removal power to permit the President to take responsibility for the conduct of the executive branch and to see that the laws are faithfully executed; the intention to make the power of removal incident to the power of appointment; and the need for the President to have full confidence in his subordinates. Nevertheless, Taft acknowledges that Congress can place certain duties in executive officers to make presidential removal inappropriate:]

... Of course there may be duties so peculiarly and specifically committed to the discretion of a particular officer as to raise a question whether the President may overrule or revise the officer's interpretation of his statutory duty in a particular instance. Then there may be duties of a quasi-judicial character imposed on executive officers and members of executive tribunals whose decisions after hearing affect interests of individuals, the discharge of which the President can not in a particular case properly influence or control. But even in such a case he may consider the decision after its rendition as a reason for removing the officer, on the ground that the discretion regularly entrusted to that officer by statute has not been on the whole intelligently or wisely exercised. Otherwise he does not discharge his own constitutional duty of seeing that the laws be faithfully executed.

. . .

For the reasons given, we must therefore hold that the provision of the law of 1876, by which the unrestricted power of removal of first class postmasters is denied to the President, is in violation of the Constitution, and invalid. This leads to an affirmance of the judgment of the Court of Claims.

. . .

MR. JUSTICE HOLMES, dissenting.

My brothers MCREYNOLDS and BRANDEIS have discussed the question before us with exhaustive research and I say a few words merely to emphasize my agreement with their conclusion.

The arguments drawn from the executive power of the President, and from his duty to appoint officers of the United States (when Congress does not vest the appointment elsewhere), to take care that the laws be faithfully executed, and to commission all officers of the United States, seem to me spider's webs inadequate to control the dominant facts.

We have to deal with an office that owes its existence to Congress and that Congress may abolish tomorrow. Its duration and the pay attached to it while it lasts depend on Congress alone. Congress alone confers on the President the power to appoint to it and at any time may transfer the power to other hands. With such power over its own creation, I have no more trouble in believing that Congress has power to prescribe a term of life for it free from any interference than I have in accepting the undoubted power of Congress to decree its end. I have equally little trouble in accepting its power to prolong the tenure of an incumbent until Congress or the Senate shall have assented to his removal. The duty of the President to see that the laws be executed is a duty that does not go beyond the laws or require him to achieve more than Congress sees fit to leave within his power.

The separate opinion of MR. JUSTICE MC-REYNOLDS.

[In this 62-page dissent, McReynolds reviews the succession of statutes that have limited the President's power of removal: civil service reforms; the laws creating commissions, boards, the Comptroller General, and the Board of Tax Appeals; and the general history of congressional control over postal affairs. He also refutes Taft's claim that a majority of the First Congress believed that the President's removal power was a constitutional grant. McReynolds pulls together his critique in the following section:]

X.

Congress has long and vigorously asserted its right to restrict removals and there has been no common executive practice based upon a contrary view. The President has often removed, and it is admitted that he may remove, with either the express or implied assent of Congress; but the present theory is that he may override the declared will of that body. This goes far beyond any practice heretofore approved or followed; it conflicts with the history of the Constitution, with the ordinary rules of interpretation, and with the construction approved by Congress since the beginning and emphatically sanctioned by this court. To adopt it would be revolutionary.

MR. JUSTICE BRANDEIS, dissenting.

[Brandeis followed with a 56-page dissent, spelling out in great detail the power of Congress to fix the tenure of inferior officers and to limit the President's power of removal. Some of the statutes provided that removal shall be made only for specified causes. Others provided for removal only after a hearing. Congress also

passed legislation restricting the President's power of nomination.]

. . .

The separation of the powers of government did not make each branch completely autonomous. It left each, in some measure, dependent upon the others, as it left to each power to exercise, in some respects, functions in their nature executive, legislative and judicial. Obviously the President cannot secure full execution of the laws, if Congress denies to him adequate means of doing so. Full execution may be defeated because Congress declines to create offices indispensable for that purpose. Or, because Congress, having created the office, declines to make the indispensable appropriation. Or, because Congress, having both created the office and made the appropriation, prevents, by restrictions which it imposes, the appointment of officials who in quality and character are indispensable to the efficient execution of the law.

. . .

Checks and balances were established in order that this should be "a government of laws and not of men." . . . The doctrine of the separation of powers was adopted by the Convention of 1787, not to promote efficiency but to preclude the exercise of arbitrary power. The purpose was, not to avoid friction, but, by means of the inevitable friction incident to the distribution of the governmental powers among three departments, to save the people from autocracy. . . .

Humphrey's Executor v. United States

295 U.S. 602 (1935)

William E. Humphrey, nominated by President Hoover for the Federal Trade Commission in 1931, was confirmed by the Senate. The Federal Trade Commission (FTC) Act allowed the President to remove a commissioner only for "inefficiency, neglect of duty, or malfeasance in office." In 1933 President Franklin D. Roosevelt asked Humphrey to resign, explaining that the administration's policies could be carried out only with commissioners supportive of Roosevelt's goals. When Humphrey refused to resign, Roosevelt removed him for policy reasons rather than the "for cause" reasons specified in the FTC Act. Humphrey's heirs brought suit to recover his salary. In this decision, the Court reviews and qualifies its broad ruling in *Myers* regarding the scope of the President's removal power.

MR. JUSTICE SUTHERLAND delivered the opinion of the Court.

Plaintiff brought suit in the Court of Claims against the United States to recover a sum of money alleged to be due the deceased for salary as a Federal Trade Commissioner from October 8, 1933, when the President undertook to remove him from office, to the time of his death on February 14, 1934. . . .

William E. Humphrey, the decedent, on December 10, 1931, was nominated by President Hoover to succeed himself as a member of the Federal Trade Commission, and was confirmed by the United States Senate. He was duly commissioned for a term of seven years expiring September 25, 1938; and, after taking the required oath of office, entered upon his duties. On July 25, 1933, President Roosevelt addressed a letter to the commissioner asking for his resignation, on the ground "that the aims and purposes of the Administration with respect to the work of the Commission can be carried out most effectively with personnel of my own selection," but disclaiming any reflection upon the commissioner personally or upon his services. The commissioner replied, asking time to consult his friends. After some further correspondence upon the subject, the President on August 31, 1933, wrote the commissioner expressing the hope that the resignation would be forthcoming and saying:

"You will, I know, realize that I do not feel that your mind and my mind go along together on either the policies or the administering of the Federal Trade Commission, and, frankly, I think it is best for the people of this country that I should have a full confidence."

The commissioner declined to resign; and on October 7, 1933, the President wrote him:

"Effective as of this date you are hereby removed

from the office of Commissioner of the Federal Trade Commission."

Humphrey never acquiesced in this action, but continued thereafter to insist that he was still a member of the commission, entitled to perform its duties and receive the compensation provided by law at the rate of $10,000 per annum....

The Federal Trade Commission Act ... creates a commission of five members to be appointed by the President by and with the advice and consent of the Senate, and § 1 provides[*that a commissioner*] "may be removed by the President for inefficiency, neglect of duty, or malfeasance in office...."

First. The question first to be considered is whether, by the provisions of § 1 of the Federal Trade Commission Act already quoted, the President's power is limited to removal for the specific causes enumerated therein. The negative contention of the government is based principally upon the decision of this court in *Shurtleff* v. *United States,* 189 U. S. 311. [*That case involved the President's power to remove a general appraiser of merchandise. An 1890 statute provided for the appointment of nine general appraisers of merchandise, who "may be removed from office at any time by the President for inefficiency, neglect of duty, or malfeasance in office." The President removed Shurtleff without giving a reason. The Court of Claims dismissed Shurtleff's petition to recover salary, upholding the President's power to remove for causes other than those stated in the law. The Supreme Court acknowledged that Congress can restrict the President's removal power to specified causes, but only if the statute used "plain language" to limit the President's general power of removal. An uncertainly in the 1890 statute was the lack of a fixed term for the general appraiser.*]

... The situation here presented is plainly and wholly different. The statute fixes a term of office, in accordance with many precedents. The first commissioners appointed are to continue in office for terms of three, four, five, six, and seven years, respectively; and their successors are to be appointed for terms of seven years—any commissioner being subject to removal by the President for inefficiency, neglect of duty, or malfeasance in office. The words of the act are definite and unambiguous.

... [I]f the intention of Congress that no removal should be made during the specified term except for one or more of the enumerated causes were not clear upon the face of the statute, as we think it is, it would be made clear by a consideration of the character of the commission and the legislative history which accompanied and preceded the passage of the act.

The commission is to be non-partisan; and it must, from the very nature of its duties, act with entire impartiality. It is charged with the enforcement of no policy except the policy of the law. Its duties are neither political nor executive, but predominantly quasi-judicial and quasi-legislative....

[*The legislative reports in both Houses reflected the view that a fixed term was necessary to the effective and fair administration of the law. The term of office at seven years anticipated commissioners who would have experience and knowledge of both the public requirements and the practical affairs of industry. The long terms gave commissioners an opportunity to acquire expertise. Unlike the Bureau of Corporations (an executive subdivision in the Department of Commerce abolished by the act), the FTC would be independent and less open to the suspicion of partisan direction.*]

The debates in both houses demonstrate that the prevailing view was that the commission was not to be "subject to anybody in the government but ... only to the people of the United States"; free from "political domination or control" or the "probability or possibility of such a thing"; to be "separate and apart from any existing department of the government—not subject to the orders of the President."

More to the same effect appears in the debates, which were long and thorough and contain nothing to the contrary....

Thus, the language of the act, the legislative reports, and the general purposes of the legislation as reflected by the debates, all combine to demonstrate the Congressional intent to create a body of experts who shall gain experience by length of service—a body which shall be independent of executive authority, *except in its selection,* and free to exercise its judgment without the leave or hindrance of any other official or any department of the government. To the accomplishment of these purposes, it is clear that Congress was of opinion that length and certainty of tenure would vitally contribute. And to hold that, nevertheless, the members of the commission continue in office at the mere will of the President, might be to thwart, in large measure, the very ends which Congress sought to realize by definitely fixing the term of office.

We conclude that the intent of the act is to limit the executive power of removal to the causes enumerated, the existence of none of which is claimed here; and we pass to the second question.

Second. To support its contention that the removal provision of § 1, as we have just construed it, is an unconstitutional interference with the executive power of the President, the government's chief reliance is *Myers* v. *United States,* 272 U.S. 52 ... [T]he narrow point actually decided was only that the President had power to remove a postmaster of the first class, without the advice and consent of the Senate as required by act of Congress....

The office of a postmaster is so essentially unlike the office now involved that the decision in the *Myers* case cannot be accepted as controlling our decision here. A postmaster is an executive officer restricted to the performance of executive functions. He is charged with no duty at all related to either the legislative or judicial power....

The Federal Trade Commission is an administrative body created by Congress to carry into effect legislative policies embodied in the statute in accordance with the legislative standard therein prescribed, and to perform other specified duties as a legislative or as a judicial aid. Such a body cannot in any proper sense be characterized as an arm or an eye of the executive. Its duties are performed without executive leave and, in the contemplation of the statute, must be free from executive control. In administering the provisions of the statute ... the commission acts in part quasi-legislatively and in part quasi-judicially. In making investigations and reports thereon for the information of Congress under § 6, in aid of the legislative power, it acts as a legislative agency....

We think it plain under the Constitution that illimitable power of removal is not possessed by the President in respect of officers of the character of those just named....

... A reading of the debates [*in 1789*] shows that the President's illimitable power of removal was not considered in respect of other than executive officers....

The result of what we now have said is this: Whether the power of the President to remove an officer shall prevail over the authority of Congress to condition the power by fixing a definite term and precluding a removal except for cause, will depend upon the character of the office; the *Myers* decision, affirming the power of the President alone to make the removal, is confined to purely executive officers; and as to officers of the kind here under consideration, we hold that no removal can be made during the prescribed term for which the officer is appointed, except for one or more of the causes named in the applicable statute.

To the extent that, between the decision in the *Myers* case, which sustains the unrestrictable power of the President to remove purely executive officers, and our present decision that such power does not extend to an office such as that here involved, there shall remain a field of doubt, we leave such cases as may fall within it for future consideration and determination as they may arise.

In accordance with the foregoing, the questions submitted are answered.

Question No. 1, Yes. Question No. 2, Yes.

Mr. Justice McReynolds agrees that both questions should be answered in the affirmative. A separate opinion in *Myers* v. *United States,* 272 U. S. 178, states his views concerning the power of the President to remove appointees.

Free Enterprise Fund v. Public Company Accounting Oversight Board

561 U.S. ___ (2010)

After several accounting scandals involving major corporations, most notably the collapse of energy giant Enron, Congress enacted the Sarbanes-Oxley Act of 2002. The Act required tighter regulation of the accounting industry under a new Public Company Accounting Oversight Board. The Board is composed of five members, appointed to staggered 5 year terms by the Securities and Exchange Commission. A Nevada accounting firm under investigation by the Board sued the Board and its members, seeking a declaratory judgment that the Board is unconstitutional and an injunction preventing the Board from exercising its powers. The District Court granted summary judgment to the Board and a divided (2–1) Court of Appeals affirmed. Note the majority's adoption of the "unitary executive" argument and the dissent's insistence on a more functionalist approach.

CHIEF JUSTICE ROBERTS delivered the opinion of the Court.

Our Constitution divided the "powers of the new

Federal Government into three defined categories, Legislative, Executive, and Judicial." *INS v. Chadha,* 462 U.S. 919, 951 (1983). Article II vests "[t]he executive Power ... in a President of the United States of America," who must "take Care that the Laws are faithfully executed." ... In light of "[t]he impossibility that one man should be able to perform all the great business of the State," the Constitution provides for executive officers to "assist the supreme Magistrate in discharging the duties of his trust." 30 Writings of George Washington 334 (J. Fitzpatrick ed. 1939).

Since 1789, the Constitution has been understood to empower the President to keep these officers accountable—by removing them from office, if necessary. See generally *Myers v. United States*, 272 U.S. 52 (1926). This Court has determined, however, that this authority is not without limit. In *Humphrey's Executor v. United States*, 295 U.S. 602 (1935), we held that Congress can, under certain circumstances, create independent agencies run by principal officers appointed by the President, whom the President may not remove at will but only for good cause. Likewise, in *United States v. Perkins*, 116 U.S. 483 (1886), and *Morrison v. Olson*, 487 U.S. 654 (1988), the Court sustained similar restrictions on the power of principal executive officers—themselves responsible to the President—to remove their own inferiors. The parties do not ask us to reexamine any of these precedents, and we do not do so.

We are asked, however, to consider a new situation not yet encountered by the Court. The question is whether these separate layers of protection can be combined. May the President be restricted in his ability to remove a principal officer, who is in turn restricted in his ability to remove an inferior officer, even though the inferior officer determines the policy and enforces the laws of the United States?

We hold that such multilevel protection from removal is contrary to Article II's vesting of the executive power in the President. The President cannot "take Care that the Laws be faithfully executed" if he cannot oversee the faithfulness of the officers who execute them. Here the President cannot remove an officer who enjoys more than one level of good-cause protection, even if the President determines that the officer is neglecting his duties or discharging them improperly. That judgment is instead committed to another officer, who may or may not agree with the President's determination, and whom the President cannot remove simply because that officer disagrees with him. This contravenes the President's "constitutional obligation to ensure the faithful execution of the laws." ...

III

We hold that the dual for-cause limitations on

the removal of Board members contravene the Constitution's separation of powers.

A

The Constitution provides that "[t]he executive Power shall be vested in a President of the United States of America." ... As Madison stated on the floor of the First Congress, "if any power whatsoever is in its nature Executive, it is the power of appointing, overseeing, and controlling those who execute the laws." 1 Annals of Cong. 463 (1789).

The removal of executive officers was discussed extensively in Congress when the first executive departments were created. The view that that "prevailed, as most consonant to the text of the Constitution" and "to the requisite responsibility and harmony in the Executive Department," was that the executive power included a power to oversee executive officers through removal; because that traditional executive power was not "expressly taken away, it remained with the President." Letter from James Madison to Thomas Jefferson (June 30, 1789), 16 Documentary History of the First Federal Congress 893 (2004). "This Decision of 1789 provides contemporaneous and weighty evidence of the Constitution's meaning since many of the Members of the First Congress had taken part in framing that instrument." *Bowsher* v. *Synar*, 478 U. S. 714, 723–724 (1986).... And it soon became the "settled and well understood construction of the Constitution." *Ex parte Hennen*, 13 Pet. 230, 259 (1839).

The landmark case of *Myers* v. *United States* reaffirmed the principle that Article II confers on the President "the general administrative control of those executing the laws." 272 U. S., at 164....

Nearly a decade later in *Humphrey's Executor*, this Court held that *Myers* did not prevent Congress from conferring good-cause tenure on the principal officers of certain independent agencies....

Humphrey's Executor did not address the removal of inferior officers, whose appointment Congress may vest in heads of departments. If Congress does so, it is ordinarily the department head, rather than the President, who enjoys the power of removal. See *Myers, supra,* at 119, 127; *Hennen, supra,* at 259–260. This Court has upheld for-cause limitations on that power as well....

B

As explained, we have previously upheld limited restrictions on the President's removal power. In those cases, however, only one level of protected tenure separated the President from an officer exercising executive power. It was the President—or a subordinate he could remove at will—who decided whether the officer's conduct merited removal under the good-cause standard.

The Act before us does something quite different. It not only protects Board members from removal except for good cause, but withdraws from the President any decision on whether that good cause exists. That decision is vested instead in other tenured officers—the Commissioners—none of whom is subject to the President's direct control. The result is a Board that is not accountable to the President, and a President who is not responsible for the Board.

The added layer of tenure protection makes a difference. Without a layer of insulation between the Commission and the Board, the Commission could remove a Board member at any time, and therefore would be fully responsible for what the Board does. The President could then hold the Commission to account for its supervision of the Board, to the same extent that he may hold the Commission to account for everything else it does.

A second level of tenure protection changes the nature of the President's review. Now the Commission cannot remove a Board member at will. The President therefore cannot hold the Commission fully accountable for the Board's conduct, to the same extent that he may hold the Commission accountable for everything else that it does. The Commissioners are not responsible for the Board's actions. They are only responsible for their own determination of whether the Act's rigorous good-cause standard is met. And even if the President disagrees with their determination, he is powerless to intervene—unless that determination is so unreasonable as to constitute "inefficiency, neglect of duty, or malfeasance in office." *Humphrey's Executor*, 295 U. S., at 620....

This novel structure does not merely add to the Board's independence, but transforms it. Neither the President, nor anyone directly responsible to him, nor even an officer whose conduct he may review only for good cause, has full control over the Board. The President is stripped of the power our precedents have preserved, and his ability to execute the laws—by holding his subordinates accountable for their conduct—is impaired.

. . .

Indeed, if allowed to stand, this dispersion of responsibility could be multiplied. If Congress can shelter the bureaucracy behind two layers of good-cause tenure, why not a third? ... The officers of such an agency—safely encased within a Matryoshka doll of tenure protections—would be im-

mune from Presidential oversight, even as they exercised power in the people's name....

The diffusion of power carries with it a diffusion of accountability. The people do not vote for the "Officers of the United States." ... They instead look to the President to guide the "assistants or deputies ... subject to his superintendence." The Federalist No. 72, p. 487 (J. Cooke ed. 1961) (A. Hamilton). Without a clear and effective chain of command, the public cannot "determine on whom the blame or the punishment of a pernicious measure, or series of pernicious measures ought really to fall." *Id.* No. 70, at 476 (same)....

C

... No one doubts Congress's power to create a vast and varied federal bureaucracy. But where, in all this, is the role for oversight by an elected President? The Constitution requires that a President chosen by the entire Nation oversee the execution of the laws. And the "'fact that a given law or procedure is efficient, convenient, and useful in facilitating functions of government, standing alone, will not save it if it is contrary to the Constitution,'" for "'[c]onvenience and efficiency are not the primary objectives—or the hallmarks—of democratic government.'" *Bowsher*, 478 U. S., at 736 (quoting *Chadha*, 462 U. S., at 944).

One can have a government that functions without being ruled by functionaries, and a government that benefits from expertise without being ruled by experts. Our Constitution was adopted to enable the people to govern themselves, through their elected leaders. The growth of the Executive Branch, which now wields vast power and touches almost every aspect of daily life, heightens the concern that it may slip from the Executive's control, and thus from that of the people. This concern is largely absent from the dissent's paean to the administrative state.... The point is not to take issue with for-cause limitations in general; we do not do that. The question here is far more modest. We deal with the unusual situation, never before addressed by the Court, of two layers of for-cause tenure....

... In its pursuit of a "workable government," Congress cannot reduce the Chief Magistrate to a cajoler-in-chief....

IV

Petitioners' complaint argued that the Board's "freedom from Presidential oversight and control" rendered it "and all power and authority exercised by it" in violation of the Constitution.... We reject such a broad holding. Instead, we agree with the Government that the unconstitutional tenure provisions are severable from the remainder of the statute.

[T]he existence of the Board does not violate the separation of powers, but the substantive removal restrictions imposed by §§ 7211(e)(6) and 7217(d)(3) do.... Concluding that the removal restrictions are invalid leaves the Board removable by the Commission at will, and leaves the President separated from Board members by only a single level of good-cause tenure....

The Sarbanes-Oxley Act remains "'fully operative as a law'" with these tenure restrictions excised....

V

[*The Court rejects three additional appointments clause claims made by petitioner (The Free Enterprise Fund). It finds that the members of the Board are "inferior officers," that the SEC is a "Department" for the purposes of the Appointments Clause, and that a multimember body like the SEC can be considered a "Head" of a Department for appointment of inferior officers.*]

. . .

The judgment of the United States Court of Appeals for the District of Columbia Circuit is affirmed in part and reversed in part, and the case is remanded for further proceedings consistent with this opinion.

It is so ordered.

Justice Breyer, with whom Justice Stevens, Justice Ginsburg, and Justice Sotomayor join, dissenting.

... I agree that the Accounting Board members are inferior officers.... But in my view the statute does not significantly interfere with the President's "executive Power." Art. II, § 1. It violates no separation-of-powers principle. And the Court's contrary holding threatens to disrupt severely the fair and efficient administration of the laws. I consequently dissent.

[I. A]

The legal question before us arises at the intersection of two general constitutional principles. On the one hand, Congress has broad power to enact statutes "necessary and proper" to the exercise of its specifically enumerated constitutional authority. Art. I, § 8, cl. 18. As Chief Justice Marshall wrote for the Court nearly 200 years ago, the Necessary and Proper Clause reflects the Framers' efforts to create a Constitution that would "endure for ages to come." *McCulloch* v. *Maryland*, 4 Wheat. 316, 415 (1819). It

embodies their recognition that it would be "unwise" to prescribe "the means by which government should, in all future time, execute its powers." *Ibid.* Such "immutable rules" would deprive the Government of the needed flexibility to respond to future "exigencies which, if foreseen at all, must have been seen dimly." *Ibid.* Thus the Necessary and Proper Clause affords Congress broad authority to "create" governmental "'offices'" and to structure those offices "as it chooses." ... And Congress has drawn on that power over the past century to create numerous federal agencies in response to "various crises of human affairs" as they have arisen....

On the other hand, the opening sections of Articles I, II, and III of the Constitution separately and respectively vest "all legislative Powers" in Congress, the "executive Power" in the President, and the "judicial Power" in the Supreme Court (and such "inferior Courts as Congress may from time to time ordain and establish"). In doing so, these provisions imply a structural separation-of-powers principle. See, *e.g.*, *Miller* v. *French*, 530 U. S. 327, 341–342 (2000). And that principle, along with the instruction in Article II, § 3 that the President "shall take Care that the Laws be faithfully executed," limits Congress' power to structure the Federal Government ... Indeed, this Court has held that the separation-of-powers principle guarantees the President the authority to dismiss certain Executive Branch officials at will. *Myers* v. *United States*, 272 U. S. 52 (1926).

But neither of these two principles is absolute in its application to removal cases. The Necessary and Proper Clause does not grant Congress power to free *all* Executive Branch officials from dismissal at the will of the President. *Ibid.* Nor does the separation-of-powers principle grant the President an absolute authority to remove *any and all* Executive Branch officials at will. Rather, depending on, say, the nature of the office, its function, or its subject matter, Congress sometimes may, consistent with the Constitution, limit the President's authority to remove an officer from his post. See *Humphrey's Executor* v. *United States*, 295 U. S. 602 (1935), overruling in part *Myers*, *supra*; *Morrison* v. *Olson*, 487 U. S. 654 (1988). And we must here decide whether the circumstances surrounding the statute at issue justify such a limitation.

. . .

B

When previously deciding this kind of nontextual question, the Court has emphasized the importance of examining how a particular provision, taken in context, is likely to function....

It is not surprising that the Court in these circumstances has looked to function and context, and not to bright-line rules. For one thing, that approach embodies the intent of the Framers. As Chief Justice Marshall long ago observed, our Constitution is fashioned so as to allow the three coordinate branches, including this Court, to exercise practical judgment in response to changing conditions and "exigencies," which at the time of the founding could be seen only "dimly," and perhaps not at all. *McCulloch,* 4 Wheat., at 415.

For another, a functional approach permits Congress and the President the flexibility needed to adapt statutory law to changing circumstances.... Indeed, the Federal Government at the time of the founding consisted of about 2,000 employees and served a population of about 4 million.... Today, however, the Federal Government employs about *4.4 million workers* who serve a Nation of more than 310 million people living in a society characterized by rapid technological, economic, and social change....

Federal statutes now require or permit Government officials to provide, regulate, or otherwise administer, not only foreign affairs and defense, but also a wide variety of such subjects as taxes, welfare, social security, medicine, pharmaceutical drugs, education, highways, railroads, electricity, natural gas, nuclear power, financial instruments, banking, medical care, public health and safety, the environment, fair employment practices, consumer protection and much else besides. Those statutes create a host of different organizational structures ...

The upshot is that today vast numbers of statutes governing vast numbers of subjects, concerned with vast numbers of different problems, provide for, or foresee, their execution or administration through the work of administrators organized within many different kinds of administrative structures, exercising different kinds of administrative authority, to achieve their legislatively mandated objectives. And,

given the nature of the Government's work, it is not surprising that administrative units come in many different shapes and sizes.

The functional approach required by our precedents recognizes this administrative complexity and, more importantly, recognizes the various ways presidential power operates within this context—and the various ways in which a removal provision might affect that power.... If the President seeks to regulate through impartial adjudication, then insulation of the adjudicator from removal at will can help him achieve that goal. And to free a technical decision maker from the fear of removal without cause can similarly help create legitimacy with respect to that official's regulatory actions by helping to insulate his technical decisions from nontechnical political pressure....

These practical reasons not only support our precedents' determination that cases such as this should examine the specific functions and context at issue; they also indicate that judges should hesitate before second-guessing a "for cause" decision made by the other branches.... Compared to Congress and the President, the Judiciary possesses an inferior understanding of the realities of administration, and the manner in which power, including and most especially political power, operates in context....

Thus, here, as in similar cases, we should decide the constitutional question in light of the provision's practical functioning in context. And our decision should take account of the Judiciary's comparative lack of institutional expertise.

[II.D]

[*Breyer notes the myriad administrative arrangements, including the civil service system and military appointments, that are called into question by the Court's ruling. A lengthy Appendix attached to his opinion lists the various agencies and regulatory arrangements that have unique and potentially questionable appointment arrangements.*]

· · ·

E. DELEGATION OF LEGISLATIVE POWER

The boundaries between the legislative and executive branches are often obscured by large grants of power delegated by Congress. This delegation supposedly violates a fundamental principle, dating back to John Locke. The legislature "cannot transfer the power of making laws to any other hands, for it being but a delegated power from the people, they who have it cannot pass it over to others." John Locke, Second Treatise on Civil Government, § 141. This concept is embodied in the ancient maxim *delegata potestas non potest delegari* ("delegated power cannot be delegated").

The non-delegation principle is essential at least in preventing Congress from transferring its leg-

---

Standardless Delegations

Broad delegations have been upheld in many cases because of the structure provided for independent commissions. They operate on a multimember (collegial) basis, which supplies a check on possible abuses. Moreover, the term of commissioners are lengthy and staggered. Congress limits the number of commissioners who may belong to the same political party and restricts the ability of the President to remove commissioners. Finally, standardless delegations have been upheld when the accumulated customs of a regulated industry and the practices developed by states have served to narrow the discretion of a federal agency. Fahey v. Mallonee, 332 U.S. 245, 250, 253 (1947). See also Chapter 5 of

Louis Fisher, The Politics of Shared Power (1998).

Standardless delegations have been upheld when the legislative history supplies guidelines for administrative action. A massive delegation of wage-price controls to President Nixon in 1970 was justified by guidelines placed in committee reports and the legislative history. A three-judge court claimed that whether legislative purposes are included in committee reports or the public law "is largely a matter of drafting style." Amalgamated Meat Cutters & Butcher Work. v. Connally, 337 F.Supp. 737, 750 (D.D.C. 1971) (three-judge court). However, agencies are not as tightly bound by legislative history and nonstatutory controls.

---

islative power to private groups. In 1936 the Supreme Court struck down a statute partly because it delegated power to representatives of the coal industry to set up a code of mandatory regulations. This was "legislative delegation in its most obnoxious form; for it is not even delegation to an official or an official body, presumptively disinterested, but to private persons whose interests may be and often are adverse to the interests of others in the same business." Carter v. Carter Coal Co., 298 U.S. 238, 311 (1936).

With the exception of two cases handed down in 1935, Congress has encountered little opposition from the courts in delegating legislative power to the President, executive agencies, and independent commissions. In sustaining these delegations, the judiciary typically waxes eloquent about the serious breach were Congress ever to transfer its legislative power to other parties, after which it finds a way to uphold the delegation. Field v. Clark, 143 U.S. 649, 692 (1891) and HAMPTON & CO. v. UNITED STATES 276 U.S. 394, 406 (1928).

The courts justify vast delegations of legislative power after satisfying themselves that the powers are confined either by congressional guidelines or procedural safeguards. Statutory guidelines are often absent, however, when Congress orders the Interstate Commerce Commission to protect the "public interest," directs the Federal Trade Commission to police "unfair methods of competition," supplies the standard of "public convenience, interest, or necessity" for the Federal Communications Commission, and requires the Securities and Exchange Commission to ensure that corporations do not "unduly or unnecessarily complicate the structure" or "unfairly or inequitably distribute voting power among security holders."[11] The structure of these commissions supplies some built-in safeguards (see box).

The NIRA Cases

On two occasions the Supreme Court struck down a delegation of legislative authority to the President. Both cases involved the National Industrial Recovery Act (NIRA), which authorized industrial

---

11. The "public interest" guideline was upheld in ICC v. Goodrich Transit Co., 224 U.S. 194, 214–15 (1912), Intermountain Rate Cases, 234 U.S. 476, 486–88 (1914), Avent v. United States, 266 U.S. 127, 130 (1924), and N.Y. Central Securities Co. v. United States, 287 U.S. 12, 24–25 (1932). "Unfair method of competition" passed muster in FTC v. Gratz, 253 U.S. 421, 427–28 (1920), while "public convenience" survived judicial scrutiny in FCC v. Pottsville Broadcasting Co., 309 U.S. 134, 137–88 (1940). The SEC guideline was upheld in American Power Co. v. SEC, 329 U.S. 90, 104–06 (1946).

and trade associations to draw up codes that minimized competition, raised prices, and restricted production. If the President found the codes unacceptable, he could prescribe his own and enforce them as law. In the first case, the Court held that Congress had failed to establish guidelines or congressional policy to control the President's actions. Panama Refining v. Ryan, 293 U.S. 388 (1935). Although Justice Cardozo argued in the first decision that Congress had supplied adequate standards, in the second he protested: "This is delegation running riot." SCHECHTER CORP. v. UNITED STATES, 295 U.S. at 553. The drafting of the NIRA was dominated by industries and trade associations; executive officials appeared to have little interest in constitutional questions or procedural safeguards. Peter H. Irons, The New Deal Lawyers 22–107 (1982).

During the course of this litigation, the Court discovered that the government had brought an indictment and taken an appeal only to learn, to its embarrassment, that the regulation justifying this action had been repealed by an executive order. Panama Refining Co. v. Ryan, 293 U.S. at 412–13. The House Judiciary Committee in 1935 condemned the "utter chaos" regarding the publication and distribution of administrative rules and pronouncements. H. Rept. No. 280, 74th Cong., 1st Sess. 1–2 (1935). Congress passed legislation that year to provide for publication in a "Federal Register" of all presidential and agency documents having the effect of law. 49 Stat. 500 (1935).

Delegation after the New Deal

After the New Deal conflict between the Court and the other branches, the Court became much more deferential on issues of delegation. Rather than striking down delegations, courts and Congress became more active in oversight of the decisionmaking of executive agencies. Some reforms are embodied in the Administrative Procedure Act (APA) of 1946, which establishes standards for agency rulemaking to assure fairness and openness. Agencies are required to give notice and a hearing before issuing a rule or regulation. Findings of fact are supplied for the record; procedures exist for appeal. Through such procedural standards, Congress tries to eliminate or minimize the opportunity for executive caprice and arbitrariness. The APA relies on the doctrine of separated powers by prohibiting investigative or prosecuting personnel from participating in agency adjudications. 5 U.S.C. §§ 553–54 (2000).

The standards for delegation need not be stricter when the power to tax is involved. Skinner v. Mid-America Pipeline Co., 490 U.S. 212 (1989). Also in 1989, eight of the nine Justices rejected a claim that Congress had delegated excessively in creating the U.S. Sentencing Commission, with only Justice Scalia dissenting. Mistretta v. United States, 488 U.S. 361 (1989). Unanimous decisions in 1991 and 1996 dismissed the argument that Congress had unconstitutionally delegated its legislative power. Touby v. United States, 500 U.S. 160 (1991); Loving v. United States, 517 U.S. 748 (1996).

In 1999, the D.C. Circuit held that language in the Clean Air Act resulted in an unconstitutional delegation of legislative power to the Environmental Protection Agency. American Trucking Associations v. U.S. E.P.A., 175 F.3d 1027 (D.C. Cir. 1999). After the EPA issued final rules, the D.C. Circuit could not yet determine whether the nondelegation doctrine had been satisfied. American Trucking Associations, Inc. v. E.P.A., 195 F.3d 4 (D.C. Cir. 1999). When the Supreme Court decided the case in 2001, it ruled that the transfer of authority to EPA was not an unconstitutional delegation of legislative power. Whitman v. American Trucking Associations, 531 U.S. 457 (2001).

In the midst of the financial crisis of 2008 Congress passed the Emergency Economic Stabilization Act of 2008, which included a "bailout" of the financial industry through TARP (Troubled Assets Relief Program) and delegated significant authority to the executive branch to implement the program. Conservative critics of the legislation argued that the act provided no "intelligible principle" to guide executive decision making and that the non-delegation doctrine was violated. Legal experts on both sides of the aisle doubted that the Court would find the delegation unconstitutional. "Some Ask if Bailout is Unconstitutional." New York Times, 16 January 2009, A16.

Presidential Legislation

Agency regulations are not supposed to be a substitute for the general policy-making that Congress supplies in the form of a public law. 6 Op. Att'y Gen. 10 (1853). Agency rulemaking draws its authority from power granted directly or indirectly by Congress.[12] The situation may be different when the President "legislates" by issuing executive orders and proclamations. Here the President draws not necessarily on statutory authority but on power he believes is his under the Constitution.

Executive orders and proclamations are subject to legislative and judicial controls. When Congress objected to an executive order used by President Nixon to rejuvenate the Subversive Activities Control Board, Congress used its power of the purse to prohibit the agency from using any funds to carry out the order. As a result, the agency eventually disappeared. Fisher, Constitutional Conflicts between Congress and the President, 112–13. The federal courts have also been active in declaring proclamations and executive orders illegal.[13]

Hampton & Co. v. United States

276 U.S. 394 (1928)

The Tariff Act of 1922 empowered the President to increase or decrease duties in order to equalize the differences between the costs of production at home and the costs in competing foreign countries. The Act established certain criteria to be taken into account in determining the differences, fixed the limits for increases and decreases, and required the Tariff Commission to first investigate before any duties could be changed. The major issue before the Court was whether the Act constituted an invalid delegation of legislative power to the President. J.W. Hampton, Jr. & Company, an importer, challenged the Constitutionality of this statute.

MR. CHIEF JUSTICE TAFT delivered the opinion of the Court.

J. W. Hampton, Jr., & Company made an importation into New York of barium dioxide, which the collector of customs assessed at the dutiable rate of six cents per pound. This was two cents per pound more than that fixed by statute.... The rate was raised by the collector by virtue of the proclamation of the President ... issued under, and by authority of, § 315 of Title III of the Tariff Act of September 21, 1922 ... which is the so-called flexible tariff provision. Protest was made and an appeal was taken

under § 514, ... The pertinent parts of § 315 of Title III ... are as follows:

"Section 315(a). That in order to regulate the foreign commerce of the United States and to put into force and effect the policy of the Congress by this Act intended, whenever the President, upon investigation of the differences in costs of production of articles wholly or in part the growth or product of the United States and of like or similar articles wholly or in part the growth or product of competing foreign countries, shall find it thereby shown that the duties fixed in this Act do not equalize the said differences

---

12. Chrysler Corp. v. Brown, 441 U.S. 281, 306–08 (1979). See Lincoln Electric Co. v. Commissioner of Int. Rev., 190 F.2d 326, 330 (6th Cir. 1951); American Broadcasting Co. v. United States, 110 F.Supp. 374, 384 (S.D. N.Y. 1953), aff'd, 347 U.S. 284 (1954); and Independent Meat Packers Ass'n v. Butz, 526 F.2d 228, 234–36 (8th Cir. 1975), cert. denied, 424 U.S. 966 (1976).

13. Chamber of Commerce of U.S. v. Reich, 74 F.3d 1322 (D.C. Cir. 1996); Independent Gasoline Marketers Council v. Duncan, 492 F.Supp. 614, 620–21 (D.D.C. 1980); Kaplan v. Johnson, 409 F.Supp. 190, 206 (N.D.Ill. 1976); Cole v. Young, 351 U.S. 536, 555 (1956); Youngstown Co. v. Sawyer, 343 U.S. 579 (1952); Schechter Corp. v. United States, 295 U.S. 495, 525–26 (1935); Panama Refining Co. v. Ryan, 293 U.S. 388, 433 (1935); United States v. Symonds, 120 U.S. 46 (1887); Little v. Barreme, 6 U.S. (2 Cr.) 170 (1804). See Adam L. Warber, Executive Orders and the Modern Presidency (2006); Phillip J. Cooper, By Order of the President (2002); Kenneth R. Mayer, With the Stroke of a Pen (2001); Louis Fisher, Constitutional Conflicts Between Congress and the President 102–14 (2007).

in costs of production in the United States and the principal competing country he shall, by such investigation, ascertain said differences and determine and proclaim the changes in classifications or increases or decreases in any rate of duty provided in this Act shown by said ascertained differences in such costs of production necessary to equalize the same. Thirty days after the date of such proclamation or proclamations, such changes in classification shall take effect, … the total increase or decrease of such rates of duty shall not exceed 50 per centum of the rates specified in Title I of this Act, or in any amendatory Act....

"(c). That in ascertaining the differences in costs of production, under the provisions of subdivisions (a) and (b) of this section, the President, in so far as he finds it practicable, shall take into consideration (1) the differences in conditions in production, including wages, costs of material, and other items in costs of production of such or similar articles in the United States and in competing foreign countries; (2) the differences in the wholesale selling prices of domestic and foreign articles in the principal markets of the United States; (3) advantages granted to a foreign producer by a foreign government, or by a person, partnership, corporation, or association in a foreign country; and (4) any other advantages or disadvantages in competition.

"Investigations to assist the President in ascertaining differences in costs of production under this section shall be made by the United States Tariff Commission, and no proclamation shall be issued under this section until such investigation shall have been made. The commission shall give reasonable public notice of its hearings and shall give reasonable opportunity to parties interested to be present, to produce evidence, and to be heard. The commission is authorized to adopt such reasonable procedure, rules, and regulations as it may deem necessary."

. . .

✒ [*The petitioners*] argue that the section is invalid in that it is a delegation to the President of the legislative power, which by Article I, § 1 of the Constitution, is vested in Congress, the power being that declared in § 8 of Article I, that the Congress shall have power to lay and collect taxes, duties, imposts and excises....

First. It seems clear what Congress intended by § 315. Its plan was to secure by law the imposition of customs duties on articles of imported merchandise which should equal the difference between the cost of producing in a foreign country the articles in question and laying them down for sale in the United States, and the cost of producing and selling like or similar articles in the United States, so that the duties not only secure revenue but at the same time enable domestic producers to compete on terms of equality with foreign producers in the markets of the United States. It may be that it is difficult to fix with exactness this difference, but the difference which is sought in the statute is perfectly clear and perfectly intelligible. Because of the difficulty in practically determining what that difference is, Congress seems to have doubted that the information in its possession was such as to enable it to make the adjustment accurately, and also to have apprehended that with changing conditions the difference might vary in such a way that some readjustments would be necessary to give effect to the principle on which the statute proceeds....

The well-known maxim *"Delegata potestas non potest delegari,"* applicable to the law of agency in the general and common law, is well understood and has had wider application in the construction of our Federal and State Constitutions than it has in private law. The Federal Constitution and State Constitutions of this country divide the governmental power into three branches.... [I]t is a breach of the National fundamental law if Congress gives up its legislative power and transfers it to the President, or to the Judicial branch, or if by law it attempts to invest itself or its members with either executive power or judicial power....

The field of Congress involves all and many varieties of legislative action, and Congress has found it frequently necessary to use officers of the Executive Branch, within defined limits, to secure the exact effect intended by its acts of legislation, by vesting discretion in such officers to make public regulations interpreting a statute and directing the details of its execution, even to the extent of providing for penalizing a breach of such regulations....

Congress may feel itself unable conveniently to determine exactly when its exercise of the legislative power should become effective, because dependent on future conditions, and it may leave the determination of such time to the decision of an Executive, …

Again, one of the great functions conferred on Congress by the Federal Constitution is the regulation of interstate commerce and rates to be exacted by interstate carriers for the passenger and merchandise traffic. The rates to be fixed are myriad. If Congress were to be required to fix every rate, it would be impossible to exercise the power at all....

… If Congress shall lay down by legislative act an

intelligible principle to which the person or body authorized to fix such rates is directed to conform, such legislative action is not a forbidden delegation of legislative power....

... What the President was required to do was merely in execution of the act of Congress. It was not the making of law. He was the mere agent of the lawmaking department to ascertain and declare the event upon which its expressed will was to take effect.

. . .

Affirmed.

Schechter Corp. v. United States

295 U.S. 495 (1935)

In *Panama Refining Co. v. Ryan,* 293 U.S. 388 (1935), the Supreme Court struck down part of the National Industrial Recovery Act as an invalid delegation of legislative power from Congress to the President. The statute placed upon industrial and trade associations the responsibility for drawing up codes to minimize competition, raise prices, and restrict production. If the President regarded the codes as unacceptable, he could prescribe his own codes and enforce them by law. *Panama Refining* held that a section of the statute governing controls on petroleum production failed to establish criteria to govern the President's course. Only Justice Cardozo dissented. In *Schechter,* the "sick chicken" case, the Court examines the constitutionality of the rest of the statute.

Mr. Chief Justice Hughes delivered the opinion of the Court.

Petitioners ... were convicted in the District Court of the United States for the Eastern District of New York on eighteen counts of an indictment charging violations of what is known as the "Live Poultry Code," and on an additional count for conspiracy to commit such violations. By demurrer to the indictment and appropriate motions on the trial, the defendants contended (1) that the Code had been adopted pursuant to an unconstitutional delegation by Congress of legislative power; (2) that it attempted to regulate intrastate transactions which lay outside the authority of Congress; and (3) that in certain provisions it was repugnant to the due process clause of the Fifth Amendment.

[*The Court described New York City as the largest live-poultry market in the United States, with 96 percent of the poultry coming from other states. The Schechter Corporation usually purchased their live poultry from a market in New York City or at the railroad terminals serving the City, but occasionally they bought in Philadelphia. They trucked the poultry to their slaughterhouse markets in Brooklyn for sale to retail dealers and butchers. They did not sell the poultry in interstate commerce.*]

The "Live Poultry Code" was promulgated under § 3 of the National Industrial Recovery Act. That section ... authorizes the President to approve "codes of fair competition." Such a code may be approved for a trade or industry, upon application by one or more trade or industrial associations or groups, if the President finds (1) that such associations or groups "impose no inequitable restrictions on admission to membership therein and are truly representative," and (2) that such codes are not designed "to promote monopolies or to eliminate or oppress small enterprises and will not operate to discriminate against them, and will tend to effectuate the policy" of Title I of the Act. Such codes "shall not permit monopolies or monopolistic practices." ... Where such a code has not been approved, the President may prescribe one, either on his own motion or on complaint. Violation of any provision of a code (so approved or prescribed) "in any transaction in or affecting interstate or foreign commerce" is made a misdemeanor punishable by a fine of not more than $500 for each offense, and each day the violation continues is to be deemed a separate offense.

The "Live Poultry Code" was approved by the President on April 13, 1934....

[*The Code fixed the number of hours for workdays, the minimum pay, the minimum number of employees, and prohibited the employment of any person under 16 years of age. The Code was administered through an "industry advisory committee" selected by trade associations and members of the industry. A "code supervisor" was appointed with the approval of the committee by agreement between the Secretary of Agriculture and the Administrator for Industrial Recovery.*]

First. Two preliminary points are stressed by the

Government with respect to the appropriate approach to the important questions presented. We are told that the provision of the statute authorizing the adoption of codes must be viewed in the light of the grave national crisis with which Congress was confronted. Undoubtedly, the conditions to which power is addressed are always to be considered when the exercise of power is challenged. Extraordinary conditions may call for extraordinary remedies. But the argument necessarily stops short of an attempt to justify action which lies outside the sphere of constitutional authority. Extraordinary conditions do not create or enlarge constitutional power. The Constitution established a national government with powers deemed to be adequate, as they have proved to be both in war and peace, but these powers of the national government are limited by the constitutional grants....

The further point is urged that the national crisis demanded a broad and intensive coöperative effort by those engaged in trade and industry, and that this necessary coöperation was sought to be fostered by permitting them to initiate the adoption of codes. But the statutory plan is not simply one for voluntary effort. It does not seek merely to endow voluntary trade or industrial associations or groups with privileges or immunities. It involves the coercive exercise of the lawmaking power....

Second. The question of the delegation of legislative power. We recently had occasion to review the pertinent decisions and the general principles which govern the determination of this question. *Panama Refining Co.* v. *Ryan*, 293 U.S. 388.... The Congress is not permitted to abdicate or to transfer to others the essential legislative functions with which it is thus vested. We have repeatedly recognized the necessity of adapting legislation to complex conditions involving a host of details with which the national legislature cannot deal directly. We pointed out in the *Panama Company* case that the Constitution has never been regarded as denying to Congress the necessary resources of flexibility and practicality, which will enable it to perform its function in laying down policies and establishing standards, while leaving to selected instrumentalities the making of subordinate rules within prescribed limits and the determination of facts to which the policy as declared by the legislature is to apply. But we said that the constant recognition of the necessity and validity of such provisions, and the wide range of administrative authority which has been developed by means of them, cannot be allowed to obscure the limitations of the authority to delegate, if our constitutional system is to be maintained. *Id.*, p. 421.

⚓ Accordingly, we look to the statute to see whether Congress has overstepped these limitations,—

whether Congress in authorizing "codes of fair competition" has itself established the standards of legal obligation, thus performing its essential legislative function, or, by the failure to enact such standards, has attempted to transfer that function to others.

The aspect in which the question is now presented is distinct from that which was before us in the case of the *Panama Company.* There, the subject of the statutory prohibition was defined. National Industrial Recovery Act, § 9 (c). That subject was the transportation in interstate and foreign commerce of petroleum and petroleum products which are produced or withdrawn from storage in excess of the amount permitted by state authority. The question was with respect to the range of discretion given to the President in prohibiting that transportation. *Id.*, pp. 414, 415, 430. As to the "codes of fair competition," under § 3 of the Act, the question is more fundamental. It is whether there is any adequate definition of the subject to which the codes are to be addressed.

What is meant by "fair competition" as the term is used in the Act? Does it refer to a category established in the law, and is the authority to make codes limited accordingly? Or is it used as a convenient designation for whatever set of laws the formulators of a code for a particular trade or industry may propose and the President may approve (subject to certain restrictions), or the President may himself prescribe, as being wise and beneficent provisions for the government of the trade or industry in order to accomplish the broad purposes of rehabilitation, correction and expansion which are stated in the first section of Title I?

The Act does not define "fair competition." ...

... [W]ould it be seriously contended that Congress could delegate its legislative authority to trade or industrial associations or groups so as to empower them to enact the laws they deem to be wise and beneficent for the rehabilitation and expansion of their trade or industries? Could trade or industrial associations or groups be constituted legislative bodies for that purpose because such associations or groups are familiar with the problems of their enterprises? And, could an effort of that sort be made valid by such a preface of generalities as to permissible aims as we find in section 1 of title I? The answer is obvious. Such a delegation of legislative power is unknown to our law and is utterly inconsistent with the constitutional prerogatives and duties of Congress.

... Section 3 of the Recovery Act is without precedent. It supplies no standards for any trade, industry or activity. It does not undertake to prescribe rules of conduct to be applied to particular states of fact determined by appropriate administrative procedure. Instead of prescribing rules of conduct, it authorizes the making of codes to prescribe them. For that legislative undertaking, §3 sets up no standards, aside from the statement of the general aims of rehabilitation, correction and expansion described in section one. In view of the scope of that broad declaration, and of the nature of the few restrictions that are imposed, the discretion of the President in approving or prescribing codes, and thus enacting laws for the government of trade and industry throughout the country, is virtually unfettered. We think that the code-making authority thus conferred is an unconstitutional delegation of legislative power.

. . .

Mr. Justice Cardozo, concurring.

The delegated power of legislation which has found expression in this code is not canalized within banks that keep it from overflowing. It is unconfined and vagrant, if I may borrow my own words in an earlier opinion. *Panama Refining Co.* v. *Ryan*, 293 U.S. 388, 440.

This court has held that delegation may be unlawful though the act to be performed is definite and single, if the necessity, time and occasion of performance have been left in the end to the discretion of the delegate. *Panama Refining Co.* v. *Ryan, supra.* I thought that ruling went too far. I pointed out in an opinion that there had been "no grant to the Executive of any roving commission to inquire into evils and then, upon discovering them, do anything he pleases." ... Here, in the case before us, is an attempted delegation not confined to any single act nor to any class or group of acts identified or described by reference to a standard. Here in effect is a roving commission to inquire into evils and upon discovery correct them.

... This is delegation running riot. No such plenitude of power is susceptible of transfer....

I am authorized to state that Mr. Justice Stone joins in this opinion.

F. CONGRESSIONAL OVERSIGHT

Congress maintains control over delegated power through a variety of methods: the power to appropriate funds, changes in authorization language, reliance on nonstatutory controls, and different forms of the "legislative veto" (which retains some vitality even after the Supreme Court declared it unconstitutional in 1983). Another form of control, the power to investigate, is covered in the next section.

Power of the Purse

In Federalist No. 58, James Madison regarded the power of the purse as the "most complete and effectual weapon with which any constitution can arm the immediate representatives of the people, for obtaining a redress of every grievance, and for carrying into effect every just and salutary measure." Article I, Section 9, of the Constitution places this weapon squarely in the hands of Congress: "No Money shall be drawn from the Treasury, but in Consequence of Appropriations made by Law."

There are relatively few restrictions on this power of the purse. Congress cannot lawfully use its funding power to establish a religion.[14] It may not diminish the compensation of federal judges. It may neither increase nor decrease the compensation of the President during his term in office. It may not include language in appropriations bills to deny funds to named "subversives," for such legislative punishment is a bill of attainder prohibited by Article III, Section 3. United States v. Lovett, 328 U.S. 303 (1946); Blitz v. Donovan, 538 F.Supp. 1119 (D.D.C. 1982). A proviso in an appropriations bill may not interfere with the President's power to issue a pardon or prescribe for the judiciary the effect of a pardon. United States v. Klein, 13 Wall. 128 (1872); Hart v. United States, 118 U.S. 62 (1886).

For the most part, Congress may invoke the power of the purse to control almost every facet of executive activity. Appropriations can be lump sum or itemized. If lump sum (to give administrators

---

14. U.S. Constitution, Amend. I; Flast v. Cohen, 392 U.S. 83, 104–05 (1968). However, plaintiffs who challenge federal assistance to religious institutions may be unable to establish standing as a litigant; Valley Forge College v. Americans United, 454 U.S. 464 (1982).

discretion), congressional committees can insist on an informal veto over certain agency actions. Congress can attach "riders" or conditions to appropriations bills to prohibit the use of funds for specified purposes. Executive officials may object to "micromanagement" by legislators, but Congress has the constitutional authority to control administrative activity in minute detail.

Presidents share the power of the purse in several ways. The Budget and Accounting Act of 1921 directed the President to submit a national budget each year. Through this submission the President has an important means of setting the legislative agenda for Congress. Moreover, Presidents and their assistants are generally given some discretion in withholding funds (impoundment), transferring funds from one appropriation account to another, and "reprogramming" funds within an account. Louis Fisher, Presidential Spending Power (1975).

In response to abuses by the Nixon administration, Congress passed the Impoundment Control Act of 1974 to limit presidential actions to two types of impoundment: *rescission* (terminating funds), which requires the approval of Congress within 45 days of continuous session, and *deferral* (delay of spending), subject to disapproval by either House. When the legislative veto was invalidated by INS v. CHADHA, 462 U.S. 919, in 1983, it was later decided that the President's authority to make policy deferrals disappeared with the legislative veto because the authority and the veto were inseverable. City of New Haven v. United States, 809 F.2d 900 (D.C. Cir. 1987). This decision restricted the President to submitting routine deferrals to Congress.

The Item Veto

In 1996, Congress passed the Line Item Veto Act to strengthen the President's power to rescind funds. Instead of requiring the approval of Congress (the procedure established in 1974), presidential rescissions would take effect within 30 days unless Congress passed a bill or joint resolution of disapproval. The President could then veto the disapproval legislation, forcing each House to muster a two-thirds majority to override the veto. It is actually a misnomer to call this statute an "item veto." Presidents would still be left with the same choice they have had since 1789: either sign the whole bill or veto the whole bill. If the President signed a bill, the new procedure became available to cancel not only appropriated funds but also new entitlements and limited tax benefits.

In 1997, a constitutional challenge to the statute was turned back by the Supreme Court, which held that the plaintiffs (members of Congress) lacked standing to bring the suit. Raines v. Byrd, 521 U.S. 811 (1997). (See the reading on this decision in Chapter 1.) A year later the Court granted standing to other plaintiffs and ruled that the Line Item Veto Act violated the Presentment Clause. CLINTON v. CITY OF NEW YORK, 524 U.S. 417 (1998). The item veto could return in some other form (see box on next page). Both the House and the Senate were active in 2006 and 2007 in considering item veto legislation that would survive the *Clinton* test. Interest in an item veto returned in 2010 and 2012, when proposed legislation passed the House but not the Senate.

Enactment of Authorizations

With the exception of the offices of the President, the Vice President, and the Supreme Court, every other agency of government depends on Congress for its existence. In creating an agency, Congress determines its mission, structure, personnel, and ceilings for appropriations. It is for Congress to decide whether the agency has a permanent authorization or must return to Congress every year or every few years for reauthorization. Through its action on authorization bills, Congress can redirect agency activities, require reports to Congress, redefine missions, or reorganize the agency out of existence.

Nonstatutory Controls

Although agencies are subject to authorization and appropriation actions through public law, much of the congressional control is maintained outside the statutory process. Committee reports, com-

The Item Veto: Will It Return?

By a 6–3 vote, the Supreme Court decided that the Line Item Veto Act of 1996 was unconstitutional because it violated the Presentment Clause. Clinton v. City of New York, 524 U.S. 417 (1998). That central part of the decision suggests that the issue was essentially procedural: to cancel law, the two branches have to follow the standard legislative process, including presentment of a bill to the President for his signature or veto. In a sense, the Court adhered to language in *Chadha*: "Amendment and repeal of statutes, no less than enactment, must conform with Art. I." 462 U.S. at 954. But *Chadha* was about Congress intervening in the executive process without complying with the lawmaking requirements of bicameralism and presentment. The item veto statute represented a grant of power to the President with no congressional interference other than an opportunity to disapprove the President's cancellations, and the disapproval measure complied fully with bicameralism and presentment.

The Court admitted, as it had to, that previous legislation had delegated to the President substantial authority to suspend and alter statutory language, particularly in tariffs and duties. Conceding the point, the Court noted that the statutes identified "all relate to foreign trade, and this Court has recognized that in the foreign affairs arena" the President has considerable discretion. The argument appears to turn from strict procedural matters (Presentment Clause) to the substance of law being altered (foreign versus domestic policy).

The Court ends by saying that any presidential power to alter legislation must come not by legislation but by constitutional amendment. However, there are a number of statutory options to create a new type of "item veto" that would comply fully with presentment. One is "separate enrollment" (breaking large appropriations bills into separate pieces). Another is to appropriate sums "not exceeding" a specified amount, allowing the President to withhold much or all of the money. Another option: a statute directs the President to carry out a program unless he certifies that it is unnecessary or not in the national interest.

mittee hearings, correspondence from review committees, and other nonstatutory techniques allow Congress to monitor and direct agency activity without passing another public law. Because these controls are informal and not legally binding, the system functions on a "keep the faith" attitude. Agencies receive lump-sum funds and broad authority from Congress; in return, they acquiesce to a multitude of nonstatutory controls. Agencies follow these controls for practical, not legal, reasons. Violation of congressional trust may result in budget cutbacks, restrictive statutory language, and line-item appropriations.

Legislative Vetoes

During the 1930s, executive officials wanted to "make law" without passage of a statute. President Hoover obtained authority to reorganize the executive branch without having to submit a bill to Congress for hearings, amendments, and enactment by both Houses. Congress agreed only on the condition that either House could reject a reorganization plan by passing a resolution of disapproval. Through this accommodation was born the "legislative veto." Congress experimented with the one-House veto, the two-House veto (passage of a concurrent resolution), and even a committee veto. Fisher, Constitutional Conflicts between Congress and the President, at 137–45 (5th ed.).

This procedure obviously departs from the Presentment Clause in Article I, Section 7, which provides that "Every Order, Resolution, or Vote to which the Concurrence of the Senate and House of Representatives may be necessary (except on a question of Adjournment)" shall be presented to the President. Legislative vetoes are not presented to the President. President Hoover accepted the compromise because it facilitated executive reorganization. This quid pro quo was extended to other areas, including immigration, arms sales, the war power, impoundment, and agency regulations. Eventually, the Justice Department and the White House decided that the bargain no longer favored the executive branch. A test case, involving an immigration statute, was soon on its way to the Supreme Court.

In the 1930s the executive branch had prevailed upon Congress to delegate discretionary authority over the deportation of aliens. Congress agreed to allow the Attorney General to suspend deportations provided that the suspensions were subject to a one-House legislative veto. Congress exercised this power on numerous occasions. The test case arose in 1975 when the House of Representatives disapproved the suspension of deportation for six aliens, including Jagdish Rai Chadha. After exhausting his administrative remedies in the Immigration and Naturalization Service, he won a court victory in the Ninth Circuit in 1980. The Supreme Court granted cert and twice heard the case on oral argument.

INS v. Chadha

In a sweeping decision issued in 1983, the Supreme Court declared the legislative veto unconstitutional. All legislative vetoes were unconstitutional because they violated the Presentment Clause. In addition, the one-House veto was unconstitutional because it violated the principle of bicameralism (which requires action by both Houses). Chief Justice Burger, writing for the majority, said that whenever congressional action has the "purpose and effect of altering the legal rights, duties and relations of persons" outside the legislative branch, Congress must act through both Houses in a bill presented to the President. INS v. CHADHA, 462 U.S. 919 (1983).

The Court's opinion is shallow in many ways. It claimed that the convenience of the legislative veto could not overcome the framers' view that efficiency was not a primary objective or hallmark of democratic government, and yet the framers ranked efficiency highly. The Court also argued that the legislative veto threatened the independence of the President by evading his veto power, but Presidents encouraged the legislative veto to obtain greater authority. Under the legislative veto procedure, Congress could not amend a President's proposal. The general veto was therefore not needed for presidential self-defense. More importantly, the decision did not, and could not, eliminate the political conditions that gave rise to the legislative veto: the desire of executive officials for broad delegations of power, and the insistence of Congress that it control those delegations without having to pass another public law. The executive-legislative accommodations that prevailed before *Chadha* continue to exist, sometimes in forms that are indistinguishable from the legislative veto supposedly struck down by the Court (see Fisher reading).

Disputes after *Chadha*

In 1989, the Bush administration entered into an accommodation with Congress which was criticized as an unconstitutional legislative veto. To obtain funds for the Nicaraguan contras, Secretary of State James A. Baker, III agreed to give four committees of Congress and congressional leaders a veto power over the release of some of the funds. White House Counsel C. Boyden Gray objected that the agreement appeared to be unconstitutional under *Chadha,* as did former federal judge Robert H. Bork. However, Baker's agreement did not appear in a public law. It was an informal, nonstatutory, "side agreement" that is not covered by *Chadha* (see box on next page). Four members of the House of Representatives challenged the "Baker Accord" as unconstitutional, but their suit was dismissed by a federal district court. Burton v. Baker, 723 F.Supp. 1550 (D.D.C. 1990).

In 1991, the Court relied on *Chadha* to strike down a statutory provision enacted by Congress that gave a board of review (composed of nine members of Congress) a veto over decisions made by a regional authority responsible for two airports serving the District of Columbia. The Court held that the veto power violated the doctrine of separation of powers. Metropolitan Washington Airports Auth. v. Noise Abatement Citizens, 501 U.S. 252 (1991). Congress enacted remedial legislation later that year, reconstituting the board of review and giving it the power to recommend but not to veto. The new statute authorized Congress to pass a joint resolution of disapproval to reject actions by the regional authority. Joint resolutions satisfy the requirements of *Chadha* (bicameralism and present-

The Baker Accord

APRIL 28, 1989

Dear Mr. Speaker:

Pursuant to the bipartisan agreement on Central America between the Executive and the Congress, the Congress has now voted to extend humanitarian assistance to the Nicaraguan Resistance at current levels through February 28, 1990. This assistance has been authorized and appropriated but will not be obligated beyond November 30, 1989, except in the context of consultation among the Executive, the Senate Majority and Minority leaders, the Speaker of the House of Representatives and the Majority and Minority leaders, and the relevant authorization and appropriation committees, and only if affirmed via letters from the Bipartisan Leadership of Congress and the relevant House and Senate authorization and appropriations committees.

This bipartisan accord on Central America represents a unique agreement between the Executive and Legislative Branches. Thus, it is the intention of the parties that this agreement in no way establishes any precedent for the Executive or the Legislative Branch regarding the authorization and appropriation process.

Sincerely yours,
James A. Baker, III

ment). 105 Stat. 2197, Title VII (1991). This new law didn't satisfy the courts either. The D.C. Circuit held that the board of review acted as an agent of Congress and that it exercised federal power in violation of the separation of powers doctrine. When this ruling was appealed to the Supreme Court, cert was denied. Hechinger v. Metro. Wash. Airports Authority, 36 F.3d 97 (D.C. Cir. 1994), cert. denied, 513 U.S. 1126 (1995).

Clinton v. City of New York

524 U.S. 417 (1998)

After President Clinton had exercised his authority under the Line Item Veto Act by canceling certain items, two plaintiffs claiming injury challenged the constitutionality of the statute. A district court ruled that the Act's cancellation procedures violated the Presentment Clause. Having granted the plaintiffs standing, the Supreme Court turned to the constitutional question: May Congress grant the President discretionary authority to amend or cancel certain provisions in budget legislation?

JUSTICE STEVENS delivered the opinion of the Court.

The Line Item Veto Act (Act) ... was enacted in April 1996 and became effective on January 1, 1997....

[*In Sections I, II, and III, Stevens reviews the canceled items that were at issue in this case, states the injuries claimed by the plaintiffs, decides that the plaintiffs (the City of New York and a farmers' cooperative) were "individuals" entitled to bring an expedited matter to the Court, and concludes that the plaintiffs had standing.*]

IV

The Line Item Veto Act gives the President the power to "cancel in whole" three types of provisions that have been signed into law: "(1) any dollar amount of discretionary budget authority; (2) any item of new direct spending; or (3) any limited tax benefit." ... It is undisputed that the New York case involves an "item of new direct spending" and that the Snake River case involves a "limited tax benefit" as those terms are defined in the Act....

The Act requires the President to adhere to precise procedures whenever he exercises his cancellation authority. In identifying items for cancellation he must consider the legislative history, the purposes, and other relevant information about the items.... He must determine, with respect to each cancellation, that it will "(i) reduce the Federal budget deficit; (ii) not impair any essential Government functions; and (iii) not harm the national interest." ... Moreover, he must transmit a special message to Congress notifying it of each cancellation within five calendar days (excluding Sundays) after the enactment of the canceled provision....

A cancellation takes effect upon receipt by Congress of the special message from the President.... If, however, a "disapproval bill" pertaining to a special message is enacted into law, the cancellations set forth in that message become "null and void." ...

The effect of a cancellation is plainly stated in §691e, which defines the principal terms used in the Act. With respect to both an item of new direct spending and a limited tax benefit, the cancellation prevents the item "from having legal force or effect." ...

In both legal and practical effect, the President has amended two Acts of Congress by repealing a portion of each. "[R]epeal of statutes, no less than enactment, must conform with Art. I." *INS v. Chadha*, 462 U.S. 919, 954 (1983). There is no provision in the Constitution that authorizes the President to enact, to amend, or to repeal statutes. Both Article I and Article II assign responsibilities to the President that directly relate to the lawmaking process, but neither addresses the issue presented by these cases....

There are important differences between the President's "return" of a bill pursuant to Article I, §7, and the exercise of the President's cancellation authority pursuant to the Line Item Veto Act. The constitutional return takes place *before* the bill becomes law; the statutory cancellation occurs *after* the bill becomes law. The constitutional return is of the entire bill; the statutory cancellation is of only a part. Although the Constitution expressly authorizes the President to play a role in the process of enacting statutes, it is silent on the subject of unilateral Presidential action that either repeals or amends parts of duly enacted statutes.

There are powerful reasons for construing constitutional silence on this profoundly important issue as equivalent to an express prohibition. The procedures governing the enactment of statutes set forth in the text of Article I were the product of the great debates and compromises that produced the Constitution itself. Familiar historical materials provide abundant support for the conclusion that the power to enact statutes may only "be exercised in accord with a single, finely wrought and exhaustively considered, procedure." *Chadha*, 462 U.S., at 951. Our first President understood the text of the Presentment Clause as requiring that he either "approve all the parts of a Bill, or reject it in toto." What has emerged in these cases from the President's exercise of his statutory cancellation powers, however, are truncated versions of two bills that passed both Houses of Congress. They are not the product of the "finely wrought" procedure that the Framers designed....

V

The Government advances two related arguments to support its position that despite the unambiguous provisions of the Act, cancellations do not amend or repeal properly enacted statutes in violation of the Presentment Clause. First, relying primarily on *Field v. Clark*, 143 U.S. 649 (1892), the Government contends that the cancellations were merely exercises of discretionary authority granted to the President by the Balanced Budget Act and the Taxpayer Relief Act read in light of the previously enacted Line Item Veto Act. Second, the Government submits that the substance of the authority to cancel tax and spending items "is, in practical effect, no more and no less than the power to 'decline to spend' specified sums of money, or to 'decline to implement' specified tax measures." ... Neither argument is persuasive.

In *Field v. Clark*, the Court upheld the constitutionality of the Tariff Act of 1890. [*The statute contained a "free list" of almost 300 specific articles that were exempted from import duties, but authorized the President to suspend the exemption for certain articles whenever he decided that the country exporting those products imposed duties on the agricultural products of the United States that he deemed to be "reciprocally unequal and unreasonable." Stevens identifies what he considered to be three critical differences between the President's power to suspend the exemption from import duties and the President's power under the Line Item Veto Act.*] First, the exercise of the suspension power was contingent upon a condition that did not exist when the Tariff Act was passed: the imposition of "reciprocally unequal and unreasonable" import duties by other countries. In contrast, the exercise of the cancellation power within five days after the enactment of the Balanced Budget and Tax Reform Acts necessarily was based on the same conditions that Congress evaluated when it passed those statutes. Second, under the Tariff Act, when the President determined that the contingency had arisen, he had a duty to suspend; in contrast, while it is true that the President was required by the Act to make three determinations before he canceled a provision, ... those determinations did not qualify his discretion to cancel or not to cancel. Finally, whenever the President suspended an exemption under the Tariff Act, he was executing the policy that Congress had embodied in the statute. In contrast, whenever the President cancels an item of new direct spending or a limited tax benefit he is rejecting the policy judgment made by Congress and relying on his own policy judgment....

The cited statutes all relate to foreign trade, and this Court has recognized that in the foreign affairs arena, the President has "a degree of discretion and freedom from statutory restriction which would not be admissible were domestic affairs alone involved." *United States v. Curtiss-Wright Export Corp.*, 299 U.S. 304, 320 (1936)....

Neither are we persuaded by the Government's contention that the President's authority to cancel new direct spending and tax benefit items is no greater than his traditional authority to decline to spend appropriated funds. The Government has reviewed in some detail the series of statutes in which Congress has given the Executive broad discretion over the expenditure of appropriated funds. For example, the First Congress appropriated "sum[s] not exceeding" specified amounts to be spent on various Government operations.... In those statutes, as in later years, the President was given wide discretion with respect to both the amounts to be spent and how the money would be allocated among different functions. It is argued that the Line Item Veto Act merely confers comparable discretionary authority over the expenditure of appropriated funds. The critical difference between this statute and all of its predecessors, however, is that unlike any of them, this Act gives the President the unilateral power to change the text of duly enacted statutes. None of the Act's predecessors could even arguably have been construed to authorize such a change.

VI

. . .

If there is to be a new procedure in which the President will play a different role in determining the final text of what may "become a law," such change must come not by legislation but through the amendment procedures set forth in Article V of the Constitution....

The judgment of the District Court is affirmed.

It is so ordered.

Justice Kennedy, concurring.

[*Kennedy emphasized the structural issues present in this case. "Liberty is always at stake when one or more of the branches seek to transgress the separation of pow-*

ers." Concentration of power in the hands of branch "is a threat to liberty." Liberty is protecte. only by the Bill of Rights but by the principles of se ration of powers, federalism, and checks and balances.]

It is no answer, of course, to say that Congress surrendered its authority by its own hand; nor does it suffice to point out that a new statute, signed by the President or enacted over his veto, could restore to Congress the power it now seeks to relinquish. That a congressional cession of power is voluntary does not make it innocuous. The Constitution is a compact enduring for more than our time, and one Congress cannot yield up its own powers, much less those of other Congresses to follow.... Abdication of responsibility is not part of the constitutional design....

Justice Scalia, with whom Justice O'Connor joins, and with whom Justice Breyer joins as to Part III, concurring in part and dissenting in part.

... [U]nlike the Court I find the President's cancellation of spending items to be entirely in accord with the Constitution.

. . .

Insofar as the degree of political, "law-making" power conferred upon the Executive is concerned, there is not a dime's worth of difference between Congress's authorizing the President to *cancel* a spending item, and Congress's authorizing money to be spent on a particular item at the President's discretion. And the latter has been done since the Founding of the Nation. From 1789–1791, the First Congress made lump-sum appropriations for the entire Government— "sum[s] not exceeding" specified amounts for broad purposes.... From a very early date Congress also made permissive individual appropriations, leaving the decision whether to spend the money to the President's unfettered discretion....

The short of the matter is this: Had the Line Item Veto Act authorized the President to "decline to spend" any item of spending contained in the Balanced Budget Act of 1997, there is not the slightest doubt that authorization would have been constitutional. What the Line Item Veto Act does instead— authorizing the President to "cancel" an item of spending—is technically different. But the technical difference does *not* relate to the technicalities of the Presentment Clause, which have been fully complied with; and the doctrine of unconstitutional delegation, which *is* at issue here, is preeminently *not* a doctrine of technicalities. The title of the Line Item

Veto Act, which was perhaps designed to simplify for public comprehension, or perhaps merely to comply with the terms of a campaign pledge, has succeeded in faking out the Supreme Court. The President's action it authorizes in fact is not a line-item veto and thus does not offend Art. I, § 7; and insofar as the substance of that action is concerned, it is no different from what Congress has permitted the President to do since the formation of the Union....

JUSTICE BREYER, with whom JUSTICE O'CONNOR and JUSTICE SCALIA join as to Part III, dissenting.

I agree with the Court that the parties have standing, but I do not agree with its ultimate conclusion. In my view the Line Item Veto Act does not violate any specific textual constitutional command, nor does it violate any implicit Separation of Powers principle. Consequently, I believe that the Act is constitutional....

III

... When the President "canceled" the two appropriation measures now before us, he did not *repeal* any law nor did he *amend* any law. He simply *followed* the law, leaving the statutes, as they are literally written, intact....

INS v. Chadha

462 U.S. 919 (1983)

Congress authorized the Attorney General to suspend the deportation of aliens. Suspensions, however, were subject to the disapproval of either House. Along with a list of 340 names, the Attorney General suspended the deportation of Jagdish Rai Chadha, an East Indian born in Kenya and who held a British passport. In 1975 the House of Representatives adopted a resolution disapproving six names, including that of Chadha. He moved to suspend the deportation proceedings on the ground that the portion of the statute giving Congress a one-House veto was unconstitutional. In 1980 the Ninth Circuit held that the legislative veto violated the doctrine of separation of powers. The Supreme Court twice held oral argument before deciding the case.

CHIEF JUSTICE BURGER delivered the opinion of the Court.

We granted certiorari [*to consider*] a challenge to the constitutionality of the provision in § 244(c)(2) ... authorizing one House of Congress, by resolution, to invalidate the decision of the Executive Branch, pursuant to authority delegated by Congress to the Attorney General of the United States, to allow a particular deportable alien to remain in the United States.

I

Chadha is an East Indian who was born in Kenya and holds a British passport. He was lawfully admitted to the United States in 1966 on a nonimmigrant student visa. His visa expired on June 30, 1972. On October 11, 1973, the District Director of the Immigration and Naturalization Service ordered Chadha to show cause why he should not be deported for having "remained in the United States for a longer time than permitted." ... Chadha conceded that he was deportable for overstaying his visa and the hearing was adjourned to enable him to file an application for suspension of deportation under § 244(a)(1) of the Act....

[*The immigration judge suspended Chadha's deportation, and a report of the suspension was transmitted. Acting under § 244(c)(2), and without debate or recorded vote, the House of Representatives disapproved Chadha's suspension. Before addressing the constitutionality of the one-House veto, the Court concluded that (1) it had jurisdiction to entertain the INS appeal, (2) the legislative veto could be severed from the Act without affecting the Attorney General's authority to suspend deportations, (3) Chadha had standing to bring the suit, (4) there was no reason to avoid the constitutional issue because Chadha might have alternative means of relief, (5) the Ninth Circuit had jurisdiction to decide the case, (6) the case represented a genuine case or controversy with the necessary concrete adverseness, and (7) the case did not constitute a nonjusticiable political question.*]

III

A

We turn now to the question whether action of one House of Congress under § 244(c)(2) violates strictures of the Constitution. We begin, of course, with the presumption that the challenged statute is valid....

By the same token, the fact that a given law or procedure is efficient, convenient, and useful in facilitating functions of government, standing alone, will not save it if it is contrary to the Constitution. Convenience and efficiency are not the primary objectives—or the hallmarks—of democratic government and our inquiry is sharpened rather than blunted by the fact that congressional veto provisions are appearing with increasing frequency in statutes which delegate authority to executive and independent agencies:

"Since 1932, when the first veto provision was enacted into law, 295 congressional veto-type procedures have been inserted in 196 different statutes as follows: from 1932 to 1939, five statutes were affected; from 1940–49, nineteen statutes; between 1950–59, thirty-four statutes; and from 1960–69, forty-nine. From the year 1970 through 1975, at least one hundred sixty-three such provisions were included in eighty-nine laws." Abourezk, The Congressional Veto: A Contemporary Response to Executive Encroachment on Legislative Prerogatives, 52 Ind. L. Rev. 323, 324 (1977).

. . .

Explicit and unambiguous provisions of the Constitution prescribe and define the respective functions of the Congress and of the Executive in the legislative process. Since the precise terms of those familiar provisions are critical to the resolution of these cases, we set them out verbatim. Article I provides:

"All legislative Powers herein granted shall be vested in a Congress of the United States, which shall consist of a Senate *and* House of Representatives." Art. I, § 1. (Emphasis added.)

"Every Bill which shall have passed the House of Representatives *and* the Senate, *shall,* before it becomes a law, be presented to the President of the United States ..." Art. I, § 7, cl. 2. (Emphasis added.)

"*Every* Order, Resolution, or Vote to which the Concurrence of the Senate and House of Representatives may be necessary (except on a question of Adjournment) *shall be* presented to the President of the United States; and before the Same shall take Effect, *shall be* approved by him, or being disapproved by him, *shall be* repassed by two thirds of the Senate and House of Representatives, according to the Rules and Limitations prescribed in the Case of a Bill." Art. I, § 7, cl. 3. (Emphasis added.)

. . .

B
THE PRESENTMENT CLAUSES

The records of the Constitutional Convention reveal that the requirement that all legislation be presented to the President before becoming law was uniformly accepted by the Framers. Presentment to the President and the Presidential veto were considered so imperative that the draftsmen took special pains to assure that these requirements could not be circumvented. During the final debate on Art. I, § 7, cl. 2, James Madison expressed concern that it might easily be evaded by the simple expedient of calling a proposed law a "resolution" or "vote" rather than a "bill." 2 Farrand 301–302. As a consequence, Art. I, § 7, cl. 3 ... was added....

C
BICAMERALISM

The bicameral requirement of Art. I, §§ 1, 7, was of scarcely less concern to the Framers than was the Presidential veto and indeed the two concepts are interdependent. By providing that no law could take effect without the concurrence of the prescribed majority of the Members of both Houses, the Framers reemphasized their belief, already remarked upon in connection with the Presentment Clauses, that legislation should not be enacted unless it has been carefully and fully considered by the Nation's elected officials....

... It emerges clearly that the prescription for legislative action in Art. I, §§ 1, 7, represents the Framers' decision that the legislative power of the Federal Government be exercised in accord with a single, finely wrought and exhaustively considered, procedure.

IV

. . .

Examination of the action taken here by one House pursuant to § 244(c)(2) reveals that it was essentially legislative in purpose and effect. In purporting to exercise power defined in Art. I, § 8, cl. 4, to "establish an uniform Rule of Naturalization," the House took action that had the purpose and effect of altering the legal rights, duties, and relations of persons, including the Attorney General, Executive Branch officials and Chadha, all outside the Legislative Branch. Section 244(c)(2) purports to authorize one House of Congress to require the Attorney General to deport an individual alien whose deportation otherwise would be canceled under § 244. The one-House veto operated in these cases to overrule the Attorney General and mandate Chadha's deportation; absent the House action, Chadha would remain in the United States. Congress has *acted* and its action has altered Chadha's status.

[*The Court acknowledges that the Constitution in some cases authorizes one House of Congress to act alone without the check of the President's veto: the power of the House of Representatives to initiate impeachment, the Senate's power to try impeachments, the Senate's action on appointments, and the Senate's action on treaties.*]

The veto authorized by § 244(c)(2) doubtless has been in many respects a convenient shortcut; the "sharing" with the Executive by Congress of its authority over aliens in this manner is, on its face, an appealing compromise. In purely practical terms, it is obviously easier for action to be taken by one House without submission to the President; but it is crystal clear from the records of the Convention, contemporaneous writings and debates, that the Framers ranked other values higher than efficiency. The records of the Convention and debates in the states preceding ratification underscore the common desire to define and limit the exercise of the newly created federal powers affecting the states and the people. There is unmistakable expression of a determination that legislation by the national Congress be a step-by-step, deliberate and deliberative process.

The choices we discern as having been made in the Constitutional Convention impose burdens on governmental processes that often seem clumsy, inefficient, even unworkable, but those hard choices were consciously made by men who had lived under a form of government that permitted arbitrary governmental acts to go unchecked. There is no support in the Constitution or decisions of this Court for the proposition that the cumbersomeness and delays often encountered in complying with explicit constitutional standards may be avoided, either by the Congress or by the President. See *Youngstown Sheet & Tube Co.* v. *Sawyer,* 343 U.S. 579 (1952). With all the obvious flaws of delay, untidiness, and potential for abuse, we have not yet found a better way to preserve freedom than by making the exercise of power subject to the carefully crafted restraints spelled out in the Constitution.

V

We hold that the congressional veto provision in § 244(c)(2) is severable from the Act and that it is unconstitutional. Accordingly, the judgment of the Court of Appeals is

Affirmed.

JUSTICE POWELL, concurring in the judgment.

The Court's decision, based on the Presentment Clauses, Art. I, § 7, cls. 2 and 3, apparently will invalidate every use of the legislative veto. The breadth of this holding gives one pause. Congress has included the veto in literally hundreds of statutes, dating back to the 1930s. Congress clearly views this procedure as essential to controlling the delegation of power to administrative agencies. One reasonably may disagree with Congress' assessment of the veto's utility, but the respect due its judgment as a coordinate branch of Government cautions that our holdings should be no more extensive than necessary to decide these cases. In my view, the cases may be decided on a narrower ground. When Congress finds that a particular person does not satisfy the statutory criteria for permanent residence in this country it has assumed a judicial function in violation of the principle of separation of powers. Accordingly, I concur only in the judgment.

. . .

JUSTICE WHITE, dissenting.

Today the Court not only invalidates § 244(c)(2) of the Immigration and Nationality Act, but also sounds the death knell for nearly 200 other statutory provisions in which Congress has reserved a "legislative veto." For this reason, the Court's decision is of surpassing importance. And it is for this reason that the Court would have been well advised to decide the cases, if possible, on the narrower grounds of separation of powers, leaving for full consideration the constitutionality of other congressional review statutes operating on such varied matters as war powers and agency rulemaking, some of which concern the independent regulatory agencies.

The prominence of the legislative veto mechanism in our contemporary political system and its importance to Congress can hardly be overstated. It has become a central means by which Congress secures the accountability of executive and independent agencies. Without the legislative veto, Congress is faced with a Hobson's choice: either to refrain from delegating the necessary authority, leaving itself with a hopeless task of writing laws with the requisite specificity to cover endless special circumstances across the entire policy landscape, or in the alternative, to abdicate its lawmaking function of the Executive Branch and independent agencies. To choose the former leaves major national problems unresolved; to opt for the latter risks unaccountable policymaking by those not elected to fill that role. Accordingly, over the past five decades, the legislative veto has been placed in nearly 200 statutes. The device is known in every field of governmental concern: reorganization, budgets, foreign affairs, war powers, and regulation of trade, safety, energy, the environment, and the economy.

I

[*White explains that the legislative veto arose in 1929 when President Hoover sought authority to reorganize the executive branch and expressed willingness to have Congress check his actions by exercising a one-House veto. In subsequent actions, the two branches applied this quid pro quo to other areas. The result was that the President gained new authority and Congress held a legislative veto to control the delegated authority.*]

... While the President has often objected to particular legislative vetoes, generally those left in the hands of congressional Committees, the Executive has more often agreed to legislative review as the price for a broad delegation of authority. To be sure, the President may have preferred unrestricted power, but that could be precisely why Congress

thought it essential to retain a check on the exercise of delegated authority.

. . .

V

I regret that I am in disagreement with my colleagues on the fundamental questions that these cases present. But even more I regret the destructive scope of the Court's holding. It reflects a profoundly different conception of the Constitution than that held by the courts which sanctioned the modern administrative state. Today's decision strikes down in one fell swoop provisions in more laws enacted by Congress than the Court has cumulatively invalidated in its history....

JUSTICE REHNQUIST, with whom JUSTICE WHITE joins, dissenting.

[*Rehnquist states his belief that Congress did not intend the one-House veto to be severable from § 244(c)(2). Because the Court had held the legislative veto unconstitutional, Rehnquist would strike down the delegated authority as well.*]

Louis Fisher
Legislative Vetoes After *Chadha*

After the Supreme Court in *INS* v. *Chadha* (1983) held the legislative veto unconstitutional, Congress continued to place legislative vetoes in bills and Presidents continued to sign them into law. Many of these new statutory controls required executive agencies to seek the approval of specific congressional committees before implementing an agency action. The various methods available to Congress for finding substitutes for the legislative veto, and in fact for using legislative vetoes, are explored by Louis Fisher in "Judicial Misjudgments About the Lawmaking Process: The Legislative Veto Case," 45 Pub. Adm. Rev. 705 (Special Issue, November 1985). A later analysis appears in Louis Fisher, "The Legislative Veto: Invalidated, It Survives," 56 Law & Contemp. Prob. 273 (Autumn 1993).

In past years the Supreme Court has damaged its reputation by issuing decisions based on misconceptions about the political and economic system. After trying to impose archaic and mechanical concepts about federalism, the taxing power, the commerce power, and other clauses of the Constitution, the court was forced to retreat from pronouncements that were simply unacceptable for a developing nation. To minimize what Charles Evans Hughes once called the court's penchant for "self-inflicted wounds," justices evolved a number of rules to limit their exercise of judicial review. One mainstay is the principle that the court will not "formulate a rule of

constitutional law broader than is required by the precise facts to which it is to be applied."

That guideline was not followed in 1983 when the Supreme Court issued *INS* v. *Chadha*, which declared the legislative veto unconstitutional in all its forms. The court announced that future congressional efforts to alter "the legal rights, duties and relations of persons" outside the legislative branch must follow the full lawmaking process: passage of a bill or joint resolution by both Houses and presentment of that measure to the president for his signature or veto. The court lectured Congress that it could no longer rely on the legislative veto as "a convenient shortcut" to control executive agencies. Instead, "legislation by the national Congress [must] be a step-by-step, deliberate and deliberative process." According to the court, the framers insisted that "the legislative power of the Federal Government be exercised in accord with a single, finely wrought and exhaustively considered, procedure."

A HISTORY OF ACCOMMODATIONS

All three branches reached agreement long ago that the step-by-step, deliberate and deliberative process is not appropriate for each and every exercise of the legislative power. Despite occasional invocations of the non-delegation doctrine, the court itself has accepted the inevitable delegation of legislative power to executive agencies and independent commissions. Administrative bodies routinely "make law" through the rulemaking process. Efforts are made to subject this lawmaking activity to procedural safeguards, but the persistence of the Administrative State is ample proof that the theoretical model of legislative action envisioned by the framers applies only in the most general sense to the 20th [now 21st] century.

. . .

THE PERSISTENCE OF LEGISLATIVE VETOES

It came as a surprise to some observers that Congress continued to place legislative vetoes in bills after the court's decision and President Reagan continued to sign the bills into law. In the 16 months between *Chadha* and the adjournment of the 98th Congress, an additional 53 legislative vetoes were added to the books.

[*By the end of the 110th Congress, which adjourned at the end of 2008, the list of new legislative vetoes exceeded six hundred.*]

A flagrant case of non-compliance? A sign of disrespect for the courts? An alarming challenge to the time-honored belief that the Supreme Court has the last word on constitutional questions? Perhaps, but the court painted with too broad a brush and offered a simplistic solution that is unacceptable to the political branches. Its decision will be eroded by open defiance and subtle evasion. Neither consequence is attractive, but much of the responsibility for this condition belongs on the doorstep of the court.

Some of the legislative vetoes enacted since *Chadha* are easy to spot. Most of them vest control in the appropriations committees. For example, construction grants by the Environmental Protection Agency are subject to the approval of the appropriations committees (97 Stat. 226). The ap-

proval of the appropriations committees is required before exceeding certain dollar amounts in the National Flood Insurance Fund (97 Stat. 227)....

Other legislative vetoes are more subtle. A continuing resolution provided that foreign assistance funds allocated to each country "shall not exceed those provided in fiscal year 1983 or those provided in the budget estimates for each country, whichever are lower, unless submitted through the regular reprogramming procedures of the Committees on Appropriations" (97 Stat. 736). Those procedures provide for committee prior-approval. The District of Columbia Appropriation Act for fiscal 1984 prohibited funds from being obligated or spent by reprogramming "except pursuant to advance approval of the reprogramming granted according to the procedure set forth" in two House reports, both of which require prior approval by the appropriations committees (97 Stat. 827).

One year after *Chadha,* President Reagan received the HUD-Independent Agencies Appropriations bill which contained a number of committee vetoes. In his signing statement, he took note of those vetoes and asked Congress to stop adding provisions that the Supreme Court had held to be unconstitutional. He said that "the time has come, with more than a year having passed since the Supreme Court's decision in *Chadha,* to make clear that legislation containing legislative veto devices that comes to me for my approval or disapproval will be implemented in a manner consistent with the *Chadha* decision." The clear import was that the administration did not feel bound by the statutory requirements to seek the approval of congressional committees before implementing certain actions.

The House Appropriations Committee responded to the president's statement by reviewing an agreement it had entered into with NASA four years previously. Caps were set on various NASA programs, usually at the level requested in the president's budget. The agreement allowed NASA to exceed the caps with the approval of the appropriations committees. The House Appropriations Committee thought that the procedure had "worked well during the past four years, and has provided a mechanism by which the Congress and the Committee can be assured that funds are used solely for the purpose for which they were appropriated." Because of Reagan's statement and the threat to ignore committee controls, the committee said it was necessary to repeal the accommodation that had lasted for four years. Repeal language was inserted in the second supplemental bill for fiscal 1984. Both sides stood to lose. The appropriations committees would not be able to veto NASA proposals; NASA would not be able to exceed ceilings without enacting new language in a separate appropriation bill.

Neither NASA nor the appropriations committees wanted to enact a separate public law just to exceed a cap. To avoid this kind of administrative rigidity, NASA Administrator James M. Beggs wrote to both committees on August 9, 1984. His letter reveals the pragmatic sense of give-and-take that is customary between executive agencies and congressional committees. His letter also underscores the impracticality and unreality of the doctrines enunciated by the Supreme Court in *Chadha*:

"We have now operated under the present operating plan and reprogramming procedures for several years and have found them to be workable. In light of the constitutional questions raised concerning the legislative veto provisions included in P.L. 98-371 [the HUD-Independent Agencies Appropriations Act], however, the House Committee on Appropriations has proposed in H.R. 6040, the FY 1984 general supplemental, deletion of all Committee approval provisions, leaving inflexible, binding funding limitations on several programs. Without some procedure for adjustment, other than a subsequent separate legislative enactment, these ceilings could seriously impact the ability of NASA to meet unforeseen technical changes or problems that are inherent in challenging R&D programs. We believe that the present legislative procedure could be converted by this letter into an informal agreement by NASA not to exceed amounts for Committee designated programs without the approval of the Committees on Appropriations. This agreement would assume that both the statutory funding ceilings and the Committee approval mechanisms would be deleted from the FY 1985 legislation, and that it would not be the normal practice to include either mechanism in future appropriations bills. Further, the agreement would assume that future program ceiling amounts would be identified by the Committees in the Conference Report accompanying NASA's annual appropriations act and confirmed by NASA in its submission of the annual operating plan. NASA would not expend any funds over the ceilings identified in the Conference Report for these programs without the prior approval of the Committees."

In short, the agency would continue to honor legislative vetoes. But they would be informal rather than statutory. Beggs ended his letter by assuring the appropriations committees that NASA "will comply with any ceilings imposed by the Committees without the need for legislative ceilings which could cause serious damage to NASA's ongoing programs." By converting the legislative veto to an informal and non-statutory status, NASA is not legally bound by the agreement. Violation of the agreement, however, could provoke the appropriations committees to place caps in the appropriation bill and force the agency to lift them only through the enactment of another public law.

. . .

CONCLUSIONS

Through its misreading of history, congressional procedures, and executive-legislative relations, the Supreme Court has commanded the political branches to follow a lawmaking process that is impracticable and unworkable. Neither agencies nor committees want the static model of government offered by the court. The inevitable result is a record of non-compliance, subtle evasion, and a system of lawmaking that is now more convoluted, cumbersome, and covert than before. In many cases the court's decision simply drives underground a set of legislative and committee vetoes that had previously operated in plain sight. No one should be misled if the number of legislative vetoes placed in statutes gradually declines over the years. Fading from view will not mean disappearance. In one form or another legislative vetoes will remain an important method for reconciling legislative and executive interests.

G. INVESTIGATIONS AND EXECUTIVE PRIVILEGE

The impact of implied powers is nowhere more evident than in the struggle for information. Although the Constitution does not expressly give Congress the power to investigate, the Supreme Court has noted that a legislative body "cannot legislate wisely or effectively in the absence of information respecting the conditions which the legislation is intended to affect or change." McGrain v. Daugherty, 273 U.S. 135, 175 (1927). Similarly, the Constitution does not give the President the privilege of withholding information from Congress, and yet in 1974 the Court decided that the President's interest in withholding information to protect confidentiality with his advisers is implied in the Constitution:

"to the extent this interest relates to the effective discharge of a President's powers, it is constitutionally based." UNITED STATES v. NIXON, 418 U.S. 683, 711 (1974).

There is an inevitable collision when Congress attempts to carry out its investigative function and the President invokes executive privilege. Which branch should surrender to the other? Major confrontations require some type of compromise, prodded by Congress's power to punish for contempt and the judiciary's ability to steer both branches toward an acceptable accommodation.

Congressional Investigations

Congress relies on its investigative power to enact legislation; to oversee the administration of programs; to inform the public; and to protect its integrity, dignity, reputation, and privileges. To enforce each of these responsibilities, each House of Congress possesses the power to punish for contempt. Without that power, Congress would be left "exposed to every indignity and interruption that rudeness, caprice, or even conspiracy, may mediate against it." Anderson v. Dunn, 6 Wheat. 204, 228 (1821).

This decision in 1821 limited the power of Congress to punish for contempt. Each House had to exercise the least possible power adequate to the end proposed (in this case the power to imprison) and the duration of punishment could not exceed the life of the legislative body (that is, imprisonment had to terminate with congressional adjournment). Because of those restrictions, Congress decided in 1857 to use the judiciary to enforce its investigative power. Failure to appear or refusal to answer pertinent questions can lead to a contempt vote in either House, which requires a U.S. attorney to seek an indictment by a grand jury and conviction in the courts. 11 Stat. 155 (1857), codified at 2 U.S.C. §§ 192–94. This law, as amended, was upheld by the Court. In re Chapman, 166 U.S. 661 (1897). Congress created a third option in 1978. If an individual from the private sector refuses to comply with a Senate subpoena (an order requiring certain action under threat of punishment), the Senate may request a court order to require compliance with the subpoena. Failure to obey the court order can lead to civil contempt. The sanction is lifted once the individual complies with the Senate's request. 28 U.S.C. § 1364. In June 2012 the House of Representatives voted criminal and civil contempt charges against Attorney General Eric Holder for refusal to turn over documents in a failed gunrunning operation. President Obama asserted an executive privilege claim on Holder's behalf but this did not deter the House from the contempt citation. Because criminal contempt must be pursued by a federal prosecutor who works for the Department of Justice, no prosecution occurred. A civil case may be pursued but is unlikely to be resolved before Holder leaves his position.

Because of such spectacles as the McCarthy hearings of the 1950s, which deteriorated into a witch hunt for "subversives," congressional investigations are often associated with careless and damaging intrusions into personal lives. Most investigations, however, are conducted in a responsible manner and pose no threat to individual liberties or the separation of powers. In fact, congressional investigations often enhance individual liberties by challenging and exposing abuses by the executive branch or the private sector.

Prodded by the adverse publicity from the 1950s, Congress adopted a set of procedures for committee investigations to assure fairness. The courts also insisted that committee hearings be properly authorized by Congress and their scope defined. United States v. Rumely, 345 U.S. 41 (1953); Gojack v. United States, 384 U.S. 702 (1966). In 1957, in what was considered a sharp rebuke to Congress, the Court held that fundamental fairness demanded that a witness be given adequate guidance in deciding the pertinency of a question. There was no congressional power "to expose for the sake of exposure." WATKINS v. UNITED STATES, 354 U.S. 178 (1957). The tone of the decision, together with other judicial rulings during that period, triggered a groundswell of opposition from legislators. Various bills were introduced to curb the Court. In the face of this political pressure, the Supreme Court, two years later, retreated from its position. It now adopted a generous "balancing test" that allowed the government's interest in self-preservation to outweigh the individual's right to remain silent. BARENBLATT v. UNITED STATES, 360 U.S. 109 (1959).

When the activities of an organization did not raise questions of subversion and communism, at least directly, the courts were more likely to protect the rights of association. This is the teaching of a 1958 case, in which a state's attorney general attempted to obtain the membership list of a civil rights organization, the NAACP. Such publicity could have discouraged individuals from joining and participating in exposed groups. The principles announced in this case give greater support to the rights of speech, assembly, and association. NAACP v. Alabama, 357 U.S. 449 (1958). See also Gibson v. Florida Legislative Investigation Committee, 372 U.S. 539 (1963).

Immunity for Witnesses

Witnesses may invoke the Fifth Amendment privilege against self-incrimination. Quinn v. United States, 349 U.S. 155 (1955) and Emspak v. United States, 349 U.S. 190 (1955). An immunity procedure is available to force testimony while at the same time recognizing Fifth Amendment rights. Witnesses may receive full immunity or partial immunity. For the latter, a witness can be compelled to testify and later be prosecuted so long as the witness's testimony (or evidence derived from it) is not used in the prosecution.[15]

Colonel Oliver North received partial immunity—also called "use immunity"—when he testified before the Iran-Contra hearings in 1987. He was later convicted of three felonies: obstructing the investigation by Congress, mutilating government documents, and taking an illegal gratuity. The charges were subsequently dismissed because of new and more stringent standards imposed by the courts. Prosecutors now had to show that a defendant's testimony could have had no influence on the witnesses called to a trial. Otherwise, the witnesses are "tainted" and their remarks may not be used to convict (see section "Immunity" in Chapter 13).

Limits on Investigations

Over the years, the Court has attempted to establish guidelines for congressional investigations. It struck down an investigation and a contempt action because the matter was already pending before a court. Kilbourn v. Thompson, 103 U.S. 168, 182 (1881). Such a doctrine would put congressional investigations on the back burner for years while awaiting the outcome of a lawsuit. Executive agencies could sidetrack an embarrassing committee hearing simply by filing suit and pursuing appeals. Congress may decide to defer its investigation until the completion of a criminal trial or refuse to wait for the results of long, drawn-out litigation. The latter course was followed during the Reagan administration when Congress investigated corruption within the Environmental Protection Agency. In such circumstances, Congress has the right to proceed, even at the cost of postponing or jeopardizing a trial.[16]

Initially, the courts held that congressional investigations must relate to some legislative purpose. Congress should not conduct "fruitless" inquiries without the prospect of legislation. Kilbourn v. Thompson, 103 U.S. at 194–95. Later, however, the Court admitted that a "potential" for legislation is sufficient. McGrain v. Daugherty, 273 U.S. at 177. Even this is too restrictive a test. Committee efforts to oversee executive agencies may take researchers up "blind alleys" and into nonproductive enterprises: "To be a valid legislative inquiry there need be no predictable end result." Eastland v. United States Servicemen's Fund, 421 U.S. 491, 509 (1975) (see box on next page).

Former Reagan Administration Attorney General William French Smith incorrectly stated that

---

15. 18 U.S.C. §§ 6001–05. The immunity procedure, as a substitute for the Fifth Amendment, was upheld in Ullmann v. United States, 350 U.S. 422 (1956); Kastigar v. United States, 406 U.S. 441 (1972); and Application of U.S. Senate Select Com. on Pres. Cam. Act., 361 F.Supp. 1270 (D.D.C. 1973).

16. Delaney v. United States, 199 F.2d 107, 114–15 (1st Cir. 1952). See also Hutcheson v. United States, 369 U.S. 599, 612–13, 623–24 (1962), Sinclair v. United States, 279 U.S. 263, 295 (1929), and Fisher, Constitutional Conflicts Between Congress and the President 155–66 (2007).

Evolving Judicial Standards for Congressional Investigations

Congress could not conduct "fruitless" inquiries without the prospect for legislation. Kilbourn v. Thompson, 103 U.S. 168, 194–95 (1881)

"Potential" for legislation is sufficient. McGrain v. Daugherty, 273 U.S. 135, 177 (1927)

Witnesses must understand the pertinency of a question. Watkins v. United States, 354 U.S. 178 (1957)

A "balancing test" permits the government's interest in self-preservation to outweigh an individual's right to remain silent. Barenblatt v. United States, 360 U.S. 109 (1959)

Investigation can lead up "blind alleys" with no predictable legislative result. Eastland v. United States Servicemen's Fund, 421 U.S. 491, 509 (1975)

---

congressional requests for information are on stronger ground if Congress has specific legislation in mind than when it simply probes as part of a general oversight effort.[17] Oversight is not subordinate to legislation. Even if that position could be argued, lawmakers could simply introduce a bill to justify an oversight investigation.

A decision by the Supreme Court in 1995 limited the ability of the Justice Department to prosecute lawmakers and government officials for lying to Congress. Section 1001 of Title 18 criminalizes unsworn false statements in any matter within the jurisdiction of any "department or agency" of the United States. In holding that Section 1001 did not apply to federal courts, the Court also overruled a 1955 case that had applied Section 1001 to a former member of Congress who had made a false statement to the Disbursing Office of the House of Representatives. The effect of the 1995 ruling was to limit the Justice Department's ability to prosecute only those individuals who committed perjury to Congress (for lying under oath). Hubbard v. United States, 514 U.S. 695 (1995). Congress responded to *Hubbard* by enacting legislation a year later that reinstated criminal penalties for making false statements to Congress. 110 Stat. 3459 (1996).

Impeachment

The ultimate form of the investigative power is impeachment. The President, Vice President, and all civil officers of the United States shall be removed from office upon "Impeachment for, and Conviction of, Treason, Bribery, or other high Crimes and Misdemeanors" (Article II, Section 4). Treason is defined in Article III, Section 3, while bribery has a fairly clear statutory meaning. What constitutes "other high Crimes and Misdemeanors"? The framers rejected vague grounds for impeachment, such as "maladministration," because this would be equivalent to having the President serve at the pleasure of Congress. 3 Farrand 65–66, 550. However, impeachment need not require indictable crimes or specific statutory offenses. In Federalist No. 65, Alexander Hamilton included "political crimes" (abuses in office or violation of the public trust) as legitimate grounds for impeachment. Madison also supported impeachment for political abuses or neglect of office. 1 Annals of Congress 372–73 (May 19, 1789). The purpose of impeachment is to remove someone from office, not to punish for a crime. Impeachable conduct need not be criminal. That was the conclusion of the House Committee on the Judiciary during the impeachment proceedings of Richard Nixon. In 1993 the Supreme Court upheld the Senate's practice of conducting an impeachment trial in two stages: fact-finding by

---

17. "Executive Privilege: Legal Opinions Regarding Claim of President Ronald Reagan in Response to a Subpoena Issued to James G. Watt, Secretary of the Interior," prepared for the use of the House Committee on Energy and Commerce, 97th Cong., 1st Sess. 3 (Comm. Print November 1981).

a 12-member committee followed by action by the full Senate. Nixon v. United States, 506 U.S. 224 (1993). For a reading on this decision, see chapter 3.

The impeachment of President Bill Clinton highlighted several issues about the process. The House of Representatives, voting largely along party lines on December 19, 1998, adopted two articles of impeachment, one on perjury and the other on obstruction of justice. Voting on February 12, 1999, the Senate "acquitted" Clinton on both articles. With regard to the perjury article, 45 Senators voted "guilty" and 55 voted "not guilty." The vote on obstruction of justice was 50 to 50, far short of the two-thirds required for removal.

The votes were distorted because the Senate currently votes simultaneously on two separate issues: guilt and removal. From 1789 to 1936, the Senate voted first for guilt and next for removal, allowing Senators to hold someone guilty of the charges brought against them but then decide that the person should not be removed from office. After 1936 the two issues were collapsed into a single vote. Many Senators who voted "not guilty" explained that Clinton was indeed guilty.

For example, Senator Robert C. Byrd (D-W.Va.) voted "not guilty" on both articles although he thought that Clinton's behavior constituted "an impeachable offense, a political high crime or misdemeanor against the state." Not wanting to remove Clinton, Byrd had only one choice: to vote "not guilty," after judging him guilty on both counts. Other Senators, including Susan Collins (R-Me.), Olympia Snowe (R-Me.), James Jeffords (R-Vt.), Fred Thompson (R-Tenn.), Ted Stevens (R-Alas.), and Slade Gorton (R-Wash.), concluded that Clinton was guilty on one or both articles but voted "not guilty" because they thought removal was unwarranted.

Senator Snowe put it this way: "Acquittal is not exoneration." John Breaux, a Democrat from Louisiana, voted against the articles but cautioned that his vote "is not a vote on the innocence of this President. He is not innocent." Bob Kerrey, Democrat from Nebraska, added: "While there is plenty of blame to go around in this case, the person responsible for it going this far is the President of the United States."

Secondly, the votes on the two articles turned on factors that had nothing to do with the evidence presented. Some legislators cited public polls of Clinton's popularity as reason to vote against impeachment and removal. Had Clinton been less popular, would that factor (unrelated to the evidence) have been adequate grounds for supporting his impeachment and removal? Moreover, lawmakers pointed to the buoyant stock market, low unemployment, and modest inflation as reasons for keeping Clinton in office. Had economic conditions turned sour, would that have justified Clinton's impeachment and removal from office? Obviously many lawmakers found it difficult to focus on the substance of the two articles. [Impeachment of judges is covered in Chapter 4, Section D.]

Executive Privilege

President George Washington and his cabinet complied with a request by the House of Representatives in 1792 for papers regarding a military defeat but also concluded that it would be appropriate in the future to refuse documents "the disclosure of which would injure the public." 1 Writings of Thomas Jefferson 303–05 (Mem. ed. 1903). In general, Presidents agree to make papers and documents available for impeachment inquiries or congressional investigations into administrative corruption. While upholding a very broad theory of executive privilege in 1982, Attorney General Smith said he would not try to "shield documents [from Congress] which contain evidence of criminal or unethical conduct by agency officials from proper review." H. Rept. No. 968, 97th Cong., 2d Sess. 41 (1982).

If executive officials refuse congressional requests for information, a move by Congress to cite the person for contempt is often an effective way to get the official's attention and cooperation. For example, in 1982 the House of Representatives voted 259 to 105 to hold Anne Gorsuch, administrator of the Environmental Protection Agency, in contempt. In an unprecedented action, the U.S. Attorney did not take the contempt citation to the grand jury, as required by statute. Instead, the administration asked a district court to declare the House action an unconstitutional intrusion into the President's authority to withhold information from Congress. After this tactic failed, the documents were released. United States v. House of Representatives, 556 F. Supp. 150 (D.D.C. 1983). Use of subpoenas and threats of contempt citations led to the release of several documents by the Clinton administration. Louis Fisher, The Politics of Executive Privilege (2004).

The major executive privilege case—United States v. Nixon—did not involve a congressional request for executive documents. The request came from the courts as part of the effort to prosecute Watergate crimes. A unanimous Court rejected the argument that the decision to release such documents is up to the President, not the courts. To permit Nixon absolute control over the documents would have prevented the judiciary from carrying out its duties. UNITED STATES v. NIXON, 418 U.S. 683 (1974).

Conflicts between the executive and legislative branches are sometimes resolved with the assistance of federal judges. A deadlock between a House committee and the Justice Department during the 1970s, regarding the release of "national security" information, was eventually broken through the efforts of Judge Harold Leventhal. He convinced each branch that a compromise worked out between them would be better than a solution dictated by the courts. Practical accommodations are required instead of rigid abstractions about the power of Congress to investigate or the power of the President to withhold information (see readings for AT&T cases). In 2008, several claims of executive privilege led to congressional contempt citations and litigation before the courts. Former presidential advisors Karl Rove and Harriet Miers were subpoenaed to appear before hearings about the decision making behind the 2007 firings of U. S. Attorneys. Also, the House Judiciary Committee subpoenaed documents from White House Chief of Staff Joshua Bolten, who provided no materials. The House held Miers and Bolten in contempt. When Attorney General Mukasey refused to refer the matter to the grand jury for possible indictment, the House filed suit in federal court. On July 31, 2008, District Judge John D. Bates rejected the administration's claim that senior White House officials have absolute immunity from congressional process. He ordered Miers to appear before the committee and Bolten to produce privilege logs. Finally, in 2009 hundreds of White House emails were released and Miers and Rove testified in closed-door hearings about the events.

Executive branch officials may use other routes to avoid executive privilege claims. The scope of executive ability to limit access to information was explored in two lawsuits aimed at Vice President Dick Cheney. Both cases involved efforts to obtain documents related to the energy task force he chaired. Members of Congress and private groups wanted to understand how much influence non-governmental officials had on the energy bill that the administration drafted and presented to Congress. GAO initiated the first suit, which a district court dismissed on the ground that the Comptroller General lacked standing. Walker v. Cheney, 230 F.Supp.2d 51 (D.D.C. 2002); Fisher, The Politics of Executive Privilege, at 183–98. GAO decided not to appeal.

The second case came from two private groups, Judicial Watch and the Sierra Club, who claimed that the Federal Advisory Commission Act required information about the task force to be made public. The D.C. Circuit rejected the administration's argument that the President and the Vice President possessed a broad immunity against any effort, through litigation, to determine how they formulated legislative proposals. It directed the two groups to narrow their request for documents. Rather than invoke executive privilege, Cheney appealed to the Supreme Court, arguing that the FACA did not apply to the group. The Supreme Court declined to accept the administration's broad doctrine, preferring to return the case to the D.C. Circuit with instructions to seek an accommodation to protect the President from litigation that might distract from the performance of constitutional duties. Cheney v. United States District Court for D.C., 542 U.S. 367 (2004). In 2005 the U.S. Court of Appeals for the D.C. Circuit ruled that the task force was not subject to the disclosure requirements of the FACA.

Presidential Immunity

Although the Constitution does not provide an express immunity for the President, the courts have developed a doctrine of official immunity for executive officials and the President. Unless executive employees enjoyed an immunity for their official actions, they could not be expected to administer laws vigorously and effectively. Barr v. Matteo, 360 U.S. 564 (1959); Gregoire v. Biddle, 177 F.2d 579 (2d Cir. 1949). In 1982, the Supreme Court held that the President is entitled to absolute immunity, in civil suits, regarding all of his official acts. Nixon v. Fitzgerald, 457 U.S. 731 (1982). A qualified immunity is available for presidential aides. Harlow v. Fitzgerald, 457 U.S. 800 (1982); Mitchell v. Forsyth, 472 U.S. 511 (1985).

A separate question is whether the President is entitled to immunity from civil liability for *unofficial* acts: acts committed in a personal capacity rather than as President. This issue arose when Paula Corbin Jones brought a lawsuit against Bill Clinton for an incident that occurred before he became President. She claimed that in 1991, at a conference held at a hotel in Little Rock, Clinton (at that time governor of Arkansas) sexually harassed and assaulted her. Clinton's attorneys argued that the President should have a temporary immunity while serving in office and that the case should not go forward until he left office. In 1997, a unanimous Court decided that the Constitution did not afford the President temporary immunity in this case. CLINTON v. JONES, 520 U.S. 681 (1997). The case was dismissed in 1998 when a district judge held that there were "no genuine issues for trial in this case." After Jones appealed, Clinton agreed to settle the case by giving her $850,000.

The Supreme Court's prediction that the case could go forward without substantially burdening President Clinton has been much maligned. However, the resulting burden had less to do with Jones than to new allegations concerning Clinton's relationship with White House intern Monica Lewinsky and serious charges of his efforts to lie, suborn witnesses, and obstruct justice.

Watkins v. United States

354 U.S. 178 (1957)

Beginning in the early 1950s, congressional committees conducted searching inquiries into left-wing activities of American citizens. The atmosphere of the cold war permitted little toleration for "disloyal" thoughts and conduct. In this case, the House Committee on Un-American Activities called John Watkins, a labor organizer, to testify. He agreed to describe his past participation in the Communist party and identify current members, but declined to answer questions about those who had left the movement. His refusal led to conviction for contempt of Congress. A panel of the D.C. Circuit reversed the conviction, but the full bench, sitting *en banc*, affirmed the conviction.

MR. CHIEF JUSTICE WARREN delivered the opinion of the Court.

This is a review by certiorari of a conviction under 2 U.S.C. § 192 for "contempt of Congress." The misdemeanor is alleged to have been committed during a hearing before a congressional investigating committee. It is not the case of a truculent or contumacious witness who refuses to answer all questions or who, by boisterous or discourteous conduct, disturbs the decorum of the committee room. Petitioner was prosecuted for refusing to make certain disclosures which he asserted to be beyond the authority of the committee to demand. The controversy thus rests upon fundamental principles of the power of the Congress and the limitations upon that power. We approach the questions presented with conscious awareness of the far-reaching ramifications that can follow from a decision of this nature.

On April 29, 1954, petitioner appeared as a witness in compliance with a subpoena issued by a Subcommittee of the Committee on Un-American Activities of the House of Representatives. The Subcommittee elicited from petitioner a description of his background in labor union activities....

[*Watkins's name had been mentioned by two witnesses who testified that he had been active with the Communist Party. He admitted to the subcommittee that "from approximately 1942 to 1947 I cooperated with the Communist Party and participated in Communist activities to such a degree that some persons may honestly believe that I was a member of the party. I have made contributions upon occasions to Communist causes. I have signed petitions for Communist causes.*

I attended caucuses at an FE [Farm Equipment] convention at which Communist Party officials were present." However, Watkins refused to talk about other people who might have been members of the Party.]:

"I am not going to plead the fifth amendment, but I refuse to answer certain questions that I believe are outside the proper scope of your committee's activities. I will answer any questions which this committee puts to me about myself. I will also answer questions about those persons whom I knew to be members of the Communist Party and whom I believe still are. I will not, however, answer any questions with respect to others with whom I associated in the past. I do not believe that any law in this country requires me to testify about persons who may in the past have been Communist Party members or otherwise engaged in Communist Party activity but who to my best knowledge and belief have long since removed themselves from the Communist movement.

"I do not believe that such questions are relevant to the work of this committee nor do I believe that this committee has the right to undertake the public exposure of persons because of their past activities. I may be wrong, and the committee may have this power, but until and unless a court of law so holds and directs me to answer, I most firmly refuse to discuss the political activities of my past associates."

[Watkins was held in contempt by the House and sentenced to a fine of $100 and one year in prison, which was suspended. He was placed on probation. The conviction was reversed by the D.C. Circuit.]

We start with several basic premises on which there is general agreement. The power of the Congress to conduct investigations is inherent in the legislative process. That power is broad. It encompasses inquiries concerning the administration of existing laws as well as proposed or possibly needed statutes. It includes surveys of defects in our social, economic or political system for the purpose of enabling the Congress to remedy them. It comprehends probes into departments of the Federal Government to expose corruption, inefficiency or waste. But, broad as is this power of inquiry, it is not unlimited. There is no general authority to expose the private affairs of individuals without justification in terms of the functions of the Congress. This was freely conceded by the Solicitor General in his argument of this case. Nor is the Congress a law enforcement or trial agency. These are functions of the executive and judicial departments of government. No inquiry is an end in itself; it must be related to, and in furtherance

of, a legitimate task of the Congress. Investigations conducted solely for the personal aggrandizement of the investigators or to "punish" those investigated are indefensible.

It is unquestionably the duty of all citizens to cooperate with the Congress in its efforts to obtain the facts needed for intelligent legislative action. It is their unremitting obligation to respond to subpoenas, to respect the dignity of the Congress and its committees and to testify fully with respect to matters within the province of proper investigation. This, of course, assumes that the constitutional rights of witnesses will be respected by the Congress as they are in a court of justice. The Bill of Rights is applicable to investigations as to all forms of governmental action. Witnesses cannot be compelled to give evidence against themselves. They cannot be subjected to unreasonable search and seizure. Nor can the First Amendment freedoms of speech, press, religion, or political belief and association be abridged.

[The Court describes the English Parliament's abuse of its contempt power, which was immune even from judicial review. Citizens who made comments critical of Parliament could be punished, fined, and imprisoned. Parliamentary probes were eventually replaced by investigations conducted by Royal Commissions of Inquiry, comprised of experts who rarely had the authority to compel the testimony of witnesses or the production of documents.]

The history of contempt of the legislature in this country is notably different from that of England. In the early days of the United States, there lingered the direct knowledge of the evil effects of absolute power. Most of the instances of use of compulsory process by the first Congresses concerned matters affecting the qualification or integrity of their members or came about in inquiries dealing with suspected corruption or mismanagement of government officials. Unlike the English practice, from the very outset the use of contempt power by the legislature was deemed subject to judicial review.

. . .

It is not surprising, from the fact that the Houses of Congress so sparingly employed the power to conduct investigations, that there have been few cases requiring judicial review of the power. The Nation was almost one hundred years old before the first case reached this Court to challenge the use of compulsory process as a legislative device [*Kilbourn v. Thompson, 103 U.S. 168 (1881). Relatively few congressional investigations thereafter were contested in the courts.*] ...

In the decade following World War II, there appeared a new kind of congressional inquiry unknown in prior periods of American history. Principally this was the result of the various investigations into the threat of subversion of the United States Government, but other subjects of congressional interest also contributed to the changed scene. This new phase of legislative inquiry involved a broad-scale intrusion into the lives and affairs of private citizens. It brought before the courts novel questions of the appropriate limits of congressional inquiry....

We have no doubt that there is no congressional power to expose for the sake of exposure. The public is, of course, entitled to be informed concerning the workings of its government. That cannot be inflated into a general power to expose where the predominant result can only be an invasion of the private rights of individuals....

The authorizing resolution of the Un-American Activities Committee was adopted in 1938.... It defines the Committee's authority as follows:

"The Committee on Un-American Activities, as a whole or by subcommittee, is authorized to make from time to time investigations of (1) the extent, character, and objects of un-American propaganda activities in the United States, (2) the diffusion within the United States of subversive and un-American propaganda that is instigated from foreign countries or of a domestic origin and attacks the principle of the form of government as guaranteed by our Constitution, and (3) all other questions in relation thereto that would aid Congress in any necessary remedial legislation."

It would be difficult to imagine a less explicit authorizing resolution. Who can define the meaning of "un-American"? What is that single, solitary "principle of the form of government as guaranteed by our Constitution"? There is no need to dwell upon the language, however. At one time, perhaps, the resolution might have been read narrowly to confine the Committee to the subject of propaganda. The events that have transpired in the fifteen years before the interrogation of petitioner make such a construction impossible at this date.

The members of the Committee have clearly demonstrated that they did not feel themselves restricted in any way to propaganda in the narrow sense of the word. Unquestionably the Committee conceived of its task in the grand view of its name. Un-American activities were its target, no matter how or where manifested....

Combining the language of the resolution with the construction it has been given, it is evident that the preliminary control of the Committee exercised by the House of Representatives is slight or non-existent. No one could reasonably deduce from the charter the kind of investigation that the Committee was directed to make.

[*The Court offers these guidelines: In order for a reviewing court to determine whether a committee investigation is fulfilling a legislative purpose, the committee's activity must be properly authorized by resolution. In order for a witness to understand the pertinency of a question directed by a committee member or committee staff, and to avoid being held in contempt, the witness must have knowledge of the subject of the inquiry and the pertinency of a question to that inquiry. This knowledge can come from the authorizing resolution, remarks by committee members, and the nature of the proceedings.*]

... Unless the subject matter has been made to appear with undisputable clarity, it is the duty of the investigative body, upon objection of the witness on grounds of pertinency, to state for the record the subject under inquiry at that time and the manner in which the propounded questions are pertinent thereto. To be meaningful, the explanation must describe what the topic under inquiry is and the connective reasoning whereby the precise questions asked relate to it.

The statement of the Committee Chairman in this case, in response to petitioner's protest, was woefully inadequate to convey sufficient information as to the pertinency of the questions to the subject under inquiry. Petitioner was thus not accorded a fair opportunity to determine whether he was within his rights in refusing to answer, and his conviction is necessarily invalid under the Due Process Clause of the Fifth Amendment.

The judgment of the Court of Appeals is reversed, and the case is remanded to the District Court with instructions to dismiss the indictment.

It is so ordered.

Mr. Justice Burton and Mr. Justice Whittaker took no part in the consideration or decision of this case.

Mr. Justice Frankfurter, concurring.

. . .

Mr. Justice Clark, dissenting.

As I see it the chief fault in the majority opinion is its mischievous curbing of the informing function of the Congress. While I am not versed in its procedures, my experience in the Executive Branch of the Government leads me to believe that the requirements laid down in the opinion for the operation of the committee system of inquiry are both unnecessary and unworkable....

Barenblatt v. United States

360 U.S. 109 (1959)

The Court's "lecture" to Congress in *Watkins* v. *United States* (1957) was one of several cases that convinced many members of Congress that the judiciary was overstepping its bounds. A number of court-curbing bills were introduced and acted upon. There is reason to believe that the Court recognized a serious collision with Congress and moved in this case, as well as others, to reduce the friction. Lloyd Barenblatt, a college professor, refused to answer certain questions put to him by a subcommittee of the House Committee on Un-American Activities. For his refusal he was convicted, fined, and sentenced to six months in prison.

MR. JUSTICE HARLAN delivered the opinion of the Court.

. . .

We here review petitioner's conviction under 2 U.S.C. § 192 for contempt of Congress, arising from his refusal to answer certain questions put to him by a Subcommittee of the House Committee on Un-American Activities during the course of an inquiry concerning alleged Communist infiltration into the field of education.

[*Section 192 provides: "Every person who having been summoned as a witness by the authority of either House of Congress to give testimony or to produce papers upon any matter under inquiry before either House, or any joint committee established by a joint or concurrent resolution of the two Houses of Congress, or any committee of either House of Congress, willfully makes default, or who, having appeared, refuses to answer any question pertinent to the question under inquiry, shall be deemed guilty of a misdemeanor, punishable by a fine of not more than $1,000 nor less than $100 and imprisonment in a common jail for not less than one month nor more than twelve months."*]

Pursuant to a subpoena, and accompanied by counsel, petitioner on June 28, 1954, appeared as a witness before this congressional Subcommittee. After answering a few preliminary questions and testifying that he had been a graduate student and teaching fellow at the University of Michigan from 1947 to 1950 and an instructor in psychology at Vassar College from 1950 to shortly before his appearance before the Subcommittee, petitioner objected generally to the right of the Subcommittee to inquire into his "political" and "religious" beliefs or any "other personal and private affairs" or "associational activities," upon grounds set forth in a previously prepared memorandum which he was allowed to file with the Subcommittee. Thereafter petitioner specifically declined to answer each of the following five questions:

"Are you now a member of the Communist Party? [Count One.]

"Have you ever been a member of the Communist Party? [Count Two.]

"Now, you have stated that you knew Francis Crowley. Did you know Francis Crowley as a member of the Communist Party? [Count Three.]

"Were you ever a member of the Haldane Club of the Communist Party while at the University of Michigan? [Count Four.]

"Were you a member while a student of the University of Michigan Council of Arts, Sciences, and Professions?" [Count Five.]

In each instance the grounds of refusal were those set forth in the prepared statement. Petitioner expressly disclaimed reliance upon "the Fifth Amendment."

... As we conceive the ultimate issue in this case to be whether petitioner could properly be convicted of contempt for refusing to answer questions relating to his participation in or knowledge of alleged Communist Party activities at educational institutions in this country, we find it unnecessary to consider the validity of his conviction under the Third and Fifth Counts, the only ones involving questions which on their face do not directly relate to such participation or knowledge.

Petitioner's various contentions resolve themselves into three propositions: First, the compelling of testimony by the Subcommittee was neither legislatively authorized nor constitutionally permissible because of the vagueness of Rule XI of the House of Representatives, Eighty-third Congress, the charter of authority of the parent Committee. Second, petitioner was not adequately apprised of the pertinency of the Subcommittee's questions to the subject matter of the inquiry. Third, the questions petitioner refused to answer infringed rights protected by the First Amendment.

[*After deciding that Rule XI was not constitutionally infirm on the ground of vagueness, that the questions put to Barenblatt were clearly pertinent, and that he had been adequately informed, the Court turns to the First Amendment issue.*]

CONSTITUTIONAL CONTENTIONS.

Where First Amendment rights are asserted to bar governmental interrogation resolution of the issue always involves a balancing by the courts of the competing private and public interests at stake in the particular circumstances shown. These principles were recognized in the *Watkins* case, where, in speaking of the First Amendment in relation to congressional inquiries, we said (at p. 198): "It is manifest that despite the adverse effects which follow upon compelled disclosure of private matters, not all such inquiries are barred.... The critical element is the existence of, and the weight to be ascribed to, the interest of the Congress in demanding disclosures from an unwilling witness." ...

... [I]n stating in the *Watkins* case, p. 200, that "there is no congressional power to expose for the sake of exposure," we at the same time declined to inquire into the "motives of committee members," and recognized that their "motives alone would not vitiate an investigation which had been instituted by a House of Congress if that assembly's legislative purpose is being served." Having scrutinized this record we cannot say that the unanimous panel of the Court of Appeals which first considered this case was wrong in concluding that "the primary purposes of the inquiry were in aid of legislative processes." 240 F.2d, at 881. Certainly this is not a case like *Kilbourn* v. *Thompson*, 103 U.S. 168, 192, where "the House of Representatives not only exceeded the limit of its own authority, but assumed a power which could only be properly exercised by another branch of the government, because it was in its nature clearly judicial." See *McGrain* v. *Daugherty*, 273 U.S. 135, 171. The constitutional legislative power of Congress in this instance is beyond question.

· · ·

We conclude that the balance between the individual and the governmental interests here at stake must be struck in favor of the latter, and that therefore the provisions of the First Amendment have not been offended.

We hold that petitioner's conviction for contempt of Congress discloses no infirmity, and that the judgment of the Court of Appeals must be

Affirmed.

MR. JUSTICE BLACK, with whom THE CHIEF JUSTICE and MR. JUSTICE DOUGLAS concur, dissenting.

... I cannot agree with this disposition of the case for I believe that the resolution establishing the House Un-American Activities Committee and the questions that Committee asked Barenblatt violate the Constitution in several respects. (1) Rule XI creating the Committee authorizes such a sweeping, unlimited, all-inclusive and undiscriminating compulsory examination of witnesses in the field of speech, press, petition and assembly that it violates the procedural requirements of the Due Process Clause of the Fifth Amendment. (2) Compelling an answer to the questions asked Barenblatt abridges freedom of speech and association in contravention of the First Amendment. (3) The Committee proceedings were part of a legislative program to stigmatize and punish by public identification and exposure all witnesses considered by the Committee to be guilty of Communist affiliations, as well as all witnesses who refused to answer Committee questions on constitutional grounds; the Committee was thus improperly seeking to try, convict, and punish suspects, a task which the Constitution expressly denies to Congress and grants exclusively to the courts, to be exercised by them only after indictment and in full compliance with all the safeguards provided by the Bill of Rights....

II.

... I do not agree that laws directly abridging First Amendment freedoms can be justified by a congressional or judicial balancing process....

To apply the Court's balancing test under such circumstances is to read the First Amendment to say "Congress shall pass no law abridging freedom of speech, press, assembly and petition, unless Congress and the Supreme Court reach the joint conclusion that on balance the interest of the Government in stifling these freedoms is greater than the interest of the people in having them exercised." ...

But even assuming what I cannot assume, that

some balancing is proper in this case, I feel that the Court after stating the test ignores it completely. At most it balances the right of the Government to preserve itself, against Barenblatt's right to refrain from revealing Communist affiliations. Such a balance, however, mistakes the factors to be weighed. In the first place, it completely leaves out the real interest in Barenblatt's silence, the interest of the people as a whole in being able to join organizations, advocate causes and make political "mistakes" without later being subjected to governmental penalties for having dared to think for themselves. It is this right, the right to err politically, which keeps us strong as a Nation. For no number of laws against communism can have as much effect as the personal conviction which comes from having heard its arguments and rejected them, or from having once accepted its tenets and later recognized their worthlessness. Instead, the obloquy which results from investigations such as this not only stifles "mistakes" but prevents all but the most courageous from hazarding any views which might at some later time become disfavored. This result, whose importance cannot be overestimated, is doubly crucial when it affects the universities, on which we must largely rely for the experimentation and development of new ideas essential to our country's welfare. It is these interests of society, rather than Barenblatt's own right to silence, which I think the Court should put on the balance against the demands of the Government, if any balancing process is to be tolerated....

Ultimately all the questions in this case really boil down to one—whether we as a people will try fearfully and futilely to preserve democracy by adopting totalitarian methods, or whether in accordance with our traditions and our Constitution we will have the confidence and courage to be free.

I would reverse this conviction.

MR. JUSTICE BRENNAN, dissenting.

I would reverse this conviction. It is sufficient that I state my complete agreement with my Brother BLACK that no purpose for the investigation of Barenblatt is revealed by the record except exposure purely for the sake of exposure....

United States v. Nixon

418 U.S. 683 (1974)

The Special Prosecutor investigating the Watergate affair filed a motion for a subpoena to produce certain tapes and documents relating to conversations and meetings between President Nixon and others. President Nixon, claiming executive privilege, filed a motion to quash the subpoena. A district judge rejected that motion and issued an order for an *in camera* examination of the subpoenaed material. This order was stayed pending appellate review.

MR. CHIEF JUSTICE BURGER delivered the opinion of the Court.

This litigation presents for review the denial of a motion, filed in the District Court on behalf of the President of the United States, in the case of *United States* v. *Mitchell* (D. C. Crim. No. 74-110), to quash a third-party subpoena *duces tecum* issued by the United States District Court for the District of Columbia, pursuant to Fed. Rule Crim. Proc. 17 (c). The subpoena directed the President to produce certain tape recordings and documents relating to his conversations with aides and advisers....

On March 1, 1974, a grand jury of the United States District Court for the District of Columbia returned an indictment charging seven named individuals [*Attorney General John N. Mitchell, White House aides H. R. Haldeman and John D. Ehrlichman, Charles W. Colson, Robert C. Mardian, Ken-neth W. Parkinson, and Gordon Strachan. The latter four were either on the White House staff or with the Committee for the Re-election of the President.*] with various offenses, including conspiracy to defraud the United States and to obstruct justice. Although he was not designated as such in the indictment, the grand jury named the President, among others, as an unindicted coconspirator. On April 18, 1974, upon motion of the Special Prosecutor, see n. 8, *infra,* a subpoena *duces tecum* was issued pursuant to Rule 17(c) to the President by the United States District Court and made returnable on May 2, 1974. This subpoena required the production, in advance of the September 9 trial date, of certain tapes, memoranda, papers, transcripts, or other writings relating to certain precisely identified meetings between the President and others. The Special Prosecutor was able to fix the time, place, and persons present at these discussions because the White House daily logs and appointment records had been delivered to him. On April 30, the President publicly released edited transcripts of 43 conversations; portions of 20 conversations subject to subpoena in the present case were included. On May 1, 1974, the President's counsel filed a "special appearance" and a motion to quash the subpoena under Rule 17 (c). This motion was accompanied by a formal claim of privilege.

. . .

II. JUSTICIABILITY

In the District Court, the President's counsel argued that the court lacked jurisdiction to issue the subpoena because the matter was an intrabranch dispute between a subordinate and superior officer of the Executive Branch and hence not subject to judicial resolution. That argument has been renewed in this Court with emphasis on the contention that the dispute does not present a "case" or "controversy" which can be adjudicated in the federal courts. The President's counsel argues that the federal courts should not intrude into areas committed to the other branches of Government. He views the present dispute as essentially a "jurisdictional" dispute within the Executive Branch which he analogizes to a dispute between two congressional committees. Since the Executive Branch has exclusive authority and absolute discretion to decide whether to prosecute a case, ... it is contended that a President's decision is final in determining what evidence is to be used in a given criminal case. Although his counsel concedes that the President has delegated certain specific powers to the Special Prosecutor, he has not "waived nor delegated to the Special Prosecutor the President's duty to claim privilege as to all materials ... which fall within the President's inherent authority to refuse to disclose to any executive officer." ... The Special Prosecutor's demand for the items therefore presents, in the view of the President's counsel, a political question under *Baker* v. *Carr,* 369 U.S. 186 (1962), since it involves a "textually demonstrable" grant of power under Art. II.

The mere assertion of a claim of an "intrabranch dispute," without more, has never operated to defeat federal jurisdiction; justiciability does not depend on such a surface inquiry....

[*The Court reviewed the following facts: under authority of Article II, Section 2, Congress vested in the Attorney General the power to conduct criminal litigation and to appoint subordinate officers; acting pursuant to statutory authority, the Attorney General delegated authority to a Special Prosecutor with unique authority and tenure; the regulation delegating this authority gave the Special Prosecutor explicit power to contest claims of executive privilege; this regulation had the force of law and had not been amended or revoked.*]

In light of the uniqueness of the setting in which the conflict arises, the fact that both parties are officers of the Executive Branch cannot be viewed as a barrier to justiciability. It would be inconsistent with the applicable law and regulation, and the unique facts of this case to conclude other than that the Special Prosecutor has standing to bring this action and that a justiciable controversy is presented for decision....

IV. THE CLAIM OF PRIVILEGE
A

... [W]e turn to the claim that the subpoena should be quashed because it demands "confidential conversations between a President and his close advisors that it would be inconsistent with the public interest to produce." App. 48a. The first contention is a broad claim that the separation of powers doctrine precludes judicial review of a President's claim of privilege. The second contention is that if he does not prevail on the claim of absolute privilege, the court should hold as a matter of constitutional law that the privilege prevails over the subpoena *duces tecum.*

In the performance of assigned constitutional duties each branch of the Government must initially interpret the Constitution, and the interpretation of its powers by any branch is due great respect from the others. The President's counsel, as we have noted, reads the Constitution as providing an absolute privilege of confidentiality for all Presidential communications. Many decisions of this Court, however, have unequivocally reaffirmed the holding of *Marbury* v. *Madison,* 1 Cranch 137 (1803), that "[i]t is emphatically the province and duty of the judicial department to say what the law is." *Id.,* at 177.

No holding of the Court has defined the scope of judicial power specifically relating to the enforcement of a subpoena for confidential Presidential communications for use in a criminal prosecution, but other exercises of power by the Executive Branch and the Legislative Branch have been found invalid as in conflict with the Constitution. *Powell* v. *McCormack,* 395 U.S. 486 (1969); *Youngstown Sheet & Tube Co.* v. *Sawyer,* 343 U.S. 579 (1952).

Notwithstanding the deference each branch must accord the others, the "judicial Power of the United

States" vested in the federal courts by Art. III, § 1, of the Constitution can no more be shared with the Executive Branch than the Chief Executive, for example, can share with the Judiciary the veto power, or the Congress share with the Judiciary the power to override a Presidential veto. Any other conclusion would be contrary to the basic concept of separation of powers and the checks and balances that flow from the scheme of a tripartite government....

B

In support of his claim of absolute privilege, the President's counsel urges two grounds, one of which is common to all governments and one of which is peculiar to our system of separation of powers. The first ground is the valid need for protection of communications between high Government officials and those who advise and assist them in the performance of their manifold duties; the importance of this confidentiality is too plain to require further discussion. Human experience teaches that those who expect public dissemination of their remarks may well temper candor with a concern for appearances and for their own interests to the detriment of the decision-making process. Whatever the nature of the privilege of confidentiality of Presidential communications in the exercise of Art. II powers, the privilege can be said to derive from the supremacy of each branch within its own assigned area of constitutional duties. Certain powers and privileges flow from the nature of enumerated powers; the protection of the confidentiality of Presidential communications has similar constitutional underpinnings.

The second ground asserted by the President's counsel in support of the claim of absolute privilege rests on the doctrine of separation of powers. Here it is argued that the independence of the Executive Branch within its own sphere, ... insulates a President from a judicial subpoena in an ongoing criminal prosecution, and thereby protects confidential Presidential communications.

However, neither the doctrine of separation of powers, nor the need for confidentiality of high-level communications, without more, can sustain an absolute, unqualified Presidential privilege of immunity from judicial process under all circumstances. The President's need for complete candor and objectivity from advisers calls for great deference from the courts. However, when the privilege depends solely on the broad, undifferentiated claim of public interest in the confidentiality of such conversations, a confrontation with other values arises. Absent a claim of need to protect military, diplomatic, or sensitive national security secrets, we find it diffi-

cult to accept the argument that even the very important interest in confidentiality of Presidential communications is significantly diminished by production of such material for *in camera* inspection with all the protection that a district court will be obliged to provide.

The impediment that an absolute, unqualified privilege would place in the way of the primary constitutional duty of the Judicial Branch to do justice in criminal prosecutions would plainly conflict with the function of the courts under Art. III....

C

Since we conclude that the legitimate needs of the judicial process may outweigh Presidential privilege, it is necessary to resolve those competing interests in a manner that preserves the essential functions of each branch....

The expectation of a President to the confidentiality of his conversations and correspondence, like the claim of confidentiality of judicial deliberations, for example, has all the values to which we accord deference for the privacy of all citizens and, added to those values, is the necessity for protection of the public interest in candid, objective, and even blunt or harsh opinions in Presidential decisionmaking. A President and those who assist him must be free to explore alternatives in the process of shaping policies and making decisions and to do so in a way many would be unwilling to express except privately. These are the considerations justifying a presumptive privilege for Presidential communications. The privilege is fundamental to the operation of Government and inextricably rooted in the separation of powers under the Constitution....

But this presumptive privilege must be considered in light of our historic commitment to the rule of law. This is nowhere more profoundly manifest than in our view that "the twofold aim [of criminal justice] is that guilt shall not escape or innocence suffer." *Berger* v. *United States,* 295 U.S., at 88. We have elected to employ an adversary system of criminal justice in which the parties contest all issues before a court of law. The need to develop all relevant facts in the adversary system is both fundamental and comprehensive. The ends of criminal justice would be defeated if judgments were to be founded on a partial or speculative presentation of the facts. The very integrity of the judicial system and public confidence in the system depend on full disclosure of all the facts, within the framework of the rules of evidence. To ensure that justice is done, it is imperative to the function of courts that compulsory process be available for the production of evidence needed either by the prosecution or by the defense.

. . .

In this case the President challenges a subpoena served on him as a third party requiring the production of materials for use in a criminal prosecution; he does so on the claim that he has a privilege against disclosure of confidential communications. He does not place his claim of privilege on the ground they are military or diplomatic secrets. As to these areas of Art. II duties the courts have traditionally shown the utmost deference to Presidential responsibilities....

. . .

In this case we must weigh the importance of the general privilege of confidentiality of Presidential communications in performance of the President's responsibilities against the inroads of such a privilege on the fair administration of criminal justice. [*The Court, in a footnote, adds: "We are not here concerned with the balance between the President's generalized interest in confidentiality and the need for relevant evidence in civil litigation, nor with that between the confidentiality interest and congressional demands for information, nor with the President's interest in preserving state secrets. We address only the conflict between the President's assertion of a generalized privilege of confidentiality and the constitutional need for relevant evidence in criminal trials."*] The interest in preserving confidentiality is weighty indeed and entitled to great respect. However, we cannot conclude that advisers will be moved to temper the candor of their remarks by the infrequent occasions of disclosure because of the possibility that such conversations will be called for in the context of a criminal prosecution.

On the other hand, the allowance of the privilege to withhold evidence that is demonstrably relevant in a criminal trial would cut deeply into the guarantee of due process of law and gravely impair the basic function of the courts. A President's acknowledged need for confidentiality in the communications of his office is general in nature, whereas the constitutional need for production of relevant evidence in a criminal proceeding is specific and central to the fair adjudication of a particular criminal case in the administration of justice. Without access to specific facts a criminal prosecution may be totally frustrated. The President's broad interest in confidentiality of communications will not be vitiated by disclosure of a limited number of conversations preliminarily shown to have some bearing on the pending criminal cases.

We conclude that when the ground for asserting privilege as to subpoenaed materials sought for use in a criminal trial is based only on the generalized interest in confidentiality, it cannot prevail over the fundamental demands of due process of law in the fair administration of criminal justice. The generalized assertion of privilege must yield to the demonstrated, specific need for evidence in a pending criminal trial.

. . .

Since this matter came before the Court during the pendency of a criminal prosecution, and on representations that time is of the essence, the mandate shall issue forthwith.

Affirmed.

MR. JUSTICE REHNQUIST took no part in the consideration or decision of these cases.

Negotiating Executive Privilege: The AT&T Cases

Executive documents are routinely shared with Congress, including documents that are highly classified and confidential. When there is a conflict between the executive and legislative branches, accommodations are usually discovered that avoid litigation. Even when a case is brought to court, the usual resolution is to force the two branches to find an intermediate position that will satisfy executive as well as congressional interests. The two cases below, involving national-security wiretaps, illustrate the practical efforts to iron out executive-legislative collisions. In a series of steps, Judge Harold Leventhal helped resolve a dispute between the Justice Department and a congressional committee. The two cases are *United States* v. *AT&T*, 551 F.2d 384 (D.C. Cir. 1976) and *United States* v. *AT&T*, 567 F.2d 121 (D.C. Cir. 1977). The first selection is from the 1976 case.

LEVENTHAL, Circuit Judge.

This unusual case involves a portentous clash between the executive and legislative branches, the executive branch asserting its authority to maintain tight control over information related to our national security, and the legislative branch asserting its authority to gather information necessary for the formulation of new legislation.

In the name of the United States, the Justice Department sued to enjoin the American Telephone and Telegraph Co. (AT&T) from complying with a subpoena of a subcommittee of the House of Representatives issued in the course of an investigation into warrantless "national security" wiretaps. Congressman Moss, chairman of the subcommittee, intervened on behalf of the House, the real defendant in interest since AT&T, while prepared to comply with the subpoena in the absence of a protective court order, has no stake in the controversy beyond knowing whether its legal obligation is to comply with the subpoena or not. The District Court issued the injunction requested by plaintiff and Chairman Moss appeals.

The case presents difficult problems, preliminary questions of jurisdiction and justiciability (application of the political question doctrine) and the ultimate issue on the merits of resolving or balancing the constitutional powers asserted by the legislative and executive branches.

In order to avoid a possibly unnecessary constitutional decision, we suggest the outlines of a possible settlement which may meet the mutual needs of the congressional and executive parties, without requiring a judicial resolution of a head-on confrontation, and we remand without decision at this time in order to permit exploration of this solution by the parties, under District Court guidance if needed.

If the parties reach an impasse this will be reported to us by the District Court. We would then be confronted with the need to enter an order disposing of the appeal pending.

I. BACKGROUND

The controversy arose out of an investigation by the Subcommittee on Oversight and Investigations of the House Committee on Interstate and Foreign Commerce. The Subcommittee was interested in determining the nature and extent of warrantless wiretapping in the United States for asserted national security purposes. It was concerned with the possible abuse of that power and its effect on privacy and other interests of U.S. citizens, and with the possible need for limiting legislation.

The warrantless wiretaps which became the focus of this part of the investigation used facilities provided by AT&T upon its receipt from the FBI of "request" letters. Each request letter specified a target line to be tapped, identified by telephone number, address, or other numerical designation. The letter requested a "leased line" to carry the tapped communications from the target location to a designated monitoring station manned by federal agents.

On June 22, 1976, the Subcommittee authorized and the Committee Chairman issued a subpoena requiring the president of AT&T to turn over to the Subcommittee copies of all national security request letters sent to AT&T and its subsidiaries by the FBI as well as records of such taps prior to the time when the practice of sending such letters was initiated. After the subpoena was issued, AT&T stood ready to comply.

At this point the White House approached Subcommittee Chairman John Moss in search of an alternative arrangement meeting the Subcommittee's information needs. The basic thrust of the ensuing negotiations between the Subcommittee and the Justice Department was to substitute, for the request letters, expurgated copies of the backup memoranda upon which the Attorney General based his decision to authorize the warrantless taps. These memoranda, providing information on the purpose and nature of the surveillance, might have been more informative to Congress than the request letters, which merely contained numerical identification of the line to be tapped. The Justice Department agreed, at least informally and tentatively, to provide the Subcommittee staff expurgated copies of the backup memo pertaining to foreign intelligence taps, with all information which would identify the target replaced by generic description, such as "Middle Eastern diplomat." The negotiations came close to success, but broke down over the issue of verification by the Subcommittee of the accuracy of the executive's generic descriptions by inspection of a sample of the original memoranda.

[*Judge Leventhal reviewed the powers of Congress to investigate, and the President's national security powers. "Each branch of government claims that as long as it is exercising its authority for a legitimate purpose, its actions are unreviewable by the courts."*]

F. BALANCING BY THE COURTS

A court seeking to balance the legislative and executive interests asserted here would face severe problems in formulating and applying standards. Granted that the subpoenas are clearly within the proper legislative investigatory sphere, it is difficult to "weigh" Congress's need for the request letters. Congress's power to monitor executive actions is implicit in the appropriations power. Here, for instance, if the President has the inherent power claimed to block the subpoena, how is Congress to assure that appropriated funds are not being used for illegal warrantless domestic electronic surveillance?

As to the danger to national security, a court would have to consider the Subcommittee's track record for security, the likelihood of a leak if other members of the House sought access to the material. In addition to this delicate and possibly unseemly determination, the court would have to weigh the effect of a leak on intelligence activities and diplomatic relations. Finally, the court would have to consider the reasonableness of the alternatives offered by the parties and decide which would better reconcile the competing constitutional interests.

IV. REASONS FOR EXPLORATION OF SETTLEMENT

Before moving on to a decision of such nerve-center constitutional questions, we pause to allow for further efforts at a settlement. We think that suggestion is particularly appropriate in this case and may well be productive.... The legislative and executive branches have a long history of settlement of disputes that seemed irreconcilable. There was almost a settlement in 1976. It may well be attainable in 1977.

Furthermore, our own reflections may be of some assistance. As a prelude to settlement conference, it may be helpful if we review pertinent considerations:

1. This dispute between the legislative and executive branches has at least some elements of the political-question doctrine. A court decision selects a victor, and tends thereafter to tilt the scales. A compromise worked out between the branches is most likely to meet their essential needs and the country's constitutional balance.

[*1977 decision:*]

LEVENTHAL, Circuit Judge:

This case brings to us for a second time conflicting assertions by the executive and legislative branches, contentions that require the third branch to decide whether its constitutional mandate to decide controversies extends to such a conflict, and if so what measure of judicial resolution is sound and appropriate.

. . .

When we first came to the case, we developed a novel and somewhat gingerly approach for the delicate problem of accommodating the needs and powers of two coordinate branches in a situation where each claimed absolute authority.... To the extent possible, we wished to avoid a resolution that might disturb the balance of power between the two branches and inaccurately reflect their true needs....

Negotiation has narrowed but not bridged the gap between the parties. Accordingly, we must adopt a somewhat more traditional approach. We begin by deciding that complete judicial abstention on political question grounds is not warranted. In addressing the merits, however, we continue to move cautiously. Taking full account of the negotiating positions, we have chartered the course that we think is most likely to accommodate the substantial needs of the parties. Doubtless, neither will be satisfied. But in our view there is good reason to believe that the procedure set forth in this opinion will prove feasible in practice, with such adjustments and refinements as may be evolved by the parties and the district court....

The framers, rather than attempting to define and allocate all governmental power in minute detail, relied, we believe, on the expectation that where conflicts in scope of authority arose between the coordinate branches, a spirit of dynamic compromise would promote resolution of the dispute in the manner most likely to result in efficient and effective functioning of our governmental system. Under this view, the coordinate branches do not exist in an exclusively adversary relationship to one another when a conflict in authority arises. Rather, each branch should take cognizance of an implicit constitutional mandate to seek optimal accommodation through a realistic evaluation of the needs of the conflicting branches in the particular fact situation. This aspect of our constitutional scheme avoids the mischief of polarization of disputes....

[*The case was dismissed on December 21, 1978, after the Justice Department and the subcommittee amicably resolved their differences.*]

Clinton v. Jones

520 U.S. 681 (1997)

Paula Corbin Jones sued President Clinton for sexual harassment and assault for an incident that occurred in 1991, when Clinton served as governor of Arkansas. While recognizing that she

would have a right to pursue the lawsuit after he left the presidency, Clinton moved to dismiss the case on grounds of presidential immunity. A federal appellate court held that a President enjoys absolute immunity only for official, not unofficial, acts. Jones v. Clinton, 72 F.3d 1354 (8th Cir. 1996). The Supreme Court agreed to hear the case.

JUSTICE STEVENS delivered the opinion of the Court.

This case raises a constitutional and a prudential question concerning the Office of the President of the United States. Respondent, a private citizen, seeks to recover damages from the current occupant of that office based on actions allegedly taken before his term began. The President submits that in all but the most exceptional cases the Constitution requires federal courts to defer such litigation until his term ends and that, in any event, respect for the office warrants such a stay. Despite the force of the arguments supporting the President's submissions, we conclude that they must be rejected.

I

Petitioner, William Jefferson Clinton, was elected to the Presidency in 1992, and reelected in 1996. His term of office expires on January 20, 2001. In 1991 he was the Governor of the State of Arkansas. Respondent, Paula Corbin Jones, is a resident of California. In 1991 she lived in Arkansas, and was an employee of the Arkansas Industrial Development Commission.

On May 6, 1994, she commenced this action in the United States District Court for the Eastern District of Arkansas by filing a complaint naming petitioner and Danny Ferguson, a former Arkansas State Police officer, as defendants....

Those allegations principally describe events that are said to have occurred on the afternoon of May 8, 1991, during an official conference held at the Excelsior Hotel in Little Rock, Arkansas. The Governor delivered a speech at the conference; respondent— working as a state employee—staffed the registration desk. She alleges that Ferguson persuaded her to leave her desk and to visit the Governor in a business suite at the hotel, where he made "abhorrent" sexual advances that she vehemently rejected. She further claims that her superiors at work subsequently dealt with her in a hostile and rude manner, and changed her duties to punish her for rejecting those advances. Finally, she alleges that after petitioner was elected President, Ferguson defamed her by making a statement to a reporter that implied she had accepted petitioner's alleged overtures, and that various persons authorized to speak for the President publicly branded her a liar by denying that the incident had occurred.

Respondent seeks actual damages of $75,000, and punitive damages of $100,000. Her complaint contains four counts. The first charges that petitioner, acting under color of state law, deprived her of rights protected by the Constitution, in violation of Rev. Stat. § 1979, 42 U.S.C. § 1983. The second charges that petitioner and Ferguson engaged in a conspiracy to violate her federal rights, also actionable under federal law. See Rev. Stat. § 1980, 42 U.S.C. § 1985. The third is a state common law claim for intentional infliction of emotional distress, grounded primarily on the incident at the hotel. The fourth count, also based on state law, is for defamation, embracing both the comments allegedly made to the press by Ferguson and the statements of petitioner's agents....

II

In response to the complaint, petitioner promptly advised the District Court that he intended to file a motion to dismiss on grounds of Presidential immunity, and requested the court to defer all other pleadings and motions until after the immunity issue was resolved....

IV

Petitioner's principal submission—that "in all but the most exceptional cases"... the Constitution affords the President temporary immunity from civil damages litigation arising out of events that occurred before he took office—cannot be sustained on the basis of precedent.

Only three sitting Presidents have been defendants in civil litigation involving their actions prior to taking office. Complaints against Theodore Roosevelt and Harry Truman had been dismissed before they took office; the dismissals were affirmed after their respective inaugurations. Two companion cases arising out of an automobile accident were filed against John F. Kennedy in 1960 during the Presidential campaign. After taking office, he unsuccessfully argued that his status as Commander in Chief gave him a right to a stay under the Soldiers' and Sailors' Civil Relief Act of 1940, 50 U.S.C.App. §§ 501–525. The motion for a stay was denied by the District Court, and the matter was settled out of court. Thus, none of those cases sheds any light on the constitutional issue before us.

The principal rationale for affording certain public servants immunity from suits for money damages arising out of their official acts is inapplicable to unofficial conduct. In cases involving prosecutors, legislators, and judges we have repeatedly explained that the immunity serves the public interest in enabling such officials to perform their designated functions effectively without fear that a particular decision may give rise to personal liability....

This reasoning provides no support for an immunity for *unofficial* conduct....

VI

Petitioner's strongest argument supporting his immunity claim is based on the text and structure of the Constitution. He does not contend that the occupant of the Office of the President is "above the law," in the sense that his conduct is entirely immune from judicial scrutiny. The President argues merely for a postponement of the judicial proceedings that will determine whether he violated any law. His argument is grounded in the character of the office that was created by Article II of the Constitution, and relies on separation of powers principles that have structured our constitutional arrangement since the founding.

As a starting premise, petitioner contends that he occupies a unique office with powers and responsibilities so vast and important that the public interest demands that he devote his undivided time and attention to his public duties. He submits that—given the nature of the office—the doctrine of separation of powers places limits on the authority of the Federal Judiciary to interfere with the Executive Branch that would be transgressed by allowing this action to proceed.

We have no dispute with the initial premise of the argument. Former presidents, from George Washington to George Bush, have consistently endorsed petitioner's characterization of the office....

... As a factual matter, petitioner contends that this particular case—as well as the potential additional litigation that an affirmance of the Court of Appeals judgment might spawn—may impose an unacceptable burden on the President's time and energy, and thereby impair the effective performance of his office.

Petitioner's predictive judgment finds little support in either history or the relatively narrow compass of the issues raised in this particular case. As we have already noted, in the more than 200-year history of the Republic, only three sitting Presidents have been subjected to suits for their private actions.... If the past is any indicator, it seems unlikely that a deluge of such litigation will ever engulf the Presidency. As for the case at hand, if properly managed by the District Court, it appears to us highly unlikely to occupy any substantial amount of petitioner's time.

Of greater significance, petitioner errs by presuming that interactions between the Judicial Branch and the Executive, even quite burdensome interactions, necessarily rise to the level of constitutionally forbidden impairment of the Executive's ability to perform its constitutionally mandated functions. "[O]ur ... system imposes upon the Branches a degree of overlapping responsibility, a duty of interdependence as well as independence the absence of which 'would preclude the establishment of a Nation capable of governing itself effectively.'" *Mistretta*, 488 U.S., at 381 (quoting *Buckley*, 424 U.S., at 121). As Madison explained, separation of powers does not mean that the branches "ought to have no *partial agency* in, or no *controul* over the acts of each other." ...

First, we have long held that when the President takes official action, the Court has the authority to determine whether he has acted within the law. Perhaps the most dramatic example of such a case is our holding that President Truman exceeded his constitutional authority when he issued an order directing the Secretary of Commerce to take possession of and operate most of the Nation's steel mills in order to avert a national catastrophe. *Youngstown Sheet & Tube Co. v. Sawyer* 343 U.S. 579 (1952)....

Second, it is also settled that the President is subject to judicial process in appropriate circumstances....

Sitting Presidents have responded to court orders to provide testimony and other information with sufficient frequency that such interactions between the Judicial and Executive Branches can scarcely be thought a novelty. President Monroe responded to written interrogatories, ... President Nixon—as noted above—produced tapes in response to a subpoena *duces tecum,* see *United States v. Nixon,* President Ford complied with an order to give a deposition in a criminal trial, *United States v. Fromme,* 405 F.Supp. 578 (E.D.Cal.1975), and President Clinton has twice given videotaped testimony in criminal proceedings.... Moreover, sitting Presidents have also voluntarily complied with judicial requests for testimony. President Grant gave a lengthy deposition in a criminal case under such circumstances, ... and President Carter similarly gave videotaped testimony for use at a criminal trial, *ibid.*

... We therefore hold that the doctrine of separation of powers does not require federal courts to stay all private actions against the President until he leaves office.

... [W]e turn to the question whether the District Court's decision to stay the trial until after petitioner leaves office was an abuse of discretion.

VII

... Although we have rejected the argument that the potential burdens on the President violate separation of powers principles, those burdens are appropriate matters for the District Court to evaluate in its management of the case. The high respect that is owed to the office of the Chief Executive, though not justifying a rule of categorical immunity, is a matter that should inform the conduct of the entire proceeding, including the timing and scope of discovery.

Nevertheless, we are persuaded that it was an abuse of discretion for the District Court to defer the trial until after the President leaves office. Such a lengthy and categorical stay takes no account whatever of the respondent's interest in bringing the case to trial. The complaint was filed within the statutory limitations period—albeit near the end of that period—and delaying trial would increase the danger of prejudice resulting from the loss of evidence, including the inability of witnesses to recall specific facts, or the possible death of a party.

... We think the District Court may have given undue weight to the concern that a trial might generate unrelated civil actions that could conceivably hamper the President in conducting the duties of his office. If and when that should occur, the court's discretion would permit it to manage those actions in such fashion (including deferral of trial) that interference with the President's duties would not occur. But no such impingement upon the President's conduct of his office was shown here.

VIII

We add a final comment on two matters that are discussed at length in the briefs: the risk that our decision will generate a large volume of politically motivated harassing and frivolous litigation, and the danger that national security concerns might prevent the President from explaining a legitimate need for a continuance.

We are not persuaded that either of these risks is serious. Most frivolous and vexatious litigation is terminated at the pleading stage or on summary judgment, with little if any personal involvement by the defendant.... Moreover, the availability of sanctions provides a significant deterrent to litigation directed at the President in his unofficial capacity for purposes of political gain or harassment. History indicates that the likelihood that a significant number of such cases will be filed is remote....

If Congress deems it appropriate to afford the President stronger protection, it may respond with appropriate legislation....

The Federal District Court has jurisdiction to decide this case. Like every other citizen who properly invokes that jurisdiction, respondent has a right to an orderly disposition of her claims. Accordingly, the judgment of the Court of Appeals is affirmed.

It is so ordered.

[*Justice Breyer prepared a lengthy concurring opinion in which he discussed the specific situation when a President "sets forth and explains a conflict between judiciary proceeding and public duties." Under this circumstance, a federal district judge might schedule a trial in such a way that it interferes with the President's discharge of his public duties. Breyer's concurrence emphasizes the importance of the President's office and the danger of having a single judge "second guess" a President's needs.*]

H. CONGRESSIONAL MEMBERSHIP AND PREROGATIVES

Under Article I, Section 5, each House of Congress "may determine the rules of its proceedings, punish its members for disorderly behavior, and, with the concurrence of two thirds, expel a member." Each House is also "the judge of the elections, returns and qualifications of its own members." Qualifications for office are set forth in Article I, Sections 2 and 3: age (25 for Representatives and 30 for Senators), citizenship (seven years for Representatives and nine years for Senators), and residency (members must be "inhabitants" of the state in which they are chosen). The custom is for Representatives to also reside in the district for which they are elected.

On a few occasions the House of Representatives has refused to seat someone elected to office. A prominent example was Victor Berger of Wisconsin, a Socialist denied his seat in 1919 because he had been convicted for opposing World War I. A case that eventually reached the Supreme Court involved Adam Clayton Powell, a controversial black Congressman from New York. He was reelected in 1966 but the House refused to seat him, in part because of criminal proceedings against him. Many observers thought that the issue was clearly a political question to be decided solely by the House, but in 1969 the Supreme Court held that neither House could deny a seat to a duly elected member who satisfied the qualifications for office specified in the Constitution: age, citizenship, and residency. Congress could not add to that list of qualifications. POWELL v. McCORMACK, 395 U.S. 486 (1969). (See box on "The Exclusion of Adam Clayton Powell" in Chapter 3).

If the House wanted to exclude Powell, it had to first seat him and then expel him by the two-thirds majority required by the Constitution. Previously, the Court had held that the Georgia legislature had violated Julian Bond's First Amendment rights by refusing to seat him because he had expressed his opposition to the Vietnam War. Bond v. Floyd, 385 U.S. 116 (1966). In addition to expulsion, Congress may censure a member for dishonorable or disreputable behavior.

Term Limits

A number of states adopted constitutional amendments and other measures to place term limits on legislators not only in state government but in Congress as well. An amendment to the Arkansas Constitution, limiting members of Congress to three terms in the House of Representatives and two terms in the Senate, was declared unconstitutional by the Supreme Court in 1995. Relying primarily on *Powell v. McCormack*, the court held that the Arkansas provision violated the U.S. Constitution by adding to the qualifications established for members of Congress. U.S. Term Limits, Inc. v. Thornton, 514 U.S. 779 (1995).

Also in 1995, the U.S. House of Representatives voted on a constitutional amendment to limit Representatives and Senators to a certain number of terms. Some of the proposals would have limited the terms of Representatives to six years and Senators to twelve, while others imposed limits of twelve years on both chambers. All of these amendments were voted down, including the basic Republican amendment (a lifetime limit of twelve years for both Houses), which lost on a vote of 227 to 204—a two-thirds majority being required for a constitutional amendment. A constitutional amendment stalled in the Senate in 1996 because of a filibuster. Another House effort in 1997 to amend the Constitution to impose term limits attracted the support of only 217 to 211.

In 2001, the Supreme Court struck down a 1996 amendment to the Missouri constitution that required special ballot language next to the names of candidates for the U.S. Congress who did not support term limits. A unanimous Court held that the notations put the candidates at a political disadvantage and represented an unconstitutional attempt to dictate electoral outcomes. Cook v. Gralike, 531 U.S. 510 (2001).

Speech or Debate Clause

Article I, Section 6, provides that "for any Speech or Debate in either House," Senators and Representatives "shall not be questioned in any other Place." The courts have consistently held that the immunities offered by this Clause exist not simply for the personal or private benefit of members "but to protect the integrity of the legislative process by insuring the independence of individual legislators." United States v. Brewster, 408 U.S. 501, 507 (1972). It protects members from executive or judicial harassment. United States v. Johnson, 383 U.S. 177 (1966). The Clause covers not only words spoken in debate but also anything required to conduct legislative business: remarks made in the course of committee hearings; speeches printed in the *Congressional Record,* even when not delivered; and information acquired by congressional staff. Other activities, which the courts call "political" rather than "legislative," are not protected: contacts with executive agencies, assistance to constituents seeking federal contracts, the preparation of news releases and newsletters, and speeches

---

Speech or Debate Clause

Covers	*Does Not Cover*
Words spoken in debate and anything in relation to legislative business. Kilbourn v. Thompson, 103 U.S. 168, 204 (1881).	Criminal actions that are peripherally related to some legislative function. United States v. Brewster, 408 U.S. 501, 521 (1972).
Remarks in committee hearings and committee reports. Gravel v. United States, 408 U.S. 606 (1972); Doe v. McMillan, 412 U.S. 306 (1973).	"Errands" for constituents, making appointments with executive agencies, and assistance in securing federal contracts. United States v. Brewster, at 513.
Speeches in *Congressional Record,* whether delivered or not. Hutchinson v. Proxmire, 433 U.S. 111, 116 n.3 (1979).	Newsletters to constituents, news releases, and speeches delivered outside Congress. United States v. Brewster, at 513; Hutchinson v. Proxmire.
Congressional aides when carrying out legislative tasks. Gravel v. United States, 408 U.S. 606 (1972).	Private publications by members of Congress. Gravel v. United States, at 625; Doe v. McMillan, at 314–15.
Judges may not inquire into the motivation for a Congressman's speech. United States v. Johnson, 383 U.S. 169, 176–77 (1966).	Contacts with executive branch. United States v. Johnson, at 172; Gravel v. United States, at 625.

---

or documents delivered outside the Congress (see box). See Gravel v. United States, 408 U.S. 606 (1972).

To protect its prerogatives, Congress has not hesitated to engage in direct confrontations with the judiciary. In 1970, the House Committee on Internal Security prepared a report entitled "Limited Survey of Honoraria Given Guest Speakers for Engagements at Colleges and Universities." By including the names of leftist or antiwar speakers and the amounts they received, the committee hoped that alumni would complain about the use of college funds and threaten to withhold future contributions. The ACLU obtained a copy of the galleys of the committee report and asked a federal judge to issue an injunction prohibiting its publication. U.S. District Judge Gesell did just that, ordering the Public Printer and the Superintendent of Documents not to print the report or even any "fascimile" of it. He suggested that Congress could print the report in the *Congressional Record* if it wanted to. Hentoff v. Ichord, 318 F.Supp. 1175 (D.D.C. 1970).

The House of Representatives responded with a resolution that told everyone, including the courts, to get out of the way. During debate on the resolution, it was pointed out that Congress does not print committee reports in the *Congressional Record.* Supporters of the resolution argued that Judge Gesell's order violated the Speech and Debate Clause and interfered with the authority of each House to determine the rules of its proceedings and to publish them. After the resolution passed by a large bipartisan margin of 302 to 54, the report was printed without any further judicial involvement. 116 Cong. Rec. 41358–74 (1970); H. Rept. No. 1732, 91st Cong., 2d Sess. (1970).

Article I, Section 6, also provides that members of Congress "shall in all cases, except treason, felony and breach of the peace, be privileged from arrest during their attendance at the session of their respective houses, and in going to and returning from the same." Immunity from arrest during sessions of the legislature can be traced back to struggles between the English Parliament and the King.

On May 20, 2006 the Justice Department triggered a major Speech or Debate Clause issue by obtaining a search warrant and entering the Capitol Hill office of Rep. William J. Jefferson (D-La.). The search continued for 18 hours, until Sunday morning. The FBI threatened to pick the office door lock if not given immediate entry. Once inside, the FBI agents refused to permit the House General Counsel or Capitol Police to enter the office while the search was proceeding. The execution of the warrant was the first ever carried out on a congressional office in over 200 years.

The initial media issue was whether a member of Congress "was above the law." The deeper issue, however, was the use of a search warrant by the executive branch on Capitol Hill and the damage that did to the independence and coequal status of Congress. In a case brought by Jefferson and the Bipartisan Legal Advisory Group of the United States House of Representatives, a district court judge found the raid to be legal. He rejected the claim that the search violated the Constitution's Speech and Debate Clause and the separation of powers, holding that a Congressman is "generally bound to the operation of the criminal laws as are ordinary persons," and the Speech or Debate Clause does not "make Members of Congress super-citizens, immune from criminal responsibility." An appellate panel overturned this decision, ruling that the Department of Justice could not review the seized files until Jefferson had the chance to determine which ones pertained to his work as a legislator. U.S. v. Rayburn House, Rm 2113, Washington, DC, 497 F.3d 654 (D.C. Cir. 2007). In 2008 the Supreme Court denied further review. Jefferson lost his re-election bid in 2008, and was tried and convicted on corruption charges in 2009, receiving a prison sentence of 13 years.

Powell v. McCormack

395 U.S. 486 (1969)

Adam Clayton Powell had served New York's 18th Congressional District since 1945. After his reelection in 1966, the House of Representatives passed a resolution refusing to seat him. By that point Powell had been charged with a number of offenses, including misappropriation of public funds and illegal salary payments for his wife. Also, he had been held in contempt in a New York defamation suit. After the exclusion vote, Powell and 13 voters of his congressional district sued John W. McCormack, Speaker of the House, and several other House officials. A district court said it lacked jurisdiction to hear the case; the D.C. Circuit held that it had jurisdiction but that the case was nonjusticiable.

MR. CHIEF JUSTICE WARREN delivered the opinion of the Court.

In November 1966, petitioner Adam Clayton Powell, Jr., was duly elected from the 18th Congressional District of New York to serve in the United States House of Representatives for the 90th Congress. However, pursuant to a House resolution, he was not permitted to take his seat. Powell (and some of the voters of his district) then filed suit in Federal District Court, claiming that the House could exclude him only if it found he failed to meet the standing requirements of age, citizenship, and residence contained in Art. I, § 2, of the Constitution—requirements the House specifically found Powell met—and thus had excluded him unconstitutionally. The District Court dismissed petitioners' complaint "for want of jurisdiction of the subject matter." A panel of the Court of Appeals affirmed the dismissal, although on somewhat different grounds, each judge filing a separate opinion. We have determined that it was error to dismiss the complaint and that petitioner Powell is entitled to a declaratory judgment that he was unlawfully excluded from the 90th Congress.

I. FACTS.

During the 89th Congress, a Special Subcommittee on Contracts of the Committee on House Administration conducted an investigation into the expenditures of the Committee on Education and Labor, of which petitioner Adam Clayton Powell, Jr., was chairman. The Special Subcommittee issued a report concluding that Powell and certain staff employees had deceived the House authorities as to travel expenses. The report also indicated there was strong evidence that certain illegal salary payments had been made to Powell's wife at his direction.... No formal action was taken during the 89th Congress. However, prior to the organization of the 90th Congress, the Democratic members-elect met in caucus and voted to remove Powell as chairman of the Committee on Education and Labor....

When the 90th Congress met to organize in January 1967, Powell was asked to step aside while the oath was administered to the other members-elect. Following the administration of the oath to the remaining members, the House discussed the procedure to be followed in determining whether Powell was eligible to take his seat. After some debate, by a vote of 363 to 65 the House adopted House Resolution No. 1, which provided that the Speaker appoint a Select Committee to determine Powell's eligibility. 113 Cong. Rec. 26–27. Although the resolution prohibited Powell from taking his seat until the House acted on the Select Committee's report, it did provide that he should receive all the pay and allowances due a member during the period.

... [O]n February 23, 1967, the Committee issued its report, finding that Powell met the standing qualifications of Art. I § 2.... However, the Committee further reported that Powell had asserted an unwarranted privilege and immunity from the processes of the courts of New York; that he had wrongfully diverted House funds for the use of others and himself; and that he had made false reports on expenditures of foreign currency to the Committee on House Administration.... The Committee recommended that Powell be sworn and seated as a member of the 90th Congress but that he be censured by the House, fined $40,000 and be deprived of his seniority....

The report was presented to the House on March 1, 1967, and the House debated the Select Committee's proposed resolution. At the conclusion of the debate, by a vote of 222 to 202 the House rejected a motion to bring the resolution to a vote. An amendment to the resolution was then offered; it called for the exclusion of Powell and a declaration that his seat was vacant. The Speaker ruled that a majority vote of the House would be sufficient to pass the resolution if it were so amended. 113 Cong. Rec. 5020. After further debate, the amendment was adopted by a vote of 248 to 176. Then the House adopted by a vote of 307 to 116 House Resolution No. 278 in its amended form, thereby excluding Powell and directing that the Speaker notify the Governor of New York that the seat was vacant.

... While the case was pending on our docket, the 90th Congress officially terminated and the 91st Congress was seated. In November 1968, Powell was again elected as the representative of the 18th Congressional District of New York and he was seated by the 91st Congress. The resolution seating Powell also fined him $25,000....

Respondents press upon us a variety of arguments to support the court below; they will be considered in the following order. (1) Events occurring subsequent to the grant of certiorari have rendered this litigation moot. (2) The Speech or Debate Clause of the Constitution, Art. I, § 6, insulates respondents' action from judicial review. (3) The decision to exclude petitioner Powell is supported by the power granted to the House of Representatives to expel a member. (4) This Court lacks subject matter jurisdiction over petitioners' action. (5) Even if subject matter jurisdiction is present, this litigation is not justiciable either under the general criteria established by this Court or because a political question is involved.

II. MOOTNESS.

[*The House argued that the case was moot because Powell was seated as a member of the 91st Congress. The Court, however, decided that the salary withheld from Powell after his exclusion from the 90th Congress made the dispute a "case or controversy."*]

III. SPEECH OR DEBATE CLAUSE.

Respondents assert that the Speech or Debate Clause of the Constitution, Art. I, § 6, is an absolute bar to petitioners' action. This Court has on four prior occasions — *Dombrowski* v. *Eastland,* 387 U. S. 82 (1967); *United States* v. *Johnson,* 383 U.S. 169 (1966); *Tenney* v. *Brandhove,* 341 U.S. 367 (1951); and *Kilbourn* v. *Thompson,* 103 U.S. 168 (1881) — been called upon to determine if allegedly unconstitutional action taken by legislators or legislative employees is insulated from judicial review by the Speech or Debate Clause....

The Speech or Debate Clause, adopted by the Constitutional Convention without debate or opposition, finds its roots in the conflict between Parliament and the Crown culminating in the Glorious Revolution of 1688 and the English Bill of Rights of 1689. Drawing upon this history, we concluded in *United States* v. *Johnson* ... that the purpose of this clause was "to prevent intimidation [of legislators] by the executive and accountability before a possibly hostile judiciary." ...

Our cases make it clear that the legislative immunity created by the Speech or Debate Clause performs an important function in representative government. It insures that legislators are free to represent the interests of their constituents without fear that they will be later called to task in the courts for that representation....

Legislative immunity does not, of course, bar all judicial review of legislative acts....

That House employees are acting pursuant to express orders of the House does not bar judicial review of the constitutionality of the underlying legislative decision. *Kilbourn* decisively settles this question, since the Sergeant at Arms was held liable for false imprisonment even though he did nothing more than execute the House Resolution that Kilbourn be arrested and imprisoned.... [T]hough this action may be dismissed against the Congressmen petitioners are entitled to maintain their action against House employees and to judicial review of the propriety of the decision to exclude petitioner Powell....

IV. EXCLUSION OR EXPULSION.

The resolution excluding petitioner Powell was adopted by a vote in excess of two-thirds of the 434 Members of Congress—307 to 116. 113 Cong. Rec. 5037–5038. Article I, § 5, grants the House authority to expel a member "with the Concurrence of two thirds." Respondents assert that the House may expel a member for any reason whatsoever and that, since a two-thirds vote was obtained, the procedure by which Powell was denied his seat in the 90th Congress should be regarded as an expulsion, not an exclusion....

[*The Court reviewed the legislative proceedings of Powell's exclusion. The chairman of the Select Committee posed a parliamentary inquiry to determine whether a two-thirds vote was necessary. The Speaker replied that action by a majority vote would be in accordance with the rules. The Court also notes that the House has determined that a member should not be expelled for action taken during a prior Congress.*]

VI. B. POLITICAL QUESTION DOCTRINE.
1. TEXTUALLY DEMONSTRABLE CONSTITUTIONAL COMMITMENT.

[*The Court concludes that the House may not exclude someone who meets the requirements for membership expressly prescribed by the Constitution. After seating such a person, the House may expel, but only after securing the two-thirds majority required by the Constitution.*]

2. OTHER CONSIDERATIONS.

Respondents' alternate contention is that the case presents a political question because judicial resolution of petitioners' claim would produce a "potentially embarrassing confrontation between coordinate branches" of the Federal Government. But, as our interpretation of Art. I, § 5, discloses, a determination of petitioner Powell's right to sit would require no more than an interpretation of the Constitution. Such a determination falls within the traditional role accorded courts to interpret the law, and does not involve a "lack of the respect due [a] coordinate [branch] of government," nor does it involve an "initial policy determination of a kind clearly for nonjudicial discretion." *Baker* v. *Carr,* 369 U.S. 186, at 217. Our system of government requires that federal courts on occasion interpret the Constitution in a manner at variance with the construction given the document by another branch. The alleged conflict that such an adjudication may cause cannot justify the courts' avoiding their constitutional responsibility. See *United States* v. *Brown,* 381 U.S. 437, 462 (1965); *Youngstown Sheet & Tube Co.* v. *Sawyer,* 343 U.S. 579, 613–614 (1952) (Frankfurter, J., concurring); *Myers* v. *United States,* 272 U.S. 52, 293 (1926) (Brandeis, J., dissenting).

... For, as we noted in *Baker* v. *Carr, supra,* at 211, it is the responsibility of this Court to act as the ultimate interpreter of the Constitution. *Marbury* v. *Madison,* 1 Cranch 137 (1803). Thus, we conclude that petitioners' claim is not barred by the political question doctrine, and, having determined that the claim is otherwise generally justiciable, we hold that the case is justiciable.

Mr. Justice Douglas [*concurring*]....

Mr. Justice Stewart, dissenting.

I believe that events which have taken place since certiorari was granted in this case on November 18, 1968, have rendered it moot, and that the Court should therefore refrain from deciding the novel, difficult, and delicate constitutional questions which the case presented at its inception....

CONCLUSIONS

Most of the conflicts between Congress and the President are resolved through informal negotiations and accommodations. Rarely does an issue enter the judicial arena. When it does, the courts are reluctant to set hard-and-fast rules in such complex areas as executive privilege, delegation, and congressional investigations. An emphasis is placed on middle-ground remedies that protect the essential interests of each branch. Beyond the statutory framework agreed to by executive and legislative officials, the two branches have evolved an elaborate system of informal, nonstatutory agreements that satisfy the competing needs of executive flexibility and congressional control. In this important sense, the meaning of separation of powers depends heavily on nonjudicial interpretations by the executive and legislative branches. Louis Fisher, "Separation of Powers: Interpretation Outside the Courts," 18 Pepperdine L. Rev. 57 (1990).

NOTES AND QUESTIONS

1. What types of separation of powers issues are likely to be resolved without need of litigation, thus challenging the notion that federal courts are the ultimate voice in deciding the meaning of the Constitution?

2. The framers decided on a single Executive to help assure accountability and effectiveness. But in what ways is the theory of a "unitary executive" undercut by statutes that place certain executive decisions beyond the reach of the President?

3. Chief Justice Taft, in *Myers v. United States* (1926), recognized a broad removal power for the President, but at the same time acknowledged that certain duties within the executive branch could be appropriately shielded from presidential influence or control. What type of duties?

4. Congress exercises substantial control over executive decisions by means of nonstatutory controls, such as committee and subcommittee vetoes. Are those types of congressional controls likely to be successfully challenged in court? If not, why not?

SELECTED READINGS

Adler, David Gray and Michael A. Genovese, eds. The Presidency and the Law: The Clinton Legacy. Lawrence: University Press of Kansas, 2002.

Barber, Sotirios A. The Constitution and the Delegation of Congressional Power. Chicago: University of Chicago Press, 1975.

Bessette, Joseph M., and Jeffrey Tulis, eds. The Constitutional Presidency. Baltimore: Johns Hopkins University Press, 2009.

Breckenridge, Adam Carlyle. The Executive Privilege, Lincoln: University of Nebraska Press, 1974.

Calabresi, Steven G. and Christopher S. Yoo. The Unitary Executive: Presidential Power from Washington to Bush. New Haven: Yale University Press, 2008.

Campbell, tom. Separation of Powers in Practice. Palo Alto: Stanford University Press, 2004.

Corley, Pamela C. "Avoiding Advice and Consent: Recess Appointments and Presidential Power." 36 Presidential Studies Quarterly 670 (2006).

Craig, Barbara Hinkson. Chadha. New York: Oxford University Press, 1988.

Fisher, Louis. The Politics of Shared Power: Congress and the Executive. College Station, Tex.: Texas A&M University Press, 4th ed., 1998.

———. Constitutional Conflicts Between Congress and the President. Lawrence: University Press of Kansas, 5th ed., 2007.

———. The Politics of Executive Privilege. Durham: Carolina Academic Press, 2004.

———. Defending Congress and the Constitution. Lawrence: University Press of Kansas, 2011.

Glennon, Michael J. "The Use of Custom in Resolving Separation of Powers Disputes." 64 Boston University Law Review 109 (1984).

Goldwin, Robert A. and Art Kaufman, eds. Separation of Powers — Does It Still Work? Washington, D.C.: American Enterprise Institute, 1986.

Gwyn, W.B. "The Meaning of Separation of Powers." Tulane Series in Political Science, Vol. IX (1965).

Hamilton, James. The Power to Probe: A Study of Congressional Investigations. New York: Random House, 1976.

Harriger, Katy J. The Special Prosecutor in American Politics. Lawrence: University Press of Kansas, 2nd ed., rev., 2000.

———. "Executive Power and Prosecution: Lessons from the Libby Trial and the U.S. Attorney Firings." 38 Presidential Studies Quarterly 491 (2008).

Harris, Joseph P. The Advice and Consent of the Senate: A Study of the Confirmation of Appointments by the United States Senate. Berkeley: University of California Press, 1953.

Kaden, Alan Scott. "Judicial Review of Executive Action in Domestic Affairs." 80 Columbia Law Review 1535 (1980).

KAISER, FREDERICK M. "Congressional Control of Executive Actions in the Aftermath of the *Chadha* Decision." 36 Administrative Law Review 239 (1984).

MacKENZIE, JOHN P. Absolute Power: How the Unitary Executive is Undermining the Constitution. Washington, DC: Century Foundation Press, 2008.

McGOWAN, CARL "Congress, Court and Control of Delegated Powers." 77 Columbia Law Review 1119 (1977).

POSNER, RICHARD A. An Affair of State; The Investigation, Impeachment, and Trial of President Clinton. Cambridge: Harvard University Press, 1999.

ROSENBERG, MORTON. "Beyond the Limits of Executive Power: Presidential Control of Agency Rulemaking Under Executive Order 12,291." 80 Michigan Law Review 193 (1981).

ROZELL, MARK J. Executive Privilege. Lawrence: University Press of Kansas, 3d ed., 2010.

ROZELL, MARK J. AND CLYDE WILCOX, eds. The Clinton Scandal and the Future of American Government. Washington, D.C.: Georgetown University Press, 2000.

SHESOL, JEFF. Supreme Power: Franklin Roosevelt v. the Supreme Court. New York: W.W. Norton, 2010.

STATHIS, STEPHEN W. "Executive Cooperation: Presidential Recognition of the Investigative Authority of Congress and the Courts." 3 Journal of Law & Politics 183 (1986).

VILE, M.J.C. Constitutionalism and the Separation of Powers. London: Oxford University Press, 1967.

WINTERTON, GEORGE. "The Concept of Extra-Constitutional Executive Power in Domestic Affairs." 7 Hastings Constitutional Law Quarterly 1 (1979).

7

Separation of Powers: Emergencies and Foreign Affairs

The doctrine of separated powers has its share of subtleties and puzzles in domestic disputes. Even more enigmatic is the doctrine's application to external affairs and emergency powers. This chapter begins by examining efforts to distinguish between external and internal affairs. It next analyzes the scope of the "executive prerogative," which some Presidents cite as authority to exercise powers not expressly stated in the Constitution, even when their actions are contrary to laws passed by Congress. Subsequent sections explore the scope of treaties and executive agreements, the war power, and questions of citizenship.

A. EXTERNAL AND INTERNAL AFFAIRS

Those who believe that the lion's share of authority in foreign affairs belongs with the President rely heavily on Justice Sutherland's decision in *United States* v. *Curtiss-Wright Corp.* (1936). The case could have been confined to a single question: May Congress delegate to the President the authority to prohibit the shipment of arms or munitions to any country in South America whenever he decided that the material would promote domestic violence? At every stage the case was about congressional power, not presidential power. The Court agreed that legislation over the international field may accord to the President greater discretion than would be admissible for domestic affairs. But Sutherland went beyond the issue of delegation to add pages of obiter dicta to describe the far-reaching dimensions of executive power in foreign affairs. He assigned to the President a number of powers not found in the Constitution. *Curtiss-Wright* is cited frequently to justify not only broad grants of legislative power to the President but also the exercise of inherent, extraconstitutional powers. UNITED STATES v. CURTISS-WRIGHT CORP., 299 U.S. 304 (1936).

Curtiss-Wright echoed positions Sutherland had taken as a United States Senator and member of the Senate Foreign Relations Committee. It closely tracks his article, "The Internal and External Powers of the National Government," printed as Senate Document No. 417 in 1910. The article claimed that national sovereignty "inhered in the United States from the beginning" rather than in the colonies or the states. His book, *Constitutional Power and World Affairs* (1919), promoted the same themes.

In *Curtiss-Wright*, Sutherland refers to Congressman John Marshall's remark in 1800 that the President is the "sole organ of the nation in its external relations," implying that the President makes foreign policy unilaterally. That would be powerful evidence, given Marshall's elevation a year later to be Chief Justice of the Supreme Court. However, when read in context, Marshall only meant that the President communicates to other nations U.S. foreign policy *after* it has been adopted jointly by the executive and legislative branches (either by treaty or statute). Marshall clearly meant that the President was the "sole organ" in *implementing*, not formulating, foreign policy (see box on next page).

Sutherland believed that foreign and domestic affairs were fundamentally different because the powers of external sovereignty passed from the Crown "not to the colonies severally, but to the colonies in their collective and corporate capacity as the United States of America." However, from

Marshall's "Sole Organ" Remark

[*The following statement by Congressman John Marshall, during legislative debate in 1800, came in response to a proposal to impeach or censure President John Adams for interfering with judicial proceedings underway in the trial of Jonathan Robbins. Pursuant to an extradition treaty, Adams had agreed to return Robbins to England.*]

The [dispute] was in its nature a national demand made upon the nation. The parties were the two nations. They cannot come into court to litigate their claims, nor can a court decide on them. Of consequence, the demand is not a case for judicial cognizance.

The President is the sole organ of the nation in its external relations, and its sole representative with foreign nations. Of consequence, the demand of a foreign nation can only be made on him.

He possesses the whole Executive power. He holds and directs the force of the nation. Of consequence, any act to be performed by the force of the nation is to be performed through him.

He is charged to execute the laws. A treaty is declared to be a law. He must then execute a treaty, where he, and he alone, possesses the means of executing it.

The treaty, which is a law, enjoins the performance of a particular object. The person who is to perform this object is marked out by the Constitution, since the person is named who conducts the foreign intercourse, and is to take care that the laws be faithfully executed. The means by which it is to be performed, the force of the nation, are in the hands of this person. Ought not this person to perform the object, although the particular mode of using the means has not been prescribed? Congress, unquestionably, may prescribe the mode, and Congress may devolve on others the whole execution of the contract; but, till this be done, it seems the duty of the Executive department to execute the contract by any means it possesses.

SOURCE: Annals of Cong., 6th Cong. 613–14 (1800).

1774 to 1788 the colonies and states operated as sovereign entities, not as parts of a collective body. They acted free and independent of one another. The creation of the Continental Congress did not disturb the sovereign capacity of the states to make treaties, borrow money, solicit arms, lay embargoes, collect tariff duties, and conduct separate military campaigns.

Even if the power of external sovereignty had somehow passed intact from the Crown to the "United States," the Constitution divides that power between Congress and the President. The President and the Senate share the treaty power. Congress has the responsibility to raise and support military forces, to lay and collect duties on foreign trade, to regulate commerce with foreign nations, and to fund the armed services. Contemporary conditions make it increasingly difficult to draw a crisp line between external and internal affairs. Oil embargoes imposed by foreign governments immediately impact America's economy, raising the price at home and producing long lines at the neighborhood gas station. The President's decision to ship or withhold wheat from a foreign nation has a major effect on farming communities. Trade policies are both international and domestic in scope. As President Bush noted in 1991: "I guess my bottom line ... is you can't separate foreign policy from domestic." Public Papers of the Presidents, 1991, II, at 1629. President Clinton, in his first inaugural address in 1993, similarly remarked: "There is no longer a clear division between what is foreign and what is domestic." There never was.

The contemporary Supreme Court continues to look more sympathetically on delegation that involves external affairs. Even Chief Justice Rehnquist, a strong advocate of the nondelegation doctrine, adopted a different standard for international crises, "the nature of which Congress can hardly have been expected to anticipate in any detail." Dames & Moore v. Regan, 453 U.S. 654, 669 (1981). He agreed that Congress "is permitted to legislate both with greater breadth and with greater flexibility" when a statute governs military affairs. Rostker v. Goldberg, 453 U.S. 57, 66 (1981), quoting Parker

v. Levy, 417 U.S. 733, 756 (1974). More importantly, *Curtiss-Wright* is used to support the existence of independent, implied, and inherent powers for the President.[1]

Officials of the Reagan administration took a number of actions known collectively as the Iran-Contra affair: sending arms to Iran, diverting funds to the Contras in Nicaragua, and soliciting funds from private donors and foreign countries because Congress refused to appropriate funds for the Contras. Some defenders of these executive actions pointed to *Curtiss-Wright* as legal justification. A report, prepared jointly by the House and the Senate, rejects this reliance on *Curtiss-Wright* (see reading "Congress Interprets *Curtiss-Wright:* The Iran-Contra Report"). In the period following the terrorist attacks of 9/11, the Bush administration relied repeatedly on what it considered "inherent" presidential powers to act in the absence of law and sometimes against it, citing the "sole organ" doctrine of *Curtiss-Wright* among other arguments (discussed later in this chapter).

Right to Travel

Claiming both constitutional and statutory authority, Presidents and their administrations use the control over passports and visas to restrict travel by foreigners to this country and by Americans to other countries. Administrations advance a number of foreign policy and national security justifications, while opponents of restraints on foreign travel raise First Amendment issues of access to information and right of association. There is broad agreement among both groups that the government is justified in banning travel to regions affected by pestilence or war.

The interesting fact about these cases is that the Court generally decides them on statutory grounds. This keeps the door fully open for participation by Congress and the President in shaping the law on the right to travel. In 1958 the Supreme Court reviewed the State Department's action in withholding passports from several Americans because of their alleged association with the Communist Party. Although the Court referred to the right to travel as part of a citizen's constitutional "liberty" that could not be denied without due process of law, it avoided the constitutional issue and held that the Secretary of State had exceeded the authority delegated to him by Congress. Kent v. Dulles, 357 U.S. 116 (1958); Dayton v. Dulles, 357 U.S. 144 (1958). Legislation was introduced to strengthen the authority of the Secretary of State, but none of the bills passed Congress.

In 1964 the Court struck down a congressional provision that prevented individuals from applying for a passport if they belonged to a "Communist-action" or "Communist-front" organization. If they already held a passport, it would be revoked. The Court decided that the provision was too broad and indiscriminate in restricting the right to travel. Aptheker v. Secretary of State, 378 U.S. 500 (1964). A year later, the Court upheld the authority of the State Department to impose *area* restrictions (in this case, involving Cuba). The Court argued that it was permissible to deny all citizens the right to travel to a certain country, in contrast to the 1958 case which involved an individual's belief or association. Zemel v. Rusk, 381 U.S. 1 (1965).

Subsequent cases circumscribed the State Department's authority to impose area restrictions.[2] In 1978 Congress passed legislation to limit area restrictions. In the spirit of the Helsinki Accords of 1975, which encouraged the free movement of people and ideas, Congress adopted the following amendment to the Passport Act: "Unless authorized by law, a passport may not be designated as restricted for travel to or for use in any country other than a country with which the United States is at war, where armed hostilities are in progress, or where there is imminent danger to the public health or the physical safety of United States travelers." 92 Stat. 971, § 124 (1978); 22 U.S.C. § 211a.

---

1. United States v. Pink, 315 U.S. 203, 229 (1942); Knauff v. Shaughnessy, 338 U.S. 537, 542 (1950); United States v. Mazurie, 419 U.S. 544, 566–67 (1975). See Louis Fisher, "Presidential Inherent Power: The 'Sole Organ' Doctrine," 37 Pres. Stud. Q. 139 (2007).

2. On area restrictions, see also United States v. Laub, 385 U.S. 475 (1967); Travis v. United States, 385 U.S. 491 (1967); Lynd v. Rusk, 389 F.2d 940 (D.C. Cir. 1967). Congress can limit welfare payments to recipients who travel abroad for 30 days or more; Califano v. Aznavorian, 439 U.S. 170 (1978).

Recent cases have given broad support to executive restrictions on foreign travel. In 1981 the Court upheld the authority of the Secretary of State to revoke the passport of Philip Agee, a former CIA employee who had announced his intention to identify undercover CIA agents and intelligence sources in foreign countries. The Court said that the revocation inhibited Agee's actions, not his speech. The Secretary's decision was based on a departmental regulation, a broad interpretation of the 1978 amendments, and the "silence" of Congress in acquiescing to the Department's action. Specific authorization from Congress, said the Court, was not required. HAIG v. AGEE, 453 U.S. 280 (1981). The broadness of this ruling suggests that an administration may prevent the foreign travel of anyone who is apt to question or embarrass the President's foreign policy.

In 1984, the Court upheld (5 to 4) a Treasury Department regulation that prohibited general tourist and business travel to Cuba. The Reagan administration decided to retaliate against Cuba for its political and military interventions in Latin America and in Africa. Congress had passed the International Emergency Economic Powers Act in 1977 to limit the President's power, but the Court read the Act broadly to permit the sanctions against Cuba. Regan v. Wald, 468 U.S. 222 (1984).

In recent years Congress has revisited the McCarran-Walter Act of 1952, which kept aliens out of the country because of their political and economic beliefs. 66 Stat. 184–86 (1952). Under that authority, a number of noted writers and political figures have been denied entrance into the United States to speak. In 1990 Congress revised McCarran-Walter to make it more difficult to exclude aliens for their beliefs, statements, and associations. 104 Stat. 5071 (1990).

United States v. Curtiss-Wright Corp.

299 U.S. 304 (1936)

In 1935, in the *Panama Refining* and *Schechter* cases, the Supreme Court struck down the National Industrial Recovery Act and its delegation of legislative power to the President. The *Curtiss-Wright* case involves the delegation of legislative power to the President in foreign rather than domestic affairs. In 1934 Congress authorized the President to place an embargo on the sale of arms and munitions to countries engaged in armed conflict in South America if the President determined that an embargo would contribute to the establishment of peace. Justice Sutherland, writing for the Court, upheld the statute partly on the distinction he drew between external and internal affairs.

MR. JUSTICE SUTHERLAND delivered the opinion of the Court.

On January 27, 1936, an indictment was returned in the court below, the first count of which charges that appellees, beginning with the 29th day of May, 1934, conspired to sell in the United States certain arms of war, namely fifteen machine guns, to Bolivia, a country then engaged in armed conflict in the Chaco, in violation of the Joint Resolution of Congress approved May 28, 1934, and the provisions of a proclamation issued on the same day by the President of the United States pursuant to authority conferred by § 1 of the resolution.…

First. It is contended that by the Joint Resolution, the going into effect and continued operation of the resolution was conditioned (a) upon the President's judgment as to its beneficial effect upon the reestab-

lishment of peace between the countries engaged in armed conflict in the Chaco; (b) upon the making of a proclamation, which was left to his unfettered discretion, thus constituting an attempted substitution of the President's will for that of Congress; (c) upon the making of a proclamation putting an end to the operation of the resolution, which again was left to the President's unfettered discretion; and (d) further, that the extent of its operation in particular cases was subject to limitation and exception by the President, controlled by no standard. In each of these particulars, appellees urge that Congress abdicated its essential functions and delegated them to the Executive.

Whether, if the Joint Resolution had related solely to internal affairs it would be open to the challenge that it constituted an unlawful delegation of legislative power to the Executive, we find it unnecessary to determine. The whole aim of the resolution is to affect a situation entirely external to the United States, and falling within the category of foreign affairs. The determination which we are called to make, therefore, is whether the Joint Resolution, as applied to that situation, is vulnerable to attack under the rule that forbids a delegation of the lawmaking power. In other words, assuming (but not deciding) that the challenged delegation, if it were confined to internal affairs, would be invalid, may it nevertheless be sustained on the ground that its exclusive aim is to afford a remedy for a hurtful condition within foreign territory?

It will contribute to the elucidation of the question if we first consider the differences between the powers of the federal government in respect of foreign or external affairs and those in respect of domestic or internal affairs. That there are differences between them, and that these differences are fundamental, may not be doubted.

The two classes of powers are different, both in respect of their origin and their nature. The broad statement that the federal government can exercise no powers except those specifically enumerated in the Constitution, and such implied powers as are necessary and proper to carry into effect the enumerated powers, is categorically true only in respect of our internal affairs. In that field, the primary purpose of the Constitution was to carve from the general mass of legislative powers *then possessed by the states* such portions as it was thought desirable to vest in the federal government, leaving those not included in the enumeration still in the states. *Carter v. Carter Coal Co.*, 298 U.S. 238, 294. That this doctrine applies only to powers which the states had, is self evident. And since the states severally never possessed international powers, such powers could not have been carved from the mass of state powers but obviously were transmitted to the United States from some other source. During the colonial period, those powers were possessed exclusively by and were entirely under the control of the Crown. By the Declaration of Independence, "the Representatives of the United States of America" declared the United [not the several] Colonies to be free and independent states, and as such to have "full Power to levy War, conclude Peace, contract Alliances, establish Commerce and to do all other Acts and Things which Independent States may of right do."

As a result of the separation from Great Britain by the colonies acting as a unit, the powers of external sovereignty passed from the Crown not to the colonies severally, but to the colonies in their collective and corporate capacity as the United States of America. Even before the Declaration, the colonies were a unit in foreign affairs, acting through a common agency—namely the Continental Congress, composed of delegates from the thirteen colonies. That agency exercised the powers of war and peace, raised an army, created a navy, and finally adopted the Declaration of Independence. Rulers come and go; governments end and forms of government change; but sovereignty survives. A political society cannot endure without a supreme will somewhere. Sovereignty is never held in suspense. When, therefore, the external sovereignty of Great Britain in respect of the colonies ceased, it immediately passed to the Union. *See Penhallow* v. *Doane*, 3 Dall. 54, 80–81. That fact was given practical application almost at once. The treaty of peace, made on September 23, 1783, was concluded between his Brittanic Majesty and the "United States of America." 8 Stat. —European Treaties—80.

The Union existed before the Constitution, which was ordained and established among other things to form "a more perfect Union." Prior to that event, it is clear that the Union, declared by the Articles of Confederation to be "perpetual," was the sole possessor of external sovereignty and in the Union it remained without change save in so far as the Constitution in express terms qualified its exercise....

[*Sutherland neglected to point out that American states did indeed exercise sovereign powers after the break with England. The creation of the Continental Congress did not disturb the sovereign power of states to make treaties, borrow money, solicit arms, lay embargoes, collect tariff duties, and conduct separate military campaigns. The Supreme Court has recognized that the American colonies, upon their separation from England, exercised the powers of a sovereign and independent government. United States v. California, 332 U.S. 19, 31 (1947); Texas v. White, 74 U.S. 700, 725 (1869); M'Ilvaine v. Coxe's Lessee, 8 U.S. (4 Cr.) 209, 212 (1808); Ware v. Hylton, 3 U.S. (3 Dall.) 199, 222–24 (1796).*]

Not only, as we have shown, is the federal power over external affairs in origin and essential character different from that over internal affairs, but participation in the exercise of the power is significantly limited. In this vast external realm, with its important, complicated, delicate and manifold problems, the President alone has the power to speak or listen as a representative of the nation. He *makes* treaties with the advice and consent of the Senate; but he alone negotiates. Into the field of negotiation the

Senate cannot intrude; and Congress itself is power-less to invade it. As Marshall said in his great argument of March 7, 1800, in the House of Representatives, "The President is the sole organ of the nation in its external relations, and its sole representative with foreign nations." Annals, 6th Cong., col. 613....

[*Sutherland exaggerates the President's exclusive power to negotiate treaties. In his book, Constitutional Powers and World Affairs (1919), he recognized that Senators did in fact participate in the negotiation phase and that Presidents had often acceded to this "practical construction" (p. 123). Far from being a "presidential monopoly," treaty negotiation frequently includes not only Senators but members of the House. Fisher, 39 Pres. Stud. Q. 144 (2008).*]

It is important to bear in mind that we are here dealing not alone with an authority vested in the President by an exertion of legislative power, but with such an authority plus the very delicate, plenary and exclusive power of the President as the sole organ of the federal government in the field of international relations—a power which does not require as a basis for its exercise an act of Congress, but which, of course, like every other governmental power, must be exercised in subordination to the ap-plicable provisions of the Constitution. It is quite apparent that if, in the maintenance of our international relations, embarrassment—perhaps serious embarrassment—is to be avoided and success for our aims achieved, congressional legislation which is to be made effective through negotiation and inquiry within the international field must often accord to the President a degree of discretion and freedom from statutory restriction which would not be admissible were domestic affairs alone involved. Moreover, he, not Congress, has the better opportunity of knowing the conditions which prevail in foreign countries, and especially is this true in time of war....

The judgment of the court below must be reversed and the cause remanded for further proceedings in accordance with the foregoing opinion.

Reversed.

MR. JUSTICE MCREYNOLDS does not agree. He is of opinion that the court below reached the right conclusion and its judgment ought to be affirmed.

MR. JUSTICE STONE took no part in the consideration or decision of this case.

Congress Interprets *Curtiss-Wright*:
The Iran-Contra Report

Several witnesses before the Iran-Contra Committees in 1987 testified that the actions by the Reagan administration could be justified in terms of *United States* v. *Curtiss-Wright Corp.* (1936), which they claimed recognized broad powers for the President in foreign affairs. The majority report rejected this position. The passage below appeared in *Iran-Contra Affair*, H. Rept. No. 100-433, S. Rept. No. 100-216, 100th Cong., 1st Sess., 388–90 (November 1987).

In urging a broad interpretation of presidential power, various witnesses before these Committees invoked the Supreme Court's 1936 decision in *United States* v. *Curtiss-Wright Export Corporation.* Their reliance on this case is misplaced.

In *Curtiss-Wright,* Congress, by statute, had delegated to the President the power to prohibit the sale of arms to countries in an area of South America if the President believed the prohibition would promote peace. The Curtiss-Wright Corporation claimed that the power to make this determination was a legislative power that Congress could not delegate to the President.

Witnesses at the hearings misread this case to justify their claim that the President had broad inherent foreign policy powers to the virtual exclusion of Congress. *Curtiss-Wright* did not present any such issue. The case involved the question of the powers of the President in foreign policy where Congress expressly authorizes him to act; it did not involve the question of the President's foreign policy powers when Congress expressly forbids him to act.

In *Curtiss-Wright,* the Court upheld broad delegations by Congress of power to the President in matters of foreign affairs. Writing for the Court, Justice Sutherland said that legislation within "the international field must often accord to the President a degree of discretion and freedom from statutory restriction which would not be admissible were domestic affairs alone involved."

In language frequently seized on by those seeking to claim that the President's role in foreign policy is exclusive, Justice Sutherland noted that the President was acting not only with a delegation of power by the legislature, but also with certain powers the Constitution gave directly to him:

"It is important to bear in mind that we are here dealing not alone with an authority vested in the President by an exertion of legislative power, but with such an authority plus the very delicate, plenary and exclusive power of the President as the sole organ of the federal government in the field of international relations — a power which does not require as a basis for its exercise an act of Congress, but which, of course, like every other governmental power, must be exercised in subordination to applicable provisions of the Constitution."

Some have tried to interpret this passage as stating that the President may act in foreign affairs against the will of Congress. But that is not what it says. As Justice Jackson later observed, the most that can be drawn from Justice Sutherland's language is the intimation "that the President might act in external affairs without congressional authority, but not that he might act contrary to an Act of Congress." More recently, in *Dames & Moore* v. *Regan*, the Supreme Court cautioned that the broad language in *Curtiss-Wright* must be viewed only in context of that case. Writing for the majority, Justice (now Chief Justice) Rehnquist expressed the Court's view of the appropriate relationship between the executive and the legislative branches in the conduct of foreign policy:

"When the President acts pursuant to an express or implied authorization from Congress, he exercises not only his powers but also those delegated by Congress. In such a case the executive action 'would be supported by the strongest presumptions and widest latitude of judicial interpretation, and the burden of persuasion would rest heavily upon any who might attack it.'... When the President acts in the absence of congressional authorization he may enter a 'zone of twilight in which he and Congress may have concurrent authority, or in which its distribution is uncertain.'... In such a case, the analysis becomes more complicated, and the validity of the President's action, at least so far as separation-of-powers principles are concerned, hinges on a consideration of all the circumstances which might shed light on the views of the Legislative Branch toward such action, including 'congressional inertia, indifference or quiescence.'... Finally, when the President acts in contravention of the will of Congress, 'his power is at its lowest ebb' and the Court can sustain his actions 'only by disabling the Congress from action on the subject.'"

Similarly, in 1981, the D.C. Circuit cautioned against undue reliance on the quoted passage from *Curtiss-Wright:* "To the extent that denominating the President as the 'sole organ' of the United States in international affairs constitutes a blanket endorsement of plenary Presidential power over any matter extending beyond the borders of this country, we reject that characterization."

In calling the President the "sole organ" of the Nation in its relations with other countries, Justice Sutherland quoted from a speech by John Marshall in 1800 when Marshall was a Member of the House of Representatives: "As Marshall said in his great argument of March 7, 1800, in the House of Representatives, 'The President is the sole organ of the nation in its external relations, and its sole representative with foreign nations.' Annals, 6th Cong., col. 613."

The reader might assume from this passage that Marshall advocated an exclusive, independent power for the President in the area of foreign affairs, free from legislative control. When his statement is placed in the context of the "great argument of March 7, 1800," however, it is clear that Marshall regarded the President as simply carrying out the law as established by statute or treaty. The House had been debating a decision by President John Adams to turn over to England a person charged with murder. Some members thought the President should be impeached for encroaching upon the judiciary, since the case was already pending in court. Marshall replied that President Adams was executing a treaty approved by the Senate that had the force of law.

Haig v. Agee

453 U.S. 280 (1981)

In this case, the "right to travel" collides with the President's interests over foreign policy and national security. Philip Agee, a former employee of the Central Intelligence Agency, had announced a campaign to expose CIA officers and agents. His activities abroad resulted in the

identification of CIA agents and intelligence sources in foreign countries. After Secretary of State Alexander Haig revoked his passport, Agee filed suit claiming that the regulation cited by Haig had not been authorized by Congress and was impermissibly overbroad. Agee also argued that the passport revocation violated his freedom to travel and his First Amendment right to criticize governmental policies. Moreover, he charged that the failure to accord him a hearing before the revocation constituted a violation of procedural due process under the Fifth Amendment. The district court and the D.C. Circuit agreed that the regulation exceeded Haig's authority.

CHIEF JUSTICE BURGER delivered the opinion of the Court.

The question presented is whether the President, acting through the Secretary of State, has authority to revoke a passport on the ground that the holder's activities in foreign countries are causing or are likely to cause serious damage to the national security or foreign policy of the United States.

I

A

Philip Agee, an American citizen, currently resides in West Germany. From 1957 to 1968, he was employed by the Central Intelligence Agency. He held key positions in the division of the Agency that is responsible for covert intelligence gathering in foreign countries. In the course of his duties at the Agency. Agee received training in clandestine operations, including the methods used to protect the identities of intelligence employees and sources of the United States overseas. He served in undercover assignments abroad and came to know many Government employees and other persons supplying information to the United States. The relationships of many of these people to our Government are highly confidential; many are still engaged in intelligence gathering.

In 1974, Agee called a press conference in London to announce his "campaign to fight the United States CIA wherever it is operating." He declared his intent "to expose CIA officers and agents and to take the measures necessary to drive them out of the countries where they are operating." Since 1974, Agee has, by his own assertion, devoted consistent effort to that program, and he has traveled extensively in other countries in order to carry it out. To identify CIA personnel in a particular country, Agee goes to the target country and consults sources in local diplomatic circles whom he knows from his prior service in the United States Government. He recruits collaborators and trains them in clandestine techniques designed to expose the "cover" of CIA employees and sources. Agee and his collaborators have repeatedly and publicly identified individuals

and organizations located in foreign countries as undercover CIA agents, employees, or sources. The record reveals that the identifications divulge classified information, violate Agee's express contract not to make any public statements about Agency matters without prior clearance by the Agency, have prejudiced the ability of the United States to obtain intelligence, and have been followed by episodes of violence against the persons and organizations identified.

In December 1979, the Secretary of State revoked Agee's passport and delivered an explanatory notice to Agee in West Germany. The notice states in part:

"The Department's action is predicated upon a determination made by the Secretary under the provisions of [22 CFR] Section 51.70 (b)(4) that your activities abroad are causing or are likely to cause serious damage to the national security or the foreign policy of the United States...."

The notice also advised Agee of his right to an administrative hearing and offered to hold such a hearing in West Germany on 5 days' notice.

Agee at once filed suit against the Secretary. He alleged that the regulation invoked by the Secretary, 22 CFR § 51.70 (b)(4) (1980), has not been authorized by Congress and is invalid; that the regulation is impermissibly overbroad; that the revocation prior to a hearing violated his Fifth Amendment right to procedural due process; and that the revocation violated a Fifth Amendment liberty interest in a right to travel and a First Amendment right to criticize Government policies. He sought declaratory and injunctive relief, and he moved for summary judgment on the question of the authority to promulgate the regulation and on the constitutional claims.

[*The district court held that the regulation exceeded the statutory powers of the Secretary under the Passport Act and ordered the Secretary to restore Agee's passport. The D.C. Circuit held that the Secretary was required to show that Congress had authorized the regulation either by an express delegation or by an im-*

plied approval. The Court found that the regulation exceeded authority granted by Congress.]

II

The principal question before us is whether the statute authorizes the action of the Secretary pursuant to the policy announced by the challenged regulation.

A
1

Although the historical background that we develop later is important, we begin with the language of the statute.... The Passport Act of 1926 provides in pertinent part:

"The Secretary of State may grant and issue passports, and cause passports to be granted, issued, and verified in foreign countries by diplomatic representatives of the United States ... under such rules as the President shall designate and prescribe for and on behalf of the United States, and no other person shall grant, issue, or verify such passports." 22 U.S.C. § 211a (1976 ed., Supp. IV).

This language is unchanged since its original enactment in 1926.

The Passport Act does not in so many words confer upon the Secretary a power to revoke a passport. Nor, for that matter, does it expressly authorize denials of passport applications. Neither, however, does any statute expressly limit those powers. It is beyond dispute that the Secretary has the power to deny a passport for reasons not specified in the statutes. For example, in *Kent* v. *Dulles,* 357 U.S. 116 (1958), the Court recognized congressional acquiescence in Executive policies of refusing passports to applicants "participating in illegal conduct, trying to escape the toils of the law, promoting passport frauds, or otherwise engaging in conduct which would violate the laws of the United States." *Id.,* at 127. In *Zemel,* the Court held that "the weightiest considerations of national security" authorized the Secretary to restrict travel to Cuba at the time of the Cuban missile crisis. 381 U.S., at 16. Agee concedes that if the Secretary may deny a passport application for a certain reason, he may revoke a passport on the same ground.

2

Particularly in light of the "broad rule-making authority granted in the [1926] Act," *Zemel,* 381 U.S., at 12, a consistent administrative construction of that statute must be followed by the courts "'unless there are compelling indications that it is

wrong.'" *E. I. du Pont de Nemours & Co.* v. *Collins,* 432 U.S. 46, 55 (1977), quoting *Red Lion Broadcasting Co.* v. *FCC,* 395 U.S. 367, 381 (1969); see *Zemel, supra,* at 11. This is especially so in the areas of foreign policy and national security, where congressional silence is not to be equated with congressional disapproval. In *United States* v. *Curtiss-Wright Export Corp.,* 299 U.S. 304 (1936), the volatile nature of problems confronting the Executive in foreign policy and national defense was underscored....

Matters intimately related to foreign policy and national security are rarely proper subjects for judicial intervention. In *Harisiades* v. *Shaughnessy,* 342 U.S. 580 (1952), the Court observed that matters relating "to the conduct of foreign relations ... are so exclusively entrusted to the political branches of government as to be largely immune from judicial inquiry or interference." *Id.,* at 589; accord, *Chicago & Southern Air Lines, Inc.* v. *Waterman S.S. Corp.,* 333 U.S. 103, 111 (1948).

III

. . .

Revocation of a passport undeniably curtails travel, but the freedom to travel abroad with a "letter of introduction" in the form of a passport issued by the sovereign is subordinate to national security and foreign policy considerations; as such, it is subject to reasonable governmental regulation....

We reverse the judgment of the Court of Appeals and remand for further proceedings consistent with this opinion.

Reversed and remanded.

JUSTICE BLACKMUN, concurring....

JUSTICE BRENNAN, with whom JUSTICE MARSHALL joins, dissenting....

II

This is not a complicated case. The Court has twice articulated the proper mode of analysis for determining whether Congress has delegated to the Executive Branch the authority to deny a passport under the Passport Act of 1926. *Zemel* v. *Rusk,* 381 U.S. 1 (1965); *Kent* v. *Dulles,* 357 U.S. 116 (1958). The analysis is hardly confusing, and I expect that had the Court faithfully applied it, today's judgment would affirm the decision below.

... [C]learly neither *Zemel* nor *Kent* holds that a longstanding Executive *policy* or *construction* is sufficient proof that Congress has implicitly authorized the Secretary's action. The cases hold that an administrative *practice* must be demonstrated; in fact

Kent unequivocally states that mere *construction* by the Executive—no matter how longstanding and consistent—is *not* sufficient....

... Only when Congress had maintained its silence in the face of a consistent and substantial pattern of actual passport denials or revocations—

where the parties will presumably object loudly, perhaps through legal action, to the Secretary's exercise of discretion—can this Court be sure that Congress is aware of the Secretary's actions and has implicitly approved that exercise of discretion....

B. AN EXECUTIVE PREROGATIVE?

Theodore Roosevelt and William Howard Taft supposedly championed rival theories of presidential power. Roosevelt claimed it was the President's right and duty to do "anything that the needs of the Nation demanded, unless such action was forbidden by the Constitution or by the laws." Theodore Roosevelt, an Autobiography 389 (1919). Through this theory the President could enter and occupy any vacuum. In contrast, Taft maintained that the President "can exercise no power which cannot be fairly and reasonably traced to some specific grant of power or justly implied and included within such express grant as proper and necessary to its exercise. Such specific grant must be either in the Federal Constitution or in an act of Congress passed in pursuance thereof." William Howard Taft, Our Chief Magistrate and His Powers 139–40 (1916).

This passage appears to make Taft an advocate of enumerated powers, but he did not believe that every use of presidential power required a specific constitutional or statutory grant. He recognized the need for implied powers: powers that can be "fairly and reasonably traced" or "justly implied." He even adds a "necessary and proper" clause for the President. His book on the presidency promoted a broad view of executive power: incidental powers to remove officers, inferable powers to protect the lives and property of American citizens living abroad, powers created by custom, and emergency powers (such as Lincoln's suspension of the writ of habeas corpus during the Civil War). Taft concluded that executive power was limited "so far as it is possible to limit such a power consistent with that discretion and promptness of action that are essential to preserve the interests of the public in times of emergency, or legislative neglect or inaction."

Lincoln's Initiatives

Taft's formulation follows what is known as the Lockean prerogative: the executive's power to act for the public good in the absence of law and sometimes even against it. Lincoln claimed this authority in April 1861 while Congress was in recess. He issued proclamations calling forth state militias, suspended the writ of habeas corpus, and placed a blockade on the rebellious states. On July 4, 1861, he told Congress that his actions, "whether strictly legal or not," were necessary for the public good. 7 Richardson, Messages and Papers of the Presidents 3225. Congress subsequently passed a statute legalizing his proclamations "as if they had been issued and done under the previous express authority and direction of the Congress of the United States." 12 Stat. 326 (1861). Legislative sanction is an essential ingredient of the prerogative. In times of emergency, the executive may act outside the law but must submit his case to the legislature and the people for approval (see box on next page).

Lincoln's suspension of the writ of habeas corpus ran directly counter to a decision by Chief Justice Taney, sitting as a circuit judge in Baltimore. Taney concluded that Lincoln had no power to issue the writ and that the prisoner, John Merryman, should be set free. But Taney recognized that he could not prevail in a direct confrontation with the President on this issue during an emergency period. With some resignation, Taney said he exercised "all the power which the constitution and laws confer upon me, but that power has been resisted by a force too strong for me to overcome." Ex parte Merryman, 17 Fed. Case No. 9,487 (1861), at 153. Lincoln had the legal support of his Attorney General. 10 Op. Att'y Gen. 74, 81 (1861).

Lincoln's Exercise of the Emergency Power

... These measures, whether strictly legal or not, were ventured upon under what appeared to be a popular demand and a public necessity; trusting then as now that Congress would readily ratify them. It is believed that nothing has been done beyond the constitutional competency of Congress.

Soon after the first call for militia, it was considered a duty to authorize the commanding general in proper cases, according to his discretion, to suspend the privilege of the writ of *habeas corpus,* or, in other words, to arrest and detain, without resort to the ordinary processes and forms of law, such individuals as he might deem dangerous to the public safety. This authority has purposely been exercised but very sparingly. Nevertheless, the legality and propriety of what has been done under it are questioned, and the attention of the country has been called to the proposition that one who is sworn to "take care that the laws be faithfully executed" should not himself violate them. Of course some consideration was given to the questions of power and propriety before this matter was acted upon. The whole of the laws which were required to be faithfully executed were being resisted, and failing of execution in nearly one third of the States. Must they be allowed to finally fail of execution, even had it been perfectly clear that by the use of the means necessary to their execution some single law, made in such extreme tenderness of the citizen's liberty, that practically it relieves more of the guilty than of the innocent, should to a very limited extent be violated? To state the question more directly: are all the laws *but one* to go unexecuted, and the Government itself go to pieces, lest that one be violated? Even in such a case, would not the official oath be broken if the government should be overthrown, when it was believed that disregarding the single law would tend to preserve it? [*Here Lincoln explains why it was appropriate for him to suspend the writ of habeas corpus, in a "dangerous emergency," even though the language for suspension appears in Article I.*]

No more extended argument is now offered, as an opinion, at some length, will probably be presented by the Attorney General. Whether there shall be any legislation upon the subject, and if any, what, is submitted entirely to the better judgment of Congress.

SOURCE: Message to Congress, July 4, 1861.

Lincoln's use of emergency power to justify the blockade on Southern states was upheld by a sharply divided Supreme Court. In a 5 to 4 decision, the Court held that Lincoln could take the actions he did despite the absence of a declaration of war by Congress. The President was bound to meet the emergency "in the shape it presented itself, without waiting for Congress to baptize it with a name; and no name given to it by him or them could change the fact." THE PRIZE CASES, 2 Black (67 U.S.) 635, 669 (1863). Justice Grier in the decision and White House Counsel during oral argument both understood that the power to *initiate war against another country* was vested solely in Congress (see excerpts from the case reading). See also Louis Fisher, "Abraham Lincoln: Preserving the Union and the Constitution," 3 Albany Gov't L. Rev. 503 (2010).

Not until the war was over and Lincoln dead did the Supreme Court breathe some life into the privilege of the writ of habeas corpus. EX PARTE MILLIGAN, 4 Wall. (71 U.S.) 2 (1866). *Milligan* announced the principle that U.S. citizens may not be tried in military courts when civil courts are open and operating. That principle was undercut somewhat by the World War II case of *Ex parte Quirin* (see the section "Military Tribunals" under Section D in this chapter).

Although *Milligan* in contemporary times is generally considered a landmark case in defense of civil liberties, it was severely criticized at the time as a judicial threat to congressional actions taken after the Civil War as part of Reconstruction of the Southern states. In response to *Milligan,* Congress passed legislation to limit the Court's jurisdiction to hear cases involving martial law and military trials (see the section on withdrawing jurisdiction in the final chapter "Efforts to Curb the Court"). In the years immediately following the Civil War, the Court was somewhat reluctant to challenge the powers of commander in chief. Mississippi v. Johnson, 4 Wall. 475 (1867).

FDR, Truman, and Nixon

A notorious use of emergency power was President Roosevelt's decision during World War II to put a curfew on more than 100,000 Americans of Japanese descent (about two-thirds of them natural-born U.S. citizens) and later place them in detention camps. A unanimous Supreme Court sustained the curfew, although Justice Murphy remarked that it "bears a melancholy resemblance to the treatment accorded to the members of the Jewish race in Germany and in other parts of Europe." Hirabayashi v. United States, 320 U.S. 81 (1943). Putting Japanese Americans in detention camps split the Court, the Justices voting 6–3 to uphold this action. The dissents by Murphy and Jackson, objecting that the exclusion order resulted from racism, were particularly vehement. KOREMATSU v. UNITED STATES, 323 U.S. 214, 243 (1944).[3] Congress passed legislation in 1988 to offer the nation's apology for this tragic episode and to provide cash reparations to survivors and their families. 102 Stat. 903 (1988).

President Truman used the emergency power in 1952 to seize steel mills during the Korean War. The Supreme Court overturned his action, but the 6 to 3 decision revealed as many positions as there were Justices. All six Justices in the majority wrote separate opinions, each taking a slightly different view of emergency power. Only Justices Black and Douglas advocated a doctrine of express and enumerated powers. The other seven Justices, in four concurrences and three dissents, recognized that implied and emergency powers may be appropriately invoked. Jackson developed a theory of constitutional powers that had three scenarios. Presidential authority reaches its highest level when the President acts pursuant to congressional authorization. His power is at its "lowest ebb" when he takes measures incompatible with the will of Congress. In between these two categories lay a "zone of twilight" in which Congress neither grants nor denies authority. In such circumstances, "congressional inertia, indifference or quiescence may sometimes, at least as a practical matter, enable, if not invite, measures of independent presidential responsibility." YOUNGSTOWN CO. v. SAWYER, 343 U.S. 579, 637 (1952). Jackson's opinion underscores the fact that the Constitution is often shaped not by textual interpretations from the courts but by a political dialectic among the branches.

The concept of "national security" often becomes an umbrella term to justify a broad range of emergency actions by the President. The Nixon administration was especially active in invoking the term. It asked the courts to enjoin two newspapers from publishing the Pentagon Papers, a confidential report that the administration had prepared to study the origins and conduct of the Vietnam War. The report had been leaked to the newspapers, raising the question of prior restraint on a free press. The Supreme Court decided against the administration. The word "security," warned Justice Black, "is a broad, vague generality whose contours should not be invoked to abrogate the fundamental law embodied in the First Amendment." NEW YORK TIMES CO. v. UNITED STATES, 403 U.S. 713, 719 (1971). Erwin N. Griswold, who served as Solicitor General at the time of the Pentagon Papers case, and who claimed in oral argument that publication of the documents would damage national security, admitted in 1989 that no such damage had occurred (see Griswold reading). Although First Amendment freedoms were protected in the Pentagon Papers case, the Court upheld the right

---

3. See also Yasui v. United States, 320 U.S. 115 (1943); Ex parte Endo, 323 U.S. 283 (1944); Eugene V. Rostow, "The Japanese American Cases—A Disaster," 54 Yale L. J. 489 (1945); Nanette Dembitz, "Racial Discrimination and the Military Judgment: The Supreme Court's Korematsu and Endo Decisions," 45 Colum. L. Rev. 175 (1945); Peter Irons, Justice at War: The Story of the Japanese American Internment Cases (1983).

of the Central Intelligence Agency to require its employees to sign secrecy agreements promising not to publish information about the agency without the Director's prior approval. Snepp v. United States, 444 U.S. 507 (1980).

National Security Wiretaps

Beginning in the 1920s, a succession of administrations resorted to wiretapping for the purpose of controlling domestic crime and protecting national security. The Communications Act of 1934 made it a crime to intercept and divulge wire or radio communications, but President Roosevelt in 1940 instructed his Attorney General that wiretapping should continue for "grave matters involving the defense of the nation." Francis Biddle, In Brief Authority 167 (1962). The tension between the statute and Roosevelt's instruction was relieved in part by the practice of intercepting but not divulging communications or using them in court for evidence.

The Omnibus Crime Control Act of 1968 allowed domestic wiretaps if authorized by judicial warrants. The government claimed that warrantless surveillances for "national security" purposes were lawful as a reasonable exercise of presidential power. A section of the 1968 Act stated that nothing in the statute limited the President's constitutional power to protect against the overthrow of the government or against "any other clear and present danger to the structure or existence of the Government." A unanimous decision by the Supreme Court in 1972 held that the section merely disclaimed congressional intent to define presidential powers in matters affecting national security and did not authorize warrantless national security surveillances. Moreover, the Fourth Amendment required prior judicial approval for surveillances of *domestic* organizations. The Court carefully avoided the question of surveillances over foreign powers, whether within or outside the country. United States v. United States District Court, 407 U.S. 297 (1972).

Congress passed the Foreign Intelligence Surveillance Act (FISA) of 1978 to clarify the scope of presidential power. A court order was now required to engage in electronic surveillance within the United States for purposes of obtaining foreign intelligence information. A special surveillance court (the FISA Court), appointed by the Chief Justice, reviews applications submitted by government attorneys. 93 Stat. 1783 (1978). The statute specified that this process constituted the "exclusive means" for conducting national security surveillance, thus excluding any access to presidential inherent powers.

Following the terrorists attacks of 9/11 on the World Trade Center and the Pentagon, the Bush Administration requested new authority to protect the nation. The USA Patriot Act, enacted on October 26, 2001, gave federal officials new powers to track and intercept communications, both for law enforcement and foreign intelligence gathering purposes. In secret, the Administration ordered the National Security Agency (NSA) to work with private telecommunications companies to conduct a surveillance program outside of FISA, claiming inherent powers under Article II. The existence of this program was revealed by the *New York Times* in December 2005, precipitating a number of lawsuits in federal courts around the country. Congress passed legislation in 2008 to revise FISA and grant immunity to the telecoms that had cooperated with the illegal program.

The Prize Cases

2 Black (67 U.S.) 635 (1863)

Among other emergency actions in 1861, President Lincoln declared a blockade of ports controlled by persons in armed rebellion against the government. The owners of the captured ships and cargo (prize, or captured property), brought suit in federal court. To justify the blockade and seizure of neutral vessels, a state of war had to exist, but Congress had made no such dec-

laration. Under what constitutional authority did Lincoln act? Does a state of war require a formal declaration by Congress? Three Lincoln appointees—Swayne, Miller, and Davis—joined Grier and Wayne to uphold presidential power.

Mr. Justice GRIER. There are certain propositions of law which must necessarily affect the ultimate decision of these cases, and many others, which it will be proper to discuss and decide before we notice the special facts peculiar to each.

They are, 1st. Had the President a right to institute a blockade of ports in possession of persons in armed rebellion against the Government, on the principles of international law, as known and acknowledged among civilized States?

2d. Was the property of persons domiciled or residing within those States a proper subject of capture on the sea as "enemies' property?"

I. Neutrals have a right to challenge the existence of a blockade *de facto,* and also the authority of the party exercising the right to institute it. They have a right to enter the ports of a friendly nation for the purposes of trade and commerce, but are bound to recognize the rights of a belligerent engaged in actual war, to use this mode of coercion, for the purpose of subduing the enemy.

That a blockade *de facto* actually existed, and was formally declared and notified by the President on the 27th and 30th of April, 1861, is an admitted fact in these cases.

That the President, as the Executive Chief of the Government and Commander-in-chief of the Army and Navy, was the proper person to make such notification, has not been, and cannot be disputed.

The right of prize and capture has its origin in the "*jus belli,*" and is governed and adjudged under the law of nations. To legitimate the capture of a neutral vessel or property on the high seas, a war must exist *de facto,* and the neutral must have a knowledge or notice of the intention of one of the parties belligerent to use this mode of coercion against a port, city, or territory, in possession of the other.

Let us enquire whether, at the time this blockade was instituted, a state of war existed which would justify a resort to these means of subduing the hostile force.

War has been well defined to be, "That state in which a nation prosecutes its right by force."

… A civil war is never solemnly declared; it becomes such by its accidents—the number, power, and organization of the persons who originate and carry it on. When the party in rebellion occupy and hold in a hostile manner a certain portion of territory; have declared their independence; have cast off their allegiance; have organized armies; have commenced hostilities against their former sovereign, the world acknowledges them as belligerents, and the contest a *war…:*

As a civil war is never publicly proclaimed, *eo nomine,* against insurgents, its actual existence is a fact in our domestic history which the Court is bound to notice and to know.

The true test of its existence, as found in the writings of the sages of the common law, may be thus summarily stated: "When the regular course of justice is interrupted by revolt, rebellion, or insurrection, so that the Courts of Justice cannot be kept open, *civil war exists* and hostilities may be prosecuted on the same footing as if those opposing the Government were foreign enemies invading the land."

By the Constitution, Congress alone has the power to declare a national or foreign war. It cannot declare war against a State, or any number of States, by virtue of any clause in the Constitution. The Constitution confers on the President the whole Executive power. He is bound to take care that the laws be faithfully executed. He is Commander-in-chief of the Army and Navy of the United States, and of the militia of the several States when called into the actual service of the United States. He has no power to initiate or declare a war either against a foreign nation or a domestic State. [During oral argument, Richard Henry Dana, Jr. for the White House agreed that the President's power did not include "the right *to initiate a war, as a voluntary act of sovereignty.* That is vested only in Congress." 67 U.S. at 660.] But by the Acts of Congress of February 28th, 1795, and 3d of March, 1807, he is authorized to call out the militia and use the military and naval forces of the United States in case of invasion by foreign nations, and to suppress insurrection against the government of a State or of the United States.

If a war be made by invasion of a foreign nation, the President is not only authorized but bound to resist force by force. He does not initiate the war, but is bound to accept the challenge without waiting for any special legislative authority. And whether the hostile party be a foreign invader, or States organized in rebellion, it is none the less a war, … *Only*

This greatest of civil wars was not gradually developed by popular commotion, tumultuous assemblies, or local unorganized insurrections. However long may have been its previous conception, it nevertheless sprung forth suddenly from the parent brain, a Minerva in the full panoply of *war.* The President was bound to meet it in the shape it presented itself, without waiting for Congress to baptize it with a name; and no name given to it by him or them could change the fact.

. . .

Whether the President in fulfilling his duties, as Commander-in-chief, in suppressing an insurrection, has met with such armed hostile resistance, and a civil war of such alarming proportions as will compel him to accord to them the character of belligerents, is a question to be decided *by him,* and this Court must be governed by the decisions and acts of the political department of the Government to which this power was entrusted....

If it were necessary to the technical existence of a war, that it should have a legislative sanction, we find it in almost every act passed at the extraordinary session of the Legislature of 1861, which was wholly employed in enacting laws to enable the Government to prosecute the war with vigor and efficiency. And finally, in 1861, we find Congress *"ex majore cautela"* and in anticipation of such astute objections, passing an act "approving, legalizing, and making valid all the acts, proclamations, and orders of the President, &c., as if they had been *issued and done under the previous express authority* and direction of the Congress of the United States."

. . .

The objection made to this act of ratification, that it is *ex post facto,* and therefore unconstitutional and void, might possibly have some weight on the trial of an indictment in a criminal Court. But precedents from that source cannot be received as authoritative in a tribunal administering public and international law.

On this first question therefore we are of the opinion that the President had a right, *jure belli,* to institute a blockade of ports in possession of the States in rebellion, which neutrals are bound to regard.

[*The Court then decides whether the property of all persons residing within the territory of the states in rebellion, captured on the high seas, is to be treated as "enemies' property" whether the owner be in arms against the government or not.*]

Mr. Justice NELSON dissenting.

. . .

This power [*of announcing war*] in all civilized nations is regulated by the fundamental laws or municipal constitution of the country.

By our Constitution this power is lodged in Congress. Congress shall have power "to declare war, grant letters of marque and reprisal, and make rules concerning captures on land and water."

... But we are asked, what would become of the peace and integrity of the Union in case of an insurrection at home or invasion from abroad if this power could not be exercised by the President in the recess of Congress, and until that body could be assembled?

The framers of the Constitution fully comprehended this question, and provided for the contingency. Indeed, it would have been surprising if they had not, as a rebellion had occurred in the State of Massachusetts while the Convention was in session, and which had become so general that it was quelled only by calling upon the military power of the State. The Constitution declares that Congress shall have power "to provide for calling forth the militia to execute the laws of the Union, suppress insurrections, and repel invasions." Another clause, "that the President shall be Commander-in-chief of the Army and Navy of the United States, and of the militia of the several States when called into the actual service of the United States;" and, again, "He shall take care that the laws shall be faithfully executed." Congress passed laws on this subject in 1792 and 1795. 1 United States Laws, pp. 264, 424.

[*In 1807 Congress passed additional legislation authorizing the President to call forth the militia to suppress insurrection.*]

The Acts of 1795 and 1807 did not, and could not under the Constitution, confer on the President the power of declaring war against a State of this Union, or of deciding that war existed, and upon that ground authorize the capture and confiscation of the property of every citizen of the State whenever it was found on the waters.... This great power over the business and property of the citizen is reserved to the legislative department by the express words of the Constitution. It cannot be delegated or surrendered to the Executive....

... [T]his power belongs exclusively to the Congress of the United States, and, consequently, that the President had no power to set on foot a blockade under the law of nations, and that the capture of the vessel and cargo in this case, and in all cases before us in which the capture occurred before the 13th of July, 1861, for breach of blockade, or as enemies' property, are illegal and void, and that the decrees of condemnation should be reversed and the vessel and cargo restored.

Mr. Chief Justice TANEY, Mr. Justice CATRON and Mr. Justice CLIFFORD, concurred in the dissenting opinion of Mr. Justice NELSON.

Ex parte Milligan

4 Wall. (71 U.S.) 2 (1866) *After the war*

Lambdin P. Milligan, a U.S. citizen from Indiana, was arrested by the military in 1864 on charges of conspiracy, found guilty before a military tribunal, and sentenced to be hanged. He presented a petition of habeas corpus to the federal courts, asking to be discharged from unlawful imprisonment because the military had no jurisdiction over him. He insisted that he was entitled to trial by jury in a civilian court. The question was whether the President, in times of emergency, could suspend the writ of habeas corpus and declare martial law, and whether the tribunal had legal authority to punish Milligan.

Mr. Justice DAVIS delivered the opinion of the court.

On the 10th day of May, 1865, Lambdin P. Milligan presented a petition to the Circuit Court of the United States for the District of Indiana, to be discharged from an alleged unlawful imprisonment....

The controlling question in the case is this: Upon the *facts* stated in Milligan's petition, and the exhibits filed, had the military commission mentioned in it *jurisdiction,* legally, to try and sentence him? Milligan, not a resident of one of the rebellious states, or a prisoner of war, but a citizen of Indiana for twenty years past, and never in the military or naval service, is, while at his home, arrested by the military power of the United States, imprisoned, and, on certain criminal charges preferred against him, tried, convicted, and sentenced to be hanged by a military commission, organized under the direction of the military commander of the military district of Indiana. Had this tribunal the *legal* power and authority to try and punish this man?

[*The Court reviews such fundamental constitutional rights as grand jury, trial by jury, confrontation of witnesses against the accused, obtaining witnesses in the accused's favor, and assistance of counsel.*]

Time has proven the discernment of our ancestors; for even these provisions, expressed in such plain English words, that it would seem the ingenuity of man could not evade them, are *now,* after the lapse of more than seventy years, sought to be avoided. Those great and good men foresaw that troublous times would arise, when rulers and people would become restive under restraint, and seek by sharp and decisive measures to accomplish ends deemed just and proper; and that the principles of

constitutional liberty would be in peril, unless established by irrepealable law. The history of the world had taught them that what was done in the past might be attempted in the future. The Constitution of the United States is a law for rulers and people, equally in war and in peace, and covers with the shield of its protection all classes of men, at all times, and under all circumstances. No doctrine, involving more pernicious consequences, was ever invented by the wit of man than that any of its provisions can be suspended during any of the great exigencies of government. Such a doctrine leads directly to anarchy or despotism, but the theory of necessity on which it is based is false; for the government, within the Constitution, has all the powers granted to it, which are necessary to preserve its existence; as has been happily proved by the result of the great effort to throw off its just authority.

. . .

This court has judicial knowledge that in Indiana the Federal authority was always unopposed, and its courts always open to hear criminal accusations and redress grievances; and no usage of war could sanction a military trial there for any offence whatever of a citizen in civil life, in nowise connected with the military service. Congress could grant no such power; and to the honor of our national legislature be it said, it has never been provoked by the state of the country even to attempt its exercise. One of the plainest constitutional provisions was, therefore, infringed when Milligan was tried by a court not ordained and established by Congress, and not composed of judges appointed during good behavior.

. . .

* Unconstitutional

This nation, as experience has proved, cannot always remain at peace, and has no right to expect that it will always have wise and humane rulers, sincerely attached to the principles of the Constitution. Wicked men, ambitious of power, with hatred of liberty and contempt of law, may fill the place once occupied by Washington and Lincoln; and if this right is conceded, and the calamities of war again befall us, the dangers to human liberty are frightful to contemplate....

It is essential to the safety of every government that, in a great crisis, like the one we have just passed through, there should be a power somewhere of suspending the writ of *habeas corpus*.... The Constitution ... does not say after a writ of *habeas corpus* is denied a citizen, that he shall be tried otherwise than by the course of the common law; if it had intended this result, it was easy by the use of direct words to have accomplished it....

... Martial rule can never exist where the courts are open, and in the proper and unobstructed exercise of their jurisdiction....

The CHIEF JUSTICE delivered the following opinion.

[*He agrees that the civil court in Indiana had jurisdiction over Milligan, he was entitled to be released from military custody, and that the military commission had no jurisdiction.*]

But the opinion which has just been read goes further; and as we understand it, asserts not only that the military commission held in Indiana was not authorized by Congress, but that it was not in the power of Congress to authorize it; from which it may be thought to follow, that Congress has no power to indemnify the officers who composed the commission against liability in civil courts for acting as members of it.

We cannot agree to this.

We agree in the proposition that no department of the government of the United States — neither President, nor Congress, nor the Courts — possesses any power not given by the Constitution.

We assent, fully, to all that is said, in the opinion, of the inestimable value of the trial by jury, and of the other constitutional safeguards of civil liberty. And we concur, also, in what is said of the writ of *habeas corpus,* and of its suspension, with two reservations: (1.) That, in our judgment, when the writ is suspended, the Executive is authorized to arrest as well as to detain; and (2.) that there are cases in which, the privilege of the writ being suspended, trial and punishment by military commission, in states where civil courts are open, may be authorized by Congress, as well as arrest and detention.

We think that Congress had power, though not exercised, to authorize the military commission which was held in Indiana....

Mr. Justice WAYNE, Mr. Justice SWAYNE, and Mr. Justice MILLER concur with me in these views.

Korematsu v. United States

323 U.S. 214 (1944)

Under authority of President Roosevelt's Executive Order 9066 and a congressional statute enacted in 1942, the Commanding General of the Western Defense Command issued an order directing the exclusion of all Japanese-Americans from a West Coast military area. Exclusion meant imprisonment in barbed wire stockades, called assembly centers, until the individuals could be transported inland to "relocation centers" under military guard. The military order, covering both aliens and U.S. citizens, was based on the belief of Commanding General J.L. DeWitt that all individuals of Japanese descent were "subversive" and belonged to an "enemy race" whose "racial strains are undiluted." Fred Korematsu, an American citizen of Japanese descent, was convicted for violating the exclusion order. His conviction was affirmed by the Ninth Circuit.

Mr. Justice Black delivered the opinion of the Court.

The petitioner, an American citizen of Japanese descent, was convicted in a federal district court for remaining in San Leandro, California, a "Military Area," contrary to Civilian Exclusion Order No. 34 of the Commanding General of the Western Command, U. S. Army, which directed that after May 9, 1942, all persons of Japanese ancestry should be excluded from that area. No question was raised as to petitioner's loyalty to the United States. The Circuit Court of Appeals affirmed, and the importance of the constitutional question involved caused us to grant certiorari.

It should be noted, to begin with, that all legal restrictions which curtail the civil rights of a single racial group are immediately suspect. That is not to say that all such restrictions are unconstitutional. It is to say that courts must subject them to the most rigid scrutiny. Pressing public necessity may sometimes justify the existence of such restrictions; racial antagonism never can.

. . .

Exclusion Order No. 34, which the petitioner knowingly and admittedly violated, was one of a number of military orders and proclamations, all of which were substantially based upon Executive Order No. 9066, 7 Fed. Reg. 1407. That order, issued after we were at war with Japan, declared that "the successful prosecution of the war requires every possible protection against espionage and against sabotage to national-defense material, national-defense premises, and national-defense utilities...."

One of the series of orders and proclamations, a curfew order, which like the exclusion order here was promulgated pursuant to Executive Order 9066, subjected all persons of Japanese ancestry in prescribed West Coast military areas to remain in their residences from 8 P.M. to 6 A.M. As is the case with the exclusion order here, that prior curfew order was designed as a "protection against espionage and against sabotage." In *Hirabayashi* v. *United States,* 320 U.S. 81, we sustained a conviction obtained for violation of the curfew order. The Hirabayashi conviction and this one thus rest on the same 1942 Congressional Act and the same basic executive and military orders, all of which orders were aimed at the twin dangers of espionage and sabotage.

... We upheld the curfew order as an exercise of the power of the government to take steps necessary to prevent espionage and sabotage in an area threatened by Japanese attack.

In the light of the principles we announced in the *Hirabayashi* case, we are unable to conclude that it was beyond the war power of Congress and the Executive to exclude those of Japanese ancestry from the West Coast war area at the time they did. True, exclusion from the area in which one's home is located is a far greater deprivation than constant confinement to the home from 8 P.M. to 6 A.M. Nothing short of apprehension by the proper military authorities of the gravest imminent danger to the public safety can constitutionally justify either. But exclusion from a threatened area, no less than curfew, has a definite and close relationship to the prevention of espionage and sabotage. The military authorities, charged with the primary responsibility of defending our shores, concluded that curfew provided inadequate protection and ordered exclusion. They did so, as pointed out in our *Hirabayashi* opinion, in accordance with Congressional authority to the military to say who should, and who should not, remain in the threatened areas.

... [W]e are not unmindful of the hardships imposed by it upon a large group of American citizens. Cf. *Ex parte Kawato,* 317 U.S. 69, 73. But hardships are part of war, and war is an aggregation of hardships. All citizens alike, both in and out of uniform, feel the impact of war in greater or lesser measure. Citizenship has its responsibilities as well as its privileges, and in time of of war the burden is always heavier....

It is said that we are dealing here with the case of imprisonment of a citizen in a concentration camp solely because of his ancestry, without evidence or inquiry concerning his loyalty and good disposition towards the United States. Our task would be simple, our duty clear, were this a case involving the imprisonment of a loyal citizen in a concentration camp because of racial prejudice. Regardless of the true nature of the assembly and relocation centers—and we deem it unjustifiable to call them concentration camps with all the ugly connotations that term implies—we are dealing specifically with nothing but an exclusion order. To cast this case into outlines of racial prejudice, without reference to the real military dangers which were presented, merely confuses the issue. Korematsu was not excluded from the Military Area because of hostility to him or his race. He *was* excluded because we are at war with the Japanese Empire, because the properly constituted military authorities feared an invasion of our West Coast and felt constrained to take proper security measures, because they decided that the military urgency of the situation demanded that all citizens of Japanese ancestry be segregated from the West Coast temporarily, and finally, because Congress, reposing its confidence in this time of war in our military leaders—as inevitably it must—determined that they should have the power to do just this. There was evidence of disloyalty on the part of some, the military authorities considered that the need for action was great, and time was short. We cannot—by availing ourselves of the calm perspective of hindsight—now say that at that time these actions were unjustified.

Affirmed.

MR. JUSTICE FRANKFURTER, concurring.

. . .

MR. JUSTICE ROBERTS.

I dissent, because I think the indisputable facts exhibit a clear violation of Constitutional rights.

This is not a case of keeping people off the streets at night as was *Hirabayashi* v. *United States*, 320 U.S. 81, nor a case of temporary exclusion of a citizen from an area for his own safety or that of the community, nor a case of offering him an opportunity to go temporarily out of an area where his presence might cause danger to himself or to his fellows. On the contrary, it is the case of convicting a citizen as a punishment for not submitting to imprisonment in a concentration camp, based on his ancestry, and solely because of his ancestry, without evidence or inquiry concerning his loyalty and good disposition towards the United States....

MR. JUSTICE MURPHY, dissenting.

This exclusion of "all persons of Japanese ancestry, both alien and non-alien," from the Pacific Coast area on a plea of military necessity in the absence of martial law ought not to be approved. Such exclusion goes over "the very brink of constitutional power" and falls into the ugly abyss of racism.

In dealing with matters relating to the prosecution and progress of a war, we must accord great respect and consideration to the judgments of the military authorities who are on the scene and who have full knowledge of the military facts. The scope of their discretion must, as a matter of necessity and common sense, be wide. And their judgments ought not to be overruled lightly by those whose training and duties ill-equip them to deal intelligently with matters so vital to the physical security of the nation.

At the same time, however, it is essential that there be definite limits to military discretion, especially where martial law has not been declared. Individuals must not be left impoverished of their constitutional rights on a plea of military necessity that has neither substance nor support. Thus, like other claims conflicting with the asserted constitutional rights of the individual, the military claim must subject itself to the judicial process of having its reasonableness determined and its conflicts with other interests reconciled....

That this forced exclusion was the result in good measure of this erroneous assumption of racial guilt rather than bona fide military necessity is evidenced by the Commanding General's Final Report on the evacuation from the Pacific Coast area. In it he refers to all individuals of Japanese descent as "subversive," as belonging to "an enemy race" whose "racial strains are undiluted," and as constituting "over 112,000 potential enemies ... at large today" along the Pacific Coast. In support of this blanket condemnation of all persons of Japanese descent, however, no reliable evidence is cited to show that such individuals were generally disloyal....

I dissent, therefore, from this legalization of racism....

MR. JUSTICE JACKSON, dissenting.

Korematsu was born on our soil, of parents born in Japan. The Constitution makes him a citizen of the United States by nativity and a citizen of California by residence. No claim is made that he is not loyal to this country. There is no suggestion that apart from the matter involved here he is not law-abiding and well disposed. Korematsu, however, has been convicted of an act not commonly a crime. It consists merely of being present in the state whereof he is a citizen, near the place where he was born, and where all his life he has lived.

. . .

Now, if any fundamental assumption underlies our system, it is that guilt is personal and not inheritable. Even if all of one's antecedents had been convicted of treason, the Constitution forbids its penalties to be visited upon him, for it provides that "no attainder of treason shall work corruption of blood, or forfeiture except during the life of the person attained." But here is an attempt to make an otherwise innocent act a crime merely because this prisoner is the son of parents as to whom he had no choice, and belongs to a race from which there is no way to resign....

Youngstown Co. v. Sawyer

343 U.S. 579 (1952)

In April 1952, to avert a nationwide strike of steelworkers that threatened U.S. military needs in the Korean War, President Truman issued an executive order directing Secretary of Com-

merce Sawyer to seize and operate most of the steel mills. The order was not based on specific statutory authority. In fact, Truman decided not to use the statutory remedy available in the Taft-Hartley Act of 1947, which was enacted into law over his veto. In district court, the administration justified the executive order on the basis of inherent presidential power (oral argument, as a reading, in Chapter 1). The district court issued a preliminary injunction against the seizure, rejecting the theory of inherent power, but the D.C. Circuit stayed this injunction pending review by the Supreme Court.

MR. JUSTICE BLACK delivered the opinion of the Court.

We are asked to decide whether the President was acting within his constitutional power when he issued an order directing the Secretary of Commerce to take possession of and operate most of the Nation's steel mills. The mill owners argue that the President's order amounts to lawmaking, a legislative function which the Constitution has expressly confided to the Congress and not to the President. The Government's position is that the order was made on findings of the President that his action was necessary to avert a national catastrophe which would inevitably result from a stoppage of steel production, and that in meeting this grave emergency the President was acting within the aggregate of his constitutional powers as the Nation's Chief Executive and the Commander in Chief of the Armed Forces of the United States....

I.

[*The Court rejects the administration's argument that the case should be resolved on nonconstitutional grounds. The constitutional question is "ripe for determination on the record presented."*]

II.

The President's power, if any, to issue the order must stem either from an act of Congress or from the Constitution itself. There is no statute that expressly authorizes the President to take possession of property as he did here. Nor is there any act of Congress to which our attention has been directed from which such a power can fairly be implied. Indeed, we do not understand the Government to rely on statutory authorization for this seizure....

Moreover, the use of the seizure technique to solve labor disputes in order to prevent work stoppages was not only unauthorized by any congressional enactment; prior to this controversy, Congress had refused to adopt that method of settling labor disputes. When the Taft-Hartley Act was under consideration in 1947, Congress rejected an amendment which would have authorized such governmental seizures in cases of emergency. Apparently it was thought that the technique of seizure, like that

of compulsory arbitration, would interfere with the process of collective bargaining. Consequently, the plan Congress adopted in that Act did not provide for seizure under any circumstances....

It is clear that if the President had authority to issue the order he did, it must be found in some provision of the Constitution. And it is not claimed that express constitutional language grants this power to the President. The contention is that presidential power should be implied from the aggregate of his powers under the Constitution. Particular reliance is placed on provisions in Article II which say that "The executive Power shall be vested in a President ..."; that "he shall take Care that the Laws be faithfully executed"; and that he "shall be Commander in Chief of the Army and Navy of the United States."

The order cannot properly be sustained as an exercise of the President's military power as Commander in Chief of the Armed Forces. The Government attempts to do so by citing a number of cases upholding broad powers in military commanders engaged in day-to-day fighting in a theater of war. Such cases need not concern us here. Even though "theater of war" be an expanding concept, we cannot with faithfulness to our constitutional system hold that the Commander in Chief of the Armed Forces has the ultimate power as such to take possession of private property in order to keep labor disputes from stopping production. This is a job for the Nation's lawmakers, not for its military authorities.

Nor can the seizure order be sustained because of the several constitutional provisions that grant executive power to the President. In the framework of our Constitution, the President's power to see that the laws are faithfully executed refutes the idea that he is to be a lawmaker. The Constitution limits his functions in the lawmaking process to the recommending of laws he thinks wise and the vetoing of laws he thinks bad. And the Constitution is neither silent nor equivocal about who shall make laws which the President is to execute. The first section of the first article says that "All legislative Powers herein granted shall be vested in a Congress of the United States...." After granting many powers to the Congress, Article I goes on to provide that Congress may "make all Laws which shall be necessary and proper for carrying into Execution the foregoing Powers, and all other Powers vested by this Constitution in the Government of the United States, or in any Department or Officer thereof."

... The power of Congress to adopt such public policies as those proclaimed by the order is beyond question. It can authorize the taking of private property for public use. It can make laws regulating the relationships between employers and employees, prescribing rules designed to settle labor disputes, and fixing wages and working conditions in certain fields of our economy. The Constitution does not subject this lawmaking power of Congress to presidential or military supervision or control.

It is said that other Presidents without congressional authority have taken possession of private business enterprises in order to settle labor disputes. But even if this be true, Congress has not thereby lost its exclusive constitutional authority to make laws necessary and proper to carry out the powers vested by the Constitution "in the Government of the United States, or any Department or Officer thereof."

The Founders of this Nation entrusted the lawmaking power to the Congress alone in both good and bad times. It would do no good to recall the historical events, the fears of power and the hopes for freedom that lay behind their choice. Such a review would but confirm our holding that this seizure order cannot stand.

The judgment of the District Court is

Affirmed.

. . .

Mr. Justice Frankfurter, concurring.

... Not so long ago it was fashionable to find our system of checks and balances obstructive to effective government. It was easy to ridicule that system as outmoded—too easy. The experience through which the world has passed in our own day has made vivid the realization that the Framers of our Constitution were not inexperienced doctrinaires. These long-headed statesmen had no illusion that our people enjoyed biological or psychological or sociological immunities from the hazards of concentrated power. It is absurd to see a dictator in a representative product of the sturdy democratic traditions of the Mississippi Valley. The accretion of dangerous power does not come in a day. It does come, however slowly, from the generative force of unchecked disregard of the restrictions that fence in even the most disinterested assertion of authority.

... It is an inadmissibly narrow conception of American constitutional law to confine it to the words of the Constitution and to disregard the gloss which life has written upon them. In short, a systematic, unbroken, executive practice, long pursued to the knowledge of the Congress and never before questioned, engaged in by Presidents who have also sworn to uphold the Constitution, making as it were such exercise of power part of the structure of our government, may be treated as a gloss on "executive Power" vested in the President by § 1 of Art. II.

. . .

Mr. Justice Douglas, concurring....

. . .

Mr. Justice Jackson, concurring in the judgment and opinion of the Court.

. . .

A judge, like an executive adviser, may be surprised at the poverty of really useful and unambiguous authority applicable to concrete problems of executive power as they actually present themselves. Just what our forefathers did envision, or would have envisioned had they foreseen modern conditions, must be divined from materials almost as enigmatic as the dreams Joseph was called upon to interpret for Pharaoh. A century and a half of partisan debate and scholarly speculation yields no net result but only supplies more or less apt quotations from respected sources on each side of any question. They largely cancel each other. And court decisions are indecisive because of the judicial practice of dealing with the largest questions in the most narrow way.

The actual art of governing under our Constitution does not and cannot conform to judicial definitions of the power of any of its branches based on isolated clauses or even single Articles torn from context. While the Constitution diffuses power the better to secure liberty, it also contemplates that practice will integrate the dispersed powers into a workable government. It enjoins upon its branches separateness but interdependence, autonomy but reciprocity. Presidential powers are not fixed but fluctuate, depending upon their disjunction or conjunction with those of Congress. We may well begin by a somewhat over-simplified grouping of practical situations in which a President may doubt, or others may challenge, his powers, and by distinguishing roughly the legal consequences of this factor of relativity.

1. When the President acts pursuant to an express or implied authorization of Congress, his authority is at its maximum, for it includes all that he possesses in his own right plus all that Congress can delegate....

2. When the President acts in absence of either a congressional grant or denial of authority, he can only rely upon his own independent powers, but there is a zone of twilight in which he and Congress may have concurrent authority, or in which its distribution is uncertain. Therefore, congressional inertia, indifference or quiescence may sometimes, at least as a practical matter, enable, if not invite, measures on independent presidential responsibility. In this area, any actual test of power is likely to depend on the imperatives of events and contemporary imponderables rather than on abstract theories of law.

3. When the President takes measures incompatible with the expressed or implied will of Congress, his power is at its lowest ebb, for then he can rely only upon his own constitutional powers minus any constitutional powers of Congress over the matter....

We should not use this occasion to circumscribe, much less to contract, the lawful role of the President as Commander in Chief. I should indulge the widest latitude of interpretation to sustain his exclusive function to command the instruments of national force, at least when turned against the outside world for the security of our society. But, when it is turned inward, not because of rebellion but because of a lawful economic struggle between industry and labor, it should have no such indulgence....

... I have no illusion that any decision by this Court can keep power in the hands of Congress if it is not wise and timely in meeting its problems. A crisis that challenges the President equally, or perhaps primarily, challenges Congress. If not good law, there was worldly wisdom in the maxim attributed to Napoleon that "The tools belong to the man who can use them." We may say that power to legislate for emergencies belongs in the hands of Congress, but only Congress itself can prevent power from slipping through its fingers.

... With all its defects, delays and inconveniences, men have discovered no technique for long preserving free government except that the Executive be under the law, and that the law be made by parliamentary deliberations.

Such institutions may be destined to pass away. But it is the duty of the Court to be last, not first, to give them up.

MR. JUSTICE BURTON, concurring in both the opinion and judgment of the Court....

MR. JUSTICE CLARK, concurring in the judgment of the Court.

... [T]he Constitution does grant to the President extensive authority in times of grave and imperative national emergency. In fact, to my thinking, such a grant may well be necessary to the very existence of the Constitution itself....

I conclude that where Congress has laid down specific procedures to deal with the type of crisis confronting the President, he must follow those procedures in meeting the crisis; but that in the absence of such action by Congress, the President's independent power to act depends upon the gravity of the situation confronting the nation. I cannot sustain the seizure in question because here ... Congress had prescribed methods to be followed by the President in meeting the emergency at hand.

. . .

MR. CHIEF JUSTICE VINSON, with whom MR. JUSTICE REED and MR. JUSTICE MINTON join, dissenting.

. . .

I.

... In 1950, when the United Nations called upon member nations "to render every assistance" to repel aggression in Korea, the United States furnished its vigorous support. For almost two full years, our armed forces have been fighting in Korea, suffering casualties of over 108,000 men. Hostilities have not abated. The "determination of the United Nations to continue its action in Korea to meet the aggression" has been reaffirmed. Congressional support of the action in Korea has been manifested by provisions for increased military manpower and equipment and for economic stabilization, as hereinafter described.

. . .

Congress recognized the impact of these defense programs upon the economy. Following the attack in Korea, the President asked for authority to requisition property and to allocate and fix priorities for scarce goods. In the Defense Production Act of 1950, Congress granted the powers requested and, *in addition,* granted power to stabilize prices and wages and to provide for settlement of labor disputes arising in the defense program. The Defense Production Act was extended in 1951, a Senate Committee noting that in the dislocation caused by the programs for purchase of military equipment "lies the seed of an economic disaster that might well destroy the military might we are straining to build." Significantly, the Committee examined the problem "in terms of just one commodity, steel," and found "a graphic picture of the over-all inflationary danger growing out of reduced civilian supplies and rising incomes." ...

New York Times Co. v. United States

403 U.S. 713 (1971)

The Nixon administration brought action in federal court to prevent publication in the *New York Times* and the *Washington Post* of certain materials collectively called the Pentagon Papers. The documents consisted of a classified study prepared by the Defense Department, entitled "History of U.S. Decision-Making Process on Viet Nam Policy." The administration claimed that publication of the materials would be injurious to national security. The newspapers argued that the First Amendment protected against prior restraint on the right to publish.

PER CURIAM.

We granted certiorari in these cases in which the United States seeks to enjoin the New York Times and the Washington Post from publishing the contents of a classified study entitled "History of U.S. Decision-Making Process on Viet Nam Policy." ...

"Any system of prior restraints of expression comes to this Court bearing a heavy presumption against its constitutional validity." *Bantam Books, Inc.* v. *Sullivan,* 372 U.S. 58, 70 (1963); see also *Near* v. *Minnesota,* 283 U.S. 697 (1931). The Government "thus carries a heavy burden of showing justification for the imposition of such a restraint." *Organization for a Better Austin* v. *Keefe,* 402 U.S. 415, 419 (1971). The District Court for the Southern District of New York in the *New York Times* case and the District Court for the District of Columbia and the Court of Appeals for the District of Columbia Circuit in the *Washington Post* case held that the Government had not met that burden. We agree.

The judgment of the Court of Appeals for the District of Columbia Circuit is therefore affirmed. The order of the Court of Appeals for the Second Circuit is reversed and the case is remanded with directions to enter a judgment affirming the judgment of the District Court for the Southern District of New York. The stays entered June 25, 1971, by the Court are vacated. The judgments shall issue forthwith.

So ordered.

MR. JUSTICE BLACK, with whom MR. JUSTICE DOUGLAS joins, concurring.

I adhere to the view that the Government's case against the Washington Post should have been dismissed and that the injunction against the New York Times should have been vacated without oral argument when the cases were first presented to this Court. I believe that every moment's continuance of the injunctions against these newspapers amounts to a flagrant, indefensible, and continuing violation of the First Amendment. ...

... Madison and the other Framers of the First Amendment, able men that they were, wrote in language they earnestly believed could never be misunderstood: "Congress shall make no law ... abridging the freedom ... of the press. ..." Both the history and language of the First Amendment support the view that the press must be left free to publish news, whatever the source, without censorship, injunctions, or prior restraints.

In the First Amendment the Founding Fathers gave the free press the protection it must have to fulfill its essential role in our democracy. The press was to serve the governed, not the governors. The Government's power to censor the press was abolished so that the press would remain forever free to censure the Government. The press was protected so that it could bare the secrets of government and inform the people. Only a free and unrestrained press can effectively expose deception in government. And paramount among the responsibilities of a free press is the duty to prevent any part of the government from deceiving the people and sending them off to distant lands to die of foreign fevers and foreign shot and shell. ...

The word "security" is a broad, vague generality whose contours should not be invoked to abrogate the fundamental law embodied in the First Amendment. The guarding of military and diplomatic secrets at the expense of informed representative government provides no real security for our Republic. ...

MR. JUSTICE DOUGLAS, with whom MR. JUSTICE BLACK joins, concurring. ...

MR. JUSTICE BRENNAN, concurring. ...

MR. JUSTICE STEWART, with whom MR. JUSTICE WHITE joins, concurring.

... If the Constitution gives the Executive a large degree of unshared power in the conduct of foreign affairs and the maintenance of our national defense, then under the Constitution the Executive must have the largely unshared duty to determine and preserve the degree of internal security necessary to exercise that power successfully. It is an awesome responsibility, requiring judgment and wisdom of a high order. I should suppose that moral, political, and practical considerations would dictate that a very first principle of that wisdom would be an insistence upon avoiding secrecy for its own sake. For when everything is classified, then nothing is classified, and the system becomes one to be disregarded by the cynical or the careless, and to be manipulated by those intent on self-protection or self-promotion....

... I am convinced that the Executive is correct with respect to some of the documents involved. But I cannot say that disclosure of any of them will surely result in direct, immediate, and irreparable damage to our Nation or its people. That being so, there can under the First Amendment be but one judicial resolution of the issues before us. I join the judgments of the Court.

Mr. Justice White, with whom Mr. Justice Stewart joins, concurring....

Mr. Justice Marshall, concurring....

Mr. Chief Justice Burger, dissenting.

... In these cases, the imperative of a free and unfettered press comes into collision with another imperative, the effective functioning of a complex modern government and specifically the effective exercise of certain constitutional powers of the Executive. Only those who view the First Amendment as an absolute in all circumstances—a view I respect, but reject—can find such cases as these to be simple or easy.

These cases are not simple for another and more immediate reason. We do not know the facts of the cases. No District Judge knew all the facts. No Court of Appeals judge knew all the facts. No member of this Court knows all the facts.

Why are we in this posture, in which only those judges to whom the First Amendment is absolute and permits of no restraint in any circumstances or for any reason, are really in a position to act?

I suggest we are in this posture because these cases have been conducted in unseemly haste....

Mr. Justice Harlan, with whom The Chief Justice and Mr. Justice Blackmun join, dissenting.

These cases forcefully call to mind the wise ad-

monition of Mr. Justice Holmes, dissenting in *Northern Securities Co.* v. *United States,* 193 U.S. 197, 400–401 (1904):

"Great cases like hard cases make bad law. For great cases are called great, not by reason of their real importance in shaping the law of the future, but because of some accident of immediate overwhelming interest which appeals to the feelings and distorts the judgment. These immediate interests exercise a kind of hydraulic pressure which makes what previously was clear seem doubtful, and before which even well settled principles of law will bend."

With all respect, I consider that the Court has been almost irresponsibly feverish in dealing with these cases.

Both the Court of Appeals for the Second Circuit and the Court of Appeals for the District of Columbia Circuit rendered judgment on June 23. The New York Times' petition for certiorari, its motion for accelerated consideration thereof, and its application for interim relief were filed in this Court on June 24 at about 11 A.M. The application of the United States for interim relief in the *Post* case was also filed here on June 24 at about 7:15 P.M. This Court's order setting a hearing before us on June 26 at 11 A.M., a course which I joined only to avoid the possibility of even more peremptory action by the Court, was issued less than 24 hours before. The record in the *Post* case was filed with the Clerk shortly before 1 P.M. on June 25; the record in the *Times* case did not arrive until 7 or 8 o'clock that same night. The briefs of the parties were received less than two hours before argument on June 26.

This frenzied train of events took place in the name of the presumption against prior restraints created by the First Amendment. Due regard for the extraordinarily important and difficult questions involved in these litigations should have led the Court to shun such a precipitate timetable.

·   ·   ·

Mr. Justice Blackmun, dissenting....

Erwin N. Griswold
How Sensitive Were the "Pentagon Papers"?

In the administration's brief to the Supreme Court on *New York Times Co.* v. *United States,* Solicitor General Erwin N. Griswold described all of the materials in the 47 volumes as classified

"Top Secret-Sensitive," "Top Secret," or "Secret." By the time the case reached the Court, the administration wanted to bar only the publication of a smaller number of documents, the disclosure of which would pose a "grave and immediate danger to the security of the United States." During oral argument, Griswold told the Court that the broaching of one of the documents "would be of extraordinary seriousness to the security of the United States." Publication of the documents, according to Griswold, "will affect lives. It will affect the process of the termination of the war. It will affect the process of recovering prisoners of war." Later in the oral argument he warned the Court that publication would interfere with the conduct of "delicate negotiations now in process, or contemplated for the future." Yet in an article for the *Washington Post* on February 15, 1989, entitled "Secrets Not Worth Keeping" (p. A25), he admits that publication produced no trace of a threat to the national security. As he explains, the principal concern of classifiers "is not with national security, but rather with government embarrassment of one sort or another."

It may be relevant at this time to recount some details of events which attracted widespread attention several years ago. The occasion was the presentation of the Pentagon Papers case (*New York Times* v. *United States* and *United States* v. *Washington Post*) before the United States Supreme Court, and the year was 1971.

At that time, I held the office of solicitor general of the United States. The government then in office, under the presidency of Richard Nixon, was determined to do everything in its power to prevent the press from publishing some 47 volumes of mimeographed papers preserved primarily in the office of the Secretary of Defense in the Pentagon, and thus known as the Pentagon Papers. These papers were *in toto* classified as Top Secret....

It was my responsibility to represent the interests of the United States before the Supreme Court. Everything happened very fast. The U.S. Court of Appeals for the District of Columbia decided the case on Thursday, June 24, 1971. On Friday, at noon, I was advised by Chief Justice Warren Burger that the case would be heard by the Supreme Court on Saturday morning, June 26, and that "briefs will be exchanged between the parties in the courtroom immediately before the argument."

At that time, no briefs had been written, and, indeed, I had never seen the *outside* of the Pentagon Papers. I immediately arranged for a set of the papers to be brought to my office. It was obvious that I could not read all of the materials in the time available. In this situation, I arranged to have three high officials, one each from the Defense Department, the State Department and the National Security Agency come to my office. I asked them to tell me what items in the 47 volumes were really bad—what items, if disclosed, would be a real threat to the security of the United States.

This produced a total of about 40 items over which these officers expressed concern. I then read

each of these items, but quickly came to the conclusion that most of them presented no serious threat to national security, and that there was simply no prospect that the Supreme Court would ban the publication of all of these items. Eventually, I reduced the list to a total of 11 items. My deputy, Daniel M. Friedman, wrote the main or "open" brief for the United States, while I wrote the "secret" brief, contending that these 11 items presented a threat to the national security.

. . .

So, I went ahead and presented the case before the court, relying only on the 11 items. As is well known, we lost, by a six-to-three vote, with three members of the majority saying there could never be a prior restraint, while three others said that a prior restraint would be appropriate in a proper case, but that there was no adequate threat to national security in this case.

Accordingly, the newspapers printed many items from the Pentagon Papers. And within a few weeks, under the auspices of Sen. Mike Gravel of Alaska, the entire contents of all the papers were printed. I have never seen any trace of a threat to the national security from the publication. Indeed, I have never seen it even suggested that there was such an actual threat....

It quickly becomes apparent to any person who has considerable experience with classified material that there is massive overclassification and that the principal concern of the classifiers is not with national security, but rather with governmental embarrassment of one sort or another. There may be some basis for short-term classification while plans are being made, or negotiations are going on, but apart from details of weapons systems, there is very rarely any real risk to current national security from the publication of facts relating to transactions in the past, even the fairly recent past....

C. TREATIES AND EXECUTIVE AGREEMENTS

Under Article VI of the Constitution, federal statutes made pursuant to the Constitution and all treaties "shall be the supreme Law of the Land." State judges are bound by those actions, "any Thing in the Constitution or Laws of any State to the Contrary Notwithstanding." Much depends on whether the treaty is "self-executing" (does not require implementing legislation or other action) or is not self-executing. In passing legislation to carry out a treaty, Congress may act in ways that might not have been sustained in the form of a freestanding statute. See Missouri v. Holland in Chapter 8.

The President makes treaties "by and with the Advice and Consent of the Senate." The process of treaty-making need not be divided into two exclusive and sequential stages: negotiation solely by the President, followed by Senate advice and consent. When President Washington first communicated with the Senate regarding the appropriate procedure for treaties, he considered oral communications with Senators "indispensably necessary." Treaties seemed to him "of a legislative nature," inviting deliberation in the Senate's chamber. 30 Writings of Washington 373, 378. On August 22, 1789, he met with Senators to secure their advice and consent to an Indian treaty. The Senators felt uncomfortable in his presence and disliked having to rely solely on information provided by the Secretary of War, who was present. Washington returned two days later and obtained the Senate's consent, but he decided against a repeat performance.

This incident has been misinterpreted to suggest that Washington negotiated all future treaties without Senate involvement. In fact, he continued to seek the Senate's advice by written communications rather than personal appearances. In later years, Senators were asked to approve the appointment of treaty negotiators and even advise on their negotiating instructions. Far from being a "presidential monopoly," the negotiation of treaties has often been shared with the Senate in order to obtain legislative guidance, understanding, and support. Presidential insistence to "go it alone" in negotiating treaties has often had disastrous results. Fisher, Constitutional Conflicts Between Congress and the President 221–26 (2007 ed.); Fisher, 38 Pres. Stud. Q. 144 (2008).

Role of the House

Although the Senate is the only chamber of Congress with an express constitutional duty in the treaty process, the House of Representatives plays a crucial role in funding treaties. In 1793, President Washington treated the House and the Senate equally in submitting a treaty to both chambers, including sensitive documents, for the purpose of paying bribes ("tributes") to the Barbary Powers. Louis Fisher, The Politics of Executive Privilege 30–33 (2004). Three years later, members of the House of Representatives insisted that the House possessed "a discretionary power of carrying the Treaty into effect, or refusing it their sanction." Annals of Congress, 4th Cong., 1st Session. 426–28. Lawmakers decided that certain powers delegated to Congress as a whole, such as the authority to regulate foreign commerce or to set tariffs, could not be exercised through the treaty-making power. The general power of appropriating funds to execute a treaty represents a substantial constraint on the President and the Senate.

When two-thirds of the Senate fails to ratify a treaty, Presidents have at times turned to Congress as a whole to accomplish the same purpose by obtaining a simple majority vote in both Houses for a joint resolution. The annexation of Texas and Hawaii and the adoption of the St. Lawrence Seaway plan were accomplished in this manner. The position of the House of Representatives is enhanced when treaties contain language requiring that funds be made available through the normal procedures of Congress, including prior authorization and annual appropriations. This language requires action not only by the Senate Foreign Relations Committee and the House Foreign Affairs Committee but also by both Appropriations Committees.

Treaty Termination

The constitutional issue of treaty termination was raised in 1978 when President Jimmy Carter terminated a defense treaty with Taiwan. The Senate considered a resolution that would have required the approval of the Senate or both Houses of Congress before the President could terminate any defense treaty, but final action was never taken on the measure. A federal district judge decided that some form of congressional concurrence was required, either the approval of a majority of both Houses or the consent of two-thirds of the Senate. Goldwater v. Carter, 481 F.Supp. 949, 963–64 (D.D.C. 1979). This decision was rejected by an appellate court and the Supreme Court, in part because of the failure of Congress to confront the President in a direct and final way. In the words of Justice Jackson from the Steel Seizure Case of 1952, Carter had acted in a "zone of twilight." Goldwater v. Carter, 617 F.2d 697 (D.C. Cir. 1979); GOLDWATER v. CARTER, 444 U.S. 996 (1979). The Justices of the Supreme Court split along so many lines that their opinions shed little light on future treaty terminations. Congress has yet to pass legislation to define executive and legislative roles in this matter.

In 2001, President George W. Bush terminated the 1972 ABM treaty between the United States and Russia. A lawsuit, challenging his authority to terminate a treaty without congressional approval, was turned aside on grounds of standing and the political question doctrine. Kucinich v. Bush, 236 F.Supp.2d 1 (D.D.C. 2002). For further analysis of the ABM dispute, see David Gray Adler, 34 Pres. Stud. Q. 156–167 (2004).

Executive Agreements

Treaties differ from executive agreements in several regards. Treaties require the advice and consent of the Senate; executive agreements do not. Treaties (unlike executive agreements) may supersede prior conflicting statutes. United States v. Schooner Peggy, 5 U.S. (1 Cr.) 103 (1801). Otherwise, officials in the executive branch have considerable latitude in entering into international compacts either by treaty or by executive agreement. Among the more controversial executive agreements are the destroyers-bases deal with Great Britain in 1940, the Yalta and Potsdam agreements of 1945, the Vietnam peace agreement of 1973, the Sinai agreements of 1975, and military-base agreements with Spain, Diego Garcia, and Bahrain. The Bush administration in 2008 raised constitutional issues when it attempted to enter into an agreement with Iraq concerning future U.S. military bases and other matters.

The vast majority of executive agreements are based on statutory authority or treaty language. Although these agreements may lack what the Supreme Court calls the "dignity" of a treaty, since they do not require Senate approval, they are nevertheless valid international compacts. Altman & Co. v. United States, 224 U.S. 583, 600–01 (1912).[4] In addition to statutory and treaty authority, the executive branch claims four sources of constitutional authority that allow the President to enter into executive agreements: (1) his duty as chief executive to represent the nation in foreign affairs, (2) his authority to receive ambassadors and other public ministers, (3) his authority as commander in chief, and (4) his duty to "take care that the laws be faithfully executed." 11 FAM [Foreign Affairs Manual] 721.2(b)(3). The scope of these unilateral initiatives has been narrowed by judicial and congressional actions.

The State Department concedes that an executive agreement cannot be "inconsistent with legisla-

---

4. In United States v. Pink, 315 U.S. 203, 230 (1942), the Court regarded executive agreements as having a "similar dignity" with treaties. For an opinion by Acting Attorney General McGranery in 1946 upholding the legality of an executive agreement made pursuant to a joint resolution, see 40 Op. Att'y Gen. 469. In 2003, the Court divided 5 to 4 to uphold an executive agreement by noting that Congress had not taken steps to disapprove it. American Ins. Assn. v. Garamendi, 539 U.S. 396 (2003).

tion enacted by the Congress in the exercise of its constitutional authority." 11 FAM 721.2(b)(3). For example, an agreement cannot survive if it conflicts with a commercial statute concerning another country. Foreign commerce is "subject to regulation, so far as this country is concerned, by Congress alone." United States v. Guy W. Capps, Inc., 204 F.2d 655, 660 (4th Cir. 1953), aff'd on other grounds, 348 U.S. 296 (1955). Other executive agreements have been struck down because they violate the Just Compensation Clause or deprive an accused of trial by jury. Seery v. United States, 127 F.Supp. 601 (Ct. Cl. 1955); Reid v. Covert, 354 U.S. 1 (1957).

The Iranian hostage crisis of 1979 produced a series of extraordinary moves by President Carter, including the freezing of Iran's assets in America and the suspension of claims pending in American courts. Although the Supreme Court found no specific authority for the suspension of claims, legal justifications were discovered somewhere in the combination of past presidential practices to settle claims by executive agreement, the history of "implicit" congressional approval, and the failure of Congress to contest the Iranian agreement. The Court, straining to uphold an agreement it was unlikely to overturn, limited the reach of its opinion by confining it to the specific circumstances in the case. DAMES & MOORE v. REGAN, 453 U.S. 654 (1981).

In 2008, the Court decided a complex case that blended many elements: international law, presidential power, and federalism. Texas had prosecuted a Mexican foreign national and found him guilty of a crime punishable by the death penalty. It did not comply with a treaty calling for countries to notify the consulate of a foreign national. A decision by the World Court (the International Court of Justice) and a memorandum signed by President George W. Bush urged Texas not to execute the prisoner without offering him a second habeas hearing, which is not allowed under Texas law. Divided 6 to 3, the Court held that the treaty in dispute (Vienna Convention on Consular Relations) was not self-executing and therefore not binding on U.S. domestic courts. Congress would have to pass legislation making the treaty binding on the states. Thus, neither the decision by the World Court nor a presidential memorandum could preempt limitations in state law that prohibited the filing of successive habeas petitions. Medellin v. Texas, 552 U.S. 491 (2008). With regard to the reach of executive agreements, the decision did much to cut back on such decisions as *Belmont*, *Pink*, *Dames & Moore*, and *Garamendi*.

A number of secret agreements have been entered into without the knowledge of Congress. Many of these agreements were of an economic or military nature, committing the United States to various obligations (see box on next page). Legislation in 1972 (the Case Act) requires the Secretary of State to transmit to Congress within 60 days the text of "any international agreement, other than a treaty," to which the United States is a party. If the President decides that publication would be prejudicial to national security, he may transmit an agreement to the Senate Committee on Foreign Relations and the House Committee on Foreign Affairs under an injunction of secrecy removable only by the President. 86 Stat. 619 (1972); 1 U.S.C. §112b. When the executive branch circumvented the statute by calling some agreements "arrangements," Congress passed legislation to tighten the reporting statute. 91 Stat. 224, §5 (1977); 92 Stat. 993, §708 (1978). Legislative control is strengthened even more by requiring that Congress approve certain agreements or appropriate funds to carry them out.

Recognition Policy

The President has broad constitutional authority to recognize foreign governments. President Roosevelt's recognition of Soviet Russia led to the "Litvinov Assignment" in 1933 and subsequent property claims in the courts. His decision was upheld by the Supreme Court. United States v. Belmont, 301 U.S. 324 (1937); United States v. Pink, 315 U.S. 203 (1942). Left undecided is the President's power to enter into agreements that involve such constitutional provisions as the Due Process and Just Compensation Clauses of the Fifth Amendment. Under certain circumstances, the use of the recognition power by the President may invade the war prerogatives of Congress. President Andrew Jackson raised that argument in declining to recognize the independence of Texas, fearing that such

Congressional Oversight of Executive Agreements

The Committee on Foreign Relations, to which was referred the bill (S. 596) to require that international agreements other than treaties, hereafter entered into by the United States, be transmitted to the Congress within 60 days after the execution thereof, having considered the same, reports favorably thereon without amendment and recommends that the bill do pass.

· · ·

As the committee has discovered, there have been numerous agreements contracted with foreign governments in recent years, particularly agreements of a military nature, which remain wholly unknown to Congress and to the people. A number of these agreements have been uncovered by the Symington Subcommittee on Security Agreements and Commitments Abroad, including, for example, an agreement with Ethiopia in 1960, agreements with Laos in 1963, with Thailand in 1964 and again in 1967, with Korea in 1966, and certain secret annexes to the Spanish bases agreement.

Section 112(a) of title I of the United States Code now requires the Secretary of State to compile and publish all international agreements other than treaties concluded by the United States during each calendar year. The executive, however, has long made it a practice to withhold those agreements which, in its judgment, are of a "sensitive" nature. Such agreements, often involving military arrangements with foreign countries, are frequently not only "sensitive" but exceedingly significant as broadened commitments for the United States. Although they are sometimes characterized as "contingency plans," they may in practice involve the United States in war. For this reason the committee attaches the greatest importance to the establishment of a legislative requirement that all such agreements be submitted to Congress.

… Whatever objection on security grounds the executive might have to the submission of such information to Congress is met by the provision of the bill which authorizes the President, at his option, to transmit certain agreements not to the Congress as a whole, but to the two foreign affairs committees "under an appropriate injunction of secrecy to be removed only upon due notice from the President."

SOURCE: S. Rept. No. 92-591, 92d Cong., 2d Sess. (1972).

---

action would result in war with Mexico and undercut the constitutional role of Congress. Louis Fisher, *Presidential War Power* 39 (2d ed. 2004).

Article II, Section 3, provides that the President "shall receive Ambassadors and other public Ministers." From that language Presidents have claimed the exclusive right to recognize other governments, a power that has been widely exercised. Why does the express authority to receive ambassadors carry with it the right to recognize foreign governments? There is no "recorded evidence that any of the participants in the drafting and ratifying of the Constitution — Federalists and Anti-Federalists alike — understood that any provision in the Constitution *vested* such a power in the presidency, and certainly not a power that is plenary in nature." Robert J. Reinstein, "Recognition: A Case Study on the Original Understanding of Executive Power," 45 U. Rich. L. Rev. 801, 862 (2011) (emphasis in original).

Federal courts have done little to clarify the President's recognition power. A case currently in the courts, *Zivotofsky* v. *Secretary of State*, might add some clarity. The lower federal courts in the District of Columbia handled the issue poorly, eventually dismissing it as a "political question." Zivotofsky v. Secretary of State, 511 F.Supp.2d 97 (D.D.C. 2007); Zivotofsky v. Secretary of State, 571 F.3d 1227 (D.C. Cir. 2009). On March 26, 2012, the Court vacated the D.C. Circuit ruling and remanded the case for further proceedings. It specifically rejected the position of the D.C. Circuit that the political question doctrine prohibited Zivotofsky's claim. Zivotofsky v. Clinton, 566 U.S. ___, ___ (2012).

Goldwater v. Carter

444 U.S. 996 (1979)

On December 15, 1978, President Carter terminated a defense treaty with Taiwan. Under the terms of the treaty, either party could end the pact after giving the other country a year's notice. By the time the case had traveled through the district court and the appellate court, the treaty was about to be terminated. Senator Barry Goldwater argued that a treaty, being law, required legislative action for its repeal. Acting without oral argument, the Court dismissed the complaint by Goldwater. Having disposed of the issue in summary fashion, several Justices filed separate statements setting forth their individual views.

MR. JUSTICE POWELL, concurring in the judgment.

Although I agree with the result reached by the Court, I would dismiss the complaint as not ripe for judicial review.

I

This Court has recognized that an issue should not be decided if it is not ripe for judicial review. *Buckley* v. *Valeo*, 424 U.S. 1, 113–114 (1976) (*per curiam*). Prudential considerations persuade me that a dispute between Congress and the President is not ready for judicial review unless and until each branch has taken action asserting its constitutional authority. Differences between the President and the Congress are commonplace under our system. The differences should, and almost invariably do, turn on political rather than legal considerations. The Judicial Branch should not decide issues affecting the allocation of power between the President and Congress until the political branches reach a constitutional impasse. Otherwise, we would encourage small groups or even individual Members of Congress to seek judicial resolution of issues before the normal political process has the opportunity to resolve the conflict.

In this case, a few Members of Congress claim that the President's action in terminating the treaty with Taiwan has deprived them of their constitutional role with respect to a change in the supreme law of the land. Congress has taken no official action. In the present posture of this case, we do not know whether there ever will be an actual confrontation between the Legislative and Executive Branches. Although the Senate has considered a resolution declaring that Senate approval is necessary for the termination of any mutual defense treaty, see 125 Cong. Rec. 13672, 13695–13697 (1979), no final vote has been taken on the resolution. See *id.*, at 32522–32531. Moreover, it is unclear whether the resolution would have retroactive effect. See *id.*, at 13711–13721; *id.*, at 15210. It can-

not be said that either the Senate or the House has rejected the President's claim. If the Congress chooses not to confront the President, it is not our task to do so. I therefore concur in the dismissal of this case.

II

Mr. Justice Rehnquist suggests, however, that the issue presented by this case is a nonjusticiable political question which can never be considered by this Court. I cannot agree.

[*Justice Powell concludes that if this case were ready for review, it would satisfy the criteria established by Baker v. Carr (1962) for cases that the Court may properly decide.*]

III

In my view, the suggestion that this case presents a political question is incompatible with this Court's willingness on previous occasions to decide whether one branch of our Government has impinged upon the power of another. See *Buckley* v. *Valeo*, 424 U.S., at 138; *United States* v. *Nixon, supra*, at 707; *The Pocket Veto Case*, 279 U.S. 655, 676–678 (1929); *Myers* v. *United States*, 272 U.S. 52 (1926). Under the criteria enunciated in *Baker* v. *Carr*, we have the responsibility to decide whether both the Executive and Legislative Branches have constitutional roles to play in termination of a treaty. If the Congress, by appropriate formal action, had challenged the President's authority to terminate the treaty with Taiwan, the resulting uncertainty could have serious consequences for our country. In that situation, it would be the duty of this Court to resolve the issue.

MR. JUSTICE REHNQUIST, with whom THE CHIEF JUSTICE, MR. JUSTICE STEWART, and MR. JUSTICE STEVENS join, concurring in the judgment.

I am of the view that the basic question presented by the petitioners in this case is "political" and therefore nonjusticiable because it involves the authority of the President in the conduct of our country's foreign relations and the extent to which the Senate or the Congress is authorized to negate the action of the President....

The present case differs in several important respects from *Youngstown Sheet & Tube Co.* v. *Sawyer,* 343 U.S. 579 (1952), cited by petitioners as authority both for reaching the merits of this dispute and for reversing the Court of Appeals. In *Youngstown,* private litigants brought a suit contesting the President's authority under his war powers to seize the Nation's steel industry, an action of profound and demonstrable domestic impact. Here, by contrast, we are asked to settle a dispute between coequal branches of our Government, each of which has resources available to protect and assert its interests, resources not available to private litigants outside the judicial forum....

MR. JUSTICE BLACKMUN, with whom MR. JUSTICE WHITE joins, dissenting in part.

In my view, the time factor and its importance are illusory; if the President does not have the power to terminate the treaty (a substantial issue that we should address only after briefing and oral argument), the notice of intention to terminate surely has no legal effect. It is also indefensible, without further study, to pass on the issue of justiciability or on the issues of standing or ripeness. While I therefore join in the grant of the petition for certiorari, I would set the case for oral argument and give it the plenary consideration it so obviously deserves.

MR. JUSTICE BRENNAN, dissenting.

I respectfully dissent from the order directing the District Court to dismiss this case, and would affirm the judgment of the Court of Appeals in-so-far as it rests upon the President's well-established authority to recognize, and withdraw recognition from, foreign governments....

In stating that this case presents a nonjusticiable "political question," MR. JUSTICE REHNQUIST, in my view, profoundly misapprehends the political-question principle as it applies to matters of foreign relations. Properly understood, the political-question doctrine restrains courts from reviewing an exercise of foreign policy judgment by the coordinate political branch to which authority to make that judgment has been "constitutional[ly] commit[ted]." *Baker* v. *Carr,* 369 U.S. 186, 211–213, 217 (1962). But the doctrine does not pertain when a court is faced with the *antecedent* question whether a particular branch has been constitutionally designated as the repository of political decisionmaking power. Cf. *Powell* v. *McCormack,* 395 U.S. 486, 519–521 (1969). The issue of decisionmaking authority must be resolved as a matter of constitutional law, not political discretion; accordingly, it falls within the competence of the courts.

The constitutional question raised here is prudently answered in narrow terms. Abrogation of the defense treaty with Taiwan was a necessary incident to Executive recognition of the Peking Government, because the defense treaty was predicated upon the now-abandoned view that the Taiwan Government was the only legitimate political authority in China. Our cases firmly establish that the Constitution commits to the President alone the power to recognize, and withdraw recognition from, foreign regimes.... That mandate being clear, our judicial inquiry into the treaty rupture can go no further....

Dames & Moore v. Regan

453 U.S. 654 (1981)

After Iran seized American hostages in 1979, President Carter declared a national emergency and blocked the removal or transfer of all Iranian property subject to the jurisdiction of the United States. He also authorized certain judicial proceedings to handle resulting disputes brought by private parties seeking access to Iranian assets. When the American hostages were released on January 20, 1981, the United States and Iran entered into an agreement that required the termination of all legal proceedings in U.S. courts involving claims of U.S. nationals against Iran. Those claims would be submitted to binding arbitration before an Iran-United States Claims Tribunal. In this case, a private party seeks to prevent enforcement of various executive orders and regulations issued to implement the agreement with Iran. The basic question of this case is whether the administration exceeded statutory and constitutional powers. A private company, Dames & Moore, sued Secretary of the Treasury Donald Regan.

JUSTICE REHNQUIST delivered the opinion of the Court.

The questions presented by this case touch fundamentally upon the manner in which our Republic is to be governed....

[*This*] dispute involves various Executive Orders and regulations by which the President nullified attachments and liens on Iranian assets in the United States, directed that these assets be transferred to Iran, and suspended claims against Iran that may be presented to an International Claims Tribunal. This action was taken in an effort to comply with an Executive Agreement between the United States and Iran....

But before turning to the facts and law which we believe determine the result in this case, we stress that the expeditious treatment of the issues involved by all of the courts which have considered the President's actions makes us acutely aware of the necessity to rest decision on the narrowest possible ground capable of deciding the case. *Ashwander* v. *TVA*, 297 U.S. 288, 347 (1936) (Brandeis, J., concurring)....

I

On November 4, 1979, the American Embassy in Tehran was seized and our diplomatic personnel were captured and held hostage. In response to that crisis, President Carter, acting pursuant to the International Emergency Economic Powers Act, ... (hereinafter IEEPA), declared a national emergency on November 14, 1979, and blocked the removal or transfer of "all property and interests in property of the Government of Iran, its instrumentalities and controlled entities and the Central Bank of Iran which are or become subject to the jurisdiction of the United States...."... On November 15, 1979, the Treasury Department's Office of Foreign Assets Control issued a regulation providing that "[u]nless licensed or authorized ... any attachment, judgment, decree, lien, execution, garnishment, or other judicial process is null and void with respect to any property in which on or since [November 14, 1979,] there existed an interest of Iran."...

On November 26, 1979, the President granted a general license authorizing certain judicial proceedings against Iran but which did not allow the "entry of any judgment or of any decree or order of similar or analogous effect...." § 535.504 (a). On December 19, 1979, a clarifying regulation was issued stating that "the general authorization for judicial proceedings contained in § 535.504 (a) includes prejudgment attachment." § 535.418.

On December 19, 1979, petitioner Dames & Moore filed suit in the United States District Court for the Central District of California against the Government of Iran, the Atomic Energy Organization of Iran, and a number of Iranian banks. In its complaint, petitioner alleged that its wholly owned subsidiary, Dames & Moore International, S. R. L., was a party to a written contract with the Atomic Energy Organization, and that the subsidiary's entire interest in the contract had been assigned to petitioner. Under the contract, the subsidiary was to conduct site studies for a proposed nuclear power plant in Iran. As provided in the terms of the contract, the Atomic Energy Organization terminated the agreement for its own convenience on June 30, 1979. Petitioner contended, however, that it was owed $3,436,694.30 plus interest for services performed under the contract prior to the date of termination. The District Court issued orders of attachment directed against property of the defendants, and the property of certain Iranian banks was then attached to secure any judgment that might be entered against them.

On January 20, 1981, the Americans held hostage were released by Iran pursuant to an Agreement entered into the day before.... The Agreement stated that "[i]t is the purpose of [the United States and Iran] ... to terminate all litigation as between the Government of each party and the nationals of the other, and to bring about the settlement and termination of all such claims through binding arbitration."...

On January 19, 1981, President Carter issued a series of Executive Orders implementing the terms of the agreement.

[*On February 24, 1981, President Reagan issued an executive order in which he "ratified" the January 19 executive orders. Meanwhile, a federal district court awarded Dames & Moore the amount claimed under the contract plus interest. Later, the company filed an action seeking to prevent enforcement of the executive orders and Treasury Department regulations implementing the agreement with Iran.*]

II

[*In this section, Justice Rehnquist finds Justice Jackson's concurring opinion in Youngstown Co. v. Sawyer (1952), classifying presidential actions into three general categories, to be analytically useful but too general to apply. Presidential action in any particular case does not fall "neatly in one of three pigeonholes, but rather at some point along a spectrum running from explicit congressional authorization to explicit congressional prohibition. This is particularly true as respects cases such as the one before us....*"]

III

In nullifying post-November 14, 1979, attachments and directing those persons holding blocked Iranian funds and securities to transfer them to the Federal Reserve Bank of New York for ultimate transfer to Iran, President Carter cited five sources of express or inherent power. The Government, however, has principally relied on §203 of the IEEPA....

[*Dames and Moore argued that the Court should ignore the plain language of this statute and examine its legislative history and the history of the Trading With the Enemy Act (TWEA), which reveals that IEEPA "was not intended to give the President such extensive power over the assets of a foreign state during times of national emergency." The Court disagreed, refusing to read out of IEEPA the meaning of certain words. To the Court, nothing in the history of that statute or of the TWEA required such a result.*] To the contrary, we think both the legislative history and cases interpreting the TWEA fully sustain the broad authority of the Executive when acting under this congressional grant of power....

IV

Although we have concluded that the IEEPA constitutes specific congressional authorization to the President to nullify the attachments and order the transfer of Iranian assets, there remains the question of the President's authority to suspend claims pending in American courts. Such claims have, of course, an existence apart from the attachments which accompanied them. In terminating these claims through Executive Order No. 12294, the President purported to act under authority of both the IEEPA and 22 U. S. C. §1732, the so-called "Hostage Act." 46 Fed. Reg. 14111 (1981).

We conclude that although the IEEPA authorized the nullification of the attachments, it cannot be read to authorize the suspension of the claims. The claims of American citizens against Iran are not in themselves transactions involving Iranian property or efforts to exercise any rights with respect to such property.... [*The Court also ruled that the Hostage Act does not provide specific authorization to the President to suspend claims in American courts.*]

Concluding that neither the IEEPA nor the Hostage Act constitutes specific authorization of the President's action suspending claims, however, is not to say that these statutory provisions are entirely irrelevant to the question of the validity of the President's action. We think both statutes highly relevant in the looser sense of indicating congressional acceptance of a broad scope for executive action in circumstances such as those presented in this case. As noted in Part III, ... the IEEPA delegates broad authority to the President to act in times of national emergency with respect to property of a foreign country. The Hostage Act similarly indicates congressional willingness that the President have broad discretion when responding to the hostile acts of foreign sovereigns....

Although we have declined to conclude that the IEEPA or the Hostage Act directly authorizes the President's suspension of claims for the reasons noted, we cannot ignore the general tenor of Congress' legislation in this area in trying to determine whether the President is acting alone or at least with the acceptance of Congress. As we have noted, Congress cannot anticipate and legislate with regard to every possible action the President may find it necessary to take or every possible situation in which he might act. Such failure of Congress specifically to delegate authority does not, "especially ... in the areas of foreign policy and national security," imply "congressional disapproval" of action taken by the Executive. *Haig* v. *Agee, ante,* at 291. On the contrary, the enactment of legislation closely related to the question of the President's authority in a particular case which evinces legislative intent to accord the President broad discretion may be considered to "invite" "measures on independent presidential responsibility." *Youngstown,* 343 U. S., at 637 (Jackson, J., concurring). At least this is so where there is no contrary indication of legislative intent and when, as here, there is a history of congressional acquiescence in conduct of the sort engaged in by the President....

... Consistent with that principle, the United States has repeatedly exercised its sovereign authority to settle the claims of its nationals against foreign countries. Though those settlements have sometimes been made by treaty, there has also been a longstanding practice of settling such claims by executive agreement without the advice and consent of the Senate....

Crucial to our decision today is the conclusion that Congress has implicitly approved the practice of claim settlement by executive agreement....

... [T]he legislative history of the IEEPA further reveals that Congress has accepted the authority of the Executive to enter into settlement agreements. Though the IEEPA was enacted to provide for some limitation on the President's emergency powers, Congress stressed that "[n]othing in this act is intended ... to interfere with the authority of the President to [block assets], or to impede the settlement of claims of U. S. citizens against foreign countries."

S. Rep. No. 95-466, p. 6 (1977); 50 U. S. C. § 1706 (a)(1) (1976 ed., Supp. III).

... [W]e do not believe that the President has attempted to divest the federal courts of jurisdiction. Executive Order No. 12294 purports only to "suspend" the claims, not divest the federal court of "jurisdiction." As we read the Executive Order, those claims not within the jurisdiction of the Claims Tribunal will "revive" and become judicially enforceable in United States courts....

In light of all of the foregoing—the inferences to be drawn from the character of the legislation Congress has enacted in the area, such as the IEEPA and the Hostage Act, and from the history of acquiescence in executive claims settlement—we conclude that the President was authorized to suspend pending claims pursuant to Executive Order No. 12294....

Just as importantly, Congress has not disapproved of the action taken here.... We are thus clearly not confronted with a situation in which Congress has in some way resisted the exercise of Presidential authority.

Finally, we re-emphasize the narrowness of our decision. We do not decide that the President possesses plenary power to settle claims, even as against foreign governmental entities....

JUSTICE STEVENS, concurring in part.

. . .

JUSTICE POWELL, concurring in part and dissenting in part.

. . .

D. THE WAR POWER

The framers broke decisively with the British political model, which gave the Executive exclusive authority over all of external affairs, including the power to declare war. Under the U.S. Constitution, the power to take the country from a state of peace to a state of war against another country is placed in Congress, not the President. Congress is given specific power to declare war and to provide for the armed forces. Congress has declared war in five conflicts: the War of 1812 against England, the Mexican War in 1846, the Spanish-American War in 1898, World War I in 1917, and World War II in 1941.[5] Congress may also pass legislation to *authorize* military action against another nation, as it did with the Quasi-War against France in 1798, the war against Iraq in 1991, the war against Afghanistan in 2001, and the Iraq Resolution in 2002. The Supreme Court recognizes the constitutionality of undeclared wars, which it calls limited, partial, imperfect, or "quasi" wars. Bas v. Tingy, 4 U.S. (4 Dall.) 36 (1800); Talbot v. Seeman, 5 U.S. (1 Cr.) 1 (1801). In the second case, Chief Justice Marshall acknowledged the broad constitutional authority of Congress to decide to *initiate* hostilities, whether by declaration or not: "The whole powers of war being, by the constitution of the United States, vested in congress, the acts of that body can alone be resorted to as our guides in this inquiry." 5 U.S. at 28.

Article I, Section 2, makes the President "Commander in Chief of the Army and Navy of the United States, and of the Militia of the several States, when called into the actual Service of the United States." Scholars disagree whether this merely confers a title (Commander in Chief) or implies additional powers for the President. At a minimum, the title provides for unity of control. The Justice Department has also argued that the President is Commander in Chief not because he is necessarily skilled in the art of war but because it preserves civilian supremacy over the military. 10 Op. Att'y Gen. 74, 79 (1861).

The delegates at the Philadelphia Convention recognized an implied power for the President to "repel sudden attacks." When it was proposed that Congress be empowered to "make war," Charles Pinckney objected that legislative proceedings "were too slow" for the safety of the country in an emergency. Madison and Elbridge Gerry successfully inserted "declare" for "make," thereby "leaving to the Executive the power to repel sudden attacks" (see box on next page). The President's independent power was therefore limited to *defensive* actions. Offensive actions were reserved to Congress, to be

---

5. Actually, there were multiple declarations during the two world wars: two declarations for World War I (against Germany and Austria-Hungary) and six declarations for World War II (Japan, Germany, Italy, Bulgaria, Hungary, and Rumania).

The Framers Debating to "Declare War"

[*On August 17, 1787, the delegates at the Constitutional Convention debated giving Congress the power to "make war."*]

Mr Pinkney opposed the vesting this power in the Legislature. Its proceedings were too slow. It wd. meet but once a year. The Hs. of Reps. would be too numerous for such deliberations. The Senate would be the best depositary, being more acquainted with foreign affairs, and most capable of proper resolutions. If the States are equally represented in Senate, so as to give no advantage to large States, the power will notwithstanding be safe, as the small have their all at stake in such cases as well as the large States. It would be singular for one—authority to make war, and another peace.

Mr Butler. The Objections agst the Legislature lie in a great degree agst the Senate. He was for vesting the power in the President, who will have all the requisite qualities, and will not make war but when the Nation will support it.

Mr. M<adison> and Mr Gerry moved to insert "*declare*," striking out "*make*" war; leaving to the Executive the power to repel sudden attacks.

Mr Sharman thought it stood very well. The Executive shd. be able to repel and not to commence war. "Make" better than "declare" the latter narrowing the power too much.

Mr Gerry never expected to hear in a republic a motion to empower the Executive alone to declare war.

Mr Elseworth. there is a material difference between the cases of making *war,* and making *peace*. It shd. be more easy to get out of war, than into it. War also is a simple and overt declaration. peace attended with intricate & secret negociations.

Mr. Mason was agst giving the power of war to the Executive, because not <safely> to be trusted with it; or to the Senate, because not so constructed as to be entitled to it. He was for clogging rather than facilitating war; but for facilitating peace. He preferred "*declare*" to "*make*".

On the Motion to insert *declare*—in place of *Make*, <it was agreed to.>

N. H. no. Mas. abst. Cont. no.* Pa ay. Del. ay. Md. ay. Va. ay. N. C. ay. S. C. ay. Geo—ay. [Ayes—7; noes—2; absent—I.]

*On the remark by Mr. King that "*make*" war might be understood to "conduct" it which was an Executive function, Mr. Elseworth gave up his objection (and the vote of Cont was changed to—ay.)

---

decided through its deliberative processes. At the Pennsylvania ratifying convention, James Wilson expressed the prevailing sentiment that the system of checks and balances "will not hurry us into war; it is calculated to guard against it. It will not be in the power of a single man, or a single body of men, to involve us in such distress; for the important power of declaring war is vested in the legislature at large." 2 Elliot 528.

Presidents and their military advisers recognized that the decision to take the country to war lay with Congress. As President Jefferson told Congress on December 8, 1801, anything "beyond the line of defense" depended on legislative judgment. Fisher, Presidential War Power, at 32–37. Court decisions during this period acknowledged the supremacy of Congress in authorizing war and setting boundaries for the President. Little v. Barreme, 6 U.S. (2 Cr.) 169, 179 (1804); United States v. Smith, 27 Fed. Cas. 1192, 1229–30 (C.C.N.Y. 1806) (No. 16,342).

When Congress delegates to the President its power to call forth the militia to suppress insurrections or to repel invasions, the decision to use force belongs to the President, but Congress can add constraints. The Militia Act of 1792 required the President to obtain the approval of a Supreme Court Justice or a district judge before calling out the militia. In time of emergencies, Presidents must take effective action. Martin v. Mott, 25 U.S. (12 Wheat.) 19 (1827). The Supreme Court has noted that the President as Commander in Chief "is authorized to direct the movements of the naval and military forces placed by law at his command, and to employ them in the manner he may deem most effectual to harass and conquer and subdue the enemy." Fleming v. Page, 50 U.S. (9 How.) 602, 614 (1850). Notice that the power to move forces is "placed by *law* at his command." How much does the

President depend on Congress to provide the authorizations and appropriations necessary for military action? Under the Constitution, it is the responsibility of Congress to raise and support the military forces, to make military regulations, to provide for calling up the militia to suppress insurrections and to repel invasions, and to provide for the organization and disciplining of the militia. Art. I, §8.

Article I, Section 8, assigns to Congress and the states different responsibilities over the militia (the part-time fighting force). Congress provides for organizing, arming, and disciplining the militia, while the states appoint the officers and retain authority for training the militia "according to the discipline prescribed by Congress." Congress may authorize the President to order members of the National Guard to active duty for purposes of training outside the United States, during time of peace, without either the consent of state governors or the declaration of a national emergency. Perpich v. Department of Defense, 496 U.S. 334 (1990).

Bypassing Congress: UN and NATO

From 1789 to 1950, all major U.S. military operations against another country were either declared or authorized by Congress. In 1950, President Truman went to war against North Korea without ever seeking or obtaining authority from Congress. Instead, he received "authorization" from resolutions adopted by the U.N. Security Council. Nothing in the U.N. Charter of 1945, either in its express language or legislative history, indicated any intent to enable the President to use this treaty to bypass Congress. The Charter required each member state to adopt through its "constitutional processes" a resolution stating how it would provide assistance to U.N. military actions. To comply with that provision in the Charter, Congress passed legislation in 1945 called the U.N. Participation Act, stating that presidential agreements for this type of military assistance "shall be subject to the approval of the Congress by appropriate Act or joint resolution." 59 Stat. 621, sec. 6 (1945). During Senate debate on the Charter, Truman pledged that when any such agreement is negotiated "it will be my purpose to ask the Congress for appropriate legislation to approve them." 91 Cong. Rec. 8185 (1945). In acting as he did against North Korea, Truman violated not merely his personal pledge but the U.N. Participation Act. Louis Fisher, "The Korean War: On What Legal Basis Did Truman Act?," 89 Am. J. Int'l L. 21 (1995).

Over the years, other Presidents circumvented Congress by relying either on resolutions passed by the Security Council or "authorizations" adopted by NATO allies. In November 1990, President George H. W. Bush claimed that a U.N. resolution was sufficient legal authority to use military force against Iraq, but Congress in January 1991 passed legislation specifically authorizing that commitment of U.S. troops. President Clinton relied on U.N. resolutions to act militarily against Haiti in 1994 and in Bosnia in 1995. When the U.N. refused to authorize military action against Serbia, he claimed authority from NATO. Louis Fisher, "Sidestepping Congress: Presidents Acting Under the UN and NATO," 47 Case West. Res. L. Rev. 1237 (1997). In 2011, President Obama acted militarily against Libya without receiving congressional authority. He obtained a U.N. resolution and NATO support. The Justice Department issued a legal opinion stating that the action did not constitute "war" because there were no U.S. casualties (OLC reading). Under that reasoning, a strong nation could pulverize a weak nation, suffer no casualties, and deny it was engaged in war. When the military action exceeded the 60–90 day limit of the War Powers Resolution, the Obama administration announced that not only was there no war but there were no "hostilities." Louis Fisher, "Military Operations in Libya: No War? No Hostilities?," 42 Pres. Stud. Q. 176 (2012).

Military Tribunals/Guantánamo

The use of military courts during the Civil War in states where federal courts were open and operating had been curbed by *Ex parte Milligan*. The issue returned during and after World War II. A unanimous Court in 1942 held that aliens and U.S. citizens who entered the country as "unlawful combatants" could be tried by military tribunal. Those who enter in civilian clothing on behalf of an enemy are not entitled to trial by jury before a civilian court. Ex parte Quirin, 317 U.S. 1 (1942).

When looked at closely, *Quirin* provides an unattractive precedent. The Roosevelt administration, reflecting on what it did in 1942 with eight German saboteurs, decided not to follow the same procedures two years later when two more unlawful combatants arrived. Louis Fisher, Nazi Saboteurs on Trial (2003). Moreover, Court decisions upholding military tribunals during World War II are almost uniformly condemned today. For example, In re Yamishita, 327 U.S. 1 (1946). *Quirin* did not allow state governors to operate under martial law and substitute military for judicial trials of civilians who were not charged with violations of the law of war. Duncan v. Kahanamoku, 327 U.S. 304 (1946). Nor may the military arrest someone who has been honorably discharged and try that person before a court-martial. Prosecution must be conducted by civilian courts. Toth v. Quarles, 350 U.S. 11 (1955).

In 1969, the Supreme Court attempted to subject certain military questions to the jurisdiction of civilian courts. It held that to be under military jurisdiction, a crime must be "service connected." Otherwise, members of the military were entitled to a civilian trial, including the constitutional right to indictment by grand jury and trial by jury. O'Callahan v. Parker, 395 U.S. 258 (1969). So confusing was the service-connected doctrine that the Court abandoned it in 1987. Jurisdiction of a court-martial now depends solely on the accused's status as a member of the armed forces. The Court announced that Congress "has primary responsibility for the delicate task of balancing the rights of servicemen against the needs of the military." Solorio v. United States, 483 U.S. 435, 447 (1987).

On November 13, 2001, in response to terrorist attacks on the United States, President George W. Bush issued a military order authorizing the use of military tribunals. Three national security cases reached the Supreme Court in 2004, testing the limits of presidential power to detain U.S. citizens and foreign nationals without trial or some kind of process to separate the guilty from the innocent. Two of the cases involved U.S. citizens: Yaser Esam Hamdi and Jose Padilla. The third affected aliens held at the U.S. naval base in Guantánamo, Cuba. In the Padilla case, the Court divided 5–4 in deciding that his habeas petition had been filed with the wrong court. Rumsfeld v. Padilla, 542 U.S. 426 (2004). Although the Fourth Circuit ruled in favor of the government in 2005, the government switched course by bringing charges against Padilla in a criminal court in Florida. The indictment made no mention of serious charges earlier made by the government, such as a "dirty bomb" plot by Padilla. In 2007, a jury convicted him of terrorism conspiracy charges and he was sentenced to 17 years in prison.

For Hamdi, eight Justices rejected the government's central argument that the detention was quintessentially a presidential decision, not to be reevaluated or second-guessed by the courts. Four members of the plurality, joined by Justices Souter and Ginsburg, held that an enemy combatant "must receive notice of the factual basis for his classification, and a fair opportunity to rebut the Government's factual assertions before a neutral decisionmaker." The plurality emphasized such terms as "an independent tribunal," an "independent review," and an "impartial adjudication," expressing satisfaction that the review could be within the executive branch and perhaps take the form of "an appropriately authorized and properly constituted military tribunal." The plurality seemed to lose sight of how Hamdi became an "enemy combatant." The person who made that designation was President Bush. No review panel within the executive branch, much less within the military, could possibly possess the sought-for qualities of neutrality, detachment, independence, and impartiality in having to pass judgment to possibly reverse a presidential decision. HAMDI v. RUMSFELD, 542 U.S. 507 (2004). Following this decision, the government decided to transfer Hamdi to Saudi Arabia in October 2004.

The third case involved the Guantánamo detainees. The government argued that the naval base was outside the jurisdiction of federal courts to give habeas relief. A 6–3 decision rejected that position, identifying a number of differences between the prisoners at the base and those held abroad in a ruling decided a half century earlier. Johnson v. Eisentrager, 339 U.S. 763 (1950). Consequently, federal courts have jurisdiction to consider challenges to the legality of the Guantánamo detainees. Rasul v. Bush, 542 U.S. 466 (2004).

As a result of *Rasul*, dozens of legal challenges were filed by detainees in Guantánamo Bay. A major case, *Hamdan* v. *Rumsfeld*, reached the Supreme Court and was decided there on June 29, 2006. Salim Ahmed Hamdan, a driver for Osama bin Laden, had been captured on the battlefield in Afghanistan and turned over to the U.S. military base in Guantánamo. During oral argument before the Court, his attorney focused on the procedures adopted for the military tribunal that was to try Hamdan: "if the military commission complied with the rules of courts-martial, we wouldn't be here." That issue was prominent among those decided by the Court, which held that the Bush administration lacked authority to proceed with the military commission it had devised. HAMDAN v. RUMSFELD, 548 U.S. 557 (2006). The decision rejected the administration's reliance on presidential "inherent" powers to conduct the war on terrorism.

Congress responded to *Hamdan* by passing the Military Commissions Act (MCA) of 2006, providing for the first time a statutory basis for the tribunals. Lawsuits against the administration claimed that the detainees at Guantánamo were entitled to submit habeas petitions to federal courts. The D.C. Circuit denied that such rights existed for the detainees, but a dissenting judge raised the question whether the MCA offended the constitutional requirement that habeas must be formally suspended and that the Suspension Clause made no distinction between citizens and non-citizens. Boumediene v. Bush, 476 F.3d 981 (D.C. Cir. 2007). On June 12, 2008, the Supreme Court held that both the MCA and the Detainee Treatment Act of 2005 operated as an unconstitutional suspension of the writ. BOUMEDIENE v. BUSH, 553 U.S. 723 (2008).

Responding to *Boumediene*, federal district courts began granting habeas relief to a number of Guantánamo detainees, in some cases ordering their release. In each instance, however, the D.C. Circuit reversed and the Supreme Court denied review. Instead of acting as an independent branch, the D.C. Circuit regularly favored the position advanced by the executive branch. Several judges on the D.C. Circuit, including A. Raymond Randolph and Janice Rogers Brown, were openly disdainful of *Boumediene*. Rather than reassert the constitutional principles it announced in 2008, the Supreme Court chose to reject appeals brought to it, including the denial of seven certiorari on June 11, 2012. In all of these actions, not a single Justice dissented. Erwin Chemerinsky, "Losing Interest: Since the Supreme Court's latest ruling guaranteeing habeas corpus rights to Guantánamo detainees, in 2008, it has refused to hear a single detainee case," Nat'l L. J., June 25, 2012, at 34.

Obama Administration

On May 15, 2009, President Obama proposed changes to military commissions to provide additional safeguards to the accused. Legislation passed by Congress on October 28, 2009, made a number of changes to trial procedures for the commissions. 123 Stat. 2574 (2009). On January 22, 2009, Obama announced his intention to close the Guantánamo facility within a year but a combination of political, technical and budgetary problems made that impossible. During 2009 and 2010, the administration was able to release a number of detainees and transfer them to other countries. Attorney General Eric Holder decided that the remaining detainees could be prosecuted either in military commissions or in federal civil court. On July 7, 2010, a Guantánamo detainee (Qosi) pled guilty to conspiring with al Qaeda and providing material support to terrorism, the first conviction before a military commission by the Obama administration. In July 2012, he was transferred from Guantánamo to Sudan.

President Obama issued a number of national security policies on May 21, 2009. The war against terrorism required "an abiding confidence in the rule of law and due process; in checks and balances and accountability." He rejected waterboarding and other extreme techniques of interrogation. Those methods "undermine the rule of law. They alienate us in the world. They serve as a recruitment tool for terrorists, and increase the will of our enemies to fight us, while decreasing the will of others to work with America."

On June 21, 2010, the Supreme Court reviewed a statute that prohibited giving "material support" to a foreign terrorist organization. Material support included not only contributions of cash and weapons but also training, "service," and providing expert advice. Plaintiffs objected that the statute (1) violated their freedom of speech and freedom of association under the First Amendment and (2) was unconstitutionally vague. The Court, divided 6 to 3, held that the statute, which did not apply to such assistance as medicine and religious materials, was constitutional as applied. A factor in the decision, discussed also in Chapter 10 on free speech, was judicial deference to the elected branches. Holder v. Humanitarian Law Project, 561 U.S. ___ (2010).

The Bush administration used armed drones after 9/11 in an effort to kill terrorists in other countries. Pakistan regularly opposed the program because it violated their national sovereignty and resulted in the deaths of women, children, and innocent bystanders. The number of drone attacks increased during the Obama administration, leading to the administration's claim that it could place names—including U.S. citizens—on a "kill list." Efforts to challenge this program in *Al-Aulaki* v. *Obama* were dismissed on December 7, 2010, by a district court as a matter beyond the capacity of the judiciary. A Justice Department memo, providing legal grounds to defend the kill list, remains secret.

War Powers Resolution

Presidential war powers have expanded because of several developments. The idea of "defensive war" was originally limited to protective actions against the borders of the United States or ships at sea. After World War II, defensive war assumed a much broader meaning. American bases were spread throughout the world; military commitments were added to defense pacts and treaties. Under these agreements, a President could interpret an attack on an ally as an attack on the United States. Presidents used military force on numerous occasions to protect American lives and property, often stretching those objectives to achieve foreign policy or military objectives, as in the Dominican Republic in 1965, Cambodia in 1970, Grenada in 1983, and Panama in 1989. The bombing of Libya in 1986 was defended as an antiterrorist response.

The exercise of presidential war power by Lyndon Johnson and Richard Nixon provoked Congress to pass legislation in an effort to curb executive initiatives and promote collective efforts between Congress and the President. The War Powers Resolution of 1973 has three main provisions: presidential consultation with Congress, presidential reports to Congress, and congressional termination of military action. The purpose of the Resolution, as stated in §2(a), is "to insure that the collective judgment" of both branches will apply to the introduction of U.S. forces into hostilities. Yet an examination of other sections, together with executive interpretations, judicial decisions, and congressional behavior, supplies ample evidence that the statute does not assure collective judgment. WAR POWERS RESOLUTION.

The President is to consult with Congress "in every possible instance." The language obviously leaves considerable discretion to the President on both the form and timing of consultation. The framers of the resolution did not expect the President to consult with 535 legislators, but who should be contacted? The leadership? The chairmen and ranking members of designated committees? Selected advisers? It is agreed that consultation means more than being briefed. Consultation means an opportunity to influence a pending decision. H. Rept. No. 287, 93d Cong., 1st Sess. 6–7 (1973).

The resolution requires that the President, after introducing forces into hostilities, report to Congress within 48 hours. Precisely what conditions require a report is unclear from the legislation, and if a report is delayed, so are the mechanisms for congressional control. Under the Resolution, military action must terminate within 60 days after the report unless Congress (1) declares war or enacts a specific authorization, (2) extends by law the 60-day period, or (3) is physically unable to meet as a result of an armed attack on the United States. The President may extend the period by an additional 30 days if he determines that force is needed to protect and remove American troops.

Congress has two means of control: (1) a decision not to support the President during the 60-to-

90 day period or (2) passage of a concurrent resolution at any time to direct the President to remove forces engaged in hostilities. The first mechanism has little meaning because the clock for the 60-to-90 day period begins to run only when the President reports under a very specific section: Section 4(a)(1). President Ford was the only President to report under that section—in the *Mayaguez* capture in 1975—but by the time he reported the operation was over. Thus, the clock that was intended to limit the President may not tick.

The force of a concurrent resolution has been weakened by two developments. The executive branch takes the position that if the President has power to put men into combat, "that power could not be taken away by concurrent resolution because the power is constitutional in nature." "War Powers: A Test of Compliance," hearings before the House Committee on International Relations, 94th Cong., 1st Sess. 91 (1975). Executive officials argue that the President has a number of constitutional powers to use military force without congressional approval, such as rescuing Americans living abroad, rescuing foreign nationals under certain circumstances, and protecting U.S. embassies and legations. Id. at 90–91.

Moreover, the Supreme Court struck down all one-House and two-House (concurrent) resolutions as "legislative vetoes" that have no binding effect on the executive branch. INS v. Chadha, 462 U.S. 919 (1983). Still, passage of a concurrent resolution would mean that a majority of legislators in each house opposed the President's actions. It is difficult to conceive of a President persisting after that vote. Also, if Congress complied with *Chadha* by passing a joint resolution of disapproval, the President could veto that and Congress would now need a two-thirds majority in each house to stop a presidential war.

Members of Congress have gone to court to contest military initiatives by the President, but these efforts are regularly turned aside by federal judges on the ground that the determination of what constitutes hostilities or imminent hostilities is essentially a fact-finding matter reserved to Congress, not the courts. Crockett v. Reagan, 558 F.Supp. 893 (D.D.C. 1982), aff'd, 720 F.2d 1355 (D.C. Cir. 1983), cert. denied, 467 U.S. 1251 (1984).[6] When President Reagan sent ships into the Persian Gulf in 1987 without reporting to Congress under the War Powers Resolution, 110 members of the House of Representatives took the matter to court. Similar to the other cases, a district court declined to accept jurisdiction and dismissed the case. Lowry v. Reagan, 676 F.Supp. 333 (D.D.C. 1987).

The War Powers Resolution does not cover "paramilitary" (covert) operations. Beginning in 1974 and continuing through the Reagan years, Congress enacted a number of statutes and amendments to restrict covert actions. Part of the accommodation of a 1980 statute required the President to fully inform the House and Senate Intelligence Committees in a "timely fashion" of covert operations in foreign countries. Congress discovered in November 1986 that President Reagan had been sending arms to Iran for ten months, without any notification to Congress. As a result, the Senate passed legislation in 1988 to tighten the requirement so that notification could be delayed for no more than 48 hours, but the House of Representatives did not act on the bill. Legislation in 1991 clarified the reporting requirements for covert operations. Presidents are now expected to inform the intelligence committees in advance on almost all such operations. 105 Stat. 441–45 (1991).

Military Actions from 1990 to 2000

The principle of "collective judgment" contemplated in § 2(a) of the War Powers Resolution was sorely tested in 1990, when President George H. W. Bush claimed that he could mount an offensive operation against Iraq without any congressional authorization. After Iraq's invasion of Kuwait on August 2, 1990, he sent U.S. troops to Saudi Arabia to defend that country, assembled a 28-nation coalition

---

6. See also Sanchez-Espinoza v. Reagan, 568 F.Supp. 596 (D.D.C. 1983), aff'd, Sanchez-Espinoza v. Reagan, 770 F.2d 202 (D.C. Cir. 1985) (Nicaragua); Conyers v. Reagan, 578 F.Supp. 324 (D.D.C. 1984), dismissed as moot, Conyers v. Reagan, 765 F.2d 1124 (D.C. Cir. 1985) (Grenada).

against Iraq, and obtained a number of U.N. resolutions condemning Iraq. In November, Bush announced a substantial increase in the number of U.S. troops, giving him the capability of acting offensively against Iraq. The Bush administration argued that it could shift from a defensive posture to an offensive operation without first obtaining authorization from Congress. Two lawsuits challenging the constitutionality of Bush's action were avoided by two federal courts. Ange v. Bush, 752 F.Supp. 509 (D.D.C. 1990); DELLUMS v. BUSH, 752 F.Supp. 1141 (D.D.C. 1990). The latter, however, rejected many of the ambitious arguments advanced by the Justice Department with regard to presidential war powers. Perhaps with an eye to that decision, on January 8, 1991, Bush asked Congress to pass legislation supporting military action in the Persian Gulf. After three days of intense debate, Congress passed the bill. 105 Stat. 3 (1991). Because of the authorizing statute, a major constitutional crisis was averted.

In his eight years in office, President Clinton engaged in a remarkable amount of military activity without ever seeking authority from Congress. He sent cruise missiles into Iraq, conducted military operations in Somalia, threatened to invade Haiti, ordered air strikes in Bosnia, dispatched 20,000 ground troops to Bosnia, sent cruise missiles into Sudan and Afghanistan, and went to war against Yugoslavia. In each case he argued that he had no constitutional obligation other than to consult with members of Congress before taking military action. Like Bush in Iraq, he sometimes pointed to "authority" obtained from resolutions passed by the UN Security Council. In addition, he cited "authorizing" actions by the North Atlantic Council (NATO) for ordering air strikes in Bosnia.

Clinton's major military initiative was against Yugoslavia in 1999. Here there was no claim of acting in a defensive manner or to protect American lives. It was an unambiguous, unvarnished example of taking the country from a state of peace to a state of war, without ever asking Congress for authority. Congress took a number of votes; none authorized what Clinton did and none prohibited him from doing what he did. An effort by a member of Congress to litigate the constitutionality of the war in Yugoslavia was unsuccessful. CAMPBELL v. CLINTON, 203 F.3d 19 (D.C. Cir. 2000). The federal appellate court revealed different views by judges on a member's standing to bring such a case and the competence of courts to decide questions of war.

Attempts to Reform or Repeal the WPR

The War Powers Resolution has been criticized ever since it was enacted. An effort by the House of Representatives in 1995 to repeal most of it failed on a vote of 201 to 217. 142 Cong. Rec. 15209–10 (1995). Only two provisions would have been kept (consultation and reporting). Much of the motivation behind that attempt reflected the belief that the resolution interferes with the President's constitutional duties. However, some scholars support repeal because the resolution delegates to the President powers that the Constitution lodges with Congress, especially the decision to initiate war.[7]

In 2008, a private war powers commission recommended the repeal of the WPR and its replacement by a statute creating a Joint Congressional Consultation Committee consisting of 20 senior lawmakers. Headed by former Secretaries of State James A. Baker III and Warren Christopher, the commission report proposed a "practical solution" to help future Presidents and members of Congress deal with war power disputes. According to the report, the proposal "avoids clearly favoring one branch over the other." In fact, the commission recommended a procedure that would allow the President to initiate military operations simply by consulting with the committee. If Congress had not enacted a formal declaration of war or expressly authorized the military action, the consultation committee would introduce a concurrent resolution of approval within 30 days. Several weeks would elapse for the two houses to report and act on this measure. If it passed, it would have no legal effect

---

7. Louis Fisher & David Gray Adler, "The War Powers Resolution: Time to Say Goodbye," 113 Pol. Sci. Q. 1 (1998); Michael J. Glennon, "Too Far Apart: Repeal the War Powers Resolution," 50 U. Miami L. Rev. 17 (1995); Edward Keynes, "The War Powers Resolution: A Bad Idea Whose Time Has Come and Gone," 23 U. Toledo L. Rev. 343 (1992).

because concurrent resolutions are not submitted to the President. In the event the resolution of approval did not pass, a joint resolution of disapproval would be acted on. Additional time would be consumed with this procedure and joint resolutions must be presented to the President. Presumably the President would veto it, requiring Congress now to muster a two-thirds majority in each house to override the veto. In other words, the President could begin and continue a war provided he maintained the support of one-third plus one in a single house.

Response to the 9/11 Attacks

On September 11, 2001, terrorists flew two planes into the World Trade Center in New York City. Under the intense heat from interior burning the two buildings collapsed, as did a third nearby. Another aircraft hit the Pentagon in Washington, D.C., and a fourth — probably destined for the White House or the Capitol — crashed in Pennsylvania. Approximately 3,000 people, of almost every nationality, died. Congress responded with legislation that authorized U.S. armed forces against those responsible for the attacks. 115 Stat. 224 (2001). In addition, Congress passed legislation strengthening airport security and expanding the authority of law enforcement officials to deal with terrorists. The major bill, the USA Patriot Act, gave the federal government major powers over the accused. Changes in the rights of the accused and electronic surveillance are discussed in Chapters 13 and 14. On November 13, 2001, President George W. Bush issued a military order allowing the use of military tribunals to try captured terrorists.

Regarding the war power, the issue debated in 2002 was whether the statute enacted the previous year (AUMF), authorizing the use of military force against the terrorists, was sufficient authority to enable President Bush to go to war against Iraq. The 2001 statute required the President to determine that a nation, organization, or person aided in the 9/11 attacks, a link the Bush administration had not been able to establish with Iraq. However, even if a link could be determined, the financial implications of a war against Iraq (hundreds of billions of dollars) and the impact on Middle East stability convinced many members of Congress that Bush needed to return to Congress for supplemental authority before mounting a war against Iraq. That legislation was enacted. 116 Stat. 1498 (2002).

State Secrets Privilege

In addition to the NSA surveillance conducted after 9/11 — brought to light by the *New York Times* in December 2005 — the Bush administration carried out another secret program called "extraordinary rendition" (sending suspected terrorists to other countries for interrogation and torture). Efforts to challenge the NSA and rendition operations in court were met by administration claims that the cases could not proceed without the risk of disclosing sensitive "national security" information. The state secrets privilege had been recognized by the Supreme Court in *United States* v. *Reynolds*, 345 U.S. 1 (1953), but cases on state secrets in the past had not addressed major initiatives by the executive branch that credibly violated statutes, treaties, and the Constitution. Louis Fisher, The Constitution and 9/11 (2008).

In an address on May 21, 2009, President Obama stated that the state secrets privilege "is absolutely necessary in some circumstances to protect national security," although he was concerned that "it has been over-used." He adopted this principle: "We must not protect information merely because it reveals the violation of a law or embarrassment to the government." He promised to apply "a stricter legal test to material that can be protected under the state secrets privilege."

On September 23, 2009, Attorney General Eric Holder announced new procedures within the Justice Department to assess claims of the state secrets privilege advanced by executive departments and agencies. However, the Obama administration continued to invoke the state secrets privilege in cases that had originated under the George W. Bush administration. Both houses of Congress held hearings on the state secrets privilege and drafted legislation to strengthen judicial independence to evaluate state secrets claims. Although the bills were reported from committee, no floor action was taken.

Military Operations in Libya
OLC opinion

In response to U.S. military operations in Libya, which began in March 2011, the Office of Legal Counsel in the Justice Department issued an opinion regarding the constitutional authority of President Obama to direct this use of force. Could he rely solely on the basis of a U.N. resolution? Did he need authority from Congress? Was his action consistent with the War Powers Resolution of 1973? Did the military operations constitute "war"?

... For the reasons explained below, we concluded that the President had the constitutional authority to direct the use of force in Libya because he could reasonably determine that such use of force was in the national interest. We also advised that prior congressional approval was not constitutionally required to use military force in the limited operations under consideration....

The President explained in his March 21, 2011 report to Congress that the use of military force in Libya serves important U.S. interests in preventing instability in the Middle East and preserving the credibility and effectiveness of the United Nations Security Council. The President also stated that he intended the anticipated United States military operations in Libya to be limited in nature, scope, and duration. [The military operations lasted seven months.] The goal of action by the United States was to "set the stage" for further action by coalition partners in implementing UNSC Resolution 1973, particularly through destruction of Libyan military assets that could either threaten coalition aircraft policing the UNSC-declared no-fly zone or engage in attacks on civilians and civilian-populated areas. In addition, no U.S. ground forces would be deployed, except possibly for any search and rescue missions, and the risk of substantial casualties for U.S. forces would be low. As we advised you prior to the commencement of military operations, we believe that, under these circumstances, the President had constitutional authority, as Commander in Chief and Chief Executive and pursuant to his foreign affairs powers, to direct such limited military operations abroad, even without prior specific congressional approval....

We have acknowledged one possible constitutionally-based limit on this presidential authority to employ military force in defense of important national interests—a planned military engagement that constitutes a "war" within the meaning of the Declaration of War Clause may require prior congressional authorization.... In our view, determining whether a particular planned engagement constitutes a "war" for constitutional purposes instead requires a fact-specific assessment of the "anticipated nature, scope, and duration" of the planned military operations. *Haiti Deployment*, 18 Op. O.L.C. at 179. This standard generally will be satisfied only by prolonged and substantial military operations, typically involving exposure of U.S. military personnel to significant risk over a substantial period. Again, Congress's own key enactment [the War Powers Resolution] on the subject reflects this understanding. By allowing United States involvement in hostilities to continue for 60 to 90 days, Congress signaled in the WPR that it considers congressional authorization most critical for "major, prolonged conflicts such as the wars in Vietnam and Korea," not more limited engagements. *Id.* at 176.

... President Obama directed United States forces [in Libya] to "conduct[] a limited and well-defined mission in support of international efforts to protect civilians and prevent a humanitarian disaster"; American airstrikes accordingly were to be "limited in their nature, duration, and scope." ... [W]e do not think the "anticipated nature, scope, and duration" of the use of force by the United States in Libya rose to the level of a "war" in the constitutional sense, requiring the President to seek a declaration of war or other prior authorization from Congress.

Accordingly, we conclude that President Obama could rely on his constitutional power to safeguard the national interest by directing the anticipated military operation in Libya—which were limited in their nature, scope, and duration—without prior congressional authorization.

Hamdi v. Rumsfeld

542 U.S. 507 (2004)

The father of Yaser Esam Hamdi filed a writ of habeas corpus to challenge the government's custody of his son "without access to legal counsel or notice of any charges pending against him." The petition argued that Hamdi's detention was not legally authorized and that detention without charges, access to an impartial tribunal, or assistance of counsel violated the Fifth and Fourteenth Amendments. The lawsuit was directed against Secretary of Defense Donald Rumsfeld.

JUSTICE O'CONNOR announced the judgment of the Court and delivered an opinion, in which THE CHIEF JUSTICE, JUSTICE KENNEDY, and JUSTICE BREYER join.

At this difficult time in our Nation's history, we are called upon to consider the legality of the Government's detention of a United States citizen on United States soil as an "enemy combatant" and to address the process that is constitutionally owed to one who seeks to challenge his classification as such.... We hold that although Congress authorized the detention of combatants in the narrow circumstances alleged here, due process demands that a citizen held in the United States as an enemy combatant be given a meaningful opportunity to contest the factual basis for that detention before a neutral decisionmaker.

I

[*Justice O'Connor describes the enactment by Congress of the Authorization for Use of Military Force (the AUMF), which authorized the President to "use all necessary and appropriate force against those nations, organizations, or persons he determines planned, authorized, committed, or aided the terrorist attacks" of 9/11 or "harbored such organizations or persons, in order to prevent any future acts of international terrorism against the United States by such nations, organizations or persons." On the basis of that authority, President Bush ordered U.S. forces to Afghanistan, with a mission to subdue al Qaeda and quell the Taliban regime. Yaser Esam Hamdi, born in Louisiana, was seized by members of the Northern Alliance, a coalition of military groups opposed to the Taliban government, and turned over to the U.S. military. After being taken to Guantánamo Bay he was transferred to a naval brig in Norfolk, Va., and later to a brig in Charlestown, S.C. The government designated Hamdi an "enemy combatant" who could be held indefinitely, without formal charges or proceedings.*]

II

The threshold question before us is whether the Executive has the authority to detain citizens who qualify as "enemy combatants"....

The Government maintains that no explicit congressional authorization is required, because the Executive possesses plenary authority to detain pursuant to Article II of the Constitution. We do not reach the question whether Article II provides such authority, however, because we agree with the Government's alternative position, that Congress has in fact authorized Hamdi's detention, through the AUMF.

[*Justice O'Connor summarizes Hamdi's argument that his detention is forbidden by 18 U.S.C. §4001(a), enacted in 1971, providing that "[n]o citizen shall be imprisoned or otherwise detained by the United States except pursuant to an Act of Congress." She concludes that AUMF is "explicit congressional authorization for the detention of individuals in the narrow category we describe." Detention of individuals in this category "is so fundamental and accepted as an incident to war as to be an exercise of the 'necessary and appropriate force' Congress has authorized the President to use." Detention, she says, is not punishment but simply a means of preventing "the captured individual from serving the enemy."*]

Hamdi contends that the AUMF does not authorize indefinite or perpetual detention. Certainly, we agree that indefinite detention for the purpose of interrogation is not authorized....

Ex parte Milligan, 4 Wall. 2, 125 (1866), does not undermine our holding about the Government's authority to seize enemy combatants, as we define that term today. In that case, the Court made repeated reference to the fact that its inquiry into whether the military tribunal had jurisdiction to try and punish Milligan turned in large part on the fact that Milligan was not a prisoner of war, but a resident of Indiana arrested while at home there.... Had Milligan been captured while he was assisting Confederate soldiers by carrying a rifle against Union troops on a Confederate battlefield, the holding of the Court might well have been different....

Quirin ... both postdates and clarifies *Milligan*,

providing us with the most apposite precedent we have on the question of whether citizens may be detained in such circumstances....

III

[*In this section, O'Connor analyzes the writ of habeas corpus, pointing out that all sides agree that the writ —absent suspension of the writ (which "has not occurred here")—remains available to every individual detained within the United States. It is thus "undisputed that Hamdi was properly before an Article III court to challenge his detention." The Government argued that because it is "undisputed" that Hamdi's seizure took place in a combat zone, no further hearing of factfinding was necessary to settle the habeas determination. She rejects that position because the circumstances of Hamdi's seizure in Afghanistan "cannot in any way be characterized as 'undisputed.'" Hamdi was not permitted to speak for himself or even through counsel. She also rejects the argument that, under the circumstances of the case, the federal judiciary should defer to the findings of the executive branch. After weighing the government's interests against those of Hamdi, she concludes that the risk of erroneous deprivation of a detainee's liberty interest is "unacceptably high" under the Government's proposed rule.*]

We therefore hold that a citizen-detainee seeking to challenge his classification as an enemy combatant must receive notice of the factual basis for his classification, and a fair opportunity to rebut the Government's factual assertions before a neutral decisionmaker....

At the same time, the exigencies of the circumstances may demand that, aside from these core elements, enemy combatant proceedings may be tailored to alleviate their uncommon potential to burden the Executive at a time of ongoing military conflict. Hearsay, for example, may need to be accepted as the most reliable available evidence from the Government in such a proceeding. Likewise, the Constitution would not be offended by a presumption in favor of the Government's evidence, so long as that presumption remained a rebuttable one and fair opportunity for rebuttal were provided....

... The parties agree that initial captures on the battlefield need not receive the process we have discussed here; that process is due only when the determination is made to *continue* to hold those who have been seized....

In so holding, we necessarily reject the Government's assertion that separation of powers principles mandate a heavily circumscribed role for the courts in such circumstances.... We have long since made clear that a state of war is not a blank check for the President when it comes to the rights of the Nation's citizens.... Whatever power the United States Constitution envisions for the Executive in its exchanges with other nations or with enemy organizations in times of conflict, it most assuredly envisions a role for all three branches when individual liberties are at stake.... Likewise, we have made clear that, unless Congress acts to suspend it, the Great Writ of habeas corpus allows the Judicial Branch to play a necessary role in maintaining this delicate balance of governance, serving as an important judicial check on the Executive's discretion in the realm of detentions....

There remains the possibility that the standards we have articulated could be met by an appropriately authorized and properly constituted military tribunal....

IV

Hamdi asks us to hold that the Fourth Circuit also erred by denying him immediate access to counsel upon his detention and by disposing of the case without permitting him to meet with an attorney.... He unquestionably has the right to access to counsel in connection with the proceedings on remand....

The judgment of the United States Court of Appeals for the Fourth Circuit is vacated, and the case is remanded for further proceedings.

It is so ordered.

JUSTICE SOUTER, with whom JUSTICE GINSBURG, joins, concurring in part, dissenting in part, and concurring in the judgment.

[*The plurality accepted the Government's argument that the AUMF is authority under the Non-Detention Act.*] Here, I disagree and respectfully dissent. The Government has failed to demonstrate that the Force Resolution authorizes the detention complained of here even on the facts the Government claims. If the Government raises nothing further than the record now shows, the Non-Detention act entitles Hamdi to be released.

... I do not adopt the plurality's resolution of constitutional issues that I would not reach.... [N]or, of course, could I disagree with the plurality's affirmation of Hamdi's right to counsel.... On the other hand, I do not mean to imply agreement that the Government could claim an evidentiary presumption casting the burden of rebuttal on Hamdi, ... or that an opportunity to litigate before a military tribunal might obviate or truncate enquiry by a court on habeas....

JUSTICE SCALIA, with whom JUSTICE STEVENS joins, dissenting....

The very core of liberty secured by our Anglo-Saxon system of separated powers has been freedom from indefinite imprisonment at the will of the Executive....

... When the writ is suspended, the Government is entirely free from judicial oversight. It does not claim such total liberation here, but argues that it need only produce what it calls "some evidence" to satisfy a habeas court that a detained individual is an enemy combatant. [*Scalia rejects the Government's position, concluding that the "only constitutional alternatives are to charge the crime or suspend the writ."*]....

The proposition that the Executive lacks indefinite wartime detention authority over citizens is consistent with the Founders' general mistrust of military power permanently at the Executive's disposal....

IV

The Government argues that our more recent jurisprudence ratifies its indefinite imprisonment of a citizen within the territorial jurisdiction of federal courts. It places primary reliance upon *Ex parte Quirin*, 317 U.S. 1 (1942), ... The case was not this Court's finest hour....

... In *Quirin* it was uncontested that the petitioners were members of enemy forces. They were "*admitted* enemy invaders," 317 U.S., at 47 (emphasis added), and it was "undisputed" that they had landed in the United States in service of German forces, ... [P]etitioner insists that he is *not* a belligerent....

V

It follows from what I have said that Hamdi is entitled to a habeas decree requiring his release unless (1) criminal proceedings are promptly brought, or (2) Congress has suspended the writ of habeas corpus....

JUSTICE THOMAS, dissenting.

The Executive Branch, acting pursuant to the powers vested in the President by the Constitution and with explicit congressional approval, has determined that Yaser Hamdi is an enemy combatant and should be detained. This detention falls squarely within the Federal Government's war powers, and we lack the expertise and capacity to second-guess that decision. [*Justice Thomas agrees with the plurality that the AUMF authorized the President to detain U.S. citizens.*]

Hamdan v. Rumsfeld

548 U.S. 557 (2006)

Salim Ahmed Hamdan was picked up by military forces in Afghanistan after 9/11 and taken to the American naval base in Guantánamo. President George W. Bush designated him an "enemy combatant" eligible for trial by military commission. Hamdan charged that the commission lacked authority to try him and its procedures prevented him from mounting an effective defense. Bringing his action against Secretary of Defense Donald H. Rumsfeld, he prevailed in district court but lost in the D.C. Circuit.

JUSTICE STEVENS announced the judgment of the Court and delivered the opinion of the Court with respect to Parts I through IV, Parts VI through VI-D-iii, Part VI-D-v, and Part VII, and an opinion with respect to Parts V and Vi-D-iv, in which JUSTICE SOUTER, JUSTICE GINSBURG, and JUSTICE BREYER join.

Petitioner Salim Ahmed Hamdan, a Yemeni national, is in custody at an American prison in Guantanamo Bay, Cuba. In November 2001, during hostilities between the United States and the Taliban (which then governed Afghanistan), Hamdan was captured by militia forces and turned over to the U.S, military. In June 2002, he was transported to Guantanamo Bay. Over a year later, the President deemed him eligible for trial by military commission for then-unspecified crimes. After another year had passed, Hamdan was charged with one count of conspiracy "to commit ... offenses triable by military commission." ...

Hamdan filed petitions for writs of habeas corpus and mandamus to challenge the Executive Branch's intended means of prosecuting this charge. He concedes that a court-martial constituted in accordance with the Uniform Code of Military Justice (UCMJ) ... would have authority to try him. His objection is that the military commission the President has convened lacks such authority, for two principal reasons: First, neither congressional Act nor the common law of war supports trial by this commission for the crime of conspiracy—an offense that, Hamdan says, is not a violation of the law of war. Second, Hamdan contends, the procedures that the President had adopted to try him violate the most basic tenets of military and international law, including the principle that a defendant must be permitted to see and hear the evidence against him.

... [W]e conclude that the military commission convened to try Hamdan lacks power to proceed because its structure and procedures violate both the UCMJ and the Geneva Conventions. Four of us also conclude, see Part V, *infra*, that the offense with which Hamdan has been charged is not an "offens[e] that by ... the law of war may be tried by military commissions." 10 U.S.C. §821.

I

[*The charging documents contain 13 numbered paragraphs, the last two entitled "Charge: Conspiracy," containing allegations against Hamdan.*] There is no allegation that Hamdan had any command responsibilities, played a leadership role, or participated in the planning of any activity....

II–III

[*In these sections, Justice Stevens analyzed language in the Detainee Treatment Act (DTA) that prohibited federal courts from hearing habeas petitions from Guantánamo detainees, other than giving the D.C. Circuit "exclusive jurisdiction" over "any final decision" of a Combatant Status Review Tribunal (CSRT). Did the jurisdictional restrictions apply only to new claims by detainees or also to claims pending on the date the bill became law? Justice Stevens rejected the government's argument that the statute stripped the Court of jurisdiction to review a decision on Hamdan by the D.C. Circuit. He also rejected the government's contention that prior case law dictated that the Court abstain from hearing Hamdan's case until there had been a final outcome of on-going military proceedings. Concluding that none of the abstention precedents applied to Hamdan, he moved to the merits of his challenge.*]

IV

... [W]hile we assume that the AUMF activated the President's war powers, ... and that those powers include the authority to convene military commissions in appropriate circumstances, ... there is nothing in the text or legislative history of the AUMF even hinting that Congress intended to expand or alter the authorization set forth in Article 21 of the

UCMJ [which provides: "The provisions of this code conferring jurisdiction upon courts-martial shall not be construed as depriving military commissions, provost courts, or other military tribunals of concurrent jurisdiction in respect of offenders or offenses that by statute or by the law of war may be tried by such military commissions, provost courts, or other military tribunals."]....

Likewise, the DTA cannot be read to authorize this commission.... [I]t contains no language authorizing that tribunal [for Hamdan] or any other at Guantanamo Bay....

V

[*Stevens reviews the types of military commissions previously used to try defendants who violated the law of war. He finds that "[n]one of the overt acts that Hamdan is alleged to have committed violates the law of war. These facts alone cast doubt on the legality of the charge and, hence, the commission.... The offense it alleges is not triable by law-of-war military commission.... There is no suggestion that Congress has, in exercise of its constitutional authority to 'define and punish ... Offences against the Law of Nations,' U.S. Const., Art. I, §8, cl. 10, positively identified 'conspiracy' as a war crime." ... [Without explicit authority from Congress there is risk of] "concentrating in military hands a degree of adjudicative and punitive power in excess of that contemplated either by statute or by the Constitution."*]

VI

[*This section focuses on several procedural deficiencies of the commission created to try Hamdan. "The accused and his civilian counsel may be excluded from, and precluded from ever learning what evidence was presented during, any part of the proceeding that either the Appointing Authority or the presiding officer decides to 'close.'... [N]either live testimony nor witnesses' written statements need be sworn.... [A] presiding officer's determination that evidence 'would not have probative value to a reasonable person' may be overridden by a majority of the other commission members." If the government relied on a confidential informant, Hamdan would "not be permitted to hear the testimony, see the witness's face, or learn his name."*]

[*Stevens finds that "the procedures governing trials by military commission historically have been the same as those governing courts-martial.... The uniformity principle is not an inflexible one; it does not preclude all departures from the procedures dictated for use by courts-martial. But any departure must be tailored to the exigency that necessitates it. . . . The rules set forth in the Manual for Courts-Martial must apply to military commissions unless impracticable. . . . Nothing in the record before us demonstrates that it would be impracticable to apply court-martial rules in this case."]*

[Finally, Stevens concludes that Common Article 3 of the Geneva Conventions "requires that Hamdan be tried by a 'regularly constituted court affording all the judicial guarantees which are recognized as indispensable by civilized peoples.'. . . Common Article 3 obviously tolerates a great degree of flexibility in trying individuals captured during armed conflict; its requirements are general ones, crafted to accommodate a wide variety of legal systems. But requirements they are nonetheless. The commission that the President has convened to try Hamdan does not meet those requirements."]

VII

. . . Hamdan does not challenge, and we do not today address, the Government's power to detain him for the duration of active hostilities in order to prevent such harm. But in undertaking to try Hamdan and subject him to criminal punishment, the Executive is bound to comply with the Rule of Law that prevails in this jurisdiction.

The judgment of the Court of Appeals is reversed, and the case is remanded for further proceedings.

It is so ordered.

THE CHIEF JUSTICE took no part in the consideration or decision of this case [*because he participated in the case before the Court of Appeals*].

[*Justice Breyer wrote a concurrence, joined by Kennedy, Souter, and Ginsburg. Kennedy wrote a sep-*

arate concurrence, joined in part by Souter, Ginsburg, and Breyer.]

JUSTICE SCALIA, with whom JUSTICE THOMAS and JUSTICE ALITO join, dissenting.

[*Scalia finds that the DTA "unambiguously" stripped the courts of jurisdiction to hear this case. He sharply criticizes Stevens for relying on legislative history of the DTA "to buttress its implausible reading" of the statute. Scalia concludes that under the doctrine of abstention the Court should not have exercised jurisdiction over the Hamdan case until all proceedings by military authorities and lower federal courts had been exhausted.*]

JUSTICE THOMAS, with whom JUSTICE SCALIA joins, and with whom JUSTICE ALITO joins in all but Parts I, II-C-1, and III-B-2, dissenting.

[*Thomas agrees with Scalia and Alito that "this Court lacks jurisdiction" to hear Hamdan's case. He also argues that the Court "openly flouts our well-established duty to respect the Executive's judgment in matters of military operations and foreign affairs." He recognizes that Congress, "to be sure, has a substantial and essential role in both foreign affairs and national security," but having gone to Congress to obtain the AUMF, President Bush had sufficient statutory and constitutional authority to act as he did with military commissions.*]

JUSTICE ALITO, with whom JUSTICE SCALIA and JUSTICE THOMAS join in Parts I–III, dissenting.

. . . There is no reason why a court that differs in structure or composition from an ordinary military court must be viewed as having been improperly constituted. . . . The commission in *Quirin* was certainly no more independent from the Executive than the commissions at issue here. . . .

Boumediene v. Bush

553 U.S. 723 (2008)

Detainees in Guantánamo had been designated as "enemy combatants" by Combatant Status Review Tribunals at the naval base. Although captured in Afghanistan and elsewhere, they denied membership in the al Qaeda terrorist network and the Taliban regime that supported al Qaeda. They sought a writ of habeas corpus in federal court. While their appeals were pending, Congress passed the Detainee Treatment Act (DTA) of 2005 to deny habeas relief. After the Supreme Court in *Hamdan* v. *Rumsfeld* (2006) held that the DTA was inapplicable to their case, Congress passed the Military Commissions Act (MCA) of 2006 to deny the courts jurisdiction over habeas actions by detainees who had been determined to be enemy combatants.

JUSTICE KENNEDY delivered the opinion of the Court.

Petitioners are aliens designated as enemy combatants and detained at the United States Naval Station at Guantanamo Bay, Cuba. There are others detained there, also aliens, who are not parties to this suit.

Petitioners present a question not resolved by our earlier cases relating to the detention of aliens at Guantanamo: whether they have the constitutional privilege of habeas corpus, a privilege not to be withdrawn except in conformance with the Suspension Clause, Art. I, §9, cl. 2. We hold these petitioners do have the habeas corpus privilege. Congress has enacted a statute, the Detainee Treatment Act of 2005 (DTA), 119 Stat. 2739, that provides certain procedures for review of the detainees' status. We hold that those procedures are not an adequate and effective substitute for habeas corpus. Therefore §7 of the Military Commissions Act of 2006 (MCA), 28 U.S.C.A. §2241(e) (Supp. 2007), operates as an unconstitutional suspension of the writ. We do not address whether the President has authority to detain these petitioners nor do we hold that the writ must issue. These and other questions regarding the legality of the detention are to be resolved in the first instance by the District Court.

I

[Justice Kennedy explains that after the Court's decision in Hamdi, *Congress established Combatant Status Review Tribunals (CSRTs) to determine whether individuals detained at Guantanamo were "enemy combatants" as defined by the Defense Department. The administration adopted procedures to implement the CSRTs, maintaining that the procedures were designed to comply with the due process requirements identified by the plurality in* Hamdi. *Although each of the detainees in this case denied that they are a member of al Qaeda or the Taliban regime, the CSRT determined them to be an enemy combatant. Their effort to seek a writ of habeas corpus began in February 2002. Federal courts reached different conclusions on their access to habeas. While their appeals were pending, Congress passed the DTA, providing that "no court, justice, or judge shall have jurisdiction to hear or consider ... an application for a writ of habeas corpus filed by or on behalf of an alien detained by the Department of Defense at Guantanamo Bay, Cuba." The statute also provided that the D.C. Circuit would have exclusive jurisdiction to review decisions of the CSRTs. In* Hamdan, *the Court held that this provision did not apply to cases (like the one here) that were pending when Congress passed the*

DTA. Congress responded by passing the MCA. The D.C. Circuit concluded in the Boumediene *case that the MCA stripped from it, and all federal courts, jurisdiction to consider the habeas petitions presented by the petitioners.]*

II

As a threshold matter, we must decide whether MCA §7 denies the federal courts jurisdiction to hear habeas corpus actions pending at the time of its enactment. We hold that statute does deny that jurisdiction so that, if the statute is valid, petitioners' cases must be dismissed. [*Kennedy first rejects the argument of the petitioners that the MCA is not a sufficiently clear statement of congressional intent to strip the federal courts of jurisdiction in pending cases. MCA, he notes, was "a direct response to* Hamdan's *holding that the DTA's jurisdiction-stripping provision had no application to pending cases."*]

III

In deciding the constitutional questions now presented we must determine whether petitioners are barred from seeking the writ or invoking the protections of the Suspension Clause either because of their status, *i.e.*, petitioners' designation by the Executive Branch as enemy combatants, or their physical location, *i.e.*, their presence at Guantanamo Bay. The Government contends that non-citizens designated as enemy combatants and detained in territory located outside our Nation's borders have no constitutional rights and no privilege of habeas corpus....

We begin with a brief account of the history and origins of the writ. Our account proceeds from two propositions. First, protection for the privilege of habeas corpus was one of the few safeguards of liberty specified in a Constitution that, at the outset, had no Bill of Rights. In the system conceived by the Framers the writ had a centrality that must inform proper interpretation of the Suspension Clause. Second, to the extent there were settled precedents or legal commentaries in 1789 regarding the extraterritorial scope of the writ or its application to enemy aliens, those authorities can be instructive for the present case.

... The Framers viewed freedom from unlawful restraint as a fundamental precept of liberty, and they understood the writ of habeas corpus as a vital instrument to secure that freedom. [*Because the writ had frequently been abused by monarchical power, the Framers recognized the need for securing it in the Constitution. After the Magna Carta supposedly placed some constraints on the king, Parliament found it necessary in 1679 to enact additional legislation to secure the writ against executive abuse.*] The Framers' inherent distrust of governmental power was the driving force behind the constitutional plan that allocated powers among the three independent branches. [*The Constitution's structure*] protects persons as well as citizens.... We know that at common law a petitioner's status as an alien was not a categorical bar to habeas corpus relief. [*Although in England, courts were prevented from issuing the writ to such places as Scotland,*] [w]e have no reason to believe an order from a federal court would be disobeyed at Guantanamo.... [W]e take notice of the obvious and uncontested fact that the United States, by virtue of its complete jurisdiction and control over the base, maintains *de facto* sovereignty over this territory.... The Government presents no credible arguments that the military mission at Guantanamo would be compromised if habeas corpus courts had jurisdiction to hear the detainees' claims.... It is true that before today the Court has never held that noncitizens detained by our Government in territory over which another country maintains *de jure* sovereignty have any rights under our Constitution.... We hold that Art. I, § 9, cl. 2, of the Constitution has full effect at Guantanamo Bay. If the privilege of habeas corpus is to be denied to the detainees now before us, Congress must act in accordance with the requirements of the Suspension Clause.

[*Kennedy argues that a detainee needs "a meaningful opportunity" to demonstrate that he is being held erroneously and must have the right to introduce evidence to clear him. Elementary procedural safeguards, including assistance of counsel, protect both citizens and non-citizens. Because of the DTA and MCA, detainees at Guantanamo face restrictions on their access to classified evidence against them and can be found guilty on the basis of hearsay evidence. The CSRTs run "considerable risk of error in the tribunal's findings of fact." Detention at Guantanamo "may last a generation or more." Congress has allowed detainee access to the D.C. Circuit, but it appears that the court cannot consider any evidence "outside the CSRT record." On those grounds, Kennedy decides that the DTA and MCA effect "an unconstitutional suspension of the writ."*]

[*His concluding observations*]: Security subsists, too, in fidelity to freedom's first principles. Chief among these are freedom from arbitrary and unlawful restraint and the personal liberty that is secured by adherence to the separation of powers.... The laws and Constitution are designed to survive, and remain in force, in extraordinary times. Liberty and security can be reconciled; and in our system they are reconciled within the framework of the law. The Framers decided that habeas corpus, a right of first importance, must be a part of that framework, a part of that law.

JUSTICE SOUTER, with whom JUSTICE GINSBURG and JUSTICE BREYER join, concurring.

... [T]he Court in *Rasul* directly answered the very historical question that JUSTICE SCALIA says is dispositive.... But whether one agrees or disagrees with today's decision, it no bolt from the blue....

It is in fact the very lapse of four years from the time *Rasul* put everyone on notice that habeas process was available to Guantanamo detainees.... [T]oday's decision is no judicial victory, but an act of perseverance in trying to make habeas review, and the obligation of the courts to provide it, mean something of value both to prisoners and to the Nation....

CHIEF JUSTICE ROBERTS, with whom JUSTICE SCALIA, JUSTICE THOMAS, and JUSTICE ALITO join, dissenting.

Today, the Court strikes down as inadequate the most generous set of procedural protections ever afforded aliens detained by this country as enemy combatants. The political branches crafted these procedures amidst an ongoing military conflict, after much careful investigation and thorough debate. The Court rejects them today out of hand, without bothering to say what due process rights the detainees possess, without explaining how the statute fails to vindicate those rights, and before a single petitioner has even attempted to avail himself of the law's operation. And to what effect? The majority merely replaces a review system designed by the people's representatives with a set of shapeless procedures to be defined by federal courts at some future date....

... How the detainee's claims will be decided now that the DTA is gone is anybody's guess....

JUSTICE SCALIA, with whom THE CHIEF JUSTICE, JUSTICE THOMAS, and JUSTICE ALITO join, dissenting.

Today, for the first time in our Nation's history, the Court confers a constitutional right to habeas corpus on alien enemies detained abroad by our military forces in the course of an ongoing war. THE CHIEF JUSTICE's dissent, which I join, shows that the procedures prescribed by Congress in the Detainee Treatment Act provide the essential protections that habeas corpus guarantees; there has thus been no suspension of the writ, and no basis exists for judicial intervention beyond what the Act allows. My problem with today's opinion is more fundamental still: The writ of habeas corpus does not, and never has, run in favor of aliens abroad; the Suspension Clause thus has no application, and the Court's intervention in this military matter is entirely *ultra vires*....

The game of bait-and-switch that today's opinion plays upon the Nation's Commander in Chief will make the war harder on us. It will almost certainly cause more Americans to be killed....

... What competence does the Court have to second-guess the judgment of Congress and the President on such a point? None whatever....

War Powers Resolution

After several years of hearings and floor action, Congress passed legislation in 1973 to provide a framework for "collective judgment" between Congress and the President in the exercise of the war power. Although President Nixon vetoed the bill, he was overridden by both Houses and the bill became law. It establishes procedures for the introduction of U.S. forces into combat and sets forth a number of important policies in Section 8. The legislation, P.L. 93-148, is found at 87 Stat. 555 (1973) and 50 U.S.C. § 1541–48.

JOINT RESOLUTION

Concerning the war powers of Congress and the President.

Resolved by the Senate and House of Representatives of the United States of America in Congress assembled,

SHORT TITLE

Section 1. This joint resolution may be cited as the "War Powers Resolution".

PURPOSE AND POLICY

Sec. 2. (a) It is the purpose of this joint resolution to fulfill the intent of the framers of the Constitution of the United States and insure that the collective judgment of both the Congress and the President will apply to the introduction of United States Armed Forces into hostilities, or into situations where imminent involvement in hostilities is clearly indicated by the circumstances, and to the continued use of such forces in hostilities or in such situations.

(b) Under article I, section 8, of the Constitution, it is specifically provided that the Congress shall have the power to make all laws necessary and proper for carrying into execution, not only its own powers but also all other powers vested by the Constitution in the Government of the United States, or in any department or officer thereof.

(c) The constitutional powers of the President as Commander-in-Chief to introduce United States Armed Forces into hostilities, or into situations where imminent involvement in hostilities is clearly indicated by the circumstances, are exercised only pursuant to (1) a declaration of war, (2) specific statutory authorization, or (3) a national emergency created by attack upon the United States, its territories or possessions, or its armed forces.

CONSULTATION

Sec. 3. The President in every possible instance shall consult with Congress before introducing United States Armed Forces into hostilities or into situations where imminent involvement in hostilities is clearly indicated by the circumstances, and after every such introduction shall consult regularly with the Congress until United States Armed Forces are no longer engaged in hostilities or have been removed from such situations.

REPORTING

Sec. 4. (a) In the absence of a declaration of war, in any case in which United States Armed Forces are introduced—

(1) into hostilities or into situations where imminent involvement in hostilities is clearly indicated by the circumstances;

(2) into the territory, airspace or waters of a foreign nation, while equipped for combat, except for deployments which relate solely to supply, replacement, repair, or training of such forces; or

(3) in numbers which substantially enlarge United States Armed Forces equipped for combat already located in a foreign nation;

the President shall submit within 48 hours to the Speaker of the House of Representatives and to the President pro tempore of the Senate a report, in writing, setting forth—

(A) the circumstances necessitating the introduction of United States Armed Forces;

(B) the constitutional and legislative authority under which such introduction took place; and

(C) the estimated scope and duration of the hostilities or involvement....

CONGRESSIONAL ACTION

Sec. 5. (a) Each report submitted pursuant to section 4(a) (1) shall be transmitted to the Speaker of the House of Representatives and to the President pro tempore of the Senate on the same calendar day....

(b) Within sixty calendar days after a report is submitted or is required to be submitted pursuant to section 4(a) (1), whichever is earlier, the President shall terminate any use of United States Armed Forces with respect to which such report was submitted (or required to be submitted), unless the Congress (1) has declared war or has enacted a specific authorization for such use of United States Armed Forces, (2) has extended by law such sixty-day period, or (3) is physically unable to meet as a result of an armed attack upon the United States. Such sixty-day period shall be extended for not more than an additional thirty days if the President determines and certifies to the Congress in writing that unavoidable military necessity respecting the safety of United States Armed Forces requires the continued use of such armed forces in the course of bringing about a prompt removal of such forces.

(c) Notwithstanding subsection (b), at any time that United States Armed Forces are engaged in hostilities outside the territory of the United States, its possessions and territories without a declaration of war or specific statutory authorization, such forces shall be removed by the President if the Congress so directs by concurrent resolution.

CONGRESSIONAL PRIORITY PROCEDURES FOR JOINT RESOLUTION OR BILL

Sec. 6 [*Provides for expedited consideration of a joint resolution or bill introduced pursuant to Section 5(b). Deadlines are established for committee and floor action, unless the House or Senate determine otherwise by yeas and nays. The objective is to complete action not later than the expiration of the 60-day period.*]

CONGRESSIONAL PRIORITY PROCEDURES FOR CONCURRENT RESOLUTION

Sec. 7. [*Provides for expedited consideration of a concurrent resolution introduced pursuant to Section 5(c). Deadlines are established for committee and floor action, unless the House or Senate determine other-*

wise by yeas and nays. The objective is to complete action within 48 days.]

INTERPRETATION OF JOINT RESOLUTION

Sec. 8. (a) Authority to introduce United States Armed Forces into hostilities or into situations wherein involvement in hostilities is clearly indicated by the circumstances shall not be inferred—

(1) from any provision of law (whether or not in effect before the date of the enactment of this joint resolution), including any provision contained in any appropriation Act, unless such provision specifically authorizes the introduction of United States Armed Forces into hostilities or into such situations and states that it is intended to constitute specific statutory authorization within the meaning of this joint resolution; or

(2) from any treaty heretofore or hereafter ratified unless such treaty is implemented by legislation specifically authorizing the introduction of United States Armed Forces into hostilities or into such situations and stating that it is intended to constitute specific statutory authorization within the meaning of this joint resolution.

(b) Nothing in this joint resolution shall be construed to require any further specific statutory authorization to permit members of United States Armed Forces to participate jointly with members of the armed forces of one or more foreign countries in the headquarters operations of high-level military commands which were established prior to the date of enactment of this joint resolution and pursuant to the United Nations Charter or any treaty ratified by the United States prior to such date.

(c) For purposes of this joint resolution, the term "introduction of United States Armed Forces" includes the assignment of members of such armed forces to command, coordinate, participate in the movement of, or accompany the regular or irregular military forces of any foreign country or government when such military forces are engaged, or there exists an imminent threat that such forces will become engaged, in hostilities.

(d) Nothing in this joint resolution—

(1) is intended to alter the constitutional authority of the Congress or of the President, or the provisions of existing treaties; or

(2) shall be construed as granting any authority to the President with respect to the introduction of United States Armed Forces into hostilities or into situations wherein involvement in hostilities is clearly indicated by the circum-

stances which authority he would not have had in the absence of this joint resolution.

SEPARABILITY CLAUSE

Sec. 9. If any provision of this joint resolution or the application thereof to any person or circumstance is held invalid, the remainder of the joint resolution and the application of such provision to any other person or circumstance shall not be affected thereby.

EFFECTIVE DATE

Sec. 10. This joint resolution shall take effect on the date of its enactment.

Dellums v. Bush

752 F.Supp. 1141 (D.D.C. 1990)

After President George H. W. Bush introduced U.S. troops into the Persian Gulf in 1990 to create the potential for taking offensive action against Iraq, Congressman Ron Dellums and 53 other members of Congress brought suit requesting an injunction to prevent him from going to war without first securing a declaration of war or other explicit congressional authorization. Although the district court declined to issue the injunction, it issued a significant opinion rejecting many of the theories of presidential power advanced by the administration.

HAROLD H. GREENE, District Judge.

This is a lawsuit by a number of members of Congress who request an injunction directed to the President of the United States to prevent him from initiating an offensive attack against Iraq without first securing a declaration of war or other explicit congressional authorization for such action.

I

The factual background is, briefly, as follows. On August 2, 1990, Iraq invaded the neighboring country of Kuwait. President George Bush almost immediately sent United States military forces to the Persian Gulf area to deter Iraqi aggression and to preserve the integrity of Saudi Arabia. The United States, generally by presidential order and at times with congressional concurrence, also took other steps, including a blockade of Iraq, which were approved by the United Nations Security Council, and participated in by a great many other nations.

On November 8, 1990, President Bush announced a substantial increase in the Persian Gulf military deployment, raising the troop level significantly above the 230,000 then present in the area. At the same time, the President stated that the objective was to provide "an adequate *offensive* military option" should that be necessary to achieve such goals as the withdrawal of Iraqi forces from Kuwait. Secretary of Defense Richard Cheney likewise referred to the ability of the additional military forces "to conduct *offensive* military operations."

The House of Representatives and the Senate have in various ways expressed their support for the President's past and present actions in the Persian Gulf. However, the Congress was not asked for, and it did not take, action pursuant to Article I, Section 8, Clause 11 of the Constitution "to declare war" on Iraq. On November 19, 1990, the congressional plaintiffs brought this action, which proceeds on the premise that the initiation of offensive United States military action is imminent, that such action would be unlawful in the absence of a declaration of war by the Congress, and that a war without concurrence by the Congress would deprive the congressional plaintiffs of the voice to which they are entitled under the Constitution....

II POLITICAL QUESTION

It is appropriate first to sketch out briefly the constitutional and legal framework in which the current controversy arises. Article, I, Section 8, Clause 11 of the Constitution grants to the Congress the power "To declare War." To the extent that this unambiguous direction requires construction or explanation, it is provided by the framers' comments that they felt it to be unwise to entrust the momentous power to involve the nation in a war to the President alone; Jefferson explained that he desired "an effectual check to the Dog of war"; James Wilson similarly expressed the expectation that this system would guard against hostilities being initiated by a single man. Even Abraham Lincoln, while a Congressman, said more than half a century later that "*no one man* should hold the power of bringing" war upon us.

The congressional power to declare war does not

stand alone, however, but it is accompanied by powers granted to the President. Article II, Section 1, Clause 1 and Section 2 provide that "[t]he executive powers shall be vested in a President of the United States of America," and that "[t]he President shall be Commander in Chief of the Army and Navy...."

It is the position of the Department of Justice on behalf of the President that the simultaneous existence of all these provisions renders it impossible to isolate the war-declaring power....

... Indeed, the Department contends that there are no judicially discoverable and manageable standards to apply....

This claim on behalf of the Executive is far too sweeping to be accepted by the courts. If the Executive had the sole power to determine that any particular offensive military operation, no matter how vast, does not constitute war-making but only an offensive military attack, the congressional power to declare war will be at the mercy of a semantic decision by the Executive. Such an "interpretation" would evade the plain language of the Constitution, and it cannot stand.

... [T]he Department goes on the suggest that the issue in this case is still political rather than legal, because in order to resolve the dispute the Court would have to inject itself into foreign affairs, a subject which the Constitution commits to the political branches. That argument, too, must fail.

While the Constitution grants to the political branches, and in particular to the Executive, responsibility for conducting the nation's foreign affairs, it does not follow that the judicial power is excluded from the resolution of cases merely because they may touch upon such affairs. The court must instead look at "the particular question posed" in the case. *Baker v. Carr,* 369 U.S. at 211.... In fact, courts are routinely deciding cases that touch upon or even have a substantial impact on foreign and defense policy....

... [T]he Court has no hesitation in concluding that an offensive entry into Iraq by several hundred thousand United States servicemen under the conditions described above could be described as a "war" within the meaning of Article I, Section 8, Clause 11, of the Constitution. To put it another way: the Court is not prepared to read out of the Constitution the clause granting to the Congress, and to it alone, the authority "to declare war."

III STANDING

The Department of Justice argues next that the plaintiffs lack "standing" to pursue this action.

. . .

With close to 400,000 United States troops stationed in Saudi Arabia, with all troop rotation and leave provisions suspended, and with the President having acted vigorously on his own as well as through the Secretary of State to obtain from the United Nations Security Council a resolution authorizing the use of all available means to remove Iraqi forces from Kuwait, including the use of force, it is disingenuous for the Department to characterize plaintiffs' allegations as to the imminence of the threat of offensive military action for standing purposes as "remote and conjectural,".... For these reasons, the Court concludes that the plaintiffs have adequately alleged a threat of injury in fact necessary to support standing.

IV REMEDIAL DISCRETION

Another issue raised by the Department which must be addressed briefly is the application to this case of the doctrine of "remedial" discretion developed by the Court of Appeals for this Circuit. [*i.e., courts will dismiss a case brought by a congressional plaintiff who could obtain substantial relief from fellow legislators through the enactment, repeal, or amendment of a statute.*] Judge Greene concludes that the "plaintiffs in this case do not have a remedy available from their fellow legislators."

V RIPENESS

. . .

No one knows the position of the Legislative Branch on the issue of war or peace with Iraq; certainly no one, including this Court, is able to ascertain the congressional position on that issue on the basis of this lawsuit brought by fifty-three members of the House of Representatives and one member of the U.S. Senate. It would be both premature and presumptuous for the Court to render a decision on the issue of whether a declaration of war is required at this time or in the near future when the Congress itself has provided no indication whether it deems such a declaration either necessary, on the one hand, or imprudent, on the other.

... In short, unless the Congress as a whole, or by a majority, is heard from, the controversy here cannot be deemed ripe; it is only if the majority of the Congress seeks relief from an infringement on its constitutional war-declaration power that it may be entitled to receive it.

... [A]n injunction will be issued only if, the Court could find that the controversy is ripe for judicial decision. That situation does not, or at least not yet, prevail, and plaintiffs' request for a preliminary injunction will therefore not be granted.

For the reasons stated, it is this 13th day of December, 1990

ORDERED that plaintiffs' motion for preliminary injunction be and it is hereby denied.

Campbell v. Clinton

203 F.3d 19 (D.C. Cir. 2000)*

Congressman Tom Campbell, joined by several other members of Congress, filed a lawsuit seeking a declaration that President Clinton violated the War Powers Clause of the Constitution and the War Powers Resolution by committing U.S. forces to hostilities in Yugoslavia without obtaining authority from Congress. After a district court granted the President's motion to dismiss, Campbell brought this appeal. The D.C. circuit considered several issues, including Campbell's standing to bring the suit and the competence of courts to decide questions of war.

SILBERMAN, Circuit Judge: ...

On March 24, 1999, President Clinton announced the commencement of NATO air and cruise missile attacks on Yugoslav targets. Two days later he submitted to Congress a report, "consistent with the War Powers Resolution," detailing the circumstances necessitating the use of armed forces, the deployment's scope and expected duration, and asserting that he had "taken these actions pursuant to [his] authority ... as Commander in Chief and Chief Executive." On April 28, Congress voted on four resolutions related to the Yugoslav conflict: It voted down a declaration of war 427 to 2 and an "authorization" of the air strikes 213 to 213, but it also voted against requiring the President to immediately end U.S. participation in the NATO operation and voted to fund that involvement. The conflict between NATO and Yugoslavia continued for 79 days, ending on June 10 with Yugoslavia's agreement to withdraw its forces from Kosovo and allow deployment of a NATO-led peacekeeping force....

... Since we agree with the district court that the congressmen lack standing it is not necessary to decide whether there are other jurisdictional defects.

... Congress certainly could have passed a law forbidding the use of U.S. forces in the Yugoslav campaign; indeed, there was a measure—albeit only a concurrent resolution—introduced to require the President to withdraw U.S. troops. Unfortunately, however, for those congressmen who, like appellants, desired an end to U.S. involvement in Yugoslavia, this measure was *defeated* by a 139 to 290 vote. Of course, Congress always retains appropriations authority and could have cut off funds for the American role in the conflict. Again there was an effort to do so but it failed; appropriations were authorized. And there always remains the possibility of impeachment should a President act in disregard of Congress' authority on these matters.

. . .

Accordingly, the district court is affirmed; appellants lack standing.

SILBERMAN, Circuit Judge, concurring:

... [I]n my view, no one is able to bring this challenge because the two claims are not justiciable. We lack "judicially discoverable and manageable standards" for addressing them, and the War Powers Clause claim implicates the political question doctrine. See *Baker* v. *Carr*, 369 U.S. 186, 217 (1962).

... It has been held that the statutory threshold standard is not precise enough and too obviously calls for a political judgment to be one suitable for judicial determinations.... I think that is correct....

RANDOLPH, Circuit Judge, concurring in the judgment:

The majority opinion [*by Silberman and Tatel, on standing*] does not, I believe, correctly analyze plaintiffs' standing to sue. It misconceives the holding of *Raines v. Byrd* ... and conflicts with the law of this circuit. I believe plaintiffs lack standing, at least to litigate their constitutional claim, but for reasons the majority opinion neglects. I also believe that the case is moot, an optional disposition of the appeal....

---

* The text for this case was obtained in electronic form from Westlaw and is reproduced by permission of the West Group.

TATEL, Circuit Judge, concurring:

Although I agree with Judge Silberman that *Raines v. Byrd* ... as interpreted by this court in *Chenoweth v. Clinton* ... deprives plaintiffs of standing to bring this action, I do not share his view that the case poses a nonjusticiable political question....

To begin with, I do not agree that courts lack judicially discoverable and manageable standards for "determining the existence of a 'war.'" ... Whether the military activity in Yugoslavia amounted to "war" within the meaning of the Declare War Clause ... is no more standardless than any other question regarding the constitutionality of government action. Precisely what police conduct violates the Fourth Amendment guarantee "against unreasonable searches and seizures?" When does government action amount to "an establishment of religion" prohibited by the First Amendment? When is an election district so bizarrely shaped as to violate the Fourteenth Amendment guarantee of "equal protection of the laws?" Because such constitutional terms are not self-defining, standards for answering these questions have evolved, as legal standards always do, through years of judicial decisionmaking. Courts have proven no less capable of developing standards to resolve war powers challenges.

Since the earliest years of the nation, courts have not hesitated to determine when military action constitutes "war." In *Bas v. Tingy*, 4 U.S. (4 Dall.) 37 (1800), the Supreme Court had to decide whether hostilities between France and the United States amounted to a state of war in order to resolve disputes over captured ships....

... [C]ourts are competent to adjudge the existence of war and the allocation of war powers between the President and Congress....

E. RIGHTS OF CITIZENSHIP

All three branches have been active in determining questions of citizenship and aliens. Article I, Section 8, Clause 4, gives Congress the power to establish a "uniform Rule of Naturalization." Congress has conferred jurisdiction upon the courts to naturalize aliens as citizens, and the executive branch has been active in asserting its notion of prerogatives concerning both citizenship and aliens.

Part of the controversy concerns the ability of aliens to obtain citizenship if they oppose war. In 1929 the Supreme Court held that the government was entitled to deny a woman an application for naturalization because, as a pacifist, she answered that she "would not take up arms personally" to defend the country. The Court said that the duty of citizens to defend the country against enemies was a "fundamental principle" of the Constitution. United States v. Schwimmer, 279 U.S. 644, 650 (1929). In one of his famous dissents, Justice Holmes noted that the woman was more than fifty years of age and could not bear arms if she wanted to. He added:

> ... [I]f there is any principle of the Constitution that more imperatively calls for attachment than any other it is the principle of free thought—not free thought for those who agree with us but freedom for the thought that we hate.... I would suggest that the Quakers have done their share to make the country what it is, that many citizens agree with the applicant's belief and that I had not supposed hitherto that we regretted our inability to expel them because they believe more than some of us do in the teachings of the Sermon on the Mount.

Two years later, the Court again upheld the government's action in denying an application for citizenship from someone who would not promise to bear arms in defense of the United States unless he believed the war to be morally justified. He based his belief not on pacifism but on the principles of Christianity. The Court acknowledged that Congress could, as it had, relieve the conscientious objector from the obligation to bear arms, but this policy applied only to citizens, not to aliens seeking citizenship. The dissenters in this 5 to 4 decision argued that Congress had never expressly required that aliens promise to bear arms as a condition of obtaining citizenship and that courts should not act on the basis of implications. United States v. Macintosh, 283 U.S. 605, 623–24 (1931); United States v. Bland, 283 U.S. 636 (1931).

These decisions were shaken and finally overturned by cases in the 1940s. The first concerned someone who had been granted citizenship in 1927 but the government began proceedings in 1939 to cancel the citizenship, claiming that during the five years before naturalization the man had been affiliated with certain Communist organizations. The government charged that he had obtained citizenship by "fraud." The Court held that it was not enough for the government to prevail on a bare preponderance of the evidence. The evidence had to be clear, unequivocal, and convincing. The government could not sustain this higher burden. Schneiderman v. United States, 320 U.S. 118 (1943).

In 1946 the Court overruled its earlier decisions in *Schwimmer, Macintosh,* and *Bland.* It held that an alien who is willing to take the oath of allegiance and to serve in the army as a noncombatant but who, because of religious beliefs, is unwilling to bear arms in defense of the country, may be admitted nonetheless to citizenship. The Court pointed out that many citizens—nurses, engineers, doctors, chaplains, litter bearers—contribute to the war effort without bearing arms. Girouard v. United States, 328 U.S. 61, 64 (1946).

The Loss of Citizenship

In 1958, the Court decided whether a native-born American could be stripped of his citizenship because he had been convicted by court-martial for wartime desertion. The Army had sentenced him to three years of hard labor, forfeited his pay and allowances, and gave him a dishonorable discharge. When he later applied for a passport, it was denied because a congressional statute required loss of citizenship for wartime desertion or a dishonorable discharge. The Court held that a person must voluntarily renounce or abandon citizenship. Citizenship was not "a license that expires upon misbehavior." Trop v. Dulles, 356 U.S. 86, 92 (1958). Denationalization violated the Eighth Amendment because it resulted in "the total destruction of the individual's status in organized society. It is a form of punishment more primitive than torture, for it destroys for the individual the political existence that was centuries in the development." Id. at 101.

The Court divided 5 to 4 on this case and split by the same margin in a companion case that upheld the power of Congress to strip someone of citizenship if he or she votes in a foreign political election. The Court deferred to Congress on this occasion because of foreign policy considerations and the possibility of serious international embarrassment. Perez v. Brownell, 356 U.S. 44 (1958). The dissenters maintained that citizenship "*is* man's basic right for it is nothing less than the right to have rights. Remove this priceless possession and there remains a stateless person, disgraced and degraded in the eyes of his countrymen."

Another 5–4 decision in 1963 held that Congress could not use expatriation as punishment for draft evaders without providing for the procedural safeguards in the Fifth and Sixth Amendments: indictment, notice, confrontation, jury trial, assistance of counsel, and compulsory process for obtaining witnesses. Kennedy v. Mendoza-Martinez, 372 U.S. 144 (1963). Obviously, this decision was inconsistent with the result five years before in *Perez,* which permitted expatriation without criminal trial, and the Court was parting company from earlier decisions that had ruled expatriation unconstitutional under the Eighth Amendment. Another ruling in 1964 struck down a statutory provision because it favored native-born citizens over naturalized citizens. Schneider v. Rusk, 377 U.S. 163 (1964).

The confusion continued in 1967 with a 5–4 decision overruling *Perez.* This brought the Court back to where it was in 1958: citizenship could be renounced only voluntarily. Even acting under the foreign affairs power, Congress has no power to divest a person of his or her citizenship. Afroyim v. Rusk, 387 U.S. 253 (1967). However, this decision and *Schneider* were "distinguished" in 1971 when the Court allowed citizenship to be lost under certain conditions. If someone acquires citizenship by being born abroad to parents, one of whom is an American citizen, citizenship can be retained only by satisfying residency requirements established by Congress. Rogers v. Bellei, 401 U.S. 815 (1971).[8]

---

8. See also Fedorenko v. United States, 449 U.S. 490 (1981); John P. Roche, "The Expatriation Cases: 'Breathes There the Man, With Soul So Dead …'?" 1963 Sup. Ct. Rev. 325; P. Allan Dionisopoulos, "Afroyim v. Rusk: The Evolution, Uncertainty and Implications of a Constitutional Principle," 55 Minn. L. Rev. 235 (1970).

CONCLUSIONS

Much of the debate on the allocation of foreign affairs powers between Congress and the President revolves around two competing models. Under *Curtiss-Wright*, the President is blessed with extra-constitutional, inherent powers. The necessities of international affairs and diplomacy make the President the dominant figure. On the other hand, the *Steel Seizure Case* assumes that Congress is the basic lawmaker in both domestic and foreign affairs. Inherent powers are denied, although congressional inertia, silence, or acquiescence may invite independent and conclusive actions by the executive.

The lesson to be drawn from either model is that Congress has ample powers to legislate for emergencies, at home or abroad, but those powers must be exercised. Congressional influence depends on its willingness to act and take responsibility. Presidential influence, at least for long-term commitments, cannot survive on assertions of inherent power. The President needs the support and understanding of both Congress and the public. Another lesson regards the role of federal courts in participating in matters of war and foreign policy. Like Congress, judges need to show a willingness to act and take responsibility. Otherwise, presidential power operates with few checks and balances.

NOTES AND QUESTIONS

1. The framers vested in Congress the constitutional authority to take the country from a state of peace to a state of war against another country. How do the doctrines developed by Justice Sutherland in *Curtiss-Wright* undermine that constitutional value of republican government? What were his sources for inherent presidential power?

2. If his comments were dicta, why are they considered relevant and influential? Did he characterize John Marshall's "sole organ" doctrine correctly? Do dicta, if repeated often enough, become the holding?

3. The framers understood that constitutional text alone would not preserve the system of checks and balances that is so critical in protecting individual rights and liberties. How is that lesson revealed in such examples as the detention of Japanese Americans during World War II, Justice Jackson's concurrence in the Steel Seizure Case, and the treaty termination case of *Goldwater v. Carter*?

4. What basic judicial checks operated on the creation of military tribunals by President George W. Bush after 9/11? Do courts have authority and competence to participate on questions of foreign relations, the war power, and national security?

SELECTED READINGS

ADLER, DAVID GRAY, AND LARRY N. GEORGE, eds. The Constitution and the Conduct of American Foreign Policy. Lawrence, Kans.: University Press of Kansas, 1996.

BOROSAGE, ROBERT L. "Para-Legal Authority and Its Perils." 40 Law and Contemporary Problems 166 (1976).

COHEN, RICHARD. "Self-Executing Executive Agreements: A Separation of Powers Problem." 24 Buffalo Law Review 137 (1974).

EDGAR, HAROLD, AND BENNO C. SCHMIDT, JR. "Curtiss-Wright Comes Home: Executive Power and National Security Secrecy." 21 Harvard Civil Rights—Civil Liberties Law Review 349 (1986).

ELY, JOHN HART. War and Responsibility: Constitutional Lessons of Vietnam and Its Aftermath. Princeton: Princeton University Press, 1993.

FARBER, DANIEL A. "National Security, the Right to Travel, and the Courts." 1981 Supreme Court Review 263.

FISHER, LOUIS. Presidential War Power. Lawrence: University Press of Kansas, 2d ed. 2004.

———. Military Tribunals and Presidential Power. Lawrence: University Press of Kansas, 2005.

———. The Constitution and 9/11: Recurring Threats to America's Freedoms. Lawrence: University Press of Kansas, 2008.

FRANCK, THOMAS M., AND EDWARD WEISBAND. Foreign Policy by Congress. New York: Oxford University Press, 1979.

——— and Michael J. Glennon. Foreign Relations and National Security Law. St. Paul, Minn.: West, 1987.

GLENNON, MICHAEL J. Constitutional Diplomacy. Princeton: Princeton University Press, 1990.

GOLDSMITH, JACK. The Terror Presidency: Law and Judgment Inside the Bush Administration. New York: Norton, 2007.

HENKIN, LOUIS. Foreign Affairs and the Constitution. New York: Oxford University Press, 1996.

HESS, GARY R. Presidential Decisions for War: Korea, Vietnam, and the Persian Gulf. Baltimore: Johns Hopkins University Press, 2001.

HURTGEN, JAMES R. "The Case for Presidential Prerogative." 7 University of Toledo Law Review 59 (1975).

KOH, HAROLD HONGJU. The National Security Constitution. New Haven: Yale University Press, 1990.

LOFGREN, CHARLES A. "U.S. v. Curtiss-Wright Export Corporation: An Historical Reassessment." 83 Yale Law Journal 1 (1973).

———. "War-Making Under the Constitution: The Original Understanding." 81 Yale Law Journal 672 (1972).

MARCUS, MAEVA. Truman and the Steel Seizure Case: The Limits of Presidential Power. New York: Columbia University Press, 1977.

MURPHY, JOHN F. "Treaties and International Agreements Other Than Treaties: Constitutional Allocation of Power and Responsibility Among the President, the House of Representatives, and the Senate." 23 University of Kansas Law Review 221 (1975).

O'DONNELL, THOMAS A. "Illumination or Elimination of the 'Zone of Twilight'? Congressional Acquiescence and Presidential Authority in Foreign Affairs." 51 Cincinnati Law Review 95 (1982).

OHLY, D. CHRISTOPHER. "Advice and Consent: International Executive Claims Settlement Agreements." 5 Californian Western International Law Journal 271 (1975).

PAUST, JORDAN J. "Is the President Bound by the Supreme Law of the Land? — Foreign Affairs and National Security Reexamined." 9 Hastings Constitutional Law Quarterly 719 (1982).

POWELL, H. JEFFERSON. The President's Authority Over Foreign Affairs. Durham: Carolina Academic Press, 2002.

REVELEY, W. TAYLOR, III. War Powers of the President and Congress. Charlottesville: University Press of Virginia, 1981.

ROVINE, ARTHUR W. "Separation of Powers and International Executive Agreements." 52 Indiana Law Review 297 (1977).

SILVERSTEIN, GORDON. Imbalance of Powers: Constitutional Interpretation and the Making of American Foreign Policy. New York: Oxford University Press, 1997.

SOFAER, ABRAHAM D. War, Foreign Affairs and Constitutional Power: The Origins. Cambridge, Mass.: Ballinger Publishing, 1976.

STEVENS, CHARLES J. "The Use and Control of Executive Agreements: Recent Congressional Initiatives." 20 Orbis 905 (1977).

YOO, JOHN. The Powers of War and Peace: The Constitution and Foreign Affairs after 9/11. Chicago: University of Chicago Press, 2005.

8

Federal-State Relations

Federalism divides constitutional authority and political power between the national government and the states. Theories of federalism cut across almost every constitutional issue, including law enforcement, civil liberties, civil rights, sex discrimination, voting rights, reapportionment, privacy, and welfare payments. This chapter focuses on six topics: the principle of federalism, state immunity against suits, the Commerce Clause, the spending and taxing power, the doctrines of preemption and abstention, and the Incorporation Doctrine (applying the Bill of Rights to the states).

Under Chief Justice Marshall, the Supreme Court extended broad support to congressional efforts to exercise its commerce powers. By the end of the nineteenth century, the Court attempted to restrain Congress, but a variety of judicial doctrines did little more than slow the growth of national power. Congress developed its own independent view of federal-state relations. The meaning of federalism has been shaped more by Congress than by the courts. As the Supreme Court noted in 1946: "the history of judicial limitation of congressional power over commerce, when exercised affirmatively, has been more largely one of retreat than of ultimate victory." Prudential Ins. Co. v. Benjamin, 328 U.S. 408, 415.

A. THE PRINCIPLE OF FEDERALISM

In Federalist No. 39, James Madison responded to criticism that the Constitution had improperly created a national government instead of a federal form (a confederation of sovereign states). Madison identified some features of the Constitution that gave it a national character; other provisions vested power directly in the states. He concluded that the proposed Constitution "is, in strictness, neither a national nor a federal Constitution, but a composition of both."

Independence from England left the 13 American states without a central government. Under the Articles of Confederation, drafted in 1777 and ratified in 1781, each state retained "its sovereignty, freedom and independence" except for a few powers *expressly* delegated to the national government. The weakness of the confederation became of increasing concern, forcing the states to seek some form of regional cooperation to deal with commercial problems. Representatives of Virginia and Maryland met in 1785 at the home of George Washington, but it was decided that an interstate compact would be of more value if it included additional states. Consequently, all states were invited to Annapolis in 1786 to discuss commercial issues. Poor attendance and the need to address other problems led to the convention at Philadelphia the following year "to devise such further provisions as shall appear to them necessary to render the constitution of the Federal Government adequate to the exigencies of the Union."

What emerged from Philadelphia was an entirely new structure of government that divided power functionally (among three separate branches) and spatially (between the national government and the states). The Constitution rejected Montesquieu's theory that republican government could flourish only in small countries. He believed that as the size of the country increased, popular control had to be surrendered, yielding power to aristocracies in moderate-sized countries and to monarchies in large countries. Madison turned this theory on its head in Federalist No. 10 by arguing that republican government was unlikely to survive in a small territory, because a dominant faction would most likely oppress the minority. "Extend the sphere," however, "and you take in a greater variety of parties and interests; you make it less probable that a majority of the whole will have a common motive to invade the rights of other citizens." Dividing this large territory into distinct states added further stability. As Hamilton said in Federalist No. 28, the national government and the states could check the usurpations of each other: "The people, by throwing themselves into either scale, will infallibly make it preponderate. If their rights are invaded by either, they can make use of the other as the instrument of redress."

The Virginia Plan

The Virginia Plan submitted to the Philadelphia Convention called for a strong central government. The rival New Jersey Plan, espousing a confederation with power left largely to the states, attracted little support. The eventual compromise gave the central government power to collect taxes, regulate commerce, declare war, and other express functions, including the Necessary and Proper Clause to carry into effect the enumerated powers. The power of Congress was divided between two chambers: a House of Representatives elected by the people, with its membership based on population; and a Senate elected by state legislatures, with two Senators for each state. This struck an accommodation between the preference of the big states (representation by population) and the demand of the small states (equal voting power for each state).

The Virginia Plan proposed a congressional veto over all state laws "contravening in the opinion of the National Legislature the articles of Union." Although this provision was initially agreed to without debate or dissent, it was later eliminated. 1 Farrand 21, 54. Instead, the Constitution assigns specific powers to Congress, expressly prohibits the states from exercising certain powers, and allows states to exercise other powers if Congress consents (see Table 8.1).

TABLE 8.1 NATIONAL AND STATE POWERS UNDER THE CONSTITUTION*

National Powers	State Powers	Prohibited State Powers	State Powers if Congress Consents
Tax	Tax	—	—
Lay duties on imports and exports	Exercise police power	Tax articles from other states	Lay duties on imports and exports
Borrow money	Borrow money	—	—
Regulate foreign commerce	—	—	—
Regulate interstate commerce	Regulate intrastate commerce	—	—
Establish courts	Establish courts	—	—
Make treaties	—	Make treaties	Make compacts with other states
Coin money	—	Coin money	—
Emit bills of credit	—	Emit bills of credit	—
Declare war	—	Declare war	Engage in war
Raise and support military	—	—	Keep troops in time of peace
Grant letters of marque and reprisal	—	Grant letters of marque and reprisal	—

*The national powers identified above are found in Art. I, §8, and Art. II. State powers are proscribed by Art. I, §10. Under Art. I, §§9 and 10, both Congress and the states are prohibited from passing bills of attainder, ex post facto laws, and laws that grant titles of nobility. In addition, states may not pass laws that impair obligation of contracts.

New States and Territories

The Constitution provides for the admission of new states in Article IV, Section 3: "[N]o new State shall be formed or erected within the Jurisdiction of any other State; nor any State be formed by the Junction of two or more States, or Parts of States, without the consent of the legislatures of the States concerned as well as of the Congress." An exception to this provision occurred in 1861, after South Carolina fired on Fort Sumter. Several states, including Virginia, voted to secede from the Union. The western counties of Virginia nullified the Virginia ordinance of secession and agreed to form a new state. In 1863 President Lincoln issued a proclamation making West Virginia the 35th state. For territory acquired from other countries (such as from the Louisiana Purchase or the Mexican War), Congress converted those lands to territories and later to states.

The Supremacy Clause

National powers are further reinforced by the Supremacy Clause in Article IV, Section 2: "This Constitution, and the laws of the United States which shall be made in pursuance thereof; and all treaties made, or which shall be made, under the authority of the United States, shall be the supreme law of the land; and the judges in every State shall be bound thereby, anything in the constitution or laws of any State to the contrary notwithstanding." Early in its history, the Supreme Court decided that in cases of conflict between state law and a treaty, the latter prevails. Ware v. Hylton, 3 U.S. (3 Dall.) 198 (1796).

In 2000, the Supreme Court applied the Supremacy Clause to a Massachusetts law that barred state entities from buying goods or services from companies doing business with Burma (Myanmar). Congress later imposed sanctions on the country, but delegated to the President substantial discretion to lift the sanctions if the regime made progress in human rights and democracy. A nonprofit corporation, representing several companies affected by the state law, sued on the basis that Massachusetts infringed on the federal foreign affairs power, violated the Foreign Commerce Clause, and was preempted by the federal statute. The Supreme Court held that the state law was invalid under the Supremacy Clause. Crosby v. National Foreign Trade Council, 530 U.S. 363 (2000).

The Property Clause

State power is qualified by the authority of Congress under the Property Clause "to dispose of and make all needful Rules and Regulations respecting the Territory or other Property belonging to the United States" (Art. IV, § 3, Cl. 2). Under this grant of authority, Congress exercises control over vast stretches of public land located inside the states, particularly those in the West. Kleppe v. New Mexico, 426 U.S. 529 (1976).

Privileges and Immunities

State sovereignty is also limited in Article IV, § 2 by the Privileges and Immunities Clause: "The Citizens of each State shall be entitled to all Privileges and Immunities of Citizens in the several States." Along with the Commerce Clause, this was intended to create a "national economic union." Supreme Court of New Hampshire v. Piper, 470 U.S. 274, 280 (1985).[1]

The protection of privileges and immunities also appears in Section 1 of the Fourteenth Amendment: "No State shall make or enforce any law which shall abridge the privileges or immunities of citizens of the United States." In 1999, the Supreme Court resurrected that provision by striking down a California statute that limited the maximum welfare benefits available to a family that had resided

---

1. See also Hicklin v. Orbeck, 437 U.S. 518 (1978); Baldwin v. Montana Fish and Game Comm'n, 436 U.S. 371 (1978); Austin v. New Hampshire, 420 U.S. 656 (1975); Toomer v. Witsell, 334 U.S. 385 (1948).

in the state for less than twelve months. Such families would receive the amount paid by the state of their prior residence. Voting 7 to 2, the Court ruled that this durational residence requirement discriminated against citizens who were entitled to enjoy the privileges and immunities of citizens in the states that they visit. Saenz v. Roe, 526 U.S. 489 (1999). Dissenting in this case, Chief Justice Rehnquist objected to the Court "unearthing from its tomb" the Privileges and Immunities Clause of the Fourteenth Amendment.

The Privileges and Immunities Clause of the Fourteenth Amendment had little use after the Court decided the *Slaughter-House Cases* in 1873. The Court at times struck down durational residency requirements for welfare benefits, but only by finding a "right to travel" in the equal protection guarantee of the Fourteenth Amendment. Shapiro v. Thompson, 394 U.S. 618 (1969). Thirteen years later, in a concurring opinion, Justice O'Connor found a right to travel in the privileges and immunities protection of Article IV, § 2. Zobel v. Williams, 457 U.S. 55 (1982).

The National Guard

Questions of federalism also affect National Guard units. Under Article I, Section 8, Congress may call forth the "militia" (part-time military forces) to suppress insurrections and repel invasions. Congress may also provide for "organizing, arming, and disciplining" the militia and "for governing such Part of them" when called into service for the federal government. The states appoint the officers and have authority for "training the Militia according to the discipline prescribed by Congress." In 1990 a unanimous Court held that a state governor's consent is not needed for training the National Guard in foreign countries. Perpich v. Department of Defense, 496 U.S. 334 (1990). The issue of state v. federal control over the National Guard surfaced again in the aftermath of the disaster caused by Hurricane Katrina in 2005, as the state of Louisiana and the federal government argued over their deployment.

Nullification and Secession

Early in U.S. history, national powers were regularly threatened by state efforts to secede from the Union or to assert the doctrines of interposition and nullification. After the Federalist party passed the Alien and Sedition Acts, the Jeffersonian Republicans protested this exercise of national power. Jefferson's draft of the Kentucky Resolutions of 1798 stated that unauthorized actions by the federal government were "void, and of no force." Here was the doctrine of nullification. The Virginia Resolutions of 1798, which Madison helped write, used somewhat softer language. In cases where the federal government overstepped its powers, the states "have the right and are in duty bound to interpose for arresting the progress of the evil, and for maintaining within their respective limits the authorities, rights, and liberties appertaining to them." Some years later the Federalists complained about Republican policies in the national government. Meeting at the Hartford Convention of 1814, Federalists considered secession and registered the opposition of New England states to the measures taken by Republicans. In 1832 South Carolina's ordinance of nullification maintained that the tariff acts enacted by Congress were "null, void, and no law."

The spirit of nullification led eventually to the South's secession from the Union and the start of the Civil War. After the war, the Supreme Court determined that the rebel states never left the Union: "The Constitution, in all its provisions, looks to an indestructible Union, composed of indestructible States." Texas v. White, 7 Wall. (74 U.S.) 700, 725 (1869). In admitting new states to the Union, Congress cannot impose conditions that would make a state unequal to others. It cannot, for example, dictate to a state the location of its capital. Coyle v. Oklahoma, 221 U.S. 559 (1911).

The Tenth Amendment

Throughout the nineteenth and twentieth centuries, there have been efforts to promote the notion of sovereign states by misconstruing the Tenth Amendment, which provides that the powers "not dele-

---

Nonjudicial Officials Determine Constitutionality of U.S. Bank

Responding to a request by the House of Rep resentatives, Secretary of the Treasury Alexander Hamilton prepared a report on the establishment of a national bank and submitted it on December 13, 1790. 2 Annals of Cong. 2082–2112. Much of the legislative debate the following year focused on the constitutional authority of Congress to use implied powers to create the bank. The Senate acted first, passing the bank bill on January 20, 1791.

During House debate, Madison argued against the constitutionality of the bank on the ground that it was not an enumerated power of Congress, although this contradicted his position two years earlier on the Tenth Amendment. Fisher Ames challenged this theory of enumerated powers by saying that if the power to raise armies had not been given expressly to Congress, it would have been implied by other parts of the Constitution. Theodore Sedgwick reminded the House that Madison, in 1789, had convinced a majority of members that the President had the power to remove executive officials, even though that power is not specifically stated in the Constitution. 2 Annals of Cong. 1955, 1960. Elias Boudinot pointed

to Madison's essay in Federalist No. 44, which offered a broad interpretation of the Necessary and Proper Clause available to Congress to discharge its powers. Id. at 1977. The House passed the bill, 39 to 20.

After the bill cleared Congress, President George Washington asked Cabinet members to comment on the constitutionality of the legislation. Attorney General Edmund Randolph and Secretary of State Thomas Jefferson concluded that Congress lacked the constitutional power to grant a corporate charter for a national bank. Secretary of the Treasury Hamilton prepared a detailed analysis, defending the power of Congress to act in this area. Having drafted the bank bill, he was hardly in a position to claim detachment or objectivity, but Madison, Randolph, and Jefferson also had well-formed attachments and predilections. Washington decided to sign the bill. When the issue was later taken to the Supreme Court, Chief Justice Marshall borrowed wholesale from Hamilton's interpretation of implied powers, sovereignty, and the Necessary and Proper Clause. See 8 The Papers of Alexander Hamilton 97–134 (Harold C. Syrett ed. 1965).

---

gated to the United States by the Constitution, nor prohibited by it to the States, are reserved to the States respectively, or to the people." The Articles of Confederation had given greater protection to the states, which retained all powers except those "expressly delegated" to the national government. When that phrase was proposed for the Tenth Amendment, Madison objected to the word "expressly" because the functions and responsibilities of the federal government could not be delineated with such precision. It was impossible to confine a government to the exercise of express powers, for there "must necessarily be admitted powers by implication, unless the Constitution descended to recount every minutiae." 1 Annals of Cong. 761 (Aug. 18, 1789). On the strength of his argument, Congress eliminated the word "expressly." Moreover, the Necessary and Proper Clause affords Congress the power to pass laws to carry into execution the express powers.

Chief Justice Marshall relied on this legislative history and constitutional text when he upheld the power of Congress to establish a national bank, even though such power is not expressly included in the Constitution. This endorsement of incidental or implied powers signaled a major advance for both national and congressional powers. McCULLOCH v. MARYLAND, 17 U.S. 315 (1819). In upholding the national bank, Marshall followed closely the reasoning and justification first set forth by legislative and executive officials when they developed constitutional grounds for the bank in 1791 (see box).

The idea that the Tenth Amendment contains substantive powers for the states is revived on occasion when the Supreme Court tries to rewrite the Constitution by shoehorning the word "expressly" into the Tenth Amendment. Lane County v. Oregon, 74 U.S. (7 Wall.) 71, 76 (1868); Hammer v. Dagenhart, 247 U.S. 251, 275 (1918). Most decisions, however, accept the Amendment as merely declaratory of a general relationship between the federal government and the states. In 1920, the Court denied that the treaty power was restricted in any way "by some invisible radiation from the general terms of the Tenth Amendment." MISSOURI v. HOLLAND, 252 U.S. 416, 434. A decade later, the Court held that the Tenth Amendment added nothing to the Constitution as originally ratified. United States v. Sprague, 282 U.S. 716, 733 (1931). After another decade, Justice Stone dismissed the Tenth Amendment as a "truism," rephrasing it to read "that all is retained which has not been surrendered." United States v. Darby, 312 U.S. 100, 124 (1941). As a declaratory statement, however, the Amendment "is not without significance." Fry v. United States, 421 U.S. 542, 547 n.7 (1975). The Tenth Amendment has been cited in recent cases to uphold state powers (Section F).

The Eleventh Amendment

States feared lawsuits by citizens from other states or citizens from foreign countries. At the Virginia ratifying convention, Madison insisted that the Supreme Court's jurisdiction over controversies between a state and citizens of another state did not give individuals the power to call any state into court. A citizen might initiate an action, but federal courts would have jurisdiction only if a state consented to be a party. 3 Elliot 533. In Federalist No. 81, Hamilton claimed that states would be shielded by the general principle of immunity: "It is inherent in the nature of sovereignty not to be amenable to the suit of an individual *without its consent.*"

One of the first cases brought to the Supreme Court involved a suit by Dutch bankers to recover funds from Maryland. In this case, the state's Attorney General voluntarily appeared. Vanstophorst v. Maryland, 2 Dall. 401 (1791). The issue of state immunity reached explosive proportions when two citizens from South Carolina, acting as executors of a British creditor, filed suit against Georgia. In 1793 the Supreme Court decided that the suit was consistent with Article III, Section 2, which gave the federal courts jurisdiction over controversies "between a State and Citizens of another State." Chisholm v. Georgia, 2 U.S. (2 Dall.) 419. To prevent a rash of citizen suits, Congress and the states promptly overturned the Court's ruling by ratifying the Eleventh Amendment: "The Judicial power of the United States shall not be construed to extend to any suit in law or equity, commenced or prosecuted against one of the United States by Citizens of another State, or by Citizens or Subjects of any foreign state." Although the Amendment does not expressly bar suits against a state by its own citizens, the Court has consistently held that a state is subject to such suits if it consents.[2]

As interpreted by the Court, however, the Eleventh Amendment does not give states total immunity from suits filed by citizens from other states. The doctrine that a state may not be sued in its own courts without its consent does not provide absolute immunity from suits in the courts of another state. Nevada v. Hall, 440 U.S. 410 (1979). Moreover, the Eleventh Amendment has been substantially narrowed by the Fourteenth Amendment. The Eleventh Amendment only prohibits suits directed against the *states.* Suits are allowed against state *officers* who are charged with denying due process or equal protection under the Fourteenth Amendment. The theory is that an officer acting illegally is functioning as an individual rather than a state official. Ex parte Young, 209 U.S. 123 (1908); Smyth v. Ames, 169 U.S. 466, 518–519 (1898).[3] During the Rehnquist Court, however, the Eleventh Amendment protection of the states was strengthened (see Section F of this chapter).

---

2. Blatchford v. Native Village of Noatak, 501 U.S. 775 (1991). Employees v. Missouri Public Health Dept., 411 U.S. 279, 280 (1973); Great Northern Life Ins. Co. v. Read, 322 U.S. 47, 51 (1944); Duhne v. New Jersey, 251 U.S. 311 (1920); Hans v. Louisiana, 134 U.S. 1 (1890). The theory that the Eleventh Amendment forbids federal courts to hear suits against a state by a citizen of that state was rejected by four Justices in Atascadero State Hospital v. Scanlon, 473 U.S. 234 (1985) and Welch v. Texas Dept. of Highways, 483 U.S. 468 (1987).

3. See Truax v. Raich, 239 U.S. 33 (1915); William A. Fletcher, "A Historical Interpretation of the Eleventh Amendment: A Narrow Construction of an Affirmative Grant of Jurisdiction Rather than a Prohibition Against Jurisdiction," 35 Stan. L. Rev. 1033 (1983); Doyle Mathis, "The Eleventh Amendment: Adoption and Interpretation," 2 Ga. L. Rev. 207 (1968).

State Budgets

This theory of liability does not support a suit against a state official who is used simply as a conduit to recover money from the state. Even if not named in such a case, the state is the real party and is entitled to sovereign immunity. Ford Motor Co. v. Department of Treasury, 323 U.S. 459 (1945); Alabama v. Pugh, 438 U.S. 781 (1978).

State governments regularly invoke sovereign immunity to protect their budgets. In 1974, the Supreme Court held that a suit could not force a state to make retroactive payments for a program it administered for the aged, blind, and disabled. Although the suit was filed against various state officials who administered the program, the funds for retroactive payments would come from the state. The fact that the program was funded equally by state and federal funds was insufficient to establish state consent to be sued in federal courts. Edelman v. Jordan, 415 U.S. 651, 673 (1974). Two years later the Court decided that whenever there is a collision between the Eleventh Amendment and Section 5 of the Fourteenth Amendment, which grants Congress authority to enforce "by appropriate legislation" the substantive provisions of the Fourteenth Amendment, the congressional statute prevails. This policy allows suits against states even for retroactive payments from their treasuries. Fitzpatrick v. Bitzer, 427 U.S. 445 (1976).

Other Factors

Principles of federalism "that might otherwise be an obstacle to congressional authority are necessarily overridden by the power to enforce the Civil War Amendments 'by appropriate legislation.' Those Amendments were specifically designed as an expansion of federal power and an intrusion on state sovereignty." Rome v. United States, 446 U.S. 156, 179 (1980). Unless Congress expresses in unmistakable terms its intent to abrogate the Eleventh Amendment, states may not be sued in federal court without their consent. Atascadero State Hospital v. Scanlon, 473 U.S. 234 (1985); Dellmuth v. Muth, 491 U.S. 223 (1989).

Other than its enforcement powers under the Fourteenth Amendment, may Congress use its Article I powers to abrogate the Eleventh Amendment? The Court has held that Congress may use the Commerce Clause to set aside the sovereign immunity of states. Dennis v. Higgins, 498 U.S. 439 (1991); Pennsylvania v. Union Gas Co., 491 U.S. 1 (1989). As explained later in this chapter (Section F), the Court began to place some limits on the Commerce Clause during the 1990s. The Court has also ruled that the Bankruptcy Code, based on the Article I power of Congress to establish uniform laws for bankruptcies, does not abrogate the states' Eleventh Amendment immunity. Hoffman v. Connecticut Income Maint. Dept., 492 U.S. 96 (1989). A series of decisions in the 1980s and 1990s revealed a Court sharply split over the meaning and application of the Eleventh Amendment, with the Court often divided 5 to 4 (Section F).

McCulloch v. Maryland

17 U.S. 315 (1819)

Congress passed legislation in 1816 to create a Bank of the United States. The power to incorporate a national bank is not expressly granted in the Constitution. On the issue whether an implied power existed, Chief Justice Marshall supplies a broad interpretation of the meaning of the Constitution. In 1818 Maryland passed legislation to impose a tax on all banks or branches of banks in the state not chartered by the legislature. James W. McCulloch, the Bank's cashier in Baltimore, refused to pay the tax. The dispute gave Marshall an opportunity to explore the extent of state sovereignty, interpret the Necessary and Proper Clause, and judge the validity of a state tax on a federal instrumentality.

March 7th, 1819. MARSHALL Ch. J., delivered the opinion of the court. — In the case now to be determined, the defendant, a sovereign state, denies the obligation of a law enacted by the legislature of the Union....

The first question made in the cause is — has congress power to incorporate a bank? ...

The power now contested was exercised by the first congress elected under the present constitution. The bill for incorporating the Bank of the United States did not steal upon an unsuspecting legislature, and pass unobserved. Its principle was completely understood, and was opposed with equal zeal and ability. After being resisted, first, in the fair and open field of debate, and afterwards, in the executive cabinet, with as much persevering talent as any measure has ever experienced, and being supported by arguments which convinced minds as pure and as intelligent as this country can boast, it became a law. The original act was permitted to expire; but a short experience of the embarrassments to which the refusal to revive it exposed the government, convinced those who were most prejudiced against the measure of its necessity, and induced the passage of the present law....

In discussing this question, the counsel for the state of Maryland have deemed it of some importance, in the construction of the constitution, to consider that instrument, not as emanating from the people, but as the act of sovereign and independent states. The powers of the general government, it has been said, are delegated by the states, who alone are truly sovereign; and must be exercised in subordination to the states, who alone possess supreme dominion. It would be difficult to sustain this proposition. The convention which framed the constitution was indeed elected by the state legislatures. But the instrument, when it came from their hands, was a mere proposal, without obligation, or pretensions to it. It was reported to the then existing congress of the United States, with a request that it might "be submitted to a convention of delegates, chosen in each state by the people thereof, under the recommendation of its legislature, for their assent and ratification." This mode of proceeding was adopted; and by the convention, by congress, and by the state legislatures, the instrument was submitted to the *people*. They acted upon it in the only manner in which they can act safely, effectively and wisely, on such a subject, by assembling in convention. It is true, they assembled in their several states — and where else should they have assembled? ...

From these conventions, the constitution derives its whole authority. The government proceeds directly from the people; is "ordained and established," in the name of the people; and is declared to be ordained, "in order to form a more perfect union, establish justice, insure domestic tranquility, and secure the blessings of liberty to themselves and to their posterity." The assent of the states, in their sovereign capacity, is implied, in calling a convention, and thus submitting that instrument to the people. But the people were at perfect liberty to accept or reject it; and their act was final. It required not the affirmance, and could not be negatived, by the state governments. The constitution, when thus adopted, was of complete obligation, and bound the state sovereignties.

. . .

This government is acknowledged by all, to be one of enumerated powers. The principle, that it can exercise only the powers granted to it, would seem too apparent, to have required to be enforced by all those arguments, which its enlightened friends, while it was depending before the people, found it necessary to urge; that principle is now universally admitted. But the question respecting the extent of the powers actually granted, is perpetually arising, and will probably continue to arise, so long as our system shall exist....

Among the enumerated powers, we do not find that of establishing a bank or creating a corporation. But there is no phrase in the instrument which, like the articles of confederation, excludes incidental or implied powers; and which requires that everything granted shall be expressly and minutely described. Even the 10th amendment, which was framed for the purpose of quieting the excessive jealousies which had been excited, omits the word "expressly," and declares only, that the powers "not delegated to the United States, nor prohibited to the states, are reserved to the states or to the people;" thus leaving the question, whether the particular power which may become the subject of contest, has been delegated to the one government, or prohibited to the other, to depend on a fair construction of the whole instrument. The men who drew and adopted this amendment had experienced the embarrassments resulting from the insertion of this word in the articles of confederation, and probably omitted it, to avoid those embarrassments. A constitution, to contain an accurate detail of all the subdivisions of which its great powers will admit, and of all the means by which they may be carried into execution, would partake of the prolixity of a legal code, and could scarcely be embraced by the human mind. It would, probably, never be understood by the public. Its nature, therefore, requires, that only its great outlines should be marked, its important objects designated, and the minor ingredients which compose those objects, be deduced from the nature of the objects themselves. That this idea was entertained by the framers of the American constitution, is not only to be inferred from the nature of the instrument, but from the language. Why else were some of the limitations, found in the 9th section of the 1st article, introduced? It is also, in some degree, warranted, by their having omitted to use any restrictive term which might prevent its receiving a fair and just interpretation. In considering this question, then, we must never forget that it is a *constitution* we are expounding.

Although, among the enumerated powers of government, we do not find the word "bank" or "incorporation," we find the great powers, to lay and collect taxes; to borrow money; to regulate commerce; to declare and conduct a war; and to raise and support armies and navies. The sword and the purse, all the external relations, and no inconsiderable portion of the industry of the nation, are intrusted to its government. It can never be pretended, that these vast powers draw after them others of inferior importance, merely because they are inferior. Such an idea can never be advanced. But it may with great reason be contended, that a government, intrusted with such ample powers, on the due execution of which the happiness and prosperity of the nation so vitally depends, must also be intrusted with ample means for their execution....

... [T]he constitution of the United States has not left the right of congress to employ the necessary means, for the execution of the powers conferred on the government, to general reasoning. To its enumeration of powers is added, that of making "all laws which shall be necessary and proper, for carrying into execution the foregoing powers, and all other powers vested by this constitution, in the government of the United States, or in any department thereof." The counsel for the state of Maryland have urged various arguments, to prove that this clause, though, in terms, a grant of power, is not so, in effect; but is really restrictive of the general right, which might otherwise be implied, of selecting means for executing the enumerated powers. In support of this proposition, they have found it necessary to contend, that this clause was inserted for the purpose of conferring on congress the power of making laws. That, without it, doubts might be entertained, whether congress could exercise its powers in the form of legislation.

But could this be the object for which it was inserted? A government is created by the people, having legislative, executive and judicial powers. Its leg-

islative powers are vested in a congress, which is to consist of a senate and house of representatives.... Could it be necessary to say, that a legislature should exercise legislative powers, in the shape of legislation? After allowing each house to prescribe its own course of proceeding, after describing the manner in which a bill should become a law, would it have entered into the mind of a single member of the convention, that an express power to make laws was necessary, to enable the legislature to make them? That a legislature, endowed with legislative powers, can legislate, is a proposition too self-evident to have been questioned.

But the argument on which most reliance is placed, is drawn from that peculiar language of this clause. Congress is not empowered by it to make all laws, which may have relation to the powers conferred on the government, but such only as may be *"necessary and proper"* for carrying them into execution. The word *"necessary"* is considered as controlling the whole sentence, and as limiting the right to pass laws for the execution of the granted powers, to such as are indispensable, and without which the power would be nugatory. That it excludes the choice of means, and leaves to congress, in each case, that only which is most direct and simple.

Is it true, that this is the sense in which the word "necessary" is always used? Does it always import an absolute physical necessity, so strong, that one thing to which another may be termed necessary, cannot exist without that other? We think it does not. If reference be had to its use, in the common affairs of the world, or in approved authors, we find that it frequently imports no more than that one thing is convenient, or useful, or essential to another. To employ the means necessary to an end, is generally understood as employing any means calculated to produce the end, and not as being confined to those single means, without which the end would be entirely unattainable....

... This provision is made in a constitution, intended to endure for ages to come, and consequently, to be adapted to the various *crises* of human affairs. To have prescribed the means by which government should, in all future time, execute its powers, would have been to change, entirely, the character of the instrument, and give it the properties of a legal code. It would have been an unwise attempt to provide, by immutable rules, for exigencies which, if foreseen at all, must have been seen dimly, and which can be best provided for as they occur....

[*Marshall proceeds to reject Maryland's argument that*

the Necessary and Proper Clause was intended to abridge the powers of Congress.]

1st. The clause is placed among the powers of congress, not among the limitations on those powers. 2d. Its terms purport to enlarge, not to diminish the powers vested in the government. It purports to be an additional power, not a restriction on those already granted. No reason has been, or can be assigned, for thus concealing an intention to narrow the discretion of the national legislature, under words which purport to enlarge it....

We admit, as all must admit, that the powers of the government are limited, and that its limits are not to be transcended. But we think the sound construction of the constitution must allow to the national legislature that discretion, with respect to the means by which the powers it confers are to be carried into execution, which will enable that body to perform the high duties assigned to it, in the manner most beneficial to the people. Let the end be legitimate, let it be within the scope of the constitution, and all means which are appropriate, which are plainly adapted to that end, which are not prohibited, but consist with the letter and spirit of the constitution, are constitutional.

. . .

It being the opinion of the court, that the act incorporating the bank is constitutional; and that the power of establishing a branch in the state of Maryland might be properly exercised by the bank itself, we proceed to inquire—

2. Whether the state of Maryland may, without violating the constitution, tax that branch? That the power of taxation is one of vital importance; that it is retained by the states; that it is not abridged by the grant of a similar power to the government of the Union; that it is to be concurrently exercised by the two governments—are truths which have never been denied....

... [T]he counsel for the bank places its claim to be exempted from the power of a state to tax its operations. There is no express provision for the case, but the claim has been sustained on a principle which so entirely pervades the constitution, is so intermixed with the materials which compose it, so interwoven with its web, so blended with its texture, as to be incapable of being separated from it, without rending it into shreds. This great principle is, that the constitution and the laws made in pursuance thereof are supreme; that they control the constitution and laws of the respective states, and cannot be controlled by them. From this, which may be almost

termed an axiom, other propositions are deduced as corollaries, on the truth or error of which, and on their application to this case, the cause has been supposed to depend. These are, 1st. That a power to create implies a power to preserve: 2d. That a power to destroy, if wielded by a different hand, is hostile to, and incompatible with these powers to create and to preserve: 3d. That where this repugnancy exists, that authority which is supreme must control, not yield to that over which it is supreme.

... That the power of taxing [*the bank*] by the states may be exercised so as to destroy it, is too obvious to be denied. But taxation is said to be an absolute power, which acknowledges no other limits than those expressly prescribed in the constitution, and like sovereign power of every other description, is intrusted to the discretion of those who use it. But the very terms of this argument admit, that the sovereignty of the state, in the article of taxation itself, is subordinate to, and may be controlled by the constitution of the United States.... It is of the very essence of supremacy, to remove all obstacles to its action within its own sphere, and so to modify every power vested in subordinate governments, as to exempt its own operations from their own influence. This effect need not be stated in terms. It is so involved in the declaration of supremacy, so necessarily implied in it, that the expression of it could not make it more certain. We must, therefore, keep it in view, while construing the constitution.

. . .

The sovereignty of a state extends to everything which exists by its own authority, or is introduced by its permission; but does it extend to those means which are employed by congress to carry into execution powers conferred on that body by the people of the United States? We think it demonstrable, that it does not. Those powers are not given by the people of a single state. They are given by the people of the United States, to a government whose laws, made in pursuance of the constitution, are declared to be supreme. Consequently, the people of a single state cannot confer a sovereignty which will extend over them.

. . .

We are unanimously of opinion, that the law passed by the legislature of Maryland, imposing a tax on the Bank of the United States, is unconstitutional and void.

. . .

Missouri v. Holland

252 U.S. 416 (1920)

The United States and Great Britain entered into a treaty in 1916 to protect migratory birds in the United States and Canada. Congress passed legislation in 1918 to enforce the treaty, providing for prohibitions on the killing, capturing, or selling of any of the migratory birds included within the terms of the treaty, except as permitted by regulations compatible with the treaty. Ray P. Holland, U.S. Game Warden, threatened to arrest and prosecute citizens of Missouri for violating the Migratory Bird Treaty Act. Missouri claimed that the treaty and the statute invaded the rights reserved to the states by the Tenth Amendment. A federal district court upheld the congressional act.

MR. JUSTICE HOLMES delivered the opinion of the court.

This is a bill in equity brought by the State of Missouri to prevent a game warden of the United States from attempting to enforce the Migratory Bird Treaty Act of July 3, 1918, c. 128, 40 Stat. 755, and the regulations made by the Secretary of Agriculture in pursuance of the same. The ground of the bill is that the statute is an unconstitutional interference with the rights reserved to the States by the Tenth Amendment, and that the acts of the defendant done and threatened under that authority invade the sovereign right of the State and contravene its will manifested in statutes. The State also alleges a pecuniary interest, as owner of the wild birds within its borders and otherwise, admitted by the Government to be sufficient, but it is enough that the bill is a reasonable and proper means to assert the alleged quasi sovereign rights of a State....

... It is unnecessary to go into any details, because, as we have said, the question raised is the general one whether the treaty and statute are void as an interference with the rights reserved to the States.

To answer this question it is not enough to refer to the Tenth Amendment, reserving the powers not delegated to the United States, because by Article II, §2, the power to make treaties is delegated expressly, and by Article VI treaties made under the authority of the United States, along with the Constitution and laws of the United States made in pursuance thereof, are declared the supreme law of the land. If the treaty is valid there can be no dispute about the validity of the statute under Article I, §8, as a necessary and proper means to execute the powers of the Government. The language of the Constitution as to the supremacy of treaties being general, the question before us is narrowed to an inquiry into the ground upon which the present supposed exception is placed.

It is said that a treaty cannot be valid if it infringes the Constitution, that there are limits, there-fore, to the treatymaking power, and that one such limit is that what an act of Congress could not do unaided, in derogation of the powers reserved to the States, a treaty cannot do. An earlier act of Congress that attempted by itself and not in pursuance of a treaty to regulate the killing of migratory birds within the States had been held bad in the District Court. *United States* v. *Shauver,* 214 Fed. Rep. 154. *United States* v. *McCullagh,* 221 Fed. Rep. 288. Those decisions were supported by arguments that migratory birds were owned by the States in their sovereign capacity for the benefit of their people, and that under cases like *Geer* v. *Connecticut,* 161 U. S. 519, this control was one that Congress had no power to displace. The same argument is supposed to apply now with equal force.

Whether the two cases cited were decided rightly or not they cannot be accepted as a test of the treaty power. Acts of Congress are the supreme law of the land only when made in pursuance of the Constitution, while treaties are declared to be so when made under the authority of the United States. It is open to question whether the authority of the United States means more than the formal acts prescribed to make the convention. We do not mean to imply that there are no qualifications to the treaty-making power; but they must be ascertained in a different way. It is obvious that there may be matters of the sharpest exigency for the national well being that an act of Congress could not deal with but that a treaty followed by such an act could, and it is not lightly to be assumed that, in matters requiring national action, "a power which must belong to and somewhere reside in every civilized government" is not to be found. *Andrews* v. *Andrews,* 188 U.S. 14, 33. What was said in that case with regard to the powers of the States applies with equal force to the powers of the nation in cases where the States individually are incompetent to act. We are not yet discussing the particular case before us but only are considering the validity of the test proposed. With regard to that we may add that when we are dealing with words that also are a constituent act, like the Constitution of the United States, we must realize that they have called into life a being the development of which could not have been foreseen completely by the most gifted of its begetters. It was enough for them to realize or to hope that they had created an organism; it has taken a century and has cost their successors much sweat and blood to prove that they created a nation. The case before us must be considered in the light of our whole experience and not merely in that of what was said a hundred years ago. The treaty in question does not contravene any prohibitory words to be found in the Constitution. The only question is whether it is forbidden by some invisible radiation from the general terms of the Tenth Amendment. We must consider what this country has become in deciding what that Amendment has reserved.

The State as we have intimated founds its claim of exclusive authority upon an assertion of title to migratory birds, an assertion that is embodied in statute. No doubt it is true that as between a State and its inhabitants the State may regulate the killing and sale of such birds, but it does not follow that its authority is exclusive of paramount powers. To put the claim of the State upon title is to lean upon a slender reed. Wild birds are not in the possession of anyone; and possession is the beginning of ownership. The whole foundation of the State's rights is the presence within their jurisdiction of birds that yesterday had not arrived, tomorrow may be in another State and in a week a thousand miles away. If we are to be accurate we cannot put the case of the State upon higher ground than that the treaty deals with creatures that for the moment are within the state borders, that it must be carried out by officers of the United States within the same territory, and that but for the treaty the State would be free to regulate this subject itself.

As most of the laws of the United States are carried out within the States and as many of them deal with matters which in the silence of such laws the State might regulate, such general grounds are not enough to support Missouri's claim. Valid treaties of course "are as binding within the territorial limits of the States as they are elsewhere throughout the dominion of the United States." *Baldwin* v. *Franks,* 120 U. S. 678, 683. No doubt the great body of private relations usually fall within the control of the State, but a treaty may override its power....

Here a national interest of very nearly the first magnitude is involved. It can be protected only by national action in concert with that of another power. The subject-matter is only transitorily within the State and has no permanent habitat therein. But for the treaty and the statute there soon might be no birds for any powers to deal with. We see nothing in the Constitution that compels the Government to sit by while a food supply is cut off and the protectors of our forests and our crops are destroyed. It is not sufficient to rely upon the States. The reliance is vain, and were it otherwise, the question is whether the United States is forbidden to act. We are of opinion that the treaty and statute must be upheld. *Carey* v. *South Dakota,* 250 U. S. 118.

Decree affirmed.

Mr. Justice Van Devanter and Mr. Justice Pitney dissent.

B. THE COMMERCE CLAUSE

The Commerce Clause has produced many collisions between the legislative and judicial branches, often pitting the power of Congress to advance its national agenda against judicial constraints that favored business or state interests. Although the Court in many instances blocked national efforts to regulate the economy, over the long run a persistent Congress prevailed with its independent interpretation of the Commerce Clause. Today, the scope of the commerce power is left largely to Congress. Over the past half century, Congress has invoked the Commerce Clause to enact civil rights legislation, treated in Chapter 15.

Commercial friction among the states during the 1770s and 1780s generated pressure for stronger national powers. The Continental Congress had no power to raise revenue or to regulate commerce among the states. Its power to conclude treaties with foreign nations meant little unless it could control commerce coming into state ports. With each state guarding its sphere of sovereignty, thirteen conflicting systems of commercial regulation and duty schedules governed trade in the country. These commercial disputes led to the Annapolis Convention in 1786 and the Philadelphia Convention a year later. Among the enumerated duties given to Congress was the power to "regulate commerce with foreign nations, and among the several States, and with the Indian tribes." Art. I, § 8, Cl. 2.

The scope of the Commerce Clause reached the Supreme Court in *Gibbons v. Ogden* (1824). The decision by Chief Justice Marshall is significant for three reasons. First, although Marshall was a strong defender of private property and contractual rights, he advanced a broad interpretation of the power of Congress to regulate commerce. Commerce was more than discrete transactions; it was intercourse. Congress had the power to regulate economic life in the nation to promote the free flow of interstate commerce, including actions within state borders that interfered with that flow. Second, his decision averted potential economic warfare among the states, which would have revived the destructive practices operating before the Constitution. Third, the decision represents one of the most articulate rebuttals of "strict constructionism." GIBBONS v. OGDEN, 22 U.S. (9 Wheat.) 1 (1824).

Three years later, Marshall again supported national power by striking down a Maryland statute because it violated two constitutional provisions: the prohibition on states to lay a duty on imports and the power of Congress to regulate interstate commerce. To distinguish between congressional and state powers. Marshall developed the "original package" concept. States could not tax an import in its original form or package, but after the imported article became "incorporated and mixed up with the mass of property in the country," it was vulnerable to state taxes. Brown v. Maryland, 25 U.S. (12 Wheat.) 419, 441 (1827). Those decisions recognized that the national government did not have exclusive control over the commerce power. In areas where Congress had not exercised its commerce power, Marshall supported the authority of states to regulate commerce within their own borders. Willson v. Black-bird Creek Marsh Co., 27 U.S. (2 Pet.) 244 (1829).

Concurrent Powers

Other cases explored jurisdictional boundaries between the national and state governments. The broad nationalistic interpretation of Marshall was supplanted by more restrictive rulings from the Taney Court. A decision in 1837 permitted states to adopt regulations for passengers arriving from foreign countries. The Court considered packages, not people, as subjects of commerce for congressional control. States could exercise the "police power" to protect the general welfare of their citizens. New York v. Miln, 36 U.S. (11 Pet.) 102 (1837). Under this doctrine of concurrent powers, states could regulate commerce within their borders unless preempted by Congress. If Congress authorized the importation of liquor from foreign countries, states had to accept the liquor in its "original package." Once the cask became part of retail or domestic traffic, the state police power justified the imposition of taxes, licenses, or total prohibition of liquor. The same reasoning applied to liquor shipped from neighboring states. License Cases, 46 U.S. (5 How.) 504 (1847). The Supreme Court allowed states to collect "fees" from foreign vessels by distinguishing fees from the imposts and duties forbidden by Article I, Section 10. States could exercise concurrent jurisdiction over portions of the power over foreign commerce, especially when invited by Congress. COOLEY v. BOARD OF WARDENS, 53 U.S. (12 How.) 299 (1852). During this same period, however, the Court denied states the right to impose taxes on alien passengers arriving at state ports, even when states used "health" as a justification. Passenger Cases, 48 U.S. (7 How.) 282 (1849).

In some cases the Supreme Court recognized exclusive jurisdictions. Under the theory of "dual federalism," the states and the national government exercised mutually exclusive powers. "The powers which one possesses, the other does not." United States v. Cruikshank, 92 U.S. (2 Otto.) 542, 550 (1876). In 1890, the Court ruled that a state's prohibition of intoxicating liquors could not be applied to original packages or kegs. The power of Congress over commerce, even if not expressly stated in a statute, appeared to override state police powers and local options. The Court qualified its opinion by saying that the states could not exclude incoming articles "without congressional permission." Leisy v. Hardin, 135 U.S. 100, 125 (1890).

Congress promptly overturned the decision by passing legislation that made intoxicating liquors,

---

May Congress Annul a Court Decision?

Mr. Justice McLEAN dissenting....

After a very tedious and minute investigation of the facts of the case, which embraced the reports of practical engineers, depositions from the most experienced river men, statements of the stages of water in the river throughout the year, and also after a full consideration of the legal principles applicable to the matter in controversy, six of the members of this tribunal, two only dissenting, were brought to the conclusion that the bridge was a material obstruction to the navigation of the river....

The decree in the Wheeling bridge case was the result of a judicial investigation, founded upon facts ascertained in the course of the hearing. It was strictly a judicial question. The complaint was an obstruction of commerce, by the bridge, to the injury of the complainant, and the court found the fact to be as alleged in the bill. It was said by Chief Justice Marshall, many years ago, that congress could do many things, but that it could not

alter a fact. This it has attempted to do in the above act....

From the organization of the legislative power, it is unfitted for the discharge of judicial duties; and the same may be said of this court in regard to legislation. It may therefore happen, that, when either trenches upon the appropriate powers of the other, their acts are inoperative and void....

Mr. Justice GRIER....

I concur with my brother McLean, that congress cannot annul or vacate any decree of this court; that the assumption of such a power is without precedent, and, as a precedent for the future, it is of dangerous example.

Mr. Justice WAYNE....

... Whatever congress may have intended by the act of August, 1852, I do not think it admits of the interpretation given to it by the majority of the court; and if it does, then my opinion is that the act would be unconstitutional....

SOURCE: Pennsylvania v. Wheeling and Belmont Bridge Co., 18 How. (59 U.S.) 421, 437–40, 449, 450 (1856).

---

upon their arrival in a state or territory, subject to the police powers "to the same extent and in the same manner as though such liquids or liquors had been produced in such State or Territory, and shall not be exempt therefrom by reason of being introduced therein in original packages or otherwise." 26 Stat. 313 (1890). The Supreme Court upheld the constitutionality of this statute. In re Rahrer, 140 U.S. 545 (1891). Three years later, the Court reviewed a state statute that prohibited the sale of oleomargarine that had been colored to look like butter, including oleomargarine manufactured outside the state. The Court supported the statute even though Congress had previously legislated on oleomargarine. Plumley v. Massachusetts, 155 U.S. 461 (1894).

Dormant Commerce Clause

In cases where Congress does not exercise its commerce power, that authority is silent or dormant. In such situations the Court may decide that a state action is forbidden by the Commerce Clause. However, if Congress then enacts legislation to permit the state action, the Court will acquiesce to the congressional policy. For example, in 1852 the Supreme Court held that the height of a bridge in Pennsylvania made it "a nuisance." Congress quickly passed legislation declaring the bridges at issue to be "lawful structures" and the Court subsequently ruled that the bridge was no longer an unlawful obstruction.[4] In separate dissents, Justices McLean, Grier, and Wayne argued that Congress could not annul or vacate a court decree and that the 1852 statute was improperly an exercise of judicial, not legislative, power (see box).

---

4. Pennsylvania v. Wheeling &c. Bridge Co., 13 How. (54 U.S.) 518 (1852); 10 Stat. 112, § 6 (1852); Pennsylvania v. Wheeling and Belmont Bridge Co., 18 How. (59 U.S.) 421 (1856).

Those positions have never been adopted by the Court, which noted in 1946: "whenever Congress' judgment has been uttered affirmatively to contradict the Court's previously expressed view that specific action taken by the states in Congress' silence was forbidden by the commerce clause, this body has accommodated its previous judgment to Congress' expressed approval." Prudential Ins. Co. v. Benjamin, 326 U.S. 408, 425 (1946). In 1985, the Court said that when Congress "so chooses, state actions which it plainly authorizes are invulnerable to constitutional attack under the Commerce Clause."[5]

The give-and-take between Congress and the judiciary is illustrated by the insurance cases. In 1869, the Supreme Court held that states could regulate insurance because it was not a "transaction of commerce." Paul v. Virginia, 8 Wall. 168. That holding, along with 150 years of precedents, was overturned in 1944 when the Court interpreted the transaction of insurance business across state lines as interstate commerce subject to congressional regulation. The Court said that Congress had not intended to exempt the insurance business from the Sherman Antitrust Act. United States v. South-Eastern Underwriters Assn., 322 U.S. 533 (1944). Congress quickly passed the McCarran Act, reversing the Court by authorizing states to regulate insurance. 59 Stat. 33 (1945). Acting under cover of this statute, states were once again allowed to regulate and tax the business of insurance. Prudential Ins. Co. v. Benjamin, 328 U.S. 408 (1946).

Antitrust Policy

In an effort to curb the concentration of economic power after the Civil War, Congress passed the Sherman Antitrust Act in 1890 to prohibit combinations and conspiracies that restrained trade. Through a series of rulings, the Supreme Court largely nullified the law's effectiveness. In 1895 the Court held that the Act did not apply to monopolies engaged in the *manufacture* of items necessary for life. Through this reasoning the Act exempted (by judicial fiat) the "Sugar Trust": the American Sugar Refining Company, which was incorporated in New Jersey and controlled about 98 percent of the sugar refining business in the country. The Court argued that manufacturing precedes commerce and is not part of it and that the power to regulate the manufacture of a "necessary of life" belongs to the police power of the states. The Court regarded the sugar monopoly's restraint on trade as "indirect," not direct. United States v. E.C. Knight Co., 156 U.S. 1 (1895).

The Court narrowly upheld the application of the Sherman Antitrust Act to holding companies that competing railroad companies had established to combine their forces and restrain interstate commerce. Northern Securities Co. v. United States, 193 U.S. 197 (1904). The Act was gravely weakened in 1911 when the Court adopted the "rule of reason" doctrine. Previously, the Court had applied the literal and strict language of the Act, which made no exceptions. It prohibited *every* contract, combination, or conspiracy in restraint of interstate or foreign trade. *Every* person engaged in such activity was guilty of a misdemeanor. Initially the Court refused to limit the Act to "unreasonable" restraints of trade. United States v. Trans-Missouri Freight Assn., 166 U.S. 290, 327–41 (1897); United States v. Joint Traffic Assn., 171 U.S. 505, 573–78 (1898). If companies entered into contracts that restrained interstate or foreign commerce to any extent, Congress could nullify the contracts. Addyston Pipe & Steel Co. v. United States, 175 U.S. 211 (1899).

Matters changed abruptly in 1911 with the "rule of reason." The Sherman Act was judicially amended to prohibit only *unreasonable* or *undue* restraints. In a dissent, Justice Harlan condemned the use of judicial construction to amend the Constitution and rewrite statutes. Standard Oil Co. v.

---

5. Northeast Bancorp v. Board of Governors, FRS, 472 U.S. 159, 174 (1985). In a concurrence in 1995, Justices Kennedy and O'Connor conceded that "if we invalidate a state law, Congress can in effect overturn our judgment." United States v. Lopez, 514 U.S. 549, 580 (1995). See also Julian N. Eule, "Laying the Dormant Commerce Clause to Rest," 91 Yale L. J. 425 (1982); William Cohen, "Congressional Power to Validate Unconstitutional State Laws: A Forgotten Solution to an Old Enigma," 35 Stan. L. Rev. 387 (1983).

United States, 221 U.S. 1, 105 (1911); United States v. American Tobacco Co., 221 U.S. 106 (1911). Judgments of "reasonable" rates are now exercised by administrative agencies, not the judiciary. Moreover, the Court has long since abandoned the artificial separation between "manufacturing" and "commerce." Mandeville Farms v. Sugar Co., 334 U.S. 219, 229 (1948).

Gibbons v. Ogden

22 U.S. (9 Wheat.) 1 (1824)

New York granted to Robert R. Livingston and Robert Fulton the exclusive privilege to operate steamboats on all waters within the jurisdiction of the state. Other states enacted similar laws, and soon friction emerged as states required out-of-state boats to pay substantial fees to be admitted. The retaliation that resulted was similar to the commercial warfare among the states prior to the adoption of the Constitution. This case involved the issue of whether New York could require a steamboat operating between New York and New Jersey to secure a New York license. Was this within the power of a state or did it infringe on the commerce power given to Congress? Thomas Gibbons and Aaron Ogden had been partners, operating a steamboat between New Jersey and New York, but they became antagonists in this tangled suit.

March 2d, 1824. MARSHALL, Ch. J., ... The appellant contends, that this decree [*by New York*] is erroneous, because the laws which purport to give the exclusive privilege it sustains, are repugnant to ... that clause in the constitution which authorizes congress to regulate commerce [*and*] to that which authorizes congress to promote the progress of science and useful arts.

... [R]eference has been made to the political situation of these states, anterior to its formation. It has been said, that they were sovereign, were completely independent, and were connected with each other only by a league. This is true. But when these allied sovereigns converted their league into a government, ... the whole character in which the states appear, underwent a change, the extent of which must be determined by a fair consideration of the instrument by which that change was effected.

This instrument contains an enumeration of powers expressly granted by the people to their government. It has been said, that these powers ought to be construed strictly. But why ought they to be so construed? Is there one sentence in the constitution which gives countenance to this rule? In the last of the enumerated powers, that which grants, expressly, the means for carrying all others into execution, congress is authorized "to make all laws which shall be necessary and proper" for the purpose. But this limitation on the means which may be used, is not extended to the powers which are conferred; nor is there one sentence in the constitution, ... or which we have been able to discern, that prescribes this rule. We do not, therefore, think ourselves justified in adopting it. What do gentlemen mean, by a strict

construction? If they contend only against that enlarged construction, which would extend words beyond their natural and obvious import, we might question the application of the term, but should not controvert the principle. If they contend for that narrow construction which, in support of some theory not to be found in the constitution, would deny to the government those powers which the words of the grant, as usually understood, import, and which are consistent with the general views and objects of the instrument — for that narrow construction, which would cripple the government, and render it unequal to the objects for which it is declared to be instituted, and to which the powers given, as fairly understood, render it competent — then we cannot perceive the propriety of this strict construction, nor adopt it as the rule by which the constitution is to be expounded....

The words are, "congress shall have power to regulate commerce with foreign nations, and among the several states, and with the Indian tribes."

The subject to be regulated is commerce; and our constitution being, as was aptly said at the bar, one of enumeration, and not of definition, to ascertain the extent of the power, it becomes necessary to settle the meaning of the word. The counsel for the appellee would limit it to traffic, to buying and selling, or the interchange of commodities, and do not admit that it comprehends navigation. This would restrict a general term, applicable to many objects, to one of its significations. Commerce, undoubtedly, is traffic, but it is something more — it is intercourse. It describes the commercial intercourse between nations, and parts of nations, in all its branches, and is regulated by prescribing rules for carrying on that intercourse. The mind can scarcely conceive a system for regulating commerce between nations, which shall exclude all laws concerning navigation, which shall be silent on the admission of the vessels of the one nation into the ports of the other.... All America understands, and has uniformly understood, the word "commerce," to comprehend navigation. It was so understood, and must have been so understood, when the constitution was framed. The power over commerce, including navigation, was one of the primary objects for which the people of America adopted their government, and must have been contemplated in forming it. The convention must have used the word in that sense, because all have understood it in that sense; and the attempt to restrict it comes too late.

If the opinion that "commerce," as the word is used in the constitution, comprehends navigation also, requires any additional confirmation, that additional confirmation is, we think, furnished by the words of the instrument itself.... The 9th section of the last article declares, that "no preference shall be given, by any regulation of commerce or revenue, to the ports of one state over those of another." This clause cannot be understood as applicable to those laws only which are passed for the purposes of revenue, because it is expressly applied to commercial regulations; and the most obvious preference which can be given to one port over another, in regulating commerce, relates to navigation. But the subsequent part of the sentence is still more explicit. It is, "nor shall vessels bound to or from one state, be obliged to enter, clear or pay duties in another." These words have a direct reference to navigation.

The universally acknowledged power of the government to impose embargoes, must also be considered as showing, that all America is united in that construction which comprehends navigation in the word commerce....

The word used in the constitution, then, comprehends, and has been always understood to comprehend, navigation within its meaning; and a power to regulate navigation, is as expressly granted, as if that term had been added to the word "commerce."

To what commerce does this power extend? The constitution informs us, to commerce "with foreign nations, and among the several states, and with the Indian tribes."

It has, we believe, been universally admitted, that these words comprehend every species of commercial intercourse between the United States and foreign nations. No sort of trade can be carried on between this country and any other, to which this power does not extend....

If this be the admitted meaning of the word, in its application to foreign nations, it must carry the same meaning throughout the sentence, and remain a unit, unless there be some plain intelligible cause which alters it.

The subject to which the power is next applied, is to commerce, "among the several states." The word "among" means intermingled with. A thing which is among others, is intermingled with them. Commerce among the states, cannot stop at the external boundary line of each state, but may be introduced into the interior.

... [I]n regulating commerce with foreign nations, the power of congress does not stop at the jurisdictional lines of the several states. It would be a very useless power, if it could not pass those lines. The commerce of the United States with foreign nations, is that of the whole United States; every district has a right to participate in it. The deep streams which penetrate our country in every direction, pass through the interior of almost every state in the Union, and furnish the means of exercising this right. If congress has the power to regulate it, that power must be exercised whenever the subject exists. If it exists within the states, if a foreign voyage may commence or terminate at a port within a state, then the power of congress may be exercised within a state.

... Commerce among the states must, of necessity, be commerce with the states....

We are now arrived at the inquiry—what is this power?

It is the power to regulate; that is, to prescribe the rule by which commerce is to be governed. This power, like all others vested in congress, is complete in itself, may be exercised to its utmost extent, and acknowledges no limitations, other than are prescribed in the constitution. These are expressed in plain terms, and do not affect the questions which arise in this case, or which have been discussed at the bar....

The power of congress, then, comprehends navigation, within the limits of every state in the Union; so far as that navigation may be, in any manner, connected with "commerce with foreign nations, or among the several states, or with the Indian tribes." It may, of consequence, pass the jurisdictional line of New York, and act upon the very waters to which the prohibition now under consideration applies.

[*Marshall concludes that the licenses for the steamboats operated by Gibbons, which were granted under an act*

*of Congress, gave full authority to those vessels to nav-
igate the waters of the United States, notwithstanding
any law of New York to the contrary. Conflicting New
York laws were unconstitutional and void.*]

Powerful and ingenious minds, taking, as postulates, that the powers expressly granted to the government of the Union, are to be contracted, by construction, into the narrowest possible compass, and
that the original powers of the states are retained, if
any possible construction will retain them, may, by
a course of well-digested, but refined and metaphys-
ical reasoning, founded on these premises, explain
away the constitution of our country, and leave it, a
magnificent structure, indeed, to look at, but totally
unfit for use.

JOHNSON, Justice. — [*Johnson agrees with the outcome, but for different reasons.*] The "power to regulate commerce" here meant to be granted was that
power to regulate commerce which previously existed in the States.... The power of a sovereign state
over commerce therefore amounts to nothing more
than a power to limit and restrain it at pleasure. And
since the power to prescribe the limits to its freedom
necessarily implies the power to determine what
shall remain unrestrained, it follows that the power
must be exclusive; it can reside but in one potentate,
and hence the grant of this power carries with it the
whole subject, leaving nothing for the State to act
upon....

When speaking of the power of Congress over
navigation, I do not regard it as a power incidental
to that of regulating commerce; I consider it as the
thing itself, inseparable from it as vital motion is
from vital existence.

Cooley v. Board of Wardens

53 U.S. 299 (1852)

**A Pennsylvania law provided that all vessels of a certain description coming into state port
should employ pilots to assure safety. If they refused they were required to pay a pilotage fee.
Aaron Cooley argued that the state law was a regulation of foreign commerce and therefore an
action solely within the authority of Congress, which had passed legislation in 1789 regarding
the regulation of ports. Was this area of commerce within the exclusive domain of Congress, or
could states exercise concurrent jurisdiction? Did foreign commerce demand uniformity or permit local diversity?**

Mr. Justice CURTIS delivered the opinion of the
court.

. . .

We think this particular regulation concerning
half-pilotage fees, is an appropriate part of a general
system of regulations of this subject. Testing it by the
practice of commercial States and countries legislating on this subject, we find it has usually been
deemed necessary to make similar provisions. Numerous laws of this kind are cited in the learned argument of the counsel for the defendant in error;
and their fitness, as a part of a system of pilotage, in
many places, may be inferred from their existence in
so many different States and countries. Like other
laws they are framed to meet the most usual cases,
quæ frequentius accidunt; they rest upon the propriety of securing lives and property exposed to the
perils of a dangerous navigation, by taking on board
a person peculiarly skilled to encounter or avoid
them....

That the power to regulate commerce includes
the regulation of navigation, we consider settled.
And when we look to the nature of the service performed by pilots, to the relations which that service
and its compensations bear to navigation between
the several States, and between the ports of the
United States and foreign countries, we are brought
to the conclusion, that the regulation of the qualifications of pilots, of the modes and times of offering
and rendering their services, of the responsibilities
which shall rest upon them, of the powers they shall
possess, of the compensation they may demand, and
of the penalties by which their rights and duties may
be enforced, do constitute regulations of navigation,
and consequently of commerce, within the just
meaning of this clause of the Constitution.

. . .

It becomes necessary, therefore, to consider
whether this law of Pennsylvania, being a regulation
of commerce, is valid.

The act of Congress of the 7th of August, 1789,
sect. 4, is as follows:

"That all pilots in the bays, inlets, rivers, harbors, and ports of the United States shall continue to be regulated in conformity with the existing laws of the States, respectively, wherein such pilots may be, or with such laws as the States may respectively hereafter enact for the purpose, until further legislative provision shall be made by Congress."

If the law of Pennsylvania, now in question, had been in existence at the date of this act of Congress, we might hold it to have been adopted by Congress, and thus made a law of the United States, and so valid. Because this act does, in effect, give the force of an act of Congress, to the then existing State laws on this subject, so long as they should continue unrepealed by the State which enacted them.

But the law on which these actions are founded was not enacted till 1803. What effect then can be attributed to so much of the act of 1789, as declares, that pilots shall continue to be regulated in conformity, "with such laws as the States may respectively hereafter enact for the purpose, until further legislative provision shall be made by Congress"?

. . .

It is the opinion of a majority of the court that the mere grant to Congress of the power to regulate commerce, did not deprive the States of power to regulate pilots, and that although Congress has legislated on this subject, its legislation manifests an intention, with a single exception, not to regulate this subject, but to leave its regulation to the several States....

We are of opinion that this State law was enacted by virtue of a power, residing in the State to legislate; that it is not in conflict with any law of Congress; that it does not interfere with any system which Congress has established by making regulations, or by intentionally leaving individuals to their own unrestricted action; that this law is therefore valid, and the judgment of the Supreme Court of Pennsylvania in each case must be affirmed.

Mr. Justice McLean and Mr. Justice Wayne dissented; and Mr. Justice Daniel, although he concurred in the judgment of the court, yet dissented from its reasoning.

Mr. Justice McLEAN.

It is with regret that I feel myself obliged to dis-

sent from the opinion of a majority of my brethren in this case.

. . .

Why did Congress pass the act of 1789, adopting the pilot-laws of the respective States? Laws they unquestionably were, having been enacted by the States before the adoption of the Constitution....

Congress adopted the pilot-laws of the States, because it was well understood, they could have had no force, as regulations of foreign commerce or of commerce among the States, if not so adopted. By their adoption they were made acts of Congress, and ever since they have been so considered and enforced.

Each State regulates the commerce within its limits; which is not within the range of federal powers. So far, and no farther could effect have been given to the pilot laws of the States, under the Constitution. But those laws were only adopted "until further legislative provisions shall be made by Congress."

This shows that Congress claimed the whole commercial power on this subject, by adopting the pilot laws of the States, making them acts of Congress....

I think the charge of half-pilotage is correct under the circumstances, and I only object to the power of the State to pass the law. Congress, to whom the subject peculiarly belongs, should have been applied to, and no doubt it would have adopted the act of the State.

Mr. Justice DANIEL.

... The true question here is, whether the power to enact pilot-laws is appropriate and necessary, or rather most appropriate and necessary to the State or the federal governments. It being conceded that this power has been exercised by the States from their very dawn of existence; that it can be practically and beneficially applied by the local authorities only; it being conceded, as it must be, that the power to pass pilot-laws, as such, has not been in any express terms delegated to Congress, and does not necessarily conflict with the right to establish commercial regulations, I am forced to conclude that this is an original and inherent power in the States, and not one to be merely tolerated, or held subject to the sanction of the federal government.

. . .

C. NATIONALIZATION OF THE ECONOMY

Fundamental changes in economic structures after the Civil War gradually washed away many traditional boundaries between intrastate and interstate commerce. Judicial doctrines of dual federalism and concurrent powers lost ground to a gradual centralization of authority in the national government.

In 1886, the Supreme Court struck down an Illinois railroad statute because it affected, even for the part of the journey within the state, commerce among the states. Wabash, &c., Railway Co. v. Illinois, 118 U.S. 557 (1886). This decision made national regulation imperative, and Congress responded a year later by creating the Interstate Commerce Commission. Another decision allowed Congress to prohibit national and interstate traffic in lottery tickets even if its motivation—such as morality—competed with the state police power. CHAMPION v. AMES (Lottery Case), 188 U.S. 321 (1903). Two years later, a unanimous Court upheld a congressional statute that prevented a company from restraining trade even when the company's cattle came to rest within a stockyard of a particular state. The movement of cattle from state to state created a "current of commerce" subject to congressional control. Swift & Co. v. United States, 196 U.S. 375, 399 (1905). In later years, the Court evoked a similar image, calling the stockyards a temporary resting place for cattle moving interstate, serving as "a throat through which the current of commerce flows." Stafford v. Wallace, 258 U.S. 495, 516 (1922).

These decisions supported congressional regulation only in selected areas: railroads, morals, and health. For example, in 1914 the Supreme Court rejected artificial distinctions between *intrastate* and *interstate* by holding that Congress could regulate actions inside a state that were *related* to interstate commerce. Through this reasoning, it allowed a congressional commission to set railroad rates within a state. Shreveport Rate Case, 234 U.S. 342 (1914). Under the Commerce Clause, Congress could establish an eight-hour day for all railroad workers engaged in interstate commerce, especially when needed to resolve a nationwide strike. Wilson v. New, 243 U.S. 332 (1917). Other decisions upheld the power of Congress to seize and condemn prohibited articles, to forbid the interstate transportation of women engaged in prostitution, and to make it a crime to transport stolen motor vehicles in interstate or foreign commerce.[6] During time of war, many commercial operations normally regulated by the states fall within the domain of the national government.[7]

Child Labor Legislation

This pattern of sustaining congressional power did not apply to factory conditions, hours, or wages. In 1916 Congress passed legislation to prevent the products of child labor from being shipped interstate. Legislators concluded that the bill was constitutional and consistent with recent Supreme Court rulings that permitted Congress to use the Commerce Clause to regulate public health and morals. However, the Court held that the law exceeded the commerce power and invaded responsibilities left to the states. HAMMER v. DAGENHART, 247 U.S. 251 (1918). Within a matter of days, members of Congress confronted the Court by introducing new measures to regulate child labor. 56 Cong. Rec. 8341 (1918). The strategy this time was to use the taxing power by levying an excise tax on the net profits of persons employing child labor. Id. at 11560. Some members of Congress thought that the Court's decision had settled the issue and that Congress had no business reopening it. Senator Henry Cabot Lodge (R-Mass.), a leading conservative, denied that another legislative attempt at ending the "great evil" of child labor was inappropriate. 57 Cong. Rec. 611 (1918).

---

6. Hipolite Egg Co. v. United States, 220 U.S. 45 (1911) (seizing and condemning articles); Hoke v. United States, 227 U.S. 308 (1913) and Caminetti v. United States, 242 U.S. 470 (1917) (White Slave Traffic Act); Brooks v. United States, 267 U.S. 432 (1925) (stolen cars). See also Atlantic Coast Line v. Riverside Mills, 219 U.S. 186 (1911).

7. Case v. Bowles, 327 U.S. 92, 102 (1946); Dakota Cent. Tel. Co. v. South Dakota, 250 U.S. 163 (1919); Northern Pac. Ry. Co. v. North Dakota, 250 U.S. 135 (1919).

Solicitor General Beck Defends Child Labor Bill

The belief that the judiciary is fully empowered to sit in judgment upon the motives or objectives of other branches of the Government is a mischievous one, in that it so lowers the sense of constitutional morality among the people that neither in the legislative branch of the Government nor among the people is there as strong a purpose as formerly to maintain their constitution form of Government.

· · ·

The erroneous idea that this court is the sole guardian and protector of our constitutional form of government has inevitably led to an impairment, both with the people and with their representatives, of what may be called the constitutional conscience.

... The prevalent disposition seems to be to ignore constitutional questions by shifting them to the Supreme Court, in the belief that that court will exercise the full powers of revision, which I have tried to show the Framers of the Constitution did not intend this court to have. The result may be an exaltation of this court, as a tribunal of extraordinary power; but, in the matter of constitutionalism, it inevitably leads to an impairment of the powers and duties of Congress and, above all, to the impairment of the popular conscience; for, in the last analysis, the Constitution will last in substance as long as the people believe in it and are willing to struggle for it.

SOURCE: Brief on Behalf of Appellants and Plaintiff in Error, Bailey v. Drexel Furniture Co., Nos. 590, 657, U.S. Supreme Court, October Term, 1921, at 54–55; 21 Landmark Briefs 59–60.

When this statute was brought before the Supreme Court, Solicitor General James M. Beck prepared a brief that defended the tax. He also urged the Court to exercise political prudence when reviewing, and possibly overturning, the considered efforts of the coequal branches, Congress and the President (see box). Nevertheless, the Court struck down this second statute as well. Bailey v. Drexel Furniture Co. [Child Labor Tax Case], 259 U.S. 20 (1922). Not until 1941, after the composition of the Court had been drastically altered and restrictive judicial doctrines abandoned, was child labor legislation upheld. United States v. Darby, 312 U.S. 100 (1941).

Judicial efforts to curb other economic reforms adopted by Congress and the states are treated in Chapter 9. Courts restricted state use of the "police power," relied on a fictional "liberty of contract" to invalidate other statutes, and used substantive due process to strike down legislative efforts to establish maximum hours and minimum wages. These judicial doctrines came to an end in 1937.

Champion v. Ames (Lottery Case)
188 U.S. 321 (1903)

Many of the states tried to suppress the buying and selling of lottery tickets but found themselves helpless in controlling lotteries in interstate commerce. Congress passed legislation in 1895 to prohibit lottery tickets from interstate or foreign commerce. Charles Champion was charged with violating the act. The Court confronted three principal issues. Is the selling of lottery tickets subject to regulation under the Commerce Clause? Does the power to regulate commerce include the authority to prohibit it? May Congress exercise a national "police power" to protect citizens from immoral transactions, or is that responsibility reserved to the states?

MR. JUSTICE HARLAN, after making the foregoing statement of facts, delivered the opinion of the court.

The appellant insists that the carrying of lottery tickets from one State to another State by an express company engaged in carrying freight and packages from State to State, although such tickets may be contained in a box or package, does not constitute, and cannot by any act of Congress be legally made to constitute, *commerce* among the States within the meaning of the clause of the Constitution of the United States providing that Congress shall have power "to regulate commerce with foreign nations, and among the several States, and with the Indian tribes;" consequently, that Congress cannot make it an offence to cause such tickets to be carried from one State to another.

. . .

It was said in argument that lottery tickets are not of any real or substantial value in themselves, and therefore are not subjects of commerce. If that were conceded to be the only legal test as to what are to be deemed subjects of the commerce that may be regulated by Congress, we cannot accept as accurate the broad statement that such tickets are of no value. Upon their face they showed that the lottery company offered a large capital prize, to be paid to the holder of the ticket winning the prize at the drawing advertised to be held at Asuncion, Paraguay. Money was placed on deposit in different banks in the United States to be applied by the agents representing the lottery company to the prompt payment of prizes. These tickets were the subject of traffic; they could have been sold; and the holder was assured that the company would pay to him the amount of the prize drawn....

We are of opinion that lottery tickets are subjects of traffic and therefore are subjects of commerce, and the regulation of the carriage of such tickets from State to State, at least by independent carriers, is a regulation of commerce among the several States.

But it is said that the statute in question does not regulate the carrying of lottery tickets from State to State, but by punishing those who cause them to be so carried Congress in effect prohibits such carrying; that in respect of the carrying from one State to another of articles or things that are, in fact, or according to usage in business, the subjects of commerce, the authority given Congress was not to *prohibit,* but only to *regulate....*

... Are we prepared to say that a provision which is, in effect, a *prohibition* of the carriage of such articles from State to State is not a fit or appropriate mode for the *regulation* of that particular kind of commerce? If lottery traffic, *carried on through interstate commerce,* is a matter of which Congress may take cognizance and over which its power may be exerted, can it be possible that it must tolerate the traffic, and simply regulate the manner in which it may be carried on? Or may not Congress, for the protection of the people of all the States, and under the power to regulate interstate commerce, devise such means, within the scope of the Constitution, and not prohibited by it, as will drive that traffic out of commerce among the States?

. . .

If a State, when considering legislation for the suppression of lotteries within its own limits, may properly take into view the evils that inhere in the raising of money, in that mode, why may not Congress, invested with the power to regulate commerce among the several States, provide that such commerce shall not be polluted by the carrying of lottery tickets from one State to another? In this connection it must not be forgotten that the power of Congress to regulate commerce among the States is plenary, is complete in itself, and is subject to no limitations except such as may be found in the Constitution. What provision in that instrument can be regarded as limiting the exercise of the power granted? What clause can be cited which, in any degree, countenances the suggestion that one may, of right, carry or cause to be carried from one State to another that which will harm the public morals? [*The Court dismisses the argument that the constitutional provision that no person shall be deprived of liberty without due process of law implies the right to introduce into commerce an article that is injurious to the public morals.*]

If it be said that the act of 1895 is inconsistent with the Tenth Amendment, reserving to the States respectively or to the people the powers not delegated to the United States, the answer is that the power to regulate commerce among the States has been expressly delegated to Congress.

Besides, Congress, by that act, does not assume to interfere with traffic or commerce in lottery tickets carried on exclusively within the limits of any State, but has in view only commerce of that kind among the several States. It has not assumed to interfere with the completely internal affairs of any State, and has only legislated in respect of a matter which concerns the people of the United States....

... We decide nothing more in the present case than that lottery tickets are subjects of traffic among those who choose to sell or buy them; that the carriage of such tickets by independent carriers from one State to another is therefore interstate commerce; that under its power to regulate commerce among the several States Congress—subject to the limitations imposed by the Constitution upon the exercise of the powers granted—has plenary authority over such commerce, and may prohibit the carriage of such tickets from State to State; and that legislation to that end, and of that character, is not inconsistent with any limitation or restriction imposed upon the exercise of the powers granted to Congress.

The judgment is

Affirmed.

Mr. Chief Justice Fuller, with whom concur Mr. Justice Brewer, Mr. Justice Shiras and Mr. Justice Peckham, dissenting.

. . .

The power of the State to impose restraints and burdens on persons and property in conservation and promotion of the public health, good order and prosperity is a power originally and always belonging to the States, not surrendered by them to the General Government nor directly restrained by the Constitution of the United States, and essentially exclusive, and the suppression of lotteries as a harmful business falls within this power, commonly called of police. *Douglas* v. *Kentucky,* 168 U.S. 488.

It is urged, however, that because Congress is empowered to regulate commerce between the several States, it, therefore, may suppress lotteries by prohibiting the carriage of lottery matter. Congress may indeed make all laws necessary and proper for carrying the powers granted to it into execution, and doubtless an act prohibiting the carriage of lottery matter would be necessary and proper to the execution of a power to suppress lotteries; but that power belongs to the States and not to Congress. To hold that Congress has general police power would be to hold that it may accomplish objects not entrusted to the General Government, and to defeat the operation of the Tenth Amendment, declaring that: "The powers not delegated to the United States by the Constitution, nor prohibited by it to the States, are reserved to the States respectively, or to the people."

. . .

Hammer v. Dagenhart

247 U.S. 251 (1918)

In 1916, Congress passed legislation to prohibit the transportation in interstate commerce of goods made at a factory where children under the age of 14 years worked, or children between the ages of 14 and 16 worked more than eight hours a day, or more than six days a week, or after 7P.M. or before 6A.M. Roland H. Dagenhart filed this suit on his own behalf and for his two minor sons who were employed in a cotton mill. After a district court declared the statute unconstitutional, the U.S. Attorney, W.C. Hammer, brought an appeal to the Supreme Court.

Mr. Justice Day delivered the opinion of the court.

. . .

The attack upon the act rests upon three propositions: First: It is not a regulation of interstate and foreign commerce; Second: It contravenes the Tenth Amendment to the Constitution; Third: It conflicts with the Fifth Amendment to the Constitution.

The controlling question for decision is: Is it within the authority of Congress in regulating commerce among the States to prohibit the transportation in interstate commerce of manufactured goods, the product of a factory in which, within thirty days prior to their removal therefrom, children ... have been employed....

The power essential to the passage of this act, the Government contends, is found in the commerce clause of the Constitution which authorizes Congress to regulate commerce with foreign nations and among the States.

In *Gibbons* v. *Ogden,* 9 Wheat. 1, Chief Justice Marshall, speaking for this court, and defining the extent and nature of the commerce power, said, "It is the power to regulate; that is, to prescribe the rule by which commerce is to be governed." In other words, the power is one to control the means by which commerce is carried on, which is directly the contrary of the assumed right to forbid commerce from moving and thus destroy it as to particular commodities. But it is insisted that adjudged cases in this court establish the doctrine that the power to regulate given to Congress incidentally includes the authority to prohibit the movement of ordinary commodities and therefore that the subject is not open for discussion. The cases demonstrate the contrary. They rest upon the character of the particular subjects dealt with and the fact that the scope of governmental authority, state or national, possessed over them is such that the authority to prohibit is as to them but the exertion of the power to regulate.

The first of these cases is *Champion* v. *Ames,* 188 U.S. 321, the so-called *Lottery Case,* in which it was held that Congress might pass a law having the effect to keep the channels of commerce free from use in the transportation of tickets used in the promotion of lottery schemes. In *Hipolite Egg Co.* v. *United States,* 220 U.S. 45, this court sustained the power of Congress to pass the Pure Food and Drug Act which prohibited the introduction into the States by means of interstate commerce of impure foods and drugs. In *Hoke* v. *United States,* 227 U.S. 308, this court sustained the constitutionality of the so-called "White Slave Traffic Act" whereby the transportation of a woman in interstate commerce for the purpose of prostitution was forbidden....

In each of these instances the use of interstate transportation was necessary to the accomplishment of harmful results. In other words, although the power over interstate transportation was to regulate, that could only be accomplished by prohibiting the use of the facilities of interstate commerce to effect the evil intended.

This element is wanting in the present case. The thing intended to be accomplished by this statute is the denial of the facilities of interstate commerce to those manufacturers in the States who employ children within the prohibited ages. The act in its effect does not regulate transportation among the States, but aims to standardize the ages at which children may be employed in mining and manufacturing within the States. The goods shipped are of themselves harmless....

The grant of power to Congress over the subject of interstate commerce was to enable it to regulate such commerce, and not to give it authority to control the States in their exercise of the police power over local trade and manufacture.

The grant of authority over a purely federal matter was not intended to destroy the local power always existing and carefully reserved to the States in the Tenth Amendment to the Constitution.

. . .

In our view the necessary effect of this act is, by means of a prohibition against the movement in interstate commerce of ordinary commercial commodities, to regulate the hours of labor of children in factories and mines within the States, a purely state authority. Thus the act in a twofold sense is repugnant to the Constitution. It not only transcends the authority delegated to Congress over commerce but also exerts a power as to a purely local matter to which the federal authority does not extend. The far reaching result of upholding the act cannot be more plainly indicated than by pointing out that if Congress can thus regulate matters entrusted to local authority by prohibition of the movement of commodities in interstate commerce, all freedom of commerce will be at an end, and the power of the States over local matters may be eliminated, and thus our system of government be practically destroyed.

For these reasons we hold that this law exceeds the constitutional authority of Congress. It follows that the decree of the District Court must be

Affirmed.

Mr. Justice Holmes, dissenting.

... The objection urged against the power [*of Congress*] is that the States have exclusive control over their methods of production and that Congress cannot meddle with them, and taking the proposition in the sense of direct intermeddling I agree to it and suppose that no one denies it. But if an act is within the powers specifically conferred upon Congress, it seems to me that it is not made any less constitutional because of the indirect effects that it may have, however obvious it may be that it will have those effects, and that we are not at liberty upon such grounds to hold it void.

The first step in my argument is to make plain what no one is likely to dispute — that the statute in question is within the power expressly given to Congress if considered only as to its immediate effects and that if invalid it is so only upon some collateral ground. The statute confines itself to prohibiting the carriage of certain goods in interstate or foreign commerce. Congress is given power to regulate such commerce in unqualified terms. It would not be argued today that the power to regulate does not include the power to prohibit....

The question then is narrowed to whether the exercise of its otherwise constitutional power by Congress can be pronounced unconstitutional because of its possible reaction upon the conduct of the

States in a matter upon which I have admitted that they are free from direct control....

The notion that prohibition is any less prohibition when applied to things now thought evil I do not understand. But if there is any matter upon which civilized countries have agreed — far more unanimously than they have with regard to intoxicants and some other matters over which this country is now emotionally aroused — it is the evil of premature and excessive child labor. I should have thought that if we were to introduce our own moral conceptions where in my opinion they do not belong, this was preeminently a case for upholding the exercise of all its powers by the United States.

But I had thought that the propriety of the exercise of a power admitted to exist in some cases was for the consideration of Congress alone and that this Court always had disavowed the right to intrude its

judgment upon questions of policy or morals. It is not for this Court to pronounce when prohibition is necessary to regulation if it ever may be necessary — to say that it is permissible as against strong drink but not as against the product of ruined lives.

The act does not meddle with anything belonging to the States. They may regulate their internal affairs and their domestic commerce as they like. But when they seek to send their products across the state line they are no longer within their rights. If there were no Constitution and no Congress their power to cross the line would depend upon their neighbors. Under the Constitution such commerce belongs not to the States but to Congress to regulate. It may carry out its views of public policy whatever indirect effect they may have upon the activities of the States....

MR. JUSTICE MCKENNA, MR. JUSTICE BRANDEIS AND MR. JUSTICE CLARKE concur in this opinion.

D. THE NEW DEAL WATERSHED

During the New Deal, the Supreme Court at first resisted, but eventually capitulated, to a wholesale expansion of congressional power over commerce. Initially the Court prohibited Congress from regulating commercial activities that were regarded as production and manufacture, as "local" or intrastate, or that affected commerce only "indirectly." Those formulas were variations of dual federalism. By 1936 the Court began to embrace what it had accepted intermittently in the past: Congress could regulate intrastate activities that had a substantial relation to interstate commerce.

In two cases in 1935, the Court declared unconstitutional the National Industrial Recovery Act (NIRA) of 1933. A provision involving production quotas for petroleum products was struck down as an excessive delegation of legislative power to the President. Panama Refining Co. v. Ryan, 293 U.S. 388 (1935). The remainder of the NIRA was invalidated a few months later when a unanimous Court decided that the statute violated the delegation doctrine and exceeded Congress's power to regulate commerce. The Court refused to apply the "current of commerce" concept to intrastate commerce that involved purchases or transportation of goods outside the state. Once a commodity became "commingled with the mass of property within the State," the flow of interstate commerce ceased. Schechter Corp. v. United States, 295 U.S. 495, 543 (1935). A reading of *Schechter* appears in Chapter 6.

The Court struck down the Railroad Retirement Act, which transferred funds from railroad carriers to retirees. The Court, refusing to justify the statute under the Commerce Clause, treated it as a taking of property requiring just compensation. Railroad Retirement Board v. Alton R. Co., 295 U.S. 330 (1935). Also invalidated was the Bituminous Coal Conservation Act of 1935, which relied on the Commerce Clause to regulate mining and the distribution of coal. The Court said that the commerce power did not permit Congress to control the conditions in which coal is produced (such as labor conditions) before coal became an article of commerce. Labor conditions affected commerce only "indirectly." Production and manufacture did not constitute commerce, said the Court, even when done with intent to sell or transport the commodities out of the state. CARTER v. CARTER COAL CO., 298 U.S. 238 (1936). The processing tax of the Agricultural Adjustment Act was declared unconstitutional in *United States* v. *Butler* (see discussion later in this chapter).

Stages of Federalism

1. Nationalism (1789–1835). National powers are read broadly to include implied as well as explicit powers. Generous interpretation of Commerce Clause. Dominated by *McCulloch v. Maryland* (1819) and *Gibbons v. Ogden* (1824). Opportunity for states in some areas to exercise concurrent power over commerce.

2. Dual Federalism (1835–1937). National and state governments have mutually exclusive powers. Within their own spheres they are supreme and independent. Congress may not exercise power over production or manufacturing because they are "local" and intrastate. Congress could not regulate economic activities that affected commerce only "indirectly."

3. Cooperative Federalism (1937–1990). Businesses "affected with a public interest" or with a substantial relation to interstate commerce may be regulated by Congress. Relying on the spend-

ing power, Congress makes grants to states and imposes conditions on those funds. Congress may preempt state regulation but, until it does, states may regulate with standards that differ from federal requirements.

4. Dual Federalism Revived (1990–?). Beginning in the 1990s, the Supreme Court handed down a number of decisions that revitalized dual federalism. As a 5–4 decision noted in 2002: "Dual sovereignty is a defining feature of our Nation's constitutional blueprint." Fed. Maritime Com'n v. S.C. State Ports Auth., 535 U.S. 743, 751 (2002). Some decisions in 2003, 2004, and 2005 seemed to suggest that this era was waning as the makeup of the Court changed, but the Court's health care decision in 2012 contained strong rhetoric about state sovereignty, even as it upheld most of the federal statute.

The Court Switches

After Roosevelt's election in 1936 and his unsuccessful attempt to pack the judiciary, the Supreme Court began to accommodate New Deal legislation. Without a change in the Court's composition, but with Chief Justice Hughes and Justice Roberts now solidly supporting the three liberals (Brandeis, Cardozo, and Stone), the Court upheld the National Labor Relations Act. The Court accepted Congress's argument that labor disputes directly burdened or obstructed interstate or foreign commerce and could be regulated by the Commerce Clause. The Act gave employees in industry a fundamental right to organize and engage in collective bargaining. Any intrastate activity that had a close and substantial relationship to interstate commerce could be brought within the control of Congress. To enforce the Act, Congress established a National Labor Relations Board (NLRB) with the power to prevent any person from engaging in unfair labor practices "affecting commerce." NLRB v. JONES & LAUGHLIN, 301 U.S. 1 (1937).

In 1939 the Court sustained the Agricultural Adjustment Act, which used marketing controls to limit the amount of commodities that could be sold. Through the use of quotas, Congress hoped to stabilize prices and limit production. Farmers who exceeded their allotment had to pay a penalty at the warehouses, the "throat" where commodities entered "the stream of commerce." Mulford v. Smith, 307 U.S. 38, 47 (1939). Wheat marketing quotas, even for wheat not intended for commerce but for consumption on the farm, were upheld three years later by a unanimous Court. WICKARD v. FILBURN, 317 U.S. 111 (1942). The Fair Labor Standards Act of 1938 was upheld, allowing Congress to regulate the wages and hours of manufacturing employees. The Court rejected the argument that manufacturing was an intrastate activity and therefore outside the Commerce Clause. Congress could regulate intrastate activities where they have a "substantial effect" on interstate commerce. UNITED STATES V. DARBY, 312 U.S. 100, 119 (1941).

Through these decisions the United States entered into its third stage of "cooperative federalism" (see box). Although by the late 1930s the Court had largely bowed to the judgments of Congress on economic regulation and the scope of the Commerce Clause, the new Roosevelt Court signaled its intention to give greater scrutiny to constitutional provisions that protect individual rights and liberties. In a famous footnote written by Justice Stone in a 1938 case, the Court suggested that it might have a special responsibility to protect "discrete and insular minorities," especially when the political processes that supposedly safeguard minority rights have been curtailed. United States v. Carolene Products Co., 304 U.S. 144, 153 n.4 (1938). This footnote foreshadowed the Court's later activism in such areas as religious liberty, racial discrimination, and criminal rights. (The *Carolene* footnote appears in Chapter 15, Section C.)

After the Court's retreat in 1937, it continued to monitor federal-state legislation over the economy. State efforts to limit the length of railroad cars traveling interstate could not be justified for reasons of safety or the police power. Even when Congress had not regulated an area, state actions that interfered with interstate commerce were not permitted under the Commerce Clause. Southern Pacific Co. v. Arizona 325 U.S. 761 (1945). Although states may impose burdensome regulations in the interest of local health and safety, they may not restrain interstate commerce for the purpose of advancing their own commercial interests or promoting local economic advantages. Hood v. Du Mond, 336 U.S. 525 (1949). The Supreme Court has developed a number of criteria to indicate when state actions burden interstate commerce, but the enforcement and implementation of these judicial tests depend largely on congressional action. Commonwealth Edison Co. v. Montana, 453 U.S. 609 (1981).

Scope of Independent State Action

These decisions did not permit Congress to preempt every area of commerce that might affect interstate activities. States could still control local conditions and affect interstate commerce incidentally while protecting their citizens' welfare. Milk Board v. Eisenberg Co., 306 U.S. 346 (1939). Even when 90 to 95 percent of a state's product was shipped in interstate or foreign commerce, states could adopt marketing and price-stabilization programs in the interest of the "safety, health and well-being of local communities," especially when the activity "may never be adequately dealt with by Congress." Parker v. Brown, 317 U.S. 341, 362–63 (1943).[8] To protect their environmental and natural resources, states may enact regulations even when the incidental effect creates some burden on interstate commerce. Minnesota v. Clover Leaf Creamery Co., 449 U.S. 456 (1981).

The commerce power allows Congress to control such local activity as "loan sharking" (using threats and extortion to collect loans). Although local, these techniques are part of organized crime that affect interstate and foreign commerce. Perez v. United States, 402 U.S. 146 (1971). The breadth of the New Deal revolution is reflected in two decisions in 1981 that upheld congressional regulation of surface coal mining. The statute authorized states to propose a program of environmental protection to meet minimum federal standards. If states failed to prepare a program, they would be forced to adopt a federal plan. A unanimous Court upheld the statute. Hodel v. Virginia Surface Mining & Recl. Assn., 452 U.S. 264 (1981); Hodel v. Indiana, 452 U.S. 314 (1981). As explained later in Section F, several decisions by the Court beginning in the 1990s limited congressional power over the states.

Other decisions gave states substantial leeway to look for new sources of revenue. The Supreme Court held in 1991 that states may adopt a single business tax (a value-added tax) without violating the Due Process Clause or the Commerce Clause. Trinova Corp. v. Michigan Dept. of Treasury, 498 U.S. 358 (1991). A 1992 ruling marked a first step toward allowing states to force mail-order companies to collect taxes from out-of-state shoppers. Quill Corp. v. North Dakota, 504 U.S. 298 (1992). The mail-order business had grown from $2.4 billion a year in 1967, when the Court first blocked state taxes on such sales, to an estimated $183 billion by 1989. In 1994, the Court ruled that states

---

8. See also Carter v. Virginia, 321 U.S. 131 (1944) for the power of states to regulate shipments entering into and passing out of their borders, and Milk Board v. Eisenberg Co., 306 U.S. 346, 351 (1939) for the ability of states to regulate local conditions even when they incidentally or indirectly involve interstate commerce.

could tax corporations not merely on their earnings within the state but also on their worldwide income. Barclays Bank v. Franchise Tax Bd. of Cal., 512 U.S. 298 (1994).

While the Court and Congress supported these state initiatives, some state activities still run afoul of the Commerce Clause. Two decisions in 1992 limited the authority of states to dispose of hazardous waste and other materials. Chemical Waste Management, Inc. v. Hunt, 504 U.S. 334 (1992); Fort Gratiot Landfill v. Mich. Dept. of Nat. Res., 504 U.S. 353 (1992). A 1994 decision held that an Oregon law—subjecting waste generated in other states to a discriminatory surcharge approximately three times higher than that imposed on waste generated within the state—was invalid under the Commerce Clause. Oregon Waste Systems v. Dept. of Env. Quality, 511 U.S. 93 (1994). In that same year, the Court ruled that a local ordinance on solid waste discriminated against interstate commerce because it favored the local station and squelched competition. C&A Carbone, Inc. v. Clarkstown, 511 U.S. 383 (1994). A unanimous Court in 1996 ruled that a North Carolina "intangibles tax" discriminated against interstate commerce by favoring purely domestic corporations over those involved in interstate commerce. Fulton Corp. v. Faulkner, 516 U.S. 325 (1996). Another unanimous ruling in 1999 held that an Alabama franchise tax violated the Commerce Clause. South Central Bell Telephone Co. v. Alabama, 526 U.S. 160 (1999).

Carter v. Carter Coal Co.

298 U.S. 238 (1936)

After the Supreme Court in 1935 struck down the National Industrial Recovery Act, Congress relied on the Commerce Clause to pass legislation to regulate mining and the distribution of coal. The legislation authorized a commission to determine maximum and minimum prices of coal and regulate the workers engaged in coal production. Could Congress control the conditions in which coal was produced before it became an article of interstate commerce, or were production and manufacturing purely within the control of states?

MR. JUSTICE SUTHERLAND delivered the opinion of the Court.

The purposes of the "Bituminous Coal Conservation Act of 1935," involved in these suits, as declared by the title, are to stabilize the bituminous coal-mining industry and promote its interstate commerce; to provide for cooperative marketing of bituminous coal; to levy a tax on such coal and provide for a drawback under certain conditions; to declare the production, distribution, and use of such coal to be affected with a national public interest; to conserve the national resources of such coal; to provide for the general welfare, and for other purposes.... The constitutional validity of the act is challenged in each of the suits.

. . .

The general rule with regard to the respective powers of the national and the state governments under the Constitution, is not in doubt. The states were before the Constitution; and, consequently, their legislative powers antedated the Constitution. Those who framed and those who adopted that in-

strument meant to carve from the general mass of legislative powers, then possessed by the states, only such portions as it was thought wise to confer upon the federal government; and in order that there should be no uncertainty in respect of what was taken and what was left, the national powers of legislation were not aggregated but enumerated—with the result that what was not embraced by the enumeration remained vested in the states without change or impairment....

... Since the validity of the act depends upon whether it is a regulation of interstate commerce, the nature and extent of the power conferred upon Congress by the commerce clause becomes the determinative question in this branch of the case....

As used in the Constitution, the word "commerce" is the equivalent of the phrase "intercourse for the purposes of trade," and includes transportation, purchase, sale, and exchange of commodities between the citizens of the different states. And the power to regulate commerce embraces the instruments by which commerce is carried on....

That commodities produced or manufactured within a state are intended to be sold or transported outside the state does not render their production or manufacture subject to federal regulation under the commerce clause....

We have seen that the word "commerce" is the equivalent of the phrase "intercourse for the purposes of trade." Plainly, the incidents leading up to and culminating in the mining of coal do not constitute such intercourse. The employment of men, the fixing of their wages, hours of labor and working conditions, the bargaining in respect of these things—whether carried on separately or collectively—each and all constitute intercourse for the purposes of production, not of trade....

A consideration of the foregoing, and of many cases which might be added to those already cited, renders inescapable the conclusion that the effect of the labor provisions of the act, including those in respect of minimum wages, wage agreements, collective bargaining, and the Labor Board and its powers, primarily falls upon production and not upon commerce; and confirms the further resulting conclusion that production is a purely local activity. It follows that none of these essential antecedents of production constitutes a transaction in or forms any part of interstate commerce.... Everything which moves in interstate commerce has had a local origin. Without local production somewhere, interstate commerce, as now carried on, would practically disappear. Nevertheless, the local character of mining, of manufacturing and of crop growing is a fact, and remains a fact, whatever may be done with the products.

. . .

Whether the effect of a given activity or condition is direct or indirect is not always easy to determine. The word "direct" implies that the activity or condition invoked or blamed shall operate proximately—not mediately, remotely, or collaterally—to produce the effect. It connotes the absence of an efficient intervening agency or condition. And the extent of the effect bears no logical relation to its character. The distinction between a direct and an indirect effect turns, not upon the magnitude of either the cause or the effect, but entirely upon the manner in which the effect has been brought about. If the production by one man of a single ton of coal intended for interstate sale and shipment, and actually so sold and shipped, affects interstate commerce indirectly, the effect does not become direct by multiplying the tonnage, or increasing the number of men employed, or adding to the expense or complexities of the business, or by all combined. It is quite true that rules of law are sometimes qualified by considerations of degree, as the government ar-

gues. But the matter of degree has no bearing upon the question here, since that question is not—What is the *extent* of the local activity or condition, or the *extent* of the effect produced upon interstate commerce? but—What is the *relation* between the activity or condition and the effect?

Much stress is put upon the evils which come from the struggle between employers and employees over the matter of wages, working conditions, the right of collective bargaining, etc., and the resulting strikes, curtailment and irregularity of production and effect on prices; and it is insisted that interstate commerce is *greatly* affected thereby. But, in addition to what has just been said, the conclusive answer is that the evils are all local evils over which the federal government has no legislative control. The relation of employer and employee is a local relation. At common law, it is one of the domestic relations. The wages are paid for the doing of local work. Working conditions are obviously local conditions....

Separate opinion of Mr. Chief Justice Hughes.

I agree that the stockholders were entitled to bring their suits; that, in view of the question whether any part of the Act could be sustained, the suits were not premature; that the so-called tax is not a real tax, but a penalty; that the constitutional power of the Federal Government to impose this penalty must rest upon the commerce clause, as the Government concedes; that production—in this case mining—which precedes commerce, is not itself commerce; and that the power to regulate commerce among the several States is not a power to regulate industry within the State.

. . .

But that is not the whole case. The Act also provides for the regulation of the prices of bituminous coal sold in interstate commerce and prohibits unfair methods of competition in interstate commerce. Undoubtedly transactions in carrying on interstate commerce are subject to the federal power to regulate that commerce and the control of charges and the protection of fair competition in that commerce are familiar illustrations of the exercise of the power, as the Interstate Commerce Act, the Packers and Stockyards Act, and the Anti-Trust Acts abundantly show....

Whether the policy of fixing prices of commodities sold in interstate commerce is a sound policy is not for our consideration. The question of that policy, and of its particular applications, is for Congress. The exercise of the power of regulation is subject to the constitutional restriction of the due process clause, and if in fixing rates, prices or conditions of competition, that requirement is transgressed, the judicial power may be invoked to the end that the constitutional limitation may be maintained....

Upon what ground, then, can it be said that this plan for the regulation of transactions in interstate commerce in coal is beyond the constitutional power of Congress? The Court reaches that conclusion in the view that the invalidity of the labor provisions requires us to condemn the Act in its entirety. I am unable to concur in that opinion. I think that the express provisions of the Act preclude such a finding of inseparability.

. . .

Mr. Justice Cardozo (dissenting in Nos. 636, 649 and 650, and in No. 651 concurring in the result).

. . .

First: I am satisfied that the Act is within the power of the central government in so far as it provides for minimum and maximum prices upon sales of bituminous coal in the transactions of interstate commerce and in those of intrastate commerce where interstate commerce is directly or intimately affected. Whether it is valid also in other provisions that have been considered and condemned in the opinion of the court, I do not find it necessary to determine at this time....

Congress was not condemned to inaction in the face of price wars and wage wars so pregnant with disaster. Commerce had been choked and burdened; its normal flow had been diverted from one state to another; there had been bankruptcy and waste and ruin alike for capital and for labor. The liberty protected by the Fifth Amendment does not include the right to persist in this anarchic riot.... There is testimony in these records, testimony even by the assailants of the statute, that only through a system of regulated prices can the industry be stabilized and set upon the road of orderly and peaceful progress.... An evil existing, and also the power to correct it, the lawmakers were at liberty to use their own discretion in the selection of the means.

. . .

I am authorized to state that Mr. Justice Brandeis and Mr. Justice Stone join in this opinion.

NLRB v. Jones & Laughlin

301 U.S. 1 (1937)

In the National Labor Relations Act of 1935, Congress concluded that labor disputes had a direct burden on interstate or foreign commerce and could be regulated by the Commerce Clause. Even activities taking place within a state, if they had a close and substantial relationship to interstate commerce, could be brought within the control of Congress. Under the shadow of Roosevelt's court-packing plan, the Court decided whether this exertion of national power invaded the rights reserved to the states.

Mr. Chief Justice Hughes delivered the opinion of the Court.

In a proceeding under the National Labor Relations Act of 1935, the National Labor Relations Board found that the respondent, Jones & Laughlin Steel Corporation, had violated the Act by engaging in unfair labor practices affecting commerce.... The unfair labor practices charged were that the corporation was discriminating against members of the union with regard to hire and tenure of employment, and was coercing and intimidating its employees in order to interfere with their self-organization. The discriminatory and coercive action alleged was the discharge of certain employees.

The National Labor Relations Board, sustaining the charge, ordered the corporation to cease and desist from such discrimination and coercion, to offer reinstatement to ten of the employees named, to make good their losses in pay, and to post for thirty days notices that the corporation would not discharge or discriminate against members, or those desiring to become members, of the labor union....

Contesting the ruling of the Board, the respondent argues (1) that the Act is in reality a regulation of labor relations and not of interstate commerce; (2) that the Act can have no application to the respondent's relations with its production employees because they are not subject to regulation by the federal government; and (3) that the provisions of the Act violate § 2 of Article III and the Fifth and Seventh Amendments of the Constitution of the United States.

... Jones & Laughlin Steel Corporation ... is organized under the laws of Pennsylvania and has its principal office at Pittsburgh. It is engaged in the business of manufacturing iron and steel in plants situated in Pittsburgh and nearby Aliquippa, Pennsylvania. It manufactures and distributes a widely diversified line of steel and pig iron, being the fourth largest producer of steel in the United States. With its subsidiaries—nineteen in number—it is a completely integrated enterprise, owning and operating ore, coal and limestone properties, lake and river transportation facilities and terminal railroads located at its manufacturing plants. It owns or controls mines in Michigan and Minnesota. It operates four ore steamships on the Great Lakes, used in the transportation of ore to its factories. It owns coal mines in Pennsylvania. It operates towboats and steam barges used in carrying coal to its factories. It owns limestone properties in various places in Pennsylvania and West Virginia. It owns the Monongahela connecting railroad which connects the plants of the Pittsburgh works and forms an interconnection with the Pennsylvania, New York Central and Baltimore and Ohio Railroad systems. It owns the Aliquippa and Southern Railroad Company which connects the Aliquippa works with the Pittsburgh and Lake Erie, part of the New York Central system. Much of its product is shipped to its warehouses in Chicago, Detroit, Cincinnati and Memphis,—to the last two places by means of its own barges and transportation equipment. In Long Island City, New York, and in New Orleans it operates structural steel fabricating shops in connection with the warehousing of semi-finished materials sent from its works. Through one of its wholly-owned subsidiaries it owns, leases and operates stores, warehouses and yards for the distribution of equipment and supplies for drilling and operating oil and gas wells and for pipe lines, refineries and pumping stations. It has sales offices in twenty cities in the United States and a wholly-owned subsidiary which is devoted exclusively to distributing its product in Canada. Approximately 75 per cent. of its product is shipped out of Pennsylvania.

Summarizing these operations, the Labor Board concluded that the works in Pittsburgh and Aliquippa "might be likened to the heart of a self-contained, highly integrated body. They draw in the raw materials from Michigan, Minnesota, West Virginia, Pennsylvania in part through arteries and by means controlled by the respondent; they transform the materials and then pump them out to all parts of the nation through the vast mechanism which the respondent has elaborated."

. . .

First. The scope of the Act.—The Act is challenged in its entirety as an attempt to regulate all industry, thus invading the reserved powers of the States over their local concerns....

There can be no question that the commerce thus contemplated by the Act (aside from that within a Territory or the District of Columbia) is interstate and foreign commerce in the constitutional sense. The Act also defines the term "affecting commerce" (§ 2 (7)):

"The term 'affecting commerce' means in commerce, or burdening or obstructing commerce or the free flow of commerce, or having led or tending to lead to a labor dispute burdening or obstructing commerce or the free flow of commerce."

This definition is one of exclusion as well as inclusion. The grant of authority to the Board does not purport to extend to the relationship between all industrial employees and employers. Its terms do not impose collective bargaining upon all industry regardless of effects upon interstate or foreign commerce. It purports to reach only what may be deemed to burden or obstruct that commerce and, thus qualified, it must be construed as contemplating the exercise of control within constitutional bounds. It is a familiar principle that acts which directly burden or obstruct interstate or foreign commerce, or its free flow, are within the reach of the congressional power....

Second. The unfair labor practices in question.— The unfair labor practices found by the Board are those defined in § 8, subdivisions (1) and (3). These provide:

Sec. 8. It shall be an unfair labor practice for an employer—

"(1) To interfere with, restrain, or coerce employees in the exercise of the rights guaranteed in section 7."

"(3) By discrimination in regard to hire or tenure of employment or any term or condition of employment to encourage or discourage membership in any labor organization...."

Section 8, subdivision (1), refers to § 7, which is as follows:

"Sec. 7. Employees shall have the right to self-organization, to form, join, or assist labor organizations, to bargain collectively through representatives of their own choosing, and to engage in concerted activities, for the purpose of collective bargaining or other mutual aid or protection."

Thus, in its present application, the statute goes no further than to safeguard the right of employees to self-organization and to select representatives of their own choosing for collective bargaining or other mutual protection without restraint or coercion by their employer.

That is a fundamental right. Employees have as clear a right to organize and select their representatives for lawful purposes as the respondent has to organize its business and select its own officers and agents. Discrimination and coercion to prevent the free exercise of the right of employees to self-organization and representation is a proper subject for condemnation by competent legislative authority. Long ago we stated the reason for labor organizations. We said that they were organized out of the necessities of the situation; that a single employee was helpless in dealing with an employer; that he was dependent ordinarily on his daily wage for the maintenance of himself and family; that if the employer refused to pay him the wages that he thought fair, he was nevertheless unable to leave the employ and resist arbitrary and unfair treatment; that union was essential to give laborers opportunity to deal on an equality with their employer....

Third. The application of the Act to employees engaged in production. — The principle involved. — Respondent says that whatever may be said of employees engaged in interstate commerce, the industrial relations and activities in the manufacturing department of respondent's enterprise are not subject to federal regulation. The argument rests upon the proposition that manufacturing in itself is not commerce....

... Although activities may be intrastate in character when separately considered, if they have such a close and substantial relation to interstate commerce that their control is essential or appropriate to protect that commerce from burdens and obstructions, Congress cannot be denied the power to exercise that control....

Fourth. Effects of the unfair labor practice in respondent's enterprise. — Giving full weight to respondent's contention with respect to a break in the complete continuity of the "stream of commerce" by reason of respondent's manufacturing operations, the fact remains that the stoppage of those operations by industrial strife would have a most serious effect upon interstate commerce. In view of respondent's far-flung activities, it is idle to say that the ef-

fect would be indirect or remote. It is obvious that it would be immediate and might be catastrophic. We are asked to shut our eyes to the plainest facts of our national life and to deal with the question of direct and indirect effects in an intellectual vacuum....

Experience has abundantly demonstrated that the recognition of the right of employees to self-organization and to have representatives of their own choosing for the purpose of collective bargaining is often an essential condition of industrial peace. Refusal to confer and negotiate has been one of the most prolific causes of strife. This is such an outstanding fact in the history of labor disturbances that it is a proper subject of judicial notice and requires no citation of instances....

Our conclusion is that the order of the Board was within its competency and that the Act is valid as here applied. The judgment of the Circuit Court of Appeals is reversed and the cause is remanded for further proceedings in conformity with this opinion.

Reversed.

[*On the same day, the Court handed down other decisions that upheld actions by the National Labor Relations Board. The dissents below are directed against this cluster of rulings.*]

Mr. Justice McReynolds delivered the following dissenting opinion in the cases preceding:

Mr. Justice Van Devanter, Mr. Justice Sutherland, Mr. Justice Butler and I are unable to agree with the decisions just announced.

. . .

The Constitution still recognizes the existence of states with indestructible powers; the Tenth Amendment was supposed to put them beyond controversy.

We are told that Congress may protect the "stream of commerce" and that one who buys raw material without the state, manufactures it therein, and ships the output to another state is in that stream. Therefore it is said he may be prevented from doing anything which may interfere with its flow.

This, too, goes beyond the constitutional limitations heretofore enforced. If a man raises cattle and regularly delivers them to a carrier for interstate shipment, may Congress prescribe the conditions under which he may employ or discharge helpers on the ranch? The products of a mine pass daily into interstate commerce; many things are brought to it from other states. Are the owners and the miners within the power of Congress in respect of the miners' tenure and discharge? May a mill owner be prohibited from closing his factory or discontinuing his business because so to do would stop the flow of products to and from his plant in interstate commerce? May employees in a factory be restrained from quitting work in a body because this will close the factory and thereby stop the flow of commerce? May arson of a factory be made a Federal offense whenever this would interfere with such flow? If the business cannot continue with the existing wage scale, may Congress command a reduction? If the ruling of the Court just announced is adhered to these questions suggest some of the problems certain to arise.

United States v. Darby

312 U.S. 100 (1941)

The Fair Labor Standards Act of 1938 provided for minimum wages and maximum hours for employees engaged in the production of goods for interstate commerce. The statute forced the Court to rethink its doctrine on "manufacture." If manufacture is not of itself interstate commerce, would the shipment of manufactured goods interstate bring it within the authority of Congress to regulate? The statute also excluded the products of child labor from interstate commerce, requiring the Court to revisit its holding in *Hammer* v. *Dagenhart* (1918), which had struck down the use of the Commerce Clause to regulate child labor. In this case, the government prosecutes Fred W. Darby, owner of a lumber company, for violating the 1938 statute.

MR. JUSTICE STONE delivered the opinion of the Court.

The two principal questions raised by the record in this case are, *first,* whether Congress has constitutional power to prohibit the shipment in interstate commerce of lumber manufactured by employees whose wages are less than a prescribed minimum or whose weekly hours of labor at that wage are greater than a prescribed maximum, and, *second,* whether it has power to prohibit the employment of workmen in the production of goods "for interstate commerce" at other than prescribed wages and hours. A subsidiary question is whether in connection with such prohibitions Congress can require the employer subject to them to keep records showing the hours worked each day and week by each of his employees including those engaged "in the production and manufacture of goods to-wit, lumber, for 'interstate commerce.'"

. . .

The indictment charges that appellee is engaged, in the State of Georgia, in the business of acquiring raw materials, which he manufactures into finished lumber with the intent, when manufactured, to ship it in interstate commerce to customers outside the state, and that he does in fact so ship a large part of the lumber so produced. There are numerous counts charging appellee with the shipment in interstate commerce from Georgia to points outside the state of lumber in the production of which, for interstate commerce, appellee has employed workmen at less than the prescribed minimum wage or more than the prescribed maximum hours without payment to them of any wage for overtime. Other counts charge the employment by appellee of workmen in the production of lumber for interstate commerce at wages at less than 25 cents an hour or for more than the maximum hours per week without payment to them of the prescribed overtime wage. Still another count charges appellee with failure to keep records showing the hours worked each day a week by each of his employees....

The demurrer, so far as now relevant to the appeal, challenged the validity of the Fair Labor Standards Act under the Commerce Clause and the Fifth and Tenth Amendments. The district court quashed the indictment in its entirety upon the broad grounds that the Act, which it interpreted as a regulation of manufacture within the states, is unconstitutional. It declared that manufacture is not interstate commerce and that the regulation by the Fair Labor Standards Act of wages and hours of employment of those engaged in the manufacture of goods which it is intended at the time of production "may or will be" after production "sold in interstate commerce in part or in whole" is not within the congressional power to regulate interstate commerce.

. . .

The prohibition of shipment of the proscribed goods in interstate commerce....

While manufacture is not of itself interstate commerce, the shipment of manufactured goods interstate is such commerce and the prohibition of such shipment by Congress is indubitably a regulation of the commerce. The power to regulate commerce is the power "to prescribe the rule by which commerce is governed." *Gibbons* v. *Ogden,* 9 Wheat. 1, 196. It extends not only to those regulations which aid, foster and protect the commerce, but embraces those which prohibit it.... It is conceded that the power of Congress to prohibit transportation in interstate commerce includes noxious articles, ... stolen articles, ... kidnapped persons, ... and articles such as intoxicating liquor or convict made goods, traffic in which is forbidden or restricted by the laws of the state of destination....

But it is said that the present prohibition falls within the scope of none of these categories; that while the prohibition is nominally a regulation of the commerce its motive or purpose is regulation of wages and hours of persons engaged in manufacture, the control of which has been reserved to the states and upon which Georgia and some of the states of destination have placed no restriction....

... Congress, following its own conception of public policy concerning the restrictions which may appropriately be imposed on interstate commerce, is free to exclude from the commerce articles whose use in the states for which they are destined it may conceive to be injurious to the public health, morals or welfare, even though the state has not sought to regulate their use....

Such regulation is not a forbidden invasion of state power merely because either its motive or its consequence is to restrict the use of articles of commerce within the states of destination; and is not prohibited unless by other Constitutional provisions. It is no objection to the assertion of the power to regulate interstate commerce that its exercise is attended by the same incidents which attend the exercise of the police power of the states....

In the more than a century which has elapsed since the decision of *Gibbons* v. *Ogden,* these principles of constitutional interpretation have been so long and repeatedly recognized by this Court as applicable to the Commerce Clause, that there would be little occasion for repeating them now were it not for the decision of this Court twenty-two years ago

in *Hammer* v. *Dagenhart,* 247 U.S. 251. In that case it was held by a bare majority of the Court over the powerful and now classic dissent of Mr. Justice Holmes setting forth the fundamental issues involved, that Congress was without power to exclude the products of child labor from interstate commerce. The reasoning and conclusion of the Court's opinion there cannot be reconciled with the conclusion which we have reached, that the power of Congress under the Commerce Clause is plenary to exclude any article from interstate commerce subject only to the specific prohibitions of the Constitution.

Hammer v. *Dagenhart* has not been followed. The distinction on which the decision was rested that Congressional power to prohibit interstate commerce is limited to articles which in themselves have some harmful or deleterious property—a distinction which was novel when made and unsupported by any provision of the Constitution—has long since been abandoned....

The conclusion is inescapable that *Hammer* v. *Dagenhart* was a departure from the principles which have prevailed in the interpretation of the Commerce Clause both before and since the decision and that such vitality, as a precedent, as it then had has long since been exhausted. It should be and now is overruled.

. . .

Our conclusion is unaffected by the Tenth Amendment which provides: "The powers not delegated to the United States by the Constitution, nor prohibited by it to the States, are reserved to the States respectively, or to the people." The amendment states but a truism that all is retained which has not been surrendered. There is nothing in the history of its adoption to suggest that it was more than declaratory of the relationship between the national and state governments as it had been established by the Constitution before the amendment or that its purpose was other than to allay fears that the new national government might seek to exercise powers not granted, and that the states might not be able to exercise fully their reserved powers....

Reversed.

Wickard v. Filburn

317 U.S. 111 (1942)

In 1941 Congress amended the Agricultural Adjustment Act of 1938 to increase the penalty on excess production. Roscoe Filburn, a farmer, received a wheat allotment of 11 acres for his 1941

crop but sowed 23 acres, planning to use the extra crop for home consumption. He was penalized for the excess production and brought suit against Secretary of Agriculture Claude Wickard. This case examines the power of Congress to control production, even within a state, to increase the price of wheat.

Mr. Justice Jackson delivered the opinion of the Court.

. . .

II

It is urged that under the Commerce Clause of the Constitution, Article I, § 8, clause 3, Congress does not possess the power it has in this instance sought to exercise. The question would merit little consideration since our decision in *United States* v. *Darby*, 312 U.S. 100, sustaining the federal power to regulate production of goods for commerce, except for the fact that this Act extends federal regulation to production not intended in any part for commerce but wholly for consumption on the farm. The Act includes a definition of "market" and its derivatives, so that as related to wheat, in addition to its conventional meaning, it also means to dispose of "by feeding (in any form) to poultry or livestock which, or the products of which, are sold, bartered, or exchanged, or to be so disposed of." Hence, marketing quotas not only embrace all that may be sold without penalty but also what may be consumed on the premises. Wheat produced on excess acreage is designated as "available for marketing" as so defined, and the penalty is imposed thereon. Penalties do not depend upon whether any part of the wheat, either within or without the quota, is sold or intended to be sold. The sum of this is that the Federal Government fixes a quota including all that the farmer may harvest for sale or for his own farm needs, and declares that wheat produced on excess acreage may neither be disposed of nor used except upon payment of the penalty, or except it is stored as required by the Act or delivered to the Secretary of Agriculture.

Appellee says that this is a regulation of production and consumption of wheat. Such activities are, he urges, beyond the reach of Congressional power under the Commerce Clause, since they are local in character, and their effects upon interstate commerce are at most "indirect." In answer the Government argues that the statute regulates neither production nor consumption, but only marketing; and, in the alternative, that if the Act does go beyond the regulation of marketing it is sustainable as a "necessary and proper" implementation of the power of Congress over interstate commerce.

The Government's concern lest the Act be held to be a regulation of production or consumption, rather than of marketing, is attributable to a few dicta and decisions of this Court which might be understood to lay it down that activities such as "production," "manufacturing," and "mining" are strictly "local" and, except in special circumstances which are not present here, cannot be regulated under the commerce power because their effects upon interstate commerce are, as matter of law, only "indirect." Even today, when this power has been held to have great latitude, there is no decision of this Court that such activities may be regulated where no part of the product is intended for interstate commerce or intermingled with the subjects thereof. We believe that a review of the course of decision under the Commerce Clause will make plain, however, that questions of the power of Congress are not to be decided by reference to any formula which would give controlling force to nomenclature such as "production" and "indirect" and foreclose consideration of the actual effects of the activity in question upon interstate commerce.

At the beginning Chief Justice Marshall described the federal commerce power with a breadth never yet exceeded. *Gibbons* v. *Ogden*, 9 Wheat. 1, 194–195. He made emphatic the embracing and penetrating nature of this power by warning that effective restraints on its exercise must proceed from political rather than from judicial processes. *Id.* at 197.

For nearly a century, however, decisions of this Court under the Commerce Clause dealt rarely with questions of what Congress might do in the exercise of its granted power under the Clause, and almost entirely with the permissibility of state activity which it was claimed discriminated against or burdened interstate commerce. During this period there was perhaps little occasion for the affirmative exercise of the commerce power, and the influence of the Clause on American life and law was a negative one, resulting almost wholly from its operation as a restraint upon the powers of the states. In discussion and decision the point of reference, instead of being what was "necessary and proper" to the exercise by Congress of its granted power, was often some concept of sovereignty thought to be implicit in the status of statehood. Certain activities such as "production," "manufacturing," and "mining" were occasionally said to be within the province of state governments and beyond the power of Congress under the Commerce Clause.

It was not until 1887, with the enactment of the Interstate Commerce Act, that the interstate commerce power began to exert positive influence in American law and life. This first important federal resort to the commerce power was followed in 1890 by the Sherman Anti-Trust Act and, thereafter, mainly after 1903, by many others. These statutes ushered in new phases of adjudication, which required the Court to approach the interpretation of the Commerce Clause in the light of an actual exercise by Congress of its power thereunder.

When it first dealt with this new legislation, the Court adhered to its earlier pronouncements, and allowed but little scope to the power of Congress. *United States* v. *Knight Co.,* 156 U.S. 1. These earlier pronouncements also played an important part in several of the five cases in which this Court later held that Acts of Congress under the Commerce Clause were in excess of its power.

Even while important opinions in this line of restrictive authority were being written, however, other cases called forth broader interpretations of the Commerce Clause destined to supersede the earlier ones, and to bring about a return to the principles first enunciated by Chief Justice Marshall in *Gibbons* v. *Ogden, supra.*

Not long after the decision of *United States* v. *Knight Co., supra,* Mr. Justice Holmes, in sustaining the exercise of national power over intrastate activity, stated for the Court that "commerce among the States is not a technical legal conception, but a practical one, drawn from the course of business." *Swift & Co.* v. *United States,* 196 U.S. 375, 398. It was soon demonstrated that the effects of many kinds of intrastate activity upon interstate commerce were such as to make them a proper subject of federal regulation. In some cases sustaining the exercise of federal power over intrastate matters the term "direct" was used for the purpose of stating, rather than of reaching, a result; in others it was treated as synonymous with "substantial" or "material"; and in others it was not used at all. Of late its use has been abandoned in cases dealing with questions of federal power under the Commerce Clause.

In the *Shreveport Rate Cases,* 234 U.S. 342, the Court held that railroad rates of an admittedly intrastate character and fixed by authority of the state might, nevertheless, be revised by the Federal Government because of the economic effects which they had upon interstate commerce. The opinion of Mr. Justice Hughes found federal intervention constitutionally authorized because of "matters having such a close and substantial relation to interstate traffic that the control is essential or appropriate to the se-

curity of that traffic, to the efficiency of the interstate service, and to the maintenance of conditions under which interstate commerce may be conducted upon fair terms and without molestation or hindrance." *Id.* at 351.

The Court's recognition of the relevance of the economic effects in the application of the Commerce Clause, exemplified by this statement, has made the mechanical application of legal formulas no longer feasible. Once an economic measure of the reach of the power granted to Congress in the Commerce Clause is accepted, questions of federal power cannot be decided simply by finding the activity in question to be "production," nor can consideration of its economic effects be foreclosed by calling them "indirect." ...

Whether the subject of the regulation in question was "production," "consumption," or "marketing" is, therefore, not material for purposes of deciding the question of federal power before us. That an activity is of local character may help in a doubtful case to determine whether Congress intended to reach it. The same consideration might help in determining whether in the absence of Congressional action it would be permissible for the state to exert its power on the subject matter, even though in so doing it to some degree affected interstate commerce. But even if appellee's activity be local and though it may not be regarded as commerce, it may still, whatever its nature, be reached by Congress if it exerts a substantial economic effect on interstate commerce, and this irrespective of whether such effect is what might at some earlier time have been defined as "direct" or "indirect."

. . .

It is well established by decisions of this Court that the power to regulate commerce includes the power to regulate the prices at which commodities in that commerce are dealt in and practices affecting such prices. One of the primary purposes of the Act in question was to increase the market price of wheat, and to that end to limit the volume thereof that could affect the market. It can hardly be denied that a factor of such volume and variability as home-consumed wheat would have a substantial influence on price and market conditions. This may arise because being in marketable condition such wheat overhangs the market and, if induced by rising prices, tends to flow into the market and check price increases. But if we assume that it is never marketed, it supplies a need of the man who grew it which would otherwise be reflected by purchases in the open market. Home-grown wheat in this sense competes with wheat in commerce. The stimulation of commerce is a use of the regulatory function quite as definitely as prohibitions or restrictions thereon. This record leaves us in no doubt that Congress may properly have considered that wheat consumed on the farm where grown, if wholly outside the scheme

of regulation, would have a substantial effect in defeating and obstructing its purpose to stimulate trade therein at increased prices.

. . .

E. FROM *NATIONAL LEAGUE* TO *GARCIA*

A contentious issue of federalism in the late 20th Century involved the extension of federal hours-and-wages standards to state employees. The Supreme Court halted this trend toward national control in *National League of Cities* v. *Usery* (1976) but reversed itself nine years later in *Garcia* v. *San Antonio Metropolitan Transit Authority* (1985), giving Congress almost total power under the Commerce Clause. In *Garcia*, the Court announced that the protection of federalism depends largely on the political process operating within Congress.

The Fair Labor Standards Act of 1938 expressly exempted all states and their political divisions from the federal minimum-wage and overtime provisions. In 1966, Congress extended federal minimum wages and overtime pay to state-operated hospitals and schools. Two years later the Court upheld that legislation as rationally based, deciding that Congress had properly taken into account the effect on interstate competition and the promotion of labor peace. Maryland v. Wirtz, 392 U.S. 183 (1968). Building on that decision, in 1975 the Court upheld the short-term power of the President to stabilize wages and salaries of state employees. Fry v. United States, 421 U.S. 542, 549–59 (1975).

A year later, however, Justice Rehnquist attracted four other votes to his position that federal minimum-wage and maximum-hour provisions could not displace state powers in such "traditional governmental functions" as fire prevention, police protection, sanitation, public health, and parks and recreation. Amendments to the Fair Labor Standards Act in 1974 had extended the wage-and-hour provisions to almost all state employees. The 5–4 decision by Rehnquist overruled *Wirtz* by holding that the 1974 amendments threatened the independent existence of states. Justice Blackmun, in a tentative concurrence, supplied the fifth vote. The dissents were sharply worded. For the first time in four decades, the Court had invalidated a statute passed by Congress pursuant to the Commerce Clause. NATIONAL LEAGUE OF CITIES v. USERY, 426 U.S. 833 (1976).

Rehnquist's bifurcation between traditional and nontraditional governmental functions could not be applied with confidence or consistency either in the lower courts or in the Supreme Court itself. When lower courts found a function to be "traditional" and thus within the realm of state sovereignty, the Court would frequently reverse on the ground that the function was actually nontraditional and beyond the protection offered in *National League* (see box on next page).

One of the curious facts about *National League* is that when the Supreme Court remanded the case to a three-judge district court, the district court did not try to determine the difference between traditional and nontraditional functions. Instead, it asked the Labor Department to identify nontraditional state functions. It did so, providing a list of traditional functions as well. Included in the Department's list of nontraditional functions was "local mass transit systems," a decision that prompted new litigation and a challenge to *National League*.

Justice Blackmun's majority opinion in the mass transit case nullified the decision with which he had concurred less than ten years before. He pointed to the difficulty that courts had experienced in distinguishing between "traditional" and "nontraditional" state functions. The effect of his 5–4 decision was to leave the protection of federalism largely to the political process of Congress. GARCIA v. SAN ANTONIO METROPOLITAN TRANSIT AUTHORITY, 469 U.S. 528 (1985).

Garcia threatened the states with massive budgetary obligations. Most state employees were already receiving at least the minimum wage, but the cost of meeting the overtime provisions of the

The Hapless, Hopeless Effort to Implement *National League*

In 1981, a unanimous Court rejected a district court's argument that land use regulation was a "traditional governmental function" reserved to the states under *National League.* The Court held that *National League* applied to "states as states" and not to private business operations within a state. Hodel v. Virginia Surface Mining & Recl. Assn., 452 U.S. 264 (1981). A year later, a 5–4 Court rejected a district court's attempt to use *National League* to prohibit Congress from regulating retail sales of electricity and natural gas. The district court said this area of economic regulation was traditional; the Court said it was not. FERC v. Mississippi, 456 U.S. 742 (1982). In that same year, the Court rejected a Second Circuit's conclusion that a state-owned railroad engaged in interstate commerce represented a traditional governmental function. A unanimous Court said that the operation of railroads "has traditionally been a function of private industry, not state or local governments." United Transportation Union v. Long Island R. Co., 455 U.S. 678, 686 (1982).

In 1981, a federal district court held that the Age Discrimination in Employment Act passed by Congress in 1967 violated the Tenth Amendment theory articulated in *National League.* The case involved Wyoming's mandatory retirement of game wardens at the age of 55. Game wardens seemed to fit the categories of police protection, parks, and recreation, all of which *National League* specifically classified as a traditional state function. Nevertheless, a 5–4 Court reversed the district court. EEOC v. Wyoming, 460 U.S. 226 (1983). Significantly, Justice Blackmun (who had given Rehnquist a fifth vote in *National League*) provided the fifth vote in this case. Although the Wyoming case did not override *National League,* many Court-watchers concluded that little life remained in the 1976 ruling.

Fair Labor Standards Act could have reached several billion dollars, much of it for firefighters and police in local government. To prevent that cost from being transferred to the states, Congress passed legislation to postpone the effective date of *Garcia* (decided February 19, 1985) to April 15, 1986, and permitted the use of compensatory time as a substitute for paying overtime. 99 Stat. 787 (1985).

National League of Cities v. Usery

426 U.S. 833 (1976)

This case marks an effort by Justice Rehnquist to devise a doctrine to protect states' rights against federal intrusion. In 1974 Congress amended the Fair Labor Standards Act to extend minimum wage and maximum hour provisions to cover almost all employees of states and their political divisions. The National League of Cities, supported by a number of cities and states, brought an action against Secretary of Labor W.J. Usery, Jr., challenging the validity of the 1974 amendments and seeking declaratory and injunctive relief. A three-judge district court dismissed the complaint for failure to state a claim upon which relief might be granted.

MR. JUSTICE REHNQUIST delivered the opinion of the Court.

Nearly 40 years ago Congress enacted the Fair Labor Standards Act, and required employers covered by the Act to pay their employees a minimum hourly wage and to pay them at one and one-half times their regular rate of pay for hours worked in excess of 40 during a workweek....

The original Fair Labor Standards Act passed in 1938 specifically excluded the States and their political subdivisions from its coverage....

I

[*Rehnquist reviews congressional changes in the Act across a period of fifteen years.*]

... In 1974, Congress again broadened the coverage of the Act.... The Act thus imposes upon almost all public employment the minimum wage and maximum hour requirements previously restricted to employees engaged in interstate commerce....

II

It is established beyond peradventure that the Commerce Clause of Art. I of the Constitution is a grant of plenary authority to Congress. That authority is, in the words of Mr. Chief Justice Marshall in *Gibbons* v. *Ogden*, 9 Wheat. 1 (1824), "the power to regulate; that is, to prescribe the rule by which commerce is to be governed." *Id.,* at 196....

Appellants in no way challenge these decisions establishing the breadth of authority granted Congress under the commerce power. Their contention, on the contrary, is that when Congress seeks to regulate directly the activities of States as public employers, it transgresses an affirmative limitation on the exercise of its power akin to other commerce power affirmative limitations contained in the Constitution....

This Court has never doubted that there are limits upon the power of Congress to override state sovereignty, even when exercising its otherwise plenary powers to tax or to regulate commerce which are conferred by Art. I of the Constitution. In *Wirtz,* for example, the Court took care to assure the appellants that it had "ample power to prevent ... 'the utter destruction of the State as a sovereign political entity,'" which they feared. 392 U.S., at 196....

One undoubted attribute of state sovereignty is the States' power to determine the wages which shall be paid to those whom they employ in order to carry out their governmental functions, what hours those persons will work, and what compensation will be provided where these employees may be called upon to work overtime. The question we must resolve here, then, is whether these determinations are "'functions essential to separate and independent existence,'" ... so that Congress may not abrogate the States' otherwise plenary authority to make them....

[*Rehnquist observes that the Act will significantly increase the costs of state programs, including police and fire protection.*]

... Our examination of the effect of the 1974 amendments, as sought to be extended to the States and their political subdivisions, satisfies us that both the minimum wage and the maximum hour provisions will impermissibly interfere with the integral governmental functions of these bodies.... [E]ven if we accept appellee's assessments concerning the impact of the amendments, their application will nonetheless significantly alter or displace the States' abilities to structure employer-employee relationships in such areas as fire prevention, police protection, sanitation, public health, and parks and recreation. These activities are typical of those performed by state and local governments in discharging their dual functions of administering the public law and furnishing public services. Indeed, it is functions such as these which governments are created to provide, services such as these which the States have traditionally afforded their citizens. We hold that insofar as the challenged amendments operate to directly displace the States' freedom to structure integral operations in areas of traditional governmental functions, they are not within the authority granted Congress by Art. I, § 8, cl. 3....

The judgment of the District Court is accordingly reversed, and the cases are remanded for further proceedings consistent with this opinion.

So ordered.

Mr. Justice Blackmun, concurring.

The Court's opinion and the dissents indicate the importance and significance of this litigation as it bears upon the relationship between the Federal Government and our States. Although I am not untroubled by certain possible implications of the Court's opinion—some of them suggested by the dissents—I do not read the opinion so despairingly as does my Brother Brennan. In my view, the result with respect to the statute under challenge here is necessarily correct. I may misinterpret the Court's opinion, but it seems to me that it adopts a balancing approach, and does not outlaw federal power in areas such as environmental protection, where the federal interest is demonstrably greater and where state facility compliance with imposed federal standards would be essential.... With this understanding on my part of the Court's opinion, I join it.

Mr. Justice Brennan, with whom Mr. Justice White and Mr. Justice Marshall join, dissenting.

The Court concedes, as of course it must, that Congress enacted the 1974 amendments pursuant to its exclusive power under Art. I, § 8, cl. 3, of the Constitution "[t]o regulate Commerce ... among the several States." It must therefore be surprising that my Brethren should choose this bicentennial year of our independence to repudiate principles governing judicial interpretation of our Constitution settled since the time of Mr. Chief Justice John Marshall, discarding his postulate that the Constitution contemplates that restraints upon exercise by Congress of its plenary commerce power lie in the political process and not in the judicial process. For 152 years ago Mr. Chief Justice Marshall enunciated that principle to which, until today, his successors on this Court have been faithful.

"[T]he power over commerce ... is vested in Congress as absolutely as it would be in a single government, having in its constitution the same restrictions on the exercise of the power as are found in the constitution of the United States. *The wisdom and the discretion of Congress, their identity with the people, and the influence which their constituents possess at elections, are ... the sole restraints on which they have relied, to secure them from its abuse. They are the restraints on which the people must often rely solely, in all representative governments.*" *Gibbons* v. *Ogden,* 9 Wheat. 1, 197 (1824) (emphasis added).

. . .

Today's repudiation of this unbroken line of precedents that firmly reject my Brethren's ill-conceived abstraction can only be regarded as a transparent cover for invalidating a congressional judgment with which they disagree. The only analysis even remotely resembling that adopted today is found in a line of opinions dealing with the Commerce Clause and the Tenth Amendment that ultimately provoked a constitutional crisis for the Court in the 1930s. *E.g., Carter* v. *Carter Coal Co.,* 298 U.S. 238 (1936); *United States* v. *Butler,* 297 U.S. 1 (1936);

Hammer v. *Dagenhart,* 247 U.S. 251 (1918).... It may have been the eventual abandonment of that overly restrictive construction of the commerce power that spelled defeat for the Court-packing plan, and preserved the integrity of this institution....

MR. JUSTICE STEVENS, dissenting.

The Court holds that the Federal Government may not interfere with a sovereign State's inherent right to pay a substandard wage to the janitor at the state capitol. The principle on which the holding rests is difficult to perceive.

The Federal Government may, I believe, require the State to act impartially when it hires or fires the janitor, to withhold taxes from his paycheck, to observe safety regulations when he is performing his job, to forbid him from burning too much soft coal in the capitol furnace, from dumping untreated refuse in an adjacent waterway, from overloading a state-owned garbage truck, or from driving either the truck or the Governor's limousine over 55 miles an hour. Even though these and many other activities of the capitol janitor are activities of the State *qua* State, I have no doubt that they are subject to federal regulation.

I agree that it is unwise for the Federal Government to exercise its power in the ways described in the Court's opinion....

My disagreement with the wisdom of this legislation may not, of course, affect my judgment with respect to its validity. On this issue there is no dissent from the proposition that the Federal Government's power over the labor market is adequate to embrace these employees....

Garcia v. San Antonio Metro. Transit Auth.

469 U.S. 528 (1985)

The federalism doctrine of *National League of Cities* (1976) rested on a narrow 5 to 4 decision, with Justice Blackmun's concurrence supplying the fifth vote. The doctrine's attempt to distinguish between "traditional" and "nontraditional" governmental functions produced vast confusion in the lower courts. Blackmun eventually concluded that the doctrine was unsound and unworkable. By switching sides, he created a new 5 to 4 majority to overturn *National League of Cities*. The *Garcia* case began in 1979 when the Department of Labor issued an opinion that the operations of the San Antonio Metropolitan Transit Authority (SAMTA) were not immune from the minimum-wage and overtime requirements of the Fair Labor Standards Act. SAMTA filed an action in federal district court, seeking declaratory relief. On the same day, Joe G. Garcia and several other SAMTA employees brought suit against SAMTA for overtime pay under the Fair Labor Standards Act.

JUSTICE BLACKMUN delivered the opinion of the Court....

In the present cases, a Federal District Court concluded that municipal ownership and operation of a mass-transit system is a traditional governmental function and thus, under *National League of Cities,* is exempt from the obligations imposed by the FLSA. Faced with the identical question, three Federal Courts of Appeals and one state appellate court have reached the opposite conclusion.

Our examination of this "function" standard applied in these and other cases over the last eight years now persuades us that the attempt to draw the boundaries of state regulatory immunity in terms of "traditional governmental function" is not only unworkable but is also inconsistent with established principles of federalism and, indeed, with those very federalism principles on which *National League of Cities* purported to rest. That case, accordingly, is overruled.

I

[*Justice Blackmun reviews the history of public transportation in San Antonio and the funding sources that supported it.*]

II

... The District Court voiced a common concern: "Despite the abundance of adjectives, identifying which particular state functions are immune [*from regulation under the Fair Labor Standards Act*] remains difficult." 557 F. Supp., at 447. Just how troublesome the task has been is revealed by the results reached in other federal cases.... We find it difficult, if not impossible, to identify an organizing principle that places each of the cases in the first group [*protected under National League of Cities*] on one side of a line and each of the cases in the second group [*not protected*] on the other side. The constitutional distinction between licensing drivers [*protected*] and regulating traffic [*not protected*], for example, or between operating a highway authority [*protected*] and operating a mental health facility [*not protected*], is elusive at best....

We believe, however, that there is a more fundamental problem at work here.... The essence of our federal system is that within the realm of authority left open to them under the Constitution, the States must be equally free to engage in any activity that their citizens choose for the common weal, no matter how unorthodox or unnecessary anyone else— including the judiciary—deems state involvement to be. Any rule of state immunity that looks to the "traditional," "integral," or "necessary" nature of governmental functions inevitably invites an unelected federal judiciary to make decisions about which state policies it favors and which ones it dislikes.... In the words of Justice Black:

"There is not, and there cannot be, any unchanging line of demarcation between essential and non-essential governmental functions. Many governmental functions of today have at some time in the past been nongovernmental. The genius of our government provides that, within the sphere of constitutional action, the people—acting not through the courts but through their elected legislative representatives—have the power to determine as conditions demand, what services and functions the public welfare requires." *Helvering* v. *Gerhardt,* 304 U.S., at 427 (concurring opinion).

We therefore now reject, as unsound in principle and unworkable in practice, a rule of state immunity from federal regulation that turns on a judicial appraisal of whether a particular governmental function is "integral" or "traditional." ...

IV

This analysis makes clear that Congress' action in affording SAMTA employees the protections of the wage and hour provisions of the FLSA contravened no affirmative limit on Congress' power under the Commerce Clause. The judgment of the District Court therefore must be reversed.

Of course, we continue to recognize that the States occupy a special and specific position in our constitutional system and that the scope of Congress' authority under the Commerce Clause must reflect that position. But the principal and basic limit on the federal commerce power is that inherent in all congressional action—the built-in restraints that our system provides through state participation in federal governmental action. The political process ensures that laws that unduly burden the States will not be promulgated. In the factual setting of these cases the internal safeguards of the political process have performed as intended.

. . .

National League of Cities v. *Usery,* 426 U.S. 833 (1976), is overruled. The judgment of the District Court is reversed, and these cases are remanded to that court for further proceedings consistent with this opinion.

It is so ordered.

JUSTICE POWELL, with whom THE CHIEF JUS-TICE, JUSTICE REHNQUIST, and JUSTICE O'CONNOR join, dissenting....

I

There are, of course, numerous examples over the history of this Court in which prior decisions have been reconsidered and overruled. There have been few cases, however, in which the principle of *stare decisis* and the rationale of recent decisions were ignored as abruptly as we now witness....

Whatever effect the Court's decision may have in weakening the application of *stare decisis,* it is likely to be less important than what the Court has done to the Constitution itself. A unique feature of the United States is the *federal* system of government guaranteed by the Constitution and implicit in the very name of our country. Despite some genuflect-ing in the Court's opinion to the concept of federal-ism, today's decision effectively reduces the Tenth Amendment to meaningless rhetoric when Congress acts pursuant to the Commerce Clause....

[II.B]

Today's opinion does not explain how the States' role in the electoral process guarantees that particu-lar exercises of the Commerce Clause power will not infringe on residual state sovereignty. Members of Congress are elected from the various States, but once in office they are Members of the Federal Gov-ernment....

More troubling than the logical infirmities in the Court's reasoning is the result of its holding, *i.e.,* that federal political officials, invoking the Commerce Clause, are the sole judges of the limits of their own power. This result is inconsistent with the funda-mental principles of our constitutional system. See, *e.g.,* The Federalist No. 78 (Hamilton). At least since *Marbury* v. *Madison,* 1 Cranch 137, 177 (1803), it has been the settled province of the federal judiciary "to say what the law is" with respect to the constitu-tionality of Acts of Congress....

JUSTICE REHNQUIST, dissenting....

JUSTICE O'CONNOR, with whom JUSTICE POWELL and JUSTICE REHNQUIST join, dissenting.

The Court today surveys the battle scene of fed-eralism and sounds a retreat. Like JUSTICE POWELL, I would prefer to hold the field and, at the very least, render a little aid to the wounded....

... With the abandonment of *National League of Cities,* all that stands between the remaining essen-tials of state sovereignty and Congress is the latter's underdeveloped capacity for self-restraint.

· · ·

F. STATE POWERS REVIVED

Although *Garcia* shifted much of the guardian role of federalism to Congress, the Supreme Court continued to use the Tenth Amendment and other constitutional provisions to protect state powers. Whereas the Court in *Garcia* was willing to leave federalism largely to the political process, in the 1990s the Court moved aggressively to curb congressional authority and reinforce state sovereignty.

In 1991 the Court held that Missouri's constitution—providing a mandatory retirement age of 70 for most state judges—did not violate the Age Discrimination in Employment Act (ADEA) of 1967. As a sovereign state, Missouri's range of action is protected by the Tenth Amendment and the Guar-antee Clause of Art. IV, § 4. The authority of states to determine the qualification of their officials lies at the heart of representative government. This decision seemed to rest largely on constitutional grounds, and yet the Court was also involved in statutory interpretation, leaving the door open for Congress to rewrite the ADEA so that it explicitly covers state judges. Gregory v. Ashcroft, 501 U.S. 452, 467 (1991).

A year later, the Court relied on the Tenth Amendment to invalidate part of a 1985 congressional statute designed to force states to find disposal sites for low-level radioactive waste. The 6–3 decision ruled that the statutory provision (forcing states to take possession of the waste if they failed to dis-cover other solutions) represented an invalid effort by Congress to commandeer the states' legislative processes and thus inconsistent with the Tenth Amendment. The Court said that states are not "mere political subdivisions" of the United States, nor are state governments regional offices or administra-tive agencies of the federal government. New York v. United States, 505 U.S. 144, 188 (1992). In terms of public policy, the decision was not too significant. Rather than draft new legislation to satisfy the

Court, Congress decided to rely on the existing compacts that states had created to dispose of low-level radioactive waste.

Gun Controls

In 1995, the Supreme Court struck down a congressional statute that banned guns within 1,000 feet of a school. Divided 5 to 4, the Court ruled that Congress had exceeded its authority under the Commerce Clause. The majority held that the statute had nothing to do with commerce or any sort of economic enterprise. UNITED STATES v. LOPEZ, 514 U.S. 549 (1995). Some commentators regarded the decision as one of the most important rulings in recent decades, but it may have been a case where Congress simply failed to present adequate findings to show an interstate commerce link with guns on school playgrounds.

Within two weeks of the Court's decision, President Clinton submitted legislation to Congress to amend the earlier statute by requiring the federal government to prove that the firearm has "moved in or the possession of such firearm otherwise affects interstate or foreign commerce." Public Papers of the Presidents, 1995, I, at 678. Congress enacted legislation in 1996, finding that crime at the local level "is exacerbated by the interstate movement of drugs, guns, and criminal gangs," that the occurrence of violent crime in school zones has resulted in a decline in the quality of education, and that it has the power under the interstate commerce clause to enact the legislation. The statutory language provides: "It shall be unlawful for any individual knowingly to possess a firearm that has moved in or that otherwise affects interstate or foreign commerce at a place that the individual knows, or has reasonable cause to believe, is a school zone." 110 Stat. 3009–369, § 657 (1996). There have been no legal challenges to this legislation, but if someone were charged under the Act, as Lopez was, it is likely that gun rights advocates would pursue an appeal.

In another 5 to 4 ruling, the Court in 1997 relied largely on its understanding of federalism to strike down a key portion of the 1993 Brady gun control law. That statute required state and local law enforcement officers to conduct background checks on prospective handgun purchasers. Relying heavily on its 1992 decision in *New York,* the Court held that state legislatures "are *not* subject to federal direction." Printz v. United States, 521 U.S. 898 (1997). The Court cited the Tenth Amendment as ground for invalidating the statutory provision. Id. at 919. It also pointed to *New York*'s standard that Congress cannot compel the states to enact or enforce a federal regulatory program and cannot "circumvent that prohibition by conscripting the States's officers directly." Id. at 935. Concurrences by Justices O'Connor and Thomas agreed that the Brady Act violated the Tenth Amendment. The dissenters looked to Hamilton's essay in Federalist No. 27 and to statutes of the early Congresses as evidence that Congress may require state courts and other state officials to implement federal law.

The Court's decision did not have a substantial effect on governmental policy. Most states already required background checks and the federal government was already developing a system that could do the work that had been expected of local law enforcement officials. Beginning on November 30, 1998, gun dealers were required to use the National Instant Criminal Background Check System (NICS) to check the names of prospective buyers. This computerized list of offenders is prepared and managed by the FBI.

Term Limits

Federalism was an issue in the term limits case decided by the Supreme Court in 1995. A number of states had adopted constitutional amendments or other measures to place term limits on legislators not only from the states but in Congress as well. Arkansas, for example, amended its constitution to limit members of Congress to three terms in the House of Representatives and to two terms in the Senate. Relying primarily on *Powell* v. *McCormack,* 395 U.S. 486 (1969), the Court held that the Arkansas provision violated the U.S. Constitution by adding to the qualifications established for members of Congress. U.S. Term Limits, Inc. v. Thornton, 514 U.S. 779 (1995). The fifth vote in this 5 to 4 decision was supplied in a concurrence by Justice Kennedy, who invoked principles of federalism to strike down the Arkansas amendment: "That the States may not invade the sphere of federal sovereignty is as incontestable, in my view, as the corollary proposition that the Federal Government must be held within the boundaries of its own power when it intrudes upon matters reserved to the States." Id. at 841.

Lawsuits Against the States

Again divided 5 to 4, the Court in 1996 ruled that Congress lacked authority under the Indian Commerce Clause to abrogate the states' Eleventh Amendment immunity from lawsuits. At issue was the Indian Gaming Regulatory Act, which allowed Indian tribes to sue states in federal court in disputes between tribes and states regarding gaming operations. Gambling in Indian casinos had grown to a $4 billion a year business. While overruling the opinion in *Pennsylvania* v. *Union Gas Co.* (1989) that the Commerce Clause can trump state sovereign immunity, the Court left in place the holding in *Fitzpatrick* v. *Bitzer* (1976) that Congress can override state immunity when it legislates pursuant to the Fourteenth Amendment. Four Justices joined two lengthy dissents. Seminole Tribe of Florida v. Florida, 517 U.S. 44 (1996).

A trio of 5–4 decisions on June 23, 1999, placed additional curbs on congressional power to expose states to private lawsuits without state consent. Although the rulings attracted broad attention, much of the interest was directed to the continued division of Justices on federalism. Split along political lines, the majority consisted of the conservative-moderate wing (Rehnquist, O'Connor, Kennedy, Scalia, and Thomas), while the dissents came from moderate-liberals (Stevens, Souter, Ginsburg, and Breyer). Writing for the *New York Times*, Linda Greenhouse remarked that "the fault line that runs through the current Court as an all but unbridgeable gulf has to do not with the higher-profile issues of race, religion, abortion or due process, but with federalism." N.Y. Times, June 24, 1999, at A22.

Two of the decisions affected the application of federal law to states. In the first, Congress had amended the Lanham Act to subject states to suits for false and misleading advertising. The Court ruled that the statute abrogated state sovereign immunity because Florida had not expressly consented to being sued in federal court and Congress had not acted validly under its enforcement powers under the Fourteenth Amendment. College Savings Bank v. Florida Prepaid Postsecondary, 527 U.S. 666 (1999).

The second decision covered a 1992 amendment to federal law that expressly abrogated the states' sovereign immunity from claims of patent infringement. The Court ruled that this amendment could not be upheld as an exercise of Congress' power under the Fourteenth Amendment because it was not properly "remedial" and it lacked proportionality. To invoke the Fourteenth Amendment, Congress must identify state conduct that transgresses the substantive provisions of the Amendment. Florida Prepaid Postsecondary v. College Sav., 527 U.S. 627 (1999). Legislation has been introduced to allow holders of intellectual property to sue states for infringement damages. 147 Cong. Rec. S11364–68 (daily ed. Nov. 1, 2001); 148 Cong. Rec. S2078–82 (daily ed. March 19, 2002).

The decision that drew most of the interest involved a suit brought against a state for violating the overtime provision of the Fair Labor Standards Act. The Court held that any effort by Congress to authorize private actions against the states *in state court*, without the consent of the states, is an unconstitutional abrogation of state sovereign immunity. In an exceptionally long and complex decision, five members of the majority and four dissenters often cited identical historical materials but came to entirely different conclusions. Alden v. Maine, 527 U.S. 706 (1999).

Continuing its string of 5–4 decisions on federalism, in 2000 the Court ruled that state workers—discriminated against because of their age—could not sue under federal law in the states. The Eleventh Amendment, said the majority, prevented such suits against state employers. The Court held that Congress, in the Age Discrimination in Employment Act of 1967 (ADEA), had stated a clear intent to abrogate the states' immunity but that the abrogation exceeded congressional authority under Section 5 of the Fourteenth Amendment. Kimel v. Florida Bd. of Regents, 528 U.S. 62 (2000).

On the following day, in a rare unanimous decision involving federalism, the Court upheld a congressional statute (the Driver's Privacy Protection Act of 1994) that prohibited states from disclosing the personal information that drivers provide when obtaining a license. As a result of the decision, states may not sell addresses, telephone numbers, and other information included in the license application. Congress passed the 1994 statute after the death of a woman who had been killed by a stalker who had obtained her address from the motor vehicles division. The Court held that Congress acted properly under its powers to regulate interstate commerce. Reno v. Condon, 528 U.S. 141 (2000).

Another blow to congressional power came in 2000 when the Court held that a provision in the Violence Against Women Act of 1994 could not be sustained under the Commerce Clause or Section 5 of the Fourteenth Amendment. The provision permitted victims of rape, domestic violence and other crimes "motivated by gender" to sue their attackers in federal court. The Court ruled that Congress may not regulate "noneconomic, violent criminal conduct based solely on that conduct's aggregate effect on interstate commerce." Unlike the Guns in the Schoolyard Act, Congress had amassed findings and compiled a record to demonstrate the scope of the problem. Similar to other federalism rulings, the Court was split 5 to 4. UNITED STATES v. MORRISON, 529 U.S. 598 (2000).

Two other decisions, in 2001 and 2002, gave further protection to the states. In 2001, split along its usual 5–4 axis, the Supreme Court ruled that state immunity prevents state employees from suing state agencies for money damages under the federal Americans With Disabilities Act (ADA). The Court decided that Congress in such cases lacked power under Section 5 of the Fourteenth Amendment to abrogate state immunity under the Eleventh Amendment. The ADA's legislative record, said the Court, failed to identify a history and pattern of irrational employment discrimination by the states against the disabled. The Court concluded that the ADA was aimed primarily at employment discrimination in the private sector. The dissenters found about 300 examples of discrimination by state governments in the legislative record. Board of Trustees of Univ. of Ala. v. Garrett, 531 U.S. 356 (2001).

In 2002, another 5–4 decision held that the principle of state sovereignty protected states from having to respond to private complaints before federal agencies, in this case the Federal Maritime Commission. The decision applies only to agency actions against the states based on private complaints. Agencies may still go to court based on their own investigations of the states. Fed. Maritime Com'n v. S.C. State Ports Auth., 535 U.S. 743 (2002). Also struck down largely on grounds of federalism was the Religious Freedom Restoration Act of 1993, treated in Chapter 12. Boerne v. Flores, 521 U.S. 507 (1997).

Losses for the States

Federalism was at stake in 2000 when the Court reversed the Supreme Court of Florida's order for a manual recount to decide the presidential election. Although critics accused the majority of inconsistently championing federalism in most matters but not in this one, the Court was faced with issues of Art. II, § 1, cl. 2, of the United States Constitution and compliance with 3 U.S.C. § 5 (see Chapter 18 for further details). As Chief Justice Rehnquist and Justices Scalia and Thomas noted in their concurrence, the Court's "inquiry does not imply a disrespect for state *courts* but rather a respect for the constitutionally prescribed role of state *legislatures*." Bush v. Gore, 531 U.S. 98, 115 (2000).

The pattern of 5–4 decisions dominated by conservatives broke in two cases decided in 2003 and 2004. In the first, a 6–3 Court ruled that states can be sued if they violate a worker's federally guaranteed right to take time off for family emergencies. Nevada had claimed constitutional immunity from being sued under the Family and Medical Leave Act. Curiously, the author of the majority opinion was Chief Justice Rehnquist, joined by O'Connor and the liberal-moderate wing of Souter, Ginsburg, Breyer, and Stevens. Rehnquist concluded that the family leave act was more "narrowly targeted" than federal statutes challenged in previous rulings. Neither proponents nor opponents of the decision could discover much coherence or consistency in the Court's federalism rulings, especially cases concerning state immunity from lawsuit. Although the congressional statute in this case was upheld, the Court could use the occasion to highlight its belief that "it falls to this Court, not Congress, to define the substance of constitutional guarantees." Nevada Dept. of Human Resources v. Hibbs, 538 U.S. 721, 728 (2003).

Some interpreters thought the decision could be explained by the Court's "heightened scrutiny" of gender-based discrimination. However, in 2004 the Court upheld the right of disabled individuals to sue state governments that fail to provide ramps and other forms of access to their courthouses. Tennessee tried to dismiss the suit by relying on the Eleventh Amendment. The Court returned to its customary 5–4 division, but this time O'Connor joined the four liberal-moderate Justices to form the majority, with Rehnquist, Kennedy, Thomas, and Scalia dissenting. The majority ruled that the Americans With Disabilities Act provides a proper basis to allow individuals to seek money damages from states that do not accommodate their access to courthouses. O'Connor may have joined the majority decision because it was limited to "the fundamental right of access to the court" and did not involve access to other state facilities, such as hockey rinks or voting booths. Moreover, in renovating courthouses, states were not expected to assume "an undue financial or administrative burden" or threaten historic preservation interests. Tennessee v. Lane, 541 U.S. 509 (2004).

Linda Greenhouse, long-time Supreme Court reporter for *The New York Times,* suggested in 2008 that the Court had backed off from its formalistic pro-state analysis of federalism because it was "out of sync with the prevailing mood" after the events of September 11, 2001. "Suddenly, the federal government looked useful, even necessary," wrote Greenhouse. "The Supreme Court's federalism revolution had been overtaken by events." "2,691 Decisions," New York Times, July 13, 2008, at WK 4.

State Moral Issues: Wine, Marijuana, and Assisted Suicide

The ambiguity about the Court's direction in the federalism realm was heightened by decisions made in 2005–2006. State attempts to regulate the sale of wine and the use of marijuana for medical purposes were rebuffed by the Court during the 2005 Term as violations of the Commerce Clause. The Court, in a 5–4 ruling, struck down Michigan and New York laws that permitted in-state, but not out-of-state, wineries to sell directly to consumers in the state. Justice Kennedy wrote for the Court that, "in all but the narrowest circumstances, state laws violate the Commerce Clause if they mandate differential treatment of in-state and out-of-state economic interests that benefits the former and burdens the latter." The Court held that the discrimination was "neither authorized nor permitted by the Twenty-first Amendment," which grants to states the authority to regulate the importation of liquor. Granholm v. Heald, 544 U.S. 460 (2005).

In *Gonzales v. Raich,* the Court, in a 6–3 ruling, upheld congressional authority and the federal prosecution of California residents who, under state law, used medically-prescribed marijuana, in a challenge that claimed Congress had violated the Commerce Clause and the boundaries of federalism. In an opinion that relied on the reasoning of Wickard v. Filburn, 317 U.S. 111 (1942), Justice Stevens held that Congress possesses the authority to prohibit the "local cultivation and use of marijuana" as a means of regulating "purely local activities that are part of an economic 'class of activities' that have a substantial effect on interstate commerce." GONZALES v. RAICH, 545 U.S. 1 (2005).

But in 2006 the Court upheld Oregon's Death with Dignity Act, concluding that the U.S. Attorney General had overstepped his authority under the Controlled Substances Act in issuing a regulation designed to stop implementation of the state act. Justice Kennedy, writing for the six-person majority, argued that if Congress had intended to preempt the traditional state regulation of the medical profession it would have done so more clearly. The new Chief Justice Roberts joined Scalia and Thomas in dissent, finding that the congressional act was sufficiently pervasive to allow the federal regulation. Gonzales v. Oregon, 546 U.S. 243 (2006). At the very least, the loss of Rehnquist and O'Connor, two strong advocates of state power, and their replacement by Roberts and Alito, two men whose careers were largely centered in the federal government, suggested that the Court may be less "aggressive" going forward in pursuing a "rigid" notion of American federalism. Banks and Blakeman, 38 Publius 576–600 (2008).

The States Push Back

As one would expect in a dynamic federal system, state officials and voters often push back against federal power, whether it is being exercised by the Congress, the Executive Branch, or the Court. Despite the *Gonzales v. Raich* decision, 16 states and the District of Columbia have laws permitting the use of medical marijuana and some have gone further in decriminalizing the drug. An initiative on the 2010 ballot in California asked voters to decide whether or not to make marijuana legal and thus taxable. It failed, but similar ballot initiatives passed in Colorado and Washington in 2012. Arguing that the federal government is not adequately managing the flow of Mexican immigrants into the United States, states and localities have begun to pass their own immigration restrictions that challenge federal authority in this area. There has been significant state activity in response to the 2010 passage of federal health care reform legislation that will eventually require virtually everyone to have health insurance. A number of states filed lawsuits challenging the legislation on Tenth Amendment grounds, claiming that Congress has exceeded its powers over interstate commerce, invaded the traditionally state regulated area of health care, and coerced the states into participating in the expansion of Medicaid coverage. Twenty states have enacted laws either challenging or opting out of participation in the health care exchanges established by the Act. According to the National Council of State Legislatures, in more than thirty state legislatures, members have filed legislation designed to "limit, alter, or oppose" various mandates in the legislation, and some states are considering state constitutional amendments in this vein. Both the House and Senate in Idaho have adopted a bill calling for a federal constitutional amendment prohibiting legislation that mandates health care purchase. In 2012 the Supreme Court heard a consolidated set of these cases. It upheld the individual mandate but held that states must be permitted to opt out of the Medicaid expansion without forfeiting their current Medicaid funds. National Federation of Independent Business, et al. v. Sebelius, 567 U.S. ___ (2012) (Additional discussion and reading in Section G. of this chapter). The lawsuits and successful legislative efforts have been largely confined to states controlled by the Republican party, whose leaders vowed to repeal the legislation should they gain control of the Congress and White House in 2013.

United States v. Lopez

514 U.S. 549 (1995)

Congress enacted legislation in 1990 [§ 922(q)] to forbid "any individual knowingly to possess a firearm at a place that [he] knows ... is a school zone." The Fifth Circuit held that, in light of what it characterized as insufficient congressional findings and legislative history, the provision was invalid because it exceeded Congress' power under the Commerce Clause. Alfonso Lopez, Jr., a 12th-grade student, arrived at his high school carrying a concealed handgun and five bullets.

CHIEF JUSTICE REHNQUIST delivered the opinion of the Court.

In the Gun-Free School Zones Act of 1990, ... neither regulates a commercial activity nor contains a requirement that the possession be connected in any way to interstate commerce. We hold that the Act exceeds the authority of Congress "[t]o regulate Commerce ... among the several States...." U.S. Const., Art. I, § 8, cl. 3.

. . .

We start with first principles. The Constitution

creates a Federal Government of enumerated pow-ers. See Art. I, §8. As James Madison wrote, "[t]he powers delegated by the proposed Constitution to the federal government are few and defined. Those which are to remain in the State governments are numerous and indefinite." The Federalist No. 45, pp. 292–293 (C. Rossiter ed. 1961). This constitution-ally mandated division of authority "was adopted by the Framers to ensure protection of our fundamen-tal liberties." *Gregory v. Ashcroft,* 501 U. S. 452, 458 (1991) (internal quotation marks omitted)....

The Constitution delegates to Congress the power "[t]o regulate Commerce with foreign Na-tions, and among the several States, and with the In-dian Tribes." Art. I, §8, cl. 3. The Court, through Chief Justice Marshall, first defined the nature of Congress' commerce power in *Gibbons v. Ogden,* 9 Wheat. 1, 189–190 (1824):

"Commerce, undoubtedly, is traffic, but it is something more: it is intercourse. It describes the commercial intercourse between nations, and parts of nations, in all its branches, and is regulated by prescribing rules for carrying on that intercourse."

... The *Gibbons* Court, however, acknowledged that limitations on the commerce power are inherent in the very language of the Commerce Clause.

. . .

"Comprehensive as the word 'among' is, it may very properly be restricted to that commerce which con-cerns more States than one.... The enumeration presupposes something not enumerated; and that something, if we regard the language, or the subject of the sentence, must be the exclusively internal commerce of a State." *Id.,* at 194–195.

[*Chief Justice Rehnquist summarizes the Court's hold-ings in cases where state laws were seen to interfere with interstate commerce and the New Deal cases that recognized a broad power in Congress to regulate com-merce, including NLRB v. Jones & Laughlin Steel Corp. (1937), United States v. Darby (1941), and Wickard v. Filburn (1942).*]

... [W]e have identified three broad categories of activity that Congress may regulate under its com-merce power.... First, Congress may regulate the use of the channels of interstate commerce.... Second, Congress is empowered to regulate and protect the instrumentalities of interstate commerce, or persons or things in interstate commerce, even though the threat may come only from intrastate activities.... Finally, Congress' commerce authority includes the power to regulate those activities having a substan-

tial relation to interstate commerce, ... *i.e.,* those ac-tivities that substantially affect interstate com-merce, ...

Within this final category, admittedly, our case law has not been clear whether an activity must "affect" or "substantially affect" interstate commerce in order to be within Congress' power to regulate it under the Commerce Clause.... We conclude, consistent with the great weight of our case law, that the proper test requires an analysis of whether the regulated activity "substantially affects" interstate commerce.

We now turn to consider the power of Congress, in the light of this framework, ... The first two cate-gories of authority may be quickly disposed of: [the law] is not a regulation of the use of the channels of interstate commerce, nor is it an attempt to prohibit the interstate transportation of a commodity through the channels of commerce; nor can [it] be justified as a regulation by which Congress has sought to protect an instrumentality of interstate commerce or a thing in interstate commerce. Thus, if [it] is to be sustained, it must be under the third category as a regulation of an activity that substan-tially affects interstate commerce.

. . .

Section 922(q) is a criminal statute that by its terms has nothing to do with "commerce" or any sort of economic enterprise, however broadly one might define those terms. Section 922(q) is not an essential part of a larger regulation of economic ac-tivity, in which the regulatory scheme could be un-dercut unless the intrastate activity were regulated. It cannot, therefore, be sustained under our cases upholding regulations of activities that arise out of or are connected with a commercial transaction, which viewed in the aggregate, substantially affects interstate commerce.

. . .

Although as part of our independent evaluation of constitutionality under the Commerce Clause we of course consider legislative findings, and indeed even congressional committee findings, regarding ef-fect on interstate commerce, ... the Government concedes that "[n]either the statute nor its legislative history contain[s] express congressional findings re-garding the effects upon interstate commerce of gun possession in a school zone." ... We agree with the Government that Congress normally is not required to make formal findings as to the substantial burdens that an activity has on interstate commerce.... But to the extent that congressional findings would enable us to evaluate the legislative judgment that the activity in question substantially affected interstate commerce, even though no such substantial effect was visible to the naked eye, they are lacking here.

. . .

The Government's essential contention, *in fine*, is that we may determine here that § 922(q) is valid because possession of a firearm in a local school zone does indeed substantially affect interstate commerce.... The Government argues that possession of a firearm in a school zone may result in violent crime and that violent crime can be expected to affect the functioning of the national economy in two ways. First, the costs of violent crime are substantial, and, through the mechanism of insurance, those costs are spread throughout the population.... Second, violent crime reduces the willingness of individuals to travel to areas within the country that are perceived to be unsafe.... The Government also argues that the presence of guns in schools poses a substantial threat to the educational process by threatening the learning environment. A handicapped educational process, in turn, will result in a less productive citizenry. That, in turn, would have an adverse effect on the Nation's economic well-being As a result, the Government argues that Congress could rationally have concluded that § 922(q) substantially affects interstate commerce.

We pause to consider the implications of the Government's arguments. The Government admits, under its "costs of crime" reasoning, that Congress could regulate not only all violent crime, but all activities that might lead to violent crime, regardless of how tenuously they relate to interstate commerce.... Similarly, under the Government's "national productivity" reasoning, Congress could regulate any activity that it found was related to the economic productivity of individual citizens: family law (including marriage, divorce, and child custody), for example. Under the theories that the Government presents in support of § 922(q), it is difficult to perceive any limitation on federal power, even in areas such as criminal law enforcement or education where States historically have been sovereign. Thus, if we were to accept the Government's arguments, we are hard pressed to posit any activity by an individual that Congress is without power to regulate.

. . .

For the foregoing reasons the judgment of the Court of Appeals is

Affirmed.

JUSTICE KENNEDY, with whom JUSTICE O'CONNOR joins, concurring....

The statute now before us forecloses the States from experimenting and exercising their own judgment in an area to which States lay claim by right of history and expertise, and it does so by regulating an activity beyond the realm of commerce in the ordinary and usual sense of that term. The tendency of this statute to displace state regulation in areas of traditional state concern is evident from its territorial operation. There are over 100,000 elementary and secondary schools in the United States....

JUSTICE THOMAS, concurring.

... Although I join the majority, I write separately to observe that our case law has drifted far from the original understanding of the Commerce Clause. In a future case, we ought to temper our Commerce Clause jurisprudence in a manner that both makes sense of our more recent case law and is more faithful to the original understanding of that Clause....

JUSTICE STEVENS, dissenting....

JUSTICE SOUTER, dissenting.

In reviewing congressional legislation under the Commerce Clause, we defer to what is often a merely implicit congressional judgment that its regulation addresses a subject substantially affecting interstate commerce "if there is any rational basis for such a finding...."

... The modern respect for the competence and primacy of Congress in matters affecting commerce developed only after one of this Court's most chastening experiences, when it perforce repudiated an earlier and untenably expansive conception of judicial review in derogation of congressional commerce power. A look at history's sequence will serve to show how today's decision tugs the Court off course....

JUSTICE BREYER, with whom JUSTICE STEVENS, JUSTICE SOUTER, and JUSTICE GINSBURG join, dissenting.

... In my view, the statute falls well within the scope of the commerce power as this Court has understood that power over the last half century.

I

In reaching this conclusion, I apply three basic principles of Commerce Clause interpretation. First, the power to "regulate Commerce ... among the several States," ... encompasses the power to regulate local activities insofar as they significantly affect interstate commerce....

... I use the word "significant" because the word "substantial" implies a somewhat narrower power than recent precedent suggests.... But to speak of "substantial effect" rather than "significant effect" would make no difference in this case.

Second, in determining whether a local activity will likely have a significant effect upon interstate commerce, a court must consider, not the effect of an individual act (a single instance of gun possession), but rather the cumulative effect of all similar instances (*i.e.*, the effect of all guns possessed in or near schools)....

Third, the Constitution requires us to judge the connection between a regulated activity and interstate commerce, not directly, but at one remove. Courts must give Congress a degree of leeway in de-termining the existence of a significant factual connection between the regulated activity and interstate commerce—both because the Constitution delegates the commerce power directly to Congress and because the determination requires an empirical judgment of a kind that a legislature is more likely than a court to make with accuracy. The traditional words "rational basis" capture this leeway....

II

... Numerous reports and studies—generated both inside and outside government—make clear that Congress could reasonably have found the empirical connection that its law, implicitly or explicitly, asserts. [*Breyer supplies an Appendix of materials to document this point.*]

United States v. Morrison

529 U.S. 598 (2000)*

Christy Brzonkala, a student at the Virginia Polytechnic Institute, accused two students with assaulting and raping her in 1994. Although the school's Judicial Committee initially found one of the students, Antonio Morrison, guilty of sexual assault (later changing the charge to "using abusive language") and sentenced him to suspension for two semesters, the university later set aside Morrison's punishment. Brzonkala sued the students and Virginia Tech in federal court, complaining that the attack violated 42 U.S.C. § 13981 (part of the Violence Against Women Act of 1994). She also charged that Virginia Tech violated Title IX. A district court dismissed the Title IX claim and concluded that Congress lacked authority under either the Commerce Clause or Section 5 of the Fourteenth Amendment to enact § 13981. The Fourth Circuit, sitting en banc, affirmed the district court's conclusion that Congress lacked constitutional authority to enact § 13981.

CHIEF JUSTICE REHNQUIST delivered the opinion of the Court.

In these cases we consider the constitutionality of 42 U.S.C. § 13981, which provides a federal civil remedy for the victims of gender-motivated violence.... Believing that these cases are controlled by our decisions in *United States* v. *Lopez*, 514 U.S. 549 (1995), *United States* v. *Harris*, 106 U.S. 629 (1883), and the *Civil Rights Cases*, 109 U.S. 3 (1883), we affirm.

I

Petitioner Christy Brzonkala enrolled at Virginia Polytechnic Institute (Virginia Tech) in the fall of 1994. In September of that year, Brzonkala met respondents Antonio Morrison and James Crawford, who were both students at Virginia Tech and members of its varsity football team. Brzonkala alleges that, within 30 minutes of meeting Morrison and Crawford, they assaulted and repeatedly raped her....

[*Brzonkala filed a complaint against the two students. After several actions by the university's judicial committee, Virginia Tech's senior vice president and provost set aside any punishment for Morrison. After learning that Morrison would be returning to Virginia Tech, Brzonkala dropped out of the university and sued Morrison, Crawford, and Virginia Tech, claiming a violation of § 13981 and Title IX.*]

Section 13981 was part of the Violence Against

* The text for this case, obtained in electronic form from Westlaw, is reproduced by permission of the West Group.

Women Act of 1994.... It states that "[a]ll persons within the United States shall have the right to be free from crimes of violence motivated by gender."...

Section 13981 defines a "crim[e] of violence motivated by gender" as "a crime of violence committed because of gender or on the basis of gender, and due, at least in part, to an animus based on the victim's gender."...

... [S]ubsection (e)(3) provides a § 13981 litigant with a choice of forums: Federal and state courts "shall have concurrent jurisdiction" over complaints brought under the section.

... Congress explicitly identified the sources of federal authority on which it relied in enacting § 13981. It said that a "federal civil rights cause of action" is established "[p]ursuant to the affirmative power of Congress ... under section 5 of the Fourteenth Amendment to the Constitution, as well as under section 8 of Article I of the Constitution."...

II

... Brzonkala and the United States rely upon the third clause of [*section 8*], which gives Congress power "[t]o regulate Commerce with foreign Nations, and among the several States, and with the Indian Tribes."...

As we observed in *Lopez*, modern Commerce Clause jurisprudence [allows regulation in three areas, the channels of commerce, the instrumentalities of commerce, and activities that substantially affect interstate commerce]....

Petitioners do not contend that these cases fall within either of the first two of these categories of Commerce Clause regulation. They seek to sustain § 13981 as a regulation of activity that substantially affects interstate commerce.... [W]e agree that this is the proper inquiry....

With these principles underlying our Commerce Clause jurisprudence as reference points, the proper resolution of the present cases is clear. Gender-motivated crimes of violence are not, in any sense of the phrase, economic activity....

In contrast with the lack of congressional findings that we faced in *Lopez*, § 13981 is supported by numerous findings regarding the serious impact that gender-motivated violence has on victims and their families.... But the existence of congressional findings is not sufficient, by itself, to sustain the constitutionality of Commerce Clause legislation.... "'[w]hether particular operations affect interstate commerce sufficiently to come under the constitutional power of Congress to regulate them is ultimately a judicial rather than a legislative question,

and can be settled finally only by this Court.'" 514 U.S., at 557, n. 2 (quoting *Heart of Atlanta Motel*, 379 U.S., at 273 (Black, J., concurring)).

In these cases, Congress' findings are substantially weakened by the fact that they rely so heavily on a method of reasoning that we have already rejected as unworkable if we are to maintain the Constitution's enumeration of powers. Congress found that gender-motivated violence affects interstate commerce

"by deterring potential victims from traveling interstate, from engaging in employment in interstate business, and from transacting with business, and in places involved in interstate commerce; ... by diminishing national productivity, increasing medical and other costs, and decreasing the supply of and the demand for interstate products."...

... If accepted, petitioners' reasoning would allow Congress to regulate any crime as long as the nationwide, aggregated impact of that crime has substantial effects on employment, production, transit, or consumption. Indeed, if Congress may regulate gender-motivated violence, it would be able to regulate murder or any other type of violence since gender-motivated violence, as a subset of all violent crime, is certain to have lesser economic impacts than the larger class of which it is a part.

Petitioners' reasoning, moreover, will not limit Congress to regulating violence but may, as we suggested in *Lopez*, be applied equally as well to family law and other areas of traditional state regulation since the aggregate effect of marriage, divorce, and childrearing on the national economy is undoubtedly significant. Congress may have recognized this specter when it expressly precluded § 13981 from being used in the family law context....

We accordingly reject the argument that Congress may regulate noneconomic, violent criminal conduct based solely on that conduct's aggregate effect on interstate commerce. The Constitution requires a distinction between what is truly national and what is truly local.... The regulation and punishment of intrastate violence that is not directed at the instrumentalities, channels, or goods involved in interstate commerce has always been the province of the States....

III

[W]e address petitioners' alternative argument that the section's civil remedy should be upheld as an exercise of Congress' remedial power under § 5 of the Fourteenth Amendment.... The principles governing an analysis of congressional legislation under

§ 5 are well settled. Section 5 states that Congress may "'enforce,' by 'appropriate legislation' the constitutional guarantee that no State shall deprive any person of 'life, liberty or property, without due process of law,' nor deny any person 'equal protection of the laws.'" *City of Boerne* v. *Flores*, 521 U.S. 507, 517 (1997)....

Petitioners' § 5 argument is founded on an assertion that there is pervasive bias in various state justice systems against victims of gender-motivated violence. This assertion is supported by a voluminous congressional record....

... However, the language and purpose of the Fourteenth Amendment place certain limitations on the manner in which Congress may attack discriminatory conduct. These limitations are necessary to prevent the Fourteenth Amendment from obliterating the Framers' carefully crafted balance of power between the States and the National Government. Foremost among these limitations is the time-honored principle that the Fourteenth Amendment, by its very terms, prohibits only state action. [*Here Rehnquist discusses* United States v. Harris, *106 U.S. 629 (1883) and the* Civil Rights Cases, *109 U.S. 3 (1883) for the proposition that Congress' § 5 power cannot be directed exclusively against the actions of private persons. He rejects the argument that* United States v. Guest, *383 U.S. 745 (1966) and* District of Columbia v. Carter, *409 U.S. 418 (1973) overruled these longstanding limitations on Congress' § 5 authority.*]

For these reasons, we conclude that Congress' power under § 5 does not extend to the enactment of § 13981.

IV

Petitioner Brzonkala's complaint alleges that she was the victim of a brutal assault. But Congress' effort in § 13981 to provide a federal civil remedy can be sustained neither under the Commerce Clause nor under § 5 of the Fourteenth Amendment. If the allegations here are true, no civilized system of justice could fail to provide her a remedy for the conduct of respondent Morrison. But under our federal system that remedy must be provided by the Commonwealth of Virginia, and not by the United States. The judgment of the Court of Appeals is

Affirmed.

JUSTICE THOMAS, concurring....

JUSTICE SOUTER, with whom JUSTICE STEVENS, JUSTICE GINSBURG, and JUSTICE BREYER join, dissenting.

The Court says both that it leaves Commerce Clause precedent undisturbed and that the Civil Rights Remedy of the Violence Against Women Act of 1994 ... exceeds Congress's power under that Clause. I find the claims irreconcilable and respectfully dissent. [*In a footnote, Souter explains that by finding the law a valid exercise of Commerce Clause power, he has no occasion to analyze the Fourteenth Amendment claim.*]

I

Our cases, which remain at least nominally undisturbed, stand for the following propositions. Congress has the power to legislate with regard to activity that, in the aggregate, has a substantial effect on interstate commerce....

One obvious difference from *United States* v. *Lopez* ... is the mountain of data assembled by Congress, here showing the effects of violence against women on interstate commerce. Passage of the Act in 1994 was preceded by four years of hearings, which included testimony from physicians and law professors; from survivors of rape and domestic violence; and from representatives of state law enforcement and private business. The record includes reports on gender bias from task forces in 21 States, and we have the benefit of specific factual findings in the eight separate Reports issued by Congress and its committees over the long course leading to enactment....

[*The facts disclosed that three out of four American women will be victims of violent crimes sometime during their life; violence is the leading cause of injuries to women ages 15 to 44; an estimated four million American women are battered each year by their husbands or partners; and over one million women in America seek medical assistance each year for injuries sustained from their husbands or other partners. The incidence of rape rose four times as fast as the total national crime rate over the past ten years; one study concluded that close to half a million girls now in high school will be raped before they graduate; and 125,000 college women can expect to be raped during any year.*]

Congress thereby explicitly stated the predicate for the exercise of its Commerce Clause power.... [T]he sufficiency of the evidence before Congress to provide a rational basis for the finding cannot seriously be questioned....

II

The Act would have passed muster at any time between *Wickard* in 1942 and *Lopez* in 1995, a period in which the law enjoyed a stable understanding that congressional power under the Commerce

Clause, complemented by the authority of the Necessary and Proper Clause, Art. I. § 8 cl. 18, extended to all activity that, when aggregated, has a substantial effect on interstate commerce....

The fact that the Act does not pass muster before the Court today is therefore proof, to a degree that *Lopez* was not, that the Court's nominal adherence to the substantial effects test is merely that. Although a new jurisprudence has not emerged with any distinctness, it is clear that some congressional conclusions about obviously substantial, cumulative effects on commerce are being assigned lesser values than the once-stable doctrine would assign them. These devaluations are accomplished not by any express repudiation of the substantial effects test or its application through the aggregation of individual conduct, but by supplanting rational basis scrutiny with a new criterion of review....

JUSTICE BREYER, with whom JUSTICE STEVENS joins, and with whom JUSTICE SOUTER and JUSTICE GINSBURG join as to Part I-A, dissenting....

Gonzales v. Raich

545 U.S. 1 (2005)

The federal Controlled Substances Act (CSA) generally criminalizes the manufacture, distribution, or possession of marijuana. California law imposed similar prohibitions but it created an exemption from prosecution for possession for (1) physicians who recommended marijuana to patients for medical purposes, and (2) patients, and their primary caregivers, who possessed or cultivated marijuana for patients' personal medical purposes upon recommendation or approval by a physician. Angel Raich used physician-recommended marijuana for serious medical conditions and sought injunctive and declaratory relief to prohibit U.S. Attorney General Alberto Gonzales from enforcing the CSA to prevent the medical use of marijuana. She asserted that enforcement of the CSA in this context would violate the Commerce Clause. The District Court denied Raich's motion, but the Ninth Circuit reversed, holding that Congress exceeded its authority under the Commerce Clause. Note the prominence of *Wickard v. Filburn* in the Supreme Court's Opinion.

JUSTICE STEVENS delivered the opinion of the Court.

California is one of at least nine States that authorize the use of marijuana for medicinal purposes. The question presented in this case is whether the power vested in Congress by Article I, § 8, of the Constitution "[t]o make all Laws which shall be necessary and proper for carrying into Execution" its authority to "regulate Commerce with foreign Nations, and among the several States" includes the power [*through the Controlled Substances Act, or CSA*] to prohibit the local cultivation and use of marijuana in compliance with California law.

I

... In 1996, California voters passed Proposition 215, now codified as the Compassionate Use Act of 1996. The proposition was designed to ensure that "seriously ill" residents of the State have access to marijuana for medical purposes....

Respondents Angel Raich and Diane Monson are California residents who suffer from a variety of serious medical conditions and have sought to avail themselves of medical marijuana pursuant to the terms of the Compassionate Use Act. They are being treated by licensed, board-certified family practitioners, who have concluded, after prescribing a host of conventional medicines to treat respondents' conditions and to alleviate their associated symptoms, that marijuana is the only drug available that provides effective treatment....

... The case is made difficult by respondents' strong arguments that they will suffer irreparable harm because, despite a congressional finding to the contrary, marijuana does have valid therapeutic purposes. The question before us, however, is not whether it is wise to enforce the statute in these circumstances; rather, it is whether Congress' power to regulate interstate markets for medicinal substances encompasses the portions of those markets that are supplied with drugs produced and consumed locally. Well-settled law controls our answer. The CSA is a valid exercise of federal power, even as applied to the troubling facts of this case. We accordingly vacate the judgment of the Court of Appeals....

III

... [R]espondents' challenge is actually quite limited; they argue that the CSA's categorical prohibition of the manufacture and possession of marijuana as applied to the intrastate manufacture and possession of marijuana for medical purposes pursuant to California law exceeds Congress' authority under the Commerce Clause....

Our case law firmly establishes Congress' power to regulate purely local activities that are part of an economic "class of activities" that have a substantial effect on interstate commerce.... *Wickard v. Filburn*, 317 U.S. 111, 128–128 (1942). As we stated in *Wickard*, "even if appellee's activity be local and though it may not be regarded as commerce, it may still, whatever its nature, be reached by Congress if it exerts a substantial economic effect on interstate commerce."...

The similarities between this case and *Wickard* are striking. Like the farmer in *Wickard*, respondents are cultivating, for home consumption, a fungible commodity for which there is an established, albeit illegal, interstate market. Just as the Agricultural Adjustment Act was designed "to control the volume [*of wheat*] moving in interstate and foreign commerce in order to avoid surpluses ..." and consequently control the market price, ... a primary purpose of the CSA is to control the supply and demand of controlled substances in both lawful and unlawful drug markets.... In *Wickard*, we had no difficulty concluding that Congress had a rational basis for believing that, when viewed in the aggregate, leaving home-consumed wheat outside the regulatory scheme would have a substantial influence on price and market conditions. Here too, Congress had a rational basis for concluding that leaving home-consumed marijuana outside federal control would similarly affect price and market conditions.

More concretely, one concern prompting inclusion of wheat grown for home consumption in the 1938 Act was that rising market prices could draw such wheat into the interstate market, resulting in lower market prices.... The parallel concern making it appropriate to include marijuana grown for home consumption in the CSA is the likelihood that the high demand in the interstate market will draw such marijuana into that market....

In assessing the scope of Congress' authority under the Commerce Clause, we stress that the task before us is a modest one. We need not determine whether respondents' activities, taken in the aggregate, substantially affect interstate commerce in fact, but only whether a "rational basis" exists for so concluding.... Given the enforcement difficulties that attend distinguishing between marijuana cultivated locally and marijuana grown elsewhere, ... and concerns about diversion into illicit channels, we have no difficulty concluding that Congress had a rational basis for believing that failure to regulate the intrastate manufacture and possession of marijuana would leave a gaping hole in the CSA....

IV

[*In this section, Stevens reasoned that unlike* United States v. Lopez *(1995) and* United States v. Morrison *(2000), the activities regulated by the CSA "are quintessentially economic." Economics refers to "the production, distribution, and consumption of commodities." Because the CSA directly regulates economic and commercial activity, Morrison "casts no doubt on its constitutionality." The CSA designated marijuana "as contraband for* any *purpose." Congress "expressly found that the drug has no acceptable medical uses." The CSA imposed controls beyond what was required by California law. The Supremacy Clause "unambiguously provides that if there is any conflict between federal and state law, federal law shall prevail."*]

... Thus the case for the exemption comes down to the claim that a locally cultivated product that is used domestically rather than sold on the open market is not subject to federal regulation. Given the findings in the CSA and the undisputed magnitude of the commercial market for marijuana, our decisions in *Wickard v. Filburn* and the later cases endorsing its reasoning foreclose that claim....

JUSTICE SCALIA, concurring in the judgment....

JUSTICE O'CONNOR, with whom THE CHIEF JUSTICE and JUSTICE THOMAS join as to all but Part III, dissenting....

This case exemplifies the role of States as laboratories. The States' core police powers have always included authority to define criminal law and to protect the health, safety, and welfare of their citizens.... Exercising those powers, California (by ballot initiative and then by legislative codification) has come to its own conclusion about the difficult and sensitive question of whether marijuana should be available to relieve severe pain and suffering. Today the Court sanctions an application of the federal Controlled Substances Act that extinguishes that experiment, without any proof that the personal cultivation, possession, and use of marijuana for medicinal purposes, if economic activity in the first place, has a substantial effect on interstate commerce and is therefore an appropriate subject of federal regulation....

II A

... If the Court is right, then *Lopez* stands for

nothing more than a drafting guide: Congress should have described the relevant crime as "transfer or possession of a firearm anywhere in the nation"—thus including commercial and noncommercial activity, and clearly encompassing some activity with assuredly substantial effect on interstate commerce. Had it done so, the majority hints, we would have sustained its authority to regulate possession of firearms in school zones....

B

Even assuming that economic activity is at issue in this case, the Government has made no showing in fact that the possession and use of homegrown marijuana for medical purposes, in California or elsewhere, has a substantial effect on interstate commerce....

JUSTICE THOMAS, dissenting....

G. THE SPENDING AND TAXING POWERS

The pattern of federal spending and taxing powers has been similar to the Commerce Clause. The courts initially placed constraints on congressional power and offered protection to "local" activities in the states. Over time, however, these constraints have been largely removed because the judiciary recognizes the need for national powers and regulation.

The Constitution speaks clearly on only one aspect of the taxing power: "No tax or duty shall be laid on articles exported from any State" (Art. I, § 9). Other tax questions have provoked extensive litigation. Difficulties in distinguishing between direct and indirect taxes created major conflicts between Congress and the judiciary. Indirect taxes must follow the rule of uniformity: "The Congress shall have Power to lay and collect Taxes, Duties, Imposts, and Excises, to pay the Debts and provide for the common Defense and general Welfare of the United States; but all Duties, Imposts and Excises shall be uniform throughout the United States" (Art. I, § 8). The rule of uniformity protects states from discriminatory actions by the national government, although federal taxes do not have to fall equally on each state, nor is Congress barred from adopting tax exemptions for certain regions. United States v. Psasynski, 462 U.S. 74 (1983).

Direct taxes are covered in Article I, Section 9: "No capitation, or other direct, tax shall be laid, unless in proportion to the census or enumeration herein before directed to be taken." Capitation taxes, or "head taxes," have never been enacted by Congress. Other direct taxes must be levied among the states in accordance with the rule of apportionment. The question of a direct tax was first decided by the Supreme Court in 1796. A carriage tax imposed by Congress was attacked as a direct tax, requiring that it be apportioned among the states on the basis of population. A unanimous Court, however, ruled that the tax was indirect. The decision appeared to limit direct taxes to two kinds: a capitation or poll tax, imposed without regard to property, and a tax on land. Hylton v. United States, 3 Dall. 171, 175 (1796). From 1798 to 1816 the federal government imposed direct taxes on real estate and slaves. In 1861 the federal tax applied to real estate only. Veazie Bank v. Fenno, 75 U.S. (8 Wall.) 533, 543 (1869). Federal taxes on currency and bank circulation were not considered a direct tax. Id. at 546–47.

Income Tax

In 1881, a unanimous Court again limited the meaning of direct taxes to capitation taxes and taxes on real estate. The Court interpreted the federal income tax of 1864, as amended in 1865, as an indirect tax. Springer v. United States, 102 U.S. 586 (1881). In 1895, after a hundred years of agreement on the meaning of direct taxes, the Court reversed direction and struck down a federal income tax, treating it as a direct tax to be apportioned on the basis of population. The statute was invalidated in two steps. The first decision held that the tax on rents or income of real estate was a direct tax and violated the Constitution by not following the apportionment rule. Pollock v. Farmers' Loan & Trust Co., 157 U.S. 429 (1895). A second decision struck down the income tax, in part because the Court concluded that invalidation of the other taxes left a tax scheme that Congress could not have intended. Pollock v. Farmers' Loan and Trust Co., 158 U.S. 601, 637 (1895).

The Court acted under the shadow of class warfare and threats of socialism. During oral argument, Joseph H. Choate warned the Justices that the tax was "communistic in its purposes and tendencies." 157 U.S. at 532. After the first hearing, the Court split 4 to 4 on the question of the income tax. Upon rehearing, a 5 to 4 decision invalidated the tax. The member missing from the first decision, Justice Jackson, voted to *sustain* the tax in the second case. All things being equal, this should have yielded a 5–4 tally supporting the income tax. One Justice obviously switched his vote. Who he was, and why he switched, has never been revealed. Because of the vote switching and razor-thin majority, the decision became known as one of three "self-inflicted wounds" on the Court (the other two being *Dred Scott* in 1857 and the Legal Tender Cases of 1871). Charles Evans Hughes, The Supreme Court of the United States 54 (1928). It was not until 1913 that Congress and the states overrode *Pollock* by passing the Sixteenth Amendment.

The income tax cases marked an unusual setback for the power of Congress to tax. In 1904 the Court held that the judiciary would not limit the taxing power simply because it had been exercised in an unwise, oppressive, or injurious manner. Nor could the courts inquire into the motive or purpose of Congress in passing a tax, or discover a limitation in the Due Process Clause of the Fifth Amendment. Congressional abuses in such cases had to be corrected by the voters. McCray v. United States, 195 U.S. 27 (1904). In 1911 a unanimous Court upheld a corporation income tax passed by Congress. The Court called it an excise, not a direct, tax and said it complied with the rule of uniformity. Flint Stone Tracy Co., 220 U.S. 107 (1911). When Congress tried to use the taxing power to regulate matters the Court considered within the police power of the states, the congressional statute was declared invalid. BAILEY V. DREXEL FURNITURE CO. (Child Labor Tax Case), 259 U.S. 20 (1922); Hill v. Wallace, 259 U.S. 44 (1922).

New Deal Cases

The question of Congress intruding upon "local" matters within the jurisdiction of the states resulted in the invalidation of several New Deal statutes. In 1936, the Supreme Court struck down a so-called excise tax in the Bituminous Coal Conservation Act of 1935 because it coerced coal producers to submit to the price-fixing and labor provisions of the Act. Carter v. Carter Coal Co., 298 U.S. 238, 288–89 (1936). Also in 1936, the Court declared unconstitutional a "processing tax" enacted by Congress as part of the Agricultural Adjustment Act. In return for limiting their acreage and crops, farmers received payments from this tax. The Court held that the power of taxation exists to support government, not to expropriate money from one group to benefit another as part of a general regulatory scheme. Moreover, the Court held that the tax was coercive on farmers and invaded state powers by trying to regulate the "local" matter of agriculture. The decision suggests that had Congress explicitly invoked its commerce power, the Act might have been sustained. In writing the opinion for the Court, Justice Owen Roberts unveiled his famous mechanical formula for determining the constitutionality of a statute, arguing that the Court's job is to "lay the article of the Constitution which is invoked beside the statute which is challenged and to decide whether the latter squares with the former." United States v. Butler, 297 U.S. 1, 62 (1936).

Spending and Regulatory Power

Roberts abandoned his conservative brethren a year later by joining a 5 to 4 decision upholding Title IX of the Social Security Act. Congress imposed a tax on employers to support a national unemployment compensation plan. Funds from state unemployment laws were paid over to the Secretary of the Treasury and credited to an unemployment trust fund. Title IX was upheld even though it seemed to conflict with *Butler* by pressuring states to adopt unemployment compensation laws as part of a regulatory, and not merely revenue-raising, effort. STEWARD MACHINE CO. v. DAVIS, 301 U.S. 548 (1937). Congress responded to *Butler* by passing the Soil Conservation and Domestic Allotment Act of 1936 and the Agricultural Adjustment Act of 1938. Those statutes avoided the processing tax but pursued the same objective of controlling production by relying on the federal appropriations power and the Commerce Clause.

By attaching conditions to federal funds, Congress can regulate certain state activities. States acquiesce by accepting federal strings with the funds. Oklahoma v. CSC, 330 U.S. 127, 143–44 (1947). Federal grants to states have grown over the years, representing a substantial percentage of state budgets. In 1955, for example, federal grants made up about 10 percent of state budgets while they are now, on average, around 20 percent. This gives the federal government the ability to induce the states to follow national policy goals. Thus, Congress may direct the Secretary of Transportation to withhold a percentage of federal highway funds from states that allow persons under 21 to buy alcoholic beverages. SOUTH DAKOTA v. DOLE, 483 U.S. 203 (1987). The Court initially accepted the use of the spending power to impose racial and ethnic criteria as a condition attached to federal grants (a 10 percent "setaside" for minority businesses). Fullilove v. Klutznick, 448 U.S. 448 (1980), reprinted in Chapter 15. If the conditions are offensive to state interests or its constitutional values, there is no obligation to accept the funds. That decision was overturned fifteen years later in *Adarand v. Pena*, 515 U.S. 200 (1995).

The Patient Protection and Affordable Care Act of 2010 raised multiple questions with implications for federalism and led to claims that Congress had exceeded its Commerce Clause powers and its taxing and spending powers. The Commerce claim was that Congress was attempting to regulate inactivity (the failure to purchase health insurance) when it created an individual mandate to purchase health care or pay a penalty to the IRS. The taxing and spending claim was that the Medicaid expansion, which required states to participate or lose all of their Medicaid funds, was coercive, leaving states no choice in deciding whether or not to participate in the program. In June 2012, somewhat to the surprise of both supporters and opponents of the Act, the Supreme Court held that the individual mandate exceeded Congress's authority under the Commerce Clause, but was a constitutional exercise of the taxing power. In addition, it held that the Medicaid expansion did constitute coercion of the states, and that states must be permitted to opt out without losing all of their existing Medicaid funds. NATIONAL FEDERATION OF INDEPENDENT BUSINESS v. SEBELIUS, 567 U.S. ___ (2012).

The states and the federal government are generally free to exercise their taxing power if they proceed on a rational basis and do not resort to classifications that are "palpably arbitrary." Allied Stores of Ohio v. Bowers, 358 U.S. 522, 527 (1959); Lehnhausen v. Lake Shore Auto Parts Co., 410 U.S. 356 (1973). Congress has had mixed results in using the taxing power to regulate narcotics, gambling, liquor, and firearms. The application of the taxing power to narcotics has been repeatedly upheld.[9] The Court has ruled that because a federal liquor tax operated not as a tax but as a penalty, it usurped the police powers of the states. United States v. Constantine, 296 U.S. 287 (1935); United States v. Kesterson, 296 U.S. 299 (1935).

The taxing power has been used to regulate firearms, with the Court pointing out that every tax "is in some measure regulatory." Sonzinsky v. United States, 300 U.S. 506, 513 (1937). Such statutes, however, cannot force gun dealers to incriminate themselves. Haynes v. United States, 390 U.S. 85 (1968). The same issue applies to federal taxes on gambling. At first, the Court determined that federal taxes and requirements to register with the Internal Revenue Service did not violate the Self-Incrimination Clause. United States v. Kahriger, 345 U.S. 22 (1953); Lewis v. United States, 348 U.S. 419 (1955). The Court later held that such statutes unconstitutionally compel gamblers to incrimi-

9. United States v. Doremus, 249 U.S. 86 (1919); Nigro v. United States, 276 U.S. 332 (1928); United States v. Sanchez, 340 U.S. 42 (1950). Questions have been raised in some cases as to whether compliance with these laws automatically exposes someone to the risk of self-incrimination. Leary v. United States, 395 U.S. 6 (1969); United States v. Covington, 395 U.S. 57 (1969); Minor v. United States, 396 U.S. 87 (1969).

nate themselves. Marchetti v. United States, 390 U.S. 39 (1968); Grosso v. United States, 390 U.S. 62 (1968).

Bailey v. Drexel Furniture Co. (Child Labor Tax Case)

259 U.S. 20 (1922)

After the Supreme Court in *Hammer* v. *Dagenhart* (1918) struck down the attempt by Congress to use the Commerce Clause to regulate child labor, Congress passed legislation in 1919 to levy a tax on goods produced by child labor. The Court in this case reviews the power of Congress to use its taxing power as a regulatory device to eliminate the evils of child labor. J.W. Bailey, an IRS collector, assessed the Drexel Furniture Company $6,312.79 for employing a boy under the age of 14 during the 1919 tax year.

MR. CHIEF JUSTICE TAFT delivered the opinion of the court.

This case presents the question of the constitutional validity of the Child Labor Tax Law....

The law is attacked on the ground that it is a regulation of the employment of child labor in the States—an exclusively state function under the Federal Constitution and within the reservations of the Tenth Amendment. It is defended on the ground that it is a mere excise tax levied by the Congress of the United States under its broad power of taxation conferred by § 8, Article I, of the Federal Constitution....

... If it were an excise on a commodity or other thing of value we might not be permitted under previous decisions of this court to infer solely from its heavy burden that the act intends a prohibition instead of a tax. But this act is more. It provides a heavy exaction for a departure from a detailed and specified course of conduct in business. That course of business is that employers shall employ in mines and quarries, children of an age greater than sixteen years; in mills and factories, children of an age greater than fourteen years, and shall prevent children of less than sixteen years in mills and factories from working more than eight hours a day or six days in the week. If an employer departs from this prescribed course of business, he is to pay to the Government one-tenth of his entire net income in the business for a full year....

... In the light of these features of the act, a court must be blind not to see that the so-called tax is imposed to stop the employment of children within the age limits prescribed. Its prohibitory and regulatory effect and purpose are palpable. All others can see and understand this. How can we properly shut our minds to it?

It is the high duty and function of this court in cases regularly brought to its bar to decline to recognize or enforce seeming laws of Congress, dealing with subjects not entrusted to Congress but left or committed by the supreme law of the land to the control of the States. We can not avoid the duty even though it require us to refuse to give effect to legislation designed to promote the highest good. The good sought in unconstitutional legislation is an insidious feature because it leads citizens and legislators of good purpose to promote it without thought of the serious breach it will make in the ark of our covenant or the harm which will come from breaking down recognized standards. In the maintenance of local self government, on the one hand, and the national power, on the other, our country has been able to endure and prosper for near a century and a half.

Out of a proper respect for the acts of a coördinate branch of the Government, this court has gone far to sustain taxing acts as such, even though there has been ground for suspecting from the weight of the tax it was intended to destroy its subject. But, in the act before us, the presumption of validity cannot prevail, because the proof of the contrary is found on the very face of its provisions. Grant the validity of this law, and all that Congress would need to do, hereafter, in seeking to take over to its control any one of the great number of subjects of public interest, jurisdiction of which the States have never parted with, and which are reserved to them by the Tenth Amendment, would be to enact a detailed measure of complete regulation of the subject and enforce it by a so-called tax upon departures from it. To give such magic to the word "tax" would be to break down all constitutional limitation of the powers of Congress and completely wipe out the sovereignty of the States.

. . .

The analogy of the *Dagenhart Case* is clear. The congressional power over interstate commerce is, within its proper scope, just as complete and unlimited as the congressional power to tax, and the legislative motive in its exercise is just as free from judicial suspicion and inquiry. Yet when Congress threatened to stop interstate commerce in ordinary and necessary commodities, unobjectionable as subjects of transportation, and to deny the same to the people of a State in order to coerce them into compliance with Congress's regulation of state concerns, the court said this was not in fact regulation of interstate commerce, but rather that of State concerns and was invalid. So here the so-called tax is a penalty to coerce people of a State to act as Congress wishes them to act in respect of a matter completely the business of the state government under the Federal Constitution....

For the reasons given, we must hold the Child Labor Tax Law invalid and the judgment of the District Court is

Affirmed.

MR. JUSTICE CLARKE dissents.

Steward Machine Co. v. Davis

301 U.S. 548 (1937)

Title IX of the Social Security Act of 1935 imposed an "excise tax" on employers, the proceeds to go into the U.S. Treasury to establish an unemployment compensation fund. Credit against the tax (up to 90 percent) would be given to employers who contributed under a state unemployment law. Questions: Did the tax unconstitutionally attempt to coerce the states to adopt their own unemployment compensation legislation, to be approved by the Federal Government? Could Title IX be interpreted as a "cooperative plan" into which states freely entered because of benefits available to them? If the credit gave the states motive and temptation, was that the same as coercion? The Steward Machine Company brought this action against Harwell G. Davis, Collector of Internal Revenue.

MR. JUSTICE CARDOZO delivered the opinion of the Court.

The validity of the tax imposed by the Social Security Act on employers of eight or more is here to be determined....

The assault on the statute proceeds on an extended front. Its assailants take the ground that the tax is not an excise; that it is not uniform throughout the United States as excises are required to be; that its exceptions are so many and arbitrary as to violate the Fifth Amendment; that its purpose was not revenue, but an unlawful invasion of the reserved powers of the states; and that the states in submitting to it have yielded to coercion and have abandoned governmental functions which they are not permitted to surrender.

The objections will be considered seriatim with such further explanation as may be necessary to make their meaning clear.

First. The tax, which is described in the statute as an excise, is laid with uniformity throughout the United States as a duty, an impost or an excise upon the relation of employment....

The subject matter of taxation open to the power of the Congress is as comprehensive as that open to the power of the states, though the method of apportionment may at times be different. "The Congress shall have power to lay and collect taxes, duties, imposts and excises." Art. 1, § 8. If the tax is a direct one, it shall be apportioned according to the census or enumeration. If it is a duty, impost, or excise, it shall be uniform throughout the United States. Together, these classes include every form of tax appropriate to sovereignty.... Whether the tax is to be classified as an "excise" is in truth not of critical importance. If not that, it is an "impost" ... or a "duty".... A capitation or other "direct" tax it certainly is not....

2. The tax being an excise, its imposition must conform to the canon of uniformity. There has been no departure from this requirement. According to the settled doctrine the uniformity exacted is geographical, not intrinsic....

Second. The excise is not invalid under the provisions of the Fifth Amendment by force of its exemptions.

The statute does not apply, as we have seen, to employers of less than eight. It does not apply to agricultural labor, or domestic service in a private home or to some other classes of less importance. Petitioner contends that the effect of these restrictions is an arbitrary discrimination vitiating the tax....

The classifications and exemptions directed by

the statute now in controversy have support in considerations of policy and practical convenience that cannot be condemned as arbitrary....

Third. The excise is not void as involving the coercion of the States in contravention of the Tenth Amendment or of restrictions implicit in our federal form of government....

To draw the line intelligently between duress and inducement there is need to remind ourselves of facts as to the problem of unemployment that are now matters of common knowledge.... During the years 1929 to 1936, when the country was passing through a cyclical depression, the number of the unemployed mounted to unprecedented heights. Often the average was more than 10 million; at times a peak was attained of 16 million or more. Disaster to the breadwinner meant disaster to dependents. Accordingly the roll of the unemployed, itself formidable enough, was only a partial roll of the destitute or needy. The fact developed quickly that the states were unable to give the requisite relief. The problem had become national in area and dimensions. There was need of help from the nation if the people were not to starve. It is too late today for the argument to be heard with tolerance that in a crisis so extreme the use of the moneys of the nation to relieve the unemployed and their dependents is a use for any purpose narrower than the promotion of the general welfare.... The nation responded to the call of the distressed....

... Before Congress acted, unemployment compensation insurance was still, for the most part, a project and no more. Wisconsin was the pioneer. Her statute was adopted in 1931. At times bills for such insurance were introduced elsewhere, but they did not reach the stage of law. In 1935, four states (California, Massachusetts, New Hampshire and New York) passed unemployment laws on the eve of the adoption of the Social Security Act, and two others did likewise after the federal act and later in the year. The statutes differed to some extent in type, but were directed to a common end. In 1936, twenty-eight other states fell in line, and eight more the present year. But if states had been holding back before the passage of the federal law, inaction was not owing, for the most part, to the lack of sympathetic interest. Many held back through alarm lest, in laying such a toll upon their industries, they would place themselves in a position of economic disadvantage as compared with neighbors or competitors.... Two consequences ensued. One was that the freedom of a state to contribute its fair share to the solution of a national problem was paralyzed by fear. The other was that in so far as there was failure

by the states to contribute relief according to the measure of their capacity, a disproportionate burden, and a mountainous one, was laid upon the resources of the Government of the nation.

The Social Security Act is an attempt to find a method by which all these public agencies may work together to a common end. Every dollar of the new taxes will continue in all likelihood to be used and needed by the nation as long as states are unwilling, whether through timidity or for other motives, to do what can be done at home....

Who then is coerced through the operation of this statute? Not the taxpayer. He pays in fulfilment of the mandate of the local legislature. Not the state. Even now she does not offer a suggestion that in passing the unemployment law she was affected by duress.... For all that appears she is satisfied with her choice, and would be sorely disappointed if it were now to be annulled. The difficulty with the petitioner's contention is that it confuses motive with coercion.... In like manner every rebate from a tax when conditioned upon conduct is in some measure a temptation. But to hold that motive or temptation is equivalent to coercion is to plunge the law in endless difficulties....

Fourth. The statute does not call for a surrender by the states of powers essential to their quasi-sovereign existence....

... The states are at liberty, upon obtaining the consent of Congress, to make agreements with one another. Constitution, Art. I, § 10, par. 3.... We find no room for doubt that they may do the like with Congress if the essence of their statehood is maintained without impairment....

Separate opinion of Mr. Justice McReynolds.

That portion of the Social Security legislation here under consideration, I think, exceeds the power granted to Congress. It unduly interferes with the orderly government of the State by her own people and otherwise offends the Federal Constitution....

Separate opinion of Mr. Justice Sutherland.

With most of what is said in the opinion just handed down, I concur....

But the question with which I have difficulty is whether the administrative provisions of the act invade the governmental administrative powers of the several states reserved by the Tenth Amendment. A state may enter into contracts; but a state cannot, by contract or statute, surrender the execution, or a share in the execution, of any of its governmental powers either to a sister state or to the federal government, any more than the federal government can surrender the control of any of its governmental powers to a foreign nation....

MR. JUSTICE VAN DEVANTER joins in this opinion.

MR. JUSTICE BUTLER, dissenting.

I think that the objections to the challenged en-

actment expressed in the separate opinions of MR. JUSTICE MCREYNOLDS and MR. JUSTICE SUTHERLAND are well taken. I am also of opinion that, in principle and as applied to bring about and to gain control over state unemployment compensation, the statutory scheme is repugnant to the Tenth Amendment....

South Dakota v. Dole

483 U.S. 203 (1987)

Congress passed legislation in 1984 directing the Secretary of Transportation to withhold a percentage of federal highway funds from states that refuse to adopt age 21 as the minimum drinking age. An issue before the Court was the extent to which Congress can use its spending power, and more particularly conditions attached to federal funds, to achieve national objectives. South Dakota challenged the constitutionality of the statute and brought suit against Secretary of Transportation Elizabeth Dole. A district court dismissed the complaint and the Eighth Circuit affirmed.

CHIEF JUSTICE REHNQUIST delivered the opinion of the Court....

In this Court, the parties direct most of their efforts to defining the proper scope of the Twenty-first Amendment. Relying on our statement in *California Retail Liquor Dealers Assn.* v. *Midcal Aluminum, Inc.,* 445 U.S. 97, 110 (1980), that the "Twenty-first Amendment grants the States virtually complete control over whether to permit importation or sale of liquor and how to structure the liquor distribution system," South Dakota asserts that the setting of minimum drinking ages is clearly within the "core powers" reserved to the States under §2 of the Amendment....

... Despite the extended treatment of the question by the parties, however, we need not decide in this case whether that Amendment would prohibit an attempt by Congress to legislate directly a national minimum drinking age. Here, Congress has acted indirectly under its spending power to encourage uniformity in the States' drinking ages. As we explain below, we find this legislative effort within constitutional bounds even if Congress may not regulate drinking ages directly.

The Constitution empowers Congress to "lay and collect Taxes, Duties, Imposts, and Excises, to pay the Debts and provide for the common Defence and general Welfare of the United States." Art. I, §8, cl. 1. Incident to this power, Congress may attach conditions on the receipt of federal funds, and has repeatedly employed the power "to further broad policy objectives by conditioning receipt of federal moneys upon

compliance by the recipient with federal statutory and administrative directives." *Fullilove* v. *Klutznick,* 448 U.S. 448, 474 (1980) (Opinion of Burger, C.J.).... The breadth of this power was made clear in *United States* v. *Butler,* 297 U.S. 1, 66 (1936), where the Court, resolving a longstanding debate over the scope of the Spending Clause, determined that "the power of Congress to authorize expenditure of public moneys for public purposes is not limited by the direct grants of legislative power found in the Constitution." Thus, objectives not thought to be within Article I's "enumerated legislative fields," *id.,* at 65, may nevertheless be attained through the use of the spending power and the conditional grant of federal funds.

The spending power is of course not unlimited, *Pennhurst State School and Hospital* v. *Halderman,* 451 U.S. 1, 17, and n. 13 (1981), but is instead subject to several general restrictions articulated in our cases. The first of these limitations is derived from the language of the Constitution itself: the exercise of the spending power must be in pursuit of "the general welfare." ... In considering whether a particular expenditure is intended to serve general public purposes, courts should defer substantially to the judgment of Congress.... Second, we have required that if Congress desires to condition the States' receipt of federal funds, it "must do so unambiguously..., enabl[ing] the States to exercise their choice knowingly, cognizant of the consequences of their participation." ... Third, our cases have suggested (without significant elaboration) that conditions on federal grants might be illegitimate if they are unrelated "to the federal interest in particular national projects or programs." ... Finally, we have noted that other constitutional provisions may provide an independent bar to the conditional grant of federal funds....

South Dakota does not seriously claim that § 158 is inconsistent with any of the first three restrictions mentioned above.... Congress found that the differing drinking ages in the States created particular incentives for young persons to combine their desire to drink with their ability to drive, and that this interstate problem required a national solution. The means it chose to address this dangerous situation were reasonably calculated to advance the general welfare. The conditions upon which States receive the funds, moreover, could not be more clearly stated by Congress. See 23 U.S.C. § 158 (1982 ed., Supp. III). And the State itself, rather than challenging the germaneness of the condition to federal purposes, admits that it "has never contended that the congressional action was ... unrelated to a national concern in the absence of the Twenty-first Amendment." ... Indeed, the condition imposed by Congress is directly related to one of the main purposes for which highway funds are expended—safe interstate travel. See 23 U.S.C. § 101(b). This goal of the interstate highway system had been frustrated by varying drinking ages among the States. A presidential commission appointed to study alcohol-related accidents and fatalities on the Nation's highways concluded that the lack of uniformity in the States' drinking ages created "an incentive to drink and drive" because "young persons commut[e] to border States where the drinking age is lower." ...

The remaining question about the validity of § 158—and the basic point of disagreement between the parties—is whether the Twenty-first Amendment constitutes an "independent constitutional bar" to the conditional grant of federal funds....

[Previous] cases establish that the "independent constitutional bar" limitation on the spending power is not, as petitioner suggests, a prohibition on the indirect achievement of objectives which Congress is not empowered to achieve directly. Instead, we think that the language in our earlier opinions stands for the unexceptionable proposition that the power may not be used to induce the States to engage in activities that would themselves be unconstitutional. Thus, for example, a grant of federal funds conditioned on invidiously discriminatory state action or the infliction of cruel and unusual punishment would be an illegitimate exercise of the Congress' broad spending power. But no such claim can be or is made here. Were South Dakota to succumb to the blandishments offered by Congress and raise its drinking age to 21, the State's action in so doing would not violate the constitutional rights of anyone.

Our decisions have recognized that in some circumstances the financial inducement offered by Congress might be so coercive as to pass the point at which "pressure turns into compulsion." *Steward Machine Co.* v. *Davis, supra,* 301 U.S., at 590. Here, however, Congress has directed only that a State desiring to establish a minimum drinking age lower than 21 lose a relatively small percentage of certain federal highway funds. Petitioner contends that the coercive nature of this program is evident from the degree of success it has achieved. We cannot conclude, however, that a conditional grant of federal money of this sort is unconstitutional simply by reason of its success in achieving the congressional objective.

When we consider, for a moment, that all South Dakota would lose if she adheres to her chosen course as to a suitable minimum drinking age is 5% of the funds otherwise obtainable under specified highway grant programs, the argument as to coercion is shown to be more rhetoric than fact....

JUSTICE BRENNAN, dissenting.

I agree with JUSTICE O'CONNOR that regulation of the minimum age of purchasers of liquor falls squarely within the ambit of those powers reserved to the States by the Twenty-first Amendment.... Since States possess this constitutional power, Congress cannot condition a federal grant in a manner that abridges this right. The Amendment, itself, strikes the proper balance between federal and state authority. I therefore dissent.

JUSTICE O'CONNOR, dissenting.

[*The National Minimum Drinking Age Amendment*] is an attempt to regulate the sale of liquor, an attempt that lies outside Congress' power to regulate commerce because it falls within the ambit of § 2 of the Twenty-first Amendment....

... [T]he Court's application of the requirement that the condition imposed be reasonably related to the purpose for which the funds are expended, is cursory and unconvincing....

... [I]f the purpose of § 158 is to deter drunken driving, it is far too over- and under-inclusive. It is over-inclusive because it stops teenagers from drinking even when they are not about to drive on interstate highways. It is under-inclusive because teenagers pose only a small part of the drunken driving problem in this Nation. See, *e.g.*, 130 Cong. Rec. S8216 (June 26, 1984) (remarks of Sen. Humphrey) ("Eighty-four percent of all highway fatalities involving alcohol occur among those whose ages exceed 21"); *id.*, at S8219 (remarks of Sen. McClure)....

National Federation of Independent Business v. Sebelius
567 U.S. ___ (2012)

Congress passed the Patient Protection and Affordable Care Act of 2010 (ACA) in order to expand health care coverage to millions of Americans. This goal was accomplished primarily through (1) the creation of an individual mandate, which required individuals without insurance to buy it or to pay a penalty to the IRS, (2) the expansion of Medicaid, which required the states to participate or lose their existing Medicaid funds, and (3) rules requiring the coverage of persons with pre-existing conditions. Lawsuits were filed almost immediately challenging the individual mandate and the Medicaid expansion as beyond Congress's powers. Lower courts produced various outcomes, and the cases were consolidated when they arrived at the Supreme Court. In the NIFB case, the Eleventh Circuit Court of Appeals upheld the Medicaid expansion as a valid exercise of the Spending power, but found that Congress lacked authority to create the individual mandate. It found that the mandate was severable from the Act, leaving the rest of it intact.

CHIEF JUSTICE ROBERTS announced the judgment of the Court and delivered the opinion of the Court with respect to Parts I, II, and III-C, an opinion with respect to Part IV, in which JUSTICE BREYER and JUSTICE KAGAN join, and an opinion with respect to Parts III-A, III-B, and III-D.

· · ·

In our federal system, the National Government possesses only limited powers; the States and the people retain the remainder....

This case concerns [the Commerce Clause, the Taxing and Spending Clause, and the Necessary and Proper Clause:] ... powers that the Constitution does grant the Federal Government, but which must be read carefully to avoid creating a general federal authority akin to the police power [of the states].

[*Roberts notes that historically, the Court has viewed these powers as very broad.*] Our permissive reading of these powers is explained in part by a general reticence to invalidate the acts of the Nation's elected leaders.... Members of this Court are vested with the authority to interpret the law; we possess neither the expertise nor the prerogative to make policy judgments. Those decisions are entrusted to our Nation's elected leaders, who can be thrown out of office if the people disagree with them. It is not our job to protect the people from the consequences of their political choices.

· · ·

II.

[*Roberts first considers the threshold question of whether The Anti-Injunction Act, which provides that "no suit for the purpose of retraining the assessment or collection of any tax shall be maintained in any court by any person," precludes the Court from deciding the case before the individual mandate penalty goes into effect in 2014. The statute allows suits for reimbursement only after a tax has been assessed. He concludes that Congress did not intend for the Act to apply to the ACA because it called the assessment for failure to buy insurance a "penalty" rather than a "tax."*]

III. [A.1]

The Government contends that the individual mandate is within Congress's power because the failure to purchase insurance "has a substantial and deleterious effect on interstate commerce" be creating the cost-shifting problem....

Given its expansive scope, it is no surprise that Congress has employed the commerce power in a wide variety of ways to address the pressing needs of the time. But Congress has never attempted to rely on that power to compel individuals not engaged in commerce to purchase an unwanted product....

The Constitution grants Congress the power to "*regulate* Commerce." ... The power to *regulate* commerce presupposes the existence of commercial activity to be regulated....

... As expansive as our cases construing the scope

of the commerce power have been, they all have one thing in common: They uniformly describe the power as reaching "activity."

The individual mandate, however, does not regulate existing commercial activity. It instead compels individuals to *become* active in commerce by purchasing a product, on the ground that the failure to do so affects interstate commerce. Construing the Commerce Clause to permit Congress to regulate individuals precisely *because* they are doing nothing would open a new and potentially vast domain to congressional authority....

Applying the Government's logic to the familiar case of *Wickard v. Filburn* shows how far that logic would carry us from the notion of a government of limited powers....

... The farmer in *Wickard* was at least actively engaged in the production of wheat, and the Government could regulate that activity because of its effect on commerce. The Government's theory here would effectively override that limitation, by establishing that individuals may be regulated ... whenever enough of them are not doing something the government would have them do.

[*Roberts notes that unhealthy eating habits contribute significantly to health care costs in the United States. Does that mean the Government could force people to buy healthier food? It seems so to him, based on the Government's argument.*]

That is not the country the Framers of our Constitution envisioned.... Congress already enjoys vast power to regulate much of what we do. Accepting the Government's theory would give Congress the same license to regulate what we do not do, fundamentally changing the relation between the citizen and the Federal Government.

. . .

2.

[*Roberts considers and rejects the Government's claim that the individual mandate is necessary to the whole regulatory scheme of ACA and therefore should be upheld under the Necessary and Proper Clause. Even if necessary, he argues, "such an expansion of federal power is not a 'proper' means for making those reforms effective."*]

B.

That is not the end of the matter.... [I]t is necessary to turn to the Government's second argument: that the mandate may be upheld as within Congress's enumerated power to "lay and collect Taxes." ...

. . .

The text of a statute can sometimes have more than one possible meaning.... And it is well established that if a statute has two possible meanings, one of which violates the Constitution, courts should adopt the meaning that does not do so....

The most straightforward reading of the mandate is that it commands individuals to purchase insurance.... But, for the reasons explained above, the Commerce Clause does not give Congress that power. Under our precedent, it is therefore necessary to ask whether the Government's alternative reading of the statute—that it only imposes a tax on those without insurance—is a reasonable one.

Under the mandate, if an individual does not maintain health insurance, the only consequence is that he must make an additional payment to the IRS when he pays his taxes.... That, according to the Government, means the mandate can be regarded as establishing a condition—not owning health insurance—that triggers a tax—the required payment to the IRS. Under that theory, the mandate is not a legal command to buy insurance. Rather, it makes going without insurance just another thing the Government taxes, like buying gasoline or earning income....

The question is not whether that is the most natural interpretation of the mandate, but only whether it is a "fairly possible" one.... As we have explained, "every reasonable construction must be resorted to, in order to save a statute from unconstitutionality." ...

C.

The exaction the Affordable Care Act imposes on those without health insurance looks like a tax in many respects. [It] is paid into the Treasury by "taxpayer[s]" when they file their tax returns.... It does not apply to [low-income] individuals who do not pay federal income taxes.... For taxpayers who do owe the payment, the amount is determined by such familiar factors as taxable income, number of dependents, and joint filing status.... The requirement to pay is found in the Internal Revenue Code and enforced by the IRS.... This process yields the essential feature of any tax: it produces at least some revenue for the Government....

. . .

None of this is to say that the payment is not intended to affect individual conduct. Although the payment will raise considerable revenue, it is plainly designed to expand health insurance coverage. But taxes that seek to influence conduct are nothing new.... [*Roberts lists examples like taxes on cigarettes.*]

. . .

... If it is troubling to interpret the Commerce Clause as authorizing Congress to regulate those who abstain from commerce, perhaps it should be similarly troubling to permit Congress to impose a tax for not doing something.

Three considerations allay this concern. First, and most importantly, it is abundantly clear the Constitution does not guarantee that individuals may avoid taxation through inactivity. A capitation, after all, is a tax that everyone must pay simply by existing, and capitations are expressly contemplated by the Constitution....

... Sustaining the mandate as a tax depends only on whether Congress *has* properly exercised its taxing power to encourage purchasing health insurance, not whether it *can*. Upholding the individual mandate under the Taxing Clause thus does not recognize any new federal power. It determines that Congress has used an existing one.

. . .

IV. [A]

The Spending Clause grants Congress the power "to pay the Debts and provide for the ... general Welfare of the United States." ... We have long recognized that Congress may use this power to grant federal funds to the States, and may condition such a grant upon the States' "taking certain actions that Congress could not require them to take." ...

At the same time, our cases have recognized limits on Congress's power under the Spending Clause to secure state compliance with federal objectives.... The legitimacy of Congress's exercise of the spending power "thus rests on whether the State voluntarily and knowingly accepts the terms of the 'contract.'"

... [W]hen "pressure turns into compulsion," ... the legislation runs contrary to our system of federalism....

... Spending Clause programs do not pose this danger when a State has a legitimate choice whether to accept the federal conditions in exchange for federal funds. In such a situation, state officials can fairly be held politically accountable for choosing to accept or refuse the federal offer. But when the State has no choice, the Federal Government can achieve its objectives without accountability....

... Congress may attach appropriate conditions to federal taxing and spending programs to preserve its control over the use of federal funds. In the typical case we look to the States to defend their prerogatives by adopting "the simple expedient of not yielding" to federal blandishments when they ... do not want to embrace the federal policies as their own.... The States are separate and independent sovereigns. Sometimes they have to act like it.

. . .

In this case, the financial "inducement" Congress has chosen is much more than "relatively mild encouragement" [that was upheld in *South Dakota v. Dole*]—it is a gun to the head.... A State that opts out of the Affordable Care Act's expansion in health care coverage thus stands to lose not merely "a relatively small percentage" of its existing Medicaid funding, but *all* of it....

B.

Nothing in our opinion precludes Congress from offering funds under the Affordable Care Act to expand the availability of health care, and requiring that States accepting such funds comply with the conditions of their use. What Congress is not free to do is to penalize States that choose not to participate in that new program by taking away their existing Medicaid funding....

. . .

We have no way of knowing how many States will accept the terms of the expansion, but we do not believe Congress would have wanted the whole Act to fall, simply because some may choose not to participate. The other reforms Congress enacted, after all, will remain "fully operative as a law." ...

. . .

The judgment of the Court of Appeals for the Eleventh Circuit is affirmed in part and reversed in part.

It is so ordered.

JUSTICE GINSBURG, with whom JUSTICE SOTOMAYOR joins, and with whom JUSTICE BREYER and JUSTICE KAGAN join as to parts I, II, III, and IV, concurring in part, concurring in the judgment in part, and dissenting in part.

I.

[*Ginsburg begins by stating that the Chief Justice's reading of the Commerce Clause is "stunningly retro-*

gressive," "crabbed," and "should not have staying power."]

A.

[*Ginsburg reviews the "unique" nature of the health care market, citing studies that demonstrate the "high cost, its unpredictability, and its inevitability," and noting that virtually everyone enters the health care market eventually, even if they do not carry insurance. Given this reality, Congress reasonably concluded that the number of uninsured people in the market places a heavy burden on the national health care market, shifting costs to private individuals and employers, health care providers, and the state and federal governments. Individual state responses could not solve the problem, necessitating a national solution. Congress "could have taken over the health insurance market by establishing a tax and spend federal program like Social Security" but instead it enacted a program "that retains a robust role for private insurers and state governments."*]

. . .

II. A

The Commerce Clause, it is widely acknowledged, "was the Framers' response to the central problem that gave rise to the Constitution itself ... Under the Articles of Confederation, the Constitution's precursor, the regulation of commerce was left to the States. This scheme proved unworkable, because the individual States, understandably focused on their own economic interests, often failed to take actions critical to the success of the Nation as a whole....

. . .

The Framers understood that the "general Interests of the Union" would change over time, in ways they could not anticipate. Accordingly, they recognized that the Constitution was of necessity "a great outlin[e]," not a detailed blueprint, ... and that its provisions included broad concepts, to be "explained by the context or by the facts of the case," [*citing an 1831 letter from James Madison.*]

B

[*Ginsburg reviews the Court's Commerce Clause precedent, arguing that "until today" it has been consistent with the Framers' intent, emphasizing the importance of taking into account "practical considerations" and "actual experience" in interpreting the clause.*]

. . .

[D.1.A]

[Chief Justice Roberts' argument that this reading of the Commerce Clause would allow the government to force people to buy vegetables] has multiple flaws. First, more than 60% of those without insurance visit a hospital or doctor's office each year.... Nearly 90% will within five years. An uninsured's consumption of health care is thus quite proximate: It is virtually certain to occur in the next five years and more likely than not to occur this year.

. . .

Second, it is Congress' role, not the Court's to delineate the boundaries of the market the Legislature seeks to regulate.... Congress could reasonably have viewed the market from a long-term perspective, encompassing all transactions, virtually certain to occur over the next decade.

Third, ... [o]ur decisions ... acknowledge Congress's authority, under the Commerce Clause, to direct the conduct of an individual today (the farmer in *Wickard,* stopped from growing excess wheat; the plaintiff in *Raich,* ordered to cease cultivating marijuana) because of a prophesied future transaction (the eventual sale of that wheat or marijuana in the interstate market). Congress' actions are even more rational in this case, where the future activity (the consumption of medical care) is certain to occur, the sole uncertainty being the time the activity will take place.

[The Chief Justice's analogy to the car and vegetable market] is inapt. The inevitable yet unpredictable need for medical care and the guarantee that emergency care will be provided when required are conditions nonexistent in other markets.... Although an individual *might* by a car or a crown of broccoli one day, there is no certainty she will ever do so. And if she eventually wants a car or has a craving for broccoli, she will be obliged to pay at the counter before receiving the vehicle or nourishment. She will get no free ride or food, at the expense of another consumer forced to pay an inflated price.... Upholding the minimum coverage provision ... would therefore carry no implication that Congress may justify under the Commerce Clause a mandate to buy other products and services.

. . .

V.

... The spending power conferred by the Constitution, the Court has never doubted, permits Congress to define the contours of the programs financed by federal funds.... And to expand [Medicaid] coverage, Congress could have recalled the existing legislation, and replaced it with a new law making Medicaid as embracive of the poor as Congress chose.

The question posed by the 2010 Medicaid expansion, then, is essentially this: To cover a notably larger population, must Congress take the repeal/reenact route, or may it achieve the same result by amending existing law? The answer should be that Congress may expand by amendment the classes of needy persons entitled to Medicaid benefits. A ritualistic requirement that Congress repeal and reenact spending legislation in order to enlarge the population served by a federally funded program would advance no constitutional principle and would scarcely serve the interests of federalism. To the contrary, such a requirement would rigidify Congress' efforts to empower States by partnering with them in the implementation of federal programs.

... States have no entitlement to receive any Medicaid funds; they enjoy only the opportunity to accept funds on Congress' terms. Future Congresses are not bound by their predecessors' dispositions; they have authority to spend federal revenue as they see fit. The Federal Government, therefore, is not ... threatening States with the loss of "existing" funds from one spending program in order to induce them to opt into another program. Congress is simply requiring States to do what States have long been required to do to receive Medicaid funding: comply with the conditions Congress proscribes for participation.

. . .

JUSTICE SCALIA, JUSTICE KENNEDY, JUSTICE THOMAS, and JUSTICE ALITO, dissenting.

[*Scalia begins by stating that the two questions before them—the constitutionality of the mandate and the Medicaid expansion—are "difficult."*]

The case is easy and straightforward, however, in another respect. What is absolutely clear, affirmed by the text of the 1789 Constitution, by the Tenth Amendment, ratified in 1791, and by innumerable cases of ours in the 220 years since, is that there are structural limits upon federal power—upon what it can prescribe with respect to private conduct, and upon what it can impose upon the sovereign States. Whatever may be the conceptual limits upon the

Commerce Clause and upon the power to tax and spend, they cannot be such as will enable the Federal Government to regulate all private conduct and to compel the States to function as administrators of federal programs.

That clear principle carries the day here.... To go beyond [*Wickard*], and to say the *failure* to grow wheat ... nonetheless affects commerce and therefore can be federally regulated, is to make mere breathing in and out the basis for federal prescription and to extend federal power to virtually all human activity.

As for the constitutional power to tax and spend for the general welfare: The Court has long since expanded that beyond (what Madison thought it meant) taxing and spending for those aspects of the general welfare that were within the Federal Government's enumerated powers.... The principle obstacle that prevents Congress from using the tax-- and-spend power to assume all the general welfare responsibilities traditionally exercised by the States is the sheer impossibility of managing a Federal Government long enough to administer such a system. That obstacle can be overcome by granting funds to the States, allowing them to administer the program. That is fair and constitutional enough when the States freely agree to have their powers employed and their employees enlisted in the federal scheme. But it is a blatant violation of the constitutional structure when the States have no choice.

[*Scalia argues that the individual mandate and the Medicaid expansion are central to the Act and that therefore, the entire statute should be "inoperative."*]

. . .

The Court today decides to save a statute Congress did not write. It rules that what the statute declares to be a requirement with a penalty is instead an option subject to a tax. And it changes the intentionally coercive sanction of a total cut-off of Medicaid funds to a supposedly noncoercive cut-off of only the incremental funds that the Act makes available.

The Court regards its strained statutory interpretation as judicial modesty. It is not. It amounts instead to a vast judicial overreaching....

JUSTICE THOMAS, dissenting. [*Thomas insists that the "substantial effects" test "is inconsistent with the original understanding of Congress' powers."*]

H. PREEMPTION AND ABSTENTION

Federal-state relationships are shaped by two cross-cutting doctrines. Under the preemption doctrine, certain matters have such a national character that federal laws must supersede state laws. The abstention doctrine works in the opposite direction. As an exercise of discretionary authority, federal courts relinquish jurisdiction under various circumstances in order to avoid needless friction with the administration of state affairs. Both doctrines are complex and change over time.

The Preemption Doctrine

The preemption doctrine draws its force from the Supremacy Clause of Article VI of the Constitution, which declares that all laws made in pursuance to the Constitution and all treaties made under the authority of the United States shall be the "supreme Law of the Land." Federal actions of this character are superior to any conflicting provision of a state constitution or law. When Congress exercises its express powers, as it does by adopting uniform laws of bankruptcy, national legislation preempts state legislation. Perez v. Campbell, 402 U.S. 637 (1971). If compliance with both federal and state regulations in interstate commerce is a physical impossibility, federal law also preempts state law. Florida Lime & Avocado Growers, Inc. v. Paul, 373 U.S. 132, 142–43 (1963). Some of the enumerated powers of Congress are obviously exclusive, such as the power to exercise "exclusive Legislation" over the District of Columbia and the power "to coin money," which Art. I, § 10, expressly prohibits for the states.

The preemption doctrine also covers powers not expressly stated. In the area of foreign affairs, including regulation of aliens, state statutes may not stand "as an obstacle to the accomplishment and execution of the full purposes and objectives of Congress." Hines v. Davidowitz, 312 U.S. 52, 67 (1941). In 1956, the Supreme Court invalidated a state sedition law because the Smith Act, passed by Congress, regulated the same subject. The Court concluded that it had been the intent of Congress to occupy the whole field of sedition. PENNSYLVANIA v. NELSON, 350 U.S. 497, 504. As an illustration of Congress — not the Court — protecting state sovereignty, the author of the Smith Act promptly denied that he had ever intended the result reached by the Court (see box).

Smith Reacts to Court Decisions

Mr. [*Howard*] SMITH of Virginia.... I do want to make 1 or 2 comments on ... a bill of which I am an author, H.R. 3, to correct a decision of the Supreme Court of the United States in the Steve Nelson and other cases....

... [T]he Supreme Court has assumed out of a clear sky to say what the Congress intended when the Congress has not said it. If anything is to be done upon this subject, I think it is very important that we have a general law which will simply say that when Congress means to do away with State laws the Congress shall say so. [102 Cong. Rec. 6385 (1956)]

Mr. SMITH of Virginia.... This bill ... just does two things. It says to the Supreme Court —

First. Do not undertake to read the minds of the Congress; we, in the Congress, think ourselves more capable of knowing our minds than the Supreme Court has proved itself capable of in the past; and we will do our own mind reading; and we are telling you that when we get ready to repeal a State law or preempt a field, we will say so and we will not leave it to the Supreme Court to guess whether we are or not. That is No. 1.

Second. The other thing this bill does is to say that the Supreme Court must not knock down State laws unless they are in irreconcilable conflict with a Federal law.... [104 Cong. Rec. 14139–40 (1958)]

[*The House of Representatives passed legislation of this nature in 1958, but no action was taken by the Senate. The House again passed legislation in 1959, but by that time the Supreme Court, in Uphaus v. Wyman, 360 U.S. 72, had decided that states could proceed with prosecutions for sedition against the state itself.*]

Congressional committees reported legislation to permit federal-state concurrent jurisdiction in the area of sedition and subversion and to prohibit courts from using intent or implication to decide preemption.[10] Although these bills were never enacted, in the midst of their consideration the Court held that a state could investigate subversive activities against itself. To this extent state and federal sedition laws could coexist. Uphaus v. Wyman, 360 U.S. 72, 76 (1959). A potential legislative-judicial clash was thus averted.

In matters affecting foreign affairs and international relations, the courts have excluded state involvement. Zschernig v. Miller, 389 U.S. 429, 436 (1968); Crosby v. National Foreign Trade Council, 530 U.S. 363 (2000). State governments maintain direct contact with both private and government officials in foreign countries in order to promote export trade and foreign investments. But a state may not use its power to regulate insurance companies in a way that interferes with federal foreign policy making, as California discovered when it attempted to require insurance companies to assist Holocaust survivors in tracing their former property. American Ins. Assn. v. Garamendi, 539 U.S. 396 (2003).

Congress has used its preemption power to regulate major areas of environmental law. The Water Quality Act of 1965, the Air Quality Act of 1967, and the Clean Water Act of 1972 illustrate this trend toward national standards. States can attempt to forestall federal controls by forming interstate compacts to handle problems of a regional nature. These compacts, however, require the approval of Congress if they tend to increase the political power of the states or encroach upon the Supremacy Clause. Cuyler v. Adams, 449 U.S. 433, 440 (1981).

The field of nuclear energy has been largely preempted by Congress, especially over questions of safety and plant construction. States retain authority over economic questions, such as the need for additional plants, the type of facility to be licensed, land use, and setting rates. Pacific Gas & Elec. v. Energy Resources Comm'n, 461 U.S. 190, 212 (1983). The exclusive authority of the federal government over safety questions was compromised a year later when the Court allowed a jury to award punitive damages against a company in a case where Karen Silkwood, a laboratory analyst, was contaminated by plutonium. Silkwood v. Kerr-McGee Corp., 464 U.S. 238 (1984). State law claims were also allowed in a later nuclear-safety case; English v. General Electric Co., 496 U.S. 72 (1990).

In 2002, Congress used an interesting procedure in the Nuclear Waste Policy Act of 1982 to approve using Yucca Mountain, Nevada, as the site for storing high-level radioactive waste. The statute allows the governor or the state legislature to disapprove a site selected by the President. Congress then has 90 days to pass a joint resolution of approval, overriding the state. In 2002, Nevada exercised its veto, both the House and the Senate passed a resolution of approval, and President Bush signed it into law. P.L. 107-200 (July 23, 2002). Yucca Mountain continued to be a controversial issue in the presidential campaigns of 2004 and 2008 and in some state races in 2010.

A number of preemption cases involve pension plans. In response to pension benefits lost by employees because of bankruptcies, mergers, and theft, Congress passed the Employee Retirement Income Security Act of 1974 (ERISA). With certain exceptions, the statute preempts all state laws that "relate to" any employee benefit plan. The Supreme Court has given a broad reading to the statute's preemption clause.[11]

---

10. H. Rept. No. 2576, 84th Cong., 2d Sess. (1956); S. Rept. No. 2117, 84th Cong., 2d Sess. (1956); S. Rept. No. 2230, 84th Cong., 2d Sess. (1956); H. Rept. No. 1878, 85th Cong., 2d Sess. (1958); 104 Cong. Rec. 13844–65, 13993–14023, 14138–62 (1958); H. Rept. No. 422, 86th Cong., 1st Sess. (1959); 105 Cong. Rec. 11486–508, 11625–67, 11789–808 (1959).

11. Ingersoll-Rand Co. v. McClendon, 498 U.S. 133 (1990); FMC v. Holliday, 498 U.S. 52 (1990); Metropolitan Life Ins. Co. v. Massachusetts, 471 U.S. 724 (1985); Shaw v. Delta Air Lines, 463 U.S. 85 (1983); Alessi v. Raybestos-Manhattan, Inc., 451 U.S. 504 (1981). Other preemption cases include California Coastal Comm'n v. Granite Rock Co., 480 U.S. 572 (1987); Exxon Corp. v. Governor of Maryland, 437 U.S. 117 (1978); Ray v. Atlantic Richfield Co., 435 U.S. 151 (1978). For a case in which federal regulations did not preempt state and local regulation because Congress had not expressed that intent, see Hillsborough County v. Automated Medical Labs, 471 U.S. 707 (1985).

The dominant role of Congress in determining preemption was emphasized by Justice Rehnquist in 1986 during his confirmation hearings to be Chief Justice. He said that Congress "is probably the ultimate decider as to what the proper relationship between State and Federal law is in most situations.... How much is going to be Federal law in any area in which the Congress power reaches and how much is going to be State law, really in the last analysis, depends upon Congress." "Nomination of Justice William Hubbs Rehnquist," hearings before the Senate Committee on the Judiciary, 99th Cong., 2d Sess., 131 (1986). His judgment has been supported by subsequent cases.[12]

Federal preemption is also at issue in contemporary debates about immigration policy. A highly polarized Congress has been unable to agree on immigration reform and some states and localities have passed their own legislation and ordinances targeting undocumented immigrants. This conflict came to a head in 2010 when Arizona passed legislation that required local law enforcement officers to ask for documentation when they suspect a person is in the country illegally and made it a state crime to be in the country and to seek employment without documentation. In the summer of 2010 the U.S. Justice Department filed suit in federal court seeking an injunction against implementation of the Act. The government's argument was that immigration regulation is a federal responsibility, and that Arizona had acted beyond its authority if passing the legislation. In 2012 the Supreme Court agreed that most of the provisions were preempted by federal law, although it allowed the "show me your papers" provision to stand, saying that there was insufficient evidence on the record that this provision would lead to racial profiling. ARIZONA v. UNITED STATES, 567 U.S. ___ (2012). As enforcement gets underway, immigrant rights groups are likely to renew this challenge.

The Abstention Doctrine

The abstention doctrine helps puncture the periodic, apocalyptic announcement that "federalism is dead." To cultivate comity and mutual respect between the national and state levels, federal courts abstain in some areas. It would be impossible and self-destructive for federal courts to intervene in every state matter. The policy of abstention can be traced back to a congressional statute in 1793: "nor shall a writ of injunction [by federal courts] be granted to stay proceedings in any court of a state." 1 Stat. 335, § 5.

The Fourteenth Amendment opened the door to a much larger federal role. After the Supreme Court in *Ex parte Young* (1908) suggested that federal courts would intervene extensively in state affairs, Congress acted to limit judicial interference. Instead of allowing a single federal judge to strike down a state statute or enjoin its operation, Congress required a three-judge court to hear and decide such actions.[13] The policy of abstention crystallized as court doctrine in 1941. A unanimous Supreme Court held that it should withhold judgment until state courts reach a definitive construction of a state statute. Federal courts should avoid "needless friction with state policies" and promote "harmonious relation between state and federal authority" by waiting until the highest state court has dis-

---

12. American Ins. Assn. v. Garamendi, 539 U.S. 396 (2003); United States v. Locke, 529 U.S. 89 (2000) (federal law preempts state regulation of oil tankers); Barnett Bank of Marion County, N.A. v. Nelson, 517 U.S. 25 (1996) (federal statute preempts state statute that prevented a national bank from selling insurance in a small town); Cipollone v. Liggett Group, Inc., 505 U.S. 504 (1992) (federal legislation does not preempt state law damages actions, although it does preempt state mandates for particular warnings on cigarette labels or in cigarette advertisements); Gade v. National Solid Wastes Management Assn., 505 U.S. 88 (1992) (federal law prohibits states from adopting additional training requirements for workers handling hazardous waste); Morales v. Trans World Airlines, Inc., 504 U.S. 374 (1992) (federal law preempts state regulation of airline fare advertising to protect consumers); Wisconsin Public Intervenor v. Mortier, 504 U.S. 374 (1991) (federal law does not preempt regulation of pesticides by local governments); United Steelworkers of America v. Rawson, 495 U.S. 362 (1990) (federal labor law preempts tort claim in state court); California v. FERC, 495 U.S. 490 (1990) (federal law preempts states from requiring flow rates for water in hydroelectric projects that are higher than federal standards, even for the purpose of protecting fish and wildlife).

13. 36 Stat. 557, § 17 (1910); 36 Stat. 1162, § 266 (1911); 37 Stat. 1013 (1913); 38 Stat. 220 (1913). These statutes are codified at 28 U.S.C. § 2284 (2000).

posed of a constitutional issue. Railroad Commission v. Pullman, 312 U.S. 496, 500–01 (1941). Acting under this authority, the Supreme Court has returned cases to state courts to permit interpretation of questions that were not considered or resolved.[14]

Abstention is a general policy and can be waived. Abstention is inappropriate where state statutes are vulnerable on their face for abridging free expression or discouraging protected activities. Federal courts intervene in these cases to prevent state officials from invoking a statute in bad faith, with no hope for success, simply to harass minorities or their organizations. This exception to the abstention doctrine is aimed at statutes that are so vague or overbroad that they threaten First Amendment freedoms. Dombrowski v. Pfister, 380 U.S. 479 (1965); Zwickler v. Koota, 389 U.S. 241 (1967). In the case of a pending state criminal proceeding, federal courts intervene only under extraordinary circumstances: where the danger of irreparable loss is both great and immediate and where the threat to federally protected rights cannot be eliminated during the course of the trial. Younger v. Harris, 401 U.S. 37 (1971); Samuels v. Mackell, 401 U.S. 66 (1971). The policy of noninterference also applies to certain state civil proceedings. Huffman v. Pursue, Ltd., 420 U.S. 592 (1975).

Noninterference by the Supreme Court in state matters often provokes biting dissents that regard federalism as a cloak used to cover constitutional violations by state officials. Justice Brennan, for example, remarked: "Under the banner of vague, undefined notions of equity, comity, and federalism, the Court has embarked upon the dangerous course of condoning both isolated … and systematic … violations of civil liberties." Juidice v. Vail, 430 U.S. 327, 346 (1977). See also the dissents in Paul v. Davis, 424 U.S. 693 (1976), and Rizzo v. Goode, 423 U.S. 362 (1976).

Pennsylvania v. Nelson

350 U.S. 497 (1956)

Steve Nelson was convicted for violating the Pennsylvania Sedition Act. The question here is whether Congress, by passing the Smith Act of 1940, preempted the enforcement of state sedition acts.

Mr. Chief Justice Warren delivered the opinion of the Court.

The respondent Steve Nelson, an acknowledged member of the Communist Party, was convicted in the Court of Quarter Sessions of Allegheny County, Pennsylvania, of a violation of the Pennsylvania Sedition Act and sentenced to imprisonment for twenty years and to a fine of $10,000 and to costs of prosecution in the sum of $13,000. The Superior Court affirmed the conviction. 172 Pa. Super. 125, 92 A.2d 431. The Supreme Court of Pennsylvania, recognizing but not reaching many alleged serious trial errors and conduct of the trial court infringing upon respondent's right to due process of law, decided the case on the narrow issue of supersession of the state law by the Federal Smith Act. In its opinion, the court stated:

"And, while the Pennsylvania statute proscribes sedition against either the Government of the United States or the Government of Pennsylvania, it is only alleged sedition against the United States with which the instant case is concerned. Out of all the voluminous testimony, we have not found, nor has anyone pointed to, a single word indicating a seditious act or even utterance directed against the Government of Pennsylvania."

The precise holding of the court, and all that is before us for review, is that the Smith Act of 1940, as amended in 1948, which prohibits the knowing ad-

---

14. Reetz v. Bozanich, 397 U.S. 82 (1970); Henry v. Mississippi, 379 U.S. 443 (1965); Meridian v. Southern Bell T. & T. Co., 358 U.S. 639 (1959); Musser v. Utah, 333 U.S. 95 (1948).

vocacy of the overthrow of the Government of the United States by force and violence, supersedes the enforceability of the Pennsylvania Sedition Act which proscribes the same conduct....

It should be said at the outset that the decision in this case does not affect the right of States to enforce their sedition laws at times when the Federal Government has not occupied the field and is not protecting the entire country from seditious conduct. The distinction between the two situations was clearly recognized by the court below. Nor does it limit the jurisdiction of the States where the Constitution and Congress have specifically given them concurrent jurisdiction, as was done under the Eighteenth Amendment and the Volstead Act. *United States* v. *Lanza,* 260 U.S. 377. Neither does it limit the right of the State to protect itself at any time against sabotage or attempted violence of all kinds. Nor does it prevent the State from prosecuting where the same act constitutes both a federal offense and a state offense under the police power....

... In this case, we think that each of several tests of supersession is met.

First, "[t]he scheme of federal regulation [is] so pervasive as to make reasonable the inference that Congress left no room for the States to supplement it." *Rice* v. *Santa Fe Elevator Corp.,* 331 U.S., at 230. The Congress determined in 1940 that it was necessary for it to re-enter the field of antisubversive legislation, which had been abandoned by it in 1921. In that year, it enacted the Smith Act which proscribes advocacy of the overthrow of any government — federal, state or local — by force and violence and organization of and knowing membership in a group which so advocates. [*The Court also summarizes the Internal Security Act of 1950 and the Communist Control Act of 1954.*]

We examine these Acts only to determine the congressional plan. Looking to all of them in the aggregate, the conclusion is inescapable that Congress has intended to occupy the field of sedition. Taken as a whole, they evince a congressional plan which makes it reasonable to determine that no room has been left for the States to supplement it....

Second, the federal statutes "touch a field in which the federal interest is so dominant that the federal system [must] be assumed to preclude enforcement of state laws on the same subject." *Rice* v. *Santa Fe Elevator Corp.,* 331 U.S., at 230, citing *Hines* v. *Davidowitz, supra.* Congress has devised an all-embracing program for resistance to the various forms of totalitarian aggression....

Third, enforcement of state sedition acts presents a serious danger of conflict with the administration of the federal program. Since 1939, in order to avoid a hampering of uniform enforcement of its program by sporadic local prosecutions, the Federal Government has urged local authorities not to intervene in such matters, but to turn over to the federal authorities immediately and unevaluated all information concerning subversive activities....

The judgment of the Supreme Court of Pennsylvania is

Affirmed.

Mr. Justice Reed, with whom Mr. Justice Burton and Mr. Justice Minton join, dissenting....

Congress has not, in any of its statutes relating to sedition, specifically barred the exercise of state power to punish the same Acts under state law. And, we read the majority opinion to assume for this case that, absent federal legislation, there is no constitutional bar to punishment of sedition against the United States by both a State and the Nation....

First, the Court relies upon the pervasiveness of the antisubversive legislation embodied in the Smith Act of 1940, 18 U.S.C. § 2385, the Internal Security Act of 1950, 64 Stat. 987, and the Communist Control Act of 1954, 68 Stat. 775. It asserts that these Acts in the aggregate mean that Congress has occupied the "field of sedition" to the exclusion of the States....

We cannot agree that the federal criminal sanctions against sedition directed at the United States are of such a pervasive character as to indicate an intention to void state action.

Secondly, the Court states that the federal sedition statutes touch a field "in which the federal interest is so dominant" they must preclude state laws on the same subject. This concept is suggested in a comment on *Hines* v. *Davidowitz,* 312 U.S. 52, in the *Rice* case, at 230. The Court in *Davidowitz* ruled that federal statutes compelling alien registration preclude enforcement of state statutes requiring alien registration. We read *Davidowitz* to teach nothing more than that, when the Congress provided a single nation-wide integrated system of regulation so complete as that for aliens' registration (with fingerprinting, a scheduling of activities, and continuous information as to their residence), the Act bore so directly on our foreign relations as to make it evident that Congress intended only one uniform national alien registration system....

Arizona v. United States

567 U.S. ___ (2012)

In response to the large number of undocumented aliens within its borders, Arizona enacted the Support our Law Enforcement and Safe Neighborhoods Act (also known as S.B. 1070) in 2010. The United States filed suit again the Act, claiming that four of its key provisions were preempted by federal law. These included making it a violation of state law to fail to comply with federal alien-registration requirements (Section 3) and to seek or engage in work in the State if undocumented (Section 5), and authorizing state and local law enforcement officers to make warrantless arrests of persons they have probable cause to believe are deportable (Section 6) and to require the verification of a person's immigration status during a stop, detention, or arrest if they have reason to believe the person is undocumented (Section 2(B)). A federal district court issued a preliminary injunction preventing the four provisions from going into effect, and the Court of Appeals for the Ninth Circuit affirmed.

JUSTICE KENNEDY delivered the opinion of the Court.

. . .

II.

A.

The Government of the United States has broad, undoubted power over the subject of immigration and the status of aliens.... This authority rests, in part, on the National Government's constitutional power to "establish an uniform Rule of Naturalization,"... and its inherent power as sovereign to control and conduct relations with foreign nations....

The federal power to determine immigration policy is well settled. Immigration policy can affect trade, investment, tourism, and diplomatic relations for the entire Nation, as well as the perceptions and expectations of aliens in this country who seek the full protection of its laws.... Perceived mistreatment of aliens in the United States may lead to harmful reciprocal treatment of American citizens abroad....

It is fundamental that foreign countries concerned about the status, safety, and security of their nationals in the United States must be able to confer and communicate on this subject with one national sovereign, no the 50 separate states....

Federal governance of immigration and alien status is extensive and complex. [*Kennedy describes the various federal law provisions governing immigration and alien status.*]

. . .

Discretion in the enforcement of immigration law embraces immediate human concerns. Unauthorized workers trying to support their families, for example, likely pose less danger than alien smugglers or aliens who commit a serious crime. The equities of an individual case may turn on many factors, in-

cluding whether the alien has children born in the United States, long ties to the community, or a record of distinguished military service. Some discretionary decisions involve policy choices that bear on the Nation's international relations....

. . .

B

The pervasiveness of federal regulation does not diminish the importance of immigration policy to the States. [*Kennedy outlines the impact on Arizona of "[h]undreds of thousands of deportable aliens" in the state.*]

These concerns are the background for the formal legal analysis that follows. The issue is whether, under preemption principles, federal law permits Arizona to implement the state-law provisions in dispute.

III.

Federalism, central to the constitutional design, adopts the principle that both the National and State Governments have elements of sovereignty the other is bound to respect.... From the existence of two sovereigns follows the possibility that laws can be in conflict or at cross purposes. The Supremacy Clause provides a clear rule that federal law "shall be the supreme Law of the Land; and the Judges in every State shall be bound thereby, any Thing in the Constitution or Laws of any State to the Contrary notwithstanding." Art.VI, cl. 2. Under this principle, Congress has the power to preempt state law.... There is no doubt that Congress may withdraw specified powers from the States by enacting a statute containing an express preemption provision.... [*The Court reviews the tests for preemption, noting that Congress' framework of regulation may be so pervasive that it leaves no room for state regulation, that the fed-*

eral interest may be so dominant that it precludes state laws on the subject, and that state laws may interfere with the ability to enforce the federal law.]

IV.A

Section 3 ... forbids the "willful failure to complete or carry an alien registration document." ... In effect, [it] adds a state law penalty for conduct prescribed by federal law....

. . .

The framework enacted by Congress leads to the conclusion here, ... that the Federal Government has occupied the field of alien registration.... The federal statutory directives provide a full set of standards governing alien registration, including the punishment for noncompliance.... Where Congress occupies an entire field, as it has in the field of alien registration, even complementary state regulation is impermissible....

Federal law makes a single sovereign responsible for maintaining a comprehensive and unified system to keep track of aliens within the Nation's borders. If [this section] were valid, every State could give itself independent authority to prosecute federal registration violations, "diminish[ing] the [Federal Government]'s control over enforcement" and "detract[ing] from the 'integrated scheme of regulation' created by Congress." ...

B

[Section 5] enacts a state criminal prohibition where no federal counterpart exists. The provision makes it a state misdemeanor for "an unauthorized alien to knowingly apply for work, solicit work in a public place or perform work as an employee or independent contractor" in Arizona.... Violations will be punished by a $2,500 fine and incarceration for up to six months.... The United States contends that the provision upsets the balance struck by the Immigration Reform and Control Act of 1986 (IRCA) and must be preempted as an obstacle to the federal plan of regulation and control.

When there was no comprehensive federal program regulating the employment of unauthorized aliens, this Court found that a State had authority to pass its own laws on the subject.... [In *DeCanas v. Bica,* in 1976, the Court] recognized that "States possess broad authority under their police powers to regulate the employment relationship to protect workers within the State." ... At that point, however, the Federal Government had expressed no more than "a peripheral concern with [the] employment of illegal entrants." ...

. . .

The legislative background of IRCA underscores the fact that Congress made a deliberate choice not to impose criminal penalties on aliens who seek, or engage in, unauthorized employment.... In the end, IRCA's framework reflects a considered judgment that making criminals out of aliens engaged in unauthorized work — aliens who already face the possibility of employer exploitation because of their removable status — would be inconsistent with federal policy and objectives....

The ordinary principles of preemption include the well-settled proposition that a state law is preempted where it "stands as an obstacle to the accomplishment and execution of the full purposes and objectives of Congress." ... Arizona law would interfere with the careful balance struck by Congress with respect to unauthorized employment of aliens....

C.

Section 6 ... provides that a state office, "without a warrant, may arrest a person if the officer has probable cause to believe ... [the person] has committed any public offense that makes [him] removable from the United States." ... The United States argues that arrests authorized by this statute would be an obstacle to the removal system Congress created.

. . .

Section 6 attempts to provide state officers even greater authority to arrest aliens on the basis of possible removability than Congress has given to trained federal immigration officers. Under state law, officers who believe an alien is removable by reason of some "public offense" would have the power to conduct an arrest on that basis regardless of whether a federal warrant has issued or the alien is likely to escape. This state authority could be exercised without any input from the Federal Government about whether an arrest is warranted in a particular case. This would allow the State to achieve its own immigration policy. The result would be unnecessary harassment of some aliens (for instance, a veteran, college student, or someone assisting with a criminal investigation) whom federal officials determine should not be removed.

. . .

D.

Section 2(B) of S.B. 1070 requires state officers to make a "reasonable attempt ... to determine the immigration status" of any person they stop, detain, or arrest on some other legitimate basis if "reasonable suspicion exists that the person is an alien and is unlawfully present in the United States." ... The law also provides that "[a]ny person who is arrested shall have the person's immigration status determined before the person is released." ... The accepted way to perform these status checks is to contact ICE, which maintains a database of immigration records.

Three limits are built into the state provisions. First, a detainee is presumed not to be an alien unlawfully present in the United States if he or she provides a valid Arizona driver's license or similar identification. Second, officers "may not consider race, color or national origin ... except to the extent permitted by the United States [and] Arizona Constitution[s]." ... Third, the provisions must be "implemented in a manner consistent with federal law regulating immigration, protecting the civil rights of all persons and respecting the privileges and immunities of United States citizens." ...

1.

Consultation between federal and state officials is an important feature of the immigration system. Congress has made clear that no formal agreement or special training needs to be in place for state officers to "communicate with the [Federal Government] regarding the immigration status of any individual, including reporting knowledge that a particular alien is not lawfully present in the United States." ... And Congress has obligated ICE to respond to any request made by state officials for verification of a person's citizenship or immigration status.... ICE's Law Enforcement Support Center operates "24 hours a day, seven days a week, 365 days a year" and provides, among other things, "immigration status, identity information and real-time assistance to local, state, and federal law enforcement agencies." ...

. . .

Congress had done nothing to suggest it is inappropriate to communicate with ICE in these situations.... Indeed, it has encouraged the sharing of information about possible immigration violations.... The federal scheme thus leaves room for a policy requiring state officials to contact ICE as a routine matter....

2.

. . .

The nature and timing of this case counsel cau-

tion in evaluating the validity of [this section.] The Federal Government has brought suit against a sovereign State to challenge the provision even before the law has gone into effect. There is a basic uncertainty about what the law means and how it will be enforced. At this stage, without the benefit of a definitive interpretation from the state courts, it would be inappropriate to assume [the section] will be construed in a way that creates a conflict with federal law.

. . .

The judgment of the Court of Appeals for the Ninth Circuit is affirmed in part and reversed in part. The case is remanded for further proceedings consistent with this opinion.

It is so ordered.

Justice Kagan took no part in the consideration or decision in this case.

Justice Scalia, concurring in part and dissenting in part.

The United States is an indivisible "Union of Sovereign States." ... Today's opinion ... deprives States of what most would consider the defining characteristic of sovereignty: the power to exclude from the sovereign's territory people who have no right to be there. Neither the Constitution itself nor even any law passed by Congress supports this result. I dissent.

. . .

In light of the predominance of federal immigration restriction in modern times, it is easy to lose sight of the States' traditional role in regulating immigration—and to overlook their sovereign prerogative to do so. I accept as a given that State regulation is excluded by the Constitution when (1) it has been prohibited by a valid federal law, or (2) it conflicts with federal regulation—when, for example, it admits those whom federal regulation would exclude, or excludes those whom federal regulation would admit. [*Scalia thinks neither of these situations exists here.*]

[*Scalia rejects the argument that the concerns of foreign countries must be taken into account.*] Even in its international relations, the Federal Government must live with the inconvenient fact that it is a Union of independent States, who have their own sovereign powers. This is not the first time it has found that a nuisance and a bother in the conduct of foreign policy.... Though it may upset foreign powers—and even when the Federal Government desperately wants to avoid upsetting foreign powers—the States have a right to protect their borders against foreign nationals, just as they have the right to execute foreign nationals for murder.

. . .

[*Noting the federal government's claim that it needs discretion to allocate enforcement resources wisely, Scalia critiques the Obama administration's 2012 decision to stop deportation of qualified undocumented young people.*] The Court opinion's looming specter of inutterable horror—[that every state would have its own separate immigration policy]— seems to me not so horrible and even less looming. But there has come to pass, and is with us today, the specter that Arizona and the States that support it predicted: A Federal Government that does not want to enforce the immigration laws as written, and leaves the States' borders unprotected against immi-

grants whom those laws would exclude. So the issue is a stark one. Are the sovereign States at the mercy of the Federal Executive's refusal to enforce the Nation's immigration laws?

. . .

JUSTICE THOMAS concurring in part and dissenting in part.

[*Thomas sees "no conflict between the 'ordinary meanin[g]" of the relevant federal laws and that of the four provisions of Arizona law...."*]

JUSTICE ALITO, concurring in part and dissenting in part.

[*Alito agrees that Section 2(B) is not pre-empted and that Section 3 is preempted. He disagrees that Section 5(C) and Section 6 are preempted.*]

I. NATIONALIZATION OF THE BILL OF RIGHTS

Two months before the first Congress met, James Madison supported constitutional amendments to provide "for all essential rights, particularly the rights of Conscience in the fullest latitude, the freedom of the press, trials by jury, security against general warrants &c." 5 The Writings of James Madison 320 (letter to George Eve, January 2, 1789). The responsibility for moving these amendments through the House of Representatives fell to Madison, who argued that a Bill of Rights would remove apprehensions that the people felt toward the new national government. 1 Annals of Congress 431–33 (1789). He also wanted to place restrictions on the states and proposed that "[n]o State shall violate the equal rights of conscience, of the freedom of the press, or the trial by jury in criminal cases." Id. at 435. The states "are as liable to attack these invaluable privileges as the General Government...." Id. at 441. As finally drafted and ratified, however, the first ten amendments to the Constitution— the Bill of Rights—limited only the federal government.

In 1833, the Supreme Court reaffirmed that the Bill of Rights restrained only the federal government, not the states. At issue was the Just Compensation Clause of the Fifth Amendment. Barron v. Baltimore, 32 U.S. (7 Pet.) 243. The same conclusion was reached by the Court 25 years later. Withers v. Buckley, 20 How. (61 U.S.) 84, 89–90 (1858). However, the Civil War and passage of the Fourteenth Amendment in 1868 worked a fundamental change in federal-state relations. The Amendment prohibited states from making or enforcing any law "which shall abridge the privileges or immunities of citizens of the United States; nor shall any State deprive any person of life, liberty, or property, without due process of law; nor deny to any person within its jurisdiction the equal protection of the laws." The Due Process Clause would become the vehicle for applying most of the Bill of Rights to the states.

The idea of imposing a national standard on the states was rejected by the Supreme Court in 1873 when it held that the primary purpose of the Civil War amendments (the Thirteenth, Fourteenth, and Fifteenth Amendments) was to guarantee freedom for blacks. Moreover, privileges and immunities were to be protected by the states, not the national government. Slaughter-House Cases, 16 Wall. 36, 77–79. Other decisions during this period also refused to apply the Bill of Rights to the states.[15] How-

---

15. Pervear v. Commonwealth, 5 Wall. (72 U.S.) 475 (1867); Twitchell v. The Commonwealth, 7 Wall. (74 U.S.) 321 (1869); The Justices v. Murray, 9 Wall. (76 U.S.) 274 (1870); Walker v. Sauvinet, 92 U.S. (2 Otto.) 90, 92 (1876); United

ever, the Equal Protection Clause of the Fourteenth Amendment was available to prevent states from acting in a discriminatory or arbitrary manner. Yick Wo v. Hopkins, 118 U.S. 356 (1886).

The Incorporation Doctrine

By the end of the century, the Court had decided that certain portions of the Bill of Rights should be applied to the states. The Court began with the Just Compensation Clause of the Fifth Amendment, reflecting the judiciary's commitment at that time to business and corporate interests. Missouri Pacific Railway Co. v. Nebraska, 164 U.S. 403 (1896); Chicago, B. & Q. Railway Co. v. Chicago, 166 U.S. 226 (1897). Thus began the process of "incorporating" the Bill of Rights into the Due Process Clause of the Fourteenth Amendment and extending these guarantees to the states. Although in 1904 the Court held that the Confrontation Clause of the Sixth Amendment did not apply to the states (West v. Louisiana, 194 U.S. 258), and four years later refused to extend the Self-Incrimination Clause of the Fifth Amendment to the states (Twining v. New Jersey, 211 U.S. 78), within a few decades the Court began the step-by-step process of bringing the states under the Bill of Rights. Almost every provision of the Bill of Rights now covers the states (see Table 8.2). In 2010 the Court revived the incorporation doctrine when it ruled that the Second Amendment right to bear arms was applicable to the states as well as the federal government. McDonald v. Chicago, 561 U.S. ___ (2010). This process is sometimes called the doctrine of absorption or the selective incorporation of the Bill of Rights.

Selective incorporation reflects a contest between two schools of thought. The second Justice Harlan believed that courts have a duty to see that due process follows principles consistent with the people's "traditions and conscience." In re Gault, 387 U.S. 1, 67 (1967). Justice Black opposed this philosophy because it requires judges to impose personal notions of natural law. Duncan v. Louisiana, 391 U.S. 145, 168 (1968). To limit judicial activism, at least in the incremental form supported by Harlan, Black promoted the wholesale incorporation of the Bill of Rights. Adamson v. California, 332 U.S. 46, 75 (1947). Ironically, Black's activism probably exceeded Harlan's. Almost all of the Bill of Rights has been incorporated, with little opposition from contemporary members of the Supreme Court (see Rehnquist's testimony).

The selective incorporation of the Bill of Rights does not always mean that a national standard has been forced upon the states. For example, the First Amendment applies to all states, and yet court rulings on obscenity allow wide discretion to accommodate local community standards. Miller v. California, 413 U.S. 15, 30–34 (1973). The right to a jury trial applies to the states, but states are at liberty to depart from federal standards by establishing juries with less than twelve members and by accepting nonunanimous verdicts (chapter 13). Also, state courts can insulate themselves from national standards by basing their rulings not on the U.S. Constitution but on rights guaranteed in their state constitutions. State courts are able to interpret individual liberties more expansively than the federal government. PruneYard Shopping Center v. Robins, 447 U.S. 74, 81 (1980); Collins et al., 13 Hast. Const. L. Q. 599 (1986). Other chapters offer specific examples in which state courts, relying on their own constitutions, reject constitutional doctrines advanced by the U.S. Supreme Court.

States v. Cruikshank, 92 U.S. 542, 552 (1876); Hurtado v. California, 110 U.S. 516, 538 (1884); Presser v. Illinois, 116 U.S. 252, 265 (1886); Spies v. Illinois, 123 U.S. 131, 166 (1887); In re Kemmler, 136 U.S. 436, 446 (1890); McElvaine v. Brush, 142 U.S. 155, 158 (1891); O'Neil v. Vermont, 144 U.S. 323, 332 (1892). See also Maxwell v. Dow, 176 U.S. 581 (1900), which declined to apply the guarantees of the Fifth and Sixth Amendments to the states.

TABLE 8.2 INCORPORATION OF BILL OF RIGHTS

Amendment	Clause	Decision
First	Congress shall make no law respecting an establishment of religion,...	Everson v. Board of Education, 330 U.S. 1, 15 (1947).
	or prohibiting the free exercise thereof;...	Cantwell v. Connecticut, 310 U.S. 296, 303 (1940).
	or abridging the freedom of speech,...	Gitlow v. New York, 268 U.S. 652, 666 (1925); Fiske v. Kansas, 274 U.S. 380, 387 (1927).
	or of the press;...	Near v. Minnesota, 283 U.S. 697, 707 (1931). See also Gitlow v. New York, 268 U.S. 652, 666 (1925).
	or the right of the people peaceably to assemble, and to petition the Government for a redress of grievances.	DeJonge v. Oregon, 299 U.S. 352, 364 (1937).
Second	A well regulated Militia, being necessary to the security of a free State, the right of the people to keep and bear arms, shall not be infringed.	McDonald v. Chicago, 561 U.S. ___ (2010).
Third	No soldier shall, in time of peace be quartered in any house, without the consent of the Owner, nor in time of war, but in a manner to be prescribed by law.	—
Fourth	The right of the people to be secure in their persons, houses, papers, and effects, against unreasonable searches and seizures, shall not be violated, and no Warrants shall issue, but upon probable cause, supported by Oath or affirmation, and particularly describing the place to be searched, and the persons or things to be seized.	Wolf v. Colorado, 338 U.S. 25, 27–28 (1949); Mapp v. Ohio, 367 U.S. 643, 655 (1961); Ker v. California, 374 U.S. 23 (1963).
Fifth	No person shall be held to answer for a capital, or otherwise infamous crime, unless on a presentment or indictment of a Grand Jury, except in cases arising in the land or naval forces, or in the Militia, when in actual service in time of War or public danger;...	—
	nor shall any person be subject for the same offence to be twice put in jeopardy of life or limb;...	Benton v. Maryland, 395 U.S. 784, 787 (1969).
	nor shall be compelled in any Criminal Case to be a witness against himself;...	Malloy v. Hogan, 378 U.S. 1, 3 (1964).
	nor be deprived of life, liberty, or property, without due process of law;...	[Parallel to Fourteenth Amendment.]
	nor shall private property be taken for public use, without just compensation.	Missouri Pacific Railway Co. v. Nebraska, 164 U.S. 403, 417 (1896); Chicago, B. & Q. R.R. Co. v. Chicago, 166 U.S. 226, 241 (1897).

TABLE 8.2 INCORPORATION OF BILL OF RIGHTS CONTINUED

Amendment	Clause	Decision
Sixth	In all criminal prosecutions, the accused shall enjoy the right to a speedy and public trial,...	In re Oliver, 333 U.S. 257, 273 (1948) [right to public trial] and Klopfer v. North Carolina, 386 U.S. 213, 222 (1967) [right to speedy trial].
	by an impartial jury of the State and district wherein the crime shall have been committed, which district shall have been previously ascertained by law, and to be informed of the nature and cause of the accusation;...	Duncan v. Louisiana, 391 U.S. 145, 149 (1968); Parker v. Gladden, 385 U.S. 363–64 (1966). See also Irvin v. Dowd, 366 U.S. 717 (1961) and Turner v. Louisiana, 379 U.S. 466 (1965).
	to be confronted with the witness against him;...	Pointer v. Texas, 380 U.S. 400, 403 (1965).
	to have compulsory process for obtaining witnesses in his favor;...	Washington v. Texas, 388 U.S. 14, 19 (1967).
	and to have the Assistance of Counsel for his defence.	Powell v. Alabama, 287 U.S. 45, 67–68 (1932) [counsel for young and illiterate in a capital case]; Gideon v. Wainright, 372 U.S. 335, 344 (1963) [counsel for felony trials]; Douglas v. California, 372 U.S. 353, 357–58 (1963) [counsel for first appeals]; Argersinger v. Hamlin, 407 U.S. 25 (1972) [counsel for felony or misdemeanor trials involving jail term].
Seventh	In suits at common law, where the value in Controversy shall exceed twenty dollars, the right of trial by jury shall be preserved, and no fact tried by a jury, shall be otherwise re-examined in any Court of the United States, than according to the rules of the common law.	—
Eighth	Excessive bail shall not be required...	Schilb v. Kuebel, 404 U.S. 357, 365 (1971).
	nor excessive fines imposed...	—
	nor cruel and unusual punishment inflicted.	Robinson v. California, 370 U.S. 660, 666 (1962).
Ninth	The enumeration in the Constitution, of certain rights, shall not be construed to deny or disparage others retained by the people.	Griswold v. Connecticut, 381 U.S. 479 484 (1965) [also invoked other parts of the Bill of Rights].
Tenth	The powers not delegated to the United States by the Constitution, nor prohibited by it to the States, are reserved to the States respectively, or to the people.	—

The Incorporation Doctrine:
Testimony by Justice Rehnquist

In 1986, during Senate hearings for his nomination for Chief Justice of the Supreme Court, Justice Rehnquist was asked by Senator Arlen Specter about the "incorporation doctrine": the gradual incorporation of the Bill of Rights into the Due Process Clause of the Fourteenth Amendment to be applied against the states. Originally, the Bill of Rights restricted only the federal government. Attorney General Edwin Meese III, as one of the more vocal critics of the incorporation doctrine, had written that "nowhere else has the principle of Federalism been dealt such a politically violent and constitutionally suspect blow as by the theory of incorporation." Meese, "The Supreme Court of the United States: Bulwark of a Limited Constitution," 27 So. Tex. L. Rev. 455, 463–64 (1986). The testimony below comes from "Nomination of Justice William Hubbs Rehnquist," hearings before the Senate Committee on the Judiciary, 99th Cong., 2d Sess., 191–92, 350–51, 356 (1986).

Justice Rehnquist.... [I]f you are looking at the language of the due process clause, as I recall it, Senator, it says: "No State shall deprive any person of life, liberty or property without due process of law."

And the question then becomes, you know, as you know perfectly well, what is included under liberty, or, what provisions from the Bill of Rights are carried over by that language? And I would say that, from the language itself, it is not evident that any particular provisions are carried over, not inexorable; but if you look at the word liberty, and you wonder what kind of liberty are they talking about, surely one liberty was freedom of speech, freedom of the press.

So, it seems to me it is quite natural to carry those over. But I do not know that the language of the due process clause, nor necessarily, what I happen to recall about the debates, and that sort of thing, necessarily indicates that the full rigors of the first amendment as applied to Congress, necessarily were to be applied to the States.

Senator Specter. Well, the difficulty with that, it seems to me—and I am just probing to get your line of reasoning on it—is that it is so speculative. If you are picking out a portion of the first amendment, the freedom of speech—if you seek to avoid putting your own personal views, as they arise in a case, which I know you have testified in the 1971 proceedings, that you are very much opposed to—how can you really separate the various aspects of something as fundamental as speech?

Isn't it really all in there? Once you say that the due process clause incorporates freedom of speech under the first amendment, isn't that all there is to it? How can you separate any of it out as not incorporated?

Justice Rehnquist. Well, if you say that the due process clause incorporates and makes applicable against the States, the first amendment in haec verba, so to speak, the question is answered. If it does that, it does carry it over in precisely the terms that it is applicable to Congress against the State.

But I think the argument on the other side, is that—and I think this is made very well in Justice Jackson's dissent in the *Beauharnais* case—is that there was a good deal of understanding of what freedom of speech meant at the time the Constitution was adopted, that was undoubtedly applicable against the States, but that there were perhaps slightly more latitude allowed to the States than were allowed to the Federal Government.

Justice Harlan took that position in his opinion in the *Roth* case. That the States could proscribe certain kinds of obscenity but that the Federal Government could not.

Senator Specter. Mr. Justice Rehnquist, at the risk of asking questions which may come before the Court, I think these are pretty well established principles, but, there is considerable concern on the part of this Senator about the applicability of the due process clause of the 14th amendment to certain fundamental liberties, as embodied in the first 10 amendments.

And I would like to ask your view as to the inclusion of the free exercise of religion in *Cantwell* v. *Connecticut*. It was a unanimous opinion. Does that matter rest, so far as you are concerned?

Justice Rehnquist. Most certainly, yes.

Senator Specter. And the establishment clause in *Everson* v. *Board of Education*?

Justice Rehnquist. No. I think I criticized the *Everson* case in my dissent in Wallace against Jaffrey, not for the result it reached at all, but for its use of the term "wall of separation between church and state," which I felt was simply not historically justified....

Senator Specter.... Is there any question in your

mind that the due process clause of the 14th amendment incorporates freedom of speech?

Justice REHNQUIST. Other than the point I made yesterday. It, obviously, incorporates freedom of speech. I took the position in a couple of opinions I wrote in following Justice Jackson and Justice Harlan that some of the details might be different as applied against the States as opposed to the Federal Government.

Senator SPECTER. Would you repeat the distinction you see as to the scope of the due process clause incorporating the establishment clause of the first amendment?

Justice REHNQUIST. No; I think that is settled by the *Everson* case.

Senator SPECTER. All right.

There is no question that the due process clause of the 14th amendment incorporates freedom of the press under the first amendment?

Justice REHNQUIST. I do not think so.

Senator SPECTER. Are the rights of assembly and petition incorporated by the due process clause of the 14th amendment?

Justice REHNQUIST. Yes; I think they are.

Senator SPECTER. Is the search and seizure clause of the fourth amendment incorporated by the due process clause of the fourteenth amendment?

Justice REHNQUIST. That was held in *Mapp* v. *Ohio.*

Senator SPECTER. Do you agree with that? Do you believe it is a decided matter?

Justice REHNQUIST. It is certainly a settled matter, yes.

Senator SPECTER. Is double jeopardy under the fifth amendment incorporated in the due process clause of the 14th amendment?

Justice REHNQUIST. I think that was in the—Senator, I am going to draw back a little. Because in a case like *Benton* v. *Maryland* that came to the Court where—before I got there. I did not participate in that case. I have followed *Benton* v. *Maryland* many times when I have been on the Court. But to say whether I agree with a case that was decided before I came on the Court, I think it is better to phrase it that my record in voting on the case has certainly shown that I have followed that case.

Senator SPECTER. Well, I am not asking whether you agree with it. I am asking whether you consider it a settled issue that the incorporation doctrine covers that issue.

The concern I have is whether the incorporation doctrine is going to be undercut. Although I do not think that you and I have any difference of opinion on this, I just want to be sure.

Justice REHNQUIST. I think in a case—I cannot remember—a case coming up from Montana, I took the—Justice Stewart joined my opinion, I joined Justice Stewart's opinion—saying that some of the nuances of the double jeopardy clause should not apply the same to the States as to the Federal Government.

I think this was a case involving when the trial started, for the purposes of—when jeopardy attached. And the rule in the Federal cases was when a witness is first sworn. But Montana had a wholly different procedure. And it just seemed that a fair translation of the Federal rule to the State rule would not give you an identical situation....

Senator SPECTER. ... I had gone through a number of the provisions of the Bill of Rights on the incorporation doctrine, Mr. Justice Rehnquist, because I think it is important to lay to rest the conclusion that the 14th amendment due process clause does incorporate certain provisions of the Bill of Rights.

I have only gone over the ones which have been incorporated. I have not gone into the ones which have not been, because I do not want to move into a lot of areas of the law which are not settled.

There are two remaining areas I want to ask you about. Do you regard it as settled law that the speedy trial provision is incorporated under the due process clause of the 14th amendment?

Justice REHNQUIST. Yes, I think that is settled law, and my opinions reflect it.

Senator SPECTER. What about the cruel and unusual punishment provision of the eighth amendment, is that incorporated into the due process clause of the 14th amendment?

Justice REHNQUIST. Again, my opinions reflect the fact.

CONCLUSIONS

Areas in which state and local governments were once virtually supreme, including agriculture, mining, manufacturing, and labor, eventually gave way to federal controls when transportation systems and economic markets assumed a national character. Over time, much of intrastate commerce became interstate commerce. Issues long identified with local government, including education, health, welfare, and law enforcement, are now largely a matter of federal-state cooperation. The federal taxing power, magnified by the Sixteenth Amendment and the income tax, ushered in hundreds of federal grant programs.

The Supreme Court likes to characterize itself as a guardian of federalism, but its doctrines in this area are often vague and unworkable. One scholar, Mark Tushnet, remarked: "Every time the Supreme Court has wandered into the federalism forest, it has gotten lost." 47 Vand. L. Rev. 1623, 1624 (1994). Moreover, the Court's incorporation doctrine has done much to undermine state independence and to centralize national power.

Although litigation continues to define federal-state relations, it operates mostly at the margins. Basic questions of federalism are left to the determination of Congress. During his confirmation hearings in 1986 to be Associate Justice to the Supreme Court, Antonin Scalia testified that "the primary defender of the constitutional balance, the Federal Government versus the states ... the primary institution to strike the right balance is the Congress.... On the basis of the court's past decisions ... the main protection for that is in the policymaking area, is in the Congress. The court's struggles to prescribe what is the proper role of the Federal Government vis-à-vis the State have essentially been abandoned for quite a while." "Nomination of Judge Antonin Scalia," hearings before the Senate Committee on the Judiciary, 99th Cong., 2d Sess., 8182 (1986).

Scalia testified one year after the Court, in *Garcia,* seemed to signal that it would no longer intervene to police the boundaries between the national government and the states, but would leave that determination chiefly to Congress. Nonetheless, beginning in the 1990s, the Court reentered the field to challenge congressional statutes and to breathe new life into the Tenth Amendment and the Eleventh Amendment. A new era of "dual federalism" appeared to have begun, although the Court was closely divided on these questions. When Chief Justice Rehnquist died and Justice O'Connor retired, the Court lost perhaps its two strongest advocates for state power and in recent years has seemed more favorably inclined toward federal power, although the five person majority finding that the Affordable Care Act exceeded Congress's Commerce authority suggests a Court unprepared to allow that authority to expand any further.

NOTES AND QUESTIONS

1. How should we understand the "elastic nature" of the Necessary and Proper Clause, as viewed by Marshall in *McCulloch v. Maryland*? What are the implications for federalism?

2. *Gibbons v. Ogden* has been referred to as the "Magna Carta of Interstate Commerce." What accounts for its stature? Have Marshall's definitions of "commerce" weathered the passage of time? Why or why not?

3. Is *Wickard v. Filburn* consistent with Marshall's reasoning in *Gibbons* v. *Ogden*? Do both rulings rest on the concept of "plenary" congressional power over commerce, or did *Filburn* represent a departure from *Gibbons v. Ogden*? Are you persuaded that the individual mandate in the 2010 health care bill can be distinguished from the regulation in *Wickard*?

4. Explain the concept of "dual federalism." What role has it played in Supreme Court decisions? In your view, does it possess constitutional merit? What is its currency today?

5. What does it mean to say, as Chief Justice Stone does in *United States v. Darby,* that the Tenth Amendment is a "truism"?

6. Can the interpretations of Congress's Commerce power in *Gonzales v. Raich* and *National Federation of Independent Business* be reconciled? Why might traditional defenders of state's rights like Justice Scalia support federal regulation of marijuana and assisted suicide but not an individual mandate for health care?

7. Should states impacted by large numbers of undocumented immigrants be permitted to pass immigration laws like Arizona's? What are the best arguments for federal preemption and what are the best ones for allowing states to act?

SELECTED READINGS

ABRAMS, KATHRYN. "On Reading and Using the Tenth Amendment." 93 Yale Law Journal 723 (1984).

ADLER, MATTHEW D. AND SETH F. KREIMER. "The New Etiquette of Federalism: New York, Printz, and Yeskey." 1998 Supreme Court Review 71.

ALFANGE, DEAN, JR. "Congressional Regulation of the 'States Qua States': From National League of Cities to EEOC v. Wyoming." 1983 Supreme Court Review 215.

BANKS, CHRISTOPHER AND JOHN BLAKEMAN. "Chief Justice Roberts, Justice Alito, and New Federalism Jurisprudence." 38 Publius: The Journal of Federalism 576 (2008).

BRENNAN, WILLIAM J., JR. "The Bill of Rights and the States." 36 New York University Law Review 761 (1961).

BRIGHTON, ROBERT CHARLES, JR. "Separating Myth from Reality in Federalism Decisions: A Perspective of American Federalism — Past and Present." 35 Vanderbilt Law Review 161 (1982).

CORWIN, EDWARD S. The Commerce Power Versus States' Rights. Princeton, N.J.: Princeton University Press, 1936.

———. "The Passing of Dual Federalism." 36 Virginia Law Review 1 (1950).

DINAN, JOHN. "Shaping Health Care Reform: State Government Influence in the Patient Protection and Affordable Care Act." 41 Publius: The Journal of Federalism 395 (Summer 2011).

FISHER, LOUIS. "How the States Shape Constitutional Law." 15 State Legislatures 37 (August 1989).

GIBBONS, JOHN J. "The Eleventh Amendment and State Sovereign Immunity: A Reinterpretation." 83 Columbia Law Review 1889 (1983).

HOWARD, A.E. DICK. "The States and the Supreme Court." 31 Catholic University Law Review 380 (1982).

KRAMER, LARRY D. "Putting the Politics Back into the Political Safeguards of Federalism." 100 Columbia Law Review 215 (2000).

LACROIX, ALISON L. The Ideological Origins of American Federalism. Cambridge, MA: Harvard University Press, 2010.

LESSIG, LAWRENCE. "Translating Federalism: United States v. Lopez," 1995 Supreme Court Review 125.

LOFGREN, CHARLES A. "The Origins of the Tenth Amendment: History, Sovereignty, and the Problem of Constitutional Intention," in Ronald K.L. Collins, ed., Constitutional Government in America. Durham, N.C.: Carolina Academic Press, 1980.

MERRITT, DEBORAH JONES. "Commerce!," 94 Michigan Law Review 674 (1995).

MICHELMAN, FRANK I. "States' Rights and States' Roles: Permutations of 'Sovereignty' in National League of Cities v. Usery." 86 Yale Law Journal 1165 (1977).

MILLER, LISA. The Perils of Federalism: Race, Poverty, and the Politics of Crime Control. New York: Oxford University Press, 2008.

MORRISON, STANLEY. "Does the Fourteenth Amendment Incorporate the Bill of Rights?" 2 Stanford Law Review 140 (1949).

NAGEL, ROBERT F. "Federalism as a Fundamental Value: National League of Cities in Perspective." 1981 Supreme Court Review 81.

NEUBORNE, BURT. "The Myth of Parity." 90 Harvard Law Review 1105 (1977).

ROBERTSON, DAVID BRIAN. Federalism and the Making of America. New York: Routledge, 2012.

SHAPIRO, DAVID L. "Wrong Terms: The Eleventh Amendment and the Pennhurst Case." 98 Harvard Law Review 61 (1984).

VILE, M.J.C. The Structure of American Federalism. London: Oxford University Press, 1961.

WELLS, MICHAEL. "The Role of Comity in the Law of Federal Courts." 60 North Carolina Law Review 59 (1981).

WISE, CHARLES AND ROSEMARY O'LEARY. "Is Federalism Dead or Alive in the Supreme Court? Implications for Public Administrators." 52 Public Administration Review 559 (1992).

9

Economic Liberties

From the late nineteenth century to the 1930s, the courts struck down efforts by Congress and state legislatures to ease the harshness of industrial conditions. Statutes that established maximum hours or minimum wages were declared unconstitutional interferences with property rights, due process, and a judicially created "liberty of contract." State legislatures had relied on the "police power" to protect public health and safety. In many of these cases the courts held that government existed to protect life, liberty, and property, with property accorded the greatest protection. Over those decades the judiciary promoted a narrow definition of property and restricted the government's ability to protect the health and safety of citizens. This chapter analyzes two other issues involving economic rights: the Contract Clause (prohibiting states from impairing the obligation of contracts) and the Taking Clause (providing that private property shall not be taken for public use without just compensation).

A. THE MEANING OF PROPERTY

Few words evoke more powerful emotions than *property.* Pierre Proudhon, the French anarchist of the nineteenth century, equated property with theft. Jesus warned that it would be easier for a camel to pass through the eye of a needle than for a rich man to enter the kingdom of God. Others elevated property to a position of reverence and respect. Machiavelli advised a prince not to take property, for "men forget more easily the death of their father than the loss of their patrimony."

We are taught from childhood to think of property as tangible objects: land, buildings, personal property, business, and wealth. The word itself, however, suggests a larger meaning. It derives from *proprius,* which means something private or peculiar to oneself. This general concept embraces intangible possessions, including reputation, ideas, and religious opinions. As a result of court decisions in recent decades, property rights have expanded to cover welfare payments, job rights, garnishment procedures, unemployment compensation, and environmental rights. Property in America acquires specific meaning from custom, statutes, and court decisions.

Property, as a legal creation, fluctuates in meaning over time. Before the War of Independence, a landed aristocracy in America gained protection from *entail* (making land inalienable) and *primogeniture* (transferring land to the eldest son). Gradually those laws were abolished. Up until the Civil War, property extended to black slaves, who were auctioned off at the market, bought and sold as human merchandise. Congress enacted fugitive slave laws to return "property" to its owners. In the *Dred Scott* case, Chief Justice Taney said that the right of property in a slave was "distinctly and expressly affirmed in the Constitution. The right to traffic in it, like an ordinary article of merchandise and property, was guaranteed to the citizens of the United States, in every State that might desire it, for twenty years." Dred Scott v. Sandford, 60 U.S. 393, 451 (1857).

Well into the twentieth century, the courts continued to treat wives as the property of the husband. The concept of *coverture,* described by Blackstone more than two centuries ago, maintained its influence. Upon marriage, a woman's legal existence was submerged into that of the husband. Marriage made husband and wife "one person in law." Under the husband's "wing, protection, and *cover,* she performs every thing." Performance included availability for sex, making it legally impossible in some states for a man to rape his wife. Adultery with a man's wife was considered a violation of the *husband's* property rights. Tinker v. Colwell, 193 U.S. 473 (1904).

Locke and Madison

To the framers of the Constitution, property had a broad meaning. They knew that when John Locke spoke of property, he meant "lives, liberties and estates"—not simply the latter. To Locke, individuals possessed property in their persons as well as in their goods. Every man had a property in the labor of his body and the work of his hands. The act of labor invested part of one's personality in an object.

James Madison developed a comprehensive view of property. In Federalist No. 10, he spoke of the "diversity in the faculties of men, from which the rights of property originate." Because mankind consists of different and unequal faculties, different and unequal kinds of property result. But Madison did not say that the most important function of government was to protect property. Rather, the "protection of these faculties is the first object of government." Consistent with that notion, the Constitution authorizes Congress to "promote the progress of science and useful arts, by securing for limited times to authors and inventors the exclusive right to their respective writings and discoveries." Art. I, §8, Cl. 8. Madison expanded on his views in an essay written in 1792. People had property in their opinions, in the free communication of ideas, in religious beliefs, and the free use of faculties and "free choice of the objects on which to employ them." Because conscience is the "most sacred of all property," it is a greater violation to invade a man's conscience than to invade his home (see Madison reading).

This broad view of property rights was obscured by the Supreme Court during America's industrial growth in the nineteenth century. The Court invoked the Due Process Clause of the Fifth and Fourteenth Amendments to control the substantive content of federal and state legislation. In upholding the right of business to operate free of government control, the Court was said to protect property. But it did not protect property in its larger sense, including the community's interest in health and safety. Walton Hamilton and Irene Till explained that it is "incorrect to say that the judiciary protected property; rather they called that property to which they accorded protection." 12 Encycl. Soc. Sci. 536 (1934).

Property has come to represent a "bundle of rights." Kaiser Aetna v. United States, 444 U.S. 164, 176 (1979). These rights have little in common except that they are asserted by persons and enforced by government. Felix S. Cohen, for many years a gifted lecturer at the Yale Law School, underscored the enforcement aspect by proposing that the following label be affixed to all property: "To the world: 'Keep off X unless you have my permission, which I may grant or withhold.' Signed: Private citizen. Endorsed: The state." 9 Rutgers L. Rev. 347, 374 (1954). Although legislative actions and judicial decisions help determine the boundaries of property, the state does not create interests. The active, driving force behind property is the individual who remains conscious of rights and insists on their protection.

Madison's Essay on Property*

This term in its particular application means "that dominion which one man claims and exercises over the external things of the world, in exclusion of every other individual."

In its larger and juster meaning, it embraces every thing to which a man may attach a value and have a right; and *which leaves to every one else the like advantage.*

In the former sense, a man's land, or merchandize, or money is called his property.

In the latter sense, a man has property in his opinions and the free communication of them.

---

* Source: This essay, by James Madison, appeared in *The National Gazette*, March 29, 1792, and is reprinted in 6 The Writings of James Madison 101–03 (Gaillard Hunt ed.).

He has a property of peculiar value in his religious opinions, and in the profession and practice dictated by them.

He has property very dear to him in the safety and liberty of his person.

He has an equal property in the free use of his faculties and free choice of the objects on which to employ them.

In a word, as a man is said to have a right to his property, he may be equally said to have a property in his rights.

Where an excess of power prevails, property of no sort is duly respected. No man is safe in his opinions, his person, his faculties or his possessions.

Where there is an excess of liberty, the effect is the same, tho' from an opposite cause.

Government is instituted to protect property of every sort; as well that which lies in the various rights of individuals, as that which the term particularly expresses. This being the end of government, that alone is a *just* government, which *impartially* secures to every man, whatever is his *own.*

According to this standard of merit, the praise of affording a just security to property, should be sparingly bestowed on a government which, however scrupulously guarding the possessions of individuals, does not protect them in the enjoyment and communication of their opinions, in which they have an equal, and in the estimation of some, a more valuable property.

More sparingly should this praise be allowed to a government, where a man's religious rights are violated by penalties, or fettered by tests, or taxed by a hierarchy. Conscience is the most sacred of all property; other property depending in part on positive law, the exercise of that, being a natural and inalienable right. To guard a man's house as his castle, to pay public and enforce private debts with the most exact faith, can give no title to invade a man's conscience which is more sacred than his castle, or to withhold from it that debt of protection, for which the public faith is pledged, by the very nature and original conditions of the social pact.…

B. THE CONTRACT CLAUSE

The Constitution prohibits any state from passing any law "impairing the Obligation of Contracts." Art. I, § 10. Objections were raised at the Philadelphia Convention that this provision was far too broad and impractical, 2 Farrand 439–40, and so it has proven to be. Madison stated in Federalist No. 44 that the constitutional prohibitions against bills of attainder, ex post facto laws, and laws impairing the obligation of contracts were added in the interest of "personal security and private rights" and to protect the people from the "fluctuating policy which had directed the public councils." However, under the police power and emergency conditions, state actions that modify the obligation of contracts have been upheld repeatedly by the courts. As the Supreme Court noted in 1987, "it is well settled that the prohibition against impairing the obligation of contracts is not to be read literally." Keystone Bituminous Coal Assn. v. DeBenedictis, 480 U.S. 470, 502 (1987). The Contract Clause is invoked only when there has been a *substantial* impairment of a contractual relationship.[1]

The prohibition against ex post facto laws might have been used to protect contracts and property rights, but in 1798 the Court restricted this constitutional provision to criminal statutes. To the Court: "Every *ex post facto* law must necessarily be retrospective; but every retrospective law is not an *ex post facto* law." CALDER v. BULL, 3 U.S. (3 Dall.) 385, 390 (1798).

The first major case involving the Contract Clause arose in Georgia. The state legislature, in what became known as the "Yazoo Land Fraud," sold vast tracts of land in 1795 to four companies. With a single exception, every legislator voting for the measure sold his vote either for money or for shares of stock in the companies. In response to this blatant bribery, a mob marched on the state capital and threatened the lives of the lawmakers. Benjamin Wright, The Contract Clause of the Constitution 21 (1938). Public outrage forced the new legislature a year later to rescind the statute. Did this repeal of

---

1. General Motors Corp. v. Romein, 503 U.S. 181, 186 (1992); Energy Reserves Group, Inc. v. Kansas Power & Light Co., 459 U.S. 400, 411 (1983); Allied Structural Steel Co. v. Spannaus, 438 U.S. 234, 244 (1978).

Doctrine of Vested Rights

... [L]egislative acts interfering with an individual's property or diminishing its value were constitutionally suspect, and this led to the third main contribution of *Fletcher* v. *Peck,* the instrumental conclusion that courts had a duty to void state laws tampering with either private or public contracts. Marshall's opinion, to be sure, made much of the great "delicacy" of voiding a law, but it did not flinch from the "solemn obligation" to declare the repeal act unconstitutional. Together, these three assumptions—the inclusion of public grants under the limitations of the contract clause, the primacy of vested property as a constitutional value, and the judicial duty to void legislative impairments of contract rights—summarize one of the most influential doctrines of American constitutionalism. Edward S. Corwin called it the "Doctrine of Vested Rights." "Setting out with the assumption that the property right is fundamental," Corwin wrote, it "treats any law impairing *vested rights,* whatever its intention, as a bill of pains and penalties, and so, void." This doctrine, which was fully asserted for the first time in the case that grew out of the Yazoo land fraud, dominated American constitutional law during much of the nineteenth century and the first third of the twentieth.

SOURCE: C. Peter Magrath, Yazoo, Law and Politics in the New Republic: The Case of *Fletcher* v. *Peck* 103 (1966).

a corrupt statute violate the contractual rights of speculators and prospective settlers who purchased land from the companies?

Writing for the Supreme Court, Chief Justice Marshall held that the legislature of 1795 possessed constitutional authority to pass the initial statute. The innocent third parties who bought land from the companies, he said, were not responsible for legislative corruption or fraud. On a good-faith basis they had entered into contracts with the companies. Marshall further pointed out that it was inappropriate to expect courts to annul a statute by inquiring into the purity of legislative motives. FLETCHER v. PECK, 10 U.S. (6 Cr.) 87 (1810). This decision made it clear that the Contract Clause covered not only "private contracts" but "state contracts" as well (see box). Another reading of the Contract Clause in defense of property rights was announced in 1812, extending the contract clause to grants of tax immunity. New Jersey v. Wilson, 11 U.S. (7 Cr.) 164 (1812). New Jersey ignored the Court's decision and imposed the tax anyway. Tony A. Freyer, Producers Versus Capitalists: Constitutional Conflict in Antebellum America 54 (1994). Over history there has been a balancing between the right of private property and the right of government through the "police power" to regulate property for the public interest.

The Dartmouth College case of 1819 stands as a famous legal landmark. The college had been created in 1754 as a charity school to instruct Indians in the Christian religion. In 1769 it was chartered by the British crown as a private corporation. The college continued to be funded entirely by private donations. In 1816 New Hampshire passed legislation to increase the number of trustees in the college and thereby transfer control to appointees of the governor.

In his decision for the Court, Chief Justice Marshall said that the British parliament could have annulled the charter at any time. New Hampshire could have altered the charter after the break with England and before ratification of the U.S. Constitution. However, the Contract Clause prohibited the state from impairing the contract of a "private eleemosynary institution": an institution created by private parties, sustained by private funds, and devoted to charitable goals. Marshall explained that had the college been created by the legislature and supported by public funds, the state could have altered the contract. Under those circumstances the college would have existed as a public corporation to satisfy a public purpose. Dartmouth, however, had a right to continue under its private charter without interference by the state. Otherwise, Marshall warned, all charitable and educational institutions would fall under the control of government. DARTMOUTH COLLEGE v. WOODWARD, 17 U.S. (4 Wheat.) 517 (1819).

This case has few applications today. The line between "public" and "private" is less clear, and even private institutions are subject to state regulation and control. Henry J. Friendly, The Dartmouth College Case and the Public-Private Penumbra (1969). Nevertheless, the case established important limits on the power of government to interfere with academic freedom and acts of incorporation. It also reassured Federalist property holders who feared the reach of majority rule and state legislatures.

Rights of the Community

The Charles River Bridge case of 1837 illustrates that the right of contract has limits. In 1785 the legislature of Massachusetts incorporated a company to build a bridge and take tolls. About four decades later it created another company to build a bridge nearby. The second bridge took tolls for a few years and then became free. Travelers, of course, switched to the new bridge and proprietors of the first bridge complained that the legislature had impaired the obligations of a contract. The Supreme Court, balancing the rights of property against the rights reserved to the states, held that a state law may be retrospective in character and alter rights formerly vested by law without violating the Contract Clause. Although corporations are given certain rights by law, the community also has rights in a dynamic economy that offers improvements in public accommodations and travel. CHARLES RIVER BRIDGE v. WARREN BRIDGE, 36 U.S. (11 Pet.) 420 (1837).

The principle of *Charles River* has been affirmed in many cases. The Contract Clause does not prevent a state from granting a right and repealing or modifying that right in future years. A legislature may grant a monopoly and decide at a later time that it is in the interest of the state to abolish the monopoly and allow other companies to enter the field. Slaughter-House Cases, 83 U.S. (16 Wall.) 36 (1873); Butchers' Union Co. v. Crescent City Co., 111 U.S. 746 (1884). In matters affecting public health, public safety, or public morals, one legislature may not bind future legislatures.[2]

Private contracts are subject to government control. The right of an owner of a building to contract with tenants may be limited by rent-control laws. Block v. Hirsh, 256 U.S. 135 (1921). Although contracts may create rights of property, when they concern a subject matter within the control of Congress "they have a congenital infirmity." Norman v. Baltimore & Ohio R. Co., 294 U.S. 240, 307–08 (1935), cited in Connolly v. Pension Benefit Guaranty Corp., 475 U.S. 211, 223–24 (1986).

If a state passes a bankruptcy law to relieve debtors of their liabilities, does this impair the obligation of contracts? The Supreme Court in an early case decided that states are not prevented from passing bankruptcy laws unless Congress preempts the field by passing a uniform law authorized by Article I, Section 8, Clause 4. In this particular case, the Court determined that the state law did impair the obligation of contracts. Sturges v. Crowninshield, 17 U.S. (4 Wheat.) 120 (1819). The following decade the Court again held that congressional inaction on uniform bankruptcy laws permitted the states to legislate on the subject. Moreover, states could pass laws discharging a debtor from liability if the law preceded the contract. If a bankruptcy act operated prospectively, it did not violate the Contract Clause. Ogden v. Saunders, 25 U.S. (12 Wheat.) 212 (1827). Contracts are then entered into in light of the bankruptcy policy established by law.

The Minnesota Moratorium

The issue of a retrospective law reached the Supreme Court in 1934. A 5 to 4 decision upheld a Minnesota law, passed during the Great Depression, that gave homeowners a delay of up to two years in meeting their mortgage payments. Although the law clearly modified contracts entered into prior to

---

2. Stone v. Mississippi, 101 U.S. 814 (1880); Fertilizing Co. v. Hyde Park, 97 U.S. 659 (1879); Beer Co. v. Massachusetts, 97 U.S. 25 (1878).

the statute, both the state court and the Supreme Court agreed that the police power had sufficient scope in an emergency to set aside, for a limited period, the Contract Clause. HOME BLDG. & LOAN ASSN. v. BLAISDELL, 290 U.S. 398 (1934). A year later, by a 5 to 4 vote, the Court upheld the power of Congress to abrogate the "gold clauses" in private contracts. To prevent a run on the banks and the hoarding of gold, President Franklin D. Roosevelt and Congress had taken emergency actions in 1933 to prevent individuals from requiring payment in gold or a particular kind of coin.[3] In several other cases, where state actions were not restricted to an emergency period, statutes were declared invalid under the Contract Clause.[4]

The Contract Clause does not carry the same importance today as it did in the era of *Fletcher* and *Dartmouth College.* As a limitation on state power, it has been largely replaced by the Due Process and Equal Protection Clauses of the Fourteenth Amendment. There are still circumstances, however, where the Contract Clause is successfully invoked to strike down a state statute. A contemporary case involved the Port Authority of New York and New Jersey. In 1962 the two states passed a statutory covenant that prevented the Authority from subsidizing rail passenger transportation by using revenues and reserves pledged as security for bonds issued by the Authority. In 1974 the two states repealed the statutory covenant. Although the New Jersey courts upheld the repeal as a valid exercise of the police power, the Supreme Court in 1977 ruled that the repeal violated the Contract Clause by eliminating an important security provision for bondholders. United States Trust Co. v. New Jersey, 431 U.S. 1 (1977).

The dissenters in this 4–3 decision accused the Court of "dusting off" the Contract Clause and giving it a meaning broader than intended by the framers. According to their analysis and some other studies, the Contract Clause was conceived of "primarily as protection for economic transactions entered into by purely private parties, rather than obligations involving the State itself." Id. at 45. This philosophy would allow each new legislature to rescind the policies of the previous legislature. The problem is that state obligations frequently involve investments by private parties, as in the Port Authority case.

A year later, the Court struck down a Minnesota law for violating the Contract Clause, pointing out that the police power did not give the states unlimited authority to abridge existing contractual relationships. Moreover, the Minnesota law did not deal with grave economic or social emergencies, as in the 1934 *Blaisdell* case. Justices Brennan, White, and Marshall dissented from what they regarded as the Court's extension of the Contract Clause beyond its original intent. Allied Structural Steel Co. v. Spannaus, 438 U.S. 234 (1978).

Calder v. Bull

3 U.S. (3 Dall.) 385 (1798)

The Constitution prohibits any state from passing any law "impairing the Obligation of Contracts." The Constitution also prohibits states from passing ex post facto laws, which might apply to protect contracts and property rights. The issue in this case was whether the prohibition against ex post facto laws applied only to criminal statutes. Caleb Bull and his wife attempted to appeal a probate court ruling over a will, only to find that the time for their appeal had expired. After they convinced the Connecticut legislature to revise the law and lengthen the time

---

3. Norman v. B.&O. R. Co., 294 U.S. 240 (1935). For other "gold clause" cases, see Nortz v. United States, 294 U.S. 317 (1935) and Perry v. United States, 294 U.S. 330 (1935).

4. Treigle v. Acme Homestead Assn., 297 U.S. 189 (1936); Worthen Co. v. Kavanaugh, 295 U.S. 56 (1935); Worthen Co. v. Thomas, 292 U.S. 426 (1934). But see also El Paso v. Simmons, 379 U.S. 497 (1965); East New York Bank v. Hahn, 326 U.S. 230 (1945); Faitoute Co. v. Asbury Park, 316 U.S. 502 (1942); Veix v. Sixth Ward Assn., 310 U.S. 32 (1940).

for appeal, and prevailed in the lawsuit, John Calder and his wife protested that the new law violated the Ex Post Facto Clause. The opinion remains prominent for the conflicting views of the Court on the role of "natural justice" in limiting and defining governmental power.

CHASE, Justice. — The decision of one question determines (in my opinion) the present dispute....

The counsel for the plaintiffs in error contend, that the said resolution or law of the legislature of Connecticut, granting a new hearing, in the above case, is an *ex post facto* law, prohibited by the constitution of the United States; that any law of the federal government, or of any of the state government, contrary to the constitution of the United States, is void; and that this court possesses the power to declare such law void.

. . .

The effect of the resolution or law of Connecticut, above stated, is to revise a decision of one of its inferior courts....

Whether the legislature of any of the states can revise and correct by law, a decision of any of its courts of justice, although not prohibited by the constitution of the state, is a question of very great importance, and not necessary now to be determined; because the resolution or law in question does not go so far. I cannot subscribe to the omnipotence of a state legislature, or that it is absolute and without control; ... An act of the legislature (for I cannot call it a law), contrary to the great first principles of the social compact, cannot be considered a rightful exercise of legislative authority. The obligation of a law, in governments established on express compact, and on republican principles, must be determined by the nature of the power on which it is founded.

. . .

I shall endeavor to show what law is to be considered an *ex post facto* law, within the words and meaning of the prohibition in the federal constitution. The prohibition, "that no state shall pass any *ex post facto* law," necessarily requires some explanation; for, naked and without explanation, it is unintelligible, and means nothing.... [T]he plain and obvious meaning and intention of the prohibition is this: that the legislatures of the several states, shall not pass laws, after a fact done by a subject or citizen, which shall have relation to such fact, and shall punish him for having done it. The prohibition, considered in this light, is an additional bulwark in favor of the personal security of the subject, to protect his person from punishment by legislative acts, having a retrospective operation. I do not think it was inserted, to secure the citizen in his private rights of either property or contracts. The prohibitions not to make anything but gold and silver coin a tender in payment of debts, and not to pass any law impairing the obligation of contracts, were inserted to secure private rights; but the restriction not to pass any *ex post facto* law, was to secure the person of the subject from injury or punishment, in consequence of such law. If the prohibition against making *ex post facto* laws was intended to secure personal rights from being affected or injured by such laws, and the prohibition is sufficiently extensive for that object, the other restraints I have enumerated, were unnecessary, and therefore, improper; for both of them are retrospective.

I will state what laws I consider *ex post facto* laws, within the words and the intent of the prohibition. 1st. Every law that makes an action done before the passing of the law, and which was innocent when done, criminal; and punishes such action. 2d. Every law that aggravates a crime, or makes it greater than it was, when committed. 3d. Every law that changes the punishment, and inflicts a greater punishment, than the law annexed to the crime, when committed. 4th. Every law that alters the legal rules of evidence, and receives less, or different testimony, than the law required at the time of the commission of the offence, in order to convict the offender. All these, and similar laws, are manifestly unjust and oppressive. In my opinion, the true distinction is between *ex post facto* laws, and retrospective laws. Every *ex post facto* law must necessarily be retrospective; but every retrospective law is not an *ex post facto* law: the former only are prohibited. Every law that takes away or impairs rights vested, agreeable to existing laws, is retrospective, and is generally unjust, and may be oppressive; and it is a good general rule, that a law should have no retrospect: but there are cases in which laws may justly, and for the benefit of the community, and also of individuals, relate to a time antecedent to their commencement; as statutes of oblivion or of pardon. They are certainly retrospective, and literally both concerning and after the facts committed. But I do not consider any law *ex post facto*, within the prohibition, that mollifies the rigor of the criminal law: but only those that create or aggravate the crime; or increase the punishment, or change the rules of evidence, for the purpose of conviction....

I am of opinion, that the decree of the supreme court of errors of Connecticut be affirmed, with costs.

PATERSON, Justice. —

… [The framers of the Constitution] understood and used the words in their known and appropriate signification, as referring to crimes, pains and penalties, and no further.…

IREDELL, Justice. — Though I concur in the general result of the opinions which have been delivered, I cannot entirely adopt the reasons that are assigned upon the occasion.

… [T]hough, I admit, that as the authority to declare it void is of a delicate and awful nature, the court will never resort to that authority, but in a clear and urgent case. If, on the other hand, the leg-islature of the Union, or the legislature of any member of the Union, shall pass a law, within the general scope of their constitutional power, the court cannot pronounce it to be void, merely because it is, in their judgment, contrary to the principles of natural justice. The ideas of natural justice are regulated by no fixed standard: the ablest and the purest men have differed upon the subject.…

CUSHING, Justice. — The case appears to me to be clear of all difficulty, taken either way. If the act is a judicial act, it is not touched by the federal constitution: and if it is a legislative act, it is maintained and justified by the ancient and uniform practice of the state of Connecticut.

Judgment affirmed.

Fletcher v. Peck

10 U.S. (6 Cr.) 87 (1810)

In 1803 John Peck sold to Robert Fletcher a tract of land lying along the Mississippi River. The land dated back to an act of the Georgia legislature in 1795 and had changed hands often since that time. Because of corruption associated with the statute, a new legislature in 1796 rescinded the land grant. Fletcher went to court in Massachusetts, claiming a breach of contract because the legislature never had authority to sell and dispose of the land. Did the rescinding legislation nullify the contractual rights of innocent third parties who had purchased land and sold it, or were they protected by the Contract Clause?

MARSHALL, Ch. J. delivered the opinion of the court as follows:

. . .

The 2d count assigns, in substance, as a breach of this covenant, that the original grantees from the state of Georgia promised and assured divers members of the legislature, then sitting in general assembly, that if the said members would assent to, and vote for, the passing of the act, and if the said bill should pass, such members should have a share of, and be interested in, all the lands purchased from the said state by virtue of such law. And that divers of the said members, to whom the said promises were made, were unduly influenced thereby, and, under such influence, did vote for the passing of the said bill; by reason whereof the said law was a nullity, &c. and so the title of the state of Georgia did not pass to the said Peck, &c.

. . .

That corruption should find its way into the governments of our infant republics, and contaminate the very source of legislation, or that impure motives should contribute to the passage of a law, or the formation of a legislative contract, are circumstances most deeply to be deplored. How far a court of justice would, in any case, be competent, on proceedings instituted by the state itself, to vacate a contract thus formed, and to annul rights acquired, under that contract, by third persons having no notice of the improper means by which it was obtained, is a question which the court would approach with much circumspection. It may well be doubted how far the validity of a law depends upon the motives of its framers, and how far the particular inducements, operating on members of the supreme sovereign power of a state, to the formation of a contract by that power, are examinable in a court of justice. If the principle be conceded, that an act of the supreme sovereign power might be declared null by a court, in consequence of the means which procured it, still would there be much difficulty in saying to what extent those means must be applied to produce this effect. Must it be direct corruption, or would interest or undue influence of any kind be sufficient? Must the vitiating cause operate on a majority, or on what number of the members? Would the act be null, whatever might be the wish of the nation, or would its obligation or nullity depend upon the public sentiment?

If the majority of the legislature be corrupted, it may well be doubted, whether it be within the province of the judiciary to control their conduct, and, if less than a majority act from impure motives, the principle by which judicial interference would be regulated, is not clearly discerned.

... It would be indecent, in the extreme, upon a private contract, between two individuals, to enter into an inquiry respecting the corruption of the sovereign power of a state. If the title be plainly deduced from a legislative act, which the legislature might constitutionally pass, if the act be clothed with all the requisite forms of a law, a court, sitting as a court of law, cannot sustain a suit brought by one individual against another founded on the allegation that the act is a nullity, in consequence of the impure motives which influenced certain members of the legislature which passed the law.

. . .

In this case the legislature may have had ample proof that the original grant was obtained by practices which can never be too much reprobated, and which would have justified its abrogation so far as respected those to whom crime was imputable. But

the grant, when issued, conveyed an estate in fee-simple to the grantee, clothed with all the solemnities which law can bestow. This estate was transferrable; and those who purchased parts of it were not stained by that guilt which infected the original transaction....

The principle asserted is, that one legislature is competent to repeal any act which a former legislature was competent to pass; and that one legislature cannot abridge the powers of a succeeding legislature....

It is, then, the unanimous opinion of the court, that, in this case, the estate having passed into the hands of a purchaser for a valuable consideration, without notice, the state of Georgia was restrained, either by general principles which are common to our free institutions, or by the particular provisions of the constitution of the United States, from passing a law whereby the estate of the plaintiff in the premises so purchased could be constitutionally and legally impaired and rendered null and void....

JOHNSON, J. In this case I entertain, on two points, an opinion different from that which has been delivered by the court.

I do not hesitate to declare that a state does not possess the power of revoking its own grants. But I do it on a general principle, on the reason and nature of things: a principle which will impose laws even on the deity....

Dartmouth College v. Woodward

17 U.S. (4 Wheat.) 517 (1819)

Dartmouth College functioned as a private school, funded entirely by private donations. New Hampshire passed legislation in 1816 to increase the number of trustees at the college and thereby transfer control to appointees of the governor. The constitutional question was whether the Contract Clause prohibited the state from impairing the contract of a "private eleemosynary institution." The old trustees of Dartmouth College brought this suit against William H. Woodward, the secretary-treasurer of Dartmouth who sided with the new trustees. The "old" trustees appealed to the Supreme Court.

February 2d, 1819. The opinion of the court was delivered by MARSHALL, Ch. J.

. . .

It can require no argument to prove, that the circumstances of this case constitute a contract. An application is made to the crown for a charter to incorporate a religious and literary institution. In the application, it is stated, that large contributions have been made for the object, which will be conferred on the corporation, as soon as it shall be created. The

charter is granted, and on its faith the property is conveyed. Surely, in this transaction every ingredient of a complete and legitimate contract is to be found. The points for consideration are, 1. Is this contract protected by the constitution of the United States? 2. Is it impaired by the acts under which the defendant holds?

1. On the first point, it has been argued, that the word "contract," in its broadest sense, would comprehend the political relations between the government and its citizens, would extend to offices held

within a state, for state purposes, and to many of those laws concerning civil institutions, which must change with circumstances, and be modified by ordinary legislation; which deeply concern the public, and which, to preserve good government, the public judgment must control. That even marriage is a contract, and its obligations are affected by the laws respecting divorces. That the clause in the constitution, if construed in its greatest latitude, would prohibit these laws. Taken in its broad, unlimited sense, the clause would be an unprofitable and vexatious interference with the internal concerns of a state, would unnecessarily and unwisely embarrass its legislation, and render immutable those civil institutions, which are established for purposes of internal government, and which, to subserve those purposes, ought to vary with varying circumstances. That as the framers of the constitution could never have intended to insert in that instrument, a provision so unnecessary, so mischievous, and so repugnant to its general spirit, the term "contract" must be understood in a more limited sense. That it must be understood as intended to guard against a power, of at least doubtful utility, the abuse of which had been extensively felt; and to restrain the legislature in future from violating the right to property....

... If the act of incorporation be a grant of political power, if it create a civil institution, to be employed in the administration of the government, or if the funds of the college be public property, or if the state of New Hampshire, as a government, be alone interested in its transactions, the subject is one in which the legislature of the state may act according to its own judgment, unrestrained by any limitation of its power imposed by the constitution of the United States.

But if this be a private eleemosynary institution, endowed with a capacity to take property, for objects unconnected with government, whose funds are bestowed by individuals, on the faith of the charter; if the donors have stipulated for the future disposition and management of those funds, in the manner prescribed by themselves; there may be more difficulty in the case....

[After determining that the funds of Dartmouth College consisted entirely of private donations, Chief Justice Marshall raises broader issues.]

... Are the trustees and professors public officers, invested with any portion of political power, partaking in any degree in the administration of civil government, and performing duties which flow from the sovereign authority? That education is an object of national concern, and a proper subject of legislation, all admit. That there may be an institution, founded by government, and placed entirely under its immediate control, the officers of which would be public officers, amenable exclusively to government, none will deny. But is Dartmouth College such an institution? Is education altogether in the hands of government? Does every teacher of youth become a public officer, and do donations for the purpose of education necessarily become public property, so far that the will of the legislature, not the will of the donor, becomes the law of the donation? These questions are of serious moment to society, and deserve to be well considered....

From this review of the charter, it appears, that Dartmouth College is an eleemosynary institution, incorporated for the purpose of perpetuating the application of the bounty of the donors, to the specified objects of that bounty; that its trustees or governors were originally named by the founder, and invested with the power of perpetuating themselves; that they are not public officers, nor is it a civil institution, participating in the administration of government; but a charity school, or a seminary of education, incorporated for the preservation of its property, and the perpetual application of that property to the objects of its creation.

. . .

The opinion of the court, after mature deliberation, is, that this is a contract, the obligation of which cannot be impaired, without violating the constitution of the United States. This opinion appears to us to be equally supported by reason, and by the former decisions of this court.

2. We next proceed to the inquiry, whether its obligation has been impaired by those acts of the legislature of New Hampshire, to which the special verdict refers?

From the review of this charter, which has been taken, it appears that the whole power of governing the college, of appointing and removing tutors, of fixing their salaries, of directing the course of study to be pursued by the students, and of filling up vacancies created in their own body, was vested in the trustees. On the part of the crown, it was expressly stipulated, that this corporation, thus constituted, should continue for ever; and that the number of trustees should for ever consist of twelve, and no more. By this contract, the crown was bound, and could have made no violent alteration in its essential terms, without impairing its obligation.

By the revolution, the duties, as well as the powers, of government devolved on the people of New Hampshire. It is admitted, that among the latter was comprehended the transcendent power of parliament, as well as that of the executive department. It is too clear, to require the support of argument, that all contracts and rights respecting property, remained unchanged by the revolution. The obligations, then, which were created by the charter to Dartmouth College, were the same in the new, that they had been in the old government. The power of the government was also the same. A repeal of this charter, at any time prior to the adoption of the present constitution of the United States, would have been an extraordinary and unprecedented act of power, but one which could have been contested only by the restrictions upon the legislature, to be found in the constitution of the state. But the constitution of the United States has imposed this additional limitation, that the legislature of a state shall pass no act "impairing the obligation of contracts." ...

It results from this opinion, that the acts of the legislature of New Hampshire, which are stated in the special verdict found in this cause, are repugnant to the constitution of the United States; and that the judgment on this special verdict ought to have been for the plaintiffs. The judgment of the state court must, therefore, be reversed.

WASHINGTON, Justice. — [*Concurred.*]

JOHNSON, Justice, concurred, for the reasons stated by the Chief Justice.

LIVINGSTON, Justice, concurred, for the reasons stated by the Chief Justice, and Justices WASHINGTON and STORY.

STORY, JUSTICE. — [*Concurred.*]

DUVALL, Justice, dissented.

Charles River Bridge v. Warren Bridge

36 U.S. (11 Pet.) 420 (1837)

In 1650, the Massachusetts legislature granted to Harvard College authority to set up a ferry from Charleston to Boston, passing over Charles River. In 1785, the legislature incorporated a company ("The Proprietors of the Charles River Bridge") to build a bridge and accept tolls. Decades later it established "The Proprietors of the Warren Bridge" to build a bridge nearby; over the course of time this bridge became free to travelers. The first bridge company filed a lawsuit, claiming that the legislature had impaired the obligation of a contract by violating the company's implied right of exclusivity to operate a bridge across the Charles River. This significant decision by Chief Justice Taney balances the rights of private property against the public's need for economic development.

TANEY, Ch. J., delivered the opinion of the court. —

. . .

[U]pon what ground can the plaintiffs in error contend, that the ferry-rights of the college [*Harvard*] have been transferred to the proprietors of the bridge? If they have been thus transferred, it must be by some mode of transfer known to the law; and the evidence relied on to prove it, can be pointed out in the record. How was it transferred? It is not suggested, that there ever was, in point of fact, a deed of conveyance executed by the college to the bridge company. Is there any evidence in the record, from which such a conveyance may, upon legal principle, be presumed? The testimony before the court, so far from laying the foundation for such a presumption, repels it, in the most positive terms....

This brings us to the act of the legislature of

Massachusetts, of 1785, by which the plaintiffs were incorporated by the name of "The Proprietors of the Charles River Bridge;" and it is here, and in the law of 1792, prolonging their charter, that we must look for the extent and nature of the franchise conferred upon the plaintiffs. Much has been said in the argument of the principles of construction by which this law is to be expounded, and what undertakings, on the part of the state, may be implied. The court think there can be no serious difficulty on that head. It is the grant of certain franchises, by the public, to a private corporation, and in a matter where the public interest is concerned....

... [T]he object and end of all government is to promote the happiness and prosperity of the community by which it is established; and it can never be assumed, that the government intended to diminish its power of accomplishing the end for which it was created. And in a country like ours, free, active and enterprising, continually advancing in numbers and wealth, new channels of communication are daily found necessary, both for travel and trade, and are essential to the comfort, convenience and prosperity of the people. A state ought never to be presumed to surrender this power, because, like the taxing power, the whole community have an interest in preserving it undiminished. And when a corporation alleges, that a state has surrendered, for seventy years, its power of improvement and public accommodation, in a great and important line of travel, along which a vast number of its citizens must daily pass, the community have a right to insist, in the language of this court, above quoted, "that its abandonment ought not to be presumed, in a case, in which the deliberate purpose of the state to abandon it does not appear." The continued existence of a government would be of no great value, if, by implications and presumptions, it was disarmed of the powers necessary to accomplish the ends of its creation, and the functions it was designed to perform, transferred to the hands of privileged corporations.... While the rights of private property are sacredly guarded, we must not forget, that the community also have rights, and that the happiness and well-being of every citizen depends on their faithful preservation.

Adopting the rule of construction above stated as the settled one, we proceed to apply it to the charter of 1785, to the proprietors of the Charles River bridge. This act of incorporation is in the usual form, and the privileges such as are commonly given to corporations of that kind. It confers on them the ordinary faculties of a corporation, for the purpose of building the bridge; and establishes certain rates of toll, which the company are authorized to take: this is the whole grant. There is no exclusive privilege given to them over the waters of Charles river, above or below their bridge; no right to erect another bridge themselves, nor to prevent other persons from erecting one; no engagement from the state, that another shall not be erected; and no undertaking not to sanction competition, nor to make improvements that may diminish the amount of its income....

The relative position of the Warren bridge has already been described. It does not interrupt the passage over the Charles River bridge, nor make the way to it, or from it, less convenient. None of the faculties or franchises granted to that corporation, have been revoked by the legislature; and its right to take the tolls granted by the charter remains unaltered. In short, all the franchises and rights of property, enumerated in the charter, and there mentioned to have

been granted to it, remain unimpaired. But its income is destroyed by the Warren bridge; which, being free, draws off the passengers and property which would have gone over it, and renders their franchise of no value. This is the gist of the complainant; for it is not pretended, that the erection of the Warren bridge would have done them any injury, or in any degree affected their right of property, if it had not diminished the amount of their tolls. In order, then, to entitle themselves to relief, it is necessary to show, that the legislature contracted not to do the act of which they complain; and that they impaired, or in other words, violated, that contract, by the erection of the Warren bridge.

The inquiry, then, is, does the charter contain such a contract on the part of the state? Is there any such stipulation to be found in that instrument? It must be admitted on all hands, that there is none; no words that even relate to another bridge, or to the diminution of their tolls, or to the line of travel....

Indeed, the practice and usage of almost every state in the Union, old enough to have commenced the work of internal improvement, is opposed to the doctrine contended for on the part of the plaintiffs in error. Turnpike roads have been made in succession, on the same line of travel; the later ones interfering materially with the profits of the first. These corporations have, in some instances, been utterly ruined by the introduction of newer and better modes of transportation and traveling. In some cases, railroads have rendered the turnpike roads on the same line of travel so entirely useless, that the franchise of the turnpike corporation is not worth preserving. Yet in none of these cases have the corporation supposed that their privileges were invaded, or any contract violated on the part of the state....

The judgment of the supreme judicial court of the commonwealth of Massachusetts, dismissing the plaintiffs' bill, must, therefore, be affirmed, with costs.

McLEAN, Justice. [*Favored dismissing the case for lack of jurisdiction.*]

BALDWIN, Justice. — [*Concurred.*]

STORY, Justice. [*Dissenting.*]

. . .

But it has been argued, and the argument has been pressed in every form which ingenuity could suggest, that if grants of this nature are to be construed liberally, as conferring any exclusive rights on the grantees, it will interpose an effectual barrier against all general improvements of the country. For myself, I profess not to feel the cogency of this argument, either in its general application to the grant of franchises, or in its special application to the present grant. This is a subject upon which different minds may well arrive at different conclusions, both as to policy and principle.... For my own part, I can conceive of no surer plan to arrest all public improvements, founded on private capital and enterprise, than to make the outlay of that capital uncertain and questionable, both as to security and as to productiveness. No man will hazard his capital in any enterprise, in which, if there be a loss, it must be borne exclusively by himself; and if there be success, he has not the slightest security of enjoying the rewards of that success, for a single moment. If the government means to invite its citizens to enlarge the public comforts and conveniences, to establish bridges, or turnpikes, or canals, or railroads, there must be

some pledge, that the property will be safe; that the enjoyment will be co-extensive with the grant; and that success will not be the signal of a general combination to overthrow its rights and to take away its profits....

Upon the whole, my judgment is, that the act of the legislature of Massachusetts granting the charter of Warren Bridge, is an act impairing the obligation of the prior contract and grant to the proprietors of Charles River bridge; and, by the constitution of the United States, it is, therefore, utterly void....

THOMPSON, Justice. — The opinion delivered by my brother, Mr. Justice STORY, I have read over and deliberately considered. On this full consideration, I concur entirely in all the principles and reasonings contained in it; and I am of opinion, the decree of the supreme judicial court of Massachusetts should be reversed.

Home Bldg. & Loan Assn. v. Blaisdell
290 U.S. 398 (1934)

A Minnesota statute, enacted in 1933, declared that the Great Depression created an emergency demanding an exercise of the police power to protect the public and promote the general welfare. It temporarily extended the time allowed by existing law for redeeming real property from foreclosure and sale under existing mortgages. It became known as the Minnesota Mortgage Moratorium Law. At issue was Article I, § 10, of the U.S. Constitution, which provides that no state shall pass any law "impairing the Obligation of Contracts." Could this constitutional prohibition be waived during time of emergency? A married couple, John H. and Rosella Blaisdell, won a court order under the act, extending the period of redemption from the foreclosure on their property. Under the order, the Blaisdells were required to pay Home Building and Loan Assn. $40 per month. Home Building and Loan appealed to the U.S. Supreme Court claiming the act violated the Contract Clause. A key underlying question: Does the Constitution change in time of emergency?

MR. CHIEF JUSTICE HUGHES delivered the opinion of the Court.

. . .

In determining whether the provision for this temporary and conditional relief exceeds the power of the State by reason of the clause in the Federal Constitution prohibiting impairment of the obligations of contracts, we must consider the relation of emergency to constitutional power, the historical setting of the contract clause, the development of the jurisprudence of this Court in the construction of that clause, and the principles of construction which we may consider to be established.

Emergency does not create power. Emergency does not increase granted power or remove or di-

minish the restrictions imposed upon power granted or reserved. The Constitution was adopted in a period of grave emergency. Its grants of power to the Federal Government and its limitations of the power of the States were determined in the light of emergency and they are not altered by emergency. What power was thus granted and what limitations were thus imposed are questions which have always been, and always will be, the subject of close examination under our constitutional system.

While emergency does not create power, emergency may furnish the occasion for the exercise of power. "Although an emergency may not call into life a power which has never lived, nevertheless emergency may afford a reason for the exertion of a living power already enjoyed." *Wilson* v. *New*, 243

U.S. 332, 348.... [E]mergency would not permit a State to have more than two Senators in the Congress, or permit the election of President by a general popular vote without regard to the number of electors to which the States are respectively entitled, or permit the States to "coin money" or to "make anything but gold and silver coin a tender in payment of debts." But where constitutional grants and limitations of power are set forth in general clauses, which afford a broad outline, the process of construction is essential to fill in the details. That is true of the contract clause....

In the construction of the contract clause, the debates in the Constitutional Convention are of little aid. But the reasons which led to the adoption of that clause, and of the other prohibitions of Section 10 of Article I, are not left in doubt and have frequently been described with eloquent emphasis. The widespread distress following the revolutionary period, and the plight of debtors, had called forth in the States an ignoble array of legislative schemes for the defeat of creditors and the invasion of contractual obligations. Legislative interferences had been so numerous and extreme that the confidence essential to prosperous trade had been undermined and the utter destruction of credit was threatened. "The sober people of America" were convinced that some "thorough reform" was needed which would "inspire a general prudence and industry, and give a regular course to the business of society." *The Federalist*, No. 44. It was necessary to interpose the restraining power of a central authority in order to secure the foundations even of "private faith." ...

But full recognition of the occasion and general purpose of the clause does not suffice to fix its precise scope. Nor does an examination of the details of prior legislation in the States yield criteria which can be considered controlling. To ascertain the scope of the constitutional prohibition we examine the course of judicial decisions in its application. These put it beyond question that the prohibition is not an absolute one and is not to be read with literal exactness like a mathematical formula....

Not only is the constitutional provision qualified by the measure of control which the State retains over remedial processes, but the State also continues to possess authority to safeguard the vital interests of its people. It does not matter that legislation appropriate to that end "has the result of modifying or abrogating contracts already in effect." *Stephenson* v. *Binford*, 287 U.S. 251, 276.... The policy of protecting contracts against impairment presupposes the maintenance of a government by virtue of which contractual relations are worth while, — a govern-

ment which retains adequate authority to secure the peace and good order of society....

While the charters of private corporations constitute contracts, a grant of exclusive privilege is not to be implied as against the State. *Charles River Bridge* v. *Warren Bridge*, 11 Pet. 420. And all contracts are subject to the right of eminent domain. *West River Bridge* v. *Dix*, 6 How. 507. The reservation of this necessary authority of the State is deemed to be a part of the contract....

It is no answer to say that this public need was not apprehended a century ago, or to insist that what the provision of the Constitution meant to the vision of that day it must mean to the vision of our time. If by the statement that what the Constitution meant at the time of its adoption it means to-day, it is intended to say that the great clauses of the Constitution must be confined to the interpretation which the framers, with the conditions and outlook of their time, would have placed upon them, the statement carries its own refutation. It was to guard against such a narrow conception that Chief Justice Marshall uttered the memorable warning — "We must never forget that it is a *constitution* we are expounding" (*McCulloch* v. *Maryland*, 4 Wheat. 316, 407) — "a constitution intended to endure for ages to come, and consequently, to be adapted to the various *crises* of human affairs." *Id.*, p. 415. When we are dealing with the words of the Constitution, said this Court in *Missouri* v. *Holland*, 252 U.S. 416, 433, "we must realize that they have called into life a being the development of which could not have been foreseen completely by the most gifted of its begetters.... The case before us must be considered in the light of our whole experience and not merely in that of what was said a hundred years ago."

· · ·

We are of the opinion that the Minnesota statute as here applied does not violate the contract clause of the Federal Constitution. Whether the legislation is wise or unwise as a matter of policy is a question with which we are not concerned.

· · ·

MR. JUSTICE SUTHERLAND, dissenting.

... The effect of the Minnesota legislation, though serious enough in itself, is of trivial significance compared with the far more serious and dangerous inroads upon the limitations of the Constitution which are almost certain to ensue as a consequence naturally following any step beyond the boundaries fixed by that instrument....

A provision of the Constitution, it is hardly necessary to say, does not admit of two distinctly opposite interpretations. It does not mean one thing at one time and an entirely different thing at another time. If the contract impairment clause, when framed and adopted, meant that the terms of a contract for the payment of money could not be altered *in invitum* by a state statute enacted for the relief of hardly pressed debtors to the end and with the effect of postponing payment or enforcement during and because of an economic or financial emergency, it is but to state the obvious to say that it means the same now....

The provisions of the Federal Constitution, undoubtedly, are pliable in the sense that in appropriate cases they have the capacity of bringing within their grasp every new condition which falls within their meaning. But, their *meaning* is changeless; it is only their *application* which is extensible....

. . .

I am authorized to say that MR. JUSTICE VAN DEVANTER, MR. JUSTICE MCREYNOLDS and MR. JUSTICE BUTLER concur in this opinion.

C. THE TAKING CLAUSE

Under the Fifth Amendment, private property shall not "be taken for public use, without just compensation." This is referred to variously as the Taking Clause, the Public Use Clause, or the Just Compensation Clause. Under the Due Process Clause of the Fourteenth Amendment, as well as under their own constitutions, states are also forbidden from taking private property for public use without just compensation. Chicago, B. & Q. R.R. Co. v. Chicago, 166 U.S. 226, 236–37, 241 (1897). The taking of property constitutes an exercise of the power of eminent domain, which gives the sovereign the right to condemn or expropriate private property for a public purpose upon payment of just compensation.

The decision to invoke the power of eminent domain is purely a legislative function. Whether compensation is "just" or whether property has been taken for "public use" are questions that might be taken to the courts. Every deprivation of property does not require compensation. PruneYard Shopping Center v. Robins, 447 U.S. 74, 82 (1980). Even when compensation must be paid, a plethora of 5–4 decisions by the Supreme Court demonstrate fundamental disagreements about the proper method of calculating what is "just."[5]

The Scope of Property

The protections available for land are of broad and changing scope. The ancient *ad coelum* doctrine gave landowners control of their property downward to the core of the earth and upward to the heavens. A landowner's rights to the column of air above the land led to successful actions against overhanging eaves, protruding structures, and firing projectiles or stringing wires across the property. Portsmouth Co. v. United States, 260 U.S. 327 (1922). One case involved a deed under which a coal company conveyed land surface to homeowners but reserved the right to remove coal under the property. Any damages to the surface resulting from mining were waived. The homeowners tried to prevent the company from burrowing under their property and removing supporting structures for their house and land. Despite the existence of a state statute passed after the deed, forbidding mining that would cause land under a home to sink, an 8–1 decision by the Supreme Court held that the police power could not protect shortsighted homeowners who acquired only surface rights. Pennsylvania Coal Co. v. Mahon, 260 U.S. 393 (1922).

Homeowners in the vicinity of transportation systems may be entitled to some compensation for damages. Those who lived next to a railroad tunnel had no right to be compensated for normal operations (vibration from trains and the emission of smoke, cinders, and gases). However, they were entitled to the recovery of some damages if fans within the tunnel pumped additional smoke and gases

---

5. United States v. Fuller, 409 U.S. 488 (1973); Almota Farmers Elevator & Whse. Co. v. United States, 409 U.S. 470 (1973); United States v. Cors, 337 U.S. 325 (1949); United States ex rel. TVA v. Powelson, 319 U.S. 266 (1943).

onto their property. Richards v. Washington Terminal Co., 233 U.S. 546 (1914). If military bombers skim so close to a person's home and chicken farm that chickens are killed by crashing into the walls from fright and homeowners are unable to sleep, the flights constitute a "taking" of property requiring just compensation. United States v. Causby, 328 U.S. 256 (1946). See also Griggs v. Allegheny County, 369 U.S. 84 (1962).[6]

The Court remains divided on issues involving private property and environmental law. In *Rapanos* v. *United States*, 547 U.S. 715 (2006), the Court split 5–4 on the question of whether wetlands adjacent to tributaries of traditionally navigable waters are "waters of the United States" within the meaning of the Clean Water Act. 86 Stat. 816 (1972). The Army Corps of Engineers had refused to issue a permit to John Rapanos to backfill wetlands that had surface connections to tributaries of navigable waters. In the opinion of the Court, Justice Scalia denounced the federal regulators' policy towards the wetlands as "beyond parody." Justice Kennedy joined the majority, but wrote a concurring opinion that set forth a standard that seemed closer to the dissenters who, in an opinion by Justice Stevens, would have deferred to federal regulators.

War, Regulation, and Zoning

Under conditions of war, private property may be demolished to prevent use by the enemy. Compensation need not be given to the owner. United States v. Caltex, 344 U.S. 149 (1952). Through its power to regulate commerce and other matters, Congress may diminish the value of private property without triggering the Taking Clause. The Supreme Court noted in 1986 that Congress "routinely creates burdens for some that directly benefit others." In setting minimum wages, controlling prices, or regulating other actions, "it cannot be said that the Taking Clause is violated whenever legislation requires one person to use his or her assets for the benefit of another." Connolly v. Pension Benefit Guaranty Corp., 475 U.S. 211, 223 (1986). Statutes may be interpreted as merely regulatory rather than a taking. FCC v. Florida Power Corp., 480 U.S. 245 (1987).

Zoning laws that restrict, diminish, or destroy the value of property do not necessarily represent a taking. Communities use zoning ordinances as part of the police power to promote public health, safety, and morals. Restrictions are placed on the height of buildings and the materials and methods of construction. Certain industries are excluded from residential areas. These regulations usually do not represent unconstitutional deprivations of property or takings.[7] Zoning ordinances that attempted to segregate neighborhoods on the basis of race have been struck down as unconstitutional. Buchanan v. Warley, 245 U.S. 60 (1917). Moreover, zoning ordinances that arbitrarily or unreasonably interfere with a family's right to remain as a unit within their home have been declared unconstitutional. Moore v. East Cleveland, 431 U.S. 494 (1977).

Zoning ordinances apply equally to all property owners in a designated area. However, laws passed to preserve historic buildings and neighborhoods affect only particular property owners. Any alterations to these structures must be approved by local officials or commissions. In a case decided by the Supreme Court in 1978, a company claimed that the application of New York City's landmarks law to the Grand Central Terminal constituted a taking of property in violation of the Fifth and Four-

---

6. Other "taking" cases include Andrus v. Allard, 444 U.S. 51 (1979); United States v. Reynolds, 397 U.S. 14 (1970); YMCA v. United States, 395 U.S. 85 (1969); Goldblatt v. Hempstead, 369 U.S. 590 (1962); Armstrong v. United States, 364 U.S. 40 (1960); United States v. Central Eureka Mining Co., 357 U.S. 155 (1958); Berman v. Parker, 348 U.S. 26 (1954); United States v. Petty Motor Co., 327 U.S. 372 (1946); Miller v. Schoene, 276 U.S. 272 (1928); Hadacheck v. Sebastian, 239 U.S. 394 (1915).

7. San Diego Gas & Electric Co. v. San Diego, 450 U.S. 621 (1981); Agins v. City of Tiburon, 447 U.S. 255 (1980); Village of Belle Terre v. Boraas, 416 U.S. 1 (1974); Zahn v. Bd. of Public Works, 274 U.S. 325 (1927); Euclid v. Ambler Co., 272 U.S. 365 (1926); Welch v. Swasey, 214 U.S. 91 (1909). See also MacDonald, Sommer & Frates v. Yolo County, 477 U.S. 340 (1986) and Williamson Planning Comm'n v. Hamilton Bank, 473 U.S. 172 (1985), for the ripeness hurdle that can prevent courts from reaching the taking issue.

Other Taking Cases

A state may not force landlords to permit a company to install cable television in return for nominal payments (such as a one-time one-dollar payment). The permanent physical occupation of an owner's property constitutes a taking and requires just compensation.	Loretto v. Teleprompter Manhattan CATV Corp., 458 U.S. 419 (1972).
If a private developer deepens a pond to form a marina and connects it to a navigable bay used by the public, the marina loses its character as a private property. However, if the government wishes to make the marina a public aquatic park, it must pay just compensation.	Kaiser Aetna v. United States, 444 U.S. 164 (1979).
Company data supplied to the government in the form of trade secrets can be treated as property entitled to protection under the Taking Clause.	Ruckelshaus v. Monsanto Co., 467 U.S. 986 (1984).
Coal companies failed to show that a taking had occurred when a state required that 50 percent of the coal beneath statutorily protected structures had to be kept in place to provide surface support.	Keystone Bituminous Coal Assn. v. DeBenedictis, 480 U.S. 470 (1987).
"Temporary" takings are impermissible. Once a taking has been determined, government must compensate the owner for the period during which the taking was effective.	First English Evangelical Lutheran Church v. Los Angeles County, 482 U.S. 304 (1987).
As a condition for permitting someone to replace a small bungalow on their beachfront lot with a larger house, a state may not insist that the owners allow the public to pass across their beach, which was located between two public beaches.	Nollan v. California Coastal Commission, 483 U.S. 825 (1987).

teenth Amendments. The decision, which denied that property had been taken, reveals the difficulty the Court encounters when it attempts to define the meaning of the Taking Clause. Penn Central Transp. Co. v. New York City, 438 U.S. 104 (1978).

Although the Taking Clause of the Fifth Amendment applies to the states, state courts may reach a different result by deciding cases entirely upon their own constitutions. Twenty-five states have Taking Clauses that require compensation for property that is "taken or damaged." The last two words can offer a heightened or different level of constitutional protection. Robert Meltz, Dwight H. Merriam, and Richard M. Frank. The Takings Issue 20–21 (1999).

Contemporary Disputes

Recent cases highlight the complexity and broad reach of the Taking Clause (see box). In a controversial case in 1984, the Court held that the use of eminent domain to condemn land as a means of redistributing private property and combating oligarchy represented a valid "public use." HAWAII HOUSING AUTHORITY v. MIDKIFF, 467 U.S. 229 (1984). The decision underscores the degree to which the judiciary will defer to constitutional judgments by national and state legislatures.

Several cases in 1992 promised to provide greater protection to property owners under the Taking Clause, but the merits were not squarely reached. In one case a unanimous Court merely held that a rent-control ordinance did not amount to a *physical* taking of the property of owners of a mobile home park. The Court concluded that the ordinance might have caused a *regulatory* taking, but that issue was not properly before the Court. Yee v. Escondido, 503 U.S. 519 (1992). A more significant ruling that year narrowed the rights of states to rely on regulatory takings that completely deprive individuals of the economic use of their property. In this case an individual bought two oceanfront lots with the intent to build homes on them, but two years later the South Carolina legislature passed environmental regulations that prohibited development of the property. As a result of the Court's ruling, South Carolina had to identify nuisance and property laws in force at the time the oceanfront lots were purchased. To be exempt from compensating a property owner, the state would have to claim more than a general public interest or an interest in preventing serious public harm. Lucas v. South Carolina Coastal Council, 505 U.S. 1003 (1992). As explained in the next section, this case took odd turns when it went back to South Carolina.

A 1994 ruling by the Supreme Court broadened property rights by announcing that land use requirements may be "takings." The 5–4 decision dealt with the practice of local governments giving property owners a permit for building a development only on the condition that they donate part of their land for parks, bike paths, and other public purposes. These conditions will now be valid only if the local government makes "some sort of individualized determination that the required dedication is related both in nature and extent to the impact of the proposed development." Dolan v. City of Tigard, 512 U.S. 374, 391 (1994). Other recent decisions on the taking of property include Babbitt v. Youpee, 519 U.S. 234 (1997); Suitum v. Tahoe Regional Planning Agency, 520 U.S. 725 (1997); Phillips v. Washington Legal Foundation, 524 U.S. 156 (1998); Eastern Enterprises v. Apfel, 524 U.S. 498 (1998); and City of Monterey v. Del Monte Dunes, 526 U.S. 687 (1999). The last three were 5–4 decisions, underscoring the Court's inability to agree on constitutional principles.

Deep disagreements also flavored two property cases decided by the Supreme Court in 2001 and 2002. In the first case, it ruled 5 to 4 that the owner of waterfront property in Rhode Island had a right to challenge in court some development restrictions even though the restrictions existed when he bought the property. The Court held that land-use restrictions that are unreasonable "do not become less so through passage of time or title." Future generations "have a right to challenge unreasonable limitations on the use and value of land." The Court remanded under the principles set forth in *Penn Central.* Palazzolo v. Rhode Island, 533 U.S. 606, 627 (2001).

A 6–3 decision in 2002 strengthened environmental regulators against legal challenges from the property-rights movement. The Court ruled that the Constitution does not automatically require governments to pay compensation to landowners when planning agencies temporarily prohibit them from developing their property. Such disputes are to be decided case by case, weighing such factors as the length of the moratorium and the reasons offered by the government. Writing for the majority, Justice Stevens said that "the extreme categorical rule that any deprivation of all economic use, no matter how brief, constitutes a compensable taking surely cannot be sustained." Tahoe-Sierra Preserv. v. Tahoe Reg. Planning, 535 U.S. 302, 334 (2002). He confined *Lucas* to "the 'extraordinary case' in which a regulation permanently deprives property of all value." Id. at 332. Interestingly, he said that many of the key decisions on takings "should be the product of legislative rulemaking rather than adjudication." Id. at 335.

The *Kelo* Decision

A landmark 5–4 ruling in 2005 triggered nationwide controversy. The Supreme Court upheld the exercise of the governmental power of eminent domain to condemn and take, with just compensation, private property for "public use" under the Fifth Amendment but for a "public purpose." Connecticut's stated objective was to advance economic development in the New London community. In an opinion with major implications for city planners and homeowners, Justice John Paul Stevens wrote for the Court that "public use" includes "promoting economic development," even if property is seized and sold for development by private developers. KELO v. CITY OF NEW LONDON, 545 U.S. 469 (2005). He added: "we emphasize that nothing in our opinion precludes any state from placing further restrictions on its exercise of the takings power." Id. at 19. In other words, the Court was not placing a national straitjacket on the states.

Reaction to the ruling was fast and heated. More than three dozen states accepted the Court's "invitation" and imposed restrictions on the ability of local governments to seize property and turn it over to private developers. A number of voter referendums and propositions were approved in the states, placing similar restrictions on the right of eminent domain. Pamela A. MacLean, "The 'Kelo' Effect," Nat'l L. J., March 31, 2008, at 1.

Congress took two actions in 2005. On June 30, the House passed H. Res. 340 by a vote of 365 to 33, stating that it "disagrees" with *Kelo* and that its holdings "effectively negate the public use requirement of the takings clause." 151 Cong. Rec. 14982–90, 14998–99. During floor debate, lawmakers pointed out that many influential organizations, including the National Association for the Advancement of Colored People (NAACP), the American Association of Retired Persons (AARP), and the American Farm Bureau Federation, had filed briefs opposing the action of New London. The House resolution was not legally binding, but legislation was introduced (H.R. 4128) and reported from committee to have legal effect. H. Rept. 109-262, Part 2. It made states ineligible for federal economic development funds for a period of up to two years if they used eminent domain to take property from private individuals to be used for economic development. States could cure their violation of the legislation by returning property found by a court to violate congressional policy. That bill passed the House on November 3 by a vote of 401 to 11. 151 Cong. Rec. 24751–53, 24759. After action on further amendments, it passed 376 to 38. Id. at 24761–98. The Senate did not act on H.R. 4128.

As an example of coordinate construction, President George W. Bush, on June 23, 2006—the first anniversary of *Kelo*—issued an executive order that prohibited federal agencies from seizing private property, except for public projects such as medical facilities, roads, parks, and government office building and institutes. As for the land set aside for economic development in New London, in the anticipation of new jobs and increased tax revenue, it sat vacant for years in part because of the serious recession that affected the entire nation.

In February 2012, the House again passed legislation along the lines of H.R. 4128. The new bill, H.R. 1433, was reported by House Judiciary on February 17. H. Rept. 112-401. It passed under suspension of the rules without a rollcall vote. 158 Cong. Rec. H997-1003 (daily ed. Feb. 28, 2012). Floor debate explains the central issues advanced by those who supported and opposed the bill (see reading).

Recent Taking Cases

In another taking case, Lingle v. Chevron, 544 U.S. 528 (2005), the Court, in a unanimous opinion by Justice O'Connor, upheld a Hawaiian statute that capped the rent paid by gasoline dealers who lease company-owned service stations, and ruled that the legislation had not effected an unconstitutional taking. The Ninth Circuit had relied on the Court's "substantially advance" test set forth in *Agins* v. *City of Tiburon*, 447 U.S. 255, 260 (1980), to affirm a lower court ruling that declared the cap an unconstitutional taking. The *Agins* test provided that a regulation effects a Fifth Amendment taking if it does not "substantially advance" legitimate state interests. But Justice O'Connor ruled that the test was dictum and that it was not a valid method for determining whether a regulation constitutes a taking of private property. As an alternative, the Court affirmed its adherence to precedents, such as *Penn Central*, which emphasize multiple factors in determining whether a taking had been effected.

A decision in 2010 skirted the question whether there can be "judicial takings" (the taking of property as a result of a judicial ruling). Justices Scalia, Roberts, Alito, and Thomas were willing to head in that direction but could not muster a majority. All of the Justices (except Stevens, who did not participate) agreed that Florida's action of adding sand to miles of eroded beaches without giving own-ers rights to the new land did not constitute a taking. Stop the Beach Renourishment, Inc. v. Florida Dept. of Environmental Protection, 560 U.S. ___ (2010). The decision was considered a defeat by the "property interest" community that seeks compensation to private property owners for a broad array of "takings."

Following the Trail

As with other Supreme Court decisions, one never knows what gap will emerge between what the Court says and what happens next. *Lucas* v. *South Carolina Coastal Council* (1992) supposedly fea-tured a collision between two forces, with the state ("the Environmentalist") preventing David Lucas from doing any construction on his two beachfront lots. After the Court reversed and remanded, South Carolina was unable to prove that the building contemplated by Lucas would constitute a com-mon law nuisance. A settlement of $1.5 million paid Lucas $425,000 for each lot and covered his in-terest and legal fees. After deducting mortgage and costs, he walked away with less than $100,000. What did South Carolina do with the two lots? Keep them pristine and untouched by the worker's hand? Not at all. First it rejected a bid from one of Lucas's neighbors, who offered $315,000 for one of the lots to prevent any building on it. The state then accepted $392,500 per lot from a construction company which intended to develop the property, precisely what the state had prohibited Lucas from doing. Thus, a case that started out with South Carolina adamantly opposed to any construction on oceanfront property did a full reverse after the Court's opinion. Gideon Kanner, "Not with a Bang, but a Giggle: The Settlement of the Lucas Case," in David L. Callies, ed., Takings 308–11 (1996).

Congressional Action

Congress has considered legislation in recent years to require federal agencies to determine whether their regulatory activities amount to a taking of private property. The purpose is either to compel gov-ernment to compensate property owners or to force agencies to scale back their regulations. The Sen-ate passed this type of requirement in 1991, building on Executive Order 12630 issued by President Reagan in 1988, but the Senate language was not enacted. 137 Cong. Rec. 14446–54, 14456–67 (1991); 53 Fed. Reg. 8859 (1988).

The "Contract with America," announced by more than 300 Republican candidates for the U.S. House of Representatives on September 27, 1994, called for a number of reforms to limit government and expand individual rights. One of the provisions sought to protect private property owners by compensating them for all but very small reductions in the value of their property that were caused by government regulation. The draft bill provided that a private property owner "is entitled" to re-ceive compensation and the head of an agency "shall pay" a private property owner any compensa-tion required.

However, when it became apparent that full compensation for such losses would add massive amounts to the federal deficit and jeopardize other Republican goals (such as a balanced budget), the bill was modified by removing the concept of an entitlement. As passed by the House, the private property bill stated that the federal government "shall" compensate anyone whose private property had been diminished in value by at least 20 percent. Yet the government's liability was sharply reduced by other language in the bill. No compensation would be made if an agency's primary purpose was to prevent an identifiable hazard to public health or safety, or if the owner's proposed use of land would have been a nuisance. Moreover, if a citizen presented a claim, the agency had the option of paying the amount or seeking reimbursement from another agency that shared responsibility. If an agency said that it had no money to pay the claim, the only obligation at that point would be for the agency head to ask Congress for an appropriation. Congress would have no obligation (except per-haps a moral one) to appropriate anything. The Senate never acted on the bill or any variation of it.

In 1997, the House passed a bill to expedite access to the federal courts for private parties claiming a violation of the Taking Clause. 143 Cong. Rec. 22509–34 (1997). The Senate did not bring the bill up for a vote. In 1998, the House passed another version of this legislation. 144 Cong. Rec. 3329–39, 3393–98 (1998). The Senate failed to act on this bill either. Opponents objected that federal courts would end up making decisions better left to local zoning authorities and state courts. In 2000, the House passed legislation for expedited access to federal courts to challenge deprivations of private property by governmental actions. 146 Cong. Rec. 2909–34 (2000). The Senate took no action on the bill. Congressional action in response to the 2005 *Kelo* decision is covered in an earlier section.

Hawaii Housing Authority v. Midkiff

467 U.S. 229 (1984)

How much may legislatures exercise their police powers without "taking" property in violation of the Fifth and Fourteenth Amendments? Such questions necessarily involve a sharing of judgments and jurisdiction by legislatures and courts. In this case, the Hawaii Legislature enacted a land reform act in 1967 in an effort to reduce the social and economic evils of a land oligopoly that could be traced back to the early high chiefs of the Hawaiian Islands. The statute created a land condemnation scheme and provoked a suit that claimed a violation of constitutional rights. Frank Midkiff, a landowner, filed suit to have the land reform act declared unconstitutional as a violation of the Taking Clause. The Ninth Circuit agreed that it was a taking.

JUSTICE O'CONNOR delivered the opinion of the Court.

. . .

[I.A]

The Hawaiian Islands were originally settled by Polynesian immigrants from the western Pacific. These settlers developed an economy around a feudal land tenure system in which one island high chief, the ali'i nui, controlled the land and assigned it for development to certain subchiefs. The subchiefs would then reassign the land to other lower ranking chiefs, who would administer the land and govern the farmers and other tenants working it. All land was held at the will of the ali'i nui and eventually had to be returned to his trust. There was no private ownership of land....

Beginning in the early 1800s, Hawaiian leaders and American settlers repeatedly attempted to divide the lands of the kingdom among the crown, the chiefs, and the common people. These efforts proved largely unsuccessful, however, and the land remained in the hands of a few. In the mid-1960s, after extensive hearings, the Hawaii Legislature discovered that, while the State and Federal Governments owned almost 49% of the State's land, another 47% was in the hands of only 72 private landowners.... The legislature further found that 18 landholders, with tracts of 21,000 acres or more,

owned more than 40% of this land and that on Oahu, the most urbanized of the islands, 22 landowners owned 72.5% of the fee simple titles.... The legislature concluded that concentrated land ownership was responsible for skewing the State's residential fee simple market, inflating land prices, and injuring the public tranquility and welfare.

To redress these problems, the legislature decided to compel the large landowners to break up their estates.... To accommodate the needs of both lessors and lessees, the Hawaii Legislature enacted the Land Reform Act of 1967 (Act), Haw. Rev. Stat., ch. 516, which created a mechanism for condemning residential tracts and for transferring ownership of the condemned fees simple to existing lessees. By condemning the land in question, the Hawaii Legislature intended to make the land sales involuntary, thereby making the federal tax consequences less severe while still facilitating the redistribution of fees simple....

Under the Act's condemnation scheme, tenants living on single-family residential lots within developmental tracts at least five acres in size are entitled to ask the Hawaii Housing Authority (HHA) to condemn the property on which they live.... When 25 eligible tenants, or tenants on half the lots in the tract, whichever is less, file appropriate applications, the Act authorizes HHA to hold a public hearing to determine whether acquisition by the State of all or part of the tract will "effectuate the public purposes" of the Act.... If HHA finds that these public purposes will be served, it is authorized to designate some or all of the lots in the tract for acquisition. It then acquires, at prices set either by condemnation trial or by negotiation between lessors and lessees, the former fee owners' full "right, title, and interest" in the land....

After compensation has been set, HHA may sell the land titles to tenants who have applied for fee simple ownership.... If HHA does not sell the lot to the tenant residing there, it may lease the lot or sell it to someone else, provided that public notice has been given....

. . .

III

The majority of the Court of Appeals next determined that the Act violates the "public use" requirement of the Fifth and Fourteenth Amendments. On this argument, however, we find ourselves in agreement with the dissenting judge in the Court of Appeals.

A

The starting point for our analysis of the Act's constitutionality is the Court's decision in *Berman* v. *Parker*, 348 U.S. 26 (1954). In *Berman,* the Court held constitutional the District of Columbia Redevelopment Act of 1945. That Act provided both for the comprehensive use of the eminent domain power to redevelop slum areas and for the possible sale or lease of the condemned lands to private interests. In discussing whether the takings authorized by that Act were for a "public use," *id.,* at 31, the Court stated:

"We deal, in other words, with what traditionally has been known as the police power. An attempt to define its reach or trace its outer limits is fruitless, for each case must turn on its own facts. The definition is essentially the product of legislative determinations addressed to the purposes of government, purposes neither abstractly nor historically capable of complete definition. Subject to specific constitutional limitations, when the legislature has spoken, the public interest has been declared in terms well-nigh conclusive. In such cases the legislature, not the judiciary, is the main guardian of the public needs to be served by social legislation, whether it be Congress legislating concerning the District of Columbia ... or the States legislating concerning local affairs.... This principle admits of no exception merely because the power of eminent domain is involved...." *Id.,* at 32 (citations omitted).

. . .

There is, of course, a role for courts to play in reviewing a legislature's judgment of what constitutes a public use, even when the eminent domain power is equated with the police power. But the Court in *Berman* made clear that it is "an extremely narrow" one. *Id.,* at 32. The Court in *Berman* cited with approval the Court's decision in *Old Dominion Co.* v. *United States,* 269 U.S. 55, 66 (1925), which held that deference to the legislature's "public use" determination is required "until it is shown to involve an impossibility." ...

To be sure, the Court's cases have repeatedly stated that "one person's property may not be taken for the benefit of another private person without a justifying public purpose, even though compensation be paid." *Thompson* v. *Consolidated Gas Corp.,* 300 U.S. 55, 80 (1937).... Where the exercise of the eminent domain power is rationally related to a conceivable public purpose, the Court has never held a compensated taking to be proscribed by the Public Use Clause....

On this basis, we have no trouble concluding that the Hawaii Act is constitutional. The people of Hawaii have attempted, much as the settlers of the original 13 Colonies did, to reduce the perceived social and economic evils of a land oligopoly traceable to their monarchs. The land oligopoly has, according to the Hawaii Legislature, created artificial deterrents to the normal functioning of the State's residential land market and forced thousands of individual homeowners to lease, rather than buy, the land underneath their homes. Regulating oligopoly and the evils associated with it is a classic exercise of a State's police powers.... We cannot disapprove of Hawaii's exercise of this power.

. . .

B

... The fact that a state legislature, and not the Congress, made the public use determination does not mean that judicial deference is less appropriate. Judicial deference is required because, in our system of government, legislatures are better able to assess what public purposes should be advanced by an exercise of the taking power. State legislatures are as capable as Congress of making such determinations within their respective spheres of authority. See *Berman* v. *Parker,* 348 U.S., at 32. Thus, if a legislature, state or federal, determines there are substantial reasons for an exercise of the taking power, courts must defer to its determination that the taking will serve a public use.

IV

The State of Hawaii has never denied that the Constitution forbids even a compensated taking of property when executed for no reason other than to confer a private benefit on a particular private party. A purely private taking could not withstand the scrutiny of the public use requirement; it would serve no legitimate purpose of government and would thus be void. But no purely private taking is involved in these cases.... Accordingly, we reverse the judgment of the Court of Appeals, and remand these cases for further proceedings in conformity with this opinion.

It is so ordered.

JUSTICE MARSHALL took no part in the consideration or decision of these cases.

Kelo v. City of New London

545 U.S. 469 (2005)

In an effort to revitalize its ailing economy, the City of New London (through its development agent) purchased most of the property earmarked for an economic development project from willing sellers, but initiated condemnation proceedings when petitioners, the owners of the rest of the property, refused to sell. Susette Kelo and other homeowners brought a state-court action claiming that the taking of their properties would violate the "public use" restriction in the Fifth Amendment Takings Clause since their properties would not be used for a "public purpose." A trial court issued a restraining order prohibiting New London from taking some of the property, but the Connecticut Supreme Court upheld the takings. The U.S. Supreme Court's opinion is noteworthy for its emphasis on judicial self-restraint.

JUSTICE STEVENS delivered the opinion of the Court.

[II]

We granted certiorari to determine whether a city's decision to take property for the purpose of economic development satisfies the "public use" requirement of the Fifth Amendment....

III

Two polar propositions are perfectly clear. On the one hand, it has long been accepted that the sovereign may not take the property of *A* for the sole purpose of transferring it to another private party *B*, even though *A* is paid just compensation. On the other hand, it is equally clear that a State may transfer property from one private party to another if future "use by the public" is the purpose of the taking; the condemnation of land for a railroad with common-carrier duties is a familiar example. Neither of these propositions, however, determines the disposition of this case.

As for the first proposition, the City would no doubt be forbidden from taking petitioners' land for the purpose of conferring a private benefit on a particular private party. See [*Hawaii Housing Authority v.*] *Midkiff*, 467 U.S., [229] at 245.... Nor would the City be allowed to take property under the mere pretext of a public purpose, when its actual purpose was to bestow a private benefit. The takings before us, however, would be executed pursuant to a "carefully considered" development plan.... The trial judge and all the members of the Supreme Court of Connecticut agreed that there was no evidence of an illegitimate purpose in this case....

· · ·

The disposition of this case therefore turns on the question whether the City's development plan serves a "public purpose." Without exception, our cases have defined that concept broadly, reflecting our longstanding policy of deference to legislative judgments in this field.

In *Berman v. Parker*, 348 U.S. 26 (1954), this Court upheld a redevelopment plan targeting a blighted area of Washington, D. C., in which most of the housing for the area's 5,000 inhabitants was beyond repair. Under the plan, the area would be condemned and part of it utilized for the construction of streets, schools, and other public facilities. The remainder of the land would be leased or sold to private parties for the purpose of redevelopment, including the construction of low-cost housing.

The owner of a department store located in the area challenged the condemnation, pointing out that his store was not itself blighted and arguing that the creation of a "better balanced, more attractive community" was not a valid public use.... Writing for a unanimous Court, Justice Douglas refused to evaluate this claim in isolation, deferring instead to the legislative and agency judgment that the area "must be planned as a whole" for the plan to be successful....

IV

Those who govern the City were not confronted with the need to remove blight in the Fort Trumbull area, but their determination that the area was sufficiently distressed to justify a program of economic rejuvenation is entitled to our deference. The City has carefully formulated an economic development plan that it believes will provide appreciable benefits to the community, including—but by no means limited to—new jobs and increased tax revenue. As with other exercises in urban planning and development, the City is endeavoring to coordinate a variety of commercial, residential, and recreational uses of land, with the hope that they will form a whole greater than the sum of its parts. To effectuate this plan, the City has invoked a state statute that specifically authorizes the use of eminent domain to promote economic development.... Because that plan unquestionably serves a public purpose, the takings challenged here satisfy the public use requirement of the Fifth Amendment.

To avoid this result, petitioners urge us to adopt a new bright-line rule that economic development does not qualify as a public use. Putting aside the unpersuasive suggestion that the City's plan will provide only purely economic benefits, neither precedent nor logic supports petitioners' proposal. Promoting economic development is a traditional and long accepted function of government. There is, moreover, no principled way of distinguishing economic development from the other public purposes that we have recognized....

Petitioners contend that using eminent domain for economic development impermissibly blurs the boundary between public and private takings. Again, our cases foreclose this objection. Quite simply, the government's pursuit of a public purpose will often benefit individual private parties....

In affirming the City's authority to take petitioners' properties, we do not minimize the hardship that condemnations may entail, notwithstanding the payment of just compensation. We emphasize that nothing in our opinion precludes any State from placing further restrictions on its exercise of the takings power. Indeed, many States already impose "public use" requirements that are stricter than the federal baseline....

The judgment of the Supreme Court of Connecticut is affirmed.

JUSTICE KENNEDY, concurring....

JUSTICE O'CONNOR, with whom THE CHIEF JUSTICE, JUSTICE SCALIA, and JUSTICE THOMAS join, dissenting.

Over two centuries ago, just after the Bill of Rights was ratified, Justice Chase wrote:

"An ACT of the Legislature (for I cannot call it a law) contrary to the great first principles of the social compact, cannot be considered a rightful exercise of legislative authority.... A few instances will suffice to explain what I mean.... [A] law that takes property from A. and gives it to B: It is against all reason and justice, for a people to entrust a Legislature with SUCH powers; and, therefore, it cannot be presumed that they have done it." *Calder v. Bull*, 3 Dall. 386, 388 (1798) (emphasis deleted).

Today the Court abandons this long-held, basic limitation on government power. Under the banner of economic development, all private property is now vulnerable to being taken and transferred to another private owner, so long as it might be upgraded—*i.e.*, given to an owner who will use it in a way that the legislature deems more beneficial to the public—in the process. To reason, as the Court does, that the incidental public benefits resulting from the subsequent ordinary use of private property render economic development takings "for public use" is to wash out any distinction between private and public use of property—and thereby effectively to delete the words "for public use" from the Takings Clause of the Fifth Amendment. Accordingly I respectfully dissent.

. . .

II

... [W]e have read the Fifth Amendment's language to impose two distinct conditions on the exercise of eminent domain: "the taking must be for a 'public use' and 'just compensation' must be paid to the owner." ...

Where is the line between "public" and "private" property use? We give considerable deference to legislatures' determinations about what governmental activities will advantage the public. But were the political branches the sole arbiters of the public-private distinction, the Public Use Clause would amount to little more than hortatory fluff. An external, judicial check on how the public use requirement is interpreted, however limited, is necessary if this constraint on government power is to retain any meaning....

Any property may now be taken for the benefit of another private party, but the fallout from this decision will not be random. The beneficiaries are likely to be those citizens with disproportionate influence and power in the political process, including large corporations and development firms. As for the victims, the government now has license to transfer property from those with fewer resources to those with more....

JUSTICE THOMAS, dissenting.

... [T]he Court replaces the Public Use Clause with a "'[P]ublic [P]urpose'" Clause, *ante*, at 479–480 (or perhaps the "Diverse and Always Evolving Needs of Society" Clause, *ante*, at 479 (capitalization added)), a restriction that is satisfied, the Court in-

structs, so long as the purpose is "legitimate" and the means "not irrational," *ante*, at 488 (internal quotation marks omitted). This deferential shift in phraseology enables the Court to hold, against all common sense, that a costly urban-renewal project whose stated purpose is a vague promise of new jobs and increased tax revenue, but which is also suspiciously agreeable to the Pfizer Corporation, is for a "public use."

I cannot agree. If such "economic development" takings are for a "public use," any taking is, and the Court has erased the Public Use Clause from our Constitution.... Today's decision is simply the latest in a string of our cases construing the Public Use Clause to be a virtual nullity, without the slightest nod to its original meaning....

Congress Responds to *Kelo*

In reaction to *Kelo*, the House of Representatives passed two measures in 2005 to express its disagreement with the ruling and to invoke the spending power to penalize states that use the power of eminent domain to take property from private owners and give it to another party for economic development. The Senate took no action. In February 2012, the House again passed legislation to deny federal funds to states that seize private property in violation of congressional policy. The debate below occurred on February 28, 2012.

Mr. SMITH of Texas....

This legislation essentially reverses this result [in *Kelo*] and prohibits State and local governments that receive Federal economic development funds from abusing eminent domain for private economic development. It also prohibits the Federal Government from using eminent domain for economic development purposes.

This bill restores Americans' faith in their ability to build, own, and keep their property without fear of the government taking their homes, farms, or businesses to give to other people. It tells commercial developers that they should seek to obtain property through private negotiation, not by public force.

Too many Americans have lost homes and small businesses to eminent domain abuse, forced to watch as private developers replace them with luxury condominiums and other upscale uses. Local governments often approve the use of eminent domain for private economic development in order to expand their tax base....

Mr. CONYERS....

I reluctantly rise in opposition to the measure before us, the so-called Private Property Rights Protection Act. Now, while the goal of this legislation to

protect property owners and tenants from the abuse of eminent domain is laudable and important, it would, in reality, supplant the work States have already done to respond to the Supreme Court's decision in Kelo v. The City of New London in the 7 years since the Court handed down that decision.

Most importantly, whatever the concerns of my colleagues may have about the Kelo decision, the use and abuse of the power of eminent domain, I hope that every Member would look very carefully at the penalty it will impose on States, counties, cities, and towns across the country. Even if they never take a single piece of property, even if a jurisdiction never uses eminent domain at all, the mere possibility that some future administration would use eminent domain in a prohibited manner would cast a permanent cloud over the jurisdiction's finances.

The risk of the catastrophic penalties being imposed over the life of a 10-year or 20-year bond would be enough to destroy or mitigate a city or State's ability to float bonds at any time for any reason. At the very least, our cities and States would be forced to pay a risk premium that would make us envy Greece....

Mr. SENSENBRENNER....

Under the decision [in Kelo], farmers in my State

of Wisconsin are particularly vulnerable. The fair market value of farmland is less than that of residential or commercial property, which means it doesn't generate as much property tax as homes or offices. Uncle Sam can condemn one family's house only because another private entity would pay more in tax revenue....

The protection of property rights is one of the most important tenets of our government. I am mindful of the long history of eminent domain abuses, particularly in low-income and often predominantly minority neighborhoods, and of the need to stop it....

Ms. WATERS....

Few protested the Kelo ruling more ardently than the National Association for the Advancement of Colored People, the NAACP. In an amicus brief filed in the case, it argued that "the burden of eminent domain has and will continue to fall disproportionately upon racial and ethnic minorities, the elderly and economically disadvantaged." Unfettered eminent domain authority, the NAACP concluded, "is a license for government to coerce individuals on behalf of society's strongest interests."...

Ms. JACKSON-LEE of Texas....

... A 2004 study estimated that 1,600 African American neighborhoods were destroyed by municipal projects in Los Angeles. In San Jose, California, 95 percent of the properties targeted for economic redevelopment are Hispanic or Asian owned, despite the fact that only 30 percent of businesses in that area are owned by racial or ethnic minorities....

... [A]ccording to a 1989 study, 90 percent of the 10,000 families displaced by highway projects in Baltimore were African Americans....

D. THE POLICE POWER

The courts of the nineteenth century permitted legislatures and municipalities broad discretion to use the "police power" to regulate public health and safety. The power of states to "impose restraints and burdens upon persons and property in conservation and promotion of the public health, good order and prosperity, is a power originally and always belonging to the States, not surrendered by them to the general government nor directly restrained by the Constitution of the United States, and essentially exclusive." In re Rahrer, 140 U.S. 545, 554 (1891). The police power may serve malign as well as benign purposes. In 1896, the Supreme Court held that Louisiana could use its police power to provide for "separate but equal" accommodations for whites and blacks in railway coaches. Plessy v. Ferguson, 163 U.S. 537, 544 (1896).

In a major case in 1873, a 5 to 4 decision by the Supreme Court upheld a monopoly that Louisiana had granted to a slaughterhouse. The Court ruled that the statute represented a valid police regulation for the health and comfort of the people. The decision proved pivotal for two other reasons. First, it concluded that the privileges and immunities under the Fourteenth Amendment were to be protected by the states, not the national government. Second, the powerful dissents influenced future proponents of property rights and liberty of contract. SLAUGHTER-HOUSE CASES, 83 U.S. (16 Wall.) 36 (1873). Just as the police power could justify a monopoly, so could the same state a few years later invoke that power to abolish the monopoly and reintroduce competition. Butchers' Union Co. v. Crescent City Co., 111 U.S. 746 (1884).

There were some hints at the state level that legislative efforts to control business activities could be curbed by the courts. Wynehamer v. People, 13 N.Y. 378 (1856). However, the Supreme Court provided broad support for state regulatory efforts. An Illinois law setting maximum charges for storing grain in warehouses and elevators was upheld in 1877 as a legitimate exercise of state authority to regulate businesses affected with a public interest. MUNN v. ILLINOIS, 94 U.S. 113 (1877). Other cases during this period supported use of the police power for economic regulation. Fertilizing Co. v. Hyde Park, 97 U.S. 659 (1879); Patterson v. Kentucky, 97 U.S. 501 (1879); Beer Co. v. Massachusetts, 97 U.S. 25 (1878).

A unanimous decision in 1885 upheld a law prohibiting public laundries from operating from 10 P.M. to 6 A.M. Barbier v. Connolly, 113 U.S. 27. A year later, the Court upheld the power of a state rail-

The Police Power

... While this [police] power is inherent in all governments, it has doubtless been greatly expanded in its application during the past century, owing to an enormous increase in the number of occupations that are dangerous, or so far detrimental to the health of employés as to demand special precautions for their well-being and protection, or the safety of adjacent property. While this court has held ... that the police power cannot be put forward as an excuse for oppressive and unjust legislation, it may be lawfully resorted to for the purpose of preserving the public health, safety or morals, or the abatement of public nuisances, and a large discretion "is necessarily vested in the legislature to determine not only what the interests of the public require, but what measures are necessary for the protection of such interests." ...

While this power is necessarily inherent in every form of government, it was, prior to the adoption of the Constitution, but sparingly used in this country. As we were then almost purely an agricultural people, the occasion for any special protection of a particular class did not exist. Certain profitable employments, such as lotteries and the sale of intoxicating liquors, which were then considered to be legitimate, have since fallen under the ban of public opinion, and are now either altogether prohibited, or made subject to stringent police regulations. The power to do this has been repeatedly affirmed by this court....

While the business of mining coal and manufacturing iron began in Pennsylvania as early as 1716, and in Virginia, North Carolina and Massachusetts even earlier than this, both mining and manufacturing were carried on in such a limited way and by such primitive methods that no special laws were considered necessary, prior to the adoption of the Constitution, for the protection of the operatives; but, in the vast proportions which these industries have since assumed, it has been found that they can no longer be carried on with due regard to the safety and health of those engaged in them, without special protection against the dangers necessarily incident to these employments....

Source: Holden v. Hardy, 169 U.S. 366, 391–93 (1898).

road commission to fix freight and passenger rates. Railroad Commission Cases, 116 U.S. 307, 347, 353 (1886). A unanimous ruling in 1887 allowed states to prohibit the manufacture and sale of intoxicating liquors within the state. It belonged to the legislative branch "to exert what are known as the police powers of the State, and to determine, primarily, what measures are appropriate or needful for the protection of the public morals, the public health, or the public safety." Mugler v. Kansas, 123 U.S. 623, 661 (1887).

Judicial Limits

In 1890, the Supreme Court declared unconstitutional a Minnesota law not because it exceeded the police power but because the judiciary of that state had decided that the reasonableness of rates established by a railroad and warehouse commission was final and conclusive, prohibiting review by the courts. This case did not prevent regulation by the state. It merely required the courts to determine whether the rates satisfied due process of law. Chicago, Milwaukee and St. Paul Railway Co. v. Minnesota, 134 U.S. 418 (1890). Also that year, the Court invalidated a Minnesota police power statute because it interfered with commerce among the states and thus invaded the province of Congress. Minnesota v. Barber, 136 U.S. 313 (1890).

In 1897, a unanimous Supreme Court used the magic phrase "liberty to contract" to speak strongly about a citizen's right to be free to earn his livelihood. Allgeyer v. Louisiana, 165 U.S. 578, 589, 591 (1897). This general philosophy did not prevent the Court the next year from upholding an eight-hour day for workers in coal mines and smelters. The Court flatly rejected the idea that workers and employers stood on equal footing in reaching a contract. Holden v. Hardy, 169 U.S. 366, 397 (1898). The Court perceptively noted that the police power had been greatly expanded in the nineteenth century because of the growth of dangerous occupations (see box). In 1903, the Court upheld an eight-hour law in Kansas covering all persons employed by the state or local governments, including work contracted by the state. Atkin v. Kansas, 191 U.S. 207 (1903).

Slaughter-House Cases

16 Wall. 36 (1873)

The legislature of Louisiana passed an act granting to a corporation, which it created, the exclusive right for 25 years to operate slaughterhouses. The corporation operated within three parishes, including the city of New Orleans, and prohibited other persons from competing with the corporation. The constitutional issue was whether this exclusive grant of monopoly privilege was a police regulation for the health and comfort of the people or whether it violated the constitutional rights of other citizens to exercise their trade and occupation. The Supreme Court's decision is significant because it marks an important interpretation of the Civil War Amendments, especially the reach and purpose of the Fourteenth Amendment and the power of the federal government to direct state activities.

Mr. Justice MILLER, now, April 14th, 1873, delivered the opinion of the court.

. . .

It is … the slaughter-house privilege, which is mainly relied on to justify the charges of gross injustice to the public, and invasion of private right.

It is not, and cannot be successfully controverted, that it is both the right and the duty of the legislative body—the supreme power of the State or municipality—to prescribe and determine the localities where the business of slaughtering for a great city may be conducted. To do this effectively it is indispensable that all persons who slaughter animals for food shall do it in those places *and nowhere else.*

The statute under consideration defines these localities and forbids slaughtering in any other. It does not, as has been asserted, prevent the butcher from doing his own slaughtering. On the contrary, the Slaughter-House Company is required, under a heavy penalty, to permit any person who wishes to do so, to slaughter in their houses; and they are bound to make ample provision for the convenience of all the slaughtering for the entire city. The butcher then is still permitted to slaughter, to prepare, and to sell his own meats; but he is required to slaughter at a specified place and to pay a reasonable compensation for the use of the accommodations furnished him at that place.

. . .

It cannot be denied that the statute under consideration is aptly framed to remove from the more densely populated part of the city, the noxious slaughter-houses, and large and offensive collections of animals necessarily incident to the slaughtering business of a large city, and to locate them where the convenience, health, and comfort of the people require they shall be located. And it must be conceded that the means adopted by the act for this purpose are appropriate, are stringent, and effectual....

The plaintiffs in error accepting this issue, allege that the statute is a violation of the Constitution of the United States in these several particulars:

That it creates an involuntary servitude forbidden by the thirteenth article of amendment;

That it abridges the privileges and immunities of citizens of the United States;

That it denies to the plaintiffs the equal protection of the laws; and,

That it deprives them of their property without due process of law; contrary to the provisions of the first section of the fourteenth article of amendment....

. . .

[*The Court summarizes the adoption of the Fourteenth Amendment, as a response to the "black codes" used by southern states to suppress blacks, and the Fifteenth Amendment.*]

The first section of the fourteenth article, to which our attention is more specially invited, opens with a definition of citizenship....

"All persons born or naturalized in the United

States, and subject to the jurisdiction thereof, are citizens of the United States and of the State wherein they reside."

. . .

It is quite clear, then, that there is a citizenship of the United States, and a citizenship of a State, which are distinct from each other, and which depend upon different characteristics or circumstances in the individual.

We think this distinction and its explicit recognition in this amendment of great weight in this argument, because the next paragraph of this same section, which is the one mainly relied on by the plaintiffs in error, speaks only of privileges and immunities of citizens of the United States, and does not speak of those of citizens of the several States. The argument, however, in favor of the plaintiffs rests wholly on the assumption that the citizenship is the same, and the privileges and immunities guaranteed by the clause are the same.

The language is, "No State shall make or enforce any law which shall abridge the privileges or immunities of citizens of *the United States.*" It is a little remarkable, if this clause was intended as a protection to the citizen of a State against the legislative power of his own State, that the word citizen of the State should be left out when it is so carefully used, and used in contradistinction to citizens of the United States, in the very sentence which precedes it....

Fortunately we are not without judicial construction of this clause of the Constitution. The first and the leading case on the subject is that of *Corfield* v. *Coryell,* decided by Mr. Justice Washington in the Circuit Court for the District of Pennsylvania in 1823.

"The inquiry," he says, "is, what are the privileges and immunities of citizens of the several States? We feel no hesitation in confining these expressions to those privileges and immunities which are *fundamental;* which belong of right to the citizens of all free governments, and which have at all times been enjoyed by citizens of the several States which compose this Union, from the time of their becoming free, independent, and sovereign. What these fundamental principles are, it would be more tedious than difficult to enumerate. They may all, however, be comprehended under the following general heads: protection by the government, with the right to acquire and possess property of every kind, and to pursue and obtain happiness and safety, subject, nevertheless, to such restraints as the government may prescribe for the general good of the whole."

... Was it the purpose of the fourteenth amendment, by the simple declaration that no State should make or enforce any law which shall abridge the privileges and immunities of *citizens of the United States,* to transfer the security and protection of all the civil rights which we have mentioned, from the States to the Federal government? And where it is declared that Congress shall have the power to enforce that article, was it intended to bring within the power of Congress the entire domain of civil rights heretofore belonging exclusively to the States?

... [S]uch a construction followed by the reversal of the judgments of the Supreme Court of Louisiana in these cases, would constitute this court a perpetual censor upon all legislation of the States, on the civil rights of their own citizens, with authority to nullify such as it did not approve as consistent with those rights, as they existed at the time of the adoption of this amendment. The argument we admit is not always the most conclusive which is drawn from the consequences urged against the adoption of a particular construction of an instrument. But when, as in the case before us, these consequences are so serious, so far-reaching and pervading, so great a departure from the structure and spirit of our institutions; when the effect is to fetter and degrade the State governments by subjecting them to the control of Congress, in the exercise of powers heretofore universally conceded to them of the most ordinary and fundamental character; when in fact it radically changes the whole theory of the relations of the State and Federal governments to each other and of both these governments to the people; the argument has a force that is irresistible, in the absence of language which expresses such a purpose too clearly to admit of doubt.

We are convinced that no such results were intended by the Congress which proposed these amendments, nor by the legislatures of the States which ratified them.

... [I]t is sufficient to say that under no construction of that provision that we have ever seen, or any that we deem admissible, can the restraint imposed by the State of Louisiana upon the exercise of their trade by the butchers of New Orleans be held to be a deprivation of property within the meaning of that provision....

The judgments of the Supreme Court of Louisiana in these cases are

Affirmed.

Mr. Justice FIELD, dissenting: ...

The act of Louisiana presents the naked case, unaccompanied by any public considerations, where a right to pursue a lawful and necessary calling, previously enjoyed by every citizen, and in connection with which a thousand persons were daily employed, is taken away and vested exclusively for twenty-five years, for an extensive district and a large population, in a single corporation, or its exercise is for that period restricted to the establishments of the corporation, and there allowed only upon onerous conditions....

[*After reviewing a number of judicial rulings, Field concludes:*] In all these cases there is a recognition of the equality of right among citizens in the pursuit of the ordinary avocations of life, and a declaration that all grants of exclusive privileges, in contravention of this equality, are against common right, and void.

This equality of right, with exemption from all disparaging and partial enactments, in the lawful pursuits of life, throughout the whole country, is the distinguishing privilege of citizens of the United States. To them, everywhere, all pursuits, all professions, all avocations are open without other restrictions than such as are imposed equally upon all oth-

ers of the same age, sex, and condition.... [I]t is to me a matter of profound regret that its validity is not recognized by a majority of this court, for by it the right of free labor, one of the most sacred and imprescriptible rights of man, is violated....

I am authorized by the CHIEF JUSTICE, Mr. Justice SWAYNE, and Mr. Justice BRADLEY, to state that they concur with me in this dissenting opinion.

Mr. Justice BRADLEY, also dissenting:

... [I]n my judgment, the right of any citizen to follow whatever lawful employment he chooses to adopt (submitting himself to all lawful regulations) is one of his most valuable rights, and one which the legislature of a State cannot invade, whether restrained by its own constitution or not.

. . .

Mr. Justice SWAYNE, dissenting:

. . .

Munn v. Illinois

94 U.S. 113 (1877)

This case illustrates the need to balance two conflicting interests: the property rights of private individuals against the duty of the state to regulate economic conditions for the public good. Although economic regulation is sometimes regarded as a phenomenon of the twentieth century, this case makes clear that it has been customary "from time immemorial." Statutes regulating private property do not necessarily deprive an owner of his property without due process of law. When the owner of property devotes it to a use "in which the public has an interest," the owner must submit to some degree of public control. Ira Munn, owner of a number of grain warehouses, challenged a state law.

Mr. CHIEF JUSTICE WAITE delivered the opinion of the court.

The question to be determined in this case is whether the general assembly of Illinois can, under the limitations upon the legislative power of the States imposed by the Constitution of the United States, fix by law the maximum of charges for the storage of grain in warehouses at Chicago and other places in the State....

It is claimed that such a law is repugnant—

1. To that part of sect. 8, art. 1, of the Constitution of the United States which confers upon Congress the power "to regulate commerce with foreign nations and among the several States;"

2. To that part of sect. 9 of the same article which provides that "no preference shall be given by any regulation of commerce or revenue to the ports of one State over those of another;" and

3. To that part of amendment 14 which ordains that no State shall "deprive any person of life, liberty, or property, without due process of law, nor deny to any person within its jurisdiction the equal protection of the laws."

We will consider the last of these objections first.

Every statute is presumed to be constitutional. The courts ought not to declare one to be unconstitutional, unless it is clearly so. If there is doubt, the expressed will of the legislature should be sustained.

The Constitution contains no definition of the word "deprive," as used in the Fourteenth Amendment. To determine its signification, therefore, it is necessary to ascertain the effect which usage has given it, when employed in the same or a like connection.

While this provision of the amendment is new in the Constitution of the United States, as a limitation upon the powers of the States, it is old as a principle of civilized government. It is found in Magna Charta, and, in substance if not in form, in nearly or quite all the constitutions that have been from time to time adopted by the several States of the Union. By the Fifth Amendment, it was introduced into the Constitution of the United States as a limitation upon the powers of the national government, and by the Fourteenth, as a guaranty against any encroachment upon an acknowledged right of citizenship by the legislatures of the States.

... Under these [*police*] powers the government regulates the conduct of its citizens one towards another, and the manner in which each shall use his own property, when such regulation becomes necessary for the public good. In their exercise it has been customary in England from time immemorial, and in this country from its first colonization, to regulate ferries, common carriers, hackmen, bakers, millers, wharfingers, innkeepers, &c., and in so doing to fix a maximum of charge to be made for services rendered, accommodations furnished, and articles sold....

From this it is apparent that, down to the time of the adoption of the Fourteenth Amendment, it was not supposed that statutes regulating the use, or even the price of the use, of private property necessarily deprived an owner of his property without due process of law. Under some circumstances they may, but not under all....

... Looking, then, to the common law, from whence came the right which the Constitution protects, we find that when private property is "affected with a public interest, it ceases to be *juris privati* only." ... Property does become clothed with a public interest when used in a manner to make it of public consequence, and affect the community at large. When, therefore, one devotes his property to a use in which the public has an interest, he, in effect, grants to the public an interest in that use, and must submit to be controlled by the public for the common good, to the extent of the interest he has thus created....

... It remains only to ascertain whether the warehouses of these plaintiffs in error, and the business which is carried on there, come within the operation of this principle.

For this purpose we accept as true the statements of fact contained in the elaborate brief of one of the counsel of the plaintiffs in error. From these it appears that "the great producing region of the West and North-west sends its grain by water and rail to Chicago, where the greater part of it is shipped by vessel for transportation to the seaboard by the Great Lakes, and some of it is forwarded by railway to the Eastern ports.... Vessels, to some extent, are loaded in the Chicago harbor, and sailed through the St. Lawrence directly to Europe.... The quantity [of grain] received in Chicago has made it the greatest grain market in the world. This business has created a demand for means by which the immense quantity of grain can be handled or stored, and these have been found in grain warehouses, which are commonly called elevators, because the grain is elevated from the boat or car, by machinery operated by steam, into the bins prepared for its reception, and elevated from the bins, by a like process, into the vessel or car which is to carry it on...."

... [I]t is apparent that all the elevating facilities through which these vast productions "of seven or eight great States of the West" must pass on the way "to four or five of the States on the sea-shore" may be a "virtual" monopoly.

Under such circumstances it is difficult to see why, if the common carrier, or the miller, or the ferryman, or the innkeeper, or the wharfinger, or the baker, or the cartman, or the hackney-coachman, pursues a public employment and exercises "a sort of public office," these plaintiffs in error do not. They stand, to use again the language of their counsel, in the very "gateway of commerce," and take toll from all who pass. Their business most certainly "tends to a common charge, and is become a thing of public interest and use." ... Certainly, if any business can be clothed "with a public interest, and cease to be *juris privati* only," this has been. It may not be made so by the operation of the Constitution of Illinois or this statute, but it is by the facts.

We also are not permitted to overlook the fact that, for some reason, the people of Illinois, when they revised their Constitution in 1870, saw fit to make it the duty of the general assembly to pass laws "for the protection of producers, shippers, and receivers of grain and produce," art. 13, sect. 7.... This indicates very clearly that during the twenty years in which this peculiar business had been assuming its present "immense proportions," something had occurred which led the whole body of the people to suppose that remedies such as are usually employed to prevent abuses by virtual monopolies might not be inappropriate here.... Of the propriety of legislative interference within the scope of legislative power, the legislature is the exclusive judge....

We know that [*the police power*] is a power which may be abused; but that is no argument against its existence. For protection against abuses by legislatures the people must resort to the polls, not to the courts....

We come now to consider the effect upon this

statute of the power of Congress to regulate commerce.

... The warehouses of these plaintiffs in error are situated and their business carried on exclusively within the limits of the State of Illinois.... Incidentally they may become connected with inter-state commerce, but not necessarily so. Their regulation is a thing of domestic concern, and, certainly, until Congress acts in reference to their inter-state relations, the State may exercise all the powers of government over them, even though in so doing it may indirectly operate upon commerce outside its immediate jurisdiction....

Judgment affirmed.

Mr. Justice Field and Mr. Justice Strong dissented.

Mr. Justice Field....

... [I]t would seem from its opinion that the court holds that property loses something of its private character when employed in such a way as to be generally useful....

If this be sound law, if there be no protection, either in the principles upon which our republican government is founded, or in the prohibitions of the Constitution against such invasion of private rights, all property and all business in the State are held at the mercy of a majority of its legislature. The public has no greater interest in the use of buildings for the storage of grain than it has in the use of buildings for the residences of families, nor, indeed, any thing like so great an interest; and, according to the doctrine announced, the legislature may fix the rent of all tenements used for residences, without reference to the cost of their erection. ... [I]ndeed, there is hardly an enterprise or business engaging the attention and labor of any considerable portion of the community, in which the public has not an interest in the sense in which that term is used by the court in its opinion....

Mr. Justice Strong....

E. SUBSTANTIVE DUE PROCESS

By 1903, the Court had sustained an eight-hour day for the public sector and for certain industries in the private sector (coal mining and smelting). Over the next three decades the courts regularly invalidated legislative efforts to establish maximum hours or minimum wages—efforts the judiciary regarded as an unconstitutional interference with the "liberty of contract." Lawyers from the corporate sector helped translate the philosophy of laissez-faire into legal terms and constitutional doctrine. One of the intellectual pillars of this movement was Thomas M. Cooley, whose *Constitutional Limitations* appeared in 1868. Cooley emphasized limits on legislative authority in order to protect personal liberty and private property. Herbert Spencer's *Social Statics* (1851) counseled against government efforts to protect the weak, preferring instead a kind of Darwinian struggle for survival of the "fittest." Christopher G. Tiedeman's *Treatise on the Limitations of the Police Power* (1886) also developed the theory of laissez-faire and liberty of contract. See Benjamin R. Twiss, Lawyers and the Constitution (1942).

The climate of the years following the Civil War promoted the pursuit of material goals, especially after the heavy sacrifices demanded by the war. Elitism by corporate leaders could not be justified on tradition (feudalism) or the will of God (Calvinism). Neither belief system fitted an age devoted to materialist thinking, scientific discovery, and industrial capitalism. Justification took the form of Social Darwinism: the belief in ruthless individualism in which only the strongest were entitled to survive. Material success became the overriding value. The American Bar Association, founded in 1878, campaigned to limit legislative interference with property rights. The specter of "socialism" and "communism" gave added force and urgency to these efforts.

The *Lochner* Era

Judicial tolerance of the police power came to an abrupt halt in 1905 when the Supreme Court invalidated a New York law limiting bakery workers to sixty hours a week or ten hours a day. Justice Peckham, writing for a 5 to 4 majority, converted the general right to make a contract into laissez-faire rigidity. He found no "reasonable ground" to interfere with the liberty of a person to contract for as many hours of work as desired. LOCHNER v. NEW YORK, 198 U.S. 45, 57 (1905). The statute seemed to him to serve no purpose in safeguarding public health or the health of the worker. Such laws were "mere meddlesome interferences" with the rights of an individual to enter into contracts. Lawyers who opposed the law argued that it was not a health measure but rather "a labor law" to promote paternalism.

In their dissent, Justices Harlan, White, and Day reviewed previous holdings of the Court that had interpreted the police power generously to support economic regulation. They cited statistical studies to show the need for remedial legislation. Peckham's opinion was so flavored with conservative business doctrines that Justice Holmes, in his dissent, accused the majority of deciding "upon an economic theory which a large part of the country does not entertain." The Constitution, he said, is "not intended to embody a particular economic theory, whether of paternalism and the organic relation of the citizen to the state or of *laissez faire.*" The doctrine of laissez-faire never meant a pure free market. Corporations were busily involved in forming pools, trusts, "community of interests," and other devices to protect themselves from competition. The marketplace of many competing units was becoming a relic of the past.

Sociological Data

The Court equivocated on the principle of laissez-faire. In 1908 it struck down a congressional statute that made it unlawful for the railroads to fire workers because of their union membership. A 6–2 decision maintained the fiction of *Lochner* that the employer and employee had "equality of right" to enter into a contract, "and any legislation that disturbs that equality is an arbitrary interference with the liberty of contract over which no government can legally justify in a free land." Adair v. United States, 208 U.S. 161, 175 (1908). See also Coppage v. Kansas, 236 U.S. 1 (1915).

Also in 1908, however, the Court sustained Oregon's ten-hour day for women. The statistical record referred to by the dissenters in *Lochner* supplied a good tactical clue for Louis D. Brandeis, who argued the case for Oregon. His sister-in-law, Josephine Goldmark, was closely associated with the National Consumers' League, which had long advocated improved working conditions. She supervised an intensive search of library holdings and helped produce a brief of 113 pages, almost all of which consisted of copious data extracted from sociological studies supporting the need for limiting working hours for women. The Court called attention to what is now known as the "Brandeis brief": a compilation of state and foreign statutes that imposed restrictions on the hours of labor required of women, followed by extracts from more than 90 reports of committees, bureaus of statistics, commissioners of hygiene, and inspectors of factories. These studies, drawn primarily from Europe, concluded that long hours of labor "are dangerous for women, primarily because of their special physical organization." Muller v. Oregon, 208 U.S. 412, 419–20 n.1 (1908).

Could the constitutional principle announced in *Lochner* be displaced by public opinion and sociological data? The Court indulged in a bit of judicial doubletalk:

> The legislation and opinions referred to in the margin may not be, technically speaking, authorities, and in them is little or no discussion of the constitutional question presented to us for determination, yet they are significant of a widespread belief that woman's physical structure, and the functions she performs in consequence thereof, justify special legislation restricting or qualifying the conditions under which she should be permitted to toil. Constitutional questions, it is true, are not settled by even a consensus of present public opinion, for it is the peculiar value of a written constitution that it places in unchanging form limitations upon legislative action, and thus gives a permanence and stability to popular government which otherwise would be lacking. At the same time, when a question of fact is debated and debatable, and the extent to which a special constitutional limitation goes is affected by the truth in

respect to that fact, a widespread and long continued belief concerning it is worthy of consideration. We take judicial cognizance of all matters of general knowledge.[8]

"Liberty of contract" did not prevent the Court in 1911 from unanimously upholding an Iowa statute that prohibited certain contracts by railroad companies, or delivering another unanimous opinion three years later to sustain a New York law requiring certain industries to pay employees semi-monthly and in cash. Chicago, Burlington & Quincy R.R. Co. v. McGuire, 219 U.S. 543 (1911) and Erie R.R. Co. v. Williams, 233 U.S. 685 (1914). Rent-control laws were also upheld, preventing a landlord from freely contracting with his or her tenants. Block v. Hirsh, 256 U.S. 135 (1921).

In 1917, the Court upheld the constitutionality of Oregon's ten-hour day for both men and women, including a provision for overtime pay. Brandeis was now on the Court as an Associate Justice. Because of his previous involvement in litigating this type of case, he did not participate in the decision. Felix Frankfurter of the Harvard Law School argued the case for Oregon and prepared a "Brandeis brief" that contained an array of facts and statistics to demonstrate the effects of overtime on the physical and moral health of the worker. His brief reviewed industrial conditions and labor experiences in England and the United States. A 5–3 Court sustained the statute. Bunting v. Oregon, 243 U.S. 426 (1917).

Frankfurter was again lead counsel in defending a congressional statute that provided for minimum wages for women and children in the District of Columbia. Despite his lengthy sociological brief, the Court held the statute invalid. Writing for a 5–3 majority, Justice Sutherland found the mass of data compiled by Frankfurter "interesting but only mildly persuasive." ADKINS v. CHILDREN'S HOSPITAL, 261 U.S. 525, 560 (1923). Because of progress in contractual, political, and civil status of women since the *Muller* decision of 1908, Sutherland said that the continuation of protective legislation could not be justified. Although the Court had sustained statutes setting maximum hours, the minimum wage law seemed dangerous territory to the majority. What was next, Sutherland asked, maximum wages? In one of the dissents, Chief Justice Taft thought that the line drawn between hours and wages was imaginary. Justice Holmes's dissent described how the phrase "due process of law" had evolved into the "dogma, Liberty of Contract."

The Great Depression

Between 1923 and 1934, the Court repeatedly struck down statutes on the ground that the activity regulated was not "affected with a public interest."[9] At the same time, new areas of economic life were becoming national in scope and gradually brought within Congress' power over interstate commerce (see Chapter 8). Finally, the onset of the Great Depression of 1929 shattered the theory of a self-correcting free economy.

The philosophy of *Adkins* survived as late as 1936, although a decision that year striking down New York's minimum wage law for women and children could muster only a 5–4 majority. "Freedom of contract," said the Court, "is the general rule and restraint the exception." Morehead v. N.Y. ex rel. Tipaldo, 298 U.S. 587, 610–11 (1936). Chief Justice Hughes dissented, joined by Brandeis, Stone, and Cardozo. Stone, in a separate dissent, criticized the basis on which the majority had declared the New

---

8. Muller v. Oregon, 208 U.S. 412, 420–21 (1908). For unanimous rulings that upheld other state statutes setting maximum hours for women, see Bosley v. McLaughlin, 236 U.S. 385 (1915); Miller v. Wilson, 236 U.S. 373 (1915); and Riley v. Massachusetts, 232 U.S. 671 (1914). A 5–4 Court upheld a congressional statute setting an eight-hour day for railroad workers engaged in interstate commerce; Wilson v. New, 243 U.S. 332 (1917).

9. New State Ice Co. v. Liebmann, 285 U.S. 262 (1932); Williams v. Standard Oil Co., 278 U.S. 235 (1929); Ribnik v. McBride, 277 U.S. 350 (1928); Tyson & Brother v. Banton, 273 U.S. 418 (1927); Wolff Co. v. Industrial Court, 262 U.S. 522 (1923).

York law invalid: "It is difficult to imagine any grounds, other than our own personal economic predilections, for saying that the contract of employment is any the less an appropriate subject of legislation than are scores of others, in dealing with which this Court has held that legislatures may curtail individual freedom in the public interest." Stone emphasized the changes that had occurred in economic conditions: "In the years that have intervened since the *Adkins* case we have had opportunity to learn that a wage is not always the resultant of free bargaining between employers and employees; that it may be one forced upon employees by their economic necessities and upon employers by the most ruthless of their competitors.... Because of their nature and extent these are public problems. A generation ago they were for the individual to solve; today they are the burden of the nation."

Liberty-of-Contract Doctrine Abandoned

Adkins was finally overruled in 1937. Sutherland, Van Devanter, McReynolds, and Butler, who had provided four of the majority votes in *Morehead,* dissented. Roberts, the fifth member of that majority, now joined the four dissenters from *Morehead* to uphold a minimum wage law for women and minors in the state of Washington. WEST COAST HOTEL CO. v. PARRISH, 300 U.S. 379 (1937). Since the Washington case was decided about two months after President Franklin D. Roosevelt had unveiled his court-packing plan (see the section on the court-packing plan in the concluding chapter), much has been made of Roberts's "switch in time that saved nine." However, Roberts had already broken with his doctrinaire laissez-faire colleagues. He wrote the 5–4 opinion in *Nebbia* v. *New York,* 291 U.S. 502 (1934), which upheld a price-setting statute. With his support, the Court was prepared to sustain minimum wage legislation in the fall of 1936 but had delayed its ruling because Justice Stone was ill.[10]

Justice Sutherland, speaking for the four dissenters in *West Coast Hotel,* assailed the theory that decisions of the Supreme Court should be reconsidered because of economic conditions: "the meaning of the Constitution does not change with the ebb and flow of economic events." His phrase "ebb and flow" suggests a seasonal if not spasmodic quality, which seems offensive to a constitution grounded on fundamental principles. However, the record of the Court on economic regulation was decidedly one of ebb and flow. Over a period of about four decades, the Court had tried to impose a liberty-of-contract theory at a time when power was shifting dramatically from the employee to the employer. A countervailing force was needed, and the elected branches intervened to redress the imbalance. Liberals welcomed the decision in *West Coast Hotel* as did conservatives, because it averted a serious threat to the Court's independence and prestige (see box on next page).

By 1941 the composition of the Court had been radically altered, especially with Reed, Murphy, and Black replacing Sutherland, Butler, and Van Devanter. A unanimous Court that year upheld a congressional statute setting minimum wages and maximum hours for men and women. The statute was within the power of Congress to regulate interstate commerce and to protect public health, morals, and welfare. No conflict was found with the due process of law or with the rights of states under the Tenth Amendment. United States v. Darby, 312 U.S. 100 (1941). Another unanimous decision in 1941 overruled the laissez-faire doctrine of *Ribnik* v. *McBride*. Olsen v. Nebraska, 313 U.S. 236 (1941). A combination of social, economic, and political forces had finally reversed the constitutional doctrines of the Court. In the future, decisions about economic or social philosophy would be left largely to legislatures, not to the courts. FERGUSON v. SKRUPA, 372 U.S. 726 (1963). See also

---

10. Felix Frankfurter, "Mr. Justice Roberts," 104 U. Pa. L. Rev. 311 (1955); 2 Merlo J. Pusey, Charles Evans Hughes 757 (1963). For a challenge to Roberts' recollection of key events in 1936, see Clement E. Vose, Constitutional Change 228–34 (1972). See also Marian C. McKenna, Franklin Roosevelt and the Great Constitutional War 418–19, 422–23, 435–37, 536 (2002).

Political Reaction to *West Coast Hotel*

The effect of this decision was far-reaching in law and in economics, but its immediate repercussions were political. The Administration forces had to like the decision, for it was what they had long contended the law to be. It stimulated the movement in both state and nation to "put a floor under wages" and a "ceiling over hours," and a law to prescribe minimum wages and maximum hours in interstate commerce was soon proposed to Congress. But the liberals had a good deal to say about judicial strangling for fifteen years of such legislation in both state and nation by what was now conceded to be a blunder of the Court....

The conservatives liked the decision. They knew the former one [*Adkins*] took ground too reactionary to be held. The timing of the yielding was a boon to them. It removed a great deal of pressure for reform of the Court, and they made much of the argument that the Court did not need reforming, but could and would reform itself. At any rate the Court had made a bold turn in direction. The doctrine of "freedom of contract," which had menaced all types of legislation to regulate the master and servant relation, had been uprooted so definitely that it could hardly be expected to thrive again. Labor was free from the shackles of a fictitious freedom.

SOURCE: Robert H. Jackson, The Struggle for Judicial Supremacy 211–12 (1941).

Williamson v. Lee Optical Co., 348 U.S. 483, 488 (1955) and Day-Brite Lighting, Inc. v. Missouri, 342 U.S. 421 (1952).

Lochner v. New York

198 U.S. 45 (1905)

New York passed a law prohibiting employees from working in bakeries more than 60 hours a week or ten hours a day. The statute, sustained by the state courts, was similar to other labor laws passed by states to protect workers from industrial conditions that threatened health and safety. The case represented a conflict between two values: the police power of the state to regulate economic activities versus the "liberty" protected by the Fourteenth Amendment to contract without unreasonable interference by the state. Joseph Lochner, a bakery owner, claimed that the New York law violated the U.S. Constitution.

MR. JUSTICE PECKHAM, after making the foregoing statement of the facts, delivered the opinion of the court.

The indictment, it will be seen, charges that the plaintiff in error violated the one hundred and tenth section of article 8, chapter 415, of the Laws of 1897, known as the labor law of the State of New York, in that he wrongfully and unlawfully required and permitted an employé working for him to work more than sixty hours in one week.... The mandate of the statute that "no employé shall be required or permitted to work," is the substantial equivalent of an enactment that "no employé shall contract or agree to work," more than ten hours per day, and as there is no provision for special emergencies the statute is mandatory in all cases. It is not an act merely fixing

the number of hours which shall constitute a legal day's work, but an absolute prohibition upon the employer, permitting, under any circumstances, more than ten hours work to be done in his establishment. The employé may desire to earn the extra money, which would arise from his working more than the prescribed time, but this statute forbids the employer from permitting the employé to earn it.

The statute necessarily interferes with the right of contract between the employer and employés, concerning the number of hours in which the latter may labor in the bakery of the employer. The general right to make a contract in relation to his business is part of the liberty of the individual protected by the Fourteenth Amendment of the Federal Constitution. *Allgeyer* v. *Louisiana*, 165 U.S. 578. Under that provision no State can deprive any person of life, liberty or property without due process of law. The right to purchase or to sell labor is part of the liberty protected by this amendment, unless there are circumstances which exclude the right. There are, however, certain powers, existing in the sovereignty of each State in the Union, somewhat vaguely termed police powers, the exact description and limitation of which have not been attempted by the courts. Those powers, broadly stated and without, at present, any attempt at a more specific limitation, relate to the safety, health, morals and general welfare of the public....

The State, therefore, has power to prevent the individual from making certain kinds of contracts, and in regard to them the Federal Constitution offers no protection. If the contract be one which the State, in the legitimate exercise of its police power, has the right to prohibit, it is not prevented from prohibiting it by the Fourteenth Amendment. Contracts in violation of a statute, either of the Federal or state government, or a contract to let one's property for immoral purposes, or to do any other unlawful act, could obtain no protection from the Federal Constitution, as coming under the liberty of person or of free contract....

It must, of course, be conceded that there is a limit to the valid exercise of the police power by the State. There is no dispute concerning this general proposition. Otherwise the Fourteenth Amendment would have no efficacy and the legislatures of the States would have unbounded power, and it would be enough to say that any piece of legislation was enacted to conserve the morals, the health or the safety of the people; such legislation would be valid, no matter how absolutely without foundation the claim might be. The claim of the police power would be a mere pretext—become another and delusive name for the supreme sovereignty of the State to be exercised free from constitutional restraint. This is not contended for. In every case that comes before this court, therefore, where legislation of this character is concerned and where the protection of the Federal Constitution is sought, the question necessarily arises: Is this a fair, reasonable and appropriate exercise of the police power of the State, or is it an unreasonable, unnecessary and arbitrary interference with the right of the individual to his personal liberty or to enter into those contracts in relation to labor which may seem to him appropriate or necessary for the support of himself and his family? Of course the liberty of contract relating to labor includes both parties to it. The one has as much right to purchase as the other to sell labor.

This is not a question of substituting the judgment of the court for that of the legislature. If the act be within the power of the State it is valid, although the judgment of the court might be totally opposed to the enactment of such a law. But the question would still remain: Is it within the police power of the State? and that question must be answered by the court.

The question whether this act is valid as a labor law, pure and simple, may be dismissed in a few words. There is no reasonable ground for interfering with the liberty of person or the right of free contract, by determining the hours of labor, in the occupation of a baker. There is no contention that bakers as a class are not equal in intelligence and capacity to men in other trades or manual occupations, or that they are not able to assert their rights and care for themselves without the protecting arm of the State, interfering with their independence of judgment and of action. They are in no sense wards of the State. Viewed in the light of a purely labor law, with no reference whatever to the question of health, we think that a law like the one before us involves neither the safety, the morals nor the welfare of the public, and that the interest of the public is not in the slightest degree affected by such an act. The law must be upheld, if at all, as a law pertaining to the health of the individual engaged in the occupation of a baker. It does not affect any other portion of the public than those who are engaged in that occupation. Clean and wholesome bread does not depend upon whether the baker works but ten hours per day or only sixty hours a week....

. . .

We think that there can be no fair doubt that the trade of a baker, in and of itself, is not an unhealthy one to that degree which would authorize the legislature to interfere with the right to labor, and with the right of free contract on the part of the individual, either as employer or employé. In looking through statistics regarding all trades and occupations, it may be true that the trade of a baker does not appear to be as healthy as some other trades, and is also vastly more healthy than still others. To the common understanding the trade of a baker has never been regarded as an unhealthy one....

... The act is not, within any fair meaning of the term, a health law, but is an illegal interference with the rights of individuals, both employers and employés, to make contracts regarding labor upon such terms as they may think best, or which they may agree upon with the other parties to such contracts. Statutes of the nature of that under review, limiting the hours in which grown and intelligent men may labor to earn their living, are mere meddlesome interferences with the rights of the individual, and they are not saved from condemnation by the claim that they are passed in the exercise of the police power....

Mr. Justice Harlan, with whom Mr. Justice White and Mr. Justice Day concurred, dissenting.

... Whether or not this be wise legislation it is not the province of the court to inquire. Under our systems of government the courts are not concerned with the wisdom or policy of legislation.... I submit that this court will transcend its functions if it assumes to annul the statute of New York. [*Justice Harlan summarizes a number of studies that describe the health hazards of working in a bakery, including the inhalation of flour dust that causes inflammation of the lungs and the bronchial tubes.*]

Mr. Justice Holmes dissenting.

. . .

This case is decided upon an economic theory which a large part of the country does not entertain. If it were a question whether I agreed with that theory, I should desire to study it further and long before making up my mind. But I do not conceive that to be my duty, because I strongly believe that my agreement or disagreement has nothing to do with the right of a majority to embody their opinions in law. It is settled by various decisions of this court that state constitutions and state laws may regulate life in many ways which we as legislators might think as injudicious or if you like as tyrannical as this, and which equally with this interfere with the liberty to contract. Sunday laws and usury laws are ancient examples. A more modern one is the prohibition of lotteries. The liberty of the citizen to do as he likes so long as he does not interfere with the liberty of others to do the same, which has been a shibboleth for some well-known writers, is interfered with by

school laws, by the Post Office, by every state or municipal institution which takes his money for purposes thought desirable, whether he likes it or not. The Fourteenth Amendment does not enact Mr. Herbert Spencer's Social Statics. The other day we sustained the Massachusetts vaccination law. *Jacobson* v. *Massachusetts,* 197 U.S. 11. United States and state statutes and decisions cutting down the liberty to contract by way of combination are familiar to this court. *Northern Securities Co.* v. *United States,* 193 U.S. 197. Two years ago we upheld the prohibition of sales of stock on margins or for future delivery in the constitution of California. *Otis* v. *Parker,* 187 U.S. 606. The decision sustaining an eight hour law for miners is still recent. *Holden* v. *Hardy,* 169 U.S. 366. Some of these laws embody convictions or prejudices which judges are likely to share. Some may not. But a constitution is not intended to embody a particular economic theory, whether of paternalism and the organic relation of the citizen to the State or of *laissez faire*. It is made for people of fundamentally differing views, and the accident of our finding certain opinions natural and familiar or novel and even shocking ought not to conclude our judgment upon the question whether statutes embodying them conflict with the Constitution of the United States.

... I think that the word liberty in the Fourteenth Amendment is perverted when it is held to prevent the natural outcome of a dominant opinion, unless it can be said that a rational and fair man necessarily would admit that the statute proposed would infringe fundamental principles as they have been understood by the traditions of our people and our law. It does not need research to show that no such sweeping condemnation can be passed upon the statute before us. A reasonable man might think it a proper measure on the score of health. Men whom I certainly could not pronounce unreasonable would uphold it as a first instalment of a general regulation of the hours of work. Whether in the latter aspect it would be open to the charge of inequality I think it unnecessary to discuss.

Adkins v. Children's Hospital

261 U.S. 525 (1923)

In 1918, Congress passed a law setting minimum wages for women and children in the District of Columbia. As in other cases, the question was one of balancing the police power of Congress to regulate health and safety with the right of individuals to conduct their own affairs without legislative interference. Children's Hospital and a female elevator operator at a hotel brought this case to prevent enforcement of the act by Jesse C. Adkins and the two other members of a wage board.

MR. JUSTICE SUTHERLAND delivered the opinion of the Court.

The question presented for determination by these appeals is the constitutionality of the Act of September 19, 1918, providing for the fixing of minimum wages for women and children in the District of Columbia. 40 Stat. 960, c. 174. [*The act authorized a three-member wage board to investigate wages for women and minors and to order changes in wages after giving public notice and holding a public hearing. Questions of fact determined by the board could not be appealed.*]

The statute now under consideration is attacked upon the ground that it authorizes an unconstitutional interference with the freedom of contract included within the guaranties of the due process clause of the Fifth Amendment. That the right to contract about one's affairs is a part of the liberty of the individual protected by this clause, is settled by the decisions of this Court and is no longer open to question.... Within this liberty are contracts of employment of labor: In making such contracts, generally speaking, the parties have an equal right to obtain from each other the best terms they can as the result of private bargaining.

... But freedom of contract is, nevertheless, the general rule and restraint the exception; and the exercise of legislative authority to abridge it can be justified only by the existence of exceptional circumstances. [*Justice Sutherland reviews cases in which the Court upheld statutes fixing rates and charges to be exacted on businesses impressed with a public interest; statutes relating to contracts for the performance of public work; statutes prescribing the character, methods, and time for payment of wages; and statutes fixing hours of labor.*]

In the *Muller Case* the validity of an Oregon statute, forbidding the employment of any female in certain industries more than ten hours during any one day was upheld. The decision proceeded upon the theory that the difference between the sexes may justify a different rule respecting hours of labor in the case of women than in the case of men. It is pointed out that these consist in differences of physical structure, especially in respect of the maternal functions, and also in the fact that historically woman has always been dependent upon man, who has established his control by superior physical strength.... In view of the great—not to say revolutionary—changes which have taken place since that utterance, in the contractual, political and civil status of women, culminating in the Nineteenth Amendment, it is not unreasonable to say that these differences have now come almost, if not quite, to the vanishing point. In this aspect of the matter, while the physical differences must be recognized in appropriate cases, and legislation fixing hours or conditions of work may properly take them into account, we cannot accept the doctrine that women of mature age, *sui juris,* require or may be subjected to restrictions upon their liberty of contract which could not lawfully be imposed in the case of men under similar circumstances....

If now, in the light furnished by the foregoing exceptions to the general rule forbidding legislative interference with freedom of contract, we examine and analyze the statute in question, we shall see that it differs from them in every material respect. It is not a law dealing with any business charged with a public interest or with public work, or to meet and tide over a temporary emergency. It has nothing to do with the character, methods or periods of wage payments. It does not prescribe hours of labor or conditions under which labor is to be done. It is not for the protection of persons under legal disability or for the prevention of fraud. It is simply and exclusively a price-fixing law, confined to adult women (for we are not now considering the provisions relating to minors), who are legally as capable of contracting for themselves as men....

The standard furnished by the statute for the guidance of the board is so vague as to be impossible of practical application with any reasonable degree of accuracy. What is sufficient to supply the necessary cost of living for a woman worker and maintain her in good health and protect her morals is obviously not a precise or unvarying sum—not even approximately so. The amount will depend upon a variety of circumstances: the individual temperament, habits of thrift, care, ability to buy necessaries intelligently, and whether the woman live alone or with her family. To those who practice economy, a given sum will afford comfort, while to those of contrary habit the same sum will be wholly inadequate.... The relation between earnings and morals is not capable of standardization. It cannot be shown that well paid women safeguard their morals more carefully than those who are poorly paid....

It is said that great benefits have resulted from the operation of such statutes, not alone in the District of Columbia but in the several States, where they have been in force. A mass of reports, opinions of special observers and students of the subject, and the like, has been brought before us in support of this statement, all of which we have found interesting but only mildly persuasive....

Finally, it may be said that if, in the interest of the public welfare, the police power may be invoked to justify the fixing of a minimum wage, it may, when the public welfare is thought to require it, be invoked to justify a maximum wage. The power to fix high wages connotes, by like course of reasoning, the power to fix low wages. If, in the face of the guaranties of the Fifth Amendment, this form of legislation shall be legally justified, the field for the operation of the police power will have been widened to a great and dangerous degree....

It follows from what has been said that the act in question passes the limit prescribed by the Constitution, and, accordingly, the decrees of the court below are

Affirmed.

Mr. Justice Brandeis took no part in the consideration or decision of these cases.

Mr. Chief Justice Taft, dissenting.

. . .

Legislatures in limiting freedom of contract between employee and employer by a minimum wage proceed on the assumption that employees, in the class receiving least pay, are not upon a full level of equality of choice with their employer and in their necessitous circumstances are prone to accept pretty much anything that is offered. They are peculiarly subject to the overreaching of the harsh and greedy employer. The evils of the sweating system and of the long hours and low wages which are characteristic of it are well known. Now, I agree that it is a disputable question in the field of political economy how far a statutory requirement of maximum hours or minimum wages may be a useful remedy for these evils, and whether it may not make the case of the oppressed employee worse than it was before. But it is not the function of this Court to hold congressional acts invalid simply because they are passed to carry out economic views which the Court believes to be unwise or unsound. [*Chief Justice Taft cites earlier cases in which the Court upheld legislation setting maximum hours.*]

... I assume that the conclusion in this case rests on the distinction between a minimum of wages and a maximum of hours in the limiting of liberty to contract. I regret to be at variance with the Court as to the substance of this distinction. In absolute freedom of contract the one term is as important as the other, for both enter equally into the consideration given and received, a restriction as to one is not any greater

in essence than the other, and is of the same kind. One is the multiplier and the other the multiplicand.

If it be said that long hours of labor have a more direct effect upon the health of the employee than the low wage, there is very respectable authority from close observers, disclosed in the record and in the literature on the subject quoted at length in the briefs, that they are equally harmful in this regard. Congress took this view and we can not say it was not warranted in so doing....

I am not sure from a reading of the opinion whether the Court thinks the authority of *Muller* v. *Oregon* is shaken by the adoption of the Nineteenth Amendment. The Nineteenth Amendment did not change the physical strength or limitations of women upon which the decision in *Muller* v. *Oregon* rests....

I am authorized to say that Mr. Justice Sanford concurs in this opinion.

Mr. Justice Holmes, dissenting.

The question in this case is the broad one, Whether Congress can establish minimum rates of wages for women in the District of Columbia with due provision for special circumstances, or whether we must say that Congress has no power to meddle with the matter at all.... When so many intelligent persons, who have studied the matter more than any of us can, have thought that the means are effective and are worth the price, it seems to me impossible to deny that the belief reasonably may be held by reasonable men....

The earlier decisions upon the same words in the Fourteenth Amendment began within our memory and went no farther than an unpretentious assertion of the liberty to follow the ordinary callings. Later that innocuous generality was expanded into the dogma, Liberty of Contract. Contract is not specially mentioned in the text that we have to construe. It is merely an example of doing what you want to do, embodied in the word liberty. But pretty much all law consists in forbidding men to do some things that they want to do, and contract is no more exempt from law than other acts....

I confess that I do not understand the principle on which the power to fix a minimum for the wages of women can be denied by those who admit the power to fix a maximum for their hours of work. I fully assent to the proposition that here as elsewhere the distinctions of the law are distinctions of degree, but I perceive no difference in the kind or degree of interference with liberty, the only matter with which we have any concern, between the one case and the other. The bargain is equally affected whichever half you regulate. *Muller* v. *Oregon*, I take it, is as good law today as it was in 1908. It will need more than the Nineteenth Amendment to convince me that there are no differences between men and women, or that legislation cannot take those differences into account....

West Coast Hotel Co. v. Parrish
300 U.S. 379 (1937)

This case overruled *Adkins* v. *Children's Hospital* (1923) and, with it, the doctrine that courts can continually second-guess legislative judgments about the need for statutes governing minimum wages, maximum hours, and other aspects of industrial working conditions. Similarly, this case rejects the exalted notion of "liberty of contract," which presupposed an equality of power between employer and employee to work out a mutually satisfactory contract. The issue before the Court in this case was a statute of the state of Washington providing for the establishment of minimum wages for women. Elsie Parrish, an employee of the West Coast Hotel Company, sued to recover wages owed her under the state law.

MR. CHIEF JUSTICE HUGHES delivered the opinion of the Court.

. . .

The appellant relies upon the decision of this Court in *Adkins* v. *Children's Hospital*, 261 U.S. 525, which held invalid the District of Columbia Minimum Wage Act, which was attacked under the due process clause of the Fifth Amendment....

... The Supreme Court of Washington has upheld the minimum wage statute of that State. It has decided that the statute is a reasonable exercise of the police power of the State. In reaching that conclusion the state court has invoked principles long established by this Court in the application of the Fourteenth Amendment. The state court has refused to regard the decision in the *Adkins* case as determinative and has pointed to our decisions both before and since that case as justifying its position. We are of the opinion that this ruling of the state court demands on our part a reëxamination of the *Adkins* case. The importance of the question, in which many States having similar laws are concerned, the close division by which the decision in the *Adkins* case was reached, and the economic conditions which have supervened, and in the light of which the reasonableness of the exercise of the protective power of the State must be considered, make it not only appropriate, but we think imperative, that in deciding the present case the subject should receive fresh consideration.

. . .

The principle which must control our decision is not in doubt. The constitutional provision invoked is the due process clause of the Fourteenth Amendment governing the States, as the due process clause invoked in the *Adkins* case governed Congress. In each case the violation alleged by those attacking minimum wage regulation for women is deprivation of freedom of contract. What is this freedom? The Constitution does not speak of freedom of contract. It speaks of liberty and prohibits the deprivation of liberty without due process of law. In prohibiting that deprivation the Constitution does not recognize an absolute and uncontrollable liberty. Liberty in each of its phases has its history and connotation. But the liberty safeguarded is liberty in a social organization which requires the protection of law against the evils which menace the health, safety, morals and welfare of the people. Liberty under the Constitution is thus necessarily subject to the restraints of due process, and regulation which is reasonable in relation to its subject and is adopted in the interests of the community is due process....

The point that has been strongly stressed that adult employees should be deemed competent to make their own contracts was decisively met nearly forty years ago in *Holden* v. *Hardy, supra,* where we pointed out the inequality in the footing of the parties....

. . .

It is manifest that this established principle is peculiarly applicable in relation to the employment of women in whose protection the State has a special interest. That phase of the subject received elaborate consideration in *Muller* v. *Oregon* (1908), 208 U.S. 412, where the constitutional authority of the State to limit the working hours of women was sustained. [*After reviewing the dissents of Justice Holmes and Chief Justice Taft in* Adkins, *and citing cases after* Adkins *that upheld state statutes on economic regulation, the Court concludes:*]

With full recognition of the earnestness and vigor which characterize the prevailing opinion in the *Adkins* case, we find it impossible to reconcile that ruling with these well-considered declarations. What can be closer to the public interest than the health of women and their protection from unscrupulous and overreaching employers? And if the protection of women is a legitimate end of the exercise of state power, how can it be said that the requirement of the payment of a minimum wage fairly fixed in order to meet the very necessities of existence is not an admissible means to that end? The legislature of the State was clearly entitled to consider the situation of women in employment, the fact that they are in the class receiving the least pay, that their bargaining power is relatively weak, and that they are the ready victims of those who would take advantage of their necessitous circumstances....

... We may take judicial notice of the unparalleled demands for relief which arose during the recent period of depression and still continue to an alarming extent despite the degree of economic recovery which has been achieved.... The community is not bound to provide what is in effect a subsidy for unconscionable employers....

Our conclusion is that the case of *Adkins* v. *Children's Hospital, supra,* should be, and it is, overruled. The judgment of the Supreme Court of the State of Washington is

Affirmed.

MR. JUSTICE SUTHERLAND, dissenting:

MR. JUSTICE VAN DEVANTER, MR. JUSTICE MCREYNOLDS, MR. JUSTICE BUTLER and I think the judgment of the court below should be reversed.

· · ·

The suggestion that the only check upon the exercise of the judicial power, when properly invoked, to declare a constitutional right superior to an unconstitutional statute is the judge's own faculty of self-restraint, is both ill considered and mischievous. Self-restraint belongs in the domain of will and not of judgment. The check upon the judge is that imposed by his oath of office, by the Constitution and by his own conscientious and informed convictions; and since he has the duty to make up his own mind and adjudge accordingly, it is hard to see how there could be any other restraint....

It is urged that the question involved should now receive fresh consideration, among other reasons, because of "the economic conditions which have supervened"; but the meaning of the Constitution does not change with the ebb and flow of economic events. We frequently are told in more general words that the Constitution must be construed in the light of the present. If by that it is meant that the Constitution is made up of living words that apply to every new condition which they include, the statement is quite true. But to say, if that be intended, that the words of the Constitution mean today what they did not mean when written — that is, that they do not apply to a situation now to which they would have applied then — is to rob that instrument of the essential element which continues it in force as the people have made it until they, and not their official agents, have made it otherwise.

... Women today stand upon a legal and political equality with men. There is no longer any reason why they should be put in different classes in respect of their legal right to make contracts; nor should they be denied, in effect, the right to compete with men for work paying lower wages which men may be willing to accept. And it is an arbitrary exercise of the legislative power to do so....

Ferguson v. Skrupa

372 U.S. 726 (1963)

For a period of about four or five decades, ending in 1937, the Supreme Court overturned dozens of statutes enacted by Congress and state legislatures to ameliorate the conditions of industrialization. Laws establishing minimum wages and maximum hours, regulating child labor, and governing other aspects of industrial society were struck down. In this decision, the Court explains that such matters in the future will be left essentially to legislatures, not courts. Frank C. Skrupa, in the business of "debt adjusting," brought this action against the Attorney General of Kansas, William M. Ferguson.

MR. JUSTICE BLACK delivered the opinion of the Court.

In this case, properly here on appeal under 28 U.S.C. § 1253, we are asked to review the judgment of a three-judge District Court enjoining, as being in violation of the Due Process Clause of the Fourteenth Amendment, a Kansas statute making it a misdemeanor for any person to engage "in the business of debt adjusting" except as an incident to "the lawful practice of law in this state." The statute defines "debt adjusting" as "the making of a contract, express or implied, with a particular debtor whereby the debtor agrees to pay a certain amount of money periodically to the person engaged in the debt adjusting business who shall for a consideration distribute the same among certain specified creditors in accordance with a plan agreed upon."

The complaint, filed by appellee Skrupa doing business as "Credit Advisors," alleged that Skrupa was engaged in the business of "debt adjusting" as defined by the statute, that his business was a "useful and desirable" one, that his business activities were not "inherently immoral or dangerous" or in any way contrary to the public welfare, and that therefore the business could not be "absolutely prohibited" by Kansas. The three-judge court heard evidence by Skrupa tending to show the usefulness and desirability of his business and evidence by the state officials tending to show that "debt adjusting" lends itself to grave abuses against distressed debtors, particularly in the lower income brackets, and that these abuses are of such gravity that a number of States have strictly regulated "debt adjusting" or prohibited it altogether....

The only case discussed by the court below as support for its invalidation of the statute was *Commonwealth* v. *Stone*, 191 Pa. Super. 117, 155 A.2d 453 (1959), in which the Superior Court of Pennsylvania struck down a statute almost identical to the Kansas act involved here.... [T]he Pennsylvania court relied heavily on *Adams* v. *Tanner*, 244 U.S. 590 (1917), which held that the Due Process Clause forbids a State to prohibit a business which is "useful" and not "inherently immoral or dangerous to public welfare."

Both the District Court in the present case and the Pennsylvania court in *Stone* adopted the philosophy of *Adams* v. *Tanner*, and cases like it, that it is the province of courts to draw on their own views as to the morality, legitimacy, and usefulness of a particular business in order to decide whether a statute bears too heavily upon that business and by so doing violates due process. Under the system of government created by our Constitution, it is up to legislatures, not courts, to decide on the wisdom and utility of legislation. There was a time when the Due Process Clause was used by this Court to strike down laws which were thought unreasonable, that is, unwise or incompatible with some particular economic or social philosophy. In this manner the Due Process Clause was used, for example, to nullify laws prescribing maximum hours for work in bakeries, *Lochner* v. *New York*, 198 U.S. 45 (1905), outlawing "yellow dog" contracts, *Coppage* v. *Kansas*, 236 U.S. 1 (1915), setting minimum wages for women, *Adkins* v. *Children's Hospital*, 261 U.S. 525 (1923), and fixing the weight of loaves of bread, *Jay Burns Baking Co.* v. *Bryan*, 264 U.S. 504 (1924). This intrusion by the judiciary into the realm of legislative value judgments was strongly objected to at the time, particularly by Mr. Justice Holmes and Mr. Justice Brandeis....

The doctrine that prevailed in *Lochner, Coppage, Adkins, Burns,* and like cases—that due process authorizes courts to hold laws unconstitutional when they believe the legislature has acted unwisely—has long since been discarded. We have returned to the original constitutional proposition that courts do not substitute their social and economic beliefs for the judgment of legislative bodies, who are elected to pass laws....

... We conclude that the Kansas Legislature was free to decide for itself that legislation was needed to deal with the business of debt adjusting. Unquestionably, there are arguments showing that the business of debt adjusting has social utility, but such arguments are properly addressed to the legislature, not to us. We refuse to sit as a "superlegislature to weigh the wisdom of legislation," and we emphatically refuse to go back to the time when courts used the Due Process Clause "to strike down state laws, regulatory of business and industrial conditions, because they may be unwise, improvident, or out of harmony with a particular school of thought." Nor are we able or willing to draw lines by calling a law "prohibitory" or "regulatory." Whether the legislature takes for its textbook Adam Smith, Herbert Spencer, Lord Keynes, or some other is no concern of ours. The Kansas debt adjusting statute may be wise or unwise. But relief, if any be needed, lies not with us but with the body constituted to pass laws for the State of Kansas....

Reversed.

MR. JUSTICE HARLAN concurs in the judgment on the ground that this state measure bears a rational relation to a constitutionally permissible objective. See *Williamson* v. *Lee Optical Co.,* 348 U.S. 483, 491.

CONCLUSIONS

The protection of economic rights is not the province solely of the courts. Legislators and executives (at both the national and state levels) make the initial determination in balancing the rights of property owners against the interests of communities and society. The historical record demonstrates that when the judiciary invokes artificial doctrines to prevent legislative action ("liberty of contract" and other slogans), the persistence of social and political pressures has been sufficient, over time, to prevail. The main struggle over economic rights is fought out within the political branches through the electoral process. Aside from a few pivotal decisions, courts generally play a marginal role at the very edges of these conflicts.

Judicial deference to legislatures is again being challenged and may lead to some changes. In the legal arena there has been renewed interest in litigating issue of economic liberty, reflected in the rise of the Law and Economics field and by interest groups with the primary purpose of litigating against state and federal regulation of business. Beyond increased use of litigation strategies by such long-standing organizations as the Chamber of Commerce, new groups have become active, including the Washington Legal Foundation. Its Web site identifies these priorities: "free-enterprise principles, responsible government, [and] property rights." The organization actively engages in lawsuits and administrative/regulatory proceedings to promote those principles.

An artificial line between property rights and human rights continues to be drawn. With forceful prose, Justice Stewart attempted to join the two concepts: "[T]he dichotomy between personal liberties and property rights is a false one. Property does not have rights. People have rights. The right to enjoy property without unlawful deprivation, no less than the right to speak or the right to travel, is in truth a 'personal' right, whether the 'property' in question be a welfare check, a home, or a savings account. In fact, a fundamental interdependence exists between the personal right to liberty and the personal right in property. Neither could have meaning without the other." Lynch v. Household Finance Corp., 405 U.S. 538, 552 (1972).

NOTES AND QUESTIONS

1. In *Calder v. Bull*, Justices Chase and Iredell held different views on the role of "natural justice" as a limitation on governmental power. Is natural justice a constitutional or a philosophical concept? If the former, what is its source? If the latter, what are its limits? Would a "philosophical" concept be judicially enforceable? Is natural justice a synonym for substantive due process? If not, what are the differences? In your view, how does judicial resort to natural justice differ from *Lochnerizing*, if at all?

2. Chief Justice Taney's opinion in *Charles River Bridge* represented a dramatic departure from the Marshall Court's interpretation of the Contract Clause. In your view, which approach better promotes economic development in the United States? Is one approach a more accurate reflection of the constitutional norms that govern property?

3. In his opinion for the Court in *Blaisdell*, Chief Justice Hughes spoke of a distinction between "altering" and "impairing" the obligation of contracts. What is the difference? Do you agree with Hughes that alteration does not constitute impairment? Why or why not? Did the Court in *Blaisdell* have a realistic alternative to upholding the Minnesota statute? What would have been the economic and social consequences of finding the statute to be unconstitutional?

4. The *Blaisdell* Court held that emergencies do not create power. Can you articulate a constitutional theory to defend that view? May constitutional provisions, such as the Contract Clause, be suspended to meet an emergency? If so, which branch of government possesses that authority? What are the limits to such a power?

5. Can you explain the doctrine of a "business affected with a public interest"? Did the Court in

Munn v. Illinois provide an adequate explanation of the doctrine? Which businesses are not "affected with a public interest?"

6. In light of *Kelo*, what criteria should be applied to satisfy the Fifth Amendment's requirement of a "public" use? Is the Court's reasoning in *Kelo* consistent with its reasoning in *Midkiff*?

SELECTED READINGS

ACKERMAN, BRUCE. Private Property and the Constitution. New Haven, Conn.: Yale University Press, 1977.

BERGER, LAWRENCE. "A Policy Analysis of the Taking Problem." 49 New York University Law Review 165 (1974).

BLUME, LAWRENCE, AND DANIEL L. RUBINFELD. "Compensation for Takings: An Economic Analysis." 72 California Law Review 569 (1984).

BRIGHAM, JOHN. "Property & the Supreme Court: Do the Justices Make Sense?" 16 Polity 242 (1983).

CALLIES, DAVID L., et al. Cases and Materials on Land Use. St. Paul, Minn.: West Group, 1999.

———, ed. Takings: Land-Development Conditions and Regulatory Takings after *Dolan* and *Lucas*. Section of State and Local Government Law, American Bar Association, 1996.

COHEN, FELIX S. "Dialogue on Private Property." 9 Rutgers Law Review 357 (1954).

DUNHAM, ALLISON. "Griggs v. Allegheny County in Perspective: Thirty Years of Supreme Court Expropriation Law." 1962 Supreme Court Review 63.

ELY, JAMES W., JR. The Guardian of Every Other Right: A Constitutional History of Property Rights. New York: Oxford University Press, 1992.

EPSTEIN, RICHARD A. Takings: Private Property and the Power of Eminent Domain. Cambridge, Mass.: Harvard University Press, 1985.

———. Liberalism. Chicago: University of Chicago Press, 2003.

———. "Taking Stock of Takings: An Author's Retrospective," 15 William and Mary Bill of Rights Journal 407 (2006).

HALE, ROBERT L. "The Supreme Court and the Contract Clause." 57 Harvard Law Review 512, 621, 852 (1944).

HORWITZ, MORTON J. "The Transformation in the Conception of Property in American Law." 40 University of Chicago Law Review 248 (1973).

HUMBACH, JOHN A. "A Unifying Theory for the Just-Compensation Cases: Takings, Regulation and Public Use." 34 Rutgers Law Review 243 (1982).

JOHNSON, CORWIN W. "Compensation for Invalid Land-Use Regulations." 15 Georgia Law Review 559 (1981).

LERNER, MAX. "The Supreme Court and American Capitalism." 42 Yale Law Journal 668 (1933).

LEVY, LEONARD W. "Property As a Human Right." 5 Constitutional Commentary 169 (1988).

McCLOSKEY, ROBERT G. "Economic Due Process and the Supreme Court: An Exhumation and Reburial." 1962 Supreme Court Review 34.

MANDELKER, DANIEL R. "Land Use Takings: The Compensation Issue." 8 Hastings Constitutional Law Quarterly 491 (1981).

MELTZ, ROBERT, DWIGHT H. MERRIAM, AND RICHARD M. FRANK. The Takings Issue. Washington, D.C.: Island Press. 1999.

MENDELSON, WALLACE. "B.F. Wright on the Contract Clause: A Progressive Misreading of the Marshall-Taney Era," 38 Western Political Quarterly 262 (1985).

MICHELMAN, FRANK I. "Property, Utility, and Fairness: Comments on the Ethical Foundations of 'Just Compensation' Law." 80 Harvard Law Review 1165 (1967).

OAKES, JAMES L. "'Property Rights' in Constitutional Analysis Today." 56 Washington Law Review 583 (1981).

REICH, CHARLES A. "The New Property." 73 Yale Law Journal 733 (1964).

ROSE, CAROL M. "Mahon Reconsidered: Why the Takings Issue Is Still a Muddle." 57 Southern California Law Review 561 (1984).

SALLET, JONATHAN B. "Regulatory 'Takings' and Just Compensation: The Supreme Court's Search for a Solution Continues." 18 Urban Lawyer 635 (1986).

SAX, JOSEPH L. "Takings and the Police Power." 74 Yale Law Journal 36 (1964).

———. "Takings, Private Property, and Public Rights." 81 Yale Law Journal 149 (1971).

STOEBUCK, WILLIAM B. "Police Power, Takings, and Due Process." 37 Washington and Lee Law Review 1057 (1980).

WRIGHT, BENJAMIN F., JR. The Contract Clause of the Constitution. Cambridge, Mass.: Harvard University Press, 1938.

10

Free Speech in a
Democratic Society

The foundations for a free and open society are expressed in the First Amendment: "Congress shall make no law respecting an establishment of religion, or prohibiting the free exercise thereof; or abridging the freedom of speech, or of the press; or the right of the people peaceably to assemble, and to petition the Government for a redress of grievances." Through these words the framers attempted to secure the freedom of conscience and the free communication of ideas. To Justice Cardozo, the freedom of thought and speech forms "the matrix, the indispensable condition, of nearly every other form of freedom." Palko v. Connecticut, 302 U.S. 319, 327 (1937).

Free speech fulfills a number of personal, social, and political functions. In part, it strengthens individual growth and self-fulfillment. In the words of Justice Brandeis, it exists to "make men free to develop their faculties." Whitney v. California, 274 U.S. 357, 375 (1927). The First Amendment protects the "marketplace" of ideas, the promotion of knowledge, and the search for truth. Finally, the First Amendment "serves to ensure that the individual citizen can effectively participate in and contribute to our republican system of self-government." Globe Newspaper Co. v. Superior Court, 457 U.S. 596, 604 (1982). Free speech supports the full political debate needed in a vigorous and healthy democratic society.

Only by tolerating different ideas and beliefs can democracy function and survive, especially in a culture as heterogeneous and heterodox as the United States. The history of America is largely the repudiation of orthodoxy by the spirit of individualism and nonconformism. In a famous dissent in 1929, Justice Holmes said that "if there is any principle of the Constitution that more imperatively calls for attachment than any other it is the principle of free thought — not free thought for those who agree with us but freedom for the thought that we hate." United States v. Schwimmer, 279 U.S. 644, 654–55 (1929). Zechariah Chafee, Jr., a major influence on free-speech doctrines, put it differently: "The real value of freedom of speech is not to the minority that wants to talk, but to the majority that does not want to listen." Zechariah Chafee, Jr., Free Speech in the United States ix (1941).

A. FREE SPEECH AND NATIONAL SECURITY

In certain periods of our history, speech has been suppressed and punished. The heavy hand of the majority fell against sympathizers with France during the 1790s; labor organizers, anarchists, and socialists in the late nineteenth and early twentieth centuries; opponents of World War I; the Communists during and after World War II; and those who spoke out against the Vietnam War. Throughout these periods, the Supreme Court attempted to fashion doctrines to separate speech from action, activity, and advocacy. Distinctions between these categories remain opaque.

Sedition and War Protesters

In 1798 the Federalist party passed the notorious Alien and Sedition Acts to silence the opposition within the United States, particularly Jeffersonian Republicans (later called the Democratic Party) and "Francophiles." The Alien Acts increased the years of residence for aliens seeking citizenship, authorized deportation of "dangerous" aliens, and imposed other sanctions. 1 Stat. 566, 570, 577 (1798). The Sedition Act prohibited any person from printing or uttering "any false, scandalous and malicious" statement against the federal government, either House of Congress, or the President. 1 Stat. 596, § 2 (1798). This statute is analyzed more closely in the next chapter.

Not until the United States entered World War I did Congress pass another sedition act. Section 3 of the Espionage Act of 1917 prohibited acts that interfered with or obstructed military recruitment or morale. When opponents of the war released pamphlets that attacked conscription and urged opposition to the draft, the government responded with criminal prosecutions. A unanimous Supreme Court upheld the indictments on the basis of wartime conditions and circumstances. Writing for the Court, Justice Holmes penned his famous admonition against "falsely shouting fire in a theatre" and offered his "clear and present danger" test. SCHENCK v. UNITED STATES, 249 U.S. 47 (1919). Holmes offered a poor analogy. Shouting a *false statement* in a crowded theater to produce panic has nothing to do with circulating a leaflet that expresses an *opinion* about a war.

The Court issued similar rulings against war protesters that same month. Frohwerk v. United States, 249 U.S. 204 (1919); Debs v. United States, 249 U.S. 211 (1919). This line of cases developed the "bad tendency" test to curb speech that posed threats or a danger to society. Under this test, there need be no clear and present danger. The mere tendency to create evil justifies suppression.

In a penetrating critique in the *Harvard Law Review* in 1919, Zechariah Chafee, Jr., argued that the First Amendment declared a national policy "in favor of the public discussion of all public questions. Such a declaration should make Congress reluctant and careful in the enactment of all restrictions upon utterance, even though the courts will not refuse to enforce them as unconstitutional." To Chafee, the framers adopted the First Amendment to give "the right of unrestricted discussion of public affairs," not only in time of peace but especially during war (see box on next page). The First Amendment protected not merely an individual's interest in speaking out but society's interest in hearing criticism and permitting impassioned debate.

Following the appearance of Chafee's article, Holmes and Brandeis dissented in a free-speech case later that year. Five antiwar activists had been convicted for criticizing U.S. involvement in World War I, encouraging resistance, and urging workers not to produce war materials. Holmes wrote one of his memorable dissents, appealing for tolerance and the "free trade in ideas." ABRAMS v. UNITED STATES, 250 U.S. 616 (1919). The clear-and-present-danger test supposedly favors free speech more than the bad-tendency test, but these standards are applied unevenly.

The Sedition Act of 1918 made it illegal to utter "any disloyal, profane, scurrilous, or abusive language" about the form of government, the Constitution, soldiers and sailors, the flag, or uniform of the armed forces. State laws that declared it a misdemeanor to teach or advocate that citizens should not assist the United States in carrying on a war with its enemies were upheld. Gilbert v. Minnesota, 254 U.S. 325 (1920). A New York law punished persons for advocating the overthrow of government. The Court sustained the statute, treating such advocacy as "a call to action" rather than the expression of abstract doctrine. GITLOW v. NEW YORK, 268 U.S. 652 (1925). Holmes and Brandeis dissented, objecting that "[e]very idea is an incitement." In *Gitlow,* the Court also ruled that freedoms of speech and press are among the personal rights and liberties protected by the Due Process Clause of the Fourteenth Amendment and are therefore applied against the states. Just three years before, the Court had held that the Fourteenth Amendment did *not* impose upon the states an obligation to confer the right of free speech. Prudential Ins. Co. v. Cheek, 259 U.S. 530, 538, 542–43 (1922).

In two decisions in 1927, the Court tackled the issue of syndicalism: the doctrine that workers could use force to seize control of the economy and the government. A unanimous Court upheld California's statute against criminal syndicalism, but a concurrence by Justice Brandeis offered a masterful essay on the principles of free speech. WHITNEY v. CALIFORNIA, 274 U.S. 357 (1927). Another unanimous opinion that year struck down Kansas's syndicalism statute because it punished class

Free Speech During Wartime

… It is sometimes argued that the Constitution gives Congress the power to declare war, raise armies, and support a navy, that one provision of the Constitution cannot be used to break down another provision, and consequently freedom of speech cannot be invoked to break down the war power. I would reply that the First Amendment is just as much a part of the Constitution as the war clauses, and that it is equally accurate to say that the war clauses cannot be invoked to break down freedom of speech. The truth is that all provisions of the Constitution must be construed together so as to limit each other. In war as in peace, this process of mutual adjustment must include the Bill of Rights. There are those who believe that the Bill of Rights can be set aside in war time at the uncontrolled will of the government. The first ten amendments were drafted by men who had just been through a war. Two of these amendments expressly apply in war.…

The First Amendment protects two kinds of interests in free speech. There is an individual interest, the need of many men to express their opinions on matters vital to them if life is to be worth living, and a social interest in the attainment of truth, so that the country may not only adopt the wisest course of action but carry it out in the wisest way. This social interest is especially important in war time. Even after war has been declared there is bound to be a confused mixture of good and bad arguments in its support, and a wide difference of opinion as to its objects. Truth can be sifted out from falsehood only if the government is vigorously and constantly cross-examined, so that the fundamental issues of the struggle may be clearly defined, and the war may not be diverted to improper ends, or conducted with an undue sacrifice of life and liberty, or prolonged after its just purposes are accomplished. Legal proceedings prove that an opponent makes the best cross-examiner. Consequently it is a disastrous mistake to limit criticism to those who favor the war.…

SOURCE: Zechariah Chafee, Jr., "Freedom of Speech in War Time," 32 Harv. L. Rev. 932, 955, 958 (1919).

struggles unrelated to crime, violence, or other unlawful acts. Fiske v. Kansas, 274 U.S. 380 (1927). A California statute making it a felony to display a red flag to symbolize opposition to government was declared unconstitutionally vague. Stromberg v. California, 283 U.S. 359 (1931). Also on the ground of vagueness, the Court invalidated a Georgia statute that made it a crime to attempt to incite insurrection or resistance by force. Herndon v. Lowry, 301 U.S. 242 (1937).

National security interests were invoked during the Vietnam War to restrain free speech. A series of cases in 1968 and 1969 involved draft-card burning, the wearing of black arm bands to protest the war, and flag burning, all covered in a later section on symbolic speech. In addition, in 1970 a unanimous Court struck down a congressional statute that imposed criminal penalties for the unauthorized wearing of an American military uniform except for a theatrical or motion picture production that does not discredit the armed forces. The statute, applied against a skit that expressed opposition to American involvement in the Vietnam War, imposed an unconstitutional restraint on free speech by singling out for punishment productions that were unfavorable to the military. Schacht v. United States, 398 U.S. 58 (1970). (The Pentagon Papers case, one of the key decisions on national security and the First Amendment, is discussed in Chapters 7 and 11.)

The Communist Cases

Following World War II, Congress placed a number of restrictions on members of the Communist party. The Labor Management Relations Act of 1947 required union officers to file a non-Communist affidavit. 61 Stat. 146, 9(h). The purpose was to remove obstructions to commerce from "political strikes" instigated by Communists. The Court, by a 4 to 2 vote, held that the statute bore a reasonable relation to the "evil" it was designed to reach and did not interfere with speech or thought. The statute, said the Court, was designed to regulate *conduct* and "Congress, not the courts, is primarily charged with determination of the need for regulation of activities affecting interstate commerce." American Communications Assn. v. Douds, 339 U.S. 382, 400 (1950). There was no actual conduct, however. The mere threat or capability of obstructing commerce was considered adequate grounds for the statute.

A year later, the Court decided the constitutionality of the Smith Act of 1940, which made it unlawful for any person to advocate the violent overthrow of "any government in the United States" or to conspire to advocate such violence. Divided 6 to 2, the Court upheld the statute against the charge that it violated the First Amendment because of indefiniteness. Although the Smith Act was aimed at potential conduct rather than actual conduct, the Court responded to the free-speech issue by saying that the statute was "directed at advocacy, not discussion." DENNIS v. UNITED STATES, 341 U.S. 494, 502 (1951). "We hold that the statute may be applied where there is a 'clear and present danger' of the substantive evil which the legislature had the right to prevent." Id. at 512. In his concurrence, Justice Frankfurter admitted the difficulty of distinguishing between protected speech and unprotected advocacy: "It is true that there is no divining rod by which we may locate 'advocacy.' Exposition of ideas readily merges into advocacy." Id. at 545.

Dennis was severely circumscribed in 1957 when the Court reversed the convictions of 14 Communists charged with advocating and teaching the overthrow of the United States government by force and violence. The Court held that the Smith Act did not prohibit advocacy and teaching of forcible overthrow as an abstract principle. As interpreted by the Court, the statute proscribed only the "advocacy of action to that end." The meaning of that phrase remains vague, but the effect has been to extend greater protection to pure advocacy. Yates v. United States, 354 U.S. 298 (1957). The Court gave the strictest interpretation to the notion of "clear and present danger" in 1969 when it struck down a state statute that made it illegal to advocate crime or violence to accomplish reform. In this case, involving a gathering of the Ku Klux Klan, the Court held that government may not forbid advocacy unless it is directed to incite imminent lawless action. BRANDENBURG v. OHIO, 395 U.S. 444 (1969). From *Schenck* to contemporary cases, the Supreme Court experiments with a number of shifting tests and doctrines on free speech (see box on next page).

Both Congress and the courts were involved in monitoring, and finally abolishing, the Subversive Activities Control Board (SACB), which had been authorized to order groups to register with the Attorney General as a "Communist-action" organization. An effort to adjudicate the statute was turned aside in 1956 because of alleged perjuries committed by three government witnesses. Communist Party v. SACB, 351 U.S. 115 (1956). Five years later the Court, with a 5 to 4 vote, affirmed the Board's finding that the Communist party was a Communist-action organization and therefore required to register with the Attorney General. Sidestepping such constitutional issues as free speech, bill of attainder, and self-incrimination, the Court concluded that the statute was "regulatory" rather than "prohibitory." Communist Party v. SACB, 367 U.S. 1 (1961). On that same day, in two decisions, the Court held that mere membership in the Communist party did not violate the Smith Act. Punishment could be applied only against members who actively advanced the party's aims. It was therefore no longer a crime to advocate, as an abstract doctrine, the forcible overthrow of government. Scales v. United States, 367 U.S. 203 (1961); Noto v. United States, 367 U.S. 290 (1961).

Other cases during this period also relaxed the pattern of rigid anticommunism. The Court held that a congressional statute making it a crime for a Communist party member to serve as union officer constituted a bill of attainder. United States v. Brown, 381 U.S. 437 (1965). In another case, a unanimous Court struck down the registration feature as a violation of the Self-Incrimination Clause because information submitted to the Attorney General could be used as evidence toward a criminal prosecution. Albertson v. SACB, 382 U.S. 70 (1965).

Congress rejuvenated the Subversive Activities Control Board in 1968 by authorizing it to determine, through hearings, whether individuals and organizations were Communist. The following year

Free Speech Tests

Clear and Present Danger	Government may suppress speech only when it represents a clear and present danger to society. "The question in every case is whether the words used are used in such circumstances and are of such a nature as to create a clear and present danger that they will bring about the substantive evils that Congress has a right to prevent." Schenck v. United States, 249 U.S. 47, 52 (1919).
Bad Tendency	Even a "tendency" to obstruct government justifies prosecution. Debs v. United States, 249 U.S. 211, 216 (1919). Government can extinguish a spark before it becomes a flame. Gitlow v. New York, 268 U.S. 652, 669 (1925).
Preferred Position	"Freedom of press, freedom of speech, freedom of religion are in a preferred position." Murdock v. Pennsylvania, 319 U.S. 105, 115 (1943); Jones v. Opelika, 316 U.S. 584, 608 (1942) (Stone, J., dissenting).
Action, not Advocacy	Constitution permits pure advocacy and teaching of forcible overthrow of government by force and violence. What is proscribed is advocacy of action or incitement to action. Yates v. United States, 354 U.S. 298 (1957); Brandenburg v. Ohio, 395 U.S. 444, 447 (1969).
Ad Hoc Balancing	Government may suppress speech when its own interests outweigh those of an individual. Barenblatt v. United States, 360 U.S. 109 (1959).

an appellate court declared that the new procedure violated the First Amendment freedom of association. Boorda v. SACB, 421 F.2d 1142 (D.C. Cir. 1969), cert. denied, 397 U.S. 1042 (1970). With the Board facing extinction, President Nixon issued an executive order expanding its power and field of inquiry. After Congress used its power of the purse to deny funds to carry out the executive order, the Board went out of business. Fisher, Constitutional Conflicts Between Congress and the President 108–09 (2007).

Terrorism and Free Speech

In the wake of the Oklahoma City bombing by Timothy McVey, Congress passed The Antiterrorism and Effective Death Penalty Act of 1996 (AEDPA), that, among other things, prohibited the provision of "material support" to terrorist organizations, both foreign and domestic. After the terrorist acts of September 11, 2001, Congress passed the U.S.A. Patriot Act, and in 2004 elaborated on that legislation with the Intelligence Reform and Terrorism Prevention Act. All of this legislation raised significant issues involving the tension between national security concerns and various civil liberties, including free speech. In 2010 the Supreme Court addressed one such case brought by The Humanitarian Law Project, an organization involved in teaching and advocating international human rights law. The Project claimed that the material support provisions put them at risk of prosecution for their work with certain groups that had been identified by the State Department as terrorist organizations, even though the work they were doing was peaceful, focused on humanitarian ends and not on supporting terrorism. In a 6–3 decision the Court rejected their claims, finding that the provisions as they applied to this group were not unconstitutionally vague, did not violate their free speech rights, and did not violate their freedom of association. The Court did suggest, however, that there might be other applications of the statute that would create potential First Amendment problems. HOLDER v. HUMANITARIAN LAW PROJECT, 561 U.S. ___ (2010).

Schenck v. United States

249 U.S. 47 (1919)

Charles T. Schenck, general secretary of the Socialist party, was charged with violating the Espionage Act of 1917. The government claimed that the printing and circulation of 15,000 leaflets, which attacked the draft for World War I, caused insubordination in the military forces and obstructed the recruitment and enlistment of soldiers. Writing for a unanimous Court, Justice Holmes formulated his "clear and present danger" test for deciding First Amendment questions.

MR. JUSTICE HOLMES delivered the opinion of the court....

The document in question upon its first printed side recited the first section of the Thirteenth Amendment, said that the idea embodied in it was violated by the Conscription Act and that a conscript is little better than a convict. In impassioned language it intimated that conscription was despotism in its worst form and a monstrous wrong against humanity in the interest of Wall Street's chosen few. It said "Do not submit to intimidation," but in form at least confined itself to peaceful measures such as a petition for the repeal of the act. The other and later printed side of the sheet was headed "Assert Your Rights." It stated reasons for alleging that any one violated the Constitution when he refused to recognize "your right to assert your opposition to the draft," and went on "If you do not assert and support your rights, you are helping to deny or disparage rights which it is the solemn duty of all citizens and residents of the United States to retain." It described the arguments on the other side as coming from cunning politicians and a mercenary capitalist press, and even silent consent to the conscription law as helping to support an infamous conspiracy. It denied the power to send our citizens away to foreign shores to shoot up the people of other lands, and added that words could not express the condemnation such cold-blooded ruthlessness deserves, &c., &c., winding up "You must do your share to maintain, support and uphold the rights of the people of this country." Of course the document would not have been sent unless it had been intended to have some effect, and we do not see what effect it could be expected to have upon persons subject to the draft except to influence them to obstruct the carrying of it out. The defendants do not deny that the jury might find against them on this point.

But it is said, suppose that that was the tendency of this circular, it is protected by the First Amendment to the Constitution.... We admit that in many places and in ordinary times the defendants in saying all that was said in the circular would have been within their constitutional rights. But the character of every act depends upon the circumstances in which it is done. *Aikens* v. *Wisconsin,* 195 U.S. 194, 205, 206. The most stringent protection of free speech would not protect a man in falsely shouting fire in a theatre and causing a panic. It does not even protect a man from an injunction against uttering words that may have all the effect of force. *Gompers* v. *Bucks Stove & Range Co.,* 221 U.S. 418, 439. The question in every case is whether the words used are used in such circumstances and are of such a nature as to create a clear and present danger that they will bring about the substantive evils that Congress has a right to prevent. It is a question of proximity and degree. When a nation is at war many things that might be said in time of peace are such a hindrance to its effort that their utterance will not be endured so long as men fight and that no Court could regard them as protected by any constitutional right. It seems to be admitted that if an actual obstruction of the recruiting service were proved, liability for words that produced that effect might be enforced. The statute of 1917 in §4 punishes conspiracies to obstruct as well as actual obstruction. If the act, (speaking, or circulating a paper,) its tendency and the intent with which it is done are the same, we perceive no ground for saying that success alone warrants making the act a crime....

Judgments affirmed.

Abrams v. United States

250 U.S. 616 (1919)

In another prosecution under the Espionage Act, the government charged five defendants with printing and circulating leaflets that opposed U.S. involvement in World War I. The five defendants, all born in Russia, were Jacob Abrams, Hyman Lachowsky, Samuel Lipman, Hyman Rosansky, and Mollie Steimer. The dissent by Justice Holmes, considering his opinion in *Schenck* earlier in the year, is especially significant.

MR. JUSTICE CLARKE delivered the opinion of the court....

It was charged in each count of the indictment that it was a part of the conspiracy that the defendants would attempt to accomplish their unlawful purpose by printing, writing and distributing in the City of New York many copies of a leaflet or circular, printed in the English language, and of another printed in the Yiddish language, copies of which, properly identified, were attached to the indictment.

All of the five defendants were born in Russia. They were intelligent, had considerable schooling, and at the time they were arrested they had lived in the United States terms varying from five to ten years, but none of them had applied for naturalization. Four of them testified as witnesses in their own behalf and of these, three frankly avowed that they were "rebels," "revolutionists," "anarchists," that they did not believe in government in any form, and they declared that they had no interest whatever in the Government of the United States. The fourth defendant testified that he was a "socialist" and believed in "a proper kind of government, not capitalistic," but in his classification the Government of the United States was "capitalistic."

It was admitted on the trial that the defendants had united to print and distribute the described circulars and that five thousand of them had been printed and distributed about the 22d day of August, 1918.... The circulars were distributed some by throwing them from a window of a building where one of the defendants was employed and others secretly, in New York City....

The first of the two articles attached to the indictment is conspicuously headed, "The Hypocrisy of the United States and her Allies." After denouncing President Wilson as a hypocrite and a coward because troops were sent into Russia, it proceeds to assail our Government in general....

The second of the articles was printed in the Yiddish language and in the translation is headed, "Workers — Wake up." After referring to "his Majesty, Mr. Wilson, and the rest of the gang; dogs of all colors!", it continues:

"Workers, Russian emigrants, you who had the least belief in the honesty of *our* Government," which defendants admitted referred to the United States Government, "must now throw away all confidence, must spit in the face the false, hypocritic, military propaganda which has fooled you so relentlessly, calling forth your sympathy, your help, to the prosecution of the war." ...

... [T]he plain purpose of their propaganda was to excite, at the supreme crisis of the war, disaffection, sedition, riots, and, as they hoped, revolution, in this country for the purpose of embarrassing and if possible defeating the military plans of the Government in Europe. A technical distinction may perhaps be taken between disloyal and abusive language applied to the *form* of our government or language intended to bring the *form* of our government into contempt and disrepute, and language of like character and intended to produce like results directed against the President and Congress, the agencies through which that form of government must function in time of war. But it is not necessary to a decision of this case to consider whether such distinction is vital or merely formal, for the language of these circulars was obviously intended to provoke and to encourage resistance to the United States in the war, as the third count runs, and, the defendants, in terms, plainly urged and advocated a resort to a general strike of workers in ammunition factories for the purpose of curtailing the production of ordnance and munitions necessary and essential to the prosecution of the war as is charged in the fourth count. Thus it is clear not only that some evidence but that much persuasive evidence was before the jury tending to prove that the defendants were guilty as charged in both the third and fourth counts of the indictment and under the long established rule of law hereinbefore stated the judgment of the District Court must be

Affirmed.

MR. JUSTICE HOLMES dissenting....

I never have seen any reason to doubt that the

questions of law that alone were before this Court in the cases of *Schenck, Frohwerk* and *Debs,* 249 U.S. 47, 204, 211, were rightly decided. I do not doubt for a moment that by the same reasoning that would justify punishing persuasion to murder, the United States constitutionally may punish speech that produces or is intended to produce a clear and imminent danger that it will bring about forthwith certain substantive evils that the United States constitutionally may seek to prevent. The power undoubtedly is greater in time of war than in time of peace because war opens dangers that do not exist at other times.

But as against dangers peculiar to war, as against others, the principle of the right to free speech is always the same. It is only the present danger of immediate evil or an intent to bring it about that warrants Congress in setting a limit to the expression of opinion where private rights are not concerned. Congress certainly cannot forbid all effort to change the mind of the country. Now nobody can suppose that the surreptitious publishing of a silly leaflet by an unknown man, without more, would present any immediate danger that its opinions would hinder the success of the government arms or have any appreciable tendency to do so. . . .

In this case sentences of twenty years imprisonment have been imposed for the publishing of two leaflets that I believe the defendants had as much right to publish as the Government has to publish the Constitution of the United States now vainly invoked by them. Even if I am technically wrong and enough can be squeezed from these poor and puny anonymities to turn the color of legal litmus paper; I will add, even if what I think the necessary intent were shown; the most nominal punishment seems to me all that possibly could be inflicted, unless the defendants are to be made to suffer not for what the indictment alleges but for the creed that they avow — a creed that I believe to be the creed of ignorance and immaturity when honestly held, as I see no reason to doubt that it was held here, but which, although made the subject of examination at the trial, no one has a right even to consider in dealing with the charges before the Court.

Persecution for the expression of opinions seems to me perfectly logical. If you have no doubt of your premises or your power and want a certain result with all your heart you naturally express your wishes in law and sweep away all opposition. To allow opposition by speech seems to indicate that you think the speech impotent, as when a man says that he has squared the circle, or that you do not care whole-heartedly for the result, or that you doubt either your power or your premises. But when men have realized that time has upset many fighting faiths, they may come to believe even more than they believe the very foundations of their own conduct that the ultimate good desired is better reached by free trade in ideas — that the best test of truth is the power of the thought to get itself accepted in the competition of the market, and that truth is the only ground upon which their wishes safely can be carried out. That at any rate is the theory of our Constitution. It is an experiment, as all life is an experiment. Every year if not every day we have to wager our salvation upon some prophecy based upon imperfect knowledge. While that experiment is part of our system I think that we should be eternally vigilant against attempts to check the expression of opinions that we loathe and believe to be fraught with death, unless they so imminently threaten immediate interference with the lawful and pressing purposes of the law that an immediate check is required to save the country. I wholly disagree with the argument of the Government that the First Amendment left the common law as to seditious libel in force. History seems to me against the notion. I had conceived that the United States through many years had shown its repentance for the Sedition Act of 1798, by repaying fines that it imposed. . . .

MR. JUSTICE BRANDEIS concurs with the foregoing opinion.

Gitlow v. New York

268 U.S. 652 (1925)

Benjamin Gitlow, a member of the left-wing section of the Socialist party, was convicted for violating the New York laws of criminal anarchy (advocating the violent overthrow of the government). This case represents a step in the incorporation of part of the First Amendment into the Due Process Clause of the Fourteenth Amendment, thus including the freedoms of speech and press among those protected from impairment by the states.

MR. JUSTICE SANFORD delivered the opinion of the Court.

Benjamin Gitlow was indicted in the Supreme Court of New York, with three others, for the statutory crime of criminal anarchy. New York Penal Laws, §§ 160, 161. He was separately tried, convicted, and sentenced to imprisonment....

The contention here is that the statute, by its terms and as applied in this case, is repugnant to the due process clause of the Fourteenth Amendment. Its material provisions are:

"§ 160. *Criminal anarchy defined.* Criminal anarchy is the doctrine that organized government should be overthrown by force or violence, or by assassination of the executive head or of any of the executive officials of government, or by any unlawful means. The advocacy of such doctrine either by word of mouth or writing is a felony.

"§ 161. *Advocacy of criminal anarchy.* Any person who:

"1. By word of mouth or writing advocates, advises or teaches the duty, necessity or propriety of overthrowing or overturning organized government by force or violence, or by assassination of the executive head or of any of the executive officials of government, or by any unlawful means; or,

"2. Prints, publishes, edits, issues or knowingly circulates, sells, distributes or publicly displays any book, paper, document, or written or printed matter in any form, containing or advocating, advising or teaching the doctrine that organized government should be overthrown by force, violence or any unlawful means...,

"'Is guilty of a felony and punishable' by imprisonment or fine, or both."

The indictment was in two counts. The first charged that the defendant had advocated, advised and taught the duty, necessity and propriety of overthrowing and overturning organized government by force, violence and unlawful means, by certain writings therein set forth entitled "The Left Wing Manifesto"; the second that he had printed, published and knowingly circulated and distributed a certain paper called "The Revolutionary Age," containing the writings set forth in the first count advocating, advising and teaching the doctrine that organized government should be overthrown by force, violence and unlawful means....

There was no evidence of any effect resulting from the publication and circulation of the Manifesto.

No witnesses were offered in behalf of the defendant.

Extracts from the Manifesto are set forth in the margin. Coupled with a review of the rise of Socialism, it condemned the dominant "moderate Socialism" for its recognition of the necessity of the democratic parliamentary state; repudiated its policy of introducing Socialism by legislative measures; and advocated, in plain and unequivocal language, the necessity of accomplishing the "Communist Revolution" by a militant and "revolutionary Socialism," based on "the class struggle" and mobilizing the "power of the proletariat in action," through mass industrial revolts developing into mass political strikes and "revolutionary mass action," for the purpose of conquering and destroying the parliamentary state and establishing in its place, through a "revolutionary dictatorship of the proletariat," the system of Communist Socialism....

The precise question presented, and the only question which we can consider under this writ of error, then is, whether the statute, as construed and applied in this case by the state courts, deprived the defendant of his liberty of expression in violation of the due process clause of the Fourteenth Amendment....

... It is not the abstract "doctrine" of overthrowing organized government by unlawful means which is denounced by the statute, but the advocacy of action for the accomplishment of that purpose. It was so construed and applied by the trial judge, who specifically charged the jury that: "A mere grouping of historical events and a prophetic deduction from them would neither constitute advocacy, advice or teaching of a doctrine for the overthrow of government by force, violence or unlawful means. [And] if it were a mere essay on the subject, as suggested by counsel, based upon deductions from alleged historical events, with no teaching, advice or advocacy of action, it would not constitute a violation of the statute...."

The Manifesto, plainly, is neither the statement of abstract doctrine nor, as suggested by counsel, mere prediction that industrial disturbances and revolutionary mass strikes will result spontaneously in an inevitable process of evolution in the economic system. It advocates and urges in fervent language mass action which shall progressively foment industrial disturbances and through political mass strikes and revolutionary mass action overthrow and destroy organized parliamentary government. It concludes with a call to action in these words: "The proletariat revolution and the Communist reconstruction of society—*the struggle for these*—is now indispensable.... The Communist International calls the proletariat of the world to the final struggle!" This is not the expression of philosophical abstraction, the mere prediction of future events; it is the language of direct incitement....

For present purposes we may and do assume that freedom of speech and of the press—which are protected by the First Amendment from abridgment by Congress—are among the fundamental personal rights and "liberties" protected by the due process clause of the Fourteenth Amendment from impairment by the States....

By enacting the present statute the State has determined, through its legislative body, that utterances advocating the overthrow of organized government by force, violence and unlawful means, are so inimical to the general welfare and involve such danger of substantive evil that they may be penalized in the exercise of its police power. That determination must be given great weight.... The State cannot reasonably be required to measure the danger from every such utterance in the nice balance of a jeweler's scale. A single revolutionary spark may kindle a fire that, smouldering for a time, may burst into a sweeping and destructive conflagration....

And finding, for the reasons stated, that the statute is not in itself unconstitutional, and that it has not been applied in the present case in derogation of any constitutional right, the judgment of the Court of Appeals is

Affirmed.

Mr. Justice Holmes, dissenting.

Mr. Justice Brandeis and I are of opinion that this judgment should be reversed. The general principle of free speech, it seems to me, must be taken to be included in the Fourteenth Amendment, in view of the scope that has been given to the word 'liberty' as there used, although perhaps it may be accepted with a somewhat larger latitude of interpretation than is allowed to Congress by the sweeping language that governs or ought to govern the laws of the United States. If I am right, then I think that the criterion sanctioned by the full Court in *Schenck* v. *United States,* 249 U.S. 47, 52, applies. "The question in every case is whether the words used are used in such circumstances and are of such a nature as to create a clear and present danger that they will bring about the substantive evils that [the State] has a right to prevent." ... If what I think the correct test is applied, it is manifest that there was no present danger of an attempt to overthrow the government by force on the part of the admittedly small minority who shared the defendant's views. It is said that this manifesto was more than a theory, that it was an incitement. Every idea is an incitement. It offers itself for belief and if believed it is acted on unless some other belief outweighs it or some failure of energy stifles the movement at its birth. The only difference between the expression of an opinion and an incitement in the narrower sense is the speaker's enthusiasm for the result. Eloquence may set fire to reason. But whatever may be thought of the redundant discourse before us it had no chance of starting a present conflagration. If in the long run the beliefs expressed in proletarian dictatorship are destined to be accepted by the dominant forces of the community, the only meaning of free speech is that they should be given their chance and have their way.

If the publication of this document had been laid as an attempt to induce an uprising against government at once and not at some indefinite time in the future it would have presented a different question. The object would have been one with which the law might deal, subject to the doubt whether there was any danger that the publication could produce any result, or in other words, whether it was not futile and too remote from possible consequences. But the indictment alleges the publication and nothing more.

Whitney v. California

274 U.S. 357 (1927)

Charlotte Anita Whitney, a niece of Justice Stephen Field and a so-called rebel of the conservative and wealthy Field family, sought to promote the interests of the poor. She was prosecuted for violating California's Criminal Syndicalism Act, which covered efforts of trade unions and industrial workers to gain control of production through general strikes, sabotage, violence, or other criminal means. She was found guilty of having organized and participated in a group assembled to advocate, teach, aid, and abet criminal syndicalism. A unanimous Court upheld the Act, but the case is remembered primarily for the eloquent exposition of First Amendment values in the concurrence by Brandeis. Although Whitney lost her case in the Supreme Court, she

received a pardon from the Governor of California, who was reported to have been greatly influenced by Justice Brandeis's concurrence.

Mr. Justice Sanford delivered the opinion of the Court....

The order dismissing the writ of error will be vacated and set aside, and the judgment of the Court of Appeal

Affirmed.

Mr. Justice Brandeis; concurring....

This Court has not yet fixed the standard by which to determine when a danger shall be deemed clear; how remote the danger may be and yet be deemed present; and what degree of evil shall be deemed sufficiently substantial to justify resort to abridgement of free speech and assembly as the means of protection. To reach sound conclusions on these matters, we must bear in mind why a State is, ordinarily, denied the power to prohibit dissemination of social, economic and political doctrine which a vast majority of its citizens believes to be false and fraught with evil consequence.

Those who won our independence believed that the final end of the State was to make men free to develop their faculties; and that in its government the deliberative forces should prevail over the arbitrary. They valued liberty both as an end and as a means. They believed liberty to be the secret of happiness and courage to be the secret of liberty. They believed that freedom to think as you will and to speak as you think are means indispensable to the discovery and spread of political truth; that without free speech and assembly discussion would be futile; that with them, discussion affords ordinarily adequate protection against the dissemination of noxious doctrine; that the greatest menace to freedom is an inert people; that public discussion is a political duty; and that this should be a fundamental principle of the American government. They recognized the risks to which all human institutions are subject. But they knew that order cannot be secured merely through fear of punishment for its infraction; that it is hazardous to discourage thought, hope and imagination; that fear breeds repression; that repression breeds hate; that hate menaces stable government; that the path of safety lies in the opportunity to discuss freely supposed grievances and proposed remedies; and that the fitting remedy for evil counsels is good ones. Believing in the power of reason as applied through public discussion, they eschewed silence coerced by law — the argument of force in its worst form. Recognizing the occasional tyrannies of governing majorities, they amended the Constitution so that free speech and assembly should be guaranteed.

Fear of serious injury cannot alone justify suppression of free speech and assembly. Men feared witches and burnt women. It is the function of speech to free men from the bondage of irrational fears. To justify suppression of free speech there must be reasonable ground to fear that serious evil will result if free speech is practiced. There must be reasonable ground to believe that the danger apprehended is imminent. There must be reasonable ground to believe that the evil to be prevented is a serious one. Every denunciation of existing law tends in some measure to increase the probability that there will be violation of it. Condonation of a breach enhances the probability. Expressions of approval add to the probability. Propagation of the criminal state of mind by teaching syndicalism increases it. Advocacy of law-breaking heightens it still further. But even advocacy of violation, however reprehensible morally, is not a justification for denying free speech where the advocacy falls short of incitement and there is nothing to indicate that the advocacy would be immediately acted on. The wide difference between advocacy and incitement, between preparation and attempt, between assembling and conspiracy, must be borne in mind. In order to support a finding of clear and present danger it must be shown either that immediate serious violence was to be expected or was advocated, or that the past conduct furnished reason to believe that such advocacy was then contemplated.

Those who won our independence by revolution were not cowards. They did not fear political change. They did not exalt order at the cost of liberty. To courageous, self-reliant men, with confidence in the power of free and fearless reasoning applied through the processes of popular government, no danger flowing from speech can be deemed clear and present, unless the incidence of the evil apprehended is so imminent that it may befall before there is opportunity for full discussion. If there be time to expose through discussion the falsehood and fallacies, to avert the evil by the processes of education, the remedy to be applied is more speech, not enforced silence. Only an emergency can justify repression. Such must be the rule if authority is to be reconciled with freedom. Such, in my opinion, is the command of the Constitution. It is therefore always open to Americans to challenge a law abridging free speech and assembly by showing that there was no emergency justifying it....

Mr. Justice Holmes joins in this opinion.

Dennis v. United States

341 U.S. 494 (1951)

Eugene Dennis and ten other leaders of the American Communist party were indicted and found guilty under the Smith Act for willfully and knowingly conspiring to teach and advocate the overthrow of the U.S. government by force or violence. The question before the courts was whether the statute violated First Amendment rights. To do that, the Supreme Court had to give clearer meaning to the *Schenck* test of "clear and present danger." Defendants were convicted in a New York district court following a sensational trial that lasted nine months. With one exception, they were sentenced to imprisonment for five years and to a fine of $10,000 by Judge Harold Medina, who also imposed sentences ranging from thirty days to six months imprisonment on the six defense attorneys for contemptuous conduct during the trial.

Mr. Chief Justice Vinson announced the judgment of the Court and an opinion in which Mr. Justice Reed, Mr. Justice Burton and Mr. Justice Minton join.

Petitioners were indicted in July, 1948, for violation of the conspiracy provisions of the Smith Act.... We granted certiorari, 340 U.S. 863, limited to the following two questions: (1) Whether either §2 or §3 of the Smith Act, inherently or as construed and applied in the instant case, violates the First Amendment and other provisions of the Bill of Rights; (2) whether either §2 or §3 of the Act, inherently or as construed and applied in the instant case, violates the First and Fifth Amendments because of indefiniteness.

Sections 2 and 3 of the Smith Act, 54 Stat. 671, 18 U.S.C. (1946 ed.) §§10, 11 (see present 18 U.S.C. §2385), provide as follows:

"Sec. 2. (a) It shall be unlawful for any person—

"(1) to knowingly or willfully advocate, abet, advise, or teach the duty, necessity, desirability, or propriety of overthrowing or destroying any government in the United States by force or violence, or by the assassination of any officer of any such government;

"(2) with intent to cause the overthrow or destruction of any government in the United States, to print, publish, edit, issue, circulate, sell, distribute, or publicly display any written or printed matter advocating, advising, or teaching the duty, necessity, desirability, or propriety of overthrowing or destroying any government in the United States by force or violence;

"(3) to organize or help to organize any society, group, or assembly of persons who teach, advocate, or encourage the overthrow or destruction of any government in the United States by force or vio-

lence; or to be or become a member of, or affiliate with, any such society, group, or assembly of persons, knowing the purposes thereof.

"(b) For the purposes of this section, the term 'government in the United States' means the Government of the United States, the government of any State, Territory, or possession of the United States, the government of the District of Columbia, or the government of any political subdivision of any of them.

"Sec. 3. It shall be unlawful for any person to attempt to commit, or to conspire to commit, any of the acts prohibited by the provisions of this title."...

[T]he Court of Appeals held that the record supports the following broad conclusions: By virtue of their control over the political apparatus of the Communist Political Association, petitioners were able to transform that organization into the Communist Party; that the policies of the Association were changed from peaceful cooperation with the United States and its economic and political structure to a policy which had existed before the United States and the Soviet Union were fighting a common enemy, namely, a policy which worked for the overthrow of the Government by force and violence; that the Communist Party is a highly disciplined organization, adept at infiltration into strategic positions, use of aliases, and double-meaning language; that the Party is rigidly controlled; that Communists, unlike other political parties, tolerate no dissension from the policy laid down by the guiding forces, but that the approved program is slavishly followed by the members of the Party; that the literature of the Party and the statements and activities of its leaders, petitioners here, advocate, and the general goal of the Party was, during the period in question, to achieve a successful overthrow of the existing order by force and violence.

I.

[*The trial judge charged the jury that the Smith Act required an unlawful intent. The Court agreed with this interpretation.*]

II.

The obvious purpose of the statute is to protect existing Government, not from change by peaceable, lawful and constitutional means, but from change by violence, revolution and terrorism. That it is within the *power* of the Congress to protect the Government of the United States from armed rebellion is a proposition which requires little discussion. Whatever theoretical merit there may be to the argument that there is a "right" to rebellion against dictatorial governments is without force where the existing structure of the government provides for peaceful and orderly change. We reject any principle of governmental helplessness in the face of preparation for revolution, which principle, carried to its logical conclusion, must lead to anarchy. No one could conceive that it is not within the power of Congress to prohibit acts intended to overthrow the Government by force and violence. The question with which we are concerned here is not whether Congress has such *power,* but whether the *means* which it has employed conflict with the First and Fifth Amendments to the Constitution.

One of the bases for the contention that the means which Congress has employed are invalid takes the form of an attack on the face of the statute on the grounds that by its terms it prohibits academic discussion of the merits of Marxism-Leninism, that it stifles ideas and is contrary to all concepts of a free speech and a free press....

The very language of the Smith Act negates the interpretation which petitioners would have us impose on that Act. It is directed at advocacy, not discussion. Thus, the trial judge properly charged the jury that they could not convict if they found that petitioners did "no more than pursue peaceful studies and discussions or teaching and advocacy in the realm of ideas." ...

III.

No important case involving free speech was decided by this Court prior to *Schenck* v. *United States,* 249 U.S. 47 (1919). Writing for a unanimous Court, Justice Holmes stated that the "question in every case is whether the words used are used in such circumstances and are of such a nature as to create a clear and present danger that they will bring about the substantive evils that Congress has a right to prevent." 249 U.S. at 52....

In this case, we are squarely presented with the application of the "clear and present danger" test, and must decide what that phrase imports. We first note that many of the cases in which this Court has reversed convictions by use of this or similar tests have been based on the fact that the interest which the State was attempting to protect was itself too insubstantial to warrant restriction of speech.... Overthrow of the Government by force and violence is certainly a substantial enough interest for the Government to limit speech. Indeed, this is the ultimate value of any society, for if a society cannot protect its very structure from armed internal attack, it must follow that no subordinate value can be protected. If, then, this interest may be protected, the literal problem which is presented is what has been meant by the use of the phrase "clear and present danger" of the utterances bringing about the evil within the power of Congress to punish.

Obviously, the words cannot mean that before the Government may act, it must wait until the *putsch* is about to be executed, the plans have been laid and the signal is awaited. If Government is aware that a group aiming at its overthrow is attempting to indoctrinate its members and to commit them to a course whereby they will strike when the leaders feel the circumstances permit, action by the Government is required....

... [T]his analysis disposes of the contention that a conspiracy to advocate, as distinguished from the advocacy itself, cannot be constitutionally restrained, because it comprises only the preparation. It is the existence of the conspiracy which creates the danger.... If the ingredients of the reaction are present, we cannot bind the Government to wait until the catalyst is added.

IV.

[*The trial judge instructed the jury that if the defendants were found guilty of violating the Smith Act, he would determine as a matter of law that there was sufficient danger of a substantive evil that Congress has a right to prevent. The Court agreed that this was a question of law for a judge to decide.*]

V.

There remains to be discussed the question of vagueness—whether the statute as we have interpreted it is too vague, not sufficiently advising those who would speak of the limitations upon their activity. It is urged that such vagueness contravenes the First and Fifth Amendments....

We agree that the standard as defined is not a

neat, mathematical formulary. Like all verbalizations it is subject to criticism on the score of indefiniteness. But petitioners themselves contend that the verbalization "clear and present danger" is the proper standard. We see no difference, from the standpoint of vagueness, whether the standard of "clear and present danger" is one contained *in haec verba* within the statute, or whether it is the judicial measure of constitutional applicability....

We hold that §§ 2(a)(1), 2(a)(3) and 3 of the Smith Act do not inherently, or as construed or applied in the instant case, violate the First Amendment and other provisions of the Bill of Rights, or the First and Fifth Amendments because of indefiniteness. Petitioners intended to overthrow the Government of the United States as speedily as the circumstances would permit. Their conspiracy to organize the Communist Party and to teach and advocate the overthrow of the Government of the United States by force and violence created a "clear and present danger" of an attempt to overthrow the Government by force and violence. They were properly and constitutionally convicted for violation of the Smith Act. The judgments of conviction are

Affirmed.

MR. JUSTICE CLARK took no part in the consideration or decision of this case.

MR. JUSTICE FRANKFURTER, concurring in affirmance of the judgment....

[*Frankfurter discusses the need to weigh the interests of free speech against those of national security and argues that Congress, not the courts, is better suited to make these judgments.*]

MR. JUSTICE JACKSON, concurring....

While I think there was power in Congress to enact this statute and that, as applied in this case, it cannot be held unconstitutional, I add that I have little faith in the long-range effectiveness of this conviction to stop the rise of the Communist movement. Communism will not go to jail with these Communists. No decision by this Court can forestall revolution whenever the existing government fails to command the respect and loyalty of the people and sufficient distress and discontent is allowed to grow up among the masses....

MR. JUSTICE BLACK, dissenting.

... These petitioners were not charged with an attempt to overthrow the Government. They were not charged with overt acts of any kind designed to overthrow the Government. They were not even charged with saying anything or writing anything designed to overthrow the Government. The charge was that they agreed to assemble and to talk and publish certain ideas at a later date: The indictment is that they conspired to organize the Communist Party and to use speech or newspapers and other publications in the future to teach and advocate the forcible overthrow of the Government. No matter how it is worded, this is a virulent form of prior censorship of speech and press, which I believe the First Amendment forbids. I would hold § 3 of the Smith Act authorizing this prior restraint unconstitutional on its face and as applied....

MR. JUSTICE DOUGLAS, dissenting.

If this were a case where those who claimed protection under the First Amendment were teaching the techniques of sabotage, the assassination of the President, the filching of documents from public files, the planting of bombs, the art of street warfare, and the like, I would have no doubts. The freedom to speak is not absolute; the teaching of methods of terror and other seditious conduct should be beyond the pale along with obscenity and immorality. This case was argued as if those were the facts. The argument imported much seditious conduct into the record. That is easy and it has popular appeal, for the activities of Communists in plotting and scheming against the free world are common knowledge. But the fact is that no such evidence was introduced at the trial....

Brandenburg v. Ohio

395 U.S. 444 (1969)

Charles Brandenburg, a Ku Klux Klan leader, was convicted under an Ohio criminal law for advocating crime or violence as a means of accomplishing industrial or political reform. Neither the indictment nor the trial judge's instructions to the jury defined the statute's definition of the crime in terms of mere advocacy as distinguished from incitement to imminent lawless action. His conviction was affirmed by the intermediate Ohio appellate court without opinion.

PER CURIAM.

The appellant, a leader of a Ku Klux Klan group, was convicted under the Ohio Criminal Syndicalism statute for "advocat[ing] ... the duty, necessity, or propriety of crime, sabotage, violence, or unlawful methods of terrorism as a means of accomplishing industrial or political reform" and for "voluntarily assembl[ing] with any society, group, or assemblage of persons formed to teach or advocate the doctrines of criminal syndicalism." Ohio Rev. Code Ann. § 2923.13. He was fined $1,000 and sentenced to one to 10 years' imprisonment....

The record shows that a man, identified at trial as the appellant, telephoned an announcer-reporter on the staff of a Cincinnati television station and invited him to come to a Ku Klux Klan "rally" to be held at a farm in Hamilton County. With the cooperation of the organizers, the reporter and a cameraman attended the meeting and filmed the events. Portions of the films were later broadcast on the local station and on a national network.

The prosecution's case rested on the films and on testimony identifying the appellant as the person who communicated with the reporter and who spoke at the rally. The State also introduced into evidence several articles appearing in the film, including a pistol, a rifle, a shotgun, ammunition, a Bible, and a red hood worn by the speaker in the films.

One film showed 12 hooded figures, some of whom carried firearms. They were gathered around a large wooden cross, which they burned. No one was present other than the participants and the newsmen who made the film. Most of the words uttered during the scene were incomprehensible when the film was projected, but scattered phrases could be understood that were derogatory of Negroes and, in one instance, of Jews ...

The second film showed six hooded figures one of whom, later identified as the appellant, repeated a speech very similar to that recorded on the first film. The reference to the possibility of "revengeance" was omitted, and one sentence was added: "Personally, I believe the nigger should be returned to Africa, the Jew returned to Israel." Though some of the figures in the films carried weapons, the speaker did not.

The Ohio Criminal Syndicalism Statute was enacted in 1919. From 1917 to 1920, identical or quite similar laws were adopted by 20 States and two territories.... In 1927, this Court sustained the constitutionality of California's Criminal Syndicalism Act, ... the text of which is quite similar to that of the laws of Ohio. *Whitney* v. *California*, 274 U.S. 357 (1927). The Court upheld the statute on the ground that, without more, "advocating" violent means to effect political and economic change involves such danger to the security of the State that the State may outlaw it.... But *Whitney* has been thoroughly discredited by later decisions. See *Dennis* v. *United States*, 341 U.S. 494, at 507 (1951). These later decisions have fashioned the principle that the constitutional guarantees of free speech and free press do not permit a State to forbid or proscribe advocacy of the use of force or of law violation except where such advocacy is directed to inciting or producing imminent lawless action and is likely to incite or produce such action....

Measured by this test, Ohio's Criminal Syndicalism Act cannot be sustained. The Act punishes persons who "advocate or teach the duty, necessity, or propriety" of violence "as a means of accomplishing industrial or political reform"; or who publish or circulate or display any book or paper containing such advocacy; or who "justify" the commission of violent acts "with intent to exemplify, spread or advocate the propriety of the doctrines of criminal syndicalism"; or who "voluntarily assemble" with a group formed "to teach or advocate the doctrines of criminal syndicalism." Neither the indictment nor the trial judge's instructions to the jury in any way refined the statute's bald definition of the crime in terms of mere advocacy not distinguished from incitement to imminent lawless action.

Accordingly, we are here confronted with a statute which, by its own words and as applied, purports to punish mere advocacy and to forbid, on pain of criminal punishment, assembly with others merely to advocate the described type of action. Such a statute falls within the condemnation of the First and Fourteenth Amendments. The contrary teaching of *Whitney* v. *California, supra,* cannot be supported, and that decision is therefore overruled.

Reversed.

MR. JUSTICE BLACK, concurring.

I agree with the views expressed by MR. JUSTICE DOUGLAS in his concurring opinion in this case that the "clear and present danger" doctrine should have no place in the interpretation of the First Amendment. I join the Court's opinion, which, as I understand it, simply cites *Dennis* v. *United States,* 341 U.S. 494 (1951), but does not indicate any agreement on the Court's part with the "clear and present danger" doctrine on which *Dennis* purported to rely.

MR. JUSTICE DOUGLAS, concurring.

While I join the opinion of the Court, I desire to enter a *caveat.* . . .

. . . I see no place in the regime of the First Amendment for any "clear and present danger" test, whether strict and tight as some would make it, or free-wheeling as the Court in *Dennis* rephrased it.

When one reads the opinions closely and sees when and how the "clear and present danger" test has been applied, great misgivings are aroused. First, the threats were often loud but always puny and made serious only by judges so wedded to the *status quo* that critical analysis made them nervous. Second, the test was so twisted and perverted in *Dennis* as to make the trial of those teachers of Marxism an all-out political trial which was part and parcel of the cold war that has eroded substantial parts of the First Amendment. . . .

The line between what is permissible and not subject to control and what may be made impermissible and subject to regulation is the line between ideas and overt acts. . . .

Holder v. Humanitarian Law Project

561 U.S. ___ (2010)

The Antiterrorism and Effective Death Penalty Act of 1996 (AEDPA) prohibited the provision of "material support or resources" to certain foreign organizations that engage in terrorist activity. 18 U. S. C. §2339B(a)(1). Congress further elaborated on this prohibition in the U.S.A Patriot Act of 2001 and the Intelligence Reform and Terrorism Prevention Act of 2004. The Humanitarian Law Project was involved in teaching advocacy skills to several organizations in Iraq and Sri Lanka (PKK and the LTTE) identified by the State Department as terrorist organizations. Plaintiffs claimed that they wished to provide support for the humanitarian and political activities of the groups in the form of monetary contributions, other tangible aid, legal training, and political advocacy, but that they could not do so for fear of prosecution under §2339B. They claimed they were teaching only lawful, non-violent activities to the group and that application of the law to their activities violated the First Amendment rights of speech and association. They also argued that the statute was too vague, presenting Fifth Amendment due process problems. The district court agreed on the vagueness question and the Ninth Circuit Court of Appeals affirmed.

CHIEF JUSTICE ROBERTS delivered the opinion of the Court. . . . We conclude that the material-support statute is constitutional as applied to the particular activities plaintiffs have told us they wish to pursue. We do not, however, address the resolution of more difficult cases that may arise under the statute in the future.

I

. . .

In 1997, the Secretary of State designated 30 groups as foreign terrorist organizations. . . . Two of those groups are the Kurdistan Workers' Party (also known as the Partiya Karkeran Kurdistan, or PKK) and the Liberation Tigers of Tamil Eelam (LTTE). . . . The Government has presented evidence that both groups have also committed numerous terrorist attacks, some of which have harmed American citizens. . . .

II

[*In this section Chief Justice Roberts outlines the de-*

tails of the challenges presented by the plaintiffs and addresses the issue of whether the case is justiciable. He concludes that it is because "Plaintiffs face 'a credible threat of prosecution'" and "should not be required to await and undergo a criminal prosecution as the sole means of seeking relief."]

III

[*Here Roberts rejects the plaintiffs' invitation to interpret the statute in a manner that exempts their speech from coverage under the Act, contending that they are asking not for an interpretation but a revision of the statute.*]

IV

We turn to the question whether the material-support statute, as applied to plaintiffs, is impermissibly vague under the Due Process Clause of the Fifth Amendment. "A conviction fails to comport with due process if the statute under which it is obtained fails to provide a person of ordinary intelligence fair notice of what is prohibited, or is so standardless that it authorizes or encourages seriously discriminatory enforcement." *United States* v. *Williams*, 553 U.S. 285, 304 (2008).... We have said that when a statute "interferes with the right of free speech or of association, a more stringent vagueness test should apply." *Id.*, at 499....

. . .

Under a proper analysis, plaintiffs' claims of vagueness lack merit. Plaintiffs do not argue that the material-support statute grants too much enforcement discretion to the Government. We therefore address only whether the statute "provide[s] a person of ordinary intelligence fair notice of what is prohibited." *Williams*, 553 U.S., at 304....

Of course, the scope of the material-support statute may not be clear in every application. But the dispositive point here is that the statutory terms are clear in their application to plaintiffs' proposed conduct, which means that plaintiffs' vagueness challenge must fail. Even assuming that a heightened standard applies because the material support statute potentially implicates speech, the statutory terms are not vague as applied to plaintiffs....

Most of the activities in which plaintiffs seek to engage readily fall within the scope of the terms "training" and "expert advice or assistance." ... A person of ordinary intelligence would understand that instruction on resolving disputes through international law falls within the statute's definition of "training" because it imparts a "specific skill," not "general knowledge." § 2339A(b)(2). Plaintiffs' activities also fall comfortably within the scope of "expert advice or assistance": A reasonable person would recognize that teaching the PKK how to petition for humanitarian relief before the United Nations involves advice derived from, as the statute puts it, "specialized knowledge." § 2339A(b)(3). In fact, plaintiffs themselves have repeatedly used the terms "training" and "expert advice" throughout this litigation to describe their own proposed activities, demonstrating that these common terms readily and naturally cover plaintiffs' conduct....

V

A

We next consider whether the material-support statute, as applied to plaintiffs, violates the freedom of speech guaranteed by the First Amendment. Both plaintiffs and the Government take extreme positions on this question. Plaintiffs claim that Congress has banned their "pure political speech." ... It has not. Under the material-support statute, plaintiffs may say anything they wish on any topic. They may speak and write freely about the PKK and LTTE, the governments of Turkey and Sri Lanka, human rights, and international law. They may advocate before the United Nations.... Congress has not, therefore, sought to suppress ideas or opinions in the form of "pure political speech." Rather, Congress has prohibited "material-support," which most often does not take the form of speech at all. And when it does, the statute is carefully drawn to cover only a narrow category of speech to, under the direction of, or in coordination with foreign groups that the speaker knows to be terrorist organizations.

For its part, the Government takes the foregoing too far, claiming that the only thing truly at issue in this litigation is conduct, not speech.... The Government argues that the proper standard of review is therefore the one set out in United States v. O'Brien, 391 U.S. 367 (1968)....

The Government is wrong that the only thing actually at issue in this litigation is conduct, and therefore wrong to argue that *O'Brien* provides the correct standard of review. *O'Brien* does not provide the applicable standard for reviewing a content-based regulation of speech, see *R.A.V.* v. *St. Paul*, 505 U.S. 377, 385–386 (1992); *Texas* v. *Johnson*, 491 U.S. 397, 403, 406–407 (1989), and § 2339B regulates speech on the basis of its content. Plaintiffs want to speak to the PKK and the LTTE, and whether they may do so under § 2339B depends on what they say. If plaintiffs' speech to those groups imparts a "specific skill" or communicates advice derived from "specialized knowledge" — for example, training on the use of international law or advice on petitioning the United Nations — then it is barred.... On the other hand, plaintiffs' speech is not barred if it imparts only general or unspecialized knowledge.

The Government argues that § 2339B should nonetheless receive intermediate scrutiny because it *generally* functions as a regulation of conduct. That argument runs headlong into a number of our precedents, most prominently *Cohen* v. *California*, 403 U.S. 15 (1971). *Cohen* also involved a generally applicable regulation of conduct, barring breaches of the peace ... But when Cohen was convicted for wearing a jacket bearing an epithet, we did not apply *O'Brien* ... Instead, we recognized that the generally applicable law was directed at Cohen because of what his speech communicated — he violated the breach of the peace statute because of the offensive content of his particular message. We accordingly applied more rigorous scrutiny and reversed his conviction....

This suit falls into the same category. The law here may be described as directed at conduct, as the law in *Cohen* was directed at breaches of the peace, but as applied to plaintiffs the conduct triggering coverage under the statute consists of communicating a message....

B

The First Amendment issue before us is more refined than either plaintiffs or the Government would have it. It is not whether the Government may prohibit pure political speech, or may prohibit material support in the form of conduct. It is instead whether the Government may prohibit what plaintiffs want to do — provide material support to the PKK and LTTE in the form of speech.

Everyone agrees that the Government's interest in combating terrorism is an urgent objective of the highest order ... Plaintiffs' complaint is that the ban on material-support, applied to what they wish to do, is not "necessary to further that interest." ... The objective of combating terrorism does not justify prohibiting their speech, plaintiffs argue, because their support will advance only the legitimate activities of the designated terrorist organizations, not their terrorism.

Whether foreign terrorist organizations meaningfully segregate support of their legitimate activities from support of terrorism is an empirical question. When it enacted § 2339B in 1996, Congress made specific findings regarding the serious threat posed by international terrorism ... One of those findings explicitly rejects plaintiffs' contention that their support would not further the terrorist activities of the PKK and LTTE: "[F]oreign organizations that engage in terrorist activity are so tainted by their criminal conduct that *any contribution to such an organization* facilitates that conduct." § 301(a)(7) (emphasis added).

Plaintiffs argue that the reference to "any contribution" in this finding meant only monetary support. There is no reason to read the finding to be so limited, particularly because Congress expressly prohibited so much more than monetary support in § 2339B. Congress's use of the term "contribution" is best read to reflect a determination that any form of material support furnished "to" a foreign terrorist organization should be barred, which is precisely what the material-support statute does. Indeed, when Congress enacted § 2339B, Congress simultaneously removed an exception that had existed in § 2339A(a) (1994 ed.) for the provision of material support in the form of "humanitarian assistance to persons not directly involved in" terrorist activity. AEDPA § 323, 110 Stat. 1255; 205 F. 3d, at 1136. That repeal demonstrates that Congress considered and rejected the view that ostensibly peaceful aid would have no harmful effects.

. . .

Material support meant to "promot[e] peaceable, lawful conduct," ... can further terrorism by foreign groups in multiple ways. "Material support" is a valuable resource by definition. Such support frees up other resources within the organization that may be put to violent ends. It also importantly helps lend legitimacy to foreign terrorist groups — legitimacy that makes it easier for those groups to persist, to recruit members, and to raise funds — all of which facilitate more terrorist attacks....

Money is fungible, and "[w]hen foreign terrorist organizations that have a dual structure raise funds, they highlight the civilian and humanitarian ends to which such moneys could be put." ... There is evidence that the PKK and the LTTE, in particular, have not "respected the line between humanitarian and violent activities." ...

C

In analyzing whether it is possible in practice to distinguish material support for a foreign terrorist group's violent activities and its nonviolent activities, we do not rely exclusively on our own inferences drawn from the record evidence. We have before us an affidavit stating the Executive Branch's conclusion on that question. The State Department informs us that "[t]he experience and analysis of the U.S. government agencies charged with combating terrorism strongly suppor[t]" Congress's finding that all contributions to foreign terrorist organizations further their terrorism....

That evaluation of the facts by the Executive, like Congress's assessment, is entitled to deference. This litigation implicates sensitive and weighty interests of national security and foreign affairs. The PKK and the LTTE have committed terrorist acts against American citizens abroad, and the material-support statute addresses acute foreign policy concerns involving relationships with our Nation's allies ...

Our precedents, old and new, make clear that concerns of national security and foreign relations do not warrant abdication of the judicial role. We do not defer to the Government's reading of the First Amendment, even when such interests are at stake. We are one with the dissent that the Government's "authority and expertise in these matters do not automatically trump the Court's own obligation to secure the protection that the Constitution grants to individuals." ... But when it comes to collecting evidence and drawing factual inferences in this area, "the lack of competence on the part of the courts is marked," ... and respect for the Government's conclusions is appropriate.... The Government, when seeking to prevent imminent harms in the context of international affairs and national security, is not required to conclusively link all the pieces in the puzzle before we grant weight to its empirical conclusions....

This context is different from that in decisions like *Cohen*. In that case, the application of the statute turned on the offensiveness of the speech at issue. Observing that "one man's vulgarity is another's lyric," we invalidated Cohen's conviction in part because we concluded that "governmental officials cannot make principled distinctions in this area." 403 U.S., at 25. In this litigation, by contrast, Congress and the Executive are uniquely positioned to make principled distinctions between activities that will further terrorist conduct and undermine United States foreign policy, and those that will not....

All this is not to say that any future applications of the material-support statute to speech or advocacy will survive First Amendment scrutiny. It is also not to say that any other statute relating to speech and terrorism would satisfy the First Amendment. In particular, we in no way suggest that a regulation of independent speech would pass constitutional muster, even if the Government were to show that such speech benefits foreign terrorist organizations. We also do not suggest that Congress could extend the same prohibition on material support at issue here to domestic organizations. We simply hold that, in prohibiting the particular forms of support that plaintiffs seek to provide to foreign terrorist groups, § 2339B does not violate the freedom of speech.

VI

Plaintiffs' final claim is that the material-support statute violates their freedom of association under the First Amendment.... The Court of Appeals correctly rejected this claim because the statute does not penalize mere association with a foreign terrorist organization. As the Ninth Circuit put it: "The statute does not prohibit being a member of one of the designated groups or vigorously promoting and supporting the political goals of the group.... What [§ 2339B] prohibits is the act of giving material support...."...

The Preamble to the Constitution proclaims that the people of the United States ordained and established that charter of government in part to "provide for the common defence."... We hold that, in regulating the particular forms of support that plaintiffs seek to provide to foreign terrorist organizations, Congress has pursued that objective consistent with the limitations of the First and Fifth Amendments.

The judgment of the United States Court of Appeals for the Ninth Circuit is affirmed in part and re-

versed in part, and the cases are remanded for further proceedings consistent with this opinion.

It is so ordered.

JUSTICE BREYER, with whom JUSTICES GINSBURG and SOTOMAYOR join, dissenting.... I do not think this statute is unconstitutionally vague. But I cannot agree with the Court's conclusion that the Constitution permits the Government to prosecute the plaintiffs criminally for engaging in coordinated teaching and advocacy furthering the designated organizations' lawful political objectives. In my view, the Government has not met its burden of showing that an interpretation of the statute that would prohibit this speech- and association-related activity serves the Government's compelling interest in combating terrorism. And I would interpret the statute as normally placing activity of this kind outside its scope....

In my view, the Government has not made the strong showing necessary to justify under the First Amendment the criminal prosecution of those who engage in these activities. All the activities involve the communication and advocacy of political ideas and lawful means of achieving political ends. Even the subjects the plaintiffs wish to teach — using international law to resolve disputes peacefully or petitioning the United Nations, for instance — concern political speech. We cannot avoid the constitutional significance of these facts on the basis that some of this speech takes place outside the United States and is directed at foreign governments, for the activities also involve advocacy in *this* country directed to *our* government and *its* policies....

That this speech and association for political purposes is the *kind* of activity to which the First Amendment ordinarily offers its strongest protection is elementary....

... Not even the "serious and deadly problem" of international terrorism can require *automatic* forfeiture of First Amendment rights ... After all, this Court has recognized that not "'[e]ven the war power ... remove[s] constitutional limitations safeguarding essential liberties.'" *United States* v. *Robel*, 389 U.S. 258, 264 (1967) (quoting *Home Building & Loan Assn.* v. *Blaisdell*, 290 U.S. 398, 426 (1934))....
Thus, there is no general First Amendment exception that applies here. If the statute is constitutional in this context, it would have to come with a strong justification attached....

The Government does identify a compelling countervailing interest, namely, the interest in protecting the security of the United States and its nationals from the threats that foreign terrorist organizations pose by denying those organizations financial and other fungible resources. I do not dispute the importance of this interest. But I do dispute whether the interest can justify the statute's criminal prohibition. To put the matter more specifically, precisely how does application of the statute to the protected activities before us *help achieve* that important security-related end? ...

The proposition that the two very different kinds of "support" are "fungible," ... is not *obviously* true. There is no *obvious* way in which undertaking advocacy for political change through peaceful means or teaching the PKK and LTTE, say, how to petition the United Nations for political change is fungible with other resources that might be put to more sinister ends in the way that donations of money, food, or computer training are fungible. It is far from obvi-

ous that these advocacy activities can themselves be redirected, or will free other resources that can be directed, towards terrorist ends. Thus, we must determine whether the Government has come forward with evidence to support its claim.

The Government has provided us with no empirical information that might convincingly support this claim ...

In my own view, the majority's arguments stretch the concept of "fungibility" beyond constitutional limits ...

I concede that the Government's expertise in foreign affairs may warrant deference in respect to many matters, ... But it remains for this Court to decide whether the Government has shown that such an interest justifies criminalizing speech activity otherwise protected by the First Amendment....

B. ASSOCIATIONAL RIGHTS

The Constitution does not expressly provide for a right of association, even though Americans in 1787 were accustomed to work politically through groups. Gradually, the First Amendment and the "liberty" interest secured by the Fourteenth Amendment have been interpreted to protect a person's right to associate with others who share similar ideas, interests, and goals. Self-government is more than Self. In many ways, America is a nation of joiners. Americans band together to seek friendship, cooperation, and concerted action.

Associational rights were heavily litigated throughout the 1940s and 1950s, usually involving a person's membership in the Communist party or in organizations considered subversive to the national interest. For a time, these memberships were punished by government. In 1943, Congress passed legislation to deny salaries to three federal officials suspected of "subversive" activities (see reading). This statute was struck down by the Supreme Court as a bill of attainder. United States v. Lovett, 328 U.S. 303 (1946). However, the Court upheld a Maryland law requiring state candidates for office — before being placed on the ballot — to take an oath or sign an affidavit that they were not engaged in an attempt to overthrow the government by force or violence and were not knowingly members of an organization engaged in such attempts. Gerende v. Election Board, 341 U.S. 56 (1951). Municipalities could require public employees to execute affidavits disclosing whether they were, or had been, members of Communist organizations. Garner v. Los Angeles Board, 341 U.S. 716 (1951). States were allowed to bar employment in public schools for any member of an organization advocating the overthrow of government by force, violence, or unlawful means. Adler v. Board of Education, 342 U.S. 485 (1952).

These cases provoked dissents from Justices who regarded these state laws as constitutionally offensive. In part, they objected to the use of "guilt by association" to punish people, often without even a hearing. The Court did manage to strike down "loyalty oaths" that required state employees to vow that they had not been a member of "Communist front" or "subversive" organizations. Such laws violated due process because membership might have been innocent and unknowing. Wieman v. Updegraff, 344 U.S. 183 (1952). By a 5 to 4 margin, the Court invalidated a city charter that stripped city employees of their jobs if they invoked the Self-Incrimination Clause before a legislative committee inquiring into their official conduct. These summary dismissals, said the Court, violated due process and made a mockery of the Fifth Amendment. Slochower v. Board of Education, 350 U.S. 551 (1956). The Court also used the Due Process Clause to protect attorneys who were refused permission to take

Freedom of Association

... Petitioner argues that in view of the facts and circumstances shown in the record, the effect of compelled disclosure of the membership lists will be to abridge the rights of its rank-and-file members to engage in lawful association in support of their common beliefs. It contends that governmental action which, although not directly suppressing association, nevertheless carries this consequence, can be justified only upon some overriding valid interest of the State.

Effective advocacy of both public and private points of view, particularly controversial ones, is undeniably enhanced by group association, as this Court has more than once recognized by remarking upon the close nexus between the freedoms of speech and assembly.... It is beyond debate that freedom to engage in association for the advancement of beliefs and ideas is an inseparable aspect of the "liberty" assured by the Due Process Clause of the Fourteenth Amendment, which embraces freedom of speech.... Of course, it is immaterial whether the beliefs sought to be advanced by association pertain to political, economic, religious or cultural matters, and state action which may have the effect of curtailing the freedom to associate is subject to the closest scrutiny.

SOURCE: NAACP v. Alabama, 357 U.S. 449, 460–61 (1958).

the bar examination, or who were not allowed to practice after passing the bar, because of their associations with Communist organizations. Schware v. Board of Bar Examiners, 353 U.S. 232 (1957); Konigsberg v. State Bar, 353 U.S. 252 (1957).[1]

The Court's record on associational freedom for Communist and subversive organizations during this period was mixed.[2] The right of association in the NAACP was treated differently. When Alabama tried to obtain the membership list of the NAACP's state chapter, a unanimous Court held that members had a constitutional right to associate freely with others as part of the "liberty" protected by the Fourteenth Amendment (see box). Another unanimous ruling rejected compulsory disclosure of NAACP memberships as an unconstitutional interference with the freedom of association.[3] Minor parties, such as the Socialist Workers party, need not report the names of campaign contributors if it results in harassment and reprisals. Brown v. Socialist Workers '74 Campaign Comm., 459 U.S. 87 (1982).

By the 1960s, the Supreme Court was striking down loyalty oaths because they were so vague as to violate due process.[4] The objection to "guilt by association" gained a Court majority by 1966. Elfbrandt v. Russell, 384 U.S. 11 (1966). In 1967, a 6 to 2 majority struck down a congressional statute that sought to punish any worker at a defense facility who belonged to a Communist organization. The Court held that the statute abridged the right of association by reaching too broadly to include inactive members or those employed in nonsensitive jobs. United States v. Robel, 389 U.S. 258 (1967).

In 1992, an 8–1 Court held that it was unconstitutional to use a defendant's membership in a white

---

1. But see the confusing array of subsequent cases: Konigsberg v. State Bar, 366 U.S. 36 (1961); In re Anastaplo, 366 U.S. 82 (1961); Baird v. State Bar of Arizona, 401 U.S. 1 (1971); In re Stolar, 401 U.S. 23 (1971); Law Students' Research Council v. Wadmond, 401 U.S. 154 (1971); In re Primus, 436 U.S. 412 (1978).

2. Sweezy v. New Hampshire, 354 U.S. 234 (1957); Beilan v. Board of Education, 357 U.S. 399 (1958); Lerner v. Casey, 357 U.S. 468 (1958); Nelson v. Los Angeles County, 362 U.S. 1 (1960); Shelton v. Tucker, 364 U.S. 479 (1960).

3. Bates v. Little Rock, 361 U.S. 516 (1960). See also NAACP v. Button, 371 U.S. 415 (1963) and Gibson v. Florida Legislative Comm., 372 U.S. 539 (1963). In 1928 the Court allowed states to obtain the membership lists of the Ku Klux Klan, because its conduct was "inimical to personal rights and public welfare." Bryant v. Zimmerman, 278 U.S. 63, 75 (1928).

4. Cramp v. Bd. of Public Instruction, 368 U.S. 278 (1961); Baggett v. Bullitt, 377 U.S. 360 (1964); Keyishian v. Board of Regents, 385 U.S. 589 (1967).

racist gang during a sentencing proceeding unless that evidence was relevant to the crime committed. Otherwise, the introduction of that evidence violates the First Amendment right of association. In this case, the murderer was white as was the victim. Dawson v. Delaware, 503 U.S. 159 (1992).

Congress Seeks to Remove "Subversives" from FDR's Administration

In an emergency appropriations bill in 1943, Congress debated an amendment designed to withhold federal salaries from three named individuals: Goodwin B. Watson and William E. Dodd, Jr., of the Federal Communications Commission, and Robert Morse Lovett, governor of the Virgin Islands. They were among a group of federal officials labeled by Congressman Martin Dies as "irresponsible, unrepresentative, crackpot, radical bureaucrats." 89 Cong. Rec. 479 (1943). The debate in the House of Representatives shows most members willing to use the power of the purse to punish individuals for their opinions and associations. A few members opposed the amendment, regarding it as a violation of the First Amendment, a usurpation of the President's removal power, and a bill of attainder forbidden by the Constitution. The debate below is taken from 89 Cong. Rec. 4482–87, 4546–58, 4581–4605.

Mr. CELLER. Mr. Chairman, we are going to vote this afternoon, I presume, on the so-called amendment offered by the Kerr committee. In that connection, I fear that we are embarking upon something rather dangerous. We should think very deeply before we vote approval of the so-called ouster of liberals from various executive departments of the Government.

As I view it, this is an attempt to discharge certain men in the Government service because of their opinions. It is primarily just that....

Mr. OUTLAND. Mr. Chairman, this proposal to remove certain men from the Government service by means of an amendment to an appropriation bill is extremely dangerous. In my judgment, it violates our American concepts of fair play, freedom of speech, and direct action. It sets up no definite standards as to what is subversive and opens wide the path of intolerance. Under the principle here implied, for example, a Cabinet member could be removed from his position by having Congress disapprove his social or economic views, and then follow up such disapproval by an amendment such as we are discussing today....

And what is the basis for this contemplated action? It is simply that they have belonged to organizations or spoken before groups which do not meet with the approval of certain Members of Congress. Thus it becomes a matter solely of opinion, not of law, and we have prided ourselves that in this democracy of ours we are governed by laws, not by the whims of men. Such action smacks far more of the tactics of the Nazis and the Fascists, against whom we are fighting, than of the spirit of American justice and fair play....

Mr. COFFEE.... What is this crime of which these men are guilty? It is that either they have been the sponsors of some organization, have addressed some organization, donated to some organization which someone, somewhere, somehow said in his opinion was inimical or acting in a manner inimical to the best interests of the United States. There is not a finding anywhere in the report of the Kerr committee that any of the gentlemen so characterized was guilty of advocating the overthrow of the American Government by force and violence....

We in Congress are sitting here as judge, as jury, and as prosecutor.... We are attempting to do something today which is unconstitutional. We are attempting to impeach men by methods other than impeachment.... [This] has the effect of a bill of attainder, one of the fundamental things against which our colonial forefathers sought separation from the mother country 160 years ago....

Mr. DIRKSEN.... The real issue is whether or not this body, that is charged under the Constitution as the keeper of the purse, without whose action not one dollar can go out of the Federal Treasury, can, under that authority, spell out that power to determine who shall be on the pay roll and who shall not....

Their freedom of speech is not involved. Dr. Dodd can go down on Marshall Square tonight and make any kind of a speech he wants to, but I am not going to see him on the pay roll of the Federal Government, the recipient of the taxpayers' money, and do it. That is a different thing.

Mr. KERR.... This Congress has the right to say to whom the people's money shall be paid. Congress will not be denied and should never be denied that right....

Mr. HOLIFIELD.... I do not know whether these three men are loyal American citizens or not. I do not believe that such a determination is the prerog-ative of a Member of Congress or a committee thereof. The transcript of the testimony before the committee was withheld, or unavailable, to the gen-eral membership until the time of voting. We were asked to vote on a punitive legislative amendment which was directed against three individuals. In my opinion, any legislation passed by Congress should be general in its impact and not directed either for or against an individual. The civil and Federal courts are the proper places to determine the punishment of an individual....

Mr. MARCANTONIO.... We have a most fantas-tic situation. We are to vote on an amendment to an appropriation bill, to expel three people from the Fed-eral Government without a single word of the hear-ings before us. All we have before us is what we are told by the gentlemen who are on the committee....

Mr. BURDICK. Mr. Chairman, many here be-moan the fact that a few Members have seen fit to raise the question of the constitutional right of the Congress to pass a law denying the salary of an offi-cer and thus deprive him of his right to hold office....

In my opinion—and I almost feel like apologiz-ing for expressing this opinion for fear that my salary may be taken away—this Congress does not have the constitutional right to legislate any citizen out of his property, or his salary, which is the same thing, merely because he has expressed an opinion which is not approved by a majority of this Congress....

Mr. HOBBS. Mr. Chairman, I am exceedingly loath to oppose the pending amendment. I honor and respect the judgment both of our great Com-mittee on Appropriations and also the special sub-committee on whose reports this amendment stands. I am devoted to the men who compose those committees and in many cases I would bow to their superior wisdom. But in a case such as this, wherein

the amendment is clearly unconstitutional, in my opinion, I simply cannot follow their leadership, much as I would like to.

The pending amendment is a bill of pains and penalties within the meaning of the constitutional prohibition:

"No bill of attainder ... shall be passed (art. I, ... sec. 9)."

"A bill of attainder is a legislative act which in-flicts punishment without a judicial trial. If the pun-ishment be less than death, it is a bill of pains and penalties. As the term 'bill of attainder' is used in the Federal Constitution, it includes both bills of attain-der particularly, and bills of pains and penalties. (*Cummings* v. *Missouri* (71 U.S. (4 Wall.) 277, 18 L. Ed. 356); *Drehman* v. *Stifle* (75 U.S. (8 Wall.), 595, 601, 19 L. Ed. 508); *Pierce* v. *Carskadon* (83 U.S. (16 Wall.), 234, 239, 21 L.Ed. 276)."

If, then, the amendment now being considered inflicts punishment, it is a bill of pains and penalties, since there has been no judicial trial....

[*President Roosevelt signed the bill containing this amendment, but later explained that he did so because the bill provided emergency appropriations during the recess of Congress. In noting that the three individuals were being disqualified for federal employment be-cause of "political opinions" attributed to them, he re-garded the provision as "not only unwise and discrim-inatory, but unconstitutional as a bill of attainder," which he said the Supreme Court had defined as "a legislative act which inflicts punishment without judi-cial trial." Public Papers and Addresses of Franklin D. Roosevelt, 1943 Volume, at 386. It was on that ground that the provision was held unconstitutional by the Court of Claims in Lovett v. United States, 66 F.Supp. 142 (Ct. Cl. 1945), and by the Supreme Court in United States v. Lovett, 328 U.S. 303 (1946).*]

C. THE REGULATION OF SPEECH

The Free Speech Clause does not confer an absolute right. Although speech is constitutionally pro-tected, government may adopt regulations to protect other societal interests. Citizens are not at lib-erty to commit perjury, to libel, or to infringe on copyrights. There is no constitutional right to "in-sist upon a street meeting in the middle of Times Square at the rush hour as a form of freedom of speech or assembly." Cox v. Louisiana, 379 U.S. 536, 554 (1965). To prevent the clogging of sidewalks and public streets, licenses may be required for parades and public processions. Cox v. New Hamp-shire, 312 U.S. 569 (1941). Sound trucks equipped with amplifiers and capable of generating "loud and raucous noises" may be prohibited. Kovacs v. Cooper, 336 U.S. 77 (1949); Saia v. New York, 334 U.S. 558 (1948). A mailer's right to communicate stops at the mailbox of an addressee who objects to what is being sent. Rowan v. Post Office Dept., 397 U.S. 728 (1970).

Forums for Speech

Traditional public forum (example: public park)	Subject to strict scrutiny by the courts (must be narrowly drawn to achieve a compelling state interest).
Public forum designated by the government (example: state university)	Also subject to strict-scrutiny analysis.
Remaining public property (example: airport terminal)	Regulation is permitted if reasonable.

The scope of free speech depends on three variables: time, place, and manner. The Supreme Court identifies three places: the traditional public forum (public parks), a public forum designated by the government (e.g., state universities), and the nonpublic forum (such as private homes). For the first two, restrictions on free speech are subject to heightened scrutiny by the courts (see box). The right of free speech applies to public forums. I have a right to express my views at a public assembly, not in your living room. When the state applies restrictions to speech, the general rule is that they be "content neutral." Government is not supposed to be a censor of viewpoints. When regulations are imposed to limit speech, they cannot be "overbroad," pulling within their reach speech that is both protected and unprotected. Even for public parks, however, government may adopt "guidelines" to regulate the noise from rock concerts that disturbs park users and nearby apartment residents. Provided that the regulation is content neutral and narrowly tailored to serve a "significant governmental interest," reasonable limits may be imposed on speech. Ward v. Rock Against Racism, 491 U.S. 781 (1989). Similarly, cities may require groups of more than 50 people to obtain a permit before engaging in large-scale events, provided the city guidelines apply equally to all groups regardless of viewpoint. Thomas v. Chicago Park Dist., 534 U.S. 316 (2002). The Supreme Court has decided a number of cases involving access to abortion clinics (Chapter 17).

Many of these doctrines, including overbreadth, were addressed by the Supreme Court in a 2003 case. A trespass order, covering a low-income housing development, prohibited unauthorized visitors to use formerly public streets and sidewalks. The purpose was to reduce the level of violent crime that had plagued the neighborhood. The Virginia Supreme Court ruled that the policy vested too much discretion in the housing manager to determine who was "authorized" to enter, including speech that the manager found to be offensive. However, the U.S. Supreme Court held that the trespass order did not impose an unconstitutional limit to the First Amendment or to free speech. Virginia v. Hicks, 539 U.S. 113 (2003). The unanimous decision acknowledged that the trespass policy could be challenged in the future on "other grounds."

Content Neutral

The standard of "content neutral" is a central principle for monitoring free speech. When public officials issue licenses or permits to allow groups to conduct peaceful demonstrations, permission should not depend on what will be said and expressed. In 1992, a 5–4 Court struck down a Georgia law that allowed county administrators to adjust a $1,000 fee for a permit to conduct a parade or assembly on public property. The Court decided that the law was facially unconstitutional because it failed to provide standards to guide administrators and appeared to allow administrators to adjust the fee based on the content of the speech. The fee could be varied to reflect the estimated cost of maintaining public order, implying that controversial or unpopular groups might have to pay more. Forsyth County, Ga. v. Nationalist Movement, 505 U.S. 123 (1992).

Regulation and suppression "are not the same, either in purpose or result, and courts of justice can tell the difference." Poulos v. New Hampshire, 345 U.S. 395, 408 (1953). Regulation can become a code word to suppress speech that is unpopular with the majority or objectionable to local authorities. To compel labor organizers to obtain a card from a state official before soliciting memberships may simply be a guise to discourage trade unionism. Thomas v. Collins, 323 U.S. 516 (1945). It is legitimate to require speakers to fill out applications before using city parks for group meetings, but not when the applications are denied for arbitrary or discriminatory reasons, such as against a disliked minority or an objectionable speech. Under these conditions, the requirement for a license or permit constitutes forbidden censorship and prior restraint.

As a regulatory device, "breach of the peace" statutes can translate easily into suppression of speech. A 1963 case involved high school and college students who had been convicted for gathering peacefully on the grounds of the South Carolina legislature to express their grievances about state laws concerning black citizens. By an 8 to 1 vote, the Court held that the state had infringed the rights of free speech, free assembly, and freedom to petition for a redress of grievances. Edwards v. South Carolina, 372 U.S. 229 (1963).[5]

More narrowly, 5–4, the Court reversed the convictions of five black males who participated in an orderly, nondisruptive sit-in at a branch library to protest segregation. The Court protected their freedom of speech, assembly, and the right to petition. Brown v. Louisiana, 383 U.S. 131 (1966).

Speech is subject to greater restraint when the question is one not of orderly demonstrations, conducted without obstructing the functions of government, but rather disruptive sit-ins and trespasses. The Supreme Court upheld the convictions of students who demonstrated on the premises of a jail. Adderley v. Florida, 385 U.S. 39 (1966). Similarly, sit-in demonstrations, kneel-in demonstrations, and mass street parades may not continue in defiance of a temporary injunction issued by a judicial authority. Walker v. City of Birmingham, 388 U.S. 307 (1967).

Overly broad breach-of-the-peace statutes, directed against actions that "agitate" or arouse citizens "from a state of repose ... to disquiet," are by their very nature antagonistic to the First Amendment. One function of the Free Speech Clause "is to invite dispute. It may indeed best serve its high purpose when it induces a condition of unrest, creates dissatisfaction with conditions as they are, or even stirs people to anger. Speech is often provocative and challenging." Cox v. Louisiana, 379 U.S. 536, 551–52 (1965), citing Terminiello v. Chicago, 337 U.S. 1, 4 (1949). The Court carefully monitors laws that restrict the solicitation of funds (see box on next page).

Content-based restrictions on speech have been permitted only for certain categories of speech, such as incitement, obscenity, defamation, fraud, child pornography, and "fighting words." This issue reached the Court again in 2012. Congress in 2005 passed the Stolen Valor Act, making it a crime to lie about the receipt of military honors and decorations. Punishment included fines and imprisonment for up to one year. The statute was premised on the assumption that false claims diminish the value of honors justly awarded. Xavier Alvarez, a local politician in California, was charged under the Act for claiming to have received the Congressional Medal of Honor. In fact, he had never served in the military. He pled guilty and was sentenced to probation, a $5,000 fine, and community service. As part of the plea agreement he reserved the right to appeal on First Amendment grounds. The Court struck down the Act as a content-based restriction without any "legally cognizable harm" that might justify a restriction on speech. The Court said that criminalizing falsity without such a showing would have a chilling effect on speech, without a "clear limiting principle" on governmental power. It left open the possibility that Congress could rewrite the law in a more narrow way. United States v. Alvarez, 567 U.S. ___ (2012). Congress began consideration of new legislation.

---

5. See also Shuttlesworth v. Birmingham, 394 U.S. 147 (1969); Poulos v. New Hampshire, 345 U.S. 395 (1953); Fowler v. Rhode Island, 345 U.S. 67 (1953); Kunz v. New York, 340 U.S. 290 (1951); Niemotko v. Maryland, 340 U.S. 268 (1951).

Solicitation of Funds

In 1980, the Court struck down a village ordinance that required charitable organizations to use at least 75 percent of their receipts for "charitable purposes" to be eligible for door-to-door or on-street solicitation of contributions. Charitable appeals involve a variety of speech interests: communication of information, dissemination of views and ideas, and advocacy of causes. Schaumburg v. Citizens for Better Environ, 444 U.S. 620 (1980). See also Cornelius v. NAACP Legal Defense & Ed. Fund, 473 U.S. 788 (1985); Secretary of State of Md. v. J.H. Munson Co., 467 U.S. 947 (1984); Breard v. Alexandria, 341 U.S. 622 (1951); Martin v. Struthers, 319 U.S. 141 (1943).

A 5–4 Court in 1990 upheld a federal regulation that prohibits solicitation on the premises of a post office. The regulation was considered a "reasonable" restriction on First Amendment rights and was not subjected to strict-scrutiny analysis. United States v. Kokinda, 497 U.S. 720 (1990). In 1992 the Court ruled that an airport terminal operated by a public authority is not a "public forum," permitting the authority to ban solicitation of money within the terminals. Such bans need only satisfy a reasonableness standard. The airports involved in this case—Kennedy, La Guardia, and Newark—permit solicitation on the sidewalks outside the terminal buildings. Although the Court

decided 6–3 that prohibitions on solicitations were reasonable, a different 5–4 majority said that airports must permit groups to hand out literature. Some airports continue to permit solicitations within their terminals but restrict them to certain areas and hours. Int'l Society for Krishna Consciousness v. Lee, 505 U.S. 672.

Also in 1992, a 5–3 Court upheld a Tennessee law that prohibited the solicitation of votes and the display of campaign materials within 100 feet of the entrance to polling places on election day. The statute was narrowly tailored to serve a compelling state interest in preventing voter intimidation and election fraud. Burson v. Freeman, 504 U.S. 191 (1992).

In 2002, the Court decided 8 to 1 against a local ordinance that made it a crime for canvassers or solicitors to visit residents of a village in Ohio unless they had prior permission from village officials. The ordinance was so broad that it prohibited unauthorized visits not only from religious groups like the Jehovah's Witnesses but also neighbors stopping by to solicit support for political candidates or improved public services. Had the ordinance been limited to commercial solicitation it might have survived scrutiny. Watchtower Bible v. Village of Stratton, 536 U.S. 150 (2002).

Expressive Content

Freedom of speech includes the right not to support an ideology. In 1977, the Supreme Court struck down a requirement in New Hampshire that noncommercial vehicles carry license tags bearing the state motto, "Live Free or Die." Jehovah's Witnesses considered the motto repugnant to their moral, religious, and political beliefs. The Court held that a state may not force an individual to advertise an ideological message, using a car as a "mobile billboard." The First Amendment protects the freedom to speak and not to speak. Wooley v. Maynard, 430 U.S. 705 (1977). In 1995, a unanimous Court upheld the right of the organizers of Boston's St. Patrick's Day parade to exclude gay marchers. To the Court, a parade is a "public drama" to make a collective point. The organizers had a right to exclude a group that would have altered the expressive content of the parade. Hurley v. Irish-American Gay Group of Boston, 515 U.S. 557 (1995).

Hurley became the basis for deciding a conflict between a New Jersey law that prohibits discrimination against sexual orientation and the right of the Boy Scouts of America to expel an adult Scout who had announced that he is gay. The Boy Scouts, a private organization engaged in instilling its system of values in young people, asserted that homosexual conduct is inconsistent with the values it seeks to promote. James Dale, whose membership was revoked, is a gay rights activist. Unlike the unanimous ruling in *Hurley*, the Court split 5 to 4 in deciding that the New Jersey law violated the

Boy Scouts' First Amendment right of expressive association. Although the Scout Oath and Law do not mention sexuality or sexual orientation, the Court interpreted the terms "morally straight" and "clean" as opposition to homosexual conduct, a position the Boy Scouts have adopted ever since 1978. Dale's presence in the Boy Scouts would force the organization to send a message that it accepts homosexual conduct as a legitimate form of behavior. Boy Scouts of America v. Dale, 530 U.S. 640 (2000).

Justice Stevens' dissent, joined by Souter, Ginsburg, and Breyer, argued that the New Jersey law did not impose any "serious burdens" on the Boy Scouts or force the organization to communicate any message it did not want to endorse. He claimed that the Boy Scouts had never taken a clear and unequivocal position on homosexuality. Further, Stevens disagreed that Dale's membership sent a message comparable to that of the gay marchers in *Hurley.*

Although the Boy Scouts prevailed in court, it might be penalized by corporations and state governments that withdraw their support for fear that continued assistance could imply tolerance for discrimination against gays. The Clinton administration announced that it would not close federal lands to Boy Scout Jamborees. In 2002, Congress passed the "Boy Scouts of America Equal Access Act," which provides that no public school or state educational agency that receives federal funds shall deny equal access to any group officially affiliated with the Boy Scouts. Failure to allow these groups to meet on school premises before or after school hours can lead to a cut-off of federal funds. 115 Stat. 1982, § 9525). In 2012 the organization reconfirmed its policy excluding gays, after a special commission conducted a two-year review of the policy.

Dues and Fees

The Court has scrutinized various dues and fees to determine whether they present First Amendment problems. In 1977, the Court upheld a Michigan requirement that nonunion members pay a "service charge" to the union, but also placed restrictions on the use of the funds. The union could use the money for collective bargaining, contract administration, and grievance-adjustment purposes, but it could not force nonunion employees to contribute to ideological causes they oppose. Abood v. Detroit Board of Education, 431 U.S. 209 (1977).

A unanimous Court in 1990 extended the principle in *Abood* by holding that lawyers cannot be compelled to pay state bar dues used to support political or ideological causes to which they do not subscribe. Keller v. State Bar of California, 496 U.S. 1 (1990). In 1991, in a further clarification of *Abood,* the Court ruled 8 to 1 that public employee unions cannot charge nonmembers for political lobbying and public relations campaigns unless those efforts are directly related to ratification of a contract. Lehnert v. Ferris Faculty Assn., 500 U.S. 507 (1991).

Other decisions have clarified the use of dues and fees. In 1995, the Court held that the University of Virginia had denied students their right of free speech by using student fees to finance the printing of student publications while at the same time withholding funds from "Wide Awake," a Christian newspaper. Rosenberger v. University of Virginia, 515 U.S. 819 (1995). The Court was divided 5 to 4 in this case, but in 2000 it was unanimous in holding that public colleges can require students to pay an "activity fee" even when the funds are used to support political advocacy by groups and some students object to the message. Christian law students at the University of Wisconsin objected that the activity fee had been used to fund student organizations supportive of gay rights and other liberal causes. The Court argued that the fees helped promote an open dialogue among students. This type of activity fee is constitutional provided it is applied neutrally and does not favor one viewpoint over another. Board of Regents of University of Wisconsin v. Southworth, 529 U.S. 217 (2000). While not dealing directly with student fees, a 2010 case raised related questions about the conditions that public educational institutions could place on groups seeking recognition as a "Registered Student Organization (RSO)." The Court ruled that Hastings College of Law could deny the Christian Legal Society recognized status because the organization discriminated against some students on the basis of their religion and their sexual orientation. The Court found the school's rule that RSO's must accept "all-comers" to be a "reasonable, view-point neutral condition" for access to its limited public forum. Christian Legal Society v. Martinez, 561 U.S. ___ (2010).

Public Employees

The right of free speech for public employees poses unique problems. After much litigation to the contrary, it is now settled that public employees have a constitutional right to comment upon matters "of public concern." Pickering v. Board of Education, 391 U.S. 563 (1968). They do not forfeit First Amendment freedoms when they engage in private communications with their employers, even when the exchange is considered insulting, hostile, loud, and arrogant. Givhan v. Western Line Consol. School Dist., 439 U.S. 410 (1979). Public employees are prohibited by the Hatch Act from participating in certain political party activities. When Presidents Theodore Roosevelt and William Howard Taft imposed a "gag order" to prohibit federal employees from lobbying Congress, Congress responded with legislation that gave civil servants the right to petition Congress and to furnish information to either House. 37 Stat. 556, §6 (1912); 48 Cong. Rec. 4513, 5201, 5223, 5235, 10671 (1912). That statute remains part of current law. 5 U.S.C. §7211.

Beyond these general guideposts, the scope of free speech for public employees is uncertain. In 1983, a 5–4 Court upheld the removal of public employees who object to internal office conditions and attempt to organize opposition to superiors, even when the reasons for dismissal are alleged to be mistaken or unreasonable. Connick v. Myers, 461 U.S. 138 (1983). Four years later, again by a 5–4 vote, the Court overturned the removal of a public employee who remarked to a coworker, after learning of the assassination attempt on President Reagan, "If they go for him again, I hope they get him." Justice Powell, the swing vote, explained that this offhand remark by a clerical employee was insufficiently disruptive of the office to justify dismissal. Rankin v. McPherson, 483 U.S. 378 (1987).

The degree of free speech available to public workers split the Court again in 1994. In ruling that a public employer must first investigate an incident before firing someone and have "reasonable" grounds for the dismissal, the Court's plurality decision (joined by four Justices) precipitated concurrences from four colleagues and drew two dissents. Waters v. Churchill, 511 U.S. 661 (1994). In a 1995 ruling, striking down a federal law that prohibited most executive branch employees from accepting outside income for speeches and articles, three Justices dissented and a fourth dissented in part. The Court found the law especially offensive because it prevented employees from accepting compensation even when the subject of the speech or article had no connection to the employee's official duties. United States v. National Treasury Employees Union, 513 U.S. 454 (1995).[6] (Additional discussion on the First Amendment rights of public employees appears in the earlier section on associational rights.)

With regard to free speech in the armed forces, the Court generally treats the military as a separate enclave of constitutional law, permitting restrictions on speech that would be impermissible in civilian society. Elementary rights of circulating petitions and listening to speeches by political candidates are denied in the interests of military discipline and order.[7]

After protecting the free-speech rights of public employees in a number of cases that restricted the use of patronage to dismiss government workers (see note 6), the Court in 1990 extended that principle to four new personnel actions: promotion, transfer, hiring, and recall (bringing someone back

---

6. For other free speech cases involving public employees, see Branti v. Finkel, 445 U.S. 507 (1980); Mt. Healthy City Board of Ed. v. Doyle, 429 U.S. 274 (1977); Elrod v. Burns, 427 U.S. 347 (1976); Perry v. Sindermann, 408 U.S. 593 (1972). O'Hare Truck Service, Inc. v. Northlake, 518 U.S. 712 (1996), builds on *Elrod* and *Burns* to extend the right of political expression to those who contract for government services. That ruling was reinforced by Board of Comm'rs, Wabaunsee Cty. v. Umbehr, 518 U.S. 668 (1996).

7. United States v. Albertini, 472 U.S. 675 (1985); Secretary of Navy v. Huff, 444 U.S. 453 (1980); Brown v. Glines, 444 U.S. 348 (1980); Greer v. Spock, 424 U.S. 828 (1976); Parker v. Levy, 417 U.S. 733 (1974). But see Flower v. United States, 407 U.S. 197 (1972).

after a layoff). In a hotly contested 5–4 decision, the Court held that personnel actions in those areas cannot be based on party affiliation and party support. Other than cases where party affiliation is an "appropriate requirement" for the position involved (the Court gave no clue as to what that means), patronage is an impermissible infringement on public employees' First Amendment rights. It appears that this decision will have more impact on state and local governments than on the Federal Government. For the dissenters, Justice Scalia excoriated the Court for usurping a "policy question to be decided by the people's representatives." He also flagged a conspicuous irony: most Justices of the Supreme Court owe their appointment to patronage. Presidents almost always appoint judges from their own party. Rutan v. Republican Party of Illinois, 497 U.S. 62 (1990).

In 1998, a unanimous Court held that federal employees can be disciplined for lying about misconduct. Unlike in criminal trials where defendants need not testify, federal workers have an obligation to answer questions. In agency investigations, federal employees have a right to be heard but not a right to lie. LaChance v. Erickson, 522 U.S. 262 (1998).

The free speech rights of public employees were further eroded by a 5–4 Court decision in 2006, holding that when government employees make statements pursuant to their official duties, they do not speak as citizens for First Amendment purposes. For that reason, the Constitution does not insulate their communications from employer discipline. Garcetti v. Ceballos 547 U.S. 410 (2006). With this test, an employee has greater protection by going public about agency conditions than through official channels. Congress can revisit this issue by strengthening current whistleblower statutes. In 2011 the Court rejected the claim of a public employee that a grievance law suit he brought against the town he worked for was covered by the Petition Clause of the First Amendment. The Court said that the grievance over alleged retaliatory actions taken by the public employer did not give rise to a sufficient "public concern" to justify First Amendment protection, and that allowing such grievance suits to be covered would be dangerous to the "efficient and effective" operations of government. Borough of Duryea v. Guarnieri, 564 U.S. ___ (2011).

"Fighting Words"

The Supreme Court created, and subsequently altered, the "fighting-words" doctrine. A unanimous decision in 1942 upheld a state law that prohibited speech in public that is offensive or derisive of another person. The statutory purpose was to prevent a breach of the peace. Chaplinsky v. New Hampshire, 315 U.S. 568 (1942). That decision was undercut in 1949 when the Court, divided 5–4, struck down a Chicago ordinance that prohibited any breach of the peace. The trial court had interpreted the ordinance to prohibit any speech that "stirs the public to anger" and "invites disputes." The Court declared that a function of free speech is to invite disputes:

> "It may indeed best serve its high purpose when it induces a condition of unrest, creates dissatisfaction with conditions as they are, or even stirs people to anger. Speech is often provocative and challenging. It may strike at prejudices and preconceptions and have profound unsettling effects as it presses for acceptance of an idea." Terminiello v. Chicago, 337 U.S. 1, 4 (1949).

The fighting-words doctrine was kept alive two years later when the Court split 6–3 in upholding a New York statute that prohibited incitement of a breach of the peace. The Court supported intervention by the police to prevent a riot. Feiner v. New York, 340 U.S. 315 (1951). The following year, a 5–4 decision upheld an Illinois statute that made it illegal to publish anything that exposed the citizens of any race, color, creed, or religion to contempt, derision, or obloquy. At issue was the distribution of racist leaflets that portrayed blacks as depraved, criminal, and unchaste. Beauharnais v. Illinois, 343 U.S. 250 (1952).

In light of later cases, little remains of the fighting-words doctrine. In 1971, a 5–4 Court overturned the conviction of Paul Robert Cohen, who had been sentenced to 30 days for wearing, in a county courthouse, a jacket bearing the words "Fuck the Draft." Unlike its decisions in cases involving obscenity and pornography, the Court found itself unable to "distinguish this from any other offensive word." COHEN v. CALIFORNIA, 403 U.S. 15, 25 (1971).[8]

A year later, the Court agreed to set aside the conviction of someone who had said to a police officer: "White son of a bitch, I'll kill you." The Court found the state law, making it a misdemeanor to use "opprobrious words or abusive language, tending to cause a breach of the peace," unconstitutionally vague and overbroad. Gooding v. Wilson, 405 U.S. 518 (1972). When an 18-year-old at a small public gathering remarked that if inducted into the army and made to carry a rifle "the first man I want to get in my sights is L.B.J. [President Lyndon B. Johnson]," the Court held that the context of this remark made it political hyperbole rather than a knowing and willful threat against the President. Watts v. United States, 394 U.S. 705 (1969).

An issue of exceptional emotional intensity involved the request of American Nazis to march in Skokie, Illinois, a village with thousands of Holocaust survivors. They wanted to march in their uniforms, display the swastika, and distribute literature promoting hatred against Jews. After many court rulings, they eventually held a rally in Chicago's Marquette Park. National Socialist Party v. Skokie, 432 U.S. 43 (1977); Collin v. Smith, 447 F.Supp. 676 (N.D. Ill. 1978), aff'd, 578 F.2d 1197 (7th Cir. 1978), cert. denied, 439 U.S. 916 (1978). See Philippa Strum, When the Nazis Came to Skokie (1999).

Another emotional issue, decided by the Supreme Court in 1992, focused on a St. Paul, Minnesota, "hate crimes law" used to prosecute someone for burning a cross on a black family's lawn. The law prohibited the display of a symbol that one knows or has reason to know "arouses anger, alarm or resentment in others on the basis of race, color, creed, religion or gender." The Court struck down the law as a violation of free speech, but the Justices could not agree on their reasoning. R.A.V. v. ST. PAUL, 505 U.S. 377 (1992). On such free speech doctrines as "discrete categories" and "overbreadth," the Justices disagree sharply (see box on the next page). The decision cast doubt on the constitutionality of other laws that prohibit cross burning; laws that impose heavier penalties for such crimes as vandalism, arson, and assault that are motivated by racial, religious, or other bias; and campus speech codes that punish students for offensive remarks. Although the St. Paul ordinance was held invalid, individuals guilty of cross burning, swastika displays, and other actions could have been prosecuted under other Minnesota statutes that prohibit terroristic threats, arson, and criminal damage to property.

Building on R.A.V., a unanimous Court in 1993 decided that states may impose heavier prison sentences when assailants select their victims on the basis of race, religion, or other biases. In this case, a group of black teenagers in Wisconsin beat up a white youth after discussing the racially charged movie *Mississippi Burning*. The Court distinguished this case from the St. Paul ordinance by holding that the latter was explicitly directed at expression, whereas the Wisconsin law aimed only at conduct. Wisconsin v. Mitchell, 508 U.S. 476 (1993).

As another spin-off from R.A.V., the Court ruled in 2003 that a state may make it a crime to burn a cross with the intent of intimidating a person or group. Prosecutors must prove that the burning was intended as a threat, not as some form of symbolic expression. A majority of the Court found the statute, passed by Virginia in 1952, unconstitutional because it permitted a jury to infer that cross-

---

8. Yet the Court distinguishes language well enough to use code by referring to articles entitled "M—f—Acquitted" and organizations known as "Up Against the Wall, M—f—." Papish v. University of Missouri Curators, 410 U.S. 667 (1973). Similar cases include Rosenfeld v. New Jersey, 408 U.S. 901 (1972); Lewis v. City of New Orleans, 408 U.S. 913 (1972); Brown v. Oklahoma, 408 U.S. 914 (1972); Cason v. City of Columbus, 409 U.S. 1053 (1972). For other obscenity/breach-of-the-peace cases, see Hess v. Indiana, 414 U.S. 105 (1973) and Lewis v. City of New Orleans, 415 U.S. 130 (1974).

Judicial Guidelines for Free Speech Cases

The Supreme Court often uses three tests to determine the constitutionality of governmental efforts to restrict free speech:

1. Discrete Categories (content-based). Certain categories of expression may be prohibited on the basis of their content: falsely shouting fire in a crowded theatre [Schenck v. United States, 249 U.S. 47, 52 (1919)]; "fighting words" [Chaplinsky v. New Hampshire, 315 U.S. 568, 572 (1942)]; defamation [Beauharnais v. Illinois, 343 U.S. 250 (1952)]; child pornography [New York v. Ferber, 458 U.S. 747 (1982)]. In these cases the expressive content is either of no value or of de minimis value to society.

2. Overbreadth Doctrine. Governmental actions are invalid if they prohibit not only unprotected expression but protected expression as well.

Schaumburg v. Citizens for a Better Environment, 444 U.S. 620, 634 (1980). The "possible harm to society in permitting some unprotected speech to go unpunished is outweighed by the possibility that protected speech of others may be muted...." Broadrick v. Oklahoma, 413 U.S. 601, 612 (1973).

3. Void for Vagueness. A law is invalid on its face if it is so vague that persons "of common intelligence must necessarily guess at its meaning and differ as to its application." Connally v. General Construction Co., 269 U.S. 385, 391 (1926). Examples include loyalty oaths [Baggett v. Bullitt, 377 U.S. 360 (1964)] and a city ordinance that forbids three or more persons from meeting on sidewalks and acting in a manner "annoying" to persons passing by [Coates v. City of Cincinnati, 402 U.S. 611 (1971)].

burning by itself implied an intent to intimidate. Some cross-burnings are not meant to be intimidating (such as stage productions of Sir Walter Scott's "The Lady of the Lake"). Virginia v. Black, 538 U.S. 343, 366 (2003).

The Free Speech Rights of Public School Students

The Court has been asked on several occasions to determine the extent of First Amendment protection of speech by students in public high schools. Its initial foray into this realm resulted in what appeared to be a resounding win for such protection. High school students were permitted to wear black arm bands to protest the Vietnam War. Saying that students do not lose their rights simply by stepping through the school house door, the Court found the arm bands to be "closely akin to 'pure speech,'" and that the students had been quiet and nondisruptive. TINKER V. DES MOINES SCHOOL DIST., 393 U.S. 503 (1969).

Later cases qualified significantly the meaning of *Tinker*. In *Bethel School District* v. *Fraser*, 478 U.S. 675 (1986), the Court found that a student government election nominating speech that was laced with sexual innuendo could be punished by the school. The student who gave the speech was disciplined for "disruptive behavior" and the Court agreed that this speech was unprotected in the school context. A high school newspaper, published as part of a journalism class, that sought to publish stories about teenage pregnancy and birth control, was legitimately censored by the school principal. The Court said the school was not required to sponsor speech that conflicts with its "legitimate pedagogical goals." Hazelwood v. Kuhlmeier, 484 U.S. 260 (1988).

The *Fraser* and *Kuhlmeier* decisions played a significant role in the Court's 2007 decision finding that a student banner reading "BONG HiTS 4 JESUS" unfurled at a school sanctioned public event, was unprotected speech because the pro-drug use message conflicted with the school's very strong interest in prohibiting such a message. MORSE V. FREDERICK, 551 U.S. 393 (2007). While it may be the case that public school students do not lose completely their rights by attending school, it is also clearly the case that the school context permits substantially more regulation of that speech than would be permitted in the general public.

Cohen v. California

403 U.S. 15 (1971)

Paul Robert Cohen was convicted of violating a California law that prohibited "maliciously and willfully disturb[ing] the peace or quiet of any neighborhood or person ... by ... offensive conduct." In a corridor of the Los Angeles Courthouse, he wore a jacket bearing the words "Fuck the Draft." The issue before the Supreme Court was whether the state had a compelling reason to override First Amendment interests by making the display of this single four-letter expletive a criminal offense. The *Cohen* decision provides a good summary of the various categories of speech that may be regulated, while distinguishing Cohen's actions from each category.

MR. JUSTICE HARLAN delivered the opinion of the Court.

This case may seem at first blush too inconsequential to find its way into our books, but the issue it presents is of no small constitutional significance.

Appellant Paul Robert Cohen was convicted in the Los Angeles Municipal Court of violating that part of California Penal Code § 415 which prohibits "maliciously and willfully disturb[ing] the peace or quiet of any neighborhood or person ... by ... offensive conduct ..." He was given 30 days' imprisonment. The facts upon which his conviction rests are detailed in the opinion of the Court of Appeal of California, Second Appellate District, as follows:

"On April 26, 1968, the defendant was observed in the Los Angeles County Courthouse in the corridor outside of division 20 of the municipal court wearing a jacket bearing the words 'Fuck the Draft' which were plainly visible. There were women and children present in the corridor. The defendant was arrested. The defendant testified that he wore the jacket knowing that the words were on the jacket as a means of informing the public of the depth of his feelings against the Vietnam War and the draft.

"The defendant did not engage in, nor threaten to engage in, nor did anyone as the result of his conduct in fact commit or threaten to commit any act of violence. The defendant did not make any loud or unusual noise, nor was there any evidence that he uttered any sound prior to his arrest." 1 Cal.App.3d 94, 97–98, 81 Cal.Rptr. 503, 505 (1969).

In affirming the conviction the Court of Appeal held that "offensive conduct" means "behavior which has a tendency to provoke *others* to acts of violence or to in turn disturb the peace," and that the State had proved this element because, on the facts of this case, "[i]t was certainly reasonably foreseeable that such conduct might cause others to rise up to commit a violent act against the person of the defendant or attempt to forcibly remove his jacket." 1

Cal.App.3d, at 99–100, 81 Cal.Rptr., at 506. The California Supreme Court declined review by a divided vote....

I

In order to lay hands on the precise issue which this case involves, it is useful first to canvass various matters which this record does *not* present.

The conviction quite clearly rests upon the asserted offensiveness of the *words* Cohen used to convey his message to the public. The only "conduct" which the State sought to punish is the fact of communication. Thus, we deal here with a conviction resting solely upon "speech," cf. *Stromberg* v. *California,* 283 U.S. 359 (1931), not upon any separately identifiable conduct....

Appellant's conviction, then, rests squarely upon his exercise of the "freedom of speech" protected from arbitrary governmental interference by the Constitution and can be justified, if at all, only as a valid regulation of the manner in which he exercised that freedom, not as a permissible prohibition on the substantive message it conveys. This does not end the inquiry, of course, for the First and Fourteenth Amendments have never been thought to give absolute protection to every individual to speak whenever or wherever he pleases, or to use any form of address in any circumstances that he chooses. In this vein, too, however, we think it important to note that several issues typically associated with such problems are not presented here.

In the first place, Cohen was tried under a statute applicable throughout the entire State. Any attempt to support this conviction on the ground that the statute seeks to preserve an appropriately decorous atmosphere in the courthouse where Cohen was arrested must fail in the absence of any language in the statute that would have put appellant on notice that certain kinds of otherwise permissible speech or conduct would nevertheless, under California law, not be tolerated in certain places.... No fair reading of the phrase "offensive conduct" can be said sufficiently to inform the ordinary person that distinctions between certain locations are thereby created. [*Here the Court adds a footnote: "It is illuminating to note what transpired when Cohen entered a courtroom in the building. He removed his jacket and stood with it folded over his arm. Meanwhile, a policeman sent the presiding judge a note suggesting that Cohen be held in contempt of court. The judge declined to do so and Cohen was arrested by the officer only after he emerged from the courtroom."*]

In the second place, as it comes to us, this case cannot be said to fall within those relatively few categories of instances where prior decisions have established the power of government to deal more comprehensively with certain forms of individual expression simply upon a showing that such a form was employed. This is not, for example, an obscenity case. Whatever else may be necessary to give rise to the States' broader power to prohibit obscene expression, such expression must be, in some significant way, erotic. *Roth v. United States,* 354 U.S. 476 (1957). It cannot plausibly be maintained that this vulgar allusion to the Selective Service System would conjure up such psychic stimulation in anyone likely to be confronted with Cohen's crudely defaced jacket.

This Court has also held that the States are free to ban the simple use, without a demonstration of additional justifying circumstances, of so-called "fighting words," those personally abusive epithets which, when addressed to the ordinary citizen, are, as a matter of common knowledge, inherently likely to provoke violent reaction. *Chaplinsky v. New Hampshire,* 315 U.S. 568 (1942). While the four-letter word displayed by Cohen in relation to the draft is not uncommonly employed in a personally provocative fashion, in this instance it was clearly not "directed to the person of the hearer." *Cantwell v. Connecticut,* 310 U.S. 296, 309 (1940). No individual actually or likely to be present could reasonably have regarded the words on appellant's jacket as a direct personal insult. Nor do we have here an instance of the exercise of the State's police power to prevent a speaker from intentionally provoking a given group to hostile reaction.... There is, as noted above, no showing that anyone who saw Cohen was in fact violently aroused or that appellant intended such a result.

Finally, in arguments before this Court much has been made of the claim that Cohen's distasteful mode of expression was thrust upon unwilling or unsuspecting viewers, and that the State might therefore legitimately act as it did in order to protect the sensitive from otherwise unavoidable exposure to appellant's crude form of protest. Of course, the mere presumed presence of unwitting listeners or viewers does not serve automatically to justify curtailing all speech capable of giving offense. See, *e.g., Organization for a Better Austin v. Keefe,* 402 U.S. 415 (1971). While this Court has recognized that government may properly act in many situations to prohibit intrusion into the privacy of the home of unwelcome views and ideas which cannot be totally banned from the public dialogue, *e.g., Rowan v. Post Office Dept.,* 397 U.S. 728 (1970), we have at the same time consistently stressed that "we are often 'captives' outside the sanctuary of the home and subject to objectionable speech." *Id.,* at 738. The ability of government, consonant with the Constitution, to shut off discourse solely to protect others from hearing it is, in other words, dependent upon a showing that substantial privacy interests are being invaded in an essentially intolerable manner. Any broader view of this authority would effectively empower a majority to silence dissidents simply as a matter of personal predilections.

In this regard, persons confronted with Cohen's jacket were in a quite different posture than, say, those subjected to the raucous emissions of sound trucks blaring outside their residences. Those in the Los Angeles courthouse could effectively avoid further bombardment of their sensibilities simply by averting their eyes....

II

... The constitutional right of free expression is powerful medicine in a society as diverse and populous as ours. It is designed and intended to remove governmental restraints from the arena of public discussion, putting the decision as to what views shall be voiced largely into the hands of each of us, in the hope that use of such freedom will ultimately produce a more capable citizenry and more perfect polity and in the belief that no other approach would comport with the premise of individual dignity and choice upon which our political system rests. See *Whitney v. California,* 274 U.S. 357, 375–377 (1927) (Brandeis, J., concurring).

To many, the immediate consequence of this freedom may often appear to be only verbal tumult, discord, and even offensive utterance. These are, however, within established limits, in truth necessary side effects of the broader enduring values which the process of open debate permits us to achieve. That the air may at times seem filled with verbal cacophony is, in this sense, not a sign of weakness but of strength. We cannot lose sight of the fact that, in what otherwise might seem a trifling and annoying instance of individual distasteful abuse of a privilege, these fundamental societal values are truly implicated....

Against this perception of the constitutional policies involved, we discern certain more particularized considerations that peculiarly call for reversal of this conviction. First, the principle contended for by the State seems inherently boundless. How is one to distinguish this from any other offensive word? Surely the State has no right to cleanse public debate to the point where it is grammatically palatable to the most squeamish among us. Yet no readily ascertainable general principle exists for stopping short of that result were we to affirm the judgment below. For, while the particular four-letter word being litigated here is perhaps more distasteful than most others of its genre, it is nevertheless often true that one man's vulgarity is another's lyric. Indeed, we think it is largely because governmental officials cannot make principled distinctions in this area that the Constitution leaves matters of taste and style so largely to the individual.

Additionally, we cannot overlook the fact, because it is well illustrated by the episode involved here, that much linguistic expression serves a dual communicative function: it conveys not only ideas capable of relatively precise, detached explication, but otherwise inexpressible emotions as well. In fact, words are often chosen as much for their emotive as their cognitive force....

Finally, and in the same vein, we cannot indulge the facile assumption that one can forbid particular words without also running a substantial risk of suppressing ideas in the process. Indeed, governments might soon seize upon the censorship of particular words as a convenient guise for banning the expression of unpopular views....

It is, in sum, our judgment that, absent a more particularized and compelling reason for its actions, the State may not, consistently with the First and Fourteenth Amendments, make the simple public display here involved of this single four-letter expletive a criminal offense. Because that is the only arguably sustainable rationale for the conviction here at issue, the judgment below must be

Reversed.

MR. JUSTICE BLACKMUN, with whom THE CHIEF JUSTICE and MR. JUSTICE BLACK join.

I dissent, and I do so for two reasons:

1. Cohen's absurd and immature antic, in my view, was mainly conduct and little speech....

2. [*Blackmun argues that subsequent construction of the statute by the California Supreme Court removes the vagueness and overbreadth problems identified by the majority.*]

MR. JUSTICE WHITE concurs in Paragraph 2 of MR. JUSTICE BLACKMUN's dissenting opinion.

R.A.V. v. St. Paul

505 U.S. 377 (1992)

A teenager (identified here by his initials R.A.V.) and his friends were charged with burning a cross on a black family's lawn. The City of St. Paul, Minnesota, charged them under its Bias-Motivated Crime Ordinance, which prohibits the display of a symbol one knows or has reason to know "arouses anger, alarm or resentment" in others on the basis of race, color, creed, religion or gender. This language drew comparison to the fighting-words doctrine of *Chaplinsky* v. *New Hampshire* (1942) and raised questions whether the ordinance was, on its face, unconstitutional because it attempted to silence speech on the basis of its content. The case is remarkable for the deep divisions within the Court on First Amendment analysis.

JUSTICE SCALIA delivered the opinion of the Court.

In the predawn hours of June 21, 1990, petitioner and several other teenagers allegedly assembled a crudely-made cross by taping together broken chair legs. They then allegedly burned the cross inside the fenced yard of a black family that lived across the street from the house where petitioner was staying. Although this conduct could have been punished under any of a number of laws [*terroristic*

threats, arson, criminal damage to property], one of the two provisions under which respondent city of St. Paul chose to charge petitioner (then a juvenile) was the St. Paul Bias-Motivated Crime Ordinance, St. Paul, Minn. Legis. Code § 292.02 (1990), which provides:

"Whoever places on public or private property a symbol, object, appellation, characterization or graffiti, including, but not limited to, a burning cross or Nazi swastika, which one knows or has reasonable grounds to know arouses anger, alarm or resentment in others on the basis of race, color, creed, religion or gender commits disorderly conduct and shall be guilty of a misdemeanor."

Petitioner moved to dismiss this count on the ground that the St. Paul ordinance was substantially overbroad and impermissibly content-based and therefore facially invalid under the First Amendment....

I

In construing the St. Paul ordinance, we are bound by the construction given to it by the Minnesota court.... Accordingly, we accept the Minnesota Supreme Court's authoritative statement that the ordinance reaches only those expressions that constitute "fighting words" within the meaning of *Chaplinsky*.... Assuming, *arguendo,* that all of the expression reached by the ordinance is proscribable under the "fighting words" doctrine, we nonetheless conclude that the ordinance is facially unconstitutional in that it prohibits otherwise permitted speech solely on the basis of the subjects the speech addresses.

The First Amendment generally prevents government from proscribing speech, see, *e.g., Cantwell* v. *Connecticut,* 310 U.S. 296, 309–311 (1940), or even expressive conduct, see, *e.g., Texas* v. *Johnson,* 491 U.S. 397, 406 (1989), because of disapproval of the ideas expressed. Content-based regulations are presumptively invalid.... From 1791 to the present, however, our society, like other free but civilized societies, has permitted restrictions upon the content of speech in a few limited areas, which are "of such slight social value as a step to truth that any benefit that may be derived from them is clearly outweighed by the social interest in order and morality." *Chaplinsky, supra,* at 572. We have recognized that "the freedom of speech" referred to by the First Amendment does not include a freedom to disregard these traditional limitations. See, *e.g., Roth* v. *United States,* 354 U.S. 476 (1957) (obscenity); *Beauharnais* v. *Illinois,* 343 U.S. 250 (1952) (defamation); *Chaplinsky* v. *New Hampshire, supra,* ("fighting words"); ...

We have sometimes said that these categories of expression are "not within the area of constitutionally protected speech," ... or that the "protection of the First Amendment does not extend" to them ... Such statements must be taken in context, however, and are no more literally true than is the occasionally repeated shorthand characterizing obscenity "as not being speech at all," ... What they mean is that these areas of speech can, consistently with the First Amendment, be regulated *because of their constitutionally proscribable content* (obscenity, defamation, etc.) — not that they are categories of speech entirely invisible to the Constitution, so that they may be made the vehicles for content discrimination unrelated to their distinctively proscribable content. Thus, the government may proscribe libel; but it may not make the further content discrimination of proscribing *only* libel critical of the government....

II

Applying these principles to the St. Paul ordinance, we conclude that, even as narrowly construed by the Minnesota Supreme Court, the ordinance is facially unconstitutional. Although the phrase in the ordinance, "arouses anger, alarm or resentment in others," has been limited by the Minnesota Supreme Court's construction to reach only those symbols or displays that amount to "fighting words," the remaining, unmodified terms make clear that the ordinance applies only to "fighting words" that insult, or provoke violence, "on the basis of race, color, creed, religion or gender." Displays containing abusive invective, no matter how vicious or severe, are permissible unless they are addressed to one of the specified disfavored topics. Those who wish to use "fighting words" in connection with other ideas — to express hostility, for example, on the basis of political affiliation, union membership, or homosexuality — are not covered. The First Amendment does not permit St. Paul to impose special prohibitions on those speakers who express views on disfavored subjects....

In its practical operation, moreover, the ordinance goes even beyond mere content discrimination, to actual viewpoint discrimination. Displays containing some words — odious racial epithets, for example — would be prohibited to proponents of all views. But "fighting words" that do not themselves invoke race, color, creed, religion, or gender — aspersions upon a person's mother, for example — would seemingly be usable *ad libitum* in the placards of those arguing *in favor* of racial, color, etc. tolerance and equality, but could not be used by that speaker's opponents. One could hold up a sign saying, for example, that all "anti-Catholic bigots" are misbegotten; but not that all "papists" are, for that would insult and provoke violence "on the basis of religion." St. Paul has no such authority to license one side of a debate to fight freestyle, while requiring the other to follow Marquis of Queensbury Rules.

... [T]he reason why fighting words are categorically excluded from the protection of the First

Amendment is not that their content communicates any particular idea, but that their content embodies a particularly intolerable (and socially unnecessary) *mode* of expressing *whatever* idea the speaker wishes to convey. St. Paul has not singled out an especially offensive mode of expression—it has not, for example, selected for prohibition only those fighting words that communicate ideas in a threatening (as opposed to a merely obnoxious) manner. Rather, it has proscribed fighting words of whatever manner that communicate messages of racial, gender, or religious intolerance. Selectivity of this sort creates the possibility that the city is seeking to handicap the expression of particular ideas. That possibility would alone be enough to render the ordinance presumptively invalid, but St. Paul's comments and concessions in this case elevate the possibility to a certainty....

Let there be no mistake about our belief that burning a cross in someone's front yard is reprehensible. But St. Paul has sufficient means at its disposal to prevent such behavior without adding the First Amendment to the fire.

The judgment of the Minnesota Supreme Court is reversed, and the case is remanded for proceedings not inconsistent with this opinion.

It is so ordered.

JUSTICE WHITE, with whom JUSTICE BLACKMUN and JUSTICE O'CONNOR join, and with whom JUSTICE STEVENS joins except as to Part I(A), concurring in the judgment.

I agree with the majority that the judgment of the Minnesota Supreme Court should be reversed. However, our agreement ends there.

This case could easily be decided within the contours of established First Amendment law by holding, as petitioner argues, that the St. Paul ordinance is fatally overbroad because it criminalizes not only unprotected expression but expression protected by the First Amendment.... Instead, "find[ing] it unnecessary" to consider the questions upon which we granted review, ... the Court holds the ordinance facially unconstitutional on a ground that was never presented to the Minnesota Supreme Court, a ground that has not been briefed by the parties before this Court, a ground that requires serious departures from the teaching of prior cases and is inconsistent with the plurality opinion in *Burson* v. *Freeman*, 504 U. S. 191 (1992), which was joined by two of the five Justices in the majority in the present case.

... [I]n the present case, the majority casts aside long-established First Amendment doctrine without the benefit of briefing and adopts an untried theory. This is hardly a judicious way of proceeding, and the Court's reasoning in reaching its result is transparently wrong....

III

Today, the Court has disregarded two established principles of First Amendment law without providing a coherent replacement theory. Its decision is an arid, doctrinaire interpretation, driven by the frequently irresistible impulse of judges to tinker with the First Amendment. The decision is mischievous at best and will surely confuse the lower courts. I join the judgment, but not the folly of the opinion.

JUSTICE BLACKMUN, concurring in the judgment.

I regret what the Court has done in this case. The majority opinion signals one of two possibilities: it will serve as precedent for future cases, or it will not. Either result is disheartening.

In the first instance, by deciding that a State cannot regulate speech that causes great harm unless it also regulates speech that does not (setting law and logic on their heads), the Court seems to abandon the categorical approach, and inevitably to relax the level of scrutiny applicable to content-based laws. As JUSTICE WHITE points out, this weakens the traditional protections of speech. If all expressive activity must be accorded the same protection, that protection will be scant. The simple reality is that the Court will never provide child pornography or cigarette advertising the level of protection customarily granted political speech. If we are forbidden from categorizing, as the Court has done here, we shall reduce protection across the board. It is sad that in its effort to reach a satisfying result in this case, the Court is willing to weaken First Amendment protections.

In the second instance is the possibility that this case will not significantly alter First Amendment jurisprudence, but, instead, will be regarded as an aberration—a case where the Court manipulated doctrine to strike down an ordinance whose premise it opposed, namely, that racial threats and verbal assaults are of greater harm than other fighting words. I fear that the Court has been distracted from its proper mission by the temptation to decide the issue over "politically correct speech" and "cultural diversity," neither of which is presented here. If this is the meaning of today's opinion, it is perhaps even more regrettable....

JUSTICE STEVENS, with whom JUSTICE WHITE and JUSTICE BLACKMUN join as to Part I, concurring in the judgment....

... I disagree with both the Court's and part of JUSTICE WHITE's analysis of the constitutionality St. Paul ordinance. Unlike the Court, I do not believe that all content-based regulations are equally infirm and presumptively invalid; unlike JUSTICE WHITE, I do not believe that fighting words are wholly unpro-tected by the First Amendment. To the contrary, I believe our decisions establish a more complex and subtle analysis, one that considers the content and context of the regulated speech, and the nature and scope of the restriction on speech. Applying this analysis and assuming *arguendo* (as the Court does) that the St. Paul ordinance is *not* overbroad, I con-clude that such a selective, subject-matter regulation on proscribable speech is constitutional....

Tinker v. Des Moines School Dist.

393 U.S. 503 (1969)

In the midst of the Vietnam War, three public school students were suspended from school for wearing black arm bands to protest U.S. involvement. They claimed that their protest, which was quiet and nondisruptive, was protected by the Free Speech Clause of the First Amendment. The school argued that school discipline and questions of suspension were within the power and jurisdiction of school authorities. A federal district court upheld the school's policy, and that ruling was affirmed by an equally divided Eighth Circuit.

MR. JUSTICE FORTAS delivered the opinion of the Court.

Petitioner John F. Tinker, 15 years old, and peti-tioner Christopher Eckhardt, 16 years old, attended high schools in Des Moines, Iowa. Petitioner Mary Beth Tinker, John's sister, was a 13-year-old student in junior high school.

In December 1965, a group of adults and stu-dents in Des Moines held a meeting at the Eckhardt home. The group determined to publicize their ob-jections to the hostilities in Vietnam and their sup-port for a truce by wearing black armbands during the holiday season and by fasting on December 16 and New Year's Eve. Petitioners and their parents had previously engaged in similar activities, and they decided to participate in the program.

The principals of the Des Moines schools became aware of the plan to wear armbands. On December 14, 1965, they met and adopted a policy that any student wearing an armband to school would be asked to remove it, and if he refused he would be suspended until he returned without the armband. Petitioners were aware of the regulation that the school authorities adopted.

On December 16, Mary Beth and Christopher wore black armbands to their schools. John Tinker wore his armband the next day. They were all sent home and suspended from school until they would come back without their armbands. They did not re-turn to school until after the planned period for wearing armbands had expired—that is, until after New Year's Day.

I.

The District Court recognized that the wearing of an armband for the purpose of expressing certain views is the type of symbolic act that is within the Free Speech Clause of the First Amendment.... As we shall discuss, the wearing of armbands in the cir-cumstances of this case was entirely divorced from actually or potentially disruptive conduct by those participating in it. It was closely akin to "pure speech" which, we have repeatedly held, is entitled to comprehensive protection under the First Amendment....

First Amendment rights, applied in light of the special characteristics of the school environment, are available to teachers and students. It can hardly be argued that either students or teachers shed their constitutional rights to freedom of speech or expres-sion at the schoolhouse gate. This has been the un-mistakable holding of this Court for almost 50 years....

... On the other hand, the Court has repeatedly emphasized the need for affirming the comprehen-sive authority of the States and of school officials, consistent with fundamental constitutional safe-guards, to prescribe and control conduct in the schools.... Our problem lies in the area where students in the exercise of First Amendment rights collide with the rules of the school authorities.

II.

The problem posed by the present case does not relate to regulation of the length of skirts or the type of clothing, to hair style, or deportment.... It does not concern aggressive, disruptive action or even group demonstrations. Our problem involves direct, primary First Amendment rights akin to "pure speech."

... [T]he school authorities did not purport to prohibit the wearing of all symbols of political or controversial significance. The record shows that students in some of the schools wore buttons relating to national political campaigns, and some even wore the Iron Cross, traditionally a symbol of Nazism. The order prohibiting the wearing of armbands did not extend to these. Instead, a particular symbol — black armbands worn to exhibit opposition to this Nation's involvement in Vietnam — was singled out for prohibition. Clearly, the prohibition of expression of one particular opinion, at least without evidence that it is necessary to avoid material and substantial interference with schoolwork or discipline, is not constitutionally permissible.

In our system, state-operated schools may not be enclaves of totalitarianism. School officials do not possess absolute authority over their students. Students in school as well as out of school are "persons" under our Constitution. They are possessed of fundamental rights which the State must respect, just as they themselves must respect their obligations to the State. In our system, students may not be regarded as closed-circuit recipients of only that which the State chooses to communicate. They may not be confined to the expression of those sentiments that are officially approved....

As we have discussed, the record does not demonstrate any facts which might reasonably have led school authorities to forecast substantial disruption of or material interference with school activities, and no disturbances or disorders on the school premises in fact occurred. These petitioners merely went about their ordained rounds in school. Their deviation consisted only in wearing on their sleeve a band of black cloth, not more than two inches wide. They wore it to exhibit their disapproval of the Vietnam hostilities and their advocacy of a truce, to make their views known, and, by their example, to influence others to adopt them. They neither interrupted school activities nor sought to intrude in the school affairs or the lives of others. They caused discussion outside of the classrooms, but no interference with work and no disorder. In the circumstances, our Constitution does not permit officials of the State to deny their form of expression.

We express no opinion as to the form of relief which should be granted, this being a matter for the lower courts to determine. We reverse and remand for further proceedings consistent with this opinion.

Reversed and remanded.

[*Justices Stewart and White prepared separate concurring opinions.*]

MR. JUSTICE BLACK, dissenting.

The Court's holding in this case ushers in what I deem to be an entirely new era in which the power to control pupils by the elected "officials of state supported public schools ..." in the United States is in ultimate effect transferred to the Supreme Court....

... While the absence of obscene remarks or boisterous and loud disorder perhaps justifies the Court's statement that the few armband students did not actually "disrupt" the classwork, I think the record overwhelmingly shows that the armbands did exactly what the elected school officials and principals foresaw they would, that is, took the students' minds off their classwork and diverted them to thoughts about the highly emotional subject of the Vietnam war. And I repeat that if the time has come when pupils of state-supported schools, kindergartens, grammar schools, or high schools, can defy and flout orders of school officials to keep their minds on their own schoolwork, it is the beginning of a new revolutionary era of permissiveness in this country fostered by the judiciary....

... I, for one, am not fully persuaded that school pupils are wise enough, even with this Court's expert help from Washington, to run the 23,390 public school systems in our 50 States....

MR. JUSTICE HARLAN, dissenting.

I certainly agree that state public school authorities in the discharge of their responsibilities are not wholly exempt from the requirements of the Fourteenth Amendment respecting the freedoms of expression and association. At the same time I am reluctant to believe that there is any disagreement between the majority and myself on the proposition that school officials should be accorded the widest authority in maintaining discipline and good order in their institutions....

Morse v. Frederick

551 U.S. 393 (2007)

When the Olympic Torch Relay came through Juneau, Alaska in 2002, a group of students in front of the local high school unfurled a banner that read "BONG HiTS 4 JESUS." The students were observing the relay as part of a school sanctioned event. The principal, Morse, regarded the banner as promoting illegal drug use and told the students to take it down. Frederick, one of the students who created the banner, refused and Morse confiscated it and later suspended him from school. The superintendent upheld the suspension as did the school board. Frederick filed suit claiming a violation of his First Amendment rights. The District Court found that the school officials had limited immunity from such suits but the Ninth Circuit reversed, finding that the school had violated the First Amendment because Frederick's speech did not threaten a substantial disruption.

CHIEF JUSTICE ROBERTS delivered the opinion of the Court....

Our cases make clear that students do not "shed their constitutional rights to freedom of speech or expression at the schoolhouse gate." *Tinker v. Des Moines Independent Community School Dist.*, 393 U. S. 503, 506 (1969). At the same time, we have held that "the constitutional rights of students in public school are not automatically coextensive with the rights of adults in other settings," *Bethel School Dist. No. 403 v. Fraser*, 478 U. S. 675, 682 (1986), and that the rights of students "must be 'applied in light of the special characteristics of the school environment.'" *Hazelwood School Dist. v. Kuhlmeier*, 484 U. S. 260, 266 (1988) (quoting *Tinker*, supra, at 506). Consistent with these principles, we hold that schools may take steps to safeguard those entrusted to their care from speech that can reasonably be regarded as encouraging illegal drug use. We conclude that the school officials in this case did not violate the First Amendment by confiscating the pro-drug banner and suspending the student responsible for it...

I

. . .

We granted certiorari on two questions: whether Frederick had a First Amendment right to wield his banner, and, if so, whether that right was so clearly established that the principal may be held liable for damages.... We resolve the first question against Frederick, and therefore have no occasion to reach the second.

II

At the outset, we reject Frederick's argument that this is not a school speech case—as has every other authority to address the question.... The event occurred during normal school hours. It was sanctioned by Principal Morse "as an approved social event or class trip," ... and the school district's rules expressly provide that pupils in "approved social events and class trips are subject to district rules for student conduct." ... Teachers and administrators were interspersed among the students and charged with supervising them. The high school band and cheerleaders performed. Frederick, standing among other JDHS students across the street from the school, directed his banner toward the school, making it plainly visible to most students. Under these circumstances, we agree with the superintendent that Frederick cannot "stand in the midst of his fellow students, during school hours, at a school-sanctioned activity and claim he is not at school." ... There is some uncertainty at the outer boundaries as to when courts should apply school-speech precedents, ... but not on these facts.

III

The message on Frederick's banner is cryptic. It is no doubt offensive to some, perhaps amusing to others. To still others, it probably means nothing at all. Frederick himself claimed "that the words were just nonsense meant to attract television cameras." ... But Principal Morse thought the banner would be interpreted by those viewing it as promoting illegal drug use, and that interpretation is plainly a reasonable one....

We agree with Morse. At least two interpretations of the words on the banner demonstrate that the sign advocated the use of illegal drugs. First, the phrase could be interpreted as an imperative: "[Take] bong hits ..."—a message equivalent, as Morse explained in her declaration, to "smoke marijuana" or "use an illegal drug." Alternatively, the phrase could be viewed as celebrating drug use—

"bong hits [are a good thing]," or "[we take] bong hits"—and we discern no meaningful distinction between celebrating illegal drug use in the midst of fellow students and outright advocacy or promotion....

The pro-drug interpretation of the banner gains further plausibility given the paucity of alternative meanings the banner might bear. The best Frederick can come up with is that the banner is "meaningless and funny." ... Gibberish is surely a possible interpretation of the words on the banner, but it is not the only one, and dismissing the banner as meaningless ignores its undeniable reference to illegal drugs....

... [N]ot even Frederick argues that the banner conveys any sort of political or religious message. Contrary to the dissent's suggestion, ... this is plainly not a case about political debate over the criminalization of drug use or possession.

IV

The question thus becomes whether a principal may, consistent with the First Amendment, restrict student speech at a school event, when that speech is reasonably viewed as promoting illegal drug use. We hold that she may. In *Tinker*, this Court made clear that "First Amendment rights, applied in light of the special characteristics of the school environment, are available to teachers and students." 393 U. S., at 506....

[*Here the Court considers the application of precedent, distinguishing the case from* Tinker, *where the speech was clearly political and non-disruptive, and finding principles established in* Fraser *more applicable.*] First, *Fraser*'s holding demonstrates that "the constitutional rights of students in public school are not automatically coextensive with the rights of adults in other settings." ... Second, *Fraser* established that the mode of analysis set forth in *Tinker* is not absolute....

Kuhlmeier [*a more recent case permitting the school to censor articles in a school newspaper*] does not control this case because no one would reasonably believe that Frederick's banner bore the school's imprimatur. The case is nevertheless instructive because it confirms both principles cited above. *Kuhlmeier* acknowledged that schools may regulate some speech "even though the government could not censor similar speech outside the school."... And, like *Fraser*, it confirms that the rule of *Tinker* is not the only basis for restricting student speech....

[*The Court reviews cases involving the Fourth Amendment and the potential drug use in the* schools.] Even more to the point, these cases also recognize that deterring drug use by schoolchildren is an "important—indeed, perhaps compelling" interest.... Drug abuse can cause severe and permanent damage to the health and well-being of young people ...

Congress has declared that part of a school's job is educating students about the dangers of illegal drug use. It has provided billions of dollars to support state and local drug-prevention programs, ... and required that schools receiving federal funds under the Safe and Drug-Free Schools and Communities Act of 1994 certify that their drug prevention programs "convey a clear and consistent message that ... the illegal use of drugs [is] wrong and harmful." 20 U. S. C. § 7114(d)(6) (2000 ed., Supp. IV).

Thousands of school boards throughout the country—including JDHS—have adopted policies aimed at effectuating this message.... Those school boards know that peer pressure is perhaps "the single most important factor leading schoolchildren to take drugs," and that students are more likely to use drugs when the norms in school appear to tolerate such behavior.... Student speech celebrating illegal drug use at a school event, in the presence of school administrators and teachers, thus poses a particular challenge for school officials working to protect those entrusted to their care from the dangers of drug abuse.

The "special characteristics of the school environment," *Tinker*, 393 U. S., at 506, and the governmental interest in stopping student drug abuse—reflected in the policies of Congress and myriad school boards, including JDHS—allow schools to restrict student expression that they reasonably regard as promoting illegal drug use. *Tinker* warned that schools may not prohibit student speech because of "undifferentiated fear or apprehension of disturbance" or "a mere desire to avoid the discomfort and unpleasantness that always accompany an unpopular viewpoint." *Id.*, at 508, 509. The danger here is far more serious and palpable. The particular concern to prevent student drug abuse at issue here, embodied in established school policy, ... extends well beyond an abstract desire to avoid controversy....

The judgment of the United States Court of Appeals for the Ninth Circuit is reversed, and the case is remanded for further proceedings consistent with this opinion.

It is so ordered.

JUSTICE THOMAS, concurring.

... In my view, the history of public education suggests that the First Amendment, as originally understood, does not protect student speech in public schools.... If students in public schools were originally understood as having free-speech rights, one would have expected 19th-century public schools to have respected those rights and courts to have enforced them.... They did not.

... [E]arly public schools were not places for freewheeling debates or exploration of competing ideas. Rather, teachers instilled "a core of common values" in students and taught them self-control....

In short, in the earliest public schools, teachers taught, and students listened. Teachers commanded, and students obeyed. Teachers did not rely solely on the power of ideas to persuade; they relied on discipline to maintain order....

JUSTICE ALITO, with whom JUSTICE KENNEDY joins, concurring.

I join the opinion of the Court on the understanding that (a) it goes no further than to hold that a public school may restrict speech that a reasonable observer would interpret as advocating illegal drug use and (b) it provides no support for any restriction of speech that can plausibly be interpreted as commenting on any political or social issue, including speech on issues such as "the wisdom of the war on drugs or of legalizing marijuana for medicinal use." See post, at 13 (STEVENS, J., dissenting)....

The opinion of the Court does not endorse the broad argument advanced by petitioners and the United States that the First Amendment permits public school officials to censor any student speech that interferes with a school's "educational mission."... This argument can easily be manipulated in dangerous ways, and I would reject it before such abuse occurs....

JUSTICE BREYER, concurring in the judgment in part and dissenting in part.

This Court need not and should not decide this difficult First Amendment issue on the merits. Rather, I believe that it should simply hold that qual-ified immunity bars the student's claim for monetary damages and say no more....

... Students will test the limits of acceptable behavior in myriad ways better known to schoolteachers than to judges; school officials need a degree of flexible authority to respond to disciplinary challenges; and the law has always considered the relationship between teachers and students special. Under these circumstances, the more detailed the Court's supervision becomes, the more likely its law will engender further disputes among teachers and students. Consequently, larger numbers of those disputes will likely make their way from the schoolhouse to the courthouse. Yet no one wishes to substitute courts for school boards, or to turn the judge's chambers into the principal's office....

JUSTICE STEVENS, with whom JUSTICE SOUTER AND JUSTICE GINSBURG join, dissenting....

I agree with the Court that the principal should not be held liable for pulling down Frederick's banner ... I would hold, however, that the school's interest in protecting its students from exposure to speech "reasonably regarded as promoting illegal drug use,"..., cannot justify disciplining Frederick for his attempt to make an ambiguous statement to a television audience simply because it contained an oblique reference to drugs. The First Amendment demands more, indeed, much more.

... In my judgment, the First Amendment protects student speech if the message itself neither violates a permissible rule nor expressly advocates conduct that is illegal and harmful to students. This nonsense banner does neither, and the Court does serious violence to the First Amendment in upholding—indeed, lauding—a school's decision to punish Frederick for expressing a view with which it disagreed.

... Admittedly, some high school students (including those who use drugs) are dumb. Most students, however, do not shed their brains at the schoolhouse gate, and most students know dumb advocacy when they see it. The notion that the message on this banner would actually persuade either the average student or even the dumbest one to change his or her behavior is most implausible....

D. FORMS OF SPEECH

The Supreme Court recognizes categories of speech that would have been novel if not inscrutable to the framers. These forms include symbolic speech, "speech plus," commercial speech, and broadcasting rights. Several free-speech issues are covered in Chapter 18: campaign financing (the Court has decided that "money is speech") and ballot initiatives.

Symbolic Speech and Flag Desecration

Ideas spread by symbols as well as by words. A California statute made it a felony to display a red flag "as a sign, symbol or emblem of opposition to organized government." By a 7–1 majority, the Supreme Court in 1931 held the statute unconstitutionally vague and repugnant to the guaranty of liberty contained in the Fourteenth Amendment. Stromberg v. California, 283 U.S. 359 (1931). There are obvious limits to symbolic speech and "expressive conduct." As Justice Rehnquist noted in a dissent: "One who burns down the factory of a company whose products he dislikes can expect his First Amendment defense to a consequent arson prosecution to be given short shrift by the courts." Smith v. Goguen, 415 U.S. 566, 594 (1974).

A spectacular form of symbolic speech occurred in a 1968 case involving the burning of a draft card to protest the Vietnam War. The act violated a federal statute that applied to any person "who forges, alters, knowingly destroys, knowingly mutilates, or in any manner changes" a draft card. A 7–1 Court held that the statute did not unconstitutionally abridge free speech; government has a legitimate interest in preserving draft cards; and the act of burning a draft card is not "symbolic speech" protected by the First Amendment. United States v. O'Brien, 391 U.S. 367 (1968).

States and the federal government have adopted a number of laws to prohibit desecration and abuse of the American flag. A 1907 decision by the Supreme Court involved a Nebraska law that punished the desecration of the flag and the use of the flag to advertise the sale of articles. An exception was made for newspapers, periodicals, or books if disconnected from any advertisement. The Court, voting 8–1, upheld the statute's application against a company that printed the flag on a bottle of beer. Halter v. Nebraska, 205 U.S. 34 (1907). A Massachusetts law, prohibiting anyone from publicly treating the flag "contemptuously," was held void for vagueness when used to convict an individual who wore a small U.S. flag sewn to the seat of his blue jeans. Smith v. Goguen, 415 U.S. 566 (1974).

More difficult to resolve are cases where the flag is used to communicate opposition to the government and its policies. In 1967, opponents of the Vietnam War burned flags in New York City's Central Park. Congress responded the next year with legislation providing that whoever "knowingly casts contempt upon any flag of the United States by publicly mutilating, defacing, defiling, burning, or trampling upon it shall be fined not more than $1,000 or imprisoned for not more than one year, or both." 82 Stat. 291. The legislative history reveals that Congress intended to punish war protesters.

A conviction for flag burning was set aside by the Supreme Court in 1969 because the punishment was directed not only for acts against the flag but for words as well. Street v. New York, 394 U.S. 576 (1969). Another flag case involved a conviction for taping a peace symbol to an American flag and hanging it upside down to protest the Vietnam War. The purpose was to associate the flag with peace, not war. The Court, by a 6–3 majority, held that the state law infringed on protected expression: "there can be little doubt that appellant communicated through the use of symbols." Spence v. Washington, 418 U.S. 405, 410 (1974).

During the 1988 presidential campaign, George Bush and Michael Dukakis clashed on the issue of whether public school teachers could be compelled to order students to pledge allegiance to the flag. Dukakis had vetoed such a bill as governor of Massachusetts, relying on an advisory opinion by the Massachusetts Supreme Court. Bush claimed that he would have found a way to sign the bill. Thereafter the two candidates tried to see who could stand in front of more flags and sound more patriotic.

The flag issue returned with full force the next year when the Supreme Court, divided 5–4, held that a conviction for flag desecration (burning the flag during a protest) was contrary to the First Amendment. The majority regarded the action as "expressive conduct" protected by the Constitution. TEXAS v. JOHNSON, 491 U.S. 397 (1989). The decision triggered a flurry of bills and constitutional amendments, with President Bush's support, to overturn the decision.

In response to *Texas* v. *Johnson,* Congress passed the Flag Protection Act of 1989. The basic purpose was to comply with *Johnson* by making the federal statute "content neutral." The major change was to delete from the 1968 statute the words "casts contempt." The new law read: "Whoever knowingly mutilates, defaces, physically defiles, burns, maintains on the floor or ground, or tramples upon any flag of the United States shall be fined under this title or imprisoned for not more than one year, or both." 103 Stat. 777. Sponsors of this legislation argued that the Court would uphold a statute that merely protected the physical integrity of the flag by focusing solely on conduct and not on the message being conveyed by the flag burner. The bill passed the House by a vote of 380 to 38; the Senate margin was 91 to 9. On October 19, 1989, the Senate rejected a proposed constitutional amendment to permit Congress to outlaw flag desecration. The 51 to 48 margin in favor of the amendment fell 15 votes short of the required two-thirds majority.

The 1989 statute provided for expedited review by the courts: a district court decision would be appealed directly to the Supreme Court. Two district courts ruled that flag-burning represents an expression of political dissent and is protected by the First Amendment. United States v. Haggerty, 731 F.Supp. 415 (W.D. Wash. 1990); United States v. Eichman, 731 F.Supp. 1123 (D.D.C. 1990). Divided 5 to 4, the Supreme Court held the congressional statute unconstitutional. The government's interest in protecting the physical integrity of the flag could not justify its infringement on First Amendment rights. United States v. Eichman, 496 U.S. 310 (1990).

Immediately following the decision, President Bush renewed his call for a constitutional amendment to protect the flag, but the House of Representatives rejected the amendment by a vote of 254 to 177, or 34 votes shy of the necessary two-thirds. The Senate also voted down the amendment, 58 to 42, or nine votes short. The time consumed by Congress to pass the new law and have it tested in the courts was sufficient to take the steam out of the campaign to amend the Constitution and thus avoid the first alteration of the Bill of Rights. See Charles Tiefer, "The Flag-Burning Controversy of 1989–90: Congress' Valid Role in Constitutional Dialogue," 29 Harv. J. on Legis. 357 (1992).

A constitutional amendment to prohibit flag desecration passed the House in 1995, this time by more than a two-thirds margin (312 to 120). The amendment was narrowly defeated in the Senate 63 to 36 (three votes short). In 1997, more than two-thirds of the House voted for a constitutional amendment to prohibit flag desecration (310 to 114), but the Senate took no action. The Senate vote in 2000 was 63 to 37 (four votes short). Another House amendment in 2001 produced a vote of 298 to 125, or more than the required two-thirds. The Senate did not vote on the amendment. In 2005, the House passed an amendment to ban flag burning, 286 to 230, but it was narrowly defeated in the Senate, 66 to 34 (one vote short). Since then, similar amendments have been proposed but not voted on, and public opinion appears to be shifting away from support for such an amendment.

"Speech Plus"

"Speech plus" refers to speech mixed with conduct. For example, picketing is "free speech *plus,* the plus being physical activity that may implicate traffic and related matters." Amalgamated Food Employees v. Logan Valley Plaza, 391 U.S. 308, 326 (1968). To promote an idea or cause, individuals gather together and carry placards, distribute leaflets, and ask passersby to sign petitions. In 1940 the Court held that picketing is protected by the constitutional freedoms of speech, peaceable assembly, and the right to petition government for redress of grievances. Thornhill v. Alabama, 310 U.S. 88 (1940).[9] A unanimous Court in 1937 held that peaceable assembly cannot be made a crime. De Jonge v. Oregon, 299 U.S. 353 (1937). This case also applied the right of peaceable assembly, guaranteed under the federal Constitution, to the states. See also Hague v. C.I.O., 307 U.S. 496 (1939).

After the *Thornhill* decision in 1940, the Court conducted a gradual retreat from the right to picket.

---

9. Other picketing cases during this period include: New Negro Alliance v. Grocery Co., 303 U.S. 552 (1938); Milk Wagon Drivers Union v. Meadowmoor Co., 312 U.S. 287 (1941); A.F. of L. v. Swing, 312 U.S. 321 (1941); Hotel Employees' Local v. Board, 315 U.S. 437 (1942); Carpenters Union v. Ritter's Cafe, 315 U.S. 722 (1942); Allen-Bradley Local v. Board, 315 U.S. 742 (1942); Bakery Drivers Local v. Wohl, 315 U.S. 769 (1942).

The state not only could regulate picketing to protect against violence and the destruction of property but also could prohibit peaceful picketing to further state interests, especially dealing with labor conditions. Picketing could be enjoined to prevent efforts to restrain trade. Giboney v. Empire Storage, 336 U.S. 490 (1949).[10] In recent years, decisions have been more supportive of peaceful demonstrations and picketing.[11] However, when picketers concentrate on a single household, government may prohibit such picketing in order to protect the privacy of a homeowner. Frisby v. Schultz, 487 U.S. 474 (1988). But picketing at the private funeral of an Iraq war soldier is protected by the First Amendment. A church that believes that God is punishing soldiers because of the United States' tolerance of gays in the military could not be sued for "intentional infliction of emotional distress" because they were engaged in protest on public land over matters of public concern. SNYDER v. PHELPS, 562 U.S. ___ (2011).

If picketing is done on private property, which constitutional interest should prevail? An early case involved the right of a company town to require a permit before anyone could distribute literature. The Supreme Court ruled that since the town's shopping district was freely accessible to the general public, the town's public nature overshadowed its private claim. The right to distribute literature was therefore upheld. Marsh v. Alabama, 326 U.S. 501 (1946).

From this simple company-town issue came the conundrum of free speech in shopping centers. The Court might well have asked plaintively: "Oh, Founding Fathers, where are you when we need you?" In 1968, the Court divided 6–3 in ruling that peaceful picketing of a business enterprise within a shopping center did not violate property rights. The Court followed the reasoning of *Marsh* but cautioned in a footnote that its decision was limited to picketing that was directly related to shopping center activities. Amalgamated Food Employees v. Logan Valley Plaza, 391 U.S. 308, 320 n.9 (1968).

The footnote helped justify a modification in 1972. The distribution of handbills inside a shopping center was held to be a violation of property rights. The handbills (protesting the Vietnam War and the draft) had no relation to the purpose of the shopping center. Lloyd Corp. v. Tanner, 407 U.S. 551 (1972). Confusion became rampant four years later when the Court denied striking members of a union the right to enter a shopping center to picket against their employer. Presumably, this kind of picketing was protected by *Logan Valley,* but the Court said that its new doctrine was based on *statutory* grounds, even though it also reached out to dispose of constitutional issues. The Justices couldn't even agree whether *Lloyd* had overruled *Logan Valley.* Hudgens v. NLRB, 424 U.S. 507 (1976).

In 1980, the Supreme Court invited states to supply protections unavailable in federal courts. It reviewed a case in which a privately owned shopping center prohibited visitors or tenants from engaging in any publicly expressive activity (including circulation of petitions) that was not directly related to the commercial purposes of the center. The California courts upheld the rights of students to petition on unrelated matters. A unanimous Supreme Court affirmed that decision. State courts can make independent and authoritative determinations, under their own constitutions, on the balance between free speech and property rights in shopping centers. PruneYard Shopping Center v. Robins, 447 U.S. 74 (1980). Thus, rights not available through the federal courts can be protected by state courts interpreting state constitutions (see box on the next page). In 1991, the Justices of the Colorado Supreme Court reviewed the "tortuous history" of the U.S. Supreme Court's jurisprudence on free speech and decided to go their own way. They were urged to follow "the twists and turns of this federal road to the end" but declined. "We are unpersuaded by the United States Supreme Court's vari-

---

10. Injunctions against peaceful picketing were also upheld in International Brotherhood of Teamsters v. Hanke, 339 U.S. 470 (1950); Building Service Union v. Gazzam, 339 U.S. 532 (1950); and International Brotherhood of Teamsters v. Vogt, Inc., 354 U.S. 284 (1957).

11. Gregory v. Chicago, 394 U.S. 111 (1969); Coates v. City of Cincinnati, 402 U.S. 611 (1971); Police Department of Chicago v. Mosley, 408 U.S. 92 (1972); Grayned v. City of Rockford, 408 U.S. 104 (1972); Carey v. Brown, 447 U.S. 455 (1980); NAACP v. Claiborne Hardware Co., 458 U.S. 886 (1982).

Independent State Interpretations

When federal courts decide that the U.S. Constitution does not protect a contested right, state judges may protect that same right by independently interpreting their own constitutions. Although the U.S. Supreme Court has decided that the federal constitution does not guarantee the right of free speech in a shopping center, the states below have upheld free speech rights in privately owned shopping centers and private universities. State constitutions not only include the negative placed in the U.S. Constitution (no law shall abridge the freedom of speech) but also the positive. For example, the Colorado Constitution provides that "every person shall be free to speak, write or publish whatever he will on any subject" (Art. II, § 10).

California	Robins v. PruneYard Shopping Center, 592 P.2d 341 (1979).
Colorado	Bock v. Westminster Mall Co., 819 P.2d 55 (1991).
New Jersey	State v. Schmid, 423 A.2d 615 (1980).
Pennsylvania	Commonwealth v. Tate, 432 A.2d 1382 (1981).
Washington	Alderwood Assoc. v. Wash. Envir. Council, 635 P.2d 108 (1981).

ous reasonings in this line of cases.... The definitive word was left to the state courts to write." Bock v. Westminster Mall Co., 819 P.2d 55, 58 (Colo. 1991).

Texas v. Johnson

491 U.S. 397 (1989)

As a means of protesting against the policies of the Reagan administration and American corporations, Gregory Lee Johnson burned an American flag in front of Dallas City Hall in 1984. He was convicted under Texas law for desecrating a flag, but the Texas Court of Criminal Appeals reversed the conviction on the ground that it was inconsistent with the First Amendment. The Supreme Court dealt with the issue of whether Johnson's action was "expressive conduct" protected by the Constitution.

JUSTICE BRENNAN delivered the opinion of the Court....

Johnson was convicted of flag desecration for burning the flag rather than for uttering insulting words. This fact somewhat complicates our consideration of his conviction under the First Amendment. We must first determine whether Johnson's burning of the flag constituted expressive conduct, permitting him to invoke the First Amendment in challenging his conviction.... If his conduct was expressive, we next decide whether the State's regulation is related to the suppression of free expression....

The State of Texas conceded for purposes of its oral argument in this case that Johnson's conduct was expressive conduct.... Johnson burned an American flag as part — indeed, as the culmination — of a political demonstration that coincided with the convening of the Republican Party and its renomination of Ronald Reagan for President. The expressive, overtly political nature of this conduct was both intentional and overwhelmingly apparent. At his trial, Johnson explained his reasons for burning the flag as follows: "The American Flag was burned as Ronald Reagan was being renominated as President. And a more powerful statement of symbolic speech, whether you agree with it or not, couldn't have been made at that time. It's quite a just position [juxtaposition]. We had new patriotism and no patriotism." ...

II

The Government generally has a freer hand in restricting expressive conduct than it has in restricting the written or spoken word....

Thus, although we have recognized that where "'speech' and 'nonspeech' elements are combined in the same course of conduct, a sufficiently important governmental interest in regulating the nonspeech element can justify incidental limitations on First Amendment freedoms," [*United States v. O'Brien (burning of a draft card)*] we have limited the applicability of *O'Brien*'s relatively lenient standard to those cases in which "the governmental interest is unrelated to the suppression of free expression...."

In order to decide whether *O'Brien*'s test applies here, therefore, we must decide whether Texas has asserted an interest in support of Johnson's conviction that is unrelated to the suppression of expression. If we find that an interest asserted by the State is simply not implicated on the facts before us, we need not ask whether *O'Brien*'s test applies.... The State offers two separate interests to justify this conviction: preventing breaches of the peace, and preserving the flag as a symbol of nationhood and national unity. We hold that the first interest is not implicated on this record and that the second is related to the suppression of expression.

A

Texas claims that its interest in preventing breaches of the peace justifies Johnson's conviction for flag desecration. However, no disturbance of the peace actually occurred or threatened to occur because of Johnson's burning of the flag....

The State's position, therefore, amounts to a claim that an audience that takes serious offense at particular expression is necessarily likely to disturb the peace and that the expression may be prohibited on this basis. Our precedents do not countenance such a presumption. On the contrary, they recognize that a principal "function of free speech under our system of government is to invite dispute. It may indeed best serve its high purpose when it induces a condition of unrest, creates dissatisfaction with conditions as they are, or even stirs people to anger." *Terminiello* v. *Chicago,* 337 U.S. 1, 4 (1949)....

Nor does Johnson's expressive conduct fall within that small class of "fighting words" that are "likely to provoke the average person to retaliation, and thereby cause a breach of the peace." *Chaplinsky* v. *New Hampshire,* 315 U.S. 568, 574 (1942). No reasonable onlooker would have regarded Johnson's generalized expression of dissatisfaction with the policies of the Federal Government as a direct personal insult or an invitation to exchange fisticuffs....

We thus conclude that the State's interest in maintaining order is not implicated on these facts....

III

It remains to consider whether the State's interest in preserving the flag as a symbol of nationhood and national unity justifies Johnson's conviction.

... Johnson was not, we add, prosecuted for the expression of just any idea; he was prosecuted for his expression of dissatisfaction with the policies of this country, expression situated at the core of our First Amendment values....

Moreover, Johnson was prosecuted because he knew that his politically charged expression would cause "serious offense." If he had burned the flag as a means of disposing of it because it was dirty or torn, he would not have been convicted of flag desecration under this Texas law: federal law designates burning as the preferred means of disposing of a flag "when it is in such condition that it is no longer a fitting emblem for display," 36 U.S.C. § 176(k), and Texas has no quarrel with this means of disposal.... The Texas law is thus not aimed at protecting the physical integrity of the flag in all circumstances, but is designed instead to protect it only against impairments that would cause serious offense to others....

Whether Johnson's treatment of the flag violated Texas law thus depended on the likely communicative impact of his expressive conduct....

... According to Texas, if one physically treats the flag in a way that would tend to cast doubt on either the idea that nationhood and national unity are the flag's referents or that national unity actually exists, the message conveyed thereby is a harmful one and therefore may be prohibited.

If there is a bedrock principle underlying the First Amendment, it is that the Government may not prohibit the expression of an idea simply because society finds the idea itself offensive or disagreeable....

We are tempted to say, in fact, that the flag's deservedly cherished place in our community will be strengthened, not weakened, by our holding today. Our decision is a reaffirmation of the principles of freedom and inclusiveness that the flag best reflects, and of the conviction that our toleration of criticism such as Johnson's is a sign and source of our strength. Indeed, one of the proudest images of our flag, the one immortalized in our own national anthem, is of the bombardment it survived at Fort McHenry. It is the Nation's resilience, not its rigidity, that Texas sees reflected in the flag — and it is that resilience that we reassert today.

The way to preserve the flag's special role is not to punish those who feel differently about these matters. It is to persuade them that they are wrong.... We can imagine no more appropriate response to burning a flag than waving one's own, no better way to counter a flag-burner's message than by saluting the flag that burns, no surer means of preserving the dignity even of the flag that burned than by—as one witness here did—according its remains a respectful burial. We do not consecrate the flag by punishing its desecration, for in doing so we dilute the freedom that this cherished emblem represents.

IV

Johnson was convicted for engaging in expressive conduct. The State's interest in preventing breaches of the peace does not support his conviction because Johnson's conduct did not threaten to disturb the peace. Nor does the State's interest in preserving the flag as a symbol of nationhood and national unity justify his criminal conviction for engaging in political expression. The judgment of the Texas Court of Criminal Appeals is therefore

Affirmed.

JUSTICE KENNEDY, concurring.

I write not to qualify the words JUSTICE BRENNAN chooses so well, for he says with power all that is necessary to explain our ruling. I join his opinion without reservation, but with a keen sense that this case, like others before us from time to time, exacts its personal toll....

The hard fact is that sometimes we must make decisions we do not like. We make them because they are right, right in the sense that the law and the Constitution, as we see them, compel the result....

CHIEF JUSTICE REHNQUIST, with whom JUSTICE WHITE and JUSTICE O'CONNOR join, dissenting.

[*Rehnquist cites various poems, resolutions, and anthems in praise of the flag, written by Ralph Waldo Emerson, Francis Scott Key, and John Greenleaf Whittier. He reviews also the role played by the flag in World War II (with the marines raising the flag on Mount Suribachi at Iwo Jima) and in the Korean War. He further explains that Congress passed the Flag Desecration Act of 1968 because flag burnings had undermined the morale of American troops in Vietnam.*]

... Johnson was free to make any verbal denunciation of the flag that he wished; indeed, he was free to burn the flag in private. He could publicly burn other symbols of the Government or effigies of political leaders. He did lead a march through the streets of Dallas, and conducted a rally in front of the Dallas City Hall. He engaged in a "die-in" to protest nuclear weapons. He shouted out various slogans during the march, including: "Reagan, Mondale which will it be? Either one means World War III"; "Ronald Reagan, killer of the hour, Perfect example of U. S. power"; and "red, white and blue, we spit on you, you stand for plunder, you will go under."... For none of these acts was he arrested or prosecuted; it was only when he proceeded to burn publicly an American flag stolen from its rightful owner that he violated the Texas statute....

The result of the Texas statute is obviously to deny one in Johnson's frame of mind one of many means of "symbolic speech." Far from being a case of "one picture being worth a thousand words," flag burning is the equivalent of an inarticulate grunt or roar that, it seems fair to say, is most likely to be indulged in not to express any particular idea, but to antagonize others....

JUSTICE STEVENS, dissenting.

The value of the flag as a symbol cannot be measured.... [I]n my considered judgment, sanctioning the public desecration of the flag will tarnish its value—both for those who cherish the ideas for which it waves and for those who desire to don the robes of martyrdom by burning it....

Snyder v. Phelps

562 U.S. ___ (2011)

Fred Phelps is the founder of Westboro Baptist Church, a Kansas congregation that abhors what it sees as the United States' embrace of homosexuality, including in the U.S. military. As a way of calling attention to its beliefs, it pickets the funerals of soldiers killed in Iraq and Afghanistan. It chose to picket the Maryland funeral of Marine Lance Corporal Matthew Snyder, killed in Iraq, with signs reading such things as "God Hates the USA/Thank God for 9/11," "Thank God for Dead Soldiers," "God Hates Fags," and "Got Hates You." The picketing complied with local rules for demonstrations. Snyder's father successfully sued Phelps and the church for "intentional infliction of emotional distress" and "intrusion upon seclusion" and was awarded compensatory and punitive damages. Phelps appealed on the grounds that their picketing was protected by the First Amendment, and the Court of Appeals agreed.

CHIEF JUSTICE ROBERTS delivered the opinion of Court.

A jury held members of the Westboro Baptist Church liable for millions of dollars in damages for picketing near a soldier's funeral service. The picket signs reflected the church's view that the United States is overly tolerant of sin and that God kills American soldiers as punishment. The question presented is whether the First Amendment shields the church members from tort liability for their speech in this case....

II.

To succeed on a claim of intentional infliction of emotional distress in Maryland, a plaintiff must demonstrate that the defendant intentionally and recklessly engaged in extreme and outrageous conduct that caused the plaintiff to suffer severe emotional distress.... The Free Speech Clause of the First Amendment ... can serve as a defense in state tort suits, including suits for intentional infliction of emotional distress. See, *e.g. Hustler Magazine, Inc. v. Falwell*, 485 U.S. 46, 50–51(1988).

Whether the First Amendment prohibits holding Westboro liable for its speech in this case turns largely on whether that speech is of public or private concern, as determined by all the circumstances of the case. "[S]peech on 'matters of public concern'... is 'at the heart of the First Amendment protection.'"...

"[N]ot all speech is of equal First Amendment importance,'" however, and where matters of purely private significance are at issue, First Amendment protections are often less rigorous.... That is because restricting speech on purely private matters does not implicate the same constitutional concerns as limiting speech on matters of public interest....

· · ·

Speech deals with matters of public concern when it can "be fairly considered as relating to any matter of political, social, or other concern in the community,"... or when it "is a subject of legitimate news interest; that is, a subject of general interest and of value and concern to the public."... The arguably "inappropriate or controversial character of a statement is irrelevant to the question of whether it deals with a matter of public concern."....

· · ·

Deciding whether speech is of public or private concern requires us to examine the "content, form, and context" of that speech, "'as revealed by the whole record.'"...

The content of Westboro's signs plainly relates to broad issues of interest to society at large, rather than matters of "purely private concern." The placards read "God Hates the USA/Thank God for 9/11," "America is Doomed," ... "Thank God for IEDs," "Fag Troops," "Semper Fi Fags," "God Hates Fags," ... "Thank God for Dead Soldiers," "Pope in Hell," ... "God Hates You." While these messages may fall short of refined social and political commentary, the issues they highlight— the political and moral conduct of the United States and its citizens, the fate of our Nation, homosexuality in the military, and scandals involving the Catholic clergy— are matters of public import. The signs certainly convey Westboro's position on those issues in a manner designed, ... to reach as broad a public audience as possible. And even if a few of the signs—such as "You're Going to Hell" and "God Hates You"—were viewed as containing messages related to Matthew Snyder or the Snyders specifically, that would not change the fact that the overall thrust and dominant theme of Westboro's demonstration spoke to broader public issues.

[As to context,] [t]he fact that Westboro spoke in connection with a funeral ... cannot itself transform the nature of Westboro's speech. Westboro's signs, displayed on public land next to a public street, reflect the fact that the church finds much to condemn in modern society. Its speech is "fairly characterized as constitution speech on a matter of public concern," ... and the funeral setting does not alter that conclusion.

... Westboro had already been actively engaged in speaking on the subjects addressed in its picketing long before it became aware of Matthew Snyder, and there can be no serious claim that Westboro's picketing did not represent its "honestly believed" views on public issues.... There was no pre-existing relationship or conflict between Westboro and Snyder that might suggest Westboro's speech on public matters was intended to mask an attack on Snyder over a private matter....

· · ·

Westboro's choice to convey those views in conjunction with Matthew Snyder's funeral made the expression of those views particularly hurtful to many, especially Matthew's father. The record makes clear that the applicable legal term — "emotional distress" — fails to capture fully the anguish Westboro's choice added to Mr. Snyder's already incalculable grief. But Westboro conducted its picketing peacefully on matters of public concern at a public place adjacent to a public street. Such space occupies a "special position in terms of First Amendment protection."....

. . .

The record confirms that any distress occasioned by Westboro's picketing turned on the content and viewpoint of the message conveyed, rather than any interference with the funeral itself. A group of parishioners standing at the very spot where Westboro stood, holding signs that said "God Bless America" and "God Loves You" would not have been subjected to liability....

. . .

The jury here was instructed that it could hold Westboro liable for intentional infliction of emotional distress based on a finding that Westboro's picketing was "outrageous." "Outrageousness," however, is a highly malleable standard with "an inherent subjectiveness about it which would allow a jury to impose liability on the basis of the jurors' tastes or views, or perhaps on the basis of their dislike of a particular expression."....

. . .

III

The jury also found Westboro liable for the state law torts of intrusion upon seclusion and civil conspiracy....

[*Roberts rejects the argument that Snyder was a "captive audience" because "Westboro stayed well away from the memorial service. Snyder could see no more than the tops of the signs when driving to the funeral. And there is no indication that the picketing in any way interfered with the funeral service itself."*]

. . .

IV

Our holding today is narrow. We are required in First Amendment cases to carefully review the record, and the reach of our opinion here is limited by the particular facts before us....

Westboro believes that America is morally flawed; many Americans might feel the same about Westboro. Westboro's funeral picketing is certainly hurtful and its contribution to public discourse may

be negligible. But Westboro addressed matters of public import on public property, in a peaceful manner, in full compliance with the guidance of local officials....

Speech is powerful. It can stir people to action, move them to tears of both joy and sorrow, and — as it did here — inflict great pain. On the facts before us, we cannot react to that pain by punishing the speaker. As a Nation we have chosen a different course — to protect even hurtful speech on public issues to ensure that we do not stifle public debate. That choice requires that we shield Westboro from tort liability for picketing in this case.

The judgment of the United States Court of Appeals for the Fourth Circuit is affirmed.

It is so ordered.

JUSTICE BREYER, concurring.

[*Breyer emphasizes the narrowness of the Court's ruling, and the emphasis on the facts in this case, contending that it does not "hold or imply that the State is always powerless to provide private individuals with necessary protection."*]

JUSTICE ALITO, dissenting.

Our profound commitment to free and open debate is not a license for the vicious verbal assault that occurred in this case.

Petitioner Albert Snyder is not a public figure. He is simply a parent whose son ... was killed in Iraq. Mr. Snyder wanted what is surely the right of any parent who experiences such an incalculable loss: to bury his son in peace. But respondents, members of the Westboro Baptist Church, deprived him of that elementary right. They first issued a press release and thus turned Matthew's funeral into a tumultuous media event. They then appeared at the church, approached as closely as they could without trespassing, and launched a malevolent verbal attack on Matthew and his family at a time of acute emotional vulnerability. As a result, Albert Snyder suffered severe and lasting emotional injury. The Court now holds that the First Amendment protected respondents' right to brutalize Mr. Snyder. I cannot agree.

[*Alito argues that Westboro had innumerable ways in which it could get its views across without interference and that the "vicious verbal attacks" they used "made no contribution to public debate." In addition, he notes that the standard for proving intentional emotional distress are very high under Maryland law, and having met the standard, Westboro should not have been excused based on the First Amendment. He concludes that it is "not necessary to allow the brutalization of innocent   victims" in order to have free and open public debate.]*

E. COMMERCIAL SPEECH

Free speech has come to include "speech" related to commercial activities. Initially unprotected under the Constitution, commercial speech is now safeguarded by the courts. In part, this reflects the growing appreciation that commercial speech is part of the free flow of information necessary for informed choice and democratic participation.

The concept of commercial speech appeared in a 1942 case involving a municipal ordinance that prohibited the distribution in the streets of printed handbills bearing commercial advertising matter. The disputed handbill in this case was double-faced: half consisting of a protest against the city's police (protected speech), the other half containing an advertisement. The Court held unanimously that such artifices could not so easily evade the prohibition of the ordinance. Although the Constitution protects the dissemination of opinion by handbills, it "imposes no such restraint on government as respects purely commercial advertising." Valentine v. Chrestensen, 316 U.S. 52, 54 (1942).

Other cases explored the notion of commercial speech,[12] but a major step occurred in 1974 when the Supreme Court narrowly upheld (by a 5–4 vote) a city's policy of allowing commercial, religious, and civic advertising in its transit system but prohibiting ads for political candidates. The four dissenters argued that once the city opened a forum for communication by accepting ads, it could not discriminate "among forum uses solely on the basis of message content." Lehman v. City of Shaker Heights, 418 U.S. 298, 310 (1974).

Free Flow of Information

The value of commercial speech was etched sharply a year later when the Supreme Court, divided 5–4, struck down a state law that made it a misdemeanor for anyone to sell or circulate newspapers that contain ads encouraging abortions. Decided in the shadow of the abortion cases of 1973, the Court held that the statute infringed upon constitutionally protected speech. At issue was not merely the right of newspapers to publish commercial material but the right of the reader to make informed choices. Bigelow v. Virginia, 421 U.S. 809 (1975).

A similar point was made concerning the right of professionals to advertise their services. In earlier cases, the Court had sustained laws that prohibited certain occupations, such as dentists, from advertising. Semler v. Dental Examiners, 294 U.S. 608 (1935). In 1976, however, an 8–1 Supreme Court decision rejected a state law that declared it unprofessional conduct for a licensed pharmacist to advertise the prices of prescription drugs. The Court explained that it was not just a matter of trade but of health and the free flow of information. Virginia State Board of Pharmacy v. Virginia Citizens Consumer Council, 425 U.S. 748 (1976). See also Linmark Associates v. Willingboro, 431 U.S. 85 (1977).

Building on this line of cases, in 1977 the Court declared unconstitutional a state rule that prohibited attorneys from advertising in newspapers or other media. The Court protected commercial speech on these grounds: "The listener's interest is substantial; the consumer's concern for the free flow of commercial speech often may be far keener than his concern for urgent political dialogue. Moreover, significant societal interests are served by such speech. Advertising, though entirely com-

---

12. In 1972, the Supreme Court summarily affirmed a district court decision's sustaining the constitutionality of 15 U.S.C. § 1335, which prohibited the electronic media from carrying cigarette advertising. Capital Broadcasting Co. v. Acting Attorney General, 405 U.S. 1000 (1972). The district court called this form of communication commercial speech. See also Pittsburgh Press Co. v. Human Rel. Comm'n, 413 U.S. 376, 384–85 (1973).

mercial, may often carry information of import to significant issues of the day." Bates v. State Bar of Arizona, 433 U.S. 350, 364 (1977).[13] The right to advertise does not protect lawyers from being disciplined by the bar for soliciting clients in person. Ohralik v. Ohio State Bar Assn., 436 U.S. 447 (1978).

The Court showed its concern for the free flow of information in 1978. Split 5–4, it held that a Massachusetts statute violated the First Amendment because it restricted business corporations from making contributions or expenditures to influence votes on questions submitted to the people. Some of the dissenters objected that the Court should have deferred to legislatures "in the context of the political arena where the expertise of legislators is at its peak and that of judges is at its very lowest." First National Bank of Boston v. Bellotti, 435 U.S. 765, 804 (1978).

In 1983, a unanimous Court struck down a congressional statute that prohibited the mailing of unsolicited advertisements for contraceptives. The Court held that the statute violated commercial speech protected by the First Amendment: "where — as in this case — a speaker desires to convey truthful information relevant to important social issues such as family planning and the prevention of venereal disease, we have previously found the First Amendment interest served by such speech paramount." Bolger v. Youngs Drug Products Corp., 463 U.S. 60, 69 (1983).

A unanimous ruling in 1995 declared unconstitutional a federal law abridging a brewer's right to provide the public with accurate information about the alcoholic content of malt beverages. Rubin v. Coors Brewing Co., 514 U.S. 476 (1995). A year later another unanimous Court struck down a Rhode Island ban on the advertising of liquor prices, ruling that the states' authority under the 21st Amendment does not override the First Amendment free speech guarantee. Writing for the Court, Justice Stevens said that the First Amendment "directs us to be especially skeptical of regulations that seek to keep people in the dark for what the government perceives to be their own good." 44 Liquormart, Inc. v. Rhode Island, 517 U.S. 484, 503 (1996). There was no majority agreement, however, on the meaning of commercial speech.

Disagreement over how commercial speech differs from other speech surfaced on the Court again in a 2011 decision striking down Vermont's Prescription Confidentiality Law. The statute banned the sale, transmission, or use of prescriber identifiable data by pharmaceutical data mining companies without the prescriber's consent. Such data revealed the prescribing practices of individual doctors. The majority on the Court found that the law imposed "content and speaker based burdens" on these companies and thus must pass a heightened level of scrutiny. Dissenters insisted that a lower standard of review for commercial speech should be used and that Vermont had sufficient justification to pass the law. Sorrell v. IMS Health, Inc., 564 U.S. ___ (2011).

Regulating the Economy

Commercial speech may create conflicts between state efforts to regulate the economy and the interest of businesses to promote their activities. A New York law prohibited an electric utility from placing ads to encourage the use of electricity. The law reflected concern at that time over insufficient fuel supply because of Middle East oil embargoes. By an 8–1 majority, the Court held that the law violated the First Amendment. Although the utility exercised a monopoly over electricity, it faced competition from oil and gas. Central Hudson Gas & Elec. v. Public Service Comm'n, 447 U.S. 557 (1980). This case suggested that government had to use the "least restrictive means" in regulating commer-

---

13. Additional guidelines on advertising by lawyers: In re R.M.J., 455 U.S. 191 (1982); Zauderer v. Office of Disciplinary Counsel, 471 U.S. 626 (1985); Shapero v. Kentucky Bar Assn., 486 U.S. 466 (1988); Peel v. Attorney Disciplinary Comm'n of Ill., 496 U.S. 91 (1990). A ruling in 1995, splitting the Court 5 to 4, upheld a Florida bar rule that prohibited personal-injury lawyers from sending targeted direct-mail solicitations to victims or their relatives until 30 days following an accident or disaster. Florida Bar v. Went For It, Inc., 515 U.S. 618 (1995).

cial speech, but in 1989 the Court held that only a reasonable "fit" is required between the legislature's ends to regulate commercial speech and the means it chooses. Board of Trustees, State Univ. of N.Y. v. Fox, 492 U.S. 469 (1989).

In 1997, when it looked like marketing orders issued by the U.S. Agriculture Department might run afoul of the standards for commercial speech announced in *Central Hudson*, the Court held that the legal question was not free speech or the First Amendment but "rather [it] is simply a question of economic policy for Congress and the Executive to resolve," and that Congress had sufficient authority to sanction these marketing orders through its power to regulate commerce. Glickman v. Wileman Bros. & Elliott, 521 U.S. 457, 468, 476 (1997). The marketing orders required producers of certain California tree fruit to pay assessments for product advertising. Four dissenters attacked the Court for failing to follow the tests issued in *Central Hudson* and other decisions.

Revisiting the issue in 2001, this time the Court struck down a congressional statute that mandated fresh mushroom handlers to pay assessments used primarily to fund advertisements that promoted mushroom sales. Distinguishing this statute from its *Wileman* ruling four years earlier, the Court held that the statute violated the First Amendment because the mushroom handlers did not function under a cooperative marketing structure like the California tree fruit growers. United States v. United Foods, Inc., 533 U.S. 405 (2001). Three Justices, in a dissent, accused the majority of disregarding the controlling precedent of *Wileman*.

Some states have tried to regulate billboards. The city of San Diego, in an effort to eliminate dangerous distractions to pedestrians and motorists and improve the appearance of city streets, placed restrictions on billboards and outdoor advertising displays. However, it made exceptions for on-site advertising (signs on the property of the business) and twelve other categories. Because the city seemed to afford greater protection to commercial (on-site) speech than to noncommercial speech, the ordinance was held invalid. Metromedia, Inc. v. San Diego, 453 U.S. 490 (1981). Restrictions that are totally neutral, such as the prohibition against the posting of all signs on public property, have been upheld. Cities may decide that a total ban is necessary to prevent visual clutter and to reduce traffic hazards. Because the ban is total, there is no hint of censorship or suppression of particular views. City Council v. Taxpayers for Vincent, 466 U.S. 789 (1984).

Metromedia and *Vincent* guided the Court in 1994 when it unanimously struck down a city ordinance that prohibited residents from putting political or personal signs in their yards. In this case a woman placed an 8.5 by 11-inch sign in the second story window of her home stating, "For Peace in the Gulf." The Court held that the ordinance, intended to minimize the "visual clutter" associated with such signs, violated her right to free speech. Ladue, City of v. Gilleo, 512 U.S. 43 (1994).

A 1986 decision on commercial speech dealt with gambling. A Puerto Rican statute legalized certain forms of casino gambling to promote tourism but prohibited gambling rooms from advertising to the public in Puerto Rico. A sharply divided (5–4) Court sustained the statute, rejecting the argument that once Puerto Rico chose to legalize casino gambling it was prohibited by the First Amendment from restricting advertising. Posadas de Puerto Rico Assoc. v. Tourism Co., 478 U.S. 328 (1986). However, in 1999 the Court held unanimously that a federal law, prohibiting radio and TV advertising of casino gambling, could not be applied to states where such gambling is legal. Federal law in this area had become too "pierced by exemptions and inconsistencies" to be applied coherently. Greater New Orleans Broadcasting v. United States, 527 U.S. 173, 190 (1999).

In 2001, the Court placed limits on the ability of state and local governments to regulate tobacco advertising. Efforts by Massachusetts to ban tobacco ads within a 1,000-foot radius of schools and playgrounds were considered a violation of commercial speech. A large number of concurrences and dissents revealed the sharp strains within the Court. Lorillard Tobacco Co. v. Reilly, 533 U.S. 525 (2001). A year later, a divided 5–4 Court invalidated a provision in federal law that banned pharmacies from advertising drugs that pharmacists make themselves by mixing ingredients ("compounded" pharmaceuticals). The majority concluded that the government had failed to justify the restriction;

dissenters objected that the Court was giving too much protection to commercial speech. Thompson v. Western States Medical Center, 535 U.S. 357 (2002).

F. CAMPAIGN FINANCE

The issue of campaign finance is addressed extensively in Chapter 18 on Political Participation. Nonetheless it bears mentioning here because since the 1976 decision in *Buckley v. Valeo,* 424 U.S. 1 (1976) the Supreme Court has equated the spending of campaign money with speech. The Court allowed limits on campaign contributions to candidates, but struck down expenditure limits, finding that "[a] restriction on the amount of money a person or group can spend on political communication during a campaign necessarily reduces the quantity of expression by restricting the number of issues discussed, the depth of their exploration, and the size of the audience reached."

Additional congressional and state efforts to regulate campaign financing met with similarly mixed results. As mentioned earlier, a Massachusetts attempt to restrict business spending on a referendum vote was found to be invalid. First National Bank of Boston v. Bellotti, 435 U.S. 765 (1978). A Federal Election Commission regulation on issue advocacy groups was also invalidated on free speech grounds. FEC v. Massachusetts Citizens for Life, Inc., 479 U.S. 238 (1986). A similar regulation was struck down in *FEC v. Wisconsin Right to Life,* 551 U.S. 449 (2007). On the other hand, the Court upheld a Michigan law prohibiting corporations from using general treasury funds to support candidates in state elections in *Austin v. Michigan Chamber of Commerce,* 494 U.S. 652 (1990) and Congress's limitations on the use of "soft money" in the McCain-Feingold campaign finance legislation in *McConnell v. FEC,* 540 U.S. 93 (2003).

Efforts to encourage candidates to take public financing have not fared well with the Court in recent years. The "Millionaire Amendment" of the Bipartisan Campaign Reform Act of 2002 promised additional money to publicly funded presidential candidates if privately funded candidates spent more than $350,000 of their own money in the elections. The Court found that this rule imposed a burden on the speech of the privately funded candidate. Davis v. Federal Election Comm'n, 554 U.S. 724 (2008). A similar provision in Arizona's Citizens Clean Election Act was struck down in 2011. Arizona Free Enterprise Club's Freedom Club PAC v. Bennett, 564 U.S. ___ (2011).

The issue of whether corporations and unions could be legitimately limited in their independent expenditures during political campaigns came again to the Court in 2009. The case challenged an FEC ruling that a film, paid for by a non-profit corporation and casting presidential candidate Hillary Clinton in a negative light, could not be broadcast during the time of the Democratic primaries in 2008. In a 5–4 decision the Court ruled that the McCain-Feingold limitations on "electioneering communications" by corporations violated the free speech rights of these organizations. In doing so, it struck down *Austin* and parts of *McConnell.* Citizens United v. FEC, 558 U.S. 50 (2010). (See Chapter 18 for case reading.) A similar prohibition in Montana law was found to be controlled by *Citizen's United* in a per curiam opinion in 2012. American Tradition Partnership, Inc. v. Bullock, 567 U.S. ___ (2012).

G. BROADCASTING RIGHTS

In theory, there is no limit to the number of newspapers. Radio and television stations, however, competed for a finite number of public airwaves. Acting under the Commerce Clause, Congress established the Federal Communications Commission (FCC) to allocate this limited space. It grants licenses for a specific number of years, subject to various conditions supplied by statute and agency regulation. The FCC may revoke or suspend a license if a station violates these conditions. No one has a free-speech right to use public airwaves without a license. National Broadcasting Co. v. United States, 319 U.S. 190 (1943).

In 1949, the FCC developed a "fairness doctrine" to require broadcasters to present public issues and give each side of an issue fair coverage. 13 FCC 1246 (1949). Although Congress never explicitly authorized this doctrine, a unanimous Court held that the agency regulation was consistent with congressional policy and did not violate the First Amendment. Red Lion Broadcasting Co. v. FCC, 395 U.S. 367 (1969). Next, there was the question of whether broadcasters are required to accept paid editorial advertisements. The Court again deferred to the judgments of the FCC and Congress that no such requirement exists. Columbia Broadcasting System v. Democratic National Committee, 412 U.S. 94 (1973). Congress and the FCC formulated the policy, accepted by the courts, that political candidates are entitled to "reasonable access" to broadcasting stations to promote their campaigns for federal office. CBS, Inc. v. FCC, 453 U.S. 367 (1981). Some congressional initiatives were struck down, such as the requirement that stations receiving federal funds could not editorialize. FCC v. League of Women Voters of California, 468 U.S. 364 (1984).

Conditions are imposed on radio and television programs that would be intolerable for newspapers. For example, Congress requires that if one political candidate is given time on the air, opponents must receive "equal opportunities." 47 U.S.C. § 315(a). In 1970, Congress prohibited the advertisement of cigarettes on radio or television. 84 Stat. 87 (1970). It later applied the same restriction to little cigars. 15 U.S.C. § 1335. In 1986, the ban was extended to smokeless tobacco (snuff). 100 Stat. 32, § 3(f); 15 U.S.C. § 4402(f).

In 1998, the Court ruled 6 to 3 that public TV stations have the right to choose which political candidates may appear in debates that are broadcast. Ralph Forbes, a former member of the American Nazi Party who ran in 1992 as an independent candidate, was excluded from a TV debate that included Republican and Democratic candidates for Arkansas' Third Congressional District. Although Forbes lost his opportunity to present his views, the Court was concerned that requiring TV stations to invite all candidates, no matter how minor or marginal, might lead broadcasters to cancel such programs. Adopting that policy "does not promote speech but represses it." Arkansas Educ. Television Com'n v. Forbes, 523 U.S. 666, 682 (1998).

The Court gives two reasons for subjecting broadcasting to more severe restrictions than newspapers: the pervasive presence of the broadcast media and its unique access to children. The FCC was therefore allowed to prohibit the playing of "indecent" material in the afternoon (George Carlin's monologue on "seven dirty words"). The same material, in a different place or at another time, might have received First Amendment protection. FCC v. PACIFICA FOUNDATION 438 U.S. 726, 748–51 (1978). Ever since 1948, Congress has prohibited anyone from uttering "any obscene, indecent, or profane language" by means of radio communication. 18 U.S.C. § 1464.

Following the *Pacifica* decision, the FCC continued to restrict its enforcement efforts against indecent broadcasts to programs before 10 P.M. Under the Reagan administration, however, the Commission pushed the "safe harbor" period up to 12 midnight. Before that standard could be implemented, Congress intervened in 1988 to order the FCC to promulgate regulations on indecent broadcasts to cover the full 24 hours a day. 102 Stat. 2228, § 608 (1988). The Commission promulgated a new rule prohibiting all broadcasts of indecent materials, but that was declared a violation of the First Amendment. Action for Children's Television v. FCC, 932 F.2d 1504 (D.C. Cir. 1991), cert. denied, 503 U.S. 913–14 (1992). Congress passed legislation to require the FCC to promulgate regulations that will prohibit indecent programming from 6 A.M. to midnight, except for stations that go off the air before midnight, which may broadcast such material beginning at 10 P.M. 106 Stat. 954, § 16 (1992).

Several incidents during the administration of George W. Bush led to increased pressure on the FCC to restrict indecency on television. During several televised award shows, musicians used some of the same words Carlin satirized and a "wardrobe malfunction" during half-time at the Super Bowl briefly exposed the breast of performer Janet Jackson. In 2004 the FCC issued regulations imposing fines for the broadcast of "fleeting expletives," finding certain words referring to sexual acts and excrement to be always indecent. Fox Television filed suit challenging the regulations. The regulations were struck down by the Second Circuit Court of Appeals in New York in 2007 as "arbitrary and capricious." Fox Television Stations, Inc. v. FCC, 280 F.3d 1027 (2d Cir. 2007). On appeal, the Supreme

Court reversed and remanded, but avoided the issue of whether the regulations violated the First Amendment. FCC v. Fox Television Stations, Inc., 556 U.S. 502 (2009). After rehearing the case, the circuit court again struck down the regulations in July 2010, this time as being "unconstitutionally vague" in violation of the First Amendment. Fox Television v. FCC, 613 F.3d 317 (2d Cir. 2010). On June 21, 2012 the Court held that the FCC failed to give Fox and ABC fair notice prior to the broadcasts that fleeting expletives and momentary nudity could be found to be actionably indecent. Having resolved the cases on fair notice grounds under the Due Process Clause, the Court did not address the First Amendment implications or reconsider *Pacifica*. FCC v. Fox Television Stations, Inc., 567 U.S. ___ (2012).

Cable TV

Congressional legislation in 1992 to regulate cable TV led to a decision by the Supreme Court two years later holding that cable is entitled to free speech protection. However, the standard applied is not strict scrutiny but rather an intermediate level of scrutiny. The intermediate level offers greater protection than for broadcasters, who are regulated more strictly because of the scarcity of channels resulting from frequencies in the electromagnetic spectrum. Turner Broadcasting Systems, Inc. v. FCC, 512 U.S. 622 (1994).

Other parts of the 1992 statute reached the Supreme court in 1996. A deeply divided Court (six Justices dissented with parts of the Court's opinion) ruled that cable TV operators may ban indecent programming from certain commercial channels but it was inconsistent with the First Amendment to ban such material from "public access" channels used by local governments and community groups. The Court also struck down a provision that required cable operators to allow access to "patently offensive" programming only when individuals request, in writing, this material. The application of this complex ruling, particularly with fast-paced technological changes, is very uncertain. Denver Area Educ. Telecom. Consortium v. FCC, 518 U.S. 727 (1996). A year later the Court, with a 5–4 majority, held that Congress could require cable systems to carry local broadcast TV stations (the "must carry" rule). The Court rejected the cable industry's argument that the 1992 congressional statute was a form of government-compelled speech that violated the First Amendment. The majority essentially deferred to Congress in reconciling "the complex and fast-changing field of television." Turner Broadcasting Systems, Inc. v. FCC, 520 U.S. 180, 224 (1997).

In 2000, the Court ruled that congressional legislation on cable television was unconstitutional because it required providers of sexually explicit material to "fully scramble" their signals or offer the programs only when children are unlikely to be watching. Divided 5 to 4, the court found that the statute violated the First Amendment because government had failed to show that the statutory remedy was the least restrictive way of preventing children from watching such material. United States v. Playboy Entertainment Group, Inc., 529 U.S. 803 (2000). [For further details on legislation to protect children from obscene or indecent messages on the Internet, e-mails, and "virtual" child porn, see the section on obscenity in Chapter 11.]

The Fairness Doctrine

Broadcasting rights fluctuate with technology. In 1973, the Court explained that the problems of regulating broadcasting "are rendered more difficult because the broadcast industry is dynamic in terms of technological change; solutions adequate a decade ago are not necessarily so now, and those acceptable today may well be outmoded 10 years hence." Columbia Broadcasting System v. Democratic National Committee, 412 U.S. 94, 102 (1973). The fairness doctrine depends largely on the limited number of access points available to licensees. If outlets increased because of technology, the doctrine's rationale would be undermined. In a footnote to a 1984 decision, the Court recognized that the emergence of cable and satellite television created new channels for the public. However, "without some signal from Congress or the FCC" that technological development required revision of broadcasting regulation, the Court was not prepared to challenge the fairness doctrine. FCC v. League of Women Voters of California, 468 U.S. 364, 377–78 n.11 (1984). See also n.12 at 378–79.

The FCC chairman in the Reagan administration criticized the fairness doctrine as unconstitutional and threatened to abolish it. In 1985, a Commission report concluded that the doctrine violates the First Amendment and no longer serves the public interest. However, it declined to initiate a new rule to eliminate or modify the doctrine. On the basis of that report, a party brought suit and asked the D.C. Circuit to consider the constitutionality of the doctrine. The D.C. Circuit refused on the ground that the report did not constitute "agency action" subject to judicial review. Radio-Television News Directors Ass'n v. FCC, 809 F.2d 860 (D.C. Cir. 1987). On the same day, the D.C. Circuit returned a case to the FCC because it had failed to give adequate consideration to a station owner's constitutional arguments regarding the fairness doctrine. The Commission regarded Congress and the courts as more appropriate arenas for deciding the constitutional question. The D.C. Circuit, however, thought it might benefit from the FCC's analysis, even if the Commission felt political pressure from Congress to avoid a final conclusion. Meredith Corp. v. FCC, 809 F.2d 863, 872 (D.C. Cir. 1987). It noted that federal officials are not only bound by the Constitution but also take an oath to support and defend it: "To enforce a Commission-generated policy that the Commission itself believes is unconstitutional may well constitute a violation of that oath...." Id. at 874.

When Congress passed legislation in 1987 to codify the fairness doctrine, President Reagan vetoed the bill. He stated that the doctrine was antagonistic to the First Amendment and was no longer justified because of new media outlets, such as cable television. Public Papers of the Presidents, 1987, I, at 690. The FCC unanimously abolished the fairness doctrine, claiming that it represented an unconstitutional restriction on free speech. Bills have been introduced in Congress to reinstate the fairness doctrine.

FCC v. Pacifica Foundation

438 U.S. 726 (1978)

A radio station of Pacifica Foundation made an afternoon broadcast of George Carlin's satiric monologue "Filthy Words," which listed and repeated a variety of colloquial uses of "words you couldn't say on the public airwaves." A father who heard the broadcast while driving with his young son complained to the Federal Communications Commission (FCC), which later issued a declaratory order granting the complaint. Although the FCC did not impose formal sanctions, it stated that the order would be placed in the station's license file and that if subsequent complaints were received it would decide whether to invoke sanctions, including a decision not to renew the license. The FCC also announced that it had the power to regulate indecent broadcasting. The D.C. Circuit reversed the FCC's action, partly on the ground that it was censorship and the agency rule was overbroad.

MR. JUSTICE STEVENS delivered the opinion of the Court (Parts I, II, III, and IV-C) and an opinion in which THE CHIEF JUSTICE and MR. JUSTICE REHNQUIST joined (Parts IV-A and IV-B).

This case requires that we decide whether the Federal Communications Commission has any power to regulate a radio broadcast that is indecent but not obscene.

A satiric humorist named George Carlin recorded a 12-minute monologue entitled "Filthy

Words" before a live audience in a California theater. He began by referring to his thoughts about "the words you couldn't say on the public, ah, airwaves, um, the ones you definitely wouldn't say, ever." He proceeded to list those words and repeat them over and over again in a variety of colloquialisms. The transcript of the recording, which is appended to this opinion, indicates frequent laughter from the audience.

At about 2 o'clock in the afternoon on Tuesday,

October 30, 1973, a New York radio station, owned by respondent Pacifica Foundation, broadcast the "Filthy Words" monologue. A few weeks later a man, who stated that he had heard the broadcast while driving with his young son, wrote a letter complaining to the Commission....

The complaint was forwarded to the station for comment. In its response, Pacifica explained that the monologue had been played during a program about contemporary society's attitude toward language and that, immediately before its broadcast, listeners had been advised that it included "sensitive language which might be regarded as offensive to some." Pacifica characterized George Carlin as "a significant social satirist" who "like Twain and Sahl before him, examines the language of ordinary people.... Carlin is not mouthing obscenities, he is merely using words to satirize as harmless and essentially silly our attitudes towards those words." Pacifica stated that it was not aware of any other complaints about the broadcast.

On February 21, 1975, the Commission issued a declaratory order granting the complaint and holding that Pacifica "could have been the subject of administrative sanctions." 56 F.C.C. 2d 94, 99. The Commission did not impose formal sanctions, but it did state that the order would be "associated with the station's license file, and in the event that subsequent complaints are received, the Commission will then decide whether it should utilize any of the available sanctions it has been granted by Congress." [*Congress has empowered the FCC to revoke a station's license, issue a cease and desist order, or impose a monetary forfeiture. The FCC can also deny a license renewal and grant a short-term renewal.*]

In its memorandum opinion the Commission stated that it intended to "clarify the standards which will be utilized in considering" the growing number of complaints about indecent speech on the airwaves. *Id.,* at 94. Advancing several reasons for treating broadcast speech differently from other forms of expression, the Commission found a power to regulate indecent broadcasting in two statutes: 18 U.S.C. § 1464 (1976 ed.), which forbids the use of "any obscene, indecent, or profane language by means of radio communications," and 47 U.S.C. § 303(g), which requires the Commission to "encourage the larger and more effective use of radio in the public interest."

... [T]he Commission concluded that certain words [*in Carlin's broadcast*] depicted sexual and excretory activities in a patently offensive manner, noted that they "were broadcast at a time when children were undoubtedly in the audience (i.e., in the early afternoon)," and that the prerecorded language, with these offensive words "repeated over and over," was "deliberately broadcast." *Id.,* at 99. In summary, the Commission stated: "We therefore hold that the language as broadcast was indecent and prohibited by 18 U.S.C. § 1464." ...

II

The relevant statutory questions are whether the Commission's action is forbidden "censorship" within the meaning of 47 U.S.C. § 326 and whether speech that concededly is not obscene may be restricted as "indecent" under the authority of 18 U.S.C. § 1464 (1976 ed.). The questions are not unrelated, for the two statutory provisions have a common origin. Nevertheless, we analyze them separately.

Section 29 of the Radio Act of 1927 provided:

"Nothing in this Act shall be understood or construed to give the licensing authority the power of censorship over the radio communications or signals transmitted by any radio station, and no regulation or condition shall be promulgated or fixed by the licensing authority which shall interfere with the right of free speech by means of radio communications. No person within the jurisdiction of the United States shall utter any obscene, indecent, or profane language by means of radio communication." 44 Stat. 1172.

The prohibition against censorship unequivocally denies the Commission any power to edit proposed broadcasts in advance and to excise material considered inappropriate for the airwaves. The prohibition, however, has never been construed to deny the Commission the power to review the content of completed broadcasts in the performance of its regulatory duties. [*Justice Stevens explains that the courts and the Commission do not regard consideration of renewing a license as "censorship."*]

We conclude, therefore, that § 326 does not limit the Commission's authority to impose sanctions on licensees who engage in obscene, indecent, or profane broadcasting.

III

The only other statutory question presented by this case is whether the afternoon broadcast of the "Filthy Words" monologue was indecent within the meaning of § 1464....

The Commission identified several words that referred to excretory or sexual activities or organs, stated that the repetitive, deliberate use of those words in an afternoon broadcast when children are in the audience was patently offensive, and held that the broadcast was indecent. Pacifica takes issue with the Commission's definition of indecency, but does not dispute the Commission's preliminary determination that each of the components of its definition was present. Specifically, Pacifica does not quarrel with the conclusion that this afternoon broadcast was patently offensive. Pacifica's claim that the broadcast was not indecent within the meaning of the statute rests entirely on the absence of prurient appeal.

The plain language of the statute does not support Pacifica's argument. The words "obscene, indecent, or profane" are written in the disjunctive, implying that each has a separate meaning. Prurient appeal is an element of the obscene, but the normal definition of "indecent" merely refers to nonconformance with accepted standards of morality....

Because neither our prior decisions nor the language or history of § 1464 supports the conclusion that prurient appeal is an essential component of indecent language, we reject Pacifica's construction of the statute. When that construction is put to one side, there is no basis for disagreeing with the Commission's conclusion that indecent language was used in this broadcast.

IV

Pacifica makes two constitutional attacks on the Commission's order. First, it argues that the Commission's construction of the statutory language broadly encompasses so much constitutionally protected speech that reversal is required even if Pacifica's broadcast of the "Filthy Words" monologue is not itself protected by the First Amendment. Second, Pacifica argues that inasmuch as the recording is not obscene, the Constitution forbids any abridgment of the right to broadcast it on the radio.

A

The first argument fails because our review is limited to the question whether the Commission has the authority to proscribe this particular broadcast. As the Commission itself emphasized, its order was "issued in a specific factual context." 59 F.C.C.2d, at 893. That approach is appropriate for courts as well as the Commission when regulation of indecency is at stake for indecency is largely a function of context — it cannot be adequately judged in the abstract....

B

When the issue is narrowed to the facts of this case, the question is whether the First Amendment denies government any power to restrict the public broadcast of indecent language in any circumstances. For if the government has any such power, this was an appropriate occasion for its exercise.

The words of the Carlin monologue are unquestionably "speech" within the meaning of the First Amendment. It is equally clear that the Commission's objections to the broadcast were based in part on its content. The order must therefore fall if, as Pacifica argues, the First Amendment prohibits all governmental regulation that depends on the content of speech. Our past cases demonstrate, however, that no such absolute rule is mandated by the Constitution....

In this case it is undisputed that the content of Pacifica's broadcast was "vulgar," "offensive," and "shocking." Because content of that character is not entitled to absolute constitutional protection under all circumstances, we must consider its context in order to determine whether the Commission's action was constitutionally permissible....

C

We have long recognized that each medium of expression presents special First Amendment problems, *Joseph Burstyn, Inc.* v. *Wilson*, 343 U.S. 495, 502–503. And of all forms of communication, it is broadcasting that has received the most limited First Amendment protection. Thus, although other speakers cannot be licensed except under laws that carefully define and narrow official discretion, a broadcaster may be deprived of his license and his forum if the Commission decides that such an action would serve "the public interest, convenience, and necessity."...

The reasons for these distinctions are complex, but two have relevance to the present case. First, the broadcast media have established a uniquely pervasive presence in the lives of all Americans. Patently offensive, indecent material presented over the airwaves confronts the citizen, not only in public, but also in the privacy of the home, where the individual's right to be left alone plainly outweighs the First Amendment rights of an intruder. *Rowan* v. *Post Office Dept.*, 397 U.S. 728. Because the broadcast audience is constantly tuning in and out, prior warnings cannot completely protect the listener or viewer from unexpected program content....

Second, broadcasting is uniquely accessible to children, even those too young to read. Although Cohen's [*Paul Cohen, who entered a courthouse wearing a jacket with the words "Fuck the Draft"; Cohen v. California, 403 U.S. 15 (1971)*] written message might have been incomprehensible to a first grader, Pacifica's broadcast could have enlarged a child's vocabulary in an instant....

The judgment of the Court of Appeals is reversed.

It is so ordered.

Mr. Justice Powell, with whom Mr. Justice Blackmun joins, concurring in part and concurring in the judgment.

I join Parts I, II, III, and IV-C of Mr. Justice Stevens' opinion. The Court today reviews only the Commission's holding that Carlin's monologue was indecent "as broadcast" at two o'clock in the afternoon, and not the broad sweep of the Commission's opinion....

Mr. Justice Brennan, with whom Mr. Justice Marshall joins, dissenting.

I agree with Mr. Justice Stewart that, under *Hamling* v. *United States*, 418 U.S. 87 (1974), and

United States v. *12 200-ft. Reels of Film*, 413 U.S. 123 (1973), the word "indecent" in 18 U.S.C. § 1464 (1976 ed.) must be construed to prohibit only obscene speech....

Mr. Justice Stewart, with whom Mr. Justice Brennan, Mr. Justice White, and Mr. Justice Marshall join, dissenting.

... The Commission held, and the Court today agrees, that "indecent" is a broader concept than "obscene" as the latter term was defined in *Miller* v. *California*, 413 U.S. 15, because language can be "indecent" although it has social, political, or artistic value and lacks prurient appeal. 56 F.C.C.2d 94, 97–98. But this construction of § 1464, while perhaps plausible, is by no means compelled. To the contrary, I think that "indecent" should properly be read as meaning no more than "obscene." Since the Carlin monologue concededly was not "obscene," I believe that the Commission lacked statutory authority to ban it....

CONCLUSIONS

The concept of "free speech" emerged from political developments in America and the needs of self-government and self-development. From the laconic formulation in the First Amendment, the right of free speech has become more specialized and complex, expanding to include such technology as broadcasting rights. Various tests have been fashioned to draw a line between liberty and licentiousness, none with much success. There is general agreement on giving broad scope to pure advocacy of ideas, even when critical of government, and applying restrictions only when advocacy takes the form of action and conduct. For the most part, pure speech—even "fighting words"—is tolerated as part of the process of peaceful political change.

Debates on free speech frequently concentrate on the meaning of judicial rulings, but the real safeguards for free speech lie in the attitudes of the general public. As Chafee wrote: "The victories of liberty of speech must be won in the mind before they are won in the courts." Zechariah Chafee, Jr., Free Speech in the United States 325 (1941). Through his writings he "often stressed the fact that the ultimate security for free and fruitful discussion lies in the tolerance of private citizens." Id. at x.

Other dimensions of the First Amendment are examined in the next chapter: the right of a free press, the natural tensions between a free press and a fair trial, and the bedeviled areas of libel and obscenity.

NOTES AND QUESTIONS

1. Students may question the application by the Court of the "Clear and Present Danger Test" to Schenck's speech. At trial, the government adduced no evidence that any soldiers who had read Schenck's leaflet had actually abandoned their rifles and deserted the war effort. If no such evidence was introduced, how can the Court hold that Schenck's speech posed a clear and present danger that Congress may prohibit? Can you explain the elements and scope of the "Bad Tendency Test"?

2. How should the government—Congress, President and Court—balance the needs of national security with the right of free speech? May one value eclipse the other? Did Justice Louis Brandeis's emphasis on the "proximity and degree" of danger in his concurrence in *Whitney v. California* provide a workable solution?

3. Brandeis declared that the Founders "did not fear political change. They did not exalt order at the cost of liberty." Assuming that to be true, do you believe it accurate to say, historically speaking, that the American government has embraced the Founders' discipline? Why or why not?

4. It has been observed that the Court's opinion in *Brandenburg v. Ohio*, represents the most protective standard yet erected to govern "subversive speech." Does it represent an improvement over the standard established in *Schenck* and subsequent cases? If so, what about the *Brandenburg* opinion renders it superior to its predecessors?

5. Should the First Amendment protect the sort of speech that lay at the center of *Cohen v. California, Texas v. Johnson,* and *Snyder v. Phelps*? Why or why not?

6. Compare the Court's notion of student rights in *Tinker* and *Morse*. Can they be reconciled? How much freedom of speech should public high school students have?

SELECTED READINGS

ANASTAPLO, GEORGE. The Constitutionalist: Notes on the First Amendment. Dallas, Tex.: Southern Methodist University Press, 1971.

BARRON, JEROME A., AND C. THOMAS DIENES. Handbook of Free Speech and Free Press. Boston: Little, Brown, 1979.

BERNS, WALTER. Freedom, Virtue, & the First Amendment. Baton Rouge: Louisiana State University Press, 1957.

———. The First Amendment and the Future of American Democracy. Chicago: Gateway Editions, 1985.

BORK, ROBERT H. "Neutral Principles and Some First Amendment Problems." 47 Indiana Law Journal 1 (1971).

BRENNAN, WILLIAM J., JR. "The Supreme Court and the Meiklejohn Interpretation of the First Amendment." 79 Harvard Law Review 1 (1965).

CAHN, EDMUND. "Mr. Justice Black and First Amendment Absolutes: A Public Interview." 37 New York University Law Review 549 (1962).

CHAFEE, ZECHARIAH, JR. "Freedom of Speech in War Time." 32 Harvard Law Review 932 (1919).

———. FREE SPEECH IN THE UNITED STATES. Cambridge, Mass.: Harvard University Press, 1941.

EMERSON, THOMAS I. The System of Freedom of Expression. New York: Random House, 1970.

FELLMAN, DAVID. The Constitutional Right of Association. Chicago: University of Chicago Press, 1963.

FINAN, CHRISTOPHER M. From the Palmer Raids to the Patriot Act: A History of the Fight for Free Speech in America. Boston: Beacon Press, 2007.

FISS, OWEN M. The Irony of Free Speech. Cambridge, Mass.: Harvard University Press, 1996.

FRIENDLY, FRED W. The Good Guys, the Bad Guys, and the First Amendment: Free Speech vs. Fairness in Broadcasting. New York: Random House, 1975.

GOLDSTEIN, ROBERT JUSTIN. Flag Burning and Free Speech: The Case of Texas v. Johnson. Lawrence: University Press of Kansas, 2000.

GREENEWALT, KENT. Fighting Words: Individuals, Communities, and Liberties of Speech. Princeton: Princeton University Press, 1995.

HAIMAN, FRANKLYN S. Speech and Law in a Free Society. Chicago: University of Chicago Press, 1981.

HENTOFF, NAT. Free Speech for Me—But Not for Thee. New York: HarperCollins, 1992.

HEUMANN, MILTON, AND THOMAS W. CHURCH, EDS. Hate Speech on Campus: Cases, Case Studies, and Commentary. Boston: Northeastern Univ. Press, 1997.

KALVEN, HARRY, JR. "The Concept of the Public Forum: Cox v. Louisiana." 1965 Supreme Court Review 1.

———. A Worthy Tradition: Freedom of Speech in America. New York: Harper and Row, 1988.

LEWIS, ANTHONY. Freedom for the Thought We Hate: A Biography of the First Amendment. New York: Basic Books, 2007.

MEIKLEJOHN, ALEXANDER. "The First Amendment Is an Absolute." 1961 Supreme Court Review 245.

———. Political Freedom: The Constitutional Powers of the People. New York: Oxford University Press, 1965.

RABBAN, DAVID M. Free Speech in Its Forgotten Years. New York: Cambridge University Press, 1997.

SCHIRO, RICHARD. "Commercial Speech: The Demise of a Chimera." 1976 Supreme Court Review 45.

SHAPIRO, MARTIN. Freedom of Speech: The Supreme Court and Judicial Review. Englewood Cliffs, N.J.: Prentice-Hall, 1966.

SMOLLA, RODNEY A. Free Speech in an Open Society. New York: Alfred A. Knopf, 1992.

VOLOKH, EUGENE. "The Trouble with 'Public Discourse' as a Limitation on Free Speech." 97 Virginia Law Review 567 (2011)

———. "Symbolic Expression and the Original Meaning of the First Amendment." 97 Georgetown Law Journal 1057 (2009).

11

Freedom of the Press

The Supreme Court often treats free speech and free press as complementary parts of a larger value designed to promote "freedom of expression." At times it has subordinated freedom of the press to make it a right derived from freedom of speech. Such formulations distort the historical record. The right to a free press has stronger roots than the right to free speech. Of the eleven original states that adopted revolutionary constitutions, nine protected freedom of press and only one (Pennsylvania) protected speech.

Freedom of the press implies two rights: the right to publish without prior restraint, and the right to publish without prosecution or penalty for the views advanced. The first right is nearly inviolable. A heavy presumption lies against any governmental effort to restrain a publication, although there is some ambiguity about matters involving national security. The second right is more circumscribed, permitting action against publishers who print materials considered libelous or obscene. A separate issue involves the collision that occurs between the sometimes competing interests of a free press and a fair trial.

A. THE EVOLUTION OF PRESS FREEDOMS

Many of the battles for individual liberty from the sixteenth to the eighteenth centuries in England centered around the struggle for a free press. Government officials and church authorities tried to suppress writings that threatened their control. Both prosecutions and persecutions were used to silence critics and free thinkers. Authors were punished for views considered to be seditious or heretical. In time, a system of censorship developed to prevent such writings from being published. One of the early protests against censorship and prior restraint came from the pen of the poet John Milton, especially *AREOPAGITICA* (1644).

English law eventually prohibited prior restraint on publications. As explained by William Blackstone, the liberty of the press "consists in laying no *previous* restraints upon publications, and not in freedom from censure for criminal matter when published." The right to publish was protected, but if an individual published material found to be "improper, mischievous or illegal, he must take the consequence of his own temerity." 4 Blackstone, Commentaries, 151–52. English law also permitted the government to punish whoever published "seditious libel," a vague category that invites action against whoever offends or annoys the government.

Zenger's Trial

The trial of John Peter Zenger in 1735 represents a watershed in the fight for a free press in America. William Cosby, New York's royal governor, became embroiled in a local power struggle. The *New-York Weekly Journal* was established to oppose the royal newspaper, the *New-York Gazette*. Zenger, serving as the printer for the opposition newspaper, helped run the first independent journal in America. A series of articles in the *New-York Weekly Journal* promoted the theory of a free press and attacked the Cosby administration.

Cosby put Zenger in prison for seditious libel. However, a grand jury decided against indicting Zenger, and the New York Assembly refused to carry out the request of Cosby's Council that several

Andrew Hamilton's Appeal to the Jury

... Gentlemen of the Jury, it is to you we must now appeal, for Witness, to the Truth of the Facts we have offered, and are denied the Liberty to prove; ...

... I beg Leave to insist, that the Right of complaining or remonstrating is natural; And the Restraint upon this natural Right is the law only, and that those Restraints can only extend to what is *false*; For as it is Truth alone which can excuse or justify any Man for complaining of a bad Administration, I as frankly agree, that nothing ought to excuse a man who raises a false Charge or Accusation, even against a private Person, and that no manner of Allowance ought to be made to him who does so against a publick Magistrate. *Truth* ought to govern the whole Affair of Libels, ...

I am truely very unequal to such an Undertaking on many Accounts. And you see I labour under the Weight of many Years, and am born down with great Infirmities of Body; yet Old and Weak as I am, I should think of it my Duty, if required, to go to the utmost Part of the Land, where my Service could be of any Use in assisting to quench the Flame of Prosecutions upon Informations, set on Foot by the Government, to deprive a People of the Right of Remonstrating (and complaining too) of the arbitrary Attempts of Men in Power. Men who injure and oppress the People under the Administration provoke them to cry out and complain; and then make that very Complaint the Foundation for new Oppressions and Prosecutions. I wish I could say there were no Instances of this Kind. But to conclude; the Question before the Court and you, Gentlemen of the Jury, is not of small nor private Concern, it is not the Cause of a poor Printer, nor of *New-York* alone, which you are now trying: No! It may in its Consequence, affect every Freeman that lives under a British Government on the main of *America*. It is the best Cause. It is the Cause of Liberty; and I make no Doubt but your upright Conduct, this Day, will not only entitle you to the Love and Esteem of your Fellow-Citizens; but every Man who prefers Freedom to a Life of Slavery will bless and honour You, as Men who have baffled the Attempt of Tyranny; and by an impartial and uncorrupt Verdict, have laid a noble Foundation for securing to ourselves, our Posterity, and our Neighbours, That, to which Nature and the Laws of our Country have given us a Right — The Liberty — both of exposing and opposing arbitrary Power (in these Parts of the World, at least) by speaking and writing Truth.

SOURCE: Leonard W. Levy, ed., Freedom of the Press from Zenger to Jefferson 48, 54, 58–59 (1996).

issues of the *New-York Weekly Journal* be burned. Zenger was imprisoned a second time for seditious libel. Another grand jury rejected indictment. The New York attorney general relied on an information (an alternative to grand jury action) to charge Zenger for publishing "false, scandalous, malicious, and seditious" libels. Andrew Hamilton, a famous trial attorney in America, argued that Zenger's newspapers had not published "false" material. He said that Zenger had published the truth and had the right to do so. The trial judge advised Hamilton that truth was not a defense under the law; the material was libelous even if true. Hamilton appealed to the jury to uphold the cause of liberty and a free press (see box). The jury returned a verdict of not guilty. Although the law had not changed, the jury action planted a seed to make truth a defense in a libel case. The threat of seditious libel virtually disappeared in America after Zenger's trial.

The Framers' Intent

Except for brief periods in its history, America placed a high value on the importance of a free press. Leonard Levy, a leading scholar of the First Amendment, wrote an influential work in 1960 in which he challenged the prevailing belief that the framers were deeply committed to press freedoms. In *Legacy of Suppression*, Levy made three major points: the First Amendment was not intended to prevent the state from suppressing seditious libel; American legislatures, especially during the colonial period, were "far more oppressive" than common-law courts; and the Bill of Rights was more the "chance product of political expediency" than a principled commitment to personal liberties. Moreover, he concluded that the Jeffersonians, strident critics of the Sedition Act of 1798, were not much more tolerant of political dissent than the Federalists had been.

In a revised version of this work in 1985, entitled *Emergence of a Free Press*, Levy examined new evidence and concluded that the American experience with a free press was broad in scope. "Press criticism of government policies and politicians, on both state and national levels, during the war [of Independence] and in the peaceful years of the 1780s and 1790s, raged as contemptuously and scorchingly as it had against Great Britain in the period between the Stamp Act and the battle of Lexington." The presses in the states operated "as if the law of seditious libel did not exist." He explained that if one examines American *practices* rather than American law and theory, there exists not a legacy of suppression but rather a "legacy of liberty" (p. x).

The Sedition Act

A period of suppression certainly includes the Sedition Act of 1798, which provided penalties for writing, printing, uttering, or publishing "false, scandalous and malicious" statements against the federal government, either House of Congress, or the President. 1 Stat. 596, §2. Still, the principle from the Zenger trial prevailed. Any person prosecuted under the act had the right to "give in evidence in his defence, the truth of the matter contained in the publication charged as a libel." Moreover, the jury had the right to "determine the law and the fact." Id., §3. The debate on the Sedition Act demonstrates that the principle of a free press was strongly held at that time (see reading). The statute was so unpopular that it fatally wounded its sponsor, the Federalist party, and expired under its own terms in 1801.

The constitutionality of the Sedition Act was never determined in the courts. Instead, it was decided by the people in the national elections of 1800, which drove the Federalist party out of office and into oblivion. President Jefferson called the Sedition Act a "nullity" and pardoned every person prosecuted under it (see box in Chapter 1). He believed that prosecution for seditious libel could be done only by the states, not the federal government. Later, Congress pronounced the statute "unconstitutional, null, and void," and appropriated funds to reimburse those who had been subjected to fines (see reading in Chapter 1). The Supreme Court later acknowledged that the Sedition Act was struck down not by a court of law but by "the court of history." New York Times Co. v. Sullivan, 376 U.S. 254, 276 (1964).

Although Jefferson condemned the Sedition Act, once in power he was willing to use the English common law notion of seditious libel to punish Federalist newspapers that criticized his administration. Many of these cases were brought at the state level, but one case that reached the U.S. Supreme Court involved editors of a Federalist newspaper in Connecticut who were being prosecuted by the Jefferson administration. The Court noted that it was the first time it had been faced with the question whether federal courts had jurisdiction over seditious libel. It concluded that the issue had "been long since settled in public opinion," meaning that Congress had yet to establish by statute that criticism of the national government was a criminal act. In short, constitutional law was decided by the people, working through their representatives, not by the courts. Whatever the law of England, the exercise of criminal jurisdiction in common law cases was not within the implied powers of federal courts. United States v. Hudson and Goodwin, 11 U.S. (7 Cr.) 32 (1812); United States v. Coolidge, 14 U.S. (1 Wheat.) 415 (1816); Leonard W. Levy, Jefferson and Civil Liberties: The Darker Side (1963).

John Milton
Areopagitica (1644)

In this classic defense of a free press, Milton appeals to the Parliament of England to reject licenses for printing. He had learned of an order that would prohibit the printing of any book, pamphlet, or paper unless first approved and licensed. His essay is one of the most compelling arguments against using prior restraint to suppress written materials.

If ye be thus resolved, as it were injury to think ye were not, I know not what should withhold me from presenting ye with a fit instance wherein to show both that love of truth which ye eminently profess, and that uprightness of your judgment which is not wont to be partial to yourselves; by judging over again that order which ye have ordained *to regulate printing: that no book, pamphlet, or paper shall be henceforth printed, unless the same be first approved and licensed by such,* or at least one of such, as shall be thereto appointed. For that part which preserves justly every man's copy to himself, or provides for the poor, I touch not; only wish they be not made pretences to abuse and persecute honest and painful men who offend not in either of these particulars. But that other clause of licensing books, which we thought had died with his brother *quadragesimal* and *matrimonial* when the prelates expired, I shall now attend with such a homily as shall lay before ye, first, the inventors of it to be those whom ye will be loth to own; next, what is to be thought in general of reading; whatever sort the books be; and that this order avails nothing to the suppressing of scandalous, seditious, and libelous books, which were mainly intended to be suppressed; last, that it will be primely to the discouragement of all learning, and the stop of truth, not only by disexercising and blunting our abilities in what we know already, but by hindering and cropping the discovery that might be yet further made both in religious and civil wisdom.

I deny not but that it is of greatest concernment in the church and commonwealth to have a vigilant eye how books demean themselves, as well as men, and thereafter to confine, imprison, and do sharpest justice on them as malefactors. For books are not absolutely dead things, but do contain a potency of life in them to be as active as that soul was whose progeny they are; nay, they do preserve as in a vial the purest efficacy and extraction of that living intellect that bred them. I know they are as lively, and as vigorously productive, as those fabulous dragon's teeth; and being sown up and down, may chance to spring up armed men. And yet, on the other hand, unless wariness be used, as good almost kill a man as kill a good book: who kills a man kills a reasonable creature, God's image; but he who destroys a good book, kills reason itself, kills the image of God, as it were, in the eye. Many a man lives a burden to the earth; but a good book is the precious life-blood of a master spirit, embalmed and treasured up on purpose to a life beyond life....

... If we think to regulate printing, thereby to rectify manners, we must regulate all recreations and pastimes, all that is delightful to man. No music must be heard, no song be set or sung, but what is grave and Doric. There must be licensing dancers, that no gesture, motion, or deportment be taught our youth, but what by their allowance shall be thought honest; for such Plato was provided of. It will ask more than the work of twenty licensers to examine all the lutes, the violins, and the guitars in every house; they must not be suffered to prattle as they do, but must be licensed what they may say. And who shall silence all the airs and madrigals that whisper softness in chambers? ...

Next, what more national corruption, for which England hears ill abroad, than household gluttony? Who shall be the rectors of our daily rioting? And what shall be done to inhibit the multitudes that frequent those houses where drunkenness is sold and harbored? Our garments also should be referred to the licensing of some more sober work-masters, to see them cut into a less wanton garb. Who shall regulate all the mixed conversation of our youth, male and female together, as is the fashion of this country? ...

What should ye do then, should ye suppress all this flowery crop of knowledge and new light sprung up and yet springing daily in this city? Should ye set an oligarchy of twenty engrossers over it, to bring a famine upon our minds again, when we shall know nothing but what is measured to us by their bushel? Believe it, Lords and Commons, they who counsel ye to such a suppressing do as good as bid ye suppress yourselves; and I will soon show how. If it be desired to know the immediate cause of all this free writing and free speaking, there cannot be assigned a truer than your own mild and free and humane government; it is the liberty, Lords and Commons, which your own valorous and happy counsels have purchased us, liberty which is the nurse of all great wits. This is that which hath rarefied and enlightened our spirits like the influence of heaven; this is that which hath enfranchised, enlarged, and lifted up our apprehensions degrees above themselves. Ye cannot make us now less capable, less knowing, less eagerly pursuing of the truth, unless ye first make yourselves, that made us so, less the lovers, less the founders of our true liberty. We can grow ignorant again, brutish, formal, and slavish, as ye found us; but you then must first become that which ye cannot be, oppressive, arbitrary, and tyrannous, as they were from whom ye have freed us....

House Debate on the Sedition Act of 1798

When John Adams was elected President in 1796, there was concern that the United States might be drawn into war against France. To control foreigners in this country and a press that lashed out against the administration's policy, Congress passed the Alien and Sedition Acts of 1798. The Sedition Act declared that if any person "shall write, print, utter or publish ... any false, scandalous and malicious writing or writings against the government of the United States, or either house of the Congress of the United States, or the President of the United States, with intent to defame the said government, or either house of the said Congress, or the said President, or to bring them, or either of them, into contempt or disrepute; or to excite against them, or either of them, the hatred of the good people of the United States, or to stir up sedition," the person would be subject to fines and imprisonment. The debate below, from the House of Representatives, is taken from 8 Annals of Congress 2093–94, 2097, 2105, 2109, 2139–40, 2147–48, 2152, 2164. Jeffersonian Republicans are identified as Democrats. The bill passed the House, 44 to 41.

[Mr. Allen, Federalist of Connecticut] — I hope this bill will not be rejected. If ever there was a nation which required a law of this kind, it is this. Let gentlemen look at certain papers printed in this city and elsewhere, and ask themselves whether an unwarrantable and dangerous combination does not exist to overturn and ruin the Government by publishing the most shameless falsehoods against the Representatives of the people of all denominations, that they are hostile to free Governments and genuine liberty, and of course to the welfare of this country; that they ought, therefore, to be displaced, and that the people ought to raise an *insurrection* against the Government.

... Permit me to read a paragraph from "The Time-Piece," a paper printed in New York:

"When such a character attempts by antiquated and exploded sophistry, by Jesuitical arguments, to extinguish the sentiment of liberty, 'tis fit the mask should be torn off from this meaner species of aristocracy than history has condescended to record; where a person without patriotism, without philosophy, without a taste for the fine arts, building his pretensions on a gross and indigested compilation of statutes and precedents, is jostled into the Chief Magistracy by the ominous combination of old Tories with old opinions, and old Whigs with new, 'tis fit this mock Monarch, with his Court, composed of Tories and speculators, ..."

Gentlemen contend for the liberty of opinions and of the press. Let me ask them whether they seriously think the liberty of the press authorizes such publications? The President of the United States is here called "a person without patriotism, without philosophy, and a mock monarch," and the free election of the people is pronounced "a jostling him into the Chief Magistracy by the ominous combination of old Tories with old opinions, and old Whigs with new."

If this be not a conspiracy against Government and people, I know not what to understand from [*such writing*] ... The freedom of the press and opinions was never understood to give the right of publishing falsehoods and slanders, nor of exciting sedition, insurrection, and slaughter, with impunity. A man was always answerable for the malicious publication of falsehood; and what more does this bill require? ...

[Edward Livingston, Democrat from New York.] ... The gentleman ... has said, that provided the law is clear and well defined, and the trial by jury is preserved, he knew of no law which could infringe the liberty of the press. If this be true, Congress might restrict all printing at once. We have, said he, nothing to do but to make the law precise, and then we may forbid a newspaper to be printed, and make it death for any man to attempt it!

If this be the extent to which this bill goes, it is ... an abridgment of the liberty of the press, which the Constitution has said shall not be abridged....

[Albert Gallatin, Democrat from Pennsylvania.] Was the gentleman afraid, or rather was Administration afraid, that in this instance error could not be successfully opposed by truth? The American Government had heretofore subsisted, it had acquired strength, it had grown on the affection of the people, it had been fully supported without the assistance of laws similar to the bill now on the table. It had been able to repel opposition by the single weapon of argument. And at present, when out of ten presses in the country nine were employed on the side of Administration, such is their want of confidence in the purity of their own views and motives, that they even fear the unequal contest, and require the help of force in order to suppress the limited circulation of the opinions of those who did not approve all their measures....

[JOHN NICHOLAS, Democrat from Virginia] rose, he said, to ask an explanation of the principles upon which this bill is founded....

Gentlemen have said that this bill is not to restrict the liberty of the press but its licentiousness. He wished gentlemen to inform him where they drew the line between this liberty and licentiousness of which they speak; he wished to know where the one commenced and the other ended? Will they say the one is truth, and the other falsehood! Gentlemen cannot believe for a moment that such a definition will satisfy the inquiry. The great difficulty which has existed in all free Governments, would, long since, have been done away, if it could have been effected by a simple declaration of this kind. It has been the object of all regulations with respect to the press, to destroy the only means by which the people can examine and become acquainted with the conduct of persons employed in their Government....

[HARRISON GRAY OTIS, Federalist from Massachusetts.] It was, therefore, most evident to his mind, that the Constitution of the United States, prior to the amendments that have been added to it, secured to the National Government the cognizance of all the crimes enumerated in the bill, and it only remained to be considered whether those amendments divested it of this power....

... [A]lthough in several of the State constitutions, the liberty of speech and of the press were guarded by the most express and unequivocal language, the Legislatures and Judicial departments of those States had adopted the definitions of the English law, and provided for the punishment of defamatory and seditious libels....

After having given this short sketch of the features of this bill, Mr. [*Gallatin*] said ... that laws against writings of this kind had uniformly been one of the most powerful engines used by tyrants to prevent the diffusion of knowledge, to throw a veil on their folly or their crimes, to satisfy those mean passions which always denote little minds, and to perpetuate their own tyranny. The principles of the law of political libels were to be found in the rescripts of the worst Emperors of Rome, in the decisions of the Star Chamber. Princes of elevated minds, Governments actuated by pure motives, had ever despised the slanders of malice, and listened to the animadversions made on their conduct. They knew that the proper weapon to combat error was truth, and that to resort to coercion and punishments in order to suppress writings attacking their measures, was to confess that these could not be defended by any other means.

B. REGULATING THE PRESS

Like other First Amendment freedoms, the press is subject to restrictions. Initially, state actions that abridged the press were not subject to redress in the federal courts. Those matters were left to state and local judgments. Patterson v. Colorado, 205 U.S. 454 (1907); Fox v. Washington, 236 U.S. 273 (1915). In 1931, however, the Supreme Court held that a free press is within the liberty safeguarded by the Due Process Clause of the Fourteenth Amendment. The case involved Minnesota's effort to suppress the "malicious, scandalous and defamatory" articles of Jay Near, an indefatigable critic of corruption in the Minneapolis government. The effect of the state law, said the Court, was to place a publisher under censorship. Except for certain conditions that did not apply in this case, the government could not impose censorship or prior restraint on newspapers and other publications. NEAR v. MINNESOTA, 283 U.S. 697 (1931).

On the other hand, censorship and prior restraint in the movie industry has been more successful. Beginning in 1907, states created censoring boards to screen movies for possible indecent or immoral content. Blocking a film at that stage kept it from circulating in the theaters. Denied a license to show the film, producers of films could delete scenes and resubmit the movie for another review. Laura Wittern-Keller and Raymond J. Haberski, Jr., The Miracle Case: Film Censorship and the Supreme Court, 16–19 (2008).

The Court later identified other unconstitutional regulations on the press. Although publications can be taxed like any other business, taxes may not be applied to discriminate against newspapers, limit their circulation, or subject publications to penalties that amount to previous restraint. Grosjean v. American Press Co., 297 U.S. 233 (1936). The Court struck down tax systems that pose the risk of discrimination or suppression. Arkansas Writers' Project, Inc. v. Ragland, 481 U.S. 221 (1987); Minneapolis Star v. Minnesota Comm'r of Rev., 460 U.S. 575 (1983). Although states may not single out the press and apply discriminatory taxes, it may tax cable television operations while exempting newspapers and magazines provided there is no intent to censor the expressive activities of cable TV. Thus, some media may be taxed differently from others. Leathers v. Medlock, 499 U.S. 439 (1991).

In 1991, a unanimous court struck down a New York law designed to prevent criminals from profiting from books and movies about their illegal actions. The legislation placed payments received by criminals for books or other works in a fund to compensate victims of crimes. In this case, New York's "Son of Sam" law was applied to a book called *Wiseguy,* which described the activities of a Mafia foot soldier. The book was later turned into the hit movie, *GoodFellas.* The Court held that the law was "significantly overinclusive" and would have prevented the publication of such works as Thoreau's *Civil Disobedience* and Saint Augustine's *Confessions,* both of which described the author's illegal actions. Simon & Schuster v. New York Crime Victims Bd., 502 U.S. 105 (1991).

Government cannot require licenses to distribute literature; this is a form of censorship. Pamphlets and leaflets have been "historic weapons in the defense of liberty." Lovell v. Griffin, 303 U.S. 444, 452 (1938). Government may not require people to print their name and address on a handbill. Anonymity is often necessary for the communication of ideas, as witnessed by the fictitious names of those who wrote the *Federalist Papers.* Talley v. California, 362 U.S. 60, 65 (1960). The principle in *Talley* was reiterated in 1995 when the Court said that anonymous pamphleteering "is a shield from the tyranny of the majority." McIntyre v. Ohio Elections Comm'n, 514 U.S. 334, 357 (1995).

It is unconstitutional to ban the distribution of handbills on the ground that prohibition prevents littering of the streets. The purpose of keeping the streets clean "is insufficient to justify an ordinance which prohibits a person rightfully on a public street from handing literature to one willing to receive it. Any burden imposed upon the city authorities in cleaning and caring for the streets as an indirect consequence of such distribution results from the constitutional protection of the freedom of speech and press." Schneider v. State, 308 U.S. 147, 162 (1939). See also Jamison v. Texas, 318 U.S. 413 (1943). The distribution of informational literature is an essential part of a free press and a democratic society. Organization for a Better Austin v. Keefe, 402 U.S. 415 (1971). (See box on the next page for other decisions regulating the press.)

Legislatures retain some latitude in regulating the content of newspapers. In 1973, the Court upheld a Pittsburgh ordinance that prohibited newspapers from printing ads that listed job opportunities under headings of "Male Interest" and "Female Interest." Such labels perpetuated sex discrimination and unequal pay. Pittsburgh Press Co. v. Human Rel. Comm'n, 413 U.S. 376 (1973). Advertisements in newspapers can be regulated because they are "classic examples of commercial speech." Id. at 385. The Court said it had "no doubt that a newspaper constitutionally could be forbidden to publish a want ad proposing a sale of narcotics or soliciting prostitutes." Id. at 388.

A unique case arose in 1997, in which a publisher was held liable in a civil suit for publishing a hitman manual. The publisher, Paladin Press, acknowledged that it realized that its book, *Hit Man: A Technical Manual for Independent Contractors,* would be used by criminals and would-be criminals in the solicitation, planning, and commission of murder and murder for hire. A contract killer relied on the 130-page manual to kill someone's wife, eight-year-old child, and the child's nurse. The First Amendment did not bar a wrongful death action against Paladin. Rice v. Paladin Enterprises Inc., 128 F.3d 233 (4th Cir. 1997), cert. denied, 523 U.S. 1074 (1998). On March 21, 1999, Paladin Press agreed to a multi-million dollar settlement.

Regulating News Coverage

Regulation of newspaper advertisements does not permit regulation of news coverage. A unanimous Court in 1974 held that government may not compel a newspaper to print a response from a politi-

Regulating the Press

Acceptable regulations

Government may punish those who call at a home, for the purpose of distributing literature, when the occupant posts an unwillingness to be disturbed. Martin v. Struthers, 319 U.S. 141 (1943).

Uninvited door-to-door canvassing by a publisher's representative can be proscribed as an invasion of privacy. Breard v. Alexandria, 341 U.S. 622 (1951).

Publishers are not exempt from agency subpoena powers. Okla. Press Pub. Co. v. Walling, 327 U.S. 186 (1946).

Prison officials may prohibit interviews between prison inmates and reporters who attempt to investigate and publicize prison conditions. Houchins v. KQED, Inc., 438 U.S. 1 (1978); Saxbe v. Washington Post, 417 U.S. 843 (1974); Pell v. Procunier, 417 U.S. 817 (1974).

Invalid regulations

Although Congress may exclude certain materials from the mails, the Postmaster General cannot act as a censor by deciding which items are mailable and which are not. Hannegan v. Esquire, Inc., 327 U.S. 146 (1946).

Laws may not prohibit the distribution of magazines on such vague grounds that they consist of bloody and lustful criminal deeds. Winters v. New York, 333 U.S. 507 (1948).

Statutes on "corrupt practices" (prohibiting electioneering or soliciting of votes on election day) cannot be applied against newspapers that publish views on election day. Mills v. Alabama, 384 U.S. 214 (1966).

Public officials may not be given "unbridled discretion" in granting or denying applications from newspapers to place newsracks on public property. Lakewood, City of, v. Plain Dealer Pub. Co., 486 U.S. 750 (1988).

cal candidate to a critical editorial. Although "access advocates" argued that chain newspapers and nationwide wire services no longer provided a true marketplace of diverse opinions, the Court refused to permit the government to dictate to the press the contents of its news stories and editorials. Miami Herald Publishing Co. v. Tornillo, 418 U.S. 241 (1974). Another unanimous opinion in 1978 struck down a Virginia statute that made it a crime to divulge information regarding proceedings before a state judicial review commission that received complaints about judges' disability or misconduct. The Court held that the First Amendment does not permit the criminal punishment of third persons (in this case the press), who were strangers to the proceedings, from publishing truthful information. Landmark Communications, Inc. v. Virginia, 435 U.S. 829 (1978). Building on *Landmark Communications,* the Court in 1990 unanimously struck down a Florida law that prohibited witnesses before a state grand jury from ever disclosing their testimony in any manner. A reporter wanted to do a story based in part on his testimony before a grand jury. The Court held that the state law violated the First Amendment to the extent that it prohibited grand jury witnesses from disclosing their testimony after the grand jury's term had ended. Butterworth v. Smith, 494 U.S. 624 (1990).

In 1989, the Court reversed a ruling that imposed compensatory and punitive damages against a newspaper that printed the name of a rape victim. Although the publication violated a state law, the woman's full name had appeared in a police report available to the press. The Florida Star v. B.J.F. 491 U.S. 524 (1989). Similarly, a newspaper is free to publish a rape victim's name that was obtained from judicial records open to public inspection. Cox Broadcasting Co. v. Cohn, 420 U.S. 469 (1975). If an individual gives a newspaper information after receiving a promise of confidentiality and the newspaper later identifies the individual, the First Amendment does not prevent the person from suing the newspaper for damages on the ground that a promise had been breached. Cohen v. Cowles Media Co., 501 U.S. 663 (1991).

The interests of a free press suffered a major setback in 1978 when the Court decided that law enforcement officials could obtain a warrant and come onto the premises of a newspaper to conduct a search for evidence regarding a third party. The newspaper itself had committed no wrong. Zurcher v. Stanford Daily, 436 U.S. 547 (1978). After the press appealed to Congress for help, legislation was enacted in 1980 to direct police to use subpoenas as a less intrusive method of obtaining documents. The congressional response is described in greater detail in Chapter 14.

National Security

In 1931, in striking down Minnesota's law as a prior restraint on the press, the Supreme Court noted that censorship would be constitutional under certain conditions. "No one would question but that a government might prevent actual obstruction to its recruiting service or the publication of the sailing dates of transports or the number and location of troops." Near v. Minnesota, 283 U.S. 697, 716 (1931). The Nixon administration thought this type of governmental need had arrived when it sought an injunction to prevent the publication of a classified study entitled "History of U.S. Decision-Making Process on Viet Nam Policy." The administration argued that publication of these materials (the "Pentagon Papers") would be injurious to national security. However, the Supreme Court, with a 6–3 majority, held that the administration had failed to meet the "heavy burden" of justifying prior restraint on a publication. A brief per curiam opinion preceded a collection of concurrences and dissents. NEW YORK TIMES V. UNITED STATES, 403 U.S. 713 (1971).

Several years later, the Carter administration attempted to prevent the publication in *The Progressive* magazine of an article that claimed to describe the design of an H-bomb. A federal district court judge issued a preliminary injunction against the publication, recognizing that this was the first instance of prior restraint to his knowledge. Balanced against a free press was this consideration: "A mistake against the United States could pave the way for thermonuclear annihilation for us all. In that event, our right to life is extinguished and the right to publish becomes moot." United States v. Progressive, 467 F.Supp. 990, 996 (W.D. Wis. 1979). As it turned out, essentially the same material appeared in another publication, without a nuclear holocaust, and the case was dismissed. 610 F.2d 819 (7th Cir. 1979); Morland v. Sprecher, 443 U.S. 709 (1979). *The Progressive* published the article in its November 1979 issue.

Questions of press and national security are at issue when the CIA and other federal agencies require employees, as a condition of employment, to sign a statement agreeing not to publish anything relating to the agency without first submitting the manuscript and obtaining approval. This condition applies both during and after employment. Frank Snepp, a former CIA employee, published a critical evaluation of the agency without first seeking approval. Although the book contained no classified information, the Supreme Court affirmed a lower court's injunction on future writings by Snepp, requiring that he submit manuscripts to the CIA. Snepp was also ordered to give the government his earnings from the book (*Decent Interval*) he published without CIA's clearance. Instead of inviting briefs and holding oral argument to fully explore the issues, the Court quickly released an unsigned per curiam opinion. In a dissent, joined by Brennan and Marshall, Stevens objected that the Court "should not reach out to decide a question not necessarily presented to it, as it has done in this case." Snepp v. United States, 444 U.S. 507, 525 (1980).[1]

On May 11, 2006, Attorney General Alberto Gonzales raised the possibility that reporters for the *New York Times* could be prosecuted for publishing classified information about National Security Agency (NSA) eavesdropping initiated by the Bush administration after the terrorist attacks of 9/11. The newspaper had revealed the operation of the secret program in mid-December 2005. Gonzales referred to the Espionage Act of 1917 as one source of authority for such prosecutions. His remarks

---

1. See Frank Snepp, Irreparable Harm (1999); United States v. Marchetti, 466 F.2d 1309 (4th Cir. 1972), cert. denied, 409 U.S. 1063 (1972); and Knopf v. Colby, 509 F.2d 1362 (4th Cir. 1975), cert. denied, 421 U.S. 992 (1975).

Shield Law

Newspaper, radio or television broadcasting station personnel need not disclose source of information. — No person shall be compelled to disclose in any legal proceeding or trial before any court, or before any grand or petit jury, or before the presiding officer of any tribunal, or his agent or agents, or before the general assembly, or any committee thereof, or before any city or county legislative body, or any committee thereof, or elsewhere, the source of any information procured or obtained by him, and published in a newspaper or by a radio or television broadcasting station by which he is engaged or employed, or with which he is connected.

SOURCE: Kentucky Revised Statutes, Annotated, § 421.100 (1992). (§ 1649d-1: amend. Acts 1952, ch. 121.)

---

indicated that the administration might act punitively toward media actions that questioned or challenged the use of presidential power. In the end, however, no prosecution occurred.

Reporter's Privilege

A landmark ruling in 1972 involved the question whether newspaper reporters can be compelled to respond to a grand jury subpoena and answer questions. Reporters argue that their sources are privileged and cannot be revealed without destroying their access to informers who demand anonymity. They also express concern that the forced disclosure of information to grand juries will make them appear to be agents of government. However, a 5–4 Court decided that the need to investigate and prosecute criminal charges overrides a reporter's rights, including the protection of confidential sources. BRANZBURG v. HAYES, 408 U.S. 665 (1972). Some of the states already had "shield laws" to protect reporters from court orders. Other state laws protecting reporters were added after *Branzburg*. Most of the states and the District of Columbia have such laws (see box).

The Supreme Court acknowledged that Congress has the power to enact similar legislation. Id. at 706. In 2006, 2009, and 2010 Congress considered a federal shield law that sought to balance the competing claims of journalists and prosecutors in these controversies. The "Free Flow of Information Act" prohibited federal courts from compelling reporters to disclose confidential sources but allowed exceptions if the court found that alternative means of obtaining the information had been exhausted, the information was "critical" to the prosecution, and the failure to disclose was "contrary to the public interest." The privilege was denied to reporters who witnessed criminal activity or where the information was needed to prevent a death, serious bodily harm, and threats to national security. In 2008 and 2009, the House of Representatives passed the legislation and the Senate Judiciary Committee reported the legislation in 2009, but it was blocked for floor action. Critics contended that the legislation could protect unlawful leaks of classified information and that the definition of "journalist" was too broad, including bloggers and people who might pose as journalists. The legislation was introduced in the House again in September 2011 but there was little reason to believe it would gain passage given the opposition.

In 2001, Vanessa Leggett was jailed for refusing to cooperate in the investigation of a Houston homicide. In preparation for a book, she had interviewed people familiar with the suspect, the victim, and the investigation. Prosecutors wanted her notes and tape recordings. When she refused to turn them over, a federal district judge cited her for civil contempt and she remained in prison for 168 days until the grand jury disbanded on January 4, 2002. In 2004, several reporters were threatened with jail terms for refusing to disclose their sources. One dispute involved the leak of a CIA officer's identity (Valerie Plame). In July 2005, Judith Miller of the *New York Times* was jailed for refusing to testify before a grand jury on the Plame issue. She was released on September 29, 2005 and testified the following day.

A second controversy concerned reporters who refused to disclose the names of sources who might have given them information about Dr. Wen Ho Lee, a nuclear scientist once suspected of espionage. After being held in solitary confinement for nine months, he was cleared of all accusations except a single charge of illegally downloading classified information. He claimed that federal officials had violated privacy laws by leaking damaging information about him to the press. On August 14, 2004, a federal judge held reporters from four major news organizations in contempt for refusing to name their sources. Finally, in June 2006, the federal government and five media organizations agreed to give Lee $1.6 million to settle the case. Here is another example where a controversial constitutional issue is resolved and decided outside the courts.

In 2008, a court held Toni Locy (a former reporter) in contempt for refusing to name her confidential sources who had discussed the possible role of Steven Hatfill in the 2001 anthrax attacks. He was suing the government for leaking information damaging to his reputation. In June 2008, the Justice Department announced it would pay him $5.8 million to settle his lawsuit and several months later officially cleared him of any potential charges.

Free-press conflicts are not always between the government and a publisher. At times, they involve one publisher against another, with the issue decided largely on statutory, not constitutional, grounds. In one case, President Gerald Ford signed a contract with Harper & Row to publish his memoirs. Harper & Row then negotiated a prepublication agreement with *Time* magazine to print parts of the manuscript. Shortly before the scheduled release of *Time*'s article, there appeared an unauthorized article in *The Nation* magazine, including at least 300 to 400 words verbatim from the unpublished Ford manuscript. In interpreting the Copyright Act passed by Congress, the Supreme Court held that *The Nation*'s article was not a "fair use" sanctioned by the statute. Harper & Row v. Nation Enterprises, 471 U.S. 539 (1985).

Near v. Minnesota

283 U.S. 697 (1931)

A Minnesota law provided that anyone engaged in the business of publishing "a malicious, scandalous and defamatory newspaper, magazine, or other periodical" was guilty of a nuisance and subject to prosecution by the state. The periodicals could be prohibited and their publishers enjoined from future violations. The punishment of contempt was available for disobeying an injunction. The state prosecuted Jay Near for publishing the *Saturday Press,* a hardhitting newspaper that focused largely on corruption and racketeering in Minneapolis. Many of his attacks were directed at the mayor and police chief.

MR. CHIEF JUSTICE HUGHES delivered the opinion of the Court.

Chapter 285 of the Session Laws of Minnesota for the year 1925 provides for the abatement, as a public nuisance, of a "malicious, scandalous and defamatory newspaper, magazine or other periodical." Section one of the Act is as follows:

"Section 1. Any person who, as an individual, or as a member or employee of a firm, or association or organization, or as an officer, director, member or employee of a corporation, shall be engaged in the business of regularly or customarily producing, publishing or circulating, having in possession, selling or giving away.

(a) an obscene, lewd and lascivious newspaper, magazine, or other periodical, or

(b) a malicious, scandalous and defamatory newspaper, magazine or other periodical, is guilty of a nuisance, and all persons guilty of such nuisance may be enjoined, as hereinafter provided....

"In actions brought under (b) above, there shall be available the defense that the truth was published with good motives and for justifiable ends and in such actions the plaintiff shall not have the right to report *(sic)* to issues or editions of periodicals taking place more than three months before the commencement of the action."...

Under this statute, clause (b), the County Attorney of Hennepin County brought this action to enjoin the publication of what was described as a "malicious, scandalous and defamatory newspaper, magazine and periodical," known as "The Saturday Press," published by the defendants in the city of Minneapolis. The complaint alleged that the defendants, on September 24, 1927, and on eight subsequent dates in October and November, 1927, published and circulated editions of that periodical which were "largely devoted to malicious, scandalous and defamatory articles" concerning Charles G. Davis, Frank W. Brunskill, the Minneapolis Tribune, the Minneapolis Journal, Melvin C. Passolt, George E. Leach, the Jewish Race, the members of the Grand Jury of Hennepin County impaneled in November, 1927, and then holding office, and other persons, as more fully appeared in exhibits annexed to the complaint, consisting of copies of the articles described and constituting 327 pages of the record. While the complaint did not so allege, it appears from the briefs of both parties that Charles G. Davis was a special law enforcement officer employed by a civic organization, that George E. Leach was Mayor of Minneapolis, that Frank W. Brunskill was its Chief of Police, and that Floyd B. Olson (the relator in this action) was County Attorney.

Without attempting to summarize the contents of the voluminous exhibits attached to the complaint, we deem it sufficient to say that the articles charged in substance that a Jewish gangster was in control of gambling, bootlegging and racketeering in Minneapolis, and that law enforcing officers and agencies were not energetically performing their duties....

[*The state court found Near's newspaper in violation of the statute and ordered that publication be ceased.*]

This statute, for the suppression as a public nuisance of a newspaper or periodical, is unusual, if not unique, and raises questions of grave importance transcending the local interests involved in the particular action. It is no longer open to doubt that the liberty of the press, and of speech, is within the liberty safeguarded by the due process clause of the Fourteenth Amendment from invasion by state action. It was found impossible to conclude that this essential personal liberty of the citizen was left unprotected by the general guaranty of fundamental rights of person and property....

First. The statute is not aimed at the redress of individual or private wrongs. Remedies for libel remain available and unaffected.... In the present action there was no allegation that the matter published was not true. It is alleged, and the statute requires the allegation, that the publication was "malicious." But, as in prosecutions for libel, there is no requirement of proof by the State of malice in fact as distinguished from malice inferred from the mere publication of the defamatory matter. The judgment in this case proceeded upon the mere proof of publication. The statute permits the defense, not of the truth alone, but only that the truth was published with good motives and for justifiable ends. It is apparent that under the statute the publication is to be regarded as defamatory if it injures reputation, and that it is scandalous if it circulates charges of reprehensible conduct, whether criminal or otherwise, and the publication is thus deemed to invite public reprobation and to constitute a public scandal. The [*state*] court sharply defined the purpose of the statute, bringing out the precise point, in these words: "There is no constitutional right to publish a fact merely because it is true.... This law is not for the protection of the person attacked nor to punish the wrongdoer. It is for the protection of the public welfare."

Second. The statute is directed not simply at the circulation of scandalous and defamatory statements with regard to private citizens, but at the continued publication by newspapers and periodicals of charges against public officers of corruption, malfeasance in office, or serious neglect of duty. Such charges by their very nature create a public scandal....

Third. The object of the statute is not punishment, in the ordinary sense, but suppression of the offending newspaper or periodical....

Fourth. The statute not only operates to suppress the offending newspaper or periodical but to put the publisher under an effective censorship. When a newspaper or periodical is found to be "malicious, scandalous and defamatory," and is suppressed as such, resumption of publication is punishable as a contempt of court by fine or imprisonment....

The question is whether a statute authorizing such proceedings in restraint of publication is consistent with the conception of the liberty of the press as historically conceived and guaranteed. In determining the extent of the constitutional protection, it has been generally, if not universally, considered that it is the chief purpose of the guaranty to prevent previous restraints upon publication. The struggle in England, directed against the legislative power of the licenser, resulted in renunciation of the censorship of the press. The liberty deemed to be established was thus described by Blackstone: "The liberty of the press is indeed essential to the nature of a free state; but this consists in laying no *previous* restraints upon publications, and not in freedom from censure for criminal matter when published. Every freeman has an undoubted right to lay what sentiments he pleases before the public; to forbid this, is to destroy the freedom of the press; but if he publishes what is improper, mischievous or illegal, he must take the consequence of his own temerity." 4 Bl. Com. 151, 152; see Story on the Constitution, §§ 1884, 1889....

The objection has also been made that the principle as to immunity from previous restraint is stated too broadly, if every such restraint is deemed to be prohibited. That is undoubtedly true; the protection even as to previous restraint is not absolutely unlimited.... No one would question but that a government might prevent actual obstruction to its recruiting service or the publication of the sailing dates of transports or the number and location of troops. On similar grounds, the primary requirements of decency may be enforced against obscene publications. The security of the community life may be protected against incitements to acts of violence and the overthrow by force of orderly government....

The fact that for approximately one hundred and fifty years there has been almost an entire absence of attempts to impose previous restraints upon publications relating to the malfeasance of public officers is significant of the deep-seated conviction that such restraints would violate constitutional right. Public officers, whose character and conduct remain open to debate and free discussion in the press, find their remedies for false accusations in actions under libel laws providing for redress and punishment, and not in proceedings to restrain the publication of newspapers and periodicals....

... Meanwhile, the administration of government has become more complex, the opportunities for malfeasance and corruption have multiplied, crime has grown to most serious proportions, and the danger of its protection by unfaithful officials and of the impairment of the fundamental security of life and property by criminal alliances and official neglect, emphasizes the primary need of a vigilant and courageous press....

For these reasons we hold the statute, so far as it authorized the proceedings in this action under clause (b) of section one, to be an infringement of the liberty of the press guaranteed by the Fourteenth Amendment. We should add that this decision rests upon the operation and effect of the statute, without regard to the question of the truth of the charges contained in the particular periodical. The fact that the public officers named in this case, and those associated with the charges of official dereliction, may be deemed to be impeccable, cannot affect the conclusion that the statute imposes an unconstitutional restraint upon publication.

Judgment reversed.

MR. JUSTICE BUTLER, dissenting....

It is of the greatest importance that the States shall be untrammeled and free to employ all just and appropriate measures to prevent abuses of the liberty of the press....

MR. JUSTICE VAN DEVANTER, MR. JUSTICE MCREYNOLDS, and MR. JUSTICE SUTHERLAND concur in this opinion.

New York Times Co. v. United States

403 U.S. 713 (1971)

The Nixon administration brought action in federal court to prevent publication in the *New York Times* and the *Washington Post* of certain materials collectively called the Pentagon Papers. The documents consisted of a classified study prepared by the Defense Department, entitled "History of U.S. Decision-Making Process on Viet Nam Policy." The administration claimed that publication of the materials would be injurious to national security. The newspapers argued that the First Amendment protected against prior restraint on the right to publish.

PER CURIAM.

We granted certiorari in these cases in which the United States seeks to enjoin the New York Times and the Washington Post from publishing the contents of a classified study entitled "History of U.S. Decision-Making Process on Viet Nam Policy." ...

"Any system of prior restraints of expression comes to this Court bearing a heavy presumption against its constitutional validity." *Bantam Books, Inc. v. Sullivan,* 372 U.S. 58, 70 (1963); see also *Near v. Minnesota,* 283 U.S. 697 (1931). The Government "thus carries a heavy burden of showing justification for the imposition of such a restraint." *Organization for a Better Austin v. Keefe,* 402 U.S. 415, 419 (1971).

The District Court for the Southern District of New York in the *New York Times* case and the District Court for the District of Columbia and the Court of Appeals for the District of Columbia Circuit in the *Washington Post* case held that the Government had not met that burden. We agree.

The judgment of the Court of Appeals for the District of Columbia Circuit is therefore affirmed. The order of the Court of Appeals for the Second Circuit is reversed and the case is remanded with directions to enter a judgment affirming the judgment of the District Court for the Southern District of New York. The stays entered June 25, 1971, by the Court are vacated. The judgments shall issue forthwith.

So ordered.

Mr. Justice Black, with whom Mr. Justice Douglas joins, concurring.

I adhere to the view that the Government's case against the Washington Post should have been dismissed and that the injunction against the New York Times should have been vacated without oral argument when the cases were first presented to this Court. I believe that every moment's continuance of the injunctions against these newspapers amounts to a flagrant, indefensible, and continuing violation of the First Amendment....

... Madison and the other Framers of the First Amendment, able men that they were, wrote in language they earnestly believed could never be misunderstood: "Congress shall make no law ... abridging the freedom ... of the press...." Both the history and language of the First Amendment support the view that the press must be left free to publish news, whatever the source, without censorship, injunctions, or prior restraints.

In the First Amendment the Founding Fathers gave the free press the protection it must have to fulfill its essential role in our democracy. The press was to serve the governed, not the governors. The Government's power to censor the press was abolished so that the press would remain forever free to censure the Government. The press was protected so that it could bare the secrets of government and inform the people. Only a free and unrestrained press can effectively expose deception in government. And paramount among the responsibilities of a free press is the duty to prevent any part of the government from deceiving the people and sending them off to distant lands to die of foreign fevers and foreign shot and shell. In my view, far from deserving condemnation for their courageous reporting, the New York Times, the Washington Post, and other newspapers should be commended for serving the purpose that the Founding Fathers saw so clearly. In revealing the workings of government that led to the Vietnam war, the newspapers nobly did precisely that which the Founders hoped and trusted they would do....

Mr. Justice Douglas, with whom Mr. Justice Black joins, concurring....

It should be noted at the outset that the First Amendment provides that "Congress shall make no law ... abridging the freedom of speech, or of the press." That leaves, in my view, no room for governmental restraint on the press....

The dominant purpose of the First Amendment was to prohibit the widespread practice of governmental suppression of embarrassing information. It is common knowledge that the First Amendment was adopted against the widespread use of the common law of seditious libel to punish the dissemination of material that is embarrassing to the powers-that-be.... The present cases will, I think, go down in history as the most dramatic illustration of that principle. A debate of large proportions goes on in the Nation over our posture in Vietnam. That debate antedated the disclosure of the contents of the present documents. The latter are highly relevant to the debate in progress.

Secrecy in government is fundamentally anti-democratic, perpetuating bureaucratic errors. Open debate and discussion of public issues are vital to our national health. On public questions, there should be "uninhibited, robust, and wide-open" debate. *New York Times Co. v. Sullivan,* 376 U.S. 254, 269–270....

Mr. Justice Brennan, concurring.

... [O]nly governmental allegation and proof that publication must inevitably, directly, and immediately cause the occurrence of an event kindred to imperiling the safety of a transport already at sea can support even the issuance of an interim restraining order....

Mr. Justice Stewart, with whom Mr. Justice White joins, concurring.

... If the Constitution gives the Executive a large degree of unshared power in the conduct of foreign affairs and the maintenance of our national defense, then under the Constitution the Executive must have the largely unshared duty to determine and preserve the degree of internal security necessary to exercise that power successfully. It is an awesome responsibility, requiring judgment and wisdom of a high order. I should suppose that moral, political, and practical considerations would dictate that a very first principle of that wisdom would be an insistence upon avoiding secrecy for its own sake. For when everything is classified, then nothing is classified, and the system becomes one to be disregarded by the cynical or the careless, and to be manipulated by those intent on self-protection or self-promotion....

... [I]n the cases before us we are asked neither to construe specific regulations nor to apply specific laws. We are asked, instead, to perform a function that the Constitution gave to the Executive, not the Judiciary. We are asked, quite simply, to prevent the publication by two newspapers of material that the Executive Branch insists should not, in the national interest, be published. I am convinced that the Executive is correct with respect to some of the documents involved. But I cannot say that disclosure of any of them will surely result in direct, immediate, and irreparable damage to our Nation or its people. That being so, there can under the First Amendment be but one judicial resolution of the issues before us. I join the judgments of the Court.

MR. JUSTICE WHITE, with whom MR. JUSTICE STEWART joins, concurring.

... I do not say that in no circumstances would the First Amendment permit an injunction against publishing information about government plans or operations. Nor, after examining the materials the Government characterizes as the most sensitive and destructive, can I deny that revelation of these documents will do substantial damage to public interests. Indeed, I am confident that their disclosure will have that result. But I nevertheless agree that the United States has not satisfied the very heavy burden that it must meet to warrant an injunction against publication in these cases, at least in the absence of express and appropriately limited congressional authorization for prior restraints in circumstances such as these....

MR. JUSTICE MARSHALL, concurring.

The Government contends that the only issue in these cases is whether in a suit by the United States, "the First Amendment bars a court from prohibiting a newspaper from publishing material whose disclosure would pose a 'grave and immediate danger to the security of the United States.'" Brief for the United States 7. With all due respect, I believe the ultimate issue in these cases is even more basic than the one posed by the Solicitor General. The issue is whether this Court or the Congress has the power to make law....

The problem here is whether, in these particular cases, the Executive Branch has authority to invoke the equity jurisdiction of the courts to protect what it believes to be the national interest.... It would ... be utterly inconsistent with the concept of separation of powers for this Court to use its power of contempt to prevent behavior that Congress has specifically declined to prohibit. There would be a similar damage to the basic concept of these co-equal branches of Government if, when the Executive Branch has adequate authority granted by Congress to protect "national security" it can choose instead to invoke the contempt power of a court to enjoin the threatened conduct. The Constitution provides that Congress shall make laws, the President execute laws, and courts interpret laws ... It did not provide for government by injunction in which the courts and the Executive Branch can "make law" without regard to the action of Congress. It may be more convenient for the Executive Branch if it need only convince a judge to prohibit conduct rather than ask the Congress to pass a law, and it may be more convenient to enforce a contempt order than to seek a criminal conviction in a jury trial. Moreover, it may be considered politically wise to get a court to share the responsibility for arresting those who the Executive Branch has probable cause to believe are violating the law. But convenience and political considerations of the moment do not justify a basic departure from the principles of our system of government....

MR. CHIEF JUSTICE BURGER, dissenting.

... In these cases, the imperative of a free and unfettered press comes into collision with another imperative, the effective functioning of a complex modern government and specifically the effective exercise of certain constitutional powers of the Executive. Only those who view the First Amendment as an absolute in all circumstances—a view I respect, but reject—can find such cases as these to be simple or easy.

These cases are not simple for another and more immediate reason. We do not know the facts of the cases. No District Judge knew all the facts. No Court of Appeals judge knew all the facts. No member of this Court knows all the facts.

Why are we in this posture, in which only those judges to whom the First Amendment is absolute and permits of no restraint in any circumstances or for any reason, are really in a position to act?

I suggest we are in this posture because these cases have been conducted in unseemly haste....

MR. JUSTICE HARLAN, with whom THE CHIEF JUSTICE and MR. JUSTICE BLACKMUN join, dissenting.

These cases forcefully call to mind the wise admonition of Mr. Justice Holmes, dissenting in *Northern Securities Co.* v. *United States,* 193 U.S. 197, 400–401 (1904):

"Great cases like hard cases make bad law. For great cases are called great, not by reason of their real importance in shaping the law of the future, but because of some accident of immediate overwhelming interest which appeals to the feelings and distorts the judgment. These immediate interests exercise a kind of hydraulic pressure which makes what previously was clear seem doubtful, and before which even well settled principles of law will bend."

With all respect, I consider that the Court has been almost irresponsibly feverish in dealing with these cases.

Both the Court of Appeals for the Second Circuit and the Court of Appeals for the District of Columbia Circuit rendered judgment on June 23. The New York Times' petition for certiorari, its motion for accelerated consideration thereof, and its application for interim relief were filed in this Court on June 24

at about 11 a.m. The application of the United States for interim relief in the *Post* case was also filed here on June 24 at about 7:15 p.m. This Court's order setting a hearing before us on June 26 at 11 a.m., a course which I joined only to avoid the possibility of even more peremptory action by the Court, was issued less than 24 hours before. The record in the *Post* case was filed with the Clerk shortly before 1 p.m. on June 25; the record in the *Times* case did not arrive until 7 or 8 o'clock that same night. The briefs of the parties were received less than two hours before argument on June 26.

This frenzied train of events took place in the name of the presumption against prior restraints created by the First Amendment. Due regard for the extraordinarily important and difficult questions involved in these litigations should have led the Court to shun such a precipitate timetable. . . .

MR. JUSTICE BLACKMUN, dissenting. . . .

With such respect as may be due to the contrary view, this, in my opinion, is not the way to try a lawsuit of this magnitude and asserted importance. It is not the way for federal courts to adjudicate, and to be required to adjudicate, issues that allegedly concern the Nation's vital welfare. . . .

Branzburg v. Hayes

408 U.S. 665 (1972)

In this case, the needs of a free press and criminal prosecution collide. Paul M. Branzburg, a reporter with the Louisville *Courier-Journal,* was called before a county grand jury after he wrote an article describing how two men made hashish from marijuana. He refused to identify them. Also involved in this case were Paul Pappas, a reporter-cameraman, and Earl Caldwell, a reporter for the *New York Times,* who refused to testify about their coverage of the Black Panthers. This action by Branzburg is against John P. Hayes, a Kentucky trial judge.

Opinion of the Court by MR. JUSTICE WHITE, announced by THE CHIEF JUSTICE.

The issue in these cases is whether requiring newsmen to appear and testify before state or federal grand juries abridges the freedom of speech and press guaranteed by the First Amendment. We hold that it does not.

I

. . . [T]he Courier-Journal carried a story under petitioner's by-line describing in detail his observations of two young residents of Jefferson County synthesizing hashish from marihuana, an activity which, they asserted, earned them about $5,000 in three weeks. The article included a photograph of a

pair of hands working above a laboratory table on which was a substance identified by the caption as hashish. The article stated that petitioner had promised not to reveal the identity of the two hashish makers. Petitioner was shortly subpoenaed by the Jefferson County grand jury; he appeared, but refused to identify the individuals he had seen possessing marihuana or the persons he had seen making hashish from marihuana. A state trial court judge ordered petitioner to answer these questions and rejected his contention that the Kentucky reporters' privilege statute, Ky. Rev. Stat. §421.100 (1962), the First Amendment of the United States Constitution, or §§ 1, 2, and 8 of the Kentucky Constitution authorized his refusal to answer. Petitioner then sought prohibition and mandamus in the Kentucky Court of Appeals on the same grounds, but the Court of Appeals denied the petition....

The second case involving petitioner Branzburg arose out of his later story published on January 10, 1971, which described in detail the use of drugs in Frankfort, Kentucky. The article reported that in order to provide a comprehensive survey of the "drug scene" in Frankfort, petitioner had "spent two weeks interviewing several dozen drug users in the capital city" and had seen some of them smoking marihuana. A number of conversations with and observations of several unnamed drug users were recounted. Subpoenaed to appear before a Franklin County grand jury "to testify in the matter of violation of statutes concerning use and sale of drugs," petitioner Branzburg moved to quash the summons; the motion was denied, although an order was issued protecting Branzburg from revealing "confidential associations, sources or information" but requiring that he "answer any questions which concern or pertain to any criminal act, the commission of which was actually observed by [him]." Prior to the time he was slated to appear before the grand jury, petitioner sought mandamus and prohibition from the Kentucky Court of Appeals, arguing that if he were forced to go before the grand jury or to answer questions regarding the identity of informants or disclose information given to him in confidence, his effectiveness as a reporter would be greatly damaged. The Court of Appeals once again denied the requested writs....

II

Petitioners Branzburg and Pappas and respondent Caldwell press First Amendment claims that may be simply put: that to gather news it is often necessary to agree either not to identify the source of information published or to publish only part of the facts revealed, or both; that if the reporter is nevertheless forced to reveal these confidences to a grand jury, the source so identified and other confidential sources of other reporters will be measurably deterred from furnishing publishable information, all to the detriment of the free flow of information protected by the First Amendment. Although the newsmen in these cases do not claim an absolute privilege against official interrogation in all circumstances, they assert that the reporter should not be forced either to appear or to testify before a grand jury or at trial until and unless sufficient grounds are shown for believing that the reporter possesses information relevant to a crime the grand jury is investigating, that the information the reporter has is unavailable

from other sources, and that the need for the information is sufficiently compelling to override the claimed invasion of First Amendment interests occasioned by the disclosure....

We do not question the significance of free speech, press, or assembly to the country's welfare. Nor is it suggested that news gathering does not qualify for First Amendment protection; without some protection for seeking out the news, freedom of the press could be eviscerated. But these cases involve no intrusions upon speech or assembly, no prior restraint or restriction on what the press may publish, and no express or implied command that the press publish what it prefers to withhold. No exaction or tax for the privilege of publishing, and no penalty, civil or criminal, related to the content of published material is at issue here. The use of confidential sources by the press is not forbidden or restricted; reporters remain free to seek news from any source by means within the law. No attempt is made to require the press to publish its sources of information or indiscriminately to disclose them on request.

The sole issue before us is the obligation of reporters to respond to grand jury subpoenas as other citizens do and to answer questions relevant to an investigation into the commission of crime. Citizens generally are not constitutionally immune from grand jury subpoenas; and neither the First Amendment nor any other constitutional provision protects the average citizen from disclosing to a grand jury information that he has received in confidence....

... [T]he great weight of authority is that newsmen are not exempt from the normal duty of appearing before a grand jury and answering questions relevant to a criminal investigation. At common law, courts consistently refused to recognize the existence of any privilege authorizing a newsman to refuse to reveal confidential information to a grand jury....

A number of States have provided newsmen a statutory privilege of varying breadth, but the majority have not done so, and none has been provided by federal statute. Until now the only testimonial privilege for unofficial witnesses that is rooted in the Federal Constitution is the Fifth Amendment privilege against compelled self-incrimination. We are asked to create another by interpreting the First Amendment to grant newsmen a testimonial privilege that other citizens do not enjoy. This we decline to do. Fair and effective law enforcement aimed at providing security for the person and property of the individual is a fundamental function of government, and the grand jury plays an important, constitutionally mandated role in this process....

There remain those situations where a source is

not engaged in criminal conduct but has information suggesting illegal conduct by others. Newsmen frequently receive information from such sources pursuant to a tacit or express agreement to withhold the source's name and suppress any information that the source wishes not published. Such informants presumably desire anonymity in order to avoid being entangled as a witness in a criminal trial or grand jury investigation. They may fear that disclosure will threaten their job security or personal safety or that it will simply result in dishonor or embarrassment.

The argument that the flow of news will be diminished by compelling reporters to aid the grand jury in a criminal investigation is not irrational, nor are the records before us silent on the matter. But we remain unclear how often and to what extent informers are actually deterred from furnishing information when newsmen are forced to testify before a grand jury. The available data indicate that some newsmen rely a great deal on confidential sources and that some informants are particularly sensitive to the threat of exposure and may be silenced if it is held by this Court that, ordinarily, newsmen must testify pursuant to subpoenas, but the evidence fails to demonstrate that there would be a significant constriction of the flow of news to the public if this Court reaffirms the prior common-law and constitutional rule regarding the testimonial obligations of newsmen. Estimates of the inhibiting effect of such subpoenas on the willingness of informants to make disclosures to newsmen are widely divergent and to a great extent speculative....

Accepting the fact, however, that an undetermined number of informants not themselves implicated in crime will nevertheless, for whatever reason, refuse to talk to newsmen if they fear identification by a reporter in an official investigation, we cannot accept the argument that the public interest in possible future news about crime from undisclosed, unverified sources must take precedence over the public interest in pursuing and prosecuting those crimes reported to the press by informants and in thus deterring the commission of such crimes in the future....

At the federal level, Congress has freedom to determine whether a statutory newsman's privilege is necessary and desirable and to fashion standards and rules as narrow or broad as deemed necessary to deal with the evil discerned and, equally important, to refashion those rules as experience from time to time

may dictate. There is also merit in leaving state legislatures free, within First Amendment limits, to fashion their own standards in light of the conditions and problems with respect to the relations between law enforcement officials and press in their own areas. It goes without saying, of course, that we are powerless to bar state courts from responding in their own way and construing their own constitutions so as to recognize a newsman's privilege, either qualified or absolute....

Mr. Justice Powell, concurring....

Mr. Justice Douglas, dissenting in No. 70-57, *United States* v. *Caldwell.*

Caldwell, a black, is a reporter for the New York Times and was assigned to San Francisco with the hope that he could report on the activities and attitudes of the Black Panther Party. Caldwell in time gained the complete confidence of its members....

It is my view that there is no "compelling need" that can be shown which qualifies the reporter's immunity from appearing or testifying before a grand jury, unless the reporter himself is implicated in a crime. His immunity in my view is therefore quite complete, ... [I]n my view a newsman has an absolute right not to appear before a grand jury, ...

Mr. Justice Stewart, with whom Mr. Justice Brennan and Mr. Justice Marshall join, dissenting.

The Court's crabbed view of the First Amendment reflects a disturbing insensitivity to the critical role of an independent press in our society. The question whether a reporter has a constitutional right to a confidential relationship with his source is of first impression here, but the principles that should guide our decision are as basic as any to be found in the Constitution....

I

The reporter's constitutional right to a confidential relationship with his source stems from the broad societal interest in a full and free flow of information to the public. It is this basic concern that underlies the Constitution's protection of a free press, ... because the guarantee is "not for the benefit of the press so much as for the benefit of all of us." *Time, Inc.* v. *Hill,* 385 U.S. 374, 389....

C. FREE PRESS VS. FAIR TRIAL

The *Branzburg* decision, requiring reporters to testify before a grand jury, is only one of many collisions between the press and the judiciary. Another confrontation emerges when the press wants to cover a trial and a judge wants to close it. For the most part, the Supreme Court has supported the press and the public in such conflicts, but the record is filled with erratic turns and refashioned doctrines. In these contests, the Court remains sensitive to public opinion and the needs of a democratic society.

One of the early cases concerned a newspaper charged with contempt of court because of its unflattering stories about a judge's conduct in a pending case. The contempt was upheld by the Supreme Court. Toledo Newspaper Co. v. United States, 247 U.S. 402 (1918). This decision was later overturned. Nye v. United States, 313 U.S. 33 (1941). Both decisions involved efforts to interpret a congressional statute that restricted the power of judges to punish for contempt. 4 Stat. 487 (1831); 18 U.S.C. §401. The right of the press to publish comments about pending litigation without being held in contempt of court was also upheld in another case in 1941. The Court observed that the "assumption that respect for the judiciary can be won by shielding judges from published criticism wrongly appraises the character of American public opinion." Bridges v. California, 314 U.S. 252, 270 (1941).

There have been many such cases. In 1946, a unanimous Court reversed a state court's action that held a newspaper in contempt for criticizing a trial judge and impugning his integrity. Pennekamp v. Florida, 328 U.S. 331 (1946). Some judges claim that newspaper stories can obstruct the fair and impartial administration of justice in pending cases. However, the general record is to protect the freedom of the press. Craig v. Harney, 331 U.S. 367 (1947). If misleading and inflammatory newspaper stories create a prejudicial climate and make a fair trial impossible, cases can be postponed, transferred to a different place, and convictions can be reversed.[2]

The confrontation between a free press and a fair trial reaches its highest pitch when judges issue gag orders to prohibit public comment about a pending trial. In 1976, a unanimous Court reversed the decision of a Nebraska state court judge who — in anticipation of a trial for a multiple murder — restrained newspapers, broadcasters, journalists, news media associations, and national newswire services from publishing or broadcasting statements by the accused to law enforcement officers. The ban extended to statements to third parties, except members of the press. The Supreme Court held that the heavy burden imposed as a condition of prior restraint had not been met. NEBRASKA PRESS ASSN. v. STUART, 427 U.S. 539 (1976). When court proceedings are open to the public, a judge may not enjoin the news media from publishing the name or photograph of someone charged with an offense. Oklahoma Publishing Co. v. District Court, 430 U.S. 308 (1977).

From *Gannett* to *Richmond Newspapers*

The dialectic between judicial decisions and public opinion is captured vividly in two back-to-back cases in 1979 and 1980. In the first, a 5 to 4 decision by the Supreme Court supported a trial judge's ruling to close a pretrial hearing to the public and the press. The motion had been made by defendants without objection by the prosecutor. In upholding the need to protect the fair-trial rights of defendants, the Court held that the public has no constitutional right of access to pretrial proceedings. The Court said that the constitutional guarantee of a public trial is for the benefit of the defendant, not the public. Its language was much too broad: "we hold that members of the public have no constitutional right under the Sixth and Fourteenth Amendments to attend criminal trials." GANNETT CO. v. DePASQUALE, 443 U.S. 368, 391 (1979). In a concurrence, Chief Justice Burger said that the Sixth Amendment right to public trial applied strictly to the trial, not to pretrial proceedings. Two other concurrences, by Powell and Rehnquist, undercut the majority opinion.

---

2. Shepherd v. Florida, 341 U.S. 50 (1951); Estes v. Texas, 381 U.S. 532 (1965); Sheppard v. Maxwell, 384 U.S. 333 (1966).

Justices Respond to Gannett

After the decision in *Gannett Co. v. DePasquale* (1979), some judges began to close their courtrooms not only for pretrial proceedings but also for the trial itself. Several Justices of the Supreme Court made unusual appearances before the public to explain that *Gannett* was being misinterpreted. In an interview, Chief Justice Burger noted that *Gannett* was limited to pretrial proceedings and wondered whether judges around the country were "reading newspaper reports of what we said" rather than the opinion itself. In a separate appearance, Justice Powell denied that the Court had any ill feelings toward the press: "Instead of having any hostility toward you, we are dependent on you very much." In this panel session at the American Bar Association's annual meeting, Powell added: "We are totally dependent on the media to interpret what we do. That's all the public knows about

us." Justice Blackmun, who wrote a lengthy dissent in *Gannett*, told a group of federal judges in South Dakota that "despite what my colleague, the Chief Justice has said," the opinion authorized the closing of full trials. At yet a fourth public meeting, Justice Stevens conceded that the possibility that judges might be granting requests too casually to close entire trials to the public "may justify the adoption of new court rules, or even new legislation." In making this comment in Tucson, Ariz., Stevens seemed to underscore Blackmun's comment that Chief Justice Burger was reading *Gannett* too narrowly. It was remarkable, and possibly unprecedented, for four Justices to comment publicly about a Court opinion. These remarks seemed to guarantee that the Court would quickly revisit *Gannett*, which is what the Justices did in *Richmond Newspapers, Inc. v. Virginia* (1980).

Sources: New York Times, August 9, 1979, at A17; August 11, 1979, at 43; August 14, 1979, at A13; September 4, 1979, at A15; September 9, 1979, at 41.

In response to the Court's fragmented and disjointed opinion, some judges around the country began to close their courtrooms to the public, not only for pretrial proceedings but for the entire trial and even sentencing. In a few cases, they allowed the public in but kept the press out. The press mounted a vigorous counterattack. Critics of the Court's decision claimed that it denied citizens the right to keep government accountable and maintain democratic control. Members of the Supreme Court, including Burger, Powell, Blackmun, and Stevens, took the unusual step of telling audiences around the country that *Gannett* had been "misread" to permit unacceptable restraints on the press (see box).

Within a year, a 7–1 Supreme Court attempted to clarify its intentions in *Gannett* by announcing a more sympathetic understanding of the public's need to attend trials. The Court held that the public's right of access to criminal trials is implicit in the First Amendment. Open trials promote many interests: the yearning to see justice done, the public education that comes from attending a trial, the maintenance of public trust in the judicial system, and the opportunity to check the fairness and accuracy of judicial proceedings. RICHMOND NEWSPAPERS, INC. v. VIRGINIA, 448 U.S. 555 (1980). The guarantee of public proceedings in criminal trials has been extended to cover even the *voir dire* screening of potential jurors. Press-Enterprise Co. v. Superior Court of Cal., 464 U.S. 501 (1984). There is also a right of access to preliminary hearings for criminal proceedings. Press-Enterprise Co. v. Superior Court, 478 U.S. 1 (1986).

Public access has reached the point where some judicial proceedings are televised. A unanimous Supreme Court held that the Constitution does not prohibit states from experimenting with televised trials. Chandler v. Florida, 449 U.S. 560 (1981). Chief Justice Burger opposed televising Supreme Court proceedings, but some members of the Rehnquist Court seemed more supportive of this prospect. In 1988, Chief Justice Rehnquist and Justices White and Kennedy attended a brief demonstration of how filming could be done of Supreme Court proceedings, but there has been no change in the Court's policy against cameras. Lower federal courts may experiment with television coverage of civil cases.[3] That experimentation, however, is subject to review by the high court. In 2010 the Court decided, in a 5–4 decision, to stay the Ninth Circuit's experimentation with live video coverage of the Proposition 8 trial in California. Supporters of Proposition 8, in which California voters rejected gay marriage, claimed that video coverage of their testimony could lead to reprisals. The Court claimed that the lower courts had not followed federal law requiring notice and comment before changing court rules about video access. Hollingsworth v. Perry, 558 U.S. ___ (2010).

Nebraska Press Assn. v. Stuart

427 U.S. 539 (1976)

A Nebraska state trial judge, anticipating a trial involving multiple murders that had attracted widespread news coverage, entered an order that restrained newspapers, broadcasters, journalists, news media associations, and national newswire services from publishing or broadcasting accounts of confessions or admissions made by the accused to law enforcement officers or third parties. An exception was made for confessions or admissions made to the press. The question was whether the order by Judge Stuart, intended to prevent pretrial publicity that might jeopardize a fair trial, violated the constitutional guarantee of a free press.

MR. CHIEF JUSTICE BURGER delivered the opinion of the Court.

The respondent State District Judge entered an order restraining the petitioners from publishing or broadcasting accounts of confessions or admissions made by the accused or facts "strongly implicative" of the accused in a widely reported murder of six persons. We granted certiorari to decide whether the entry of such an order on the showing made before the state court violated the constitutional guarantee of freedom of the press....

III

The problems presented by this case are almost as old as the Republic. Neither in the Constitution nor in contemporaneous writings do we find that the conflict between these two important rights was anticipated, yet it is inconceivable that the authors of the Constitution were unaware of the potential conflicts between the right to an unbiased jury and the guarantee of freedom of the press....

The speed of communication and the pervasiveness of the modern news media have exacerbated these problems, however, as numerous appeals demonstrate. The trial of Bruno Hauptmann in a small New Jersey community for the abduction and murder of the Charles Lindberghs' infant child probably was the most widely covered trial up to that time, and the nature of the coverage produced widespread public reaction. Criticism was directed at the "carnival" atmosphere that pervaded the community and the courtroom itself. Responsible leaders of press and the legal profession — including other judges — pointed out that much of this sorry performance could have been controlled by a vigilant trial judge and by other public officers subject to the control of the court....

The excesses of press and radio and lack of responsibility of those in authority in the *Hauptmann* case and others of that era led to efforts to develop voluntary guidelines for courts, lawyers, press, and broadcasters.... The effort was renewed in 1965 when the American Bar Association embarked on a project to develop standards for all aspects of criminal justice, including guidelines to accommodate the right to a fair trial and the rights of a free press.... The resulting standards, approved by the Association in 1968, received support from most of the legal profession....

In practice, of course, even the most ideal guidelines are subjected to powerful strains when a case such as Simants' [*arrested for six murders in Sutherland, Neb.*] arises, with reporters from many parts of the country on the scene. Reporters from distant places are unlikely to consider themselves bound by

3. "Cameras Roll Into Federal Court Again," Legal Times, May 6, 1996, at 14; Jonathan Groner, "Who Rules? Which Rules?: Cameras-in-Court Decision Tests Power of Judicial Conference," Legal Times, March 11, 1996, at 1; Linda Greenhouse, "Reversing Course, Judicial Panel Allows Televising Appeals Courts," The New York Times, March 13, 1996, at A1; Joe Sexton, "U.S. Judge Allows Cameras at Hearing," The New York Times, March 2, 1996, at 22.

local standards. They report to editors outside the area covered by the guidelines, and their editors are likely to be guided only by their own standards....

IV

The Sixth Amendment in terms guarantees "trial, by an impartial jury ..." in federal criminal prosecutions. Because "trial by jury in criminal cases is fundamental to the American scheme of justice," the Due Process Clause of the Fourteenth Amendment guarantees the same right in state criminal prosecutions. *Duncan* v. *Louisiana*, 391 U.S. 145, 149 (1968)....

In *Irvin* v. *Dowd*, ... the defendant was convicted of murder following intensive and hostile news coverage. The trial judge had granted a defense motion for a change of venue, but only to an adjacent county, which had been exposed to essentially the same news coverage. At trial, 430 persons were called for jury service; 268 were excused because they had fixed opinions as to guilt. Eight of the 12 who served as jurors thought the defendant guilty, but said they could nevertheless render an impartial verdict. On review the Court vacated the conviction and death sentence and remanded to allow a new trial for, "[w]ith his life at stake, it is not requiring too much that petitioner be tried in an atmosphere undisturbed by so huge a wave of public passion...." 366 U.S., at 728.

Similarly, in *Rideau* v. *Louisiana*, 373 U.S. 723 (1963), the Court reversed the conviction of a defendant whose staged, highly emotional confession had been filmed with the cooperation of local police and later broadcast on television for three days while he was awaiting trial, saying "[a]ny subsequent court proceedings in a community so pervasively exposed to such a spectacle could be but a hollow formality." *Id.*, at 726. And in *Estes* v. *Texas*, 381 U.S. 532 (1965), the Court held that the defendant had not been afforded due process where the volume of trial publicity, the judge's failure to control the proceedings, and the telecast of a hearing and of the trial itself "inherently prevented a sober search for the truth." *Id.*, at 551....

V

The First Amendment provides that "Congress shall make no law ... abridging the freedom ... of the press," and it is "no longer open to doubt that the liberty of the press, and of speech, is within the liberty safeguarded by the due process clause of the Fourteenth Amendment from invasion by state action." *Near* v. *Minnesota ex rel. Olson*, 283 U.S. 697, 707 (1931). See also *Grosjean* v. *American Press Co.*,

297 U.S. 233, 244 (1936). The Court has interpreted these guarantees to afford special protection against orders that prohibit the publication or broadcast of particular information or commentary — orders that impose a "previous" or "prior" restraint on speech. None of our decided cases on prior restraint involved restrictive orders entered to protect a defendant's right to a fair and impartial jury, but the opinions on prior restraint have a common thread relevant to this case.

[*Burger reviews cases holding that any prior restraint on expression comes to the Court with a "heavy presumption" against its constitutional validity.*]

... [T]he protection against prior restraint should have particular force as applied to reporting of criminal proceedings, whether the crime in question is a single isolated act or a pattern of criminal conduct.

"A responsible press has always been regarded as the handmaiden of effective judicial administration, especially in the criminal field. Its function in this regard is documented by an impressive record of service over several centuries. The press does not simply publish information about trials but guards against the miscarriage of justice by subjecting the police, prosecutors, and judicial processes to extensive public scrutiny and criticism." *Sheppard* v. *Maxwell*, 384 U.S., at 350....

VI

We turn now to the record in this case ...

[A]

Our review of the pretrial record persuades us that the trial judge was justified in concluding that there would be intense and pervasive pretrial publicity concerning this case. He could also reasonably conclude, based on common human experience, that publicity might impair the defendant's right to a fair trial. He did not purport to say more, for he found only "a clear and present danger that pre-trial publicity *could* impinge upon the defendant's right to a fair trial." (Emphasis added.) His conclusion as to the impact of such publicity on prospective jurors was of necessity speculative, dealing as he was with factors unknown and unknowable.

B

We find little in the record that goes to another aspect of our task, determining whether measures short of an order restraining all publication would have insured the defendant a fair trial....

We have therefore examined this record to determine the probable efficacy of the measures short of prior restraint on the press and speech. There is no finding that alternative measures would not have protected Simants' rights, and the Nebraska Supreme Court did no more than imply that such measures might not be adequate. Moreover, the record is lacking in evidence to support such a finding.

C

We must also assess the probable efficacy of prior restraint on publication as a workable method of protecting Simants' right to a fair trial, and we cannot ignore the reality of the problems of managing and enforcing pretrial restraining orders. The territorial jurisdiction of the issuing court is limited by concepts of sovereignty....

... [T]he events disclosed by the record took place in a community of 850 people. It is reasonable to assume that, without any news accounts being printed or broadcast, rumors would travel swiftly by word of mouth. One can only speculate on the accuracy of such reports, given the generative propensities of rumors; they could well be more damaging than reasonably accurate news accounts. But plainly a whole community cannot be restrained from discussing a subject intimately affecting life within it.

Given these practical problems, it is far from clear that prior restraint on publication would have protected Simants' rights.

[E]

Of necessity our holding is confined to the record before us. But our conclusion is not simply a result of assessing the adequacy of the showing made in this case; it results in part from the problems inherent in meeting the heavy burden of demonstrating, in advance of trial, that without prior restraint a fair trial will be denied. The practical problems of managing and enforcing restrictive orders will always be present. In this sense, the record now before us is illustrative rather than exceptional....

... We hold that, with respect to the order entered in this case prohibiting reporting or commentary on judicial proceedings held in public, the barriers have not been overcome; to the extent that this order restrained publication of such material, it is clearly invalid. To the extent that it prohibited publication based on information gained from other sources, we conclude that the heavy burden imposed as a condition to securing a prior restraint was not met and the judgment of the Nebraska Supreme Court is therefore

Reversed.

[*Justices White and Powell wrote concurring opinions. Brennan, joined by Stewart and Marshall, concurred in the judgment. Stevens wrote a separate opinion, concurring in the judgment.*]

Gannett Co. v. DePasquale

443 U.S. 368 (1979)

At a pretrial hearing on a motion to suppress allegedly involuntary confessions and certain physical evidence, two defendants in a state prosecution for second-degree murder, robbery, and grand larceny requested that the public be excluded from the hearing. They argued that adverse publicity had jeopardized their ability to receive a fair trial. The District Attorney did not oppose the motion, nor did a reporter for the Gannett publishers. Judge DePasquale granted the motion. In response to the reporter's letter the next day asserting a right to cover the hearing and requesting access to the transcript, the judge refused to grant Gannett immediate access to the transcript, ruling that the interests of the press and the public were outweighed by defendants' right to a fair trial.

Mr. Justice Stewart delivered the opinion of the Court.

The question presented in this case is whether members of the public have an independent constitutional right to insist upon access to a pretrial judicial proceeding, even though the accused, the prosecutor, and the trial judge all have agreed to the closure of that proceeding in order to assure a fair trial.

I

[*Wayne Clapp disappeared after he had accompanied two men, Greathouse and Jones, on a fishing outing. The boat they used was laced with bullet holes, suggesting a violent death for Clapp. Two Gannett newspapers covered the story, including the arrest of Greathouse, Jones, and Greathouse's wife. The newspapers reported the indictments of the two men and the woman and their arraignments. Defense attorneys were given 90 days to file pretrial motions. During that period, Greathouse and Jones moved to suppress statements made to the police and to suppress physical evidence seized.*]

The motions to suppress came on before Judge DePasquale on November 4. At this hearing, defense attorneys argued that the unabated buildup of adverse publicity had jeopardized the ability of the defendants to receive a fair trial. They thus requested that the public and the press be excluded from the hearing. The District Attorney did not oppose the motion. Although Carol Ritter, a reporter employed by the petitioner, was present in the courtroom, no objection was made at the time of the closure motion. The trial judge granted the motion.

The next day, however, Ritter wrote a letter to the trial judge asserting a "right to cover this hearing," and requesting that "we ... be given access to the transcript." The judge responded later the same day. He stated that the suppression hearing had concluded and that any decision on immediate release of the transcript had been reserved. The petitioner then moved the court to set aside its exclusionary order.

[*The judge refused to vacate his order. The New York Supreme Court, Appellate Division, vacated the order, but the New York Court of Appeals upheld the exclusion of the press and the public from the pretrial proceeding.*]

II

[*Shortly before the entry of judgment by the Appellate Division, both defendants pleaded guilty to lesser offenses and a transcript of the suppression hearing was made available to Gannett. In this section the Court holds that, notwithstanding the availability of the transcript, the controversy is not moot.*]

III

This Court has long recognized that adverse publicity can endanger the ability of a defendant to receive a fair trial....

Publicity concerning pretrial suppression hearings such as the one involved in the present case poses special risks of unfairness. The whole purpose of such hearings is to screen out unreliable or illegally obtained evidence and insure that this evidence does not become known to the jury....

The danger of publicity concerning pretrial suppression hearings is particularly acute, because it may be difficult to measure with any degree of certainty the effects of such publicity on the fairness of the trial. After the commencement of the trial itself, inadmissible prejudicial information about a defen-

dant can be kept from a jury by a variety of means. When such information is publicized during a pretrial proceeding, however, it may never be altogether kept from potential jurors....

[IV.A]

... Among the guarantees that the [Sixth] Amendment provides to a person charged with the commission of a criminal offense, and to him alone, is the "right to a speedy and public trial, by an impartial jury." The Constitution nowhere mentions any right of access to a criminal trial on the part of the public; its guarantee, like the others enumerated, is personal to the accused....

B

While the Sixth Amendment guarantees to a defendant in a criminal case the right to a public trial, it does not guarantee the right to compel a private trial.... [T]he issue is whether members of the public have an enforceable right to a public trial that can be asserted independently of the parties in the litigation.

There can be no blinking the fact that there is a strong societal interest in public trials. Openness in court proceedings may improve the quality of testimony, induce unknown witnesses to come forward with relevant testimony, cause all trial participants to perform their duties more conscientiously, and generally give the public an opportunity to observe the judicial system....

Recognition of an independent public interest in the enforcement of Sixth Amendment guarantees is a far cry, however, from the creation of a constitutional right on the part of the public. In an adversary system of criminal justice, the public interest in the administration of justice is protected by the participants in the litigation....

V

In arguing that members of the general public have a constitutional right to attend a criminal trial, despite the obvious lack of support for such a right in the structure or text of the Sixth Amendment, the petitioner and *amici* rely on the history of the public-trial guarantee. This history, however, ultimately demonstrates no more than the existence of a common-law rule of open civil and criminal proceedings.

A

... The history upon which the petitioner and *amici* rely totally fails to demonstrate that the Framers of the Sixth Amendment intended to create a constitutional right in strangers to attend a pretrial proceeding, when all that they actually did was to confer upon the accused an explicit right to demand a public trial....

B

But even if the Sixth and Fourteenth Amendments could properly be viewed as embodying the common-law right of the public to attend criminal trials, it would not necessarily follow that the petitioner would have a right of access under the circumstances of this case. For there exists no persuasive evidence that at common law members of the public had any right to attend pretrial proceedings; indeed, there is substantial evidence to the contrary....

For these reasons, we hold that members of the public have no constitutional right under the Sixth and Fourteenth Amendments to attend criminal trials.

VI

The petitioner also argues that members of the press and the public have a right of access to the pretrial hearing by reason of the First and Fourteenth Amendments....

... [A]ny denial of access in this case was not absolute but only temporary. Once the danger of prejudice had dissipated, a transcript of the suppression hearing was made available. The press and the public then had a full opportunity to scrutinize the suppression hearing. Unlike the case of an absolute ban on access, therefore, the press here had the opportunity to inform the public of the details of the pretrial hearing accurately and completely. Under these circumstances, any First and Fourteenth Amendment right of the petitioner to attend a criminal trial was not violated.

VII

We certainly do not disparage the general desirability of open judicial proceedings. But we are not asked here to declare whether open proceedings represent beneficial social policy, or whether there would be a constitutional barrier to a state law that imposed a stricter standard of closure than the one here employed by the New York courts. Rather, we are asked to hold that the Constitution itself gave the petitioner an affirmative right of access to this pretrial proceeding, even though all the participants in the litigation agreed that it should be closed to protect the fair-trial rights of the defendants.

For all of the reasons discussed in this opinion, we hold that the Constitution provides no such right. Accordingly, the judgment of the New York Court of Appeals is affirmed.

It is so ordered.

[*Chief Justice Burger and Justices Powell and Rehnquist wrote separate concurring opinions.*]

Mr. Justice Blackmun, with whom Mr. Justice Brennan, Mr. Justice White, and Mr. Justice Marshall join, concurring in part and dissenting in part.

[*Blackmun acknowledges that the Sixth Amendment speaks only of a public "trial," but argues that the pretrial suppression hearing often is a decisive stage for the defendant and the prosecution. He concludes that the Sixth and Fourteenth Amendments prohibit a state from conducting a pretrial suppression hearing in private, even at the request of the accused, "unless full and fair consideration is first given to the public's interest, protected by the Amendments, in open trials."*]

Richmond Newspapers, Inc. v. Virginia

448 U.S. 555 (1980)

After three trials on a murder charge had been either reversed on appeal or had resulted in mistrials, a Virginia court granted the motion of the defense counsel to close the fourth trial to the public and to the press. The prosecutor did not object. Richmond Newspapers, Inc., appealed claiming a First Amendment violation.

Mr. Chief Justice Burger announced the judgment of the Court and delivered an opinion, in which Mr. Justice White and Mr. Justice Stevens joined.

The narrow question presented in this case is whether the right of the public and press to attend criminal trials is guaranteed under the United States Constitution....

II

We begin consideration of this case by noting that the precise issue presented here has not previously been before this Court for decision. In *Gannett Co.* v. *DePasquale, supra,* the Court was not required to decide whether a right of access to *trials,* as distinguished from hearings on *pre*trial motions, was constitutionally guaranteed. The Court held that the Sixth Amendment's guarantee to the accused of a public trial gave neither the public nor the press an enforceable right of access to a *pre*trial suppression hearing....

In prior cases the Court has treated questions involving conflicts between publicity and a defendant's right to a fair trial; ... But here for the first time the Court is asked to decide whether a criminal trial itself may be closed to the public upon the unopposed request of a defendant, without any demonstration that closure is required to protect the defendant's superior right to a fair trial, or that some other overriding consideration requires closure....

B

... [T]he historical evidence demonstrates conclusively that at the time when our organic laws were adopted, criminal trials both here and in England had long been presumptively open. This is no quirk of history; rather, it has long been recognized as an indispensable attribute of an Anglo-American trial. Both Hale in the 17th century and Blackstone in the 18th saw the importance of openness to the proper functioning of a trial; it gave assurance that the proceedings were conducted fairly to all concerned, and it discouraged perjury, the misconduct of participants, and decisions based on secret bias or partiality....

... The early history of open trials in part reflects the widespread acknowledgment, long before there were behavioral scientists, that public trials had significant community therapeutic value. Even without such experts to frame the concept in words, people sensed from experience and observation that, especially in the administration of criminal justice, the means used to achieve justice must have the support derived from public acceptance of both the process and its results.

When a shocking crime occurs, a community reaction of outrage and public protest often follows. See H. Weihofen, The Urge to Punish 130–131 (1956). Thereafter the open processes of justice serve an important prophylactic purpose, providing an outlet for community concern, hostility, and emotion. Without an awareness that society's responses to criminal conduct are underway, natural human reactions of outrage and protest are frustrated and may manifest themselves in some form of vengeful "self-help," as indeed they did regularly in the activities of vigilante "committees" on our frontiers....

Civilized societies withdraw both from the victim and the vigilante the enforcement of criminal laws, but they cannot erase from people's consciousness the fundamental, natural yearning to see justice done—or even the urge for retribution. The crucial prophylactic aspects of the administration of justice cannot function in the dark; ... where the trial has been concealed from public view an unexpected outcome can cause a reaction that the system at best has failed and at worst has been corrupted....

[III.A]

... In guaranteeing freedoms such as those of speech and press, the First Amendment can be read as protecting the right of everyone to attend trials so as to give meaning to those explicit guarantees....

C

The State argues that the Constitution nowhere spells out a guarantee for the right of the public to attend trials, and that accordingly no such right is protected. The possibility that such a contention could be made did not escape the notice of the Constitution's draftsmen; they were concerned that some important rights might be thought disparaged because not specifically guaranteed....

But arguments such as the State makes have not precluded recognition of important rights not enumerated. Notwithstanding the appropriate caution against reading into the Constitution rights not explicitly defined, the Court has acknowledged that certain unarticulated rights are implicit in enumerated guarantees. For example, the rights of association and of privacy, the right to be presumed innocent, and the right to be judged by a standard of proof beyond a reasonable doubt in a criminal trial, as well as the right to travel, appear nowhere in the Constitution or Bill of Rights. Yet these important but unarticulated rights have nonetheless been found to share constitutional protection in common with explicit guarantees.... [F]undamental rights, even though not expressly guaranteed, have been recognized by the Court as indispensable to the enjoyment of rights explicitly defined.

We hold that the right to attend criminal trials is implicit in the guarantees of the First Amendment; without the freedom to attend such trials, which people have exercised for centuries, important aspects of freedom of speech and "of the press could be eviscerated." *Branzburg*, 408 U.S., at 681....

Mr. Justice Powell took no part in the consideration or decision of this case.

[Justices White, Stevens, Brennan (joined by Marshall), Stewart, and Blackmun wrote concurring opinions.]

MR. JUSTICE REHNQUIST, dissenting.

In the Gilbert and Sullivan operetta "Iolanthe," the Lord Chancellor recites:

> "The Law is the true embodiment
> of everything that's excellent,
> It has no kind of fault or flaw,
> And I, my Lords, embody the Law."

It is difficult not to derive more than a little of this flavor from the various opinions supporting the judgment in this case. The opinion of THE CHIEF JUSTICE states:

"[H]ere for the first time the Court is asked to decide whether a criminal trial itself may be closed to the public upon the unopposed request of a defendant, without any demonstration that closure is required to protect the defendant's superior right to a fair trial, or that some other overriding consideration requires closure." *Ante*, at 564.

The opinion of MR. JUSTICE BRENNAN states:

"Read with care and in context, our decisions must therefore be understood as holding only that any privilege of access to governmental information is subject to a degree of restraint dictated by the nature of the information and countervailing interests in security or confidentiality." *Ante*, at 586.

For the reasons stated in my separate concurrence in *Gannett Co.* v. *DePasquale*, 443 U.S. 368, 403 (1979), I do not believe that either the First or Sixth Amendment, as made applicable to the States by the Fourteenth, requires that a State's reasons for denying public access to a trial, where both the prosecuting attorney and the defendant have consented to an order of closure approved by the judge, are subject to any additional constitutional review at our hands....

D. LIBEL LAW

The press and the media face a battery of costly suits brought by individuals who claim damage to their reputations. Making publishers fully liable for errors that cause injury would lead to self-censorship and a diminished free press. In balancing the values between the rights of a free press and safeguards against defamation, the Supreme Court recognizes that the First Amendment "requires that we protect some falsehood in order to protect speech that matters." Gertz v. Robert Welch, Inc., 418 U.S. 323, 341 (1974).

Defamation takes the form of *slander* (oral defamation) and *libel* (written defamation). In addition to defamation of a person, there can also be "product disparagement." Bose Corp. v. Consumers Unions of U.S., Inc., 466 U.S. 485 (1984). In 1998, a federal judge ruled that Texas cattlemen had no right to sue Oprah Winfrey for her televised remarks about the potential effects of "mad cow disease" on the safety of beef. In winning the case, Winfrey spent close to a million dollars in her defense.

British libel law permitted punishment of any writing that tended to bring into disrepute the government or established religion or was likely to provoke a breach of the peace. Truth was not a defense in criminal libel; "the provocation, and not the falsity, is the thing to be punished criminally." 4 Blackstone, Commentaries 150. Contemporary courts recognize truth as a defense, but libel law is engulfed by confusion and tenuous distinctions.

Public Officials

Although the relationship between malice and defamation was explored in the nineteenth century, White v. Nicholls, 44 U.S. (3 How.) 266 (1845), the benchmark libel case dates from 1964. After an advertisement in the *New York Times* charged Alabama police with acts of terrorism and violence against civil rights demonstrators, a state official responsible for the police brought a libel suit against the newspaper and four civil rights leaders. In a unanimous decision, the Court held that the official could not recover damages unless he could prove that the defamatory information in the advertisement was made with "actual malice," which the Court defined as "knowledge that it was false or with reckless disregard of whether it was false or not." NEW YORK TIMES CO. v. SULLIVAN, 376 U.S. 254, 280 (1964).

Following *Sullivan,* a series of cases have limited the reach of defamation suits. For example, a Louisiana defamation statute permitted critics of public officials to be punished not only for false statements made with ill will but even true statements made with ill will. A district attorney in Louisiana, during a news conference, accused state judges of being lazy and inefficient and of hampering his efforts to enforce the laws. He was convicted of violating the state defamation statute. A unanimous Supreme Court held that the Constitution limits state power to impose sanctions for criticism of the official conduct of public officials. Punishment applied only to false statements made with knowledge of their falsity or with reckless disregard of whether they are true or false. "Truth may not be the subject of either civil or criminal sanctions where discussion of public affairs is concerned." Garrison v. Louisiana, 379 U.S. 64, 74 (1964). Concurrences by Justices Black, Douglas, and Goldberg objected to *any* punishment for criticizing public officials. Black and Douglas claimed that fines and jail sentences for "malicious" statements marked a return to the Sedition Act of 1798 and a revival of the law of seditious libel.

In 1966, the Court reversed another libel suit that had awarded damages to an individual employed by three county commissioners. He claimed that a newspaper column accused him of fiscal mismanagement, but the Court ruled that any implication of wrongdoing had not been directed at him personally. Rosenblatt v. Baer, 383 U.S. 75 (1966). Three concurrences by Douglas, Stewart, and Black argued that the Constitution bars any libel actions against government officials.

Public Figures

Apart from libel suits involving government officials, the Supreme Court reviews cases in which private individuals seek damages for defamation or invasion of privacy. A libel suit was brought by James Hill, who had been held hostage in his home, along with his family, by escaped convicts. His ordeal helped inspire a novel and later a play, called *The Desperate Hours.* In writing about the play, *Life* magazine related it specifically to the Hill incident and called the play a reenactment. Hill was awarded damages. The Court reversed the judgment with instructions that damages could be given only upon proof that *Life* was knowingly or recklessly false. There had to be calculated falsehoods. Mere negligence, said the Court, would put an intolerable burden on the press. Time, Inc. v. Hill, 385 U.S. 374 (1967).

This case developed the public-figure doctrine by distinguishing between private citizens (like James Hill) who desired anonymity and those who, because of their prominence in sports, entertainment, and other fields, were "public figures." The latter had a reduced right of privacy. The public-figure doctrine was used in another case in 1967. Libel damages were allowed for an athletic director accused in a magazine article of "fixing" a football game. The falsehood inflicted substantial damage on his reputation and resulted from deficient investigative and reporting techniques. Curtis Publishing Co. v. Butts, 388 U.S. 130 (1967). The Court has issued other guidelines to clarify the public-figure doctrine. Harte-Hanks Communications v. Connaughton, 491 U.S. 657 (1989).

Public Concern

In 1971, a plurality of Supreme Court Justices was ready to float another doctrine. They said that the First Amendment's impact on state libel laws depended not so much on whether the plaintiff was a public official, a public figure, or a private individual, but whether the defamation concerns "an issue of public or general concern." Rosenbloom v. Metromedia, 403 U.S. 29, 44 (1971). Under the latter test, the rights of a free press require special protection and tolerance. In his concurrence, Justice White attempted to summarize the multiple and evolving doctrines of the Court. Public officers and public figures had to prove either knowing or reckless disregard of the truth. Other plaintiffs had to prove at least negligent falsehood, "but if the publication about them was in an area of legitimate public interest, then they too must prove deliberate or reckless error."

This new formulation did not sit well. Why should a private individual be forced to satisfy the rigorous requirement of knowing-or-reckless falsity simply because the defamatory falsehood became an issue of public or general interest? With what competence can courts figure out what constitutes an issue of "public or general interest?" Within a few years the Court abandoned the *Rosenbloom* doctrine because it gave insufficient protection to private individuals. The Court recognized that public officials and public figures have more opportunities to use the media to rebut defamation. Private individuals are "more vulnerable to injury, and the state interest in protecting them is correspondingly greater." GERTZ v. ROBERT WELCH, INC., 418 U.S. 323, 344 (1974). Although states must follow the knowing-or-reckless-disregard test for public officials and public figures, they "should retain substantial latitude in their efforts to enforce a legal remedy for defamatory falsehood injurious to the reputation of a private individual." In discarding the doctrine of "public or general concern," the Court doubted the wisdom of committing such tasks to the conscience of judges.

In *Gertz,* the Court suggested that statements of "opinion" might be exempt from defamation suits. In 1990, the Court focused specifically on the issue of whether a columnist can be sued for expressing an opinion. The Court denied that a dichotomy exists between fact and opinion, refusing to create a wholesale defamation exemption for anything that might be labeled an opinion. Expressions of opinion, said the Court, may often imply an assertion of objective fact. The 7–2 decision permits libel suits if opinions contain or imply "false and defamatory" facts. Milkovich v. Lorain Journal Co., 497 U.S. 1 (1990). A year later, the Court ruled that writers may be sued for fabricating quotations if the injurious words are significantly different from what was actually said. Manufactured quotations can be the basis for a libel suit if the writer makes a "material change in the meaning" of someone's statement. Under this test, writers still have substantial flexibility to alter a speaker's words without fear of a libel suit. Masson v. New Yorker Magazine, Inc., 501 U.S. 496 (1991).

This heightened solicitude for private individuals who seek damages in libel suits has been reinforced over the years. A series of cases adopted a narrow definition of "public figure," thus allowing private individuals who might be prominent locally a better chance of collecting on a libel suit.[4] However, in 1985 the Court resurrected the public-concern doctrine. Divided 5 to 4, it held that speech on matters of "purely private concern" is entitled to less First Amendment protection than speech involving public concern. Once it is determined that there is a lack of public concern in a libel action, plaintiffs may be awarded damages without having to show actual malice. Dun & Bradstreet, Inc. v. Greenmoss Builders, 472 U.S. 749 (1985). The dissenters objected that the majority had provided "almost no guidance as to what constitutes a protected matter of public concern." The public-concern doctrine was used a year later in another 5–4 decision. The Court held that when a newspaper publishes speech of public concern about a private figure, the individual cannot recover libel damages without showing that the statements are false. Philadelphia Newspapers, Inc. v. Hepps, 475 U.S. 767 (1986). Libel cases are guided by a number of doctrines (see box on next page).

Financial Burdens of Litigation

Although *Sullivan* made it more difficult for public officials and public figures to win libel verdicts against the press, nothing in that decision prevented the filing of a suit and forcing the press to exhaust funds and resources to defend itself. Celebrities claiming injury sued the press and the media for large sums. For example, General William C. Westmoreland filed a $120 million suit against CBS-TV and its weekly program "60 Minutes" for charging that he and his command had misled the public, the Congress, and the President about enemy troop strength in Vietnam in order to advance the political argument that the war was being won. Ariel Sharon, former Israeli Defense Minister, sued

---

4. Wolston v. Reader's Digest Assn., Inc., 443 U.S. 157 (1979); Hutchinson v. Proxmire, 443 U.S. 111 (1979); Time, Inc. v. Firestone, 424 U.S. 448 (1976). In *Hutchinson,* the Court noted: "Clearly, those charged with defamation cannot, by their own conduct, create their own defense by making the claimant a public figure." 443 U.S. at 135.

Libel Doctrines

1. *Actual Malice.* Public officials or public figures may recover damages if there is "actual malice" (knowledge that the statements are false or made with reckless disregard of whether they were false or not). New York Times Co. v. Sullivan, 376 U.S. 254, 280 (1964).

2. *Public Figure.* Certain individuals who are prominent in public life (because of sports, entertainment, and so forth) have a reduced right of privacy. Time, Inc. v. Hill, 385 U.S. 374, 384–86 (1967). Their defamation suits must meet a higher standard of proof than for a private citizen.

3. *Public Concern.* Libel actions are more difficult to win if the information published relates to an issue of public or general concern. Rosenbloom v. Metromedia, 403 U.S. 29, 44 (1971). The Court later backed away from that test. Gertz v. Robert Welch, Inc., 418 U.S. 323 (1974).

4. *Fact vs. Opinion.* There is no wholesale exemption for what might be called "opinion." Expressions of opinion may often imply an assertion of objective fact. Milkovich v. Lorain Journal Co., 497 U.S. 1 (1990).

Time magazine for $50 million for suggesting that he had encouraged the massacre of hundreds of Palestinians in the Sabra and Shatila refugee camps.

Westmoreland agreed to drop the case in 1985, before verdict, in return for a joint statement in which CBS expressed its respect for his "long and faithful service to his country" and Westmoreland gave his esteem for CBS's "distinguished journalistic tradition." In a separate statement, CBS said it stood by the fairness and accuracy of the program. Also in 1985, a jury in New York issued a split verdict on Sharon, concluding that *Time* had acted negligently and carelessly but not with actual malice or reckless disregard for the truth. In a separate action in Israel, Sharon and *Time* announced an out-of-court settlement in 1986 in which *Time* admitted that its story was "erroneous" and agreed to pay part of Sharon's legal fees. The legal expenses for CBS and *Time* to defend their interests were vast.

A decision by the Supreme Court in 1988 sparked an unusual amount of interest in libel law. A jury had awarded $200,000 to the Reverend Jerry Falwell, founder of the Moral Majority, for damages inflicted by an advertisement in *Hustler* magazine. The ad was a takeoff on a Campari liqueur campaign in which celebrities discussed "their first time." The parody portrays Falwell as a drunkard having sex with his mother in an outhouse. Although the jury said the ad was not libelous because it was patently unbelievable, it assessed damages for the "emotional distress" suffered by Falwell. A unanimous Court ruled that public figures and public officials unable to prove libel cannot recover damages for parodies, no matter how outrageous, that might cause emotional distress. "Outrageousness" was too subjective a test and would interfere with the free flow of ideas protected by the First Amendment. HUSTLER MAGAZINE v. FALWELL, 485 U.S. 46 (1988).

The original purpose of the actual-malice test was to safeguard the press by erecting a high shield. How does a plaintiff determine that a falsehood results from malice? What steps must be taken to show that a publisher has "knowledge" or acts with "reckless disregard" in issuing false statements? May plaintiffs interview and depose employees of a newspaper or broadcasting station to discover the state of mind of those who edit, produce, and publish stories? Would this threaten a free press? In 1979, a 6–3 Court held that the First Amendment does not prohibit a plaintiff in a libel case from inquiring into the editorial process. Herbert v. Lando, 441 U.S. 153 (1979).

A 1985 libel case offers a rare example where the Court was able to speak with a unanimous voice. In letters to President Reagan, someone had written false and derogatory statements about a person being considered for U.S. attorney. The author of the letters claimed that the Petition Clause of the First Amendment gave him absolute immunity from liability. The Court held that statements made in a petition are not entitled to greater constitutional protection than other First Amendment expressions. McDonald v. Smith, 472 U.S. 479 (1985).

The law on libel has become so confused and costly for plaintiffs and defendants that alternatives to adjudication are being explored. One approach is to bar lawsuits if a complainant receives a retraction or an opportunity to reply in a newspaper or broadcast outlet. If the complainant fails to receive that satisfaction, either side could ask a court for a declaratory judgment on the truth or falsity of the statement at issue. The objective of these reforms is to eliminate vague standards, including "actual malice" and "public figure."

New York Times Co. v. Sullivan

376 U.S. 254 (1964)

An advertisement in the *New York Times* included statements, some of them false, about actions that Alabama police had taken against civil rights demonstrators. L.B. Sullivan, who supervised the police, brought a libel action against the newspaper and four civil rights leaders. After he won a jury award in the state courts, a unanimous Supreme Court held that the law applied by the Alabama courts gave insufficient protection to free speech and free press. The Court developed the actual-malice test for recovering damages in a defamation suit.

MR. JUSTICE BRENNAN delivered the opinion of the Court.

We are required in this case to determine for the first time the extent to which the constitutional protections for speech and press limit a State's power to award damages in a libel action brought by a public official against critics of his official conduct.

Respondent L. B. Sullivan is one of the three elected Commissioners of the City of Montgomery, Alabama. He testified that he was "Commissioner of Public Affairs and the duties are supervision of the Police Department, Fire Department, Department of Cemetery and Department of Scales." He brought this civil libel action against the four individual petitioners, who are Negroes and Alabama clergymen, and against petitioner the New York Times Company, a New York corporation which publishes the New York Times, a daily newspaper. A jury in the Circuit Court of Montgomery County awarded him damages of $500,000, the full amount claimed, against all the petitioners, and the Supreme Court of Alabama affirmed. 273 Ala. 656, 144 So.2d 25.

Respondent's complaint alleged that he had been libeled by statements in a full-page advertisement that was carried in the New York Times on March 29, 1960. Entitled "Heed Their Rising Voices," the advertisement began by stating that "As the whole world knows by now, thousands of Southern Negro students are engaged in widespread non-violent demonstrations in positive affirmation of the right to live in human dignity as guaranteed by the U. S. Constitution and the Bill of Rights." It went on to charge that "in their efforts to uphold these guarantees, they are being met by an unprecedented wave of terror by those who would deny and negate that

document which the whole world looks upon as setting the pattern for modern freedom...." Succeeding paragraphs purported to illustrate the "wave of terror" by describing certain alleged events. The text concluded with an appeal for funds for three purposes: support of the student movement, "the struggle for the right-to-vote," and the legal defense of Dr. Martin Luther King, Jr., leader of the movement, against a perjury indictment then pending in Montgomery.

The text appeared over the names of 64 persons, many widely known for their activities in public affairs, religion, trade unions, and the performing arts. Below these names, and under a line reading "We in the south who are struggling daily for dignity and freedom warmly endorse this appeal," appeared the names of the four individual petitioners and of 16 other persons....

Of the 10 paragraphs of text in the advertisement, the third and a portion of the sixth were the basis of respondent's claim of libel. They read as follows:

Third paragraph:

"In Montgomery, Alabama, after students sang 'My Country, 'Tis of Thee' on the State Capitol steps, their leaders were expelled from school, and truckloads of police armed with shotguns and tear-gas ringed the Alabama State College Campus. When the entire student body protested to state authorities by refusing to re-register, their dining hall was padlocked in an attempt to starve them into submission."

Sixth paragraph:

"Again and again the Southern violators have answered Dr. King's peaceful protests with intimidation and violence. They have bombed his home almost killing his wife and child. They have assaulted his person. They have arrested him seven times—for 'speeding,' 'loitering' and similar 'offenses.' And now they have charged him with 'perjury'—a *felony* under which they could imprison him for *ten years....*"

Although neither of these statements mentions respondent by name, he contended that the word "police" in the third paragraph referred to him as the Montgomery Commissioner who supervised the Police Department, so that he was being accused of "ringing" the campus with police. He further claimed that the paragraph would be read as imputing to the police, and hence to him, the padlocking of the dining hall in order to starve the students into submission. As to the sixth paragraph, he contended that since arrests are ordinarily made by the police, the statement "They have arrested [Dr. King] seven times" would be read as referring to him; he further contended that the "They" who did the arresting would be equated with the "They" who committed the other described acts and with the "Southern violators." Thus, he argued, the paragraph would be read as accusing the Montgomery police, and hence him, of answering Dr. King's protests with "intimidation and violence," bombing his home, assaulting his person, and charging him with perjury. Respondent and six other Montgomery residents testified that they read some or all of the statements as referring to him in his capacity as Commissioner.

It is uncontroverted that some of the statements contained in the two paragraphs were not accurate descriptions of events which occurred in Montgomery. Although Negro students staged a demonstration on the State Capitol steps, they sang the National Anthem and not "My Country, 'Tis of Thee." Although nine students were expelled by the State Board of Education, this was not for leading the demonstration at the Capitol, but for demanding service at a lunch counter in the Montgomery County Courthouse on another day. Not the entire student body, but most of it, had protested the expulsion, not by refusing to register, but by boycotting classes on a single day; virtually all the students did register for the ensuing semester. The campus dining hall was not padlocked on any occasion, and the only students who may have been barred from eating there were the few who had neither signed a preregistration application nor requested temporary meal tickets. Although the police were deployed near the campus in large numbers on three occasions, they did not at any time "ring" the campus, and they were not called to the campus in connection with the demonstration on the State Capitol steps, as the third paragraph implied. Dr. King had not been arrested seven times, but only four; and although he claimed to have been assaulted some years earlier in connection with his arrest for loitering outside a courtroom, one of the officers who made the arrest denied that there was such an assault.

On the premise that the charges in the sixth paragraph could be read as referring to him, respondent was allowed to prove that he had not participated in the events described. Although Dr. King's home had in fact been bombed twice when his wife and child were there, both of these occasions antedated respondent's tenure as Commissioner, and the police were not only not implicated in the bombings, but had made every effort to apprehend those who were. Three of Dr. King's four arrests took place before respondent became Commissioner. Although Dr. King had in fact been indicted (he was subsequently acquitted) on two counts of perjury, each of which carried a possible five-year sentence, respondent had nothing to do with procuring the indictment.

Respondent made no effort to prove that he suffered actual pecuniary loss as a result of the alleged libel....

Alabama law denies a public officer recovery of punitive damages in a libel action brought on account of a publication concerning his official conduct unless he first makes a written demand for a public retraction and the defendant fails or refuses to comply. Alabama Code, Tit. 7, § 914. Respondent served such a demand upon each of the petitioners. None of the individual petitioners responded to the demand, primarily because each took the position that he had not authorized the use of his name on the advertisement and therefore had not published the statements that respondent alleged had libeled him. The Times did not publish a retraction in response to the demand, but wrote respondent a letter stating, among other things, that "we ... are somewhat puzzled as to how you think the statements in any way reflect on you," and "you might, if you desire, let us know in what respect you claim that the statements in the advertisement reflect on you." Respondent filed this suit a few days later without answering the letter. The Times did, however, subsequently publish a retraction of the advertisement upon the demand of Governor John Patterson of Alabama, who asserted that the publication charged him with "grave misconduct and ... improper actions and omissions as Governor of Alabama and

Ex-Officio Chairman of the State Board of Education of Alabama." When asked to explain why there had been a retraction for the Governor but not for respondent, the Secretary of the Times testified: "We did that because we didn't want anything that was published by The Times to be a reflection on the State of Alabama and the Governor was, as far as we could see, the embodiment of the State of Alabama and the proper representative of the State and, furthermore, we had by that time learned more of the actual facts which the ad purported to recite and, finally, the ad did refer to the action of the State authorities and the Board of Education presumably of which the Governor is the ex-officio chairman...." On the other hand, he testified that he did not think that "any of the language in there referred to Mr. Sullivan."...

II.

Under Alabama law as applied in this case, a publication is "libelous per se" if the words "tend to injure a person ... in his reputation" or to "bring [him] into public contempt"; the trial court stated that the standard was met if the words are such as to "injure him in his public office, or impute misconduct to him in his office, or want of official integrity, or want of fidelity to a public trust...."... Unless [*the defendant*] can discharge the burden of proving truth, general damages are presumed, and may be awarded without proof of pecuniary injury. A showing of actual malice is apparently a prerequisite to recovery of punitive damages, and the defendant may in any event forestall a punitive award by a retraction meeting the statutory requirements. Good motives and belief in truth do not negate an inference of malice, but are relevant only in mitigation of punitive damages if the jury chooses to accord them weight....

The question before us is whether this rule of liability, as applied to an action brought by a public official against critics of his official conduct, abridges the freedom of speech and of the press that is guaranteed by the First and Fourteenth Amendments....

... [W]e consider this case against the background of a profound national commitment to the principle that debate on public issues should be uninhibited, robust, and wide-open, and that it may well include vehement, caustic, and sometimes unpleasantly sharp attacks on government and public officials.... The present advertisement, as an expression of grievance and protest on one of the major public issues of our time, would seem clearly to qualify for the constitutional protection. The question is whether it forfeits that protection by the falsity of some of its factual statements and by its alleged defamation of respondent....

Injury to official reputation affords no more warrant for repressing speech that would otherwise be free than does factual error. Where judicial officers are involved, this Court has held that concern for the dignity and reputation of the courts does not justify the punishment as criminal contempt of criticism of the judge or his decision. *Bridges* v. *California,* 314 U.S. 252. This is true even though the utterance contains "half-truths" and "misinformation." ... If judges are to be treated as "men of fortitude, able to thrive in a hardy climate," ... surely the same must be true of other government officials, such as elected city commissioners. Criticism of their official conduct does not lose its constitutional protection merely because it is effective criticism and hence diminishes their official reputations.

If neither factual error nor defamatory content suffices to remove the constitutional shield from criticism of official conduct, the combination of the two elements is no less inadequate. This is the lesson to be drawn from the great controversy over the Sedition Act of 1798, 1 Stat. 596, which first crystallized a national awareness of the central meaning of the First Amendment....

Although the Sedition Act was never tested in this Court, the attack upon its validity has carried the day in the court of history. Fines levied in its prosecution were repaid by Act of Congress on the ground that it was unconstitutional.... Jefferson, as President, pardoned those who had been convicted and sentenced under the Act and remitted their fines....

The constitutional guarantees require, we think, a federal rule that prohibits a public official from recovering damages for a defamatory falsehood relating to his official conduct unless he proves that the statement was made with "actual malice"—that is, with knowledge that it was false or with reckless disregard of whether it was false or not....

III.

... [W]e consider that the proof presented to show actual malice lacks the convincing clarity which the constitutional standard demands, and hence that it would not constitutionally sustain the judgment for respondent under the proper rule of law. The case of the individual petitioners requires little discussion. Even assuming that they could constitutionally be found to have authorized the use of their names on the advertisement, there was no evidence whatever that they were aware of any erroneous statements or were in any way reckless in that regard. The judgment against them is thus without constitutional support.

As to the Times, we similarly conclude that the facts do not support a finding of actual malice. The statement by the Times' Secretary that, apart from the padlocking allegation, he thought the advertisement was "substantially correct," affords no constitutional warrant for the Alabama Supreme Court's conclusion that it was a "cavalier ignoring of the falsity of the advertisement [from which] the jury could not have but been impressed with the bad faith of The Times, and its maliciousness inferable therefrom."... The Times' failure to retract upon respondent's demand, although it later retracted upon the demand of Governor Patterson, is likewise not adequate evidence of malice for constitutional purposes. Whether or not a failure to retract may ever constitute such evidence, there are two reasons why it does not here. *First*, the letter written by the Times reflected a reasonable doubt on its part as to whether the advertisement could reasonably be taken to refer to respondent at all. *Second*, it was not a final refusal, since it asked for an explanation on this point—a request that respondent chose to ignore....

Finally, there is evidence that the Times published the advertisement without checking its accuracy against the news stories in the Times' own files. The mere presence of the stories in the files does not, of course, establish that the Times "knew" the advertisement was false, since the state of mind required for actual malice would have to be brought home to the persons in the Times' organization having responsibility for the publication of the advertisement. With respect to the failure of those persons to make the check, the record shows that they relied upon their knowledge of the good reputation of many of those whose names were listed as sponsors of the advertisement, and upon the letter from A. Philip Randolph, known to them as a responsible individual, certifying that the use of the names was authorized....

The judgment of the Supreme Court of Alabama is reversed and the case is remanded to that court for further proceedings not inconsistent with this opinion.

Reversed and remanded.

MR. JUSTICE BLACK, with whom MR. JUSTICE DOUGLAS joins, concurring.

... I vote to reverse exclusively on the ground that the Times and the individual defendants had an absolute, unconditional constitutional right to publish in the Times advertisement their criticisms of the Montgomery agencies and officials....

MR. JUSTICE GOLDBERG, with whom MR. JUSTICE DOUGLAS joins, concurring in the result....

In my view, the First and Fourteenth Amendments to the Constitution afford to the citizen and to the press an absolute, unconditional privilege to criticize official conduct despite the harm which may flow from excesses and abuses....

Gertz v. Robert Welch, Inc.

418 U.S. 323 (1974)

An article appearing in a magazine published by Robert Welch, Inc., claimed that a murder trial was part of a Communist conspiracy to discredit the local police. The article falsely stated that Elmer Gertz, an attorney who represented the parents of a youth killed by the police, had a criminal record and labeled him a "Communist-fronter." This case prompted the Court to revisit its holdings on the protections of private individuals who are subject to defamatory falsehoods, and the separate question of what constitutes a matter of "general or public interest."

MR. JUSTICE POWELL delivered the opinion of the Court.

This Court has struggled for nearly a decade to define the proper accommodation between the law of defamation and the freedoms of speech and press protected by the First Amendment. With this decision we return to that effort....

I

In 1968 a Chicago policeman named Nuccio shot and killed a youth named Nelson. The state authorities prosecuted Nuccio for the homicide and ultimately obtained a conviction for murder in the second degree. The Nelson family retained petitioner Elmer Gertz, a reputable attorney, to represent them in civil litigation against Nuccio.

Respondent publishes American Opinion, a monthly outlet for the views of the John Birch Society. Early in the 1960's the magazine began to warn of a nationwide conspiracy to discredit local law enforcement agencies and create in their stead a national police force capable of supporting a Communist dictatorship. As part of the continuing effort to alert the public to this assumed danger, the managing editor of American Opinion commissioned an article on the murder trial of Officer Nuccio. For this purpose he engaged a regular contributor to the magazine. In March 1969 respondent published the resulting article under the title "FRAME-UP: Richard Nuccio And The War On Police." The article purports to demonstrate that the testimony against Nuccio at his criminal trial was false and that his prosecution was part of the Communist campaign against the police.

In his capacity as counsel for the Nelson family in the civil litigation, petitioner attended the coroner's inquest into the boy's death and initiated actions for damages, but he neither discussed Officer Nuccio with the press nor played any part in the criminal proceeding. Notwithstanding petitioner's remote connection with the prosecution of Nuccio, respondent's magazine portrayed him as an architect of the "frame-up." According to the article, the police file on petitioner took "a big, Irish cop to lift." The article stated that petitioner had been an official of the "Marxist League for Industrial Democracy, originally known as the Intercollegiate Socialist Society, which has advocated the violent seizure of our government." It labeled Gertz a "Leninist" and a "Communist-fronter." It also stated that Gertz had been an officer of the National Lawyers Guild, described as a Communist organization that "probably did more than any other outfit to plan the Communist attack on the Chicago police during the 1968 Democratic Convention."

These statements contained serious inaccuracies. The implication that petitioner had a criminal record was false. Petitioner had been a member and officer of the National Lawyers Guild some 15 years earlier, but there was no evidence that he or that organization had taken any part in planning the 1968 demonstrations in Chicago. There was also no basis for the charge that petitioner was a "Leninist" or a "Communist-fronter." And he had never been a member of the "Marxist League for Industrial Democracy" or the "Intercollegiate Socialist Society."

The managing editor of American Opinion made no effort to verify or substantiate the charges against petitioner....

[*Robert Welch, Inc., asserted that Gertz was a public official or a public figure and that the article concerned an issue of public interest and concern. Relying on New York Times Co. v. Sullivan(1964), the publisher claimed that Gertz had to prove "actual malice" — that the publisher had knowledge the article was false or operated with reckless disregard whether it was false or not. The magazine's managing editor submitted an affidavit denying any knowledge of the falsity of the statements and stating that he had relied on the author's reputation for accuracy.*]

II

The principal issue in this case is whether a newspaper or broadcaster that publishes defamatory falsehoods about an individual who is neither a public official nor a public figure may claim a constitutional privilege against liability for the injury inflicted by those statements. The Court considered this question on the rather different set of facts presented in *Rosenbloom* v. *Metromedia, Inc.,* 403 U.S. 29 (1971).

... The eight Justices who participated in *Rosenbloom* announced their views in five separate opinions, none of which commanded more than three votes....

In affirming the trial court's judgment in the instant case, the Court of Appeals relied on MR. JUSTICE BRENNAN's conclusion for the *Rosenbloom* plurality that "all discussion and communication involving matters of public or general concern," 403 U.S., at 44, warrant the protection from liability for defamation accorded by the rule originally enunciated in *New York Times Co.* v. *Sullivan,* 376 U.S. 254 (1964)....

... MR. JUSTICE BRENNAN took the *New York Times* privilege one step further. He concluded that its protection should extend to defamatory falsehoods relating to private persons if the statements concerned matters of general or public interest. He abjured the suggested distinction between public officials and public figures on the one hand and private individuals on the other. He focused instead on society's interest in learning about certain issues: "If a matter is a subject of public or general interest, it cannot suddenly become less so merely because a private individual is involved, or because in some sense the individual did not 'voluntarily' choose to become involved." ...

III

We begin with the common ground. Under the First Amendment there is no such thing as a false idea. However pernicious an opinion may seem, we depend for its correction not on the conscience of judges and juries but on the competition of other ideas. But there is no constitutional value in false statements of fact....

Although the erroneous statement of fact is not worthy of constitutional protection, it is nevertheless inevitable in free debate.... And punishment of error runs the risk of inducing a cautious and restrictive exercise of the constitutionally guaranteed freedoms of speech and press. Our decisions recognize that a rule of strict liability that compels a publisher or broadcaster to guarantee the accuracy of his factual assertions may lead to intolerable self-censorship....

The need to avoid self-censorship by the news media is, however, not the only societal value at issue. If it were, this Court would have embraced long ago the view that publishers and broadcasters enjoy an unconditional and indefeasible immunity from liability for defamation....

The legitimate state interest underlying the law of libel is the compensation of individuals for the harm inflicted on them by defamatory falsehood. We would not lightly require the State to abandon this purpose, ...

... The first remedy of any victim of defamation is self-help — using available opportunities to contradict the lie or correct the error and thereby to minimize its adverse impact on reputation. Public officials and public figures usually enjoy significantly greater access to the channels of effective communication and hence have a more realistic opportunity to counteract false statements than private individuals normally enjoy. Private individuals are therefore more vulnerable to injury, and the state interest in protecting them is correspondingly greater.

More important than the likelihood that private individuals will lack effective opportunities for rebuttal, there is a compelling normative consideration underlying the distinction between public and private defamation plaintiffs. An individual who decides to seek governmental office must accept certain necessary consequences of that involvement in public affairs. He runs the risk of closer public scrutiny than might otherwise be the case....

Those classed as public figures stand in a similar position. Hypothetically, it may be possible for someone to become a public figure through no purposeful action of his own, but the instances of truly involuntary public figures must be exceedingly rare....

Even if the foregoing generalities do not obtain in every instance, the communications media are entitled to act on the assumption that public officials and public figures have voluntarily exposed themselves to increased risk of injury from defamatory

falsehood concerning them. No such assumption is justified with respect to a private individual.... [P]rivate individuals are not only more vulnerable to injury than public officials and public figures; they are also more deserving of recovery.

For these reasons we conclude that the States should retain substantial latitude in their efforts to enforce a legal remedy for defamatory falsehood injurious to the reputation of a private individual. The extension of the *New York Times* test proposed by the *Rosenbloom* plurality would abridge this legitimate state interest to a degree that we find unacceptable. And it would occasion the additional difficulty of forcing state and federal judges to decide on an *ad hoc* basis which publications address issues of "general or public interest" and which do not — to determine, in the words of Mr. Justice Marshall, "what information is relevant to self-government." *Rosenbloom* v. *Metromedia, Inc.,* 403 U.S., at 79. We doubt the wisdom of committing this task to the conscience of judges....

We hold that, so long as they do not impose liability without fault, the States may define for themselves the appropriate standard of liability for a publisher or broadcaster of defamatory falsehood injurious to a private individual....

V

[*The Court denies Welch's contention that Gertz is a "public official" or a "public figure" because of his activity in community and professional affairs.*]

Mr. Justice Blackmun, concurring....

Mr. Chief Justice Burger, dissenting.

... In today's opinion the Court abandons the traditional thread so far as the ordinary private citizen is concerned and introduces the concept that the media will be liable for negligence in publishing defamatory statements with respect to such persons....

Mr. Justice Douglas, dissenting.

The Court describes this case as a return to the struggle of "defin[ing] the proper accommodation between the law of defamation and the freedoms of speech and press protected by the First Amendment."... I would suggest that the struggle is a quite hopeless one, for, in light of the command of the First Amendment, no "accommodation" of its freedoms can be "proper" except those made by the Framers themselves....

Mr. Justice Brennan, dissenting.

... I adhere to my view expressed in *Rosenbloom*

v. *Metromedia, Inc., supra,* that we strike the proper accommodation between avoidance of media self-censorship and protection of individual reputations only when we require States to apply the *New York Times Co.* v. *Sullivan,* 376 U.S. 254 (1964), knowing-or-reckless-falsity standard in civil libel actions concerning media reports of the involvement of private individuals in events of public or general interest....

MR. JUSTICE WHITE, dissenting.

... The States must now struggle to discern the meaning of such ill-defined concepts as "liability without fault" and to fashion novel rules for the recovery of damages. These matters have not been briefed or argued by the parties and their workability has not been seriously explored....

Hustler Magazine v. Falwell

485 U.S. 46 (1988)

Jerry Falwell, a nationally known minister and commentator on politics and public affairs, filed a libel suit against the *Hustler* magazine and its publisher, Larry C. Flynt. The suit sought to recover damages for libel and intentional infliction of emotional distress arising from the publication of an advertisement parody that displayed Falwell as a drunkard having sex with his mother in an outhouse. The jury rejected the libel claim on the ground that the parody was not believable, but it ruled in Falwell's favor on the emotional distress claim. The Fourth Circuit affirmed the ruling.

CHIEF JUSTICE REHNQUIST delivered the opinion of the Court.

Petitioner Hustler Magazine, Inc., is a magazine of nationwide circulation. Respondent Jerry Falwell, a nationally known minister who has been active as a commentator on politics and public affairs, sued petitioner and its publisher, petitioner Larry Flynt, to recover damages for invasion of privacy, libel, and intentional infliction of emotional distress....

The inside front cover of the November 1983 issue of Hustler Magazine featured a "parody" of an advertisement for Campari Liqueur that contained the name and picture of respondent and was entitled "Jerry Falwell talks about his first time." This parody was modeled after actual Campari ads that included interviews with various celebrities about their "first times." Although it was apparent by the end of each interview that this meant the first time they sampled Campari, the ads clearly played on the sexual double entendre of the general subject of "first times." Copying the form and layout of these Campari ads, Hustler's editors chose respondent as the featured celebrity and drafted an alleged "interview" with him in which he states that his "first time" was during a drunken incestuous rendezvous with his mother in an outhouse. The Hustler parody portrays respondent and his mother as drunk and immoral, and suggests that respondent is a hypocrite who preaches only when he is drunk. In small print at the bottom of the page, the ad contains the disclaimer, "ad parody—not to be taken seriously." The magazine's

table of contents also lists the ad as "Fiction; Ad and Personality Parody."

Soon after the November issue of Hustler became available to the public, respondent brought this diversity action in the United States District Court for the Western District of Virginia against Hustler Magazine, Inc., Larry C. Flynt, and Flynt Distributing Co. Respondent stated in his complaint that publication of the ad parody in Hustler entitled him to recover damages for libel, invasion of privacy, and intentional infliction of emotional distress.... The jury then found against respondent on the libel claim, specifically finding that the ad parody could not "reasonably be understood as describing actual facts about [respondent] or actual events in which [he] participated." ... The jury ruled for respondent on the intentional infliction of emotional distress claim, however, and stated that he should be awarded $100,000 in compensatory damages, as well as $50,000 each in punitive damages from petitioners....

At the heart of the First Amendment is the recognition of the fundamental importance of the free flow of ideas and opinions on matters of public interest and concern.... We have therefore been particularly vigilant to ensure that individual expressions of ideas remain free from governmentally imposed sanctions....

The sort of robust political debate encouraged by the First Amendment is bound to produce speech that is critical of those who hold public office or those public figures who are "intimately involved in the resolution of important public questions or, by reason of their fame, shape events in areas of concern to society at large." ... Such criticism, inevitably, will not always be reasoned or moderate; public figures as well as public officials will be subject to "vehement, caustic, and sometimes unpleasantly sharp attacks," ...

Of course, this does not mean that *any* speech about a public figure is immune from sanction in the form of damages. Since *New York Times Co.* v. *Sullivan, supra,* we have consistently ruled that a public figure may hold a speaker liable for the damage to reputation caused by publication of a defamatory falsehood, but only if the statement was made "with knowledge that it was false or with reckless disregard of whether it was false or not." ... False statements of fact are particularly valueless; they interfere with the truth-seeking function of the marketplace of ideas, and they cause damage to an individual's reputation that cannot easily be repaired by counterspeech, however persuasive or effective.... But even though falsehoods have little value in and of themselves, they are "nevertheless inevitable in free debate," ... and a rule that would impose strict liability on a publisher for false factual assertions would have an undoubted "chilling" effect on speech relating to public figures that does have constitutional value....

Respondent argues, however, that a different standard should apply in this case because here the State seeks to prevent not reputational damage, but the severe emotional distress suffered by the person who is the subject of an offensive publication.... In respondent's view, and in the view of the Court of Appeals, so long as the utterance was intended to inflict emotional distress, was outrageous, and did in fact inflict serious emotional distress, it is of no constitutional import whether the statement was a fact or an opinion, or whether it was true or false. It is the intent to cause injury that is the gravamen of the tort, and the State's interest in preventing emotional harm simply outweighs whatever interest a speaker may have in speech of this type.

Generally speaking the law does not regard the intent to inflict emotional distress as one which should receive much solicitude, and it is quite understandable that most if not all jurisdictions have chosen to make it civilly culpable where the conduct in question is sufficiently "outrageous." But in the world of debate about public affairs, many things done with motives that are less than admirable are protected by the First Amendment....

Were we to hold otherwise, there can be little doubt that political cartoonists and satirists would be subjected to damages awards without any showing that their work falsely defamed its subject. Webster's defines a caricature as "the deliberately distorted picturing or imitating of a person, literary style, etc. By exaggerating features or mannerisms for satirical effect." ... The appeal of the political cartoon or caricature is often based on exploration of unfortunate physical traits or politically embarrassing events—an exploration often calculated to injure the feelings of the subject of the portrayal. The art of the cartoonist is often not reasoned or evenhanded, but slashing and one-sided....

Despite their sometimes caustic nature, from the early cartoon portraying George Washington as an ass down to the present day, graphic depictions and satirical cartoons have played a prominent role in public and political debate.... From the viewpoint of history it is clear that our political discourse would have been considerably poorer without them.

Respondent contends, however, that the caricature in question here was so "outrageous" as to distinguish it from more traditional political cartoons. There is no doubt that the caricature of respondent and his mother published in Hustler is at best a distant cousin of the political cartoons described above, and a rather poor relation at that. If it were possible by laying down a principled standard to separate the one from the other, public discourse would probably suffer little or no harm. But we doubt that there is any such standard, and we are quite sure that the pejorative description "outrageous" does not supply one. "Outrageousness" in the area of political and social discourse has an inherent subjectiveness about it which would allow a jury to impose liability on the basis of the jurors' tastes or views, or perhaps on the basis of their dislike of a particular expression....

Admittedly, these oft-repeated First Amendment principles, like other principles, are subject to limitations. We recognized in *Pacifica Foundation,* that speech that is " 'vulgar,' 'offensive,' and 'shocking' " is "not entitled to absolute constitutional protection under all circumstances." 438 U.S., at 747. In *Chaplinsky* v. *New Hampshire,* 315 U.S. 568 (1942), we held that a state could lawfully punish an individual for the use of insulting " 'fighting' words—those which by their very utterance inflict injury or tend to incite an immediate breach of the peace." ... But the sort of expression involved in this case does not seem to us to be governed by any exception to the general First Amendment principles stated above.

We conclude that public figure and public officials may not recover for the tort of intentional infliction of emotional distress by reason of publications such as the one here at issue without showing in addition that the publication contains a false statement of fact which was made with "actual malice," *i.e.*, with knowledge that the statement was false or with reckless disregard as to whether or not it was true....

[The "outrageous" conduct] claim cannot, consistently with the First Amendment, form a basis for the award of damages when the conduct in question is the publication of a caricature such as the ad parody involved here. The judgment of the Court of Appeals is accordingly

Reversed.

JUSTICE KENNEDY took no part in the consideration or decision of this case.

JUSTICE WHITE concurring in the judgment.

As I see it, the decision in *New York Times* v. *Sullivan*, 376 U.S. 254 (1964), has little to do with this case, for here the jury found that the ad contained no assertion of fact. But I agree with the Court that the judgment below, which penalized the publication of the parody, cannot be squared with the First Amendment.

E. OBSCENITY

One approaches judicial rulings on obscenity and pornography with heavy heart and wry amusement. Readers are unlikely to comprehend judicial declamations about prurient interest, lascivious matter, lewdness, lust, socially redeeming values, and contemporary community standards. Students are baffled to encounter plaintiffs called "12 200-ft Reels of Super 8 mm. Film." Still, this is an important area of First Amendment law, and there is some instruction in the Court's willingness to adjudicate and offer guidance for an overwhelmingly thankless task. The Court is regularly accused of delving into metaphysics and functioning like an ecclesiastical court.

Under English law, the test of obscenity was defined as the tendency of the written matter "to deprave and corrupt those whose minds are open to such immoral influences, and into whose hands a publication of this sort may fall." Regina v. Hicklin, L.R. 3 Q.B. 360, 371 (1868). In the United States, the issue of obscenity did not preoccupy the national government. It was not until 1873 that Congress passed the Comstock Act to make it illegal to sell, lend, give away, or exhibit any obscene writings or pictures. The statute also prohibited the mailing of obscene materials. 17 Stat. 598–600. These and other statutes led to several Supreme Court decisions before the century was out.[5] The Supreme Court found it necessary to distinguish between coarse and vulgar writings (not covered by the statute) and lewd, lascivious, and obscene writings which were made illegal. Swearingen v. United States, 161 U.S. 446 (1896). In addition to these prohibited categories, Congress outlawed the mailing of "filthy" books. 35 Stat. 1129, § 211 (1909); United States v. Limehouse, 285 U.S. 424 (1932). A major case in 1931, upholding the rights of a free press, said that "the primary requirements of decency may be enforced against obscene publications." Near v. Minnesota, 283 U.S. 697, 716 (1931).

Important principles were developed in the lower federal courts. In 1913, Judge Learned Hand rejected the English precedent in *Hicklin*. He did not believe that society was content in reducing "our treatment of sex to the standard of a child's library in the supposed interest of a salacious few." United States v. Kennerly, 209 F. 119, 121 (S.D.N.Y. 1913). Further driving home his point: "To put thought in leash to the average conscience of the time is perhaps tolerable, but to fetter it by the necessities of the lowest and least capable seems a fatal policy." Reacting to a legal challenge to James Joyce's *Ulysses*, a district judge held that the courts must determine whether an author *intended* a book to be obscene. The judge concluded that *Ulysses* was a sincere and honest book and that Joyce did not intend to excite sexual impulses or lustful thoughts. United States v. One Book Called "Ulysses," 5 F.Supp. 182 (S.D.N.Y. 1933). Another judge allowed a book to enter the country on the ground that a reading of

---

5. United States v. Chase, 135 U.S. 255 (1890); Grimm v. United States, 156 U.S. 604 (1895); Rosen v. United States, 161 U.S. 29 (1895); Andrews v. United States, 162 U.S. 420 (1896); Price v. United States, 165 U.S. 311 (1897); Dunlop v. United States, 165 U.S. 486 (1897).

it "would not stir the sex impulses of any person with a normal mind." United States v. One Book Entitled "Contraception," 51 F.2d 525, 528 (S.D.N.Y. 1931).

The Supreme Court's preoccupation with the issue of obscenity began in the 1950s. In a censorship case involving a New York law banning "sacrilegious" movies, a unanimous Court held that the statute violated two constitutional principles: the presumption against prior restraint and the forbidden use of religious objectives to pursue state policy. Joseph Burstyn, Inc. v. Wilson, 343 U.S. 495 (1952). In 1957 another unanimous ruling struck down a Michigan statute that sought to keep "obscene" books from the general public when the book would have a potentially deleterious effect on youth. As the Court noted, the law would "reduce the adult population of Michigan to reading only what is fit for children." Butler v. Michigan, 352 U.S. 380, 383 (1957).

Vague, Fragmented Doctrines

These two unanimous rulings encouraged the Court's foray into obscenity law, but subsequent cases scattered the Justices in different directions with conflicting theories. Justice Harlan later observed: "The subject of obscenity has produced a variety of views among the members of the Court unmatched in any other course of constitutional interpretation." Interstate Circuit v. Dallas, 390 U.S. 676 (1968). The Court split 5–4 in 1957 in upholding a state law that allowed a court, without a jury trial, to enjoin further distribution of obscene books and order their destruction. Kingsley Books, Inc. v. Brown, 354 U.S. 436 (1957). In a pivotal case the same year, the Court unveiled a set of new doctrines: obscenity is not within the area of constitutionally protected speech or press; sex and obscenity are not synonymous; the test for obscenity is whether "to the average person, applying contemporary community standards, the dominant theme of the material taken as a whole appeals to prurient interest." The dissenters attacked these obscure, open-ended standards. ROTH v. UNITED STATES, 354 U.S. 476 (1957).

To appreciate the complaint of the dissenters, look up *prurient* in the dictionary. Read also the meandering opinions, none of them attracting a majority, in Manual Enterprises v. Day, 370 U.S. 479 (1962). Justice Clark, dissenting, said of this 6 to 1 decision that "those in the majority like ancient Gaul are split into three parts." In Jacobellis v. Ohio, 378 U.S. 184 (1964), a 6–3 decision generated five opinions by those in the majority. In one of the concurrences, Justice Stewart uttered his famous test for hard-core pornography: "I know it when I see it."

In two 1959 decisions, the Court managed a unanimous ruling on one case and an 8–1 majority on the other. In the first, it held that the denial of a license to show a motion picture (*Lady Chatterly's Lover*) violated the First Amendment freedom to advocate ideas. The movie had been banned because it presented adultery as being right and desirable under certain circumstances. Kingsley Pictures Corp. v. Regents, 360 U.S. 684 (1959). In his concurrence, Justice Black said that if the nation embarked on the road of censorship, "this Court is about the most inappropriate Supreme Court of Censors that could be found." In the other case, the Court ruled that a city ordinance was unconstitutional because its effect would allow a store owner to sell only the books he had inspected. Under this scheme, restrictions affected the distribution of constitutionally protected as well as obscene literature. Smith v. California, 361 U.S. 147 (1959).

The question of prior restraint returned in 1961, producing a 5–4 decision that upheld the examination of movies before their showing. Licensing could be used to suppress ideas—not only obscene but social and political views as well. The issue was not the standards for censorship but the act of censorship itself. Times Film Corp. v. Chicago, 365 U.S. 43 (1961). The Court supported the screening of movies, a procedure that would be intolerable for newspapers or even broadcasting. The Court later offered some procedural safeguards whenever films are required to be submitted to a censor.[6]

---

6. Freedman v. Maryland, 380 U.S. 51 (1965); Teitel Film Corp. v. Cusack, 390 U.S. 139 (1968); Southeastern Promotions, Ltd. v. Conrad, 420 U.S. 546 (1975); Vance v. Universal Amusement Co., 445 U.S. 308 (1980).

Revisiting *Roth*

The tests announced in *Roth* begged for clarification. What are "contemporary community standards"? For Justices Brennan and Goldberg, the phrase referred not to state and local communities but to society at large. Jacobellis v. Ohio, 378 U.S. 184, 193 (1964). Yet Chief Justice Warren and Justice Clark, in dissent, believed that "contemporary community standards" meant community or local standards, not a national standard. Two years later, in a dissent, Justice Black said he was uncertain whether the community standards referred to were worldwide, nationwide, sectionwide, statewide, countrywide, precinctwide, or townshipwide. Ginzburg v. United States, 383 U.S. 463, 479–80 (1966).

What is obscenity? *Roth* said that sex and obscenity are not synonymous. The Court has also held that obscenity means more than vulgarity. To be obscene, an expression must be erotic. Cohen v. California, 403 U.S. 15, 20 (1971). In 1985, the Court found it necessary to distinguish between "lust," which it called a normal sexual response, and the categories of lasciviousness or prurient interest that involve a morbid interest in sex. Brockett v. Spokane Arcades, Inc., 472 U.S. 491 (1985). What is lascivious? What is prurient? What is morbid? Also, cities may not outlaw pornography on the ground that it discriminates against women by portraying them as sex objects. The state may not declare one perspective right and silence opponents. Hudnut v. American Booksellers Assn., Inc., 475 U.S. 1001 (1986); 771 F.2d 323.

Nudity, depending on the context, is not necessarily obscene.[7] The Court struck down as overbroad a state law that made it a punishable offense for a drive-in movie to exhibit films showing nudity when the screen is visible from a public street or place. The Court pointed out that the law would bar even "a baby's buttocks, the nude body of a war victim, or scenes from a culture in which nudity is indigenous." Erznoznik v. City of Jacksonville, 422 U.S. 205, 213 (1975). A 6–3 Court deferred to the states on the question of whether nude entertainment could take place simultaneously with the dispensing of liquor. The decision depended partly on the authority of states under the Twenty-First Amendment to control liquor.[8]

An interesting twist to *Roth* is that its author, Justice Brennan, later took the lead in restricting its scope. Writing an opinion in 1966 joined by Chief Justice Warren and Justice Fortas, he said that even if a book had (1) prurient appeal and (2) was patently offensive to contemporary community standards, it also had to be found (3) "*utterly* without redeeming social value" to be banned. All three elements had to be met. Memoirs v. Massachusetts, 383 U.S. 413, 418–19 (1966). In one of the dissents, Justice Harlan noted: "The central development that emerges from the aftermath of *Roth* ... is that no stable approach to the obscenity problem has yet been devised by this Court." He also doubted whether the utterly-without-redeeming test had "any meaning at all."

On the same day, a 5–4 Court affirmed the conviction of someone who had "pandered" to the erotic interests of readers by mailing literature at first from Intercourse and Blue Ball, Pennsylvania, finally settling on Middlesex, New Jersey. Ginzburg v. United States, 383 U.S. 463 (1966). These promotional and advertising techniques appeared to be the decisive factors in justifying the person's conviction. Justice Douglas, dissenting, reminded his brethren of advertisements in national magazines "chock-full of thighs, ankles, calves, bosoms, eyes, and hair, to draw the potential buyer's attention to lotions, tires, food, liquor, clothing, autos, and even insurance policies."[9]

---

7. Kois v. California, 408 U.S. 229 (1972); Jenkins v. Georgia, 418 U.S. 153, 161 (1974); Schad v. Mount Ephraim, 452 U.S. 61 (1981).

8. California v. La Rue, 409 U.S. 109 (1972). See also New York State Liquor Authority v. Bellanca, 452 U.S. 714 (1981) and Newport v. Iacobucci, 479 U.S. 92 (1986).

9. For other cases during this period, see Mishkin v. New York, 383 U.S. 502 (1966); Redrup v. New York, 386 U.S. 767 (1967); Interstate Circuit v. Dallas, 390 U.S. 676 (1968); Rabeck v. New York, 391 U.S. 462 (1968). For instructive articles on obscenity, see Harry Kalven, Jr., "The Metaphysics of the Law of Obscenity," 1960 Sup. Ct. Rev. 1; Louis Henkin, "Morals and the Constitution: The Sin of Obscenity," 63 Colum. L. Rev. 391 (1963); Earl Finbar Murphy, "The Value of Pornography," 10 Wayne L. Rev. 655 (1964); C. Peter Magrath, "The Obscenity Cases: Grapes of Roth," 1966 Sup. Ct. Rev. 7.

Obscenity Doctrines

ROTH V. UNITED STATES
(1957)

Obscenity is not within the area of constitutionally protected speech or press. The test for obscenity is whether "to the average person, applying contemporary community standards, the dominant theme of the material taken as a whole appeals to prurient interest."

MEMOIRS V. MASSACHUSETTS
(1966)

It must be established that (1) the dominant theme of the material taken as a whole appeals to a prurient interest in sex; (2) the material is patently offensive because it affronts contemporary community standards relating to the description or representation of sexual matters; and (3) the material is utterly without redeeming social value. All three elements had to be met.

MILLER V. CALIFORNIA
(1973)

Three guidelines: (1) whether the average person, applying contemporary community standards, would find that the work, taken as a whole, appeals to the prurient interest; (2) whether the work depicts or describes, in a patently offensive way, sexual conduct specifically defined by the applicable state law; and (3) whether the work, taken as a whole, lacks "serious literary, artistic, political, or scientific value."

The *Miller* Standards

By 1973, the legal meaning of *obscenity* had run in so many directions that the Court needed to formulate new standards. This it did by rejecting the *Memoirs* test that a work must be "*utterly* without redeeming social value." Moreover, the Court said it was not necessary to employ a "national standard." The values of a "forum community" (such as a state) will do. New guidelines for obscenity were announced: (1) whether the "average person, applying contemporary community standards," would find that the work, taken as a whole, appeals to the prurient interest; (2) whether the work depicts or describes, in a patently offensive way, sexual conduct specifically defined by the applicable state law; and (3) whether the work, taken as a whole, lacks "serious literary, artistic, political, or scientific value." MILLER v. CALIFORNIA, 413 U.S. 15 (1973). One of the four dissents came from Justice Brennan, author of *Roth*. He elaborated on his objections while dissenting in another case the same day. Paris Adult Theatre I v. Slaton, 413 U.S. 49 (1973). Obscenity doctrines have changed significantly from case to case (see box).

The forum-community test does not mean that a jury can operate without limits, allowing it to convict someone for showing a woman with a bare midriff. Jenkins v. Georgia, 418 U.S. 153, 161 (1974). One judge, who was reversed, told the jury that community standards on obscene films meant whatever should not be seen with their mothers sitting next to them. Liles v. Oregon, 425 U.S. 963, 966 (1975). In 1987, the Court held that only the first two prongs of the *Miller* test should be decided by juries on "contemporary community standards." Whether a work has literary, artistic, political, or scientific value need not obtain majority approval to merit protection. The value of a work does not vary from community to community. Pope v. Illinois, 481 U.S. 497 (1987).

Some of the states have refused to adopt the three tests of *Miller* v. *California*. For example, the Oregon Supreme Court said that it could not justify the prosecution of someone who failed to meet such a vague notion as contemporary standards. State citizens would be forced to guess about a future jury's estimate of contemporary state standards of "prurience." The state court also explained that the *Miller* guidelines ran counter to Oregon's political and social culture, which was "dedicated to founding a free society unfettered by the governmental imposition of some people's views of morality on the free expression of others." State v. Henry, 732 P.2d 9, 16 (Ore. 1987).

In 1969, a unanimous Court held that the private possession of obscene materials by adults at home cannot be made a crime. Adults may read and watch what they like in the privacy of their own home. Stanley v. Georgia, 394 U.S. 557 (1969) (see reading in Chapter 17). The *Stanley* doctrine does not justify the mailing of obscene materials to adults, the attempt to introduce obscene materials at a port of entry, or the importation of obscene matter intended for an adult's private use.[10] Moreover, states may outlaw the possession or viewing of child pornography even in the privacy of one's home. Osborne v. Ohio, 495 U.S. 103 (1990).

Watching obscene films at home does not create a right to watch them at public theaters. Paris Adult Theatre I v. Slaton, 413 U.S. 49 (1973). Cities may use their zoning authority to disperse adult movie theaters, even if the distinction demands content-based regulation. Young v. American Mini Theatres, 427 U.S. 50 (1976). Cities may also adopt zoning ordinances to keep adult movie theaters away from residential areas, churches, parks, and schools. Renton v. Playtime Theatres, Inc., 475 U.S. 41 (1986). A unanimous Court in 1990 held that cities may prohibit motels from renting rooms for less than ten hours, on the theory that short periods of time indicate the use of rooms for prostitution. In this same case, the Court divided 6–3 when it required city regulations on sexually oriented businesses to contain procedural safeguards to avoid violations of the First Amendment. FW/PBS, Inc. v. Dallas, 493 U.S. 215 (1990).

In 2002, the Court held that Los Angeles had provided sufficient evidence to ban more than one sex-related business from operating under the same roof. The city found that these "sex superstores" had negative side effects on the surrounding neighborhood. Because of an ambivalent concurrence by Justice Kennedy, the Court lacked a five-member majority. Justices Souter, Stevens, Ginsburg, and Breyer dissented. Los Angeles v. Alameda Books, Inc., 535 U.S. 425 (2002).

Dial-a-Porn

Congress has been active in legislating against "dial-a-porn": sexually explicit messages available over the telephone. Legislation in 1983 prohibited any party in the District of Columbia or in interstate or foreign communication from providing by telephone, either directly or through use of a recording device, "any obscene or indecent communication for commercial purposes" to any person under 18 years of age. 97 Stat. 1469, § 8. The statute had two problems. The provider of these messages had no way of knowing the age of the caller. The FCC, responsible for implementing this statute, found it nearly impossible to enforce it. Second, by permitting persons over 18 to receive these messages with their consent, the statute in effect legalized dial-a-porn.

Congress passed new legislation in 1988 to completely ban dial-a-porn services, regardless of the age of the caller. 102 Stat. 424, § 6101. The Court later held that Congress may prohibit the interstate transmission of obscene commercial telephone messages, but that the ban on *indecent* messages violated the First Amendment. There were no legislative findings to justify the conclusion that Congress was unable to devise constitutionally acceptable and less restrictive means to achieve the government's legitimate interest in protecting minors. The statute, therefore, was not drawn in a sufficiently narrow manner. Sable Communications of Cal. v. FCC, 492 U.S. 115 (1989).

In response, Congress rewrote the statute to require telephone companies to block access to sexually explicit messages unless customers ask in writing to receive them. Dial-a-porn companies attacked the statute as a violation of free press, but in 1992 the Supreme Court refused to hear a challenge to an appellate court that upheld the amended statutory language. Dial Information Services Corp. of New York v. Barr, 502 U.S. 1072 (1992); 938 F.2d 1535 (2d Cir. 1991).

---

10. United States v. Reidel, 402 U.S. 351 (1971); United States v. Thirty-Seven Photographs, 402 U.S. 363 (1971); United States v. 12 200-ft Reels of Super 8 mm. Film, 413 U.S. 123 (1973); United States v. Orito, 413 U.S. 139 (1973).

NEA Grants

Congress passed legislation in 1989 in response to public outcries against the use of public funds to support exhibits (showing the work of Robert Mapplethorpe and Andres Serrano) that many found to be obscene and sacrilegious. Under the terms of the statute, funds appropriated to the National Endowment for the Arts (NEA) and the National Endowment for the Humanities (NEH) could not be used to promote materials considered by the endowments to be obscene *and,* taken as a whole, lacking in serious literary, artistic, political, or scientific value. Substantial debate in both Houses of Congress resulted in adopting statutory language that would avoid government censorship and violation of the First Amendment. 103 Stat. 741, §304 (1989). The restriction was removed the following year.

In two highly controversial cases in 1990, juries in Cincinnati, Ohio, and Fort Lauderdale, Florida, decided that an art gallery and the rap band 2 Live Crew were not guilty of obscenity charges. These cases underscore the point that "obscenity" often depends more on the intuition and judgment of jurors than on Supreme Court guidelines. Regardless of what standards are announced by the Court, jurors have the "final word" in deciding whether a book, movie, art exhibit, or musical production belongs in their neighborhood.

The issue of NEA funding returned to the Court in 1998. Legislation passed by Congress in 1990 required the agency to ensure that "artistic excellence and artistic merit are the criteria by which [grant] applications are judged, taking into consideration general standards of decency and respect for the diverse beliefs and values of the American public." The Ninth Circuit held that this language, on its face, impermissibly discriminated on the basis of viewpoint and was void for vagueness under the First and Fifth Amendments. The Supreme Court, however, found that the language was facially valid and did not interfere with First Amendment rights or violate vagueness principles. An 8–1 Court held that the statutory provision merely added "considerations" and did not prevent awards to projects that might be "indecent" or "disrespectful." As for vagueness, the Court noted that all NEA grants are inescapably subjective, including giving awards for "artistic excellence" and "artistic merit." Many government programs that award scholarships and grants depend on general criteria such as "excellence" and "superior ability." National Endowment for Arts v. Finley, 524 U.S. 569 (1998). In their concurrence, Justices Scalia and Thomas said that the statutory language was constitutional even if it was viewpoint discrimination. They pointed out that the four individuals denied funding by the NEA may pursue their free expression at any time, but without the public paying for it.

Nude Dancing

In 1991, the Court splintered in several directions in passing judgment on an Indiana law that required public dancers in entertainment establishments to wear pasties and a G-string. A 5–4 majority upheld the statute but could not offer coherent reasons for doing so. Chief Justice Rehnquist, joined by O'Connor and Kennedy, concluded that the state's police power (protecting public health, safety, and morals) was sufficient to override whatever expressive conduct the dancers hoped to achieve under the First Amendment. They said the statute was directed at public nudity, not erotic dancing. Souter, in a concurrence, agreed that there was a First Amendment issue but offered different reasons for upholding the statute. The fifth member of the majority, Scalia, denied that the statute implicated a First Amendment interest. Barnes v. Glen Theatre, Inc., 501 U.S. 560 (1991). It was uncertain how the majority would react to the prosecution of those who produce *Hair* or *Equus,* two plays that feature totally nude scenes.

The Court revisited this issue in 2000, ruling that cities and states may ban nude dancing to combat crime and "other negative secondary effects." The 6 to 3 opinion upheld a city ordnance that required dancers in clubs to wear pasties and a G-string. Writing for a plurality of four, Justice O'Connor said that the ordinance—*on its face*—represented a general prohibition on public nudity and therefore regulated conduct, not expression. It did not, she said, specifically target nudity that contained an erotic message. However, statements by the city attorney and other city officials indicated that the ordinance was aimed at nude dancing in clubs and was not intended to apply to "legitimate" theater productions. O'Connor concluded that the city's interest in combating negative secondary effects overrode whatever expressive message there might be in nude dancing. Scalia and Thomas, concurring in the judgment, regarded the case as moot but pointed out that the ordinance did not contain any exception for productions like *Hair* or *Equus*; nevertheless, the city was unlikely to enforce the ban on such plays. Scalia and Thomas would have upheld an ordinance directed solely at nude dancing without trying to identify "secondary effects." Souter dissented in part, concluding that the city's evidentiary record failed to justify the ordinance. In their dissent, Stevens and Ginsburg objected to the secondary-effects test to ban what they considered to be protected First Amendment expression, and pointed to the case record to show that the ordinance was targeting nude dancing and not public nudity in general. City of Erie v. Pap's A.M., 529 U.S. 277 (2000).

Child Pornography

One of the few areas of agreement in obscenity law is the need to treat children differently from adults. States may restrict minors under 17 years of age from reading materials that are not obscene for adults. Ginsberg v. New York, 390 U.S. 629 (1968). Literature can be restricted if there is a "tendency of widely circulated books of this category to reach the impressionable young and have a continuing impact." Kaplan v. California, 413 U.S. 115, 120 (1973). There are continuing disputes as to how booksellers should be required to display sexual publications harmful to juveniles. Virginia v. American Booksellers Assn., 484 U.S. 383 (1988).

In one of the rare unanimous decisions on obscenity, in 1982 the Court upheld a state law directed at child pornography. The statute prohibited persons from knowingly promoting a "sexual performance" by a child under 16 by distributing material describing such a performance. Sexual performance was defined as actual or simulated sexual intercourse, deviate sexual intercourse, sexual bestiality, masturbation, sado-masochistic abuse, or lewd exhibition of the genitals. NEW YORK v. FERBER, 458 U.S. 747 (1982). Congress passed legislation in 1978 to make it a federal crime to use children under 16 for the production of pornographic materials. The law applies to the sale and distribution of obscene materials, mailed or transported in interstate or foreign commerce, that depict children in sexually explicit conduct. 92 Stat. 7. Those restrictions were strengthened in 1984 by raising the age to 18 and relying on *Ferber* to remove the requirement in existing law that child pornography be proven "obscene" before convictions could be obtained. 98 Stat. 204. Amendments in 1986 and 1988 further tightened the statutory prohibitions against child pornography. 100 Stat. 3510; 102 Stat. 4485–4503 (Subtitle N).

The 1988 legislation was struck down because the requirements for recordkeeping by producers of visual materials of sexually explicit conduct placed an excessive burden on First Amendment rights. Records had to be kept for all models, regardless of age. American Library Ass'n v. Thornburgh, 713 F.Supp. 469 (D.D.C. 1989). Congress rewrote the statute in 1990, but the revised language was also found unconstitutional, again on the ground that the record-keeping requirement was not narrowly tailored. American Library Ass'n v. Barr, 794 F.Supp. 412 (D.D.C. 1992).

In 1990, a 6–3 decision by the Supreme Court broadened state power to curb child pornography. States may now outlaw the possession or viewing of child pornography even in the privacy of one's own home. The majority concluded that a law passed by Ohio was a legitimate effort to protect the victims of child pornography by eliminating the market at all levels of the distribution chain. All fifty states and the District of Columbia now make it illegal to possess, produce, and/or distribute child pornography. In their dissent, Justices Brennan, Marshall, and Stevens regarded the Ohio statute as overbroad, permitting prosecution for innocuous and constitutionally protected conduct. The majority conceded that such instances could arise because the statute "may have been imprecise at its fringes." Nevertheless, they rejected the overbreadth challenge, partly on the ground that state courts have the ability to narrow state statutes so that they apply only to unprotected conduct. Osborne v. Ohio, 495 U.S. 103 (1990).

The Internet

By passing the Communications Decency Act of 1996, Congress tried to protect children from obscene or indecent messages on the Internet. The Court held that two provisions of the statute violated the First Amendment. One provision prohibited the knowing transmission on the Internet of obscene or indecent messages to any recipient under 18 years of age. The other provision prohibited the knowing sending or displaying of patently offensive messages in a manner that made it available to anyone under 18. The Court, with a 7 to 2 majority, decided that Congress had suppressed speech that adults had a constitutional right to receive. RENO v. ACLU, 521 U.S. 844 (1997). The statutory provisions were struck down partly because of alternatives that exist: software programs ("filters") that allow parents to screen out objectionable material.

In 1999, the Court affirmed a lower court ruling that upheld a federal law that makes it a crime to transmit e-mails that are obscene, lewd, or intended to annoy other people. The statute was upheld with the understanding that the Justice Department would prosecute only cases of obscenity and not messages that are indecent or merely annoying. ApolloMedia Corp., 526 U.S. 1061 (1999).

After *Reno v. ACLU*, Congress passed more narrowly crafted legislation (the Child Online Protection Act, or COPA) to prevent children from gaining access to sexual material on the Internet. In 2002, the Court ruled that the statutory reliance on the notion of "community standards" (drawn from *Miller* v. *California*) to define the material in cyberspace "harmful to minors" did not, on its face, violate the First Amendment. A lower appellate court had expressed concern that the provision would give the most conservative communities in the country a veto over sexual content on the Internet. Only Justice Stevens dissented. Ashcroft v. American Civil Liberties Union, 535 U.S. 564 (2002).

Upon remand, a district court held that enforcement of COPA would likely violate the First Amendment. Once again the Court, divided 5 to 4, ruled that there were plausible, less restrictive alternatives available to Congress, especially given the development of filtering technologies. Ashcroft v. American Civil Liberties Union, 542 U.S. 656 (2004). With the case heading back to district court, the burden was on the government to demonstrate that COPA was constitutionally acceptable. After a trial that began in 2006, the district court held in 2007 that the government had not met that burden and struck down the statute as a facial violation of the First and Fifth amendments. The Third Circuit affirmed that ruling in the summer of 2008. The U.S. Justice Department appealed to the Supreme Court but in January 2009 the Court refused to hear the appeal. Mukasey v. ACLU, 555 U.S. 1337 (2009).

In 2003, the Supreme Court (split 6 to 3) upheld a congressional statute that restricts access to Internet pornography in libraries. The Children's Internet Protection Act requires libraries that receive federal funds to use filtering software to block Internet pornography. The majority disagreed that the software's capacity to "overblock" created a constitutional defect. Under the law, adults may ask the library to remove the filtering software. United States v. American Library Assn., 539 U.S. 194 (2003).

"Virtual" Child Porn

Congress passed legislation in 1996 to prohibit computer-generated child pornography. The statute made it a criminal offense to distribute or possess images that "appear to be" of minors engaged in sexually explicit conduct. It also prohibited sexual activity by adults who look like minors. In 2002, a 6–3 Court struck down the law as overbroad. The Court noted that *Ferber* prohibited only child pornography using *actual* children, and that the congressional statute did not comply with *Miller* requirements. According to the Court, the statute would have prohibited such contemporary films as

"Traffic" and "American Beauty," which feature actors portrayed as under 18 engaged in sex. Left standing in the law is a provision that bans "morphing" (where a photograph of an actual child is manipulated on a computer to make it appear that the child is engaged in sex). Ashcroft v. Free Speech Coalition, 535 U.S. 234 (2002).

In response to this decision, Congress passed legislation covering the pandering and solicitation of child pornography. The provisions were challenged in the lower courts as overbroad under the First Amendment and impermissibly vague under the Due Process Clause of the Fifth Amendment. In 2008, the Supreme Court upheld the provisions. United States v. Williams, 553 U.S. 285 (2008). Writing for a 7 to 2 Court, Justice Scalia denied that the legislation could plausibly lead to the prosecution of grandparents who proudly share photos of "little Janie in the bath." He left open for future cases the possible prosecution of documentaries that cover atrocities committed in foreign countries, such as soldiers raping young children.

"Crush Videos" and Video Games

In 1999, Congress passed legislation criminalizing the commercial production, sale, or possession of depictions of cruelty to animals with the intent of placing the depictions into interstate commerce. 18 U.S.C. §48. A 2004 prosecution of a man indicted for creating and selling dog fight videos led to United States v. Stevens, 559 U.S. ___ (2010), where the Court struck down the provision as "substantially overbroad." Congress had been targeting "crush videos," a variety of pornography that usually involves women in stiletto heels stepping on small animals, but the Court, with an 8–1 ruling, found the statute to be so general that it could be used to punish scenes of hunting or butchering animals for food production.

The day after the ruling a new bill was introduced in Congress, responding to the Court's concern about overbreadth. The Animal Crush Video Prohibition Act of 2010 (H.R. 5566) narrowed the focus of the act to target only the "crush video" market. This bill became law on December 9, 2010 (P.L. 111-294). (See Reading "The House Responds to *Stevens*.")

The Court relied on its analysis in *Stevens* in 2011 when it struck down California's effort to regulate the sale of violent video games to minors. The statute prohibited the sale of video games that involved "killing, maiming, dismembering or sexual assaulting an image of a human being." In an effort to protect the legislation from legal challenge, the state adopted language from the Court's earlier decisions upholding restrictions on sales of pornography to minors, stating that the law applied to video games that were "patently offensive," lacked "serious literary, artistic, political or scientific value," and that appealed "to deviant or morbid interest." Writing for the majority, Justice Scalia argued that video games "communicate ideas ... through many familiar literary devises" and that there was no tradition in the United States of restricting children's access to violence. He noted the violence in Grimm's Fairy Tales as evidence. Scalia also rejected the argument that violence was like obscenity. "[S]peech about violence is not obscene," he argued, and the attempt to track the language of the earlier obscenity cases did not change that. Brown v. Entertainment Merchants Assn., 564 U.S. ___ (2011).

Search and Seizure

Some of the efforts to combat obscenity raise Fourth Amendment issues. Police officers may not make ad hoc decisions to search newsstands and seize "obscene" materials.[11] Before issuing a warrant to seize allegedly obscene materials, a magistrate must make some kind of inquiry into the factual basis for the allegation. Lee Art Theatre v. Virginia, 392 U.S. 636 (1968). However, an adversary hearing is not required prior to a seizure. Heller v. New York, 413 U.S. 483 (1973).

---

11. Marcus v. Search Warrant, 367 U.S. 717 (1961); A Quantity of Books v. Kansas, 378 U.S. 205 (1964); Roade v. Kentucky, 413 U.S. 496 (1973).

Roth v. United States

354 U.S. 476 (1957)

In this decision, the Supreme Court for the first time sets forth major doctrines regarding obscenity. Two cases are involved. The *Roth* case (referred to as No. 582) concerns the constitutionality of a federal statute used to convict Roth for mailing an obscene book and obscene circulars and advertising. The companion case, *Alberts* v. *California* (No. 61), deals with a California law that made it a misdemeanor to keep for sale or to advertise material that is "obscene or indecent."

MR. JUSTICE BRENNAN delivered the opinion of the Court.

The constitutionality of a criminal obscenity statute is the question in each of these cases. In *Roth,* the primary constitutional question is whether the federal obscenity statute violates the provision of the First Amendment that "Congress shall make no law … abridging the freedom of speech, or of the press.…" In *Alberts,* the primary constitutional question is whether the obscenity provisions of the California Penal Code invade the freedoms of speech and press as they may be incorporated in the liberty protected from state action by the Due Process Clause of the Fourteenth Amendment.…

The dispositive question is whether obscenity is utterance within the area of protected speech and press. Although this is the first time the question has been squarely presented to this Court, either under the First Amendment or under the Fourteenth Amendment, expressions found in numerous opinions indicate that this Court has always assumed that obscenity is not protected by the freedoms of speech and press.…

The guaranties of freedom of expression in effect in 10 of the 14 States which by 1792 had ratified the Constitution, gave no absolute protection for every utterance. Thirteen of the 14 States provided for the prosecution of libel, and all of those States made either blasphemy or profanity, or both, statutory crimes. As early as 1712, Massachusetts made it criminal to publish "any filthy, obscene, or profane song, pamphlet, libel or mock sermon" in imitation or mimicking of religious services.… Thus, profanity and obscenity were related offenses.

… [I]mplicit in the history of the First Amendment is the rejection of obscenity as utterly without redeeming social importance.… We hold that obscenity is not within the area of constitutionally protected speech or press.

… [S]ex and obscenity are not synonymous. Obscene material is material which deals with sex in a manner appealing to prurient interest. The portrayal of sex, *e.g.,* in art, literature and scientific works, is not itself sufficient reason to deny material the constitutional protection of freedom of speech and press. Sex, a great and mysterious motive force in human life, has indisputably been a subject of absorbing interest to mankind through the ages; …

The early leading standard of obscenity allowed material to be judged merely by the effect of an isolated excerpt upon particularly susceptible persons. *Regina* v. *Hicklin,* [1868] L. R. 3 Q. B. 360. Some American courts adopted this standard but later decisions have rejected it and substituted this test: whether to the average person, applying contemporary community standards, the dominant theme of the material taken as a whole appeals to prurient interest. The *Hicklin* test, judging obscenity by the effect of isolated passages upon the most susceptible persons, might well encompass material legitimately treating with sex, and so it must be rejected as unconstitutionally restrictive of the freedoms of speech and press. On the other hand, the substituted standard provides safeguards adequate to withstand the charge of constitutional infirmity.

Both trial courts below sufficiently followed the proper standard. Both courts used the proper definition of obscenity. In addition, in the *Alberts* case, in ruling on a motion to dismiss, the trial judge indicated that, as the trier of facts, he was judging each item as a whole as it would affect the normal person, and in *Roth,* the trial judge instructed the jury as follows:

"… The test is not whether it would arouse sexual desires or sexual impure thoughts in those comprising a particular segment of the community, the young, the immature or the highly prudish or would leave another segment, the scientific or highly educated or the so-called worldly-wise and sophisticated indifferent and unmoved.…

"The test in each case is the effect of the book, picture or publication considered as a whole, not upon any particular class, but upon all those whom it is likely to reach. In other words, you determine its impact upon the average person in the community. The books, pictures and circulars must be judged as a whole, in their entire context, and you are not to consider detached or separate portions in reaching a conclusion. You judge the circulars, pictures and publications which have been put in evidence by present-day standards of the community. You may ask yourselves does it offend the common conscience of the community by present-day standards....

"In this case, ladies and gentlemen of the jury, you and you alone are the exclusive judges of what the common conscience of the community is, and in determining that conscience you are to consider the community as a whole, young and old, educated and uneducated, the religious and the irreligious — men, women and children."

... [W]e hold that these statutes, applied according to the proper standard for judging obscenity, do not offend constitutional safeguards against convictions based upon protected material, or fail to give men in acting adequate notice of what is prohibited....

The judgments are

Affirmed.

MR. CHIEF JUSTICE WARREN, concurring in the result.

I agree with the result reached by the Court in these cases, but, because we are operating in a field of expression and because broad language used here may eventually be applied to the arts and sciences and freedom of communication generally, I would limit our decision to the facts before us and to the validity of the statutes in question as applied....

MR. JUSTICE HARLAN, concurring in the result in No. 61, and dissenting in No. 582.

I regret not to be able to join the Court's opinion....

I.

My basic difficulties with the Court's opinion are threefold. First, the opinion paints with such a broad brush that I fear it may result in a loosening of the tight reins which state and federal courts should hold upon the enforcement of obscenity statutes. Second, the Court fails to discriminate between the different factors which, in my opinion, are involved in the constitutional adjudication of state and federal obscenity cases. Third, relevant distinctions between the two obscenity statutes here involved, and the Court's own definition of "obscenity," are ignored....

We are faced here with the question whether the federal obscenity statute, as construed and applied in this case, violates the First Amendment to the Constitution. To me, this question is of quite a different order than one where we are dealing with state legislation under the Fourteenth Amendment. I do not think it follows that state and federal powers in this area are the same, and that just because the State may suppress a particular utterance, it is automatically permissible for the Federal Government to do the same....

MR. JUSTICE DOUGLAS, with whom MR. JUSTICE BLACK concurs, dissenting....

By these standards punishment is inflicted for thoughts provoked, not for overt acts nor antisocial conduct. This test cannot be squared with our decisions under the First Amendment....

The tests by which these convictions were obtained require only the arousing of sexual thoughts. Yet the arousing of sexual thoughts and desires happens every day in normal life in dozens of ways. Nearly 30 years ago a questionnaire sent to college and normal school women graduates asked what things were most stimulating sexually. Of 409 replies, 9 said "music"; 18 said "pictures"; 29 said "dancing"; 40 said "drama"; 95 said "books"; and 218 said "man." ...

Miller v. California

413 U.S. 15 (1973)

After thrashing about in a number of cases on obscenity and pornography, the Court in this case sets forth general principles that have helped guide subsequent decisions. An interesting feature of this case is that Justice Brennan, author of *Roth* v. *United States,* dissents in both *Miller* and the companion case, *Paris Adult Theatre I.* In those dissents Brennan argues that judicial standards for obscenity have not protected First Amendment rights and that the concept of obscenity cannot be defined with sufficient specificity by the courts to provide fair notice to persons vulnerable to prosecution. California prosecuted Marvin Miller for distributing obscene matter.

MR. CHIEF JUSTICE BURGER delivered the opinion of the Court.

This is one of a group of "obscenity-pornography" cases being reviewed by the Court in a re-examination of standards enunciated in earlier cases....

I

This case involves the application of a State's criminal obscenity statute to a situation in which sexually explicit materials have been thrust by aggressive sales action upon unwilling recipients who had in no way indicated any desire to receive such materials....

... [I]t is useful for us to focus on two of the landmark cases in the somewhat tortured history of the Court's obscenity decisions. In *Roth* v. *United States,* 354 U.S. 476 (1957), the Court sustained a conviction under a federal statute punishing the mailing of "obscene, lewd, lascivious or filthy...." materials. The key to that holding was the Court's rejection of the claim that obscene materials were protected by the First Amendment....

Nine years later, in *Memoirs* v. *Massachusetts,* 383 U.S. 413 (1966), the Court veered sharply away from the *Roth* concept and, with only three Justices in the plurality opinion, articulated a new test of obscenity. The plurality held that under the *Roth* definition

"as elaborated in subsequent cases, three elements must coalesce: it must be established that (a) the dominant theme of the material taken as a whole appeals to a prurient interest in sex; (b) the material is patently offensive because it affronts contemporary community standards relating to the description or representation of sexual matters; and (c) the material is utterly without redeeming social value." ...

While *Roth* presumed "obscenity" to be "utterly without redeeming social importance," *Memoirs* required that to prove obscenity it must be affirmatively established that the material is *"utterly* without redeeming social value." Thus, even as they repeated the words of *Roth,* the *Memoirs* plurality produced a drastically altered test that called on the prosecution to prove a negative, *i.e.,* that the material was *"utterly* without redeeming social value"—a burden virtually impossible to discharge under our criminal standards of proof....

The case we now review was tried on the theory that the California Penal Code § 311 approximately incorporates the three-stage *Memoirs* test, *supra.* But now the *Memoirs* test has been abandoned as unworkable by its author [*Brennan*], and no Mem-

ber of the Court today supports the *Memoirs* formulation.

II

... [W]e now confine the permissible scope of such regulation to works which depict or describe sexual conduct. That conduct must be specifically defined by the applicable state law, as written or authoritatively construed. A state offense must also be limited to works which, taken as a whole, appeal to the prurient interest in sex, which portray sexual conduct in a patently offensive way, and which, taken as a whole, do not have serious literary, artistic, political, or scientific value.

The basic guidelines for the trier of fact must be: (a) whether "the average person, applying contemporary community standards" would find that the work, taken as a whole, appeals to the prurient interest, ... (b) whether the work depicts or describes, in a patently offensive way, sexual conduct specifically defined by the applicable state law; and (c) whether the work, taken as a whole, lacks serious literary, artistic, political, or scientific value. We do not adopt as a constitutional standard the *"utterly without redeeming social value"* test of *Memoirs* v. *Massachusetts,* ...

We emphasize that it is not our function to propose regulatory schemes for the States. That must await their concrete legislative efforts. It is possible, however, to give a few plain examples of what a state statute could define for regulation under part (b) of the standard announced in this opinion, *supra:*

(a) Patently offensive representations or descriptions of ultimate sexual acts, normal or perverted, actual or simulated.

(b) Patently offensive representations or descriptions of masturbation, excretory functions, and lewd exhibition of the genitals....

... [T]oday, for the first time since *Roth* was decided in 1957, a majority of this Court has agreed on concrete guidelines to isolate "hard core" pornography from expression protected by the First Amendment....

III

Under a National Constitution, fundamental First Amendment limitations on the powers of the States do not vary from community to community, but this does not mean that there are, or should or can be, fixed, uniform national standards of precisely what appeals to the "prurient interest" or is "patently offensive." These are essentially questions of fact, and our Nation is simply too big and too diverse for this Court to reasonably expect that such standards could be articulated for all 50 States in a single formulation, even assuming the prerequisite consensus exists....

IV

The dissenting Justices sound the alarm of repression. But, in our view, to equate the free and robust exchange of ideas and political debate with commercial exploitation of obscene material demeans the grand conception of the First Amendment and its high purposes in the historic struggle for freedom....

In sum, we (a) reaffirm the *Roth* holding that obscene material is not protected by the First Amendment; (b) hold that such material can be regulated by the States, subject to the specific safeguards enunciated above, without a showing that the material is *"utterly* without redeeming social value"; and (c) hold that obscenity is to be determined by applying "contemporary community standards," ... not "national standards." ...

Vacated and remanded.

Mr. Justice Douglas, dissenting....

Obscenity cases usually generate tremendous emotional outbursts. They have no business being in the courts. If a constitutional amendment authorized censorship, the censor would probably be an administrative agency. Then criminal prosecutions could follow as, if, and when publishers defied the censor and sold their literature. Under that regime a publisher would know when he was on dangerous ground. Under the present regime—whether the old standards or the new ones are used—the criminal law becomes a trap. A brand new test would put a publisher behind bars under a new law improvised by the courts after the publication....

Mr. Justice Brennan, with whom Mr. Justice Stewart and Mr. Justice Marshall join, dissenting.

In my dissent in *Paris Adult Theatre I* v. *Slaton, post,* p. 73, decided this date, I noted that I had no occasion to consider the extent of state power to regulate the distribution of sexually oriented material to juveniles or the offensive exposure of such material to unconsenting adults. In the case before us, appellant was convicted of distributing obscene matter in violation of California Penal Code § 311.2, on the basis of evidence that he had caused to be mailed unsolicited brochures advertising various books and a movie. I need not now decide whether a statute might be drawn to impose, within the requirements of the First Amendment, criminal penalties for the precise conduct at issue here. For it is clear that under my dissent in *Paris Adult Theatre I,* the statute under which the prosecution was brought is unconstitutionally overbroad, and therefore invalid on its face....

New York v. Ferber

458 U.S. 747 (1982)

A New York statute prohibited persons from knowingly promoting a sexual performance by a child under the age of 16 by distributing material that depicts such a performance. The statute defined "sexual performance." Paul Ira Ferber was convicted for selling films depicting young boys masturbating. The highest New York court reversed the conviction by holding that the statute violated the First Amendment because it was both underinclusive and overbroad.

Justice White delivered the opinion of the Court.

At issue in this case is the constitutionality of a New York criminal statute which prohibits persons from knowingly promoting sexual performances by children under the age of 16 by distributing material which depicts such performances.

I

In recent years, the exploitive use of children in the production of pornography has become a serious national problem. The Federal Government and 47 States have sought to combat the problem with statutes specifically directed at the production of child pornography. At least half of such statutes do not require that the materials produced be legally obscene. Thirty-five States and the United States Congress have also passed legislation prohibiting the distribution of such materials; 20 States prohibit the distribution of material depicting children engaged in sexual conduct without requiring that the material be legally obscene.

New York is one of the 20. In 1977, the New York Legislature enacted Article 263 of its Penal Law....

Section 263.05 criminalizes as a class C felony the use of a child in a sexual performance:

"A person is guilty of the use of a child in a sexual performance if knowing the character and content thereof he employs, authorizes or induces a child less than sixteen years of age to engage in a sexual performance or being a parent, legal guardian or custodian of such child, he consents to the participation by such child in a sexual performance."

A "[s]exual performance" is defined as "any performance or part thereof which includes sexual conduct by a child less than sixteen years of age." § 263.00(1). "Sexual conduct" is in turn defined in § 263.00(3):

"'Sexual conduct' means actual or simulated sexual intercourse, deviate sexual intercourse, sexual bestiality, masturbation, sado-masochistic abuse, or lewd exhibition of the genitals."

A performance is defined as "any play, motion picture, photograph or dance" or "any other visual representation exhibited before an audience." § 263.00(4).

At issue in this case is § 263.15, defining a class D felony:

"A person is guilty of promoting a sexual performance by a child when, knowing the character and content thereof, he produces, directs or promotes any performance which includes sexual conduct by a child less than sixteen years of age." ...

II

The Court of Appeals proceeded on the assumption that the standard of obscenity incorporated in § 263.10, which follows the guidelines enunciated in *Miller* v. *California*, 413 U.S. 15 (1973), constitutes the appropriate line dividing protected from unprotected expression by which to measure a regulation directed at child pornography. It was on the premise that "nonobscene adolescent sex" could not be singled out for special treatment that the court found § 263.15 "strikingly underinclusive." Moreover, the assumption that the constitutionally permissible regulation of pornography could not be more extensive with respect to the distribution of material depicting children may also have led the court to conclude that a narrowing construction of § 263.15 was unavailable.

The Court of Appeals' assumption was not unreasonable in light of our decisions. This case, however, constitutes our first examination of a statute directed at and limited to depictions of sexual activity involving children. We believe our inquiry should begin with the question of whether a State has somewhat more freedom in proscribing works which portray sexual acts or lewd exhibitions of genitalia by children....

B

The *Miller* standard, like its predecessors, was an accommodation between the State's interests in protecting the "sensibilities of unwilling recipients" from exposure to pornographic material and the dangers of censorship inherent in unabashedly content-based laws. Like obscenity statutes, laws directed at the dissemination of child pornography run the risk of suppressing protected expression by allowing the hand of the censor to become unduly heavy. For the following reasons, however, we are persuaded that the States are entitled to greater leeway in the regulation of pornographic depictions of children.

First. It is evident beyond the need for elaboration that a State's interest in "safeguarding the physical and psychological well-being of a minor" is "compelling." *Globe Newspaper Co.* v. *Superior Court,* 457 U.S. 596, 607 (1982). "A democratic society rests, for its continuance, upon the healthy, well-rounded growth of young people into full maturity as citizens." *Prince* v. *Massachusetts,* 321 U.S. 158, 168 (1944)....

... The legislative judgment, as well as the judgment found in the relevant literature, is that the use of children as subjects of pornographic materials is harmful to the physiological, emotional, and mental health of the child. That judgment, we think, easily passes muster under the First Amendment.

Second. The distribution of photographs and films depicting sexual activity by juveniles is intrinsically related to the sexual abuse of children in at least two ways. First, the materials produced are a permanent record of the children's participation and the harm to the child is exacerbated by their circulation. Second, the distribution network for child pornography must be closed if the production of material which requires the sexual exploitation of children is to be effectively controlled. Indeed, there is no serious contention that the legislature was unjustified in believing that it is difficult, if not impossible, to halt the exploitation of children by pursuing only those who produce the photographs and movies. While the production of pornographic materials is a low-profile, clandestine industry, the need to market the resulting products requires a visible apparatus of distribution. The most expeditious if not the only practical method of law enforcement may be to dry up the market for this material by imposing severe criminal penalties on persons selling, advertising, or otherwise promoting the product....

... The *Miller* standard, like all general definitions of what may be banned as obscene, does not reflect the State's particular and more compelling interest in prosecuting those who promote the sexual exploitation of children. Thus, the question under the *Miller* test of whether a work, taken as a whole, appeals to the prurient interest of the average person bears no connection to the issue of whether a child has been physically or psychologically harmed in the production of the work....

Third. The advertising and selling of child pornography provide an economic motive for and are thus an integral part of the production of such materials, an activity illegal throughout the Nation....

Fourth. The value of permitting live performances and photographic reproductions of children engaged in lewd sexual conduct is exceedingly modest, if not *de minimis.* We consider it unlikely that visual depictions of children performing sexual acts or lewdly exhibiting their genitals would often constitute an important and necessary part of a literary performance or scientific or educational work....

Fifth. Recognizing and classifying child pornography as a category of material outside the protection of the First Amendment is not incompatible with our earlier decisions. When a definable class of material, such as that covered by § 263.15, bears so heavily and pervasively on the welfare of children engaged in its production, we think the balance of competing interests is clearly struck and that it is permissible to consider these materials as without the protection of the First Amendment....

III

It remains to address the claim that the New York statute is unconstitutionally overbroad because it would forbid the distribution of material with serious literary, scientific, or educational value

or material which does not threaten the harms sought to be combated by the State. Respondent prevailed on that ground below, and it is to that issue that we now turn.

... [W]e hold that § 263.15 is not substantially overbroad. We consider this the paradigmatic case of a state statute whose legitimate reach dwarfs its arguably impermissible applications. New York, as we have held, may constitutionally prohibit dissemination of material specified in § 263.15. While the reach of the statute is directed at the hard core of child pornography, the Court of Appeals was understandably concerned that some protected expression, ranging from medical textbooks to pictorials in the National Geographic would fall prey to the statute. How often, if ever, it may be necessary to employ children to engage in conduct clearly within the reach of § 263.15 in order to produce educational, medical, or artistic works cannot be known with certainty. Yet we seriously doubt, and it has not been suggested, that these arguably impermissible applications of the statute amount to more than a tiny fraction of the materials within the statute's reach....

IV

Because § 263.15 is not substantially overbroad, it is unnecessary to consider its application to material that does not depict sexual conduct of a type that New York may restrict consistent with the First Amendment. As applied to Paul Ferber and to others who distribute similar material, the statute does not violate the First Amendment as applied to the States through the Fourteenth. The judgment of the New York Court of Appeals is reversed, and the case is remanded to that court for further proceedings not inconsistent with this opinion.

So ordered.

[*Blackmun concurs in the result, O'Connor concurs, Brennan (joined by Marshall) concurs in the judgment, and Stevens concurs in the judgment.*]

Reno v. ACLU

521 U.S. 844 (1997)

Congress passed the Communications Decency Act (CDA) of 1996 to protect minors from harmful material on the Internet. Several parties, including the ACLU, brought this suit against Attorney General Janet Reno. A three-judge panel entered a preliminary injunction against enforcement of the statutory provisions challenged under the First Amendment. Under the special review provisions of the CDA, the government appealed the case directly to the Supreme Court.

JUSTICE STEVENS delivered the opinion of the Court.

At issue is the constitutionality of two statutory provisions enacted to protect minors from "indecent" and "patently offensive" communications on the Internet. Notwithstanding the legitimacy and importance of the congressional goal of protecting children from harmful materials, we agree with the three-judge District Court that the statute abridges "the freedom of speech" protected by the First Amendment.

I

The District Court made extensive findings of fact, most of which were based on a detailed stipulation prepared by the parties....

The Internet

The Internet is an international network of interconnected computers. It is the outgrowth of what began in 1969 as a military program called "ARPANET,"...

The internet has experienced "extraordinary growth." The number of "host" computers—those that store information and relay communications—increased from about 300 in 1981 to approximately 9,400,000 by the time of the trial in 1996. Roughly 60% of these hosts are located in the United States. About 40 million people used the Internet at the time of trial, a number that is expected to mushroom to 200 million by 1999.

Individuals can obtain access to the Internet from many different sources, generally hosts themselves or entities with a host affiliation. Most colleges and universities provide access for their students and faculty; many corporations provide their employees with access through an office network; many communities and local libraries provide free access; and an increasing number of storefront "computer coffee shops" provide access for a small hourly fee. Several major national "online services" such as America Online, CompuServe, the Microsoft Network, and Prodigy offer access to their own extensive proprietary network as well as a link to the much larger resources of the Internet. These commercial online services had almost 12 million individual subscribers at the time of trial.

Anyone with access to the Internet may take advantage of a wide variety of communication and information retrieval methods. These methods are constantly evolving and difficult to categorize precisely. But, as presently constituted, those most relevant to this case are electronic mail ("e-mail"), automatic mailing list services ("mail exploders,"

sometimes referred to as "listservs"), "newsgroups," "chat rooms," and the "World Wide Web." All of these methods can be used to transmit text; most can transmit sound, pictures, and moving video images....

Sexually Explicit Material

Sexually explicit material on the Internet includes text, pictures, and chat and "extends from the modestly titillating to the hardest-core." ...

Some of the communications over the Internet that originate in foreign countries are also sexually explicit.

Though such material is widely available, users seldom encounter such content accidentally. "A document's title or a description of the document will usually appear before the document itself ... and in many cases the user will receive detailed information about a site's content before he or she need take the step to access the document. Almost all sexually explicit images are preceded by warnings as to the content." For that reason, the "odds are slim" that a user would enter a sexually explicit site by accident. Unlike communications received by radio or television, "the receipt of information on the Internet requires a series of affirmative steps more deliberate and directed than merely turning a dial. A child requires some sophistication and some ability to read to retrieve material and thereby to use the Internet unattended."

Systems have been developed to help parents control the material that may be available on a home computer with Internet access. A system may either limit a computer's access to an approved list of sources that have been identified as containing no adult material, it may block designated inappropriate sites, or it may attempt to block messages containing identifiable objectionable features. "Although parental control software currently can screen for certain suggestive words or for known sexually explicit sites, it cannot now screen for sexually explicit images." Nevertheless, the evidence indicates that "a reasonably effective method by which parents can prevent their children from accessing sexually explicit and other material which parents may believe is inappropriate for their children will soon be available."

Age Verification

The problem of age verification differs for different uses of the Internet. The District Court categorically determined that there "is no effective way to determine the identity or the age of a user who is accessing material through e-mail, mail exploders, newsgroups or chat rooms." The Government offered no evidence that there was a reliable way to screen recipients and participants in such fora for age. Moreover, even if it were technologically feasible to block minors' access to newsgroups and chat rooms containing discussions of art, politics or other subjects that potentially elicit "indecent" or "patently offensive" contributions, it would not be possible to block their access to that material and "still allow them access to the remaining content, even if the overwhelming majority of that content was not indecent."

Technology exists by which an operator of a Web site may condition access on the verification of requested information such as a credit card number or an adult password. Credit card verification is only feasible, however, either in connection with a commercial transaction in which the card is used, or by payment to a verification agency. Using credit card possession as a surrogate for proof of age would impose costs on non-commercial Web sites that would require many of them to shut down.... Moreover, the imposition of such a requirement "would completely bar adults who do not have a credit card and lack the resources to obtain one from accessing any blocked material."

Commercial pornographic sites that charge their users for access have assigned them passwords as a method of age verification. The record does not contain any evidence concerning the reliability of these technologies. Even if passwords are effective for commercial purveyors of indecent material, the District Court found that an adult password requirement would impose significant burdens on non-commercial sites, both because they would discourage users from accessing their sites and because the cost of creating and maintaining such screening systems would be "beyond their reach."...

II

[*Title V of the Telecommunications Act of 1996— known as the Communications Decency Act (CDA)— contained two provisions challenged in this case.*]

The first, 47 U.S.C.A. §223(a) (Supp. 1997), prohibits the knowing transmission of obscene or indecent messages to any recipient under 18 years of age. [*The statute provided for fines and up to two years in prison.*]

The breadth of these prohibitions is qualified by two affirmative defenses.... One covers those who take "good faith, reasonable, effective, and appropriate actions" to restrict access by minors to the prohibited communications. §223(e)(5)(A). The

other covers those who restrict access to covered material by requiring certain designated forms of age proof, such as a verified credit card or an adult identification number or code. §223(e)(5)(B)....

IV

In arguing for reversal, the Government contends that the CDA is plainly constitutional under three of our prior decisions: (1) *Ginsberg v. New York*, 390 U.S. 629 (1968); (2) *FCC v. Pacifica Foundation*, 438 U.S. 726 (1978); and (3) *Renton v. Playtime Theatres, Inc.*, 475 U.S. 41 (1986). A close look at these cases, however, raises—rather than relieves—doubts concerning the constitutionality of the CDA.

In *Ginsberg,* we upheld the constitutionality of a New York statute that prohibited selling to minors under 17 years of age material that was considered obscene as to them even if not obscene as to adults. [*The Court gives four reasons why the statute upheld in* Ginsberg *was narrower than the CDA: the New York prohibition did not bar parents from purchasing the magazines for their children; the New York statute applied only to commercial transactions whereas the CDA contained no such limitation; the New York statute cabined its definition of material that is harmful to minors with the requirement that it be "utterly without redeeming social importance for minors," whereas the CDA failed to provide any definition of the term "indecent" and omitted any requirement that the "patently offensive" material lack serious literary, artistic, political, or scientific value; and the New York statute defined a minor as a person under the age of 17, whereas the CDA applied to those under 18.*]

In *Pacifica,* we upheld a declaratory order of the Federal Communications Commission, holding that the broadcast of a recording of a 12-minute monologue entitled "Filthy Words" that had previously been delivered to a live audience "could have been the subject of administrative sanctions." [*The Court found these distinctions between* Pacifica *and the CDA: the order in* Pacifica *targeted a specific broadcast whereas the CDA's broad categorical prohibition is not limited to particular times; unlike the CDA, the FCC's declaratory order was not punitive; the FCC's order applied to a medium that had received the most limited First Amendment protection. The Internet has no comparable history.*]

In *Renton,* we upheld a zoning ordinance that kept adult movie theatres out of residential neighborhoods. The ordinance was aimed, not at the content of the films shown in the theaters, but rather at the "secondary effects"—such as crime and deteriorating property values—that these theaters fostered: "It is th[e] secondary effect which these zoning ordinances attempt to avoid, not the dissemination of 'offensive' speech." 475 U.S. at 49 (quoting *Young v. American Mini Theatres, Inc.*, 427 U.S. 50, 71, n.34 (1976). According to the Government, the CDA is constitutional because it constitutes a sort of "cyberzoning" on the Internet. But the CDA applies broadly to the entire universe of cyberspace. And the purpose of the CDA is to protect children from the primary effects of "indecent" and "patently offensive" speech, rather than any "secondary" effect of such speech. Thus, the CDA is a content-based blanket restriction on speech, and, as such, cannot be "properly analyzed as a form of time, place, and manner regulation." 475 U.S., at 46....

V

[*Here the Court explains that the Internet is not as "invasive" as radio and television. Users seldom encounter content "by accident." Also, unlike congressional regulation of the broadcast spectrum, the Internet cannot be considered a "scarce" expressive commodity.*]

VI

Regardless of whether the CDA is so vague that it violates the Fifth Amendment, the many ambiguities concerning the scope of its coverage render it problematic for purposes of the First Amendment. For instance, each of the two parts of the CDA uses a different linguistic form. The first uses the word "indecent," 47 U.S.C.A. § 223(a) (Supp.1997), while the second speaks of material that "in context, depicts or describes, in terms patently offensive as measured by contemporary community standards, sexual or excretory activities or organs," § 223(d). Given the absence of a definition of either term, this difference in language will provoke uncertainty among speakers about how the two standards relate to each other and just what they mean....

The vagueness of the CDA is a matter of special concern for two reasons. First, the CDA is a content-based regulation of speech. The vagueness of such a

regulation raises special First Amendment concerns because of its obvious chilling effect on free speech.... Second, the CDA is a criminal statute. In addition to the opprobrium and stigma of a criminal conviction, the CDA threatens violators with penalties including up to two years in prison for each act of violation. The severity of criminal sanctions may well cause speakers to remain silent rather than communicate even arguably unlawful words, ideas, and images....

VII

We are persuaded that the CDA lacks the precision that the First Amendment requires when a statute regulates the content of speech. In order to deny minors access to potentially harmful speech, the CDA effectively suppresses a large amount of speech that adults have a constitutional right to receive and to address to one another....

X

[*In this section the Court declines the government's invitation for the Court to sever from the CDA the words or phrases that the Court finds unconstitutional. Drawing on language from an earlier decision, it says that it "will not rewrite a ... law to conform it to constitutional requirements."*]

For the foregoing reasons, the judgment of the district court is affirmed.

It is so ordered.

JUSTICE O'CONNOR with whom THE CHIEF JUSTICE joins, concurring in the judgment in part and dissenting in part.

[*The dissenters agree with the Court that the "display" provision cannot pass muster but conclude that the "indecency transmission" and "specific person" provisions would not be unconstitutional in all of their applications. They would sustain those provisions "to the extent they apply to the transmission of Internet communications where the party initiating the communication knows that all of the recipients are minors."*]

The House Responds to *Stevens* (2010)

Demonstrating that the Court does not have the final word on issues of obscenity, Congress quickly responded to the Court's 2010 decision in *U.S.* v. *Stevens.* In that case the Court found that Congress's attempt to regulate pornography depicting animal cruelty was overbroad. Shortly after that opinion was issued, The Prevention of Interstate Commerce in Animal Crush Videos Act of 2010 was introduced in Congress. The bill made clear that depictions of "customary and normal veterinary or animal husbandry practices" and "hunting, trapping, and fishing" were excluded from coverage under the Act. The following excerpt comes from the floor debate in the House of Representatives. 156 Cong. Rec. H5788–5791 (daily ed. July 20, 2010).

Mr. Scott of Virginia.... [T]his legislation addresses a disturbing subject in need of congressional action.

In the late 1990's Congress was made aware of a growing market of videotapes and still photographs depicting animals, typically small animals, being slowly and sadistically crushed to death. These depictions are commonly referred to as "crush videos." Much of the material features women inflicting torture with their bare feet or while wearing high-heeled shoes. The depictions often appeal to people with a very specific sexual fetish.

Even in States where harming the animals in such a way violates State laws prohibiting cruelty to animals, prosecutors have difficulty obtaining convictions. For example, the faces of the persons inflicting the torture were often not shown in the videos; and the locations, times and dates of the acts could not be ascertained from the depictions themselves. So defendants were often able to successfully assert as a defense that the State could not prove its jurisdiction over the place where the acts occurred nor that it could prove that the actions took place within the statute of limitations.

. . .

So Congress enacted a new law prohibiting the creation, sale, and possession of the depictions of such acts.... The motivation for passing the law was to address the sale of crush videos, but the statute was written in such a way that it also could be read, in some circumstances, to apply to more mainstream material, such as videos depicting hunting and fishing and other activity protected by the First Amendment of the Constitution.

Because of this susceptibility to a broader reading, in April the United States Supreme Court invalidated the entire statute in the case United States v. Stevens ... The Court made it clear, however, it did not rule out the possibility of Congress' adopting a bill that would hold up under constitutional scrutiny....

Mr. Gallegly [of California].... The district attorney of Ventura County, California, first brought this issue to my attention back in 1999. He explained that, although crush videos were illegal under State laws, the crime was difficult to prosecute because video producers moved their goods through interstate commerce to avoid prosecution.

The FBI, the U.S. Department of Education, and the U.S. Department of Justice consider animal cruelty to be one of the early warning signs of potential violent youth. The Boston Strangler, the Unabomber, Jeffrey Dahmer, and Ted Bundy all tortured animals before they began to murder people.

Everyone agrees that these disgusting videos must be stopped. My first bill passed the House in 1999 by a bipartisan vote of 372–42, by unanimous consent in the Senate, and was signed into law by then President Bill Clinton ...

. . .

Immediately after the 1999 bill became law, the crush video business virtually disappeared. It has recently reemerged in light of the court ruling. Quick passage of H.R. 5566 will once again stop these revolting videos that depict the torture of animals and killing of defenseless animals....

. . .

Mr. Moran of Virginia.... Quite simply, animal crush videos contain some of the vilest treatment of animals imaginable.... A law was passed by Congress 11 years ago that [made it possible to prosecute people trafficking in these videos], but earlier this year the Supreme Court struck down that law, claiming it could be used to violate free speech rights.

While I didn't agree with that decision, it was clear that Congress could not just stand by while these videos once again proliferated on the Internet....

As demonstrated by its long list of bipartisan cosponsors and its unanimous passage out of Committee, this bill represents a good faith effort by Members of both parties to maintain the effectiveness of the original law while addressing the constitutional concerns raised by the Court.

. . .

The Speaker pro tempore (Mr. Himes). The question is on the motion offered by the gentleman from Virginia ... that the House suspend the rules and pass the bill, H.R. 5566, as amended.

The question was taken.

The Speaker pro tempore. In the opinion of the Chair, two-thirds being in the affirmative, the ayes have it. [*Later the House passed the bill on a rollcall vote of 416 to 3.*]

CONCLUSIONS

The decision by the Court in *New York Times Co.* v. *Sullivan* (1964) appeared to be a ringing endorsement for a free press. Debate on public issues was to be "uninhibited, robust, and wide-open." However, the language and rationale of *Sullivan* paved the way for a series of rulings by the Court that exposed the press to costly settlements and lawsuits in libel cases. There continues to be a presumption against prior restraint, but some self-censorship by the press is a possible consequence of expensive litigation. Moreover, the Court held that newsrooms could be searched by law enforcement officials (*Zurcher* in 1978) and reporters could be jailed for refusing to disclose confidential sources (*Branzburg* in 1972). With some starts and stops, the Court generally supported press freedoms with regard to open trials and access to court proceedings. Questions of obscenity and pornography continue to perplex and divide the Court.

Freedom of the press depends on the relationship that exists between the government and the citizen. Does government extend the right of a free press to the people or do the people instruct the government on its rights and powers? Remarks by James Madison during House debate in 1794 provide an important context for this question. The House was considering a censure of certain societies involved in an insurrection in western Pennsylvania (the Whiskey Rebellion). Madison warned that opinions could not be the object of legislation. Congressional resolutions of censure might extend improperly to the liberties of speech and of the press, he said, and then concluded: "If we advert to the nature of Republican Government, we shall find that the censorial power is in the people over the Government, and not in the Government over the people." 4 Annals of Congress 934 (1794).

NOTES AND QUESTIONS

1. What were the major arguments by John Milton, in *Areopagitica* (1644), against censorship and prior restraint? Do they still make sense in the 21st Century? Why or why not?

2. What are the risks of "seditious libel" to democratic government? Are there limits to the criticism that democratic governments should tolerate?

3. What constitutional interests are served when the press and the public follow a trial?

4. Do libel doctrines adequately protect a free press, public access to information, and personal privacy?

5. The Supreme Court has attempted to articulate standards for what is obscene. In the end, the decisive voice is for jurors and local communities. Does this standard make sense to you? Why or why not?

SELECTED READINGS

ANDERSON, DAVID A. "The Origins of the Press Clause." 30 UCLA Law Review 455 (1983).

BARRON, JEROME A. Freedom of the Press for Whom? Bloomington: Indiana University Press, 1973.

BATES, STEPHEN."The Reporter's Privilege, Then and Now." 38 Society 41 (2001).

BERNS, WALTER. "Freedom of the Press and the Alien and Sedition Laws: A Reappraisal." 1970 Supreme Court Review 109.

BEZANSON, RANDALL P., ET AL. Libel Law and the Press: Myth and Reality. New York: The Free Press, 1987.

BLANCHARD, MARGARET A. "The Institutional Press and its First Amendment Privileges." 1978 Supreme Court Review 225.

BLASI, VINCENT. "Toward a Theory of Prior Restraint: The Central Linkage." 66 Minnesota Law Review 11 (1981).

BURANELLI, VINCENT. The Trial of Peter Zenger. New York: New York University Press, 1957.

EMERSON, THOMAS I. "The Doctrine of Prior Restraint." 20 Law and Contemporary Problems 648 (1955).

EMERY, EDWIN. The Press and America. Englewood Cliffs, N.J.: Prentice-Hall, 1984.

FRIENDLY, FRED W. Minnesota Rag. New York: Random House, 1981.

GERALD, J. EDWARD. The Press and the Constitution, 1931–1947. Minneapolis, Minn.: University of Minnesota Press, 1948. ANDERSEN JONES, RONNELL. "Media Subpoenas: Impact, Perception, and Legal Protection in the Changing World of American Journalism." 84 Washington Law Review 317 (2009).

JONES, RONNELL ANDERSEN. "Media Subpoenas: Impact, Perception, and Legal Protection in the Changing World of American Journalism." 84 Washington Law Review 317 (2009).

KALVEN, HARRY, JR. "The Reasonable Man and the First Amendment: Hill, Butts, and Walker." 1967 Supreme Court Review 267.

———. "The New York Times Cases: A Note on the 'Central Meaning of the First Amendment.'" 1964 Supreme Court Review 191.

KING, ELLIOT. Free for All: The Internet's Transformation of Journalism. Evanston, IL: Northwestern University Press, 2010.

LAWHORNE, CLIFTON O. Defamation and Public Officials. Carbondale: Southern Illinois University Press, 1971.

———. The Supreme Court and Libel. Carbondale: Southern Illinois University Press, 1981.

LEVY, LEONARD W. Emergence of a Free Press. New York: Oxford University Press, 1985.

———, ED. Freedom of the Press from Zenger to Jefferson. Durham, N.C.: Carolina Academic Press, 1996.

LEWIS, ANTHONY. Make No Law: The Sullivan Case and the First Amendment. New York: Vintage Books, 1991.

LINDE, HANS. "Courts and Censorship." 66 Minnesota Law Review 171 (1981).

LOFTON, JOHN. The Press as Guardian of the First Amendment. Columbia: University of South Carolina Press, 1980.

MACKINNON, CATHERINE A. Only Words. Cambridge, Mass.: Harvard University Press, 1993.

MURPHY, PAUL L. "Near v. Minnesota in the Context of Historical Developments." 66 Minnesota Law Review 95 (1981).

NELSON, HAROLD L., ED. Freedom of the Press: From Hamilton to the Warren Court. Indianapolis, Ind.: Bobbs-Merrill, 1967.

SHAPIRO, MARTIN, ED. The Pentagon Papers and the Courts: A Study in Foreign Policy-Making and Freedom of the Press. San Francisco: Chandler Publishing, 1972.

SMITH, JAMES MORTON. Freedom's Fetters: The Alien and Sedition Laws and American Civil Liberties. Ithaca, N.Y.: Cornell University Press, 1956.

SMITH, JEFFERY A. War and Press Freedom: The Problem of Prerogative Power. New York: Oxford University Press, 1999.

SNEPP, FRANK. Irreparable Harm. Lawrence: University Press of Kansas, 2001.

UNGAR, SANFORD J. The Papers & The Papers. New York: Dutton, 1972.

12

Religious Freedom

The religion clauses in the First Amendment contain two distinct objectives: "Congress shall make no law respecting an establishment of religion or prohibiting the free exercise thereof." These clauses—the Establishment Clause and the Free Exercise Clause—sometimes overlap and compete. Satisfying one clause may violate the other. If Congress grants a tax exemption for church property, is that establishment of religion? Taxing the property, however, would interfere with free exercise. When Congress provides chaplains for soldiers in the armed forces, is that an act of establishment? Yet denying soldiers access to ministers, rabbis, or Muslim clerics would interfere with free exercise, especially for soldiers assigned to remote outposts. It is well settled that government may accommodate religious practices in various ways without violating the Establishment Clause.

These complexities are not resolved by invoking metaphors about the "wall of separation" between church and state. In upholding state assistance of transportation to parochial schools, Justice Black claimed that the First Amendment "has erected a wall between church and state. That wall must be kept high and impregnable. We could not approve the slightest breach. New Jersey has not breached it here." Everson v. Board of Education, 330 U.S. 1, 18 (1947). In fact, a breach occurred in that case. A year later, in a concurring opinion, Justice Jackson questioned the Court's reasoning and predicted correctly that the Court would make "the legal 'wall of separation between church and state' as winding as the famous serpentine wall designed by Mr. Jefferson for the University he founded." McCollum v. Board of Education, 333 U.S. 203, 238 (1948). Justice Reed advised: "A rule of law should not be drawn from a figure of speech." Id. at 247.

A complete wall between church and state is neither possible nor desirable. Religious organizations have a right to lobby and petition government for various programs and activities. Ministers may serve in the legislature and hold other public offices. McDaniel v. Paty, 435 U.S. 618 (1978). Sectarian schools are obliged to teach the secular subjects specified by the state and must adhere to state health and safety standards. "Some relationship between government and religious organizations is inevitable.... Fire inspections, building and zoning regulations, and state requirements under compulsory school-attendance laws are examples of necessary and permissible contacts." Lemon v. Kurtzman, 403 U.S. 602, 614 (1971).

How should the religion clauses be interpreted? On several occasions the Supreme Court has recognized that the clauses "had the same objective and were intended to provide the same protection against governmental intrusion on religious liberty as the Virginia statute." Everson v. Board of Education, 330 U.S. at 13. See also Reynolds v. United States, 98 U.S. 145, 162–64 (1878). The Virginia Statute for Establishing Religious Freedom—the handiwork of Thomas Jefferson and James Madison—provides valuable guidance in understanding the motivations behind the religion clauses. However, six states (Connecticut, Georgia, Maryland, Massachusetts, New Hampshire, and South Carolina) continued to provide assistance to established churches after 1786. In 1833, Massachusetts became the last state to end support to established religions. When the first Congress enacted the Northwest Territory Ordinance, Article III provided: "Religion, morality, and knowledge, being necessary to good government and the happiness of mankind, schools and the means of education shall forever be encouraged." 1 Stat. 52 (1789).

A. THE VIRGINIA STATUTE

Religious liberties, part of the foundation for political and social rights, had their origin in the long struggle to separate church and state. The three-volume study by Anson Phelps Stokes documents this development: "the study of American history shows that this actual separation, especially in the states, was generally the precursor, and always the surest support of public opinion in guaranteeing freedom of conscience and worship." 1 Stokes, Church and State in the United States 646 (1950). The Virginia statute of 1786 declared "that no man shall be compelled to frequent or support any religious worship, place, or ministry whatsoever, nor shall be enforced, restrained, molested, or burthened in his body or goods, nor shall otherwise suffer on account of his religious opinions or belief...." The preamble stated: "to compel a man to furnish contributions of money for the propagation of opinions which he disbelieves, is sinful and tyrannical." The author of the statute was Jefferson; Madison shepherded it into Virginia law. Both men regarded religion and its free exercise as a fundamental human right forever free from state intrusion. Wrote Jefferson: "our rulers can have authority over such natural rights, only as we have submitted to them. The rights of conscience we never submitted, we could not submit." 3 Writings of Thomas Jefferson 263 (Ford ed.).

Religious liberty did not reach America on the wings of court decisions. The active, driving force for creating and preserving religious liberty has been the political—not the judicial—process. No court rulings guided the early settlers, who drew inspiration from their hearts and minds. Independent and headstrong pioneers were willing to confront authority, suffer punishment and persecution, and face exile. Louis Fisher, Religious Liberty in America (2002).

Neither Madison nor Jefferson had patience for sectarian battles, narrow creeds, or doctrinal wrangling. For them, religion was more of a general moral code to be practiced, not preached. "On the dogmas of religion," wrote Jefferson, "as distinguished from moral principles, all mankind, from the beginning of the world to this day, have been quarrelling, fighting, burning and torturing one another, for abstractions unintelligible to themselves and to all others, and absolutely beyond the comprehension of the human mind. Were I to enter on that arena, I should only add an unit to the number of Bedlamites." 10 Writings of Thomas Jefferson 67–68 (Ford ed.).

As with other colonies, Virginians suffered from religious cruelty and intolerance among different sects. Madison deplored the "diabolical, hell-conceived principle of persecution" that raged about him in 1774. 1 Writings of James Madison 21 (Hunt ed.). Baptists, Presbyterians, Catholics, Quakers, and other minority groups were whipped, fined, imprisoned, and forced to support the established Anglican Church. Between 1776 and 1786, Virginia moved a step at a time to establish religious freedom. The state Bill of Rights in 1776 proclaimed that religion "can be directed only by reason and conviction, not by force or violence, and therefore all men are equally entitled to the free exercise of religion, according to the dictates of conscience."

General Assessment Bill

Oppressive laws against dissenters nevertheless remained on the books. In December 1776, Virginia repealed its laws directed against heretics and nonattendance and exempted dissenters from giving financial support to the Anglican Church. Another step toward disestablishment occurred in 1779 when Virginia repealed all laws requiring even the members of the Anglican Church to support their own ministry. As a substitute for this preferential treatment, the Anglican Church pressed for a general tax to benefit all Christian religions. Bills were introduced to obtain public funds for teachers of Christianity. The final version allowed taxpayers to designate which church should receive their share of the tax and even gave the nonreligious taxpayer the option of directing taxes to general educational purposes.

Proponents of the general assessment claimed that Christianity and public morals would suffer without state financial aid, but the Baptists and some Presbyterians, who would have benefited financially from the bill, opposed the general assessment. Madison, in his famous "Memorial and Remonstrance Against Religious Assessments," insisted that religion be left to the conviction and conscience of the individual. Religion consisted in voluntary acts "wholly exempt" from the state's jurisdiction. He protested against religious assessments partly because "experience witnesseth that ecclesiastical establishments, instead of maintaining the purity and efficacy of Religion, have had a contrary operation. . . . What have been its fruits? More or less in all places, pride and indolence in the Clergy; ignorance and servility in the laity; in both, superstition, bigotry and persecution." 2 Writings of James Madison 187 (Hunt ed.).

The force and logic of Madison's detailed attack, emphasizing the inherent incompatibility between private religious beliefs and public financial support, led to the defeat of the general assessment bill. Virginia thereby prohibited religious aid even on a nonpreferential basis. Madison seized the opportunity to reintroduce Jefferson's Statute for Establishing Religious Freedom, which passed in January 1786 (see reading on Virginia statute). Many of those principles appear in the House debate in 1789 on the Bill of Rights (see reading). Years later, in evaluating religious institutions in Virginia after they had been denied public funds, Madison remarked that "it is impossible to deny that Religion prevails with more zeal, and a more exemplary priesthood than it ever did when established and patronised by Public authority." 9 Writings of James Madison 102 (Hunt ed.). A resolution passed by Congress in 1988 contains this Madisonian sentiment: "religion is most free when it is observed voluntarily at private initiative, uncontaminated by Government interference and unconstrained by majority preference." 102 Stat. 1772 (1988).

Oath or Affirmation

Debate at the constitutional convention in Philadelphia contained few comments about religion. On May 29, 1787, Charles Pinckney's draft constitution included a provision that the national legislature "shall pass no law on the subject of Religion." 3 Farrand 599. However, his plan was never acted upon. The subject of religion was not addressed except for debate on a national university and two provisions in Article VI. Three days before adjournment, Madison and Pinckney moved to give Congress the power "to establish an University, in which no preferences or distinctions should be allowed on account of religion." With little discussion the motion was defeated, 6 to 4, with one state divided. 2 Farrand 616.

Article VI provides that members of Congress, members of state legislatures, and all executive and judicial officers — both federal and state — "shall be bound by Oath or Affirmation, to support this Constitution; but no religious Test shall ever be required as a Qualification to any Office or public Trust under the United States." Unlike affirmation, an oath is generally understood to be directed to a deity or divine authority. Quakers, Mennonites, and other denominations objected to oaths on various grounds, including the Biblical injunction "Swear not at all" (Matthew 5:34). Offering affirmation as an option accommodated their religious beliefs.

Whereas the oath/affirmation requirement applies to all public officials — state and federal — the test ban covers only federal officials. Several state constitutions included a religious test, requiring officeholders to profess faith in Jesus Christ, God, Protestantism, or the Christian religion. Many of those religious tests were removed from the state constitutions from 1789 to 1793. A religious test in Maryland's constitution reached the Supreme Court in 1961. Roy Torcaso, appointed to the office of Notary Public, refused to comply with the constitutional requirement that he declare a belief in the existence of God. The Court held that the religious test invaded his "freedom of belief and religion and therefore cannot be enforced against him." Torcaso v. Watkins, 367 U.S. 488, 496 (1961).

Virginia Statute for Establishing Religious Freedom (1786)

James Madison, Thomas Jefferson, and George Mason were in the forefront of Virginians who challenged the established Anglican Church and sought to secure religious liberty for all citizens. For them, religious belief was a natural right entrusted to the conscience of the individual and could not be subjected to state interference or coercion. That principle was included in the state Bill of Rights in 1776. Three years later, Virginia repealed its law requiring members of the Anglican Church to support their own ministry. The Church advocated a general tax to benefit all Christian religions, but Madison and others were successful in defeating the bill. Madison was then able to pass, in 1786, Jefferson's Statute for Establishing Religious Freedom. The bill is reproduced from 12 William Waller Hening, The Statutes at Large: Being a Collection of All the Laws of Virginia 84–86 (1823).

I. WHEREAS Almighty God hath created the mind free; that all attempts to influence it by temporal punishments or burthens, or by civil incapacitations, tend only to beget habits of hypocrisy and meanness, and are a departure from the plan of the Holy author of our religion, who being Lord both of body and mind, yet chose not to propagate it by coercions on either, as was in his Almighty power to do; that the impious presumption of legislators and rulers, civil as well as ecclesiastical, who being themselves but fallible and uninspired men, have assumed dominion over the faith of others, setting up their own opinions and modes of thinking as the only true and infallible, and as such endeavouring to impose them on others, hath established and maintained false religions over the greatest part of the world, and through all time; that to compel a man to furnish contributions of money for the propagation of opinions which he disbelieves, is sinful and tyrannical; that even the forcing him to support this or that teacher of his own religious persuasion, is depriving him of the comfortable liberty of giving his contributions to the particular pastor, whose morals he would make his pattern, and whose powers he feels most persuasive to righteousness, and is withdrawing from the ministry those temporary rewards, which proceeding from an approbation of their personal conduct, are an additional incitement to earnest and unremitting labours for the instruction of mankind; that our civil rights have no dependence on our religious opinions, any more than our opinions in physics or geometry; that therefore the proscribing any citizen as unworthy the public confidence by laying upon him an incapacity of being called to offices of trust and emolument, unless he profess or renounce this or that religious opinion, is depriving him injuriously of those privileges and advantages to which in common with his fellow-citizens he has a natural right; that it tends only to corrupt the principles of that religion it is meant to encourage, by bribing with a monopoly of wordly honours and emoluments, those who will externally profess and conform to it; that though indeed these are criminal who do not withstand such temptation, yet neither are those innocent who lay the bait in their way; that to suffer the civil magistrate to intrude his powers into the field of opinion, and to restrain the profession or propagation of principles on supposition of their ill tendency, is a dangerous fallacy, which at once destroys all religious liberty, because he being of course judge of that tendency will make his opinions the rule of judgment, and approve or condemn the sentiments of others only as they shall square with or differ from his own; that it is time enough for the rightful purposes of civil government, for its officers to interfere when principles break out into overt acts against peace and good order; and finally, that truth is great and will prevail if left to herself, that she is the proper and sufficient antagonist to error, and has nothing to fear from the conflict, unless by human interposition disarmed of her natural weapons, free argument and debate, errors ceasing to be dangerous when it is permitted freely to contradict them:

II. *Be it enacted by the General Assembly,* That no man shall be compelled to frequent or support any religious worship, place, or ministry whatsoever, nor shall be enforced, restrained, molested, or burthened in his body or goods, nor shall otherwise suffer on account of his religious opinions or belief; but that all men shall be free to profess, and by argument to maintain, their opinion in matters of religion, and that the same shall in no wise diminish, enlarge, or affect their civil capacities.

III. And though we well know that this assembly elected by the people for the ordinary purposes of legislation only, have no power to restrain the acts of succeeding assemblies, constituted with powers equal to our own, and that therefore to declare this act to be irrevocable would be of no effect in law; yet we are free to declare, and do declare, that the rights hereby asserted are of the natural rights of mankind, and that if any act shall be hereafter passed to repeal the present, or to narrow its operation, such act will be an infringement of natural right.

House Debate on the Religion Clauses (1789)

On June 8, 1789, Congressman James Madison proposed the following language as part of a list of amendments to the Constitution: "The civil rights of none shall be abridged on account of religious belief or worship, nor shall any national religion be established, nor shall the full and equal rights of conscience be in any manner, or on any pretext, infringed." He also recommended the following restriction on the states: "No State shall violate the equal rights of conscience, or the freedom of the press, or the trial by jury in criminal cases." 1 Annals of Congress 434, 435. After Madison's proposals were reworked by a special committee, on August 15 the House debated the Religion Clauses. The passages below are taken from 1 Annals of Congress 729–31, 766, 913.

The House again went into a Committee of the Whole on the proposed amendments to the Constitution, Mr. BOUDINOT in the Chair.

The fourth proposition being under consideration, as follows:

Article 1. Section 9. Between paragraphs two and three insert "no religion shall be established by law, nor shall the equal rights of conscience be infringed."

Mr. SYLVESTER had some doubts of the propriety of the mode of expression used in this paragraph. He apprehended that it was liable to a construction different from what had been made by the committee. He feared it might be thought to have a tendency to abolish religion altogether.

Mr. VINING suggested the propriety of transposing the two members of the sentence.

Mr. GERRY said it would read better if it was, that no religious doctrine shall be established by law.

Mr. SHERMAN thought the amendment altogether unnecessary, inasmuch as Congress had no authority whatever delegated to them by the Constitution to make religious establishments; he would, therefore, move to have it struck out.

Mr. CARROLL — As the rights of conscience are, in their nature, of peculiar delicacy, and will little bear the gentlest touch of governmental hand; and as many sects have concurred in opinion that they are not well secured under the present Constitution, he said he was much in favor of adopting the words. He thought it would tend more towards conciliating the minds of the people to the Government than almost any other amendment he had heard proposed. He would not contend with gentlemen about the phraseology, his object was to secure the substance in such a manner as to satisfy the wishes of the honest part of the community.

Mr. MADISON said, he apprehended the meaning of the words to be, that Congress should not establish a religion, and enforce the legal observation of it by law, nor compel men to worship God in any manner contrary to their conscience. Whether the words are necessary or not, he did not mean to say, but they had been required by some of the State Conventions, who seemed to entertain an opinion that under the clause of the Constitution, which gave power to Congress to make all laws necessary and proper to carry into execution the Constitution, and the laws made under it, enabled them to make laws of such a nature as might infringe the rights of conscience, and establish a national religion; to prevent these effects he presumed the amendment was intended, and he thought it was well expressed as the nature of the language would admit.

Mr. HUNTINGTON said that he feared, with the gentleman first up on this subject, that the words might be taken in such latitude as to be extremely hurtful to the cause of religion. He understood the amendment to mean what had been expressed by the gentleman from Virginia; but others might find it convenient to put another construction upon it. The ministers of their congregations to the Eastward were maintained by the contributions of those who belonged to their society; the expense of building meeting-houses was contributed in the same manner. These things were regulated by by-laws. If an action was brought before a Federal Court on any of these cases, the person who had neglected to perform his engagements could not be compelled to do it; for a support of ministers or building of places of worship might be construed into a religious establishment.

By the charter of Rhode Island, no religion could be established by law; he could give a history of the effects of such a regulation; indeed the people were now enjoying the blessed fruits of it. He hoped, therefore, the amendment would be made in such a way as to secure the rights of conscience, and a free exercise of the rights of religion, but not to patronise those who professed no religion at all.

Mr. MADISON thought, if the word "national" was inserted before religion, it would satisfy the minds of honorable gentlemen. He believed that the people feared one sect might obtain a preeminence, or two combine together, and establish a religion to which they would compel others to conform. He thought if the word "national" was introduced, it would point the amendment directly to the object it was intended to prevent.

Mr. LIVERMORE was not satisfied with that amendment; but he did not wish them to dwell long on the subject. He thought it would be better if it were altered, and made to read in this manner, that Congress shall make no laws touching religion, or infringing the rights of conscience.

Mr. GERRY did not like the term national, proposed by the gentleman from Virginia, and he hoped it would not be adopted by the House. It brought to his mind some observations that had taken place in the conventions at the time they were considering the present Constitution. It had been insisted upon by those who were called anti-federalists, that this form of Government consolidated the Union; the honorable gentleman's motion shows that he considers it in the same light. Those who were called anti-federalists at that time, complained that they had injustice done them by the title, because they were in favor of a Federal Government, and the others were in favor of a national one; the federalists were for ratifying the Constitution as it stood, and the others not until amendments were made. Their names then ought not to have been distinguished by federalists and anti-federalists, but rats and anti-rats.

Mr. MADISON withdrew his motion, but observed that the words "no national religion shall be established by law," did not imply that the Government was a national one; the question was then taken on Mr. LIVERMORE's motion, and passed in the affirmative, thirty-one for, and twenty against it.

[*August 20, 1789:*]

On motion of Mr. AMES, the fourth amendment was altered so as to read "Congress shall make no law establishing religion, or to prevent the free exercise thereof, or to infringe the rights of conscience." This being adopted.

[*The Senate considered a number of changes and also combined the clauses of religion, speech, press, assembly, and petition to produce this language: "Congress shall make no law establishing articles of faith or a mode of worship, or prohibiting the free exercise of religion, or abridging the freedom of speech, or the press, or the right of the people peaceably to assemble, and petition the government for the redress of grievances."*]

[*September 24, 1789:*]

The House proceeded to consider the report of a Committee of Conference, on the subject-matter of the amendments depending between the two Houses to the several articles of amendment to the Constitution of the United States, as proposed by this House: whereupon, it was resolved, that they recede from their disagreement to all the amendments; provided that the two articles, which, by the amendments of the Senate, are now proposed to be inserted as the third and eighth articles, shall be amended to read as follows:

"Art. 3. Congress shall make no law respecting an establishment of religion, or prohibiting a free exercise thereof, or abridging the freedom of speech, or of the press, or the right of the people peaceably to assemble, and to petition the Government for a redress of grievances."

B. FREE EXERCISE CLAUSE

Does government have a positive duty to promote religion? Is the purpose of the First Amendment to extend religious rights only to the believer and the orthodox? What of nonbelievers or agnostics? A treaty with Tripoli in 1796 stated that the United States "is not in any sense founded on the Christian religion." 8 Stat. 155, Art. XI. Dicta from a few decisions of the Supreme Court suggest the contrary. The history of the country, said the Court in 1892, confirms that "this is a Christian nation." Church of the Holy Trinity v. United States, 143 U.S. 457, 471. Writing for the Court a half century later, Justice Douglas said "We are a religious people whose institutions presuppose a Supreme Being." Zorach v. Clauson, 343 U.S. 306, 313 (1952). The religious complexity of the United States has led some speakers to refer to "Judeo-Christian" values, but even that term excludes increasingly large populations of Moslems, Hindus, Buddhists, and other religions.

Free Exercise of Religion

Protected (Belief)

The truth of a religious belief (avoiding heresy trials). United States v. Ballard, 322 U.S. 78 (1944).

Property disputes that turn on the question of church doctrine or ecclesiastical law, an area that is beyond the bounds of civil courts. Watson v. Jones, 13 Wall. 679 (1872); Jones v. Wolf, 443 U.S. 595 (1979); Presbyterian Church v. Hull Church, 393 U.S. 440, 449 (1969).

Government may not interfere with the selection of clergy to head a church. Nedroff v. St. Nicholas Cathedral, 344 U.S. 94 (1952); Serbian Orthodox Diocese v. Milovojevich, 426 U.S. 696 (1976).

Unprotected (Practice)

Mormon's belief in polygamy. Reynolds v. United States, 98 U.S. 145 (1878); Davis v. Beason, 133 U.S. 333 (1890); Mormon Church v. United States, 136 U.S. 1 (1890).

Transporting a woman across state lines to enter into a plural marriage, even if motivated by religious belief. Cleveland v. United States, 329 U.S. 14 (1946).

Handling poisonous reptiles as part of a church service. Lawson v. Commonwealth, 164 S.W.2d 972 (Ky. 1942); State v. Massey, 51 S.E.2d 179 (N.C. 1949), appeal dismissed for want of a substantial federal question sub nom. Bunn v. North Carolina, 336 U.S. 942 (1949); State ex rel. Swann v. Pack, 527 S.W.2d 99 (Tenn. 1975), cert. denied, 424 U.S. 954 (1976).

"In God We Trust" Motto

Congressional statutes have endorsed religious belief. Congress has required the inscription "In God We Trust" on coins and paper money.[1] After World War II, Congress engaged in ideological fencing with Soviet Russia by promoting spiritualism over materialism and theism over atheism. It directed the President to "set aside and proclaim a suitable day each year, other than a Sunday, as a National Day of Prayer, on which the people of the United States may turn to God in prayer and meditation at churches, in groups, and as individuals." 66 Stat. 64 (1952); 36 U.S.C. § 169h. Two years later it added the words "under God" to the pledge of allegiance. 68 Stat. 249 (1954); 36 U.S.C. § 172. This flourish of religiosity culminated in a law making "In God We Trust" the national motto. 70 Stat. 732 (1956); 36 U.S.C. § 186. An appellate court concluded that the national motto and the slogan on coinage and currency merely reflected a patriotic or ceremonial quality and had "no theological or ritualistic impact." Aronow v. United States, 432 F.2d 242, 243 (9th Cir. 1970).[2]

The executive branch joined in this quest for piety. In 1955, President Eisenhower advised the American Legion: "Without God, there could be no American form of Government, nor an American way of life. Recognition of the Supreme Being is the first—the most basic—expression of Americanism." 1955 Public Papers of the Presidents 274. Recent Presidents, from Richard Nixon to George W. Bush, have actively used their office to promote religion and prayer. In 2002, the Ninth Circuit held that the words "under God" in the Pledge of Allegiance violated the Establishment Clause. Newdow v. U.S. Congress, 292 F.3d 597 (9th Cir. 2002). Two years later the Supreme Court decided that the plaintiff, Michael Newdow, lacked standing to bring the case. Elk Grove Unified School Dist. v. Newdow, 542 U.S. 1 (2004). Although the Court disposed of his case, the combination of the majority opinion and the various concurrences (some of them actually dissents) revealed deep disagreement on questions of standing and the Establishment Clause.

---

1. E.g., 13 Stat. 518, § 5 (1865); 35 Stat. 164 (1908); 69 Stat. 290 (1955); 31 U.S.C. §§ 5112(d)(1), 5114(b).

2. See also O'Hair v. Blumenthal, 462 F.Supp. 19 (W.D. Tex. 1978); Louis Fisher and Nada Sabbah-Mourtada, "Adopting 'In God We Trust' as the U.S. National Motto," 44 J. Church & State 671 (Autumn 2002).

In response to the Ninth Circuit ruling, legislation was introduced in the House to strip lower federal courts of jurisdiction to hear any case involving the Pledge of Allegiance (H.R. 2028). Under this legislation, any challenge to the phrase "under God" in the Pledge would be heard only by state courts. This House effort is discussed in greater detail in Chapter 19.

Congressional and presidential affirmations of religion have been tempered by court decisions calling for neutrality on the part of government — not just between religions but between religion and irreligion. "The law knows no heresy, and is committed to the support of no dogma, the establishment of no sect." Watson v. Jones, 13 Wall. 679, 728 (1872). Neither a state nor the federal government "can force [or] influence a person to go to or to remain away from church against his will or force him to profess a belief or disbelief in any religion. No person can be punished for entertaining or professing religious beliefs or disbeliefs, for church attendance or non-attendance." Everson v. Board of Education, 330 U.S. 1, 15–16 (1947). Justice Jackson, who sent his own children to sectarian schools, warned that the "day that this country ceases to be free for irreligion it will cease to be free for religion — except for the sect that can win political power." Zorach v. Clauson, 343 U.S. at 325 (dissenting opinion).

Chaplains

Beginning in 1774, the Continental Congress authorized Rev. Jacob Duché to open Congress with prayers. Congress appropriated funds to pay him and his successors, as well as chaplains to serve military troops and to assist in military hospitals. The First Congress built on those precedents by electing chaplains to serve in the House and Senate. Chaplains provide pastoral care and counseling for federal and state prisoners. In 1862, Congress changed a denomination-specific provision for military chaplains (required to be drawn from a "Christian denomination") to a non-specific category (from "some religious denomination"). 12 Stat. 270, § 9 (1861), 12 Stat. 288, § 7 (1861); 12 Stat. 595, § 5 (1862).

Conscientious Objectors

In requiring citizens to serve in the militia, colonies and early state governments made exceptions for individuals who presented religious objections. The First Congress also considered giving an exemption from military service for conscientious objectors. In the militia bill of 1790, lawmakers debated exempting persons conscientiously scrupulous of bearing arms, allowing them to pay a certain amount in lieu of military service. After considerable discussion, it was decided to shift that issue to the states. 1 Annals of Cong. 1869–73, 1874–75 (1790). In what became the Second Amendment, the House added this provision: "but no one religiously scrupulous of bearing arms shall be compelled to render military service in person." However, the Senate deleted that language. 1 S. Journal 63–64, 71, 77 (1789).

Congress passed legislation in 1917 to exempt ministers of religion and theological students from military service. Conscientious objectors were relieved from military action but had to serve in a noncombatant role. The Court held that these laws did not violate the religion clauses. Selective Draft Law Cases, 245 U.S. 366 (1918). State universities were permitted to require male students to take a course in military science and tactics, even if such courses offended the beliefs of conscientious and religious objectors. The Court reasoned that the students were not compelled to attend a state university. If they chose to matriculate, they had to comply with the conditions imposed. Hamilton v. Regents, 293 U.S. 245 (1934).

As a result of subsequent statutes and decisions, an individual can now be exempt from combat duty without professing a belief in a Supreme Being. Congress excused from military combat persons whose religious training and belief made them conscientiously opposed to participating in war in any form. As used in the statute, religious training and belief meant "an individual's belief in a relation to a Supreme Being involving duties superior to those arising from any human relation, but [not including] essentially political, sociological or philosophical views or a merely personal code." 62 Stat. 613 (1948). The Court held that the test of "religious belief" is whether it is a sincere and meaningful belief occupying in the individual's life a place parallel to that filled by the God of those explicitly eligible for the exemption. United States v. Seeger, 380 U.S. 163 (1965). Congress rewrote the statute two years later by eliminating the phrase "a relation to a Supreme Being involving duties superior to those arising from any human relation." 81 Stat. 104 (1967); 50 U.S.C. app. § 456(j). Persons may be classified as conscientious objectors even when they do not affirm or deny belief in a Supreme Being.[3]

The congressional requirement that a religious objector be conscientiously opposed to war "in any form" does not apply to a Jehovah's Witness who indicates a willingness to fight in defense of "his ministry, Kingdom Interests and ... his fellow brethren." The weapons of this warfare are spiritual, not carnal. He is willing to engage in a "theocratic war" if Jehovah so commands. The congressional statute refers to military conflicts in our time, not a fight at Armageddon. Sicurella v. United States, 348 U.S. 385 (1955).

The Flag-Salute Cases

Periodically, government has prosecuted and harassed religious minorities. For example, a number of states in the 1930s adopted laws that compelled school children to salute the flag. The Jehovah's Witnesses complained that saluting a secular symbol offended their religious faith. They took literally the language of Exodus 20: 4–5: "Thou shalt not make unto thee any graven image ... [or] bow down thyself to them, nor serve them." Nonetheless, the compulsory flag salute survived several test cases.[4]

In 1937, a federal district judge in Pennsylvania found these statutes unconstitutional. If someone on the basis of sincere religious beliefs defied a statute, the individual's rights would prevail unless the state demonstrated that the statute was necessary for the public safety, health, morals, property, or personal rights. The district judge distinguished between the compulsory military courses in state universities sanctioned by Regents v. Hamilton, 293 U.S. 245 (1934), and the compulsory flag salute imposed on children in grade school and high school. Students attend state universities on their own volition; attendance at the elementary and secondary school level is mandatory. The judge appealed to the heritage of his state: "We may well recall that William Penn, the founder of Pennsylvania, was expelled from Oxford University for his refusal for conscience' sake to comply with regulations not essentially dissimilar [to the compulsory flag salute], and suffered, more than once, imprisonment in England because of his religious convictions. The commonwealth he founded was intended as a haven for all those persecuted for conscience' sake." Gobitis v. Minersville School Dist., 21 F.Supp. 581, 585 (E.D. Pa. 1937). This judgment was supported by another decision from the same judge, Gobitis v. Minersville School Dist., 24 F.Supp. 271 (1938), and a federal appellate court, Minersville School Dist. v. Gobitis, 108 F.2d 683 (3d Cir. 1939).

The Supreme Court granted certiorari to review the Pennsylvania flag-salute case. Before issuing a decision, in another case it upheld the right of a Jehovah's Witness who had been prosecuted for violating a state law that prohibited the solicitation of money, services, subscriptions "or any valuable thing" unless approved in advance by a public official. Jesse Cantwell had gone from house to house to solicit money, sell books, and play records on a portable phonograph. Some of the records included attacks on Roman Catholics. A unanimous Court struck down the state law as a violation of the free exercise of religion. The Court also held that the religion clauses in the First Amendment applied to the states. Cantwell v. Connecticut, 310 U.S. 296, 303 (1940).

---

3. Welsh v. United States, 398 U.S. 333, 337 (1970). See also Gillette v. United States, 401 U.S. 437 (1971) and Clay v. United States, 403 U.S. 698 (1971). Inconsistent statements can cast legitimate doubt on the sincerity of a religious objector. Witmer v. United States, 348 U.S. 375 (1955).

4. Leoles v. Landers, 192 S.E. 218; 302 U.S. 656 (1937); Hering v. State Board of Education, 189 A. 629; 303 U.S. 624 (1938); Gabrielli v. Knickerbocker, 82 P.2d 391; 306 U.S. 621 (1939); Johnson v. Deerfield, 25 F.Supp. 918; 306 U.S. 621 (1939).

Two weeks later, the Supreme Court upheld Pennsylvania's flag-salute law. Justice Frankfurter, writing for an 8–1 majority, wrote a decision deeply flawed by contradictions, ipse dixits, and double-talk. The logic appeared to rest on two assumptions: liberty requires unifying sentiments, and national unity promotes national security. Only Justice Stone dissented. Several Justices in the majority would soon wish they had. MINERSVILLE SCHOOL DISTRICT v. GOBITIS, 310 U.S. 586 (1940).

The decision was excoriated by law journals, the press, and religious organizations. Roman Catholics, although often the prime target of attacks from Jehovah's Witnesses, found Frankfurter's opinion intolerable. A few months after Frankfurter's decision, Justice Douglas told Frankfurter that Justice Black was having second thoughts. Sarcastically, Frankfurter asked whether Black had spent the summer reading the Constitution. "No," Douglas replied, "he has been reading the papers." H. N. Hirsch, The Enigma of Felix Frankfurter 152 (1981).

By 1942 three members of the *Gobitis* majority publicly apologized for their votes. Justices Black, Douglas, and Murphy now announced that the 1940 case "was wrongly decided." Jones v. Opelika, 316 U.S. 584, 624 (1942). Frankfurter's decision thus commanded at best a slim majority, and two members of the *Gobitis* Court had been replaced by Justices Jackson and Rutledge. The 8–1 majority evaporated so quickly that a federal district judge in 1942 determined that *Gobitis* was no longer binding even though it had yet to be overruled. He calculated that of the seven remaining Justices on the Supreme Court who had participated in *Gobitis*, "four have given public expression to the view that it is unsound." Barnette v. West Virginia State Board of Ed., 47 F.Supp. 251, 253 (S.D. W.Va. 1942).

The Court overruled *Gobitis* in 1943, almost three years to the date that it was announced. Justice Jackson wrote for a 6–3 majority. Only Justices Roberts and Reed agreed with Frankfurter that *Gobitis* was properly decided. In a lengthy and passionate dissent, Frankfurter sought to vindicate his views. WEST VIRGINIA STATE BOARD OF EDUCATION v. BARNETTE, 319 U.S. 624 (1943). Jackson wrote a moving and powerful defense of religious freedom and the Bill of Rights, but credit for the liberalized decision belongs to citizens who refused to accept the Court's 1940 pronouncements on the meaning of the Constitution, minority rights, and religious liberty.

Accommodating Religious Beliefs

While deciding the flag-salute cases in the 1940s, the Court confronted other issues of religious freedom. A Jehovah's Witness had been convicted for violating a Texas ordinance that required a permit to solicit orders and sell books. The Court held unanimously that the ordinance represented "administrative censorship in an extreme form" and abridged the freedom of religion, press, and speech guaranteed by the Fourteenth Amendment. Largent v. Texas, 318 U.S. 418, 422 (1943). Similarly, it struck down a Pennsylvania ordinance requiring a license tax for those who canvass or solicit orders for books, paintings, pictures, wares, or merchandise. Once again a Jehovah's Witness had been convicted. The Court held that these constraints on missionary evangelism violated the constitutional liberties of speech, press, and religion. Murdock v. Pennsylvania, 319 U.S. 105 (1943). Other state efforts to impose a license tax on the selling of religious merchandise or to require a town's permission before "peddling" religious literature were struck down.[5] A state may not permit one religious organization to conduct services in a public park while denying that same privilege to another religious group. Fowler v. Rhode Island, 345 U.S. 67 (1953).

The state's interest in regulating religious activity may be strengthened when a child is involved. In 1944 the Court upheld a Massachusetts statute that prohibited minors (boys under 12, girls under 18) from selling newspapers, magazines, or other articles in public places. A nine-year-old had helped in the distribution of Jehovah's Witness literature. By a 5–4 vote, the Court upheld the conviction of the youth's guardian on the ground that the state has a special interest in protecting children from such

---

5. Douglas v. Jeannette, 319 U.S. 157 (1943); Follett v. McCormick, 321 U.S. 573 (1944); Tucker v. Texas, 326 U.S. 517 (1946).

duties. Prince v. Massachusetts, 321 U.S. 158 (1944). As the child matures, however, the state's interest declines. In 1972, the Supreme Court decided the case of members of the Amish religious order who had been convicted for violating Wisconsin's requirement that children attend school until age 16. The parents argued that sending their children to public or private schools after the eighth grade endangered the salvation of both parent and child by exposing the children to material, competitive, and modern values. The Court found that the religious interests of the Amish outweighed the interests of the state. Wisconsin v. Yoder, 406 U.S. 205 (1972).

Congress exempts self-employed Amish from paying social security taxes because they have a religiously based obligation to provide for their fellow members. 26 U.S.C. § 1402(g). The Supreme Court held that the exemption applied only to self-employed individuals, not to all employers and employees who are Amish. To the Court, the accommodation in the *Yoder* case was less disruptive than allowing various exceptions to the social security system. "Because the broad public interest in maintaining a sound tax system is of such a high order, religious belief in conflict with the payment of taxes affords no basis for resisting the tax." United States v. Lee, 455 U.S. 252, 260 (1982). Congress, finding the Court's interpretation too narrow, broadened the exemption for the Amish. 102 Stat. 3781–83, § 8007 (1988).

The question of taxing religious organizations returned in 1990, when a unanimous Court held that it was constitutional for California to subject religious materials sold by a Louisiana religious organization to two taxes: a sales tax for sales within California, and a use tax for mail-order sales. The Court regarded the taxes not as a tax on the right to disseminate religious information, ideas, or beliefs, but rather as a neutral tax on retail purchases, just as Bibles sold in a secular bookstore are taxed. The Louisiana organization (operated by Jimmy Swaggart) was not being singled out for special or burdensome treatment. Swaggart Ministries v. Cal. Bd. of Equalization, 493 U.S. 378 (1990).

Other cases illustrate the constant need to reach accommodations between state interests and religious belief. Minnesota required religious organizations at a state fair to sell and distribute religious literature and to solicit funds only at an assigned location within the fairgrounds. Members of those organizations were free to walk around and discuss religious matters in face-to-face contacts. A Krishna group claimed that the rule restricted its religious practices and its ability to proselytize for new members and financial support. The Court agreed that a state, in an effort to control the flow of crowds at a large fair, can restrict the sale of literature and solicitation of funds. Heffron v. Int'l Soc. for Krishna Consciousness, 452 U.S. 640 (1981).

A 1986 decision again illustrates how the First Amendment is shaped not merely by court opinions but by legislative action. An Air Force regulation provided that headgear may not be worn indoors except by armed security police in the performance of their duties. An Air Force officer (an Orthodox Jew and ordained rabbi) claimed that the regulation prevented him from wearing his yarmulke (skullcap) and therefore infringed on his freedom to exercise his religious beliefs. The Supreme Court, split 5–4, upheld the regulation as necessary for military discipline, unity, and order. In one of the dissents, Justice Brennan claimed that the Court's response "is to abdicate its role as primary expositor of the Constitution and protector of individual liberties in favor of credulous deference to unsupported assertions of military necessity." GOLDMAN v. WEINBERGER, 475 U.S. 503, 514 (1986). Fortunately, other institutions of government are capable of protecting individual liberties, Congress among them. As Brennan noted: "Guardianship of this precious liberty [*of religious freedom*] is not the exclusive domain of federal courts. It is the responsibility as well of the States and of the other branches of the Federal Government." Id. at 523. Congress passed legislation in 1987 to permit military personnel to wear conservative, unobtrusive religious apparel indoors, provided that it does not interfere with their military duties (see reading of floor debate).

A number of state laws governing Sunday worship and Sunday closings implicate both religion clauses: free exercise and establishment. In one of these cases, *Employment Division* v. *Smith* (1990), the Court abandoned its usual test that states must show a "compelling governmental interest" in restricting the free exercise of religion. Congress passed legislation in 1993 to challenge that decision, but in 1997 the Court held this statute to be unconstitutional. Congress enacted new legislation in 2000. This issue is addressed in Section C.

Minersville School District v. Gobitis
310 U.S. 586 (1940)

Pennsylvania required students in public schools to participate in a daily ceremony of saluting the national flag while reciting in unison a pledge of allegiance to it "and to the Republic for which it stands; one Nation indivisible, with liberty and justice for all." Failure to abide by this requirement resulted in the expulsion of Jehovah's Witnesses, who believed that this gesture of respect for the flag was forbidden by Biblical commands. Two students, Lillian and William Gobitis (misspelled by the Court as Gobitis), brought this case with their father against school authorities.

MR. JUSTICE FRANKFURTER delivered the opinion of the Court.

A grave responsibility confronts this Court whenever in course of litigation it must reconcile the conflicting claims of liberty and authority. But when the liberty invoked is liberty of conscience, and the authority is authority to safeguard the nation's fellowship, judicial conscience is put to its severest test. Of such a nature is the present controversy.

... The Gobitis family are affiliated with "Jehovah's Witnesses," for whom the Bible as the Word of God is the supreme authority. The children had been brought up conscientiously to believe that such a gesture of respect for the flag was forbidden by command of Scripture. [*A footnote refers to these verses from Chapter 20 of Exodus: "3. Thou shalt have no other gods before me. 4. Thou shalt not make unto thee any graven image, or any likeness of any thing that is in heaven above, or that is in the earth beneath, or that is in the water under the earth. 5. Thou shalt not bow down thyself to them, nor serve them: ..."*]

The Gobitis children were of an age for which Pennsylvania makes school attendance compulsory. Thus they were denied a free education, and their parents had to put them into private schools. To be relieved of the financial burden thereby entailed, their father, on behalf of the children and in his own behalf, brought this suit. He sought to enjoin the authorities from continuing to exact participation in the flag-salute ceremony as a condition of his children's attendance at the Minersville school....

We must decide whether the requirement of participation in such a ceremony, exacted from a child who refuses upon sincere religious grounds, infringes without due process of law the liberty guaranteed by the Fourteenth Amendment.

... When does the constitutional guarantee [*of re-*

ligious freedom] compel exemption from doing what society thinks necessary for the promotion of some great common end, or from a penalty for conduct which appears dangerous to the general good? ...

... Our present task, then, as so often the case with courts, is to reconcile two rights in order to prevent either from destroying the other. [*Frankfurter refers to earlier cases in which political authority was upheld over conscientious scruples, including laws against bigamy (contrary to Mormonism), drafting conscientious objectors for noncombatant roles, and requiring military training for all male university students.*]

... Even if it were assumed that freedom of speech goes beyond the historic concept of full opportunity to utter and to disseminate views, however heretical or offensive to dominant opinion, and includes freedom from conveying what may be deemed an implied but rejected affirmation, the question remains whether school children, like the Gobitis children, must be excused from conduct required of all the other children in the promotion of national cohesion. We are dealing with an interest inferior to none in the hierarchy of legal values. National unity is the basis of national security. To deny the legislature the right to select appropriate means for its attainment presents a totally different order of problem from that of the propriety of subordinating the possible ugliness of littered streets to the free expression of opinion through distribution of handbills....

The wisdom of training children in patriotic impulses by those compulsions which necessarily pervade so much of the educational process is not for our independent judgment. Even were we convinced of the folly of such a measure, such belief would be no proof of its unconstitutionality. For ourselves, we might be tempted to say that the deepest patriotism is best engendered by giving unfettered scope to the most crochety beliefs. Perhaps it is best, even from the standpoint of those interests which ordinances like the one under review seek to promote, to give to the least popular sect leave from conformities like those here in issue. But the courtroom is not the arena for debating issues of educational policy. It is not our province to choose among competing considerations in the subtle process of securing effective loyalty to the traditional ideals of democracy, while respecting at the same time individual idiosyncrasies among a people so diversified in racial origins and religious allegiances. So to hold would in effect make us the school board for the country. That authority has not been given to this Court, nor should we assume it....

What the school authorities are really asserting is the right to awaken in the child's mind considerations as to the significance of the flag contrary to those implanted by the parent....

Judicial review, itself a limitation on popular government, is a fundamental part of our constitutional scheme. But to the legislature no less than to courts is committed the guardianship of deeply-cherished liberties.... Where all the effective means of inducing political changes are left free from interference, education in the abandonment of foolish legislation is itself a training in liberty. To fight out the wise use of legislative authority in the forum of public opinion and before legislative assemblies rather than to transfer such a contest to the judicial arena, serves to vindicate the self-confidence of a free people.

Reversed.

Mr. Justice McReynolds concurs in the result.

Mr. Justice Stone, dissenting:

... We have previously pointed to the importance of a searching judicial inquiry into the legislative judgment in situations where prejudice against discrete and insular minorities may tend to curtail the operation of those political processes ordinarily to be relied on to protect minorities. See *United States* v. *Carolene Products Co.,* 304 U.S. 144, 152, note 4.... Here we have such a small minority entertaining in good faith a religious belief, which is such a departure from the usual course of human conduct, that most persons are disposed to regard it with little toleration or concern. In such circumstances careful scrutiny of legislative efforts to secure conformity of belief and opinion by a compulsory affirmation of the desired belief, is especially needful if civil rights are to receive any protection. Tested by this standard, I am not prepared to say that the right of this small and helpless minority, including children having a strong religious conviction, whether they understand its nature or not, to refrain from an expression obnoxious to their religion, is to be overborne by the interest of the state in maintaining discipline in the schools....

West Virginia State Board of Education v. Barnette

319 U.S. 624 (1943)

Justice Frankfurter's opinion in *Gobitis* provoked strong criticism from the legal community, the press, civil liberties groups, and religious organizations. In *Jones* v. *Opelika* (1942), three members of Frankfurter's 8 to 1 majority stated that the decision "was wrongly decided." That reduced the majority to 5 to 4, and changes in the Court's composition since *Gobitis* pointed to a probable overturning of Frankfurter's decision. One of the new members of the Court, Robert H. Jackson, wrote for a 6 to 3 majority striking down the compulsory flag salute. Walter Barnette, a Jehovah's Witness, challenged a West Virginia statute on the ground that it violated his and his children's religious beliefs.

Mr. Justice Jackson delivered the opinion of the Court....

The Board of Education on January 9, 1942, adopted a resolution containing recitals taken largely from the Court's *Gobitis* opinion and ordering that the salute to the flag become "a regular part of the program of activities in the public schools," that all teachers and pupils "shall be required to participate in the salute honoring the Nation represented by the Flag; provided, however, that refusal to salute the Flag be regarded as an act of insubordination, and shall be dealt with accordingly."

The resolution originally required the "commonly accepted salute to the Flag" which it defined. Objections to the salute as "being too much like Hitler's" were raised by the Parent and Teachers Association, the Boy and Girl Scouts, the Red Cross, and the Federation of Women's Clubs. Some modification appears to have been made in deference to these objections, but no concession was made to Jehovah's Witnesses. What is now required is the "stiff-arm" salute, the saluter to keep the right hand raised with palm turned up while the following is repeated: "I pledge allegiance to the Flag of the United States of America and to the Republic for which it stands; one Nation, indivisible, with liberty and justice for all."

Failure to conform is "insubordination" dealt with by expulsion. Readmission is denied by statute until compliance. Meanwhile the expelled child is "unlawfully absent" and may be proceeded against as a delinquent. His parents or guardians are liable to prosecution, and if convicted are subject to fine not exceeding $50 and jail term not exceeding thirty days....

The freedom asserted by these appellees does not bring them into collision with rights asserted by any other individual. It is such conflicts which most frequently require intervention of the State to determine where the rights of one end and those of another begin. But the refusal of these persons to participate in the ceremony does not interfere with or deny rights of others to do so. Nor is there any question in this case that their behavior is peaceable and orderly. The sole conflict is between authority and rights of the individual....

[*Jackson analyzes several premises that formed the foundation for* Gobitis.]

1. It was said that the flag-salute controversy confronted the Court with "the problem which Lincoln cast in memorable dilemma: 'Must a government of necessity be too *strong* for the liberties of its people, or too *weak* to maintain its own existence?'" and that the answer must be in favor of strength. *Minersville School District* v. *Gobitis, supra,* at 596.

We think these issues may be examined free of pressure or restraint growing out of such considerations.

It may be doubted whether Mr. Lincoln would have thought that the strength of government to maintain itself would be impressively vindicated by our confirming power of the State to expel a handful of children from school. Such oversimplification, so handy in political debate, often lacks the precision necessary to postulates of judicial reasoning. If validly applied to this problem, the utterance cited would resolve every issue of power in favor of those in authority....

2. It was also considered in the *Gobitis* case that functions of educational officers in States, counties

and school districts were such that to interfere with their authority "would in effect make us the school board for the country." ...

The Fourteenth Amendment, as now applied to the States, protects the citizen against the State itself and all of its creatures—Boards of Education not excepted. These have, of course, important, delicate, and highly discretionary functions, but none that they may not perform within the limits of the Bill of Rights. That they are educating the young for citizenship is reason for scrupulous protection of Constitutional freedoms of the individual, if we are not to strangle the free mind at its source and teach youth to discount important principles of our government as mere platitudes....

3. The *Gobitis* opinion reasoned that this is a field "where courts possess no marked and certainly no controlling competence," that it is committed to the legislatures as well as the courts to guard cherished liberties and that it is constitutionally appropriate to "fight out the wise use of legislative authority in the forum of public opinion and before legislative assemblies rather than to transfer such a contest to the judicial arena," since all the "effective means of inducing political changes are left free." ...

The very purpose of a Bill of Rights was to withdraw certain subjects from the vicissitudes of political controversy, to place them beyond the reach of majorities and officials and to establish them as legal principles to be applied by the courts. One's right to life, liberty, and property, to free speech, a free press, freedom of worship and assembly, and other fundamental rights may not be submitted to vote; they depend on the outcome of no elections....

4. Lastly, and this is the very heart of the *Gobitis* opinion, it reasons that "National unity is the basis of national security," that the authorities have "the right to select appropriate means for its attainment," and hence reaches the conclusion that such compulsory measures toward "national unity" are constitutional.... Upon the verity of this assumption depends our answer in this case.

National unity as an end which officials may foster by persuasion and example is not in question. The problem is whether under our Constitution compulsion as here employed is a permissible means for its achievement.

Struggles to coerce uniformity of sentiment in support of some end thought essential to their time and country have been waged by many good as well as by evil men. Nationalism is a relatively recent phenomenon but at other times and places the ends have been racial or territorial security, support of a dynasty or regime, and particular plans for saving souls. As first and moderate methods to attain unity have failed, those bent on its accomplishment must resort to an ever-increasing severity. As governmental pressure toward unity becomes greater, so strife becomes more bitter as to whose unity it shall be. Probably no deeper division of our people could proceed from any provocation than from finding it necessary to choose what doctrine and whose program public educational officials shall compel youth to unite in embracing. Ultimate futility of such attempts to compel coherence is the lesson of every such effort from the Roman drive to stamp out Christianity as a disturber of its pagan unity, the Inquisition, as a means to religious and dynastic unity, the Siberian exiles as a means to Russian unity, down to the fast failing efforts of our present totalitarian enemies. Those who begin coercive elimination of dissent soon find themselves exterminating dissenters. Compulsory unification of opinion achieves only the unanimity of the graveyard.

It seems trite but necessary to say that the First Amendment to our Constitution was designed to avoid these ends by avoiding these beginnings. There is no mysticism in the American concept of the State or of the nature or origin of its authority. We set up government by consent of the governed, and the Bill of Rights denies those in power any legal opportunity to coerce that consent. Authority here is to be controlled by public opinion, not public opinion by authority.

The case is made difficult not because the principles of its decision are obscure but because the flag involved is our own. Nevertheless, we apply the limitations of the Constitution with no fear that freedom to be intellectually and spiritually diverse or even contrary will disintegrate the social organization. To believe that patriotism will not flourish if patriotic ceremonies are voluntary and spontaneous instead of a compulsory routine is to make an unflattering estimate of the appeal of our institutions to free minds. We can have intellectual individualism and the rich cultural diversities that we owe to exceptional minds only at the price of occasional eccentricity and abnormal attitudes. When they are so harmless to others or to the State as those we deal with here, the price is not too great. But freedom to differ is not limited to things that do not matter much. That would be a mere shadow of freedom. The test of its substance is the right to differ as to things that touch the heart of the existing order.

If there is any fixed star in our constitutional constellation, it is that no official, high or petty, can prescribe what shall be orthodox in politics, nationalism, religion, or other matters of opinion or force citizens to confess by word or act their faith therein. If there are any circumstances which permit an exception, they do not now occur to us.

We think the action of the local authorities in compelling the flag salute and pledge transcends constitutional limitations on their power and invades the sphere of intellect and spirit which it is the purpose of the First Amendment to our Constitution to reserve from all official control.

The decision of this Court in *Minersville School District* v. *Gobitis* and the holdings of those few *per curiam* decisions which preceded and foreshadowed it are overruled, and the judgment enjoining enforcement of the West Virginia Regulation is

Affirmed.

MR. JUSTICE ROBERTS and MR. JUSTICE REED adhere to the views expressed by the Court in *Minersville School District* v. *Gobitis,* 310 U.S. 586, and are of the opinion that the judgment below should be reversed.

MR. JUSTICE BLACK and MR. JUSTICE DOUGLAS, concurring: . . .

MR. JUSTICE MURPHY, concurring: . . .

MR. JUSTICE FRANKFURTER, dissenting:

One who belongs to the most vilified and persecuted minority in history is not likely to be insensible to the freedoms guaranteed by our Constitution. Were my purely personal attitude relevant I should wholeheartedly associate myself with the general libertarian views in the Court's opinion, representing as they do the thought and action of a lifetime. But as judges we are neither Jew nor Gentile, neither Catholic nor agnostic. We owe equal attachment to the Constitution and are equally bound by our judicial obligations whether we derive our citizenship from the earliest or the latest immigrants to these shores. As a member of this Court I am not justified in writing my private notions of policy into the Constitution, no matter how deeply I may cherish them or how mischievous I may deem their disregard. The duty of a judge who must decide which of two claims before the Court shall prevail, that of a State to enact and enforce laws within its general competence or that of an individual to refuse obedience because of the demands of his conscience, is not that of the ordinary person. It can never be emphasized too much that one's own opinion about the wisdom or evil of a law should be excluded altogether when one is doing one's duty on the bench. The only opinion of our own even looking in that direction that is material is our opinion whether legislators could in reason have enacted such a law. In the light of all the circumstances, including the history of this question in this Court, it would require more daring than I possess to deny that reasonable legislators could have taken the action which is before us for review....

Goldman v. Weinberger

475 U.S. 503 (1986)

Captain Goldman, an Orthodox Jew and an ordained rabbi, brought suit against Secretary of Defense Weinberger, claiming that an Air Force regulation prevented him from wearing his yarmulke (skullcap) indoors and infringed on his First Amendment freedom to exercise his religious belief. A federal district court granted an injunction against the Air Force, prohibiting it from denying Goldman the right to wear a yarmulke while in uniform; the D.C. Circuit reversed the decision.

Justice Rehnquist delivered the opinion of the Court.

Petitioner S. Simcha Goldman contends that the Free Exercise Clause of the First Amendment to the United States Constitution permits him to wear a yarmulke while in uniform, notwithstanding an Air Force regulation mandating uniform dress for Air Force personnel....

Until 1981, petitioner was not prevented from wearing his yarmulke on the base. He avoided controversy by remaining close to his duty station in the health clinic and by wearing his service cap over the yarmulke when out of doors. But in April 1981, after he testified as a defense witness at a court-martial wearing his yarmulke but not his service cap, opposing counsel lodged a complaint with Colonel Joseph Gregory, the Hospital Commander, arguing that petitioner's practice of wearing his yarmulke was a violation of Air Force Regulation (AFR) 35-10. This regulation states in pertinent part that "[h]eadgear will not be worn ... [w]hile indoors except by armed security police in the performance of their duties." AFR 35-10, ¶ 1-6.h(2)(f) (1980).

Colonel Gregory informed petitioner that wearing a yarmulke while on duty does indeed violate AFR 35-10, and ordered him not to violate this regulation outside the hospital. Although virtually all of petitioner's time on the base was spent in the hospital, he refused. Later, after petitioner's attorney protested to the Air Force General Counsel, Colonel Gregory revised his order to prohibit petitioner from wearing the yarmulke even in the hospital....

Petitioner argues that AFR 35-10, as applied to him, prohibits religiously motivated conduct and should therefore be analyzed under the standard enunciated in *Sherbert* v. *Verner*, 374 U.S. 398, 406 (1963).... But we have repeatedly held that "the mil-

itary is, by necessity, a specialized society separate from civilian society." *Parker* v. *Levy,* 417 U.S. 733, 743 (1974)....

Our review of military regulations challenged on First Amendment grounds is far more deferential than constitutional review of similar laws or regulations designed for civilian society. The military need not encourage debate or tolerate protest to the extent that such tolerance is required of the civilian state by the First Amendment; to accomplish its mission the military must foster instinctive obedience, unity, commitment, and esprit de corps....

The considered professional judgment of the Air Force is that the traditional outfitting of personnel in standardized uniforms encourages the subordination of personal preferences and identities in favor of the overall group mission. Uniforms encourage a sense of hierarchical unity by tending to eliminate outward individual distinctions except for those of rank....

To this end, the Air Force promulgated AFR 35-10, a 190-page document, which states that "Air Force members will wear the Air Force uniform while performing their military duties, except when authorized to wear civilian clothes on duty." AFR § 35-10, ¶ 1-6 (1980). The rest of the document describes in minute detail all of the various items of apparel that must be worn as part of the Air Force uniform. It authorizes a few individualized options with respect to certain pieces of jewelry and hair style, but even these are subject to severe limitations....

Petitioner Goldman contends that the Free Exercise Clause of the First Amendment requires the Air Force to make an exception to its uniform dress requirements for religious apparel unless the accoutrements create a "clear danger" of undermining discipline and esprit de corps. He asserts that in general, visible but "unobtrusive" apparel will not create such a danger and must therefore be accommodated. He argues that the Air Force failed to prove that a specific exception for his practice of wearing an unobtrusive yarmulke would threaten discipline. He contends that the Air Force's assertion to the contrary is mere *ipse dixit,* with no support from actual experience or a scientific study in the record, and is contradicted by expert testimony that religious exceptions to AFR 35-10 are in fact desirable and will increase morale by making the Air Force a more humane place.

But whether or not expert witnesses may feel that religious exceptions to AFR 35-10 are desirable is quite beside the point. The desirability of dress regulations in the military is decided by the appropriate military officials, and they are under no constitutional mandate to abandon their considered professional judgment.... The Air Force has drawn the line essentially between religious apparel which is visible and that which is not, and we hold that those portions of the regulations challenged here reasonably and even-handedly regulate dress in the interest of the military's perceived need for uniformity. The First Amendment therefore does not prohibit them from being applied to petitioner even though their effect is to restrict the wearing of the headgear required by his religious beliefs.

The judgment of the Court of Appeals is

Affirmed.

JUSTICE STEVENS, with whom JUSTICE WHITE and JUSTICE POWELL join, concurring....

... The very strength of Captain Goldman's

claim creates the danger that a similar claim on behalf of a Sikh or a Rastafarian might readily be dismissed as "so extreme, so unusual, or so faddish an image that public confidence in his ability to perform his duties will be destroyed." ... The Air Force has no business drawing distinctions between such persons when it is enforcing commands of universal application.

As the Court demonstrates, the rule that is challenged in this case is based on a neutral, completely objective standard — visibility. It was not motivated by hostility against, or any special respect for, any religious faith. An exception for yarmulkes would represent a fundamental departure from the true principle of uniformity that supports that rule. For that reason, I join the Court's opinion and its judgment.

JUSTICE BRENNAN, with whom JUSTICE MARSHALL joins, dissenting.

Simcha Goldman invokes this Court's protection of his First Amendment right to fulfill one of the traditional religious obligations of a male Orthodox Jew — to cover his head before an omnipresent God. The Court's response to Goldman's request is to abdicate its role as principal expositor of the Constitution and protector of individual liberties in favor of credulous deference to unsupported assertions of military necessity. I dissent....

JUSTICE BLACKMUN, dissenting....

JUSTICE O'CONNOR, with whom JUSTICE MARSHALL joins, dissenting....

Congress Reverses *Goldman*

After the Supreme Court's decision in *Goldman* v. *Weinberger* (1986), legislation was immediately introduced to permit members of the armed forces to wear religious apparel indoors if the item is neat and conservative. The legislation permitted the Secretary of Defense to prohibit the wearing of an item of religious apparel if it interfered with the performance of military duties. The House passed the legislation in 1986, but it failed in the Senate. Both Houses acted on the legislation in 1987, and the provision was enacted into law. 101 Stat. 1086–87, § 508 (1987). Excerpts from the congressional debate appear below. 133 Cong. Rec. 11851–53, 25250–60 (1987).

[*House action:*]

Mrs. SCHROEDER....

Mr. Chairman, the amendment permits the wearing of "neat and conservative" religious apparel — that is, Jewish yarmulkes and Sikh turbans — so long as the apparel does not interfere with the performance of military duties.

The "neat and conservative" standard was drawn from existing Air Force regulations, which use that term to define what jewelry members of the military may wear.

The military services have opposed any such legislation....

Mr. DORNAN of California. Mr. Chairman, I rise in support of this amendment.

I cannot think of any religious devotion more unobtrusive than wearing a yarmulke. There are people who have more hair, times 10, than a tiny little skull cap and it can be worn under jet fighter helmets, under garrison hats, under helmets, it can even be worn under a regular flight cap....

Is there some specificity in this where it leaves— I would like to ask the gentlewoman to respond— where it leaves the military some leeway, Rastafarian hair or something, but where we can be specific in our legislative dialog that this has nothing to do with restricting something as precious, but as tiny and small, as the wearing of a yarmulke by orthodox people?

I yield to the gentlewoman from Colorado.

Mrs. SCHROEDER....

Yes, indeed, what we are saying here is that the Secretary concerned may prohibit the wearing of any item of religious apparel if the circumstances are that the Secretary determines that the wearing of the item would interfere with the performance of the Member's military duties....

Mr. SOLARZ....

I think it is important for the Members to know that the armed forces of Canada, the armed forces of the United Kingdom, the armed forces of New Zealand, all permit people in their military not only to wear yarmulkes, but also, if they are Sikhs, to wear turbans.

I need hardly remind you that the most effective military force in the Middle East, the Israel Defense Forces, permits its members to wear yarmulkes. I do not think it has handicapped their ability to overcome their enemies in battle....

The CHAIRMAN. The question is on the amendment offered by the gentlewoman from Colorado [Mrs. SCHROEDER].

The amendment was agreed to.

[*Senate action:*]

Mr. LAUTENBERG.

... [T]his amendment, and this issue, is broader than any one religion. It concerns the right of people of all faiths to serve their country without having to forsake their religious beliefs and practices, it would affirm the religious and ethnic diversity that have made America strong, not weak.

The primary philosophical objection to this amendment has been that wearing visible items of religious apparel may threaten the military uniformity necessary in building unit cohesion. While I appreciate and agree with the importance of unit cohesion and esprit de corps in the Armed Forces, I do not believe that wearing neat and conservative religious apparel threatens this principle.

To the contrary, it would strengthen morale by affirming that the military is a humane and tolerant institution....

Although uniformity is claimed as an important value, the services easily permit other manifestations of religious diversity. Service members attend Christian, Islamic, Jewish, and other religious services. Barracks mates see Mormons wearing temple garments, and Catholics wearing crosses and scapulars. It is obvious that our services are made up of people from different faiths and ethnic backgrounds, and that diversity is America's greatest asset. It is no secret, nor should it be....

Some of the services have argued that the neat and conservative standard will be hard to apply, forcing them to make delicate and difficult distinctions between religious garb. But the services have a successful record of using the neat and conservative standard to distinguish acceptable from unacceptable jewelry. If we can make this distinction for neat and conservative jewelry, why can't we make it for religious apparel....

Certainly, the wearing of apparel central to the practice of one's religious beliefs is more important and worthy of review than the wearing of jewelry....

Mr. MURKOWSKI....

Mr. President, I rise as the ranking minority member of the Committee on Veterans' Affairs. At the request of numerous organizations representing service members and veterans of all faiths, I feel compelled to express my concern regarding the amendment of the Senator from New Jersey, which would allow service members to wear religious apparel while in uniform. The American Legion, with over 2.5 million members, and the Military Coalition, representing 16 of the largest organizations for military personnel, do not support the amendment of the Senator from New Jersey....

Mr. GLENN. [*In announcing his decision to vote against the amendment, Senator Glenn placed in the Record a letter from the Secretary of Defense, Caspar Weinberger, opposing the amendment on the ground that it would force commanders to apply subjective criteria ("neat and conservative") in distinguishing among religious apparel. Senator Glenn also placed in the Record a "20-star letter" from the Joint Chiefs of Staff, opposing the amendment. The letter, signed by the chairman of the Joint Chiefs, the general of the Air Force, the general of the Army, the general of the Marine Corps, and the admiral of the Navy, adds up to five four-star officers.*]

Mr. ADAMS.... I have to tell you that I was shocked by the level of lobbying that has gone on about this issue. I have had more calls from constituents on this issue than I had on SDI [*Strategic Defense Initiative*]; I had more requests for visits from DOD on this issue than I did on a comprehensive test ban. There are some really vital issues that need to be addressed in this bill—and while this issue is important, the fate of the nation does not hang on it....

[*After defeating a motion to table the amendment, which lost 42 to 55, the Senate agreed to the amendment, 55 to 42, and the bill became law.*]

C. ESTABLISHMENT CLAUSE

The church-state docket since the 1940s has been dominated by two issues: (1) the appropriation of public funds to support sectarian schools, and (2) government encouragement of prayer and religious instruction in public schools. Other cases, however, helped define the boundaries of the Establishment Clause.

In 1899, the Supreme Court upheld the appropriation of funds by Congress to a hospital operated by the Catholic Church. The Court denied that the statute violated the Establishment Clause. Religious ownership did not, by itself, make the hospital religious or sectarian. The character of an institution is measured by the charter creating it. There was no allegation that the hospital was confined to members of the Catholic Church or that the hospital had violated its charter to serve the poor. Bradfield v. Roberts, 175 U.S. 291 (1899). The Court also held that a congressional appropriation to educate Indians in sectarian schools did not violate the Establishment Clause. The tribal and trust funds used for this purpose were not general public moneys. They belonged to the Indians as compensation for lands that they had ceded to the United States. Quick Bear v. Leupp, 210 U.S. 50 (1908).

A series of cases from 1947 to 1970 tested the extent to which government could provide financial assistance to sectarian schools (section D in this chapter). By 1971, the Court was ready to develop what is called the "*Lemon* test" to guide its rulings on church-state questions (see box).

Equal Access

In a 1981 case, a state university allowed student secular groups to meet in university buildings but denied the same privilege to student religious groups. The university reasoned that giving permission to the latter would violate the Establishment Clause. The Supreme Court, voting 8–1, disagreed. State efforts to comply with the Establishment Clause do not permit discrimination against the religious speech of the student group seeking access to buildings for their meetings. Widmar v. Vincent, 454 U.S. 263 (1981).

The *Lemon* Test

In *Lemon v. Kurtzman*, 403 U.S. 602, 61213 (1971), the Court established a three-prong test to determine the constitutionality of legislation regarding church-state relations, especially the Establishment Clause. These three principles are quite broad, giving the Court substantial discretion in applying them. For some erosion of the *Lemon* test, see the box in Section D.

1. The statute must have a secular legislative purpose.

2. Its principal or primary effect must be one that neither advances nor inhibits religion.

3. It must not foster excessive entanglement with religion.

In response to *Widmar,* Congress passed the "Equal Access" bill to prohibit any public secondary school receiving federal funds from denying equal access to students who wish to conduct a meeting devoted to religious objectives. Such meetings are to be voluntary, student-initiated, and without sponsorship by the school. If schools allow one or more non-curricular clubs (clubs unrelated to regular courses) to meet on school property during noninstructional time, they cannot refuse other groups to meet simply because of "the religious, political, philosophical, or other content of the speech at such meetings." 98 Stat. 1302 (1984). In 1990, the Court upheld this statute against challenges that it violated the Establishment Clause. Eight Justices agreed that, in this case, a public high school had allowed such clubs as Subsurfers and a chess group to meet after school and should not have prohibited a Christian club from meeting. Westside Community Bd. of Ed. v. Mergens, 496 U.S. 226 (1990). If states permit school property to be used after hours for social, civic, and recreational purposes, they may not discriminate on the basis of religious viewpoint. Lamb's Chapel v. Center Moriches School Dist., 508 U.S. 384 (1993).

Building on *Widmar* and *Lamb's Chapel,* the Court in 1995 held that the University of Virginia denied students their right of free speech when it helped finance the printing of student publications but withheld payment from "Wide Awake," a Christian newspaper. The university argued that funding the newspaper would have violated the Establishment Clause, but a 5–4 majority ruled that no violation exists when a university subsidizes publications on a religion-neutral basis. The Court found it significant that the financial assistance came from student fees rather than from a tax levied by the State, but admitted that the payment of student fees is also mandatory. Rosenberger v. University of Virginia, 515 U.S. 819 (1995).

Another extension of equal access came in 2001, when the Court ruled that public elementary schools must open their doors to after-school religious activities. The 6–3 decision applied to these schools the same principle that had covered public high schools and universities. Good News Club v. Milford Central School, 533 U.S. 98 (2001). When the city of Tucson, Ariz., charged a religious gathering a $130 fee for municipal services that it provided free to other groups sponsoring events in the city's parks, and was upheld by the Ninth Circuit, the Court vacated the judgment and returned it to the Ninth Circuit for further consideration in the light of *Good News Club.* Gentala v. Tucson, 534 U.S. 946 (2001).

The treatment of student groups was again at issue in 2010 with a case from Hastings College of the Law, a school within the University of California public-school system. The school extended official recognition to student groups, offering benefits in the form of school funds, facilities, channels of communication, and Hastings's name and logo. These groups had to comply with the school's nondiscrimination policy. The Christian Legal Society (CLS) was therefore barred because it believes that sexual activity should not occur outside of marriage and must be between a man and a woman. Excluded from the CLS would be individuals who engage in "unrepentant homosexual activity." The Court, divided 5 to 4, held that the school's all-comers policy is a reasonable, viewpoint-neutral condition and does not transgress on First Amendment limitations. Christian Legal Society v. Martinez, 561 U.S. ___ (2010).

Other Conflicts

A Minnesota law provided that only religious organizations receiving more than half of their total contributions from members or affiliated organizations would be exempt from the registration and reporting requirements of a charitable solicitation statute. A 5–4 Supreme Court held that the statute violated the Establishment Clause because it set up an official denominational preference. The 50 percent rule was not "closely fitted" to the state's asserted interest in preventing fraudulent solicitations. Moreover, the statute presented too great a risk of politicizing religion. Different religious organizations would jockey for support within the legislature to obtain exemptions. Larson v. Valente, 456 U.S. 228 (1982).

In that same year the Court held that a Massachusetts statute violated the Establishment Clause by vesting in the governing bodies of churches the power to prevent issuance of liquor licenses within a 500-foot radius of the churches. The Court regarded the statute as a delegation of legislative zoning power to a nongovernmental entity. Not only was the churches' power under the statute standardless, calling for no reasons or findings for action, but the "mere appearance of a joint exercise of legislative authority by Church and State provides a significant symbolic benefit to religion in the minds of some by reason of the power conferred." Larkin v. Grendel's Den, Inc., 459 U.S. 116, 125–26 (1982).

The Continuing Saga of Kiryas Joel

In 1994, the Court relied on *Larkin* to strike down a public school district that New York had created solely for the disabled children of a small village of Hasidic Jews. New York drew the school district to coincide with the population of Kiryas Joel, a Satmar Hasidic enclave about 40 miles north of New York City. The Court, divided 6 to 3, ruled that the school district violated the Establishment Clause. Board of Ed. of Kiryas Joel v. Grumet, 512 U.S. 687 (1994). New York responded by passing a statute that allowed any municipality meeting certain criteria to form its own school district. Kiryas Joel met the criteria. In fact, out of 1,546 municipalities in New York State, it was the *only* one to qualify. In 1995, a state trial court upheld the new law but was reversed a year later by the State Appellate Division. The state's highest court, the Court of Appeals, also struck down this second attempt to create a district for Kiryas Joel. Defying the courts, the state legislature passed legislation on August 4, 1997, creating a special public school district for the Hasidic sect. The legislators said that the new legislation was applicable to other municipalities, not just Kiryas Joel, but the benefits appeared to favor only Kiryas Joel. "Defying Courts, Lawmakers Approve School District for Hasidim," New York Times, August 5, 1997, at A19. This third attempt to preserve the Hasidic school district was also rejected by New York courts. In 1999, the Supreme Court refused to hear an appeal from Kiryas Joel. Pataki v. Grumet, 528 U.S. 946 (1999).

Crèches and Menorahs

The Court has left a confusing trail of decisions on whether public officials can erect crèches and menorahs on public property. In 1984, the Court split 5–4 in reviewing a crèche case from the city of Pawtucket, Rhode Island, which annually erected a Christmas display, including a crèche, or Nativity scene. In upholding the city, the Court offended some religious groups by reasoning that the crèche could be displayed because it had a "secular purpose." LYNCH v. DONNELLY, 465 U.S. 668 (1984). The decision opened the door to other governmental practices. The issue returned to the Court in 1989 in two forms: the constitutionality of a crèche on the grand staircase of the Allegheny County Courthouse and an 18-foot Chanukah menorah (candelabrum) plus a 45-foot decorated Christmas tree placed just outside the City-County Building. In a muddled decision, offering few intelligible principles to guide the lower courts (or state legislatures), the Court struck down the crèche display by the vote of 5 to 4 and upheld the menorah/Christmas tree display 6 to 3. ALLEGHENY COUNTY v. GREATER PITTSBURGH ACLU, 492 U.S. 573 (1989).

To reach this result, the majority concluded that the combination of a Jewish menorah and a Christmas tree somehow produced "cultural diversity," with little appreciation that the attempt to transform a religious symbol to a cultural event would offend many Jews. By noting that Christmas and Chanukah "are part of the same winter-holiday season, which has attained a secular status in our society," Justice Blackmun's opinion for the majority appeared to secularize, if not Christianize, a Jewish holiday. As to the crèche display, Blackmun argued that it offended the Constitution in part because it stood alone, surrounded by a floral decoration, whereas the crèche in *Lynch* v. *Donnelly* was mixed with a Santa Claus house, reindeer pulling Santa's sleigh, candy-striped poles, a Christmas tree, carolers, and cutout figures representing such characters as a clown, an elephant, and a teddy bear. Would the addition of some of those objects have saved the crèche in Pittsburgh? No one knows. It is not even clear whether the menorah/Christmas tree combination would be constitutional had the two symbols been transposed, placing the menorah directly in front of the entrance to the City-County Building with the Christmas tree positioned to the side, or making the menorah 45-feet high alongside a smaller Christmas tree. Finally, if municipalities are free to celebrate Christian and Jewish holidays, what of other sects and of nonbelievers? Does the goal of "cultural diversity" require representation for those groups? Instead of disposing of such questions, the Court virtually invited any number of variations to revisit the judiciary.

One such variation, decided by the Court in 1995, involved Ohio prohibiting the Ku Klux Klan from placing a large wooden cross in front of the state capitol. In the past, state officials had allowed in that public forum the display of a Christmas tree and a menorah. The state argued that the Klan's cross, given the proximity to the seat of government, might imply that the cross bore the state's approval. The Court decided that the Klan's display was private religious speech entitled to protection under the First Amendment. However, the plurality opinion by Justice Scalia (joined by Rehnquist, Kennedy, and Thomas) was followed by three concurrences: one by Thomas, another by O'Connor (joined by Souter and Breyer) and a third by Souter (joined by O'Connor and Breyer), making it difficult to locate agreement on any general principles that might guide future cases. Stevens and Ginsburg wrote separate dissenting opinions. Capitol Sq. Review Bd. v. Pinette, 515 U.S. 753 (1995).

The crèche/menorah issue continued to percolate in the lower courts. City officials of Jersey City, N.J., erected on the city hall plaza a holiday display containing a crèche and menorah. After a federal district court issued an injunction against the display, it was modified by adding plastic figures of Frosty the Snowman and Santa Claus and a red wooden sled. That satisfied the district judge, who decided that the secular figures somehow "demystified" and "desanctified" the religious meaning of the crèche and menorah. The Third Circuit, however, ruled that the display violated the Establishment Clause. ACLU v. Schundler, 104 F.3d 1435 (3d Cir. 1997), cert. denied, 520 U.S. 1265 (1997).

The San Diego Cross

A dispute in San Diego centered around a 29-foot cross standing on top of Mount Soledad in the La Jolla neighborhood. Built in 1954, it had stood as a memorial to veterans of the Korean War before being challenged in court as a violation of the Establishment Clause. After many efforts to resolve the dispute had failed, President Bush on August 14, 2006 signed a bill transferring the cross to the federal government to be maintained as a veterans memorial (P.L. 109-272, 120 Stat. 770). This action invited continued legal challenges. In 2008, a federal judge ruled that the plaintiffs who had sued to have the cross taken down had failed to demonstrate that its primary purpose was religious. At the base of the memorial, arranged in six concentric rings, are some 2,400 plaques paying tribute to war veterans. For the judge, the primary effect was patriotic and nationalistic. The Ninth Circuit heard argument on December 9, 2009 and ruled in 2011 that the cross violated the Establishment Clause. However, it remanded the case to the district court to fashion an appropriate remedy. As a result, on June 25, 2012, the Supreme Court declined to hear the dispute because the lower courts had yet to reach a binding decision. Mount Soledad Memorial Association v. Trunk, 567 U.S. ___ (2012).

The Mojave Cross

In 1934, members of the Veterans of Foreign Wars (VFW) placed a six-foot white cross on federal land in the Mojave National Preserve in California to honor American soldiers who died in World War I.

In January 2002, Congress designated the cross a national memorial and authorized $10,000 to install a memorial plaque on the cross. 115 Stat. 2278, sec. 8137. Six months later a district court held that plaintiffs objecting to the placement of a religious symbol on federal property had standing to sue and that the cross violated the Establishment Clause because it represented governmental endorsement of religion. Congress responded in September 2003 with a land swap: transferring the property and the cross to a private party (the VFW) in exchange for privately-owned land given to the Preserve. 117 Stat. 1100, sec. 8121.

After various appeals the dispute reached the Supreme Court, which issued a 5 to 4 decision in 2010 reversing lower court holdings that had enjoined the government from implementing the land-transfer statute. The case was remanded to the Ninth Circuit for further proceedings. Salazar v. Buono, 559 U.S. ___ (2010). The Court's guidance in this case was confused because of multiple opinions. The decision was a plurality ruling (Kennedy wrote for the Court, joined by Roberts and Alito). Roberts added a short concurrence. Alito prepared a longer concurrence. Scalia and Thomas, representing the fourth and fifth votes of the majority, concurred only in the judgment, not the reasoning. A dissent by Stevens was joined by Ginsburg and Sotomayor. Breyer wrote a separate dissent. The lower courts now have to decide if the congressional remedy is constitutional.

Sunday Worship

In laws governing Sunday worship and Sunday closings, state interests are balanced against an individual's preference to worship on a day other than Sunday (so-called Sabbatarians). In one case, a Seventh-Day Adventist had been fired because she would not work on Saturday, the Sabbath day of her faith. She was later denied unemployment compensation benefits on the ground that she would not accept suitable work when offered. The Court held that the state law violated her religious freedoms. This law was vulnerable on First Amendment grounds because the state expressly saved the Sunday worshipper from having to make the kind of choice faced by the Seventh-Day Adventist. Sherbert v. Verner, 374 U.S. 398, 406 (1963). Government may not put an employee in the predicament of choosing between fidelity to religious beliefs and access to public benefits. Hobbie v. Unemployment Appeals Comm'n of Fla., 480 U.S. 136 (1987); Thomas v. Review Bd., Ind. Empl. Sec. Div., 450 U.S. 707 (1981). It is not necessary to belong to an established religious sect that forbids work on Sundays. A sincere, personal religious belief is sufficient. Frazee v. Employment Security Dept., 489 U.S. 829 (1989).

These cases were decided on constitutional grounds. Other cases revolve around statutory questions, including the intent of Congress when it passes legislation to prohibit religious discrimination. One provision states that employers have an obligation to "reasonably accommodate to an employee's ... religious observance or practice without undue hardship on the conduct of the employer's business." 42 U.S.C. § 2000e(j). Congress added this provision after courts had "come down on both sides" of the rights of Sabbatarians. The language was intended to "resolve by legislation ... that which the courts apparently have not resolved." 118 Cong. Rec. 70506 (1972). These cases turn on questions of what burden of proof should be placed on the employee to prove discrimination. Ansonia Board of Education v. Philbrook, 479 U.S. 60 (1986). Congress also exempted religious organizations from the prohibition on religious discrimination in employment. 42 U.S.C. § 2000e-1. The purpose was to shield religious organizations from liability in the case of employment suits. A unanimous Court in 1987 held that this exemption does not offend the Establishment Clause. Corporation of Presiding Bishop v. Amos, 483 U.S. 327 (1987).

Although states may not discriminate against Sabbatarians, they might err by going in the opposite direction to promote their religious practice. In 1985, the Court held that a Connecticut law violated the Establishment Clause because it provided that no person "who states that a particular day of the week is observed as his Sabbath may be required by his employer to work on such day. An employee's refusal to work on his Sabbath shall not constitute grounds for his dismissal." The Court struck down the statute because it lacked neutrality in religious matters. Estate of Thornton v. Caldor, Inc., 472 U.S. 703. What began as an effort to accommodate the free exercise of religion ended up violating the Establishment Clause.

Religious Freedom Restoration Act (RFRA)

A decision by the Court in 1990, regarding unemployment compensation benefits, undercut the protections promised in *Sherbert* v. *Verner*. Congress passed legislation in 1993 to override the decision, but four years later the Court declared the statute to be unconstitutional, pushing the matter back to Congress to consider alternative legislation.

The 1990 decision concerned two members of the Native American Church who had been fired by a private organization because they ingested peyote, a hallucinogenic drug. They took the drug as part of a religious, sacramental exercise. Eating the peyote plant, which embodies their deity, is an act of worship and communion. Their application for unemployment compensation was denied by Oregon under a state law that disqualifies employees who are fired for work-related "misconduct." Remaining drug-free was a condition of their employment.

The Court, divided 6 to 3, held that the Free Exercise Clause permits a state to prohibit sacramental peyote use and to deny unemployment benefits to persons fired for such use. State law may prohibit the possession and use of a drug even if it incidentally prohibits a religious practice. The Court distinguished this case from other unemployment-benefit cases by noting that the religious conduct in those cases was not prohibited by law. Oregon law made it a criminal offense to possess or use peyote. Four Justices—O'Connor in her concurrence and Blackmun, Brennan, and Marshall in their dissents—rejected the Court's opinion that states need not demonstrate a "compelling government interest" to justify general prohibitions that affect the free exercise of religion. Oregon remained free to make an exemption for the use of peyote by members of the Native American Church. About two dozen states had statutory or judicially-crafted exemptions for the religious use of peyote. EMPLOYMENT DIVISION v. SMITH, 494 U.S. 872 (1990). The Oregon legislature repaired some of the damage of the Court's decision by enacting a bill that protects the sacramental use of peyote by the Native American Church. Oregon Laws, Chap. 329, June 24, 1991.

Smith provided a framework for the Court to analyze ordinances that a Florida city council passed to prohibit the Santeria religion from sacrificing animals as a form of devotion. Adherents of this religion kill animals to nurture a personal relationship with spirits. Since the ordinances were aimed specifically at the Santeria religion the *Smith* test did not apply. The ordinances were not general and neutral. Thus, the ordinances had to be justified by a compelling governmental interest and had to be narrowly tailored to advance that interest. A unanimous Court found the ordinances to be overbroad and underinclusive. Even were the governmental interests compelling, the ordinances were not drawn narrowly enough to accomplish those purposes. To the Court, the ordinances were aimed at suppressing a religious exercise. Church of Lukumi Babalu Aye v. Hialeah, 508 U.S. 520 (1993).

A number of religious and civil liberties groups urged Congress to pass legislation that would grant greater religious freedom than recognized in *Smith*. The purpose was to reinstate the previous *Sherbert* standard (compelling governmental interest) for testing federal, state, and local laws. Proponents of the bill believed that the Court's ruling threatened a number of religious practices, including the use of ceremonial wine, the practice of kosher slaughter, and the Hmong (Laotian) religious objection to autopsy. In 1993, Congress passed the Religious Freedom Restoration Act (RFRA). (See reading for congressional debate.)

RFRA provided that governments may substantially burden a person's religious exercise only if they demonstrate a compelling interest and use the least restrictive means of furthering that interest. The statute restored the compelling interest test of *Sherbert* and *Wisconsin* v. *Yoder*. 107 Stat. 1488 (1993). A year later, Congress passed legislation to legalize the use of peyote by Native Americans for ceremonial purposes. No Indian may be penalized or discriminated against for such use, including the denial of benefits under public assistance programs. 108 Stat. 3125 (1994).

Whatever the Court decided to do with RFRA, it would acknowledge the central role of majoritarian politics in protecting religious rights. If it upheld the statute, it would recognize that religious groups, in concert with Congress, could define religious freedom more generously than the Court. If it struck it down, it would merely reaffirm the 1990 *Smith* holding, which itself depended on the majoritarian process to protect religion. As the Court noted in *Smith*: "It may fairly be said that leaving accommodation to the political process will place at a relative disadvantage those religious practices that are not widely engaged in; but that unavoidable consequence of democratic government must be preferred to a system in which each conscience is a law unto itself or in which judges weigh the social importance of all laws against the centrality of all religious beliefs." 494 U.S. at 890.

In 1997, the Court ruled that Congress exceeded the scope of its enforcement power under Section 5 of the Fourteenth Amendment in enacting RFRA. In many ways, Congress had asked for a black eye by attempting to reimpose a constitutional standard (*Sherbert*) that the Court itself had rejected in *Smith*. The Court could not sit still and have Congress ram *Sherbert* down its throat. But the reasoning and premises in the Court's decision were superficial, unpersuasive, and internally inconsistent (see box). They invite continued challenges and legislative activity. Although the Court strongly hinted that it has the last and final word in deciding the meaning of the Constitution, it in fact left the door wide open for future congressional action. BOERNE v. FLORES, 521 U.S. 507 (1997). Federal courts have held that RFRA is constitutional as applied to the federal government. Kikumura v. Hurley, 242 F.3d 950 (10th Cir. 2001); In re Young, 141 F.3d 854 (8th Cir. 1998), cert. denied, sub nom. Christians v. Crystal Evangelical Free Church, 525 U.S. 811 (1998).

"Son of RFRA"

On June 9, 1998, a "Son of RFRA" bill was introduced, relying this time on congressional powers over spending and commerce. The bill passed the House the following year by a vote of 306 to 118. By the time the bill cleared both chambers, it had been restricted to provide two kinds of protections. First, it offers religious groups protection in land-use disputes, such as zoning issues (the kind that triggered *Boerne* v. *Flores*). Second, the bill makes it easier for prisoners or other persons confined in state-run institutions to practice their faith. The bill applies to any organization that receives federal money, including state and local prisons that get federal construction and maintenance funds. Finally, the bill relies on congressional power over interstate commerce, because construction materials are shipped between states for the renovation of buildings owned by religious organizations. 114 Stat. 803 (2000). There have been no effective legal challenges to this statute.

Sunday Closing Laws

Sunday closing laws (or "blue laws") were challenged in court as a violation of the Establishment Clause. A major case involved a Maryland law that prohibited the sale on Sunday of all merchandise except the retail sale of tobacco products, confectionaries, milk, bread, fruit, gasoline, oils, greases, drugs, medicines, newspapers, and periodicals. After litigation began, the state legislature allowed other exceptions. In reviewing the history of Sunday closing laws, an 8–1 majority for the Supreme Court found that the original motivation had gradually changed from a religious character to a secular purpose in setting aside a day for rest and recreation. The fact that the day was Sunday, "a day of particular significance for the dominant Christian sects, does not bar the State from achieving its secular goals." McGowan v. Maryland, 366 U.S. 420, 445 (1961). The secularization of Sunday was evident in the repeal of earlier laws that had a distinctly religious purpose, such as banning bingo games, pinball machines, slot machines, dancing, and the sale of alcoholic beverages. Id. at 423–24, 448.

State Closing Laws

Although the U.S. Supreme Court upheld Sunday closing laws, some of the states changed their laws to permit businesses to operate on Sunday if religious convictions forced them to close on another day. The Supreme Court of Pennsylvania concluded that state laws on Sunday closings were so "riddled with exception after exception" that they violated the equal protection of the laws. Kroger Co. v. O'Hara Tp., 392 A.2d 266, 273 (Pa. 1978). The Supreme Court of Pennsylvania could find no fair and substantial relationship between the objective of providing a uniform day of rest and recreation and in "permitting the sale of novelties but not Bibles and bathing suits; in permit-ting the sale of fresh meat patties but not frozen meat patties; or in permitting the installation of an electric meter but not a T.V. antenna." Id. at 275.

The Supreme Court of Connecticut found the state's Sunday closing laws too arbitrary, discriminatory, and unreasonable to satisfy the requirements of equal protection and due process. It cited a comic strip showing a customer at a drugstore buying a snow shovel, a roll of film, a hairnet, and a box of candy. When the customer asked whether the store had any wood stoves the proprietor replied indignantly: "Wood Stoves? … in a DRUG store?" Caldor's, Inc. v. Bedding Barn, Inc., 417 A.2d 343, 353 n.9 (Conn. 1979).

Corporations, claiming economic injury, were unsuccessful in challenging the Sunday closing laws. Two Guys v. McGinley, 366 U.S. 582 (1961). The effect of those laws raised more difficult questions when applied to Jewish businesses that closed Friday evening and all day Saturday to observe the Sabbath. The state forced them to close on Sunday as well. Dividing 6–3 on this issue, the Court reasoned that the law did not inconvenience all members of the Orthodox Jewish faith, but only those who chose to work on Sunday. Dodging the question of why Sunday would be selected as the official day of rest, the Court argued that any law was likely to result in an economic disadvantage to some religious sect. Braunfeld v. Brown, 366 U.S. 599 (1961). A Massachusetts law allowing kosher markets to sell kosher meats until 10 A.M. on Sunday was upheld 6–3, even though plaintiffs argued that it was economically impractical for them to stay open from Saturday at sundown until 10 A.M. on Sunday. These laws were saved, said the Court, because they had lost their original religious character. Gallagher v. Crown Kosher Market, 366 U.S. 617 (1961). See also Arlan's Dept. Store v. Kentucky, 371 U.S. 218 (1962). The doctrinal confusion of these federal rulings convinced some state legislatures and state courts to adopt more coherent policies under their own constitutions (see box on next page).

Teenage Chastity

In 1988, the Supreme Court decided an important case involving the use of federal funds to discourage adolescent, premarital sex. The statute, known formally as the Adolescent Family Life Act of 1981 and informally as the Teenage Chastity Act, authorized federal grants to public and private groups, including religious organizations. The Court acknowledged that some of the funds had been spent by religious groups impermissibly to promote religious doctrines. Nevertheless, a 5 to 4 Court held that the statute, *on its face,* did not violate the Establishment Clause. It remanded the case to the district court to determine whether the Act, *as applied,* violates the Clause. Bowen v. Kendrick, 487 U.S. 589 (1988).

The remand put pressure on the government to negotiate with the plaintiffs to show that the law, as applied, had no *Lemon* problems. The government took time for this review. The plaintiffs were in no hurry. They wanted the government to do whatever was necessary to avoid constitutional violations. The district judge, hoping to resolve the dispute without a judicial ruling, gave the government time to negotiate draft settlement agreements with the plaintiffs. Finally, in 1993, the parties reached agreement out of court.

Lynch v. Donnelly

465 U.S. 668 (1984)

Each year the city of Pawtucket, R.I., set up a Christmas display in a park owned by a nonprofit organization and located in the city's shopping district. In addition to such objects as a Santa Clause house, a Christmas tree, and a banner that read "SEASONS GREETINGS," the display included a crèche (nativity scene). The crèche had been included in this display for four decades. Daniel Donnelly brought an action in federal court, challenging the inclusion of the crèche as a violation of the Establishment Clause. The defendant was Dennis Lynch, Mayor of Pawtucket. The district court upheld the challenge and permanently enjoined the city from including the crèche in the display. The First Circuit affirmed.

CHIEF JUSTICE BURGER delivered the opinion of the Court.

We granted certiorari to decide whether the Establishment Clause of the First Amendment prohibits a municipality from including a crèche, or Nativity scene, in its annual Christmas display.

I

... The Pawtucket display comprises many of the figures and decorations traditionally associated with Christmas, including, among other things, a Santa Claus house, reindeer pulling Santa's sleigh, candy-striped poles, a Christmas tree, carolers, cutout figures representing such characters as a clown, an elephant, and a teddy bear, hundreds of colored lights, a large banner that reads "SEASONS GREETINGS," and the crèche at issue here. All components of this display are owned by the city.

The crèche, which has been included in the display for 40 or more years, consists of the traditional figures, including the Infant Jesus, Mary and Joseph, angels, shepherds, kings, and animals, all ranging in height from 5" to 5'. In 1973, when the present crèche was acquired, it cost the city $1,365; it now is valued at $200. The erection and dismantling of the crèche costs the city about $20 per year; nominal expenses are incurred in lighting the crèche. No money has been expended on its maintenance for the past 10 years....

[II.B]

The Court's interpretation of the Establishment Clause has comported with what history reveals was the contemporaneous understanding of its guarantees. A significant example of the contemporaneous understanding of that Clause is found in the events of the first week of the First Session of the First Congress in 1789. In the very week that Congress approved the Establishment Clause as part of the Bill of Rights for submission to the states, it enacted legislation providing for paid Chaplains for the House and Senate. In *Marsh* v. *Chambers,* 463 U.S. 783 (1983), we noted that 17 Members of that First Congress had been Delegates to the Constitutional Convention where freedom of speech, press, and religion and antagonism toward an established church were subjects of frequent discussion. We saw no conflict with the Establishment Clause when Nebraska employed members of the clergy as official legislative Chaplains to give opening prayers at sessions of the state legislature....

C

[*Burger provides other examples of official acknowledgment of religion: making Thanksgiving, with its religious overtones, a national holiday; giving federal employees a holiday for Christmas; putting "In God We Trust" on currency; including "One nation under God" in the Pledge of Allegiance; using public revenue to display religious paintings in art galleries; decorating the Supreme Court with religious motifs; and having Congress direct the President to proclaim a National Day of Prayer.*]

III

... The District Court plainly erred by focusing almost exclusively on the crèche. When viewed in the proper context of the Christmas Holiday season, it is apparent that, on this record, there is insufficient evidence to establish that the inclusion of the crèche is a purposeful or surreptitious effort to express some kind of subtle governmental advocacy of a particular religious message....

The narrow question is whether there is a secular purpose for Pawtucket's display of the crèche....

... [T]o conclude that the primary effect of including the crèche is to advance religion in violation of the Establishment Clause would require that we view it as more beneficial to and more an endorsement of religion, for example, than expenditure of large sums of public money for textbooks supplied throughout the country to students attending church-sponsored schools, *Board of Education* v. *Allen, supra;* expenditure of public funds for transportation of students to church-sponsored schools, *Everson* v. *Board of Education, supra;* federal grants for college buildings of church-sponsored institutions of higher education combining secular and religious education, *Tilton* v. *Richardson,* 403 U.S. 672 (1971); noncategorical grants to church-sponsored colleges and universities, *Roemer* v. *Board of Public Works,* 426 U.S. 736 (1976); and the tax exemptions for church properties sanctioned in *Walz* v. *Tax Comm'n,* 397 U.S. 664 (1970). It would also require that we view it as more of an endorsement of religion than the Sunday Closing Laws upheld in *McGowan* v. *Maryland,* 366 U.S. 420 (1961); the release time program for religious training in *Zorach* v. *Clauson,* 343 U.S. 306 (1952); and the legislative prayers upheld in *Marsh* v. *Chambers,* 463 U.S. 783 (1983).

[IV]

The Court has acknowledged that the "fears and political problems" that gave rise to the Religion Clauses in the 18th century are of far less concern today. *Everson,* 330 U.S., at 8. We are unable to perceive the Archbishop of Canterbury, the Bishop of Rome, or other powerful religious leaders behind every public acknowledgment of the religious heritage long officially recognized by the three constitutional branches of government. Any notion that these symbols pose a real danger of establishment of a state church is farfetched indeed.

V

That this Court has been alert to the constitutionally expressed opposition to the establishment of religion is shown in numerous holdings striking down statutes or programs as violative of the Establishment Clause.... Taken together these cases abundantly demonstrate the Court's concern to protect the genuine objectives of the Establishment Clause. It is far too late in the day to impose a crabbed reading of the Clause on the country.

VI

We hold that, notwithstanding the religious significance of the crèche, the city of Pawtucket has not violated the Establishment Clause of the First Amendment. Accordingly, the judgment of the Court of Appeals is reversed.

It is so ordered.

JUSTICE O'CONNOR, concurring....

JUSTICE BRENNAN, with whom JUSTICE MARSHALL, JUSTICE BLACKMUN, and JUSTICE STEVENS join, dissenting.

[IA]

Applying the three-part [*Lemon*] test to Pawtucket's crèche, I am persuaded that the city's inclusion of the crèche in its Christmas display simply does not reflect a "clearly secular ... purpose." ...

... [A]s was true in *Larkin* v. *Grendel's Den, Inc.,* 459 U.S. 116, 123–124 (1982), all of Pawtucket's "valid secular objectives can be readily accomplished by other means." Plainly, the city's interest in celebrating the holiday and in promoting both retail sales and goodwill are fully served by the elaborate display of Santa Claus, reindeer, and wishing wells that are already a part of Pawtucket's annual Christmas display. More importantly, the nativity scene, unlike every other element of the Hodgson Park display, reflects a sectarian exclusivity that the avowed purposes of celebrating the holiday season and promoting retail commerce simply do not encompass....

Finally, it is evident that Pawtucket's inclusion of a crèche as part of its annual Christmas display does pose a significant threat of fostering "excessive entanglement." ... Jews and other non-Christian groups, prompted perhaps by the Mayor's remark that he will include a Menorah in future displays, can be expected to press government for inclusion of their symbols, and faced with such requests, government will have to become involved in accommodating the various demands....

JUSTICE BLACKMUN, with whom JUSTICE STEVENS joins, dissenting....

Allegheny County v. Greater Pittsburgh ACLU

492 U.S. 573 (1989)

Two holiday displays on public property in downtown Pittsburgh prompted this lawsuit: a crèche depicting the Christian nativity scene (placed on the Grand Staircase of the Allegheny County Courthouse) and an 18-foot Chanukah menorah, or candelabrum, (placed just outside

the City-County Building next to the city's 45-foot decorated Christmas tree). The crèche was donated by the Holy Name Society, a Roman Catholic group, and the menorah is owned by Chabad, a Jewish group. The ACLU objected that the displays violated the Establishment Clause. The District Court denied relief, relying on *Lynch* v. *Donnelly* (1984), but the Third Circuit reversed. This case is of interest because of the continuing inability of the Court to present a coherent doctrine governing these displays.

JUSTICE BLACKMUN announced the judgment of the Court and delivered the opinion of the Court with respect to Parts III-A, IV, and V, an opinion with respect to Parts I and II, in which JUSTICE STEVENS and JUSTICE O'CONNOR join, an opinion with respect to Part III-B, in which JUSTICE STEVENS joins, an opinion with respect to Part VII, in which JUSTICE O'CONNOR joins, and an opinion with respect to Part VI....

I

A

The county courthouse is owned by Allegheny County and is its seat of government....

The crèche in the county courthouse, like other crèches, is a visual representation of the scene in the manger in Bethlehem shortly after the birth of Jesus, as described in the Gospels of Luke and Matthew. The crèche includes figures of the infant Jesus, Mary, Joseph, farm animals, shepherds, and wise men, all placed in or before a wooden representation of a manger, which has at its crest an angel bearing a banner that proclaims "Gloria in Excelsis Deo!"

During the 1986–1987 holiday season, the crèche was on display on the Grand Staircase from November 26 to January 9.... It had a wooden fence on three sides and bore a plaque stating: "This Display Donated by the Holy Name Society." Sometime during the week of December 2, the county placed red and white poinsettia plants around the fence.... The county also placed a small evergreen tree, decorated with a red bow, behind each of the two endposts of the fence.... These trees stood alongside the manger backdrop and were slightly shorter than it was. The angel thus was at the apex of the crèche display. Altogether, the crèche, the fence, the poinsettias, and the trees occupied a substantial amount of space on the Grand Staircase. No figures of Santa Claus or other decorations appeared on the Grand Staircase....

B

The City-County Building is separate and a block removed from the county courthouse and, as the name implies, is jointly owned by the city of Pittsburgh and Allegheny County....

For a number of years, the city has had a large Christmas tree under the middle arch outside the Grant Street entrance. Following this practice, city employees on November 17, 1986, erected a 45-foot tree under the middle arch and decorated it with lights and ornaments.... A few days later, the city placed at the foot of the tree a sign bearing the mayor's name and entitled "Salute to Liberty." Beneath the title, the sign stated:

"During this holiday season, the city of Pittsburgh salutes liberty. Let these festive lights remind us that we are the keepers of the flame of liberty and our legacy of freedom." JEV 41.

At least since 1982, the city has expanded its Grant Street holiday display to include a symbolic representation of Chanukah, an 8-day Jewish holiday that begins on the 25th day of the Jewish lunar month of Kislev.... The 25th of Kislev usually occurs in December, and thus Chanukah is the annual Jewish holiday that falls closest to Christmas Day each year. In 1986, Chanukah began at sundown on December 26....

According to Jewish tradition, on the 25th of Kislev in 164 B.C.E. (before the common era (165 B.C.)), the Maccabees rededicated the Temple of Jerusalem after recapturing it from the Greeks.... [*The Talmud explains that the Temple housed a seven-branch menorah, to be kept burning continuously. When the Maccabees rededicated the Temple they had oil for only one day, but it miraculously lasted for eight days. To celebrate this miracle, the Talmud designates it as a mitzvah (a religious deed or commandment) and Jews place a lamp with eight lights in a front window during the eight days of Chanukah.*]

Chanukah, like Christmas, is a cultural event as well as a religious holiday.... Indeed, the Chanukah story always has had a political or national, as well as a religious, dimension: it tells of national heroism in addition to divine intervention. Also, Chanukah, like Christmas, is a winter holiday; according to some historians, it was associated in ancient times with the winter solstice. Just as some Americans celebrate Christmas without regard to its religious significance, some nonreligious American Jews celebrate Chanukah as an expression of ethnic identity, and "as a cultural or national event, rather than as a specifically religious event." ...

... [S]ome have suggested that the proximity of Christmas accounts for the social prominence of Chanukah in this country. Whatever the reason, Chanukah is observed by American Jews to an extent greater than its religious importance would indicate: in the hierarchy of Jewish holidays, Chanukah ranks fairly low in religious significance. This socially heightened status of Chanukah reflects its cultural or secular dimension....

IV

We turn first to the county's crèche display. There is no doubt, of course, that the crèche itself is capable of communicating a religious message.... Indeed, the crèche in this lawsuit uses words, as well as the picture of the nativity scene, to make its religious meaning unmistakably clear. "Glory to God in the Highest!" says the angel in the crèche — Glory to God because of the birth of Jesus. This praise to God in Christian terms is indisputably religious — indeed sectarian — just as it is when said in the Gospel or in a church service.

Under the Court's holding in *Lynch,* the effect of a crèche display turns on its setting. Here, unlike in *Lynch,* nothing in the context of the display detracts from the crèche's religious message. The *Lynch* display comprised a series of figures and objects, each group of which had its own focal point. Santa's house and his reindeer were objects of attention separate from the crèche, and had their specific visual story to tell. Similarly, whatever a "talking" wishing well may be, it obviously was a center of attention separate from the crèche. Here, in contrast, the crèche stands alone: it is the single element of the display on the Grand Staircase....

In sum, *Lynch* teaches that government may celebrate Christmas in some manner and form, but not in a way that endorses Christian doctrine. Here, Allegheny County has transgressed this line. It has chosen to celebrate Christmas in a way that has the effect of endorsing a patently Christian message: Glory to God for the birth of Jesus Christ. Under *Lynch,* and the rest of our cases, nothing more is required to demonstrate a violation of the Establishment Clause....

VI

The display of the Chanukah menorah in front of the City-County Building may well present a closer constitutional question....

... [T]he menorah here stands next to a Christmas tree and a sign saluting liberty. While no challenge has been made here to the display of the tree and the sign, their presence is obviously relevant in determining the effect of the menorah's display. The necessary result of placing a menorah next to a Christmas tree is to create an "overall holiday setting" that represents both Christmas and Chanukah — two holidays, not one....

... Because government may celebrate Christmas as a secular holiday, it follows that government may also acknowledge Chanukah as a secular holiday. Simply put, it would be a form of discrimination against Jews to allow Pittsburgh to celebrate Christmas as a cultural tradition while simultaneously disallowing the city's acknowledgment of Chanukah as a contemporaneous cultural tradition.

Accordingly, the relevant question for Establishment Clause purposes is whether the combined display of the tree, the sign, and the menorah has the effect of endorsing both Christian and Jewish faiths, or rather simply recognizes that both Christmas and Chanukah are part of the same winter-holiday season, which has attained a secular status in our society. Of the two interpretations of this particular display, the latter seems far more plausible and is also in line with *Lynch.*

... [A] 40-foot Christmas tree was one of the objects that validated the crèche in *Lynch.* The widely accepted view of the Christmas tree as the preeminent secular symbol of the Christmas holiday season serves to emphasize the secular component of the message communicated by other elements of an accompanying holiday display, including the Chanukah menorah.

The tree, moreover, is clearly the predominant element in the city's display. The 45-foot tree occupies the central position beneath the middle archway in front of the Grant Street entrance to the City-County Building; the 18-foot menorah is positioned to one side....

VII

Lynch v. *Donnelly* confirms, and in no way repudiates, the longstanding constitutional principle that government may not engage in a practice that has the effect of promoting or endorsing religious beliefs. The display of the crèche in the county courthouse has this unconstitutional effect. The display of the menorah in front of the City-County Building, however, does not have this effect, given its "particular physical setting."

The judgment of the Court of Appeals is affirmed in part and reversed in part, and the cases are remanded for further proceedings.

It is so ordered.

[*O'Connor, joined by Brennan and Stevens in Part II of her opinion, concurs in part and concurs in the judgment of Blackmun's opinion for the Court. Brennan, joined by Marshall and Stevens, writes a separate opinion concurring in part and dissenting in part. He would have held both displays in violation of the Establishment Clause.*]

JUSTICE KENNEDY, with whom THE CHIEF JUSTICE, JUSTICE WHITE, and JUSTICE SCALIA join, concurring in the judgment in part and dissenting in part.

The majority holds that the County of Allegheny violated the Establishment Clause by displaying a crèche in the county courthouse, ... This view of the Establishment Clause reflects an unjustified hostility toward religion, a hostility inconsistent with our history and our precedents, and I dissent from this holding. The crèche display is constitutional....

Employment Division v. Smith

494 U.S. 872 (1990)

Oregon law prohibited sacramental use of the drug peyote. Alfred Smith and Galen Black were fired from their jobs because they ingested peyote at a ceremony of the Native American Church. Their application for unemployment compensation was denied on the ground that they had been discharged for work-related "misconduct." Divided 6 to 3, the Supreme Court upheld the state's action against the charge that it violated the Free Exercise Clause. Four Justices—three dissenters and Justice O'Connor in her concurrence—objected to the Court dismissing the compelling interest test. The Oregon Supreme Court held that the statutory prohibition was invalid under the Free Exercise Clause.

JUSTICE SCALIA delivered the opinion of the Court.

This case requires us to decide whether the Free Exercise Clause of the First Amendment permits the State of Oregon to include religiously inspired peyote use within the reach of its general criminal prohibition on use of that drug, and thus permits the State to deny unemployment benefits to persons dismissed from their jobs because of such religiously inspired use....

II

Respondents' claim for relief rests on our decisions in *Sherbert* v. *Verner, supra, Thomas* v. *Review Board, Indiana Employment Security Div., supra,* and *Hobbie* v. *Unemployment Appeals Comm'n of Florida,* 480 U.S. 136 (1987), in which we held that a State could not condition the availability of unemployment insurance on an individual's willingness to forgo conduct required by his religion. As we observed in *Smith I* [485 U.S. 660 (1988)], however, the conduct at issue in those cases was not prohibited by law.... Now that the Oregon Supreme Court has confirmed that Oregon does prohibit the religious use of peyote, we proceed to consider whether that prohibition is permissible under the Free Exercise Clause.

A

... The free exercise of religion means, first and foremost, the right to believe and profess whatever religious doctrine one desires....

But the "exercise of religion" often involves not only belief and profession but the performance of (or abstention from) physical acts: assembling with others for a worship service, participating in sacramental use of bread and wine, proselytizing, abstaining from certain foods or certain modes of transportation. It would be true, we think (though no case of ours has involved the point), that a state would be "prohibiting the free exercise [of religion]" if it sought to ban such acts or abstentions only when they are engaged in for religious reasons, or only because of the religious belief that they display. It would doubtless be unconstitutional, for example, to ban the casting of "statutes that are to be used for worship purposes," or to prohibit bowing down before a golden calf.

Respondents in the present case, however, seek to carry the meaning of "prohibiting the free exercise [of religion]" one large step further. They contend that their religious motivation for using peyote places them beyond the reach of a criminal law that is not specifically directed at their religious practice, and that is concededly constitutional as applied to those who use the drug for other reasons.... As a textual matter, we do not think the words must be given that meaning. It is no more necessary to regard the collection of a general tax, for example, as "prohibiting the free exercise [of religion]" by those citizens who believe support of organized government to be sinful, than it is to regard the same tax as "abridging the freedom ... of the press" of those publishing companies that must pay the tax as a condition of staying in business. It is a permissible reading of the text, in the one case as in the other, to say that if prohibiting the exercise of religion (or burdening the activity of printing) is not the object of the tax but merely the incidental effect of a generally applicable and otherwise valid provision, the First Amendment has not been offended....

Our decisions reveal that the latter reading is the correct one. We have never held that an individual's religious beliefs excuse him from compliance with an otherwise valid law prohibiting conduct that the State is free to regulate. [*Here Justice Scalia refers to* Reynolds *v.* United States, *98 U.S. 145 (1879), which rejected the claim that criminal laws against polygamy could not be constitutionally applied to those whose religion commanded the practice.*]

... There being no contention that Oregon's drug law represents an attempt to regulate religious beliefs, the communication of religious beliefs, or the raising of one's children in those beliefs, the rule to which we have adhered ever since *Reynolds* plainly controls....

B

Respondents argue that even though exemption from generally applicable criminal laws need not automatically be extended to religiously motivated actors, at least the claim for a religious exemption must be evaluated under the balancing test set forth in *Sherbert* v. *Verner,* 374 U.S. 398 (1963). Under the *Sherbert* test, governmental actions that substantially burden a religious practice must be justified by a compelling governmental interest.... Applying that test we have, on three occasions, invalidated state unemployment compensation rules that conditioned the availability of benefits upon an applicant's willingness to work under conditions forbidden by his religion.... We have never invalidated any governmental action on the basis of the *Sherbert* test except the denial of unemployment compensation.... In recent years we have abstained from applying the *Sherbert* test (outside the unemployment compensation field) at all. [*Scalia cites* Bowen v. Roy, *476 U.S. 693 (1986),* Lyng v. Northwest Indian Cemetery Protective Assn., *485 U.S. 439 (1988),* Goldman v. Weinberger, *475 U.S. 503 (1986), and* O'Lone v. Estate of Shabazz, *482 U.S. 342 (1987).*]

Even if we were inclined to breathe into *Sherbert* some life beyond the unemployment compensation

field, we would not apply it to require exemptions from a generally applicable criminal law....

The "compelling governmental interest" requirement seems benign, because it is familiar from other fields [*such as race and speech*]. What it produces in those other fields — equality of treatment, and an unrestricted flow of contending speech — are constitutional norms; what it would produce here — a private right to ignore generally applicable laws — is a constitutional anomaly.

Nor is it possible to limit the impact of respondents' proposal by requiring a "compelling state interest" only when the conduct prohibited is "central" to the individual's religion. Cf. *Lyng* v. *Northwest Indian Cemetery Protective Assn.,* 485 U.S., at 474–476 (BRENNAN, J., dissenting). It is no more appropriate for judges to determine the "centrality" of religious beliefs before applying a "compelling interest" test in the free exercise field, than it would be for them to determine the "importance" of ideas before applying the "compelling interest" test in the free speech field....

Because respondents' ingestion of peyote was prohibited under Oregon law, and because that prohibition is constitutional, Oregon may, consistent with the Free Exercise Clause, deny respondents unemployment compensation when their dismissal results from use of the drug. The decision of the Oregon Supreme Court is accordingly reversed.

It is so ordered.

JUSTICE O'CONNOR, with whom JUSTICE BRENNAN, JUSTICE MARSHALL, and JUSTICE BLACKMUN join as to Parts I and II, concurring in the judgment....

[*O'Connor concludes that Oregon has a compelling interest in prohibiting the possession of peyote by its citizens and that granting a selective exemption for Native Americans "would seriously impair" Oregon's compelling interest.*]

JUSTICE BLACKMUN, with whom JUSTICE BRENNAN and JUSTICE MARSHALL join, dissenting....

The State proclaims an interest in protecting the health and safety of its citizens from the dangers of unlawful drugs. It offers, however, no evidence that the religious use of peyote has ever harmed anyone....

The State also seeks to support its refusal to make an exception for religious use of peyote by invoking its interest in abolishing drug trafficking. There is, however, practically no illegal traffic in peyote....

Congress Reacts to *Smith*

In response to *Employment Division* v. *Smith* (1990), members of Congress introduced the Religious Freedom Restoration Act (RFRA) to give greater protection to religious liberty than afforded by the Supreme Court. In 1993, Congress passed the bill. Excerpts of the floor debate in the House of Representatives, demonstrating that the "majoritarian" branch of Congress can often be more sensitive and protective of minority rights than the Court, are included below. Source: 139 Cong. Rec. 9680–82 (1993).

Mr. [*Jack*] BROOKS [*chairman of the House Judiciary Committee*]....

Mr. Speaker, H.R. 1308, the Religious Freedom Restoration Act of 1993, reflects a commitment to one of our most cherished freedoms—the right to practice one's faith without undue interference at the hands of the Government. It will restore the standard for addressing claims under the free exercise clause of the first amendment as it was prior to the Supreme Court's Smith decision in 1990. Under longstanding constitutional principles, any governmental burden on the free exercise of religion was subject to the strictest test of constitutional scrutiny. In order to satisfy the free exercise clause, Government had to demonstrate that it had a compelling State interest in burdening the free exercise of religion and that it used the least restrictive means of furthering that interest.

In Smith, the Supreme Court abandoned the compelling State interest test in favor of a much weaker standard of review. H.R. 1308 statutorily reinstates the strict test that was in place prior to Smith.

The Supreme Court's decision 3 years ago transformed a most hallowed liberty into a mundane concept with little more status than a fishing license—thus subjecting religious freedom to the whims of Government officials. That, indeed, has been the sorry legacy of the Court's view of this matter. Passage of this legislation is the only means to restore substance to the constitutional guarantee of religious freedom.

... I want to note the unprecedented coalition of religious denominations and civil rights groups who have united to stand up for the liberty given meaning by this bill. I am proud of how such marvelous diversity was united by a shared view of the place and role of religion in our society. I urge the approval of this legislation....

Mr. [*Hamilton*] FISH. Mr. Speaker, the ability of men and women of faith to freely practice their religion as guaranteed by the first amendment was seriously threatened by the 1990 decision of the U.S. Supreme Court in Employment Services Division versus Smith. In response to the Smith decision, a broad and unprecedented coalition of religious groups including the American Jewish Congress, the Church of Jesus Christ of Latter-day Saints, the Christian Life Commission of the Southern Baptist Convention, and the National Council of Churches have come together to support enactment of the Religious Freedom Restoration Act....

Since Smith was decided in 1990, individuals seeking to practice their religion, unhampered by Government action, have largely been without recourse. The Religious Freedom Restoration Act will provide them with a means to challenge Government regulations which unnecessarily burden the free exercise of religion....

Mr. [*Don*] EDWARDS of California....

This is a very, very important bill. People say, "Well, why is it so important?"

Let me just point out things that have happened that violate religious freedom, since the 1990 Smith decision.

Autopsies have been unnecessarily and wrongly performed upon the Hmong and Jewish deceased in violation of strong religious feelings that autopsies should not be performed.

For example, the Amish in Minnesota. It is an important part of their religious freedom that their buggies—we have seen them, Mr. Speaker, the buggies of the Amish, driving along the country roads—be very plain. That has religious significance to the Amish.

And yet the State of Minnesota, I believe, or maybe it was the local ordinance, required the Amish to put a light on the buggies, a fluorescent light, in violation of the religious freedom of the Amish people. And they had to finally seek State help, the State constitution, to rescue them from this violation.

And so here is another case. I think it is important to see the examples of why this bill is needed. A Federal investigator was fired because it was against his religion to do a certain investigation of a pacifist group....

Mr. [*Henry*] HYDE....

A major issue of contention in the 102d Congress was whether the bill was a true restoration of the law as it existed prior to Smith or whether it sought to impose a more stringent statutory standard. Of course, the label restoration is inappropriate in this context since the Congress writes laws—it does not and cannot overrule the Supreme Court's interpretation of the Constitution. [*What prevents Congress, by statute, from protecting religious liberties left unprotected by the Court? Justice Scalia's decision in* Smith *invited legislative action. Throughout history Congress has engaged in constitutional interpretation, often reaching decisions in opposition to court rulings.*]

Boerne v. Flores

521 U.S. 507 (1997)

Local zoning authorities in Boerne, Texas, denied a Catholic Archbishop a building permit to enlarge a church subject to an ordinance governing historic preservation. P. F. Flores, the Archbishop, brought this suit to challenge the ordinance under the Religious Freedom Restoration Act (RFRA). A district court held that Congress had exceeded the scope of its enforcement power under Section 5 of the Fourteenth Amendment, but that decision was reversed by the Fifth Circuit, which found RFRA to be constitutional.

JUSTICE KENNEDY delivered the opinion of the Court.

... The case calls into question the authority of Congress to enact RFRA. We conclude the statute exceeds Congress' power....

II

[*Kennedy reviews the ruling in* Employment Division v. Smith *(1990) and the decision by Congress to enact RFRA in response to* Smith.]

III
A

Under our Constitution, the Federal Government is one of enumerated powers. *M'Culloch v. Maryland,* 4 Wheat. 316, 405 (1819).... The judicial authority to determine the constitutionality of laws, in cases and controversies, is based on the premise that the "powers of the legislature are defined and limited; and that those limits may not be mistaken, or forgotten, the constitution is written." *Marbury v. Madison,* 1 Cranch 137, 176 (1803).

Congress relied on its Fourteenth Amendment enforcement power in enacting the most far reaching and substantial of RFRA's provisions, ... The Fourteenth Amendment provides, in relevant part:

"Section 1.... No State shall make or enforce any law which shall abridge the privileges or immunities of citizens of the United States; nor shall any State deprive any person of life, liberty, or property, without due process of law; nor deny to any person within its jurisdiction the equal protection of the laws.

. . .

"Section 5. The Congress shall have power to en-force, by appropriate legislation, the provisions of this article."

The parties disagree over whether RFRA is a proper exercise of Congress' § 5 power "to enforce" by "appropriate legislation" the constitutional guarantee that no State shall deprive any person of "life, liberty, or property, without due process of law" nor deny any person "equal protection of the laws."...

Congress' power under § 5, however, extends only to "enforc[ing]" the provisions of the Fourteenth Amendment. The Court has described this power as "remedial," *South Carolina v. Katzenbach, supra,* at 326. The design of the Amendment and the text of § 5 are inconsistent with the suggestion that Congress has the power to decree the substance of the Fourteenth Amendment's restrictions on the States. Legislation which alters the meaning of the Free Exercise Clause cannot be said to be enforcing the Clause. Congress does not enforce a constitutional right by changing what the right is. It has been given the power "to enforce," not the power to determine what constitutes a constitutional violation. Were it not so, what Congress would be enforcing would no longer be, in any meaningful sense, the "provisions of [the Fourteenth Amendment]."

While the line between measures that remedy or prevent unconstitutional actions and measures that make a substantive change in the governing law is not easy to discern, and Congress must have wide latitude in determining where it lies, the distinction exists and must be observed. There must be a congruence and proportionality between the injury to be prevented or remedied and the means adopted to that end....

1

The Fourteenth Amendment's history confirms the remedial, rather than substantive, nature of the Enforcement Clause. [*Here Kennedy reviews the work of the Joint Committee on Reconstruction, which drafted what would become the Fourteenth Amendment in January 1866. Floor debate criticized the draft for giving Congress the power to intrude into traditional areas of state sovereignty. The House voted to table the proposal. The Joint Committee drafted new language. Instead of the original language, giving Congress the power "to make all laws which shall be necessary and proper to secure to the citizens of each State all privileges and immunities of citizens in the several States, and to all persons in the several States equal protection in the rights of life, liberty, and property," the revised text provided that Congress "shall have power to enforce, by appropriate legislation, the provisions of this article." According to Kennedy, Congress' power "was no longer plenary but remedial." In the words of a study by Horace E. Flack,* The Adoption of the Fourteenth Amendment *(1908), the early draft gave "Congress, and not the courts, [the power] to judge whether or not any of the privileges or immunities were not secured to citizens in the several States."*]

2

The remedial and preventive nature of Congress' enforcement power, and the limitation inherent in the power, were confirmed in our earliest cases on the Fourteenth Amendment. In the *Civil Rights Cases,* 109 U.S. 3 (1883), the Court invalidated sections of the Civil Rights Act of 1875 which prescribed criminal penalties for denying to any person "the full enjoyment of" public accommodations and conveyances, on the grounds that it exceeded Congress' power by seeking to regulate private conduct....

[*Kennedy proceeds to analyze such cases as* South Carolina v. Katzenbach *to explain the remedial nature of Section 5 in dealing with racial discrimination. In such cases Congress had before it a historical record of discriminatory treatment of racial minorities.*]

3

. . .

If Congress could define its own powers by altering the Fourteenth Amendment's meaning, no longer would the Constitution be "superior paramount law, unchangeable by ordinary means." it would be "on a level with ordinary legislative acts, and, like other acts, ... alterable when the legislature shall please to alter it." *Marbury v. Madison,* 1 Cranch, at 177. Under this approach, it is difficult to conceive of a principle that would limit congressional power.... Shifting legislative majorities could change the Constitution and effectively circumvent the difficult and detailed amendment process contained in Article V....

B

Respondent contends that RFRA is a proper exercise of Congress' remedial or preventive power....

While preventive rules are sometimes appropriate remedial measures, there must be a congruence between the means used and the ends to be achieved....

A comparison between RFRA and the Voting Rights Act is instructive. In contrast to the record which confronted Congress and the judiciary in the voting rights cases, RFRA's legislative record lacks examples of modern instances of generally applicable laws passed because of religious bigotry. The history of persecution in the country detailed in the hearings mentions no episodes occurring in the past 40 years....

Regardless of the state of the legislative record, RFRA cannot be considered remedial, preventive legislation, if those terms are to have any meaning. RFRA is so out of proportion to a supposed remedial or preventive object that it cannot be understood as responsive to, or designed to prevent, unconstitutional behavior. It appears, instead, to attempt a substantive change in constitutional protections....

Our national experience teaches that the Constitution is preserved best when each part of the government respects both the Constitution and the proper actions and determinations of the other branches. When the Court has interpreted the Constitution, it has acted within the province of the Judicial Branch, which embraces the duty to say what the law is. *Marbury v. Madison,* 1 Cranch, at 177. When the political branches of the Government act against the background of a judicial interpretation of the Constitution already issued, it must be understood that in later cases and controversies the Court will treat its precedents with the respect due them under settled principles, including *stare decisis,* and contrary expectations must be disappointed. RFRA was designed to control cases and controversies, such as the one before us; but as the provisions of the federal statute here invoked are beyond congressional authority, it is this Court's precedent, not RFRA, which must control....

... The judgment of the Court of Appeals sustaining the Act's constitutionality is reversed.

It is so ordered

JUSTICE STEVENS, concurring.

JUSTICE SCALIA, with whom JUSTICE STEVENS joins, concurring in part....

JUSTICE O'CONNOR, with whom JUSTICE BREYER joins except as to a portion of Part I, dissenting....

... As the Court's careful and thorough historical analysis shows, Congress lacks the "power to decree the *substance* of the Fourteenth Amendment's restrictions on the States." ... (emphasis added)....

JUSTICE SOUTER, dissenting.

To decide whether the Fourteenth Amendment gives Congress sufficient power to enact the Religious Freedom Restoration Act, the Court measures the legislation against the free-exercise standard of *Employment Div., Dept. of Human Resources of Oregon v. Smith,* ... I have serious doubts about the precedential value of the *Smith* rule and its entitlement to adherence....

JUSTICE BREYER, dissenting.

I agree ... that the Court should direct the parties to brief the question whether *Employment Div., Dept. of Human Resources of Oregon v. Smith,* ... was correctly decided, and set this case for reargument....

D. FINANCIAL ASSISTANCE TO SECTARIAN SCHOOLS

Before the *Everson* case of 1947, litigation on sectarian schools was limited to such questions as their right to exist. Pierce v. Society of Sisters, 268 U.S. 510 (1925). Other cases dealt with the liberty of private schools to teach certain subjects, such as German. Meyer v. Nebraska, 262 U.S. 390 (1923). Financial aid became an issue when Louisiana used public funds to supply school books to children in private schools, including sectarian schools. A unanimous Supreme Court sustained this legislation on the ground that the books were not religious (they were the same books used by public school students) and that the books benefited children and the state, not the religious schools. The state's interest in education, said the Court, justified the assistance. Cochran v. Board of Education, 281 U.S. 370 (1930). This "child-benefit" theory became the basis for upholding other forms of state assistance to sectarian schools. In time, the Court came to recognize that this theory opened the door to almost unlimited public funding of religious schools.

Transportation, Textbooks, and Tax Exemptions

In 1947, a sharply divided Supreme Court upheld a New Jersey statute that reimbursed parents for the cost of sending their children to parochial schools on public buses. The 5–4 decision also declared that the Establishment Clause was applicable to the states, just as *Cantwell* in 1940 had applied the Free Exercise Clause to the states. Justice Black's opinion for the Court made unrealistic claims about separating church and state. He said neither a state nor the federal government "can pass laws which aid one religion, aid all religions, or prefer one religion over another." EVERSON v. BOARD OF EDUCATION, 330 U.S. 1, 15. Yet *Cochran* had supported the purchase of school books for religious schools, and the New Jersey statute aided parochial schools by reimbursing transportation costs. Congress has passed laws to assist particular religions, such as the social security exemption for the Amish. Black also asserted: "No tax in any amount, large or small, can be levied to support any religious activities or institutions...." In fact, taxpayer funds were used to provide transportation to religious institutions. Finally, Black claimed that neither a state nor the federal government "can, openly or secretly, participate in the affairs of any religious organizations or groups and *vice versa*." That, too, was incorrect. Government may establish health, safety, and curricula standards for sectarian schools, and religious organizations may lobby legislatures, the courts, and the agencies. Justice Douglas, who joined with Black, later admitted doubts about *Everson.* Engel v. Vitale, 370 U.S. 421, 443 (1962); Walz v. Tax Commission, 397 U.S. 664, 703 (1970).

The next step in supporting financial assistance to sectarian schools came in 1968. A New York law required textbooks to be "lent" free of charge to all students in grades 7 through 12, including children attending private and sectarian schools. A 6–3 decision by the Court held that the statute was constitutional because the benefit was to parents and children, not to schools. Board of Education v. Allen, 392 U.S. 236 (1968). The child-benefit theory would look less appealing five years later when the Court struck down a Mississippi law that authorized the lending of books to all-white, nonsectarian private schools. The state argued that the statute benefitted children, not schools. The Court dismissed this effort as a way to rationalize state assistance to segregated schools. Norwood v. Harrison, 413 U.S. 455 (1973).

Interestingly, the opinion for the Court in *Allen* defended the textbook assistance partly on the basis of *Everson,* and yet Black, the author of *Everson,* dissented along with Douglas and Fortas. Black now realized what he had invited with his child-benefit theory in the transportation case: "It requires no prophet to foresee that on the argument used to support this law others could be upheld providing for state or federal government funds to buy property on which to erect religious school buildings or to erect the buildings themselves, to pay the salaries of the religious school teachers, and finally to have the sectarian religious groups cease to rely on voluntary contributions of members of their sects while waiting for the Government to pick up all the bills for the religious schools." 392 U.S. at 253. A number of state courts, interpreting highly specific and restrictive language in their constitutions, refused to uphold transportation and textbook assistance to sectarian schools. They specifically rejected the child-benefit theory embraced by the Supreme Court (see box on next page).

In 1970, the Court upheld tax exemptions to religious organizations for properties used solely for religious worship. The Court decided 8–1 that the exemption was not aimed at establishing, sponsoring, or supporting religion; tax exemption created only a minimal and remote involvement between church and state; and government involvement would be far greater with taxation. Apparently decisive for the Court was the persistence of tax exemptions to religious bodies for almost two centuries. Walz v. Tax Commission, 397 U.S. 664, 677 (1970). The thrust of *Walz* was limited in 1989 when the Court struck down as a violation of the Establishment Clause a Texas law that exempted religious publications from sales taxes. The meaning of this decision was diluted by several concurring opinions. Texas Monthly, Inc. v. Bullock, 489 U.S. 1 (1989). Two years earlier the Court had held that tax systems may not be used to discriminate or suppress. Arkansas Writers' Project, Inc. v. Ragland, 481 U.S. 221 (1987).

Seeking Limits on Assistance

In 1971, the Court attempted to stem the flow of financial assistance to sectarian schools by striking down laws in two states. Pennsylvania had given state funds to nonpublic elementary and secondary schools by reimbursing teachers' salaries, textbooks, and institutional materials in secular subjects. Rhode Island paid teachers in nonpublic elementary schools a supplement of 15 percent of their annual salaries. By a 7–0 vote in the Pennsylvania case and a 7–1 vote in the Rhode Island case, the Court found that those forms of assistance violated the religion clauses. Three tests were developed to determine constitutionality: (1) the statute must have a secular legislative purpose, (2) its principal or primary effect must be one that neither advances nor inhibits religion, and (3) it must not foster excessive entanglement with religion. LEMON v. KURTZMAN, 403 U.S. 602, 612–13 (1971). This three-prong test is frequently waived or ignored by the courts.

On the same day that the Court struck down the Pennsylvania and Rhode Island statutes, it upheld 5 to 4 a congressional statute that provided construction grants for church-related colleges and universities. The money was spent for buildings that had a nonreligious purpose: libraries; a science building; a language laboratory; and a music, drama, and arts building. The Court decided there was less religious indoctrination in colleges than in elementary and secondary schools, where student minds are more impressionable. It ruled, however, that the congressional provision allowing the re-

The States Limit Assistance

A number of states have refused to accept decisions by the U.S. Supreme Court upholding public assistance to sectarian schools (transportation in *Everson v. Board of Education* and textbooks in *Board of Education v. Allen*). State constitutions are frequently quite specific in prohibiting the appropriation of public funds for any religious worship or instruction. The Alaska Supreme Court dismissed the U.S. Supreme Court's decision in *Everson* as "unpersuasive." Matthews v. Quinton, 362 P.2d 932, 936 (Alas. 1961). Many state courts rejected the doctrinal basis for upholding public assistance to sectarian schools: the "child-benefit" theory. The California Supreme Court said that in most instances this theory "leads to results which are logically indefensible." California Teachers Ass'n v. Riles, 632 P.2d 953, 962 (Cal. 1981). Other state courts, despite restrictive language in their constitutions, have upheld transportation and textbooks for sectarian schools. The following states have invalidated such assistance:

Alaska	Matthews v. Quinton, 362 P.2d 932 (1961), cert. denied, 368 U.S. 517 (1962) (transportation).
California	California Teachers Ass'n v. Riles, 632 P.2d 953 (1981) (textbooks).
Delaware	Opinion of the Justices, 216 A.2d 668 (1966) (transportation).
Hawaii	Spears v. Honda, 449 P.2d 130 (1969) (transportation).
Idaho	Epeldi v. Engelking, 488 P.2d 860 (1971), cert. denied, 406 U.S. 957 (1972) (transportation).
Kentucky	Fannin v. Williams, 655 S.W.2d 480 (1983) (textbooks); Fiscal Court of Jefferson City v. Brady, 885 S.W.2d 681 (1994) (transportation).
Massachusetts	Bloom v. School Committee of Springfield, 379 N.E.2d 578 (1978) (textbooks).
Michigan	In re Advisory Op. re Const. of 1974 PA 242, 228 N.W.2d 772 (1975) (textbooks).
Missouri	McVey v. Hawkins, 258 S.W.2d 927 (1953) (transportation); Paster v. Tussey, 512 S.W.2d 97 (1974), cert. denied sub nom. Reynolds v. Paster, 419 U.S. 1111 (1975) (textbooks).
Nebraska	Gaffney v. State Department of Education, 220 N.W.2d 550 (1974) (textbooks).
Oklahoma	Board of Education for Ind. Sch. Dist. No. 52 v. Antone, 384 P.2d 911 (1963); Gurney v. Ferguson, 122 P.2d 1002 (1941), cert. denied, 317 U.S. 588 (1942), rehearing denied, 317 U.S. 707 (1942) (transportation).
Oregon	Dickman v. School District No. 62C, 366 P.2d 533 (1961), cert. denied, 371 U.S. 823 (1962) (textbooks).
South Dakota	McDonald v. School Bd. of Yankton, Etc., 246 N.W.2d 93 (1976) (textbooks).
Washington	Visser v. Nooksack Valley School Dist. No. 506, 207 P.2d 198 (1949) (transportation).
Wisconsin	State v. Nusbaum, 115 N.W.2d 761 (1962); State v. Milquet, 192 N.W. 392 (1923) (transportation).

ligious use of these buildings after 20 years constituted a violation of the religion clauses. Tilton v. Richardson, 403 U.S. 672, 683–84 (1971).

New forms of financial assistance to sectarian schools appeared. New York appropriated $28 million to reimburse nonpublic schools for expenses related to examinations, record keeping, and reports mandated by the state. The Court held that this aid contravened the Establishment Clause. There was no audit to determine whether state payments exceeded costs by the schools, nor any evaluation to see whether the tests were free of religious instruction. The schools had argued that the state should be permitted to pay for any activity mandated by state law or regulation, but the Court rejected this theory because it could require state payments for minimum lighting or sanitary facilities for all school buildings. Levitt v. Committee for Public Education, 413 U.S. 472, 481 (1973). A later effort by New York to reimburse nonpublic schools for expenses incurred before the Court's decision was declared unconstitutional. New York v. Cathedral Academy, 434 U.S. 125 (1977).

A case in 1973 concerned a South Carolina statute that authorized revenue bonds to benefit a Baptist-controlled college. Using *Lemon*'s three-part test, the Court held 6–3 that the statute had a secular purpose (benefiting higher education), its primary effect did not advance or inhibit religion, and there was no excessive entanglement with religion. *Tilton* was cited to support state assistance to schools at the university level. The Court found that the Baptist college had no significant religious orientation. The three dissenters viewed the state as deeply involved in the fiscal affairs of the college, even to the extent of fixing tuition rates as part of the state's duty to assure sufficient revenues to meet bond and interest obligations. Hunt v. McNair, 413 U.S. 734, 753 (1973).

Tuition Assistance

A New York statute provided direct money grants to qualifying nonpublic schools. The money was used to maintain and repair facilities and equipment, to reimburse low-income parents who sent their children to nonpublic elementary and secondary schools, and to provide tax relief for parents failing to qualify for tuition reimbursement. The Supreme Court held that all three forms of assistance violated the Establishment Clause, even if the tuition grants went to the parents rather than directly to the schools. All of the Justices agreed that the maintenance and repair provision was unconstitutional. Chief Justice Burger and Justices White and Rehnquist would have upheld the reimbursement and tax relief provisions. Committee for Public Education v. Nyquist, 413 U.S. 756 (1973).

The Court tried to explain why tax exemptions were permissible in *Walz* (they were "indirect and incidental") while the tax credits at stake in the New York statutes were unconstitutional. The decisive element was that the granting of new tax benefits, in contrast to the extension of tax exemptions, "would tend to increase rather than limit the involvement between Church and State." The Court had to weigh the "potentially divisive political effect of an aid program." Support for maintenance and repair and the grants for tuition would require appropriations each year, opening the door to continuing strife between church and state. Id. at 793–97.

In short, the Court had to make a political judgment about the level of tension and confrontation likely to result from government assistance to sectarian schools. It was for this reason that it also struck down a Pennsylvania statute that reimbursed parents for a portion of tuition expenses incurred in sending their children to nonpublic schools. More than 90 percent of the nonpublic schools were sectarian. The Court rejected the contention that tuition assistance went to parents rather than to schools. Sloan v. Lemon, 413 U.S. 825 (1973).

Vouchers

Waiting in the wings was another constitutional issue. May government provide parents with vouchers to subsidize their children's education at private and sectarian schools? State and federal courts handed down a number of decisions, some upholding vouchers, others striking them down.

Congress considered several amendments in 2001 to authorize school vouchers. The House voted 273 to 155 against an amendment that would have given students who attended unsafe or failing public schools a $1,500 voucher for private school tuition. By a vote of 241 to 186, it defeated a pilot voucher program for five schools. 147 Cong. Rec. 9247-54, 9259 (2001). The Senate, voting 58 to 41, rejected a proposal to allow private school vouchers for low-income students. 147 Cong. Rec. 10400-29 (2001).

In 2002, a 5–4 Supreme Court upheld a Cleveland voucher plan that permits the use of public money for religious school tuition. ZELMAN v. SIMMONS-HARRIS, 536 U.S. 639 (2002). Although the decision removed one of the constitutional arguments against vouchers for sectarian schools, state courts may still invalidate the use of vouchers as contrary to the state constitution. Six weeks after the Court's decision, a state judge in Tallahassee ruled that Florida's school voucher program was impermissible under the Florida Constitution, which was "clear and unambiguous" in barring the use of public money for sectarian education. On August 16, 2004, the Florida District Court of Appeal also found the school voucher program a violation of the state constitution (*Bush* v. *Holmes*). Most state constitutions have similarly restrictive language. Proponents of vouchers have gone to court to challenge some of these provisions in state constitutions.

"Lending" Textbooks and School Equipment

Other decisions involving financial assistance to sectarian schools split the Court 6–3 or 5–4. Lengthy concurrences made it difficult to chart the positions of individual Justices. A 1975 decision responded to a Pennsylvania statute that authorized "auxiliary services" and textbook loans to all children enrolled in nonpublic elementary and secondary schools. The state could loan instructional materials and equipment. Auxiliary services included counseling, testing, psychological services, and speech and hearing therapy; instructional materials included periodicals, photographs, maps, charts, recordings, and films; instructional equipment embraced such items as projectors, recorders, and laboratory paraphernalia. A 6–3 Court, made more complex by Justices concurring in part and dissenting in part, held that everything but textbook loans violated the Establishment Clause. The Court continued to believe that textbook loans benefitted parents and children, not schools. Meek v. Pittenger, 421 U.S. 349, 361 (1975). To the extent that *Meek* assumed that placing public employees on parochial school grounds inevitably results in state-sponsored indoctrination or constitutes a symbolic union between government and religion, it was overruled by Agostini v. Felton, 521 U.S. 203, 223 (1997).

Would it have made a constitutional difference if instructional materials and equipment had been "lent" to parents and children rather than to schools? Justice Brennan, joined by Justices Douglas and Marshall, said it was "pure fantasy" in *Meek* to treat the textbook program as a loan to students: "The whole business is handled by the school and public authorities and neither parents nor children have a say. The guidelines make crystal clear that the nonpublic school, not its pupils, is the motivating force behind the textbook loan, and that virtually the entire loan transaction is to be, and is in fact, conducted between officials of the nonpublic school, on the one hand, and officers of the State on the other."

A year later the Court, divided 5–4, upheld a Maryland grant of state funds to colleges and universities that refrained from awarding "only seminarian or theological degrees." Funds could not be used for sectarian purposes. The four colleges were affiliated with the Roman Catholic Church. The federal district court had found that the religious colleges were not "pervasively sectarian" or substantially involved in indoctrination. In one of the dissents, Justice Stevens expressed concern about "the pernicious tendency of a state subsidy to tempt religious schools to compromise their religious mission without wholly abandoning it." Roemer v. Maryland Public Works Bd., 426 U.S. 736, 775 (1976).

Ohio authorized various forms of aid to nonpublic schools, most of which were sectarian. Splitting in various directions, the Court upheld the provisions extending assistance for secular textbooks, standardized testing and scoring, diagnostic services, and therapeutic and remedial services. It struck down the portions of the law relating to instructional materials, instructional equipment, and providing transportation and services for field trips. The state statute "loaned" the instructional materials and equipment to the pupils or their parents, but the Court dismissed this mechanism as a patent effort to exploit the *Meek* holding. Parents and students were being used as a conduit to funnel assistance to the schools. Wolman v. Walter, 433 U.S. 229, 250 (1977). Justice Marshall, who had voted with the majority in *Allen* to uphold textbook loans, now announced that it should be overruled and a new line drawn between church and state.

Reimbursements

In 1980, the Supreme Court reviewed a New York law similar to the payment system declared unconstitutional in *Levitt* in 1973. The law directed payment to nonpublic schools for their costs in complying with certain state-mandated requirements, including testing, reporting, and recordkeeping. The new law provided for state auditing to assure that public funds would be used only for secular purposes (a safeguard absent from the law struck down in *Levitt*). A 5–4 decision held that the statute did not violate the Establishment Clause. Blackmun's dissent, joined by Brennan and Marshall, pointed out that the "state-mandated" requirements would have been performed by the schools, with or without reimbursement. Stevens, also dissenting, said the Court's rationale could be used to justify state subsidies for fire drills or the construction and maintenance of fireproof classrooms. He advised that "the entire enterprise of trying to justify various types of subsidies to nonpublic schools should be abandoned." Committee for Public Education v. Regan, 444 U.S. 646, 671 (1980).

A Parade of 5–4 Decisions

Two decisions in 1985 underscore the profound disagreements within the Court on public assistance to sectarian schools. One decision, with Justices divided 5–4, held invalid a New York program that used federal funds to pay the salaries of public school employees who taught in parochial schools. Although the state monitored the content of federally funded classes to avoid the advancement of religion (part of the *Lemon* test), the Court held that this very involvement produced excessive entanglement of church and state. Aguilar v. Felton, 473 U.S. 402 (1985). Twelve years later the Court (again divided 5 to 4) decided that *Aguilar* erred in concluding that New York City's program resulted in an excessive entanglement between church and state. In the years following *Aguilar,* the parties affected by that decision told the Court that the 1985 ruling could not be squared with subsequent changes to Establishment Clause jurisprudence. In 1997, the Court agreed that *Aguilar* was no longer good law and reversed it. Agostini v. Felton, 521 U.S. 203 (1997).

Why did the Court reverse itself between 1985 and 1997? The switch is explained partly by changing composition. Of the five Justices in the *Aguilar* majority, only Stevens remained on the Court in 1997. Joining him on the dissenting side in 1997 were three newcomers: Souter, Ginsburg, and Breyer. Of the four dissenters in 1985, two remained to decide *Agostini*: Rehnquist and O'Connor. They formed a majority by combining with three new members of the Court: Scalia, Kennedy, and Thomas.

But it was more than a change in composition. From the start, *Aguilar* never made much sense. By prohibiting public school teachers from entering parochial schools, the Court created the need for mobile classrooms, other "neutral sites," and a reliance on computer and telecommunications technologies, all of which were more costly. Starting in 1988, Congress appropriated "capital expenses" to finance this alternative instruction. Instead of limiting public assistance to parochial schools, *Aguilar* led to greater expenditures. *Agostini* again raises questions about the utility of the three-prong *Lemon* test (see box on next page).

Another decision from 1985 involved a complicated Michigan program that used public funds to teach nonpublic school students in classrooms located in and leased from nonpublic schools. A "shared time" program offered secular classes during the regular school day. The teachers were full-time employees of the public schools, but a "significant portion" had previously taught in nonpublic schools. A second program, called "community education," was voluntary and offered secular classes after school. These teachers were part-time public school employees generally employed in the nonpublic schools in which the classes were held. Most of the nonpublic schools were sectarian religious schools. A 5–4 decision held that both programs had the primary effect of advancing religion. Grand

Problems with the *Lemon* Test

In Lemon v. Kurtzman, 403 U.S. 602, 612–13 (1971), the Court established a three-prong test for determining church-state issues, especially the Establishment Clause: (1) the statute must have a secular legislative purpose, (2) its principal or primary effect must be one that neither advances nor inhibits religion, and (3) it must not foster excessive entanglement with religion.

On some church-state issues, such as the use of chaplains by legislative bodies, the Court would have had to strike down the practice had it followed *Lemon*. Instead, the Court simply ignored the three-part test and relied on historical precedents to uphold the use of chaplains in legislatures. Marsh v. Chambers, 463 U.S. 783 (1983).

In a dissent in 1985, Justice Rehnquist pointed to problems with the first and third prongs. The secular purpose test "has proved mercurial in application" in part because it depends upon what legislators put in the legislative history and what they leave out. That is, legislative purpose can be easily manipulated to hide intentions. The entanglement test, he said, can create an "insoluble paradox" because the Court requires that aid to parochial schools be closely watched so that it is not put to sectarian use, and yet the very effort to supervise might create an entanglement issue. Wallace v. Jaffree, 472 U.S. 38, 108–09. Justice O'Connor has also questioned the utility of the entanglement test. Aguilar v. Felton, 473 U.S. 402, 422 (1983).

In upholding public aid to sectarian schools in 1997, the Court submerged the entanglement test into the primary effect test. Instead of separate guidelines, the two tests were combined. Agostini v. Felton, 521 U.S. 203, 232–33 (1997).

In recent decisions, the Court has resolved a number of Establishment Clause cases with little or no reference to the *Lemon* test. Rosenberger v. University of Virginia, 515 U.S. 819 (1995); Capitol Square Review Bd. v. Pinette, 515 U.S. 753 (1995); Board of Education of Kiryas Joel v. Grumet, 512 U.S. 687 (1994); Zobrest v. Catalina Foothills Sch. Dist., 509 U.S. 1 (1993); Lee v. Weisman, 505 U.S. 577 (1992).

Rapids School District v. Ball, 473 U.S. 373 (1985). In deciding *Agostini* in 1997, another 5–4 decision said that it was abandoning the presumption in *Ball* that placing public employees on parochial school grounds inevitably results in state-sponsored indoctrination or constitutes a symbolic union between government and religion. 521 U.S. at 223.

In 2000, the Court was again badly divided on the issue of providing financial assistance to sectarian schools. Six Justices agreed that it was constitutional to provide computers and related instructional materials to religious schools, but two of those Justices objected to the breadth of the opinion written by the other four. Three Justices prepared a lengthy dissent. Mitchell v. Helms, 530 U.S. 793 (2000).

Other Disputes

Federal assistance to sectarian schools may also implicate the Property Clause, which empowers Congress "to dispose of and make all needful Rules and Regulations respecting the Territory or other Property belonging to the United States." Art. IV, § 3, Cl. 2. Pursuant to this Clause, Congress passed a law governing the disposition of surplus federal property and the government transferred a military hospital to a church-related college. An organization favoring church-state separation filed suit on the ground that the transfer violated the Establishment Clause. A 5–4 decision by the Supreme Court held that the organization lacked standing to bring the suit. Moreover, the Court reasoned that the transfer was not pursuant to the Taxing and Spending Clause, under which the parties might have had standing, but under the Property Clause. Relying on a legal fiction, the majority claimed that the source of the complaint was not a congressional action but rather an agency action to transfer a parcel of federal property. Through this rationale the parties were unable to challenge the action under the Establishment Clause. The dissenters accused the majority of engaging in a "dissembling exercise." Valley Forge College v. Americans United, 454 U.S. 464, 493 (1982).

Tax deductions are another source of state assistance to sectarian schools. A Minnesota law allowed taxpayers, in computing their state income tax, to deduct expenses incurred in providing tuition, textbooks, and transportation for their children attending elementary and secondary schools, including schools of a sectarian nature. Another 5–4 decision by the Supreme Court held that the statute did not violate the Establishment Clause. It met the three-part *Lemon* test, even though the law helped fund sectarian textbooks. Mueller v. Allen, 463 U.S. 388 (1983).

In 1986, in a rare unanimous ruling regarding government assistance to sectarian schools, the Court held that state aid under a rehabilitation program to finance an individual's training at a Christian college did not advance religion in a way inconsistent with the Establishment Clause. The assistance was defended on the ground that it went to the student, who then transmitted it to an institution of his or her choice. The majority opinion made no mention of *Mueller,* which four concurring Justices thought should have formed the basis for the decision. Witters v. Wash. Dept. of Services for Blind, 474 U.S. 481 (1986). When the case went back to the state of Washington, the state supreme court reached the opposite conclusion. Looking to the state constitution, which prohibits the use of any public monies for religious instruction, it held that the funds could not go to the student. Witters v. State Com'n for the Blind, 771 P.2d 1119 (Wash. 1989). The kinds of assistance that are permitted to religious institutions and those that are prohibited form a complicated and often incomprehensible pattern (see box on next page).

Building on *Witters,* in 1993 the Court (divided 5–4) ruled that the Establishment Clause does not prevent a public school from providing a sign-language interpreter to a deaf child enrolled in a sectarian high school. Even when a sectarian school receives a financial benefit, the government program is permissible if it neutrally provides benefits to a broad class of citizens defined without reference to religion. Zobrest v. Catalina Foothills School Dist., 509 U.S. 1 (1993). The four dissenters objected that the majority should have returned the case to the lower courts to decide statutory and regulatory questions first before reaching the constitutional issue.

In 2004, the Court ruled that states are not obliged to give students preparing for careers in the clergy the same access to taxpayer-funded college aid available to other students. Voting 7 to 2, the Court upheld Washington state's program that offered cash assistance to academically qualified low-income college students, provided they were not majoring in theology. Locke v. Davey, 540 U.S. 712 (2004). Including Washington, 36 state constitutions contain specific restrictions on public aid to religious education.

In 2012, a unanimous Court held that a Lutheran Church had full authority to fire a school teacher who had fallen ill and was on disability leave. The Court agreed that her status as "minister" gave the church sufficient grounds to fire her and she had no grounds to seek financial compensation through the EEOC. The decision reinforced that a ministerial exception exists for the Religion Clauses. Tabor Evangelical Lutheran Church and School v. EEOC, 565 U.S. ___ (2012).

Faith-Based Initiatives

By executive order, President George W. Bush created a White House office and several centers within federal agencies to ensure that faith-based community groups were eligible to compete for federal financial support. Congress provided no authority for this initiative and did not enact specific appropriations to support it. An organization sued, claiming that the program violated the Establishment Clause. The Supreme Court held that the plaintiffs lacked standing. Hein v. Freedom From Religion Foundation, 551 U.S. 557 (2007). Depending on how the votes are counted, the decision was either 5 to 4 or 3–2–4. Two concurring Justices (Scalia and Thomas) referred to the three writing for the Court as "the plurality." Oddly, the Court decided that a plaintiff could get standing only if the injury came from a statute passed by Congress. An unauthorized presidential initiative could not be chal-

Court Decisions Involving Financial Assistance to Sectarian Schools

Assistance Sustained

Transportation. Everson v. Board of Education, 330 U.S. 1 (1947).

Textbooks. Board of Education v. Allen, 392 U.S. 236 (1968).

Tax exemptions. Walz v. Tax Commission, 397 U.S. 664 (1970).

Construction grants for colleges. Tilton v. Richardson, 403 U.S. 672 (1971).

Revenue bonds for colleges. Hunt v. McNair, 413 U.S. 734 (1973).

State grants to colleges. Roemer v. Maryland Public Works Bd., 426 U.S. 736 (1976).

Standardized testing and scoring; diagnostic services; therapeutic and remedial services. Wolman v. Walter, 433 U.S. 229 (1977).

Testing, reporting, and record keeping (with state auditing). Committee for Public Education v. Regan, 444 U.S. 646 (1980).

"Surplus" federal property for colleges. Valley Forge College v. Americans United, 454 U.S. 464 (1982).

Tax deductions for expenses incurred in providing tuition, textbooks, and transportation. Mueller v. Allen, 463 U.S. 388 (1983).

State aid under a rehabilitation program used to finance training at a Christian college. Witters v. Wash. Dept. of Services for Blind, 474 U.S. 481 (1986).

Providing sign-language interpreter to a deaf child enrolled in a sectarian high school. Zobrest v. Catalina Foothills School Dist., 509 U.S. 1 (1993).

Salaries for public school employees teaching in parochial schools. Agostini v. Felton, 521 U.S. 203 (1997).

Computers and related instructional materials. Mitchell v. Helms, 530 U.S. 793 (2000).

School vouchers. Zelman v. Simmons-Harris, 536 U.S. 639 (2002).

Assistance Invalidated

Teachers' salaries. Lemon v. Kurtzman, 403 U.S. 602 (1971).

Examinations, record keeping, and reports (without state auditing). Levitt v. Committee for Public Education, 413 U.S. 472 (1973).

Maintenance and repair of facilities and equipment; reimbursements for low-income parents; tax relief for parents not qualifying for tuition reimbursement. Committee for Public Education v. Nyquist, 413 U.S. 756 (1973).

Reimbursements for tuition expenses. Sloan v. Lemon, 413 U.S. 825 (1973).

Counseling, testing, psychological services, and speech and hearing therapy; instructional materials including periodicals, photographs, maps, charts, recordings, and films; instructional equipment including projectors, recorders, and laboratory paraphernalia. Meek v. Pittenger, 421 U.S. 349 (1975). To the extent that *Meek* assumes that placing public employees on parochial school grounds inevitably results in state-sponsored indoctrination or constitutes a symbolic union between government and religion, *Meek* is overruled by Agostini v. Felton, 521 U.S. 203, 223 (1997). *Meek* was also weakened by *Mitchell* v. *Helms*, 530 U.S. 793 (2000).

Instructional materials, instructional equipment, and transportation and services for field trips. Wolman v. Walter, 433 U.S. 229 (1977). *Wolman* was weakened by *Mitchell* v. *Helms*, 530 U.S. 793 (2000).

lenged in court. Justice Souter, writing for the four dissenters, observed: "the controlling opinion closes the door on these taxpayers because the Executive Branch, and not the Legislative Branch, caused their injury. I see no basis for this distinction in either logic or precedent, and respectfully dissent." He said that when executive agencies spend money for religious purposes, "no less than when Congress authorizes the same thing, taxpayers suffer injury."

Flast v. *Cohen* Weakened

Divided 5 to 4, the Court in 2011 substantially limited the reach of *Flast* v. *Cohen*, a 1968 ruling that gave taxpayers standing to challenge government assistance to religious organizations (reading in Chapter 3). Written broadly to apply to all "taxing and spending programs, *Flast* provided an exception to the general rule that denies taxpayers to sue the government. At stake in the 2011 case was not a direct expenditure or appropriation to benefit religion but rather a tax credit. An Arizona law allowed taxpayers to obtain tax credits of up to $500 per person and $1,000 per married couple to contribute to school tuition organizations (STOs). The contributions, amounting to an estimated annual value of $50 million, were used to provide scholarships to students attending both private sectarian and religious schools. Writing for the majority, Justice Kennedy held that *Flast* provided taxpayer standing only for government expenditures, not tax credits.

In the dissent, joined by Justices Ginsburg, Breyer, and Sotomayor, Justice Kagan objected that the "novel distinction in standing law between appropriations and tax expenditures has as little basis in principle as it has in our precedent." Cash grants and targeted tax breaks, she said, provide financial support from the government. The "effective demise" of taxpayer standing for tax credits "will diminish the Establishment Clause's force and meaning." The distinction drawn by the majority "finds no support in case law, and just as little in reason." Previous taxpayer standing cases did not distinguish between appropriations and tax expenditures. For Kagan, the two categories "are readily interchangeable; what is a cash grant today can be a tax break tomorrow." Arizona Christian School Tuition Organization v. Winn, 563 U.S. ___ (2011).

Everson v. Board of Education

330 U.S. 1 (1947)

Acting under a New Jersey statute, the township of Ewing reimbursed parents for money spent in transporting their children to school. Part of the money went to children attending Catholic schools. Arch R. Everson, a taxpayer in the local school district, filed suit challenging the right of the Board of Education of the township to reimburse parents of parochial school students. The New Jersey Supreme Court held the statute unconstitutional, but was reversed by the New Jersey Court of Errors and Appeals.

MR. JUSTICE BLACK delivered the opinion of the Court.

[*Everson charged that the statute and township resolution violated the Due Process Clause of the Fourteenth Amendment by authorizing the state to tax the private property of some and bestow it upon others, to be used for their own private purposes. Black rejects this argument and turns to the question of the Establishment Clause.*]

... The First Amendment ... commands that a state "shall make no law respecting an establishment of religion, or prohibiting the free exercise thereof...." ...

The "establishment of religion" clause of the First Amendment means at least this: Neither a state nor the Federal Government can set up a church. Neither can pass laws which aid one religion, aid all re-

ligions, or prefer one religion over another. Neither can force nor influence a person to go to or to remain away from church against his will or force him to profess a belief or disbelief in any religion. No person can be punished for entertaining or professing religious beliefs or disbeliefs, for church attendance or nonattendance. No tax in any amount, large or small, can be levied to support any religious activities or institutions, whatever they may be called, or whatever form they may adopt to teach or practice religion. Neither a state nor the Federal Government can, openly or secretly, participate in the affairs of any religious organizations or groups and *vice versa*. In the words of Jefferson, the clause against establishment of religion by law was intended to erect "a wall of separation between church and State." *Reynolds* v. *United States, supra* at 164.

... New Jersey cannot consistently with the "establishment of religion" clause of the First Amendment contribute tax-raised funds to the support of an institution which teaches the tenets and faith of any church. On the other hand, other language of the amendment commands that New Jersey cannot hamper its citizens in the free exercise of their own religion.... While we do not mean to intimate that a state could not provide transportation only to children attending public schools, we must be careful, in protecting the citizens of New Jersey against state-established churches, to be sure that we do not inadvertently prohibit New Jersey from extending its general state law benefits to all its citizens without regard to their religious belief.

Measured by these standards, we cannot say that the First Amendment prohibits New Jersey from spending tax-raised funds to pay the bus fares of parochial school pupils as a part of a general program under which it pays the fares of pupils attending public and other schools. It is undoubtedly true that children are helped to get to church schools. There is even a possibility that some of the children might not be sent to the church schools if the parents were compelled to pay their children's bus fares out of their own pockets when transportation to a public school would have been paid for by the State. The same possibility exists where the state requires a local transit company to provide reduced fares to school children including those attending parochial schools, or where a municipally owned transportation system undertakes to carry all school children free of charge. Moreover, state-paid policemen, detailed to protect children going to and from church schools from the very real hazards of traffic, would serve much the same purpose and accomplish much the same result as state provisions intended to guarantee free transportation of a kind which the state deems to be best for the school children's welfare. And parents might refuse to risk their children to the serious danger of traffic accidents going to and from parochial schools, the approaches to which were not protected by policemen. Similarly, parents might be reluctant to permit their children to attend schools which the state had cut off from such general government services as ordinary police and fire protection, connections for sewage disposal, public highways and sidewalks. Of course, cutting off church schools from these services, so separate and so indisputably marked off from the religious function, would make it far more difficult for the schools to operate. But such is obviously not the purpose of the First Amendment. That Amendment requires the state to be a neutral in its relations with groups of religious believers and non-believers; it does not re-

quire the state to be their adversary. State power is no more to be used so as to handicap religions than it is to favor them.

This Court has said that parents may, in the discharge of their duty under state compulsory education laws, send their children to a religious rather than a public school if the school meets the secular educational requirements which the state has power to impose. See *Pierce* v. *Society of Sisters*, 268 U.S. 510. It appears that these parochial schools meet New Jersey's requirements. The State contributes no money to the schools. It does not support them. Its legislation, as applied, does no more than provide a general program to help parents get their children, regardless of their religion, safely and expeditiously to and from accredited schools.

The First Amendment has erected a wall between church and state. That wall must be kept high and impregnable. We could not approve the slightest breach. New Jersey has not breached it here.

Affirmed.

Mr. Justice Jackson, dissenting.

I find myself, contrary to first impressions, unable to join in this decision. I have a sympathy, though it is not ideological, with Catholic citizens who are compelled by law to pay taxes for public schools, and also feel constrained by conscience and discipline to support other schools for their own children. Such relief to them as this case involves is not in itself a serious burden to taxpayers and I had assumed it to be as little serious in principle. Study of this case convinces me otherwise. The Court's opinion marshals every argument in favor of state aid and puts the case in its most favorable light, but much of its reasoning confirms my conclusions that there are no good grounds upon which to support the present legislation. In fact, the undertones of the opinion, advocating complete and uncompromising separation of Church from State, seem utterly discordant with its conclusion yielding support to their commingling in educational matters. The case which irresistibly comes to mind as the most fitting precedent is that of Julia who, according to Byron's reports, "whispering 'I will ne'er consent,'—consented."....

Mr. Justice Frankfurter joins in this opinion.

Mr. Justice Rutledge, with whom Mr. Justice Frankfurter, Mr. Justice Jackson, and Mr. Justice Burton agree, dissenting....

... New Jersey's statute sustained is the first, if indeed it is not the second breach to be made by this

Court's action. That a third, and a fourth, and still others will be attempted, we may be sure. For just as *Cochran* v. *Board of Education,* 281 U.S. 370, has opened the way by oblique ruling [*supplying secular textbooks to religious schools*] for this decision, so will the two make wider the breach for a third. Thus with time the most solid freedom steadily gives way before continuing corrosive decision.

Lemon v. Kurtzman

403 U.S. 602 (1971)

A number of states passed legislation providing financial assistance to church-related elementary and secondary schools, going far beyond the initial support of transportation and textbooks. These state initiatives required the Court to establish guidelines and principles to distinguish permissible from impermissible aid. This case involves legislation enacted by Rhode Island and Pennsylvania. In the lead case, Alton J. Lemon, a citizen and taxpayer of Pennsylvania as well as a parent of a child attending a public school in Pennsylvania, brought suit against David H. Kurtzman, Superintendent of Public Instruction of Pennsylvania. A three-judge federal court held that the Pennsylvania law violated neither the Establishment nor the Free Exercise Clause of the First Amendment.

MR. CHIEF JUSTICE BURGER delivered the opinion of the Court....

Pennsylvania has adopted a statutory program that provides financial support to nonpublic elementary and secondary schools by way of reimbursement for the cost of teachers' salaries, textbooks, and instructional materials in specified secular subjects. Rhode Island has adopted a statute under which the State pays directly to teachers in nonpublic elementary schools a supplement of 15% of their annual salary. Under each statute state aid has been given to church-related educational institutions. We hold that both statutes are unconstitutional.

I
THE RHODE ISLAND STATUTE

The Rhode Island Salary Supplement Act was enacted in 1969. It rests on the legislative finding that the quality of education available in nonpublic elementary schools has been jeopardized by the rapidly rising salaries needed to attract competent and dedicated teachers. The Act authorizes state officials to supplement the salaries of teachers of secular subjects in nonpublic elementary schools by paying directly to a teacher an amount not in excess of 15% of his current annual salary. As supplemented, however, a nonpublic school teacher's salary cannot exceed the maximum paid to teachers in the State's public schools, and the recipient must be certified by the state board of education in substantially the same manner as public school teachers.

In order to be eligible for the Rhode Island salary supplement, the recipient must teach in a nonpublic school at which the average per-pupil expenditure on secular education is less than the average in the State's public schools during a specified period. Appellant State Commissioner of Education also requires eligible schools to submit financial data. If this information indicates a per-pupil expenditure in excess of the statutory limitation, the records of the school in question must be examined in order to assess how much of the expenditure is attributable to secular education and how much to religious activity.

The Act also requires that teachers eligible for salary supplements must teach only those subjects that are offered in the State's public schools. They must use "only teaching materials which are used in the public schools." Finally, any teacher applying for a salary supplement must first agree in writing "not to teach a course in religion for so long as or during such time as he or she receives any salary supplements" under the Act....

A three-judge federal court ... found that Rhode Island's nonpublic elementary schools accommodated approximately 25% of the State's pupils. About 95% of these pupils attended schools affiliated with the Roman Catholic church. To date some 250 teachers have applied for benefits under the Act. All of them are employed by Roman Catholic schools....

THE PENNSYLVANIA STATUTE

Pennsylvania has adopted a program that has some but not all of the features of the Rhode Island program....

The statute authorizes appellee state Superintendent of Public Instruction to "purchase" specified "secular educational services" from nonpublic schools. Under the "contracts" authorized by the statute, the State directly reimburses nonpublic schools solely for their actual expenditures for teachers' salaries, textbooks, and instructional materials. A school seeking reimbursement must maintain prescribed accounting procedures that identify the "separate" cost of the "secular educational service." These accounts are subject to state audit....

There are several significant statutory restrictions on state aid. Reimbursement is limited to courses "presented in the curricula of the public schools." It is further limited "solely" to courses in the following "secular" subjects: mathematics, modern foreign languages, physical science, and physical education. Textbooks and instructional materials included in the program must be approved by the state Superintendent of Public Instruction. Finally, the statute prohibits reimbursement for any course that contains "any subject matter expressing religious teaching, or the morals or forms of worship of any sect."

... The State has now entered into contracts with some 1,181 nonpublic elementary and secondary schools with a student population of some 535,215 pupils—more than 20% of the total number of students in the State. More than 96% of these pupils attend church-related schools, and most of these schools are affiliated with the Roman Catholic church.

[II]

Every analysis in this area must begin with consideration of the cumulative criteria developed by the Court over many years. Three such tests may be gleaned from our cases. First, the statute must have a secular legislative purpose; second, its principal or primary effect must be one that neither advances nor inhibits religion, *Board of Education* v. *Allen,* 392 U.S. 236, 243 (1968); finally, the statute must not foster "an excessive government entanglement with religion." *Walz, supra,* at 674.

Inquiry into the legislative purposes of the Pennsylvania and Rhode Island statutes affords no basis for a conclusion that the legislative intent was to advance religion. On the contrary, the statutes themselves clearly state that they are intended to enhance the quality of the secular education in all schools covered by the compulsory attendance laws. There is no reason to believe the legislatures meant anything else....

The two legislatures, however, have also recognized that church-related elementary and secondary schools have a significant religious mission and that a substantial portion of their activities is religiously oriented. They have therefore sought to create statutory restrictions designed to guarantee the separation between secular and religious educational functions and to ensure that State financial aid supports only the former. All these provisions are precautions taken in candid recognition that these programs approached, even if they did not intrude upon, the forbidden areas under the Religion Clauses. We need not decide whether these legislative precautions restrict the principal or primary effect of the programs to the point where they do not offend the Religion Clauses, for we conclude that the cumulative impact of the entire relationship arising under the statutes in each State involves excessive entanglement between government and religion.

III
[(A) RHODE ISLAND PROGRAM]

We need not and do not assume that teachers in parochial schools will be guilty of bad faith or any conscious design to evade the limitations imposed by the statute and the First Amendment. We simply recognize that a dedicated religious person, teaching in a school affiliated with his or her faith and operated to inculcate its tenets, will inevitably experience great difficulty in remaining religiously neutral. Doctrines and faith are not inculcated or advanced by neutrals....

... The State must be certain, given the Religion Clauses, that subsidized teachers do not inculcate religion—indeed the State here has undertaken to do so. To ensure that no trespass occurs, the State has therefore carefully conditioned its aid with pervasive restrictions. An eligible recipient must teach only those courses that are offered in the public schools and use only those texts and materials that are found in the public schools. In addition the teacher must not engage in teaching any course in religion.

A comprehensive, discriminating, and continuing state surveillance will inevitably be required to ensure that these restrictions are obeyed and the First Amendment otherwise respected. Unlike a book, a teacher cannot be inspected once so as to determine the extent and intent of his or her personal beliefs and subjective acceptance of the limitations imposed by the First Amendment. These prophylactic contacts will involve excessive and enduring entanglement between state and church.

There is another area of entanglement in the Rhode Island program that gives concern. The statute excludes teachers employed by nonpublic schools whose average per-pupil expenditures on secular education equal or exceed the comparable figures for public schools. In the event that the total expenditures of an otherwise eligible school exceed this norm, the program requires the government to examine the school's records in order to determine how much of the total expenditures is attributable to secular education and how much to religious activity. This kind of state inspection and evaluation of the religious content of a religious organization is fraught with the sort of entanglement that the Constitution forbids....

(B)

Pennsylvania Program [*The Court found similar problems of excessive entanglement: providing state aid to sectarian schools established to propagate a particular religious faith; state restrictions and surveillance to ensure that teachers play a strictly nonideological role; reimbursement contingent on state approval of courses and teaching materials; and state auditing of a parochial school's financial records.*]

MR. JUSTICE MARSHALL took no part in the consideration or decision of No. 89 [*the Pennsylvania case*].

MR. JUSTICE DOUGLAS, whom MR. JUSTICE BLACK joins, concurring....

MR. JUSTICE MARSHALL, who took no part in the consideration or decision of No. 89, ... while intimating no view as to the continuing vitality of *Everson v. Board of Education,* 330 U.S. 1 (1947), concurs in MR. JUSTICE DOUGLAS' opinion covering Nos. 569 and 570 [*the Rhode Island cases*].

MR. JUSTICE BRENNAN [*concurring*]....

MR. JUSTICE WHITE, concurring in the judgments in No. 153 [*Tilton v. Richardson, which sustained federal construction grants to sectarian universities*] and No. 89 and dissenting in Nos. 569 and 570....

The Court thus creates an insoluble paradox for the State and the parochial schools. The State cannot finance secular instruction if it permits religion to be taught in the same classroom; but if it exacts a promise that religion not be so taught—a promise the school and its teachers are quite willing and on this record able to give—and enforces it, it is then entangled in the "no entanglement" aspect of the Court's Establishment Clause jurisprudence....

Zelman v. Simmons-Harris

536 U.S. 639 (2002)

Doris Simmons-Harris and other state taxpayers challenged Ohio's voucher program as a violation of the Establishment Clause. The program offered a $2,250 tuition grant for each student from a low-income family enrolled in a private school within the Cleveland district. The private school could be religious or nonreligious. The majority of students who participated in the program enrolled in religiously affiliated schools. The district court granted the taxpayers summary judgment, and the Sixth Circuit affirmed. The defendant in this case is Susan Tave Zelman, Superintendent of Public Instruction of Ohio.

CHIEF JUSTICE REHNQUIST delivered the opinion of the Court.

The State of Ohio has established a pilot program designed to provide educational choices to families with children who reside in the Cleveland City School District. The question presented is whether this program offends the Establishment Clause of the United States Constitution. We hold that it does not.

There are more than 75,000 children enrolled in the Cleveland City School District. The majority of these children are from low-income and minority families. Few of these families enjoy the means to

send their children to any school other than an inner-city public school. For more than a generation, however, Cleveland's public schools have been among the worst performing public schools in the Nation.... More than two-thirds of high school students either dropped or failed out before graduation. Of those students who managed to reach their senior year, one of every four still failed to graduate....

It is against this backdrop that Ohio enacted ... its Pilot Project Scholarship Program.... The program provides financial assistance to families in any Ohio school district that is or has been "under federal court order requiring supervision and operational management of the district by the state superintendent." ... Cleveland is the only Ohio school district to fall within that category. [*Any suburban district that agreed to participate in the program would receive a $2,250 tuition grant plus the ordinary allotment of per-pupil state funding for each program student enrolled. If parents selected a private school, the checks would be made payable to the parents, who then endorse the checks to the school. In the 1999–2000 school year, 56 private schools participated in the program, and 46 (or 82%) had a religious affiliation.*]

The Establishment Clause of the First Amendment, applied to the States through the Fourteenth Amendment, prevents a State from enacting laws that have the "purpose" or "effect" of advancing or inhibiting religion.... There is no dispute that the program challenged here was enacted for the valid secular purpose of providing educational assistance to poor children in a demonstrably failing public school system. Thus, the question presented is whether the Ohio program nonetheless has the forbidden "effect" of advancing or inhibiting religion.

To answer that question, our decisions have drawn a consistent distinction between government programs that provide aid directly to religious schools, ... and programs of true private choice, in which government aid reaches religious schools only as a result of private individuals.... [*Rehnquist discusses the Minnesota tax deduction program for various educational expenses, including private school costs*, Mueller v. Allen, 463 U.S. 388 (1983); *the vocational scholarship program that provided tuition aid to a blind student*, Witters v. Washington Dept. of Servs. for Blind, 474 U.S. 481 (1986); *and a federal program that permitted sign-language interpreters to assist deaf children enrolled in religious schools*, Zobrest v. Catalina Foothills School Dist., 509 U.S. 1 (1993).]

Mueller, Witters, and *Zobrest* thus make clear that where a government aid program is neutral with respect to religion, and provides assistance directly to a broad class of citizens who, in turn, direct government aid to religious schools wholly as a result of their own genuine and independent private choice, the program is not readily subject to challenge under the Establishment Clause.... The incidental advancement of a religious mission, or the perceived endorsement of a religious message, is reasonably attributable to the individual recipient, not to the government, whose role ends with the disbursement of benefits....

We believe that the program challenged here is a program of true private choice ... and thus constitutional.... [T]he Ohio program is neutral in all respects toward religion. It is part of a general and multifaceted undertaking by the State of Ohio to provide educational opportunities to the children of a failed school district. It confers educational assistance directly to a broad class of individuals defined without reference to religion, *i.e.*, any parent of a school-age child who resides in the Cleveland City School District. The program permits the participation of *all* schools within the district, religious or nonreligious....

... The program here in fact creates financial *dis*incentives for religious schools, with private schools receiving only half the government assistance given to community schools and one-third the assistance given to magnet schools.... Families too have a financial disincentive to choose a private religious school over other schools. Parents that choose to participate in the scholarship program and then to enroll their children in a private school (religious or nonreligious) must copay a portion of the school's tuition. Families that choose a community school, magnet school, or traditional public school pay nothing....

... It is true that 82% of Cleveland's participating private schools are religious schools, but it is also true that 81% of private schools in Ohio are religious schools....

Respondents and JUSTICE SOUTER claim that even if we do not focus on the number of participating schools that are religious schools, we should attach constitutional significance to the fact that 96% of scholarship recipients have enrolled in religious schools.... We need not consider this argument in detail, since it was flatly rejected in *Mueller*, where we found it irrelevant that 96% of parents taking deductions for tuition expenses paid tuition at religious schools....

... [W]e hold that the program does not offend the Establishment Clause.

The judgment of the Court of Appeals is reversed.

It is so ordered.

[*Justices O'Connor and Thomas wrote separate concurring opinions.*]

JUSTICE STEVENS, dissenting....

JUSTICE SOUTER, with whom JUSTICE STEVENS, JUSTICE GINSBURG, and JUSTICE BREYER join, dissenting.

... The occasion for the legislation thus upheld is the condition of public education in the city of Cleveland. The record indicates that the schools are failing to serve their objective, and the vouchers in issue here are said to be needed to provide adequate alternatives to them. If there were an excuse for giving short shrift to the Establishment Clause, it would probably apply here. But there is no excuse. Constitutional limitations are placed on government to preserve constitutional values in hard cases, like these....

[*In Section II, Souter objects that the majority has misused the twin standards of neutrality and free choice. There is "no way to interpret the 96.6% of current voucher money going to religious schools as reflecting a free and genuine choice by the families that apply for vouchers. The 96.6% reflects, instead, the fact that too few nonreligious school desks are available and few but religious schools can afford to accept more than a handful of voucher students."*]

JUSTICE BREYER, with whom JUSTICE STEVENS and JUSTICE SOUTER join, dissenting....

... The [Ohio] program also insists that no participating school "advocate or foster unlawful behavior or teach hatred of any person or group on the basis of race, ethnicity, national origin, or religion." ... And it requires the State to "revoke the registration of any school if, after a hearing, the superintendent determines that the school is in violation" of the program's rules.... As one *amicus* argues, "it is difficult to imagine a more divisive activity" than the appointment of state officials as referees to determine whether a particular religious doctrine "teaches hatred or advocates lawlessness." ...

E. RELIGIOUS INSTRUCTION AND PRAYERS

Beginning in 1948, the Supreme Court has had to referee an extraordinarily divisive and emotional issue: efforts to introduce religious instruction and prayers into public schools. Especially with regard to the prayer issue, the Supreme Court has been vilified for "driving God out of the classroom," but these critiques often misunderstand the Court's rulings.

Religious Instruction

A 1948 case dealt with an Illinois law that allowed religious teachers to give religious instruction in public school buildings once a week. Parents could excuse their children from secular classes to attend religious instruction. The Court held, 8–1, that use of the state's tax-supported public schools for compulsory education to enable sectarian groups to give religious instruction to students in public school buildings violated the religion clauses. In a concurring opinion, joined by Justices Jackson, Rutledge, and Burton, Justice Frankfurter spoke about the dangers of coercing children: "The law of imitation operates, and non-conformity is not an outstanding characteristic of children. The result is an obvious pressure upon children to attend." McCollum v. Board of Education, 333 U.S. 203, 227 (1948).

Advocates of religious instruction next proposed that it be done outside the school building. New York City permitted its public schools to release students during school hours, on written requests from their parents, to go to religious centers for religious instruction or devotional exercises. Students not released stayed in the public school classrooms. The churches providing the instruction reported the names of children released for instruction but who failed to appear. The Supreme Court, divided 6–3, held that the "released time" program did not violate the religion clauses. When the state "encourages religious instruction or cooperates with religious authorities by adjusting the schedule of public events to sectarian needs, it follows the best of our traditions. For it then respects the religious nature of our people and accommodates the public service to their spiritual needs." Zorach v. Clauson, 343 U.S. 306, 313–14 (1952).

Justice Black, who had adopted the accommodationist position when he upheld reimbursement of transportation costs in *Everson,* dissented in the released-time case. He accused the Court of abandoning the neutrality principle by endorsing a law that helped "religious sects get attendants presumably too unenthusiastic to go unless moved to do so by the pressure of this state machinery." Frankfurter, dissenting, agreed with this criticism of the majority's opinion. Jackson, in the third dissent, put the matter forcefully: "Here schooling is more or less suspended during the 'released time' so the nonreligious attendants will not forge ahead of the churchgoing absentees. But it serves as a temporary jail for a pupil who will not go to Church. It takes more subtlety of mind than I possess to deny that this is governmental constraint in support of religion."

Prayers in Public Schools

If the Court attempted to accommodate religious groups in *Zorach,* in 1962 it set off a storm still raging by holding that a New York "Regents' Prayer" was unconstitutional. State law directed that the following prayer be said aloud by each class of a public school at the beginning of each day: "Almighty God, we acknowledge our dependence upon Thee, and we beg Thy blessings upon us, our parents, our teachers and our Country." The 6–1 decision, written by Black, argued that the Establishment Clause "must at least mean that in this country it is no part of the business of government to compose official prayers for any group of the American people to recite as a part of a religious program carried on by government." ENGEL v. VITALE, 370 U.S. 421, 425 (1962). Douglas' concurrence offered unfortunate and unnecessary speculations about the use of prayers in opening the business of the Supreme Court and of Congress. Those practices were not at issue. Stewart's dissent also strayed from the dispute before the Court. He did not want to deny school children their "wish" to recite the prayer or to interfere with those "who want to begin their day by joining in prayer," but the issue was not the desire of children to pray on their own initiative. It was the constitutionality of a state composing an official prayer mandated for minors in public schools.

A number of newspapers incorrectly reported that the Court had banned prayer, when in fact it had banned *official* prayer. There was strong pressure to pass a constitutional amendment to nullify the Court's decision. That movement stalled when congressional hearings revealed broad support by Protestant, Catholic, and Jewish organizations for the Court's ruling (see reading).

A year later, the Court decided 8–1 that states may not require that passages from the Bible be read or that the Lord's Prayer be recited in the public schools at the beginning of each day, even if individual students may be excused upon written request of their parents. The Court did not bar the study of the Bible or of religion "when presented objectively as part of a secular program of education." Abington School Dist. v. Schempp, 374 U.S. 203, 225 (1963). Stewart was again the lone dissenter.

Evolutionism vs. Creationism

States have been active in prohibiting the teaching of evolution in the schools. Tennessee's "monkey law," adopted in 1925, led to the famous *Scopes* case in 1927. Scopes v. State, 289 S.W. 363 (Tenn. 1927). When the issue of anti-evolution laws reached the Supreme Court in 1968, a unanimous Court struck down Arkansas's statute making it unlawful for a teacher in any state-supported school or university to teach or use a textbook that claimed that mankind evolved from a lower order of animals. The statute violated the Establishment Clause because a particular religious group considered the evolution theory in conflict with the Book of Genesis. Epperson v. Arkansas, 393 U.S. 97 (1968).

In 1987, a 7–2 Court held invalid Louisiana's "Creationism Act," which prohibited the teaching of the theory of evolution in public elementary and secondary schools unless accompanied by instruction in the theory of "creation science." The latter, based on the Book of Genesis, opposes the theory of evolution. The Court rejected the state's assertion that the statute furthered "academic freedom." The legislative record revealed a bias in favor of religious doctrine. Edwards v. Aguillard, 482 U.S. 578 (1987). Other cases in the lower courts concerned challenges to textbooks that allegedly promote the "religion" of secular humanism.[6] In 1999, the Kansas Board of Education voted to delete any mention

---

6. A federal judge in Tennessee held that a state requirement for all students in grades 1 through 8 to use a prescribed set of reading textbooks was unconstitutional because the books contained "secular humanist" teachings that offended

of evolution from the state's science curriculum and from any state assessment test. The curriculum allowed for the teaching of "micro-evolution" (genetic adaptation). However, elections in 2000 to the Kansas school board led to a reinstatement of the teaching of evolution in 2001. In 2002, the Ohio state school board voted 18 to 0 to require the teaching of evolution, while allowing students to fully critique it. Battles over the teaching of evolution continued to be fought from 2003 to 2008 in Georgia, Kansas, Kentucky, Ohio, and Pennsylvania.

Ten Commandments

The votes on these cases show a remarkable strength for the majority of the Supreme Court: 8–1 in *McCollum,* 6–1 in *Engel,* 8–1 in *Abington,* unanimous in *Epperson,* and 7–2 in *Edwards.* Only in *Zorach* was the Court seriously divided (6–3). No such agreement marks other decisions on religious instruction and prayer. In 1980, the Court split 5 to 4 in holding that a Kentucky statute requiring the posting of a copy of the Ten Commandments on the wall of each public school classroom violated the Establishment Clause. Although the copies were purchased with private funds, the mere posting provided official state support for religion. Portions of the Ten Commandments could have been regarded as secular in purpose (the parts concerning honoring one's parents, killing, adultery, stealing, false witness, and covetousness), but other sections were clearly religious in nature (worshiping the Lord God alone, avoiding idolatry, not using the Lord's name in vain, and observing the Sabbath). Stone v. Graham, 449 U.S. 39, 41–42 (1980). The dissenters were Burger, Blackmun, Stewart, and Rehnquist. In 2001, the Court let stand a Seventh Circuit decision that ruled against the city of Elkhart, Indiana, for keeping a 6-foot-tall granite pillar engraved with the Ten Commandments on the lawn of the town hall. Elkhart v. Books, 532 U.S. 1058 (2001).

In 2001, Chief Justice Roy Moore of the Alabama Supreme Court precipitated a nationwide furor when he moved a 5,280-pound monument of the holy tablets into his courthouse. A federal district court ruled the monument unconstitutional. When Moore defied the order an ad hoc Alabama Supreme Court (of retired judges) voted 7 to 0 for his removal. All regular members of the Court had recused themselves from the case. The U.S. Supreme Court refused to hear the case on appeal from the Eleventh Circuit. Moore v. Glassroth, 540 U.S. 1000 (2003).

In 2005, the Court divided 5–4 in two Ten Commandments cases. In Van Orden v. Perry, 545 U.S. 677 (2005), the Court upheld the placement of a six-foot Ten Commandments monument amidst 21 historical markers and 17 other monuments in a 22-acre park surrounding the Texas State Capital in Austin, Texas, against an Establishment Clause challenge. In an opinion for a plurality that included Justices Scalia, Kennedy and Thomas, Chief Justice Rehnquist acknowledged the religious nature of the Ten Commandments, but "[s]imply having religious content or promoting a message consistent with a religious doctrine does not run afoul of the Establishment Clause." Rehnquist distinguished the "passive" nature of the display, which represented a part of the state's political and legal history, and which was largely ignored by passersby, from the posting of the Ten Commandments in public schoolrooms, at issue in *Stone,* since they "confronted" students. Justice Breyer filed a concurring opinion. Justices Stevens, O'Connor, Souter, and Ginsburg dissented

In McCREARY COUNTY v. ACLU, 545 U.S. 844 (2005), the Court held as a violation of the Establishment Clause the installation in two county courthouses of large copies of the King James Version of the Ten Commandments. The display was not saved by the subsequent addition of historical

Christian beliefs. Mozert v. Hawkins County Public Schools, 647 F.Supp. 1194 (E.D. Tenn. 1986). His decision was overturned by a unanimous panel of the Sixth Circuit; 827 F.2d 1058 (6th Cir. 1987), cert. denied, 484 U.S. 1066 (1988). A federal judge in Alabama also banned textbooks from public schools in the state because they promoted the "religion" of secular humanism. Smith v. Board of Com'rs of Mobile County, 655 F.Supp. 939 (S.D. Ala. 1987). His decision was reversed by the Eleventh Circuit; 827 F.2d 684 (11th Cir. 1987).

documents since the Court discerned in it a "religious purpose" that unconstitutionally advanced religion. O'Connor wrote a concurring opinion. Scalia, Rehnquist, Kennedy and Thomas dissented.

In 2009, a "unanimous" Supreme Court opinion on a Ten Commandments case managed to fracture into four separate concurring opinions, offering substantially different views of the Establishment Clause. A public park in Pleasant Grove City in Utah included a monument with the Ten Commandments. A religion called "Summum" (formed in 1975) insisted that its monument listing seven aphorisms of ethical principles be placed in the park. The Court held that the Ten Commandments monument was a form of "government speech" and not subject to scrutiny under the Free Speech Clause. Pleasant Grove City v. Summum, 555 U.S. 460 (2009). Delivering the opinion of the Court, Alito wrote: "The Free Speech Clause restricts government regulation of private speech; it does not regulate government speech." But he added: "This does not mean that there are no restraints on government speech." Whatever those restraints, for Alito they did not apply in this case. Stevens, joined by Ginsburg, concurred but found the "recently minted government speech doctrine" to be "of doubtful merit." Scalia, joined by Thomas, wrote a concurrence. Breyer and Souter wrote separate concurrences. The latter expressed "qualms" about the position that public monuments are "government speech categorically."

Chaplains

In 1983, the Court divided 6–3 in upholding the practice of the Nebraska legislature to begin each of its sessions with a prayer by a chaplain paid by the state with the legislature's approval. The Court noted that Congress had followed the same practice without interruption for almost 200 years, and that precedents dating back to the First Congress, which drafted the Bill of Rights, shed important light on what the framers intended by the Establishment Clause. Marsh v. Chambers, 463 U.S. 783 (1983). As Justice Brennan noted in his dissent, the historical analogy allowed the Court to violate *Lemon*'s three-part test. The Nebraska statute had a religious, not a secular, purpose; its principal or primary effect advanced religion; and it fostered government entanglement with religion.

While the Nebraska chaplain case was wending its way through the courts, a separate challenge concerned chaplains in the U.S. Senate and the U.S. House of Representatives. A district judge held in 1981 that the taxpayer had no standing to bring the suit. Murray v. Morton, 505 F.Supp. 144 (D.D.C. 1981). However, the appellate court reinstated the suit and sent the case back to the trial judge for a decision on the merits. Murray v. Buchanan, 674 F.2d 14 (D.C. Cir. 1982). Three weeks later the House of Representatives passed a resolution viewing with "deep concern" the appellate court decision and expressing in strong terms the constitutional power of the House "to determine the rules of its proceedings, to select officers, and otherwise to control its internal affairs." The resolution also stated that the decision of the appellate court "implies a lack of respect due a coordinate branch concerning matters committed to it by the Constitution." The resolution passed by the vote of 388 to zero. 128 Cong. Rec. 5890–96 (1982). The case was then heard by the D.C. Circuit, sitting en banc. Because of the Supreme Court's decision in *Marsh v. Chambers,* the D.C. Circuit held that the complaint against the House and Senate chaplains "retains no vitality" and dismissed the case. Murray v. Buchanan, 720 F.2d 689 (D.C. Cir. 1983) (en banc).

Moment of Silence

A 1985 decision saw the Court again badly fractured on questions of prayer. The case concerned Alabama's one-minute period of silence in all public schools "for meditation or voluntary prayer." A 6–3 Court, this time using the *Lemon* test, found that the state law violated the religion clauses because the purpose of the statute was to advance religion. WALLACE v. JAFFREE, 472 U.S. 38 (1985). Alabama continued to try other forms of public school prayers, but eventually conceded that school officials may not prescribe prayer or allow state employees to lead, participate in, or otherwise endorse prayer of any type during curricular or extracurricular events. The constitutional ban was against *state* prayer, not prayer. Genuinely student-initiated religious activity is permitted at appropriate times and places. Chandler v. Siegelman, 230 F.3d 1313 (11th Cir. 2000); Chandler v. Siegelman, 533 U.S. 916 (2001).

A New Jersey "moment of silence" statute reached the Supreme Court in 1987, but the case was dismissed because the parties bringing the case no longer had standing. Karcher v. May, 484 U.S. 72 (1987). In 2001, the Fourth Circuit upheld a Virginia statute that provided for a minute of silence. Students were advised that they could use the time to either pray or meditate. The court regarded the statute as "at most a minor and nonintrusive accommodation of religion." Brown v. Gilmore, 258 F.3d 265, 278 (4th Cir. 2001), cert. denied, 534 U.S. 996 (2001).

Graduation Prayers

The constitutionality of graduation prayers split the Court 5–4 in 1992. The case involved the practice in Rhode Island middle and high schools of inviting members of the clergy to give invocations and benedictions at school graduation ceremonies. School officials advised speakers that the invocations and benedictions should be nonsectarian. Because of that fact, the Court concluded that state officials were directing the performance of a formal religious exercise, resulting in a state-sponsored and state-directed activity. The school principal selected the religious participant and provided guidelines on the content of the prayer. Such activities were proscribed by *Engel* v. *Vitale* and earlier decisions. The fact that graduation exercise were "voluntary" did not permit school officials to use indirect coercion against students and parents who wanted to attend a very significant event but objected to religious exercises. The Court distinguished between the school prayers at issue in this case (involving young people subject to indoctrination and peer pressure) with the prayers earlier allowed in adult institutions such as the Nebraska legislature and the U.S. Congress. LEE v. WEISMAN, 505 U.S. 577 (1992).

Student-Led Prayers

States continued to use other methods to bring prayers into graduation exercises. A Texas school district permitted public high school seniors to choose student volunteers to deliver nonsectarian, non-proselytizing invocations at their graduation ceremonies. Unlike *Lee* v. *Weisman,* outside clergy were not invited nor did school officials become involved in directing or monitoring the content of these prayers. The Fifth Circuit upheld the Texas practice in 1992; a year later the Supreme Court let this decision stand without comment. Jones v. Clear Creek Independent School Dist., 977 F.2d 963 (5th Cir. 1992), cert. denied, 508 U.S. 967 (1993). The District of Columbia decided in 1993 to permit student-led prayers at graduation exercises. Washington Post, June 17, 1993, at D1.

The issue of school prayer returned to the Court in 2000 when it ruled, 6 to 3, that prayers led by students at high school football games are unconstitutional when they are officially sanctioned. Rejecting the arguments that the prayers were voluntary and private, the Court regarded the prayers as "authorized by a government policy and take place on government property at government-sponsored school-related events." SANTA FE INDEPENDENT SCHOOL DIST. v. DOE, 530 U.S. 290 (2000). Although school authorities cannot organize student-led prayers to be given over the public address system, nothing can stop students from standing up to give prayers at the start of a football game, or other sporting event, if the prayers seem spontaneous and undirected.

Responses by the Elected Branches

Although President Reagan lost no time in 1981 in stating that the Court had "ruled wrongly" on school prayer, his administration never directly challenged the Court on *Engel*. Instead, Justice Department officials merely argued in favor of a moment of silence or voluntary prayer. Reagan never embraced state-mandated school prayers. While remarking in 1982 that "God should [never] have been expelled from the classroom," his constitutional amendment simply proposed that nothing should be construed to prohibit individual or group prayer in public schools and that no person

President Clinton's Memorandum on Religious Expression in Public Schools

I share the concern and frustration that many Americans feel about situations where the protections accorded by the First Amendment are not recognized or understood. This problem has manifested itself in our Nation's public schools. It appears that some school officials, teachers and parents have assumed that religious expression of any type is either inappropriate, or forbidden altogether, in public schools.

As our courts have affirmed, however, nothing in the First Amendment converts our public schools into religion-free zones, or requires all religious expression to be left behind at the schoolhouse door. While the government may not use schools to coerce the consciences of our students, or to convey official endorsement of religion, the government's schools also may not discriminate against private religious expression during the school day.

I have been advised by the Department of Justice and the Department of Education that the First Amendment permits—and protects—a greater degree of religious expression in public schools than many Americans may now understand.... The following principles are among those that apply to religious expression in our schools:

Student prayer and religious discussion: The Establishment Clause of the First Amendment does not prohibit purely private religious speech by students. Students therefore have the same right to engage in individual or group prayer and religious instruction during the school day as they do to engage in other comparable activity. For example, students may read their Bibles or other scriptures, say grace before meals, and pray before tests to the same extent they may engage in comparable non-disruptive activities. Local school authorities possess substantial discretion to impose rules of order and other pedagogical restrictions on student activities, but they may not structure or administer such rules to discriminate against religious activity or speech.

Generally, students may pray in a nondisruptive manner when not engaged in school activities or instruction, and subject to the rules that normally pertain to the applicable setting. Specifically, students in informal settings, such as cafeterias and hallways, may pray and discuss their religious views with each other, subject to the same rules or order as apply to other student activities and speech. Students may also speak to, and attempt to persuade, their peers about religious topics just as they do with regard to political topics. School officials, however, should intercede to stop student speech that constitutes harassment aimed at a student or a group of students....

Graduation prayer and baccalaureates: Under current Supreme Court decisions, school officials may not mandate or organize prayer at graduation, nor organize religious baccalaureate ceremonies. If a school generally opens its facilities to private groups, it must make its facilities available on the same terms to organizers of privately sponsored religious baccalaureate services. A school may not extent preferential treatment to baccalaureate ceremonies and may in some instances be obliged to disclaim official endorsement of such ceremonies.

Official neutrality regarding religious activity: Teachers and school administrators, when acting in those capacities, are representatives of the state and are prohibited by the establishment clause from soliciting or encouraging religious activity, and from participating in such activity with students. Teachers and administrators also are prohibited from discouraging activity because of its religious content, and from soliciting or encouraging antireligious activity.

Teaching about religion: Public schools may not provide religious instruction, but they may teach *about* religion, including the Bible or other scripture: the history of religion, comparative religion, the Bible (or other scripture)-as-literature, and the role of religion in the history of the United States and other countries are all permissible public school subjects....

SOURCE: Public Papers of the Presidents, 1995, II, 1083–85. See also 68 Fed. Reg. 9645 (2003).

should be required to participate in prayer. Public Papers of the Presidents, 1982, I, 603, 647–48. This language did not repudiate *Engel*; it supported it.

When Reagan's constitutional amendment was reported by the Senate Judiciary Committee in 1984, it included this language: "Neither the United States nor any state shall compose the words of any prayer to be said in public schools." That language echoed *Engel*. The committee amendment was accepted 96 to zero, but the amendment as a whole received a vote of only 56–44, or eleven votes short of the required two-thirds. 130 Cong. Rec. 4318, 5421, 5919 (1984).

Several times Congress has considered legislation to permit voluntary prayer by school children. These bills sometimes propose that federal courts be denied jurisdiction to enter any judgment, decree, or order denying or restricting voluntary prayer in any public school. Such bills have never been adopted. In 1971, the House of Representatives voted 240 to 162 for a constitutional amendment to permit voluntary prayer or meditation in public buildings. The vote was 28 votes shy of the two-thirds needed. Reagan's proposed constitutional amendment for voluntary prayer failed in 1984, eleven votes short. In June 1998, the House of Representatives voted 224 to 203 for a constitutional amendment to permit voluntary prayer. The effort failed by 61 votes. The proposed language was fully consistent with *Engel* because government was not to "initiate or designate school prayers." For all the fulmination against the Court's ruling in 1962, religious groups remain largely in support of that decision.

In 1995, in an effort to take some of the steam out of a proposed school prayer amendment, President Bill Clinton issued a memorandum to clarify the rights of public school children to religious expression. Children may engage in individual or group prayer and religious discussion during the school day and participate in events, before and after school, with religious content (see box on previous page). Studies indicate that students in public schools are active in prayer clubs and other religious activities, and a number of public schools offer classes that study the Bible as history and literature. In 2003, the Bush administration released similar guidelines on school prayer, but warned that schools could lose federal funds if they fail to comply with the instructions. 68 Fed. Reg. 9645 (2003).

Engel v. Vitale

370 U.S. 421 (1962)

After the New York Board of Regents composed a prayer to be recited in public schools, a group of parents brought action against the state. The parent named first in the suit was Steven I. Engel, who sued William J. Vitale and other members of the Board of Education of Union Free School District. The New York courts upheld the "Regents' prayer," provided that pupils were not compelled to join in the prayer over their objections or the objections of their parents.

MR. JUSTICE BLACK delivered the opinion of the Court.

The respondent Board of Education of Union Free School District No. 9, New Hyde Park, New York, acting in its official capacity under state law, directed the School District's principal to cause the following prayer to be said aloud by each class in the presence of a teacher at the beginning of each school day:

"Almighty God, we acknowledge our dependence upon Thee, and we beg Thy blessings upon us, our parents, our teachers and our Country."

This daily procedure was adopted on the recommendation of the State Board of Regents, a govern-

mental agency created by the State Constitution to which the New York Legislature has granted broad supervisory, executive, and legislative powers over the State's public school system. These state officials composed the prayer....

We think that by using its public school system to encourage recitation of the Regents' prayer, the State of New York has adopted a practice wholly inconsistent with the Establishment Clause. There can, of course, be no doubt that New York's program of daily classroom invocation of God's blessings as prescribed in the Regents' prayer is a religious activity. It is a solemn avowal of divine faith and supplication for the blessings of the Almighty....

The petitioners contend among other things that

the state laws requiring or permitting use of the Regents' prayer must be struck down as a violation of the Establishment Clause because that prayer was composed by governmental officials as a part of a governmental program to further religious beliefs. For this reason, petitioners argue, the State's use of the Regents' prayer in its public school system breaches the constitutional wall of separation between Church and State. We agree with that contention since we think that the constitutional prohibition against laws respecting an establishment of religion must at least mean that in this country it is no part of the business of government to compose official prayers for any group of the American people to recite as a part of a religious program carried on by government.

It is a matter of history that this very practice of establishing governmentally composed prayers for religious services was one of the reasons which caused many of our early colonists to leave England and seek religious freedom in America. The Book of Common Prayer, which was created under governmental direction and which was approved by Acts of Parliament in 1548 and 1549, set out in minute detail the accepted form and content of prayer and other religious ceremonies to be used in the established, tax-supported Church of England. The controversies over the Book and what should be its content repeatedly threatened to disrupt the peace of that country as the accepted forms of prayer in the established church changed with the views of the particular ruler that happened to be in control at the time....

It is an unfortunate fact of history that when some of the very groups which had most strenuously opposed the established Church of England found themselves sufficiently in control of colonial governments in this country to write their own prayers into law, they passed laws making their own religion the official religion of their respective colonies....

... Neither the fact that the prayer may be denominationally neutral nor the fact that its observance on the part of the students is voluntary can serve to free it from the limitations of the Establishment Clause.... When the power, prestige and financial support of government is placed behind a particular religious belief, the indirect coercive pressure upon religious minorities to conform to the prevailing officially approved religion is plain. But the purposes underlying the Establishment Clause go much further than that. Its first and most immediate purpose rested on the belief that a union of government and religion tends to destroy government and to degrade religion. The history of governmentally established religion, both in England and in this country, showed that whenever government had allied itself with one particular form of religion, the inevitable result had been that it had incurred the hatred, disrespect and even contempt of those who held contrary beliefs....

It has been argued that to apply the Constitution in such a way as to prohibit state laws respecting an establishment of religious services in public schools is to indicate a hostility toward religion or toward prayer. Nothing, of course, could be more wrong. The history of man is inseparable from the history of religion.... It is neither sacrilegious nor antireligious to say that each separate government in this country should stay out of the business of writing or sanctioning official prayers and leave that purely religious function to the people themselves and to those the people choose to look to for religious guidance....

The judgment of the Court of Appeals of New York is reversed and the cause remanded for further proceedings not inconsistent with this opinion.

Reversed and remanded.

MR. JUSTICE FRANKFURTER took no part in the decision of this case.

MR. JUSTICE WHITE took no part in the consideration or decision of this case.

MR. JUSTICE DOUGLAS, concurring....

What New York does on the opening of its public schools is what we do when we open court. Our Crier has from the beginning announced the convening of the Court and then added "God save the United States and this Honorable court." That utterance is a supplication, a prayer in which we, the judges, are free to join, but which we need not recite any more than the students need recite the New York prayer.

What New York does on the opening of its public schools is what each House of Congress does at the opening of each day's business....

In New York the teacher who leads in prayer is on the public payroll; and the time she takes seems minuscule as compared with the salaries appropriated by state legislatures and Congress for chaplains to conduct prayers in the legislative halls. Only a bare fraction of the teacher's time is given to reciting this short 22-word prayer, about the same amount of time that our Crier spends announcing the opening of our sessions and offering a prayer for this Court. Yet for me the principle is the same, no matter how briefly the prayer is said, for in each of the instances given the person praying is a public official on the public payroll, performing a religious exercise in a governmental institution....

Mr. Justice Stewart, dissenting.

... I cannot see how an "official religion" is established by letting those who want to say a prayer say it. On the contrary, I think that to deny the wish of these school children to join in reciting this prayer is to deny them the opportunity of sharing in the spiritual heritage of our Nation.

The Court's historical review of the quarrels over the Book of Common Prayer in England throws no light for me on the issue before us in this case. England had then and has now an established church. Equally unenlightening, I think, is the history of the early establishment and later rejection of an official church in our own States. For we deal here not with the establishment of a state church, which would, of course, be constitutionally impermissible, but with whether school children who want to begin their day by joining in prayer must be prohibited from doing so....

Congressional Hearings on School Prayer (1964)

After the Supreme Court decided *Engel* v. *Vitale* (1962), many members of Congress introduced constitutional amendments to permit school prayer. Some legislators may have assumed that their initiative would appeal to organized religion, but hearings conducted in 1964 by the House Judiciary Committee revealed broad opposition by Protestant, Catholic, and Jewish organizations. The groups testifying against a constitutional amendment included the American Baptist Convention, the American Jewish Congress, the American Lutheran Church, the Episcopal Church, the National Council of Churches of Christ, the Synagogue Council of America, and the United Presbyterian Church. The testimony below is by Dr. Edwin H. Tuller, General Secretary, American Baptist Convention, speaking on behalf of the National Council of Churches. These hearings underscore the linkage between constitutional law and the attitudes, values, and participation of the private sector.

Dr. Tuller: ... As a result of the Supreme Court decision on the regents' prayer, many constitutional amendments had been proposed by Members of Congress at the time the general board [*of the National Council of Churches*] met, which do not differ appreciably from those now before this committee. In reference to such efforts to rewrite the first amendment, the general board said:

"We express the conviction that the first amendment to our Constitution *in its present wording* has provided the framework within which responsible citizens and our courts have been able to afford maximum protection for the religious liberty of all our citizens." [Emphasis added.]

The general board did not single out a specific proposed amendment for comment, but they were in effect rejecting the current proposals to rewrite the first amendment.

Many people assume that church leaders would of course favor anything designed to "aid religion," and some do not understand why they do not favor prayer and Bible reading in public schools. "What harm can it do"? they ask. It is not possible to know the mind of all members of the general board, but some of them expressed their convictions in debate or discussion on such points as these:

(*a*) Public institutions belong to all citizens, whatever their religious beliefs or lack of them; it is not right for the majority to impose religious beliefs or practices on the minority in public institutions when adequate provisions are available for those who desire to do so to express such beliefs and follow such practices in nonpublic settings with others of like mind;

(*b*) Because of American religious variety, our public schools are particularly inappropriate places for corporate religious exercises. Young and impressionable children from a wide variety of religious backgrounds and from no religious background at all, are present not by choice, but by compulsion of law and are not genuinely free to decide for themselves whether or not they will participate....;

(*c*) In such a setting, children are almost always not given a genuinely free choice by glib use of the words "voluntary participation," when the whole atmosphere of the classroom is one of compliance and conformity to group activities.

When the teacher (or a group of pupils) selects a

prayer or Bible reading, and all or most of the class members participate in it, at a time and in a procedure instituted by the teacher as the adult bearer of the authority of the public school, it is a rare child indeed who will isolate himself from his fellows by declining to participate. Thus a subtle but no less effective form of duress is present which should never blight the act of worship....;

(d) Who is to compose the prayers, and who is to select the Scriptures? What form of the Lord's Prayer will be used, and which version of the Bible? In those who take their faith seriously, these things are important. They do not consider all prayers or Scriptures interchangeable....;

(e) What a nonsectarian theistic majority can require today in the way of a regents prayer or Bible reading "without comment" a sectarian majority can require tomorrow in the way of an Augsburg Confession, a "Hail, Mary" or a theistic tract. These things are best not subject to a majority decision, but left to the free choice of each person at the time and place his conscience directs;

(f) Religious practices that are nonsectarian are too vague and generalized to have much meaning or

effect for character development or moral motivation; ...

(g) Protestants believe that prayer can be effectively addressed to God by any believer at any time and in any place. It does not have to be oral or formal, it does not have to be in unison or collective, it does not require a set garb or posture. Any and all children can pray to God in public schools or anywhere else at any time, and no one can stop them.

It is not necessary, however, that the children who happen to be assigned to the same classroom should stop what they are doing to pray with them. God will hear and answer the prayer of one child, though his petition be uttered in the secret places of his inmost self. The effectiveness and the availability of prayer are not enhanced by the intervention of the agencies of the public school or government; in fact, the reverse is as likely to be the case.

(h) Many Christians see in routine formal corporate rituals in public schools at least the danger against which their Lord warned in the Sermon on the Mount—that what begins as a spontaneous and sincere outpouring of devotion can become a public display of hypocrisy, making a show of piety....

Wallace v. Jaffree

472 U.S. 38 (1985)

Alabama passed legislation authorizing a one-minute period of silence in all public schools "for meditation or voluntary prayer." It also authorized teachers to lead "willing students" in a prescribed prayer to "Almighty God ... the Creator and Supreme Judge of the world." A federal district court upheld the statute, concluding that Alabama could establish a state religion if it wanted to. That ruling was reversed by the Eleventh Circuit. Ishmael Jaffree, a citizen of Alabama and parent of children in public schools, initiated the suit. The appellant is George C. Wallace, Governor of Alabama.

JUSTICE STEVENS delivered the opinion of the Court.

At an early stage of this litigation, the constitutionality of three Alabama statutes was questioned: (1) § 16-1-20, enacted in 1978, which authorized a 1-minute period of silence in all public schools "for meditation"; (2) § 16-1-20.1, enacted in 1981, which authorized a period of silence "for meditation or voluntary prayer"; and (3) § 16-1-20.2, enacted in 1982, which authorized teachers to lead "willing students" in a prescribed prayer to "Almighty God ... the Creator and Supreme Judge ... of the world."

... [T]he narrow question for decision is whether § 16-1-20.1, which authorizes a period of silence for "meditation or voluntary prayer," is a law respecting

the establishment of religion within the meaning of the First Amendment.

III

It is the first of these three [*Lemon*] criteria that is most plainly implicated by this case. As the District Court correctly recognized, no consideration of the second or third criteria is necessary if a statute does not have a clearly secular purpose. For even though a statute that is motivated in part by a religious purpose may satisfy the first criterion, ... the First Amendment requires that a statute must be invalidated if it is entirely motivated by a purpose to advance religion.

In applying the purpose test, it is appropriate to

ask "whether government's actual purpose is to endorse or disapprove of religion." In this case, the answer to that question is dispositive. For the record not only provides us with an unambiguous affirmative answer, but it also reveals that the enactment of § 16-1-20.1 was not motivated by any clearly secular purpose — indeed, the statute had *no* secular purpose.

IV

The sponsor of the bill that became § 16-1-20.1, Senator Donald Holmes, inserted into the legislative record — apparently without dissent — a statement indicating that the legislation was an "effort to return voluntary prayer" to the public schools. Later Senator Holmes confirmed this purpose before the District Court. In response to the question whether he had any purpose for the legislation other than returning voluntary prayer to public schools, he stated: "No, I did not have no other purpose in mind." The State did not present evidence of *any* secular purpose.

The unrebutted evidence of legislative intent contained in the legislative record and in the testimony of the sponsor of § 16-1-20.1 is confirmed by a consideration of the relationship between this statute and the two other measures that were considered in this case. The District Court found that the 1981 statute and its 1982 sequel had a common, nonsecular purpose. The wholly religious character of the later enactment is plainly evident from its text. When the differences between § 16-1-20.1 and its 1978 predecessor, § 16-1-20, are examined, it is equally clear that the 1981 statute has the same wholly religious character.

There are only three textual differences between § 16-1-20.1 and § 16-1-20: (1) the earlier statute applies only to grades one through six, whereas § 16-1-20.1 applies to all grades; (2) the earlier statute uses the word "shall" whereas § 16-1-20.1 uses the word "may"; (3) the earlier statute refers only to "meditation" whereas § 16-1-20.1 refers to "meditation or voluntary prayer." The first difference is of no relevance in this litigation because the minor appellees were in kindergarten or second grade during the 1981–1982 academic year. The second difference would also have no impact on this litigation because the mandatory language of § 16-1-20 continued to apply to grades one through six. Thus, the only significant textual difference is the addition of the words "or voluntary prayer."

The legislative intent to return prayer to the public schools is, of course, quite different from merely protecting every student's right to engage in voluntary prayer during an appropriate moment of silence during the schoolday. The 1978 statute already protected that right, containing nothing that prevented any student from engaging in voluntary prayer during a silent minute of meditation. Appellants have not identified any secular purpose that was not fully served by § 16-1-20 before the enactment of § 16-1-20.1. Thus, only two conclusions are consistent with the text of § 16-1-20.1: (1) the statute was enacted to convey a message of State endorsement and promotion of prayer; or (2) the statute was enacted for no purpose. No one suggests that the statute was nothing but a meaningless or irrational act.

We must, therefore, conclude that the Alabama Legislature intended to change existing law and that it was motivated by the same purpose that the Governor's answer to the second amended complaint expressly admitted; that the statement inserted in the legislative history revealed; and that Senator Holmes' testimony frankly described. The legislature enacted § 16-1-20.1, despite the existence of § -16-1-20 for the sole purpose of expressing the State's endorsement of prayer activities for one minute at the beginning of each schoolday. The addition of "or voluntary prayer" indicates that the State intended to characterize prayer as a favored practice. Such an endorsement is not consistent with the established principle that the government must pursue a course of complete neutrality toward religion....

The judgment of the Court of Appeals is affirmed.

It is so ordered.

JUSTICE POWELL, concurring.

... I agree fully with JUSTICE O'CONNOR's assertion that some moment-of-silence statutes may be constitutional, a suggestion set forth in the Court's opinion as well....

JUSTICE O'CONNOR, concurring in the judgment.

... I write separately to identify the peculiar features of the Alabama law that render it invalid, and to explain why moment of silence laws in other States do not necessarily manifest the same infirmity....

CHIEF JUSTICE BURGER, dissenting.

... To suggest that a moment-of-silence statute that includes the word "prayer" unconstitutionally endorses religion, while one that simply provides for a moment of silence does not, manifests not neutrality but hostility toward religion....

Curiously, the opinions do not mention that *all* of the sponsor's statements relied upon — including the statement "inserted" into the Senate Journal—were made *after* the legislature had passed the statute; indeed, the testimony that the Court finds critical was given well over a year after the statute was enacted. As even the appellees concede, ... there is not a shred of evidence that the legislature as a whole shared the sponsor's motive or that a majority in either house was even aware of the sponsor's view of the bill when it was passed....

JUSTICE WHITE, dissenting.

... [I]t is apparent that in my view the First Amendment does not proscribe either (1) statutes authorizing or requiring in so many words a moment of silence before classes begin or (2) a statute that provides, when it is initially passed, for a moment of silence for meditation or prayer....

JUSTICE REHNQUIST, dissenting.

[*Rehnquist concludes that the First Amendment was designed to prohibit the establishment of a national religion, and perhaps to prevent discrimination among sects, but did not require neutrality on the part of government between religion and irreligion. He also critiques the three-part test of* Lemon v. Kurtzman.]

Lee v. Weisman

505 U.S. 577 (1992)

Principals of the public middle and high schools in Providence, R.I., were permitted to invite members of the clergy to give invocations and benedictions at school graduation ceremonies. Robert E. Lee, a principal, invited a rabbi to offer prayers at a middle school graduation. Daniel Weisman, father of a daughter (Deborah) scheduled to graduate at those exercises, filed a suit to prevent school officials from including prayers in that ceremony. After that motion was denied, Daniel Weisman sought a permanent injunction to bar Lee and other public school officials from inviting clergy to deliver invocations and benedictions at future graduations, including Deborah's high school graduation. A federal district court enjoined Lee from continuing the practice on the ground that it violated the Establishment Clause, and the First Circuit affirmed.

JUSTICE KENNEDY delivered the opinion of the Court.

[I.A]

It has been the custom of Providence school officials to provide invited clergy with a pamphlet entitled "Guidelines for Civic Occasions," prepared by the National Conference of Christians and Jews. The Guidelines recommend that public prayers at non-sectarian civic ceremonies be composed with "inclusiveness and sensitivity," though they acknowledge that "[p]rayer of any kind may be inappropriate on some civic occasions." ... The principal gave Rabbi Gutterman the pamphlet before the graduation and advised him the invocation and benediction should be nonsectarian....

Rabbi Gutterman's prayers were as follows:

"INVOCATION

"God of the Free, Hope of the Brave:

"For the legacy of America where diversity is celebrated and the rights of minorities are protected, we thank You. May these young men and women grow up to enrich it.

"For the liberty of America, we thank You. May these new graduates grow up to guard it.

"For the political process of America in which all its citizens may participate, for its court system where all may seek justice we thank You. May those we honor this morning always turn to it in trust.

"For the destiny of America we thank You. May the graduates of Nathan Bishop Middle School so live that they might help to share it.

"May our aspirations for our country and for these young people, who are our hope for the future, be richly fulfilled.

AMEN"

"BENEDICTION

"O God, we are grateful to You for having endowed us with the capacity for learning which we have celebrated on this joyous commencement.

"Happy families give thanks for seeing their children achieve an important milestone. Send Your blessings upon the teachers and administrators who helped prepare them.

"The graduates now need strength and guidance for the future, help them to understand that we are not complete with academic knowledge alone. We must each strive to fulfill what You require of us all: To do justly, to love mercy, to walk humbly.

"We give thanks to You, Lord, for keeping us alive, sustaining us and allowing us to reach this special, happy occasion.

AMEN"

. . .

II

These dominant facts mark and control the confines of our decision: State officials direct the performance of a formal religious exercise at promotional and graduation ceremonies for secondary schools. Even for those students who object to the religious exercise, their attendance and participation in the state-sponsored religious activity are in a fair and real sense obligatory, though the school district does not require attendance as a condition for receipt of the diploma.

... [T]he controlling precedents as they relate to prayer and religious exercise in primary and secondary public schools compel the holding here that the policy of the city of Providence is an unconstitutional one.... The government involvement with religious activity in this case is pervasive, to the point of creating a state-sponsored and state-directed religious exercise in a public school....

That involvement is as troubling as it is undenied. A school official, the principal, decided that an invocation and a benediction should be given; this is a choice attributable to the State, and from a constitutional perspective it is as if a state statute decreed that the prayers must occur. The principal chose the religious participant, here a rabbi, and that choice is also attributable to the State. The reason for the choice of a rabbi is not disclosed by the record, but the potential for divisiveness over the choice of a particular member of the clergy to conduct the ceremony is apparent.

Divisiveness, of course, can attend any state decision respecting religions, and neither its existence nor its potential necessarily invalidates the State's attempts to accommodate religion in all cases. The potential for divisiveness is of particular relevance here though, because it centers around an overt religious exercise in a secondary school environment where, as we discuss below, ... subtle coercive pressures exist and where the student had no real alternative which would have allowed her to avoid the fact or appearance of participation.

The State's role did not end with the decision to include a prayer and with the choice of clergyman.

Principal Lee provided Rabbi Gutterman with a copy of the "Guidelines for Civic Occasions," and advised him that his prayers should be nonsectarian. Through these means the principal directed and controlled the content of the prayer.... It is a cornerstone principle of our Establishment Clause jurisprudence that "it is no part of the business of government to compose official prayers for any group of the American people to recite as a part of a religious program carried on by government," *Engel* v. *Vitale*, 370 U.S. 421, 425 (1962), and that is what the school officials attempted to do.

... The question is not the good faith of the school in attempting to make the prayer acceptable to most persons, but the legitimacy of its undertaking that enterprise at all when the object is to produce a prayer to be used in a formal religious exercise which students, for all practical purposes, are obliged to attend.

... There can be no doubt that for many, if not most, of the students at the graduation, the act of standing or remaining silent was an expression of participation in the Rabbi's prayer. That was the very point of the religious exercise. It is of little comfort to a dissenter, then, to be told that for her the act of standing or remaining in silence signifies mere respect, rather than participation. What matters is that, given our social conventions, a reasonable dissenter in this milieu could believe that the group exercise signified her own participation or approval of it.

... Research in psychology supports the common assumption that adolescents are often susceptible to pressure from their peers towards conformity, and that the influence is strongest in matters of social convention....

There was a stipulation in the District Court that attendance at graduation and promotional ceremonies is voluntary.... Petitioners and the United States, as *amicus*, made this a center point of the case, arguing that the option of not attending the graduation excuses any inducement or coercion in the ceremony itself. The argument lacks all persuasion. Law reaches past formalism. And to say a teenage student has a real choice not to attend her high school graduation is formalistic in the extreme. True, Deborah could elect not to attend commencement without renouncing her diploma; but we shall not allow the case to turn on this point. Everyone knows that in our society and in our culture high school graduation is one of life's most significant occasions.... Graduation is a time for family and those closest to the student to celebrate success and express mutual wishes of gratitude and respect, all to the end of impressing upon the young person the role that it is his or her right and duty to assume in the community and all of its diverse parts.

... The Constitution forbids the State to exact religious conformity from a student as the price of attending her own high school graduation....

For the reasons we have stated, the judgment of the Court of Appeals is

Affirmed.

JUSTICE BLACKMUN, with whom JUSTICE STEVENS and JUSTICE O'CONNOR join, concurring....

JUSTICE SOUTER, with whom JUSTICE STEVENS and JUSTICE O'CONNOR join, concurring....

JUSTICE SCALIA, with whom THE CHIEF JUSTICE, JUSTICE WHITE, and JUSTICE THOMAS join, dissenting.

... In holding that the Establishment Clause prohibits invocations and benedictions at public-school graduation ceremonies, the Court—with nary a mention that it is doing so—lays waste a tradition that is as old as public-school graduation ceremonies themselves, and that is a component of an even more long-standing American tradition of nonsectarian prayer to God at public celebrations generally. As its instrument of destruction, the bulldozer of its social engineering, the Court invents a boundless, and boundlessly manipulable, test of psychological coercion....

Santa Fe Independent Sch. Dist. v. Doe

530 U.S. 290 (2000)*

In Texas, before each home varsity football game, a student of Santa Fe High School delivered a prayer. Mormon and Catholic students, along with their mothers, challenged this practice as a violation of the Establishment Clause. While the suit was pending, the school district altered the procedure for deciding whether a prayer should be delivered. A district court ruled that the prayer must be nonsectarian and nonproselytizing. The Fifth Circuit held that the student-led and student-initiated prayer, even as modified, was invalid.

JUSTICE STEVENS delivered the opinion of the Court.

Prior to 1995, the Santa Fe High School student who occupied the school's elective office of student council chaplain delivered a prayer over the public address system before each varsity football game for the entire season. This practice, along with others, was challenged in District Court as a violation of the Establishment Clause of the First Amendment. While these proceedings were pending in the District Court, the school district adopted a different policy that permits, but does not require, prayer initiated and led by a student at all home games. The District Court entered an order modifying that policy to permit only nonsectarian, nonproselytizing prayer. The Court of Appeals held that, even as modified by the District Court, the football prayer policy was invalid. We granted the school district's petition for certiorari to review that holding.

I

The Santa Fe Independent School District (District) is a political subdivision of the State of Texas, ... Respondents are two sets of current or former students and their respective mothers. One family is Mormon and the other is Catholic. The District Court permitted respondents (Does) to litigate anonymously to protect them from intimidation or harassment.

... In their complaint the Does alleged that the District had engaged in several proselytizing practices, such as promoting attendance at a Baptist revival meeting, encouraging membership in religious clubs, chastising children who held minority religious beliefs, and distributing Gideon Bibles on school premises. They also alleged that the District allowed students to read Christian invocations and benedictions from the stage at graduation ceremonies, and to deliver overtly Christian prayers over the public address system at home football games.

---

* The text for this case was obtained in electronic form from Westlaw and is reproduced by permission from West Group.

[*The district court entered an interim order, requiring that prayer at graduation exercises be "non-denominational" and that it be presented by a senior student or students selected by members of the graduating class.*] The text of the prayer was to be determined by the students, without scrutiny or preapproval by school officials. References to particular religious figures "such as Mohammed, Jesus, Buddha, or the like" would be permitted "as long as the general thrust of the prayer is non-proselytizing." ...

[*The district court subsequently adopted other procedures, including the use of a secret ballot to decide whether to include an invocation and benediction as part of a graduation exercise, and to elect by secret ballot, from a list of student volunteers, students to deliver nonsectarian, nonproselytizing invocations and benedictions. Similar guidelines were provided for prayer at football games. The court later eliminated the requirement that invocations, benedictions, and prayers be nonsectarian and nonproselytizing, and substituted "messages" and "statements" for the word "prayer." Fifth Circuit precedents held that student-led prayer that was approved by a vote of the students and was nonsectarian and nonproselytizing was permissible at high school graduation ceremonies. However, the Fifth Circuit regarded school-encouraged prayer at school-related sporting events as constitutionally impermissible for two reasons: they were far less solemn and far more frequent.*]

II

... Santa Fe's student election system ensures that only those messages deemed "appropriate" under the District's policy may be delivered. That is, the majoritarian process implemented by the District guarantees, by definition, that minority candidates will never prevail and that their views will be effectively silenced....

Moreover, the District has failed to divorce itself from the religious content in the invocations. It has not succeeded in doing so, either by claiming that its policy is "'one of neutrality rather than endorsement'" or by characterizing the individual student as the "circuit-breaker" in the process. Contrary to the District's repeated assertions that it has adopted a "hands-off" approach to the pregame invocation, the realities of the situation plainly reveal that its policy involves both perceived and actual endorsement of religion. In this case, as we found in *Lee*, the "degree of school involvement" makes it clear that the pregame prayers bear "the imprint of the State and thus put school-age children who objected in an untenable position." 505 U.S., at 590.

The District has attempted to disentangle itself from the religious messages by developing the two-step student election process. The text of the October policy, however, exposes the extent of the school's entanglement. The elections take place at all only because the school "board *has chosen to permit* students to deliver a brief invocation and/or message." App. 104 (emphasis added). The elections thus "shall" be conducted "by the high school student council" and "[u]pon advice and direction of the high school principal." *Id.*, at 104–105. The decision whether to deliver a message is first made by majority vote of the entire student body, followed by a choice of the speaker in a separate, similar majority election. Even though the particular words used by the speaker are not determined by those votes, the policy mandates that the "statement or invocation" be "consistent with the goals and purposes of this policy," which are "to solemnize the event, to promote good sportsmanship and student safety, and to establish the appropriate environment for the competition." *Ibid.*

In addition to involving the school in the selection of the speaker, the policy, by its terms, invites and encourages religious messages. The policy itself states that the purpose of the message is "to solemnize the event." A religious message is the most obvious method of solemnizing an event. Moreover, the requirements that the message "promote good citizenship" and "establish the appropriate environment for competition" further narrow the types of message deemed appropriate, suggesting that a solemn, yet nonreligious, message, such as commentary on United States foreign policy, would be prohibited. Indeed, the only type of message that is expressly endorsed in the text is an "invocation"—a term that primarily describes an appeal for divine assistance....

III

The District next argues that its football policy is distinguishable from the graduation prayer in *Lee* because it does not coerce students to participate in religious observances. Its argument has two parts: first, that there is no impermissible government coercion because the pregame messages are the product of student choices; and second, that there is really no coercion at all because attendance at an extracurricular event, unlike a graduation ceremony, is voluntary.

... Attendance at a high school football game, unlike showing up for class, is certainly not required in order to receive a diploma. Moreover, we may assume that the District is correct in arguing that the informal pressure to attend an athletic event is not as strong as a senior's desire to attend her own graduation ceremony.

There are some students, however, such as cheerleaders, members of the band, and, of course, the team members themselves, for whom seasonal commitments mandate their attendance, sometimes for class credit. The District also minimizes the importance to many students of attending and participating in extracurricular activities as part of a complete educational experience....

... [N]othing in the Constitution as interpreted by this Court prohibits any public school student from voluntarily praying at any time before, during, or after the schoolday....

The judgment of the Court of Appeals is, accordingly, affirmed.

It is so ordered.

CHIEF JUSTICE REHNQUIST, with whom JUSTICE SCALIA and JUSTICE THOMAS join, dissenting....

... [W]ith respect to the policy's purpose, the Court holds that "the simple enactment of this policy, with the purpose and perception of school endorsement of student prayer, was a constitutional violation." ... But the policy itself has plausible secular purposes: "[T]o solemnize the event, to promote good sportsmanship and student safety, and to establish the appropriate environment for the competition." ... Where a governmental body "expresses a plausible secular purpose" for an enactment, "courts should generally defer to that stated intent." *Wallace, supra,* at 74–75 (O'CONNOR, J., concurring in judgment); ... The Court grants no deference to—and appears openly hostile toward—the policy's stated purposes, and wastes no time in concluding that they are a sham....

McCreary County v. ACLU

545 U.S. 844 (2005)

Two Kentucky counties, McCreary and Pulaski, publicly posted two large copies of the Ten Commandments. The American Civil Liberties Union (ACLU) brought suit, arguing that the displays violated the First Amendment's Establishment Clause. In response, the Counties adopted resolutions stating that the Ten Commandments represent the "precedent legal code" of Kentucky, and requiring the addition of historical documents that included religious references, such as the Declaration of Independence's "endowed by their Creator" language. A federal district court held that the exhibits violated the First Amendment, and the Counties responded by adding additional secular documents, including the Magna Carta and lyrics from "The Star Spangled Banner." The third exhibit of the Ten Commandments, challenged once more by the ACLU, failed to pass constitutional muster, and a federal district court ordered its removal. The Sixth Circuit affirmed the lower court, denying the Counties's claim that the displays possessed a secular and educational purpose. McCreary County appealed to the Supreme Court.

JUSTICE SOUTER delivered the opinion of the Court....

II

Twenty-five years ago in a case prompted by posting the Ten Commandments in Kentucky's public schools, this Court recognized that the Ten Commandments "are undeniably a sacred text in the Jewish and Christian faiths" and held that their display in public classrooms violated the First Amendment's bar against establishment of religion. *Stone* [*v. Graham*], 449 U.S. [39], at 41. *Stone* found a predominantly religious purpose in the government's posting of the Commandments, given their prominence as "'an instrument of religion,'"....

A

... When the government acts with the ostensible and predominant purpose of advancing religion, it violates that central Establishment Clause value of official religious neutrality, there being no neutrality when the government's ostensible object is to take sides....

[B–C]

[*The Court rejects the Counties' argument that Lemon's purpose test should be abandoned, that "purpose" is unknowable and that it is invoked by courts in a selective and unpredictable manner. The Court notes that purpose is a traditional tool for both statutory and constitutional interpretation, and that it has been used in numerous Establishment Clause cases*].

Lemon said that government action must have "a secular ... purpose," 403 U.S., at 612, and after a host of cases it is fair to add that although a legislature's stated reasons will generally get deference, the secular purpose required has to be genuine, not a sham, and not merely secondary to a religious objective....

[III.]

Once the Counties were sued, they modified the exhibits and invited additional insight into their purpose in a display that hung for about six months. [*The Court recounts the various additions—historical documents with references to God and Christianity—and determines that the displays' clear focus was the promotion of religion*].... The display's unstinting focus was on religious passages, showing that the Counties were posting the Commandments precisely because of their sectarian content. That demonstration of the government's objective was enhanced by serial religious references and the accompanying resolution's claim about the embodiment of ethics in Christ. Together, the display and resolution presented an indisputable, and undisputed, showing of an impermissible purpose....

... [T]he sectarian spirit of the common resolution found enhanced expression in the third display, which quoted more of the purely religious language of the Commandments than the first two displays had done ... ("I the LORD thy God am a jealous God") (text of Second Commandment in third display); ("the LORD will not hold him guiltless that taketh his name in vain") (from text of Third Commandment); and ("that thy days may be long upon the land which the LORD thy God giveth thee") (text of Fifth Commandment). No reasonable observer could swallow the claim that the Counties had cast off the objective so unmistakable in the earlier displays....

IV

... [T]he principle of neutrality has provided a good sense of direction: the government may not favor one religion over another, or religion over irreligion, religious choice being the prerogative of individuals under the Free Exercise Clause. The principle has been helpful simply because it responds to one of the major concerns that prompted adoption of the Religion Clauses. The Framers and the citizens of their time intended not only to protect the integrity of individual conscience in religious matters, *Wallace v. Jaffree*, 472 U.S., at 52–54, ... but to

guard against the civic divisiveness that follows when the Government weighs in on one side of religious debate; nothing does a better job of roiling society, a point that needed no explanation to the descendants of English Puritans and Cavaliers (or Massachusetts Puritans and Baptists).... A sense of the past thus points to governmental neutrality as an objective of the Establishment Clause, and a sensible standard for applying it....

V

... [W]e affirm the Sixth Circuit in upholding the preliminary injunction.

JUSTICE O'CONNOR, concurring.

... At a time when we see around the world the violent consequences of the assumption of religious authority by government, Americans may count themselves fortunate: Our regard for constitutional boundaries has protected us from similar travails, while allowing private religious exercise to flourish....

JUSTICE SCALIA, with whom THE CHIEF JUSTICE and JUSTICE THOMAS join, and with whom JUSTICE KENNEDY joins as to Parts II and III, dissenting.

... [H]ow can the Court *possibly* assert that "'the First Amendment mandates governmental neutrality between ... religion and nonreligion,'" ... and that "[m]anifesting a purpose to favor ... adherence to religion generally," ... is unconstitutional? Who says so? Surely not the words of the Constitution. Surely not the history and traditions that reflect our society's constant understanding of those words....

Besides appealing to the demonstrably false principle that the government cannot favor religion over irreligion, today's opinion suggests that the posting of the Ten Commandments violates the principle that the government cannot favor one religion over another.... That is indeed a valid principle where public aid or assistance to religion is concerned, ... or where the free exercise of religion is at issue, ... but it necessarily applies in a more limited sense to public acknowledgment of the Creator. If religion in the public forum had to be entirely nondenominational, there could be no religion in the public forum at all....

[*Scalia concludes that neither the first nor the second displays evidence an intent to advance religious practices.*]

... [T]he Court has identified no evidence of a purpose to advance religion in a way that is inconsistent with our cases. The Court may well be correct

in identifying the third displays as the fruit of a desire to display the Ten Commandments, … but nei-

ther our cases nor our history support its assertion
that such a desire renders the fruit poisonous.…

F. NINE JUSTICES IN SEARCH OF A MODEL

The Court has experimented with a number of tests and models in trying to referee church-state disputes. The child-benefit theory, adopted in *Everson,* was partly abandoned after states used it to justify an increasing array of financial assistance to sectarian schools. The three-part *Lemon* test has been
somewhat more durable, because its generality allows the Court to reshape it or ignore it for individual cases. Does a statute have a "secular legislative purpose"? "Secular" is often redefined to meet
the case at hand. Is the "principal or primary effect" of a statute such that it neither "advances nor inhibits" religion? Does the statute foster "excessive entanglement" with religion? These formulations
give the Court ample room to maneuver. The tests can even conflict. As Chief Justice Rehnquist noted
in one dissent, the entanglement test presents a "Catch-22" paradox. Aid must be supervised by the
state to avoid religious content in state-funded secular classes, "but the supervision itself is held to
cause an entanglement." Aguilar v. Felton, 473 U.S. at 421. If the *Lemon* test presents difficulties for
the Court, it can switch to a different model and justify a religious practice on the historical record.
It used this approach in upholding tax exemptions in *Walz* and state chaplains in *Marsh.*

Another test is to distinguish between state aid to primary and secondary schools and state aid to
colleges and universities. A more tolerant judicial attitude toward the latter, on the ground that college students are less likely to be indoctrinated to a particular religious creed, was used to sustain financial assistance in *Tilton, Hunt,* and *Roemer.* It was on this basis that the Court in *Lee* v. *Weisman*
held invalid invocations and benedictions by clergy at public middle and high schools, while recognizing that adults are frequently exposed to prayers at public ceremonies.

The Court has not consistently adopted a policy of "neutrality" toward religions. The majority in
several cases openly follows a principle of supporting religious belief. Justice Douglas justified the
released-time program in *Zorach* because it "encourages religious instruction" and therefore "follows
the best of our traditions." When Chief Justice Burger wrote the opinion in 1970 upholding tax exemptions to religious organizations, he claimed that the exemption was "neither the advancement nor
the inhibition of religion; it is neither sponsorship nor hostility." Yet, a page later, he explained that
the state has an "affirmative policy" to consider religious groups "as beneficial and stabilizing influences in community life.…" Walz v. Tax Commission, 397 U.S. 664, 672–73. An affirmative and supportive attitude is also reflected in his commitment to a "benevolent neutrality" toward churches and
religious exercises. Id. at 676–77.

Justice Black warned in *Engel* v. *Vitale* that a union of government and religion injures both parties
because it "tends to destroy government and to degrade religion." To qualify for state and federal funds,
religious schools are tempted to surrender some autonomy and to dilute the sectarian content of their
courses. Secularization has reduced the phrase "In God We Trust" (found on coins, in the national anthem, and in the national motto) to patriotic rather than theological significance. According to the reasoning in *Lynch* v. *Donnelly,* even the crèche has been secularized as part of the Christmas season. Pressure for prayer in public schools risks the formulation of bland language to satisfy all sects.

NOTES AND QUESTIONS

1. In *Engel v. Vitale*, the Court ruled that "it is no part of the business of government to compose
official prayers for any group of people to recite as part of a religious program carried on by the government." It was clear to the Court that under such a practice, students who did not share the beliefs

embodied in the prayer might well choose not to participate, but in that event, they risked being viewed as an outsider. Or, they might compromise their beliefs and choose to participate so as to avoid the outsider label. The feature of coercion was conspicuous. Which subsequent opinions have embraced this rationale? Has the Court departed from this rationale? In your opinion, has the Court exhibited sufficient concern for nonconformists or outsiders?

2. In *McCreary*, Justice Souter observed that the "principle of neutrality" is a workable guide in religion cases. Do you agree? What problems arise from the employment of this standard?

3. In *Marsh v. Chambers*, 463 U.S. 783 (1983), the Court upheld the practice of legislative prayer. If that position is sustainable, does it follow that a National Day of Prayer would be constitutional? Consider what is involved in the course of legislative prayer, and who the target audience is. Who is the target audience of a National Day of Prayer? Would the government violate the principle of neutrality if it sponsored such an event?

4. Describe the Court's treatment of the *Lemon* test. Does it remain intact? Does it supply a workable constitutional theory?

5. By what reasoning did the Court save the nativity scene in *Lynch v. Donnelly*? How should the Court distinguish secular from religious activities?

6. *Goldman v. Weinberger* illustrates the hazards of viewing the judiciary as the branch of government best-positioned to protect civil liberties. After the Court rejected Captain Goldman's free exercise challenge, Congress passed legislation securing his right to wear a yarmulke indoors while on duty. In your view, what other cases may be advanced to further illustrate the duty of elected branches to independently interpret the Constitution?

7. In *Gobitis*, Justice Frankfurter rejected the argument that religious freedom compels exemption from civic duties. In your view, does the Free Exercise Clause compel such exemptions? Why or why not?

8. In light of *Smith* and *Boerne*, what remains of the use of the compelling government interest test in cases involving the religious clauses?

SELECTED READINGS

BLANCHARD, PAUL. God and Man in Washington. Boston: Beacon Press, 1960.

BROWN, ERNEST. "Quis Custodiet Ipsos Custodes?—The School-Prayer Cases." 1963 Supreme Court Review 1.

CHOPER, JESSE. "The Religion Clauses of the First Amendment: Reconciling the Conflict." 41 University of Pittsburgh Law Review 673 (1980).

CORD, ROBERT L. Separation of Church and State: Historical Fact and Current Fiction. New York: Lambeth Press, 1982.

DOLBEARE, KENNETH M. AND PHILLIP E. HAMMOND. The School Prayer Decisions. Chicago: University of Chicago Press, 1971.

EVANS, BETTE NOVIT. Interpreting the Free Exercise of Religion: The Constitution and American Pluralism. Chapel Hill, N.C.: University of North Carolina Press, 1997.

FISHER, LOUIS. Religious Liberty in America: Political Safeguards. Lawrence: University Press of Kansas, 2002.

———. "Statutory Exemptions for Religious Freedom," 44 Journal of Church and State 291 (2002).

———. "Nonjudicial Safeguards for Religious Liberty," 70 University of Cincinnati Law Review 31 (2001).

FOWLER, ROBERT, ALLEN HERTZE, LAURA OLSON, AND KEVIN DEN DULK. Religion and Politics in America. Boulder, Colo.: Westview Press, 2d ed., 2004.

GIANNELLA, DONALD A. "Religious Liberty, Nonestablishment, and Doctrinal Development: The Religious Liberty Guarantee." 80 Harvard Law Review 1381 (1967).

———. "Religious Liberty, Nonestablishment, and Doctrinal Development: The Nonestablishment Principle." 81 Harvard Law Review 513 (1968).

———. "Lemon and Tilton: The Bitter and the Sweet of Church-State Entanglement." 1971 Supreme Court Review 147.

GREENAWALT, KENT. Does God Belong in Public Schools? Princeton: Princeton University Press, 2005.

———. "Quo Vadis: The Status and Prospects of 'Tests' Under the Religion Clauses," 1995 Supreme Court Review 323.

HAMBURGER, PHILIP. Separation of Church and State. Cambridge: Harvard University Press, 2002.

KATZ, WILBUR G. "Radiations from Church Tax Exemption." 1970 Supreme Court Review 93.

KAUPER, PAUL G. Religion and the Constitution. Baton Rouge: Louisiana State University Press, 1964.

———. "Church Autonomy and the First Amendment: The Presbyterian Church Case." 1969 Supreme Court Review 347.

KELLY, DEAN M., ED. Government Intervention in Religious Affairs. New York: Pilgrim Press, 1982.

KURLAND, PHILIP B. Religion and the Law: Of Church and State and the Supreme Court. Chicago: Aldine Publishing, 1962.

———. "The Regents' Prayer Case: "Full of Sound and Fury, Signifying…'" 1962 Supreme Court Review 1.

LEVY, LEONARD W. The Establishment Clause: Religion and the First Amendment. Chapel Hill, N.C.: University of North Carolina Press, 1994.

MORGAN, RICHARD E. The Supreme Court and Religion. New York: The Free Press, 1972.

———. "The Establishment Clause and Sectarian Schools: A Final Installment?" 1973 Supreme Court Review 57.

OAKS, DALLIN H., ed. The Wall between Church and State. Chicago: University of Chicago Press, 1963.

PETERS, SHAWN FRANCIS. Judging Jehovah's Witnesses: Religious Persecution and the Dawn of the Rights Revolution. Lawrence: University Press of Kansas, 2000.

PFEFFER, LEO. Church, State, and Freedom. Boston: Beacon Press, 1967.

SORAUF, FRANK J. The Wall of Separation: The Constitutional Politics of Church and State. Princeton, N.J.: Princeton University Press, 1976.

STOKES, ANSON PHELPS. Church and State in the United States. 3 vols. New York: Harper & Row, 1950.

VAN ALSTYNE, William W. "Constitutional Separation of Church and State: The Quest for a Coherent Position." 57 American Political Science Review 865 (1963).

WITTE, JOHN JR. Religion and the American Constitutional Experiment. Boulder, Colo.: Westview Press, 2d ed., 2005.

13

Due Process
of Law

Probably no area of constitutional law harbors as many public misconceptions and suspicions as the rights available to the accused. The public wonders how many rights flow from the Constitution and how many from the pen of a judge. The right to a jury trial is generally understood and supported. Juries form an independent check between the government and the defendant. The writ of habeas corpus provides constitutional protection for those unlawfully detained by government. The Bill of Rights contains additional safeguards for defendants: use of a grand jury to indict suspects; protections against double jeopardy and self-incrimination; the right to a speedy and public trial by an impartial jury; the right to confront witnesses and obtain witnesses; the right to counsel; and prohibitions against excessive bail, excessive fines, and cruel and unusual punishment. Still other rights derive from congressional statutes and judicial decisions.

To the popular mind, "legal technicalities" permit known criminals to go free. Public fears and ignorance are easily exploited during political campaigns dominated by law-and-order themes. Candidates routinely attack the courts for handcuffing the police. Strong emotions thus cast a dark shadow across basic values of procedural due process and the right to a fair trial. Although Americans are quick to condemn violations of human rights in other countries, they often attack the operation of due process at home. Yet Justice Felix Frankfurter reminded us that "the history of liberty has largely been the history of observance of procedural safeguards." McNabb v. United States, 318 U.S. 332, 347 (1943). Justice Robert Jackson said he would rather live under Soviet law enforced by American procedures than under American law enforced by Soviet procedures. Leonard W. Levy, The Origins of the Fifth Amendment ix (1986 ed.).

Criminal litigation is largely a matter for state courts. The vast bulk of criminal offenses are handled at the state, not the national, level. This chapter reviews developments of criminal law by Congress, the executive branch, and the federal courts. It also identifies areas in which state courts either took the lead or rejected standards announced by federal courts.

A. THE CONCEPT OF DUE PROCESS

Due process can be traced to the Magna Carta of 1215, in which the English king promised not to proceed against a freeman "unless by the lawful judgment of his peers or by the law of the land." Due process became equivalent to the laws passed by the English Parliament. In America, however, legislative enactments are subjected to the scrutiny of the courts. Murray's Lessee v. Hoboken Land & Improvement Co., 18 How. 272, 276 (1856).

Due process relies partly on the written guarantees in the Constitution. Under the Fifth Amendment, which originally applied only to the federal government, no person shall be "deprived of life, liberty, or property, without due process of law." The Fourteenth Amendment applies the same standard to the states. At a minimum, "due process" means that an accused must be given notice of a charge and adequate opportunity to appear and be heard.[1] Other amendments, from the Fourth through the Eighth, supply additional substance to due process, and most were made applicable to the states through the process of "selective incorporation" of the Bill of Rights. On a case by case basis the Court considered whether protections such as a jury trial and access to counsel were "implicit in the concept of ordered liberty" and therefore incorporated by the term "liberty" in the due process clause of the Fourteenth Amendment. (For a more detailed discussion of this development see the chapter on Federalism).

Due process also depends on American values of fairness. The Constitution does not specify the standards required to convict, but the requirement that guilt of a criminal charge be proved "beyond a reasonable doubt" is part of custom dating back to the early years of our nation. In re Winship, 397 U.S. 358, 361 (1970). The reasonable-doubt standard "is indispensable to command the respect and confidence of the community in applications of the criminal law. It is critical that the moral force of the criminal law not be diluted by a standard of proof that leaves people in doubt whether innocent men are being condemned." Id. at 364. The requirement of proof beyond a reasonable doubt in a criminal case is "bottomed on a fundamental value determination of our society that it is far worse to convict an innocent man than to let a guilty man go free." Id. at 372 (Harlan, J., concurring). Civil litigation, on the other hand, permits proof by a preponderance of the evidence. Id. at 371. Also, a presumption of innocence favors the accused. A defendant is innocent until proved guilty. The burden of establishing guilt rests on the prosecution "from the beginning to the end of the trial." Agnew v. United States, 165 U.S. 36, 49–50 (1897).

A fair trial cannot be conducted in the presence of a mob-dominated jury. A jury is unable to deliberate fairly and reach a just conclusion when threatened by violence from a mob bent on lynching the accused. Such trials violate fundamental notions of due process. A case decided by the Supreme Court in 1915 concerned Leo Frank, who had been charged with the murder of a 13-year-old girl. Angry crowds, chanting "Hang the Jew," dominated the trial. After the Supreme Court upheld the conduct of his trial, he was taken from prison by an armed mob and lynched. Frank v. Mangum, 237 U.S. 309 (1915). In 1986, the Georgia Board of Pardons and Paroles granted Frank a posthumous pardon. Even before assistance of counsel was recognized as a constitutional right in state criminal cases, the Supreme Court held in 1932 that due process required counsel for a defendant facing a death sentence. POWELL v. ALABAMA, 287 U.S. 45 (1932).

In addition to judicial guidance, due process is defined by legislative actions that revise the criminal code. Through statutory action, Congress and state legislatures provide standards for culpability; identifies grounds (such as insanity) to defend against prosecution; establishes a structure for sentencing; and sets forth the rules for pretrial and trial procedures, admissibility of evidence, and contempt of court. Congress reviews the Federal Rules of Criminal Procedure submitted by the Supreme Court. These rules, governing such matters as alibis, plea bargaining, and pretrial motions, may be revised or delayed by Congress. Rules of evidence, dealing with privileges, witnesses, and testimony, are also subject to congressional review and action.

In 2009, the Supreme Court deferred to the states and Congress on rules governing access to DNA evidence. An Alaska man convicted of a brutal crime claimed that the district attorney's office was violating his due process rights by refusing to provide him with DNA evidence from the case. He claimed that advanced DNA testing was not available at the time of his conviction and such testing would provide proof of his innocence. The Court said that the task of devising rules "to harness DNA's power to prove innocence" belonged with the legislative branch and noted that 46 states and Congress had all enacted statutes creating rules about access to such evidence. District Atty's Office for Third Jud. Dist. v. Osborne, 557 U.S. 52 (2009).

---

1. In a series of rulings, the Supreme Court has held that due process does not in every instance require advance notice and hearing. For example, see Gilbert v. Homar, 520 U.S. 924 (1997), decided by a unanimous Court.

Three years later, the Court again gave guidance on DNA evidence. Skinner v. Switzer, 562 U.S. ___ (2011). In 2012, the Court noted that eyewitness misidentification is the single greatest cause of wrongful convictions. Of the first 250 convictions overturned due to DNA evidence, 76% involved eyewitness misidentification. Perry v. New Hampshire, 565 U.S. ___ (2012).

Habeas Corpus

Under Article I, Section 9, the privilege of the writ of habeas corpus "shall not be suspended, unless when in Cases of Rebellion or Invasion the public Safety may require it." Through use of this "great writ," judges may determine whether someone is being imprisoned illegally. Authorities who receive the writ (*habeas corpus* means "you have the body") must justify the legality of a detention. Over time, the purpose of the writ has been expanded from protecting rights before conviction to giving relief after conviction. The Warren Court used the writ to enforce Bill of Rights protections in state courts, both broadening federal power over the states and adding substantially to the Court's workload. Fay v. Noia, 372 U.S. 391 (1963). The Burger Court attempted to cut back the scope of the writ. Wainwright v. Sykes, 433 U.S. 72 (1977); Francis v. Henderson, 425 U.S. 536 (1976). Congress has passed legislation to limit the availability of habeas corpus relief for state and federal prisoners. The Court has also been active in limiting the opportunity for prisoners to obtain habeas corpus relief. Restrictions have been placed on death row inmates who want their claims heard in federal court after unsuccessful appeals in state court (addressed at the end of this chapter).

Entrapment

Due process is an issue in questions of entrapment, when law enforcement officers instigate a crime by trickery and deception. Through such actions they help manufacture or stimulate a crime that might not have occurred without their intervention. Entrapment tactics should not be confused with "sting" operations, in which law officers use deceit to ensnare those who have *already* committed a crime.

As an example of entrapment, government officials lured a citizen into violating the law by making repeated and persistent solicitations, taking advantage of sentiment and friendship to encourage and provoke a crime. The Supreme Court held that the officials implanted in the mind of an innocent person the disposition to commit an offense. Sorrells v. United States, 287 U.S. 435 (1932). In another case, the Court limited law enforcement to the prevention of crime and the apprehension of criminals: "Manifestly, that function does not include the manufacturing of crime." Sherman v. United States, 356 U.S. 369, 372 (1958). The Court attempts to distinguish between two tests: subjective (the defendant's predisposition to commit a crime) and objective (the tactics used by law enforcement officers to instigate a crime). The Supreme Court has offered the vague standard that entrapment is no defense unless the government's conduct "is so outrageous" as to violate due process. United States v. Russell, 411 U.S. 423, 431 (1973). This decision, parting company with *Sorrells* and *Sherman,* opened the door to governmental abuses.

In 1992, the Court returned to the traditional test by holding that the government must prove beyond a reasonable doubt that the accused was predisposed to commit a crime. Government agents may not excite someone's interest in illegal pornographic material and pressure that person into purchasing the literature. Jacobson v. United States, 503 U.S. 540 (1992). The Court has devised many technical definitions of entrapment, some of them quite subtle and vague in determining "predisposition." But if a juror decides that prosecutors have abused their powers by encouraging someone to commit a crime that would not have happened without the government's intervention, the last word on the meaning of entrapment (at least in that case) is with the juror.

The *Brady* Violation

In 1963, the Supreme Court divided 7 to 2 in holding that due process is violated whenever the prosecution suppresses evidence favorable to an accused who has requested it and the evidence is material either to guilt or to punishment, irrespective of the good faith or bad faith of the prosecution. In this case, an accused charged with murder was denied a statement in which his accomplice to a crime admitted to the actual homicide. It did not come to his notice until after he had been tried, convicted, sentenced, and his sentence had been affirmed. Brady v. Maryland, 373 U.S. 83 (1963). The Court in 2012 reversed a conviction because the prosecution failed to disclose evidence that contradicted statements by an eyewitness. Smith v. Cain, 565 U.S. ___ (2012). Although *Brady* remains a constitutional principle that requires prosecutors to provide the accused exculpatory evidence, failure to abide by that principle may not result in any liability or penalties for members of the prosecution team, even when the withholding of evidence is deliberate. Connick v. Thompson, 563 U.S. ___ (2011).

Powell v. Alabama

287 U.S. 45 (1932)

In this famous trial known as the "Scottsboro case," Ozie Powell and several other black youths in Alabama were charged with raping two white girls. The boys were found guilty and given the death sentence. The case involves basic questions of due process, including the right to a fair trial, assistance of counsel, and the exclusion of blacks from the jury.

Mr. Justice Sutherland delivered the opinion of the Court....

In this court the judgments are assailed upon the grounds that the defendants, and each of them, were denied due process of law and the equal protection of the laws, in contravention of the Fourteenth Amendment, specifically as follows: (1) they were not given a fair, impartial and deliberate trial; (2) they were denied the right of counsel, with the accustomed incidents of consultation and opportunity of preparation for trial; and (3) they were tried before juries from which qualified members of their own race were systematically excluded....

The only one of the assignments which we shall consider is the second, in respect of the denial of counsel; ...

The record shows that on the day when the offense is said to have been committed, these defendants, together with a number of other negroes, were upon a freight train on its way through Alabama. On the same train were seven white boys and the two white girls. A fight took place between the negroes and the white boys, in the course of which the white boys, with the exception of one named Gilley, were thrown off the train. A message was sent ahead, reporting the fight and asking that every negro be gotten off the train. The participants in the fight, and the two girls, were in an open gondola car. The two girls testified that each of them was assaulted by six different negroes in turn, and they identified the seven defendants as having been among the number. None of the white boys was called to testify, with the exception of Gilley, who was called in rebuttal.

Before the train reached Scottsboro, Alabama, a sheriff's posse seized the defendants and two other negroes. Both girls and the negroes then were taken to Scottsboro, the county seat....

First. The record shows that immediately upon the return of the indictment defendants were arraigned and pleaded not guilty. Apparently they were not asked whether they had, or were able to employ, counsel, or wished to have counsel appointed; or whether they had friends or relatives who might assist in that regard if communicated with. That it would not have been an idle ceremony to have given the defendants reasonable opportunity to communicate with their families and endeavor to obtain counsel is demonstrated by the fact that, very soon after conviction, able counsel appeared in their behalf. This was pointed out by Chief Justice Anderson in the course of his dissenting opinion. "They were non-residents," he said, "and had little time or opportunity to get in touch with their families and friends who were scattered throughout two other states, and time has demonstrated that they could or would have been represented by able counsel had a better opportunity been given by a reasonable delay in the trial of the cases, judging from the number and activity of counsel that appeared immediately or shortly after their conviction." ...

It is hardly necessary to say that, the right to counsel being conceded, a defendant should be afforded a fair opportunity to secure counsel of his own choice. Not only was that not done here, but such designation of counsel as was attempted was either so indefinite or so close upon the trial as to amount to a denial of effective and substantial aid in that regard. ...

It thus will be seen that until the very morning of the trial no lawyer had been named or definitely designated to represent the defendants. Prior to that time, the trial judge had "appointed all the members of the bar" for the limited "purpose of arraigning the defendants." Whether they would represent the defendants thereafter if no counsel appeared in their behalf, was a matter of speculation only, or, as the judge indicated, of mere anticipation on the part of the court. Such a designation, even if made for all purposes, would, in our opinion, have fallen far short of meeting, in any proper sense, a requirement for the appointment of counsel. How many lawyers were members of the bar does not appear; but, in the very nature of things, whether many or few, they would not, thus collectively named, have been given that clear appreciation of responsibility or impressed with that individual sense of duty which should and naturally would accompany the appointment of a selected member of the bar, specifically named and assigned.

... The defendants, young, ignorant, illiterate, surrounded by hostile sentiment, haled back and forth under guard of soldiers, charged with an atrocious crime regarded with especial horror in the community where they were to be tried, were thus put in peril of their lives within a few moments after counsel for the first time charged with any degree of responsibility began to represent them. ...

What, then, does a hearing include? Historically and in practice, in our own country at least, it has always included the right to the aid of counsel when desired and provided by the party asserting the right. The right to be heard would be, in many cases, of little avail if it did not comprehend the right to be heard by counsel. Even the intelligent and educated layman has small and sometimes no skill in the sci-

ence of law. If charged with crime, he is incapable, generally, of determining for himself whether the indictment is good or bad. He is unfamiliar with the rules of evidence. Left without the aid of counsel he may be put on trial without a proper charge, and convicted upon incompetent evidence, or evidence irrelevant to the issue or otherwise inadmissible. He lacks both the skill and knowledge adequately to prepare his defense, even though he have a perfect one. He requires the guiding hand of counsel at every step in the proceedings against him. Without it, though he be not guilty, he faces the danger of conviction because he does not know how to establish his innocence. If that be true of men of intelligence, how much more true is it of the ignorant and illiterate, or those of feeble intellect. ...

In the light of the facts outlined in the forepart of this opinion—the ignorance and illiteracy of the defendants, their youth, the circumstances of public hostility, the imprisonment and the close surveillance of the defendants by the military forces, the fact that their friends and families were all in other states and communication with them necessarily difficult, and above all that they stood in deadly peril of their lives—we think the failure of the trial court to give them reasonable time and opportunity to secure counsel was a clear denial of due process.

... Whether this would be so in other criminal prosecutions, or under other circumstances, we need not determine. All that it is necessary now to decide, as we do decide, is that in a capital case, where the defendant is unable to employ counsel, and is incapable adequately of making his own defense because of ignorance, feeble mindedness, illiteracy, or the like, it is the duty of the court, whether requested or not, to assign counsel for him as a necessary requisite of due process of law; ...

The judgments must be reversed and the causes remanded for further proceedings not inconsistent with this opinion.

Judgments reversed.

Mr. Justice Butler, dissenting. ...

Mr. Justice McReynolds concurs in this opinion.

B. DUE PROCESS FOR JUVENILES

For most of our history, juvenile rights depended on a paternalistic system. Under the doctrine *parens patriae* (with the government taking the role as parent), juvenile courts were supposed to serve as guardians for youthful offenders. Procedural rights and protections were considered unnecessary because it was assumed that the judge would act in the best interest of the child. In many cases, however, judges acted arbitrarily and harshly toward juveniles, meting out periods of incarceration that exceeded penalties imposed on adults for the same offense.

Congress passed several statutes during the 1960s to deal with the mounting problem of juvenile delinquency. 75 Stat. 572 (1961); 82 Stat. 462 (1968). Beginning in 1971, the Senate Judiciary Committee held a series of hearings on juvenile delinquency and the methods used for treatment and rehabilitation. The hearings revealed widespread inadequacies in correctional facilities. For example, eight-year-old youths were placed in these institutions for several years at a time. Initial efforts to protect the constitutional rights of juveniles centered on procedural safeguards but later spread to free speech, privacy, and other elements of due process.

Criminal Procedures

How many procedural safeguards available to adults should protect the rights of juveniles? A 1948 case involved a 15-year-old boy who was arrested about midnight on a charge of murder. He was questioned by relays of police from that point until about 5 a.m., without benefit of counsel or friends to advise him. After the police said his friends had confessed to the crime, he signed a confession and was later convicted. He was not taken before a magistrate and formally charged with a crime until three days after his confession. A lawyer tried to see him twice but the police refused. The Court held his confession inadmissible. Haley v. Ohio, 332 U.S. 596 (1948). Similar circumstances led the Court 14 years later to declare inadmissible the confession of a 14-year-old boy held for five days without seeing a lawyer, parent, or other friendly adult, although his mother twice tried to see him. Gallegos v. Colorado, 370 U.S. 49 (1962).

After these cases, the Court began to challenge some conventional notions about the protections accorded by juvenile courts. In theory, juvenile courts acted toward a child in a "parental" relationship and not as adversary. Since the proceedings were civil in nature and not criminal, the youth had no opportunity to complain that basic rights of criminal law had been denied.

A major breakthrough came in 1966. A 16-year-old was accused of housebreaking, robbery, and rape. He was committed to the juvenile court unless it waived jurisdiction after "full investigation" and assigned his case to a federal court. Jurisdiction was waived; he was indicted and convicted. The Supreme Court held that such waivers were invalid unless the juvenile received a hearing and his counsel had access to social records and probation reports. Moreover, the juvenile court had to give reasons for a waiver. Under the system existing at that time, a child received "the worst of both worlds: that he gets neither the protections accorded to adults nor the solicitous care and regenerative treatment postulated for children." Kent v. United States, 383 U.S. 541, 556 (1966).

After these ad hoc efforts to protect the rights of juveniles, the Court took a more comprehensive approach in 1967. Gerald Gault, a 15-year-old, was taken into custody for allegedly making obscene phone calls. No notice was left at his home for his parents. After hearings, a juvenile court committed him to the State Industrial School until he reached majority (a commitment of almost six years). No appeal was permitted by state law for juvenile cases. The Supreme Court held that minors are entitled to certain procedural rights: adequate notice, right to counsel, privilege against self-incrimination, and the rights of confrontation and sworn testimony. IN RE GAULT, 387 U.S. 1 (1967). Many of the requirements of *Gault* are not being met in contemporary juvenile courts (see box on next page).

Closely resembling this case was the decision of a state family court to place a 12-year-old boy in a "training school" for up to six years for stealing $112 from a woman's pocketbook. The Supreme Court held that when a juvenile is charged with an act that would constitute a crime if committed by an adult, due process requires proof beyond a reasonable doubt during the adjudicatory phase. The family court had relied on a preponderance of the evidence. In re Winship, 397 U.S. 358 (1970).

Juvenile Rights after *Gault*

In 1967 the Supreme Court ruled that juveniles are entitled to such basic procedural rights as adequate notice, right to counsel, privilege against self-incrimination, and the rights of confrontation and sworn testimony. In re Gault, 387 U.S.1 (1967). As explained by Paul Marcotte in "Criminal Kids," 76 A.B.A.J. 60, 62–63 (1990), state procedures often fall short of these Supreme Court standards:

"Despite *In Re Gault*, kids often are not represented by lawyers. About half of the youths who appeared before juvenile courts in Minnesota, Nebraska and North Dakota were not represented by counsel, according to [research by Barry Feld, a University of Minnesota law professor.] In another study last year, he found that one-third of Minnesota juveniles removed from their homes and one-fourth incarcerated in training schools never saw a lawyer.

"The Arkansas Supreme Court's removal of exclusive jurisdiction over juveniles from the county courts in 1987 also illustrates this problem. *Walker v. Arkansas Department of Human Resources*, 722 S.W.2d 558. The *Gault* requirements were not being met. County courts did not have the 'same judicial safeguards as other state courts.... County courts, by their very nature, have been unable to ensure the proper disposition of juvenile delinquency cases,' the opinion states.

"... States were beginning the campaign to revise their juvenile codes. New laws required youths with a history of misbehavior to be tried as adults. Other laws excluded certain crimes from the authority of juvenile judges. Prosecutors also were given more authority to charge youths directly in adult court.

"For example, Delaware requires a mandatory waiver for juveniles charged with certain violent crimes. Florida requires a waiver hearing for youths charged with violent crimes who committed a prior crime against the person. California requires juveniles to show that they should be in juvenile court rather than adult court.

"Vermont permits juvenile judges to waive kids as young as 10 into criminal court. In Montana it's 12, and in Georgia, Illinois and Mississippi it's 13, according to a 1987 survey. Many laws set age limits by type of offense. In New York, 14-year-olds are regularly tried as adults."

More Contemporary Rulings

Other rights have been recognized for juveniles. A case in 1975 involved a youth who had been prosecuted as an adult following a finding in juvenile court that he violated a criminal law and was unfit for treatment as a juvenile. The Supreme Court held that the procedure violated the Double Jeopardy Clause. Breed v. Jones, 421 U.S. 519 (1975). Questions also concern the *Miranda* warning, Fare v. Michael C., 442 U.S. 707 (1979), and pretrial detention for juvenile delinquents, Schall v. Martin, 467 U.S. 253 (1984).

In extending these rights to juveniles, the Court decided that a jury trial is not constitutionally required for a state juvenile court delinquency proceeding. At least in this area, the Court was "reluctant to disallow the States to experiment further and to seek in new and different ways the elusive answers to the problems of the young." McKeiver v. Pennsylvania, 403 U.S. 528, 547 (1971). In 1988, the Supreme Court vacated the death sentence of someone who had participated in a murder at age 15. However, a majority of the Court did not agree that the Constitution prohibits the execution of persons who were under 16 at the time of the offense. Although a national consensus appeared to be developing against executing such minors, the Court allowed state legislatures leeway in determining standards and punishment. Thompson v. Oklahoma, 487 U.S. 815 (1988).

A year later, five Justices of the Supreme Court affirmed the death sentence for Kevin Stanford (17 at the time he committed murder) and Heath Wilkins (16 when he committed murder). In its search for objective criteria to decide the constitutional issue, the Court looked to statutes passed by state legislatures. As Justice Scalia noted with his usual crisp style: "The audience for these arguments, in other words, is not this Court but the citizenry of the United States. It is they, not we, who must be persuaded.... [O]ur job is to *identify* the 'evolving standards of decency'; to determine, not what they *should* be, but what they *are.*" Justice O'Connor joined the majority but wrote a concurrence rejecting Scalia's deference to majority opinion. The Court, she said, has a constitutional obligation to determine that a punishment is proportional to the crime. Stanford v. Kentucky, 492 U.S. 361 (1989). In 2002, four Justices (Stevens, Souter, Ginsburg, and Breyer) stated their opposition to executing juvenile offenders. In re Stanford, 537 U.S. 868 (2002).

In 2005, the Supreme Court voted 5 to 4 to abolish capital punishment for juvenile offenders. Citing a "national consensus," the Court ruled that it was unconstitutional to sentence anyone to death for a crime he or she committed while younger than 18. At the time of the Court's decision, 20 states permitted the death penalty for juveniles under 18 (five fewer states than in 1989 when the Court decided *Stanford v. Kentucky*). The new Justices joining the majority in 2005 were Breyer, Ginsburg, and Souter. Roper v. Simmons, 543 U.S. 551 (2005). In a 6–3 decision in 2010 the Court went a step further, holding that juveniles who commit crimes in which no one is killed may not be sentenced to life in prison without the possibility of parole. Graham v. Florida, 560 U.S. ___ (2010). In 2012, a 5–4 Court held that a mandatory term of life imprisonment for two 14-year-olds, without the possibility of parole, violated the Eighth Amendment. Miller v. Alabama, 567 U.S. ___ (2012).

Juvenile justice experts believe that Supreme Court decisions since 2005 reflect similar trends in the states. The pattern of treating violent juveniles like adults in terms of sentencing and incarceration has been challenged by neurological evidence that adolescent brains are not fully developed. A majority of the Court appears to believe that juveniles are sufficiently different from adults regarding culpability and must be treated by separate standards in deciding on punishment. There is also the problem of prison overcrowding.

In re Gault

387 U.S. 1 (1967)

Gerald Gault, 15 years old, was taken into custody for allegedly making obscene phone calls to a woman. The police did not notify his parents. After hearings before a juvenile court judge, he was ordered committed to the State Industrial School as a juvenile delinquent until he reached the age of majority (age 21). His parents challenged the constitutionality of the Arizona Juvenile Code and the procedures used in Gerald's case. The Supreme Court of Arizona concluded that the proceedings that led to Gault's commitment did not offend due process requirements.

MR. JUSTICE FORTAS delivered the opinion of the Court....

I.

On Monday, June 8, 1964, at about 10 a.m., Gerald Francis Gault and a friend, Ronald Lewis, were taken into custody by the Sheriff of Gila County. Gerald was then still subject to a six months' probation order which had been entered on February 25, 1964, as a result of his having been in the company of another boy who had stolen a wallet from a lady's purse. The police action on June 8 was taken as the result of a verbal complaint by a neighbor of the boys, Mrs. Cook, about a telephone call made to her in which the caller or callers made lewd or indecent remarks. It will suffice for purposes of this opinion to say that the remarks or questions put to her were of the irritatingly offensive, adolescent, sex variety.

At the time Gerald was picked up, his mother and father were both at work. No notice that Gerald was being taken into custody was left at the home. No other steps were taken to advise them that their son had, in effect, been arrested. Gerald was taken to the Children's Detention Home. When his mother arrived home at about 6 o'clock, Gerald was not there. Gerald's older brother was sent to look for him at the trailer home of the Lewis family. He apparently learned then that Gerald was in custody. He so informed his mother. The two of them went to the Detention Home. The deputy probation officer, Flagg, who was also superintendent of the Detention Home, told Mrs. Gault "why Jerry was there" and said that a hearing would be held in Juvenile Court at 3 o'clock the following day, June 9.

Officer Flagg filed a petition with the court on the hearing day, June 9, 1964. It was not served on the Gaults. Indeed, none of them saw this petition until the habeas corpus hearing on August 17, 1964. The petition was entirely formal. It made no reference to any factual basis for the judicial action which it initiated. It recited only that "said minor is under the age of eighteen years, and is in need of the protection of this Honorable Court; [and that] said minor is a delinquent minor." It prayed for a hearing and an order regarding "the care and custody of said minor." Officer Flagg executed a formal affidavit in support of the petition.

On June 9, Gerald, his mother, his older brother, and Probation Officers Flagg and Henderson appeared before the Juvenile Judge in chambers. Gerald's father was not there. He was at work out of the city. Mrs. Cook, the complainant, was not there. No one was sworn at this hearing. No transcript or recording was made. No memorandum or record of the substance of the proceedings was prepared. Our information about the proceedings and the subsequent hearing on June 15, derives entirely from the testimony of the Juvenile Court Judge, Mr. and Mrs. Gault and Officer Flagg at the habeas corpus proceeding conducted two months later. From this, it appears that at the June 9 hearing Gerald was questioned by the judge about the telephone call. There was conflict as to what he said. His mother recalled that Gerald said he only dialed Mrs. Cook's number and handed the telephone to his friend, Ronald. Officer Flagg recalled that Gerald had admitted making the lewd remarks. Judge McGhee testified that Gerald "admitted making one of these [lewd] statements." At the conclusion of the hearing, the judge said he would "think about it." Gerald was taken back to the Detention Home. He was not sent to his own home with his parents. On June 11 or 12, after having been detained since June 8, Gerald was released and driven home. There is no explanation in the record as to why he was kept in the Detention Home or why he was released. At 5 p.m. on the day of Gerald's release, Mrs. Gault received a note signed by Officer Flagg. It was on plain paper, not letterhead. Its entire text was as follows:

"Mrs. Gault:
"Judge McGhee has set Monday June 15, 1964 at 11:00 a.m. as the date and time for further Hearings on Gerald's delinquency

"/s/Flagg"

At the appointed time on Monday, June 15, Gerald, his father and mother, Ronald Lewis and his father, and Officers Flagg and Henderson were present before Judge McGhee.... Again, the complainant, Mrs. Cook, was not present.... The judge did not speak to Mrs. Cook or communicate with her at any time....

At this June 15 hearing a "referral report" made by the probation officers was filed with the court, although not disclosed to Gerald or his parents. This listed the charge as "Lewd Phone Calls." At the conclusion of the hearing, the judge committed Gerald as a juvenile delinquent to the State Industrial School "for the period of his minority [that is, until 21], unless sooner discharged by due process of law."...

No appeal is permitted by Arizona law in juvenile cases....

[II.]

From the inception of the juvenile court system, wide differences have been tolerated—indeed insisted upon—between the procedural rights accorded to adults and those of juveniles. In practically all jurisdictions, there are rights granted to adults which are withheld from juveniles. In addition to the specific problems involved in the present case, for example, it has been held that the juvenile is not entitled to bail, to indictment by grand jury, to a public trial or to trial by jury....

If Gerald had been over 18, he would not have been subject to Juvenile Court proceedings. For the particular offense immediately involved, the maximum punishment would have been a fine of $5 to $50, or imprisonment in jail for not more than two months. Instead, he was committed to custody for a maximum of six years. If he had been over 18 and had committed an offense to which such a sentence might apply, he would have been entitled to substantial rights under the Constitution of the United States as well as under Arizona's laws and constitution. The United States Constitution would guarantee him rights and protections with respect to arrest, search and seizure, and pretrial interrogation. It would assure him of specific notice of the charges and adequate time to decide his course of action and to prepare his defense. He would be entitled to clear advice that he could be represented by counsel, and, at least if a felony were involved, the State would be required to provide counsel if his parents were unable to afford it. If the court acted on the basis of his confession, careful procedures would be required to assure its voluntariness. If the case went to trial, confrontation and opportunity for cross-examination would be guaranteed....

[Justice Fortas itemized the rights that must be extended to juveniles: (1) notice "must be given sufficiently in advance of scheduled court proceedings so

that reasonable opportunity to prepare will be afforded," and it must be specific about the alleged misconduct; (2) in proceedings to determine delinquency that may result in commitment to an institution, the child and the parents must be notified of the child's right to be represented by counsel retained by them, or if they are unable to afford counsel, counsel will be appointed to represent the child; (3) the constitutional privilege against self-incrimination applies to juveniles as it does to adults. There may be "some differences in technique — but not in principle — depending upon the age of the child and the presence and competence of parents." Care must be taken to assure that a child's admission of wrongdoing is voluntary, not coerced or suggested, and not "the product of ignorance of rights or of adolescent fantasy, fright or despair." As to Mrs. Cook not being present during the proceedings, unless there is a valid confession adequate to support the determination of the Juvenile Court, confrontation and sworn testimony by witnesses available for cross-examination are essential to find "delinquency" and commit Gerald to a state institution for a maximum of six years. Fortas found no need to rule on a requirement for appellate review, the failure to provide a transcript or recording of the hearings, or the failure of the Juvenile Judge to give grounds for his conclusion.]

For the reasons stated, the judgment of the Supreme Court of Arizona is reversed and the cause remanded for further proceedings not inconsistent with this opinion.

It is so ordered.

MR. JUSTICE BLACK, concurring....

MR. JUSTICE WHITE, concurring. [*He joins the Court's opinion except for the part on confrontation, self-incrimination, and cross-examination.*]

MR. JUSTICE HARLAN, concurring in part and dissenting in part. [*He also disagreed with the Court's analysis of confrontation, self-incrimination, and cross-examination.*]

MR. JUSTICE STEWART, dissenting.

The Court today uses an obscure Arizona case as a vehicle to impose upon thousands of juvenile courts throughout the Nation restrictions that the Constitution made applicable to adversary criminal trials. I believe the Court's decision is wholly unsound as a matter of constitutional law, and sadly unwise as a matter of judicial policy.

Juvenile proceedings are not criminal trials. They are not civil trials. They are simply not adversary proceedings....

C. GRAND JURIES AND JURY TRIALS

Procedural safeguards include indictment by a grand jury and trial by regular (petit) jury. The Fifth Amendment provides that "no person shall be held for a capital, or otherwise infamous crime, unless on a presentment or indictment of a grand jury, except in cases arising in the land or naval forces, or in the militia, when in actual service in time of war or public danger." Definitions of "infamous" vary from one time period to another. An offense punishable by death must be prosecuted by indictment; offenses punishable by imprisonment exceeding one year must also be prosecuted by indictment unless the defendant waives indictment and requests prosecution by "information" (taken at the initiative of a prosecutor under sworn oath). The grand jury procedure in the Fifth Amendment is one of the few provisions in the Bill of Rights that has not been incorporated into the Due Process Clause of the Fourteenth Amendment and applied against the states.

The Grand Jury

Grand juries are meant to check government. In England, they acquired an independence "free from control by the Crown or judges." Costello v. United States, 350 U.S. 359, 362 (1956). Before initiating a criminal trial in America, a federal prosecutor must convince a body of lay persons (usually 23 members) that sufficient evidence exists to try a suspect. If satisfied by the evidence, 12 or more jurors may indict, which is a formal charge recommending that the person be brought to trial. A trial is limited to the charges identified in the indictment. A trial judge may not broaden the charges and allow a jury to decide questions outside the scope of the indictment.

State grand juries vary in size. The requirement for a grand jury applies only to the federal government. In 1884, the Supreme Court held that the Due Process Clause of the Fourteenth Amendment cannot be used to require states to indict by grand jury. Instead, states may prosecute upon a district attorney's "information," which consists of a prosecutor's accusation under oath.[2]

Grand juries do not follow the same procedural or evidentiary rules as a trial court. Witnesses, asked questions under oath, are not accompanied by their attorney. A judge is not present in the grand jury room. The rules of evidence, which normally require that questions be relevant and material, do not apply in the grand jury room. The public and the press are excluded. Records, transcripts, and materials are largely secret.[3] The proceedings are not adversary hearings to adjudicate guilt or innocence. They merely determine whether criminal proceedings should be instituted.

Witnesses before a grand jury may invoke the Fifth Amendment privilege against self-incrimination. Counselman v. Hitchcock, 142 U.S. 547 (1892). This privilege is overridden if the government grants immunity to the witness (discussed later in this chapter). Witnesses who then refuse to answer questions may be jailed for contempt of court. Witnesses may not refuse to answer because questions are based on illegally obtained evidence. United States v. Calandra, 414 U.S. 338 (1974). The First Amendment does not protect newspaper reporters from responding to a grand jury subpoena and answering questions. Branzburg v. Hayes, 408 U.S. 665 (1972). This judicial doctrine can be modified by Congress, but Congress has yet to pass such legislation. A number of states have enacted shield laws to protect reporters from grand jury inquiries.

Grand juries are supposed to be independent checks on a prosecutor's allegations, but at times they become pawns in the hands of zealous and politically motivated prosecutors. Justice Douglas once said in dissent: "It is, indeed, common knowledge that the grand jury, having been conceived as a bulwark between the citizen and the Government, is now a tool of the Executive." United States v. Mara, 410 U.S. 19, 23 (1973). Indiscriminate use of grand juries can smear the reputation of an individual targeted by an administration. At times, the grand jury can be unleashed against radical, nonconformist, and unpopular groups, and exploited to harass and intimidate political opposition. But federal prosecutors must marshal sufficient information to gain the support of grand juries, and service on a grand jury allows citizens to feel that they are part of government decisions, understand them, and can check abusive prosecutors.

Jury Trials

Article III, Section 2, provides that the "Trial of all Crimes, except in Cases of Impeachment, shall be by Jury." Under the Sixth Amendment, for all criminal prosecutions the accused is entitled to "an impartial jury." Although the system of jury trials is often under attack, it offers a valuable opportunity for ordinary citizens to participate in the administration of justice. Their involvement can prevent the government's use of arbitrary power. Alexis de Tocqueville praised the jury for its ability to educate people in civic affairs: "By obliging men to turn their attention to other affairs than their own, it rubs off that private selfishness which is the rust of society." 1 Democracy in America 295 (Bradley ed. 1951).

An accused may waive the right to a jury trial and be tried by the court. A defendant waives a jury trial in writing with the approval of the court and the consent of the government. Due process is denied when a suspect is tried before a judge who has a direct, personal, substantial, and pecuniary interest in deciding against the defendant. Tumey v. Ohio, 272 U.S. 510 (1927). Defendants may forgo a trial by entering into a "plea bargain" with the prosecutor. Most criminal cases are disposed of in

---

2. Hurtado v. California, 110 U.S. 516 (1884); Maxwell v. Dow, 176 U.S. 581 (1900); Lem Wood v. Oregon, 229 U.S. 586 (1913).

3. Under the general rule of secrecy of Rule 6(e) of the Federal Rules of Criminal Procedure, access to grand jury materials is severely restricted, even for government attorneys. United States v. Baggot, 463 U.S. 476 (1983); United States v. Sells Engineering, Inc., 463 U.S. 418 (1983).

this manner. By pleading guilty to a lesser charge, the defendant avoids the risk of a heavier sentence if convicted at trial. Plea bargaining places great power in the hands of a prosecutor, who can use this tool in a coercive and arbitrary manner by threatening to indict for a higher crime if the accused refuses to plead guilty.

Federal juries "shall be of 12," but a verdict may be rendered with less than 12 if one or more jurors are excused after the trial begins. A jury verdict in federal courts must be unanimous. State juries may follow different procedures. The constitutional guarantee of trial by jury does not require a state to provide an accused with a jury of 12 for noncapital cases. The Supreme Court regards 12 as a common-law number and a "historical accident." Williams v. Florida, 399 U.S. 78, 88–89 (1970). However, a jury for a criminal trial in the states must number at least six. BALLEW v. GEORGIA, 435 U.S. 223 (1978).

For noncapital cases, states may allow non-unanimous jury verdicts. APODACA v. OREGON, 406 U.S. 404 (1972). Currently, only two states (Louisiana and Oregon) allow non-unanimous verdicts for some criminal cases. If the jury consists of only six persons, a non-unanimous verdict in a state criminal trial for nonpetty offenses violates the Sixth and Fourteenth Amendments. Burch v. Louisiana, 441 U.S. 130 (1979).

The right to a jury trial does not extend to every criminal proceeding. Offenses that are "petty" (as defined by congressional statute) are tried without a jury. The right to a jury trial usually depends on the potential penalty, not the category of offense. Thus, if someone faces a two-year prison sentence for a "misdemeanor," a jury trial is required. DUNCAN v. LOUISIANA, 391 U.S. 145 (1968). Some decisions hold that an offense cannot be regarded as "petty" if imprisonment of more than six months is authorized. Baldwin v. New York, 399 U.S. 66 (1970); Blanton v. North Las Vegas, 489 U.S. 538 (1989). However, in 1996 the Court (divided 5 to 4) held that someone is not entitled to a jury trial even when facing an aggregate prison term greater than six months. What counts, said the Court, was the legislature's judgment that the offense is petty. Lewis v. United States, 518 U.S. 343 (1996).

Criminal Sentencing

In 2004, the Supreme Court faced the question whether judges or juries should have the predominant say on criminal sentencing. A 5 to 4 ruling held that a system that allows judges to make findings that increase a convicted defendant's sentence beyond the maximums suggested by statutory guidelines represented a violation of the right to trial by jury. The facts supporting an increased sentence must be found by the jury. Blakely v. Washington, 542 U.S. 296 (2004). This decision was based on earlier rulings on the death penalty (see the heading "Juries vs. Judges" in Section G of this chapter). *Blakely* raised questions about the constitutionality of sentencing guidelines, forcing the Court six weeks later to agree to take up that question at the next term. It did so in 2005, deciding that the guidelines were advisory, not mandatory. The result gave federal judges greater discretion in deciding sentences. United States v. Booker, 543 U.S. 220 (2005).

In 2007, the Supreme Court in two cases invited federal judges to disagree with sentencing guidelines that gave much longer sentences for offenses involving crack cocaine than for crimes involving cocaine in its powdered form. Congress treated every gram of crack cocaine as the equivalent of 100 grams of powder cocaine (the 100–1 rule), concluding that crack users were more likely to be involved in violent crime. Most crack offenders were black; powdered cocaine was more widely used by whites. Kimbrough v. United States, 552 U.S. 85 (2007); Gall v. United States, 552 U.S. 38 (2007). Following those decisions, the federal government began to reduce the sentences of crack cocaine offenders and release some prisoners who had received heavy sentences for crack convictions. "Government Starts Cutting Sentences of Crack Inmates," Washington Post, March 5, 2008, A2. In a rare example of bipartisan agreement, Congress passed and the President signed into law the Fair Sentencing Act of 2010. Among other things, the act reduced substantially the disparity between amounts of crack and cocaine from 100–1 to 18–1. The Court in 2012 held that Congress intended the more lenient sentences for crack offenders to begin immediately, even for those who committed their crimes before the bill was enacted. *Dorsey v. United States*, 567 U.S. ___ (2012).

Jury Nullification

For the most part, jurors follow the law as explained by prosecutors and judges. On some occasions — and often highly important ones — jurors rely on their own conscience in deciding what is constitutional and proper. In their own way, jurors sense and articulate what is due process, equal protection, free speech, obscenity, unreasonable searches and seizures, and cruel and unusual punishments. In exercising independent judgment, jurors at various times have represented the best and the worst of democracy. Jeffrey Abramson, *We, the Jury* (1994). Jurors help draw a line around permissible governmental behavior, no matter what legislators enact, prosecutors bring, or judges decide.

"Jury nullification" remains a controversial issue. The term means that jurors may acquit even when they are convinced that the defendant is guilty as charged. At such times, jurors refuse to be bound by the facts of the case or the judge's instruction of the law, and instead vote their conscience. Members of a minority might do this to protest majority policy. But the philosophy of jury nullification is broader than that. In the words of one study, juries "might be the last outpost of a skeptical citizenry that is wary of too much power in the hands of public officials, and nullification introduces a degree of unpredictability that requires prosecutors always to remember who has the last word about who is punished." Leipold, 82 Va. L. Rev. 253, 324 (1996).

The Seventh Amendment

The Seventh Amendment provides: "In suits at common law, where the value in controversy shall exceed twenty dollars, the right of trial by jury shall be preserved...." The purpose was to guarantee a jury not only for criminal trials but for civil trials as well. Nevertheless, the reach of the Seventh Amendment has been severely limited. First, it has not been applied to the states. *Walker v. Sauvinet*, 92 U.S. (2 Otto.) 90, 92 (1876). Second, the trial of civil cases may be conducted before a jury of six persons rather than the 12 required for other federal trials. *Colgrove v. Battin*, 413 U.S. 149 (1973). Third, the Seventh Amendment does not prevent Congress from assigning to an administrative agency the task of adjudicating violations of federal statutes that create new "public rights" involving the government in its sovereign capacity. The Seventh Amendment "preserved" only the rights to a jury trial in existence at that time. *Atlas Roofing Co. v. Occupational Safety Comm'n*, 430 U.S. 442 (1977). More than a hundred federal statutes allow civil penalties to be imposed in excess of $20 without a jury trial. 132 Cong. Rec. 24867–69 (1986). Fourth, there is no Seventh Amendment right to a jury trial against the federal government. *Galloway v. United States*, 319 U.S. 372, 388 (1943).[4] Fifth, the Seventh Amendment right to a jury trial does not extend to patent claims. The Court regards judges as better suited than juries to give meaning to patent terms. *Markman v. Westview Instruments, Inc.*, 517 U.S. 370 (1996).

Discrimination in Jury Selection

Racial and gender discrimination in jury formation has been a persistent problem in America. Congress passed legislation in 1875 to prohibit the use of race as a factor in selecting jurors. 18 Stat. 336, §4; 18 U.S.C. §243. The Court upheld that statute and has continued to strike down the systematic

---

4. Other important Seventh Amendment cases include *Gasperini v. Center for Humanities, Inc.*, 518 U.S. 415 (1996); *Granfinanciera v. Nordberg*, 492 U.S. 33 (1989); *Tull v. United States*, 481 U.S. 412 (1987); *Lehman v. Nakshian*, 453 U.S. 156 (1981); and *Dimick v. Schiedt*, 293 U.S. 474 (1935). For a critique of adjudication by executive agencies rather than by Article III courts, see Sun, "Congressional Delegation of Adjudicatory Power to Federal Agencies and the Right to Trial by Jury," 1988 Duke L. J. 539.

exclusion of blacks from grand juries.[5] Exclusion of Mexican-Americans from grand juries and regular juries is unconstitutional. Hernandez v. Texas, 347 U.S. 475 (1954). Even inadequate representation of a class, such as Mexican-Americans, is unconstitutional. Castaneda v. Partida, 430 U.S. 482 (1977).

The Supreme Court has held that due process is denied when blacks are consistently and wholly excluded from jury service. Norris v. Alabama, 294 U.S. 587 (1935). Although these principles existed for almost a century, Congress had to pass legislation in 1968 to supply additional safeguards against discrimination in the selection of jurors (both grand and petit). 82 Stat. 54. Yet the problem of racial exclusion continued.[6] It was not until 1975 that the Supreme Court held that the exclusion of women from petit juries violated the right to a jury trial. Taylor v. Louisiana, 419 U.S. 522 (1975).

Peremptory Strikes

In 1965, the Supreme Court reviewed the practice of prosecutors who use "peremptory strikes" (eliminating potential jurors without stating a reason). The Court held that a prosecutor's reliance on peremptory challenges to strike all six blacks, even though it produced an all-white jury, did not constitute racial discrimination unless it could be shown that the prosecutor had engaged in this practice for many years. Swain v. Alabama, 380 U.S. 202 (1965). The Court's ruling provoked strong critiques in the law reviews and was rejected by a number of state courts, which put a much heavier burden on prosecutors to justify peremptory challenges along racial lines (see box on next page). In 1983, in a case denying certiorari to revisit *Swain,* two Justices dissented and three other Justices appeared ready to reconsider the merits of *Swain,* especially in light of its unfriendly reception in the states. Justice Stevens noted: "In my judgment it is a sound exercise of discretion for the Court to allow the various States to serve as laboratories in which the issue receives further study before it is addressed by this Court." McCray v. New York, 461 U.S. 961, 963 (1983).

Under these pressures, the Court decided to overturn *Swain* in 1986. The Court held that a prosecutor may not use racial reasons and peremptory challenges to strike all black persons to produce an all-white jury. A prosecutor may not use peremptory challenges on the assumption that black jurors cannot impartially consider a state's case against a black. It is no longer necessary, as under *Swain,* for the defendant to prove discrimination by the prosecutor. If a minority defendant objects to a prosecutor's peremptory challenges, the burden falls on the prosecutor to convince the judge that the exclusions are not racially motivated. Batson v. Kentucky, 476 U.S. 79 (1986).

Refinements to *Batson*

A case in 1990 involved a *white* defendant who objected to the exclusion of blacks from his jury. The Court, split 5 to 4, held that white defendants have standing to object to peremptory challenges that exclude blacks from a jury, but that the Sixth Amendment's "fair cross section" requirement does not prevent either side from using peremptory strikes to exclude racial or other groups. The Court said that the Sixth Amendment does not assure a *representative* jury but rather an *impartial* one. Because the petitioner in this case was a white man, an equal protection issue was not raised. Holland v. Illinois, 493 U.S. 474 (1990).[7]

---

5. E.g., Ex parte Virginia, 100 U.S. 339 (1880); Strauder v. West Virginia, 100 U.S. 303, 308 (1880). See also Vasquez v. Hillery, 474 U.S. 254 (1986); Rose v. Mitchell, 443 U.S. 545 (1979); Alexander v. Louisiana, 405 U.S. 625 (1972); Arnold v. North Carolina, 376 U.S. 773 (1964); Eubanks v. Louisiana, 356 U.S. 584 (1958); Pierre v. Louisiana, 306 U.S. 354 (1939).

6. See McCray v. New York, 461 U.S. 961 (1983); Peters v. Kiff, 407 U.S. 493 (1972); Carter v. Jury Commission, 396 U.S. 320 (1970).

7. In 1991, the Court held that state courts could not rule that a defendant's allegation of an equal protection violation under *Swain* failed to raise a *Batson* claim, nor could state courts adopt a procedural rule after a defendant's trial that prohibited federal judicial review of an equal protection claim. Ford v. Georgia, 498 U.S. 411 (1991).

State Courts Reject *Swain*

Following the Supreme Court's decision in *Swain v. Alabama* (1965), several state courts regarded the ruling as defective, unworkable, and too prejudicial to the rights of defendants. They decided that prosecutors should have a much heavier burden when they use peremptory challenges to affect the racial composition of a jury.

The Supreme Court of California announced that Swain "provides less protection to California residents than the rule we now adopt." People v. Wheeler, 583 P.2d 748, 767 (Cal. 1978). The 1965 decision furnished "no protection whatsoever" to the first defendant who suffered discrimination, and subsequent defendants had little likelihood of collecting the evidence needed to show a pattern of prosecutorial abuse. Research would not reveal which of the excused jurors were black. Id. at 767–68.

The Supreme Judicial Court of Massachusetts, persuaded by California's decision, noted that *Swain* imposed "Sisyphean burdens" on defen-

dants. Commonwealth v. Soares, 387 N.E.2d 499, 509 n.10 (Mass. 1979), cert. denied, 444 U.S. 881 (1979). In light of the extensive criticism of *Swain* in the law reviews "and in recognition of the negligible protection that decision offers to a defendant asserting the right to trial by jury of peers, we take this opportunity to depart from applying its rule perfunctorily, and choose instead to examine this problem from a new vantage point." Id. at 510 n.12.

The Supreme Court of Florida concluded that the *Swain* test was so burdensome that it "has seldom if ever been met." State v. Neil, 457 So.2d 481, 483 (Fla. 1984). While not embracing fully either the California or the Massachusetts approach, the Florida court decided that "an alternative to *Swain* is needed." Id. at 485. The New Mexico Court of Appeals indicated that two alternatives were available: *Swain* or the California-Massachusetts rationale supported by the New Mexico Constitution. State v. Crespin, 612 P.2d 716 (N.M. 1980).

Note: The U.S. Supreme Court overturned *Swain* in Batson v. Kentucky, 476 U.S. 79 (1986).

In 1991, the Court revisited the question of excluding black jurors from a white person's trial. This time, a 7–2 Court held that a white person has a right under the Equal Protection Clause to object to the state's use of peremptory challenges to remove blacks from a jury. It no longer matters whether the defendant and the excluded jurors are of the same race. Reaching back to the Civil Rights Act passed by Congress in 1875, which prohibited the exclusion of blacks from juries, the Court said that racial discrimination in jury selection casts doubt on the integrity of the judicial process. Powers v. Ohio, 499 U.S. 400 (1991). That decision was later reinforced when the Court, divided 6–3, held that private litigants in civil cases cannot exclude potential jurors because of their race. *Batson* applied to peremptory strikes by the prosecution; it now applies to the defendant's attorney as well. Edmonson v. Leeville Concrete Co., 500 U.S. 614 (1991). That broader principle was extended to criminal cases in 1992. Georgia v. McCollum, 505 U.S. 42 (1992).

As a further clarification of *Batson,* the Court in 1991 explained that prosecutors may use peremptory challenges to exclude Hispanics from jury service when the prosecutor can explain that the basis for the exclusion was race-neutral. There may be legitimate reasons for excluding potential jurors who happen to be Hispanic or of some other race. Hernandez v. New York, 500 U.S. 352 (1991). Another peremptory challenge case was decided in Trevino v. Texas, 503 U.S. 562 (1992).

Lawyers may not use gender to exclude people from serving on a jury. Sex stereotyping (women on juries are likely to vote a certain way on accused rapists, paternity suits, etc.) is no longer permissible. J.E.B. v. Alabama ex rel. T.B., 511 U.S. 127 (1994). The Court also ruled that prosecutors may strike potential jurors for reasons that do not make sense so long as the action is race-neutral (e.g., striking jurors because they have long hair, a mustache, or a goatee type beard). Purkett v. Elem, 514 U.S. 765 (1995). In 1998, the Court ruled that white criminal defendants who have been indicted by grand juries from which black people have been excluded may challenge the constitutionality of the indictment. Campbell v. Louisiana, 523 U.S. 392 (1998). In 2003, the Court ruled 8 to 1 that a black prisoner, sentenced to death, was entitled to a new hearing because out of eleven blacks entitled to serve on his jury, ten were excluded. Miller-El v. Cockrell, 537 U.S. 322 (2003). Two years later it overturned this individual's conviction because of racial discrimination in jury selection. Miller-El v. Dretke, 545 U.S. 231 (2005). In 2009, a unanimous Court agreed that since the Constitution does not require states to provide peremptory challenges, "if a defendant is tried before a qualified jury composed of individuals not challengeable for cause, the loss of a peremptory challenge due to a state court's good faith error is not a matter of federal constitutional concern." Rivera v. Illinois, 556 U.S. 148 (2009).

Duncan v. Louisiana
391 U.S. 145 (1968)

Gary Duncan was sentenced to 60 days in prison and fined $150 for simple battery. Louisiana law made simple battery a misdemeanor punishable by a maximum of two years in prison. Dunan's request for a jury trial was denied. In this case, the Court decides whether trial by jury in criminal cases is so fundamental to the American scheme of justice that it must be available in state courts as well as federal courts.

Mr. Justice White delivered the opinion of the Court.

Appellant, Gary Duncan, was convicted of simple battery in the Twenty-fifth Judicial District Court of Louisiana. Under Louisiana law simple battery is a misdemeanor, punishable by a maximum of two years' imprisonment and a $300 fine. Appellant sought trial by jury, but because the Louisiana Constitution grants jury trials only in cases in which capital punishment or imprisonment at hard labor may be imposed, the trial judge denied the request. Appellant was convicted and sentenced to serve 60 days in the parish prison and pay a fine of $150....

I

The Fourteenth Amendment denies the States the power to "deprive any person of life, liberty, or property, without due process of law." In resolving conflicting claims concerning the meaning of this spacious language, the Court has looked increasingly to the Bill of Rights for guidance; many of the rights guaranteed by the first eight Amendments to the Constitution have been held to be protected against state action by the Due Process Clause of the Fourteenth Amendment....

The test for determining whether a right extended by the Fifth and Sixth Amendments with respect to federal criminal proceedings is also protected against state action by the Fourteenth Amendment has been phrased in a variety of ways in the opinions of this Court. The question has been asked whether a right is among those "'fundamental principles of liberty and justice which lie at the base of all our civil and political institutions,'" *Powell* v. *Alabama*, 287 U.S. 45, 67 (1932); whether it is "basic in our system of jurisprudence," *In re Oliver*, 333 U.S. 257, 273 (1948); and whether it is "a fundamental right, essential to a fair trial," *Gideon* v. *Wainwright*, 372 U.S. 335, 343–344 (1963).... The claim before us is that the right to trial by jury guaranteed by the Sixth Amendment meets these tests. The position of Louisiana, on the other hand, is that the Constitution imposes upon the States no duty to give a jury trial in any criminal case, regardless of the seriousness of the crime or the size of the punishment which may be imposed. Because we believe that trial by jury in criminal cases is fundamental to the American scheme of justice, we hold that the Fourteenth Amendment guarantees a right of jury trial in all criminal cases which — were they to be tried in a federal court — would come within the Sixth Amendment's guarantee. Since we consider the appeal before us to be such a case, we hold that the Constitution was violated when appellant's demand for jury trial was refused.

The history of trial by jury in criminal cases has been frequently told. It is sufficient for present purposes to say that by the time our Constitution was written, jury trial in criminal cases had been in existence in England for several centuries and carried impressive credentials traced by many to Magna Carta. Its preservation and proper operation as a protection against arbitrary rule were among the major objectives of the revolutionary settlement which was expressed in the Declaration and Bill of Rights of 1689....

Jury trial came to America with English colonists, and received strong support from them. Royal interference with the jury trial was deeply resented. Among the resolutions adopted by the First Congress of the American Colonies (the Stamp Act Congress) on October 19, 1765 — resolutions deemed by their authors to state "the most essential rights and liberties of the colonists" — was the declaration:

"That trial by jury is the inherent and invaluable right of every British subject in these colonies."

The First Continental Congress, in the resolve of October 14, 1774, objected to trials before judges dependent upon the Crown alone for their salaries and to trials in England for alleged crimes committed in the colonies; the Congress therefore declared:

"That the respective colonies are entitled to the common law of England, and more especially to the great and inestimable privilege of being tried by their peers of the vicinage, according to the course of that law."

The Declaration of Independence stated solemn objections to the King's making "Judges dependent on his Will alone, for the tenure of their offices, and the amount and payment of their salaries," to his "depriving us in many cases, of the benefits of Trial by Jury," and to his "transporting us beyond Seas to be tried for pretended offenses." The Constitution itself, in Art. III, § 2, commanded:

"The Trial of all Crimes, except in Cases of Impeachment, shall be by Jury; and such Trial shall be held in the State where the said Crimes shall have been committed."

Objections to the Constitution because of the absence of a bill of rights were met by the immediate submission and adoption of the Bill of Rights. Included was the Sixth Amendment which, among other things, provided:

"In all criminal prosecutions, the accused shall enjoy the right to a speedy and public trial, by an impartial jury of the State and district wherein the crime shall have been committed."

The constitutions adopted by the original States guaranteed jury trial. Also, the constitution of every State entering the Union thereafter in one form or another protected the right to jury trial in criminal cases. Even such skeletal history is impressive support

for considering the right to jury trial in criminal cases to be fundamental to our system of justice....

II.

Louisiana's final contention is that even if it must grant jury trials in serious criminal cases, the conviction before us is valid and constitutional because here the petitioner was tried for simple battery and was sentenced to only 60 days in the parish prison. We are not persuaded. It is doubtless true that there is a category of petty crimes or offenses which is not subject to the Sixth Amendment jury trial provision and should not be subject to the Fourteenth Amendment jury trial requirement here applied to the States. Crimes carrying possible penalties up to six months do not require a jury trial if they otherwise qualify as petty offenses, *Cheff* v. *Schnackenberg*, 384 U.S. 373 (1966). But the penalty authorized for a particular crime is of major relevance in determining whether it is serious or not and may in itself, if severe enough, subject the trial to the mandates of the Sixth Amendment. *District of Columbia* v. *Clawans*, 300 U.S. 617 (1937)....

In determining whether the length of the authorized prison term or the seriousness of other punishment is enough in itself to require a jury trial, we are counseled by *District of Columbia* v. *Clawans*, *supra*, to refer to objective criteria, chiefly the existing laws and practices in the Nation. In the federal system, petty offenses are defined as those punishable by no more than six months in prison and a $500 fine. In 49 of the 50 States crimes subject to trial without a jury, which occasionally include simple battery, are punishable by no more than one year in jail.... We need not, however, settle in this case the exact location of the line between petty offenses and serious crimes. It is sufficient for our purposes to hold that a crime punishable by two years in prison is, based on past and contemporary standards in this country, a serious crime and not a petty offense. Consequently, appellant was entitled to a jury trial and it was error to deny it.

The judgment below is reversed and the case is remanded for proceedings not inconsistent with this opinion.

[*Fortas wrote a concurring opinion. Black, joined by Douglas, wrote a concurrence disputing the position taken in Harlan's dissent, which objects to the selective incorporation of the Bill of Rights into the Fourteenth Amendment and prefers reliance on the Due Process Clause. Black objects to this approach because due process has "no permanent meaning [and shifts] from time to time in accordance with judges' predilections and understandings of what is best for the country."*]

MR. JUSTICE HARLAN, whom MR. JUSTICE STEWART joins, dissenting.

... The Due Process Clause of the Fourteenth Amendment requires that those procedures be fundamentally fair in all respects. It does not, in my view, impose or encourage nationwide uniformity for its own sake; it does not command adherence to forms that happen to be old; and it does not impose on the States the rules that may be in force in the federal courts except where such rules are also found to be essential to basic fairness.

The Court's approach to this case is an uneasy and illogical compromise among the views of various Justices on how the Due Process Clause should be interpreted. The Court does not say that those who framed the Fourteenth Amendment intended to make the Sixth Amendment applicable to the States. And the Court concedes that it finds nothing unfair about the procedure by which the present appellant was tried. Nevertheless, the Court reverses his conviction: it holds, for some reason not apparent to me, that the Due Process Clause incorporates the particular clause of the Sixth Amendment that requires trial by jury in federal criminal cases — including, as I read its opinion, the sometimes trivial accompanying baggage of judicial interpretation in federal contexts....

Apodaca v. Oregon

406 U.S. 404 (1972)

After the Court had agreed in *Duncan* v. *Louisiana* (1968) that a criminal defendant is entitled to a jury trial in the states, the Court faced a related issue. Could jury verdicts be less than unanimous, even though unanimity is required in the federal courts? Distinctions were necessary between capital and noncapital crimes. Robert Apodaca and two other men were convicted by Oregon jurors who returned less-than-unanimous verdicts.

MR. JUSTICE WHITE announced the judgment of the Court and an opinion in which THE CHIEF JUSTICE, MR. JUSTICE BLACKMUN, and MR. JUSTICE REHNQUIST joined.

... [A]ll three sought review in this Court upon a claim that conviction of crime by a less-than-unanimous jury violates the right to trial by jury in criminal cases specified by the Sixth Amendment and made applicable to the States by the Fourteenth. See *Duncan* v. *Louisiana*, 391 U.S. 145 (1968). We granted certiorari to consider this claim, 400 U.S. 901 (1970), which we now find to be without merit.

In *Williams* v. *Florida*, 399 U.S. 78 (1970), we had occasion to consider a related issue: whether the Sixth Amendment's right to trial by jury requires that all juries consist of 12 men. After considering the history of the 12-man requirement and the functions it performs in contemporary society, we concluded that it was not of constitutional stature. We reach the same conclusion today with regard to the requirement of unanimity.

I

Like the requirement that juries consist of 12 men, the requirement of unanimity arose during the Middle Ages and had become an accepted feature of the common-law jury by the 18th century. But, as we observed in *Williams,* "the relevant constitutional history casts considerable doubt on the easy assumption ... that if a given feature existed in a jury at common law in 1789, then it was necessarily preserved in the Constitution." *Id.,* at 92–93. The most salient fact in the scanty history of the Sixth Amendment, which we reviewed in full in *Williams,* is that, as it was introduced by James Madison in the House of Representatives, the proposed Amendment provided for trial

"by an impartial jury of freeholders of the vicinage, with the requisite of unanimity for conviction, of the right of challenge, and other accustomed requisites...." 1 Annals of Cong. 435 (1789).

Although it passed the House with little alteration, this proposal ran into considerable opposition in the Senate, particularly with regard to the vicinage requirement of the House version. The draft of the proposed Amendment was returned to the House in considerably altered form, and a conference committee was appointed. That committee refused to accept not only the original House language but also an alternate suggestion by the House conferees that juries be defined as possessing "the accustomed requisites." Letter from James Madison to Edmund Pendleton, Sept. 23, 1789, in 5 Writings of James

Madison 424 (G. Hunt ed. 1904). Instead, the Amendment that ultimately emerged from the committee and then from Congress and the States provided only for trial

"by an impartial jury of the State and district wherein the crime shall have been committed, which district shall have been previously ascertained by law...."

As we observed in *Williams,* one can draw conflicting inferences from this legislative history. One possible inference is that Congress eliminated references to unanimity and to the other "accustomed requisites" of the jury because those requisites were thought already to be implicit in the very concept of jury. A contrary explanation, which we found in *Williams* to be the more plausible, is that the deletion was intended to have some substantive effect. See 399 U.S., at 96–97. Surely one fact that is absolutely clear from this history is that, after a proposal had been made to specify precisely which of the common-law requisites of the jury were to be preserved by the Constitution, the Framers explicitly rejected the proposal and instead left such specification to the future....

II

Our inquiry must focus upon the function served by the jury in contemporary society.... As we said in *Duncan,* the purpose of trial by jury is to prevent oppression by the Government by providing a "safeguard against the corrupt or overzealous prosecutor and against the compliant, biased, or eccentric judge." *Duncan* v. *Louisiana,* 391 U.S., at 156. "Given this purpose, the essential feature of a jury obviously lies in the interposition between the accused and his accuser of the commonsense judgment of a group of laymen...." *Williams* v. *Florida, supra,* at 100. A requirement of unanimity, however, does not materially contribute to the exercise of this commonsense judgment. As we said in *Williams,* a jury will come to such a judgment as long as it consists of a group of laymen representative of a cross section of the community who have the duty and the opportunity to deliberate, free from outside attempts at intimidation, on the question of a defendant's guilt. In terms of this function we perceive no difference between juries required to act unanimously and those permitted to convict or acquit by votes of 10 to two or 11 to one. Requiring unanimity would obviously produce hung juries in some situations where nonunanimous juries will convict or acquit. But in either case, the interest of the defendant in having the judgment of his peers interposed between himself and the officers of the State who prosecute and judge him is equally well served....

IV

[*White rejects the argument that the requirement that a jury panel reflects the cross-section of a community necessarily requires a unanimous vote. There is no constitutional requirement that "every distinct voice" in the community has a right to prevent conviction.*]

We also cannot accept petitioners' second assumption—that minority groups, even when they are represented on a jury, will not adequately represent the viewpoint of those groups simply because they may be outvoted in the final result. They will be present during all deliberations, and their views will be heard. We cannot assume that the majority of the jury will refuse to weigh the evidence and reach a decision upon rational grounds, just as it must now do in order to obtain unanimous verdicts, or that a majority will deprive a man of his liberty on the basis of prejudice when a minority is presenting a reasonable argument in favor of acquittal. We simply find no proof for the notion that a majority will disregard its instructions and cast its votes for guilt or innocence based on prejudice rather than the evidence.

We accordingly affirm the judgment of the Court of Appeals of Oregon.

It is so ordered.

[*Blackmun and Powell wrote concurring opinions. Douglas, Brennan, and Marshall wrote dissenting opinions.*]

Mr. Justice Stewart, with whom Mr. Justice Brennan and Mr. Justice Marshall join, dissenting.

In *Duncan* v. *Louisiana,* 391 U.S. 145, the Court squarely held that the Sixth Amendment right to trial by jury in a federal criminal case is made wholly applicable to state criminal trials by the Fourteenth Amendment. Unless *Duncan* is to be overruled, therefore, the only relevant question here is whether the Sixth Amendment's guarantee of trial by jury embraces a guarantee that the verdict of the jury must be unanimous. The answer to that question is clearly "yes," as my Brother Powell has cogently demonstrated in that part of his concurring opinion that reviews almost a century of Sixth Amendment adjudication.

Until today, it has been universally understood

that a unanimous verdict is an essential element of a Sixth Amendment jury trial....

I would follow these settled Sixth Amendment precedents and reverse the judgment before us.

Ballew v. Georgia

435 U.S. 223 (1978)

In 1972, in *Apodaca* v. *Oregon,* the Supreme Court decided that jury verdicts in the states need not be unanimous as in federal courts. The Court also had to resolve questions about the *size* of a jury. *Williams* v. *Florida* (1970) determined that jury trials in the states need not follow the common-law number of twelve. It could be six. Could it be less than six? What was the magic minimum number for a constitutional trial by jury? In this case, Claude Davis Ballew argued that Georgia's law allowing a jury of five for a criminal trial was unconstitutional.

MR. JUSTICE BLACKMUN announced the judgment of the Court and delivered an opinion in which MR. JUSTICE STEVENS joined.

This case presents the issue whether a state criminal trial to a jury of only five persons deprives the accused of the right to trial by jury guaranteed to him by the Sixth and Fourteenth Amendments....

[I]

Petitioner [*Ballew*] was brought to trial in the Criminal Court of Fulton County. After a jury of 5 persons had been selected and sworn, petitioner moved that the court impanel a jury of 12 persons.... That court, however, tried its misdemeanor cases before juries of five persons pursuant to Ga. Const., Art. 6 § 16, ¶ 1, ... and to ... Ga. Laws.... Petitioner contended that for an obscenity trial, a jury of only five was constitutionally inadequate to assess the contemporary standards of the community.... He also argued that the Sixth and Fourteenth Amendments required a jury of at least six members in criminal cases....

The motion for a 12-person jury was overruled, and the trial went on to its conclusion before the 5-person jury that had been impaneled....

... Because we now hold that the five-member jury does not satisfy the jury trial guarantee of the Sixth Amendment, as applied to the States through the Fourteenth, we do not reach the other issues.

II

The Fourteenth Amendment guarantees the right of trial by jury in all state nonpetty criminal cases. *Duncan* v. *Louisiana,* 391 U.S. 145, 159–162 (1968). The Court in *Duncan* applied this Sixth Amendment right to the States because "trial by jury in criminal cases is fundamental to the American scheme of justice." *Id.,* at 149. The right attaches in the present case because the maximum penalty for violating § 26-2101, as it existed at the time of the alleged offenses, exceeded six months' imprisonment....

In *Williams* v. *Florida,* 399 U.S., at 100, the Court reaffirmed that the "purpose of the jury trial, as we noted in *Duncan,* is to prevent oppression by the Government. 'Providing an accused with the right to be tried by a jury of his peers gave him an inestimable safeguard against the corrupt or overzealous prosecutor and against the compliant, biased, or eccentric judge.' *Duncan* v. *Louisiana,* [391 U.S.,] at 156."....

Williams held that these functions and this purpose could be fulfilled by a jury of six members. As the Court's opinion in that case explained at some length, *id.,* at 86–90, common-law juries included 12 members by historical accident, "unrelated to the great purposes which gave rise to the jury in the first place." *Id.,* at 89–90. The Court's earlier cases that had *assumed* the number 12 to be constitutionally compelled were set to one side because they had not considered history and the function of the jury. *Id.,* at 90–92. Rather than requiring 12 members, then, the Sixth Amendment mandated a jury only of sufficient size to promote group deliberation, to insulate members from outside intimidation, and to provide a representative cross-section of the community. *Id.,* at 100. Although recognizing that by 1970 little empirical research had evaluated jury performance, the Court found no evidence that the reliability of jury verdicts diminished with six-member panels....

III

... Recent empirical data suggest that progressively smaller juries are less likely to foster effective group deliberation. At some point, this decline leads to inaccurate fact-finding and incorrect application of the common sense of the community to the facts. Generally, a positive correlation exists between group size and the quality of both group performance and group productivity. A variety of explanations have been offered for this conclusion. Several are particularly applicable in the jury setting. The smaller the group, the less likely are members to make critical contributions necessary for the solution of a given problem. Because most juries are not permitted to take notes ... memory is important for accurate jury deliberations. As juries decrease in size, then, they are less likely to have members who remember each of the important pieces of evidence or argument. Furthermore, the smaller the group, the less likely it is to overcome the biases of its members to obtain an accurate result....

Second, the data now raise doubts about the accuracy of the results achieved by smaller and smaller panels. Statistical studies suggest that the risk of convicting an innocent person (Type I error) rises as the size of the jury diminishes. Because the risk of not convicting a guilty person (Type II error) increases with the size of the panel, an optimal jury size can be selected as a function of the interaction between the two risks. Nagel and Neef concluded that the optimal size, for the purpose of minimizing errors, should vary with the importance attached to the two types of mistakes. After weighting Type I error as 10 times more significant than Type II, perhaps not an unreasonable assumption, they concluded that the optimal jury size was between six and eight. As the size diminished to five and below, the weighted sum of errors increased because of the enlarging risk of the conviction of innocent defendants.

[*Here Blackmun draws extensively on statistical studies that relate jury size to "correct" decisions, hung juries, and representation on the jury by minority groups in the community.*]

IV

While we adhere to, and reaffirm our holding in *Williams* v. *Florida*, these studies, most of which

have been made since *Williams* was decided in 1970, lead us to conclude that the purpose and functioning of the jury in a criminal trial is seriously impaired, and to a constitutional degree, by a reduction in size to below six members. We readily admit that we do not pretend to discern a clear line between six members and five. But the assembled data raise substantial doubt about the reliability and appropriate representation of panels smaller than six. Because of the fundamental importance of the jury trial to the American system of criminal justice, any further reduction that promotes inaccurate and possibly biased decisionmaking, that causes untoward differences in verdicts, and that prevents juries from truly representing their communities, attains constitutional significance....

Petitioner, therefore, has established that his trial on criminal charges before a five-member jury deprived him of the right to trial by jury guaranteed by the Sixth and Fourteenth Amendments.

VI

The judgment of the Court of Appeals is reversed, and the case is remanded for further proceedings not inconsistent with this opinion.

It is so ordered.

[*Stevens and White wrote concurring opinions.*]

Mr. Justice Powell, with whom The Chief Justice and Mr. Justice Rehnquist join, concurring in the judgment.

... I have reservations as to the wisdom — as well as the necessity — of Mr. Justice Blackmun's heavy reliance on numerology derived from statistical studies. Moreover, neither the validity nor the methodology employed by the studies cited was subjected to the traditional testing mechanisms of the adversary process. The studies relied on merely represent unexamined findings of persons interested in the jury system.

For these reasons I concur only in the judgment.

Mr. Justice Brennan, with whom Mr. Justice Stewart and Mr. Justice Marshall join....

D. FUNDAMENTALS OF A FAIR TRIAL

Procedural protections are essential checks against governmental abuses and arbitrary action. The procedural safeguards treated in this section include a speedy and public trial, protections against double jeopardy, and the right to confront witnesses and call witnesses for the defense.

Speedy and Public Trial

The Sixth Amendment provides that in all criminal prosecutions the accused "shall enjoy the right to a speedy and public trial, by an impartial jury of the State and district wherein the crime shall have been committed, which district shall have been previously ascertained by law, and to be informed of the nature and cause of the accusation...." The needs of public justice may require delays, however. "While justice should be administered with dispatch, the essential ingredient is orderly expedition and not mere speed." Smith v. United States, 360 U.S. 1, 10 (1959).

When a trial is repeatedly and indefinitely postponed, an indicted person is subjected to public scorn without an opportunity to be exonerated in the courts. Under such conditions, a defendant is denied a speedy trial, a right now applied against the states. Klopfer v. North Carolina, 386 U.S. 213 (1967). In cases in which defendants failed to assert the right to a speedy trial and delays did not seriously prejudice their case, five years could elapse between an arrest and a trial without violating the Speedy Trial Clause. Barker v. Wingo, 407 U.S. 514 (1972).

Congress passed the Speedy Trial Act in 1974 in an effort to prevent extensive delays in federal court. Charges can be dismissed unless the person is brought to trial within 100 days of arrest. The statute establishes deadlines for indictment and arraignment. Certain delays can be excluded in computing the 100 days. 88 Stat. 2076 (1975); 18 U.S.C. §§ 3161–74 (2000). Congress later required a criminal trial to begin within 70 days after a defendant is charged or makes an initial appearance. The Court has held that the time during which an accused is not under indictment or under official restraint (subject to bail or in jail) is excluded when determining a speedy trial claim. Under these tests, the government has been permitted to prosecute charges that are ten years old. United States v. Loud Hawk, 474 U.S. 302 (1986). In some jurisdictions, such as the District of Columbia, suspects have been held a year or more in jail while awaiting trial. Washington Post, April 4, 1987, p. A1. In 1992, a 5–4 Court ruled that the government may not bring a person to trial eight and one-half years after indictment, particularly when the government is to blame for the delay. Doggett v. United States, 505 U.S. 647 (1992). See Zedner v. United States, 547 U.S. 489 (2006).

The constitutional right to a "public trial" protects an individual from secret proceedings where there is no opportunity to secure counsel, prepare a defense, cross-examine witnesses, or summon witnesses for the accused. The Anglo-American distrust of secret trials has been traced to the Spanish Inquisition, the English Star Chamber, and the French *lettre de cachet*. In re Oliver, 333 U.S. 257, 268–69 (1948). Public trials restrain potential abuses of judicial power. Id. at 270. This constitutional protection in the Bill of Rights has been applied to the states. Id. at 273. There is a constant tension between a judge's interest in closing a trial and the right of the public and the press to be present (see Chapter 11).

Military Tribunals

After the 9/11 terrorist attacks on the United States, the Justice Department argued that "enemy combatants" could be held indefinitely without access to counsel, formal charges, trial, or judicial review. According to the department, U.S. citizens (Yaser Esam Hamdi and Jose Padilla) could be treated in this manner, as could detainees at Guantánamo Bay, Cuba. In 2004, the Supreme Court rejected those broad assertions, insisting that the executive branch must create a process that allows detainees and enemy combatants an opportunity to challenge the government's claims against them. Hamdi v. Rumsfeld, 542 U.S. 507 (2004); Rasul v. Bush, 542 U.S. 466 (2004). In 2006, the Court again objected to the procedures the Bush Administration adopted for military tribunals. Hamdan v. Rumsfeld, 548 U.S. 557 (2006). Congress responded to *Hamdan* by passing the Military Commissions Act (MCA) of 2006, providing for the first time a statutory basis for the tribunals. Lawsuits against the administration claimed that the detainees at Guantánamo were entitled to submit habeas petitions to federal courts. On June 12, 2008, the Supreme Court held that both the MCA and the Detainee Treatment

Act of 2005 operated as an unconstitutional suspension of the writ. Boumediene v. Bush, 553 U.S. 723 (2008). Portions of *Hamdi, Hamdan,* and *Boumediene* decisions are reprinted in Chapter 7.

Double Jeopardy

Under the Fifth Amendment, a person shall not be subject "for the same offense to be twice put in jeopardy of life or limb." Litigation exposes a raft of complex issues. What is the "same offense"? How do we define "jeopardy"? The law of double jeopardy consists of several rules, each rule "marooned in a sea of exceptions." 75 Yale L. J. 262, 263 (1965). The Supreme Court admits that its decisions in this area are "a veritable Sargasso Sea." Albernaz v. United States, 450 U.S. 333, 343 (1981).

As first proposed by Madison in 1789, the Double Jeopardy Clause provided: "No person shall be subject, except in cases of impeachment, to more than one punishment or one trial for the same offence." 1 Annals of Congress 434. Some members of the House of Representatives objected that the limitation of "one trial" would prevent a convicted person from obtaining a second trial if the first was deficient. Id. at 753. The Senate changed the language to its present form. S. Jour., 1st Cong., 1st Sess. 71, 77.

The underlying purpose of the Double Jeopardy Clause is to prohibit the government from making repeated attempts to convict an individual, "subjecting him to embarrassment, expense and ordeal and compelling him to live in a continuing state of anxiety and insecurity." Green v. United States, 355 U.S. 184, 187 (1957). Acquittal acts as an absolute bar on a second trial. United States v. DiFrancesco, 449 U.S. 117, 129 (1980). The meaning of "acquittal," however, often divides the Court.[8]

There is no double jeopardy in trying someone twice for the same offense if the jury is unable to reach a verdict and the jury is discharged. In 2001, a D.C. jury deadlocked for the fourth time in the trial of Corey A. Moore. After four mistrials in four years, the government decided to drop the charges. In 2012, the Court upheld the retrial of an Arkansas man on capital murder charges after a jury unanimously agreed he was not guilty of either capital or first-degree murder, but was unable to reach a verdict on whether he had committed manslaughter. The judge declared a mistrial and discharged the jury. Because the jury did not acquit him in a final sense, but only in the forewoman's report to the judge, the Court said his retrial for capital murder and first-degree murder did not constitute double jeopardy. Blueford v. Arkansas, 566 U.S. ___ (2012).

There is no double jeopardy when an appeals court returns the case to the trial court because of defects in the original indictment.[9] Even so, by the time a judge discharges the jury the accused might already have been placed in "jeopardy." When does jeopardy attach? When the jury is empaneled and sworn? The first witness sworn? The first evidence introduced? On such questions the Court splinters to produce 5–4 and 6–3 decisions.[10]

Double Jeopardy and Sovereignty

Other difficulties spring from jurisdictional questions. May a state and the federal government (two sovereigns) prosecute someone for the same act? In three unanimous rulings, the Supreme Court held that a person may be prosecuted for the same act under federal law and state law. The theory is that there are two distinct offenses, tried in two separate sovereign governments, rather than the "same offense" under the Fifth Amendment.[11]

---

8. United States v. Scott, 437 U.S. 82 (1978); United States v. Sisson, 399 U.S. 267 (1970).

9. United States v. Ball, 163 U.S. 662, 672 (1896); Thompson v. United States, 155 U.S. 271 (1894); Logan v. United States, 144 U.S. 263, 297–98 (1892).

10. Crist v. Bretz, 437 U.S. 28 (1978); Illinois v. Somerville, 410 U.S. 458 (1973); United States v. Jorn, 400 U.S. 470 (1971); Downum v. United States, 372 U.S. 734 (1963); Gori v. United States, 367 U.S. 364 (1961).

11. Jerome v. United States, 318 U.S. 101 (1943); Herbert v. Louisiana, 272 U.S. 312 (1926); United States v. Lanza, 260 U.S. 377 (1922).

When this theory was reaffirmed in 1959, the Court split 5–4. The dissenters regarded double prosecutions as constitutionally repulsive when the federal government, after losing a case, helps a state try the person for the same offense. Bartkus v. Illinois, 359 U.S. 121 (1959). Because of inherent tribal sovereignty, an Indian can be tried in Tribal Court and in federal court for the same incident. United States v. Wheeler, 435 U.S. 313 (1978). Two states may prosecute a person for the same criminal activity. Heath v. Alabama, 474 U.S. 82 (1985). This theory of "dual sovereignty" does not allow double prosecutions *within* a state: first by the state and next by a municipality. Cities are not sovereign entities. Waller v. Florida, 406 U.S. 916 (1972).

In 1997, a unanimous Court held that the Double Jeopardy Clause permitted the government to fine someone for fraud or other regulatory wrongdoing and later resort to the criminal process to prosecute the person for the same offense. The first action was civil, the second criminal. Hudson v. United States, 522 U.S. 93 (1997). Similarly, although O. J. Simpson was acquitted in a criminal trial for the deaths of Nicole Brown Simpson and Ronald Goldman, their families successfully brought a civil suit charging Simpson with wrongful death. Lemrick Nelson, Jr., was cleared in 1992 of state criminal charges that he killed Yankel Rosenbaum in Brooklyn. Five years later he was convicted of violating Rosenbaum's civil rights. See Yale Kamisar, "Call It Double Jeopardy," New York Times, February 14, 1997, at A37. Martha Stewart, after serving prison time for obstructing justice regarding the sale of stocks, faced a civil case brought by the Securities and Exchange Commission in 2006.

Decisions on double jeopardy initially dealt with the federal government or its territories.[12] In 1937, the Court reviewed a *state* prosecution of an individual who had been sentenced to life imprisonment but, upon retrial, was sentenced to death. The Court denied that double jeopardy represented a fundamental principle of liberty and justice that must be applied against the states. PALKO v. CONNECTICUT, 302 U.S. 319 (1937). This decision was overturned in 1969 when the Court held that the double jeopardy provision in the Fifth Amendment is fundamental to America's constitutional heritage and enforceable against the states through the Fourteenth Amendment. Benton v. Maryland, 395 U.S. 784 (1969). Other decisions attempted to define the confused contours of the Double Jeopardy Clause, raising issues of exquisite complexity and subtlety (see box on next page).

Double Jeopardy and Sentencing

The issue of imposing a more severe sentence when a defendant is convicted in a second trial has occupied both Congress and the courts. In 1969, the Supreme Court decided that there is no constitutional bar to imposing a more severe sentence on reconviction, provided the sentencing judge is not motivated by vindictiveness. The guarantee against double jeopardy, however, requires that punishment already exacted must be fully credited to the new sentence. North Carolina v. Pearce, 395 U.S. 711, 718 (1969); Chaffin v. Stynchcombe, 412 U.S. 17 (1973). If someone is convicted and successfully moves for a new trial because of prosecutorial misconduct, upon reconviction the judge may impose a heavier sentence. Texas v. McCullough, 475 U.S. 134 (1986).

These cases deal with new sentences after a new trial. In 1970, Congress authorized increases in an *existing* sentence; appellate courts may review and increase a trial court's sentence for "dangerous special offenders." 84 Stat. 950, § 3576. The Supreme Court upheld this procedure in United States v. DiFrancesco, 449 U.S. 117 (1980). Legislation in 1984 permits appellate courts to increase existing sentences for offenses in areas other than organized crime. 98 Stat. 2011, § 3742 (1984). The basis for such statutes is that the scope of punishment is a matter for legislatures, not courts. Missouri v. Hunter, 459 U.S. 359, 368 (1983). Legislatures may authorize multiple punishments and consecutive sentences. Although a person may not be punished more than once for the same offense, a single in-

---

12. Diaz v. United States, 223 U.S. 442 (1912); Serra v. Mortiga, 204 U.S. 470 (1907); Kepner v. United States, 195 U.S. 100 (1904); United States v. Ball, 163 U.S. 662 (1896).

Double Jeopardy Rulings

1. If someone is found guilty and an appeals court orders a new trial, the trial court may not impose a stiffer penalty than the one the defendant received the first time. Arizona v. Rumsey, 467 U.S. 203 (1984); Price v. Georgia, 398 U.S. 323 (1970); Green v. United States, 355 U.S. 184 (1957).

2. If someone is charged with robbing six poker players and is acquitted in a trial involving one of the players, the government may not proceed to prosecute him for robbing one of the other players. Ashe v. Swenson, 397 U.S. 436 (1970). See also Simpson v. Florida, 403 U.S. 384 (1971).

3. The federal government may introduce at trial the statement of someone who testified at an earlier trial against the same defendant, even though the defendant was acquitted in the first trial. Dowling v. United States, 493 U.S. 342 (1990).

4. An individual pleaded guilty to driving while intoxicated and failing to keep to the right of the median. Later he was indicted for man-slaughter, homicide, and assault. To prove those charges, the government had to depend on the charges for which he had already pled guilty. The Court held that the Double Jeopardy Clause bars a subsequent prosecution if, to establish an essential element of an offense charged, the government will seek to prove conduct for which the defendant has already been prosecuted. Grady v. Corbin, 495 U.S. 508 (1990). Three years later the Court reversed *Grady* to permit the prosecution of a man charged with assaulting his wife even though he had been earlier convicted of contempt of court for the same attack. United States v. Dixon, 509 U.S. 688 (1993).

5. Someone was found guilty of attempting to manufacture an illegal drug based on evidence concerning the shipment of chemicals and equipment to him. The person was later charged with conspiracy, relying in part on the earlier conviction. The Court held that the Double Jeopardy Clause does not bar the prosecution of two crimes different in time and place. United States v. Felix, 503 U.S. 378 (1992).*

---

* For other recent rulings, in 1994 the Court split 5 to 4 in holding that Montana could not convict marijuana farmers of drug crimes and later use the state law to collect an estimated $900,000 in taxes on the marijuana grown. Montana Dept. of Revenue v. Kurth Ranch, 511 U.S. 767 (1994). The Court agreed 8 to 1 that double jeopardy principles do not prevent prosecution for a crime even if the same criminal behavior had been used to increase the defendant's prison sentence for a different offense. Witte v. United States, 515 U.S. 389 (1995). A rare unanimous Court held that a district court had erred in sentencing someone to concurrent life sentences for the same offense. Rutledge v. United States, 517 U.S. 292 (1996). The Court held (8 to 1) that civil forfeiture is not "punishment" for double jeopardy purposes. Government may both prosecute someone for criminal violations and later seize their property. United States v. Ursery, 518 U.S. 267 (1996). See also Monge v. California, 524 U.S. 721 (1998).

cident can violate more than one statutory provision and lead to cumulative punishment. These statutes do not violate double jeopardy.[13]

In 2003, the Court revisited the issue of heavier sentences at a second trial. After a Pennsylvania jury deadlocked on the question of life or death, the judge followed state law by giving the defendant a life sentence. He challenged his conviction and won a second trial, where he was found guilty and sentenced to death. Split 5 to 4, the Court upheld the death penalty. It reasoned that because the life sentence was not an acquittal, the death penalty did not constitute double jeopardy. Defendants who

---

13. Jones v. Thomas, 491 U.S. 376 (1989); Garrett v. United States, 471 U.S. 773 (1985); Albernaz v. United States, 450 U.S. 333 (1981); Illinois v. Vitale, 447 U.S. 410 (1980); Whalen v. United States, 445 U.S. 684 (1980).

challenge a lighter sentence run the risk of receiving a heavier one. Sattazahn v. Pennsylvania, 537 U.S. 101 (2003).

Megan's Law

"Megan's Law," named after a 7-year-old girl raped and murdered by a twice-convicted sex offender, is a New Jersey statute that requires authorities to notify communities of convicted persons who move to their neighborhoods. Other states, including the District of Columbia, have adopted similar statutes. The claim that these laws impose a second punishment and violate the Double Jeopardy Clause was rejected by the Third Circuit in 1997. W.P. v. Verniero, 127 F.3d 298 (3d Cir. 1997), cert. denied, 522 U.S. 1109–10 (1998). In 1997, a 5–4 ruling by the Supreme Court held that locking up a repeat sex offender in a mental institution does not violate the double-jeopardy protection. Kansas v. Hendricks, 521 U.S. 346 (1997).

In 2001, New Jersey's highest court ruled that children found guilty of sexual offenses before age 14 are not automatically subject to having the public warned about them and their crimes. The ruling was an effort to reconcile the public impact of Megan's Law with the privacy protections that are part of juvenile justice. In 2002, the Supreme Court reinforced its ruling in *Hendricks* by holding that a state may keep a convicted sexual offender in extended civil confinement after the criminal penalties expire. States retain substantial leeway in defining the personality disorders that justify commitment to an institution. Kansas v. Crane, 534 U.S. 407 (2002).

Several challenges in the lower courts to the constitutionality of Megan's laws led to two Court decisions in 2003. In one, a 6 to 3 ruling upheld Alaska's policy of posting a registry of convicted sex offenders on the Internet, including those who were convicted before the state Megan law took effect. The Court decided that the posting, considered civil and nonpunitive, did not violate the constitutional prohibition against ex post facto legislation. Smith v. Doe, 538 U.S. 84 (2003). The second ruling dealt with a Connecticut law that posted offenders' photographs and information on the Internet, explicitly disclaiming any effort to predict their future dangerousness. A unanimous Court upheld that procedure. Connecticut Dept. of Public Safety v. Doe, 538 U.S. 1 (2003). The opinion did not foreclose future challenges on other grounds.

Right of Confrontation

The Sixth Amendment provides that in all criminal prosecutions the accused has the right to "be confronted with the witnesses against him [and] to have compulsory process for obtaining witnesses in his favor." In 1965, the Supreme Court held that the right of confrontation and cross-examination is a fundamental right made obligatory on the states by the Fourteenth Amendment. Pointer v. Texas, 380 U.S. 400 (1965); Douglas v. Alabama, 380 U.S. 415 (1965). Two years later, the Court also applied against the states the right of an accused to have compulsory process for obtaining witnesses. Washington v. Texas, 388 U.S. 14 (1967). The Confrontation and Compulsory Process Clauses give an accused a fair opportunity to present a defense.[14]

In 1988, the Court struck down a state law permitting children who claim they are victims of sexual abuse to testify in court behind screens. Coy v. Iowa, 487 U.S. 1012 (1988). Two years later a 5–4 Court upheld a Maryland law that allowed a child witness in a sexual abuse case to testify against a defendant at trial, outside the defendant's physical presence, by one-way closed circuit television. The child, prosecutor, and defense counsel were in another room; the defendant remained in electronic communication with counsel. The Court held that the Confrontation Clause does not guarantee criminal defendants an absolute right to a face-to-face meeting with the witnesses against them at

---

14. Pennsylvania v. Ritchie, 480 U.S. 39 (1987); Crane v. Kentucky, 476 U.S. 683 (1986); Lee v. Illinois, 476 U.S. 530 (1986).

trial. The Maryland procedure passed constitutional muster because it was necessary to further an important public policy (protecting children from courtroom trauma) and it otherwise assured the testimony's reliability. Writing for the dissenters, Justice Scalia accused the Court of using cost-benefit analysis to read out of the Constitution an explicit guarantee. Maryland v. Craig, 497 U.S. 836 (1990). The Court also divided 5–4 in deciding that a two-and-one-half-year-old girl's statement to her pediatrician that her father sexually abused her could not be used at trial. The Court concluded that there was no guarantee that the pediatrician's hearsay testimony was trustworthy. Idaho v. Wright, 497 U.S. 805 (1990). In 1992, the Court again explored the necessity of producing children (victims of a sexual assault) at trial. White v. Illinois, 502 U.S. 346 (1992).

In 1991, the Court divided 7–2 in upholding Michigan's rape-shield statute that requires defendants to give notice ten days in advance of an intent to introduce evidence of a defendant's past sexual conduct with the victim. Although the statute implicates the Sixth Amendment to the extent that it diminishes a defendant's ability to present evidence and confront adverse witnesses, the Court held that the statute serves a valid legislative purpose that rape victims are protected against surprise, harassment, and unnecessary invasions of privacy. Michigan v. Lucas, 500 U.S. 145 (1991).

Under certain circumstances, a disruptive defendant may be removed from the courtroom without violating his constitutional right to be present and to confront witnesses against him. Illinois v. Allen, 397 U.S. 337 (1970). A trial court's ruling in violation of the Confrontation Clause may even be tolerated if the Supreme Court finds the error "harmless." Delaware v. Van Arsdall, 475 U.S. 673 (1986). Other exceptions to the Confrontation Clause include the use of out-of-court statements in conspiracy trials (permitting hearsay evidence).[15]

In 1980, the Court held that it was possible to admit prior-recorded testimony at a trial without the opportunity for confrontation if two conditions are met: the evidence is reliable and the state has made an effort to locate the witness. Ohio v. Roberts, 448 U.S. 56 (1980). However, in 2004 the Court overturned that case as inconsistent with the Sixth Amendment, which enables the accused in all criminal prosecutions "to be confronted with the witnesses against him." Permitting out-of-court testimonial statements violates the historical purpose of the Sixth Amendment. Crawford v. Washington, 541 U.S. 36 (2004). In 2006, the Court applied its *Crawford* ruling to statements made to law enforcement personnel during a 911 call. Davis v. Washington, 547 U.S. 813 (2006). Two years later, a 6 to 3 Court vacated and remanded the conviction of a man accused of murdering his ex-girlfriend because he could not challenge an incriminating account she gave the police shortly before her death. The Court said that the lower court was required to find that Giles had committed the murder to keep her from testifying against him, in order to conclude that he had forfeited his Sixth Amendment right of confrontation. Giles v. California, 554 U.S. 353 (2008).

In a far reaching opinion with major consequences for the prosecution, the Court ruled in 2009 that crime laboratory reports cannot be used at trial unless the lab analyst responsible for creating the report is available for testimony and cross-examination. Melendez-Diaz v. Massachusetts, 557 U.S. 305 (2009). The four dissenters in the case predicted major negative consequences for the criminal justice system and legal analysts and prosecutors seemed to agree. One defense attorney called it "the biggest case for the defense since *Miranda*." "Lab Analyst Decision Complicates Prosecutions," Washington Post, July 15, 2009, A1. In 2011, the Court held that a scientific report could not be used as evidence unless the analyst who prepared and certified the report was subject to confrontation and cross-examination in court. Bullcoming v. New Mexico, 564 U.S. ___ (2011).

In 2012, the Court backtracked from *Melendez-Diaz* and *Bullcoming* by holding that a defendant's right to confront and cross-examine an expert witness is not violated when the scientific report relied on by the expert did not specifically target the defendant. During her testimony in court, the expert

---

15. Bourjaily v. United States, 483 U.S. 171 (1987); United States v. Inadi, 475 U.S. 387 (1986); Dutton v. Evans, 400 U.S. 74 (1970).

confirmed that she did not conduct or observe any of the testing of vaginal swabs taken from a rape victim, and had not seen any of the calibrations or work performed by a firm that found a male DNA profile in the swabs. The decision consisted of a plurality of four (Alito, Roberts, Kennedy, and Breyer) plus a concurrence by Thomas, but Thomas in his necessary fifth vote said he shared the dissent's view of the plurality's "flawed analysis." The dissent by Kagan pointed to a trial in 1995 where an expert witness subject to cross-examination admitted under questioning that the DNA on a sweatshirt did not match the defendant, as she had earlier testified, but rather the victim. Kagan's dissent was joined by Scalia, Ginsburg, and Sotomayor. Williams v. Illinois, 567 U.S. ___ (2012).

In the case of Zacarias Moussaoui, indicted for being part of the al Qaeda conspiracy to kill and maim persons and destroy structures in the United States, the Justice Department denied that the Sixth Amendment could be extended overseas to potential witnesses who are "enemy combatants." Any effort to interrogate them, according to the government, would "change the course of a military operation." Louis Fisher, Military Tribunals and Presidential Power 214–16 (2005). Moussaoui's access to al Qaeda witnesses in U.S. custody was litigated. The district court judge ruled that the government must provide him access to witnesses that could provide potentially exonerating testimony. The Court of Appeals agreed that Moussaoui had a Sixth Amendment right to access to these witnesses but allowed the government to provide summaries from interviews and interrogations rather than having them testify in person. U.S. v. Moussaoui, 383 F.3d 453 (4th Cir. 2004). In 2005, the Supreme Court rejected an appeal without comment and Moussaoui was sentenced to life imprisonment.

Palko v. Connecticut

302 U.S. 319 (1937)

In this opinion on the Double Jeopardy Clause, Justice Cardozo looks more broadly to determine the respective responsibilities of the federal government and the states and to identify the individual rights "found to be implicit in the concept of ordered liberty." Frank Palko was found guilty of second-degree murder and sentenced to life imprisonment. Upon retrial, he was convicted of first-degree murder and sentenced to be executed. In this opinion the Court lays out the argument in support of the selective incorporation of certain Bill of Rights protections by the 14th Amendment due process clause while others are not incorporated.

MR. JUSTICE CARDOZO delivered the opinion of the Court....

[*Palko was indicted*] for the crime of murder in the first degree. A jury found him guilty of murder in the second degree, and he was sentenced to confinement in the state prison for life. Thereafter the State of Connecticut, with the permission of the judge presiding at the trial, gave notice of appeal to the Supreme Court of Errors.... [T]he Supreme Court of Errors reversed the judgment and ordered a new trial.... It found that there had been error of law to the prejudice of the state (1) in excluding testimony as to a confession by defendant; (2) in excluding testimony upon cross-examination of defendant to impeach his credibility, and (3) in the instructions to the jury as to the difference between first and second degree murder.

Pursuant to the mandate of the Supreme Court of Errors, defendant was brought to trial again. Before a jury was impaneled and also at later stages of

the case he made the objection that the effect of the new trial was to place him twice in jeopardy for the same offense, and in so doing to violate the Fourteenth Amendment of the Constitution of the United States. Upon the overruling of the objection the trial proceeded. The jury returned a verdict of murder in the first degree, and the court sentenced the defendant to the punishment of death. The Supreme Court of Errors affirmed the judgment of conviction....

1. The execution of the sentence will not deprive appellant of his life without the process of law assured to him by the Fourteenth Amendment of the Federal Constitution.

The argument for appellant is that whatever is forbidden by the Fifth Amendment is forbidden by the Fourteenth also. The Fifth Amendment, which is not directed to the states, but solely to the federal government, creates immunity from double jeopardy. No person shall be "subject for the same offense to be twice put in jeopardy of life or limb." The Fourteenth Amendment ordains, "nor shall any State deprive any person of life, liberty, or property, without due process of law." To retry a defendant, though under one indictment and only one, subjects him, it is said, to double jeopardy in violation of the Fifth Amendment, if the prosecution is one on behalf of the United States. From this the consequence is said to follow that there is a denial of life or liberty without due process of law, if the prosecution is one on behalf of the People of a State.…

We have said that in appellant's view the Fourteenth Amendment is to be taken as embodying the prohibitions of the Fifth. His thesis is even broader. Whatever would be a violation of the original bill of rights (Amendments I to VIII) if done by the federal government is now equally unlawful by force of the Fourteenth Amendment if done by a state. There is no such general rule.

The Fifth Amendment provides, among other things, that no person shall be held to answer for a capital or otherwise infamous crime unless on presentment or indictment of a grand jury. This court has held that, in prosecutions by a state, presentment or indictment by a grand jury may give way to informations at the instance of a public officer. [*The Court summarizes the provisions of the Fourth, Fifth, and Sixth Amendments.*]

… [T]he due process clause of the Fourteenth Amendment may make it unlawful for a state to abridge by its statutes the freedom of speech which the First Amendment safeguards against encroachment by the Congress, … or the like freedom of the press, … or the free exercise of religion, … or the right of peaceable assembly, without which speech would be unduly trammeled, … or the right of one accused of crime to the benefit of counsel, *Powell* v. *Alabama,* 287 U.S. 45. In these and other situations immunities that are valid as against the federal government by force of the specific pledges of particular amendments have been found to be implicit in the concept of ordered liberty, and thus, through the Fourteenth Amendment, become valid as against the states.

… There emerges the perception of a rationalizing principle which gives to discrete instances a proper order and coherence. The right to trial by jury and the immunity from prosecution except as the result of an indictment may have value and importance. Even so, they are not of the very essence of a scheme of ordered liberty. To abolish them is not to violate a "principle of justice so rooted in the traditions and conscience of our people as to be ranked as fundamental." *Snyder* v. *Massachusetts, supra,* p.

105; *Brown* v. *Mississippi, supra,* p. 285; *Hebert* v. *Louisiana,* 272 U.S. 312, 316. Few would be so narrow or provincial as to maintain that a fair and enlightened system of justice would be impossible without them. What is true of jury trials and indictments is true also, as the cases show, of the immunity from compulsory self-incrimination. *Twining* v. *New Jersey, supra.* This too might be lost, and justice still be done.…

We reach a different plane of social and moral values when we pass to the privileges and immunities that have been taken over from the earlier articles of the federal bill of rights and brought within the Fourteenth Amendment by a process of absorption. These in their origin were effective against the federal government alone. If the Fourteenth Amendment has absorbed them, the process of absorption has had its source in the belief that neither liberty nor justice would exist if they were sacrificed. *Twining* v. *New Jersey, supra,* p. 99. This is true, for illustration, of freedom of thought, and speech. Of that freedom one may say that it is the matrix, the indispensable condition, of nearly every other form of freedom. With rare aberrations a pervasive recognition of that truth can be traced in our history, political and legal. So it has come about that the domain of liberty, withdrawn by the Fourteenth Amendment from encroachment by the states, has been enlarged by latter-day judgments to include liberty of the mind as well as liberty of action. The extension became, indeed, a logical imperative when once it was recognized, as long ago it was, that liberty is something more than exemption from physical restraint, and that even in the field of substantive rights and duties the legislative judgment, if oppressive and arbitrary, may be overridden by the courts.… Fundamental too in the concept of due process, and so in that of liberty, is the thought that condemnation shall be rendered only after trial.… The hearing, moreover, must be a real one, not a sham or a pretense.… For that reason, ignorant defendants in a capital case were held to have been condemned unlawfully when in truth, though not in form, they were refused the aid of counsel. *Powell* v. *Alabama, supra,* pp. 67, 68.…

Our survey of the cases serves, we think, to justify the statement that the dividing line between them, if not unfaltering throughout its course, has been true for the most part to a unifying principle. On which side of the line the case made out by the appellant has appropriate location must be the next inquiry and the final one. Is that kind of double jeopardy to which the statute has subjected him a hardship so acute and shocking that our polity will not endure it? Does it violate those "fundamental principles of liberty and justice which lie at the base of all our civil and political institutions"? *Hebert* v. *Louisiana, supra.* The answer surely must be "no." ... The state is not attempting to wear the accused out by a multitude of cases with accumulated trials. It asks no more than this, that the case against him shall go on until there shall be a trial free from the corrosion of substantial legal error....

2. The conviction of appellant is not in derogation of any privileges or immunities that belong to him as a citizen of the United States.

There is argument in his behalf that the privileges and immunities clause of the Fourteenth Amendment as well as the due process clause has been flouted by the judgment.

Maxwell v. *Dow, supra,* p. 584, gives all the answer that is necessary.

The judgment is

Affirmed.

Mr. Justice Butler dissents.

E. SELF-INCRIMINATION

Procedural due process includes other protections for the accused: prompt arraignment before a magistrate and the privilege against self-incrimination. Those issues triggered some of the most bitterly contested rulings by the Supreme Court: *Mallory* v. *United States* (1957), *Escobedo* v. *Illinois* (1964), and *Miranda* v. *Arizona* (1966). The last two cases are analyzed in the next section on "Assistance of Counsel."

Prompt Arraignment

Congress and state legislatures require police officers to take an accused to the nearest judicial officer to plead to charges (arraignment). If officers ignore this procedure and detain the suspect for days in order to extract a confession, the evidence can be excluded by the courts. McNabb v. United States, 318 U.S. 332 (1943). These rulings conform to legislative policy, such as the rule adopted by Congress that requires an arrested person to be taken before a committing magistrate "without unnecessary delay." Mallory v. United States, 354 U.S. 449 (1957). Federal law officers arrested Andrew Mallory on charges of rape and proceeded to question him until he confessed seven hours later.

Congress responded to *Mallory* by making confessions admissible if the defendant is arraigned within six hours. 82 Stat. 210 (1968); 18 U.S.C. § 3501(c). Lower courts disagreed on how to apply the federal rule. In 2009 a closely divided Court upheld the McNabb-Mallory rule and said that the best reading of the statute is that long delays between arrest and arraignment make confessions obtained during that time suspect. In this case the confession began after the defendant had been in custody almost ten hours and he was not arraigned until almost thirty hours had passed. Corley v. United States, 556 U.S. 303 (2009).

At the state level, persons arrested without a warrant were expected to be brought before a neutral magistrate, who would determine whether there was probable cause for detention. Gerstein v. Pugh, 420 U.S. 103 (1975). That standard was clarified in 1991 by a 5–4 Court. Persons arrested without a warrant may be held for up to 48 hours before being brought before a magistrate. A delay of that length can be challenged if the arrested person can prove that the delay was unreasonable. Riverside, County of, v. McLaughlin, 500 U.S. 44 (1991). The Court later held that the 48-hour rule applied retroactively to all pending cases at the time of *McLaughlin*. Powell v. Nevada, 511 U.S. 79 (1994).

Coerced Testimony

Due process is denied when witnesses are whipped and tortured until they testify against the accused. Moore v. Dempsey, 261 U.S. 86, 89 (1923). Confessions have been extorted by law officers who used violence and brutality. In one case, a black suspect was repeatedly hanged by a rope to the limb of a tree and tied to the tree and whipped until he confessed. Other defendants were stripped and beaten to obtain confessions. Their convictions were reversed on the ground that coerced confessions are inherently suspect as evidence. Brown v. Mississippi, 297 U.S. 278 (1936).

Even if a confession can be corroborated by independent evidence, the state violates due process if it uses methods that are inquisitorial and threatening. Rogers v. Richmond, 365 U.S. 534 (1961). These forms of persecution are generally inflicted upon "the poor, the ignorant, the numerically weak, the friendless, and the powerless." Chambers v. Florida, 309 U.S. 227, 237–38 (1940). Coercion can involve psychological compulsion, not merely physical beatings. Miller v. Fenton, 474 U.S. 104 (1985). Confessions might result improperly from a "truth serum" administered by a police physician. Townsend v. Sain, 372 U.S. 293 (1963).[16]

Privilege against Self-Incrimination

The Fifth Amendment provides that no person "shall be compelled in any Criminal Case to be a witness against himself." The purpose of this privilege is to prevent repressive and arbitrary methods of prosecution, such as "the horror of Star Chamber proceedings" in England. Quinn v. United States, 349 U.S. 155, 161 (1955). Government officials may not pry incriminating evidence from the lips of the accused. Prosecutors are "forced to search for independent evidence instead of relying upon proof extracted from individuals by force of law." United States v. White, 322 U.S. 694, 698 (1944).

The privilege against self-incrimination is not automatic or self-executing. It can be waived if a witness does not assert it in a timely manner. Although the privilege can be waived, even vague and ambiguous references to the "Fifth Amendment" are sufficient to invoke its protection.[17] If a defendant voluntarily takes the stand, he or she may be cross-examined as any other witness, thereby risking the disclosure of incriminating information. Brown v. United States, 356 U.S. 148 (1958). Once a defendant offers to be a witness, "his credibility may be impeached, his testimony may be assailed, and is to be weighed as that of any other witness." Reagan v. United States, 157 U.S. 301, 305 (1895).

In federal proceedings, an accused may request the court to instruct the jury that a defendant's failure to testify does not create a presumption of guilt and must not be used by the jury against him or her. In some of the states, however, courts and prosecutors were allowed to comment on a defendant's failure to explain or to deny evidence against him or her. The court or the jury could take that into consideration. Adamson v. California, 332 U.S. 46 (1947) (reprinted in Chapter 8). In this case and in *Twining* v. *New Jersey,* 211 U.S. 78 (1908), the Court applied the Self-Incrimination Clause only to the federal government, not to the states. In 1964, the Court held that the privilege against self-incrimination is incorporated in the Due Process Clause of the Fourteenth Amendment and therefore applicable to the states. Malloy v. Hogan, 378 U.S. 1 (1964). Subsequent cases have attempted to explain when it is appropriate to comment on a defendant's failure to testify.[18]

Problems of federalism provoked the extension of the Self-Incrimination Clause to the states. In 1944, the Court held that a person could be compelled under a state immunity statute to give testimony and the information could be used later in federal court to convict him. Feldman v. United States, 322 U.S. 487 (1944). This placed the witness in a no-win situation. Agreeing to testify could bring conviction in federal court; refusal to testify risked state imprisonment for contempt of court. This dilemma was resolved in 1964 when a unanimous Court held that one jurisdiction within the federal system may not compel a witness (granted immunity) to give testimony that might incrim-

---

16. For examples of other coerced confessions that were overturned, see Arizona v. Fulminante, 499 U.S. 279 (1991); Clewis v. Texas, 386 U.S. 707 (1967); Haynes v. Washington, 373 U.S. 503 (1963); and Culombe v. Connecticut, 367 U.S. 568 (1961).

17. Quinn v. United States, 349 U.S. at 162–64; Emspak v. United States, 349 U.S. 190 (1955).

18. If the defendant's attorney is concerned about jury misconceptions regarding the defendant's silence, the judge has an obligation, upon the attorney's request, to instruct the jury that the accused's decision not to testify cannot be used as an inference of guilt. Carter v. Kentucky, 450 U.S. 288 (1981). Instruction can possibly stimulate adverse inferences by calling attention to a defendant's silence. Lakeside v. Oregon, 435 U.S. 333 (1978).

inate him under the laws of another jurisdiction. Murphy v. Waterfront Comm'n, 378 U.S. 52 (1964).

What Does the Privilege Protect?

An early case held that seizure of a person's private books and papers, to be used as evidence in court, was the same as compelling the person to be a witness against himself or herself. Boyd v. United States, 116 U.S. 616 (1886). This sweeping interpretation was narrowed by subsequent decisions. Official or business records, including union records, are not protected by the Fourth or Fifth Amendments. The privilege against self-incrimination is a personal one and applies only to natural individuals, not to corporations or organizations.[19] Individuals cannot refuse to file a tax return simply because the government might discover income from criminal activities.

Drivers involved in an accident can be required to stop and provide their name and address, even at the risk of criminal liability. California v. Byers, 402 U.S. 424 (1971). Initially, the Court decided that federal requirements that gamblers register with the IRS did not violate the Self-Incrimination Clause. United States v. Kahriger, 345 U.S. 22 (1953); Lewis v. United States, 348 U.S. 419 (1955). The Court later reversed itself and held that such statutes unconstitutionally compel gamblers to incriminate themselves. Marchetti v. United States, 390 U.S. 39 (1968); Grosso v. United States, 390 U.S. 62 (1968). It is unconstitutional to require a group to register and file a list of its members if that information can be used as evidence toward a criminal prosecution. Albertson v. SACB, 382 U.S. 70 (1965). Witnesses may not be asked to exercise this constitutional privilege at the cost of losing their jobs.[20]

In 1998, the Court held that a resident alien cannot invoke the Self-Incrimination Clause to withhold information from the U.S. government out of fear that disclosure might lead to prosecution by a foreign nation. Although an alien is a "person" under the Fifth Amendment, the Clause applies to prosecution of criminal cases in the United States, not in foreign countries. United States v. Balsys, 524 U.S. 666 (1998).

Nontestimonial Evidence

Novel issues suggest the difficulty of relying solely on "framers' intent." The Court has held that the extraction of blood by a physician in a hospital does not offend due process. A blood sample, containing alcohol, can be used to convict someone for involuntary manslaughter. Breithaupt v. Abram, 352 U.S. 432 (1957). A blood test, regarded as "physical or real" evidence rather than testimonial evidence, is unprotected by the Fifth Amendment. Blood may be extracted even if the patient refuses. Schmerber v. California, 384 U.S. 757 (1966). If someone arrested for drunk driving refuses to take a blood-alcohol test, the refusal may be used against him at trial without offending the Self-Incrimination Clause. South Dakota v. Neville, 459 U.S. 553 (1983). Police may videotape drunk-driving suspects and use evidence of their slurred speech against them at trial without first advising them of their constitutional rights. The Court considers the evidence of slurred-speech to be "nontestimonial" and therefore unprotected by the Self-Incrimination Clause and not requiring a *Miranda* warning. Pennsylvania v. Muniz, 496 U.S. 582 (1990). Handwriting samples may be taken of a sus-

---

19. Braswell v. United States, 487 U.S. 99 (1988); United States v. Doe, 465 U.S. 605 (1984); Fisher v. United States, 425 U.S. 391 (1976).

20. Lefkowitz v. Turley, 414 U.S. 70 (1973); Sanitation Men v. Sanitation Comm'n, 392 U.S. 280 (1968); Gardner v. Broderick, 392 U.S. 273 (1968); Garrity v. New Jersey, 385 U.S. 493 (1967); Slochower v. Board of Education, 350 U.S. 551 (1956). Lawyers who invoke their privilege against self-incrimination should not face disbarment as a result. Sperack v. Klein, 385 U.S. 511 (1967), overturning Cohen v. Hurley, 366 U.S. 117 (1961).

pect without violating the Self-Incrimination Clause. Gilbert v. California, 388 U.S. 263 (1967). An accused may be compelled to be present at a police lineup and utter the words of the person who committed the crime. United States v. Wade, 388 U.S. 218, 221–23 (1967).

A 1990 case concerned a woman held in civil contempt for refusing to produce to state authorities her infant son, who had been the subject of child abuse. The state feared that the child was abused or even dead. She claimed that the contempt order violated the Self-Incrimination Clause. A 7–2 Court held that she could not invoke the Clause under these circumstances, but did not decide whether the state could use her refusal in a subsequent criminal proceeding. Baltimore Dept. of Soc. Serv. v. Bouknight, 493 U.S. 549 (1990).

Immunity

Congress has enacted legislation to compel persons to testify by granting them immunity from prosecution. The Interstate Commerce Act of 1887 compelled persons to testify and produce documents. The claim of a witness that such testimony or evidence "may tend to criminate ... shall not excuse such witness from testifying," but the evidence or testimony "shall not be used against such person on the trial of any criminal proceeding." 24 Stat. 383, § 12 (1887). The statute was revised two years later. 25 Stat. 858, § 3.

The Supreme Court held that this procedure did not conform to the Self-Incrimination Clause because it did not give a witness *absolute* immunity against future prosecution. Counselman v. Hitchcock, 142 U.S. 547 (1892). Congress rewrote the statute to provide that no person compelled to testify "shall be prosecuted or subjected to any penalty or forfeiture for or on account of any transaction, matter or thing, concerning which he may testify...." 27 Stat. 443 (1893). This is called "transactional immunity," offering complete immunity for the transaction (offense). In a 5–4 decision, the Supreme Court upheld this statute and rejected a literal interpretation of the Constitution. It concluded that compelled testimony, in the company of absolute immunity, met the essential purpose of the Self-Incrimination Clause, even if the testimony exposed the witness to public disgrace. Brown v. Walker, 161 U.S. 591, 595 (1896).[21]

In 1954, Congress authorized the granting of immunity by a grand jury. The authority could also be granted by a majority of one House or by a two-thirds majority of a congressional committee. Applications are made for a court order to compel testimony. Refusal to testify can result in contempt of court and imprisonment. 68 Stat. 745. The Court upheld this statute in Ullmann v. United States, 350 U.S. 422 (1956). The immunity procedure was codified in 1970 (84 Stat. 926) and appears in 18 U.S.C. §§ 6001–05. The immunity offered is called "use immunity" or "limited immunity." No testimony or other information compelled under a court order, or any information "directly or indirectly" derived from the testimony or other information, "may be used against the witness in any criminal case." 18 U.S.C. § 6002.

Use immunity provides less protection than transactional immunity. A witness given use immunity may still be prosecuted for the crime on the basis of evidence obtained from independent sources. However, as the Iran-Contra cases of Lt. Col. Oliver North and Vice Admiral John Poindexter illustrate, the granting of limited immunity by Congress for the purpose of taking testimony at hearings makes it extremely difficult for the prosecution to demonstrate that the testimony of witnesses at trial has not been tainted by the compelled testimony (see box). The Supreme Court has held that the scope

---

21. Under certain statutes, if a witness appears in response to a subpoena and gives testimony, this action by itself may provide total immunity and prevent prosecution regardless of whether the witness claims the privilege against self-incrimination. United States v. Monia, 317 U.S. 424 (1943). See also Smith v. United States, 337 U.S. 137 (1949); Shapiro v. United States, 335 U.S. 1 (1948); United States v. Hoffman, 335 U.S. 77 (1948).

Compelled Testimony and Tainted Witnesses

In 1972, the Supreme Court held that Congress can compel testimony from an unwilling witness who invokes the Self-Incrimination Clause by conferring "use" (limited) immunity. However, the prosecution has the burden of proving affirmatively that evidence introduced at trial is derived from a legitimate source "wholly independent" of the compelled testimony. The prosecutor may not rely on information that is "directly or indirectly" derived from compelled testimony. Kastigar v. United States, 406 U.S. 441, 453, 460 (1972). At a "*Kastigar* hearing," trial judges must determine whether testimony given in court is tainted by immunized testimony presented to Congress.

The convictions of Lt. Col. Oliver North and Vice Admiral John Poindexter, stemming from the Iran-Contra affair, were overturned on appeal because independent counsel Lawrence E. Walsh had failed to show that the testimony of witnesses at the trials had not been impermissibly tainted by exposure to the immunized testimony of North and Poindexter to Congress.

In the North case, the D.C. Circuit adopted a heightened standard for use immunity. It held that a prohibited "use" occurs whenever a witness's testimony is in any way "shaped, altered, or affected" by immunized testimony. United States v. North, 910 F.2d 843, 863 (D.C. Cir. 1990). It returned the case to the trial court, requiring it to review the testimony of each witness "line-by-line and item-by-item." Id. at 872. That standard proved too onerous for the prosecution, and North's conviction was thrown out.

Poindexter's conviction was also overturned because the D.C. Circuit decided that independent counsel Walsh had not carried his burden of showing that Poindexter's compelled testimony was not used against him at his trial. When North testified at Poindexter's trial, he said he could not separate in his mind (1) what he knew after watching Poindexter's immunized testimony to Congress and (2) what he knew before from his own unrefreshed memory. United States v. Poindexter, 951 F.2d 369 (D.C. Cir. 1991), cert. denied, 506 U.S. 1021 (1992).

of use immunity under Section 6002 is coextensive with the Self-Incrimination Clause. Kastigar v. United States, 406 U.S. 441 (1972).

F. ASSISTANCE OF COUNSEL

The Sixth Amendment entitles a person "to have the Assistance of Counsel for his defence." Without counsel, an accused is unable to exercise effectively the rights available in the Constitution: the privilege to remain silent, to cross-examine witnesses, to challenge biased jurors, and a variety of subtle questions of law that tax the resourcefulness even of seasoned lawyers. "A layman is usually no match for the skilled prosecutor whom he confronts in the court room. He needs the aid of counsel lest he be the victim of overzealous prosecutors, of the law's complexity, or his own ignorance or bewilderment." Williams v. Kaiser, 323 U.S. 471, 476 (1945). A defendant may proceed without counsel if the decision is voluntary and the defendant is aware of the dangers and disadvantages of self-representation.[22]

The question of providing an attorney for indigent defendants was decided partly by the Supreme Court in 1932 when it held that the Due Process Clause of the Fourteenth Amendment requires the appointment of counsel for someone accused of a capital crime. If a defendant is incapable of making his own defense because of "ignorance, feeblemindedness, illiteracy, or the like, it is the duty of

---

22. Faretta v. California, 422 U.S. 806 (1975); McKaskle v. Wiggins, 465 U.S. 168 (1984). Under certain circumstances, judges may deny the defendant's choice of lawyer. Wheat v. United States, 486 U.S. 153 (1988).

the court, whether requested or not, to assign counsel for him as a necessary requisite of due process of law." Powell v. Alabama, 287 U.S. 45, 71 (1932). Six years later, the Court held that indigents charged with a crime in a federal court are entitled by the Sixth Amendment to have the assistance of counsel unless that right is intelligently and competently waived. Johnson v. Zerbst, 304 U.S. 458 (1938).

From *Betts* to *Gideon*

The question of how to provide counsel in a state court vexed the Court for more than two decades. In 1942 it ruled that a state's refusal to appoint counsel for an indigent in a criminal proceeding did not deny due process. Betts v. Brady, 316 U.S. 455 (1942). The Court divided 6–3 in this case, and dozens and dozens of subsequent decisions whittled away at the majority position. The denial of counsel in a state court brought four dissents in 1946. Carter v. Illinois, 329 U.S. 173 (1946). The Court agreed unanimously in 1954 that due process was violated when a state judge denied a defendant the opportunity to obtain counsel on a separate accusation regarding his habitual criminal record. Chandler v. Fretag, 348 U.S. 3(1954). The Court split 5 to 4 in two cases in the late 1950s in which counsel had been denied in a state proceeding. In re Groban, 352 U.S. 330 (1957); Anonymous v. Baker, 360 U.S. 287 (1959).

In 1960, the Court held that lack of counsel for an indigent in a state case deprived the accused of due process. As the two dissenters noted, the Court did not even mention *Betts* v. *Brady,* although the decision "cuts serious inroads into that holding." Hudson v. North Carolina, 363 U.S. 697, 704 (1960). A year later a unanimous Court ruled that due process had been violated by denying counsel to an indigent, ignorant, and mentally ill black. This was a noncapital felony case. Again, the opinion of the Court made no mention of *Betts.* McNeal v. Culver, 365 U.S. 109, 117 (1961). In two other noncapital felony cases, a unanimous Court held that the denial of counsel violated due process. Chewning v. Cunningham, 368 U.S. 443 (1962); Carnley v. Cochran, 369 U.S. 506 (1962). *Betts,* left dangling by a thread, was allowed to fall in 1963. A unanimous Court held that the Sixth Amendment right of assistance of counsel is incorporated in the Due Process Clause of the Fourteenth Amendment and applied against the states. GIDEON v. WAINWRIGHT, 372 U.S. 335 (1963). This decision provoked other rulings on the right of counsel (see box on next page).

The Supreme Court received great credit for issuing *Gideon,* yet it lagged behind many states that had already recognized that government has a constitutional responsibility to provide counsel for indigents prosecuted by the state. The Supreme Court of Indiana in 1854 held that a "civilized community" could not put a citizen in jeopardy and withhold counsel from the poor. Webb v. Baird, 6 Ind. 13 (1854). In 1859, the Wisconsin Supreme Court called it a "mockery" to promise a pauper a fair trial and then tell him he must employ his own counsel. Carpenter v. Dane, 9 Wis. 249 (1859). Congress passed legislation in 1892 to provide counsel to represent poor persons and extended that provision in 1910. 27 Stat. 252 (1892); 36 Stat. 866 (1910).

No sooner had the Court forged a unanimous front to produce *Gideon,* than it split 5–4 on a case that still divides the nation. Danny Escobedo was held in police headquarters for questioning regarding the fatal shooting of his brother-in-law. Although he asked to see his lawyer who was in the building, the police rejected his request and eventually obtained a damaging statement. The Court held that Escobedo had been denied the assistance of counsel in violation of the Sixth and Fourteenth Amendments. ESCOBEDO v. ILLINOIS, 378 U.S. 478 (1964).

The Court continues to issue 5–4 decisions on assistance of counsel. In 2011, it divided by that margin in ruling that an individual in a civil contempt proceeding—facing a year in prison for failing to supply child support—must receive "alternative procedures" to assistance of counsel, such as being informed that ability to pay is a key issue in contempt proceedings. Moreover, the individual needs to be told it is necessary for the state to obtain relevant financial information. Failure to provide that instruction violates due process. Turner v. Rogers, 564 U.S. ___ (2011).

Assistance of Counsel

The Supreme Court's decision in *Gideon v. Wainwright* (1963), requiring states to appoint counsel for indigent defendants, precipitated a number of other decisions to define at what stage of a prosecution the assistance of counsel is needed.

Required

Assistance of counsel for a first appeal. Douglas v. California, 372 U.S. 353 (1963); Evitts v. Lucey, 469 U.S. 387 (1985).

Post-indictment lineups. United States v. Wade, 388 U.S. 218 (1967); Gilbert v. California, 388 U.S. 263 (1967).

Preliminary hearings. Coleman v. Alabama, 399 U.S. 1 (1970). This includes any adversary proceeding before trial in which the government seeks incriminating testimony. Brewer v. Williams, 430 U.S. 387, 401 (1977); Maine v. Moulton, 474 U.S. 159, 170 (1985).

Post-trial proceedings, such as sentencing. Mempa v. Rhay, 389 U.S. 128 (1967).

Assistance of counsel is needed if a sentence involves some imprisonment, whether the offense is classified as felony, misdemeanor, or petty. Argersinger v. Hamlin, 407 U.S. 25 (1972); Scott v. Illinois, 440 U.S. 367 (1979).

Assistance of psychiatrist for indigents whose main defense is insanity. Ake v. Oklahoma, 470 U.S. 68 (1985).

Assistance is required when the state activates a suspended sentence upon an indigent's violation of probation terms. Alabama v. Shelton, 535 U.S. 654 (2002).

Assistance of counsel for plea bargains. Missouri v. Frye, 566 U.S. ___ (2012); Lafler v. Cooper, 566 U.S. ___ (2012).

Not required

Counsel for additional appeals, such as a petition for certiorari to the U.S. Supreme Court. Ross v. Moffitt, 417 U.S. 600 (1974).

Pre-indictment "showup" at police station. Kirby v. Illinois, 406 U.S. 682 (1972).

Under certain circumstances, a suspect may be brought before a witness for the purpose of identification without the assistance of counsel. Stovall v. Denno, 388 U.S. 293 (1967); Kirby v. Illinois, 406 U.S. 682 (1972). This is not allowed, however, if the prosecutor uses a suggestive manner in presenting a suspect to the witness. Moore v. Illinois, 434 U.S. 220 (1971).

The right to counsel is not violated when an attorney refuses to agree to a defendant's desire to present perjured testimony. Nix v. Whiteside, 475 U.S. 157 (1986).

Counsel for death-row inmates seeking postconviction relief. Murray v. Giarrantano, 492 U.S. 1 (1989).

Post-indictment photographic display to allow witness to identify offender. United States v. Ash, 413 U.S. 300 (1973).

Providing Effective Counsel

Recent cases have explored the criteria needed for "effective" assistance of counsel.[23] In 2002, the Supreme Court let stand an appellate court ruling that a Texas death row inmate was entitled to a new trial because his lawyer slept repeatedly during the initial trial. Cockrell v. Burdine, 535 U.S. 1120

---

23. Lockhart v. Fretwell, 506 U.S. 364 (1993); Lozada v. Deeds, 498 U.S. 430 (1991); Burger v. Kemp, 483 U.S. 776 (1987); Strictland v. Washington, 466 U.S. 688 (1984); United States v. Cronic, 466 U.S. 648 (1984); Jones v. Barnes, 463 U.S. 745 (1983); Wainwright v. Torna, 455 U.S. 586 (1982); Cuyler v. Sullivan, 446 U.S. 335 (1980); Holloway v. Arkansas, 435 U.S. 475 (1978).

(2002). The previous week, however, an 8–1 Court overturned an appellate court ruling that a defense lawyer's failure to call witnesses or make a closing statement at his client's sentencing hearing marked a deficiency so serious that it invalidated the death sentence. Bell v. Cone, 535 U.S. 685 (2002). The next year, the Court overturned a death sentence because of the poor performance of defense lawyers. Wiggins v. Smith, 539 U.S. 510 (2003). Counties, complaining that they lack funds to defend the poor, have sued states for financial relief, and some states try to require indigents to pay minimal amounts for legal representation.

In two cases in 2012, a sharply divided Court (5–4) insisted on effective counsel for defendants during plea bargain negotiations. Missouri v. Frye, 566 U.S. ___ (2012); Lafler v. Cooper, 566 U.S. ___ (2012). Divided 7–2 in a third case, it found ineffective assistance of counsel given to someone who was sentenced to death for murder. He had been represented by two appointed lawyers but they left the law firm without informing him. Maples v. Thomas, 565 U.S. ___ (2012).

The *Miranda* Warning

Building on cases involving coerced confessions, self-incrimination, and right to counsel, the Supreme Court in 1966 handed down the controversial *Miranda* ruling. The decision announced a cluster of constitutional rights for defendants who are held in police custody and cut off from the outside world. The atmosphere and environment of incommunicado interrogation was held to be inherently intimidating and hostile to the privilege against self-incrimination. To prevent compulsion by law enforcement officials, the person in custody must be clearly informed—before interrogation—of the following: the right to remain silent, anything said may be used in court, the right to consult with an attorney and to have a lawyer present during interrogation, and the right to have a lawyer appointed if the accused is indigent. MIRANDA v. ARIZONA, 384 U.S. 436 (1966).

The decision did not rest solely on constitutional grounds. The Court invited Congress to contribute its handiwork: "Our decision in no way creates a constitutional straitjacket which will handicap sound efforts at reform, nor is it intended to have this effect. We encourage Congress and the States to continue their laudable search for increasingly effective ways of protecting the rights of the individual while promoting efficient enforcement of our criminal laws." Id. at 467. Congress passed legislation in 1968 to allow for the admissibility of confessions if voluntarily given. Trial judges would determine the issue of voluntariness after taking into consideration all the circumstances surrounding the confession, including five elements identified by Congress. 82 Stat. 210 (1968); 18 U.S.C. § 3501(a)(b).

Miranda has been bitterly attacked for restricting the efforts of law enforcement officials. However, the Supreme Court correctly noted that its holding was not "an innovation in our jurisprudence." 384 U.S. at 442. Indeed, *Miranda*-type warnings had been given routinely by federal agents in the past. McNabb v. United States, 318 U.S. 332, 336 (1943). They had been given by state officials, as the Court noted in *Michigan* v. *Tucker,* 417 U.S. 433, 447 (1974). Long before *Miranda,* state police recognized that an individual has a constitutional right to remain silent and that suspects must be told that anything said could be used against them in court. Haley v. Ohio, 332 U.S. 596, 598, 604 (1948).

Miranda and *Escobedo* were not given full retroactivity. Johnson v. New Jersey, 384 U.S. 719 (1966). When applied to future prosecutions, the reversal of a conviction because of a *Miranda* violation does not mean that the suspect goes free. The state can try the case again without the tainted evidence. Orozco v. Texas, 394 U.S. 324 (1969).

In 1999, the Fourth Circuit held that *Miranda* was not a constitutional holding and that the statute Congress enacted in 1968 was the final say on the question of admissibility of a defendant's statement. The Supreme Court reversed the Fourth Circuit in 2000, ruling that *Miranda* was a constitutional decision and could not be overruled by Congress. DICKERSON v. UNITED STATES, 530 U.S. 428 (2000).

In 2011, the Court divided 5 to 4 in holding that age must be taken into account when deciding to issue a *Miranda* warning. In this case, a 13-year-old was questioned for more than 30 minutes by a uniformed police officer and school administrators, eventually admitting to being involved in two home break-ins. The dissenters objected that allowing age to be a factor weakened the "clear and certain" standards of *Miranda*. J.D.B. v. North Carolina, 564 U.S. ___ (2011).

When Is Someone in Custody?

Since 1966, *Miranda* has been modified by a lengthening list of exceptions. Although an accused's statement to police may be rendered inadmissible under *Miranda,* it can be used to impeach the credibility of an accused who chooses to take the stand in his or her own defense. *Miranda* is not a license to commit perjury. Harris v. New York, 401 U.S. 222 (1971); Oregon v. Hass, 420 U.S. 714 (1975). If a defendant takes the stand and tells the jury a story that is inconsistent with what he told the police after being given *Miranda* warnings, cross-examination may probe these conflicting statements. Anderson v. Charles, 447 U.S. 404 (1980).

The reach of the *Miranda* rule is circumscribed by specific conditions. It does not apply to testimony before a grand jury. United States v. Mandujano, 425 U.S. 564 (1976). It applies only after a person is taken into custody. The Court admits that the definition of custody is "a slippery one" and presents "murky and difficult questions" of when it begins. Oregon v. Elstad, 470 U.S. 298, 309, 316 (1985). Although a person in custody is entitled to *Miranda* rights regardless of the nature of the offense (felony or misdemeanor), there is no need to read these rights for routine roadside stops by traffic cops. Berkemer v. McCarty, 468 U.S. 420 (1984). Moreover, if incriminating information can be obtained before a person is taken into custody and given the *Miranda* warning, the information is admissible as evidence. Oregon v. Mathiason, 429 U.S. 492 (1977). Police therefore have an incentive to talk to a suspect without placing him under arrest and reading the *Miranda* rights, in the hopes of uncovering incriminating evidence or eliciting a confession. California v. Beheler, 463 U.S. 1121 (1983). Convicted felons who are required to report to probation officers and be truthful "in all matters" are not considered "in custody." Therefore, any statements they make of an incriminating nature may be used against them in court. Minnesota v. Murphy, 465 U.S. 420 (1984).[24]

Police questioning in the absence of a *Miranda* warning, even when overbearing, is allowed under certain circumstances. In one case the police questioned a suspect at the hospital while he was undergoing treatment for gunshot wounds. The information they obtained was not used in a criminal proceeding. Because of multiple concurrences in this case, it is difficult to find a guiding principle for *Miranda*. The suspect in this case was allowed to pursue a civil rights suit against the office on due process grounds. Chavez v. Martinez, 538 U.S. 760 (2003). In 2012, a 6–3 Court ruled that a prison inmate did not require *Miranda* warnings when meeting with a corrections officer and two sheriff's deputies in a conference room, where he was questioned for five to seven hours. At various times he was told he was free to leave and return to his cell. During the questioning he confessed to an earlier crime. Howes v. Fields, 565 U.S. ___ (2012).

Once in Custody

Even after a person is in custody and advised of his *Miranda* rights, police officers may engage in a conversation between themselves that leads to an incriminating statement from the suspect. Such conversations are permissible if they are not "interrogations" (questioning intended to elicit an incriminating response). Rhode Island v. Innis, 446 U.S. 291 (1980). How do the courts distinguish between

---

24. In 1995, the Court reviewed a confession of murder that resulted from a two-hour, tape-recorded session at Alaska state trooper headquarters. The state trial and appellate courts determined that the suspect was not "in custody" when he confessed. Statutory law provides that state-court fact findings shall be presumed to be correct, but the Court held that the issue whether a suspect is "in custody" (and therefore entitled to *Miranda* warnings) presents a mixed question of law and fact warranting independent review by federal courts. Thompson v. Keohane, 516 U.S. 99 (1995).

conversations and interrogations and decide whether the police intended to provoke an incriminating response?

Police questioning may expand for other reasons. After a suspect is given a *Miranda* warning and declines to comment, police may suspend questioning for a "significant" period, give another warning, and obtain incriminating information that is admissible as evidence. Michigan v. Mosley, 423 U.S. 96 (1975). Once an accused asks for counsel, the police may not return and interrogate him without counsel unless he voluntarily "initiates" the communication. Edwards v. Arizona, 451 U.S. 477 (1981).[25]

Edwards led to some confusion in the lower courts. Did *Edwards* only protect an accused between the time he invokes his right to counsel and consults counsel but not afterward? Is the protection of *Edwards* terminated or suspended simply because a suspect consults with counsel? In 1991 the Court ruled that the protection does not end but continues. It does not pass "in and out of existence." Minnick v. Mississippi, 498 U.S. 146, 154 (1991). But in 2010 the Court decided to create a "bright line rule" about how long the protection lasts after police custody ends. In a case involving a prisoner who was interrogated two and a half years after he first invoked his *Miranda* rights, the Court concluded that that invocation was no longer in force. In the interest of providing clarity for police, Justice Scalia's opinion concluded that fourteen days was sufficient time for the protection to continue. Maryland v. Shatzer, 559 U.S. ___ (2010).

Further Erosion of *Miranda*

The opportunity for the police to question a suspect split the Court 5 to 4 in 1990. After a suspect told the police that he did not know whether he should talk to his lawyer, an officer said that it was unnecessary. He then made a statement that was later used to impeach his testimony, a procedure the Court upheld. Michigan v. Harvey, 494 U.S. 344 (1990). Another decision in 1990 held that the police may place an undercover agent in jail, posing as a fellow inmate, and it is not necessary to give *Miranda* warnings to a cellmate before eliciting an incriminating response. The essential ingredients that require *Miranda* warnings are a "police dominated atmosphere," coercion, and compulsion. An 8–1 Court decided that those conditions are not present in a jail cell block. Illinois v. Perkins, 496 U.S. 292 (1990).

In another *Miranda* interpretation in 1991, a 6–3 Court distinguished between the Fifth Amendment right to counsel set forth in *Miranda* and the Sixth Amendment right to counsel required by the Constitution. Thus, a suspect who is represented in court triggers the Sixth Amendment right to counsel but not the Fifth Amendment right. The Sixth Amendment right is "offense-specific." As a result, someone represented by a lawyer in court for one crime may be questioned by the police about a separate offense. Representation for one crime does not prevent the police from advising the suspect of his *Miranda* rights and obtaining incriminating statements about another crime. McNeil v. Wisconsin, 501 U.S. 171 (1991). In the future, counsel for defendants will have to state specifically that they are invoking their clients' *Miranda* rights.

There is also a "public safety" exception to the *Miranda* rule. Its literal language may be waived if there is concern for the public safety. When an officer frisks a suspect and discovers an empty shoulder holster, it is appropriate to ask where the gun is before making formal arrest and reading the *Miranda* rights. New York v. Quarles, 467 U.S. 649 (1984). Moreover, a 5–4 Court decided that the warning need not be given in the exact form described in *Miranda*, but simply must reasonably con-

---

25. See also Michigan v. Jackson, 475 U.S. 625 (1986); Shea v. Louisiana, 470 U.S. 51 (1985); Smith v. Illinois, 469 U.S. 91 (1984); Solem v. Stumes, 465 U.S. 638 (1984); Wyrick v. Fields, 459 U.S. 42 (1982). Further refinements depend on what kind of communication the accused "initiates": a substantive discussion about the crime or merely a routine request for a drink of water or use of the telephone. Oregon v. Bradshaw, 462 U.S. 1039 (1983). A refusal to make a written statement without counsel need not be interpreted to exclude an oral statement that is incriminating. Connecticut v. Barrett, 479 U.S. 523 (1987). See also Colorado v. Spring, 479 U.S. 564 (1987).

vey to a suspect his or her rights. Informing a suspect that an attorney would be appointed "if and when you go to court" does not render the warning inadequate. Duckworth v. Eagan, 492 U.S. 195 (1989).

Efforts to Clarify *Miranda*

In a major weakening of the *Miranda* doctrine in 1985, the Court held that if police officers violate *Miranda* procedures by obtaining a confession before reading a suspect his rights, the mistake may be cured by reading the rights later and obtaining a confession a second time. The suspect, having let the "cat out of the bag" with the first confession, may be more inclined to repeat it. OREGON v. ELSTAD, 470 U.S. 298 (1985). A year later, the Court clarified that the involuntariness of a confession after a *Miranda* warning derives only from police coercion, not from a defendant's mental condition (such as being told by the "voice of God" to confess). Colorado v. Connolly, 479 U.S. 157 (1986).

Two Court decisions in 2004 attempted to clarify *Miranda*, but in each case the Justices split 5 to 4, underscoring the lack of a general consensus on basic principles. In the first case, the Court placed limits on the widespread practice of police who question a suspect without a *Miranda* warning in order to obtain incriminating evidence, followed by a second round of questioning under *Miranda*. The ruling rejected this procedure as an obvious attempt to "get a confession the suspect would not make if he understood his rights at the outset." Missouri v. Seibert, 542 U.S. 600 (2004). Statements repeated after a warning in such circumstances are now inadmissible, but the Court did not overrule *Elstad*. Thus, police may continue to use the two-step procedure if they manage a decisive and clear break between the interrogations. In the second case, the Court held that physical evidence gathered because of a suspect's statement, without a *Miranda* warning, can be used in court. The majority decided that excluding the physical evidence would be an unlawful extension of *Miranda*. United States v. Patane, 542 U.S. 630 (2004). The majority of five in this case represented an opinion by three Justices joined by two who concurred. In a third decision in 2004, a unanimous Court held that police cannot "deliberately elicit" incriminating statements from someone under indictment without a waiver of counsel. This case involved the Sixth Amendment right to counsel rather than the Fifth Amendment custodial-interrogation standard (*Elstad*). Fellers v. United States, 540 U.S. 519 (2004).

Gideon v. Wainwright

372 U.S. 335 (1963)

In *Betts* v. *Brady* (1942), the Supreme Court held that an indigent defendant was not entitled to be appointed counsel for noncapital cases. That doctrine was undercut repeatedly in subsequent cases. Clarence Earl Gideon, sentenced to five years in the Florida state prison, had to defend himself at the trial without benefit of counsel. From his prison cell, with a handwritten note, he petitioned the Supreme Court to overturn *Betts*.

MR. JUSTICE BLACK delivered the opinion of the Court.

Petitioner was charged in a Florida state court with having broken and entered a poolroom with intent to commit a misdemeanor. This offense is a felony under Florida law. Appearing in court without funds and without a lawyer, petitioner asked the court to appoint counsel for him, whereupon the following colloquy took place:

"THE COURT: Mr. Gideon, I am sorry, but I can-

not appoint Counsel to represent you in this case. Under the laws of the State of Florida, the only time the Court can appoint Counsel to represent a Defendant is when that person is charged with a capital offense. I am sorry, but I will have to deny your request to appoint Counsel to defend you in this case.

"THE DEFENDANT: The United States Supreme Court says I am entitled to be represented by Counsel."

Put to trial before a jury, Gideon conducted his

defense about as well as could be expected from a layman. He made an opening statement to the jury, cross-examined the State's witnesses, presented witnesses in his own defense, declined to testify himself, and made a short argument "emphasizing his innocence to the charge contained in the Information filed in this case." The jury returned a verdict of guilty, and petitioner was sentenced to serve five years in the state prison.... To give this problem another review here, we granted certiorari. 370 U.S. 908. Since Gideon was proceeding *in forma pauperis,* we appointed counsel to represent him and requested both sides to discuss in their briefs and oral arguments the following: "Should this Court's holding in *Betts* v. *Brady,* 316 U.S. 455, be reconsidered?"

I.

The facts upon which Betts claimed that he had been unconstitutionally denied the right to have counsel appointed to assist him are strikingly like the facts upon which Gideon here bases his federal constitutional claim. Betts was indicted for robbery in a Maryland state court. On arraignment, he told the trial judge of his lack of funds to hire a lawyer and asked the court to appoint one for him. Betts was advised that it was not the practice in that county to appoint counsel for indigent defendants except in murder and rape cases. He then pleaded not guilty, had witnesses summoned, cross-examined the State's witnesses, examined his own, and chose not to testify himself. He was found guilty by the judge, sitting without a jury, and sentenced to eight years in prison. Like Gideon, Betts sought release by habeas corpus, alleging that he had been denied the right to assistance of counsel in violation of the Fourteenth Amendment. Betts was denied any relief, and on review this Court affirmed. It was held that a refusal to appoint counsel for an indigent defendant charged with a felony did not necessarily violate the Due Process Clause of the Fourteenth Amendment, ...

II.

The Sixth Amendment provides, "In all criminal prosecutions, the accused shall enjoy the right ... to have the Assistance of Counsel for his defence." We have construed this to mean that in federal courts counsel must be provided for defendants unable to employ counsel unless the right is competently and intelligently waived. Betts argued that this right is extended to indigent defendants in state courts by the Fourteenth Amendment. In response the Court stated that, while the Sixth Amendment laid down "no rule for the conduct of the States, the question recurs whether the constraint laid by the Amend-

ment upon the national courts expresses a rule so fundamental and essential to a fair trial, and so, to due process of law, that it is made obligatory upon the States by the Fourteenth Amendment." 316 U.S., at 465....

We accept *Betts* v. *Brady's* assumption, based as it was on our prior cases, that a provision of the Bill of Rights which is "fundamental and essential to a fair trial" is made obligatory upon the States by the Fourteenth Amendment. We think the Court in *Betts* was wrong, however, in concluding that the Sixth Amendment's guarantee of counsel is not one of these fundamental rights. Ten years before *Betts* v. *Brady,* this Court, after full consideration of all the historical data examined in *Betts,* had unequivocally declared that "the right to the aid of counsel is of this fundamental character." *Powell* v. *Alabama,* 287 U.S. 45, 68 (1932). While the Court at the close of its *Powell* opinion did by its language, as this Court frequently does, limit its holding to the particular facts and circumstances of that case, its conclusions about the fundamental nature of the right to counsel are unmistakable. Several years later, in 1936, the Court reemphasized what it had said about the fundamental nature of the right to counsel in this language:

"We concluded that certain fundamental rights, safeguarded by the first eight amendments against federal action, were also safeguarded against state action by the due process of law clause of the Fourteenth Amendment, and among them the fundamental right of the accused to the aid of counsel in a criminal prosecution." *Grosjean* v. *American Press Co.,* 297 U.S. 233, 243–244 (1936).

And again in 1938 this Court said:

"[The assistance of counsel] is one of the safeguards of the Sixth Amendment deemed necessary to insure fundamental human rights of life and liberty.... The Sixth Amendment stands as a constant admonition that if the constitutional safeguards it provides be lost, justice will not 'still be done.'" *Johnson* v. *Zerbst,* 304 U.S. 458, 462 (1938). To the same effect, see *Avery* v. *Alabama,* 308 U.S. 444 (1940), and *Smith* v. *O'Grady,* 312 U.S. 329 (1941).

In light of these and many other prior decisions of this Court, it is not surprising that the *Betts* Court, when faced with the contention that "one charged with crime, who is unable to obtain counsel, must be furnished counsel by the State," conceded that "[e]xpressions in the opinions of this court lend color to the argument...." 316 U.S., at 462–463. The fact is that in deciding as it did—that "appointment of counsel is not a fundamental right, essential to a fair trial" — the Court in *Betts* v. *Brady* made an abrupt break with its own well-considered precedents. In returning to these old precedents, sounder we believe than the new, we but restore constitutional principles established to achieve a fair system of justice. Not only these precedents but also reason and reflection require us to recognize that in our adversary system of criminal justice, any person hauled into court, who is too poor to hire a lawyer, cannot be assured a fair trial unless counsel is provided for him. This seems to us to be an obvious truth. Governments, both state and federal, quite properly spend vast sums of money to establish machinery to try defendants accused of crime. Lawyers to prosecute are everywhere deemed essential to protect the public's interest in an orderly society. Similarly, there are few defendants charged with crime, few indeed, who fail to hire the best lawyers they can get to prepare and present their defenses. That government hires lawyers to prosecute and defendants who have the money hire lawyers to defend are the strongest indications of the widespread belief that lawyers in criminal courts are necessities, not luxuries. The right of one charged with crime to counsel may not be deemed fundamental and essential to fair trials in some countries, but it is in ours. From the very beginning, our state and national constitutions and laws have laid great emphasis on procedural and substantive safeguards designed to assure fair trials before impartial tribunals in which every defendant stands equal before the law. This noble ideal cannot be realized if the poor man charged with crime has to face his accusers without a lawyer to assist him....

The Court in *Betts* v. *Brady* departed from the sound wisdom upon which the Court's holding in *Powell* v. *Alabama* rested. Florida, supported by two other States, has asked that *Betts* v. *Brady* be left intact. Twenty-two States, as friends of the Court, argue that *Betts* was "an anachronism when handed down" and that it should now be overruled. We agree.

The judgment is reversed and the cause is remanded to the Supreme Court of Florida for further action not inconsistent with this opinion.

Reversed.

[*Douglas, Clark, and Harlan wrote separate concurring opinions.*]

Escobedo v. Illinois

378 U.S. 478 (1964)

Danny Escobedo, a 22-year-old of Mexican extraction, was arrested in connection with the fatal shooting of his brother-in-law. Although his lawyer was in police headquarters, the lawyer was denied access to see his client. The question was whether the refusal by the police to allow Escobedo to consult with his lawyer constituted a denial of the right to counsel.

MR. JUSTICE GOLDBERG delivered the opinion of the Court.

The critical question in this case is whether, under the circumstances, the refusal by the police to honor petitioner's request to consult with his lawyer during the course of an interrogation constitutes a denial of "the Assistance of Counsel" in violation of the Sixth Amendment to the Constitution as "made obligatory upon the States by the Fourteenth Amendment," *Gideon* v. *Wainwright,* 372 U.S. 335, 342, and thereby renders inadmissible in a state criminal trial any incriminating statement elicited by the police during the interrogation.

On the night of January 19, 1960, petitioner's brother-in-law was fatally shot. In the early hours of the next morning, at 2:30 a.m., petitioner was arrested without a warrant and interrogated. Petitioner made no statement to the police and was re-leased at 5 that afternoon pursuant to a state court writ of habeas corpus obtained by Mr. Warren Wolfson, a lawyer who had been retained by petitioner.

On January 30, Benedict DiGerlando, who was then in police custody and who was later indicted for the murder along with petitioner, told the police that petitioner had fired the fatal shots. Between 8 and 9 that evening, petitioner and his sister, the widow of the deceased, were arrested and taken to police headquarters. En route to the police station, the police "had handcuffed the defendant behind his back," and "one of the arresting officers told defendant that DiGerlando had named him as the one who shot" the deceased. Petitioner testified, without contradiction, that the "detectives said they had us pretty well, up pretty tight, and we might as well admit to this crime," and that he replied, "I am sorry but I would like to have advice from my lawyer." A police officer testified that although petitioner was not formally charged "he was in custody" and "couldn't walk out the door."

Shortly after petitioner reached police headquarters, his retained lawyer arrived. The lawyer described the ensuing events in the following terms:

"On that day I received a phone call [from "the mother of another defendant"] and pursuant to that phone call I went to the Detective Bureau at 11th and State. The first person I talked to was the Sergeant on duty at the Bureau Desk, Sergeant Pidgeon. I asked Sergeant Pidgeon for permission to speak to my client, Danny Escobedo.... Sergeant Pidgeon made a call to the Bureau lockup and informed me that the boy had been taken from the lockup to the Homicide Bureau. This was between 9:30 and 10:00 in the evening. Before I went anywhere, he called the Homicide Bureau and told them there was an attorney waiting to see Escobedo. He told me I could not see him. Then I went upstairs to the Homicide Bureau. There were several Homicide Detectives around and I talked to them. I identified myself as Escobedo's attorney and asked permission to see him. They said I could not.... The police officer told me to see Chief Flynn who was on duty. I identified myself to Chief Flynn and asked permission to see my client. He said I could not.... I think it was approximately 11:00 o'clock. He said I couldn't see him because they hadn't completed questioning.... [F]or a second or two I spotted him in an office in the Homicide Bureau. The door was open and I could see through the office.... I waved to him and he waved back and then the door was closed, by one of the officers at Homicide. There were four or five officers milling around the Homicide Detail that night. As to whether I talked to Captain Flynn any later that day, I waited around for another hour or two and went back again and renewed by [sic] request to see my client. He again told me I could not.... I filed an official complaint with Commissioner Phelan of the Chicago Police Department. I had a conversation with every police officer I could find. I was told at Homicide that I couldn't see him and I would have to get a writ of habeas corpus. I left the Homicide Bureau and from the Detective Bureau at 11th and State at approximately 1:00 A.M. [Sunday morning] I had no opportunity to talk to my client that night. I quoted to Captain Flynn the Section of the Criminal Code which allows an attorney the right to see his client."

Petitioner testified that during the course of the interrogation he repeatedly asked to speak to his lawyer and that the police said that his lawyer "didn't want to see" him. The testimony of the po-

lice officers confirmed these accounts in substantial detail.

Notwithstanding repeated requests by each, petitioner and his retained lawyer were afforded no opportunity to consult during the course of the entire interrogation.

[*During the interrogation, Escobedo made an incriminating statement and was later convicted of murder.*]

The interrogation here was conducted before petitioner was formally indicted. But in the context of this case, that fact should make no difference. When petitioner requested, and was denied, an opportunity to consult with his lawyer, the investigation had ceased to be a general investigation of "an unsolved crime." *Spano* v. *New York,* 360 U.S. 315, 327 (STEWART, J., concurring). Petitioner had become the accused, and the purpose of the interrogation was to "get him" to confess his guilt despite his constitutional right not to do so. At the time of his arrest and throughout the course of the interrogation, the police told petitioner that they had convincing evidence that he had fired the fatal shots. Without informing him of his absolute right to remain silent in the face of this accusation, the police urged him to make a statement....

It is argued that if the right to counsel is afforded prior to indictment, the number of confessions obtained by the police will diminish significantly, because most confessions are obtained during the period between arrest and indictment, and "any lawyer worth his salt will tell the suspect in no uncertain terms to make no statement to police under any circumstances." *Watts* v. *Indiana,* 338 U.S. 49, 59 (Jackson, J., concurring in part and dissenting in part). This argument, of course, cuts two ways. The fact that many confessions are obtained during this period points up its critical nature as a "stage when legal aid and advice" are surely needed.... Our Constitution, unlike some others, strikes the balance in favor of the right of the accused to be advised by his lawyer of his privilege against self-incrimination....

... No system worth preserving should have to *fear* that if an accused is permitted to consult with a lawyer, he will become aware of, and exercise, these rights. If the exercise of constitutional rights will thwart the effectiveness of a system of law enforcement, then there is something very wrong with that system.

We hold, therefore, that where, as here, the investigation is no longer a general inquiry into an unsolved crime but has begun to focus on a particular suspect, the suspect has been taken into police custody, the police carry out a process of interrogations that lends itself to eliciting incriminating statements, the suspect has requested and been denied an opportunity to consult with his lawyer, and the police have not effectively warned him of his absolute constitutional right to remain silent, the accused has been denied "the Assistance of Counsel" in violation of the Sixth Amendment to the Constitution as "made obligatory upon the States by the Fourteenth Amendment," *Gideon* v. *Wainwright,* 372 U.S., at 342, and that no statement elicited by the police during the interrogation may be used against him at a criminal trial....

The judgment of the Illinois Supreme Court is reversed and the case remanded for proceedings not inconsistent with this opinion.

Reversed and remanded.

Mr. Justice Harlan, dissenting.

... I think the rule announced today is most ill-conceived and that it seriously and unjustifiably fetters perfectly legitimate methods of criminal law enforcement.

Mr. Justice Stewart, dissenting....

Mr. Justice White, with whom Mr. Justice Clark and Mr. Justice Stewart join, dissenting....

... The only "inquisitions" the Constitution forbids are those which compel incrimination. Escobedo's statements were not compelled and the Court does not hold that they were.

This new American judges' rule, which is to be applied in both federal and state courts, is perhaps thought to be a necessary safeguard against the possibility of extorted confessions. To this extent it reflects a deep-seated distrust of law enforcement officers everywhere, unsupported by relevant data or current material based upon our own experience. Obviously law enforcement officers can make mistakes and exceed their authority, as today's decision shows that even judges can do, but I have somewhat more faith than the Court evidently has in the ability and desire of prosecutors and of the power of the appellate courts to discern and correct such violations of the law.

Miranda v. Arizona
384 U.S. 436 (1966)

Prior to 1966, Supreme Court decisions had established a number of rights for individuals taken into police custody: defendants had to be arraigned before a neutral magistrate; indigent defendants had a right to court-appointed counsel; confessions could not be coerced. In this landmark decision, the Court announced the rights available to an accused during police interrogation to protect his or her constitutional privilege against self-incrimination. Ernesto Miranda confessed to a crime during police interrogation without requesting the assistance of counsel.

Mr. Chief Justice Warren delivered the opinion of the Court....

I.

The constitutional issue we decide in each of these cases is the admissibility of statements obtained from a defendant questioned while in custody or otherwise deprived of his freedom of action in any significant way. In each, the defendant was questioned by police officers, detectives, or a prosecuting attorney in a room in which he was cut off from the outside world. In none of these cases was the defendant given a full and effective warning of his rights at the outset of the interrogation process. In all the cases, the questioning elicited oral admissions, and in three of them, signed statements as well which were admitted at their trials. They all thus share salient features—incommunicado interrogation of

individuals in a police-dominated atmosphere, resulting in self-incriminating statements without full warnings of constitutional rights.

An understanding of the nature and setting of this in-custody interrogation is essential to our decisions today. The difficulty in depicting what transpires at such interrogations stems from the fact that in this country they have largely taken place incommunicado. From extensive factual studies undertaken in the early 1930's, including the famous Wickersham Report to Congress by a Presidential Commission, it is clear that police violence and the "third degree" flourished at that time. In a series of cases decided by this Court long after these studies, the police resorted to physical brutality—beating, hanging, whipping—and to sustained and protracted questioning incommunicado in order to extort confessions....

The examples given above are undoubtedly the exception now, but they are sufficiently widespread to be the object of concern. Unless a proper limitation upon custodial interrogation is achieved—such as these decisions will advance—there can be no assurance that practices of this nature will be eradicated in the foreseeable future....

Again we stress that the modern practice of in-custody interrogation is psychologically rather than physically oriented. As we have stated before, "Since *Chambers* v. *Florida,* 309 U.S. 227, this Court has recognized that coercion can be mental as well as physical, and that the blood of the accused is not the only hallmark of an unconstitutional inquisition." *Blackburn* v. *Alabama,* 361 U.S. 199, 206 (1960)....

The officers are told by the manuals that the "principal psychological factor contributing to a successful interrogation is *privacy*—being alone with the person under interrogation." The efficacy of this tactic has been explained as follows:

"If at all practicable, the interrogation should take place in the investigator's office or at least in a room of his own choice. The subject should be deprived of every psychological advantage. In his own home he may be confident, indignant, or recalcitrant. He is more keenly aware of his rights and more reluctant to tell of his indiscretions or criminal behavior within the walls of his home. Moreover his family and other friends are nearby, their presence lending moral support. In his own office, the investigator possesses all the advantages. The atmosphere suggests the invincibility of the forces of the law."

To highlight the isolation and unfamiliar surroundings, the manuals instruct the police to display an air of confidence in the suspect's guilt and from outward appearance to maintain only an interest in confirming certain details. The guilt of the subject is to be posited as a fact. The interrogator should direct his comments toward the reasons why the subject committed the act, rather than court failure by asking the subject whether he did it. Like other men, perhaps the subject has had a bad family life, had an unhappy childhood, had too much to drink, had an unrequited desire for women. The officers are instructed to minimize the moral seriousness of the offense, to cast blame on the victim or on society. These tactics are designed to put the subject in a psychological state where his story is but an elaboration of what the police purport to know already—that he is guilty....

... The current practice of incommunicado interrogation is at odds with one of our Nation's most cherished principles—that the individual may not be compelled to incriminate himself. Unless adequate protective devices are employed to dispel the compulsion inherent in custodial surroundings, no statement obtained from the defendant can truly be the product of his free choice....

III.

... We have concluded that without proper safeguards the process of in-custody interrogation of persons suspected or accused of crime contains inherently compelling pressures which work to undermine the individual's will to resist and to compel him to speak where he would not otherwise do so freely. In order to combat these pressures and to permit a full opportunity to exercise the privilege against self-incrimination, the accused must be adequately and effectively apprised of his rights and the exercise of those rights must be fully honored.

It is impossible for us to foresee the potential alternatives for protecting the privilege which might be devised by Congress or the States in the exercise of their creative rule-making capacities. Therefore we cannot say that the Constitution necessarily requires adherence to any particular solution for the inherent compulsions of the interrogation process as it is presently conducted. Our decision in no way creates a constitutional straitjacket which will handicap sound efforts at reform, nor is it intended to have this effect. We encourage Congress and the States to continue their laudable search for increasingly effective ways of protecting the rights of the individual while promoting efficient enforcement of our criminal laws. However, unless we are shown other procedures which are at least as effective in apprising accused persons of their right of silence and in assuring a continuous opportunity to exercise it, the following safeguards must be observed.

At the outset, if a person in custody is to be subjected to interrogation, he must first be informed in clear and unequivocal terms that he has the right to remain silent....

The warning of the right to remain silent must be accompanied by the explanation that anything said can and will be used against the individual in court....

... It is necessary to warn him not only that he has the right to consult with an attorney, but also that if he is indigent a lawyer will be appointed to represent him. Without this additional warning, the admonition of the right to consult with counsel would often be understood as meaning only that he can consult with a lawyer if he has one or has the funds to obtain one....

Over the years the Federal Bureau of Investigation has compiled an exemplary record of effective law enforcement while advising any suspect or arrested person, at the outset of an interview, that he is not required to make a statement, that any statement may be used against him in court, that the individual may obtain the services of an attorney of his own choice and, more recently, that he has a right to free counsel if he is unable to pay....

MR. JUSTICE CLARK, dissenting in Nos. 759, 760, and 761, and concurring in the result in No. 584.

... I am unable to join the majority because its opinion goes too far on too little, while my dissenting brethren do not go quite far enough. Nor can I join in the Court's criticism of the present practices of police and investigatory agencies as to custodial interrogation. The materials it refers to as "police manuals" are, as I read them, merely writings in this field by professors and some police officers. Not one is shown by the record here to be the official manual of any police department, much less in universal use in crime detection....

MR. JUSTICE HARLAN, whom MR. JUSTICE STEWART and MR. JUSTICE WHITE join, dissenting.

I believe the decision of the Court represents poor constitutional law and entails harmful consequences for the country at large. How serious these consequences may prove to be only time can tell....

... There can be little doubt that the Court's new code would markedly decrease the number of confessions. To warn the suspect that he may remain silent and remind him that his confession may be used in court are minor obstructions. To require also an express waiver by the suspect and an end to questioning whenever he demurs must heavily handicap questioning. And to suggest or provide counsel for the suspect simply invites the end of the interrogation....

MR. JUSTICE WHITE, with whom MR. JUSTICE HARLAN and MR. JUSTICE STEWART join, dissenting.

... There is, in my view, every reason to believe that a good many criminal defendants who otherwise would have been convicted on what this Court has previously thought to be the most satisfactory kind of evidence will now, under this new version of the Fifth Amendment, either not be tried at all or will be acquitted if the State's evidence, minus the confession, is put to the test of litigation....

Dickerson v. United States

530 U.S. 428 (2000)

Charles Thomas Dickerson was charged with conspiracy to commit bank robbery and other offenses. His motion, to suppress a statement he had made on the ground that it was obtained in violation of *Miranda*, was granted by a district court. The Fourth Circuit reversed the suppression order. It agreed with the district court that Dickerson had not received *Miranda* warnings before making his statement, but also held that *Miranda* was not a constitutional holding and that a statute enacted by Congress to modify *Miranda* was the final say on the question of admissibility of the statement.

CHIEF JUSTICE REHNQUIST delivered the opinion of the Court.

In *Miranda* v. *Arizona*, 384 U.S. 436 (1966), we held that certain warnings must be given before a suspect's statement made during custodial interrogation could be admitted in evidence. In the wake of that decision, Congress enacted 18 U.S.C. § 3501, which in essence laid down a rule that the admissibility of such statements should turn only on whether or not they were voluntarily made. We hold that *Miranda*, being a constitutional decision of this Court, may not be in effect overruled by an Act of Congress, and we decline to overrule *Miranda* ourselves....

Two years after *Miranda* was decided, Congress enacted § 3501. That section provides, in relevant part:

"(a) In any criminal prosecution brought by the United States or by the District of Columbia, a confession ... shall be admissible in evidence if it is voluntarily given. Before such confession is received in evidence, the trial judge shall, out of the presence of the jury, determine any issue as to voluntariness. If the trial judge determines that the confession was voluntarily made it shall be admitted in evidence and the trial judge shall permit the jury to hear relevant evidence on the issue of voluntariness and shall instruct the jury to give such weight to the confession as the jury feels it deserves under all the circumstances.

"(b) The trial judge in determining the issue of voluntariness shall take into consideration all the circumstances surrounding the giving of the confession, ..."

... Congress may not legislatively supersede our decisions interpreting and applying the Constitution. See, *e.g., City of Boerne* v. *Flores*, 521 U.S. 507, 517–521 (1997). This case therefore turns on whether the *Miranda* Court announced a constitutional rule or merely exercised its supervisory authority to regulate evidence in the absence of congressional direction. Recognizing this point, the Court of Appeals surveyed *Miranda* and its progeny to determine the constitutional status of the *Miranda* decision.... Relying on the fact that we have created several exceptions to *Miranda*'s warnings requirement and that we have repeatedly referred to the *Miranda* warnings as "prophylactic," *New York* v. *Quarles*, 467 U.S. 649, 653 (1984), and "not themselves rights protected by the Constitution," *Michigan* v. *Tucker*, 417 U.S. 433, 444 (1974), the Court of Appeals concluded that the protections announced in *Miranda* are not constitutionally required....

We disagree with the Court of Appeals' conclusion, although we concede that there is language in some of our opinions that supports the view taken by that court....

The *Miranda* opinion itself begins by stating that the Court granted certiorari "to explore some facets of the problems ... of applying the privilege against self-incrimination to in-custody interrogation, *and to give concrete constitutional guidelines for law enforcement agencies and courts to follow.*" 384 U.S., at 441–442 (emphasis added). In fact, the majority opinion is replete with statements indicating that the majority thought it was announcing a constitutional rule....

Additional support for our conclusion that *Miranda* is constitutionally based is found in the *Miranda* Court's invitation for legislative action to protect the constitutional right against coerced self-incrimination. After discussing the "compelling pressures" inherent in custodial police interrogation, the *Miranda* Court concluded that, "[i]n order to combat these pressures and to permit a full opportunity to exercise the privilege against self-incrimination, the accused must be adequately and effectively appraised of his rights and the exercise of those rights must be fully honored." *Id.*, at 467. However, the Court emphasized that it could not foresee "the potential alternatives for protecting the privilege which might be devised by Congress or the

States," and it accordingly opined that the Constitution would not preclude legislative solutions that differed from the prescribed *Miranda* warnings but which were "at least as effective in apprising accused persons of their right of silence and in assuring a continuous opportunity to exercise it." *Ibid.*

[*Note 6 provides: The Court of Appeals relied in part on our statement that the* Miranda *decision in no way "creates a 'constitutional straightjacket.'" ... However, a review of our opinion in* Miranda *clarifies that this disclaimer was intended to indicate that the Constitution does not require police to administer the particular* Miranda *warnings, not that the Constitution does not require a procedure that is effective in securing Fifth Amendment rights.*]

The Court of Appeals also relied on the fact that we have, after our *Miranda* decision, made exceptions from its rule in cases such as *New York* v. *Quarles* ... and *Harris* v. *New York* ... But we have also broadened the application of the *Miranda* doctrine in cases such as *Doyle* v. *Ohio* ... and *Arizona* v. *Roberson*, ... These decisions illustrate the principle—not that *Miranda* is not a constitutional rule—but that no constitutional rule is immutable....

Whether or not we would agree with *Miranda*'s reasoning and its resulting rule, were we addressing the issue in the first instance, the principles of *stare decisis* weigh heavily against overruling it now....

We do not think there is such justification for overruling *Miranda*. *Miranda* has become embedded in routine police practice to the point where the warnings have become part of our national culture....

In sum, we conclude that *Miranda* announced a constitutional rule that Congress may not supersede legislatively. Following the rule of *stare decisis*, we decline to overrule *Miranda* ourselves. The judgment of the Court of Appeals is therefore

Reversed.

JUSTICE SCALIA, with whom JUSTICE THOMAS joins, dissenting.

Those to whom judicial decisions are an unconnected series of judgments that produce either favored or disfavored results will doubtless greet today's decision as a paragon of moderation, since it declines to overrule *Miranda* v. *Arizona*, 384 U.S. 436 (1966). Those who understand the judicial process will appreciate that today's decision is not a reaffirmation of *Miranda*, but a radical revision of the most significant element of *Miranda* (as of all cases): the rationale that gives it a permanent place in our jurisprudence.

Marbury v. *Madison* ... held that an Act of Congress will not be enforced by the courts if what it prescribes violates the Constitution of the United States. That was the basis on which *Miranda* was decided. One will search today's opinion in vain, however, for a statement (surely simple enough to make) that what 18 U.S.C. § 3501 prescribes—the use at trial of a voluntary confession, even when a *Miranda* warning or its equivalent has failed to be given—violates the Constitution. The reason the statement does not appear is not only (and perhaps not so much) that it would be absurd, inasmuch as § 3501 excludes from trial precisely what the Constitution excludes from trial, viz., compelled confessions; but also that Justices whose votes are needed to compose today's majority are on record as believing that a violation of *Miranda* is *not* a violation of the Constitution.... And so, to justify today's agreed-upon result, the Court must adopt a significant *new*, if not entirely comprehensible, principle of constitutional law. As the Court chooses to describe that principle, statutes of Congress can be disregarded, not only when what they prescribe violates the Constitution, but when what they prescribe contradicts a decision of this Court that "announced a constitutional rule," ... As I shall discuss in some detail, the only thing that can possibly mean in the context of this case is that this Court has the power, not merely to apply the Constitution but to expand it, imposing what it regards as useful "prophylactic" restrictions upon Congress and the States. That is an immense and frightening antidemocratic power, and it does not exist.

[II]

The issue ... is not whether court rules are "mutable"; they assuredly are. It is not whether, in the light of "various circumstances," they can be "modifi[ed]"; they assuredly can. The issue is whether, *as mutated and modified*, they must *make sense*. The requirement that they do so is the only thing that prevents this Court from being some sort of nine-headed Caesar, giving thumbs-up or thumbs-down to whatever outcome, case by case, suits or offends its collective fancy....

IV

... I am not convinced by petitioner's argument that *Miranda* should be preserved because the decision occupies a special place in the "public's consciousness." ... As far as I am aware, the public is not under the illusion that we are infallible. I see little harm in admitting that we made a mistake in taking away from the people the ability to decide for themselves what protections (beyond those required by the Constitution) are reasonably affordable in the criminal investigatory process....

Today's judgment converts *Miranda* from a milestone of judicial overreaching into the very Cheops' Pyramid (or perhaps the Sphinx would be a better analogue) of judicial arrogance....

I dissent from today's decision, and, until § 3501 is repealed, will continue to apply it in all cases where there has been a sustainable finding that the defendant's confession was voluntary.

G. THE EIGHTH AMENDMENT

The Eighth Amendment, borrowing language from the English Bill of Rights of 1689, provides that "[e]xcessive bail shall not be required, nor excessive fines imposed, nor cruel and unusual punishments inflicted." The first two clauses produce relatively few cases for the Supreme Court. The last six words have generated a massive caseload on the death penalty, an issue that is extraordinarily complex and divisive.

Excessive Bail

To gain freedom while awaiting trial, a defendant may have to put up money for a bail bond to guarantee his presence at the trial. Meeting bail allows the accused to prepare a defense and prevents the infliction of punishment prior to conviction. Excessive bail destroys both rights. The level of bail is monitored by criminal rules adopted by Congress and judicial rulings. Stack v. Boyle, 342 U.S. 1 (1952).

Bail may be denied totally for capital cases. Even for noncapital cases, there are instances where bail is refused. Carlson v. Landon, 342 U.S. 524 (1952). In 1966, Congress passed legislation to remove the inequity of holding persons too poor to raise bail. Defendants charged with noncapital offenses shall be released on their own "personal recognizance" unless a court determines that release will not assure the defendant's later appearance in court. 80 Stat. 214 (1966); 18 U.S.C. §§ 3141–56. Additional legislation in 1984 requires courts to keep suspects in jail if the government demonstrates by clear and convincing evidence that release will not "reasonably assure" the safety of the community. 98 Stat. 1978–80. This statute on pretrial detention ("preventive detention") was upheld in *United States* v. *Salerno*, 481 U.S. 739 (1987). With a 6–3 majority in 1990, the Court held that the failure of the government to comply with the prompt-hearing provision of the Bail Reform Act of 1984 does not require the release of a person who should be, under the terms of that statute, detained. United States v. Montalvo-Murillo, 495 U.S. 711 (1990). The question of excessive bail is sometimes addressed not in terms of the Eighth Amendment but on grounds of equal protection and due process. Schilb v. Kuebel, 404 U.S. 357 (1971).

Excessive Fines

This section of the Constitution was rarely litigated in the past. For example, see Ex parte Watkins, 7 Pet. 568 (1833). In contemporary times, the question of excessive fines is more likely attacked under the Equal Protection and Due Process Clauses. In 1970 the Supreme Court unanimously struck down on equal protection grounds a state statute that subjected indigents to additional imprisonment if they failed to pay a fine. Williams v. Illinois, 399 U.S. 235 (1970). See also Tate v. Short, 401 U.S. 395 (1971).

A 7–2 ruling by the Supreme Court in 1989 held that the Excessive Fines Clause does not protect businesses against multimillion dollar awards of punitive damages in civil disputes brought by private parties. The Clause is restricted to cases in which the government prosecutes a case and has an interest in recovering damages. Every member of the Court (the majority opinion by Blackmun, the concurrence by Brennan and Marshall, and the partial dissent by O'Connor and Stevens) indicated that punitive damage awards may still be limited under the Due Process Clause of the Fourteenth Amendment. Browning-Ferris Industries v. Kelco Disposal, 492 U.S. 257 (1989).

In 1991, the Court provided some guidelines on due process restrictions on punitive damages awards. Pacific Mutual Life Ins. Co. v. Haslip, 499 U.S. 1 (1991). Two years later it upheld a jury's award of $10 million in punitive damages when there had been actual damages of only $19,000. Although six Justices sustained the large punitive damages award, they could not form a majority of the Court behind any particular reasoning. TXO Production Corp. v. Alliance Resources Corp., 509 U.S. 443 (1993). Also in 1993, the Court ruled that the Excessive Fines Clause limits the power of the federal government to seize homes and businesses (civil forfeiture proceedings) to combat illegal drug trafficking. Austin v. United States, 509 U.S. 602 (1993). Since that time, the Court has decided that other federal government seizures violate the Excessive Fines Clause (see section in next chapter or civil forfeitures).

In 1994, the Court held that Oregon's constitution, which prohibited judicial review of the amount of punitive damages awarded by a jury "unless the Court can affirmatively say there is no evidence to support the verdict," violated the Due Process Clause. Honda Motor Co. v. Oberg, 512 U.S. 415 (1994). Two years later the Court for the first time overturned a punitive-damage award. An Alabama physician, after purchasing a new BMW automobile, discovered that the car had been repainted. A jury awarded him $4 million as punishment to BMW for fraud and breach of contract for failing to disclose the repainting; an appeals court lowered the amount to $2 million. The Supreme Court, divided 5 to 4, ruled that the $2 million punitive damages award was grossly excessive and violated the Due Process Clause. BMW of North America, Inc. v. Gore, 517 U.S. 559 (1996).

The decision raised the expectation that Congress would revisit the issue of establishing national standards for punitive damages. On May 2, 1996, President Clinton vetoed a bill passed by the Republican Congress to limit the liability of companies that make faulty products. He argued that the bill intruded on state authority over tort law and disadvantaged consumers. The House sustained the veto. In 2003, a 6 to 3 Court announced new guidelines for punitive damages. It decided that an award of $145 million in punitive damages, with compensatory damages set at $1 million, violated the Due Process Clause. Without imposing a specific ratio between compensatory and punitive damages, it warned that few awards exceeding a single-digit ratio would satisfy due process. It further cautioned that the wealth of a defendant cannot justify an otherwise unconstitutional punitive damages award. State Farm Mut. Automobile Ins. Co. v. Campbell, 538 U.S. 408 (2003).

These prior cases focused on punitive damage awards in state courts. In the summer of 2008 the Court announced another significant decision cutting back on punitive damages awards, this time in a case involving federal maritime jurisdiction. The 1989 wreck of the Exxon Valdez in Alaska's Prince William Sound spilled eleven million barrels of oil. The Court reduced the punitive damage award of $2.5 billion dollars to $507.5 million, based on federal common law rules about excessive damages. Exxon Shipping Co. v. Baker, 554 U.S. 471 (2008). The dissenters criticized the majority for showing a lack of restraint, suggesting that rules of this sort should be made by Congress, not the Court. The litigation continued into 2011. "22 Years Later, the Exxon Valdez Case Is Back in Court," New York Times, March 4, 2011, at A15.

In 2007, the Court divided 5 to 4 in overturning an Oregon jury's award of $79.5 million in punitive damages against Philip Morris, concluding that jurors might have decided to punish the cigarette maker rather than the man whose widow brought the case. Philip Morris USA v. Williams, 549 U.S. 346 (2007). The case turned on whether the trial court should have instructed the jury that it could not punish Philip Morris for injury to persons not before the court.

Cruel and Unusual Punishments

The meaning of "cruel and unusual" varies over time in American culture. A congressional statute in 1790 required the death penalty for forgery. 1 Stat. 115, §14. Today, that penalty would be considered grossly disproportionate to the crime. In 1879, the Supreme Court decided that public shooting was not cruel and unusual, although forms of torture (dragged to the place of execution, disembowelled alive, beheaded, quartered, or burned alive) exceeded constitutional limits. Wilkerson v. Utah, 99 U.S. 130 (1879). The framers would have regarded electrocution as "unusual," if not inconceivable, but in 1890 the Court found it constitutionally inoffensive. In re Kemmler, 136 U.S. 436 (1890). Throughout this period the Court held consistently that the states were not bound by the Eighth Amendment.[26]

Even for most of the twentieth century, the Eighth Amendment added little to the Supreme Court's docket. It invoked the amendment in 1910 to strike down the sentence of someone given 15 years at hard labor and kept in chains day and night for falsifying a public document. The Court said that punishment must be graduated and proportioned to the offense committed. Weems v. United States, 217 U.S. 349 (1910). In 1947, the Court held that states could make a second effort to electrocute someone after they had bungled the first effort. To the 5–4 majority, a second attempt was neither double jeopardy nor cruel and unusual punishment. Francis v. Resweber, 329 U.S. 459 (1947).

The extent to which "cruel and unusual" is culturally determined and varies with the times can be seen in two cases decided in 1958 and 1962. In the first, the Court interpreted the Eighth Amendment in light of the "evolving standards of decency that mark the progress of a maturing society." Trop v. Dulles, 356 U.S. 86, 101 (1958). Stripping a native-born American of his citizenship because of wartime desertion constituted cruel and unusual punishment. Four years later the Court, guided by "contemporary human knowledge," decided it was cruel and unusual to punish someone for the mere status of being a narcotics addict when the person was not under the influence of narcotics at the time of arrest. Robinson v. California, 370 U.S. 660, 666 (1962). This decision incorporated the Cruel and Unusual Punishment Clause into the Fourteenth Amendment and applied it to the states. In 1968,

---

26. O'Neil v. Vermont, 144 U.S. 323 (1892); In re Kemmler, 136 U.S. 436 (1890); Pervear v. The Commonwealth, 5 Wall. (72 U.S.) 475 (1867).

the Court refused to extend the narcotics decision to strike down a conviction for public drunkenness. It distinguished being drunk in public from the general status of having a narcotics addiction. Powell v. Texas, 392 U.S. 514, 532 (1968).

In 1992, the Court rejected the claim that execution by cyanide gas, which takes eight to ten minutes before the victim dies by suffocation, is cruel and unusual punishment. Gomez v. U.S. Dist. Court for N.D. of Cal., 503 U.S. 653 (1992). In 1999, the Court denied cert to a constitutional challenge against Florida's use of the electric chair as the sole means of execution. The chair had malfunctioned a number of times. Lopez v. Singletary, 525 U.S. 1116 (1999). The next year Florida passed legislation to provide death by lethal injection as an alternative procedure. In 2001, the Georgia Supreme Court held that electrocution is an unconstitutionally cruel and unusual punishment. The state now uses lethal injection.

In 2006, a unanimous U.S. Supreme Court allowed a challenge to lethal injections to go forward, without deciding whether this form of execution is constitutional. The challenge concerned the mix of three chemicals used in the injection. Does this particular mix produce unnecessary and gratuitous pain? Hill v. McDonough, 547 U.S. 573(2006). In Baze v. Rees, 553 U.S. 35 (2008) the Court answered this question, finding that Kentucky's use of a similar method of lethal injection did not violate the Eighth Amendment because that amendment encompassed no requirement that a method of execution avoid all risk of pain. Only two Justices joined Chief Justice Roberts' opinion for the 7 to 2 Court. Five concurring opinions offered different constitutional standards, inviting continued litigation on the issue.

A Growing Workload

The overwhelming number of cases on the Eighth Amendment have been decided since 1970. In a series of cases from 1970 to 1973, the Court held that a guilty plea is not invalid or coerced simply because the accused wants to avoid a possible death penalty.[27] In 1971, the Court handed down the first of many long-winded, discursive explorations of the death penalty, deciding in this case that juries could be given absolute discretion to choose between life imprisonment and death and that juries can decide both guilt and punishment (death) in a single unitary proceeding. Due process did not require a bifurcated trial. McGautha v. California, 402 U.S. 183 (1971).

The number of prisoners executed declined sharply in the 1950s and 1960s. By the late 1960s and early 1970s, there were no persons executed in any of the states. In 1972, the Supreme Court of California declared the death penalty a violation of the state constitutional ban against cruel or unusual punishments. Within nine months, however, the voters of California amended the state constitution to reinstate the death penalty. People v. Anderson, 493 P.2d 880 (Cal. 1972), cert. denied, 406 U.S. 958 (1972); Cal. Const. Art. I, § 27. This collision between a judicial ruling and public opinion in California would soon occur at the national level.

The *Furman* Challenge

In 1972, the Court abruptly struck down death-penalty statutes in Georgia and Texas as cruel and unusual because of the erratic nature of their application. A brief one-page per curiam—announcing the result—served as a preface for more than two hundred pages of concurrences and dissents. Only two Justices (Brennan and Marshall) regarded the death penalty unconstitutional in all cases. The opinions for the 5–4 majority focused on the arbitrariness and inequalities in state practices: the in-

---

27. Tollett v. Henderson, 411 U.S. 258 (1973); North Carolina v. Alford, 400 U.S. 25 (1970); Parker v. North Carolina, 397 U.S. 790 (1970); Brady v. North Carolina, 397 U.S. 742 (1970).

creasing rarity of executions and the application of that punishment to blacks more than whites, to men more than women, and to the poor more than the rich. FURMAN v. GEORGIA, 408 U.S. 238 (1972).

The Court's holding challenged explicit language in the Constitution, which acknowledges the death penalty four times. The Fifth Amendment requires a presentment or indictment by grand jury for persons accused of a "capital, or otherwise infamous crime." The Double Jeopardy Clause refers to taking "life or limb." Also in the Fifth Amendment, no person shall be deprived of "life, liberty, or property" without due process of law. Under the Fourteenth Amendment, no state shall deprive any person of "life, liberty, or property" without due process of law. One could argue that *acknowledging* the death penalty in the Constitution does not mandate it or even favor it.

The Public Responds

Following the *Furman* decision, the majority of states immediately reinstituted the death penalty for certain kinds of crime. This public endorsement of capital punishment put pressure on the Court to modify *Furman*. In the first of five decisions handed down on July 2, 1976, the Court reviewed the changes in Georgia's statute following *Furman* and upheld, 7–2, the new procedure. GREGG v. GEORGIA, 428 U.S. 153 (1976). The Court noted that the position of Justices Brennan and Marshall in *Furman* that the Eighth Amendment prohibits the death penalty had been "undercut substantially" by state actions from 1972 to 1976 to enact statutes calling for the death penalty. Id. at 179. Moreover, in 1974 Congress enacted legislation providing the death penalty for aircraft piracy that results in death. Id. at 179–80. The "evolving standards of decency" (Warren's language in *Trop v. Dulles*) still tolerated and supported executions. In this and the companion cases, the Court attempted to identify the factors and criteria that are necessary for states to invoke the death penalty. Proffitt v. Florida, 428 U.S. 242 (1976); Jurek v. Texas, 428 U.S. 262 (1976); Woodson v. North Carolina, 428 U.S. 280 (1976); Roberts v. Louisiana, 428 U.S. 325 (1976). These cases require states to establish a capital-sentencing procedure that weighs aggravating factors against mitigating factors.

Although the death penalty is once again available, executions are often postponed or avoided because the Court finds defects in sentencing procedures or discovers due process problems.[28] The Court has gradually broadened the scope of the death penalty to include not only those who intend to kill but also those who serve as accomplices to a murder. Compare Tison v. Arizona, 481 U.S. 137 (1987) with Cabana v. Bullock, 474 U.S. 376 (1986) and Enmund v. Florida, 458 U.S. 782 (1982).

Aggravating and Mitigating Factors

The Court is often divided 5 to 4 on how judges and juries should weigh and reweigh aggravating and mitigating circumstances in reaching a death sentence. Clemons v. Mississippi, 494 U.S. 738 (1990); Boyde v. California, 494 U.S. 370 (1990); Blystone v. Pennsylvania, 494 U.S. 299 (1990). Two other death penalty cases in 1990 produced 5–4 splits on the Court. Lewis v. Jeffers, 497 U.S. 764 (1990); Walton v. Arizona, 497 U.S. 639 (1990). Even after David Souter replaced William Brennan on the

---

28. In 2004, the Court reversed a death sentence because prosecutors had withheld key information from the defendant. Banks v. Dretke, 540 U.S. 668 (2004). The previous year, the Court threw out a death sentence because of the poor performance of defense attorneys. Wiggins v. Smith, 539 U.S. 510 (2003). In 1994 the Court, split 5 to 4, held that federal judges may stop a scheduled execution to give a state prisoner time to obtain a lawyer to challenge the constitutionality of a sentence. McFarland v. Scott, 512 U.S. 849 (1994). The Court divided 5 to 4 a year later in holding that state prosecutors had wrongly suppressed evidence favorable to a defendant, who was sentenced to death. He was entitled to a new trial. Kyles v. Whitley, 514 U.S. 419 (1995).

Court, the Justices remain divided 5–4 on some death penalty cases. A decision in 1991 held that the Florida Supreme Court had failed to consider whether mitigating circumstances in a case would have resulted in a life sentence rather than a death penalty. Parker v. Dugger, 498 U.S. 308 (1991). Another 5–4 decision held that the sentencing procedure followed by a state judge violated the Due Process Clause. Lankford v. Idaho, 500 U.S. 110 (1991).

The 1992 Court included Clarence Thomas as a replacement for Thurgood Marshall, who, along with Justice Brennan, had been a steadfast opponent of the death penalty. A 1992 decision, with Scalia, Rehnquist, and Thomas dissenting, ruled that a murder defendant in a capital case has the right to question potential jurors whether they would automatically impose a death sentence if they returned a guilty verdict. Such jurors must be excluded: "A juror who will automatically vote for the death penalty in every case will fail in good faith to consider the evidence of aggravating and mitigating circumstances as the instructions require him to do." Morgan v. Illinois, 504 U.S. 719, 729 (1992). The Court had previously, in *Witherspoon* v. *Illinois,* 391 U.S. 510 (1968), given prosecutors the same right to question jurors. The Court divided 5–4 in 1993 in holding that a judge had properly instructed a jury on the future dangerousness of a youthful defendant, who was later sentenced to death. Johnson v. Texas, 509 U.S. 350 (1993).

In 1994, the Court held that a sentencing jury, in choosing between death or life imprisonment, must be told that if sentenced to life the defendant would not be eligible for parole under state law. Otherwise, the jury might more readily accept the prosecutor's argument that the defendant is so dangerous that he must be executed. That argument is undercut when jurors understand that the defendant will not be released on parole. Simmons v. South Carolina, 512 U.S. 154 (1994).

What happens when state law provides for the imposition of the death penalty when aggravating circumstances are equally matched by mitigating circumstances? Does this create an impermissible presumption in favor of death, violating the Eighth Amendment? The Supreme Court split 5 to 4 in 2006 in denying any such violation. Kansas v. Marsh, 548 U.S. 163 (2006).

Juries vs. Judges

In 1990, the Court held that Arizona's sentencing scheme — allowing a judge to weigh aggravating and mitigating circumstances to impose a death sentence — did not violate the Sixth Amendment right to a jury trial. Walton v. Arizona, 497 U.S. 639 (1990). That ruling was undermined in 2000 when the Court ruled that any fact increasing the penalty for a crime beyond the prescribed statutory maximum (other than the fact of a prior conviction) must be submitted to a jury and proved beyond a reasonable doubt. Apprendi v. New Jersey, 530 U.S. 466 (2000). The conflict between these two rulings forced the Court two years later to overrule *Walton*. The Court now held that decisions on the death penalty must be made by juries, not judges. Ring v. Arizona, 536 U.S. 584 (2002). This decision cast doubt on over a hundred death sentences, but two years later the court held that *Ring* did not apply retroactively. Schriro v. Summerlin, 542 U.S. 348 (2004). On non-capital cases, the Court allows a judge to increase mandatory minimum sentences without proof to a jury and to find facts that lead to imposing consecutive sentences. Harris v. United States, 536 U.S. 545 (2002); Oregon v. Ice, 555 U.S. 160 (2009). In *Oregon* v. *Ice* the dissenters insisted that *Apprendi* should control. In 2012, the Court ruled that *Apprendi* applies to the imposition of criminal fines. Southern Union Co. v. United States, 567 U.S. ___ (2012).

Proportionality and Three-Strikes Laws

At times, the Court decides whether executions are justified for a certain class of crimes. In 1977, it found the death penalty disproportionate punishment for the crime of raping an adult woman. The gradual abandonment of that penalty by most states was accepted by the Court as persuasive evidence of contemporary public judgment. Coker v. Georgia, 433 U.S. 584, 593–96 (1977). In 2008, a closely divided court (5 to 4) decided that a Louisiana law permitting the death penalty for rape of a child under 12 was unconstitutional. Kennedy v. Louisiana, 554 U.S.407 (2008). Under the principle of proportionality, life imprisonment for certain nonviolent crimes contravenes the Eighth Amendment. Solem v. Helm, 463 U.S. 277 (1983).

Solem was weakened in 1991 when a 5–4 Court decided that a mandatory life term in prison, without possibility of parole, for possessing about one and a half pounds of cocaine was not unconstitutional. Two members of the majority, Scalia and Rehnquist, supported the overriding of *Solem* and declaring that the Eighth Amendment contains no proportionality guarantee. Sentencing would be purely a matter of legislative prerogative. The other three members of the majority (Kennedy, O'Connor, and Souter) continued to recognize a proportionality principle but concluded it was not breached in this case. Harmelin v. Michigan, 501 U.S. 957 (1991). In affirming a death sentence, state courts are not required to compare the sentence to others to determine if it is disproportionate. The Court tolerates what it calls "aberrational outcomes" in the application of the death penalty. Pulley v. Harris, 465 U.S. 37, 54 (1984).

Questions of cruel and unusual punishment sometimes concern unusually heavy sentences. The Supreme Court held that conviction for three felonies totaling $229.11 could be punished by a mandatory life sentence. Rummel v. Estelle, 445 U.S. 263 (1980). Following the policy of deferring to the legislature for the level of punishment, the Court sustained a 40-year sentence for someone convicted of possessing and selling marijuana. Hutto v. Davis, 454 U.S. 370 (1982).

Relying on *Rummel*, the Court in 2003 upheld California's "Three Strikes and You're Out" law. Divided 5 to 4, it held that a sentence of 25 years to life for stealing three golf clubs represented a defensible policy of a state's effort to fight crime, was not grossly disproportional, and did not constitute cruel and unusual punishment. Prior to the theft of golf clubs the defendant had been found guilty or pled guilty on ten occasions. Ewing v. California, 538 U.S. 11 (2003). In a second three-strikes case, the Court divided 5 to 4 again in upholding a 50-year sentence for someone whose last crime was stealing nine videotapes worth about $150. Previous to this incident he had been convicted a half dozen times. Lockyer v. Andrade, 538 U.S. 63 (2003).

Victims' Rights

A death penalty case in 1991 split the court 6 to 3 with regard to the introduction of "victim-impact" evidence about the character of a murder and its effects on family members and survivors. In two earlier 5–4 decisions—Booth v. Maryland, 482 U.S. 497 (1987) and South Carolina v. Gaithers, 490 U.S. 805 (1989)—the Court had ruled such evidence inadmissible at a capital sentencing hearing. Yet the Court in 1991 decided that the Eighth Amendment does not prohibit juries, in considering the death penalty, from hearing victim-impact evidence. Prosecutors may now describe the emotional impact of a murder on the victim's family. Payne v. Tennessee, 501 U.S. 808 (1991).

Congress passed legislation in 1997 to allow certain relatives of the victims of the 1995 Oklahoma City bombing to attend the trial of the accused bombers. The law prevented federal judges from barring from the courtroom individuals who planned to testify during the sentencing phase of the trial. 111 Stat. 12 (1997). Judge Richard Matsch, the presiding judge in the Oklahoma case, had previously ruled that people who intended to testify at sentencing time could not sit in on the trial. Legislation in 1996 also dealt with the victims of crimes. 110 Stat. 1227–47 (1996).

Executing the Retarded

The Court has held that the execution of prisoners who are insane violates the Eighth Amendment. Ford v. Wainwright, 477 U.S. 399 (1986). The issue of executing the retarded or mentally incapacitated divides the nation and the judiciary. A 5–4 decision by the Supreme Court in 1989 held that the Eighth Amendment does not categorically bar execution of the mentally retarded. The majority cited a lack of "objective indicators" from society to prohibit such executions. The "clearest and most reliable objective evidence of contemporary values," it said, are the statutes passed by legislative bodies in this country. The Court also looked to data concerning the actions of sentencing jurors. Penry v. Lynaugh, 492 U.S. 302, 331 (1989). The individual in this case, Johnny Paul Penry, was not executed because the Court ruled in 2001 that his jurors received flawed instructions about how they should consider his retardation. Penry v. Johnson, 532 U.S. 782 (2001).

The next year, the Court overturned its 1989 Penry ruling by reviewing changes in public attitudes as reflected in legislative judgments at the state level. In 1989, only two states (Georgia and Maryland) prohibited execution of the mentally retarded. By 2002, the number of states exempting the mentally retarded from the death penalty had grown to 18, prompting the Court to remark: "it is fair to say that a national consensus has developed against it." ATKINS v. VIRGINIA, 536 U.S. 304, 316 (2002). Rehnquist, Scalia, and Thomas dissented. In part, they objected to the majority's reliance on foreign laws, the views of professional and religious organizations, and opinion polls. In determining contemporary social attitudes, they would have relied solely on the work of state legislatures and the practices of juries when sentencing offenders.

The Court's ruling decided the general issue but not its specific application. The 20 states that allowed for the execution of retarded persons now had to define by statute who is retarded. Standards of measurement generally refer to subaverage intelligence or particular I.Q. scores. Also, statutes often require proof that the disability appeared by a certain age, such as 18 to 22.

Racial Bias

Statistics demonstrate that the death penalty is applied disproportionately to blacks who kill whites, compared to whites who kill blacks or each race killing one of its own. Nevertheless, the Court refused in 1987 to find a constitutional violation to this pattern. Discretion in sentencing need not mean discrimination. Discretionary judgments by jurors, even when they reveal a strong racial bias at an aggregate level, did not convince the Court that racial discrimination exists for a *particular* case. The Court held that legislatures are better qualified to evaluate and respond to statistical studies regarding racial discrimination in sentencing. McCleskey v. Kemp, 481 U.S. 278, 319 (1987). In response to this decision, Congress considered legislation that would create a federal right to be free from race discrimination in cases of capital punishment. Language was included in a 1994 statute to ensure that race is not considered by jurors in deciding a death sentence. 108 Stat. 1996 (1994). In 2001, Attorney General John Ashcroft released the findings of a new study that showed "no evidence of racial bias in the administration of the federal death penalty." Washington Post, June 7, 2001, at A29. In 2003, the Supreme Court ruled 8 to 1 that a black prisoner on death row in Texas should receive a new hearing because of alleged racial bias at his trial. Of eleven blacks eligible to serve on his jury, ten were excluded. Miller-El v. Cockrell, 537 U.S. 322 (2003).

Application to Juveniles

In 2012, the Court split 5 to 4 in a case involving two 14-year-olds sentenced to a mandatory term of life imprisonment after their conviction for murder, with no possibility of parole. The Court held that the sentencing violated the Eighth Amendment's prohibition of "cruel and unusual punishments." In dissent were Roberts, Scalia, Thomas, and Alito. Miller v. Alabama, 567 U.S. ___ (2012).

Legislative Procedures

Congress has considered a number of bills to establish procedures for imposing the death penalty. At the time of *Furman v. Georgia* (1972), federal law authorized capital punishment for such crimes as espionage and treason. Congress tried to pass legislation to remove arbitrary and capricious results. In 1988, Congress passed legislation to provide constitutional procedures for implementing the death penalty in cases involving certain drug-related murders and the killing of law enforcement officers. 102 Stat. 4387 (1988). The Federal Death Penalty Act of 1994 authorized capital punishment for dozens of federal crimes. The procedures under this statute were upheld by the Supreme Court in 1999, divided 5 to 4. Jones v. United States, 527 U.S. 373 (1999). Other procedures are included in the Antiterrorism and Effective Death Penalty Act of 1996. 110 Stat. 1214. The record shows that questions of the death penalty are largely in the hands of legislatures and public opinion (see Powell reading).

A unanimous Court in 1996 upheld the constitutionality of the military's death penalty. At the same time, it found nothing objectionable in terms of separation of powers for Congress to delegate to the President the discretion to identify aggravating factors in capital murder cases. Loving v. United States, 517 U.S. 748 (1996).

State Options

Operating under their own constitutions, states have a range of choices in supporting or prohibiting capital punishment. Thirty-five states have a death penalty, but most of the executions occur in a handful of states, particularly Texas, Virginia, Florida, Missouri, and Louisiana. The use of new evidence to exonerate death-row inmates prompted a number of states to review their capital punishment procedures. In 2000, Governor George H. Ryan of Illinois announced that he would block executions until the procedures in his state were thoroughly investigated. After reviewing the cases of inmates on the state's death row, in 2003 he commuted the death sentences of 167 people to life in prison, concluding that capital punishment was "haunted by the demons of error." Legislatures in some states have voted down moratoriums on capital punishment but three states have eliminated the death penalty either through court decisions which have not been challenged by the legislature (New York in 2007) or state legislative action (New Jersey in 2007, New Mexico in 2009). The Connecticut legislature passed repeal legislation in 2009 but it was vetoed by the governor.

Habeas Corpus Relief

The death penalty continues to preoccupy Congress, the Court, and the states. Recent decisions have made it more difficult for death row inmates to seek federal review of their conviction in state courts. The result is that prisoners are less likely to obtain habeas corpus relief and the pace of executions has quickened (see box on next page).

The Antiterrorism and Effective Death Penalty Act of 1996 includes a provision that cuts back on inmates' ability to appeal to the Supreme Court in successive habeas petitions. After their first appeal, prisoners would need the approval of a three-judge panel before presenting their habeas petition to a trial court. 110 Stat. 1217–26 (1996). This part of the law was challenged as an unconstitutional restriction on the appellate jurisdiction of the Supreme Court. A unanimous Court held that the statute did not violate the Constitution because the Court could still entertain original habeas petitions (those filed in the first instance with the Court). Under Court rules, petitions for an original writ of habeas corpus are granted only under "exceptional circumstances." The Act only removed the Court's authority to consider an appeal or a cert petition to review a decision of the three-judge panel. Felker v. Turpin, 518 U.S. 651 (1996).

Two years later the Court held that the 1996 statute does not prevent an inmate from claiming he is insane and should not be executed. This type of habeas corpus petition is not limited to a single appeal. Stewart v. Martinez-Villareal, 523 U.S. 637 (1998). In 2000, the Court offered further guidance in interpreting the 1996 statute and the scope of federal court review of state court actions in capital cases. Williams v. Taylor, 529 U.S. 362 (2000); Williams v. Taylor, 529 U.S. 420 (2000). A decision in 2003 ruled that the 1996 statutory limits on appeals in death penalty cases apply even to cases that were in a preliminary stage before the law took effect. Woodford v. Garceau, 538 U.S. 202 (2003).

Habeas Corpus Relief for Death-Row Inmates

A series of Supreme Court rulings beginning in 1990 have limited the ability of death-row inmates to use the writ of habeas corpus to seek federal review of state court convictions. Three decisions in 1990 curbed prisoner access to federal review. Those decisions, building on Teague v. Lane, 489 U.S. 288 (1989), involve the issue of whether "new rules" by the Court can be applied retroactively to challenge a conviction. Divided 5 to 4 in these cases, the Court refused to apply new rules retroactively to overturn convictions for a capital crime. Butler v. McKellar, 494 U.S. 407 (1990); Saffle v. Parks, 494 U.S. 484 (1990); Sawyer v. Smith, 497 U.S. 227 (1990). Another 5–4 decision in 1996 used the new-rule analysis to deny a death-row inmate the right to have his conviction reviewed in federal court. Gray v. Netherland, 518 U.S. 152 (1996).

In 1991, the Court clarified its standards for determining when a petitioner abuses the writ of habeas corpus. To disprove abuse, a petitioner must explain why a claim was not raised at an earlier time and must identify the prejudice that would result in denying the writ, such as a fundamental miscarriage of justice or the conviction of an innocent person. McCleskey v. Zant, 499 U.S. 467 (1991). A year later, the Court turned aside the effort of a death-row prisoner to get a second chance in federal court to prove that he did not deserve the death penalty for his crimes. Sawyer v. Whitley, 505 U.S. 333 (1992).

In 1993, a 6–3 Court held that prisoners who have exhausted their appeals and later produce new evidence, have no right to be heard in a federal court unless the evidence offers a truly persuasive claim of their innocence. Herrera v. Collins, 506 U.S. 390 (1993).

A 5–4 decision in 1995 permitted a state prisoner to file a second federal habeas petition to avoid a sentence of death. He was allowed to introduce new evidence that he was wrongly convicted. Schlup v. Delo, 513 U.S. 298 (1995). In 1996, a unanimous Court held that a federal court had erred in dismissing a death row inmate's first federal appeal alleging violation of constitutional rights. The Court said that if a district judge cannot dismiss a first habeas petition on the merits before the scheduled execution, the court must postpone the execution and address the merits. Lonchar v. Thomas, 517 U.S. 314 (1996). In 1998, the Court split 5 to 4 in holding that a lower court had erroneously granted habeas corpus relief to a death-row inmate. Calderon v. Coleman, 525 U.S. 141 (1998).

Furman v. Georgia

408 U.S. 238 (1972)

William Henry Furman was convicted of murder in Georgia and sentenced to death. Another petitioner was sentenced to death after being convicted of rape in Georgia. A third petitioner was sentenced to death in Texas for the crime of rape. The Court was asked whether the death penalty in these cases constituted cruel and unusual punishment and was therefore unconstitutional. Note Chief Justice Burger's advice to state legislatures in his dissent.

PER CURIAM.

... Certiorari was granted limited to the following question: "Does the imposition and carrying out of the death penalty in [these cases] constitute cruel and unusual punishment in violation of the Eighth and Fourteenth Amendments?" 403 U.S. 952 (1971). The Court holds that the imposition and carrying out of the death penalty in these cases constitute cruel and unusual punishment in violation of the Eighth and Fourteenth Amendments. The judgment in each case is therefore reversed insofar as it leaves undisturbed the death sentence imposed, and the cases are remanded for further proceedings.

So ordered.

MR. JUSTICE DOUGLAS, MR. JUSTICE BRENNAN, MR. JUSTICE STEWART, MR. JUSTICE WHITE, and MR. JUSTICE MARSHALL have filed separate opinions in support of the judgments. THE CHIEF JUSTICE, MR. JUSTICE BLACKMUN, MR. JUSTICE POWELL, and MR. JUSTICE REHNQUIST have filed separate dissenting opinions.

Mr. Justice Douglas, concurring....

The words "cruel and unusual" certainly include penalties that are barbaric. But the words, at least when read in light of the English proscription against selective and irregular use of penalties, suggest that it is "cruel and unusual" to apply the death penalty—or any other penalty—selectively to minorities whose numbers are few, who are outcasts of society, and who are unpopular, but whom society is willing to see suffer though it would not countenance general application of the same penalty across the board....

There is increasing recognition of the fact that the basic theme of equal protection is implicit in "cruel and unusual" punishments. "A penalty ... should be considered 'unusually' imposed if it is administered arbitrarily or discriminatorily." The same authors add that "[t]he extreme rarity with which applicable death penalty provisions are put to use raises a strong inference of arbitrariness." ...

Mr. Justice Brennan, concurring.

[II]

In determining whether a punishment comports with human dignity, we are aided also by a second principle inherent in the Clause—that the State must not arbitrarily inflict a severe punishment. This principle derives from the notion that the State does not respect human dignity when, without reason, it inflicts upon some people a severe punishment that it does not inflict upon others....

[III]

In comparison to all other punishments today, then, the deliberate extinguishment of human life by the State is uniquely degrading to human dignity. I would not hesitate to hold, on that ground alone, that death is today a "cruel and unusual" punishment, were it not that death is a punishment of longstanding usage and acceptance in this country. I therefore turn to the second principle—that the State may not arbitrarily inflict an unusually severe punishment.

The outstanding characteristic of our present practice of punishing criminals by death is the infrequency with which we resort to it. The evidence is conclusive that death is not the ordinary punishment for any crime.

There has been a steady decline in the infliction of this punishment in every decade since the 1930's, the earliest period for which accurate statistics are available. In the 1930's, executions averaged 167 per year; in the 1940's, the average was 128; in the 1950's, it was 72; and in the years 1960–1962, it was

48. There have been a total of 46 executions since then, 36 of them in 1963–1964. Yet our population and the number of capital crimes committed have increased greatly over the past four decades....

Mr. Justice Stewart, concurring.

The penalty of death differs from all other forms of criminal punishment, not in degree but in kind. It is unique in its total irrevocability. It is unique in its rejection of rehabilitation of the convict as a basic purpose of criminal justice. And it is unique, finally, in its absolute renunciation of all that is embodied in our concept of humanity.

For these and other reasons, at least two of my Brothers have concluded that the infliction of the death penalty is constitutionally impermissible in all circumstances under the Eighth and Fourteenth Amendments. Their case is a strong one. But I find it unnecessary to reach the ultimate question they would decide....

These death sentences are cruel and unusual in the same way that being struck by lightning is cruel and unusual. For, of all the people convicted of rapes and murders in 1967 and 1968, many just as reprehensible as these, the petitioners are among a capriciously selected random handful upon whom the sentence of death has in fact been imposed ...

Mr. Justice White, concurring....

The imposition and execution of the death penalty are obviously cruel in the dictionary sense. But the penalty has not been considered cruel and unusual punishment in the constitutional sense because it was thought justified by the social ends it was deemed to serve. At the moment that it ceases realistically to further these purposes, however, the emerging question is whether its imposition in such circumstances would violate the Eighth Amendment. It is my view that it would, for its imposition would then be the pointless and needless extinction of life with only marginal contributions to any discernible social or public purposes....

Mr. Justice Marshall concurring.

[*After rejecting the traditional purposes conceivably served by capital punishment (retribution, deterrence, prevention of repetitive criminal acts, encouragement of guilty pleas and confessions, eugenics, and economy), Marshall turns to other considerations.*]

VI

... [C]apital punishment is imposed discriminatorily against certain identifiable classes of people; there is evidence that innocent people have been executed before their innocence can be proved; and the death penalty wreaks havoc with our entire criminal justice system....

Regarding discrimination, it has been said that "[i]t is usually the poor, the illiterate, the underprivileged, the member of the minority group—the man who, because he is without means, and is defended by a court-appointed attorney—who becomes society's sacrificial lamb...." Indeed, a look at the bare statistics regarding executions is enough to betray much of the discrimination. A total of 3,859 persons have been executed since 1930, of whom 1,751 were white and 2,066 were Negro. Of the executions, 3,334 were for murder; 1,664 of the executed murderers were white and 1,630 were Negro; 455 persons, including 48 whites and 405 Negroes, were executed for rape. It is immediately apparent that Negroes were executed far more often than whites in proportion to their percentage of the population. Studies indicate that while the higher rate of execution among Negroes is partially due to a higher rate of crime, there is evidence of racial discrimination....

There is also overwhelming evidence that the death penalty is employed against men and not women. Only 32 women have been executed since 1930, while 3,827 men have met a similar fate....

MR. CHIEF JUSTICE BURGER, with whom MR. JUSTICE BLACKMUN, MR. JUSTICE POWELL, and MR. JUSTICE REHNQUIST join, dissenting.

[I]

If we were possessed of legislative power, I would either join with MR. JUSTICE BRENNAN and MR. JUSTICE MARSHALL or, at the very least, restrict the use of capital punishment to a small category of the most heinous crimes. Our constitutional inquiry, however, must be divorced from personal feelings as to the morality and efficacy of the death penalty, and be confined to the meaning and applicability of the uncertain language of the Eighth Amendment....

... [I]t disregards the history of the Eighth Amendment and all the judicial comment that has followed to rely on the term "unusual" as affecting the outcome of these cases. Instead, I view these cases as turning on the single question whether capital punishment is "cruel" in the constitutional sense. The term "unusual" cannot be read as limiting the ban on "cruel" punishments or as somehow expanding the meaning of the term "cruel." For this reason I am unpersuaded by the facile argument that since capital punishment has always been cruel in the everyday sense of the word, and has become unusual

due to decreased use, it is, therefore, now "cruel and unusual."...

[V]

Today the Court has not ruled that capital punishment is per se violative of the Eighth Amendment; nor has it ruled that the punishment is barred for any particular class or classes of crimes.... This much, however, seems apparent: if the legislatures are to continue to authorize capital punishment for some crimes, juries and judges can no longer be permitted to make the sentencing determination in the same manner they have in the past ...

While I would not undertake to make a definitive statement as to the parameters of the Court's ruling, it is clear that if state legislatures and the Congress wish to maintain the availability of capital punishment, significant statutory changes will have to be made. Since the two pivotal concurring opinions turn on the assumption that the punishment of death is now meted out in a random and unpredictable manner, legislative bodies may seek to bring their laws into compliance with the Court's ruling by providing standards for juries and judges to follow in determining the sentence in capital cases or by more narrowly defining the crimes for which the penalty is to be imposed....

MR. JUSTICE BLACKMUN, dissenting.

[*Blackman expresses his "abhorrence" for the death penalty and states that if he were a legislator he would vote against the death penalty and that if he were a governor he would be "sorely tempted" to exercise executive clemency. But he concludes that the Court oversteps its constitutional duties by striking down the Georgia and Texas statutes.*]

MR. JUSTICE POWELL, with whom THE CHIEF JUSTICE, MR. JUSTICE BLACKMUN, and MR. JUSTICE REHNQUIST join, dissenting....

In terms of the constitutional role of this Court, the impact of the majority's ruling is all the greater because the decision encroaches upon an area squarely within the historic prerogative of the legislative branch—both state and federal—to protect the citizenry through the designation of penalties for prohibitable conduct. It is the very sort of judgment that the legislative branch is competent to make and for which the judiciary is ill-equipped....

MR. JUSTICE REHNQUIST, with whom THE CHIEF JUSTICE, MR. JUSTICE BLACKMUN, and MR. JUSTICE POWELL join, dissenting.

... The most expansive reading of the leading

constitutional cases does not remotely suggest that this Court has been granted a roving commission, either by the Founding Fathers or by the framers of the Fourteenth Amendment, to strike down laws that are based upon notions of policy or morality suddenly found unacceptable by a majority of this Court....

Gregg v. Georgia

428 U.S. 153 (1976)

After the Supreme Court in *Furman* v. *Georgia* (1972) declared the death penalty unconstitutional as practiced in Georgia and Texas, more than 30 states reinstituted the death penalty. But these states added new procedures in an effort to minimize the arbitrariness of the death sentence. On July 2, 1976, the Court handed down five decisions that reviewed these new state laws. In this case, Troy Leon Gregg was charged with committing armed robbery and murder. He was convicted, and the jury returned a sentence of death.

Judgment of the Court, and opinion of MR. JUSTICE STEWART, MR. JUSTICE POWELL, and MR. JUSTICE STEVENS, announced by MR. JUSTICE STEWART.

The issue in this case is whether the imposition of the sentence of death for the crime of murder under the law of Georgia violates the Eighth and Fourteenth Amendments.

I

The petitioner, Troy Gregg, was charged with committing armed robbery and murder. In accordance with Georgia procedure in capital cases, the trial was in two stages, a guilt stage and a sentencing stage. [*The jury found Gregg guilty of two counts of armed robbery and two counts of murder. At the penalty stage, which took place before the same jury, neither the prosecutor nor Gregg's lawyer offered any additional evidence. The trial judge instructed the jury that it could recommend either a death sentence or a life prison sentence on each count. The jury could consider the facts and circumstances, if any, presented by the parties in mitigation or aggravation. To impose the death penalty, the jury had to first find beyond a reasonable doubt one of these aggravating circumstances: (1) that the murder was committed while Gregg was engaged in the armed robbery, (2) that Gregg committed the offense of murder for the purpose of receiving money and the automobile taken during the murder, or (3) the offense of murder was "outrageously and wantonly vile, horrible and inhuman" in that it involved the "depravity" of Gregg's mind.*]

[*The jury found the first and second of these circumstances and returned verdicts of death on each count. The Supreme Court of Georgia affirmed the convictions and the imposition of the death sentences for murder.*]

III

We address initially the basic contention that the punishment of death for the crime of murder is, under all circumstances, "cruel and unusual" in violation of the Eighth and Fourteenth Amendments of the Constitution. In Part IV of this opinion, we will consider the sentence of death imposed under the Georgia statutes at issue in this case.

[B]

... [I]n assessing a punishment selected by a democratically elected legislature against the constitutional measure, we presume its validity. We may not require the legislature to select the least severe penalty possible so long as the penalty selected is not cruelly inhumane or disproportionate to the crime involved. And a heavy burden rests on those who would attack the judgment of the representatives of the people.

This is true in part because the constitutional test is intertwined with an assessment of contemporary standards and the legislative judgment weighs heavily in ascertaining such standards. "[I]n a democratic society legislatures, not courts, are constituted to respond to the will and consequently the moral values of the people." *Furman* v. *Georgia, supra,* at 383 (BURGER, C. J., dissenting)....

C

In the discussion to this point we have sought to identify the principles and considerations that guide a court in addressing an Eighth Amendment claim. We now consider specifically whether the sentence of death for the crime of murder is a *per se* violation of the Eighth and Fourteenth Amendments to the Constitution. We note first that history and precedent strongly support a negative answer to this question....

The most marked indication of society's endorsement of the death penalty for murder is the legislative response to *Furman*. The legislatures of at least 35 States have enacted new statutes that provide for the death penalty for at least some crimes that result in the death of another person. And the Congress of the United States, in 1974, enacted a statute providing the death penalty for aircraft piracy that results in death. These recently adopted statutes have attempted to address the concerns expressed by the Court in *Furman* primarily (i) by specifying the factors to be weighed and the procedures to be followed in deciding when to impose a capital sentence, or (ii) by making the death penalty mandatory for specified crimes. But all of the post-*Furman* statutes make clear that capital punishment itself has not been rejected by the elected representatives of the people.

In the only statewide referendum occurring since *Furman* and brought to our attention, the people of California adopted a constitutional amendment that authorized capital punishment, in effect negating a prior ruling by the Supreme Court of California in *People* v. *Anderson,* 6 Cal.3d 628, 493 P.2d 880, cert. denied, 406 U.S. 958 (1972), that the death penalty violated the California Constitution.

The jury also is a significant and reliable objective index of contemporary values because it is so directly involved.... [T]he actions of juries in many States since *Furman* are fully compatible with the legislative judgments, reflected in the new statutes, as to the continued utility and necessity of capital punishment in appropriate cases....

... Considerations of federalism, as well as respect for the ability of a legislature to evaluate, in terms of its particular State, the moral consensus concerning the death penalty and its social utility as a sanction, require us to conclude, in the absence of more convincing evidence, that the infliction of death as a punishment for murder is not without justification and thus is not unconstitutionally severe....

IV

We now consider whether Georgia may impose the death penalty on the petitioner in this case.

A

... [T]he concerns expressed in *Furman* that the penalty of death not be imposed in an arbitrary or capricious manner can be met by a carefully drafted statute that ensures that the sentencing authority is given adequate information and guidance. As a general proposition these concerns are best met by a system that provides for a bifurcated proceeding at which the sentencing authority is apprised of the in-

formation relevant to the imposition of sentence and provided with standards to guide its use of the information.

... [W]e have embarked upon this general exposition to make clear that it is possible to construct capital-sentencing systems capable of meeting *Furman*'s constitutional concerns.

B

We now turn to consideration of the constitutionality of Georgia's capital-sentencing procedures. In the wake of *Furman*, Georgia amended its capital punishment statute, but chose not to narrow the scope of its murder provisions.... Thus, now as before *Furman*, in Georgia "[a] person commits murder when he unlawfully and with malice aforethought, either express or implied, causes the death of another human being." ... All persons convicted of murder "shall be punished by death or by imprisonment for life." ...

Georgia did act, however, to narrow the class of murderers subject to capital punishment by specifying 10 statutory aggravating circumstances, one of which must be found by the jury to exist beyond a reasonable doubt before a death sentence can ever be imposed. In addition, the jury is authorized to consider any other appropriate aggravating or mitigating circumstances.... The jury is not required to find any mitigating circumstance in order to make a recommendation of mercy that is binding on the trial court, ... but it must find a *statutory* aggravating circumstance before recommending a sentence of death.

These procedures require the jury to consider the circumstances of the crime and the criminal before it recommends sentence. No longer can a Georgia jury do as Furman's jury did: reach a finding of the defendant's guilt and then, without guidance or direction, decide whether he should live or die. Instead, the jury's attention is directed to the specific circumstances of the crime: Was it committed in the course of another capital felony? Was it committed for money? Was it committed upon a peace officer or judicial officer? Was it committed in a particularly heinous way or in a manner that endangered the lives of many persons? In addition, the jury's attention is focused on the characteristics of the person who committed the crime: Does he have a record of prior convictions for capital offenses? Are there any special facts about this defendant that mitigate against imposing capital punishment (*e.g.,* his youth, the extent of his cooperation with the police, his emotional state at the time of the crime)....

As an important additional safeguard against arbitrariness and caprice, the Georgia statutory scheme provides for automatic appeal of all death sentences to the State's Supreme Court. That court is required by statute to review each sentence of death and determine whether it was imposed under the influence of passion or prejudice, whether the evidence supports the jury's finding of a statutory aggravating circumstance, and whether the sentence is disproportionate compared to those sentences imposed in similar cases....

V

... [W]e hold that the statutory system under which Gregg was sentenced to death does not violate the Constitution. Accordingly, the judgment of the Georgia Supreme Court is affirmed.

It is so ordered.

MR. JUSTICE WHITE, with whom THE CHIEF JUSTICE and MR. JUSTICE REHNQUIST join, concurring in the judgment....

Statement of THE CHIEF JUSTICE and MR. JUSTICE REHNQUIST: ...

MR. JUSTICE BLACKMUN, concurring in the judgment....

MR. JUSTICE BRENNAN, dissenting....

The fatal constitutional infirmity in the punishment of death is that it treats "members of the human race as nonhumans, as objects to be toyed with and discarded. [It is] thus inconsistent with the fundamental premise of the Clause that even the vilest criminal remains a human being possessed of common human dignity." ...

MR. JUSTICE MARSHALL, dissenting.

In *Furman* v. *Georgia*, 408 U.S. 238, 314 (1972) (concurring opinion), I set forth at some length my views on the basic issue presented to the Court in these cases. The death penalty, I concluded, is a cruel and unusual punishment prohibited by the Eighth and Fourteenth Amendments. That continues to be my view.

Atkins v. Virginia

536 U.S. 304 (2002)

Daryl Renard Atkins, convicted of abduction, armed robbery, and murder, was sentenced to death. At issue was whether he was mentally retarded, forcing the Court to revisit its ruling in *Penry* v. *Lynaugh* (1989). It was not sufficient for the Court to analyze constitutional text, framers' intent, and its own prior holdings. It also found it necessary to examine changes in public attitudes and legislation passed by the states. What "consensus" had emerged since *Penry*?

JUSTICE STEVENS delivered the opinion of the Court.

Those mentally retarded persons who meet the law's requirements for criminal responsibility should be tried and punished when they commit crimes. Because of their disabilities in areas of reasoning, judgment, and control of their impulses, however, they do not act with the level of moral culpability that characterizes the most serious adult criminal conduct. Moreover, their impairments can jeopardize the reliability and fairness of capital proceedings against mentally retarded defendants. Presumably for these reasons, in the 13 years since we decided Penry v. Lynaugh, 492 U.S. 302 (1989), the American public, legislators, scholars, and judges have deliberated over the question whether the death penalty should ever be imposed on a mentally retarded criminal. The consensus reflected in those deliberations informs our answer to the question

presented by this case: whether such executions are "cruel and unusual punishments" prohibited by the Eighth Amendment to the Federal Constitution.

I

[*Atkins, accompanied by William Jones, abducted Eric Nesbitt, robbed him of the money on his person, and drove him to an automated teller machine to withdraw additional cash. Taken to an isolated location, Nesbitt was shot eight times and killed. Atkins and Jones stated that the other had shot and killed Nesbitt. The prosecution permitted Jones to plead guilty to first-degree murder in exchange for his testimony against Atkins. As a result of the plea, Jones was ineligible to receive the death penalty. The testimony by Jones was more coherent and credible than Atkins. The prosecution relied on Atkins' prior felony convictions. A witness for the defense, Dr. Evan Nelson, a forensic psychologist, evaluated Atkins before trial and concluded he was "mildly mentally retarded." A standard intelligence test indicated that Adkins had a full scale IQ of 59. The test measures an intelligence range from 45 to 155. The mean score of the test is 100, which means that a person receiving a score of 100 is considered to have an average level of cognitive functioning. It is estimated that between 1 and 3 percent of the population has an IQ between 70 and 75 or lower, which is typically considered the cutoff IQ score for defining mental retardation. The prosecution presented Dr. Stanton Samenow as an expert rebuttal witness. He expressed the opinion that Atkins was not mentally retarded but rather of "average intelligence, at least." He diagnosed him as having an anti-social personality disorder. Samenow did not administer an intelligence test.]*

Because of the gravity of the concerns expressed by the dissenters, and in light of the dramatic shift in the state legislative landscape that has occurred in the past 13 years, we granted certiorari to revisit the issue that we first addressed in the *Penry* case....

II

The Eighth Amendment succinctly prohibits "[e]xcessive" sanctions....

A claim that punishment is excessive is judged not by the standards that prevailed in 1685 when Lord Jeffreys presided over the "Bloody Assizes" or when the Bill of Rights was adopted, but rather by those that currently prevail....

Proportionality review under those evolving standards should be informed by "'objective factors to the maximum possible extent,'" see *Harmelin* [v. *Michigan*], 501 U.S., at 1000 (quoting *Rummel* v. *Estelle*, 445 U.S. 263, 274–275 (1980)). We have pinpointed that the "clearest and most reliable objective evidence of contemporary values is the legislation enacted by the country's legislatures." *Penry*, 492 U.S., at 331....

Guided by our approach in these cases, we shall first review the judgment of legislatures that have addressed the suitability of imposing the death penalty on the mentally retarded and then consider reasons for agreeing or disagreeing with their judgment.

III

The parties have not called our attention to any state legislative consideration of the suitability of imposing the death penalty on mentally retarded offenders prior to 1986. In that year, the public reaction to the mentally retarded murderer in Georgia apparently led to the enactment of the first state statute prohibiting such executions. In 1988, when Congress enacted legislation reinstating the federal

death penalty, it expressly provided that a "sentence of death shall not be carried out upon a person who is mentally retarded." In 1989, Maryland enacted a similar prohibition. It was in that year that we decided *Penry*, and concluded that those two state enactments, "even when added to the 14 States that have rejected capital punishment completely, do not provide sufficient evidence at present of a national consensus." 492 U.S. at 334.

Much has changed since then. Responding to the national attention received by the Bowden execution [*Jerome Bowden in the Georgia case had an IQ of 65*] and our decision in *Penry*, state legislatures across the country began to address the issue. In 1990, Kentucky and Tennessee enacted statutes similar to those in Georgia and Maryland, as did New Mexico in 1991, and Arkansas, Colorado, Washington, Indiana, and Kansas in 1993 and 1994. In 1995, when New York reinstated its death penalty, it emulated the Federal Government by expressly exempting the mentally retarded. Nebraska followed suit in 1998.... in 2000 and 2001 six more States—South Dakota, Arizona, Connecticut, Florida, Missouri, and North Carolina—joined the procession. The Texas Legislature unanimously adopted a similar bill, and bills have passed at least one house in other States, including Virginia and Nevada.

It is not so much the number of these States that is significant, but the consistency of the direction of change.... Moreover, even in those States that allow the execution of mentally retarded offenders, the practice is uncommon.... The practice, therefore, has become truly unusual, and it is fair to say that a national consensus has developed against it. [Note 21 refers to position taken by the American Psychological Association, various religious communities, polling data, and the European Union.]

IV

The consensus unquestionably reflects widespread judgment about the relative culpability of mentally retarded offenders, and the relationship between mental retardation and the penological purposes served by the death penalty....

With respect to deterrence—the interest in preventing capital crimes by prospective offenders—"it seems likely that 'capital punishment can serve as a deterrent only when murder is the result of premeditation and deliberation,'" *Enmund* [v. *Florida*], 458 U.S., at 799. Exempting the mentally retarded from that punishment will not affect the "cold calculus that precedes the decision" of other potential murderers. *Gregg* [v. *Georgia*], 428 U.S., at 186....

... Mentally retarded defendants may be less able

to give meaningful assistance to their counsel and are typically poor witnesses, and their demeanor may create an unwarranted impression of lack of remorse for their crimes.... Mentally retarded defendants in the aggregate face a special risk of wrongful execution.

Our independent evaluation of the issue reveals no reason to disagree with the judgment of "the legislatures that have recently addressed the matter" and concluded that death is not a suitable punishment for a mentally retarded criminal. We are not persuaded that the execution of mentally retarded criminals will measurably advance the deterrent or the retributive purpose of the death penalty....

CHIEF JUSTICE REHNQUIST, with whom JUSTICE SCALIA and JUSTICE THOMAS, join, dissenting.

The question presented by this case is whether a national consensus deprives Virginia of the constitutional power to impose the death penalty on capital murder defendants like petitioner, *i.e.*, those defendants who indisputably are competent to stand trial, aware of the punishment they are about to suffer and why, and whose mental retardation has been found an insufficiently compelling reason to lessen their individual responsibility for the crime. The Court pronounces the punishment cruel and unusual primarily because 18 States have recently passed laws limiting the death eligibility of certain defendants based on mental retardation alone, despite the fact that the laws of 19 other States besides Virginia continue to leave the question of proper punishment to the individuated consideration of sentencing judges or juries familiar with the particular offender and his or her crime....

I agree with JUSTICE SCALIA ... that the Court's assessment of the current legislative judgment regarding the execution of defendants like petitioner more resembles a *post hoc* rationalization for the majority's subjectively preferred result rather than any objective effort to ascertain the content of an evolving standard of decency. I write separately, however, to call attention to the defects in the Court's decision to place weight on foreign laws, the views of professional and religious organizations, and opinion polls in reaching its conclusion.... [*Rehnquist agrees on the Court ascribing "primacy to legislative enactments." It follows "from the constitutional role legislatures play in expressing policy of a State." He also looked to sentencing jury determinations for guidance on the constitutional issue. He objected particularly to reliance on policies adopted by foreign countries.*]

JUSTICE SCALIA, with whom THE CHIEF JUSTICE and JUSTICE THOMAS join, dissenting.

Today's decision is the pinnacle of our Eighth Amendment death-is-different jurisprudence. Not only does it, like all of that jurisprudence, find no support in the text or history of the Eighth Amendment; it does not even have support in current social attitudes regarding the conditions that render an otherwise death penalty inappropriate. Seldom has an opinion of this Court rested so obviously upon nothing but the personal views of its Members.

II

. . .

The Court makes no pretense that execution of the mildly mentally retarded would have been considered "cruel and unusual" in 1791. Only the *severely* or *profoundly* mentally retarded, commonly known as "idiots," enjoyed any special status under the law at that time. They, like lunatics, suffered a "deficiency in will" rendering them unable to tell right from wrong. 4 W. Blackstone, Commentaries on the Laws of England 24 (1769).... [*Scalia cites a source saying that idiots had an IQ of 25 or below.*] Mentally retarded offenders with less severe impairments — those who were not "idiots" — suffered criminal prosecution and punishment, including capital punishment....

The Court is left to argue, therefore, that execution of the mildly retarded is inconsistent with the "evolving standards of decency that mark the progress of a maturing society." *Trop v. Dulles*, 356 U.S. 86, 101 (1958) (plurality opinion) (Warren, C.J.). Before today, our opinions consistently emphasized that Eighth Amendment judgments regarding the existing of social "standards" "should be informed by objective factors to the maximum possible extent" and "should not be, or appear to be, merely the subjective views of individual Justices." *Coker v. Georgia*, 433 U.S. 584, 592 (1977) (plurality opinion).... "First" among these objective factors are the "statutes passed by society's elected representatives," ... because it "will rarely if ever be the case that the Members of this Court will have a better sense of the evolution in views of the American people than do their elected representatives," *Thompson* [v. *Oklahoma*, 487 U.S. 815 (1986)], at 865 (SCALIA, J., dissenting).

The Court pays lipservice to these precedents as it miraculously extracts a "national consensus" forbidding execution of the mentally retarded ... from the fact that 18 States — less than *half* (47%) of the

38 States that permit capital punishment (for whom the issue exists)—have very recently enacted legislation barring execution of the mentally retarded. Even that 47% figure is a distorted one. If one is to say, as the Court does today, that *all* executions of the mentally retarded are so morally repugnant as to violate our national "standards of decency," surely the "consensus" it points to must be one that has sets its righteous face against *all* such executions. Not 18 States, but only 7–18% of death penalty jurisdictions—have legislation of that scope. Eleven of those that the Court counts enacted statutes prohibiting execution of mentally retarded defendants *convicted after, or convicted of crimes committed after, the effective date* of the legislation; those already on death row, or consigned there before the statute's effective date, or even (in those States using the date of the crime as the criterion of retroactivity) tried in the future for murders committed many years ago, could be put to death. That is not a statement of absolute moral repugnance, but one of current preference between two tolerable approaches....

But let us accept, for the sake of argument, the Court's faulty count. That bare number of States alone—*18*—should be enough to convince any reasonable person that no "national consensus" exists. How is it possible that agreement among 47% of the death penalty jurisdictions amounts to "consensus"? Our prior cases have generally required a much higher degree of agreement before finding a punishment cruel and unusual on "evolving standards" grounds. In *Coker* [v. *Georgia*, 433 U.S. 584 (1977)], at 595–596, we proscribed the death penalty for rape of an adult woman after finding

that only one jurisdiction, Georgia, authorized such a punishment....

Moreover, a major factor that the Court entirely disregards is that the legislation of all 18 States it relies on is still in its infancy. The oldest of the statutes is only 14 years old; five were enacted last year; over half were enacted within the past eight years. Few, if any, of the States have had sufficient experience with these laws to know whether they are sensible in the long term....

The Court attempts to bolster its embarrassingly feeble evidence of "consensus" with the following: "It is not so much the number of these States that is significant, but the *consistency* of the direction of change." *Ante*, at 315 (emphasis added). But in what *other* direction *could we possibly* see change? Given that 14 years ago *all* the death penalty statutes included the mentally retarded, *any* change (except precipitate undoing of what had just been done) was *bound to be* in the one direction the Court finds significant enough to overcome the lack of real consensus....

But the Prize for the Court's Most Feeble Effort to fabricate "national consensus" must go to its appeal (deservedly relegated to a footnote) to the views of assorted professional and religious organizations, members of the so-called "world community," and respondents to opinion polls.... I agree with THE CHIEF JUSTICE, *ante*, at 325–328 (dissenting opinion), that the views of professional and religious organizations and the results of opinion polls are irrelevant. Equally irrelevant are the practices of the "world community," whose notions of justice are (thankfully) not always those of our people....

Justice Lewis Powell, Jr.
The Death Penalty and Public Opinion

Following his retirement from the Supreme Court, Justice Lewis Powell, Jr., delivered a speech on capital punishment on August 7, 1988, at the American Bar Association's annual meeting in Toronto. He cited language from the Constitution and statutes from the First Congress to indicate that the Founding Fathers approved capital punishment. After summarizing the Court's holdings in *Furman* v. *Georgia* (1972) and *Gregg* v. *Georgia* (1976), he concluded that the decision on capital punishment was basically in the hands of legislatures and public opinion. The excerpts below are taken from "Death Penalty? Society Has Ruled," *Legal Times,* August 15, 1988, pp. 12, 13.

Since *Gregg,* the Supreme Court has decided—with full opinions—a number of capital cases. In view of the finality of capital punishment, appellate courts—including the Supreme Court—have re-

viewed each case with great care. Although protective refinements have been enunciated, *Gregg* remains the law. We have recognized, in accordance with Chief Justice Warren's opinion in *Trop* v. *Dulles,* that the Eighth Amendment "must draw its meaning from evolving standards of decency that mark the progress of a maturing society."

Thus, our constitutional decisions have been informed by contemporary judgments of society as evidenced by decisions of state legislatures and sentencing decisions of juries. Thirty-seven states now have capital punishment statutes enacted since the *Furman* decision. In 33 of these states, death sentences have been imposed. Although no federal death sentences have been imposed in recent years, several federal criminal statutes authorize a penalty of death, and Congress has recently been considering imposition of the death penalty for certain murders committed in connection with drug violations. And juries continue to impose the sentence of death.

The evidence, therefore, is compelling that a large majority of our people consider that for certain crimes, capital punishment is appropriate. In the face of this evidence, it would be difficult for a court—even the Supreme Court—to conclude that the legislatures of a great majority of the states and the Congress are mistaken as to contemporary standards of decency in our society.

... As a co-author of *Gregg* and recently the author of *McCleskey* [v. *Kemp*], I adhere to the view that the death penalty lawfully may be imposed under our Constitution. My concerns relate to the way the system malfunctions and to the shocking murder rate that prevails in our country. In view of the unambiguous public support for capital punishment, one would think that the time has come for Congress to give thoughtful consideration to making reasonable changes in the federal law governing review of criminal convictions. It is now evident that our unique system of multiple and dual collateral review is abused, particularly in capital cases. If capital punishment cannot be enforced, even where innocence is not an issue and the fairness of the trial is not seriously questioned, perhaps Congress and the state legislatures should take a serious look at whether retention of a punishment that is not being enforced is in the public interest.

H. PRISONERS' RIGHTS

Prisoners and inmates of mental institutions were long kept in a constitutional backwater. Legislators had little incentive to provide adequate funds for shelter, food, clothing, and medical care. Constituents were content, perhaps out of ignorance, to have public funds spent elsewhere.[29] Congressman Robert Kastenmeier reflected on his service as chairman of the Subcommittee on Corrections of the House Judiciary Committee: "[F]ew organizations have lobbied for prison reform. This apparent lack of interest creates little external pressure for action, while there is growing and vocal opposition to penal reform based on the widespread sentiment that high crime rates can only be reduced by long and harsh incarceration."[30] Because of the crimes they committed, prisoners were considered undeserving of even minimal care. At one time in our history, an inmate in a penitentiary was considered "the slave of the State." Ruffin v. Commonwealth, 62 Va. 790, 796 (1871).

Litigation has been the chief instrument for initiating prison reform. In the 1960s, professional journals began to focus on the primitive conditions in mental hospitals and prisons. Out of these studies came the concept of a right to treatment for institutionalized persons. U.S. Judge David Bazelon pioneered some of the reforms in mental hospitals, ruling in 1966 that a failure to provide suitable treatment would justify a patient's release. Rouse v. Cameron, 373 F.2d 451 (D.C. Cir. 1966). A few years later, U.S. Judge Frank Johnson held that inadequate treatment for institutionalized persons represented a violation of the basic fundamentals of due process. Wyatt v. Stickney, 325 F.Supp. 781 (M.D. Ala. 1971). It is difficult to criticize Johnson's efforts as an exercise in "judicial activism." The counsel for the state admitted in open court that the evidence conclusively established violations of

---

29. For basic cases on the rights of inmates in mental institutions, see Foucha v. Louisiana, 504 U.S. 71 (1992); Youngberg v. Romeo, 457 U.S. 307 (1982); Mills v. Rogers, 457 U.S. 291 (1982); Vitek v. Jones, 445 U.S. 480 (1980); Secretary of Public Welfare v. Institutionalized Juveniles, 442 U.S. 640 (1979); Parham v. J.R., 442 U.S. 584 (1979); O'Connor v. Donaldson, 422 U.S. 563 (1975).

30. Robert W. Kastenmeier, "The Legislator and the Legislature: Their Roles in Prison Reform," in Michele G. Hermann and Marilyn G. Haft, eds., Prisoners' Rights Sourcebook 456 (1973).

the Eighth Amendment rights of prisoners. Pugh v. Locke, 406 F.Supp. 318, 322, 329 n.13 (M.D. Ala. 1976). (For additional material on Johnson's efforts, see Chapter 1.)

Even before the attention to prisoner rights in recent years, certain rights were conceded. States cannot impair a prisoner's right to apply to the federal courts for a writ of habeas corpus.[31] Prisoners must be given a reasonable opportunity to pursue their religious faith, but prison officials are not expected to sacrifice their legitimate objectives in accommodating every religious need.[32] Prisoners may not be segregated by race. Lee v. Washington, 390 U.S. 333 (1968). States may not initially assign inmates to racially segregated cells without demonstrating that it has no race-neutral method of preventing interracial violence. Johnson v. California, 543 U.S. 499 (2005). A prisoner's desire to marry may not be prevented by prison regulations that rely on an exaggerated and unreasonable concern for security.[33]

Due Process Protections

Beginning in the early 1970s, the Supreme Court announced a series of new rights for prisoners and parolees. Authorities may no longer revoke paroles and return a person to prison without an informal hearing. The parolee must be given written notice of claimed violations, the evidence against him, an opportunity to be heard, to present witnesses and evidence, and to confront and cross-examine adverse witnesses. Morrissey v. Brewer, 408 U.S. 471 (1972). These procedural protections also apply to those under the status of "pre-parole" (persons released to reduce prison overcrowding). Young v. Harper, 520 U.S. 143 (1997). Parole *revocation* is a serious deprivation of liberty, requiring procedural protections, but the possible *granting* of parole does not create the same entitlement of due process. Greenholtz v. Nebraska Penal Inmates, 442 U.S. 1 (1979). The Fourth Amendment does not prohibit a police officer from conducting a suspicionless search of a parolee. Samson v. California, 547 U.S. 843 (2006).

Due process does not require a state prisoner to be given a hearing simply because he is being transferred to a prison with less favorable conditions. Meachum v. Fano, 427 U.S. 215 (1976); Montanye v. Haymes, 427 U.S. 236 (1976); Olim v. Wakinekona, 461 U.S. 238 (1983). Only informal, nonadversary review is required before placing a prisoner in confinement, provided he receives notice of the charges and has an opportunity to present his views. Hewitt v. Helms, 459 U.S. 460 (1983).

If a state creates the right to "good time" credits (to reduce a sentence), a prisoner is entitled to minimal procedures to ensure that this right is not arbitrarily abrogated. The prisoner must be given advance written notice of the claimed violation, a statement of the evidence, and the reasons for the disciplinary action. The inmate has a right to call witnesses and to present evidence; there is no right of confrontation and cross-examination. Wolff v. McDonnell, 418 U.S. 539 (1974). The *Wolff* standards divided the Court 5 to 4 in 1995 when it held that prison officials could deny prisoners the right to present witnesses during a disciplinary hearing that led to segregated confinement. Sandin v. Conner, 515 U.S. 472 (1995).

In 1990, the Court divided 6 to 3 in holding that mentally ill prisoners are not entitled to a judicial hearing before the state administers antipsychotic drugs against their will. These drugs can have

---

31. Ex parte Hull, 312 U.S. 546 (1941); Johnson v. Avery, 393 U.S. 483 (1969). States must even assist inmates in preparing and filing legal papers by providing adequate law libraries and assistance from persons trained in the law. Bounds v. Smith, 430 U.S. 817 (1977). The Court restricted *Bounds* in 1996 by holding that prisoners who seek access to a law library or legal assistance must demonstrate that they are pursuing a nonfrivolous legal claim. Inmates do not have a right to file any and every type of legal claim. They need only the tools to attack their sentences and to challenge the conditions of their confinement. Lewis v. Casey, 518 U.S. 343 (1996).

32. O'Lone v. Estate of Shabazz, 482 U.S. 342 (1987); Cruz v. Beto, 405 U.S. 319 (1972); Cooper v. Pate, 378 U.S. 333 (1968). See also Cutter v. Wilkinson, 544 U.S. 709 (2005).

33. Turner v. Safley, 482 U.S. 78 (1987); Butler v. Wilson, 415 U.S. 953 (1974), aff'g, Johnson v. Rockefeller, 365 F.Supp. 377 (S.D. N.Y. 1973).

serious, even fatal, side effects. Prisoners are entitled to certain rights from prison officials, such as the right to notice of a hearing on the decision to administer the drugs and the right to attend, present evidence, and cross-examine witnesses. Washington v. Harper, 494 U.S. 210 (1990). In 1992, a 7–2 Court held that a state judge erred in forcing a criminal defendant to take an antipsychotic drug during a trial, in which his insanity defense was unsuccessful. The error was a narrow one; the Court only insisted that the judge should have made a determination of the need for the medication and should have made findings about reasonable alternatives. Riggins v. Nevada, 504 U.S. 127 (1992).

In 2002, a 5–4 Court upheld a prison rehabilitative program designed for sex offenders. Inmates who chose to participate in the program were required to reveal previously undisclosed crimes at the risk of facing new prosecution for those offenses. Although participation was voluntary, a refusal (such as on self-incrimination grounds) could result in being moved to a maximum security cell and losing some privileges. McKune v. Lile, 536 U.S. 24 (2002). In a case that centered on Congress's authority under the necessary and proper clause, the Court held in 2010 that Congress could allow the continued civil commitment of sexually dangerous federal prisoners who had completed their criminal sentences. Prison officials must provide a judge "clear and convincing evidence" that the prisoner is sexually violent, mentally ill, or lacks self control. United States v. Comstock, 560 U.S. ___ (2010).

Prison Conditions

Prisoners do not have the same rights as other citizens regarding privacy and First Amendment freedoms. Their letters may be turned over and given to government officials. Stroud v. United States, 251 U.S. 15 (1919). Prison officials may censor or restrict personal correspondence if necessary for security, order, and the rehabilitation of inmates. Turner v. Safley, 482 U.S. 78 (1987); Procunier v. Martinez, 416 U.S. 396 (1974). The Supreme Court defers considerably to prison officials who monitor and exclude incoming publications that they find detrimental to the "security, good order, or discipline" of the institution. Prisoners have greater First Amendment rights with regard to *outgoing* correspondence because it presents less of a risk to institutional security. Thornburgh v. Abbott, 490 U.S. 401 (1989). Prisoners have no right to "contact visits" (physical touching) with their spouses, relatives, children, or friends. This privilege may be denied by prison officials concerned about the introduction of drugs, weapons, and other contraband. Block v. Rutherford, 468 U.S. 576 (1984). In deciding which visitors to exclude, prison officials are not bound by the Due Process Clause (such as providing a hearing before the exclusion). Kentucky Dept. of Corrections v. Thompson, 490 U.S. 454 (1989).

Conversations may be monitored and intercepted through electronic listening devices. Lanza v. New York, 370 U.S. 139 (1962). Because the Court holds that prisoners have no reasonable expectation of privacy in their prison cells, they are not entitled to Fourth Amendment protections against unreasonable searches. Hudson v. Palmer, 468 U.S. 517 (1984); Block v. Rutherford, 468 U.S. 576 (1984). Although the press has an interest in reporting on prison conditions, the government may prohibit interviews between news reporters and inmates in medium-security and maximum-security prisons.[34]

In 2011, the Court divided 5 to 4 in holding that a court-ordered population limit in California's prisons was necessary to remedy the violation of prisoners' constitutional rights under the Eighth Amendment. The majority found specific authority in the Prison Litigation Reform Act of 1995. To the dissenters (Scalia, Roberts, Alito, Thomas) the majority's decision violated the statute, ignored limitations on Article III judges, and took federal courts beyond their institutional capacity. Brown v. Plata, 563 U.S. ___ (2011).

A 5–4 Court in 2012 decided that prison officials may strip search individuals arrested for minor, non-indictable offenses, in this case failure to pay a fine that had actually been paid. The police ar-

---

34. Houchins v. KQED, Inc., 438 U.S. 1 (1978); Saxbe v. Washington Post, 417 U.S. 843 (1974); Pell v. Procunier, 417 U.S. 817 (1974).

Prisoners' Rights

Through a series of rulings in recent decades, the Supreme Court has gradually outlined the basic rights that are available to prisoners and detainees. The table below identifies some of the fundamental issues.

Protected rights:	Permissible actions:
Prisoners may not be segregated by race. Lee v. Washington, 390 U.S. 333 (1968).	Double-bunking in detention centers. Bell v. Wolfish, 441 U.S. 520 (1979).
Procedural protections for parole *revocation.* Morrissey v. Brewer, 408 U.S. 471 (1972).	No procedural protections for *granting* parole. Greenholtz v. Nebraska Penal Inmates, 442 U.S. 1 (1979).
Detainees may not be punished prior to adjudication of guilt. Bell v. Wolfish, 441 U.S. 520 (1979).	Searches and seizures unrestricted by Fourth Amendment. Hudson v. Palmer, 468 U.S. 517 (1984).
Limits on time in isolation cells. Hutto v. Finney, 437 U.S. 678 (1978).	No right to contact visits. Block v. Rutherford, 468 U.S. 576 (1984).
Reasonable opportunity to pursue religious faith. O'Lone v. Estate of Shabazz, 482 U.S. 342 (1987).	Strip search, exposing body cavities, after contact visits. Bell v. Wolfish, 441 U.S. 520 (1979).
Freedom from excessive physical force even when there is no serious injury. Hudson v. McMillian, 503 U.S. 1 (1992).	Restrictions on incoming mail and packages. Thornburgh v. Abbott, 490 U.S. 401 (1989).

---

resting him relied on a computer database that was in error about the fine. The strip search was visual. It did not involve the search of body cavities. Prison officials justified a strip search to look for body markings, wounds, and contraband. In dissent: Breyer, Ginsburg, Sotomayor, Kagan. Florence v. Board of Chosen Freeholders of County of Burlington, 566 U.S. ___ (2012).

Cruel and Unusual Punishment

Federal courts have intervened to put pressure on states to upgrade their prison facilities. The Supreme Court upheld a court order placing a maximum limit of 30 days in Arkansas' isolation cells. Confinement beyond that period constituted cruel and unusual punishment. Conditions in the Arkansas prisons, with a history of overcrowding, physical violence, and malnutrition, were described as "a dark and evil world completely alien to the free world." Hutto v. Finney, 437 U.S. 678, 681 (1978). Conditions in the Attica, N.Y., prison led to riots in 1971. By the end of the five-day uprising, eleven guards and 32 prisoners had died. After decades of litigation, New York agreed in 2000 to set aside $12 million: $8 million for the former inmates and $4 million for lawyers' fees.

For the most part, the judiciary defers to prison officials on questions of "double-bunking," body-cavity searches, and restrictions on incoming packages. Bell v. Wolfish, 441 U.S. 520 (1979). Prison rules and regulations are not subject to strict-scrutiny analysis. The Court applies a lesser and more lenient standard of scrutiny. Turner v. Safley, 482 U.S. 78 (1987). The Court recognizes that running a prison "is an inordinately difficult undertaking that requires expertise, planning, and the commitment of resources, all of which are peculiarly within the province of the legislative and executive branches of government." Id. at 84–85 (see box).

In 1991, a 5–4 Court ruled that prisoners who file lawsuits regarding conditions in prison must overcome two hurdles: that the conditions constitute cruel and unusual punishment in violation of the Eighth Amendment, and that prison officials exhibited "deliberate indifference." As the dissenters pointed out, this two-part test may mean that inhumane prison conditions cannot be effectively challenged if they are the result of insufficient funding by state legislators rather than deliberate indifference by prison officials. Wilson v. Seiter, 501 U.S. 294 (1991).

In 1992, the Court divided 7–2 in holding that excessive physical force against a prisoner may constitute cruel and unusual punishment even though the prisoner does not suffer serious injury. The prisoner, placed in handcuffs and shackles, was punched in the mouth, eyes, chest, and stomach by one guard while another guard kicked and punched him from behind. The prison supervisor watched the beating and told the guards "not to have too much fun." The prisoner suffered minor bruises and swelling of his face, mouth, and lip. The blows also loosened his teeth and cracked his partial dental plate. Hudson v. McMillian, 503 U.S. 1 (1992).

Also in 1992, the Court made it easier for state and local officials to modify court settlements that required them to improve conditions in prisons and other public institutions. For example, judicial requirements for single-cell occupancy in jails can be lifted if the state demonstrates that significant changes in circumstances (such as financial constraints) warrant revision of a consent decree. Rufo v. Inmates of Suffolk County Jail, 502 U.S. 367 (1992). A decision by the Court in 1993 allowed prisoners to sue prison officials on the ground that smoking by a cellmate posed health hazards and constituted cruel and unusual punishment under the Eighth Amendment. Helling v. McKinney, 509 U.S. 25 (1993). A year later a unanimous Court held that a prison official may be held liable for acting with "deliberate indifference" to inmate health or safety, but only if he knows that inmates face a substantial risk of serious harm and fails to take reasonable measures to abate the risk. In this case a transsexual prisoner was transferred from a correctional institution to a penitentiary, where he was beaten and raped. Farmer v. Brennan, 511 U.S. 825 (1994). In 2002, the Court called cruel and unusual Alabama's practice of chaining disruptive prisoners to outdoor "hitching" posts. The 6–2 decision allowed the prisoner to sue three prison guards who carried out this form of punishment. Hope v. Pelzer, 536 U.S. 730 (2002).

Congressional Legislation

In 1995, Congress passed legislation to restrict the ability of prisoners to sue over their living conditions and to limit the scope of court-ordered settlements in such lawsuits. In a case that reached the Supreme Court, inmates at a correctional facility brought a class action and a district court found that living conditions at the prison violated both state and federal law, including the Cruel and Unusual Punishment Clause. The Seventh Circuit issued a remedial order concerning overcrowding, quality of food, and other issues. The statute allowed a defendant (such as the state or prison official) to file for the immediate termination of any prospective relief and required the court to make certain findings to continue the relief. The Seventh Circuit ruled that the statutory procedure was unconstitutional because it allowed court orders to be set aside by legislative determination, violating the separation of powers. However, the Supreme Court interpreted the statute to avoid constitutional problems. Congress could set up a procedure triggering an automatic stay of a court order for prospective relief, and prohibit the continuation of the relief unless the court finds that the relief is narrowly drawn, extends no further than necessary to correct the violation of the federal right, and is the least intrusive means to correct the violation. Miller v. French, 530 U.S. 327 (2000).

I. THE RIGHT TO BEAR ARMS

The right to bear arms may seem to fit awkwardly in a chapter devoted to the rights of the accused. However, challenges to gun regulation often arise out of criminal cases and some gun regulations are criminal statutes for which people can be prosecuted for violations. The Second Amendment is debated so widely, and with such intensity and emotion, that it requires analysis. What was the purpose of this amendment? Is the right to bear arms so fundamental that government is powerless to regulate it? What types of restrictions on guns are appropriate and constitutional?

Adoption of the Second Amendment

At face value, the Second Amendment appears to protect a *collective* right (a well-regulated militia), not a personal right: "A well regulated Militia, being necessary to the security of a free State, the right of the people to keep and bear Arms, shall not be infringed." However, that issue is confused somewhat by the legislative history of the amendment. Madison's proposal on June 8, 1789, starts with individual rights: "The right of the people to keep and bear arms shall not be infringed; a well armed and well regulated militia being the best security of a free country; but no person religiously scrupulous of bearing arms shall be compelled to render military service in person." 1 Annals of Cong. 434 (1789).

Through this language, Madison drew upon principles from English history and the American states. Individuals needed arms to participate as citizen-soldiers in a well-regulated militia. These temporary fighting forces, created in periods of emergency, were intended to avoid the dangers of a standing army. Joyce Lee Malcolm, To Keep and Bear Arms 1–3, 146–49 (1996 ed.). This argument has little application to the contemporary reliance on a standing army.

Madison's language changed as it moved through Congress. By the time his proposal emerged from a select committee, the emphasis had shifted from personal rights to individuals operating within a militia: "A well regulated militia, composed of the body of the people, being the best security of a free state, the right of the people to keep and bear arms shall not be infringed; but no person religiously scrupulous shall be compelled to bear arms." 1 Annals of Cong. 749. The Senate dropped the provision on conscientious objectors and perfected other language. 1 Journal of the First Session of the Senate 71, 77 (1820).

It could be argued that the purpose of the Bill of Rights as a whole is to protect *personal* rights, not collective rights.[35] Even if one accepts that position, however, the individual rights identified in the first ten amendments are not absolute. Various limits operate on speech, press, religion, and other rights. The right to bear arms does not mean that every individual may possess a howitzer or rocket launcher; there is no constitutional right to bring a handgun into a classroom, hospital, or police station.

Federal Legislation and Executive Action

In 1934, Congress passed legislation to restrict the transportation of sawed-off shotguns (with a barrel less than 18 inches long) in interstate commerce. 48 Stat. 1236 (1934). A unanimous Court upheld that statute against the claim that it violated the Second Amendment. The Court found no evidence that sawed-off shotguns had "some reasonable relationship to the preservation or efficiency of a well regulated militia." United States v. Miller, 307 U.S. 174, 178 (1939). The Court related the Second Amendment to the power of Congress, in Article I, to call forth the militia and to see that it is properly organized, armed, and disciplined. The rest of the decision focused on the right to bear arms as a collective responsibility rather than an individual right to use weapons for hunting or other purposes.

Congress has passed other legislation to control firearms. A major gun control bill was enacted in 1968, following the fatal shootings of Martin Luther King, Jr. and Robert F. Kennedy. 82 Stat. 1213 (1968). A separate statute, the Omnibus Crime Control and Safe Streets Act, included a section on firearms. 82 Stat. 225–35 (1968). Two decades later, during the Reagan administration, Congress passed the Firearms Owners' Protection Act, which eased somewhat the restrictions in the 1968 legislation. 100 Stat. 449 (1986). See also 100 Stat. 766 (1986). In 1993, the Brady bill provided a five-day waiting period for handgun purchases. 107 Stat. 1536 (1993). Legislation in 1994 added a ban on

---

35. William Van Alstyne, "The Second Amendment and the Personal Right to Arms," 43 Duke L. J. 1236 (1994); 1 Laurence H. Tribe, American Constitutional Law 897–98 n.211 (2000).

semiautomatic weapons. 108 Stat. 1996–2010 (1994). Because of the paucity of federal court decisions on the Second Amendment, the scope of "gun rights" was left largely to the elected branches operating at the national level and in the states.

Under the George W. Bush administration, the Justice Department moved in several directions to
establish an individual right to own guns. In a May 17, 2001 letter to the National Rifle Association,
Attorney General John Ashcroft stated that the Second Amendment gives individuals a right to
firearms. In October of that year, the Fifth Circuit held that while the federal government may regulate gun possession, the constitutional guarantee to have a gun extends to the individual. United States
v. Emerson, 270 F.3d 203 (5th Cir. 2001). The Supreme Court decided not to hear that case or another one decided by the Tenth Circuit. Emerson v. United States, 536 U.S. 907 (2002); Haney v.
United States, 536 U.S. 907 (2002).

On May 6, 2002, in a brief filed with the Supreme Court, the Justice Department argued that the
Second Amendment protects an individual's right to possess a firearm, and that the right is not related solely to maintaining a state militia. The brief acknowledged that the right is subject to "reasonable restrictions designed to prevent possession by unfit persons or to restrict the possession of
types of firearms that are particularly suited to criminal misuse." On December 10, 2002, the Court
reviewed a case brought by a licensed firearms dealer who lost his gun privileges after his conviction
for transporting ammunition from Texas into Mexico. A unanimous Court held that he had no right
to ask federal courts to review inaction by the Bureau of Alcohol, Tobacco and Firearms (ATF) on his
application to have his gun privilege restored. By statute, Congress had denied ATF any funds to
process such applications. United States v. Beans, 537 U.S. 71 (2002). The gun dealer had earlier asked
the Court to rule that the Second Amendment protects an individual's right to bear arms, but the
Court's decision did not address that issue. The Supreme Court decided in 2005 that the 1968 statute
did not apply to felons convicted by courts in foreign countries. Small v. United States, 544 U.S. 385
(2005).

New Directions in Second Amendment Law

Efforts to get the Court to change Second Amendment law eventually succeeded. Washington, D.C.
had perhaps the strictest gun regulations in the country, banning handguns in the home. In a landmark ruling in 2008 the Court (5 to 4) struck down these provisions as violations of the Second
Amendment. DISTRICT OF COLUMBIA v. HELLER, 554 U.S. 570 (2008). Since *Heller* dealt with a
regulation in the federal enclave of the District of Columbia, it left open the question of whether the
Second Amendment applied to the states. After *Heller* some challenges to state and local regulations
were filed and the first to reach the Court involved Chicago's ban on most handgun possessions. The
lower courts upheld the ban based on an earlier precedent interpreting the amendment as applying
only to the national government. In 2010 the Supreme Court held that the individual right identified
in *Heller* was "fundamental to the National scheme of ordered liberty" and was thus applicable to the
states via the due process clause of the Fourteenth Amendment. McDonald v. Chicago, 561 U.S. ___
(2010). The Court repeated its assertion in *Heller* that the right is not unlimited and that there are
reasonable regulations of handguns that could withstand scrutiny.

District of Columbia v. Heller

554 U.S. 570 (2008)

Dick Heller, a D.C. special police officer, sought to register a handgun to keep at his home. His
request was refused because D.C. law prohibited the possession of usable handguns in the home.
It also made it a crime to carry an unregistered firearm and required owners of registered
firearms to have them unloaded, dissembled or trigger-locked, in their homes. Heller challenged

the prohibitions on Second Amendment grounds, seeking to enjoin the city from enforcement of its ban on registering handguns and on keeping "functional firearms" in the home. The District Court dismissed the complaint. The D.C. Circuit reversed, agreeing with Heller that the Second Amendment was violated by these prohibitions. All nine Justices sought guidance from the framers' intent but split on the merits, 5 to 4.

JUSTICE SCALIA delivered the opinion of the Court.

We consider whether a District of Columbia prohibition on the possession of usable handguns in the home violates the Second Amendment to the Constitution....

II

We turn first to the meaning of the Second Amendment.

A

The Second Amendment provides: "A well regulated Militia, being necessary to the security of a free State, the right of the people to keep and bear Arms, shall not be infringed." ...

The two sides in this case have set out very different interpretations of the Amendment. Petitioners and today's dissenting Justices believe that it protects only the right to possess and carry a firearm in connection with militia service.... Respondent argues that it protects an individual right to possess a firearm unconnected with service in a militia, and to use that arm for traditionally lawful purposes, such as self-defense within the home....

The Second Amendment is naturally divided into two parts: its prefatory clause and its operative clause. The former does not limit the latter grammatically, but rather announces a purpose.... Although this structure of the Second Amendment is unique in our Constitution, other legal documents of the founding era, particularly individual-rights provisions of state constitutions, commonly included a prefatory statement of purpose....

1. Operative Clause.

a. "Right of the People." The first salient feature of the operative clause is that it codifies a "right of the people." The unamended Constitution and the Bill of Rights use the phrase "right of the people" two other times, in the First Amendment's Assembly-and-Petition Clause and in the Fourth Amendment's Search-and-Seizure Clause. The Ninth Amendment uses very similar terminology ("The enumeration in the Constitution, of certain rights, shall not be construed to deny or disparage others retained by the people"). All three of these instances unambiguously refer to individual rights, not "collective" rights, or rights that may be exercised only through participation in some corporate body.

Three provisions of the Constitution refer to "the people" in a context other than "rights"—the famous preamble ("We the people"), § 2 of Article I (providing that "the people" will choose members of the House), and the Tenth Amendment (providing that those powers not given the Federal Government remain with "the States" or "the people"). Those provisions arguably refer to "the people" acting collectively—but they deal with the exercise or reservation of powers, not rights. Nowhere else in the Constitution does a "right" attributed to "the people" refer to anything other than an individual right.

What is more, in all six other provisions of the Constitution that mention "the people," the term unambiguously refers to all members of the political community, not an unspecified subset....

This contrasts markedly with the phrase "the militia" in the prefatory clause. As we will describe below, the "militia" in colonial America consisted of a subset of "the people"—those who were male, able bodied, and within a certain age range. Reading the Second Amendment as protecting only the right to "keep and bear Arms" in an organized militia therefore fits poorly with the operative clause's description of the holder of that right as "the people."

We start therefore with a strong presumption that the Second Amendment right is exercised individually and belongs to all Americans.

b. "Keep and bear Arms." We move now from the holder of the right—"the people"—to the substance of the right: "to keep and bear Arms."

Before addressing the verbs "keep" and "bear," we interpret their object: "Arms." The 18th-century meaning is no different from the meaning today....

... The term was applied, then as now, to weapons that were not specifically designed for military use and were not employed in a military capacity.... Although one founding-era thesaurus limited "arms" (as opposed to "weapons") to "instruments of offence *generally* made use of in war," even that source stated that all firearms constituted "arms." ...

We turn to the phrases "keep arms" and "bear arms." Johnson defined "keep" as, most relevantly, "[t]o retain; not to lose," and "[t]o have in custody." Johnson 1095. Webster defined it as "[t]o hold; to retain in one's power or possession." No party has apprised us of an idiomatic meaning of "keep Arms." Thus, the most natural reading of "keep Arms" in the Second Amendment is to "have weapons." ...

... "Keep arms" was simply a common way of referring to possessing arms, for militiamen *and everyone else....*

... Nine state constitutional provisions written in the 18th century or the first two decades of the 19th, ... enshrined a right of citizens to "bear arms in defense of themselves and the state" or "bear arms in defense of himself and the state." ...

c. Meaning of the Operative Clause. Putting all of these textual elements together, we find that they guarantee the individual right to possess and carry weapons in case of confrontation. This meaning is strongly confirmed by the historical background of the Second Amendment. We look to this because it has always been widely understood that the Second Amendment, like the First and Fourth Amendments, codified a pre-existing right. The very text of the Second Amendment implicitly recognizes the pre-existence of the right and declares only that it "shall not be infringed." ...

By the time of the founding, the right to have arms had become fundamental for English subjects.... Blackstone, whose works, we have said, "constituted the preeminent authority on English law for the founding generation," *Alden v. Maine*, 527 U. S. 706, 715 (1999), cited the arms provision of the Bill of Rights as one of the fundamental rights of Englishmen. See 1 Blackstone 136, 139–140 (1765). His description of it cannot possibly be thought to tie it to militia or military service. It was, he said, "the natural right of resistance and self-preservation," *id.*, at 139, and "the right of having and using arms for self-preservation and defence," *id.*, at 140; ...

There seems to us no doubt, on the basis of both text and history, that the Second Amendment conferred an individual right to keep and bear arms. Of course the right was not unlimited, just as the First Amendment's right of free speech was not, ... Thus, we do not read the Second Amendment to protect the right of citizens to carry arms for *any sort* of confrontation, just as we do not read the First Amendment to protect the right of citizens to speak for *any purpose....*

2. Prefatory Clause.

The prefatory clause reads: "A well regulated Militia, being necessary to the security of a free State...."

a. "Well-Regulated Militia." In *United States v. Miller*, 307 U. S. 174, 179 (1939), we explained that "the Militia comprised all males physically capable of acting in concert for the common defense." That definition comports with founding-era sources....

Although we agree with petitioners' interpretive assumption that "militia" means the same thing in Article I and the Second Amendment, we believe that petitioners identify the wrong thing, namely, the organized militia. Unlike armies and navies, which Congress is given the power to create ... the militia is assumed by Article I already to be *in existence....*

Finally, the adjective "well-regulated" implies nothing more than the imposition of proper discipline and training....

b. "Security of a Free State." The phrase "security of a free state" meant "security of a free polity," not security of each of the several States ... Joseph Story wrote in his treatise on the Constitution that "the word 'state' is used in various senses [and in] its most enlarged sense, it means the people composing a particular nation or community." ... It is true that the term "State" elsewhere in the Constitution refers to individual States, but the phrase "security of a free state" and close variations seem to have been terms of art in 18th-century political discourse, meaning a "'free country'" or free polity....

3. Relationship between Prefatory Clause and Operative Clause.

We reach the question, then: Does the preface fit with an operative clause that creates an individual right to keep and bear arms? It fits perfectly, once one knows the history that the founding generation knew and that we have described above. That history showed that the way tyrants had eliminated a militia consisting of all the able-bodied men was not by banning the militia but simply by taking away the people's arms, enabling a select militia or standing army to suppress political opponents. This is what had occurred in England that prompted codification of the right to have arms in the English Bill of Rights.

The debate with respect to the right to keep and bear arms, as with other guarantees in the Bill of Rights, was not over whether it was desirable (all agreed that it was) but over whether it needed to be codified in the Constitution. During the 1788 ratification debates, the fear that the federal government would disarm the people in order to impose rule through a standing army or select militia was pervasive in Antifederalist rhetoric....

... The prefatory clause does not suggest that preserving the militia was the only reason Americans valued the ancient right; most undoubtedly thought it even more important for self-defense and hunting....

D

... As we will show, virtually all interpreters of the Second Amendment in the century after its enactment interpreted the amendment as we do. [*In this section Scalia discusses scholarly analysis of the amendment during the post-ratification period, case law from the nineteenth century, and the fact that the post-Reconstruction Congress included among the rights to be protected for new black citizens "the right to bear arms."*]

E

We now ask whether any of our precedents forecloses the conclusions we have reached about the meaning of the Second Amendment.

United States v. Cruikshank, 92 U. S. 542, in the course of vacating the convictions of members of a white mob for depriving blacks of their right to keep and bear arms, held that the Second Amendment does not by its own force apply to anyone other than the Federal Government. The opinion explained that the right "is not a right granted by the Constitution [or] in any manner dependent upon that instrument for its existence. The second amendment ... means no more than that it shall not be infringed by Congress." 92 U. S., at 553. States, we said, were free to restrict or protect the right under their police powers. The limited discussion of the Second Amendment in *Cruikshank* supports, if anything, the individual-rights interpretation.... [*In a footnote, Scalia notes that the question of whether incorporation makes the Second Amendment applicable to the states was not before the Court.*]

III

Like most rights, the right secured by the Second Amendment is not unlimited. From Blackstone through the 19th-century cases, commentators and courts routinely explained that the right was not a right to keep and carry any weapon whatsoever in any manner whatsoever and for whatever purpose.... [N]othing in our opinion should be taken to cast doubt on longstanding prohibitions on the possession of firearms by felons and the mentally ill, or laws forbidding the carrying of firearms in sensitive places such as schools and government buildings, or laws imposing conditions and qualifications on the commercial sale of arms.

We also recognize another important limitation on the right to keep and carry arms. *Miller* said, as we have explained, that the sorts of weapons protected were those "in common use at the time." 307 U. S., at 179. We think that limitation is fairly supported by the historical tradition of prohibiting the carrying of "dangerous and unusual weapons." ...

IV

We turn finally to the law at issue here....

... The handgun ban amounts to a prohibition of an entire class of "arms" that is overwhelmingly chosen by American society for that lawful purpose. The prohibition extends, moreover, to the home, where the need for defense of self, family, and property is most acute. Under any of the standards of scrutiny that we have applied to enumerated constitutional rights, banning from the home "the most preferred firearm in the nation to 'keep' and use for protection of one's home and family," 478 F. 3d, at 400, would fail constitutional muster.

Few laws in the history of our Nation have come close to the severe restriction of the District's handgun ban....

We must also address the District's requirement (as applied to respondent's handgun) that firearms in the home be rendered and kept inoperable at all times. This makes it impossible for citizens to use them for the core lawful purpose of self-defense and is hence unconstitutional....

In sum, we hold that the District's ban on handgun possession in the home violates the Second Amendment, as does its prohibition against rendering any lawful firearm in the home operable for the purpose of immediate self-defense. Assuming that Heller is not disqualified from the exercise of Second Amendment rights, the District must permit him to register his handgun and must issue him a license to carry it in the home.

. . .

We are aware of the problem of handgun violence in this country, and we take seriously the concerns raised by the many *amici* who believe that prohibition of handgun ownership is a solution. The Constitution leaves the District of Columbia a variety of tools for combating that problem, including some measures regulating handguns,.... But ... it is not the role of this Court to pronounce the Second Amendment extinct.

We affirm the judgment of the Court of Appeals.

It is so ordered.

Justice Stevens, with whom Justice Souter, Justice Ginsburg, and Justice Breyer join, dissenting.

The question presented by this case is not whether the Second Amendment protects a "collective right" or an "individual right." Surely it protects a right that can be enforced by individuals. But a conclusion that the Second Amendment protects an individual right does not tell us anything about the scope of that right.

Guns are used to hunt, for self-defense, to commit crimes, for sporting activities, and to perform military duties. The Second Amendment plainly does not protect the right to use a gun to rob a bank; it is equally clear that it *does* encompass the right to use weapons for certain military purposes. Whether it also protects the right to possess and use guns for nonmilitary purposes like hunting and personal self-defense is the question presented by this case. The text of the Amendment, its history, and our decision in *United States v. Miller*, 307 U. S. 174 (1939), provide a clear answer to that question.

The Second Amendment was adopted to protect the right of the people of each of the several States to maintain a well-regulated militia. It was a response to concerns raised during the ratification of the Constitution that the power of Congress to disarm the state militias and create a national standing army posed an intolerable threat to the sovereignty of the several States. Neither the text of the Amendment nor the arguments advanced by its proponents evidenced the slightest interest in limiting any legislature's authority to regulate private civilian uses of firearms. Specifically, there is no indication that the Framers of the Amendment intended to enshrine the common-law right of self-defense in the Constitution.

... The view of the Amendment we took in *Miller*—that it protects the right to keep and bear arms for certain military purposes, but that it does not curtail the Legislature's power to regulate the nonmilitary use and ownership of weapons—is both the most natural reading of the Amendment's text and the interpretation most faithful to the history of its adoption.

Since our decision in *Miller*, hundreds of judges have relied on the view of the Amendment we endorsed there; we ourselves affirmed it in 1980.... No new evidence has surfaced since 1980 supporting the view that the Amendment was intended to curtail the power of Congress to regulate civilian use or misuse of weapons. Indeed, a review of the drafting history of the Amendment demonstrates that its Framers *rejected* proposals that would have broadened its coverage to include such uses....

Even if the textual and historical arguments on both sides of the issue were evenly balanced, respect for the well-settled views of all of our predecessors on this Court, and for the rule of law itself, ... would prevent most jurists from endorsing such a dramatic upheaval in the law....

When each word in the text is given full effect, the Amendment is most naturally read to secure to the people a right to use and possess arms in conjunction with service in a well-regulated militia. So far as appears, no more than that was contemplated by its drafters or is encompassed within its terms....

Indeed, not a word in the constitutional text even arguably supports the Court's overwrought and novel description of the Second Amendment as "elevat[ing] above all other interests" "the right of law-abiding, responsible citizens to use arms in defense of hearth and home."...

For these reasons, I respectfully dissent.

JUSTICE BREYER, with whom JUSTICE STEVENS, JUSTICE SOUTER, and JUSTICE GINSBURG join, dissenting....

The majority's conclusion is wrong for two independent reasons. The first reason is that set forth by JUSTICE STEVENS ...

The second independent reason is that the protection the Amendment provides is not absolute. The Amendment permits government to regulate the interests that it serves. Thus, irrespective of what those interests are—whether they do or do not include an independent interest in self-defense—the majority's view cannot be correct unless it can show that the District's regulation is unreasonable or inappropriate in Second Amendment terms. This the majority cannot do.

... [T]he District's law is consistent with the Second Amendment even if that Amendment is interpreted as protecting a wholly separate interest in individual self-defense....

... The law is tailored to the urban crime problem in that it is local in scope and thus affects only a geographic area both limited in size and entirely urban; the law concerns handguns, which are specially linked to urban gun deaths and injuries, and which are the overwhelmingly favorite weapon of armed criminals; and at the same time, the law imposes a burden upon gun owners that seems proportionately no greater than restrictions in existence at the time the Second Amendment was adopted. In these circumstances, the District's law falls within the zone that the Second Amendment leaves open to regulation by legislatures....

With respect, I dissent.

NOTES AND QUESTIONS

1. Is it fair that someone can be prosecuted for the same crime in both federal and state courts? Why doesn't this violate the Double Jeopardy Clause?

2. Should the government be able to seize blood samples, handwriting samples, and compel presence at a police lineup? Should this be a violation of the Self-Incrimination Clause? Why or why not?

3. Why is compelled testimony, in the company of absolute immunity, not a violation of the Self-Incrimination Clause?

4. *Miranda* provides certain constitutional rights for someone held in police custody. What opportunities do law enforcement officials nonetheless have for obtaining incriminating evidence? Should they have those opportunities?

5. Should the meaning of the Eighth Amendment, particularly "cruel and unusual punishments," essentially be defined by public opinion and legislative action rather than by the U.S. Supreme Court? Does the "evolving standards of decency" test make sense to you?

6. Did the Court make the right decision in *D.C.* v. *Heller*? Do you think the Second Amendment should protect a collective right or a personal right? Are there any gun regulations that should be permitted?

SELECTED READINGS

ABRAMSON, JEFFREY. We the Jury: The Jury System and the Ideal of Democracy. Cambridge, MA: Harvard University Press, 2000.

AMAR, AKHIL REED. The Constitution and Criminal Procedure: First Principles. New Haven, Conn.: Yale University Press, 1997.

BEDAU, HUGO ADAM. ed. The Death Penalty in America. New York: Oxford University Press, 1982.

BLACK, CHARLES L. Capital Punishment: The Inevitability of Caprice and Mistake. New York: Norton, 1974.

BODENHAMER, DAVID J. Fair Trial: Rights of the Accused in American History. New York: Oxford University Press, 1992.

CLUTE, PENELOPE D. The Legal Aspects of Prisons and Jails. Springfield, Ill.: Charles C. Thomas, 1980.

EDWARDS, GEORGE J., JR. The Grand Jury. New York: AMS Press, 1973. Originally published in 1906.

FAIR, DARYL R. "Prison Reform by the Courts," in Richard A. L. Gambitta et al. Governing Through Courts. Beverley Hills, Calif.: Sage Publications, 1981.

FEELEY, MALCOLM M., AND EDWARD L. RUBIN. Judicial Policy Making and the Modern State: How the Courts Reformed America's Prisons. New York: Cambridge University Press, 1999.

FOX, SANFORD J. The Law of Juvenile Courts. St. Paul, Minn.: West, 1984.

FRANKEL, MARVIN E., AND GARY P. NAFTALIS. The Grand Jury. New York: Hill and Wang, 1975.

GOLDSTEIN, ABRAHAM S. The Passive Judiciary: Prosecutorial Discretion and the Guilty Plea. Baton Rouge: Louisiana State University Press, 1981.

GRAHAM, FRED P. The Self-Inflicted Wound. New York: Macmillan, 1970.

HALLIDAY, PAUL D. Habeas Corpus: From England to Empire. Cambridge, MA and London: The Belknap Press of Harvard University Press, 2010.

LEVY, LEONARD W. Origins of the Fifth Amendment. New York: Macmillan, 1986.

———. Against the Law: The Nixon Court and Criminal Justice. New York: Harper Torchbooks, 1976.

———. The Palladium of Justice: Origins of Trial by Jury. Chicago: Ivan R. Dee, 1999.

LEWIS, ANTHONY. Gideon's Trumpet. New York: Vintage, 1964.

MALCOLM, JOYCE LEE. To Keep and Bear Arms. Cambridge: Harvard University Press, 1996 ed.

MANFREDI, CHRISTOPHER P. The Supreme Court and Juvenile Justice. Lawrence: University Press of Kansas, 1998.

MANSFIELD, JOHN H. "The Albertson Case: Conflict between the Privilege Against Self-Incrimination and the Government's Need for Information." 1966 Supreme Court Review 103.

MELTSNER, MICHAEL. Cruel and Unusual: The Supreme Court and Capital Punishment. New York: William Morrow, 1974.

ORTH, JOHN V. Due Process of Law: A Brief History. Lawrence, KS: University Press of Kansas, 2003.

PAULSEN, MONRAD G. "The Constitutional Domestication of the Juvenile Court." 1967 Supreme Court Review 233.

POLSBY, DANIEL D. "The Death of Capital Punishment? Furman v. Georgia." 1972 Supreme Court Review 1.

SELLIN, THORSTEN. The Penalty of Death. Beverly Hills, Calif.: Sage Publications, 1980.

SIEGLER, ALISON AND BARRY SULLIVAN, "'Death is Different' No Longer: *Graham* v. *Florida* and the Future of Eighth Amendment Challenges to Noncapital Sentences." 2010 Supreme Court Review 327.

SIGLER, JAY A. Double Jeopardy: The Development of a Legal and Social Policy. Ithaca, N.Y.: Cornell University Press, 1969.

SPERLICH, PETER W. "Trial by Jury: It May Have a Future." 1978 Supreme Court Review 191.

SPITZER. ROBERT J. The Politics of Gun Control, 4th ed. Washington, DC: CQ Press, 2008.

WALKER, THOMAS G. Eligible for Execution: The Story of the Daryl Atkins Case. Washington, DC: CQ Press, 2009.

WESTEN, PETER, AND RICHARD DRUBEL. "Toward a General Theory of Double Jeopardy." 1978 Supreme Court Review 81.

WRIGHTSMAN, LAWRENCE S. AND MARY L. PITMA. The Miranda Ruling: Its Past, Present, and Future. New York: Oxford University Press, 2010.

14

Search and Seizure

No area of constitutional law is more unsettled, and unsettling, than Supreme Court decisions on search and seizure. The Court must apply eighteenth-century principles to such contemporary practices as automobile and aerial searches, the use of trained dogs to detect drugs, wiretaps of phone calls, heat-sensing devices, GPS devices, and increasingly sophisticated methods of electronic eavesdropping. Congress has had to legislate to protect the privacy of communication by cellular phones. What privacy should exist for computers, Internet service providers, software, and e-mail? All three branches of government have been active in defining the contours and content of the Fourth Amendment.

A. EXPECTATIONS OF PRIVACY

Several statutes passed by the First Congress affected what we know today as Fourth Amendment interests, but the Amendment itself was not ratified until 1791. Indeed, it would be years before the federal courts handed down decisions interpreting the Fourth Amendment. In the meantime, Congress formed its own judgments on the permissible limits of governmental searches and seizures.

Congress did not have to wait for the drafting of the Fourth Amendment to understand private citizens' resentment of governmental intrusion. The insistence on privacy in the home, captured in the maxim "a man's house is his castle," had been expressed for thousands of years.[1] The expectation of privacy within one's home is found in biblical law, the *Talmud,* and the *Code of Hammurabi.* The members of the First Congress understood this heritage. The Fourth Amendment specifically refers to the right of the individuals to be secure in their "houses."

The amendment is difficult to interpret in isolation because it often implicates other sections of the Constitution. The Fourth and Fifth Amendments "throw great light on each other. For the 'unreasonable searches and seizures' condemned in the Fourth Amendment are almost always made for the purpose of compelling a man to give evidence against himself, which in criminal cases is condemned by the Fifth Amendment...." Boyd v. United States, 116 U.S. 616, 633 (1886). The two Amendments sometimes "run almost into each other." Id. at 630. Cases lie at the "crossroads" of the Fourth and Fifth Amendments. Brown v. Illinois, 422 U.S. 590, 591 (1975). Searches and seizures also invoke more general constitutional interests, such as the privacy of the individual. In 1965 the Court asked: "Would we allow the police to search the sacred precincts of marital bedrooms for telltale signs of the use of contraceptives? The very idea is repulsive to the notions of privacy surrounding the marriage relationship." Griswold v. Connecticut, 381 U.S. 479, 485–86 (1965).

These complexities are compounded by the language of the Fourth Amendment: "The right of the people to be secure in their persons, houses, papers, and effects, against unreasonable searches and seizures, shall not be violated and no Warrants shall issue, but upon probable cause, supported by Oath or affirmation, and particularly describing the place to be searched, and the persons or things to be seized." It is more than a problem of defining "unreasonable" and "probable cause." Should the

---

1. Nelson B. Lasson, The History and Development of the Fourth Amendment to the United States Constitution 13 (1937).

Amendment be taken as a unit, requiring warrants for every search and seizure to make them reasonable? There are too many exceptions to the warrant requirement to accept that construction.

Does the Amendment split into two discrete halves, allowing warrantless searches and seizures (provided they are "reasonable") in the first clause, followed by a second clause that describes warrants if used? Some Justices appear to emphasize the first clause to the exclusion of the second, insisting on "reasonableness" but not warrants. These interpretations overlook the decisive break by America with British and colonial practices. Justice Bradley summarized the conditions that preceded the rupture with England:

> In order to ascertain the nature of the proceedings intended by the Fourth Amendment to the Constitution under the terms "unreasonable searches and seizures," it is only necessary to recall the contemporary or then recent history of the controversies on the subject, both in this country and in England. The practice had obtained in the colonies of issuing writs of assistance to the revenue officers, empowering them, in their discretion, to search suspected places for smuggled goods, which James Otis pronounced "the worst instrument of arbitrary power, the most destructive of English liberty, and the fundamental principles of law, that ever was found in an English law book;" since they placed "the liberty of every man in the hands of every petty officer." This was in February, 1761, in Boston, and the famous debate in which it occurred was perhaps the most prominent event which inaugurated the resistance of the colonies to the oppressions of the mother country. "Then and there," said John Adams, "then and there was the first scene of the first act of opposition to the arbitrary claims of Great Britain. Then and there the child Independence was born." Boyd v. United States, 116 U.S. 616, 625 (1886).

In 1772, a Committee of Correspondence in Boston prepared *The Rights of the Colonists* and added a long list of British actions that had infringed those rights. Collectors and other "petty officers" boarded vessels and entered homes and shops in the search for illegal merchandise: "Our houses and even our bed chambers, are exposed to be ransacked, our boxes chests & trunks broke open ravaged and plundered by wretches, whom no prudent man would venture to employ even as menial servants." 1 The Roots of the Bill of Rights 206 (Bernard Schwartz ed. 1980). By the time of independence, American states had begun to adopt their own bills of rights to include protections against unreasonable searches and seizures (see box on next page).

Although Americans were outraged by writs of assistance and the general search warrant, it has been settled practice throughout our history that warrants are not required for every search and seizure. Various exceptions exist, and the list lengthens with each passing decade. The following sections cover the warrant requirement, the exceptions to it, the technological problems of electronic eavesdropping, and the Court's doctrine of excluding illegally obtained evidence (the exclusionary rule).

B. ARREST AND SEARCH WARRANTS

It is customary for the Court to reiterate that "searches conducted outside the judicial process, without prior approval by judge or magistrate, are *per se* unreasonable under the Fourth Amendment— subject only to a few specifically established and well-delineated exceptions." Katz v. United States, 389 U.S. 347, 357 (1967). These "exceptions" have grown rapidly over the years.

For most of the Court's history, it has been axiomatic that the safeguards built into the Fourth Amendment depend upon warrants issued upon probable cause "by a neutral and detached magistrate." Constitutional liberties are not secure when relying on the judgments of the officer "engaged in the often competitive enterprise of ferreting out crime." To allow warrantless action by a law enforcement officer "would reduce the Amendment to a nullity and leave the people's homes secure only in the discretion of police officers." Johnson v. United States, 333 U.S. 10, 14 (1948). Searches and

---

Early State Provisions on Search and Seizure

The Virginia Bill of Rights of 1776: "general warrants, whereby an officer or messenger may be commanded to search suspected places without evidence of a fact committed, or to seize any person or persons not named, or whose offence is not particularly described and supported by evidence, are grievous and oppressive, and ought not to be granted."

The Declaration of Rights issued by Pennsylvania in 1776: "[T]he people have a right to hold themselves, their houses, papers, and possessions free from search and seizure, and therefore warrants without oaths or affirmation first made, affording a sufficient foundation for them, and whereby any officer or messenger may be commanded or required to search suspected places, or to seize any person or persons, his or their property, not particularly described are contrary to that right, and ought not to be granted."

The Massachusetts Declaration of Rights of 1780: "Every subject has a right to be secure from all unreasonable searches, and seizures, of his person, his houses, his papers, and all his possessions. All warrants, therefore, are contrary to this right, if the cause or foundation of them be not previously supported by oath or affirmation, and if the order in the warrant to a civil officer, to make search in suspected places, or to arrest one or more suspected persons, or to seize their property, be not accompanied with a special designation of the persons or objects of search, arrest, or seizure; and no warrant ought to be issued but in cases, and with the formalities prescribed by the laws."

The early constitutions of Maryland, New Hampshire, North Carolina, and Vermont also included safeguards against arbitrary searches and seizures.

---

seizures inside a house without a warrant "are presumptively unreasonable." Brigham City v. Stuart, 547 U.S. 398, 403 (2006), quoting Groh v. Ramirez, 540 U.S. 551, 559 (2004).

Grounds for Issuing a Warrant

To obtain a search warrant, a law enforcement officer must state in an affidavit the reasons for the search. The reasons must show probable cause; mere suspicion or belief is insufficient ground. If an affidavit merely asserts an officer's belief in the truth of statements made by others, without adequate reason to support the statements, the affidavit does not justify a search warrant. Before authorizing a warrant, a magistrate is required to find probable cause from facts or circumstances presented in the affidavit. These standards were substantially weakened in 1984 when the Court adopted the "good-faith" test that allowed the admission of evidence obtained from a search warrant even after it was later found to be unsupported by probable cause. United States v. Leon, 468 U.S. 897 (1984), discussed later in Section E.

Since searches are sometimes conducted incident to an arrest, an arrest warrant must also be based on an officer's personal knowledge and belief that someone has committed a crime. Giordenello v. United States, 357 U.S. 480 (1958). In determining probable cause and reasonable grounds, warrants may be based on information and hearsay supplied by informers who have a record of providing reliable tips and when officers verify the information through their own observations.[2] If a warrant is

---

2. Draper v. United States, 358 U.S. 307 (1959); Rugendorf v. United States, 376 U.S. 528 (1964). The magistrate must understand some of the underlying circumstances relied on by the informer and some of the underlying circumstances that prompt an officer to conclude that an informer is creditable and his or her information reliable. Aguilar v. Texas, 378 U.S. 108 (1964); United States v. Harris, 403 U.S. 573 (1971). A magistrate cannot authorize a warrant simply by accepting an informer's unsubstantiated tip. Spinelli v. United States, 393 U.S. 410 (1969); Whiteley v. Warden, 401 U.S. 560 (1971). Also on the importance of corroborating an informer's tip: Florida v. J.L., 529 U.S. 266 (2000); Alabama v. White, 496 U.S. 325 (1990).

deficient in some respect, the resulting search and seizure can be declared invalid. If law enforcement officers violate the terms of a warrant, the information obtained through the search can be held inadmissible in court. United States v. Jones, 565 U.S. ___ (2012).

The Fourth Amendment requires that a search warrant "particularly describe" the items to be seized. A magistrate may not authorize an open-ended search warrant and leave to the discretion of officials (even when he accompanies them) the decision of what objects to seize when they arrive. The warrant must specify the things to be seized at the time the warrant is issued, not after the search and seizure are complete. Lo-Ji Sales, Inc. v. New York, 442 U.S. 319 (1979). Under some circumstances, a defective warrant can nonetheless produce a valid conviction. In one case, several men transported stolen goods to a retail store, which was searched under a defective warrant. The men were unable to contest the admission of the seized evidence because they had no legitimate expectation of privacy or interest of any kind in the store. Brown v. United States, 411 U.S. 223 (1973). Law enforcement officers may be sued if their warrants are found lacking in what courts call objective reasonableness. Messerschmidt v. Millender, 565 U.S. ___ (2012); Groh v. Ramirez, 540 U.S. 551 (2004).

"Exigent Circumstances"

In 1980, the Supreme Court struck down a New York law that authorized police officers to enter a private residence without a warrant and using force, if necessary, to make a routine felony arrest. The statute allowed them to seize evidence after entry. The Court held that, absent "exigent circumstances," officers may not enter a home without a warrant. (Exigent refers to the need for immediate action, including the need to prevent destruction of evidence.) It is a basic principle of the Fourth Amendment that searches and seizures inside a home without a warrant are "presumptively unreasonable." Payton v. New York, 445 U.S. 573, 586 (1980). The Supreme Court cited *Payton* in a 1990 decision in holding, 7 to 2, that the police had no exigent circumstances to justify their warrantless entry into a house where a robbery suspect was an overnight guest. There was no risk that he would escape and he had a legitimate expectation of privacy as a guest. Minnesota v. Olson, 495 U.S. 91 (1990). *Payton* was weakened in another 1990 decision, *New York* v. *Harris*, discussed in Section E.

Although an overnight guest is protected by the Fourth Amendment, the same privilege does not extend to someone who is present in a person's house or apartment for a couple of hours (to bag cocaine). Minnesota v. Carter, 525 U.S. 83 (1998). In 2001, the Court held 8 to 1 that it was reasonable for police, while waiting for a search warrant, to briefly prevent a suspect from entering his house without a police escort. Illinois v. McArthur, 531 U.S. 326 (2001).

A warrantless nighttime entry into a home to arrest someone for a noncriminal, nonjailable traffic offense is prohibited by the Fourth Amendment. Welsh v. Wisconsin, 466 U.S. 740 (1984). Without consent or exigent circumstances, a law enforcement officer with an arrest warrant may not legally search for that person in the home of a third party (a party not suspected of a crime) without first obtaining a search warrant. The Court explained the broad potential for abuse. In one case the police, armed with an arrest warrant for two fugitives, searched 300 homes. Steagald v. United States, 451 U.S. 204, 215 (1981). A decision by the Court in 2011 further explored the meaning of "exigent circumstances." Kentucky v. King, 563 U.S. ___ (2011).

Congressional Safeguards

The question of third-party searches arose in a 1978 case involving a police search of a student newspaper that had taken photographs of a clash between demonstrators and police. A search warrant was issued to enter the newspaper offices to obtain the photographs and learn the identities of those who had assaulted police officers. The Court held that police are not prevented from issuing a search warrant simply because the owner of a place is not reasonably suspected of criminal involvement. Zurcher v. Stanford Daily, 436 U.S. 547 (1978). The Court invited the elected branches to participate by noting that the Fourth Amendment "does not prevent or advise against legislative or executive efforts to establish nonconstitutional protections against possible abuses of the search warrant procedure." Id. at 567. (The use of "nonconstitutional" is a judicial conceit that anything of a constitutional nature is exclusively for the courts.) Although Congress could not pass legislation to weaken the Fourth Amendment, it could act to strengthen its protections. S. Rept. No. 96-874, at 4.

The Court's decision was denounced by newspapers as "a first step toward a police state," an assault that "stands on its head the history of both the first and the fourth amendments" and posed a threat to the "privacy rights of the law-abiding." S. Rept. No. 96-874, at 5. In an amicus brief, Solicitor General Wade H. McCree argued that the use of a warrant to search third parties was constitutional and that there was no need to adopt a "subpoena-first" policy to obtain materials, even if the parties were newspapers with a First Amendment interest. After the uproar that greeted the Court's decision, the Carter administration realized it had miscalculated. McCree had a hobby of composing clever limericks. Robert J. Havel, at that time Deputy Director of Public Information for the Justice Department, applied his own hand to this craft:

> A solicitor known fondly as Wade
> Filed a brief supporting a raid
> By police on the premises
> Of a newspaper nemesis
> Said the press, what a big egg Wade laid.

Congress responded by passing a bill that limited newsroom searches. With certain exceptions, it required the use of a subpoena instead of a search warrant to obtain documentary materials from those who disseminate newspapers, books, broadcasts, or other similar forms of public communication. 94 Stat. 1879 (1980). The "dialogue" between Congress and the Court on constitutional matters is captured nicely in the floor debates (see reading).

The subpoena-first policy offers several advantages to newspapers. A subpoena involves a court hearing where the newspaper can state its case; search warrants are issued without any possibility of influence by a newspaper. Moreover, a subpoena allows the newspaper to produce the specific document requested, rather than having police officers enter the premises of a newsroom and disrupt operations while searching through file cabinets, desks, and wastebaskets.

Subpoenas have been used to obtain microfilms of checks, deposit slips, and other records from a bank account. In 1976, the Supreme Court held that a Fourth Amendment challenge in court could not prevail over this type of subpoena. The Court treated the materials as business records of a bank, not private papers of a person. The Court did not consider checks as confidential communications. The depositor took the risk that third parties could convey sensitive information to the government. United States v. Miller, 425 U.S. 435 (1976).

In short, private parties could not look to the courts for the protection of Fourth Amendment interests. Justice Brennan noted in a dissent that a depositor "reveals many aspects of his personal affairs, opinions, habits and associations. Indeed, the totality of bank records provides a virtual current biography." See also California Bankers Assn. v. Shultz, 416 U.S. 21 (1974). To protect citizens, Congress passed the Right to Financial Privacy Act of 1978. The statute allows notice to depositors before access is given to governmental agencies to review their financial records; gives the depositor an opportunity to challenge governmental access; and sets forth requirements for administrative subpoena or summons, search warrants, and judicial subpoena. The government can delay notice to the depositor only by obtaining an order from a judge or magistrate. 92 Stat. 3697. In this manner, certain Fourth Amendment safeguards rendered unavailable by the Supreme Court were secured by congressional action. The congressional debate on the Financial Privacy Act is reprinted in Chapter 17.

Congress Responds to *Zurcher*

In *Zurcher* v. *Stanford Daily*, 436 U.S. 547 (1978), the Supreme Court upheld the right of law enforcement officers to use a search warrant on the premises of a newspaper. The newspaper was not a suspected party to a crime. It was a "third party," and in previous cases third-party searches were subject to substantial restraints. This use of a search warrant against a newspaper created a collision between two values: First Amendment rights versus law enforcement needs. In response to *Zurcher,* Congress passed legislation in 1980 to offer greater protection to First Amendment interests. The debate below, from the House of Representatives, is taken from 126 Cong. Rec. 26561–64, 26567 (1980).

Mr. KASTENMEIER. Mr. Speaker, I move to suspend the rules and pass the bill (H.R. 3486) to limit governmental search and seizure of materials possessed by persons involved in first amendment activities, …

Mr. Speaker, sometimes a longstanding principle of constitutional jurisprudence is thrown into doubt by a decision of the Supreme Court which — while it may answer a narrow question based on specific facts — leaves Government officials and members of the public in doubt as to how to interpret the law. When this occurs it is often best for Congress to step in to fill the void, rather than to await the results of many years of potential litigation which will again redefine the principle. This is the case with respect to the matter before us today — legislation to redefine a portion of the law of search and seizure in response to the Supreme Court's decision in Zurcher against Stanford Daily in 1978.

Prior to Stanford Daily, the long established interpretation of the fourth amendment had held that a search warrant was considered to meet the constitutional ban on general searches only if the evidence sought constituted contraband, or fruits or instrumentalities of a crime. This rule was modified in 1967 in Warden against Hayden to permit searches for mere evidence, but the facts of that case involved evidence obtained incidental to an arrest.

In the Stanford Daily case the Supreme Court swept away 200 years of jurisprudence greatly limiting searches directed against innocent third parties. The opinion of the Court, delivered by Mr. Justice White, set forth a new theory governing third party searches — identifying the standard to be applied in issuing such warrants as one of "reasonableness." Further, while recognizing that any reasonableness requirement must be established with "scrupulous exactitude," where a newspaper was involved, the Court's opinion did not conclude that the first amendment placed any additional restraints on such searches.

The public and congressional response to the Supreme Court's decision was immediate. Newspaper editorials appeared all over the country condemning the Court's decision. And in Congress numerous members, of every ideological and political stripe, introduced remedial legislation. Meanwhile, the President ordered the Attorney General to study the issue and make a legislative recommendation to him. After consultation with constitutional scholars, civil libertarians, law enforcement authorities, and Cabinet officers, the President recommended H.R. 3486, the bill before us today.

As introduced the bill before you protected third parties from arbitrary searches only where first amendment interests were involved. However, with the exception of the Department of Justice, not a single witness in favor of the legislation testified that the protections of the bill should be limited to the press alone. In fact, the representatives of media organizations were among the strongest proponents of expanding the legislation to protect all innocent third parties from arbitrary search and seizure. A great deal of apprehension was expressed about singling out the press for special treatment.

As a result, when the committee met for markup it was agreed that the legislation should be extended to provide guidance to Federal law enforcement officials as to the circumstances under which search warrants should be used to obtain information from innocent third parties other than those engaged in first amendment activities. However, because of the constitutional and policy implications of regulating the police powers of State and local authorities, the committee decided to limit the applicability of any broader third party provisions of the bill to searches by Federal officials only. Of course, we would hope that State legislatures would follow suit, and indeed eight States have already enacted similar legislation. With respect to searches directed against persons preparing materials for broadcast or publication, we retained the features of the original bill — which apply to State and local as well as Federal officials. The justification involved is the historic obligation of the Federal Government to protect the free speech values of the first amendment....

Mr. HYDE. Mr. Speaker, I rise in reluctant support of this legislation. Since the moment it emerged from the Subcommittee on Courts, Civil Liberties, and the Administration of Justice, I opposed a provision then contained in section 3 of the bill and which was designed to extend the "subpena-first" rule to "all innocent third parties." At that time, I offered an amendment to strike that section and fully intended to join with my colleague from the other side, Mr. DANIELSON from California, in offering an amendment on the floor to remove that portion of the bill. The Justice Department has since withdrawn its support for this amendment and so I will not offer it.

As has been stated, this legislation is principally designed to protect the public's right to know. It is not designed to make a sweeping change in constitutional law regarding the probable cause standard contained in the fourth amendment. In Zurcher against Stanford Daily, 436 U.S. 597 (1978), the Court held that the fourth amendment's minimal requirement for the issuance of a search warrant is probable cause to believe the evidence exists where you wish to search. Congress, of course, has the power to broaden and build upon that standard. This is what we have done with the creation of the "subpena first" rule now contained in the bill. By this procedure, law enforcement authorities must seek a subpena first before resorting to the issuance of a search warrant....

C. EXCEPTIONS TO THE WARRANT REQUIREMENT

As already explained, law enforcement officials may make warrantless arrests and searches by relying on "exigent circumstances." There are eleven other exceptions: (1) border searches, (2) consent, (3) "hot pursuit" and no-knock entry, (4) the "plain-view" doctrine, (5) automobiles, (6) "stop and frisk," (7) search incident to arrest, (8) administrative inspections, (9) drug tests, (10) students, and (11) civil forfeiture. Each exception has its own unique, evolutionary history of complex line drawing.

Border Searches

Long before the Supreme Court discovered exceptions to the warrant requirement, Congress and the executive branch decided that warrants were not necessary for border searches. As the Supreme Court noted in 1985: "Since the founding of our Republic, Congress has granted the Executive plenary authority to conduct routine searches and seizures at the border, without probable cause or a warrant, in order to regulate the collection of duties and to prevent the introduction of contraband into this country." United States v. Montoya de Hernandez, 473 U.S. 531, 535 (1985). A statute in 1789 authorized federal officials to enter any ship or vessel suspected of having concealed goods or merchandise and to search and seize such goods. 1 Stat. 43, § 24. Under contemporary law, any officer authorized to board or search vessels may examine any person on whom he "shall suspect there is merchandise which is subject to duty, or shall have been introduced into the United States in any manner contrary to law ... and to search any trunk or envelope, wherever found, in which he may have a reasonable cause to suspect there is merchandise which was imported contrary to law." Such merchandise shall be seized and held for trial. 19 U.S.C. § 482.

These laws reflect the judgment of the legislative and executive branches that the expectation of privacy in the interior of the country does not apply to the borders where smuggling and illegal entry are chronic problems. The authority of the United States to search baggage "of arriving international travelers is based on its inherent sovereign authority to protect its territorial integrity." Torres v. Puerto Rico, 442 U.S. 465, 472–73 (1979). Common carriers (such as airlines) have a right to inspect packages to assure that they do not contain contraband or explosive substances. Illinois v. Andreas, 463 U.S. 765, 769 n.1 (1983). (Border searches for illegal aliens are also discussed in the section entitled "Automobiles.")

The First Congress established a number of precedents for warrantless searches and seizures at the border. 1 Stat. 164, § 31; 19 U.S.C. § 1581(a). Upon reviewing the constitutionality of a statute that authorized warrantless border searches, Justice Rehnquist traced the law back to 1790 and agreed that "the enactment of this statute by the same Congress that promulgated the constitutional Amendments that ultimately became the Bill of Rights gives the statute an important historical pedigree." United States v. Villamonte-Marquez, 462 U.S. 579, 585 (1983). Acting under this statutory authority, customs officials may board vessels without any suspicion of wrongdoing. All persons coming into the United States from foreign countries "shall be liable to detention and search" by authorized federal officers or agents. 19 U.S.C. § 1582.

Border officials must now contend with smugglers who swallow drug capsules or cocaine-filled balloons and condoms. When officials suspected one woman of being a "balloon swallower," attempting what is called alimentary canal smuggling, they held her for 16 hours during which time they considered sending her home, performing an x-ray (which she refused), and conducting a test to check her claim of being pregnant (the test proved negative). Nature eventually took its course. Over a four-day period she discharged 88 cocaine-filled balloons. The Court regarded the officials' actions as permissible under the Fourth Amendment. United States v. Montoya de Hernandez, 473 U.S. 531 (1985).

Search and Seizure Abroad. A decision by the Supreme Court in 1990 addressed the question of whether the Fourth Amendment applies to a search and seizure by U.S. agents in a foreign country. The Drug Enforcement Administration (DEA), working with Mexican officials, searched the Mexican residences of a Mexican suspect and seized certain documents. A 6–3 Court held that the Fourth Amendment does not apply to searches and seizures by U.S. agents of property owned by a nonresident alien and located in a foreign country. Although no judicial remedies are available to limit these actions by U.S. agents, the Court noted: "If there are to be restrictions on searches and seizures which occur incident to such American action, they must be imposed by the political branches through diplomatic understanding, treaty, or legislation." United States v. Verdugo-Urquidez, 494 U.S. 259 (1990).

Two years later the Court decided whether the U.S. government may kidnap people from foreign countries to bring them here for trial. In what is called the Ker-Frisby doctrine, the Court had earlier tolerated illegal abductions from abroad for the purpose of bringing a suspect to trial in a U.S. court. Ker v. Illinois, 119 U.S. 436 (1886); Frisbie v. Collins, 342 U.S. 519 (1952). The case in 1992 concerned kidnapping someone from Mexico. Voting 6–3, the Court concluded that the abduction did not violate an extradition treaty between the United States and Mexico. Writing for the majority, Chief Justice Rehnquist noted that the treaty "says nothing about the obligations of the United States and Mexico to refrain from forcible abductions of people from the territory of the other nation, or the consequences under the Treaty if such an abduction occurs." United States v. Alvarez-Machain, 504 U.S. 655, 663 (1992). Under this interpretation, the treaty would have to prohibit kidnappings explicitly. In his dissent, Justice Stevens said that Rehnquist's reasoning would permit the United States "to torture or simply to execute a person rather than to attempt extradition," because those actions are not explicitly prohibited by the treaty either. Stevens warned that the U.S. example invites other countries to attempt their own kidnappings. The decision provoked the charge from domestic critics and foreign countries that U.S. Presidents could act in defiance of international law, an impression that the Bush and Clinton administrations attempted to dispel (see box on next page).

Alvarez-Machain sued the United States and a Mexican police officer for his kidnapping. The Court held that foreigners have a right to seek compensation in federal court for abuses that occur abroad, but announced guidelines to limit judicial interference with foreign affairs. A unanimous Court ruled that Alvarez-Machain could not sue the federal government for false arrest under the Federal Tort Claims Act, but split 6 to 3 in upholding civil suits under the Alien Tort Statute, first enacted in 1789. Sosa v. Alvarez-Machain, 542 U.S. 692 (2004).

Consent

Fourth Amendment protections may be waived if a person's consent is voluntary and without coercion. Johnson v. United States, 333 U.S. 10, 13 (1948). In one case, government agents entered a sus-

Elected Branch Response to *Alvarez-Machain*

On the very day that the Supreme Court decided *Alvarez-Machain*, Press Secretary Marlin Fitzwater attempted to defuse the impact of the ruling by announcing that the United States strongly believes in "fostering respect for international rules of law, including in particular the principles of respect for territorial integrity and sovereign equality of states." Neither Alvarez-Machain's arrest nor the Court's decision reflected any change in U.S. policy "to cooperate with foreign states in achieving law enforcement objectives." Public Papers of the Presidents, 1992–93, I, at 940–41.

Within a week of the Court's ruling, a subcommittee of the House Judiciary Committee held hearings on the legality of abducting foreign nationals. The experts who testified were strongly critical of the Court's decision and the practice of transborder abductions. "Kidnapping Suspects Abroad," hearings before the Subcommittee on Civil and Constitutional Rights of the House

Committee on the Judiciary, 102d Cong., 2d Sess. (1992). Legislation was proposed to prohibit international kidnapping. Because of the critical response to the Court's ruling, negotiations began between U.S. and Mexican government officials. President Bush announced to the Mexican government that the United States would not engage in transborder abductions, although leaving open the possibility that abductions might occur in extreme cases.

Negotiations between the United States and Mexico continued with the Clinton administration, resulting on November 24, 1994, in the Treaty to Prohibit Transborder Abductions. However, the treaty was never submitted to the U.S. Senate. For further details, see William J. Aceves, "The Legality of Transborder Abductions: A Study of *United States* v. *Alvarez-Machain*," 3 Southwestern Journal of Law & Trade in the Americas 101 (1996).

pect's home without a search warrant or arrest warrant but with his wife's permission. The Court held that his constitutional rights had not been waived when his wife, under implied coercion, allowed the agents to enter. Amos v. United States, 255 U.S. 313 (1921). Under other circumstances the Court has allowed a wife or third party to admit officers to make a full search and find incriminating evidence if consent has been given voluntarily. United States v. Matlock, 415 U.S. 164 (1974).

Following the reasoning in *Matlock,* a 6–3 Court in 1990 decided that evidence from a warrantless search could be introduced at trial if the police were allowed to enter a home by someone they "reasonably believed" had authority to consent to the search, even if it was later discovered that the person *lacked* authority. Illinois v. Rodriguez, 497 U.S. 177 (1990). In a 2006 case, the police seized evidence in a home with the permission of one occupant (the wife), but the other occupant (the husband) refused consent. Unlike *Matlock* and other cases, the co-tenant here was present and expressly withheld his consent. On that ground the Court held the warrantless search to be unreasonable. Georgia v. Randolph, 547 U.S. 103 (2006).

In 1991, another 6–3 decision by the Court held that police officers looking for illicit drugs may board buses and ask passengers for permission to search their bags. The Court considered such encounters "consensual" if passengers felt free to disregard the police and go about their business. The dissenters argued that passengers would feel intimidated by the police and unable to assert their constitutional rights fully. Florida v. Bostick, 501 U.S. 429 (1991).

On the other hand, the Court has held that bus passengers have a legitimate expectation of privacy that their carry-on bags will not be manipulated by law enforcement officers in their search for contraband. Bond v. United States, 529 U.S. 334 (2000). Building on *Bostick*, the Court later held that police officers, in seeking to search and question passengers on public buses, need not tell them they have a right to refuse to cooperate. A 6–3 Court concluded that a "reasonable person" would know that refusal was allowed. United States v. Drayton, 536 U.S. 194 (2002). The dissenters said that such searches are reasonable at airports, because of terrorist threats, but less justified for ground transportation.

The use of undercover agents complicates the notion of consent. A federal narcotics agent, by misrepresenting his identity and expressing his willingness to buy narcotics, was invited into the home of a drug dealer. There was no question of entrapment; the agent did not encourage or stimulate a crime. The Court decided that the dealer, by opening his home as a place of illegal business, had surrendered any expectation of privacy. Lewis v. United States, 385 U.S. 206 (1966).

"Hot Pursuit" and No-Knock Entry

A 1967 decision by the Supreme Court dealt with an armed robbery suspect who, police learned, had entered a certain house. The police arrived minutes later and were told at the door of the house, by the suspect's wife, that she had no objection to their searching the house. Her consent alone did not justify the resulting search. The police acted reasonably by entering the house and searching for the suspect and for weapons he had used in the robbery or might use against them. The Fourth Amendment did not require the police to delay the investigation and endanger their lives or the lives of others. "Speed here was essential, and only a thorough search of the house for persons and weapons could have insured that [the suspect] was the only man present and that the police had control of all weapons which could be used against them or to effect an escape." Warden v. Hayden, 387 U.S. 294, 298–99 (1967).

The Court also expanded the police power by rejecting the "mere evidence" rule. Previous decisions had allowed police to seize the instrumentalities of a crime (weapons, stolen property) but prohibited the seizure of "merely evidentiary materials." The Court now rejected that distinction by allowing the officers to seize certain clothing items that were later used to convict the suspect. The Court held that privacy is not disturbed to any greater degree by a search directed to a purely evidentiary object than by a search directed to an instrumentality or contraband. Id. at 301–02.

Another case concerned a woman suspected of selling narcotics. When the police approached her to make an arrest, she was standing in the doorway holding a paper bag. As she retreated into the house they followed, finding envelopes containing heroin and marked money. The Court held that standing in the doorway put her in a "public place" with no expectation of privacy. United States v. Santana, 427 U.S. 38 (1976).

The Court recognizes that under some circumstances (e.g., the belief that evidence might be destroyed if advance notice is given) the "knock and announce" principle is not always required. Wilson v. Arkansas, 514 U.S. 927 (1995). No-knock entry may be necessary to prevent the destruction of evidence, Richards v. Wisconsin, 520 U.S. 385 (1997), even when property is damaged by the entry, United States v. Ramirez, 523 U.S. 65 (1998).

The Court split 5 to 4 in 2006 in deciding that violation of the "knock and announce" rule does not require suppression of evidence found in a search. Hudson v. Michigan, 547 U.S. 586 (2006). This decision is further discussed at the end of Section E on the exclusionary rule. Also in 2006, a unanimous Court supported another exception to the knock-and-announce rule. Brigham City v. Stuart, 547 U.S. 398 (2006).

"Plain-View" Doctrine

Following a brutal murder of a 14-year-old girl, the police went to the suspect's home to question him. On later visits they questioned his wife and eventually arrested him. The police searched his car without a warrant, arguing that it was an instrumentality of the crime and could be seized on his property "because it was in plain view." The Supreme Court reviewed previous holdings on the plain-view doctrine and concluded that the police officer in each of them had a justification for an intrusion "in the course of which he came inadvertently across a piece of evidence incriminating the accused." There has to be some valid reason for the officer's presence, for otherwise the doctrine would invite a general exploratory search without a warrant. When the police know in advance the location of the evidence and intend to seize it, a warrant should be obtained. In this case the police had ample oppor-

State Courts Dispute the Merits of *Greenwood*

After the Supreme Court in *California* v. *Greenwood*(1988) upheld a police search of trash left out for a pickup, some state courts required law enforcement officials to obtain a warrant first before searching garbage. In reaching that conclusion in 1990, the New Jersey Supreme Court noted that when it interprets the state constitution, "we look for direction to the United States Supreme Court, ... But although that Court may be a polestar that guides us as we navigate the New Jersey Constitution, we bear ultimate responsibility for the safe passage of our ship. Our eyes must not be so fixed on that star that we risk the welfare of our passengers on the shoals of constitutional doctrine. In interpreting the New Jersey Constitution, we must look in front of us as well as above us."

The New Jersey Supreme Court pointed out that for "most of our country's history, the primary source of protection of individual rights has been state constitutions, not the federal Bill of Rights." Whenever the U.S. Constitution offers citizens less protection than a state constitution, "we have not merely the authority to give full effect to the State protection, we have a duty to do so." State v. Hempele, 576 A.2d 793, 800 (N.J. 1990). The Supreme Court of Washington also held, contrary to *Greenwood*, that the removal of garbage by law enforcement officials for the purpose of obtaining evidence is an unreasonable intrusion upon private affairs. State v. Boland, 800 P.2d 1112 (Wash. 1990).

tunity to obtain a warrant and failed to do so, making the seizure and subsequent search of the car unconstitutional. COOLIDGE v. NEW HAMPSHIRE, 403 U.S. 443, 464–73 (1971).

The issue of "inadvertence" in *Coolidge* was replayed in 1990 in a 7–2 opinion of the Court. A police officer, having obtained a search warrant to look for property stolen during an armed robbery, did not find the goods but saw weapons in plain view and seized them. The Court held that the Fourth Amendment does not prohibit the warrantless seizure of evidence in plain view even though the discovery of the evidence was not inadvertent. The Court reached this conclusion despite the Fourth Amendment requirement that warrants "particularly describ[e] the place to be searched, and the persons or things to be seized." Horton v. California, 496 U.S. 128 (1990).

The plain-view doctrine allows limited searches and seizures following a fire. In one case, after a fire had been brought under control, firefighters discovered containers of a flammable liquid. A police detective took some pictures, and the fire chief and the detective removed the containers. Subsequent visits produced additional evidence and information. At no time was there a warrant. The Supreme Court upheld the removal of the containers without a warrant, as well as materials taken the following morning, but later visits (some coming a month later) required a warrant. A burning building is "an exigency of sufficient proportions" to permit a warrantless entry, and once inside the building firefighters "may seize evidence of arson that is in plain view." Michigan v. Tyler, 436 U.S. 499, 509 (1978). Some state courts have rejected the U.S. Supreme Court's doctrine on "plain view" (see the box in Chapter 1, Section G)

Trash. In 1988, the Court ruled that police do not need a warrant to look through trash left on a curb for a pickup, and through that examination discover evidence that supports a search warrant for narcotics use. The owner of the trash has no reasonable expectation of privacy. California v. Greenwood, 486 U.S. 35 (1988). Some state courts, interpreting their own constitutions, decided that *Greenwood* intrudes too much on privacy interests (see box).

Open Fields. Related to the plain-view exception is the "open-field" doctrine, which permits police officers to enter and search a field without a warrant. Hester v. United States, 265 U.S. 57 (1924). The term "effects" in the Fourth Amendment is considered less inclusive than property, permitting law enforcement officers to bypass locked gates and "No Trespassing" signs to discover marijuana growing in open fields. The Court reasons that open fields are accessible to the public and to the police in ways that a home, office, or commercial structure are not. Oliver v. United States, 466 U.S. 170 (1984). Similarly, police may cross a series of fences to look in a barn that is not considered to be protected by the Fourth Amendment. United States v. Dunn, 480 U.S. 294 (1987).

Aerial Searches. Two cases in 1986 expanded the government's authority under the open-field or plain-view doctrines. In one, the Court upheld the authority of the Environmental Protection Agency to use aerial observation and photography to implement the Clean Air Act. Without a warrant, EPA agents took aerial photographs of an industrial plant complex. Dow Chemical Co. v. United States, 476 U.S. 227 (1986). In the second, law enforcement officers flew over a suspect's house at an altitude of 1,000 feet and identified marijuana plants growing in the yard. On the basis of these observations, they obtained a search warrant. The Court, divided 5–4, ruled that the suspect had no expectation of privacy from *all* observations of his backyard. CALIFORNIA v. CIRAOLO, 476 U.S. 207 (1986). This case invited variations on the theme, such as flying over at even lower altitudes or using police helicopters to hover over a suspect's home or outside an apartment window. In 1989 the Court (again divided 5–4) upheld the use of police helicopters to conduct surveillance from a height of 400 feet above a greenhouse in a residential backyard. Florida v. Riley, 488 U.S. 445 (1989).

Automobiles

No exception to the warrant requirement contains as many permutations and perturbations as the exception for automobiles. The automobile exception illustrates how the constitutionality of an issue can be shaped by the executive and legislative branches. From an early date, congressional statutes and Attorney General opinions agreed that government agents could make warrantless searches and seizures of ships, automobiles, and other vehicles that could be easily moved outside the jurisdiction of an officer by the time he obtained a warrant. 1 Stat. 43, §24 (1789); 26 Op. Att'y Gen. 243 (1907). This justification appears in the first Supreme Court decision on automobile searches. If law enforcement officers had probable cause to stop a car, they could search it without a warrant and seize its contents without violating the Fourth Amendment. The Court regarded its decision as consistent with the intent of Congress in the National Prohibition Act.[3]

The Court struggled to find reasonable boundaries for car searches. If evidence is in plain sight of an officer who has a right to be in a position of viewing it, the material can be introduced in evidence without a warrant.[4] Incriminating evidence can be taken from the exterior of an automobile without a search warrant. Cardwell v. Lewis, 417 U.S. 583 (1974). Even when a car is impounded at a police station or towed to a garage, with no risk of its being moved or its contents taken, a warrantless search of the *interior* is valid. The Court reasons that such searches are necessary to inventory the vehicle's contents and to prevent dangerous weapons or materials from falling into the hands of vandals.[5] If inventory searches are insufficiently regulated to prevent "a general rummaging in order to discover incriminating evidence," the evidence will be suppressed. Florida v. Wells, 495 U.S. 1 (1990).

Leather Briefcases vs. Cardboard Boxes. Some decisions suggested that the right to privacy in automobiles exists for such items as personal luggage, especially when fortified by double locks. United States v. Chadwick, 433 U.S. 1 (1977); Arkansas v. Sanders, 442 U.S. 753 (1979). That line of argument, however, was ill-fated. Justice Blackmun warned that left "hanging in limbo, and probably soon to be litigated, are the briefcase, the wallet, the package, the paper bag, and every other kind of con-

---

3. Carroll v. United States, 267 U.S. 132 (1925). See also Husty v. United States, 282 U.S. 694 (1931) and Brinegar v. United States, 338 U.S. 160 (1949). If a car could have been searched on the streets, officers may follow it into a garage and search it there. Scher v. United States, 305 U.S. 251 (1938).

4. Texas v. Brown, 460 U.S. 730 (1983); Colorado v. Bannister, 449 U.S. 1 (1980); Harris v. United States, 390 U.S. 234 (1968).

5. See Colorado v. Bertine, 479 U.S. 367 (1987); Illinois v. Lafayette, 462 U.S. 640 (1983); Michigan v. Thomas, 458 U.S. 259 (1982); South Dakota v. Opperman, 428 U.S. 364, 369 (1976); Texas v. White, 423 U.S. 67 (1975); Cady v. Dombrowski, 413 U.S. 433, 448 (1973); Chambers v. Maroney, 399 U.S. 42 (1970).

The *Ross* Doctrine

Police with probable cause stopped a car, searched the driver, and searched the interior of the car. After arresting the driver, they opened the car's trunk and discovered a closed brown paper bag. Inside they found glassine bags containing a white powder, later determined to be heroin. They drove the car to police headquarters and conducted another warrantless search, opening a zippered leather pouch.

The Supreme Court held that police officers who have legitimately stopped an automobile and have probable cause to believe that it contains contraband may conduct a warrantless search that is as thorough as a magistrate could authorize by warrant. United States v. Ross, 456 U.S. 798 (1982). The Court insisted that the decision was "faithful to the interpretation of the Fourth Amendment that the Court has followed with substantial consistency throughout our history." Id. at 824. And yet it effectively repealed the Fourth Amendment warrant requirement for automobile searches and the traditional reliance on a neutral and detached magistrate. The Court did not explain why a search warrant could not be obtained after arresting a suspect and immobilizing the car.

In 1999, the Court (divided 7 to 2) upheld the search of an automobile when police had probable cause that it contained illegal drugs. Under those circumstances, it was not necessary to obtain a search warrant, even if there was time. Maryland v. Dyson, 527 U.S. 465 (1999).

States may reject the *Ross* doctrine by adopting standards that offer owners of automobiles greater protection against searches and seizures. E.g., State v. Ringer, 674 P.2d 1240 (Wash. 1983).

---

tainer." 442 U.S. at 768. Within a few years the Court decided that officers needed a search warrant before opening packages wrapped in green opaque plastic. Clearly the Court did not want to make what might appear to be class distinctions, upholding the right of privacy for a leather briefcase but denying it for a cardboard box: "What one person may put into a suitcase, another may put into a paper bag." Robbins v. California, 453 U.S. 420, 426 (1981). Justice Powell criticized the law on automobile searches as "intolerably confusing." Id. at 430.

The latitude for automobile searches continues to widen. As an incident to a lawful arrest, a police officer may reach into the interior of a car, remove a jacket, and unzip one of the pockets to discover cocaine. The search was valid because incident to a lawful custodial arrest. New York v. Belton, 453 U.S. 454 (1981). However, if a police officer stopped a car without probable cause or reasonable suspicion, the seizure of contraband—even if in plain view—was unreasonable under the Fourth Amendment. Delaware v. Prouse, 440 U.S. 648 (1979). If passengers in an automobile are unable to show ownership of the car or its contents, they have no standing to raise vicarious Fourth Amendment challenges to a search. Rakas v. Illinois, 439 U.S. 128 (1978). The major expansion of automobile searches came in 1982 (see box). UNITED STATES v. ROSS, 456 U.S. 798.

In 1991, a 6–3 court held that when a police search extends only to a container within an automobile and police have probable cause to believe that the container holds contraband or evidence, they may search the container without a warrant. California v. Acevedo, 500 U.S. 565 (1991). Another 1991 decision ruled that when an individual gives a police officer consent to search a car, the officer may search all items within the car, including a folded paper bag. Florida v. Jimeno, 500 U.S. 248 (1991). In 1991, the Supreme Court of Vermont rejected *Acevedo* and held that the type of seizure at issue in that case was impermissible under the state constitution. State v. Savva, 616 A.2d 774 (Vt. 1991).

The Court allows the government to seize trucks suspected of containing marijuana and, three days later, search the packages without a search warrant. United States v. Johns, 469 U.S. 478 (1985). When police have probable cause to believe that an automobile contains contraband and it is sitting in a public place, they may seize it without a warrant. Florida v. White, 526 U.S. 559 (1999). The freedom of police officers to search a car extends to mobile motor homes parked in a lot. The Court has largely replaced the mobility rationale of *Carroll* with the argument that the expectation of privacy in a car or motor home is significantly less than for a home or office. New York v. Class, 475 U.S. 106 (1986); California v. Carney, 471 U.S. 386 (1985).

In 2009, a 5–4 Court ruled that law enforcement officers had been misinterpreting *New York* v. *Belton* (1981) to permit the search of a suspect's car after he had been arrested and held in custody outside his vehicle. Following the reasoning in *Chimel* v. *California*(1969), discussed later in the section "Search Incident to Arrest," the Court held that the police may search incident to arrest only the space within an arrestee's "immediate control." The majority consisted of an unusual alliance of Justices: Stevens joined by Scalia, Souter, Thomas, and Ginsburg. Arizona v. Gant, 556 U.S. 332 (2009).

Minor Traffic Violations. In 1996, a unanimous Court ruled that police officers may stop motorists for minor traffic violations and use that opportunity to search for evidence of drug trafficking. The drugs can be seized and used for prosecution even if the officers had no probable cause to suspect illegal drug-dealing activity. Whren v. United States, 517 U.S. 805 (1996). Two years later a unanimous Court held that police may not stop a motorist for speeding and use that occasion to conduct a full search of the car. Knowles v. Iowa, 526 U.S. 113 (1998). The next year the Court reviewed a case in which a patrol officer stopped someone for speeding and driving with a faulty break light. The officer noticed a hypodermic syringe in the shirt pocket of the driver, who admitted that he used the syringe to take drugs. At that point the officer had probable cause to search the automobile. He looked into the passenger's purse and found drugs and drug paraphernalia. Divided 6 to 3, the Court upheld looking into the purse, reading *Ross* broadly to permit the police to discover contraband. Wyoming v. Houghton, 526 U.S. 295 (1999). In 2001, the Court split 5 to 4 in holding that the police may arrest a motorist for a minor offense (failure to wear a seat belt) and use that occasion to search the vehicle. Atwater v. Lago Vista, 532 U.S. 318 (2001).

In 1996, the Court held that when police officers stop motorists for speeding violations they need not tell them they are "free to go" before questioning them on other matters or searching their cars for drugs. Ohio v. Robinette, 519 U.S. 33 (1996). Justice Ginsburg in a concurrence and Justice Stevens in a dissent pointed out that states, in interpreting their constitutions, could prevent the type of search condoned by the Supreme Court. When a car is lawfully stopped, a police officer may not only order the driver to step out of the car but the passengers as well. Maryland v. Wilson, 519 U.S. 408 (1997); Pennsylvania v. Mimms, 434 U.S. 106 (1977).

After delivering hints in such cases as Delaware v. Prouse (1979), United States v. Hensley (1985), California v. Hodari D. (1991), and Whren v. United States (1996), a unanimous Court in 2007 held that when police make a traffic stop, a passenger in the car, like the driver, is seized for Fourth Amendment purposes and may challenge the stop's constitutionality. Brendlin v. California, 551 U.S. 249 (2007).

Checkpoints. Several automobile cases concern the use of roving patrols and checkpoints near the Mexican border to discover contraband or illegal aliens. Unless there is probable cause or consent, a roving patrol may not conduct a warrantless search of a car 25 air miles north of the Mexican border. Almeida-Sanchez v. United States, 413 U.S. 266 (1973). A roving patrol may not stop vehicles near the Mexican border and question the occupants about their citizenship and immigration status simply because they appear to be of Mexican ancestry. If an officer's observations lead him to suspect that a vehicle contains illegal aliens, he may stop a car briefly and investigate the circumstances that provoked his suspicion. United States v. Brignoni-Ponce, 422 U.S. 873 (1975); United States v. Cortez, 449 U.S. 411 (1981).

Fixed checkpoints present a different issue. Patrol officers at these sites, located away from the border, may stop vehicles and inquire about citizenship without consent or probable cause, but may not search the interior of a vehicle. United States v. Ortiz, 422 U.S. 891 (1975); United States v. Martinez-Fuerte, 428 U.S. 543 (1976). When vehicles use side roads to avoid a checkpoint, and other facts indicate likely drug smuggling, Border Patrol agents have reasonable cause to stop the vehicle. United States v. Arvizu, 534 U.S. 266 (2002).

In 1990, a 6–3 decision by the Court held that highway sobriety checkpoints are constitutional. Although roadblocks to catch drunk drivers are seizures under the Fourth Amendment, they are a "reasonable" technique for responding to "alcohol-related death and mutilation on the Nation's roads." Michigan State Police Dept. v. Sitz, 496 U.S. 444, 451 (1990). However, a decade later a 6–3 Court held that government could not create checkpoints— as part of a drug-interdiction effort— and stop all cars without a basis to suspect individual wrongdoing. The purpose of the checkpoint in *Sitz* (ensuring roadway safety) was not present here. Indianapolis v. Edmond, 531 U.S. 32 (2000).

GPS Devices. In 2012, the Court held that when the government installs on a suspect's automobile a Global-Positioning-System (GPS) tracking device, it constitutes a Fourth Amendment "search." These devices permit the government to minutely monitor an individual's public movements, revealing trips that may be of a very private and embarrassing nature, including to an abortion clinic, an AIDS treatment center, a strip club, a by-the-hour motel, and a gay bar. Citing an earlier ruling, the Court concluded that a vehicle is an "effect" as that term is used in the amendment. United States v. Jones, 565 U.S. ___, ___ (2012). Although the government obtained a warrant to install the device, it failed to abide by the magistrate's order. Therefore, the information the government recovered from the device could not be used at trial against the accused. There were no dissents in this decision, but five Justices in their concurrences offered substantially different interpretations about the Fourth Amendment's application to this type of governmental intrusion into personal vehicles.

"*Terry* Stops"

A police officer has a right to "stop and frisk" an individual who is behaving suspiciously, even though there is no probable cause to make an arrest. Whenever a "reasonably prudent officer" believes that his safety or that of others is endangered, he may make a reasonable search for weapons of the person he thinks armed and dangerous. He need not have probable cause for arrest or an absolute certainty that the individual is armed. The Court recognizes that officers on the beat may have to take swift action and make on-the-spot decisions. TERRY v. OHIO, 392 U.S. 1 (1968).[6]

Terry now permits "protective sweeps" in private homes when the searching officer acts with an arrest warrant and has reasonable belief that the areas to be swept may harbor individuals posing a danger to the police. Maryland v. Buie, 494 U.S. 325 (1990). A *Terry* investigatory stop is permissible when based on an anonymous tip corroborated by independent police work. Alabama v. White, 496 U.S. 325 (1990). A unanimous Court upheld a *Terry*-stop to seize non-threatening contraband. Minnesota v. Dickerson, 508 U.S. 366 (1993).

The Fourth Amendment limits on-the-spot decisions by police who use deadly force against unarmed, fleeing suspects. Here the suspect was shot in the back of the head running away. Tennessee v. Garner, 471 U.S. 1 (1985). In 2007, the Court held 8 to 1 that a police officer who rammed a fleeing suspect's car, forcing it to crash, was acting reasonably in part because the suspect's conduct posed a substantial risk to others on the road. Scott v. Harris, 550 U.S. 372 (2007).

Brief stops to question a suspect are allowed if police have a reasonable suspicion that is grounded in specific and articulable facts. Reid v. United States, 448 U.S. 438 (1980); United States v. Hensley, 469 U.S. 221 (1985). Individuals suspected of criminal activity can be detained for periods up to 40 minutes when the delay is attributable mainly to their evasive actions. United States v. Sharpe, 470 U.S. 675 (1985). Detentions of 90 minutes are not justified as a *Terry*-type investigative stop, United States v. Place, 462 U.S. 696 (1983), but detention can last for much longer periods at the border when smuggling is suspected, United States v. Montoya de Hernandez, 473 U.S. 531 (1985). These deci-

---

6. See also United States v. Sokolow, 490 U.S. 1 (1989); Michigan v. Long, 463 U.S. 1032 (1983); Michigan v. Summers, 452 U.S. 692 (1981); Pennsylvania v. Mimms, 434 U.S. 106 (1977); Adams v. Williams, 407 U.S. 143 (1972).

Independent Standards under the Constitution of Hawaii

... [W]e decline to adopt the definition of seizure employed by the United States Supreme Court in *Hodari D.* and, instead, choose to afford greater protection to our citizens....

We cannot allow the police to randomly "encounter" individuals without any objective basis for suspecting them of misconduct and then place them in a coercive environment in order to develop reasonable suspicion to justify their detention. This investigative technique is based on the proposition that an otherwise innocent person, who comes under police scrutiny for no good reason, is not innocent unless he or she convinces the police that he or she is. Such a procedure is anathema to our constitutional freedoms. For these reasons, we hold that the police conduct violated [the defendant's] right to be secure against unreasonable seizures guaranteed by article I, section 7 of the Hawaii Constitution.

SOURCE: State v. Quino, 840 P.2d 358, 362, 365 (Hawaii 1992).

---

sions do not justify detaining a suspect or bringing him or her to police headquarters on less than probable cause with the hope of discovering incriminating evidence.[7]

Suspicious activities and furtive movements may be sufficient reason for an officer to apprehend someone and frisk the suspect for possible weapons or burglar's tools. Sibron v. New York, 392 U.S. 40, 66 (1968). However, unless there is reasonable suspicion based on objective facts that an individual is engaged or has engaged in criminal conduct, the Court initially held that an officer may not require someone to identify himself or herself and may not make an arrest if identification is refused.[8] In 2004, a 5 to 4 Court upheld a Nevada law that made it a crime to refuse to tell the police one's name when stopped for suspicious behavior. The Court reasoned that obtaining a suspect's name "in the course of a *Terry* stop serves important government interests." Hiibel v. Sixth Judicial Dist. Court of Nev., 542 U.S. 177, 186 (2004). This decision marks an exception to the *Miranda* warning: "You have the right to remain silent."

May the police pursue a fleeing suspect and introduce as evidence drugs discarded by him during the chase? The Court held that the fleeing suspect was not "seized" when he dropped the drugs. Assuming that the officer's pursuit constituted a "show of authority" ordering the person to stop, the person did not comply with the order and therefore was not seized until finally tackled. Because the suspect did not submit to the officer's authority, the abandoned drugs were not the fruit of a seizure and could be introduced as evidence. California v. Hodari D., 499 U.S. 621 (1991). A year later, the Supreme Court of Hawaii declined to adopt this definition of seizure, preferring to give greater protection to Hawaiian citizens (see box).

Two decisions in 2000 add refinements to *Terry*. The Court held that a defendant's unprovoked flight from police, in an area of heavy narcotics trafficking, supported a reasonable suspicion that he was involved in criminal activity. His behavior justified a stop and frisk. Illinois v. Wardlow, 528 U.S. 119 (2000). In the second decision, the Court ruled that police may not stop and frisk someone merely on the basis of an anonymous tip that he is carrying a gun. The Court left open the door to accepting anonymous tips in other situations: tips about someone carrying a bomb, and conditions in airports, schools, and other public places. Florida v. J.L., 529 U.S. 266 (2000).

---

7. Florida v. Royer, 460 U.S. 491 (1983); Taylor v. Alabama, 457 U.S. 687 (1982); Dunaway v. New York, 442 U.S. 200 (1979); Morales v. New York 396 U.S. 102 (1969).

8. Kolender v. Lawson, 461 U.S. 352 (1983); Michigan v. DeFillippo, 443 U.S. 31 (1979); Brown v. Texas, 443 U.S. 47 (1979).

In 2010, the Court declined to take a case from Virginia where an individual's drunk-driving conviction was reversed because the police relied solely on an anonymous tip without independent corroboration. Chief Justice Roberts, joined by Scalia, dissented from this denial of cert, saying the effect was to grant drunk drivers "one free swerve" before arrest. Virginia v. Harris, 558 U.S. ___ (2010).

Search Incident to Arrest

Police officers may conduct a search incident to a valid arrest and seize articles in plain view. However, allowing a warrantless search and seizure whenever there is an arrest risks swallowing the general principle of the Fourth Amendment in an exception. Trupiano v. United States, 334 U.S. 699, 708 (1948). Otherwise, the government could justify an arrest because of a search and a search because of an arrest. Johnson v. United States, 333 U.S. 10, 16–17 (1948).

What are the limits of a search for articles that are not in plain view? An arrest should not be used as a pretext to conduct a general and exploratory search for incriminating information. Nevertheless, in 1947 the Supreme Court allowed an arrest warrant to justify a five-hour search of an apartment. Beneath clothes in a bedroom bureau drawer, federal agents found a sealed envelope marked "personal papers." They tore it open and found several draft cards used to convict the suspect. The Court claimed that the search was incident to the arrest, although the draft cards were unrelated to the crimes for which the suspect had been arrested. Harris v. United States, 331 U.S. 145 (1947). Three years later the Court allowed government agents with an arrest warrant to search a suspect's desk, safe, and file cabinets to seize 573 forged stamps. The search and seizure were considered incident to a lawful arrest. United States v. Rabinowitz, 339 U.S. 56 (1950). These decisions were overturned in *Chimel* (1969), discussed below.

A search incident to an arrest must be closely connected in time and place. A warrantless search is not incident to an arrest that occurs two days later, Stoner v. California, 376 U.S. 483 (1964); or when an arrest occurs in one place and the police attempt to use it to search a home blocks away, James v. Louisiana, 382 U.S. 36 (1965); or when the police arrest a person outside the individual's house and take the person inside for the purpose of conducting a warrantless search, Shipley v. California, 395 U.S. 818 (1969) and Vale v. Louisiana, 399 U.S. 30 (1970). However, when a formal arrest quickly follows a search, it may not be "particularly important that the search preceded the arrest rather than vice versa." Rawlings v. Kentucky, 448 U.S. 98, 111 (1980).

In 1969, the Supreme Court limited the reach of searches that are incident to an arrest. The case involved police officers who arrived at a home with an arrest warrant but not a search warrant. The suspect's wife allowed them to enter. When the suspect arrived, he was arrested but he specifically denied the police the right to "look around." They did so anyway, searching the entire house, attic, garage, and small workshop. The Court reversed the conviction, holding that an arresting officer may search a person to discover and remove weapons and may search the area within the immediate control of the suspect, who might grab a weapon or destroy evidence. A broader search requires a search warrant. CHIMEL v. CALIFORNIA, 395 U.S. 752 (1969).

When a suspect is detained with probable cause, even though not arrested, it is permissible for the police in the course of questioning at a station house to take samples from the person's fingernails. Although there was no search warrant and the suspect objected, the search was considered an appropriate action to preserve highly evanescent evidence. Cupp v. Murphy, 412 U.S. 291 (1973). In the case of a lawful custodial arrest, a full search of the person is reasonable under the Fourth Amendment. Police may search outer clothing to remove weapons, search elsewhere for evidence, and inventory possessions as part of the process of booking someone.[9]

---

9. United States v. Robinson, 414 U.S. 218 (1973); Gustafson v. Florida, 414 U.S. 260 (1973); United States v. Edwards, 415 U.S. 800 (1974); Illinois v. Lafayette, 462 U.S. 640 (1983).

Administrative Inspections

Congressional statutes authorize many types of warrantless inspections by federal officers, and in almost every case of a challenged statute the Supreme Court has upheld the legislative judgment. Beginning with the First Congress, statutes have required certain businesses to have their records available for federal inspectors. Legislation in 1791 provided that the books of distilleries shall "lie open" for inspection officers to take notes. 1 Stat. 207, § 35. Contemporary law authorizes federal inspectors to enter distilleries during business hours to examine records and documents. 26 U.S.C. § 5146(b). The Narcotics Drug Act of 1914 required persons who dispensed narcotics to prepare orders on IRS (Internal Revenue Service) forms and make them available to official inspectors. United States v. Doremus, 249 U.S. 86 (1919). During business hours, federal inspectors may enter the premises of any firearms or ammunition importer, manufacturer, dealer, or collector to examine records and documents. 18 U.S.C. § 923(g).

With the growth of federal regulatory activities, the courts began to monitor the scope of agency inspections. In 1924, the Supreme Court rejected the argument of the Federal Trade Commission that it had unlimited right of access to company records. The spirit and letter of the Fourth Amendment counseled against the belief that Congress intended to authorize a "fishing expedition" into private papers on the possibility that they may disclose a crime. FTC v. American Tobacco Co., 264 U.S. 298 (1924). However, when federal agents used heavy-handed tactics to investigate a black market operation in gasoline, the Court sustained the warrantless search because the agents found gasoline ration coupons, which the Court regarded as public documents, not private property. Davis v. United States, 328 U.S. 582 (1946). Similarly, the Court held that the terms of a government contract allowed federal agents to audit a contractor's books at any time during business hours. Zap v. United States, 328 U.S. 624 (1946).

Private Homes. Beginning in 1950, the Supreme Court upheld the right of government inspectors to enter private homes to inspect for unsanitary conditions. District of Columbia v. Little, 339 U.S. 1 (1950). Home owners who refused to allow health inspectors to enter could be convicted. This meant that someone suspected of criminal activity had a constitutional right to object to warrantless searches of his home, while no such right existed for those not suspected of crime but who objected to health inspectors entering. Frank v. Maryland, 359 U.S. 360, 378 (1959). See also Ohio ex rel. Eaton v. Price, 360 U.S. 246 (1959), and Eaton v. Price, 364 U.S. 263 (1960). A few years later the Court began placing some limits on administrative inspections of homes and businesses, but adopted lowered standards to justify a warrant (see box).

Standards for Administrative Inspections

In 1967, the Supreme Court placed restrictions on warrantless inspections of homes and businesses. The Court pointed out that inspections by city officials were not merely "civil" in nature. A refusal to allow an inspection, combined with the discovery of conditions that violate local ordinances, rendered the person subject to criminal process. Unless an emergency required immediate access, owners of homes and businesses had a constitutional right to insist that inspectors first obtain a search warrant. Nevertheless, the warrant need not conform to the Fourth Amendment standard of probable cause. "Reasonableness" or a "suitable" warrant would suffice. Camera v. Municipal Court, 387 U.S. 523 (1967); See v. City of Seattle, 387 U.S. 541 (1967). Although government employees are entitled to Fourth Amendment protections and have a legitimate expectation of privacy in their office, desk, and file cabinets, employers may, without a warrant, conduct a search of the office if there are reasonable grounds related to work or work-related misconduct. O'Connor v. Ortega, 480 U.S. 709 (1987).

Liquor and Firearms. Certain businesses are particularly susceptible to warrantless inspections. The Court acknowledges that Congress "has broad authority to fashion standards of reasonableness for searches and seizures" in the liquor industry. Colonnade Catering Corp. v. United States, 397 U.S. 72, 77 (1970). Congress also authorized warrantless searches of firearms stores during business hours, and the Court upheld this provision against the charge that it violated the Fourth Amendment. United States v. Biswell, 406 U.S. 311 (1972). Without a warrant, state health inspectors may enter a corporation's outdoor premises in the daylight, without its knowledge or consent, for the purpose of conducting tests of smoke emitted from chimneys. Air Pollution Variance Bd. v. Western Alfalfa, 416 U.S. 861 (1974).

OSHA Inspections. Judicial support for congressional judgments on administrative inspections came to a sudden halt in 1978 when a 5–3 Court held that warrantless inspections of company work areas, in search of safety and health hazards, intruded on Fourth Amendment rights. The Court struck down these OSHA (Occupational Safety and Health Administration) inspections in part because they affected every industry involved in interstate commerce, in contrast to such specific industries as liquor and firearms. The Court held that OSHA inspectors require a warrant, though probable cause was not necessary. Marshall v. Barlow's, Inc., 436 U.S. 307 (1978). The dissenters (Stevens, Blackmun, and Rehnquist) maintained that the Fourth Amendment had no application to "routine, regulatory inspections of commercial premises" and objected to the Court's substituting its judgment for Congress' on the inspection procedure needed to implement the statute.

The rationale in *Barlow's* was quickly tested by litigation on the Federal Mine Safety and Health Amendments Act of 1977. The statute required federal officials to inspect underground mines at least four times a year and surface mines at least twice a year to ensure compliance with safety and health standards. Inspectors had a right to enter without advance notice and did not need a warrant. A federal court, relying on *Barlow's*, held that the statute violated the rights of private companies, who could refuse entry to federal inspectors. Marshall v. Dewey, 493 F.Supp. 963 (E.D. Wis. 1980).

The district court's trust in Supreme Court precedents was misplaced. An 8–1 majority of the Supreme Court reversed, holding that Congress had properly determined that warrantless searches were needed to further the regulatory scheme for mine inspections. Congress had "broad authority" to regulate commercial enterprises engaged in interstate commerce. In language that appeared to undermine its holding in *Barlow's,* the Court maintained that its previous decisions on administrative inspections

> make clear that a warrant may not be constitutionally required when Congress has reasonably determined that warrantless searches are necessary to further a regulatory scheme and the federal regulatory presence is sufficiently comprehensive and defined that the owner of commercial property cannot help but be aware that his property will be subject to periodic inspections undertaken for specific purposes. Donovan v. Dewey, 452 U.S. 594, 600 (1981).

The scope of warrantless inspections of "closely regulated" industries was extended in 1987 to permit police officers to enter junkyards to discover stolen automobiles and parts. New York v. Burger, 482 U.S. 691 (1987).

Businesses open to the general public do not have the same expectations of privacy as people who live at home or work in offices. Detectives may enter a bookstore, purchase a magazine, and use that as evidence to arrest the owner for selling obscene materials. Examining the books and magazines offered for sale is not a "search" nor is the purchase a "seizure." The bookstore owner had no "reasonable expectation of privacy in areas of the store where the public was invited to enter and to transact business." Maryland v. Macon, 472 U.S. 463, 469 (1985).

Drug Tests

Mandatory drug tests for government employees have been reviewed by the courts for compliance with the Fourth Amendment. Three decisions in 1989 began the process of establishing some boundaries. In the first case, decided by a 7–2 majority, the Supreme Court upheld federal regulations that require blood and urine tests for railroad employees following major train accidents. Such tests are considered reasonable even though they are warrantless and there is no reasonable suspicion that any particular employee is impaired. Skinner v. Railway Labor Executives' Assn., 489 U.S. 602 (1989). In the second case, the Court divided 5–4 in upholding a Customs Service requirement of urine tests for all employees seeking transfer or promotion to positions having a direct involvement in drug interdiction or that involve the carrying of firearms. National Treasury Employees Union v. Von Raab, 489 U.S. 656 (1989). In 1989, the Court also upheld Conrail's policy of requiring its employees to undergo physical examinations periodically and upon return from leave. Urinalysis drug screening is part of the exam. Consol. Rail Corp. v. Railway Labor Executives, 491 U.S. 299 (1989).

In 1990, the Court refused to review challenges to two lower-court decisions that upheld random drug testing of two groups of federal workers. The first case involved the Army's compulsory drug-testing program for drug counselors. National Federation of Federal Employees v. Cheney, 493 U.S. 1056 (1990); National Federation of Federal Employees v. Cheney, 884 F.2d 603 (D.C. Cir. 1989). The second involved a program in the Justice Department to perform random drug testing of employees who hold top secret, national-security clearances. Bell v. Thornburgh, 493 U.S. 1056 (1990); Harmon v. Thornburgh, 878 F.2d 484 (D.C. Cir. 1989). In 1995, the Court upheld an Oregon school district's policy that required junior high boys and girls who wanted to participate in sports to provide urine samples as a method for determining drug use. Vernonia School Dist. v. Acton, 515 U.S. 646 (1995).

In 1997, the Court decided a case in which candidates for high office in Georgia challenged the constitutionality of a statute that required them to submit to and pass drug tests to qualify for state office. Divided 8 to 1, the Court held that the state law did not fit within the category of constitutionally permissible suspicionless searches. Previous exceptions (drug testing for those involved in drug interdiction, the carrying of firearms, student athletics, customs employees, railway employees, and other areas) did not apply here. Chandler v. Miller, 520 U.S. 305 (1997). A year later the Court denied an appeal by two government economists who objected to a policy that required them to take random drug tests because they had access to the Old Executive Office Building, which is on White House grounds. Stigile v. Clinton, 110 F.3d 801 (D.C. Cir. 1997), cert. denied, 522 U.S. 1147 (1998).

A public hospital in Charleston, S.C. conducted a warrantless drug-testing program on maternity patients to stop drug use by pregnant women and avoid "crack babies." A 6–3 Court held that the tests were unconstitutional if performed without a warrant or the patient's consent. The central purpose of the hospital's policy was not law enforcement. Ferguson v. Charleston, 532 U.S. 67 (2001).

Text Messaging

Building on the two 1989 drug-test cases of *Skinner* and *Von Raab*, the Court in 2010 decided another case on the scope of search and seizure for government officials over employees. The Ontario Police Department in California hired Jeff Quon as a police sergeant and gave him and other officers a pager capable of sending and receiving text messages. Under the city's service contract with Arch Wireless, each pager was allotted a limited number of characters sent or received each month. Usage beyond that amount resulted in an additional fee. The city announced a computer policy that applied to all employees, specifying that the city reserved the right to monitor and log all network activity including e-mail and Internet use, with or without notice. Users would have no expectation of privacy or confidentiality. Quon signed a statement acknowledging that he had read and understood that policy.

This policy did not expressly apply to text messaging, which relied on pagers under the contract with Arch Wireless. E-mails were sent through the city's own data servers. Text messages did not pass through city computers. However, the city explained to Quon and other officers that it considered messages sent on pagers to be e-mail messages. Quon was advised that if he exceeded his character limit he could reimburse the city, which he chose to do. He might have assumed that if he paid the overage the contents of his messages would remain private.

Eventually the city decided to get transcripts of text messages sent by Quon and others who exceeded the character allowance. Some of his messages on the pager were not work related and some were sexually explicit. Quon sued, charging that the city violated his Fourth Amendment rights and privacy rights under state law (the Stored Communications Act). Writing for the Court, Justice Kennedy recognized that cell phone and text messages arc so pervasive that individuals might have an expectation of privacy. He also recognized that the devices are generally affordable, making it possible for employees to purchase their own to assure privacy. Even if Quon had a reasonable expectation of privacy in his text messages, the city "did not necessarily violate the Fourth Amendment by obtaining and reviewing the transcripts."

Although warrantless searches are "*per se* unreasonable," exceptions exist, including the "special needs" of the workplace. The city's review of Quon's transcripts was reasonable and not "excessively intrusive," especially when the city redacted all messages that he sent while off duty. Under the circumstances, a reasonable employee (especially a law enforcement officer like Quon) "would be aware that sound management principles might require the audit of messages to determine whether the pager was being appropriately used." Even if Arch Wireless violated state law by giving the city the transcripts, that issue was not before the Court and did not make the city's action unreasonable. The Court found it unnecessary to resolve another question: were the Fourth Amendment rights of those who text messaged with Quon violated? Two Justices (Stevens and Scalia) wrote concurring opinions. There were no dissents. Ontario v. Quon, 560 U.S. ___ (2010).

Students

What standards apply to search and seizure of school students? In 1985, the Court decided that the Fourth Amendment applies to minors on public school property, but relaxed standards are necessary to permit school authorities to discover drugs and other contraband. Teachers need not obtain a warrant or adhere to the probable-cause requirement. NEW JERSEY v. T.L.O, 469 U.S. 325 (1985). For the use of German shepherds to perform "sniff tests" while searching students for drugs in junior and senior high schools, see *Doe* v. *Renfrow,* 451 U.S. 1022 (1981).

T.L.O. was further developed in 1995 when the Court upheld an Oregon school district's policy that required junior high students interested in participating in sports to provide urine samples as a means of testing for drug use. Athletes are tested at the beginning of the season for their sport and thereafter on a random basis. No suspicion of drug use is necessary. Safeguards are taken to protect student privacy. The Court sustained the Oregon policy because (1) it applies to children and (2) the children are committed to the temporary custody of the State as schoolmaster. As the Court noted, Fourth Amendment rights, "no less than First and Fourteenth Amendment rights, are different in public schools than elsewhere." Vernonia School Dist. v. Acton, 515 U.S. 646 (1995). In 1997, the Court let stand an Eleventh Circuit ruling that second-graders may be strip-searched to investigate the theft of $7 from a classmate. Jenkins v. Herring, 522 U.S. 966 (1997).

School drug testing has expanded to include nonatheletes. In 2002, the Court (split 5 to 4) approved random drug testing of public high school students engaged in such extracurricular activities as band, chess, choir, and quiz teams. The urinalysis test is designed to detect drugs like amphetamines, marijuana, cocaine, opiates, and barbiturates, not authorized prescription medications. Board of Ed. of Independent School Dist. v. Earls, 536 U.S. 822 (2002).

The issue of searching students returned to the Court in 2009. School authorities suspected a 13-year-old girl of giving drugs to fellow students. After searching her backpack and finding no pills, she was taken to the school nurse's office and asked to remove her outer clothing, again disclosing no drugs. At that point she was asked to pull her bra out and shake it and pull out the elastic on her underpants, exposing her breasts and pelvic area. The Court held that the search was reasonable with regard to the backpack and outer clothing but not of underwear, in part because of the intrusive and degrading procedure. The Court also held that the school officials were protected from liability because of qualified immunity. Safford Unified School Dist. #1 v. Redding, 557 U.S. ___ (2009). Justices Stevens and Ginsburg dissented on the question of immunity. A dissent by Thomas concluded that the search did not violate the Fourth Amendment.

Civil Forfeiture

Congress and the Supreme Court have begun to place some restrictions on the government's ability to seize property (with or without a warrant) as part of civil forfeiture procedures used in the war on drugs. Unlike criminal forfeiture, civil forfeiture does not require criminal conviction of the property owner. In fact, an owner's acquittal does not prevent the government from seizing houses, automobiles, boats, and other property. Under civil forfeiture proceedings, the government did not adhere to constitutionally required safeguards needed in criminal prosecutions. The standard for civil forfeiture was guilty until proven innocent. The burden of proof was on the property owner, not the government. Law enforcement agencies began relying on civil forfeiture as a source of revenue to relieve strained budgets.

A 1993 ruling now requires a hearing before U.S. marshals can seize property. United States v. James Daniel Good Real Property, 510 U.S. 43 (1993). Other restrictions have been imposed by the Court: United States v. Parcel of Rumson, N.J., Land, 507 U.S. 111 (1993); Austin v. United States, 509 U.S. 602 (1993). However, in 1996 the Court (divided 5 to 4) held that a state may use forfeiture proceedings to seize a car used by a husband for sexual activities with a prostitute even though the car was jointly owned by the husband and his wife. The Court ruled that she was not entitled to innocent owner defense, nor was the forfeiture of her interest in the car a taking of private property for public use in violation of the Taking Clause. Bennis v. Michigan, 516 U.S. 442 (1996). Also in 1996, the Court ruled that the government may prosecute someone for criminal violations and also seize their property without violating the constitutional provision regarding double jeopardy. Even though the civil forfeiture arose from the same offense leading to criminal prosecution, the Court (divided 8 to 1) found no constitutional objection. Civil forfeiture, it said, is not "punishment" for double jeopardy purposes. United States v. Ursery, 518 U.S. 267 (1996).

Divided 5–4 in 1998, the Court ruled that the federal government could not seize and keep the money of someone who tried to take funds out of the country simply because the person failed to fill out a Customs Service form properly. A Syrian immigrant tried to take $357,000 out of the country without declaring it on the form that requires someone to report the carrying of more than $10,000 outside the United States. The Court held that the forfeiture violated the Excessive Fines Clause. United States v. Bajakajian, 524 U.S. 321 (1998).

In 2000, Congress passed the Civil Asset Forfeiture Reform Act, which places restrictions on law enforcement officials. A coalition of civil libertarians, business executives, and conservatives argued that too many innocent citizens had their rights violated by the campaign against drugs and other crimes. Government prosecutors must now satisfy a burden of proof (preponderance of the evidence) before seizing property, and indigent defendants will receive free representation. The government must also reimburse property owners for their legal expenses if they successfully challenge the seizure of their assets. 114 Stat. 202 (2000).

Coolidge v. New Hampshire
403 U.S. 443 (1971)*

This case involves what the Court called a "particularly brutal murder" of a 14-year-old girl. Edward Coolidge was charged with the murder. The case illustrates the need to have warrants is-

---

* Parts II-A, II-B, and II-C of this opinion are joined only by Mr. Justice Douglas, Mr. Justice Brennan, and Mr. Justice Marshall.

sued by a "neutral and detached magistrate" and to have searches and seizures conducted pursuant to judicial process. Also discussed in this case is the plain-view doctrine and the scope of searches and seizures that are incident to an arrest. The Court divided 5–4 on most of the issues, but a precise count is impossible because several of the Justices never discussed or joined in sections of the majority opinion.

Mr. Justice Stewart delivered the opinion of the Court....

Pamela Mason, a 14-year-old girl, left her home in Manchester, New Hampshire, on the evening of January 13, 1964, during a heavy snowstorm, apparently in response to a man's telephone call for a babysitter. Eight days later, after a thaw, her body was found by the side of a major north-south highway several miles away. She had been murdered. The event created great alarm in the area, and the police immediately began a massive investigation.

On January 28, having learned from a neighbor that the petitioner, Edward Coolidge, had been away from home on the evening of the girl's disappearance, the police went to his house to question him. They asked him, among other things, if he owned any guns, and he produced three, two shotguns and a rifle. They also asked whether he would take a lie-detector test concerning his account of his activities on the night of the disappearance. He agreed to do so on the following Sunday, his day off....

[*Coolidge traveled to Concord, N.H. for the lie-detector test. That evening, two plainclothes policemen arrived at his house. They were not the two who had visited the house earlier. The men told Mrs. Coolidge that her husband was in "serious trouble" and obtained from her four guns belonging to Coolidge, plus some clothes she thought her husband might have been wearing on the evening of Pamela Mason's disappearance. After accumulating other evidence to support the belief that Coolidge killed her, the Manchester police chief applied for arrest and search warrants, particularly the search of his Pontiac automobile. The warrants were signed and issued by the Attorney General, acting as a justice of the peace. Under New Hampshire law, all justices of the peace were authorized to issue search warrants.*]

The police arrested Coolidge in his house on the day the warrant issued [*February 19*].... [A]bout two and a half hours after Coolidge had been taken into custody the cars were towed to the police station. It appears that at the time of the arrest the cars were parked in the Coolidge driveway, and that although dark had fallen they were plainly visible both from the street and from inside the house where Coolidge was actually arrested. The 1951 Pontiac

was searched and vacuumed on February 21, two days after it was seized, again a year later, in January 1965, and a third time in April 1965.

At Coolidge's subsequent jury trial on the charge of murder, vacuum sweepings, including particles of gun powder, taken from the Pontiac were introduced in evidence against him, as part of an attempt by the State to show by microscopic analysis that it was highly probable that Pamela Mason had been in Coolidge's car. Also introduced in evidence was one of the guns taken by the police on their Sunday evening visit to the Coolidge house—a .22-caliber Mossberg rifle, which the prosecution claimed was the murder weapon. Conflicting ballistics testimony was offered on the question whether the bullets found in Pamela Mason's body had been fired from this rifle. Finally, the prosecution introduced vacuum sweepings of the clothes taken from the Coolidge house that same Sunday evening, and attempted to show through microscopic analysis that there was a high probability that the clothes had been in contact with Pamela Mason's body. Pretrial motions to suppress all this evidence were referred by the trial judge to the New Hampshire Supreme Court, which ruled the evidence admissible ... The jury found Coolidge guilty and he was sentenced to life imprisonment. The New Hampshire Supreme Court affirmed the judgment of conviction, ...

I

The petitioner's first claim is that the warrant authorizing the seizure and subsequent search of his 1951 Pontiac automobile was invalid because not issued by a "neutral and detached magistrate." Since we agree with the petitioner that the warrant was invalid for this reason, we need not consider his further argument that the allegations under oath supporting the issuance of the warrant were so conclusory as to violate relevant constitutional standards....

The classic statement of the policy underlying the warrant requirement of the Fourth Amendment is that of Mr. Justice Jackson, writing for the Court in *Johnson v. United States,* 333 U.S. 10, 13–14:

"The point of the Fourth Amendment, which often is not grasped by zealous officers, is not that it denies law enforcement the support of the usual inferences which reasonable men draw from evidence. Its protection consists in requiring that those inferences be drawn by a neutral and detached magistrate instead of being judged by the officer engaged in the often competitive enterprise of ferreting out crime.... When the right of privacy must reasonably yield to the right of search is, as a rule, to be decided by a judicial officer, not by a policeman or government enforcement agent." ...

In this case, the determination of probable cause was made by the chief "government enforcement agent" of the State—the Attorney General—who was actively in charge of the investigation and later was to be chief prosecutor at the trial....

II

The State proposes three distinct theories to bring the facts of this case within one or another of the exceptions to the warrant requirement....

A

The State's first theory is that the seizure on February 19 and subsequent search of Coolidge's Pontiac were "incident" to a valid arrest. [*The Court found the State's position "untenable" because a warrantless search "incident to a lawful arrest" generally extends to the area in the immediate vicinity of the arrest and is contemporaneous with the arrest. Coolidge's arrest inside the house did not permit the search of his car outside.*]

B

The second theory put forward by the State to justify a warrantless seizure and search of the Pontiac car is that under *Carroll* v. *United States*, 267 U.S. 132, the police may make a warrantless search of an automobile whenever they have probable cause to do so, and, under our decision last Term in *Chambers* v. *Maroney*, 399 U.S. 42, whenever the police may make a legal contemporaneous search under *Carroll*, they may also seize the car, take it to the police station, and search it there. But even granting that the police had probable cause to search the car, the application of the *Carroll* case to these facts would extend it far beyond its original rationale....

The word "automobile" is not a talisman in whose presence the Fourth Amendment fades away and disappears. And surely there is nothing in this case to invoke the meaning and purpose of the rule of *Carroll* v. *United States*—no alerted criminal bent on flight, no fleeting opportunity on an open highway after a hazardous chase, no contraband or stolen goods or weapons, no confederates waiting to move the evidence, not even the inconvenience of a special police detail to guard the immobilized automobile. In short, by no possible stretch of the legal imagination can this be made into a case where "it is not practicable to secure a warrant," *Carroll, supra,* at 153, and the "automobile exception," despite its label, is simply irrelevant....

C

The State's third theory in support of the warrantless seizure and search of the Pontiac car is that the car itself was an "instrumentality of the crime," and as such might be seized by the police on Coolidge's property because it was in plain view. Supposing the seizure to be thus lawful, the case of *Cooper* v. *California,* 386 U.S. 58, is said to support a subsequent warrantless search at the station house, with or without probable cause. Of course, the distinction between an "instrumentality of crime" and "mere evidence" was done away with by *Warden* v. *Hayden,* 387 U.S. 294, and we may assume that the police had probable cause to seize the automobile. But, for the reasons that follow, we hold that the "plain view" exception to the warrant requirement is inapplicable to this case....

What the "plain view" cases have in common is that the police officer in each of them had a prior justification for an intrusion in the course of which he came inadvertently across a piece of evidence incriminating the accused. The doctrine serves to supplement the prior justification—whether it be a warrant for another object, hot pursuit, search incident to lawful arrest, or some other legitimate reason for being present unconnected with a search directed against the accused—and permits the warrantless seizure. Of course, the extension of the original justification is legitimate only where it is immediately apparent to the police that they have evidence before them; the "plain view" doctrine may not be used to extend a general exploratory search from one object to another until something incriminating at last emerges....

In the light of what has been said, it is apparent that the "plain view" exception cannot justify the police seizure of the Pontiac car in this case. The police had ample opportunity to obtain a valid warrant; they knew the automobile's exact description and location well in advance; they intended to seize it when they came upon Coolidge's property. And this is not a case involving contraband or stolen goods or objects dangerous in themselves.

The seizure was therefore unconstitutional, and so was the subsequent search at the station house. Since evidence obtained in the course of the search was admitted at Coolidge's trial, the judgment must be reversed and the case remanded to the New Hampshire Supreme Court. *Mapp* v. *Ohio*, 367 U.S. 643.

[*Justice Harlan wrote a concurring opinion, and Chief Justice Burger dissented in part and concurred in part.*]

MR. JUSTICE BLACK, concurring and dissenting.

... Believing that the search and seizure here was reasonable and that the Fourth Amendment properly construed contains no such exclusionary rule, I dissent....

MR. JUSTICE BLACKMUN joins MR. JUSTICE BLACK in Parts II and III of this opinion and in that portion of Part I thereof which is to the effect that the Fourth Amendment supports no exclusionary rule.

MR. JUSTICE WHITE, with whom THE CHIEF JUSTICE joins, concurring and dissenting.

I would affirm the judgment. In my view, Coolidge's Pontiac was lawfully seized as evidence of the crime in plain sight and thereafter was lawfully searched under *Cooper* v. *California*, 386 U.S. 58 (1967)....

California v. Ciraolo

476 U.S. 207 (1986)

California police received an anonymous telephone tip that Dante Ciraolo was growing marijuana in his backyard, which was enclosed by two fences and shielded from view at ground level. Using a private airplane, the police flew over his house at an altitude of 1,000 feet and readily identified marijuana plants growing in the yard. After obtaining a search warrant, the marijuana plants were seized. The California trial court denied Ciraolo's motion to suppress the evidence of the search, but the California Court of Appeal reversed on the ground that the warrantless aerial observation violated the Fourth Amendment. This case illustrates how the Court determines constitutionality based not on the text, intent, or history of the Constitution, but on what "society is willing to recognize" as a reasonable expectation of privacy.

CHIEF JUSTICE BURGER delivered the opinion of the Court....

I

On September 2, 1982, Santa Clara Police received an anonymous telephone tip that marijuana was growing in respondent's backyard. Police were unable to observe the contents of respondent's yard from ground level because of a 6-foot outer fence and a 10-foot inner fence completely enclosing the yard. Later that day, Officer Shutz, who was assigned to investigate, secured a private plane and flew over respondent's house at an altitude of 1,000 feet, within navigable airspace; he was accompanied by Officer Rodriguez. Both officers were trained in marijuana identification. From the overflight, the officers readily identified marijuana plants 8 feet to 10 feet in height growing in a 15- by 25-foot plot in respondent's yard; they photographed the area with a standard 35mm camera.

On September 8, 1982, Officer Shutz obtained a search warrant on the basis of an affidavit describing the anonymous tip and their observations; a photograph depicting respondent's house, the backyard, and neighboring homes was attached to the affidavit as an exhibit. The warrant was executed the next day

and 73 plants were seized; it is not disputed that these were marijuana....

II

The touchstone of Fourth Amendment analysis is whether a person has a "constitutionally protected reasonable expectation of privacy." *Katz* v. *United States*, 389 U.S. 347, 360 (1967) (Harlan, J., concurring). *Katz* posits a two-part inquiry: first, has the individual manifested a subjective expectation of privacy in the object of the challenged search? Second, is society willing to recognize that expectation as reasonable? See *Smith* v. *Maryland*, 442 U.S. 735, 740 (1979).

Clearly—and understandably—respondent has met the test of manifesting his own subjective intent and desire to maintain privacy as to his unlawful agricultural pursuits. However, we need not address that issue, for the State has not challenged the finding of the California Court of Appeal that respondent had such an expectation. It can reasonably be assumed that the 10-foot fence was placed to conceal the marijuana crop from at least street-level views....

Yet a 10-foot fence might not shield these plants from the eyes of a citizen or a policeman perched on the top of a truck or a 2-level bus. Whether respondent therefore manifested a subjective expectation of privacy from *all* observations of his backyard, or whether instead he manifested merely a hope that no one would observe his unlawful gardening pursuits, is not entirely clear in these circumstances. Respondent appears to challenge the authority of government to observe his activity from any vantage point or place if the viewing is motivated by a law enforcement purpose, and not the result of a casual, accidental observation.

We turn, therefore, to the second inquiry under *Katz, i.e.,* whether that expectation is reasonable. In pursuing this inquiry, we must keep in mind that "[t]he test of legitimacy is not whether the individual chooses to conceal assertedly 'private' activity," but instead "whether the government's intrusion infringes upon the personal and societal values protected by the Fourth Amendment." *Oliver, supra,* at 181–183.

Respondent argues that because his yard was in the curtilage of his home, no governmental aerial observation is permissible under the Fourth Amendment without a warrant. The history and genesis of the curtilage doctrine is instructive. "At common law, the curtilage is the area to which extends the intimate activity associated with the 'sanctity of a man's home and the privacies of life.'" *Oliver, supra,* at 180 (quoting *Boyd* v. *United States,* 116 U.S. 616, 630 (1886)). See 4 Blackstone, Commentaries *225. The protection afforded the curtilage is essentially a protection of families and personal privacy in an area intimately linked to the home, both physically and psychologically, where privacy expectations are most heightened. The claimed area here was immediately adjacent to a suburban home, surrounded by high double fences. This close nexus to the home would appear to encompass this small area within the curtilage. Accepting, as the State does, that this yard and its crop fall within the curtilage, the question remains whether naked-eye observation of the curtilage by police from an aircraft lawfully operating at an altitude of 1,000 feet violates an expectation of privacy that is reasonable.

That the area is within the curtilage does not itself bar all police observation. The Fourth Amendment protection of the home has never been extended to require law enforcement officers to shield their eyes when passing by a home on public thoroughfares. Nor does the mere fact that an individual has taken measures to restrict some views of his activities preclude an officer's observations from a public vantage point where he has a right to be and which renders the activities clearly visible.... The observations by Officers Shutz and Ro-

driguez in this case took place within public navigable airspace, see 49 U.S.C. App. § 1304, in a physically nonintrusive manner; from this point they were able to observe plants readily discernible to the naked eye as marijuana.... Such observation is precisely what a judicial officer needs to provide a basis for a warrant. Any member of the public flying in this airspace who glanced down could have seen everything that these officers observed. On this record, we readily conclude that respondent's expectation that his garden was protected from such observation is unreasonable and is not an expectation that society is prepared to honor....

Reversed.

JUSTICE POWELL with whom JUSTICE BRENNAN, JUSTICE MARSHALL, and JUSTICE BLACKMUN join, dissenting.

Concurring in *Katz* v. *United States,* 389 U.S. 347 (1967), Justice Harlan warned that any decision to construe the Fourth Amendment as proscribing only physical intrusions by police onto private property "is, in the present day, bad physics as well as bad law, for reasonable expectations of privacy may be defeated by electronic as well as physical invasion." *Id.,* at 362. Because the Court today ignores that warning in an opinion that departs significantly from the standard developed in *Katz* for deciding when a Fourth Amendment violation has occurred, I dissent....

The Court's holding ... must rest solely on the fact that members of the public fly in planes and may look down at homes as they fly over them.... The Court does not explain why it finds this fact to be significant. One may assume that the Court believes that citizens bear the risk that air travelers will observe activities occurring within backyards that are open to the sun and air. This risk, the Court appears to hold, nullifies expectations of privacy in those yards even as to purposeful police surveillance from the air....

This line of reasoning is flawed. First, the actual risk to privacy from commercial or pleasure aircraft is virtually nonexistent. Travelers on commercial flights, as well as private planes used for business or personal reasons, normally obtain at most a fleeting, anonymous, and nondiscriminating glimpse of the landscape and buildings over which they pass. The risk that a passenger on such a plane might observe private activities, and might connect those activities with particular people, is simply too trivial to protect against. It is no accident that, as a matter of common experience, many people build fences around their residential areas, but few build roofs over their backyards....

United States v. Ross

456 U.S. 798 (1982)

Police officers conducted a warrantless search of the interior of a car belonging to Albert Ross, even after the car had been taken to police headquarters and impounded. After a federal district court denied Ross's motion to suppress the evidence found in the car, he was convicted for possessing heroin with intent to distribute it. The Court of Appeals reversed by holding that the officers had probable cause to stop and search the car, including its trunk, without a warrant, but they should not have opened a paper bag or leather pouch discovered in the trunk.

JUSTICE STEVENS delivered the opinion of the Court.

In *Carroll* v. *United States,* 267 U.S. 132, the Court held that a warrantless search of an automobile stopped by police officers who had probable cause to believe the vehicle contained contraband was not unreasonable within the meaning of the Fourth Amendment. The Court in *Carroll* did not explicitly address the scope of the search that is permissible. In this case, we consider the extent to which police officers—who have legitimately stopped an automobile and who have probable cause to believe that contraband is concealed somewhere within it—may conduct a probing search of compartments and containers within the vehicle whose contents are not in plain view. We hold that they may conduct a search of the vehicle that is as thorough as a magistrate could authorize in a warrant "particularly describing the place to be searched."

I

In the evening of November 27, 1978, an informant who had previously proved to be reliable telephoned Detective Marcum of the District of Columbia Police Department and told him that an individual known as "Bandit" was selling narcotics kept in the trunk of a car parked at 439 Ridge Street. The informant stated that he had just observed "Bandit" complete a sale and that "Bandit" had told him that additional narcotics were in the trunk. The informant gave Marcum a detailed description of "Bandit" and stated that the car was a "purplish maroon" Chevrolet Malibu with District of Columbia license plates.

Accompanied by Detective Cassidy and Sergeant Gonzales, Marcum immediately drove to the area and found a maroon Malibu parked in front of 439 Ridge Street. A license check disclosed that the car was registered to Albert Ross; a computer check on Ross revealed that he fit the informant's description and used the alias "Bandit." ...

The officers returned five minutes later and observed the maroon Malibu turning off Ridge Street onto Fourth Street. They pulled alongside the Malibu, noticed that the driver matched the informant's description, and stopped the car. Marcum and Cassidy told the driver—later identified as Albert Ross, the respondent in this action—to get out of the vehicle. While they searched Ross, Sergeant Gonzales discovered a bullet on the car's front seat. He searched the interior of the car and found a pistol in the glove compartment. Ross then was arrested and handcuffed. Detective Cassidy took Ross' keys and opened the trunk, where he found a closed brown paper bag. He opened the bag and discovered a number of glassine bags containing a white powder. Cassidy replaced the bag, closed the trunk, and drove the car to headquarters.

At the police station Cassidy thoroughly searched the car. In addition to the "lunch-type" brown paper bag, Cassidy found in the trunk a zippered red leather pouch. He unzipped the pouch and discovered $3,200 in cash. The police laboratory later determined that the powder in the paper bag was heroin. No warrant was obtained.

Ross was charged with possession of heroin with intent to distribute, in violation of 21 U.S.C. § 841(a). Prior to trial, he moved to suppress the heroin found in the paper bag and the currency found in the leather pouch. After an evidentiary hearing, the District Court denied the motion to suppress. The heroin and currency were introduced in evidence at trial and Ross was convicted.

A three-judge panel of the Court of Appeals reversed the conviction. It held that the police had probable cause to stop and search Ross' car and that, under *Carroll* v. *United States, supra,* and *Chambers* v. *Maroney,* 399 U.S. 42, the officers lawfully could search the automobile—including its trunk—without a warrant. The court considered separately, however, the warrantless search of the two containers found in the trunk. On the basis of *Arkansas* v. *Sanders,* 442 U.S. 753, the court concluded that the constitutionality of a warrantless search of a container found in an automobile depends on whether the owner possesses a reasonable expectation of privacy in its contents. Applying that test, the court held that the warrantless search of the paper bag was valid but the search of the leather pouch was not. The court remanded for a new trial at which the items taken from the paper bag, but not those from the leather pouch, could be admitted.

The entire Court of Appeals then voted to rehear the case en banc. A majority of the court rejected the panel's conclusion that a distinction of constitutional significance existed between the two containers found in respondent's trunk; it held that the police should not have opened either container without first obtaining a warrant....

The en banc Court of Appeals considered, and rejected, the argument that it was reasonable for the police to open both the paper bag and the leather pouch because they were entitled to conduct a warrantless search of the entire vehicle in which the two containers were found....

IV

In *Carroll* itself, the whiskey that the prohibition agents seized was not in plain view. It was discovered only after an officer opened the rumble seat and tore open the upholstery of the lazyback. The Court did not find the scope of the search unreasonable. Having stopped Carroll and Kiro on a public road and subjected them to the indignity of a vehicle search — which the Court found to be a reasonable intrusion on their privacy because it was based on probable cause that their vehicle was transporting contraband — prohibition agents were entitled to tear open a portion of the roadster itself. The scope of the search was no greater than a magistrate could have authorized by issuing a warrant based on the probable cause that justified the search. Since such a warrant could have authorized the agents to open the rear portion of the roadster and to rip the upholstery in their search for concealed whiskey, the search was constitutionally permissible....

A lawful search of fixed premises generally extends to the entire area in which the object of the search may be found and is not limited by the possibility that separate acts of entry or opening may be required to complete the search. Thus, a warrant that authorizes an officer to search a home for illegal weapons also provides authority to open closets, chests, drawers, and containers in which the weapon might be found. A warrant to open a footlocker to search for marihuana would also authorize the opening of packages found inside. A warrant to search a vehicle would support a search of every part of the vehicle that might contain the object of the search. When a legitimate search is under way, and

when its purpose and its limits have been precisely defined, nice distinctions between closets, drawers, and containers, in the case of a home, or between glove compartments, upholstered seats, trunks, and wrapped packages, in the case of a vehicle, must give way to the interest in the prompt and efficient completion of the task at hand.

This rule applies equally to all containers, as indeed we believe it must. One point on which the Court was in virtually unanimous agreement in [*Robbins v. California, 453 U.S. 420 (1981)*] was that a constitutional distinction between "worthy" and "unworthy" containers would be improper. Even though such a distinction perhaps could evolve in a series of cases in which paper bags, locked trunks, lunch buckets, and orange crates were placed on one side of the line or the other, the central purpose of the Fourth Amendment forecloses such a distinction. For just as the most frail cottage in the kingdom is absolutely entitled to the same guarantees of privacy as the most majestic mansion, so also may a traveler who carries a toothbrush and a few articles of clothing in a paper bag or knotted scarf claim an equal right to conceal his possessions from official inspection as the sophisticated executive with the locked attaché case.

... [A]n individual's expectation of privacy in a vehicle and its contents may not survive if probable cause is given to believe that the vehicle is transporting contraband. Certainly the privacy interests in a car's trunk or glove compartment may be no less than those in a movable container. An individual undoubtedly has a significant interest that the upholstery of his automobile will not be ripped or a hidden compartment within it opened. These interests must yield to the authority of a search, however, which — in light of *Carroll* — does not itself require the prior approval of a magistrate....

V

... We hold that the scope of the warrantless search authorized by that exception is no broader and no narrower than a magistrate could legitimately authorize by warrant. If probable cause justifies the search of a lawfully stopped vehicle, it justifies the search of every part of the vehicle and its contents that may conceal the object of the search.

The judgment of the Court of Appeals is reversed. The case is remanded for further proceedings consistent with this opinion.

It is so ordered.

[*Blackmun and Powell wrote separate concurring opinions.*]

JUSTICE WHITE, dissenting.

... I would ... affirm the judgment of the Court of Appeals. I also agree with much of JUSTICE MARSHALL's dissent in this case.

JUSTICE MARSHALL, with whom JUSTICE BRENNAN joins, dissenting.

The majority today not only repeals all realistic limits on warrantless automobile searches, it repeals the Fourth Amendment warrant requirement itself. By equating a police officer's estimation of probable cause with a magistrate's, the Court utterly disregards the value of a neutral and detached magistrate....

Terry v. Ohio

392 U.S. 1 (1968)

The Fourth Amendment standard of probable cause for searches and seizures was relaxed in this case to permit a "stop and frisk" of three individuals who had been behaving suspiciously. The patdown by the police officer produced concealed weapons used to convict John Terry and his companion. The Ohio Supreme Court dismissed their appeal. As a result of this case and subsequent holdings, the *Terry*-stop has become a legitimate technique available for law enforcement officers.

MR. CHIEF JUSTICE WARREN delivered the opinion of the Court....

Petitioner Terry was convicted of carrying a concealed weapon and sentenced to the statutorily prescribed term of one to three years in the penitentiary. Following the denial of a pretrial motion to suppress, the prosecution introduced in evidence two revolvers and a number of bullets seized from Terry and a codefendant, Richard Chilton, by Cleveland Police Detective Martin McFadden. At the hearing on the motion to suppress this evidence, Officer McFadden testified that while he was patrolling in plain clothes in downtown Cleveland at approximately 2:30 in the afternoon of October 31, 1963, his attention was attracted by two men, Chilton and Terry, standing on the corner of Huron Road and Euclid Avenue. He had never seen the two men before, and he was unable to say precisely what first drew his eye to them. However, he testified that he had been a policeman for 39 years and a detective for 35 and that he had been assigned to patrol this vicinity of downtown Cleveland for shoplifters and pickpockets for 30 years. He explained that he had developed routine habits of observation over the years and that he would "stand and watch people or walk and watch people at many intervals of the day." He added: "Now, in this case when I looked over they didn't look right to me at the time."

His interest aroused, Officer McFadden took up a post of observation in the entrance to a store 300 to 400 feet away from the two men. "I get more purpose to watch them when I seen their movements," he testified. He saw one of the men leave the other one and walk southwest on Huron Road, past some stores. The man paused for a moment and looked in a store window, then walked on a short distance, turned around and walked back toward the corner, pausing once again to look in the same store window. He rejoined his companion at the corner, and the two conferred briefly. Then the second man went through the same series of motions, strolling down Huron Road, looking in the same window, walking on a short distance, turning back, peering in the store window again, and returning to confer with the first man at the corner. The two men repeated this ritual alternately between five and six times apiece—in all, roughly a dozen trips. At one point, while the two were standing together on the corner, a third man approached them and engaged them briefly in conversation. This man then left the two others and walked west on Euclid Avenue. Chilton and Terry resumed their measured pacing, peering, and conferring. After this had gone on for 10 to 12 minutes, the two men walked off together, heading west on Euclid Avenue, following the path taken earlier by the third man.

By this time Officer McFadden had become thoroughly suspicious. He testified that after observing their elaborately casual and oft-repeated reconnaissance of the store window on Huron Road, he suspected the two men of "casing a job, a stick-up," and that he considered it his duty as a police officer to investigate further. He added that he feared "they may have a gun." Thus, Officer McFadden followed Chilton and Terry and saw them stop in front of Zucker's store to talk to the same man who had conferred with them earlier on the street corner. Deciding that the situation was ripe for direct action, Officer McFadden approached the three men, identified himself as a police officer and asked for their names. At this point his knowledge was confined to what he had observed. He was not acquainted with any of the three men by name or by sight, and he had received no information concerning them from any other source. When the men "mumbled something" in response to his inquiries, Officer McFadden grabbed petitioner Terry, spun him around so that they were facing the other two, with Terry between McFadden and the others, and patted down the outside of his clothing. In the left breast pocket of Terry's overcoat Officer McFadden felt a pistol. He reached inside the overcoat pocket, but was unable to remove the gun. At this point, keeping Terry between himself and the others, the officer ordered all three men to enter Zucker's store. As they went in, he removed Terry's overcoat completely, removed a .38-caliber revolver from the pocket and ordered all three men to face the wall with their hands raised. Officer McFadden proceeded to pat down the outer clothing of Chilton and the third man, Katz. He discovered another revolver in the outer pocket of Chilton's overcoat, but no weapons were found on Katz. The officer testified that he only patted the men down to see whether they had weapons, and that he did not put his hands beneath the outer garments of either Terry or Chilton until he felt their guns. So far as appears from the record, he never placed his hands beneath Katz' outer garments. Officer McFadden seized Chilton's gun, asked the proprietor of the store to call a police wagon, and took all three men to the station, where Chilton and Terry were formally charged with carrying concealed weapons....

I.

... [W]e turn our attention to the quite narrow question posed by the facts before us: whether it is always unreasonable for a policeman to seize a person and subject him to a limited search for weapons unless there is probable cause for an arrest....

II.

Our first task is to establish at what point in this encounter the Fourth Amendment becomes relevant. That is, we must decide whether and when Officer McFadden "seized" Terry and whether and when he conducted a "search." There is some suggestion in the use of such terms as "stop" and "frisk" that such police conduct is outside the purview of the Fourth Amendment because neither action rises to the level of a "search" or "seizure" within the meaning of the Constitution. We emphatically reject this notion. It is quite plain that the Fourth Amendment governs "seizures" of the person which do not

eventuate in a trip to the station house and prosecution for crime—"arrests" in traditional terminology. It must be recognized that whenever a police officer accosts an individual and restrains his freedom to walk away, he has "seized" that person. And it is nothing less than sheer torture of the English language to suggest that a careful exploration of the outer surfaces of a person's clothing all over his or her body in an attempt to find weapons is not a "search."...

In this case there can be no question, then, that Officer McFadden "seized" petitioner and subjected him to a "search" when he took hold of him and patted down the outer surfaces of his clothing. We must decide whether at that point it was reasonable for Officer McFadden to have interfered with petitioner's personal security as he did....

III.

If this case involved police conduct subject to the Warrant Clause of the Fourth Amendment, we would have to ascertain whether "probable cause" existed to justify the search and seizure which took place. However, that is not the case.... [W]e deal here with an entire rubric of police conduct—necessarily swift action predicated upon the on-the-spot observations of the officer on the beat—which historically has not been, and as a practical matter could not be, subjected to the warrant procedure....

Our evaluation of the proper balance that has to be struck in this type of case leads us to conclude that there must be a narrowly drawn authority to permit a reasonable search for weapons for the protection of the police officer, where he has reason to believe that he is dealing with an armed and dangerous individual, regardless of whether he has probable cause to arrest the individual for a crime. The officer need not be absolutely certain that the individual is armed; the issue is whether a reasonably prudent man in the circumstances would be warranted in the belief that his safety or that of others was in danger....

IV.

... We think on the facts and circumstances Officer McFadden detailed before the trial judge a reasonably prudent man would have been warranted in believing petitioner was armed and thus presented a threat to the officer's safety while he was investigating his suspicious behavior. The actions of Terry and Chilton were consistent with McFadden's hypothesis that these men were contemplating a daylight robbery—which, it is reasonable to assume, would be likely to involve the use of weapons—and nothing in their conduct from the time he first noticed them until the time he confronted them and identified himself as a police officer gave him sufficient reason to negate that hypothesis....

V.

We conclude that the revolver seized from Terry was properly admitted in evidence against him. At the time he seized petitioner and searched him for weapons, Officer McFadden had reasonable grounds to believe that petitioner was armed and dangerous, and it was necessary for the protection of himself and others to take swift measures to discover the true facts and neutralize the threat of harm if it materialized.... Such a search is a reasonable search under the Fourth Amendment, and any weapons seized may properly be introduced in evidence against the person from whom they were taken.

Affirmed.

Mr. Justice Black concurs in the judgment....

[*Harlan and White write separate concurring opinions.*]

Mr. Justice Douglas, dissenting....

To give the police greater power than a magistrate is to take a long step down the totalitarian path. Perhaps such a step is desirable to cope with modern forms of lawlessness. But if it is taken, it should be the deliberate choice of the people through a constitutional amendment....

Chimel v. California

395 U.S. 752 (1969)

In this decision, the Supreme Court attempted to limit the scope of a search that is made incident to an arrest. Police officers, armed with an arrest warrant but not a search warrant, were admitted to Ted Steven Chimel's home by his wife. They served him with the arrest warrant when he arrived and proceeded to search the entire house, finding evidence that led to his conviction for burglary. The conviction was upheld by the state courts.

Mr. Justice Stewart delivered the opinion of the Court.

This case raises basic questions concerning the permissible scope under the Fourth Amendment of a search incident to a lawful arrest.

The relevant facts are essentially undisputed. Late in the afternoon of September 13, 1965, three police officers arrived at the Santa Ana, California, home of the petitioner with a warrant authorizing his arrest for the burglary of a coin shop. The officers knocked on the door, identified themselves to the petitioner's wife, and asked if they might come inside. She ushered them into the house, where they waited 10 or 15 minutes until the petitioner returned home from work. When the petitioner entered the house, one of the officers handed him the arrest warrant and asked for permission to "look around." The petitioner objected, but was advised that "on the basis of the lawful arrest," the officers would nonetheless conduct a search. No search warrant had been issued.

Accompanied by the petitioner's wife, the officers then looked through the entire three-bedroom house, including the attic, the garage, and a small workshop. In some rooms the search was relatively cursory. In the master bedroom and sewing room, however, the officers directed the petitioner's wife to open drawers and "to physically move contents of the drawers from side to side so that [they] might view any items that would have come from [the] burglary." After completing the search, they seized numerous items—primarily coins, but also several medals, tokens, and a few other objects. The entire search took between 45 minutes and an hour.

At the petitioner's subsequent state trial on two charges of burglary, the items taken from his house were admitted into evidence against him, over his objection that they had been unconstitutionally seized. He was convicted, and the judgments of conviction were affirmed by both the California Court of Appeal ... and the California Supreme Court.... Both courts accepted the petitioner's contention that the arrest warrant was invalid because the supporting affidavit was set out in conclusory terms, but held that since the arresting officers had procured the warrant "in good faith," and since in any event they had had sufficient information to constitute probable cause for the petitioner's arrest, that arrest had been lawful. From this conclusion the appellate courts went on to hold that the search of the petitioner's home had been justified, despite the absence of a search warrant, on the ground that it had been incident to a valid arrest....

Without deciding the question, we proceed on the hypothesis that the California courts were correct in holding that the arrest of the petitioner was valid under the Constitution. This brings us directly to the question whether the warrantless search of the petitioner's entire house can be constitutionally justified as incident to that arrest. The decisions of this Court bearing upon that question have been far from consistent, as even the most cursory review makes evident....

In 1950 ... came *United States* v. *Rabinowitz,* 339 U.S. 56, the decision upon which California primarily relies in the case now before us. In *Rabinowitz,* federal authorities had been informed that the defendant was dealing in stamps bearing forged overprints. On the basis of that information they secured a warrant for his arrest, which they executed at his one-room business office. At the time of the arrest, the officers "searched the desk, safe, and file cabinets in the office for about an hour and a half," *id.,* at 59, and seized 573 stamps with forged overprints. The stamps were admitted into evidence at the defendant's trial, and this Court affirmed his conviction, rejecting the contention that the warrantless search had been unlawful. The Court held that the search in its entirety fell within the principle giving law enforcement authorities "[t]he right 'to search the place where the arrest is made in order to find and seize things connected with the crime....'" *Id.,* at 61....

Rabinowitz has come to stand for the proposition, *inter alia,* that a warrantless search "incident to a lawful arrest" may generally extend to the area that is considered to be in the "possession" or under the "control" of the person arrested. And it was on the basis of that proposition that the California courts upheld the search of the petitioner's entire house in this case. That doctrine, however, at least in the broad sense in which it was applied by the California courts in this case, can withstand neither historical nor rational analysis.

... Mr. Justice Frankfurter wisely pointed out in his *Rabinowitz* dissent that the Amendment's proscription of "unreasonable searches and seizures" must be read in light of "the history that gave rise to the words"—a history of "abuses so deeply felt by the Colonies as to be one of the potent causes of the Revolution...." 339 U.S., at 69. The Amendment was in large part a reaction to the general warrants and warrantless searches that had so alienated the colonists and had helped speed the movement for independence....

Only last Term in *Terry* v. *Ohio,* 392 U.S. 1, we emphasized that "the police must, whenever practicable, obtain advance judicial approval of searches and seizures through the warrant procedure,"... and that "[t]he scope of [a] search must be 'strictly tied to and justified by' the circumstances which rendered its initiation permissible." ... The search undertaken by the officer in that "stop and frisk" case was sustained under that test, because it was no more than a "protective ... search for weapons."...

A similar analysis underlies the "search incident to arrest" principle, and marks its proper extent. When an arrest is made, it is reasonable for the arresting officer to search the person arrested in order to remove any weapons that the latter might seek to use in order to resist arrest or effect his escape. Otherwise, the officer's safety might well be endangered, and the arrest itself frustrated. In addition, it is entirely reasonable for the arresting officer to search for and seize any evidence on the arrestee's person in order to prevent its concealment or destruction. And the area into which an arrestee might reach in order to grab a weapon or evidentiary items must, of course, be governed by a like rule. A gun on a table or in a drawer in front of one who is arrested can be as dangerous to the arresting officer as one concealed in the clothing of the person arrested. There is ample justification, therefore, for a search of the arrestee's person and the area "within his immediate control"—construing that phrase to mean the area from within which he might gain possession of a weapon or destructible evidence.

There is no comparable justification, however, for routinely searching any room other than that in which an arrest occurs—or, for that matter, for searching through all the desk drawers or other closed or concealed areas in that room itself. Such searches, in the absence of well-recognized exceptions, may be made only under the authority of a search warrant. The "adherence to judicial processes" mandated by the Fourth Amendment requires no less....

Application of sound Fourth Amendment principles to the facts of this case produces a clear result. The search here went far beyond the petitioner's person and the area from within which he might have obtained either a weapon or something that could have been used as evidence against him. There was no constitutional justification, in the absence of a search warrant, for extending the search beyond that area. The scope of the search was, therefore, "unreasonable" under the Fourth and Fourteenth Amendments, and the petitioner's conviction cannot stand.

Reversed.

Mr. Justice Harlan, concurring....

Mr. Justice White, with whom Mr. Justice Black joins, dissenting.

Few areas of the law have been as subject to shifting constitutional standards over the last 50 years as that of the search "incident to an arrest." There has been a remarkable instability in this whole area, which has seen at least four major shifts in emphasis. Today's opinion makes an untimely fifth....

New Jersey v. T.L.O.

469 U.S. 325 (1985)

T.L.O., a 14-year-old high school freshman, was caught smoking in the school bathroom. After being taken to the Principal's office, she denied that she had been smoking and claimed that she did not smoke at all. The Assistant Vice Principal opened her purse, found a pack of cigarettes, cigarette rolling papers commonly associated with the use of marijuana, some marijuana, money, and documents that implicated her in marijuana dealing. The state of New Jersey brought delinquency charges against her in Juvenile Court. After denying her motion to suppress the evidence found in her purse, the court held that the Fourth Amendment applied to searches by school officials but that the search in question was a reasonable one. The Appellate Division of the New Jersey Superior Court affirmed that there had been no Fourth Amendment violation. The New Jersey Supreme Court reversed and ordered the suppression of the evidence on the ground that the search of the purse was unreasonable.

Justice White delivered the opinion of the Court.

We granted certiorari in this case to examine the appropriateness of the exclusionary rule as a remedy for searches carried out in violation of the Fourth Amendment by public school authorities. Our consideration of the proper application of the Fourth Amendment to the public schools, however, has led us to conclude that the search that gave rise to the case now before us did not violate the Fourth Amendment. Accordingly, we here address only the questions of the proper standard for assessing the legality of searches conducted by public school officials and the application of that standard to the facts of this case.

I

On March 7, 1980, a teacher at Piscataway High School in Middlesex County, N.J., discovered two girls smoking in a lavatory. One of the two girls was the respondent T.L.O., who at that time was a 14-year-old high school freshman. Because smoking in the lavatory was a violation of a school rule, the teacher took the two girls to the Principal's office, where they met with Assistant Vice Principal Theodore Choplick. In response to questioning by Mr. Choplick, T.L.O.'s companion admitted that she had violated the rule. T.L.O., however, denied that she had been smoking in the lavatory and claimed that she did not smoke at all.

Mr. Choplick asked T.L.O. to come into his private office and demanded to see her purse. Opening the purse, he found a pack of cigarettes, which he removed from the purse and held before T.L.O. as he accused her of having lied to him. As he reached into the purse for the cigarettes, Mr. Choplick also noticed a package of cigarette rolling papers. In his experience, possession of rolling papers by high school students was closely associated with the use of marihuana. Suspecting that a closer examination of the purse might yield further evidence of drug use, Mr. Choplick proceeded to search the purse thoroughly. The search revealed a small amount of marihuana, a pipe, a number of empty plastic bags, a substantial quantity of money in one-dollar bills, an index card that appeared to be a list of students who owed T.L.O. money, and two letters that implicated T.L.O. in marihuana dealing.

Mr. Choplick notified T.L.O.'s mother and the police, and turned the evidence of drug dealing over to the police. At the request of the police, T.L.O.'s mother took her daughter to police headquarters, where T.L.O. confessed that she had been selling marihuana at the high school. On the basis of the confession and the evidence seized by Mr. Choplick, the State brought delinquency charges against T.L.O. in the Juvenile and Domestic Relations Court of Middlesex County. Contending that Mr. Choplick's search of her purse violated the Fourth Amendment, T.L.O. moved to suppress the evidence found in her purse as well as her confession, ...

II

In determining whether the search at issue in this

case violated the Fourth Amendment, we are faced initially with the question whether that Amendment's prohibition on unreasonable searches and seizures applies to searches conducted by public school officials. We hold that it does.

... [T]he State of New Jersey has argued that the history of the Fourth Amendment indicates that the Amendment was intended to regulate only searches and seizures carried out by law enforcement officers; accordingly, although public school officials are concededly state agents for purposes of the Fourteenth Amendment, the Fourth Amendment creates no rights enforceable against them.

It may well be true that the evil toward which the Fourth Amendment was primarily directed was the resurrection of the pre-Revolutionary practice of using general warrants or "writs of assistance" to authorize searches for contraband by officers of the Crown.... But this Court has never limited the Amendment's prohibition on unreasonable searches and seizures to operations conducted by the police. Rather, the Court has long spoken of the Fourth Amendment's strictures as restraints imposed upon "governmental action"—that is, "upon the activities of sovereign authority." ...

III

To hold that the Fourth Amendment applies to searches conducted by school authorities is only to begin the inquiry into the standards governing such searches....

Although this Court may take notice of the difficulty of maintaining discipline in the public schools today, the situation is not so dire that students in the schools may claim no legitimate expectations of privacy....

... Students at a minimum must bring to school not only the supplies needed for their studies, but also keys, money, and the necessaries of personal hygiene and grooming. In addition, students may carry on their persons or in purses or wallets such nondisruptive yet highly personal items as photographs, letters, and diaries. Finally, students may have perfectly legitimate reasons to carry with them articles of property needed in connection with extracurricular or recreational activities. In short, schoolchildren may find it necessary to carry with them a variety of legitimate, noncontraband items, and there is no reason to conclude that they have necessarily waived all rights to privacy in such items merely by bringing them onto school grounds.

Against the child's interest in privacy must be set the substantial interest of teachers and administrators in maintaining discipline in the classroom and on school grounds. Maintaining order in the classroom has never been easy, but in recent years, school disorder has often taken particularly ugly forms: drug use and violent crime in the schools have become major social problems....

... It is evident that the school setting requires some easing of the restrictions to which searches by public authorities are ordinarily subject. The warrant requirement, in particular, is unsuited to the school environment: requiring a teacher to obtain a warrant before searching a child suspected of an infraction of school rules (or of the criminal law) would unduly interfere with the maintenance of the swift and informal disciplinary procedures needed in the schools....

The school setting also requires some modification of the level of suspicion of illicit activity needed to justify a search. Ordinarily, a search—even one that may permissibly be carried out without a warrant—must be based upon "probable cause" to believe that a violation of the law has occurred.... However, "probable cause" is not an irreducible requirement of a valid search. The fundamental command of the Fourth Amendment is that searches and seizures be reasonable....

... Determining the reasonableness of any search involves a twofold inquiry: first, one must consider "whether the ... action was justified at its inception," *Terry* v. *Ohio*, 392 U.S., at 20; second, one must determine whether the search as actually conducted "was reasonably related in scope to the circumstances which justified the interference in the first place," *ibid.* Under ordinary circumstances, a search of a student by a teacher or other school official will be "justified at its inception" when there are reasonable grounds for suspecting that the search will turn up evidence that the student has violated or is violating either the law or the rules of the school....

IV

... T.L.O. had been accused of smoking, and had denied the accusation in the strongest possible terms when she stated that she did not smoke at all. Surely it cannot be said that under these circumstances, T.L.O.'s possession of cigarettes would be irrelevant to the charges against her or to her response to those charges....

Our conclusion that Mr. Choplick's decision to open T.L.O.'s purse was reasonable brings us to the question of the further search for marihuana once the pack of cigarettes was located.... The discovery of the rolling papers concededly gave rise to a reasonable suspicion that T.L.O. was carrying marihuana as well as cigarettes in her purse. This suspicion justified further exploration of T.L.O.'s purse, which turned up more evidence of drug-related activities: a pipe, a number of plastic bags of the type commonly used to store marihuana, a small quantity of marihuana, and a fairly substantial amount of money. Under these circumstances, it was not unreasonable to extend the search to a separate zippered compartment of the purse; and when a search of that compartment revealed an index card containing a list of "people who owe me money" as well as two letters, the inference that T.L.O. was involved in marihuana trafficking was substantial enough to justify Mr. Choplick in examining the letters to determine whether they contained any further evidence. In short, we cannot conclude that the search for marihuana was unreasonable in any respect.

Because the search resulting in the discovery of the evidence of marijuana dealing by T.L.O. was reasonable, the New Jersey Supreme Court's decision to exclude that evidence from T.L.O.'s juvenile delinquency proceedings on Fourth Amendment grounds was erroneous. Accordingly, the judgment of the Supreme Court of New Jersey is

Reversed.

Justice Powell, with whom Justice O'Connor joins, concurring....

Justice Blackmun, concurring in the judgment....

Justice Brennan, with whom Justice Marshall joins, concurring in part and dissenting in part. [*Agrees that teachers, like other government officials, must conform their conduct to the Fourth Amendment's protections of personal privacy and personal security, but rejects the standard of "reasonableness" as "unclear, unprecedented, and unnecessary."*]

Justice Stevens, with whom Justice Marshall joins, and with whom Justice Brennan joins as to Part I, concurring in part and dissenting in part. [*Objects that the Court "unnecessarily and inappropriately" reached out to decide a constitutional question, and that the decision "will permit school administrators to search students suspected of violating only the most trivial school regulations and guidelines for behavior."*]

D. ELECTRONIC EAVESDROPPING

The framers understood how eavesdropping could intrude upon personal privacy. The use of *electronic* eavesdropping, however, forced Congress and the Supreme Court to interpret eighteenth-century language in the Fourth Amendment in light of the latest technological advances. The use of wiretapping by law enforcement officials requires the active involvement of all three branches.

The Court first confronted electronic eavesdropping when it considered the use of wiretaps by prohibition agents in the 1920s to monitor and intercept telephone calls. Small wires were inserted in telephone wires leading from residences. Taps could be made in the streets near the houses or in the basement of large office buildings. In a bitterly divided 5–4 decision, the Court reasoned that there was no violation of the Fourth Amendment because the taps did not *enter* the premises. Hence, there was neither "search" nor "seizure." This wooden assessment provoked a scathing dissent from Justice Brandeis, who accurately predicted that technology would overwhelm the Fourth Amendment unless the Court met the challenge with open eyes. OLMSTEAD v. UNITED STATES, 277 U.S. 438 (1928).

Chief Justice Taft, writing for the majority, invited Congress to establish boundaries for wiretapping: "Congress may of course protect the secrecy of telephone messages by making them, when intercepted, inadmissible in evidence in federal criminal trials, by direct legislation, and thus depart from the common law of evidence." Id. at 465–66. Section 605 of the Federal Communications Act of 1934 was intended to fill that gap by making it a crime to intercept or to use any wire or radio communication. Because of that statute, the government could not introduce as trial evidence any information obtained from a wiretap.[10] This restriction, however, did not prevent the government from using wiretaps to "induce" people whose conversations had been overheard to turn state's evidence and appear as witnesses for the government. Goldstein v. United States, 316 U.S. 114 (1942).

---

10. Nardone v. United States, 302 U.S. 379 (1937); Weiss v. United States, 308 U.S. 321 (1939); Nardone v. United States, 308 U.S. 338 (1939).

Roosevelt's Confidential Memo on Wiretapping

[To Attorney General Robert H. Jackson, May 21, 1940]

I am convinced that the Supreme Court never intended any dictum in the particular case which it decided to apply to grave matters involving the defense of the Nation.

It is, of course, well known that certain other nations have been engaged in the organization of propaganda of so-called "fifth columns" in other countries and in preparation for sabotage, as well as in actual sabotage.

You are, therefore, authorized and directed in such cases as you may approve, after investigation of the need in each case, to authorize the necessary investigating agents that they are at liberty to secure information by listening devices direct to the conversation or other communications of persons suspected of subversive activities against the Government of the United States, including suspected spies. You are requested furthermore to limit these investigations so conducted to a minimum and to limit them in so far as possible to aliens.

SOURCE: Francis Biddle, In Brief Authority 167 (1962).

Executive Practices

In the 1930s, the executive branch followed a divided policy on wiretapping. The Bureau of Investigation (later the Federal Bureau of Investigation) regarded wiretapping as unethical and impermissible under the regulations of the Attorney General. The Bureau of Prohibition, located within the Department of the Treasury, freely admitted to using wiretapping. Congress considered, but never passed, statutory prohibitions on wiretapping by the Bureau of Prohibition. The Bureau was abolished after the states ratified the Twenty-First Amendment in 1933, repealing the constitutional prohibition on liquor.

In the early 1940s, committee reports from the House of Representatives recommended that certain federal agencies be authorized to wiretap for purposes of national security, including investigations into sabotage, treason, seditious conspiracy, espionage, and violations of the neutrality law. The House passed such a bill in 1940, but the Senate took no action. After the attack on Pearl Harbor on December 7, 1941, the House passed legislation to authorize wiretapping for national security purposes. Again, the Senate did not take up the bill.

Denied statutory authority for wiretapping, the executive branch took matters into its own hands. On March 18, 1940, Attorney General Robert H. Jackson issued the following order to the Bureau of Investigation: "Wire tapping: Telephone or telegraph wires shall not be tapped unless prior authorization of the Director of the Bureau has been secured." 86 Cong. Rec. A1471 (1940). On May 21, 1940, President Franklin D. Roosevelt sent a confidential memorandum to Jackson that permitted wiretapping in selected areas (see box).

Technological Advances

Until *Olmstead* was overturned in 1967, the Court wrestled with new forms of technological intrusion. Federal agents used a "detectaphone" to overhear telephone conversations. This instrument, placed against the wall of a room, could pick up sound waves on the other side of the wall. A receiver amplified the sound waves and allowed agents to listen to phone conversations. The Court held that there was neither a "communication" nor an "interception" within the meaning of Section 605. Relying on *Olmstead*, the Court found no violation of the Fourth Amendment. Goldman v. United States, 316 U.S. 129 (1942). Undercover agents, equipped with a radio transmitter, were allowed to stand in a laundry and engage a suspect in conversation. His self-incriminating statements were picked up by a radio receiver and used to convict him. The Court ruled that there was neither "search" nor "seizure" because the government did not trespass when it entered the suspect's store. On Lee v. United States, 343 U.S. 747 (1952).

The ingenuity of investigators and police easily outpaced the Court's interpretation of the Fourth Amendment. Using a key made by a locksmith, state police entered the home of a suspect and installed a concealed microphone in the hall. A hole was bored in the roof to allow wires to transmit sounds to a neighboring garage. The police returned later and moved the microphone to a bedroom and came back a third time to move it to a closet. Although a trespass and probably a burglary had been committed, the Court found no violation of Section 605 and upheld the action. Irvine v. California, 347 U.S. 128 (1954). The Court blithely noted: "All that was heard through the microphone was what an eavesdropper, hidden in the hall, the bedroom, or the closet, might have heard." All that and nothing more!

Other variations of electronic eavesdropping blossomed. Police officers used an extension phone in an adjoining room to listen to a conversation. They had the consent of the subscriber (who was a party to the conversation) but not the consent of the sender, which Section 605 required. Nevertheless, the Court held that the contents of the communication were admissible in a federal criminal trial because there was no "interception" within the meaning of Section 605. The Court remarked that every party to a telephone conversation takes the risk that the other party may have an extension phone, allowing others to overhear the conversation. Rathbun v. United States, 355 U.S. 107, 111 (1957). A decade later the Court held that the use of a four-party line, with one line connected to a phone that permits the police to hear and record all conversations without lifting the receiver, violated Section 605 because it intercepted and divulged a communication. Lee v. Florida, 392 U.S. 378 (1968). The police deliberately arranged to have the four-party line connected to a suspect's house, whereas in *Rathbun* the extension phone had not been installed just for the police.

In another case, government agents pushed an electronic listening device through the wall of an adjoining house until it touched the heating duct of a suspect's house. Through the use of this "spike mike," officers with earphones listened to conversations taking place on both floors of the house. The Court held that this physical penetration into the suspect's house violated the Fourth Amendment. Silverman v. United States, 365 U.S. 505 (1961). Three years later, the Court reversed a state court decision that had upheld the use of evidence obtained by a small microphone that had been stuck in a wall, penetrating to the depth of a thumb tack. Clinton v. Virginia, 377 U.S. 158; 130 S.E.2d 437.

On some occasions federal judges were asked to authorize an electronic device to record conversations. For example, a lawyer was suspected of wanting to bribe a prospective member of a federal jury. He had hired a Nashville policeman to investigate backgrounds of potential jurors, unaware that the policeman had also agreed to report to federal agents any illegal activities he observed. The district court authorized the placement of a tape recorder on the policeman to record future conversations about bribe efforts. The Court upheld the admissibility of these conversations, which led to the lawyer's conviction. Osborn v. United States, 385 U.S. 323 (1966).

Judicial Restrictions

Two decisions in 1967 placed major constraints on electronic eavesdropping. A New York law was struck down because it permitted the installation of recording devices without requiring the police to specify that a particular crime had been or was being committed. Also, the police failed to particularly describe the conversations sought. The broad sweep of the statute violated the Fourth Amendment. Berger v. New York, 388 U.S. 41 (1967). Also in 1967, the Court finally overturned the "trespass" doctrine of *Olmstead* and *Goldman*. By a 7–1 vote, the Court declared unconstitutional the placing of electronic listening and recording devices on the outside of public telephone booths to obtain incriminating evidence. Although there was no physical entrance into the area occupied by the suspect, he had a legitimate expectation of privacy within the phone booth. In a broadly principled decision capable of accommodating technological ingenuity, the Court held that the Fourth Amendment "protects people, not places." KATZ v. UNITED STATES, 389 U.S. 347, 351 (1967).

In response to *Katz,* Congress passed legislation in 1968 requiring law enforcement officers to obtain a warrant before placing taps on phones or installing bugs (concealed microphones). If an "emergency" exists, communications can be intercepted for up to 48 hours without a warrant in cases involving organized crime or national security. Warrants are limited to specific periods of time. After a wire intercept is terminated, the person monitored is informed of the fact and date of the entry. 82 Stat. 212; 18 U.S.C. §§ 2510–20.

Judicial activity after 1968 concentrated more on statutory construction than on constitutional interpretation. A number of cases examined the government's compliance with the wiretap statute.[11] The Court decided that the Fourth Amendment and congressional legislation protect the *content* of communications, not the numbers dialed from a phone. Smith v. Maryland, 442 U.S. 735 (1979). Although the wiretap law does not explicitly authorize covert entry to install bugging equipment, the Court has held that the language and purpose of the statute implicitly authorize such action without violating the Fourth Amendment. Dalia v. United States, 441 U.S. 238 (1979). (For judicial and congressional action on electronic surveillance for "national security" purposes, see Chapter 7.)

High-Tech Surveillance

Court doctrines and congressional statutes are periodically tested and outstripped by new technology. "Beepers" (battery-operated radio transmitters) allow law enforcement officers to follow cars and locate illegal operations. United States v. Knotts, 460 U.S. 276 (1983). The use of a beeper to monitor the movement of articles within a private residence, however, is not permitted under the Fourth Amendment. United States v. Karo, 468 U.S. 705 (1984). Other developments include electronic mail, cellular and cordless phones, night vision cameras, parabolic microphones to pick up conversations in homes or offices, satellite communication systems, and closed-circuit video cameras.

In 2001, a 5–4 Court decided that thermal imaging constituted a "search" within the meaning of the Fourth Amendment. The device allows police officers outside a home to measure heat emanating from the inside (such as heat needed to grow marijuana plants). Kyllo v. United States, 533 U.S. 27 (2001). The majority limited its ruling to technology that "is not in general public use." What happens when such devices are available at local stores?

Technological innovations made it necessary for Congress to rethink and rewrite the law on electronic eavesdropping. Federal judges appealed to Congress to pass legislation that would clarify Fourth Amendment law. United States v. Torres, 751 F.2d 875, 885–86 (7th Cir. 1984). Congress passed legislation in 1986 to modernize the restrictions on electronic eavesdropping. During the debate in the House of Representatives, the floor manager, Congressman Robert Kastenmeier, noted: "We may provide the forum to balance the privacy rights of citizens with the legitimate law enforcement needs of the Government; or we abdicate that role to ad hoc decisions made by the courts and the executive branch." 132 Cong. Rec. 14886 (1986). Congress passed additional legislation in 1994 to help police wiretappers keep pace with advancing technology. 108 Stat. 4279 (1994).

USA Patriot Act

After the 9/11 terrorist attacks, Congress enacted the USA Patriot Act in 2001 to give federal officials greater authority to track and intercept communications. The statute expands the powers of both law

---

11. E.g., United States v. Ojeda Rios, 495 U.S. 257 (1990); Scott v. United States, 436 U.S. 128 (1978); United States v. New York Telephone Co., 434 U.S. 159 (1977); United States v. Donovan, 429 U.S. 413 (1977); United States v. Chavez, 416 U.S. 562 (1974); United States v. Giordano, 416 U.S. 505 (1974); United States v. Kahn, 415 U.S. 143 (1974).

enforcement and foreign intelligence investigators. Section 219 authorizes nationwide service of search warrants in terrorism investigations. A single judge, having authorized the first warrant, may grant future warrants in other jurisdictions. Section 206 provides for roving wiretaps under the Foreign Intelligence Surveillance Act. This provision allows surveillance to follow a person, thus avoiding the need for a separate court order that identifies each telephone company every time the target of investigation changes phones. Section 213, referred to as "sneak and peak," authorizes surreptitious search warrants and seizures without the previous requirement to immediately notify a person of the entry and the seized items. Law enforcement officers may therefore enter someone's home without giving immediate notice, which may be delayed for "a reasonable period."

The FISA Court

The Foreign Intelligence Surveillance Act (FISA) of 1978 created a statutory framework for using electronic surveillance to gather foreign intelligence. Congress rejected the previous practice of administrations that conducted warrantless surveillance of U.S. citizens and domestic organizations. The statute created a special court (the FISA court) to review applications of the federal government for this type of surveillance. The USA Patriot Act of 2001 increased the number of judges from 7 to 11 and also changed the requirements placed on federal officers when applying for a search order. The 1978 legislation required the government to certify that "the purpose" of the surveillance was to obtain foreign intelligence information. The 2001 amendment allows application if a "significant purpose" is to obtain foreign intelligence information. The new language blurs the line between the use of surveillance for gathering foreign intelligence (the central objective of the 1978 statute) and using it more broadly for criminal law enforcement purposes.

From the operation of FISA in May 1979 to 2002, the FISA court approved almost all of the government's applications for a search order. That pattern changed on May 17, 2002, when the court released its first published opinion. It now challenged the government's argument that FISA can be used "primarily for a law enforcement purpose, so long as a significant foreign intelligence purpose remains." While sidestepping that question, the court disclosed that the Clinton administration had included errors in 75 FISA applications, and that additional errors appeared in applications submitted by the George W. Bush administration.

The court was particularly troubled by an inadequate "wall" between FISA information-gathering and criminal investigations. It charged that procedures adopted by the administration in March 2002 "appear to be designed to amend the law." The court objected not to information-sharing but to the capacity of law enforcement investigators to give advice to FISA searches. To the court, *coordination* between intelligence and criminal investigations had been replaced by the *subordination* of both investigations to law enforcement objectives. In re All Matters to Foreign Intelligence Surveil., 218 F.Supp.2d 611 (Foreign Intel. Surv. Ct. 2002). A three-judge FISA appeals court reversed the May 17 ruling and upheld the authority of criminal prosecutors to be actively involved in foreign intelligence wiretaps. The court did not find in the 1978 statute, or in any litigation since that time, a requirement that a "wall" be maintained between the acquisition of intelligence and the needs of criminal law enforcement. In re Sealed Case, 310 F.3d 717 (Foreign Intel. Surv. Ct. of Rev. 2002).

Bush's NSA Surveillance

In December 2005, a story in the *New York Times* revealed the existence of a secret surveillance program carried out by the National Security Agency after the terrorist attacks of 9/11. President Bush and other administration officials, admitting the operation of a warrantless eavesdropping program, explained that it was directed only at listening to and intercepting international phone and e-mail communications between someone in the United States and another person suspected of ties to al Qaeda and related terrorist organizations. The administration offered statutory and constitutional arguments to defend the legality of the program. In May 2006, *USA Today* described a separate eavesdropping activity by the administration, this one involving the collection and monitoring of phone numbers rather than actual conversations. The administration neither confirmed nor denied this program, and several telephone companies denied that they had given customer calling records to the NSA.

On July 25, 2006, a district judge in Illinois dismissed a class-action lawsuit against this second program. The judge noted that "no executive branch official has officially confirmed or denied the existence of any program to obtain large quantities of customer telephone records." By invoking the state secrets privilege, the government prevented the plaintiffs from seeking additional facts or documents to establish that they had been harmed or would suffer harm in the future. Consequently, the judge ruled that the plaintiffs could not seek relief in the courts and would have to seek redress from the political branches.

Litigation on the first program led to different results. On July 20, 2006, a district judge in California refused to dismiss a lawsuit against AT&T. The state secrets privilege, said the judge, did not apply in this case because the administration had publicly acknowledged the program and defended its legality. On August 17, 2006, a district court in Michigan ruled that the warrantless surveillance of international communications violated the Constitution and federal statutes. Like the judge in California, the court took note of the fact that the program had been admitted by the administration. The Michigan court was reversed by the Sixth Circuit and the Supreme Court refused to hear the case. Dozens of other lawsuits contested the legality of NSA eavesdropping. In 2008, as part of revisions to the FISA legislation, Congress granted immunity to the telecoms. See Louis Fisher, The Constitution and 9/11, at 285–320 (2008).

Olmstead v. United States

277 U.S. 438 (1928)

Roy Olmstead and several accomplices were convicted of violating the National Prohibition Act by importing and selling liquor. On the basis of evidence obtained by wiretapping telephone conversations, indictments were handed down against more than seventy individuals involved in an extensive operation that reached across the Canadian border. The Ninth Circuit upheld the convictions.

Mr. Chief Justice Taft delivered the opinion of the Court....

The information which led to the discovery of the conspiracy and its nature and extent was largely obtained by intercepting messages on the telephones of the conspirators by four federal prohibition officers. Small wires were inserted along the ordinary telephone wires from the residences of four of the petitioners and those leading from the chief office. The insertions were made without trespass upon any property of the defendants. They were made in the basement of the large office building. The taps from house lines were made in the streets near the houses.

The gathering of evidence continued for many months. Conversations of the conspirators of which refreshing stenographic notes were currently made, were testified to by the government witnesses. They revealed the large business transactions of the part-

ners and their subordinates. Men at the wires heard the orders given for liquor by customers and the acceptances; they became auditors of the conversations between the partners. All this disclosed the conspiracy charged in the indictment. Many of the intercepted conversations were not merely reports but parts of the criminal acts. The evidence also disclosed the difficulties to which the conspirators were subjected, the reported news of the capture of vessels, the arrest of their men and the seizure of cases of liquor in garages and other places. It showed the dealing by Olmstead, the chief conspirator, with members of the Seattle police, the messages to them which secured the release of arrested members of the conspiracy, and also direct promises to officers of payments as soon as opportunity offered....

The [*Fourth*] Amendment itself shows that the search is to be of material things—the person, the house, his papers or his effects. The description of the warrant necessary to make the proceeding lawful, is that it must specify the place to be searched and the person or *things* to be seized.

It is urged that the language of Mr. Justice Field in *Ex parte Jackson* ... offers an analogy to the interpretation of the Fourth Amendment in respect of wire tapping. But the analogy fails. The Fourth Amendment may have proper application to a sealed letter in the mail because of the constitutional provision for the Postoffice Department and the relations between the Government and those who pay to secure protection of their sealed letters. See Revised Statutes, §§ 3978 to 3988, whereby Congress monopolizes the carriage of letters and excludes from that business everyone else, and § 3929 which forbids any postmaster or other person to open any letter not addressed to himself. It is plainly within the words of the Amendment to say that the unlawful rifling by a government agent of a sealed letter is a search and seizure of the sender's papers or effects. The letter is a paper, an effect, and in the custody of a Government that forbids carriage except under its protection.

The United States takes no such care of telegraph or telephone messages as of mailed sealed letters. The Amendment does not forbid what was done here. There was no searching. There was no seizure. The evidence was secured by the use of the sense of hearing and that only. There was no entry of the houses or offices of the defendants.

... The language of the Amendment can not be extended and expanded to include telephone wires reaching to the whole world from the defendant's house or office. The intervening wires are not part of his house or office any more than are the highways along which they are stretched.

This Court in *Carroll* v. *United States,* 267 U.S. 132, 149, declared:

"The Fourth Amendment is to be construed in the light of what was deemed an unreasonable search and seizure when it was adopted and in a manner which will conserve public interests as well as the interests and rights of individual citizens." ...

Congress may of course protect the secrecy of telephone messages by making them, when intercepted, inadmissible in evidence in federal criminal trials, by direct legislation, and thus depart from the common law of evidence. But the courts may not adopt such a policy by attributing an enlarged and unusual meaning to the Fourth Amendment. The reasonable view is that one who installs in his house a telephone instrument with connecting wires in-

tends to project his voice to those quite outside, and that the wires beyond his house and messages while passing over them are not within the protection of the Fourth Amendment....

A standard which would forbid the reception of evidence if obtained by other than nice ethical conduct by government officials would make society suffer and give criminals greater immunity than has been known heretofore....

The judgments of the Circuit Court of Appeals are affirmed. The mandates will go down forthwith under Rule 31.

Affirmed.

MR. JUSTICE HOLMES:

... It is desirable that criminals should be detected, and to that end that all available evidence should be used. It also is desirable that the Government should not itself foster and pay for other crimes, when they are the means by which the evidence is to be obtained.... We have to choose, and for my part I think it a less evil that some criminals should escape than that the Government should play an ignoble part....

MR. JUSTICE BRANDEIS, dissenting....

When the Fourth and Fifth Amendments were adopted, "the form that evil had theretofore taken," had been necessarily simple. Force and violence were then the only means known to man by which a Government could directly effect self-incrimination.... Subtler and more far-reaching means of invading privacy have become available to the Government. Discovery and invention have made it possible for the Government, by means far more effective than stretching upon the rack, to obtain disclosure in court of what is whispered in the closet.

Moreover, "in the application of a constitution, our contemplation cannot be only of what has been but of what may be." The progress of science in furnishing the Government with means of espionage is not likely to stop with wire-tapping. Ways may some day be developed by which the Government, without removing papers from secret drawers, can reproduce them in court, and by which it will be enabled to expose to a jury the most intimate occurrences of the home. Advances in the psychic and related sciences may bring means of exploring unexpressed beliefs, thoughts and emotions....

The protection guaranteed by the [*Fourth and Fifth*] Amendments is much broader in scope. The makers of our Constitution undertook to secure conditions favorable to the pursuit of happiness. They recognized the significance of man's spiritual nature, of his feelings and of his intellect. They knew that only a part of the pain, pleasure and satisfactions of life are to be found in material things. They sought to protect Americans in their beliefs, their thoughts, their emotions and their sensations. They conferred, as against the Government, the right to be let alone—the most comprehensive of rights and the right most valued by civilized men. To protect that right, every unjustifiable intrusion by the Government upon the privacy of the individual, whatever the means employed, must be deemed a violation of the Fourth Amendment. And the use, as evidence in a criminal proceeding, of facts ascertained by such intrusion must be deemed a violation of the Fifth.

Applying to the Fourth and Fifth Amendments the established rule of construction, the defendants' objections to the evidence obtained by wire-tapping must, in my opinion, be sustained. It is, of course, immaterial where the physical connection with the telephone wires leading into the defendants' premises was made. And it is also immaterial that the intrusion was in aid of law enforcement. Experience should teach us to be most on our guard to protect liberty when the Government's purposes are beneficent. Men born to freedom are naturally alert to repel invasion of their liberty by evil-minded rulers. The greatest dangers to liberty lurk in insidious encroachment by men of zeal, well-meaning but without understanding. . . .

Decency, security and liberty alike demand that government officials shall be subjected to the same rules of conduct that are commands to the citizen. In a government of laws, existence of the government will be imperilled if it fails to observe the law scrupulously. Our Government is the potent, the omnipresent teacher. For good or for ill, it teaches the whole people by its example. Crime is contagious. If the Government becomes a lawbreaker, it breeds contempt for law; it invites every man to become a law unto himself; it invites anarchy. To declare that in the administration of the criminal law the end justifies the means—to declare that the Government may commit crimes in order to secure the conviction of a private criminal—would bring terrible retribution. Against that pernicious doctrine this Court should resolutely set its face.

[Butler and Stone wrote separate dissenting opinions.]

Katz v. United States

389 U.S. 347 (1967)

Charles Katz was convicted for transmitting information on bets and wagers by telephone across state lines. FBI agents overheard his phone conversations by attaching an electronic listening and recording device to the top of a public telephone booth he used. The Ninth Circuit affirmed his conviction, finding that there was no Fourth Amendment violation since there was "no physical entrance into the area occupied by" Katz.

Mr. Justice Stewart delivered the opinion of the Court.

. . . [T]he parties have attached great significance to the characterization of the telephone booth from which the petitioner placed his calls. The petitioner has strenuously argued that the booth was a "constitutionally protected area." The Government has maintained with equal vigor that it was not. But this effort to decide whether or not a given "area," viewed in the abstract, is "constitutionally protected" deflects attention from the problem presented by this case. For the Fourth Amendment protects people, not places. What a person knowingly exposes to the public, even in his own home or office, is not a subject of Fourth Amendment protection. . . . But what he seeks to preserve as private, even in an area accessible to the public, may be constitutionally protected. . . .

The Government stresses the fact that the telephone booth from which the petitioner made his calls was constructed partly of glass, so that he was as visible after he entered it as he would have been if he had remained outside. But what he sought to exclude when he entered the booth was not the intruding eye—it was the uninvited ear. He did not shed his right to do so simply because he made his calls from a place where he might be seen. No less than an individual in a business office, in a friend's apartment, or in a taxicab, a person in a telephone booth may rely upon the protection of the Fourth Amendment. One who occupies it, shuts the door behind him, and pays the toll that permits him to place a call is surely entitled to assume that the words he utters into the mouthpiece will not be broadcast to the world. To read the Constitution more narrowly is to ignore the vital role that the public telephone has come to play in private communication.

The Government contends, however, that the activities of its agents in this case should not be tested by Fourth Amendment requirements, for the surveillance technique they employed involved no physical penetration of the telephone booth from which the petitioner placed his calls. It is true that the absence of such penetration was at one time thought to foreclose further Fourth Amendment inquiry, *Olmstead* v. *United States,* 277 U.S. 438, 457, 464, 466; *Goldman* v. *United States,* 316 U.S. 129, 134–136, for that Amendment was thought to limit only searches and seizures of tangible property. But "[t]he premise that property interests control the right of the Government to search and seize has been discredited." *Warden* v. *Hayden,* 387 U.S. 294, 304. Thus, although a closely divided Court supposed in *Olmstead* that surveillance without any trespass and without the seizure of any material object fell outside the ambit of the Constitution, we have since departed from the narrow view on which that decision rested. Indeed, we have expressly held that the Fourth Amendment governs not only the seizure of tangible items, but extends as well to the recording of oral statements, overheard without any "technical trespass under … local property law." *Silverman* v. *United States,* 365 U.S. 505, 511. Once this much is acknowledged, and once it is recognized that the Fourth Amendment protects people — and not simply "areas" — against unreasonable searches and seizures, it becomes clear that the reach of that Amendment cannot turn upon the presence or absence of a physical intrusion into any given enclosure.

We conclude that the underpinnings of *Olmstead* and *Goldman* have been so eroded by our subsequent decisions that the "trespass" doctrine there enunciated can no longer be regarded as controlling. The Government's activities in electronically listening to and recording the petitioner's words violated the privacy upon which he justifiably relied while using the telephone booth and thus constituted a "search and seizure" within the meaning of the Fourth Amendment. The fact that the electronic device employed to achieve that end did not happen to penetrate the wall of the booth can have no constitutional significance.

The question remaining for decision, then, is whether the search and seizure conducted in this case complied with constitutional standards. In that regard, the Government's position is that its agents acted in an entirely defensible manner: They did not begin their electronic surveillance until investigation of the petitioner's activities had established a strong probability that he was using the telephone in question to transmit gambling information to persons in other States, in violation of federal law. Moreover, the surveillance was limited, both in scope and in duration, to the specific purpose of establishing the contents of the petitioner's unlawful telephonic communications. The agents confined their surveillance to the brief periods during which he used the telephone booth, and they took great care to overhear only the conversations of the petitioner himself.

Accepting this account of the Government's actions as accurate, it is clear that this surveillance was so narrowly circumscribed that a duly authorized magistrate, properly notified of the need for such investigation, specifically informed of the basis on which it was to proceed, and clearly apprised of the precise intrusion it would entail, could constitutionally have authorized, with appropriate safeguards, the very limited search and seizure that the Government asserts in fact took place....

The Government urges that, because its agents relied upon the decisions in *Olmstead* and *Goldman,* and because they did no more here than they might properly have done with prior judicial sanction, we should retroactively validate their conduct. That we cannot do. It is apparent that the agents in this case acted with restraint. Yet the inescapable fact is that this restraint was imposed by the agents themselves, not by a judicial officer. They were not required, before commencing the search, to present their estimate of probable cause for detached scrutiny by a neutral magistrate. They were not compelled, during the conduct of the search itself, to observe precise limits established in advance by a specific court order. Nor were they directed, after the search had been completed, to notify the authorizing magistrate in detail of all that had been seized. In the absence of such safeguards, this Court has never sustained a search upon the sole ground that officers reasonably expected to find evidence of a particular crime and voluntarily confined their activities to the least intrusive means consistent with that end.... [S]earches conducted outside the judicial process, without prior approval by judge or magistrate, are *per se* unreasonable under the Fourth Amendment — subject only to a few specifically established and well-delineated exceptions.

It is difficult to imagine how any of those exceptions could ever apply to the sort of search and seizure involved in this case. Even electronic surveillance substantially contemporaneous with an individual's arrest could hardly be deemed an "incident" of that arrest. Nor could the use of electronic surveillance without prior authorization be justified on grounds of "hot pursuit." And, of course, the very nature of electronic surveillance precludes its use pursuant to the suspect's consent.

The Government does not question these basic principles. Rather, it urges the creation of a new exception to cover this case. It argues that surveillance of a telephone booth should be exempted from the usual requirement of advance authorization by a magistrate upon a showing of probable cause. We cannot agree....

... Wherever a man may be, he is entitled to know that he will remain free from unreasonable searches and seizures.... Because the surveillance here failed to meet that condition, and because it led to the petitioner's conviction, the judgment must be reversed.

It is so ordered.

MR. JUSTICE MARSHALL took no part in the consideration or decision of this case.

MR. JUSTICE DOUGLAS, with whom MR. JUSTICE BRENNAN joins, concurring.

While I join the opinion of the Court, I feel compelled to reply to the separate concurring opinion of my Brother WHITE, which I view as a wholly unwarranted green light for the Executive Branch to resort to electronic eavesdropping without a warrant in cases which the Executive Branch itself labels "national security" matters.

Neither the President nor the Attorney General is a magistrate. In matters where they believe national security may be involved they are not detached, disinterested, and neutral as a court or magistrate must be....

MR. JUSTICE HARLAN, concurring....

MR. JUSTICE WHITE, concurring.

... We should not require the warrant procedure and the magistrate's judgment if the President of the United States or his chief legal officer, the Attorney General, has considered the requirements of national security and authorized electronic surveillance as reasonable.

MR. JUSTICE BLACK, dissenting ...

Tapping telephone wires, of course, was an unknown possibility at the time the Fourth Amendment was adopted. But eavesdropping (and wiretapping is nothing more than eavesdropping by telephone) ... There can be no doubt that the Framers were aware of this practice, and if they had desired to outlaw or restrict the use of evidence obtained by eavesdropping, I believe that they would have used the appropriate language to do so in the Fourth Amendment. They certainly would not have left such a task to the ingenuity of language--stretching judges....

E. THE EXCLUSIONARY RULE

The "exclusionary rule" refers to a general doctrine that excludes illegally obtained evidence from trial. The rule is shaped by Court doctrine as well as by congressional and executive actions. Sometimes the Court invites action by Congress. Olmstead v. United States, 277 U.S. 438, 465–66 (1928). The wiretap statute of 1968 prohibited the admissibility of any evidence "in any trial, hearing, or other proceeding in or before any court, grand jury, department, officer, agency, regulatory body, legislative committee, or other authority of the United States, a State, or a political subdivision thereof" if the disclosure of that information violated the statute. 82 Stat. 216 (1968).

The exclusion of coerced confessions dates back to common-law practice; the exclusion of evidence and documents obtained by illegal searches and seizures is largely a development of the past century. The practice at the state level allowed pertinent evidence even if law enforcement officers had acted illegally. Courts did not take notice of how documents or articles were seized. Judges considered only the competence of the evidence, not the method by which it was obtained. Adams v. New York, 192 U.S. 585 (1904). There were some exceptions at the state level. The Iowa Supreme Court announced in 1903 that the admission of evidence illegally obtained would "emasculate" the constitutional guaranty in the state constitution against unreasonable searches and seizures. State v. Sheridan, 96 N.W. 730, 731 (Iowa 1903).

The Federal Exclusionary Rule

The exclusionary rule originated at the federal level in 1914, when the Supreme Court ruled unanimously that papers illegally seized by federal officers may not be introduced in court as evidence. The details of the case demonstrate that the Court was reacting to the record of law enforcement officials who were willing and able to convict people by any means: unlawful seizures, forced confessions, and other violations of constitutional rights. WEEKS v. UNITED STATES, 232 U.S. 383 (1914).

Because the decision did not address papers illegally seized by private parties or state and local officers, federal agents could still profit from violations committed by others. When private parties stole documents and gave them to the federal government for prosecution, a suit had to be directed against the private party. On the theory that the government was not responsible for the wrongful seizure, it could use the stolen papers for grand jury action. Burdeau v. McDowell, 256 U.S. 465 (1921). Similarly, federal agents could use the fruits of an illegal search and seizure committed by state officers as long as the federal government did not participate or cooperate in the illegal actions. Byars v. United States, 273 U.S. 28 (1927); Gambino v. United States, 275 U.S. 310 (1927). The crux of the Court's doctrine was "that a search is a search by a federal official if he had a hand in it; it is not a search by a federal official if evidence secured by state authorities is turned over to the federal authorities on a silver platter." Lustig v. United States, 338 U.S. 74, 79 (1949).

When federal officers violated congressional policy by failing to take suspects to the nearest U.S. commissioner or judicial officer for arraignment, and instead held them for several days to obtain incriminating evidence, the Court set aside the convictions and held that the illegally obtained information was inadmissible. McNabb v. United States, 318 U.S. 332 (1943). These convictions were overturned because federal agents violated the Federal Rules of Criminal Procedure devised by Congress to assure that an arrested person is taken before a committing magistrate "without unnecessary delay." Mallory v. United States, 354 U.S. 449 (1957).

Applying *Weeks* to the States?

In 1949, the Court held squarely that the doctrine of *Weeks,* which made illegally obtained evidence inadmissible in federal courts, was not imposed on the states by the Fourteenth Amendment. In a strange opinion, Justice Frankfurter spoke eloquently about an individual's constitutional right to be protected from arbitrary intrusions by state police; he offered little, however, in the way of practical relief. He suggested two ways to restrain the states from making illegal searches and seizures: "the remedies of private action" against the offending officer, and "the internal discipline of the police, under the eyes of an alert public opinion." He also thought that Congress could pass a statute under Section 5 of the Fourteenth Amendment to make *Weeks* binding on the states. Wolf v. Colorado, 338 U.S. 25, 33 (1949). In his dissenting opinion, Justice Murphy dismissed Frankfurter's remedies as unrealistic. Murphy, who had served previously as Attorney General under President Franklin D. Roosevelt, remarked: "Little need be said concerning the possibilities of criminal prosecution. Self-scrutiny is a lofty ideal, but its exaltation reaches new heights if we expect a District Attorney to prosecute himself or his associates for well-meaning violations of the search and seizure clause during a raid the District Attorney or his associates have ordered." Murphy concluded that only one remedy existed to deter violations of the Fourth Amendment: a rule to exclude illegally obtained evidence. In a separate dissent, Justice Rutledge agreed that without the exclusionary rule the Fourth Amendment was "a dead letter."

Two years later, the Supreme Court advised lower federal courts not to intervene in state criminal proceedings to suppress evidence even when there were claims that the evidence had been obtained by unlawful search and seizure. Stefanelli v. Minard, 342 U.S. 117 (1951). But when state officers used methods that seemed to the Court "too close to the rack and the screw," evidence was excluded as a violation of the Due Process Clause. The actions of county sheriffs in entering a home without a warrant, forcing their way into a suspect's bedroom, struggling with him to extract capsules he had placed in his mouth, and then taking him to a hospital where "stomach pumping" caused him to vomit two capsules containing morphine, seemed to the Court "conduct that shocks the conscience." Rochin v. California, 342 U.S. 165, 172 (1952). Nevertheless, local police continued to obtain evidence that would have been inadmissible in federal court. Schwartz v. Texas, 344 U.S. 199 (1952); Irvine v. California, 347 U.S. 128 (1954). The practical result was that the Court applied the exclusionary rule in ad hoc fashion to the states whenever a majority of the Court felt sufficiently revolted by local police actions.

A 1960 decision laid the groundwork for overturning *Wolf* and applying *Weeks* to the states. State law enforcement officers had conducted an illegal search and seizure. Because federal agents were not involved, evidence admitted in federal court was used to convict the defendant. The Supreme Court decided that the silver-platter doctrine had become intolerable and that it did not matter to the victim of police abuse "whether his constitutional right has been invaded by a federal agent or by a state officer." Elkins v. United States, 364 U.S. 206, 215 (1960). The decision responded to practical problems of federalism. If the fruit of an unlawful search by state agents could not be admitted in a federal trial, there would be no inducement "to subterfuge and evasion with respect to federal-state cooperation in criminal investigation." Id. at 222.

Mapp v. Ohio

A year later the Court applied the exclusionary rule to the states. Prior to the *Wolf* case in 1949, about one-third of the states supported the exclusionary rule. By 1961, additional states had conceded that the only effective remedy to official lawlessness was the exclusion of evidence illegally obtained. The remedies offered by Frankfurter in *Wolf* now seemed to the Court an exercise in "obvious futility." MAPP v. OHIO, 367 U.S. 643, 652 (1961). The Court applied the exclusionary rule to the states for several reasons: to deter unlawful conduct by the government; to provide effective protection to a person's constitutional right to privacy under the Fourth Amendment; to eliminate the double standard practiced by the federal government and the states; and to preserve judicial integrity by forcing the government to obey its own laws.

Mapp was criticized for placing a federal straitjacket on the diverse needs of state police and prosecutors. In fact, *Mapp* has accommodated a variety of circumstances and conditions at both the state and federal level. In 1971, the Court held that a defendant's statement, although ruled inadmissible as evidence, could nevertheless be used by the state to impeach a suspect's credibility if he or she chose to testify. The exclusionary rule does not give a defendant the right to commit perjury. Harris v. New York, 401 U.S. 222 (1971). In 1974, the Court denied that a grand jury witness could invoke the exclusionary rule as grounds for not testifying. When a grand jury subpoenas an individual for questioning, the person cannot refuse because the evidence at issue was seized illegally. The Court considered the deterrent effect on police misconduct too speculative and minimal to impede the grand jury's role. United States v. Calandra, 414 U.S. 338 (1974).

Erosion of Exclusionary Rule

The largest loophole in the exclusionary rule is the "good faith" defense, which has been actively explored by all three branches. In 1976, the Court held that evidence seized by a state officer acting in good faith (who nonetheless violated the Fourth and Fourteenth Amendments) is admissible in a *civil* proceeding by the federal government. The Court, pointing out that the exclusionary rule was intended to deter state officers from overzealous criminal investigations, questioned the deterrent effect of excluding evidence at a federal civil proceeding. The societal cost of excluding the evidence seemed too high to the Court. The supervision of law enforcement "is properly the duty of the Executive and Legislative Branches." United States v. Janis, 428 U.S. 433, 459 (1976). Justice Stewart, dis-

Exceptions to Exclusionary Rule

1. "Good faith" actions for civil cases. United States v. Janis, 428 U.S. 433 (1976).

2. "Good faith" actions for criminal cases. United States v. Leon, 468 U.S. 897 (1984); Segura v. United States, 468 U.S. 796 (1984); Illinois v. Krull, 480 U.S. 340 (1987). (States may reject good-faith doctrine.)

3. Habeas corpus petitions appealing state convictions are denied if the exclusionary rule issue has been fully litigated in the state courts. Stone v. Powell, 428 U.S. 465 (1976).

4. Illegally obtained evidence may be used to impeach a witness's credibility. United States v. Havens, 446 U.S. 620 (1978). That doctrine does not apply to the testimonies of all defense witnesses. James v. Illinois, 493 U.S. 307 (1990).

5. Illegally obtained evidence taken from a third person may be used to convict someone else. United States v. Payner, 447 U.S. 727 (1980); United States v. Salvucci, 448 U.S. 83 (1980).

6. Use of illegally obtained information may be used when it would have been discovered anyway (the "inevitable discovery" exception). Nix v. Williams, 467 U.S. 431 (1984).

7. Second confessions are allowed after a first confession is illegally obtained. New York v. Harris, 495 U.S. 14 (1990).

8. Grand jury witnesses may not invoke the exclusionary rule and refuse to testify because the evidence at issue was seized illegally. United States v. Calandra, 414 U.S. 338 (1974).

9. Exclusionary rule does not apply in parole revocation hearings. Pennsylvania Bd. of Probation v. Scott, 524 U.S. 357 (1998).

senting, expressed concern that the Court was reviving the silver-platter doctrine. On the same day, the Court reviewed a number of state court criminal convictions based on evidence that allegedly was illegally obtained. Notwithstanding the fact that the Fourth Amendment claims might have been meritorious had they been asserted originally, the Court held that federal courts should not consider such petitions when a defendant has already been afforded an opportunity to litigate that claim in a state court. Stone v. Powell, 428 U.S. 465 (1976).

Opportunities to circumvent the exclusionary rule are evident in other cases. After federal agents had participated in a break-in and theft of papers belonging to a third party, the government used this evidence to convict someone else of falsifying his federal income tax. The Court held that the convicted person had no standing to contest the illegal and unconstitutional search of another party. United States v. Payner, 447 U.S. 727 (1980). Similarly, the Court discarded an earlier ruling that persons charged with crimes of possession had "automatic standing" to challenge illegal searches, without regard to whether they had an expectation of privacy in the place searched. The Court now held that defendants charged with crimes of possession may only claim the benefits of the exclusionary rule if their own Fourth Amendment rights had been violated. United States v. Salvucci, 448 U.S. 83 (1980).

United States v. Leon

The Court continues to carve out other exceptions to the exclusionary rule. If information is obtained from a suspect in violation of the constitutional right to have counsel and that information would have been discovered anyway without a constitutional violation, the evidence is admissible. Under this "inevitable discovery" standard, prosecutors need not prove good faith of police or the absence of bad faith. Nix v. Williams, 467 U.S. 431, 445 (1984). When a search results from a defective warrant, the incriminating evidence obtained from that search is admissible on the ground that the mistake was made by the judge issuing the warrant, not the police officer. The Court reasoned that suppression of the evidence would have no deterrent effect on the police who thought they were acting in "good faith" that the warrant was valid. Massachusetts v. Shepperd, 468 U.S. 981 (1984); UNITED STATES v. LEON, 468 U.S. 897 (1984). The same reasoning applies to a search conducted by police pursuant to a statute later found to be unconstitutional. Illinois v. Krull, 480 U.S. 340 (1987). Illegal police conduct in the form of a warrantless entry is effectively excused unless it can be shown that the officers acted in bad faith by purposely delaying the obtaining of a warrant. Segura v. United States, 468 U.S. 796 (1984).

The Court divided 5 to 4 in a 1990 case involving a warrantless entry by police into a suspect's home. The suspect was read his *Miranda* rights and made an admission of guilt. After arrest and a trip to the police station, he was read his *Miranda* rights again and made another statement of guilt. The Court held that the second statement could be admitted into evidence, even though the first was obtained in violation of *Payton* v. *New York,* 445 U.S. 573 (1980). The majority denied that admission of the second statement provided an incentive for the police to violate *Payton.* New York v. Harris, 495 U.S. 14 (1990). In 1995, the Court held that the exclusionary rule does not require the suppression of evidence seized in violation of the Fourth Amendment when the error results from clerical mistakes by court employees. Similar to the reasoning in *Leon,* the Court said that the purpose of the exclusionary rule is to deter misconduct by police, not court employees, and that since court employees are not direct adjuncts to law enforcement officers devoted to ferreting out crimes, court employees have no stake in the outcome of particular prosecutions. Arizona v. Evans, 514 U.S. 1 (1995).

The exclusionary rule has been narrowed by the Supreme Court to the point where it exists solely to deter police misconduct. United States v. Leon, 468 U.S. at 916. Largely ignored are other important objectives of the rule identified so carefully in *Weeks* and *Mapp:* protecting an individual's right to privacy; eliminating the double standard between the federal government and the states; shielding the judiciary from the taint of official lawlessness; and forcing the government to obey its own laws. As the Court gradually dilutes the meaning of the exclusionary rule, constitutional rights are now more likely to be protected at the state level. A number of state courts have refused to adopt the *Leon* good-faith doctrine for the state constitution (see box).

By grounding the exclusionary rule almost exclusively on the rationale that it deters unlawful police conduct, the doctrine is simply a judicial choice of remedies cast in the form of a rule of evidence rather than a doctrine that is constitutionally anchored. Congress may therefore pass legislation to modify the rule. In 1995, the House passed the Exclusionary Rule Reform Act, which incorporated the good-faith exception. 141 Cong. Rec. 4064–85 (1995). However, the Senate did not act on the bill. Enactment of this exception would place an extraordinary and unrealistic demand on the sensitivity of law enforcement officers to respect constitutional rights and limits. Law enforcers would have to police themselves instead of having their actions monitored by a neutral and detached magistrate. Unless Congress can pass an effective tort remedy to punish officers who violate constitutional rights, the exclusionary rule will remain a necessary constraint on official lawlessness.[12]

Scalia's Decision in *Hudson*

In 2006, a five-Justice majority seemed to question the value and usefulness of the exclusionary rule. Writing for the Court, Justice Scalia concluded that a violation of the "knock and announce" rule did

---

12. In 1971, the Supreme Court held that violations of the Fourth Amendment by federal agents give rise to a cause of action for damages resulting from unconstitutional conduct. Bivens v. Six Unknown Fed. Narcotics Agents, 403 U.S. 388 (1971). Even the Attorney General acting in the realm of national security is not absolutely immune for violating the Fourth Amendment. Mitchell v. Forsyth, 472 U.S. 511 (1985). Other cases on the liability of law enforcement officers for damages include Malley v. Briggs, 475 U.S. 335 (1986) and Anderson v. Creighton, 483 U.S. 635 (1987). In 1999, the Court held that police can be sued for allowing media "ride-alongs" with law enforcement officers, particularly when reporters and photographers enter private homes. Wilson v. Layne, 526 U.S. 603 (1999). For cases involving lawsuits against police officers who prepared what plaintiffs regarded as defective warrants: Groh v. Ramirez, 540 U.S. 551 (2004) and Messerschmidt v. Millender, 565 U.S. ___ (2012).

not require suppression of evidence found in a search. Hudson v. Michigan, 547 U.S. 586 (2006). A decade earlier, in *Wilson* v. *Arkansas* (1995), a unanimous Court held that the Fourth Amendment normally requires law enforcement officers to knock and announce their presence before entering a dwelling. Exceptions exist, such as when evidence might be destroyed by a suspect if the police gave advance notice. The purpose of "knock and announce" is to avoid the violence that might occur when residents react in self-defense to an unannounced entry. Also, the knock-and-announce rule gives individuals the opportunity to comply with the law and avoid the destruction of doors and property that comes from a forcible entry.

In deciding to allow the use of evidence obtained in the search, Justice Scalia argued that conditions have changed fundamentally since *Mapp* v. *Ohio* (1961). He spoke about the costs of the exclusionary rule, amounting "in many cases to a get-out-of-jail-free card." The original purpose of the exclusionary rule, he explained, was to act as a deterrent against police abuses. "Viewed from this perspective, deterrence of knock-and-announce violations is not worth a lot." Excluding evidence to convict a suspect "would be forcing the public today to pay for the sins and inadequacies of a legal regime that existed almost half a century ago." Dollree Mapp at that time could not file a civil suit against violations by law enforcement officers, as is possible today. Also, Scalia noted that over the past half-century there has developed a new deterrent against civil rights violations: "the increasing professionalism of police forces, including a new emphasis on internal police discipline."

In a concurrence, Justice Kennedy cautioned that the Court's decision "should not be interpreted as suggesting that violations of the [knock-and-announce] requirement are trivial or beyond the law's concern." It was his judgment that "continued operation of the exclusionary rule, as settled and defined by our precedents, is not in doubt." Yet the addition of John Roberts and Samuel Alito to the Court in 2006, with both joining Scalia in the majority in *Hudson*, suggests that support for the exclusionary rule may be waning. Breyer, joined by Stevens, Souter, and Ginsburg, warned that Scalia's opinion represented "a significant departure from the Court's precedents" and "weakens, perhaps destroys, much of the practical value of the Constitution's knock-and-announce protection." To Breyer, Scalia's reference to the "substantial social costs" that result from excluding evidence "is an argument against the Fourth Amendment's exclusionary principle itself."

Exclusion Because Precedents Change?

In 2011, the Supreme Court, divided 5 to 4, held that a police search of a car was conducted in reasonable reliance on judicial rulings at that time, and that a subsequent ruling (Arizona v. Gant, 556 U.S. 332 (2005)) did not warrant the exclusion of evidence. It was inappropriate to retroactively apply *Gant* to this automobile search. Davis v. United States, 564 U.S. ___ (2011).

Weeks v. United States

232 U.S. 383 (1914)

Without a search warrant, police entered the home of Fremont Weeks and took certain papers used to convict him of transporting lottery tickets through the mails. Weeks filed a petition for the return of his private papers and possessions. The Supreme Court confronted the question of whether illegal and unauthorized actions by the government could produce evidence admissible in a criminal prosecution. A federal district court required the return to Weeks of property that was not pertinent to the charge against him but permitted the District Attorney to retain papers to be used in evidence in the trial.

Mr. Justice Day delivered the opinion of the court.

... [P]olice officers had gone to the house of the defendant and being told by a neighbor where the key was kept, found it and entered the house. They searched the defendant's room and took possession of various papers and articles found there, which were afterwards turned over to the United States Marshal. Later in the same day police officers returned with the Marshal, who thought he might find additional evidence, and, being admitted by someone in the house, probably a boarder, in response to a rap, the Marshal searched the defendant's room and carried away certain letters and envelopes found in the drawer of a chiffonier. Neither the marshal nor the police officers had a search warrant....

Upon the introduction of such papers during the trial, the defendant objected on the ground that the papers had been obtained without a search warrant and by breaking open his home, in violation of the Fourth and Fifth Amendments to the Constitution of the United States, which objection was overruled by the court. Among the papers retained and put in evidence were a number of lottery tickets and statements with reference to the lottery, taken at the first visit of the police to the defendant's room, and a number of letters written to the defendant in respect to the lottery, taken by the Marshal upon his search of defendant's room....

The history of [*the Fourth*] Amendment is given with particularity in the opinion of Mr. Justice Bradley, speaking for the court in *Boyd* v. *United States* 116 U.S. 616. As was there shown, it took its origin in the determination of the framers of the Amendments to the Federal Constitution to provide for that instrument a Bill of Rights, securing to the American people, among other things, those safeguards which had grown up in England to protect the people from unreasonable searches and seizures, such as were permitted under the general warrants issued under authority of the Government by which there had been invasions of the home and privacy of the citizens and the seizure of their private papers in support of charges, real or imaginary, made against them. Such practices had also received sanction under warrants and seizures under the so-called writs of assistance, issued in the American colonies.... Resistance to these practices had established the principle which was enacted into the fundamental law in the Fourth Amendment, that a man's house was his castle and not to be invaded by any general authority to search and seize his goods and papers....

The effect of the Fourth Amendment is to put the courts of the United States and Federal officials, in the exercise of their power and authority, under limitations and restraints as to the exercise of such power and authority, and to forever secure the people, their persons, houses, papers and effects against

all unreasonable searches and seizures under the guise of law. This protection reaches all alike, whether accused of crime or not, and the duty of giving to it force and effect is obligatory upon all entrusted under our Federal system with the enforcement of the laws. The tendency of those who execute the criminal laws of the country to obtain conviction by means of unlawful seizures and enforced confessions, the latter often obtained after subjecting accused persons to unwarranted practices destructive of rights secured by the Federal Constitution, should find no sanction in the judgments of the courts which are charged at all times with the support of the Constitution and to which people of all conditions have a right to appeal for the maintenance of such fundamental rights.

What then is the present case? Before answering that inquiry specifically, it may be well by a process of exclusion to state what it is not. It is not an assertion of the right on the part of the Government, always recognized under English and American law, to search the person of the accused when legally arrested to discover and seize the fruits or evidences of crime. This right has been uniformly maintained in many cases.... Nor is it the case of testimony offered at a trial where the court is asked to stop and consider the illegal means by which proofs, otherwise competent, were obtained — of which we shall have occasion to treat later in this opinion. Nor is it the case of burglar's tools or other proofs of guilt found upon his arrest within the control of the accused.

The case in the aspect in which we are dealing with it involves the right of the court in a criminal prosecution to retain for the purposes of evidence the letters and correspondence of the accused, seized in his house in his absence and without his authority, by a United States Marshal holding no warrant for his arrest and none for the search of his premises.... If letters and private documents can thus be seized and held and used in evidence against a citizen accused of an offense, the protection of the Fourth Amendment declaring his right to be secure against such searches and seizures is of no value, and, so far as those thus placed are concerned, might as well be stricken from the Constitution. The efforts of the courts and their officials to bring the guilty to punishment, praiseworthy as they are, are not to be aided by the sacrifice of those great principles established by years of endeavor and suffering which have resulted in their embodiment in the fundamental law of the land. The United States Marshal could only have invaded the house of the accused when armed with a warrant issued as required by the Constitution, upon sworn information and describing with reasonable particularity the thing for which the search was to be made. Instead, he acted without sanction of law, doubtless prompted by the desire to bring further proof to the aid of the Government, and under color of his office undertook to make a seizure of private papers in direct violation of the constitutional prohibition against such action. Under such circumstances, without sworn information and particular description, not even an order of court would have justified such procedure, much less was it within the authority of the United States Marshal to thus invade the house and privacy of the accused....

We therefore reach the conclusion that the letters in question were taken from the house of the accused by an official of the United States acting under color of his office in direct violation of the constitutional rights of the defendant; that having made a seasonable application for their return, which was heard and passed upon by the court, there was involved in the order refusing the application a denial of the constitutional rights of the accused, and that the court should have restored these letters to the accused. In holding them and permitting their use upon the trial, we think prejudicial error was committed. As to the papers and property seized by the policemen, it does not appear that they acted under any claim of Federal authority such as would make the Amendment applicable to such unauthorized seizures. The record shows that what they did by way of arrest and search and seizure was done before the finding of the indictment in the Federal court, under what supposed right or authority does not appear. What remedies the defendant may have against them we need not inquire, as the Fourth Amendment is not directed to individual misconduct of such officials. Its limitations reach the Federal Government and its agencies. *Boyd Case,* 116 U.S., *supra,* and see *Twining* v. *New Jersey,* 211 U. S. 78.

It results that the judgment of the court below must be reversed, and the case remanded for further proceedings in accordance with this opinion.

Reversed.

Mapp v. Ohio

367 U.S. 643 (1961)

Dollree Mapp was convicted for possessing obscene materials. Cleveland police arrived at her home looking for a bombing suspect. Without a search warrant, they forced their way in and proceeded to search the entire house, including dresser drawers, suitcases, photo albums, personal papers, and a trunk in the basement. Although the Supreme Court of Ohio admitted that the materials had been "unlawfully seized during an unlawful search," it upheld her conviction.

MR. JUSTICE CLARK delivered the opinion of the Court....

On May 23, 1957, three Cleveland police officers arrived at appellant's residence in that city pursuant to information that "a person [was] hiding out in the home, who was wanted for questioning in connection with a recent bombing, and that there was a large amount of policy paraphernalia being hidden in the home." Miss Mapp and her daughter by a former marriage lived on the top floor of the two-family dwelling. Upon their arrival at that house, the officers knocked on the door and demanded entrance but appellant, after telephoning her attorney, refused to admit them without a search warrant. They advised their headquarters of the situation and undertook a surveillance of the house.

The officers again sought entrance some three hours later when four or more additional officers arrived on the scene. When Miss Mapp did not come to the door immediately, at least one of the several doors to the house was forcibly opened and the policemen gained admittance. Meanwhile Miss Mapp's attorney arrived, but the officers, having secured their own entry, and continuing in their defiance of the law, would permit him neither to see Miss Mapp nor to enter the house.... She demanded to see the search warrant. A paper, claimed to be a warrant, was held up by one of the officers. She grabbed the "warrant" and placed it in her bosom. A struggle ensued in which the officers recovered the piece of paper and as a result of which they handcuffed appellant because she had been "belligerent" in resisting their official rescue of the "warrant" from her person. Running roughshod over appellant, a policeman "grabbed" her, "twisted [her] hand," and she "yelled [and] pleaded with him" because "it was hurting." Appellant, in handcuffs, was then forcibly taken upstairs to her bedroom where the officers searched a dresser, a chest of drawers, a closet and some suitcases. They also looked into a photo album and through personal papers belonging to the appellant. The search spread to the rest of the second floor including the child's bedroom, the living room, the kitchen and a dinette. The basement of the building and a trunk found therein were also searched. The obscene materials for possession of which she was ultimately convicted were discovered in the course of that widespread search.

At the trial no search warrant was produced by the prosecution, nor was the failure to produce one explained or accounted for....

The State says that even if the search were made without authority, or otherwise unreasonably, it is not prevented from using the unconstitutionally seized evidence at trial, citing *Wolf* v. *Colorado,* 338 U.S. 25 (1949), in which this Court did indeed hold "that in a prosecution in a State court for a State crime the Fourteenth Amendment does not forbid the admission of evidence obtained by an unreasonable search and seizure."...

I.

Seventy-five years ago, in *Boyd* v. *United States,* 116 U.S. 616, 630 (1886), considering the Fourth and Fifth Amendments as running "almost into each other" on the facts before it, this Court held that the doctrines of those Amendments

"apply to all invasions on the part of the government and its employés of the sanctity of a man's home and the privacies of life. It is not the breaking of his doors, and the rummaging of his drawers, that constitutes the essence of the offence; but it is the invasion of his indefeasible right of personal security, personal liberty and private property.... Breaking into a house and opening boxes and drawers are circumstances of aggravation; but any forcible and compulsory extortion of a man's own testimony or of his private papers to be used as evidence to convict him of crime or to forfeit his goods, is within the condemnation ... [of those Amendments]."

The Court noted that

"constitutional provisions for the security of person and property should be liberally construed.... It is the duty of courts to be watchful for the constitutional rights of the citizen, and against any stealthy encroachments thereon."....

II.

In 1949, 35 years after *Weeks* was announced, this Court, in *Wolf* v. *Colorado, supra,* again for the first time, discussed the effect of the Fourth Amendment upon the States through the operation of the Due Process Clause of the Fourteenth Amendment. It said:

"[W]e have no hesitation in saying that were a State affirmatively to sanction such police incursion into privacy it would run counter to the guaranty of the Fourteenth Amendment." At p. 28.

Nevertheless, after declaring that the "security of one's privacy against arbitrary intrusion by the police" is "implicit in 'the concept of ordered liberty' and as such enforceable against the States through the Due Process Clause," cf. *Palko* v. *Connecticut,* 302 U.S. 319 (1937), and announcing that it "stoutly adhere[d]" to the *Weeks* decision, the Court decided that the *Weeks* exclusionary rule would not then be imposed upon the States as "an essential ingredient of the right." 338 U.S., at 27–29....

... While in 1949, prior to the *Wolf* case, almost two-thirds of the States were opposed to the use of the exclusionary rule, now, despite the *Wolf* case, more than half of those since passing upon it, by their own legislative or judicial decision, have wholly or partly adopted or adhered to the *Weeks* rule.... Significantly, among those now following the rule is California, which, according to its highest court, was "compelled to reach that conclusion because other remedies have completely failed to secure compliance with the constitutional provisions...." *People* v. *Cahan,* 44 Cal.2d 434, 445, 282 P.2d 905, 911 (1955). In connection with this California case, we note that the second basis elaborated in *Wolf* in support of its failure to enforce the exclusionary doctrine against the States was that "other means of protection" have been afforded "the right to privacy." 338 U.S., at 30. The experience of California that such other remedies have been worthless and futile is buttressed by the experience of other States....

V.

Moreover, our holding that the exclusionary rule is an essential part of both the Fourth and Fourteenth Amendments is not only the logical dictate of prior cases, but it also makes very good sense. There is no war between the Constitution and common sense. Presently, a federal prosecutor may make no use of evidence illegally seized, but a State's attorney across the street may, although he supposedly is operating under the enforceable prohibitions of the same Amendment.... If the fruits of an unconstitutional search had been inadmissible in both state and federal courts, this inducement to evasion would have been sooner eliminated....

There are those who say, as did Justice (then Judge) Cardozo, that under our constitutional exclusionary doctrine "[t]he criminal is to go free because the constable has blundered." *People* v. *Defore*, 242 N.Y., at 21, 150 N.E., at 587. In some cases this will undoubtedly be the result. But, as was said in *Elkins*, "there is another consideration — the imperative of judicial integrity." 364 U.S., at 222. The criminal goes free, if he must, but it is the law that sets him free. Nothing can destroy a government more quickly than its failure to observe its own laws, or worse, its disregard of the charter of its own existence.... Nor can it lightly be assumed that, as a practical matter, adoption of the exclusionary rule fetters law enforcement. Only last year this Court expressly considered that contention and found that "pragmatic evidence of a sort" to the contrary was not wanting. *Elkins* v. *United States, supra*, at 218. The Court noted that

"The federal courts themselves have operated under the exclusionary rule of *Weeks* for almost half a century; yet it has not been suggested either that the Federal Bureau of Investigation has thereby been rendered ineffective, or that the administration of criminal justice in the federal courts has thereby been disrupted. Moreover, the experience of the states is impressive.... The movement towards the rule of exclusion has been halting but seemingly inexorable." *Id.*, at 218–219.

The ignoble shortcut to conviction left open to the State tends to destroy the entire system of constitutional restraints on which the liberties of the people rest. Having once recognized that the right to privacy embodied in the Fourth Amendment is enforceable against the States, and that the right to be secure against rude invasions of privacy by state officers is, therefore, constitutional in origin, we can no longer permit that right to remain an empty promise. Because it is enforceable in the same manner and to like effect as other basic rights secured by the Due Process Clause, we can no longer permit it to be revocable at the whim of any police officer who, in the name of law enforcement itself, chooses to suspend its enjoyment....

The judgment of the Supreme Court of Ohio is reversed and the cause remanded for further proceedings not inconsistent with this opinion.

Reversed and remanded.

[*Black and Douglas write separate concurring opinions.*]

Memorandum of MR. JUSTICE STEWART....

MR. JUSTICE HARLAN, whom MR. JUSTICE FRANKFURTER and MR. JUSTICE WHITTAKER join, dissenting....

United States v. Leon

468 U.S. 897 (1984)

The question in this case is whether the exclusionary rule covers the actions of law enforcement officers who believe they are acting in "good faith" by obtaining a search warrant but later discover that the warrant is invalid. The search involved drug trafficking by Alberto Leon and his associates. The District Court rejected the government's good-faith defense and suppressed the evidence against Leon. The Ninth Circuit affirmed.

JUSTICE WHITE delivered the opinion of the Court.

This case presents the question whether the Fourth Amendment exclusionary rule should be modified so as not to bar the use in the prosecution's case in chief of evidence obtained by officers acting in reasonable reliance on a search warrant issued by a detached and neutral magistrate but ultimately found to be unsupported by probable cause....

I

In August 1981, a confidential informant of unproven reliability informed an officer of the Burbank Police Department that two persons known to him as "Armando" and "Patsy" were selling large quanti-

ties of cocaine and methaqualone from their residence at 620 Price Drive in Burbank, Cal. The informant also indicated that he had witnessed a sale of methaqualone by "Patsy" at the residence approximately five months earlier and had observed at that time a shoebox containing a large amount of cash that belonged to "Patsy." He further declared that "Armando" and "Patsy" generally kept only small quantities of drugs at their residence and stored the remainder at another location in Burbank.

On the basis of this information, the Burbank police initiated an extensive investigation focusing first on the Price Drive residence and later on two other residences as well. Cars parked at the Price Drive residence were determined to belong to respondents Armando Sanchez, who had previously been arrested for possession of marihuana, and Patsy Stewart, who had no criminal record. During the course of the investigation, officers observed an automobile belonging to respondent Ricardo Del Castillo, who had previously been arrested for possession of 50 pounds of marihuana, arrive at the Price Drive residence. The driver of that car entered the house, exited shortly thereafter carrying a small paper sack, and drove away. A check of Del Castillo's probation records led the officers to respondent Alberto Leon, whose telephone number Del Castillo had listed as his employer's. Leon had been arrested in 1980 on drug charges, and a companion had informed the police at that time that Leon was heavily involved in the importation of drugs into this country. Before the current investigation began, the Burbank officers had learned that an informant had told a Glendale police officer that Leon stored a large quantity of methaqualone at his residence in Glendale. During the course of this investigation, the Burbank officers learned that Leon was living at 716 South Sunset Canyon in Burbank.

Subsequently, the officers observed several persons, at least one of whom had prior drug involvement, arriving at the Price Drive residence and leaving with small packages; observed a variety of other material activity at the two residences as well as at a condominium at 7902 Via Magdalena; and witnessed a variety of relevant activity involving respondents' automobiles. The officers also observed respondents Sanchez and Stewart board separate flights for Miami. The pair later returned to Los Angeles together, consented to a search of their luggage that revealed only a small amount of marihuana, and left the airport. Based on these and other observations summarized in the affidavit, App. 34, Officer Cyril Rombach of the Burbank Police Department, an experienced and well-trained narcotics investigator, prepared an application for a warrant to search 620 Price Drive, 716 South Sunset Canyon, 7902 Via Magdalena, and automobiles registered to each of the respondents for an extensive list of items believed to be related to respondents' drug-trafficking activities. Officer Rombach's extensive application was reviewed by several Deputy District Attorneys.

A facially valid search warrant was issued in September 1981 by a State Superior Court Judge. The ensuing searches produced large quantities of drugs at the Via Magdalena and Sunset Canyon addresses and a small quantity at the Price Drive residence. Other evidence was discovered at each of the residences and in Stewart's and Del Castillo's automo-biles. Respondents were indicted by a grand jury in the District Court for the Central District of California and charged with conspiracy to possess and distribute cocaine and a variety of substantive counts.

The respondents then filed motions to suppress the evidence seized pursuant to the warrant....

[IIA]

The substantial social costs exacted by the exclusionary rule for the vindication of Fourth Amendment rights have long been a source of concern. "Our cases have consistently recognized that unbending application of the exclusionary sanction to enforce ideals of governmental rectitude would impede unacceptably the truth-finding functions of judge and jury." *United States* v. *Payner*, 447 U.S. 727, 734 (1980). An objectionable collateral consequence of this interference with the criminal justice system's truth-finding function is that some guilty defendants may go free or receive reduced sentences as a result of favorable plea bargains. Particularly when law enforcement officers have acted in objective good faith or their transgressions have been minor, the magnitude of the benefit conferred on such guilty defendants offends basic concepts of the criminal justice system....

[IIIA]

... To the extent that proponents of exclusion rely on its behavioral effects on judges and magistrates [*to authorize proper warrants*], their reliance is misplaced. First, the exclusionary rule is designed to deter police misconduct rather than to punish the errors of judges and magistrates. Second, there exists no evidence suggesting that judges and magistrates are inclined to ignore or subvert the Fourth Amendment or that lawlessness among these actors requires application of the extreme sanction of exclusion.

... [M]ost important, we discern no basis, and are offered none, for believing that exclusion of evidence seized pursuant to a warrant will have a significant deterrent effect on the issuing judge or magistrate.... Judges and magistrates are not adjuncts to the law enforcement team; as neutral judicial officers, they have no stake in the outcome of particular criminal prosecutions. The threat of exclusion thus cannot be expected significantly to deter them....

[IIIB]

... Suppressing evidence obtained pursuant to a technically defective warrant supported by probable cause also might encourage officers to scrutinize more closely the form of the warrant and to point out suspected judicial errors. We find such arguments speculative and conclude that suppression of evidence obtained pursuant to a warrant should be ordered only on a case-by-case basis and only in those unusual cases in which exclusion will further the purposes of the exclusionary rule.

... Penalizing the officer for the magistrate's error, rather than his own, cannot logically contribute to the deterrence of Fourth Amendment violations.

C

Suppression ... remains an appropriate remedy if the magistrate or judge in issuing a warrant was misled by information in an affidavit that the affiant knew was false or would have known was false except for his reckless disregard of the truth.... The exception we recognize today will also not apply in cases where the issuing magistrate wholly abandoned his judicial role in the manner condemned in *Lo-Ji Sales, Inc.* v. *New York*, 442 U.S. 319 (1979); in such circumstances, no reasonably well trained officer should rely on the warrant. Nor would an officer manifest objective good faith in relying on a warrant based on an affidavit "so lacking in indicia of probable cause as to render official belief in its existence entirely unreasonable." ... Finally, depending on the circumstances of the particular case, a warrant may be so facially deficient — *i.e.,* in failing to particularize the place to be searched or the things to be seized — that the executing officers cannot reasonably presume it to be valid....

Accordingly, the judgment of the Court of Appeals is

Reversed.

JUSTICE BLACKMUN, concurring....

JUSTICE BRENNAN, with whom JUSTICE MARSHALL joins, dissenting.

... [I]n case after case, I have witnessed the Court's gradual but determined strangulation of the rule. It now appears that the Court's victory over the Fourth Amendment is complete....

The Court seeks to justify this result on the ground that the "costs" of adhering to the exclusionary rule in cases like those before us exceed the "benefits." But the language of deterrence and of cost/benefit analysis, if used indiscriminately, can have a narcotic effect. It creates an illusion of technical precision and ineluctability. It suggests that not only constitutional principle but also empirical data support the majority's result. When the Court's analysis is examined carefully, however, it is clear that we have not been treated to an honest assessment of the merits of the exclusionary rule, but have instead been drawn into a curious world where the "costs" of excluding illegally obtained evidence loom to exaggerated heights and where the "benefits" of such exclusion are made to disappear with a mere wave of the hand....

JUSTICE STEVENS ... dissenting ...

CONCLUSIONS

From 1789 to the present, members of Congress and Presidents have been deeply involved in the development of Fourth Amendment law. Often they had to explore search and seizure issues without guidance from judicial rulings. With few exceptions, the courts have accepted congressional judgments as consistent with the Fourth Amendment. On some occasions, even after the Supreme Court has decided a Fourth Amendment issue, Congress has reentered the field and significantly modified what the Court has done. In these areas the "law" of search and seizure is defined as much by the *United States Code* as by the *United States Reports*.

While it is important to understand the purpose of the Fourth Amendment in restricting governmental searches, reliance on the "framers' intent" offers only limited assistance. The framers did not anticipate or discuss the types of cases that now bedevil the courts. Is it a permissible search and seizure to extract blood from someone to prove intoxication? Breithaupt v. Abram, 352 U.S. 432 (1957); Schmerber v. California, 384 U.S. 757 (1966). May a state force a suspect to undergo surgery to remove a bullet lodged in his chest and then introduce the bullet into evidence? Winston v. Lee, 470 U.S. 753 (1985). Answers to these questions ("yes" for the first, "no" for the second) require the Court each time to balance individual and government rights within the particular fact patterns of a case.

The scope of the Fourth Amendment has broadened considerably since the framers first drafted the language. Although the Amendment refers to the "right of the people" to be secure, it also protects corporations from unlawful search and seizure.[13] Through a series of decisions, the Amendment now applies to the states.

Over the years, the Court has adopted a balancing test that weighs a suspect's right against the needs of government and society. As the Court noted in 1983: "We must balance the nature and quality of the intrusion on the individual's Fourth Amendment interests against the importance of the governmental interests alleged to justify the intrusion." United States v. Place, 462 U.S. 696, 703. This attitude severely weakens the Fourth Amendment. Instead of serving as a restriction on government, which was the original purpose, the contemporary test is whether the government's interest or society's interest will prevail over a particular suspect. An individual can expect little protection from the Constitution when the odds are so heavily stacked. A more appropriate balance is not one suspect against the government or against society but rather the interest of society against governmental misconduct and overreaching. To the extent that a court balances an individual's interest against society's interest in law enforcement, it performs essentially a legislative judgment, inviting a sharing of power with Congress and the executive.

As with other branches, Congress can make major mistakes when it interprets the Fourth Amendment. However, the impulsiveness with which Congress sometimes moves in wrong directions allows it just as easily to reverse course and repeal the offending statute. For example, in 1970 Congress passed two ill-considered measures that authorized law enforcement officers to break and enter private dwellings and businesses. 84 Stat. 630–31; 84 Stat. 1274, § 509. Serious doubts about the constitutionality of these bills, combined with shocking reports of federal agents breaking into the wrong homes, prompted Congress four years later to repeal both provisions. 88 Stat. 1455, §§ 3, 4. Compare that performance with the 12 years it took the Court in *Mapp* to overturn *Wolf*, or the 39 years needed for *Katz* to reverse *Olmstead*.

NOTES AND QUESTIONS

1. The study of constitutional law has become very case-centered. Give some examples where Congress recognized exceptions to the warrant requirement long before courts ruled on such issues.

2. How does the *Zurcher* case explain how Congress can respond to a Supreme Court ruling and provide greater protections to individual privacy and press freedoms?

3. *Alvarez-Machain* illustrates in what way the constructive dialogue that occurs in Congress and the executive branch after Supreme Court announces a constitutional decision?

4. Give some examples where states, interpreting their own constitutions, reject decisions by the U.S. Supreme Court and adopt independent positions on constitutional standards in the area of search and seizure.

5. Explain how *Olmstead* on electronic surveillance demonstrates not merely changes in constitutional law in response to new challenges but independent interpretations by Congress and the President.

6. Regarding the exclusionary rule, provide some examples where states showed their independence not only by acting long before the U.S. Supreme Court but also after the Court has issued a ruling.

---

13. G.M. Leasing Corp. v. United States, 429 U.S. 338, 353 (1977); Essgee Co. v. United States, 262 U.S. 151 (1923); Silverthorne Lumber Co. v. United States, 251 U.S. 385 (1920).

SELECTED READINGS

ALLEN, FRANCIS A. "Federalism and the Fourth Amendment: A Requiem for Wolf." 1961 Supreme Court Review 1.

AMSTERDAM, ANTHONY G. "Perspectives on the Fourth Amendment." 58 Minnesota Law Review 349 (1974).

ERVIN, SAM J., JR. "The Exclusionary Rule: An Essential Ingredient of the Fourth Amendment." 1983 Supreme Court Review 283.

FISHER, EDWARD C. Search and Seizure. Evanston, Ill.: Northwestern University Press, 1970.

FISHER, LOUIS. "Congress and the Fourth Amendment." 21 Georgia Law Review 107 (Special Issue 1986).

KAMISAR, YALE. "Is the Exclusionary Rule an 'Illogical' or 'Unnatural' Interpretation of the Fourth Amendment?" 62 Judicature 66 (1978).

———. "The Exclusionary Rule in Historical Perspective: The Struggle to Make the Fourth Amendment More Than 'An Empty Blessing.'" 62 Judicature 337 (1979).

KAPLAN, JOHN. "The Limits of the Exclusionary Rule." 26 Stanford Law Review 1027 (1974).

KITCH, EDMUND W. "Katz v. United States: The Limits of the Fourth Amendment." 1968 Supreme Court Review 133.

LAFAVE, WAYNE R. "'Case-by-Case Adjudication' Versus 'Standardized Procedures': The Robinson Dilemma." 1974 Supreme Court Review 127.

———. Search and Seizure: A Treatise on the Fourth Amendment. 6 vols. St. Paul, Minn.: Thomson West, 2004.

LANDYNSKI, JACOB W. Search and Seizure and the Supreme Court. Baltimore: Johns Hopkins University Press, 1966.

LEVY, LEONARD W. A License to Steal: The Forfeiture of Property. Chapel Hill, N.C.: University of North Carolina Press, 1996.

———. "Origins of the Fourth Amendment." 114 Political Science Quarterly 79 (1999).

LICHTBLAU, ERIC. Bush's Law: The Remaking of American Justice. New York: Pantheon Books, 2008.

LONG, CAROLYN N. Mapp v. Ohio: Guarding Against Unreasonable Searches and Seizures. Lawrence: University Press of Kansas, 2006.

OAKS, DALLIN H. "Studying the Exclusionary Rule in Search and Seizure." 37 University of Chicago Law Review 665 (1970).

POSNER, RICHARD A. "Rethinking the Fourth Amendment." 1981 Supreme Court Review 49.

SCHLESINGER, STEVEN R. Exclusionary Injustice. New York: Marcel Dekker, 1977.

SKLANSKY, DAVID A. "Traffic Stops, Minority Motorists, and the Future of the Fourth Amendment." 1997 Supreme Court Review 271.

STEWART, POTTER. "The Road to Mapp v. Ohio and Beyond: The Origins, Development and Future of the Exclusionary Rule in Search-and-Seizure Cases." 83 Columbia Law Review 1365 (1983).

TRAYNOR, ROGER J. "Mapp v. Ohio at Large in the Fifty States." 1962 Duke Law Journal 319.

U.S. CONGRESS. "The Exclusionary Rule Bills." Hearings before the Senate Committee on the Judiciary, 97th Cong., 1st and 2d Sess. (1981, 1982).

WILKEY, MALCOLM RICHARD. "The Exclusionary Rule: Why Suppress Valid Evidence?," 62 Judicature 214 (1978).

———. "A Call for Alternatives to the Exclusionary Rule: Let Congress and the Courts Speak." 62 Judicature 351 (1979).

15

Racial Discrimination

No issue has dominated American constitutional law as much as the question of race, beginning with slavery and discrimination against blacks, followed by recent efforts to heal the wounds of racism. Race was an important issue in the consideration of the sit-in and demonstration cases (Chapter 10), jury composition and the death penalty (Chapter 13), and voting rights and reapportionment (discussed in Chapter 18). This chapter concentrates on slavery, the Civil War amendments, school desegregation, racial discrimination in housing, desegregation of public facilities, and issues of employment and affirmative action.

A. SLAVERY

At the time the framers met at the Philadelphia Convention, slavery was an established institution in the southern states and some in the North. Recognizing that reality while laying the groundwork for abolishing slavery represented a matter of delicate tactics and compromise in drafting the Constitution. How could the framers reconcile slavery with the principles in the Declaration of Independence? A nation could not proclaim that "all men are created equal" and at the same time condone slavery. Thomas Jefferson's original draft of the Declaration of Independence contained a sharp condemnation of slavery:

> [*King George III*] has waged cruel war against human nature itself, violating its most sacred rights of life & liberty in the persons of a distant people who never offended him, captivating & carrying them into slavery in another hemisphere, or to incur miserable death in their transportation thither, this piratical warfare, the opprobrium of *infidel* powers, is the warfare of the CHRISTIAN king of Great Britain, determined to keep open a market where MEN should be bought & sold, he has prostituted his negative [*veto*] for suppressing every legislative attempt to prohibit or to restrain this execrable commerce: and that this assemblage of horrors might want no fact of distinguished die, he is now exciting those very people to rise in arms among us, and to purchase that liberty of which *he* has deprived them, by murdering the people upon whom *he* also obtruded them; thus paying off former crimes committed against the *liberties* of one people, with crimes which he urges them to commit against the *lives* of another.

Because of opposition from southern delegates in the Continental Congress, that passage was struck from Jefferson's draft. However, the Northwest Ordinance of 1787, which governed the territory northwest of the Ohio River, contained this forthright declaration in Article 6: "There shall be neither slavery nor involuntary servitude in the said territory, otherwise than in the punishment of crimes whereof the party shall have been duly convicted." However, it added this proviso: "That any person escaping into the same, from whom labor or service is lawfully claimed in any of the original States, such fugitive may be lawfully reclaimed and conveyed to the person claiming his or her labor or service as aforesaid."

Constitutional Language

Although the word "slavery" does not appear in the Constitution drafted at Philadelphia in 1787, its existence is recognized in several places. First, Article V provides that no amendment to the Constitution prior to 1808 "shall in any Manner affect the first and fourth Clauses in the Ninth Section of the first Article." The first clause in Section 9 states that the "Migration or Importation of such Persons as any of the States now existing shall think proper to admit" shall not be prohibited by Congress before 1808. This grace period for the slave trade prompted Madison to remark: "Twenty years will produce all the mischief that can be apprehended from the liberty to import slaves. So long a term will be more dishonorable to the National Character than to say nothing about it in the Constitution." 2 Farrand 415. The first clause in Section 9 also permitted a tax or duty on imported slaves "not exceeding ten dollars for each Person." The delegates divided on the merits of this language. Some regarded it as offensive to tax slaves as though they were incoming goods or articles of merchandise. Others thought that a tax might discourage the importation of slaves. The modest level of the tax suggests that the objective was revenue more than prohibition. 2 Farrand 416. Madison "thought it wrong to admit in the Constitution the idea that there could be property in men." 2 Farrand 417.

Slavery also became mixed with the question of apportioning taxes and Representatives among the states. The fourth clause in Section 9 prohibits capitation or other direct taxes unless in proportion to population. How was population to be measured? Should slaves be counted like whites, giving the southern states additional representation because of their "peculiar institution"? Alternatively, should representation be based solely on free inhabitants? William Paterson of New Jersey, objecting to any credit to the south for slaves, did not want to give "an indirect encouragemt. of the slave trade." 1 Farrand 561.

As with other matters, the framers reached a compromise. Under Article I, Representatives and direct taxes were apportioned among the states "according to their respective Numbers, which shall be determined by adding to the whole Number of free Persons, including those bound to Service for a Term of Years, and excluding Indians not taxed, three fifths of all other Persons." The three-fifths formula had been devised by the Continental Congress to deal with taxes. As picked up by the framers, the formula seems to imply that they regarded blacks as three-fifths of a person, or subhuman, but the fraction had a different effect. It actually penalized the states for practicing slavery. Their number of Representatives was reduced from what it would have been by freeing blacks. Maximum human dignity would have counted each slave not as one but as zero.

Finally, Article IV, Section 2, provided that persons "held to Service or Labour" in one state shall be delivered back to that state in case they escaped to another. At the Virginia ratifying convention, Madison explained that this clause was inserted to "enable owners of slaves to reclaim them." 3 Farrand 325. This part of the Constitution became the basis for the fugitive slave laws passed by Congress.

Early Legislation

The 1790 census showed 757,363 blacks in the United States, or 19.3 percent of the population. Of these, 59,466 were free. States in excess of 20 percent slaves included South Carolina, Virginia, Georgia, Maryland, North Carolina, and Delaware. Slave-holding plantations were not profitable, but the situation changed dramatically in 1793 with Eli Whitney's invention of the cotton gin. The machine made it easier to separate the fiber from the seed, allowing plantation owners to export much greater quantities. Beginning in 1794, Congress passed various bills to regulate and restrict the slave trade. It enacted legislation in 1807 to stop the slave trade altogether, effective January 1, 1808. However, slaves continued to enter the country illegally, requiring additional legislation.[1]

Opposition to slavery came from the public, not from judicial, executive, or legislative actions. Individual Americans, untutored in the fine points of constitutional law, viewed slavery as repugnant to fundamental political and legal principles, especially those embedded in the Declaration of Independence. The essential antislavery documents were private writings and speeches, not court decisions or legislative statutes. William M. Wiecek, The Sources of Antislavery Constitutionalism in

---

1. 1 Stat. 347 (1794); 2 Stat. 70 (1800); 2 Stat. 205 (1803); 2 Stat. 426 (1807). Additional legislation was needed after 1808: 3 Stat. 450 (1818); 3 Stat. 532 (1819); 3 Stat. 600, §§ 4, 5 (1820).

America, 1760–1848 (1977). Citizens felt a strong duty to express their opinions on constitutional rights. They deferred neither to courts nor legislatures. Americans of the mid-nineteenth century "were not inclined to leave to private lawyers any more than to public men the conception, execution, and interpretation of public law. The conviction was general that no aristocracy existed with respect to the Constitution. Like politics, with which it was inextricably joined, the Constitution was everyone's business." Harold M. Hyman, A More Perfect Union 6 (1975).

Legislation in the early decades contained conflicting positions on slavery. Naturalization was permitted only for "free white person[s]." 1 Stat. 103, §1 (1790); 1 Stat. 414, §1 (1795). However, several early statutes governing the territories of Mississippi and Louisiana prohibited slavery. 1 Stat. 550, §7 (1798); 2 Stat. 286, §10 (1804).

Congress passed legislation to implement the constitutional provision on runaway slaves. The Fugitive Slave Act of 1793 authorized the return of slaves to their owners. 1 Stat. 302. The Supreme Court decided that congressional action preempted fugitive slave laws passed by the states. Prigg v. Pennsylvania, 16 Pet. 539 (1842). In response, many of the northern states repealed their laws, making it more difficult to capture runaways and forcing Congress to amend the Fugitive Slave Act in 1850. 9 Stat. 462. A unanimous Court upheld the constitutionality of this statute. Ableman v. Booth, 21 How. 506 (1859).

During this period, Congress attempted to maintain a balance between free states and slave states. The Ordinance of 1787 had prohibited slavery in the Northwest Territory (the Ohio country). Land acquired by the Louisiana Purchase threatened to upset the delicate ratio between slave and nonslave states. As a remedy, the Missouri Compromise Act of 1820 admitted Missouri as a slave state but prohibited slavery in future states north of the 36°30' line.

That compromise was upended when the United States acquired a vast tract of new territory after the Mexican War (1848). In response, Congress enacted the Compromise of 1850, but the statute largely dodged the issue of slavery. Senator Stephen Douglas reignited the issue by proposing that states unable under the 1820 Missouri Compromise Act to have slaves could elect to have them if their citizens so chose. The resulting Kansas-Nebraska Act of 1854 repealed the Missouri Compromise and left the decision of slavery to the new territories (and future states), a policy known as the doctrine of congressional noninterference or "popular sovereignty." Political leadership was desperately needed at the national level to moderate the passions, but neither Congress nor the President was willing to confront the matter. Instead, they tossed the smoldering issue to the Supreme Court, encouraging it to resolve the dispute.

The Dred Scott Case

Elected President in 1856, James Buchanan wanted to mention the subject of slavery in his inaugural address but was uncertain of the Court's plans to decide the pending case of *Dred Scott* v. *Sandford.* In an extraordinary revelation of internal Court proceedings, Justices Catron and Grier wrote to Buchanan that the Court was indeed ready to decide the matter and that Buchanan should mention that fact in his address. Catron advised Buchanan to say that because of the "high and independent character" of the Court, "it will decide & settle a controversy which has so long and seriously agitated the country, and which *must* ultimately be decided by the Supreme Court." In a separate letter, Grier even gave Buchanan details on how the Court would split and along what lines. 10 The Works of James Buchanan 106–08 (J. Moore ed. 1910). Fortified by these confidential communications, Buchanan included within his inaugural address the naive expectation that the explosive issue of slavery could be decided solely and finally by the Supreme Court (see box on next page).

Dred Scott, a slave from Missouri, argued that he had become free by following his master to a free state (Illinois) and to a free territory (Upper Louisiana). The principal issue was whether Scott, after returning to Missouri, was a citizen capable of suing in the federal courts. Did his stay on free soil give him this right? The Court held that Scott (and all other black slaves and their descendants) was not a citizen of the United States or of Missouri. Chief Justice Taney refused to allow contemporary social

---

Buchanan's Inaugural Address (1857)
(Excerpts)

We have recently passed through a Presidential contest in which the passions of our fellow-citizens were excited to the highest degree by questions of deep and vital importance; but when the people proclaimed their will the tempest at once subsided and all was calm.

The voice of the majority, speaking in the manner prescribed by the Constitution, was heard, and instant submission followed. Our own country could alone have exhibited so grand and striking a spectacle of the capacity of man for self-government.

What a happy conception, then, was it for Congress to apply this simple rule, that the will of the majority shall govern, to the settlement of the question of domestic slavery in the Territories! Congress is neither "to legislate slavery into any Territory or State nor to exclude it therefrom, but to leave the people thereof perfectly free to form and regulate their domestic institutions in their own way, subject only to the Constitution of the United States."

As a natural consequence, Congress has also prescribed that when the Territory of Kansas shall be admitted as a State it "shall be received into the Union with or without slavery, as their constitution may prescribe at the time of their admission."

A difference of opinion has arisen in regard to the point of time when the people of a Territory shall decide this question for themselves.

This is, happily, a matter of but little practical importance. Besides, it is a judicial question, which legitimately belongs to the Supreme Court of the United States, before whom it is now pending, and will, it is understood, be speedily and finally settled. To their decision, in common with all good citizens, I shall cheerfully submit, whatever this may be....

---

beliefs to change the meaning of the Constitution by making citizens of blacks. No one, he said, "supposes that any change in public opinion or feeling, in relation to this unfortunate race, in the civilized nations of Europe or in this country, should induce the court to give to the words of the Constitution a more liberal construction in their favor than they were intended to bear when the instrument was framed and adopted." DRED SCOTT v. SANDFORD, 19 How. 393, 426 (1857). Taney also ruled that Congress was without power to prevent the spread of slavery to the territories in the West.

The press divided widely in their response to Taney's decision. The *New York Tribune* remarked: "The decision, we need hardly say, is entitled to just as much moral weight as would be the judgment of a majority of those congregated in any Washington bar-room." Newspapers in the south accepted Taney's decision as the last word. According to the *Louisville Democrat*, the decision "is right, and the argument unanswerable, we presume, but whether or not, what this tribunal decides the Constitution to be, that it is; and all patriotic men will acquiesce."

Unlike Buchanan, who expressed a willingness to accept any decision of the Court, regardless of its merits, the people took sides. A historic challenge came in Illinois in 1858, when Senator Douglas debated a largely unknown challenger, Abraham Lincoln. Douglas supported *Dred Scott* without reservation. Lincoln accepted the decision only as it affected the particular parties; he repudiated the larger policy questions decided by the Court (see reading in Chapter 1).

The Court had miscalculated wildly. Concurring in Taney's opinion, Justice Wayne referred to the constitutional issues as so divisive "that the peace and harmony of the country required the settlement of them by judicial decision." Id. at 455. In his inaugural address, Buchanan had spoken confidently that the Dred Scott case was at the Supreme Court, where the issue of slavery would be "speedily and finally settled." Instead, the country lurched into a bloody civil war that left, out of a population of about 30 million, more than 600,000 dead and another 400,000 wounded.

A recent study by Mark Graber concludes that *Dred Scott* "may" have been constitutionally correct and that Stephen Douglas "understood the antebellum constitutional order better than Abraham Lincoln." Taney's opinion that "slavery could not be banned in the territories and that former slaves could not be American citizens was constitutionally as plausible as the contrary views detailed in the dissents in Dred Scott." Taney's decision was "consistent" with the "majority will" and his constitutional claims, Graber notes, "were well within the mainstream of antebellum constitutional thought." Mark A. Graber, *Dred Scott* and the Problem of Constitutional Evil (2006).

Dred Scott v. Sandford

60 U.S. (19 How.) 393 (1857)

Dred Scott, a Negro slave, belonged to Dr. Emerson, who in 1834 took him from Missouri to the free state of Illinois. In 1836 Dr. Emerson brought Dred Scott to a military post in the territory known as Upper Louisiana, situated north of 36 degrees, 30 minutes, also a free territory. In 1838 they returned to Missouri. Dred Scott and his wife and two daughters were later sold to John F.A. Sanford (incorrectly spelled in the case as Sandford). Dred Scott filed a lawsuit in the Circuit Court of the United States, claiming that as a result of his stay in free territory he was a citizen of Missouri capable of suing for his freedom. The case might have been confined to the question whether the Circuit Court had jurisdiction to hear the case or whether Dred Scott was a citizen. Instead, the issues were broadened to include the power of Congress to exclude slavery in the territories.

Mr. Chief Justice TANEY delivered the opinion of the Court....

The question is simply this: Can a negro, whose ancestors were imported into this country, and sold as slaves, become a member of the political community formed and brought into existence by the Constitution of the United States, and as such become entitled to all the rights, and privileges, and immunities, guarantied by that instrument to the citizen? One of which rights is the privilege of suing in a court of the United States in the cases specified in the Constitution.

It will be observed, that the plea applies to that class of persons only whose ancestors were negroes of the African race, and imported into this country, and sold and held as slaves. The only matter in issue before the court, therefore, is, whether the descendants of such slaves, when they shall be emancipated, or who are born of parents who had become free before their birth, are citizens of a State, in the sense in which the word citizen is used in the Constitution of the United States....

In discussing this question, we must not confound the rights of citizenship which a State may confer within its own limits, and the rights of citizenship as a member of the Union. It does not by any means follow, because he has all the rights and privileges of a citizen of a State, that he must be a citizen of the United States. He may have all of the rights and privileges of the citizen of a State, and yet not be entitled to the rights and privileges of a citizen in any other State. For previous to the adoption of the Constitution of the United States, every State had the undoubted right to confer on whomsoever it pleased the character of citizen, and to endow him with all its rights....

The question then arises, whether the provisions of the Constitution, in relation to the personal rights and privileges to which the citizen of a State should be entitled, embraced the negro African race, at that time in this country, or who might afterwards be imported, who had then or should afterwards be made free in any State; and to put it in the power of a single State to make him a citizen of the United States, and endue him with the full rights of citizenship in every other State without their consent? Does the Constitution of the United States act upon him whenever he shall be made free under the laws of a State, and raised there to the rank of a citizen, and immediately clothe him with all the privileges of a citizen in every other State, and in its own courts?

The court think the affirmative of these propositions cannot be maintained. And if it cannot, the plaintiff in error could not be a citizen of the State of Missouri, within the meaning of the Constitution of the United States, and, consequently, was not entitled to sue in its courts....

It becomes necessary, therefore, to determine who were citizens of the several States when the Constitution was adopted. And in order to do this, we must recur to the Governments and institutions of the thirteen colonies, when they separated from Great Britain and formed new sovereignties, and took their places in the family of independent nations. We must inquire who, at that time, were recognized as the people or citizens of a State, whose rights and liberties had been outraged by the English Government; and who declared their independence, and assumed the powers of Government to defend their rights by force of arms.

In the opinion of the court, the legislation and histories of the times, and the language used in the Declaration of Independence, show, that neither the class of persons who had been imported as slaves, nor their descendants, whether they had become free or not, were then acknowledged as a part of the people, nor intended to be included in the general words used in that memorable instrument.

It is difficult at this day to realize the state of public opinion in relation to that unfortunate race, which prevailed in the civilized and enlightened portions of the world at the time of the Declaration of Independence, and when the Constitution of the United States was framed and adopted. But the public history of every European nation displays it in a manner too plain to be mistaken.

They had for more than a century before been regarded as beings of an inferior order, and altogether unfit to associate with the white race, either in social or political relations; and so far inferior, that they had no rights which the white man was bound to respect; and that the negro might justly and lawfully be reduced to slavery for his benefit. He was bought and sold, and treated as an ordinary article of merchandise and traffic, whenever a profit could be made by it. This opinion was at that time fixed and universal in the civilized portion of the white race....

[*The Declaration of Independence*] proceeds to say: "We hold these truths to be self-evident: that all men are created equal; that they are endowed by their Creator with certain unalienable rights; that among them is life, liberty, and the pursuit of happiness; that to secure these rights, Governments are instituted, deriving their just powers from the consent of the governed."

The general words above quoted would seem to embrace the whole human family, and if they were used in a similar instrument at this day would be so understood. But it is too clear for dispute that the enslaved African race were not intended to be included, and formed no part of the people who framed and adopted this declaration; ...

[*Taney states that the words "people" and "citizens" in the U.S. Constitution excluded the negro race and refers to the provisions permitting the slave trade until 1808 and requiring states to return escaped persons held in labor or service. He also discusses the move-*

ment in some states, after 1787, to abolish slavery, and the persistence of laws in slaveholding states treating blacks as an inferior class. He cites a law passed by Congress in 1790 limiting the right of becoming citizens "to aliens being free white persons."]

No one, we presume, supposes that any change in public opinion or feeling, in relation to this unfortunate race, in the civilized nations of Europe or in this country, should induce the court to give to the words of the Constitution a more liberal construction in their favor than they were intended to bear when the instrument was framed and adopted. Such an argument would be altogether inadmissible in any tribunal called on to interpret it. If any of its provisions are deemed unjust, there is a mode prescribed in the instrument itself by which it may be amended; but while it remains unaltered, it must be construed now as it was understood at the time of its adoption. It is not only the same in words, but the same in meaning, and delegates the same powers to the Government, and reserves and secures the same rights and privileges to the citizen; and as long as it continues to exist in its present form, it speaks not only in the same words, but with the same meaning and intent with which it spoke when it came from the hands of its framers, and was voted on and adopted by the people of the United States. Any other rule of construction would abrogate the judicial character of this court, and make it the mere reflex of the popular opinion or passion of the day....

... [T]he court is of opinion, that ... Dred Scott was not a citizen of Missouri within the meaning of the Constitution of the United States, and not entitled as such to sue in its courts; and, consequently, that the Circuit Court had no jurisdiction of the case ...

[*Taney next turns to the question whether Dred Scott became free by living in a free state or territory. This raised the issue whether Congress was empowered to pass legislation to exclude slavery from certain lands.*]

In considering this part of the controversy, two questions arise: 1. Was he, together with his family, free in Missouri by reason of the stay in the territory of the United States herein-before mentioned? And 2. If they were not, is Scott himself free by reason of his removal to Rock Island, in the State of Illinois, as stated in the above admission?

We proceed to examine the first question.

The act of Congress, upon which the plaintiff relies, declares that slavery and involuntary servitude, except as a punishment for crime, shall be forever prohibited in all that part of the territory ceded by France, under the name of Louisiana, which lies north of thirty-six degrees thirty minutes north latitude, and not included within the limits of Missouri [*the Missouri Compromise Act of 1820*]. And the difficulty which meets us at the threshold of this part of the inquiry is, whether Congress was authorized to pass this law under any of the powers granted to it by the Constitution; for if the authority is not given by that instrument, it is the duty of this court to declare it void and inoperative, and incapable of conferring freedom upon any one who is held as a slave under the laws of any one of the States.

The counsel for the plaintiff has laid much stress upon that article in the Constitution which confers on Congress the power "to dispose of and make all needful rules and regulations respecting the territory or other property belonging to the United States;" but, in the judgment of the court, that provision has no bearing on the present controversy, and the power there given, whatever it may be, is confined, and was intended to be confined, to the territory which at that time belonged to, or was claimed by, the United States, and was within their boundaries as settled by the treaty with Great Britain, and can have no influence upon a territory afterwards acquired from a foreign Government....

The language used in the clause, the arrangement and combination of the powers, and the somewhat unusual phraseology it uses, when it speaks of the political power to be exercised in the government of the territory, all indicate the design and meaning of the clause to be such as we have mentioned. It docs not speak of *any* territory, nor of *Territories,* but uses language which, according to its legitimate meaning, points to a particular thing. The power is given in relation only to *the* territory of the United States—that is, to a territory then in existence, and then known or claimed as the territory of the United States....

Upon these considerations, it is the opinion of the court that the act of Congress which prohibited a citizen from holding and owning property of this kind in the territory of the United States north of the line therein mentioned, is not warranted by the Constitution, and is therefore void; and that neither Dred Scott himself, nor any of his family, were made free by being carried into this territory; even if they had been carried there by the owner, with the intention of becoming a permanent resident....

[*Justices Wayne, Nelson, Grier, Daniel, Campbell, and Catron wrote separate concurring opinions.*]

Mr. Justice McLEAN dissenting....

In the argument, it was said that a colored citizen would not be an agreeable member of society. This is more a matter of taste than of law. Several of the States have admitted persons of color to the right of suffrage, and in this view have recognised them as citizens; and this has been done in the slave as well as the free States. On the question of citizenship, it must be admitted that we have not been very fastidious. Under the late treaty with Mexico, we have made citizens of all grades, combinations, and colors. The same was done in the admission of Louisiana and Florida....

... [I]f we are to turn our attention to the dark ages of the world, why confine our view to colored slavery? On the same principles, white men were made slaves. All slavery has its origin in power, and is against right.

The power of Congress to establish Territorial Governments, and to prohibit the introduction of slavery therein, is the next point to be considered....

The prohibition of slavery north of thirty-six degrees thirty minutes, and of the State of Missouri, contained in the act admitting that State into the Union, was passed by a vote of 134, in the House of Representatives, to 42. Before Mr. Monroe signed the act, it was submitted by him to his Cabinet, and they held the restriction of slavery in a Territory to be within the constitutional powers of Congress....

But this law of Congress, which prohibits slavery north of Missouri and of thirty-six degrees thirty minutes, is declared to have been null and void by my brethren. And this opinion is founded mainly, as I understand, on the distinction drawn between the [*Northwest*] ordinance of 1787 and the Missouri compromise line. In what does the distinction consist? The ordinance, it is said, was a compact entered into by the confederated States before the adoption of the Constitution; and that in the cession of territory authority was given to establish a Territorial Government.

It is clear that the ordinance did not go into operation by virtue of the authority of the Confederation, but by reason of its modification and adoption by Congress under the Constitution. It seems to be supposed, in the opinion of the court, that the articles of cession placed it on a different footing from territories subsequently acquired. I am unable to perceive the force of this distinction. That the ordinance was intended for the government of the Northwestern Territory, and was limited to such Territory, is admitted. It was extended to Southern Territories, with modifications, by acts of Congress, and to some Northern Territories. But the ordinance was made valid by the act of Congress, and without such act could have been of no force. It rested for its validity on the act of Congress, the same, in my opinion, as the Missouri compromise line.

If Congress may establish a Territorial Government in the exercise of its discretion, it is a clear principle that a court cannot control that discretion. This being the case, I do not see on what ground the act is held to be void....

Mr. Justice CURTIS dissenting.

... It has already been shown that in five of the thirteen original States, colored persons then possessed the elective franchise, and were among those by whom the Constitution was ordained and established. If so, it is not true, in point of fact, that the Constitution was made exclusively by the white race....

I dissent, therefore, from that part of the opinion of the majority of the court, in which it is held that a person of African descent cannot be a citizen of the United States; and I regret I must go further, and dissent both from what I deem their assumption of authority to examine the constitutionality of the act of Congress commonly called the Missouri compromise act, and the grounds and conclusions announced in their opinion.

... On so grave a subject as this, I feel obliged to say that, in my opinion, such an exertion of judicial power transcends the limits of the authority of the court, ...

B. CIVIL WAR AMENDMENTS

During the war, Congress and President Lincoln took steps to eradicate slavery and its evils. Many of their actions in 1862 and 1863 eviscerated the two main principles announced by Chief Justice Taney in *Dred Scott:* Congress could not prohibit slavery in the territories, and blacks could not be citizens. Several years later that decision was formally overturned by the three Civil War amendments, ratified from 1865 to 1870. But Congress and the Attorney General acted before those amendments.

In 1862, Congress passed a number of statutes directed against slavery. It offered financial compensation to states that agreed to gradually abolish slavery, abolished slavery in the District of Columbia, and prohibited slavery in the territories (thus rejecting a central tenet of *Dred Scott*). 12 Stat. 617, 376, 432 (1862). During debate on the latter statute, no one even referred to the Court's decision. Congress never doubted its own independent constitutional power to prohibit slavery in the territories, with or without the Court. Congress also passed legislation that freed slaves from all those who committed treason against the United States or incited or engaged in any rebellion or insurrection against the United States. 12 Stat. 589 (1862). On January 1, 1863, Lincoln issued his Emancipation Proclamation.

The second main element of *Dred Scott* was discredited in 1862 when Attorney General Bates released a long opinion stating that neither color nor race could deny American blacks the right of citizenship. He pointed out that "freemen of all colors" had voted in some of the states. The idea of denying citizenship on the ground of color was received by other nations "with incredulity, if not disgust." The Constitution, Bates said, was "silent about *race* as it is about *color.*" With regard to *Dred Scott,* he held that the case, "as it stands of record, does not determine, nor purport to determine," the question of blacks to be citizens. What Chief Justice Taney said about citizenship was pure dicta and "of no authority as a judicial decision." Bates concluded: "the *free man of color,* ... if born in the United States, is a citizen of the United States." 10 Op. Att'y Gen. 382 (1862).

Constitutional Amendments

Following the war, Congress passed the Thirteenth Amendment, adopted in 1865, to abolish the institution of slavery. The Fourteenth Amendment, ratified in 1868, provided for the equality of whites and blacks before the law. The Fifteenth Amendment, which became effective in 1870, gave blacks the right to vote. Under the express language of these Amendments, Congress was empowered to enforce them "by appropriate legislation."

The Fourteenth Amendment had been foreshadowed by the Civil Rights Act of 1866. After passage of the Thirteenth Amendment, a number of southern states enacted "Black Codes" to keep the newly freed slaves in a subordinate status economically, politically, and culturally. The 1866 statute made all persons born in the United States, excluding Indians not taxed, citizens of the United States. Such citizens, "of every race and color," had the same right in every state and territory "to make and enforce contracts, to sue, be parties, and give evidence, to inherit, purchase, lease, sell, hold, and convey real and personal property, and to full and equal benefit of all laws and proceedings for the security of person and property, as is enjoyed by white citizens." 14 Stat. 27, § 1 (1866). President Andrew Johnson vetoed the bill, claiming that the power to confer the right of state citizenship "is just as exclusively with the several States as the power to confer the right of Federal citizenship is with Congress." He objected to forcing this policy on the southern states and questioned whether blacks, newly emerged from slavery, had the "requisite qualifications to entitle them to all the privileges and immunities of citizens of the United States." Congress overrode the veto, making the Civil Rights Act law on April 9, 1866. Similar objectives were incorporated in the Fourteenth Amendment, passed by Congress on June 13, 1866, and ratified by the states on July 20, 1868.

Public Accommodations

Legislation in 1875 attempted to close the gap between the Declaration of Independence and the Constitution. The preamble of the statute read: "Whereas, it is essential to just government we recognize the equality of all men before the law...." 18 Stat. 335. The statute provided for equality of all races in using public accommodations: inns, "conveyances" (transportation), theaters, and other places of public amusement. One of the sponsors, Congressman Benjamin Butler (R-Mass.), forcefully rejected the argument of opponents who claimed that the bill attempted to impose a national standard of "social equality" among blacks and whites (see box on next page). This landmark legislation would be struck down by the Supreme Court in 1883 as a federal encroachment on the states and an interference with private relationships.

Before issuing that decision, the Court handled other questions of race. State efforts to deny blacks the right to participate as jurors were struck down as a violation of the Equal Protection Clause of the Fourteenth Amendment. In doing so, however, the Court betrayed a prevailing attitude: "the colored race, as a race, was abject and ignorant, and in that condition was unfitted to command the respect of those who had superior intelligence. Their training had left them mere children, and as such they needed the protection which a wise government extends to those who are unable to protect themselves." Strauder v. West Virginia, 100 U.S. 303, 306 (1880). The Equal Protection Clause was available to offer that protection. As the Court later admitted, however, that Clause was "[v]irtually strangled in infancy by post-civil-war judicial reactionism." Regents of the University of California v. Bakke, 438 U.S. 265, 291 (1978), quoting with approval a law review article.

The Court recognized the authority of Congress, under Section 5 of the Fourteenth Amendment, to enact appropriate legislation to enforce the amendment. State judges who excluded blacks from grand and petit juries could be indicted for violating federal law. The purpose of the Civil War amendments was to "raise the colored race from that condition of inferiority and servitude in which most of them had previously stood, into perfect equality of civil rights with all other persons within the jurisdiction of the States." Ex parte Virginia, 100 U.S. 339, 344–45 (1880). When states excluded blacks from grand juries on the ground that they were "utterly unqualified by want of intelligence, experience, or moral integrity," the Court dismissed the indictments issued by the grand jury. Neal v. Delaware, 103 U.S. 370, 394 (1880). However, when Alabama prohibited interracial cohabitation or marriage and imposed heavier penalties for interracial cohabitation than for cohabitation by those of the same race, a unanimous Court discovered no violation of the Equal Protection Clause of the Fourteenth Amendment. Pace v. Alabama, 106 U.S. 583 (1883).

Equal Access and "Social Equality"

Opponents of the Civil Rights Act of 1875 claimed that the goal of giving blacks equal access to public accommodations was meant to enforce "social equality" among the races. Congressman Benjamin Butler (R-Mass.) eloquently rejected that claim, but it was later used by the Supreme Court in the *Civil Rights Cases* (1883) to declare the legislation unconstitutional.

Mr. BUTLER.... It seems to me wholly illogical, as I know it to be wholly unjust and wrong [to deny blacks equal access to public accommodations]. The colored men are either American citizens or they are not. The Constitution, for good or for evil, for right or for wrong, has made them American citizens; and the moment they were clothed with that attribute of citizenship they stood on a political and legal equality with every other citizen, be he whom he may. And I repel and repudiate the idea that there is any intention by the provisions of any one of these bills to make any social equality. That is simply an argument to the prejudice.

Social equality is not effected or affected by law. It can only come from the voluntary will of each person. Each man can in spite of the law, and does in spite of the law, choose his own associates.

But it is said we put them into the cars. The men that are put into the cars and the women that are put into the cars I trust are not my associates. There are many white men and white women whom I should prefer not to associate with who have a right to ride in the cars. That is not a question of society at all; it is a question of a common right in a public conveyance.

And so in regard of places of amusement, in regard to theaters. I do not understand that a theater is a social gathering. I do not understand that men gather there for society, except the society they choose to make each for himself. So in regard to inns....

... There is not a white man [in] the South that would not associate with the negro—all that is required by this bill—if that negro were his servant. He would eat with him, suckle from her, play with her or him as children, be together with them in every way, provided they were slaves. There never has been an objection to such an association. But the moment that you elevate this black man to citizenship from a slave, then immediately he becomes offensive. That is why I say that this prejudice is foolish, unjust, illogical, and ungentlemanly.

SOURCE: 3 Cong. Rec. 939–40 (1875).

Civil Rights Cases (1883)

The major case from this period was the Court's decision to strike down the Civil Rights Act of 1875, which had made all public accommodations available regardless of race. The Court held that Section 5 of the Fourteenth Amendment empowered Congress only to enforce the prohibitions placed upon the states. Congress could regulate only "state action," not discrimination by private parties. The Court's decision prevented the Fourteenth Amendment from providing an effective barrier against racial discrimination. In effect, the "system of 'white supremacy' was mainly beyond federal control." Alfred H. Kelly and Winfred Harbison, The American Constitution 491 (1948). The Court suggested that Congress might invoke the commerce power to regulate rights in public conveyances passing from one state to another, but that question was not before the Court. Justice Harlan issued the sole dissent, pointing out that for centuries the common law had prohibited private parties from acting in a discriminatory fashion toward travelers who needed access to inns and restaurants. Because of the Court's action, what could have been accomplished in 1875 had to await the Civil Rights Act of 1964. CIVIL RIGHTS CASES, 109 U.S. 3 (1883).

The Court initially believed that the "one pervading purpose" of the Civil War amendments was to free enslaved blacks and protect their freedoms. Slaughter-House Cases, 16 Wall. 36, 71 (1873), reprinted in Chapter 9. Although the Fourteenth Amendment appeared to give limited protection to blacks, a unanimous Court in 1886 declared a San Francisco ordinance discriminatory against Chinese operators of laundries. Announced as a fire-prevention measure, the ordinance required all laundries in wooden buildings to obtain a permit. Local authorities denied permission to a majority of Chinese, but all of the non-Chinese laundries, except for one, were allowed to continue. The Court found the ordinance "purely arbitrary" and a violation of the Equal Protection Clause of the Fourteenth Amendment. Yick Wo v. Hopkins, 118 U.S. 356 (1886).

Yick Wo illustrates that the Fourteenth Amendment, intended to grant rights to newly freed blacks, applies literally to "all persons"(see Chapter 16). Yick Wo was not a U.S. citizen; he was still a subject of the Emperor of China. However, the Fourteenth Amendment protects all persons, not all citizens. As the nation filled with immigrants, the Equal Protection Clause of the Fourteenth Amendment was extended "to all ethnic groups seeking protection from official discrimination": Celtic Irish, Chinese, Austrian resident aliens, Japanese, and Mexican-Americans. Regents of the University of California v. Bakke, 438 U.S. at 292. Similarly, although Congress passed civil rights legislation in 1866 and 1870 to protect blacks (currently §§ 1981 and 1982), those statutory provisions apply to all groups subjected to discrimination solely because of their ancestry or ethnic characteristics, including Jews and Arabs. Shaare Tefila Congregation v. Cobb, 481 U.S. 615 (1987); Saint Francis College v. Al-Khazraji, 481 U.S. 604 (1987).

Separate but Equal

The Fourteenth Amendment extended civil rights to blacks, but a number of states (not only in the South) invoked the police power to require separate facilities. Racial segregation applied to transportation, education, housing, parks, hospitals, restaurants, hotels, theaters, waiting rooms, and bathrooms. Statutes and ordinances even required separate phone booths for blacks and whites and separate textbooks. Black and white prostitutes had to be kept in separate districts. Regents of the University of California v. Bakke, 438 U.S. at 393.

When states attempted to require shared accommodations for public transportation, a unanimous Court held that these statutes, to the extent that they regulated interstate commerce, were unconstitutional and void. Hall v. DeCuir, 95 U.S. 485 (1878). Mississippi passed a law in 1888 that required all railroads (other than streetcars) carrying passengers within the state to provide equal, but separate, accommodations for whites and blacks. A 7–2 Court ruled that the statute did not violate the Commerce Clause because the law applied solely to commerce within the state. Louisville &c. Railway Co. v. Mississippi, 133 U.S. 587 (1890).

In 1896, the Supreme Court upheld a Louisiana statute that required railroads to provide equal, but separate, accommodations for white and black passengers. At that time, the tide of public opinion ran strongly against the policy of shared accommodations. The Court said that "in the nature of things" it could not have been intended to force the commingling of the two races. Laws requiring their separation "do not necessarily imply the inferiority of either race to the other" and were within the police power of the states. Justice Harlan penned the sole dissent. PLESSY v. FERGUSON, 163 U.S. 537, 544 (1896).

The separate-but-equal doctrine saddled state governments with heavy financial costs, requiring duplicate facilities for whites and blacks. In 1914, a unanimous Court upheld an Oklahoma statute that required separate-but-equal train accommodations for whites and blacks. As it was restricted to intrastate commerce, the Court found no constitutional infirmity. However, it rejected the railroads' contention that they could provide dining and Pullman (sleeper) cars for whites only, because there were insufficient blacks to justify separate cars. States had to bear the expense of separate facilities. McCabe v. A., T. & S.F. Ry. Co., 235 U.S. 151 (1914).

Bus and train systems changed from intrastate to interstate, making it difficult for states to defend a separate-but-equal policy. In 1941 a unanimous Court held that the treatment of a black on an interstate journey—denying him the right to use an available seat in a Pullman car after he had paid a first-class fare and requiring him to leave that car and ride in a second-class car—was unjust and violated the Interstate Commerce Act. Moreover, the Court found that the accommodations for black passengers were substantially inferior to those for white passengers. Mitchell v. United States, 313 U.S. 80 (1941).

A Virginia statute required all passenger motor vehicle carriers, both interstate and intrastate, to separate the races. A black was convicted for refusing to move to the back of an interstate bus that traveled from Virginia through the District of Columbia to Baltimore, Maryland. A 7–1 Court held the statute invalid because it interfered with interstate commerce and disrupted the uniformity and convenience required for national travel. To comply with the Virginia law, black passengers traveling from the north would have to change their seats once they entered Virginia. Morgan v. Virginia, 328 U.S. 373 (1946). Finally, a unanimous Court in 1950 decided that an interstate railroad's separation of races in the dining car violated the Interstate Commerce Act, which made it unlawful for a railroad in interstate commerce "to subject any particular person ... to any undue or unreasonable prejudice or disadvantage in any respect whatsoever." The Court thus disposed of this issue on statutory, not constitutional, grounds. Henderson v. United States, 339 U.S. 816 (1950). Therefore, before the Court handed down its Desegregation Decision in 1954, a combination of factors had chipped away at the policy of separate-but-equal facilities for transportation. The next section on school desegregation identifies other decisions, before 1954, that undermined the separate-but-equal doctrine.

Civil Rights Cases

109 U.S. 3 (1883)

Congress passed the Civil Rights Act of 1875 to extend to blacks the full and equal enjoyment of public accommodations, including inns, transportation on land and water, theaters, and other places of amusement. The statute also provided penalties for anyone who denied these privileges to black people. Five cases from New Jersey, Tennessee, Missouri, Kansas and California, were consolidated and decided by the court in the Civil Rights Cases. Owners of hotels, theaters, and a railroad were indicted. The question for the Court was whether the Thirteenth and Fourteenth Amendments prohibited only state action or private action as well.

Mr. Justice Bradley delivered the opinion of the court ...

Has Congress constitutional power to make such a law? Of course, no one will contend that the power to pass it was contained in the Constitution before the adoption of the last three amendments. The power is sought, first, in the Fourteenth Amendment, ...

The first section of the Fourteenth Amendment (which is the one relied on), after declaring who shall be citizens of the United States, and of the several States, is prohibitory in its character, and prohibitory upon the States. It declares that:

"No State shall make or enforce any law which shall abridge the privileges or immunities of citizens of the United States; nor shall any State deprive any person of life, liberty, or property without due process of law; nor deny to any person within its jurisdiction the equal protection of the laws."

It is State action of a particular character that is prohibited. Individual invasion of individual rights is not the subject-matter of the amendment. It has a deeper and broader scope. It nullifies and makes void all State legislation, and State action of every kind, which impairs the privileges and immunities of citizens of the United States, or which injures them in life, liberty or property without due process of law, or which denies to any of them the equal protection of the laws. It not only does this, but, in order that the national will, thus declared, may not be a mere *brutum fulmen,* the last section of the amendment invests Congress with power to enforce it by appropriate legislation. To enforce what? To enforce the prohibition. To adopt appropriate legislation for correcting the effects of such prohibited State laws and State acts, and thus to render them effectually null, void, and innocuous. This is the legislative power conferred upon Congress, and this is the whole of it. It does not invest Congress with power to legislate upon subjects which are within the domain of State legislation; but to provide modes of relief against State legislation, or State action, of the kind referred to. It does not authorize Congress to create a code of municipal law for the regulation of private rights; but to provide modes of redress against the operation of State laws, and the action of State officers executive or judicial, when these are subversive of the fundamental rights specified in the amendment....

We have discussed the question presented by the law on the assumption that a right to enjoy equal accommodation and privileges in all inns, public conveyances, and places of public amusement, is one of the essential rights of the citizen which no State can abridge or interfere with. Whether it is such a right, or not, is a different question which, in the view we have taken of the validity of the law on the ground already stated, it is not necessary to examine.

We have also discussed the validity of the law in reference to cases arising in the States only; and not in reference to cases arising in the Territories or the District of Columbia, which are subject to the plenary legislation of Congress in every branch of municipal regulation. Whether the law would be a valid one as applied to the Territories and the District is not a question for consideration in the cases before us; they all being cases arising within the limits of States. And whether Congress, in the exercise of its power to regulate commerce amongst the several States, might or might not pass a law regulating rights in public conveyances passing from one State to another, is also a question which is not now before us, as the sections in question are not conceived in any such view.

But the power of Congress to adopt direct and primary, as distinguished from corrective legislation, on the subject in hand, is sought, in the second place, from the Thirteenth Amendment, which abolishes slavery. This amendment declares "that neither slavery, nor involuntary servitude, except as a punishment for crime, whereof the party shall have been duly convicted, shall exist within the United States, or any place subject to their jurisdiction;" and it gives Congress power to enforce the amendment by appropriate legislation.

... [I]t is assumed, that the power vested in Congress to enforce the article by appropriate legislation, clothes Congress with power to pass all laws necessary and proper for abolishing all badges and inci-

dents of slavery in the United States: and upon this assumption it is claimed, that this is sufficient authority for declaring by law that all persons shall have equal accommodations and privileges in all inns, public conveyances, and places of amusement; the argument being, that the denial of such equal accommodations and privileges is, in itself, a subjection to a species of servitude within the meaning of the amendment....

Now, conceding, for the sake of the argument, that the admission to an inn, a public conveyance, or a place of public amusement, on equal terms with all other citizens, is the right of every man and all classes of men, is it any more than one of those rights which the states by the Fourteenth Amendment are forbidden to deny to any person? And is the Constitution violated until the denial of the right has some State sanction or authority? Can the act of a mere individual, the owner of the inn, the public conveyance or place of amusement, refusing the accommodation, be justly regarded as imposing any badge of slavery or servitude upon the applicant, or only as inflicting an ordinary civil injury, properly cognizable by the laws of the State, and presumably subject to redress by those laws until the contrary appears?

... [W]e are forced to the conclusion that such an act of refusal has nothing to do with slavery or involuntary servitude, and that if it is violative of any right of the party, his redress is to be sought under the laws of the State; ...

When a man has emerged from slavery, and by the aid of beneficent legislation has shaken off the inseparable concomitants of that state, there must be some stage in the progress of his elevation when he takes the rank of a mere citizen, and ceases to be the special favorite of the laws, and when his rights as a citizen, or a man, are to be protected in the ordinary modes by which other men's rights are protected. There were thousands of free colored people in this country before the abolition of slavery, enjoying all the essential rights of life, liberty and property the same as white citizens; yet no one, at that time, thought that it was any invasion of his personal status as a freeman because he was not admitted to all the privileges enjoyed by white citizens, or because he was subjected to discriminations in the enjoyment of accommodations in inns, public conveyances and places of amusement. Mere discriminations on account of race or color were not regarded as badges of slavery. If, since that time, the enjoyment of equal rights in all these respects has become established by constitutional enactment, it is not by force of the Thirteenth Amendment (which merely abolishes slavery), but by force of the Thirteenth and Fifteenth Amendments.

... [T]he answer to be given will be that the first and second sections of the act of Congress of March 1st, 1875, entitled "An Act to protect all citizens in their civil and legal rights," are unconstitutional and void, and that judgment should be rendered upon the several indictments in those cases accordingly.

And it is so ordered.

Mr. Justice Harlan dissenting.

... [W]hat are the legal rights of colored persons in respect of the accommodations, privileges and facilities of public conveyances, inns and places of public amusement?

First, as to public conveyances on land and water. [*Earlier cases ruled that*] railroads are public highways, established by authority of the State for the public use; that they are none the less public highways, because controlled and owned by private corporations; that it is a part of the function of government to make and maintain highways for the conveyance of the public; that no matter who is the agent, or what is the agency, the function performed is *that of the State;* ...

Second, as to inns. The same general observations which have been made as to railroads are applicable to inns. The word "inn" has a technical legal signification. It means, in the act of 1875, just what it meant at common law. A mere private boarding-house is not an inn, nor is its keeper subject to the responsibilities, or entitled to the privileges of a common innkeeper. "To constitute one an innkeeper, within the legal force of that term, he must keep a house of entertainment or lodging for all travellers or wayfarers who might choose to accept the same, being of good character or conduct." Redfield on Carriers, etc., § 575....

... [A] keeper of an inn is in the exercise of a quasi public employment. The law gives him special privileges and he is charged with certain duties and responsibilities to the public. The public nature of his employment forbids him from discriminating against any person asking admission as a guest on account of the race or color of that person.

Third. As to places of public amusement.... [P]laces of public amusement, within the meaning of the act of 1875, are such as are established and maintained under direct license of the law. The authority to establish and maintain them comes from the public. The colored race is a part of that public. The local government granting the license represents them as well as all other races within its jurisdiction....

... I agree that government has nothing to do with social, as distinguished from technically legal, rights of individuals. No government ever has brought, or ever can bring, its people into social intercourse against their wishes. Whether one person will permit or maintain social relations with another is a matter with which government has no concern. I agree that if one citizen chooses not to hold social intercourse with another, he is not and cannot be made amenable to the law for his conduct in that regard; for no legal right of a citizen is violated by the refusal of others to maintain merely social relations with him, even upon grounds of race. What I affirm is that no State, nor the officers of any State, nor any corporation or individual wielding power under State authority for the public benefit or the public convenience, can, consistently either with the freedom established by the fundamental law, or with that equality of civil rights which now belongs to every citizen, discriminate against freemen or citizens, in those rights, because of their race, or because they once labored under the disabilities of slavery imposed upon them as a race. The rights which Congress, by the act of 1875, endeavored to secure and protect are legal, not social rights....

Plessy v. Ferguson

163 U.S. 537 (1896)

After the Civil War, and despite the Thirteenth and Fourteenth Amendments, some of the states began to adopt segregationist policies by creating "separate-but-equal" facilities for blacks and whites. Eventually, the policy extended to schools, transportation, parks, and other public accommodations. This case involved a Louisiana law, enacted in 1890, that required separate railway cars for whites and blacks. Homer A. Plessy, one-eighth black, was arrested for attempting to sit in a railroad coach reserved for whites. He appealed an order by a state judge, John Ferguson.

Mr. Justice Brown, after stating the case, delivered the opinion of the court....

The constitutionality of this act is attacked upon the ground that it conflicts both with the Thirteenth

Amendment of the Constitution, abolishing slavery, and the Fourteenth Amendment, which prohibits certain restrictive legislation on the part of the States.

1. That it does not conflict with the Thirteenth Amendment, which abolished slavery and involuntary servitude, except as a punishment for crime, is too clear for argument. Slavery implies involuntary servitude — a state of bondage; the ownership of mankind as a chattel, or at least the control of the labor and services of one man for the benefit of another, and the absence of a legal right to the disposal of his own person, property and services. This amendment was said in the *Slaughter-house cases,* 16 Wall. 36, to have been intended primarily to abolish slavery, as it had been previously known in this country, and that it equally forbade Mexican peonage or the Chinese coolie trade, when they amounted to slavery or involuntary servitude, and that the use of the word "servitude" was intended to prohibit the use of all forms of involuntary slavery, of whatever class or name....

A statute which implies merely a legal distinction between the white and colored races — a distinction which is founded in the color of the two races, and which must always exist so long as white men are distinguished from the other race by color — has no tendency to destroy the legal equality of the two races, or reëstablish a state of involuntary servitude. Indeed, we do not understand that the Thirteenth Amendment is strenuously relied upon by the plaintiff in error in this connection.

2. By the Fourteenth Amendment, all persons born or naturalized in the United States, and subject to the jurisdiction thereof, are made citizens of the United States and of the State wherein they reside; and the States are forbidden from making or enforcing any law which shall abridge the privileges or immunities of citizens of the United States, or shall deprive any person of life, liberty or property without due process of law, or deny to any person within their jurisdiction the equal protection of the laws.

The proper construction of this amendment was first called to the attention of this court in the *Slaughter-house cases,* 16 Wall. 36, which involved, however, not a question of race, but one of exclusive privileges. The case did not call for any expression of opinion as to the exact rights it was intended to secure to the colored race, but it was said generally that its main purpose was to establish the citizenship of the negro; to give definitions of citizenship of the United States and of the States, and to protect from the hostile legislation of the States the privileges and immunities of citizens of the United

States, as distinguished from those of citizens of the States.

The object of the amendment was undoubtedly to enforce the absolute equality of the two races before the law, but in the nature of things it could not have been intended to abolish distinctions based upon color, or to enforce social, as distinguished from political equality, or a commingling of the two races upon terms unsatisfactory to either. Laws permitting, and even requiring, their separation in places where they are liable to be brought into contact do not necessarily imply the inferiority of either race to the other, and have been generally, if not universally, recognized as within the competency of the state legislatures in the exercise of their police power. The most common instance of this is connected with the establishment of separate schools for white and colored children, which has been held to be a valid exercise of the legislative power even by courts of States where the political rights of the colored race have been longest and most earnestly enforced.

... [T]he case reduces itself to the question whether the statute of Louisiana is a reasonable regulation, and with respect to this there must necessarily be a large discretion on the part of the legislature. In determining the question of reasonableness it is at liberty to act with reference to the established usages, customs and traditions of the people, and with a view to the promotion of their comfort, and the preservation of the public peace and good order. Gauged by this standard, we cannot say that a law which authorizes or even requires the separation of the two races in public conveyances is unreasonable, or more obnoxious to the Fourteenth Amendment than the acts of Congress requiring separate schools for colored children in the District of Columbia, the constitutionality of which does not seem to have been questioned, or the corresponding acts of state legislatures.

We consider the underlying fallacy of the plaintiff's argument to consist in the assumption that the enforced separation of the two races stamps the colored race with a badge of inferiority. If this be so, it is not by reason of anything found in the act, but solely because the colored race chooses to put that construction upon it. The argument necessarily assumes that if, as has been more than once the case, and is not unlikely to be so again, the colored race should become the dominant power in the state legislature, and should enact a law in precisely similar terms, it would thereby relegate the white race to an inferior position. We imagine that the white race, at least, would not acquiesce in this assumption. The argument also assumes that social prejudices may be overcome by legislation, and that equal rights cannot be secured to the negro except by an enforced commingling of the two races. We cannot accept this proposition. If the two races are to meet upon terms of social equality, it must be the result of natural affinities, a mutual appreciation of each other's merits and a voluntary consent of individuals.... If the civil and political rights of both races be equal one cannot be inferior to the other civilly or politically. If one race be inferior to the other socially, the Constitution of the United States cannot put them upon the same plane.

It is true that the question of the proportion of colored blood necessary to constitute a colored person, as distinguished from a white person, is one upon which there is a difference of opinion in the different States, some holding that any visible admixture of black blood stamps the person as belonging to the colored race, ... ; others that it depends upon the preponderance of blood, ... ; and still others that the predominance of white blood must only be in the proportion of three fourths.... But these are questions to be determined under the laws of each State and are not properly put in issue in this case. Under the allegations of his petition it may undoubtedly become a question of importance whether, under the laws of Louisiana, the petitioner belongs to the white or colored race.

The judgment of the court below is, therefore,

Affirmed.

Mr. Justice Harlan dissenting....

That a railroad is a public highway, and that the corporation which owns or operates it is in the exercise of public functions, is not, at this day, to be disputed....

In respect of civil rights, common to all citizens, the Constitution of the United States does not, I think, permit any public authority to know the race of those entitled to be protected in the enjoyment of such rights. Every true man has pride of race, and under appropriate circumstances when the rights of others, his equals before the law, are not to be affected, it is his privilege to express such pride and to take such action based upon it as to him seems proper. But I deny that any legislative body or judicial tribunal may have regard to the race of citizens when the civil rights of those citizens are involved....

It was said in argument that the statute of Louisiana does not discriminate against either race, but prescribes a rule applicable alike to white and colored citizens. But this argument does not meet the difficulty. Every one knows that the statute in question had its origin in the purpose, not so much to exclude white persons from railroad cars occupied by blacks, as to exclude colored people from coaches occupied by or assigned to white persons....

The white race deems itself to be the dominant race in this country. And so it is, in prestige, in achievements, in education, in wealth and in power. So, I doubt not, it will continue to be for all time, if it remains true to its great heritage and holds fast to the principles of constitutional liberty. But in view of the Constitution, in the eye of the law, there is in this country no superior, dominant, ruling class of citizens. There is no caste here. Our Constitution is color-blind, and neither knows nor tolerates classes among citizens. In respect of civil rights, all citizens are equal before the law....

In my opinion, the judgment this day rendered will, in time, prove to be quite as pernicious as the decision made by this tribunal in the *Dred Scott case....* Sixty millions of whites are in no danger from the presence here of eight millions of blacks. The destinies of the two races, in this country, are indissolubly linked together, and the interests of both require that the common government of all shall not permit the seeds of race hate to be planted under the sanction of law. What can more certainly arouse race hate, what more certainly create and perpetuate a feeling of distrust between these races, than state enactments, which, in fact, proceed on the ground that colored citizens are so inferior and degraded that they cannot be allowed to sit in public coaches occupied by white citizens? ...

There is a race so different from our own that we do not permit those belonging to it to become citizens of the United States. Persons belonging to it are, with few exceptions, absolutely excluded from our country. I allude to the Chinese race. But by the statute in question, a Chinaman can ride in the same passenger coach with white citizens of the United States, while citizens of the black race in Louisiana, many of whom, perhaps, risked their lives for the preservation of the Union, who are entitled, by law, to participate in the political control of the State and nation, who are not excluded, by law or by reason of their race, from public stations of any kind, and who have all the legal rights that belong to white citizens, are yet declared to be criminals, liable to imprisonment, if they ride in a public coach occupied by citizens of the white race....

The arbitrary separation of citizens, on the basis of race, while they are on a public highway, is a badge of servitude wholly inconsistent with the civil freedom and the equality before the law established by the Constitution. It cannot be justified upon any legal grounds.

If evils will result from the commingling of the two races upon public highways established for the benefit of all, they will be infinitely less than those that will surely come from state legislation regulating the enjoyment of civil rights upon the basis of race. We boast of the freedom enjoyed by our people above all other peoples. But it is difficult to rec-

oncile that boast with a state of the law which, practically, puts the brand of servitude and degradation upon a large class of our fellow-citizens, our equals before the law. The thin disguise of "equal" accommodations for passengers in railroad coaches will not mislead any one, nor atone for the wrong this day done....

Mr. Justice Brewer did not hear the argument or participate in the decision of this case.

C. SCHOOL DESEGREGATION

Like transportation, the policy of separate-but-equal in education became increasingly impractical. Various forces helped erode this practice long before the Court struck it down in 1954. Part of the shift toward desegregation reflected a mobile society, with each state receiving new visitors and new challenges to its customs. Another factor was foreign policy. Competition with international communism after World War II put pressure on the United States to abolish segregation and bring practices in line with American ideals.

Plessy reinforced the separate-but-equal doctrine in many fields, including education. A unanimous Court in 1899 ruled that schools, even if segregated, were a matter belonging to the states. The opinion was written by Justice Harlan, the lone dissenter in *Plessy*. Cumming v. Board of Education, 175 U.S. 528 (1899). States were permitted to outlaw integrated education in private colleges. Berea College v. Kentucky, 211 U.S. 45 (1908). A unanimous ruling held that states had discretion to assign Chinese children to attend public schools with blacks. Gong Lum v. Rice, 275 U.S. 78 (1927).

Opponents of *Plessy* decided to file lawsuits to attack the most vulnerable area: segregated graduate schools. The timing was propitious. During the late 1930s, the courts began to abandon use of the Due Process Clause to protect property interests ("substantive due process") and rely more on the Equal Protection Clause to defend individual rights. Regents of the University of California v. Bakke, 438 U.S. at 291–92. This attitude was expressed most forcefully in a famous footnote by Justice Stone. In reviewing the standards for judicial review and the choice between activism and restraint, he suggested that the courts might have a special responsibility for protecting "discrete and insular minorities," particularly when political processes relied upon to protect minorities have been curtailed (see box on next page). This footnote expressed a solicitude that captures much of the Court's work in racial discrimination since 1938.

Beginning in 1936, Court decisions on the separate-but-equal policy in higher education gradually painted *Plessy* into an ever-narrowing corner. In one case, black applicants were denied admission to the law school at the University of Maryland. As compensation, the state offered to pay their tuition to a law school outside the state. A unanimous appellate court in Maryland ruled that this policy violated the Equal Protection Clause. Blacks would encounter greater costs traveling to another state and paying additional living expenses. Moreover, an education outside the state would not adequately prepare blacks who intended to practice in Maryland. Pearson v. Murray, 182 A. 593 (Md. 1936). Missouri also wanted to pay black students their tuition costs for a law school education in an adjacent state. The Supreme Court, divided 7–2, held that this policy violated the Equal Protection Clause by creating a privilege for white law students (able to attend the Missouri law school) that was denied to blacks. Missouri ex rel. Gaines v. Canada, 305 U.S. 337 (1938). See also Sipuel v. Board of Regents, 332 U.S. 631 (1948) and Fisher v. Hurst, 333 U.S. 147 (1948).

The next effort to preserve *Plessy* was to create a separate law school for blacks within the state. A unanimous Court in 1950 concluded that the school for blacks did not satisfy the separate-but-equal

The *Carolene* Footnote

[*In 1938, at a time when the Supreme Court was withdrawing its scrutiny of economic regulation, Justice Stone wrote a footnote indicating that the Court had a special duty to safeguard minority rights. United States v. Carolene Products Co., 304 U.S. 144, 153 n.4 (1938). His formulation later evolved into a "strict scrutiny" analysis for protecting fundamental rights, including issues of race discrimination.*]

There may be narrower scope for operation of the presumption of constitutionality when legislation appears on its face to be within a specific prohibition of the Constitution, such as those of the first ten amendments, which are deemed equally specific when held to be embraced within the Fourteenth....

It is unnecessary to consider now whether legislation which restricts those political processes which can ordinarily be expected to bring about repeal of undesirable legislation, is to be subjected to more exacting judicial scrutiny under the general prohibitions of the Fourteenth Amendment than are most other types of legislation [*restrictions upon the right to vote, to disseminate information, and interferences with political organizations and peaceable assembly*].

Nor need we enquire whether similar considerations enter into the review of statutes directed at particular religious ... or national ... or racial minorities ... ; whether prejudice against discrete and insular minorities may be a special condition, which tends seriously to curtail the operation of those political processes ordinarily to be relied upon to protect minorities, and which may call for a correspondingly more searching judicial inquiry....

standard. The University of Texas Law School, attended by whites, was superior in terms of its professional staff, library, law review, moot court facilities, scholarship funds, distinguished alumni, tradition, and prestige. Sweatt v. Painter, 339 U.S. 629 (1950). Oklahoma agreed to admit blacks to the state university but separated them from white students. Blacks had to sit in a special seat in the classroom, a special table in the library, and a special table in the cafeteria. Once again, a unanimous Court found this in violation of the Equal Protection Clause. The restrictions on the black student impaired and inhibited "his ability to study, to engage in discussions and exchange views with other students, and, in general, to learn his profession." McLaurin v. Oklahoma State Regents, 339 U.S. 637 (1950). Clearly, *Plessy*'s days were numbered.

Brown v. Board of Education

These cases laid part of the groundwork for the desegregation case of 1954. Other influences were important. The horrors of racism in Nazi Germany, sending millions of Jews to their death in gas chambers and concentration camps, showed the results of preaching a "master race." After the war, President Truman took steps to eliminate discrimination in federal government and to abolish segregation in the armed forces. The United States, which emerged as a world leader after World War II, could not fight world communism effectively while maintaining racial segregation at home. The NAACP's brief observed: "Survival of our country in the present international situation is inevitably tied to resolution of this domestic issue." The federal government's amicus brief in 1952 explained in great detail the harmful effects of American segregation on the foreign policy of the executive branch. Racial discrimination affected American blacks and dark-skinned visitors from other countries, furnishing "grist for the Communist propaganda mills" (see reading).

By the time of the desegregation case of 1954, 17 states and the District of Columbia required segregated schools. Four other states permitted segregation as a local option. The Supreme Court admitted that in approaching the problem of school segregation "we cannot turn the clock back to 1868 when the [Fourteenth] Amendment was adopted, or even to 1896 when *Plessy* v. *Ferguson* was written." BROWN v. BOARD OF EDUCATION, 347 U.S. 483, 492 (1954). The unanimous decision was

Building a Unanimous Court

In 1952 and through most of 1953, the Supreme Court appeared to be split down the middle on the constitutionality of segregated schools. Four Justices (Black, Douglas, Burton, and Minton) were ready to overrule *Plessy*. Five Justices (Vinson, Reed, Frankfurter, Jackson, and Clark) either supported *Plessy* or were loath to abandon it. Chief Justice Vinson died on September 8, 1953, and was replaced by Earl Warren. There now seemed to be a 5–4 majority to reverse *Plessy*. Moreover, Clark indicated he was ready to shift sides, giving Warren a 6–3 majority. What could Warren do to attract Reed, Frankfurter, and Jackson and present a united front?

Two of the Southerners on the Court (Clark and Reed) indicated they might join a unanimous decision if enforcement could be done in different ways, and different times, by the states. Jackson and Frankfurter also wanted a flexible remedy. Frankfurter recalled a phrase from Justice Holmes and used it to argue that states could enforce *Brown* "with all deliberate speed" (close to an oxymoron). These vague formulations, helpful in producing a unanimous ruling, also encouraged years of minimal compliance from the states. The broad constitutional rights announced in 1954 were undermined a year later in the implementing decision.

SOURCES: S. Sidney Ulmer, "Earl Warren and the *Brown* Decision," 33 J. Pol. 689, 691–92 (1971); Richard Kluger, Simple Justice 589–614, 682–87, 696–99, 742–45 (1975); William O. Douglas, The Court Years 113 (1980); Bernard Schwartz, Super Chief, 72–127 (1983); and Philip Elman, "The Solicitor General's Office, Justice Frankfurter, and Civil Rights Litigation, 1946–1960: An Oral History," 100 Harv. L. Rev. 817, 842–43 (1987).

the result of much internal bargaining (see box). Segregation, said the Court, generated a feeling of inferiority among black children: "Whatever may have been the extent of psychological knowledge at the time of *Plessy* v. *Ferguson,* this finding [of inequality] is amply supported by modern authority." Following this sentence was a famous footnote, the wisdom of which has been extensively debated, citing seven psychological and sociological studies on the effects of discrimination and segregation on children.[2]

In striking down segregated schools in the states, the Court relied on the Equal Protection Clause of the Fourteenth Amendment. What could be used to overturn segregation in the nation's capital? The Fifth Amendment, applicable to the District of Columbia, does not contain an equal protection clause. It would have been intolerable for the Court to invalidate segregated schools in the states and allow them to operate in the District of Columbia. The Court finessed the problem by holding that racial segregation in the D.C. public schools denied black children the due process of law guaranteed by the Fifth Amendment. The concepts of equal protection and due process, "both stemming from our American ideal of fairness, are not mutually exclusive." BOLLING v. SHARPE, 347 U.S. 497, 499 (1954).

In 1955, the Court announced guidelines for implementing its desegregation decision. How quickly were states to make the transition? The answer: No great hurry. The Court largely deferred to local school authorities in determining the appropriate course, leaving to federal courts the duty of considering whether school authorities were acting in good faith to comply with desegregation. Several phrases from the Court—including "practical flexibility," "as soon as practicable," "a prompt and

---

2. See Abraham L. Davis, The United States Supreme Court and the Uses of Social Science Data 48–61, 65–74, 95–118 (1973); William B. Ball, "Lawyers and Social Sciences—Guiding the Guides," 5 Vill. L. Rev. 215 (1959–60); Kenneth B. Clark, "The Desegregation Cases: Criticism of the Social Scientist's Role," 5 Vill. L. Rev. 224 (1959–60); Herbert Garfinkel, "Social Science Evidence and the School Desegregation Cases," 21 J. Pol. 37 (1959); Jack Greenberg, "Social Scientists Take the Stand," 54 Mich. L. Rev. 953 (1956); Edmond Cahn, "Jurisprudence," 30 N.Y.U. L. Rev. 150 (1955).

reasonable start," and "all deliberate speed"—gave a green light to obstruction and procrastination. BROWN v. BOARD OF EDUCATION, 349 U.S. 294 (1955).

Political Resistance

In issuing its desegregation decision, the Supreme Court obviously did not have the last word. The Justice Department had given strong encouragement to the Court to strike down segregated schools, but that was during the Truman administration. The amicus brief filed by the Justice Department after Dwight D. Eisenhower became President was not as strong. Eisenhower failed to give full support to the *Brown* decision, perhaps reflecting his belief in states' rights and limited government. In any event, the record after 1954 was marred by massive state resistance and acts of violence against blacks. A major confrontation occurred in Arkansas, when Governor Orval Faubus defied three court orders to integrate the Little Rock Central High School. On September 24, 1957, President Eisenhower sent in armed troops to prevent the obstruction of justice. In a radio and television address to the nation, Eisenhower spoke of the harm done to America's prestige and influence in the world, noting that "enemies are gloating over this incident." Public Papers of the Presidents, 1957, at 694. In 1958, after calling a special term in August, the Court affirmed the lower court orders in the Little Rock crisis. COOPER v. AARON, 358 U.S. 1 (1958).

The Court's insistence on desegregation in 1954 and its announcement of judiciary supremacy in 1958 did little to integrate public schools. As late as 1964, the Court complained that there "has been entirely too much deliberation and not enough speed" in enforcing *Brown*. Griffin v. School Bd., 377 U.S. 218, 229 (1964). Reaching finality needed more than a Court decision. Resolution required the concerted action of the elected branches: Congress and the President. A federal appellate court noted in 1966: "A national effort, bringing together Congress, the executive and the judiciary may be able to make meaningful the right of Negro children to equal educational opportunities. *The courts acting alone have failed.*" United States v. Jefferson County Board of Education, 372 F.2d 836, 847 (5th Cir. 1966) (emphasis in original). Three federal statutes, passed in 1957, 1960, and 1964, put the nation on course in eliminating segregation in public facilities. [The Voting Rights Act of 1965 is analyzed in Chapter 18.]

Federal Legislation

The Civil Rights Act of 1957 marked the first civil rights measure passed since 1875. It established a Commission on Civil Rights to investigate allegations of discrimination, authorized the President to appoint an additional Assistant Attorney General to head a new Civil Rights Division in the Justice Department, and set fines for those convicted in cases arising from the statute. 71 Stat. 634. The broad investigative powers of the Commission were upheld by the Supreme Court. Hannah v. Larche, 363 U.S. 420 (1960). The Civil Rights Act of 1960 strengthened existing laws on obstruction of court orders, provided criminal penalties for acts of violence and destruction, and authorized court-appointed "referees" to monitor voting rights. 74 Stat. 86.

The major step was the Civil Rights Act of 1964, the most far-reaching civil rights statute since the Reconstruction Era. Public pressure for legislative action included sit-ins, demonstrations, picketing, and boycotts. For the first time on a civil rights bill, Senators were able to vote cloture and stop a filibuster. The legislation passed by top-heavy majorities of 289–126 in the House and 73–27 in the Senate. Bipartisan support was solid. The House voted 153–91 Democrat and 136–35 Republican. The party split in the Senate: 46–21 for Democrats and 27–6 for Republicans. Major factions throughout the country had united to give the final word. 78 Stat. 241.

The statute provided new guarantees for black voters and created a Community Relations Service to help resolve civil rights problems. The most significant sections concerned public accommodations, termination of federal funds, and discrimination in employment. Title IV dealt with desegregation of public education, including elementary, secondary, and higher education. Title VI provided for nondiscrimination in federally assisted programs. If parties receiving federal funds refused to voluntarily comply with the statute, agencies could terminate funds. Termination of assistance was subject to judicial review. Title VII, on equal employment opportunity, outlawed employment practices based on race, color, religion, sex, or national origin. The Act created the Equal Employment Opportunity Commission (EEOC) to enforce the law.

Title VI, threatening a cutoff of federal funds from states that continued racial discrimination in schools, became more significant as the level of federal assistance increased. The Elementary and Secondary Education Act of 1965 provided large federal grants to school districts. It was the first general school aid in the nation's history. School districts now had to decide what they wanted most: segregated schools or federal funds.

De Facto Segregation and Busing

For much of the 1950s and 1960s, smug northerners pretended that segregation was a problem only for the South. Little notice was taken of northern school systems that were segregated in fact (de facto) rather than by law (de jure). Increasingly, inner-city blacks were encircled by white suburbs. What was to be done when segregated schools resulted not from state laws but from residential patterns and family income?

Busing was one possibility. Although busing today is associated with efforts to integrate schools, it can be used just as easily to promote segregation. In eastern Virginia, where there was little residential segregation, school buses were used heavily to criss-cross students from one corner of the county to another to maintain all-white and all-black schools. Green v. County School Board, 391 U.S. 430, 432 (1968).

In 1971, a unanimous Court held that district courts had broad power to fashion remedies for desegregated schools. To achieve greater racial balance, judges could alter school district zones, reassign teachers, and bus students. SWANN v. CHARLOTTE-MECKLENBURG BD. OF ED., 402 U.S. 1 (1971). A unanimous Court also struck down state antibusing laws. North Carolina State Board of Education v. Swann, 402 U.S. 43 (1971).

These rulings appeared to clash with language in the Civil Rights Act of 1964, which defined *desegregation* as the assignment of students to public schools without regard to their race, color, religion, or national origin, and stated that desegregation "shall not mean the assignment of students to public schools in order to overcome racial imbalance." 78 Stat. 246, §401(b). In fact, race was regularly taken into account by courts to devise desegregation plans. The Civil Rights Act of 1964 did not empower any federal official or court "to issue any order seeking to achieve a racial balance in any school by requiring the transportation of pupils." 78 Stat. 248, §407(a). The Court sidestepped this potential conflict by arguing that the busing provision in the statute was directed at de facto, not de jure, segregation. Swann v. Charlotte-Mecklenburg, 402 U.S. at 17–18.

Busing Orders Outside the South

Within a few years busing was used to integrate schools in non-southern states. A Supreme Court decision in 1973 involved the school system in Denver, Colorado. Parents of black children charged that the school board maintained a segregated system through the use of student attendance zones, school-site selection, and a neighborhood school policy. A 7–1 Court found that the school board intended school segregation in one area, thereby practicing de jure segregation, and that the burden appropriately shifted to the board to prove that other segregated schools were not also the result of intentional actions. Several Justices dismissed the difference between de jure and de facto segregation, preferring that whenever segregated public schools exist there is prima facie evidence of a constitutional violation by the school board. This test avoided the question of whether segregation resulted from "intent" (de jure) or "effect" (de facto). Keyes v. School District No. 1, Denver, Colo., 413 U.S. 189 (1973).

Another non-southern school system scrutinized by the Court was in Detroit. Black families claimed that schools had been racially segregated because of official policies. The lower courts concluded that a Detroit-only solution was inadequate; widespread busing, reaching to outlying districts, would be necessary. The string of unanimous or near-unanimous decisions by the Supreme Court on school segregation now shattered. Divided 5 to 4, the Court dismissed the remedies adopted by the lower courts. It decided that a cross-district busing plan would disrupt school district lines, violate the tradition of local school control, and thrust judges into the role of "school superintendent" for which they are unqualified. The district court had ordered the school board to obtain at least 295 school buses, with the cost borne by the state. The Court concluded that a metropolitan area remedy punished outlying districts with no showing that they had committed constitutional violations. MIL-LIKEN v. BRADLEY, 418 U.S. 717 (1974). In a follow-up case for Detroit, a unanimous Court agreed that lower courts can order compensatory or remedial educational programs for schoolchildren subjected to past acts of de jure segregation. Assistance included reading instruction, in-service teacher training, testing, and counseling. Milliken v. Bradley, 433 U.S. 267 (1977).

The Supreme Court scrutinized two other northern school systems, in Columbus and Dayton, Ohio. The Court decided that because there had been de jure segregation, officials had to take affirmative steps to desegregate the school system. Chief Justice Burger agreed that it "is becoming increasingly doubtful that massive public transportation really accomplishes the desirable objectives sought." Columbus Board of Education v. Penick, 443 U.S. 449, 469 (1979). In a dissent, Powell warned that parents resentful of court-ordered integration might withdraw their children from public schools by relocating their families ("white flight") or turning to private schools. Either choice would produce resegregation of public schools. Id. at 484. See also Dayton Board of Education v. Brinkman, 433 U.S. 406 (1977), and Dayton Board of Education v. Brinkman, 443 U.S. 526 (1979).

Opposition to Busing and Other Resistance

In addition to placing antibusing language in the Civil Rights Act of 1964, Congress prohibited the use of appropriated funds to bus students for racial balance. However, these restrictions generally controlled federal agencies, not the courts. Statutory limitations prohibited agencies from forcing states to bus students as a condition for receiving federal funds.[3] In prohibiting the forced busing of students, Congress sometimes softened the language by adding: "Except as required by the Constitution." 84 Stat. 48, §§ 408, 409 (1970). Congress stated that its actions were "not intended to modify or diminish the authority" of U.S. courts to enforce the Fifth and Fourteenth Amendments. 88 Stat. 515, § 203(b) (1974), codified at 20 U.S.C. § 1702(b) (2000). Some limitations applied directly to the courts. 88 Stat. 517, § 215 (1974), codified at 20 U.S.C. § 1714 (2000). The riders on appropriations bills expired at the end of each fiscal year; other restrictions on busing became part of permanent law.[4]

In 1982, the Court reviewed a statewide initiative in Washington designed to prohibit the use of mandatory busing to achieve integrated public schools. Split 5 to 4, the Court held that the initiative violated the Equal Protection Clause. Washington v. Seattle School Dist. No. 1, 458 U.S. 457 (1982). A combination of dissenting Justices, public opposition, and restrictions by Congress eventually forced the courts to abandon widespread busing as a remedy for desegregation. Black parents as well as white parents objected to having their children transported on buses for long distances. They pre-

---

3. 81 Stat. 441, § 16 (1967); 82 Stat. 995, § 409 (1968); 84 Stat. 805, §§ 209, 210 (1970); 85 Stat. 107, §§ 309, 310 (1971); 90 Stat. 21–22, §§ 207–09 (1976); 90 Stat. 1433–34, §§ 206–08 (1976); 92 Stat. 1585–86, §§ 207–09 (1978).

4. 80 Stat. 1264, § 205(f) (1966), codified at 42 U.S.C. § 3335(f) (2000); 84 Stat. 169, § 422 (1970), codified at 20 U.S.C. § 1232a (2000); 86 Stat. 371–73, Title VIII (1972), codified at 20 U.S.C. §§ 1651–56 (2000); 88 Stat. 514–21, Title II (1974), codified at 20 U.S.C. §§ 1701–58 (2000).

ferred other solutions, including "compensatory schools" or "magnet schools" that offered extra teachers, computers, better laboratories, and other resources. With the support of the Supreme Court, some cities abandoned busing as a means of racially integrating their schools. Riddick v. School Bd. of City of Norfolk, 784 F.2d 521 (4th Cir. 1986) (en banc), cert. denied, 479 U.S. 938 (1986). In 1998, a federal judge in Maryland finally ordered an end to mandatory busing in Prince George's County, a 26-year-old policy that had been opposed by both white and black parents. By 1996, nearly 92 percent of bused students were black, and many were sent to predominantly black schools outside their neighborhoods. In 1999, in the area where busing began, a federal judge ruled that busing was no longer necessary for the Charlotte-Mecklenburg School District because evidence of intentional discrimination had disappeared. Capacchione v. Charlotte-Mecklenberg Schools, 57 F.Supp. 2d 228 (WDNC 1999).

Desegregation was frustrated by other tactics. "Freedom of choice" plans permitted whites to attend all-black schools and blacks to attend all-white schools. Predictably, whites did not attend black schools, and few blacks attended white schools. The Court struck down these plans as inadequate remedies for desegregation.[5] "Transfer plans" allowed students to transfer from a school where they would be in a racial minority back to a former segregated school. A unanimous Court declared this procedure invalid. Goss v. Board of Education, 373 U.S. 683 (1963). Also, states were not permitted to create new school districts that had the effect of producing a refuge for white students. United States v. Scotland Neck Bd. of Educ., 407 U.S. 484 (1972).

A Return to Segregated Schools?

In 1991 the Supreme Court, divided 5–3, reversed an appellate court order that made it difficult for schools to terminate desegregation decrees. The Court held that district courts, in determining whether a school board had complied with a desegregation decree, must decide whether the board complied in good faith with the decree since it was entered and whether, in light of every facet of school operations, the vestiges of past de jure segregation had been eliminated to the extent practicable. Under this ruling, desegregation decrees could be lifted even if a school district is heading toward a more segregated, dual system. Board of Ed. of Oklahoma City v. Dowell, 498 U.S. 237 (1991).

The trend toward accepting largely all-white or all-black schools was reinforced by a 1992 unanimous ruling by the Supreme Court. It held that when racial imbalance in schools is the result of population shifts, school districts and federal judges are not required to adopt "awkward, inconvenient, and even bizarre" measures (language borrowed from Swann v. Charlotte-Mecklenburg) to achieve integrated schools. Massive busing was not considered a viable option by either of the parties, the district court, or the Supreme Court. A school district has a duty to eliminate segregation that is de jure, not de facto. Federal courts may relinquish supervision and control of school districts even if full compliance with desegregation plans has not been achieved in every area of school operations. Freeman v. Pitts, 503 U.S. 467 (1992).

In 1990, the Court issued an extraordinary decision that empowered federal judges to order local governmental bodies to increase taxes to pay for a court-ordered school desegregation plan. Missouri v. Jenkins, 495 U.S. 33 (1990). This 5 to 4 decision was undercut five years later when the Court, divided again 5 to 4, held that a federal judge had exceeded his authority in ordering pay raises for school personnel and increased funding for remedial programs in inner-city public schools, the same schools at issue in the 1990 ruling. The judge had ordered extra spending on the predominantly black Kansas City public schools so that they might attract white students from the suburbs. Missouri v. Jenkins, 515 U.S. 70 (1995). In 1997, a federal appellate court scrapped a wide-ranging school desegregation decree because many of its remedies were unjustified and an abuse of judicial discretion. People Who

---

5. Wright v. Council of City of Emporia, 407 U.S. 451 (1972); Monroe v. Board of Commissioners, 391 U.S. 450 (1968); Raney v. Board of Education, 391 U.S. 443 (1968); Green v. County School Board, 391 U.S. 430 (1968).

A Return to "Separate but Equal"?

Because of neighborhood housing patterns, a retreat from busing, and court decisions that are dismantling desegregation plans, public schools are returning to a de facto segregated status. Researchers at the Harvard Graduate School of Education found that from 1991 to 1994, the percentage of minority students in schools with a substantial white enrollment fell appreciably. That trend has continued. Hispanic students are now more likely than black students to be isolated in schools that are largely minority and poor. Segre-gated schools are developing in the suburbs just as they did in the inner cities.

Some analysts believe that the trend toward re-segregation reflects the view of many parents and educators, both white and minority, that integrated schools are no longer a paramount educational goal. Some minority parents seek out ethnic identification for their children or put the emphasis on safety, neighborhood schools, and good education rather than an integrated environment.

SOURCES: "Schools See Re-Emergence of 'Separate but Equal,'" New York Times, April 8, 1997, at A10. See also "After 45 Years, Resegregation Emerges In Schools, Study Finds," New York Times, June 13, 1999, at 31, and "Schools' Racial Isolation Growing," Washington Post, July 18, 2001, at A3; "Schools Resegregate, Study Finds," New York Times, January 21, 2003, at A14.

Care v. Rockford Bd. of Ed., 111 F.3d 528 (7th Cir. 1997); see also People Who Care v. Rockford Bd. of Ed., 171 F.3d 1083 (7th Cir. 1999).

The withdrawal of the district courts from oversight of school desegregation answered the question of how long school districts could be forced to make efforts to desegregate. But what about school systems that adopted voluntary plans to keep their schools diverse? This question came to the Court in 2007. As part of their school choice plans, school districts in Seattle, Washington and Jefferson County, Kentucky adopted voluntary plans that used race as one of the factors in school assignment for over-subscribed schools. A closely divided (5 to 4) Court concluded that these plans violated the Fourteenth Amendment because they failed to show that the plans were "narrowly tailored" to meet a "compelling state interest." Dissenters claimed that the spirit of *Brown v. the Board of Education* had been abandoned by the decision. PARENTS INVOLVED IN COMMUNITY SCHOOLS V. SEATTLE SCHOOL DISTRICT NO. 1, 551 U.S. 701 (2007). Recent studies show a return to segregated schools (see box).

Private Schools

Southern states attempted to avoid integrated education by closing public schools with white and black enrollment and setting up "private schools" operated for white students only. County funds provided tuition funds for the private schools, euphemistically called a "freedom of choice" program. Federal courts prohibited the counties from paying tuition grants or giving tax credits as long as public schools remained closed. The Supreme Court supported those rulings and announced, in 1964, that its slogan "all deliberate speed" had produced too much deliberation and not enough speed. Griffin v. School Board, 377 U.S. 218, 229 (1964). The time for deliberate speed "has run out." Id. at 234.[6] The IRS denied tax-exempt status to private schools with racially discriminatory admissions policies. Prince Edward School Foundation v. Commissioner of Internal Revenue, 478 F.Supp. 107 (D.D.C.

---

6. Other rejections of the "all deliberate speed" formula include Alexander v. Board of Education, 396 U.S. 1218 (1969); Keyes v. Denver School District, 396 U.S. 1215 (1969); Alexander v. Board of Education, 396 U.S. 19 (1969).

1979), cert. denied, 450 U.S. 944 (1981). Some of these schools, such as the Prince Edward Academy in Virginia, regained tax-exempt status after announcing that they were open to all races.

In Mississippi, the number of virtually all-white private secular schools increased substantially after the desegregation ruling in 1954. In 1973, a unanimous Court held that Mississippi could not give free textbooks to private schools that practiced racial or other invidious discrimination. Norwood v. Harrison, 413 U.S. 455 (1973). Another ruling involved private schools that had been set up in Virginia shortly after the 1954 desegregation decision. These schools excluded qualified children solely because they were black. A 7–2 Court held that federal law prohibited racial discrimination in the making and enforcement of private contracts practiced by these schools. Runyon v. McCrary, 427 U.S. 160 (1976).

In 1970, the IRS announced that it would not give tax-exempt status to private schools that practiced racial discrimination. That policy persisted until 1982 when the Reagan administration said that the IRS had exceeded its statutory powers. A year later, an 8–1 Court sustained the IRS. The national policy of nondiscrimination could not support the granting of tax exemption to institutions that adopt racial policies. Tax exemption is a benefit given to organizations that provide a public benefit. Bob Jones University v. United States, 461 U.S. 574 (1983). In other cases, suits brought against the IRS for failing to deny tax-exempt status to racially discriminatory private schools have been set aside for lack of standing by plaintiffs. Allen v. Wright, 468 U.S. 737 (1984).

Desegregation in Higher Education

At the university level, the Court continued to put pressure on state schools to eliminate racial segregation. An 8–1 ruling in 1992 required state officials to do more than simply declare the historically white and black colleges are open to students of any race. A race-neutral admissions policy does not necessarily satisfy a state's obligation. Certain policies, such as setting a higher minimum test scores at white colleges or providing less state funding for black colleges, may have the effect of perpetuating segregated institutions. This case involved Mississippi, where more than 99 percent of white students attended five large white colleges (averaging between 80 and 91 percent white students), and the racial composition of three other colleges ranged from 92 to 99 percent black. Other states were affected by this ruling. United States v. Fordice, 505 U.S. 717 (1992).

Government's Brief in *Brown*

In an amicus brief filed December 1952 in the case of *Brown* v. *Board of Education,* the Justice Department explained the interest of the President and the executive branch in abolishing racial discrimination. The importance of civil rights transcended domestic politics. The persistence of segregation in America undermined its claim to democratic values and provided an easy target for exploitation by communist nations. The selection below is from 49 Landmark Briefs 116–21.

... The cases at bar do not involve isolated acts of racial discrimination by private individuals or groups. On the contrary, it is contended in these cases that public school systems established in the states of Kansas, South Carolina, Virginia, and Delaware, and in the District of Columbia, unconstitutionally discriminate against Negroes solely because of their color.

This contention raises questions of the first importance in our society. For racial discriminations imposed by law, or having the sanction or support of government, inevitably tend to undermine the

foundations of a society dedicated to freedom, justice, and equality. The proposition that all men are created equal is not mere rhetoric. It implies a rule of law—an indispensable condition to a civilized society—under which all men stand equal and alike in the rights and opportunities secured to them by their government. Under the Constitution every agency of government, national and local, legislative, executive, and judicial, must treat each of our people as an *American,* and not as a member of a particular group classified on the basis of race or some other constitutional irrelevancy. The color of a man's skin—like his religious beliefs, or his political attachments, or the country from which he or his ancestors came to the United States—does not diminish or alter his legal status or constitutional rights. "Our Constitution is color-blind, and neither knows nor tolerates classes among citizens."

The problem of racial discrimination is particularly acute in the District of Columbia, the nation's capital. This city is the window through which the world looks into our house. The embassies, legations, and representatives of all nations are here, at the seat of the Federal Government. Foreign officials and visitors naturally judge this country and our people by their experiences and observations in the nation's capital; and the treatment of colored persons here is taken as the measure of our attitude toward minorities generally. The President has stated that "The District of Columbia should be a true symbol of American freedom and democracy for our own people, and for the people of the world." Instead, as the President's Committee on Civil Rights found, the District of Columbia "is a graphic illustration of a failure of democracy." The Committee summarized its findings as follows:

"For Negro Americans, Washington is not just the nation's capital. It is the point at which all public transportation into the South becomes 'Jim Crow.' If he stops in Washington, a Negro may dine like other men in the Union Station, but as soon as he steps out into the capital, he leaves such democratic practices behind. With very few exceptions, he is refused service at downtown restaurants, he may not attend a downtown movie or play, and he has to go into the poorer section of the city to find a night's lodging. The Negro who decides to settle in the District must often find a home in an overcrowded, substandard area. He must often take a job below the level of his ability. He must send his children to the inferior public schools set aside for Negroes and entrust his family's health to medical agencies which give inferior service. In addition, he must endure the countless daily humiliations that the system of segregation imposes upon the one-third of Washington that is Negro....

"The shamefulness and absurdity of Washington's treatment of Negro Americans is highlighted by the presence of many dark-skinned foreign visitors. Capital custom not only humiliates colored citizens, but is a source of considerable embarrassment to these visitors.... Foreign officials are often mistaken for American Negroes and refused food, lodging and entertainment. However, once it is established that they are not Americans, they are accommodated."

It is in the context of the present world struggle between freedom and tyranny that the problem of racial discrimination must be viewed. The United States is trying to prove to the people of the world, of every nationality, race, and color, that a free democracy is the most civilized and most secure form of government yet devised by man. We must set an example for others by showing firm determination to remove existing flaws in our democracy.

The existence of discrimination against minority groups in the United States has an adverse effect upon our relations with other countries. Racial discrimination furnishes grist for the Communist propaganda mills, and it raises doubts even among friendly nations as to the intensity of our devotion to the democratic faith....

Brown v. Board of Education

347 U.S. 483 (1954)

After chipping away at the foundations of *Plessy* v. *Ferguson,* a unanimous Court in this case resolved that the "separate but equal" doctrine has no place in the field of education. In deciding that the history of the Fourteenth Amendment is inconclusive as to its intended effect on public education, the Court held that the use of race to segregate white and black children in the public schools is a denial to black children of the equal protection of the laws guaranteed by the Fourteenth Amendment. In this case, Linda Brown was prohibited from attending a white public school in Topeka, Kansas. She was one of several plaintiffs from the states of Kansas, South Carolina, Virginia and Delaware.

MR. CHIEF JUSTICE WARREN delivered the opinion of the Court....

In each of the cases, minors of the Negro race, through their legal representatives, seek the aid of the courts in obtaining admission to the public schools of their community on a nonsegregated basis. In each instance, they had been denied admission to schools attended by white children under laws requiring or permitting segregation according to race. This segregation was alleged to deprive the plaintiffs of the equal protection of the laws under the Fourteenth Amendment. In each of the cases other than the Delaware case, a three-judge federal district court denied relief to the plaintiffs on the so-called "separate but equal" doctrine announced by this Court in *Plessy* v. *Ferguson,* 163 U.S. 537. Under that doctrine, equality of treatment is accorded when the races are provided substantially equal facilities, even though these facilities be separate. In the Delaware case, the Supreme Court of Delaware adhered to that doctrine, but ordered that the plaintiffs be admitted to the white schools because of their superiority to the Negro schools.

The plaintiffs contend that segregated public schools are not "equal" and cannot be made "equal," and that hence they are deprived of the equal protection of the laws. Because of the obvious importance of the question presented, the Court took jurisdiction. Argument was heard in the 1952 Term, and reargument was heard this Term on certain questions propounded by the Court.

Reargument was largely devoted to the circumstances surrounding the adoption of the Fourteenth Amendment in 1868. It covered exhaustively consideration of the Amendment in Congress, ratification by the states, then existing practices in racial segregation, and the views of proponents and opponents of the Amendment. This discussion and our own investigation convince us that, although these sources cast some light, it is not enough to resolve the problem with which we are faced. At best, they are inconclusive. The most avid proponents of the post-War Amendments undoubtedly intended them to remove all legal distinctions among "all persons born or naturalized in the United States." Their opponents, just as certainly, were antagonistic to both the letter and the spirit of the Amendments and wished them to have the most limited effect. What others in Congress and the state legislatures had in mind cannot be determined with any degree of certainty.

An additional reason for the inconclusive nature of the Amendment's history, with respect to segregated schools, is the status of public education at that time. In the South, the movement toward free common schools, supported by general taxation, had not yet taken hold. Education of white children was largely in the hands of private groups. Education of Negroes was almost nonexistent, and practi-

cally all of the race were illiterate. In fact, any education of Negroes was forbidden by law in some states. Today, in contrast, many Negroes have achieved outstanding success in the arts and sciences as well as in the business and professional world. It is true that public school education at the time of the Amendment had advanced further in the North, but the effect of the Amendment on Northern States was generally ignored in the congressional debates. Even in the North, the conditions of public education did not approximate those existing today. The curriculum was usually rudimentary; ungraded schools were common in rural areas; the school term was but three months a year in many states; and compulsory school attendance was virtually unknown. As a consequence, it is not surprising that there should be so little in the history of the Fourteenth Amendment relating to its intended effect on public education.

In the first cases in this Court construing the Fourteenth Amendment, decided shortly after its adoption, the Court interpreted it as proscribing all state-imposed discriminations against the Negro race. The doctrine of "separate but equal" did not make its appearance in this Court until 1896 in the case of *Plessy* v. *Ferguson, supra,* involving not education but transportation. American courts have since labored with the doctrine for over half a century. In this Court, there have been six cases involving the "separate but equal" doctrine in the field of public education. In *Cumming* v. *County Board of Education,* 175 U.S. 528, and *Gong Lum* v. *Rice,* 275 U.S. 78, the validity of the doctrine itself was not challenged. In more recent cases, all on the graduate school level, inequality was found in that specific benefits enjoyed by white students were denied to Negro students of the same educational qualifications. *Missouri ex rel. Gaines* v. *Canada,* 305 U.S. 337; *Sipuel* v. *Oklahoma,* 332 U.S. 631; *Sweatt* v. *Painter,* 339 U.S. 629; *McLaurin* v. *Oklahoma State Regents,* 339 U.S. 637. In none of these cases was it necessary to re-examine the doctrine to grant relief to the Negro plaintiff. And in *Sweatt* v. *Painter, supra,* the Court expressly reserved decision on the question whether *Plessy* v. *Ferguson* should be held inapplicable to public education.

In the instant cases, that question is directly presented. Here, unlike *Sweatt* v. *Painter,* there are findings below that the Negro and white schools involved have been equalized, or are being equalized, with respect to buildings, curricula, qualifications and salaries of teachers, and other "tangible" factors. Our decision, therefore, cannot turn on merely a comparison of these tangible factors in the Negro and white schools involved in each of the cases. We must look instead to the effect of segregation itself on public education.

In approaching this problem, we cannot turn the clock back to 1868 when the Amendment was adopted, or even to 1896 when *Plessy* v. *Ferguson* was written. We must consider public education in the light of its full development and its present place in American life throughout the Nation. Only in this way can it be determined if segregation in public schools deprives these plaintiffs of the equal protection of the laws.

Today, education is perhaps the most important function of state and local governments. Compulsory school attendance laws and the great expenditures for education both demonstrate our recognition of the importance of education to our democratic society. It is required in the performance of our most basic public responsibilities, even service in the armed forces. It is the very foundation of good citizenship. Today it is a principal instrument in awakening the child to cultural values, in preparing him for later professional training, and in helping him to adjust normally to his environment. In these days, it is doubtful that any child may reasonably be expected to succeed in life if he is denied the opportunity of an education. Such an opportunity, where the state has undertaken to provide it, is a right which must be made available to all on equal terms.

We come then to the question presented: Does segregation of children in public schools solely on the basis of race, even though the physical facilities and other "tangible" factors may be equal, deprive the children of the minority group of equal educational opportunities? We believe that it does.

In *Sweatt* v. *Painter, supra,* in finding that a segregated law school for Negroes could not provide them equal educational opportunities, this Court relied in large part on "those qualities which are incapable of objective measurement but which make for greatness in a law school." In *McLaurin* v. *Oklahoma State Regents, supra,* the Court, in requiring that a Negro admitted to a white graduate school be treated like all other students, again resorted to intangible considerations: " ... his ability to study, to engage in discussions and exchange views with other students, and, in general, to learn his profession." Such considerations apply with added force to children in grade and high schools. To separate them from others of similar age and qualifications solely because of their race generates a feeling of inferiority as to their status in the community that may affect their hearts and minds in a way unlikely ever to be undone. The effect of this separation on their educational opportunities was well stated by a finding

in the Kansas case by a court which nevertheless felt compelled to rule against the Negro plaintiffs:

"Segregation of white and colored children in public schools has a detrimental effect upon the colored children. The impact is greater when it has the sanction of the law; for the policy of separating the races is usually interpreted as denoting the inferiority of the negro group. A sense of inferiority affects the motivation of a child to learn. Segregation with the sanction of law, therefore, has a tendency to [retard] the educational and mental development of negro children and to deprive them of some of the benefits they would receive in a racial[ly] integrated school system."

Whatever may have been the extent of psychological knowledge at the time of *Plessy* v. *Ferguson,* this finding is amply supported by modern authority. [*Here the Court adds its famous footnote 11: K. B. Clark, Effect of Prejudice and Discrimination on Personality Development (Midcentury White House Conference on Children and Youth, 1950); Witmer and Kotinsky, Personality in the Making (1952), c. VI; Deutscher and Chein, The Psychological Effects of Enforced Segregation: A Survey of Social Science Opinion, 26 J. Psychol. 259 (1948); Chein, What are the Psychological Effects of Segregation Under Conditions of Equal Facilities?, 3 Int. J. Opinion and Attitude Res. 229 (1949); Brameld, Educational Costs, in Discrimination and National Welfare (MacIver, ed., 1949), 4448; Frazier, The Negro in the United States (1949), 674681. And see generally Myrdal, An American Dilemma (1944).*] Any language in *Plessy* v. *Ferguson* contrary to this finding is rejected.

We conclude that in the field of public education the doctrine of "separate but equal" has no place. Separate educational facilities are inherently unequal. Therefore, we hold that the plaintiffs and others similarly situated for whom the actions have been brought are, by reason of the segregation complained of, deprived of the equal protection of the laws guaranteed by the Fourteenth Amendment. This disposition makes unnecessary any discussion whether such segregation also violates the Due Process Clause of the Fourteenth Amendment.

Because these are class actions, because of the wide applicability of this decision, and because of the great variety of local conditions, the formulation of decrees in these cases presents problems of considerable complexity. On reargument, the consideration of appropriate relief was necessarily subordinated to the primary question — the constitutionality of segregation in public education. We have now announced that such segregation is a denial of the equal protection of the laws. In order that we may have the full assistance of the parties in formulating decrees, the cases will be restored to the docket, and the parties are requested to present further argument on Questions 4 and 5 previously propounded by the Court for the reargument this Term. The Attorney General of the United States is again invited to participate. The Attorneys General of the states requiring or permitting segregation in public education will also be permitted to appear as *amici curiae* upon request to do so by September 15, 1954, and submission of briefs by October 1, 1954.

It is so ordered.

Bolling v. Sharpe
347 U.S. 497 (1954)

In *Brown* v. *Board of Education* (1954), the Supreme Court struck down "separate but equal" public schools in the states, relying on the Equal Protection Clause of the Fourteenth Amendment. What was to be done about segregated schooling in the District of Columbia, which is not subject to the Fourteenth Amendment? The Court could invoke the Fifth Amendment, which did apply to the District of Columbia, but the Fifth Amendment lacks an Equal Protection Clause. Politically, the Court could not invalidate segregated schools in the states and allow them to operate in D.C. In this case the Court discovers a solution. Spottswood Thomas Bolling and other students from a junior high school brought this action against C. Melvin Sharpe and the other members of the D.C. Board of Education.

MR. CHIEF JUSTICE WARREN delivered the opinion of the Court.

This case challenges the validity of segregation in the public schools of the District of Columbia ...

We have this day held that the Equal Protection Clause of the Fourteenth Amendment prohibits the states from maintaining racially segregated public schools. The legal problem in the District of Columbia is somewhat different, however. The Fifth Amendment, which is applicable in the District of Columbia, does not contain an equal protection clause as does the Fourteenth Amendment which applies only to the states. But the concepts of equal protection and due process, both stemming from our American ideal of fairness, are not mutually exclusive. The "equal protection of the laws" is a more explicit safeguard of prohibited unfairness than "due process of law," and, therefore, we do not imply that the two are always interchangeable phrases. But, as this Court has recognized, discrimination may be so unjustifiable as to be violative of due process.

Classifications based solely upon race must be scrutinized with particular care, since they are contrary to our traditions and hence constitutionally suspect. As long ago as 1896, this Court declared the principle "that the Constitution of the United States, in its present form, forbids, so far as civil and political rights are concerned, discrimination by the General Government, or by the States, against any citizen because of his race." And in *Buchanan* v. *Warley*, 245 U.S. 60, the Court held that a statute which limited the right of a property owner to convey his property to a person of another race was, as an unreasonable discrimination, a denial of due process of law.

Although the Court has not assumed to define "liberty" with any great precision, that term is not confined to mere freedom from bodily restraint. Liberty under law extends to the full range of conduct which the individual is free to pursue, and it cannot be restricted except for a proper governmental objective. Segregation in public education is not reasonably related to any proper governmental objective, and thus it imposes on Negro children of the District of Columbia a burden that constitutes an arbitrary deprivation of their liberty in violation of the Due Process Clause.

In view of our decision that the Constitution prohibits the states from maintaining racially segregated public schools, it would be unthinkable that the same Constitution would impose a lesser duty on the Federal Government. We hold that racial segregation in the public schools of the District of Columbia is a denial of the due process of law guaranteed by the Fifth Amendment to the Constitution....

It is so ordered.

Brown v. Board of Education

349 U.S. 294 (1955)

In the first Brown case, called Brown I, the Court held that racial discrimination in public schools is unconstitutional. Having announced the constitutional principle, the Court had to issue instructions on the means used to implement its ruling. This case, called Brown II, has been heavily criticized for deferring too much to local school districts and thus delaying implementation of Brown I.

MR. CHIEF JUSTICE WARREN delivered the opinion of the Court.

These cases were decided on May 17, 1954. The opinions of that date, declaring the fundamental principle that racial discrimination in public education is unconstitutional, are incorporated herein by reference. All provisions of federal, state, or local law requiring or permitting such discrimination must yield to this principle. There remains for consideration the manner in which relief is to be accorded.

Because these cases arose under different local conditions and their disposition will involve a variety of local problems, we requested further argument on the question of relief. In view of the nationwide importance of the decision, we invited the Attorney General of the United States and the Attorneys General of all states requiring or permitting racial discrimination in public education to present their views on that question. The parties, the United States, and the States of Florida, North Carolina, Arkansas, Oklahoma, Maryland, and Texas filed briefs and participated in the oral argument.

These presentations were informative and helpful to the Court in its consideration of the complexities arising from the transition to a system of public education freed of racial discrimination. The presentations also demonstrated that substantial steps to eliminate racial discrimination in public schools have already been taken, not only in some of the communities in which these cases arose, but in some of the states appearing as *amici curiae,* and in other states as well. Substantial progress has been made in the District of Columbia and in the communities in Kansas and Delaware involved in this litigation. The defendants in the cases coming to us from South Carolina and Virginia are awaiting the decision of this Court concerning relief.

Full implementation of these constitutional principles may require solution of varied local school problems. School authorities have the primary responsibility for elucidating, assessing, and solving these problems; courts will have to consider whether the action of school authorities constitutes good faith implementation of the governing constitutional principles. Because of their proximity to local conditions and the possible need for further hearings, the courts which originally heard these cases can best perform this judicial appraisal. Accordingly, we believe it appropriate to remand the cases to those courts.

In fashioning and effectuating the decrees, the courts will be guided by equitable principles. Traditionally, equity has been characterized by a practical flexibility in shaping its remedies and by a facility for adjusting and reconciling public and private needs. These cases call for the exercise of these traditional attributes of equity power. At stake is the personal interest of the plaintiffs in admission to public schools as soon as practicable on a nondiscriminatory basis. To effectuate this interest may call for elimination of a variety of obstacles in making the transition to school systems operated in accordance with the constitutional principles set forth in our May 17, 1954, decision. Courts of equity may properly take into account the public interest in the elimination of such obstacles in a systematic and effective manner. But it should go without saying that the vitality of these constitutional principles cannot be allowed to yield simply because of disagreement with them.

While giving weight to these public and private considerations, the courts will require that the defendants make a prompt and reasonable start toward full compliance with our May 17, 1954, ruling. Once such a start has been made, the courts may find that additional time is necessary to carry out the ruling in an effective manner. The burden rests upon the defendants to establish that such time is necessary in the public interest and is consistent with good faith compliance at the earliest practicable date. To that end, the courts may consider problems related to administration, arising from the physical condition of the school plant, the school transportation system, personnel, revision of school districts and attendance areas into compact units to achieve a system of determining admission to the public schools on a nonracial basis, and revision of local laws and regulations which may be necessary in solving the foregoing problems. They will also consider the adequacy of any plans the defendants may propose to meet these problems and to effectuate a transition to a racially nondiscriminatory school system. During this period of transition, the courts will retain jurisdiction of these cases.

The judgments below, except that in the Delaware case, are accordingly reversed and the cases are remanded to the District Courts to take such proceedings and enter such orders and decrees consistent with this opinion as are necessary and proper to admit to public schools on a racially nondiscriminatory basis with all deliberate speed the parties to these cases. The judgment in the Delaware case — ordering the immediate admission of the plaintiffs to schools previously attended only by white children — is affirmed on the basis of the principles stated in our May 17, 1954, opinion, but the case is remanded to the Supreme Court of Delaware for such further proceedings as that Court may deem necessary in light of this opinion.

It is so ordered.

Cooper v. Aaron

358 U.S. 1 (1958)

Federal courts approved a plan of gradual desegregation of the races in the public schools in Little Rock, Arkansas, to admit black children to a previously all-white high school at the beginning of the 1957–58 school year. The state legislature and Governor Orval Faubus opposed the plan, leading to threats of mob violence. John Aaron, a black student prevented from attending the high school, brought this case against William G. Cooper, a member of the Board of Directors of the Little Rock school district.

Opinion of the Court by THE CHIEF JUSTICE, MR. JUSTICE BLACK, MR. JUSTICE FRANKFURTER, MR. JUSTICE DOUGLAS, MR. JUSTICE BURTON, MR. JUSTICE CLARK, MR. JUSTICE HARLAN, MR. JUSTICE BRENNAN, and MR. JUSTICE WHITTAKER.

As this case reaches us it raises questions of the highest importance to the maintenance of our federal system of government. It necessarily involves a claim by the Governor and Legislature of a State that there is no duty on state officials to obey federal court orders resting on this Court's considered interpretation of the United States Constitution. Specifically it involves actions by the Governor and Legislature of Arkansas upon the premise that they are not bound by our holding in *Brown v. Board of Education,* 347 U.S. 483....

On May 20, 1954, three days after the first *Brown* opinion the Little Rock District School Board adopted, and on May 23, 1954, made public, a statement of policy entitled "Supreme Court Decision — Segregation in Public Schools." In this statement the Board recognized that

"It is our responsibility to comply with Federal Constitutional Requirements and we intend to do so when the Supreme Court of the United States outlines the method to be followed."

[*The board instructed the superintendent of schools to prepare a plan for desegregation, and approved the plan on May 24, 1955, seven days before the second* Brown *opinion. The plan provided first for desegregation at the senior high school level (grades 10 through 12), with desegregation at the junior high and elementary levels to follow. Desegregation at the high school level would begin in the fall of 1957, leading to complete desegregation of the school system by 1963. The board reached the conclusion that "a large majority of the residents" of Little Rock were of "the belief ... that the Plan, although objectionable in principle," from the point of view of those supporting segregated schools, "was still the best for the interests of all pupils in the District." After a group of black plaintiffs sought more rapid desegregation, a district court upheld the school board's plan. Aaron v. Cooper, 143 F.Supp. 855. The Court of Appeals affirmed, 243 F.2d 361. Review of that judgment was not taken to the Supreme Court.*]

While the School Board was thus going forward with its preparation for desegregating the Little Rock school system, other state authorities, in contrast, were actively pursuing a program designed to perpetuate in Arkansas the system of racial segregation which this Court had held violated the Fourteenth Amendment. First came, in November 1956, an amendment to the State Constitution flatly commanding the Arkansas General Assembly to oppose "in every Constitutional manner the Unconstitutional desegregation decisions of May 17, 1954 and May 31, 1955 of the United States Supreme Court," Ark. Const., Amend. 44, and, through their initiative, a pupil assignment law, … relieving school children from compulsory attendance at racially mixed schools, …

The School Board and the Superintendent of Schools nevertheless continued with preparations to carry out the first stage of the desegregation program. Nine Negro children were scheduled for admission in September 1957 to Central High School, which has more than two thousand students. Various administrative measures, designed to assure the smooth transition of this first stage of desegregation, were undertaken.

[*On September 2, 1957, the day before the black students were to enter Central High, Faubus dispatched units of the Arkansas National Guard and placed the school "off limits" to black students. The district court made these findings. As of September 2, no crowds had gathered about Central High School, no acts of violence or threats of violence occurred, and school authorities frequently conferred with the Mayor and Chief of Police of Little Rock about appropriate steps to prevent any possible disturbances or acts of violence. The Mayor concluded that the Little Rock police force could cope with any incidents that might occur, and there was no need to request assistance from Governor Faubus or state representatives. Faubus did not consult with Little Rock authorities about the capacity of Little Rock police to handle the situation or with stationing Arkansas National Guard at the high school. Aaron v. Cooper, 156 F.Supp. 220, 225.*]

The Board's petition for postponement in this proceeding states: "The effect of that action [of the Governor] was to harden the core of opposition to the Plan and cause many persons who theretofore had reluctantly accepted the Plan to believe there was some power in the State of Arkansas which, when exerted, could nullify the Federal law and permit disobedience of the decree of this [District] Court, and from that date hostility to the Plan was increased and criticism of the officials of the [School] District has become more bitter and unrestrained." …

[*For three weeks, state military guards prevented the nine black students from entering the school building. The district court found that the school board's plan had been obstructed by Faubus and enjoined him from further interference.*]

The next school day was Monday, September 23, 1957. The Negro children entered the high school that morning under the protection of the Little Rock Police Department and members of the Arkansas State Police. But the officers caused the children to

be removed from the school during the morning because they had difficulty controlling a large and demonstrating crowd which had gathered at the high school. 163 F.Supp., at 16. On September 25, however, the President of the United States dispatched federal troops to Central High School and admission of the Negro students to the school was thereby effected. Regular army troops continued at the high school until November 27, 1957. They were then replaced by federalized National Guardsmen who remained throughout the balance of the school year. Eight of the Negro students remained in attendance at the school throughout the school year.

[*On February 20, 1958, the school board and the superintendent of schools requested from the district court a two and a half years postponement of their program for desegregation. The black students were to be withdrawn and sent to segregated schools. After the district court granted the relief requested by the school board, the Eighth Circuit reversed. The Supreme Court convened in special term on August 28, 1958, to hear oral argument. On September 12, the Court affirmed the judgment of the Eighth Circuit.*]

The controlling legal principles are plain. The command of the Fourteenth Amendment is that no "State" shall deny to any person within its jurisdiction the equal protection of the laws. "A State acts by its legislative, its executive, or its judicial authorities. It can act in no other way. The constitutional provision, therefore, must mean that no agency of the State, or of the officers or agents by whom its powers are exerted, shall deny to any person within its jurisdiction the equal protection of the laws.…

What has been said, in the light of the facts developed, is enough to dispose of the case. However, we should answer the premise of the actions of the Governor and Legislature that they are not bound by our holding in the *Brown* case. It is necessary only to recall some basic constitutional propositions which are settled doctrine.

Article VI of the Constitution makes the Constitution the "supreme Law of the Land." In 1803, Chief Justice Marshall, speaking for a unanimous Court, referring to the Constitution as "the fundamental and paramount law of the nation," declared in the notable case of *Marbury* v. *Madison*, 1 Cranch 137, 177, that "It is emphatically the province and duty of the judicial department to say what the law is." This decision declared the basic principle that the federal judiciary is supreme in the exposition of the law of the Constitution, and that principle has ever since been respected by this Court and the Country as a permanent and indispensable feature of our constitutional system. It follows that the interpretation of the Fourteenth Amendment enunciated by this Court in the *Brown* case is the supreme law of the land, and Art. VI of the Constitution makes it of binding effect on the States "any Thing in the Constitution or Laws of any State to the Contrary notwithstanding." Every state legislator and executive and judicial officer is solemnly committed by oath taken pursuant to Art. VI, cl. 3, "to support this Constitution."...

No state legislator or executive or judicial officer can war against the Constitution without violating his undertaking to support it. Chief Justice Marshall spoke for a unanimous Court in saying that: "If the legislatures of the several states may, at will, annul the judgments of the courts of the United States, and destroy the rights acquired under those judgments, the constitution itself becomes a solemn mockery...." *United States v. Peters,* 5 Cranch 115, 136. A Governor who asserts a power to nullify a federal court order is similarly restrained....

It is, of course, quite true that the responsibility for public education is primarily the concern of the States, but it is equally true that such responsibilities, like all other state activity, must be exercised consistently with federal constitutional requirements as they apply to state action....

Concurring opinion of MR. JUSTICE FRANKFURTER....

Swann v. Charlotte-Mecklenburg Bd. of Ed.

402 U.S. 1 (1971)

By 1971, there had been little progress in desegregating public schools, despite the Supreme Court's historic decision in 1954. School boards were under pressure from the courts to come forward with desegregation plans *now*. Here the Court focuses on remedies available to federal courts to produce a school system free of state-imposed segregation, and makes what comes to be a very important distinction between de jure and de facto segregation. While the decision is known for its approval of busing as one legitimate remedy available for accomplishing desegregation, at its core it is about the extent of the power of federal district court judges to fashion remedies. James Swann and other black students challenged the desegregation plans of the Charlotte-Mecklenberg school district in N.C.

MR. CHIEF JUSTICE BURGER delivered the opinion of the Court.

We granted certiorari in this case to review important issues as to the duties of school authorities and the scope of powers of federal courts under this Court's mandates to eliminate racially separate public schools established and maintained by state action. *Brown v. Board of Education,* 347 U.S. 483 (1954) *(Brown I).*

... These cases present us with the problem of defining in more precise terms than heretofore the scope of the duty of school authorities and district courts in implementing *Brown I* and the mandate to eliminate dual systems and establish unitary systems at once....

[*Litigation produced a number of desegregation plans by the school board; by a court-appointed expert; by the U.S. Department of Health, Education, and Welfare; and by four members of the school board. From these plans the Court issued new guidelines for school authorities and courts.*]

[III]

The school authorities argue that the equity powers of federal district courts have been limited by Title IV of the Civil Rights Act of 1964, 42 U.S.C. § 2000c.... Section 2000c (b) defines "desegregation" as it is used in Title IV:

"'Desegregation' means the assignment of students to public schools and within such schools without regard to their race, color, religion, or national origin, but 'desegregation' shall not mean the assignment of students to public schools in order to overcome racial imbalance."

Section 2000c-6, authorizing the Attorney General to institute federal suits, contains the following proviso:

"[N]othing herein shall empower any official or court of the United States to issue any order seeking to achieve a racial balance in any school by requiring the transportation of pupils or students from one school to another or one school district to another in order to achieve such racial balance, or otherwise enlarge the existing power of the court to insure compliance with constitutional standards."

On their face, the sections quoted purport only to insure that the provisions of Title IV of the Civil Rights Act of 1964 will not be read as granting new powers. The proviso in § 2000c-6 is in terms designed to foreclose any interpretation of the Act as expanding the *existing* powers of federal courts to enforce the Equal Protection Clause. There is no suggestion of an intention to restrict those powers or withdraw from courts their historic equitable remedial powers.... [T]here is nothing in the Act that provides us material assistance in answering the question of remedy for state-imposed segregation in violation of *Brown I.* The basis of our decision must be the prohibition of the Fourteenth Amendment that no State shall "deny to any person within its jurisdiction the equal protection of the laws." [*The Civil Rights Act only limits the ability of federal judges to remedy de facto segregation. Because Charlotte-Mecklenburg had a history of de jure segregation, and the Court concluded that the school system had not yet created a unitary system, the federal judge had broad discretion to fashion an appropriate remedy to the constitutional violation.*]

[IV–V]

✴ [*The Court reviews the major principles identified in previous cases regarding remedies for segregated school systems: (1) racial balances or racial quotas, (2) eliminating one-race schools, and (3) altering school districts and attendance zones. It then focused on a fourth remedy.*]

(4) *Transportation of Students.*

The scope of permissible transportation of students as an implement of a remedial decree has never been defined by this Court and by the very nature of the problem it cannot be defined with precision. No rigid guidelines as to student transportation can be given for application to the infinite variety of problems presented in thousands of situations....

... The District Court's conclusion that assignment of children to the school nearest their home serving their grade would not produce an effective dismantling of the dual system is supported by the record.

Thus the remedial techniques used in the District Court's order were within that court's power to provide equitable relief; implementation of the decree is well within the capacity of the school authority.

The decree provided that the buses used to implement the plan would operate on direct routes. Students would be picked up at schools near their homes and transported to the schools they were to attend. The trips for elementary school pupils average about seven miles and the District Court found that they would take "not over 35 minutes at the most." This system compares favorably with the transportation plan previously operated in Charlotte under which each day 23,600 students on all grade levels were transported an average of 15 miles one way for an average trip requiring over an hour....

VI

✴ The Court of Appeals, searching for a term to define the equitable remedial power of the district courts, used the term "reasonableness." In *Green,* ... this Court used the term "feasible" and by implication, "workable," "effective," and "realistic" in the mandate to develop "a plan that promises realistically to work, and ... to work *now.*" On the facts of this case, we are unable to conclude that the order of the District Court is not reasonable, feasible and workable....

For the reasons herein set forth, the judgment of the Court of Appeals is affirmed as to those parts in which it affirmed the judgment of the District Court. The order of the District Court, dated August 7, 1970, is also affirmed.

It is so ordered.

Milliken v. Bradley

418 U.S. 717 (1974)

Ronald Bradley and other parents and students in Detroit, Michigan, brought an action against Governor William G. Milliken. They alleged that the Detroit public school system was racially segregated as a result of the official policies and actions of state and city officials. A district court, concluding that official acts had created and perpetuated school segregation, ordered the Detroit Board of Education to submit Detroit-only desegregation plans. The court also ordered

the state officials to submit desegregation plans encompassing the three-county metropolitan area, despite the fact that the 85 outlying school districts in these three counties were not parties to the action and there was no claim that they had committed constitutional violations. The district court ruled that Detroit-only plans were inadequate to accomplish desegregation and that it was proper to consider metropolitan plans. The Sixth Circuit affirmed that a metropolitan plan was the only feasible solution and was within the district court's equity powers.

MR. CHIEF JUSTICE BURGER delivered the opinion of the Court.

We granted certiorari in these consolidated cases to determine whether a federal court may impose a multidistrict, areawide remedy to a single-district *de jure* segregation problem absent any finding that the other included school districts have failed to operate unitary school systems within their districts....

I

[*After the case bounced back and forth between the district court and the Sixth Circuit, the district court concluded that governmental actions had contributed to residential segregation and therefore school segregation. Moreover, school segregation had been perpetuated by optional attendance zones created by the Detroit Board of Education, allowing white students to escape black schools. Busing was used to transport black students to distant black schools rather than have them attend closer white schools. With one exception, created by the burning of a white school, white children were not bused to predominantly black schools. As a remedy, the district court designated 53 of the 85 suburban school districts plus Detroit as the "desegregation area" and ordered the Detroit Board of Education to purchase or lease "at least" 295 school buses to produce a desegregation plan for the metropolitan area. The Sixth Circuit agreed that any solution less comprehensive than a metropolitan area plan would be ineffective.*]

II

... [A]n interdistrict remedy might be in order where the racially discriminatory acts of one or more school districts caused racial segregation in an adjacent district, or where district lines have been deliberately drawn on the basis of race. In such circumstances an interdistrict remedy would be appropriate to eliminate the interdistrict segregation directly caused by the constitutional violation. Conversely, without an interdistrict violation and interdistrict effect, there is no constitutional wrong calling for an interdistrict remedy.

The record before us, voluminous as it is, contains evidence of *de jure* segregated conditions only in the Detroit schools; indeed, that was the theory on which the litigation was initially based and on which the District Court took evidence.... With no showing of significant violation by the 53 outlying school districts and no evidence of any interdistrict violation or effect, the court went beyond the original theory of the case as framed by the pleadings and mandated a metropolitan area remedy....

[IV]

We conclude that the relief ordered by the District Court and affirmed by the Court of Appeals was based upon an erroneous standard and was unsupported by record evidence that acts of the outlying districts effected the discrimination found to exist in the schools of Detroit. Accordingly, the judgment of the Court of Appeals is reversed and the case is remanded for further proceedings consistent with this opinion leading to prompt formulation of a decree directed to eliminating the segregation found to exist in Detroit city schools, a remedy which has been delayed since 1970.

Reversed and remanded.

MR. JUSTICE STEWART, concurring....

MR. JUSTICE DOUGLAS, dissenting....

When we rule against the metropolitan area remedy we take a step that will likely put the problems of the blacks and our society back to the period that antedated the "separate but equal" regime of *Plessy* v. *Ferguson,* 163 U.S. 537. The reason is simple.

The inner core of Detroit is now rather solidly black; and the blacks, we know, in many instances are likely to be poorer, just as were the Chicanos in *San Antonio School District* v. *Rodriguez,* 411 U.S. 1. By that decision the poorer school districts must pay their own way. It is therefore a foregone conclusion that we have now given the States a formula whereby the poor must pay their own way.

Today's decision, given *Rodriguez,* means that there is no violation of the Equal Protection Clause though the schools are segregated by race and though the black schools are not only "separate" but "inferior." ...

MR. JUSTICE WHITE, with whom MR. JUSTICE

Douglas, Mr. Justice Brennan, and Mr. Justice Marshall join, dissenting.

☀ The District Court and the Court of Appeals found that over a long period of years those in charge of the Michigan public schools engaged in various practices calculated to effect the segregation of the Detroit school system. The Court does not question these findings, nor could it reasonably do so. Neither does it question the obligation of the federal courts to devise a feasible and effective remedy. But it promptly cripples the ability of the judiciary to perform this task, ...

[*White argues that once a violation by the state is shown, precedent imposes "the affirmative duty to take whatever steps might be necessary to convert to a unitary system in which racial discrimination would be eliminated root and branch, ..."*].

Mr. Justice Marshall, with whom Mr. Justice Douglas, Mr. Justice Brennan, and Mr. Justice White join, dissenting.

☀ In *Brown* v. *Board of Education,* 347 U.S. 483 (1954), this Court held that segregation of children in public schools on the basis of race deprives minority group children of equal educational opportunities and therefore denies them the equal protection of the laws under the Fourteenth Amendment....

After 20 years of small, often difficult steps toward that great end, the Court today takes a giant step backwards. Notwithstanding a record showing widespread and pervasive racial segregation in the educational system provided by the State of Michigan for children in Detroit, this Court holds that the District Court was powerless to require the State to remedy its constitutional violation in any meaningful fashion....

Parents Involved in Community Schools v. Seattle School District No. 1

551 U.S. 701 (2007)

School districts in Seattle, Washington and Jefferson County, Kentucky voluntarily adopted school assignment plans that relied on race in order to maintain integrated schools. Seattle classified children as white and non-white for the purposes of assignment and used this classification as a "tiebreaker" to allocate slots in particularly popular high schools. Jefferson County, which had been under a court-ordered desegregation plan, adopted its plan after the district court released it from the earlier decree. Its plan classified students as black or other for elementary school assignments and all transfer requests. Petitioners, whose children were affected by the plans, sued, arguing that the use of race in the assignment plans violated the Fourteenth Amendment. The school districts won in the district and circuit courts.

Chief Justice Roberts announced the judgment of the Court, and delivered the opinion of the Court with respect to Parts I, II, III-A, and III-C, and an opinion with respect to Parts III-B and IV, in which Justices Scalia, Thomas, and Alito join....

I

Both cases present the same underlying legal question—whether a public school that had not operated legally segregated schools or has been found to be unitary may choose to classify students by race and rely upon that classification in making school assignments ...

A

[*Seattle used the race classification as the second tiebreaker if too many students wanted admission to a*

particular high school. The first tie breaker was whether you had a sibling at the school.] In the district's public schools approximately 41 percent of enrolled students are white; the remaining 59 percent, comprising all other racial groups, are classified by Seattle for assignment purposes as nonwhite.... If an oversubscribed school is not within 10 percentage points of the district's overall white/nonwhite racial balance, it is what the district calls "integration positive," and the district employs a tiebreaker that selects for assignment students whose race "will serve to bring the school into balance." ...

Seattle has never operated segregated schools—legally separate schools for students of different races—nor has it ever been subject to court-ordered desegregation. It nonetheless employs the racial tiebreaker in an attempt to address the effects of racially identifiable housing patterns on school assignments....

B

[*Jefferson County Public Schools had been under a segregation court order since 1973. When the district court released them from that order in 2000 it adopted its plan, which required non-magnet schools to have a minimum black enrollment of 15% and a maximum enrollment of 50%. In order to keep schools within this range, the racial classification was used in school assignments.*] Approximately 34 percent of the district's 97,000 students are black; most of the remaining 66 percent are white ...

III

A

It is well established that when the government distributes burdens or benefits on the basis of individual racial classifications, that action is reviewed under strict scrutiny.... As the Court recently reaffirmed, "'racial classifications are simply too pernicious to permit any but the most exact connection between justification and classification.'" *Gratz v. Bollinger*, 539 U. S. 244, 270 (2003) ... In order to satisfy this searching standard of review, the school districts must demonstrate that the use of individual racial classifications in the assignment plans hereunder review is "narrowly tailored" to achieve a "compelling" government interest ...

Without attempting in these cases to set forth all the interests a school district might assert, it suffices to note that our prior cases, in evaluating the use of racial classifications in the school context, have recognized two interests that qualify as compelling. The first is the compelling interest of remedying the effects of past intentional discrimination.[*Neither school district relies on this argument.*] ...

The second government interest we have recognized as compelling for purposes of strict scrutiny is the interest in diversity in higher education upheld in *Grutter*, 539 U. S., at 328. The specific interest found compelling in *Grutter* was student body diversity "in the context of higher education." Ibid. The diversity interest was not focused on race alone but encompassed "all factors that may contribute to student body diversity." Id., at 337....

The entire gist of the analysis in *Grutter* was that the admissions program at issue there focused on each applicant as an individual, and not simply as a member of a particular racial group. The classification of applicants by race upheld in *Grutter* was only as part of a "highly individualized, holistic review," 539 U. S., at 337....

In the present cases, by contrast, race is not considered as part of a broader effort to achieve "exposure to widely diverse people, cultures, ideas, and viewpoints," *ibid.*; race, for some students, is determinative standing alone.... [*The Court concludes:*] "The present cases are not governed by *Grutter*."

B

Perhaps recognizing that reliance on *Grutter* cannot sustain their plans, both school districts assert additional interests, distinct from the interest upheld in *Grutter*, to justify their race-based assignments.... Seattle contends that its use of race helps to reduce racial concentration in schools and to ensure that racially concentrated housing patterns do not prevent nonwhite students from having access to the most desirable schools.... Jefferson County has articulated a similar goal, phrasing its interest in terms of educating its students "in a racially integrated environment." ... Each school district argues that educational and broader socialization benefits flow from a racially diverse learning environment, and each contends that because the diversity they seek is racial diversity—not the broader diversity at issue in *Grutter*—it makes sense to promote that interest directly by relying on race alone.

The parties and their *amici* dispute whether racial diversity in schools in fact has a marked impact on test scores and other objective yardsticks or achieves intangible socialization benefits. The debate is not one we need to resolve, however, because it is clear that the racial classifications employed by the districts are not narrowly tailored to the goal of achieving the educational and social benefits asserted to flow from racial diversity. In design and operation, the plans are directed only to racial balance, pure and simple, an objective this Court has repeatedly condemned as illegitimate....

Accepting racial balancing as a compelling state interest would justify the imposition of racial proportionality throughout American society, contrary to our repeated recognition that "[a]t the heart of the Constitution's guarantee of equal protection lies the simple command that the Government must treat citizens as individuals, not as simply components of a racial, religious, sexual or national class." *Miller v. Johnson*, 515 U. S. 900, 911 (1995)....

The principle that racial balancing is not permitted is one of substance, not semantics. Racial balancing is not transformed from "patently unconstitutional" to a compelling state interest simply by relabeling it "racial diversity." ...

... To the extent the objective is sufficient diversity so that students see fellow students as individuals rather than solely as members of a racial group, using means that treat students solely as members of a racial group is fundamentally at cross-purposes with that end.

IV

[*The Court takes issue with Justice Breyer's dissent, contending that he misreads and misapplies precedent and exaggerates the consequences of the majority opinion. It also rejects the argument that the school districts' good motives in using the assignment plans distinguish them from past cases where race classification was used to separate students.*]

Before *Brown*, schoolchildren were told where they could and could not go to school based on the color of their skin. The school districts in these cases have not carried the heavy burden of demonstrating that we should allow this once again — even for very different reasons. For schools that never segregated on the basis of race, such as Seattle, or that have removed the vestiges of past segregation, such as Jefferson County, the way "to achieve a system of determining admission to the public schools on a nonracial basis," *Brown II*, 349 U. S., at 300–301, is to stop assigning students on a racial basis. The way to stop discrimination on the basis of race is to stop discriminating on the basis of race.

The judgments of the Courts of Appeals for the Sixth and Ninth Circuits are reversed, and the cases are remanded for further proceedings.

It is so ordered.

JUSTICE THOMAS, concurring.

[*Thomas rejects Breyer's claim in his dissent that the school districts are trying to avoid "resegregation." Racial imbalance that is not caused by state rules is not unconstitutional he argues, and there is no compelling interest in diverse education given the conflicting social science evidence about the effects of diversity on educational outcomes. He contends that the dissenters' deference to local officials and discomfort with the notion of a "color-blind" constitution puts them in the company of the segregationist position in* Plessy *and* Brown.]

JUSTICE KENNEDY, concurring in part and concurring in the judgment....

I agree with THE CHIEF JUSTICE ... and join Parts I and II of the Court's opinion. I also join Parts III-A and III-C for reasons provided below. My views do not allow me to join the balance of the opinion by THE CHIEF JUSTICE, which seems to me to be inconsistent in both its approach and its implications

with the history, meaning, and reach of the Equal Protection Clause.... [*Kennedy argues that diversity is a compelling interest of the state and school districts that they may pursue through properly constructed assignment plans.*] ...

Our Nation from the inception has sought to preserve and expand the promise of liberty and equality on which it was founded. Today we enjoy a society that is remarkable in its openness and opportunity. Yet our tradition is to go beyond present achievements, however significant, and to recognize and confront the flaws and injustices that remain. This is especially true when we seek assurance that opportunity is not denied on account of race. The enduring hope is that race should not matter; the reality is that too often it does.

This is by way of preface to my respectful submission that parts of the opinion by THE CHIEF JUSTICE imply an all-too-unyielding insistence that race cannot be a factor in instances when, in my view, it may be taken into account. The plurality opinion is too dismissive of the legitimate interest government has in ensuring all people have equal opportunity regardless of their race.... Fifty years of experience since *Brown v. Board of Education*, 347 U. S. 483 (1954), should teach us that the problem before us defies so easy a solution. School districts can seek to reach *Brown's* objective of equal educational opportunity. The plurality opinion is at least open to the interpretation that the Constitution requires school districts to ignore the problem of *de facto* resegregation in schooling. I cannot endorse that conclusion. To the extent the plurality opinion suggests the Constitution mandates that state and local school authorities must accept the status quo of racial isolation in schools, it is, in my view, profoundly mistaken....

... If school authorities are concerned that the student-body compositions of certain schools interfere with the objective of offering an equal educational opportunity to all of their students, they are free to devise race-conscious measures to address the problem in a general way and without treating each student in different fashion solely on the basis of a systematic, individual typing by race....

With this explanation I concur in the judgment of the Court.

JUSTICE STEVENS, dissenting.

While I join JUSTICE BREYER's eloquent and unanswerable dissent in its entirety, it is appropriate to add these words.

There is a cruel irony in THE CHIEF JUSTICE's reliance on our decision in *Brown v. Board of Educa-*

tion, 349 U. S. 294 (1955). The first sentence in the concluding paragraph of his opinion states: "Before *Brown*, schoolchildren were told where they could and could not go to school based on the color of their skin." *Ante*, at 40. This sentence reminds me of Anatole France's observation: "[T]he majestic equality of the la[w], forbid[s] rich and poor alike to sleep under bridges, to beg in the streets, and to steal their bread." THE CHIEF JUSTICE fails to note that it was only black schoolchildren who were so ordered; indeed, the history books do not tell stories of white children struggling to attend black schools. In this and other ways, THE CHIEF JUSTICE rewrites the history of one of this Court's most important decisions....

JUSTICE BREYER, with whom JUSTICE STEVENS, JUSTICE SOUTER, and JUSTICE GINSBURG join, dissenting.

I

[*Justice Breyer argues that Brown and Swann encouraged state and local government to take primary responsibility for integrating the schools and permitted them to experiment with different ways to accomplish this goal. He details the history of both Seattle and Louisville, contending that in both places the starting point was segregation by race. Seattle settled lawsuits in order to avoid a court order forcing integration and Louisville was under court order from the early seventies. He contends that in both cases their current efforts reflect recognition of that history. Breyer cites Supreme Court and lower federal court decisions from the 1960's and 1970's that permitted school districts wide latitude in fashioning remedies that insured integration. He goes on to argue that a compelling state interest exists and that the programs are narrowly tailored to accomplish that interest.*]

VI
CONCLUSIONS

... The plans before us satisfy the requirements of the Equal Protection Clause. And it is the plurality's opinion, not this dissent that "fails to ground the result it would reach in law." ...

Four basic considerations have led me to this view. First, the histories of Louisville and Seattle reveal complex circumstances and a long tradition of conscientious efforts by local school boards to resist racial segregation in public schools. Segregation at the time of *Brown* gave way to expansive remedies that included busing, which in turn gave rise to fears of white flight and resegregation. For decades now, these school boards have considered and adopted and revised assignment plans that sought to rely less upon race, to emphasize greater student choice, and to improve the conditions of all schools for all students, no matter the color of their skin, no matter where they happen to reside. The plans under review — which are less burdensome, more egalitarian, and more effective than prior plans — continue in that tradition....

Second, since this Court's decision in *Brown*, the law has consistently and unequivocally approved of both voluntary and compulsory race-conscious measures to combat segregated schools. The Equal Protection Clause, ratified following the Civil War, has always distinguished in practice between state action that excludes and thereby subordinates racial minorities and state action that seeks to bring together people of all races....

Third, the plans before us, subjected to rigorous judicial review, are supported by compelling state interests and are narrowly tailored to accomplish those goals. Just as diversity in higher education was deemed compelling in *Grutter*, diversity in public primary and secondary schools — where there is even more to gain — must be, *a fortiori*, a compelling state interest. Even apart from *Grutter*, five Members of this Court agree that "avoiding racial isolation" and "achiev[ing] a diverse student population" remain today compelling interests. *Ante*, at 17–18 (opinion of KENNEDY, J.). These interests combine remedial, educational, and democratic objectives....

Fourth, the plurality's approach risks serious harm to the law and for the Nation. Its view of the law rests either upon a denial of the distinction between exclusionary and inclusive use of race-conscious criteria in the context of the Equal Protection Clause, or upon such a rigid application of its "test" that the distinction loses practical significance. Consequently, the Court's decision today slows down and sets back the work of local school boards to bring about racially diverse schools....

Indeed, the consequences of the approach the Court takes today are serious. Yesterday, the plans under review were lawful. Today, they are not. Yesterday, the citizens of this Nation could look for guidance to this Court's unanimous pronouncements concerning desegregation. Today, they cannot. Yesterday, school boards had available to them a full range of means to combat segregated schools. Today, they do not.

The Court's decision undermines other basic institutional principles as well. What has happened to *stare decisis*? The history of the plans before us, their educational importance, their highly limited use of race—all these and more—make clear that the compelling interest here is stronger than in *Grutter*. The plans here are more narrowly tailored than the law school admissions program there at issue. Hence, applying *Grutter*'s strict test, their lawfulness follows *a fortiori*. To hold to the contrary is to transform that test from "strict" to "fatal in fact"—the very opposite of what *Grutter* said. And what has happened to *Swann*? To *McDaniel*? To *Crawford*? To *Harris*? To *School Committee of Boston*? To *Seattle School Dist. No. 1*? After decades of vibrant life, they would all, under the plurality's logic, be written out of the law.

And what of respect for democratic local decisionmaking by States and school boards? For several decades this Court has rested its public school decisions upon *Swann*'s basic view that the Constitution grants local school districts a significant degree of leeway where the inclusive use of race-conscious criteria is at issue. Now localities will have to cope with the difficult problems they face (including resegregation) deprived of one means they may find necessary.

And what of law's concern to diminish and peacefully settle conflict among the Nation's people? Instead of accommodating different good-faith visions of our country and our Constitution, today's holding upsets settled expectations, creates legal uncertainty, and threatens to produce considerable further litigation, aggravating race-related conflict.

And what of the long history and moral vision that the Fourteenth Amendment itself embodies? The plurality cites in support those who argued in *Brown* against segregation, and JUSTICE THOMAS likens the approach that I have taken to that of segregation's defenders.... But segregation policies did not simply tell schoolchildren "where they could and could not go to school based on the color of their skin,"... ; they perpetuated a caste system rooted in the institutions of slavery and 80 years of legalized subordination....

Finally, what of the hope and promise of *Brown*? For much of this Nation's history, the races remained divided. It was not long ago that people of different races drank from separate fountains, rode on separate buses, and studied in separate schools. In this Court's finest hour, *Brown v. Board of Education* challenged this history and helped to change it. For *Brown* held out a promise. It was a promise embodied in three Amendments designed to make citizens of slaves. It was the promise of true racial equality—not as a matter of fine words on paper, but as a matter of everyday life in the Nation's cities and schools. It was about the nature of a democracy that must work for all Americans. It sought one law, one Nation, one people, not simply as a matter of legal principle but in terms of how we actually live.

... [T]he very school districts that once spurned integration now strive for it. The long history of their efforts reveals the complexities and difficulties they have faced. And in light of those challenges, they have asked us not to take from their hands the instruments they have used to rid their schools of racial segregation, instruments that they believe are needed to overcome the problems of cities divided by race and poverty. The plurality would decline their modest request.

... This is a decision that the Court and the Nation will come to regret.

I must dissent.

D. DESEGREGATING OTHER ACTIVITIES

Aside from schools and transportation, other facilities and activities available to the public were the subject of segregation laws: housing, parks and playgrounds, golf courses, swimming pools, beaches, courtrooms, restaurants, and marriage. All three branches have searched for remedies.

Race and Housing

Public schools remain segregated because of housing patterns, both within the city and between the city and the suburbs. Some of these patterns result from discriminatory actions by public officials and private homeowners. The process of breaking down racial barriers depends on a combination of judicial rulings, presidential leadership, congressional enactments, state initiatives, and racial tolerance by private homeowners.

Compared to the tenacious hold of the separate-but-equal doctrine in the fields of education, transportation, and public accommodations, it is surprising to find a number of early judicial rulings squarely against segregated housing. In *Buchanan* v. *Warley* (1917), a unanimous Court struck down a city ordinance that prohibited blacks from occupying houses in blocks controlled by whites. Such restrictions, said the Court, exceeded the police power and invaded the Fourteenth Amendment's right to acquire, enjoy, and use property. The case was not so much a vindication of racial equality; rather, it supported the freedom of whites to sell their property without interference. The Court based its decision not only on the Fourteenth Amendment but also on the Civil Rights Acts passed by Congress in 1866 and 1870.[7]

Of major importance is a unanimous opinion by the Court in 1948. Private parties in St. Louis, Missouri, agreed to exclude blacks from buying or occupying residences. The Court held that the agreements (restrictive covenants) did not themselves violate the Fourteenth Amendment. However, it would be a constitutional violation for the state courts to enforce them. SHELLEY v. KRAEMER, 334 U.S. 1 (1948). See also Hurd v. Hodge, 334 U.S. 25 (1948), and Barrows v. Jackson, 346 U.S. 249 (1953).

The principle of *Shelley* also prohibited discrimination against blacks in state-owned buildings. A restaurant in a building owned by Delaware refused to serve blacks. The building, constructed with public funds for public purposes, was owned and operated by the state, which leased part of it to a private operator for a restaurant. To the Court, this made the state a joint participant in operating the restaurant. The proscriptions of the Fourteenth Amendment applied to the restaurant just as though they were "binding covenants" written into the lease itself. Burton v. Wilmington Pkg. Auth., 365 U.S. 715 (1961).

The Fair Housing Act

In 1962, President Kennedy issued Executive Order 11063 to prohibit racial, ethnic, and religious discrimination in federally owned and assisted housing. The Civil Rights Act of 1964 prohibited racial discrimination in federally assisted programs, including public housing. In 1968, Congress passed the Fair Housing Act to prohibit the use of race, color, religion, or national origin in the sale or rental of most housing. Passage came in the turmoil of urban riots and widespread violence. 82 Stat. 81 (1968). One week before the House took its final vote to support open housing, Martin Luther King, Jr., was assassinated.

While Congress debated this legislation, an open-housing case reached the Supreme Court. An interracial couple had been denied the right to buy a house in suburban St. Louis. Two months after enactment of the fair housing bill, a 7–2 Court held that federal law (dating back to the Civil Rights Act of 1866) prohibited every racially motivated refusal to rent or sell property. The Court ruled that Congress had authority under the Thirteenth Amendment to pass the 1866 legislation. The Amendment forbade not only slavery but also the "badges and the incidents of slavery." Congress may prohibit both state action and private action that restrict the right of blacks to purchase, lease, and use property. Jones v. Mayer,Co., 392 U.S. 409 (1968).

A year later, the Court held that questions of fair housing may not be put to voters for approval. The rights of minorities cannot be delegated to referenda results. Hunter v. Erickson, 393 U.S. 385 (1969). When the issue is not fair housing but simply low-rent public housing, states may put such matters to the people in the form of a referendum. The question here is not racial but rather income class (poor versus rich). James v. Valtierra, 402 U.S. 137 (1971). The Court also held that "private social clubs" may not use racial discrimination to prevent white owners from leasing their homes to blacks. These practices violate congressional policy dating back to 1866. Sullivan v. Little Hunting Park, 396 U.S. 229 (1969).

---

7. Buchanan v. Warley, 245 U.S. 60, 78–79 (1917). See also Corrigan v. Buckley, 271 U.S. 323 (1926); Benjamin v. Tyler, 273 U.S. 668 (1927); Richmond, City of v. Deans, 281 U.S. 704 (1930).

Enforcing Fair Housing

Statutes and judicial rulings do not by themselves assure justice. Segregated housing persists through-out the country. Studies conducted by sending white, black, and Hispanic "testers" to real estate of-fices reveal that discrimination continued to be practiced against blacks and dark-skinned Hispanics. Havens Realty Corp. v. Coleman, 455 U.S. 363 (1982). The Fair Housing Act of 1968 was never ef-fectively enforced. To strengthen the Act, Congress passed legislation in 1988 to give the executive branch new authority to bring lawsuits when mediation efforts fail. The law permits government to seek large monetary damages for victims of housing discrimination. 102 Stat. 1619 (1988). The 1988 statute removed a $1,000 limit on punitive damage awards in housing bias cases. As a result, a settle-ment in Maryland in 1990 resulted in the payment of $225,000 by a development company, while a settlement earlier that year in California produced a payment of $450,000 by a Los Angeles apartment complex. Washington Post, April 13, 1990, at B1; February 20, 1990, at A2. In 1995, a Wisconsin property insurer accused of discriminating against minorities agreed to pay a record $14.5 million to seven black plaintiffs — the first time the Justice Department used the Fair Housing Act against prop-erty insurers. Washington Post, April 8, 1995, at E1.

In 1990, the Court placed limits on federal judges who tried to force compliance with a housing de-segregation plan. Split 5–4, the Court held that a district judge had abused his power by levying indi-vidual fines against four members of the city council of Yonkers, N.Y., for refusing to pass legislation needed to settle the discrimination suit. The majority decided that the fines would be permissible only if a much larger fine against the *city* proved ineffective. Spallone v. United States, 493 U.S. 265 (1990).

Public Accommodations

Following *Brown* v. *Board of Education,* federal courts struck down a number of laws that discrimi-nated on the basis of race. These cases affected public beaches and bathhouses, golf courses and parks, buses, courtrooms, and restaurants (see box). Blacks sat at lunch counters to challenge the policy of owners to deny them service. A cluster of cases pushed restaurants in the direction of abandoning that policy, but these cases also implied that the final word on this issue would have to come from legisla-tures, not courts.[8]

Mounting pressure for action finally culminated in passage of the Civil Rights Act of 1964. One of its sections on public accommodations barred discrimination on grounds of race, color, religion, or

---

Integrated Public Facilities

Beaches and bathhouses. Dawson v. Mayor, 220 F.2d 386 (4th Cir. 1955), aff'd, 350 U.S. 877 (1955).

Golf courses, parks, playgrounds, community centers. Holmes v. City of Atlanta, 223 F.2d 93 (5th Cir. 1955), aff'd, 350 U.S. 879 (1955); Wat-son v. Memphis, 373 U.S. 526 (1963).

Buses. Browder v. Gayle, 142 F.Supp. 707 (M.D. Ala. 1956), aff'd, 352 U.S. 903 (1956) [explicitly overruling *Plessy* v. *Ferguson*].

Courtrooms. Johnson v. Virginia, 373 U.S. 61 (1963).

Bus terminal restaurants (interstate). Boynton v. Virginia, 364 U.S. 454 (1960).

Public accommodations covered by the Civil Rights Act of 1964. Heart of Atlanta Motel v. United States, 379 U.S. 241 (1964); Katzenbach v. McClung, 379 U.S. 294 (1964).

---

8. Bouie v. City of Columbia, 378 U.S. 347 (1964); Bell v. Maryland, 378 U.S. 226 (1964); Avent v. North Carolina, 373 U.S. 375 (1963); Gober v. City of Birmingham, 373 U.S. 374 (1963); Lombard v. Louisiana, 373 U.S. 267 (1963); Shut-tlesworth v. City of Birmingham, 373 U.S. 262 (1963); Peterson v. City of Greenville, 373 U.S. 244 (1963); Turner v. City of Memphis, 369 U.S. 350 (1962); Garner v. Louisiana, 368 U.S. 157 (1961).

national origin if the operations affected interstate commerce or discrimination was supported by state action. Activities covered within this section included restaurants, cafeterias, lunchrooms, lunch counters, soda fountains, gas stations, movies, theaters, concert halls, sports arenas, stadiums, or any inn, hotel, motel, or lodging house for transient guests other than units with five or less rooms. This section did not apply to private clubs. Congressional action on public accommodations appeared to contradict the *Civil Rights Cases* of 1883, which had never been overruled by the Supreme Court. Congress avoided a potential conflict by basing the statute not only on the Civil War amendments but also on the Commerce Clause (see reading).

In two unanimous rulings the Supreme Court sustained the public accommodation section. The first involved a large motel in Atlanta, Georgia, used by interstate travelers. The Court supported the public accommodation provision as a valid exercise of congressional power under the Commerce Clause. HEART OF ATLANTA MOTEL v. UNITED STATES, 379 U.S. 241 (1964). The second case concerned a restaurant in Birmingham, Alabama. Although it catered to local white customers and provided a take-out service for blacks, it served food obtained from interstate commerce and was therefore within the reach of the Commerce Power as exercised by Congress. The Act specifically covers restaurants where "a substantial portion" of the food served "has moved in commerce." Katzenbach v. McClung, 379 U.S. 294 (1964).

Private Facilities

The public accommodations title of the Civil Rights Act of 1964 did not apply to "a private club or other establishment not in fact open to the public," other than the facilities specifically covered by the title (Section 201(e)). Several decisions fleshed out the scope of that section. Even when a facility is privately owned, action by the state to enforce a private policy of racial segregation violates the Equal Protection Clause of the Fourteenth Amendment. Griffin v. Maryland, 378 U.S. 130 (1964). When private individuals or groups exercise powers or perform functions governmental in nature, such as establishing a park for whites only, they become agencies or instrumentalities of the state and are subject to the restrictions of the Fourteenth Amendment. Evans v. Newton, 382 U.S. 296 (1966).

As with school segregation, opponents of racial equality tried a number of tactics. Residents of Virginia opened playground facilities and a community park for whites only. A 6–3 Court held that this nonstock corporation, acting as a "private social club," practiced racial discrimination in violation of federal law. Sullivan v. Little Hunting Park, 396 U.S. 229 (1969). A unanimous Court in 1973 ruled that a recreational association violated congressional policy by limiting the use of its swimming pool to white members and their white guests. The Court considered this case indistinguishable from *Sullivan.* Tillman v. Wheaton-Haven Recreation Assn., 410 U.S. 431 (1973).

The Court reached a different result in a 1972 case. A black guest at a private club had been denied service in the dining room and bar solely because of his race. Did the issuance of a state liquor license make the discriminatory practices "state action"? The Court, divided 6–3, relied on the *Civil Rights Cases* of 1883 to distinguish between discriminatory action by the state, which is prohibited by the Equal Protection Clause, and discriminatory action by private parties, against which the Clause erects no shield. The Court was reluctant to conclude that the provision of state benefits or services, including such necessities as electricity, water, and police and fire protection, sufficiently implicated the state to automatically convert a private entity into state action. Moose Lodge No. 107 v. Irvis, 407 U.S. 163 (1972). Private companies and schools that receive almost all of their funds from public sources do not necessarily perform a "state action." Randell-Baker v. Kohn, 457 U.S. 830 (1982).

Marriage and Cohabitation

In 1955, the Court received a miscegenation case from Virginia. Rather than strike down a law against mixed marriages, the Court decided to dodge this socially explosive issue. The Court's ruling on desegregation in 1954 prompted opponents to predict that integrated schools would produce "mongrelization" of the white race. A state court, in upholding the Virginia statute, said that natural law forbade interracial marriage: "the social amalgamation which leads to a corruption of races is as clearly divine as that which imparted to them different natures." Naim v. Naim, 87 S.E.2d 749, 752 (Va. 1955). State regulation of marriages was necessary to prevent "a mongrel breed of citizens." Id. at 756.

The Supreme Court quickly returned the case to Virginia, giving time for its ruling on desegregation to establish itself as the law of the land. Naim v. Naim, 350 U.S. 891 (1955). A decade later, a unanimous ruling held that Florida's statute prohibiting the cohabitation of unmarried interracial couples, singling them out for punishment, was a denial of equal protection. McLaughlin v. Florida, 379 U.S. 184 (1964). By 1967, with the Civil Rights Act of 1964 in place, the Court was prepared to strike down miscegenation laws and did so unanimously. It pointed out that 14 states in the previous 15 years had repealed laws prohibiting interracial marriages. Contemporary public opinion, operating through legislatures, thus played a part. The Court rejected the argument that the state law should be upheld because the framers of the Fourteenth Amendment did not intend to prohibit miscegenation laws. "Under our Constitution, the freedom to marry, or not marry, a person of another race resides with the individual and cannot be infringed by the State." Loving v. Virginia, 388 U.S. 1, 12 (1967).

Shelley v. Kraemer

334 U.S. 1 (1948)

Private agreements, known as restrictive covenants, were used in Missouri to prevent blacks from owning property. Private agreements, standing alone, usually do not violate the Fourteenth Amendment, which is directed against actions by state governments. The question in this case was whether a connection existed between private agreements and the state of Missouri. The Kraemers, a couple in the neighborhood subject to the terms of the restrictive covenant, brought suit to prevent the Shelleys, a black couple, from taking possession of property. The trial court denied the relief but was reversed by the Supreme Court of Missouri. The Shelley's appeal represented a test case for the NAACP Legal Defense Fund. The appeal was brought by the NAACP's lead counsel, Charles Houston and Thurgood Marshall.

MR. CHIEF JUSTICE VINSON delivered the opinion of the Court.

These cases present for our consideration questions relating to the validity of court enforcement of private agreements, generally described as restrictive covenants, which have as their purpose the exclusion of persons of designated race or color from the ownership or occupancy of real property. Basic constitutional issues of obvious importance have been raised.

The first of these cases comes to this Court on certiorari to the Supreme Court of Missouri. On February 16, 1911, thirty out of a total of thirty-nine owners of property fronting both sides of Labadie Avenue between Taylor Avenue and Cora Avenue in the city of St. Louis, signed an agreement, which was subsequently recorded....

On August 11, 1945, pursuant to a contract of sale, petitioners Shelley, who are Negroes, for valuable consideration received from one Fitzgerald a warranty deed to the parcel in question. The trial court found that petitioners had no actual knowledge of the restrictive agreement at the time of the purchase.

On October 9, 1945, respondents, as owners of other property subject to the terms of the restrictive covenant, brought suit in the Circuit Court of the city of St. Louis praying that petitioners Shelley be restrained from taking possession of the property and that judgment be entered divesting title out of petitioners Shelley and revesting title in the immediate grantor or in such other person as the court should direct....

I.

Whether the equal protection clause of the Fourteenth Amendment inhibits judicial enforcement by state courts of restrictive covenants based on race or color is a question which this Court has not heretofore been called upon to consider. Only two cases have been decided by this Court which in any way have involved the enforcement of such agreements. The first of these was the case of *Corrigan* v. *Buckley*, 271 U.S. 323 (1926). There, suit was brought in the courts of the District of Columbia to enjoin a threatened violation of certain restrictive covenants relating to lands situated in the city of Washington. [*This case did not present a Fourteenth Amendment issue, because "that Amendment by its terms applies only to the States."*]

The second of the cases involving racial restrictive covenants was *Hansberry* v. *Lee*, 311 U.S. 32 (1940). [*As disposed of by the Court, the issues presented by* Shelley v. Kraemer *were not reached.*]

It is well, at the outset, to scrutinize the terms of the restrictive agreements involved in these cases. In the Missouri case, the covenant declares that no part of the affected property shall be "occupied by any person not of the Caucasian race, it being intended hereby to restrict the use of said property ... against the occupancy as owners or tenants of any portion of said property for resident or other purpose by people of the Negro or Mongolian Race." Not only does the restriction seek to proscribe use and occupancy of the affected properties by members of the excluded class, but as construed by the Missouri courts, the agreement requires that title of any person who uses his property in violation of the restriction shall be divested....

It cannot be doubted that among the civil rights intended to be protected from discriminatory state action by the Fourteenth Amendment are the rights to acquire, enjoy, own and dispose of property. Equality in the enjoyment of property rights was regarded by the framers of that Amendment as an essential pre-condition to the realization of other basic civil rights and liberties which the Amendment was intended to guarantee. Thus, § 1978 of the Revised Statutes, derived from § 1 of the Civil Rights Act of 1866 which was enacted by Congress while the Fourteenth Amendment was also under consideration, provides:

"All citizens of the United States shall have the same right, in every State and Territory, as is enjoyed by white citizens thereof to inherit, purchase, lease, sell, hold, and convey real and personal property."

This Court has given specific recognition to the same principle. *Buchanan* v. *Warley*, 245 U.S. 60 (1917).

It is likewise clear that restrictions on the right of occupancy of the sort sought to be created by the private agreements in these cases could not be squared with the requirements of the Fourteenth Amendment if imposed by state statute or local ordinance....

... [T]he present cases ... do not involve action by state legislatures or city councils. Here the particular patterns of discrimination and the areas in which the restrictions are to operate, are determined, in the first instance, by the terms of agreements among private individuals. Participation of the State consists in the enforcement of the restrictions so defined. The crucial issue with which we are here confronted is whether this distinction removes these cases from the operation of the prohibitory provisions of the Fourteenth Amendment.

Since the decision of this Court in the *Civil Rights Cases*, 109 U.S. 3 (1883), the principle has become firmly embedded in our constitutional law that the action inhibited by the first section of the Fourteenth Amendment is only such action as may fairly be said to be that of the States. That Amendment erects no shield against merely private conduct, however discriminatory or wrongful.

We conclude, therefore, that the restrictive agreements standing alone cannot be regarded as violative of any rights guaranteed to petitioners by the Fourteenth Amendment. So long as the purposes of those agreements are effectuated by voluntary adherence to their terms, it would appear clear that there has been no action by the State and the provisions of the Amendment have not been violated....

But here there was more. These are cases in which the purposes of the agreements were secured only by judicial enforcement by state courts of the restrictive terms of the agreements....

II.

That the action of state courts and judicial officers in their official capacities is to be regarded as action of the State within the meaning of the Fourteenth Amendment, is a proposition which has long been established by decisions of this Court....

The short of the matter is that from the time of the adoption of the Fourteenth Amendment until the present, it has been the consistent ruling of this Court that the action of the States to which the Amendment has reference includes action of state courts and state judicial officials....

[III.]

We hold that in granting judicial enforcement of the restrictive agreements in these cases, the States have denied petitioners the equal protection of the laws and that, therefore, the action of the state courts cannot stand....

For the reasons stated, the judgment of the

Supreme Court of Missouri and the judgment of the Supreme Court of Michigan must be reversed.

Reversed.

Mr. Justice Reed, Mr. Justice Jackson, and Mr. Justice Rutledge took no part in the consideration or decision of these cases.

Congress Interprets the Commerce Clause

Congressional action on the public accommodations section of the Civil Rights Act of 1964 was jeopardized by the Supreme Court's decision in the *Civil Rights Cases* of 1883. In that case, the Court struck down an earlier congressional effort, based on the Fourteenth Amendment, to pass legislation on public accommodations. Rather than risk a head-on collision with the Court, Congress selected another instrument to achieve its ends: the Commerce Clause. The language below is from Senate Report No. 872, 88th Cong., 2d Sess. 12–14 (1964).

At the outset a formidable obstacle to a favorable determination on S. 1732 appeared to be an 1883 decision by the U.S. Supreme Court holding unconstitutional an 1875 statute providing criminal penalties for denials of service by public facilities or accommodations on account of race, color, or religion. This 1875 law was expressly based on the 14th amendment, but the Supreme Court could not find the requisite "State action" in denials of service by privately owned establishments. There is a large body of legal thought that believes the Court would either reverse the earlier decision if the question were again presented or that changed circumstances in the intervening 80 years would make it possible for the earlier decision to be distinguished. That question, however, was not before the committee, for the instant measure is based on the commerce clause (art. 1, sec. 8, clause 3) of the Constitution. The majority opinion of the Court in the 1883 decision carefully stated that they were not foreclosing a statute based on the broad powers of Congress such as are found in the commerce clause. Mr. Justice Bradley wrote:

"Of course, these remarks do not apply to those cases in which Congress is clothed with direct and plenary powers of legislation over the whole subject, accompanied with an express or implied denial of such power to the States, as in the regulation of commerce with foreign nations, and among the several States and with the Indian tribes, the coining of money, the establishment of post offices and post roads, the declaring of war, etc. In these cases Congress has power to pass laws for regulating the subjects specified in every detail, and the conduct and transactions of individuals in respect thereof." (109 U.S. 3, 18 (1883))

Attached as an appendix to this report is a brief prepared at the request of the committee by Prof. Paul Freund of the Harvard Law School, a noted authority on the Constitution. In this document Professor Freund concludes that the law proposed by S. 1732 is consistent with the Constitution and the decisions thereunder by the Supreme Court. In the judgment of the committee it would be upheld on review. Similar conclusions were reached by almost all legal scholars or practitioners consulted by the committee or inquired of by witnesses appearing before the committee. Professor Freund wrote: "The commerce power is clearly adequate and appropriate. No impropriety need be felt in using the commerce clause as a response to a deep moral concern." Where social injustices occur in commercial activities the commerce clause has been used to prevent discrimination; it has been used to prohibit racial discrimination; and it has been used to reach intrastate activities if they have a substantial effect (individually or cumulatively) upon commerce. The committee concludes that there is sufficient authority in the Constitution to uphold S. 1732.

Congress, in the exercise of its plenary power over interstate commerce, may regulate commerce or that which affects it for other than purely economic goals.

"The motive and purpose of a regulation of interstate commerce are matters for the legislative judgment upon the exercise of which the Constitution places no restriction and over which the courts are given no control." (Mr. Justice Stone in *United States* v. *Darby,* 312 U.S. 100, 115 (1941))

The fact that S. 1732 would accomplish socially oriented objectives by aid of the commerce clause powers would not detract from its validity. There are many instances in which Congress has discouraged practices which it deems evil, dangerous, or unwise by a regulation of interstate commerce. Examples of this are found in Federal legislation keeping the channels of commerce free from the transportation of tickets used in lottery schemes, sustained in *Champion* v. *Ames*, 188 U.S. 321 (1903); the Pure Food and Drug Act, sustained in *Hipolite Egg Co.* v. *United States*, 220 U.S. 45 (1911); the "White Slave Traffic Act," upheld in *Hoke* v. *United States*, 227 U.S. 308 (1913); strict regulation of the transportation of intoxicating liquors, sustained in *Clark Distilling Co.* v. *Western Maryland Railway Co.*, 242 U.S. 311 (1917); and the Fair Labor Standards Act, imposing wages and hours requirements, sustained in *United States* v. *Darby*, 312 U.S. 100 (1941).

Heart of Atlanta Motel v. United States

379 U.S. 241 (1964)

Title II of the Civil Rights Act of 1964 prohibits racial discrimination in places of public accommodation affecting interstate commerce. Establishments covered by the Act include inns, hotels, restaurants, cafeterias, and movie theaters. The appellant in this case, the Heart of Atlanta Motel located in Atlanta, Georgia, restricted its clientele to white persons. The motel claimed that the statute exceeded Congress' power under the Commerce Clause and violated other parts of the Constitution. A three-judge court upheld the constitutionality of Title II.

MR. JUSTICE CLARK delivered the opinion of the Court....

1. THE FACTUAL BACKGROUND AND CONTENTIONS OF THE PARTIES.

The case comes here on admissions and stipulated facts. Appellant owns and operates the Heart of Atlanta Motel which has 216 rooms available to transient guests. The motel is located on Courtland Street, two blocks from downtown Peachtree Street. It is readily accessible to interstate highways 75 and 85 and state highways 23 and 41. Appellant solicits patronage from outside the State of Georgia through various national advertising media, including magazines of national circulation; it maintains over 50 billboards and highway signs within the State, soliciting patronage for the motel; it accepts convention trade from outside Georgia and approximately 75% of its registered guests are from out of State. Prior to passage of the Act the motel had followed a practice of refusing to rent rooms to Negroes, and it alleged that it intended to continue to do so. In an effort to perpetuate that policy this suit was filed.

The appellant contends that Congress in passing this Act exceeded its power to regulate commerce under Art. I, §8, cl. 3, of the Constitution of the United States; that the Act violates the Fifth Amendment because appellant is deprived of the right to choose its customers and operate its business as it wishes, resulting in a taking of its liberty and property without due process of law and a taking of its property without just compensation; and, finally, that by requiring appellant to rent available rooms to Negroes against its will, Congress is subjecting it to involuntary servitude in contravention of the Thirteenth Amendment.

The appellees counter that the unavailability to Negroes of adequate accommodations interferes significantly with interstate travel, and that Congress, under the Commerce Clause, has power to remove such obstructions and restraints; that the Fifth Amendment does not forbid reasonable regulation and that consequential damage does not constitute a "taking" within the meaning of that amendment; that the Thirteenth Amendment claim fails because it is entirely frivolous to say that an amendment directed to the abolition of human bondage and the removal of widespread disabilities associated with slavery places discrimination in public accommodations beyond the reach of both federal and state law....

3. TITLE II OF THE ACT.

This Title is divided into seven sections beginning with §201(a) which provides that:

"All persons shall be entitled to the full and equal enjoyment of the goods, services, facilities, privileges, advantages, and accommodations of any place of public accommodation, as defined in this section, without discrimination or segregation on the ground of race, color, religion, or national origin." [*Section 201(b) lists four classes of business establishments, each of which "serves the public" and "is a place of public accommodation" within the meaning of §201(a) "if its operations affect commerce, or if discrimination or segregation by it is supported by State action." The first class covered "(1) any inn, hotel, motel, or other establishment which provides lodging to transient guests, other than an establishment located within a building which contains not more than five rooms for rent or hire and which is actually occupied by the proprietor of such establishment as his residence."*]

Section 201(c) defines the phrase "affect commerce" as applied to the above establishments. It first declares that "any inn, hotel, motel, or other establishment which provides lodging to transient guests" affects commerce *per se*. Restaurants, cafeterias, etc., in class two affect commerce only if they serve or offer to serve interstate travelers or if a substantial portion of the food which they serve or products which they sell have "moved in commerce." ...

4. APPLICATION OF TITLE II TO HEART OF ATLANTA MOTEL.

It is admitted that the operation of the motel brings it within the provisions of § 201(a) of the Act and that appellant refused to provide lodging for transient Negroes because of their race or color and that it intends to continue that policy unless restrained.

The sole question posed is, therefore, the constitutionality of the Civil Rights Act of 1964 as applied to these facts. The legislative history of the Act indicates that Congress based the Act on § 5 and the Equal Protection Clause of the Fourteenth Amendment as well as its power to regulate interstate commerce under Art. I, § 8, cl. 3, of the Constitution.

The Senate Commerce Committee made it quite clear that the fundamental object of Title II was to vindicate "the deprivation of personal dignity that surely accompanies denials of equal access to public establishments." At the same time, however, it noted that such an objective has been and could be readily achieved "by congressional action based on the commerce power of the Constitution." S. Rep. No. 872, *supra*, at 16–17. Our study of the legislative record, made in the light of prior cases, has brought us to the conclusion that Congress possessed ample power in this regard, and we have therefore not considered the other grounds relied upon. This is not to say that the remaining authority upon which it acted was not adequate, a question upon which we do not pass, but merely that since the commerce power is sufficient for our decision here we have considered it alone. ...

5. THE CIVIL RIGHTS CASES, 109 U.S. 3 (1883), AND THEIR APPLICATION.

In light of our ground for decision, it might be well at the outset to discuss the *Civil Rights Cases, supra*, which declared provisions of the Civil Rights Act of 1875 unconstitutional. 18 Stat. 335, 336. We think that decision inapposite, and without precedential value in determining the constitutionality of the present Act. Unlike Title II of the present legislation, the 1875 Act broadly proscribed discrimination in "inns, public conveyances on land or water, theaters, and other places of public amusement," without limiting the categories of affected businesses to those impinging upon interstate commerce. In contrast, the applicability of Title II is carefully limited to enterprises having a direct and substantial relation to the interstate flow of goods and people, except where state action is involved. Further, the fact that certain kinds of businesses may not in 1875 have been sufficiently involved in interstate commerce to warrant bringing them within the ambit of the commerce power is not necessarily dispositive of the same question today. Our populace had not reached its present mobility, nor were facilities, goods and services circulating as readily in interstate commerce as they are today. ...

6. THE BASIS OF CONGRESSIONAL ACTION.

While the Act as adopted carried no congressional findings the record of its passage through each house is replete with evidence of the burdens that discrimination by race or color places upon interstate commerce. ... This testimony included the fact that our people have become increasingly mobile with millions of people of all races traveling from State to State; that Negroes in particular have been the subject of discrimination in transient accommodations, having to travel great distances to secure the same; that often they have been unable to obtain accommodations and have had to call upon friends to put them up overnight ... ;

7. THE POWER OF CONGRESS OVER INTERSTATE TRAVEL.

The power of Congress to deal with these obstructions depends on the meaning of the Commerce Clause. ...

It is said that the operation of the motel here is of a purely local character. But, assuming this to be true, "[i]f it is interstate commerce that feels the pinch, it does not matter how local the operation which applies the squeeze." *United States* v. *Women's Sportswear Mfrs. Assn.,* 336 U.S. 460, 464 (1949). ...

Nor does the Act deprive appellant of liberty or property under the Fifth Amendment. The commerce power invoked here by the Congress is a specific and plenary one authorized by the Constitution itself. The only questions are: (1) whether Congress had a rational basis for finding that racial discrimination by motels affected commerce, and (2) if it had such a basis, whether the means it selected to eliminate that evil are reasonable and appropriate. If they are, appellant has no "right" to select its guests as it sees fit, free from governmental regulation....

We find no merit in the remainder of appellant's contentions, including that of "involuntary servitude." As we have seen, 32 States prohibit racial discrimination in public accommodations. These laws but codify the common-law innkeeper rule which long predated the Thirteenth Amendment....

We, therefore, conclude that the action of the Congress in the adoption of the Act as applied here to a motel which concededly serves interstate travelers is within the power granted it by the Commerce Clause of the Constitution, as interpreted by this Court for 140 years....

Affirmed.

[*Justices Black, Douglas, and Goldberg wrote separate concurring opinions.*]

E. EMPLOYMENT AND AFFIRMATIVE ACTION

Racial segregation persists because of a number of interlocking cycles. Segregated housing contributes to segregated education; segregated education is a factor in segregated employment. One way to combat racial segregation is through job opportunities. Blacks and Hispanics with stable jobs and higher incomes have greater choices in deciding where to live and where to send their children to school. To broaden their choices, the government has relied on the controversial tools of quotas and affirmative action (usually called "reverse discrimination" by opponents).

Executive Orders

From 1941 to 1958, Presidents Roosevelt, Truman, and Eisenhower issued a number of Executive Orders to improve employment opportunities for blacks. Under pressure from civil rights activists who protested discrimination in hiring, Roosevelt issued an Executive Order in 1941 to establish the Committee on Fair Employment Practices. The purpose was to increase black employment in the defense industry. Executive Order 8802 declared that "there shall be no discrimination in the employment of workers in defense industries or government because of race, creed, color, or national origin." Outbreaks of racial violence after World War II prompted Truman, in 1946, to issue Executive Order 9808 to establish the President's Committee on Civil Rights. The Committee attacked segregation and the separate-but-equal doctrine as morally wrong and economically wasteful. In a major address to Congress on February 2, 1948, Truman set forth an agenda for civil rights. The goals he established, including a commission to prevent unfair discrimination in employment, had to await passage of the civil rights bills from 1957 to 1964.

In the meantime, President Kennedy issued Executive Order 10925 in 1961 to establish the President's Committee on Equal Employment Opportunity. There were two goals: equal access to employment within the government and equal opportunity for those who receive government contracts. As a condition for receiving federal contracts, private companies had to agree to nondiscriminatory policies. Executive Order 11114, issued in 1963, extended the Committee's authority to include federally assisted construction. President Johnson issued Executive Order 11246 in 1965, vesting in the Secretary of Labor the responsibility for ensuring nondiscrimination by government contractors.

Legislative Action

Title VII of the Civil Rights Act of 1964 prohibits employment practices based on race, color, religion, sex, or national origin. Congress created the Equal Employment Opportunity Commission (EEOC) to oversee this title but gave the Commission authority only to conciliate complaints of job bias. It had no power to issue cease-and-desist orders to employers or to file suit in court. Enforcement powers were strengthened in 1972 by authorizing the EEOC to take discrimination cases to federal court if conciliation efforts fail. 86 Stat. 103 (1972). The 1972 amendments also extended Title VII coverage to state and local government employees.

In 1971, a unanimous Court interpreted Title VII to prohibit the use of hiring practices that are not job-related and that operate to exclude blacks. In this case, a company required a high school diploma and the taking of an intelligence test. The Court said it was immaterial whether the employer had a discriminatory intent. Griggs v. Duke Power Co., 401 U.S. 424 (1971). The *Griggs* test appeared to require an employee to prove only disparate *results,* not the employer's *intent.*

Another case on employment tests was decided in 1976. Two blacks, after being rejected as police officers, claimed that the written personnel tests bore no relation to job performance and were racially discriminatory. Although the police department had made affirmative efforts to recruit black officers, the tests excluded a disproportionately high number of black applicants. The tests measured verbal ability, vocabulary, reading, and comprehension. The Court, by a 7–2 vote, held that the tests were not unconstitutional solely because they had a racially disproportionate impact. In an apparent conflict with *Griggs,* the Court said that there must be a purpose (intent) to discriminate. The Court justified a different conclusion because this was not a Title VII case. The plaintiffs asserted that the tests violated their rights under the Due Process Clause of the Fifth Amendment, under 42 U.S.C. § 1981, and under the D.C. Code. Washington v. Davis, 426 U.S. 229 (1976).

Localities trying to navigate the Court's and Congress's actions in the area of disparate impact may feel "damned if they do and damned if they don't." The city of New Haven, Connecticut was worried about a disparate impact lawsuit when it threw out the results of an exam used to determine promotions in the fire department. No black firefighters scored high enough on the exam to gain promotion. Seventeen white and two Hispanic firefighters who had scored higher on the exam sued the city for violating Title VII. They lost in the lower courts but the Supreme Court reversed those holdings, finding that the city had discriminated on the basis of race in throwing out the test results. Ricci v. DeStefano, 557 U.S. 557 (2009). The case became a cause célèbre when one of the Court of Appeals judges who ruled against the firefighters, Sonia Sotomayor, was nominated for a seat on the Supreme Court by President Barack Obama.

Affirmative Action

A number of government and private programs give preferential treatment to certain races. Congressional attitudes and policy on "affirmative action" have been inconsistent and often contradictory (see box). Lit-

Congressional Policy on "Affirmative Action"

Civil rights legislation appeared to prohibit racial discrimination in any form, For example, Section 703 of Title VII of the Civil Rights Act of 1964 makes it unlawful to "discriminate ... because of ... race" in hiring and in the selection of apprentices for training programs. Moreover, Section 703(j) states that nothing in Title VII shall be interpreted to require "preferential treatment" to any individual for reasons of race or color. On the other hand, Section 706(g) authorized a court to order "such affirmative action as may be appropriate, which may include reinstatement or hiring of employees, with or without backpay." This au-

thority was strengthened in 1972 to read: "such affirmative action as may be appropriate, which may include, but is not limited to, reinstatement or hiring of employees, with or without back pay ... or any other equitable relief as the court deems appropriate." 86 Stat. 107. Senator Ervin in 1972 offered an amendment to prohibit any federal agency or office from requiring employees to practice "discrimination in reverse." His amendment was rejected by the decisive margin of 44 to 22, in part because it would deprive courts of their power to remedy cases of discrimination. 118 Cong. Rec. 1661–76 (1972).

tle opposition exists to programs that make special efforts to recruit minorities, assuring that a sufficient number will be in the pool of candidates. But should race be a factor in making the selections? Can employers prefer, for reasons of race, a minority over an equally qualified white? Does affirmative action allow the hiring of a minority who is less qualified? Is racial discrimination an appropriate means to compensate for past injuries and injustices? Should quotas or "goals" be established to guarantee the acceptance of a specific number of blacks, Hispanics, and other minorities?

Initially, the judiciary interpreted congressional policy to require a standard of racial neutrality in hiring. Race was not to be a factor. In 1971, a unanimous Court stated that Congress did not, in Title VII of the Civil Rights Act of 1964, command "that the less qualified be preferred over the better qualified simply because of minority origins. Far from disparaging job qualifications as such, Congress has made such qualifications the controlling factor, so that race, religion, nationality, and sex become irrelevant." Griggs v. Duke Power Co., 401 U.S. at 436. Congress prohibited discriminatory preference "for any group, minority or majority." Id. at 431. A unanimous Court in 1976 held that Title VII prohibits racial discrimination whether the victim is black or white. Employers could not dismiss whites for an offense and retain a black who committed the same offense. McDonald v. Santa Fe Trail Transp. Co., 427 U.S. 273 (1976).

Yet various administrations used race as a criterion in overseeing the award of federal contracts. Under the Philadelphia Plan, developed by the Nixon administration, contractors had to set specific goals for hiring members of minority groups as a condition for working on federally assisted projects. Federal courts upheld the legality of the plan in 1970 and 1971, as well as the Executive Order that placed it in operation.[9]

The question of affirmative action confronted the Court in 1974. Marco DeFunis, Jr., a white applicant to the University of Washington Law School, was denied admission. He claimed that the school's policy discriminated against him. Out of 150 openings for first-year students, the school set aside a specific number of places for minority applicants (blacks, Chicanos, American Indians, and Filipinos). DeFunis scored higher than most of the minorities accepted. Had the minority applicants been considered under the same procedure applied to him, none of those eventually enrolled would have been admitted.

After a state trial court upheld DeFunis' claim of discrimination, he was admitted to the law school. The trial court was reversed by the Washington Supreme Court, but by that time DeFunis was in his second year. The U.S. Supreme Court, reviewing his appeal when he was in his final year, held the case moot. DeFunis v. Odegaard, 416 U.S. 312 (1974). Among the questions the Court was able to avoid: If positions are reserved for blacks, Chicanos, Native Americans, and Filipinos, why not Asians and other "minorities"? How can courts draw and justify such lines? Excerpts of this decision are reprinted in Chapter 3.

The *Bakke* Case

Within a few years the issue of affirmative action returned to the Court, this time involving Allan Bakke's application to the medical school at the University of California at Davis. The school had two admissions programs: a regular admissions program (for Bakke and other nonminority candidates) and a special admissions program for "disadvantaged" minorities (blacks, Chicanos, Asians, and Native Americans). Disadvantaged whites were not admitted to the special program, although many applied. Out of 100 openings for entering students, 16 were reserved for special admissions. Bakke was

---

9. Contractors Ass'n of Eastern Pa. v. Secretary of Labor, 442 F.2d 159 (3d Cir. 1971), cert. denied, 404 U.S. 854 (1971). See also Contractors Ass'n of Eastern Pa. v. Secretary of Labor, 311 F.Supp. 1002 (E.D. Pa. 1970); Robert P. Schuwerk, "The Philadelphia Plan: A Study in the Dynamics of Executive Power," 39 U. Chi. L. Rev. 723 (1972); and "Committee Analysis of Executive Order 11246 (The Affirmative Action Program)," prepared by the Senate Committee on Labor and Human Resources, 97th Cong., 2d Sess. (Comm. Print April 1982).

rejected twice; minorities with significantly lower scores were admitted under the special program. The Supreme Court decided that Bakke should be admitted to the medical school and that the special admissions program was invalid. However, it reversed the judgment of lower courts that race could not be taken into account in an admissions program. Race would be a permissible factor in promoting diverse student bodies. The judgment of the Court, concurrences, and separate opinions filled 156 rambling pages. Eight Justices found fault with parts of the opinion of the Court written by Powell. REGENTS OF THE UNIVERSITY OF CALIFORNIA v. BAKKE, 438 U.S. 265 (1978).

The following year, a 5–2 Court supported the use of affirmative action for private employment. It had been the practice in some industries to hire as craftworkers only persons with prior craft experience; blacks were usually excluded from craft unions. To open up opportunities for the well-paying craft jobs, Kaiser Aluminum and the United Steelworkers union agreed upon an affirmative action plan. Fifty percent of craft-training openings were reserved for black employees until the percentage of black craftworkers equaled the percentage of blacks in the local labor force. The most senior black trainee had less seniority than several whites who were rejected. One of the whites, Brian Weber, filed a class action claiming that the plan violated Title VII by discriminating on the basis of race. The Court held that Title VII does not prohibit private, voluntary, race-conscious affirmative action programs to overcome past discrimination. Chief Justice Burger and Justice Rehnquist dissented, accusing the majority of rewriting Title VII. Justice Blackmun, in a concurrence, pointed out that if the Court "has misperceived the political will, it has the assurance that because the question is statutory Congress may set a different course if it so chooses." United Steelworkers v. Weber, 443 U.S. 193, 216 (1979).

Set-Asides

Although language in some of the civil rights acts appeared to announce a race-neutral policy, other statutes endorsed preferential treatment. Two years before *Weber,* Congress passed legislation to set aside 10 percent of public works funds for "minority business enterprises." The statute defined minority group members as U.S. citizens "who are Negroes, Spanish-speaking, Orientals, Indians, Eskimos, and Aleuts." 91 Stat. 117. Congressional action had been preceded by several Executive Orders during the Nixon administration directing federal agencies to increase the proportion of procurement contracts to minority business enterprises.[10]

A 6–3 Court found the set-aside an acceptable exercise of congressional authority under the spending power. The Court said the statute could also be justified on the basis of congressional power under the Commerce Clause or Section 5 of the Fourteenth Amendment. The use of racial and ethnic criteria as a condition attached to a federal grant did not violate the equal protection component of the Due Process Clause of the Fifth Amendment. FULLILOVE v. KLUTZNICK, 448 U.S. 448 (1980).

Fullilove supported the use of set-asides by Congress. Could states and cities adopt that policy? In 1989, a 6–3 Court struck down a city of Richmond plan that required contractors receiving city construction contracts to subcontract at least 30 percent of the funds to "minority business enterprises" (blacks, Hispanics, Asians, Native Americans, Eskimos, and Aleuts). The Court rejected *Fullilove* as an acceptable precedent, pointing out that the Fourteenth Amendment authorizes Congress, not cities or states, to act against racial discrimination. Also, the plan was not narrowly tailored to accomplish a remedial purpose. With regard to the set-aside for such groups as the Aleuts, the Court remarked: "The gross overinclusiveness of Richmond's racial preference strongly impugns the city's claim of remedial motivation." RICHMOND v. CROSON CO., 488 U.S. 469, 506 (1989).

---

10. Executive Order 11458, 34 Fed. Reg. 4937 (1969); Executive Order 11518, 35 Fed. Reg. 4939 (1970); Executive Order 11625, 36 Fed. Reg. 19967 (1971); Public Papers of the Presidents, 1969, at 197–98; 994–95; Public Papers of the Presidents, 1970, at 284–88.

The difference between the use of race-conscious remedies by Congress (as in *Fullilove*) and by the states (as in *Croson*) is highlighted by a 5–4 decision in 1990. The Federal Communications Commission (FCC) adopted two minority preference policies in awarding licenses and ownership of radio and television broadcast stations. These policies were part of FCC's effort to promote diversification of programming. After the filing of a lawsuit that challenged the FCC policy, Congress enacted legislation prohibiting the agency from spending any appropriated funds to examine or change its minority policies. The Supreme Court upheld the minority-preference policies because they bear the "imprimatur" of longstanding congressional support and direction and were substantially related to the achievement of the important government objective of broadcast diversity. Metro Broadcasting, Inc. v. FCC, 497 U.S. 547 (1990). This ruling would be reexamined and revised within a few years.

Title VII Disputes

After resolving the question of congressional power in *Fullilove*, the Court turned to a Title VII case in 1984. Two black members of a Memphis, Tennessee, fire department filed a complaint of racial discrimination. A district court issued a consent decree (incorporating the agreement of the two parties) to remedy the department's hiring and promotion practices. When budget deficits required the release of some city employees, the court enjoined the department from following its seniority system to decide layoffs. A modified layoff plan resulted in white employees, with more seniority than black employees, being laid off. A 6–3 Court held that the injunction exceeded the consent decree, which had made no mention of layoffs, demotions, or departures from the seniority system. Firefighters v. Stotts, 467 U.S. 561 (1984).

Two years later, the Court affirmed a lower court's judgment that established a 29 percent nonwhite membership goal in a union, based on the percentage of nonwhites in the local labor force. The decision is significant because the Court agreed that race-conscious relief can be granted to benefit individuals who are not identified victims of unlawful discrimination. The Justice Department, and the Justices who dissented, argued that the legislative history of Title VII indicates that Congress intended that affirmative relief could benefit only those who had been identified as victims of past discrimination. Sheet Metal Workers v. EEOC, 478 U.S. 421 (1986). In a second case issued that day, the Court decided that Title VII does not preclude consent decrees that benefit individuals who were not the actual victims of discriminatory practices. Firefighters v. Cleveland, 478 U.S. 501 (1986).

Although the Court has deferred to congressional actions that benefit minorities and has supported private efforts to hire minorities or admit them to universities, a more stringent review is applied to the use of racial classification for layoffs. Nonminority school teachers in Michigan challenged a provision in a collective bargaining agreement that allowed the school board to give preferential protection to minorities in case of layoffs. A 5–4 decision held that the agreement violated the Fourteenth Amendment. The Court reasoned that when affirmative action is used for hiring goals, the burden on innocent individuals is diffused among society generally, whereas layoffs represent a greater and more intrusive loss to specific employees. Wygant v. Jackson Bd. of Educ., 476 U.S. 267 (1986). Throughout recent decades the three branches have developed basic principles for affirmative action (see box on next page).

The general support for some form of affirmative action is underscored by a 1987 decision. For almost four decades, Alabama had excluded blacks as state troopers. District court orders were ineffective in hiring blacks. Finally, under court order, the state promoted eight blacks and eight whites. A 5–4 Court affirmed this remedy, citing the long and systematic exclusion of blacks, the continuous practice of discrimination, and the state's record of delay and resistance. United States v. Paradise, 480 U.S. 149 (1987). Also in 1987, the Court approved affirmative action to increase promotional opportunities for women. Johnson v. Transportation Agency, 480 U.S. 616 (1987), discussed in Chapter 16.

Affirmative Action Principles

A series of Supreme Court decisions, congressional statutes, and presidential policies have established several general guidelines for permissible affirmative action:

1. Presidents used such policies as the Philadelphia Plan to require governmental contractors to set specific goals for hiring members of minority groups as a condition for receiving federal funds. Contractors Ass'n of Eastern Pa. v. Secretary of Labor, 442 F.2d 159 (3d Cir. 1971), cert. denied, 404 U.S. 854 (1971).

2. Affirmative action programs must be narrowly tailored to meet a legitimate governmental objective.

3. Race or gender may be included as one of several factors in determining admission to a university or for employment. Regents of the University of California v. Bakke, 438 U.S. 265 (1978) (race); Johnson v. Transportation Agency, 480 U.S. 616 (1987) (gender); Grutter v. Bollinger, 539 U.S. 306 (2003) (race and ethnicity).

4. Voluntary initiatives by the private sector may be race-conscious for employment decisions. United Steelworkers v. Weber, 443 U.S. 193 (1979).

5. Congress supported preferential treatment for minorities, through set-asides and other programs, but states and localities must meet a higher standard. Fullilove v. Klutznick, 448 U.S. 448 (1980); Metro Broadcasting, Inc. v. FCC, 497 U.S. 547 (1990); Richmond v. Croson Co., 488 U.S. 506 (1989). In 1995, the Court adopted a high standard (strict scrutiny) for federal programs. Adarand Constructors, Inc. v. Pena, 515 U.S. 200 (1995).

6. It is more difficult to defend affirmative action in court when used for layoffs than for hiring. Firefighters v. Stotts, 467 U.S. 561 (1984); Wygant v. Jackson Bd. of Educ., 476 U.S. 267 (1986).

7. Quotas may be used when employers are intransigent and refuse to comply with repeated court orders. United States v. Paradise, 480 U.S. 149 (1987) (constitutional question); Sheet Metal Workers v. EEOC, 478 U.S. 421 (1986) (Title VII question).

8. Congress has remedied societal discrimination (Fullilove v. Klutznick) and promoted diversity (Metro Broadcasting, Inc. v. FCC). Those programs must now satisfy the strict-scrutiny standard of *Adarand*.

The *Adarand* Decision

The holdings in *Fullilove* and *Metro Broadcasting* were revisited by the Court in 1995 when it decided a case involving federal agency contracts that gave prime contractors a financial incentive to hire subcontractors who are black, Hispanic, or belong to other minorities. Split 5 to 4, the Court ruled that federal race-based policies must now satisfy the same judicial standard—"strict scrutiny"—applied to state and local programs. Such programs must serve a compelling governmental interest and be narrowly tailored to address identifiable past discrimination. Writing for the Court, Justice O'Connor said that the Constitution protects "*persons,* not *groups.*" To the extent that *Fullilove* and *Metro Broadcasting* are inconsistent with the Court's new standard, they are overruled. The decision required federal courts, Congress, and federal agencies to reassess affirmative action programs. ADARAND CONSTRUCTORS, INC. v. PENA, 515 U.S. 200 (1995).

On July 19, 1995, President Clinton summarized his administration's five-month review of federal affirmative action programs. Acknowledging problems in some programs, such as set-asides, he concluded: "We should reaffirm the principle of affirmative action and fix the practices. We should have a simple slogan: Mend it, but don't end it." Public Papers of the Presidents, 1995, II, at 1113. On the same day he issued a memorandum to departments and agencies, stating that policy principles must be eliminated or reformed if they (1) create a quota, (2) create preferences for unqualified individuals, (3) create reverse discrimination, or (4) continue even after its equal opportunity purposes have been achieved. Id. at 1114. In 1996, the Clinton administration announced a three-year moratorium on set-aside programs for minority and women-owned companies. Nevertheless, the administration said it would allow federal agencies, if they can justify it, to use other kinds of preferences, such as giving price breaks and extra points in evaluating contract bids by minority and female-headed firms. The moratorium was later reduced to two years.

Trying to Implement *Adarand*

The impact of *Adarand* is still unclear. In deciding the case, the Court remanded it for further proceedings consistent with the Court's opinion. The matter ended up with a district court judge, who ruled in 1997 that the highway project at issue satisfied the compelling governmental interest test of strict scrutiny but was not narrowly tailored. Adarand Constructors, Inc. v. Pena, 965 F.Supp. 1556 (D. Colo. 1997). The Clinton administration appealed that decision to the Tenth Circuit, which ruled that Colorado's certification of Adarand as a DBE (disadvantaged business enterprise) mooted its constitutional challenge to federal subcontractor preferences. Rocked by the litigation, Colorado had modified its DBE regulations to eliminate the automatic presumption of social and economic disadvantage for racial and ethnic minorities. The sole inquiry would be whether the head of a company was *socially* disadvantaged. Adarand Constructors, Inc. v. Slater, 169 F.3d 1292 (10th Cir. 1999). Under this modified regulation, Adarand (headed by a white male) was certified as a DBE.

The story kept going. The Supreme Court in 2000 held that Colorado's certification of Adarand as a DBE did *not* moot the case. The Tenth Circuit's decision was therefore reversed and remanded. Adarand Constructors, Inc. v. Slater, 528 U.S. 216 (2000). The Tenth Circuit then held that, by virtue of DBE's revised regulatory framework, the program passed constitutional muster. Adarand Constructors, Inc. v. Slater, 228 F.3d 1147 (10th Cir. 2000). The Supreme Court granted cert, but—because of changes in the posture of the case—later dismissed the writ of cert as improvidently granted. Adarand Constructors, Inc. v. Mineta, 534 U.S. 103 (2001). Not to be lost sight of in these multiple decisions is that Colorado was pressured to change its regulation to remove the preferences for racial and ethnic minorities.

Another potentially hot issue was headed to the Supreme Court in 1997, involving a white schoolteacher who was laid off by a Piscataway, N.J., school board that wanted to preserve the job of a black teacher. Had the Court decided the case, it would have likely overruled the decision as in violation of *Wygant* and might have announced other standards restrictive of affirmative action. Before the Court could decide, however, the parties settled out of court. A black civil rights group put up about 70 percent of the $433,500 needed to pay the white teacher's back salary and legal bills. She had already been rehired by the school.

Civil Rights Act of 1991

After Anthony Kennedy replaced Lewis Powell in 1988, the Court began to backtrack from its previous positions on civil rights. This pattern became pronounced during the spring of 1989, when the Court issued a series of stunning rulings. One decision shifted the burden to employees to prove that racial disparities in the work force result from employment practices and are not justified by business needs. This new test conflicted with the *Griggs* ruling in 1971, which appeared to require an employee to demonstrate disparate results, not intent. Wards Cove Packing Co. v. Atonio, 490 U.S. 642 (1989). Since this decision was a statutory interpretation of Title VII, Congress could rewrite the statute and overturn the Court.

Another decision limited the reach of a civil rights statute passed in 1866, codified at 42 U.S.C. § 1981. The law gives blacks the same right to "make and enforce contracts" as whites. Brenda Patterson, a black woman, claimed that her employer had harassed her, withheld promotion, and discharged her for reasons of race. The Court decided that Section 1981 is limited to prohibiting discriminatory actions *before* someone is hired, not after, and advised Patterson that she should have acted under Title VII. Patterson v. McLean Credit Union, 491 U.S. 164 (1989). Although Title VII is not a full substitute for Section 1981, nothing prevented Congress from changing this statute to prohibit racial harassment on the job.

A third decision gave white men new authority to challenge consent decrees that embody court-approved affirmative action plans. To avoid future challenges, consent decrees had to reach out to all groups that might be affected. Martin v. Wilks, 490 U.S. 755 (1989). Since the Court decided the case by interpreting the Federal Rules of Civil Procedure, Congress could enter the fray and reverse the Court. Also during the spring of 1989 the Court handed down two other rulings restrictive of Title VII rights: Independent Fed. of Flight Attendants v. Zipes, 491 U.S. 754 (1989), and Lorance v. AT&T Technologies, Inc., 490 U.S. 900 (1989).

The Civil Rights Act of 1991 reversed or modified nine Court rulings dealing with employment discrimination: (1) *Wards Cove Packing Co.* v. *Atonio* (by returning to the employer the burden of proving that a discriminatory practice is a business necessity); (2) *Patterson* v. *McLean Credit Union* (by prohibiting discrimination on the job); (3) *Martin* v. *Wilks* (by providing notice to interested non-parties and giving them an opportunity to be heard when a consent decree is proposed); (4) *Lorance* v. *AT&T Technologies, Inc.* (by allowing challenges to a discriminatory action when a person is actually harmed); (5) *Price Waterhouse* v. *Hopkins* (once a plaintiff proves that race, color, religion, national origin, or sex was a "motivating factor" in an employer's decision, the employer is liable for a Title VII violation); (6) *EEOC* v. *Aramco* (by protecting from federal job discrimination U.S. citizens working for American companies abroad); (7) *West Virginia University Hospitals* v. *Casey* (by reversing this 1991 decision that denied successful civil rights plaintiffs the right to recover the costs of hiring expert witnesses); (8) *Crawford Fitting Co.* v. *J.T. Gibbons* (a 1987 case that also denied the costs of hiring expert witnesses); and (9) *Library of Congress* v. *Shaw* (by allowing parties in bias cases against the federal government to recover interest to compensate for delays in obtaining payment).

The most controversial change was the response to *Wards Cove*. Critics claimed that shifting the burden to employers would force them to adopt racial quotas, a charge that supporters of the bill denied. The administration endorsed portions of the bill (the response to *Patterson* and *Lorance*), but President Bush vetoed the bill in 1990 and Congress failed to override. Congress revised the bill slightly in 1991. Bush, facing a probable override, signed it.

In passing the Civil Rights Act of 1991, Congress equivocated on whether it would be retroactive. Parts of the legislative history said yes; others said no. In two rulings decided in 1994, the Supreme Court held that the statute did not apply to complaints that were pending at the time the statute was enacted. Landgraf v. USI Film Products, 511 U.S. 244 (1994); Rivers v. Roadway Exp. Inc., 511 U.S. 298 (1994).

State Initiatives

Affirmative action programs were attacked in court in a number of states, including California, Texas, Georgia, and Michigan (see box on next page). Following California's lead, the state of Washington passed a referendum in 1998 banning preferential treatment on the basis of race, sex, color, ethnicity, or national origin. In 2000, the Ninth Circuit ruled that race may be considered in admissions decisions at the University of Washington law school. The Supreme Court declined to review that decision. Smith v. University of Washington Law School, 233 F.3d 1188 (9th Cir. 2000), cert. denied, 532 U.S. 1051 (2001). The Florida legislature passed anti-affirmative action legislation in 2000, as part of Governor Jeb Bush's "One Florida" initiative. In 2008 two states, Nebraska and Colorado, had anti-affirmative action initiatives on the ballot. The initiative passed in Nebraska but failed in Colorado.

Bilingual Education

In other state initiatives, California voters in 1998 supported Proposition 227 to end bilingual education. Immigrant students would receive one year of English immersion before moving into regular

Challenges from the States

At the state level, a number of governmental programs that gave preferences to race and gender were openly and often successfully challenged:

California. In 1996, the citizens of California passed a state constitutional amendment that banned affirmative action in public employment, public education, or public contracting. After a federal district judge issued an injunction to prevent state officials from implementing the amendment, that decision was reversed on appeal. In a bow to the force of public opinion, the Ninth Circuit remarked: "A system which permits one judge to block with the stroke of a pen what 4,736,180 state residents voted to enact as law tests the integrity of our constitutional democracy." Coalition for Economic Equity v. Wilson, 110 F.3d 1431, 1437 (9th Cir. 1997). After the 9th Circuit refused to rehear the case en banc, the Supreme Court denied cert. 122 F.3d 692 (9th Cir. 1997), cert. denied, 522 U.S. 963 (1997). Statistics released in 2002 indicate that the University of California system is admitting more minority students than it did in the days of race-based admissions policies.

Texas. Cheryl J. Hopwood, a white female, along with three white males, sued the University of Texas School of Law for its affirmative action admissions program. They said the law school discriminated against them by using a system of "targets" to favor less qualified black and Mexican American applicants. A federal district court held that the program, though needed to achieve compelling governmental interests, was not narrowly tailored. Hopwood v. State of Tex., 861 F.Supp. 551 (W.D. Tex. 1994). On appeal, the Fifth Circuit agreed that the admissions program — by using racial preferences to discriminate in favor of minority applicants — violated the Equal Protection Clause because the law school had presented no compelling justification for the program. The appellate court ruled that the law school "may not use race as a factor in law school admissions."

Hopwood v. State of Tex., 78 F.3d 932, 935 (5th Cir. 1996), cert. denied, 518 U.S. 1033 (1996).

After the Fifth Circuit's decision, the Texas legislature adopted an alternative plan that granted automatic admission to the flagship public colleges to all state high school students who graduated in the top 10 percent of their classes. Although the plan did not mention race, it has increased the number of blacks, Hispanics, and other minorities who are now enrolled in the Texas university system. A similar plan has been adopted by Florida, which in 2000 abolished affirmative action in favor of guaranteeing a spot in one of ten state universities to Florida high school students who rank in the top 20 percent of their class and complete a college preparatory curriculum. California, moving in the same direction as Texas and Florida, guaranteed provisional admission to the top 12.5 percent of students at every high school, provided that they take a college preparatory curriculum. These fixed-percentage solutions are criticized for overlooking the different quality of students who graduate from more demanding high schools.

Georgia. Jennifer L. Johnson and two other white females sued the University of Georgia because its admissions policy gave bonus points to nonwhite applicants. In 2001, the Eleventh Circuit ruled that the university policy was unconstitutional. It concluded that race was not the only, or best, criterion for assuring a diverse student body. Johnson v. University of Georgia, 263 F.3d 1234 (11th Cir. 2001).

Michigan. Jennifer Gratz, a white applicant to the University of Michigan's undergraduate program, sued the school in 1997 to challenge its admission policy. Her challenge reached the Supreme Court in 2003, which allowed race to be a factor in law school admissions at the University of Michigan but found invalid the affirmative action policy in the undergraduate program (see subsection "The Michigan Cases of 2003").

---

classes unless their parents obtained a waiver. Progress varies from one school district to the next. The transition to full English was expected to take several years to accomplish. There have also been initiatives in Arizona, Colorado, and Massachusetts to halt bilingual education.

In 2002, the Ninth Circuit upheld California's initiative, concluding that the replacement of bilingual education with English-only instruction was motivated by education reform, not racial animus.

The reform did not violate the Equal Protection Clause. Valeria v. Davis, 307 F.3d 1036 (9th Cir. 2002). A petition for panel rehearing was denied. Valeria v. Davis, 320 F.3d 1014 (9th Cir. 2003).

The Michigan Cases of 2003

Jennifer Gratz, a white applicant to the University of Michigan undergraduate program, sued the university when she was not accepted. She graduated from high school with a 3.765 grade point average and was student council leader, a math tutor, an aide to senior citizens, and a homecoming queen. She was denied entry while minorities with lower grades and fewer extracurricular activities were accepted. In response to her lawsuit the university eliminated a two-tiered admission procedure that operated as an impermissible quota system. However, relying on *Bakke*, the university adopted a new policy that gave minority applicants 20 points towards a 150-point maximum. The new system was upheld by a federal district court in 2000. Gratz v. Bollinger, 122 F.Supp.2d 811 (E.D. Mich. 2000). After a different district court held unconstitutional a race-conscious admissions system at the University of Michigan's law school in 2001, that decision was overturned by the Sixth Circuit, which argued that a race-conscious system was needed to produce a "critical mass" of minority students. Grutter v. Bollinger, 288 F.3d 732 (6th Cir. 2002).

These cases were decided by the Supreme Court in 2003. A 5 to 4 opinion upheld the Michigan law school approach, but a 6 to 3 majority rejected the affirmative action program adopted by the undergraduate school. Relying on *Adarand*'s strict-scrutiny analysis, the Court found that giving members of "unrepresented" groups an automatic 20 points was not narrowly tailored. GRATZ v. BOLLINGER, 539 U.S. 244 (2003). The law school admission policy tried to avoid this quantitative stigma. It focused on a student's academic ability coupled with an assessment of talent, experience, potential, letters of recommendation, and the applicant's essay that described how acceptance would contribute to the life and diversity of the law school. The school's commitment to diversity made special reference to blacks, Hispanics, and Native Americans, with a goal of enrolling a "critical mass" of underrepresented minority students. The school did not quantify critical mass in terms of numbers of percentages, which would have produced a quota system unacceptable to the Court, but the dissenters regarded the school's record of achieving numerical goals as indistinguishable from quotas.

Barbara Grutter, a white Michigan resident with a 3.8 GPA and 161 LSAT score, brought the case against the law school after being denied admission. The Court held that the school adopted a narrowly tailored approach to further a compelling interest, and that student body diversity promoted the educational experience and offered important opportunities for future leaders in public and private life. GRUTTER v. BOLLINGER, 539 U.S. 306 (2003). The 5–4 decision underscored the difficulty of applying *Bakke*. Justices on both sides, however, expressed the belief that race-conscious admission policies should have no place in national policy after 25 years. Three years later, Michigan voters rejected the use of affirmative action in public colleges and government contracting in a 2006 ballot initiative.

In 2012, the Supreme Court agreed to hear a case arising out of a challenge to the admission's practices of the University of Texas at Austin. The University followed the race-neutral statewide policy of admitting students who finished in the top 10% of their high school class (see box). In addition, it has a complicated system for reviewing the applications of those who don't make the automatic cut-off, where race is considered as a factor but is not given a quantified weight. Abigail Fisher, a white student who failed to make the 10% cut-off sued the school in 2008, arguing that the state was not permitted to supplement its race neutral process with one that took race into account. A federal district court and the Fifth Circuit ruled for the state, finding the practice within the allowable limits set by *Grutter*. Fisher v. University of Texas at Austin, 645 F.Supp. 2d 587 (W.D. Tex. 2009); 631 F.3d 213 (5th Cir. 2011). With Justice O'Connor having been replaced with Justice Alito since the 5–4 *Grutter* decision was made, many legal scholars believe that the *Grutter* rule will be overturned much sooner than the 25 years Justice O'Connor suggested in her opinion in that case.

Regents of the University of California v. Bakke

438 U.S. 265 (1978)

Allan Bakke, a white applicant to the medical school at the University of California at Davis, was twice rejected by the regular admissions program. "Disadvantaged" applicants from minority groups (blacks, Chicanos, Asians, and American Indians) were screened by a special admissions program. Although some of these minorities had lower grade point averages from undergraduate school and scored lower on the medical admissions test, they were accepted to fill 16 out of 100 openings for first-year students. The California Supreme Court, while agreeing that increasing the number of minorities in the medical profession was a compelling state interest, concluded that the special admissions program was not the least intrusive means of achieving that goal. It held that the Equal Protection Clause of the Fourteenth Amendment required that "no applicant may be rejected because of his race, in favor of another who is less qualified, as measured by standards applied without regard to race." When the University conceded its inability to prove that Bakke would not have been admitted even in the absence of a special admissions program, the California court directed that Bakke be admitted. That order was stayed pending review by the Supreme Court. "Petitioner" in this case is the University of California; the "respondent" is Bakke.

MR. JUSTICE POWELL announced the judgment of the Court....

For the reasons stated in the following opinion, I believe that so much of the judgment of the California court as holds petitioner's special admissions program unlawful and directs that respondent be admitted to the Medical School must be affirmed. For the reasons expressed in a separate opinion, my Brothers THE CHIEF JUSTICE, MR. JUSTICE STEWART, MR. JUSTICE REHNQUIST, and MR. JUSTICE STEVENS concur in this judgment.

I also conclude for the reasons stated in the following opinion that the portion of the court's judgment enjoining petitioner from according any consideration to race in its admissions process must be reversed. For reasons expressed in separate opinions, my Brothers MR. JUSTICE BRENNAN, MR. JUSTICE WHITE, MR. JUSTICE MARSHALL, and MR. JUSTICE BLACKMUN concur in this judgment.

Affirmed in part and reversed in part.

I

The Medical School of the University of California at Davis opened in 1968 with an entering class of 50 students. In 1971, the size of the entering class was increased to 100 students, a level at which it remains. No admissions program for disadvantaged or minority students existed when the school opened, and the first class contained three Asians but no blacks, no Mexican-Americans, and no American Indians. Over the next two years, the faculty devised a special admissions program to increase the representation of "disadvantaged" students in each Med-

ical School class. The special program consisted of a separate admissions system operating in coordination with the regular admissions process.

Under the regular admissions procedure, a candidate could submit his application to the Medical School beginning in July of the year preceding the academic year for which admission was sought.... Because of the large number of applications, the admissions committee screened each one to select candidates for further consideration. Candidates whose overall undergraduate grade point averages fell below 2.5 on a scale of 4.0 were summarily rejected.... About one out of six applicants was invited for a personal interview.... Following the interviews, each candidate was rated on a scale of 1 to 100 by his interviewers and four other members of the admissions committee. The rating embraced the interviewers' summaries, the candidate's overall grade point average, grade point average in science courses, scores on the Medical College Admissions Test (MCAT), letters of recommendation, extracurricular activities, and other biographical data.... The ratings were added together to arrive at each candidate's "benchmark" score. Since five committee members rated each candidate in 1973, a perfect score was 500; in 1974, six members rated each candidate, so that a perfect score was 600. The full committee then reviewed the file and scores of each applicant and made offers of admission on a "rolling" basis. The chairman was responsible for placing names on the waiting list. They were not placed in strict numerical order; instead, the chairman had discretion to include persons with "special skills." ...

The special admissions program operated with a

separate committee, a majority of whom were members of minority groups.... On the 1973 application form, candidates were asked to indicate whether they wished to be considered as "economically and/or educationally disadvantaged" applicants; on the 1974 form the question was whether they wished to be considered as members of a "minority group," which the Medical School apparently viewed as "Blacks," "Chicanos," "Asians," and "American Indians." ... If these questions were answered affirmatively, the application was forwarded to the special admissions committee. No formal definition of "disadvantaged" was ever produced, ... but the chairman of the special committee screened each application to see whether it reflected economic or educational deprivation.... [S]pecial candidates did not have to meet the 2.5 grade point average cutoff applied to regular applicants....

From the year of the increase in class size—1971—through 1974, the special program resulted in the admission of 21 black students, 30 Mexican-Americans, and 12 Asians, for a total of 63 minority students. Over the same period, the regular admissions program produced 1 black, 6 Mexican-Americans, and 37 Asians, for a total of 44 minority students. Although disadvantaged whites applied to the special program in large numbers, ... none received an offer of admission through that process. Indeed, in 1974, at least, the special committee explicitly considered only "disadvantaged" special applicants who were members of one of the designated minority groups....

Allan Bakke is a white male who applied to the Davis Medical School in both 1973 and 1974. In both years Bakke's application was considered under the general admissions program, and he received an interview.... Despite a strong benchmark score of 468 out of 500, Bakke was rejected. His application had come late in the year, and no applicants in the general admissions process with scores below 470 were accepted after Bakke's application was completed.

[*Bakke was also rejected in 1974, after scoring 549 out of 600. In both years, applicants were admitted under the special program with grade point averages, MCAT scores, and benchmark scores significantly lower than Bakke's.*]

[III.B]

Petitioner urges us to adopt for the first time a more restrictive view of the Equal Protection Clause and hold that discrimination against members of the white "majority" cannot be suspect if its purpose can be characterized as "benign." The clock of our liberties, however, cannot be turned back to 1868.... It is far too late to argue that the guarantee of equal protection to *all* persons permits the recognition of special wards entitled to a degree of protection greater than that accorded others....

Once the artificial line of a "two-class theory" of the Fourteenth Amendment is put aside, the difficulties entailed in varying the level of judicial review according to a perceived "preferred" status of a particular racial or ethnic minority are intractable. The concepts of "majority" and "minority" necessarily reflect temporary arrangements and political judgments. As observed above, the white "majority" itself is composed of various minority groups, most of which can lay claim to a history of prior discrimination at the hands of the State and private individuals. Not all of these groups can receive preferential treatment and corresponding judicial tolerance of distinctions drawn in terms of race and nationality, for then the only "majority" left would be a new minority of white Anglo-Saxon Protestants. There is no principled basis for deciding which groups would merit "heightened judicial solicitude" and which would not. Courts would be asked to evaluate the extent of the prejudice and consequent harm suffered by various minority groups.... The kind of variable sociological and political analysis necessary to produce such rankings simply does not lie within the judicial competence—even if they otherwise were politically feasible and socially desirable....

[V.A]

It has been suggested that an admissions program which considers race only as one factor is simply a subtle and more sophisticated—but no less effective—means of according racial preference than the Davis program. A facial intent to discriminate, however, is evident in petitioner's preference program and not denied in this case. No such facial infirmity exists in an admissions program where race or ethnic background is simply one element—to be weighed fairly against other elements—in the selection process....

B

In summary, it is evident that the Davis special admissions program involves the use of an explicit racial classification never before countenanced by this Court. It tells applicants who are not Negro, Asian, or Chicano that they are totally excluded from a specific percentage of the seats in an entering class. No matter how strong their qualifications, quantitative and extracurricular, including their own potential for contribution to educational diversity, they are never afforded the chance to compete with applicants from the preferred groups for the special admissions seats. At the same time, the preferred applicants have the opportunity to compete for every seat in the class.

... [W]hen a State's distribution of benefits or imposition of burdens hinges on ancestry or the color of a person's skin, that individual is entitled to a demonstration that the challenged classification is necessary to promote a substantial state interest. Petitioner has failed to carry this burden. For this reason, that portion of the California court's judgment holding petitioner's special admissions program invalid under the Fourteenth Amendment must be affirmed.

C

In enjoining petitioner from ever considering the race of any applicant, however, the courts below failed to recognize that the State has a substantial interest that legitimately may be served by a properly devised admissions program involving the competitive consideration of race and ethnic origin. For this reason, so much of the California court's judgment as enjoins petitioner from any consideration of the race of any applicant must be reversed.

VI

With respect to respondent's entitlement to an injunction directing his admission to the Medical School, petitioner has conceded that it could not carry its burden of proving that, but for the existence of its unlawful special admissions program, respondent still would not have been admitted. Hence, respondent is entitled to the injunction, and that portion of the judgment must be affirmed....

Opinion of MR. JUSTICE BRENNAN, MR. JUSTICE WHITE, MR. JUSTICE MARSHALL, and MR. JUSTICE BLACKMUN, concurring in the judgment in part and dissenting in part.

The Court today, in reversing in part the judgment of the Supreme Court of California, affirms the constitutional power of Federal and State Governments to act affirmatively to achieve equal opportunity for all. The difficulty of the issue presented — whether government may use race-conscious programs to redress the continuing effects of past discrimination — and the mature consideration which each of our Brethren has brought to it have resulted in many opinions, no single one speaking for the Court. But this should not and must not mask the central meaning of today's opinions: Government may take race into account when it acts not to demean or insult any racial group, but

to remedy disadvantages cast on minorities by past racial prejudice, at least when appropriate findings have been made by judicial, legislative, or administrative bodies with competence to act in this area....

MR. JUSTICE WHITE....

MR. JUSTICE MARSHALL.

I agree with the judgment of the Court only insofar as it permits a university to consider the race of an applicant in making admissions decisions. I do not agree that petitioner's admissions program violates the Constitution. For it must be remembered that, during most of the past 200 years, the Constitution as interpreted by this Court did not prohibit the most ingenious and pervasive forms of discrimination against the Negro. Now, when a State acts to remedy the effects of that legacy of discrimination, I cannot believe that this same Constitution stands as a barrier....

[III.A]

It is plain that the Fourteenth Amendment was not intended to prohibit measures designed to remedy the effects of the Nation's past treatment of Negroes. The Congress that passed the Fourteenth Amendment is the same Congress that passed the 1866 Freedmen's Bureau Act, an Act that provided many of its benefits only to Negroes....

MR. JUSTICE BLACKMUN....

I yield to no one in my earnest hope that the time will come when an "affirmative action" program is unnecessary and is, in truth, only a relic of the past. I would hope that we could reach this stage within a decade at the most. But the story of *Brown* v. *Board of Education,* 347 U.S. 483 (1954), decided almost a quarter of a century ago, suggests that that hope is a slim one....

[II]

It is worth noting, perhaps, that governmental preference has not been a stranger to our legal life. We see it in veterans' preferences. We see it in the aid-to-the-handicapped programs. We see it in the progressive income tax. We see it in the Indian programs.... [I]n the admissions field ... educational institutions have always used geography, athletic ability, anticipated financial largess, alumni pressure, and other factors of that kind.

... In order to get beyond racism, we must first take account of race. There is no other way. And in order to treat some persons equally, we must treat them differently....

Mr. Justice Stevens, with whom The Chief Justice, Mr. Justice Stewart, and Mr. Justice Rehnquist join, concurring in the judgment in part and dissenting in part....

III

Section 601 of the Civil Rights Act of 1964, 78 Stat. 252, 42 U.S.C. § 2000d, provides:

"No person in the United States shall, on the ground of race, color, or national origin, be excluded from participation in, be denied the benefits of, or be subjected to discrimination under any program or activity receiving Federal financial assistance."

The University, through its special admissions policy, excluded Bakke from participation in its program of medical education because of his race. The University also acknowledges that it was, and still is, receiving federal financial assistance. The plain language of the statute therefore requires affirmance of the judgment below....

Fullilove v. Klutznick

448 U.S. 448 (1980)

Congress passed legislation in 1977 providing that at least 10 percent of federal funds granted for local public works projects must be used to obtain services or supplies from businesses owned by minority groups, defined as United States citizens "who are Negroes, Spanish-speaking, Orientals, Indians, Eskimos, and Aleuts." H. Earl Fullilove and several associations of construction contractors and subcontractors filed suit for declaratory and injunctive relief in federal district court, alleging that they had sustained economic injury due to enforcement of the statute. They claimed that the provision for minority businesses violated, on its face, the Equal Protection Clause of the Fourteenth Amendment and the equal protection component of the Due Process Clause of the Fifth Amendment. The district court upheld the statute; the Second Circuit affirmed. Defending the statute was Philip M. Klutznick, Secretary of Commerce.

Mr. Chief Justice Burger announced the judgment of the Court and delivered an opinion, in which Mr. Justice White and Mr. Justice Powell joined.

We granted certiorari to consider a facial constitutional challenge to a requirement in a congressional spending program that, absent an administrative waiver, 10% of the federal funds granted for local public works projects must be used by the state or local grantee to procure services or supplies from businesses owned and controlled by members of statutorily identified minority groups. 441 U.S. 960 (1979).

I

In May 1977, Congress enacted the Public Works Employment Act of 1977, ... The 1977 amendments authorized an additional $4 billion appropriation for federal grants to be made by the Secretary of Commerce, acting through the Economic Development Administration (EDA), to state and local governmental entities for use in local public works projects. Among the changes made was the addition of the provision that has become the focus of this liti-

gation. Section 103 (f)(2) of the 1977 Act, referred to as the "minority business enterprise" or "MBE" provision, requires that:

"Except to the extent that the Secretary determines otherwise, no grant shall be made under this Act for any local public works project unless the applicant gives satisfactory assurance to the Secretary that at least 10 per centum of the amount of each grant shall be expended for minority business enterprises. For purposes of this paragraph, the term 'minority business enterprise' means a business at least 50 per centum of which is owned by minority group members or, in case of a publicly owned business, at least 51 per centum of the stock of which is owned by minority group members. For the purposes of the preceding sentence, minority group members are citizens of the United States who are Negroes, Spanish-speaking, Orientals, Indians, Eskimos, and Aleuts."

[The Secretary promulgated regulations to implement the grant program and the EDA issued supplementary guidelines. A district court and the Second Circuit upheld the statute against constitutional challenge on equal protection grounds.]

II

A

[*The 10 percent provision for minorities originated as an amendment in the House of Representatives, where it was argued that in fiscal year 1976 less than 1 percent of all federal procurement was concluded with minority business enterprises, although minorities comprised 15 to 18 percent of the population. It was also stated that the concept of a set-aside for minorities had been used for ten years in the Small Business Administration. The House Committee on Small Business issued a lengthy report pointing out discriminatory practices against minorities in the economy. Minorities had difficulties gaining access to government contracting opportunities at the federal, state, and local levels. The Senate adopted the amendment, slightly modified, without debate.*]

III

... A program that employs racial or ethnic criteria, even in a remedial context, calls for close examination; yet we are bound to approach our task with appropriate deference to the Congress, a co-equal branch charged by the Constitution with the power to "provide for the ... general Welfare of the United States" and "to enforce, by appropriate legislation," the equal protection guarantees of the Fourteenth Amendment....

A(1)

In enacting the MBE provision, it is clear that Congress employed an amalgam of its specifically delegated powers. The Public Works Employment Act of 1977, by its very nature, is primarily an exercise of the Spending Power. U.S. Const., Art. I, § 8, cl. 1. This Court has recognized that the power to "provide for the ... general Welfare" is an independent grant of legislative authority, distinct from other broad congressional powers.... Congress has frequently employed the Spending Power to further broad policy objectives by conditioning receipt of federal moneys upon compliance by the recipient with federal statutory and administrative directives. This Court has repeatedly upheld against constitutional challenge the use of this technique to induce governments and private parties to cooperate voluntarily with federal policy....

(2)

We turn first to the Commerce Power. U.S. Const., Art. I, § 8, cl. 3. Had Congress chosen to do so, it could have drawn on the Commerce Clause to regulate the practices of prime contractors on federally funded public works projects.... The legislative history of the MBE provision shows that there was a rational basis for Congress to conclude that the subcontracting practices of prime contractors could perpetuate the prevailing impaired access by minority businesses to public contracting opportunities, and that this inequity has an effect on interstate commerce. Thus Congress could take necessary and proper action to remedy the situation....

(3)

In certain contexts, there are limitations on the reach of the Commerce Power to regulate the actions of state and local governments.... To avoid such complications, we look to § 5 of the Fourteenth Amendment for the power to regulate the procurement practices of state and local grantees of federal funds.... A review of our cases persuades us that the objectives of the MBE program are within the power of Congress under § 5 "to enforce, by appropriate legislation," the equal protection guarantees of the Fourteenth Amendment.

... Congress had abundant evidence from which it could conclude that minority businesses have been denied effective participation in public contracting opportunities by procurement practices that perpetuated the effects of prior discrimination....

B

We now turn to the question whether, as a *means* to accomplish these plainly constitutional objectives, Congress may use racial and ethnic criteria, in this limited way, as a condition attached to a federal grant....

Here we deal ... not with the limited remedial powers of a federal court, for example, but with the broad remedial powers of Congress. It is fundamental that in no organ of government, state or federal, does there repose a more comprehensive remedial power than in the Congress, expressly charged by the Constitution with competence and authority to enforce equal protection guarantees. Congress not only may induce voluntary action to assure compliance with existing federal statutory or constitutional antidiscrimination provisions, but also, where Congress has authority to declare certain conduct unlawful, it may, as here, authorize and induce state action to avoid such conduct....

IV

Congress, after due consideration, perceived a pressing need to move forward with new approaches in the continuing effort to achieve the goal of equality of economic opportunity.... That the program may press the outer limits of congressional authority affords no basis for striking it down....

... The MBE provision of the Public Works Employment Act of 1977 does not violate the Constitution.

Affirmed.

MR. JUSTICE POWELL, concurring....

MR. JUSTICE MARSHALL, with whom MR. JUSTICE BRENNAN and MR. JUSTICE BLACKMUN join, concurring in the judgment....

MR. JUSTICE STEWART, with whom MR. JUSTICE REHNQUIST joins, dissenting.

"Our Constitution is color-blind, and neither knows nor tolerates classes among citizens.... The law regards man as man, and takes no account of his surroundings or of his color...." Those words were written by a Member of this Court 84 years ago. *Plessy* v. *Ferguson,* 163 U. S. 537, 559 (Harlan, J., dissenting). His colleagues disagreed with him, and held that a statute that required the separation of people on the basis of their race was constitutionally valid because it was a "reasonable" exercise of legislative power and had been "enacted in good faith for the promotion [of] the public good...." ... Today, the Court upholds a statute that accords a preference to citizens who are "Negroes, Spanish-speaking, Orientals, Indians, Eskimos, and Aleuts," for much the same reasons. I think today's decision is wrong for the same reason that *Plessy* v. *Ferguson* was wrong, and I respectfully dissent....

MR. JUSTICE STEVENS, dissenting....

Even if we assume that each of the six racial subclasses has suffered its own special injury at some time in our history, surely it does not necessarily follow that each of those subclasses suffered harm of identical magnitude. Although "the Negro was dragged to this country in chains to be sold in slavery," *Bakke, supra,* at 387 (opinion of MARSHALL, J.), the "Spanish-speaking" subclass came voluntarily, frequently without invitation, ...

Richmond v. Croson Co.

488 U.S. 469 (1989)

Following the precedent established by Congress and upheld by the Court in *Fullilove*, the city of Richmond, Virginia, adopted a Minority Business Utilization Plan requiring prime contractors of city construction contracts to subcontract at least 30 percent of the dollar amount of each contract to one or more "Minority Business Enterprises" (MBEs). The Plan defined an MBE as a business from anywhere in the country at least 51 percent of which is owned and controlled by black, Spanish-speaking, Oriental, Indian, Eskimo, or Aleut citizens. The issue here is whether the city could identify evidence and legal justification to refute the claim by a firm, J.A. Croson Company, that there had been discrimination in violation of the Equal Protection Clause.

JUSTICE O'CONNOR announced the judgment of the Court and delivered the opinion of the Court with respect to Parts I, III-B, and IV, an opinion with respect to Part II, in which THE CHIEF JUSTICE and JUSTICE WHITE join, and an opinion with respect to Parts III-A and V, in which THE CHIEF JUSTICE, JUSTICE WHITE, and JUSTICE KENNEDY join.

In this case, we confront once again the tension between the Fourteenth Amendment's guarantee of equal treatment to all citizens, and the use of race-based measures to ameliorate the effects of past discrimination on the opportunities enjoyed by members of minority groups in our society....

What [*Richmond*] ignores is that Congress, unlike any State or political subdivision, has a specific constitutional mandate to enforce the dictates of the Fourteenth Amendment. The power to "enforce" may at times also include the power to define situations which *Congress* determines threaten principles of equality and to adopt prophylactic rules to deal with those situations.... The Civil War Amendments themselves worked a dramatic change in the balance between congressional and state power over matters of race....

That Congress may identify and redress the effects of society-wide discrimination does not mean that, *a fortiori*, the States and their political subdivisions are free to decide that such remedies are appropriate. Section 1 of the Fourteenth Amendment is an explicit *constraint* on state power, and the States must undertake any remedial efforts in accordance with that provision....

It would seem equally clear, however, that a state or local subdivision (if delegated the authority from the State) has the authority to eradicate the effects of private discrimination within its own legislative jurisdiction. This authority must, of course, be exercised within the constraints of § 1 of the Fourteenth Amendment.... As a matter of state law, the city of Richmond has legislative authority over its procurement policies, and can use its spending powers to remedy private discrimination, if it identifies that discrimination with the particularity required by the Fourteenth Amendment....

Thus, if the city could show that it had essentially become a "passive participant" in a system of racial exclusion practiced by elements of the local construction industry, we think it clear that the city could take affirmative steps to dismantle such a system. It is beyond dispute that any public entity, state or federal, has a compelling interest in assuring that public dollars, drawn from the tax contributions of all citizens, do not serve to finance the evil of private prejudice....

While there is no doubt that the sorry history of both private and public discrimination in this country has contributed to a lack of opportunities for black entrepreneurs, this observation, standing alone, cannot justify a rigid racial quota in the awarding of public contracts in Richmond, Virginia....

It is sheer speculation how many minority firms there would be in Richmond absent past societal discrimination, ...

These defects are readily apparent in this case. The 30% quota cannot in any realistic sense be tied to any injury suffered by anyone....

... [N]one of the evidence presented by the city points to any identified discrimination in the Richmond construction industry. We, therefore, hold that the city has failed to demonstrate a compelling interest in apportioning public contracting opportunities on the basis of race. To accept Richmond's claim that past societal discrimination alone can serve as the basis for rigid racial preferences would be to open the door to competing claims for "remedial relief" for every disadvantaged group....

The foregoing analysis applies only to the inclusion of blacks within the Richmond set-aside program. There is *absolutely no evidence* of past discrimination against Spanish-speaking, Oriental, Indian, Eskimo, or Aleut persons in any aspect of the Richmond construction industry. The District Court took judicial notice of the fact that the vast majority of "minority" persons in Richmond were black.... It may well be that Richmond has never had an Aleut or Eskimo citizen. The random inclusion of racial groups that, as a practical matter, may never have suffered from discrimination in the construction industry in Richmond suggests that perhaps the city's purpose was not in fact to remedy past discrimination.

If a 30% set-aside was "narrowly tailored" to compensate black contractors for past discrimination, one may legitimately ask why they are forced to share this "remedial relief" with an Aleut citizen who moves to Richmond tomorrow? The gross overinclusiveness of Richmond's racial preference strongly impugns the city's claim of remedial motivation....

V

Nothing we say today precludes a state or local entity from taking action to rectify the effects of identified discrimination within its jurisdiction. If the city of Richmond had evidence before it that nonminority contractors were systematically excluding minority businesses from subcontracting opportunities, it could take action to end the discriminatory exclusion....

[*Justices Stevens and Kennedy wrote separate opinions, concurring in part and concurring in the judgment.*]

JUSTICE SCALIA, concurring in the judgment.

I agree with much of the Court's opinion, and, in particular, with JUSTICE O'CONNOR's conclusion that strict scrutiny must be applied to all governmental classification by race, whether or not its asserted purpose is "remedial" or "benign." ... I do not agree, however, with JUSTICE O'CONNOR's dictum suggesting that, despite the Fourteenth Amendment, state and local governments may in some circumstances discriminate on the basis of race in order (in a broad sense) "to ameliorate the effects of past discrimination." ... The benign purpose of compensating for social disadvantages, whether they have been acquired by reason of prior discrimination or otherwise, can no more be pursued by the illegitimate means of racial discrimination than can other assertedly benign purposes we have repeatedly rejected....

JUSTICE MARSHALL, with whom JUSTICE BRENNAN and JUSTICE BLACKMUN join, dissenting....

JUSTICE BLACKMUN, with whom JUSTICE BRENNAN joins, dissenting....

Adarand Constructors, Inc. v. Pena

515 U.S. 200 (1995)

Federal agency contracts contain a subcontractor compensation clause, giving a prime contractor a financial incentive to hire subcontractors certified as small businesses controlled by socially and economically disadvantaged individuals, and require the contractor to presume that such individuals include minorities or any other individuals found to be disadvantaged by the Small Business Administration. The prime contractor in this case awarded a subcontract to a company that was certified as a small disadvantaged business. Adarand Constructors, Inc., submitted the low bid on the subcontract but was not a certified business. It filed this suit against Federico Pena, the Secretary of Transportation, claiming that the race-based presumptions used in these subcontractor clauses violated the equal protection component of the Fifth Amendment's Due Process Clause. The Tenth Circuit upheld the federal contracts under the lenient standard of Fullilove v. Klutznick (1980) and Metro Broadcasting, Inc. v. FCC (1990).

JUSTICE O'CONNOR announced the judgment of the Court and delivered an opinion with respect to Parts I, II, III-A, III-B, III-D, and IV, which is for the Court except insofar as it might be inconsistent with the views expressed in JUSTICE SCALIA's concurrence, and an opinion with respect to Part III-C in which JUSTICE KENNEDY joins.

Petitioner Adarand Constructors, Inc., claims that the Federal Government's practice of giving general contractors on Government projects a financial incentive to hire subcontractors controlled by "socially and economically disadvantaged individuals," and in particular, the Government's use of race-based presumptions in identifying such individuals, violates the equal protection component of the Fifth Amendment's Due Process Clause. The Court of Appeals rejected Adarand's claim. We conclude, however, that courts should analyze cases of this kind under a different standard of review than the one the Court of Appeals applied. We therefore vacate the Court of Appeals' judgment and remand the case for further proceedings.

I

In 1989, the Central Federal Lands Highway Division (CFLHD), which is part of the United States Department of Transportation (DOT), awarded the prime contract for a highway construction project in Colorado to Mountain Gravel & Construction Company. Mountain Gravel then solicited bids from subcontractors for the guardrail portion of the contract. Adarand, a Colorado-based highway construction company specializing in guardrail work, submitted the low bid. Gonzales Construction Company also submitted a bid.

The prime contract's terms provide that Mountain Gravel would receive additional compensation if it hired subcontractors certified as small businesses controlled by "socially and economically disadvantaged individuals," ... Gonzales is certified as such a business; Adarand is not. Mountain Gravel awarded the subcontract to Gonzales, despite Adarand's low bid, and Mountain Gravel's Chief Estimator has submitted an affidavit stating that Mountain Gravel would have accepted Adarand's bid, had it not been for the additional payment it received by hiring Gonzales instead.... Federal law requires that a subcontracting clause similar to the one used here must appear in most federal agency contracts, and it also requires the clause to state that "[t]he contractor shall presume that socially and economically disadvantaged individuals include Black Americans, Hispanic Americans, Native Americans, Asian Pacific Americans, and other minorities, or any other individual found to be disadvantaged by the [Small Business] Administration pursuant to section 8(a) of the Small Business Act." ... Adarand claims that the presumption set forth in that statute discriminates on the basis of race in violation of the Federal Government's Fifth Amendment obligation not to deny anyone equal protection of the laws.

[*Here the Court reviews the federal statutes and regulations that guide federal agencies in awarding contracts to small business and economically disadvantaged individuals. The dispute in this case arose from the Surface Transportation and Uniform Relocation Assistance Act of 1987, which contained a provision that "not less than 10 percent" of the appropriated funds "shall be expended with small business concerns owned and controlled by socially and economically disadvantaged individuals." The record does not reveal how Gonzales obtained its certification as a small dis-*]

advantaged business. In Section II of this decision, the Court concludes that Adarand has standing to bring this suit.]

III

Respondents urge that "[t]he Subcontracting Compensation Clause program is ... a program based on *disadvantage,* not on race," and thus that it is subject only to "the most relaxed judicial scrutiny." ... To the extent that the statutes and regulations involved in this case are race neutral, we agree. Respondents concede, however, that "the race-based rebuttable presumption used in some certification determinations under the Subcontracting Compensation Clause" is subject to some heightened level of scrutiny.... The parties disagree as to what that level should be....

B

[*This section reviews the inability of the Court, in decisions like* Bakke, Fullilove, *and* Wygant, *to produce a majority opinion on the level of scrutiny required for racial classifications. Repeatedly, the Court issued plurality opinions in debating the choice between strict scrutiny and less stringent standards.*]

With *Croson,* the Court finally agreed that the Fourteenth Amendment requires strict scrutiny of all race-based action by state and local governments. But *Croson* of course had no occasion to declare what standard of review the Fifth Amendment requires for such action taken by the Federal Government.... Thus, some uncertainty persisted with respect to the standard of review for federal racial classifications ...

Despite lingering uncertainty in the details, however, the Court's cases through *Croson* had established three general propositions with respect to governmental racial classifications. First, skepticism: "'Any preference based on racial or ethnic criteria must necessarily receive a most searching examination,'" *Wygant,* 476 U.S., at 273 (plurality opinion of Powell, J.);.... Second, consistency: "[T]he standard of review under the Equal Protection Clause is not dependent on the race of those burdened or benefited by a particular classification," *Croson,* 488 U.S., at 494 (plurality opinion); ... *i.e.,* all racial classifications reviewable under the Equal Protection Clause must be strictly scrutinized. And third, congruence: "Equal protection analysis in the Fifth Amendment area is the same as that under the Fourteenth Amendment," *Buckley* v. *Valeo,* 424 U.S., at 93;.... Taken together, these three propositions lead to the conclusion that any person, of whatever race, has the right to demand that any governmental actor

subject to the Constitution justify any racial classification subjecting that person to unequal treatment under the strictest judicial scrutiny....

[*The Court acknowledges in this section that Metro Broadcasting took "a surprising turn" by holding that "benign" federal racial classifications need only satisfy intermediate scrutiny, after Croson had decided that such classifications enacted by a state must satisfy strict scrutiny. Metro Broadcasting, said the Court, rejected the proposition of congruence and undermined the propositions of skepticism and consistency.*]

The three propositions undermined by *Metro Broadcasting* all derive from the basic principle that the Fifth and Fourteenth Amendments to the Constitution protect *persons,* not *groups,* It follows from that principle that all governmental action based on race—a *group* classification long recognized as "in most circumstances irrelevant and therefore prohibited," *Hirabayashi,* 320 U.S., at 100—should be subjected to detailed judicial inquiry to ensure that the *personal* right to equal protection of the laws has not been infringed.... Accordingly, we hold today that all racial classifications, imposed by whatever federal, state, or local governmental actor, must be analyzed by a reviewing court under strict scrutiny. In other words, such classifications are constitutional only if they are narrowly tailored measures that further compelling governmental interests. To the extent that *Metro Broadcasting* is inconsistent with that holding, it is overruled....

JUSTICE STEVENS ... claims that we have ignored any difference between federal and state legislatures. But requiring that Congress, like the States, enact racial classifications only when doing so is necessary to further a "compelling interest" does not contravene any principle of appropriate respect for a co-equal branch of the Government....

[D]

Finally, we wish to dispel the notion that strict scrutiny is "strict in theory, but fatal in fact." *Fullilove, supra,* at 519 (Marshall, J., concurring in judgment). The unhappy persistence of both the practice and the lingering effects of racial discrimination against minority groups in this country is an unfortunate reality, and government is not disqualified from acting in response to it.... When race-based action is necessary to further a compelling interest, such action is within constitutional constraints if it satisfies the "narrow tailoring" test this Court has set out in previous cases.

IV

Because our decision today alters the playing

field in some important respects, we think it best to remand the case to the lower courts for further consideration in light of the principles we have announced. The Court of Appeals, following *Metro Broadcasting* and *Fullilove,* analyzed the case in terms of intermediate scrutiny....

Accordingly, the judgment of the Court of Appeals is vacated, and the case is remanded for further proceedings consistent with this opinion.

It is so ordered.

Justice Scalia, concurring in part and concurring in the judgment.

I join the opinion of the Court, except Part III-C, and except insofar as it may be inconsistent with the following: In my view, government can never have a "compelling interest" in discriminating on the basis of race in order to "make up" for past racial discrimination in the opposite direction.... Individuals who have been wronged by unlawful racial discrimination should be made whole; but under our Constitution there can be no such thing as either a creditor or a debtor race. That concept is alien to the Constitution's focus upon the individual, see Amdt. 14, § 1 ("[N]or shall any State ... deny to *any person*" the equal protection of the laws) (emphasis added), ...

Justice Thomas, concurring in part and concurring in the judgment.

... So-called "benign" discrimination teaches many that because of chronic and apparently immutable handicaps, minorities cannot compete with them without their patronizing indulgence. Inevitably, such programs engender attitudes of superiority or, alternatively, provoke resentment among those who believe that they have been wronged by the government's use of race. These programs stamp minorities with a badge of inferiority and may cause them to develop dependencies or to adopt an attitude that they are "entitled" to preferences....

Justice Stevens, with whom Justice Ginsburg joins, dissenting....

Justice Souter, with whom Justice Ginsburg and Justice Breyer join, dissenting.

... I agree with Justice Stevens's conclusion that *stare decisis* compels the application of *Fullilove....*

Justice Ginsburg, with whom Justice Breyer joins, dissenting.

For the reasons stated by Justice Souter, and in view of the attention the political branches are currently giving the matter of affirmative action, I see no compelling cause for the intervention the Court has made in this case. I further agree with Justice Stevens that, in this area, large deference is owed by the Judiciary to "Congress' institutional competence and constitutional authority to overcome historic racial subjugation." ...

Gratz v. Bollinger

539 U.S. 244 (2003)

Jennifer Gratz was a Caucasian who was denied undergraduate admission to the University of Michigan. She sued the university under the Equal Protection Clause of the 14th Amendment, arguing that the admissions process discriminated on the basis of race. The admissions office used a "selection index" that allowed applicants to score a maximum of 150 points. Applicants receiving 100 or above on the index were admitted automatically. Points were awarded for GPA, standardized test scores, strength of the high-school curriculum, in-state residency, alumni relationship, personal essay, personal achievement, and leadership. In addition, applicants who were from underrepresented racial or ethnic minorities received 20 points. A federal district court upheld the admissions plan.

Chief Justice Rehnquist delivered the opinion of the Court....

II[B]

Petitioners ... contend that this Court has only sanctioned the use of racial classifications to rem-

edy identified discrimination, a justification on which respondents have never relied. Petitioners further argue that "diversity as a basis for employing racial preferences is simply too open-ended, ill-defined, and indefinite to constitute a compelling interest capable of supporting narrowly-tailored means." But for the reasons set forth today in *Grut-*

ter v. Bollinger, the Court has rejected these arguments of petitioners.

Petitioners alternatively argue that even if the University's interest in diversity can constitute a compelling state interest, the District Court erroneously concluded that the University's use of race in its current freshman admission policy is narrowly tailored to achieve such an interest. Petitioners argue that the guidelines the University began using in 1999 do not "remotely resemble the kind of consideration of race and ethnicity that Justice Powell endorsed in *Bakke*." ...

It is by now well established that "all racial classifications reviewable under the Equal Protection Clause must be strictly scrutinized." ... This "standard of review ... is not dependent on the race of those burdened or benefitted by a particular classification." ...

To withstand our strict scrutiny analysis, respondents must demonstrate that the University's use of race in its current admission program employs "narrowly tailored measures that further compelling governmental interests." ... We find that the University's policy, which automatically distributes 20 points, or one-fifth of the points needed to guarantee admission, to every single "underrepresented minority" applicant solely because of race, is not narrowly tailored to achieve the interest in educational diversity that respondents claim justifies this program....

Justice Powell's opinion in *Bakke* emphasized the importance of considering each particular applicant as an individual, assessing all of the qualities that individual possesses, and in turn, evaluating that individual's ability to contribute to the unique setting of higher education. The admissions program Justice Powell described, however, did not contemplate that any single characteristic automatically ensured a specific and identifiable contribution to a university's diversity....

[Michigan's] policy does not provide such individualized consideration.... [The] automatic distribution of 20 points has the effect of making "the factor of race ... decisive" for virtually every minimally qualified underrepresented minority applicant....

Respondents contend that "[t]he volume of applications and the presentation of applicant information make it impractical ... to use the ... admissions system" upheld by the Court today in *Grutter*. But the fact that the implementation of a program capable of providing individualized consideration might present administrative challenges does not render constitutional an otherwise problematic system.... Nothing in Justice Powell's opinion in *Bakke* signaled that a university may employ whatever means it desires to achieve the stated goal of diversity, without regard to the limits imposed by our strict scrutiny analysis.

We conclude, therefore, that because the University's use of race in its current freshman admission policy is not narrowly tailored to achieve respondents' asserted compelling interest in diversity, the admissions policy violates the Equal Protection Clause of the Fourteenth Amendment [and federal civil rights law.] Accordingly, we reverse the [decision of the District Court] and remand the case for proceedings consistent with this opinion.

It is so ordered.

[Justices O'Connor, Breyer, and Thomas concurred with separate opinions. Justices Souter, Ginsburg, and Stevens dissented with separate opinions].

Grutter v. Bollinger

539 U.S. 306 (2003)

The Court considered with *Gratz* a challenge to the University of Michigan Law School's admission policy by Barbara Grutter, a white student denied admission to the law school. The law school's admissions policy used "a flexible assessment of applicants' talents, experiences" and the contribution they make to the diversity of the overall class. Applicants were evaluated individually with no guaranteed admissions for anyone, even those with the highest test scores. The policy gave "substantial weight" to the ability of an applicant to contribute to the diversity of the class, but it defined diversity very broadly to include not only race and ethnicity but also such things as economic class, talents, and unusual life experiences. As to race and ethnicity, it sought to ensure a "critical mass" of students from underrepresented groups in order to avoid tokenism and ensure "their ability to make unique contributions to the character of the Law School." The 6th Circuit Court of Appeals upheld the plan.

JUSTICE O'CONNOR delivered the opinion of the Court....

II
A

We last addressed the use of race in public higher education over 25 years ago ... Since this Court's splintered decision in *Bakke,* Justice Powell's opinion announcing the judgment of the Court has served as the touchstone for constitutional analysis of race-conscious admissions policies.... [T]oday we endorse Justice Powell's view that student body diversity is a compelling state interest that can justify the use of race in university admissions.

B

. . .

Context matters when reviewing race-based governmental action under the Equal Protection Clause.... Not every decision influenced by race is equally objectionable and strict scrutiny is designed to provide a framework for carefully examining the importance and the sincerity of the reasons advanced by the governmental decisionmaker for the use of race in that particular context.

III
A

With these principles in mind, we turn to the question whether the Law School's use of race is justified by a compelling state interest. Before this Court, as they have throughout this litigation, respondents assert only one justification for their use of race in the admissions process: obtaining "the educational benefits that flow from a diverse student body." ... In other words, the Law School asks us to recognize, in the context of higher education, a compelling state interest in student body diversity ...

The Law School's educational judgment that such diversity is essential to its educational mission is one to which we defer. The Law School's assessment that diversity will, in fact, yield educational benefits is substantiated by respondents and their amici.... Our conclusion that the Law School has a compelling interest in a diverse student body is informed by our view that attaining a diverse student body is at the heart of the Law School's proper educational mission, and that "good faith" on the part of the university is "presumed" absent "a showing to the contrary." ...

As part of its goal of "assembling a class that is both exceptionally academically qualified and broadly diverse," the Law School seeks to "enroll a 'critical mass' of minority students." The Law School's interest is not simply "to assure within its student body some specified percentage of a particular group merely because of its race or ethnic origin." ... That would amount to outright racial balancing, which is patently unconstitutional.... Rather, the Law School's concept of critical mass is defined by reference to the educational benefits that diversity is designed to produce....

The Law School's claim of compelling interest is further bolstered by its amici, who point to the educational benefits that flow from student body diversity. In addition to the expert studies and reports entered into evidence at trial, numerous studies show that student body diversity promotes learning outcomes, and "better prepares students for an increasingly diverse workforce and society, and better prepares them as professionals." ...

These benefits are not theoretical but real, as major American businesses have made clear that the skills needed in today's increasingly global marketplace can only be developed through exposure to widely diverse people, cultures, ideas, and viewpoints.... What is more, high-ranking retired officers and civilian leaders of the United States military assert that "[b]ased on [their] decades of experience," a "highly qualified, racially diverse officer corps ... is essential to the military's ability to fulfill its principle mission to provide national security." ... At present, "the military cannot achieve an officer corps that is both highly qualified and racially diverse unless the service academies and the ROTC used limited race-conscious recruiting and admissions policies." ...

In order to cultivate a set of leaders with legitimacy in the eyes of the citizenry, it is necessary that the path to leadership be visibly open to talented and qualified individuals of every race and ethnicity. All members of our heterogeneous society must have confidence in the openness and integrity of the educational institutions that provide this training....

B

. . .

We find that the Law School's admissions program bears the hallmarks of a narrowly tailored plan. As Justice Powell made clear in *Bakke*, truly individualized consideration demands that race be used in a flexible, nonmechanical way. It follows from this mandate that universities cannot establish quotas for members of certain racial groups or put members of those groups on separate admissions tracks.... Nor can universities insulate applicants who belong to certain racial or ethnic groups from the competition for admission.... Universities can, however, consider race or ethnicity more flexibly as a "plus" factor in the context of individualized consideration of each and every applicant.... ...

Here, the Law School engages in a highly individualized, holistic review of each applicant's file, giving serious consideration to all the ways in which an applicant might contribute to a diverse educational environment. The Law School affords this individualized consideration to applicants of all races. There is no policy, either de jure or de facto, of automatic acceptance or rejection based on any single "soft" variable. Unlike the program at issue in *Gratz v. Bollinger* ... the Law School awards no mechanical, predetermined diversity "bonuses" ...

[L]ike the Harvard plan Justice Powell referred to in *Bakke*, the Law School's race-conscious admissions program adequately insures that all factors that may contribute to student body diversity are meaningfully considered alongside race in admissions decisions. With respect to the use of race itself, all underrepresented minority students admitted by the Law School have been deemed qualified. By virtue of our Nation's struggle with racial inequality, such students are both likely to have experiences of particular importance to the Law School's mission, and less likely to be admitted in meaningful numbers on criteria that ignore those experiences.

[*O'Connor rejects the petitioners argument that there are race neutral approaches like a lottery or a top 10% model that it could adopt.*] ... Narrow tailoring does not require exhaustion of every conceivable race-neutral alternative. Nor does it require a university to choose between maintaining a reputation for excellence or fulfilling a commitment to provide educational opportunities to members of all racial groups....

. . .

We are satisfied that the Law School's admissions program does not [unduly burden white applicants]. Because the Law School considers "all pertinent elements of diversity," it can (and does) select nonminority applicants who have greater potential to enhance student body diversity over underrepresented minority applicants....

. . .

We take the Law School at its word that it would "like nothing better than to find a race-neutral admissions formula" and will terminate its race-conscious admissions program as soon as practicable.... It has been 25 years since Justice Powell first approved the use of race to further an interest in student body diversity in the context of public higher education. Since that time, the number of minority applicants with high grades and test scores has indeed increased. We expect that 25 years from now, the use of racial preferences will no longer be necessary to further the interest approved today....

[*There were multiple concurring and dissenting opinions. Ginsburg and Breyer concurred. Chief Justice Rehnquist, and Justices Kennedy, Scalia, and Thomas dissented. The common concern among dissenters was that the "critical mass" approach operated, in effect, as a quota.*]

CONCLUSIONS

The preoccupation with race in American constitutional law continues with little interruption. The first effort to reconcile the Declaration of Independence and the Constitution came from Congress, which passed the three Civil War amendments (the Thirteenth, Fourteenth, and Fifteenth) and the Civil Rights Acts of 1866 and 1875. The nation then turned its back on problems of racism for decades. During the 1930s and 1940s, the courts and the President began to take some initiatives to eliminate discrimination against blacks. America's contribution in World War II to combat racism in Europe made it imperative, after the war, for America to honor its democratic ideals. That was important to prevent communist leaders from taunting the United States for its betrayal of democratic principles. All of those forces produced the political momentum for *Brown* v. *Board of Education*.

Since 1954, the effort to eradicate racism has collided with stubborn counterforces: state resistance, housing patterns, and job discrimination. Despite a series of court orders, beginning in 1954 and stretching over the next decade, little was accomplished toward desegregation until Congress and the

President in the Civil Rights Act of 1964 confronted the injustices of racism. Judicial remedies in the form of school busing proved controversial and were curtailed. Although substantial progress has been achieved in recent decades, the policy of affirmative action has created major strains in a society that wants to eliminate racial discrimination without abandoning the merit principle or the principle that the Constitution protects individuals, not groups. Precisely how to implement affirmative action, and for how long, is a task that remains unsettled and unresolved. There seems to be a growing consensus that affirmative action is justified not on race or gender alone but on economic class. This policy would support preferential action for individuals, whether white or black, from poor families.

NOTES AND QUESTIONS

1. In your view, what was the long-term impact of the Court's reasoning in the *Civil Rights Cases* of 1883 and *Plessy v. Ferguson* of 1896 on the hopes and aspirations of African-Americans?

2. Justice Brown concluded in *Plessy* that if "the enforced separation of the two races stamps the colored race with a badge of inferiority ... it is not by reason of anything found in the act, but solely because the colored race chooses to put that interpretation on it." Was that accurate? How would that assessment be viewed in light of the sociological data advanced in *Brown v. Bd. of Education*? Is the inclusion of sociological data a desirable factor for judges to take into consideration?

3. What was the basis of the Court's opinion in *Brown*? Did the Court assign sufficient weight to legal considerations?

4. In his famous dissent in *Plessy*, Justice Harlan stated: "Our Constitution is color-blind." Is race ever a permissible basis for distributing public benefits or burdens? If so, when? Under what circumstances? Apply your views to the issues in *Bakke* and other affirmative action cases. What are the results?

5. How compelling was the Court's ruling in *Heart of Atlanta* that the commerce power could be used to prohibit discrimination in public accommodations? Why didn't the Court rely on the Fourteenth Amendment to accomplish that end?

6. How important is diversity to the educational mission of K–12 public schools? To undergraduate and professional higher education?

SELECTED READINGS

ANDERSON, JAMES D. "Race-Conscious Educational Policies Versus a 'Color-Blind Constitution': A Historical Perspective." 36 Educational Researcher 249 (2007).

BICKEL, ALEXANDER M. "The Original Understanding and the Segregation Decision." 69 Harvard Law Review 1 (1955).

BOGER, JOHN CHARLES, AND GARY ORFIELD, Ed. School Resegregation: Must the South Turn Back? Chapel Hill: University of North Carolina Press, 2005.

DUDZIAK, MARY L. Cold War and Civil Rights: Race and the Image of American Democracy. Princeton: Princeton University Press, 2000.

ELY, JOHN HART. "The Constitutionality of Reverse Racial Discrimination." 41 University of Chicago Law Review 723 (1974).

FALLON, RICHARD H., JR., AND PAUL C. WEILER. "Firefighters v. Stotts: Conflicting Models of Racial Justice." 1984 Supreme Court Review 1.

FINCH, MINNIE. The NAACP: Its Fight for Justice. Metuchen, N.J.: Scarecrow Press, 1981.

FRANKLIN, JOHN HOPE. From Slavery to Freedom: A History of Negro Americans. New York: Knopf, 1980.

FREED, MAYER G., AND DANIEL D. POLSBY. "Race, Religion, and Public Policy: Bob Jones University v. United States." 1983 Supreme Court Review 1.

GLAZER, NATHAN. Affirmative Discrimination. New York: Basic Books, 1975.

GRAGLIA, LINO A. Disaster by Decree: The Supreme Court's Decisions on Race and the Schools. Ithaca, N.Y.: Cornell University Press, 1976.

GRAHAM, HUGH DAVIS. The Civil Rights Era: Origins and Development of National Policy, 1960–1972. New York: Oxford University Press, 1990.

GREENAWALT, KENT. Discrimination and Reverse Discrimination. New York: Knopf, 1983.

GREENBERG, JACK. Crusaders in the Courts. How a Dedicated Band of Lawyers Fought for the Civil Rights Revolution. New York: Basic Books, 1994.

HAMILTON, CHARLES V. The Bench and the Ballot: Southern Federal Judges and Black Voters. New York: Oxford University Press, 1973.

IRONS, PETER. Jim Crow's Children: The Broken Promise of the *Brown* Decision. New York: Viking Press, 2002.

KITCH, EDMUND W. "The Return of Color-Consciousness to the Constitution: Weber, Dayton and Columbus." 1979 Supreme Court Review. 1.

KLUGER, RICHARD. Simple Justice. New York: Knopf, 1976.

MINOW, MARTHA. In *Brown's* Wake: Legacies of America's Educational Landmark. New York: Oxford University Press, 2010.

MORGAN, RUTH. The President and Civil Rights: Policy-Making by Executive Order. New York: St. Martin's Press, 1970.

PACELLI, KIMBERLY A. "*Fisher v. University of Texas at Austin*: Navigating the Narrows Between *Grutter* and *Parents Involved*." 63 Maine Law Review 570 (2011).

PELTASON, JACK. Fifty-Eight Lonely Men: Southern Federal Judges and School Desegregation. New York: Harcourt, Brace & World, 1961.

POSNER, RICHARD A. "The DeFunis Case and the Constitutionality of Preferential Treatment of Racial Minorities." 1974 Supreme Court Review 1.

RUTHERGLEN, GEORGE. "Ricci v. DeStefano: Affirmative Action and the Lessons of Adversity." 2009 The Supreme Court Review 83.

SINDLER, ALLAN P. Bakke, DeFunis, and Minority Admissions. New York: Longman, 1978.

STRAUSS, DAVID A. "The Myth of Colorblindness." 1986 The Supreme Court Review 99.

———. "Affirmative Action and the Public Interest," 1995 The Supreme Court Review 1.

VOSE, CLEMENT E. Causasians Only: The Supreme Court, the NAACP, and the Restrictive Covenant Cases. Berkeley: University of California Press, 1959.

WILKINSON, J. HARVIE, III. From Brown to Bakke: The Supreme Court and School Integration. New York: Oxford University Press, 1979.

WILLIAMS, JUAN. Thurgood Marshall: American Revolutionary. New York: Times Books, 1998.

WOLK, ALLAN. The Presidency and Black Civil Rights: Eisenhower to Nixon. Cranbury, N.J.: Fairleigh Dickinson University Press, 1971.

16

The Expansion of Equal Protection

Building on the rights established for black Americans, women pressed for fundamental changes in their rights. From this period of "rights consciousness" emerged other efforts to secure rights for Hispanics, Indians, aliens, the indigent, the aged, the handicapped, juveniles, illegitimate children, institutionalized persons, and gays and lesbians. This extension of individual rights placed heavy demands on Congress and the judiciary as well as state and local governments but led to an understanding of equal protection far more inclusive of all of the "persons" protected by the Fourteenth Amendment.

Several groups are studied in this chapter. Women, legal and undocumented aliens, poor people, and gays and lesbians have all fought for equal protection of the laws. In each case they had to overcome entrenched ideas and customs and in some cases they continue to struggle against them. People within groups have constitutional rights as *individuals* and should not be deprived of rights simply because they fall within the category of women, aliens, the poor, or homosexuals. Many issues of equal protection are covered elsewhere, such as Chapter 17 on privacy and Chapter 18 on political participation.

A. THE STRUGGLE FOR WOMEN'S RIGHTS

When the framers proclaimed in the Declaration of Independence that "all men are created equal," they meant men literally, and not even all men. Blacks were excluded from equal treatment, as were nonpropertied white males. Although the phrase "all men are created equal" did not protect women, blacks, or nonpropertied white males in 1776, it is best understood as a fundamental principle meant to apply to all human beings, even if the aspiration was unfulfilled at the time of the framers and for many years to come.

On March 31, 1776, Abigail Adams appealed to her husband, John Adams, who was busily engaged with the Continental Congress in Philadelphia. She urged that "in the new code of laws which I suppose it will be necessary for you to make, I desire you would remember the ladies and be more generous and favorable to them than your ancestors. Do not put such unlimited power into the hands of the husbands. Remember, all men would be tyrants if they could." His curt reply mirrored the attitude of the times: "As to your extraordinary code of laws, I cannot but laugh." C. F. Adams, ed., Familiar Letters of John Adams and His Wife Abigail Adams During the Revolution 149–50, 155 (1876).

The customs of 1776 included the ancient doctrine of *coverture*, which placed women in a subordinate position to men. Blackstone, the great English jurist, stated that marriage made husband and wife "one person in law: that is, the very being or legal existence of the woman is suspended during the marriage, or at least is incorporated and consolidated into that of the husband: under whose wing, protection, and *cover,* she performs every thing." 2 Commentaries *442. The legal status of women inspired a scene in Charles Dickens' *Oliver Twist.* Mr. Bumble, trying to dissociate himself from his wife's theft, is told that he is "the more guilty of the two, in the eye of the law; for the law supposes that your wife acts under your direction." Bumble explodes: "If the law supposes that, the law is a ass — a idiot. If that's the eye of the law, the law is a bachelor; and the worst I wish the law is, that his eye may be opened by experience — by experience."

The Right to Practice Law

Blackstone's philosophy animates the early Supreme Court rulings on women's rights. A prominent example is *Bradwell* v. *State* (1873). Myra Bradwell had a law degree but needed the approval of a panel of judges (all men, of course) to practice law in Illinois. They turned her down solely because she was a woman. The Supreme Court denied that her rejection violated the privileges and immunities of the Fourteenth Amendment. The *Slaughter-House Cases*, announced earlier that year, left those questions to the states, not the federal government. Eight Justices voted against Mrs. Bradwell; only Chief Justice Chase (without a written opinion) dissented.

Significantly, Mrs. Bradwell prevailed at the state level as a result of *legislative* action. The Supreme Court of Illinois rejected her application for a license to practice law partly on "the deference and delicacy with which it is the pride of our ruder sex to treat her," but largely because the state legislature had not explicitly authorized women to practice law. The state court clearly invited the legislature to act. In re Bradwell, 55 Ill. 535, 542 (1869). Three years later the state legislature passed a bill stating that no person "shall be precluded or debarred from any occupation, profession or employment (except military) on account of sex." Illinois Laws, 1871–72, at 578. The issue before the U.S. Supreme Court in 1873 was, therefore, Bradwell's *national* right under the Privileges or Immunities Clause.

The concurrence by Justice Bradley in *Bradwell* claimed that the "natural and proper timidity and delicacy which belongs to the female sex evidently unfits it for many of the occupations of civil life." A woman's responsibility to domestic life and to the family institution made it "repugnant" for her to adopt a career independent from that of her husband. Bradley recognized that his argument was irrelevant for unmarried women, but he regarded them as exceptions to the general rule: "The paramount destiny and mission of woman are to fulfill the noble and benign offices of wife and mother. This is the law of the Creator. And the rules of civil society must be adapted to the general constitution of things, and cannot be based on exceptional cases." BRADWELL v. STATE, 83 U.S. (16 Wall.) 130 (1873). Similar stereotypes appear in an 1875 decision by the Supreme Court of Wisconsin (see box on next page).

After Myra Bradwell lost her case in the U.S. Supreme Court in 1873, congressional action was possible. A rule adopted by the Court prohibited women from practicing there. In 1878, Congress began consideration of a bill "to relieve certain legal disabilities of women." The bill provided that any woman who shall have been a member of the bar of the highest court of any state or territory or of the Supreme Court of the District of Columbia for three years, and who qualified on moral character, may be admitted to the Supreme Court of the United States. The bill passed the House of Representatives on February 21, 1878, by a vote of 169 to 87. 7 Cong. Rec. 1235 (1878). The Senate Judiciary Committee reported the bill adversely, concluding that such matters should be left to the Court through its own rules. Id. at 1821. During Senate debate, members recognized that women were entering a number of professions, including law and medicine, and appeared to take the *Bradwell* case of 1873 as an invitation to Congress to act. Id. at 2704.

When the bill was debated the following year, Senator Aaron Sargent argued: "No man has a right to put a limit to the exertions or the sphere of woman. That is a right which only can be possessed by that sex itself. . . . The enjoyment of liberty, the pursuit of happiness in her own way, is as much the birthright of woman as of man. In this land man has ceased to dominate over his fellow — let him cease to dominate over his sister; for he has no higher right to do the latter than the former" (see reading). The bill, after passing the Senate 39 to 20, was enacted into law. 20 Stat. 292 (1879). Thus, an all-male legislative body provided impressive support and understanding for women's rights — rights unavailable from the Court.

As a result of that statute, Belva Lockwood became the first woman admitted to practice before the U.S. Supreme Court. When she later appealed to the U.S. Supreme Court for the right to practice in Virginia, a unanimous Court deferred to the Supreme Court of Virginia in construing the statute that

Prohibiting Women from Practicing Law

[R. Lavinia Goodell requested permission to practice law before the Wisconsin Supreme Court. Unlike Myra Bradwell, Goodell was not married. Nonetheless, the court denied her motion, arguing that the "law of nature" destines women to bear and nurture children, take care of the custody of homes, and love and honor their husbands. In re Goodell, 39 Wis. 232 (1875).]

RYAN, C.J.... we find no statutory authority for the admission of females to the bar of any court of this state. And, with all the respect and sympathy for this lady which all men owe to all good women, we cannot regret that we do not. We cannot but think the common law wise in excluding women from the profession of the law. The profession enters largely into the well being of society; and to be honorably filled and safely to society, exacts the devotion of life. The law of nature destines and qualifies the female sex for the bearing and nurture of the children of our race and for the custody of the homes of the world and their maintenance in love and honor. And all lifelong callings of women, inconsistent with these radical and sacred duties of their sex, as is the profession of the law, are departures from the order of nature; and when voluntary, treason against it.... There are many employments in life not unfit for female character. The profession of the law is surely not one of these. The peculiar qualities of womanhood, its gentle graces, its quick sensibility, its tender susceptibility, its purity, its delicacy, its emotional impulses, its subordination of hard reason to sympathetic feeling, are surely not qualifications for forensic strife. Nature has tempered woman as little for the juridical conflicts of the court room, as for the physical conflicts of the battle field. Womanhood is moulded for gentler and better things. And it is not the saints of the world who chiefly give employment to our profession. It has essentially and habitually to do with all that is selfish and malicious, knavish and criminal, coarse and brutal, repulsive and obscene in human life. It would be revolting to all female sense of the innocence and sanctity of their sex, shocking to man's reverence for womanhood and faith in woman, on which hinge all the better affections and humanities of life, that woman should be permitted to mix professionally in all the nastiness of the world which finds its way into courts of justice; all the unclean issues, all the collateral questions of sodomy, incest, rape, seduction, fornication, adultery, pregnancy, bastardy, legitimacy, prostitution, lascivious cohabitation, abortion, infanticide, obscene publications, libel and slander of sex, impotence, divorce: all the nameless catalogue of indecencies, *la chronique scandaleuse* of all the vices and all the infirmities of all society, with which the profession has to deal, and which go towards filling judicial reports which must be read for accurate knowledge of the law. This is bad enough for men....

authorized persons to practice in the state. The interpretation of the Privileges or Immunities Clause was again at stake. In re Lockwood, 154 U.S. 116 (1894).

Voting Rights

Within two years of *Bradwell*, the judiciary delivered another major blow against women's rights. A lawsuit by Mrs. Virginia Minor argued that she was a "citizen" within the meaning of the Constitution and therefore entitled to vote as one of the privileges and immunities protected by the Fourteenth Amendment. A unanimous Court agreed that women are citizens but denied that the Fourteenth Amendment added substantive rights to previous privileges and immunities. According to the Court, Section 2 of the Fourteenth Amendment limited suffrage to male inhabitants. Indeed, it took the Fifteenth Amendment to give blacks the right to vote. The Court ruled that women, like children, were "citizens" and "persons" in the constitutional sense, but that status did not automatically entitle either to vote. Minor v. Happersett, 88 U.S. (21 Wall.) 162 (1875). Women did not gain the right to vote until ratification of the Nineteenth Amendment in 1920. Although women, nationwide, had to await the ratification of Nineteenth Amendment to vote in federal elections, in a number of states they were already voting in both state and federal elections. M. Margaret Conway, et al., Women and Political Participation 8–9 (1997).

Protective Legislation

Although women later won important cases in the courts, the victories were often premised on their inferiority, not their equality. A decision in 1908, in which the Supreme Court unanimously upheld Oregon's ten-hour day for women, helped perpetuate the stereotype of women advanced in *Bradwell*. Speaking for the Court, Justice Brewer remarked: "Still again, history discloses the fact that woman has always been dependent upon man. He established his control at the outset by superior physical strength, and this control in various forms, with diminishing intensity, has continued to the present." Muller v. Oregon, 208 U.S. 412, 421 (1908). Despite new opportunities for women to acquire knowledge, "it is still true that in the struggle for subsistence she is not an equal competitor with her brother. Though limitations upon personal and contractual rights may be removed by legislation, there is that in her disposition and habits of life which will operate against a full assertion of those rights." Id. at 422. Acknowledging that individual exceptions existed, Brewer felt confident that even with the elimination of political and contractual restrictions "it would still be true that she is so constituted that she will rest upon and look to him for protection." Blackstone still reigned.

By 1923 the Court concluded that protective legislation for women was no longer necessary because of the Nineteenth Amendment and changes in statutory and contractual law. Adkins v. Children's Hospital, 261 U.S. 525, 553 (1923). Chief Justice Taft, in one of the dissents, wondered whether the majority believed that previous Court doctrines had been invalidated by the Nineteenth Amendment, which "did not change the physical strength or limitations of women upon which the decision in *Muller* v. *Oregon* rests." Id. at 567. A dissent by Justice Holmes wryly observed: "It will need more than the Nineteenth Amendment to convince me that there are no differences between men and women, or that legislation cannot take those differences into account." Id. at 569–70.

The Court continued to support certain types of protective legislation for women. In 1924, it upheld a New York law that prohibited women in large cities from working between 10 P.M. and 6 A.M. Radice v. New York, 264 U.S. 292 (1924). But the spirit of *Adkins* survived through 1936 when the Court (divided 5–4) struck down New York's minimum wage law for women and minors. The Court saw no justification for protective legislation for women when men "in need of work are as likely as women to accept the low wages offered by unscrupulous employers." Morehead v. N.Y. ex rel. Tipaldo, 298 U.S. 587, 616 (1936). *Adkins* was overturned the next year. A 5–4 majority accepted minimum wage legislation for women. States were entitled to consider "the fact that they are in the class receiving the least pay, that their bargaining power is relatively weak, and that they are the ready victims of those who would take advantage of their necessitous circumstances." West Coast Hotel Co. v. Parrish, 300 U.S. 379, 398 (1937). The Court also took "judicial notice" of the public relief needed during the Great Depression. Inadequate wages for women had placed demands on state agencies for public assistance: "The community is not bound to provide what is in effect a subsidy for unconscionable employers." Id. at 399.

Bartenders, Conspiracies, and Jury Duty

Court doctrines had not advanced very far by 1948, when the Supreme Court upheld a Michigan law that prohibited female bartenders unless they were the wife or daughter of the male owner. Attitudes in state legislatures and the judiciary had not changed much since *Bradwell*. By a 6–3 vote, the Court decided that Michigan had not violated the Equal Protection Clause of the Fourteenth Amendment. Frankfurter's opinion for the majority has a smug quality: "Beguiling as the subject is, it need not detain us for long. To ask whether or not the Equal Protection of the Laws Clause of the Fourteenth Amendment barred Michigan from making the classification the State has made between wives and

No Wrestling for Women

In 1956, the Supreme Court of Oregon upheld a state statute that prohibited women from participating in wrestling exhibitions. In sustaining the statute, the court poked fun at the legislators. After taking judicial notice that the legislative assembly that enacted the statute was predominantly male, the court speculated on what might have driven the lawmakers:

It seems to us that its purpose, although somewhat selfish in nature, stands out in the statute like a sore thumb. Obviously it intended that there should be at least one island on the sea of life reserved for man that would be impregnable to the assault of woman.... She had already invaded practically every activity formerly considered suitable and appropriate for men only.... In these circumstances, is it any wonder that the legislative assembly took advantage of the police power of the state in its decision to halt this ever-increasing feminine encroachment upon what for ages had been considered strictly as manly arts and privileges? State v. Hunter, 300 P.2d 455, 458 (Ore. 1956).

These statutory efforts to halt the "assault of woman" gave way in time to female participation not only in wrestling but boxing as well.

daughters of owners of liquor places and wives and daughters of non-owners, is one of those rare instances where to state the question is in effect to answer it." Goeseart v. Cleary, 335 U.S. 464, 465 (1948). So much for judicial reasoning. Frankfurter concluded that Michigan could, "beyond question," forbid all women from working behind a bar. To the three dissenters, Michigan's statute arbitrarily discriminated between men and women.

In 1960, Frankfurter wrote an opinion rejecting the "medieval view" that husband and wife are one person with but a single will and, therefore, legally incapable of entering into a criminal conspiracy. To the extent that this outmoded doctrine of coverture rested on a legal fiction, three dissenters preferred that it be corrected by Congress, not the judiciary. United States v. Dege, 364 U.S. 51 (1960). Medieval thinking triumphed in 1961, when the Court agreed unanimously that women could be largely exempted from jury service because they are "still regarded as the center of home and family life." Hoyt v. Florida, 368 U.S. 57, 62 (1961). Remnants of the law of coverture persisted until 1966. United States v. Yazell, 382 U.S. 341 (1966).

Abolishing Sexual Stereotypes

Judicial attitudes on sex discrimination did not change until long after the desegregation case of 1954. Judges, at both the federal and state level, held fast to anachronous legal doctrines. Yet World War II had done much to change public attitudes about the kind of work that was suitable for women. During the war, women filled many jobs previously associated with "men's work": machine tools, aircraft production, shipbuilding, and munitions. The dainty image of women gave way to "Rosie the Riveter." Women began entering a number of professions that were new to them. An amusing case came out of Oregon, where the legislature voted to exclude women from wrestling exhibitions (see box).

Not until 1971 did the U.S. Supreme Court issue a decision striking down sex discrimination. The judicial record before 1971 was deplorable. According to one study: "Our conclusion, independently reached, but completely shared, is that by and large the performance of American judges in the area of sex discrimination can be succinctly described as ranging from poor to abominable." Johnston & Knapp, "Sex Discrimination by Law: A Study in Judicial Perspective," 46 N.Y.U.L. Rev. 675, 676 (1971).

Progress came primarily from the legislative and executive branches, which showed a much greater capacity to recognize wrongs and to right them. Using its constitutional power to regulate commerce, Congress passed the Equal Pay Act in 1963 to prohibit employers in the private sector from discriminating on the basis of sex. 77 Stat. 56. The debate demonstrates how Congress can respond to constitutional inequities before they are addressed, or redressed, by the courts (see reading).

Title VII of the Civil Rights Act of 1964 made it illegal for any employer to discriminate against anyone with respect to "compensation, terms, conditions, or privileges of employment" because of the person's sex. 42 U.S.C. § 2000e-2(a)(1) (2000). It is sometimes claimed that the word "sex" was added to the bill to ridicule and perhaps sabotage the enactment of a civil rights bill. However, the debate suggests a different motivation. By prohibiting discrimination on the basis of race, members of Congress were concerned that a white woman applying for a job would be at a disadvantage, legally, to a black woman (see reading). No doubt the person who offered the amendment prohibiting gender discrimination, Congressman Howard Smith (D-Va.), was well-known for his opposition to civil rights. Yet he was also a supporter of the Equal Rights Amendment and had the backing of women's groups. The National Women's Party (NWP) objected to the civil rights bill because it only prohibited discrimination on the basis of race, color, religion, or national origin. The NWP said that the bill gave no protection "to a *White Woman*, a *Woman of the Christian Religion*, or a *Woman of United States origin*." The NWP worked with Smith on his amendment to the Civil Rights Act. Cynthia Harrison, On Account of Sex 21, 176–77 (1988).

Congress established the Equal Employment Opportunity Commission (EEOC) to investigate claims of discrimination. Much of the agency's workload deals with cases of sex discrimination. Upholding congressional policy and EEOC regulations, the Court held that a company could not deny employment to a woman because she had preschool-aged children if the company agreed to hire men with preschool-aged children. Phillips v. Martin Marietta Corp., 400 U.S. 542 (1971). In another initiative, Congress passed Title IX of the Education Amendments of 1972 to withdraw federal financial assistance from any educational institution that practices sex discrimination. 86 Stat. 373 (1972).

Bradwell v. State

83 U.S. 130 (1873)

Myra Bradwell, a resident of Illinois, applied to the judges of the Illinois Supreme Court for a license to practice law. It rejected her application. In taking her case to the U.S. Supreme Court, she asserted that she was entitled to the license by virtue of the privileges and immunities guaranteed to U.S. citizens under Section 2 of Article IV and under Section 1 of the Fourteenth Amendment. With only one Justice dissenting, the Court found no merit to her argument. The concurrence by Justice Bradley is of special interest because of his view about the "mission of woman."

Mr. Justice MILLER delivered the opinion of the court.

The record in this case is not very perfect, but it may be fairly taken that the plaintiff asserted her right to a license on the grounds, among others, that she was a citizen of the United States, and that having been a citizen of Vermont at one time, she was, in the State of Illinois, entitled to any right granted to citizens of the latter State.

The court having overruled these claims of right founded on the clauses of the Federal Constitution before referred to, those propositions may be considered as properly before this court.

As regards the provision of the Constitution that citizens of each State shall be entitled to all the privileges and immunities of citizens in the several States, the plaintiff in her affidavit has stated very clearly a case to which it is inapplicable.

The protection designed by that clause, as has been repeatedly held, has no application to a citizen of the State whose laws are complained of. If the plaintiff was a citizen of the State of Illinois, that provision of the Constitution gave her no protection against its courts or its legislation.

The plaintiff seems to have seen this difficulty, and attempts to avoid it by stating that she was born in Vermont.

While she remained in Vermont that circumstance made her a citizen of that State. But she states, at the same time, that she is a citizen of the

United States, and that she is now, and has been for many years past, a resident of Chicago, in the State of Illinois.

The fourteenth amendment declares that citizens of the United States are citizens of the State within which they reside; therefore the plaintiff was, at the time of making her application, a citizen of the United States and a citizen of the State of Illinois.

We do not here mean to say that there may not be a temporary residence in one State, with intent to return to another, which will not create citizenship in the former. But the plaintiff states nothing to take her case out of the definition of citizenship of a State as defined by the first section of the fourteenth amendment.

In regard to that amendment counsel for the plaintiff in this court truly says that there are certain privileges and immunities which belong to a citizen of the United States as such; otherwise it would be nonsense for the fourteenth amendment to prohibit a State from abridging them, and he proceeds to argue that admission to the bar of a State of a person who possesses the requisite learning and character is one of those which a State may not deny.

In this latter proposition we are not able to concur with counsel. We agree with him that there are privileges and immunities belonging to citizens of the United States, in that relation and character, and that it is these and these alone which a State is forbidden to abridge. But the right to admission to practice in the courts of a State is not one of them. This right in no sense depends on citizenship of the United States. It has not, as far as we know, ever been made in any State, or in any case, to depend on citizenship at all. Certainly many prominent and distinguished lawyers have been admitted to practice, both in the State and Federal courts, who were not citizens of the United States or of any State. But, on whatever basis this right may be placed, so far as it can have any relation to citizenship at all, it would seem that, as to the courts of a State, it would relate to citizenship of the State, and as to Federal courts, it would relate to citizenship of the United States.

The opinion just delivered in the *Slaughter-House Cases* renders elaborate argument in the present case unnecessary; for, unless we are wholly and radically mistaken in the principles on which those cases are decided, the right to control and regulate the granting of license to practice law in the courts of a State is one of those powers which are not transferred for its protection to the Federal government, and its exercise is in no manner governed or controlled by citizenship of the United States in the party seeking such license.

It is unnecessary to repeat the argument on which the judgment in those cases is founded. It is sufficient to say they are conclusive of the present case.

Judgment affirmed.

Mr. Justice BRADLEY:

I concur in the judgment of the court in this case, by which the judgment of the Supreme Court of Illinois is affirmed, but not for the reasons specified in the opinion just read.

The claim of the plaintiff, who is a married woman, to be admitted to practice as an attorney and counsellor-at-law, is based upon the supposed right of every person, man or woman, to engage in any lawful employment for a livelihood. The Supreme Court of Illinois denied the application on the ground that, by the common law, which is the basis of the laws of Illinois, only men were admitted to the bar, and the legislature had not made any change in this respect, ...

The claim that, under the fourteenth amendment of the Constitution, which declares that no State shall make or enforce any law which shall abridge the privileges and immunities of citizens of the United States, the statute law of Illinois, or the common law prevailing in that State, can no longer be set up as a barrier against the right of females to pursue any lawful employment for a livelihood (the practice of law included), assumes that it is one of the privileges and immunities of women as citizens to engage in any and every profession, occupation, or employment in civil life.

It certainly cannot be affirmed, as an historical fact, that this has ever been established as one of the fundamental privileges and immunities of the sex. On the contrary, the civil law, as well as nature herself, has always recognized a wide difference in the respective spheres and destinies of man and woman. Man is, or should be, woman's protector and defender. The natural and proper timidity and delicacy which belongs to the female sex evidently unfits it for many of the occupations of civil life. The constitution of the family organization, which is founded in the divine ordinance, as well as in the nature of things, indicates the domestic sphere as that which properly belongs to the domain and functions of womanhood. The harmony, not to say identity, of interests and views which belong, or should belong, to the family institution is repugnant to the idea of a woman adopting a distinct and independent career from that of her husband. So firmly fixed was this sentiment in the founders of the common law that it became a maxim of that system of jurisprudence that a woman had no legal existence separate from her husband, who was regarded as her head and representative in the social state; and, notwithstanding some recent modifications of this civil status, many of the special rules of law flowing from and dependent upon this cardinal principle still exist in full force in most States. One of these is, that a married woman is incapable, without her husband's consent, of making contracts which shall be binding on her or him. This very incapacity was one circumstance which the Supreme Court of Illinois deemed important in rendering a married woman incompetent fully to perform the duties and trusts that belong to the office of an attorney and counsellor.

It is true that many women are unmarried and not affected by any of the duties, complications, and incapacities arising out of the married state, but these are exceptions to the general rule. The paramount destiny and mission of woman are to fulfil the noble and benign offices of wife and mother. This is the law of the Creator. And the rules of civil society must be adapted to the general constitution of things, and cannot be based upon exceptional cases.

... It is the prerogative of the legislator to prescribe regulations founded on nature, reason, and experience for the due admission of qualified persons to professions and callings demanding special skill and confidence. This fairly belongs to the police power of the State; and, in my opinion, in view of the peculiar characteristics, destiny, and mission of woman, it is within the province of the legislature to ordain what offices, positions, and callings shall be filled and discharged by men, and shall receive the benefit of those energies and responsibilities, and that decision and firmness which are presumed to predominate in the sterner sex.

For these reasons I think that the laws of Illinois now complained of are not obnoxious to the charge of abridging any of the privileges and immunities of citizens of the United States.

Mr. Justice SWAYNE and Mr. Justice FIELD concurred in the foregoing opinion of Mr. Justice BRADLEY.

The CHIEF JUSTICE dissented from the judgment of the court, and from all the opinions.

Congress Responds to *Bradwell*

Congress passed legislation in 1879 to permit women to practice before the U.S. Supreme Court (20 Stat. 292), thus explicitly rejecting the principles and reasoning announced by the Court in *Bradwell* v. *State* (1873). Instead of following the contemporary attitude of courts, which concluded that women were temperamentally unfitted to practice law and engage in other professional activities, legislators at both the national and state level decided to remove legal impediments that interfered with the right of women to pursue a legal career. The following passages appear at 7 Cong. Rec. 2704 (1878) and 8 Cong. Rec. 1084 (1879).

[Senator Aaron] SARGENT [R-Cal.]. Mr. President, the best evidence that members of the legal profession have no jealousy against the admission of women to the bar who have the proper learning is shown by that document which I hold in my hand, signed by one hundred and fifty-five lawyers of the District of Columbia, embracing the most eminent men in the ranks of that profession, [exhibiting a petition.] That there is no jealousy or consideration of impropriety on its part in the various States is shown by the fact that the Legislatures of many of the States have recently admitted women to the bar; and my own State, California, has passed such a law within the last week or two. Illinois has done the same thing: so have Michigan, Minnesota, Missouri, and North Carolina; and Wyoming, Utah, and the District of Columbia among the Territories have also

done it. There is no reason in principle why women should not be admitted to this profession or the profession of medicine, provided they have the learning to enable them to be useful in those professions, and useful to themselves. Where is the propriety in opening our colleges, our higher institutions of learning, or any institutions of learning to women, and then when they have acquired in the race with men the cultivation for higher employment to shut them out? There certainly is none....

Mr. SARGENT.... The medical universities of the world are receiving women and instructing them in medicine and surgery, and there are many women engaged in these studies and practicing this profession. In France the universities are open to them. The prejudice in England has been gradually overcome in this direction, and the London Medical College receives them. They are admitted into the Scotch schools and into some of the best medical schools of the United States, and they are making their way in them all. There are in the various States of the Union women lawyers; and women in literature have won a very high place. No man has a right to put a limit to the exertions or the sphere of woman. That is a right which only can be possessed by that sex itself.

I say again, men have not the right, in contradiction to the intentions, the wishes, the ambition, of women, to say that their sphere shall be circumscribed, that bounds shall be set which they cannot pass. The enjoyment of liberty, the pursuit of happiness in her own way, is as much the birthright of woman as of man. In this land man has ceased to dominate over his fellow—let him cease to dominate over his sister; for he has no higher right to do that latter than the former. It is mere oppression to say to the bread-seeking woman, you shall labor only in certain narrow ways for your living, we will hedge you out by law from profitable employments, and monopolize them for ourselves....

[Senator George] HOAR [R-Mass.].... Mr. President, I understand the brief statement which was made I think during the last session by the majority of the Judiciary Committee in support of their opposition to this bill, did not disclose that the majority of the committee were opposed to permitting women to engage in the practice of law or to be admitted to practice it in the Supreme Court of the United States, but the point they made was that the legislation of the United States left to the Supreme Court the power of determining by rule who should be admitted to practice before that tribunal, and that we ought not by legislation to undertake to interfere with their rules. Now, with the greatest respect for that tribunal, I conceive that the law-making and not the law-expounding power in this Government ought to determine the question what class of citizens shall be clothed with the office of the advocate....

Now, Mr. President, this bill is not a bill merely to admit women to the privilege of engaging in a particular profession; it is a bill to secure to the citizen of the United States the right to select his counsel, and that is all. At present a case is tried and decided in the State courts of any State of this Union which may be removed to the Supreme Court of the United States. In the courts of the State women are permitted to practice as advocates, and a woman has been the advocate under whose direction and care and advocacy the case has been won in the court below. Is it tolerable that the counsel who has attended the case from its commencement to its successful termination in the highest court of the State should not be permitted to attend upon and defend the rights of that client when the case is transferred to the Supreme Court of the United States? Everybody knows, at least every lawyer of experience knows the impossibility of transferring with justice to the interests of a client a cause from one counsel to another....

Equal Pay Act of 1963: Congressional Debate

The federal government had prohibited discrimination on the basis of sex for federal salaries, but the private sector was at liberty to pay women less than men for the same job. Congress passed legislation in 1963 to place restrictions on private employers. Although the bill permitted some exceptions, Congress used its power over commerce to bring a measure of fairness and justice to private wages. The debate below occurred in the House of Representatives on May 23, 1963.

Mrs. ST. GEORGE. Mr. Speaker, ... this resolution, House Resolution 362, makes in order the consideration of H.R. 6060 to prohibit discrimination on account of sex in the payment of wages by employers engaged in commerce or in the production of goods for commerce....

For those who fear this legislation—and there are some—I would like to point out that all women are by no means covered in this act. As a matter of fact, we see, according to the supplemental views in the report, that the prohibition against discrimination because of sex is placed under the Fair Labor Standards Act, with the act's established coverage of employers and employees. All of the Fair Labor Standards exemptions apply; and, this is very noteworthy, agriculture, hotels, motels, restaurants, and laundries are excluded. Also all professional, managerial, and administrative personnel and outside salesmen are excluded. So, a very great quantity of women will not be covered in this act, especially because it considers hotels, motels, restaurants, and laundries, where women are by far the majority of the workers. They will not be included.

Mr. Speaker, I have always felt that these bills would come to us from now on, and I hope that they will, but in every instance it is only one bite of the cherry. In other words, we are just nibbling away at a thing that could have been completely covered by an amendment to the Constitution simply giving women equal rights and letting it go at that. That apparently has not been the will of the House so far. I hope someday that it will be. However, in the meantime, we are going to have to have these bills which will help, which will do a little, which will get a foot in the door, and they will have to continue to come to us....

Mr. COLMER. Mr. Speaker, ... I recognize that this bill is going to pass. It is going to pass overwhelmingly, I suspect, because it has an appeal to a minority or special group. It deals with women. I recognize the seeming popular appeal and then, too, Mr. Speaker, I recognize in addition to the futility of my stating my position the politically unwise situation in which I find myself. I certainly do not want to be put in the position of opposing the women of this country, and I could dwell at some length on that subject. I am not so sure that the women want this bill. However, I am opposed to this proposal because I think it is basically unsound, just as I have opposed proposals here that were aimed at other minority or special groups.

I doubt seriously, Mr. Speaker, if this bill is constitutional. I do not like the idea of pointing out women here as if they are an inferior group and that the Federal Government with its strong arm must step in and try to protect them. I think they can stand on their own. They have been doing that for many, many generations.

Mr. Speaker, there are many instances where women are entitled to more pay than the opposite sex and why should we just put them on an equal basis? This strikes at the merit system....

Mrs. FRANCES P. BOLTON. Mr. Speaker, as a long-time advocate of the principle of equal pay for equal work, I am very glad to speak in favor of H.R. 6060. I am very much interested in the remarks of the previous speaker because it is some time since the women of this country have been in the minority. We are rather far ahead of you in that regard, my distinguished colleague. Of course, if you care to be the spokesman for the actual minority. Equal pay legislation has been introduced in every Congress since 1945 by Members of both parties, a truly bipartisan effort....

It is a matter of simple justice to pay a woman the same rate as a man when she is performing the same duties. We have had equal pay in the Government for some years through the Federal classified civil service. Some 22 States have enacted equal-pay laws, but let me say right there that in many of these they do not work too well. However, a Federal law is needed to give complete and adequate coverage....

Mr. POWELL....

This principle of equality has been endorsed by labor, by leaders in both political parties, and by numerous business organizations and spokesmen. The International Labor Organization — of which we are a member and which I shall attend next week — provides in its constitution that "men and women should receive equal remuneration for work of equal value." Thirty-eight countries have ratified an ILO Convention which sets up standards and procedures for establishing equal pay in fact as well as in principle. The European Common Market agreement, the Rome Treaty, also carries a specific provision for equal pay.

Civil Rights Act of 1964: Congressional Debate

During debate on the Civil Rights Act of 1964, Congressman Howard Smith of Virginia offered an amendment to prohibit discrimination not only on the basis of race but also on "sex" as well. This amendment has been widely interpreted as an effort by a Southern opponent of civil rights to jeopardize the entire bill by weighing it down with a ludicrous amendment. But the concerns of Congressman Smith and his colleagues from the South were real. If Congress only prohibited discrimination on the basis of race, white women would consistently lose out to black women in the competition for jobs. Employers would tend to favor black women as a way of avoiding discrimination suits. An alternative motivation for the amendment — defending the interests of white women — comes out strongly in the debate, taken from 110 Cong. Rec. 2577–84 (1964).

Mr. SMITH of Virginia. Mr. Chairman, I offer an amendment.

The Clerk read as follows:

"Amendment offered by Mr. SMITH of Virginia: On page 68, line 23, after the word 'religion,' insert the word 'sex.'

"On page 69, line 10, after the word 'religion,' insert the word 'sex.'

"On page 69, line 17, after the word 'religion,' insert the word 'sex.'

"On page 70, line 1, after the word 'religion,' insert the word 'sex.'

"On page 71, line 5, after the word 'religion,' insert the word 'sex.'"

Mr. SMITH of Virginia. Mr. Chairman, this amendment is offered to the fair employment practices title of this bill to include within our desire to prevent discrimination against another minority group, the women, but a very essential minority group, in the absence of which the majority group would not be here today.

Now, I am very serious about this amendment. It has been offered several times before, but it was offered at inappropriate places in the bill. Now, this is the appropriate place for this amendment to come in. I do not think it can do any harm to this legislation; maybe it can do some good. I think it will do some good for the minority sex.

I think we all recognize and it is indisputable fact that all throughout industry women are discriminated against in that just generally speaking they do not get as high compensation for their work as do the majority sex. Now, if that is true, I hope that the committee chairman will accept this amendment....

Mrs. GRIFFITHS. Mr. Chairman, ... I rise in support of the amendment primarily because I feel as a white woman when this bill has passed this House and the Senate and has been signed by the President that white women will be last at the hiring gate.

... I come from a city in which there is a university. It is my understanding that there has never been a woman political scientist employed at that university to teach political science. Suppose a colored woman political scientist applied for a job. Could she or could she not invoke the act?

Mr. CELLER. Of course, we are addressing ourselves to business activity. It is conceivable that colleges might be covered. There again, if there were discrimination then there would be a violation.

Mrs. GRIFFITHS. Could a white woman turned away from the college or from the restaurant where all the employees were white invoke the act? Would a white woman have any recourse under the act?

Mr. CELLER. I think we covered that in colloquies we had in the earlier part of the afternoon. There could be discrimination against white people and there could be against colored people.

Mrs. GRIFFITHS. Mr. Chairman, you know well and good if every employee of that restaurant were white, that that woman cannot go to the FEPC or to a district attorney and say, "I was turned away from there because I was white," because every employee is white there....

Now, Mr. Chairman, I would like to proceed to some of the arguments I have heard on this floor against adding the word "sex." In some of the arguments, I have heard the comment that the chairman is making, which is, that this makes it an equal rights bill. Of course it does not even approach making it an equal rights bill. This is equal employment rights. In one field only—employment. And if you do not add sex to this bill, I really do not believe there is a reasonable person sitting here who does not by now understand perfectly that you are going to have white men in one bracket, you are going to try to take colored men and colored women and give them equal employment rights, and down at the bottom of the list is going to be a white woman with no rights at all....

Mr. ANDREWS of Alabama ... I rise in support of this amendment offered by the gentleman from Virginia [Mr. Smith]. Unless this amendment is adopted, the white women of this country would be drastically discriminated against in favor of a Negro woman.

If a white woman and a Negro woman applied for the same job, and each woman had the identical qualifications, the chances are about 99 to 1 that the Negro woman would be given the job because if the employer did not give the job to the Negro woman he could be prosecuted under this bill. Failure to employ the white woman would not subject the employer to such action.

Commonsense tells us that the employer would hire the Negro woman to avoid prosecution. The white woman will be at a great disadvantage in the business world unless this amendment is adopted.

Mr. RIVERS of South Carolina. I rise in support of the amendment offered by the gentleman from Virginia [Mr. SMITH] making it possible for the white Christian woman to receive the same consideration for employment as the colored woman. It is incredible to me that the authors of this monstrosity—whomever they are—would deprive the white woman of mostly Anglo-Saxon or Christian heritage equal opportunity before the employer. I know this Congress will not be a party to such an evil.

Mr. SMITH of Virginia.... I put a question to you in behalf of the white women of the United States. Let us assume that two women apply for the same job and both of them are equally eligible, one a white woman and one a Negro woman. The first thing that employer will look at will be the provision with regard to the records he must keep. If he does not employ that colored woman and has to make that record, that employer will say, "Well, now, if I hire the colored woman I will not be in any trouble, but if I do not hire the colored woman and hire the white woman, then the Commission is going to be looking down my throat and will want to know why I did not. I may be in a lawsuit."

That will happen as surely as we are here this afternoon. You all know it....

The CHAIRMAN. The question is on the amendment offered by the gentleman from Virginia [Mr. SMITH].

Mrs. GRIFFITHS. Mr. Chairman, on that I demand tellers.

Tellers were ordered, and the Chairman appointed as tellers Mr. CELLER and Mrs. GRIFFITHS.

The Committee divided, and the tellers reported that there were—ayes 168, noes 133.

So the amendment was agreed to.

B. CONTEMPORARY GENDER ISSUES

Supreme Court doctrines began to shift after Warren Burger replaced Earl Warren as Chief Justice in 1969. A major pressure for this change came from Congress and the country during debate on the Equal Rights Amendment, which passed the House in 1970 by the top-heavy margin of 350–15. After Senate action, the language submitted to the states for ratification read: "Equality of rights under the law shall not be denied or abridged by the United States or by any State on account of sex." Members of the House argued strongly that a constitutional amendment was necessary because the Supreme Court had failed to protect the rights of women. Representative Martha Griffiths, a leader behind the ERA, put the matter bluntly in October 1971: "Mr. Chairman, what the equal rights amendment seeks to do, and all it seeks to do, is to say to the Supreme Court of the United States, 'Wake up! This is the 20th century. Before it is over, judge women as individual human beings.'" 117 Cong. Rec. 35323 (1971). (See box in Chapter 19, Section A)

A month later, a unanimous Supreme Court struck down an Idaho law that preferred men over women in administering estates. The statute, the Court held, arbitrarily discriminated on the basis of sex and violated the Equal Protection Clause of the Fourteenth Amendment. Reed v. Reed, 404 U.S. 71 (1971). Since that time, a flood of cases has gradually challenged and eliminated sexual stereotypes of an earlier age. In 1973, the Court said that sex discrimination had survived in America as "romantic paternalism," whereas the practical effect was to put women "not on a pedestal, but in a cage." Statutes were "laden with gross, stereotyped distinctions between the sexes." Frontiero v. Richardson, 411 U.S. 677, 684–85 (1973).[1] Customs of earlier times were "no longer tenable" to exclude women from juries. Taylor v. Louisiana, 419 U.S. 522, 537 (1975). The Court rejected "old notions" about a man's primary responsibility to provide a home. Stanton v. Stanton, 421 U.S. 7, 10 (1975). In 1994, the Court prohibited lawyers from using gender to exclude people from a jury. Stereotypes regarding sex (that men or women jurors are likely to vote a certain way) may not be used. J.E.B. v. Alabama ex rel. T.B., 511 U.S. 127 (1994).

The Supreme Court had an opportunity in 1973 to declare sex a "suspect classification," as it had done with race and alienage. Under this classification, the strict-scrutiny test is applied to governmental actions that discriminate and the government must show a compelling interest to support its policy and be narrowly tailored. The more lenient standard permits a legislature to make classifications if the statute is rational and furthers an important governmental interest (see box on next page).

---

1. The clever pedestal-cage image was lifted from a 1971 decision by the Supreme Court of California: "The pedestal upon which women have been placed has all too often, upon closer examination, been revealed as a cage." Sail'er Inn, Inc. v. Kirby, 485 P.2d 529, 541 (Cal. 1971).

Standards of Review

The Supreme Court uses different standards when reviewing governmental actions. The three tests below are general guidelines. Actual application in a given case can vary widely from the theoretical model. For example, the intermediate standard applied to sex discrimination often approaches strict-scrutiny analysis.

Rational basis — Legislation is valid if the legislature's purpose is legitimate and the law is "rationally" related to that purpose. Following the post-1937 period, this standard governs review of economic regulation.

Intermediate — A position between the customary two-tiered analysis (rational basis and strict scrutiny). Governmental action is valid if it serves an "important" purpose and is "substantially related" to that purpose. Often applied in cases of sex discrimination and commercial speech.

Strict scrutiny — A heightened standard used to review legislation that discriminates against fundamental interests (examples: race, voting, marriage). This category is sometimes called a suspect classification. To satisfy this test, a legislative classification must be necessary to achieve a compelling governmental interest and be narrowly tailored to satisfy that interest.

The case before the Court in 1973 involved a congressional statute that permitted a serviceman to claim his wife as a "dependent" even if she was not dependent on him. In contrast, a female member of the armed forces could not claim her husband as a dependent (and therefore obtain increased housing allowances and medical and dental benefits) unless he relied on her for more than one-half of his support. An 8–1 majority found the statute unconstitutional. Justice Brennan was one of four members of the Court who urged that sex be made a suspect classification. Other Justices thought that the Court should defer to the workings of the constitutional amendment process under way with the ERA. FRONTIERO v. RICHARDSON, 411 U.S. 677 (1973).[2]

In *Frontiero,* Justice Brennan took note of the fact that Congress had passed the ERA and submitted it to the states for ratification: "Thus, Congress itself has concluded that classifications based upon sex are inherently invidious, and this conclusion of a coequal branch of Government is not without significance to the question presently under consideration." Id. at 687–88.

When the ERA failed to be ratified by the end of the seven-year period specified in the amendment, Congress extended the deadline to June 30, 1982. Even with this extra time, the amendment fell short of the necessary states. The ERA failed for a number of reasons. Some women were concerned that they might lose traditional benefits from divorce settlements or be subject to the military draft. The major setback, however, was the Supreme Court's decision in *Roe* v. *Wade* (1973), upholding a woman's right to have an abortion in the first two trimesters of pregnancy (reprinted in Chapter 17). ERA proponents had tried to keep abortion as a separate issue. *Roe* seemed to link ERA with the pro-

---

2. Two years later, the Court accepted a congressional decision to establish different periods of tenure for servicemen and servicewomen before forcing them out. Male officers were subject to mandatory discharge after nine years unless they were promoted; female officers faced that test after thirteen years. The Court decided that the legislative classification was rational because Congress had taken into account the restrictions placed upon women with regard to combat duty and sea service. Schlesinger v. Ballard, 419 U.S. 498 (1975). Another congressional decision was accepted in *Mathews* v. *De Castro*, 429 U.S. 181 (1976), which concluded that it was not irrational for Congress in the Social Security Act to grant monthly benefits to a married woman under 62 whose husband retires or becomes disabled and she has a minor or dependent child in her care, whereas a divorced woman under 62 whose ex-husband retires or becomes disabled receives no such benefits. Congress recognized that divorced couples typically live separate lives, giving the divorced woman greater financial independence.

choice philosophy. Moreover, it appeared throughout the 1970s that many of the goals of the feminist movement could be accomplished by legislative action and judicial decisions rather than by constitutional amendment.

Statutory Standards

In 1966, EEOC permitted employers to place want ads that had "Male" or "Female" headings. 31 Fed. Reg. 6414 (1966). EEOC's decision ran counter to language in Section 704(b) of Title VII making it "an unlawful employment practice ... to print or publish ... any notice or advertisement relating to employment ... indicating any preference, limitation, specification, or discrimination, based on race, color, religion, sex, or national origin," other than for bfoq's (bona fide occupational qualifications, such as male and female actors, male and female models, and so forth). Representative Martha Griffiths assailed the EEOC both for its "Jane Crow" policy and its attitudes about women. 112 Cong. Rec. 13689, 13693 (1966). The next year the EEOC changed its policy to clearly oppose sex-based want ads. 32 Fed. Reg. 5999 (1967).

Not until six years later did the Supreme Court agree that a city could prohibit a newspaper from printing ads that listed job opportunities under "Male Interest" and "Female Interest" headings. Pittsburgh Press Co. v. Human Rel. Comm'n, 413 U.S. 376 (1973). Two years later the Court held that the systematic exclusion of women from jury panels violates the right to a jury trial in the Sixth Amendment. Taylor v. Louisiana, 419 U.S. 522 (1975), overruling Hoyt v. Florida, 368 U.S. 57 (1961).

Discrepancies in the age of majority (21 for men and 18 for women) were declared unconstitutional. Old notions of viewing men as the breadwinners, requiring additional years to obtain an education and training before assuming the position as head of the house, were rejected by the Court as justification for the difference between 21 and 18. The Court noted that women are increasingly involved in education, business, the professions, and government. Stanton v. Stanton, 421 U.S. 7, 15 (1975). State laws describing the husband as "head and master" and giving him unilateral power to sell jointly owned property were struck down as a violation of the Equal Protection Clause. Kirchberg v. Feenstra, 450 U.S. 455 (1981).

Increased professional activity by women produced other changes. Women lawyers denied partnership in their firm may take a sex discrimination claim to court. Hishon v. King & Spalding, 467 U.S. 69 (1984). It is still uncertain how much evidence is required to prove discrimination under Title VII. It is clear that employers may not rely on sex-based considerations in denying a woman a promotion. However, a 6–3 decision by the Supreme Court held that when a woman shows that gender played a motivating part in an unfavorable employment decision, the employer may avoid a finding of liability by proving that it would have made the same decision even if it had not allowed gender to play a role. The plurality of four, plus a concurrence by Justice O'Connor, agreed that employers have to prove their case by a preponderance of the evidence. Price Waterhouse v. Hopkins, 490 U.S. 228 (1989). As part of the Civil Rights Act of 1991 (see Chapter 15, Section E), Congress gave a statutory response to *Price Waterhouse:* Once a plaintiff proves that race, color, religion, national origin, or sex was a motivating factor in an employer's decision, the employer would be liable for a Title VII violation. In 2009 Congress corrected another Court interpretation of Title VII. Lilly Ledbetter sued Goodyear Tire and Rubber Company because she discovered, at retirement, that her salary over the years was substantially lower than that of her male peers. The case hinged on the interpretation of a provision of Title VII requiring plaintiffs to file their suits within 180 days of the discriminatory action taken by the employer. In Ledbetter's case, the salary inequity was the product of years of salary decisions that she did not discover until her retirement. In a 5–4 decision, the Court said that she had not filed her complaint within the time limit imposed by the statute. Ledbetter v. Goodyear Tire and Rubber Co., 550 U.S. 618 (2007). Congress passed the Lilly Ledbetter Fair Pay Act of 2009 which allowed for suits like Ledbetter's (See Chapter 19 for reading).

Title VII is not limited to economic or "tangible" discrimination. A claim of "hostile environment" because of sexual harassment by a supervisor is a valid basis for a lawsuit. Meritor Savings Bank v. Vinson, 477 U.S. 57 (1986). A unanimous Court in 1993 ruled that a woman need not prove psychological injury to win money damages for a claim of sexual harassment. A hostile or abusive work environment is sufficient to sustain a claim. Harris v. Forklift Systems, Inc., 510 U.S. 17 (1993). Title VII was further addressed by two Court decisions in 1998. In one case, the Court ruled that sexual harassment can exist even when the employee — subject to unwelcome and threatening sexual advances by a supervisor — suffers no adverse, tangible job consequences. Burlington Industries, Inc. v. Ellerth, 524 U.S. 742 (1998). In the second case, the Court provided additional guidelines in determining employer liability for sexual discrimination by a supervisor. Faragher v. Boca Raton, 524 U.S. 775 (1998). In 2006, a unanimous Court adopted an employee-friendly definition of the type of retaliation that is prohibited under Title VII, deciding that a company's suspension for 37 days of a female employee (the only woman working in the company's railyard) constituted retaliation. Burlington North. & Santa Fe Ry. Co. v. White, 548 U.S. 53 (2006).

Private Clubs

Although some private clubs and organizations have the constitutional freedom of association to exclude women, organizations can be required to accept women when the organizational purpose concerns economic advancement of its members through the use of commercial programs and benefits. Roberts v. United States Jaycees, 468 U.S. 609, 626 (1984). Rotary Clubs, because of their assistance to businesses and professions, have been forced to admit women as members. Bd. of Dirs. of Rotary Int'l v. Rotary Club, 481 U.S. 537 (1987). Other organizations, including the Kiwanis International and the Lions Club International, now accept female members. In 1988 a unanimous court upheld a New York City law that prohibited discrimination based on sex in any private club with more than 400 members involved directly or indirectly in furthering trade or business. New York State Club Assn. v. New York City, 487 U.S. 1 (1988). As a result of the Court's decision in 1991 not to review a New Jersey holding, the last remaining all-male eating club at Princeton University was forced to admit women as members. Tiger Inn v. Frank, 498 U.S. 1073 (1991).

Discrimination against Men

Sex discrimination may injure men as well as women. In 1972, the Court struck down an Illinois law that took children from the custody of an unwed father without a hearing, although a hearing was required for an unwed mother. Under state law, his fitness as a father was irrelevant. This procedure violated the Equal Protection Clause. Stanley v. Illinois, 405 U.S. 645 (1972). In cases where an unwed father fails to legitimate a child or take responsibility for the child's care, states can use a "best interests of the child" standard in permitting only the mother's consent for the adoption of an illegitimate child. Quilloin v. Walcott, 434 U.S. 246 (1978); Lehr v. Robertson, 463 U.S. 248 (1983). Variations on this issue can send the Court scattering in various directions. Compare Caban v. Mohammed, 441 U.S. 380 (1979) with Parham v. Hughes, 441 U.S. 347 (1979).[3]

Under a social security law struck down by a unanimous Court in 1975, a man's benefits went to both the widow and the children. If the wife died, the benefits went only to the children, not to the

---

3. In 1968, the Supreme Court ruled that an illegitimate child is a "person" under the Fourteenth Amendment and capable of challenging practices and laws as a denial of equal protection. Levy v. Louisiana, 391 U.S. 68 (1968). The rights of illegitimate children have been further explored and defined in Glona v. American Guarantee Co., 391 U.S. 73 (1968); Labine v. Vincent, 401 U.S. 532 (1971); Weber v. Aetna Casualty & Surety Co., 406 U.S. 164 (1972); Gomez v. Perez, 409 U.S. 535 (1973); New Jersey Welfare Rights Org. v. Cahill, 411 U.S. 619 (1973); Jimenez v. Weinberger, 417 U.S. 628 (1974); Mathews v. Lucas, 427 U.S. 495 (1976); Norton v. Mathews, 427 U.S. 524 (1976); Trimble v. Gordon, 430 U.S. 762 (1977); Mills v. Habluetzel, 456 U.S. 91 (1982); Pickett v. Brown, 462 U.S. 1 (1983).

Widowers, Alimony, and Nurses

A Missouri law was struck down because it denied a widower the benefits from his wife's work-related death unless he was mentally or physically incapacitated or could prove dependence on the wife's earnings. No such test was required for widows. Wengler v. Druggists Mutual Ins. Co., 446 U.S. 142 (1980). Alimony laws were successfully challenged. In 1979, the Court held that an Alabama statute violated the Equal Protection Clause by requiring husbands, but not wives, to pay alimony. Although assisting needy spouses is "a legitimate and important governmental objective," needy males along with needy females can be helped "with little if any additional burden on the States." Orr v. Orr, 440 U.S. 268, 280–81 (1979). In 1982, the Court held that a state-supported university could not limit its nursing school to women. The school attempted to justify its admission policy as compensation for past discrimination against women, but the Court concluded that the policy merely perpetuated the stereotype that nursing is exclusively a woman's job. The decision applied only to professional nursing school; other single-sex colleges were not affected by the ruling. Mississippi University for Women v. Hogan, 458 U.S. 718 (1982).

widower. This law violated the Equal Protection Clause by giving a female wage earner and the male survivor less protection. Weinberger v. Wiesenfeld, 420 U.S. 636 (1975). In another social security case, Congress provided benefits to the widow regardless of dependency. However, if the wife died, the widower received benefits only if he was receiving at least half of his support from her. The Court held this an invidious and unconstitutional discrimination. Califano v. Goldfarb, 430 U.S. 199 (1977). In that same year, however, the Court upheld a social security law in which Congress deliberately used classification by gender to compensate for previous economic discrimination against women. Califano v. Webster, 430 U.S. 313 (1977).

An Oklahoma law was invalidated in 1976 on equal protection grounds. It prohibited the sale of 3.2 percent beer to males under 21 while allowing females at age 18 to purchase the beer. The Court dismissed as inconsequential the slight percentage difference between females and males arrested for drunk driving. CRAIG v. BOREN, 429 U.S. 190 (1976). Other traditional laws—governing widowers, alimony, and nurses—were also struck down (see box).

Some sexual stereotypes persist. In 1974, the Court upheld a Florida statute that granted widows an annual $500 property tax exemption but denied widowers the same benefit. According to the Court, the law was reasonably designed to further the state's policy of cushioning the financial impact when a spouse dies. The Court accepted the generalization that widows are more needy than widowers, even if some heiresses and rich widows have no need for largesse from the state. Kahn v. Shevin, 416 U.S. 351 (1974).

A state law that defined "statutory rape" as sexual intercourse with a female under 18 who is not the wife of the perpetrator was upheld, even though it discriminate on the basis of gender. Men alone were criminally liable. These laws were based on the premise that young women (but not young men) are legally incapable of consenting to sex. In a California case challenging such a law, Justice Rehnquist argued that young women had a "natural" disincentive to engage in pre-marital sex (pregnancy) while young men had no such deterrent. Thus, a state could reasonably create a deterrent for men only in the law. MICHAEL M. v. SONOMA COUNTY SUPERIOR COURT, 450 U.S. 464 (1981). By the year 2000, however, all fifty states had gender neutral statutory rape laws.

In another decision in 1981, the Court again placed its imprimatur on discrimination between men and women. By a 6–3 majority it upheld the decision of Congress to require registration of males, but not females, for possible military service. The Court deferred to congressional judgment on this constitutional question, claiming unconvincingly that the exemption for women was not the "accidental byproduct of a traditional way of thinking about females." Rostker v. Goldberg, 453 U.S. 57, 74 (1981).[4] (The issue of women in the military is explored more fully later in this chapter.)

In 1998, a unanimous Court held that Title VII's prohibition against sex discrimination on the job covers misconduct even when the victim and the harasser are of the same sex. In this case, a male worker was sexually harassed by other men. Oncale v. Sundowner Offshore Services, 523 U.S. 75 (1998). Another case in 1998, relying on a sexual stereotype to favor mothers over fathers in citizenship cases, split the Court 6 to 3. Federal law automatically grants citizenship to a child born out of wedlock in a foreign country if the mother is American, but adopts a higher standard if the father is the American. In upholding the law, the Court reasoned that there is a closer connection between a mother and her child than a father and his child. Actually, the six Justices in the majority could not agree on their reasoning. Stevens, joined by Rehnquist, wrote for the Court. O'Connor, joined by Kennedy, wrote one concurrence. Scalia, joined by Thomas, wrote another concurrence. The three dissenters (Ginsburg, Souter, and Breyer) accused the Court of needlessly perpetuating a stereotype, especially after the availability of DNA paternity tests. Miller v. Albright, 523 U.S. 420 (1998).

Preferential Hiring

Despite efforts to eliminate gender-based employment, a person's sex may still be a factor in hiring decisions. In 1979, the Court upheld a Massachusetts law that gave a lifetime preference to veterans for state jobs. Although a woman received higher test scores than her male competitors, they were entitled under state laws to be considered first if they were veterans. The Court rationalized that the law distinguished between veterans and nonveterans, not men and women. While necessarily admitting that the statute "today benefits an overwhelmingly male class," the Court announced that the law was "neutral on its face." PERSONNEL ADMINISTRATOR OF MASS. v. FEENEY, 442 U.S. 256, 269, 274 (1979).

In 1987, the Court issued a major decision that supported affirmative action programs to hire women. An agency in California had employed 238 workers in a skilled craft position; all had been men. The company took gender into account in selecting the first woman, even though a man had scored slightly higher during an interview. The Court allowed employers to consider as one factor the sex of a qualified applicant. JOHNSON v. TRANSPORTATION AGENCY, 480 U.S. 616 (1987).

Pregnancy

The rights of pregnant women have proved particularly troublesome for Congress and the courts. Total elimination of gender-based discrimination would make it impossible to address the special needs of pregnant workers. In 1974, by a 7–2 majority, the Court struck down the policy of requiring pregnant teachers to quit their jobs without pay several months before expecting a child. Some states forced teachers to quit as much as five months before the delivery date, all done on the quaint notion that schoolchildren should be spared the sight of a pregnant woman. Cleveland Board of Education v. LaFleur, 414 U.S. 632 (1974).

The question of paying benefits to pregnant women was more difficult to resolve. A California law paid benefits to persons temporarily disabled from working and not covered by workers' compensation. Payment was not made for certain disabilities attributable to pregnancy. The Court upheld the statute in *Geduldig* v. *Aiello,* 417 U.S. 484 (1974). Building on this precedent, two years later the Court supported a company's disability plan that gave benefits for nonoccupational sickness and accidents but not for disabilities arising from pregnancy. The Court decided that the plan did not violate Title VII of the Civil Rights Act of 1964. General Electric Co. v. Gilbert, 429 U.S. 125 (1976). This decision

---

4. On the question of granting wives a portion of their husbands' military retired pay (required by certain state laws), the Court has held that federal law preempts state action. McCarty v. McCarty, 453 U.S. 210 (1981).

was "distinguished" a year later when the Court held that a company policy on leave of absence for pregnant workers violated Title VII. Nashville Gas Co. v. Satty, 434 U.S. 136 (1977).

Congress passed the Pregnancy Discrimination Act of 1978 to reverse *Gilbert.* The statute amended Title VII to prohibit employment discrimination on the basis of pregnancy and to require fringe benefit and insurance plans to cover pregnant workers. 92 Stat. 2076 (1978). When a company responded to this statute by amending its health insurance plan to provide female workers with hospitalization benefits for pregnancy-related conditions, it provided less extensive pregnancy benefits for the wives of male employees. The Court held that this plan discriminated against male employees in violation of Title VII of the Civil Rights Act of 1964. Newport News Shipbuilding & Dry Dock v. EEOC, 462 U.S. 669 (1983).

In 1987, the Court upheld state laws that require employers to give female workers an unpaid pregnancy disability leave and guarantee them their jobs when they return. The Court ruled that these laws, granting greater benefits to pregnant women than under the 1978 congressional statute, are not preempted by federal action. Moreover, the state laws necessarily discriminate on the basis of sex because pregnant women are given preferential treatment not available to other workers. California Federal S. & L. v. Guerra, 479 U.S. 272 (1987). See also Wimberly v. Labor & Industrial Rel. Comm'n, 479 U.S. 511 (1987). A decision by the Court in 1991 examined the policy of some companies to prohibit fertile women from working in certain hazardous jobs for the purpose of protecting a potential fetus. The Court held that such policies violate the Pregnancy Discrimination Act of 1978. AUTO-MOBILE WORKERS v. JOHNSON CONTROLS, 499 U.S. 187 (1991).

In 1993, Congress passed the Family and Medical Leave Act, requiring employers with 50 or more employees to provide workers with up to 12 weeks of unpaid leave for the birth or adoption of a child or the illness of a close family member. The option is available to both fathers and mothers. In the findings section of the law, Congress noted the importance of "fathers and mothers" participating in early childrearing, although the primary responsibility for family caretaking "often falls on women." Yet the purpose of the statute was to promote "the goal of equal employment opportunity for women and men." 107 Stat. 7. If both spouses work for the same employer, the aggregate number of weeks is limited to twelve.

Title IX Actions

By enacting Title IX of the Education Amendments of 1972, Congress announced that it would withdraw federal financial assistance from any educational institution that practiced sex discrimination. The Court interprets Title IX broadly to apply not only to students but to employees as well. North Haven Board of Education v. Bell, 456 U.S. 512 (1982). Enforcement of Title IX depends largely on the executive branch, but private parties have a right of action to bring disputes to the courts. Cannon v. University of Chicago, 441 U.S. 677 (1979). In 1992, a unanimous Court expanded the rights of students who are victims of sexual harassment by giving them, for the first time, the right to win money damages in Title IX suits. Franklin v. Gwinnett County Public Schools, 503 U.S. 60 (1992). Legislation by Congress in 1986 helped push the Court in this direction. 100 Stat. 1845, § 1003 (1986). In 1998, the Court held that students may not be awarded money damages in a sexual harassment suit unless a district school official knows of the misconduct and does nothing about it. Gebser v. Lago Vista Independent School Dist., 524 U.S. 274 (1998).

In 1984, the Court construed Title IX narrowly. An educational institution, Grove City College, did not accept direct federal assistance, but some of its students received federal grants. The Court held that the student aid triggered Title IX. However, it declined to make the coverage institution-wide. Title IX therefore applied only to the financial aid program, not to other activities at the college. Grove City College v. Bell, 465 U.S. 555 (1984). This meant that Title IX could be used to withhold funds only from the particular program or activity that practiced sex discrimination; federal funds would continue to flow to other programs and activities at the school. Congress tried repeatedly to pass legislation to reverse the decision, but action was stalled by numerous complications, especially language dealing with abortion. In 1988 Congress managed to pass legislation overturning *Grove City,* thereby enacting broad coverage for civil rights. President Reagan vetoed the bill but was overridden. 102 Stat. 28 (1988).

The Court split 5 to 4 in 1999 in deciding that public schools receiving Title IX funds can be sued and forced to pay damages when they fail to stop sexual harassment by one student against another. Damages are not available for simple acts of teasing and name-calling, but only when schools act with "deliberate indifference" to severe acts of harassment that effectively bar a student's access to an educational opportunity or benefit. Davis v. Monroe County Bd. of Educ., 526 U.S. 629 (1999).

Women in the Military

The requirements of World War II pulled approximately 350,000 women into the armed forces. In 1948 Congress limited women to two percent of the total enlisted strength and prohibited women in the Navy and the Air Force from being involved in combat. In 1967 Congress removed the two-percent limit and the statutory limits that restricted promotions for women. Both changes resulted from the need for women to serve in the Vietnam War. 81 Stat. 376 (1967). The decision in 1970 to end the draft (which actually terminated in 1973) created new demands for women in the military. The percentage of women in the armed forces eventually reached more than 10 percent. Congress passed legislation in 1975 to permit women to enter the service academies: the Military Academy at West Point, New York; the Naval Academy at Annapolis, Maryland; and the Air Force Academy at Colorado Springs, Colorado. 89 Stat. 537, § 803 (1975).

Job opportunities within the military also expanded for women. Before 1970, women could participate in about 35 percent of military jobs. By 2010 the proportion of jobs open to women in the military had grown substantially: Coast Guard (100 percent), Air Force (99 percent), Navy (96 percent), Marine Corps (94 percent), and Army (93 percent).

Combat Roles for Women

The issue of using women in combat divided the nation. During debate in 1972, Senator Marlow Cook (R-Ky.) denied that combat necessarily meant marching across the fields in France and Germany: "Combat today may be a lady sitting at a computer at a missile site in North Dakota." 118 Cong. Rec. 9349 (1972). Nurses served in combat zones during the Vietnam War and were paid combat pay. Women in the Navy brought suit in federal court to object to the statutory ban on assigning female personnel to duty on navy vessels other than hospital ships and transports. They claimed that this limited their opportunities for assignments and promotions. A federal district judge ruled that the restriction abridged the equal protection guarantee embodied in the Due Process Clause of the Fifth Amendment. Owens v. Brown, 455 F.Supp. 291 (D.D.C. 1978). In response to this decision, Congress gave some slight ground. 92 Stat. 1623, § 808 (1978); S. Rept. No. 826, 95th Cong., 2d Sess. 119–21 (1978).

The Soviet Union's invasion of Afghanistan in 1979 put pressure on the Carter administration to reconsider military registration as a supplement to the volunteer force. The male-only nature of this registration led to a challenge in court. A three-judge court concluded that the principal reason given by Congress for male-only registration was military flexibility, and yet flexibility was "in fact limited by the complete exclusion of women." Goldberg v. Rostker, 509 F.Supp. 586, 605 (E.D. Pa. 1980). This court held that male-only registration unconstitutionally discriminated between males and females, but the Supreme Court reversed and sustained the congressional policy. ROSTKER v. GOLDBERG, 453 U.S. 57 (1981).

By the late 1980s, the issue of women in the military returned, in part because the U.S. invasion of Panama in December 1989 included 800 Army women, some of whom saw combat. When U.S. forces were sent to the Persian Gulf in August 1990 to resist Iraq's invasion of Kuwait, approximately 26,000 women were in the deployment. More than 40,000 American female soldiers served in the Persian Gulf. They flew helicopters to transport personnel, directed artillery, drove trucks, and served with Patriot missile battalions in Saudi Arabia, Israel, and Turkey. Among the 123 U.S. troops killed in action, five were women. Eight other women were killed in accidents.

In 1991, the House Armed Services Committee voted to repeal the statutory limitation on assigning women to combat aircraft. A floor amendment to retain the statutory prohibition on women in combat was rejected. The Senate Armed Services Committee opposed any change in the statutory prohibition, but the full Senate voted overwhelmingly to allow women to fly combat missions (see reading). In conference, the two Houses agreed to repeal the statutory limitations on the assignment of women to combat aircraft. The statute also established a commission to assess the laws and policies restricting the assignment of women to military duties. 105 Stat. 2365–70 (1991). The commission's report, released during the first Bush administration, was generally critical of using women in combat, but the issue was explored anew during the Clinton administration. In 1993, Congress enacted legislation to repeal the statutory restriction on the assignment of women to combat in the Navy and Marine Corps. 107 Stat. 1659, § 541. An effort was made in Congress in 2005 to ban women from combat, but the restrictive language was removed. A Pentagon review in 2012 led to the opening of about 14,000 combat-related positions to women, but 238,000 other positions, mostly in the Army and Marine Corps, remained male only. As of August 2012, 140 U.S. female soldiers had died in Iraq or Afghanistan. This constituted 2.1% of the casualties.

The constitutional issue of women in combat has been debated and resolved almost entirely outside the courts. Legislators and executive officials analyzed the constitutional options under heavy pressure from interest groups. The decisive factors were nonjudicial: the government's need for women to serve in the military, technological changes in the meaning of "combat," and a fundamental rethinking within American society of the opportunities that should be made available to women.

Women at Military Academies

As a result of congressional legislation in 1975, women entered the service academies at West Point, the Naval Academy, and the Air Force Academy. They were barred, however, from other military academies. In a closely-watched case, in 1996 the Court held that the exclusion of women from the state-supported Virginia Military Institute (VMI) was unconstitutional. The state had offered a parallel program for women at Mary Baldwin College, but the Court ruled that this alternative did not provide equal tangible and intangible benefits. UNITED STATES v. VIRGINIA, 518 U.S. 515 (1996). Following the Court's decision, the Citadel (the only other all-male, public military college, located in South Carolina) announced that it would begin accepting women. VMI also accepted women.

Frontiero v. Richardson

411 U.S. 677 (1973)

> Sharron Frontiero, a lieutenant in the U.S. Air Force, sought increased allowances for quarters and housing and medical benefits for her husband on the ground that he was her "dependent." The law provided that wives of servicemen automatically were treated as dependents, but husbands of servicewomen were not dependents unless they depended on their wives for more than one-half their support. Lt. Frontiero and her husband brought suit on the ground that the congressional statute deprived servicewomen of due process under the Fifth Amendment (in which the Court had found an equal protection requirement applicable to the federal government in the same way the Fourteenth Amendment equal protection clause is applicable to the states).

Mr. Justice Brennan announced the judgment of the Court and an opinion in which Mr. Justice Douglas, Mr. Justice White, and Mr. Justice Marshall join.

The question before us concerns the right of a female member of the uniformed services to claim her spouse as a "dependent" for the purposes of obtaining increased quarters allowances and medical and dental benefits ... on an equal footing with male members. Under these statutes, a serviceman may claim his wife as a "dependent" without regard to whether she is in fact dependent upon him for any part of her support.... A servicewoman, on the other hand, may not claim her husband as a "dependent" under these programs unless he is in fact dependent upon her for over one-half of his support....

[I]

Appellant Sharron Frontiero, a lieutenant in the United States Air Force, sought increased quarters allowances, and housing and medical benefits for her husband, appellant Joseph Frontiero, on the ground that he was her "dependent." Although such benefits would automatically have been granted with respect to the wife of a male member of the uniformed services, appellant's application was denied because she failed to demonstrate that her husband was dependent on her for more than one-half of his support.... In essence, appellants asserted that the discriminatory impact of the statutes is twofold: first, as a procedural matter, a female member is required to demonstrate her spouse's dependency, while no such burden is imposed upon male members; and, second, as a substantive matter, a male member who does not provide more than one-half of his wife's support receives benefits, while a similarly situated female member is denied such benefits....

Although the legislative history of these statutes sheds virtually no light on the purposes underlying the differential treatment accorded male and female members, a majority of the three-judge District Court surmised that Congress might reasonably have concluded that, since the husband in our society is generally the "breadwinner" in the family — and the wife typically the "dependent" partner — "it would be more economical to require married female members claiming husbands to prove actual dependency than to extend the presumption of dependency to such members." 341 F.Supp., at 207. Indeed, given the fact that approximately 99% of all members of the uniformed services are male, the District Court speculated that such differential treatment might conceivably lead to a "considerable saving of administrative expense and manpower." *Ibid.*

II

At the outset, appellants contend that classifica-

tions based upon sex, like classifications based upon race, alienage, and national origin, are inherently suspect and must therefore be subjected to close judicial scrutiny. We agree and, indeed, find at least implicit support for such an approach in our unanimous decision only last Term in *Reed* v. *Reed*, 404 U.S. 71 (1971).

In *Reed*, the Court considered the constitutionality of an Idaho statute providing that, when two individuals are otherwise equally entitled to appointment as administrator of an estate, the male applicant must be preferred to the female....

... [T]he Court held the statutory preference for male applicants unconstitutional. In reaching this result, the Court implicitly rejected appellee's apparently rational explanation of the statutory scheme, and concluded that, by ignoring the individual qualifications of particular applicants, the challenged statute provided "dissimilar treatment for men and women who are ... similarly situated." ... The Court therefore held that, even though the State's interest in achieving administrative efficiency "is not without some legitimacy," "[t]o give a mandatory preference to members of either sex over members of the other, merely to accomplish the elimination of hearings on the merits, is to make the very kind of arbitrary legislative choice forbidden by the [Constitution]...." ...

... [O]ur statute books gradually became laden with gross, stereotyped distinctions between the sexes and, indeed, throughout much of the 19th century the position of women in our society was, in many respects, comparable to that of blacks under the pre-Civil War slave codes. Neither slaves nor women could hold office, serve on juries, or bring suit in their own names, and married women traditionally were denied the legal capacity to hold or convey property or to serve as legal guardians of their own children.... And although blacks were guaranteed the right to vote in 1870, women were denied even that right — which is itself "preservative of other basic civil and political rights" — until adoption of the Nineteenth Amendment half a century later.

... [S]ince sex, like race and national origin, is an immutable characteristic determined solely by the accident of birth, the imposition of special disabilities upon the members of a particular sex because of their sex would seem to violate "the basic concept of our system that legal burdens should bear some relationship to individual responsibility...." *Weber* v. *Aetna Casualty & Surety Co.*, 406 U.S. 164, 175 (1972). And what differentiates sex from such nonsuspect statuses as intelligence or physical disability, and aligns it with the recognized suspect criteria, is that the sex characteristic frequently bears no relation to ability to perform or contribute to society. As a result, statutory distinctions between the sexes often have the effect of invidiously relegating the entire class of females to inferior legal status without regard to the actual capabilities of its individual members.

We might also note that, over the past decade, Congress has itself manifested an increasing sensitivity to sex-based classifications. [*The Court refers to Title VII of the Civil Rights Act of 1964, the Equal Pay Act of 1963, and the Equal Rights Amendment.*] Thus, Congress itself has concluded that classifications based upon sex are inherently invidious, and this conclusion of a coequal branch of Government is not without significance to the question presently under consideration....

With these considerations in mind, we can only conclude that classifications based upon sex, like classifications based upon race, alienage, or national origin, are inherently suspect, and must therefore be subjected to strict judicial scrutiny. Applying the analysis mandated by that stricter standard of review, it is clear that the statutory scheme now before us is constitutionally invalid....

Reversed.

MR. JUSTICE STEWART concurs in the judgment, agreeing that the statutes before us work an invidious discrimination in violation of the Constitution. *Reed* v. *Reed*, 404 U.S. 71.

MR. JUSTICE REHNQUIST dissents for the reasons stated by Judge Rives in his opinion for the District Court, *Frontiero* v. *Laird*, 341 F.Supp. 201 (1972).

MR. JUSTICE POWELL, with whom THE CHIEF JUSTICE and MR. JUSTICE BLACKMUN join, concurring in the judgment.

I agree that the challenged statutes constitute an unconstitutional discrimination against servicewomen in violation of the Due Process Clause of the Fifth Amendment, but I cannot join the opinion of MR. JUSTICE BRENNAN, which would hold that all classifications based upon sex, "like classifications based upon race, alienage, and national origin," are "inherently suspect and must therefore be subjected to close judicial scrutiny."... It is unnecessary for the Court in this case to characterize sex as a suspect classification, with all of the far-reaching implications of such a holding....

There is another, and I find compelling, reason for deferring a general categorizing of sex classifications as invoking the strictest test of judicial scrutiny. The Equal Rights Amendment, which if adopted will resolve the substance of this precise question, has been approved by the Congress and submitted for ratification by the States. If this Amendment is duly adopted, it will represent the will of the people accomplished in the manner prescribed by the Constitution. By acting prematurely and unnecessarily, as I view it, the Court has assumed a decisional responsibility at the very time when state legislatures, functioning within the traditional democratic process, are debating the proposed Amendment....

... [D]emocratic institutions are weakened, and confidence in the restraint of the Court is impaired, when we appear unnecessarily to decide sensitive issues of broad social and political importance at the very time they are under consideration within the prescribed constitutional processes.

Craig v. Boren

429 U.S. 190 (1976)

Curtis Craig, a male then between 18 and 21 years old, together with a licensed vendor of 3.2 percent beer, brought an action in federal court for declaratory and injunctive relief, claiming that an Oklahoma law constituted a gender-based discrimination in violation of the Equal Protection Clause. The law prohibited the sale of "nonintoxicating" 3.2 percent beer to males under the age of 21 and to females under the age of 18. A three-judge court held that the state's statistical evidence regarding young males' drunk-driving arrests and traffic injuries demonstrated that the gender-based discrimination was substantially related to the achievement of traffic safety on Oklahoma roads. David Boren was governor of Oklahoma.

MR. JUSTICE BRENNAN delivered the opinion of the Court.

The interaction of two sections of an Oklahoma statute ... prohibits the sale of "nonintoxicating"

3.2% beer to males under the age of 21 and to females under the age of 18. The question to be decided is whether such a gender-based differential constitutes a denial to males 18–20 years of age of the equal protection of the laws in violation of the Fourteenth Amendment.

[*In Section I, the Court addressed the preliminary question of standing. Craig had turned 21 by the time the Court noted probable jurisdiction. Since only declaratory and injunctive relief against enforcement of the gender-based differential had been sought, the controversy was moot as to Craig. However, the Court held that the licensed vendor (Whitener) who had joined the case with Craig, had standing to raise an equal protection challenge to the Oklahoma law.*]

[II.A]

Analysis may appropriately begin with the reminder that *Reed* emphasized that statutory classifications that distinguish between males and females are "subject to scrutiny under the Equal Protection Clause." 404 U.S., at 75. To withstand constitutional challenge, previous cases establish that classifications by gender must serve important governmental objectives and must be substantially related to achievement of those objectives....

... We turn then to the question whether, under *Reed,* the difference between males and females with respect to the purchase of 3.2% beer warrants the differential in age drawn by the Oklahoma statute. We conclude that it does not.

[C]

The appellees introduced a variety of statistical surveys. First, an analysis of arrest statistics for 1973 demonstrated that 18–20-year-old male arrests for "driving under the influence" and "drunkenness" substantially exceeded female arrests for that same age period. Similarly, youths aged 17–21 were found to be overrepresented among those killed or injured in traffic accidents, with males again numerically exceeding females in this regard. [*A footnote by the Court explains that this survey did not draw a correlation between the accident figures for any age group and levels of intoxication found in those killed or injured.*] Third, a random roadside survey in Oklahoma City revealed that young males were more inclined to drive and drink beer than were their female counterparts. Fourth, Federal Bureau of Investigation nationwide statistics exhibited a notable increase in arrests for "driving under the influence." [*The Court notes that the FBI did not attempt to relate the arrest figures either to beer drinking or to an 18–21 age differential.*] Finally, statistical evidence gathered

in other jurisdictions, particularly Minnesota and Michigan, was offered to corroborate Oklahoma's experience by indicating the pervasiveness of youthful participation in motor vehicle accidents following the imbibing of alcohol. Conceding that "the case is not free from doubt," 399 F.Supp., at 1314, the District Court nonetheless concluded that this statistical showing substantiated "a rational basis for the legislative judgment underlying the challenged classification." *Id.,* at 1307.

Even were this statistical evidence accepted as accurate, it nevertheless offers only a weak answer to the equal protection question presented here. The most focused and relevant of the statistical surveys, arrests of 18–20-year-olds for alcohol-related driving offenses, exemplifies the ultimate unpersuasiveness of this evidentiary record. Viewed in terms of the correlation between sex and the actual activity that Oklahoma seeks to regulate—driving while under the influence of alcohol—the statistics broadly establish that .18% of females and 2% of males in that age group were arrested for that offense. While such a disparity is not trivial in a statistical sense, it hardly can form the basis for employment of a gender line as a classifying device. Certainly if maleness is to serve as a proxy for drinking and driving, a correlation of 2% must be considered an unduly tenuous "fit." Indeed, prior cases have consistently rejected the use of sex as a decisionmaking factor even though the statutes in question certainly rested on far more predictive empirical relationships than this.

Moreover, the statistics exhibit a variety of other shortcomings that seriously impugn their value to equal protection analysis. Setting aside the obvious methodological problems, the surveys do not adequately justify the salient features of Oklahoma's gender-based traffic-safety law. None purports to measure the use and dangerousness of 3.2% beer as opposed to alcohol generally, a detail that is of particular importance since, in light of its low alcohol level, Oklahoma apparently considers the 3.2% beverage to be "nonintoxicating." ... Moreover, many of the studies, while graphically documenting the unfortunate increase in driving while under the influence of alcohol, make no effort to relate their findings to age-sex differentials as involved here. Indeed, the only survey that explicitly centered its attention upon young drivers and their use of beer—albeit apparently not of the diluted 3.2% variety—reached results that hardly can be viewed as impressive in justifying either a gender or age classification.

... Suffice to say that the showing offered by the appellees does not satisfy us that sex represents a legitimate, accurate proxy for the regulation of drinking and driving....

We hold, therefore, that under *Reed,* Oklahoma's 3.2% beer statute invidiously discriminates against males 18–20 years of age.

D

[*In this section, the Court considers Oklahoma's contention that Sections 241 and 245 enforce state policies concerning the sale and distribution of alcohol and by force of the Twenty-first Amendment should therefore be held to withstand the equal protection challenge. The Court holds that the Amendment does not save the invidious gender-based discrimination from invalidation.*]

We conclude that the gender-based differential contained in Okla. Stat., Tit. 37, § 245 (1976 Supp.) constitutes a denial of the equal protection of the laws to males aged 18–20 and reverse the judgment of the District Court.

It is so ordered.

MR. JUSTICE POWELL, concurring.

[*In a footnote, Powell refers to the dissatisfaction with the Court's "two-tier" analysis of the Equal Protection Clause, adopting a strict-scrutiny test for discrimination in cases of race and alienage and a more lenient test that permits a legislature to make classifications if the statute is rational and furthers an important governmental interest. He even suggests that the holding in the Oklahoma case implies a "middle-tiered" approach.*]

MR. JUSTICE STEVENS, concurring.

There is only one Equal Protection Clause. It requires every State to govern impartially. It does not direct the courts to apply one standard of review in some cases and a different standard in other cases. Whatever criticism may be leveled at a judicial opinion implying that there are at least three such standards applies with the same force to a double standard....

MR. JUSTICE BLACKMUN, concurring in part.

I join the Court's opinion except Part II-D thereof. I agree, however, that the Twenty-first Amendment does not save the challenged Oklahoma statute.

MR. JUSTICE STEWART, concurring in the judgment....

MR. CHIEF JUSTICE BURGER, dissenting.

I am in general agreement with MR. JUSTICE REHNQUIST's dissent, ...

MR. JUSTICE REHNQUIST, dissenting.

The Court's disposition of this case is objectionable on two grounds. First is its conclusion that *men* challenging a gender-based statute which treats them less favorably than women may invoke a more stringent standard of judicial review than pertains to most other types of classifications. Second is the Court's enunciation of this standard, without citation to any source, as being that "classifications by gender must serve *important* governmental objectives and must be *substantially* related to achievement of those objectives." *Ante,* at 197 (emphasis added). The only redeeming feature of the Court's opinion, to my mind, is that it apparently signals a retreat by those who joined the plurality opinion in *Frontiero* v. *Richardson,* 411 U.S. 677 (1973), from their view that sex is a "suspect" classification for purposes of equal protection analysis. I think the Oklahoma statute challenged here need pass only the "rational basis" equal protection analysis ... and I believe that it is constitutional under that analysis.

[I]

The Court's conclusion that a law which treats males less favorably than females "must serve important governmental objectives and must be substantially related to achievement of those objectives" apparently comes out of thin air. The Equal Protection Clause contains no such language, and none of our previous cases adopt that standard. I would think we have had enough difficulty with the two standards of review which our cases have recognized—the norm of "rational basis," and the "compelling state interest" required where a "suspect classification" is involved—so as to counsel weightily against the insertion of still another "standard" between those two. How is this Court to divine what objectives are important? How is it to determine whether a particular law is "substantially" related to the achievement of such objective, rather than related in some other way to its achievement? Both of the phrases used are so diaphanous and elastic as to invite subjective judicial preferences or prejudices relating to particular types of legislation, masquerading as judgments whether such legislation is directed at "important" objectives or, whether the relationship to those objectives is "substantial" enough.

Michael M. v. Sonoma County Superior Court

450 U.S. 464 (1981)

Michael M., a 17-year-old male, was charged with violating California's "statutory rape" law, which defines unlawful sexual intercourse as "an act of sexual intercourse accomplished with a female not the wife of the perpetrator, where the female is under the age of 18 years." He sued on the ground that the statute unlawfully discriminated on the basis of gender since men alone were criminally liable. The Supreme Court of California held that the classification, when subjected to "strict scrutiny," was justified by the state's compelling interest to avoid the cost of illegitimate teenage pregnancies, abortions, and teenage childbearing.

JUSTICE REHNQUIST announced the judgment of the Court and delivered an opinion, in which THE CHIEF JUSTICE, JUSTICE STEWART, and JUSTICE POWELL joined.

The question presented in this case is whether California's "statutory rape" law ... violates the Equal Protection Clause of the Fourteenth Amendment. Section 261.5 defines unlawful sexual intercourse as "an act of sexual intercourse accomplished with a female not the wife of the perpetrator, where the female is under the age of 18 years." The statute thus makes men alone criminally liable for the act of sexual intercourse....

We are satisfied not only that the prevention of illegitimate pregnancy is at least one of the "purposes" of the statute, but also that the State has a strong interest in preventing such pregnancy. At the risk of stating the obvious, teenage pregnancies, which have increased dramatically over the last two decades, have significant social, medical, and economic consequences for both the mother and her child, and the State. Of particular concern to the State is that approximately half of all teenage pregnancies end in abortion. And of those children who are born, their illegitimacy makes them likely candidates to become wards of the State.

We need not be medical doctors to discern that young men and young women are not similarly situated with respect to the problems and the risks of sexual intercourse. Only women may become pregnant, and they suffer disproportionately the profound physical, emotional, and psychological consequences of sexual activity. The statute at issue here protects women from sexual intercourse at an age when those consequences are particularly severe.

The question thus boils down to whether a State may attack the problem of sexual intercourse and teenage pregnancy directly by prohibiting a male from having sexual intercourse with a minor female. We hold that such a statute is sufficiently related to the State's objectives to pass constitutional muster.

Because virtually all of the significant harmful and inescapably identifiable consequences of teenage pregnancy fall on the young female, a legislature acts well within its authority when it elects to punish only the participant who, by nature, suffers few of the consequences of his conduct. It is hardly unreasonable for a legislature acting to protect minor females to exclude them from punishment. Moreover, the risk of pregnancy itself constitutes a substantial deterrence to young females. No similar natural sanctions deter males. A criminal sanction imposed solely on males thus serves to roughly "equalize" the deterrents on the sexes....

There remains only petitioner's contention that the statute is unconstitutional as it is applied to him because he, like Sharon, was under 18 at the time of sexual intercourse. Petitioner argues that the statute is flawed because it presumes that as between two persons under 18, the male is the culpable aggressor. We find petitioner's contentions unpersuasive. Contrary to his assertions, the statute does not rest on the assumption that males are generally the aggressors. It is instead an attempt by a legislature to prevent illegitimate teenage pregnancy by providing an additional deterrent for men. The age of the man is irrelevant since young men are as capable as older men of inflicting the harm sought to be prevented....

Accordingly the judgment of the California Supreme Court is

Affirmed.

JUSTICE STEWART, concurring....

JUSTICE BLACKMUN, concurring in the judgment....

JUSTICE BRENNAN, with whom JUSTICES WHITE and MARSHALL join, dissenting.

... [T]he experience of other jurisdictions, and California itself, belies the plurality's conclusion that a gender-neutral statutory rape law "may well be incapable of enforcement." There are now at least 37

States that have enacted gender-neutral statutory rape laws. Although most of these laws protect young persons (of either sex) from the sexual exploitation of older individuals, the laws of Arizona, Florida, and Illinois permit prosecution of both minor females and minor males for engaging in mutual sexual conduct. California has introduced no evidence that those States have been handicapped by the enforcement problems the plurality finds so persuasive....

... [E]ven assuming that a gender-neutral statute would be more difficult to enforce, the State has still not shown that those enforcement problems would make such a statute less effective than a gender-based statute in deterring minor females from engaging in sexual intercourse. Common sense, however, suggests that a gender-neutral statutory rape law is potentially a *greater* deterrent of sexual activity than a gender-based law, for the simple reason that a gender-neutral law subjects both men and women to criminal sanctions and thus arguably has a deterrent effect on twice as many potential violators....

JUSTICE STEVENS, dissenting.

... [T]he fact that a female confronts a greater risk of harm than a male is a reason for applying the prohibition to her—not a reason for granting her a license to use her own judgment on whether or not to assume the risk. Surely, if we examine the problem from the point of view of society's interest in preventing the risk-creating conduct from occurring at all, it is irrational to exempt 50% of the potential violators....

Personnel Administrator of Mass. v. Feeney
442 U.S. 256 (1979)

Under a Massachusetts statute, all veterans who qualify for state civil service positions must be considered for appointment ahead of any qualifying nonveteran. The statute made the preference available to "any person, male or female, including a nurse," who was honorably discharged from the United States armed forces after at least 90 days of active service, at least one day of which was during "wartime." Helen B. Feeney, who was not a veteran, passed a number of open competitive civil service examinations but, because of the veterans' preference law, was ranked below male veterans who had lower test scores. A three-judge district court held that the veterans' preference statute violated the Equal Protection Clause.

MR. JUSTICE STEWART delivered the opinion of the Court.

This case presents a challenge to the constitutionality of the Massachusetts veterans' preference statute, ... on the ground that it discriminates against women in violation of the Equal Protection Clause of the Fourteenth Amendment. Under ch. 31, § 23, all veterans who qualify for state civil service positions must be considered for appointment ahead of any qualifying nonveterans. The preference operates overwhelmingly to the advantage of males.

The appellee Helen B. Feeney is not a veteran. She brought this action pursuant to 42 U.S.C. § 1983, alleging that the absolute-preference formula established in ch. 31, § 23, inevitably operates to exclude women from consideration for the best Massachusetts civil service jobs and thus unconstitutionally denies them the equal protection of the laws....

[I.A]

The Federal Government and virtually all of the States grant some sort of hiring preference to veterans. The Massachusetts preference, which is loosely termed an "absolute lifetime" preference, is among the most generous. It applies to all positions in the State's classified civil service, which constitute approximately 60% of the public jobs in the State. It is available to "any person, male or female, including a nurse," who was honorably discharged from the United States Armed Forces after at least 90 days of active service, at least one day of which was during "wartime."...

... All applicants for employment must take competitive examinations. Grades are based on a formula that gives weight both to objective test results and to training and experience. Candidates who pass are then ranked in the order of their respective scores on an "eligible list." Chapter 31, § 23, requires, however, that disabled veterans, veterans, and surviving spouses and surviving parents of veterans be ranked—in the order of their respective scores—above all other candidates.

... Under formulas prescribed by civil service rules, a small number of candidates from the top of an appropriate list, three if there is only one vacancy, are certified. The appointing agency is then required to choose from among these candidates. Although the veterans' preference thus does not guarantee that a veteran will be appointed, it is obvious that the preference gives to veterans who achieve passing scores a well-nigh absolute advantage.

[B]

During her 12-year tenure as a public employee, Ms. Feeney took and passed a number of open competitive civil service examinations. On several she did quite well, receiving in 1971 the second highest score on an examination for a job with the Board of Dental Examiners, and in 1973 the third highest on a test for an Administrative Assistant position with a mental health center. Her high scores, however, did not win her a place on the certified eligible list. Because of the veterans' preference, she was ranked sixth behind five male veterans on the Dental Examiner list. She was not certified, and a lower scoring veteran was eventually appointed. On the 1973 examination, she was placed in a position on the list behind 12 male veterans, 11 of whom had lower scores....

C

The veterans' hiring preference in Massachusetts, as in other jurisdictions, has traditionally been justified as a measure designed to reward veterans for the sacrifice of military service, to ease the transition from military to civilian life, to encourage patriotic service, and to attract loyal and well-disciplined people to civil service occupations....

III
A

The question whether ch. 31, § 23, establishes a classification that is overtly or covertly based upon gender must first be considered. The appellee has conceded that ch. 31, § 23, is neutral on its face. She has also acknowledged that state hiring preferences for veterans are not *per se* invalid, for she has limited her challenge to the absolute lifetime preference that Massachusetts provides to veterans....

... Veteran status is not uniquely male. Although few women benefit from the preference, the non-veteran class is not substantially all female. To the contrary, significant numbers of nonveterans are men, and all nonveterans—male as well as female—are placed at a disadvantage. Too many men are affected by ch. 31, § 23, to permit the inference that the statute is but a pretext for preferring men over women.

... The distinction made by ch. 31, § 23, is, as it seems to be, quite simply between veterans and non-veterans, not between men and women.

[B1]

The contention that this veterans' preference is "inherently nonneutral" or "gender-biased" presumes that the State, by favoring veterans, intentionally incorporated into its public employment policies the panoply of sex-based and assertedly discriminatory federal laws that have prevented all but a handful of women from becoming veterans. There are two serious difficulties with this argument. First, it is wholly at odds with the District Court's central finding that Massachusetts has not offered a preference to veterans for the purpose of discriminating against women. Second, it cannot be reconciled with the assumption made by both the appellee and the District Court that a more limited hiring preference for veterans could be sustained. Taken together, these difficulties are fatal....

2

... [N]othing in the record demonstrates that this preference for veterans was originally devised or subsequently re-enacted because it would accomplish the collateral goal of keeping women in a stereotypic and predefined place in the Massachusetts Civil Service....

IV

Veterans' hiring preferences represent an awkward—and, many argue, unfair—exception to the widely shared view that merit and merit alone should prevail in the employment policies of government. After a war, such laws have been enacted virtually without opposition. During peacetime, they inevitably have come to be viewed in many quarters as undemocratic and unwise. Absolute and permanent preferences, as the troubled history of this law demonstrates, have always been subject to the objection that they give the veteran more than a square deal.... The substantial edge granted to veterans by ch. 31, § 23, may reflect unwise policy. The appellee, however, has simply failed to demonstrate that the law in any way reflects a purpose to discriminate on the basis of sex.

The judgment is reversed, and the case is remanded for further proceedings consistent with this opinion.

It is so ordered.

MR. JUSTICE STEVENS, with whom MR. JUSTICE WHITE joins, concurring....

MR. JUSTICE MARSHALL, with whom MR. JUS-TICE BRENNAN joins, dissenting.

... In my judgment, Massachusetts' choice of an absolute veterans' preference system evinces purposeful gender-based discrimination....

II

... [T]here are a wide variety of less discrimina-tory means by which Massachusetts could effect its compensatory purposes. For example, a point preference system, such as that maintained by many States and the Federal Government, ... or an absolute preference for a limited duration would reward veterans without excluding all qualified women from upper level civil service positions....

Johnson v. Transportation Agency

480 U.S. 616 (1987)

Paul E. Johnson, a male employee, was passed over for promotion to the position of road dispatcher. Instead, the Transportation Agency selected a female employee, Diane Joyce. Both were rated as well qualified for the job, but Joyce was picked in part because the Agency took into account her gender as a factor. Johnson filed suit, claiming that the Agency had violated Title VII of the Civil Rights Act of 1964. The district court agreed; the Ninth Circuit reversed.

JUSTICE BRENNAN delivered the opinion of the Court.

[I.A.]

In December 1978, the Santa Clara County Transit District Board of Supervisors adopted an Affirmative Action Plan (Plan) for the County Transportation Agency. The Plan implemented a County Affirmative Action Plan, which had been adopted, declared the County, because "mere prohibition of discriminatory practices is not enough to remedy the effects of past practices and to permit attainment of an equitable representation of minorities, women and handicapped persons." ... Relevant to this case, the Agency Plan provides that, in making promotions to positions within a traditionally segregated job classification in which women have been significantly underrepresented, the Agency is authorized to consider as one factor the sex of a qualified applicant.

In reviewing the composition of its work force, the Agency noted in its Plan that women were represented in numbers far less than their proportion of the county labor force in both the Agency as a whole and in five of seven job categories. Specifically, while women constituted 36.4% of the area labor market, they composed only 22.4% of Agency employees. Furthermore, women working at the Agency were concentrated largely in EEOC job categories traditionally held by women: women made up 76% of Office and Clerical Workers, but only 7.1% of Agency Officials and Administrators, 8.6% of Professionals, 9.7% of Technicians, and 22% of Service and Maintenance workers. As for the job classification relevant to this case, none of the 238 Skilled Craft Worker positions was held by a woman....

B

On December 12, 1979, the Agency announced a vacancy for the promotional position of road dispatcher in the Agency's Roads Division. Dispatchers assign road crews, equipment, and materials, and maintain records pertaining to road maintenance jobs.... The position requires at minimum four years of dispatch or road maintenance work experience for Santa Clara County. The EEOC job classification scheme designates a road dispatcher as a Skilled Craft worker.

Twelve County employees applied for the promotion, including Joyce and Johnson. Joyce had worked for the County since 1970, serving as an account clerk until 1975. She had applied for a road dispatcher position in 1974, but was deemed ineligible because she had not served as a road maintenance worker. In 1975, Joyce transferred from a senior account clerk position to a road maintenance worker position, becoming the first woman to fill such a job.... During her four years in that position, she occasionally worked out of class as a road dispatcher.

Petitioner Johnson began with the county in 1967 as a road yard clerk, after private employment that included working as a supervisor and dispatcher. He had also unsuccessfully applied for the road dispatcher opening in 1974. In 1977, his clerical position was downgraded, and he sought and received a transfer to the position of road maintenance worker.... He also occasionally worked out of class as a dispatcher while performing that job.

Nine of the applicants, including Joyce and Johnson, were deemed qualified for the job, and were interviewed by a two-person board. Seven of the applicants scored above 70 on this interview, which meant that they were certified as eligible for selection by the appointing authority. The scores awarded ranged from 70 to 80. Johnson was tied for second with score of 75, while Joyce ranked next with a score of 73. A second interview was conducted by three Agency supervisors, who ultimately recommended that Johnson be promoted. Prior to the second interview, Joyce had contacted the County's Affirmative Action Office because she feared that her application might not receive disinterested review. The Office in turn contacted the Agency's Affirmative Action Coordinator, whom the Agency's Plan makes responsible for, *inter alia,* keeping the Director informed of opportunities for the Agency to accomplish its objectives under the Plan. At the time, the Agency employed no women in any Skilled Craft position, and had never employed a woman as a road dispatcher. The Coordinator recommended to the Director of the Agency, James Graebner, that Joyce be promoted.

... After deliberation, Graebner concluded that the promotion should be given to Joyce. As he testified: "I tried to look at the whole picture, the combination of her qualifications and Mr. Johnson's qualifications, their test scores, their expertise, their background, affirmative action matters, things like that ... I believe it was a combination of all those."...

... Graebner testified that he did not regard as significant the fact that Johnson scored 75 and Joyce 73 when interviewed by the two-person board....

[II]

... [I]t was plainly not unreasonable for the Agency to determine that it was appropriate to consider as one factor the sex of Ms. Joyce in making its decision. The promotion of Joyce thus satisfies the first requirement enunciated in *Weber* [Steelworkers v. Weber, 443 U.S. 193 (1979)], since it was undertaken to further an affirmative action plan designed to eliminate Agency work force imbalances in traditionally segregated job categories.

We next consider whether the Agency Plan unnecessarily trammeled the rights of male employees or created an absolute bar to their advancement. In contrast to the plan in *Weber,* which provided that 50% of the positions in the craft training program

were exclusively for blacks, and to the consent decree upheld last term in *Firefighters* v. *Cleveland,* 478 U.S. 501 (1986), which required the promotion of specific numbers of minorities, the Plan sets aside no positions for women.... As the Agency Director testified, the sex of Joyce was but one of numerous factors he took into account in arriving at his decision....

III

. . .

We therefore hold that the Agency appropriately took into account as one factor the sex of Diane Joyce in determining that she should be promoted to the road dispatcher position.... Accordingly, the judgment of the Court of Appeals is

Affirmed.

JUSTICE STEVENS, concurring....

JUSTICE O'CONNOR, concurring in the judgment....

JUSTICE WHITE, dissenting....

JUSTICE SCALIA, with whom THE CHIEF JUSTICE joins, and with whom JUSTICE WHITE joins in Parts I and II, dissenting.

... Title VII of the Civil Rights Act of 1964 declares:

"It shall be an unlawful employment practice for an employer—
"(1) to fail or refuse to hire or to discharge any individual, or otherwise to discriminate against any individual with respect to his compensation, terms, conditions, or privileges, of employment, because of such individual's race, color, religion, sex, or national origin; or
"(2) to limit, segregate, or classify his employees or applicants for employment in any way which would deprive or tend to deprive any individual of employment opportunities or otherwise adversely affect his status as an employee, because of such individual's race, color, religion, sex, or national origin." 42 U.S.C. § 2000e-2(a).

The Court today completes the process of converting this from a guarantee that race or sex will *not* be the basis for employment determinations, to a guarantee that it often *will....*

Automobile Workers v. Johnson Controls

499 U.S. 187 (1991)

Johnson Controls, a manufacturer of batteries, prohibited fertile women from working in jobs that would expose them to lead and possible health hazards to the fetus a woman might conceive. The question for the Court was whether the company's policy was barred by the Pregnancy Discrimination Act of 1978, which amended the sex discrimination provision in the Civil Rights Act of 1964. The Court was unanimous in deciding that Johnson Controls had discriminated against women, but the Justices who concurred disagreed with the majority's analysis of congressional policy.

JUSTICE BLACKMUN delivered the opinion of the Court.

In this case we are concerned with an employer's gender-based fetal-protection policy. May an employer exclude a fertile female employee from certain jobs because of its concern for the health of the fetus the woman might conceive?

I

Respondent Johnson Controls, Inc., manufactures batteries. In the manufacturing process, the element lead is a primary ingredient. Occupational exposure to lead entails health risks, including the risk of harm to any fetus carried by a female employee.

Before the Civil Rights Act of 1964, 78 Stat. 241, became law, Johnson Controls did not employ any woman in a battery-manufacturing job. In June 1977, however, it announced its first official policy concerning its employment of women in lead-exposure work:

"[P]rotection of the health of the unborn child is the immediate and direct responsibility of the prospective parents. While the medical profession and the company can support them in the exercise of this responsibility, it cannot assume it for them without simultaneously infringing their rights as persons....

"... Since not all women who can become mothers wish to become mothers (or will become mothers), it would appear to be illegal discrimination to treat all who are capable of pregnancy as though they will become pregnant."...

Consistent with that view, Johnson Controls "stopped short of excluding women capable of bearing children from lead exposure,"... but emphasized that a woman who expected to have a child should not choose a job in which she would have such exposure. The company also required a woman who wished to be considered for employment to sign a

statement that she had been advised of the risk of having a child while she was exposed to lead....

Five years later, in 1982, Johnson Controls shifted from a policy of warning to a policy of exclusion [*of pregnant women or women capable of bearing children*]....

II

[*Petitioners included a woman who had chosen to be sterilized in order to avoid losing her job, a woman who had suffered a loss in compensation when she was transferred out of a job where she was exposed to lead, and a man who had been denied a request for a leave of absence for the purpose of lowering his lead level because he intended to become a father.*]

III

The bias in Johnson Controls' policy is obvious. Fertile men, but not fertile women, are given a choice as to whether they wish to risk their reproductive health for a particular job. Section 703(a) of the Civil Rights Act of 1964, ... prohibits sex-based classifications in terms and conditions of employment, in hiring and discharging decisions, and in other employment decisions that adversely affect an employee's status. Respondent's fetal-protection policy explicitly discriminates against women on the basis of their sex....

... Respondent does not seek to protect the unconceived children of all its employees. Despite evidence in the record about the debilitating effect of lead exposure on the male reproductive system, Johnson Controls is concerned only with the harms that may befall the unborn offspring of its female employees.... Johnson Controls' policy is facially discriminatory because it requires only a female employee to produce proof that she is not capable of reproducing.

Our conclusion is bolstered by the Pregnancy Discrimination Act of 1978 (PDA), ... in which Congress explicitly provided that, for purposes of

Title VII, discrimination "on the basis of sex" includes discrimination "because of or on the basis of pregnancy, childbirth, or related medical conditions." "The Pregnancy Discrimination Act has now made clear that, for all Title VII purposes, discrimination based on a woman's pregnancy is, on its face, discrimination because of her sex." *Newport News Shipbuilding & Dry Dock Co. v. EEOC,* 462 U.S. 669, 684 (1983). In its use of the words "capable of bearing children" in the 1982 policy statement as the criterion for exclusion, Johnson Controls explicitly classifies on the basis of potential for pregnancy. Under the PDA, such a classification must be regarded, for Title VII purposes, in the same light as explicit sex discrimination. Respondent has chosen to treat all its female employees as potentially pregnant; that choice evinces discrimination on the basis of sex....

... We hold that Johnson Controls' fetal-protection policy is sex discrimination forbidden under Title VII unless respondent can establish that sex is a "bona fide occupational qualification."

IV

Under § 703(e)(1) of Title VII, an employer may discriminate on the basis of "religion, sex, or national origin in those certain instances where religion, sex, or national origin is a bona fide occupational qualification reasonably necessary to the normal operation of that particular business or enterprise." ... We therefore turn to the question whether Johnson Controls' fetal-protection policy is one of those "certain instances" that come within the BFOQ exception.

The BFOQ defense is written narrowly, and this Court has read it narrowly....

We conclude that the language of both the BFOQ provision and the PDA which amended it, as well as the legislative history and the case law, prohibit an employer from discriminating against a woman because of her capacity to become pregnant unless her reproductive potential prevents her from performing the duties of her job....

V

We have no difficulty concluding that Johnson Controls cannot establish a BFOQ. Fertile women, as far as appears in the record, participate in the manufacture of batteries as efficiently as anyone else. Johnson Controls' professed moral and ethical concerns about the welfare of the next generation do not suffice to establish a BFOQ of female sterility. Decisions about the welfare of future children must be left to the parents who conceive, bear, support, and raise them rather than to the employers who hire those parents....

[VII]

The judgment of the Court of Appeals is reversed and the case is remanded for further proceedings consistent with this opinion.

It is so ordered.

JUSTICE WHITE, with whom THE CHIEF JUSTICE and JUSTICE KENNEDY join, concurring in part and concurring in the judgment.

[*Disagrees with the Court's holding that the BFOQ defense is so narrow that it could never justify a sex-specific fetal protection policy. A fetal protection policy would be justified if an employer showed that "exclusion of women from certain jobs was reasonably necessary to avoid substantial tort liability."*]

JUSTICE SCALIA, concurring in the judgment....

[*Agrees with White's concurrence.*]

Rostker v. Goldberg

453 U.S. 57 (1981)

In 1980, Congress reactivated the registration process for military service but denied President Carter the authority he requested to permit the registration and conscription of women as well as men. After President Carter ordered the registration of specified groups of young men, several men, including Robert L. Goldberg, brought a lawsuit challenging the statute's constitutionality. A three-judge district court held that the statute's gender-based discrimination violated the Due Process Clause of the Fifth Amendment and enjoined registration under the statute. Bernard Rostker, Director of Selective Service, brought this appeal to the Supreme Court.

JUSTICE REHNQUIST delivered the opinion of the Court.

The question presented is whether the Military Selective Service Act ... violates the Fifth Amendment to the United States Constitution in authorizing the President to require the registration of males and not females.

I

Congress is given the power under the Constitution "To raise and support Armies," "To provide and maintain a Navy," and "To make Rules for the Government and Regulation of the land and naval Forces." ... Pursuant to this grant of authority Congress has enacted the Military Selective Service Act [*MSSA*].... Section 3 of the Act ... empowers the President, by proclamation, to require the registration of "every male citizen" and male resident aliens between the ages of 18 and 26. The purpose of this registration is to facilitate any eventual conscription....

II

Whenever called upon to judge the constitutionality of an Act of Congress — "the gravest and most delicate duty that this Court is called upon to perform." ... the Court accords "great weight to the decisions of Congress." ... The Congress is a coequal branch of government whose Members take the same oath we do to uphold the Constitution of the United States....

This is not, however, merely a case involving the customary deference accorded congressional decisions. The case arises in the context of Congress' authority over national defense and military affairs, and perhaps in no other area has the Court accorded Congress greater deference. In rejecting the registration of women, Congress explicitly relied upon its constitutional powers under Art. I, § 8, cls. 12–14. The "specific findings" section of the Report of the Senate Armed Services Committee, later adopted by both Houses of Congress, began by stating:

"Article I, section 8 of the Constitution commits exclusively to the Congress the powers to raise and support armies, provide and maintain a Navy, and make rules for Government and regulation of the land and naval forces, and pursuant to these powers it lies within the discretion of the Congress to determine the occasions for expansion of our Armed Forces, and the means best suited to such expansion should it prove necessary." ...

⌐ Not only is the scope of Congress' constitutional power in this area broad, but the lack of competence on the part of the courts is marked. In *Gilligan* v. *Morgan*, 413 U.S. 1, 10 (1973), the Court noted:

"[I]t is difficult to conceive of an area of governmental activity in which the courts have less

competence. The complex, subtle, and professional decisions as to the composition, training, equipping, and control of a military force are essentially professional military judgments, subject *always* to civilian control of the Legislative and Executive Branches." ...

None of this is to say that Congress is free to disregard the Constitution when it acts in the area of military affairs. In that area, as any other, Congress remains subject to the limitations of the Due Process Clause, ... [B]ut the tests and limitations to be applied may differ because of the military context. We of course do not abdicate our ultimate responsibility to decide the constitutional question, but simply recognize that the Constitution itself requires such deference to congressional choice....

III

... The question of registering women for the draft not only received considerable national attention and was the subject of wide-ranging public debate, but also was extensively considered by Congress in hearings, floor debate, and in committee. Hearings held by both Houses of Congress in response to the President's request for authorization to register women adduced extensive testimony and evidence concerning the issue....

The MSSA established a plan for maintaining "adequate armed strength ... to insure the security of [the] Nation." 50 U.S.C. App. § 451 (b). Registration is the first step "in a united and continuous process designed to raise an army speedily and efficiently," ... "A functioning registration system is a vital part of any mobilization plan." ...

Women as a group, however, unlike men as a group, are not eligible for combat. The restrictions on the participation of women in combat in the Navy and Air Force are statutory....

The existence of the combat restrictions clearly indicates the basis for Congress' decision to exempt women from registration. The purpose of registration was to prepare for a draft of combat troops. Since women are excluded from combat, Congress concluded that they would not be needed in the event of a draft, and therefore decided not to register them....

In light of the foregoing, we conclude that Congress acted well within its constitutional authority when it authorized the registration of men, and not women, under the Military Selective Service Act. The decision of the District Court holding otherwise is accordingly

Reversed.

JUSTICE WHITE, with whom JUSTICE BRENNAN joins, dissenting....

JUSTICE MARSHALL, with whom JUSTICE BRENNAN joins, dissenting.

The Court today places its imprimatur on one of the most potent remaining public expressions of "ancient canards about the proper role of women,"

Phillips v. *Martin Marietta Corp.,* 400 U.S. 542, 545 (1971) (MARSHALL, J., concurring). It upholds a statute that requires males but not females to register for the draft, and which thereby categorically excludes women from a fundamental civic obligation. Because I believe the Court's decision is inconsistent with the Constitution's guarantee of equal protection of the laws, I dissent....

Senate Debates Women in Combat

During action on the defense authorization bill in 1991, the Senate considered an amendment to remove the statutory prohibition on using women in combat roles. The debate, reflecting the performance of women soldiers in the Persian Gulf War, shows how changing political attitudes affect constitutional discourse. Much of the support voiced by Senators for women in combat, especially as combat aviators, would have been inconceivable decades earlier. Source: 137 Cong. Rec. 20710–11, 20713, 20722 (1991).

Mr. [William V.] ROTH [R-Del.]. Mr. President, the amendment which Senator Kennedy and I will propose later is not about gender, but about excellence. It is not about women pilots flying combat missions, but about the best pilots flying combat missions.

The readiness and preparedness of our military defense is a serious matter. When our Nation's future is at stake—and the future of free nations is at stake—we want the most skilled and seasoned men and women on the job.

Make no mistake—military excellence must be our first priority. Our Secretary of Defense must have the greatest flexibility and maneuverability to marshall the forces at his command. We want the best and brightest pilots in the air, not on the ground. We want the best person in the cockpit of a Stealth fighter or a B-1 bomber—not the second best.

Mr. President, America is with us on this issue. A Newsweek poll released just this week shows that 63 percent of Americans favor allowing women to fly combat aircraft. The American people know that what is good for our military defense is also good for the country. And what is good for the country is excellence, readiness, preparedness, strength, and flexibility.

Forty years ago Congress imposed a rule which now prevents women from serving as combat pilots. This congressional restriction is as old and outdated in today's military as a World War II propeller plane....

In removing the ban, we give women the opportunity to compete for these positions as DOD sees fit—nothing more and nothing less. And, we give

the military the opportunity to make the best use of its talent.

The Senate Armed Services Committee—instead of adopting my proposal—has called for a study commission. We do not need a commission to study the issue. A commission will not tell us anything we do not already know about the performance of women pilots in battle.

Women have proven themselves—the documentation is clear and well-documented. The best arguments are performance, experience, and aptitude—and women military pilots have come through with flying colors on all three counts.

For anyone who thinks we need more studies, more evidence, I say, look at the record. Women have been pulling G's in high performance aircraft for over 15 years now. Women aviators train our male combat pilots. They test the newest generation aircraft. They fly the space shuttle. Women pilots test FA-18's and C-27's, they fly transport planes and refueling planes, they fly AWACS and helicopters. In fact, women have flown just about every plane that the Pentagon has built in the past three decades. There is no question about their performance, or their experience, in this regard.

But women have proven themselves, not only in the instructor's seat and in the test pilot's seat, but in battle conditions and in the line of fire. Their aptitude and ability may have been proven here at home—but their courage and mettle were proven in the skies over Saudi Arabia, Kuwait, and Iraq....

Mr. [Edward] KENNEDY [D-Mass.]. Mr. President, I commend my friend and colleague, the Senator from Delaware [Mr. Roth] for the leadership he has provided on this issue and I am delighted to have the chance to join with him, Senator McConnell, Senator Leahy, and Senator Bingaman in support of our amendment to repeal the statutes that bar women from serving in combat aircraft. These exclusionary statutes are relics of the 1940's that Congress should have repealed long ago.

The Armed Forces claim that they are an equal opportunity employer, and they are, partly. They have made great strides in opening up all branches of the service to racial minorities.

But the same cannot be said with regard to sex discrimination, because archaic statutes still in the books deny equal opportunity to women.

Barriers based on sex discrimination are coming down in every part of our society. The Armed Forces should be no exception. Women should be allowed to play a full role in our national defense, free of any arbitrary and discriminatory restrictions. The only fair and proper test of a women's role is not gender but ability to do the job....

Mr. Roth....

What about women in ground combat? Some have raised that specter, that fear, that the Kennedy and Roth amendment will lead women down the slippery slope into the trenches of ground combat. That is an unfounded fear, and it is an unnecessary fear. Our amendment is surgical, precise, circumscribed, and only germane to the role of women combat aviators; nothing more, nothing less. We are not establishing a dangerous precedent here.

Legal experts agree that lifting the combat aircraft restriction will not mean a dramatic change in the woman's role in the military.

They raise a question about unit cohesion and bonding. Just let me point out that something like 35,000 women served in the Persian Gulf, and military leader after military leader including Mr. Cheney [Secretary of Defense], have said women pilots are successful members of aircraft crews. As one woman pilot said, "The old so-called male bonding of former days was replaced with unit bonding in the gulf." We have the testimony of male pilots who have verified the team spirit of their women colleagues. So, once again, we see [stalking] horses being raised just to be knocked down.

What about gender norming, lower standards for women pilots? Some say allowing women to fly as combat pilots will result in a double standard and will place less capable women in critical positions. If anyone reads the testimony of the Chiefs of Staff before the Armed Services Subcommittee a few short days ago, it will become very clear by what the Chief of Staff, for example, of the Air Force said:

"There would be no lowering of the standard. What we are really doing is permitting the military to do what is in the best interests of the national defense."

United States v. Virginia

518 U.S. 515 (1996)

Virginia Military Institute (VMI) operated as the sole single-sex school among Virginia's public institutions of higher learning. The distinctive mission of the school was to produce "citizen-soldiers," men prepared for leadership in civilian life and in military service. Only about 15% of VMI cadets entered career military service. The United States sued Virginia and VMI on the ground that the school's exclusively male admission policy violated the Fourteenth Amendment's Equal Protection Clause. The district court ruled in VMI's favor; the Fourth Circuit reversed. To remedy the constitutional problem, Virginia proposed a parallel program for women: Virginia Women's Institute for Leadership (VWIL), located at Mary Baldwin College, a private liberal arts school for women. The district court and the Fourth Circuit found that this proposal satisfied the equal protection requirement.

Justice Ginsburg delivered the opinion of the Court.

Virginia's public institutions of higher learning include an incomparable military college, Virginia Military Institute (VMI). The United States maintains that the Constitution's equal protection guarantee precludes Virginia from reserving exclusively to men the unique educational opportunities VMI affords. We agree.

I

Founded in 1839, VMI is today the sole single-sex school among Virginia's 15 public institutions of higher learning. VMI's distinctive mission is to produce "citizen-soldiers," men prepared for leadership in civilian life and in military service. VMI pursues this mission through pervasive training of a kind not available anywhere else in Virginia. Assigning prime place to character development, VMI uses an "adversative method" modeled on English public schools and once characteristic of military instruction. VMI constantly endeavors to instill physical and mental discipline in its cadets and impart to them a strong moral code....

Neither the goal of producing citizen-soldiers nor VMI's implementing methodology is inherently unsuitable to women. And the school's impressive record in producing leaders has made admission desirable to some women. Nevertheless, Virginia has elected to preserve exclusively for men the advantages and opportunities a VMI education affords.

II

A

From its establishment in 1839 as one of the Nation's first state military colleges, ... VMI has remained financially supported by Virginia and "subject to the control of the [Virginia] General Assembly," ...

[VMI has a special mission to produce educated men prepared for civil life, "imbued with love of learning, confident in the functions and attitudes of leadership, possessing a high sense of public service, advocates of the American democracy and free enterprise system, and ready as citizen-soldiers to defend their country in time of national peril." 766 F.Supp. 1407, 1425 (WD Va. 1991) (quoting Mission Study Committee of the VMI Board of Visitors, Report, May 16, 1986). In contrast to federal service academies that prepare cadets for career service in the armed forces, VMI's program is directed at both military and civilian life. Only about 15% of VMI cadets enter career military service.]

VMI cadets live in spartan barracks where surveillance is constant and privacy nonexistent; they wear uniforms, eat together in the mess hall, and regularly participate in drills.... Entering students are incessantly exposed to the rat line, "an extreme form of the adversative model," comparable in intensity to Marine Corps boot camp.... Tormenting and punishing, the rat line bonds new cadets to their fellow sufferers and, when they have completed the 7-month experience, to their former tormentors....

B

[In the two years preceding the lawsuit, VMI received inquiries from 347 women but responded to none. It was established that some women were capable of the activities required of VMI cadets, and that the admission of women would provide better training in dealing with a mixed-gender army. Some aspects of VMI's distinctive method would be altered if women were admitted: changes in personal privacy, altering physical education requirements, and modification of the adversative environment.]

[The district court concluded that the goal of producing citizen soldiers and VMI's methodology were not inherently unsuitable to women. In remanding the case, the Fourth Circuit suggested these options for Virginia: Admit women to VMI, establish parallel institutions or programs, or abandon state support and let VMI function as a private institution. Virginia proposed a Virginia Women's Institute for Leadership (VWIL), a 4-year, state-sponsored undergraduate program located at Mary Baldwin College, a private liberal arts school for women. VWIL would share VMI's mission (to produce "citizen-soldiers"), but the program would differ in academic offerings, methods of education, and financial resources. The district court decided that the plan satisfied the Equal Protection Clause. A divided Fourth Circuit affirmed.]

IV

... [W]e conclude that Virginia has shown no "exceedingly persuasive justification" for excluding all women from the citizen-soldier training afforded by VMI. We therefore affirm the Fourth Circuit's initial judgment, which held that Virginia had violated the Fourteenth Amendment's Equal Protection Clause. Because the remedy proffered by Virginia— the Mary Baldwin VWIL program—does not cure the constitutional violation, i.e., it does not provide equal opportunity, we reverse the Fourth Circuit's final judgment in this case.

V

... Virginia ... asserts two justifications in defense of VMI's exclusion of women. First, the Commonwealth contends, "single-sex education provides important educational benefits," ... and the option of single-sex education contributes to "diversity in educational approaches," ... Second, the Commonwealth argues, "the unique VMI method of character development and leadership training," the school's adversative approach, would have to be modified were VMI to admit women.... We consider these two justifications in turn.

A

... [I]t is not disputed that diversity among public educational institutions can serve the public good. But Virginia has not shown that VMI was established, or has been maintained, with a view to diversifying, by its categorical exclusion of women, educational opportunities within the Commonwealth....

Neither recent nor distant history bears out Virginia's alleged pursuit of diversity through single-sex educational options.[*Excluded from universities in Virginia, women were admitted to a state seminary in 1884 and to women's colleges in 1908 and 1910. In 1972, women were admitted to the University of Virginia.*]

B

Virginia next argues that VMI's adversative method of training provides educational benefits that cannot be made available, unmodified, to women. Alterations to accommodate women would necessarily be "radical," so "drastic," Virginia asserts, as to transform, indeed "destroy," VMI's program....

... [I]t is uncontested that women's admission would require accommodations, primarily in arranging housing assignments and physical training programs for female cadets.... It is also undisputed, however, that "the VMI methodology could be used to educate women." ... and "some women," the expert testimony established, "are capable of all of the individual activities required of VMI cadets," ...

VI

In the second phase of the litigation, Virginia presented its remedial plan—maintain VMI as a male-only college and create VWIL as a separate program for women....

[A]

VWIL affords women no opportunity to experience the rigorous military training for which VMI is famed.... Instead, the VWIL program "deemphasize[s]" military education ... and uses a "cooperative method" of education "which reinforces self-esteem," ...

VWIL students participate in ROTC and a "largely ceremonial" Virginia Corps of Cadets, ... but Virginia deliberately did not make VWIL a military institute. The VWIL House is not a military-style residence and VWIL students need not live together throughout the 4-year program, eat meals together, or wear uniforms during the school day.... VWIL students thus do not experience the "barracks" life "crucial to the VMI experience," the spartan living arrangements designed to foster an "egalitarian ethic." ...

... The Task Force charged with developing the leadership program for women, drawn from the staff and faculty at Mary Baldwin College, "determined that a military model and, especially VMI's adversative method, would be wholly inappropriate for educating and training *most women*." ...

As earlier stated, ... generalizations about "the way women are," estimates of what is appropriate for *most women,* no longer justify denying opportunity to women whose talent and capacity place them outside the average description. Notably, Virginia never asserted that VMI's method of education suits *most men....*

B

In myriad respects other than military training, VWIL does not qualify as VMI's equal. VWIL's student body, faculty, course offerings, and facilities hardly match VMI's. Nor can the VWIL graduate anticipate the benefits associated with VMI's 157-year history, the school's prestige, and its influential alumni network.

Mary Baldwin College, whose degree VWIL students will gain, enrolls first-year women with an average combined SAT score about 100 points lower than the average score for VMI freshmen.... The Mary Baldwin faculty holds "significantly fewer Ph.D.'s" ... and receives substantially lower salaries....

Mary Baldwin does not offer a VWIL student the range of curricular choices available to a VMI cadet. VMI awards baccalaureate degrees in liberal arts, biology, chemistry, civil engineering, electrical and computer engineering, and mechanical engineering.... VWIL students attend a school that "does not have a math and science focus," ... [T]hey cannot take at Mary Baldwin any courses in engineering or the advanced math and physics courses VMI offers....

Although Virginia has represented that it will provide equal financial support for in-state VWIL students and VMI cadets, ... and the VMI Foundation has agreed to endow VWIL with $5.4625 million, ... the difference between the two schools' financial reserves is pronounced. Mary Baldwin's endowment, currently about $19 million, will gain an additional $35 million based on future commitments; VMI's current endowment, $131 million—the largest public college per-student endowment in the Nation—will gain $220 million....

The VWIL student does not graduate with the advantage of a VMI degree. Her diploma does not unite her with the legions of VMI "graduates [who] have distinguished themselves" in military and civilian life...." [VMI] alumni are exceptionally close to the school," and that closeness accounts, in part, for

VMI's success in attracting applicants.... A VWIL graduate cannot assume that the "network of business owners, corporations, VMI graduates and non-graduate employers ... interested in hiring VMI graduates" ... will be equally responsive to her search for employment, ...

C

[*The Court describes the "deferential review" used by the Fourth Circuit in accepting the VWIL plan as a remedy and regards it as inconsistent with "the more exacting standard our precedent requires." Contemporary gender-based classifications require "heightened scrutiny."*] In sum, Virginia's remedy does not match the constitutional violation; the Commonwealth has shown no "exceedingly persuasive justification" for withholding from women qualified for the experience premier training of the kind VMI affords.

[VII]

For the reasons stated, the initial judgment of the Court of Appeals, 976 F.2d 890 (CA4 1992), is affirmed, the final judgment of the Court of Appeals, 44 F.3d 1229 (CA4 1995), is reversed, and the case is remanded for further proceedings consistent with this opinion.

It is so ordered.

JUSTICE THOMAS took no part in the consideration or decision of this case.

CHIEF JUSTICE REHNQUIST, concurring in the judgment.

[*While agreeing with the Court's conclusions, he objects to the requirement that Virginia must demonstrate an "exceedingly persuasive justification" to support a gender-based classification. He would have adhered more closely to the traditional standard that a gender-based classification "must bear a close and substantial relationship to important governmental objectives." Although VMIL failed as a remedy because it was no match for VMI, Rehnquist states that Virginia could*

have remedied the problem by creating a single-sex institution for women had it offered the same quality of education and the same overall caliber.]

JUSTICE SCALIA, dissenting

Today the Court shuts down an institution that has served the people of the Commonwealth of Virginia with pride and distinction for over a century and a half. To achieve that desired result, it rejects (contrary to our established practice) the factual findings of two courts below, sweeps aside the precedents of this Court, and ignores the history of our people. As to facts: It explicitly rejects the finding that there exist "gender-based developmental differences" supporting Virginia's restriction of the "adversative" method to only a men's institution, and the finding that the all-male composition of the Virginia Military Institute (VMI) is essential to that institution's character. As to precedent: It drastically revises our established standards for reviewing sex-based classifications. And as to history: It counts for nothing the long tradition, enduring down to the present, of men's military colleges supported by both States and the Federal Government.

... The virtue of a democratic system with a First Amendment is that it readily enables the people, over time, to be persuaded that what they took for granted is not so, and to change their laws accordingly. That system is destroyed if the smug assurances of each age are removed from the democratic process and written into the Constitution. So to counterbalance the Court's criticism of our ancestors, let me say a word in their praise: They left us free to change. The same cannot be said of this most illiberal Court, which has embarked on a course of inscribing one after another of the current preferences of the society (and in some cases only the countermajoritarian preferences of the society's law-trained elite) into our Basic Law. Today it enshrines the notion that no substantial educational value is to be served by an all-men's military academy ...

C. RIGHTS OF ALIENS

Immigration law involves a tangled web of legal issues that range from issues of federalism and congressional preemption to due process rights and equal protection. We discuss the rights of aliens, both legal and undocumented, because developments in the law reflect the way in which the Court has expanded equal protection of the laws beyond the question of race. In fact, it is clear that the framers of the Fourteenth Amendment were aware that the broad general language of the Amendment would encompass more than just the newly freed slaves. The record of the congressional debate shows that Senator John Conness of California discussed the discrimination that Chinese immigrants in his state experienced and believed that the Amendment would provide them some long overdue protection of their rights. McClain, In Search of Equality: The Chinese Struggle Against Discrimination in Nineteenth-Century America 34 (California, 1994). Chinese immigrants were particularly active in claiming the protection of the Fourteenth Amendment during the nineteenth century and their litigation laid the groundwork for the notion that states could not arbitrarily discriminate against non-citizens in their laws.

Early Cases on Immigrant Rights

Until 1875 Congress passed no restrictive immigration legislation and at the federal level this is generally seen as a time when we had an "open door" policy toward immigration. States and localities, however, began early on to pass legislation and ordinances designed to control the flow of migration into their areas. For example, California imposed taxes on miners coming from abroad. New York and Massachusetts required alien passengers arriving at their ports to pay landing fees that were justified as a way for the states to cover the costs of alien paupers. The Court struck these fees down in *Passenger Cases*, 48 U.S. (7 How.) 282 (1849) as state interference with interstate commerce, but upheld a New York law that required the provision of a list of every passenger on board and the posting of a bond to protect against any of the passengers becoming wards of the city by finding this regulation to be within the police powers of the state. New York v. Miln, 36 U.S. (11 Pet.) 102 (1837).

The first opportunities to apply the Fourteenth Amendment to immigrants arose in the context of discriminatory state and local ordinances targeted at the Chinese population on the West Coast. It is interesting that in the same month that the amendment officially became part of the U.S. Constitution, the U.S. signed "The Burlingame Treaty" with China, one part of which promised that "Chinese subjects visiting or residing in the United States, shall enjoy the same privileges, immunities, and exemptions in respect to travel or residence, as may there be enjoyed by the citizens or subjects of the most favored nation." The Burlingame Treaty, art. VI, 16 Stat. 740. This treaty and the Fourteenth Amendment encouraged Chinese immigrants to pursue federal court protection of their rights.

State regulation of the laundry trade, which was dominated by the Chinese in California, was a key area of litigation. State and local regulators claimed that Chinese laundries were more fire prone and a threat to the whole city in which they operated. In San Francisco an ordinance prohibited laundries unless they were in brick or stone buildings and imposed fines and imprisonment for failure to comply. Existing wooden laundries had to seek permits from the supervisors who possessed broad discretionary authority. While the language of the ordinance was neutral, the reality was that city supervisors clearly intended the regulations to affect only Chinese laundries, which tended to be in small wood structures. No Chinese laundries were given permits while wooden laundries operated by whites were allowed to continue to operate. Enforcement of the ordinances, and the increasingly restrictive ones that followed, was left to the discretion of the Board of Supervisors. Challenges to the broad regulation of the laundry business were upheld as within the police powers of the state. Barbier v. Connolly, 113 U.S. 27 (1885) and Soon Hing v. Crowley 113 U.S. 703 (1885). Litigation against the selective enforcement of the building codes for laundries met with more success. In 1886 the Court agreed with two Chinese laundrymen that the selective enforcement of a law that interfered with their ability to pursue their livelihood violated the equal protection clause of the Fourteenth Amendment. It was the first time that the Court found legislation that was race neutral on its face to be discriminatory because of the way in which was enforced. YICK WO v. HOPKINS 118 U.S. 356 (1886). This decision was significant because it acknowledged that aliens were "persons" entitled to protection under the equal protection clause of the Fourteenth Amendment.

Congress's Power and Issues of Federal Preemption

While the Court was willing to impose limits on state and local governments' treatment of aliens, it was far more deferential to Congress. Gerald Neuman argues that "normal constitutional reasoning" does not apply when it comes to immigration law. In the late nineteenth century the Court adopted the notion from international law that recognizes the sovereign right of nations to decide whom to allow to enter and whom to expel from the country. Neuman contends that the Court "transformed this characterization of international law into a constitutional doctrine of Congress's 'plenary power' to exclude or expel aliens, unconstrained by any judicially enforceable limits." Strangers to the Constitution 14 (1996). Consequently, at the same time that the Court was extending equal protection guarantees against state actions, it was granting almost unlimited power to Congress to make and enforce immigration law at its will. Henderson v. New York, 92 U.S. 259 (1876); Chy Lung v. Freeman, 92 U.S. 275 (1876); Chinese Exclusion Case, 130 U.S. 581 (1889). It was not until the 1970's that the Court began to impose a "minimal rationality" test upon federal immigration policy. Kleindienst v. Mandel, 408 U.S. 753 (1972); Fiallo v. Bell, 430 U.S. 787 (1977).

The issue of federal preemption remains a significant limitation on the ability of state and local governments to regulate undocumented workers in their communities. Federal preemption was one of the issues considered by the Court when it struck down Arizona's efforts to impose residency requirements on legal aliens before they could become eligible for state benefits. Graham v. Richardson, 403 U.S. 365 (1971). When Texas attempted to restrict access to public education for the children of undocumented aliens, the Court found that in addition to the Equal Protection violation, the statute did not "mirror" federal policy. Plyler v. Doe, 457 U.S. 202 (1982). When California voters passed Proposition 187 in 1994 they sought to restrict access by illegal immigrants to social services, health care, and public education. A federal district court issued a temporary injunction finding that the state had intruded into the federal realm of immigration regulation. A later decision found that in addition to the federal preemption problem, Proposition 187 violated both the due process clause and the equal protection clause of the Fourteenth Amendment. LULAC v. Wilson, 997 F.Supp. 1244 (S.D. Cal. 1997).

The Supreme Court has not been completely hostile to state efforts, particularly in the area of employment law. In 1976 it upheld a California law that imposed sanctions on employers who hired undocumented workers, finding that federal law was compatible with the state regulation and that the regulation of employment relationships in order to protect state workers was within the police powers of the state. De Canas v. Bica, 424 U.S. 351 (1976).

Reflecting the local frustration with the failure of federal immigration policy to effectively stem the tide of illegal immigration, states and localities have begun another round of efforts to regulate and limit access to government services, employment, and housing by undocumented aliens. The National Conference of State Legislatures has documented the huge increase in state legislative efforts. Court challenges followed on both pre-emption and equal protection grounds. The city of Hazleton, Pennsylvania, got considerable national attention when it imposed one of the first of a series of restrictive local ordinances governing access to housing and employment. A federal district court struck down the ordinance on federal preemption grounds in 2007. Lozano v. Hazleton, 496 F.Supp.2d 477 (M.D. Pa. 2007). Also in 2007 Arizona passed the Legal Arizona Workers Act, targeted at employers who hire undocumented workers. It threatened the revocation of state business licenses for violators of the law. A facial challenge to the law by business and immigrant groups was unsuccessful. Chicanos Por La Causa, Inc. v. Napolitano, 544 F.3d 976 (9th Cir. 2008). In 2011 the U.S. Supreme Court upheld the legislation, finding that it was not pre-empted by federal law. Chamber of Commerce v. Whiting, 563 U.S. ___ (2011). In 2010 Arizona passed legislation that called for local police officers to check the immigration status of persons stopped in the process of enforcing other laws and required immigrants to prove their status when asked or face state criminal charges. The Obama administration challenged the statute in federal court on preemption grounds and in June 2012 the Court struck down three parts of the statute on preemption grounds, but upheld the "show me your papers" policy as consistent with federal policy. It left open the question of whether actual implementation of the provision might lead to racial profiling, which could be challenged on due process and equal protection grounds if proven. United States v. Arizona, 567 U.S. ___ (2012). (Reading in Chapter 8 on Federalism.)

Equal Protection and Social Services

In the realm of equal protection analysis the Court has issued two decisions of particular importance dealing with the equal protection rights associated with alienage. In the first, the Court found that alienage is a "suspect classification" like race and that state legislation using such classifications must be subjected to strict scrutiny. Arizona's attempt to limit access to government benefits to those who had lived in the state five years or more was found not to withstand such scrutiny. Graham v. Richardson, 403 U.S. 365 (1971). When it came to state legislation targeted particularly at undocumented aliens, however, the Court backed away from the strict scrutiny standard. In *Plyler v. Doe* it suggested that only the rational basis test may be necessary for legislation that targets adults illegally in the country. But the Texas legislation in this case was directed toward the children of illegals who were not themselves responsible for the violation of law. Here the Court suggested that because it was children and because of the central place of education in our society, some level of heightened scrutiny was merited. PLYLER v. DOE, 457 U.S. 202 (1982).

Employment and the "Political Community"

Despite *Graham v. Richardson*, the Court has allowed states to make distinctions between aliens and citizens in the area of public service employment. In a series of cases involving state limitations on the ability of legal aliens to obtain state and locally funded jobs, the Court has held that states may have a sufficiently strong interest in having these jobs done by citizens who have demonstrated their commitment to the political community. A New York state law that restricted all competitive civil service jobs to citizens was struck down by the Court in 1973 as overly broad in its reach. But the Court did say that states might be able to show that *some kinds* of jobs were best restricted to citizens in the same way that participation in the electoral process was legitimately restricted. The Court suggested a lower level of scrutiny would be warranted in cases where the state could show that "citizenship bears some rational relationship to the special demands of the particular position." Sugarman v. Dougall, 413 U.S. 634, 646–49 (1973). Following this decision the Court permitted citizenship requirements for state troopers, public school teachers, and probation officers. Foley v. Connelie, 435 U.S. 291 (1978); Ambach v. Norwick, 441 U.S. 68 (1979); Cabell v. Chavez-Salido, 454 U.S. 432 (1982).

Yick Wo v. Hopkins

118 U.S. 356 (1886)

Yick Wo was one of several plaintiffs to challenge a municipal ordinance in California designed to regulate public laundries. As implemented by the Board of Supervisors, eighty white owners received licenses to operate but licenses were denied to two hundred Chinese-owned laundries. Could law be administered in such a discriminatory fashion? For the first time, the Court had to decide the meaning of "persons" in the Fourteenth Amendment. Did the word apply both to citizens and aliens? Peter Hopkins was the sheriff of the city and county of San Francisco.

Mr. JUSTICE MATTHEWS delivered the opinion of the court. . . .

The rights of the petitioners, as affected by the proceedings of which they complain, are not less because they are aliens and subjects of the Emperor of China. By the third article of the treaty between this Government and that of China, concluded November 17, 1880, 22 Stat. 827, it is stipulated: "If Chinese laborers, or Chinese of any other class, now either permanently or temporarily residing in the territory of the United States, meet with ill treatment at the hands of any other persons, the Government of the United States will exert all its powers to devise measures for their protection, and to secure to them the same rights, privileges, immunities and exemptions as may be enjoyed by the citizens or subjects of the most favored nation, and to which they are entitled by treaty."

The Fourteenth Amendment to the Constitution is not confined to the protection of citizens. It says: "Nor shall any State deprive any person of life, liberty, or property without due process of law; nor deny to any person within its jurisdiction the equal protection of the laws." These provisions are universal in their application to all persons within the territorial jurisdiction, without regard to any differences of race, of color, or of nationality, and the equal protection of the laws is a pledge of the protection of equal laws. It is accordingly enacted by § 1977 of the Revised Statutes, that "all persons within the jurisdiction of the United States shall have the same right in every State and Territory to make and enforce contracts, to sue, be parties, give evidence, and to the full and equal benefit of all laws and proceedings for the security of persons and property as is enjoyed by white citizens and shall be subject to like punishment, pains, penalties, taxes, licenses, and exactions of every kind, and to no other." The questions we have to consider and decide in these cases, therefore, are to be treated as involving the rights of every citizen of the United States equally with those of the strangers and aliens who now invoke the jurisdiction of the court.

It is contended on the part of the petitioners, that the ordinances for violations of which they are severally sentenced to imprisonment, are void on their face, as being within the prohibitions of the Fourteenth Amendment; and, in the alternative, if not so, that they are void by reason of their administration, operating unequally so as to punish in the present petitioners what is permitted to others as lawful, without any distinction of circumstances — an unjust and illegal discrimination, it is claimed, which, though not made expressly by the ordinances, is made possible by them.

When we consider the nature and the theory of our institutions of government, the principles upon which they are supposed to rest, and review the his-

tory of their development, we are constrained to conclude that they do not mean to leave room for the play and action of purely personal and arbitrary power. Sovereignty itself is, of course, not subject to law, for it is the author and source of law; but in our system, while sovereign powers are delegated to the agencies of government, sovereignty itself remains with the people, by whom and for whom all government exists and acts. And the law is the definition and limitation of power. It is, indeed, quite true, that there must always be lodged somewhere, and in some person or body, the authority of final decision; and in many cases of mere administration the responsibility is purely political, no appeal lying except to the ultimate tribunal of the public judgment, exercised either in the pressure of opinion or by means of the suffrage. But the fundamental rights to life, liberty, and the pursuit of happiness, considered as individual possessions, are secured by those maxims of constitutional law which are the monuments showing the victorious progress of the race in securing to men the blessings of civilization under the reign of just and equal laws, so that, in the famous language of the Massachusetts Bill of Rights, the government of the commonwealth "may be a government of laws and not of men." For the very idea that one man may be compelled to hold his life, or the means of living, or any material right essential to the enjoyment of life at the mere will of another, seems to be intolerable in any country where freedom prevails, as being the essence of slavery itself....

... In the present cases we are not obliged to reason from the probable to the actual, and pass upon the validity of the ordinances complained of, as tried merely by the opportunities which their terms afford, of unequal and unjust discrimination in their administration. For the cases present the ordinances in actual operation, and the facts shown establish an administration directed so exclusively against a particular class of persons as to warrant and require the conclusion, that, whatever may have been the intent of the ordinances as adopted, they are applied by the public authorities charged with their administration, and thus representing the State itself, with a mind so unequal and oppressive as to amount to a practical denial by the State of that equal protection of the laws which is secured to the petitioners, as to all other persons, by the broad and benign provisions of the Fourteenth Amendment to the Constitution of the United States. Though the law itself be fair on its face and impartial in appearance, yet, if it is applied and administered by public authority with an evil eye and an unequal hand, so as practically to make unjust and illegal discriminations between persons in similar circumstances, material to their rights, the denial of equal justice is still within the prohibition of the Constitution....

The present cases, as shown by the facts disclosed in the record, are within this class. It appears that both petitioners have complied with every requisite, deemed by the law or by the public officers charged with its administration, necessary for the protection of neighboring property from fire, or as a precaution against injury to the public health. No reason whatever, except the will of the supervisors, is assigned why they should not be permitted to carry on, in the accustomed manner, their harmless and useful occupation, on which they depend for a livelihood. And while this consent of the supervisors is withheld from them and from two hundred others who have also petitioned, all of whom happen to be Chinese subjects, eighty others, not Chinese subjects, are permitted to carry on the same business under sim-

ilar conditions. The fact of this discrimination is admitted. No reason for it is shown, and the conclusion cannot be resisted, that no reason for it exists except hostility to the race and nationality to which the petitioners belong, and which in the eye of the law is not justified. The discrimination is, therefore, illegal, and the public administration which enforces it is a denial of the equal protection of the laws and a violation of the Fourteenth Amendment of the Constitution. The imprisonment of the petitioners is, therefore, illegal, and they must be discharged. To this end,

The judgment of the Supreme Court of California in the case of Yick Wo, and that of the Circuit Court of the United States for the District of California in the case of Wo Lee, are severally reversed, and the cases remanded, each to the proper court, with directions to discharge the petitioners from custody and imprisonment.

Plyler v. Doe

457 U.S. 202 (1982)

In 1975 Texas revised its education laws to withhold state education funds from children who were not "legally admitted" to the United States. It authorized school districts to deny admission or charge tuition to students who could not prove their legal status. This suit was brought on behalf of children, contending that the Texas law violated the Equal Protection Clause of the Fourteenth Amendment. The federal district court and court of appeals agreed and ruled against the state. James Plyler was the Superintendent of Tyler Independent School District and its Board of Trustees.

JUSTICE BRENNAN delivered the opinion of the Court.

. . .

II

The Fourteenth Amendment provides that "[n]o State shall ... deprive any person of life, liberty, or property, without due process of law; nor deny to *any person within its jurisdiction* the equal protection of the laws." (Emphasis added.) Appellants argue at the outset that undocumented aliens, because of their immigration status, are not "persons within the jurisdiction" of the State of Texas, and that they therefore have no right to the equal protection of Texas law. We reject this argument. Whatever his status under the immigration laws, an alien is surely a "person" in any ordinary sense of that term. Aliens, even aliens whose presence in this country is unlawful, have long been recognized as "persons" guaran-

teed due process of law by the Fifth and Fourteenth Amendments....

Appellants seek to distinguish our prior cases, emphasizing that the Equal Protection Clause directs a State to afford its protection to persons *within its jurisdiction*, while the Due Process Clauses of the Fifth and Fourteenth Amendments contain no such assertedly limiting phrase. In appellants' view, persons who have entered the United States illegally are not "within the jurisdiction" of a State even if they are present within a State's boundaries and subject to its laws. Neither our cases nor the logic of the Fourteenth Amendment supports that constricting construction of the phrase "within its jurisdiction." We have never suggested that the class of persons who might avail themselves of the equal protection guarantee is less than coextensive with that entitled to due process. To the contrary, we have recognized that both provisions were fashioned to protect an identical class of persons, and to reach every exercise of state authority ...

In concluding that "all persons within the territory of the United States," including aliens unlawfully present, may invoke the Fifth and Sixth Amendments to challenge actions of the Federal Government, we reasoned from the understanding that the Fourteenth Amendment was designed to afford its protection to all within the boundaries of a State....

There is simply no support for appellants' suggestion that "due process" is somehow of greater stature than "equal protection," and therefore available to a larger class of persons. To the contrary, each aspect of the Fourteenth Amendment reflects an elementary limitation on state power. To permit a State to employ the phrase "within its jurisdiction" in order to identify subclasses of persons whom it would define as beyond its jurisdiction, thereby relieving itself of the obligation to assure that its laws are designed and applied equally to those persons, would undermine the principal purpose for which the Equal Protection Clause was incorporated in the Fourteenth Amendment. The Equal Protection Clause was intended to work nothing less than the abolition of all caste-based and invidious class-based legislation. That objective is fundamentally at odds with the power the State asserts here to classify persons subject to its laws as nonetheless excepted from its protection....

Use of the phrase "within its jurisdiction" thus does not detract from, but rather confirms, the understanding that the protection of the Fourteenth Amendment extends to anyone, citizen or stranger, who is subject to the laws of a State, and reaches into every corner of a State's territory. That a person's initial entry into a State, or into the United States, was unlawful, and that he may for that reason be expelled, cannot negate the simple fact of his presence within the State's territorial perimeter. Given such presence, he is subject to the full range of obligations imposed by the State's civil and criminal laws. And until he leaves the jurisdiction—either voluntarily, or involuntarily in accordance with the Constitution and laws of the United States—he is entitled to the equal protection of the laws that a State may choose to establish....

III

The Equal Protection Clause directs that "all persons similarly circumstanced shall be treated alike." ... But so too, "[t]he Constitution does not require things which are different in fact or opinion to be treated in law as though they were the same." ... The initial discretion to determine what is "different" and what is "the same" resides in the legislatures of the States. A legislature must have substantial latitude to establish classifications that roughly approximate the nature of the problem perceived, that accommodate competing concerns both public and private, and that account for limitations on the practical ability of the State to remedy every ill. In applying the Equal Protection Clause to most forms of state action, we thus seek only the assurance that the classification at issue bears some fair relationship to a legitimate public purpose.

But we would not be faithful to our obligations under the Fourteenth Amendment if we applied so deferential a standard to every classification. The Equal Protection Clause was intended as a restriction on state legislative action inconsistent with elemental constitutional premises. Thus, we have treated as presumptively invidious those classifications that disadvantage a "suspect class," or that impinge upon the exercise of a "fundamental right." With respect to such classifications, it is appropriate to enforce the mandate of equal protection by requiring the State to demonstrate that its classification has been precisely tailored to serve a compelling governmental interest. In addition, we have recognized that certain forms of legislative classification, while not facially invidious, nonetheless give rise to recurring constitutional difficulties; in these limited circumstances we have sought the assurance that the classification reflects a reasoned judgment consistent with the ideal of equal protection by inquiring whether it may fairly be viewed as furthering a substantial interest of the State. We turn to a consideration of the standard appropriate for the evaluation of [*the Texas law*].

A

Sheer incapability or lax enforcement of the laws barring entry into this country, coupled with the failure to establish an effective bar to the employment of undocumented aliens, has resulted in the creation of a substantial "shadow population" of illegal migrants—numbering in the millions—within our borders. This situation raises the specter of a permanent caste of undocumented resident aliens, encouraged by some to remain here as a source of cheap labor, but nevertheless denied the benefits that our society makes available to citizens and lawful residents. The existence of such an underclass presents most difficult problems for a Nation that prides itself on adherence to principles of equality under law.

The children who are plaintiffs in these cases are special members of this underclass. Persuasive arguments support the view that a State may withhold its beneficence from those whose very presence within the United States is the product of their own unlawful conduct. These arguments do not apply with the same force to classifications imposing disabilities on the minor *children* of such illegal entrants. At the least, those who elect to enter our territory by stealth and in violation of our law should be prepared to bear the consequences, including, but not limited to, deportation. But the children of those illegal entrants are not comparably situated. Their "parents have the ability to conform their conduct to societal norms," and presumably the ability to remove themselves from the State's jurisdiction; but the children who are plaintiffs in these cases "can affect neither their parents' conduct nor their own status." Even if the State found it expedient to control the conduct of adults by acting against their children, legislation directing the onus of a parent's misconduct against his children does not comport with fundamental conceptions of justice....

Of course, undocumented status is not irrelevant to any proper legislative goal. Nor is undocumented status an absolutely immutable characteristic since it is the product of conscious, indeed unlawful, action. But § 21.031 [*the Texas law*] is directed against children, and imposes its discriminatory burden on the basis of a legal characteristic over which children can have little control. It is thus difficult to conceive of a rational justification for penalizing these children for their presence within the United States. Yet that appears to be precisely the effect of § 21.031.

Public education is not a "right" granted to individuals by the Constitution. *San Antonio Independent School Dist. v. Rodriguez*, 411 U.S. 1, 35 (1973). But neither is it merely some governmental "benefit" indistinguishable from other forms of social welfare legislation. Both the importance of education in maintaining our basic institutions and the lasting impact of its deprivation on the life of the child, mark the distinction ... In addition, education provides the basic tools by which individuals might lead economically productive lives to the benefit of us all. In sum, education has a fundamental role in maintaining the fabric of our society. We cannot ignore the significant social costs borne by our Nation when select groups are denied the means to absorb the values and skills upon which our social order rests.

... Illiteracy is an enduring disability. The inability to read and write will handicap the individual deprived of a basic education each and every day of his life. The inestimable toll of that deprivation on the social, economic, intellectual, and psychological well-being of the individual, and the obstacle it poses to individual achievement, make it most difficult to reconcile the cost or the principle of a status-based denial of basic education with the framework of equality embodied in the Equal Protection Clause....

B

These well-settled principles allow us to determine the proper level of deference to be afforded § 21.031. Undocumented aliens cannot be treated as a suspect class because their presence in this country in violation of federal law is not a "constitutional irrelevancy." Nor is education a fundamental right; a State need not justify by compelling necessity every variation in the manner in which education is provided to its population.... But more is involved in these cases than the abstract question whether § 21.031 discriminates against a suspect class, or whether education is a fundamental right. Section 21.031 imposes a lifetime hardship on a discrete class of children not accountable for their disabling status. The stigma of illiteracy will mark them for the rest of their lives. By denying these children a basic education, we deny them the ability to live within the structure of our civic institutions, and foreclose any realistic possibility that they will contribute in even the smallest way to the progress of our Nation. In determining the rationality of § 21.031, we may appropriately take into account its costs to the Nation and to the innocent children who are its victims. In light of these countervailing costs, the discrimination contained in § 21.031 can hardly be considered rational unless it furthers some substantial goal of the State.

IV

[*The Court rejects the State's argument that its policy is consistent with federal immigration policy, arguing that it finds no evidence that Congress intended "to withhold from these children, for so long as they are present in this country through no fault of their own, access to a basic education."*]

V

[*The Court reviews each of the State's asserted interests (largely about managing resources) and finds none of them justify the burden placed on these children.*]

VI

If the State is to deny a discrete group of innocent children the free public education that it offers to other children residing within its borders, that denial must be justified by a showing that it furthers some substantial state interest. No such showing was made here. Accordingly, the judgment of the Court of Appeals in each of these cases is

Affirmed.

JUSTICE MARSHALL concurring.

While I join the Court opinion, I do so without in any way retreating from my opinion in *San Antonio Independent School District v. Rodriguez*, 411 U.S. 1, 70–133 (1973) (dissenting opinion). I continue to believe that an individual's interest in education is fundamental, and that this view is amply supported "by the unique status accorded public education by our society, and by the close relationship between education and some of our most basic constitutional values."

JUSTICE BLACKMUN, concurring....

Because I believe that the Court's carefully worded analysis recognizes the importance of the equal protection and preemption interests I consider crucial, I join its opinion as well as its judgment.

JUSTICE POWELL, concurring.

[*Powell emphasizes "the unique character of the cases before us" and admonishes Congress for its failure to address the rising number of undocumented workers in the country.*]

CHIEF JUSTICE BURGER, with whom JUSTICE WHITE, JUSTICE REHNQUIST, and JUSTICE O'CONNOR join, dissenting.

Were it our business to set the Nation's social policy, I would agree without hesitation that it is senseless for an enlightened society to deprive any children—including illegal aliens—of an elementary education. I fully agree that it would be folly—and wrong—to tolerate creation of a segment of society made up of illiterate persons, many having a limited or no command of our language. However, the Constitution does not constitute us as "Platonic Guardians," nor does it vest in this Court the authority to strike down laws because they do not meet our standards of desirable social policy, "wisdom," or "common sense."... We trespass on the assigned function of the political branches under our structure of limited and separated powers when we assume a policymaking role as the Court does today.

The Court makes no attempt to disguise that it is acting to make up for Congress' lack of "effective leadership" in dealing with the serious national problems caused by the influx of uncountable millions of illegal aliens across our borders.... The failure of enforcement of the immigration laws over more than a decade and the inherent difficulty and expense of sealing our vast borders have combined to create a grave socioeconomic dilemma. It is a dilemma that has not yet even been fully assessed, let alone addressed. However, it is not the function of the Judiciary to provide "effective leadership" simply because the political branches of government fail to do so.

The Court's holding today manifests the justly criticized judicial tendency to attempt speedy and wholesale formulation of "remedies" for the failures—or simply the laggard pace—of the political processes of our system of government. The Court employs, and, in my view, abuses, the Fourteenth Amendment in an effort to become an omnipotent and omniscient problem solver. That the motives for doing so are noble and compassionate does not alter the fact that the Court distorts our constitutional function to make amends for the defaults of others.

I

. . .

I have no quarrel with the conclusion that the Equal Protection Clause of the Fourteenth Amendment *applies* to aliens who, after their illegal entry into this country, are indeed physically "within the jurisdiction" of a state. However, as the Court concedes, this "only begins the inquiry."... The Equal Protection Clause does not mandate identical treatment of different categories of persons....

The dispositive issue in these cases, simply put, is whether, for purposes of allocating its finite resources, a state has a legitimate reason to differentiate between persons who are lawfully within the state and those who are unlawfully there. The distinction the State of Texas has drawn—based not only upon its own legitimate interests but on classifications established by the Federal Government in its immigration laws and policies—is not unconstitutional.

Without laboring what will undoubtedly seem obvious to many, it simply is not "irrational" for a state to conclude that it does not have the same responsibility to provide benefits for persons whose very presence in the state and this country is illegal as it does to provide for persons lawfully present. By definition, illegal aliens have no right whatever to be here, and the state may reasonably, and constitutionally, elect not to provide them with governmental services at the expense of those who are lawfully in the state....

D. RIGHTS OF THE POOR

The full realization of constitutional rights often depends on personal income. The Sixth Amendment guarantees that the accused may have the assistance of counsel. It did not require the government to provide counsel to a defendant unable to afford an attorney. Not until 1963, in *Gideon* v. *Wainwright,* did the Supreme Court rule that the government must provide a lawyer if an indigent person is accused of a felony. As explained in Chapter 13, this right has been expanded by subsequent decisions. Similarly, in 1966, the Court struck down the poll tax, concluding that lines drawn on the basis of wealth or property, like those of race, "are traditionally disfavored." Harper v. Virginia Board of Elections, 383 U.S. 663 (1966).

The fact that these decisions did not come until the 1960s suggests a quite different conclusion: tradition has very much favored the distribution of justice on the basis of wealth. Anatole France made his famous remark about the law, "in all its majestic equality," prohibiting both rich and poor from sleeping under bridges, begging in the streets, and stealing bread. Even with a court-appointed attorney, an indigent defendant is unlikely to fare as well as the wealthy defendant who hires three or four attorneys from a major law firm. By creating the Legal Services Corporation in 1974, Congress attempted to provide financial support for legal assistance for low-income people, but this program is designed only for noncriminal proceedings and is funded at modest levels.

Welfare Benefits

There is no constitutional right to receive welfare payments or other forms of public assistance for the indigent. The extent of public funding for these purposes is determined by legislative action. Once granted, however, assistance may be terminated only by observing procedural safeguards. In 1970, the Supreme Court held that individuals receiving financial aid under the federally assisted Aid to Families with Dependent Children (AFDC) program or under New York's general home-relief program could not have their assistance terminated without prior notice and hearing. Goldberg v. Kelly, 397 U.S. 254 (1970). In the case of disability benefits, the Court has ruled that an evidentiary hearing is not required before the initial termination of benefits. The Court distinguished *Goldberg* on the ground that welfare recipients have greater financial need than the disabled. Mathews v. Eldridge, 424 U.S. 319 (1976).

The Court has reviewed state restrictions that make people ineligible for welfare benefits. One-year residency requirements were struck down as an unconstitutional interference with the right of interstate movement. SHAPIRO v. THOMPSON, 394 U.S. 618 (1969). Applying the same principle, states may not require a year's residence in a county as a condition for an indigent to receive nonemergency hospitalization or medical care at the county's expense. Memorial Hospital v. Maricopa County, 415 U.S. 250 (1974).

For the most part, judges confine their review of welfare rights to questions of statutory interpretation and congressional intent, not constitutional law. The Supreme Court decided that an Alabama regulation, denying AFDC payments to the children of a mother who kept "a man in the house," was inconsistent with federal law. King v. Smith, 392 U.S. 309 (1968). On the other hand, state efforts to impose a ceiling on AFDC payments, regardless of family size or need, have been sustained as not prohibited by federal law. Dandridge v. Williams, 397 U.S. 471 (1970). The "intractable economic, social, and even philosophical problems presented by public welfare assistance programs are not the business of this Court." Id. at 487.

In 1971, the Court confronted the sensitive issue of caseworkers entering the home of a welfare recipient. New York required caseworkers to visit beneficiaries during working hours and prohibited forcible entry and snooping. A beneficiary under the AFDC program refused to admit caseworkers, contending that home visitation amounted to a search and required either consent or a warrant supported by probable cause. The Court, divided 6–3, decided that constitutional rights had not been violated. Home visitation is not a search within the traditional criminal law context of the Fourth Amendment. Wyman v. James, 400 U.S. 309 (1971).

In that same year the Court, with only Justice Black dissenting, ruled that due process is denied by refusing indigents (including welfare recipients) access to the courts to dissolve a marriage simply because of their inability to pay court fees and costs. Such a policy amounts to denying them an opportunity to be heard. Boddie v. Connecticut, 401 U.S. 371 (1971). On other matters the Court has upheld filing fees for indigents when the fee "does not rise to the same constitutional level" as in *Boddie*, especially where alternative procedures are available without payment of a fee. Ortwein v. Schwab, 410 U.S. 656 (1973); United States v. Kras, 409 U.S. 434 (1973). In 1995, the Court ruled that a state may not refuse to hear a mother's appeal of a court decision terminating her parental rights to her two minor children just because she cannot pay court fees. M.L.B. v. S.L.J., 519 U.S. 102 (1996).

In 1999, the Supreme Court ruled that state welfare programs may not restrict new residents to the welfare benefits they were entitled to receive in the state from which they moved. Instead of relying on the "right to travel" (language not found in the Constitution), the 7 to 2 decision exhumed the Fourteenth Amendment's Privileges or Immunities Clause, which provides: "No State shall make or enforce any law which shall abridge the privileges or immunities of citizens of the United States." The last time the Court relied on that clause was in 1935, but that ruling was overturned five years later. Colgate v. Harvey, 296 U.S. 404 (1935); Madden v. Kentucky, 309 U.S. 83, 90–93 (1940). To find full discussion of the clause one has to go back to the *Slaughter-House Cases* of 1873. In a dissent to the 1999 ruling, Rehnquist spoke of "unearthing from its tomb the right to become a state citizen and to be treated equally in the new State of residence." Saenz v. Roe, 526 U.S. 489, 516 (1999).

School Financing

The Supreme Court split 5–4 on a major case in 1973 involving the financing of public schools. In Texas, half of the revenues for public elementary and secondary schools came from a state-funded program. Each district then supplemented that amount through an ad valorem tax on property within its jurisdiction. The higher the value of the properties, the higher the supplement. Rich communities could therefore support better schools than poor neighborhoods. A class action brought by Mexican-American parents argued that the system violated the Equal Protection Clause by favoring students in more affluent districts. The Court held that the system did not disadvantage any suspect class. The fundamental right of education is not interfered with, said the Court, if state-supported revenues assure at least a minimum education. With respect to wealth, the Court announced that the Equal Protection Clause does not require absolute equality of precisely equal advantages. SAN ANTONIO SCHOOL DISTRICT v. RODRIGUEZ, 411 U.S. 1 (1973). Justice Marshall, penning one of the dissents, pointed to the inconsistency between this decision and the cases on desegregation that invalidated inequality in educational facilities. However, the Court may have concluded that it lacked the political legitimacy or power to dictate funding levels in public schools throughout the states.

State courts have reached different results. The Supreme Court of New Jersey reviewed the state's system of financing public education, which relied heavily on local taxation to cover public school costs and created substantial variations in spending per pupil. The court held that the system violated the provision in the state constitution that requires the state to furnish "thorough and efficient" public schooling. The New Jersey court explained why it could be more demanding on the question of equal protection than the U.S. Supreme Court: "For one thing, there is absent the principle of federalism which cautions against too expansive a view of a federal constitutional limitation upon the power and opportunity of the several States to cope with their own problems in the light of their own circumstances." Robinson v. Cahill, 303 A.2d 273, 282 (N.J. 1973), cert. denied, sub nom. Dickey v. Robinson, 414 U.S. 976 (1973). Other state courts have struck down systems of financing public schools because they violated equal protection (see box on next page). State legislatures have restructured their financing systems to provide more equitable funding for schools in poorer communities, but litigation

State Litigation on School Financing

In *San Antonio School District* v. *Rodriguez* (1973), the Supreme Court held that school financing systems that provided greater funding for affluent districts did not violate the Equal Protection Clause. Since that time a number of state courts have upheld such systems. Other state courts have declared that disparate financing schemes are invalid under the state constitution, often because state charters contain explicit requirements and standards for public education. For example, Art X, § 1, of the Montana constitution provides: "Equality of educational opportunity is guaranteed to each person of the state." When state legislatures responded with inadequate funding and reforms, state courts issued additional rulings. The following state courts have invalidated school financing systems because they discriminate against poorer districts and deny equal education:

Arizona	Roosevelt Elem. Sch. Dist. v. Bishop, 877 P.2d 806 (1994); Hull v. Albrecht, 960 P.2d 634 (1998).
Arkansas	Dupree v. Alma School Dist. No. 30, 651 S.W.2d 90 (1983).
California	Serrano v. Priest, 557 P.2d 929 (1977).
Connecticut	Horton v. Meskill, 376 A.2d 359 (1977); Sheff v. O'Neill, 678 A.2d 1267 (1996). Sheff v. O'Neill, 733 A.2d 925 (1999), held that the state had complied with the 1996 decision.
Kentucky	Rose v. Council for Better Educ., Inc., 790 S.W.2d 186 (1989).
Massachusetts	McDuffy v. Sec'y of Exec. Off. of Educ., 615 N.E.2d 516 (1993).
Montana	Helena Elementary School Dist. v. State, 769 P.2d 684 (1989).
New Jersey	Robinson v. Cahill, 303 A.2d 273 (1973), cert. denied, sub nom. Dickey v. Robinson, 414 U.S. 976 (1973); Robinson v. Cahill, 355 A.2d 129 (1976); Abbott v. Burke, 575 A.2d 359 (1990); Abbott ex rel. Abbott v. Burke, 751 A.2d 1032 (2000).
Ohio	DeRolph v. State, 677 N.E.2d 733 (1997).
Tennessee	Tenn. Small School Systems v. McWherter, 851 S.W.2d 139 (1993), 894 S.W.2d 734 (1995).
Texas	Edgewood Indep. School Dist. v. Kirby, 777 S.W.2d 391 (1989); Edgewood Indep. Sch. Dist. v. Kirby, 804 S.W.2d 491 (1991).
Vermont	Brigham v. State, 692 A.2d 384 (1997).
Washington	Seattle Sch. Dist. No. 1 of King Cty. v. State, 585 P.2d 71 (1978).
West Virginia	Pauley v. Kelly, 255 S.E.2d 859 (1979).
Wyoming	Washakie Co. Sch. Dist. No. One v. Herschler, 606 P.2d 310 (1980), cert. denied, 449 U.S. 824 (1980).

continues to test the constitutionality of school financing. Although suits of this nature are often brought by blacks and Mexican-Americans, plaintiffs can also be overwhelmingly white and rural.

Abortion

In 1980, the Supreme Court upheld the Hyde Amendment, passed by Congress to deny public funds for abortions except to save the mother's life or in cases of rape or incest. Harris v. McRae, 448 U.S. 297 (1980). As with the school financing cases, state courts reached different conclusions. In California, Connecticut, Massachusetts, Michigan, New Jersey, and Oregon, state courts struck down state versions of the Hyde Amendment. They held that states have no obligation to provide medical care to the poor, but that it is a violation of the state constitution to give money to indigent women wanting to bear a child and deny funds to those who seek an abortion. This issue is explored more fully in Chapter 17.

Shapiro v. Thompson

394 U.S. 618 (1969)

A number of states, citing budgetary reasons, established a one-year waiting period before residents could qualify for welfare assistance. In this dispute, Vivian Marie Thompson moved from Massachusetts to Connecticut and applied for welfare benefits under the Aid to Families with Dependent Children (AFDC) program. Denied assistance, she sued the Commissioner of Welfare, Bernard Shapiro. This case, implicating the constitutional right to travel, also involved residency requirements in Pennsylvania and the District of Columbia. A three-judge district court held that residency requirements violate the Equal Protection Clause of the Fourteenth Amendment (covering the states) and the Due Process Clause of the Fifth Amendment (covering D.C.).

MR. JUSTICE BRENNAN delivered the opinion of the Court....

I.

In No. 9, the Connecticut Welfare Department invoked § 17-2d of the Connecticut General Statutes to deny the application of appellee Vivian Marie Thompson for assistance under the program for Aid to Families with Dependent Children (AFDC). She was a 19-year-old unwed mother of one child and pregnant with her second child when she changed her residence in June 1966 from Dorchester, Massachusetts, to Hartford, Connecticut, to live with her mother, a Hartford resident. She moved to her own apartment in Hartford in August 1966, when her mother was no longer able to support her and her infant son. Because of her pregnancy, she was unable to work or enter a work training program. Her application for AFDC assistance, filed in August, was denied in November solely on the ground that, as required by § 17-2d, she had not lived in the State for a year before her application was filed....

II.

There is no dispute that the effect of the waiting-period requirement in each case is to create two classes of needy resident families indistinguishable from each other except that one is composed of residents who have resided a year or more, and the second of residents who have resided less than a year, in the jurisdiction. On the basis of this sole difference the first class is granted and the second class is denied welfare aid upon which may depend the ability of the families to obtain the very means to subsist — food, shelter, and other necessities of life....

III.

Primarily, appellants justify the waiting-period requirement as a protective device to preserve the fiscal integrity of state public assistance programs. It is asserted that people who require welfare assistance during their first year of residence in a State are likely to become continuing burdens on state welfare programs....

We do not doubt that the one-year waiting-period device is well suited to discourage the influx of poor families in need of assistance. An indigent who desires to migrate, resettle, find a new job, and start a new life will doubtless hesitate if he knows that he must risk making the move without the possibility of falling back on state welfare assistance during his first year of residence, when his need may be most acute. But the purpose of inhibiting migration by needy persons into the State is constitutionally impermissible.

This Court long ago recognized that the nature of our Federal Union and our constitutional concepts of personal liberty unite to require that all citizens be free to travel throughout the length and breadth of our land uninhibited by statutes, rules, or regulations which unreasonably burden or restrict this movement....

We have no occasion to ascribe the source of this right to travel interstate to a particular constitutional provision. It suffices that, as MR. JUSTICE STEWART said for the Court in *United States* v. *Guest,* 383 U.S. 745, 757–758 (1966):

"The constitutional right to travel from one State to another ... occupies a position fundamental to the concept of our Federal Union. It is a right that has been firmly established and repeatedly recognized.

"... [T]he right finds no explicit mention in the Constitution. The reason, it has been suggested, is that a right so elementary was conceived from the beginning to be a necessary concomitant of the stronger Union the Constitution created. In any event, freedom to travel throughout the United States has long been recognized as a basic right under the Constitution."

Thus, the purpose of deterring the in-migration of indigents cannot serve as justification for the classification created by the one-year waiting period, since that purpose is constitutionally impermissible....

We recognize that a State has a valid interest in preserving the fiscal integrity of its programs. It may legitimately attempt to limit its expenditures, whether for public assistance, public education, or any other program. But a State may not accomplish such a purpose by invidious distinctions between classes of its citizens. It could not, for example, reduce expenditures for education by barring indigent children from its schools. Similarly, in the cases before us, appellants must do more than show that denying welfare benefits to new residents saves money. The saving of welfare costs cannot justify an otherwise invidious classification.

... For the reasons we have stated in invalidating the Pennsylvania and Connecticut provisions, the District of Columbia provision is also invalid—the Due Process Clause of the Fifth Amendment prohibits Congress from denying public assistance to poor persons otherwise eligible solely on the ground that they have not been residents of the District of Columbia for one year at the time their applications are filed.

Accordingly, the judgments in Nos. 9, 33, and 34 are

Affirmed.

Mr. Justice Stewart, concurring....

Mr. Chief Justice Warren, with whom Mr. Justice Black joins, dissenting.

In my opinion the issue before us can be simply stated: May Congress, acting under one of its enumerated powers, impose minimal nationwide residence requirements or authorize the States to do so? Since I believe that Congress does have this power and has constitutionally exercised it in these cases, I must dissent.

I.

The Court insists that § 402 (b) of the Social Security Act "does not approve, much less prescribe, a one-year requirement." ... From its reading of the legislative history it concludes that Congress did not intend to authorize the States to impose residence requirements. An examination of the relevant legislative materials compels, in my view, the opposite conclusion, *i.e.,* Congress intended to authorize state residence requirements of up to one year....

Mr. Justice Harlan, dissenting.

[II.]

... In light of this undeniable relation of residence requirements to valid legislative aims, it cannot be said that the requirements are "arbitrary" or "lacking in rational justification." Hence, I can find no objection to these residence requirements under the Equal Protection Clause of the Fourteenth Amendment or under the analogous standard embodied in the Due Process Clause of the Fifth Amendment.

III.

... Today's decision, it seems to me, reflects to an unusual degree the current notion that this Court possesses a peculiar wisdom all its own whose capacity to lead this Nation out of its present troubles is contained only by the limits of judicial ingenuity in contriving new constitutional principles to meet each problem as it arises....

San Antonio School Dist. v. Rodriguez

411 U.S. 1 (1973)

Elementary and secondary schools in Texas are financed by state and local contributions. In this case, almost half of the revenues came from the state in order to provide a basic minimum for schools. Supplemental funds were derived from a property tax adopted by each school district. A class action was brought on behalf of schoolchildren from members of poor families, who claimed that the Texas system of relying on local property taxes favored the more affluent neighborhoods and violated the Equal Protection Clause. A federal district court relied on strict judicial scrutiny to conclude that Texas needed to show a compelling state interest to justify the financing system. Demetrio Rodriguez and other Mexican-American parents brought this suit.

MR. JUSTICE POWELL delivered the opinion of the Court.

[I]

Recognizing the need for increased state funding to help offset disparities in local spending and to meet Texas' changing educational requirements, the state legislature in the late 1940's undertook a thorough evaluation of public education with an eye toward major reform. In 1947, an 18-member committee, composed of educators and legislators, was appointed to explore alternative systems in other States and to propose a funding scheme that would guarantee a minimum or basic educational offering to each child and that would help overcome interdistrict disparities in taxable resources. The Committee's efforts led to the … Texas Minimum Foundation School Program. Today, this Program accounts for approximately half of the total educational expenditures in Texas.

The Program calls for state and local contributions to a fund earmarked specifically for teacher salaries, operating expenses, and transportation costs. The State, supplying funds from its general revenues, finances approximately 80% of the Program, and the school districts are responsible — as a unit — for providing the remaining 20%. The districts' share, known as the Local Fund Assignment, is apportioned among the school districts under a formula designed to reflect each district's relative taxpaying ability. The Assignment is first divided among Texas' 254 counties pursuant to a complicated economic index that takes into account the relative value of each county's contribution to the State's total income from manufacturing, mining, and agricultural activities. It also considers each county's relative share of all payrolls paid within the State and, to a lesser extent, considers each county's share of all property in the State. Each county's assignment is then divided among its school districts on the basis of each district's share of assessable property within the county. The district, in turn, finances its share of the Assignment out of revenues from local property taxation.

[*Demetrio Rodriguez and other appellees lived in the Edgewood Independent School District, one of seven public school districts in the metropolitan area. Approximately 90% of the student population was Mexican-American and over 6% black. The average assessed property value and the median family income were the lowest in the metropolitan area. The district* contributed $26 to the education of each child for the 1967–1968 school year, the Foundation Program contributed $222 per pupil, and federal funds added $108, or a total of $356 per pupil. In contrast, Alamo Heights, the most affluent school district in San Antonio, had a predominantly "Anglo" school population. The assessed property value per pupil was eight times that in Edgewood. In 1967–1968 the local tax rate yielded $333 per pupil. Combined with $225 from the Foundation Program, the district was able to supply $558 per student. Federal funds of $36 per pupil brought the total to $594 per pupil. For the 1970–1971 school year, the Foundation School Program allotment for Edgewood was $356 per pupil, and for Alamo Heights, $491 per pupil. Alamo Heights, because of its relative wealth, was required to contribute from local property tax collections approximately $100 per pupil. Edgewood paid only $8.46 per pupil.*]

Texas virtually concedes that its historically rooted dual system of financing education could not withstand the strict judicial scrutiny that this Court has found appropriate in reviewing legislative judgments that interfere with fundamental constitutional rights or that involve suspect classifications.…

II

The District Court's opinion … conclud[*ed*] that strict judicial scrutiny was required [*and*] relied on decisions dealing with the rights of indigents to equal treatment in the criminal trial and appellate processes, and on cases disapproving wealth restrictions on the right to vote.…

… [F]or the several reasons that follow, we find neither the suspect-classification nor the fundamental-interest analysis persuasive.

A

… Apart from the unsettled and disputed question whether the quality of education may be determined by the amount of money expended for it, a sufficient answer to appellees' argument is that, at least where wealth is involved, the Equal Protection Clause does not require absolute equality or precisely equal advantages. Nor, indeed, in view of the infinite variables affecting the educational process, can any system assure equal quality of education except in the most relative sense.…

B

In *Brown v. Board of Education*, 347 U.S. 483

(1954), a unanimous Court recognized that "education is perhaps the most important function of state and local governments." *Id.,* at 493. What was said there in the context of racial discrimination has lost none of its vitality with the passage of time....

Nothing this Court holds today in any way detracts from our historic dedication to public education. We are in complete agreement with the conclusion of the three-judge panel below that "the grave significance of education both to the individual and to our society" cannot be doubted. But the importance of a service performed by the State does not determine whether it must be regarded as fundamental for purposes of examination under the Equal Protection Clause....

Education, of course, is not among the rights afforded explicit protection under our Federal Constitution. Nor do we find any basis for saying it is implicitly so protected. As we have said, the undisputed importance of education will not alone cause this Court to depart from the usual standard for reviewing a State's social and economic legislation....

C

... This case represents far more than a challenge to the manner in which Texas provides for the education of its children. We have here nothing less than a direct attack on the way in which Texas has chosen to raise and disburse state and local tax revenues....

In addition to matters of fiscal policy, this case also involves the most persistent and difficult questions of educational policy, another area in which this Court's lack of specialized knowledge and experience counsels against premature interference with the informed judgments made at the state and local levels....

[*In Section III, the Court holds that the Texas school finance system rationally furthers a legitimate state purpose or interest and therefore satisfies the Equal Protection Clause.*]

IV

... The consideration and initiation of fundamental reforms with respect to state taxation and education are matters reserved for the legislative processes of the various States, and we do no violence to the values of federalism and separation of powers by staying our hand. We hardly need add that this Court's action today is not to be viewed as placing its judicial imprimatur on the status quo. The need is apparent for reform in tax systems which may well have relied too long and too heavily on the local property tax.... But the ultimate solutions must come from the lawmakers and from the democratic pressures of those who elect them.

Reversed.

MR. JUSTICE STEWART, concurring....

MR. JUSTICE BRENNAN, dissenting.

Although I agree with my Brother WHITE that the Texas statutory scheme is devoid of any rational basis, and for that reason is violative of the Equal Protection Clause, I also record my disagreement with the Court's rather distressing assertion that a right may be deemed "fundamental" for the purposes of equal protection analysis only if it is "explicitly or implicitly guaranteed by the Constitution."...

... [T]here can be no doubt that education is inextricably linked to the right to participate in the electoral process and to the rights of free speech and association guaranteed by the First Amendment.... This being so, any classification affecting education must be subjected to strict judicial scrutiny, and since even the State concedes that the statutory scheme now before us cannot pass constitutional muster under this stricter standard of review, I can only conclude that the Texas school-financing scheme is constitutionally invalid.

MR. JUSTICE WHITE, with whom MR. JUSTICE DOUGLAS and MR. JUSTICE BRENNAN join, dissenting....

MR. JUSTICE MARSHALL, with whom MR. JUSTICE DOUGLAS concurs, dissenting.

The Court today decides, in effect, that a State may constitutionally vary the quality of education which it offers its children in accordance with the amount of taxable wealth located in the school districts within which they reside. The majority's decision represents an abrupt departure from the mainstream of recent state and federal court decisions concerning the unconstitutionality of state educational financing schemes dependent upon taxable local wealth. More unfortunately, though, the majority's holding can only be seen as a retreat from our historic commitment to equality of educational opportunity and as unsupportable acquiescence in a system which deprives children in their earliest years of the chance to reach their full potential as citizens....

E. EQUAL PROTECTION FOR GAYS AND LESBIANS

The rights of gays and lesbians are also discussed in Chapter 17 on the right to privacy. But any consideration of the expansion of equal protection must include some discussion of the struggle of gays and lesbians to obtain the equal protection of the laws. As was the case with race, gender and alienage, it has taken an organized litigation strategy in state and federal courts, along with activism in states and local communities to bring about change in the law. In 1972 attorney Bill Thom modeled the Lambda Legal Defense and Education Fund after the NAACP Legal Defense and Educational Fund with the goal of providing legal services in cases involving the legal rights of homosexuals and educating them about their legal rights. His initial application for permission to practice law as a voluntary association was denied by a three-judge panel of a New York court assembled to review it. The judges distinguished Lambda from other groups that had been approved, contending that while homosexuals "too faced widespread discrimination, the difficulties they had in securing legal representation merely reflected 'a matter of taste' on the part of individual lawyers." Thom successfully challenged this ruling on First and Fourteenth Amendment grounds and Lambda was incorporated. As Ellen Ann Andersen argues in her study of Lambda's litigation strategy, the story of Lambda's beginnings demonstrates that in the early 1970's "[T]he notion that homosexuals had the 'right' to be free of discrimination based on their sexuality seemed absurd to many. The notion is still a contested one today, but in the intervening years the issue has moved from the fringes of American social consciousness to a central position." Out of the Closets and Into the Courts 2–3 (2005).

The mobilization of legal resources to fight discrimination has led to a backlash in the political arena. There has been widespread use of ballot initiatives to pass anti-gay legislation. Perhaps the most famous, because it resulted in litigation before the Supreme Court, was Amendment 2, passed by Colorado voters in 1992. The amendment forbade municipalities and departments of the state government from including sexual orientation among the groups to be protected in anti-discrimination laws. In 1996 the Court, in a 6–3 decision, struck down the amendment on equal protection grounds, finding that the amendment was based on irrational "animus" toward gays. ROMER v. EVANS, 517 U.S. 620 (1996).

While the decision was a significant victory for gay rights, there was disappointment that the Court was not prepared to impose strict scrutiny as the test for classifications based on sexual orientation. Instead the Court applied the lowest tier of analysis, finding no rational basis for Colorado's law. This led to a debate in the legal community among those working on gay rights cases as to the legitimacy of the three-tiered class based approach to equal protection analysis. Evan Gerstmann, for example, contends that the three-tiered approach forces groups to make claims of being "suspect" in order to gain strict scrutiny at a time when the Court has pulled back from a willingness to impose this level of scrutiny. He claims the small window of opportunity for claiming "suspectness" was in the 1970's and that since that time a more conservative court has sought to pull back from aggressive enforcement of equal protection. The Constitutional Underclass: Gays, Lesbians and the Failure of Class-Based Equal Protection (1999).

Defense of Marriage Act and Same-Sex Marriage

Litigation in Hawaii challenged a state marriage law that prohibited same-sex couples from obtaining marriage licenses. Under pressure from this lawsuit, Congress passed the Defense of Marriage Act (DOMA) in 1996, which allowed states to refuse to recognize such marriages performed in other states and also prohibited federal recognition of same-sex marriages. The latter provision prevents gay couples from filing joint tax returns or gaining access to spousal benefits under Social Security and other federal programs. President Clinton signed the legislation without comment. 110 Stat. 2419 (1996). Congress acted under Section 1 of Article IV: "Full Faith and Credit shall be given in each State to the public Acts, Records, and judicial Proceedings of every other State; And the Congress may by general

Laws prescribe the Manner in which such Acts, Records and Proceedings shall be proved, and the Effect thereof." The House passed legislation in 2004 to strip from federal courts their ability to rule on DOMA (see Section D in Chapter 19). The Senate took no action on the bill.

After enactment of DOMA, gay rights organizations sought to convince state courts and state legislatures to legalize same-sex unions. In Vermont, a 1997 lawsuit challenging the state's prohibition of same-sex marriages led to state legislation in 2000 that allowed gays to form a "civil union," giving them the same benefits, protections, and responsibilities granted to spouses in a marriage. Baker v. State, 744 A.2d 864 (Vt. 1999). Other states adopted explicit prohibitions on same-sex marriages in either statutes or constitutional amendments. The Supreme Court's decision in *Lawrence* v. *Texas* (2003), striking down a Texas sodomy law, encouraged some states to grant same-sex couples rights previously recognized only for traditional couples. In November 2003, the Massachusetts Supreme Judicial Court ruled that same-sex couples have a right under the state constitution to civil marriages. In February 2004, the court amplified its earlier ruling by holding that the state legislature may not offer "civil union" instead of marriage for same-sex couples. By 2012, six states and the District of Columbia permitted gay marriage and several others recognized such marriages even though they did not permit them to be performed in the state.

As a reaction to developments in the states, some conservative legal scholars drafted an amendment to the U.S. Constitution to define marriage as the union of a man and a woman. President Bush, referring to the actions by the Massachusetts court, supported the amendment. In a radio address on July 10, 2004, he explained: "When judges insist on imposing their arbitrary will on the people, the only alternative left to the people is an amendment to the Constitution—the only law a court cannot overturn." Four days later the Senate voted 48 to 50 against bringing the amendment to the floor for a vote. On September 30, the House voted 227 to 186 in favor of the amendment, well below the 290 votes needed to reach the required two-thirds majority.

On May 15, 2008, the California Supreme Court by a 4 to 3 vote ruled that gays have a constitutional right to marry. Gay couples began to wed, but the issue was put before California voters in the November 2008 elections in the form of Proposition 8, an amendment to the state constitution. The voters by a 52 percent margin supported a ban on same-sex marriages. In May 2009 the California Supreme Court, six to one, upheld the ban, noting that same-sex couples retained a right to civil unions. The dispute then moved to federal court. On August 4, 2010, District Judge Vaughn Walker ruled that Proposition 8 violates the Equal Protection Clause of the U.S. Constitution because it failed "to advance any rational basis in singling out gay men and lesbians for denial of a marriage license." Tradition alone or moral disapproval, he said, could not form a rational basis for law. Perry v. Schwarzenegger, 704 F.Supp.2d 921(N.D. Cal. 2010). On appeal, the Ninth Circuit affirmed the decision, but on substantially narrower grounds, limiting the reach of the opinion to only the state of California. Perry v. Brown, 671 F.3d 1052 (9th Cir. 2012).

In 2011 the Obama Administration notified Congress that while it would continue to enforce DOMA, it would no longer defend it in Court. In a letter to Speaker of the House John Boehner, Attorney General Eric Holder wrote that he and the President had determined that Section 3 of DOMA, denying federal benefits to legally married same-sex couples, could not withstand heightened scrutiny under equal protection analysis. (See Attorney General Letter reading.) A number of federal courts have found Section 3 of DOMA (which denies federal benefits to legally married same-sex couples) to be unconstitutional on both equal protection and federalism grounds, and both the Obama Department of Justice and supporters of DOMA have asked the Supreme Court to review these decisions. Gill v. Office of Personnel Management, 699 F.Supp.2d 374 (D. Mass. 2010); aff'd, 682 F.3d 1 (1st Cir. 2012); Massachusetts v. U.S. Dept. of Health and Human Services, 698 F.Supp.2d 234 (D. Mass. 2010); Windsor v. U.S., 833 F.Supp.2d 394 (S.D. N.Y. 2012); Golinski v. Office of Personnel Management, 824 F.Supp.2d 968 (N.D. Cal. 2012).

Romer v. Evans

517 U.S. 620 (1996)

In 1992 Colorado voters, through a statewide referendum, adopted Amendment 2 to their constitution prohibiting any state entity from including sexual orientation in any of their antidiscrimination laws. Several municipalities that had such ordinances and several individuals affected by the law filed suit in state court. The trial court granted a preliminary injunction to stay enforcement and the decision was appealed to the Supreme Court of Colorado. That court sustained the injunction and held that the amendment was subject to strict scrutiny under the Fourteenth Amendment because it denied the rights of gays and lesbians to participate in the political process. The trial court held that the amendment was not narrowly tailored to meet a compelling interest and struck it down. The state supreme court affirmed and the state appealed to the U.S. Supreme Court. Although affirming the judgment of the lower court, note that the Court adopts a different rationale for its decision. Richard G. Evans brought this case against Governor Roy Romer.

JUSTICE KENNEDY delivered the opinion of the Court.

One century ago, the first Justice Harlan admonished this Court that the Constitution "neither knows nor tolerates classes among citizens." *Plessy* v. *Ferguson,* 163 U.S. 537, 559 (1896) (dissenting opinion). Unheeded then, those words now are understood to state a commitment to the law's neutrality where the rights of persons are at stake. The Equal Protection Clause enforces this principle and today requires us to hold invalid a provision of Colorado's Constitution.

I

The enactment challenged in this case is an amendment to the Constitution of the State of Colorado, adopted in a 1992 statewide referendum. The parties and the state courts refer to it as "Amendment 2," its designation when submitted to the voters. The impetus for the amendment and the contentious campaign that preceded its adoption came in large part from ordinances that had been passed in various Colorado municipalities. For example, the cities of Aspen and Boulder and the city and County of Denver each had enacted ordinances which banned discrimination in many transactions and activities, including housing, employment, education, public accommodations, and health and welfare services.... What gave rise to the statewide controversy was the protection the ordinances afforded to persons discriminated against by reason of their sexual orientation.... Amendment 2 repeals these ordinances to the extent they prohibit discrimination on the basis of "homosexual, lesbian or bisexual orientation, conduct, practices or relationships." Colo. Const., Art. II, § 30b.

Yet Amendment 2, in explicit terms, does more than repeal or rescind these provisions. It prohibits all legislative, executive or judicial action at any level of state or local government designed to protect the named class, a class we shall refer to as homosexual persons or gays and lesbians. The amendment reads:

"No Protected Status Based on Homosexual, Lesbian or Bisexual Orientation. Neither the State of Colorado, through any of its branches or departments, nor any of its agencies, political subdivisions, municipalities or school districts, shall enact, adopt or enforce any statute, regulation, ordinance or policy whereby homosexual, lesbian or bisexual orientation, conduct, practices or relationships shall constitute or otherwise be the basis of or entitle any person or class of persons to have or claim any minority status, quota preferences, protected status or claim of discrimination. This Section of the Constitution shall be in all respects self-executing."....

II

The State's principal argument in defense of Amendment 2 is that it puts gays and lesbians in the same position as all other persons. So, the State says, the measure does no more than deny homosexuals special rights. This reading of the amendment's language is implausible. We rely not upon our own interpretation of the amendment but upon the authoritative construction of Colorado's Supreme Court. The state court, deeming it unnecessary to determine the full extent of the amendment's reach, found it invalid even on a modest reading of its implications. The critical discussion of the amendment, set out in *Evans I,* is as follows:

"The immediate objective of Amendment 2 is, at a minimum, to repeal existing statutes, regulations, ordinances, and policies of state and local entities that barred discrimination based on sexual orientation....

"The 'ultimate effect' of Amendment 2 is to prohibit any governmental entity from adopting similar, or more protective statutes, regulations, ordinances, or policies in the future unless the state constitution is first amended to permit such measures." ...

Sweeping and comprehensive is the change in legal status effected by this law. So much is evident from the ordinances the Colorado Supreme Court declared would be void by operation of Amendment 2. Homosexuals, by state decree, are put in a solitary class with respect to transactions and relations in both the private and governmental spheres. The amendment withdraws from homosexuals, but no others, specific legal protection from the injuries caused by discrimination, and it forbids reinstatement of these laws and policies.

The change Amendment 2 works in the legal status of gays and lesbians in the private sphere is far reaching, both on its own terms and when considered in light of the structure and operation of modern antidiscrimination laws. That structure is well illustrated by contemporary statutes and ordinances prohibiting discrimination by providers of public accommodations. "At common law, innkeepers, smiths, and others who 'made profession of a public employment,' were prohibited from refusing, without good reason, to serve a customer." *Hurley* v. *Irish-American Gay, Lesbian and Bisexual Group of Boston, Inc.,* 515 U. S. 557, 571 (1995). The duty was a general one and did not specify protection for particular groups. The common-law rules, however, proved insufficient in many instances, and it was settled early that the Fourteenth Amendment did not give Congress a general power to prohibit discrimination in public accommodations, *Civil Rights Cases,* 109 U.S. 3, 25 (1883). In consequence, most States have chosen to counter discrimination by enacting detailed statutory schemes.... Colorado's state and municipal laws typify this emerging tradition of statutory protection and follow a consistent pattern. The laws first enumerate the persons or entities subject to a duty not to discriminate ...

These statutes and ordinances also depart from the common law by enumerating the groups or persons within their ambit of protection. Enumeration is the essential device used to make the duty not to discriminate concrete and to provide guidance for those who must comply. In following this approach, Colorado's state and local governments have not limited antidiscrimination laws to groups that have so far been given the protection of heightened equal protection scrutiny under our cases.... Rather, they set forth an extensive catalog of traits which cannot be the basis for discrimination, including age, military status, marital status, pregnancy, parenthood, custody of a minor child, political affiliation, physical or mental disability of an individual or of his or her associates—and, in recent times, sexual orientation....

Amendment 2 bars homosexuals from securing protection against the injuries that these public-accommodations laws address. That in itself is a severe consequence, but there is more. Amendment 2, in addition, nullifies specific legal protections for this targeted class in all transactions in housing, sale of real estate, insurance, health and welfare services, private education, and employment....

Not confined to the private sphere, Amendment 2 also operates to repeal and forbid all laws or policies providing specific protection for gays or lesbians from discrimination by every level of Colorado government.... The repeal of these measures and the prohibition against their future reenactment demonstrate that Amendment 2 has the same force and effect in Colorado's governmental sector as it does elsewhere and that it applies to policies as well as ordinary legislation.

Amendment 2's reach may not be limited to specific laws passed for the benefit of gays and lesbians. It is a fair, if not necessary, inference from the broad language of the amendment that it deprives gays and lesbians even of the protection of general laws and policies that prohibit arbitrary discrimination in governmental and private settings.... At some point in the systematic administration of these laws, an official must determine whether homosexuality is an arbitrary and, thus, forbidden basis for decision. Yet a decision to that effect would itself amount to a policy prohibiting discrimination on the basis of homosexuality, and so would appear to be no more valid under Amendment 2 than the specific prohibitions against discrimination the state court held invalid.

If this consequence follows from Amendment 2, as its broad language suggests, it would compound the constitutional difficulties the law creates.... In any event, even if, as we doubt, homosexuals could find some safe harbor in laws of general application, we cannot accept the view that Amendment 2's prohibition on specific legal protections does no more than deprive homosexuals of special rights. To the contrary, the amendment imposes a special disability upon those persons alone. Homosexuals are forbidden the safeguards that others enjoy or may seek without constraint. They can obtain specific protection against discrimination only by enlisting the citizenry of Colorado to amend the State Constitution or perhaps, on the State's view, by trying to pass helpful laws of general applicability. This is so no matter how local or discrete the harm, no matter how public and widespread the injury. We find nothing special in the protections Amendment 2 withholds. These are protections taken for granted by most people either because they already have them or do not need them; these are protections against exclusion from an almost limitless number of transactions and endeavors that constitute ordinary civic life in a free society.

III

The Fourteenth Amendment's promise that no person shall be denied the equal protection of the laws must coexist with the practical necessity that most legislation classifies for one purpose or another, with resulting disadvantage to various groups or persons.... We have attempted to reconcile the principle with the reality by stating that, if a law neither burdens a fundamental right nor targets a suspect class, we will uphold the legislative classification so long as it bears a rational relation to some legitimate end.... Amendment 2 fails, indeed defies, even this conventional inquiry. First, the amendment has the peculiar property of imposing a broad and undifferentiated disability on a single named group, an exceptional and, as we shall explain, invalid form of legislation. Second, its sheer breadth is so discontinuous with the reasons offered for it that the amendment seems inexplicable by anything but animus toward the class it affects; it lacks a rational relationship to legitimate state interests.

Taking the first point, even in the ordinary equal protection case calling for the most deferential of standards, we insist on knowing the relation between the classification adopted and the object to be attained.... In the ordinary case, a law will be sustained if it can be said to advance a legitimate government interest, even if the law seems unwise or works to the disadvantage of a particular group, or if the rationale for it seems tenuous.... By requiring that the classification bear a rational relationship to an independent and legitimate legislative end, we ensure that classifications are not drawn for the purpose of disadvantaging the group burdened by the law....

Amendment 2 confounds this normal process of judicial review. It is at once too narrow and too broad. It identifies persons by a single trait and then denies them protection across the board. The resulting disqualification of a class of persons from the right to seek specific protection from the law is unprecedented in our jurisprudence....

It is not within our constitutional tradition to enact laws of this sort. Central both to the idea of the rule of law and to our own Constitution's guarantee of equal protection is the principle that government and each of its parts remain open on impartial terms to all who seek its assistance.... Respect for this principle explains why laws singling out a certain class of citizens for disfavored legal status or general hardships are rare. A law declaring that in general it shall be more difficult for one group of citizens than for all others to seek aid from the government is itself a denial of equal protection of the laws in the most literal sense....

A second and related point is that laws of the kind now before us raise the inevitable inference that the disadvantage imposed is born of animosity toward the class of persons affected.... Even laws enacted for broad and ambitious purposes often can be explained by reference to legitimate public policies which justify the incidental disadvantages they impose on certain persons. Amendment 2, however, in making a general announcement that gays and lesbians shall not have any particular protections from the law, inflicts on them immediate, continuing, and real injuries that outrun and belie any legitimate justifications that may be claimed for it. We conclude that, in addition to the far-reaching deficiencies of Amendment 2 that we have noted, the principles it offends, in another sense, are conventional and venerable; a law must bear a rational relationship to a legitimate governmental purpose ... and Amendment 2 does not.

The primary rationale the State offers for Amendment 2 is respect for other citizens' freedom of association, and in particular the liberties of landlords or employers who have personal or religious objections to homosexuality. Colorado also cites its interest in conserving resources to fight discrimination against other groups. The breadth of the amendment is so far removed from these particular justifications that we find it impossible to credit them. We cannot say that Amendment 2 is directed to any identifiable legitimate purpose or discrete objective. It is a status-based enactment divorced from any factual context from which we could discern a relationship to legitimate state interests; it is a classification of persons undertaken for its own sake, something the Equal Protection Clause does not permit....

We must conclude that Amendment 2 classifies homosexuals not to further a proper legislative end but to make them unequal to everyone else. This Colorado cannot do. A State cannot so deem a class of persons a stranger to its laws. Amendment 2 violates the Equal Protection Clause, and the judgment of the Supreme Court of Colorado is affirmed.

It is so ordered.

Justice Scalia, with whom Chief Justice Rehnquist and Justice Thomas join, dissenting.

The Court has mistaken a Kulturkampf for a fit of spite. The constitutional amendment before us here is not the manifestation of a "'bare ... desire to harm'" homosexuals ... but is rather a modest attempt by seemingly tolerant Coloradans to preserve traditional sexual mores against the efforts of a politically powerful minority to revise those mores through use of the laws. That objective, and the means chosen to achieve it, are not only unimpeachable under any constitutional doctrine hitherto pronounced (hence the opinion's heavy reliance upon principles of righteousness rather than judicial holdings); they have been specifically approved by the Congress of the United States and by this Court.

In holding that homosexuality cannot be singled out for disfavorable treatment, the Court contradicts a decision, unchallenged here, pronounced only 10 years ago, see *Bowers* v. *Hardwick*, 478 U. S. 186 (1986), and places the prestige of this institution behind the proposition that opposition to homosexu-

ality is as reprehensible as racial or religious bias. Whether it is or not is *precisely* the cultural debate that gave rise to the Colorado constitutional amendment (and to the preferential laws against which the amendment was directed). Since the Constitution of the United States says nothing about this subject, it is left to be resolved by normal democratic means, including the democratic adoption of provisions in state constitutions. This Court has no business imposing upon all Americans the resolution favored by the elite class from which the Members of this institution are selected, pronouncing that "animosity" toward homosexuality ... is evil. I vigorously dissent.

. . .

Today's opinion has no foundation in American constitutional law, and barely pretends to. The people of Colorado have adopted an entirely reasonable provision which does not even disfavor homosexuals in any substantive sense, but merely denies them preferential treatment. Amendment 2 is designed to prevent piecemeal deterioration of the sexual morality favored by a majority of Coloradans, and is not only an appropriate means to that legitimate end, but a means that Americans have employed before. Striking it down is an act, not of judicial judgment, but of political will. I dissent.

Attorney General Letter to Congress Regarding DOMA

The Defense of Marriage Act (DOMA) was passed by Congress and signed into law by President Bill Clinton in 1996. The law said that no state was required to recognize the marriage of a same-sex couple who had been permitted to marry in their own state. In addition, Section 3 of the ACT denied those same couples access to any federal benefit associated with marriage. At the time the Act was passed, this possibility was merely hypothetical because no state had legalized gay marriage. Once states began to do so, the Act raised equal protection issues that were brought to federal courts. In February 2011, when the Obama administration notified Congress that it would no longer defend DOMA, several lawsuits had been filed arguing that classifications based on sexual orientation required heightened scrutiny and could not be justified under this level of review. Note that the argument is based on the Fifth Amendment concept of equal protection articulated by the Court in *Bolling v. Sharp* (see reading in Chapter 15). The House Bipartisan Legal Advisory Group hired outside lawyers to defend the statute.

The Honorable John A. Boehner
Speaker
U.S. House of Representatives
Washington, DC 20515

Re: <u>Defense of Marriage Act</u>

Dear Mr. Speaker:

After careful consideration, including a review of a recommendation from me, the President of the United States has made the determination that Section 3 of the Defense of Marriage Act ... as applied to same-sex couples who are legally married under state law, violates the equal protection component of the Fifth Amendment ... I am writing to advise you of the Executive Branch's determination and to inform you of the steps the Department will take in two pending DOMA cases to implement that determination.

While the Department has previously defended DOMA against legal challenges involving legally married same-sex couples, recent lawsuits that challenge the constitutionality of DOMA Section 3 have caused the President and the Department to conduct a new examination of the defense of this provision.... Previously, the Administration has defended Section 3 in jurisdictions where circuit courts have already held that classifications based on sexual orientation are subject to rational basis review, and it has advanced arguments to defend DOMA Section 3 under the binding standard that has applied in those cases.

These new lawsuits, by contrast, will require the Department to take an affirmative position on the level of scrutiny that should be applied to DOMA Section 3 in a circuit without binding precedent on the issue. As described more fully below, the President and I have concluded that classifications based on sexual orientation warrant heightened scrutiny and that, as applied to same-sex couples legally married under state law, Section 3 of DOMA is unconstitutional.

Standard of Review

The Supreme Court has yet to rule on the appropriate level of scrutiny for classifications based on sexual orientation. It has, however, rendered a number of decisions that set forth the criteria that should inform this and any other judgment as to whether heightened scrutiny applied: (1)whether the group in question has suffered a history of discrimination; (2) whether individuals "exhibit obvious, immutable, or distinguishing characteristics that define them as a discrete group"; (3)whether the group is a minority or is politically powerless; and (4)whether the characteristics distinguishing the group have little relation to legitimate policy objectives or to an individual's "ability to perform or contribute to society." ...

Each of these factors counsels in favor of being suspicious of classifications based on sexual orientation....

... [Neither *Lawrence v. Texas* nor *Romer v. Evans*] reached, let alone resolved, the level of scrutiny issue because in both the Court concluded that the laws could not even survive the more deferential rational basis standard.

Application to Section 3 of DOMA

In reviewing a legislative classification under heightened scrutiny, the government must establish that the classification is "substantially related to an important government objective." ... Under heightened scrutiny, "a tenable justification must describe actual state purposes, not rationalizations for actions in fact differently grounded...."

In other words, under heightened scrutiny, the United States cannot defend Section 3 by advancing hypothetical rationales, independent of the legislative record, as it has done in circuits where precedent mandated application of rational basis review. Instead, the United States can defend Section 3 only by invoking Congress' actual justification for the law.

Moreover, the legislative record underlying DOMA's passage contains discussion and debate that undermines any defense under heightened scrutiny. The record contains numerous expressions reflecting moral disapproval of gays and lesbians and their intimate and family relationships—precisely the kind of stereotype-based thinking and animus the Equal Protection Clause is designed to guard against....

Application to Second Circuit cases

... [T]he President has instructed the Department not to defend the statute in *Windsor* and *Pedersen,* now pending in the Southern District of New York and the District of Connecticut. I concur in the determination.

Notwithstanding this determination, the President has informed me that Section 3 will continue to be enforced by the Executive Branch. To that end, the President has instructed Executive agencies to continue to comply with Section 3 of DOMA, consistent with the Executives obligation to take care that the laws be faithfully executed, unless and until Congress repeals Section 3 or the judicial branch renders a definitive verdict against the law's constitutionality. This course of action respects the actions of the prior Congress that enacted DOMA, and it recognizes the judiciary as the final arbiter of the constitutional claims raised....

In light of the forgoing, I will instruct the Department's lawyers to immediately inform the district courts in *Windsor* and *Pedersen* of the Executive Branch's view that heightened scrutiny is the appropriate standard of review and that, consistent with that standard, Section 3 of DOMA may not be constitutionally applied to same-sex couples whose marriages are legally recognized under state law....

Sincerely yours,
Eric H. Holder, Jr.
Attorney General

CONCLUSIONS

The cases and issues studied in this chapter illustrate the strong social forces and customs that help shape constitutional law. They also highlight the pressures applied to legislative and judicial bodies, with one branch or the other initiating action in response to changing conditions. Although the courts take the lead in some instances, the section on women's rights shows that Congress and the President were more important and took the initiative earlier. The section on school financing demonstrates that judges are cautious in ordering remedies that involve vast appropriations and that state courts are often avenues for change when the U.S. Supreme Court is not. Such allocations of state or federal funds are left generally to legislative action and the priorities established by the two political branches. State courts are demonstrating increasing independence in interpreting constitutional values through their own state charters.

NOTES AND QUESTIONS

1. How did the Court in *Bradwell* v. *State* distinguish the privileges of state citizenship from the privileges derived from national citizenship? What are the privileges of national citizenship?

2. The *Bradwell* Court's condescending attitude toward women was overridden by the comparatively enlightened attitude of Congress toward women, when it passed legislation in 1879 to permit women to practice before the U.S. Supreme Court. Can you think of other examples in which Congress, and not the courts, better protected citizens's rights and liberties?

3. In your view, should sex-based classifications be treated as "suspect"? Are gender classifications any more invidious or any less benign than race-based classifications?

4. In light of the Court's ruling in *Craig v. Boren*, are there grounds for applying the strict scrutiny test to statutes that discriminate against men? Why or why not?

5. All of the Justices in *Rostker* seemed to agree that it is constitutionally permissible for the armed services to exclude women from combat military roles. Do you agree with the Court? Why or why not?

6. In *Plyler v. Doe* the Court applies heightened scrutiny to state laws affecting the children of undocumented aliens but suggests that their parents are not due the same level of protection. Is this a distinction that makes sense? Do you think the Court has given sufficient weight to the state's concerns in this case?

7. What is the appropriate standard of review for legislation that discriminates against gays and lesbians? Is it "heightened scrutiny" as the Obama administration contends? Why or why not?

SELECTED READINGS

ANDERSEN, ELLEN ANN. Out of the Closet and into the Courts: Legal Opportunity Structure and Gay Rights Litigation. Ann Arbor: University of Michigan Press, 2005.

BABCOCK, BARBARA A., et al. Sex Discrimination and the Law. Boston: Little, Brown, 1975.

BAER, JUDITH. "Sexual Equality and the Burger Court." 31 Western Political Quarterly 470 (1978).

BENNETT, ROBERT W. "The Burger Court and the Poor," in Vincent Blasi, ed. The Burger Court: The Counter-Revolution That Wasn't. New Haven, Conn.: Yale University Press, 1983.

DINAN, JOHN. "Can State Courts Produce Social Reform? School Finance Equalization in Kentucky, Texas, and New Jersey." 24 Southeastern Political Review 431 (1996).

GERSTMANN, EVAN. The Constitutional Underclass: Gays, Lesbians, and the Failure of Class-Based Equal Protection. Chicago: University of Chicago Press, 1999.

GETMAN, JULIUS. "The Emerging Constitutional Principle of Sexual Equality." 1972 Supreme Court Review 157.

GINSBURG, RUTH BADER. "Gender in the Supreme Court: The 1973 and 1974 Terms." 1975 Supreme Court Review 1.

———. "The Burger Court's Grapplings with Sex Discrimination," in Vincent Blasi, ed. The Burger Court: The Counter-Revolution That Wasn't. New Haven, Conn.: Yale University Press, 1983.

HAPPERLE, WINIFRED, AND LAURA CRITES. Women in the Courts. Williamsburg, Va.: National Center for State Court, 1978.

HULL, ELIZABETH. Without Justice for All: The Constitutional Rights of Aliens. Westport, CT: Greenwood Press, 1985.

KANOWITZ, LEO. Women and the Law. Albuquerque: University of New Mexico Press, 1969.

MANSBRIDGE, JANE J. Why We Lost the ERA. Chicago: University of Chicago Press, 1986.

McCLAIN, CHARLES J. In Search of Equality: The Chinese Struggle Against Discrimination in Nineteenth-Century America. Berkeley: University of California Press, 1994.

O'CONNOR, KAREN. Women's Organizations' Use of the Courts. Lexington, Mass.: Lexington Books, 1980.

RODRIGUEZ, CRISTINA. "The Significance of the Local in Immigration Regulation." 106 Michigan Law Review 567 (2008).

SCHEINGOLD, STUART. The Politics of Rights. New Haven, Conn.: Yale University Press, 1974.

STEINER, GILBERT Y. Constitutional Inequality: The Political Fortunes of the Equal Rights Amendment. Washington, D.C.: The Brookings Institution, 1985.

WELLS, MIRIAM J. "The Grassroots Reconfiguration of U.S. Immigration Policy." 38 International Migration Review 1308 (Winter 2004).

17

Rights of Privacy

The right to privacy is invoked repeatedly by Congress, the President, federal courts, and the states to uphold basic rights of individual conduct and choice. If privacy includes the right of a person to prevent intrusion into certain thoughts and activities, privacy is protected by the First Amendment (freedom of speech, religion, and association), the Third Amendment (quartering of troops in private homes), the Fourth Amendment (freedom from unreasonable searches and seizures), and the Fifth Amendment (freedom from self-incrimination). Some privacy advocates rely on the Ninth Amendment, which states that the "enumeration in the Constitution, of certain rights, shall not be construed to deny or disparage others retained by the people." The Due Process and Equal Protection Clauses provide other shields for privacy interests, and a number of state constitutions include express rights of privacy.

A. DIMENSIONS OF PRIVACY

In contemporary times, privacy has a special urgency because of industrialization, urbanization, electronic surveillance methods, computer data banks, and technological advances. The U.S. Constitution does not mention privacy, and yet a zone of autonomy is implicit in the framers' support for individual rights and limited government. The notion of privacy is part of our pre-societal "natural rights." Areas of private conduct and thought in America have always sought protection from state intrusion. James Madison felt strongly that people had a property interest in their opinions, the free communication of ideas, religious beliefs, and conscience (first reading in Chapter 9).

The Declaration of Independence attacked England's practice of "quartering large bodies of armed troops among us." In response, the Third Amendment provides that no soldier shall, "in time of peace be quartered in any house, without the consent of the owner, nor in time of war, but in a manner to be prescribed by law." The Fourth Amendment was adopted to prevent the hated general warrants and writs of assistance used by England to invade the homes and businesses of American colonists. In a famous dissent in 1928, Justice Brandeis interpreted the trilogy in the Declaration of Independence — life, liberty, and the pursuit of happiness — in these terms:

> The makers of our Constitution undertook to secure conditions favorable to the pursuit of happiness. They recognized the significance of man's spiritual nature, of his feelings and of his intellect. They knew that only a part of his pain, pleasure and satisfactions of life are to be found in material things. They sought to protect Americans in their beliefs, their thoughts, their emotions and their sensations. They conferred, as against the Government, the right to be let alone — the most comprehensive of rights and the right most valued by civilized men. Olmstead v. United States, 277 U.S. 438, 478 (1928).

The phrase "the right to be let alone" appeared earlier in an article published by Brandeis and Samuel D. Warren in 1890. Building on Judge Thomas Cooley's treatise on torts, they concluded that the right to privacy evolved from transformations that had occurred in property rights: from tangible to intangible interests; from actual bodily injury (battery) to the mere threat of injury (assault). Protections were extended to reputation (slander and libel) and to intellectual property (copyright, trademarks, and trade secrets). Brandeis and Warren were especially offended by reporters and photographers who invaded "the sacred precincts of private and domestic life." 4 Harv. L. Rev. 193, 195 (1890).

The right of citizens to conduct their own lives was protected by the Supreme Court in 1923 when it struck down a Nebraska law prohibiting the teaching in any school of any modern language other than English to any child who had not passed the eighth grade. The statute, reflecting an anti-German bias following World War I, interfered with the liberty of individuals to pursue their interests: "the right of the individual to contract, to engage in any of the common occupations of life, to acquire useful knowledge, to marry, to establish a home and bring up children, to worship God according to the dictates of his own conscience, and generally to enjoy those privileges long recognized at common law as essential to the orderly pursuit of happiness by free men." Meyer v. Nebraska, 262 U.S. 390, 399 (1923).

Two years later, the Court invalidated an Oregon law that required all children between the ages of eight and 16 to attend public school. A Roman Catholic orphanage and a military academy brought suit to defend the rights of parents to send their children to private schools. Following the doctrine of *Meyer* v. *Nebraska,* the Court held that the Oregon statute unreasonably interfered with the liberty of parents and guardians to direct the upbringing and education of their children: "The child is not the mere creature of the State; those who nurture him and direct his destiny have the right, coupled with the high duty, to recognize and prepare him for additional obligations." Pierce v. Society of Sisters, 268 U.S. 510, 535 (1925).[1]

Sterilization

At the same time that the Supreme Court defended the right to teach foreign languages and operate private schools, it endorsed a major governmental intrusion into individual privacy: sterilization of the "unfit." Some of the early decisions by federal courts rejected state efforts to sterilize prisoners for eugenic reasons. In 1914, a federal district court struck down a law in Iowa that required a vasectomy for criminals convicted twice of a felony (even if "felonies" consisted of breaking an electric globe or unfastening a strap on a harness). The court regarded vasectomy as a cruel and unusual punishment that "belongs to the Dark Ages." Davis v. Berry, 216 Fed. 413, 416 (S.D. Iowa 1914). A Nevada law on sterilization was struck down in 1918 because it gave judges too much discretion. Mickle v. Henrichs, 262 Fed. 687 (D. Nev. 1918).

A Virginia court in 1925 upheld the states's sterilization law as a proper use of the police power to prevent the transmission of insanity, idiocy, imbecility, epilepsy, and crime. Buck v. Bell, 143 Va. 310 (1925). The case involved Carrie Buck, committed to a state institution at the age of 18. Her mother had been committed to the same institution, and Carrie had just given birth to an illegitimate child that the state claimed was of "defective mentality."

By an 8–1 majority, a three-page opinion by Justice Holmes affirmed the state law. The decision is marred by illogic, hasty assumptions of unproved assertions, and a judgment that is harsh if not cruel. Holmes dashed off one of his famous aphorisms: "Three generations of imbeciles are enough." BUCK v. BELL, 274 U.S. 200, 207 (1927). In fact, Carrie's child was not mentally impaired and there is doubt that her mother was "enfeebled."[2] The Court handed down its decision in an environment that believed that crime and other social problems could be controlled by sterilization (see box on next page).

Buck v. *Bell* has never been explicitly overruled. However, its tenets were challenged by the Supreme Court in 1942 when it struck down an Oklahoma law that provided for the sterilization of "habitual

---

1. For historical background and analysis of *Meyer* and *Pierce,* see William G. Ross, Forging New Freedoms: Nativism, Education, and the Constitution, 1917–1927 (1994).

2. For good critiques of *Buck* v. *Bell,* see J. David Smith and K. Ray Nelson, The Sterilization of Carrie Buck: Was She Feebleminded or Society's Pawn? (1989); Paul A. Lombardo, "Three Generations, No Imbeciles: New Light on *Buck* v. *Bell*," 60 N.Y.U. L. Rev. 30 (1985); Clement E. Vose, Constitutional Change 5–20 (1972); James B. O'Hara and T. Howland Sanks, "Eugenic Sterilization," 45 Geo. L. J. 20 (1956); Walter Berns, "*Buck* v. *Bell:* Due Process of Law?," 6 West. Pol. Q. 762 (1953).

Controlling Crime with Eugenics

An 1877 study by Richard Louis Dugdale, *The Jukes*, popularized the notion that crime was largely hereditary. Cesare Lombroso's *Criminal Man* (1896–97) identified anthropological features that supposedly marked the born criminal. A study published in 1893 claimed that "it is established beyond controversy that criminals and paupers, both, are degenerate; the imperfect, knotty, knurly, worm-eated, half-rotten fruit of the race" (Henry M. Boies, *Prisoners and Paupers*, p. 266). The eugenics movement had the remedy: sterilization.

In the hands of reformers and progressives, eugenics became a respected argument for opposing mixed marriages and for excluding "lower stock" immigrants from Mediterranean countries, Eastern Europe, and Russia. Experts proposed that sterilization be directed against such vague categories as the feeble-minded, the criminalistic

(including the delinquent and the "wayward"), the epileptic, inebriates and drug users, the diseased (including tuberculosis, syphilis, and leprosy), the blind (including seriously impaired vision), the deaf (including seriously impaired hearing), the deformed (including the crippled), and dependents, "including orphans, ne'er-do-wells, the homeless, tramps, and paupers" (Harry Hamilton Laughlin, Eugenical Stcrilization in the United States 446–47 (1922)).

The Supreme Court's decision in *Buck* v. *Bell* preceded by a few years Nazi Germany's biological experiments and its extermination of millions of Jews, Poles, gypsies, and other groups, all part of a plan to produce a "master race." Today, instead of sterilization's being forced on the "unfit," the operation is submitted to voluntarily each year by thousands of fit adults for the purpose of population control.

criminals." A unanimous opinion held that the state statute violated the Equal Protection Clause of the Fourteenth Amendment by making an invidious distinction. Under the statute, someone who stole more than $20 three times would be sterilized, whereas someone who embezzled that amount three times was exempt, even though both crimes were a felony under state law.

The Court did not define the scope of the police power to mandate sterilization. It did note that the case involved "one of the basic civil rights of man. Marriage and procreation are fundamental to the very existence and survival of the race." Skinner v. Oklahoma, 316 U.S. 535, 541 (1942). Chief Justice Stone, concurring, thought that a state could, after appropriate inquiry, sterilize someone "to prevent the transmission by inheritance of his socially injurious tendencies." Justice Jackson, also concurring, insisted that there are limits to the extent that legislatures "may conduct biological experiments at the expense of the dignity and personality and natural powers of a minority—even those who have been guilty of what the majority defines as crimes." Jackson's concerns have been underscored by more recent cases involving the rights of marriage, family, and privacy.

In 2002, Virginia Gov. Mark Warner formally apologized for the state's policy of eugenics, under which some 8,000 people were involuntarily sterilized from 1927 to 1979. Reflecting the views of the state legislature, he said the eugenics movement "was a shameful effort in which state government never should have been involved." Nationwide, the practice affected an estimated 65,000 Americans.

Privacy and Family

In 1967, the Supreme Court issued an important decision that recognized the essential value of privacy in the Fourth Amendment. After decades of tortured reasoning on what constitutes a "search," the Court finally came to terms with an individual's constitutional right to preserve certain activities as private, even in an area accessible to the public. Katz v. United States, 389 U.S. 347 (1967), reprinted in Chapter 14.

Two years later, a unanimous Supreme Court held that the private possession of obscene materials by an adult cannot constitutionally be made a crime. State claims that the materials are obscene cannot override an individual's liberty: "If the First Amendment means anything, it means that a State has no business telling a man, sitting alone in his own house, what books he may read or what films he may watch. Our whole constitutional heritage rebels at the thought of giving government the power to control men's minds." STANLEY v. GEORGIA, 394 U.S. 557, 565 (1969). *Stanley* was qualified by the Court in 1990 when it upheld state efforts to prohibit the possession or viewing of child pornography, even in the privacy of one's home. Osborne v. Ohio, 495 U.S. 103 (1990).

The relationship between privacy and the choice of family and marriage has been explored in other decisions. A zoning case in 1977 involved a local ordinance that denied a woman the right to remain in her house because she lived with her son and two grandsons (who were first cousins). Because of the latter, she did not qualify under the definition of "family" included in the ordinance. The Court held that the ordinance arbitrarily interfered with the family unit. The Constitution "protects the sanctity of the family precisely because the institution of the family is deeply rooted in this Nation's history and tradition." Moore v. East Cleveland, 431 U.S. 494 (1977). In that same year, a unanimous Court upheld a New York law that provided for expedited procedures for removing a child from foster parents and placing the child with the natural parents. The liberty interest in family privacy "has its source, and its contours are ordinarily to be sought, not in state law, but in intrinsic human rights...." Smith v. Organization of Foster Families, 431 U.S. 816, 845 (1977).

In 2000, the Court ruled that a Washington state law providing for court-ordered visitation rights for grandparents and "any person" was constitutionally overbroad and violated the rights of parents to make fundamental decisions about their children. Writing for a 6 to 3 Court, Justice O'Connor held that a Washington state judge improperly granted visitation rights to grandparents of two young girls against the wishes of their mother. The Court decided that the statute violated the Due Process Clause of the Fourteenth Amendment. Troxel v. Granville, 530 U.S. 57 (2000).

The right to marry supports an individual's decision to make without governmental interference, other than establishing minimum ages. Loving v. Virginia, 388 U.S. 1, 12 (1967). A Wisconsin statute prohibited a certain class of state resident from marrying without first obtaining a court order granting permission. The class was anyone with a child not in his custody and whom he is obligated to support by court order or judgment. An 8–1 Court held that the statute violated the Due Process Clause by interfering with the fundamental right to marry. The decision to marry is "among the personal decisions protected by the right of privacy." Zablocki v. Redhail, 434 U.S. 374, 384 (1978).

Reputation

Part of intangible property is reputation. The precious quality of this commodity is captured in Shakespeare's *Othello:* "Good name in man and woman, dear my lord, is the immediate jewel of their souls: who steals my purse steals trash; 'tis something, nothing; 'twas mine, 'tis his, and has been slave to thousands; but he that filches from me my good name robs me of that which not enriches him, but makes me poor indeed."

A case in 1971 involved the action of a Wisconsin police chief who posted a notice in all retail stores forbidding for one year the sale of liquor to a woman. State law required these postings—without notice or hearing—whenever a designated official decided that the sale of liquor to a particular person would endanger the community or place the individual or the individual's family in a state of want. The Supreme Court, by a 6–3 majority, held that notice and an opportunity to be heard are essential safeguards whenever a person's name, reputation, honor, or integrity is at stake. Wisconsin v. Constantineau, 400 U.S. 433, 437 (1971).

The Court decided a similar case in 1976, but this time left the individual's reputation unprotected. The police in Kentucky authorized the preparation and distribution of a flyer containing the names and mug shots of persons described as "subjects known to be active in this criminal field" of shoplifting. About 800 flyers were distributed to merchants and businesspeople in downtown Louisville. A newspaper photographer was arrested (but not convicted) of shoplifting. Although the charges against him were eventually dropped, his name and photograph appeared in the flyer. He filed suit, claiming injury to reputation and impairment of earning ability. The Sixth Circuit rejected the idea that police chiefs can determine the guilt or innocence of an accused. However, a 5–3 Court—distinguishing this case from *Constantineau*—reversed the Sixth Circuit by holding that distribution of the flyer did not deprive the plaintiff of any "liberty" or "property" rights secured against state deprivation by the Fourteenth Amendment. Paul v. Davis, 424 U.S. 693 (1976). The Court declined to elevate a state issue to the federal level.

FOIA Exemptions

The Freedom of Information Act (FOIA) gives the public broad access to documents held by the federal government. 5 U.S.C. § 552 (2006). However, a number of exemptions allow the government to withhold documents if they fall within certain categories identified in the statute. Exemption 7(C) covers "records or information compiled for law enforcement purposes" if their production "could reasonably be expected to constitute an unwarranted invasion of personal privacy." In 2004, the Supreme Court interpreted that exemption to prevent the release of police photographs of former Deputy White House Counsel Vincent W. Foster, who the government concluded committed suicide by gunshot. National Archives and Records Admin. v. Favish, 541 U.S. 157 (2004).

Buck v. Bell

274 U.S. 200 (1927)

A Virginia statute provided for the sexual sterilization of inmates in state institutions who were found to be afflicted with a hereditary form of insanity or imbecility. The state intended to perform on Carrie Buck the operation of salpingectomy, which consists of opening the abdominal cavity and cutting the Fallopian tubes. The statute, upheld by the Virginia Supreme Court of Appeals, provided for a hearing before the operation could be performed. The defendant in this case was Dr. J. H. Bell, Superintendent of the Colony for Epileptics and Feeble Minded.

Mr. JUSTICE HOLMES delivered the opinion of the Court ...

Carrie Buck is a feeble minded white woman who was committed to the State Colony [*for Epileptics and Feeble Minded*] in due form. She is the daughter of a feeble minded mother in the same institution, and the mother of an illegitimate feeble minded child. She was eighteen years old at the time of the trial of her case in the Circuit Court, in the latter part of 1924. An Act of Virginia, approved March 20, 1924, recites that the health of the patient and the welfare of society may be promoted in certain cases by the sterilization of mental defectives, under careful safeguard, &c.; that the sterilization may be effected in males by vasectomy and in females by salpingectomy, without serious pain or substantial danger to life; that the Commonwealth is supporting in various institutions many defective persons who if now discharged would become a menace but if incapable of procreating might be discharged with safety and become self-supporting with benefit to themselves and to society; and that

experience has shown that heredity plays an important part in the transmission of insanity, imbecility, &c. The statute then enacts that whenever the superintendent of certain institutions including the above named State Colony shall be of opinion that it is for the best interests of the patients and of society that an inmate under his care should be sexually sterilized, he may have the operation performed upon any patient afflicted with hereditary forms of insanity, imbecility, &c., on complying with the very careful provisions by which the act protects the patients from possible abuse.

The superintendent first presents a petition to the special board of directors of his hospital or colony, stating the facts and the grounds for his opinion, verified by affidavit. Notice of the petition and of the time and place of the hearing in the institution is to be served upon the inmate, and also upon his guardian, and if there is no guardian the superintendent is to apply to the Circuit Court of the County to appoint one. If the inmate is a minor notice also is to be given to his parents if any with a copy of the petition. The board is to see to it that the inmate may attend the hearings if desired by him or his guardian. The evidence is all to be reduced to writing, and after the board has made its order for or against the operation, the superintendent, or the inmate, or his guardian, may appeal to the Circuit Court of the County. The Circuit Court may consider the record of the board and the evidence before it and such other admissible evidence as may be offered, and may affirm, revise, or reverse the order of the board and enter such order as it deems just. Finally any party may apply to the Supreme Court of Appeals, which, if it grants the appeal, is to hear the case upon the record of the trial in the Circuit Court and may enter such order as it thinks the Circuit Court should have entered. There can be no doubt that so far as procedure is concerned the rights of the patient are most carefully considered, and as every step in this case was taken in scrupulous compliance with the statute and after months of observation, there is no doubt that in that respect the plaintiff in error has had due process of law.

The attack is not upon the procedure but upon the substantive law. It seems to be contended that in no circumstances could such an order be justified. It certainly is contended that the order cannot be justified upon the existing grounds. The judgment finds the facts that have been recited and that Carrie Buck "is the probable potential parent of socially inadequate offspring, likewise afflicted, that she may be sexually sterilized without detriment to her general health and that her welfare and that of society will be promoted by her sterilization," and thereupon makes the order. In view of the general declarations of the legislature and the specific findings of the Court, obviously we cannot say as matter of law that the grounds do not exist, and if they exist they justify the result. We have seen more than once that the public welfare may call upon the best citizens for their lives. It would be strange if it could not call upon those who already sap the strength of the State for these lesser sacrifices, often not felt to be such by those concerned, in order to prevent our being swamped with incompetence. It is better for all the world, if instead of waiting to execute degenerate offspring for crime, or to let them starve for their imbecility, society can prevent those who are manifestly unfit from continuing their kind. The principle that sustains compulsory vaccination is broad enough to cover cutting the Fallopian tubes. *Jacobson* v. *Massachusetts,* 197 U.S. 11. Three generations of imbeciles are enough.

But, it is said, however it might be if this reasoning were applied generally, it fails when it is confined to the small number who are in the institutions named and is not applied to the multitudes outside. It is the usual last resort of constitutional arguments to point out shortcomings of this sort. But the answer is that the law does all that is needed when it does all that it can, indicates a policy, applies it to all within the lines, and seeks to bring within the lines all similarly situated so far and so fast as its means allow. Of course so far as the operations enable those who otherwise must be kept confined to be returned to the world, and thus open the asylum to others, the equality aimed at will be more nearly reached.

Judgment affirmed.

MR. JUSTICE BUTLER dissents.

Stanley v. Georgia

394 U.S. 557 (1969)

Law enforcement officers obtained a warrant to search Robert Eli Stanley's home for evidence of alleged bookmaking activities. While conducting this search, they found some films in his bedroom, used a projector to view the films, and judged them to be obscene. He was later convicted for violating a Georgia law that prohibits the possession of obscene matter. The conviction was confirmed by the Georgia Supreme Court.

MR. JUSTICE MARSHALL delivered the opinion of the Court....

Appellant raises several challenges to the validity of his conviction. We find it necessary to consider only one. Appellant argues here, and argued below, that the Georgia obscenity statute, insofar as it punishes mere private possession of obscene matter, violates the First Amendment, as made applicable to the States by the Fourteenth Amendment. For reasons set forth below, we agree that the mere private possession of obscene matter cannot constitutionally be made a crime.

... The State and appellant both agree that the question here before us is whether "a statute imposing criminal sanctions upon the mere [knowing] possession of obscene matter" is constitutional. In this context, Georgia concedes that the present case appears to be one of "first impression ... on this exact point," but contends that since "obscenity is not within the area of constitutionally protected speech or press," *Roth* v. *United States,* 354 U.S. 476, 485 (1957), the States are free, subject to the limits of other provisions of the Constitution, see, *e.g., Ginsberg* v. *New York,* 390 U.S. 629, 637–645 (1968), to deal with it any way deemed necessary, just as they may deal with possession of other things thought to be detrimental to the welfare of their citizens. If the State can protect the body of a citizen, may it not, argues Georgia, protect his mind?

It is true that *Roth* does declare, seemingly without qualification, that obscenity is not protected by the First Amendment.... However, neither *Roth* nor any subsequent decision of this Court dealt with the precise problem involved in the present case. Roth was convicted of mailing obscene circulars and advertising, and an obscene book, in violation of a federal obscenity statute. The defendant in a companion case, *Alberts* v. *California,* 354 U.S. 476 (1957), was convicted of "lewdly keeping for sale obscene and indecent books, and [of] writing, composing and publishing an obscene advertisement of them...." *Id.,* at 481. None of the statements cited by the Court in *Roth* for the proposition that "this Court has always assumed that obscenity is not protected by the freedoms of speech and press" were made in the context of a statute punishing mere private possession of obscene material; the cases cited deal for the most part with use of the mails to distribute objectionable material or with some form of public distribution or dissemination. Moreover, none of this Court's decisions subsequent to *Roth* involved prosecution for private possession of obscene materials. Those cases dealt with the power of the State and Federal Governments to prohibit or regulate certain public actions taken or intended to be taken with respect to obscene matter. Indeed, with one exception, we have been unable to discover any case in which the issue in the present case has been fully considered....

It is now well established that the Constitution protects the right to receive information and ideas. "This freedom [of speech and press] ... necessarily protects the right to receive...." *Martin* v. *City of Struthers,* 319 U.S. 141, 143 (1943); ... [t]his right to receive information and ideas, regardless of their social worth, see *Winters* v. *New York,* 333 U.S. 507, 510 (1948), is fundamental to our free society. Moreover, in the context of this case—a prosecu-

tion for mere possession of printed or filmed matter in the privacy of a person's own home—that right takes on an added dimension. For also fundamental is the right to be free, except in very limited circumstances, from unwanted governmental intrusions into one's privacy....

These are the rights that appellant is asserting in the case before us. He is asserting the right to read or observe what he pleases—the right to satisfy his intellectual and emotional needs in the privacy of his own home. He is asserting the right to be free from state inquiry into the contents of his library. Georgia contends that appellant does not have these rights, that there are certain types of materials that the individual may not read or even possess. Georgia justifies this assertion by arguing that the films in the present case are obscene. But we think that mere categorization of these films as "obscene" is insufficient justification for such a drastic invasion of personal liberties guaranteed by the First and Fourteenth Amendments. Whatever may be the justifications for other statutes regulating obscenity, we do not think they reach into the privacy of one's own home. If the First Amendment means anything, it means that a State has no business telling a man, sitting alone in his own house, what books he may read or what films he may watch. Our whole constitutional heritage rebels at the thought of giving government the power to control men's minds....

... Georgia asserts that exposure to obscene materials may lead to deviant sexual behavior or crimes of sexual violence. There appears to be little empirical basis for that assertion. But more important, if the State is only concerned about printed or filmed materials inducing antisocial conduct, we believe that in the context of private consumption of ideas and information we should adhere to the view that "[a]mong free men, the deterrents ordinarily to be applied to prevent crime are education and punishment for violations of the law...." *Whitney* v. *California,* 274 U.S. 357, 378 (1927) (Brandeis, J., concurring). See Emerson, Toward a General Theory of the First Amendment, 72 Yale L. J. 877, 938 (1963). Given the present state of knowledge, the State may no more prohibit mere possession of obscene matter on the ground that it may lead to antisocial conduct than it may prohibit possession of chemistry books on the ground that they may lead to the manufacture of homemade spirits.

It is true that in *Roth* this Court rejected the necessity of proving that exposure to obscene material would create a clear and present danger of antisocial conduct or would probably induce its recipients to such conduct. 354 U.S., at 486–487. But that case dealt with public distribution of obscene materials and such distribution is subject to different objections. For example, there is always the danger that obscene material might fall into the hands of children, see *Ginsberg* v. *New York, supra,* or that it might intrude upon the sensibilities or privacy of the general public. See *Redrup* v. *New York,* 386 U.S. 767, 769 (1967). No such dangers are present in this case.

Finally, we are faced with the argument that prohibition of possession of obscene materials is a necessary incident to statutory schemes prohibiting distribution. That argument is based on alleged difficulties of proving an intent to distribute or in producing evidence of actual distribution. We are not convinced that such difficulties exist, but even if they did we do not think that they would justify infringement of the individual's right to read or observe what he pleases. Because that right is so fundamental to our scheme of individual liberty, its restriction may not be justified by the need to ease

the administration of otherwise valid criminal laws. See *Smith* v. *California,* 361 U.S. 147 (1959).

We hold that the First and Fourteenth Amendments prohibit making mere private possession of obscene material a crime. *Roth* and the cases following that decision are not impaired by today's holding. As we have said, the States retain broad power to regulate obscenity; that power simply does not extend to mere possession by the individual in the privacy of his own home. Accordingly, the judgment of the court below is reversed and the case is remanded for proceedings not inconsistent with this opinion.

It is so ordered.

Mr. Justice Black, concurring ...

Mr. Justice Stewart, with whom Mr. Justice Brennan and Mr. Justice White join, concurring in the result....

B. USE OF CONTRACEPTIVES

Family and marriage cases rely heavily on a landmark case in 1965 regarding the right to privacy. A Connecticut law made it a crime for any person to use any drug or article to prevent conception. This type of statute can be traced to the Comstock Act of 1873, which Congress passed to suppress the circulation of obscene literature and "immoral" articles. The statute prohibited selling, giving away, exhibiting, possessing, or promoting "any drug or medicine, or any article whatever, for the prevention of conception" and prohibited the mailing of any article designed to prevent conception. 17 Stat. 598, §§ 1, 2 (1873).

The constitutional issue of using contraceptives did not reach the Supreme Court until 1943, when it dismissed a case on the ground that the physician bringing it lacked standing to challenge a Connecticut statute. Tileston v. Ullman, 318 U.S. 44 (1943). The Court avoided the issue again in 1961, arguing that the case lacked ripeness because the plaintiff had not been prosecuted. However, two of the four dissents argued that the statute invaded the right to privacy. To Justice Douglas, the Connecticut law "touches the relationship between man and wife [and] reaches into the intimacies of the marriage relationship." Poe v. Ullman, 367 U.S. 497, 519 (1961). Efforts to enforce the law would mark "an invasion of the privacy that is implicit in a free society." Id. at 521.

Justice Harlan's dissent also invoked the right of privacy to condemn the Connecticut law: "I believe that a statute making it a criminal offense for *married couples* to use contraceptives is an intolerable and unjustifiable invasion of privacy in the conduct of the most intimate concerns of an individual's life." Id. at 539. The law was "grossly offensive to this privacy" and forced the machinery of criminal law "into the very heart of marital privacy." Id. at 549, 553. *Poe* v. *Ullman* is reprinted in Chapter 3.

The Griswold Case

By 1965, the Supreme Court was prepared to decide the constitutionality of the Connecticut statute. An administrator and physician had been convicted for giving married persons information and medical advice on how to prevent conception and prescribing a contraceptive device for the wife's use. Writing for the Court, Justice Douglas held that the law violated the Due Process Clause of the Four-

Unenumerated Privacy Rights

In a 1971 article, Robert Bork used *Griswold* v. *Connecticut* to illustrate the problems of judge-made law. He thought that *Griswold* embodied the Warren Court's tendency to make its own value choices supreme and thereby displace elected government. For Bork, *Griswold* was "an unprincipled decision" that "fails every test of neutrality." Robert H. Bork, "Neutral Principles and Some First Amendment Problems," 47 Ind. L. J. 1 (1971). The Senate's rejection of Bork as nominee to the Supreme Court relied heavily on his views on privacy and his objection to privacy rights that were not enumerated in the Constitution.

Bork's defeat made it unlikely that subsequent judicial nominees would challenge privacy and unenumerated rights. Anthony Kennedy, nominated to replace Bork, was quick to embrace privacy at his confirmation hearing. Kennedy noted that "the concept of liberty in the due process clause is quite expansive, quite sufficient, to protect the values of privacy that Americans legitimately think are part of their constitutional heritage." Kennedy was confirmed by a unanimous Senate.

The next nominee to the Supreme Court, David Souter, told the Senate Judiciary Committee that he believed that "the due process clause of the 14th amendment does recognize and does protect an unenumerated right of privacy." In his first day of hearings as nominee to the Court, Clarence Thomas said that it was his view "that there is a right to privacy in the Fourteenth Amendment." Clinton nominees Ruth Bader Ginsburg and Stephen Breyer also embraced privacy rights at their confirmation hearings.

teenth Amendment, "emanations" and "penumbras" from the First Amendment (including association and privacy), and other privacy values derived from the Third, Fourth, Fifth, and Ninth Amendments. Justice Goldberg, joined by Chief Justice Warren and Justice Brennan, relied primarily on the Ninth Amendment. GRISWOLD v. CONNECTICUT, 381 U.S. 479 (1965). Robert Bork's critique of *Griswold* was a major factor in the Senate's decision to reject him in 1987 as a nominee to the Supreme Court. Subsequent nominees to the Court recognized that there do exist unenumerated privacy rights (see box).

Single People

The next question was whether contraceptives could be denied to single people. In 1972, the Court struck down a Massachusetts law that made it a felony to give away a drug, medicine, instrument, or article for the prevention of conception except when registered physicians or registered pharmacists gave them to married persons. A 6–1 Court held that the statute violated the rights of single persons. "If the right of privacy means anything, it is the right of the *individual,* married or single, to be free from unwarranted governmental intrusion into matters so fundamentally affecting a person as the decision whether to bear or beget a child." Eisenstadt v. Baird, 405 U.S. 438, 453 (1972).

Minors

Having sustained the use of contraceptives by adults, whether married or single, the next issue waiting to be resolved concerned the use of contraceptives by minors. New York argued that the cases striking down state prohibitions on the *use* of contraceptives did not prevent states from prohibiting the *sale* and *manufacture* of contraceptives. This fine distinction did not convince the Court, which held that the New York law prohibiting the selling or distribution of any contraceptive to a minor under the age of 16 was unconstitutional as it applied to nonprescription contraceptives. Restrictions on the distribution of contraceptives necessarily interfered with their use. The Court also struck down New York's prohibition of any advertisement or display of contraceptive devices. The law was considered unreasonable in part because New York allowed girls to marry at the age of 14 with parental consent. Carey v. Population Services International, 431 U.S. 678 (1977).

In 1983, the Supreme Court reviewed a law passed by Congress that prohibited the mailing of unsolicited advertisements for contraceptives. A unanimous decision held that the statute violated the First Amendment: "where—as in this case—a speaker desires to convey truthful information relevant to important social issues such as family planning and the prevention of venereal disease, we have previously found the First Amendment interest served by such speech paramount." Bolger v. Youngs Drug Products Corp., 463 U.S. 60, 69 (1983). The law was also defective because it denied parents information bearing on their ability to discuss birth control and make informed decisions. Id. at 74.

Griswold v. Connecticut

381 U.S. 479 (1965)

Estelle Griswold, the executive director of the Planned Parenthood League of Connecticut, was convicted for giving married persons information on how to prevent conception. C. Lee Buxton, medical director of the League, was convicted for giving medical advice on conception and for prescribing a contraceptive device for a married woman. A Connecticut statute made it a crime for any person to use any drug or article to prevent conception.

Mr. Justice Douglas delivered the opinion of the Court....

The statutes whose constitutionality is involved in this appeal are §§ 53-32 and 54-196 of the General Statutes of Connecticut (1958 rev.). The former provides:

"Any person who uses any drug, medicinal article or instrument for the purpose of preventing conception shall be fined not less than fifty dollars or imprisoned not less than sixty days nor more than one year or be both fined and imprisoned."

Section 54-196 provides:

"Any person who assists, abets, counsels, causes, hires or commands another to commit any offense may be prosecuted and punished as if he were the principal offender."

The appellants were found guilty as accessories and fined $100 each, against the claim that the accessory statute as so applied violated the Fourteenth Amendment....

We think that appellants have standing to raise the constitutional rights of the married people with whom they had a professional relationship.... Here those doubts are removed by reason of a criminal conviction for serving married couples in violation of an aiding-and-abetting statute....

Coming to the merits, we are met with a wide range of questions that implicate the Due Process Clause of the Fourteenth Amendment. Overtones of some arguments suggest that Lochner v. New York, 198 U.S. 45, should be our guide. But we decline that invitation.... We do not sit as a super-legislature to determine the wisdom, need, and propriety of laws that touch economic problems, business affairs, or social conditions. This law, however, operates directly on an intimate relation of husband and wife and their physician's role in one aspect of that relation.

The association of people is not mentioned in the Constitution nor in the Bill of Rights. The right to educate a child in a school of the parents' choice—whether public or private or parochial—is also not mentioned. Nor is the right to study any particular subject or any foreign language. Yet the First Amendment has been construed to include certain of those rights....

The foregoing cases suggest that specific guarantees in the Bill of Rights have penumbras, formed by emanations from those guarantees that help give them life and substance. See Poe v. Ullman, 367 U.S. 497, 516–522 (dissenting opinion). Various guarantees create zones of privacy. The right of association contained in the penumbra of the First Amendment is one, as we have seen. The Third Amendment in its prohibition against the quartering of soldiers "in any house" in time of peace without the consent of the owner is another facet of that privacy. The Fourth Amendment explicitly affirms the "right of the people to be secure in their persons, houses, papers, and effects, against unreasonable searches and seizures." The Fifth Amendment in its Self-Incrimination Clause enables the citizen to create a zone of privacy which government may not force him to surrender to his detriment. The Ninth Amendment provides: "The enumeration in the Constitution, of certain rights, shall not be construed to deny or disparage others retained by the people."

The Fourth and Fifth Amendments were described in *Boyd* v. *United States,* 116 U.S. 616, 630, as protection against all governmental invasions "of the sanctity of a man's home and the privacies of life." We recently referred in *Mapp* v. *Ohio,* 367 U.S. 643, 656, to the Fourth Amendment as creating a "right to privacy, no less important than any other right carefully and particularly reserved to the people."...

The present case, then, concerns a relationship lying within the zone of privacy created by several fundamental constitutional guarantees. And it concerns a law which, in forbidding the *use* of contraceptives rather than regulating their manufacture or sale, seeks to achieve its goals by means having a maximum destructive impact upon that relationship.... Would we allow the police to search the sacred precincts of marital bedrooms for telltale signs of the use of contraceptives? The very idea is repulsive to the notions of privacy surrounding the marriage relationship.

We deal with a right of privacy older than the Bill of Rights—older than our political parties, older than our school system. Marriage is a coming together for better or for worse, hopefully enduring, and intimate to the degree of being sacred. It is an association that promotes a way of life, not causes; a harmony in living, not political faiths; a bilateral loyalty, not commercial or social projects. Yet it is an association for as noble a purpose as any involved in our prior decisions.

Reversed.

MR. JUSTICE GOLDBERG, whom THE CHIEF JUSTICE and MR. JUSTICE BRENNAN join, concurring....

The Ninth Amendment reads, "The enumeration in the Constitution, of certain rights, shall not be construed to deny or disparage others retained by the people." The Amendment is almost entirely the work of James Madison. It was introduced in Congress by him and passed the House and Senate with little or no debate and virtually no change in language. It was proffered to quiet expressed fears that a bill of specifically enumerated rights could not be sufficiently broad to cover all essential rights and that the specific mention of certain rights would be interpreted as a denial that others were protected.

In presenting the proposed Amendment, Madison said:

"It has been objected also against a bill of rights, that, by enumerating particular exceptions to the grant of power, it would disparage those rights which were not placed in that enumeration; and it might follow by implication, that those rights which were not singled out, were intended to be assigned into the hands of the General Government, and were consequently insecure. This is one of the most plausible arguments I have ever heard urged against the admission of a bill of rights into this system; but, I conceive, that it may be guarded against. I have attempted it, as gentlemen may see by turning to the last clause of the fourth resolution [the Ninth Amendment]." I Annals of Congress 439 (Gales and Seaton ed. 1834)....

... To hold that a right so basic and fundamental and so deep-rooted in our society as the right of privacy in marriage may be infringed because that right is not guaranteed in so many words by the first eight amendments to the Constitution is to ignore the Ninth Amendment and to give it no effect whatsoever....

MR. JUSTICE HARLAN, concurring in the judgment....

In my view, the proper constitutional inquiry in this case is whether this Connecticut statute infringes the Due Process Clause of the Fourteenth Amendment because the enactment violates basic values "implicit in the concept of ordered liberty," *Palko* v. *Connecticut,* 302 U.S. 319, 325. For reasons stated at length in my dissenting opinion in *Poe* v. *Ullman, supra,* I believe that it does. While the relevant inquiry may be aided by resort to one or more of the provisions of the Bill of Rights, it is not dependent on them or any of their radiations....

MR. JUSTICE WHITE, concurring in the judgment.

In my view this Connecticut law as applied to married couples deprives them of "liberty" without due process of law, as that concept is used in the Fourteenth Amendment. I therefore concur in the judgment of the Court reversing these convictions under Connecticut's aiding and abetting statute....

MR. JUSTICE BLACK, with whom MR. JUSTICE STEWART joins, dissenting.

... I get nowhere in this case by talk about a constitutional "right of privacy" as an emanation from one or more constitutional provisions. I like my privacy as well as the next one, but I am nevertheless compelled to admit that government has a right to invade it unless prohibited by some specific constitutional provision. For these reasons I cannot agree with the Court's judgment and the reasons it gives for holding this Connecticut law unconstitutional....

[*Black argues that if the Constitution must be changed it should be done by amendment, not by judicial interpretations of the Due Process Clause, the Ninth Amendment, "or any mysterious and uncertain natural law concept."*]

MR. JUSTICE STEWART, whom MR. JUSTICE BLACK joins, dissenting.

Since 1879 Connecticut has had on its books a law which forbids the use of contraceptives by anyone. I think this is an uncommonly silly law. As a practical matter, the law is obviously unenforceable, except in the oblique context of the present case. As a philosophical matter, I believe the use of contraceptives in the relationship of marriage should be left to personal and private choice, based upon each individual's moral, ethical, and religious beliefs. As a matter of social policy, I think professional counsel about methods of birth control should be available to all, so that each individual's choice can be meaningfully made. But we are not asked in this case to say whether we think this law is unwise, or even asinine. We are asked to hold that it violates the United States Constitution. And that I cannot do.

... If, as I should surely hope, the law before us does not reflect the standards of the people of Connecticut, the people of Connecticut can freely exercise their true Ninth and Tenth Amendment rights to persuade their elected representatives to repeal it....

C. REPRODUCTIVE FREEDOM

No contemporary issue has inflamed the country, Congress, and the courts more than the right of a woman to abort her pregnancy. What balance should be struck between a woman's interest in deciding to have an abortion and the state's interest in protecting the health and life of the mother and child? If a wife decides to abort, must the husband first consent? Does government have an obligation to fund abortions? Do abortion rights extend to minors? Must women under the age of 18 notify their parents? Is a fetus a "person" entitled to constitutional protection under the Fourteenth Amendment? These and other emotional issues bombard the courts, executive agencies, and legislatures.

The question that reached the Supreme Court in 1973 was not the abstract issue of whether abortions would be performed. The record was abundantly clear that they would take place, with or without the law. In states that had prohibited or severely restricted abortion, some women attempted self-abortion by using coat hangers and other life-threatening techniques. Others placed their life and health in the hands of whoever was willing, with or without medical training, to do the job. Women with higher incomes had more options. They could travel to another state or country for the operation. The issue before the Court in 1973 was politically complex: How could abortions be performed within a legal structure that satisfied the conflicting values of those who wanted abortion on demand and those who believed equally strongly in the right to life?

Roe v. Wade

In 1973, the Supreme Court attempted to steer a middle course by rejecting both abortion on demand and the absolute right to life. If it hoped to avoid criticism it miscalculated. The Court held that state laws permitting abortions only to save the mother's life violated due process, which the Court said protects the right to privacy and a woman's *qualified* right to terminate her pregnancy. The state has legitimate interests in protecting both the pregnant woman's health and the potential life of the fetus. Each of those interests grows and reaches a "compelling" point at later stages of the woman's pregnancy. Over the first three months (the first trimester), the decision to abort is left to the woman and her physician. Later, states may regulate the abortion procedure in ways that are reasonably related to the health of the mother. After the fetus becomes viable (about seven months), the state may prohibit abortion except where necessary to preserve the life or health of the mother. ROE v. WADE, 410 U.S. 113 (1973).

This decision was widely condemned (by both liberals and conservatives) as the work of an activist Court conducting itself like a legislature, even to the extent of identifying the particular stages of pregnancy where the state's interest prevails over the woman's. The Court had difficulty in identifying its source of authority. In discussing the right of privacy, the Court pointed to the First, Fourth, Fifth, and Ninth Amendments; "the penumbras of the Bill of Rights;" and the "concept of liberty guaranteed by the first section of the Fourteenth Amendment." Precisely where to anchor the decision did not seem to matter: "This right of privacy, whether it be founded in the Fourteenth Amendment's concept of personal liberty and restrictions upon state action, as we feel it is, or, as the District Court determined, in the Ninth Amendment's reservation of rights to the people, is broad enough to encompass a woman's decision whether or not to terminate her pregnancy." Id. at 153.

The Court specifically rejected the argument that a fetus is a "person" within the language and meaning of the Fourteenth Amendment. After examining the various instances in the Constitution where the word *person* is used, the Court concluded that they apply only postnatally. The constitutional meaning of person "does not include the unborn." Id. at 157–58.

The constitutional issue was mixed with factual questions. The ruling depended on "the light of present medical knowledge." Id. at 163. The "compelling" point for state intervention, said the Court, is viability, a condition that is not fixed but varies with medical competence and technology. As the Court noted in a subsequent case, viability is "a matter of medical judgment, skill, and technical ability, and we preserved the flexibility of the term." Planned Parenthood of Missouri v. Danforth, 428 U.S. 52, 64 (1976). As medical knowledge advanced, the Court's identification of trimester stages would provide less guidance. In fact, the Court later struck down a Pennsylvania statute that required doctors to determine first the viability of a fetus. If the fetus was viable, the statute mandated that the doctor exercise the same care to preserve the fetus' life and health as would be necessary for a regular birth. The Court held the statute void for vagueness. Colautti v. Franklin, 439 U.S. 379 (1979).

The companion case to *Roe v. Wade* reviewed the requirement in Georgia's law that abortion be performed in a hospital accredited by a joint commission. The Court determined that the statute was unconstitutional because it unduly restricted a woman's rights, particularly the indigent married woman who brought the case. The state law also required that the abortion procedure be approved by a hospital committee, a condition the Court again found too restrictive on a woman's rights. Finally, by requiring that her doctor's judgment be confirmed by two other licensed physicians, the state law infringed impermissibly on a doctor's right to practice. Doe v. Bolton, 410 U.S. 179 (1973).

Although the Court had announced its constitutional decision, full compliance with the ruling was not forthcoming. Dr. Kenneth Edelin, a physician in Boston, was indicted in 1974 for performing an abortion and subsequently found guilty of manslaughter. His conviction was later overturned, but the opposition to *Roe v. Wade* intensified. Over the following years, right-to-lifers would bomb abortion clinics, send letter bombs through the mails, murder physicians, and use other tactics to intimidate and harass women and their doctors.

The Court addressed other issues in 1976. It upheld Missouri's requirement that a woman consent to an abortion in writing and certify that her consent is freely given. However, the state's requirement for a written consent from the woman's spouse (unless the physician certified that an abortion was necessary to save her life) was struck down. Also, a blanket requirement for parental consent for minors was declared unconstitutional. Planned Parenthood of Missouri v. Danforth, 428 U.S. 52 (1976). See also Bellotti v. Baird, 443 U.S. 622 (1979).

Public Funding

Were states required to provide public funds for abortion? Acting under its interpretation of federal law, Pennsylvania denied women medical assistance for nontherapeutic abortions. State regulations limited assistance to abortion certified by physicians as medically necessary. The Court, split 6–3, held that federal law did not require the funding of nontherapeutic abortions as a condition for states to participate in the federal Medicaid program. This decision turned on statutory construction, not constitutional interpretation. Beal v. Doe, 432 U.S. 438 (1977). Evidently the Court regarded these issues as moral questions to be resolved by legislatures, not the judiciary. It recognized the risk of trying to direct legislatures how to spend public funds, at least in this area. On the same day, the Court held that the Constitution does not obligate states to pay the pregnancy-related medical expenses of indigent women. Maher v. Roe, 432 U.S. 464 (1977). See also Poelker v. Doe, 432 U.S. 519 (1977).

The major challenge came from the Hyde Amendment, first passed by Congress in 1976 (see reading). In the version that eventually came to the Supreme Court, the language provided that

> ... none of the funds provided by this joint resolution shall be used to perform abortions except where the life of the mother would be endangered if the fetus were carried to term; or except for such medical procedures necessary for the victims of rape or incest when such rape or incest has been reported promptly to a law enforcement agency or public health service. 93 Stat. 926, § 109 (1979).

A federal district court, without deciding the constitutional issue, first enjoined the Secretary of Health, Education, and Welfare from enforcing the Hyde Amendment. The court order required the Secretary to continue providing federal reimbursement for abortions. McRae v. Mathews, 421 F.Supp. 533 (E.D. N.Y. 1976). The Supreme Court vacated the injunction and remanded the case for reconsideration in light of its holdings. In 1980, the district court held that the Hyde Amendment impermissibly used appropriation language to change substantive (legislative) language in federal law, violated an individual's liberty to terminate pregnancy for medical reasons, and unreasonably denied funds for medically necessary abortions. McRae v. Califano, 491 F.Supp. 630 (E.D. N.Y. 1980).

Clearly a major collision loomed between Congress and the judiciary. In 1980, by a 5–4 vote, the Supreme Court upheld the Hyde Amendment. According to the Court, government may not place obstacles in the path of a woman's decision to choose abortion, but neither has it an obligation to remove obstacles it did not create (such as being poor). Poverty, standing alone, was not considered a suspect classification. The Court concluded that the Hyde Amendment, by encouraging childbirth except in the most urgent circumstances, was rationally related to legitimate governmental objectives of protecting potential life. HARRIS v. McRAE, 448 U.S. 297 (1980). In a companion decision, the Court (again split 5–4) upheld the right of state legislatures to limit public funds for abortions. Williams v. Zbaraz, 448 U.S. 358 (1980). When the issue of public funding is framed entirely as a state matter to be decided under the state constitution, the results can differ from *Harris* v. *McRae* (see box on next page).

Chronic Challenges

Roe v. *Wade* was not accepted as the last word on the rights of abortion. Legislative efforts by state and local bodies put constant pressure on the Court to clarify and modify the boundaries of its 1973 ruling. A 1981 case involved Utah's statute requiring a physician to notify, if possible, the parents or guardian of a minor facing an abortion. Concluding that the statute did not amount to a parental veto, the Court upheld the law as a legitimate opportunity for parents to supply essential medical and other information to the physician. Three members of the *Roe* majority (Marshall, Brennan, and Blackmun) dissented. H.L. v. Matheson, 450 U.S. 398 (1981).

A cluster of three cases in 1983 raised new issues. An Akron, Ohio, ordinance set forth five requirements: (1) abortions after the first trimester had to be performed in a hospital, (2) abortions were prohibited for unmarried minors under the age of 15 without parental consent or court order, (3) the physician had to inform the woman of various facts concerning the operation, (4) abortions were delayed for at least 24 hours after the woman's consent, and (5) the physician had to ensure that fetal remains were disposed of in a "humane and sanitary manner." The Court found each provision unconstitutional. Justices White and Rehnquist continued to dissent from the *Roe* doctrine, but Justice O'Connor, added to the Court in 1981, now joined them by penning a major critique of the

Independent State Action

Although Congress (with the Hyde Amendment) withheld federal funds for abortion and the Supreme Court sustained this legislation, some of the states followed a different course in interpreting their constitutions. California restricted the circumstances under which public funds would be authorized to pay for abortions for Medi-Cal recipients. The California courts struck down these statutes as unconstitutional, holding that the state has no constitutional obligation to provide medical care to the poor, but that once it does it bears the heavy burden of justifying a provision that withholds benefits from otherwise qualified individuals solely because they chose to exercise their constitutional right to have an abortion. Committee to Defend Reprod. Rights v. Myers, 625 P.2d 779 (Cal. 1981). Similar decisions were issued by the New Jersey and Massachusetts courts, overturning state laws that restricted public funding for abortions. Right to Choose v. Byrne, 450 A.2d 925 (N.J. 1982); Moe v. Secretary of Administration, 417 N.E.2d 387 (Mass. 1981).

State regulations denying funds for abortion were also declared invalid under other state constitutions. An agency regulation in Oregon, restricting funds to indigent women seeking abortions, was struck down by a state court as a violation of the state constitution's privileges and immunities clause. Planned Parenthood Ass'n v. Dept. of Human Res., 663 P.2d 1247 (Or. App. 1983). A Connecticut court invalidated a state agency's rule that restricted funding of abortion for indigent women unless to save their lives. The regulation exceeded the statutory authority of the agency and violated various provisions of the state constitution. Dating back to 1650, Connecticut had compiled a record of almost 350 years of paying for all necessary expenses for the poor. Doe v. Maher, 515 A.2d 134, 143 (Conn. Super. 1986).

premises supporting *Roe*. AKRON v. AKRON CENTER FOR REPRODUCTIVE HEALTH, 462 U.S. 416 (1983).

Two other decisions handed down the same day as *Akron* explored additional restrictions on abortion rights. A Missouri statute required that abortions, after 12 weeks of pregnancy, be performed in a hospital. Consistent with previous rulings, the Court struck down the hospital requirement, but sustained three other requirements in the Missouri law: a pathology report for each abortion, the presence of a second physician for abortions performed after viability, and either parental or court consent for minors. The latter marked a major departure from past rulings. Planned Parenthood Ass'n v. Ashcroft, 462 U.S. 476 (1983). The 7–2 majority from *Roe* had clearly evaporated. Four Justices (Blackmun, Brennan, Marshall, and Stevens) dissented from the Court's support for pathology reports, second physicians, and parental or court consent.

In the second case, the Court upheld Virginia's law that second trimester abortions be performed either in hospitals or licensed outpatient clinics. The requirement furthered the state's interest in protecting the health of a woman after the end of the first trimester. Justice Stevens was the sole dissenter. Simopoulos v. Virginia, 462 U.S. 506 (1983).

Reexamining *Roe*

In 1986, the Supreme Court faced another major case. A Pennsylvania statute required that a woman be informed of the following: the physician who would perform the abortion; the "particular medical risks" of the abortion procedure, including physical and psychological effects; the medical assistance benefits available for prenatal care, childbirth, and care immediately after birth; the father's liability to provide financial support for the child; and printed materials that describe fetal characteristics at two-week intervals and that list agencies offering alternatives to abortion. The state also required other procedures, such as the presence of a second physician during an abortion performed when viability is possible. The responsibility of the second physician was to take all reasonable steps to preserve the child's life and health.

The States Respond to *Webster*

Pennsylvania enacted new restrictions on abortion, leading immediately to challenges in the courts. Idaho and Louisiana passed restrictive statutes in 1990, but the governors vetoed them. In 1991, the governor of Louisiana again vetoed a restrictive abortion statute, but this time the legislature overrode him. An antiabortion law enacted by Guam was regarded as unconstitutional by the territory's attorney general, a federal district judge, and the Ninth Circuit. Connecticut in 1990 became the first state to give women the legal right to abortion, even if *Roe* v. *Wade* were overturned. Maryland passed a similar law in 1991; that law survived a statewide referendum vote in November 1992. In 1991, the governor of North Dakota vetoed what would have been the strictest antiabortion bill in the nation. Utah passed a stringent antiabortion law. A Michigan appeals court invalidated a voter-approved ban on state-paid abortions for poor women.

In 1990, a 5–4 Court struck down as unconstitutional a Minnesota law that prohibited an abortion performed on a woman under 18 years of age until at least 48 hours after notifying *both* of her parents. The Court found the provision too restrictive in part because nine percent of the minors in Minnesota lived with neither parent, 33 percent lived with only one parent, and only 50 percent resided with both biological parents. Justice O'Connor supplied the fifth vote, casting her first vote to strike down an antiabortion restriction. Dissenters were Scalia, Kennedy, Rehnquist, and White. O'Connor voted with those four in holding that it would be constitutional if minors had the option of asking a judge to waive the notification requirement. Hodgson v. Minnesota, 497 U.S. 417 (1990). In a second ruling, the Court voted 6 to 3 to uphold an Ohio law requiring a physician to notify one parent of a pregnant minor's intent to have an abortion. Ohio provided for a judicial bypass but required the minor to prove by "clear and convincing" evidence that she should not be forced to notify a parent. Ohio v. Akron Center for Reproductive Health, 497 U.S. 502 (1990).

With a 5–4 majority, the Court invalidated the statute. It held that states are not free, under the guise of protecting maternal health or potential life, to intimidate women into continuing their pregnancies. The statute impermissibly intruded upon a decision to be made by the woman and her physician. The dissent by Chief Justice Burger was significant, since he formed part of the 7–2 majority in *Roe* v. *Wade.* He agreed with the dissenters that "we should reexamine *Roe.*" Three other dissenters (White, Rehnquist, and O'Connor) were much more emphatic in rejecting the premises of *Roe.* Thornburgh v. American Coll. of Obst. & Gyn., 476 U.S. 747 (1986).

Support for *Roe* v. *Wade* continued to erode. With Antonin Scalia replacing Burger in 1986 and Anthony Kennedy taking Powell's seat in 1988, the Court was positioned to overhaul and possibly overrule *Roe.* The opportunity came in 1989, when the Court reviewed a Missouri statute that imposed a number of restrictions on a woman's decision to have an abortion. Without overruling *Roe,* four Justices rejected the trimester framework (Justice O'Connor, who declined to join that part of the Court's decision, had criticized the trimester concept in previous opinions). The 5–4 decision upheld key portions of the Missouri statute and allowed governmental regulation that would have been prohibited under earlier decisions. Webster v. Reproductive Health Services, 492 U.S. 490 (1989). *Webster* triggered a flurry of legislative activity by the states (see box).

Jettisoning Trimester Framework

In 1992 the Court decided the constitutionality of a Pennsylvania statute that restricted abortions. With David Souter succeeding William Brennan and Clarence Thomas replacing Thurgood Marshall, it was thought that the Court might overturn *Roe* v. *Wade.* However, the Court managed to hold on to what it called the "central holding" of *Roe:* the constitutional liberty of women to have some freedom to terminate pregnancies. In so deciding, the Court rejected *Roe*'s trimester framework and announced an "undue burden" standard that would hold a law invalid if its purpose or effect is to place substantial obstacles in the path of a woman seeking an abortion before the fetus attains viability. That position was accepted by only a three-Justice plurality: O'Connor, Kennedy, and Souter. Using this standard, most of the Pennsylvania statute was held constitutional. A provision requiring a woman to notify her husband was struck down. PLANNED PARENTHOOD v. CASEY, 505 U.S. 833 (1992).

Following this decision, Congress began work on the Freedom of Choice Act (FOCA) to codify many of the protections originally announced in *Roe*. Pro-choice groups, previously dependent on the courts to advance their agenda, now turned to Congress for their protection. NARAL (National Abortion Rights Action League) sent a "Supreme Court Alert" to its membership on June 27, 1991, stating a new outlook: "Clearly Congress is our Court of Last Resort. All hope of protecting our constitutional rights to choose depends upon our elected representatives in Congress responding to the will of the American people." In urging support for FOCA, the Religious Coalition for Abortion Rights also called Congress "our court of last resort."

FOCA was never enacted, but it represented the efforts of political groups—both liberal and conservative—to seek legislative solutions. In an address delivered in 1993, Judge (now Justice) Ruth Bader Ginsburg argued that *Roe* v. *Wade* failed to recognize that judicial decisions must work in concert with the coequal executive and legislative branches at the national level and with state authorities (see box on next page).

Access to Abortion Clinics

Pro-life groups have been active in trying to block access to abortion clinics. In 1993, the Supreme Court held that abortion clinics and abortion rights organizations could not use a civil rights statute (passed in 1871 to curb the Ku Klux Klan) to find a private conspiracy against the members of Operation Rescue, which organized demonstrations to block access to abortion clinics. Bray v. Alexandria Women's Health Clinic, 506 U.S. 263 (1993). Congress responded by passing legislation to make it a federal crime to obstruct the entrance to an abortion clinic. 108 Stat. 694 (1994). The Fourth Circuit upheld the constitutionality of this statute (against a First Amendment challenge) and the Supreme Court denied cert. Woodall v. Reno, 515 U.S. 1141 (1995).

In 1994, a unanimous Court held that abortion clinics may use a federal racketeering law (RICO) to sue protesters who conspire to shut them down. No proof was needed that the racketeering enterprise was motivated by an economic purpose. National Organization for Women, Inc. v. Scheidler, 510 U.S. 249 (1994). Also in 1994, the Court ruled that judges may prevent demonstrators from coming within 36 feet of abortion clinics. The purpose of this buffer zone is to prevent intimidation and to ensure clinic access. Madsen v. Women's Health Center, Inc., 512 U.S. 753 (1994). In 1997, the Court refined its position on buffer zones by holding that it was permissible to place a 15-foot buffer around clinic entrances but that a "floating buffer zone" (a 15-foot shield around patients and clinic staff) interfered with the free speech rights of abortion opponents. Schenck v. Pro-Choice Network of Western New York, 519 U.S. 357 (1997). In 2000, the Court upheld a Colorado law that requires opponents of abortion to stay at least eight feet away from people entering health care facilities. Hill v. Colorado, 530 U.S. 703 (2000).

In 2003, the Court revisited the issue of whether abortion rights supporters could use RICO to sue pro-life organizations for their campaigns against abortion clinics. The Court decided that the statutory language "extortion" did not apply to abortion protesters. Eight Justices joined the ruling because they understood the implications not just for pro-life demonstrations but for any type of political protest. Scheidler v. National Organization for Women, 537 U.S. 393 (2004).

Late-Term Abortions

In 1996, President Clinton vetoed a bill that would have prohibited late-term abortions except to save the life of a woman. He said he opposed late-term abortions but insisted on another exception to cover

Ruth Bader Ginsburg on *Roe* v. *Wade*

[*In the following address, Judge (now Justice) Ruth Bader Ginsburg said that the Supreme Court's ruling in* Roe v. Wade *(1973) was too broadly decided and failed to take proper account of other political institutions involved in shaping constitutional law*]:

In *The Federalist* No. 78, Alexander Hamilton said that federal judges, in order to preserve the people's rights and privileges, must have authority to check legislation and acts of the executive for constitutionality. But he qualified his recognition of that awesome authority. The judiciary, Hamilton wrote, from the very nature of its functions, will always be "the least dangerous" branch of government, for judges hold neither the sword nor the purse of the community; ultimately, they must depend upon the political branches to effectuate their judgments....

... [J]udges play an interdependent part in our democracy. They do not alone shape legal doctrine but, as I suggested at the outset, they participate in a dialogue with other organs of government, and with the people as well....

The seven to two judgment in *Roe* v. *Wade* declared "violative of the Due Process Clause of the Fourteenth Amendment" a Texas criminal abortion statute that intolerably shackled a woman's autonomy; the Texas law "except[ed] from criminality only a *life-saving* procedure on behalf of the [pregnant] woman." Suppose the Court had stopped there, rightly declaring unconstitutional the most extreme brand of law in the nation, and

had not gone on, as the Court did in *Roe,* to fashion a regime blanketing the subject, a set of rules that displaced virtually every state law then in force. Would there have been the twenty-year controversy we have witnessed, reflected most recently in the Supreme Court's splintered decision in *Planned Parenthood* v. *Casey*? A less encompassing *Roe,* one that merely struck down the extreme Texas law and went no further ... might have served to reduce rather than to fuel controversy.

[In a series of cases involving gender discrimination, the Court] opened a dialogue with the political branches of government. In essence, the Court instructed Congress and state legislatures: rethink ancient positions on these questions....

The ball, one might say, was tossed by the Justices back into the legislators' court, where the political forces of the day could operate. The Supreme Court wrote modestly, it put forward no grand philosophy; but by requiring legislative reexamination of once customary sex-based classifications, the Court helped to ensure that laws and regulations would "catch up with a changed world."

Roe v. *Wade,* in contrast, invited no dialogue with legislators. Instead, it seemed to remove the ball from the legisators' court. In 1973, when *Roe* was issued, abortion law was in a state of change across the nation. As the Supreme Court itself noted, there was a marked trend in state legislatures "toward liberalization of abortion statutes." ...

SOURCE: Ruth Bader Ginsburg, "Speaking in a Judicial Voice," 67 N.Y.U. L. Rev. 1185 (1992) (footnotes omitted).

adverse health consequences. The bill would have made it a federal crime for a doctor to perform the procedure, also known as "partial birth" abortion. Although the House overrode the veto, the Senate was nine votes short. In 1997, Clinton vetoed a similar bill. The Senate delayed the override effort until 1998 to attract additional votes, but it fell three votes short. Lower courts struck down Ohio's ban on late-term abortions. When the dispute was appealed to the Supreme Court, it denied cert. Voinovich v. Women's Medical Professional Corporation, 523 U.S. 1036 (1998).

About 30 states passed legislation to prohibit late-term abortions, with a number of the statutes struck down by federal courts on the grounds that they were vague and placed an undue burden on a woman's right to decide on an abortion. Nebraska's law, banning "partial birth abortions," was struck down by the Supreme Court in 2000. Divided 5 to 4, the Court split in many directions: an opinion written by Justice Breyer, separate concurrences by Stevens, O'Connor, and Ginsburg, and dissenting opinions by Rehnquist, Scalia, Kennedy, and Thomas. STENBERG v. CARHART, 530 U.S. 914

(2000). States began redrafting these bills to place prohibitions on partial-birth abortion in a manner designed to withstand constitutional scrutiny.

Responding to *Stenberg*, Congress in 2002 passed the Born-Alive Infants Protection Act, which provides that the words "person," "human being," "child," and "individual" shall include every infant born alive at any stage of development. "Born alive" is defined as "the complete expulsion or extraction from his or her mother of that member, at any stage of development, who after such expulsion or extraction breathes or has a beating heart, pulsation of the umbilical cord, or definite movement of voluntary muscles, regardless of whether the umbilical cord has been cut, and regardless of whether the expulsion or extraction occurs as a result of natural or induced labor, cesarean section, or induced abortion." The purpose of the statute is to protect a child that emerges from the mother as a live baby. If a fetus were to survive an abortion procedure, it would be considered a person under federal law. The statute provides that it should not be construed to affirm, deny, expand, or contract any legal right to abortion. 116 Stat. 296 (2002).

Congress followed this with the Partial-Birth Abortion Ban Act of 2003, which finds that a moral, medical, and ethical consensus exists that the practice of performing a partial-birth abortion "is never medically necessary and should be prohibited." The law provides for fines and imprisonment for physicians who violate the statute. Relying on facts unavailable to the *Stenberg* Court, Congress rejected the position that in some circumstances partial-birth abortion would be the safest procedure on abortion. The statute does not totally prohibit partial-birth abortion. It allows the procedure when "necessary to save the life of a mother whose life is endangered by a physical disorder, physical illness, or physical injury, including a life-endangering physical condition caused by or arising from the pregnancy itself." 117 Stat. 1201, 1206 (2003).

On April 18, 2007, the Supreme Court upheld the statute. Divided 5 to 4, the Court distinguished the federal statute from the Nebraska law at issue in *Stenberg*. An important change in the Court was Samuel Alito replacing Sandra Day O'Connor. He was part of the five-Justice majority. In *Stenberg*, she had voted to strike down the Nebraska law. GONZALES v. CARHART, 550 U.S. 124 (2007).

Unborn-Victims Bill

In 2004, Congress passed the Unborn Victims of Violence Act, treating attacks on a pregnant woman as separate crimes against her and the fetus. An offense under the statute does not require proof that the person who committed the crime "had knowledge or should have had knowledge that the victim of the underlying offense was pregnant." 118 Stat. 568 (2004).

Post-*Casey* Record

Other than *Stenberg* and *Carhart*, the pattern since *Casey* has been for the Supreme Court to decline to hear major abortion cases. In 1993, it let stand a Mississippi law that required women under 18 to obtain *both* parents' permission before having an abortion. The state law allows the permission of only one parent in case of divorce, separation, and other factors. Barnes v. Mississippi, 510 U.S. 976 (1993). In 1996, the Court refused to review a South Dakota law that had been invalidated by the Eighth Circuit. The federal appeals court struck down a parental notice statute that required teenagers seeking abortions to notify a parent 48 hours in advance. Janklow v. Planned Parenthood, 517 U.S. 1174 (1996). Also in 1996, the Court relied on a procedural dispute to revive a Utah law that prohibits abortion after the twentieth week of pregnancy. The Tenth Circuit had declared that prohibition invalid because it was not severable from another provision struck down, but the Court ruled that the Utah Code required courts to analyze statutory provisions independently. Under this severability analysis, the prohibition on abortion after the twentieth week survived. Four Justices dissented. Leavitt v. Jane L., 518 U.S. 137 (1996). In 2006, the Court gave further guidance to parental involvement for minors seeking an abortion. Ayotte v. Planned Parenthood of Northern New Eng., 546 U.S. 320 (2006). The

Abortion Regulations

Ever since the Supreme Court issued *Roe* v. *Wade* (1973), it has ruled on the permissibility of state regulations that affect a woman's decision to have an abortion.

Permissible regulations

Assuring that woman's consent is freely given. Planned Parenthood of Mo. v. Danforth (1976).

A pathology report prepared for each abortion. Planned Parenthood Ass'n v. Ashcroft (1983).

Presence of a second physician for abortions after viability. Planned Parenthood Ass'n v. Ashcroft (1983).

Performance of second-trimester abortions either in hospitals or in licensed outpatient clinics. Simopoulos v. Virginia (1983).

Viability test at 20 weeks or more. Webster v. Reproductive Health Services (1989).

"Informed consent" requirements to advise a woman about fetal developments and alternatives to abortion, including adoption. Planned Parenthood v. Casey (1992).

24-hour wait between informed consent and the procedure for abortion. Planned Parenthood v. Casey (1992).

Prohibiting use of public facilities or public employees to perform abortion. Webster v. Reproductive Health Services (1989).

The Partial-Birth Abortion Ban Act of 2003 does not impose a "substantial obstacle" to late-term abortions as prohibited by the *Casey* plurality. Gonzales v. Carhart (2007).

Impermissible regulations

Consent from a woman's spouse. Planned Parenthood of Mo. v. Danforth (1976).

Parental consent for minors; must provide option for consent by a judge. Planned Parenthood of Mo. v. Danforth (1976).

Performance of abortion after first trimester in a hospital. Akron v. Akron Center for Reproductive Health (1983).

Performance of abortion after 12 weeks in a hospital. Planned Parenthood Ass'n v. Ashcroft (1983).

Notification of both parents by women under the age of 18. Hodgson v. Minnesota (1990).

[Informed-consent requirements had been invalidated earlier. Akron v. Akron Center (1983); Thornburgh v. American Coll. of Obst. & Gyn. (1986).]

[24-hour delays had been held invalid in earlier cases, such as Akron v. Akron Center for Reproductive Health (1983).]

Requiring women under the age of 18 to notify both parents. Hodgson v. Minnesota (1990).

Requiring women to notify their spouses. Planned Parenthood v. Casey (1992).

Prohibitions on "partial birth abortion." Stenberg v. Carhart (2000).

judicial record from 1973 to the present consists of a number of rulings that sustain some regulations on abortion while disallowing others (see box).

The Gag Rule

The Reagan administration took steps to limit the use of federal funds for family-planning activities and for abortion counseling. Congress had passed legislation in 1970 to provide funds for family planning, specifying that none of the funds "shall be used in programs where abortion is a method of family planning." 84 Stat. 1508, § 1008. On September 1, 1987, the Department of Health and Human Services issued a proposed rule prohibiting family-planning clinics from using federal funds to counsel women on abortions or referring them to a doctor for abortion, even if women requested the information. Congress placed language in a conference report stating that changes in existing law must be achieved through the regular legislative process and not through executive regulations. H. Rept. No. 100-498, at 943. Nevertheless, the Reagan administration made the regulations final in 1988.

In 1991, a 5–4 decision by the Supreme Court upheld the regulations, which had been challenged as a violation of congressional intent and of constitutional rights available under the First and Fifth Amendments. Rust v. Sullivan, 500 U.S. 173 (1991). Both Houses of Congress began drafting legislation to reverse *Rust*. Language in an appropriation bill prohibited the use of funds to enforce the rule that barred abortion counseling, but President Bush vetoed the bill on November 19, 1991. Shortly before his veto, Bush prepared a memorandum stating that there was no Gag Rule to interfere with the doctor-patient relationship. In implementing the regulation, nothing should prevent a woman from receiving complete medical information about her condition from a physician. However, since abortion counseling in family-planning clinics is done largely by nurses and other nonphysician health-care personnel, the Gag Rule still retained its restrictive force. Late in 1992, the D.C. Circuit nullified the Gag Rule because when the administration modified it (to permit physicians to counsel patients on abortion), it had failed to submit the regulation for public notice and comment. National Family Planning and Reproductive Health Ass'n, Inc. v. Sullivan, 979 F.2d 227 (D.C. Cir. 1992).

During the 1992 presidential campaign, Bill Clinton promised to cancel the Gag Rule if elected. On January 22, 1993, he ordered the Department of Health and Human Services to suspend the Gag Rule through notice and comment procedures. The counseling policy appeared at 65 Fed. Reg. 41278–80 (July 3, 2000). He also directed the Agency for International Development to reverse the "Mexico City Policy" (followed by Presidents Reagan and Bush) that prohibited the use of federal funds for abortion and family-planning counseling overseas. When President George W. Bush took office in 2001, one of his first actions was to overturn Clinton's order on the "Mexico City Policy." Congressional efforts to block Bush's order failed. One of the first initiatives by President Obama in January 2009 was to rescind the Bush order.

Stem Cell Research

On July 19, 2006, President George W. Bush exercised his first veto since assuming the presidency when he rejected legislation to expand federally supported embryonic stem cell research. The measure would have allowed taxpayer-financed research on embryos scheduled for destruction at fertility clinics. The veto defied the Republican-controlled Congress, which had sent to him legislation that would have overturned research restrictions he had imposed in 2001. President Bush's veto of H.R. 810 survived an override effort by House members. The vote, 235 to 193, fell 51 votes short of the two-thirds majority required. Fifty-one Republican and 183 Democrats joined one independent in the override attempt. Sheryl Gay Stolberg, "First Bush Veto Maintains Limits on Stem Cell Use," New York Times, July 20, 2006, p. A1.On June 20, 2007, Bush vetoed another stem-cell bill, explaining that he continued to support research on stem cells lines derived from embryos that had already been destroyed.

President Obama on March 9, 2009, issued Executive Order 13505, "Removing Barriers to Responsible Research Involving Human Stem Cells." In a ruling on August 23, 2010, District Judge Royce Lamberth blocked the administration from funding human embryonic stem cell research, concluding that the research violated a federal law barring the use of taxpayer money for experiments that destroy human embryos. In April 2011, the D.C. Circuit reversed his ruling. On July 27, 2011, Judge Lamberth dismissed a challenge to NIH (National Institutes of Health) funding for human embryonic stem cell research.

Roe v. Wade

410 U.S. 113 (1973)

Using the pseudonym "Jane Roe," a pregnant single woman brought a class action challenging the constitutionality of a Texas law that made it a criminal offense to attempt an abortion except for the purpose of saving the mother's life. A three-judge district court declared the Texas

law void as vague and infringing the rights under the Ninth and Fourteenth Amendments. Henry Wade, the District Attorney of Dallas County, cross-appealed on the district court's grant of declaratory relief to Roe and to a physician who intervened, while Roe appealed on the district court's ruling to bar injunctive relief.

MR. JUSTICE BLACKMUN delivered the opinion of the Court....

We forthwith acknowledge our awareness of the sensitive and emotional nature of the abortion controversy, of the vigorous opposing views, even among physicians, and of the deep and seemingly absolute convictions that the subject inspires. One's philosophy, one's experiences, one's exposure to the raw edges of human existence, one's religious training, one's attitudes toward life and family and their values, and the moral standards one establishes and seeks to observe, are all likely to influence and to color one's thinking and conclusions about abortion.

In addition, population growth, pollution, poverty, and racial overtones tend to complicate and not to simplify the problem.

Our task, of course, is to resolve the issue by constitutional measurement, free of emotion and of predilection....

I

The Texas statutes that concern us here are Arts. 1191–1194 and 1196 of the State's Penal Code. These make it a crime to "procure an abortion," as therein defined, or to attempt one, except with respect to "an abortion procured or attempted by medical advice for the purpose of saving the life of the mother." Similar statutes are in existence in a majority of the States....

II

["Jane Roe," a single woman residing in Dallas County, Texas, brought this federal action against the District Attorney of the county. James Hubert Hallford, a licensed physician, intervened in her action, alleging that he had been arrested previously for violating the Texas abortion statutes and that two prosecutions were pending against him. John and Mary Doe [pseudonyms], a married couple, joined in the action also. They had postponed having children because of her "neural-chemical" disorder. If she became pregnant, she would want to terminate the pregnancy by an abortion performed by a competent, licensed physician under safe, clinical conditions. After deciding that Jane Roe had standing to sue, that she presented a justiciable controversy, that the termination of her 1970 pregnancy did not render the case moot, and that neither Hallford nor the Does had

standing, the Court moved to the merits and substance of the case.]

VI

It perhaps is not generally appreciated that the restrictive criminal abortion laws in effect in a majority of States today are of relatively recent vintage. Those laws, generally proscribing abortion or its attempt at any time during pregnancy except when necessary to preserve the pregnant woman's life, are not of ancient or even of common-law origin. Instead, they derive from statutory changes effected, for the most part, in the latter half of the 19th century.

[The Court devotes 17 pages to explain ancient attitudes toward abortion, the Hippocratic oath, the common law, English statutory law, American law, and the positions of the American Medical Association, the American Public Health Association, and the American Bar Association.]

VII

[The Court reviews three reasons for the enactment of criminal abortion laws in the 19th century and their continued existence. One reason relied on a Victorian social concern to discourage illicit sexual conduct, but Texas did not advance that justification in this case. The second reason relates to medical procedures. When most criminal abortion laws were first enacted, procedures were hazardous for the woman. Modern medical techniques for abortion in early pregnancy (prior to the end of the first trimester) have become relatively safe. The third reason is the state's interest in protecting prenatal life, based partly on the theory that a new human life is present from the moment of conception. Under this concept, only when the life of the pregnant mother is at stake should the interest of the fetus not prevail.]

VIII

The Constitution does not explicitly mention any right of privacy. In a line of decisions, however, going back perhaps as far as Union Pacific R. Co. v. Botsford, 141 U.S. 250, 251 (1891), the Court has recognized that a right of personal privacy, or a guarantee of certain areas or zones of privacy, does exist under the Constitution ...

This right of privacy, whether it be founded in the Fourteenth Amendment's concept of personal liberty and restrictions upon state action, as we feel it is, or, as the District Court determined, in the Ninth Amendment's reservation of rights to the people, is broad enough to encompass a woman's decision whether or not to terminate her pregnancy. The detriment that the State would impose upon the pregnant woman by denying this choice altogether is apparent. Specific and direct harm medically diagnosable even in early pregnancy may be involved. Maternity, or additional offspring, may force upon the woman a distressful life and future. Psychological harm may be imminent. Mental and physical health may be taxed by child care. There is also the distress, for all concerned, associated with the unwanted child, and there is the problem of bringing a child into a family already unable, psychologically and otherwise, to care for it. In other cases, as in this one, the additional difficulties and continuing stigma of unwed motherhood may be involved. All these are factors the woman and her responsible physician necessarily will consider in consultation.

On the basis of elements such as these, appellant and some *amici* argue that the woman's right is absolute and that she is entitled to terminate her pregnancy at whatever time, in whatever way, and for whatever reason she alone chooses. With this we do not agree.... The Court's decisions recognizing a right of privacy also acknowledge that some state regulation in areas protected by that right is appropriate....

We, therefore, conclude that the right of personal privacy includes the abortion decision, but that this right is not unqualified and must be considered against important state interests in regulation....

IX

[*This section analyzes whether a fetus is a "person" within the language and meaning of the Fourteenth Amendment. The Constitution refers to "person" in the Fourteenth Amendment, the Due Process and Equal Protection Clauses, and elsewhere, but "in nearly all these instances, the use of the word is such that it has application only postnatally. None indicates, with any assurance, that it has any possible pre-natal application." Texas argued that life begins at conception and is present throughout pregnancy, and that it has a compelling interest in protecting the fetus from and after conception. "We need not resolve the difficult question of when life begins. When those trained in the respective disciplines of medicine, philosophy, and theology are unable to arrive at any consensus, the judiciary, at this point in the development of man's knowledge, is not in a position to speculate as to the answer."*]

X

... We repeat ... that the State does have an important and legitimate interest in preserving and protecting the health of the pregnant woman, ... These interests are separate and distinct. Each grows in substantiality as the woman approaches term and, at a point during pregnancy, each becomes "compelling."

With respect to the State's important and legitimate interest in the health of the mother, the "compelling" point, in the light of present medical knowledge, is at approximately the end of the first trimester. This is so because of the now-established medical fact ... that until the end of the first trimester mortality in abortion may be less than mortality in normal childbirth. It follows that, from and after this point, a State may regulate the abortion procedure to the extent that the regulation reasonably relates to the preservation and protection of maternal health. Examples of permissible state regulation in this area are requirements as to the qualifications of the person who is to perform the abortion; as to the licensure of that person; as to the facility in which the procedure is to be performed, that is, whether it must be a hospital or may be a clinic or some other place of less-than-hospital status; as to the licensing of the facility; and the like.

This means, on the other hand, that, for the period of pregnancy prior to this "compelling" point, the attending physician, in consultation with his patient, is free to determine, without regulation by the State, that, in his medical judgment, the patient's pregnancy should be terminated. If that decision is reached, the judgment may be effectuated by an abortion free of interference by the State.

With respect to the State's important and legitimate interest in potential life, the "compelling" point is at viability. This is so because the fetus then presumably has the capability of meaningful life outside the mother's womb. State regulation protective of fetal life after viability thus has both logical and biological justifications. If the State is interested in protecting fetal life after viability, it may go so far as to proscribe abortion during that period, except when it is necessary to preserve the life or health of the mother.

Measured against these standards, Art. 1196 of the Texas Penal Code, in restricting legal abortions to those "procured or attempted by medical advice for the purpose of saving the life of the mother," sweeps too broadly. The statute makes no distinction between abortions performed early in pregnancy and those performed later, and it limits to a single reason, "saving" the mother's life, the legal justification for the procedure. The statute, therefore, cannot survive the constitutional attack made upon it here....

XI

To summarize and to repeat ...

(a) For the stage prior to approximately the end of the first trimester, the abortion decision and its effectuation must be left to the medical judgment of the pregnant woman's attending physician.

(b) For the stage subsequent to approximately the end of the first trimester, the State, in promoting its interest in the health of the mother, may, if it chooses, regulate the abortion procedure in ways that are reasonably related to maternal health.

(c) For the stage subsequent to viability, the State in promoting its interest in the potentiality of human life may, if it chooses, regulate, and even proscribe, abortion except where it is necessary, in appropriate medical judgment, for the preservation of the life or health of the mother....

[*Chief Justice Burger and Justices Douglas and Stewart wrote separate concurring opinions.*]

Mr. Justice Rehnquist, dissenting....

... If the Texas statute were to prohibit an abortion even where the mother's life is in jeopardy, I have little doubt that such a statute would lack a rational relation to a valid state objective.... But the Court's sweeping invalidation of any restrictions on abortion during the first trimester is impossible to justify under that standard, and the conscious weighing of competing factors that the Court's opin-ion apparently substitutes for the established test is far more appropriate to a legislative judgment than to a judicial one....

... The decision here to break pregnancy into three distinct terms and to outline the permissible restrictions the State may impose in each one, for example, partakes more of judicial legislation than it does of a determination of the intent of the drafters of the Fourteenth Amendment....

Mr. Justice White, with whom Mr. Justice Rehnquist joins, dissenting.

... I find nothing in the language or history of the Constitution to support the Court's judgment. The Court simply fashions and announces a new constitutional right for pregnant mothers and, with scarcely any reason or authority for its action, invests that right with sufficient substance to override most existing state abortion statutes. The upshot is that the people and the legislatures of the 50 States are constitutionally disentitled to weigh the relative importance of the continued existence and development of the fetus, on the one hand, against a spectrum of possible impacts on the mother, on the other hand. As an exercise of raw judicial power, the Court perhaps has authority to do what it does today; but in my view its judgment is an improvident and extravagant exercise of the power of judicial review that the Constitution extends to this Court....

Hyde Amendment of 1976: Congressional Debate

As an amendment to the Labor-HEW appropriations bill for fiscal 1977, Cong. Henry J. Hyde (R-Ill.) offered language to prohibit any of the funds appropriated in the bill "to pay for abortions or to promote or encourage abortions." His amendment passed in the Committee of the Whole, 207-167, and again in the full House, 199-165. After action by the Senate and conference committee, the enacted language read: "None of the funds contained in this Act shall be used to perform abortions except where the life of the mother would be endangered if the fetus were carried to term." 90 Stat. 1434, § 209 (1976).

Mr. HYDE. Mr. Chairman, I offer an amendment.

The Clerk read as follows:

"Amendment offered by Mr. HYDE: On page 36, after line 9, add the following new section:
'Sec. 209. None of the funds appropriated under this Act shall be used to pay for abortions or to promote or encourage abortions.'"

Mr. HYDE.... [T]there are those of us who be-lieve it is to the everlasting shame of this country that in 1973 approximately 800,000 legal abortions were performed in this country—and so it is fair to assume that this year over a million human lives will be destroyed because they are inconvenient to someone.

The unborn child facing an abortion can best be classified as a member of the innocently inconvenient and since the pernicious doctrine that some lives are more important than others seems to be persuasive with the pro-abortion forces, we who seek to protect that most defenseless and innocent of human lives, the unborn—seek to inhibit the use of Federal funds to pay for and thus encourage abortion as an answer to the human and compelling problem of an unwanted child.

We are all exercised at the wanton killing of the porpoise, the baby seal. We urge big game hunters to save the tiger, but we somehow turn away at the specter of a million human beings being violently destroyed because this great, society does not want them.

And make no mistake, an abortion is violent.

I think in the final analysis, you must determine whether or not the unborn person is human. If you think it is animal or vegetable then, of course, it is disposable like an empty beer can to be crushed and thrown out with the rest of the trash.

But medicine, biology, embryology, say that growing living organism is not animal or vegetable or mineral—but it is a human life.

And if you believe that human life is deserving of due process of law—of equal protection of the laws, then you cannot in logic and conscience help fund the execution of these innocent defenseless human lives....

We hear the claim that the poor are denied a right available to other women if we do not use tax money to fund abortions.

Well, make a list of all the things society denies poor women and let them make the choice of what we will give them.

Don't say "poor women, go destroy your young, and we will pay for it."

An innocent, defenseless human life, in a caring and humane society deserves better than to be flushed down a toilet or burned in an incinerator.

The promise of America is that life is not just for the privileged, the planned, or the perfect....

Mr. FLOOD. Mr. Chairman, I rise in opposition to the amendment.

... [E]verybody knows my position for many years with respect to abortion. I believe it is wrong, with a capital "W". It violates the most basic rights, the right of the unborn child, the right to life.

It is for that reason that I have supported for many, many years constitutional amendments which would address this very serious matter, and the Members know it. So, what am I doing down here now? Well, I will tell you. I oppose this amendment, and I will tell you why. Listen. This is blatantly discriminatory; that is why.

The Members do not like that? Of course they do not. It does not prohibit abortion. No, it does not prohibit abortion. It prohibits abortion for poor people. That is what it does.... It does not require any change in the practice of the middle-income and the upper-income people. Oh, no. They are able to go to their private practitioners and get the service done for a fee. But, it does take away the option from those of our citizens who must rely on medicaid—and other public programs for medical care....

This is not the place, on an appropriation bill, to address that kind of issue. This is not. Mr. Chairman, this is an appropriation bill. This is not a constitutional amendment....

Mr. BAUMAN....

The gentleman from Pennsylvania objects to using an appropriation bill for the purpose of making public policy, but no question was raised against the form of this amendment, and none could be, because it is a legitimate limit on the expenditure of Federal funds.

The gentleman raises an interesting, but I think answerable, point on the grounds that this would discriminate against poor people. The answer is that we have not been able to pass a constitutional amendment that would permit the right to life, regardless of poverty or wealth....

I think the unborn children whose lives are being snuffed out, even though they may not be adults have a right to live, too, regardless of the mistaken and immoral Supreme Court decision. I do not think the taxpayers of the United States have any obligation to permit their money to be used in this manner for federally financed abortions. That is the only issue here today....

Ms. ABZUG. Mr. Chairman, ... the issue confronting this body is whether it will conduct itself with respect for the normal processes in which we engage and for which we were sent here. The issue being discussed here today is irrelevant, nongermane, and inappropriate as it relates to this measure, because the relief that is being sought by those who have a very particular point of view cannot be accomplished by this amendment....

The implementation of this amendment or an amendment like this, if agreed to in this House, will mean only one thing, and that will be, as was pointed out by the subcommittee chairman, to deny to some people the rights the majority have in this country.

Harris v. McRae

448 U.S. 297 (1980)

Since 1976, versions of the Hyde Amendment passed by Congress severely limited the use of any federal funds to reimburse the cost of abortions under the Medicaid program. Cora McRae brought an action in federal court, challenging the Hyde Amendment on the ground that it violated the Due Process Clause of the Fifth Amendment and the Religion Clauses of the First Amendment. The defendant was Patricia R. Harris, Secretary of Health and Human Services. The district court held that the Amendment violated the equal protection component of the Fifth Amendment's Due Process Clause and the Free Exercise Clause of the First Amendment.

MR. JUSTICE STEWART delivered the opinion of the Court.

This case presents statutory and constitutional questions concerning the public funding of abortions under Title XIX of the Social Security Act, commonly known as the "Medicaid" Act, and recent annual Appropriations Acts containing the so-called "Hyde Amendment." The statutory question is whether Title XIX requires a State that participates in the Medicaid program to fund the cost of medically necessary abortions for which federal reimbursement is unavailable under the Hyde Amendment. The constitutional question, which arises only if Title XIX imposes no such requirement, is whether the Hyde Amendment, by denying public funding for certain medically necessary abortions, contravenes the liberty or equal protection guarantees of the Due Process Clause of the Fifth Amendment, or either of the Religion Clauses of the First Amendment.

I

The Medicaid program was created in 1965, when Congress added Title XIX to the Social Security Act ... for the purpose of providing federal financial assistance to States that choose to reimburse certain costs of medical treatment for needy persons. Although participation in the Medicaid program is entirely optional, once a State elects to participate, it must comply with the requirements of Title XIX....

II–III

[*The Court concludes that Title XIX does not require a participating state to include in its plan any service for which Congress has withheld federal funding. It next considers the constitutional validity of the Hyde Amendment.*]

[III.A]

We address first the appellees' argument that the Hyde Amendment, by restricting the availability of certain medically necessary abortions under Medic-

aid, impinges on the "liberty" protected by the Due Process Clause as recognized in *Roe* v. *Wade*, 410 U.S. 113, and its progeny....

[*In* Maher v. Roe, *432 U.S. 464 (1977), the Court held that the constitutional freedom recognized in* Roe v. Wade *did not prevent a state from making a value judgment by providing funds to favor childbirth over abortion. A state has no constitutional obligation to subsidize abortions.*]

... [R]egardless of whether the freedom of a woman to choose to terminate her pregnancy for health reasons lies at the core or the periphery of the due process liberty recognized in *Wade*, it simply does not follow that a woman's freedom of choice carries with it a constitutional entitlement to the financial resources to avail herself of the full range of protected choices. The reason why was explained in *Maher:* although government may not place obstacles in the path of a woman's exercise of her freedom of choice, it need not remove those not of its own creation. Indigency falls in the latter category....

... Whether freedom of choice that is constitutionally protected warrants federal subsidization is a question for Congress to answer, not a matter of constitutional entitlement. Accordingly, we conclude that the Hyde Amendment does not impinge on the due process liberty recognized in *Wade*.

B

The appellees also argue that the Hyde Amendment contravenes rights secured by the Religion Clauses of the First Amendment. It is the appellees' view that the Hyde Amendment violates the Establishment Clause because it incorporates into law the doctrines of the Roman Catholic Church concerning the sinfulness of abortion and the time at which life commences. Moreover, insofar as a woman's decision to seek a medically necessary abortion may be a product of her religious beliefs under certain Protestant and Jewish tenets, the appellees assert that the funding limitations of the Hyde Amendment impinge on the freedom of religion guaranteed by the Free Exercise Clause.

1

... [I]t does not follow that a statute violates the Establishment Clause because it "happens to coincide or harmonize with the tenets of some or all religions." *McGowan* v. *Maryland,* 366 U.S. 420, 442. That the Judaeo-Christian religions oppose stealing does not mean that a State or the Federal Government may not, consistent with the Establishment Clause, enact laws prohibiting larceny....

C

It remains to be determined whether the Hyde Amendment violates the equal protection component of the Fifth Amendment. This challenge is premised on the fact that, although federal reimbursement is available under Medicaid for medically necessary services generally, the Hyde Amendment does not permit federal reimbursement of all medically necessary abortions. The District Court held, and the appellees argue here, that this selective subsidization violates the constitutional guarantee of equal protection.

The guarantee of equal protection under the Fifth Amendment is not a source of substantive rights or liberties....

1

For the reasons stated above, we have already concluded that the Hyde Amendment violates no constitutionally protected substantive rights. We now conclude as well that it is not predicated on a constitutionally suspect classification. In reaching this conclusion, we again draw guidance from the Court's decision in *Maher* v. *Roe....*

It is our view that the present case is indistinguishable from *Maher* in this respect. Here, as in *Maher,* the principal impact of the Hyde Amendment falls on the indigent. But that fact does not itself render the funding restriction constitutionally invalid, for this Court has held repeatedly that poverty, standing alone, is not a suspect classification....

2

The remaining question then is whether the Hyde Amendment is rationally related to a legitimate governmental objective. It is the Government's position that the Hyde Amendment bears a rational relationship to its legitimate interest in protecting the potential life of the fetus. We agree....

IV

... Accordingly, the judgment of the District Court is reversed, and the case is remanded to that court for further proceedings consistent with this opinion.

It is so ordered.

MR. JUSTICE WHITE, concurring....

MR. JUSTICE BRENNAN, with whom MR. JUSTICE MARSHALL and MR. JUSTICE BLACKMUN join, dissenting.

... *Roe* and its progeny established that the pregnant woman has a right to be free from state interference with her choice to have an abortion—a right which, at least prior to the end of the first trimester, absolutely prohibits any governmental regulation of that highly personal decision.... The Hyde Amendment's denial of public funds for medically necessary abortions plainly intrudes upon this constitutionally protected decision, for both by design and in effect it serves to coerce indigent pregnant women to bear children that they would otherwise elect not to have....

MR. JUSTICE MARSHALL, dissenting....

The consequences of today's opinion—consequences to which the Court seems oblivious—are not difficult to predict. Pregnant women denied the funding necessary to procure abortions will be restricted to two alternatives. First, they can carry the fetus to term—even though that route may result in severe injury or death to the mother, the fetus, or both. If that course appears intolerable, they can resort to self-induced abortions or attempt to obtain illegal abortions—not because bearing a child would be inconvenient, but because it is necessary in order to protect their health....

MR. JUSTICE BLACKMUN, dissenting.

I join the dissent of MR. JUSTICE BRENNAN and agree wholeheartedly with his and MR. JUSTICE STEVENS' respective observations....

MR. JUSTICE STEVENS, dissenting....

Having decided to alleviate some of the hardships of poverty by providing necessary medical care, the government must use neutral criteria in distributing benefits. It may not deny benefits to a financially and medically needy person simply because he is a Republican, a Catholic, or an Oriental—or because he has spoken against a program the government has a legitimate interest in furthering. In sum, it may not create exceptions for the sole purpose of furthering a governmental interest that is constitutionally subordinate to the individual interest that the entire program was designed to protect....

Akron v. Akron Center for Reproductive Health

462 U.S. 416 (1983)

An Akron, Ohio, ordinance required all abortions after the first trimester of pregnancy to be performed in a hospital. The ordinance also established other requirements, including regulations for abortion on an unmarried minor, counseling of the patient by the physician, a 24-hour delay in performing an abortion after a pregnant woman signed a consent form, and procedures for disposing of the fetal remains. A federal district court invalidated some of the requirements and upheld others. The Sixth Circuit sustained some of the lower court's rulings but reversed others.

JUSTICE POWELL delivered the opinion of the Court.

In this litigation we must decide the constitutionality of several provisions of an ordinance enacted by the city of Akron, Ohio, to regulate the performance of abortions....

III

Section 1870.03 of the Akron ordinance requires that any abortion performed "upon a pregnant woman subsequent to the end of the first trimester of her pregnancy" must be "performed in a hospital."...

... [W]e now hold that § 1870.03 is unconstitutional....

There can be no doubt that § 1870.03's second-trimester hospitalization requirement places a significant obstacle in the path of women seeking an abortion. A primary burden created by the requirement is additional cost to the woman. The Court of Appeals noted that there was testimony that a second-trimester abortion costs more than twice as much in a hospital as in a clinic.... Moreover, the court indicated that second-trimester abortions were rarely performed in Akron hospitals.... Thus, a second-trimester hospitalization requirement may force women to travel to find available facilities, resulting in both financial expense and additional health risk....

Akron does not contend that § 1870.03 imposes only an insignificant burden on women's access to abortion, but rather defends it as a reasonable health regulation. This position had strong support at the time of *Roe* v. *Wade,* as hospitalization for second-trimester abortions was recommended by the American Public Health Association (APHA) ... and the American College of Obstetricians and Gynecologists (ACOG).... Since then, however, the safety of second-trimester abortions has increased dramatically.

... The evidence is strong enough to have convinced the APHA to abandon its prior recommendation of hospitalization for all second-trimester abortions....

Similarly, the ACOG no longer suggests that all second-trimester abortions be performed in a hospital....

IV

We turn next to § 1870.05(B), the provision prohibiting a physician from performing an abortion on a minor pregnant woman under the age of 15 unless he obtains "the informed written consent of one of her parents or her legal guardian" or unless the minor obtains "an order from a court having jurisdiction over her that the abortion be performed or induced." ... [*The Court holds this unconstitutional, pointing to earlier holdings (as in* Planned Parenthood of Missouri *v.* Danforth, *428 U.S. 52 (1976)) that ruled against parental consent for minors without an option for consent by a judge.*]

V

The Akron ordinance provides that no abortion shall be performed except "with the informed written consent of the pregnant woman, ... given freely and without coercion." § 1870.06(A). Furthermore, "in order to insure that the consent for an abortion is truly informed consent," the woman must be "orally informed by her attending physician" of the status of her pregnancy, the development of her fetus, the date of possible viability, the physical and emotional complications that may result from an abortion, and the availability of agencies to provide her with assistance and information with respect to birth control, adoption, and childbirth. § 1870.06(B)....

B

... [W]e believe that § 1870.06(B) attempts to extend the State's interest in ensuring "informed consent" beyond permissible limits. First, it is fair to say that much of the information required is designed not to inform the woman's consent but rather to persuade her to withhold it altogether. Subsection

(3) requires the physician to inform his patient that "the unborn child is a human life from the moment of conception," a requirement inconsistent with the Court's holding in *Roe* v. *Wade* that a State may not adopt one theory of when life begins to justify its regulation of abortions.... [S]ubsection (5), that begins with the dubious statement that "abortion is a major surgical procedure" and proceeds to describe numerous possible physical and psychological complications of abortion, is a "parade of horribles" intended to suggest that abortion is a particularly dangerous procedure....

C

Section 1870.06(C) presents a different question. Under this provision, the "attending physician" must inform the woman

"of the particular risks associated with her own pregnancy and the abortion technique to be employed including providing her with at least a general description of the medical instructions to be followed subsequent to the abortion in order to insure her safe recovery, and shall in addition provide her with such other information which in his own medical judgment is relevant to her decision as to whether to have an abortion or carry her pregnancy to term."

The information required clearly is related to maternal health and to the State's legitimate purpose in requiring informed consent. Nonetheless, the Court of Appeals determined that it interfered with the physician's medical judgment "in exactly the same way as section 1870.06(B). It requires the doctor to make certain disclosures in all cases, regardless of his own professional judgment as to the desirability of doing so." ...

... [W]e believe that it is unreasonable for a State to insist that only a physician is competent to provide the information and counseling relevant to informed consent. We affirm the judgment of the Court of Appeals that § 1870.06(C) is invalid.

VI

The Akron ordinance prohibits a physician from performing an abortion until 24 hours after the pregnant woman signs a consent form. § 1870.07.... The Court of Appeals reversed, finding that the inflexible waiting period had "no medical basis," and that careful consideration of the abortion decision by the woman "is beyond the state's power to require." ... We affirm the Court of Appeals' judgment.

The District Court found that the mandatory 24-hour waiting period increases the cost of obtaining an abortion by requiring the woman to make two separate trips to the abortion facility....

VII

Section § 1870.16 of the Akron ordinance requires physicians performing abortions to "insure that the remains of the unborn child are disposed of in a humane and sanitary manner." The Court of Appeals found that the word "humane" was impermissibly vague as a definition of conduct subject to criminal prosecution. The court invalidated the entire provision, declining to sever the word "humane" in order to uphold the requirement that disposal be "sanitary." ... We affirm this judgment....

VIII

We affirm the judgment of the Court of Appeals invalidating those sections of Akron's "Regulations of Abortions" ordinance that deal with parental consent, informed consent, a 24-hour waiting period, and the disposal of fetal remains. The remaining portion of the judgment, sustaining Akron's requirement that all second-trimester abortions be performed in a hospital, is reversed.

It is so ordered.

JUSTICE O'CONNOR, with whom JUSTICE WHITE and JUSTICE REHNQUIST join, dissenting....

... The decision of the Court today graphically illustrates why the trimester approach is a completely unworkable method of accommodating the conflicting personal rights and compelling state interests that are involved in the abortion context.

As the Court indicates today, the State's compelling interest in maternal health changes as medical technology changes, and any health regulation must not "depart from accepted medical practice." ... In applying this standard, the Court holds that "the safety of second-trimester abortions has increased dramatically" since 1973, when *Roe* was decided....

It is not difficult to see that despite the Court's purported adherence to the trimester approach adopted in *Roe,* the lines drawn in that decision have now been "blurred" because of what the Court accepts as technological advancement in the safety of abortion procedure....

Just as improvements in medical technology inevitably will move *forward* the point at which the State may regulate for reasons of maternal health, different technological improvements will move *backward* the point of viability at which the State may proscribe abortions except when necessary to preserve the life and health of the mother.

In 1973, viability before 28 weeks was considered unusual.... However, recent studies have demonstrated increasingly earlier fetal viability. It is certainly reasonable to believe that fetal viability in the first trimester of pregnancy may be possible in the not too distant future....

The *Roe* framework, then, is clearly on a collision course with itself....

Planned Parenthood v. Casey

505 U.S. 833 (1992)

Five provisions of the Pennsylvania Abortion Control Act required that a woman give her informed consent, receive certain information at least 24 hours before the abortion, required a minor to receive the informed consent of one parent (subject to a judicial bypass procedure), required women to first notify their husband (with some exceptions), and imposed certain reporting requirements on facilities providing abortion services. A three-Justice plurality (O'Connor, Kennedy, and Souter) joined with Stevens and Blackmun to preserve a central principle of *Roe* v. *Wade* and to strike down the provision for spousal notification.

JUSTICE O'CONNOR, JUSTICE KENNEDY, and JUSTICE SOUTER announced the judgment of the Court and delivered the opinion of the Court with respect to Parts I, II, III, V-A, V-C, and VI, an opinion with respect to Part V-E, in which JUSTICE STEVENS joins, and an opinion with respect to Parts IV, V-B, and V-D.

I

Liberty finds no refuge in a jurisprudence of doubt. Yet 19 years after our holding that the Constitution protects a woman's right to terminate her pregnancy in its early stages, *Roe* v. *Wade*, 410 U.S. 113 (1973), that definition of liberty is still questioned. Joining the respondents as *amicus curiae*, the United States, as it has done in five other cases in the last decade, again asks us to overrule *Roe*....

After considering the fundamental constitutional questions resolved by *Roe*, principles of institutional integrity, and the rule of *stare decisis*, we are led to conclude this: the essential holding of *Roe* v. *Wade* should be retained and once again reaffirmed.

It must be stated at the outset and with clarity that *Roe*'s essential holding, the holding we reaffirm, has three parts. First is a recognition of the right of the woman to choose to have an abortion before viability and to obtain it without undue interference from the State. Before viability, the State's interests are not strong enough to support a prohibition of abortion or the imposition of a substantial obstacle to the woman's effective right to elect the procedure. Second is a confirmation of the State's power to restrict abortions after fetal viability, if the law contains exceptions for pregnancies which endanger a woman's life or health. And third is the principle that the State has legitimate interests from the outset of the pregnancy in protecting the health of the woman and the life of the fetus that may become a child. These principles do not contradict one another; and we adhere to each....

[III.A.2]

The inquiry into reliance [*by women on* Roe] counts the cost of a rule's repudiation as it would fall on those who have relied reasonably on the rule's continued application....

... [F]or two decades of economic and social developments, people have organized intimate relationships and made choices that define their views of themselves and their places in society, in reliance on the availability of abortion in the event that contraception should fail. The ability of women to participate equally in the economic and social life of the Nation has been facilitated by their ability to control their reproductive lives....

4

We have seen how time has overtaken some of *Roe*'s factual assumptions: advances in maternal health care allow for abortions safe to the mother later in pregnancy than was true in 1973, ... and advances in neonatal care have advanced viability to a point somewhat earlier.... But these facts go only to the scheme of time limits on the realization of competing interests, and the divergences from the factual premises of 1973 have no bearing on the validity of *Roe*'s central holding, that viability marks the earliest point at which the State's interest in fetal life is constitutionally adequate to justify a legislative ban on nontherapeutic abortions. The soundness or unsoundness of that constitutional judgment in no sense turns on whether viability occurs at approximately 28 weeks, as was usual at the time of *Roe,* at 23 to 24 weeks, as it sometimes does today, or at some moment even slightly earlier in pregnancy, as it may if fetal respiratory capacity can somehow be enhanced in the future....

5

The sum of the precedential inquiry to this point shows *Roe*'s underpinnings unweakened in any way affecting its central holding.... Within the bounds of normal *stare decisis* analysis, then, and subject to the considerations on which it customarily turns, the stronger argument is for affirming *Roe*'s central holding, with whatever degree of personal reluctance any of us may have, not for overruling it.

B

[*O'Connor contrasts* Roe *with two earlier decisions eventually overruled in full by the Court:* Lochner v. New York *(1905), which limited the authority of government to regulate health and welfare; and* Plessy v. Ferguson *(1896), which upheld legislatively mandated racial segregation in public transportation. She concludes that* Lochner *represented a "fundamentally false factual assumption" about the capacity of an unregulated market to satisfy minimal levels of human welfare, while it was clear at least by 1954 that legally sanctioned segregation stigmatized blacks with a "badge of inferiority" (an assertion denied by the* Plessy *Court). She also stated that* Plessy *"was wrong the day it was decided."*]

C

... [O]nly the most convincing justification under accepted standards of precedent could suffice to demonstrate that a later decision overruling the first was anything but a surrender to political pressure, and an unjustified repudiation of the principle on which the Court stakes its authority in the first instance. So to overrule under fire in the absence of the most compelling reason to reexamine a watershed decision would subvert the Court's legitimacy beyond any serious question....

IV

[*O'Connor states that it is the duty of the Court to draw a line to determine a woman's right to terminate her pregnancy.*]

We conclude the line should be drawn at viability, so that before that time the woman has a right to choose to terminate her pregnancy. We adhere to this principle for two reasons. First, as we have said, is the doctrine of *stare decisis....*

The second reason is that the concept of viability,

as we noted in *Roe,* is the time at which there is a realistic possibility of maintaining and nourishing a life outside the womb, so that the independent existence of the second life can in reason and all fairness be the object of state protection that now overrides the rights of the woman.... The viability line also has, as a practical matter, an element of fairness. In some broad sense it might be said that a woman who fails to act before viability has consented to the State's intervention on behalf of the developing child....

Though the woman has a right to choose to terminate or continue her pregnancy before viability, it does not at all follow that the State is prohibited from taking steps to ensure that this choice is thoughtful and informed. Even in the earliest stages of pregnancy, the State may enact rules and regulations designed to encourage her to know that there are philosophic and social arguments of great weight that can be brought to bear in favor of continuing the pregnancy to full term and that there are procedures and institutions to allow adoption of unwanted children as well as a certain degree of state assistance if the mother chooses to raise the child herself....

We reject the trimester framework, which we do not consider to be part of the essential holding of *Roe....* The trimester framework suffers from these basic flaws: in its formulation it misconceives the nature of the pregnant woman's interest; and in practice it undervalues the State's interest in potential life, as recognized in *Roe....*

A finding of an undue burden is a shorthand for the conclusion that a state regulation has the purpose or effect of placing a substantial obstacle in the path of a woman seeking an abortion of a nonviable fetus. A statute with this purpose is invalid because the means chosen by the State to further the interest in potential life must be calculated to inform the woman's free choice, not hinder it.

... In our considered judgment, an undue burden is an unconstitutional burden....

V

[*O'Connor applies the undue burden standard to the Pennsylvania statute, which defines medical emergency as "[t]hat condition which, on the basis of the physician's good faith clinical judgment, so complicates the medical condition of a pregnant woman as to necessitate the immediate abortion of her pregnancy to avert her death or for which a delay will create serious risk of substantial and irreversible impairment of a major bodily function." She accepts this interpretation of "serious risk" by the Court of Appeals: "we read the medical emergency exception as intended by the Pennsylvania legislature to assure that compliance with its abortion regulations would not in any way pose a significant threat to the life or health of a woman." Under that interpretation, the medical emergency definition "imposes no undue burden on a woman's abortion right."*]

[*Second: O'Connor considers the informed consent requirement. Except in a medical emergency, at least 24 hours before performing an abortion a physician must inform the woman of the nature of the procedure, the health risks of abortion and childbirth, and the "probable gestational age of the unborn child." She must be informed about the availability of printed materials describing the fetus and providing information about medical assistance for childbirth, information about child support from the father, and a list of agencies that provide adoption and other services as alternatives to abortion. An abortion may not be performed unless the woman certifies in writing that she has been informed of the availability of these printed materials and has been provided them if she chooses to view them. O'Connor decides that a constitutional violation does not exist when the government requires the giving of truthful, nonmisleading information about the nature of the procedure, the attendant health risks and those of childbirth, and the "probable gestational age" of the fetus.*]

[*Third: except in cases of medical emergency, a married woman must provide a signed statement that she has notified her husband that she is about to undergo an abortion. She may provide an alternative signed statement certifying that her husband is not the man who impregnated her, that he could not be located, that the pregnancy is the result of spousal sexual assault that she has reported, or that the woman believes that notifying her husband will cause him or someone else to inflict bodily injury upon her. O'Connor reviews professional studies that suggest that from one-fifth to one-third of all women are physically assaulted by a partner or ex-partner during their lifetime, and notes that many victims of domestic violence remain with their abusers, because they see no alternative. She concludes that the spousal notification requirement is invalid because it imposes a substantial obstacle for many women.*]

[*Fourth: except in a medical emergency, a woman under 18 may not obtain an abortion unless she and one of her parents (or guardian) provides informed consent. If neither a parent nor guardian provides consent, a court may authorize an abortion after determining that the woman is mature and capable of giving informed consent and has in fact given her informed consent, or that an abortion would be in her best interests. O'Connor reaffirms that a state may require a minor seeking an abortion to obtain the consent of a parent or guardian, provided that there is an adequate judicial bypass procedure.*]

[*Finally: when recordkeeping and reporting requirements are reasonably directed to preserving maternal health and properly respect a patient's confidentiality and privacy, they are constitutional except for the provision of spousal notice, which places an undue burden on a woman's choice.*]

JUSTICE STEVENS, concurring in part and dissenting in part. [*Stevens agreed with the three-judge plurality with two exceptions. He regarded the provision for informed consent and the 24-hour waiting period as invalid. Although he agreed that the parental-consent requirement was valid, he did not join that part of the plurality's opinion.*]

JUSTICE BLACKMUN, concurring in part, concurring in the judgment in part, and dissenting in part.

I join parts I, II, III, V-A, V-C, and VI of the joint opinion of JUSTICES O'CONNOR, KENNEDY, and SOUTER, *ante*. [*While agreeing with those parts of the plurality opinion, Blackmun held that the statute was invalid with regard to recordkeeping, informed consent, the 24-hour waiting period, and parental consent. He also disagreed with much of the analysis in Part IV regarding viability, the trimester approach, and the undue burden test.*]

CHIEF JUSTICE REHNQUIST, with whom JUSTICE WHITE, JUSTICE SCALIA, and JUSTICE THOMAS join, concurring in the judgment in part and dissenting in part.

The joint opinion, following its newly-minted variation on *stare decisis,* retains the outer shell of *Roe* v. *Wade,* 410 U.S. 113 (1973), but beats a wholesale retreat from the substance of that case. We believe that *Roe* was wrongly decided, and that it can and should be overruled consistently with our traditional approach of the plurality in *Webster* v. *Reproductive Health Services,* 492 U.S. 490 (1989), and uphold the challenged provisions of the Pennsylvania statute in their entirety.

[*Rehnquist objects to the "undue burden" standard because it is based "even more on a judge's subjective determinations than was the trimester framework" and will "do nothing to prevent 'judges from roaming at large in the constitutional field' guided only by their personal views."*]

JUSTICE SCALIA, with whom THE CHIEF JUSTICE, JUSTICE WHITE, and JUSTICE THOMAS join, concurring in the judgment in part and dissenting in part....

... [B]y foreclosing all democratic outlet for the deep passions this issue arouses, by banishing the issue from the political forum that gives all participants, even the losers, the satisfaction of a fair hearing and an honest fight, by continuing the imposition of a rigid national rule instead of allowing for regional differences, the Court merely prolongs and intensifies the anguish.

We should get out of this area, where we have no right to be, and where we do neither ourselves nor the country any good by remaining.

Stenberg v. Carhart

530 U.S. 914 (2000)

Dr. Leroy Carhart, a physician, brought this lawsuit against Attorney General Don Stenberg of Nebraska, charging that Nebraska's law banning "partial birth abortion" violated the Federal Constitution. The District Court held the statute unconstitutional, the Eighth Circuit affirmed, and the Supreme Court granted cert to decide whether the statute, under the guidelines of *Planned Parenthood* v. *Casey* (1992), constituted an "undue burden" on a woman's right to choose to have an abortion. Much of the opinion by Justice Breyer turns on the legislative intent of the Nebraska statute.

JUSTICE BREYER delivered the opinion of the Court.

We again consider the right to an abortion. We understand the controversial nature of the problem. Millions of Americans believe that life begins at conception and consequently that an abortion is akin to causing the death of an innocent child; they recoil at the thought of a law that would permit it. Other millions fear that a law that forbids abortion would condemn many American women to lives that lack dignity, depriving them of equal liberty and leading those with least resources to undergo illegal abortions with the attendant risks of death and suffering....

Three established principles determine the issue before us. We shall set them forth in the language of the joint opinion in *Casey*. First, before "viability ... the woman has a right to choose to terminate her pregnancy." ...

Second, "a law designed to further the State's interest in fetal life which imposes an undue burden on the woman's decision before fetal viability" is unconstitutional....

Third, "'subsequent to viability, the State in promoting its interest in the potentiality of human life may, if it chooses, regulate, and even proscribe, abortion except where it is necessary, in appropriate medical judgment, for the preservation of the life or health of the mother.'" ...

We apply these principles to a Nebraska law banning "partial birth abortion." The statute reads as follows:

"No partial birth abortion shall be performed in this state, unless such procedure is necessary to save the life of the mother whose life is endangered by a physical disorder, physical illness, or physical injury, including a life-endangering physical condition caused by or arising from the pregnancy itself." ... [*The statute defines "partial birth abortion" as "an abortion procedure in which the person performing the abortion partially delivers vaginally a living unborn child before killing the unborn child and completing the delivery." It defines "partially delivers vaginally a living unborn child before killing the unborn child" to mean "deliberately and intentionally delivering into the vagina a living unborn child, or a substantial portion thereof, for the purpose of performing a procedure that the person performing such procedure knows will kill the unborn child and does kill the unborn child."*]

The law classifies violation of the statute as a "Class III felony" carrying a prison term of up to 20 years, and a fine of up to $25,000.... It also provides for the automatic revocation of a doctor's license to practice medicine in Nebraska....

We hold that this statute violates the Constitution.

[I.B]

Because Nebraska law seeks to ban one method of aborting a pregnancy, we must describe and then discuss several different abortion procedures....

[*About 90% of abortions performed in the United States occur during the first trimester (before 12 weeks). During this period the predominant method is "vacuum aspiration": inserting a vacuum tube (can-*

nula) into the uterus to evacuate the contents. The remaining 10% of abortions are performed during the second trimester (12 to 24 weeks). The most common procedure is "dilation and evacuation" (D&E), relying on a modified form of vacuum aspiration.]

[Between 13 and 15 weeks, D&E is similar to vacuum aspiration except that the cervix is dilated more widely to remove larger pieces of tissue. Because fetal tissue is easily broken, the fetus may not be removed intact. After 15 weeks, the fetus is larger (particularly the head) and bones are more rigid. Dismemberment or other destructive procedures are therefore more likely to be required. After 20 weeks, some physicians use potassium chloride or digoxin to kill the fetus to facilitate evacuation. D&E carries certain risks. The use of instruments within the uterus may cause accidental perforation and damage neighboring organs. Sharp fetal bone fragments create dangers. Fetal tissue accidentally left behind may cause infection and other complications.]

[A variation of D&E, referred to as an "intact D&E," begins with induced dilation of the cervix and removal of the fetus from the uterus through the cervix "intact" (in one pass rather than in several passes). It is used after 16 weeks. Vacuum aspiration is ineffective because the fetal skull is too large to pass through the cervix. If the fetus comes head first, the doctor collapses the skull and extracts the entire fetus through the cervix. If the fetus comes feet first, the doctor pulls the fetal body through the cervix, collapses the skull, and extracts the fetus through the cervix. The breech extraction version of the intact D&E is also known as "dilation and extraction" (D&X).]

II

The question before us is whether Nebraska's statute, making criminal the performance of a "partial birth abortion," violates the Federal Constitution, as interpreted in *Planned Parenthood of Southeastern Pa. v. Casey* ... and *Roe* v. *Wade*.... We conclude that it does for at least two independent reasons. First, the law lacks any exception "'for the preservation of the ... health of the mother.'" *Casey*, 505 U.S., at 879 (joint opinion of O'CONNOR, KENNEDY, and SOUTER, JJ.). Second, it "imposes an undue burden on a woman's ability" to choose a D&E abortion, thereby unduly burdening the right to choose abortion itself....

[A.2–3]

[Nebraska, along with supporting amici, said that D&X is "little-used" and only by "a handful of doctors." Breyer agrees that D&E is infrequently used, "but the health exception question is whether protect-

ing women's health requires an exception for those infrequent occasions." Nebraska argued that D&E and labor induction are at all times "safe alternative procedures." The District Court agreed that alternatives, such as D&E and induced labor, are "safe" but found that D&X was significantly safer in certain circumstances. Nebraska emphasized that no medical studies established the safety of the partial-birth/D&X procedure and no medical studies compared the relative safety of partial-birth/D&X to other abortion procedures. Breyer agrees that there "are no general medical studies documenting comparative safety."]

4

... Nebraska has not convinced us that a health exception is "never necessary to preserve the health of women." ... Rather, a statute that altogether forbids D&X creates a significant health risk. The statute consequently must contain a health exception. This is not to say, as JUSTICE THOMAS and JUSTICE KENNEDY claim, that a State is prohibited from proscribing an abortion procedure whenever a particular physician deems the procedure preferable. By no means must a State grant physicians "unfettered discretion" in their selection of abortion methods....

B

. . .

Our earlier discussion of the D&E procedure ... shows that it falls within the statutory prohibition. The statute forbids "deliberately and intentionally delivering into the vagina a living unborn child, or a substantial portion thereof, for the purpose of performing a procedure that the person performing such procedure knows will kill the unborn child." ... We do not understand how one could distinguish, using this language, between D&E (where a foot or arm is drawn through the cervix) and D&X (where the body up to the head is drawn through the cervix)....

Even if the statute's basic aim is to ban D&X, its language makes clear that it also covers a much broader category of procedures. The language does not track the medical differences between D&E and D&X—though it would have been a simple matter, for example, to provide an exception for the performance of D&E and other abortion procedures....

[Breyer does not accept Stenberg's argument that the statute differentiates between the two procedures and that the statutory words "substantial portion" mean "the child up to the head." The two lower courts rejected Stenberg's narrowing interpretation and so does Breyer. Stenberg points to the legislature's debates, but Breyer finds that the debates "hurt his argument more *than they help it," because some lawmakers understood "substantial" to mean as small a portion of the fetus as a foot.*]

In sum, using this law some present prosecutors and future Attorneys General may choose to pursue physicians who use D&E procedures, the most commonly used method for performing previability second trimester abortions. All those who perform abortion procedures using that method must fear prosecution, conviction, and imprisonment. The result is an undue burden upon a woman's right to make an abortion decision. We must consequently find the statute unconstitutional.

The judgment of the Court of Appeals is

Affirmed.

JUSTICE STEVENS, with whom JUSTICE GINSBURG joins, concurring.

Although much ink is spilled today describing the gruesome nature of late-term abortion procedures, that rhetoric does not provide me a reason to believe that the procedure Nebraska here claims it seeks to ban is more brutal, more gruesome, or less respectful of "potential life" than the equally gruesome procedure Nebraska claims it still allows....

[*Justice O'Connor wrote a separate concurrence, as did Justice Ginsburg (joined by Justice Stevens.)*]

CHIEF JUSTICE REHNQUIST, dissenting.

I did not join the joint opinion in *Planned Parenthood of Southeastern Pa.* v. *Casey* ... and continue to believe that case is wrongly decided. Despite my disagreement with the opinion, ... the *Casey* joint opinion represents the holding of the Court in that case. I believe JUSTICE KENNEDY and JUSTICE THOMAS have correctly applied *Casey*'s principles and join their dissenting opinions.

JUSTICE SCALIA, dissenting.

... [*The decision*] has been arrived at by precisely the process *Casey* promised—a democratic vote by nine lawyers, not on the question whether the text of the Constitution has anything to say about this subject (it obviously does not); nor even on the question (also appropriate for lawyers) whether the legal traditions of the American people would have sustained such a limitation upon abortion (they obviously would); but upon the pure policy question whether this limitation upon abortion is "undue"— *i.e.*, goes too far.

... [T]hose who believe that a 5-to-4 vote on a policy matter by unelected lawyers should not overcome the judgment of 30 state legislatures have a problem, not with the application of *Casey*, but with its existence. *Casey* must be overruled.

... If only for the sake of its own preservation, the Court should return this matter to the people— where the Constitution, by its silence on the subject, left it—and let them decide, State by State, ...

JUSTICE KENNEDY, with whom THE CHIEF JUSTICE joins, dissenting.

... When the Court [in *Casey*] reaffirmed the essential holding of *Roe*, a central premise was that the States retain a critical and legitimate role in legislating on the subject of abortion, as limited by the woman's right the Court restated and again guaranteed.... The political processes of the State are not to be foreclosed from enacting laws to promote the life of the unborn and to ensure respect for all human life and its potential....

JUSTICE THOMAS, with whom THE CHIEF JUSTICE and JUSTICE SCALIA join, dissenting.

... Nothing in our Federal Constitution deprives the people of this country of the right to determine whether the consequences of abortion to the fetus and to society outweigh the burden of an unwanted pregnancy on the mother....

[*In analyzing the statutory language, Thomas concludes that it is "highly doubtful that the statute could be applied to ordinary D&E." He argues that "there is no doubt that the Nebraska statute is susceptible of a narrowing construction by Nebraska courts that would preserve a physician's ability to perform D&E."*]

Gonzales v. Carhart

550 U.S. 124 (2007)

Dr. Carhart brought this lawsuit against Attorney General Gonzales, charging that the Partial-Birth Abortion Ban Act of 2003 was unconstitutional on various grounds, including vagueness and imposing an undue burden on a woman's right to abortion. The Court compared the congressional statute with the Nebraska statute struck down in *Stenberg* v. *Carhart*(2000).

JUSTICE KENNEDY delivered the opinion of the Court.

... Compared to the state statute at issue in *Stenberg*, the Act is more specific concerning the instances to which it applies and in this respect is more precise in its coverage. We conclude the Act should be sustained against the objections lodged by the broad, facial attack brought against it.

[*In describing abortion procedures in the second trimester, Justice Kennedy uses very powerful and graphic language: "After sufficient dilation the surgical operation can commence. The woman is placed under general anesthesia or conscious sedation. The doctor, often guided by ultrasound, inserts grasping forceps through the woman's cervix and into the uterus to grab the fetus. The doctor grips a fetal part with the forceps and pulls it back through the cervix and vagina, continuing to pull even after meeting resistance from the cervix. The friction causes the fetus to tear apart. For example, a leg might be ripped off the fetus as it is pulled through the cervix and out of the woman. The process of evacuating the fetus piece by piece continues until it has been completely removed." Relying on one doctor's description, when the fetus' head cannot pass through the cervix, the surgeon forces the scissors into the base of the skull, spreads the scissors to enlarge the opening, and introduces a suction catheter into the hole to evacuate the skull contents. A nurse offered this account: "The doctor opened up the scissors, stuck a high-powered suction tube into the opening, and sucked the baby's brains out. Now the baby went completely limp ... He cut the umbilical cord and delivered the placenta. He threw the baby in a pan, along with the placenta and the instruments he had just used." Other doctors pulled the fetus out of the woman "until it disarticulates at the neck, in effect decapitating it."*]

[I.B.]

... [*The congressional statute*] responded to *Stenberg* in two ways. First, Congress made factual findings. Congress determined that this Court in *Stenberg* "was required to accept the very questionable findings issued by the district court judge," ... but that Congress was "not bound to accept the same factual findings." ... Congress found, among other things, that "[a] moral, medical, and ethical consensus exists that the practice of performing a partial-birth abortion ... is a gruesome and inhumane procedure that is never medically necessary and should be prohibited." ...

Second, and more relevant here, the Act's language differs from that of the Nebraska statute

struck down in *Stenberg*. The operative provisions of the Act provide in relevant part:

"(a) Any physician who, in or affecting interstate or foreign commerce, knowingly performs a partial-birth abortion and thereby kills a human fetus shall be fined under this title or imprisoned not more than 2 years, or both. This subsection does not apply to a partial-birth abortion that is necessary to save the life of a mother whose life is endangered by a physical disorder, physical illness, or physical injury, including a life-endangering physical condition caused by or arising from the pregnancy itself." [*The statute defines partial-birth abortion as deliberately and intentionally vaginally delivering a living fetus. In a head-first presentation, the entire fetal head is outside the body of the mother. In the case of breech presentation, any part of the fetal trunk past the navel is outside the mother's body. The physician knows that the procedure will kill the partially delivered living fetus. A woman subject to partial-birth abortion may not be prosecuted under this law.*]

[*The Eighth Circuit invalidated the statute by asking "whether 'substantial medical authority' supports the medical necessity of the banned procedure" (quoting* Stenberg*). It reasoned that "when a lack of consensus exists in the medical community, the Constitution requires legislatures to err on the side of protecting women's health by including a health exception," which was absent in the congressional statute. The Ninth Circuit agreed with a district court decision that the statute posed an undue burden on a woman's ability to choose a second trimester abortion, was unconstitutionally vague, and required a health exception as set forth in* Stenberg.*]

II

... Whatever one's views concerning the *Casey* joint opinion, it is evident a premise central to its conclusion—that the government has a legitimate and substantial interest in preserving and promoting fetal life—would be repudiated were the Court now to affirm the judgments of the Courts of Appeal....

III

[*Kennedy rejects the position of the appellate courts that the statute is void for vagueness and imposes an undue burden on a woman. The statute applies only to vaginal deliveries and to an overt act by a physician that causes the fetus' death separate from delivery. The physician must act deliberately and intentionally. "If a living fetus is delivered past the critical point by accident or inadvertence, the Act is inapplicable." The statute "sets forth 'relatively clear guide-*

lines as to prohibited conduct' and provides 'objective criteria' to evaluate whether a doctor has performed a prohibited procedure." Unlike the Nebraska law in Stenberg *"that prohibited the delivery of a 'substantial portion' of the fetus— where a doctor might question how much of the fetus is a substantial portion— the Act defines the line between potentially criminal conduct on the one hand and lawful abortion on the other." As to undue burden, Kennedy concludes that the statute prohibits "intact D&E" but "does not prohibit the D&E procedure in which the fetus is removed in parts" within the woman's body. "The Court in* Stenberg *interpreted 'substantial portion' of the fetus to include an arm or a leg." The congressional statute clarifies that "the removal of a small portion of the fetus is not prohibited." The fetus must be delivered "so that it is partially 'outside the body of the mother.'" In case the cervix dilates to an unexpected degree so that the fetus can be removed largely intact, partially outside the body, Kennedy states that a doctor under those circumstances would not have the intent to violate the statute. A lack of intent would "preclude liability from attaching to an accidental intact D&E."]*

The evidence also supports a legislative determination that an intact delivery is almost always a conscious choice rather than a happenstance. Doctors, for example, may remove the fetus in a manner than will increase the chances of an intact delivery.... And intact D&E is usually described as involving some manner of serial dilation.... Doctors who do not seek to obtain this serial dilation perform an intact D&E on far fewer occasions.... This evidence belies any claim that a standard D&E cannot be performed without intending or foreseeing an intact D&E.

Many doctors who testified on behalf of respondents [*Dr. Carhart and other physicians*], and who objected to the Act, do not perform an intact D&E by accident. On the contrary, they begin every D&E abortion with the objective of removing the fetus as intact as possible.... This does not prove, as respondents suggest, that every D&E might violate the Act and that the Act therefore imposes an undue burden. It demonstrates only that those doctors who intend to perform a D&E that would involve delivery of a living fetus to one of the Act's anatomical landmarks must adjust their conduct to the law by not attempting to deliver the fetus to either of those points....

IV

[*Kennedy in this section denies that the statute imposes a substantial obstacle to "late-term, but previability," abortions. "The Act does not on its face impose a sub-*

stantial obstacle, and we reject this further facial challenge to its validity."]

Respect for human life finds an ultimate expression in the bond of love the mother has for her child. The Act recognizes this reality as well. Whether to have an abortion requires a difficult and painful moral decision.... While we find no reliable data to measure the phenomenon, it seems unexceptionable to conclude some women come to regret their choice to abort the infant life they once created and sustained.... Severe depression and loss of esteem can follow....

It is objected that the standard D&E is in some respects as brutal, if not more, than the intact D&E, so that the legislation accomplishes little. What we have already said, however, shows ample justification for the regulation. Partial-birth abortion, as defined by the Act, differs from a standard D&E because the former occurs when the fetus is partially outside the mother to the point of one of the Act's anatomical landmarks. It was reasonable for Congress to think that partial-birth abortion, more than standard D&E, "undermines the public's perception of the appropriate role of a physician during the delivery process, and perverts a process during which life is brought into the world." Congressional Findings ...

Respondents have not demonstrated that the Act, as a facial matter, is void for vagueness, or that it imposes an undue burden on a woman's right to abortion based on its overbreadth or lack of a health exception. For those reasons the judgments of the Courts of Appeals for the Eight and Ninth Circuits are reversed.

It is so ordered.

JUSTICE THOMAS, with whom JUSTICE SCALIA joins, concurring.

I join the Court's opinion because it accurately applies current jurisprudence, including *Planned Parenthood of Southeastern Pa.* v. *Casey*, 505 U.S. 833 (1992). I write separately to reiterate my view that the Court's abortion jurisprudence, including *Casey* and *Roe* v. *Wade*, 410 U.S. 113 (1973), has no basis in the Constitution....

JUSTICE GINSBURG, with whom JUSTICE STEVENS, JUSTICE SOUTER, and JUSTICE BREYER join, dissenting.

In *Planned Parenthood of Southeastern Pa.* v. *Casey*, 505 U.S. 833, 844 (1992), the Court declared that "[l]iberty finds no refuge in a jurisprudence of doubt." There was, the Court said, an "imperative" need to dispel doubt as to "the meaning and reach" of the Court's 7-to-2 judgment, rendered nearly two decades earlier in *Roe* v. *Wade*, 410 U.S. 113 (1973)....

Today's decision is alarming. It refuses to take *Casey* and *Stenberg* seriously. It tolerates, indeed applauds, federal intervention to ban nationwide a procedure found necessary and proper in certain cases by the American College of Obstetricians and Gynecologists (ACOG). It blurs the line, firmly drawn in *Casey*, between previability and postviability abortions. And, for the first time since *Roe*, the Court blesses a prohibition with no exceptions safeguarding a woman's health....

In *Stenberg*, we expressly held that a statute banning intact D&E was unconstitutional in part because it lacked a health exception. 530 U.S., at 930, 937. We noted that there existed a "division of medical opinion" about the relative safety of intact D&E, *id.*, at 937, but we made clear that as long as "substantial medical authority supports the proposition that banning a particular abortion procedure could endanger women's health," a health exception is required, ...

Thus, we reasoned, division in medical opinion "at most means uncertainty, a factor that signals the presence of risk, not its absence." ..."[A] statute that altogether forbids [intact D&E] ... consequently must contain a health exception." ... [*Note 4 provides: "The Act's sponsors left no doubt that their intention was to nullify our ruling in* Stenberg, *530 U.S. 914. See, e.g., 149 Cong. Rec. 5731 (2003) (statement of Sen. Santorum) ("Why are we here? We are here because the Supreme Court defended the indefensible.... We have responded to the Supreme Court."). See also 148 Cong. Rec. 14273 (2002) (statement of Rep. Linder) (rejecting proposition that Congress has "no right to legislate a ban on this horrible practice because the Supreme Court says* [*it*] *cannot").*]

As another reason for upholding the ban, the Court emphasizes that the Act does not proscribe the nonintact D&E procedure.... But why not, one might ask. Nonintact D&E could equally be characterized as "brutal," ... involving as it does "tear[ing] [a fetus] apart" and "ripp[ing] off" its limbs, ..."[T]he notion that either of these two equally gruesome procedures ... is more akin to infanticide than the other, or that the State furthers any legitimate interest by banning one but not the other, is simply irrational." *Stenberg*, 530 U.S., at 946–947 (STEVENS, J., concurring).

Delivery of an intact, albeit nonviable, fetus warrants special condemnation, the Court maintains, because a fetus that is not dismembered resembles an infant.... But so, too, does a fetus delivered intact after it is terminated by injection a day or two before the surgical evacuation, ... or a fetus delivered through medical induction or cesarean....

[*Ginsburg challenges Kennedy's reliance on "moral concerns" by pointing to his own decision for the Court in* Lawrence v. Texas *(2003), regarding homosexual conduct, where he said the purpose of the Court "is to define the liberty of all, not to mandate our own moral code." As to Kennedy's statement that women who have abortions may come to regret their choice and suffer from severe depression and loss of esteem, and the "bond of love the mother has for her child," she finds that way of thinking reflective of "ancient notions about women's place in the family and under the Constitution—ideas that have long since been discredited" (citing cases about protective legislation and the* Bradwell *case on women practicing law*).]

... The Court's hostility to the right *Roe* and *Casey* secured is not concealed. Throughout, the opinion refers to obstetrician-gynecologists and surgeons who perform abortions not by the titles of their medical specialists, but by the pejorative label "abortion doctor." ... A fetus is described as an "unborn child," and as a "baby." ... second-trimester, previability abortions are referred to as "late-term,"....

D. THE RIGHT TO DIE

Questions of privacy include the right to die for the elderly and for patients who survive solely because of life-support systems with no hope of recovery. An especially tragic case concerned Karen Ann Quinlan, who at 22 years of age lay in a New Jersey hospital in what the state court called a "vegetative existence." Her parents wanted to withdraw the life-sustaining mechanism and allow her to die naturally. After lengthy and anguished litigation, they gained that right. Matter of Quinlan, 355 A.2d 647 (N.J. 1976) (see box on next page).

The issue in the Quinlan case reached the U.S. Supreme Court in 1990. The Court divided 5–4 in deciding that the federal constitution does not forbid Missouri to require "clear and convincing" ev-

The Karen Ann Quinlan Case

The father of Karen Ann Quinlan, a 22-year-old in a persistent vegetative state, asked the state to discontinue all extraordinary procedures for sustaining her life. The Supreme Court of New Jersey, concluding that "she can *never* be restored to cognitive or sapient life," granted his request. Excerpts from the court's decision appear below. Matter of Quinlan, 355 A.2d 647, 662–64 (N.J. 1976).

HUGHES, C.J....

It is the issue of the constitutional right of privacy that has given us most concern, in the exceptional circumstances of this case....

The claimed interests of the State in this case are essentially the preservation and sanctity of human life and defense of the right of the physician to administer medical treatment according to his best judgment. In this case the doctors say that removing Karen from the respirator will conflict with their professional judgment. The plaintiff answers that Karen's present treatment serves only a maintenance function; that the respirator cannot cure or improve her condition but at best can only prolong her inevitable slow deterioration and death; and that the interests of the patient, as seen by her surrogate, the guardian, must be evaluated by the court as predominant, even in the face of an opinion *contra* by the present attending physicians. Plaintiff's distinction is significant. The nature of Karen's care and the realistic changes of her recovery are quite unlike those of the patients discussed in many of the cases where treatments were ordered. In many of those cases the medical procedure required (usually a transfusion) constituted a minimal body invasion and the chances of recovery and return to functioning life were very good. We think that the State's interest *contra* weakens and the individual's right to privacy grows as the degree of bodily invasion increases and the prognosis dims. Ultimately there comes a point at which the individual's rights overcome the State interest. It is for that reason that we believe Karen's choice, if she were competent to make it, would be vindicated by the law....

Our affirmation of Karen's independent right of choice, however, would ordinarily be based upon her competency to assert it. The sad truth, however, is that she is grossly incompetent and we cannot discern her supposed choice based on the testimony of her previous conversations with friends, where such testimony is without sufficient probative weight.... Nevertheless, we have concluded that Karen's right of privacy may be asserted on her behalf by her guardian under the peculiar circumstances here present.

idence that an incompetent, permanently unconscious person wishes the withdrawal of life-support systems. The Court also held that a competent person has a constitutional right to refuse such systems. Other states may adopt more liberal laws than Missouri's, and individuals may protect their privacy rights to some extent by signing "living wills" that express their desire to reject life-support systems. CRUZAN v. DIRECTOR, MISSOURI DEPT. OF HEALTH, 497 U.S. 261 (1990). Six months after the Court's ruling, a Missouri court ruled that clear and convincing evidence justified the withdrawal of food and water from Nancy Cruzan. She died on December 26, 1990.

In response to *Cruzan*, Congress passed the Patient Self-Determination Act to require health-care providers in Medicare and Medicaid programs to give patients information about living wills and to educate staff about rights and procedures under state law. For example, patients must be informed about their right to grant power of attorney to someone else to make such a decision. 104 Stat. 1388-117, § 4027 (1990).

Assisted Suicide

At the state level, legal questions were raised about individuals who assisted others to commit suicide. Jack Kevorkian, a retired pathologist, used a machine that allowed terminally ill patients to inhale carbon monoxide. By 1993 he had assisted 19 people with such procedures. Murder charges brought by

Michigan prosecutors were dropped because the state had no law against assisted suicide. Although Michigan passed legislation in 1992 to make assisted suicide a felony, Kevorkian continued to defy the law. In several subsequent prosecutions, Kevorkian was acquitted, but he was sentenced to prison in 1999. His appeal to the Supreme Court was rejected in 2002 when the Court denied cert to hear his case. Kervokian v. Michigan, 537 U.S. 881 (2002).

In 1996, the Second Circuit struck down New York's law making it a crime for a physician to assist in a suicide. The Court reasoned that if patients may ask physicians to withdraw life support systems, they also have a right for physicians to prescribe drugs to hasten death. Quill v. Vacco, 80 F.3d 716 (2d Cir. 1996). The Second Circuit's ruling was similar to an earlier decision by the Ninth Circuit. Compassion in Dying v. State of Wash., 79 F.3d 790 (9th Cir. 1996).

A year later those issues reached the Supreme Court, which overturned the Second and Ninth Circuits by holding that there was no right, under the U.S. Constitution, to assisted suicide. The effect was to reinstate the New York and Washington laws that made it a crime for doctors to give lethal drugs to dying patients who wanted to end their lives. But the Court's ruling also allowed other states to permit physician-assisted suicide, shifting the matter from courts to state legislatures. The Court found a fundamental difference between patients refusing life-support systems (at issue in *Cruzan*) and doctors intervening with lethal medications. Although all of the Justices agreed to uphold the New York and Washington statutes, a number of concurring opinions offered a wide variety of views and recognized that some patients, in extreme cases, might seek assisted suicide. Washington v. Glucksberg, 521 U.S. 702 (1997); VACCO v. QUILL, 521 U.S. 793 (1997).

Oregon's Death with Dignity Act

The scope for variety among the states was made evident later in the year when the Supreme Court denied cert on a case out of Oregon that had upheld a law allowing physician-assisted suicide. Oregon voters adopted the Death With Dignity Act in 1994 in a statewide referendum. An injunction delayed implementation of the law until 1997, when voters again supported the policy. Under the Oregon law, a mentally competent adult suffering from a terminal illness may receive a lethal dose of medication after consulting with two physicians and waiting 15 days. Lee v. Harcleroad, 522 U.S. 927 (1997). Just as Congress had passed the Hyde Amendment to limit federal funding of abortions, so did it in 1997 pass legislation to ban federal funding for assisted suicide. The statute had more of a preventive quality, because existing federal programs did not provide any funds for assisted suicide. The statute bans the funding of assisted suicide, euthanasia, or mercy killing, and prohibits the use of federal taxpayer funds to subsidize legal assistance or other forms of advocacy to support assisted suicide, euthanasia, or mercy killing. 111 Stat. 23 (1997). Any risk that doctors who used the Oregon law to prescribe lethal drugs to terminally ill patients would be prosecuted by the federal government under the Controlled Substances Act was removed in 1998 when Attorney General Janet Reno announced that states may enact and implement such laws without federal interference.

On November 6, 2001, Attorney General John Ashcroft authorized federal agents to prosecute doctors in Oregon who prescribed lethal drugs for terminally ill patients. After Oregon sued, a federal district court blocked Ashcroft's policy, by ruling that his order exceeded his authority under the Controlled Substances Act. Oregon v. Ashcroft, 192 F.Supp.2d 1077 (D. Or. 2002). Two years later the Ninth Circuit agreed that Ashcroft's order attempted to control an area of law traditionally reserved to the states, and that he acted without congressional authority. Oregon v. Ashcroft, 368 F.3d 118 (9th Cir. 2004). The Supreme Court affirmed. Gonzales v. Oregon, 546 U.S. 243 (2006). This decision is discussed, with a reading, in Section F of Chapter 8.

Other states, including Washington in 2008, have passed legislation authorizing doctor-assisted suicide. Terminally ill patients must be Washington residents who have less than six months to live. In May 2009, Linda Fleming of Sequim, Wash., became the first person in that state to die under the legislative procedures.

Terri Schiavo

Another controversy involved Terri Schiavo, who lay in a coma-like state for over a decade after suffering a heart attack in 1990. Her husband, acting as guardian, regarded her condition as irreversible and said she would not have wanted to be kept on life support. Her parents wanted the feeding tube kept in place. After Florida courts supported the husband, the state legislature intervened in 2003 to authorize Governor Jeb Bush to prevent the withholding of nutrition and hydration. The feeding tube was reinserted. On May 6, 2004, a state circuit judge struck down "Terri's Law" as an unconstitutional attempt to authorize the governor to deprive Florida citizens of their right to privacy. On September 23, 2004, the Florida Supreme Court ruled unanimously that the law encroached upon the judiciary and violated separation of powers. On March 21, 2005, Congress passed legislation to transfer jurisdiction over the case to federal courts. After some delay, the feeding tube was removed and Terri Schiavo died on March 31, 2005.

Cruzan v. Director, Missouri Dept. of Health

497 U.S. 261 (1990)

The parents of Nancy Cruzan, a 32-year-old woman in a "persistent vegetative state," wanted to remove her life-support systems against the wishes of the state of Missouri. This case explores complex moral and ethical questions. Is there a "right to die"? Who decides that question for someone legally incompetent and therefore unable to express a preference? What criteria guide that choice? What of infants in a vegetative state, never able to express a preference?

CHIEF JUSTICE REHNQUIST delivered the opinion of the Court.

Petitioner Nancy Beth Cruzan was rendered incompetent as a result of severe injuries sustained during an automobile accident. Co-petitioners Lester and Joyce Cruzan, Nancy's parents and co-guardians, sought a court order directing the withdrawal of their daughter's artificial feeding and hydration equipment after it became apparent that she had virtually no chance of recovering her cognitive faculties. The Supreme Court of Missouri held that because there was no clear and convincing evidence of Nancy's desire to have life-sustaining treatment withdrawn under such circumstances, her parents lacked authority to effectuate such a request....

... The Missouri trial court in this case found that permanent brain damage generally results after 6 minutes in an anoxic state; it was estimated that Cruzan was deprived of oxygen from 12 to 14 minutes. She remained in a coma for approximately three weeks and then progressed to an unconscious state in which she was able to orally ingest some nutrition. In order to ease feeding and further the recovery, surgeons implanted a gastrostomy feeding and hydration tube in Cruzan with the consent of her then husband. Subsequent rehabilitative efforts proved unavailing. She now lies in a Missouri state hospital in what is commonly referred to as a persis-

tent vegetative state: generally, a condition in which a person exhibits motor reflexes but evinces no indications of significant cognitive function. The State of Missouri is bearing the cost of her care.

[*The state trial court found that a person in Nancy's condition had a fundamental right under the state and federal constitutions to refuse or direct the withdrawal of "death prolonging procedures," and that her conversation at age 25 with a housemate friend indicated she would not wish to live unless she could live at least halfway normally. The Supreme Court of Missouri reversed, deciding that the Missouri Living Will statute embodied a state policy strongly favoring the preservation of life. Nancy's statement to her roommate was considered unreliable. Chief Justice Rehnquist reviewed right-to-die holdings in New Jersey, Massachusetts, New York, California, Minnesota, and Illinois.*]

As these cases demonstrate, the common-law doctrine of informed consent is viewed as generally encompassing the right of a competent individual to refuse medical treatment. Beyond that, these decisions demonstrate both similarity and diversity in their approach to what all agree is a perplexing question with unusually strong moral and ethical overtones. State courts have available to them for decision a number of sources—state constitutions, statutes, and common law—which are not available to us. In this Court, the question is simply and starkly whether the United States Constitution prohibits Missouri from choosing the rule of decision which it did....

The Fourteenth Amendment provides that no State shall "deprive any person of life, liberty, or property, without due process of law." The principle that a competent person has a constitutionally protected liberty interest in refusing unwanted medical treatment may be inferred from our prior decisions....

But determining that a person has a "liberty interest" under the Due Process Clause does not end the inquiry; "whether respondent's constitutional rights have been violated must be determined by balancing his liberty interests against the relevant state interests."...

Petitioners insist that under the general holdings of our cases, the forced administration of life-sustaining medical treatment, and even of artificially-delivered food and water essential to life, would implicate a competent person's liberty interest. Although we think the logic of the cases discussed above would embrace such a liberty interest, the dramatic consequences involved in refusal of such treatment would inform the inquiry as to whether the deprivation of that interest is constitutionally permissible. But for purposes of this case, we assume that the United States Constitution would grant a competent person a constitutionally protected right to refuse lifesaving hydration and nutrition.

Petitioners go on to assert that an incompetent person should possess the same right in this respect as is possessed by a competent person....

The difficulty with petitioners' claim is that in a sense it begs the question: an incompetent person is not able to make an informed and voluntary choice to exercise a hypothetical right to refuse treatment or any other right. Such a "right" must be exercised for her, if at all, by some sort of surrogate. Here, Missouri has in effect recognized that under certain circumstances a surrogate may act for the patient in electing to have hydration and nutrition withdrawn in such a way as to cause death, but it has established a procedural safeguard to assure that the action of the surrogate conforms as best it may to the wishes expressed by the patient while competent. Missouri requires that evidence of the incompetent's wishes as to the withdrawal of treatment be proved by clear and convincing evidence. The question, then, is whether the United States Constitution forbids the establishment of this procedural requirement by the State. We hold that it does not.

Whether or not Missouri's clear and convincing

evidence requirement comports with the United States Constitution depends in part on what interests the State may properly seek to protect in this situation. Missouri relies on its interest in the protection and preservation of human life, and there can be no gainsaying this interest....

In our view, Missouri has permissibly sought to advance these interests through the adoption of a "clear and convincing" standard of proof to govern such proceedings....

... We believe that Missouri may permissibly place an increased risk of an erroneous decision on those seeking to terminate an incompetent individual's life-sustaining treatment. An erroneous decision not to terminate results in a maintenance of the status quo; the possibility of subsequent developments such as advancements in medical science, the discovery of new evidence regarding the patient's intent, changes in the law, or simply the unexpected death of the patient despite the administration of life-sustaining treatment, at least create the potential that a wrong decision will eventually be corrected or its impact mitigated. An erroneous decision to withdraw life-sustaining treatment, however, is not susceptible of correction....

[*Rehnquist points out that most states, if not all, forbid oral testimony in determining the wishes of parties in such transactions as contracts and the making of wills. Nancy Cruzan's statements to her housemate about a year before her accident were not, to the Court, clear and convincing evidence.*]

No doubt is engendered by anything in this record but that Nancy Cruzan's mother and father are loving and caring parents. If the State were required by the United States Constitution to repose a right of "substituted judgment" with anyone, the Cruzans would certainly qualify. But we do not think the Due Process Clause requires the State to repose judgment on these matters with anyone but the patient herself.... All of the reasons previously discussed for allowing Missouri to require clear and convincing evidence of the patient's wishes lead us to conclude that the State may choose to defer only to those wishes, rather than confide the decision to close family members.

The judgment of the Supreme Court of Missouri is

Affirmed.

JUSTICE O'CONNOR, concurring.

[*O'Connor provides separate reasons why a protected*

liberty interest in refusing unwanted medical treatment, including artificially delivered food and water, may be inferred from prior decisions.]

JUSTICE SCALIA, concurring.

[*Scalia would have preferred that the Court announce "that the federal courts have no business in this field." The point at which life becomes "worthless" and the point at which efforts to preserve life are "inappropriate," Scalia says, "are neither set forth in the Constitution nor known to the nine Justices of this Court any better than they are known to nine people picked at random from the Kansas City telephone directory." He would have left the issue to the citizens of Missouri to decide through their elected representatives.*]

JUSTICE BRENNAN, with whom JUSTICE MARSHALL and JUSTICE BLACKMUN join dissenting.

... Because I believe that Nancy Cruzan has a fundamental right to be free of unwanted artificial nutrition and hydration, which right is not out-weighed by any interests of the State, and because I find that the improperly biased procedural obstacles imposed by the Missouri Supreme Court impermissibly burden that right, I respectfully dissent. Nancy Cruzan is entitled to choose to die with dignity.

[*Brennan argues that the right to die is a fundamental right and therefore can be set aside only if Missouri identifies sufficiently important state interests and closely tailors its remedies to effectuate those interests.*]

JUSTICE STEVENS, dissenting.

... [I]f Nancy Cruzan has no interest in continued treatment, and if she has a liberty interest in being free from unwanted treatment, and if the cessation of treatment would have no adverse impact on third parties, and if no reason exists to doubt the good faith of Nancy's parents, then what possible basis could the State have for insisting upon continued medical treatment? ...

Vacco v. Quill

521 U.S. 793 (1997)

Physicians brought this action challenging the constitutionality of a New York statute making it a crime to aid persons in committing suicide or attempting to commit suicide. Timothy E. Quill was one of the physicians bringing this case against Dennis C. Vacco, Attorney General of New York. The district court found no constitutional defect to the statute, but the Second Circuit reversed.

CHIEF JUSTICE REHNQUIST delivered the opinion of Court.

In New York, as in most States, it is a crime to aid another to commit or attempt suicide, but patients may refuse even lifesaving medical treatment. The question presented by this case is whether New York's prohibition on assisting suicide therefore violates the Equal Protection Clause of the Fourteenth Amendment. We hold that it does not.

Petitioners are various New York public officials. Respondents Timothy E. Quill, Samuel C. Klagsbrun, and Howard A. Grossman are physicians who practice in New York ... Respondents, and three gravely ill patients who have since died, sued the State's Attorney General in the United States District Court. They urged that because New York permits a competent person to refuse life-sustaining medical treatment, and because the refusal of such treatment is "essentially the same thing" as physician-assisted suicide, New York's assisted-suicide ban violates the Equal Protection Clause. *Quill v. Koppell,* 870 F.Supp. 78, 84–85 (S.D.N.Y. 1994).

[*The district court disagreed, concluding that "it is hardly unreasonable or irrational for the State to recognize a difference between allowing nature to take its course, even in the most severe situations, and intentionally using an artificial death-producing device." Id, at 84. The Second Circuit reversed, ruling that the statute did not treat equally all competent persons in the final stages of fatal illness. Those on life-support systems were allowed to hasten their deaths by directing the removal of such systems, but those not on life-sustaining equipment lacked that choice. The Second Circuit also decided that the statute was not rationally related to any legitimate state interest.*]

The Equal Protection Clause commands that no State shall "deny to any person within its jurisdiction the equal protection of the laws." This provision creates no substantive rights.... Instead, it embodies a general rule that States must treat like cases alike but may treat unlike cases accordingly.... If a legislative classification or distinction "neither burdens a fundamental right nor targets a suspect class, we will uphold [it] so long as it bears a rational relation to some legitimate end." *Romer v. Evans*, 517 U.S. 620, 631 (1996).

New York's statutes outlawing assisting suicide affect and address matters of profound significance to all New Yorkers alike. They neither infringe fundamental rights nor involve suspect classifications.... These laws are therefore entitled to a "strong presumption of validity." *Heller v. Doe*, 509 U.S. 312, 319 (1993).

On their faces, neither New York's ban on assisting suicide nor its statutes permitting patients to refuse medical treatment treat anyone differently than anyone else or draw any distinctions between persons. *Everyone*, regardless of physical condition, is entitled, if competent, to refuse unwanted lifesaving medical treatment; *no one* is permitted to assist a suicide. Generally speaking, laws that apply evenhandedly to all "unquestionably comply" with the Equal Protection Clause....

The Court of Appeals, however, concluded that some terminally ill people—those who are on life-support systems—are treated differently than those who are not, in that the former may "hasten death" by ending treatment, but the latter may not "hasten death" through physician-assisted suicide. 80 F.3d, at 729. This conclusion depends on the submission that ending or refusing lifesaving medical treatment "is nothing more nor less than assisted suicide." *Ibid.* Unlike the Court of Appeals, we think the distinction between assisting suicide and withdrawing life-sustaining treatment, a distinction widely recognized and endorsed in the medical profession and in our legal traditions, is both important and logical; it is certainly rational....

The distinction comports with fundamental legal principles of causation and intent. First, when a patient refuses life-sustaining medical treatment, he dies from an underlying fatal disease or pathology; but if a patient ingests lethal medication prescribed by a physician, he is killed by that medication....

Given these general principles, it is not surprising that many courts, including New York courts, have carefully distinguished refusing life-sustaining treatment from suicide.... In fact, the first state-court decision explicitly to authorize withdrawing lifesaving treatment noted the "real distinction be-

tween the self-infliction of deadly harm and a self-determination against artificial life support" *In re Quinlan*, 70 N.J. 10, 43, 52, and n. 9, 355 A.2d 647, 665, 670, and n. 9, cert. denied *sub nom. Garger v. New Jersey*, 429 U.S. 922 (1976)....

Similarly, the overwhelming majority of state legislatures have drawn a clear line between assisting suicide and withdrawing or permitting the refusal of unwanted lifesaving medical treatment by prohibiting the former and permitting the latter ... Thus, even as the States move to protect and promote patients' dignity at the end of life, they remain opposed to physician-assisted suicide.

New York is a case in point. The State enacted its current assisted-suicide statutes in 1965. Since then, New York has acted several times to protect patients' common-law right to refuse treatment.... In so doing, however, the State has neither endorsed a general right to "hasten death" nor approved physician-assisted suicide. Quite the opposite: The State has reaffirmed the line between "killing" and "letting die." ...

This Court has also recognized, at least implicitly, the distinction between letting a patient die and making that patient die. In *Cruzan v. Director, Mo. Dept. of Health,* 497 U.S. 261, 278 (1990), we concluded that "[t]he principle that a competent person has a constitutionally protected liberty interest in refusing unwanted medical treatment may be inferred from our prior decisions," and we assumed the existence of such a right for purposes of that case, *id.*, at 279. But our assumption of a right to refuse treatment was grounded not, as the Court of Appeals supposed, on the proposition that patients have a general and abstract "right to hasten death," 80 F.3d, at 727–728, but on well established, traditional rights to bodily integrity and freedom from unwanted touching, *Cruzan*, 497 U.S., at 278–279; *id.*, at 287–288 (O'CONNOR, J., concurring). In fact, we observed that "the majority of States in this country have laws imposing criminal penalties on one who assists another to commit suicide." *Id.*, at 280. *Cruzan* therefore provides no support for the notion that refusing life-sustaining medical treatment is "nothing more nor less than suicide."

For all these reasons, we disagree with respondents' claim that the distinction between refusing lifesaving medical treatment and assisted suicide is "arbitrary" and "irrational." ... By permitting everyone to refuse unwanted medical treatment while prohibiting anyone from assisting a suicide, New York law follows a longstanding and rational distinction.

New York's reasons for recognizing and acting on this distinction — including prohibiting intentional killing and preserving life; preventing suicide; maintaining physicians' role as their patients' healers; protecting vulnerable people from indifference, prejudice, and psychological and financial pressure to end their lives; and avoiding a possible slide towards euthanasia — are discussed in greater detail in our opinion in *Glucksberg, ante.*...

The judgment of the Court of Appeals is reversed.

It is so ordered.

[*O'Connor writes a concurring opinion, as do Stevens, Ginsburg, and Breyer. They are placed in the companion case of* Washington v. Glucksberg, 521 US. 702 (1997). *Souter's concurrence is placed in* Vacco v. Quill.]

E. GAY RIGHTS

States have attempted to criminalize homosexuality by passing laws that prohibit "crimes against nature," "buggery," "deviancy," and sodomy. States sometimes borrowed from English common law to define the offense as "the abominable and detestable crime against nature, either with mankind or with beast." Frequently these laws were challenged as vague, unenforceable, and an invasion of privacy. It was often unclear whether the laws applied only to homosexuals or to married couples as well.

Opponents of those laws generally limited their attack to governmental efforts to control private, consensual sex acts between adults. For cases in which the activity concerned married couples and there was no issue of force or coercion, legal action was successful in striking down the statute or reversing a conviction. Buchanan v. Batchelor, 308 F.Supp. 729 (N.D. Tex. 1970); Cotner v. Henry, 394 F.2d 873 (7th Cir. 1968). However, a state sodomy statute proscribing "the abominable and detestable crime against nature, either with mankind or with beast," was held to be not unconstitutionally vague when applied to two adult males. Wainwright v. Stone, 414 U.S. 21 (1973).

Opponents of sodomy statutes acknowledged that states had certain legitimate interests if the activity involved minors, unwilling participants, or actions that occurred in public.[3] If the activity involved two males, one of them a minor, a conviction was likely to stand. State v. Crawford, 478 S.W.2d 314 (Mo. 1972), appeal dismissed for want of substantial federal question, 409 U.S. 811 (1972). Similarly, if consenting adults committed sodomy in private and allowed their activity to become known to a minor, the state could convict them on that ground. Lovisi v. Slayton, 363 F.Supp. 620 (E.D. Va. 1973).

A major case involving adults was decided by a federal court in 1975. A lawsuit claimed that a Virginia statute deprived adult males, engaging in homosexual relations consensually and in private, of their constitutional rights to due process, freedom of expression, and privacy. The court upheld the statute by distinguishing between the right of privacy in *Griswold* (the use of contraceptives by married couples in private) and the practices of adultery, homosexuality, and other sexual intimacies, which the state may forbid. Interestingly, the court relied on the *dissenting* opinion of Justice Harlan in *Poe* v. *Ullman* in making this distinction. Doe v. Commonwealth, 403 F.Supp. 1199, 1201 (E.D. Va. 1975), aff'd, 425 U.S. 901 (1976). In a dissent, District Judge Merhige read *Griswold* and the abortion cases to stand for the principle that "every individual has a right to be free from unwarranted governmental intrusion into one's decisions on private matters of individual concern." More particularly, he said: "A mature individual's choice of an adult sexual partner, in the privacy of his or her own home, would appear to me to be a decision of the utmost private and intimate concern. Private con-

---

3. "Statement as to Jurisdiction," Buchanan v. Wade, U.S. Supreme Court, October Term, 1969, at 8.

sensual sex acts between adults are matters, absent evidence that they are harmful, in which the state has no legitimate interest." 403 F.Supp. at 1203.

Michael Hardwick

In 1986, the Supreme Court narrowly sustained—by a 5–4 vote—the constitutionality of a Georgia statute that criminalized sodomy. Michael Hardwick was arrested for committing sodomy with another male adult in the bedroom of his home. After the district attorney decided not to present the matter to the grand jury, Hardwick challenged the statute as it applied to private, consensual sodomy. A majority of Justices held that the Constitution does not confer a fundamental right upon gays to engage in sodomy. BOWERS v. HARDWICK, 478 U.S. 186 (1986). Justice Powell, concurring in the opinion, suggested that had Hardwick been "tried, much less convicted and sentenced" and had he raised the Eighth Amendment, he might have decided differently. Powell later admitted that he switched his vote to create the majority upholding Georgia's statute. Washington Post, August 13, 1986, at A4; Washington Post, July 13, 1986, at A1.

The Court did not pretend to have the last word on consensual sodomy. It emphasized that its decision "raises no question about the right or propriety of state legislative decisions to repeal their laws that criminalize homosexual sodomy, or of state-court decisions invalidating those laws on state constitutional grounds." 478 U.S. at 190. A number of state courts have invalidated state statutes that criminalize consensual sodomy. People v. Onofre, 415 N.E.2d 936 (N.Y. 1980); Commonwealth v. Bonadio, 415 A.2d 47 (Pa. 1980); Commonwealth v. Wasson, 842 S.W.2d 487 (Ky. 1992); State v. Morales, 826 S.W.2d 201 (Tex. App. 1992); City of Dallas v. England, 846 S.W.2d 957 (Tex. App. 1993); Campbell v. Sundquist, 926 S.W.2d 250 (Tenn. App. 1996) [the state supreme court denied appeal without an opinion]; Gryczan v. State, 942 P.2d 112 (Mont. 1997); Powell v. State, 510 S.E.2d 18 (Ga. 1998); Jegley v. Picado, 80 S.W.3d 332 (Ark. 2002). (For excerpts from Kentucky decision, see box on next page.) In recent years, several dozen states have repealed their sodomy laws, as has the District of Columbia.

In 2003, the Supreme Court reversed *Hardwick* by striking down Texas's ban on private consensual sex between adults of the same sex. Five Justices ruled that the state had violated the "liberty of the person both in its spatial and more transcendent dimensions." In a separate opinion, Justice O'Connor also voted to strike down the law, but on separate grounds. She found an equal protection violation because the law punished homosexuals while allowing the same conduct by heterosexuals. LAWRENCE v. TEXAS, 539 U.S. 558 (2003).

Civil Rights Protections

In 1996, the Supreme Court struck down a provision of the Colorado Constitution that nullified existing civil rights protections for homosexuals in the state. The constitutional language prohibited all legislative, executive, or judicial action at any level of state or local government designed to protect the status of persons based on their "homosexual, lesbian or bisexual orientation, conduct, practices or relationships." Several cities in the state had adopted ordinances to prohibit discrimination against gays. The 6 to 3 decision stated that the constitutional provision, by placing the state's homosexuals "in a solitary class" and singling them out, had violated the U.S. Constitution's equal protection guarantee. The Colorado provision, said the Court, failed to show a rational relationship to a legitimate governmental purpose. The Court rejected the argument that the provision merely took away "special rights," not equal rights. The Court made no mention of *Bowers v. Hardwick* (1986). Romer v. Evans, 517 U.S. 620 (1996). [In 1995, the Court decided a case involving the exclusion of gay marchers in a parade; see discussion under "Expressive Content" in Section C of Chapter 10.]

Two years after the Court's decision in *Romer*, the Court denied cert on a Sixth Circuit ruling that upheld a Cincinnati anti-gay initiative that was quite similar to Colorado's provision. Cincinnati's city

Kentucky Court Invalidates Sodomy Law

In 1992, the Supreme Court of Kentucky held that the state's criminal statute prohibiting consensual homosexual sodomy violates the privacy and equal protection guarantees of the Kentucky Constitution. Commonwealth v. Wasson, 842 S.W.2d 487 (Ky. 1992). Below are excerpts from the decision by Justice Leibson.

Appellee, Jeffrey Wasson, is charged with having solicited an undercover Lexington policeman to engage in deviate sexual intercourse. KRS 510.100 punishes "deviate sexual intercourse with another person of the same sex" as a criminal offense, and specifies "consent of the other person shall not be a defense." Nor does it matter that the act is private and involves a caring relationship rather than a commercial one. [*The sexual activity was intended to have taken place in Wasson's home by consenting adults; no money was offered or solicited.*]

... [W]e hold the guarantees of individual liberty provided in our 1891 Kentucky Constitution offer greater protection of the right of privacy than provided by the Federal Constitution as interpreted by the United States Supreme Court, and that the statute in question is a violation of such rights; and, further, we hold that the statute in question violates rights of equal protection as guaranteed by our Kentucky Constitution.

I. RIGHTS OF PRIVACY

No language specifying "rights or privacy," *as such,* appears in either the Federal or State Constitution. The Commonwealth recognizes such rights exist, but takes the position that, since they are implicit rather than explicit, our Court should march in lock step with the United States Supreme Court in declaring when such rights exist. Such is not the formulation of federalism. On the contrary, under our system of dual sovereignty, it is our responsibility to interpret and apply our state constitution independently. We are not bound by decisions of the United States Supreme Court when deciding whether a state statute impermissibly infringes upon individual rights guaranteed in the State Constitution so long as state constitutional protection does not fall below the federal *floor.* ...

The clear implication is that immorality in private which does "not operate to the detriment of others," is placed beyond the reach of state action by the guarantees of liberty in the Kentucky Constitution.

. . .

... The statute before us is in violation of Kentucky constitutional protection in Section Three that "all men (persons), when they form a social compact, are equal," and in Section Two that "absolute and arbitrary power over the lives, liberty and property of free men (persons) exist nowhere in a republic, not even in the largest majority." We have concluded that it is "arbitrary" for the majority to criminalize sexual activity solely on the basis of majoritarian sexual preference, and that it denied "equal" treatment under the law when there is no rational basis, as this term is used and applied in our Kentucky cases.

---

charter amendment removed gays, lesbians, and bisexuals from protections of municipal antidiscrimination ordinances. The Sixth Circuit held that the charter amendment was rationally related to the city's valid interest in conserving public costs that accrue from investigating and adjudicating sexual orientation discrimination complaints. Equality Foundation v. City of Cincinnati, 128 F.3d 289 (6th Cir. 1997), cert. denied, 525 U.S. 943 (1998). Justices Stevens, Souter and Ginsburg played down the cert denial, explaining that the Court may simply have concluded that the Cincinnati case did "not constitute an appropriate forum in which to decide a significant case."

Boy Scouts Case

In 2000, the Court ruled that the Boy Scouts of America had a right to expel an adult Scout leader after he announced he was gay. Although he sued under a New Jersey law that prohibits discrimination in public places based on sexual orientation, the Court held that the Boy Scouts have a First

Amendment right of "expressive association" to control the message and values it directs to the public. Boy Scouts of America v. Dale, 530 U.S. 640 (2000). For further discussion of the First Amendment issue, see Chapter 10, Section C, "Expressive Content."

After the ruling, there was some concern that corporations and state governments might withdraw their support from the Boy Scouts for fear that continued assistance might imply tolerance for discrimination against gays. Responding to the Court's decision, Congress passed legislation in 2002 called "Boy Scouts of America Equal Access Act." It provides that public elementary and secondary schools, local educational agencies, and state educational agencies that receive federal funds shall not deny equal access or a fair opportunity to meet to any group officially affiliated with the Boy Scouts of America. 115 Stat. 1981, §9525 (2002). Failure to comply with the statute might lead to a loss of federal funds. In 2007, because of its position on homosexuality, the Boy Scouts of America lost its lease on a building in Philadelphia. City policy required that any organization renting property from it on a subsidized basis agree to nondiscriminatory language in its lease. Ian Urbina, "Boy Scouts Lose Philadelphia Lease in Gay-Rights Fight," N.Y. Times, Dec. 6, 2007, at A16.

Defense of Marriage Act

Under pressure from a lawsuit in Hawaii, Congress passed the Defense of Marriage Act (DOMA) in 1996, permitting states to refuse to recognize such marriages performed in other states. Access to federal benefits were also affected by the statute. Subsequent actions, including the decision by President Obama in 2011 not to defend the constitutionality of DOMA, are treated in Chapter 16. The House passed legislation in 2004 to strip from federal courts their ability to rule on DOMA (see Section D in Chapter 19). The Senate took no action on the bill.

Gays in the Military

President Clinton inherited an issue that had been simmering for decades: the rights of gay soldiers. In an early case, a Navy officer, discharged for homosexual conduct, brought an action seeking to be reinstated in the service. He acknowledged engaging in homosexual acts in a Navy barracks. In 1984 a federal appellate court held that the Navy's policy of mandatory discharge for homosexual conduct did not violate constitutional rights to privacy or equal protection. If government may proscribe homosexual conduct in a civilian context, as in Doe v. Commonwealth, "then such a regulation is certainly sustainable in a military context" where discipline and good order justify restrictions "that go beyond the needs of civilian society." Dronenberg v. Zech, 741 F.2d 1388, 1392 (D.C. Cir. 1984).

In 1990, the Supreme Court refused to consider constitutional challenges to the military's policy of excluding persons who acknowledge they are gay, even if there is no evidence of actual homosexual conduct. One case involved a woman who had been discharged from the Army because of homosexual tendencies but was reinstated under court order. After her enlistment terminated, she sought reenlistment, admitting that she is a lesbian, but the Army opposed her entry. Ben-Shalom v. Stone, 494 U.S. 1004 (1990); Ben-Shalom v. Marsh, 881 F.2d 454 (7th Cir. 1989). The other case involved a man who was accepted into Navy flight school after acknowledging that he had homosexual tendencies. He was released from active duty when he visited the officer's club in the company of an enlisted man who was awaiting discharge because of homosexuality. Woodward v. United States, 494 U.S. 1003 (1990); Woodward v. United States, 871 F.2d 1068 (Fed. Cir. 1989).

During the 1992 presidential campaign, Bill Clinton promised to end the U.S. prohibition on gay people in the armed services. Throughout the 1980s, an average of 1,500 men and women were discharged from the military because of their homosexuality. After Clinton's election, the Supreme Court let stand a lower court ruling that gay status, by itself, is insufficient justification to exclude homosexuals from the military. The burden is on the military to show that discrimination against homosexuals is rationally related to a permissible governmental purpose. Cheney v. Pruitt, 506 U.S. 1020 (1993); Pruitt v. Cheney, 963 F.2d 1160 (9th Cir. 1991).

"Don't Ask/Don't Tell"

President Clinton ordered the Defense Department to draft an executive order and departmental directives by July 15, 1993. The resulting policy was characterized as "don't ask/don't tell." The Pentagon would no longer ask volunteers whether they are gay or bisexual. Military personnel would not be asked to disclose their sexual orientation when they apply for security clearances. However, they could be discharged for homosexual conduct. A lower court ruling prohibited the Pentagon from discriminating against gays, but the Supreme Court lifted that order. The Court's action permitted full implementation of the Clinton policy, including discharge for homosexual conduct. U.S. Department of Defense v. Meinhold, 510 U.S. 939 (1993). In the meantime, Congress legislated on the issue, establishing conditions for gays in the military that were more stringent than the policy envisioned in the Clinton administration regulations. 107 Stat. 1670, §571 (1993).

In 1996, the Fourth Circuit upheld the Clinton administration's "don't ask/don't tell" policy. A Navy lieutenant was dismissed after giving a letter to his commanding officer stating "I am gay." The court held that the statute does not target speech declaring homosexuality; it targets homosexual acts and the propensity or intent to engage in homosexual acts, and permissibly uses speech as evidence. Thomasson v. Perry, 80 F.3d 915 (4th Cir. 1996), cert. denied, 519 U.S. 948 (1996). Other federal appellate court decisions also upheld the "don't ask, don't tell" policy.[4]

Although the Clinton policy was adopted to make it easier for homosexuals to serve in the military, more gay service members were discharged than before it took effect. In a number of cases military officials directly asked members about their sexual orientation. The Defense Department explained that the discharges were due to an increasing number of voluntary statements to commanders by homosexuals who wanted to leave the military.[5] In 1999, Clinton concluded that his policy on gays in the military is "out of whack now" and that it wasn't being implemented "as it was announced and as it was intended." Public Papers of the Presidents, 1999, II, at 2293. In 2000, the Pentagon issued new guidelines to enforce Clinton's policy.

In his State of the Union Address of January 27, 2010, President Barack Obama promised to work with Congress and the military "to finally repeal the law that denies gay Americans the right to serve the country they love because of who they are." The military announced it would no longer aggressively pursue disciplinary action against gay service members whose orientation had been revealed against their will by third parties. The Pentagon stated it would ease enforcement of the statutory policy by ignoring anonymous complaints about gay soldiers and requiring that those who file complaints do so under oath. On May 27, 2010, the House voted 234 to 194 to repeal "don't ask, don't tell" and the repeal became law in the lame-duck session at the end of the year. The formal repeal took effect on September 21, 2011. From 1993 to the ban, the military had discharged more than 13,000 service members for violating the service policy. Ed O'Keefe, "A Day, At Last, Open and Fear-Free," Washington Post, September 20, 2011, at B1. As of June 2012, an estimated 66,000 gay and lesbian troops were on active duty. Lisa Rein, "After Repeal of 'Don't Ask, Don't Tell,' a Celebration," Washington Post, June 27, 2012, at A15.

---

4. E.g., Richenberg v. Perry, 97 F.3d 256 (8th Cir. 1996), cert. denied, 522 U.S. 807 (1997); Philips v. Perry, 106 F.3d 1420 (9th Cir. 1997); Holmes v. California Army National Guard, 124 F.3d 1126 (9th Cir. 1997).

5. "Study Says Discharges Continue Under Don't Ask, Don't Tell," New York Times, March 24, 2004, at A14; "Military Discharges of Gays Rise, and So Do Bias Incidents," The New York Times, March 14, 2002, at A24; "Military's Discharges of Gays Increased 17 Percent in 2000," The New York Times, June 2, 2001, at A9; "Number of Recruits Discharged for Being Gay Increases for Fifth Year," Washington Post, January 23, 1999, at A5; "Military Discharges of Homosexuals Soar," The New York Times, April 7, 1998, at A24; "Military, Despite Policy Shift, Discharged More Gays in '95," Washington Post, February 28, 1996, at A2.

Bowers v. Hardwick

478 U.S. 186 (1986)

Michael Hardwick was charged with violating Georgia law by committing sodomy with another adult male in the bedroom of his home. After the district attorney decided not to present the matter to the grand jury, Hardwick brought suit in federal court to have the statute declared unconstitutional because it criminalized consensual sodomy. A district court granted the state's motion to dismiss; the Eleventh Circuit reversed, holding that the statute violated Hardwick's fundamental rights. The defendant in this case is Michael J. Bowers, Attorney General of Georgia. John and Mary Doe joined Hardwick as plaintiffs in the action, claiming that they wished to engage in sexual activity proscribed by the statute. The Court examined only Hardwick's challenge and expressed no opinion on the constitutionality of the Georgia statute as applied to other acts of sodomy.

JUSTICE WHITE delivered the opinion of the Court....

Because other Courts of Appeals have arrived at judgments contrary to that of the Eleventh Circuit in this case, we granted the State's petition for certiorari questioning the holding that its sodomy statute violates the fundamental rights of homosexuals. We agree with the State that the Court of Appeals erred, and hence reverse its judgment.

This case does not require a judgment on whether laws against sodomy between consenting adults in general, or between homosexuals in particular, are wise or desirable. It raises no question about the right or propriety of state legislative decisions to repeal their laws that criminalize homosexual sodomy, or of state court decisions invalidating those laws on state constitutional grounds. The issue presented is whether the Federal Constitution confers a fundamental right upon homosexuals to engage in sodomy and hence invalidates the laws of the many States that still make such conduct illegal and have done so for a very long time. The case also calls for some judgment about the limits of the Court's role in carrying out its constitutional mandate.

We first register our disagreement with the Court of Appeals and with respondent that the Court's prior cases have construed the Constitution to confer a right of privacy that extends to homosexual sodomy and for all intents and purposes have decided this case. The reach of this line of cases was sketched in *Carey* v. *Population Services International,* 431 U.S. 678, 685 (1977). *Pierce* v. *Society of Sisters,* 268 U.S. 510 (1925), and *Meyer* v. *Nebraska,* 262 U.S. 390 (1923), were described as dealing with child rearing and education; *Prince* v. *Massachusetts,* 321 U.S. 158 (1944), with family relationships; *Skinner* v. *Oklahoma ex rel. Williamson,* 316 U.S. 535 (1942), with procreation; *Loving* v. *Virginia,* 388 U.S. 1 (1967), with marriage; *Griswold* v. *Connecticut, supra,* and *Eisenstadt* v. *Baird, supra,* with contraception; and *Roe* v. *Wade,* 410 U.S. 113 (1973), with abortion. The latter three cases were interpreted as construing the Due Process Clause of the Fourteenth Amendment to confer a fundamental individual right to decide whether or not to beget or bear a child....

... [W]e think it evident that none of the rights announced in those cases bears any resemblance to the claimed constitutional right of homosexuals to engage in acts of sodomy that is asserted in this case. No connection between family, marriage, or procreation on the one hand and homosexual activity on the other has been demonstrated, either by the Court of Appeals or by respondent. Moreover, any claim that these cases nevertheless stand for the proposition that any kind of private sexual conduct between consenting adults is constitutionally insulated from state proscription is unsupportable....

Precedent aside, however, respondent would have us announce, as the Court of Appeals did, a fundamental right to engage in homosexual sodomy. This we are quite unwilling to do. It is true that despite the language of the Due Process Clauses of the Fifth and Fourteenth Amendments, which appears to focus only on the processes by which life, liberty, or property is taken, the cases are legion in which those Clauses have been interpreted to have substantive content, subsuming rights that to a great extent are immune from federal or state regulation or proscription. Among such cases are those recognizing rights that have little or no textual support in the constitutional language. *Meyer, Prince,* and *Pierce* fall in this category, as do the privacy cases from *Griswold* to *Carey.*

Striving to assure itself and the public that announcing rights not readily identifiable in the Constitution's text involves much more than the imposition of the Justices' own choice of values on the States and the Federal Government, the Court has sought to identify the nature of the rights qualifying for heightened judicial protection. In *Palko* v. *Connecticut,* 302 U.S. 319, 325, 326, (1937), it was said that this category includes those fundamental liberties that are "implicit in the concept of ordered liberty," such that "neither liberty nor justice would exist if [they] were sacrificed." A different description of fundamental liberties appeared in *Moore* v. *East Cleveland,* 431 U.S. 494, 503, (1977) (opinion of POWELL, J.), where they are characterized as those liberties that are "deeply rooted in this Nation's history and tradition." *Id.,* at 503, (POWELL, J.). See also *Griswold* v. *Connecticut,* 381 U.S., at 506.

It is obvious to us that neither of these formulations would extend a fundamental right to homosexuals to engage in acts of consensual sodomy. Proscriptions against that conduct have ancient roots.... Sodomy was a criminal offense at common law and was forbidden by the laws of the original thirteen States when they ratified the Bill of Rights. In 1868, when the Fourteenth Amendment was ratified, all but 5 of the 37 States in the Union had criminal sodomy laws. In fact, until 1961, all 50 States outlawed sodomy, and today, 24 States and the District of Columbia continue to provide criminal penalties for sodomy performed in private and between consenting adults.... Against this background, to claim that a right to engage in such conduct is "deeply rooted in this Nation's history and tradition" or "implicit in the concept of ordered liberty" is, at best, facetious.

Nor are we inclined to take a more expansive view of our authority to discover new fundamental rights imbedded in the Due Process Clause. The Court is most vulnerable and comes nearest to illegitimacy when it deals with judge-made constitutional law having little or no cognizable roots in the language or design of the Constitution....

Even if the conduct at issue here is not a fundamental right, respondent asserts that there must be a rational basis for the law and that there is none in this case other than the presumed belief of a majority of the electorate in Georgia that homosexual sodomy is immoral and unacceptable. This is said to be an inadequate rationale to support the law. The law, however, is constantly based on notions of morality, and if all laws representing essentially moral choices are to be invalidated under the Due Process Clause, the courts will be very busy indeed. Even respondent makes no such claim, but insists that majority sentiments about the morality of homosexuality should be declared inadequate. We do not agree, and are un-

persuaded that the sodomy laws of some 25 States should be invalidated on this basis.

Accordingly, the judgment of the Court of Appeals is

Reversed.

CHIEF JUSTICE BURGER, concurring....

JUSTICE POWELL, concurring.

I join the opinion of the Court. I agree with the Court that there is no fundamental right—*i.e.,* no substantive right under the Due Process Clause—such as that claimed by respondent, and found to exist by the Court of Appeals. This is not to suggest, however, that respondent may not be protected by the Eighth Amendment of the Constitution. The Georgia statute at issue in this case, Ga.Code Ann. § 16-6-2, authorizes a court to imprison a person for up to 20 years for a single private, consensual act of sodomy. In my view, a prison sentence for such conduct—certainly a sentence of long duration—would create a serious Eighth Amendment issue....

In this case, however, respondent has not been tried, much less convicted and sentenced. Moreover, respondent has not raised the Eighth Amendment issue below. For these reasons this constitutional argument is not before us.

JUSTICE BLACKMUN, with whom JUSTICE BRENNAN, JUSTICE MARSHALL, and JUSTICE STEVENS join, dissenting.

This case is no more about "a fundamental right to engage in homosexual sodomy," as the Court purports to declare ... than *Stanley* v. *Georgia,* 394 U.S. 557 (1969), was about a fundamental right to watch obscene movies, or *Katz* v. *United States,* 389 U.S. 347 (1967), was about a fundamental right to place interstate bets from a telephone booth. Rather, this case is about "the most comprehensive of rights and the right most valued by civilized men," namely, "the right to be let alone." *Olmstead* v. *United States,* 277 U.S. 438, 478 (1928) (Brandeis, J., dissenting).

The statute at issue ... denies individuals the right to decide for themselves whether to engage in particular forms of private, consensual sexual activity. The Court concludes that § 16-6-2 is valid essentially because "the laws of ... many States ... still make such conduct illegal and have done so for a very long time." ... But the fact that the moral judgments expressed by statutes like § 16-6-2 may be "natural and familiar ... ought not to conclude our judgment upon the question whether statutes embodying them conflict with the Constitution of the United States." *Roe* v. *Wade,* 410 U.S. 113, 117

(1973), quoting *Lochner* v. *New York,* 198 U.S. 45, 76 (1905) (Holmes J., dissenting)....

JUSTICE STEVENS, with whom JUSTICE BRENNAN and JUSTICE MARSHALL join, dissenting.

Like the statute that is challenged in this case, the rationale of the Court's opinion applies equally to the prohibited conduct regardless of whether the parties who engage in it are married or unmarried, or are of the same or different sexes....

Our prior cases make two propositions abundantly clear. First, the fact that the governing majority in a State has traditionally viewed a particular practice as immoral is not a sufficient reason for up-holding a law prohibiting the practice; neither history nor tradition could save a law prohibiting miscegenation from constitutional attack. Second, individual decisions by married persons, concerning the intimacies of their physical relationship, even when not intended to produce offspring, are a form of "liberty" protected by the Due Process Clause of the Fourteenth Amendment. *Griswold* v. *Connecticut,* 381 U.S. 479 (1965). Moreover, this protection extends to intimate choices by unmarried as well as married persons. *Carey* v. *Population Services International,* 431 U.S. 678 (1977); *Eisenstadt* v. *Baird,* 405 U.S. 438 (1972)....

Lawrence v. Texas

539 U.S. 558 (2003)

Responding to a reported weapons disturbance in a private residence, the police entered the apartment of John Geddes Lawrence and saw him with another adult man, Tyron Garner, engaging in a private, consensual sexual act (anal sex). The right of the police to enter does not seem to have been questioned. The two men were arrested and convicted of deviate sexual intercourse in violation of a Texas statute that forbade two persons of the same sex to engage in certain intimate sexual conduct. The State Court of Appeals, relying on *Bowers* v. *Hardwick,* held that the statute was not unconstitutional.

JUSTICE KENNEDY delivered the opinion of the Court.

Liberty protects the person from unwarranted government intrusions into a dwelling or other private places. In our tradition the State is not omnipresent in the home. And there are other spheres of our lives and existence, outside the home, where the State should not be a dominant presence. Freedom extends beyond spatial bounds. Liberty presumes an autonomy of self that includes freedom of thought, belief, expression, and certain intimate conduct. The instant case involves liberty of the person both in its spatial and more transcendent dimensions.

[II]

We conclude the case should be resolved by determining whether the petitioners were free as adults to engage in the private conduct in the exercise of their liberty under the Due Process Clause of the Fourteenth Amendment to the Constitution. For this inquiry we deem it necessary to reconsider the Court's holding in *Bowers....*

[*Kennedy explains that the Georgia statute prohibited the conduct whether or not the participants were of the same sex; the Texas statute applied only to participants of the same sex. Hardwick was not prosecuted, but he sued in federal court to declare the state statute in violation of his constitutional rights.*]

The Court began its substantive discussion in *Bowers* as follows: "The issue presented is whether the Federal Constitution confers a fundamental right upon homosexuals to engage in sodomy and hence invalidates the laws of the many States that still make such conduct illegal and have done so for a very long time." *Id.* at 190. That statement, we now conclude, discloses the Court's own failure to appreciate the extent of the liberty at stake. To say that the issue in *Bowers* was simply the right to engage in certain sexual conduct demeans the claim the individual put forward, just as it would demean a married couple were it to be said marriage is simply about the right to have sexual intercourse. The laws involved in *Bowers* and here are, to be sure, statutes that purport to do no more than prohibit a particular sexual act. Their penalties and purposes, though, have more far-reaching consequences, touching upon the most private human conduct, sexual behavior, and in the most private of places, the home. The statutes do seek to control a personal relationship that, whether or not entitled to formal recognition in the law, is within the liberty of persons to choose without being punished as criminals.

This, as a general rule, should counsel against attempts by the State, or a court, to define the meaning of a relationship or to set its boundaries absent injury to a person or abuse of an institution the law protects. It suffices for us to acknowledge that adults may choose to enter upon this relationship in the confines of their homes and their own private lives and still retain their dignity as free persons. When sexuality finds overt expression in intimate conduct with another person, the conduct can be but one element in a personal bond that is more enduring. The liberty protected by the Constitution allows homosexual persons the right to make this choice.

[*Kennedy reviews the history of sodomy laws, noting that prohibitions of sodomy derived from English criminal laws included relations between men and women as well as relations between men. Law prohibiting sodomy "do not seem to have been enforced against consenting adults acting in private." Prosecutions and convictions were "for predatory acts against those who could not or did not consent, as in the case of a minor or the victim of an assault." The infrequency of prosecutions "makes it difficult to say that society approved of a rigorous and systematic punishment of the consensual acts committed in private and by adults." Far from possessing "ancient roots," as the* Bowers *decision claimed, American laws "targeting same-sex couples did not develop until the last third of the 20th century." Only nine states (Ark., Kan., Ky., Mo., Mont., Nev., Tenn., Tex., and Okla.) singled out same-sex relations for criminal prosecution, and five of those in recent years abolished them (Ark., Mont., Tenn., Ky. and Nev.)*]

... These references show an emerging awareness that liberty gives substantial protection to adult persons in deciding how to conduct their private lives in matters pertaining to sex....

This emerging recognition should have been apparent when *Bowers* was decided....

Of even more importance, almost five years before *Bowers* was decided the European Court of Human Rights considered a case with parallels to *Bowers* and to today's case. An adult male resident in Northern Ireland alleged he was a practicing homosexual who desired to engage in consensual homosexual conduct. The laws of Northern Ireland forbade him that right. He alleged that he had been questioned, his home had been searched, and he feared criminal prosecution. The court held [*in 1981*] that the laws proscribing the conduct were invalid under the European Convention on Human Rights.... Authoritative in all countries that are members of the Council of Europe (21 nations then,

45 nations now), the decision is at odds with the premise in *Bowers* that the claim put forward was insubstantial in our Western civilization.

[*Kennedy points to two cases after* Bowers *that cast its holding "into even more doubt":* Planned Parenthood v. Casey *(1992) and* Romer v. Evans *(1996). The latter raised the question whether the Texas sodomy statute should be held invalid under the Equal Protection Clause. In that case, would a state prohibition on sodomy be valid if it applied to both same-sex and different-sex participants? Kennedy chooses to look at the continuing validity of* Bowers.]

The stigma this criminal statute imposes, moreover, is not trivial. The offense, to be sure, is but a class C misdemeanor, a minor offense in the Texas legal system. Still, it remains a criminal offense with all that imports for the dignity of the persons charged....

Bowers was not correct when it was decided, and it is not correct today. It ought not to remain binding precedent. *Bowers v. Hardwick* should be and now is overruled....

The judgment of the Court of Appeals for the Texas Fourteenth District is reversed, and the case is remanded for further proceedings not inconsistent with this opinion.

It is so ordered.

JUSTICE O'CONNOR, concurring in the judgment. [*She does not join the Court in overruling* Bowers *but agreed that the Texas statute banning same-sex sodomy is unconstitutional. Instead of relying on the Due Process Clause, however, she based her conclusion on the Equal Protection Clause. "The statute at issue here makes sodomy a crime only if a person 'engages in deviate sexual intercourse with another individual of the same sex.'... Sodomy between opposite-sex partners, however, is not a crime in Texas. That is, Texas treats the same conduct differently based solely on the participants." She did not attempt to decide whether a sodomy law "that is neutral both in effect and application" would violate the substantive component of the Due Process Clause.*]

JUSTICE SCALIA, with whom THE CHIEF JUSTICE and JUSTICE THOMAS join, dissenting.

[*Scalia contrasts the "surprising readiness" of the Court to overturn* Bowers, *without worrying about stare decisis, with the Court's behavior in* Planned Parenthood v. Casey, *where stare decisis was heavily relied on to preserve the central tenet in* Roe v. Wade.]

Today's approach to *stare decisis* invites us to

overrule an erroneously decided precedent (including an "intensely divisive" decision) *if* (1) its foundations have been "ero[ded]" by subsequent decisions, *ante*, at 576; (2) it has been subject to "substantial and continuing" criticism, *ibid.*; and (3) it has not induced "individual or societal reliance" that counsels against overturning, *ante*, at 577. The problem is that *Roe* itself—which today's majority surely has no disposition to overrule—satisfies these conditions to at least the same degree as *Bowers*.

II

. . .

Bowers held, first, that criminal prosecutions of homosexual sodomy are not subject to heightened scrutiny because they do not implicate a "fundamental right" under the Due Process Clause, ...

The Court today does not overrule this holding. Not once does it describe homosexual sodomy as a "fundamental right" or a "fundamental liberty interest," not does it subject the Texas statute to strict scrutiny. Instead, ... the Court concludes that the application of Texas's statute to petitioners' conduct fails the rational-basis test, and overrules *Bowers*' holding to the contrary....

III

[*Scalia faults the majority for this statement: "[W]e think that our laws and traditions in the past half century are of most relevance here. These references show an emerging awareness that liberty gives substantial protection to adult persons in deciding how to conduct their private lives in matters pertaining to sex." To Scalia, an "emerging awareness" does not establish a "fundamental right." "Constitutional entitlements do not spring into existence because some States choose to lessen or eliminate criminal sanctions on certain behavior. Much less do they spring into existence, as the*

Court seems to believe, because foreign nations decriminalize conduct."]

IV

[*Scalia rejects the majority's contention that no rational basis exists for the Texas statute. "The Texas statute undeniably seeks to further the belief of its citizens that certain forms of sexual behavior are 'immoral and unacceptable,'... the same interest furthered by criminal laws against fornication, bigamy, adultery, adult incest, bestiality, and obscenity.... If, as the Court asserts, the promotion of majoritarian sexual morality is not even a* legitimate *state interest, none of the above-mentioned laws can survive rational-basis review."*]

V

[*Differing with O'Connor's analysis, Scalia concludes that even if the Texas did deny equal protection to "homosexuals as a class," the denial need not be justified by "anything more than a rational basis, which our cases show is satisfied by the enforcement of traditional notions of sexual morality."*]

Let me be clear that I have nothing against homosexuals, or any other group, promoting their agenda through normal democratic means. Social perceptions of sexual and other morality change over time, and every group has the right to persuade its fellow citizens that its view of such matters is the best.... But persuading one's fellow citizens is one thing, and imposing one's views in absence of democratic majority will is something else. I would no more *require* a State to criminalize homosexual acts—or, for that matter, display *any* moral disapproval of them—than I would *forbid* it to do so. What Texas has chosen to do is well within the range of traditional democratic action, and its hand should not be stayed through the invention of a brand-new "constitutional right" by a Court that is impatient of democratic change....

Justice Thomas, dissenting....

F. DEFINING THE LIMITS OF PRIVACY

Privacy has a multitude of meanings. In part, it preserves an individual's interest in seclusion or solitude. At other times it protects against the public disclosure of embarrassing private facts or avoids placing someone in a "false light" in the public eye. On other occasions, it prevents the appropriation of one's name or likeness. Prosser, 48 Cal. L. Rev. 383, 389 (1960).

Alan Westin, in *Privacy and Freedom* (1967), recommended that personal information (the right of decision over one's private personality) be defined as a property right. A citizen would be entitled to have due process of law before his "property" could be taken and misused, including access to information in the person's file and a right to challenge its accuracy. By passing the Fair Credit Reporting Act of 1970, Congress supplied that type of protection. Credit agencies are required to disclose to a consumer information about that person in their files, including the sources of the information. If a consumer successfully challenges the completeness or accuracy of any item in the file, the information must be promptly deleted. 84 Stat. 1127 (1970).

Congress intervened to protect the privacy interests of bank depositors. In 1976, the Supreme Court held that a Fourth Amendment interest could not be vindicated in court by challenging a government subpoena for microfilms of checks, deposit slips, and other records in a bank. The Court treated the materials as business records of a bank, not private papers of a person. Justice Brennan noted in a dissent that a depositor "reveals many aspects of his personal affairs, opinions, habits and associations. Indeed, the totality of bank records provides a virtual current biography." United States v. Miller, 425 U.S. 435, 451 (1976). Two years later Congress passed the Right to Financial Privacy Act, giving depositors certain procedural rights and protections that were unavailable from the Court. 92 Stat. 3697 (1978). The legislative debate illustrates that privacy interests left unprotected by the judiciary can be secured by congressional action (see reading).

In 1978, the Supreme Court upheld the right of law enforcement officers to use warrants to come onto the premises of a newspaper. Zurcher v. Stanford Daily, 436 U.S. 547 (1978). In quick response, Congress passed the Privacy Protection Act of 1980. With certain exceptions, the statute requires the use of a subpoena instead of a search warrant to obtain documentary materials from those who disseminate newspapers, books, broadcasts, or other similar forms of public communication. 94 Stat. 1879 (1980). The effect is to protect the privacy rights of those engaged in First Amendment activities. Here, too, the congressional debate is instructive (Chapter 14, Section B).

During hearings in 1987 on the nomination of Judge Robert H. Bork to be Associate Justice of the Supreme Court, a reporter obtained from a local video store a list of the movies that Bork and his family had rented. After the list was published in a newspaper, this invasion of Bork's privacy was roundly condemned. Congress responded by enacting the Video Privacy Protection Act of 1988, which makes video stores liable for actions forbidden by the statute. With certain exceptions, stores may be sued for disclosing the videotapes rented by customers. 102 Stat. 3195 (1988).

The Right to Publish

The right to privacy does not carry with it a comprehensive right to be "let alone." Legitimate actions by private agencies and government may intrude upon the individual. Carried to its extreme, the right to privacy would practically extinguish the freedom of the press. No one would dare publish or broadcast anything for fear of a lawsuit from an aggrieved citizen or public official. Even when state law prohibits the broadcasting of a rape victim's name, this right to privacy yields to the freedom of the press to publish accurately names obtained from judicial records that are open to public inspection. Cox Broadcasting v. Cohn, 420 U.S. 469 (1975). Newspapers may not be punished for publishing the name of a rape victim if the woman's full name appeared in a police report available to the press. The Florida Star v. B.J.F., 491 U.S. 524 (1989).

There are many anomalies to the right of privacy. Entertainers demand both the right to privacy and the desire for publicity. In the same year that Congress substantially strengthened the Freedom of Information Act of 1974, which gave the public access to federal agency records, it also passed the Privacy Act. This statute prohibits access by the public to certain materials in agency records. It also provides U.S. citizens the right to examine their own federal agency files and correct erroneous entries.

Governmental Powers

Although one may object to vaccination and regard it as a deprivation of personal liberty, states may invoke their police power to make it compulsory in order to prevent the spread of contagious diseases, such as smallpox. Jacobson v. Massachusetts, 197 U.S. 11 (1905). Playing radio programs on bus and streetcar systems may seem an invasion of privacy to some passengers, but the Supreme Court did not

Anthony Kennedy on Privacy

[*During his confirmation hearings in 1987 to become Associate Justice of the Supreme Court, Anthony M. Kennedy testified that he believed that a right of privacy is implicit in the U.S. Constitution.*]

Now, how far can you continue that inquiry away from the words of the text? Your question is whether or not there are unenumerated rights. To begin with, most of the inquiries that the Supreme Court has conducted in cases of this type have centered around the word "liberty." Now, the framers had that, what I call "spacious phrase," both in the fifth amendment, almost contemporaneous with the Constitution, and again in the 14th amendment they reiterated it.

The framers had an idea which is central to Western thought.

... It is central to our American tradition. It is central to the idea of the rule of law. That is there is a zone of liberty, a zone of protection, a line that is drawn where the individual can tell the Government: Beyond this line you may not go.

... It seems to me that most Americans, most lawyers, most judges, believe that liberty includes protection of a value that we call privacy....

SOURCE: "Nomination of Anthony M. Kennedy to be Associate Justice of the Supreme Court of the United States," hearings before the Senate Committee on the Judiciary, 100th Cong., 1st Sess. 86, 88 (1987).

find the practice offensive to the Constitution. Public Utilities Comm'n v. Pollak, 343 U.S. 451 (1952). However, the state does have a right to protect citizens assaulted by raucous loudspeakers. Kovacs v. Cooper, 336 U.S. 77 (1949).

In criminal law, a defendant can expect no success when invoking the right of privacy for certain activities, such as incest. Criminal procedures often affect sensitive areas of privacy, particularly those involving the body. Suspects accused of drunk driving can be subjected to compulsory blood tests and breath tests. Breithaupt v. Abram, 352 U.S. 432 (1957); Schmerber v. California, 384 U.S. 757 (1966). The Court has held that no one has an expectation of privacy if law enforcement officers decide to fly over their backyard and take photographs of marijuana plants. California v. Ciraolo, 476 U.S. 207 (1986); Florida v. Riley, 488 U.S. 445 (1989).

There are, of course, limits on the search for evidence. The police cannot use stomach pumps on a narcotics suspect to recover forbidden substances. Rochin v. California, 342 U.S. 165 (1952). States have been prohibited from compelling an armed robbery suspect to undergo surgery to remove a bullet lodged in his chest. Winston v. Lee, 470 U.S. 753 (1985). Individuals arrested and booked for misdemeanors may not be subjected to the indignity of strip searches and body-cavity searches, regardless of whether they are reasonably suspected of concealing contraband. Weber v. Dell, 804 F.2d 796 (2d Cir. 1986), cert. denied, 483 U.S. 1020 (1987).

Justice Douglas' decision in *Griswold* v. *Connecticut,* discovering a right of privacy in various "emanations" and "penumbras" in the Constitution, has been the target of harsh critiques and ridicule. However, the nation's commitment to privacy is not grounded in ephemeral judicial doctrine. Citizens harbor a natural resistance to government intrusions. The Senate 1987 hearings on the ill-fated nomination of Robert Bork to the Supreme Court underscore the deep roots of privacy in America (see reading). After Bork was rejected by the Senate, the next nominee, Anthony M. Kennedy, was forthright in recognizing an implicit right of privacy in the Constitution (see box).

Financial Privacy Act of 1978: Congressional Debate

In *United States* v. *Miller,* 425 U.S. 435 (1976), the Supreme Court held that bank depositors were not protected by the Fourth Amendment when the government wanted to gain access to microfilms of checks, deposit slips, or other bank records. These materials were regarded as business records of a bank, not the private papers of a person. Congress responded by passing legislation — the Right to Financial Privacy Act — that gave depositors certain procedural rights and protections. The debate in the House of Representatives illustrates how members of Congress are involved in deciding questions of Fourth Amendment rights and privacy interests. The excerpts below come from 124 Cong. Rec. 33310–11, 33818–19, 33835 (1978).

Mr. WHALEN. Mr. Chairman, the legislation now before us, the Financial Institution's Regulatory Act, is a complex bill, for the most part dealing with relatively esoteric questions of banking regulation. One title, however, is of direct and immediate concern to every American and is one with which I have been involved personally.

I am referring, of course, to title XI, the Right to Financial Privacy Act of 1968.

Title XI represents an enormous step forward in the protection of the rights to privacy of American citizens. I am delighted to see this legislation come to the floor of the House.

During the 93rd Congress, Senator CHARLES MATHIAS of Maryland first proposed the Bill of Rights Procedures Act. Its primary purpose was to prevent warrantless Government searches of bank, credit, medical, telephone toll billing, and other records that reveal the nature of one's private affairs. This was the first legislative proposal ever to address the problem of access to third party records.

At the start of the 94th Congress, Senator MATHIAS reintroduced the Bill of Rights Procedures Act with our former colleague, the Honorable Charles A. Mosher, serving as the chief House sponsor. I was pleased to join as a cosponsor of that measure (H.R. 214). The bill underwent more than 40 days of hearings and markup in the House Judiciary Subcommittee on Courts, Civil Liberties and the Administration of Justice, but was reported out of subcommittee too late to reach the floor in 1976....

... [T]he new legislation preserves our basic principle that third party records of a personal nature, in this case bank and credit records, should not be accessed by Government agents except with the knowledge of the subject individual or else with the supervision of the courts.

This is a crucial concept. It returns to the individual some measure of control over dissemination of records that contain very detailed information about one's daily life. And it puts the courts into a proper role of resolving conflicts between a citizen's rights to privacy and society's needs for information.

Moreover, it also restores the record holders, the banks, and credit card companies to their proper role as impartial custodians of records. I know that the financial community welcomes this opportunity to get out of the middle of disputes between customers and Government. And they surely will welcome being able once again to assure their clients that they can have a reasonable expectation that the confidentiality of their records will be maintained. Surely, everyone will benefit from the establishment of a clear set of rules and procedures....

Mr. LA FALCE. Mr. Chairman, ...

The overriding purpose of this title is to let an individual know when the Federal Government is seeking access to his financial records and what use is made of those records after the Government acquires them. The individual is given an opportunity to challenge the access to his records if he thinks that there is no legitimate reason for the Government to be seeking them. The first step is that the Government informs the individual that it wishes to review his records for a given purpose. The individual is also given a form to fill out which will enable him to challenge the Government's access to the records.

It is then up to the Government to show that the records are relevant to the investigation and that the investigation itself is a legitimate one, and not being conducted to harass an individual for political reasons, to intimidate a witness, or for other bad faith motives. The important point to remember is that we are dealing here with the preliminary stages of an investigation and, especially in cases of white collar crime, financial records are the best, if not the only evidence of the crime. At the beginning of investigations into alleged embezzlement, bribery, public corruption, extortion, drug trafficking and the like, financial records provide the information needed to begin or continue the investigation, and it is not the intent of the framers of this title to inhibit these legitimate activities of Government law enforcement authorities. To require excessively detailed demonstrations of the basis for the investigation at this point in the process would lead to the courts making preliminary decisions on investigations rather than prosecutors, and would be a violation of the separation of powers doctrine.

Some very limited exceptions are included in the

title to allow for situations in which prior notice to the individual would cause serious harm to that individual, another person, or to the investigation. In these cases, the Government is required to demonstrate the potential harm to a court, and the individual is notified after the fact that the records have been obtained, and may challenge the access if it was improper. Notice is also given to the individual of transfers of his records between Government agencies, so that at all times, unless there is a compelling reason not to disclose the transfer, he or she will know which agencies in the Federal Government have reviewed the bank records....

Mr. PATTISON of New York....

Many of us on both sides of the aisle strongly believe that individual bank records must be afforded basic privacy rights. Furthermore, it is our belief that the framers of the Constitution intended to provide protection for all individual records. At the time the fourth amendment to the Constitution was drafted, however, almost all personal records were kept at home. Protecting those records actually in the possession of the individual citizen was an adequate safeguard. In this century, however, increasingly financial records have been held by banks and other financial institutions. Furthermore, advances in communications and recordkeeping technology

now allow financial institutions to store and quickly retrieve vast amounts of information.

These records can tell a complete story about the customer's life and lifestyle: His religious and political affiliations, what medical services he requires, how much he drinks, and a vast array of his personal habits.

Despite their personal nature, these records are not afforded privacy protections. In its 1976 Miller decision, the Supreme Court ruled that, under current law, records held by a financial institution are the property of the institution, rather than the customer's. These records are therefore not entitled to safeguards from unwarranted government access. Therefore, under Miller, a citizen does not have "standing" to sue to prevent unreasonable access to those records.

Clearly, it is an empty gesture to protect individual records held in the home when a much richer store of information is readily available at the individual's bank. This inconsistency led the Privacy Protection Study Commission, in its 1977 report entitled "Personal Privacy in an Information Society," to call for the creation of "a legitimate, enforceable expectation of confidentiality."

The legislation before us today is based on the premise that bank customers have a right to reasonable expectation of privacy....

The Right to Privacy: The Bork Hearings

During the hearings in 1987 on the nomination of Robert H. Bork to be Associate Justice of the U.S. Supreme Court, questions zeroed in on Bork's position on privacy. The questioning below is directed by the Chairman of the Senate Judiciary Committee, Joseph R. Biden, Jr., followed by questions from Senator Alan K. Simpson. These passages come from "Nomination of Robert H. Bork to be Associate Justice of the Supreme Court of the United States," hearings before the Senate Committee on the Judiciary, 100th Cong., 1st Sess. 114–21, 240–42 (Part 1 of 5 Parts) (1987).

The CHAIRMAN. Well, let's talk about another case. Let's talk about the *Griswold* case. Now, while you were living in Connecticut, that State had a law—I know you know this, but for the record—that it made it a crime for anyone, even a married couple, to use birth control. You indicated that you thought that law was "nutty," to use your words and I quite agree. Nevertheless, Connecticut, under that "nutty" law, prosecuted and convicted a doctor and the case finally reached the Supreme Court.

The Court said that the law violated a married couple's constitutional right to privacy. You criticized this opinion in numerous articles and speeches, beginning in 1971 and as recently as July

26th of this year. In your 1971 article, "Neutral Principles and Some First Amendment Problems," you said that the right of married couples to have sexual relations without fear of unwanted children is no more worthy of constitutional protection by the courts than the right of public utilities to be free of pollution control laws.

You argued that the utility company's right or gratification, I think you referred to it, to make money and the married couple's right or gratification to have sexual relations without fear of unwanted children, as "the cases are identical." Now, I am trying to understand this. It appears to me that you are saying that the government has as much right to control a married couple's decision about choosing to have a child or not, as that government has a right to control the public utility's right to pollute the air. Am I misstating your rationale here?

Judge BORK. With due respect, Mr. Chairman, I think you are. I was making the point that where the Constitution does not speak—there is no provision in the Constitution that applies to the case—then a judge may not say, I place a higher value upon a marital relationship than I do upon an economic freedom. Only if the Constitution gives him some reasoning. Once the judge begins to say economic rights are more important than marital rights or vice versa, and if there is nothing in the Constitution, the judge is enforcing his own moral values, which I have objected to. Now, on the *Griswold* case itself—

The CHAIRMAN. Can we stick with that point a minute to make sure I understand it?

Judge BORK. Sure.

The CHAIRMAN. So that you suggest that unless the Constitution, I believe in the past you used the phrase, textually identifies, a value that is worthy of being protected, then competing values in society, the competing value of a public utility, in the example you used, to go out and make money—that economic right has no more or less constitutional protection than the right of a married couple to use or not use birth control in their bedroom. Is that what you are saying?

Judge BORK. No, I am not entirely, but I will straighten it out. I was objecting to the way Justice Douglas, in that opinion, *Griswold* v. *Connecticut*, derived this right. It may be possible to derive an objection to an anti-contraceptive statute in some other way. I do not know.

But starting from the assumption, which is an assumption for purposes of my argument, not a proven fact, starting from the assumption that there is nothing in the Constitution, in any legitimate method of constitutional reasoning about either subject, all I am saying is that the judge has no way to prefer one to the other and the matter should be left to the legislatures who will then decide which competing gratification, or freedom, should be placed higher.

The CHAIRMAN. Then I think I do understand it, that is, that the economic gratification of a utility company is as worthy of as much protection as the sexual gratification of a married couple, because neither is mentioned in the Constitution.

Judge BORK. All that means is that the judge may not choose.

The CHAIRMAN. Who does?

Judge BORK. The legislature.

The CHAIRMAN. Well, that is my point, so it is not a constitutional right. I am not trying to be picky here. Clearly, I do not want to get into a debate with a professor, but it seems to me that what you are saying is what I said and that is, that the Constitution—if it were a constitutional right, if the Constitution said anywhere in it, in your view, that a married couple's right to engage in the decision of having a child or not having a child was a constitutionally-protected right of privacy, then you would rule that that right exists. You would not leave it to a legislative body no matter what they did.

Judge BORK. That is right.

The CHAIRMAN. But you argue, as I understand it, that no such right exists.

Judge BORK. No, Senator, that is what I tried to clarify. I argued that the way in which this unstructured, undefined right of privacy that Justice Douglas elaborated, that the way he did it did not prove its existence.

The CHAIRMAN. You have been a professor now for years and years, everybody has pointed out and I have observed, you are one of the most well-read and scholarly people to come before this committee. In all your short life, have you come up with any other way to protect a married couple, under the Constitution, against an action by a government telling them what they can or cannot do about birth control in their bedroom? Is there any constitutional right, anywhere in the Constitution?

Judge BORK. I have never engaged in that exercise....

The CHAIRMAN.

... Does a State legislative body, or any legislative body, have a right to pass a law telling a married couple, or anyone else, that behind—let's stick with the married couple for a minute—behind their bedroom door, telling them they can or cannot use birth control? Does the majority have the right to tell a couple that they cannot use birth control?

Judge BORK. There is always a rationality standard in the law, Senator. I do not know what rationale the State would offer or what challenge the married couple would make. I have never decided that case. If it ever comes before me, I will have to decide it. All I have done was point out that the right of privacy, as defined or undefined by Justice Douglas, was a free-floating right that was not derived in a principled fashion from constitutional materials. That is all I have done.

The CHAIRMAN. Judge, I agree with the rationale offered in the case. Let me just read it to you and it went like this. I happen to agree with it. It said, in part, "would we allow the police to search the sacred precincts of marital bedrooms for telltale signs of contraceptives? The very idea is repulsive to the notions of privacy surrounding the marriage relationship. We deal with the right of privacy older than the Bill of Rights. Marriage is a coming together for better or worse, hopefully enduring, and intimate to the degree of being sacred. The association promotes a way of life, not causes. A harmony of living, not political [faiths]. A bilateral loyalty, not a commercial or social projects."

Obviously, that Justice believes that the Constitution protects married couples, anyone.

Judge Bork. I could agree with almost every—I think I could agree with every word you read but that is not, with respect, Mr. Chairman, the rationale of the case. That is the rhetoric at the end of the case. What I objected to was the way in which this right of privacy was created and that was simply this. Justice Douglas observed, quite correctly, that a number of provisions of the Bill of Rights protect aspects of privacy and indeed they do and indeed they should.

But he went on from there to say that since a number of the provisions did that and since they had emanations, by which I think he meant buffer zones to protect the basic right, he would find a penumbra which created a new right of privacy that existed where no provision of the Constitution applied, so that he—

The Chairman. What about the ninth amendment?

Judge Bork. Wait, let me finish with Justice Douglas.

The Chairman. All right.

Judge Bork. He did not rest on the ninth amendment. That was Justice Goldberg.

The Chairman. Right. That is what I was talking about.

Judge Bork. Yes. And I want to discuss first Justice Douglas and then I would be glad to discuss Justice Goldberg.

The Chairman. OK.

Judge Bork. Now you see, in that way, he could have observed, equally well, the various provisions of the Constitution protect individual freedom and therefore, generalized a general right of freedom that would apply where no provision of the Constitution did. That is exactly what Justice Hugo Black criticized in dissent in that case, in some heated terms—and Justice Potter Stewart also dissented in that case.

So, in observing that *Griswold* v. *Connecticut* does not sustain its burden, the judge's burden of

showing that the right comes from constitutional materials, I am by no means alone. A lot of people, including Justices, have criticized that decision.

The Chairman. I am not suggesting whether you are alone or in the majority. I am just trying to find out where you are. As I hear you, you do not believe that there is a general right of privacy that is in the Constitution.

Judge Bork. Not one derived in *that* fashion. There may be other arguments and I do not want to pass upon those....

Senator Simpson ...

I want to ask you if it is fair to say that you believe that privacy is protected under the Constitution, but that you just do not believe that there is a general and unspecified right that protects everything including homosexual conduct, incest, whatever—and you mentioned that yesterday. Is that correct?

Judge Bork. That is correct, Senator. I think the fact that I did not get everything I wanted to say out was my fault because I was trying to discuss with Senator Biden and others the constitutional problem. But I think it requires a fuller answer than that and that is this: No civilized person wants to live in a society without a lot of privacy in it. And the framers, in fact, of the Constitution protected privacy in a variety of ways.

The first amendment protects free exercise of religion. The free speech provision of the first amendment has been held to protect the privacy of membership lists and a person's associations in order to make the free speech right effective. The fourth amendment protects the individual's home and office from unreasonable searches and seizures, and usually requires a warrant. The Fifth amendment has a right against self-incrimination.

There is much more. There is a lot of privacy in the Constitution. *Griswold,* in which we were talking about a Connecticut statute which was unenforced against any individual except the birth control clinic, *Griswold* involved a Connecticut statute which banned the use of contraceptives. And Justice Douglas entered that opinion with a rather eloquent statement of how awful it would be to have the police pounding into the marital bedroom. And it would be awful, and it would never happen because there is the fourth amendment.

Nobody ever tried to enforce that statute, but the police simply could not get into the bedroom without a warrant, and what magistrate is going to give the police a warrant to go in to search for signs of the use of contraceptives? I mean it is a wholly bizarre and imaginary case.

... [T]he only reason that Connecticut statute stayed on the statute book—it was an old, old statute, dating back from the days when Connecticut was entirely a Yankee State—the only reason it stayed on the statute book was that it was not enforced. If anybody had tried to enforce that against a married couple, he would have been out of office instantly and the law would have been repealed....

CONCLUSIONS

Although not expressly mentioned in the U.S. Constitution, the right of privacy is strongly defended by all sectors of society, liberal and conservative, even though their notions of privacy may differ. The framers cherished privacy as an essential condition for the development of the mind and the foundation for religious liberty. Precisely where the right of privacy ends and the power of government begins is a complex process in which all three branches of government are engaged with the general public.

In its decisions on privacy, the Court initially adopted sweeping and ambitious theories of fundamental rights (*Griswold* and *Roe*). Under heavy criticism from the public—raising core questions of illegitimate judicial power—the Court was forced to carve out a more modest role for itself while recognizing a larger function for elected branches and the states. Having overstepped in *Roe*, the Court was not about to recognize a fundamental constitutional right to die (*Glucksberg* and *Vacco*).

Some of the privacy issues are perennial topics of debate, such as reputation and the scope of the Fourth Amendment. Other issues, including the quartering of troops proscribed by the Third Amendment, seem archaic. A number of the privacy issues of recent decades are controversies brought about by technology, ranging from electronic surveillance to medical advances that affect the right of abortion and the right to die. On all these issues the announcement of what constitutes privacy may originate at first as an agency regulation, congressional statute, or court decision, with no branch having the final say. Increasingly, state legislatures, governors, and state courts are pursuing their own concepts of privacy, as seen under state constitutions. A number of state constitutions expressly provide for the right of privacy. The driving force behind these governmental actions, whether at the national or state level, are the individuals and the groups pressing their particular principles of privacy.

NOTES AND QUESTIONS

1. Justice Douglas's opinion for the Court in *Griswold v. Connecticut* asserts a general right to privacy grounded in the "penumbras and emanations" of the Bill of Rights. Explain his argument. Is it persuasive? Why or why not? What limitations may be imposed on this approach? Do some constitutional provisions more readily lend themselves to this approach than others? Which ones?

2. In *Griswold*, Justice Goldberg cited the Ninth Amendment as the source of a right to privacy. Is his approach persuasive? Why or why not? How can the language of the Ninth Amendment be read to support Goldberg's claim? In your view, who is responsible for determining the existence of "others retained by the people"? May the Court create new rights? If so, can you articulate a constitutional theory to support your position?

3. Has the Court's reaffirmation of the core of *Roe v. Wade* created a precedent that is "too late" to be disturbed? What weight should be attached to Justice Cardozo's view, as endorsed and explained by Justice O'Connor's opinion in *Planned Parenthood v. Casey*, that the Court's work would suffer if "it eyed each issue afresh in every case that raised it"? Has the "undue burden" test provided a workable standard that satisfies concerns about the Court's abortion jurisprudence?

4. In *Texas v. Lawrence*, Justice Kennedy sought to illuminate the issues in the case by drawing attention to a parallel case in Northern Ireland decided by the European Court of Human Rights. In

your opinion, is it appropriate for the Court to utilize foreign cases in its interpretation of U.S. law? Why or why not?

5. To what extent has the Court applied Justice Brandeis's insight in *Olmstead v. United States* that the Constitution embodies and protects the "right to be let alone"? Which particular cases promote that belief? Why didn't the Court embrace that approach in *Bowers v. Hardwick*?

SELECTED READINGS

BERGER, RAOUL. "The Ninth Amendment." 66 Cornell Law Review 1 (1980).

BLOUSTEIN, EDWARD J. "Privacy as an Aspect of Human Dignity: An Answer to Dean Prosser." 39 New York University Law Review 962 (1964).

BRECKINRIDGE, ADAM CARLYLE. The Right to Privacy. Lincoln: University of Nebraska Press, 1970.

CAPLAN, RUSSELL L. "The History and Meaning of the Ninth Amendment." 69 Virginia Law Review 223 (1983).

CRAVEN, J. BRAXTON, JR. "Personhood: The Right to Be Let Alone," 1976 Duke Law Journal 699.

DEVINS, NEAL. Shaping Constitutional Values: Elected Government, the Supreme Court, and the Abortion Debate. Baltimore, Md.: Johns Hopkins University Press, 1996.

ELY, JOHN HART. "The Wages of Crying Wolf: A Comment on Roe v. Wade." 82 Yale Law Journal 920 (1973).

EPSTEIN, LEE AND JOSEPH F. KOBYLKA. The Supreme Court and Legal Change: Abortion and the Death Penalty. Chapel Hill: University of North Carolina Press, 1992.

EPSTEIN, RICHARD A. "Substantive Due Process by Any Other Name: The Abortion Cases." 1973 Supreme Court Review 159.

FRIED, CHARLES. "Privacy." 77 Yale Law Journal 475 (1968).

GARROW, DAVID J. Liberty and Sexuality: The Right to Privacy and the Making of Roe v. Wade. New York: Macmillan, 1994.

HENKIN, LOUIS. "Privacy and Autonomy." 74 Columbia Law Review 1410 (1974).

LUKER, KRISTIN. Abortion and the Politics of Motherhood. Berkeley: University of California Press, 1984.

MAYER, MICHAEL. Rights of Privacy. New York: Law-Arts Publishers, 1972.

McCLELLAN, GRANT S., ed. The Right to Privacy. New York: H.W. Wilson, 1976.

MILLER, ARTHUR R. The Assault on Privacy. Ann Arbor: University of Michigan Press, 1971.

O'BRIEN, DAVID M. Privacy, Law, and Public Policy. New York: Praeger, 1979.

PEMBER, DON R. Privacy and the Press. Seattle: University of Washington Press, 1972.

PENNOCK, J. ROLAND, AND JOHN W. CHAPMAN, eds. Privacy. New York: Atherton, 1971.

PROSSER, WILLIAM L. "Privacy." 48 California Law Review 383 (1960).

REHNQUIST, WILLIAM H. "Is an Expanded Right of Privacy Consistent with Fair and Effective Law Enforcement? Or, Privacy, You've Come a Long Way, Baby." 23 University of Kansas Law Review 1 (1974).

RUBIN, EVA R. Abortion, Politics, and the Courts: Roe v. Wade and Its Aftermath. New York: Greenwood Press, 1987.

SHATTUCK, JOHN H. F. Rights of Privacy. Skokie, Ill.: National Textbook Co., 1977.

STEINER, GILBERT Y., ed. The Abortion Dispute and the American System. Washington, D.C.: The Brookings Institution, 1983.

WARREN, SAMUEL D., AND LOUIS D. BRANDEIS. "The Right to Privacy." 4 Harvard Law Review 193 (1890).

WESTIN, ALAN F. Privacy and Freedom. New York: Atheneum, 1967.

18

Political Participation

Democratic systems depend on public participation at every level: national, state, and local. Citizens need to be involved throughout the year, not merely on election day. All three branches have helped shape the rights and privileges of the political process. Previous chapters discussed political participation in terms of free speech, free press, the right of petition, and freedom of assembly. This chapter focuses on presidential elections, voting rights, primaries and general elections, reapportionment, campaign financing, and lobbying.

A. PRESIDENTIAL ELECTIONS

The framers decided against a direct election for the President. Instead, they chose an indirect method that depends on a body of electors equal to the "whole Number of Senators and Representatives to which the State may be entitled in the Congress" (Art. II, § 1). This system is not "anti-democratic" or at odds with the popular will. It seeks to balance the needs of the national government and the individual states. Citizens still vote for the President, but their choices are state by state rather than expressed though a national referendum. Second, the formula offers an advantage to small states. No matter how small in population, each state has at least three electors. Third, in addition to this initial advantage to small states, the Electoral College offers benefits to populous states and to concentrations of voters within states because electoral votes are generally awarded on a winner-take-all basis. Fourth, since most states follow the winner-take-all principle, the existing system favors the two principal political parties over the interests of minor parties. Direct election of the President would likely produce stronger third parties and reduce the voting strength of the winning candidate.

In the early years, state legislatures generally chose the electors but all states now provide for popular election of electors. Voters actually choose a slate of electors for a presidential candidate, even though the names of electors usually do not appear on the ballot. Congress passed legislation to require electors to meet in their state capitals on the first Monday after the second Wednesday in December to cast their votes for President and Vice President. In 2000, that date came on December 18. A successful presidential candidate must garner a majority of the Electoral College (270 out of 538 votes). Winning the popular vote may be personally gratifying but it does not automatically take a candidate to the White House.

Twelfth Amendment

If no presidential candidate wins a majority of electoral votes, the selection goes to the House of Representatives, with each state delegation given a single vote. The Constitution provided that the electors "vote by Ballot for two Persons." If a political party voted in a disciplined way for President and Vice President, each person would receive the identical number of electoral votes. That happened in 1800 when every Democratic-Republican (the current Democratic Party) elector cast their votes for the two party nominees: Thomas Jefferson and Aaron Burr. The intent was to elect Jefferson as President and Burr as Vice President, but each ended up with 73 electoral votes. After 36 ballots over a six-day period, the House selected Jefferson as President. The Twelfth Amendment, adopted in1804, fixed this problem by requiring electors to vote not for "two persons" but to vote "by ballot for President and Vice President." Another problem arose in 1824 when electoral votes were split among four candidates: Andrew Jackson, William Crawford, John Quincy Adams, and Henry Clay, throwing the matter into the House again, which elected Adams on the first ballot.

Statutory Remedies (3 U.S.C. § 5)

A candidate who wins a majority of electoral votes may fail to win a majority of the popular vote and may even receive a smaller popular vote than the losing candidate. In 1876, Democrat Samuel J. Tilden polled 4,287,670 votes against 4,035,924 for Republican Rutherford B. Hayes. A majority of the Electoral College at that time was 185. Tilden had 184 to Hayes's 165. After an Electoral Commission created by Congress gave Hayes 20 disputed votes, he was declared President. See Michael F. Holt, By One Vote: The Disputed Presidential Election of 1876 (2008). In 1887, Congress passed legislation in an effort to prevent a repetition of what happened a decade earlier. Congress set up a system that encouraged states to pass legislation for the appointment of electors. If the states followed specified procedures, their decisions would be treated as "conclusive" on Congress when it met to receive electoral votes. 24 Stat. 373, sec. 2 (1887). That provision is now codified at 3 U.S.C. § 5 (analyzed later).

The 2000 Election

Presidential elections worked fairly smoothly until 2000. For 35 excruciating days—from election day November 7 to December 12—the contest between Al Gore and George W. Bush maintained a dizzying pace. At issue were 25 crucial electoral votes in Florida. One could scarcely leave the house for three hours without discovering, upon one's return, that the legal landscape had (once again) been dramatically altered. At various times rulings were handed down by lower courts in Florida, federal district courts, the Eleventh Circuit, the Florida Supreme Court (four times), and the U.S. Supreme Court (twice). Sitting in the wings were other political institutions waiting to exercise their constitutional duties: the Florida Legislature and the U.S. Congress. On December 12, the U.S. Supreme Court ruled against a recount of Florida votes requested by Gore and the following day he gave his concession speech. On January 6, 2001, a joint session of Congress officially tallied the electoral votes that made Bush the next President.

This extraordinary election raised many questions. Why did the U.S. Supreme Court take the case? Was its decision persuasive? Who might have won had the recount been allowed to go forward? Why not let the decision be decided by Congress through established statutory procedures? Were voters (as some claimed) "disenfranchised"? Should the Electoral College be abolished? The controversy provided an educational primer on the election process and the deficiencies of voting machines and ballots. Everyone added a word to their vocabulary: *chad* (the piece of paper punched out of a ballot).

High-Stakes Litigation[1]

On the evening of election day, November 7, television networks first projected Gore as the winner in Florida (and therefore President). By early morning, the networks switched to announce Bush as

---

1. For some of the literature analyzing the Florida election, see Charles L. Zelden, Bush v. Gore: Exposing the Hidden Crisis in American Democracy (2008); Howard Gillman, The Votes That Counted: How the Court Decided the 2000 Presidential Election (2001); Samuel Issacharoff et al., When Elections Go Bad; The Law of Democracy and the Presidential Election of 2000 (2001); Kathleen Hall Jamieson and Paul Waldman, eds., Electing the President, 2000: The Insiders' View (2001); Richard A. Posner, Breaking Deadlock: The 2000 Election, the Constitution, and the Courts (2001); Jack N. Rakove, ed., The Unfinished Election of 2000: Leading Scholars Examine America's Strangest Election (2001); Cass R. Sunstein and Richard A. Epstein, eds., The Vote: Bush, Gore and the Supreme Court (2001). An article in the October 2004 issue of *Vanity Fair* offers a few insights by law clerks who served at the time of *Bush* v. *Gore*, but the authors concede that the story from these clerks "is admittedly skewed" and "may at times be lopsided, partisan, speculative, and incomplete." David Margolick et al., "The Path to Florida," Vanity Fair, October 2004, at 310, 320.

"Protest" and "Contest" Procedures in Florida

102.166. Protest of election returns

Any candidate for nomination or election has the right to protest election returns "as being erroneous" by filing with the appropriate canvassing board a sworn, written protest. The protest must be filed prior to the time the canvassing board certifies the results for the office being protested or within 5 days after midnight of the date the election is held, whichever occurs later. Requests for a manual recount may also be made by political committees and political parties.

The county canvassing board "may authorize a manual recount," which must include at least three precincts and at least one percent of the total votes cast for such candidate or issue. If the manual recount indicates an error in the vote tabulation "which could affect the outcome of the election," the county canvassing board shall (a) correct the error and recount the remaining precincts with the vote tabulation system; (b) request the Department of State to verify the tabulation software; or (c) manually recount all ballots. If a counting team "is unable to determine *a voter's intent* in casting a ballot, the ballot shall be presented to the county canvassing board for it to determine *the voter's intent*" (emphasis supplied).

102.168. Contest of election

The certification of election, nomination, or the result of any referendum question "may be contested in the circuit court by any unsuccessful candidate for such office or nomination thereto or by any elector qualified to vote in the election related to such candidacy, or by any taxpayer, respectively." A contestant shall file a complaint with the clerk of the circuit court within 10 days after midnight of the date the last county canvassing board certifies the results of the election being contested, or within 5 days after midnight of the date the last county canvassing board certifies the results of that particular election following a protest pursuant to 102.166, whichever occurs later.

The grounds for contesting an election include (a) misconduct, fraud, or corruption on the part of any election official or any member of the canvassing board "sufficient to change or *place in doubt* the result of the election" (emphasis supplied); (b) ineligibility of the successful candidate for the nomination or office in dispute; (c) receipt of a number of illegal votes or rejection of a number of legal votes "sufficient to change or *place in doubt* the result of the election" (emphasis supplied). The circuit judge handling the contest "may fashion such orders as he or she deems necessary to ensure that each allegation in the complaint is investigated, examined, or checked, to prevent or correct any alleged wrong, and to provide any relief appropriate under such circumstances."

---

the winner. Bush's lead in Florida on November 8 stood at 1,784 votes. Because that margin was less than one-half of one percent of the total votes cast, state law mandated an automatic machine recount in all 67 counties. The recount cut Bush's lead to 327.

Florida law offered candidates two ways to challenge election results: one before certification of the election results, the other after. For the first, candidates may file a "protest" with the canvassing board, which has authority to call for a manual recount. An initial test recount is conducted in at least three precincts. After certification, unsuccessful candidates may "contest" an election by filing a lawsuit in circuit court. The complaint must establish grounds to show that the result of the election can be changed or "place[d] in doubt." (See box for details of these two procedures.)

On November 9, the Florida Democratic Executive Committee exercised the protest option by requesting manual recounts in four counties: Miami-Dade, Broward, Palm Beach, and Volusia. Bush went to federal district court to bar the manual recount, but the court on November 13 denied his request. Siegel v. Lepore, 120 F.Supp.2d 1041 (S.D. Fla. 2000), aff'd, 234 F.3d 1163 (11th Cir. 2000). Legal action was also started by Democrats to challenge the counting of absentee ballots in Seminole County. With the manual and machine recounts underway, Florida law required that all county returns be certified by 5 P.M. on the seventh day after an election, unless the Secretary of State exercised statutory discretion to accept ballots (such as overseas ballots) counted after the deadline. On November 13, Florida Secretary of State Katherine Harris announced that she would ignore returns of manual recounts received after the statutory deadline of November 14 at 5 P.M.

The Volusia County Canvassing Board filed suit in Florida court, claiming it was not bound by her decision; the Florida Democratic Party joined as intervenors. On November 14, Judge Terry Lewis ruled that the deadline was mandatory and that he had no authority to "rewrite the Statute" creating another deadline. McDermott v. Harris, Case No. 00-2700 (Nov. 14, 2000). Subsequent to his order, Harris instructed Florida's Supervisors of Elections to submit to her by 2 P.M. on November 15 why they should be allowed to amend certified returns previously filed. After considering their reasons in light of specific criteria, she announced on November 15 that the amended returns would not be accepted and that she would certify the results of the presidential election on November 18.

Florida Supreme Court (I)

After Judge Lewis denied Gore relief, the Florida Supreme Court on November 21 issued a unanimous ruling in his favor, directed in part by "the will of the people" as the "guiding principle in election cases." The Court concluded that Harris was required to accept returns after the seven-day deadline set forth in Florida law. It moved the November 14 certification deadline to 5 P.M. on November 26. Palm Beach County Canvassing Board v. Harris, 772 So.2d 1220 (Fla. 2000).

U.S. Supreme Court (I)

The U.S. Supreme Court on November 24 granted Bush's motion for expedited consideration of a cert petition to consider two questions: (1) whether the Florida Supreme Court, by effectively changing elector appointment procedures after the election day, violated the Due Process Clause or 3 U.S.C. §5, and (2) whether the Florida Supreme Court changed the manner in which the state's electors are to be selected, in violation of the state legislature's power under the U.S. Constitution, Art. II, §1, cl. 2:

> Each State shall appoint, in such Manner as the Legislature thereof may direct, a Number of Electors, equal to the whole Number of Senators and Representatives to which the State may be entitled in the Congress: …

The Court added another question: (3) what would be the consequences of finding that the Florida Supreme Court's decision does not comply with 3 U.S.C. §5? That provision of federal law offers a "safe harbor" for electors appointed in accordance with state law enacted prior to the election day by making their appointment—completed six days before the time fixed for the meeting of the electors—"conclusive" on Congress. In 2000, that meant that states should appoint electors by December 12 (six days before the electors met on December 18). 3 U.S.C. §5 provides:

> If any State shall have provided, by laws enacted prior to the day fixed for the appointment of the electors, for its final determination of any controversy or contest concerning the appointment of all or any of the electors of such State, by judicial or other methods or procedures, and such determination shall have been made at least six days before the time fixed for the meeting of the electors, such determination made pursuant to such law so existing on said day, and made at least six days prior to said time of meeting of the electors, shall be conclusive, and shall govern in the counting of the electoral votes as provided in the Constitution, and as hereinafter regulated, so far as the ascertainment of the electors appointed by such State is concerned.

During oral argument on December 1, several Justices sharply questioned the ruling of the Florida Supreme Court (see box on next page).

With a unanimous per curiam order on December 4, the Supreme Court vacated the judgment of the Florida Supreme Court. Acknowledging that the U.S. Supreme Court generally defers to a state court's interpretation of a state statute, the per curiam noted that in the selection of presidential elec-

Justices Uneasy about Florida Ruling

Responding to the Florida Supreme Court's use of equitable power to extend a statutory deadline, Kennedy asked: "Isn't that such an amorphous, general, abstract standard that it can't possibly be said to be law that was enacted and in place at the time of the election?" Also on altering the deadline, O'Connor remarked: "Well, but certainly the date changed. That is a dramatic change. The date for certification. Right?" She later asked: "who would have thought that the [Florida] Legislature was leaving open the date for change by the court? Who would have thought that?" Gore's attorney, Laurence Tribe, appeared to make light of the change in deadlines, saying that "it is part of the popular culture to talk about how unfair it is to change the rules of the game." He dismissed the change in deadlines as "nothing extraordinary. It's not like suddenly moving Heartbreak Hill or adding a mile or subtracting a mile from a marathon." Kennedy jumped in with some sarcasm: "In fact, we can change the rules after the game; it's not important. Popular culture."

The Deputy Attorney General of Florida noted that § 102.166 authorizes manual recounts, but

Scalia corrected him: "That's different from requires." On a different point, Scalia asked Tribe: "Can I ask you why you think the Florida Legislature delegated to the Florida Supreme Court the authority to interpose the Florida Constitution?" Rehnquist made the same point: "It seems to me a federal question arises if the Florida Supreme Court, in its opinion, rather clearly says that we're using the Florida Constitution to reach the result we reach in construing the statute," referring to *McPherson* v. *Blacker*, 146 U.S. 1 (1892) for the proposition that Art. II, § 1, cl. 2, gives plenary power to the state legislature to appoint electors.

Some Justices were inclined to leave the matter to other political institutions. Ginsburg argued that the Court has generally deferred to state courts when they interpret state law: "I mean, in case after case, we have said we owe the highest respect to what the State Supreme Court says is the state's law." Souter suggested it might be better to let Congress resolve the dispute under 5 U.S.C. § 15, which explains how Congress will count electoral votes. Breyer wondered whether the issue was too speculative to warrant intervention by the Court.

SOURCE: Oral argument of December 1, 2000.

tors the Florida legislature was not acting solely under state authority but also by virtue of authority granted under Art. II, § 2, cl. 2, of the U.S. Constitution. Bush v. Palm Beach County Canvassing Board, 531 U.S. 70 (2000). The underlying message: Try again, but this time be more careful. Interestingly, nothing in the grant of cert on November 24 or in the per curiam of December 4 mentioned what would later be the key issue: the Equal Protection Clause.

Judge Sauls' Ruling

While the U.S. Supreme Court was considering its case, Judge N. Sanders Sauls of Leon County Circuit Court presided over a case brought by Gore, who contested the state certification of Bush as erroneous. Much of the two-day trial focused on the legitimacy of counting indented ("dimpled") ballots—where the voter had not punched through the ballot. Were these votes being discovered or manufactured? On December 4, Sauls announced that he found "no credible statistical evidence, and no other competent substantial evidence to establish by a preponderance of a reasonable probability that the results of the statewide election in the State of Florida would be different from the result which had been certified by the State Elections Canvassing Commission." He found no evidence of illegality, dishonesty, gross negligence, improper influence, coercion, or fraud in the balloting and counting procedures. He also concluded that Gore's request for a partial recount would create "a two-tier situation within one county, as well as with respect to other counties," treating voters differently depending on the county they voted in. A recount would require a review of all ballots in all of the counties. Gore v. Harris, Case No. CV 00-2808 (Dec. 4, 2000).

Florida Supreme Court (II)

In reviewing Sauls' ruling, a 4 to 3 Florida Supreme Court on December 8 agreed that any recount would have to be done statewide, not just the counties selected by Gore. However, it reversed Sauls by granting Gore a manual recount in all Florida counties. The Court held that Sauls had failed to apply the proper standard in determining Gore's burden under the contest statute. Sauls required a "preponderance of a reasonable probability," but under 102.168 it was enough for Gore to show that the results of the election had been "placed in doubt." Chief Justice Charles T. Wells and two other Justices issued strong dissents. By failing to provide a meaningful standard for counting ballots, they reasoned, the majority created equal protection problems. Gore v. Harris, 772 So.2d 1243 (Fla. 2000). On the evening of December 8, Judge Terry Lewis ordered the counting of ballots to begin at 8 A.M. the following day (Saturday) and be concluded by 2 P.M. on Sunday, December 10. He left it up to the canvassing boards to determine the standards for judging the "clear indication of the intent of the voter." Any disagreements would be returned to him for final determination. Gore v. Harris, Case No. 00-2808 (Dec. 9, 2000). In this manner, Judge Lewis promised to supply a single, impartial standard to review these contested ballots. However, this uniform standard would be imposed *afterwards*, not before.

U.S. Supreme Court (II)

Early on the afternoon of December 9, while ballots were being segregated into different categories in Florida and some votes were counted, the U.S. Supreme Court ordered a stay to the recount process. In a concurrence, Scalia highlighted the issue that troubled a number of his colleagues: "the propriety, indeed the constitutionality, of letting the standard for determination of voters' intent—dimpled chads, hanging chads, etc.—vary from county to county, as the Florida Supreme Court opinion, as interpreted by the Circuit Court, permits." He also expressed concern that "each manual recount produces a degradation of the ballots, which renders a subsequent recount inaccurate." Bush v. Gore, 531 U.S. 1046 (2000). Stevens, joined by Souter, Ginsburg, and Breyer, dissented. The case was set for oral argument on Monday, December 11, at 11 A.M.

During oral argument, O'Connor said she found it "troublesome" that the Florida Supreme Court had not responded to the remand by the U.S. Supreme Court on December 4: "It just seemed to kind of bypass it and assume that all those changes and deadlines were just fine and they'd go ahead and adhere to them." Later that day, the Florida Supreme Court released its opinion (No. III) in response to the remand. It reviewed its arguments on the "shall" versus "may" statutory conflict and maintained that the November 26 deadline it established on November 11 "was not a new 'deadline' and has no effect in future elections." Footnote 17 indicated that manual recounts were circumscribed by 3 U.S.C. §5, "which sets December 12, 2000 as the date for final determination to be given conclusive effect in Congress." Palm Beach County Canvassing Board v. Harris, 772 So.2d 1273 (Fla. 2000). If December 12 was indeed the deadline, how could the Florida Supreme Court on December 8 have set in motion a recount procedure that was almost certainly impossible (given inevitable appeals) to complete by December 12?

At oral argument, six Justices expressed concern about the inadequate standards for recounting votes in Florida: Breyer, Kennedy, O'Connor, Rehnquist, Scalia, and Souter. Because Thomas had joined the stay order, he was likely the seventh Justice troubled by the lack of standards. When Kennedy asked whether the "intent of the voter" standard could vary from county to county, Gore attorney David Boies admitted it "can vary from individual to individual."

At about 10 P.M. on December 12, the Court released its opinion reversing the Florida Supreme

Court. The per curiam opinion, finding a violation of the Equal Protection Clause because of the standardless manual recounts, said a state "may not, by later arbitrary and disparate treatment, value one person's vote over that of another." Seven Justices found constitutional problems with the recount ordered by the Florida Supreme Court, but Souter and Breyer would have returned the matter to Florida with instructions to establish uniform acceptable standards. Rehnquist wrote a concurrence, joined by Scalia and Thomas. Stevens, Souter, Ginsburg, and Breyer issued separate dissenting opinions. BUSH v. GORE, 531 U.S. 98 (2000).

The per curiam suggests that the December 12 deadline came from *the Florida Supreme Court*: "The Supreme Court of Florida has said that the legislature intended the State's electors to 'participat[e] fully in the federal electoral process,' as provided in 3 U.S.C. §5." The per curiam contains conflicting statements about whether the Florida Supreme Court, or a Florida trial judge, could have issued uniform standards. At one place the per curiam states that for purposes of resolving the equal protection challenge "it is not necessary to decide whether the Florida Supreme Court had the authority under the legislative scheme for resolving whether disputes to define what a legal vote is and to mandate a manual recount implementing that decision." A few pages later, however, the per curiam remarks: "we are presented with a situation where a state court with the power to assure uniformity has ordered a statewide recount with minimal procedural safeguards. When a court orders a statewide remedy, there must be at least some assurance that the rudimentary requirements of equal treatment and fundamental fairness are satisfied." This seems like a pretty clear rebuke to the Florida judiciary, and yet, given the remand of December 4 by the U.S. Supreme Court, Florida courts were no doubt leery of crafting standards that might be taken as the creation of "new law" and thus invite further reversals.

Options for the U.S. Supreme Court

Serious issues were created by the Florida Supreme Court when it (1) established a new deadline for issuing the certification, (2) performed a strained statutory interpretation of the conflict between "shall" and "may," and (3) called for a statewide manual recount without uniform standards. Changing the statutory deadline from November 14 to November 26 looked too much like creation of new law. On statutory interpretation, it is true there was a conflict between two statutory provisions. 102.111 directed that the Secretary of State "shall" ignore county returns not received by 5 P.M. of the seventh day following an election; 102.112 said that late returns "may" be ignored. It was proper for the Court to treat 102.112 as controlling, because it was added in 1989; 102.111 dated back to 1951. However, the Court created a third category: the Secretary "must" accept late returns up to the Court's November 26 deadline. It transformed statutory discretion ("may") to a mandate. Regarding the lack of uniform standards, the Florida Supreme Court may have been gun-shy about "creating new law" and running afoul of 3 U.S.C. §5.

In reversing the Florida Supreme Court, the U.S. Supreme Court relied heavily on the December 12 deadline. For several reasons, this analysis was artificial and unconvincing. First, states can forgo the "safe harbor" of 3 U.S.C. §5 and submit their results on December 18 and even later. Second, the ballots probably could have been counted by December 12 had the Court not issued its stay on December 9. Of course, any result of the manual recount announced by December 12 would have been subject to legal challenges, with the case going back to the Florida Supreme Court and probably to the U.S. Supreme Court.

It might have been more persuasive if the Court had issued this ruling: "The standardless manual recount provisions in place in Florida for the presidential election violate fundamental principles of equal protection. We have no authority to create new standards in the middle of the game. Neither does the Florida Supreme Court, a Florida trial judge, or the Florida Legislature. The Florida Legislature has authority to create uniform standards that will satisfy equal protection guarantees, but those standards would necessarily govern future elections, not this one." Instead of relying on the December 12 deadline, the Court could have emphasized the inability of any political institution (judicial, executive, or legislative) to change the rules in the middle of an election contest. Moreover, by stating that it had no authority to issue such standards, it would have looked less "activist" and less intent on arrogating power that belongs in the hands of other political bodies.

Other options were available. The U.S. Supreme Court, by a 7–2 margin, could have given Florida until December 18 to develop acceptable standards for the recount. Florida courts would have had to hear testimony in creating those standards, let the recount go forward, permit Gore and Bush to object to particular ballots, and then allow judicial review by the Florida Supreme Court and the U.S. Supreme Court. This process could not have been completed by December 18, but the spotlight would have been taken off the U.S. Supreme Court and redirected to the impossibility of Florida correcting inadequacies in its system.

Florida Supreme Court (IV)

On December 22, the Florida Supreme Court responded to the remand of December 12. It explained that the "intent of the voter" standard it ordered on December 8 was the legislative standard in place as of November 7, 2000, and that "a more expansive ruling would have raised an issue as to whether this Court would be substantially rewriting the Code after the election, in violation of article II, section 1, clause 2 of the United States Constitution and 3 U.S.C. § 5 (1994)." It explained in detail the technical and legal problems of conducting a manual recount. To cope with those problems, it was necessary to adopt statewide standards, the Court concluded that the development of those standards belonged to a different political body: the Florida Legislature. Gore v. Harris, 773 So.2d 524 (Fla. 2000).

Some Mopping Up

On January 5, 2001, the U.S. Supreme Court denied cert on several issues that had been decided by lower courts. One involved an Eleventh Circuit decision rejecting a challenge to absentee ballots cast by overseas voters. The other concerned a suit arguing that George W. Bush and Richard B. Cheney were both "inhabitants" of Texas and thus in violation of the Twelfth Amendment, which prohibits the President and Vice President from being inhabitants of the same state. The Fifth Circuit had ruled that Cheney, who had a home in Dallas, Texas, was a resident of Wyoming. Harris v. Florida Elections Canvassing Commission, 531 U.S. 1062 (2001); Jones v. Bush, 531 U.S. 1062 (2001).

Issues Along the Way

Suspicions about the Florida election were inflamed by some extraordinary factors. The governor of Florida, Jeb Bush, was the brother of George W. Bush. The Florida Secretary of State, Katherine Harris, had co-chaired the Bush campaign committee in Florida. The Florida legislature threatened to appoint its own electors (for Bush) if Gore won a recount. Divisions were rampant on all sides. The national vote for Bush and Gore was close to 50:50. The U.S. Senate was evenly divided, 50 Democrats and 50 Republicans, while the Republicans held a narrow margin in the House of Representatives. The Florida Supreme Court consisted of six Democratic Justices plus a seventh jointly agreed to by Democratic Governor Lawton Chiles and the incoming governor, Jeb Bush. The court delivered a unanimous opinion on November 21, favoring Gore, but split 4 to 3 on December 8. The U.S. Supreme Court divided 5 to 4 with its December 12 ruling. Everyone was aware that if neither Gore nor Bush gained 270 electoral votes, the issue would go to the U.S. House of Representatives. Under the Constitution, each state would cast a single vote. Because of the makeup of state delegations, the House would have selected Bush.

Critics argued that the U.S. Supreme Court, by speaking broadly about equal protection, invited thousands of lawsuits raising questions about disparate treatment of voters. Some of the language in the per curiam on December 12 was indeed broad: "Having once granted the right to vote on equal terms, the State may not, by later arbitrary and disparate treatment, value one person's vote over that of another." However, the per curiam also noted that "[o]ur consideration is limited to the present circumstances." In other words, whatever constitutional principles were at play were for that day only, not to be relied on in the future.

The front page story in the *New York Times* on December 13 said that the Court "effectively handed the presidential election to George W. Bush tonight." A more balanced lead might have read: "The Supreme Court sustained the election of George W. Bush by turning back, on equal protection grounds, an effort by Al Gore to manually recount ballots in Florida without an adequate standard." Bush won because he was able, through the popular vote, to gain the necessary 270 electoral votes. He won in Florida, won after the automatic machine recount, and was still winning after manual recounts in heavily Democratic districts. Had Gore been elected on the basis of a Florida recount, it would have been just as inaccurate to say the Florida Supreme Court "effectively handed him the election."

Gore and his supporters made much of the fact that he won the popular vote by over 300,000 votes (eventually reaching over 500,000). An interesting statistic, but it has no bearing on the presidential contest. Both Gore and Bush knew that what mattered was gaining 270 electoral votes, and they organized their campaigns accordingly to deliver the only constitutional result that matters.

Were Voters "Disenfranchised"?

The Florida Supreme Court, in the concluding section of its December 8 ruling, referred three times to "uncounted votes." That careless phrase revealed poor judgment, if not demagoguery. All votes *were* counted: at least two times by machines. Many were counted a third time by hand. Justice Stevens' dissent on December 12 accused the majority of "effectively order[ing] the disenfranchisement of an unknown number of voters whose ballots reveal their intent — and are therefore legal under state law — but were for some reason rejected by ballot-counting machines." That argument is disingenuous. To determine whether ballots reveal "intent" raises the question of a lack of standards that troubled seven of Stevens' colleagues.

The issue was not *uncounted votes*. It was "undervotes" and "overvotes." An undervote occurs when a voter registers decisions on a number of issues on the ballot, but does not record (at least to the machine) a vote for President. That is not unusual. Approximately two percent of the voters in America do not indicate a preference for President. They vote on other races and issues. An overvote happens when someone votes for both presidential candidates. The machine does not count such votes (nor should it).

Many voters (white, black, and Hispanic) complained that they were unable to vote, but it was never demonstrated in court that election officials committed fraud or took any other illegal act to invalidate a vote. The Justice Department collected the various charges of voter intimidation and disenfranchisement and had all the political incentive (under a Clinton administration) to take legal action. It never did, presumably because the evidence was insufficient or unpersuasive. The quality and reliability of voting machines did vary from county to county. Investigations by Florida, the U.S. Civil Rights Commission, and other organizations highlighted the difficulties experienced by voters and suggested ways of alleviating those problems in the future.

More tangible than the "disenfranchisement" issue were the 2,000 or so votes that were illegal and never should have been counted. These votes came from unregistered voters, ineligible felons, and some citizens who voted absentee first and then voted again at the local precinct after claiming that they had not voted. Some people voted in one county but lived in another. "Fla. Officials Urge Uniform Voting Technology," Wash. Post, Jan. 24, 2001, at A5.

Objections were raised to the form of the "butterfly" ballot used in Palm Beach County. To assist the elderly, the names of presidential candidates were placed on two pages in large type. Pat Buchanan, a candidate, was placed on the opposite page between Gore and Bush, possibly leading some voters to select Buchanan rather than their intended choice, Gore. Appellants claimed that the ballot was defective on its face, confusing to voters, and may have forced citizens to cast a vote for a candidate other than the one they intended to support. As a remedy, they wanted a re-vote. The trial court denied relief, as did a unanimous Florida Supreme Court. Fladell v. Palm Beach County Canvassing Board, 772 So.2d 1240 (Fla. 2000).

Democratic voters filed suit to throw out nearly 25,000 absentee ballots in Martin and Seminole counties. They argued that the ballots, which favored Bush over Gore by about 2 to 1, should be discarded because election officials allowed Republican workers to fix Republican ballot applications by adding voter identification numbers. Judges Terry Lewis and Nikki Clark agreed that the changes to the ballot applications violated state law, but found no evidence of fraud, gross negligence, intentional wrongdoing, or partisan misconduct. Election officials treated Republicans and Democrats differently, but that was because a number of Republican request forms had missing or incorrect voter identification number on them, while there were no similar problems with the Democratic request forms. The two judges decided that the voters were qualified, registered, and had cast valid absentee ballots that should be counted. Taylor v. Martin County Canvassing Board, Case No. 00-2850 (Dec. 8, 2000); Jacobs v. Seminole County Canvassing Board, Case No. CV-00-2816 (Dec. 8, 2000). Their rulings were affirmed by the Florida Supreme Court. Taylor v. Martin County Canvassing Board, 773 So.2d 517 (Fla. 2000); Jacobs v. Seminole County Canvassing Board, 773 So.2d 519 (Fla. 2000).

Some Lessons Learned

Many experts and citizens expressed dismay that the Florida courts and the U.S. Supreme Court had become involved in "politics." Writing for the *Washington Post* on December 14 (A25), Robert Kaiser remarked: "Observers on all sides agreed that *Bush* v. *Gore* represented a departure from past Supreme Courts' great reluctance to interfere in purely political issues." In the *New York Times* on December 11 (A22), Linda Greenhouse warned that the Court could lose credibility by "stepping over the fine but nonetheless distinct line that separates law and politics." Why these concerns? The courts are a part of government and regularly decide political matters, including abortion, affirmative action, federalism, public funding of sectarian schools, race-based districting, campaign financing, and reapportionment.

Courts have a legitimate right to participate in election contests to review accusations of misconduct, fraud, and other charges. The Florida trial courts did an excellent job of airing complaints and educating citizens. Each side brought in experts and statisticians, trying to prove a case. Judges Lewis and Clark ventilated the dispute over absentee ballots, showing convincingly that the irregularities committed by elected officials did not invalidate the votes. Although Judge Sauls was reversed by the Florida Supreme Court, his position that manual recounts had to be done on a statewide basis—and not by selected counties—was accepted both by the Florida Supreme Court and the U.S. Supreme Court. Legitimate objections can be aimed at the U.S. Supreme Court for using strained analysis (good for this day only) to settle the matter rather than let the issue be resolved by Congress pursuant to statutory procedures.

Hand counts and litigation spotlighted the variations in voting machine quality from county to county. Across the country, voting systems varied from punch cards to optical scanners to lever machines. Other counties used electronic machines that rely on keyboards or touch-screens to record votes, or paper ballots marked with pen or pencil. In 2002, Congress passed legislation to provide $3.9 billion to overhaul the nation's election system and to replace punch-card machines that had been discredited because of the chad problem. The funding will establish statewide voter databases to make it easier to register voters and detect fraud.

Just as Gore supporters objected to the accuracy of the results because they failed to include undervotes, so did Bush supporters warn about inaccuracies produced by standardless manual recounts. What everyone learned from the 2000 presidential election is that voting results are *approximate*. Machine and human errors make it impossible to produce a totally accurate result.

Because Gore won the popular vote and lost the election, many people wanted to abolish the Electoral College and elect Presidents directly by popular vote. Adopting that reform could create other problems. In a close presidential contest with a popular vote system, it would be necessary to do a hand count not only in one state, like Florida, but for the entire country. Not an appealing prospect. Also, depending on the system used for a direct election, the nation is likely to move from a two-party system to a multi-party system. Some people may want that, but they have to think it through. After some initial interest in 2000–2001 to eliminate the Electoral College, those proposals were quickly shelved.

Bush v. Gore

531 U.S. 98 (2000)

The Florida Supreme Court, divided 4 to 3, ordered an immediate manual recount of all ballots where no vote for Al Gore or George W. Bush for President had been recorded by machines. On the following day, the U.S. Supreme Court issued a stay on the manual recount. Lawyers for Bush claimed that the manual recount violated the constitutional guarantee for equal protection. The Gore legal team argued the importance of counting every legal vote.

PER CURIAM.

[I]

The petition presents the following questions: whether the Florida Supreme Court established new standards for resolving Presidential election contests, thereby violating Art. II, §1, cl. 2, of the United States Constitution and failing to comply with 3 U.S.C. §5, and whether the use of standardless manual recounts violates the Equal Protection and Due Process Clauses. With respect to the equal protection question, we find a violation of the Equal Protection Clause.

[II.B]

The individual citizen has no constitutional right to vote for electors for the President of the United States unless and until the state legislature chooses a statewide election as the means to implement its power to appoint members of the Electoral College....

The right to vote is protected in more than the initial allocation of the franchise. Equal protection applies as well to the manner of its exercise. Having once granted the right to vote on equal terms, the State may not, by later arbitrary and disparate treatment, value one person's vote over that of another....

Much of the controversy seems to revolve around ballot cards designed to be perforated by a stylus but which, either through error or deliberate omission, have not been perforated with sufficient precision for a machine to count them. In some cases a piece of the card—a chad—is hanging, say by two corners. In other cases there is no separation at all, just an indentation [a "dimpled" ballot].

The Florida Supreme Court has ordered that the intent of the voter be discerned from such ballots. For purposes of resolving the equal protection challenge, it is not necessary to decide whether the Florida Supreme Court had the authority under the legislative scheme for resolving election disputes to define what a legal vote is and to mandate a manual recount implementing that definition. The recount mechanisms implemented in response to the decisions of the Florida Supreme Court do not satisfy the minimum requirement for non-arbitrary treatment of voters necessary to secure the fundamental right. Florida's basic command for the count of legally cast votes is to consider the "intent of the voter."... This is unobjectionable as an abstract proposition and a starting principle. The problem inheres in the absence of specific standards to ensure its equal application. The formulation of uniform rules to determine intent based on these recurring circumstances is practicable and, we conclude, necessary.

... Our consideration is limited to the present circumstances, for the problem of equal protection in election processes generally presents many complexities.

The question before the Court is not whether local entities, in the exercise of their expertise, may develop different systems for implementing elections. Instead, we are presented with a situation where a state court with the power to assure uniformity has ordered a statewide recount with minimal procedural safeguards. When a court orders a statewide remedy, there must be at least some assurance that the rudimentary requirements of equal treatment and fundamental fairness are satisfied.

... [I]t is obvious that the recount cannot be conducted in compliance with the requirements of equal protection and due process without substantial additional work. It would require not only the adoption (after opportunity for argument) of adequate statewide standards for determining what is a legal vote, and practicable procedures to implement them, but also orderly judicial review of any disputed matters that might arise....

The Supreme Court of Florida has said that the legislature intended the State's electors to "participat[e] fully in the federal electoral process," as provided in 3 U.S.C. § 5.... That statute, in turn, requires that any controversy or contest that is designed to lead to a conclusive selection of electors be completed by December 12. That date is upon us, and there is no recount procedure in place under the State Supreme Court's order that comports with minimal constitutional standards. Because it is evident that any recount seeking to meet the December 12 date will be unconstitutional for the reasons we have discussed, we reverse the judgment of the Supreme Court of Florida ordering a recount to proceed.

Seven Justices of the Court agree that there are constitutional problems with the recount ordered by the Florida Supreme Court that demand a remedy [*referring to dissenting opinions by Souter and Breyer*].... The only disagreement is as to the remedy. Because the Florida Supreme Court has said that the Florida Legislature intended to obtain the safe-harbor benefits of 3 U.S.C. § 5, JUSTICE BREYER's proposed remedy—remanding to the Florida Supreme Court for its ordering of a constitutionally proper contest until December 18—contemplates action in violation of the Florida election code, and hence could not be part of an "appropriate" order authorized by Fla. Stat. § 102.168(8) (2000)....

None are more conscious of the vital limits on judicial authority than are the members of this Court, and none stand more in admiration of the Constitution's design to leave the selection of the President to the people, through their legislatures, and to the political sphere. When contending parties invoke the process of the courts, however, it becomes our unsought responsibility to resolve the federal and constitutional issues the judicial system has been forced to confront.

The judgment of the Supreme Court of Florida is reversed, and the case is remanded for further proceedings not inconsistent with this opinion....

It is so ordered.

CHIEF JUSTICE REHNQUIST, with whom JUSTICE SCALIA and JUSTICE THOMAS join, concurring.

[I]

In most cases, comity and respect for federalism compel us to defer to the decisions of state courts on issues of state law. That practice reflects our understanding that the decisions of state courts are definitive pronouncements of the will of the States as sovereigns.... But there are a few exceptional cases in which the Constitution imposes a duty or confers a power on a particular branch of a State's government. This is one of them....

... Isolated sections of the [*state*] code may well admit of more than one interpretation, but the general coherence of the legislative scheme may not be altered by judicial interpretation so as to wholly change the statutorily provided apportionment of responsibility among these various bodies. In any election but a Presidential election, the Florida Supreme Court can give as little or as much deference to Florida's executives as it chooses, so far as Article II is concerned, and this Court will have no cause to question the court's actions....

This inquiry does not imply a disrespect for state *courts* but rather a respect for the constitutionally prescribed role of state *legislatures*. To attach definitive weight to the pronouncement of a state court, when the very question at issue is whether the court has actually departed from the statutory meaning, would be to abdicate our responsibility to enforce the explicit requirements of Article II.

II

[*The first decision by the Florida Supreme Court on November 21, 2000*] extended the 7-day statutory certification deadline established by the legislature. This modification of the code, by lengthening the protest period, necessarily shortened the contest period for Presidential elections....

... [T]he court's interpretation of "legal vote," and hence its decision to order a contest-period recount, plainly departed from the legislative scheme....

III

Surely when the Florida Legislature empowered the courts of the State to grant "appropriate" relief, it must have meant relief that would have become final by the cutoff date of 3 U.S.C. § 5. In light of the inevitable legal challenges and ensuing appeals to the Supreme Court of Florida and petitions for certiorari to this Court, the entire recounting process could not possibly be completed by that date....

For these reasons, in addition to those given in the *per curiam*, we would reverse.

JUSTICE STEVENS, with whom JUSTICE GINSBURG and JUSTICE BREYER join, dissenting....

... Neither § 5 nor Article II grants federal judges any special authority to substitute their views for those of the state judiciary on matters of state law....

Admittedly, the use of differing substandards for determining voter intent in different counties employing similar voting systems may raise serious concerns. Those concerns are alleviated—if not eliminated—by the fact that a single impartial magistrate [*Judge Terry Lewis*] will ultimately adjudicate all objections arising from the recount process....

Even assuming that aspects of the remedial scheme might ultimately be found to violate the Equal Protection Clause, I could not subscribe to the majority's disposition of the case.... [T]he appropriate course of action would be to remand to allow more specific procedures for implementing the legislature's uniform general standard to be established.

... Although we may never know with complete certainty the identity of the winner of this year's Presidential election, the identity of the loser is perfectly clear. It is the Nation's confidence in the judge as an impartial guardian of the rule of law.

I respectfully dissent.

JUSTICE SOUTER, with whom JUSTICE BREYER joins and with whom JUSTICE STEVENS and JUSTICE GINSBURG join with regard to all but Part C, dissenting.

[III]

It is only on the third issue before us [*equal protection or due process*] that there is a meritorious argument for relief, as this Court's *per curiam* opinion recognizes....

It is an issue that might well have been dealt with adequately by the Florida courts if the state proceedings had not been interrupted, and if not disposed of at the state level it could have been considered by the Congress in any electoral vote dispute....

In deciding what to do about this, we should take account of the fact that electoral votes are due to be cast in six days. I would therefore remand the case to the courts of Florida with instructions to establish uniform standards for evaluating the several types of ballots that have prompted differing treat-

ments, to be applied within and among counties when passing on such identical ballots in any further recounting (or successive recounting) that the courts might order.

Unlike the majority, I see no warrant for this Court to assume that Florida could not possibly comply with this requirement before the date set for the meeting of electors, December 18....

I respectfully dissent.

JUSTICE GINSBURG, with whom JUSTICE STEVENS joins, and with whom JUSTICE SOUTER and JUSTICE BREYER join as to Part I, dissenting.

[I]

No doubt there are cases in which the proper application of federal law may hinge on interpretations of state law. Unavoidably, this Court must sometimes examine state law in order to protect federal rights....

The extraordinary setting of this case has obscured the ordinary principle that dictates its proper resolution: Federal courts defer to state high courts' interpretations of their state's own law. This principle reflects the core of federalism, on which all agree.... Were the other members of this Court as mindful as they generally are of our system of dual sovereignty, they would affirm the judgment of the Florida Supreme Court....

JUSTICE BREYER, with whom JUSTICE STEVENS and JUSTICE GINSBURG join except as to Part I-A-1, and with whom JUSTICE SOUTER joins as to Part I, dissenting.

The Court was wrong to take this case. It was wrong to grant a stay. It should now vacate that stay and permit the Florida Supreme Court to decide whether the recount should resume.

[I.A.2]

... [T]here is no justification for the majority's remedy, which is simply to reverse the lower court and halt the recount entirely. An appropriate remedy would be, instead, to remand this case with instructions that, even at this late date, would permit the Florida Supreme Court to require recounting *all* undercounted votes in Florida ... and to do so in accordance with a single uniform substandard....

B. VOTING RIGHTS

The right to vote would seem inherent in the republican form of government envisaged in the Constitution. "The United States shall guarantee to every State in this Union a Republican Form of Government." Art. IV, §4. Nevertheless, it took the Fifteenth Amendment, ratified in 1870, to establish the right of blacks to vote. A unanimous Supreme Court in 1875, announcing that the Constitution "does not confer the right of suffrage upon any one," denied that women were entitled to vote as a privilege and immunity protected by the Constitution. Minor v. Happersett, 88 U.S. 162, 178 (1875). Yet in 1886 a unanimous opinion of the Court could refer to voting as "a fundamental political right, because preservative of all rights." Yick Wo v. Hopkins, 118 U.S. 356, 370 (1886). Not until 1920, with the Nineteenth Amendment, did women gain the *general* right to vote. (They had previously voted in some states.)

Voting rights in America have been hammered out by state action, judicial decisions, congressional initiatives, and constitutional amendments. Members of the House of Representatives are chosen directly by the people. Senators were originally selected by state legislatures but are now elected directly by the people as a result of the Seventeenth Amendment, ratified in 1913. The time, place, and manner of elections of Representatives and Senators are left to the states; Congress may alter state regulations except as to the place of choosing Senators. Art. I, §4, Cl. 1; Amend. XVII.

Fifteenth Amendment

In the same year that the states ratified the Fifteenth Amendment, Congress passed the Enforcement Act of 1870 to guarantee blacks the right to vote in state elections. 16 Stat. 140. Using a strict dual-federalism model, the Supreme Court held that the statute was not "appropriate legislation" under Section 2 of the Fifteenth Amendment. Remarkably, it said that the Amendment "does not confer the right of suffrage upon any one." United States v. Reese, 92 U.S. 214, 217 (1876). To the Court, the Amendment merely prohibited government from preventing the vote because of race, color, or previous condition of servitude. Another decision further undermined the Enforcement Act by holding that jurisdiction and sovereignty to bring indictments under the statute rested solely with the states. United States v. Cruikshank, 92 U.S. 542 (1876). The Court did sustain the power of Congress—in elections for U.S. Representatives—to enact penalties for those who stuff the ballot box. Ex parte Siebold, 100 U.S. 371 (1880).

A few years later, a unanimous Court upheld a congressional statute that prohibited two or more persons from conspiring to threaten or intimidate any citizen (in this case a black) from exercising the right to vote for national office. The Court stated that the Fifteenth Amendment conferred upon blacks the right to vote "and Congress has the power to protect and enforce that right." Ex parte Yarbrough, 110 U.S. 651, 665 (1884). See also United States v. Mosley, 238 U.S. 383 (1915); Swafford v. Templeton, 185 U.S. 487 (1902); Wiley v. Sinkler, 179 U.S. 58 (1900).

States tried to nullify the Fifteenth Amendment by adopting a "Grandfather Clause"—extending voting rights only to those who were entitled to vote before the Amendment. Not until 1915 did the Court overturn those tactics. Guinn v. United States, 238 U.S. 347; Myers v. Anderson, 238 U.S. 368. Oklahoma changed its law to provide that those who had voted in 1914 automatically remained qualified voters. This requirement affected only blacks, forcing them to apply between April 30 and May 11, 1916, or risk permanent disfranchisement. The Court held the statute unconstitutional, remarking that the Fifteenth Amendment "nullifies sophisticated as well as simple-minded modes of discrimination." Lane v. Wilson, 307 U.S. 268, 275 (1939).

In 2000, the Court relied on the Fifteenth Amendment to strike down a Hawaiian voting restriction designed to benefit persons whose ancestry qualified them as either a "Hawaiian" or "native Hawaiian." Using ancestry as a proxy for race represented a prohibited race-based voting qualification. In this case the Fifteenth Amendment was used to safeguard the rights of a white man. Rice v. Cayetano, 528 U.S. 495 (2000).

Primaries

In some states, winning a primary election assures victory in the general election. Although the Fifteenth Amendment protected the right of blacks to vote, some states restricted that right to the general election and used different methods to bar blacks from participating in primary elections. In the "white primary" cases, the Supreme Court reviewed a Texas statute that barred blacks from voting in the Democratic party primary for U.S. Senator and Representatives. A unanimous Court held that this violated the Fourteenth Amendment. Texas claimed that the suit was political and hence inappropriate for the courts, an objection Justice Holmes called "little more than a play upon words." Nixon v. Herndon, 273 U.S. 536, 540 (1927).

Texas tried a different tactic. It gave state political parties the power to prescribe qualifications for party membership, including the right to vote. The Democratic party adopted a resolution that allowed only white Democrats to participate in primaries. By a 5–4 vote, the Court held the statute in violation of the Fourteenth Amendment. It rejected the argument that the Amendment operates only against the states, not private parties (in this case, officials of the Democratic party). The Court pointed out that the statute lodged the power to determine voter qualification in the executive committee of each party; to that extent the parties functioned as organs of the state. Nixon v. Condon, 286 U.S. 73 (1932).

Three years later, however, a unanimous Court agreed that a county clerk in Texas could refuse to give a ballot to a black who wanted to vote in the Democratic party primary. The party convention, acting on its own without state legislation, had voted to restrict party membership to whites. The Court decided that the clerk was not a state officer, there was no "state action," and the conduct did not violate the federal Constitution. Grovey v. Townsend, 295 U.S. 45 (1935). In 1941, the Court backed away from *Grovey* by holding that election officials in a Louisiana primary (conducted at public expense) acted "under color of" state law in altering and falsely counting ballots. Voters had a right under the U.S. Constitution to cast their ballots and have them counted. United States v. Classic, 313 U.S. 299 (1941). *Grovey* was finally overruled by the Court in 1944, when it declared (8 to 1) that Texas could not exclude blacks by limiting participation in state conventions to white citizens. This was held to be state action in violation of the Fifteenth Amendment. SMITH v. ALLWRIGHT, 321 U.S. 649 (1944).

This ruling did not exhaust the bag of tricks. Texas excluded blacks from participating in elections conducted by the Jaybird Democratic Association, which selected candidates for county offices. These candidates were invariably the ones nominated to run in the Democratic primary and elected to office. The Jaybirds claimed that their association was not a political party but a self-governing voluntary club. Although the elections for candidates were not governed by state laws and did not use state machinery or state funds, an 8–1 Court held that the process violated the Fifteenth Amendment. The Democratic primary and the general election became "no more than the perfunctory ratifiers of the choice that has already been made in Jaybird elections from which Negroes have been excluded." Terry v. Adams, 345 U.S. 461, 469 (1953).

In 2008, a unanimous Supreme Court reviewed a New York requirement that political parties select their nominees for state Supreme Court Justices at a convention of delegates chosen by members in a primary election. Did this law violate the First Amendment rights of prospective party candidates? The Court held that a political party has a First Amendment right to limit its membership, subject to certain limits. For example, a party's racially discriminatory policy may become state action that violates the Fifteenth Amendment. But the Court found no First Amendment violations. New York State Bd. of Elections v. Lopez Torres, 552 U.S. 196 (2008).

Poll Taxes

Another technique for restricting or discouraging the black vote was to require payment of a poll tax before a person could register to vote. This type of tax was upheld by the Court in Breedlove v. Suttles, 302 U.S. 277 (1937). A later case involved the Virginia Constitution, which required a poll tax to vote. Although some members of the state constitutional convention expressed a desire to eliminate the black vote in Virginia, a three-judge federal court in 1951 found insufficient evidence that the state requirement discriminated against blacks. Butler v. Thompson, 97 F.Supp. 17, 21 (E.D. Va. 1951). A per curiam ruling by the Supreme Court affirmed this judgment. Only Justice Douglas dissented. Butler v. Thompson, 341 U.S. 937 (1951).

Congress took steps to eliminate the poll tax in federal elections. By 1962, when both the House and the Senate passed the Twenty-fourth Amendment, only five states used the tax: Alabama, Arkansas, Mississippi, Texas, and Virginia. The Amendment, ratified in 1964, provides that the right of the U.S. citizens to vote in any primary or other election for federal office "shall not be denied or abridged by the United States or any State by reason of failure to pay any poll tax or other tax."

States were still permitted to use poll taxes for state and local elections. In another congressional initiative, the Voting Rights Act of 1965 declared that the poll tax placed an unreasonable hardship on voter rights and did not bear a reasonable relationship to any legitimate state interest. It also authorized the Attorney General to institute actions against state poll taxes and gave federal courts jurisdiction to decide these cases. Attorney General Katzenbach supported a challenge to the poll tax brought by Annie E. Harper. With this case as the vehicle, the Supreme Court declared Virginia's poll tax for its elections a violation of the Equal Protection Clause of the Fourteenth Amendment. Writing for the Court, Justice Douglas said that voter qualifications "have no relation to wealth nor to paying or not paying this or any other tax." HARPER v. VIRGINIA BOARD OF ELECTIONS, 383 U.S. 663, 666 (1966).

In 1996, the Court held that the Voting Rights Act gives the Justice Department authority to review changes in the rules that state parties adopt for nominating conventions. The change at issue in this case was the imposition of a $35 or $45 registration fee to attend the Republican party convention in Virginia that selected the 1994 U.S. Senate nominee, Oliver L. North. The fee, which had not been previously charged, was challenged by three law students as equivalent to a poll tax. A three-judge federal court ruled that the preclearance requirement of Section 5 of the Voting Rights Act did not apply to party conventions, and that the challenge to the poll-tax provisions could be brought only by the government, not by individuals. The Court, split 5 to 4, overturned both of those conclusions. Morse v. Republican Party of Virginia, 517 U.S. 186 (1996). The issue of a "poll tax" returned to the Supreme Court in 2008 with Indiana's requirement for a voter ID, discussed later in this section.

Literacy Tests

Still another contrivance to limit the black vote was the literacy test. A unanimous Court in 1959 held that states may apply a literacy test to all voters irrespective of race or color. The particular statute at issue, a North Carolina law, required that the prospective voter "be able to read and write any section of the Constitution of North Carolina in the English language." The Court concluded that the law did not, on its face, violate the Fifteenth Amendment. Lassiter v. Northampton Election Bd., 360 U.S. 45 (1959).

The Voting Rights Act of 1965 placed temporary suspensions on the use of literacy tests. This provision was upheld in South Carolina v. Katzenbach, 383 U.S. 301 (1966). In 1965, a unanimous Court held that election commissioners and voting registrars in Mississippi could be sued for using literacy tests and other devices to disfranchise blacks. State techniques had reduced the percentage of black "qualified" voters from over 50 percent to about 5 percent. To register for voting, a citizen of Mississippi had to read and copy any section of the state constitution, *and* give a reasonable interpretation of that section to the county registrar, *and* demonstrate to the registrar "a reasonable understanding of the duties and obligations of citizenship under a constitutional form of government." The opportunities for racial discrimination and abuse were immense. United States v. Mississippi, 380 U.S. 128 (1965). The use of these "interpretation tests" gave the state unbridled discretion to keep blacks from voting. Blacks, even those "with the most advanced education and scholarship, were declared by voting registrars with less education to have an unsatisfactory understanding of the Constitution of Louisiana or of the United States. This is not a test but a trap, sufficient to stop even the most brilliant man on his way to the voting booth." Louisiana v. United States, 380 U.S. 145, 153 (1965).

In the Voting Rights Act Amendments of 1970, Congress enacted a five-year ban on literacy tests for the entire nation. These tests had been used to restrict the registration of blacks, Spanish-Americans, and Indians. The ban was upheld by every member of the Supreme Court. Oregon v. Mitchell, 400 U.S. 112, 131–34, 144–47, 216–17, 231–36, 282–84 (1970).

Residency Requirements

In other cases, the Court ruled that states may not discriminate against members of the armed forces by denying them the right to vote if they moved their home to another state. Carrington v. Rush, 380 U.S. 89 (1965). Residency requirements were also subject to congressional restrictions. In 1970, Congress abolished residency requirements as a precondition to vote for President and Vice President. Such restrictions, it said, bore no "reasonable relationship to any compelling State interest." 84 Stat. 316. This provision was upheld by eight Justices in Oregon v. Mitchell, 400 U.S. 112, 134, 147–50, 236–39, 285–87 (1970). In 1972, the Court struck down residency requirements in excess of 30 days as a prerequisite to register for voting. Such provisions violated the Equal Protection Clause and were not necessary to further a compelling state interest. Dunn v. Blumstein, 405 U.S. 330 (1972). A year later, the Court upheld a 50-day residency requirement. Marston v. Lewis, 410 U.S. 679 (1973); Burns v. Fortson, 410 U.S. 686 (1973).

Civil Rights Statutes

Congress passed the Civil Rights Act of 1957 to protect the voting rights of blacks. If someone was about to engage in any practice to deprive a person of the right to vote, the U.S. Attorney General could seek an injunction. 71 Stat. 637, § 131. This provision was upheld by a unanimous Court. United States v. Raines, 362 U.S. 17 (1960). The Civil Rights Act of 1960 adopted additional measures, including the appointment of "voting referees" by federal judges to protect the right of blacks to register and vote. 74 Stat. 86. The voting-rights provision was strengthened again in Title I of the Civil Rights Act of 1964. 78 Stat. 241.

The Voting Rights Act of 1965 represents the most comprehensive measure since 1870 to protect the voting rights of blacks. The statute suspended literacy tests, authorized the appointment of federal voting examiners, and created federal machinery to supervise voter registration. These statutes, in combination with other political forces, have led to a dramatic increase in the election of black officials. In 1970, the number of elected black officials in the nation (federal, state, county, municipal, judicial/law enforcement, and education) was 1,469. Three decades later the number exceeded 9,000. To increase the number of Puerto Rican voters in New York, Congress prohibited a state from conditioning the right to vote on the ability to read, write, understand, or interpret any matter in the English language. The statute waived English language literacy requirements for persons who had completed the sixth grade in a school under the American flag (including the Commonwealth of Puerto Rico) where the language of instruction was other than English.

South Carolina filed an original suit to test the validity of the Voting Rights Act. The state claimed that Congress exceeded its constitutional powers and invaded states' rights. Twenty-one states filed amici briefs supporting the statute; five Southern states joined with South Carolina in opposition. With Justice Black dissenting in part, an 8–1 Court upheld all challenged provisions of the Act. The decision gives broad recognition to the power of Congress to enforce the Fifteenth Amendment. SOUTH CAROLINA v. KATZENBACH, 383 U.S. 301 (1966).

Another case challenged a provision that waived the English language requirement for Puerto Ricans. A 7–2 Supreme Court held that the waiver was "a proper exercise of the powers granted to Congress by § 5 of the Fourteenth Amendment." Fact-finding was a legislative, not a judicial, responsibility. "It was for Congress, as the branch that made this judgment, to assess and weigh the various conflicting considerations.... It is not for us to review the congressional resolution of these factors. It is enough that we be able to perceive a basis upon which the Congress might resolve the conflict as it did." Morgan v. Katzenbach, 384 U.S. 641, 653 (1966).

Voting at Age Eighteen

In 1970, Congress extended the Voting Rights Act and lowered the voting age to 18 for federal, state, and local elections. In signing the bill, President Nixon said that this provision for an 18-year-old vote was unconstitutional because Congress lacked authority to extend the suffrage by statute. The issue was taken directly to the Supreme Court, as a case of original jurisdiction, where a 5–4 decision held that the voting age provision was constitutional as applied to national elections but invalid for state and local contests. Oregon v. Mitchell, 400 U.S. 112 (1970). The cost and confusion of dual voting rolls (one for the federal government and another for state and local elections) created sufficient incentive to override the Court. The Twenty-sixth Amendment quickly passed the House and the Senate and was ratified on July 1, 1971, imposing the 18-year-old vote for all national, state, and local elections.

Purpose vs. Effect

Section 2 of the Voting Rights Act provides that voting qualifications or practices may not deny or abridge the voting rights of any U.S. citizen on account of race or color. Is discriminatory impact alone sufficient to find a violation of the statute? In 1980, a plurality of the Court held that states are prohibited only from *purposefully* discriminating against the voting rights of blacks. Abridgement of voting rights had to be intentional, not incidental. To be held invalid, the voting plan had to be conceived for the purpose of furthering racial discrimination. MOBILE v. BOLDEN, 446 U.S. 55 (1980).

Nevertheless, on the same day, the Court upheld the power of Congress to go beyond discriminatory purpose to include discriminatory *effect*. At issue was Section 5 of the Voting Rights Act, which requires that changes in state voting practices be submitted for preclearance to the U.S. Attorney General or a federal judge. Section 5 provides that the Attorney General may clear a voting practice only if it "does not have the purpose and will not have the effect of denying or abridging the right to vote on account of race or color." A 6–3 Court held that Congress had deliberately used the conjunctive (purpose *and* effect) and that this objective was within its power to enact "appropriate legislation" to enforce the Fifteenth Amendment. City of Rome v. United States, 446 U.S. 156 (1980).

Congress responded to *Mobile* v. *Bolden* by amending the Voting Rights Act to allow plaintiffs to show discrimination solely on the *effects* of a voting plan (see reading). The statute borrowed language from an earlier opinion by the Court in *White* v. *Regester,* 412 U.S. 755 (1973). 96 Stat. 134, § 3 (1982). The Court accepted the statute's "results test" to invalidate districting plans that have the effect of diluting the black vote, whether intended by the state or not. Thornburgh v. Gingles, 478 U.S. 30 (1986).[2] Sections 2 and 5 of the Voting Rights Act are litigated with great frequency (see box on next page).

More Recent Cases

In three decisions in 1991, the Court broadened the Voting Rights Act to cover judicial elections. In the first, a unanimous Court ruled that Section 5 of the Act requires states to seek approval from the U.S. Attorney General before they proceed with elections for state judges. The case was brought by

---

2. For earlier cases on preclearance under Section 5, see McCain v. Lybrand, 465 U.S. 236 (1984); Lockhart v. United States, 460 U.S. 125 (1983); Port Arthur v. United States, 459 U.S. 159 (1982); McDaniel v. Sanchez, 452 U.S. 130 (1981).

Voting Rights Act of 1965

The Voting Rights Act of 1965 suspended the use of literacy tests and authorized the appointment of federal voting examiners to order the registration of blacks in certain states and counties. The Supreme Court upheld the constitutionality of the Act in such cases as South Carolina v. Katzenbach, 383 U.S. 301 (1966) and Morgan v. Katzenbach, 384 U.S. 641 (1966). The two sections of the statute most litigated are Section 2 and Section 5:

Section 2. Provides that voting qualifications or practices may not deny or abridge the voting rights of any U.S. citizen on account of race or color. In Mobile v. Bolden, 446 U.S. 55 (1980), the Court held that abridgement of voting rights had to be *intentional,* not incidental. In response to that decision, Congress amended the Voting Rights Act in 1982 to allow plaintiffs to show that discrimination exists solely on the *effects* (not in-

tent) of a voting plan. The Court accepted this "results test" in Thornburgh v. Gingles, 478 U.S. 30 (1986).

Section 5. Requires that changes in voting practices in certain states be first submitted to the U.S. Attorney General or to a federal district judge in the District of Columbia Circuit. By declaratory judgment a court may approve the change in voting practice. As an alternative, a state may submit the change to the Attorney General, who has sixty days to review it. The Attorney General may clear a voting practice only if it "does not have the purpose and will not have the effect of denying or abridging the right to vote on account of race or color...." In City of Rome v. United States, 446 U.S. 156 (1980), the Court reasoned that Congress had used the conjunctive (purpose *and* effect) to prohibit voting plans that have the *effect* of discrimination.

SOURCE: 42 U.S.C. §§ 1973(a), 1973c (2000).

black voters in Louisiana who claimed that the state's electoral scheme diluted minority voting strength. Clark v. Roemer, 500 U.S. 646 (1991). Earlier, in a summary affirmance of a district court decision, the Court had indicated that Section 5 applied to judges. Martin v. Haith, 477 U.S. 901 (1986), aff'g, Haith v. Martin, 618 F.Supp. 410 (E.D. N.C. 1985).

The other two decisions involved Section 2 of the Voting Rights Act. As amended in 1982, the statute refers to the ability of minority voters to elect "representatives" of their choice. Divided 6 to 3, the Court held that judicial elections are covered by Section 2. The word "representatives" describes the winners of representative, popular elections, including elected judges. Chisom v. Roemer, 501 U.S. 380 (1991). A companion case also concerned a challenge to the election of state judges. Houston Lawyers' Assn. v. Texas Attorney Gen., 501 U.S. 419 (1991). Both decisions are expected to increase the number of black and Hispanic state judges.

In 1992, the Court split 6 to 3 in deciding that Section 5 of the Voting Rights Act did not apply to an Alabama system that relied on county commissioners to supervise and control the maintenance, repair, and construction of county roads. In 1986, for the first time in modern history, three blacks were elected as county commissioners, but resolutions were subsequently adopted that prevented the three blacks from exercising the decision-making authority traditionally associated with their offices. The Court denied that the changes brought about by the resolutions were "with respect to voting" within the meaning of Section 5. The resolutions concerned only the internal operations of an elected body and did not have a direct relation to voting. Thus, the changes were not subject to judicial or administrative preclearance. Presley v. Etowah County Com'n, 502 U.S. 491 (1992).

The Court decided in 1994 that a Florida reapportionment plan, which created single-member districts in the two houses of the state legislature, did not violate Section 2 of the Voting Rights Act. "One may suspect vote dilution from political famine, but one is not entitled to suspect (must less infer) dilution from mere failure to guarantee a political feast." Johnson v. DeGrandy, 512 U.S. 997,

1017 (1994). On the same day, the Court held that a single-commissioner form of government in Georgia did not dilute the influence of blacks. The size of a governing authority, said the Court, is not subject to a vote-dilution challenge under Section 2 of the Voting Rights Act. Holder v. Hall, 512 U.S. 874 (1994).

The preclearance procedure was examined by the Court in 2009. A small utility district in Texas, with an elected board, was required by Section 5 of the Voting Rights Act to seek federal preclearance before it could change anything about its elections, even though no evidence existed that it ever discriminated on the basis of race. A section of the statute permits a "bailout" from preclearance. Given the fact that the statute was more than four decades old, the Court said it raised serious constitutional concerns, especially with regard to federalism. But instead of declaring the statute unconstitutional, an 8 to one Court settled the matter on statutory grounds, deciding that the district was eligible for the bailout provision. Justice Thomas concurred in the judgment but dissented on the ground that the bailout provision did not provide the county full relief and it was therefore necessary for the Court to reach the constitutional question. Northwest Austin Municipal Util. Dist. No. One v. Holder, 557 U.S. 193 (2009). The Court's ruling is expected to stimulate new challenges to the preclearance requirement.

Also in 2009, a divided Court (5 to 4) narrowed the scope of the Voting Rights Act by ruling that it does not require states to create "crossover districts" (where minorities are not the majority but may join forces with whites to elect a candidate of their choice). In this case, North Carolina redrew its district lines in 2003 by creating a district with 39 percent voting-age population. It divided a county into two districts, which the state constitution prohibits. The state argued that the Voting Rights Act required it to act as it did. Writing for the Court, Justice Kennedy concluded that the Act is concerned only with creating districts in which minorities are a majority and does not require crossover districts. In dissent, Justice Souter argued that crossover districts are an effective method of increasing minority representation. In a separate dissent, Justice Ginsburg noted that the Court's decision "returns the ball to Congress' court." Bartlett v. Strickland, 556 U.S. 1 (2009). Congress is considering amending the Voting Rights Act to make it clear that is supports crossover districts.

Voter Identification

In 2008, the Supreme Court upheld an Indiana law that required citizens voting in person to present a government-issued photo identification. Was a photo necessary to combat voter fraud and protect the integrity of elections? Would such laws discourage or effectively disenfranchise people who lacked driver's licenses, passports, or other acceptable photos? Republicans generally favored the requirement. Many Democrats thought it would limit voting by their supporters. A district court upheld the law. A divided Seventh Circuit affirmed, rejecting the argument that the law should be judged by the same standard as the poll tax struck down in the 1966 *Harper* case.

Writing for a 6 to 3 Court, Justice Stevens concluded that the Indiana law was not enough of a burden to violate the Constitution. He explained that the law did not apply to absentee ballots submitted by mail and it contained an exception for persons living and voting in a state-licensed facility (such as a nursing home). Voters who were indigent or objected on religious grounds to be photographed could cast a provisional ballot to be counted only if the person executed an affidavit before a circuit court clerk within ten days following the election.

Two congressional statutes (National Voter Registration Act of 1993 and the Help America Vote Act of 2002) may have encouraged Indiana to require photo IDs to determine voter qualification. The state's list of required voters included the names of thousands of persons who had either moved, died, or were ineligible to vote because of felony convictions. No evidence had been presented of voter fraud at polling places in Indiana, although such incidents had occurred in other states where individuals impersonated a registered voter.

Stevens acknowledged that voter fraud can occur with absentee ballots. He said that *Harper* would present an issue if Indiana required voters to pay for a photo ID, but it was provided by Indiana's Bureau of Motor Vehicles (BMV) without cost. To obtain a photo ID card, it is necessary to present a "primary" document, such as a birth certificate. Indiana charges a fee ($3 to $12) to obtain a copy of one's birth certificate. Passports are a primary document, but they can cost up to $100. In casting a provisional ballot, voters might face other expenses in traveling to the circuit court.

Based in part on a recently decided case about primary election procedures — Washington State Grange v. Washington State Republican Party, 552 U.S. 442 (2008) — Stevens decided that the plaintiffs had failed to sustain their pre-election, facial attack on the Indiana law. The small number of voters who might experience a burden did not outweigh Indiana's interest in protecting election integrity. Crawford v. Marion County Election Board, 553 U.S. 181 (2008).

A concurrence by Scalia, Thomas, and Alito described the burden as "minimal and justified," eliminating the need for a balancing test. They said Indiana had already weighed the costs and benefits and its judgment prevailed unless the law imposed a severe and unjustified burden. A dissent by Souter and Ginsburg said that because Indiana's law "threatens to impose nontrivial burdens" on the right to vote, the balancing test was the proper judicial principle. The required trip to the BMV by poor, old, and disabled voters who do not drive a car may be "prohibitive." The number of BMV offices are far fewer than polling places, and public transportation in the state is limited. A county has several polling places and BMV offices, but only one county seat to sign affidavits for absentee voting. In a separate dissent, Breyer regarded the statute as unconstitutional because it imposed an excessive burden on eligible voters. He called attention to less restrictive photo ID requirements in Florida and Georgia.

When the case returned to Indiana, a state appellate court in September 2009 held that the voter ID law violated the Indiana Constitution because it did not treat voters equally. It did not require mail-in voters and residents of nursing homes to produce state-approved identification. That ruling is under appeal. The Obama administration challenged a number of state requirements that voters produce IDs, claiming that the documents can be costly to obtain and create substantial difficulties for those who have no cars to reach state offices that can be a hundred miles away. Krissah Thompson, "10 States' ID Laws Create Barriers for Some Voters, Study Finds," Washington Post, July 18, 2012, at A7. In December 2011, the Justice Department blocked a South Carolina law that required voters to present photo IDs, concluding that the law would particularly suppress voting by minorities.

On August 15, 2012, a lower state court in Pennsylvania upheld a state law that requires voters to show IDs. That ruling will be appealed to the Pennsylvania Supreme Court. This dispute differs from challenges to voter IDs in such states as South Carolina and Texas, where changes in voting laws must be approved by federal authorities or courts.

Identifying Names on Ballots

In 2010, the Court decided a case about people who sign petitions to put referenda on state ballots. Do they have a First Amendment right to prevent their names from being made public? Suppose they sign petitions designed to oppose gay rights? Would they fear harassment and retaliation if their names were posted on the Internet? The case that reached the Court arose in Washington State, which allows voters to reject state legislation through a referendum. The issue was a state domestic partnership law called the "everything but marriage" act, supporting civil unions but not marriage for same-sex couples. Divided 8 to one, the Supreme Court held that there was no general First Amendment right to anonymity for those who sign ballot petitions. Moreover, public disclosure can help prevent some kinds of fraud, such as when an individual signs a petition based on a misrepresentation of the underlying issue. Doe v. Reed, 561 U.S. ___ (2010). Although eight Justices agreed that no general First Amendment right existed, they split in different directions. Chief Justice Roberts wrote the opinion for the Court. It was followed by separate concurrences from Breyer, Alito, Sotomayor, Stevens, and Scalia. Thomas dissented, holding that voters were entitled to privacy. The Court decided to send back to the lower courts the more difficult issue: Do petitions concerning controversial measures warrant privacy?

Ballot Initiatives

A number of states allow citizens to make laws directly through initiatives placed on election ballots. These initiatives often express positions on constitutional values. In 1999, the Court reviewed three conditions that Colorado placed on the ballot-initiative process: (1) initiative-petition circulators had to be registered voters, (2) they had to wear an identification badge showing their name; and (3) proponents of an initiative had to report the names and the addresses of all paid circulators and the amount paid to each circulator. The Court struck down the conditions on the ground that they significantly inhibited communication with voters about proposed political change and were not warranted by the state's interests. Buckley v. American Constitutional Law Foundation, 525 U.S. 182 (1999).

(The Supreme Court's 1995 decision regarding term limits is treated in Chapter 6. A number of voting rights issues are covered in the next section on reapportionment.)

Smith v. Allwright

321 U.S. 649 (1944)

The statutes of Texas provided for primary elections for U.S. Senators, U.S. Representatives, and state officers. The Democratic party of Texas, which the Texas Supreme Court called a "voluntary association," adopted in a state convention a resolution permitting only white citizens of the state to participate in the Democratic primary. The issue in this case was whether the resolution constituted "state action" in violation of the Fifteenth Amendment. Lonnie Smith, a black, sued an election judge, S.E. Allwright.

MR. JUSTICE REED delivered the opinion of the Court.

This writ of certiorari brings here for review a claim for damages in the sum of $5,000 on the part of petitioner, a Negro citizen of the 48th precinct of Harris County, Texas, for the refusal of respondents, election and associate election judges respectively of that precinct, to give petitioner a ballot or to permit him to cast a ballot in the primary election of July 27, 1940, for the nomination of Democratic candidates for the United States Senate and House of Representatives, and Governor and other state officers. The refusal is alleged to have been solely because of the race and color of the proposed voter....

The State of Texas by its Constitution and statutes provides that every person, if certain other requirements are met which are not here in issue, qualified by residence in the district or county "shall be deemed a qualified elector." ... Primary elections for United States Senators, Congressmen and state officers are provided for by Chapters Twelve and Thirteen of the statutes. Under these chapters, the Democratic party was required to hold the primary which was the occasion of the alleged wrong to petitioner....

The Democratic party of Texas is held by the Supreme Court of that State to be a "voluntary association," ... protected by § 27 of the Bill of Rights, Art. 1, Constitution of Texas, from interference by the State except that:

"In the interest of fair methods and a fair expression by their members of their preferences in the selection of their nominees, the State may regulate such elections by proper laws." ...

The Democratic party on May 24, 1932, in a state convention adopted the following resolution, which has not since been "amended, abrogated, annulled or avoided":

"Be it resolved that all white citizens of the State of Texas who are qualified to vote under the Constitution and laws of the State shall be eligible to membership in the Democratic party and, as such, entitled to participate in its deliberations."

It was by virtue of this resolution that the respondents refused to permit the petitioner to vote.

Texas is free to conduct her elections and limit her electorate as she may deem wise, save only as her action may be affected by the prohibitions of the United States Constitution or in conflict with powers delegated to and exercised by the National Government. The Fourteenth Amendment forbids a State from making or enforcing any law which abridges the privileges or immunities of citizens of the United States and the Fifteenth Amendment specifically interdicts any denial or abridgement by a State of the right of citizens to vote on account of color. Respondents appeared in the District Court and the Circuit Court of Appeals and defended on the ground that the Democratic party of Texas is a voluntary organization with members banded together for the purpose of selecting individuals of the group representing the common political beliefs as candidates in the general election. As such a voluntary organization, it was claimed, the Democratic party is free to select its own membership and limit to whites participation in the party primary. Such action, the answer asserted, does not violate the Fourteenth, Fifteenth or Seventeenth Amendment as officers of government cannot be chosen at primaries and the Amendments are applicable only to general elections where governmental officers are actually elected. Primaries, it is said, are political party affairs, handled by party, not governmental, officers....

The right of a Negro to vote in the Texas primary has been considered heretofore by this Court. The first case was *Nixon* v. *Herndon*, 273 U.S. 536. At that time, 1924, the Texas statute ... declared "in no event shall a Negro be eligible to participate in a Democratic Party primary election in the State of Texas." *[The Court held that the statute violated the Equal Protection Clause of the Fourteenth Amendment, after which the legislature of Texas gave the State Executive Committee of a party the power to prescribe the voting qualifications of its members. In* Nixon *v.* Condon, *286 U.S. 73 (1932), the Court held that the Committee action was state action and invalid as discriminatory under the Fourteenth Amendment. In* Grovey *v.* Townsend, *295 U.S. 45 (1935), the Court decided that the refusal of a county clerk in Texas to give a black an absentee ballot, for reasons only of race, was permissible because the clerk was not a state officer and there was no "state action." After* Grovey, *the Court held in* United States *v.* Classic, *313 U.S. 299 (1941), that Section 4 of Article I of the Constitution authorized Congress to regulate primary as well as general elections.]*

... The fusing by the *Classic* case of the primary and general elections into a single instrumentality for choice of officers has a definite bearing on the permissibility under the Constitution of excluding Negroes from primaries. This is not to say that the *Classic* case cuts directly into the rationale of *Grovey* v. *Townsend.* This latter case was not mentioned in the opinion. *Classic* bears upon *Grovey* v. *Townsend* not because exclusion of Negroes from primaries is any more or less state action by reason of the unitary character of the electoral process but because the

recognition of the place of the primary in the electoral scheme makes clear that state delegation to a party of the power to fix the qualifications of primary elections is delegation of a state function that may make the party's action the action of the State....

It may now be taken as a postulate that the right to vote in such a primary for the nomination of candidates without discrimination by the State, like the right to vote in a general election, is a right secured by the Constitution.... By the terms of the Fifteenth Amendment that right may not be abridged by any State on account of race. Under our Constitution the great privilege of the ballot may not be denied a man by the State because of his color.

We are thus brought to an examination of the qualifications for Democratic primary electors in Texas, to determine whether state action or private action has excluded Negroes from participation....

Primary elections are conducted by the party under state statutory authority. The county executive committee selects precinct election officials and the county, district or state executive committees, respectively, canvass the returns. These party committees or the state convention certify the party's candidates to the appropriate officers for inclusion on the official ballot for the general election. No name which has not been so certified may appear upon the ballot for the general election as a candidate of a political party. No other name may be printed on the ballot which has not been placed in nomination by qualified voters who must take oath that they did not participate in a primary for the selection of a candidate for the office for which the nomination is made.

The state courts are given exclusive original jurisdiction of contested elections and of mandamus proceedings to compel party officers to perform their statutory duties.

We think that this statutory system for the selection of party nominees for inclusion on the general election ballot makes the party which is required to follow these legislative directions an agency of the State in so far as it determines the participants in a primary election. The party takes its character as a state agency from the duties imposed upon it by state statutes; the duties do not become matters of private law because they are performed by a political party.... This is state action within the meaning of the Fifteenth Amendment....

The United States is a constitutional democracy. Its organic law grants to all citizens a right to participate in the choice of elected officials without restriction by any State because of race. This grant to the people of the opportunity for choice is not to be nullified by a State through casting its electoral process in a form which permits a private organization to practice racial discrimination in the election. Constitutional rights would be of little value if they could be thus indirectly denied. *Lane* v. *Wilson,* 307 U.S. 268, 275.

... In reaching this conclusion we are not unmindful of the desirability of continuity of decision in constitutional questions. However, when convinced of former error, this Court has never felt constrained to follow precedent. In constitutional questions, where correction depends upon amendment and not upon legislative action this Court throughout its history has freely exercised its power to reex-

amine the basis of its constitutional decisions.... *Grovey* v. *Townsend* is overruled.

Judgment reversed.

Mr. Justice Frankfurter concurs in the result.

Mr. Justice Roberts: ...

... [T]he instant decision, overruling that announced about nine years ago, tends to bring adjudications of this tribunal into the same class as a restricted railroad ticket, good for this day and train only. I have no assurance, in view of current decisions, that the opinion announced today may not shortly be repudiated and overruled by justices who deem they have new light on the subject....

Harper v. Virginia Board of Elections

383 U.S. 663 (1966)

Annie E. Harper and other residents of Virginia brought this action to have Virginia's poll tax declared unconstitutional. A three-judge district court dismissed the complaint. The Supreme Court decided whether the poll tax violated the Equal Protection Clause of the Fourteenth Amendment. The three dissenters (Douglas, Harlan and Stewart) believed that the decision to invalidate the poll tax at the state level should have been left to Congress or to the states, not to the courts.

Mr. Justice Douglas delivered the opinion of the Court.

These are suits by Virginia residents to have declared unconstitutional Virginia's poll tax. The three-judge District Court, feeling bound by our decision in *Breedlove* v. *Suttles,* 302 U.S. 277, dismissed the complaint....

While the right to vote in federal elections is conferred by Art. I, § 2, of the Constitution ... the right to vote in state elections is nowhere expressly mentioned. It is argued that the right to vote in state elections is implicit, particularly by reason of the First Amendment and that it may not constitutionally be conditioned upon the payment of a tax or fee. Cf. *Murdock* v. *Pennsylvania,* 319 U.S. 105, 113. We do not stop to canvass the relation between voting and political expression. For it is enough to say that once the franchise is granted to the electorate, lines may not be drawn which are inconsistent with the Equal Protection Clause of the Fourteenth Amendment. That is to say, the right of suffrage "is subject to the imposition of state standards which are not discriminatory and which do not contravene any restriction that Congress, acting pursuant to its constitutional powers, has imposed." *Lassiter* v.

Northampton Election Board, 360 U.S. 45, 51. We were speaking there of a state literacy test which we sustained, warning that the result would be different if a literacy test, fair on its face, were used to discriminate against a class. *Id.,* at 53. But the *Lassiter* case does not govern the result here, because, unlike a poll tax, the "ability to read and write ... has some relation to standards designed to promote intelligent use of the ballot." *Id.,* at 51.

We conclude that a State violates the Equal Protection Clause of the Fourteenth Amendment whenever it makes the affluence of the voter or payment of any fee an electoral standard. Voter qualifications have no relation to wealth nor to paying or not paying this or any other tax. Our cases demonstrate that the Equal Protection Clause of the Fourteenth Amendment restrains the States from fixing voter qualifications which invidiously discriminate....

We say the same whether the citizen, otherwise qualified to vote, has $1.50 in his pocket or nothing at all, pays the fee or fails to pay it. The principle that denies the State the right to dilute a citizen's vote on account of his economic status or other such factors by analogy bars a system which excludes those unable to pay a fee to vote or who fail to pay.

It is argued that a State may exact fees from citizens for many different kinds of licenses; that if it can demand from all an equal fee for a driver's license, it can demand from all an equal poll tax for voting. But we must remember that the interest of the State, when it comes to voting, is limited to the power to fix qualifications. Wealth, like race, creed, or color, is not germane to one's ability to participate intelligently in the electoral process. Lines drawn on the basis of wealth or property, like those of race (*Korematsu* v. *United States,* 323 U.S. 214, 216), are traditionally disfavored.... To introduce wealth or payment of a fee as a measure of a voter's qualifications is to introduce a capricious or irrelevant factor....

We have long been mindful that where fundamental rights and liberties are asserted under the Equal Protection Clause, classifications which might invade or restrain them must be closely scrutinized and carefully confined....

Those principles apply here. For to repeat, wealth or fee paying has, in our view, no relation to voting qualifications; the right to vote is too precious, too fundamental to be so burdened or conditioned.

Reversed.

Mr. Justice Black, dissenting.

[Black points out that the Court in *Breedlove* v. *Suttles,* 302 U.S. 277 (1937), and *Butler* v. *Thompson,* 341 U.S. 937 (1951), upheld poll taxes.]

Since the *Breedlove* and *Butler* cases were decided the Federal Constitution has not been amended in the only way it could constitutionally have been, that is, as provided in Article V of the Constitution. I would adhere to the holding of those cases. The Court, however, overrules *Breedlove* in part, but its opinion reveals that it does so not by using its limited power to interpret the original meaning of the Equal Protection Clause, but by giving that clause a new meaning which it believes represents a better governmental policy. From this action I dissent.

... All voting laws treat some persons differently from others in some respects. Some bar a person from voting who is under 21 years of age; others bar those under 18. Some bar convicted felons or the insane, and some have attached a freehold or other property qualification for voting. The *Breedlove* case

upheld a poll tax which was imposed on men but was not equally imposed on women and minors, and the Court today does not overrule that part of *Breedlove* which approved those discriminatory provisions. And in *Lassiter* v. *Northampton Election Board,* 360 U.S. 45, this Court held that state laws which disqualified the illiterate from voting did not violate the Equal Protection Clause. From these cases and all the others decided by this Court interpreting the Equal Protection Clause it is clear that some discriminatory voting qualifications can be imposed without violating the Equal Protection Clause.

... State poll tax legislation can "reasonably," "rationally" and without an "invidious" or evil purpose to injure anyone be found to rest on a number of state policies including (1) the State's desire to collect its revenue, and (2) its belief that voters who pay a poll tax will be interested in furthering the State's welfare when they vote. Certainly it is rational to believe that people may be more likely to pay taxes if payment is a prerequisite to voting....

Mr. Justice Harlan, whom Mr. Justice Stewart joins, dissenting.

... In substance the Court's analysis of the equal protection issue goes no further than to say that the electoral franchise is "precious" and "fundamental,"... and to conclude that "[t]o introduce wealth or payment of a fee as a measure of a voter's qualifications is to introduce a capricious or irrelevant factor,"... These are of course captivating phrases, but they are wholly inadequate to satisfy the standard governing adjudication of the equal protection issue: Is there a rational basis for Virginia's poll tax as a voting qualification? I think the answer to that question is undoubtedly "yes."...

Property and poll-tax qualifications ... are not in accord with current egalitarian notions of how a modern democracy should be organized. It is of course entirely fitting that legislatures should modify the law to reflect such changes in popular attitudes. However, it is all wrong, in my view, for the Court to adopt the political doctrines popularly accepted at a particular moment of our history and to declare all others to be irrational and invidious, barring them from the range of choice by reasonably minded people acting through the political process....

South Carolina v. Katzenbach

383 U.S. 301 (1966)

By passing the Voting Rights Act of 1965, Congress acted against states that used various tests and devices to prevent blacks from registering and voting. The statute authorized federal examiners to qualify applicants for registration, entitling them to vote in elections. South Carolina filed suit to have the Act declared unconstitutional as an encroachment on states' rights and a violation of due process protections. The case was one of original jurisdiction, with South Carolina supported by Alabama, Georgia, Louisiana, Mississippi, and Virginia, while the states supporting Attorney General Katzenbach included California, Illinois, and Massachusetts, joined by Hawaii, Indiana, Iowa, Kansas, Maine, Maryland, Michigan, Montana, New Hampshire, New Jersey, New York, Oklahoma, Oregon, Pennsylvania, Rhode Island, Vermont, West Virginia, and Wisconsin.

MR. CHIEF JUSTICE WARREN delivered the opinion of the Court.

By leave of the Court, 382 U.S. 898, South Carolina has filed a bill of complaint, seeking a declaration that selected provisions of the Voting Rights Act of 1965 violate the Federal Constitution, and asking for an injunction against enforcement of these provisions by the Attorney General....

The Voting Rights Act was designed by Congress to banish the blight of racial discrimination in voting, which has infected the electoral process in parts of our country for nearly a century. The Act creates stringent new remedies for voting discrimination where it persists on a pervasive scale, and in addition the statute strengthens existing remedies for pockets of voting discrimination elsewhere in the country. Congress assumed the power to prescribe these remedies from § 2 of the Fifteenth Amendment, which authorizes the National Legislature to effectuate by "appropriate" measures the constitutional prohibition against racial discrimination in voting. We hold that the sections of the Act which are properly before us are an appropriate means for carrying out Congress' constitutional responsibilities and are consonant with all other provisions of the Constitution. We therefore deny South Carolina's request that enforcement of these sections of the Act be enjoined.

I.

The constitutional propriety of the Voting Rights Act of 1965 must be judged with reference to the historical experience which it reflects. Before enacting the measure, Congress explored with great care the problem of racial discrimination in voting. The House and Senate Committees on the Judiciary each held hearings for nine days and received testimony from a total of 67 witnesses. More than three full days were consumed discussing the bill on the floor of the House, while the debate in the Senate covered

26 days in all. At the close of these deliberations, the verdict of both chambers was overwhelming. The House approved the bill by a vote of 328–74, and the measure passed the Senate by a margin of 79–18.

Two points emerge vividly from the voluminous legislative history of the Act contained in the committee hearings and floor debates. First: Congress felt itself confronted by an insidious and pervasive evil which had been perpetuated in certain parts of our country through unremitting and ingenious defiance of the Constitution. Second: Congress concluded that the unsuccessful remedies which it had prescribed in the past would have to be replaced by sterner and more elaborate measures in order to satisfy the clear commands of the Fifteenth Amendment....

The Fifteenth Amendment to the Constitution was ratified in 1870. Promptly thereafter Congress passed the Enforcement Act of 1870, which made it a crime for public officers and private persons to obstruct exercise of the right to vote. The statute was amended in the following year to provide for detailed federal supervision of the electoral process, from registration to the certification of returns. As the years passed and fervor for racial equality waned, enforcement of the laws became spotty and ineffective, and most of their provisions were repealed in 1894. The remnants have had little significance in the recently renewed battle against voting discrimination.

Meanwhile, beginning in 1890, the States of Alabama, Georgia, Louisiana, Mississippi, North Carolina, South Carolina, and Virginia enacted tests still in use which were specifically designed to prevent Negroes from voting. Typically, they made the ability to read and write a registration qualification and also required completion of a registration form. These laws were based on the fact that as of 1890 in each of the named States, more than two-thirds of the adult Negroes were illiterate while less than one-quarter of the adult whites were unable to read or write. At the same time, alternate tests were prescribed in all of the named States to assure that white illiterates would not be deprived of the franchise. These included grandfather clauses, property qualifications, "good character" tests, and the requirement that registrants "understand" or "interpret" certain matter.

The course of subsequent Fifteenth Amendment litigation in this Court demonstrates the variety and persistence of these and similar institutions designed to deprive Negroes of the right to vote. [*A series of decisions struck down grandfather clauses, procedural hurdles, white primaries, improper challenges, racial gerrymandering, and discriminatory application of voting tests.*]

According to the evidence in recent Justice Department voting suits, the latter stratagem is now the principal method used to bar Negroes from the polls.... White applicants for registration have often been excused altogether from the literacy and understanding tests or have been given easy versions, have received extensive help from voting officials, and have been registered despite serious errors in their answers. [*A footnote observes that a white applicant in Louisiana satisfied the registrar of his ability to interpret the state constitution by writing, "FRDUM FOOF SPETGH," while another white applicant in Alabama who had not completed the first grade was enrolled after the registrar filled out the entire form for him.*] ...

... According to estimates by the Attorney General during hearings on the Act, registration of voting-age Negroes in Alabama rose only from 14.2% to 19.4% between 1958 and 1964; in Louisiana it barely inched ahead from 31.7% to 31.8% between 1956 and 1965; and in Mississippi it increased only from 4.4% to 6.4% between 1954 and 1964. In each instance, registration of voting-age whites ran roughly 50 percentage points or more ahead of Negro registration....

II.

The Voting Rights Act of 1965 reflects Congress' firm intention to rid the country of racial discrimination in voting.... The first of the remedies, contained in § 4(a), is the suspension of literacy tests and similar voting qualifications for a period of five years from the last occurrence of substantial voting discrimination. Section 5 prescribes a second remedy, the suspension of all new voting regulations pending review by federal authorities to determine whether their use would perpetuate voting discrimination. The third remedy ... is the assignment of

federal examiners on certification by the Attorney General to list qualified applicants who are thereafter entitled to vote in all elections....

COVERAGE FORMULA.

The remedial sections of the Act assailed by South Carolina automatically apply to any State, or to any separate political subdivision such as a county or parish, for which two findings have been made: (1) the Attorney General has determined that on November 1, 1964, it maintained a "test or device," and (2) the Director of the Census has determined that less than 50% of its voting-age residents were registered on November 1, 1964, or voted in the presidential election of November 1964. [*Under this Section 4(b) procedure, coverage was extended to Alabama, Alaska, Georgia, Louisiana, Mississippi, South Carolina, Virginia, 26 counties in North Carolina, three counties in Arizona, one county in Hawaii, and one county in Idaho.*]

III.

These provisions of the Voting Rights Act of 1965 are challenged on the fundamental ground that they exceed the powers of Congress and encroach on an area reserved to the States by the Constitution....

... § 2 of the Fifteenth Amendment expressly declares that "Congress shall have power to enforce this article by appropriate legislation." By adding this authorization, the Framers indicated that Congress was to be chiefly responsible for implementing the rights created in § 1....

We ... reject South Carolina's argument that Congress may appropriately do no more than to forbid violations of the Fifteenth Amendment in general terms — that the task of fashioning specific remedies or of applying them to particular localities must necessarily be left entirely to the courts. Congress is not circumscribed by any such artificial rules under § 2 of the Fifteenth Amendment....

IV.

Congress exercised its authority under the Fifteenth Amendment in an inventive manner when it enacted the Voting Rights Act of 1965. First: The measure prescribes remedies for voting discrimination which go into effect without any need for prior adjudication. This was clearly a legitimate response to the problem, for which there is ample precedent under other constitutional provisions.... Congress had found that case-by-case litigation was inadequate to combat widespread and persistent discrimination in voting, because of the inordinate amount of time and energy required to overcome the obstructionist tactics invariably encountered in these lawsuits. After enduring nearly a century of systematic resistance to the Fifteenth Amendment, Congress might well decide to shift the advantage of time and inertia from the perpetrators of the evil to its victims....

[The Court upholds the sections on coverage formula, suspension of tests, review of new rules, and federal examiners.]

... We may finally look forward to the day when truly "[t]he right of citizens of the United States to vote shall not be denied or abridged by the United States or by any State on account of race, color, or previous condition of servitude."

The bill of complaint is

Dismissed.

MR. JUSTICE BLACK, concurring and dissenting.

... I agree with most of the Court's conclusions, [*but*] dissent from its holding that every part of § 5 of the Act is constitutional. Section 4(a), to which § 5 is linked, suspends for five years all literacy tests and similar devices in those States coming within the formula of § 4(b). Section 5 goes on to provide that a State covered by § 4(b) can in no way amend its constitution or laws relating to voting without first trying to persuade the Attorney General of the United States or the Federal District Court for the District of Columbia that the new proposed laws do not have the purpose and will not have the effect of denying the right to vote to citizens on account of

their race or color. I think this section is unconstitutional on at least two grounds.

(a) The Constitution gives federal courts jurisdiction over cases and controversies only. If it can be said that any case or controversy arises under this section which gives the District Court for the District of Columbia jurisdiction to approve or reject state laws or constitutional amendments, then the case or controversy must be between a State and the United States Government. But it is hard for me to believe that a justiciable controversy can arise in the constitutional sense from a desire by the United States Government or some of its officials to determine in advance what legislative provisions a State may enact or what constitutional amendments it may adopt....

(b) My second and more basic objection to § 5 is that Congress has here exercised its power under § 2 of the Fifteenth Amendment through the adoption of means that conflict with the most basic principles of the Constitution.... Section 5, by providing that some of the States cannot pass state laws or adopt state constitutional amendments without first being compelled to beg federal authorities to approve their policies, so distorts our constitutional structure of government as to render any distinction drawn in the Constitution between state and federal power almost meaningless.... Certainly if all the provisions of our Constitution which limit the power of the Federal Government and reserve other power to the States are to mean anything, they mean at least that the States have power to pass laws and amend their constitutions without first sending their officials hundreds of miles away to beg federal authorities to approve them....

Mobile v. Bolden

446 U.S. 55 (1980)

In this case the Court decides whether voting practices must discriminate *purposefully* or only *in effect*. Wiley L. Bolden and other residents of Mobile, Alabama, brought a class action in federal court against the city on behalf of all black citizens in the city. They alleged that the practice of electing city commissioners at-large unfairly diluted the voting strength of blacks in violation of the Fourteenth and Fifteenth Amendments and Section 2 of the Voting Rights Act of 1965. Although finding that blacks registered and voted "without hindrance," the district court held that the at-large electoral system violated the Fifteenth Amendment and invidiously discriminated against blacks in violation of the Equal Protection Clause of the Fourteenth Amendment. The Fifth Circuit affirmed.

MR. JUSTICE STEWART announced the judgment of the Court and delivered an opinion, in which THE CHIEF JUSTICE, MR. JUSTICE POWELL, and MR. JUSTICE REHNQUIST joined.

The city of Mobile, Ala., has since 1911 been governed by a City Commission consisting of three members elected by the voters of the city at large. The question in this case is whether this at-large system of municipal elections violates the rights of Mobile's Negro voters in contravention of federal statutory or constitutional law....

I

In Alabama, the form of municipal government a city may adopt is governed by state law. Until 1911, cities not covered by specific legislation were limited to governing themselves through a mayor and city council. In that year, the Alabama Legislature authorized every large municipality to adopt a commission form of government. Mobile established its City Commission in the same year, and has maintained that basic system of municipal government ever since.

The three Commissioners jointly exercise all legislative, executive, and administrative power in the municipality. They are required after election to designate one of their number as Mayor, a largely ceremonial office, but no formal provision is made for allocating specific executive or administrative duties among the three. As required by the state law enacted in 1911, each candidate for the Mobile City Commission runs for election in the city at large for a term of four years in one of three numbered posts, and may be elected only by a majority of the total vote....

II

[Bolden's claim that the Mobile electoral system violated Section 2 of the Voting Rights Act of 1965 was not adjudicated by the Court. It concluded that the claim added nothing to the complaint because Section 2 does no more than elaborate upon the Fifteenth Amendment.]

III

The Court's early decisions under the Fifteenth Amendment established that it imposes but one limitation on the powers of the States. It forbids them to discriminate against Negroes in matters having to do with voting....

Our decisions, moreover, have made clear that action by a State that is racially neutral on its face violates the Fifteenth Amendment only if motivated by a discriminatory purpose. [Guinn v. United States, 238 U.S. 347 (1915)]...

The Court's more recent decisions confirm the principle that racially discriminatory motivation is a necessary ingredient of a Fifteenth Amendment violation. [Gomillion v. Lightfoot, 364 U.S. 339 (1960)]... [Bolden argued that the at-large system was unconstitutional because the effect of racially polarized voting in Mobile was the same as that of a racially exclusionary primary.]

The answer to the appellees' argument is that, as the District Court expressly found, their freedom to vote has not been denied or abridged by anyone. The Fifteenth Amendment does not entail the right to have Negro candidates elected, and neither Smith v. Allwright nor Terry v. Adams contains any implication to the contrary. That Amendment prohibits only purposefully discriminatory denial or abridgment by government of the freedom to vote "on account of race, color, or previous condition of servitude."...

[IV.A]

Despite repeated constitutional attacks upon multimember legislative districts, the Court has consistently held that they are not unconstitutional per se, ... We have recognized, however, that such legislative apportionments could violate the Fourteenth Amendment if their purpose were invidiously to minimize or cancel out the voting potential of racial or ethnic minorities.... To prove such a purpose it is not enough to show that the group allegedly discriminated against has not elected representatives in proportion to its numbers.... A plaintiff must prove that the disputed plan was "conceived or operated as [a] purposeful devic[e] to further racial ... discrimination," id., at 149....

[The Court noted that no black had been elected to the Mobile City Commission. However, blacks had the only active "slating" organization in the city. "It may be that Negro candidates have been defeated, but that fact alone does not work a constitutional deprivation."]

V

The judgment is reversed, and the case is remanded to the Court of Appeals for further proceedings.

It is so ordered.

MR. JUSTICE BLACKMUN, concurring in the result....

MR. JUSTICE STEVENS, concurring in the judgment....

MR. JUSTICE BRENNAN, dissenting.

I dissent because I agree with MR. JUSTICE MARSHALL that proof of discriminatory impact is sufficient in these cases....

MR. JUSTICE WHITE, dissenting.

In *White v. Regester,* 412 U.S. 755 (1973), this

Court unanimously held the use of multimember districts for the election of state legislators in two counties in Texas violated the Equal Protection Clause of the Fourteenth Amendment because, based on a careful assessment of the totality of the circumstances, they were found to exclude Negroes and Mexican-Americans from effective participation in the political processes in the counties. Without questioning the vitality of *White* v. *Regester* and our other decisions dealing with challenges to multimember districts by racial or ethnic groups, the Court today inexplicably rejects a similar holding based on meticulous factual findings and scrupulous application of the principles of these cases by both the District Court and the Court of Appeals. The Court's decision is flatly inconsistent with *White* v. *Regester* and it cannot be understood to flow from our recognition in *Washington* v. *Davis*, 426 U.S. 229 (1976), that the Equal Protection Clause forbids only purposeful discrimination. Both the District Court and the Court of Appeals properly found that an invidious discriminatory purpose could be inferred from the totality of facts in this case....

Mr. Justice Marshall, dissenting....

The plurality concludes that our prior decisions establish the principle that proof of discriminatory intent is a necessary element of a Fifteenth Amendment claim. In contrast, I continue to adhere to my conclusion in *Beer* v. *United States*, 425 U.S., at 148, n. 4 (dissenting opinion), that "[t]he Court's decisions relating to the relevance of purpose-and/or-effect analysis in testing the constitutionality of legislative enactments are somewhat less than a seamless web." As I there explained, at various times

the Court's decisions have seemed to adopt three inconsistent approaches: (1) that purpose alone is the test for unconstitutionality; (2) that effect alone is the test; and (3) that purpose or effect, either alone or in combination, is sufficient to show unconstitutionality. *Ibid.* In my view, our Fifteenth Amendment jurisprudence on the necessity of proof of discriminatory purpose is no less unsettled than was our approach to the importance of such proof in Fourteenth Amendment racial discrimination cases prior to *Washington* v. *Davis*, 426 U.S. 229 (1976). What is called for in the present cases is a fresh consideration—similar to our inquiry in *Washington* v. *Davis, supra,* with regard to Fourteenth Amendment discrimination claims—of whether proof of discriminatory purpose is necessary to establish a claim under the Fifteenth Amendment....

... [I]t is beyond dispute that a standard based solely upon the motives of official decisionmakers creates significant problems of proof for plaintiffs and forces the inquiring court to undertake an unguided, tortuous look into the minds of officials in the hope of guessing why certain policies were adopted and others rejected.... An approach based on motivation creates the risk that officials will be able to adopt policies that are the products of discriminatory intent so long as they sufficiently mask their motives through the use of subtlety and illusion....

I continue to believe, then, that under the Fifteenth Amendment an "[e]valuation of the purpose of a legislative enactment is just too ambiguous a task to be the sole tool of constitutional analysis.... [A] demonstration of effect ordinarily should suffice....

Congress Reverses *Mobile* v. *Bolden*

In *Mobile* v. *Bolden*, 446 U.S. 55 (1980), the Supreme Court held that the Voting Rights Act of 1965 only prohibits states from purposefully discriminating against the voting rights of blacks. There had to be an *intent* on the part of states to abridge voting rights. In 1982, Congress amended the Act to allow plaintiffs to show discrimination solely on the *effects* of a voting plan. As explained in the congressional debate, members of Congress borrowed language that had appeared in an earlier decision by the Supreme Court, in *White* v. *Regester*, 412 U.S. 755 (1973). The selections below come from 128 Cong. Rec. 14100, 14111, 14113–15, 14936 (1982).

Mr. DeCONCINI. Mr. President, for the past several months the attention of the Nation's civil rights community, this Congress, and of the Nation itself has been focused upon the extension of the Voting Rights Act of 1965. I join in this concern, for as the Supreme Court noted almost a century ago,

"the political franchise of voting is ... a fundamental political right, because preservative of all rights." ...

In the years since the passage of the Voting Rights Act, many subtle and complex means have been developed to avoid inclusion of minority persons in the political process. With the recent Supreme Court decision of *Mobile* v. *Bolden,* 446 U.S. 55 (1980), which requires a finding of discriminatory intent to establish a violation of the 15th amendment, a new statutory tool became necessary to avoid the consequences of such subtle discriminatory mechanisms. S. 1992 would establish a "results" test in section 2 of the act, ...

In the course of the debate over a "results" versus an "intent" test for section 2 of the act, opponents of "results" have asserted that intent to discriminate is, and always has been, the standard of proof in civil rights law. This assertion involves a number of misunderstandings of the history of civil rights law.

First, while intentional discrimination has always been clearly prohibited by the 14th and 15th amendments to the Constitution, it has not always been understood to be the sole standard by which discrimination could be attacked under those provisions. Indeed, it was entirely consistent for Attorney General Katzenbach to state in 1965 that section 2 would reach any practice or procedure "if its purpose or effect was to deny or abridge the right to vote on account of race or color," and to agree with Senator Dirksen's assertion that section 2 was "a restatement, in effect, of the 15th amendment." That same year, the Supreme Court had held that multimember district systems would be unconstitutional if it were shown that—

"designedly or otherwise, a multi-member constituency scheme ... would operate to minimize or cancel out the voting strength of racial ... elements of the voting population." *Fortson* v. *Dorsey,* 379 U.S. 433 at 439 (1965). (Emphasis added.)

Intent has been expressly required by the Supreme Court as a necessary element of a 14th amendment equal protection case only since 1976. It has been expressly required in 15th amendment cases only since the Mobile against Bolden decision in 1980.

Second, "effect" standards have been used, and are being used today, in civil rights law. Both title VII of the Civil Rights Act of 1964 and section 5 of the Voting Rights Act employ effects-based standards. It is true that the proposed "results" standards of S. 1992 would not be identical to these standards, however. S. 1992 employs language designed to assure that the mere numbers of minorities elected to office would not, by themselves, provide a basis for alleging a violation of section 2 nor provide a standard for remedies of adjudicated violations of section 2. In other words, the section 2

"results" test would be a more difficult test under which to establish a violation than either the section 5 or title VII "effects" tests.

A "results" test would be superior to the present "intent" test for a variety of reasons. First and most fundamentally, "results" language in section 2 of the act would reimpose the standard which most Federal courts used in vote dilution cases prior to the Bolden decision in 1980. This standard was arrived at through interpretation of a number of landmark Supreme Court decisions over the past two decades.... These Supreme Court decisions did not create a standard of proof which required discriminatory intent; ...

[*Almost two dozen federal cases from 1972 to 1979*] are extremely important in the evaluation of a "results" test which would incorporate their standards into statutory law. It is important to note, for instance, that in these 23 cases, the defendants prevailed 13 times. Thus, a "results" test would not mean automatic victory for plaintiffs in vote dilution cases....

Mr. MATHIAS. [*This bill would amend the Voting Rights Act*] to prohibit any voting practice or procedure which results in voting discrimination. This amendment is designed to make clear that proof of discriminatory intent is not required to establish a violation of section 2....

... In Bolden, a plurality of the Supreme Court broke with precedent and substantially increased the burden on plaintiffs by requiring proof of discriminatory intent. As noted in the committee report, the Bolden intent test is unacceptable for a number of reasons.

First, the intent test asks the wrong question. Rather than focusing on the crucial question of whether or not minority voters now have a fair chance to participate in the electoral process, the intent test diverts the inquiry to an analysis of the subjective motives of public officials. Thus the intent test requires Federal judges to engage in protracted, burdensome inquiries into the motives of lawmakers, which often have little or no bearing on the ability of minority voters to participate in their electoral process. For example, on remand, following the Supreme Court's decision in Bolden, the district court was required to make an inquiry into the motives of legislators to determine if the system was devised or maintained for a discriminatory purpose. In order to comply with Bolden, the district court was forced to recreate events shedding light on the motivation of politicians who held office during the several crucial periods under investigation between 1814 and the present.

Second, as Arthur Flemming, former Chairman of the U.S. Commission on Civil Rights, told the Subcommittee on the Constitution that inquiries under the intent test "can only be divisive, threatening to destroy any existing racial progress in a community."

Third, the intent test places an unacceptable burden on plaintiffs in voting discrimination cases. It creates the risk that electoral systems will be free from challenge even where there is overwhelming evidence of unequal access to the political process. . . .

C. REAPPORTIONMENT

Activism by the Warren Court revolutionized many areas of constitutional law: criminal rights, desegregation, reapportionment, church and state, and other sensitive issues. Of all these initiatives and innovations, it is widely assumed that the desegregation case of *Brown* v. *Board of Education* (1954) was the most important decision. Chief Justice Warren, author of the 1954 ruling, disagreed. The "accolade," he said, should go to *Baker* v. *Carr* (1962), which opened the door to the "one person, one vote" rule for reapportionment. This decision helped return power to the people, giving them a direct means of protecting their rights and responsibilities through representative government. The Memoirs of Earl Warren 306–08 (1977).

Taking the Census

The Constitution requires that every ten years there be a national counting of the people. On the basis of those counts the Census Bureau reports the state populations and they are used to reapportion the seats in the House of Representatives. Because of substantial errors and undercounts in the 1990 census, the Census Bureau planned to use statistical sampling for the 2000 census. However, in 1999 the Supreme Court ruled that the Census Act prohibits the use of statistical sampling for the apportionment of House seats. The Court did not foreclose statistical sampling for other purposes, such as drawing political boundaries or allocating federal funds to the states. Dept. of Commerce v. U.S. House of Representatives, 525 U.S. 316 (1999). Three years later, the Court divided 5 to 4 in deciding that the Census Bureau could use an "imputational" statistical method to award a congressional seat to North Carolina rather than to Utah. The method supplemented census data but did not, said the majority, amount to sampling. Utah v. Evans, 536 U.S. 452 (2002).

Apportioning Legislative Seats

The first major reapportionment case appeared in 1946, involving congressional districts in Illinois. Because of changes in population and the state's failure to reapportion districts for forty years, the districts ranged from a low of 112,116 to a high of 914,053. Voters in the most populous district therefore had one-ninth the voting power of those in the smallest district. A 4–3 decision by the Supreme Court dismissed the complaint. Justice Frankfurter said it was "hostile to a democratic system to involve the judiciary in the politics of the people." COLEGROVE v. GREEN, 328 U.S. 549, 554 (1946). Although nothing in previous decisions suggested that reapportionment was outside the jurisdiction of the courts,[3] Frankfurter warned that courts "ought not to enter this political thicket" and counseled that the ultimate remedy lay with the people to insist on fair apportionment. How citizens could protect their interests when disfranchised by malapportioned districts he never explained.

In a concurrence that supplied the fourth vote, Rutledge rejected Frankfurter's position that reapportionment was nonjusticiable. Rutledge believed that the Court had jurisdiction to decide the case, but that the shortness of time remaining before the election (a few months off) prevented judicial ac-

---

3. See Wood v. Broom, 287 U.S. 1 (1932); Smiley v. Holm, 285 U.S. 355 (1932); Koenig v. Flynn, 285 U.S. 375 (1932); Carroll v. Becker, 285 U.S. 380 (1932).

tion. Thus, a majority of Justices (4–3) agreed that the Court could take jurisdiction in reapportionment cases. Because of Rutledge's position, Frankfurter had actually written a *minority* opinion on the question of jurisdiction. However, the circumstances of the Illinois case did not allow sufficient time to draw new district lines. Declaring them invalid would have forced candidates to run at-large on a statewide ticket. The pressure of an impending election also dictated the Court's decision two years later to refuse jurisdiction. MacDougall v. Green, 335 U.S. 281 (1948).

In a 1950 case, the Court regarded Georgia's apportionment law a political matter unfit for judicial review. South v. Peters, 339 U.S. 276 (1950). Georgia allotted each county a number of unit votes, giving residents of the less populous rural counties an advantage over the more populous counties in the cities. The vote in the least populous county was worth more than 120 times the vote of residents in the most populous county (Fulton County). The system did more than disfranchise urban voters. The large cities had a heavy black population. In their dissent, Justices Douglas and Black pointed out that the County Unit System "has indeed been called the 'last loophole' around our decisions holding that there must be no discrimination because of race in primary as well as in general elections." Id. at 278. With regard to the issue of nonjusticiability, Douglas and Black assumed that the Court would strike down state efforts to reduce the votes of blacks, Catholics, or Jews "so that each got only one-tenth of a vote." Id. at 277.

In 1960, a unanimous Court agreed to strike down the political boundaries drawn by the Alabama legislature for the city of Tuskegee. Black citizens challenged the legislature's decision to change the boundaries from a square to an irregular 28-sided figure. Through this process of gerrymandering, the state eliminated all but four or five of the city's 400 black voters without eliminating a single white voter. The Court invalidated the redistricting, but not on the general ground of the Equal Protection Clause. It disposed of the case on the specific commands of the Fifteenth Amendment, which forbids a state to deprive any citizen of the right to vote because of race. Justice Whittaker, concurring, would have decided the case on equal protection grounds. Gomillion v. Lightfoot, 364 U.S. 339 (1960).

Baker v. Carr

With *Gomillion*, the Court stepped gingerly into the "political thicket" of redistricting. Two years later it completed the journey. Tennessee had failed to reapportion its state legislature since 1900, despite massive population shifts over the course of six census takings. A single vote in Moore County was worth 19 votes in Hamilton County. Basing its decision on the Equal Protection Clause, a 6–2 Court held that (1) it possessed jurisdiction over reapportionment; (2) plaintiffs could obtain appropriate relief in the courts; and (3) plaintiffs had standing to challenge the Tennessee apportionment statutes. The particular remedy was left to the district court. BAKER v. CARR, 369 U.S. 186 (1962). Justice Frankfurter wrote an impassioned dissent (see box on next page).

The Court explained that the question in the Tennessee case was "the consistency of state action with the Federal Constitution. We have no question decided, or to be decided, by a political branch of government coequal with this Court." 369 U.S. at 226. However, two years later the Court accepted a case involving *congressional* districts and held that it had jurisdiction, plaintiffs had standing, and relief could be granted by the courts. Drawing upon constitutional history and the framers' intent, the Court concluded that the U.S. House of Representatives was bound by the principle of equal representation for equal numbers of people. Although it might not be possible to draw congressional districts with "mathematical precision," the principle of "one person, one vote" applied to the House. WESBERRY v. SANDERS, 376 U.S. 1 (1964). In a dissent, Justice Harlan calculated that the decision impugned the validity of 398 Representatives, leaving a "constitutional" House of 37 members.

In 1968, the Court extended the one-person, one-vote principle to any legislative or administrative body in the state subject to popular election, including units of local government with general governmental powers over the entire geographical area served by the body. Avery v. Midland County, 390 U.S. 474 (1968). In a separate case, the Court rejected the idea of limiting equal apportionment

Frankfurter's Dissent in *Baker*

Having argued in *Colegrove* that courts should not take jurisdiction in reapportionment cases, Frankfurter insisted in *Baker* v. *Carr* that the remedy for malapportionment should be left not to the courts but to the political process, "to an informed, civically militant electorate. In a democratic society like ours, relief must come through an aroused popular conscience that sears the conscience of the people's representatives." 369 U.S. at 270. However, a concurrence by Justice Clark pointed out that there were no practical means by which voters could correct malapportionment. Tennessee had no initiative or referendum. Constitutional con-

ventions could be called only by the legislature. Appeal to the state courts had been futile. Clark concluded that the majority of voters "have been caught up in a legislative strait jacket." Id. at 259. When the Court, during oral argument, asked whether there was any remedy in the courts of Tennessee for the citizens of that state, the response from state's counsel was refreshingly candid: "[O]n the present status of the case law in Tennessee and of the views held as to the constitutional law in Tennessee, ... this right, this alleged right, is not enforceable in any of the courts of Tennessee to any degree whatsoever." 56 Landmark Briefs 54 (1975).

to "important" elections. "In some instances the election of a local sheriff may be far more important than the election of a United States Senator." Hadley v. Junior College District, 397 U.S. 50, 55 (1970). On the other hand, nonlegislative state or local officials need not be chosen by election. Their selection is not governed by the one-person, one-vote requirement. Sailors v. Board of Education, 387 U.S. 105 (1967). The Court also refused to extend the one-person, one-vote principle to specialized state agencies that govern limited jurisdictions.[4]

A unanimous Court struck down New York City's Board of Estimate in 1989. The Board consisted of the Mayor, the comptroller, and the president of the City Council (all elected citywide and each with two votes on the Board), plus the elected presidents of the city's five boroughs (each casting one vote). This arrangement gave Brooklyn's 2.2 million people, about half of them minorities, the same voting strength on the Board as the 400,000 residents of Staten Island, which was mostly white. The Board exercises major powers with respect to zoning, franchises, sewer and water rates, and city contracts. Although the city offered various arguments to justify the composition of the Board, including efforts to accommodate natural and political boundaries, the Court found that the Board violated the Equal Protection Clause. Board of Estimate of City of New York v. Morris, 489 U.S. 688 (1989).

Federal and state courts often exercise concurrent jurisdiction over redistricting disputes. When this occurs, federal judges are expected to defer consideration whenever a state (through either its legislative or judicial branch) has begun to address the controversy. Growe v. Emison, 507 U.S. 25 (1993).

Single-Member Districts

In requiring a population-based formula for redistricting, the Supreme Court allows state legislatures to experiment with other variations. For example, the Court does not insist that state legislators be selected from single-member districts. Some districts can be multimember.[5] However, when federal courts are forced to fashion an apportionment plan, single-member districts are generally preferred.[6]

---

4. Ball v. James, 451 U.S. 355 (1982); Salyer Land Co. v. Tulare Lake Basin Water Storage Dist., 410 U.S. 719 (1973); Associated Enterprises, Inc. v. Toltec District, 410 U.S. 743 (1973).

5. Reynolds v. Sims, 377 U.S. 533, 577 (1964). See also Fortson v. Dorsey, 379 U.S. 433 (1965) and Burns v. Richardson, 384 U.S. 73, 88–89 (1966). The merits and demerits of multimember voting were explored more fully in Whitcomb v. Chavis, 403 U.S. 124 (1971).

6. Growe v. Emison, 507 U.S. 25, 40 (1993); Connor v. Finch, 431 U.S. 407, 415 (1977); East Carroll Parish School Bd. v. Marshall, 424 U.S. 636 (1976); Chapman v. Meier, 420 U.S. 1 (1975); Connor v. Johnson, 402 U.S. 690 (1971). For further analysis of single-member versus at-large elections, see also Branch v. Smith, 538 U.S. 254 (2003).

Under certain conditions, multimember districts are declared unconstitutional if they discriminate against minorities and ethnic groups. The capacity of these groups to elect one of their own is diluted when their votes are cast in a large, multimember district controlled by whites. White v. Regester, 412 U.S. 755 (1973).

The problem is similar with an at-large electoral system, where voters of an entire county elect a multimember governing board. If at-large voting discriminates against blacks or other groups, the county may have to be divided into districts to avoid vote dilution. Rogers v. Lodge, 458 U.S. 613 (1982). These cases generally required plaintiffs to prove that an at-large system was designed with the *intent* to further racial discrimination. There had to be not only a discriminatory effect but also a discriminatory purpose. Mobile v. Bolden, 446 U.S. 55 (1980). The distinction between effect and purpose was also explored in City of Rome v. United States, 446 U.S. 156 (1980).

In response to *Bolden,* Congress amended the Voting Rights Act in 1982 to provide that a violation could be proved by showing discriminatory effect alone. The new language adopted the "results test." 96 Stat. 134, § 3. This amendment has been used to challenge and overturn multimember districting that impairs black voting, but blacks are not automatically guaranteed seats in the legislature because of their percentage of the population. Thornburgh v. Gingles, 478 U.S. 30 (1986). Congress specifically provided that there is no right "to have members of a protected class elected in numbers equal to their proportion of the population." 96 Stat. 134, § 3.

Equality in Population

Over the years, Congress has adopted different policies on the question of making election districts equal in population. The text of the Constitution contradicted the principle of equality of representation. In counting the "whole Number of free Persons," certain Indians were excluded and only "three-fifths of all other Persons" (blacks) were added to the total. Art. I, § 2. The Civil War Amendments eliminated these constitutional supports for racism. In 1872 Congress required Representatives to be elected from districts "containing as nearly as practicable an equal number of inhabitants." 17 Stat. 28, § 2. That standard was continued in 1882, 1891, 1901, and 1911, dropped in 1929, and not revived by subsequent statutes.[7]

In 1963, the Supreme Court held that the concept of political equality could mean only one thing with regard to apportionment systems: "one person, one vote." Gray v. Sanders, 372 U.S. 368, 381 (1963). A year later it announced a softer standard. The constitutional command of Article I, Section 2, that members of the U.S. House of Representatives be chosen "by the People of the several States," means that "as nearly as is practicable one man's vote in a congressional election is to be worth as much as another's." Wesberry v. Sanders, 376 U.S. at 8. In 1964, the Court said that "mathematical nicety is not a constitutional requisite." Reynolds v. Sims, 377 U.S. 533, 568 (1964).

Although states are not compelled to achieve mathematical exactness in population among districts, a failure to articulate acceptable reasons for variations can result in the invalidation of a reapportionment plan. In cases involving *congressional* districts, population variations, no matter how small, have to be justified by the state.[8] Even variations of less than one percent from the ideal must be justified by good-faith efforts to achieve population equality. Karcher v. Daggett, 462 U.S. 725 (1983). Efforts to preserve intact whole regions of less populous counties are unacceptable justifications for population variations. Wells v. Rockefeller, 394 U.S. 542 (1969). Yet the Court recognizes some flexibility (see box on next page).

In a 1992 case, Montana wanted the minimum population variations of *Wesberry* v. *Sanders* (1964) applied to congressional districts after the most recent census. The 1990 census revealed a population

---

7. 22 Stat. 6, § 3 (1882); 26 Stat. 735, § 3 (1891); 31 Stat. 734, § 3 (1901); 37 Stat. 14, § 3 (1911); 46 Stat. 26, § 22 (1929).

8. Kirkpatrick v. Preisler, 394 U.S. 526 (1969); White v. Weiser, 412 U.S. 783 (1973). Population variations in state legislatures also had to be explained: Swann v. Adams, 385 U.S. 440 (1967); Kilgarin v. Hill, 386 U.S. 120 (1967).

Deviations from Mathematical Exactness

With regard to apportioning seats in a state legislature, the Court permits some population variations in an effort to preserve the integrity of political subdivision lines. Mahan v. Howell, 410 U.S. 315 (1973); Gaffney v. Cummings, 412 U.S. 735 (1973). When state constitutions ensure that each county (no matter how small its population) will have one representative in the state legislature, the Court has upheld population deviations as large as 16 percent as necessary to maintain political subdivisions. Brown v. Thomson, 462 U.S. 835 (1983). The Court tolerates "slightly greater percentage deviations" for local government apportionment schemes than for state and national counterparts. Abate v. Mundt, 403 U.S. 182, 185 (1971). When courts devise a reapportionment plan, they are held to a higher standard than legislatures in making districts as nearly of equal populations as is practicable. Connor v. Finch, 431 U.S. 407 (1997).

of 803,655 for Montana and an average size of 572,466 for the 435 congressional districts. A single district would have put Montana 231,189 above the average size, while an allotment of two seats would have placed Montana 170,638 below the average size. Montana was awarded one seat. A three-judge district court held that this allocation violated *Wesberry,* but a unanimous Supreme Court ruled that the quest for mathematical equality can run into insuperable hurdles at the federal level. U.S. Dept. of Commerce v. Montana, 503 U.S. 442 (1992).[9]

Bicameralism

The federal Constitution provides for a House of Representatives based on population and a Senate that gives two Senators to each state regardless of population. In the states, this "federal analogy" was invoked to argue for a population-based lower house, while allowing for factors other than population to determine seats in the other house.

In 1964, the Supreme Court extended the principle of equal representation to both houses of a state legislature. Relying on the Equal Protection Clause, the Court held that seats in both houses of a bicameral state legislature must be apportioned substantially on a population basis. The Court found the federal analogy irrelevant. Whereas the original states surrendered some of their sovereignty to form the Union and insisted on equal representation in the Senate as part of the Grand Compromise, counties did not form the states. They are creatures of the state and were never sovereign entities. REYNOLDS v. SIMS, 377 U.S. 533 (1964).[10] It mattered not to the Court whether the voters of a state specifically supported a constitutional amendment to allow one house of a state legislature to be apportioned on a basis other than population. The constitutional meaning of the Equal Protection Clause does not depend on majority vote. Lucas v. Colorado Gen. Assembly, 377 U.S. 713, 736–37 (1964).

---

9. In 1992, the Court accepted as constitutional the decision of the Secretary of Commerce to allocate the Defense Department's overseas employees to particular states for reapportionment purposes in the 1990 decision. The result was to shift a Representative from Massachusetts to Washington State. Franklin v. Massachusetts, 505 U.S. 788 (1992). In 1996, a unanimous Court rejected a challenge to the Secretary of Commerce's decision not to statistically adjust the 1990 census for differential underaccounting. The Court held that the Secretary's decisions were not subject to heightened scrutiny and were well within constitutional bounds of discretion over the conduct of the federal census. Wisconsin v. City of New York, 517 U.S. 1 (1996).

10. The Court also struck down New York's apportionment law, which gave greater representation to the less populous counties for both houses of the state legislature. WMCA, Inc. v. Lomenzo, 377 U.S. 633 (1964). The Court held that both houses of Maryland's legislature must be apportioned substantially on a population basis. Maryland Committee v. Tawes, 377 U.S. 656 (1964). The same standard was applied to the two houses of the legislatures in Virginia and in Delaware. Davis v. Mann, 377 U.S. 678 (1964); Roman v. Sincock, 377 U.S. 695 (1964).

Senator Everett Dirksen, Republican from Illinois, took the lead in trying to reverse the Court's ruling that both houses of a state legislature must be based on population. The Republican National Convention adopted a platform plank in 1964 in support of a constitutional amendment to allow one house to be based on other than population. Congressman William Tuck (D-Va.) introduced a bill to strip the federal courts of jurisdiction to hear apportionment cases. After a pitched battle, these and other court-curbing efforts were defeated.[11]

Compactness and Gerrymandering

The term *gerrymander* originates from an election district in Massachusetts so tortured in shape that it resembled a salamander. The district lines were drawn by Governor Elbridge Gerry, a member of the Jeffersonian party. The Federalist party complained that the district was configured in this odd way intentionally to disadvantage them. Congress passed legislation to limit gerrymandering. In 1842, it provided that members of the House of Representatives be elected from districts of "contiguous territory." 5 Stat. 491. Over the years, this requirement was periodically dropped and reinstated.[12]

In *Gomillion* (1960), the Supreme Court struck down a gerrymandered district because it deprived blacks of their voting rights. In 1964, however, the Court decided a case in which gerrymandering was used in New York City to *promote* the interests of black voters. The evidence strongly suggests that district lines had been drawn to segregate white voters from black and Puerto Rican voters. The result was a white congressional district and a nonwhite congressional district, giving black voters control over the latter. A 7–2 Court decided that a district court's ruling—that plaintiffs had failed to show that the apportionment was motivated by racial considerations—"was not clearly erroneous." The dissent by Douglas and Goldberg claimed that New York supported segregation not on the "separate but equal" theory of *Plessy* v. *Ferguson* but on the theory of "separate but better off." Wright v. Rockefeller, 376 U.S. 52, 62 (1964).

With the Court applying constant pressure on state legislatures to attain mathematical equivalence in the population among districts, states were tempted to create strange configurations through gerrymandering. As Justice Harlan noted in one dissent: "The fact of the matter is that the rule of absolute equality is perfectly compatible with 'gerrymandering' of the worst sort." Wells v. Rockefeller, 394 U.S. at 542, 551 (1969). Justice Stevens remarked in 1983 that advances in computer technology since the time Harlan wrote "have made the task of the gerrymander even easier." Karcher v. Daggett, 462 U.S. 725, 752 (1983).

In the Voting Rights Act of 1965, Congress directed that states were not to adopt practices or procedures that have the purpose or effect "of denying or abridging the right to vote on account of race or color." 79 Stat. 439, §5 (1965); 42 U.S.C. §1973c. These practices and procedures include redistricting that discriminates against blacks. Allen v. State Board of Elections, 393 U.S. 544, 569–70 (1969). Although race may not be used to deny or abridge voting rights, it may be used to enhance voting power (see box on next page).[13]

In addition to gerrymanders along racial lines, the Court has reviewed gerrymanders that favor

---

11. Richard C. Cortner, The Apportionment Cases 236–46 (1970); Robert G. Dixon, Jr., Democratic Representation 385–435 (1968); Royce Hanson, The Political Thicket 82–101 (1966).

12. The requirement of "contiguous territory" was dropped in 1850, 9 Stat. 432, §25, and reinstated in 1862, 1872, 1882, and 1891. 12 Stat. 572 (1862); 17 Stat. 28, §2 (1872); 22 Stat. 6, §3 (1882); 26 Stat. 735, §3 (1891). The language in 1901 and 1911 became "contiguous and compact territory." 31 Stat. 734, §3 (1901); 37 Stat. 14, §3 (1911). This requirement was dropped in 1929. 46 Stat. 26, §22 (1929).

13. Race is also a factor when cities annex nearby counties to reduce the percentage of the black population. Part of the compromise may be the creation of wards with substantial black populations. City of Richmond v. United States, 422 U.S. 358 (1975); Georgia v. United States, 411 U.S. 526 (1973); Perkins v. Matthews, 400 U.S. 379 (1971). See also Beer v. United States, 425 U.S. 130 (1976). When cities try to annex only white areas, they may be unable to obtain either the approval of the Attorney General or a federal judge. City of Pleasant Grove v. United States, 479 U.S. 462 (1987).

Support for Racial Gerrymandering

In 1964, the Supreme Court supported racial gerrymandering in New York City, which divided citizens in such a way as to create a white congressional district and a nonwhite congressional district. Wright v. Rockefeller, 376 U.S. 52 (1964). Race was also used in Brooklyn to divide the Hasidic Jewish community in order to maintain certain percentages in the white and nonwhite districts. In upholding this reapportionment, the Second Circuit reasoned that the Voting Rights Act contemplated that the Attorney General and the state legislature would have "to think in racial terms" to satisfy the Act, which "necessarily deals with race or color." The Supreme Court affirmed this judgment. United Jewish Organizations v. Carey, 430 U.S. 144, 154–55 (1977). Compliance with the Act in apportionment cases "would often necessitate the use of racial considerations in drawing district lines." Id. at 159. The Court recognized that New York "deliberately increased the nonwhite majorities in certain districts in order to enhance the opportunity for election of nonwhite representatives from those districts." Id. at 165. In the l990s, the Court would begin to place curbs on racial gerrymandering.

one political party over another. In 1983, it sidestepped a New Jersey political gerrymandering case by deciding it on grounds of equal population. Karcher v. Daggett, 462 U.S. 725 (1983). A political gerrymandering case decided by the Court in 1986 involved the Indiana legislature: a 100-member House of Representatives and a 50-member Senate. Following the 1980 census, the legislature (controlled by Republicans) reapportioned the districts. The Democrats claimed that the reapportionment plan constituted a political gerrymander that violated their right to equal protection. In a decision marked by confusion of gigantic proportions (see political cartoon), a badly fractured Court agreed that it had jurisdiction over political gerrymandering. The standards it established, however, were remarkably vague. Davis v. Bandemer, 478 U.S. 109 (1986).

In 2006, the Supreme Court ruled on a unique political gerrymandering case. After a court-ordered reapportionment in 2001 following the census, the Texas legislature redrew the congressional district lines two years later to favor Republican candidates. As a result, the Republicans gained six seats in the 2004 elections to increase their majority in the House of Representatives. The Court upheld most of the legislature's plan, but also ruled that a West Texas district violated the Voting Rights Act by diluting the voting power of Latinos. Justice Kennedy announced the judgment for a 5–4 Court. Concurrences and dissents by the other eight Justices offered a wide range of conflicting tests and values on the standards that should guide political gerrymandering. League of United Latin American Citizens v. Perry, 548 U.S. 399 (2006).

Revisting Racial Redistricting

Two Supreme Court decisions in 1993 gave further thought to race-conscious redistricting. In one case, an Ohio apportionment board adopted a plan to create several districts in which racial minorities would predominate. A unanimous Court held that the plan did not violate Section 2 of the Voting Rights Act. Opponents of the plan argued that packing black voters in a few districts diluted their voting power elsewhere. The Court concluded that the plaintiffs had failed to satisfy one prong of the vote-dilution test: they did not demonstrate that the white majority voted in such a bloc to frustrate the election of a minority group's candidate. There was no proof of racially polarized voting. Voinovich v. Quilter, 507 U.S. 146 (1993).

The second case concerned North Carolina's Twelfth congressional district that snaked 160 miles through the state in search of a black majority. For much of its length it followed Interstate 85 and was no wider than the highway's corridor. One state legislator remarked that "[i]f you drove down the interstate with both car doors open, you'd kill most of the people in the district." Divided 5–4, the

Court held that white voters may challenge the constitutionality of "bizarre" redistricting plans that are designed to separate voters by race. In returning the case to the district court for further proceedings, the Court said that state officials must demonstrate a "compelling" reason in order to meet the constitutionality of equal protection of the laws. Writing for the majority, Justice O'Connor warned that racial gerrymandering may "balkanize" the United States into competing racial factions, reinforce racial stereotypes, and undermine representative democracy by signaling to elected officials that they represent only a particular racial group rather than the constituency as a whole. SHAW v. RENO, 509 U.S. 630 (1993).

The decision cast doubt about the constitutionality of a number of other odd-looking congressional districts that were drawn after the 1990 census. Other than a plea that districts be made more compact in shape, the ruling gave little guidance on what states must do to avoid invalid "bizarre" shapes. Politicians are torn on the value of race-based districting. Packing blacks into particular districts may increase their chance of winning those seats, but it also dilutes their strength in other districts and gives Republicans a better chance of prevailing in districts formerly held by Democrats.

The Court gave further definition to *Shaw v. Reno* in 1995 when it rejected a race-based redistricting plan in Georgia. The initial plan by the state legislature provided for two congressional districts drawn in a way to elect two blacks. The Justice Department denied clearance on that plan, and the legislature redrew the lines to provide for three blacks (out of a total of eleven congressional seats).

NORTH CAROLINA'S 12TH CONGRESSIONAL DISTRICT

Divided 5 to 4, the Court held that a congressional district, regardless of its shape, could be unconstitutional if race was the prominent factor in drawing its lines. By subjecting redistricting plans to strict scrutiny, the Court requires states to show that it had a compelling governmental interest in adopting the plan, and that the plan was narrowly tailored to meet that interest. It is clear from this decision that complying with preclearance mandates from the Justice Department does not constitute a compelling interest, but the Court's decision (including the concurrence by Justice O'Connor) permits race to continue to be a factor in redistricting. MILLER v. JOHNSON, 515 U.S. 900 (1995).

On the same day as the Georgia case, a unanimous Court held that voters in Louisiana lacked standing to challenge a redistricting plan as a racial gerrymander because they lived in a different district. United States v. Hays, 515 U.S. 737 (1995). In summary action the Court affirmed a California redistricting plan for state legislators and members of Congress that considered race but also other factors, including population equality, geographic compactness, contiguity, political boundaries, and the presence or absence of a sense of community. DeWitt v. Wilson, 515 U.S. 1170 (1995); 856 F.Supp. 1409 (D. Cal. 1994).

From Broad Doctrine to the Nitty-Gritty

In 1996, the Supreme Court issued two more decisions on race-based districting, invalidating the 12th congressional district in North Carolina and three in Texas but failed again to provide clear guidelines for the acceptable use of race in drawing district lines. The decisions are becoming as twisted and disjointed as the districts the Court reviews. There was no majority opinion in the Texas case. O'Connor wrote a plurality opinion for herself, Rehnquist, and Kennedy. Thomas and Scalia agreed that the Texas districts were unconstitutional but refused to sign her opinion because it suggested that race could be legitimately used as one factor in deciding the boundaries of a district. O'Connor recognized that race was not the only factor for the Texas districts, but rejected the state's explanation that old-fashioned partisan politics and the traditional goal of protecting incumbents were the overriding objectives. Pointing out that Texas used a computer program that provided racial data on a block-by-block basis while other data such as party registration and past voting records were available only at the precinct-by-precinct level, she concluded that race was the dominant motivation. Bush v. Vera, 517 U.S. 952 (1996).

The North Carolina case, also splitting the Justices 5 to 4, allowed the Court to revisit the district it had called "bizarre" in *Shaw v. Reno* (1993). The Court decided that the contours of the skinny, 160-mile district were still not "narrowly tailored" to achieve the state's goal. Shaw v. Hunt, 517 U.S. 899 (1996). The district, redrawn to make it more compact, returned to the Court in 1999. The Court was persuaded by an expert's analysis that the state was motivated primarily by political, not racial, considerations in drawing the district lines. The state could engage in constitutional political gerrymandering even when it is conscious that most loyal Democrats happen to be black Democrats. The Court reversed a summary judgment by a three-judge district court that the district was an unconstitutional racial gerrymander. Hunt v. Cromartie, 526 U.S. 541 (1999). In other words, the Court would wink at political gerrymandering and give greater scrutiny to racial gerrymandering. States learned how to finesse the Court's decisions.

When the case went back to the district court, it declared the 12th district an unconstitutional racial gerrymander. However, the Supreme Court set aside that ruling to allow the congressional primaries to take place as scheduled with the redrawn district. Hunt v. Cromartie, 529 U.S. 1014 (2000). A year later, a 5–4 Court upheld the 12th district. Race is allowed in redistricting as long as it is not the predominant and controlling factor. Easley v. Cromartie, 532 U.S. 234 (2001). Clearly, states have an incentive to hide racial motivations. The four dissenters stated that the district court's ruling—that race was predominant—should not have been overturned unless the lower court was in clear error, which they said had not been established.

Racial districting was challenged elsewhere. In 1996, a three-judge court ruled unconstitutional a horseshoe-shaped congressional district in Florida that had been drawn to assure the election of a black. The district was redrawn. In 1997, federal judges invalidated an Hispanic-majority congressional district in New York City (represented by Democratic Rep. Nydia M. Velazquez), prompting a redrawing of the district.

On a separate issue, the Supreme Court made it easier for the Justice Department to approve state redistricting as part of the preclearance procedure without insisting on extreme measures to maximize the representation of minorities. Reno v. Bossier Parish School Bd., 520 U.S. 471 (1997). That decision was reinforced in 2000 when the Court held that the Voting Rights Act prevents nothing but "backsliding" (putting minority voters in a worse position than before), and preclearance affirms nothing but the absence of backsliding. Reno v. Bossier Parish School Bd., 528 U.S. 320 (2000).

By a vote of 5 to 4, the Court upheld a redrawn Georgia district map that contained only one majority-black district. The districting plan that had been struck down by the Court two years earlier, in *Miller v. Johnson*, had provided for three black-minority districts. Abrams v. Johnson, 521 U.S. 74 (1997). In another 1997 development, a three-judge court in Virginia held that the 3rd congressional district had been racially gerrymandered in violation of equal protection and the Supreme Court affirmed that judgment. Moon v. Meadows, 952 F.Supp. 1141 (D. Va. 1997) (three-judge court), aff'd sub nom. Harris v. Moon, 521 U.S. 1113 (1997).

Continued Judicial Division

In 2003, the Supreme Court gave further encouragement to racial redistricting by holding that when states draw new legislative boundaries they may take into account the minority's influence in various districts. After the 2000 census, Democrats in several states put substantial numbers of black voters in districts in order to support the election changes of white Democrats. They chose to reduce the number of majority-minority districts in order to increase the number of elected Democrats. The 5–4 decision involved a redistricting plan in Georgia. Writing for the majority, Justice O'Connor took note of the substantial overlap between political and racial gerrymandering: "The State may choose, consistent with § 5, that it is better to risk having fewer minority representatives in order to achieve greater overall representation of a minority group by increasing the number of representatives sympathetic to the interests of minority voters." Georgia v. Ashcroft, 539 U.S. 461, 483 (2003).

Another 5–4 decision, in 2004, upheld a congressional redistricting plan in Pennsylvania that was designed to benefit the Republican Party. The majority decided that there were insufficient grounds to conclude that politics had so dominated the plan that it denied the Democrats equal protection under state law. Writing for the Court, Justice Scalia said that "no judicially discernable and manageable standards for adjudicating political gerrymandering claims have emerged." Vieth v. Jubelirer, 541 U.S. 267, 281(2004). A concurrence by Kennedy, combined with the four dissenters, suggested that political gerrymandering might be adjudicated in the future, but the decision seemed to shift the battle from the courts to the regular political process.

An 8–1 decision in 2004, upholding a lower-court decision on a Georgia redistricting plan, appeared to reflect a broad consensus among the Justices. However, the top-heavy majority was possible only because the Court chose to issue a summary affirmance to support the district court judgment. Cox v. Larios, 542 U.S. 947 (2004). Had the Court issued a full opinion to spell out its judicial rationale, the positions of Justices would likely have scattered in several directions.

Colegrove v. Green
328 U.S. 549 (1946)

Congressional districts in Illinois varied widely in population, ranging from 112,116 to 914,000. Kenneth W. Colegrove and two other citizens of Illinois qualified to vote in the upcoming congressional elections brought suit in federal court under the Declaratory Judgments Act to restrain state officers from arranging for an election. They alleged that the congressional districts lacked compactness of territory and approximate equality of population, violating various provisions of the federal Constitution and the Reapportionment Act of 1911. The district court dismissed the complaint. The defendant was Dwight H. Green, an Illinois election official.

MR. JUSTICE FRANKFURTER announced the judgment of the Court and an opinion in which MR. JUSTICE REED and MR. JUSTICE BURTON concur.

... The District Court, feeling bound by this Court's opinion in Wood v. Broom, 287 U.S. 1, dismissed the complaint. 64 F.Supp. 632.

The District Court was clearly right in deeming itself bound by Wood v. Broom, supra, and we could also dispose of this case on the authority of Wood v. Broom. The legal merits of this controversy were settled in that case, inasmuch as it held that the Reapportionment Act of June 18, 1929, 46 Stat. 21, as amended, 2 U.S.C. § 2 (a), has no requirements "as to the compactness, contiguity and equality in population of districts." 287 U.S. at 8. The Act of 1929 still governs the districting for the election of Representatives.... Nothing has now been adduced to lead us to overrule what this Court found to be the requirements under the Act of 1929, the more so since seven Congressional elections have been held under the Act of 1929 as construed by this Court. No man-

ifestation has been shown by Congress even to question the correctness of that which seemed compelling to this Court in enforcing the will of Congress in Wood v. Broom.

But we also agree with the four Justices (Brandeis, Stone, Roberts, and Cardozo, JJ.) who were of opinion that the bill in Wood v. Broom, supra, should be "dismissed for want of equity." ...

We are of opinion that the appellants ask of this Court what is beyond its competence to grant. This is one of those demands on judicial power which cannot be met by verbal fencing about "jurisdiction." It must be resolved by considerations on the basis of which this Court, from time to time, has refused to intervene in controversies. It has refused to do so because due regard for the effective working of our Government revealed this issue to be of a peculiarly political nature and therefore not meet for judicial determination.

... In effect this is an appeal to the federal courts to reconstruct the electoral process of Illinois in order that it may be adequately represented in the councils of the Nation. Because the Illinois legislature has failed to revise its Congressional Representative districts in order to reflect great changes, during more than a generation, in the distribution of its population, we are asked to do this, as it were, for Illinois.

Of course no court can affirmatively re-map the Illinois districts so as to bring them more in conformity with the standards of fairness for a representative system. At best we could only declare the existing electoral system invalid. The result would be to leave Illinois undistricted and to bring into operation, if the Illinois legislature chose not to act, the choice of members for the House of Representatives on a state-wide ticket. The last stage may be worse than the first. The upshot of judicial action may defeat the vital political principle which led Congress, more than a hundred years ago, to require districting.... Nothing is clearer than that this controversy concerns matters that bring courts into immediate and active relations with party contests. From the determination of such issues this Court has traditionally held aloof. It is hostile to a democratic system to involve the judiciary in the politics of the people. And it is not less pernicious if such judicial intervention in an essentially political contest be dressed up in the abstract phrases of the law.

... The short of it is that the Constitution has conferred upon Congress exclusive authority to secure fair representation by the States in the popular House and left to that House determination whether States have fulfilled their responsibility. If Congress failed in exercising its powers, whereby standards of fairness are offended, the remedy ultimately lies with the people....

To sustain this action would cut very deep into the very being of Congress. Courts ought not to enter this political thicket. The remedy for unfairness in districting is to secure State legislatures that will apportion properly, or to invoke the ample powers of Congress. The Constitution has many commands that are not enforceable by courts because they clearly fall outside the conditions and purposes that circumscribe judicial action....

Dismissal of the complaint is affirmed.

MR. JUSTICE JACKSON took no part in the consideration or decision of this case.

MR. JUSTICE RUTLEDGE.

I concur in the result. But for the ruling in *Smiley* v. *Holm*, 285 U.S. 355, I should have supposed that the provisions of the Constitution, Art. I, §4, that "The Times, Places and Manner of holding Elections for ... Representatives, shall be prescribed in each State by the Legislature thereof; but the Congress may at any time by Law make or alter such Regulations ..."; Art. I, §2, vesting in Congress the duty of apportionment of representatives among the several states "according to their respective Numbers"; and Art. I, §5, making each House the sole judge of the qualifications of its own members, would remove the issues in this case from justiciable cognizance. But, in my judgment, the *Smiley* case rules squarely to the contrary, save only in the matter of degree.

... [T]his Court has power to afford relief in a case of this type as against the objection that the issues are not justiciable....

The shortness of the time remaining makes it doubtful whether action could, or would, be taken in time to secure for petitioners the effective relief they seek. To force them to share in an election at large might bring greater equality of voting right. It would also deprive them and all other Illinois citizens of representation by districts which the prevailing policy of Congress commands....

I think, therefore, the case is one in which the Court may properly, and should, decline to exercise its jurisdiction. Accordingly, the judgment should be affirmed and I join in that disposition of the cause.

MR. JUSTICE BLACK, dissenting.

... It is my judgment that the District Court had jurisdiction; that the complaint presented a justiciable case and controversy; and that appellants had standing to sue, since the facts alleged show that they have been injured as individuals....

MR. JUSTICE DOUGLAS and MR. JUSTICE MURPHY join in this dissent.

Baker v. Carr

369 U.S. 186 (1962)

Charles W. Baker and other residents of Tennessee brought this suit against Joe C. Carr, the Secretary of State of Tennessee. They alleged that a state statute passed in 1901 arbitrarily and capri-

ciously apportioned the seats in the General Assembly among the state's 95 counties and the state failed to reapportion the seats notwithstanding substantial growth and redistribution of the state's population. Through this "debasement of their votes" they claimed they were denied the equal protection of the laws guaranteed by the Fourteenth Amendment. After dismissing the argument that the matter constituted a "political question" (see the portion of the decision reprinted on pages 104–06), the Court decided whether the issue was justiciable.

MR. JUSTICE BRENNAN delivered the opinion of the Court.

... The Tennessee Constitution provides in Art. II as follows:

"Sec. 3. Legislative authority — Term of office. — The Legislative authority of this State shall be vested in a General Assembly, which shall consist of a Senate and House of Representatives, both dependent on the people; who shall hold their offices for two years from the day of the general election.

"Sec. 4. Census. — An enumeration of the qualified voters, and an apportionment of the Representatives in the General Assembly, shall be made in the year one thousand eight hundred and seventy-one, and within every subsequent term of ten years.

"Sec. 5. Apportionment of representatives. — The number of Representatives shall, at the several periods of making the enumeration, be apportioned among the several counties or districts, according to the number of qualified voters in each; and shall not exceed seventy-five, until the population of the State shall be one million and a half, and shall never exceed ninety-nine; Provided, that any county having two-thirds of the ratio shall be entitled to one member.

"Sec. 6. Apportionment of senators. — The number of Senators shall, at the several periods of making the enumeration, be apportioned among the several counties or districts according to the number of qualified electors in each, and shall not exceed one-third the number of representatives. In apportioning the Senators among the different counties, the fraction that may be lost by any county or counties, in the apportionment of members to the House of Representatives, shall be made up to such county or counties in the Senate, as near as may be practicable. When a district is composed of two or more counties, they shall be adjoining; and no county shall be divided in forming a district."

Thus, Tennessee's standard for allocating legislative representation among her counties is the total number of qualified voters resident in the respective counties, subject only to minor qualifications. Decennial reapportionment in compliance with the constitutional scheme was effected by the General Assembly each decade from 1871 to 1901. The 1871 apportionment was preceded by an 1870 statute requiring an enumeration. The 1881 apportionment involved three statutes, the first authorizing an enumeration, the second enlarging the Senate from 25 to 33 members and the House from 75 to 99 members, and the third apportioning the membership of both Houses. In 1891 there were both an enumeration and an apportionment. In 1901 the General Assembly abandoned separate enumeration in favor of reliance upon the Federal Census and passed the Apportionment Act here in controversy. In the more than 60 years since that action, all proposals in both Houses of the General Assembly for reapportionment have failed to pass....

We come, finally, to the ultimate inquiry whether our precedents as to what constitutes a nonjusticiable "political question" bring the case before us under the umbrella of that doctrine. A natural beginning is to note whether any of the common characteristics which we have been able to identify and label descriptively are present. We find none: The question here is the consistency of state action with the Federal Constitution. We have no question decided, or to be decided, by a political branch of government coequal with this Court. Nor do we risk embarrassment of our government abroad, or grave disturbance at home if we take issue with Tennessee as to the constitutionality of her action here challenged. Nor need the appellants, in order to succeed in this action, ask the Court to enter upon policy determinations for which judicially manageable standards are lacking. Judicial standards under the Equal Protection Clause are well developed and familiar, and it has been open to courts since the enactment of the Fourteenth Amendment to determine, if on the particular facts they must, that a discrimination reflects *no* policy, but simply arbitrary and capricious action....

We conclude that the complaint's allegations of a denial of equal protection present a justiciable constitutional cause of action upon which appellants are entitled to a trial and a decision. The right asserted is within the reach of judicial protection under the Fourteenth Amendment.

The judgment of the District Court is reversed and the cause is remanded for further proceedings consistent with this opinion.

Reversed and remanded.

MR. JUSTICE WHITTAKER did not participate in the decision of this case....

MR. JUSTICE DOUGLAS, concurring....

MR. JUSTICE CLARK, concurring.

... I would not consider intervention by this Court into so delicate a field if there were any other relief available to the people of Tennessee. But the majority of the people of Tennessee have no "practical opportunities for exerting their political weight at the polls" to correct the existing "invidious discrimination." Tennessee has no initiative and referendum. I have searched diligently for other "practical opportunities" present under the law. I find none other than through the federal courts. The majority of the voters have been caught up in a legislative strait jacket. Tennessee has an "informed, civically militant electorate" and "an aroused popular conscience," but it does not sear "the conscience of the people's representatives."... We therefore must conclude that the people of Tennessee are stymied and without judicial intervention will be saddled with the present discrimination in the affairs of their state government....

MR. JUSTICE STEWART, concurring....

MR. JUSTICE FRANKFURTER, whom MR. JUSTICE HARLAN joins, dissenting.

The Court today reverses a uniform course of decision established by a dozen cases, including one by which the very claim now sustained was unanimously rejected only five years ago. The impressive body of rulings thus cast aside reflected the equally uniform course of our political history regarding the relationship between population and legislative representation—a wholly different matter from denial of the franchise to individuals because of race, color, religion or sex. Such a massive repudiation of the experience of our whole past in asserting destructively novel judicial power demands a detailed analysis of the role of this Court in our constitutional scheme. Disregard of inherent limits in the effective exercise of the Court's "judicial Power" not only presages the futility of judicial intervention in the essentially political conflict of forces by which the relation between population and representation has time out of mind been and now is determined. It may well impair the Court's position as the ultimate organ of "the supreme Law of the Land" in that vast range of legal problems, often strongly entangled in popular feeling, on which this Court must pronounce. The Court's authority—possessed of neither the purse nor the sword—ultimately rests on sustained public confidence in its moral sanction. Such feeling must be nourished by the Court's complete detachment, in fact and in appearance, from political entanglements and by abstention from injecting itself into the clash of political forces in political settlements.

... Appeal must be to an informed, civically militant electorate. In a democratic society like ours, relief must come through an aroused popular conscience that sears the conscience of the people's representatives. In any event there is nothing judicially more unseemly nor more self-defeating than for this Court to make *in terrorem* pronouncements, to indulge in merely empty rhetoric, sounding a word of promise to the ear, sure to be disappointing to the hope....

Dissenting opinion of MR. JUSTICE HARLAN, whom MR. JUSTICE FRANKFURTER joins.

... [I]n my opinion, appellants' allegations, accepting all of them as true, do not, parsed down or as a whole, show an infringement by Tennessee of any rights assured by the Fourteenth Amendment. Accordingly, I believe the complaint should have been dismissed for "failure to state a claim upon which relief can be granted."...

Wesberry v. Sanders

376 U.S. 1 (1964)

After the Court decided in *Baker* v. *Carr* (1962) to accept jurisdiction in reapportionment cases, it had to determine whether judicial scrutiny would cover only malapportionment in state legislatures or in Congress as well. This case involved Georgia's Fifth Congressional District, which had a population two to three times greater than some other congressional districts in the state. A three-judge district court dismissed the complaint filed by James P. Wesberry, Jr., a citizen of Fulton County, for "want of equity." The defendant was Carl E. Sanders, Governor of Georgia.

MR. JUSTICE BLACK delivered the opinion of the Court.

Appellants are citizens and qualified voters of Fulton County, Georgia, and as such are entitled to vote in congressional elections in Georgia's Fifth Congressional District. That district, one of ten created by a 1931 Georgia statute, includes Fulton, DeKalb, and Rockdale Counties and has a population according to the 1960 census of 823,680. The average population of the ten districts is 394,312, less than half that of the Fifth. One district, the Ninth, has only 272,154 people, less than one-third as many as the Fifth. Since there is only one Congressman for each district, this inequality of population means that the Fifth District's Congressman has to represent from two to three times as many people as do Congressmen from some of the other Georgia districts.

Claiming that these population disparities deprived them and voters similarly situated of a right under the Federal Constitution to have their votes for Congressmen given the same weight as the votes of other Georgians, the appellants brought this action under 42 U.S.C. §§ 1983 and 1988 and 28 U.S.C. § 1343 (3) asking that the Georgia statute be declared invalid and that the appellees, the Governor and Secretary of State of Georgia, be enjoined from conducting elections under it. The complaint alleged that appellants were deprived of the full benefit of their right to vote, in violation of (1) Art. I, § 2, of the Constitution of the United States, which provides that "The House of Representatives shall be composed of Members chosen every second Year by the People of the several States ..."; (2) the Due Process, Equal Protection, and Privileges and Immunities Clauses of the Fourteenth Amendment; and (3) that part of Section 2 of the Fourteenth Amendment which provides that "Representatives shall be apportioned among the several States according to their respective numbers...."

I.

[The Court summarizes its holding in *Baker* v. *Carr* (1962), concluding that the district court erred in dismissing the complaint.]

II.

This brings us to the merits. We agree with the District Court that the 1931 Georgia apportionment grossly discriminates against voters in the Fifth Congressional District. A single Congressman represents from two to three times as many Fifth District voters as are represented by each of the Congressmen from the other Georgia congressional districts. The apportionment statute thus contracts the value of some votes and expands that of others. If the Federal Constitution intends that when qualified voters elect members of Congress each vote be given as much weight as any other vote, then this statute cannot stand.

We hold that, construed in its historical context, the command of Art. I, § 2, that Representatives be chosen "by the People of the several States" means that as nearly as is practicable one man's vote in a congressional election is to be worth as much as another's. This rule is followed automatically, of course, when Representatives are chosen as a group on a statewide basis, as was a widespread practice in the first 50 years of our Nation's history. It would be extraordinary to suggest that in such statewide elections the votes of inhabitants of some parts of a State, for example, Georgia's thinly populated Ninth District, could be weighted at two or three times the value of the votes of people living in more populous parts of the State, for example, the Fifth District around Atlanta. Cf. *Gray* v. *Sanders,* 372 U.S. 368. We do not believe that the Framers of the Constitution intended to permit the same vote-diluting discrimination to be accomplished through the device of districts containing widely varied numbers of inhabitants. To say that a vote is worth more in one district than in another would not only run counter to our fundamental ideas of democratic government, it would cast aside the principle of a House of Representatives elected "by the People," a principle tenaciously fought for and established at the Constitutional Convention. The history of the Constitution, particularly that part of it relating to the adoption of Art. I, § 2, reveals that those who framed the Constitution meant that, no matter what the mechanics of an election, whether statewide or by districts, it was population which was to be the basis of the House of Representatives....

The question of how the legislature should be constituted precipitated the most bitter controversy of the Convention. One principle was uppermost in the minds of many delegates: that, no matter where he lived, each voter should have a voice equal to that of every other in electing members of Congress. In support of this principle, George Mason of Virginia

"argued strongly for an election of the larger branch by the people. It was to be the grand depository of the democratic principle of the Govt."

James Madison agreed, saying "If the power is not immediately derived from the people, in proportion to their numbers, we may make a paper confederacy, but that will be all." Repeatedly, delegates rose to make the same point: that it would be unfair, unjust, and contrary to common sense to give a small number of people as many Senators or Representatives as were allowed to much larger groups — in short, as James Wilson of Pennsylvania put it, "equal numbers of people ought to have an equal no. of representatives . . ." and representatives "of different districts ought clearly to hold the same proportion to each other, as their respective constituents hold to each other."

[The Court describes the fear of small states that they would be overwhelmed in a legislature based only on population. As part of the Grand Compromise, each state would have two Senators, elected by the state legislatures, while members of the House of Representatives would be chosen directly by the people and "apportioned among the several States . . . according to their respective Numbers."]

It would defeat the principle solemnly embodied in the Great Compromise — equal representation in the House for equal numbers of people — for us to hold that, within the States, legislatures may draw the lines of congressional districts in such a way as to give some voters a greater voice in choosing a Congressman than others. The House of Representatives, the Convention agreed, was to represent the people as individuals, and on a basis of complete equality for each voter. The delegates were quite aware of what Madison called the "vicious representation" in Great Britain whereby "rotten boroughs" with few inhabitants were represented in Parliament on or almost on a par with cities of greater population. Wilson urged that people must be represented as individuals, so that America would escape the evils of the English system under which one man could send two members to Parliament to represent the borough of Old Sarum while London's million people sent but four. . . .

While it may not be possible to draw congressional districts with mathematical precision, that is no excuse for ignoring our Constitution's plain objective of making equal representation for equal numbers of people the fundamental goal for the House of Representatives. That is the high standard

of justice and common sense which the Founders set for us.

Reversed and remanded.

Mr. Justice Clark, concurring in part and dissenting in part. . . .

Mr. Justice Harlan, dissenting.

[In reviewing the 1962 elections, Harlan notes that in all but five States the difference between the largest and smallest districts exceeded 100,000 persons, which he presumed was not equality among districts "as nearly as is practicable."] Thus, today's decision impugns the validity of the election of 398 Representatives from 37 States, leaving a "constitutional" House of 37 members now sitting.

Only a demonstration which could not be avoided would justify this Court in rendering a decision the effect of which, inescapably as I see it, is to declare constitutionally defective the very composition of a coordinate branch of the Federal Government. The Court's opinion not only fails to make such a demonstration, it is unsound logically on its face and demonstrably unsound historically.

[Harlan believes that it is unlikely that "most or many" delegates to the Constitutional Convention would have subscribed to the one-person, one-vote principle; that state legislatures had plenary power to district, subject only to the supervisory power of Congress; and that the Court is not simply undertaking to exercise a power which the Constitution reserves to Congress but is also overruling congressional judgment expressed in previous statutes and legislative history. He warns that the "promise of judicial intervention in matters of this sort cannot but encourage popular inertia in efforts for political reform through the political process, with the inevitable result that the process is itself weakened."]

Mr. Justice Stewart.

. . . I think Mr. Justice Harlan has unanswerably demonstrated that Art. I, § 2, of the Constitution gives no mandate to this Court or to any court to ordain that congressional districts within each State must be equal in population.

Reynolds v. Sims

377 U.S. 533 (1964)

In this case, the Court faces the question whether the principle of equal representation applies to both houses of a state legislature, or whether one house — following the federal model (the

U.S. Senate) — may be apportioned on a basis other than population. M.O. Sims and other voters from Alabama brought suit to challenge the apportionment of the state legislature as a violation of the Equal Protection Clause of the Fourteenth Amendment and the Alabama Constitution. They sued B. A. Reynolds, judge of probate of Dallas County, Alabama. Under the state constitution, each county was entitled to at least one state representative, no matter how small the population. A three-judge federal court refused to order the May 1962 primary election to be held at large, stating that it should not act until the legislature had an opportunity to take corrective action before the general election. After the legislature acted, the district court held that neither of the two apportionment plans fashioned by the legislature would cure the violation of the Equal Protection Clause and proceeded to combine features of the two plans to produce a more equitable apportionment. The state appealed, claiming that a federal court lacks power to apportion a legislature.

MR. CHIEF JUSTICE WARREN delivered the opinion of the Court.

[I.]

The complaint stated that the Alabama Legislature was composed of a Senate of 35 members and a House of Representatives of 106 members. It set out relevant portions of the 1901 Alabama Constitution, which prescribed the number of members of the two bodies of the State Legislature and the method of apportioning the seats among the State's 67 counties, and provide as follows:

[Each county was entitled to at least one representative. The state was to be divided into as many senatorial districts as there were senators, with each district as "nearly equal" to each other in population. Representation in the legislature "shall be based upon population." Although the state constitution required that the legislature be apportioned every ten years, the last apportionment was based on the 1900 census. Population-variance ratios of up to about 41-to-1 existed in the Senate and up to about 16-to-1 in the House.]

II.

... The right to vote freely for the candidate of one's choice is of the essence of a democratic society, and any restrictions on that right strike at the heart of representative government. And the right of suffrage can be denied by a debasement or dilution of the weight of a citizen's vote just as effectively as by wholly prohibiting the free exercise of the franchise. *[The Court reviews the holdings in* Baker *v.* Carr *(1962),* Gray *v.* Sanders *(1963), and* Wesberry *v.* Sanders *(1964).]*

III.

A predominant consideration in determining whether a State's legislative apportionment scheme constitutes an invidious discrimination violative of rights asserted under the Equal Protection Clause is that the rights allegedly impaired are individual and personal in nature....

Legislators represent people, not trees or acres. Legislators are elected by voters, not farms or cities or economic interests. As long as ours is a representative form of government, and our legislatures are those instruments of government elected directly by and directly representative of the people, the right to elect legislators in a free and unimpaired fashion is a bedrock of our political system. It could hardly be gainsaid that a constitutional claim had been asserted by an allegation that certain otherwise qualified voters had been entirely prohibited from voting for members of their state legislature. And, if a State should provide that the votes of citizens in one part of the State should be given two times, or five times, or 10 times the weight of votes of citizens in another part of the State, it could hardly be contended that the right to vote of those residing in the disfavored areas had not been effectively diluted....

... A citizen, a qualified voter, is no more nor no less so because he lives in the city or on the farm. This is the clear and strong command of our Constitution's Equal Protection Clause. This is an essential part of the concept of a government of laws and not men. This is at the heart of Lincoln's vision of "government of the people, by the people, [and] for the people." The Equal Protection Clause demands no less than substantially equal state legislative representation for all citizens, of all places as well as of all races.

IV.

We hold that, as a basic constitutional standard, the Equal Protection Clause requires that the seats in both houses of a bicameral state legislature must be apportioned on a population basis. Simply stated, an individual's right to vote for state legislators is unconstitutionally impaired when its weight is in a substantial fashion diluted when compared with votes of citizens living in other parts of the State. Since, under neither the existing apportionment provisions nor either of the proposed plans was either of the houses of the Alabama Legislature apportioned on a population basis, the District Court correctly held that all three of these schemes were constitutionally invalid....

V.

Since neither of the houses of the Alabama Legislature, under any of the three plans considered by the District Court, was apportioned on a population basis, we would be justified in proceeding no further. However, one of the proposed plans, that contained in the so-called 67-Senator Amendment, at least superficially resembles the scheme of legislative representation followed in the Federal Congress. Under this plan, each of Alabama's 67 counties is allotted one senator, and no counties are given more than one Senate seat. Arguably, this is analogous to the allocation of two Senate seats, in the Federal Congress, to each of the 50 States, regardless of population. Seats in the Alabama House, under the proposed constitutional amendment, are distributed by giving each of the 67 counties at least one, with the remaining 39 seats being allotted among the more populous counties on a population basis. This scheme, at least at first glance, appears to resemble that prescribed for the Federal House of Representatives, where the 435 seats are distributed among the States on a population basis, although each State, regardless of its population, is given at least one Congressman. Thus, although there are substantial differences in underlying rationale and result, the 67-Senator Amendment, as proposed by the Alabama Legislature, at least arguably presents for consideration a scheme analogous to that used for apportioning seats in Congress....

The system of representation in the two Houses of the Federal Congress is one ingrained in our Constitution, as part of the law of the land. It is one conceived out of compromise and concession indispensable to the establishment of our federal republic. Arising from unique historical circumstances, it is based on the consideration that in establishing our type of federalism a group of formerly independent States bound themselves together under one national government. Admittedly, the original 13 States surrendered some of their sovereignty in agreeing to join together "to form a more perfect Union."...

Political subdivisions of States—counties, cities, or whatever—never were and never have been considered as sovereign entities. Rather, they have been traditionally regarded as subordinate governmental instrumentalities created by the State to assist in the carrying out of state governmental functions.... The relationship of the States to the Federal Government could hardly be less analogous....

VI.

By holding that as a federal constitutional requisite both houses of a state legislature must be apportioned on a population basis, we mean that the Equal Protection Clause requires that a State make an honest and good faith effort to construct districts, in both houses of its legislature, as nearly of equal population as is practicable. We realize that it is a practical impossibility to arrange legislative districts so that each one has an identical number of residents, or citizens, or voters. Mathematical exactness or precision is hardly a workable constitutional requirement....

... [W]e affirm the judgment below and remand the cases for further proceedings consistent with the views stated in this opinion.

It is so ordered.

MR. JUSTICE CLARK, concurring in the affirmance....

MR. JUSTICE STEWART....

MR. JUSTICE HARLAN, dissenting.

In these cases the Court holds that seats in the legislatures of six States are apportioned in ways that violate the Federal Constitution. Under the Court's ruling it is bound to follow that the legislatures in all but a few of the other 44 States will meet the same fate. These decisions, with *Wesberry* v. *Sanders,* 376 U.S. 1, involving congressional districting by the States, and *Gray* v. *Sanders,* 372 U.S. 368, relating to elections for statewide office, have the effect of placing basic aspects of state political systems under the pervasive overlordship of the federal judiciary. Once again, I must register my protest. *[Harlan proceeds to set forth a detailed account of the proposal and ratification of the Fourteenth Amendment, concluding that Congress deliberately excluded from the Amendment any restriction on the states' power "to control voting rights because it believed that if such restrictions were included," the Amendment would not have been adopted.]*

Shaw v. Reno
509 U.S. 630 (1993)

As a result of the 1990 census, North Carolina increased its number of seats in Congress from eleven to twelve. The Justice Department rejected an initial state plan that provided for only one majority black congressional district (the state was about 20 percent black). The Justice Department approved a subsequent plan that provided for two majority black districts. Five white voters sued North Carolina lawmakers and the Justice Department, claiming that the state's racial separation of voters violated their constitutional right to participate in "color-blind" elections. Ruth O. Shaw, one of the plaintiffs, sued Attorney General Janet Reno and state officials.

JUSTICE O'CONNOR delivered the opinion of the Court.

This case involves two of the most complex and sensitive issues this Court has faced in recent years: the meaning of the constitutional "right" to vote, and the propriety of race-based state legislation designed to benefit members of historically disadvantaged racial minority groups.... Appellants allege that the revised plan, which contains district boundary lines of dramatically irregular shape, constitutes an unconstitutional racial gerrymander. The question before us is whether appellants have stated a cognizable claim.

I

The voting age population of North Carolina is approximately 78% white, 20% black, and 1% Native American; the remaining 1% is predominantly Asian.... The black population is relatively dispersed; blacks constitute a majority of the general population in only 5 of the State's 100 counties....

[The General Assembly's first redistricting plan contained one majority-black district centered in the eastern coastal plain. After the Attorney General objected, the General Assembly revised the plan to create a second majority-black district.]

The second majority-black district, District 12, is even more unusually shaped. It is approximately 160 miles long and, for much of its length, no wider than the I-85 corridor. It winds in snake-like fashion through tobacco country, financial centers, and manufacturing areas "until it gobbles in enough enclaves of black neighborhoods." 808 F.Supp., at 476–477 (Voorhees, C.J., concurring in part and dissenting in part). Northbound and southbound drivers on I-85 sometimes find themselves in separate districts in one county, only to "trade" districts when they enter the next county....

... Appellants alleged not that the revised plan constituted a political gerrymander, nor that it violated the "one person, one vote" principle, see

Reynolds v. *Sims,* 377 U.S. 533, 558 (1964), but that the State had created an unconstitutional *racial* gerrymander [*to assure the election of two black representatives to Congress*]....

[II.A]

[In this section O'Connor reviews how the essential right to vote had been denied to blacks in the past—despite the Fifteenth Amendment—through a variety of tactics including literacy tests, Grandfather Clauses, "good character" provisos, and racial gerrymandering. One result was the Voting Rights Act of 1965.]

B

It is against this background that we confront the questions presented here. In our view, the District Court properly dismissed appellants' claims against the federal appellees. Our focus is on appellants' claim that the State engaged in unconstitutional racial gerrymandering. That argument strikes a powerful historical chord: It is unsettling how closely the North Carolina plan resembles the most egregious racial gerrymanders of the past....

Despite their invocation of the ideal of a "color-blind" Constitution, see *Plessy* v. *Ferguson,* 163 U.S. 537, 559 (1896) (Harlan, J., dissenting), appellants appear to concede that race-conscious redistricting is not always unconstitutional.... That concession is wise: This Court never has held that race-conscious state decisionmaking is impermissible in *all* circumstances. What appellants object to is redistricting legislation that is so extremely irregular on its face that it rationally can be viewed only as an effort to segregate the races for purposes of voting, without regard for traditional districting principles and without sufficiently compelling justification....

[III.A]

The Equal Protection Clause provides that "[n]o State shall ... deny to any person within its jurisdiction the equal protection of the laws." U.S. Const.,

Amdt. 14, § 1. Its central purpose is to prevent the States from purposefully discriminating between individuals on the basis of race....

B

Appellants contend that redistricting legislation that is so bizarre on its face that it is "unexplainable on grounds other than race," *Arlington Heights, supra,* at 266, demands the same close scrutiny that we give other state laws that classify citizens by race. Our voting rights precedents support that conclusion. *[O'Connor reviews the Court's holdings in previous racial gerrymandering cases, including* Gomillion v. Lightfoot *(1960) and* Wright v. Rockefeller *(1964), and explains the burden of proof needed by plaintiffs to successfully challenge a redistricting plan.]*

The difficulty of proof, of course, does not mean that a racial gerrymander, once established, should receive less scrutiny under the Equal Protection Clause than other state legislation classifying citizens by race. Moreover, it seems clear to us that proof sometimes will not be difficult at all. In some exceptional cases, a reapportionment plan may be so highly irregular that, on its face, it rationally cannot be understood as anything other than an effort to "segregat[e] ... voters" on the basis of race. *Gomillion, supra,* at 341. *Gomillion,* in which a tortured municipal boundary line was drawn to exclude black voters, was such a case. So, too, would be a case in which a State concentrated a dispersed minority population in a single district by disregarding traditional districting principles such as compactness, contiguity, and respect for political subdivisions. We emphasize that these criteria are important not because they are constitutionally required—they are not, cf. *Gaffney* v. *Cummings,* 412 U.S. 735, 752, n. 18 (1973)—but because they are objective factors that may serve to defeat a claim that a district has been gerrymandered on racial lines....

Put differently, we believe that reapportionment is one area in which appearances do matter. A reapportionment plan that includes in one district individuals who belong to the same race, but who are otherwise widely separated by geographical and political boundaries, and who may have little in common with one another but the color of their skin, bears an uncomfortable resemblance to political apartheid. It reinforces the perception that members of the same racial group—regardless of their age, education, economic status, or the community in which they live—think alike, share the same political interests, and will prefer the same candidates at the polls. We have rejected such perceptions elsewhere as impermissible racial stereotypes....

The message that such districting sends to elected representatives is equally pernicious. When a district obviously is created solely to effectuate the perceived common interests of one racial group, elected officials are more likely to believe that their primary obligation is to represent only the members of that group, rather than their constituency as a whole. This is altogether antithetical to our system of representative democracy....

For these reasons, we conclude that a plaintiff challenging a reapportionment statute under the Equal Protection Clause may state a claim by alleging that the legislation, though race-neutral on its face, rationally cannot be understood as anything other than an effort to separate voters into different districts on the basis of race, and that the separation lacks sufficient justification. It is unnecessary for us to decide whether or how a reapportionment plan that, on its face, can be explained in nonracial terms successfully could be challenged. Thus, we express no view as to whether "the intentional creation of majority-minority districts, without more" always gives rise to an equal protection claim. *Post,* at 668 (WHITE, J., dissenting). We hold only that, on the facts of this case, plaintiffs have stated a claim sufficient to defeat the state appellees' motion to dismiss.

C

[Here O'Connor states that (1) nothing in case law compels the conclusion that racial and political gerrymanders are subject to precisely the same constitutional scrutiny, (2) racial gerrymandering is not automatically acceptable simply because it favors the minority, and (3) nothing in *United Jewish Organizations* dictates the results in the North Carolina case. For example, the districts in *UJO* were basically compact, unlike the district challenged here.]

V

... Racial gerrymandering, even for remedial purposes, may balkanize us into competing racial factions; it threatens to carry us further from the goal of a political system in which race no longer matters—a goal that the Fourteenth and Fifteenth Amendments embody, and to which the Nation continues to aspire....

... Accordingly, we reverse the judgment of the District Court and remand the case for further proceedings consistent with this opinion.

It is so ordered.

JUSTICE WHITE, with whom JUSTICE BLACKMUN and JUSTICE STEVENS join, dissenting.

[They argue that the facts in the North Carolina case

"mirror" those presented in *UJO*. With regard to the compelling-interest standard, they conclude that the North Carolina plan was narrowly tailored to meet that test. Finally, they raise a number of questions about the manner in which states will engage in "narrow tailoring" in response to this decision: "Is it more 'narrowly tailored' to create an irregular majority-minority district as opposed to one that is compact but harms other State interests such as incumbency protection or the representation of rural interests?"]

[Justices Blackmun, Stevens, and Souter wrote separate dissenting opinions.]

Miller v. Johnson

515 U.S. 900 (1995)

After the 1990 census increased the number of congressional seats in Georgia from ten to eleven, the state legislature prepared a districting plan that provided for two majority-black districts. The Justice Department refused to clear this plan, and the legislature eventually redrew the lines to provide for three black seats. Here the Court applies the general principles from *Shaw v. Reno* to determine whether the Georgia redistricting plan is valid under the Equal Protection Clause. Plaintiffs Davida Johnson and others brought this action against Governor Zell Miller.

JUSTICE KENNEDY delivered the opinion of the Court.

The constitutionality of Georgia's congressional redistricting plan is at issue here. In *Shaw v. Reno,* 509 U.S. 630 (1993), we held that a plaintiff states a claim under the Equal Protection Clause by alleging that a state redistricting plan, on its face, has no rational explanation save as an effort to separate voters on the basis of race. The question we now decide is whether Georgia's new Eleventh District gives rise to a valid equal protection claim under the principles announced in *Shaw,* and, if so, whether it can be sustained nonetheless as narrowly tailored to serve a compelling governmental interest.

[I.B]

[In 1965, the Attorney General designated Georgia a covered jurisdiction under the Voting Rights Act, requiring Georgia to obtain either administrative preclearance from the Attorney General or approval by the U.S. District Court for the District of Columbia of any change in "standard, practice, or procedure with respect to voting." Between 1980 and 1990, one of Georgia's ten congressional districts was a majority-black district (where a majority of the district's voters were black). The 1990 census entitled Georgia to an additional eleventh congressional seat. At the time of this case, 27% of the population in Georgia was black.]

[Georgia's legislature submitted a congressional redistricting plan to the Attorney General for preclearance. The plan contained two majority-black districts, the Fifth and Eleventh, and an additional district, the Second, in which blacks comprised just over 35% of the voting age population. The Justice Department refused

preclearance and also rejected a new plan that increased the black populations in the Second, Fifth, and Eleventh Districts. The Department supported an alternative plan of three majority-black districts. As the trial court noted, the third plan from the legislature contained "all the signs [of the Justice Department's] involvement." The populations of the Eleventh "are centered around four discrete, widely spaced urban centers that have absolutely nothing to do with each other, and stretch the district hundreds of miles across rural counties and narrow swamp corridors." In the 1992 elections, black candidates were elected to Congress from all three majority-black districts. Five white voters from the Eleventh filed an action against various state officials, alleging that the district was a racial gerrymander and violated the Equal Protection Clause. A three-judge court ruled that the Eleventh was invalid under Shaw, *with one judge dissenting.]*

[II.A]

... [T]he District Court held that race was the predominant, overriding factor in drawing the Eleventh District.... Appellants do not take issue with the court's factual finding of this racial motivation. Rather, they contend that evidence of a legislature's deliberate classification of voters on the basis of race cannot alone suffice to state a claim under *Shaw*. They argue that, regardless of the legislature's purposes, a plaintiff must demonstrate that a district's shape is so bizarre that it is unexplainable other than on the basis of race, and that appellees failed to make that showing here. Appellants' conception of the constitutional violation misapprehends our holding in *Shaw* and the Equal Protection precedent upon which *Shaw* relied.

Shaw recognized a claim "analytically distinct" from a vote dilution claim.... Whereas a vote dilution claim alleges that the State has enacted a particular voting scheme as a purposeful device "to minimize or cancel out the voting potential of racial or ethnic minorities," *Mobile v. Bolden,* 446 U.S. 55, 56 (1980) (citing cases) an action disadvantaging voters of a particular race, the essence of the equal protection claim recognized in *Shaw* is that the State has used race as a basis for separating voters into districts. Just as the State may not, absent extraordinary justification, segregate citizens on the basis of race in [*its public parks, buses, golf courses, beaches, and schools*] so did we recognize in *Shaw* that it may not separate its citizens into different voting districts on the basis of race....

Our observation in *Shaw* of the consequences of racial stereotyping was not meant to suggest that a district must be bizarre on its face before there is a constitutional violation. Nor was our conclusion in *Shaw* that in certain instances a district's appearance (or, to be more precise, its appearance in combination with certain demographic evidence) can give rise to an equal protection claim, 509 U.S., at 649, a holding that bizarreness was a threshold showing, as appellants believe it to be. Our circumspect approach and narrow holding in *Shaw* did not erect an artificial rule barring accepted equal protection analysis in other redistricting cases. Shape is relevant not because bizarreness is a necessary element of the constitutional wrong or a threshold requirement of proof, but because it may be persuasive circumstantial evidence that race for its own sake, and not other districting principles, was the legislature's dominant and controlling rationale in drawing its district lines. The logical implication, as courts applying *Shaw* have recognized, is that parties may rely on evidence other than bizarreness to establish race-based districting....

B

... Redistricting legislatures will, for example, almost always be aware of racial demographics; but it does not follow that race predominates in the redistricting process.... The plaintiff's burden is to show, either through circumstantial evidence of a district's shape and demographics or more direct evidence going to legislative purpose, that race was the predominant factor motivating the legislature's decision to place a significant number of voters within or without a particular district. To make this showing, a plaintiff must prove that the legislature subordinated traditional race-neutral districting principles, including but not limited to compactness, contiguity, and respect for political subdivisions or communities defined by actual shared interests, to racial considerations....

In our view, the District Court applied the correct analysis, and its finding that race was the predominant factor motivating the drawing of the Eleventh District was not clearly erroneous.... The District Court had before it considerable additional evidence showing that the General Assembly was motivated by a predominant, overriding desire to assign black populations to the Eleventh District and thereby permit the creation of a third majority-black district in the Second....

III

... There is little doubt that the State's true interest in designing the Eleventh District was creating a third majority-black district to satisfy the Justice Department's preclearance demands....

... One of the two Department of Justice line attorneys overseeing the Georgia preclearance process himself disclosed that "'what we did and what I did specifically was to take a ... map of the State of Georgia shaded for race, shaded by minority concentration, and overlay the districts that were drawn by the State of Georgia and see how well those lines adequately reflected black voting strength.'"...

The judgment of the District Court is affirmed, and the case is remanded for further proceedings consistent with this decision.

It is so ordered.

JUSTICE O'CONNOR, concurring....

JUSTICE STEVENS, dissenting.

... Neither in *Shaw* itself nor in the cases decided today has the Court coherently articulated what injury this cause of action is designed to redress. Because respondents have alleged no legally cognizable injury, they lack standing, and these cases should be dismissed....

JUSTICE GINSBURG, with whom JUSTICE STEVENS and JUSTICE BREYER join, and with whom JUSTICE SOUTER joins except as to Part III-B, dissenting.

... District lines are drawn to accommodate a myriad of factors—geographic, economic, historical, and political—and state legislatures, as arenas of compromise and electoral accountability, are best positioned to mediate competing claims; courts, with a mandate to adjudicate, are ill equipped for the task.

[II.B]

The record before us does not show that race ... overwhelmed traditional districting practices in

Georgia. Although the Georgia General Assembly prominently considered race in shaping the Eleventh District, race did not crowd out all other factors, as the Court found it did in North Carolina's delineation of the *Shaw* district.

In contrast to the snake-like North Carolina district inspected in *Shaw,* Georgia's Eleventh District is hardly "bizarre," "extremely irregular," or "irrational on its face." ...

D. CAMPAIGN FINANCING

As a result of court rulings, elections now operate under the broad doctrine of "one person, one vote." This superficial equality, giving equal weight to each voter, is seriously skewed by large campaign contributions from individuals, corporations, unions, and political action committees (PACs). Congress has attempted to regulate campaign spending to remove the most serious abuses, but these efforts have been circumscribed and limited by court rulings. The one-person, one-vote principle collides with the reality of wealthy and powerful financial contributors. Moreover, the Democratic and Republican parties have been creative in locating major loopholes in statutory constraints.

Legislation on Corrupt Practices

Congress has to juggle two conflicting interests: (1) the right of private citizens to make financial contributions to elections and (2) the need to protect campaigns from corrupting influences. One of the first efforts to reconcile this conflict came in 1907, when Congress responded to large corporate contributions to political candidates. Legislation that year prohibited any national bank or any corporation created by Congress from contributing money for political elections. 34 Stat. 864. The Federal Corrupt Practices Act of 1910 limited the amount of money that congressional candidates could contribute to their own nomination or election. Political committees had to record their contributions and make regular reports to Congress. 36 Stat. 822 (1910); 37 Stat. 25 (1911).

The Supreme Court held that the corrupt practices statute, to the extent that it covered primaries, was unconstitutional. Although Article I, Section 4, empowers Congress to alter state regulations concerning the "Manner of holding Elections" for U.S. Senators and Representatives, four members of the Court ruled that elections in the constitutional sense meant "the final choice of an officer." Pushing original intent and strict construction to an extreme limit, the Court said that primaries "were then unknown" at the time of the Constitution. Primaries were "in no sense elections for an office." Newberry v. United States, 256 U.S. 232, 250 (1921). As applied to primaries and nominating conventions, therefore, the statute under this reading usurped state power. Justice McKenna joined the four Justices in setting aside the conviction but offered no opinion on the constitutional issue.

In one of the dissents, Chief Justice White denounced the appeal to original intent as "suicidal." Id. at 262. To underscore his point, he reviewed the framers' expectation that members of the electoral college would be free agents, capable of exercising discretion when choosing the President. In 1876, however, when James Russell Lowell was urged to exercise independence and vote for Tilden, he refused on the ground that "whatever the first intent of the Constitution was, usage had made the presidential electors strictly the instruments of the party which chose them." Id. at 266. White concluded that whatever case could have been made for state autonomy in matters of national elections had evaporated in 1913 with the Seventeenth Amendment, which provided for the election of U.S. Senators by the people rather than by state legislatures. Justice Pitney, joined by Justices Brandeis and Clarke, also repudiated the Court's foray into strict construction. Pitney wrote: "It is said primaries were unknown when the Constitution was adopted. So were the steam railway and the electric telegraph. But the authority of Congress to regulate commerce among the several States extended over these instrumentalities...." Id. at 282.

Congress rewrote the Federal Corrupt Practices Act to conform to the Court's ruling but also strengthened several provisions in the statute. 43 Stat. 1070 (1925). The Court upheld the power of Congress to require political committees to keep detailed accounts of all financial contributions and to file with Congress a statement containing the name and address of each contributor to a federal election. The Court denied that the statute invaded state power. The operation of the statute was confined to situations which, "if not beyond the power of the state to deal with at all, are beyond its power to deal with adequately." The authority of Congress to safeguard federal elections comes from "the power of self protection." Burroughs v. United States, 290 U.S. 534, 544–45 (1934). In the Hatch Act, Congress enacted additional legislation in 1939 and 1940 to protect campaigns from corruption and "pernicious political activities." 53 Stat. 1147; 54 Stat. 767. The Hatch Act was liberalized in 1993 to permit federal employees to participate in a greater range of political activities, including managing campaigns, raising funds, and holding positions within political parties. Some restrictions on political activities by federal employees remain. 107 Stat. 1001 (1993).

Newberry Reversed

Although the Court in *Newberry* had denied Congress the power to regulate primary elections, the Justice Department challenged the Court's decision. The government argued that the right of voters in congressional primaries is secured by Article I, Section 2, calling for the choice of Representatives "by the People," as well as the Times, Places, and Manner Clause of Section 4. Richard Claude, The Supreme Court and the Electoral Process 33 (1970). Under these pressures and with a reconstituted membership, the Court reversed *Newberry* and held that congressional power embraced not merely the final election but primaries as well. Even the three dissenters, Douglas, Black, and Murphy, rejected *Newberry*'s conclusion that Congress had no power to control primary elections. United States v. Classic, 313 U.S. 299, 329–30 (1941).

PACs

The prohibition that Congress had placed on corporate and national bank campaign contributions was later extended to cover labor organizations. 57 Stat. 167, § 9 (1943); 61 Stat. 159, § 304 (1947). Labor unions responded by creating political action committees (PACs) to pursue campaign goals. Initially, union members had to contribute to these political funds, which were used to support the campaigns of candidates friendly to the labor cause. These funds were later replaced by a "voluntary" organization, with funds segregated from union dues. Congress authorized this type of fund in 1972 by stating that the prohibition on labor contributions did not include "the establishment, administration, and solicitation of contributions to a separate segregated fund to be utilized for political purposes by a corporation or labor organization." 86 Stat. 10, § 205 (1972). Partly on the basis of this law, the Supreme Court upheld political funds operated by labor unions. Pipefitters v. United States, 407 U.S. 385 (1972).

As explained later in this chapter, PACs would be followed by "Super PACs" and the Supreme Court in *Citizens United* (2010) would strike down the authority of Congress to place limits on campaign expenditures as a means of acting against corrupt practices.

Campaign Finance Reform

The high cost of federal campaigns, especially for TV ads, led to the Federal Election Campaign Act of 1971. New limits were placed on campaign contributions and expenditures. 86 Stat. 3. Congress created the Presidential Election Campaign Fund in 1971 to provide public subsidies for presidential candidates in the general election. 85 Stat. 562–74. On the heels of the Watergate scandal, which exposed widespread corruption during the presidential campaign of 1972, Congress enacted new legislation. The Federal Election Campaign Act Amendments of 1974 placed limits on contributions and expenditures, created the Federal Election Commission (FEC) to enforce the law, and provided optional public funding for presidential elections. 88 Stat. 1263.

A strange alliance challenged the constitutionality of the 1974 amendments. Opponents of the legislation included conservative Senator James L. Buckley, liberal Senator Eugene J. McCarthy, the Conservative party of New York State, the Libertarian party, the New York Civil Liberties Union, and *Human Events,* a conservative publication. They argued that the limits on campaign contributions and expenditures represented a violation of the First Amendment right of expression, both by contributors and candidates.

In *Buckley* v. *Valeo* (1976), the Court upheld limits on how much individuals and political action committees may contribute to candidates. The limits serve the important governmental interest of preventing corruption of the political process. However, the contribution limits on a candidate's personal funds (or family funds) were declared invalid constraints on the ability of persons to become engaged in protected First Amendment expression. The Court upheld the statute's disclosure-recordkeeping provisions and the public financing of presidential campaigns. If presidential candidates accept public funds, expenditure limits are imposed on campaign costs. The Court upheld those limits. Other limits on campaign expenditures were struck down as a violation of the freedoms of speech and association protected by the First Amendment. The Court made a key distinction between contributions and expenditures, concluding that the risk of corruption is greater in *giving,* rather than *spending,* money. Quid pro quos, said the Court, pose a more serious threat with contributions than with expenditures—a point that has been widely disputed. Finally, the Court found the composition of the FEC to be unconstitutional (an issue addressed in Chapter 6). BUCKLEY v. VALEO, 424 U.S. 1 (1976).

Congress corrected the defect in the FEC (Chapter 6) and adopted other reforms, but years of effort have been unsuccessful in providing public funding for congressional campaigns or limiting the amount spent by PACs. Members of Congress and committees are directly influenced by PAC spending. Dairy PACs give money to members of the agriculture committees, corporate PACs contribute to members of the tax committees, and other PACs donate funds to committee members that have jurisdiction over their activities. These issues of *influence* are not covered by the Court's preoccupation with *corruption.* In other cases the Court has expressed concern not only about electoral corruption but the *integrity* of the electoral process.[14]

The cost of running for Congress continues to spiral upward. The average expenditure (in current dollars) by the winning House candidate rose from an estimated $87,000 in 1976 to about $1.4 million in 2010. Comparable figures for the winning Senate candidate: $609,000 and $8.9 million. As the cost of campaigns soars, qualified candidates are less able to enter the race. Instead of the "robust debate" promised by the Supreme Court in *Buckley,* including enhanced protection to First Amendment values, the high cost of campaigning reduces the field of candidates to an ever-narrowing band of wealthy politicians or those skilled in raising large sums of money. Also, members of Congress spend about one-fourth of their time raising money for their campaigns and for their party, taking precious time from their legislative duties.

Adjudication After *Buckley*

The basic thrust of *Buckley* has been sustained in subsequent decisions. Congress may set limits on how much presidential candidates spend as a condition on their receiving public funds. Republican National Committee v. FEC, 445 U.S. 955 (1980), 487 F.Supp. 280 (S.D.N.Y. 1980) (three-judge court) and 616 F.2d 1 (2d Cir. 1980) (en banc). Congress can place limits on some contributions. California Medical Assn. v. FEC, 453 U.S. 182 (1982). However, the Court has held that other restrictions on contributions run afoul of First Amendment freedoms. In 1978, a 5–4 Court held that Massachusetts violated the First Amendment by prohibiting business corporations from contributing funds to in-

---

14. For example, Storer v. Brown, 415 U.S. 724 (1974); Kusper v. Pontikes, 414 U.S. 51 (1973); Rosario v. Rockefeller, 410 U.S. 752 (1973); Bullock v. Carter, 405 U.S. 134 (1972); Williams v. Rhodes, 393 U.S. 23 (1968).

Controls on Independent Expenditures

"Independent expenditures" consist of the expenses of a person or political committee free of any coordination with a candidate's official campaign committee. The Federal Election Campaign Act amendments of 1974 imposed a $1,000 limit on independent expenditures, but the Court struck down that limit in *Buckley*. As a result, while federal law limits contributions made directly to political candidates, no such restraints operate on independent expenditures. A three-judge court in 1980 ruled that the $1,000 limit on independent expenditures of political committees was facially unconstitutional under the First Amendment. Common Cause v. Schmitt, 512 F. Supp. 489 (D.D.C. 1980). This ruling was affirmed by an equally divided (4–4) Supreme Court in a per curiam decision. 455 U.S. 129 (1982). In 1986, a 5–4 Court struck down FEC's regulation that prohibited political expenditures by nonprofit advocacy groups that take positions on abortion, busing, gun control, and other issues. Under the Court's reading of the First Amendment, those groups may take out advertisements urging voters to support or oppose specific candidates. These independent expenditures are not subject to federal limits. FEC v. Massachusetts Citizens for Life, Inc., 479 U.S. 238 (1986).

Massachusetts Citizens invalidated a federal restriction on independent expenditures by nonprofit, advocacy groups such as an antiabortion

organization. In 1990, the Court refused to extend that protection to business-oriented organizations. At issue was a Michigan law that prohibited corporations (other than media corporations, such as newspapers and broadcasting stations) from using general treasury funds to make independent expenditures in connection with candidates in state elections. Corporations had to establish segregated funds or political action committees to support these political purposes. The Court, divided 6 to 3, held that although the requirement burdened a corporation's freedom of expression, it was justified by a compelling state interest: preventing corruption (or the appearance of corruption) in the political arena. Austin v. Michigan Chamber of Commerce, 494 U.S. 652 (1990).

In their dissents, Justices Scalia, Kennedy, and O'Connor issued vigorous objections to the Court's validation of "censorship" of speech. Scalia said that if there was a compelling state need to prevent corporate wealth from skewing the political debate, media corporations should be included, not excluded. Kennedy and O'Connor also criticized the exception for media corporations: "The web of corporate ownership that links media and nonmedia corporations is difficult to untangle for the purpose of any meaningful distinction. Newspapers, television networks, and other media may be owned by parent corporations with multiple business interests."

fluence a referendum. The "speech" protected, of course, was not by natural persons but by artificial entities created in the form of corporations. In a dissent, Justice White warned that in the area of campaign financing "the expertise of legislators is at its peak and that of judges is at its very lowest." First National Bank of Boston v. Bellotti, 435 U.S. 765, 804 (1978). Members of the Court have expressed increasing difficulty in understanding the contribution/expenditure distinction in *Buckley*. See the dissents in FEC v. National Conservative PAC, 470 U.S. 480 (1985). A crucial issue of campaign financing is how to control "independent expenditures" (see box).[15]

In addition to the loophole for independent expenditures, other techniques were devised to circumvent restrictions in federal law. One method was "soft money": contributions to political parties for administrative costs and party-building activities (such as voter registration drives). These con-

---

15. Government cannot compel minor political parties, such as the Socialist Workers party, to report the names and addresses of campaign contributors and recipients of campaign disbursements if disclosure is likely to result in harassment and reprisals. Brown v. Socialist Workers '74 Campaign Comm., 459 U.S. 87 (1982); Buckley v. Valeo, 424 U.S. at 64–74. Other questions of campaign financing are explored in FEC v. National Right to Work Committee, 459 U.S. 197 (1982) and Citizens Against Rent Control v. Berkeley, 454 U.S. 290 (1981).

tributions from individuals and corporations could far exceed the original statutory limits of $1,000 for individual contributions to a candidate per election and $20,000 a year from individuals to a national party committee. Using soft money, contributions in excess of $100,000 were not unusual. Soft-money contributions came to support not just party-building activities but support for particular candidates.

In 1991, the Court grappled with a sensitive issue: When does a politician's plea for campaign contributions become extortion punishable by federal law? Simply receiving money and providing assistance is insufficient grounds for proving extortion. "Serving constituents and supporting legislation that will benefit the district and individuals and groups therein is the everyday business of a legislator." McCormick v. United States, 500 U.S. 257, 272 (1991). Candidates are constantly soliciting funds and making promises in return. Criminal conduct occurs only when contributions are accepted with an explicit promise to perform an official act.

McCain-Feingold Legislation

About a half-billion dollars of "soft money" entered the 2000 political campaign. What would be called the McCain-Feingold bill—after Senators John McCain (R-Ariz.) and Russ Feingold (D-Wis.)—passed Congress in 2002. The new law prohibits the national political parties from raising and spending soft money, but places no such restrictions on independent groups (PACs). 116 Stat. 81 (2002). Opponents argued that attempts to redirect campaign contributions from political parties to outside groups would weaken the ability of parties to function generally as moderating influences, and place soft money in the hands of organizations that have special interests (ranging from abortion to the environment to tobacco).

How this worked in practice depended greatly on FEC regulations. One issue was whether state political parties could use soft money to run TV ads that promote, support, or attack a federal candidate. The authors of McCain-Feingold thought they had prohibited that practice by eliminating "issue ads" that are thinly veiled attacks on a candidate. The FEC sustained that prohibition, but opened a new loophole by allowing state political parties broader use of soft money.

The constitutionality of McCain-Feingold was challenged in court, especially the law's prohibition on using soft money for radio and TV commercials that "promote, support, attack or oppose" federal candidates. Was that an invalid restriction on free speech? In 2003 the Supreme Court, divided 5 to 4, upheld the ban on soft money and by the same margin upheld restrictions on broadcast ads by corporations and labor unions that mention candidates. The Justices were unanimous in upholding the statute's increase in the maximum allowable campaign donations (increasing individual contributions from $1,000 to $2,000) and indexing them to inflation. Also unanimously, the Court struck down a ban on contributions from individuals younger than 18. McConnell v. FEC, 540 U.S. 93 (2003).

In 2007, a reconstituted Supreme Court (especially the replacement of Sandra Day O'Connor by Samuel Alito) took another look at "issue ads." By a margin of 5 to 4, the Court held that the prohibition against the use of a candidate's name in television ads in the days before an election was an unconstitutional restriction on the rights of corporations and unions to advocate their positions on public issues. The Court decided that the ads in question were genuine issue ads concerning legislative policy. The ads did not specifically praise or criticize a candidate, even though they urged viewers to contact two named U.S. Senators and oppose a filibuster. Three Justices (Scalia, Kennedy, and Thomas) concurred with the majority but found its standards unacceptably vague. The four dissenters denied that an acceptable line could be drawn between genuine issue ads and political/partisan advocacy. In the case of the issue ad on the filibuster, they pointed out that the website listed on the TV ad left no doubt about the organization's intent to criticize and defeat Senator Russ Feingold. Federal Election Comm'n v. Wisconsin Right to Life, Inc., 551 U.S. 449 (2007).

Part of McCain-Feingold provided special fund-raising opportunities for congressional candidates who ran against wealthy opponents. Called the "Millionaire's Amendment," it allowed less wealthy candidates to accept triple the maximum donation ($2,300 in 2008) when their opponents spent more than $350,000 of their own money. Divided 5 to 4, the Supreme Court in 2008 found the provision unconstitutional because it forced rich candidates to "choose between the First Amendment right to engage in unfettered political speech and subjection to discriminatory fundraising limitations." Writing one of the dissents, Stevens said the Amendment "quiets no speech at all. On the contrary, it does no more than assist the opponent of a self-funding candidate in his attempts to make his voice heard." Davis v. Federal Election Comm'n, 554 U.S. 724 (2008).

"527" Organizations

The Bush-Kerry presidential race in 2004 highlighted another source of campaign funds: "527" organizations. These groups, established under Section 527 of the Internal Revenue Code, are given tax-exempt status for certain political expenditures. Exempt functions include influencing or attempting to influence the selection, nomination, election or appointment of an individual to a federal, state, or local public office, to an office in a political organization, or as a presidential or vice-presidential elector. 26 U.S.C. § 527(e)(2). These organizations may fund a hard-hitting political advertising agenda provided they do not coordinate their efforts with the candidate or the candidate's party. There is no limit on the amount of money that an individual can donate. A published list of top donors in 2004 shows individual contributions ranging from $1,057,500 to $23,250,000. Washington Post, October 17, 2004, at A14.

One of the 527 groups in 2004, "Swift Boat Veterans for Truth," initiated a damaging campaign against the Vietnam record of Democratic presidential candidate, Senator John Kerry. The accuracy of those accusations has been repeatedly challenged. "Veterans Rebut Swift Boat Charges Against Kerry," New York Times, June 22, 2008, at 18. Concerns about a repeat of a smear campaign in 2008 by independent groups prompted Democratic presidential candidate Senator Barack Obama to decide against public financing in the general election. He was the first major party candidate to reject public financing and its associated spending limits.

Rethinking *Buckley*

Over the years, in a series of rulings, the Supreme Court gradually set forth criteria on limitations established on campaign funding, upholding some while invalidating others (see box on next page). In 1995, the Court decided whether Ohio's election law could prohibit the distribution of anonymous campaign literature. The Court held that Ohio had failed to justify the ban as necessary to prevent fraudulent and libelous statements. McIntyre v. Ohio Elections Comm'n, 514 U.S. 334 (1995). A year later, the Court ruled that the First Amendment prohibits the Federal Government from placing limits on the amounts that political parties can spend independently on congressional candidates. In disposing of this narrow question, the multiple opinions of the Justices raised the question whether the Court would reexamine the soundness of *Buckley* v. *Valeo*. Colorado Republican Campaign Comm. v. FEC, 518 U.S. 604 (1996). This decision left open the question whether the First Amendment permits limits on spending by political parties in *coordination* with their congressional candidates. A 5–4 Court in 2001 upheld these limits by treating coordinated party spending as similar to contributions from individuals and PACs. FEC v. Colorado Republican Federal Campaign Comm., 533 U.S. 431 (2001).

At the state level, a Cincinnati ordinance enacted in 1995 posed a direct challenge to *Buckley* by imposing a $140,000 political spending cap on candidates for city council. The restriction was overturned by a federal judge and later by the Sixth Circuit in 1998 as an unconstitutional restriction on free speech. Kruse v. City of Cincinnati, 142 F.3d 907 (6th Cir. 1998), cert. denied, 525 U.S. 1001 (1998). Thirty-three states filed briefs supporting Cincinnati's position.

Federal and State Controls on Campaign Funding

Limits	Court Response
$1,000 limit on contributions by individuals and groups to candidates and authorized campaign committees	Upheld in Buckley v. Valeo (1976)
$5,000 limit on contributions to a candidate by political committees	Upheld in Buckley
$25,000 limit on total contributions by an individual during any calendar year	Upheld in Buckley
Expenditure ceilings on candidates, their campaigns, and political parties in connection with election campaigns	Held invalid in Buckley
Limits on independent expenditures	Held invalid in Buckley
Public financing of presidential election campaigns	Upheld in Buckley
Limits on expenditures by candidates from personal or family resources	Held invalid in Buckley
Prohibition by Massachusetts of business corporations from contributing funds to influence a referendum	Held invalid in First National Bank of Boston v. Bellotti (1978)
Prohibition by FEC regulation of political expenditures by nonprofit advocacy groups that take positions on public issues	Held invalid in FEC v. Massachusetts Citizens for Life, Inc. (1986)
Prohibition by Michigan of corporations (other than media corporations) from using general treasury funds to assist candidates in state elections	Upheld in Austin v. Michigan Chamber of Commerce (1990)
Prohibition on soft money	Upheld in McConnell v. FEC (2003)
Prohibition on "issue ads"	Held invalid in FEC v. Wisconsin Right to Life (2007)
The "Millionaire's Amendment"	Held invalid in Davis v. FEC (2008)
Limits on corporate and union spending	Held invalid in Citizens United (2010)

(In 2002, Congress enacted legislation raising some of the dollar limits, such as increasing individual contributions from $1,000 to $2,000.)

Challenges continue to come from other states. In 2000, the Court upheld Missouri's ceiling of $1,000 on political contributions, rejecting the argument that the $1,000 limit upheld in *Buckley* was now too low because of inflation. *Nixon v. Shrink Missouri Government PAC*, 528 U.S. 377 (2000). Several opinions for the 6 to 3 majority indicated that a number of Justices were troubled by *Buckley* and ready to reexamine and possibly reject it. In a concurrence, Justice Stevens said that "Money is property; it is not speech." A concurrence by Breyer, with Ginsburg joining, remarked that the decision to make a campaign contribution is a First Amendment concern "not because money *is* speech (it is not); but because it *enables* speech." He also thought that campaign finance was "a difficult question best left, in the main, to the political branches," and recognized that if *Buckley* denied the political branches sufficient leeway to enact comprehensive solutions, the Court should reconsider *Buckley*. In a dissent, Kennedy accused the Court in *Buckley* of creating "covert speech" that "mocks the First Amendment," said that *Buckley* "has not worked," and urged that it be overruled to free Congress and state legislatures to attempt new solutions. A dissent by Thomas, joined by Scalia, spoke of the "analytic fallacies of our flawed decision" in *Buckley* and recommended that it be overruled. When the Supreme Court upheld McCain-Feingold, Scalia again announced that *Buckley* was "wrongly decided" and rejected the notion that "money is speech." McConnell v. FEC, 540 U.S. 93, 250–55 (2003).

In 2006, the Court struck down state restrictions on campaign contributions and spending. Vermont had passed legislation in 1997 to deliberately challenge *Buckley*, placing a limit of $200 on contributions for a state representative, $300 for a state senator, and $400 for governor and lieutenant governor. The Court ruled that Vermont's limits on the amount a candidate may spend in a campaign violated the free speech guarantees. Three sets of concurrences and two separate dissents fuzzed up whatever principles the Court might have wanted to announce. Several Justices analyzed the weaknesses in *Buckley's* treatment of expenditure limits, the distinction between contributions and expenditures, and the problem of equating money with speech, Randall v. Sorrell, 548 U.S. 230 (2006).

Judicial Elections

In 2002, a 5–4 Court held that under the First Amendment states may not prohibit candidates in judicial elections from taking stands on disputed legal or political issues. Would full discussion by these candidates help educate the public on significant issues, or instead give advance notice of how, once elected, the candidates would decide a case? States will have to redraft their codes to meet the Court's test. Republican Party of Minnesota v. White, 536 U.S. 765 (2002).

Citizens United

In 2010, the Court issued an extraordinary decision on campaign finance — extraordinary in its breadth, in the deep divisions among the Justices, and the votes of two members of the 5–4 majority (Roberts and Alito) who in recent confirmation hearings pledged to respect Congress as the lawmaking body and decide issues narrowly to limit the Court's policymaking role. Also, the issues before the Court were not included in the questions originally presented to the litigants. The Court reached broad issues because it ordered the case to be reargued without guidance from fact-finding by lower courts. To an unusual degree, the majority relied heavily on plurality and dissenting opinions in earlier cases. The Court overruled *Austin* v. *Michigan Chamber of Commerce* (1990) and part of *McConnell* v. *FEC* (2003), which had sustained the McCain-Feingold ban on corporate and union "electioneering communications" 30 days before a presidential primary and 60 days before a general election. The majority left room for Congress to legislate disclaimer and disclosure requirements. CITIZENS UNITED v. FEDERAL ELECTION COMM'N, 558 U.S. ___ (2010). With six Justices seated before him at the State of the Union, President Obama said: "With all due deference to separation of powers, last week the Supreme Court reversed a century of law that I believe will open the floodgates for special interests — including foreign corporations — to spend without limit in our elections. I don't think American elections should be bankrolled by America's most powerful interests, or worse, by foreign entities."

The decision reopened two fundamental issues. First, what does it mean to call corporations "persons"? Corporations are not the same as natural persons. They do not exist until government creates them, can live indefinitely, and have no capacity to speak other than through corporate officers. Do shareholders join in corporate speech? Second, why is money "speech" in terms of the First Amendment? Justice Kennedy, writing for the majority, observed: "Speech is an essential mechanism of democracy, for it is the means to hold officials accountable to the people." Yet unregulated campaign spending, with unlimited funds from corporations, can make officials less accountable to the people.

Other questions arise. In regulating campaign finance, is Congress restricted to what the Court set forth: merely disclaimer and disclosure requirements? May it not look broadly as the law-making body to determine the extent to which the level of campaign expenditures corrupts the political system, drains power from the people, and weakens Congress as an independent branch?

Although some critics of *Citizens United* proposed a constitutional amendment to override the Court, Congress focused narrowly on legislation to improve disclaimers and disclosure. The general purpose is to force corporate and union officials to disclose their identities in ads, just as federal politicians are required to do. Legislation would also restrict political activity for companies that receive federal contracts and place limits on campaign-related spending by foreign-owned companies. The House approved the bill in June 2010 but it encountered delays in the Senate. Efforts in 2012 to enact disclosure legislation also failed. More ambitious would be some form of public financing to eliminate the dependence of lawmakers on private and corporate contributions.

"Super PACs"

As a result of *Citizens United*, campaign organizations emerged to spend unlimited corporate and union funds. Known as "super PACs," these entities are not supposed to contribute funds directly to political candidates or parties, but their partisan identity and purpose are clearly known. During the 2012 Republican primaries, the "Restore Our Future" super PAC was dedicated to Mitt Romney, the "Red, White and Blue Fund" supported Rick Santorum, "Winning Our Future" backed Newt Gingrich, and so forth. Sheldon Adelson, a casino magnate, gave Gingrich a check for $5 million and later wrote a check for the same amount to promote Gingrich's campaign. Extremely wealthy donors formed the backbone of these super PACs. Although ostensibly independent of the candidates, super PACs are generally staffed by former aides of the candidates. Dan Eggen, "Super PACs Outspend Campaigns 2 to 1 in S.C.," Washington Post, January 17, 2012, at A6. A super PAC called "Priorities USA Action" supported the reelection effort of President Obama.

Challenges to *Citizens United*

The Supreme Court would have several opportunities to reconsider the constitutional principles it announced in *Citizens United*, especially the majority's conclusion "that independent expenditures, including those made by corporations, do not give rise to corruption or the appearance of corruption." The Court offered no evidence to support that assertion. Several state laws and cases directly challenged its claim.

One opportunity to revisit *Citizens United* came from Arizona, which created a system to fund primary and general elections for state office. Under the Arizona Citizens Clean Elections Act, candidates could agree to receive public funds for their campaigns on the condition they accepted certain conditions. They had to limit personal spending to $500. Other states, including Connecticut, Florida, Maine, Minnesota, and North Carolina, adopted similar public financing systems. Part of the motivation behind these laws was to reduce the power of money in elections and limit corruption or the appearance of corruption. Arizona's law responded to a record of corruption in its elections.

On June 27, 2011, the Supreme Court held that the law substantially burdened political speech and was not sufficiently justified by a compelling state interest to survive First Amendment scrutiny. To the Court, an interest in combating campaign corruption was inadequate. As with *Citizens United*, the Court divided 5 to 4 and reflected the same array of Justices in the majority. They decided that *Davis* v. *Federal Election Comm'n* (2008) "largely controlled" the outcome, although the issue with the "Millionaire's Amendment" was quite different. With Arizona's law, candidates who chose not to participate could spend as much money as they had or could raise. Writing for the Court, Chief Justice Roberts argued that the law "burdens" a candidate's expenditure of his own funds, but that limit is entirely voluntary. He concluded that the law inhibited "robust and wide-open political debate without sufficient justification." Arizona Free Enterprise Club's Freedom Club PAC v. Bennett, 564 U.S. ___ (2011).

Kagan's dissent, joined by Ginsburg, Breyer, and Sotomayor, defended Arizona's right to act against corruption by creating a public financing program. She agreed with the majority that the First Amendment's "core purpose is to foster a healthy, vibrant political system full of robust discussion and debate," but found nothing in Arizona's law to violate that constitutional protection. The Court in *Buckley* v. *Valeo* had recognized that large private contributions may result in "political *quid pro quo[s]*" to undermine the integrity of democracy. She pointed out that almost one-third of the states have adopted some form of public financing. *Buckley* declared that public financing of presidential elections was constitutional, provided it is voluntary. Arizona acted after the state suffered "the worst public corruption scandal in its history," with nearly ten percent of state legislators caught accepting campaign contributions or bribes in exchange for supporting particular legislative objectives. To Kagan, Arizona had a compelling interest in preventing corruption and its matching funds provision "does not restrict, but instead subsidizes, speech."

A second opportunity to reconsider *Citizens United* came from a Montana law enacted in 1912 that prohibited a corporation from making "an expenditure in connection with a candidate or a political committee that supports or opposes a candidate of a political party." The law was flatly inconsistent with *Citizens United*, but on December 30, 2011, the Montana Supreme Court rejected the claim that the statute violated the First Amendment. The state had acted in the context of campaign corruption dating back a century, especially from powerful copper interests. More than 20 states filed briefs supporting Montana's position.

The procedural handling of this case is of special interest. On February 17, 2012, the U.S. Supreme Court granted a stay on the Montana Supreme Court's decision. It did so pending the filing and disposition of a petition for a writ of certiorari. Had the writ been granted, the U.S. Supreme Court could have ordered briefs, heard oral argument, and considered the reasons that prompted Montana to prohibit corporate expenditures. The state's legislature and judiciary had supported this policy after reviewing corrupting forces within the state. Unlike the mere assertion in *Citizens United* that corporate expenditures "do not give rise to corruption or the appearance of corruption," Montana possessed substantial evidence to make the connection between corporate spending and campaign corruption. When the Court granted the stay on February 17, 2012, Ginsburg and Breyer noted that Montana's "experience, and experience elsewhere since this Court's decision in *Citizens United* ... make it exceedingly difficult to maintain that independent expenditures by corporations" do not give rise to corruption or the appearance of corruption. A petition of certiorari "will give the Court an opportunity to consider whether, in light of the huge sums currently deployed to buy candidates' allegiance, *Citizens United* should continue to hold sway." By accepting the Montana case for full briefing and argument, the Court could have considered detailed evidence and reached an informed position on campaign spending.

Instead, on June 25, 2012, the Court issued a short per curiam stating: "The question presented in this case is whether the holding of *Citizens United* applies to the Montana state law. There can be no serious doubt that it does. See U.S. Const., Art. VI, cl. 2." This clause in Article VI merely states that the Constitution, federal laws, and treaties "shall be the supreme Law of the Land; and the Judges in every State shall be bound thereby, any Thing in the Constitution or Laws of any State to the Contrary notwithstanding." That language has never been read to invalidate every state law that conflicts with national policy. Such a claim would eliminate all elements of state sovereignty. The per curiam continued: "Montana's arguments in support of the judgment below either were already rejected in *Citizens United*, or fail to meaningfully distinguish that case. The petition for certiorari is granted. The judgment of the Supreme Court of Montana is reversed." American Tradition Partnership, Inc. v. Bullock, 567 U.S. ___ (2012).

By issuing this per curiam, the Court decided against reviewing any evidence or hearing any argument that might raise substantive questions about *Citizens United*. Dissenting from the per curiam were Breyer, Ginsburg, Sotomayor, and Kagan. They expressed their agreement with the dissent by Justice Stevens in *Citizens United* that "technically independent expenditures can be corrupting in much the same way as direct contributions." They further stated that *Citizens United* "should not bar the Montana Supreme Court's finding, made on the record before it, that independent expenditures by corporations did in fact lead to corruption or the appearance of corruption in Montana." Given its history and political experience, the state "had a compelling interest in limiting independent expenditures by corporations." The dissenters would have preferred granting the petition for certiorari in order to reconsider *Citizens United*, but given the controlling votes of the majority they did not see "a significant possibility of reconsideration" and therefore voted to deny the petition.

[The issue of corporate contributions has little to do with the remarkable level of spending by super PACs in the period after *Citizens United*. Most of the campaign contributions come from wealthy individuals, not from corporations.]

A third opportunity for the Court to reconsider *Citizens United* could come from congressional action—not from disclosure legislation, which the Court specifically supported, but from hearings and findings that dispute central constitutional arguments offered by the Court. On July 24, 2012, a subcommittee of the Senate Judiciary Committee held a hearing on "Taking Back Our Democracy: Responding to *Citizens United* and the Rise of Super PACs." Testimony by Lawrence Lessig of the Harvard Law School identified a number of claims by the Court with regard to campaign financing that he finds deficient both in law and in politics (see reading).

Buckley v. Valeo

424 U.S. 1 (1976)

In response to the scandals uncovered by the Watergate affair, Congress rewrote campaign finance laws to impose stricter limits on contributions and expenditures. The Federal Election Campaign Act amendments of 1974 also created a Federal Election Commission (FEC) to enforce the statute. The Supreme Court considered the objectives of Congress in light of First Amendment freedoms of speech and association. It concluded that the restrictions on contributions were legitimate means to accomplish the purpose of combating campaign corruption, but held that the limits on expenditures violated the First Amendment. James L. Buckley, U.S. Senator, was the lead plaintiff in filing this case against Francis R. Valeo, Secretary of the Senate.

PER CURIAM.

These appeals present constitutional challenges to the key provisions of the Federal Election Campaign Act of 1971 (Act), and related provisions of the Internal Revenue Code of 1954, all as amended in 1974.

[After determining that the lawsuit constituted a "case or controversy" within the meaning of Article III of the Constitution, the Court turned to the merits. The Court examined limits on individual political contributions and expenditures, reporting and disclosure requirements, public funding of presidential campaigns, and the establishment of a Federal Election Commission (an issue dealt with in Chapter 6).]

I. CONTRIBUTION AND EXPENDITURE LIMITATIONS

The intricate statutory scheme adopted by Con-

gress to regulate federal election campaigns includes restrictions on political contributions and expenditures that apply broadly to all phases of and all participants in the election process....

A. GENERAL PRINCIPLES

The Act's contribution and expenditure limitations operate in an area of the most fundamental First Amendment activities. Discussion of public issues and debate on the qualifications of candidates are integral to the operation of the system of government established by our Constitution....

A restriction on the amount of money a person or group can spend on political communication during a campaign necessarily reduces the quantity of expression by restricting the number of issues discussed, the depth of their exploration, and the size of the audience reached. This is because virtually every means of communicating ideas in today's mass society requires the expenditure of money. The distribution of the humblest handbill or leaflet entails printing, paper, and circulation costs. Speeches and rallies generally necessitate hiring a hall and publicizing the event. The electorate's increasing dependence on television, radio, and other mass media for news and information has made these expensive modes of communication indispensable instruments of effective political speech.

The expenditure limitations contained in the Act represent substantial rather than merely theoretical restraints on the quantity and diversity of political speech....

By contrast with a limitation upon expenditures for political expression, a limitation upon the amount that any one person or group may contribute to a candidate or political committee entails only a marginal restriction upon the contributor's ability to engage in free communication. A contribution serves as a general expression of support for the candidate and his views, but does not communicate the underlying basis for the support....

In sum, although the Act's contribution and expenditure limitations both implicate fundamental First Amendment interests, its expenditure ceilings impose significantly more severe restrictions on protected freedoms of political expression and association than do its limitations on financial contributions.

B. CONTRIBUTION LIMITATIONS

[The Court upholds the $1,000 limitation on contributions by individuals and groups to candidates and authorized campaign committees: "It is unnecessary to look beyond the Act's primary purpose — to limit the actuality and appearance of corruption resulting from large individual financial contributions — in order to find a constitutionally sufficient justification for the $1,000 contribution limitation.... To the extent that large contributions are given to secure a political quid pro quo from current and potential office holders, the integrity of our system of representative democracy is undermined." On similar grounds the Court upholds the $5,000 limitation on contributions by political committees, the limitations on volunteers' incidental expenses, and the $25,000 limitation on total contributions during any calendar year.]

C. EXPENDITURE LIMITATIONS

The Act's expenditure ceilings impose direct and substantial restraints on the quantity of political speech. The most drastic of the limitations restricts individuals and groups, including political parties

that fail to place a candidate on the ballot, to an expenditure of $1,000 "relative to a clearly identified candidate during a calendar year." § 608(e)(1). Other expenditure ceilings limit spending by candidates, § 608(a), their campaigns, § 608(c), and political parties in connection with election campaigns, § 608(f). It is clear that a primary effect of these expenditure limitations is to restrict the quantity of campaign speech by individuals, groups, and candidates....

[The Court found the $1,000 limitation on expenditures "Relative to a Clearly Identified Candidate" an inadequate governmental interest in preventing corruption and the appearance of corruption, and thus unconstitutional under the First Amendment. Similarly unconstitutional was the limitation on expenditures by candidates from personal or family resources. The ceiling on personal expenditures "imposes a substantial restraint on the ability of persons to engage in protected First Amendment expression. The candidate, no less than any other person, has a First Amendment right to engage in the discussion of public issues and vigorously and tirelessly to advocate his own election and the election of other candidates." The governmental interest in preventing actual and apparent corruption does not apply to the expenditure of personal funds. Indeed, "the use of personal funds reduces the candidate's dependence on outside contributions and thereby counteracts the coercive pressures and attendant risks of abuse to which the Act's contribution limitations are directed." Finally, the Court found unconstitutional the limitations on campaign expenditures. The government's interest in "alleviating the corrupting influence of large contributions is served by the Act's contribution limitations and disclosure provisions rather than ... campaign expenditure ceilings.]

II. REPORTING AND DISCLOSURE REQUIREMENTS

... [T]he disclosure requirements of the Act ... are not challenged by appellants as *per se* unconstitutional restrictions on the exercise of First Amendment freedoms of speech and association.

[Each political committee is required to register with the FEC and keep detailed records of contributions and expenditures. The records are subject to periodic FEC audits and field investigations. " ... we find no constitutional infirmities in the recordkeeping, reporting, and disclosure provisions of the Act."]

III. PUBLIC FINANCING OF PRESIDENTIAL ELECTION CAMPAIGNS

[Individual taxpayers, on their tax returns, may authorize payment to a Presidential Election Campaign Fund of one dollar. Two dollars are authorized for a joint return. Each major candidate may spend up to $20 million (adjusted for inflation) from this fund during the general election campaign. In receiving these funds, presidential candidates agree not to exceed the ceiling. The Court found no merit to the contention that the legislation violates the First and Fifth Amendments.]

MR. JUSTICE STEVENS took no part in the consideration or decision of these cases....

MR. CHIEF JUSTICE BURGER, concurring in part and dissenting in part.

For reasons set forth more fully later, I dissent from those parts of the Court's holding sustaining the statutory provisions (a) for disclosure of small contributions, (b) for limitations on contributions, and (c) for public financing of Presidential campaigns. In my view, the Act's disclosure scheme is impermissibly broad and violative of the First Amendment as it relates to reporting contributions in excess of $10 and $100. The contribution limitations infringe on First Amendment liberties and suffer from the same infirmities that the Court correctly sees in the expenditure ceilings....

MR. JUSTICE WHITE, concurring in part and dissenting in part.

[He dissents from the Court's view that the expenditure limits violate the First Amendment.]

It would make little sense to me, and apparently made none to Congress, to limit the amounts an individual may give to a candidate or spend with his approval but fail to limit the amounts that could be spent on his behalf. Yet the Court permits the former while striking down the latter limitation....

I also disagree with the Court's judgment that § 608(a), which limits the amount of money that a candidate or his family may spend on his campaign, violates the Constitution.... By limiting the importance of personal wealth, § 608(a) helps to assure that only individuals with a modicum of support from others will be viable candidates. This in turn would tend to discourage any notion that the outcome of elections is primarily a function of money. Similarly, § 608(a) tends to equalize access to the political arena, encouraging the less wealthy, unable to bankroll their own campaigns, to run for political office....

MR. JUSTICE MARSHALL, concurring in part and dissenting in part. *[Also disagrees with the Court's invalidation of § 608(a)].*

MR. JUSTICE BLACKMUN, concurring in part and dissenting in part.

I am not persuaded that the Court makes, or indeed is able to make, a principled constitutional distinction between the contribution limitations, on the one hand, and the expenditure limitations, on the other, that are involved here. *[Blackmun also dissented from the Court's responses to limits on contributions, limits on incidental expenditures by volunteers, and the definition of "political committee."]*

MR. JUSTICE REHNQUIST, concurring in part and dissenting in part. *[He dissented from the Court's opinion that certain aspects of the statutory treatment of minor parties and independent candidates are constitutionally valid.]*

Citizens United v. FEC

558 U.S. ___ (2010)

In January 2008, Citizens United, a nonprofit corporation, released a documentary film critical of then-Senator Hillary Clinton, a presidential candidate. With plans to make the movie available on cable television within 30 days of the primary, Citizens United produced TV ads to run on broadcast and cable TV. Concerned about possible civil and criminal penalties for violating federal election law, it sought declaratory and injunctive relief, arguing that the law was unconstitutional. A district court denied the preliminary injunction and granted the Federal Election Commission summary judgment. The Supreme Court ordered that the case be reargued to consider broader issues of constitutional law, particularly the chilling of political speech under the First Amendment.

PER CURIAM.

JUSTICE KENNEDY delivered the opinion of the Court.

Federal law prohibits corporations and unions from using their general treasury funds to make independent expenditures for speech defined as an "electioneering communication" or for speech expressly advocating the election or defeat of a candidate. 2 U.S.C. § 441b. Limits on electioneering communications were upheld in *McConnell* v. *Federal Election Comm'n*, 540 U.S. 93, 203–209 (2003). The holding in *McConnell* rested to a large extent on an earlier case, *Austin* v. *Michigan Chamber of Commerce*, 494 U.S. 652 (1990). *Austin* had held that political speech may be banned based on the speaker's corporate identity.

In this case we are asked to reconsider *Austin* and, in effect, *McConnell*. It has been noted that "*Austin* was a significant departure from ancient First Amendment principles," *Federal Election Comm'n* v. *Washington Right to Life, Inc.*, 551 U.S. 449, 490 (2007) (WRTL) (SCALIA, J., concurring in part and concurring in judgment). We agree with that conclusion and hold that *stare decisis* does not compel the continued acceptance of *Austin*. The Government may regulate corporate political speech through disclaimer and disclosure requirements, but it may not suppress that speech altogether. We turn to the case now before us.

I
A

Citizens United is a nonprofit corporation. It brought this action in the United States District Court for the District of Columbia. A three-judge court later convened to hear the cause. The resulting judgment gives rise to this appeal.

Citizens United has an annual budget of about $12 million. Most of its funds are from donations by individuals; but, in addition, it accepts a small portion of its funds from for-profit corporations.

In January 2008, Citizens United released a film entitled *Hillary: The Movie*. We refer to the film as *Hillary*. It is a 90-minute documentary about then-Senator Hillary Clinton, who was a candidate in the Democratic Party's 2008 Presidential primary elections. *Hillary* mentions Senator Clinton by name and depicts interviews with political commentators and other persons, most of them quite critical of Senator Clinton. *Hillary* was released in theaters and on DVD, but Citizens United wanted to increase distribution by making it available through video-on-demand.

Video-on-demand allows digital cable subscribers to select programming from various menus, including movies, television shows, sports, news, and music. The viewer can watch the program at any time and can elect to rewind or pause the program. In December 2007, a cable company offered, for a payment of $1.2 million, to make *Hillary* available on a video-on-demand channel called "Elections '08."...

To implement the proposal, Citizens United was prepared to pay for the video-on-demand; and to promote the film, it produced two 10-second ads and one 30-second ad for *Hillary*. Each ad includes a short (and, in our view, pejorative) statement about Senator Clinton, followed by the name of the movie and the movie's Website address....

B

Before the Bipartisan Campaign Reform Act of 2002 (BCRA), federal law prohibited—and still does prohibit—corporations and unions from using general treasury funds to make direct contributions to candidates or independent expenditures that expressly advocate the election or defeat of a candidate, through any form of media, in connection with certain qualified federal elections.... An electioneering communication is defined as "any broadcast, cable, or satellite communication" that "refers to a clearly identified candidate for Federal office" and is made within 30 days of a primary or 60 days of a general election.... The Federal Election Commission's (FEC) regulations further define an electioneering communication as a communication that is "publicly distributed."... "In the case of a candidate for President ... *publicly distributed* means" that the communication "[c]an be received by 50,000 or more persons in a State where a primary election ... is being held within 30 days."... Corporations and unions are barred from using their general treasury funds for express advocacy or electioneering communications. They may establish, however, a "separate segregated fund" (known as a political action committee, or PAC) for these purposes....

C

[Citizens United wanted to make *Hillary* available through video-on-demand within 30 days of the 2008 primary elections. Fearing that both the film and the ads would subject them to civil and criminal penalties, it sought declaratory and injunctive relief against the FEC. The district court denied their motion and granted FEC summary judgment. The Court noted probable jurisdiction and had the case reargued, asking the parties whether it should overrule *Austin* and part of *McConnell.*]

II

Before considering whether *Austin* should be overruled, we first address whether Citizens United's claim that § 441b cannot be applied to *Hillary* may be resolved on other, narrower grounds. [*The Supreme Court concludes that efforts to interpret the statute narrowly are unpersuasive.*] The First Amendment does not permit laws that force speakers to retain a campaign finance attorney, conduct demographic marketing research, or seek declaratory rulings before discussing the most salient political issues of the day. Prolix laws chill speech for the same reason that vague laws chill speech: People "of common intelligence must necessarily guess at [the law's] meaning and differ as to its application." [*In this section the Court concludes that "there is no reasonable interpretation of* Hillary *other than an appeal to vote against Senator Clinton."*] ...

E

As the foregoing analysis confirms, the Court cannot resolve this case on a narrower ground without chilling political speech, ... It is not judicial restraint to accept an unsound, narrow argument just so the Court can avoid another argument with broader implications....

III

The First Amendment provides that "Congress shall make no law ... abridging the freedom of speech." Law enacted to control or suppress speech may operate at different points in the speech process....

The law before us is an outright ban, backed by criminal sanctions. Section 441b makes it a felony for all corporations—including nonprofit advocacy corporations—either to expressly advocate the election or defeat of candidates or to broadcast electioneering communications within 30 days of a primary election and 60 days of a general election.... These prohibitions are classic examples of censorship.

Section 441b is a ban on corporate speech notwithstanding the fact that a PAC created by a corporation can still speak.... A PAC is a separate association from the corporation.... Even if a PAC could somehow allow a corporation to speak—and it does not—the option to form PACs does not alleviate the First Amendment problems with § 441b. PACs are burdensome alternatives; they are expensive to administer and subject to extensive regulations....

Speech is an essential mechanism of democracy, for it is the means to hold officials accountable to the people. See *Buckley, supra,* at 14–15 ("In a republic where the people are sovereign, the ability of the citizenry to make informed choices among candidates for office is essential"). The right of citizens to inquire, to hear, to speak, and to use information to reach consensus is a precondition to enlightened self-government and a necessary means to protect it....

[A.1]

The Court has recognized that First Amendment protections extends to corporations. [*Long string citation of 23 Court decisions.*] ...

This protection has been extended by explicit holdings to the context of political speech....

[B.1]

If the First Amendment has any force, it prohibits Congress from finding or jailing citizens, or associations of citizens, for simply engaging in political speech....

There is simply no support for the view that the First Amendment, as originally understood, would permit the suppression of political speech by media corporations.... The First Amendment was certainly not understood to condone the suppression of political speech in society's most salient market.... The great debates between the Federalists and the Anti-Federalists over our founding document were published and expressed in the most important means of mass communication of that era—newspapers owned by individuals....

... Factions will necessarily form in our Republic, but the remedy of "destroying the liberty" of some factions is "worse than the disease." The Federalist No. 10, p. 130 (B. Wright ed. 1961) (J. Madison). Factions should be checked by permitting them all to speak....

A single footnote in *Bellotti* purported to leave open the possibility that corporate independent expenditures could be shown to cause corruption. 435 U.S. at 788, n. 26. For the reasons explained above, we now conclude that independent expenditures, including those made by corporations, do not give rise to corruption or the appearance of corruption....

The appearance of influence or access, furthermore, will not cause the electorate to lose faith in our democracy.... The fact that a corporation, or any other speaker, is willing to spend money to try to persuade voters presupposes that the people have the ultimate influence over elected officials....

... When Congress finds that a problem exists, we must give that finding due deference; but Congress may not choose an unconstitutional remedy.... We must give weight to attempts by Congress to seek to dispel either the appearance or reality of these influences. The remedies enacted into law, however, must comply with the First Amendment; and, it is our law and our tradition that more speech, not less, is the governing rule....

C

... [i]t must be concluded that *Austin* was not well reasoned.... *Austin* abandoned First Amendment principles, ...

Due consideration leads to this conclusion: *Austin*, 494 U.S. 652, should be and now is overruled.... [*The Court also overrules the part of* McConnell *that upheld BCRA § 203's extension of § 441b's restriction on corporate independent expenditures.*]

CHIEF JUSTICE ROBERTS, with whom JUSTICE ALITO joins, concurring.

[*This concurrence is devoted primarily to explain why the principle of* stare decisis *does not apply to the overruling of* Austin *and* McConnell.] ... It should go without saying, however, that we cannot embrace a narrow ground of decision simply because it is narrow; it must also be right.... There is a difference between judicial restraint and judicial abdication.

... When considering whether to reexamine a prior erroneous holding, we must balance the importance of having constitutional questions *decided* against the importance of having them *decided right.*...

JUSTICE SCALIA, with whom JUSTICE ALITO joins, and with whom JUSTICE THOMAS joins in part, concurring....

JUSTICE STEVENS, with whom JUSTICE GINSBURG, JUSTICE BREYER, and JUSTICE SOTOMAYOR join, concurring in part and dissenting in part.

... The conceit that corporations must be treated identically to natural persons in the political sphere is not only inaccurate but also inadequate to justify the Court's disposition of this case.

In the context of election to public office, the distinction between corporate and human speakers is significant. Although they make enormous contributions to our society, corporations are not actually members of it. They cannot vote or run for office. Because they may be managed and controlled by nonresidents, their interests may conflict in fundamental respects with the interests of eligible voters. The financial resources, legal structure, and instrumental orientation of corporations raise

legitimate concerns about their role in the electoral process. Our lawmakers have a compelling constitutional basis, if not also a democratic duty, to take measures designed to guard against the potentially deleterious effects of corporation spending in local and national races.

... I concur in the Court's decision to sustain BCRA's disclosure provisions and join Part IV of its opinion ...

I

The Court's ruling threatens to undermine the integrity of elected institutions across the Nation. The path it has taken to reach its outcome will, I fear, do damage to this institution....

... [T]he question was not properly brought before us. In declaring § 203 of BCRA facially unconstitutional on the ground that corporations' electoral expenditures may not be regulated any more stringently than those of individuals, the majority decides this case on a basis relinquished below, not included in the questions presented to us by the litigants, and argued here only in response to the Court's invitation....

Setting the case for reargument was a constructive step, but it did not cure this fundamental problem. Essentially, five Justices were unhappy with the limited nature of the case before us, so they changed the case to give themselves an opportunity to change the law.

... In this case, the record is not simply incomplete or unsatisfactory; it is nonexistent. Congress crafted BCRA in response to a virtual mountain of research on the corruption that previous legislation has failed to avert. The Court now negates Congress' efforts without a shred of evidence on how § 203 or its state-law counterparts have been affecting any entity other than Citizens United....

II

The final principle of judicial process that the majority violates is the most transparent: *stare decisis.* I am not an absolutist when it comes to *stare decisis*, in the campaign finance area or in any other. No one is. But if this principle is to do any meaningful work in supporting the rule of law, it must at least demand a significant justification, beyond the preferences of five Justices, for overturning settled doctrine....

... I am perfectly willing to concede that if one of our precedents were dead wrong in is reasoning or irreconcilable with the rest of our doctrine, there would be a compelling basis for revisiting it. But neither is true of *Austin*, ...

... The Court proclaims that "*Austin* is undermined by experience since its announcement." ... This is a curious claim to make in a case that lacks a developed record. The majority has no empirical evidence with which to substantiate the claim; we just have its *ipse dixit* that the real world has not been kind to *Austin*....

... The only relevant thing that has changed since *Austin* and *McConnell* is the composition of this Court....

IV

. . .

The fact that corporations are different from human beings might seem to need no elaboration, except that the majority opinion almost completely elides it. *Austin* set forth some of the basic differences. Unlike natural persons, corporations have "limited liability" for their owners and managers, "perpetual life," separation of ownership and control, "and favorable treatment of the accumulation and distribution of assets ... that enhance their ability to attract capital and to deploy their resources in ways that maximize the return of their shareholders' investments." 494 U.S., at 658–659. Unlike voters in U.S. elections, corporations may be foreign controlled....

It might also be added that corporations have no consciences, no beliefs, no feelings, no thoughts, no desires. Corporations help structure and facilitate the activities of human beings, to be sure, and their "personhood" often serves as a legal fiction. But they are not themselves members of "We the People" by whom and for whom our Constitution was established....

It is an interesting question "who" is even speaking when a business corporation places an advertisement that endorses or attacks a particular candidate. Presumably it is not the customers or employees, who typically have no say in such matters. It cannot realistically be said to be the shareholders, who tend to be far removed from the day-to-day decisions of the firm and whose political preferences may be opaque to management. Perhaps the officers or directors of the corporation have the best claim to be the ones speaking, except their fiduciary duties generally prohibit them from using corporate funds for personal ends....

The Court's blinkered and aphoristic approach to the First Amendment may well promote corporate power at the cost of the individual and collective self-expression the Amendment was meant to serve. It will undoubtedly cripple the ability of ordinary citizens, Congress, and the States to adopt even limited measures to protect against corporate domination of the electoral process. Americans may be forgiven if they do not feel the Court has advanced the cause of self-government today....

JUSTICE THOMAS, concurring in part and dissenting in part.

[He holds that the disclosure, disclaimer, and reporting requirements in BCRA §§ 201 and 311 are unconstitutional.] I cannot endorse a view of the First Amendment that subjects citizens of this Nation to death threats, ruined careers, damaged or defaced property, or pre-emptive and threatening warning letters as the price for engaging in "core political speech, the 'primary object of First Amendment protection,'" *McConnell*, 540 U.S. at 264 (THOMAS, J., concurring in part, and dissenting in part) (quoting *Nixon* v. *Shrink Missouri Government PAC*, 528 U.S. 377, 410–411 (2000) (THOMAS, J., dissenting)....

Testimony by Lawrence Lessig

During a hearing on July 24, 2012, Harvard Law School Professor Lawrence Lessig told a subcommittee of the Senate Judiciary Committee that the majority's ruling in *Citizens United* was constitutionally defective and requires Congress to pass remedial legislation. He said the Court's support for unlimited expenditures, including by corporations and unions, constituted a major threat to representative democracy and popular control.

Mr. Chairman, and Members of the Committee, my name is Lawrence Lessig, and I am the Roy L. Furman Professor of Law and Leadership at Harvard Law School.... Before teaching, I clerked for Judge Richard Posner of the Seventh Circuit Court of Appeals, and Justice Antonin Scalia.

I commend this Committee, and its Chairman, for holding this hearing, a celebration of the extraordinary grassroots movement that has developed to demand the reversal of *Citizens United*, and an end to a system for funding elections that leads most Americans to believe that this government is corrupt. Hundreds of thousands of citizens have gotten hundreds of cities, and now a half dozen states, to pass resolutions calling on Congress to correct the Supreme Court's mistake. It has been a century since we have seen such anti-corruption activism, and it is a testament to the leadership of the many new grassroots organizations, such as *Free Speech for People*, and *Move to Amend*, that in just two years, they have achieved so much.

Yet this hearing is just the beginning of the serious work that will be required to address the problem in America's democracy that *Citizens United* has come to represent. That problem can be simply stated:

THE PEOPLE HAVE LOST FAITH IN THEIR GOVERNMENT.

They have lost the faith that their government is responsive to them, because they have become convinced that their government is more responsive to those who fund your campaigns. As all of you, Democrats, Republicans, and Independents alike, find yourselves forced into a cycle of perpetual fundraising—spending, according to the estimates in the academic literature, anywhere between 30% and 70% of your time raising money to get back into office or to get your party back into power—you become, or at least most Americans believe you become, responsive to the will of "the Funders." But "the Funders" are not "the People": .26% of Americans give more than $200 in a congressional campaign; .05% give the maximum amount to any congressional candidate; and .01%—the 1% of the 1%—give more than $10,000 in an election cycle. We have *up-sourced* the funding of your campaigns to the tiniest fraction of the 1%; America has grown cynical in response.

Citizens United has only made this problem worse, as it has further and predictably concentrated funding in an even smaller slice of America. In the current presidential election cycle, .000063% of America—that's 196 citizens—have funded 80% of Super PAC spending. 22 Americans—that's 7 one-millionths of 1%—account for 50% of that funding. *Citizens United* has thus further shifted the sources of campaign funding toward an ever shrinking few.

This, Senators, is corruption. Not "corruption" in the criminal sense. I am not talking about bribery or quid pro quo influence peddling. It is instead "corruption" in a sense that our Framers would certainly and easily have recognized: They architected a government that in this branch at least was to be, as Federalist 52 puts it, "dependent upon the People alone." You have evolved a government that is not dependent upon the People *alone*, but that is also dependent upon the Funders. That different and conflicting dependence is a corruption of our Framers' design, now made radically worse by the errors of *Citizens United*.

As the Supreme Court has now doubled down on its deeply flawed decision, it is both appropriate and necessary for this Congress to consider how best to respond. [By "doubling-down," Lessig refers to the Court's 2012 ruling in the Montana case.]

But in considering this response, you should not lose sight of this one critical fact: On January 20, 2010, the day before *Citizens United* was decided, our democracy was already broken. *Citizens United* may have shot the body, but the body was already cold. And any response to *Citizens United* must also respond to that more fundamental corruption. We must find a way to restore a government "dependent upon the People alone," so that we give "the People" a reason again to have confidence in their government....

This is not to say that before *Citizens United*, large contributions or expenditures did not matter. Of course they did. But *Citizens United* and its progeny have changed the way that large expenditures did matter. And that change in turn has inspired an explosion of the level—both the amount and the size—of such contributions....

There are some who believe that any problem that *Citizens United* created could be remedied simply by more effective disclosure. It is critical that this Committee recognize that however important disclosure is, disclosure alone *could not* reveal the actual influence of unlimited independent expenditures. [Lessig explains that an incumbent could fear that 30 days before an election, a super PAC could threaten to spend $1 million for an attack ad unless the incumbent supported the super PAC's legislative agenda. If the incumbent acquiesced, there would be no expenditure by the super PAC and nothing to disclose. Lessig says: "This is the economy of a protection racket."] ...

The Framers gave us a "Republic." But by a Republic, they meant a "representative democracy." And by a "representative democracy," they meant a government with a branch that would be "dependent upon the people alone."

... simply reversing *Citizens United* would not achieve this end. Indeed, returning America to the democracy that existed before *Citizens United* would still leave us with a democracy in which Congress was dependent upon the tiniest slice of the 1% to fund its elections.... [In that sense, it appears that

Lessig is taking aim at the 1976 case of *Buckley* v. *Valeo*, in which the Court held that political money is political speech and therefore Congress may not limit campaign expenditures.]

E. LOBBYING

A variety of interest groups maintain regular contacts with members of Congress, congressional committees, and executive agencies, supplying advice and information they hope will influence government policy. The pejorative term *lobbying* is often applied to these activities, but it is healthy and appropriate in a democracy for private groups to intervene in the process of government. As the Supreme Court remarked in 1961, "the whole concept of representation depends upon the ability of the people to make their wishes known to their representatives." Eastern Railroad Presidents Conference v. Noerr Motors, Inc., 365 U.S. 127, 137 (1961). The First Amendment recognizes the right of citizens to petition their government for a redress of grievances. How can this activity be regulated through constitutional means?

It is difficult to conceive of a democratic government operating in a sterile environment never contaminated by private lobbyists. However, the activity of interest groups has been cast in negative terms from the start. In Federalist No. 10, Madison defined *faction* as a number of citizens "united and actuated by some common impulse of passion, or of interest, adverse to the rights of other citizens, or to the permanent and aggregate interests of the community." Under his definition, almost every interest group in America is rendered suspect. Although Madison disapproved of factions, he did not urge that they be abolished. The remedy was not in removing the cause of faction but in "controlling its effects" (see reading).

Regulatory Efforts

In 1919, Congress passed legislation to prevent executive officials from using appropriated funds to stimulate grassroots lobbying against Congress. Officials had used telephones, telegrams, letters, and other forms of communication to drum up pressure against Congress from the private sector. Legislation prohibited this practice and the restriction remains part of current law. 41 Stat. 68, § 6 (1919); 18 U.S.C. § 1913. In 1934, Congress amended the tax code to restrict expenditures by charitable organizations for lobbying. The amendment applied to organizations covered by Section 501(c)(3) of the Internal Revenue Code, which gives tax-exempt status to various groups. As a condition attached to this tax benefit, Congress required that "no substantial part" of the activities of tax-exempt groups should consist of "carrying on propaganda, or otherwise attempting, to influence legislation." 48 Stat. 690 (1934); 26 U.S.C. § 501(c)(3) (2000).

A year later, Congress required representatives of public utility holding companies to file a report with the Securities and Exchange Commission (SEC) before attempting to influence Congress, the SEC, or the Federal Power Commission. 49 Stat. 825 (1935). Similar requirements were applied in 1936 to lobbyists for the merchant marine and in 1938 to agents of foreign governments. 49 Stat. 2014, § 807 (1936); 52 Stat. 631 (1938).

The Lobbying Act

The most extensive effort to control lobbying is the Federal Regulation of Lobbying Act of 1946, which required lobbyists to register with Congress and file quarterly reports of their activities. 60 Stat. 839 (1946); 2 U.S.C. §§ 261–70 (2000). The statute was criticized for using vague language to cover activities that carried criminal penalties for violations. The statute has limited reach. It applies only to lobbyists whose "principal purpose" is to influence Congress. A more general critique is that the Act

---

Federal Lobbying

By virtually all indications, the activities of lobbyists and pressure groups have increased significantly in the last two decades. This increase is reflected in many areas: the numbers of corporations that have opened offices in Washington, the numbers of trade and other non-profit associations that have either made Washington their headquarters or opened offices here, the numbers of out-of-town law firms that have opened offices in Washington, and the numbers of public relations firms new to Washington.

Where once most Washington lobbying centered around economic interests, the last twenty years have witnessed the development of an array of groups representing social, environmental, philosophical and ideological interests.

While there is no single theory to account for this activity, a number of factors are clearly involved: growth of the Federal Government and the expansion of its influence—often as manager and provider; increased levels of relative affluence and education; advances in communications

technology; and changes in Congress and in the elections process. These factors create a fertile environment for pressure group politics.

Not surprisingly, as Congress delegated decision-making authority to the executive agencies, so the agencies became the focus of increasing pressure group activity. At the same time that groups made heightened efforts to influence agency policies, the agencies themselves were making efforts to open up their decision-making processes to public scrutiny and involvement.

Although Congress periodically sought to control pressure group activities, mostly through registration and reporting requirements, none of its actions was particularly effective. In the past twenty years, the growth in numbers and diversity of pressure groups saw a similar rise in allegations of abuse of the lobbying process, claims that "secrecy" in the lobbying process was inimical to democratic government, and the belief of many that certain lobbying activities should be restricted or at least disclosed....

SOURCE: "Congress and Pressure Groups: Lobbying in a Modern Democracy," S. Prt. 99-161, 99th Cong., 2d Sess. 39 (1986).

---

interferes with the First Amendment freedom to petition government. National Ass'n of Mfrs. v. McGrath, 103 F.Supp. 510 (D.D.C. 1952), vacated as moot, 344 U.S. 804 (1952). Moreover, a large number of lobbyists, consultants, and trade associations never register, even though they meet regularly with members of Congress and seek to influence legislation. For years Congress tried to revise and strengthen the lobbying act (see box).

Section 307 of the Lobbying Act covered persons who, "directly or indirectly," solicit, collect, or receive money to influence Congress. In 1953, the Supreme Court restricted the reach of the lobbying statute to "direct" appeals to members of Congress, rather than the more general definition of influencing the thinking of the community. United States v. Rumely, 345 U.S. 41, 47 (1953). A year later the Court dismissed the charge of vagueness leveled against the statute but agreed with *Rumely* that the statute covered only direct communications with members of Congress. As to the First Amendment challenge, the Court held that Congress is not forbidden to require the disclosure of lobbying activities. United States v. Harriss, 347 U.S. 612 (1954).

The Lobbying Disclosure Act of 1995—the first general lobbying statute since 1946—tightens registration requirements for those who lobby members of Congress and their staff, the White House, and federal agencies. Lobbyists have to disclose the issue they lobbied on, the specific legislative or executive agency they contacted, and the amount of money they spent on the effort. 109 Stat. 691 (1995). The previous law covered only those who lobbied members of Congress.

The Internal Revenue Code, as interpreted by Treasury Department regulations, forbids the deduction of sums expended for "the promotion or defeat of legislation." In upholding these regulations, a unanimous Court held that they apply to expenditures made in connection with efforts to promote or defeat legislation by persuasion of the general public (as in initiative measures and referenda), as well as efforts to influence legislative bodies directly through "lobbying." Cammarano v. United States, 358 U.S. 498 (1959). In granting tax exemptions to certain nonprofit organizations on the condition that "no substantial part" of their activities involve propaganda or attempts to influence legislation, Congress does not violate the First Amendment. Members of Congress may legitimately choose not to subsidize lobbying activities. Regan v. Taxation With Representation of Wash., 461 U.S. 540 (1983).

Current Lobbying Disputes

The Supreme Court has recognized a broad right of citizens to demonstrate against governmental policies, including those of the Court itself and also foreign governments. A congressional statute prohibited the display of any flag, banner, or device in the Supreme Court or on its grounds "to bring into public notice any party, organization, or movement." The purpose was to insulate the Court from direct lobbying, but in 1983 the Court held that the acts of distributing leaflets and carrying picket signs on the public sidewalk around the building were protected by the First Amendment. United States v. Grace, 461 U.S. 171 (1983).

Five years later, in a case involving demonstrations against foreign governments, the Court issued a decision that illustrates the dialogue between Congress and the judiciary on constitutional questions. The D.C. government made it unlawful for individuals, within 500 feet of a foreign embassy, to display any sign that tended to bring the foreign government into "public odium" or "public disrepute." Congress had also passed an antipicketing provision to protect foreign officials, but repealed it in 1976 because of First Amendment concerns. In 1986 Congress passed legislation to suggest that the D.C. law on demonstrations near foreign missions may be inconsistent with First Amendment rights. The D.C. government repealed the law, contingent on Congress's extending to the District the federal law on foreign embassies. Against this background, the Court held that the D.C. law violated the First Amendment because it represented a content-based restriction on political speech in a public forum. Boos v. Barry, 485 U.S. 312 (1988).

In 2001, the Court (5–4) struck down a congressional 1996 statute that prohibited federally subsidized attorneys in the Legal Services Corporation from raising legal or constitutional challenges on behalf of clients who claimed benefits under federal welfare laws. The Court held that Congress had unconstitutionally limited the free speech rights of those attorneys. Legal Services Corp. v. Velazquez, 531 U.S. 533 (2001). A year later, a federal appellate court struck down a 30-year-old prohibition against protesters who gather at the House and Senate entrances to the Capitol. The court held that the demonstration ban violated First Amendment rights. Lederman v. United States, 291 F.3d 36 (D.C. Cir. 2002).

On January 21, 2009, President Obama issued Executive Order 13490 to place limits on the ability of lobbyists to serve in Government positions related to their prior lobbying activities. The administration also placed restrictions on individual lobbyists to obtain economic recovery funds and to serve on agency advisory boards and commissions. The line between permissible and impermissible activities was not always easy to discern.

Madison's Views on Factions

In Federalist No. 10, James Madison defined *faction* as citizens "united and actuated by some common impulse of passion, or of interest, adverse to the rights of other citizens, or to the permanent and aggregate interests of the community." As a very rough and often unfair characterization, the definition could apply to interest groups or the even more pejorative "lobbyists." In a careful and insightful analysis, Madison reconciles the activity of factions to democratic government.

Among the numerous advantages promised by a well-constructed Union, none deserves to be more accurately developed than its tendency to break and control the violence of faction. The friend of popular governments never finds himself so much alarmed for their character and fate, as when he contemplates their propensity to this dangerous vice. He will not fail, therefore, to set a due value on any plan which, without violating the principles to which he is attached, provides a proper cure for it....

By a faction, I understand a number of citizens, whether amounting to a majority or minority of the whole, who are united and actuated by some common impulse of passion, or of interest, adverse to the rights of other citizens, or to the permanent and aggregate interests of the community.

There are two methods of curing the mischiefs of faction: the one, by removing its causes; the other, by controlling its effects.

There are again two methods of removing the causes of faction: the one, by destroying the liberty which is essential to its existence; the other, by giving to every citizen the same opinions, the same passions, and the same interests.

It could never be more truly said than of the first remedy, that it was worse than the disease. Liberty is to faction what air is to fire, an aliment without which it instantly expires. But it could not be less folly to abolish liberty, which is essential to political life, because it nourishes faction, than it would be to wish the annihilation of air, which is essential to animal life, because it imparts to fire its destructive agency.

The second expedient is as impracticable as the first would be unwise. As long as the reason of man continues fallible, and he is at liberty to exercise it, different opinions will be formed. As long as the connection subsists between his reason and his self-love, his opinions and his passions will have a reciprocal influence on each other: and the former will be objects to which the latter will attach themselves. The diversity in the faculties of men, from which the rights of property originate, is not less an insuperable obstacle to a uniformity of interests. The protection of these faculties is the first object of government....

It is in vain to say that enlightened statesmen will be able to adjust these clashing interests, and render them all subservient to the public good. Enlightened statesmen will not always be at the helm. Nor, in many cases, can such an adjustment be made at all without taking into view indirect and remote considerations, which will rarely prevail over the immediate interest which one party may find in disregarding the rights of another or the good of the whole.

The inference to which we are brought is, that the *causes* of faction cannot be removed, and that relief is only to be sought in the means of controlling its *effects*.

If a faction consists of less than a majority, relief is supplied by the republican principle, which enables the majority to defeat its sinister views by regular vote. It may clog the administration, it may convulse the society; but it will be unable to execute and mask its violence under the forms of the Constitution. When a majority is included in a faction, the form of popular government, on the other hand, enables it to sacrifice to its ruling passion or interest both the public good and the rights of other citizens. To secure the public good and private rights against the danger of such a faction, and at the same time to preserve the spirit and the form of popular government, is then the great object to which our inquiries are directed....

By what means is this object attainable? Evidently by one of two only. Either the existence of the same passion or interest in a majority at the same time must be prevented, or the majority, having such coexistent passion or interest, must be rendered, by their number and local situation, unable to concert and carry into effect schemes of oppression. If the impulse and the opportunity be suffered to coincide, we well know that neither moral nor religious motives can be relied on as an adequate control. They are not found to be such on the injustice and violence of individuals, and lose their efficacy in proportion to the number combined together, that is, in proportion as their efficacy becomes needful.

From this view of the subject it may be concluded that a pure democracy, by which I mean a society consisting of a small number of citizens, who assemble and administer the government in person, can admit of no cure for the mischiefs of faction. A common passion or interest will, in almost every case, be felt by a majority of the whole; a communication and concert result from the form of government itself; and there is nothing to check the inducements to sacrifice the weaker party or an obnoxious individual. Hence it is that such democracies have ever been spectacles of turbulence and contention....

A republic, by which I mean a government in which the scheme of representation takes place, opens a different prospect, and promises the cure for which we are seeking. Let us examine the points in which it varies from pure democracy, and we shall comprehend both the nature of the cure and the efficacy which it must derive from the Union.

The two great points of difference between a democracy and a republic are: first, the delegation of the government, in the latter, to a small number of citizens elected by the rest; secondly, the greater number of citizens, and greater sphere of country, over which the latter may be extended....

The other point of difference is, the greater number of citizens and extent of territory which may be brought within the compass of republican than of democratic government; and it is this circumstance principally which renders factious combinations less to be dreaded in the former than in the latter. The smaller the society, the fewer probably will be the distinct parties and interests composing it; the fewer the distinct parties and interests, the more frequently will a majority be found of the same party; and the smaller the number of individuals composing a majority, and the smaller the compass within which they are placed, the most easily will they concert and execute their plans of oppression. Extend the sphere, and you take in a greater variety of parties and interests; you make it less probable that a majority of the whole will have a common motive to invade the rights of other citizens; or if such a common motive exists, it will be more difficult for all who feel it to discover their own strength, and to act in unison with each other....

Hence, it clearly appears, that the same advantage which a republic has over a democracy, in controlling the effects of faction, is enjoyed by a large over a small republic, — is enjoyed by the Union over the States composing it. Does the advantage consist in the substitution of representatives whose enlightened views and virtuous sentiments render them superior to local prejudices and to schemes of injustice? It will not be denied that the representation of the Union

will be most likely to possess these requisite endowments. Does it consist in the greater security afforded by a greater variety of parties, against the event of any one party being able to outnumber and oppress the rest? In an equal degree does the increased variety of parties comprised within the Union, increase this security. Does it, in fine, consist in the greater obstacles opposed to the concert and accomplishment of the secret wishes of an unjust and interested majority? Here, again, the extent of the Union gives it the most palpable advantage.

The influence of factious leaders may kindle a flame within their particular States, but will be unable to spread a general conflagration through the other States. A religious sect may degenerate into a political faction in a part of the Confederacy; but the variety of sects dispersed over the entire face of it must secure the national councils against any danger from that source. A rage for paper money, for an abolition of debts, for an equal division of property, or for any other improper or wicked project, will be less apt to pervade the whole body of the Union than a particular member of it; in the same proportion as such a malady is more likely to taint a particular county or district, than an entire State.

In the extent and proper structure of the Union, therefore, we behold a republican remedy for the diseases most incident to republican government. And according to the degree of pleasure and pride we feel in being republicans, ought to be our zeal in cherishing the spirit and supporting the character of Federalists.

PUBLIUS

CONCLUSIONS

This chapter provides further examples of the essentially shared nature of constitutional interpretation, calling upon the combined efforts of legislators, executive officials, judges, states, and the general public. The responsibility for keeping the political process free and open is not entrusted to a single branch. Members of the judiciary must exercise careful judgment in deciding which cases to accept and resolve. Harold Leventhal, for many years a distinguished federal judge on the D.C. Circuit, recognized that the "political thicket" did not constitute a flat ban on judicial involvement: "For me the 'thicket' sign does not mean out of bounds, but a caution to walk carefully in the work of interpreting and determining the validity of the legislature's efforts to structure the political process." 77 Colum. L. Rev. 345, 346 (1977). The Court in *Buckley* and *Citizens United* waded deep into the political thicket and is now in the process of deciding whether it overstepped and should allow the elected branches more leeway in fashioning a solution to the problems of campaign finance. Other constraints on judicial activism are addressed in the next chapter.

NOTES AND QUESTIONS

1. Consider the impact of the Court's ruling in *Buckley v. Valeo* on such democratic values as equality, participation, autonomy and accountability. Paul Brest observed: "'Those who are better off participate more, and by participating more they exercise more influence on government officials.' Unequal resources produce unequal influence in determining which issues get on the political [agenda]. Campaign finance regulations barely begin to remedy the systematic ways in which inequalities of wealth distort the political process." Brest, "Further Beyond the Republican Revival," 97 Yale L.J. 1623, 1627 (1988). Is Professor Brest right? If so, what is the proper response to the Court's ruling *Buckley*?

2. To what extent should campaign contributions be viewed as an exercise of free speech? In *Buckley*, the conservative Senator James L. Buckley and the liberal Senator Eugene McCarthy joined forces in arguing that limits on campaign contributions and expenditures constituted a violation of the First Amendment right of expression of both contributors and candidates. Do you agree with them? Why or why not? Should the Court view money as property, rather than speech? Would it make a difference? What light is shed on these questions by *Citizens United* v. *FEC* (2010)?

3. The Warren Court's decisions revolutionized many areas of constitutional law: rights of the accused, desegregation, reapportionment, church and states, and other sensitive issues. Of all these innovations, it is widely assumed that the desegregation case of *Brown v. Board of Education* (1954) was the most important decision. Yet, Chief Justice Warren, who authored the *Brown* opinion, disagreed. The "accolade," he said, should go to *Baker v. Carr* (1962), which opened the door to the "one person, one vote" rule for reapportionment. In your view, what are the implications of that ruling for democracy and constitutional government?

4. In *Colegrove*, Justice Frankfurter argued that courts should not take jurisdiction in reapportionment cases. The remedy for malapportionment, he argued, lay in the political, not the judicial, process. In your opinion, was he right?

5. In your view, did the Supreme Court act appropriately when it assumed jurisdiction in *Bush v. Gore*? Did the Court avert a crisis by taking the appeal? What would have happened had the Court decided to return the matter once again to Florida and let it search for a solution? In your view, will the decision have any precedential value?

6. In *Citizens United,* the Supreme Court ruled against expenditure limits by arguing that corporations are "persons" and money is "speech." What do you think of those arguments?

SELECTED READINGS

ALEXANDER, HERBERT E. Financing Politics: Money, Elections, and Political Reform. Washington, D.C.: Congressional Quarterly, 1992.

ALFANGE, DEAN, JR. "Gerrymandering and the Constitution: Into the Thorns of the Thicket at Last." 1986 Supreme Court Review 175.

AUERBACH, CARL A. "The Reapportionment Cases: One Person, One Vote—One Vote, One Value." 1964 Supreme Court Review 1.

BAKER, GORDON E. The Reapportionment Revolution. New York: Random House, 1966.

BALL, HOWARD. The Warren Court's Conceptions of Democracy: An Evaluation of the Supreme Court's Apportionment Cases. Rutherford, N.J.: Fairleigh Dickinson University Press, 1971.

BICKEL, ALEXANDER. "The Voting Rights Cases." 1966 Supreme Court Review 79.

BUTLER, KATHARINE INGLIS. "Racial Fairness and Traditional Districting Standards: Observations on the Impact of the Voting Rights Act on Geographic Representation." 57 South Carolina Law Review 749 (2006).

———. "Redistricting in a Post-*Shaw* era: A Small Treatise Accompanied by Districting Guidelines for Legislators, Litigants, and Courts." 36 University of Richmond Law Review 137 (2002).

CAIN, BRUCE E. The Reapportionment Puzzle. Berkeley: University of California Press, 1984.

CLAUDE, RICHARD. The Supreme Court and the Electoral Process. Baltimore, Md.: Johns Hopkins University Press, 1970.

CORRADO, ANTHONY., et al., eds., Campaign Finance Reform: A Sourcebook. Washington, D.C.: Brookings Institution Press, 1997.

CORTNER, RICHARD C. The Apportionment Cases. Knoxville: University of Tennessee Press, 1970.

DIXON, ROBERT G., JR. Democratic Representation: Reapportionment in Law and Politics. New York: Oxford University Press, 1968.

———. "The Warren Court Crusade for the Holy Grail of 'One Man-One Vote.'" 1969 Supreme Court Review 219.

DWORKIN, RONALD. "The Decision That Threatens American Democracy," New York Review of Books, May 13, 2010, pp. 63–67.

EDWARDS, GEORGE C. III. Why the Electoral College Is Bad for America. New Haven: Yale University Press, 2004.

ELLIOTT, WARD. "Prometheus, Proteus, Pandora, and Procrustes Unbound: The Political Consequences of Reapportionment." 37 University of Chicago Law Review 474 (1970).

FISHER, LOUIS. "Saying what the law is: On campaign finance, it's not just for the Court; Congress has a co-equal say." National Law Journal, February 22, 2010, at 38.

———. "Bush v. Gore: Too Political?," in Nada Mourtada-Sabbah and Bruce E. Cain, eds. The Political Question Doctrine and the Supreme Court of the United States. Lanham, Md.: Lexington Books, 2007.

HAMILTON, HOWARD D., ed. Legislative Reapportionment: Key to Power. New York: Harper & Row, 1964.

HANSON, ROYCE. The Political Thicket: Reapportionment and Constitutional Democracy. Englewood Cliffs, N.J.: Prentice-Hall, 1966.

LEVENTHAL, HAROLD. "Courts and Political Thickets." 77 Columbia Law Review 345 (1977).

LEWIS, ANTHONY. "Legislative Apportionment and the Federal Courts." 71 Harvard Law Review 1057 (1958).

NEAL, PHIL C. "Baker v. Carr: Politics in Search of Law." 1962 Supreme Court Review 252.

PENNOCK, J. ROLAND, AND JOHN W. CHAPMAN, eds. Representation. New York: Atherton Press, 1968.

POLSBY, DANIEL D. "Buckley v. Valeo: The Special Nature of Political Speech." 1976 Supreme Court Review 1.

POLSBY, NELSON W., ed. Reapportionment in the 1970s. Berkeley: University of California Press, 1971.

RYDEN, DAVID K., ed. The U.S. Supreme Court and the Electoral Process. Washington, D.C.: Georgetown University Press, 2002.

SCHER, RICHARD K., et al. Voting Rights and Democracy: The Law and Politics of Districting. Chicago: Nelson-Hall Publishers, 1997.

SCHRAM, MARTIN. Speaking Freely: Former Members of Congress Talk About Money in Politics. Washington, D.C.: Center for Responsive Politics, 1995.

SORAUF, FRANK J. "Caught in a Political Thicket: The Supreme Court and Campaign Finance." 3 Constitutional Commentary 97 (1986).

———. Inside Campaign Finance: Myths and Realities. New Haven, Conn.: Yale University Press, 1992.

TAPER, BERNARD. Gomillion versus Lightfoot: Apartheid in Alabama. New York: McGraw-Hill, 1967.

WRIGHT, J. SKELLY. "Money and the Pollution of Politics: Is the First Amendment an Obstacle to Political Equality?" 82 Columbia Law Review 609 (1982).

19

Efforts to Curb the Court

Justice Stone once chided his brethren: "the only check upon our own exercise of power is our own sense of self-restraint." United States v. Butler, 297 U.S. 1, 79 (1936). While that is an important check, it is by no means the only one. Judges act within a political environment that constantly tests the reasonableness and acceptability of their rulings. Courts issue the "last word" only for an instant, for after the release of an opinion the process of interaction begins: with Congress, the President, executive agencies, states, professional associations, law journals, and the public at large.

Earlier chapters identified some of the constraints that operate on the judiciary: the President's power to appoint; the Senate's power to confirm; congressional powers over the purse, impeachment, and court jurisdiction; the force of public opinion, the press, and scholarly studies. Other restraints, covered in this chapter, include constitutional amendments, statutory reversals, changing the number of Justices (court packing), withdrawing jurisdiction, and noncompliance with court rulings.

Court-curbing periods at the national level often emerge when the judiciary nullifies statutes passed by Congress. The judiciary can also create enemies by *upholding* legislation, such as the broad nationalist rulings issued by Chief Justice John Marshall. To restrain the courts, members of Congress introduce a variety of legislative bills and constitutional amendments. Hearings are held to explore ways to curb the judiciary. State legislatures prepare petitions of protest; state judges draft resolutions of "concern," if not condemnation. Citizens pass initiatives, propositions, and take other positions on constitutional issues. To reduce the tension, the federal judiciary may decide to conduct a partial and possibly graceful retreat.

Judicial-congressional confrontations were especially sharp between 1858 and 1869 (reflecting the *Dred Scott* case and congressional efforts to protect Reconstruction legislation), from 1935 to 1937 (reacting to the Court's nullification of New Deal legislation), and from 1955 to 1959 (triggered by decisions involving desegregation, congressional investigations, and national security).[1] A new round of court-curbing efforts began in the late 1970s to challenge judicial rulings on school prayer, school busing, abortion, and affirmative action. The Court's decisions in *Bush* v. *Gore* in 2000 and *Citizens United* in 2010 provoked deep concerns about judicial power and legal reasoning.

The judiciary is most likely to be out of step with Congress or the President during periods of electoral and partisan realignment, when the country is undergoing sharp shifts in political directions while the courts retain the orientation of an age gone by.[2] During earlier periods, attacks on the judiciary generally came from liberal groups: Jeffersonians, Jacksonians, Radical Republicans, LaFollette Republicans, and New Deal Democrats. Conservatives dominated the 1955–59 confrontation and have inspired most of the court-curbing efforts since then.

---

1. See Stuart S. Nagel, "Court-Curbing Periods in American History," 18 Vand. L. Rev. 925 (1965). For a review of proposals to remedy judicial activism, see Charles Grove Haines, The American Doctrine of Judicial Supremacy 467–99 (1932).

2. Richard Funston, "The Supreme Court and Critical Elections," 69 Am. Pol. Sci. Rev. 795 (1975); David Adamany, "Legitimacy, Realigning Elections, and the Supreme Court," 1973 Wisc. L. Rev. 790.

A. CONSTITUTIONAL AMENDMENTS

Whenever two-thirds of both houses of Congress deem it necessary, they may propose amendments to the Constitution. Ratification requires three-fourths of the states. Alternatively, two-thirds of the states may call a convention for constitutional amendment, but thus far all successful amendments have been initiated by Congress. The process of amending the Constitution is extraordinarily difficult and time-consuming. On only four occasions has Congress successfully used constitutional amendments to reverse Supreme Court decisions.

The Eleventh Amendment responded to *Chisholm* v. *Georgia,* 2 U.S. (2 Dall.) 419 (1793), which decided that a state could be sued in federal court by a plaintiff from another state. The lower house of the Georgia legislature adopted the modest proposal that any federal marshal attempting to enforce that ruling would be guilty of a felony and hanged until death "without the benefit of the clergy." To protect states from a flood of costly citizen suits, Congress quickly passed a constitutional amendment. Although a sufficient number of states ratified it by 1795, not until 1798 did President John Adams notify Congress that the amendment was effective. The Eleventh Amendment reads: "The Judicial power of the United States shall not be construed to extend to any suit in law or equity, commenced or prosecuted against one of the United States by Citizens of another State, or by Citizens or Subjects of any Foreign States."

The Fourteenth Amendment nullified the Supreme Court's decision in *Dred Scott* v. *Sandford,* 60 U.S. (19 How.) 393 (1857), which held that blacks as a class were not citizens protected under the Constitution. After the nation had fought a bloody civil war, North against South, the Fourteenth Amendment was ratified in 1868. Section 1 provides: "All persons born or naturalized in the United States and subject to the jurisdiction thereof, are citizens of the United States and of the State wherein they reside." *Dred Scott* had been partially reversed by statute in 1862 when Congress passed legislation to prohibit slavery in the territories. 12 Stat. 432.

The Sixteenth Amendment overruled *Pollock* v. *Farmers' Loan and Trust Co.,* 158 U.S. 601 (1895), which struck down a federal income tax. The need to finance national expansion and new international responsibilities, combined with a desire to reduce the dependence on high tariffs as the main source of revenue, triggered the drive for a constitutional amendment. Ratified in 1913, the Sixteenth Amendment gave Congress the power "to lay and collect taxes on incomes, from whatever source derived, without apportionment among the several States, and without regard to any census or enumeration."

The Twenty-sixth Amendment was ratified in 1971 to overturn *Oregon* v. *Mitchell,* 400 U.S. 112 (1970), a Supreme Court decision of the previous year that had voided a congressional effort to lower the minimum voting age in state elections to 18. Proponents of lowering the voting age argued that if 18-year-olds could be drafted to fight in wars, they were old enough to vote in elections. As a way to encourage youths to participate constructively in the political process and to avoid the cost and confusion of a dual registration system of 18 years for national elections and 21 years for state and local elections, Congress sent a constitutional amendment to the states. In record time, three months later, a sufficient number of states ratified this language: "The right of citizens of the United States, who are eighteen years of age or older, to vote shall not be denied or abridged by the United States or any State on account of age."

Other Amendment Efforts

Other constitutional amendments, driven by seemingly irresistible political forces, have fallen by the wayside. A successful amendment process requires an extraordinary combination of social, economic, and political forces. If any one of these factors is absent, an amendment may fail. For example, Congress made a concerted effort in 1964 to amend the Constitution to overturn the Supreme Court's decisions in the reapportionment and school prayer cases. Because of delays by House committees and filibusters on the Senate side, these efforts were unsuccessful.

Debate on Equal Rights Amendment

[During House debate in 1970 and 1971, Congresswoman Martha Griffiths used the proposed Equal Rights Amendment as a vehicle for attacking the Supreme Court for its failure to address laws and practices that discriminated against women. These debates helped provoke the Court to act in Reed v. Reed, *404 U.S. 71 (1971).]*

Mrs. GRIFFITHS.... We will show you that the Supreme Court which has readily moved to change the boundaries of your District and the boundaries of your school district has on not one single occasion granted to women the basic protection of the fifth or 14th amendment. The only right guaranteed to women today by the Constitution of the United States is the right to vote and to hold public office.

It is time, Mr. Speaker, that in this battle with the Supreme Court, that this body and the legislatures of the States come to the aid of women by passing this amendment....

Mr. Speaker, this is not a battle between the sexes — nor a battle between this body and women. This body and State legislatures have supported women. This is a battle with the Supreme Court of the United States.

... Let me repeat again and again that the States, their legislatures and frequently their courts or Federal district courts have shown more sense than the Supreme Court ever has....

Mr. Chairman, what the equal rights amendment seeks to do, and all it seeks to do, is to say to the Supreme Court of the United States, "Wake up! This is the 20th century. Before it is over, judge women as individual human beings. They, too, are entitled to the protection of the Constitution, the basic fundamental law of this country."

Source: 116 Cong. Rec. 28000, 28004, 28005 (1970); 117 Cong. Rec. 35323 (1971).

Even when Congress reacts against a Court decision by clearing an amendment for ratification by the states, the hurdles are immense. After the Supreme Court in 1918 and 1922 denied Congress the right to regulate child labor conditions, opponents of the Court rulings tried unsuccessfully to reverse them by constitutional amendment. Hammer v. Dagenhart, 247 U.S. 251 (1918); Bailey v. Drexel Furniture Co., 259 U.S. 20 (1922). In 1924, both houses of Congress passed a constitutional amendment to give Congress the power to "limit, regulate and prohibit the labor of persons under 18 years of age." By 1937 only 28 of the necessary 36 states had ratified the amendment. The issue became moot after Congress regulated child labor through the Fair Labor Standards Act of 1938 and the Supreme Court upheld the statute three years later. United States v. Darby, 312 U.S. 100 (1941).

Unsuccessful constitutional amendments can sometimes prod the Court to address neglected issues. In 1970, the House of Representatives passed the Equal Rights Amendment. After Senate action, the language sent to the states for ratification read: "Equality of rights under the law shall not be denied or abridged by the United States or by any State on account of sex." The ERA was never ratified, even with an extension by Congress to June 30, 1982, but the debate on the amendment had an obvious impact on the Court. Congresswoman Martha Griffiths, during debate in October 1971, said that the whole purpose of the ERA was to tell the Supreme Court "Wake up! This is the 20th century." 117 Cong. Rec. 35323 (1971). A month later the Court invalidated an Idaho law that preferred men over women in administering estates, the first time in its history that the Court had struck down sex discrimination on constitutional grounds (see box).

Once the Constitution is successfully amended to overturn a Court decision, there is no guarantee that the judiciary will interpret the amendment consistent with the intent of the framers and ratifiers. Although the Thirteenth, Fourteenth, and Fifteenth Amendments were meant to overturn *Dred Scott* and protect the rights of blacks, such decisions as the *Civil Rights Cases,* 109 U.S. 3 (1883) and *Plessy* v. *Ferguson,* 163 U.S. 537 (1896), were more in line with racial attitudes that flourished before the Civil War.

In addition to constitutional amendments aimed at particular decisions, other proposals attempt to curb the Court's strength by imposing procedural requirements. These amendments have never been successful. Of recurring interest are the following: requiring more than a majority of Justices to strike down a statute; subjecting the Court's decisions to another tribunal, such as the Senate or a judicial body consisting of a judge from each state; submitting the Court's decisions to popular referenda; allowing Congress by two-thirds vote to override a Court decision just as it does a presidential veto; and making laws held unconstitutional by the Court valid if reenacted by Congress.

Other amendments are directed at the Court's tenure and qualifications: allowing the removal of Supreme Court Justices and other federal judges by majority vote of each house of Congress; restricting the term of a Justice to a set number of years; having Justices retire at the age of 75; requiring direct election from the judicial districts; itemizing the qualifications for Justices, such as requiring prior judicial service in the highest court of a state or excluding anyone who has, within the preceding five years, served in the executive or legislative branch; and vesting the appointment of Justices in judges from the highest state courts.[3] Although unsuccessful in every case, these amendments serve the purpose of venting popular and professional resentment toward Court decisions and may even temper future rulings.

The Court held in 1921 that constitutional amendments must be ratified within some reasonable time after their submission to the states. Ratification "must be sufficiently contemporaneous in that number of States to reflect the will of the people in all sections at relatively the same period." Dillon v. Gloss, 256 U.S. 368, 375 (1921). However, in 1939 the Court declined to be the judge of what constituted a reasonable period for ratification. Coleman v. Miller, 307 U.S. 433, 452 (1939). In 1992, Congress agreed that 202 years were not too long to ratify a constitutional amendment proposed in 1789. That language, now the Twenty-seventh Amendment, reads: "No law, varying the compensation for the services of the Senators and Representatives, shall take effect, until an election of Representatives shall have intervened."

B. STATUTORY REVERSALS

When decisions turn on the interpretation of federal statutes, Congress may overturn a ruling simply by passing a new statute to clarify legislative intent. The private sector often uses Congress as an "appellate court" to reverse judicial interpretations of a statute. At a congressional hearing in 1959, Congressman Wilbur Mills leaned across the witness table and told a company president: "It seems that it is becoming more and more almost a full-time job of the Congress to correct the Supreme Court's desire to legislate." The company president, seeking to have a major Supreme Court decision modified to his advantage, nodded his agreement. Emmette S. Redford, et al., Politics and Government in the United States 518 (1965).

In 1969, the Supreme Court struck down a joint operating agreement by two newspapers on the ground that it violated the Antitrust Act. Citizen Publishing Co. v. United States, 394 U.S. 131 (1969). Congress responded within a year with the Newspaper Preservation Act, specifically exempting from the Act any authorizing agreement needed to prevent newspapers from going out of business. 84 Stat. 466 (1970).

Judicial-legislative conversations helped shape the meaning of the Freedom of Information Act (FOIA). In one case, 33 members of the House of Representatives went to court to obtain documents prepared for President Nixon concerning an underground nuclear test. In 1973, the Supreme Court decided that it had no authority to examine the documents *in camera* to sift out "non-secret compo-

---

3. Maurice S. Culp, "A Survey of the Proposals to Limit or Deny the Power of Judicial Review by the Supreme Court of the United States," 4 Ind. L. J. 386 (1929); Shelden D. Elliott, "Court-Curbing Proposals in Congress," 33 Notre Dame Lawyer 597, 606 (1958).

nents" for their release. EPA v. Mink, 410 U.S. 73 (1973). Congress passed legislation a year later to authorize federal courts to examine sensitive records in judges' chambers. 88 Stat. 1562, §4(B) (1974).

The *Grove City* Confrontation

Another successful congressional effort concerned the case of *Grove City College* v. *Bell*, 465 U.S. 555 (1984). Title IX of the Education Amendments of 1972 prohibited sex discrimination in any education program or activity that received federal financial assistance. After the Reagan administration had issued statements indicating that its interpretation of Title IX was not as broad as rulings from previous administrations, the House of Representatives on November 16, 1983, passed a resolution by a vote of 414–8 opposing the administration's position. The resolution stated the sense of the House that Title IX and regulations issued pursuant to the title "should not be amended or altered in any manner which will lessen the comprehensive coverage of such statute in eliminating gender discrimination throughout the American educational system." The resolution, of course, was not legally binding, but it was passed because the Supreme Court was about to hear oral argument on the *Grove City* case. As Congressman Paul Simon noted: "Passing this resolution the House can send the Court a signal that we believe that no institution should be allowed to discriminate on the basis of sex if it receives Federal funds." 129 Cong. Rec. 33105 (1983).

The issue before the Court was whether Title IX required federal funds to be terminated only for specific programs in which discrimination occurs or for the entire educational institution. The Supreme Court adopted the narrow interpretation. Justices Brennan and Marshall dissented in part, stating that the Court was ignoring congressional intent for institution-wide coverage. Within four months the House of Representatives, by a vote of 375–32, passed legislation to amend not only Title IX but also three other statutes to adopt broad coverage of the antidiscrimination provisions. 130 Cong. Rec. 18880 (1984). The Senate resisted action that year, and subsequent efforts were complicated by questions of church-state and abortion. Finally, in 1988, Congress was able to forge a compromise. President Reagan vetoed the measure, but both houses overrode the veto to enact the broader coverage for civil rights that had been rejected in *Grove City*.

Continued Challenges

In 1988, Congress passed two other statutes to reverse the Supreme Court. In one decision, the Court ruled that federal employees could be sued for common law torts committed on the job. They were not entitled to absolute immunity from lawsuit. However, the Court remarked: "Congress is in the best position to provide guidance for the complex and often highly empirical inquiry into whether absolute immunity is warranted in a particular context." Westfall v. Erwin, 484 U.S. 292, 300 (1988). Congress passed legislation to overturn this decision by protecting federal employees from personal liability for common law torts committed within the scope of their employment. The statute provides the injured person with a remedy against the United States government. Thus, compensation would come from the U.S. Treasury, not the employee's pocketbook. 102 Stat. 4563 (1988).

The other statutory reversal in 1988 concerned a Supreme Court decision that accepted the definition of the Veterans Administration that alcoholism results from "willful misconduct" rather than from a disease. For those who regarded the Court's position as erroneous, they were advised that their arguments would be "better presented to Congress than to the courts." Traynor v. Turnage, 485 U.S. 535 (1988). Legislation enacted by Congress recognized that veterans seeking education or rehabilitation would not be denied those benefits under the willful-misconduct standard. 102 Stat. 4170, §109 (1988).

The Jencks Bill

These cases involve matters of statutory interpretation, an area in which Congress can ultimately prevail. However, even in cases where constitutional rights are present, Congress may pass legislation to modify a Court ruling. A 1957 case involved access by defendants to government files bearing on their trial. On the basis of statements by two informers for the FBI, the government prosecuted Clifford Jencks for failing to state that he was a member of the Communist Party. He asked that the FBI reports be turned over to the trial judge for examination to determine whether they had value in impeaching the statements of the two informers. The Supreme Court went beyond Jencks' request by ordering the government to produce for *his* inspection all FBI reports "touching the events and activities" at issue in the trial. Jencks v. United States, 353 U.S. 657, 668 (1957). The Court specifically rejected the option of producing government documents only to the trial judge for his determination of relevancy and materiality. Id. at 669.

In their concurrence, Justices Burton and Harlan believed that Jencks was only entitled to have the records submitted to the trial judge. A dissent by Justice Clark agreed that the documents should be delivered solely to the trial judge. In a remarkable statement he urged Congress to act: "Unless the Congress changes the rule announced by the Court today, those intelligence agencies of our Government engaged in law enforcement may as well close up shop, for the Court has opened their files to the criminal and thus afforded him a Roman holiday for rummaging through confidential information as well as vital national secrets."

The Court announced its decision on June 3, 1957. Both houses of Congress quickly held hearings and reported remedial legislation. The Jencks Bill (after much redrafting) passed the Senate by voice vote on August 26 and cleared the House on August 27, 351 to 17. The conference report was adopted with huge majorities: 74–2 in the Senate and 315–0 in the House. The bill became law on September 2, 1957. The statute provides that in any federal criminal prosecution, no statement or report in the possession of the government "which was made by a Government witness or prospective Government witness (other than the defendant) to an agent of the Government shall be the subject of subpoena, discovery, or inspection unless said witness has testified on direct examination in the trial of the case." If a witness testifies, statements may be delivered to the defendant for examination and use unless the United States claims that the statement contains irrelevant matter, in which case the statement shall be inspected by the court *in camera*. The judge may excise irrelevant portions of the statement before submitting it to the defendant. 71 Stat. 595 (1957); 18 U.S.C. § 3500.

Contemporary Reversals

Congress has resorted to statutory reversals with greater frequency in recent years. A single statute in 1991 overturned or modified nine Supreme Court decisions (see the heading "Civil Rights Act of 1991" in Section E of Chapter 15). In 1995, Congress passed legislation to overturn the Supreme Court's opinion in *Dole* v. *United Steelworkers of America*, 494 U.S. 26 (1990), which had restricted OMB's authority to review and countermand agency regulations. The new legislation (P.L. 104-13) made all paperwork requirements subject to OMB review. Both houses were active in considering legislation to overturn a Court decision regarding a pay discrimination suit brought by Lilly Ledbetter. Ledbetter v. Goodyear Tire & Rubber Co., 550 U.S. 618 (2007). The bill overriding the Court became the second statute passed at the start of the Obama administration, enacted into law on January 29, 2009. Section 2 states that the Court's decision "significantly impairs statutory protections against discrimination in compensation that Congress established and that have been bedrock principles of American law for decades" (123 Stat. 5). (See reading.)

Statutory Reversal: Lilly Ledbetter

Lilly Ledbetter filed a claim against Goodyear Tire for pay discrimination on grounds of gender. A jury found for her and awarded backpay and damages. On May 29, 2007, the Supreme Court (divided 5 to 4) decided she had filed her claim too late. The Court held that, to comply with statutory policy, she should have filed her charge within 180 days after the allegedly discriminatory pay decision was made and communicated to her. The dissenters objected that management often hides comparative pay information from employees and that Congress had never intended to immunize discriminatory pay differentials unchallenged within the 180-day period. Members of Congress debated legislation to ensure that employees in the future would not be limited by the results in *Ledbetter*. House and Senate debate occurred between January 9 and January 27, 2009.

Mr. GEORGE MILLER of California....

Madame Speaker, the 2007 Ledbetter v. Goodyear Supreme Court ruling was a painful step backwards in the civil rights of this country. Today, the House will vote once again to say that the ruling is unacceptable and must not stand.

Nondiscrimination in the workplace is a sacred American principle. Workers should be paid based upon their merits and their responsibilities, not on the employer's prejudices. Yet, more than 40 years after the passage of the Civil Rights Act of 1964, the Supreme Court decided to dramatically turn back the clock.

Lilly Ledbetter worked for Goodyear for nearly two decades. Just as she was retiring as supervisor in 1998, she found out that her salary was 20 percent, 20 percent lower than that of the lowest paid male supervisor. Not only was Ms. Ledbetter earning nearly $400 a month less than her male colleagues, she also retired with substantially smaller pension and Social Security benefits. A jury found that Goodyear in fact had discriminated against Ms. Ledbetter because she was a woman. She was awarded $3.8 million in back pay and damages. This amount was reduced to $360,000 because of the damage gap of title VII of the Civil Rights Act.

... The practical result, the practical result of the decision by this court, would be that as long as [management] could continue to hide the act, if they could get past the 180 days, Ms. Ledbetter could be discriminated against and she would not be able to recover anything....

The court's misguided decision is already having very harmful consequences far beyond Ms. Ledbetter's case. According to The New York Times, the Ledbetter decision has been cited in over 300 cases in the last 19 months that have denied people the opportunity to provide for recovery....

Mr. [ROBERT E.] ANDREWS....

The Supreme Court, with all due respect, turned this law into a trap and a game. Today, we are recorrecting that law, restoring the notion that when a woman goes to work in this country, she should be compensated on how good she is at her job, not her gender.... [The House passed the bill on January 9, 2009, 247 to 171. Senate debate began January 15.]

Mr. [PATRICK] LEAHY.

... The Justice Department has advocated a position that has set back the progress we had made toward eliminating workplace discrimination. This was a mistake. Unfortunately, five Justices on the Supreme Court adopted the Justice Department's erroneous interpretation of congressional intent. That decision necessitates our action here today. We must pass legislation so that employers are not rewarded for deceiving workers about their illegal conduct....

Mrs. [KAY BAILEY] HUTCHISON.... [M]y amendment ... is a substitute for the underlying bill that is now before us, S. 181. I hope we will, now that we have taken up the bill, fully discuss and hopefully have some amendments that will make the Fair Pay Act a bill that will serve all of the needs of our country. Paramount is the right of an employee to have redress, if that employee is experiencing discrimination. We also need to make sure that our small businesses and medium-sized businesses know what their underlying liabilities might be. That is part of business planning.

I have certainly been a person who has known discrimination. I want everyone who believes they have a cause of action to have that right.

I have also been a business owner. I know how important it is that our businesses know what their potential liabilities are. That is why statutes of limitation were put into the laws of the country, so that one could have a defense, so that there would be timely filings of claims, so that there would be witnesses who would have the memory or the records or the documents to defend against a claim

My substitute amendment allows the person who is aggrieved, when that person knows or should have known that there was discrimination, to have 180 days, approximately six months, to file that claim so that there will be records, there will be notice, and there will be the ability for a defense and for the person to have the fair trial with the people who would be relevant to her or his case....

Mr. [RICHARD] DURBIN....

We are saying to the Supreme Court, wake up to reality. You don't know what the person next to you is being paid. They don't publish it on a bulletin board. Maybe they do for public employees such as us, and that is right. But in the private sector, that doesn't happen. That is what this is all about. That is what the battle is all about....

Ms. [BARBARA] MIKULSKI....

The Senator from Texas [Hutchison] says her amendment would bring balance to our discrimination laws, but in reality it imposes a very unreasonable standard on workers—a standard that would be almost impossible for someone to meet.

Under the Hutchison framework, a worker would have to prove not only that she did not know she was being discriminated against but also she "should not have been expected to have had enough information to support a reasonable suspicion of discrimination."

How can workers prove what someone else expects of them? How does a worker prove a double negative, that she didn't suspect that something in the workplace wasn't quite right. And—again quoting the Hutchison recommendation—what is a "reasonable suspicion of discrimination"? That phrase ... is vague, and fuzzy, and I am concerned would even add to the already legal burdens. There is no similar standard in any other discrimination law....

[Hutchison's substitute amendment failed on a vote of 40 to 55. Two amendments by Arlen Specter were tabled, 53 to 43 and 55 to 39. The same procedure was used to table amendments by Michael Enzi, Jim DeMint, Johnny Isakson, and David Vitter. The bill then passed the Senate, 61 to 36. Subsequent action by the two chambers was necessary to pass an identical bill.]

[As enacted, the bill states that the Court's decision in Ledbetter "significantly impairs statutory protections against discrimination in compensation that Congress established and that have been bedrock principles of American law for decades. The Ledbetter decision undermines those statutory protections by unduly restricting the time period in which victims of discrimination can challenge and recover for discriminatory compensation decisions or other practices, contrary to the intent of Congress." The new legislation provides that "an unlawful employment practice occurs, with respect to discrimination in compensation in violation of this title [VII], when a discriminatory compensation decision or other practice is adopted, when an individual becomes subject to a discriminatory compensation decision or other practice, or when an individual is affected by application of a discriminatory compensation decision or other practice, including each time wages, benefits, or other compensation is paid, resulting in whole or in part from such a decision or other practice." Public Law 111-2, 123 Stat. 6, January 29, 2009.]

C. COURT PACKING

Congress has altered the number of Justices on the Supreme Court throughout its history. It authorized six Justices in 1789, lowered that number to five in 1801, returned to six a year later, and increased the size of the Court in subsequent years to keep pace with the creation of new circuits. From 1869 to the present the number of Justices has remained fixed at nine. Appointments to the Court have often produced marked changes in judicial policy, as witnessed by the abrupt shift in the Legal Tender Cases from 1870 to 1871. In none of these earlier examples was the alteration of court size linked so blatantly to changing judicial policy as in FDR's court-packing plan.

In his inaugural address in 1933, Franklin D. Roosevelt struck a confident note for presidential-judicial relations. He said the Constitution "is so simple and practical that it is possible always to meet extraordinary needs by changes in emphasis and arrangement without loss of essential form." Privately, he tempered that public optimism with the knowledge that most members of the Supreme Court were conservative, business-oriented, and opposed to his legislative goals.

Black Monday

Presidential hopes were routed on "Black Monday," May 27, 1935, when the Supreme Court unanimously struck down the National Industrial Recovery Act (NIRA). Schechter Corp. v. United States, 295 U.S. 495 (1935). On that same day it ruled that Presidents could remove members of independent regulatory commissions only by following the statutory reasons for removal, and it held unconstitutional a statute for the relief of farm mortgagors. Humphrey's Executor v. United States, 295 U.S. 602 (1935); Louisville Bank v. Radford, 295 U.S. 555 (1935). Feeling betrayed by the liberal members on the Court, Roosevelt asked plaintively: "Well, where was Ben Cardozo? And what about old Isaiah [Brandeis]?"[4] Direct attacks on the Court were shelved after the public reacted unfavorably to Roosevelt's sneering accusation at a press conference that the Justices had adopted a "horse-and-buggy definition of interstate commerce." At a cabinet meeting in December 1935, Roosevelt reviewed several methods of restraining the Court. The notion of packing the Court, Interior Secretary Harold Ickes recorded in his diary, "was a distasteful idea." 1 The Secret Diary of Harold L. Ickes 495 (1953).

Roosevelt's patience was tested again on January 6, 1936, when the Court struck down the processing tax in the Agricultural Adjustment Act. The ruling divided the Court, 6 to 3, with Justice Stone penning a stinging dissent. He reminded the other Justices that they were not the only branch of government assumed to have the capacity to govern. United States v. Butler, 297 U.S. at 87. This time there appeared to be a groundswell of public support for adding younger Justices more attuned to the temper of the times. Yet Roosevelt bided his time, not wanting to give his opponents in an election year the opportunity to rally behind the Constitution and the Court. Other decisions in 1936, striking down federal and state laws, provided extra incentives to curb the Court. Some of those decisions attracted three or four dissents.[5] The climate for curbing the Court was encouraged by the national popularity of The Nine Old Men (1936), a caustic portrait of the Justices written by Drew Pearson and Robert Allen. Peppered by such chapters as "The Lord High Executioners," the book charged that "justice has no relation whatsoever to popular will. Administrations may come and go, the temper of the people may reverse itself, economic conditions may be revolutionalized, the Nine Old Men sit on."

Roosevelt's landslide victory in 1936, capturing all but two states, paved the way for a direct assault on the Court. Constitutional amendments seemed to him wholly impracticable. They were difficult to frame and nearly impossible to pass. Statutory remedies, such as requiring a unanimous or 8-to-1 decision in the Supreme Court to invalidate a law, were of doubtful constitutionality. After rejecting a number of alternatives, he considered court packing the only feasible solution.

Roosevelt Shows His Hand

Working closely with his Attorney General and Solicitor General, but without the advice of congressional leaders, Roosevelt ordered preparation of a draft bill. The President would be authorized to nominate Justices to the Supreme Court whenever an incumbent over the age of 70 declined to resign or retire. The same procedure would apply to federal lower courts, limiting the number of additional appointments to 50 and setting the maximum size of the Supreme Court at 15. Under this scenario, Roosevelt could name as many as six new Justices to the Supreme Court.

When he submitted his proposal to Congress on February 5, 1937, he attempted to disguise it primarily as an economy and efficiency measure. Additional Justices and judges would help relieve the delay and congestion he claimed resulted from aged or infirm judges. FDR's "indirection" (a euphemism for his deception and deviousness) offended some potential supporters. Roosevelt soon revealed his real purpose: to pack the Supreme Court with liberal Justices. In a "fireside chat" on March 9, 1937, he told the country that he wanted a Supreme Court that "will enforce the Constitution as written." But a mechanical application of that document by six additional Justices would not automatically alleviate the problems Roosevelt faced. Later in that address he called for judges "who will bring to the Courts a present-day sense of the Constitution." What did he recommend? The Constitution as written in 1787 or as applied in 1937? He wanted "younger men who have had personal experience and contact with modern facts and circumstances." More concretely, he promised to appoint

4. William E. Leuchtenburg, "The Origins of Franklin D. Roosevelt's 'Court-Packing' Plan," 1966 Sup. Ct. Rev. 347, 357.

5. Jones v. SEC, 298 U.S. 1 (1936) (Cardozo, Brandeis, Stone dissenting); St. Joseph Stock Yards Co. v. United States, 298 U.S. 38 (1936) (Cardozo, Brandeis, and Stone dissenting in part); Carter v. Carter Coal Co., 298 U.S. 238 (1936) (Hughes, Cardozo, Brandeis, Stone disagreeing in part; Morehead v. New York ex rel. Tipaldo, 298 U.S. 587 (1936) (Hughes, Brandeis, Stone, Cardozo dissenting).

Justices "who will not undertake to override the judgment of the Congress on legislative policy." The result of this reform, he said plainly, would be a "reinvigorated, liberal-minded Judiciary."

Repudiation by the Senate

The Senate Judiciary Committee denounced Roosevelt's bill. Its report methodically and mercilessly shreds the bill's premises, structure, content, and motivation. This searing indictment constituted an extraordinary determination on the part of the committee to pulverize Roosevelt's creation and bury it forever. The first of six reasons for rejecting the plan bluntly noted: "the bill does not accomplish any one of the objectives for which it was originally offered." S. Rept. No. 711, 75th Cong., 1st Sess., 3 (1937). Among other points in this scathing attack, the committee said that the courts "with the oldest judges have the best records in the disposition of business." The bill called for retirement only for judges who had served for ten years (penalizing not age itself but age combined with experience). Nothing in the bill prevented Roosevelt from nominating someone 69 years and eleven months of age without prior judicial service. A possible result: a Court of 15 members, all of them older than 70. To the committee, the bill had one purpose and one purpose only: to apply force to the judiciary.

The committee condemned the bill as a "needless, futile, and utterly dangerous abandonment of constitutional principle." The report's harsh language (see reading) was designed to repudiate the bill so emphatically "that its parallel will never again be presented to the free representatives of the free people of America." The committee's position was reinforced by a letter from Chief Justice Hughes stating that the Court was "fully abreast of its work" and there was "no congestion of cases upon our calendar" (see box on next page).

A number of unexpected developments sealed the fate of the court-packing bill. Senate Majority Leader Joe Robinson, who Roosevelt hoped would steer the bill through the Senate, died on July 14 after a week of debate in the sweltering capital. By that time the Court had already begun to modify some of its earlier rulings. On March 29, 1937, it upheld a state law establishing a minimum wage law for women, basically reversing a decision handed down ten months earlier.[6] This reversal occurred because of a change in position by Justice Roberts, leading some to refer to the "switch in time that saved nine." However, before FDR submitted his court-packing plan Roberts had already broken with his laissez-faire colleagues. He wrote the opinion for a 5–4 Court in *Nebbia v. New York,* 291 U.S. 502 (1934), upholding a New York price-setting statute. With his support, the Court was prepared to sustain minimum-wage legislation in the fall of 1936 but delayed its ruling because of Justice Stone's illness. Late in 1936, Roberts voted with the liberals to affirm a state unemployment insurance law.[7]

Other decisions in 1937 confirmed that the Court had become more accepting of New Deal programs. Roosevelt remarked with obvious relish: "The old minority of 1935 and 1936 had become the majority of 1937—without a single new appointment of a justice!"[8] Because Congress finally passed legislation early in 1937 to provide full judicial pay during retirement, Justice Van Devanter stepped down on June 2, 1937, giving Roosevelt his first chance in more than four years to nominate a Justice to the Supreme Court. Other retirements were imminent. Within a matter of months, the need for

---

6. West Coast Hotel Co. v. Parrish, 300 U.S. 379 (1937), overturning Adkins v. Children's Hospital, 261 U.S. 525 (1923) and "distinguishing" (in fact reversing) Morehead v. New York ex rel. Tipaldo, 298 U.S. 587 (1936).

7. W. H. H. Chamberlin, Inc. v. Andrews, 299 U.S. 515, decided November 23, 1936. The Court was equally divided. For Roberts' vote, see John W. Chambers, "The Big Switch: Justice Roberts and the Minimum-Wage Cases," 10 Labor Hist. 44, 57 (1969). See also Felix Frankfurter, "Mr. Justice Roberts," 104 U. Pa. L. Rev. 311 (1955); 2 Merlo J. Pusey, Charles Evans Hughes 757 (1963). For a challenge to Roberts' recollection of key events in 1936, see Clement E. Vose, Constitutional Change: Amendment Politics and Supreme Court Litigation Since 1900, 228–34 (1972).

8. 6 Public Papers and Addresses of Franklin D. Roosevelt lxviii (1941). See also Virginian Ry. v. Federation, 300 U.S. 515 (1937); Wright v. Vinton Branch, 300 U.S. 440 (1937); NLRB v. Jones & Laughlin, 301 U.S. 1 (1937); NLRB v. Fruehauf Co., 301 U.S. 49 (1937); NLRB v. Clothing Co., 301 U.S. 58 (1937); Steward Machine Co. v. Davis, 301 U.S. 548 (1937); Helvering v. Davis, 301 U.S. 619 (1937).

Chief Justice Hughes Writes to Congress

March 21, 1937

Hon. Burton K. Wheeler
United States Senate
Washington, D.C.

My Dear Senator Wheeler: In response to your in-quiries, I have the honor to present the following statement with respect to the work of the Supreme Court:

1. The Supreme Court is fully abreast of its work. When we rose on March 15 (for the present recess) we had heard argument in cases in which certiorari had been granted only 4 weeks before—February 15.

During the current term, which began last Oc-tober and which we call "October term, 1936", we have heard argument on the merits in 150 cases (180 numbers) and we have 28 cases (30 num-bers) awaiting argument. We shall be able to hear all these cases, and such others as may come up for argument, before our adjournment for the term. There is no congestion of cases upon our calendar.

This gratifying condition has been obtained for several years. We have been able for several terms to adjourn after disposing of all cases which are ready to be heard. [*Hughes supplies statistics for six years on total cases on docket (original and ap-pellate), cases disposed of during term, and cases re-maining on dockets.*]

7. An increase in the number of Justices of the Supreme Court, apart from any question of pol-icy, which I do not discuss, would not promote the efficiency of the Court. It is believed that it would impair that efficiency so long as the Court acts as a unit. There would be more judges to hear, more judges to confer, more judges to discuss, more judges to be convinced and to decide....

I understand that it has been suggested that with more Justices the Court could hear cases in divisions. It is believed that such a plan would be impracticable. A large proportion of the cases we hear are important and a decision by a part of the Court would be unsatisfactory.

I may also call attention to the provisions of article III, section 1, of the Constitution that the judicial power of the United States shall be vested "in one Supreme Court" and in such inferior courts as the Congress may from time to time or-dain and establish. The Constitution does not ap-pear to authorize two or more Supreme Courts or two or more parts of a supreme court functioning in effect as separate courts.

On account of the shortness of time I have not been able to consult with the members of the Court generally with respect to the foregoing statement, but I am confident that it is in accord with the views of the Justices. I should say, how-ever, that I have been able to consult with Mr. Jus-tice Van Devanter and Mr. Justice Brandeis, and I am at liberty to say that the statement is approved by them.

I have the honor to remain,
Respectfully yours,

Charles E. Hughes
Chief Justice of the Supreme Court

SOURCE: S. Rept. No. 711, 75th Cong., 1st Sess. 38–40 (1937).

the court-packing plan had evaporated. President Roosevelt would be able to "reorganize" the Court through the regular appointment process.

FDR's Court-Packing Plan: Senate Report

President Roosevelt submitted to Congress on February 5, 1937, a proposal for "judicial reor-ganization." In actual fact, the plan would have allowed him to pack the Supreme Court and lower federal courts with liberal judges. Because of top-heavy Democratic majorities in both houses, he hoped for quick passage. His expectations were permanently dashed on June 7, when the Senate Judiciary Committee reported the bill adversely and so excoriated the President's idea that any parallels to it would "never again be presented to the free representatives of the free people of America." S. Rept. No. 711, 75th Cong., 1st Sess. (1937).

The Committee on the Judiciary, to whom was referred the bill (S. 1392) to reorganize the judicial branch of the Government, after full consideration, having unanimously amended the measure, hereby report the bill adversely with the recommendation that it do not pass....

THE ARGUMENT

The committee recommends that the measure be rejected for the following primary reasons:

I. The bill does not accomplish any one of the objectives for which it was originally offered.

II. It applies force to the judiciary and in its initial and ultimate effect would undermine the independence of the courts.

III. It violates all precedents in the history of our Government and would in itself be a dangerous precedent for the future.

IV. The theory of the bill is in direct violation of the spirit of the American Constitution and its employment would permit alteration of the Constitution without the people's consent or approval; it undermines the protection our constitutional system gives to minorities and is subversive of the rights of individuals.

V. It tends to centralize the Federal district judiciary by the power of assigning judges from one district to another at will.

VI. It tends to expand political control over the judicial department by adding to the powers of the legislative and executive departments respecting the judiciary.

. . .

BILL FAILS OF ITS PURPOSE

In the first place, as already pointed out, the bill does not provide for any increase of personnel unless judges of retirement age fail to resign or retire. Whether or not there is to be an increase of the number of judges, and the extent of the increase if there is to be one, is dependent wholly upon the judges themselves and not at all upon the accumulation of litigation in any court. To state it another way the increase of the number of judges is to be provided, not in relation to the increase of work in any district or circuit, but in relation to the age of the judges and their unwillingness to retire.

In the second place, as pointed out in the President's message, only 25 of the 237 judges serving in the Federal courts on February 5, 1937, were over 70 years of age. Six of these were members of the Supreme Court at the time the bill was introduced.... Moreover, the facts indicate that the courts with the oldest judges have the best records in the disposition of business....

QUESTION OF AGE NOT SOLVED

The next question is to determine to what extent "the persistent infusion of new blood" may be expected from this bill.

... The man on the bench may be 80 years of age, but this bill will not authorize the President to appoint a new judge to sit beside him unless he has served as a judge for 10 years. In other words, age itself is not penalized; the penalty falls only when age is attended with experience.

No one should overlook the fact that under this bill the President, whoever he may be and whether or not he believes in the constant infusion of young blood in the courts, may nominate a man 69 years and 11 months of age to the Supreme Court, or to any court, and, if confirmed, such nominee, if he never had served as a judge, would continue to sit upon the bench unmolested by this law until he had attained the ripe age of 79 years and 11 months.

We are told that "modern complexities call also for a constant infusion of new blood in the courts, just as it is needed in executive functions of the Government and in private business." Does this bill provide for such? The answer is obviously no....

THE BILL APPLIES FORCE TO THE JUDICIARY

The [bill] applies force to the judiciary. It is an attempt to impose upon the courts a course of action, a line of decision which, without that force, without that imposition, the judiciary might not adopt.

Can there be any doubt that this is the purpose of the bill? Increasing the personnel is not the object of this measure; infusing young blood is not the object; for if either one of these purposes had been in the minds of the proponents, the drafters would not have written the following clause to be found on page 2, lines 1 to 4, inclusive:

"*Provided*, That no additional judge shall be appointed hereunder if the judge who is of retirement age dies, resigns, or retires prior to the nomination of such additional judge."

... For the protection of the people, for the preservation of the rights of the individual, for the maintenance of the liberties of minorities, for maintaining the checks and balances of our dual system, the three branches of the Government were so constituted that the independent expression of honest difference of opinion could never be restrained in the people's servants and no one branch could overawe or subjugate the others. That is the American system. It is immeasurably more important, immeasurably more sacred to the people of America, indeed, to the people of all the world than the immediate adoption of any legislation however beneficial....

A PRECEDENT OF LOYALTY TO THE CONSTITUTION

. . .

This is the first time in the history of our country that a proposal to alter the decisions of the court by enlarging its personnel has been so boldly made. Let us meet it. Let us now set a salutary precedent that will never be violated. Let us, of the Seventy-fifth Congress, in words that will never be disregarded by any succeeding Congress, declare that we would rather have an independent Court, a fearless Court, a Court that will dare to announce its honest opinions in what it believes to be the defense of the liberties of the people, than a Court that, out of fear or sense of obligation to the appointing power, or factional passion, approves any measure we may enact. We are not the judges of the judges. We are not above the Constitution.

Even if every charge brought against the so-called "reactionary" members of this Court be true, it is far better that we await orderly but inevitable change of

personnel than that we impatiently overwhelm them with new members....

SUMMARY

We recommend the rejection of this bill as a needless, futile, and utterly dangerous abandonment of constitutional principle.

It was presented to the Congress in a most intricate form and for reasons that obscured its real purpose.

It would not banish age from the bench nor abolish divided decisions.

It would not affect the power of any court to hold laws unconstitutional nor withdraw from any judge the authority to issue injunctions.

It would not reduce the expense of litigation nor speed the decision of cases.

It is a proposal without precedent and without justification.

It would subjugate the courts to the will of Congress and the President and thereby destroy the independence of the judiciary, the only certain shield of individual rights....

Its ultimate operation would be to make this Government one of men rather than one of law, and its practical operation would be to make the Constitution what the executive or legislative branches of the Government choose to say it is—an interpretation to be changed with each change of administration.

It is a measure which should be so emphatically rejected that its parallel will never again be presented to the free representatives of the free people of America.

D. WITHDRAWING JURISDICTION

During the past several decades, Congress has been under strong pressure to withdraw the Supreme Court's jurisdiction to hear appeals in cases of abortion, school busing, school prayer, and other issues on the conservatives' "social agenda." This strategy is based on language in Article III of the Constitution: "The Supreme Court shall have appellate jurisdiction, both as to law and fact, with such exceptions, and under such regulations, as the Congress shall make." The Exceptions Clause, it is argued, gives Congress plenary power to determine the Court's appellate jurisdiction.

Although this approach appears to be grounded on constitutional language, the Exceptions Clause must be read in concert with other provisions in the Constitution. An aggressive use of the Exceptions Clause by Congress would make an exception the rule and deny citizens access to the Supreme Court to vindicate constitutional rights. Stripping the Supreme Court of jurisdiction to hear certain issues would vest ultimate judicial authority in the lower federal and state courts, producing contradictory and conflicting legal doctrines.

A more radical proposal would prevent even the lower federal courts from ruling on specific social issues. Under Article III, the judicial power is vested in a Supreme Court "and in such inferior Courts as the Congress may from time to time ordain and establish." Because Congress creates the lower courts, it may by statute confer, define, and withdraw jurisdiction. Sheldon v. Sill, 49 U.S. (8 How.) 441, 449 (1850). Although Congress has withdrawn jurisdiction to adjudicate certain issues, the exercise of that power "is subject to compliance with at least the requirements of the Fifth Amendment. That is to say, while Congress has the undoubted power to give, withhold, and restrict the jurisdiction of courts other than the Supreme Court, it must not so exercise that power as to deprive any person of life, liberty, or property without due process of law or to take private property without just compensation." Battaglia v. General Motors Corp., 169 F.2d 254, 257 (2d Cir. 1948), cert. denied, 335 U.S. 887 (1948). To deny the lower federal courts jurisdiction to hear claims arising under the Constitution would upset the system of checks and balances, alter the balance of power between the national government and the states, and strengthen the force of majority rule over individual rights (see reading on ABA report).

Withdrawing appellate jurisdiction from the Supreme Court and withdrawing jurisdiction from the lower federal courts would also undercut the Supremacy Clause in Article VI, which states that the Constitution and federal laws "made in Pursuance thereof ... shall be the supreme Law of the Land; and the Judges in every State shall be bound thereby, any Thing in the Constitution or Laws of any State to the contrary notwithstanding." In 1982, the chief justices of the highest state courts issued a unanimous resolution expressing "serious concerns" about bills introduced in Congress to give the states sole authority to decide certain social issues. Among other objections, the chief justices pointed out that the result of such legislation would be contrary to what conservatives professed to be their goal. Instead of overturning Supreme Court decisions, they would be "cast in stone" when state judges continued to honor their oaths to obey the federal Constitution and to give full force (pursuant to the Supremacy Clause) to Supreme Court precedents. The practical effect, therefore, would be to place a body of legal doctrine outside the reach of federal courts or state courts either to alter or overrule. 128 Cong. Rec. 689–90 (1982).

Members of Congress have also attempted to use their power to enforce the Fourteenth Amendment as a lever to alter the jurisdiction of the federal courts. Section 5 of the Fourteenth Amendment gives Congress the power "to enforce, by appropriate legislation," the provisions of that Amendment. In 1981, the Senate Judiciary Committee held hearings on a bill that looked to Section 5 as the vehicle for overturning the Supreme Court's 1973 abortion decision. The hearings covered the scope of Section 5, the issue of whether Congress would be exercising judgments over "facts" or "law," and a possible shift of balance of power between the national government and the states (see reading).

The *McCardle* Case

In a number of early decisions, the Supreme Court recognized the power of Congress to make exceptions and to regulate the Court's appellate jurisdiction.[9] For example, in 1847 the Court stated that it possessed "no appellate power in any case, unless conferred upon it by act of Congress; nor can it, when conferred be exercised in any other form, or by any other mode of proceeding than that which the law prescribes." Barry v. Mercein, 5 How. 103, 119 (1847). These early decisions defined the congressional power too broadly, as will be shown.

The leading case for empowering Congress to withdraw appellate jurisdiction from the Supreme Court is *Ex parte McCardle* (1869). In 1868, Congress withdrew the Court's jurisdiction to review circuit court judgments on habeas corpus actions. The clear purpose was to prevent the Court from deciding a case on the constitutionality of the Reconstruction military government in the South, even though the Court had already heard oral argument in the case of William McCardle. He had been

---

9. Wiscart v. Dauchy, 3 Dall. 321 (1796); Durousseau v. United States, 10 U.S. (6 Cr.) 306 (1810); Daniels v. Railroad Co., 70 U.S. (3 Wall.) 250, 254 (1866).

held in custody awaiting trial by military commission, charged with publishing articles that incited "insurrection, disorder, and violence." Under an act of February 5, 1867, he petitioned a federal circuit court for a writ of habeas corpus. The writ was issued, directing the military commander to deliver McCardle to a federal marshal. After the commander complied with the writ (having denied that the restraint was unlawful), the circuit court rejected McCardle's petition.

At that point McCardle appealed to the Supreme Court. On February 17, 1868, the Court dismissed the government's argument that the Court lacked jurisdiction to hear the case. 73 U.S. (6 Wall.) 318 (1868). The case was argued March 2, 3, 4, and 9. However, before the Court could meet in conference to decide the case, Congress passed legislation to nullify McCardle's relief under the act of February 5, 1867. The new legislation provided that the portion of the 1867 statute that authorized an appeal from the judgment of the circuit court to the Supreme Court, "or the exercise of any such jurisdiction by said Supreme Court on appeals which have been or may hereafter be taken, be, and the same is, hereby repealed." 15 Stat. 44 (1868). Congress wanted to sweep McCardle's case from the docket, fearing that the Court might use it to invalidate the Reconstruction laws.

In a unanimous opinion upholding the repeal statute, Chief Justice Chase stated that the Court was "not at liberty to inquire into the motives of the legislature. We can only examine into its power under the Constitution; and the power to make exceptions to the appellate jurisdiction of this court is given by express words." EX PARTE McCARDLE, 74 U.S. (7 Wall.) 506, 514 (1869). The Court dismissed the case for want of jurisdiction. The Court might have used Section 14 of the Judiciary Act of 1789 to review habeas corpus actions. 1 Stat. 81–82, § 14. To do that in the face of the repeal statute would have invited a major collision with Congress. The House of Representatives had already passed legislation to require a two-thirds majority of the Court to invalidate a federal statute, and some of the more rambunctious Radicals wanted to further trim the power of the Supreme Court.

There is some question whether Congress acted under the Exceptions Clause, even though it forms the basis for the Court's decision. Congress may have merely repealed a special statutory right of access that it had previously granted. As the Court noted a year later, Congress did not repeal alternative rights of access, such as under the Judiciary Act of 1789 and later statutes that expanded the writ of habeas corpus. Ex parte Yerger, 75 U.S. (8 Wall.) 85, 101–02 (1869).

During this same period, Congress passed legislation to remove from federal and state courts their jurisdiction to hear other cases arising from the Civil War. The legislation responded to the Supreme Court's decision in *Ex parte Milligan* (1866), holding that military courts could not function in states where federal courts had been open and operating. Although cases were already pending with regard to the conduct of U.S. officials during and immediately after the war, Congress gave indemnity to all officials who implemented presidential proclamations from March 4, 1861, to June 30, 1866, with respect to martial law and military trials. The statute adds: "And no civil court of the United States, or of any State, or of the District of Columbia, or of any district or territory of the United States, shall have or take jurisdiction of, or in any manner reverse any of the proceedings had or acts done as aforesaid...." 14 Stat. 432, 433 (1867). Legislative debate underscored the determination of Congress to limit the jurisdiction of the courts (see box on next page).

Refinements to *McCardle*

McCardle remains in a shadowy realm, surrounded by conflicting cases that both limit and legitimate congressional power under the Exceptions Clause. Shortly after *McCardle,* the Supreme Court decided *United States* v. *Klein* (1872), which involved a congressional attempt to use the appropriations power to nullify the President's power to pardon. The Court said that Congress had exceeded its authority, first by trying to limit a presidential power granted by the Constitution, and second by preventing a presidential pardon or amnesty from being admitted as evidence in court. The statute was meant to strip the Supreme Court of its jurisdiction over such cases. The Court agreed that the Exceptions Clause gave Congress the power to deny the right of appeal in a particular class of cases, but

Congress Responds to *Milligan*

[James Falconer Wilson, floor manager of this bill for the House Judiciary Committee, explains why Congress had not only the authority but also the obligation to respond to the Court's decision in Ex parte Milligan*]:*

Mr. WILSON, of Iowa....

The object of this part of the bill cannot be mistaken. It is alleged that the President of the United States, in regard to the various matters here enumerated, has acted without authority of law, and that all who have been in any manner associated with him, as instruments in rendering effective his acts, proclamations, and orders, are guilty of infractions of the law, for which they may be indicted, convicted, punished, and subjected to civil actions for the recovery of damages. Many officers and soldiers of the United States have already been made defendants in civil and criminal actions for acts which it is proposed to cover by the broad mantle of this bill....

[*Wilson reviews congressional and judicial precedents that support the pending bill.*] The legislative and judicial action of the Government presents no difficulty in this regard until we reach the recent decision of the Supreme Court in the Milligan case, and even that case interposes no real and valid objection to the passage of this bill. It is true that a majority of the court, in the opinion announced by Mr. Justice Davis, declares that Congress could grant no power to try, in the State of Indiana, a citizen in civil life, in nowise connected with the military service, by a court-martial or military commission, and in so far as this goes the court stands in opposition to this bill. But this is a piece of judicial impertinence which we are not bound to respect. No such question was before the court in the Milligan case, and that tribunal wandered beyond the record in treating of it. Its discussion by the court was out of place, uncalled for, and wholly unjustifiable....

The purpose of the bill is very plainly indicated in its terms, and that is to deprive the civil courts of the United States of all jurisdiction in relation to the acts of military commissions and courts-martial.

SOURCE: Congressional Globe, 39th Cong., 2d Sess. 1484, 1487 (1867).

it could not withhold appellate jurisdiction "as a means to an end" if the end was forbidden under the Constitution. In this case, the effect of withholding appellate jurisdiction was to prescribe impermissible rules of decision for the judiciary in a pending case. 80 U.S. (13 Wall.) 128, 146 (1872).

Other considerations place limits on the Exceptions Clause. For example, Congress could not extend certain rights and then attempt, through the Exceptions Clause, to exclude a particular race or religious group. Such actions would violate the Due Process Clause and the First Amendment. As noted by Laurence H. Tribe, Congress could not deny access to federal courts "to all but white Anglo-Saxon Protestants, or to all who voted in the latest election for a losing candidate." 127 Cong. Rec. 13360 (1981).

The Supreme Court has announced in cases following *McCardle* and *Klein* that its appellate jurisdiction "is confined within such limits as Congress sees fit to prescribe." The "Francis Wright," 105 U.S. 381, 385 (1881). However, the establishment of exceptions and regulations must give "due regard to all the provisions of the Constitution." United States v. Bitty, 208 U.S. 393, 399–400 (1908). For district and appellate courts, Congress "may give, withhold or restrict such jurisdiction at its discretion, provided it be not extended beyond the boundaries fixed by the Constitution." Kline v. Burke Const. Co., 260 U.S. 226, 234 (1922). Precisely what those boundaries are is never said, which is probably prudent. The Court has allowed Congress to limit the availability of certain judicial remedies, such as prohibiting district courts from issuing injunctions to control labor disputes or the enforcement of price regulations. Lauf v. E.G. Shinner & Co., 303 U.S. 323 (1938); Lockerty v. Phillips, 319 U.S. 182 (1942).

Contemporary Issues

An appropriations bill enacted in 1989 raised a possible violation of *Klein*. The bill stated that Congress determined and directed that the management of forests covered by previous legislation was "adequate consideration for the purpose of meeting the statutory requirements" that served as the basis for two pending lawsuits. The Ninth Circuit held that the language in the appropriations bill was unconstitutional under *Klein* because it attempted to direct courts to reach a particular decision. A unanimous Supreme Court disagreed, concluding that the language in the appropriations bill merely changed the law underlying the litigation. Robertson v. Seattle Audubon Soc., 503 U.S. 429 (1992).

Although not technically an issue of withdrawing jurisdiction, in 1995 the Supreme Court referred to the *Klein* and *Seattle Audubon* cases in determining that Congress cannot pass legislation that has the effect of reopening cases that had been dismissed in response to a Supreme Court ruling. The congressional statute was considered a violation of separation of powers. Plaut v. Spendthrift Farm, Inc., 514 U.S. 211 (1995).

A 1996 decision by the Supreme Court directly concerned a possible challenge to the Exceptions Clause. In a unanimous opinion, the Court upheld a congressional statute that placed limits on prisoners who seek to make successive habeas petitions to the Court. After the first appeal, prisoners would need the approval of a three-judge panel before presenting a habeas petition to a trial judge. Felker v. Turpin, 518 U.S. 651 (1996).

These precedents cannot be read to justify the exclusion of whole areas of constitutional law from the Supreme Court.[10] The mere existence of a power does not mean that it may be used without limit. Such a construction runs counter to basic principles of constitutionalism, separation of powers, and checks and balances. The President has the "power" to withhold documents and appropriations, but we live under a system that recognizes limits on executive privilege and impoundment. The Court has the "power" to declare presidential and congressional acts unconstitutional, but it can exercise that power effectively only by acknowledging the limits imposed on it by the political system. The use of the Exceptions Clause must take due regard of an independent judiciary, the Supremacy Clause, and the constitutional rights available to citizens.

Disputes from 2004 to 2012

Twice in 2004 the House voted to strip federal courts of their ability to rule on the constitutionality of certain issues. On July 22, the House voted 233 to 194 to limit federal court jurisdiction over questions under the Defense of Marriage Act (DOMA). The bill language, cross-referencing to DOMA, reads: "No court created by Act of Congress shall have any jurisdiction, and the Supreme Court shall have no appellate jurisdiction, to hear or decide any question pertaining to the interpretation of, or the validity under the Constitution of, section 1738C or this section." 150 Cong. Rec. H6561–69, 6580–13 (daily ed. July 22, 2004); H. Rept. No. 108-614, 108th Cong., 2d sess. (2004). The Senate took no action on the bill.

The second House effort involved the emotional issue of placing the words "under God" in the Pledge of Allegiance. Although the Supreme Court in *Elk Grove Unified School Dist.* v. *Newdow*, 542 U.S. 1 (2004) had held that the plaintiff in this case lacked standing to challenge the constitutionality of this language in the Pledge, the House decided that federal courts should have no future opportu-

---

10. For studies cautioning unbounded use of the Exceptions Clause, see Lawrence Gene Sager, "The Supreme Court, 1980 Term—Foreword: Constitutional Limitations on Congress' Authority to Regulate the Jurisdiction of the Federal Courts," 95 Harv. L. Rev. 17 (1981); Leonard G. Ratner, "Congressional Power over the Appellate Jurisdiction of the Supreme Court," 109 U. Pa. L. Rev. 157 (1960); and Henry M. Hart, Jr., "The Power of Congress to Limit the Jurisdiction of Federal Courts: An Exercise in Dialectic," 66 Harv. L. Rev. 1362 (1953).

nities to rule on the issue. On September 23, voting 247 to 173, the House barred federal courts from hearing this type of Pledge case. The bill language: "No court created by Act of Congress shall have any jurisdiction, and the Supreme Court shall have no appellate jurisdiction, to hear or decide any question pertaining to the interpretation of, or the validity under the Constitution of, the Pledge of Allegiance, as defined in section 4 of title 4, or its recitation." The limitation would not apply to the Superior Court of the District of Columbia or the District of Columbia Court of Appeals. 150 Cong. Rec. H7391–95, 7451–78 (daily ed. Sept. 22–23, 2004); H. Rept. No. 108-691, 108th Cong., 2d Sess. (2004). The Senate did not act on that measure either.

In 2005 and 2006, Congress took several steps in an effort to strip federal courts of jurisdiction to hear cases brought by detainees held at the U.S. naval base in Guantánamo Bay, Cuba. The first appeared in the Detainee Treatment Act of 2005, which placed restrictions on the jurisdiction of federal courts to hear habeas petitions filed by the detainees. P.L. 109-148, 119 Stat. 2741–43 (2005). However, the Supreme Court in *Hamdan v. Rumsfeld*, 548 U.S. 557 (2006) interpreted the statutory language narrowly to permit the detainee in this case to have his appeal heard and decided by the Court. In response, Congress adopted more specific language in the Military Commissions Act of 2006. Section 7 provides that no federal court "shall have jurisdiction to hear or consider an application for a writ of habeas corpus filed by or on behalf of an alien detained by the United States who has been determined by the United States to have been properly detained as an enemy combatant or is awaiting such determination." The D.C. Circuit would have exclusive jurisdiction to determine the validity of any *final decision* rendered by a military commission.

On June 12, 2008, the Supreme Court held that the procedures in the Detainee Treatment Act and the Military Commissions Act, regarding the right of detainees to have their cases heard by federal courts, operated as an unconstitutional suspension of the writ of habeas corpus. The Court emphasized the importance of habeas as a check on arbitrary and unlawful restraint by the executive branch. Boumediene v. Bush, 553 U.S. 723 (2008).

Jurisdiction-Stripping Proposals: ABA Report

Congress has authority under Article III of the Constitution to regulate the jurisdiction of federal district and appellate courts and to make "exceptions" to the appellate jurisdiction of the Supreme Court. That authority, however, must be placed in the context of other constitutional principles and restrictions, an issue discussed below by the Association of the Bar of the City of New York, "Jurisdiction-Stripping Proposals in Congress: The Threat to Judicial Constitutional Review," December 1981. Footnotes omitted.

... There are pending in both houses of Congress at least 25 bills that, if enacted and upheld as constitutional, would have the effect of scrapping the federal courts' historical role in the system of checks and balances. These bills ... would divest the federal courts of all original and appellate jurisdiction to hear cases relating to (1) the constitutionality of programs of "voluntary" prayer in the public schools or other public places, (2) the constitutionality of laws or regulations affecting abortions, (3) busing as a remedy for school segregation, and (4) the constitutionality of treating men and women differently in connection with the armed forces or the draft. One bill, H.R. 114, may be read to go even further—to eliminate all federal judicial review of state court decisions.

In this Report, we do not address the merits of the various federal court decisions on these subjects that have prompted the proposed legislation, nor do we analyze the individual bills in detail. Rather, we address a question that is raised by all such proposals: Is the elimination of federal court jurisdiction to hear constitutional claims a lawful and appropriate response to judicial decisions of which a current majority in Congress disapproves? That question is fundamental to the structure of our government because, if Congress can legitimately curtail the federal courts' jurisdiction to hear constitutional claims concerning such specific issues as school prayer, abortion, and desegregation, then there is no principled limitation on Congress' power effectively to eliminate the judicial branch as a check on the other branches of the federal government or the states. By enacting any of the present bills, Congress would necessarily be claiming the power, should it so choose, to forbid the federal courts to hear *any* claim asserted under the Bill of Rights or under any other provision of the Constitution.

Although most of the proponents of these bills generally style themselves as "conservatives," our review of the historical record reveals that their proposals are *radical* in the most extreme sense of that word. They would not only cast doubt upon the abortion, school prayer, and busing decisions of the past few years, but two centuries of historical development and constitutional doctrine. For the reasons set forth below, we conclude that this radical departure from the system of checks and balances that has served our nation well for the past two centuries is unwise and probably unconstitutional....

Article III of the Constitution does grant Congress power to regulate the jurisdiction of the federal courts.... But, as the following analysis shows, this power cannot fairly be construed to permit Congress to deprive the courts of jurisdiction to hear claims arising under the Constitution itself, particularly on an issue-by-issue basis. If Congress' power were so extensive, it would undo the elaborate system of checks and balances that the Framers of the Constitution so carefully crafted. First, it would upset the checks and balances among the three coordinate

branches of the federal government, eliminating the judiciary as a check upon unconstitutional actions of the political branches by the simple expedient of removing their jurisdiction to consider challenges to such actions. Second, it would disrupt the allocation of power between the federal government and the states, by eliminating the power of the federal judiciary to restrain acts of the states that violate the Constitution. Third, and perhaps most significant, it would alter the constitutional balance between individual rights and majority will, since the judiciary is the only organ of government that is institutionally suited to protect the rights that our Constitution guarantees to individuals against the wishes of a strong-willed majority.

Another serious objection to legislation of the sort currently proposed is that it is undesirable to deal with complex and controversial social issues, particularly those of constitutional dimension, by eliminating the opportunity for full airing and debate in the federal judiciary. Indeed, one of the ironies of the present bills is that the constitutional interpretations with which the bills' sponsors differ would remain frozen as the supreme law of the land forever, binding upon the state courts under the Supremacy Clause and the doctrine of *stare decisis*, without any possibility of change through the evolution of legal thought or a change in judicial (particularly Supreme Court) personnel....

Human Life Bill: Senate Hearings

In response to the Supreme Court's abortion decision in *Roe* v. *Wade,* 410 U.S. 113 (1973), members of Congress looked for ways to overturn the ruling. Possible approaches: define *person* in the Fourteenth Amendment to include life beginning at conception, allow states to enact antiabortion laws, and prevent lower federal courts from striking down those state laws. Members looked for authority to Section 5 of the Fourteenth Amendment, under which Congress may "enforce, by appropriate legislation, the provisions of this article." This approach was defended by Stephen H. Galebach, attorney for Covington & Burling, and opposed by Professor Laurence H. Tribe of the Harvard Law School. "The Human Life Bill," hearings before the Senate Committee on the Judiciary, 97th Cong., 1st Sess. (1981).

STEPHEN H. GALEBACH:

In its 1973 abortion decision, the Supreme Court declared that it was unable to determine whether unborn children were human beings. The Court also held that unborn children were not persons within the meaning of the 14th amendment and that a woman's right to privacy took precedence over the State's right to protect potential life until a fetus had become viable.

The Supreme Court thus left unresolved the fundamental question of whether unborn children are human beings. The answer to this question necessarily influences the proper resolution of the abortion issue. However, if the Supreme Court is unable to decide when human life begins, who can make that decision? I submit that under the Constitution, Congress can make that decision.

The 5th and 14th amendments to the Constitution provide that no person may be deprived of life without due process of law. The 14th amendment expressly authorizes Congress to enforce its protections by appropriate legislation.

If Congress examines the question the Supreme Court was unable to answer and concludes that unborn children are human beings, then the Court's conclusion that they are not persons would be subject to change, and Congress would have the power to enforce the 14th amendment by declaring that unborn children are persons within the meaning of that amendment.

In my law review article, I explained the constitutional justification of the human life bill in terms of two leading theories advanced by Supreme Court Justices concerning the power of Congress to enforce 14th amendment rights.

The first theory is found in Justice Brennan's majority opinion in the landmark case of *Katzenbach* v. *Morgan*. Under this theory, Congress has broad power to define the scope and meaning of the 14th amendment rights so long as it acts to expand those rights.

The second theory is found in Justice Harlan's dissenting opinion in *Katzenbach* v. *Morgan*. Justice Harlan took a narrower view of Congress power, allowing Congress to make legislative findings that influence constitutional determinations, but reserving to the Court the authority to make the ultimate constitutional decision.

The majority opinion in *Katzenbach* v. *Morgan* is controversial because it confers on Congress such broad power to redefine the 14th amendment rights and to force its view on the Supreme Court. There is serious question whether the Court would or should reaffirm such a broad precedent today.

However, the constitutionality of the human life bill does not depend on the validity of such a broad theory of Congress power. The narrow enforcement power described by Justice Harlan is sufficient to justify the human life bill.

... The key sentence in Justice Harlan's opinion in *Katzenbach* v. *Morgan* is as follows:

"To the extent 'legislative facts' are relevant to a judicial determination, Congress is well equipped to investigate them, and such determinations are of course entitled to due respect."

According to this theory, congressional findings influence the Supreme Court, but do not necessarily control the Court's decisions. For example, in the 1965 and 1970 Voting Rights Acts, Congress influenced the Supreme Court to conclude that literacy tests for voting were racially discriminatory, even though in 1959 the Court held them not to be discriminatory. The Supreme Court was not persuaded, on the other hand, by Congress finding that equal protection requires the extension of voting rights to 18-year-olds in State elections.

. . .

... [T]he Supreme Court will have to reevaluate the proper balance between the privacy right and the right to life of unborn children. The Supreme Court will still have the final say. The human life bill does not dictate what the result must be. All the bill does is ask the Court to look at the issue again in light of Congress' answer to the question that the Court said it could not resolve, namely, when does human life begin.

LAURENCE H. TRIBE:

The fact that a question is profound and important does not mean that Government must tell us how to answer it. The whole point of the Supreme Court's decision in 1973 was not simply one of judicial incapacity, for right after the Court said that it was unable to answer the question of when human life begins, the Court explained that what it really meant was that no State, by adopting its own answer to that question — choosing one theory of life rather than another — could be permitted to override the fundamental right of the pregnant woman to give an answer for herself.

One may disagree with that view. One may disagree with the view that this fundamental question must be left to the woman. However, if one disagrees with that view, one is not disagreeing on a question of fact — What is the fetus? What is a human being? — but on a basic proposition of constitutional law.

The only way to undo a proposition of constitutional law announced by the Court is by constitutional amendment, not by legislative redefinition of constitutional language and not by waving the magic wand of section 5 of the 14th amendment and saying, "We will now inform the Court as to what the fertilized ovum is." ...

Let me close with a concern that I have that would persist even if this law were to be upheld, even if it were deemed to be constitutional.

I believe that S. 158 is inherently and unavoidably defective as measured by its own aims. I think the chairman stated the reasonable aims in a way that I found almost compelling when he said that we are simply trying to return to the States a matter that perhaps ought never to have been taken over by the

Federal Government in the first place. If these matters are divisive, if they are unclear, why try to resolve them nationally? Why not decentralize?

However, observe that that is not, despite its intentions, what this law does. To begin with, on the matter of State and local funding for abortions, the law leaves States no choice. In Massachusetts and in California, the State constitutions require public funds to be expended without discrimination against abortion. Under this law, spending on abortion would be forbidden because that would, if this law were upheld, amount to State action which destroys the lives of persons.

To that degree at least, the matter is suddenly nationalized and not restored to its condition as it was in 1973....

It seems to me this measure is clearly unconstitutional. That it would be so held by the Supreme Court is not a matter of guesswork. It is not a responsible thing, however well-intentioned, for this Congress to do. I would regard it as a very sad day were this very serious, difficult issue to become the occasion for futile confrontation between the Congress and the Supreme Court, with a predictable outcome—one that would not enhance respect for either body, and one that would not advance the cause either of women or of unborn life.

Ex Parte McCardle

74 U.S. (7 Wall.) 506 (1869)

William H. McCardle, a Southern editor, had been arrested under the Reconstruction Acts and tried before a military commission for publishing articles considered incendiary and libelous. After his petition for a writ of habeas corpus was denied by a federal circuit court in Mississippi, the Supreme Court accepted jurisdiction and held oral argument. It was widely speculated that the Court might hold the Reconstruction Acts unconstitutional. Congress had begun the impeachment of President Andrew Johnson, partly for his opposition to the Reconstruction Acts. To prevent a decision on the constitutionality of the Reconstruction Acts, Congress passed legislation to withdraw the appellate jurisdiction of the Supreme Court in McCardle's case.

The CHIEF JUSTICE delivered the opinion of the court.

The first question necessarily is that of jurisdiction; for, if the act of March, 1868, takes away the jurisdiction defined by the act of February, 1867, it is useless, if not improper, to enter into any discussion of other questions.

It is quite true, as was argued by the counsel for the petitioner, that the appellate jurisdiction of this court is not derived from acts of Congress. It is, strictly speaking, conferred by the Constitution. But it is conferred "with such exceptions and under such regulations as Congress shall make."

It is unnecessary to consider whether, if Congress had made no exceptions and no regulations, this court might not have exercised general appellate jurisdiction under rules prescribed by itself. For among the earliest acts of the first Congress, at its first session, was the act of September 24th, 1789, to establish the judicial courts of the United States. That act provided for the organization of this court; and prescribed regulations for the exercise of its jurisdiction.

The source of that jurisdiction, and the limitations of it by the Constitution and by statute, have been on several occasions subjects of consideration here. In the case of *Durousseau* v. *The United States,* particularly, the whole matter was carefully examined, and the court held, that while "the appellate powers of this court are not given by the judicial act, but are given by the Constitution," they are, nevertheless, "limited and regulated by that act, and by such other acts as have been passed on the subject." The court said, further, that the judicial act was an exercise of the power given by the Constitution to Congress "of making exceptions to the appellate jurisdiction of the Supreme Court." "They have described affirmatively," said the court, "its jurisdiction, and this affirmative description has been understood to imply a negation of the exercise of such appellate power as is not comprehended within it."

The principle that the affirmation of appellate jurisdiction implies the negation of all such jurisdiction not affirmed having been thus established, it was an almost necessary consequence that acts of Congress, providing for the exercise of jurisdiction, should come to be spoken of as acts granting jurisdiction, and not as acts making exceptions to the constitutional grant of it.

The exception to appellate jurisdiction in the case before us, however, is not an inference from the affirmation of other appellate jurisdiction. It is made in terms. The provision of the act of 1867, affirming the appellate jurisdiction of this court in cases of *habeas corpus* is expressly repealed. It is hardly possible to imagine a plainer instance of positive exception.

We are not at liberty to inquire into the motives of the legislature. We can only examine into its power under the Constitution; and the power to make exceptions to the appellate jurisdiction of this court is given by express words.

What, then, is the effect of the repealing act upon the case before us? We cannot doubt as to this. Without jurisdiction the court cannot proceed at all in any cause. Jurisdiction is power to declare the law, and when it ceases to exist, the only function remaining to the court is that of announcing the fact and dismissing the cause. And this is not less clear upon authority than upon principle.

Several cases were cited by the counsel for the petitioner in support of the position that jurisdiction of this case is not affected by the repealing act. But none of them, in our judgment, afford any support to it. They are all cases of the exercise of judicial power by the legislature, or of legislative interference with courts in the exercising of continuing jurisdiction.

On the other hand, the general rule, supported by the best elementary writers, is, that "when an act of the legislature is repealed, it must be considered, except as to transactions past and closed, as if it never existed." And the effect of repealing acts upon suits under acts repealed, has been determined by the adjudications of this court. The subject was fully considered in *Norris* v. *Crocker,* and more recently in *Insurance Company* v. *Ritchie.* In both of these cases it was held that no judgment could be rendered in a suit after the repeal of the act under which it was brought and prosecuted.

It is quite clear, therefore, that this court cannot proceed to pronounce judgment in this case, for it has no longer jurisdiction of the appeal; and judicial duty is not less fitly performed by declining ungranted jurisdiction than in exercising firmly that which the Constitution and the laws confer.

Counsel seemed to have supposed, if effect be given to the repealing act in question, that the whole appellate power of the court, in cases of *habeas corpus,* is denied. But this is an error. The act of 1868 does not except from that jurisdiction any cases but appeals from Circuit Courts under the act of 1867. It does not affect the jurisdiction which was previously exercised.

The appeal of the petitioner in this case must be

Dismissed for want of jurisdiction.

E. NONCOMPLIANCE

In a masterful phrase, rendered almost hypnotic by its elegance, Justice Jackson said: "We are not final because we are infallible, but we are infallible only because we are final." Brown v. Allen, 344 U.S. 443, 540 (1953). The historical record demonstrates convincingly that the Supreme Court is neither infallible nor final. The lack of finality is evident in the fluid quality of its decisions, reshaped over the years by all three branches. Furthermore, the Court often experiences substantial difficulty in obtaining full compliance with decisions when they are handed down. Noncompliance is a direct threat to the Court's dignity, authority, legitimacy, and reputation (see reading "Sustaining Public Confidence").

In theory, judicial opinions are binding on the public and the other branches of government. In practice, judicial opinions are implemented with varying degrees of fidelity by local and federal officials. Noncompliance sometimes results from deliberate evasion, as in the South's "massive resistance" to the desegregation cases. Unintentional violations may also occur, but they can be relieved by adequate education and clear judicial rulings. Between these two positions are various shades of avoidance and evasion.

In 1983, the Supreme Court held that the "legislative veto," used by Congress for 50 years to control executive actions, was unconstitutional. INS v. Chadha, 462 U.S. 919 (1983). Over the following years, however, Congress passed more than 600 additional legislative vetoes, all signed into law by Presidents Reagan, Bush I, Clinton, Bush II, and Obama. Moreover, Congress continued to exercise other instruments of control that are the functional equivalent of the legislative veto. Although the Court had announced one of the most important separation of powers cases of all time, the practical effect was not nearly as sweeping as the Court's decision (see readings on legislative veto in Chapter 6).

One source of noncompliance is poor communication of judicial opinions. Scholars have found that most people do not know or understand decisions rendered by the courts. Instead, the public receives abbreviated interpretations, often erroneous, from the media and local officials. For a variety of reasons, the media have difficulty providing adequate coverage of the courts.

Second, the sheer force of inertia limits compliance. Court decisions must pass through the perceptual screens of citizens who believe that current practices can persist with only slight modifications. A half century after *Engel* v. *Vitale*, 370 U.S. 421 (1962), which struck down state-sponsored prayers in public schools, school authorities continue to set aside time during the day for students to say prayers (see reading). Local officials may prefer to reinterpret judicial decisions on church-state separation to minimize the level of conflict and dissension within their communities.[11]

Lower-Court Implementation

Decisions by the Supreme Court and federal appellate courts are filtered through U.S. district courts and state courts. Lower courts, legislatures, and administrators have a number of ways to avoid full compliance. Lower courts can reinterpret rulings. Parties can relitigate to delay implementation or appeal to legislators to reverse a ruling that turns on statutory interpretation. When the Supreme Court reverses a lower court decision, it may remand the case for disposition "not inconsistent with this opinion." In this new round, the litigant who found success at the Supreme Court level may lose out in the lower courts. 67 Harv. L. Rev. 1251 (1954). For a specific example of this surprise reversal, see the box in Section G of Chapter 1.

If the Court's opinion is a patchwork quilt, stitched together from disparate strands of conflicting views in the majority, the leeway for lower courts and elected officials will be substantial. Ambiguities can result from "inadvertence, or because of a deliberate fudging or vagueness built into the opinion to secure the support of a wavering colleague." Davis & Reynolds, 1974 Duke L. J. 59, 71. When the Supreme Court is unable to muster a majority of Justices behind a decision and instead merely releases a plurality opinion, a confused message is sent to lower courts (state and federal) and to the legislative and executive branches.

Judges in the lower courts have substantial latitude in applying Supreme Court doctrines. Justice Thurgood Marshall, after dissenting in a case that reversed the Second Circuit, later met with the judges from that circuit and urged them to read the Court's decision narrowly (see box).

In 1985, Justice Brennan said that the Court's rulings on *Miranda*-type cases "have led nearly every lower court to reject its simplistic reasoning." Oregon v. Elstad, 470 U.S. 298, 320 (1985) (dissenting opinion). He pointed out that the Court's reasoning "is sufficiently obscured and qualified as to leave state and federal courts with continued authority to combat obvious flouting by the authorities of the privilege against self-incrimination. I am confident that lower courts will exercise this authority responsibly, as they have for the most part prior to this Court's intervention." Id. at 346.

After the Supreme Court handed down its Desegregation Decision in 1954, lower court judges followed different paths in implementing the ruling. Some were faithful; others were defiant or evasive. Many federal judges were torn between the edict of the High Court and the sentiments and customs of their local communities. It has been said that the Constitution is what the Supreme Court says it is, but Supreme Court decisions often mean what district courts say they mean. Jack W. Peltason, Federal Courts in the Political Process 14 (1955).

---

11. Kenneth M. Dolbeare and Phillip E. Hammond, The School Prayer Decisions: From Court Policy to Local Practice (1971); Frank J. Sorauf, "*Zorach* v. *Clauson*: The Impact of a Supreme Court Decision," 53 Am. Pol. Sci. Rev. 777 (1959); Gordon Patric, "The Impact of a Court Decision: Aftermath of the McCollum Case," 6 J. Pub. L. 455 (1957).

Justice Thurgood Marshall Encourages Lower Courts to Protect Rights More Expansively than Supreme Court

Dissenting in *Bell* v. *Wolfish* (1979), a case involving the rights of prisoners, Justice Marshall argued that the lower courts were correct the first time when they concluded that pretrial detainees should not be subjected to certain procedures (such as body-cavity searches) while in jail awaiting trial. As part of his responsibilities for supervising the Second Circuit (which had been reversed in this case), Marshall gave an address before the judges of that circuit and said that he "can only hope that district and appellate judges will read the [Court's] decision narrowly." His conclusion produced gasps from the audience: "Ill-conceived reversals should be considered as no more than temporary interruptions." The New York Times, May 28, 1979, at A1, A11.

As noted by political scientist Sotirios Barber: "Justice Marshall's remarks attracted an unusual amount of public attention, for this was not the kind of talk one usually hears from members of the Supreme Court.... Surely, a measure of shock was understandable; here was a top judicial official appearing to exhort the judges of his circuit to take advantage of whatever opportunities they might have to undermine the will of the Supreme Court. Justice Marshall knew that his advice could have an effect on the course of decision in the lower courts." Sotirios A. Barber, On What the Constitution Means 3 (1984).

Sustaining Public Confidence

In *Baker* v. *Carr,* 369 U.S. 186 (1962), the Supreme Court accepted jurisdiction to decide the politically volatile issue of legislative reapportionment. Justice Frankfurter, who had written the Court's opinion in *Colegrove* v. *Green,* 328 U.S. 549 (1946), describing reapportionment as "of a peculiarly political nature and therefore not meet for judicial determination," dissented in *Baker.* Although he proved to be a false prophet by overstating the difficulties of judicial remedies to malapportionment, his dissent explains that the Court's ultimate authority is not its status as the "court of last resort" but rather its ability to sustain public confidence in the moral force of its opinions.

MR. JUSTICE FRANKFURTER, whom MR. JUSTICE HARLAN joins, dissenting.

The Court today reverses a uniform course of decision established by a dozen cases, including one by which the very claim now sustained was unanimously rejected only five years ago. The impressive body of rulings thus cast aside reflected the equally uniform course of our political history regarding the relationship between population and legislative representation—a wholly different matter from denial of the franchise to individuals because of race, color, religion or sex. Such a massive repudiation of the experience of our whole past in asserting destructively novel judicial power demands a detailed analysis of the role of this Court in our constitutional scheme. Disregard of inherent limits in the effective exercise of the Court's "judicial Power" not only presages the futility of judicial intervention in the essentially political conflict of forces by which the relation between

population and representation has time out of mind been and now is determined. It may well impair the Court's position as the ultimate organ of "the supreme Law of the Land" in that vast range of legal problems, often strongly entangled in popular feeling, on which this Court must pronounce. The Court's authority—possessed of neither the purse nor the sword—ultimately rests on sustained public confidence in its moral sanction. Such feeling must be nourished by the Court's complete detachment, in fact and in appearance, from political entanglements and by abstention from injecting itself into the clash of political forces in political settlements.

... [T]here is not under our Constitution a judicial remedy for every political mischief, for every undesirable exercise of legislative power. The Framers carefully and with deliberate forethought refused so to enthrone the judiciary. In this situation, as in others of like nature, appeal for relief does not belong here. Appeal must be to an informed, civically militant electorate. In a democratic society like ours, relief must come through an aroused popular conscience that sears the conscience of the people's representatives. In any event there is nothing judi-cially more unseemly nor more self-defeating than for this Court to make *in terrorem* pronouncements, to indulge in merely empty rhetoric, sounding a word of promise to the ear, sure to be disappointing to the hope.

Prayers in Public Schools

In *Engel* v. *Vitale,* 370 U.S. 421 (1962), the Supreme Court struck down state-sponsored prayers in public schools. Nevertheless, school authorities across the nation permitted prayers to continue, sometimes by acquiescing to the initiatives of individual teachers, sometimes by directly intervening to assure a daily prayer. The following extracts are from an article by David E. Rosenbaum, "Prayer in Many Schoolrooms Continues Despite '62 Ruling," *The New York Times*, March 11, 1984, Section 1, pp. 1, 32.

The 31 children in Alvenia P. Hunter's second-grade class at the Pratt Elementary School in Birmingham, Ala., began the school day Thursday as they do every day, by bowing their heads for prayer.

In unison, they recited: "O, help me please each day to find new ways of just being kind. At home, at work, at school and play, please help me now and every day. Amen."

Mrs. Hunter's class is one of many across the nation where, despite the Supreme Court's prohibition of organized prayer in the schools more than 20 years ago, students continue to recite prayers, sing hymns or read the Bible aloud.

Many more students observe a period of silence in which they can pray if they want, a practice the Supreme Court has neither upheld nor rejected.

There is no organized worship in most of the country's public schools. In the main, educators have accepted the Supreme Court's doctrine that prayer prescribed by government or led by a teacher, a government employee, violates the First Amendment sanction against "establishment of religion." ...

A spot check of schools in communities from coast to coast last week revealed practices ranging from that in Iowa, where few schools had organized prayers even before the Supreme Court outlawed them in 1962, a practice that continues, to that in North Carolina, where a survey found regular prayer

recitation and Bible readings in 39 of the state's 100 counties.

Mrs. Hunter, who has been a teacher for 18 years, said she had never heard an objection to her classroom prayer from a parent or a principal. "I believe in doing things right," she said. "I have been given the strength to come here and the ability to teach. This way I am thanking my God for enabling me to come here to work."

Louis Dale, president of the Birmingham School Board, said that the board had an official policy against organized prayer in the schools but that the policy was not enforced. He said he was personally of two minds about the matter.

. . .

In some places, parents who complained about prayers in the schools have been ostracized, or worse.

Three years ago, two mothers sued to stop organized prayers in the schools in Little Axe, Okla., a rural community southeast of Oklahoma City. One of the women, JoAnn Bell, a member of the Church of the Nazarene, argued that other people should not tell her children how to pray. She said last week that after she won her suit in Federal court, she was beaten by a school worker and her home was set afire, so she moved.

F. CONSTITUTIONAL DIALOGUES

"Judicial sacrosanctity" can be a useful rallying cry to protect the independence of the courts from external attacks. The concept is a powerful talisman for warding off major court-curbing efforts, such as court-packing or the withdrawal of appellate jurisdiction. However, it is ineffective in preventing Congress from passing laws to reverse statutory interpretations by the courts. No one doubts the right of Congress to pass legislation that overturns what it considers to be judicial misinterpretations of statutes. But even when the courts render a constitutional interpretation, it is usually only a matter of time before Congress prevails. Through changes in the composition of courts or adjustments in the attitudes of judges who continue to sit, a determined majority in Congress is likely to have its way. At some point a similar statute, struck down in the past as unconstitutional, will find acceptance in the courts. That pattern has been evident in such areas as commerce, federalism, and civil rights.

Do these congressional challenges to the Court threaten to usurp judicial responsibilities? If the Constitution could be interpreted in mechanical fashion, left unchanged over the years and with few dissenting or even concurring opinions, and if the record revealed precious few instances of the Court reversing itself, this argument might have merit. But if the function of the Supreme Court is to apply the general language of the Constitution to changing needs, and if the Constitution is developmental rather than static in meaning, there can be no doubt about the propriety of legislation that prompts the Court to reconsider its decisions.

When the Supreme Court struck down the first effort by Congress to regulate child labor, Congress shifted the basis for national legislation from the commerce power to the taxing power. That effort was also invalidated by the Supreme Court. By 1938 Congress had returned to the commerce power, and this time the legislation was upheld by a unanimous court. United States v. Darby, 312 U.S. 100 (1941). Similar examples can be cited. Congress decided to pass the Civil Rights Act of 1964, despite its apparent collision with the *Civil Rights Cases*, 109 U.S. 3 (1883). This conflict between judicial doctrine and legislative aspirations did not prevent Congress from acting. It avoided a direct confrontation with the judiciary by basing the statute not only on the Fourteenth Amendment but also on the Commerce Clause. The Supreme Court promptly upheld the Act as a valid exercise of congressional power. Heart of Atlanta Motel v. United States, 379 U.S. 241 (1964); Katzenbach v. McClung, 379 U.S. 294 (1964).

The "Continuing Colloquy"

Through what Alexander Bickel once called the Court's "continuing colloquy" with the political branches and society at large, the judiciary's search for constitutional principles can be reconciled with democratic values. Bickel, The Least Dangerous Branch 240 (1962). An open dialogue between Congress and the courts is a more fruitful avenue for constitutional interpretation than simply believing that the judiciary possesses unequaled skills and authority.

No one doubts that Congress, like the Court, can reach unconstitutional results. As Justice Brennan said in a 1983 dissent: "Legislators, influenced by the passions and exigencies of the moment, the pressure of constituents and colleagues, and the press of business, do not always pass sober constitutional judgment on every piece of legislation they enact." Marsh v. Chambers, 463 U.S. 783, 814 (1983). Yet if we count the times that Congress has been "wrong" about the Constitution and compare those lapses with the occasions when the Court has been "wrong" by its own later admissions, the results make a compelling case for legislative confidence and judicial modesty. George Anastaplo has noted that "in the great crises over the past two hundred years, when Congress and the Supreme Court have differed on major issues, Congress has been correct." Center Magazine, November/December 1986, at 15.

There is no justification for deferring automatically to the judiciary because of its doctrinal announcements and political independence. Each decision by a court is subject to scrutiny and rejection by private citizens and public officials. What is "final" at one stage of political development may be reopened at some later date, leading to revisions, fresh interpretations, and reversals of Court decisions. Through this process of interaction among the branches, all three institutions are able to expose weaknesses, hold excesses in check, and gradually forge a consensus on constitutional issues. Also through that process, the public has an opportunity to add a legitimacy and a meaning to what might otherwise be an alien and short-lived document.

Arguments for Judicial Finality

At certain moments in U.S. constitutional history, there has been a compelling need for an authoritative and binding decision by the Supreme Court. The unanimous ruling in 1958, signed by each Justice, was essential in dealing with the Little Rock crisis. Cooper v. Aaron, 358 U.S. 1 (1958). Another unanimous decision in 1974 disposed of the confrontation between President Nixon and the judiciary regarding the Watergate tapes. United States v. Nixon, 418 U.S. 683 (1974). These moments are rare. Usually the Court makes a series of exploratory movements followed by backing and filling—a necessary and sensible tactic for resolving constitutional issues that have profound political, social, and economic ramifications.

For the most part, Court decisions are tentative and reversible like other political events. The Court is not the Constitution. To accept the two as equivalent is to relinquish individual responsibility and the capacity for self-government. Popular sovereignty should not be made subordinate to judicial supremacy. Constitutional determinations are not exclusively for the courts. Individuals outside the courts have their own judgments to make. They cannot abdicate the duty to think for themselves. What is constitutional or unconstitutional must be left for citizens to explore, ponder, and come to terms with. Attorney General Edwin Meese III presented a controversial speech in 1986, in which he challenged the belief that the Constitution is equivalent to Supreme Court decisions (see reading). The "finality" of Supreme Court decisions was examined during Senate hearings in 1986 on William Rehnquist's nomination as Chief Justice and a year later on Anthony Kennedy's nomination as Associate Justice. Their attitudes were fundamentally different (see reading).

An "activist" member of the judiciary, Earl Warren, explained the limits of the courts. In times of political stress, the courts may acquiesce to actions that we later deplore. Commenting on the Court's role in upholding the treatment of Japanese-Americans during World War II, he said: "the fact that the Court rules in a case like *Hirabayashi* that a given program is constitutional, does not necessarily answer the question whether, in a broader sense, it actually is." The underlying message: a judicial failure to strike down a governmental action does not mean that constitutional standards have been followed. The habit of looking automatically to the courts to protect constitutional liberties is ill-advised. Warren concluded that under our political system the judiciary must play a limited role: "In our democracy it is still the Legislature and the elected Executive who have the primary responsibility for fashioning and executing policy consistent with the Constitution" (see box on next page).

The belief in judicial supremacy imposes a burden that the Court cannot carry. It sets up expectations that invite disappointment if not disaster. A President once reassured his country in an inaugural address that an issue deeply dividing the nation "legitimately belongs to the Supreme Court of the United States, before whom it is now pending, and will, it is understood, be speedily and finally settled." The President was James Buchanan. The case about to be decided: *Dred Scott* v. *Sandford*, 60 U.S. (19 How.) 393 (1857).[12]

In her book, *The Majesty of the Law* (2003), Justice Sandra Day O'Connor examined the assertion that the judiciary's word on the meaning of the Constitution is final. She said that if "one looks at the history of the Court, the country, and the Constitution over a very long period, the relationship appears to be more of a dialogue than a series of commands." As to the Court's decision in *Roe v. Wade*, 410 U.S. 113 (1973), she points out that it did not end the debate over abortion rights: "A nation that docilely and unthinkingly approved every Supreme Court decision as infallible and immutable would, I believe, have severely disappointed our founders" (pp. 44, 45).

---

12. Judicial supremacy on constitutional issues was recently endorsed by Larry Alexander and Frederick Schauer, "On Extrajudicial Constitutional Interpretation," 110 Harv. L. Rev. 1359 (1997). For a rebuttal, see Neal Devins and Louis Fisher, "Judicial Exclusivity and Political Instability," 84 Va. L. Rev. 83 (1998). See also: Devins and Fisher, The Democratic Constitution (2004).

Chief Justice Warren Disputes Judicial Supremacy

Whatever may be the correct view of the specific holding of these cases [regarding the rights of Japanese-Americans during World War II], their importance for present purposes lies in a more general consideration. These decisions demonstrate dramatically that there are some circumstances in which the Court will, in effect, conclude that it is simply not in a position to reject descriptions by the Executive of the degree of military necessity. Thus, in a case like *Hirabayashi*, only the Executive is qualified to determine whether, for example, an invasion is imminent....

The consequence of the limitations under which the Court must sometimes operate in this area is that other agencies of government must bear the primary responsibility for determining whether specific actions they are taking are consonant with our Constitution. To put it another way, the fact that the Court rules in a case like *Hirabayashi* that a given program is constitutional, does not necessarily answer the question whether, in a broader sense, it actually is....

In concluding, I must say that I have, of course, not touched upon every type of situation having some relation to our military establishment which the Court considers. Those to which I have pointed might suggest to some that the Court has at times exceeded its role in this area. My view of the matter is the opposite. I see how limited is the role that the courts can truly play in protecting the heritage of our people against military supremacy. In our democracy it is still the Legislature and the elected Executive who have the primary responsibility for fashioning and executing policy consistent with the Constitution. Only an occasional aberration from norms of operation is brought before the Court by some zealous litigant. Thus we are sometimes provided with opportunities for reiterating the fundamental principles on which our country was founded and has grown mighty. But the day-to-day job of upholding the Constitution really lies elsewhere. It rests, realistically, on the shoulders of every citizen.

SOURCE: Earl Warren, "The Bill of Rights and the Military," 37 N.Y.U. L. Rev. 181, 192–93, 202 (1962).

The Last-Word Doctrine

Although constitutional law and constitutional values have never been monopolized by the courts over the past two centuries, many scholars, judges, reporters and other observers continue to say that the Supreme Court has the final word on constitutional disputes. Such statements fail to address the following realities.

1. The fact that the Supreme Court upholds the constitutionality of a measure, as when it sustained the U.S. Bank in *McCulloch v. Maryland*, 17 U.S. (4 Wheat.) 315 (1819), places no obligation on executive and legislative branches to agree with that judgment. Congress was free to discontinue the Bank. If it passed legislation to renew it, President Jackson was within his rights to veto the bill. A decision by the Supreme Court did not relieve the other branches of their duty or freedom to reach independent interpretations.

2. A decision by the Supreme Court that a certain practice is not prohibited by the Constitution, such as the use of search warrants in *Zurcher* v. *Stanford Daily*, 436 U.S. 547 (1978) or access to bank records in *United States* v. *Miller*, 425 U.S. 435 (1976), does not prevent the other branches from passing legislation to prohibit or restrict these practices. Rights unprotected by the courts may be secured by Congress and the President.

3. When the Supreme Court concludes that an action has no constitutional protection in the federal courts—for example, distributing petitions in a shopping center, as in *PruneYard Shopping Center* v. *Robins*, 447 U.S. 74 (1980)—the states are not inhibited in any way from protecting those actions through their own constitutional interpretations. Decisions by the Supreme Court set a floor,

or minimum, for constitutional rights. States may exceed those rights through independent interpretations of their own constitutions and unique cultures.

4. Many constitutional issues are resolved through rules of evidence, statutes, customs, and accommodations—a common-law method of settling disputes. Through these techniques, institutions outside the courts play a decisive role in shaping not only constitutional values but also constitutional doctrines.

5. There are occasions when Supreme Court rulings strike such a discordant note in the body politic that they will be tested again and again with new variations on the same theme. Court decisions are entitled to respect, not adoration. When the Court issues its judgment, we should not suspend ours. These challenges and collisions help keep the constitutional dialogue open and vigorous. In the search for a harmony between constitutional law and self-government, we must all participate.

6. It is unrealistic to expect the Court to "settle" an important issue at a single stroke. Typically, the Court tackles one slice of an issue, leaving the rest for subsequent court decisions and nonjudicial actions. Justice Ginsburg put it this way: "In our system of adjudication, matters seldom can be fully settled 'on the basis of one or two cases'; they generally 'require a closer working out,' often involving responses by, or a continuing dialogue with, other branches of government, the States, or the private sector." Ginsburg, 83 Geo. L. J. 2119, 2125 (1995), citing language from Roscoe Pound.

7. The Court generally announces broad guidelines: "undue burden," "compelling governmental interest," "narrowly tailored," "all deliberate speed," and "prurient" material. It is up to elected officials (and juries) to apply those general principles to particular cases. The Court defines the edges; nonjudicial actors fill in the important middle.

8. Through the use of threshold doctrines and prudential considerations, the courts often duck constitutional issues and leave them to the regular political process. For example, the meaning of the Statement and Account Clause for covert spending by the intelligence community was decided by the legislative and executive branches.

9. Judicial decisions are not pure creative acts. They build on precedents and values established by other actors, both at the national and state levels. Long before *Gideon* v. *Wainwright*, 372 U.S. 335 (1963), many states had decided that due process required that attorneys be appointed to represent indigent defendants. Federal courts often look for guidance to state practices and congressional judgments.

10. In many cases the Court does have finality, of a sort. In the summer of 1998, when Chief Justice Rehnquist turned down a White House effort to prevent the Office of Independent Counsel from questioning Secret Service agents about Monica Lewinsky's visits to President Clinton, within two hours the agents were called to testify in the grand jury room. However, Congress may reopen the issue by enacting legislation that gives Secret Service agents greater privilege not to testify about presidential activities. Thus, there are interim points of finality. On complex and overarching issues, like abortion, affirmative action, religious freedom, and the death penalty, there is no finality until a consensus is reached by all of the branches and society at large.

In 2008, Linda Greenhouse summed up 30 years of legal reporting for the *New York Times*. What she witnessed over that period was not a Supreme Court occupying a dominant position in deciding constitutional law, but rather Justices engaged "in the ceaseless American dialogue about constitutional values." Judicial rulings were not accepted as the "final voice" about a dispute. Elected leaders at the national and state level could respond by trying to do indirectly what the Court had just said it could not do directly, producing a "constitutional Ping-Pong match." The Court, she cautioned, "can only do so much. It can lead, but the country does not necessarily follow." The Court often found itself following nonjudicial decisions. It "ratifies or consolidates changes rather than propelling it." As a result, Justices "live in constant dialogue with other institutions, formal and informal." Judicial rulings can collide with policies adopted by legitimate participants outside the Court. On those occasions "it is often the court that eventually retreats when it finds itself out of sync with the prevailing mood." Linda Greenhouse, "2,691 Decisions," New York Times, July 13, 2008, WK 1, 4.

Is the Supreme Court the Constitution?

On October 21, 1986, Attorney General Edwin Meese III presented an address at Tulane University called "The Law of the Constitution." He referred to the Constitution as fundamental law, capable of change only by constitutional amendment, and contrasted that "higher law" to the body of law developed by the Supreme Court. He quoted from constitutional historian Charles Warren that "however the Court may interpret the provisions of the Constitution, it is still the Constitution which is the law, not the decisions of the Court." Meese's address sent shock waves across the country. Some columnists called the speech a "stink bomb" that showed disrespect for the Court. One newspaper column claimed that the speech invited anarchy. Other commentators predicted "enormous chaos" if Meese's view ever prevailed. His speech provides an important backdrop for the next reading, which is a colloquy between Senator Arlen Specter and Judge Anthony Kennedy on the Court's authority and power to issue the "final word" in constitutional law.

. . .

Since becoming Attorney General, I have had the pleasure to speak about the Constitution on several occasions. I have tried to examine it from many angles. I have discussed its moral foundations. I have also addressed on separate occasions its great structural principles—federalism and separation of powers. Tonight I would like to look at it from yet another perspective and try to develop further some of the views that I have already expressed. Specifically, I would like to consider a distinction that is essential to maintaining our limited form of government. That is the necessary distinction between the Constitution and constitutional law. The two are not synonymous.

What, then, is this distinction?

The Constitution is—to put it simply but, one hopes, not simplistically—the Constitution. It is a document of our most fundamental law. It begins "We the People of the United States, in Order to form a more perfect Union ..." and ends up, some 6,000 words later, with the 26th Amendment. It creates the institutions of our government, it enumerates the powers those institutions may wield, and it cordons off certain areas into which government may not enter. It prohibits the national authority, for example, from passing *ex post facto* laws while it prohibits the states from violating the obligations of contracts.

The Constitution is, in brief, the instrument by which the consent of the governed—the fundamental requirement of any legitimate government—is transformed into a government complete with "the powers to act and a structure designed to make it act wisely or responsibly." Among its various "internal contrivances" (as James Madison called them) we find federalism, separation of powers, bicameralism, representation, an extended commercial republic, an energetic executive, and an independent judiciary. Together, these devices form the machinery of our popular form of government and secure the rights of the people. The Constitution, then, is the Constitution, and as such it is, in its own words, "the supreme Law of the Land."

Constitutional law, on the other hand, is that body of law which has resulted from the Supreme Court's adjudications involving disputes over constitutional provisions or doctrines. To put it a bit more simply, constitutional law is what the Supreme Court says about the Constitution in its decisions resolving the cases and controversies that come before it.

And in its limited role of offering judgment, the Court has had a great deal to say. In almost two hundred years, it has produced nearly 500 volumes of *Reports* of cases. While not all these opinions deal with constitutional questions, of course, a good many do. This stands in marked contrast to the few, slim paragraphs that have been added to the original Constitution as amendments. So, in terms of sheer bulk, constitutional law greatly overwhelms the Constitution. But in substance, it is meant to support and not overwhelm the Constitution whence it is derived.

And this body of law, this judicial handiwork, is, in a fundamental way, unique in our scheme. For the Court is the only branch of our government that routinely, day in and day out, is charged with the awesome task of addressing the most basic, the most enduring political questions: What *is* due process of law? How *does* the idea of separation of powers affect the Congress in certain circumstances? And so forth. The answers the Court gives are very important to the stability of the law so necessary for good government. But as constitutional historian Charles Warren once noted, what's most important to remember is that "however the Court may interpret the provisions of the Constitution, it is still the Constitution which is the law, not the decisions of the Court."

By this, of course, Charles Warren did not mean that a constitutional decision by the Supreme Court lacks the character of law. Obviously it does have binding quality: It binds the parties in a case and also the executive branch for whatever enforcement is necessary. But such a decision does not establish a "supreme Law of the Land" that is binding on all persons and parts of government, henceforth and forevermore.

This point should seem so obvious as not to need elaboration. Consider its necessity in particular reference to the Court's own work. The Supreme Court would face quite a dilemma if its own constitutional decisions really were "the supreme Law of the Land" binding on all persons and governmental entities, including the Court itself, for then the Court would not be able to change its mind. It could not overrule itself in a constitutional case. Yet we know that the Court has done so on numerous occasions....

... If a constitutional decision is not the same as the Constitution itself, if it is not binding in the same way that the Constitution is, we as citizens may respond to a decision we disagree with. As Lincoln in effect pointed out, we can make our responses through the presidents, the senators, and the representatives we elect at the national level. We can also make them through those we elect at the state and local levels....

Once we understand the distinction between constitutional law and the Constitution, once we see that constitutional decisions need not be seen as the last words in constitutional construction, once we comprehend that these decisions do not necessarily determine future public policy—once we see all of this, we can grasp a correlative point: that constitutional interpretation is not the business of the Court only, but also, and properly, the business of all branches of government....

... [A]s Justice Felix Frankfurter once said, "The ultimate touchstone of constitutionality is the Constitution itself and not what we have said about it."

The "Finality" of Supreme Court Decisions: Senate Hearings

During the hearings in 1986 on the nomination of William Hubbs Rehnquist as Chief Justice of the U.S. Supreme Court, Senator Arlen Specter referred to the "binding precedent" of *Marbury* v. *Madison* (1803). Specter claimed that the Supreme Court "is the final arbiter, the final decisionmaker of what the Constitution means." Asked whether he agreed with that assessment, Rehnquist responded: "Unquestionably" (p. 187 of Rehnquist's 1986 hearings). A year later, when Senator Specter put that same question to Anthony M. Kennedy during his confirmation hearings for appointment as Associate Justice of the U.S. Supreme Court, Kennedy did not agree that the Court is the final arbiter of all constitutional issues. Instead, Kennedy develops an interesting picture of the constant interaction between the Court and the political branches (pp. 221–225 of Kennedy's 1987 hearings).

Senator SPECTER. There was a comment in a speech you made before the Los Angeles Patent Lawyers Association back in February of 1982, which I would like to call to your attention and ask you about.

Quote: As I have pointed out, the Constitution, in some of its most critical aspects, is what the political branches of the government have made it, whether the judiciary approves or not.

By making that statement, you didn't intend to undercut, to any extent at all, your conviction that the Supreme Court of the United States has the final word on the interpretation of the Constitution?

Judge KENNEDY. That is my conviction. And I think that the Court has an important role to play in umpiring disputes between the political branches.

Senator SPECTER. What did you mean by that, that in most critical aspects, it is what the political branches of the government have made it, whether the judiciary approves or not?

Judge KENNEDY. I was thinking in two different areas. One in this area of separation of powers and the growth of the office of the presidency. The courts just have had nothing to do with that.

Second, and even more importantly, is the shape of federalism. It seems to me that the independence of the States, or their nonindependence, as the case may be, is really largely now committed to the Congress of the United States, in the enactment of its grants-in-aid programs, and in the determination whether or not to impose conditions that the States must comply with in order to receive federal monies; that kind of thing.

Senator SPECTER. Well, this is a very important subject. And I want to refer you to a comment which was made by Attorney General Meese in a speech last year at Tulane, and ask for your reaction to it.

He said this:

"But as constitutional historian Charles Warren once noted, what is most important to remember is that, quote, however the Court may interpret the provisions of the Constitution, it is still the Constitution which is the law, not the decisions of the Court.

"By this, of course, Charles Warren did not mean that a constitutional decision by the Supreme Court lacks the character of law. Obviously it does have binding quality. It binds the parties in a case, and also the executive branch for whatever enforcement is necessary.

"But such a decision does not establish a supreme law of the land that is binding on all persons and parts of government henceforth and evermore."

Do you agree with that?

Judge KENNEDY. Well, I am not sure—I am not sure I read that entire speech. But if we can just take it as a question, whether or not I agree that the decisions of the Supreme Court are or are not the law of the land. They are the law of the land, and they must be obeyed.

I am somewhat reluctant to say that in all circumstances each legislator is immediately bound by the full consequences of a Supreme Court decree.

Senator SPECTER. Why not?

Judge KENNEDY. Well, as I have indicated before, the Constitution doesn't work very well if there is not a high degree of voluntary compliance, and, in the school desegregation cases, I think, it was not permissible for any school board to refuse to implement *Brown* v. *Board of Education* immediately.

On the other hand, without specifying what the situations are, I can think of instances, or I can accept the proposition that a chief executive or a Congress might not accept as doctrine the law of the Supreme Court.

Senator SPECTER. Well, how can that be if the Supreme Court is to have the final word?

Judge KENNEDY. Well, suppose that the Supreme Court of the United States tomorrow morning in a sudden, unexpected development were to overrule in *New York Times* v. *Sullivan*. Newspapers no longer have protection under the libel laws. Could you, as a legislator, say I think that decision is constitutionally wrong and I want to have legislation to change

it? I think you could. And I think you should.

Senator SPECTER. Well, there could be legislation—

Judge KENNEDY. And I think you could make that judgment as a constitutional matter.

Senator SPECTER. Well, there could be legislation in the hypothetical you suggest which would give the newspapers immunity for certain categories of writings.

Judge KENNEDY. But I think you could stand up on the floor of the U.S. Senate and say I am introducing this legislation because in my view the Supreme Court of the United States is 180 degrees wrong under the Constitution. And I think you would be fulfilling your duty if you said that.

Senator SPECTER. Well, you can always say it, but the issue is whether or not I would comply with it.

Judge KENNEDY. Well, I am just indicating that it doesn't seem to me that just because the Supreme Court has said it legislators cannot attempt to affect its decision in legitimate ways.

Senator SPECTER. Well, but the critical aspect about the final word that the Supreme Court has is that there is a significant school of thought in this country that the Supreme Court does not have the final word. That the President has the authority to interpret the Constitution as the President chooses and the Congress has the authority to interpret the Constitution as the Congress chooses, and there is separate but equal and the Supreme Court does not have the final word.

And, if *Marbury* v. *Madison* is to have any substance, then it seems to me that we do have to recognize the Supreme Court as the final arbiter of the Constitution, just as rockbed.

Judge KENNEDY. Well, as I have indicated earlier in my testimony, I think it was a landmark in constitutional responsibility for the Presidents in the *Youngstown* case and the *Nixon* case to instantly comply with the Court's decisions. I think that was an exercise of the constitutional obligation on their part. I have no problem with that at all.

Senator SPECTER. Well, there has been compliance because it has been accepted that the Supreme Court is the final arbiter. I just want to be sure that you agree with that proposition.

Judge KENNEDY. Yes, but there just may be instances in which I think it is consistent with constitutional morality to challenge those views. And I am not saying to avoid those views or to refuse to obey a mandate.

Senator SPECTER. Well, I think it is fine to challenge them. You can challenge them by constitutional amendment, you can challenge by taking another case to the Supreme Court. But, as long as the Court has said what the Court concludes the Constitution means, then I think it is critical that there be an acceptance that that is the final word.

Judge KENNEDY. I would agree with that as a general proposition. I am not sure there are not exceptions.

Senator SPECTER. But you can't think of any at the moment?

Judge KENNEDY. Not at the moment.

Senator SPECTER. Okay. If you do think of any between now and the time we vote, would you let me know?

Judge KENNEDY. I will let you know, Senator.

Senator SPECTER. Let me pick up some specific issues on executive power and refer to a speech that you presented in Salzburg, Austria, back in November of 1980, where you talk about the extensive discretion saying, "The blunt fact is that American Presidents have in the past had a significant degree of discretion in defining their constitutional powers."

Then you refer to, "The President in the international sphere can commit us to a course of conduct that is all but irrevocable despite the authority of Congress to issue corrective instructions in appropriate cases." Then you refer to President Truman, saying he committed thousands of troops to Korea without a congressional declaration. And then you say, "My position has always been that as to some fundamental constitutional questions it is best not to insist on definitive answers."

And you say further, "I am not one who believes that all of the important constitutional declarations of most important constitutional evolutions come from pronouncements of the courts."

And, without asking you for a specific statement on the War Powers Act, that is a matter of enormous concern that engulfs us with frequency. Major questions arise under the authority of the Congress to require notice from the President on covert operations coming out of the Iran-contra hearings. What is the appropriate range of redress for the Congress? Do we cut off funding for military action in the Persian Gulf? Do we cut off funding for covert operations? Are these justiciable issues which we can ex-

pect the Supreme Court of the United States to decide?

Judge KENNEDY. Well, whether or not they are justiciable issues, of course, depends on the peculiar facts of the case, and I would not like to commit myself on that. But the very examples you gave indicate to me that there are within the political powers of the Congress, within its great arsenal of powers under article I of the Constitution, very strong remedies that it can take to bring a chief executive into compliance with its will, and this is the way the political system was designed to work.

The framers knew about fighting for turf. I don't think they knew that term, but they deliberately set up a system wherein each branch would compete somewhat with the other in an orderly constitutional fashion for control over key policy areas. And these are the kinds of things where the political branches of the government may have a judgment that is much better than that of the courts.

Senator SPECTER. But isn't it unrealistic, Judge Kennedy, to expect the Congress to respond by cutting off funds for U.S. forces in the Persian Gulf? If you accept the proposition that the President can act to involve us in war without a formal declaration, and the President and the Congress ought to decide those questions for themselves, isn't that pretty much an abdication of the Supreme Court's responsibility to be the arbiter and the interpreter of the Constitution?

Judge KENNEDY. Well, I don't know if it is an abdication of responsibility for a nominee not to say that under all circumstances he thinks the Court can decide that broad of an issue. If the issue is presented in a manageable judicial form, in a manageable form, I have no objection to the Court being the umpire between the branches.

On the other hand, I point out that having to rely on the courts may infer, or may imply an institutional weakness on the part of the Congress that is ultimately debilitating. It seems to me that in some instances Congress is better off standing on its own feet and making its position known and then its strength in the federal system will be greater than if it had relied on the assistance of the courts.

CONCLUSIONS

Judicial review fits our constitutional system because we like to fragment power. We feel safer with checks and balances, even when an unelected Court tells an elected legislature or elected President they have overstepped. This very preference for fragmented power denies the Supreme Court an authoritative and final voice for deciding constitutional questions. We do not accept the concentration of legislative power in Congress or executive power in the President. For the same reason, we cannot permit constitutional interpretation to reside only in the courts. Supremacy in a single branch should be subordinate to the higher value placed on freedom, discourse, democracy, and limited government. The dialogue that takes place between the Court, elected government, and the American people is not merely inevitable and a conspicuous part of our history. It is also constructive and stabilizing because this dynamic adds to public understanding and public support of constitutional values.

We all have a need to respect procedure and our institutions. Nevertheless, respect for the judiciary does not mean blind deference and an unwillingness by other actors to think independently and critically. Congress can respect the President's duties in foreign affairs without abdicating its own constitutionally assigned powers. The history of American law provides convincing evidence that national policies hammered out jointly by two or more branches is superior to singlehanded and often misguided actions by a single branch. Each branch should be exposed to penetrating critiques from the other two. From such scrutiny no branch is immune.

NOTES AND QUESTIONS

1. Rulings on such controversial issues as abortion, school busing and school prayers, among others, have triggered calls for Congress to strip the Supreme Court of some of its appellate jurisdiction. Advocates of this strategy have invoked the Exceptions Clause of Article III. What are the implications of court-stripping? Consider the impact on efforts by citizens to vindicate their rights and liberties in the Supreme Court. How is due process affected? Would lower federal courts exercise the final "judicial word" on the meaning of the Constitution?

2. Did the Court surrender its "judicial power" in *Ex parte McCardle* (1869) when it upheld congressional legislation to withdraw the appellate jurisdiction of the Court in McCardle's case? Or was this a temporary, strategic retreat? Consider the distinction between "jurisdiction" and "judicial power." When does a case move from the realm of jurisdiction to the realm of judicial power?

3. In theory, judicial opinions are binding on the public and other branches of government. In practice, of course, judicial opinions are implemented with varying degrees of fidelity by governmental officials. In your view, what are the implications of noncompliance for the enterprise of constitutional government? Is the Rule of Law undermined? Are there circumstances in which noncompliance is permissible, even desirable, and perhaps warranted? If so, when, and why? Recall the reaction by the executive and legislative branches to the Court's ruling in *INS v. Chadha*.

4. Having come to the end of your course, you are in a position to assess the oft-quoted observation that the Supreme Court has the final word on constitutional disputes. Does that assertion capture the realities of constitutional dialogue in the United States? If not, how would you explain the American process of resolving constitutional issues?

SELECTED READINGS

ALEXANDER, LARRY, AND FREDERICK SCHAUER. "On Extrajudicial Constitutional Interpretation." 110 Harvard Law Review 1359 (1997).

BECKER, THEODORE L., AND MALCOLM M. FEELEY, eds. The Impact of Supreme Court Decisions. New York: Oxford University Press, 1973.

BRECKENRIDGE, ADAM CARLYLE. Congress Against the Court. Lincoln: University of Nebraska Press, 1970.

CULP, MAURICE S. "A Survey of the Proposals to Limit or Deny the Power of Judicial Review by the Supreme Court of the United States." 4 Indiana Law Journal 386, 474 (1929).

DEVINS, NEAL, AND LOUIS FISHER. "Judicial Exclusivity and Political Instability." 84 Virginia Law Review 83 (1998).

———. The Democratic Constitution. New York: Oxford University Press, 2004.

DEVINS, NEAL, AND KEITH E. WHITTINGTON, EDS. Congress and the Constitution. Durham: Duke University Press, 2005.

"Efforts in the Congress to Curtail the Federal Courts: Pro & Con." Congressional Digest, May 1982.

ELLIOTT, SHELDEN D. "Court-Curbing Proposals in Congress." 33 Notre Dame Lawyer 597 (1958).

ESKRIDGE, WILLIAM N., JR. "Overriding Supreme Court Statutory Interpretation Decisions." 101 Yale Law Journal 331 (1991).

FISHER, LOUIS. "One of the Guardians Some of the Time," in Is the Supreme Court the Guardian of the Constitution? (Robert A. Licht, ed. Washington, D.C.: American Enterprise Institute, 1993).

———. "Statutory Construction: Keeping a Respectful Eye on Congress," 53 SMU Law Review 49 (2000).

———. The Supreme Court and Congress: Rival Interpretations. Washington, D.C.: CQ Press, 2009.

GEYH, CHARLES GARDNER. When Courts and Congress Collide: The Struggle for Control of America's Judicial System. Ann Arbor: University of Michigan Press, 2006.

HALPER, THOMAS. "Supreme Court Responses to Congressional Threats: Strategy and Tactics." 19 Drake Law Review 292 (1970).

HANDBERG, ROGER, AND HAROLD F. HILL, JR. "Court Curbing, Court Reversals, and Judicial Review: The Supreme Court Versus Congress." 14 Law & Society Review 309 (1980).

HARRIGER, KATY J., ED. Separation of Powers: Documents and Commentary. Washington, D.C.: CQ Press, 2003.

HENSCHEN, BETH. "Statutory Interpretations of the Supreme Court: Congressional Responses." 11 American Politics Quarterly 441 (1983).

IGNAGNI, JOSEPH AND JAMES MEERNIK. "Explaining Congressional Attempts to Reverse Supreme Court Decisions." 47 Political Research Quarterly 353 (1994).

KYVIG, DAVID E. Explicit and Authentic Acts: Amending the U.S. Constitution, 1776–1995. Lawrence, Kansas: University Press of Kansas, 1996.

LEUCHTENBURG, WILLIAM E. "The Origins of Franklin D. Roosevelt's 'Court-Packing' Plan." 1966 Supreme Court Review 347.

LICHT, ROBERT A. Is the Supreme Court the Guardian of the Constitution? Washington, D.C.: American Enterprise Institute, 1993.

LYTLE, CLIFFORD M. "Congressional Response to Supreme Court Decisions in the Aftermath of the School Desegregation Cases." 12 Journal of Public Law 290 (1963).

McDOWELL, GARY L. Curbing the Courts: The Constitution and the Limits of Judicial Power. Baton Rouge: Louisiana State University Press, 1988.

McKENNA, MARIAN C. Franklin Roosevelt and the Great Constitutional War: The Court-Packing Crisis of 1937. New York: Fordham University Press, 2002.

MIKVA, ABNER J., AND JEFF BLEICH. "When Congress Overrules the Court." 79 California Law Review 729 (1991).

MURPHY, WALTER F. Congress and the Court. Chicago: University of Chicago Press, 1962.

———. "Lower Court Checks on Supreme Court Power." 53 American Political Science Review 1017 (1959).

NAGEL, STUART S. "Court-Curbing Periods in American History." 18 Vanderbilt Law Review 925 (1965).

NICHOLS, EGBERT RAY, ED. Congress or the Supreme Court: Which Shall Rule America? New York: Noble and Noble, 1935.

NOTE. "Congressional Reversal of Supreme Court Decisions: 1945–1957." 71 Harvard Law Review 1324 (1958).

———. "Tension Between Judicial and Legislative Powers as Reflected in Confrontations Between Congress and the Courts." 13 Georgia Law Review 1513 (1979).

PASCHAL, RICHARD A. "The Continuing Colloquy: Congress and the Finality of the Supreme Court." 8 Journal of Law & Politics 143 (1991).

PRITCHETT, C. HERMAN. Congress Versus the Supreme Court: 1957–1960. Minneapolis: University of Minnesota Press, 1961.

QUIRK, WILLIAM J. Courts and Congress: America's Unwritten Constitution. New Brunswick, N.J.: Transaction Publishers, 2008.

ROSS, WILLIAM G. A Muted Fury: Populists, Progressives, and Labor Unions Confront the Courts, 1890–1937. Princeton, N.J.: Princeton University Press, 1994.

SCHMIDHAUSER, JOHN R., AND LARRY L. BERG. The Supreme Court and Congress: Conflict and Interaction, 1945–1968. New York: The Free Press, 1972.

SOLIMINE, MICHAEL E., AND JAMES L. WALKER. "The Next Word: Congressional Response to Supreme Court Statutory Decisions." 65 Temple Law Review 425 (1992).

STUMPF, HARRY P. "Congressional Response to Supreme Court Rulings: The Interaction of Law and Politics." 14 Journal of Public Law 377 (1965).

TUSHNET, MARK. Taking the Constitution Away from the Courts. Princeton, N.J.: Princeton University Press, 1999.

VOSE, CLEMENT E. Constitutional Change: Amendment Politics and Supreme Court Litigation Since 1900. Lexington, Mass.: D.C. Heath, 1972.

WARREN, CHARLES. "Legislative and Judicial Attacks on the Supreme Court of the United States—A History of the Twenty-Fifth Section of the Judiciary Act." 47 American Law Review 1, 161 (1913).

Appendix 1

The Constitution of the United States

We the People of the United States, in Order to form a more perfect Union, establish Justice, insure domestic Tranquility, provide for the common defence, promote the general Welfare, and secure the Blessings of Liberty to ourselves and our Posterity, do ordain and establish this Constitution for the United States of America.

ARTICLE 1

Section 1.   All legislative Powers herein granted shall be vested in a Congress of the United States, which shall consist of a Senate and House of Representatives.

Section 2.   The House of Representatives shall be composed of Members chosen every second Year by the People of the several States, and the Electors in each State shall have the Qualifications requisite for Electors of the most numerous Branch of the State Legislature.

No Person shall be a Representative who shall not have attained to the Age of twenty five Years, and been seven Years a Citizen of the United States, and who shall not, when elected, be an Inhabitant of that State in which he shall be chosen.

[Representatives and direct Taxes shall be apportioned among the several States which may be included within this Union, according to their respective Numbers, which shall be determined by adding to the whole Number of free Persons, including those bound to Service for a Term of Years, and excluding Indians not taxed, three fifths of all other Persons.][1] The actual Enumeration shall be made within three Years after the first Meeting of the Congress of the United States, and within every subsequent Term of ten Years, in such Manner as they shall by Law direct. The Number of Representatives shall not exceed one for every thirty Thousand, but each State shall have at Least one Representative; and until such enumerations shall be made, the State of New Hampshire shall be entitled to chuse three, Massachusetts eight, Rhode-Island and Providence Plantations one, Connecticut five, New-York six, New Jersey four, Pennsylvania eight, Delaware one, Maryland six, Virginia ten, North Carolina five, South Carolina five, and Georgia three.

When vacancies happen in the Representation from any State, the Executive Authority thereof shall issue Writs of Election to fill such Vacancies.

The House of Representatives shall chuse their speaker and other Officers; and shall have the sole Power of Impeachment.

Section 3.   The Senate of the United States shall be composed of two Senators from each State, [chosen by the Legislature thereof,][2] for six Years; and each Senator shall have one Vote.

Immediately after they shall be assembled in Consequence of the first Election, they shall be divided as equally as may be into three Classes. The Seats of the Senators of the first Class shall be va-

---

1. Changed by Section 2 of the Fourteenth Amendment.
2. Changed by the Seventeenth Amendment.

cated at the Expiration of the second Year, of the second Class at the Expiration of the fourth Year, and of the third Class at the Expiration of the sixth Year, so that one third may be chosen every second Year; [and if Vacancies happen by Resignation, or otherwise, during the Recess of the Legislature of any State, the Executive thereof may make temporary Appointments until the next Meeting of the Legislature, which shall then fill such Vacancies.][3]

No Person shall be a Senator who shall not have attained to the Age of thirty Years, and been nine Years a Citizen of the United States, and who shall not, when elected, be an Inhabitant of that State for which he shall be chosen.

The Vice President of the United States shall be President of the Senate, but shall have no Vote, unless they be equally divided.

The Senate shall chuse their other Officers, and also a President pro tempore, in the Absence of the Vice President, or when he shall exercise the Office of President of the United States.

The Senate shall have the sole Power to try all Impeachments. When sitting for that Purpose, they shall be on Oath or Affirmation. When the President of the United States is tried, the Chief Justice shall preside: And no Person shall be convicted without the concurrence of two thirds of the Members present. Judgment in Cases of Impeachment shall not extend further than to removal from Office, and disqualification to hold and enjoy any Office of honor, Trust or Profit under the United States: but the Party convicted shall nevertheless be liable and subject to Indictment, Trial, Judgment and Punishment, according to law.

Section 4. The Times, Places and Manner of holding Elections for Senators and Representatives, shall be prescribed in each State by the Legislature thereof; but the Congress may at any time by Law make or alter such Regulations, except as to the Places of chusing Senators.

The Congress shall assemble at least once in every Year, and such Meeting shall be [on the first Monday in December,][4] unless they shall by Law appoint a different Day.

Section 5. Each House shall be the Judge of the Elections, Returns and Qualifications of its own Members, and a Majority of each shall constitute a Quorum to do business; but a smaller Number may adjourn from day to day, and may be authorized to compel the Attendance of absent Members, in such Manner, and under such Penalties as each House may provide.

Each House may determine the Rules of its Proceedings, punish its Members for disorderly Behaviour, and, with the Concurrence of two thirds, expel a Member.

Each House shall keep a Journal of its Proceedings, and from time to time publish the same, excepting such Parts as may in their Judgment require Secrecy; and the yeas and Nays of the Members of either House on any question shall, at the Desire of one fifth of those Present, be entered on the Journal.

Neither House, during the Session of Congress, shall, without the Consent of the other, adjourn for more than three days, nor to any other place than that in which the two Houses shall be sitting.

Section 6. The Senators and Representatives shall receive a Compensation for their Services, to be ascertained by Law, and paid out of the Treasury of the United States. They shall in all Cases, except Treason, Felony and Breach of the Peace, be privileged from Arrest during their Attendance at the Session of their respective Houses, and in going to and returning from the same; and for any Speech or Debate in either House, they shall not be questioned in any other Place.

No Senator or Representative shall, during the Time for which he was elected, be appointed to any civil Office under the Authority of the United States, which shall have been created, or the Emoluments whereof shall have been encreased during such time; and no Person holding any Office under the United States, shall be a Member of either House during his Continuance in Office.

3. Changed by the Seventeenth Amendment.
4. Changed by Section 2 of the Twentieth Amendment.

Section 7. All Bills for raising Revenue shall originate in the House of Representatives; but the Senate may propose or concur with Amendments as on other Bills.

Every Bill which shall have passed the House of Representatives and the Senate, shall, before it become a Law, be presented to the President of the United States; If he approve he shall sign it, but if not he shall return it, with his Objections to that House in which it shall have originated, who shall enter the Objections at large on their Journal, and proceed to reconsider it. If after such Reconsideration two thirds of that House shall agree to pass the Bill, it shall be sent, together with the Objections, to the other House, by which it shall likewise be reconsidered, and if approved by two thirds of that House, it shall become a Law. But in all such Cases the Votes of both Houses shall be determined by yeas and Nays, and the Names of the Persons voting for and against the Bill shall be entered on the Journal of each House respectively. If any Bill shall not be returned by the President within ten Days (Sundays excepted) after it shall have been presented to him, the Same shall be a Law, in like Manner as if he had signed it, unless the Congress by their Adjournment prevent its Return, in which Case it shall not be a Law.

Every Order, Resolution, or Vote to which the Concurrence of the Senate and House of Representatives may be necessary (except on a question of Adjournment) shall be presented to the President of the United States; and before the Same shall take Effect, shall be approved by him, or being disapproved by him, shall be repassed by two thirds of the Senate and House of Representatives, according to the Rules and Limitations prescribed in the Case of a Bill.

Section 8. The Congress shall have Power To lay and collect Taxes, Duties, Imposts and Excises, to pay the Debts and provide for the common Defence and general Welfare of the United States; but all duties, Imposts and Excises shall be uniform throughout the United States;

To borrow Money on the Credit of the United States;

To regulate Commerce with foreign Nations, and among the several States, and with the Indian Tribes;

To establish an uniform Rule of Naturalization, and uniform Laws on the subject of Bankruptcies throughout the United States;

To coin Money, regulate the Value thereof, and of foreign Coin, and fix the Standard of Weights and Measures;

To provide for the Punishment of counterfeiting the Securities and current Coin of the United States;

To establish Post Offices and post Roads;

To promote the Progress of Science and useful Arts, by securing for limited Times to Authors and Inventors exclusive Right to their respective Writings and Discoveries;

To constitute Tribunals inferior to the supreme Court;

To define and punish Piracies and Felonies committed on the high Seas, and Offences against the Law of Nations;

To declare War, grant Letters of Marque and Reprisal, and make rules concerning Captures on Land and Water;

To raise and support Armies, but no Appropriation of Money to that Use shall be for a longer Term than two Years;

To provide and maintain a Navy;

To make rules for the Government and Regulation of the land and naval Forces;

To provide for calling forth the Militia to execute the Laws of the Union, suppress Insurrections and repel Invasions;

To provide for organizing, arming, and disciplining, the Militia, and for governing such Part of them as may be employed in the Service of the United States, reserving to the States respectively, the Appointment of the Officers, and the Authority of training the Militia according to the discipline prescribed by Congress;

To exercise exclusive Legislation in all Cases whatsoever, over such District (not exceeding ten Miles square), as may, by Cession of particular States, and the Acceptance of Congress, become the Seat of the Government of the United States, and to exercise like Authority over all Places purchased by the Consent of the Legislature of the State in which the Same shall be for the Erection of Forts, Magazines, Arsenals, dock-Yards, and other needful Buildings;—And

To make all Laws which shall be necessary and proper for carrying into Execution the foregoing Powers, and all other Powers vested by this Constitution in the Government of the United States, or in any Department or Officer thereof.

Section 9.   The Migration or Importation of such Persons as any of the States now existing shall think proper to admit, shall not be prohibited by the Congress prior to the Year one thousand eight hundred and eight, but a Tax or duty may be imposed on such Importation, not exceeding ten dollars for each Person.

The Privilege of the Writ of Habeas Corpus shall not be suspended, unless when in Cases of Rebellion or Invasion the public Safety may require it.

No Bill of Attainder or ex post facto Law shall be passed.

[No Capitation, or other direct, Tax shall be laid, unless in Proportion to the Census or Enumeration herein before directed to be taken.][5]

No Tax or Duty shall be laid on Articles exported from any State.

No Preference shall be given by any Regulation of Commerce or Revenue to the Ports of one State over those of another: nor shall Vessels bound to, or from, one State, be obliged to enter, clear, or pay Duties in another.

No money shall be drawn from the Treasury, but in Consequence of Appropriations made by Law; and a regular Statement and Account of the Receipts and Expenditures of all public Money shall be published from time to time.

No Title of Nobility shall be granted by the United States: And no Person holding any Office of Profit or Trust under them, shall, without the Consent of the Congress, accept of any present, Emolument, Office, or Title, of any kind whatever, from any King, Prince, or foreign State.

Section 10.   No State shall enter into any Treaty, Alliance, or Confederation; grant Letters of Marque and Reprisal; coin Money; emit Bills of Credit; make any Thing but gold and silver Coin a Tender in Payment of Debts; pass any Bill of Attainder, ex post facto Law, or Law impairing the Obligation of Contracts, or grant any Title of Nobility.

No State shall, without the Consent of the Congress, lay any Imposts or Duties on Imports or Exports, except what may be absolutely necessary for executing it's inspection Laws: and the net Produce of all Duties and Imposts, laid by any State on Imports or Exports, shall be for the Use of the Treasury of the United States; and all such Laws shall be subject to the Revision and Controul of the Congress.

No State shall, without the Consent of Congress, lay any Duty of Tonnage, keep Troops, or Ships of War in time of Peace, enter into any Agreement or Compact with another State, or with a foreign Power, or engage in War, unless actually invaded, or in such imminent Danger as will not admit of delay.

ARTICLE II

Section 1.   The executive Power shall be vested in a President of the United States of America. He shall hold his Office during the Term of four Years, and, together with the Vice President, chosen for the same term, be elected, as follows:

---

5. Changed by the Sixteenth Amendment.

Each State shall appoint, in such Manner as the Legislature thereof may direct, a Number of Electors, equal to the whole Number of Senators and Representatives to which the State may be entitled in the Congress: but no Senator or Representative, or Person holding an Office of Trust or Profit under the United States, shall be appointed an Elector.

[The Electors shall meet in their respective States, and vote by Ballot for two Persons, of whom one at least shall not be an Inhabitant of the same State with themselves. And they shall make a List of all the Persons voted for, and of the Number of Votes for each; which List they shall sign and certify, and transmit sealed to the Seat of the Government of the United States, directed to the President of the Senate. The President of the Senate shall, in the Presence of the Senate and House of Representatives, open all the Certificates, and the Votes shall then be counted. The Person having the greatest Number of Votes shall be the President, if such Number be a Majority of the whole Number of Electors appointed; and if there be more than one who have such Majority, and have an equal Number of Votes, then the House of Representatives shall immediately chuse by Ballot one of them for President: and if no Person have a Majority, then from the five highest on the List the said House shall in like Manner chuse the President. But in chusing the President, the Votes shall be taken by States, the Representation from each State having one Vote; A quorum for this Purpose shall consist of a Member or Members from two thirds of the States, and a Majority of all the States shall be necessary to a Choice. In every Case, after the Choice of the President, the Person having the greatest Number of Votes of the Electors shall be the Vice President. But if there should remain two or more who have equal Votes, the Senate shall chuse from them by Ballot the Vice President.][6]

The Congress may determine the Time of chusing the Electors, and the Day on which they shall give their Votes; which Day shall be the same throughout the United States.

No Person except a natural born Citizen, or a Citizen of the United States, at the time of the Adoption of this Constitution, shall be eligible to the Office of President; neither shall any Person be eligible to that Office who shall not have attained to the Age of thirty five Years, and been fourteen Years a Resident within the United States.

[In Case of the Removal of the President from Office, or of his Death, Resignation, or Inability to discharge the Powers and Duties of the said Office, the Same shall devolve on the Vice President, and the Congress may by Law provide for the Case of Removal, Death, Resignation or Inability, both of the President and Vice President, declaring what Officer shall then act as President, and such Officer shall act accordingly, until the Disability be removed, or a President shall be elected.][7]

The President shall, at stated Times, receive for his Services, a Compensation, which shall neither be encreased nor diminished during the Period for which he shall have been elected, and he shall not receive within that Period any other Emolument from the United States, or any of them.

Before he enter on the Execution of his Office, he shall take the following Oath or Affirmation: — "I do solemnly swear (or affirm) that I will faithfully execute the Office of President of the United States, and will to the best of my Ability, preserve, protect and defend the Constitution of the United States."

Section 2.   The President shall be Commander in Chief of the Army and Navy of the United States, and of the Militia of the several States, when called into the actual Service of the United States; he may require the Opinion, in writing, of the principal Officer in each of the executive Departments, upon any Subject relating to the Duties of their respective Offices, and he shall have Power to grant Reprieves and Pardons for Offences against the United States, except in Cases of Impeachment.

He shall have Power, by and with the Advice and Consent of the Senate, to make Treaties, provided

---

6. Changed by the Twelfth Amendment.
7. Changed by the Twenty-Fifth Amendment.

two thirds of the Senators present concur; and he shall nominate, and by and with the Advice and Consent of the Senate, shall appoint Ambassadors, other public Ministers and Consuls, Judges of the supreme Court, and all other Officers of the United States, whose Appointments are not herein otherwise provided for, and which shall be established by Law; but the Congress may by Law vest the Appointment of such inferior Officers, as they think proper, in the President alone, in the Courts of Law, or in the Heads of Departments.

The President shall have Power to fill up all Vacancies that may happen during the Recess of the Senate, by granting Commissions which shall expire at the End of their next Session.

Section 3.   He shall from time to time give to the Congress Information of the State of the Union, and recommend to their Consideration such Measures as he shall judge necessary and expedient; he may, on extraordinary Occasions, convene both Houses, or either of them, and in Case of Disagreement between them, with Respect to the Time of Adjournment, he may adjourn them to such Time as he shall think proper; he shall receive Ambassadors and other public Ministers; he shall take Care that the Laws be faithfully executed, and shall Commission all the Officers of the United States.

Section 4.   The President, Vice President and all civil Officers of the United States, shall be removed from Office on Impeachment for, and Conviction of, Treason, Bribery, or other High Crimes and Misdemeanors.

ARTICLE III

Section 1.   The judicial Power of the United States, shall be vested in one supreme Court, and in such inferior Courts as the Congress may from time to time ordain and establish. The Judges, both of the supreme and inferior Courts, shall hold their Offices during good Behaviour, and shall, at stated Times, receive for their Services, a Compensation, which shall not be diminished during their Continuance in Office.

Section 2.   The judicial Power shall extend to all Cases, in Law and Equity, arising under this Constitution, the Laws of the United States, and Treaties made, or which shall be made, under their Authority;—to all Cases affecting Ambassadors, other public Ministers and Consuls;—to all Cases of admiralty and maritime Jurisdiction;—to Controversies to which the United States shall be a Party;—to Controversies between two or more States; [between a State and Citizens of another State;][8]—between Citizens of different States;—between Citizens of the same State claiming Lands under Grants of different States, [and between a State, or the Citizens thereof, and foreign States, Citizens or Subjects.][9]

In all Cases affecting Ambassadors, other public Ministers and Consuls, and those in which a State shall be Party, the supreme Court shall have original Jurisdiction. In all the other Cases before mentioned, the supreme Court shall have appellate Jurisdiction, both as to Law and Fact, with such Exceptions, and under such Regulations as the Congress shall make.

The Trial of all Crimes, except in Cases of Impeachment, shall be by Jury; and such Trial shall be held in the State where the said Crimes shall have been committed; but when not committed within any State, the Trial shall be at such Place or Places as the Congress may by Law have directed.

Section 3.   Treason against the United States, shall consist only in levying War against them, or in adhering to their Enemies, giving them Aid and Comfort. No Person shall be convicted of Treason unless on the Testimony of two Witnesses to the same overt Act, or on Confession in open Court.

The Congress shall have Power to declare the Punishment of Treason, but no Attainder of Treason shall work Corruption of Blood, or Forfeiture except during the Life of the Person attainted.

---

8. Changed by the Eleventh Amendment.
9. Changed by the Eleventh Amendment.

ARTICLE IV

Section 1.   Full Faith and Credit shall be given in each State to the public Acts, Records, and judicial Proceedings of every other State. And the Congress may by general Laws prescribe the Manner in which such Acts, Records and Proceedings shall be proved, and the Effect thereof.

Section 2.   The Citizens of each State shall be entitled to all Privileges and Immunities of Citizens in the several States.

A Person charged in any State with Treason, Felony, or other Crime, who shall flee from Justice, and be found in another State, shall on Demand of the executive Authority of the State from which he fled, be delivered up, to be removed to the State having Jurisdiction of the Crime.

[No person held to Service or Labour in one State, under the Laws thereof, escaping into another, shall, in Consequence of any Law or Regulation therein, be discharged from such Service or Labour, but shall be delivered up on Claim of the Party to whom such Service or Labour may be due.][10]

Section 3.   New States may be admitted by the Congress into this Union; but no new State shall be formed or erected within the Jurisdiction of any other State; nor any State be formed by the Junction of two or more States, or Parts of States, without the Consent of the Legislatures of the States concerned as well as of the Congress.

The Congress shall have Power to dispose of and make all needful Rules and Regulations respecting the Territory or other Property belonging to the United States; and nothing in this Constitution shall be so construed as to Prejudice any Claims of the United States, or of any particular State.

Section 4.   The United States shall guarantee to every State in this Union a Republican Form of Government, and shall protect each of them against Invasion; and on Application of the Legislature, or of the Executive (when the Legislature cannot be convened) against domestic Violence.

ARTICLE V

The Congress, whenever two thirds of both Houses shall deem it necessary, shall propose Amendments to this Constitution, or, on the Application of the Legislatures of two thirds of the several States, shall call a Convention for proposing Amendments, which, in either Case, shall be valid to all Intents and Purposes, as Part of this Constitution, when ratified by the Legislatures of three fourths of the several States, or by Conventions in three fourths thereof, as the one or the other Mode of Ratification may be proposed by the Congress; Provided that no Amendment which may be made prior to the Year One thousand eight hundred and eight shall in any Manner affect the first and fourth Clauses in the Ninth Section of the first Article; and that no State, without its Consent, shall be deprived of its equal Suffrage in the Senate.

ARTICLE VI

All Debts contracted and Engagements entered into, before the Adoption of this Constitution, shall be as valid against the United States under this Constitution, as under the Confederation.

This Constitution, and the Laws of the United States which shall be made in Pursuance thereof; and all Treaties made, or which shall be made, under the Authority of the United States, shall be the supreme Law of the Land; and the Judges in every State shall be bound thereby, any Thing in the Constitution or Laws of any State to the Contrary notwithstanding.

The Senators and Representatives before mentioned, and the Members of the several State Legislatures, and all executive and judicial Officers, both of the United States and of the several States, shall be bound by Oath or Affirmation, to support this Constitution; but no religious Test shall ever be re-

---

10. Changed by the Thirteenth Amendment.

quired as a Qualification to any Office or public Trust under the United States.

ARTICLE VII

The Ratification of the Conventions of nine States, shall be sufficient for the Establishment of this Constitution between the States so ratifying the Same.

AMENDMENTS

[The first 10 Amendments were ratified December 15, 1791, and form what is known as the "Bill of Rights."]

AMENDMENT 1

Congress shall make no law respecting an establishment of religion, or prohibiting the free exercise thereof; or abridging the freedom of speech, or of the press; or the right of the people peaceably to assemble, and to petition the Government for a redress of grievances.

AMENDMENT 2

A well regulated Militia, being necessary to the security of a free State, the right of the people to keep and bear Arms, shall not be infringed.

AMENDMENT 3

No Soldier shall, in time of peace be quartered in any house, without the consent of the Owner, nor in time of war, but in a manner to be prescribed by law.

AMENDMENT 4

The right of the people to be secure in their persons, houses, papers, and effects, against unreasonable searches and seizures, shall not be violated, and no Warrants shall issue, but upon probable cause, supported by Oath or affirmation, and particularly describing the place to be searched, and the persons or things to be seized.

AMENDMENT 5

No person shall be held to answer for a capital, or otherwise infamous crime, unless on a presentment or indictment of a Grand Jury, except in cases arising in the land or naval forces, or in the Militia, when in actual service in time of War or public danger; nor shall any person be subject for the same offence to be twice put in jeopardy of life or limb; nor shall be compelled in any criminal case to be a witness against himself, nor be deprived of life, liberty, or property, without due process of law; nor shall private property be taken for public use, without just compensation.

AMENDMENT 6

In all criminal prosecutions, the accused shall enjoy the right to a speedy and public trial, by an impartial jury of the State and district wherein the crime shall have been committed, which district shall have been previously ascertained by law, and to be informed of the nature and cause of the accusation; to be confronted with the witnesses against him; to have compulsory process for obtaining witnesses in his favor, and to have the Assistance of Counsel for his defence.

AMENDMENT 7

In Suits at common law, where the value in controversy shall exceed twenty dollars, the right of trial by jury shall be preserved, and no fact tried by a jury, shall be otherwise re-examined in any Court of the United States, than according to the rules of the common law.

AMENDMENT 8

Excessive bail shall not be required, nor excessive fines imposed, nor cruel and unusual punishments inflicted.

AMENDMENT 9

The enumeration in the Constitution, of certain rights, shall not be construed to deny or disparage others retained by the people.

AMENDMENT 10

The powers not delegated to the United States by the Constitution, nor prohibited by it to the States, are reserved to the States respectively, or to the people.

AMENDMENT 11
(Ratified February 7, 1795)

The Judicial power of the United States shall not be construed to extend to any suit in law or equity, commenced or prosecuted against one of the United States by Citizens of another State, or by Citizens or Subjects of any Foreign State.

AMENDMENT 12
(Ratified July 27, 1804)

The Electors shall meet in their respective states and vote by ballot for President and Vice-President, one of whom, at least, shall not be an inhabitant of the same state with themselves; they shall name in their ballots the person voted for as President, and in distinct ballots the person voted for as Vice-President, and they shall make distinct lists of all persons voted for as President, and of all persons voted for as Vice-President, and of the number of votes for each, which lists they shall sign and certify, and transmit sealed to the seat of the government of the United States, directed to the President of the Senate; — The President of the Senate shall, in the presence of the Senate and House of Representatives, open all the certificates and the votes shall then be counted; — The person having the greatest number of votes for President, shall be the President, if such number be a majority of the whole number of Electors appointed; and if no person have such majority, then from the persons having the highest numbers not exceeding three on the list of those voted for as President, the House of Representatives shall choose immediately, by ballot, the President. But in choosing the President, the votes shall be taken by states, the representation from each state having one vote; a quorum for this purpose shall consist of a member or members from two-thirds of the states, and a majority of all the states shall be necessary to a choice. [And if the House of Representatives shall not choose a President whenever the right of choice shall devolve upon them, before the fourth day of March next following, then the Vice-President shall act as President, as in the case of the death or other constitutional disability of the President. —]* The person having the greatest number of votes as Vice-

---

* Superseded by Section 3 of the Twentieth Amendment.

President, shall be the Vice-President, if such number be a majority of the whole number of Electors appointed, and if no person have a majority, then from the two highest numbers on the list, the Senate shall choose the Vice-President; a quorum for the purpose shall consist of two-thirds of the whole number of Senators, and a majority of the whole number shall be necessary to a choice. But no person constitutionally ineligible to the office of President shall be eligible to that of Vice-President of the United States.

AMENDMENT 13
(Ratified December 6, 1865)

Section 1.   Neither slavery nor involuntary servitude, except as a punishment for crime whereof the party shall have been duly convicted, shall exist within the United States, or any place subject to their jurisdiction.

Section 2.   Congress shall have power to enforce this article by appropriate legislation.

AMENDMENT 14
(Ratified July 9, 1868)

Section 1.   All persons born or naturalized in the United States, and subject to the jurisdiction thereof, are citizens of the United States and of the State wherein they reside. No State shall make or enforce any law which shall abridge the privileges or immunities of citizens of the United States; nor shall any State deprive any person of life, liberty, or property, without due process of law; nor deny to any person within its jurisdiction the equal protection of the laws.

Section 2.   Representatives shall be apportioned among the several States according to their respective numbers, counting the whole number of persons in each State, excluding Indians not taxed. But when the right to vote at any election for the choice of electors for President and Vice President of the United States, Representatives in Congress, the Executive and Judicial officers of a State, or the members of the Legislature thereof, is denied to any of the male inhabitants of such State, being twenty-one years of age, and citizens of the United States, or in any way abridged, except for participation in rebellion, or other crime, the basis of representation therein shall be reduced in the proportion which the number of such male citizens shall bear to the whole number of male citizens twenty-one years of age in such State.

Section 3.   No person shall be a Senator or Representative in Congress, or elector of President and Vice President, or hold any office, civil or military, under the United States, or under any State, who, having previously taken an oath, as a member of Congress, or as an officer of the United States, or as a member of any State legislature, or as an executive or judicial officer of any State, to support the Constitution of the United States, shall have engaged in insurrection or rebellion against the same, or given aid or comfort to the enemies thereof. But Congress may by a vote of two-thirds of each House, remove such disability.

Section 4.   The validity of the public debt of the United States, authorized by law, including debts incurred for payment of pensions and bounties for services in suppressing insurrection or rebellion, shall not be questioned. But neither the United States nor any State shall assume or pay any debt or obligation incurred in aid of insurrection or rebellion against the United States, or any claim for the loss or emancipation of any slave; but all such debts, obligations and claims shall be held illegal and void.

Section 5.   The Congress shall have power to enforce, by appropriate legislation, the provisions of this article.

AMENDMENT 15
(Ratified February 3, 1870)

Section 1. The right of citizens of the United States to vote shall not be denied or abridged by the United States or by any State on account of race, color, or previous condition of servitude.

Section 2. The Congress shall have power to enforce this article by appropriate legislation.

AMENDMENT 16
(Ratified February 3, 1913)

The Congress shall have power to lay and collect taxes on incomes, from whatever source derived, without apportionment among the several States, and without regard to any census or enumeration.

AMENDMENT 17
(Ratified April 8, 1913)

The Senate of the United States shall be composed of two Senators from each State, elected by the people thereof for six years; and each Senator shall have one vote. The electors in each State shall have the qualifications requisite for electors of the most numerous branch of the State legislatures.

When vacancies happen in the representation of any State in the Senate, the executive authority of such State shall issue writs of election to fill such vacancies: *Provided,* That the legislature of any State may empower the executive thereof to make temporary appointments until the people fill the vacancies by election as the legislature may direct.

This amendment shall not be so construed as to affect the election or term of any Senator chosen before it becomes valid as part of the Constitution.

AMENDMENT 18
(Ratified January 16, 1919. Repealed December 5, 1933 by Amendment 21)

Section 1. After one year from the ratification of this article the manufacture, sale, or transportation of intoxicating liquors within, the importation thereof into, or the exportation thereof from the United States and all territory subject to the jurisdiction thereof for beverage purposes is hereby prohibited.

Section 2. The Congress and the several States shall have concurrent power to enforce this article by appropriate legislation.

Section 3. This article shall be inoperative unless it shall have been ratified as an amendment to the Constitution by the legislatures of the several States as provided in the Constitution, within seven years from the date of the submission hereof to the States by the Congress.

AMENDMENT 19
(Ratified August 18, 1920)

The right of citizens of the United States to vote shall not be denied or abridged by the United States or by any State on account of sex.

Congress shall have power to enforce this article by appropriate legislation.

AMENDMENT 20
(Ratified January 23, 1933)

Section 1. The terms of the President and Vice President shall end at noon on the 20th day of January, and the terms of Senators and Representatives at noon on the 3d day of January, of the years in which such terms would have ended if this article had not been ratified; and the terms of their successors shall then begin.

Section 2. The Congress shall assemble at least once in every year, and such meeting shall begin at noon on the 3d day of January, unless they shall by law appoint a different day.

Section 3. If, at the time fixed for the beginning of the term of the President, the President elect shall have died, the Vice President elect shall become President. If a President shall not have been chosen before the time fixed for the beginning of his term, or if the President elect shall have failed to qualify, then the Vice President elect shall act as President until a President shall have qualified; and the Congress may by law provide for the case wherein neither a President elect nor a Vice President elect shall have qualified, declaring who shall then act as President, or the manner in which one who is to act shall be selected, and such person shall act accordingly until a President or Vice President shall have qualified.

Section 4. The Congress may by law provide for the case of the death of any of the persons from whom the House of Representatives may choose a President whenever the right of choice shall have devolved upon them, and for the case of the death of any of the persons from whom the Senate may choose a Vice President whenever the right of choice shall have devolved upon them.

Section 5. Sections 1 and 2 shall take effect on the 15th day of October following the ratification of this article.

Section 6. This article shall be inoperative unless it shall have been ratified as an amendment to the Constitution by the legislatures of three-fourths of the several States within seven years from the date of its submission.

AMENDMENT 21
(Ratified December 5, 1933)

Section 1. The eighteenth article of amendment to the Constitution of the United States is hereby repealed.

Section 2. The transportation or importation into any State, Territory, or possession of the United States for delivery or use therein of intoxicating liquors, in violation of the laws thereof, is hereby prohibited.

Section 3. This article shall be inoperative unless it shall have been ratified as an amendment to the Constitution by conventions in the several States, as provided in the Constitution, within seven years from the date of the submission hereof to the States by the Congress.

AMENDMENT 22
(Ratified February 27, 1951)

Section 1. No person shall be elected to the office of the President more than twice, and no person who has held the office of President, or acted as President, for more than two years of a term to which some other person was elected President shall be elected to the office of the President more than once. But this Article shall not apply to any person holding the office of President when this Article was proposed by the Congress, and shall not prevent any person who may be holding the office of President, or acting as President, during the term within which this Article becomes operative from holding the office of President or acting as President during the remainder of such term.

Section 2. This article shall be inoperative unless it shall have been ratified as an amendment to the Constitution by the legislatures of three-fourths of the several States within seven years from the date of its submission to the States by the Congress.

AMENDMENT 23
(Ratified March 29, 1961)

Section 1.   The District constituting the seat of Government of the United States shall appoint in such manner as the Congress may direct:

A number of electors of President and Vice President equal to the whole number of Senators and Representatives in Congress to which the District would be entitled if it were a State, but in no event more than the least populous State; they shall be in addition to those appointed by the States, but they shall be considered, for the purposes of the election of President and Vice President, to be electors appointed by a State; and they shall meet in the District and perform such duties as provided by the twelfth article of amendment.

Section 2.   The Congress shall have power to enforce this article by appropriate legislation.

AMENDMENT 24
(Ratified January 23, 1964)

Section 1.   The right of citizens of the United States to vote in any primary or other election for President or Vice President, for electors for President or Vice President, or for Senator or Representative in Congress, shall not be denied or abridged by the United States or any State by reason of failure to pay any poll tax or other tax.

Section 2.   The Congress shall have power to enforce this article by appropriate legislation.

AMENDMENT 25
(Ratified February 10, 1967)

Section 1.   In case of the removal of the President from office or of his death or resignation, the Vice President shall become President.

Section 2.   Whenever there is a vacancy in the office of the Vice President, the President shall nominate a Vice President who shall take office upon confirmation by a majority vote of both Houses of Congress.

Section 3.   Whenever the President transmits to the President pro tempore of the Senate and the Speaker of the House of Representatives his written declaration that he is unable to discharge the powers and duties of his office, and until he transmits to them a written declaration to the contrary, such powers and duties shall be discharged by the Vice President as Acting President.

Section 4.   Whenever the Vice President and a majority of either the principal officers of the executive departments or of such other body as Congress may by law provide, transmit to the President pro tempore of the Senate and the Speaker of the House of Representatives their written declaration that the President is unable to discharge the powers and duties of his office, the Vice President shall immediately assume the powers and duties of the office as Acting President.

Thereafter, when the President transmits to the President pro tempore of the Senate and the Speaker of the House of Representatives his written declaration that no inability exists, he shall resume the powers and duties of his office unless the Vice President and a majority of either the principal officers of the executive department or of such other body as Congress may by law provide, transmit within four days to the President pro tempore of the Senate and the Speaker of the House of Representatives their written declaration that the President is unable to discharge the powers and duties of his office. Thereupon Congress shall decide the issue, assembling within forty-eight hours for that purpose if not in session. If the Congress, within twenty-one days after receipt of the latter written declaration, or, if Congress is not in session, within twenty-one days after Congress is required to assemble, determines by two-thirds vote of both Houses that the President is unable to discharge the powers and duties of his office, the Vice President shall continue to discharge the same as Acting President; otherwise, the President shall resume the powers and duties of his office.

AMENDMENT 26
(Ratified July 1, 1971)

Section 1.   The right of citizens of the United States, who are eighteen years of age or older, to vote shall not be denied or abridged by the United States or by any State on account of age.

Section 2.   The Congress shall have the power to enforce this article by appropriate legislation.

AMENDMENT 27
(Ratified May 7, 1992)

No law, varying the compensation for the services of the Senators and Representatives, shall take effect, until an election of Representatives shall have intervened.

Appendix 2

Justices of the Supreme Court (1789–2012)

Year	Chief Justice	Associate Justices								
1789	Jay	Rutledge	Cushing	Wilson	Blair					
1790	Jay	Rutledge	Cushing	Wilson	Blair	Iredell				
1791	Jay	Johnson	Cushing	Wilson	Blair	Iredell				
1793	Jay	Paterson	Cushing	Wilson	Blair	Iredell				
1795	Rutledge	Paterson	Cushing	Wilson	Blair	Iredell				
1796	Ellsworth	Paterson	Cushing	Wilson	Chase	Iredell				
1798	Ellsworth	Paterson	Cushing	Washington	Chase	Iredell				
1799	Ellsworth	Paterson	Cushing	Washington	Chase	Moore				
1801	Marshall	Paterson	Cushing	Washington	Chase	Moore				
1804	Marshall	Paterson	Cushing	Washington	Chase	Johnson				
1806	Marshall	Livingston	Cushing	Washington	Chase	Johnson				
1807	Marshall	Livingston	Cushing	Washington	Chase	Johnson	Todd			
1811	Marshall	Livingston	Story	Washington	Duvall	Johnson	Todd			
1823	Marshall	Thompson	Story	Washington	Duvall	Johnson	Todd			
1826	Marshall	Thompson	Story	Washington	Duvall	Johnson	Trimble			
1829	Marshall	Thompson	Story	Washington	Duvall	Johnson	McLean			
1830	Marshall	Thompson	Story	Baldwin	Duvall	Johnson	McLean			
1835	Marshall	Thompson	Story	Baldwin	Duvall	Wayne	McLean			
1836	Taney	Thompson	Story	Baldwin	Barbour	Wayne	McLean			
1837	Taney	Thompson	Story	Baldwin	Barbour	Wayne	McLean	McKinley		Catron
1841	Taney	Thompson	Story	Baldwin	Daniel	Wayne	McLean	McKinley		Catron
1845	Taney	Nelson	Woodbury	Baldwin	Daniel	Wayne	McLean	McKinley		Catron
1846	Taney	Nelson	Woodbury	Grier	Daniel	Wayne	McLean	McKinley		Catron
1851	Taney	Nelson	Curtis	Grier	Daniel	Wayne	McLean	McKinley		Catron
1853	Taney	Nelson	Curtis	Grier	Daniel	Wayne	McLean	Campbell		Catron
1858	Taney	Nelson	Clifford	Grier	Daniel	Wayne	McLean	Campbell		Catron
1862	Taney	Nelson	Clifford	Grier	Miller	Wayne	Swayne	Davis		Catron
1863	Taney	Nelson	Clifford	Grier	Miller	Wayne	Swayne	Davis	Field	Catron
1864	Chase	Nelson	Clifford	Grier	Miller	Wayne	Swayne	Davis	Field	Catron
1865	Chase	Nelson	Clifford	Grier	Miller	—	Swayne	Davis	Field	Catron
1867	Chase	Nelson	Clifford	Grier	Miller	—	Swayne	Davis	Field	—
1870	Chase	Nelson	Clifford	Strong	Miller	Bradley	Swayne	Davis	Field	
1872	Chase	Hunt	Clifford	Strong	Miller	Bradley	Swayne	Davis	Field	
1874	Waite	Hunt	Clifford	Strong	Miller	Bradley	Swayne	Davis	Field	
1877	Waite	Hunt	Clifford	Strong	Miller	Bradley	Swayne	Harlan	Field	
1880	Waite	Hunt	Clifford	Woods	Miller	Bradley	Swayne	Harlan	Field	
1881	Waite	Hunt	Gray	Woods	Miller	Bradley	Matthews	Harlan	Field	
1882	Waite	Blatchford	Gray	Woods	Miller	Bradley	Matthews	Harlan	Field	
1888	Fuller	Blatchford	Gray	Lamar	Miller	Bradley	Matthews	Harlan	Field	
1889	Fuller	Blatchford	Gray	Lamar	Miller	Bradley	Brewer	Harlan	Field	
1890	Fuller	Blatchford	Gray	Lamar	Brown	Bradley	Brewer	Harlan	Field	
1892	Fuller	Blatchford	Gray	Lamar	Brown	Shiras	Brewer	Harlan	Field	
1893	Fuller	Blatchford	Gray	Jackson	Brown	Shiras	Brewer	Harlan	Field	
1894	Fuller	White	Gray	Jackson	Brown	Shiras	Brewer	Harlan	Field	
1895	Fuller	White	Gray	Peckham	Brown	Shiras	Brewer	Harlan	Field	
1898	Fuller	White	Gray	Peckham	Brown	Shiras	Brewer	Harlan	McKenna	
1902	Fuller	White	Holmes	Peckham	Brown	Shiras	Brewer	Harlan	McKenna	
1903	Fuller	White	Holmes	Peckham	Brown	Day	Brewer	Harlan	McKenna	
1906	Fuller	White	Holmes	Peckham	Moody	Day	Brewer	Harlan	McKenna	
1909	Fuller	White	Holmes	Lurton	Moody	Day	Brewer	Harlan	McKenna	

1910	White	Van Devanter	Holmes	Lurton	Lamar	Day	Hughes	Harlan	McKenna
1912	White	Van Devanter	Holmes	Lurton	Lamar	Day	Hughes	Pitney	McKenna
1914	White	Van Devanter	Holmes	McReynolds	Lamar	Day	Hughes	Pitney	McKenna
1916	White	Van Devanter	Holmes	McReynolds	Brandeis	Day	Clarke	Pitney	McKenna
1921	Taft	Van Devanter	Holmes	McReynolds	Brandeis	Day	Clarke	Pitney	McKenna
1922	Taft	Van Devanter	Holmes	McReynolds	Brandeis	Butler	Sutherland	Pitney	McKenna
1923	Taft	Van Devanter	Holmes	McReynolds	Brandeis	Butler	Sutherland	Sanford	McKenna
1925	Taft	Van Devanter	Holmes	McReynolds	Brandeis	Butler	Sutherland	Sanford	Stone
1930	Hughes	Van Devanter	Holmes	McReynolds	Brandeis	Butler	Sutherland	Roberts	Stone
1932	Hughes	Van Devanter	Cardozo	McReynolds	Brandeis	Butler	Sutherland	Roberts	Stone
1937	Hughes	Black	Cardozo	McReynolds	Brandeis	Butler	Sutherland	Roberts	Stone
1938	Hughes	Black	Cardozo	McReynolds	Brandeis	Butler	Reed	Roberts	Stone
1939	Hughes	Black	Frankfurter	McReynolds	Douglas	Butler	Reed	Roberts	Stone
1940	Hughes	Black	Frankfurter	McReynolds	Douglas	Murphy	Reed	Roberts	Stone
1941	Stone	Black	Frankfurter	Byrnes	Douglas	Murphy	Reed	Roberts	Jackson
1943	Stone	Black	Frankfurter	Rutledge	Douglas	Murphy	Reed	Roberts	Jackson
1945	Stone	Black	Frankfurter	Rutledge	Douglas	Murphy	Reed	Burton	Jackson
1946	Vinson	Black	Frankfurter	Rutledge	Douglas	Murphy	Reed	Burton	Jackson
1949	Vinson	Black	Frankfurter	Minton	Douglas	Clark	Reed	Burton	Jackson
1953	Warren	Black	Frankfurter	Minton	Douglas	Clark	Reed	Burton	Jackson
1955	Warren	Black	Frankfurter	Minton	Douglas	Clark	Reed	Burton	Harlan
1956	Warren	Black	Frankfurter	Brennan	Douglas	Clark	Reed	Burton	Harlan
1957	Warren	Black	Frankfurter	Brennan	Douglas	Clark	Whittaker	Burton	Harlan
1958	Warren	Black	Frankfurter	Brennan	Douglas	Clark	Whittaker	Stewart	Harlan
1962	Warren	Black	Goldberg	Brennan	Douglas	Clark	White	Stewart	Harlan
1965	Warren	Black	Fortas	Brennan	Douglas	Clark	White	Stewart	Harlan
1967	Warren	Black	Fortas	Brennan	Douglas	Marshall	White	Stewart	Harlan
1969	Burger	Black	Fortas	Brennan	Douglas	Marshall	White	Stewart	Harlan
1970	Burger	Black	Blackmun	Brennan	Douglas	Marshall	White	Stewart	Harlan
1972	Burger	Powell	Blackmun	Brennan	Douglas	Marshall	White	Stewart	Rehnquist
1975	Burger	Powell	Blackmun	Brennan	Stevens	Marshall	White	Stewart	Rehnquist
1981	Burger	Powell	Blackmun	Brennan	Stevens	Marshall	White	O'Connor	Rehnquist
1986	Rehnquist	Powell	Blackmun	Brennan	Stevens	Marshall	White	O'Connor	Scalia
1988	Rehnquist	Kennedy	Blackmun	Brennan	Stevens	Marshall	White	O'Connor	Scalia
1990	Rehnquist	Kennedy	Blackmun	Souter	Stevens	Marshall	White	O'Connor	Scalia
1991	Rehnquist	Kennedy	Blackmun	Souter	Stevens	Thomas	White	O'Connor	Scalia
1993	Rehnquist	Kennedy	Blackmun	Souter	Stevens	Thomas	Ginsburg	O'Connor	Scalia
1994	Rehnquist	Kennedy	Breyer	Souter	Stevens	Thomas	Ginsburg	O'Connor	Scalia
2005	Roberts	Kennedy	Breyer	Souter	Stevens	Thomas	Ginsburg	O'Connor	Scalia
2006	Roberts	Kennedy	Breyer	Souter	Stevens	Thomas	Ginsburg	Alito	Scalia
2009	Roberts	Kennedy	Breyer	Sotomayer	Stevens	Thomas	Ginsburg	Alito	Scalia
2010	Roberts	Kennedy	Breyer	Sotomayer	Kagan	Thomas	Ginsburg	Alito	Scalia

Appendix 3

Glossary of Legal Terms

Abstention doctrine   Permits a federal court to relinquish jurisdiction where necessary to avoid needless friction with the state's administration of its own affairs.

Acquittal   Certifying the innocence of a person charged with a crime.

Advisory opinion   An opinion rendered by a court indicating how the court would rule on a matter; an interpretation of a law without binding effect. Federal courts do not issue advisory opinions.

Affidavit   A written statement of facts, made voluntarily and confirmed by oath or affirmation before a judge or magistrate.

Affirm   To declare that a lower court's judgment is valid and right. This is done by an appellate court.

Amicus curiae   "Friend of the court." A person or group, not a party to a case, that submits a brief detailing its views on a case.

Ante   "Before."

Appeal   A review by a superior court of an inferior court's decision. There may also be levels of appeal within an administrative agency.

Appellant   The party appealing a case.

Appellate jurisdiction   The power of an appellate court to review and revise the judicial action of an inferior court; distinguished from *original jurisdiction*.

Appellee   The party responding to a case brought by an appellant; sometimes called "respondent."

Arraignment   Bringing an accused before a court, stating the criminal charge against him or her and calling on him or her to enter a plea.

Article I court   See *legislative court*.

Article III court   See *constitutional court*.

Aver   In a pleading, to declare, assert, or allege.

Balancing test   A constitutional doctrine in which a court weighs an individual's rights with the rights or powers of the state.

Battery   The unlawful use of force, either bodily injury or offensive touching, against another person.

Bill of attainder   A legislative act that inflicts punishment without judicial proceeding.

Brandeis brief   A brief that includes, along with legal citations and principles, references to economic and social surveys. It takes its name from Louis D. Brandeis, who used such practices before joining the Supreme Court.

Brief   A written statement prepared by the counsel arguing a case in court.

Case   A general term for an action, cause, suit, or controversy, at law or in equity.

Case law   The aggregate of reported cases that forms a body of jurisdiction; distinguished from statutory law.

Case or controversy   A constitutional prerequisite, from Article III, that determines the justiciability of a question before a federal court.

Cause of action   The facts that give a person a right of judicial relief.

Certification, writ of   A method of taking a case from a federal appellate court to the Supreme Court. The appellate court may certify any question of law on which it requests instruction from the Court.

Certiorari, writ of   An order by the Supreme Court when it exercises discretion to hear an appeal. It may grant or deny "cert."

Circuit courts   Federal appellate courts with jurisdiction over several states.

Civil law   The body of law that is concerned with private rights and remedies; distinguished from *criminal law.*

Class action   A suit brought by a person or group of persons to represent the interests of a class.

Collateral estoppel   The doctrine that prevents relitigation of the same issue in a suit upon a different claim or cause of action.

Common law   The body of law that derives its authority from usages and customs or from court decrees regarding these usages and customs; distinguished from law created by legislative enactments (statutory law).

Compelling state interest   The term used to uphold state action in the area of Equal Protection or First Amendment rights because of an overriding need for state action.

Concurrent powers   Powers that may be exercised independently by Congress and state legislatures on the same subject matter.

Concurring opinion   An opinion that agrees with the decision of the majority but offers separate reasons for reaching that decision.

Consent decree   A decree entered by a judge expressing the consent of both parties in resolving their dispute; a contract by the parties made under the sanction of the court.

Constitutional court   A court protected by Article III rights (life tenure and no diminution of salary). See *legislative court.*

Criminal law   The body of law created to prevent harm to society; distinguished from *civil law.*

Curtilage   The land and buildings immediately adjacent to a home.

Declaratory judgment   A binding adjudication of the legal rights of litigants but with no award of relief.

De facto   "In fact"; in reality; distinguished from *de jure.*

Defendant   The party against whom relief is sought in an action or suit; the accused in a criminal case.

De jure   "By law"; the result of official action; distinguished from *de facto.* For example, de jure segregation is mandated by law; de facto segregation exists but is not officially sanctioned.

Demurrer   A defendant admits the facts of a complaint but states that they are insufficient to proceed upon or to oblige the defendant to answer.

De novo   "From the beginning."

Dicta   Expressions in a court opinion that go beyond the necessities of the case and are not binding. Singular is *dictum.* See *obiter dictum.*

Dissenting opinion   A disagreement with the majority opinion. A dissent may or may not be accompanied by an opinion.

Distinguish   A court's explanation of why a previous decision does not apply.

District courts   Trial courts. Each state has one or more federal judicial districts.

Diversity jurisdiction   The jurisdiction of federal courts over cases between citizens of different states.

Docket   The list of cases set to be tried at a specified term.

Eleemosynary   Devoted to charity.

En banc   The full bench of an appellate court, as distinguished from a panel of three judges.

Enjoin   To require or command; specifically, to require a person to perform or desist from some act. See *injunction.*

Eo nomine   "Under that name."

Equity   Justice administered according to fairness rather than the stricter rules of common law.

Estop   To stop, bar, or prevent.

Exclusionary rule   A rule that prohibits the introduction in a criminal trial of evidence obtained by illegal means, such as from a search or seizure that violates the Fourth Amendment.

Ex parte   "On one side only"; by or for one party.

Ex post facto   "After the fact."

Ex post facto law   A law that inflicts punishment on a person for an act done which, at the time committed, was not illegal. This is forbidden by the U.S. Constitution.

Express   Clear; definite; explicit; set forth in words; distinguished from *implied.*

Ex proprio vigore   "By their own force."

Federal question   A case arising under the U.S. Constitution, federal statutes, or treaties. It generally involves a significant or major issue.

Grand jury   A jury of inquiry to hear accusations in criminal cases and find bills of indictment when it is satisfied that the accused should be tried. See *petit jury.*

Habeas corpus "You have the body." A writ commanding a law officer to bring a party before a court or judge. The purpose is to release someone from unlawful imprisonment.

Harmless error An error that is not prejudicial to the substantial rights of a person convicted. It does not provide grounds for granting a new trial.

Implied Not manifested by explicit and direct words. The meaning is gathered by necessary deduction; distinguished from *express*.

Inalienable rights Rights that are not capable of being surrendered without the consent of the person possessing such rights.

In camera "In chambers"; in private. In camera hearings occur in the judge's private chambers or when all spectators are excluded from the courtroom.

Indictment An accusation in writing presented by a grand jury. It charges the person named with an act that is a public offense.

In forma pauperis (I.F.P.) "In the character or manner of a pauper." Permission is given to a poor person to proceed without liability for court fees or costs.

Information An accusation against a person for some criminal offense. It differs from indictment in that it is presented by a public officer instead of by a grand jury.

Infra "Below."

Injunction A prohibitive remedy issued by a court that forbids the defendant to do some act.

In re "In the matter of."

Ipse dixit "He himself said it." A bare assertion resting on an individual's authority.

Judicial Conference The policy-making organization of the federal judiciary. Annual meetings consist of the Chief Justice of the United States, the chief judge of each judicial circuit, and a district judge from each judicial circuit.

Judicial council The meeting of judges of each circuit to assure expeditious and effective administration of the business of the courts.

Judicial review A court's authority to review the constitutionality of legislative and executive acts.

Jure belli "By the law of war."

Jurisdiction The authority, the right, or the power by which courts take cognizance of and decide cases. This term embraces every kind of judicial action.

Jurisprudence The philosophy of law; the science that treats the principles of law.

Jury A body of persons sworn to inquire into matters of fact and to declare the truth upon evidence laid before them.

Jus belli "The law of war."

Justiciable A matter appropriate for court review.

Legislative court Courts created by Congress (Article I courts) in contrast to those created by the Constitution (Article III courts). See *constitutional court*.

Litigant A party to a lawsuit.

Magistrate A person, such as a public civil officer, invested with executive or judicial power.

Mandamus "We command." The name of a writ issued from a court and commanding the performance of a particular act.

Mandatory jurisdiction The jurisdiction that a court must accept.

Moot A question is moot when it presents no actual controversy or where the issues have ceased to exist or have become academic or dead.

Motion An application made to a court or judge for the purpose of obtaining a rule or order.

Natural law A universal system of rules and principles that guide human conduct. It applies to all nations and people; distinguished from *positive law*. Also called "*jus naturale*."

Natural rights Rights that grow out of the nature of human beings; distinguished from rights created by *positive law*.

Obiter dictum "A remark by the way." A statement in an opinion that is not essential to the case at hand. Plural is *dicta*.

Order A direction of a court or judge made in writing but not included in the judgment.

Original jurisdiction The jurisdiction in the first instance; distinguished from *appellate jurisdiction*.

Overbreadth doctrine The requirement that a statute be aimed specifically at evils within the allowable area of governmental control. A statute cannot reach conduct that is constitutionally protected.

Per curiam   "By the court." An unsigned opinion reflecting a majority of the court.

Perjury   False, material statement under oath or equivalent affirmation.

Petitioner   The party filing a petition seeking action or relief from a court.

Petit jury   Trial jury; the ordinary jury to try civil or criminal action.

Plaintiff   The party bringing an action to obtain relief for a claimed injury.

Plurality opinion   An opinion of an appellate court that has the support of less than a majority of judges.

Police power   The power of government to protect the health, safety, welfare, and morals of its citizens.

Political question   An issue that must be resolved by the nonjudicial branches.

Positive law   A law enacted by a governmental body; distinguished from *natural law.*

Post   "After."

Preemption   The doctrine adopted by the U.S. Supreme Court holding that certain matters are of such a national character that federal laws take precedence over state laws.

Prima facie   "At first sight." A fact presumed to be true unless disproved by contrary evidence.

Pro se   "For himself." One who appears in court without legal representation.

Quash   To overthrow, vacate, annul; to make void.

Recuse   For a judge to disqualify himself or herself from hearing a case because of interest or prejudice.

Remand   To send a case back to a lower court with instructions to correct specified irregularities. This is done by an appellate court.

Respondent   One who answers. When the Supreme Court grants a writ of certiorari, the party seeking review is the petitioner and the party responding is the respondent.

Reverse   To overthrow or set aside. An appellate court may send a case back to a lower court with instructions to change the result reached.

Ripeness   The doctrine that requires a court to consider whether a case has matured or developed into a controversy worthy of adjudication.

Saving clause   The clause that returns to the states the power to enforce state laws not preempted by federal law. It is often used in federal statutes that preempt state action. Also refers to an exception for a particular provision in a statute that distinguishes it from the rest of the statute (see *severability clause,* which is a specific form of a saving clause).

Scienter   "Knowingly." Used to signify the defendant's guilty knowledge.

Seriatim   "One after another." Initially, each Justice of the Supreme Court prepared a separate opinion rather than have one Justice write for the majority.

Severability clause   Language in a statute providing that in the event one or more provisions are declared unconstitutional, the balance of the statute remains valid. Also called *separability clause.*

Standing   A position from which one may assert legal rights. To have standing to sue, a person must have a sufficient stake in a controversy to merit judicial resolution.

Stare decisis   "Stand by things decided." To abide by, or adhere to, decided cases.

State action   A term used to determine whether an action complained of has its source in state authority or policy.

Statutory law   Law created by legislative enactments.

Stay   To stop, arrest, or hold in abeyance.

Strict constructionism   A close or rigid reading and interpretation of a law or constitutional provision.

Sua sponte   "On its own initiative."

Sub nomine   "Under the name of."

Suborn   To procure or persuade another person to commit perjury.

Subpoena   "Under pain." A command to appear at a certain time and place. A *subpoena duces tecum* requires the production of books, papers, or objects. A *subpoena ad testificandum* requires testimony.

Sub silentio   "Under silence"; without notice taken.

Summary judgment   A short opinion written by the Court without receiving briefs or oral argument.

Supra   "Above."

Temporary restraining order (TRO) An emergency remedy issued by a court until it can hear arguments or evidence on a controversy.

Three-judge court A panel that combines federal district and appellate judges to expedite the review of a challenged action.

Trial court The first court to consider litigation.

Trover A remedy for any wrongful interference with or detention of the goods of another.

Ultra vires "Beyond powers." Acts in excess of powers granted.

Underinclusiveness The challenge that a statute is invalid because it limits benefits to a specified group rather than making them available to all groups.

Uttering To circulate counterfeit notes.

Vacate To annul; to set aside.

Vel non "Or not." For example, the Court might say, "We now judge the merits vel non of this claim."

Venire "To come." This is used in summoning a jury.

Vested rights Rights so settled in a person that they cannot be taken or diminished without the person's consent.

Vicinage Neighborhood; vicinity.

Voir dire "To speak the truth." Preliminary examination by a court to determine competency and impartiality of a witness or juror.

Warrant A writ issued by a judge or magistrate authorizing a law officer to make an arrest, a search, or a seizure or to perform other acts in the administration of justice. An *arrest warrant,* made on behalf of the state, commands a law enforcement officer to arrest a person and bring him before a magistrate. A *search warrant,* issued in writing by a judge or magistrate, directs a law enforcement officer to search for and seize specified property.

Writ An order issued from a court requiring the performance of a specified act.

Appendix 4

How to Research the Law

When a bill passes Congress and is signed by the President, or is vetoed by the President and Congress overrides the veto, the bill is printed either as a public law or a private law. The latter series is reserved for legislation intended for the relief of private parties, especially bills dealing with claims against the United States, the waiver of claims by the government against individuals, and exceptions for individuals subject to certain immigration and naturalization requirements.

The enacted bill first appears as a "slip law." The heading indicates the public law number, date of approval, and bill number. For example, the Civil Rights Restoration Act of 1987, which originated as S. 557, was enacted on March 22, 1988, and designated Public Law 100-259 (the 259th public law of the One Hundredth Congress). The heading also indicates the volume and page in the *U.S. Statutes at Large*, where the public law will appear. For the Civil Rights Restoration Act of 1987, the citation is 102 Stat. 28 (Volume 102, page 28). At the end of the slip law is a convenient legislative history that refers to the House and Senate reports and floor debates that preceded the bill's enactment. Private laws are numbered by a separate series, also prefixed by the Congress. Thus, a bill for the relief of Miriama Jones, enacted October 28, 1978, was called Private Law 95-110.

Bound volumes, called the *U.S. Statutes at Large,* contain public laws, private laws, reorganization plans, joint resolutions, concurrent resolutions, and proclamations issued by the President. There is little practical difference between a bill and a joint resolution. Both forms of legislation must be presented to the President for his signature; both are legally binding. Concurrent resolutions, adopted by the House and the Senate, are not presented to the President and do not have the force of law. Nor are simple resolutions, adopted either by the House or the Senate.

Beginning with Volume 52 (1938), each volume of the *Statutes at Large* contains the laws enacted during a calendar year. After Volume 64, treaties and other international agreements were no longer printed in the *Statutes.* They are printed in a new series of volumes, published by the State Department, called *United States Treaties and Other International Agreements.* The documents first appear in pamphlet form numbered in the "Treaties and Other International Acts Series" (TIAS). Citations are usually given to both the TIAS number and the volume of *United States Treaties and Other International Agreements,* as in 30 UST 617, TIAS 9207 (1978).

Treaties may supersede prior conflicting statutes.[1] By virtue of Article VI, Section 2, the Constitution, statutes, and treaties are collectively called "the supreme Law of the Land." On the other hand, executive agreements cannot be "inconsistent with legislation enacted by Congress in the exercise of its constitutional authority."[2] In cases where executive agreements violate rights secured by the Constitution, they have been struck down by the courts.[3]

As laws are modified or repealed by subsequent enactments of Congress, the need arises for a publication that consolidates the permanent body of law. The first codification of U.S. laws, enacted June 22, 1874, appeared in the *Revised Statutes.* A second edition was published in 1878, followed by sup-

---

1. United States v. Schooner Peggy, 5 U.S. (1 Cr.) 103 (1801).
2. 11 Foreign Affairs Manual [FAM] 721.2(b)(3) (1974); United States v. Guy W. Capps, Inc., 204 F.2d 655, 660 (4th Cir. 1953), aff'd on other grounds, 348 U.S. 296 (1955).
3. Seery v. United States, 127 F.Supp. 601, 606 (Ct. Cl. 1955); Reid v. Covert, 354 U.S. 1, 16 (1956).

plements. In 1926, Congress passed a law to provide for a code intended to embrace the laws of the United States that are general and permanent in their character. The first volume, reflecting the laws in force as of December 7, 1925, was printed as Volume 44, Part I, of the *Statutes at Large*. This series is now known as the *United States Code*. New editions of the code appeared in 1934 and every six years thereafter. Supplements to the code are issued after each session of Congress. The code consists of fifty titles organized by subject matter (Agriculture, Highways, Money and Finance, and so forth). Index references are to title, section, and year, as in 7 U.S.C. § 443 (1982) and 10 U.S.C. § 1437 (Supp. IV, 1986).

Administrative Legislation

Unless superseded by federal statute or invalidated by the courts, presidential proclamations, executive orders, and regulations are other sources of law. Not until 1935 did Congress pass legislation to provide for the custody and publication of these administrative rules and pronouncements. This publication, the *Federal Register,* includes all presidential proclamations and executive orders that have general applicability and legal effect, as well as agency regulations and orders that prescribe a penalty. Based partly on the statutory authority vested in him by the Federal Register Act, President Franklin D. Roosevelt issued an executive order in 1936 that vested in the Bureau of the Budget (now Office of Management and Budget) the responsibility for reviewing all proposed executive orders and proclamations.[4]

The *Federal Register* is published daily, Monday through Friday, except for official holidays. A typical citation is 46 Fed. Reg. 36707 (1981). The rules, regulations, and orders that constitute the current body of administrative regulations are arranged under fifty titles (generally parallel to those of the *United States Code*) and printed as the *Code of Federal Regulations*. Citations are by title and section, as in 50 C.F.R. § 17.13 (1980).

There is continuing controversy over the range and legal effect of executive orders and proclamations. Executive orders cannot supersede a statute or override contradictory congressional expressions,[5] but the latitude for presidential lawmaking is still substantial and a source of concern.[6] Proclamations also operate in a twilight zone of legality. When a statute prescribes a specific procedure and the President elects to follow a different course, a proclamation by him is illegal and void.[7] Proclamations have been upheld, however, with only tenuous ties to statutory authority.[8]

How to Brief a Case

At its heart, a case brief summarizes the facts, questions, holding, and impact of a court opinion. A well-written brief can help a student organize the relevant arguments of a case, thus making it easier

---

4. 49 Stat. 500, § 5 (1935). Roosevelt's Executive Order 7298, February 18, 1936, appeared too early for the first volume of the Federal Register. It is reprinted in James Hart, "The Exercise of Rule-Making Power," the President's Committee on Administrative Management 355 (1937).

5. Marks v. CIA, 590 F.2d 997, 1003 (D.C. Cir. 1978); Weber v. Kaiser Aluminum & Chemical Corp., 563 F.2d 216, 227 (5th Cir. 1977), rev'd on other grounds, Steelworkers v. Weber, 443 U.S. 193 (1979). The judiciary has struck down executive orders that exceed presidential authority; for example, Youngstown Co. v. Sawyer, 343 U.S. 579 (1952) and Panama Refining Co. v. Ryan, 293 U.S. 388, 433 (1935). See Louis Fisher, "Laws Congress Never Made," Constitution, Fall 1993, pp. 59–66.

6. Note, "Judicial Review of Executive Action in Domestic Affairs," 80 Colum. L. Rev. 1535 (1980); "Presidential Control of Agency Rulemaking: An Analysis of Constitutional Issues That May be Raised by Executive Order 12291," a Report Prepared for the Use of the House Committee on Energy and Commerce, 97th Cong., 1st Sess. (Comm. Print, June 15, 1981).

7. Schmidt Pritchard & Co. v. United States, 167 F.Supp. 272 (Cust. Ct. 1958); Carl Zeiss, Inc. v. United States, 76 F.2d 412 (Ct. Cust. & Pa. App. 1935).

8. United States v. Yoshida Intern., Inc., 526 F.2d 560 (Ct. Cust. & Pat. App. 1975); Louis Fisher, Constitutional Conflicts between Congress and the President 103–05 (5th ed. 2007).

to understand. There are many ways to brief a case, but standard elements include: (1) name and date of the case, (2) major facts of the dispute, including the litigation history, (3) legal and constitutional issues at stake, (4) the holding of the court that answers the questions presented, (5) how the court analyzed and justified its holding, (6) effect of the case on precedents and policy, and (7) concurring and dissenting opinions.

It is important to look for consistency (or inconsistency) in the majority's reasoning. Do you find it persuasive or strained? Do you think the concurrences or dissents have the better argument? If so, why? Can you think of issues that merited analysis but were left unexplored? Perhaps the court did not reach substantive issues because it decided it lacked jurisdiction for a number of reasons, including standing, mootness, ripeness, and the political question doctrine.

If you find the opinion difficult to follow, it may not be your fault. Properly written, a judicial opinion explains the legal dispute, analyzes alternative interpretations, and presents clear reasons for the proper resolution. Many rulings fail those elementary objectives. Frequently they provide little focus or clarity, leaving not only students puzzled but also lower courts, federal agencies, Congress, and the legal profession. At the level of the Supreme Court or any multi-member judicial body, the need to stitch together a majority may create some incoherence by incorporating various arguments that can be at cross-purposes or not centrally relevant. See Orin S. Kerr, "How to Read a Legal Opinion," 11 Green Bag 2d 51 (2007).

Constitutional Interpretation

As a general guide to constitutional powers, students can consult what has become known as the "Annotated Constitution." The actual title is *The Constitution of the United States of America: Analysis and Interpretation,* prepared periodically by the Congressional Research Service of the Library of Congress and printed as a Senate document. Edward S. Corwin wrote the 1952 edition, which is revised every ten years. Other basic sources include *The Records of the Federal Convention of 1787,* a four-volume work edited by Max Farrand and published by Yale University Press in 1937, and the *Federalist Papers* of Hamilton, Jay, and Madison, a prominent edition of which was published by Harvard University Press in 1966 under the guidance of Benjamin Fletcher Wright and reissued in 2002 by MetroBooks.

Other than brief accounts that appear in daily newspapers announcing major decisions by the Supreme Court, a researcher must rely on more specialized sources to keep track of legal interpretations—especially lower-court decisions. Decisions by federal district and appellate courts are important for two reasons: (1) they are the first step in shaping constitutional and statutory law and (2) often they are the last step, for few of their rulings are reviewed by the Supreme Court.

This huge body of material is conveniently organized by the *United States Law Week,* which consists of four major sections: (1) a summary and analysis of major decisions, with page references to more extended treatment in the *Law Week;* (2) congressional and agency actions; (3) Supreme Court proceedings, including oral arguments before the Court, reviews granted, summary actions, reviews denied, cases recently filed, and special articles summarizing and analyzing the most significant Supreme Court opinions rendered for each term; and (4) Supreme Court opinions. The *Law Week* is published by the Bureau of National Affairs. Citations are by volume, page, and year, as in *Maher* v. *Roe,* 45 U.S.L.W. [or L.W.] 4787 (1977).

The *National Law Journal,* published weekly, contains stories on appointments to the federal agencies, personnel actions, departmental politics, budget cutbacks, executive-legislative clashes, regulatory policy, and administrative law. This periodical provides incisive, sophisticated, and well-written accounts on current developments.

Supreme Court decisions are printed first in the form of "slip opinions" and are available from the Court's webpage: www.supremecourt.gov. The full decisions are republished in paperbacks called "preliminary prints" and finally in bound volumes of the *United States Reports.* Citations take this form: *Ohio* v. *Roberts,* 448 U.S. 56 (1980), which indicates that the decision may be found in Volume 448, beginning on page 56.

The first ninety volumes of the *Reports* were named after court reporters. Volumes 1 through 4 (1790–1800) were named after Dallas. Later volumes, 5 through 90, carry the names of Cranch, Wheaton, Peters, Howard, Black, and Wallace. Volumes 91–107 (1875–1882) are designated "1 to 17 Otto" as well as "United States Reports 91–107." Reprints of Volumes 1 through 90 generally have a dual numbering system to the *Reports* and to court reporters, requiring such citations as *Marbury* v. *Madison,* 5 U.S. (1 Cr.) 137 (1803).

The full text of each Supreme Court decision also appears in the *Supreme Court Reporter,* issued by West Publishing Company. The citations for these decisions are in the form *Maryland* v. *Louisiana,* 101 S.Ct. 2114 (1981). Another source of Supreme Court decisions is *United States Supreme Court Reports, Lawyers' Edition,* published by the Lawyers Co-Operative Publishing Company. A unique feature of the *Lawyers' Edition* is a summary of the arguments in each case for the majority of the Court and for justices who concur and dissent. The first series of the *Lawyers' Edition,* consisting of 100 volumes, covers the period from 1790 to 1956. There is now a second series. A typical citation is *Steagald* v. *United States,* 68 L.Ed. 2d 38 (1981).

Briefs and oral arguments to the Supreme Court, for major cases, are published in *Landmark Briefs and Arguments of the Supreme Court of the United States: Constitutional Law,* edited by Gerald Gunther and Gerhard Casper and published by University Publications of America. Oral arguments are also available from the Supreme Court's webpage.

Significant decisions by federal district courts are printed in the *Federal Supplement,* issued first in a paper edition and later in bound volumes. The citation shows the volume, page, state, and year, as in *United States* v. *Mandel,* 505 F.Supp. 189 (D. Md. 1981). The "D" in parentheses indicates that the decision occurred at the district court level. For decisions that are not reported in the *Federal Supplement,* or in situations where immediate access to a decision is needed, a researcher may call the judge's chamber and receive a copy of the memorandum decision from a law clerk or filing clerk.

To follow appeals of district court decisions, the source is the *Federal Reporter.* The first series (F. or Fed.) stopped with Volume 300; the second series (F.2d) ended with Volume 999. The *Federal Reporter* is now in its third series (F.3d). Typical citations are *Rowe* v. *Drohen,* 262 F. 15 (2d Cir. 1919) and *Romeo* v. *Youngberg,* 644 F.2d 147 (3d Cir. 1980). These decisions are initially available as slip opinions and in memorandum form either from the court or libraries.

Finding Citations

Various databases, including LEXIS and WESTLAW, are used to find citations to statutes, administrative legislation, and court decisions. *U.S. Code Congressional and Administrative News*, published by West, reprints the full text of public laws and selected House and Senate documents, as well as presidential proclamations, executive orders, presidential messages, and federal regulations. The *CIS/ Index* provides citations to all congressional publications, including reports, hearings, and other legislative documents.

The "citator" or citation book tells the student whether a decision is still valid and authoritative. A decision by a lower court may be affirmed, reversed, or modified. *Shepard's Citations,* a widely used sourcebook, has spawned such words as *Shepardize* and *Shepardizing* to describe the process of determining the current state of the law. *Shepard's United States Citations* includes citations to Supreme Court decisions, U.S. statutes, treaties, and court rules for federal courts. *Shepard's Federal Citations,* covering decisions by federal courts below the Supreme Court, is issued in two series. One series covers the *Federal Supplement,* and the other the *Federal Reporter.*

DOJ and GAO

Many of the issues that come before the courts have been first explored by the Justice Department and the General Accounting Office (now the Governmental Accountability Office). These analyses are published in *Official Opinions of the Attorneys General* and *Decisions of the Comptroller General*. Among his other duties, the Attorney General rendered important opinions on legal issues presented to him by Presidents and departmental heads. Citations to these opinions are by volume, page, and year, as in 40 Ops. Att'y Gen. 469 (1946). Legal opinions are now issued by the Office of Legal Counsel within the Justice Department (Ops. O.L.C.) and are available from the Department's webpage: www.justice.gov/olc/opinions.htm.

The Comptroller General determines the legality of payments of appropriated funds by federal officials. This function was vested in the Treasury Department from 1817 to 1921 but passed thereafter to the Comptroller General as the head of the newly created General Accounting Office. The decisions are cited as 49 Comp. Gen. 59 (1969). In 1969, the Comptroller General and the Attorney General disagreed completely about the legality of the Nixon administration's "Philadelphia Plan," designed to increase the number of minority workers in federally assisted contracts.[9] In this dispute the courts sided with the Attorney General's interpretation.[10]

General Literature

An indispensable guide to the literature is the *Index to Legal Periodicals,* published by the H.W. Wilson Company. Currently covering more than 400 legal periodicals, it indexes the articles under subject and author. Entries of special interest include administrative agencies, administrative law, administrative procedure, delegation of powers, discrimination, executive agreements, executive power, federalism, freedom of information, freedom of religion, freedom of speech, freedom of the press, government, judicial review, legislation, political science, politics, public finance, separation of powers, United States: Congress, United States: President, and United States: Supreme Court. Legal periodicals can also be accessed through *Current Law Index,* published by Information Access Company, InfoTrac/LegalTrac Database, a computerized system offered by Information Access Company, and HeinOnline.

State Decisions

Decisions by state courts are reported in volumes published by each state. They are also published in seven regional reporters. For example, decisions by Connecticut, Delaware, the District of Columbia, Maine, Maryland, New Hampshire, New Jersey, Pennsylvania, Rhode Island, and Vermont appear in the *Atlantic Reporter.* The citation for the second series is A.2d. Other state court decisions appear in the following reporters, with citations given to the second series: *North Eastern Reporter* (N.E.2d; Illinois, Indiana, Massachusetts, New York, Ohio); *North Western Reporter* (N.W.2d; Iowa, Michigan, Minnesota, Nebraska, North Dakota, South Dakota, Wisconsin); *Pacific Reporter* (P.2d; Alaska, Arizona, California, Colorado, Hawaii, Idaho, Kansas, Montana, Nevada, New Mexico, Oklahoma, Oregon, Utah, Washington, Wyoming); *South Eastern Reporter* (S.E.2d; Georgia, North Carolina, South Carolina, Virginia, West Virginia); *Southern Reporter* (So.2d; Alabama, Florida, Louisiana, Mississippi); and *South Western Reporter* (S.W.2d; Arkansas, Kentucky, Missouri, Tennessee, Texas).

---

9. 49 Comp. Gen. (1969); 42 Ops. Att'y Gen. 405 (1969).

10. Contractors Ass'n of Eastern Pa. v. Secretary of Labor, 442 F.2d 159 (3d Cir. 1971), cert. denied, 404 U.S. 854 (1971).

Table of Cases

Index